ANNUAL BIBLIOGRAPHY OF ENGLISH LANGUAGE AND LITERATURE FOR 1996

ANNUAL

BIBLIOGRAPHY

OF

ENGLISH LANGUAGE AND LITERATURE

FOR 1996

VOLUME 71

EDITOR
GERARD LOWE

AMERICAN EDITOR
JAMES R. KELLY

W.E.B. Du Bois Library, University of Massachusetts at Amherst

ASSOCIATE AMERICAN EDITOR
BRUCE T. SAJDAK

Neilson Library, Smith College, Northampton, MA

Published by

W. S. Maney & Son Ltd

for the

Modern Humanities Research Association

1998

The *Annual Bibliography*
of English Language and Literature
may be ordered from the Hon. Treasurer MHRA
King's College, Strand, London wc2r 2ls, England

Unsolicited offprints, photocopies or other material for reporting, and correspondence about such matters ought to be sent direct to the Editor, *Annual Bibliography of English Language and Literature*, University Library, West Road, Cambridge cb3 9dr, England
(E-mail: abell@ula.cam.ac.uk)
(WWW: http://www.lib.cam.ac.uk/MHRA/ABELL/)

isbn 0 901 286 93 1
issn 0066-3786

Printed in Great Britain by
W.S. MANEY & SON LIMITED
HUDSON ROAD LEEDS LS9 7DL

PREFACE

In the preface to Volume 70 I drew attention to the fact that it was the largest volume of the Bibliography to have been published; Volume 71, however, is considerably larger still.

Our attempt to provide a comprehensive record of scholarship in the field of English studies would not be possible without the dedication of our regular contributors whom I would like to take this opportunity to thank warmly. Once again I am pleased to welcome our new contributors and to express my sincere gratitude to Jacek Fisiak, O.B.E., and David R. Cheney, who retire this year, having contributed to 29 volumes and 38 volumes of the Bibliography respectively.

I am, as always, very grateful to our Academic Advisers for their expert advice and guidance. I am also greatly indebted to our American Editor, James R. Kelly, for the huge contribution which he makes to the Bibliography. With this volume Bruce T. Sajdak becomes Associate American Editor, and his energy, enthusiasm and hard work have been unstinting. It is a pleasure to have such colleagues on the project.

ABELL continues to be published online and is available via the World Wide Web. The first CD-ROM, covering volumes 1920–1995, is now published too. Further details are available from the address given opposite.

Finally, I am always keen to hear from potential contributors, and to hear of errors and omissions.

GERARD LOWE

Contributors — *continued*

Sweden: SVEN BÄCKMAN, Lund University

Syria: SULEIMAN M. AHMAD, University of Damascus

UK and
Republic of
Ireland: MICHAEL C. HEAD

    PRISCILLA SCHLICKE

    RUTH SMITH

    JOHN TURNER, University College of Wales, Aberystwyth

USA: STEPHEN ADAMS, Westfield State College, Westfield, MA

    MARLIN E. BLAINE, University of North Texas, Denton

    DAVID R. CHENEY, University of Toledo, OH

    RUTH COPANS, Lucy Scribner Library, Skidmore College, Saratoga Springs, NY

    G. RONALD DOBLER, Morehead State University, Morehead, KY

    LAURA S. FUDERER, Notre Dame University, Notre Dame, IN

    MARC GLASSER, Morehead State University, Morehead, KY

    LILA M. HARPER, Central Washington State University, Ellensburg, WA

    STYRON HARRIS, East Tennessee State University, Johnson City, TN

    RICHARD HENRY, State University of New York, Potsdam

    CRAIG HOWES, University of Hawaii, Honolulu

    CECILE M. JAGODZINSKI, Illinois State University, Normal

    SIGRID KELSEY, Penrose Memorial Library, Whitman College, Walla Walla, WA

    DIANE MAHER, University of San Diego, CA

    MARGARET K. POWELL, Yale University Library, New Haven, CT

    SUSAN P. REILLY, Brown University, Providence, RI

    GLENN ELLEN STARR, Appalachian State University, Boone, NC

    STEPHEN L. THOMPSON, Rockefeller Library, Brown University, Providence, RI

    JOHN THOMSON, Dodge City Community College, Dodge City, KS

    MARKEL D. TUMLIN, University of San Diego, San Diego, CA

    KEVIN A. WARD, SSAI, NASA Goddard Space Flight Center, Greenbelt, MD

    KELLIE DONOVAN WIXSON, Tufts University, Medford, MA

    and the editorial staff of the *Annual Bibliography*

CONTENTS

SOURCES AND ABBREVIATIONS
1996

What follows is a list of the periodicals consulted in the compilation of the Bibliography; an asterisk indicates that relevant items have been found and are indexed in this volume. The editors are always glad to hear of journals requiring coverage.

In many cases journals are referred to in this volume by their main titles alone (e.g. Ariel) without this title being shown separately below as an abbreviation.

13th Moon: a feminist literary magazine (Dept of English, SUNY at Albany)
*1650–1850: ideas, aesthetics, and inquiries (New York)
*AAA   Arbeiten aus Anglistik und Amerikanistik (Inst. für Anglistik, Univ. of Graz, Austria) (Tübingen)
*AAR   African American Review (Indiana State Univ., Terre Haute). *Formerly* Black American Literature Forum
A/B   A/B: Auto/Biography Studies (Univ. of Kansas, Lawrence)
ABPR   American Book Publishing Record (New Providence, NJ)
*ABR   American Benedictine Review (Assumption Abbey, Richardton, ND)
*Acme: annali della Facoltà di Lettere e Filosofia dell'Università degli Studi di Milano
*Àcoma (Florence)
ACPQ   American Catholic Philosophical Quarterly (American Catholic Philosophical Assn, Washington, DC). *Formerly* New Scholasticism
*Acta Universitatis Lodziensis: Folia Litteraria Anglica (Łódź)
*AD   Armchair Detective: a quarterly journal devoted to the appreciation of mystery, detective, and suspense fiction (New York)
ADE Bulletin (Assn of Depts of English, New York)
*AEB   Analytical and Enumerative Bibliography (Bibliographical Soc. of Northern Illinois, DeKalb)
*Æstel (Seattle, WA)
*Aevum: rassegna di scienze storiche linguistiche e filologiche (Università Cattolica del Sacro Cuore, Milan)
*Agni (Boston Univ., Boston, MA)
*AH   American Heritage: the magazine of history (Soc. of American Historians, New York)
*AHR   American Historical Review (American Historical Assn, Washington, DC)
*AI   American Imago: a psychoanalytic journal for culture, science and the arts (Assn for Applied Psychoanalysis) (Baltimore, MD)
*AICRJ   American Indian Culture and Research Journal (UCLA American Indian Studies Center, Los Angeles, CA)
AIQ   American Indian Quarterly (Southwestern American Indian Soc.; Soc. for American Indian Studies & Research) (Lincoln, NB)
*AJ   Age of Johnson (New York)
*AJH   American Jewish History (American Jewish Historical Soc.) (Baltimore, MD)
*AJSem   American Journal of Semiotics (Semiotic Soc. of America) (Bloomington, IN)
*AL   American Literature: a journal of literary history, criticism, and bibliography (Durham, NC)
*AlaR   Alabama Review: a quarterly journal of Alabama history (Alabama Historical Assn, Tuscaloosa)
Albina (Bucharest)
*Albion: a quarterly journal concerned with British studies (Dept of History, Appalachian State Univ., Boone, NC; North American Conference on British Studies)
*Allegorica: a journal of medieval and Renaissance literature (Texas A&M Univ., College Station)
*ALR   American Literary Realism (Dept of English, Univ. of New Mexico) (Jefferson, NC). *Formerly* American Literary Realism 1870–1910

*Alternation (Centre for the Study of Southern African Literature and Languages, Durban)
*AmDr American Drama (Univ. of Cincinnati, OH)
*American Literary Scholarship: an annual (Durham, NC)
*AmJ American Journalism (American Journalism Historians Assn, Univ. of Georgia, Athens)
*AmLH American Literary History (Cary, NC)
*AmP American Periodicals: a journal of history, criticism, and bibliography (Research Soc. for American Periodicals, Denton, TX)
*AmQ American Quarterly (American Studies Assn) (Baltimore, MD)
*AmS American Studies (Mid-America American Studies Assn, Univ. of Kansas, Lawrence)
*AmSS American Studies in Scandinavia (Copenhagen)
*Amst Amerikastudien/American Studies (Johannes Gutenberg-Univ., Mainz)
*Anaïs: an international journal (Anaïs Nin Foundation, Los Angeles, CA)
*Analecta Husserliana: the yearbook of phenomenological research (Dordrecht)
*Ang Anglia: Zeitschrift für englische Philologie (Tübingen)
*Angelaki (London)
*Anglica Wratislaviensia (Wrocław, Poland)
*Anglo-Norman Studies (Woodbridge, Suffolk)
*Annales de l'Université de Savoie (Chambéry)
*Annales UMCS Annales Universitatis Mariae Curie-Sklodowska (Lublin)
*Annali anglistica (Istituto Universitario Orientale, Naples)
*AnnS Annals of Scholarship: an international quarterly in the humanities and social sciences (Detroit, MI)
*ANQ: a quarterly journal of short articles, notes, and reviews (Univ. of Kentucky, Lexington)
*Antaeus (Hopewell, NJ)
*AntR Antigonish Review (St Francis Xavier Univ., Antigonish, N.S.)
AnUILingv Analele ştiinţifice ale Universităţii 'Al. I. Cuza' din Iaşi, Serie nouă, Sectiunea III.e. Lingvistică) (Jassy, Romania)
*AP Acta Philologica (Warsaw)
*APHA APHA Newsletter (American Printing History Assn, New York)
*APJPH American Presbyterians: journal of Presbyterian history (Presbyterian Historical Soc., Philadelphia, PA)
Apostrof (Bucharest)
*AppalJ Appalachian Journal: a regional studies review (Appalachian State Univ., Boone, NC)
*AQ Arizona Quarterly: a journal of American literature, culture, and theory (Univ. of Arizona, Tucson)
*AR Antioch Review (Yellow Springs, OH)
Arca (Bucharest)
*arcadia: Zeitschrift für allgemeine und vergleichende Literaturwissenschaft (Berlin)
*Archiv Archiv für das Studium der neueren Sprachen und Literaturen (Berlin)
*ARCS American Review of Canadian Studies (Assn for Canadian Studies in the United States, Washington, DC)
*Argumentation: an international journal on reasoning (European Centre for the Study of Argumentation, Dordrecht)
Ariadne (Univ. of Crete School of Philosophy, Rethymno)
*ArizEB Arizona English Bulletin (Arizona English Teachers Assn, Tempe)
*ArsL Ars Lyrica: journal of Lyrica, Society for Word–Music Relations (Guilford, CT)
ArthL Arthurian Literature (Cambridge; Rochester, NY)
*Arthuriana (International Arthurian Soc.; Southern Methodist Univ., Dallas, TX). Formerly Quondam et Futurus
*ARV: Nordic Yearbook of Folklore (Royal Gustavus Adolphus Academy, Uppsala)
*AS American Speech: a quarterly of linguistic usage (American Dialect Soc., Duke Univ., NC)
*ASch American Scholar (Washington, DC)
*Aschkenas: Zeitschrift für Geschichte und Kultur der Juden (Vienna)
*ASE Anglo-Saxon England (Cambridge)

*Assays: critical approaches to medieval and Renaissance texts (Pittsburgh, PA)
 Ateneu (Bacău, Romania)
*Atlanta Review (Atlanta, GA)
*Atlantis: journal of the Spanish Association for Anglo-American Studies (Univ. de
 La Laguna, Tenerife)
*ATQ   American Transcendental Quarterly: 19th century American
                          literature and culture (Univ. of Rhode Island, Kingston)
*AUMLA: journal of the Australasian Universities Language and Literature Association:
 a journal of literary criticism and linguistics (Christchurch, New Zealand)
*AUNC   Acta Universitatis Nicolai Copernici: English Studies (Toruń,
                          Poland)
*AUR   Aberdeen University Review (Alumnus Assn, Univ. of Aberdeen)
*Australian Folklore (Univ. of New England) (Armidale, N.S.W.)
*BALF   Black American Literature Forum. *See* AAR
 Balkan Studies (Inst. for Balkan Studies, Salonika)
*BB   Bulletin of Bibliography (Westport, CT)
*BC   Book Collector (London)
*Biblio (Eugene, OR)
*Biblion: the bulletin of the New York Public Library (New York; Westport, CT)
*Bibliotheck: a Scottish journal of bibliography and allied topics (National Library of
 Scotland, Edinburgh)
*BJCS   British Journal of Canadian Studies (British Assn for Canadian
                          Studies, Univ. of Edinburgh)
*BJECS   British Journal for Eighteenth-Century Studies (Voltaire
                          Foundation, Oxford)
*BJJ   Ben Jonson Journal: literary contexts in the age of Elizabeth,
                          James and Charles (Reno, NV)
*BJRL   Bulletin of the John Rylands University Library of Manchester
*BkIA   Books at Iowa (Friends of the Univ. of Iowa Libraries, Univ. of
                          Iowa, Iowa City)
*BkW   Book World (Washington, DC). *Variant title* Washington Post
                          Book World
 Black Renaissance (Bloomington, IN)
*Blake: an illustrated quarterly (Rochester Univ., Rochester, NY)
*BLR   Bodleian Library Record (Oxford)
 Blueline (Potsdam College, Potsdam, NY)
*BNB   British National Bibliography (London)
*Book: Newsletter of the Program in the History of the Book in American Culture
 (American Antiquarian Soc., Worcester, MA)
*Boundary 2: an international journal of literature and culture (Durham, NC)
 BPJ   Beloit Poetry Journal (Ellsworth, ME)
 BPN   Barbara Pym Newsletter (St Bonaventure, NY)
 BR   Bilingual Review/La revista bilingüe (Hispanic Research Center,
                          Arizona State Univ., Tempe)
*Bracket: a journal of graduate studies (Dept of English, Univ. of Cape Town)
*Brno Studies in English (Univ. Masarykova, Brno) (Prague)
 Broadsheet: New Zealand feminist magazine (Auckland)
*BSEAA   Bulletin de la Société d'Études Anglo-Américaines des XVIIe et
                          XVIIIe siècles (Paris)
*BSJ   Baker Street Journal: an irregular quarterly of Sherlockiana
                          (Baker Street Irregulars, Hanover, PA)
*BST   Brontë Society Transactions (Brontë Soc., Haworth)
 Buletin ştiintific Universitătea Baia Mare. Seria A, fasc. filologie (Baia Mare, Romania)
*Bulletin de la Société de Linguistique de Paris (Paris)
*Bunyan Studies (London)
*BWR   Black Warrior Review (Univ. of Alabama, Tuscaloosa)
*BYUS   Brigham Young University Studies (Provo, UT)
*Callaloo (Univ. of Virginia, Charlottesville)
*CamQ   Cambridge Quarterly (Cambridge Quarterly Assn, Clare
                          College, Cambridge) (Oxford)
*CanL   Canadian Literature/Littérature canadienne: a quarterly of
                          criticism and review (Univ. of British Columbia, Vancouver)
 CanMLR   Canadian Modern Language Review/Revue canadienne des
                          langues vivantes (North York, Ont.)

*CanRCL	Canadian Review of Comparative Literature/Revue canadienne de littérature comparée (Canadian Comparative Literature Assn/Assn canadienne de littérature comparée, Downsview, Ont.)
*CanTR	Canadian Theatre Review (North York, Ont.)
*CathS	Cather Studies (Lincoln, NB)
*CC	Cross Currents (Assn for Religion and Intellectual Life, Pearl River, NY)
*CCTE	Proceedings of the Conference of College English Teachers at Texas (Commerce)
*CEACrit	CEA Critic: an official journal of the College English Association (Rock Hill, SC)
CEAF	CEA Forum (College English Assn, Youngstown State Univ., Youngstown, OH)
*CEl	Cahiers élisabéthains: late medieval and Renaissance English studies (Centre d'Études et de Recherches Élisabéthaines de l'Univ. Paul-Valéry, Montpellier)
CFM	Canadian Fiction Magazine (Kingston, Ont.)
*ChauR	Chaucer Review: a journal of medieval studies and literary criticism (Pennsylvania State Univ., University Park)
*ChauY	Chaucer Yearbook: a journal of late medieval studies (Cambridge)
*ChesR	Chesterton Review (Chesterton Soc., Saskatoon, Sask.)
*ChildLit	Children's Literature: annual of the Modern Language Association Division on Children's Literature and the Children's Literature Association (New Haven, CT)
*ChrisL	Christianity and Literature (Conference on Christianity and Literature, West Georgia College, Carrollton)
*ChronOkla	Chronicles of Oklahoma (Oklahoma Historical Soc., Oklahoma City)
*CI	Critical Inquiry (Chicago Univ.)
*CimR	Cimarron Review (Dept of English, Oklahoma State Univ., Stillwater)

*Cineaste: America's leading magazine on the art and politics of the cinema (New York)

*CinJ	Cinema Journal (Soc. for Cinema Studies) (Austin, TX)

*Cithara: essays in the Judaeo-Christian tradition (St Bonaventure Univ., NY)

CJa	Cizí jazyky ve škole (Prague)
*CJIS	Canadian Journal of Irish Studies (Canadian Assn for Irish Studies, Saskatchewan, Sask.)
CJL	Canadian Journal of Linguistics/Revue canadienne de linguistique (Canadian Linguistic Assn, Downsview, Ont.)
*CL	Comparative Literature (Oregon Univ., Eugene)
*CLAJ	CLA Journal (College Language Assn, Morehouse College, Atlanta, GA)
*CLAQ	Children's Literature Association Quarterly (Battle Creek, MI)
CLC	Columbia Library Columns (Columbia Univ., New York)

*CLIO: a journal of literature, history, and the philosophy of history (Indiana Univ.–Purdue Univ., Fort Wayne)

*CLS	Comparative Literature Studies (Pennsylvania State Univ., University Park)
*ČMF	Časopis pro moderní filologii (Czech Academy of Sciences) (Amsterdam; Philadelphia, PA)
*CML	Classical and Modern Literature: a quarterly (Terre Haute, IN)
*ColbyQ	Colby Quarterly (Colby College, Waterville, ME)
ColJR	Columbia Journalism Review (Columbia Univ., New York)
*ColLit	College Literature (West Chester Univ., West Chester, PA)

*Comitatus: a journal of medieval and Renaissance studies (Center for Medieval and Renaissance Studies, Univ. of California, Los Angeles)

*CommEd	Communication Education (Speech Communication Assn, Annandale, VA)

*Comparatist: journal of the Southern Comparative Literature Association (Virginia Commonwealth Univ., Richmond)

*CompCrit	Comparative Criticism: an annual journal (Cambridge)
*CompLing	Computational Linguistics (Assn for Computational Linguistics) (Cambridge, MA)

*ComQ   Communication Quarterly (Eastern Communication Assn,
                             Univ. of New Haven, West Haven, CT)
*Configurations: a journal of literature, science and technology (Baltimore, MD)
*ConLit   Contemporary Literature (Univ. of Wisconsin, Madison)
*ConnHSB   Connecticut Historical Society Bulletin (Hartford)
*Conradiana: a journal of Joseph Conrad studies (Texas Tech Univ., Lubbock)
 Contemporanul Ideea Europeana (Bucharest). *Formerly* Contemporanul
*CPR   Cumberland Poetry Review (Nashville, TN)
*CR   Centennial Review (Michigan State Univ., East Lansing)
*Cresset: a review of literature, the arts and public affairs (Valparaiso Univ.,
     Valparaiso, IN)
*Critic: a Catholic review of culture and the arts (Thomas More Assn, Chicago)
*Criticism: a quarterly for literature and the arts (Detroit, MI)
*CritM   Critical Matrix: the Princeton journal of women, gender, and
                             culture (Princeton Univ., Princeton, NJ)
*CritQ   Critical Quarterly (Oxford)
*CritR   Critical Review: an interdisciplinary journal (San Francisco, CA)
*CritS   Critical Survey (Oxford)
 Cronica: renastere romaneascǎ, integrare europeanǎ (Jassy, Romania)
*CSL: the bulletin of the New York C. S. Lewis Society (New York)
*CSLL   Cardozo Studies in Law and Literature (Jacob Burns Inst. for
                             Advanced Legal Studies, Benjamin N. Cardozo School of Law
                             of Yeshiva Univ.)
*CultA   Cultural Anthropology: journal of the Society for Cultural
                             Anthropology (American Anthropological Assn, Arlington,
                             VA)
*Current Writing: text and reception in Southern Africa (Univ. of Natal, Durban)
 Cuvantul Liber (Giurgiu, Romania)
*CVE   Cahiers victoriens et édouardiens (Univ. Paul-Valéry,
                             Montpellier)
*Cweal   Commonweal (Commonweal Foundation, New York)
*CWH   Civil War History: a journal of the Middle Period (Dept of
                             History, Kent State Univ., OH)
*CWPL   Calgary Working Papers in Linguistics (Graduate Student Assn,
                             Univ. of Calgary, Calgary, Alta)
*DA   Dissertation Abstracts International (Ann Arbor, MI)
*Daedalus: journal of the American Academy of Arts and Sciences (Cambridge, MA)
*De Gids (Amsterdam)
*De Proverbio: electronic journal of international proverb studies (Univ. of Tasmania)
*DHLR   D. H. Lawrence Review (Univ. of Delaware, Newark)
*Diacritics: a review of contemporary criticism (Dept of Romance Studies, Cornell Univ.,
     Ithaca, NY)
*Dialog: miesięcznik poświęcony dramaturgii współczesnej: teatralnej, filmowej, radiowej,
     telewizyjnej (Warsaw)
*Diavazo: mēniaia epitheōrēsē tou bibliou (Athens)
*DickQ   Dickens Quarterly: a scholarly journal devoted to the study of the
                             life, times, & works of Charles Dickens (Univ. of Massachusetts,
                             Amherst)
 Dilema (Bucharest)
*Dionysos: the literature and addiction triquarterly (Addiction Studies Program,
     Seattle Univ., Seattle, WA)
*DNR   Dime Novel Roundup: a magazine devoted to the collecting,
                             preservation and study of old-time dime and nickel novels,
                             popular story papers, series books, and pulp magazines (Happy
                             Hours Brotherhood, Dundas, MN)
 Dodona: University of Ioannina School of Philosophy yearbook (Ioannina, Greece)
*DQ   Denver Quarterly: a journal of modern culture (Dept of English,
                             Univ. of Denver, CO)
*DreiS   Dreiser Studies (Dept of English, Indiana State Univ., Terre
                             Haute)
*DSA   Dickens Studies Annual: essays on Victorian fiction (Graduate
                             Center, City Univ. of New York)
*DUJ   Durham University Journal (Dept of English Studies,
                             Univ. of Durham)
*EA   Études anglaises: Grande-Bretagne, États-Unis (Paris)

*EAL   Early American Literature (Chapel Hill, NC)
*Early Medieval Europe (Harlow)
*EAS   Essays and Studies (English Assn) (Cambridge)
*EC   Essays in Criticism: a quarterly journal founded by F. W.
                             Bateson (Oxford)
*ECanW   Essays on Canadian Writing (Canadian Literary Research
                             Foundation, Toronto)
*ECent   Eighteenth Century: theory and interpretation (Texas Tech
                             Univ., Lubbock)
*ECF   Eighteenth-Century Fiction (McMaster Univ., Hamilton, Ont.)
*ECL   Eighteenth-Century Life (College of William and Mary,
                             Williamsburg, VA)
*ECS   Eighteenth-Century Studies (American Soc. for Eighteenth
                             Century Studies, Univ. of North Carolina, Chapel Hill)
*Edda: nordisk tidsskrift for litteraturforskning/Scandinavian Journal of Literary
   Research (Oslo; Elmont, NY)
*Edinburgh Bibliographical Society Transactions
*Edinburgh Review
*editio: international yearbook of scholarly editing (Tübingen)
*EDJ   Emily Dickinson Journal (Niwot, CO)
*EEM   European English Messenger (European Soc. for the Study of
                             English, Basle)
*EGN   Ellen Glasgow Newsletter (Ellen Glasgow Soc.) (Austin, TX)
*EHR   English Historical Review (Oxford)
*EI   Éire-Ireland: a journal of Irish studies (Irish American Cultural
                             Inst., St Paul, MN)
*EIUC   Estudios ingleses de la Universidad Complutense (Madrid)
*ELH: journal of English literary history (Baltimore, MD)
*ELit   Essays in Literature (Western Illinois Univ., Macomb)
*ELN   English Language Notes (Univ. of Colorado, Boulder)
*ELR   English Literary Renaissance (Univ. of Massachusetts, Amherst)
*ELT   English Literature in Transition (1880–1920) (Univ. of North
                             Carolina, Greensboro)
*Emblematica: an interdisciplinary journal of emblem studies (Pittsburgh Univ., PA)
   (New York)
*EMLS   Early Modern Literary Studies: a journal of sixteenth- and
                             seventeenth-century English literature (Univ. of British
                             Columbia, Vancouver)
*Eng   English (English Assn, Univ. of Leicester)
*EngA   English in Africa (Inst. for the Study of English in Africa, Rhodes
                             Univ., Grahamstown, South Africa)
*English Academy Review (English Academy of South Africa, Wits)
*English Dance and Song (English Folk Dance and Song Soc., London)
*English Today: the international review of the English language (Cambridge)
*EngS   English Studies: a journal of English language and literature
                             (Lisse, The Netherlands)
*EngSt   English Studies (Seoul National Univ.)
*Enlightenment and Dissent (Univ. of Wales, Aberystwyth)
*EOR   Eugene O'Neill Review (Eugene O'Neill Soc.; Suffolk Univ.,
                             Boston, MA). Formerly Eugene O'Neill Newsletter
*EP   Essays in Poetics: the journal of the British Neo-Formalist Circle
                             (Univ. of Keele)
*Epoch: a magazine of contemporary literature (Cornell Univ., Ithaca, NY)
*ER   Elizabethan Review (Kew Gardens, NY)
ERec   English Record (New York State English Council) (Albany, NY)
*ERev   English Review (Oxford Univ.)
Erevna (Athens)
*ERGS   ETC: a review of general semantics (International Soc. for
                             General Semantics, Concord, CA)
*ERR   European Romantic Review (North American Soc. for the Study
                             of Romanticism, San Francisco, CA)
*ESA   English Studies in Africa: a journal of the humanities (Univ. of
                             the Witwatersrand, South Africa)
*ESCan   English Studies in Canada (Carleton Univ., Ottawa)
ESQ: a journal of the American renaissance (Pullman, WA)

Esquire: the magazine for men (New York)
*Essays in Theatre/Études théâtrales (Univ. of Guelph, Ont.)
*Ethics: an international journal of social, political, and legal philosophy
    (Univ. of Chicago)
*Ethnologia Europaea: journal of European ethnology (Copenhagen)
*Études Écossaises (Grenoble)
*Études Lawrenciennes (Univ. Paris-X, Nanterre)
*Études littéraires (Univ. Laval, Quebec)
Euphorion: Zeitschrift für Literaturgeschichte (Heidelberg)
*Europe: revue littéraire mensuelle (Paris)
*EWeltyN   Eudora Welty Newsletter (Univ. of Toledo, OH)
*EWR   Edith Wharton Review (Edith Wharton Soc., Long Island Univ.,
                     Brooklyn, NY)
*EWW   English World-Wide: a journal of varieties of English
                     (Amsterdam; Philadelphia, PA)
*Exemplaria: a journal of theory in medieval and Renaissance studies (State Univ. of
    New York, Binghamton)
*Exp   Explicator (Helen Dwight Reed Educational Foundation,
                     Washington, DC)
*ExRC   Explorations in Renaissance Culture (South-Central
                     Renaissance Conference; Southwest Missouri State Univ.,
                     Springfield, MO)
*Extrapolation: a journal of science fiction and fantasy (Kent, OH)
*Fabula: Zeitschrift für Erzählforschung (Berlin; New York)
Familia (Oradea, Romania)
*FCS   Fifteenth-Century Studies (Univ. of Virginia, Charlottesville)
                     (Columbia, SC)
*Feminist Issues (Rutgers Univ., New Brunswick, NJ)
*Feminist Studies (Univ. of Maryland, College Park)
*FF   Folklore Forum (Bloomington, IN)
*FHQ   Florida Historical Quarterly (Florida Historical Soc., Melbourne)
*Field: contemporary poetry and poetics (Oberlin College, OH)
*FilCo   Film Comment (Film Soc. of Lincoln Center, New York)
*FilCr   Film Criticism (Allegheny College, Meadville, PA)
*FilmH   Film & History (Historians Film Committee, New Jersey Inst. of
                     Technology, Newark)
*Film History: an international journal (London)
*FilmQ   Film Quarterly (Berkeley, CA)
FilmR   Films in Review (National Board of Review of Motion Pictures,
                     New York)
*Filologia e critica (Rome)
*FiveP   Five Points (Georgia State Univ., Atlanta)
*FJ   Faulkner Journal (Univ. of Akron, OH)
*FL   Folia Linguistica: acta Societatis Linguisticae Europaeae (Berlin)
Flyway (Dept of English, Iowa State Univ., Ames). *Formerly* Poet and Critic
*FMJ   Folk Music Journal: the journal of traditional music and dance
                     (London)
*FNS   Frank Norris Studies (Frank Norris Soc., Tallahassee, FL)
*FOB   Flannery O'Connor Bulletin (Georgia College,
                     Milledgeville, GA)
*Folk Life: journal of ethnological studies (Soc. for Folk Life Studies, Leeds)
*Folklore (Journal of the Folklore Soc., University College, London)
*Fontanus: from the collections of McGill University (Montreal)
Forum: internationale Zeitschrift für kulturelle Freiheit, politische Gleichheit und
    solidarische Arbeit (Vienna)
*Forum modernes Theater (Tübingen)
*Foundation: the review of science fiction (Science Fiction Foundation, Liverpool)
*Franco-British Studies: journal of the British Institute in Paris
*Frank: an international journal of contemporary writing and art (Paris)
*Frontiers: a journal of women studies (Niwot, CO)
FS   Faulkner Studies (Kyoto, Japan)
*Fund og forskning i det Kongelige Biblioteks Samlinger (Copenhagen)
*GaHQ   Georgia Historical Quarterly (Georgia Historical Soc.,
                     Savannah)
*Gaskell Society Journal (Univ. of Manchester)

*GateH   Gateway Heritage (Missouri Historical Soc., St Louis, MO).
                          Formerly Missouri Historical Society Bulletin
*Gazette du livre médiéval (Villejuif)
*Genre: forms of discourse and culture (Dept of English, Univ. of Oklahoma, Norman)
  Germanica Olomucensia (Prague)
*GetR   Gettysburg Review (Gettysburg College, PA)
*GGA   Göttingische gelehrte Anzeigen: unter Aufsicht der Akademie
                          der Wissenschaften (Göttingen)
*GHJ   George Herbert Journal (Sacred Heart Univ., Fairfield, CT)
*Ghosts and Scholars (Hoole, Chester)
  Giornale storico della letteratura italiana (Turin)
*GissJ   Gissing Journal (Bradford)
*GL   General Linguistics (State Univ. of New York, Binghamton)
*Glossologia: a Greek annual for general and historical linguistics (Univ. of Athens)
*GPQ   Great Plains Quarterly (Center for Great Plains Studies, Univ. of
                          Nebraska at Lincoln)
*GR   Germanic Review (Washington, DC)
*Gramma: periodiko theorias & kritikes (Dept of English, Univ. of Thessaloniki)
*Gravesiana: the journal of the Robert Graves Society (Oxford)
*Green Mountains Review (Johnson State College, Johnson, VT)
  Greensboro Review (English Dept, Univ. of North Carolina at Greensboro)
*Greyfriar: Siena studies in literature (Siena College, Loudonville, NY)
*Griffithiana: journal of film history: la rivista della Cineteca del Friuli (Gemona, Italy)
*Griot: official journal of the Southern Conference on Afro-American Studies
  (Black Cultural Center, Berea College, KY) (Houston, TX)
*GRM   Germanisch-romanische Monatsschrift (Heidelberg)
*GSB   General Semantics Bulletin (Inst. of General Semantics,
                          Englewood, NJ)
*HC   Hollins Critic (Hollins College, Roanoke, VA)
  Helios (Classical Assn of the Southwestern US, Lubbock, TX)
  Hellēnika: philologikon, historikon kai laographikon periodikon syngramma (Salonika)
*HemR   Hemingway Review (Hemingway Soc., Grand Forks, ND)
  Historian: a journal of history (Phi Alpha Theta International Honor Soc. in History,
  Michigan State Univ., East Lansing)
  Historical News. *See* History Now
*Historiographia Linguistica: international journal for the history of the language sciences
  (Amsterdam; Philadelphia, PA)
  History Now: te pae tawito o te wa (History Dept, Univ. of Canterbury, Christchurch,
  New Zealand). *Formerly* Historical News
*HJR   Henry James Review (Henry James Soc., Univ. of Louisville, KY)
*HopQ   Hopkins Quarterly (International Hopkins Assn, Hamilton, Ont.)
*HT   History Today (London)
*Humanist (American Humanist Assn, Amherst, NY)
*ICAME Journal: International Computer Archive of Modern English (Norwegian
  Computing Centre for the Humanities, Bergen)
  IHB   Indiana History Bulletin (Indiana Historical Bureau,
                          Indianapolis)
*IJL   International Journal of Lexicography (Oxford)
  Illusions: a New Zealand magazine of film, television and theatre criticism (Wellington)
*Imaginaires (Reims)
*In-between: essays & studies in literary criticism (Dept of English, RLA College,
  Univ. of New Delhi)
*IndL   Indian Literature: Sahitya Akademi's bi-monthly journal
                          (New Delhi)
*IndS   Independent Shavian (Bernard Shaw Soc., New York)
*IowaR   Iowa Review (Univ. of Iowa, Iowa City)
*Irish Literary Supplement (Selden, NY)
*Irish Review (Inst. of Irish Studies, Queen's Univ. of Belfast)
*Isis: international review devoted to the history of science and its cultural influences
  (History of Science Soc., Chicago)
*IUR   Irish University Review: a journal of Irish studies (University
                          College, Dublin)
*JAAL   Journal of Adolescent and Adult Literacy (International Reading
                          Assn, Newark, DE). *Formerly* Journal of Reading

*JAC	Journal of American Culture: studies of a civilization (American Culture Assn, Bowling Green State Univ., OH)
JACJ	JAC: a journal of composition theory (Assn of Teachers of Advanced Composition, Ames, IA)
*JADT	Journal of American Drama and Theatre (Graduate School, City Univ. of New York)
*JAE	Journal of Aesthetic Education (Univ. of Illinois at Urbana-Champaign)
*JAF	Journal of American Folklore: journal of the American Folklore Society (Arlington, VA)
*JAML	Journal of Arts Management, Law, and Society (Helen Dwight Reed Educational Foundation, Washington, DC). *Formerly* Journal of Arts Management and Law
*JAR	Journal of Anthropological Research (Univ. of New Mexico, Albuquerque)
*JAStud	Journal of American Studies (Cambridge)
*JBecS	Journal of Beckett Studies (Florida State Univ., Tallahassee)
*JBS	Journal of British Studies (Chicago Univ.)
*JCanStud	Journal of Canadian Studies/Revue d'études canadiennes (Trent Univ., Peterborough, Ont.)
JCarL	Journal of Caribbean Literatures (Univ. of Northern Iowa, Cedar Falls)
*JCG	Journal of Cultural Geography (Bowling Green State Univ., OH)
*JCL	Journal of Commonwealth Literature (London)
*JCP	Journal of Canadian Poetry (Nepean, Ont.)
*JCS	Journal of Caribbean Studies (Assn of Caribbean Studies, Lexington, KY)
*JCSJ	John Clare Society Journal (Helpston, Peterborough)
*JDJ	John Donne Journal: studies in the age of Donne (John Donne Soc., Raleigh, NC)
*JDTC	Journal of Dramatic Theory and Criticism (Univ. of Kansas, Lawrence)
*JEL	Journal of English Linguistics (Univ. of Georgia, Athens)
*JELL	Journal of English Language and Literature (Seoul)
*JELLC	Journal of English Language and Literature (Chongju, Korea)
*JFA	Journal of the Fantastic in the Arts (Assn for the Fantastic in the Arts, Stow, OH)
*JfD	Journal für Druckgeschichte/Journal of Printing History (Munich)
*JFR	Journal of Folklore Research (Indiana Univ. Folklore Inst., Bloomington)
*JFV	Journal of Film and Video (University Film and Video Assn, Georgia State Univ., Atlanta)
JGE	Journal of General Education (University Park, PA)
*JGLS	Journal of the Gypsy Lore Society (Cheverly, MD)
*JJQ	James Joyce Quarterly (Univ. of Tulsa, OK)
*JLJ	Jack London Journal (Chicago)
*JLS	Journal of Literary Studies/Tydskrif vir Literaturswetenskap (Pretoria)
*JLSem	Journal of Literary Semantics: an international review (Heidelberg)
*JMCQ	Journalism and Mass Communication Quarterly (Assn for Education in Journalism & Mass Communication, Univ. of South Carolina, Columbia). *Formerly* Journalism Quarterly
*JMEMS	Journal of Medieval and Early Modern Studies (Durham, NC). *Formerly* Journal of Medieval and Renaissance Studies
*JML	Journal of Modern Literature (Temple Univ., Philadelphia, PA)
*JMMLA	Journal of the Midwest Modern Language Association (Univ. of Iowa, Iowa City)
JMRS	Journal of Medieval and Renaissance Studies. *See* JMEMS

John Dos Passos Newsletter (Dept of English, Univ. of Kansas, Lawrence)
Journal of Narrative and Life History (Mahwah, NJ)
*Journal of the Southwest (Southwest Center, Univ. of Arizona, Tucson)
*Journalism History (Greenspun School of Communication, Univ. of Nevada, Las Vegas)

*JPC	Journal of Popular Culture (Popular Culture Center, Bowling Green State Univ., OH)
*JPCL	Journal of Pidgin and Creole Languages (Southern Illinois Univ., Carbondale) (Amsterdam; Philadelphia, PA)
*JPFT	Journal of Popular Film and Television (Popular Culture Center, Bowling Green State Univ., OH) (Washington, DC)
*JPhon	Journal of Phonetics (London)
*JPHS	Journal of the Printing Historical Society (London)
JPRS	Journal of Pre-Raphaelite Studies (Lethbridge, Alta)
JQ	Journalism Quarterly. See JMCQ
*JRead	Journal of Reading (International Reading Assn, Newark, DE)
*JRS	Journal of Ritual Studies (Pittsburgh, PA)
*JSA	Joyce Studies Annual (Austin, TX)
*JSAL	Journal of South Asian Literature (Asian Studies Center, Michigan State Univ., East Lansing)
*JSchP	Journal of Scholarly Publishing (Univ. of Toronto)
*JSSE	Journal of the Short Story in English (Univ. d'Angers; Belmont Univ., Nashville, TN)
*JTD	Journal of Theatre and Drama (Faculty of Humanities, Univ. of Haifa, Mount Carmel)

Jump Cut: a review of contemporary media (Berkeley, CA)

*JWCI	Journal of the Warburg and Courtauld Institutes (Univ. of London)
*JWest	Journal of the West: an illustrated quarterly of Western American history and culture (Manhattan, KS)
*KenR	Kentucky Review (Univ. of Kentucky Library Associates, Lexington, KY)

*Kenyon Review (Kenyon College, Gambier, OH)
Kirke og kultur (Oslo)

*KJ	Kipling Journal (Kipling Soc., London)
KN	Kwartalnik Neofilologiczny (Warsaw)

*Krieg und Literatur: Beiträge zur Erforschung der Kriegs- und Antikriegsliteratur/ War and Literature: international research papers on war and anti-war literature (Osnabrück)

*KSJ	Keats–Shelley Journal: Keats, Shelley, Byron, Hunt, and their circles (Keats–Shelley Assn of America, New York)

*Landfall: New Zealand arts and letters (Dunedin)

*LangL	Language and Literature: journal of the Poetics and Linguistics Association (Harlow)

*Language & Communication: an interdisciplinary journal (Exeter)
*Language and Speech (London)
Language, Culture and Curriculum (Linguistics Inst. of Ireland, Dublin)
*Language in Society (New York)
*Legacy: a journal of American women writers (University Park, PA)
*Letteratura d'America: rivista trimestrale (Rome)
Lexi (Athens)

*LH	Lincoln Herald: magazine of Lincoln and the Civil War (Lincoln Memorial Univ., Harrogate, TN)
*LHR	Langston Hughes Review (Langston Hughes Soc.; Inst. for African American Studies, Univ. of Georgia, Athens)
*LI	Linguistic Inquiry (Cambridge, MA)

*Libraries & Culture: a journal of library history (Univ. of Texas)
*Library Review (Bradford)
*Libri: international journal of libraries and information services (Copenhagen)
*Linguist: journal of the Institute of Linguists (London)
*Linguistic Analysis (Dept of Linguistics, Univ. of Washington, Seattle)
*Linguistica Pragensia (Czech Academy of Sciences) (Amsterdam; Philadelphia, PA)
*Linguistics: an interdisciplinary journal of the language sciences (Berlin)
*Linguistics in The Netherlands (Amsterdam; Philadelphia, PA)
*Links & Letters (Dept de Filologia Anglesa i de Germanística, Univ. Autònoma de Barcelona)
*Literator: tydskrif vir besondere en vergelykende taal- en literatuurstudie/ journal of literary criticism, comparative linguistics and literary studies (Potschefstroom, South Africa)
*Literatura na Świecie (Warsaw)

*Literature and History (Manchester Univ.)
*LitFQ   Literature/Film Quarterly (Salisbury State Univ., MD)
*LitMed   Literature and Medicine (Baltimore, MD)
*LitPs   Literature and Psychology (National Assn for Psychoanalytic
                      Criticism; Rhode Island Univ., Providence)
*LitR   Literary Review: an international review of contemporary
                      writing (Fairleigh Dickinson Univ., Madison, NJ)
*Litteraria Pragensia: studies in literature and culture (Center for Comparative Studies,
   Charles Univ., Prague) (Amsterdam)
*LitTheol   Literature & Theology: an interdisciplinary journal of theory and
                      criticism (Oxford)
*Livres du mois (Paris)
*LJGG   Literaturwissenschaftliches Jahrbuch im Auftrage der Görres-
                      Gesellschaft (Görres-Gesellschaft zur Pflege der Wissenschaft,
                      Cologne) (Berlin)
*LLM   Language and Linguistics in Melanesia: journal of the Linguistic
                      Society of Papua New Guinea and the Society on Pidgins and
                      Creoles in Melanesia (Ukarumpa via Lae, Papua New Guinea)
*LMN   Lubelskie Materiały Neofilologiczne (Lublin, Poland)
*Long Room: Ireland's journal for the history of the book (Friends of Trinity College
   Library, Dublin)
*LRB   London Review of Books
*LRC   Literary Review of Canada: a review of Canadian books on
                      culture, politics and society (Toronto)
*LU   Lion and the Unicorn: a critical journal of children's literature
                      (Mankato State Univ., MN) (Baltimore, MD)
   Luceafărul (Bucharest)
*LVC   Language Variation and Change (Cambridge)
*LWU   Literatur in Wissenschaft und Unterricht (Englisches Seminar,
                      Univ. of Kiel) (Würzburg)
*MÆ   Medium Ævum (Soc. for the Study of Medieval Languages and
                      Literature, Oxford)
*Mail & Guardian (Johannesburg)
*MalaR   Malahat Review (Univ. of Victoria, Victoria, B.C.)
*MalLR   Malcolm Lowry Review (Dept of English, Wilfrid Laurier Univ.,
                      Waterloo, Ont.)
   Mānoa: a Pacific journal of international writing (Honolulu, HI)
*MatC   Material Culture: journal of the Pioneer American Society
                      (Wilmington, NC)
*Meanjin (Univ. of Melbourne, Parkville, Vic.)
*Med   Mediævistik: internationale Zeitschrift für interdisziplinäre
                      Mittelalterforschung (Frankfurt)
*MedRen   Medieval & Renaissance Drama in England: an annual
                      gathering of research, criticism and reviews (New York)
*MedStud   Mediaeval Studies (Pontifical Inst. of Mediaeval Studies,
                      Toronto)
*MelSE   Melville Society Extracts (Melville Soc. of America)
                      (Texas A&M Univ., College Station, TX)
   MELUS: the journal of the Society for the Study of the Multi-Ethnic Literature of the
   United States (Univ. of Massachusetts, Amherst)
   Mentalities/Mentalités (Hamilton, New Zealand)
*MESN   Medieval English Studies Newsletter (Centre for Medieval
                      English Studies, Univ. of Tokyo)
*Metro (Auckland)
*MFS   Modern Fiction Studies (Purdue Univ., West Lafayette, IN)
*MFSJ   Missouri Folklore Society Journal (Columbia, MO)
*MichH   Michigan History Magazine (Dept of State, Michigan Historical
                      Center, Lansing)
*MichQR   Michigan Quarterly Review (Univ. of Michigan, Ann Arbor)
*MidAF   Mid-America Folklore (Mid-America Folklore Soc.,
                      Lyon College, Batesville, AR)
*Midamerica (Soc. for the Study of Midwestern Literature, East Lansing, MI)
*MidF   Midwestern Folklore (Hoosier Folklore Soc.; Indiana
                      State Univ., Terre Haute, IN)

*MidM	Midwestern Miscellany (Soc. for the Study of Midwestern Literature, Michigan State Univ., East Lansing, MI)
*MidQ	Midwest Quarterly: a journal of contemporary thought (Pittsburg State Univ., KS)
*MinnR	Minnesota Review: a journal of committed writing: fiction, poetry, essays, reviews (Dept of English, East Carolina Univ., Greenville, NC)
*Misc	Miscelánea: a journal of English and American Studies (Zaragoza Univ.)

Missouri Historical Society Bulletin. *See* GateH

*MLQ	Modern Language Quarterly: a journal of literary history (Duke Univ., Durham, NC)
*MLR	Modern Language Review (London)
*MLS	Modern Language Studies (Northeast Modern Language Assn; Brown Univ.) (Potsdam, NY)
*ModAge	Modern Age: a quarterly review (Intercollegiate Studies Inst., Bryn Mawr, PA)
*ModDr	Modern Drama (Graduate Centre for Study of Drama, Univ. of Toronto) (Downsview, Ont.)

*Moderne Sprachen (Salzburg)
*Modernism/Modernity (Baltimore, MD)

*MP	Modern Philology: a journal devoted to research in medieval and modern literature (Univ. of Chicago)
*MQ	Milton Quarterly (Milton Soc. of America; Ohio Univ., Athens)
*MS	Moderna språk (Riksfœreningen fœr Lærarna i Moderna Språk/Modern Language Teachers' Assn of Sweden) (Visingsœ)
MsM	Ms (New York)
*MSS	Manuscripts (Manuscript Soc., Burbank, CA)
*MStud	Milton Studies (Pittsburgh, PA)

*Music in the Air (Palmerston North, New Zealand)
*Mythlore: a journal of J. R. R. Tolkien, C. S. Lewis, Charles Williams, and the genres of myth and fantasy studies (Mythopoeic Soc., Altadena, CA)
*Mythprint (Mythopoeic Soc., Altadena, CA)

*NADS	Newsletter of the American Dialect Society (MacMurray College, Jacksonville, IL)

*Natural Language and Linguistic Theory (Dordrecht)

*NCarF	North Carolina Folklore Journal (North Carolina Folklore Soc.; Appalachian State Univ., Boone, NC)
*NCL	Notes on Contemporary Literature (West Georgia College, Carrollton)
*NCLR	North Carolina Literary Review (Dept of English, East Carolina Univ., Greenville)
*NCS	Nineteenth-Century Studies (Nineteenth-Century Studies Assn, The Citadel, Charleston, SC)
NDEJ	Notre Dame English Journal. *See* ReLit
NDH	North Dakota History: journal of the Northern plains (State Historical Soc. of North Dakota, Bismarck)
*NDQ	North Dakota Quarterly (Univ. of North Dakota, Grand Forks)

*Nea Hestia (Athens)
Nea Poreia (Thessaloniki, Greece)
*NELM News (National English Literary Museum, Grahamstown, South Africa)
*NELS: Proceedings of the North East Linguistic Society (Amherst, MA)
*Neohelicon: acta comparationis litterarum universarum (Akadémiai Kiadó, Budapest)
*Neophilologus: an international journal of modern and mediaeval language and literature (Dordrecht; Boston, MA; London)

*NEQ	New England Quarterly: a historical review of New England life and letters (Northeastern Univ., Boston, MA)
NER	New England Review: Middlebury Series (Middlebury College) (Hanover, NH)

*Nestroyana (Vienna)

*NETJ	New England Theatre Journal (New England Theatre Conference, Boston, MA)

*New Coin (Inst. for the Study of English in Africa, Rhodes Univ., Grahamstown).
  Formerly New Coin Poetry
*New Contrast: South African literary journal (Cape Town)
*New Courant (Dept of English, Univ. of Helsinki)
*NewL   New Leader: a bi-weekly of news and opinion (American Labor
                    Conference on International Affairs, New York)
*New Letters: a magazine of writing and art (Univ. of Missouri, Kansas City)
*New Zealand Books (Wellington)
  New Zealand Journal of French Studies (Massey Univ., Palmerston North)
*New Zealand National Bibliography (National Library of New Zealand, Wellington)
*New Zealand Speech-Language Therapists' Journal (New Zealand Speech-Language
  Therapists' Assn, Christchurch)
  New Zealand Studies (Wellington). *Formerly* Stout Centre Review
*NF   Northeast Folklore (Maine Folklife Center, Univ. of Maine,
                    Orono)
*NHR   Nathaniel Hawthorne Review (Nathaniel Hawthorne Soc.;
                    Duquesne Univ., Pittsburgh, PA)
NiemR   Nieman Reports (Nieman Foundation, Harvard Univ.,
                    Cambridge, MA)
*NIF   Newsletter on Intellectual Freedom (American Library Assn,
                    Chicago)
  Nimrod: international journal of prose and poetry (Arts and Humanities Council of
  Tulsa, OK)
*NineL   Nineteenth-Century Literature (Berkeley; Los Angeles, CA)
NJH   New Jersey History: a magazine of New Jersey history (New
                    Jersey Historical Soc., Newark)
*NLH   New Literary History: a journal of theory and interpretation
                    (Univ. of Virginia, Charlottesville) (Baltimore, MD)
*NM   Neuphilologische Mitteilungen: bulletin de la Société
                    Néophilologique/ bulletin of the Modern Language Society
                    (Helsinki)
*NMAS   Newsletter of the Margaret Atwood Society (Tampa, FL)
*NNER   Northern New England Review (Franklin Pierce College,
                    Rindge, NH)
*NoB   Namn och bygd: tidskrift för nordisk ortnamnsforskning/journal
                    for Nordic place-name research (Uppsala)
*NOR   New Orleans Review (Loyola Univ., New Orleans, LA)
*Northwest Review (Univ. of Oregon, Eugene)
*Notes on Modern Irish Literature (Butler, PA)
  Novel: a forum on fiction (Brown Univ., Providence, RI)
*NOWELE: North-Western European Language Evolution (Odense)
*NQ   Notes and Queries: for readers and writers, collectors and
                    librarians (Oxford)
*NS   Neueren Sprachen (Frankfurt am Main)
NSch   New Scholasticism. *See* ACPQ
*NTrans   Notes on Translation (Summer Inst. of Linguistics, Dallas, TX)
NwOQ   Northwest Ohio Quarterly (Maumee Valley Historical Soc.,
                    Maumee, OH)
*NWSAJ   NWSA Journal (National Women's Studies Assn,
                    College Park, MD)
*NYF   New York Folklore (New York Folklore Soc., Newfield, NY)
*NYTM   New York Times Magazine (New York)
*NZEJ   New Zealand English Journal (Univ. of Canterbury,
                    Christchurch). *Formerly* New Zealand English Newsletter
*NZJH   New Zealand Journal of History (Univ. of Auckland)
*NZLib   New Zealand Libraries (New Zealand Library and
                    Information Assn, Wellington)
*NZList   New Zealand Listener (Wellington)
*NZSAL   New Zealand Studies in Applied Linguistics (English
                    Language Inst., Victoria Univ., Wellington)
*Ob   Obsidian II: Black literature in review (North Carolina
                    State Univ., Raleigh)
*OhioanaQ   Ohioana Quarterly (Ohioana Library Assn, Columbus, OH)
*OnS   On-Stage Studies (Dept of Theatre & Dance, Univ. of Colorado,
                    Boulder)

*Onthebus (Los Angeles, CA)
*OntR   Ontario Review (Princeton, NJ)
*Oral Tradition (Univ. of Missouri, Columbia)
 OreHQ   Oregon Historical Quarterly (Oregon Historical Soc., Portland)
*Pacific Way (Auckland)
*PADS   Publications of the American Dialect Society (University, AL)
*Paideuma: a journal devoted to Ezra Pound scholarship (Univ. of Maine, Orono)
*Parergon: bulletin of the Australian and New Zealand Association for Medieval and
     Early Modern Studies (Sydney)
 Parousia (Univ. of Athens)
*PBSA   Papers of the Bibliographical Society of America (New York)
*PCR   Popular Culture Review (Far West Popular and American
                             Culture Assns; Univ. of Nevada, Las Vegas)
*PeakeS   Peake Studies (Orzens, Vaud, Switzerland)
*Persuasions (Jane Austen Soc. of North America, New York)
*PH   Przeglad Humanistyczny (Warsaw)
*Philologike Protochronia (Athens)
*Philosophy (Royal Inst. of Philosophy, Cambridge)
*Playboy (Chicago)
*PLL   Papers on Language & Literature: a journal for scholars and
                             critics of language and literature (Southern Illinois Univ.,
                             Edwardsville)
*Ploughshares: a journal of new writing (Emerson College, Boston, MA)
*PMLA: Publications of the Modern Language Association of America (New York)
*PMPA   Publications of the Missouri Philological Association (Central
                             Missouri State Univ., Warrensburg)
*PN Review (Manchester)
*PoeM   Poe Messenger (Poe Foundation, Richmond, VA)
 PoeSAN   Poe Studies Association Newsletter (Worcester, MA)
*PoetA   Poetica: Zeitschrift für Sprach- und Literaturwissenschaft
                             (Fachgruppe Literaturwissenschaft der Univ. Konstanz)
                             (Munich)
 PoetC   Poet and Critic. See Flyway
*Poet's Voice (Salzburg)
*PoetT   Poetica: an international journal of linguistic-literary studies
                             (Tokyo)
*PolAS   Polish–Anglo-Saxon Studies (Adam Mickiewicz Univ., Poznań,
                             Poland)
*PowJ   Powys Journal (Powys Soc., Bath)
*Pragmatics, Ideology, and Contacts Bulletin (Helsinki)
 Prairie Journal (Calgary, Alta)
*Pre/Text: a journal of rhetorical theory (Univ. of Texas, Arlington)
*Pretexts: studies in writing and culture (Univ. of Cape Town)
*PrH   Printing History: journal of the American Printing History
                             Association (New York)
*Printout (Norwell, MA)
*Prism(s): essays in Romanticism (American Conference on Romanticism,
     Brigham Young Univ., Provo, UT)
*Prose Studies: history, theory, criticism (London)
*Proteus: a journal of ideas (Shippensburg Univ., Shippensburg, PA)
*Proverbium: yearbook of international proverb scholarship (Univ. of Vermont,
     Burlington)
 PrS   Prairie Schooner (Univ. of Nebraska, Lincoln)
*PS   Post Script: essays in film and the humanities (East Texas
                             State Univ., Commerce)
*PSiCL   Papers and Studies in Contrastive Linguistics (Adam
                             Mickiewicz Univ., Poznań, Poland)
*PT   Poetics Today: international journal for theory and analysis of
                             literature and communication (Durham, NC) (Porter Inst. for
                             Poetics and Semiotics, Tel Aviv Univ.)
*PTFS   Publications of the Texas Folklore Society (Nacogdoches)
*PULC   Princeton University Library Chronicle (Princeton, NJ)
*Pynchon Notes (Miami Univ., Hamilton, OH; English Dept, Univ. of Wisconsin,
     Eau Claire)

*QCH   Queen City Heritage (Cincinnati Historical Soc.,
                     Cincinnati, OH)
*QLLSM   Quaderni del Dipartimento di Lingue e Letterature Straniere
                     Moderne (Univ. of Genoa)
*QRFV   Quarterly Review of Film and Video (New York)
*Quaderni di lingue e letterature (Univ. degli Studi di Verona)
*Quondam et Futurus: a journal of Arthurian interpretations (Southern Methodist Univ.,
   Dallas, TX)
*Quote Unquote (Auckland)
*Q/W/E/R/T/Y: arts, littératures & civilisations du monde anglophone (Pau Univ.)
*RAEI   Revista alicantina de estudios ingleses (Alicante Univ.)
*RAL   Research in African Literatures (Bloomington, IL)
   Ramuri (Craiova, Romania)
*RANAM   Recherches anglaises et nord-américaines (Univ. des Sciences
                     Humaines de Strasbourg)
*Raritan: a quarterly review (Rutgers Univ., New Brunswick, NJ)
*RCEI   Revista canaria de estudios ingleses (Laguna Univ., Tenerife)
*Reader: essays in reader-oriented theory, criticism, and pedagogy (Michigan
   Technological Univ., Houghton)
*REAL   RE:AL, the Journal of Liberal Arts (College of Liberal Arts,
                     Stephen F. Austin State Univ., Nacogdoches, TX)
*RecL   Recovering Literature: a journal of contextualist criticism
                     (Alpine, CA)
*ReLit   Religion and Literature (Univ. of Notre Dame, IN). *Formerly*
                     Notre Dame English Journal
*Ren   Renascence: essays on value in literature (Marquette Univ.,
                     Milwaukee, WI)
*RenD   Renaissance Drama (Evanston, IL)
*RenP   Renaissance Papers (Southeastern Renaissance Conference,
                     North Carolina State Univ., Raleigh)
*Representations (Univ. of California, Berkeley)
*RES   Review of English Studies: a quarterly journal of English
                     literature and the English language (Oxford)
*Review (Charlottesville, VA)
*RFR   Robert Frost Review (Robert Frost Soc.; Dept of English,
                     Winthrop Univ., Rock Hill, SC)
*RhR   Rhetoric Review (Univ. of Arizona, Tucson)
   RITL   Revista de istorie si teorie literară (Bucharest)
*RMRLL   Rocky Mountain Review of Language and Literature (Rocky
                     Mountain Modern Language Assn, Boise, ID)
*Romantist (F. Marion Crawford Memorial Soc., Nashville, TN)
*RomLit   România literară: săptăminal de literatură si artă editat de
                     Uniunea Scriitorilor din Republica Socialistă România
                     (Bucharest)
*RR   Romanic Review (Dept of French & Romance Philology,
                     Columbia Univ., NY)
   RRL   Revue roumaine de linguistique (Bucharest). *Includes* Cahiers de
                     linguistique théorique et appliquée
*RSAJ   Rivista di Studi Nord-Americani (Florence)
   RSAP Newsletter (Research Soc. for American Periodicals, Denton, TX)
*RSQ   Rhetoric Society Quarterly (Rhetoric Soc. of America, St Cloud,
                     MN)
*RT   Radical Teacher: a news journal of socialist theory and practice
                     (Boston Women's Teachers' Group, Cambridge, MA)
*Ruch Literacki (Polish Academy of Sciences, Warsaw)
*Ruskin Gazette (Oxford)
*RWT   Readerly/Writerly Texts: essays on literature, literary/textual
                     criticism, and pedagogy (Eastern New Mexico Univ., Portales)
   SAB   South Atlantic Bulletin. *See* SAtlR
*SAC   Studies in the Age of Chaucer (New Chaucer Soc.,
                     Ohio State Univ., Columbus)
*SAF   Studies in American Fiction (Dept of English,
                     Northeastern Univ., Boston, MA)
*Sagetrieb: a journal devoted to poets in the Imagist/Objectivist tradition
   (National Poetry Foundation; Univ. of Maine, Orono)

*SAH   Studies in American Humor (Southwest Texas State Univ.,
                        San Marcos)
*SAIL   Studies in American Indian Literatures: the journal of the
                        Association for the Study of American Indian Literatures
                        (Richmond, VA)
*SAJMRS   Southern African Journal of Medieval and Renaissance
                        Studies/Suider-Afrikaanse Tydskrif vir Middeleeuse en
                        Renaissancestudies (Rand-Afrikaans Univ., Johannesburg)
*SA Journal of Linguistics   South African Journal of Linguistics/Suid-Afrikaanse
                        Tydskrif vir Taalkunde (Linguistics Soc. of Southern
                        Africa, Pretoria)
*Salmagundi: a quarterly of the humanities & social sciences (Skidmore College,
    Saratoga Springs, NY)
  Samtiden: tidsskrift for politikk, litteratur og samfunnsspørsmål (Oslo)
*Samuel Beckett Today/aujourd'hui (Amsterdam)
*SAP   Studia Anglica Posnaniensia: an international review of English
                        studies (Adam Mickiewicz Univ., Poznań, Poland)
*SARB   Southern African Review of Books (Ulm, Germany)
*SATJ   South African Theatre Journal (Uniedal)
*SAtlR   South Atlantic Review (South Atlantic Modern Language Assn;
                        Georgia State Univ., Atlanta). *Formerly* South Atlantic Bulletin
*SB   Studies in Bibliography: papers of the Bibliographical Society of
                        the University of Virginia (Charlottesville)
*SBJ   Saul Bellow Journal (West Bloomfield, MI)
*SCJ   Southern Communication Journal (Southern States
                        Communication Assn, Univ. of Memphis, TN). *Formerly*
                        Southern Speech Communication Journal
*Scriblerian   Scriblerian and the Kit-Cats (Temple Univ., Philadelphia, PA)
*Scrutiny2 (Dept of English, Univ. of South Africa, Pretoria). *Formerly* UNISA
    English Studies
*SCS   Studies in Contemporary Satire: a creative and critical journal
                        (Univ. of Nebraska at Kearney)
*SDR   South Dakota Review (Univ. of South Dakota, Vermillion)
*SECOLR   SECOL Review: Southeastern Conference on Linguistics
                        (Memphis State Univ., Memphis, TN)
  Secolul 20: revista de literatura universala (Uniunea Scriitorilor din România, Bucharest)
*SEL   Studies in English Literature/Eibungaku kenkyu (English
                        Literary Soc. of Japan/Nihon Eibungakkai, Tokyo)
  Selecta: journal of the Pacific Northwest Council on Foreign Languages (Corvallis, OR)
*SELIM   Revista de la Sociedad Española de Lengua y Literatura Inglesa
                        Medieval (Oviedo Univ.)
*SELit   Studies in English Literature 1500–1900 (Rice Univ.,
                        Houston, TX)
*SEVEN: an Anglo-American literary review (Wheaton College, IL)
*SF   Southern Folklore (Lexington, KY)
*Shakespeare Society of Southern Africa: Newsletter and Occasional Papers and Reviews
    (Rhodes Univ., Grahamstown, South Africa)
*Shakespeare Yearbook (Lewiston, NY)
*Shandean: an annual volume devoted to Laurence Sterne and his works (Laurence
    Sterne Trust, Amsterdam)
*SHARP News (Soc. for the History of Authorship, Reading and Publishing, Drew Univ.,
    Madison, NJ)
*Shaw (University Park, PA)
*ShB   Shakespeare Bulletin: a journal of performance criticism and
                        scholarship, incorporating Shakespeare on Film Newsletter
                        (Lafayette College, Easton, PA)
*Shen   Shenandoah: the Washington and Lee University review
                        (Lexington, VA)
*SHogg   Studies in Hogg and His World (Univ. of Stirling)
*ShR   Shakespeare Review (Seoul)
*SHum   Studies in the Humanities (Indiana Univ. of Pennsylvania)
*Signal: approaches to children's books (Stroud)
*Signs: journal of women in culture and society (Chicago)
  Sites: a journal for radical perspectives on culture (Palmerston North, New Zealand)

*SJ	Shakespeare Jahrbuch (Deutsche Shakespeare-Gesellschaft, Bochum)
*Skrift (Univ. of Oslo)	
*SL	Studies in Language: international journal sponsored by the foundation 'Foundations of Language' (Amsterdam; Philadelphia, PA)
*SLang	Scottish Language (Assn for Scottish Literary Studies, Aberdeen Univ.)
*SLI	Studies in the Literary Imagination (Georgia State Univ., Atlanta)
*SLJ	Scottish Literary Journal (Assn for Scottish Literary Studies, Aberdeen Univ.)
*SM	Studia Mystica (Skidmore College; Texas A&M Univ.) (Sacramento, CA)
Small Press Review/Small Magazine Review (Paradise, CA)	
*SN	Studia Neophilologica: a journal of Germanic and Romance languages and literature (Oslo; Cambridge, MA)
*SNL	Shakespeare Newsletter (Dept of English, Iona College, New Rochelle, NY)
*SoCR	South Carolina Review (Clemson Univ., Clemson, SC)
SoHR	Southern Humanities Review (Auburn Univ., AL)
*SoLJ	Southern Literary Journal (Chapel Hill, NC)
Something Quarterly (Gauteng, South Africa)	
*SoQ	Southern Quarterly: a journal of the arts in the South (Univ. of Southern Mississippi, Hattiesburg)
*Soundings: an interdisciplinary journal (Soc. for Values in Higher Education, Georgetown Univ., Washington, DC; Univ. of Tennessee, Knoxville)	
*South African Journal of Library and Information Science (South African Inst. for Librarianship and Information Science, Pretoria)	
*Southfields (London)	
*SP	Studies in Philology (Univ. of North Carolina, Chapel Hill)
*Span: journal of the South Pacific Association for Commonwealth Literature and Language Studies (Murdoch, W. Australia)	
*Spectakel (Salzburg)	
*SPELL	Swiss Papers in English Language and Literature (Tübingen)
*SpenN	Spenser Newsletter (Dept of English, Kansas State Univ., Manhattan)
*Sport (Christchurch, New Zealand)	
SPR	Southern Poetry Review (Dept of English, Univ. of North Carolina, Charlotte)
*Spr	Sprachkunst: Beiträge zur Literaturwissenschaft (Bundesministerium für Wissenschaft und Forschung, Vienna)
*Spring: the journal of the e. e. cummings Society (Flushing, NY)	
*SQ	Shakespeare Quarterly (Folger Shakespeare Library, Washington, DC)
*SR	Studies in Romanticism (Boston Univ., MA)
*SRASP	Shakespeare and Renaissance Association of West Virginia: selected papers (Marshall Univ., Huntington, VA)
*SRev	Southwest Review (Southern Methodist Univ., Dallas, TX)
*SSA	Shakespeare in Southern Africa: journal of the Shakespeare Society of Southern Africa (Rhodes Univ., Grahamstown)
SSCJ	Southern Speech Communication Journal. See SCJ
*SSF	Studies in Short Fiction (Newberry College, Newberry, SC)
*SSL	Studies in Scottish Literature (Univ. of South Carolina, Columbia)
*SSMLN	Society for the Study of Midwestern Literature Newsletter (Michigan State Univ., East Lansing)
*SSp	Studies in Spirituality (Kampen, The Netherlands)
*SSQ	Social Science Quarterly (Southwestern Social Science Assn) (Austin, TX)
*SStud	Shakespeare Studies (Madison, NJ)
*SStudT	Shakespeare Studies (Shakespeare Soc. of Japan, Tokyo)
*StAD	Studies in American Drama, 1945–Present (Columbus, OH)
*StAL	Studies in American Literature/Amerika bungaku kenkyu (Kobe)

Stanford Humanities Review (Stanford Humanities Center, Stanford, CA)
*Steaua (Bucharest)
SteiN   Steinbeck Newsletter (San Jose State Univ., CA)
*SteiQ   Steinbeck Quarterly (International Steinbeck Soc.;
                        Ball State Univ., Muncie, IN)
StUCNPhil   Studia Universitatis Babes-Bolyai. Series Philologia
                        (Cluj-Napoca, Romania)
*StudAJL   Studies in American Jewish Literature (Dept of English,
                        Pennsylvania State Univ., University Park)
*StudAR   Studies in the American Renaissance (Charlottesville, VA)
*StudCanL   Studies in Canadian Literature/Études en littérature canadienne
                        (Univ. of New Brunswick, Fredericton)
*StudLS   Studies in the Linguistic Sciences (Dept of Linguistics & School
                        of Humanities, Univ. of Illinois, Urbana)
*StudME   Studies in Medieval English Language and Literature (Japan
                        Soc. for Medieval English Studies, Tokyo)
*StudN   Studies in the Novel (Univ. of North Texas, Denton)
*Style (Northern Illinois Univ., DeKalb)
*Takahe (Christchurch, New Zealand)
*Talisman: a journal of contemporary poetry and poetics (Jersey City, NJ)
*Tampa Review (Tampa Univ., FL)
*TCL   Twentieth Century Literature: a scholarly and critical journal
                        (Hofstra Univ., Hempstead, NY)
TDR/The Drama Review: a journal of performance studies (Tisch School of the Arts;
   New York Univ.) (Cambridge, MA)
*Teaching and Learning (Joensuu)
*Te Reo: journal of the Linguistic Society of New Zealand (Auckland)
*TexPres   Text & Presentation: the journal of the Comparative Drama
                        Conference (Dept of Classics, Univ. of Florida, Gainesville)
*TexR   Texas Review (Dept of English, Sam Houston State Univ.,
                        Huntsville, TX)
*Text: transactions of the Society for Textual Scholarship (Ann Arbor, MI)
*Textures (Univ. of Orange Free State, South Africa)
*Textus: English studies in Italy (Genoa)
*TFSB   Tennessee Folklore Society Bulletin (Middle Tennessee
                        State Univ., Murfreesboro)
*THC   Theatre History in Canada (Assn for Canadian Theatre
                        Research, Graduate Centre for Study of Drama, Univ. of
                        Toronto)
*Theater (Yale School of Drama; Yale Repertory Theater, New Haven, CT)
*Theoria: a journal of studies in the arts, humanities and social sciences (Univ. of Natal,
   Pietermaritzburg)
*THJ   Thomas Hardy Journal (Thomas Hardy Soc., Dorchester)
*ThN   Thackeray Newsletter (Mississippi State Univ., Starkville)
THS   Theatre History Studies (Mid-America Theatre Conference,
                        Central College, Pella, IA)
*TJ   Theatre Journal (Assn for Theatre in Higher Education)
                        (Baltimore, MD)
*TLR   Turnbull Library Record (Alexander Turnbull Library,
                        Wellington)
*TLS   Times Literary Supplement (London)
*Topic: a journal of the liberal arts (Washington & Jefferson College, Washington, PA)
TPAPA   Transactions and Proceedings of the American Philological
                        Society (Case Western Reserve Univ., Cleveland, OH)
*TPB   Tennessee Philological Bulletin: proceedings of the annual
                        meeting of the Tennessee Philological Association
                        (Univ. of Tennessee at Chattanooga)
TPQ   Text and Performance Quarterly (Speech Communication Assn,
                        Annandale, VA)
*TransR   Translation Review (American Literary Translators Assn;
                        Univ. of Texas at Dallas, Richardson)
*TRB   Tennyson Research Bulletin (Tennyson Soc., Lincoln)

*TRC   Theatre Research in Canada/Recherches théâtrales au Canada (Assn for Canadian Theatre Research, Graduate Centre for Study of Drama, Univ. of Toronto). *Formerly* Theatre History in Canada

*TRI   Theatre Research International (International Federation for Theatre Research) (Oxford; Cary, NC)

*Tristania: a journal devoted to Tristan studies (Tristan Soc., Chattanooga, TN)

*TSB   Thoreau Society Bulletin: devoted to the life and writings of Henry David Thoreau (Thoreau Soc.; Dept of English, East Carolina Univ., Breenville, NC)

*TSL   Tennessee Studies in Literature (Univ. of Tennessee, Knoxville)

*TSLL   Texas Studies in Literature and Language (Univ. of Texas, Austin)

*TSWL   Tulsa Studies in Women's Literature (Univ. of Tulsa, OK)

*TT   Theatre Topics (Assn for Theatre in Higher Education) (Baltimore, MD)

*Twainian (Mark Twain Research Foundation, Hannibal LaGrange College, Hannibal, MO)

*TWR   Thomas Wolfe Review (Thomas Wolfe Soc.; Dept of English, Univ. of Akron, OH)

*Tygiel Kultury (Łódź)

*UC   Upstart Crow: a Shakespeare journal (Drury College, Springfield, MO)

*UDR   University of Dayton Review (Dayton, OH)

*UES   UNISA English Studies. *See* Scrutiny2

*University Calendars (New Zealand)

*Utopian Studies (Soc. for Utopian Studies, Univ. of Missouri, St Louis)

*UTQ   University of Toronto Quarterly: a Canadian journal of the humanities (Toronto)

Vatra: lunar social-cultural (Tîrgu-Mures, Romania)

*Verbatim: the language quarterly (Indianapolis, IN; Aylesbury)

*VH   Vermont History (Vermont Historical Soc., Montpelier)

*Viator: medieval and Renaissance studies (Center for Medieval and Renaissance Studies, Univ. of California, Los Angeles)

*VIEWS: Vienna English Working Papers

*VIJ   Victorians Institute Journal (Chapel Hill, NC)

Vinduet (Oslo)

*VLC   Victorian Literature and Culture (Browning Inst., New York). *Formerly* Browning Institute Studies

VLT   Velvet Light Trap: review of cinema (Austin, TX)

*VP   Victorian Poetry (West Virginia Univ., Morgantown)

*VPR   Victorian Periodicals Review (Niwot, CO)

*VS   Victorian Studies: a journal of the humanities, arts and sciences (Indiana Univ., Bloomington)

*WCL   West Coast Line: a journal of contemporary writing and criticism (Simon Fraser Univ., Burnaby, B.C.). *Formerly* West Coast Review

*WCPMN   Willa Cather Pioneer Memorial Newsletter (Willa Cather Pioneer Memorial & Educational Foundation, Red Cloud, NB)

WCR   West Coast Review. *See* WCL

*WCWR   William Carlos Williams Review (Univ. of Texas, Austin)

*WD   Writer's Digest (Cincinnati, OH)

*WE   Winesburg Eagle: the official publication of the Sherwood Anderson Society (Blacksburg, VA)

*WebS   Weber Studies: an interdisciplinary humanities journal (Weber State Univ., Ogden, UT)

*WHR   Western Humanities Review (Dept of English, Univ. of Utah, Salt Lake City)

*Wide Angle: a quarterly journal of film history, theory, criticism & practice (Ohio Univ. School of Film, Athens)

*WLA   War, Literature, and the Arts (US Air Force Academy, Colorado Springs, CO)

*WLR   World Literary Review (Dept of English, Univ. College, Thiruvananthapuram, India)

*WLT   World Literature Today: a literary quarterly of the University of
                  Oklahoma (Norman)
*WMQ   William and Mary Quarterly: a magazine of early American
                  history and culture (Inst. of Early American History and
                  Culture, Williamsburg, VA)
   Women's Studies Journal (Auckland)
*WorldE   World Englishes: journal of English as an international and
                  intranational language (Urbana, IL)
*WP   Women & Performance: a journal of feminist theory (Women &
                  Performance Project, New York)
*WS   Women's Studies: an interdisciplinary journal (New York)
*WVH   West Virginia History (Charleston, VA)
*WWPL   Wellington Working Papers in Linguistics
*WWQR   Walt Whitman Quarterly Review (Whitman Studies Assn, Univ.
                  of Iowa, Iowa City)
*Yearbook of Morphology (Dordrecht)
   Year's Work in Dime Novels, Series Books, and Pulp Magazines (Happy Hours
   Brotherhood, Dundas, MN). *Supp. to* DNR
*Yeats Annual (Basingstoke)
*YES   Yearbook of English Studies (Modern Humanities
                  Research Assn) (Leeds)
*YJC   Yale Journal of Criticism (New Haven, CT)
*YJLH   Yale Journal of Law & the Humanities (New Haven, CT)
*YLS   Yearbook of Langland Studies (College of Arts and Letters,
                  Michigan State Univ., East Lansing)
*YREAL   REAL: the yearbook of research in English and American
                  literature (Inst. für Anglistik & Amerikanistik der
                  Univ. Giessen)
*YTM   Yearbook for Traditional Music (International Council for
                  Traditional Music, Columbia Univ., New York)
*YWCCT   Year's Work in Critical and Cultural Theory (English Assn)
                  (Oxford)
*YWES   Year's Work in English Studies (London)
*ZAA   Zeitschrift für Anglistik und Amerikanistik (Tübingen)
*ZNWO   Zeszyty Naukowe Wyższej Szkoły Pedagogicznej w Opolu:
                  Filologia Angielska (Opole, Poland)
*ZRL   Zagadnienia Rodzajów Literackich: woprosy literaturnych
                  żanrov/les problèmes des genres littéraires (Łódź, Poland)

ANNUAL BIBLIOGRAPHY OF ENGLISH LANGUAGE AND LITERATURE
1996
FESTSCHRIFTEN AND OTHER COLLECTIONS

African-American Autobiography

1. ANDREWS, WILLIAM L. (ed.). African-American autobiography: a collection of critical essays. Englewood Cliffs, NJ: Prentice Hall, 1992. pp. viii, 231. (New century views.)

ANDREWS, WILLIAM L. The representation of slavery and the rise of Afro-American literary realism 1865–1920. 77–89

CARBY, HAZEL V. 'Hear my voice, careless daughters': narratives of slave and free women before Emancipation. 59–76

DAVIS, CHARLES T. From experience to eloquence: Richard Wright's *Black Boy* as art. 138–50

GATES, HENRY LOUIS, JR. James Gronniosaw and the trope of the talking book. 8–25

KENT, GEORGE E. Maya Angelou's *I Know Why the Caged Bird Sings* and Black autobiographical tradition. 162–70

LIONNET, FRANÇOISE. Autoethnography: the an-archic style of *Dust Tracks on a Road*. 113–37

McDOWELL, DEBORAH E. In the first place: making Frederick Douglass and the Afro-American narrative tradition. 36–58

OLNEY, JAMES. The value of autobiography for comparative studies: African *vs* Western autobiography. 212–23

PAQUET, SANDRA POUCHET. West Indian autobiography. 196–211

STEPTO, ROBERT B. Narration, authentication, and authorial control in Frederick Douglass' *Narrative* of 1845. 26–35

STONE, ALBERT E. After *Black Boy* and *Dusk of Dawn*: patterns in recent Black autobiography. 171–95

AIDS: the Literary Response

2. NELSON, EMMANUEL S. (ed.). AIDS: the literary response. New York: Twayne; Toronto; Oxford: Maxwell Macmillan, 1992. pp. ix, 233.

BERGMAN, DAVID. Larry Kramer and the rhetoric of AIDS. 175–86

BRODSLEY, LAUREL. Defoe's *The Journal of the Plague Year*: a model for stories of plagues. 11–22

BROWNING, BARBARA.   Babaluaiyé: searching for the text of a pandemic. 76–87

DEWEY, JOSEPH.   Music for a closing: responses to AIDS in three American novels. 23–38

HARTY, KEVIN J.   'All the elements of a good movie': cinematic responses to the AIDS pandemic. 114–30

LAWSON, D. S.   Rage and remembrance: the AIDS plays. 140–54

PASTORE, JUDITH LAURENCE.   Suburban AIDS: Alice Hoffman's *At Risk.* 39–49

SHATZKY, JOEL.   AIDS enters the American theater: *As Is* and *The Normal Heart.* 131–9

WEBER, MYLES.   When a risk group is not a risk group: the absence of AIDS panic in Peter Cameron's fiction. 69–75

WOODS, GREGORY.   AIDS to remembrance: the uses of elegy. 155–66

WRIGHT, LES.   Gay genocide as literary trope. 50–68

American Women Short-Story Writers

3. BROWN, JULIE (ed.).   American women short-story writers: a collection of critical essays. New York; London: Garland, 1995. pp. xxx, 367. (Garland reference library of the humanities, 1737.) (Wellesley studies in critical theory, literary history, and culture, 8.)

ANDERSON, DOUGLAS.   Displaced abjection and states of grace: Denise Chávez's *The Last of the Menu Girls.* 235–50

BRANSON, STEPHANIE.   Ripe fruit: fantastic elements in the short fiction of Ellen Glasgow, Edith Wharton, and Eudora Welty. 61–71

BURGAN, MARY.   The 'feminine' short story in America: historicizing epiphanies. 267–80

FADERMAN, LILLIAN.   Lesbian magazine fiction in the early twentieth century. 99–120

GARVEY, ELLEN GRUBER.   Representations of female authorship in turn-of-the-century American magazine fiction. 85–98

HUBBARD, DOLAN.   Society and self in Alice Walker's *In Love and Trouble.* 209–33

JOHNSON, KEN.   Dorothy Parker's perpetual motion. 251–65

KARELL, LINDA K.   *Lost Borders* and blurred boundaries: Mary Austin as storyteller. 153–66

KELLEY, MARGOT.   Gender and genre: the case of the novel-in-stories. 295–310

KOPPELMAN, SUSAN.   Fannie Hurst's short stories of working women – *Oats for the Woman, Sob Sister,* and contemporary reader responses: a meditation. 137–52

LINKON, SHERRY LEE.   Fiction as political discourse: Rose Terry Cooke's antisuffrage short stories. 17–31

MILLS, BRUCE.   Literary excellence and social reform: Lydia Maria Child's ultraisms for the 1840s. 3–16

MORRIS, TIMOTHY.   Elizabeth Stoddard: an examination of her work as pivot between exploratory fiction and the modern short story. 33–44

MULLEN, BILL.   'A revolutionary tale': in search of African-American women's short-story writing. 191–207

PATRICK, BARBARA.   Lady terrorists: nineteenth-century American women writers and the ghost story. 73–84

ROZGA, MARGARET.   Joyce Carol Oates: reimagining the masters; or, A woman's place is in her own fiction. 281–94

RUOFF, A. LAVONNE BROWN.   Ritual and renewal: Keres traditions in the short fiction of Leslie Silko. 167–89

SHOLLAR, BARBARA.   Martha Wolfenstein's *Idyls of the Gass* and the dilemma of ethnic self-representation. 121–36

SMITH, GAIL K.   Who was that masked woman? Gender and form in Louisa May Alcott's confidence stories. 45–59

The Beat Generation Writers

4.   LEE, A. ROBERT (ed.).   The Beat Generation writers. London; East Haven, CT: Pluto Press, 1996. pp. 225.

BUSH, CLIVE.   'Why do we always say angel?': Herbert Huncke and Neal Cassady. 128–57

ELLIS, R. J.   'I am only a jolly storyteller': Jack Kerouac's *On the Road* and *Visions of Cody*. 37–60

FRIEDMAN, AMY L.   'I say my new name': women writers of the Beat Generation. 200–16

HAMILTON, CYNTHIA S.   The prisoner of self: the work of John Clellon Holmes. 114–27

INGRAM, DAVID.   William Burroughs and language. 95–113

LEE, A. ROBERT.   Black Beats: the signifying poetry of LeRoi Jones/Amiri Baraka, Ted Joans and Bob Kaufman. 158–77

LEE, A. ROBERT.   Introduction. 1–9

MCNEIL, HELEN.   The archaeology of gender in the Beat Movement. 178–99

MUCKLE, JOHN.   The names: Allen Ginsberg's writings. 10–36

PHILIP, JIM.   Journeys in the mindfield: Gregory Corso reconsidered. 61–73

WISKER, ALISTAIR.   An anarchist among the floorwalkers: the poetry of Lawrence Ferlinghetti. 74–94

Between 'Race' and Culture

5. CHEYETTE, BRYAN (ed.).   Between 'race' and culture: representations of 'the Jew' in English and American literature. Stanford, CA: Stanford UP, 1996. pp. xiv, 222. (Stanford studies in Jewish history and culture.)

BAUMGARTEN, MURRAY.   Seeing double: Jews in the fiction of F. Scott Fitzgerald, Charles Dickens, Anthony Trollope, and George Eliot. 44–61

ELLMANN, MAUD.   The imaginary Jew: T. S. Eliot and Ezra Pound. 84–91

FREEDMAN, JONATHAN.   Henry James and the discourses of anti-Semitism. 62–83

GALPERIN, WILLIAM.   Romanticism and/or anti-Semitism. 16–26

GILMAN, SANDER L.   Mark Twain and the diseases of the Jews. 27–43

HOMBERGER, ERIC.   Some uses for Jewish ambivalence: Abraham Cahan and Michael Gold. 165–80

LASSNER, PHYLLIS.   'The milk of our mother's kindness has ceased to flow': Virginia Woolf, Stevie Smith, and the representation of the Jew. 129–44

LOWENSTEIN, ANDREA FREUD.   The protection of masculinity: Jews as projective pawns in the texts of William Gerhardi [*sic*] and George Orwell. 145–64

REIZBAUM, MARILYN.   A nightmare of history: Ireland's Jews and Joyce's *Ulysses*. 102–13

ROSE, JACQUELINE.   Dorothy Richardson and the Jew. 114–28

Beyond Representation

6. ELDRIDGE, RICHARD (ed.).   Beyond representation: philosophy and poetic imagination. Cambridge; New York: CUP, 1996. pp. xii, 306. (Cambridge studies in philosophy and the arts.)

ALTIERI, CHARLES.   The values of articulation: aesthetics after the aesthetic ideology. 66–89

BATTERSBY, CHRISTINE.   Her blood and his mirror: Mary Coleridge, Luce Irigaray, and the female self. 249–72

FISCHER, MICHAEL.   Wordsworth and the reception of poetry. 197–215

JOHNSTON, KENNETH R.   Self-consciousness, social guilt, and Romantic poetry: Coleridge's Ancient Mariner and Wordsworth's Old Pedlar. 216–48

Biographies of Books

7. BARBOUR, JAMES; QUIRK, TOM (eds).   Biographies of books: the compositional histories of notable American writings. Columbia; London: Missouri UP, 1996. pp. 334.

Blurred Boundaries

RAATZ, VOLKER.   'My own use': Henry David Thoreau and techno-logical progress. 27–40

SAWYER, DAVID.   'Yet why not say what happened?' Boundaries of the self in Raymond Carver's fiction and Robert Altman's *Short Cuts*. 195–219

Bodies of Writing, Bodies in Performance

9. FOSTER, THOMAS C.; SIEGEL, CAROL; BERRY, ELLEN E. (eds).   Bodies of writing, bodies in performance. New York; London: New York UP, 1996. pp. vi, 338. (Genders, 23.)

FREEDGOOD, ELAINE.   E. M. Forster's queer nation: taking the closet to the colony in *A Passage to India*. 123–44

HANNON, CHARLES.   *The Ballad of the Sad Café* and other stories of women's wartime labor. 97–119

HOWELL, AMANDA.   Lost boys and angry ghouls: Vietnam's undead. 297–334

MONK, LELAND.   A terrible beauty is born: Henry James, aestheti-cism, and homosexual panic. 247–65

RESTUCCIA, FRANCES L.   Literary representations of battered women: spectacular domestic punishment. 42–71

WILCOX, JANELLE.   Resistant silence, resistant subject: (re)reading Gayl Jones's *Eva's Man*. 72–96

Body & Text in the Eighteenth Century

10. KELLY, VERONICA; VON MÜCKE, DOROTHEA (eds).   Body & text in the eighteenth century. Stanford, CA: Stanford UP, 1994. pp. x, 349. Rev. by J.F. in TLS, 12 May 1995, 22; by Marshall Brown in ECF (8:1) 1995, 143–4; by Robert W. Jones in BJECS (19:2) 1996, 246.

CULLENS, CHRIS.   Mrs Robinson and the masquerade of womanliness. 266–89

DE BOLLA, PETER.   The charm'd eye. 89–111

KELLY, VERONICA.   Locke's eyes, Swift's spectacles. 68–85

LYNCH, DEIRDRE.   Overloaded portraits: the excesses of character and countenance. 112–43

SACCAMANO, NEIL.   Wit's breaks. 45–67

Bright Is the Ring of Words

11. POLLNER, CLAUSDIRK; ROHLFING, HELMUT; HAUSMANN, FRANK-RUTGER (eds).   *Bright is the ring of words*: Festschrift für Horst Weinstock zum 65. Geburtstag. Bonn: Romanistischer Verlag, 1996. pp. iv, 372. (Abhandlungen zur Sprache und Literatur, 85.)

ANON. (comp.).   Schriftenverzeichnis Horst Weinstock. 363–70

CASSIDY, FREDERIC G.   The Anglo-Saxon interjection. 45–8

ERZGRÄBER, WILLI.   The Wife of Bath and Molly Bloom: self-portrait of two women. 75–82

GERRITSEN, JOHAN.   Preserved abroad: some notes on *STC*-books in Holland and Germany. 101–8

HUSSEY, STANLEY.   Persuasion in *Othello*. 127–43

KIRBY, IAN J.   First in the field? A 'new-old' word in Laȝamon's *Brut*. 163–6

KNIEZSA, VERONIKA.   The orthography of Older Scots: the manuscripts of Barbour's *The Bruce*. 167–82

LIBERMAN, ANATOLY.   The 'icy' ship of Scyld Scefing: *Beowulf* 33. 183–94

LINDBERG, CONRAD.   The Wyclif Bible in Scots. 195–203

MÜLLER, WOLFGANG G.   Drei Formen des Wortspiels bei Shakespeare: Paronomasie, Paronymie, Polyptoton. 205–24

PLETT, HEINRICH F.   Utopias Aporien: Ansichten einer prekären Literaturform. 225–40

POLLNER, CLAUSDIRK.   A royal gift – the *Basilikon Doron* of James VI. 241–9

RIDLEY, FLORENCE H.   The *Canterbury Tales*: questions and an answer. 251–7

ROT, SÁNDOR.   Periphrastic verbal constructions in Middle English. 273–82

SAUER, HANS.   Die Exkommunikationsriten aus Wulfstans Handbuch und Liebermanns Gesetze. 283–307

SCHREYER, RÜDIGER.   The invisible hand in the history of language. 309–23

VIERECK, WOLFGANG.   Some notes on possessives. 325–31

WEINSTOCK, CAROLA; WEINSTOCK, ALEXANDER; WEINSTOCK, CONSTANZE. Alphabetum auctoris emeriti. 333–62

Camp Grounds
12.   BERGMAN, DAVID (ed.).   Camp grounds: style and homosexuality. Amherst: Massachusetts UP, 1993. pp. ix, 300.

BABUSCIO, JACK.   Camp and gay sensibility. 19–38

BERGMAN, DAVID.   Strategic camp: the art of gay rhetoric. 92–109

CLARK, WILLIAM LANE.   Degenerate personality: deviant sexuality and race in Ronald Firbank's novels. 134–55

FRANK, MARCIE.   The critic as performance artist: Susan Sontag's writing and gay culture. 173–84

KELLER, KARL.   Walt Whitman camping. 113–20

KOPELSON, KEVIN.   Fake it like a man. 259–67

Long, Scott.   The loneliness of camp. 78–91

Newton, Esther.   Role models. 39–53

Robertson, Pamela.   'The kinda comedy that imitates me': Mae West's identification with the feminist camp. 156–72

Román, David.   'It's my party and I'll die if I want to!': gay men, AIDS, and the circulation of camp in US theater. 206–33

Ross, Andrew.   Uses of camp. 54–77

Roth, Marty.   Homosexual expression and homophobic censorship: the situation of the text. 268–81

Viegener, Matias.   'Kinky escapades, bedroom techniques, un-bridled passion, and secret sex codes'. 234–56

Canadian Canons

13. Lecker, Robert.   Canadian canons: essays in literary value. Toronto; Buffalo, NY; London: Toronto UP, 1991. pp. 251. Rev. by Arnold E. Davidson in ARCS (23:2) 1993, 311–13; by Barbara Drennan in TRC (14:1) 1993, 106–8; by Richard Plant in CanTR (79/80) 1994, 154–7.

Bennett, Donna.   Conflicted vision: a consideration of canon and genre in English-Canadian literature. 131–49

Gerson, Carole.   The canon between the wars: field-notes of a feminist archaeologist. 46–56

Knowles, Richard Paul.   Voices (off): deconstructing the modern English-Canadian dramatic canon. 91–111

Lecker, Robert.   Introduction. 3–16

McCarthy, Dermot.   Early Canadian literary histories and the function of a canon. 30–45

Mathews, Lawrence.   Calgary, canonization, and class: de-ciphering List B. 150–66

Salter, Denis.   The idea of a national theatre. 71–90

Scobie, Stephen.   Leonard Cohen, Phyllis Webb, and the end(s) of Modernism. 57–70

Surette, Leon.   Creating the Canadian canon. 17–29

Weir, Lorraine.   Normalizing the subject: Linda Hutcheon and the English-Canadian postmodern. 180–95

Class and Gender in Early English Literature

14. Harwood, Britton J.; Overing, Gillian R. (eds).   Class and gender in early English literature: intersections. Bloomington: Indiana UP, 1994. pp. xiii, 156.

Aers, David.   Class, gender, medieval criticism and *Piers Plowman*. 59–75

Bennett, Helen T.   Exile and the semiosis of gender in Old English elegies. 43–58

FRANTZEN, ALLEN J.   The Pardoner's Tale, the pervert, and the price of order in Chaucer's world. 131–47

HARWOOD, BRITTON J.   Building class and gender into Chaucer's *Hous.* 95–111

HUDSON, HARRIET E.   Construction of class, family, and gender in some Middle English popular romances. 76–94

LEES, CLARE A.   Gender and exchange in *Piers Plowman.* 112–30

LOCHRIE, KARMA.   Gender, sexual violence, and the politics of war in the Old English *Judith.* 1–20

TANKE, JOHN W.   *Wonfeax wale*: ideology and figuration in the sexual riddles of the Exeter Book. 21–42

Comparative Studies in Merlin

15.   GOLLNICK, JAMES (ed.).   Comparative studies in Merlin from the Vedas to C. G. Jung. Lewiston, NY; Queenston, Ont.; Lampeter: Mellen Press, 1991. pp. v, 131. (Papers presented at the 23rd International Congress on Medieval Studies, Western Michigan Univ., 1988.)

DEAN, CHRISTOPHER.   The metamorphosis of Merlin: an examination of the protagonist of *The Crystal Cave* and *The Hollow Hills.* 63–75

ECKHARDT, CAROLINE D.   The figure of Merlin in Middle English chronicles. 21–39

GOLLNICK, JAMES.   Merlin as psychological symbol: a Jungian view. 111–31

GOODRICH, PETER H.   The alchemical Merlin. 91–110

KELLMAN, MARTIN.   T. H. White's Merlyn: a flawed prophet. 55–61

THUNDY, ZACHARIAS P.   Merlin in the Indo-European tradition. 79–90

WALTON, BRAD.   Merlin and the divine machinery of Dryden's *King Arthur.* 41–52

Craft and Tradition

16.   DE GROOT, H. B.; LEGGATT, ALEXANDER (eds).   Craft and tradition: essays in honour of William Blissett. Calgary, Alta: Calgary UP, 1990. pp. xvii, 334. Rev. by David A. Blostein in UTQ (62:1) 1992, 133–6; by John LeVay in ChesR (19:1) 1993, 85–7; by Barbara Carman Garner in ESCan (21:1) 1995, 121–4.

CHAMBERLIN, J. E.   The languages of contemporary West Indian poetry. 295–309

DAVENPORT, GUY.   Stanley Spencer and David Jones. 259–68

DE QUEHEN, A. H.   *The Silent Woman* in the Restoration. 137–46

DILWORTH, THOMAS.   *In Parenthesis*: the displacement of chronicle. 229–40

GRAZIANI, RENÉ.   Donne's *Anniversaries* and the beatification of Elizabeth Drury by poetic licence. 59–80

HAMILTON, A. C.   Closure in Spenser's *The Faerie Queene.* 23–34

HERENDEEN, WYMAN H.   Ben Jonson and the play of words. 123–36

KANE, SEAN.   Spenser's broken symmetries. 13–22

KEITH, W. J.   'Intermixed lingo': listening to David Jones. 251–8

KIRKHAM, MICHAEL.   The high Modernism of F. T. Prince. 281–94

LEGGATT, ALEXANDER.   The hidden hero: Shakespeare's *Coriolanus* and Eliot's *Coriolan.* 89–98

MARGESON, JOHN.   Individualism and order in the *Byron* plays of Chapman and Jonson's *Catiline.* 111–21

PARKER, R. B.   *King Lear*, Sir Donald Wolfit, and *The Dresser.* 99–109

QUINN, KENNETH.   The sound of verse. 311–23

SADDLEMYER, ANN.   Vision and design in *The Playboy of the Western World.* 203–16

SHERRY, VINCENT.   David Jones and literary Modernism: the use of the dramatic monologue. 241–9

TESKEY, GORDON.   Positioning Spenser's *Letter to Raleigh.* 35–46

TUCKER, JOHN.   *The Waste Land*, order and myth. 217–27

WARKENTIN, GERMAINE.   Spenser at the still point: a schematic device in *Epithalamion.* 47–57

WHITAKER, THOMAS R.   H.D.'s *Trilogy* and the poetics of passage. 269–80

ZITNER, S. P.   Zigzag in *Hamlet* I.v. 81–8

Criticism and Dissent in the Middle Ages

17.   COPELAND, RITA (ed.).   Criticism and dissent in the Middle Ages. Cambridge; New York: CUP, 1996. pp. xii, 332.

BECKWITH, SARAH.   *Sacrum signum*: sacramentality and dissent in York's theatre of Corpus Christi. 264–88

CAMILLE, MICHAEL.   The dissenting image: a postcard from Matthew Paris. 115–50

HANNA, RALPH, III.   *Vae octuplex*, Lollard socio-textual ideology, and Ricardian–Lancastrian prose translation. 244–63

JUSTICE, STEVEN.   Inquisition, speech, and writing: a case from late medieval Norwich. 289–322

SIMPSON, JAMES.   Desire and the scriptural text: Will as reader in *Piers Plowman.* 215–43

Cultural Politics at the *Fin de Siècle*

18.   LEDGER, SALLY; McCRACKEN, SCOTT (eds).   Cultural politics at the *fin de siècle*. Cambridge; New York: CUP, 1995. pp. xv, 329. Rev. by

Isobel Murray in SLJ (supp. 43) 1995, 26–8; by Michael Whitworth in NQ (43:1) 1996, 110–11.

CHRISMAN, LAURA. Empire, 'race' and feminism at the *fin de siècle*: the work of George Egerton and Olive Schreiner. 45–65

COHEN, ED. The double lives of man: narration and identification in late nineteenth-century representations of ec-centric masculinities. 85–114

EAGLETON, TERRY. The flight to the real. 11–21

GAGNIER, REGENIA. Is market society the *fin* of history? 290–310

HALBERSTAM, JUDITH. Technologies of monstrosity: Bram Stoker's *Dracula*. 248–66

HAPGOOD, LYNNE. Urban utopias: socialism, religion and the city, 1880 to 1900. 184–201

IAN, MARCIA. Henry James and the spectacle of loss: psychoanalytic metaphysics. 115–36

JANOWITZ, ANNE. *The Pilgrims of Hope*: William Morris and the dialectic of Romanticism. 160–83

LEDGER, SALLY. The New Woman and the crisis of Victorianism. 22–44

LEDGER, SALLY; McCRACKEN, SCOTT. Introduction. 1–10

McCRACKEN, SCOTT. Postmodernism, a *Chance* to reread? 267–89

REGAN, STEPHEN. W. B. Yeats and Irish cultural politics in the 1890s. 66–84

ROBBINS, RUTH. 'A very curious construction': masculinity and the poetry of A. E. Housman and Oscar Wilde. 137–59

WARWICK, ALEXANDRA. Vampires and the Empire: fears and fictions of the 1890s. 202–20

WILLIAMS, CAROLYN. *Utopia, Limited*: nationalism, empire and parody in the comic operas of Gilbert and Sullivan. 221–47

Cultural Power/Cultural Literacy

19. BRAENDLIN, BONNIE (ed.). Cultural power/cultural literacy: selected papers from the Fourteenth Annual Florida State University Conference on Literature and Film. Tallahassee: Florida State UP, 1991. pp. vii, 202.

BAUER, DALE. The figure of the film critic as virile poet: Delmore Schwartz at the *New Republic* in the 1930s. 110–19

BENDER, EILEEN T. Repossessing *Uncle Tom's Cabin*: Toni Morrison's *Beloved*. 129–42

BOOZER, JACK. *Wall Street*: the commodification of perception. 76–95

CURRY, RENÉE R. To star is to mean: the casting of John Waters's *Hairspray*. 167–78

DeCroix, Rick.   'Once upon a time in idealized America ...': simulated utopia and the Hardy Family series. 152–66

Giffone, Tony.   Disoriented in the Orient: the representation of the Chinese in two contemporary mystery novels. 143–51

Kalson, Albert.   From agitprop to SRO: the political drama of David Edgar. 96–109

Kaplan, E. Ann.   Popular culture, politics, and the canon: cultural literacy in the postmodern age. 12–31

Luhr, William.   *Ordinary People*: feminist psychotherapy on a see-saw. 50–60

Rockett, Will.   Jason dreams of Freddy: genre, supertext, and the production of meaning through pop-cultural literacy. 179–98

Welsch, Janice.   Canon (re)formation: a feminist perspective. 32–49

Wilson, Charles E., Jr.   Chesnutt's *Baxter's 'Procrustes'*: cultural fraud as link to cultural identity. 120–8

Cultural Readings of Restoration and Eighteenth-Century English Theater

20.   Canfield, J. Douglas; Payne, Deborah C. (eds).   Cultural readings of Restoration and eighteenth-century English theater. Athens; London: Georgia UP, 1995. pp. vi, 320. Rev. by David Roberts in NQ (43:3) 1996, 355–6.

Braverman, Richard.   The rake's progress revisited: politics and comedy in the Restoration. 140–68

Burke, Helen.   'Law-suits', 'love-suits', and the family property in Wycherley's *The Plain Dealer*. 89–113

Canfield, J. Douglas.   Shifting tropes of ideology in English serious drama, late Stuart to early Georgian. 195–227

Green, Susan.   A cultural reading of Charlotte Lennox's *Shakespear Illustrated*. 228–57

Kroll, Richard.   Instituting imperialism: Hobbes's *Leviathan* and Dryden's *Marriage à la Mode*. 39–66

Markley, Robert.   'Be impudent, be saucy, forward, bold, touzing, and leud': the politics of masculine sexuality and feminine desire in Behn's Tory comedies. 114–40

Payne, Deborah C.   Reified object or emergent professional? Retheorizing the Restoration actress. 24–38

Peters, J. S.   The novelty; or, Print, money, fashion, getting, spending, and glut. 169–94

Straub, Kristina.   Actors and homophobia. 258–80

Thompson, James.   'Sure I have seen that face before': representation and value in eighteenth-century drama. 281–308

WEBER, HAROLD.   Carolinean sexuality and the Restoration stage: reconstructing the royal phallus in *Sodom*. 67–88

Culture and Society in the Stuart Restoration

21. MacLean, Gerald (ed.).   Culture and society in the Stuart Restoration: literature, drama, history. Cambridge; New York: CUP, 1995. pp. xvi, 292. Rev. by John Ross in AUMLA (86) 1996, 115–17; by David Womersley in NQ (43:3) 1996, 349–50; by Susan J. Owen in Eng (45:182) 1996, 150–3.

FERGUSON, MOIRA.   Seventeenth-century Quaker women: displacement, colonialism, and anti-slavery discourse. 221–40

HOBBY, ELAINE.   A woman's best setting out is silence: the writings of Hannah Wolley. 179–200

ILIFFE, ROBERT.   'Is he like other men?': the meaning of the *Principia Mathematica*, and the author as idol. 159–76

KEEBLE, N. H.   Obedient subjects? The loyal self in some later seventeenth-century Royalist women's memoirs. 201–18

MacLean, Gerald.   Literature, culture, and society in Restoration England. 3–27

MAGUIRE, NANCY KLEIN.   Factionary politics: John Crowne's *Henry VI*. 70–92

MONTAÑO, JOHN PATRICK.   The quest for consensus: the Lord Mayor's Day shows in the 1670s. 31–51

TURNER, JAMES GRANTHAM.   Pepys and the private parts of monarchy. 95–110

WALKLING, ANDREW R.   Politics and the Restoration masque: the case of *Dido and Aeneas*. 52–69

WORDEN, BLAIR.   Milton, *Samson Agonistes*, and the Restoration. 111–36

ZWICKER, STEVEN N.   Milton, Dryden, and the politics of literary controversy. 137–58

De gustibus

22. FOLEY, JOHN MILES (ed.); WOMACK, CHRIS; WOMACK, WHITNEY A. (asst eds).   *De gustibus*: essays for Alain Renoir. New York; London: Garland, 1992. pp. xiv, 596. (Garland reference library of the humanities, 1482.) (Albert Bates Lord studies in oral tradition, 2.)

AMODIO, MARK C.   Old-English oral-formulaic tradition and Middle-English verse. 1–20

ANDERSON, THEODORE M.   The speeches in the *Waldere* fragments. 21–9

BENSON, C. DAVID.   The lost honor of Sir Gawain. 30–9

CHERNISS, MICHAEL D.   The oral-tradition opening theme in the poems of Cynewulf. 40–65

CLARK, GEORGE.   Maldon: history, poetry, and truth. 66–84

CREED, ROBERT PAYSON.   Beowulf's fourth act. 85–109

DAVIS, ADAM.   *Agon* and *gnomon*: forms and functions of the Anglo-Saxon riddles. 110–50

FEENY, SARAH J.   The funeral pyre theme in *Beowulf*. 185–200

FRY, DONALD K.   Exeter Riddle 31: feather-pen. 234–49

LORD, ALBERT B.   *Beowulf* and the Russian *Byliny*. 304–23

MORLAND, LAURA.   Cædmon and the Germanic tradition. 324–58

NILES, JOHN D.   Toward an Anglo-Saxon oral poetics. 359–77

OSBORN, MARIJANE.   'Verbal sea charts' and Beowulf's approach to Denmark. 441–55

PARKS, WARD.   The traditional narrator in *Beowulf* and Homer. 456–79

RAUCH, IRMENGARD.   Another Old English–Old Saxon isogloss: (REM) activity. 480–93

SCHAEFER, URSULA.   'From an aesthetic point of view ...': receptional aspects of Old English poetry. 494–541

THORMANN, JANET.   The poetics of absence: 'The Lament of the Sole Survivor' in *Beowulf*. 542–50

TYLER, LEE EDGAR.   The heroic oath of Hildebrand. 551–85

Dialogues = *Dialogi*

23.   AIKEN, SUSAN HARDY, *et al.*   Dialogues = *Dialogi*: literary and cultural exchanges between (ex)Soviet and American women. Durham, NC; London: Duke UP, 1994. pp. xviii, 415. Rev. by Barbara Evans Clements in NWSAJ (7:3) 1995, 142–7; by Stephanie Sandler in MFS (42:1) 1996, 205–8; by Nina Pelikan Straus in Signs (21:2) 1996, 482–7.

AIKEN, SUSAN HARDY.   Stages of dissent: Olsen, Grekova, and the politics of creativity. 120–40

AIKEN, SUSAN HARDY.   Telling the other('s) story; or, The blues in two languages. 206–23

BARKER, ADELE MARIE.   Crossings. 340–53

BARKER, ADELE MARIE.   The world of our mothers. 253–65

KORENEVA, MAYA.   Children of the sixties. 191–205

KORENEVA, MAYA.   Hopes and nightmares of the young. 266–78

STETSENKO, EKATERINA.   Retelling the legends. 327–39

STETSENKO, EKATERINA.   Revolutions from within. 141–57

Disorderly Eaters

24.   FURST, LILIAN R.; GRAHAM, PETER W. (eds).   Disorderly eaters: texts in self-empowerment. (Cf. bibl. 1994, 2335, where collection not analysed.)

COHEN, PAULA MARANTZ.   The anorexic syndrome and the nineteenth-century domestic novel. 125–39

CORTI, LILIAN.   *Medea* and *Beloved*: self-definition and abortive nurturing in literary treatments of the infanticidal mother. 61–77

GAINOR, J. ELLEN.   'The slow-eater-tiny-bite-taker': an eating disorder in Betty MacDonald's *Mrs Piggle-Wiggle*. 29–41

GRAHAM, PETER W.   The order and disorder of eating in Byron's *Don Juan*. 113–23

GUTIERREZ, NANCY A.   Double standard in the flesh: gender, fasting, and power in English Renaissance drama. 79–93

KESTER, GUNILLA THEANDER.   The forbidden fruit and female disorderly eating: three versions of Eve. 231–8

LASHGARI, DEIRDRE.   What some women can't swallow: hunger as protest in Charlotte Brontë's *Shirley*. 141–52

NETTELS, ELSA.   New England indigestion and its victims. 167–84

NICHOLSON, MERVYN.   Magic food, compulsive eating, and power poetics. 43–60

Earthly Words

25.   COOLEY, JOHN (ed.).   Earthly words: essays on contemporary American nature and environmental writers. Ann Arbor: Michigan UP, 1994. pp. xii, 270.

ABBEY, EDWARD.   'Mr Krutch'. 105–18

BAILEY, THOMAS C.   John McPhee: the making of a meta-naturalist. 195–213

BERRY, WENDELL.   A few words in favor of Edward Abbey. 19–28

COOLEY, JOHN.   Matthiessen's voyages on the River Styx: deathly waters, endangered peoples. 167–92

FOLSOM, ED.   Gary Snyder's descent to Turtle Island: searching for fossil love. 217–36

HICKS, JACK.   Wendell Berry's husband to the world: a place on earth. 51–66

McCLINTOCK, JAMES I.   'Pray without ceasing': Annie Dillard among the nature writers. 69–86

McILROY, GARY.   *Pilgrim at Tinker Creek* and the legacy of *Walden*. 87–101

MURPHY, PATRICK D.   Penance or perception: spirituality and land in the poetry of Gary Snyder and Wendell Berry. 237–49

RUCKERT, WILLIAM H.   Barry Lopez and the search for a dignified and honorable relationship with nature. 137–64

TALLMADGE, JOHN.   Anatomy of a classic. 119–34

WAKOSKI, DIANE.   Edward Abbey: joining the visionary 'inhumanists'. 29–36

WEILAND, STEVEN.   Wendell Berry resettles America: fidelity, education, and culture. 37–49

The Endless Knot

26. TAVORMINA, M. TERESA; YEAGER, R. F. (eds).   The endless knot: essays on Old and Middle English in honor of Marie Borroff. Cambridge; Rochester, NY: Brewer, 1995. pp. ix, 252.

ARCHIBALD, ELIZABETH.   Contextualizing Chaucer's Constance: romance modes and family values. 161–75

BARNEY, STEPHEN A.   Langland's prosody: the state of study. 65–85

BURROW, J. A.   Elvish Chaucer. 105–11

CARRUTHERS, MARY J.   Invention, mnemonics, and stylistic ornament in *Psychomachia* and *Pearl*. 201–13

FURROW, MELISSA M.   Latin and affect. 29–41

GINSBERG, WARREN.   Chaucer's disposition. 129–40

HANNA, RALPH, III.   Defining Middle English alliterative poetry. 43–64

HIGGINS, ANNE.   Alceste the washerwoman. 113–27

KIRK, ELIZABETH D.   The anatomy of a mourning: reflections on the *Pearl* dreamer. 215–25

LAWLER, TRAUGOTT.   Conscience's dinner. 87–103

LEICESTER, H. MARSHALL, JR.   Piety and resistance: a note on the representation of religious feeling in the *Canterbury Tales*. 151–60

REAMES, SHERRY L.   Artistry, decorum, and purpose in three Middle English retellings of the Cecilia legend. 177–99

ROBINSON, FRED C.   Eight letters from Elizabeth Elstob. 241–52

STANLEY, ERIC.   Paradise lost of the Old English dual. 1–27

TAVORMINA, M. TERESA.   '*Lo, swilk a complyn*': musical topicality in the Reeve's and Miller's Tales. 141–50

YEAGER, R. F.   Ben Jonson's *English Grammar* and John Gower's reception in the seventeenth century. 227–39

English Historical Linguistics 1994

27. BRITTON, DEREK (ed.).   English historical linguistics 1994. Papers from the 8th International Conference on English Historical Linguistics (Edinburgh, 19–23 September 1994). Amsterdam; Philadelphia, PA: Benjamins, 1996. pp. viii, 403. (Amsterdam studies in the theory and history of linguistic science, IV: Current issues in linguistic theory, 135.)

BEAL, JOAN.   The Jocks and the Geordies: modified standards in eighteenth-century pronouncing dictionaries. 363–82

DENISON, DAVID.   The case of the unmarked pronoun. 287–99

FISCHER, OLGA.   Verbal complementation in early ME: how do the infinitives fit in? 247–70

GÖRLACH, MANFRED. Morphological standardization: the strong verb in Scots. 161–81

HOGG, RICHARD M. Tertiary stress in Old English: some reflections on explanatory inadequacy. 3–12

KASTOVSKY, DIETER. Verbal derivation in English: a historical survey; or, Much ado about nothing. 93–117

KOOPMAN, WILLEM F. Evidence for clitic adverbs in Old English: an evaluation. 223–45

LÓPEZ COUSO, MARÍA JOSÉ. A look at *that/zero* variation in Restoration English. 271–86

MCMAHON, APRIL M. S. On the use of the past to explain the present: the history of /r/ in English and Scots. 73–89

MINKOVA, DONKA. Verse structure as evidence for prosodic reconstruction in Old English. 13–37

MOSKOWICH, ISABEL; SEOANE, ELENA. Scandinavian loans and processes of word-formation in ME: some preliminary considerations. 185–98

NEVALAINEN, TERTTU; RAUMOLIN-BRUNBERG, HELENA. Social stratification in Tudor English? 303–26

OGURA, MIEKO; WANG, WILLIAM S.-Y. Snowball effect in lexical diffusion: the development of *-s* in the third-person singular present indicative in English. 119–41

PERCY, CAROL. Eighteenth-century normative grammar in practice: the case of Captain Cook. 339–62

SCHENDL, HERBERT. The 3rd-person plural present indicative in early modern English – variation and linguistic contact. 143–60

SCHNEIDER, EDGAR W. Towards syntactic isomorphism and semantic dissimilation: the semantics and syntax of prospective verbs in early modern English. 199–220

STOCKWELL, ROBERT P. Old English short diphthongs and the theory of glide emergence. 57–72

SUZUKI, SEIICHI. On the syllable weight of -VC# in Old English: a metrical perspective. 39–55

TIEKEN-BOON VAN OSTADE, INGRID. Social network theory and eighteenth-century English: the case of Boswell. 327–37

English Romanticism and Modern Fiction

28. CHAVKIN, ALLAN (ed.). English Romanticism and modern fiction: a collection of critical essays. New York: AMS Press, 1993. pp. 205. (AMS studies in modern literature, 21.)

BUCKWALD, CRAIG. Journeying westward: Romantic nature rhetoric and lyric structure for Joyce's *The Dead*. 7–37

CHAVKIN, ALLAN. The Romantic imagination of Saul Bellow. 113–38

HUTCHINGS, WILLIAM.   Proletarian Byronism: Alan Sillitoe and the Romantic tradition. 83–112

LISCIO, LORRAINE.   Marilynne Robinson's *Housekeeping*: misreading *The Prelude*. 139–62

MOSES, JOHN W.   Orlando's 'caricature value': Virginia Woolf's portrait of the artist as a Romantic poet. 39–81

SCHEICK, WILLIAM J.   Romantic tradition in recent post-nuclear holocaust fiction. 162–91

The Epic Cosmos

29.   ALLUMS, LARRY (ed.).   The epic cosmos. Introd. by Louise Cowan. Dallas, TX: Dallas Inst. of Humanities and Culture, 1992. pp. xi, 378. (Studies in genre.)

COWAN, BAINARD.   America between two myths: *Moby-Dick* as epic. 217–46

HENDERSON, KATHLEEN.   Caroline Gordon's *Green Centuries*: the end of the epic journey. 273–97

MUMBACH, MARY.   The figural action of sacrifice in *Go Down, Moses*. 247–72

SLATTERY, DENNIS.   The narrative play of memory in epic. 331–52

STEWART, MARILYN.   Human dreams and angelic visions: world-making in *Paradise Lost*. 185–215

Eroticism and Containment

30.   SIEGEL, CAROL; KIBBEY, ANN (eds).   Eroticism and containment: notes from the flood plain. New York; London: New York UP, 1994. pp. vi, 338. (Genders, 20.)

BOXWELL, D. A.   In formation: male homosocial desire in Willa Cather's *One of Ours*. 285–310

CHATTMAN, LAUREN.   Diagnosing the domestic woman in *The Woman in White* and *Dora*. 123–53

GRAHAM, WENDY.   Henry James's thwarted love. 66–95

HARRIS, ANDREA L.   The third sex: figures of inversion in Djuna Barnes's *Nightwood*. 233–59

MCRUER, ROBERT.   Boys' own stories and new spellings of my name: coming out and other myths of queer positionality. 260–84

RAY, SANGEETA.   Gender and the discourse of nationalism in Anita Desai's *Clear Light of Day*. 96–119

ROMÁN, DAVID.   Shakespeare out of Portland: Gus Van Sant's *My Own Private Idaho*, homoneurotics, and boy actors. 311–33

Famous Last Words

31.   BOOTH, ALISON (ed.).   Famous last words: changes in gender and narrative closure. Afterword by U. C. Knoepflmacher. Charlottesville:

Virginia UP, 1993. pp. viii, 393. (Feminist issues.) Rev. by Walter Kendrick in VLC (22) 1994, 312–13; by Deirdre d'Albertis in VS (39:1) 1995, 76–7.

ARATA, STEPHEN D.   Object lessons: reading the museum in *The Golden Bowl*. 199–229

ARDIS, ANN.   Toward a redefinition of 'experimental writing': Netta Syrett's realism, 1908–12. 259–79

BENSTOCK, SHARI.   'The word which made all clear': the silent close of *The House of Mirth*. 230–58

BOOTH, ALISON.   The silence of great men: statuesque femininity and the ending of *Romola*. 110–34

DAVIE, SHARON.   'Reader, my story ends with freedom': Harriet Jacobs's *Incidents in the Life of a Slave Girl*. 86–109

JADWIN, LISA.   Clytemnestra rewarded: the double conclusion of *Vanity Fair*. 35–61

JONES, SUZANNE W.   Reading the endings in Katherine Anne Porter's *Old Mortality*. 280–99

KNOEPFLMACHER, U. C.   Afterword: endings as beginnings. 347–68

KRUEGER, CHRISTINE L.   'Speaking like a woman': how to have the last word on *Sylvia's Lovers*. 135–53

PETERSON, CARLA L.   Unsettled frontiers: race, history, and romance in Pauline Hopkins's *Contending Forces*. 177–96

RABINOWITZ, PETER J.   'Reader, I blew him away': convention and transgression in Sue Grafton. 326–44

RODY, CAROLINE.   Burning down the house: the revisionary paradigm of Jean Rhys's *Wide Sargasso Sea*. 300–26

TUCKER, HERBERT F.   *Aurora Leigh*: epic solutions to novel ends. 63–85

ZIMMERMAN, BONNIE.   George Eliot's sacred chest of language. 154–76

The Female Tradition in Southern Literature

32. MANNING, CAROL S. (ed.).   The female tradition in Southern literature. Urbana: Illinois UP, 1993. pp. 290. Rev. by Shirley A. Leckie in FHQ (73:3) 1995, 395–6.

BETTS, DORIS.   Daughters, Southerners, and Daisy. 259–76

BROOKHART, MARY HUGHES.   Spiritual daughters of the Black American South. 125–39

COOPER, JAN.   Zora Neale Hurston was always a Southerner too. 57–69

DAVIS, THADIOUS M.   Women's art and authorship in the Southern region: connections. 15–36

Feminism, Bakhtin, and the Dialogic

33. BAUER, DALE M.; McKINSTRY, SUSAN JARET (eds).   Feminism, Bakhtin, and the dialogic. Albany: New York State UP, 1991. pp. vi, 259. (SUNY series in feminist criticism and theory.) Rev. by Veronica Stewart in MinnR (41/42) 1993/94, 133–8.

SIPPLE, SUSAN.   'Witness [to] the suffering of women': poverty and sexual transgression in Meridel Le Sueur's *Women on the Breadlines*. 135–53

STEVENSON, SHERYL.   Language and gender in transit: feminist extensions of Bakhtin. 181–98

YELIN, LOUISE.   Problems of Gordimer's poetics: dialogue in *Burger's Daughter*. 219–38

Forked Tongues?

34. MASSA, ANN; STEAD, ALISTAIR (eds).   Forked tongues? Comparing twentieth-century British and American literature. London; New York: Longman, 1994. pp. xxiii, 384. Rev. by R. J. Dingley in NQ (43:3) 1996, 372–3.

BROWN, RICHARD.   Postmodern Americas in the fiction of Angela Carter, Martin Amis and Ian McEwan. 92–110

CHEYETTE, BRYAN.   Philip Roth and Clive Sinclair: representations of an 'imaginary homeland' in postwar British and American-Jewish literature. 355–73

COHN, RUBY.   States of the artist: the plays of Edward Bond and Sam Shepard. 169–87

EGRI, PETER.   American variations on a British theme: Giles Cooper and Edward Albee. 135–51

HARDING, BRIAN.   Comparative metafictions of history: E. L. Doctorow and John Fowles. 253–72

JARMAN, MARK.   Brer Rabbit and Brer Possum: the Americanness of Ezra Pound and T. S. Eliot. 21–37

JOHNSEN, WILLIAM A.   The treacherous years of postmodern poetry in English. 75–91

KENYON, OLGA.   Alice Walker and Buchi Emecheta rewrite the myth of motherhood. 336–54

LEE, HERMIONE.   Cather's bridge: Anglo-American crossings in Willa Cather. 38–56

MASSA, ANN.   Theatre of manners, theatre of matters: British and American theatre between the wars. 57–74

MOTTRAM, ERIC.   American poetry and the British poetry revival 1960–75. 152–68

NEWMAN, JUDIE.   Paleface into Redskin: cultural transformations in Alison Lurie's *Foreign Affairs*. 188–205

PALMER, PAULINA.   The city in contemporary women's fiction. 315–35

PECK, DAVID.   'The morning that is yours': American and British literary cultures in the thirties. 214–31

SCOBIE, BRIAN.   Carver country. 273–87

SEED, DAVID.   Party-going: the Jazz Age novels of Evelyn Waugh, Wyndham Lewis, F. Scott Fitzgerald and Carl Van Vechten. 117–34

STEAD, ALISTAIR.   Pastoral sexuality in British and American fiction. 295–314

TUMA, KEITH.   Is there a British Modernism? 232–52

Framing Elizabethan Fictions

35. RELIHAN, CONSTANCE C. (ed.).   Framing Elizabethan fictions: contemporary approaches to early modern narrative prose. Kent, OH; London: Kent State UP, 1996. pp. ix, 274.

ALWES, DEREK B.   Elizabethan dreaming: fictional dreams from Gascoigne to Lodge. 153–67

BURNETT, MARK THORNTON.   Henry Chettle's *Piers Plainness: Seven Years' Prenticeship*: contexts and consumers. 169–86

DAVIS, WALTER R.   Silenced women. 187–209

LINTON, JOAN PONG.   The Humanist in the market: gendering exchange and authorship in Lyly's *Euphues* romances. 73–97

NEWCOMB, LORI HUMPHREY.   The romance of service: the simple history of *Pandosto*'s servant readers. 117–39

PORIES, KATHLEEN.   The intersection of Poor Laws and literature in the sixteenth century: fictional and factual categories. 17–40

PRENDERGAST, MARIA TERESA MICAELA.   Philoclea parsed: prose, verse, and femininity in Sidney's *Old Arcadia*. 99–116

RELIHAN, CONSTANCE C.   Introduction: framing Elizabethan fictions. 1–15

RELIHAN, CONSTANCE C.   Rhetoric, gender, and audience construction in Thomas Nashe's *The Unfortunate Traveller*. 141–52

STAUB, SUSAN C.   The Lady Frances did watch: Gascoigne's voyeuristic narrative. 41–54

STOCKTON, SHARON.   Making men: visions of social mobility in *A Petite Pallace of Pettie His Pleasure*. 55–72

Functions of the Fantastic

36. SANDERS, JOE (ed.).   Functions of the fantastic: selected essays from the Thirteenth International Conference on the Fantastic in the Arts. Westport, CT; London: Greenwood Press, 1995. pp. ix, 230. (Contributions to the study of science fiction and fantasy, 65.)

ATTEBERY, BRIAN.   The closing of the final frontier: science fiction after 1960. 205–13

BORCHARDT, EDITH.   Criminal artists and artisans in mysteries by E. T. A. Hoffman, Dorothy Sayers, Ernesto Sábato, Patrick Süskind, and Thomas Harris. 125–34

BUFFINGTON, NANCY.   What about Bob? Doubles and demons in *Twin Peaks*. 101–6

EURIDGE, GARETH M.   The company we keep: comic function in M. G. Lewis's *The Monk*. 83–90

FOOTE, BUD.   Assuming the present in SF: Sartre in a new dimension. 161–7

GEARY, ROBERT F.   The corpse in the dung cart: *The Night-Side of Nature* and the Victorian supernatural tale. 47–53

HALLAB, MARY Y.   Carter and Blake: the dangers of innocence. 177–83

HENDRIX, LAUREL L.   'A world of glas': the heroine's quest for identity in Spenser's *Faerie Queene* and Stephen R. Donaldson's *Mirror of Her*. 91–100

HOLLINGER, VERONICA.   Travels in hyperreality: Jean Baudrillard's *America* and J. G. Ballard's *Hello America*. 185–93

KLINE, BARBARA.   Duality, reality, and magic in *Sir Gawain and the Green Knight*. 107–14

KRIPS, VALERIE.   Finding one's place in the fantastic: Susan Cooper's *The Dark Is Rising*. 169–75

LATHAM, ROB.   The men who walked on the moon: images of America in the 'new wave' science fiction of the 1960s and 1970s. 195–203

O'BRIEN, DENNIS.   Shoring fragments: how CBS's *Beauty and the Beast* adapts consensus reality to shape its magical world. 37–46

PENNINGTON, JOHN.   Reader response and fantasy literature: the uses and abuses of interpretation in *Queen Victoria's Alice in Wonderland*. 55–65

ROWEN, NORMA.   Reinscribing Cinderella: Jane Austen and the fairy tale. 29–36

SENIOR, WILLIAM.   Oliphaunts in the perilous realm: the function of internal wonder in fantasy. 115–23

WEBB, SARAH JO.   Culture as spiritual metaphor in Le Guin's *Always Coming Home*. 155–60

ZIPES, JACK.   Recent trends in the contemporary American fairy tale. 1–17

Gender, Culture, and the Arts

37. DOTTERER, RONALD; BOWERS, SUSAN (eds).   Gender, culture, and the arts: women, the arts, and society. Selinsgrove, PA: Susquehanna UP; London; Toronto: Assoc. UPs, 1993. pp. 175. (Susquehanna Univ. studies.) Rev. by Susan McClary in *Signs* (21:1) 1995, 168–72.

BETSINGER, SUE ANN.   *Jane Eyre*: the ascent of woman. 74–86

BLEND, BENAY.   'I have heard the spinning woman of the sky': Alice Corbin, poet and art critic (1881–1949). 128–42

BRYAN, T. J.   Women poets of the Harlem renaissance. 99–114

DICKERSON, VANESSA D.   Angels, money, and ghosts: Victorian female writers of the supernatural. 87–98

PAVLIDES, MEROPE.   Poetics of women's writing: dramatic tragedy. 11–21

RESS, LISA.   From Futurism to feminism: the poetry of Mina Loy. 115–27

VARHUS, SARA B.   The 'solitary philosopher' and 'nature's favourite': gender and identity in the *Rambler*. 61–73

Gender, I-deology

38.   CORNUT-GENTILLE D'ARCY, CHANTAL; GARCÍA LANDA, JOSÉ ÁNGEL (eds).   Gender, I-deology: essays on theory, fiction and film. Amsterdam; Atlanta, GA: Rodopi, 1996. pp. 465. (Postmodern studies, 16.)

ARIZTI MARTÍN, BÁRBARA.   Female spectatorship in *The Purple Rose of Cairo*. 387–97

ASENSIO ARÓSTEGUI, MARÍA DEL MAR.   Subversion of sexual identity in Jeanette Winterson's *The Passion*. 265–79

BARRIOS, OLGA.   Formulating the aesthetics of African-American women playwrights: the resonance of the Black Liberation and the Black Theatre movements. 121–30

COLLADO RODRÍGUEZ, FRANCISCO.   Complexity/controversy: some aspects of contemporary Women's Studies in America. 107–20

CORNUT-GENTILLE D'ARCY, CHANTAL.   Who's afraid of the *femme fatale* in *Breakfast at Tiffany's*? Exposure and implications of a myth. 371–85

DE LA CONCHA, ANGELES.   The female body: a resonant voice in the multicultural scene. 55–72

DE LEYTO ALCALA, CELESTINO.   Regulating desire: castration and fantasy in Blake Edwards' *Switch*. 419–37

DEL RÍO ÁLVARO, CONSTANZA.   Misogyny in Flann O'Brien's *The Third Policeman*. 207–24

FLORÉN SERRANO, CELIA.   A reading of Margaret Atwood's dystopia, *The Handmaid's Tale*. 253–64

FRAILE MURLANCH, ISABEL.   The silent woman: silence as subversion in Angela Carter's *The Magic Toyshop*. 239–52

GARCÍA LANDA, JOSÉ ÁNGEL.   Introduction: gender, I-deology and addictive representation: the film of familiarity. 13–54

GONZÁLEZ ÁBALOS, SUSANA.   Winterson's *Sexing the Cherry*: rewriting 'woman' through fantasy. 281–95

HERRERO GRANADO, MARÍA DOLORES.   George Egerton's *Wedlock*: unlocking closed doors, searching for a key of one's own. 165–80

HIDALGO, PILAR.   The New Historicism and its female discontents. 131–48

Loyo Gómez, Hilaria. Dietrich's androgyny and gendered spectatorship. 317–32

Martínz Alegre, Sara. Not Oedipus' sister: the redefinition of female rites of passage in the screen adaptation of Thomas Harris's *The Silence of the Lambs.* 439–50

Nadal Blasco, Marita. 'The death of a beautiful woman is, unquestionably, the most poetical topic in the world': poetic and parodic treatment of women in Poe's tales. 151–63

Neff van Aertselaer, JoAnne. Fear, desire and masculinity. 73–87

Olsen, Vickie. The subordination of gender to race issues in the film musical *South Pacific.* 345–58

Onega Jaén, Susana. Jeanette Winterson's politics of uncertainty in *Sexing the Cherry.* 297–313

Penas Ibáñez, Beatriz. Kristeva's *Desire in Language*: a feminist semiotic perspective on language and literature. 95–105

Plo Alastrué, Ramón. Gender and genre conventions in *When Harry Met Sally.* 399–418

Romero Guillén, María Dolores. Woman's death and patriarchal closure in Fritz Lang's *The Big Heat.* 333–44

Rudnick, Lois. Feminist utopian visions and the 'New Woman': Jane Addams and Charlotte Perkins Gilman. 181–93

Sargent, Pamela. Women and science fiction. 225–37

Shinn, Thelma J. Gender images and patterns from novel to film. 451–9

Suárez Sánchez, Juan A. The rear view: paranoia and homosocial desire in Alfred Hitchcock's *Rear Window.* 359–69

Zamorano, Ana. 'Adrift on an unknown sea': androgyny and writing with particular reference to *Echo* by Violet Trefusis. 195–206

Gendered Modernisms

39. Dickie, Margaret; Travisano, Thomas J. (eds). Gendered Modernisms: American women poets and their readers. Philadelphia: Pennsylvania UP, 1996. pp. xvi, 321.

Chisholm, Dianne. Pornopoeia, the Modernist canon, and the cultural capital of sexual literacy: the case of H.D. 69–94

Clark, Suzanne. *Jouissance* and the sentimental daughter: Edna St Vincent Millay. 143–69

Daniels, Kate. Muriel Rukeyser and her literary critics. 247–63

Dickie, Margaret. Recovering the repression in Stein's erotic poetry. 3–25

Flynn, Richard. 'The buried life and the body of waking': Muriel Rukeyser and the politics of literary history. 264–79

HEUVING, JEANNE.   Laura (Riding) Jackson's 'really new' poem. 191–213

LAITY, CASSANDRA.   H.D. , Modernism, and the transgressive sexualities of Decadent–Romantic Platonism. 45–68

LINDBERG, KATHRYNE V.   Whose canon? Gwendolyn Brooks: founder at the center of the 'margins'. 283–311

LOEFFELHOLZ, MARY.   History as conjugation: Stein's *Stanzas in Meditation* and the literary history of the Modernist long poem. 26–42

SCHULZE, ROBIN GAIL.   *The Frigate Pelican*'s progress: Marianne Moore's multiple versions and Modernist practice. 117–39

STEINMAN, LISA M.   'So as to be one having some way of being one having some way of working': Marianne Moore and literary tradition. 97–116

TRAVISANO, THOMAS.   The Elizabeth Bishop phenomenon. 217–44

WALKER, CHERYL.   Antimodern, modern, and postmodern Millay: contexts of revaluation. 170–88

Heirs of Fame

40. SWISS, MARGO; KENT, DAVID A. (eds).   Heirs of fame: Milton and writers of the English Renaissance. Lewisburg, PA: Bucknell UP; London; Toronto: Assoc. UPs, 1995. pp. viii, 317. Rev. by Michael G. Brennan in NQ (43:3) 1996, 344–5.

BENET, DIANA TREVIÑO.   The genius of the wood and the prelate of the grove: Milton and Marvell. 230–46

CANTALUPO, CHARLES.   'By art is created that great ... state': Milton's *Paradise Lost* and Hobbes's *Leviathan*. 184–207

CREASER, JOHN.   Milton: the truest of the sons of Ben. 158–83

DANIELSON, DENNIS.   Milton, Bunyan, and the clothing of Truth and Righteousness. 247–69

DOHERTY, M. J.   Beyond androgyny: Sidney, Milton, and the phoenix. 34–65

PARRISH, PAUL A.   Milton and Crashaw: the Cambridge and Italian years. 208–29

REVARD, STELLA P.   Myth, masque, and marriage: *Paradise Lost* and Shakespeare's romances. 114–34

ROCHE, THOMAS P., JR.   Spenser, Milton, and the representation of evil. 14–33

RØSTVIG, MAREN-SOFIE.   The craftsmanship of God: some structural contexts for the *Poems of Mr John Milton* (1645). 85–113

STANWOOD, P. G.   Of prelacy and polity in Milton and Hooker. 66–84

SWISS, MARGO.   *Lachrymae Christi*: the theology of tears in Milton's *Lycidas* and Donne's sermon *Jesus Wept*. 135–57

ZWICKER, STEVEN.   Milton, Dryden, and the politics of literary controversy. 270–89

High and Low Moderns

41. DiBATTISTA, MARIA; McDIARMID, LUCY (eds).   High and low moderns: literature and culture, 1889–1939. New York; Oxford: OUP, 1996. pp. x, 259.

BROMWICH, DAVID.   T. S. Eliot and Hart Crane. 49–64

DiBATTISTA, MARIA.   Introduction. 3–19

DiBATTISTA, MARIA.   The lowly art of murder: Modernism and the case of the free woman. 176–93

DICKSON, JAY.   Surviving Victoria. 23–46

FOSTER, R. F.   Love, politics, and textual corruption: Mrs O'Shea's *Parnell*. 197–211

GoGWILT, CHRIS.   Broadcasting news from nowhere: R. B. Cunninghame Graham and the geography of politics in the 1890s. 235–54

GRENE, NICHOLAS.   The Edwardian Shaw; or, The Modernist that never was. 135–47

LITZ, A. WALTON.   Florence Farr: a 'transitional' woman. 85–106

LONGLEY, EDNA.   'The business of the earth': Edward Thomas and ecocentrism. 107–31

McDIARMID, LUCY.   The demotic Lady Gregory. 212–34

MENAND, LOUIS.   Kipling in the history of forms. 148–65

MENDELSON, EDWARD.   How Lawrence corrected Wells; how Orwell refuted Lawrence. 166–75

TERES, HARVEY.   Remaking Marxist criticism: *Partisan Review*'s Eliotic Leftism, 1934–1936. 65–84

A History of Women in the West

42. DAVIS, NATALIE ZEMON; FARGE, ARLETTE (eds).   A history of women in the West: vol. III, Renaissance and Enlightenment paradoxes. Cambridge, MA: Harvard UP; Belknap Press, 1992. pp. x, 595.

DESAIVE, JEAN-PAUL.   The ambiguities of literature. 261–94

DULONG, CLAUDE.   From conversation to creation. 395–419

GELBART, NINA RATTNER.   Female journalists. 420–43

NICHOLSON, ERIC A.   The theater. 295–314

Home Ground: Southern Autobiography

43. BERRY, J. BILL (ed.).   Home ground: Southern autobiography. Columbia; London: Missouri UP, 1991. pp. viii, 201. (Cf. bibl. 1992, 3235, where collection not analysed.)

ANDREWS, WILLIAM L.   Booker T. Washington, Belle Kearney, and the Southern patriarchy. 85–97

BLOOM, LYNN Z.   Coming of age in the segregated South: autobiographies of twentieth-century childhoods, Black and White. 110–22

CORE, GEORGE.   Life's bright parenthesis: Warren's example and one man's pedagogy. 48–60

COX, JAMES M.   Beneath my father's name. 13–30

FOSTER, FRANCES SMITH.   Parents and children in autobiography by Southern Afro-American writers. 98–109

OLNEY, JAMES.   Parents and children in Robert Penn Warren's autobiography. 31–47

SIMPSON, LEWIS P.   The autobiographical impulse in the South. 63–84

SULLIVAN, WALTER.   Strange children: Caroline Gordon and Allen Tate. 123–30

Image and Ideology in Modern/Postmodern Discourse

44. DOWNING, DAVID B.; BAZARGAN, SUSAN (eds).   Image and ideology in modern/postmodern discourse. Albany: New York State UP, 1991. pp. ix, 394.

BALSAMO, GIAN.   The narrative text as historical artifact: the case of John Fowles. 127–52

BURNS, MARGIE.   A good rose is hard to find: Southern gothic as signs of social dislocation in Faulkner and O'Connor. 105–23

BUZARD, JAMES M.   Faces, photos, mirrors: image and ideology in the novels of John le Carré. 153–79

CARAHER, BRIAN G.   A Modernist allegory of narration: Joseph Conrad's *Youth* and the ideology of the image. 47–68

DOWNING, DAVID B.; BAZARGAN, SUSAN.   Image and ideology: some preliminary histories and polemics. 3–44

MACASKILL, BRIAN.   Figuring rupture: iconology, politics, and the image. 249–71

MESMER, MICHAEL W.   Apostle to the techno/peasants: word and image in the work of John Berger. 199–227

PEARCE, RICHARD.   Virginia Woolf's struggle with author-ity. 69–83

STRAUB, KRISTINA.   Feminist politics and postmodernist style. 274–86

WACKER, NORMAN.   Ezra Pound and the visual: notations for new subjects in *The Cantos*. 85–104

Image of India in the Indian Novel in English 1960–1985

45. PANDEY, SUDHAKAR; RAO, R. RAJ (eds).   Image of India in the Indian novel in English 1960–1985. Hyderabad: Orient Longman, 1993. pp. xix, 143.

CHINDHADE, SHIRISH V. The triumph of timeless India: Rama Mehta's *Inside the Haveli*. 84–91

DHAWAN, R. K. Destiny of a nation: Arun Joshi's *The Apprentice*. 51–60

DNYATE, RAMESH. The hothouse cactus: a note on R. K. Narayan's *The Painter of Signs*. 61–8

EZEKIEL, NISSIM. An image of India in Shouri Daniels' *A City of Children*. 135–40

KIRPAL, VINEY. The perfect bubble: a study of Anita Desai's *In Custody*. 123–34

MADGE, V. M. Rise of the *demos*: a study of Malgonkar's *The Princes*. 12–20

MATHUR, O. P. A metaphor of reality: a study of the protagonist of *Midnight's Children*. 113–22

NABAR, VRINDA. The four-dimensional reality: Anita Desai's *Clear Light of Day*. 102–12

PANDEY, SUDHAKAR; RAO, R. RAJ. Introduction. xi–xix

PARANJAPE, MAKARAND. Critique of Communism in Raja Rao's *Comrade Kirillov*. 69–83

SHAHANE, VASANT A. Fictional montage in Anita Desai's *Fire on the Mountain*. 92–101

SHIRWADKAR, K. R. Literature as ideology: Raja Rao's *The Serpent and the Rope*. 1–11

SINGH, R. S. West meets East: a study of Kamala Markandaya's *Possession*. 21–35

WANDREKAR, KALPANA. The ailing aliens: Anita Desai's *Bye Bye Blackbird* as a symptomatic study in schizophrenia. 36–50

Images of Persephone

46. HAYES, ELIZABETH T. (ed.). Images of Persephone: feminist readings in Western literature. Gainesville: Florida UP, 1994. pp. xi, 224. Rev. by Jack Stewart in DHLR (25:1–3) 1993/94, 248–50.

DOLL, MARY A. Ghosts of themselves: the Demeter women in Beckett. 121–35

GREGORY, EILEEN. Dark Persephone and Margaret Atwood's *Procedures for Underground*. 136–52

HARLEY, MARTA POWELL. Chaucer's use of the Proserpina myth in the Knight's Tale and the Merchant's Tale. 20–31

HAYES, ELIZABETH T. 'Like seeing you buried': Persephone in *The Bluest Eye*, *Their Eyes Were Watching God*, and *The Color Purple*. 170–94

HYDE, VIRGINIA. 'Lost' girls: D. H. Lawrence's versions of Persephone. 99–120

LAFFRADO, LAURA.   The Persephone myth in Hawthorne's *Tanglewood Tales*. 75–83

PENNELL, MELISSA MCFARLAND.   Through the Golden Gate: madness and the Persephone myth in Gertrude Atherton's *The Foghorn*. 84–98

WOLF, JANET S.   'Like an old tale still': Paulina, 'triple Hecate', and the Persephone myth in *The Winter's Tale*. 32–44

Imagining Romanticism

47. COLEMAN, DEIRDRE; OTTO, PETER (eds).   Imagining Romanticism: essays on English and Australian Romanticisms. West Cornwall, CT: Locust Hill Press, 1992. pp. xxiv, 300. (Locust Hill literary studies, 10.) Rev. by Heidi Van de Veire in AUMLA (82) 1994, 132–4; by Horst Priessnitz in Archiv (231:2) 1994, 410–12.

BARBOUR, JUDITH.   Dr John William Polidori: author of *The Vampyre*. 85–110

BEER, JOHN.   Is the Romantic imagination our imagination? 25–48

DAVIES, J. M. Q.   Blake's *Paradise Lost* designs reconsidered. 143–81

HASKELL, DENNIS.   Landscape at the edge of a promise: Australian Romanticism and John Shaw Neilson. 203–15

HILTON, NELSON.   Keats, teats, and the fane of poesy. 49–72

KING, FRANCIS.   Wordsworth's Italian Alps. 111–24

MCCREDDEN, LYN.   Mastering Romanticism: the struggle for vocation in the texts of James McAuley. 265–73

MEAD, PHILIP.   Charles Harpur's disfiguring origins: allegory in colonial poetry. 217–40

MEE, JON.   William Blake and John Wright: two ex-Swedenborgians. 73–84

PRICKETT, STEPHEN.   *Biographia Literaria*: Chapter Thirteen. 3–23

REID, IAN.   The instructive imagination: English with tears. 241–64

TAYLOR, ANDREW.   A case of Romantic disinheritance. 185–201

TAYLOR, ANDREW.   Postmodern Romantic: the imaginary in David Malouf's *An Imaginary Life*. 275–90

TOLLEY, MICHAEL J.   'Words standing in chariots': the literalism of Blake's imagination. 125–42

Infant Tongues

48. GOODENOUGH, ELIZABETH; HEBERLE, MARK A.; SOKOLOFF, NAOMI B. (eds).   Infant tongues: the voice of the child in literature. Foreword by Robert Coles. Detroit, MI: Wayne State UP, 1994. pp. ix, 331.

AVERY, GILLIAN.   The voice of the child, both godly and unregenerate, in early modern England. 16–27

BOTTIGHEIMER, RUTH B.   The child-reader of children's Bibles, 1656–1753. 44–56

GALBRAITH, MARY. Pip as 'infant tongue' and as adult narrator in Chapter One of *Great Expectations*. 123–41

GOODENOUGH, ELIZABETH. 'We haven't the words': the silence of children in the novels of Virginia Woolf. 184–201

HEBERLE, MARK A. 'Innocent prate': *King John* and Shakespeare's children. 28–43

JOHNSON, ALEXANDRA. The drama of imagination: Marjory Fleming and her diaries. 80–109

MCHALE, BRIAN. Child as ready-made: baby-talk and the language of Dos Passos's children in *USA*. 202–24

MYERS, MITZI. Reading Rosamond reading: Maria Edgeworth's 'Wee-Wee Stories' interrogate the canon. 57–79

RAHN, SUZANNE. The changing language of Black child characters in American children's books. 225–58

SKLENICKA, CAROL; SPILKA, MARK. A womb of his own: Lawrence's passional/paternal view of childhood. 164–83

SOKOLOFF, NAOMI. Childhood lost: children's voices in Holocaust literature. 259–74

TATAR, MARIA. Is anybody out there listening? Fairy tales and the voice of the child. 275–83

International Aspects of Irish Literature

49. FUROMOTO, TOSHI, *et al.* (eds). International aspects of Irish literature. Gerrards Cross: Smythe, 1996. pp. viii, 450. (Irish literary studies, 44.) (IASAIL-Japan, 5.) Rev. by Norman Vance in TLS, 27 Sept. 1996, 13.

ARNDT, MARIE. Sean O'Faolain: an advocate for women? 356–61

CHADWICK, JOSEPH. Yeats: colonialism and responsibility. 107–14

COLDWELL, JOAN. The anxiety of influence: feminist response to father Yeats. 362–8

CONNOR, STEVEN. Beckett's interdictions. 313–22

CORBALLIS, RICHARD. Some echoes of Ireland in New Zealand literature, 1890–1990. 45–58

CROGHAN, MARTIN J. Maria Edgeworth and the tradition of Irish semiotics. 340–8

DALSIMER, ADELE M. 'Knocknagow is no more', but when was it? 189–95

DEVY, GANESH N. The Indian Yeats. 93–106

D'HAEN, THEO. Irish regionalism, magic realism and post-modernism. 59–68

DILLON MERCIER, EILÍS. Beckett's Irishness. 328–35

DILLON MERCIER, EILÍS.   Folk memory as history – the Irish tradition. 1–13

HEANEY, SEAMUS.   Keeping time: Irish poetry and contemporary society. 247–62

HUBER, WERNER.   Irish novels in a German court library of the early 19th century. 37–44

HUGHES, CLAIR.   'Hound voices': the Big House in three novels by Anglo-Irish women writers. 349–55

KENNEALLY, MICHAEL.   The transcendent impulse in contemporary Irish drama. 272–82

KONDO, MASAKI.   The self vanishing into impersonal staring into the void. 323–7

KOSOK, HEINZ.   Ta-ra-ra-boom-dee-ay *vs* the *Noh*: Sean O'Casey and William Butler Yeats. 211–27

McMILLAN, PETER.   The literary criticism of Lafcadio Hearn. 201–10

McNAMARA, LEO.   The plays of Jack B. Yeats. 228–34

MORI, NAOYA.   Beckett's brief dream: Dante in *Mal vu mal dit* and *Stirrings Still*. 283–91

MORRISON, KRISTIN.   Child murder as metaphor of colonial exploitation in Toni Morrison's *Beloved*, *The Silence in the Garden*, and *The Killeen*. 292–300

MURRAY, CIARAN.   The Japanese garden and the mystery of Swift. 159–68

Ó H-EIDIRSCEOIL, SEÁN.   A Shavian interlude. 180–8

OLINDER, BRITTA.   Hewitt's region in a post-colonial perspective. 301–10

ROBINSON, PETER.   Joyce's lyric poetry. 151–8

RONAN, SEAN G.   Hearn's Irish background. 196–200

RONSLEY, JOSEPH.   Initial response to Denis Johnston's *The Moon in the Yellow River*. 235–46

SADDLEMYER, ANN.   Reading Yeats's *A Prayer for My Daughter* – yet again. 69–81

SCOTT, BONNIE KIME.   Joyce's post-modern return to Ireland. 123–34

SUZUKI, TAKASHI.   Regionalism in *Ulysses*: a trap. 115–22

TANIGAWA, FUYUJI.   The deconstructive impulse: Seamus Heaney's poetics in 'kinship'. 263–71

WEINTRAUB, STANLEY.   'The Hibernian School': Oscar Wilde and Bernard Shaw. 169–79

WELCH, ROBERT. 'He rests. He has travelled.' Movement in Joyce. 135–50

YAMAZAKI, HIROYUKI. Yeats and Orientalism. 82–92

International Women's Writing

50. BROWN, ANNE E.; GOOZÉ, MARJANNE E. (eds). International women's writing: new landscapes of identity. Westport, CT; London: Greenwood Press, 1995. pp. xxv, 289. (Contributions in women's studies, 147.)

BARNES, FIONA R. Dismantling the master's houses: Jean Rhys and West Indian identity. 150–61

BAZIN, NANCY TOPPING. Southern Africa and the theme of madness: novels by Doris Lessing, Bessie Head, and Nadine Gordimer. 137–49

ELKINS, MARILYN. Expatriate Afro-American women as exotics. 264–73

GOLDMAN, MARLENE. Naming the unspeakable: the mapping of female identity in Maxine Hong Kingston's *The Woman Warrior*. 223–32

KEHDE, SUZANNE. Colonial discourse and female identity: Bharati Mukherjee's *Jasmine*. 70–7

MADDEN, DEANNA. Wild child, tropical flower, mad wife: female identity in Jean Rhys's *Wide Sargasso Sea*. 162–74

NIESEN DE ABRUÑA, LAURA. The ambivalence of mirroring and female bonding in Paule Marshall's *Brown Girl, Brownstones*. 245–52

PORTER, SUSAN. The 'imaginative space' of Medbh McGuckian. 86–101

SHEN, GLORIA. Born of a stranger: mother–daughter relationships and storytelling in Amy Tan's *The Joy Luck Club*. 233–44

Intertextuality in Literature and Film

51. CANCALON, ELAINE DAVIS; SPACAGNA, ANTOINE (eds). Intertextuality in literature and film: selected papers from the Thirteenth Annual Florida State University Conference on Literature and Film. Gainesville: Florida UP, 1994. pp. vi, 176.

FEBLES, JORGE. A character's indictment of authorial subterfuge: the parody of texts in Roberto G. Fernández. 21–35

FOSTER, JOHN BURT, JR. Starting with Dostoevsky's double: Bakhtin and Nabokov as intertextualists. 9–20

KNEE, ADAM. The compound genre film: *Billy the Kid versus Dracula* meets *The Harvey Girls*. 141–56

LAWLOR, MARY. Placing source in *Greed* and *McTeague*. 93–104

LAWSON, BENJAMIN SHERWOOD. Federated fancies: Balzac's *Lost Illusions* and Melville's *Pierre*. 37–47

MIRAGLIA, ANNE MARIE.   Texts engendering texts: a Québécois writing of American novels. 49–60

Irish Writers and Their Creative Process

52. GENET, JACQUELINE; HELLEGOUARC'H, WYNNE (eds).   Irish writers and their creative process. Gerrards Cross: Smythe, 1996. pp. vii, 151. (Irish literary studies, 48.) Rev. by Norman Vance in TLS, 27 Sept. 1996, 13.

BANVILLE, JOHN.   The personae of summer. 118–22

CRONIN, JOHN.   John McGahern: a new image? 110–17

HARMON, MAURICE.   Seamus Heaney and the gentle flame. 17–29

HEANEY, SEAMUS.   The frontier of writing. 3–16

HENDERSON, LYNDA.   Men, women and the life of the spirit in Tom Murphy's plays. 87–99

IMHOF, RÜDIGER.   In search of the Rosy Grail: the creative process in the novels of John Banville. 123–36

KILROY, THOMAS.   From page to stage. 55–62

McGAHERN, JOHN.   Reading and writing. 103–9

MARTIN, AUGUSTINE.   John Montague: passionate contemplative. 37–51

MONTAGUE, JOHN.   The sweet way. 30–6

MURPHY, TOM.   The creative process. 78–86

MURRAY, CHRISTOPHER.   Thomas Kilroy's world elsewhere. 63–77

Jacobean Drama as Social Criticism

53. HOGG, JAMES (ed.).   Jacobean drama as social criticism. Lewiston, NY; Lampeter: Mellen Press, 1995. pp. iv, 365. (Salzburg studies in English literature: Jacobean drama studies, 101.)

BAUMANN, UWE.   The presentation of the Roman imperial court in Jacobean tragedy. 73–93

BORN-LECHLEITNER, ILSE.   Implicit social criticism in *The Witch of Edmonton*. 261–74

BROOKE, NICHOLAS.   Performance structures as social criticism in English classic drama. 21–6

BURNS, EDWARD.   The sharp spectator. 193–203

CORBIN, PETER.   'A dog's obeyed in office': kingship and authority in Jacobean tragedy. 59–71

DAPHINOFF, DIMITER.   How conservative was John Ford? 231–8

DE SILVA, D. M.   Society, politics, and the aesthetic life of Massinger's plays. 239–59

DORANGEON, SIMONE.   Beaumont and Fletcher, or a self-subverting praise of virtue in an impure society. 275–84

FARLEY-HILLS, DAVID.   The audience implications of some Paul's and Blackfriars' plays. 205–15

HOGG, JAMES.   Court satire in John Webster's *The White Devil*. 147–65

HOGG, JAMES.   An ephemeral hit: Thomas Middleton's *A Game at Chess*. 285–318

HOGG, JAMES.   William Hayley's *Marcella* and Thomas Middleton and William Rowley's *The Changeling*: a watered-down Jacobean masterpiece. 319–61

HONIGMANN, E. A. J.   Social questioning in Elizabethan and Jacobean plays, with special reference to *Othello*. 3–11

HUSSEY, STANLEY.   Social stratification by language. 179–91

KISS, ATTILA.   Abjection and power: the semiotics of violence in Jacobean tragedy. 95–105

LORANT, ANDRÉ.   Social criticism in *Hamlet* and *The Revenger's Tragedy*. 13–19

MAHLER, ANDREAS.   A lost world, no new-found land – disorientation and immobility as social criticism in early seventeenth-century tragedy. 27–43

SCHMITZ, GÖTZ.   Satirical elements in Latin comedies acted on the occasion of royal visits to Cambridge University. 217–30

SCOTT, MICHAEL.   Confrontational comedy. 167–77

SORGE, THOMAS.   Baroque theatricality and anxiety in the drama of John Ford. 125–45

SZÖNYI, GYÖRGY E.   'My charms are all o'erthrown': the social and ideological context of the magician in Jacobean drama. 107–23

WYMER, ROWLAND.   Jacobean pageant or Elizabethan *fin-de-siècle*? The political context of early seventeenth-century tragedy. 45–58

Keeping the Victorian House

54. DICKERSON, VANESSA D. (ed.).   Keeping the Victorian house: a collection of essays. New York; London: Garland, 1995. pp. xxxi, 369. (Garland reference library of the humanities, 1818.) (Origins of Modernism, 7.)

ALEXANDER, LYNN M.   Loss of the domestic idyll: shop workers in Victorian fiction. 291–311

CONNELL, EILEEN.   Playing house: Frances Hodgson Burnett's Victorian fairy tale. 149–71

DANAHAY, MARTIN A.   Housekeeping and hegemony in Dickens's *Bleak House*. 3–25

FASICK, LAURA.   God's house, women's place. 75–103

FENNELL, FRANCIS L.; FENNELL, MONICA A.   'Ladies – loaf givers': food, women, and society in the novels of Charlotte Brontë and George Eliot. 235–58

GERARD, JESSICA.   The chatelaine: women of the Victorian landed classes and the country house. 175–206

GERGITS, JULIA M.   Women artists at home. 105–29

IVES, MAURA.   Housework, mill work, women's work: the functions of cloth in Charlotte Brontë's *Shirley*. 259–89

LOGAN, THAD.   Decorating domestic space: middle-class women and Victorian interiors. 207–34

MORSE, DEBORAH DENENHOLZ.   Stitching repentance, sewing rebellion: seamstress and fallen woman in Elizabeth Gaskell's fiction. 27–73

SHAFFER, BRIAN W.   Domestic ironies: housekeeping as mankeeping in Conrad's *The Secret Agent*. 313–29

STANLEY, SANDRA KUMAMOTO.   Female acquisition in *The Spoils of Poynton*. 131–48

Language and Literature in the African-American Imagination

55. BLACKSHIRE-BELAY, CAROL AISHA (ed.).   Language and literature in the African-American imagination. Westport, CT; London: Greenwood Press, 1992. pp. x, 210. (Contributions in Afro-American and African studies, 154.) Rev. by Toya A. Wyatt in JPCL (9:2) 1994, 345–51; by Edmund Bamiro in WorldE (13:2) 1994, 276–8.

ABARRY, ABU SHARDOW.   Afrocentric aesthetics in selected Harlem renaissance poetry. 133–46

ASANTE, MOLEFI KETE.   Locating a text: implications of Afrocentric theory. 9–20

BLACKSHIRE-BELAY, CAROL AISHA.   Afrocentricity and literary theory: the maturing imagination. 3–7

DE LANCEY, FRANZELLA ELAINE.   Refusing to be boxed in: Sonia Sanchez's transformation of the haiku form. 21–36

HOLMES, CAROLYN L.   Reassessing African-American literature through an Afrocentric paradigm: Zora N. Hurston and James Baldwin. 37–51

JENNINGS, REGINA B.   The blue/black poetics of Sonia Sanchez. 119–32

JOHNSON, LONNELL E.   Dilemma of the dutiful servant: the poetry of Jupiter Hammon. 105–17

JONES, KIRKLAND C.   Folk idiom in the literary expression of two African-American authors: Rita Dove and Yusef Komunyakaa. 149–65

LESEUR, GETA.   From nice colored girl to womanist: an explanation of development in Ntozake Shange's writings. 167–80

MARSHALL, BARBARA J.   Kitchen table talk: J. California Cooper's use of *nommo* – female bonding and transcendence. 91–102

MAZRUI, ALAMIN. African languages in the African-American experience. 75–90

Late-Medieval Religious Texts and Their Transmission

56. MINNIS, A. J. (ed.). Late-medieval religious texts and their transmission: essays in honour of A. I. Doyle. Cambridge; Rochester, NY: Brewer, 1994. pp. ix, 198. (York Manuscripts Conference proceedings, III.) Rev. by Tim William Machan in YLS (9) 1995, 169–73; by Thorlac Turville-Petre in SAC (18) 1996, 254–7; by Wendy Scase in NQ (43:1) 1996, 73–4.

DUNCAN, THOMAS G. Two Middle English penitential lyrics: sound and scansion. 55–65

EDWARDS, A. S. G. The transmission and audience of Osbern Bokenham's *Legendys of Hooly Wummen*. 157–67

FLETCHER, ALAN J. A hive of industry or a hornets' nest? MS Sidney Sussex 74 and its scribes. 131–55

GILLESPIE, VINCENT. Thy will be done: *Piers Plowman* and the Paternoster. 95–119

HANNA, RALPH, III. 'Meddling with makings' and Will's work. 85–94

HUDSON, ANNE. Aspects of the 'publication' of Wyclif's Latin sermons. 121–9

MILLETT, BELLA. *Mouvance* and the medieval author: re-editing *Ancrene Wisse*. 9–20

PICKERING, O. S. The outspoken *South English Legendary* poet. 21–37

POWELL, SUE. The transmission and circulation of *The Lay Folks' Catechism*. 67–84

THOMPSON, JOHN J. Another look at the religious texts in Lincoln, Cathedral Library, MS 91. 169–87

WOGAN-BROWNE, JOCELYN. The apple's message: some post-Conquest hagiographic accounts of textual transmission. 39–53

Laurence Sterne in Modernism and Postmodernism

57. PIERCE, DAVID; DE VOOGD, PETER (eds). Laurence Sterne in Modernism and postmodernism. Amsterdam; Atlanta, GA: Rodopi, 1996. pp. 210. (Postmodern studies, 15.) Rev. by Anne Bandry in Shandean (8) 1996, 139–42.

BALLESTEROS GONZÁLEZ, ANTONIO. Digression and intertextual parody in Thomas Nashe, Laurence Sterne and James Joyce. 55–64

BELL, MICHAEL. Laurence Sterne and the twentieth century. 39–54

DESCARGUES, MADELEINE. Sterne, Nabokov and the happy (non)ending of biography. 167–78

DUPAS, JEAN-CLAUDE. A sun-dial in a grave: the founding gesture. 99–108

Göbel, Walter; Grint, Damian.   Salman Rushdie's silver medal. 87–98

Hart, Michael.   'Many planes of narrative': a comparative perspective on Sterne and Joyce. 65–80

Klein, Herbert.   Identity reclaimed: the art of being Tristram. 123–32

Laudando, Carla Maria.   Deluge of fragments: Rabelais's *Fourth Book*, Sterne's *Fragment* and Beckett's *Fizzles*. 157–65

Milesi, Laurent.   Have you not forgot to wind up the clock? Tristram Shandy and Jacques *le fataliste* on the (post?)modern psychoanalytic couch. 179–95

Parnell, Tim.   Sterne and Kundera: the novel of variations and the 'noisy foolishness of human certainty'. 147–55

Pegenaute, Louis.   Three trapped tigers in Shandy Hall. 133–45

Pierce, David.   Introduction. 7–17

Rademacher, Jörg W.   Totalized (auto-)biography as fragmented intertextuality: Shakespeare – Sterne – Joyce. 81–6

Sim, Stuart.   'All that exist are "islands of determinism"': Shandean sentiment and the dilemma of postmodern physics. 109–21

Watts, Carol.   The modernity of Sterne. 19–38

Learning the Trade

58. Fleming, Deborah (ed.).   Learning the trade: essays on W. B. Yeats and contemporary poetry. West Cornwall, CT: Locust Hill Press, 1993. pp. xxxi, 313. (Locust Hill literary studies, 11.) Rev. by Joseph M. Hassett in EI (29:4) 1994, 189–92.

Allison, Jonathan.   Questioning Yeats: Paul Muldoon's *7, Middagh Street*. 3–20

Burris, Sidney.   Pastoral nostalgia and the poetry of W. B. Yeats and Seamus Heaney. 195–201

De La Vars, Gordon J.   Contrasting landscapes: John Hewitt's rural vision and Yeats's Irish world. 39–45

Engle, John.   A modest refusal: Yeats, MacNeice, and Irish poetry. 71–88

Gray, Cecile.   Medbh McGuckian: imagery wrought to its uttermost. 165–77

Horowitz, Steven.   W. B. Yeats's Ireland and James Wright's Ohio. 237–51

Knowles, Sebastian.   Interview with Desmond Egan. 89–111

Lense, Edward.   An influence survived: Roethke and Yeats. 253–64

Libby, Anthony.   Angels in the bone shop. 281–301

Mahon, Ellen.   Eavan Boland's journey with the muse. 179–94

MOLONEY, KAREN MARGUERITE. Re-envisioning Yeats's *The Second Coming*: Desmond O'Grady and the Charles River. 135–47

REECE, ERIK. Detour to the 'alltombing womb': Amiri Baraka's assault on Yeats's muse. 219–35

REVIE, LINDA L. The little red fox, emblem of the Irish peasant in poems by Yeats, Tynan and Ní Dhomhnaill. 113–33

SAILER, SUSAN SHAW. Time against time: myth and the poetry of Yeats and Heaney. 202–17

SCHRICKER, GALE C. From Yeats's *Great Wheel* to O'Siadhail's *Image Wheel*. 149–64

TANNEHILL, ARLENE. 'No saint or hero ... / Brings dangerous tokens to the new era': Derek Mahon and Tess Gallagher's revisions of Yeats's *The Magi*. 47–69

WILSON, WILLIAM A. Yeats, Muldoon, and heroic history. 21–38

ZIMMERMAN, LEE. Self-delighting souls, self-enclosed egos: Yeats and Galway Kinnell. 265–79

Listening to Silences

59. HEDGES, ELAINE; FISHKIN, SHELLEY FISHER (eds). Listening to silences: new essays in feminist criticism. New York; Oxford: OUP, 1994. pp. viii, 326. Rev. by Barbara Frey Waxman in TSWL (15:1) 1996, 167–70; by Paula S. Berggren in AL (68:1) 1996, 276–7.

ADAMS, KATE. Northamerican silences: history, identity, and witness in the poetry of Gloria Anzaldúa, Cherríe Moraga, and Leslie Marmon Silko. 130–45

ALARCÓN, NORMA. Cognitive desires: an allegory of/for Chicana critics. 260–73

BRAXTON, JOANNE M.; ZUBER, SHARON. Silences in Harriet 'Linda Brent' Jacobs's *Incidents in the Life of a Slave Girl*. 146–55

CHEUNG, KING-KOK. Attentive silence in Joy Kogawa's *Obasan*. 113–29

COINER, CONSTANCE. 'No one's private ground': a Bakhtinian reading of Tillie Olsen's *Tell Me a Riddle*. 71–93

DIZARD, ROBIN. Filling in the silences: Tillie Olsen's reading lists. 295–309

FISHKIN, SHELLEY FISHER. Reading, writing, and arithmetic: the lessons *Silences* has taught us. 23–48

KAPLAN, CARLA. Reading feminist readings: recuperative reading and the silent heroine of feminist criticism. 168–94

LAURENCE, PATRICIA. Women's silence as a ritual of truth: a study of literary expressions in Austen, Brontë, and Woolf. 156–67

MIDDLEBROOK, DIANE. Circle of women artists: Tillie Olsen and Anne Sexton at the Radcliffe Institute. 17–22

PETERSON, CARLA L.   'Further liftings of the veil': gender, class, and labor in Frances E. W. Harper's *Iola Leroy*. 97–112

ROSENFELT, DEBORAH SILVERTON.   Rereading *Tell Me a Riddle* in the age of deconstruction. 49–70

SENSIBAR, JUDITH L.; WITTENBERG, JUDITH BRYANT.   Silences in the in-between: feminist women critics and the canon. 274–86

Literary Inter-Relations

60. MASSOUD, MARY (ed.).   Literary inter-relations: Ireland, Egypt, and the Far East. Gerrards Cross: Smythe, 1996. pp. x, 426. (Irish literary studies, 47.) Rev. by Norman Vance in TLS, 27 Sept. 1996, 13.

BASTA, SAMIRA.   The factual and the imaginary in Thomas Moore's Egyptian tale, *The Epicurean*. 125–32

BOWER, MARTHA.   Regionalism and cultural marginalism: the New England Irish in O'Neill's late plays. 154–9

CAVE, RICHARD ALLEN.   The city *versus* the village. 281–96

COTTREAU, DEBORAH.   Friel and Beckett: the politics of language. 160–9

CROGHAN, MARTIN J.   Swift & Conrad: gamekeepers make great poachers. 208–21

EAGLETON, TERRY.   Form and ideology in the Anglo-Irish novel. 135–46

ELBANNA, ETAF A.   The autobiography of an Irish rebel: Brendan Behan's *Borstal Boy*. 170–6

FAHIM, SHADIA S.   The city and the crisis of identity in the *Bildungsromane* of Mahfouz and O'Faolain. 335–44

FREITAG, BARBARA.   *The Untilled Field*: harvesting the seeds of discontent. 327–34

FUROMOTO, TOSHI.   Contemporary poetry of Northern Ireland: recovery of political interest and social concern. 177–81

GRENE, NICHOLAS.   Shaw, Egypt and the Empire. 201–7

HAFEZ, AZIZA S.   The use of myth, parable and folk tale in Flann O'Brien's *At Swim-Two-Birds* and Etedal Othman's *The Sun's Tattoo*. 62–72

EL-HALAWANY, MONA.   The spatial role of the village and the city in Thomas Murphy's *Bailegangaire* and Yussuf Idris's *Al-Naddaha*. 358–70

HAROUN, MAGDA.   Donald O'Nery and Goha in folktales of Ireland and Egypt. 91–6

HASHEM, EVINE.   The re-enactment of colonialism in James Joyce's *A Portrait of the Artist as a Young Man*. 235–43

KHALLAF, NADIA.   Colonialism in Honor Tracy's 'Irish' novel, *A Number of Things*. 222–7

KHOLOUSSY, SAMIA. Cracks in the edifice of national consciousness: Tawfik El Hakim's *Bird of the East* and Elizabeth Bowen's *The Last September*. 266–77

KIBERD, DECLAN. Yeats and the national longing for form. 185–200

KIERNAN, MAUREEN. Paradise revisited: representation of the rural in Irish & Egyptian film. 309–18

KOSOK, HEINZ. Charles Robert Maturin and colonialism. 228–34

KULLMANN, THOMAS. Irish mythology, Eastern philosophy and literary Modernism in James Stephens' *The Crock of Gold*. 53–61

LAYIWOLA, DELE. Irish folktales and Beckett's *Molloy*: a study in tropism. 78–82

MASSOUD, MARY M. F. Literary parallels: eighteenth-century Anglo-Irish literature and twentieth-century Egyptian literature. 3–22

MAZHAR, AMAL ALY. The symbolic significance of place in Brian Friel's *Philadelphia, Here I Come* and Mahmoud Diab's *A Messenger from the Village of Temira*. 345–57

MEIHUIZEN, NICHOLAS. The nature of the beast: Yeats and the shadow. 105–11

MONÈS, MONA H. George Moore's *Muslin* and Abdel Rahman Al-Sharqawi's *The Earth*: novels of social protest. 252–65

MURPHY, MAUREEN. Folk narrative motifs in Egyptian, Irish and Native-American folklore and literature. 39–52

MURSI, NAWAL. Death in urban and rural poems of Thomas Kinsella. 297–308

MURSI, WAFFIA. The Big House in Mahfouz's *The Count Down* and Jennifer Johnston's *Fool's Sanctuary*. 23–36

ONO, MOTOKO. Portraits of a mask: Wilde, Joyce and Mishima. 112–16

PERSSON, ÅKE. The heroic ideal in Brendan Kennelly's poetry. 97–104

RIYADH, MUSTAFA. The provincial scene in Edward Martyn's *The Heather Field* and *Maeve*. 319–26

ROSS, MÍCEÁL. Androgynous Bloom: forerunners in Irish and Egyptian folk tradition. 83–90

SMYTHE, COLIN. The Gregorys and Egypt, 1855–56 and 1881–82. 147–53

TALLONE, GIOVANNA. *Odi et amo*: Deirdre, Grania and Lady Gregory. 117–24

WATARAI, YOSHIICHI. Lafcadio Hearn's *kwaidan* and Japanese mythologies of the dead. 73–7

WESSELS, J. A. Irish nationalism and the Anglo-Irish: historical and literary parallels to Afrikanerdom. 244–51

Literature and Religion in the Later Middle Ages

61. NEWHAUSER, RICHARD G.; ALFORD, JOHN A. (eds). Literature and religion in the later Middle Ages: philological studies in honor of Siegfried Wenzel. Binghamton, NY: Medieval & Renaissance Texts & Studies, 1995. pp. 414. (Medieval & Renaissance Texts & Studies, 118.) Rev. by Peter Whiteford in Parergon (13:2) 1996, 282–4.

ALFORD, JOHN A. Langland's exegetical drama: the sources of the banquet scene in *Piers Plowman*. 97–117

BLYTHE, JOAN HEIGES. Sins of the tongue and rhetorical prudence in *Piers Plowman*. 119–42

BOITANI, PIERO. 'My tale is of a cock'; or, The problems of literal interpretation. 25–42

DOYLE, A. I. '*Lectulus noster floridus*': an allegory of the penitent soul. 179–90

HANNA, RALPH, III. Robert the Ruyflare and his companions. 81–96

HARTUNG, ALBERT E. The Parson's Tale and Chaucer's penance. 61–80

IRVING, EDWARD B., JR. Heroic worlds: the Knight's Tale and *Beowulf*. 43–59

NEWHAUSER, RICHARD. '*Strong it is to flitte*' – a Middle English poem on death and its pastoral context. 319–36

REICHL, KARL. '*No more ne willi wiked be*': religious poetry in a Franciscan manuscript (Digby 2). 297–317

STEMMLER, THEO. Chaucer's ballade *To Rosemounde* – a parody? 11–23

VON NOLCKEN, CHRISTINA. A 'certain sameness' and our response to it in English Wycliffite texts. 191–208

Literature and Science

62. BRUCE, DONALD; PURDY, ANTHONY (eds). Literature and science. Amsterdam; Atlanta, GA: Rodopi, 1994. pp. 179. (Rodopi perspectives on modern literature, 14.) Rev. by June Deery in Utopian Studies (7:2) 1996, 225–6; by Ronald Bogue in CanRCL (23:4) 1996, 1236–8.

HAYLES, N. KATHERINE. Deciphering the rules of unruly disciplines: a modest proposal for literature and science. 25–48

PURDY, ANTHONY. Introduction: on science and social discourse. 5–24

WALL, ANTHONY. Developing a taste for metaphors. 49–72

WINTHROP-YOUNG, GEOFFREY. Undead networks: information processing and media boundary conflicts in *Dracula*. 107–29

Literature and the Political Imagination

63. HORTON, JOHN; BAUMEISTER, ANDREA T. (eds). Literature and the political imagination. London; New York: Routledge, 1996. pp. viii, 260.

ARBLASTER, ANTHONY.   Literature and moral choice. 129–44

CANOVAN, MARGARET.   'Breathes there the man, with soul so dead ...': reflections on patriotic poetry and liberal principles. 170–97

GILBERT, PAUL.   The idea of a national literature. 198–217

HORTON, JOHN.   Life, literature and ethical theory: Martha Nussbaum on the role of the literary imagination in ethical thought. 70–97

HORTON, JOHN; BAUMEISTER, ANDREA T.   Literature, philosophy and political theory. 1–31

INGLE, STEPHEN.   The anti-imperialism of George Orwell. 218–37

SARGISSON, LUCY.   Contemporary feminist utopianism: practising utopia on utopia. 238–55

SEABRIGHT, PAUL.   The aloofness of liberal politics: can imaginative literature furnish a private space? 145–69

WARNER, MARTIN.   Modes of political imagining. 98–128

WHITEBROOK, MAUREEN.   Taking the narrative turn: what the novel has to offer political theory. 32–52

Look Who's Laughing

64. FINNEY, GAIL (ed.).   Look who's laughing: gender and comedy. Langhorne, PA; Yverdon, Switzerland: Gordon & Breach, 1994. pp. xii, 363. (Studies in humor and gender, 1.)

BIAMONTE, GLORIA A.   Funny isn't it? Testing the boundaries of gender and genre in women's detective fiction. 231–54

BLOOM, DONALD A.   Dwindling into wifehood: the romantic power of the witty heroine in Shakespeare, Dryden, Congreve, and Austen. 53–79

BLUEMEL, KRISTIN.   The feminine laughter of no return: James Joyce and Dorothy Richardson. 161–71

BLY, MARY.   Imagining consummation: women's erotic language in comedies of Dekker and Shakespeare. 35–52

DRESNER, ZITA Z.   Alice Childress's *Like One of the Family*: domestic and undomesticated domestic humor. 221–9

FINNEY, GAIL.   Unity in difference? An introduction. 1–13

GINDELE, KAREN C.   When women laugh wildly and (gentle)men roar: Victorian embodiments of laughter. 139–60

ISIKOFF, ERIN.   Masquerade, modesty, and comedy in Hannah Cowley's *The Belle's Stratagem*. 99–117

IVANOV, ANDREA J.   Mae West was not a man: sexual parody and genre in the plays and films of Mae West. 275–97

KINNEY, SUZ-ANNE.   Confinement sharpens the invention: Aphra Behn's *The Rover* and Susanna Centlivre's *The Busie Body*. 81–98

LASSNER, PHYLLIS.   'Between the gaps': sex, class and anarchy in the British comic novel of World War II. 205–19

MCWHIRTER, DAVID.   Feminism/gender/comedy: Meredith, Woolf, and the reconfiguration of comic distance. 189–204

MONROE, BARBARA.   Courtship, comedy, and African-American expressive culture in Zora Neale Hurston's fiction. 173–88

ROHSE, CORINNA SUNDARARAJAN.   The sphinx goes wild(e): Ada Leverson, Oscar Wilde, and the gender equipollence of parody. 119–36

YOUNG, KAY.   Hollywood, 1934: 'inventing' romantic comedy. 257–74

Louisiana Women Writers

65. BROWN, DOROTHY H.; EWELL, BARBARA C. (eds).   Louisiana women writers: new essays and a comprehensive bibliography. (Cf. bibl. 1993, 6474, where collection not analysed.)

BRADY, PATRICIA.   Mollie Moore Davis: a literary life. 98–118

BROWN, DOROTHY H.   Louisiana women writers: a bibliography. 213–334

BRYAN, VIOLET HARRINGTON.   Race and gender in the early works of Alice Dunbar-Nelson. 120–38

COLEMAN, LINDA S.   At odds: race and gender in Grace King's short fiction. 32–55

ISKANDER, SYLVIA PATTERSON.   Setting and local color in the young adult novels of Berthe Amoss. 184–92

JUNCKER, CLARA.   Behind Confederate lines: Sarah Morgan Dawson. 16–30

MEESE, ELIZABETH.   What the old ones know: Ada Jack Carver's Cane River stories. 140–52

OLEKSY, ELZBIETA.   The keepers of the house: Scarlett O'Hara and Abigail Howland. 168–82

PEEL, ELLEN.   Semiotic subversion in *Désirée's Baby*. 56–73

SKAGGS, MERRILL.   The Louisianas of Katherine Anne Porter's mind. 154–67

WOODLAND, J. RANDAL.   'New people in the old museum of New Orleans': Ellen Gilchrist, Sheila Bosworth, and Nancy Lemann. 194–210

Mapping American Culture

66. FRANKLIN, WAYNE; STEINER, MICHAEL (eds).   Mapping American culture. Iowa City: Iowa UP, 1992. pp. viii, 310. (American land & life.)

ALLEN, RAY.   Back home: Southern identity and African-American gospel quartet performance. 112–35

MEYER, KINERETH. Possessing America: William Carlos Williams's *Paterson* and the politics of appropriation. 152–67

SCHEESE, DON. Thoreau's *Journal*: the creation of a sacred place. 139–51

SCHULTZ, APRIL. 'To lose the speakable': folklore and landscape in O. E. Rølvaag's *Giants in the Earth*. 89–111

WALLACE, KATHLEEN R. 'Roots, aren't they supposed to be buried?' The experience of place in Midwestern women's autobiographies. 168–87

Marketing Modernisms

67. DETTMAR, KEVIN J. H.; WATT, STEPHEN (eds). Marketing Modernisms: self-promotion, canonization, rereading. Ann Arbor: Michigan UP, 1996. pp. x, 374.

BLACKMER, CORINNE E. Selling taboo subjects: the literary commerce of Gertrude Stein and Carl Van Vechten. 221–52

BOSCAGLI, MAURIZIA; DUFFY, ENDA. Joyce's face. 133–59

DIEPEVEEN, LEONARD. 'I can have more than enough power to satisfy me': T. S. Eliot's construction of his audience. 37–60

FORD, KAREN JACKSON. Making poetry pay: the commodification of Langston Hughes. 275–96

GREEN, BARBARA. Advertising feminism: ornamental bodies/docile bodies and the discourse of suffrage. 191–220

KALAIDJIAN, WALTER. Marketing modern poetry and the Southern public sphere. 297–319

MATERER, TIMOTHY. Make it sell! Ezra Pound advertises Modernism. 17–36

MORRIS, DANIEL. A taste of fortune: *In the Money* and Williams's New Directions phase. 161–87

MOTT, CHRISTOPHER M. The art of self-promotion; or, Which self to sell? The proliferation and disintegration of the Harlem renaissance. 253–74

MURPHY, MICHAEL. 'One hundred per cent Bohemia': pop decadence and the aestheticization of commodity in the rise of the slicks. 61–89

NELSON, CARY. The fate of gender in modern American poetry. 321–60

WEXLER, JOYCE. Selling sex as art. 91–108

WICKE, JENNIFER. Coterie consumption: Bloomsbury, Keynes, and Modernism as marketing. 109–32

Middle English Miscellany

68. FISIAK, JACEK (ed.). Middle English miscellany: from vocabulary to linguistic variation. Poznań: Motivex, 1996. pp. 238. (Papers from the

International Conference on Middle English held at Rydzyna, Poland, 13–16 April 1994.)

BATELY, JANET.   Towards a Middle English thesaurus: some terms relating to fortune, fate and chance. 69–82

COLEMAN, JULIE.   The treatment of sexual vocabulary in Middle English dictionaries. 183–206

COLMAN, FRAN.   Morphology: Old and Middle English – derivational and inflectional. 3–28

DE LA CRUZ, JUAN.   Complex locative expressions in Middle English. A study of structural complexity and ambivalence. 207–32

DIENSBERG, BERNHARD.   French transplanted: a re-evaluation of the importance of Anglo-French in the development of the English language during the Middle English period. 253–66

DILLER, HANS-JÜRGEN.   *Joy* and *mirth* in Middle English and a little bit in Old: a plea for the consideration of genre in historical semantics. 83–105

KASTOVSKY, DIETER.   Categorial restructuring of the weak verbs in late Old English and Middle English. 29–45

KRYGIER, MARCIN.   Plural markers of the Old English nouns of relationship in the two manuscripts of Laʒamon's *Brut*. 47–68

NAGUCKA, RUTA.   Spatial relations in Chaucer's *Treatise on the Astrolabe*. 233–44

NORRI, JUHANI.   On the origins of plant names in fifteenth-century English. 159–81

ROBERTS, JANE.   Laʒamon's plain words. 107–22

SAUER, HANS.   English plant names in the thirteenth century: the trilingual Harley vocabulary. 135–58

STACZEK, JOHN.   Ðin in late Middle English and its contemporary reflex in instructional settings. 245–52

SYLVESTER, LOUISE.   Procedures in classifying Middle English vocabulary: some preliminary observations. 123–33

WEŁNA, JERZY.   The Middle English source of a present-day dialectal distinction. 267–80

Modernist Writers and the Marketplace

69. WILLISON, IAN; GOULD, WARWICK; CHERNAIK, WARREN (eds). Modernist writers and the marketplace. Basingstoke: Macmillan; New York: St Martin's Press, 1996. pp. xviii, 331.

BISHOP, EDWARD.   Re:covering Modernism – format and function in the little magazines. 287–319

CARACCIOLO, PETER L.   The metamorphoses of Wyndham Lewis's *The Human Age*: medium, intertextuality, genre. 258–86

FERRER, DANIEL. Joyce's notebooks: publicizing the private sphere of writing. 202–22

GOULD, WARWICK. 'Playing at treason with Miss Maud Gonne': Yeats and his publishers in 1900. 36–80

HAMPSON, ROBERT. Conrad, Curle and the *Blue Peter.* 89–104

HORNE, PHILIP. Henry James and the economy of the short story. 1–35

MARCUS, LAURA. Virginia Woolf and the Hogarth Press. 124–50

SCHUCHARD, RONALD. American publishers and the transmission of T. S. Eliot's prose: a sociology of English and American editions. 171–201

SHARPE, TONY. T. S. Eliot and ideas of *oeuvre.* 151–70

TAYLOR, RICHARD. Towards a textual biography of *The Cantos.* 223–57

WATTS, CEDRIC. Marketing Modernism: how Conrad prospered. 81–8

WILLISON, IAN. Introduction. xii–xviii

WORTHEN, JOHN. D. H. Lawrence and the 'expensive edition business'. 105–23

Modes of the Fantastic

70. LATHAM, ROBERT A.; COLLINS, ROBERT A. (eds). Modes of the fantastic: selected essays from the Twelfth International Conference on the Fantastic in the Arts. Westport, CT; London: Greenwood Press, 1995. pp. xxi, 233. (Contributions to the study of science fiction and fantasy, 66.)

AIRAUDI, JESSE T. Fantasia for sewercovers and drainpipes: T. S. Eliot, Abram Tertz, and the surreal quest for *pravda.* 21–7

ANDRIANO, JOSEPH. The masks of Gödel: math and myth in Thomas Pynchon's *Gravity's Rainbow.* 14–20

BOSKY, BERNADETTE. Charles Williams: occult fantasies/occult fact. 176–85

BURELBACH, FREDERICK M. Totemic animals in some Shakespeare plays. 155–60

CHEEVER, LEONARD A. Fantasies of sexual hell: Manuel Puig's *Pubis Angelical* and Margaret Atwood's *The Handmaid's Tale.* 110–21

ELPHINSTONE, MARGARET. Contemporary feminist fantasy in the Scottish literary tradition. 84–92

GRUESSER, JOHN. Pauline Hopkins' *Of One Blood*: creating an Afrocentric fantasy for a Black middle class audience. 74–83

HELDRETH, LILLIAN M. The mercy of the torturer: the paradox of compassion in Gene Wolfe's world of the new sun. 186–94

LATHAM, ROBERT A. Collage as critique and invention in the fiction of William S. Burroughs and Kathy Acker. 29–37

MALKKI, TARYA. The marriage metaphor in the works of Ursula K. Le Guin. 100–9

MERRILL, CATHERINE. Defining the fantastic grotesque: Nathanael West's *The Dream Life of Balso Snell*. 64–73

MICHAELSEN, SCOTT. Twain's *The American Claimant* and the figure of Frankenstein: a reading in rhetorical hermeneutics. 195–203

PALUMBO, DONALD E. The politics of entropy: revolution *vs* evolution in George Pal's film version of H. G. Wells's *The Time Machine*. 204–11

PHARR, MARY. Different shops of horrors: from Roger Corman's cult classic to Frank Oz's mainstream musical. 212–19

SPONSLER, CLAIRE. William Gibson and the death of cyberpunk. 47–55

WILLS, DEBORAH. The madwoman in the matrix: Joanna Russ's *The Two of Them* and the psychiatric postmodern. 93–9

Money: Lure, Lore, and Literature

71. DiGAETANI, JOHN LOUIS (ed.). Money: lure, lore, and literature. Westport, CT; London: Greenwood Press, 1994. pp. xix, 268. (Contributions to the study of world literature, 55.)

BAUBLES, RAYMOND L., JR. Displaced persons: the cost of speculation in Charles Dickens' *Martin Chuzzlewit*. 245–52

DICKERSON, VANESSA D. Feminine transactions: money and nineteenth-century British women writers. 227–43

DiGAETANI, JOHN LOUIS. Metrical experimentation in Swift's *Wood's Halfpence Poems*. 217–25

FISCHER, SANDRA K. 'Cut my heart in sums': Shakespeare's economics and *Timon of Athens*. 187–95

KRIEG, JOANN P. Health capital: Henry James' *The Wings of the Dove*. 111–20

LEONARD, ROBERT A. Money and language. 3–13

MORRISSEY, LEE. *Robinson Crusoe* and South Sea trade, 1710–1720. 209–15

POWERS-BECK, JEFFREY. The fusion of 'social eminence with divine eminence': George Herbert and the king's stamp. 197–207

SMART, ROBERT A. Blood and money in Bram Stoker's *Dracula*: the struggle against monopoly. 253–60

ULRICH, JOHN. Giving Williams some credit: money and language in *Paterson*, Book Four, Part II. 121–9

Monster Theory

72. COHEN, JEFFREY JEROME (ed.).   Monster theory: reading culture. Minneapolis; London: Minnesota UP, 1996. pp. xiii, 315.

CAMPBELL, MARY BAINE.   *Anthropometamorphosis*: John Bulwer's monsters of cosmology and the science of culture. 202–22

CLARK, DAVID L.   Monstrosity, illegibility, denegation: de Man, bp Nichol and the resistance to postmodernism. 40–71

COHEN, JEFFREY JEROME.   Monster culture (seven theses). 3–25

HIRSCH, DAVID A. HEDRICH.   Liberty, equality, monstrosity: revolutionizing Mary Shelley's *Frankenstein*. 115–40

O'NEILL, JOHN.   Dinosaurs-R-Us: the (un)natural history of *Jurassic Park*. 292–308

PENDER, STEPHEN.   'No monsters in the resurrection': inside some conjoined twins. 143–67

PINGREE, ALLISON.   America's 'United Siamese Brothers': Chang and Eng and nineteenth-century ideologies of democracy and domesticity. 92–114

PRESCOTT, ANNE LAKE.   The odd couple: Gargantua and Tom Thumb. 75–91

WATERHOUSE, RUTH.   *Beowulf* as palimpsest. 26–39

Mündliches Wissen in neuzeitlicher Literatur

73. GOETSCH, PAUL (ed.).   Mündliches Wissen in neuzeitlicher Literatur. Tübingen: Narr, 1990. pp. 305. (ScriptOralia, 18.) Rev. by Wilhelm Füger in GRM (42:1) 1992, 110–13.

BOSENBERG, EVA.   Das Überleben der Sprache in der Stille: zur Adaptation mündlicher Erzähltraditionen in drei Werken zeitgenössischer afro-amerikanischer Autorinnen. 229–50

BREINIG, HELMBRECHT.   Macht und Gegenmacht: mündliches Wissen und Schriftlichkeit in Mark Twains *A Connecticut Yankee in King Arthur's Court*. 121–35

DRESCHER, HORST W.   Sir Walter Scott: Geschichte, Überlieferung und die Erfahrung nationaler Identität. 95–104

ERZGRÄBER, WILLI.   Mündlich tradiertes Wissen in *Finnegans Wake*. 149–69

GOETSCH, PAUL.   Mündliches Wissen in neuzeitlicher Literatur. 17–35

GOETSCH, PAUL.   Die Rolle der mündlichen Tradition bei der literarischen Konstruktion sozialer Identität. 289–302

GROSS, KONRAD.   Mündliches Wissen in Leslie Silkos *Storyteller*. 217–27

HERMANN, ELISABETH.   Elemente mündlichen Erzählens im erzählerischen Werk von Leslie Marmon Silko und Paula Gunn Allen. 203–15

HOCHBRUCK, WOLFGANG.   'Black Elk speaks': Ansprüche und Grenzen bei der Verwendung indianischen mündlichen Wissens in literarischen Texten. 185–201

SIEMERLING, WINFRIED.   Das andere Toronto: mündliches Wissen in Michael Ondaatjes *In the Skin of a Lion*. 171–83

WIESENFARTH, JOSEPH.   'Schreibe, wie du sprichst': *Ford Madox Ford's fiction*. 137–48

WINKGENS, MEINHARD.   Mündlichkeit zwischen sozialer Traditionsstiftung und '*gossip*': zur Ambivalenz der Bewertung mündlichen Wissens in George Eliots frühen Regionalromanen. 105–19

Muscular Christianity: Embodying the Victorian Age

74. HALL, DONALD E. (ed.).   Muscular Christianity: embodying the Victorian age. Cambridge; New York: CUP, 1994. pp. xiii, 244. (Cambridge studies in nineteenth-century literature and culture, 2.) Rev. by Andrew Michael Roberts in Eng (44:180) 1995, 272–7; by Lawrence Frank in DickQ (13:2) 1996, 113–17.

ADAMS, JAMES ELI.   Pater's muscular aestheticism. 215–38

ALLEN, DENNIS W.   Young England: muscular Christianity and the politics of the body in *Tom Brown's Schooldays*. 114–32

FASICK, LAURA.   Charles Kingsley's scientific treatment of gender. 91–113

FAULKNER, DAVID.   The confidence man: empire and the deconstruction of muscular Christianity in *The Mystery of Edwin Drood*. 175–93

HALL, DONALD E.   On the making and unmaking of monsters: Christian Socialism, muscular Christianity, and the metaphorization of class conflict. 45–65

PENNINGTON, JOHN.   Muscular spirituality in George MacDonald's Curdie books. 133–49

ROBERSON, SUSAN L.   'Degenerate effeminacy' and the making of a masculine spirituality in the sermons of Ralph Waldo Emerson. 150–72

ROSEN, DAVID.   The volcano and the cathedral: muscular Christianity and the origins of primal manliness. 17–44

SREBRNIK, PATRICIA.   The re-subjection of 'Lucas Malet': Charles Kingsley's daughter and the response to muscular Christianity. 194–214

WEE, C. J. W.-L.   Christian manliness and national identity: the problematic construction of a racially 'pure' nation. 66–88

The New Nineteenth Century

75. HARMAN, BARBARA LEAH; MEYER, SUSAN (eds).   The new nineteenth century: feminist readings of underread Victorian fiction. New York; London: Garland, 1996. pp. xxxvii, 286. (Garland reference library of the humanities, 1700.) (Wellesley studies in critical theory, literary history and culture, 10.)

ANDERSON, NANCY FIX.   Eliza Lynn Linton: *The Rebel of the Family* (1880) and other novels. 117–33

DAVID, DEIRDRE.   Rewriting the male plot in Wilkie Collins's *No Name* (1862): Captain Wragge orders an omelette and Mrs Wragge goes into custody. 33–44

HALL, JASMINE YONG.   Solicitors soliciting: the dangerous circulation of professionalism in *Dracula* (1897). 97–116

HARMAN, BARBARA LEAH.   Joy behind the screen: the problem of 'presentability' in George Gissing's *The Nether World* (1889). 181–94

HELLER, TAMAR.   The vampire in the house: hysteria, female sexuality, and female knowledge in Le Fanu's *Carmilla* (1872). 77–95

KOROBKIN, LAURA HANFT.   Silent woman, speaking fiction: Charles Reade's *Griffith Gaunt* (1866) at the adultery trial of Henry Ward Beecher. 45–62

KUCICH, JOHN.   Curious dualities: *The Heavenly Twins* (1893) and Sarah Grand's belated Modernist aesthetics. 195–204

McCULLOUGH, KATE.   Mapping the '*terra incognita*' of woman: George Egerton's *Keynotes* (1893) and New Woman fiction. 205–23

MEYER, SUSAN.   Words on 'great vulgar sheets': writing and social resistance in Anne Brontë's *Agnes Grey* (1847). 3–16

MITCHELL, JUDITH.   Naturalism in George Moore's *A Mummer's Wife* (1885). 159–79

NEETENS, WIM.   Problems of a 'democratic text': Walter Besant's impossible story in *All Sorts and Conditions of Men* (1882). 135–57

O'MEALY, JOSEPH H.   Mrs Oliphant, *Miss Marjoribanks* (1866), and the Victorian canon. 63–76

PAXTON, NANCY L.   Mobilizing chivalry: rape in Flora Annie Steel's *On the Face of the Waters* (1896) and other British novels about the Indian uprising of 1857. 247–75

ROSEN, JUDITH.   At home upon a stage: domesticity and genius in Geraldine Jewsbury's *The Half Sisters* (1848). 17–32

WILT, JUDITH.   'Transition time': the political romances of Mrs Humphry Ward's *Marcella* (1894) and *Sir George Tressady* (1896). 225–46

New Readings of Late Medieval Love Poems

76. CHAMBERLAIN, DAVID (ed.).   New readings of late medieval love poems. (Cf. bibl. 1995, 3876, where collection not analysed.) Rev. by Barrie Ruth Straus in SAC (18) 1996, 190–5; by Teresa Kennedy in FCS (22) 1996, 226–8.

BROWN, MELISSA L.   The hope for 'pleasaunce': Richard Ross' translation of Alain Chartier's *La Belle Dame sans Mercy*. 119–43

CHAMBERLAIN, DAVID.   Clanvowe's cuckoo. 41–65

CROCKETT, BRYAN.   Venus unveiled: Lydgate's *Temple of Glas* and the religion of love. 67–93

EBERLY, SUSAN SCHOON.   '*Under the schadow of ane hawthorne grene*': the hawthorn in medieval love literature. 15–39

FRIEDMAN, BONITA.   In love's thrall: *The Court of Love* and its captives. 173–90

JAMES, CLAIR F.   *The Kingis Quair*: the plight of the courtly lover. 95–118

SNYDER, CYNTHIA LOCKARD.   *The Floure and the Leafe*: an alternative approach. 145–71

The Nightmare Considered

77.   ANISFIELD, NANCY (ed.).   The nightmare considered: critical essays on nuclear war literature. Bowling Green, OH: Bowling Green State Univ. Popular Press, 1991. pp. 201. Rev. by Clair James in Configurations (2:2) 1994, 367–8.

ANISFIELD, NANCY.   'Under the wheat': an analysis of options and ethical components. 140–5

BARRY, JAN.   The end of art: poetry and nuclear war. 85–94

BRANSCOMB, JACK.   Knowledge and understanding in *Riddley Walker*. 106–13

BRIANS, PAUL.   Nuclear family/nuclear war. 151–8

CAPUTI, JANE.   Psychic numbing, radical futurelessness, and sexual violence in the nuclear film. 58–70

CLIFTON, MERRITT.   A flash of light: the evolution of anti-nuclear consciousness in an alternative literary journal (*Samisdat*, 1973–1990). 27–51

DORRIS, MICHAEL; ERDRICH, LOUISE.   The day after tomorrow: novelists at Armageddon. 52–7

FRANKLIN, H. BRUCE.   Fatal fiction: a weapon to end all wars. 5–14

HEARRON, TOM.   The theme of guilt in Vonnegut's cataclysmic novels. 186–92

JASKOSKI, HELEN.   Thinking woman's children and the bomb. 159–76

KLINKOWITZ, JEROME.   Kurt Vonnegut's ultimate. 193–8

LENZ, MILLICENT.   Reinventing a world: myth in Denis Johnson's *Fiskadoro*. 114–22

SCHEICK, WILLIAM J.   Post-nuclear holocaust re-minding. 71–84

SCHLEY, JIM.   News. 97–105

SCHUTH, H. WAYNE.   *Testament*: to deserve the children. 146–50

SCHWENINGER, LEE.   Ecofeminism, nuclearism, and O'Brien's *The Nuclear Age*. 177–85

SMETAK, JACQUELINE R.   Sex and death in nuclear holocaust literature of the 1950s. 15–26

ZINS, DANIEL F.   Waging nuclear war rationally: strategic 'thought' in Arthur Kopit's *End of the World*. 129–39

Oral Poetics in Middle English Poetry

78.   AMODIO, MARK C. (ed.); MILLER, SARAH GRAY (asst ed.).   Oral poetics in Middle English poetry. New York; London: Garland, 1994. pp. xii, 289. (Garland reference library of the humanities, 1595.) (Albert Bates Lord studies in oral tradition, 13.) Rev. by Carl Lindahl in SAC (18) 1996, 167–70.

AMODIO, MARK C.   Introduction: oral poetics in post-Conquest England. 1–28

ARNOVICK, LESLIE K.   Dorigen's promise and scholars' premise: the orality of the speech act in the Franklin's Tale. 125–47

BRADBURY, NANCY MASON.   Literacy, orality, and the poetics of Middle English romance. 39–69

GANIM, JOHN M.   The Devil's writing lessons. 109–23

HARWOOD, BRITTON J.   The alliterative *Morte Arthure* as a witness to epic. 241–86

HENDERSON, DAVE.   Tradition and heroism in the Middle English romances. 89–107

LERER, SETH.   '*Now holde youre mouth*': the romance of orality in the 'Thopas–Melibee' section of the *Canterbury Tales*. 181–205

OLSEN, ALEXANDRA HENNESSEY.   Oral tradition in the Middle English romance: the case of *Robert of Cisyle*. 71–87

PARKS, WARD.   Oral tradition and the *Canterbury Tales*. 149–79

RONDOLONE, DONNA LYNNE.   *Wyrchipe*: the clash of oral-heroic and literate-Ricardian ideals in the alliterative *Morte Arthure*. 207–39

Order in Variety

79.   CRUMP, R. W. (ed.).   Order in variety: essays and poems in honor of Donald E. Stanford. Newark: Delaware UP; London; Toronto: Assoc. UPs, 1991. pp. 221.

ADAMS, PERCY G.   Edward Taylor's love affair with sounding language. 12–31

BRADBROOK, M. C.   The Kensington Quartets. 143–57

BROOKS, CLEANTH.   The humanities: liberator of mind and spirit. 162–75

BROWN, ASHLEY.   Prose into poetry: D. H. Lawrence's *The Rainbow*. 133–42

EMERSON, EVERETT.   Mark Twain's quarrel with God. 32–48

LENSING, GEORGE S.   The early readers of Wallace Stevens. 49–73

MIDDLETON, DAVID.   The classic mind restored: the achievemnt of Donald Stanford – poet, editor, mentor. 192–211

PHILLIPS, CATHERINE.   Robert Bridges and the English musical renaissance. 89–103

POWELL, GROSVENOR.   T. Sturge Moore and Yeats's golden bird. 104–16

TRIMPI, WESLEY.   Whose worth's unknown, although his height be taken. 79–88

An Other Tongue

80. ARTEAGA, ALFRED (ed.).   An other tongue: nation and ethnicity in the linguistic borderlands. Durham, NC; London: Duke UP, 1994. pp. x, 295.

ALARCÓN, NORMA.   Conjugating subjects: the heteroglossia of essence and resistance. 125–38

ARTEAGA, ALFRED.   Bonding in difference: an interview with Gayatri Chakravorty Spivak. 273–85

ARTEAGA, ALFRED.   An other tongue. 9–33

BRUCE-NOVOA.   Dialogical strategies, monological goals, Chicano literature. 225–45

CANDELARIA, CORDELIA CHÁVEZ.   *Différance* and the discourse of 'community' in writings in and about the ethnic other(s). 185–202

COOKE, MICHAEL G.   A rhetoric of obliquity in African and Caribbean women writers. 169–84

LLOYD, DAVID.   Adulteration and the nation: monologic nationalism and the colonial hybrid. 53–92

NIRANJANA, TEJASWINI.   Colonialism and the politics of translation. 35–52

SAVIN, ADA.   Bilingualism and dialogism: another reading of Lorna Dee Cervantes's poetry. 215–23

TODOROV, TZVETAN.   Dialogism and schizophrenia. Trans. by Michael B. Smith. 203–14

TORRES, LUIS A.   Bilingualism as satire in nineteenth-century Chicano poetry. 247–62

VIZENOR, GERALD.   The ruins of representation: shadow survivance and the literature of dominance. 139–67

Out of the Kumbla

81. DAVIES, CAROLE BOYCE; FIDO, ELAINE SAVORY (eds).   Out of the Kumbla: Caribbean women and literature. Trenton, NJ: Africa World Press, 1990. pp. xxiii, 399. Rev. by Maria Helena Lima in Feminist Studies (21:1) 1995, 115–28.

CARNEGIE, JENIPHIER R.   Selected bibliography of criticism and related works. 373–94

COBHAM, RHONDA. Women in Jamaican literature 1900–1950. 195–222

COOPER, CAROLYN. Afro-Jamaican folk elements in Brodber's *Jane and Louisa Will Soon Come Home*. 279–88

COVI, GIOVANNA. Jamaica Kincaid and the resistance to canons. 345–54

DAVIES, CAROLE BOYCE. 'Woman is a nation …': women in Caribbean oral literature. 165–93

DAVIES, CAROLE BOYCE. Writing home: gender and heritage in the works of Afro-Caribbean/American women writers. 59–73

DAVIES, CAROLE BOYCE; FIDO, ELAINE SAVORY. Introduction: women and literature in the Caribbean: an overview. 1–24

DAVIES, CAROLE BOYCE; FIDO, ELAINE SAVORY. Preface: talking it over: women, writing and feminism. ix–xx

FIDO, ELAINE SAVORY. Finding a way to tell it: methodology and commitment in theatre about women in Barbados and Jamaica. 331–43

FIDO, ELAINE SAVORY. Textures of Third World reality in the poetry of four African-Caribbean women. 29–44

JOHNSON, LEMUEL A. A-beng: (re)calling the body in(to) question. 111–42

LIDDELL, JANICE LEE. The narrow enclosure of motherdom/martyrdom: a study of Gatha Randall Barton in Sylvia Wynter's *The Hills of Hebron*. 321–30

McWATT, MARK A. Wives and other victims: women in the novels of Roy A. K. Heath. 223–35

O'CALLAGHAN, EVELYN. Interior schisms dramatised: the treatment of the 'mad' woman in the work of some female Caribbean novelists. 89–109

PHILIP, MARLENE NOURBESE. The absence of writing; or, How I almost became a spy. 271–8

STEWART, JOYCE. Woman as life or 'spirit of place': Wilson Harris's *Companions of the Day and Night*. 237–47

WYNTER, SYLVIA. Afterword: *Beyond Miranda's Meanings: Un/Silencing the 'Demonic Ground' of Caliban's 'Woman'*. 355–72

Passing and the Fictions of Identity

82. GINSBERG, ELAINE K. (ed.). Passing and the fictions of identity. Durham, NC: Duke UP, 1996. pp. vii, 298. (New Americanists.)

CUTTER, MARTHA J. Sliding significations: passing as a narrative and textual strategy in Nella Larsen's fiction. 75–100

INGS, KATHARINE NICHOLSON. Blackness and the literary imagination: uncovering *The Hidden Hand*. 131–50

KAWASH, SAMIRA. *The Autobiography of an Ex-Coloured Man*: (passing for) Black passing for White. 59–74

ROHY, VALERIE. Displacing desire: passing, nostalgia, and *Giovanni's Room*. 218–33

RUST, MARION. The subaltern as imperialist: speaking of Olaudah Equiano. 21–36

STERN, JULIA. Spanish masquerade and the drama of racial identity in *Uncle Tom's Cabin*. 103–30

WALD, GAYLE. 'A most disagreeable mirror': reflections on White identity in *Black like Me*. 151–77

WEINAUER, ELLEN M. 'A most respectable looking gentleman': passing, possession, and transgression in *Running a Thousand Miles for Freedom*. 37–56

YOUNG, ELIZABETH. Confederate counterfeit: the case of the cross-dressed Civil War soldier. 181–216

The Performance of Power

83. CASE, SUE-ELLEN; REINELT, JANELLE (eds). The performance of power: theatrical discourse and politics. Iowa City: Iowa UP, 1991. pp. xix, 284. (Studies in theatre history and culture.) Rev. by Alan Filewod in ModDr (36:1) 1993, 170–2; by Susan Bennett in TJ (45:2) 1993, 263–4; by Diana Devlin in YES (24) 1994, 359–60.

AUERBACH, NINA. Victorian players and sages. 183–98

BREDBECK, GREGORY W. Constructing Patroclus: the high and low discourses of Renaissance sodomy. 77–91

CARLISLE, JANICE. Spectacle as government: Dickens and the working-class audience. 163–80

GAINOR, J. ELLEN. Bernard Shaw and the drama of imperialism. 56–74

GOLUB, SPENCER. Charlie Chaplin, Soviet icon. 199–220

HALL, KIM F. Sexual politics and cultural identity in *The Masque of Blackness*. 3–18

MCCONACHIE, BRUCE A. New Historicism and American theater history: toward an interdisciplinary paradigm for scholarship. 265–71

MASON, JEFFREY D. The politics of *Metamora*. 92–110

REINELT, JANELLE. Theorizing utopia: Edward Bond's war plays. 221–32

ROACH, JOSEPH. The artificial eye: Augustan theater and the empire of the visible. 131–45

SAVRAN, DAVID. Revolution ... history ... theater: the politics of the Wooster Group's second trilogy. 41–55

WITHAM, BARRY B. The playhouse and the committee. 146–62

Performing Feminisms

84. CASE, SUE-ELLEN (ed.). Performing feminisms: feminist critical theory and theatre. Baltimore, MD; London: Johns Hopkins UP, 1990. pp. 327.

BUTLER, JUDITH. Performative acts and gender constitution: an essay in phenomenology and feminist theory. 270–82

COOK, CAROL. Unbodied figures of desire. 177–95

DE LAURETIS, TERESA. Sexual indifference and lesbian representation. 17–39

DIAMOND, ELIN. Refusing the romanticism of identity: narrative interventions in Churchill, Benmussa, Duras. 92–105

DICKERSON, GLENDA. The cult of true womanhood: toward a womanist attitude in African-American theatre. 109–18

DOLAN, JILL. 'Lesbian' subjectivity in realism: dragging at the margins of structure and ideology. 40–53

EATON, SARA. Beatrice-Joanna and the rhetoric of love in *The Changeling*. 237–48

FINKE, LAURIE A. Painting women: images of femininity in Jacobean tragedy. 223–36

FORTE, JEANIE. Women's performance art: feminism and postmodernism. 251–69

FREEDMAN, BARBARA. Frame-up: feminism, psychoanalysis, theatre. 54–76

HELMS, LORRAINE. Playing the woman's part: feminist criticism and Shakespearean performance. 196–206

HERMANN, ANNE. Travesty and transgression: transvestism in Shakespeare, Brecht, and Churchill. 294–315

PATRAKA, VIVIAN M. Feminism and the Jewish subject in the plays of Sachs, Atlan, and Schenkar. 160–74

RACKIN, PHYLLIS. Anti-historians: women's roles in Shakespeare's histories. 207–22

REINELT, JANELLE. Beyond Brecht: Britain's new feminist drama. 150–9

STEPHENS, JUDITH L. Gender ideology and dramatic convention in Progressive Era plays, 1890–1920. 283–93

WILKERSON, MARGARET B. *A Raisin in the Sun*: anniversary of an American classic. 119–30

The Playwright's Art

85. BRYER, JACKSON R. (ed.). The playwright's art: conversations with contemporary American dramatists. New Brunswick, NJ: Rutgers UP, 1995. pp. xx, 317.

BRYER, JACKSON R. Lanford Wilson. 277–96

BRYER, JACKSON R.   Neil Simon. 221–40

COE, RICHARD L.   Jerome Lawrence. 168–81

FROCKT, DEBORAH.   David Henry Hwang. 123–46

JACOBSON, LESLIE.   Wendy Wasserstein. 257–76

JOSELOVITZ, ERNEST.   Robert Anderson. 24–47

MAGUIRE, ROBERT.   Alice Childress. 48–69

MASHON, LAURENCE.   Edward Albee. 1–23

MONDELLO, BOB.   Larry L. King. 147–67

PLUNKA, GENE A.   Jean-Claude van Itallie. 241–56

ROSE, LLOYD.   John Guare. 70–85

SPONBERG, ARVID E.   A. R. Gurney. 86–101

WASHINGTON, MARY HELEN.   Ntozake Shange. 205–20

WIMMER-MOUL, CYNTHIA.   Beth Henley. 102–22

ZINOMAN, JOY.   Terrence McNally. 182–204

Poetry in Contemporary Irish Literature

86. KENNEALLY, MICHAEL (ed.).   Poetry in contemporary Irish literature. Gerrards Cross: Smythe, 1995. pp. xiv, 462. (Irish literary studies, 43.) (Studies in contemporary Irish literature, 2.) Rev. by Anthony Bradley in ConLit (37:3) 1996, 486–9.

ANDREWS, ELMER.   Tom Paulin: underground resistance fighter. 329–43

BRANDES, RAND.   A shaping music: Richard Murphy's *The Price of Stone*. 190–203

BRENNAN, RORY.   Contemporary Irish poetry: an overview. 1–27

BROWN, TERENCE.   Telling tales: Kennelly's *Cromwell*, Muldoon's *The More a Man Has the More a Man Wants*. 144–57

CAVE, RICHARD ALLEN.   John Montague: poetry of the depersonalised self. 216–37

CLYDE, TOM.   The echo chamber: some emerging Ulster poets. 114–29

DAWE, GERALD.   Poetry as example: Kinsella's Peppercanister poems. 204–15

DENMAN, PETER.   Ways of saying: Boland, Carson, McGuckian. 158–73

ELLIOTT, MAURICE.   Paul Durcan – Duarchain. 304–28

GRENNAN, EAMON.   The American connection: an influence on modern and contemporary Irish poetry. 28–47

LONGLEY, EDNA.   Derek Mahon: extreme religion of art. 280–303

McCRACKEN, KATHLEEN.   Ciaran Carson: unravelling the conditional, mapping the provisional. 356–72

McDONALD, PETER.   Seamus Heaney as a critic. 174–89

MARKEN, RON.   Michael Foley, Robert Johnstone and Frank Ormsby: three Ulster poets in the *GO* situation. 130–43

MEANEY, GERARDINE.   History gasps: myth in contemporary Irish women's poetry. 99–113

O'DONOGHUE, BERNARD.   'The half-said thing to them is dearest': Paul Muldoon. 400–18

O'DRISCOLL, DENNIS.   Foreign relations: Irish and international poetry. 48–60

PEACOCK, ALAN.   Michael Longley: poet between worlds. 263–79

SMITH, STAN.   The language of displacement in contemporary Irish poetry. 61–83

TRACY, ROBERT.   Into an Irish Free State: Heaney, Sweeney and clearing away. 238–62

WILLS, CLAIR.   Voices from the nursery: Medbh McGuckian's plantation. 373–99

Politics, Gender, and the Arts

87. DOTTERER, RONALD; BOWERS, SUSAN (eds).   Politics, gender, and the arts: women, the arts, and society. Selinsgrove, PA: Susquehanna UP, 1992. pp. 210. (Susquehanna Univ. studies.)

BRIGANTI, CHIARA.   Austen's shackles and feminine filiation. 130–49

DOSKOW, MINNA.   *Herland*: utopic in a different voice. 53–63

DYER, JOYCE.   The historical dimensions of Mary Lee Settle's *The Scapegoat*: Appalachia, labor, and Mother Jones. 166–84

HANKINS, LESLIE K.   The thwarting of the artist as a young woman: gender and class acts in Eudora Welty's *The Golden Apples*. 158–65

HIRSHFIELD, CLAIRE.   The actress as social activist: the case of Lena Ashwell. 72–86

STANNARD, KATHERINE.   Technology and the female in the *Doctor Who* series: companions or competitors? 64–71

WARREN, JOYCE W.   The gender of American individualism: Fanny Fern, the novel, and the American dream. 150–7

The Power of Culture

88. FOX, RICHARD WIGHTMAN; LEARS, T. J. JACKSON (eds).   The power of culture: critical essays in American history. Chicago: Chicago UP, 1993. pp. vi, 292.

FOX, RICHARD WIGHTMAN.   Intimacy on trial: cultural meanings of the Beecher–Tilton affair. 103–32

HALTUNEN, KAREN.   Early American murder narratives: the birth of horror. 67–101

LEARS, T. J. JACKSON.   Sherwood Anderson: looking for the white spot. 13–37

RUBIN, JOAN SHELLEY.   Between culture and consumption: the mediations of the middlebrows. 163–91

WILSON, CHRISTOPHER P.   Unlimn'd they disappear: recollecting *Yonnondio: from the Thirties.* 39–63

Privileging Gender in Early Modern England

89. BRINK, JEAN R. (ed.).   Privileging gender in early modern England. Kirksville, MO: Sixteenth Century Journal, 1993. pp. vi, 250. (Sixteenth century essays & studies, 23.)

BLECKI, CATHERINE LA COURREYE.   An intertextual study of Volumnia: from legend to character in Shakespeare's *Coriolanus.* 81–91

BRINK, JEAN R.   Domesticating the Dark Lady. 93–108

DOWNS-GAMBLE, MARGARET.   The taming-school: *The Taming of the Shrew* as lesson in Renaissance Humanism. 65–78

ERLER, MARY.   The books and lives of three Tudor women. 5–17

FLEMING, JULIET.   Dictionary English and the female tongue. 175–204

FOSTER, DONALD W.   Resurrecting the author: Elizabeth Tanfield Cary. 141–73

GARDINER, JUDITH KEGAN.   Re-gendering individualism: Margaret Fell Fox and Quaker rhetoric. 205–24

HANNAY, MARGARET P.   'Unlock my lipps': the *Miserere mei Deus* of Anne Vaughan Lok and Mary Sidney Herbert, Countess of Pembroke. 19–36

HOWARD, JEAN E.   Forming the commonwealth: including, excluding, and criminalizing women in Heywood's *Edward IV* and Shakespeare's *Henry IV.* 109–21

LUSSIER, MARK S.   'Marrying that hated object': the carnival of desire in Behn's *The Rover.* 225–39

RACKIN, PHYLLIS.   Historical difference/sexual difference. 37–63

WARNICKE, RETHA.   Private and public: the boundaries of women's lives in early Stuart England. 123–40

The Production of English Renaissance Culture

90. MILLER, DAVID LEE; O'DAIR, SHARON; WEBER, HAROLD (eds). The production of English Renaissance culture. Ithaca, NY; London: Cornell UP, 1994. pp. viii, 326. Rev. by John Gouws in NQ (43:1) 1996, 84–5.

BARKER, FRANCIS.   Treasures of culture: *Titus Andronicus* and death by hanging. 226–61

BOEHRER, BRUCE THOMAS. Bestial buggery in *A Midsummer Night's Dream*. 123–50

FERGUSON, MARGARET. News from the New World: miscegenous romance in Aphra Behn's *Oroonoko* and *The Widow Ranter*. 151–89

HALPERN, RICHARD. 'The picture of Nobody': White cannibalism in *The Tempest*. 262–92

HULSE, CLARK. Dead man's treasure: the cult of Thomas More. 190–225

KENDRICK, CHRISTOPHER. Agons of the manor: *Upon Appleton House* and agrarian capitalism. 13–55

LOEWENSTEIN, JOSEPH F. Legal proofs and corrected readings: press-agency and the new bibliography. 93–122

MILLER, DAVID LEE; O'DAIR, SHARON; WEBER, HAROLD. Introduction: criticism and cultural production. 1–12

TESKEY, GORDON. Allegory , materialism, violence. 293–318

The Profession of Eighteenth-Century Literature

91. DAMROSCH, LEO (ed.). The profession of eighteenth-century literature: reflections on an institution. Madison; London: Wisconsin UP, 1992. pp. vi, 234. Rev. by William B. Warner in ECS (27:3) 1994, 497–501; by Deirdre Coleman in AUMLA (83) 1995, 119–20; by J. Paul Hunter in MP (92:3) 1995, 371–5; by Katherine A. Armstrong in BJECS (19:1) 1996, 105–6.

BENDER, JOHN. A new history of the Enlightenment? 62–83

BRAUDY, LEO. Varieties of literary affection. 26–41

BROWN, MARSHALL. Commentary. 211–20

DAMROSCH, LEO. Reaching mid-career in 'the eighteenth century': some personal reflections. 200–10

DOWLING, WILLIAM C. Ideology and the flight from history in eighteenth-century poetry. 135–53

EPSTEIN, WILLIAM H. Professing Gray: the resumption of authority in eighteenth-century studies. 84–94

FABRICANT, CAROLE. Swift in his own time and ours: some reflections on theory and practice in the profession. 113–34

LANDRY, DONNA. Commodity feminism. 154–74

LIPKING, LAWRENCE. Inventing the eighteenth centuries: a long view. 7–25

MCKEON, MICHAEL. Cultural crisis and dialectical method: destabilizing Augustan literature. 42–61

MORRIS, DAVID B. Samuel H. Monk and a scholar's life: humanism as praxis. 175–99

RICHETTI, JOHN. The legacy of Ian Watt's *The Rise of the Novel*. 95–112

Professions of Desire

92. HAGGERTY, GEORGE E.; ZIMMERMAN, BONNIE (eds).   Professions of desire: lesbian and gay studies in literature. New York: Modern Language Assn of America, 1995. pp. xii, 246. Rev. by Robert Kaplan in RMRLL (50:1) 1996, 72–6.

BENNETT, PAULA.   Lesbian poetry in the United States, 1890–1990: a brief overview. 98–110

CLARKE, CHERYL.   Race, homosocial desire, and 'Mammon' in *Autobiography of an Ex-Coloured Man*. 84–97

FADERMAN, LILLIAN.   What is lesbian literature? Forming a historical canon. 49–59

FARWELL, MARILYN R.   The lesbian narrative: 'the pursuit of the inedible by the unspeakable'. 156–80

JAY, KARLA.   Lesbian Modernism: (trans)forming the (c)anon. 72–83

MOON, MICHAEL.   Memorial rags. 233–40

NUNOKAWA, JEFFREY.   The disappearance of the homosexual in *The Picture of Dorian Gray*. 183–90

SEDGWICK, EVE KOSOFSKY.   Tales of the avunculate: queer tutelage in *The Importance of Being Earnest*. 191–209

Queering the Renaissance

93. GOLDBERG, JONATHAN (ed.).   Queering the Renaissance. Durham, NC; London: Duke UP, 1994. pp. vi, 388. (Series Q.) Rev. by Peter L. Rudnytsky in MedRen (8) 1996, 248–52.

BRAY, ALAN.   Homosexuality and the signs of male friendship in Elizabethan England. 40–61

FRANK, MARCIE.   Fighting women and loving men: Dryden's representation of Shakespeare in *All for Love*. 310–29

GOLDBERG, JONATHAN.   *Romeo and Juliet*'s open *R*s. 218–35

HAMMILL, GRAHAM.   The epistemology of expuragtion: Bacon and *The Masculine Birth*. 236–52

MAGER, DONALD M.   John Bale and early Tudor sodomy discourse. 140–61

MASTEN, JEFF.   My two dads: collaboration and the reproduction of Beaumont and Fletcher. 280–309

PITTENGER, ELIZABETH.   'To serve the queere': Nicholas Udall, Master of Revels. 162–89

RAMBUSS, RICHARD.   Pleasure and devotion: the body of Jesus and seventeenth-century religious lyric. 253–79

TRAUB, VALERIE.   The (in)significance of 'lesbian' desire in early modern England. 62–83

WARNER, MICHAEL.   New English Sodom. 330–58

A Question of Identity

94.   BENJAMIN, MARINA (ed.).   A question of identity: women, science, and literature. New Brunswick, NJ: Rutgers UP, 1993. pp. xiii, 248. Rev. by Jane Donawerth in Utopian Studies (6:2) 1995, 140–1; by Anne Fausto-Sterling in Signs (21:1) 1995, 172–5.

CALDER, JENNI.   Science and the supernatural in the stories of Margaret Oliphant. 173–91

COSSLETT, TESS.   The aseptic male obstetrician and the filthy peasant crone: contemporary women writers' accounts of birth. 74–96

HAYLES, N. KATHERINE.   The life cycle of cyborgs: writing the posthuman. 152–70

MULLAN, JOHN.   Gendered knowledge, gendered minds: women and Newtonianism, 1690–1760. 41–56

ROBERTS, MARIE MULVEY.   The male scientist, man-midwife, and female monster: appropriation and transmutation in *Frankenstein*. 59–73

SHUTTLEWORTH, SALLY.   'Preaching to the nerves': psychological disorder in sensation fiction. 192–222

SQUIER, SUSAN.   Conceiving difference: reproductive technology and the construction of identity in two contemporary fictions. 97–115

Questioning Romanticism

95.   BEER, JOHN (ed.).   Questioning Romanticism. Baltimore, MD; London: Johns Hopkins UP, 1995. pp. xiv, 319.

ASKE, MARTIN.   Critical disfigurings: the 'jealous leer malign' in Romantic criticism. 49–70

BEER, JOHN.   Fragmentations and ironies. 234–64

BONE, DRUMMOND.   The question of a European Romanticism. 121–32

BURWICK, FREDERICK.   The Romantic concept of mimesis: *idem et alter*. 179–208

GOODSON, A. C.   Romantic theory and the critique of language. 3–28

LEASK, NIGEL.   Toward a universal aesthetic: De Quincey on murder as carnival and tragedy. 92–120

MARTIN, PHILIP.   Authorial identity and the critical act: John Clare and Lord Byron. 71–91

MELLOR, ANNE K.   A criticism of their own: Romantic women literary critics. 29–48

NEWLYN, LUCY.   'Questionable shape': the aesthetics of indeterminacy. 209–33

RAJAN, TILOTTAMA.   Phenomenology and Romantic theory: Hegel and the subversion of aesthetics. 155–78

WOLFSON, SUSAN J.   Romanticism and the question of poetic form. 133–54

Reading and Writing Women's Lives

96. BOWERS, BEGE K.; BROTHERS, BARBARA (eds).   Reading and writing women's lives: a study of the novel of manners. Ann Arbor: Michigan UP, 1990. pp. xi, 236. (Challenging the literary canon.) Rev. by Ann Owens Weekes in RMRLL (45:4) 1991, 250–2; by Joyce Zonana in VPR (25:3) 1992, 137–9.

BOWERS, BEGE K.   George Eliot's *Middlemarch* and the 'text' of the novel of manners. 105–17

BROTHERS, BARBARA.   Love, marriage, and manners in the novels of Barbara Pym. 153–70

DUNLEAVY, JANET EGLESON.   Maria Edgeworth and the novel of manners. 49–65

GROSS, GLORIA SYBIL.   Jane Austen and psychological realism: 'What does a woman want?' 19–33

HEILBRUN, CAROLYN G.   The detective novel of manners. 187–97

HUSSEY, MARK.   'I' rejected, 'we' substituted: self and society in *Between the Acts*. 141–52

KINCAID, JAMES R.   Anthony Trollope and the unmannerly novel. 87–104

MEYERSOHN, MARYLEA.   Jane Austen's garrulous speakers: social criticism in *Sense and Sensibility*, *Emma*, and *Persuasion*. 35–48

REDDY, MAUREEN T.   Men, women, and manners in *Wives and Daughters*. 67–83

SISNEY, MARY F.   The view from the outside: Black novels of manners. 171–85

WIESENFARTH, JOSEPH.   *The Portrait of a Lady*: gothic manners in Europe. 119–39

WILKINSON, JOHN.   Conventions of comedies of manners and British novels of academic life. 199–213

Reconfigured Spheres

97. HIGONNET , MARGARET R.; TEMPLETON, JOAN (eds).   Reconfigured spheres: feminist explorations of literary space. Amherst: Massachusetts UP, 1994. pp. x, 212. Rev. by Deborah Clarke in Legacy (13:2) 1996, 159–61.

CASTILLO, DEBRA A.   Borderliners: Federico Campbell and Ana Castillo. 147–70

HIGONNET, MARGARET R.   Mapping the text: critical metaphors. 194–212

HIGONNET, MARGARET R.   New cartographies: an introduction. 1–19

KARAMCHETI, INDIRA.   The geographics of marginality: place and textuality in Simone Schwarz-Bart and Anita Desai. 125–46

KOMAR, KATHLEEN L.   Feminist curves in contemporary literary space. 89–107

MARCUS, JANE.   Registering objections: grounding feminist alibis. 171–93

PETERSON, CARLA L.   Secular and sacred space in the spiritual autobiographies of Jarena Lee. 37–59

STADLER, EVA MARIA.   Addressing social boundaries: dressing the female body in early realist fiction. 20–36

VLASOPOLOS, ANCA.   Staking claims for no territory: the sea as woman's space. 72–88

Reconsidering the Renaissance

98. DI CESARE, MARIO A. (ed.).   Reconsidering the Renaissance: papers from the twenty-first annual conference. Binghamton, NY: Medieval & Renaissance Texts & Studies, 1992. pp. xiv, 528. (Medieval & Renaissance Texts & Studies, 93.)

BUSHNELL, REBECCA.   Tyranny and effeminacy in early modern England. 339–54

CALLAGHAN, DYMPNA.   Wicked women in *Macbeth*: a study of power, ideology, and the production of motherhood. 355–69

CAMPBELL, GORDON.   Popular traditions of God in the Renaissance. 501–20

CORTHELL, RONALD J.   Milton and the possibilities of theory. 489–99

ENGLE, LARS.   Milton, Bakhtin, and the unit of analysis. 476–88

FRIEDMAN, DONALD.   Bottom, Burbage, and the birth of tragedy. 315–26

GREEN, DOUGLAS E.   Shakespeare's violation: 'One face, one voice, one habit, and two persons'. 327–38

JACOBUS, LEE A.   Milton: the rhetorical gesture of monody. 447–60

KREVANS, NITA.   Print and the Tudor poets. 301–13

LECHTER-SIEGEL, AMY.   Isabella's silence: the consolidation of power in *Measure for Measure*. 471–80

ODABASHIAN, BARBARA.   Thomas Wyatt and the rhetoric of change. 287–300

RUBIN, DEBORAH.   'Let your death be my *Iliad*': Classical allusion and Latin in George Herbert's *Memoriae Matris Sacrum*. 429–45

SHOAF, R. A.   'Our names are debts': Messiah's account of himself. 461–73

SINGH, JYOTSNA.   The influence of feminist criticism/theory on Shakespeare studies 1976–1986. 381–93

TRICOMI, ALBERT H.   Shakespeare, Chapman, and the Julius Caesar play in Renaissance Humanist drama. 395–412

WILTENBURG, ROBERT.   Donne's dialogue of one: the self and the soul. 413–27

Redefining the Political Novel

99. HARRIS, SHARON M. (ed.).   Redefining the political novel: American women writers, 1797–1901. Knoxville: Tennessee UP, 1995. pp. xxiii, 200.

BAYM, LINDA.   Reinventing Sigourney. 66–85

BERKSON, DOROTHY.   'A goddess behind a sordid veil': the domestic heroine meets the labor novel in Mary E. Wilkins Freeman's *The Portion of Labor*. 149–68

CASTIGLIA, CHRISTOPHER.   Susanna Rowson's *Reuben and Rachel*: captivity, colonization, and the domestication of Columbus. 23–42

HAMILTON, KRISTIE.   The politics of survival: Sara Parton's *Ruth Hall* and the literature of labor. 86–108

HARRIS, SHARON M.   Hannah Webster Foster's *The Coquette*: critiquing Franklin's America. 1–22

PAMPLIN, CLAIRE.   'Race' and identity in Pauline Hopkins's *Hagar's Daughter*. 169–83

RIGSBY, MARY.   'So like women!': Louisa May Alcott's *Work* and the ideology of relations. 109–27

SUKSANG, DUANGRUDI.   A world of their own: the separatist utopian vision of Mary E. Bradley Lane's *Mizora*. 128–48

ZAGARELL, SANDRA A.   Expanding 'America': Lydia Sigourney's *Sketch of Connecticut*, Catharine Sedgwick's *Hope Leslie*. 43–65

Rethinking Class

100. DIMOCK, WAI CHEE; GILMORE, MICHAEL T. (eds).   Rethinking class: literary studies and social formations. New York: Columbia UP, 1994. pp. vi, 285. (Social foundations of aesthetic forms.)

BRODHEAD, RICHARD H.   Regionalism and the upper class. 150–74

DIMOCK, WAI CHEE.   Class, gender, and a history of metonymy. 57–104

GILMORE, MICHAEL T.   Hawthorne and the making of the middle class. 215–38

GUILLORY, JOHN.   Literary critics as intellectuals: class analysis and the crisis of the humanities. 107–49

JANOWITZ, ANNE.   Class and literature: the case of Romantic Chartism. 239–66

LANG, AMY SCHRAGER.   The syntax of class in Elizabeth Stuart Phelps's *The Silent Partner*. 267–85

LOTT, ERIC.   White kids and no kids at all: languages of race in ante-bellum US working-class culture. 175–211

Rethinking the Henrician Era

101. HERMAN, PETER C. (ed.).   Rethinking the Henrician era: essays on early Tudor texts and contexts. Urbana: Illinois UP, 1994. pp. 312. Rev. by Carole Levin in MedRen (8) 1996, 252–6.

BLANCHARD, W. SCOTT.   Skelton: the voice of the mob in sanctuary. 123–44

ESTRIN, BARBARA L.   Wyatt's unlikely likenesses; or, Has the lady read Petrarch? 219–39

GREENE, ROLAND.   The colonial Wyatt: contexts and openings. 240–66

HALASZ, ALEXANDRA.   Wyatt's David. 193–218

HERMAN, PETER C.   Introduction: rethinking the Henrician era. 1–15

HERMAN, PETER C.   Leaky ladies and droopy dames: the grotesque realism of Skelton's *The Tunnynge of Elynour Rummynge*. 145–67

HOWARD, SKILES.   'Ascending the riche mount': performing hierarchy and gender in the Henrician masque. 16–39

KASTAN, DAVID SCOTT.   'Holy wurdes' and 'slypper wit': John Bale's *King Johan* and the poetics of propaganda. 267–82

KING, JOHN N.   Henry VIII as David: the king's image and Reformation politics. 78–92

MUELLER, JANEL.   'The whole island like a single family': positioning women in Utopian patriarchy. 93–122

READINGS, BILL.   When did the Renaissance begin? The Henrician court and the Shakespearean stage. 283–302

REMLEY, PAUL G.   Mary Shelton and her Tudor literary milieu. 40–77

SESSIONS, W. A.   Surrey's Wyatt: autumn 1542 and the new poet. 168–92

'Return' in Post-Colonial Writing

102. MIHAILOVICH-DICKMAN, VERA.   'Return' in post-colonial writing: a cultural labyrinth. Amsterdam; Atlanta, GA: Rodopi, 1994. pp. xv, 173. (Cross/cultures: readings in the post/colonial literatures in English, 12.)

COAD, DAVID.   Platonic return in Patrick White's *The Eye of the Storm*. 51–5

DAVIS, GEOFFREY V.   'When it's all over, and we all return': Matsemela Manaka's play *Ekhaya – Going Home*. 123–38

FRASER, ROBERT.   Mental travellers: myths of return in the poetry of Walcott and Brathwaite. 7–13

FUCHS, ANNE.   Turn again, Whittington! Signs of re-turn to form in the work of South African praise poets. 139–52

GALLE, ETIENNE.   Soyinka's twisted circle: a return with a difference. 77–84

GIBBS, JAMES.   'Marshal Ky of African culture' or 'heir to the tradition'? Wole Soyinka's position on his return to Nigeria in 1960. 85–99

HARRIS, WILSON.   Living absences and presences. 1–5

INNES, C. L.   Reversal and return in fiction by Bessie Head and Ama Ata Aidoo. 69–75

JONES, BRIDGET.   Duppies and other revenants, with particular reference to the use of the supernatural in Jean D'Costa's work. 23–32

LINDFORS, BERNTH.   Future returns. 153–62

MUNNICK, JAMES.   Back to the roots: Mphahlele's return to South Africa. 101–9

RAINES, GAY.   'Return' in Australian fiction. 41–9

SANTAOLALLA, ISABEL.   A fictitious return to the past: Saleem Sinai's autobiographical journey in *Midnight's Children*. 163–70

Re-Visioning Romanticism

103. WILSON, CAROL SHINER; HAEFNER, JOEL (eds).   Re-visioning Romanticism: British women writers, 1776–1837. Philadelphia: Pennsylvania UP, 1994. pp. xii, 329, (plates) 4.

AARON, JANE.   The way above the world: religion in Welsh and Anglo-Welsh women's writing, 1780–1830. 111–27

BURROUGHS, CATHERINE B.   English Romantic women writers and theatre theory: Joanna Baillie's Prefaces to the *Plays on the Passions*. 274–96

CURRAN, STUART.   Mary Robinson's *Lyrical Tales* in context. 17–35

ELLISON, JULIE.   The politics of fancy in the age of sensibility. 228–55

FORD, SUSAN ALLEN.   'A name more dear': daughters, fathers, and desire in *A Simple Story*, *The False Friend*, and *Mathilda*. 51–71

HAEFNER, JOEL.   The Romantic scene(s) of writing. 256–73

McGANN, JEROME J.   Literary history, Romanticism, and Felicia Hemans. 210–27

PASCOE, JUDITH.   Female botanists and the poetry of Charlotte Smith. 193–209

PETERSON, LINDA H.   Becoming an author: Mary Robinson's *Memoirs* and the origin of woman artist's autobiography. 36–50

ROGERS, KATHARINE M.   Romantic aspirations, restricted possibilities: the novels of Charlotte Smith. 72–88

ROSS, MARLON B.   Configurations of feminist reform: the woman writer and the tradition of dissent. 91–110

WILSON, CAROL SHINER. Lost needles, tangled threads: stitchery, domesticity, and the artistic enterprise in Barbauld, Edgeworth, Taylor, and Lamb. 167–90

WOLFSON, SUSAN J. 'Domestic affections' and 'the spear of Minerva': Felicia Hemans and the dilemma of gender. 128–66

Romance Reading on the Book

104. FELLOWS, JENNIFER, *et al.* (eds). Romance reading on the book: essays on medieval narrative presented to Maldwyn Mills. Cardiff: UP of Wales, 1996. pp. x, 307.

ALLEN, ROSAMUND. *The Awntyrs off Arthure*: jests and jousts. 129–42

BARRON, W. R. J. *The Wars of Alexander*: from reality to romance. 22–35

BLANCHFIELD, LYNNE S. Rate revisited: the compilation of the narrative works in MS Ashmole 61. 208–20

FELLOWS, JENNIFER. *Bevis redivivus*: the printed editions of *Sir Bevis of Hampton*. 251–68

FIELD, P. J. C. Malory's Mordred and the *Morte Arthure*. 77–93

HUWS, DANIEL. MS Porkington 10 and its scribes. 188–207

MEALE, CAROL M. '*Prenes: engre*': an early sixteenth-century presentation copy of *The Erle of Tolous*. 221–36

PEARSALL, DEREK. Madness in *Sir Orfeo*. 51–63

ROGERS, GILLIAN. '*Illuminat vith lawte, and with lufe lasit*': Gawain gives Arthur a lesson in magnanimity. 94–111

SHEPHERD, STEPHEN H. A. No poet has his travesty alone: *The Weddynge of Sir Gawen and Dame Ragnell*. 112–28

SIMONS, JOHN. Robert Parry's *Moderatus*: a study in Elizabethan romance. 237–50

SPEED, DIANE. The pattern of Providence in *Chevelere Assigne*. 143–54

THOMPSON, JOHN J. Looking behind the book: MS Cotton Caligula A.ii, part 1, and the experience of its texts. 171–87

WILLIAMS, ELIZABETH. '*A damsell by herselfe alone*': images of magic and femininity from *Lanval* to *Sir Lambewell*. 155–70

Rough Justice: Essays on Crime in Literature

105. FRIEDLAND, M. L. (ed.). Rough justice: essays on crime in literature. Toronto; Buffalo, NY; London: Toronto UP, 1991. pp. xxix, 248. Rev. by Tone Sundt Urstad in UTQ (63:1) 1993, 163–5.

BAIRD, JOHN D. Criminal elements: Fielding's *Jonathan Wild*. 76–94

BLAKE, CAESAR R. On Richard Wright's *Native Son*. 187–99

CHAMBERLIN, J. E. Oscar Wilde. 141–56

DUFFY, DENNIS. Wiebe's real Riel? *The Scorched-Wood People* and its audience. 200–13

EBERLE, PATRICIA J.   Crime and justice in the Middle Ages: cases from the *Canterbury Tales* of Geoffrey Chaucer. 19–51

HAYNE, BARRIE.   Dreiser's *American Tragedy*. 170–86

MILLGATE, JANE.   Scott and the law: *The Heart of Midlothian*. 95–113

MILLGATE, MICHAEL.   Undue process: William Faulkner's *Sanctuary*. 157–69

PARKER, BRIAN.   *A Fair Quarrel* (1617), the duelling code, and Jacobean law. 52–75

ROBSON, JOHN M.   Crime in *Our Mutual Friend*. 114–40

SADDLEMYER, ANN.   Crime in literature: Canadian drama. 214–30

ŠKVORECKÝ, JOSEF.   Detective stories: some notes on *Fingerprints*. 231–48

Rural Ireland, Real Ireland?

106.   GENET, JACQUELINE (ed.).   Rural Ireland, real Ireland? Gerrards Cross: Smythe, 1996. pp. 245. (Irish literary studies, 49.) Rev. by Norman Vance in TLS, 27 Sept. 1996, 13.

AGOSTINI, RENÉ.   J. M. Synge's 'celestial peasants'. 159–73

BRIHAULT, JEAN.   Lady Morgan: deep furrows. 71–81

CARPENTIER, GODELEINE.   The peasantry in Kickham's tales and novels: an epitome of the writer's realism, idealism and ideology. 93–107

ESCARBELT, BERNARD.   William Chaigneau's Jack Connor: a literary image of the Irish peasant. 51–7

FIEROBE, CLAUDE.   The peasantry in the Irish novels of Maria Edgeworth. 59–69

GENET, JACQUELINE.   Introduction. 9–17

GENET, JACQUELINE.   Yeats and the myth of rural Ireland. 139–57

HARMON, MAURICE.   Kavanagh's old peasant. 213–22

JACQUIN, DANIELLE.   '*Cerveaux lucides* is good begob': Flann O'Brien and the world of peasants. 223–34

KEARNEY, COLBERT.   Daniel Corkery: a priest and his people. 201–12

KIBERD, DECLAN.   Decolonizing the mind: Douglas Hyde and Irish Ireland. 121–37

MACDONOGH, CAROLINE.   Augusta Gregory: a portrait of a lady. 109–20

MARTIN, AUGUSTINE.   The past and the peasant in the stories of Seumas O'Kelly. 185–200

MEIR, COLIN.   Status and style in Carleton's *Traits and Stories of the Irish Peasantry*. 83–91

Sacred and Profane

107.   WILCOX, HELEN; TODD, RICHARD; MACDONALD, ALASDAIR (eds). Sacred and profane: secular and devotional interplay in early modern British literature. Amsterdam: VU UP, 1996. pp. xiii, 345. Rev. by Daniel W. Doerksen in GHJ (19:1/2) 1995/96, 116–20.

BAKER-SMITH, DOMINIC.   John Donne as medievalist. 185–93

BERGE, MARK.   Milton's Orphic harmony: Ovidian imitation and Christian revelation in *The Nativity Ode* and *The Passion*. 259–74

BURNS, EDWARD.   Rochester, Behn and the martyrdom of lust. 329–36

CORNS, THOMAS N.   'Varnish on a harlot's cheek': John Milton and the hierarchies of secular and divine literature. 275–81

FRANSSEN, PAUL J. C. M.   Donne's jealous God and the concept of sacred parody. 151–62

GRAHAM, ELSPETH.   'Lewd, profane swaggerers' and charismatic preachers: John Bunyan and George Fox. 307–18

GUIBBORY, ACHSAH.   The Gospel according to Aemilia: women and the sacred in Aemilia Lanyer's *Salve Deus Rex Judaeorum*. 105–26

HEALE, ELIZABETH.   Lute and harp in Wyatt's poetry. 3–15

HESTER, M. THOMAS.   'Let me love': reading the sacred 'currant' of Donne's profane lyrics. 129–50

HOBBY, ELAINE.   The politics of women's prophecy in the English Revolution. 295–306

JOHNSON, JEFFREY.   'Til we mix wounds': liturgical paradox and Crashaw's Classicism. 251–8

KINNEY, ARTHUR F.   Re-historicising *Macbeth*. 93–103

KORSTEN, FRANS.   The Restoration poetry of John Norris. 319–28

MACDONALD, A. A.   *Contrafacta* and the *Gude and Godlie Ballatis*. 33–44

MAULE, JEREMY.   Donne and the past. 203–21

MONNICKENDAM, ANDREW.   Epic ends and novel beginnings in *Paradise Lost*. 283–94

ROBERTS, JOHN R.; ROBERTS, LORRAINE.   'To weave a new webbe in their owne loome': Robert Southwell and Counter-Reformation poetics. 63–77

SAWDAY, JONATHAN.   Poison and honey: the politics of the sacred and the profane in Spenser's *Fowre Hymnes* (1596). 79–92

SELLIN, PAUL R.   The mimetic poetry of Jack and John Donne: a field theory for the amorous and the divine. 163–72

SESSIONS, W. A.   Surrey's Psalms in the Tower. 17–31

STANWOOD, P. G.   Donne's reinvention of the Fathers: sacred truths suitably expressed. 195–201

STRINGER, GARY A.   Some sacred and profane con-texts of John Donne's *Batter My Hart.* 173–83

VAN HEIJNSBERGEN, THEO.   The sixteenth-century Scottish love lyric. 45–61

WARWICK, CLAIRE.   'Love thou art absolute': Richard Crashaw and the discourse of human and divine love. 237–50

San Francisco in Fiction

108. FINE, DAVID; SKENAZY, PAUL (eds).   San Francisco in fiction: essays in a regional literature. Albuquerque: New Mexico UP, 1995. pp. 243.

BLANKLEY, ELYSE.   Clear-cutting the Western myth: beyond Joan Didion. 177–97

CHEUSE, ALAN.   Double wonder: the novelistic achievement of James D. Houston. 144–59

FINE, DAVID.   Jack London's Sonoma Valley: finding the way home. 56–72

HASLAN, GERALD.   William Saroyan and San Francisco: emergence of a genius (self-proclaimed). 111–25

KOWALEWSKI, MICHAEL.   Jack Kerouac and the Beats in San Francisco. 126–43

McCLURE, CHARLOTTE S.   Gertrude Atherton and her San Francisco: a wayward writer and a wayward city in a wayward paradise. 73–95

McELRATH, JOSEPH R., JR.   Beyond San Francisco: Frank Norris's invention of Northern California. 35–55

MORGAN, NINA Y.   The Chinatown aesthetic and the architecture of radical identity. 217–37

NELSON, NANCY OWEN.   Land lessons in an 'unhistoried' West: Wallace Stegner's California. 160–76

SCHARNHORST, GARY.   Mark Twain, Bret Harte, and the literary construction of San Francisco. 21–34

SKENAZY, PAUL.   Borders and bridges, doors and drugstores: toward a geography of time. 198–216

SKENAZY, PAUL.   The 'heart field': Dashiell Hammett's anonymous territory. 96–110

Sexuality, the Female Gaze, and the Arts

109. DOTTERER, RONALD; BOWERS, SUSAN (eds).   Sexuality, the female gaze, and the arts: women, the arts, and society. Selinsgrove, PA: Susquehanna UP; London; Toronto: Assoc. UPs, 1992. pp. 191. (Susquehanna Univ. studies.)

AUGUSTINE, JANE.   Bisexuality in Hélène Cixous, Virginia Woolf, and H.D.: an aspect of *l'écriture féminine.* 11–18

BOWERS, SUSAN R.   The witch's garden: the feminist grotesque. 19–36

ELIAS, KAREN.   The pain of the body's world: women, poetry, and society in the work of Adrienne Rich. 115–26

FUCHS, CYNTHIA J.   Desperately seeking a subject: postmodern sexuality, Seidelman, and Madonna. 37–52

HUMPHREYS, DEBRA.   The discursive construction of women's sexuality and madness in mainstream cinema. 64–74

LEVINE-KEATING, HELANE.   The bright shadow: images of the double in women's poetry. 166–84

MORLIER, MARGARET M.   She for God in her: Elizabeth Barrett Browning's new Eve. 127–44

SCHOFIELD, MARY ANNE.   Romance subversion: eighteenth-century feminine fiction. 75–86

Shakespeare, Aphra Behn and the Canon

110.   OWENS, W. R.; GOODMAN, LIZBETH (eds).   Shakespeare, Aphra Behn and the canon. London; New York: Routledge in assn with Open Univ., 1996. pp. v, 346. (Approaching literature.)

CLARKE, KATE; GOODMAN, LIZBETH.   Reading *As You Like It.* 193–250

DAY, ROGER.   Reading *Othello.* 89–130

ELIOT, SIMON.   An English history play: reading and studying *Henry V.* 35–88

GOODMAN, LIZBETH.   The idea of the canon. 3–19

OWENS, W. R.   Shakespeare: theatre poet. 21–33

OWENS, W. R.; GOODMAN, LIZBETH.   Remaking the canon: Aphra Behn's *The Rover.* 131–91

Shakespeare and the Christian Tradition

111.   BATSON, E. BEATRICE (ed.).   Shakespeare and the Christian tradition. Lewiston, NY; Lampeter: Mellen Press, 1994. pp. xviii, 189.

BASNEY, LIONEL.   Is a Christian perspective on Shakespeare productive and/or necessary? 19–35

BATTENHOUSE, ROY.   Shakespeare's *Henry VIII* reconsidered in the light of Boethian and biblical commonplaces. 51–82

BEVINGTON, DAVID.   Shakespeare and recent criticism: issues for a Christian approach to teaching. 1–18

COX, JOHN D.   Shakespeare: New Criticism, New Historicism, and the Christian story. 37–50

HASSEL, R. CHRIS, JR.   Which is the Christian here, and which the Jew? Christian patterns in *The Merchant of Venice.* 103–19

HOWARD, THOMAS.   'Peace, Paulina,' 'My charms are all o'erthrown': Christian patterns in *The Winter's Tale* and *The Tempest.* 163–75

NOLL, MARK A.   The Reformation and Shakespeare: focus on *Henry VIII*. 83–101

SIMONDS, PEGGY MUÑOZ.   The iconography of transformed fish in Shakespeare's *Pericles*: a study of the rusty armor *topos* in the English Renaissance. 121–61

A Small Nation's Contribution to the World

112. MORSE, DONALD E.; BERTHA, CSILLA; PÁLFFY, ISTVÁN (eds). A small nation's contribution to the world: essays on Anglo-Irish literature and language. Debrecen: Lajos Kossuth Univ.; Gerrards Cross: Smythe, 1993. pp. xiii, 248. (Irish literary studies, 45.)

BERTHA, CSILLA.   'The harmony of reality and fantasy': the fantastic in Irish drama. 28–42

BOURKE, EOIN.   Poetic outrage: aspects of social criticism in modern Irish poetry. 88–106

BURKE, PATRICK.   'Both heard and imagined': music as structuring principle in the plays of Brian Friel. 43–52

CROGHAN, MARTIN J.   Maria Edgeworth and the tradition of Irish semiotics. 194–206

FLEISCHMANN, RUTH.   Knowledge of the world as the forbidden fruit: Canon Sheehan and Joyce on the *sacrificium intellectus*. 127–37

HARMON, MAURICE.   Ancient lights in Austin Clarke and Thomas Kinsella. 70–87

HUBER, WERNER.   Myth and motherland: Edna O'Brien's *Mother Ireland*. 175–81

KNIEZSA, VERONIKA.   'Proper words in proper places': Jonathan Swift on language. 182–93

KURDI, MÁRIA.   The ways of twoness: pairs, parallels and contrasts in Stewart Parker's *Spokesong*. 61–9

MORSE, DONALD E.   Starting from the earth, starting from the stars: the fantastic in Samuel Beckett's plays and James Joyce's *Ulysses*. 6–18

NIEL, RUTH.   Speech and silence: beyond the religious in Brian Moore's novels. 161–74

RÁCZ, ISTVÁN D.   Mask lyrics in the poetry of Paul Muldoon and Derek Mahon. 107–18

RAIZIS, MARIUS BYRON.   Yeats's preoccupation with spiritualism and his Byzantium poems. 119–26

SARBU, ALADÁR.   Romantic and modern: vision and form in Yeats, Shaw and Joyce. 19–27

SCHRANK, BERNICE.   'Death is here and death is there, death is busy everywhere': temporality and the desire for transcendence in O'Casey's *The Shadow of a Gunman*. 53–60

SWANN, JOSEPH.   Banville's Faust: *Doctor Copernicus, Kepler, The Newton Letter* and *Mefisto* as stories of the European mind. 148–60

UNGAR, ANDRÁS P.   Ulysses in *Ulysses*: what the Nolan said. 138–47

Social and Political Change in Literature and Film

113.   CHAPPLE, RICHARD (ed.).   Social and political change in literature and film: selected papers from the Sixteenth Annual Florida State University Conference on Literature and Film. Gainesville: Florida UP, 1994. pp. 136.

MASON, CAROL.   *Rear Window*'s Lisa Freemont: masochistic female spectator or post-war socioeconomic threat? 109–21

ODABASHIAN, BARBARA.   Double vision: Scorsese and Hitchcock. 21–35

PAGAN, NICHOLAS O.   Decentering the subject: David Hare's *Wetherby*. 53–63

ROSE, BRIAN.   Transformations of terror: reading changes in social attitudes through film and television adaptations of Stevenson's *Dr Jekyll and Mr Hyde*. 37–52

STONEBACK, H. R.   Fiction into film: 'Is dying hard, daddy?' Hemingway's *Indian Camp*. 93–108

VAN OOSTRUM, DUCO.   Wim Wenders' Euro-American construction site: *Paris, Texas* or Texas, Paris. 7–20

WILSON, CHARLES, JR.   Revolution as theme in John Oliver Killens' *Youngblood*. 123–32

Studies in English Language and Literature

114.   TOSWELL, M. J.; TYLER, E. M. (eds).   Studies in English language and literature. 'Doubt wisely': papers in honour of E. G. Stanley. London; New York: Routledge, 1996. pp. xiii, 545.

ALAMICHEL, MARIE-FRANÇOISE.   Doubt and time in Laȝamon's *Brut*. 219–39

BAKER, PETER S.   Textual boundaries in Anglo-Saxon works on time (and in some Old English poems). 445–56

BREMMER, ROLF H., JR.   Grendel's arm and the law. 121–32

COLMAN, FRAN.   Names will never hurt me. 13–28

FISCHER, ANDREAS.   The vocabulary of very late Old English. 29–41

FRANZEN, CHRISTINE.   Late copies of Anglo-Saxon charters. 42–70

FURROW, MELISSA.   Unscholarly Latinity and Margery Kempe. 240–51

GAMESON, FIONA; GAMESON, RICHARD.   *Wulf and Eadwacer, The Wife's Lament*, and the discovery of the individual in Old English verse. 457–74

GRIFFITH, MARK S.   Does *wyrd bið ful aræd* mean 'Fate is wholly inexorable'? 133–56

HARBUS, ANTONINA.   Old English *swefn* and *Genesis B* line 720. 157–74

HARVEY, E. RUTH.   The swallow's nest and the spider's web. 327–41

HEALEY, ANTONETTE DIPAOLO.   Reasonable doubt, reasoned choice: the letter *A* in the *Dictionary of Old English*. 71–84

HERBISON, IVAN.   The idea of the 'Christian epic': towards a history of an Old English poetic genre. 342–61

HILL, JOYCE.   Ælfric's sources reconsidered: some case studies from the *Catholic Homilies*. 362–86

IRVINE, SUSAN.   Ulysses and Circe in King Alfred's *Boethius*: a Classical myth transformed. 387–401

MCNELIS, JAMES I., III.   The sword mightier than the pen? Hrothgar's hilt, theory, and philology. 175–85

MOMMA, H.   Metrical stress on alliterating finite verbs in clause-initial *a*-verses: 'some doubts and no conclusions'. 186–98

MUGGLESTONE, L. C.   Alexander Ellis and the virtues of doubt. 85–98

OGURA, MICHIKO.   Old English *habban* + past participle of a verb of motion. 199–214

ORCHARD, ANDY.   Poetic inspiration and prosaic translation: the making of *Cædmon's Hymn*. 402–22

SAUNDERS, CORINNE J.   '*Symtyme the fende*': questions of rape in *Sir Gowther*. 286–303

SOLOPOVA, ELIZABETH.   The metre of the *Ormulum*. 423–39

THOMPSON, PAULINE A.   St Æthelthryth: the making of history from hagiography. 475–92

TOSWELL, M. J.   Tacitus, Old English heroic poetry, and ethnographic preconceptions. 493–507

TYLER, ELIZABETH M.   How deliberate is deliberate verbal repetition? 508–30

WALLS, KATHRYN.   Medieval 'allegorical imagery' in *c*.1630: Will. Baspoole's revision of *The Pilgrimage of the Lyfe of the Manhode*. 304–22

WRIGHT, LAURA.   About the evolution of Standard English. 99–115

Studies in Scottish Fiction: 1945 to the Present

115.   HAGEMANN, SUSANNE (ed.).   Studies in Scottish fiction: 1945 to the present. New York; Frankfurt; Bern; Paris: Lang, 1996. pp. 281. (Scottish studies: pubs of the Scottish Studies Centre of the Johannes Gutenberg Universität Mainz in Germersheim, 19.) Rev. by Martin McQuillan in SLJ (supp. 45) 1996, 35–9.

BAKER, SIMON.   'Wee stories with a working-class theme': the reimagining of urban realism in the fiction of James Kelman. 235–50

BELL, IAN A.   Imagine living there: form and ideology in contemporary Scottish fiction. 217–33

CAMPBELL, IAN.   Beside Brown's ocean of time. 263–74

CAROLAN-BROZY, SANDRA; HAGEMANN, SUSANNE. 'There is such a place' – is there? Scotland in Margaret Laurence's *The Diviners*. 145–58

DIXON, KEITH. 'No fairies. No monsters. Just people.' Resituating the work of William McIlvanney. 187–98

FREEMAN, ALAN. Ghosts in sunny Leith: Irvine Welsh's *Trainspotting*. 251–62

GIFFORD, DOUGLAS. Imagining Scotlands: the return to mythology in modern Scottish fiction. 17–49

HAGEMANN, SUSANNE. Introduction. 7–15

HARVIE, CHRISTOPHER. North Sea oil and Scottish culture. 159–85

MACLACHLAN, CHRISTOPHER. Muriel Spark and gothic. 125–44

MALZAHN, MANFRED. 'Yet at the start of every season hope springs up': Robin Jenkins's *The Thistle and the Grail* (1954). 85–96

MONNICKENDAM, ANDREW. Beauty or beast? Landscape in the fiction of Jessie Kesson. 109–23

PITTIN, MARIE ODILE. Alasdair Gray: a strategy of ambiguity. 199–215

RIACH, ALAN. Nobody's children: orphans and their ancestors in popular Scottish fiction after 1945. 51–83

SELLIN, BERNARD. Commitment and betrayal: Robin Jenkins' *A Very Scotch Affair*. 97–108

Subjects on the World's Stage

116. ALLEN, DAVID G.; WHITE, ROBERT A. (eds). Subjects on the world's stage: essays on British literature of the Middle Ages and the Renaissance. Newark: Delaware UP; London; Toronto: Assoc. UPs, 1995. pp. 319. (Revised versions of papers originally presented at the Seventh Citadel Conference on Literature, Charleston, SC, 1991.)

BEVINGTON, DAVID. All's well that plays well. 162–80

BROWN, TED. Pride and pastoral in *The Shepheardes Calendar*. 101–15

COINER, NANCY. Galathea and the interplay of voices in Skelton's *Speke, Parrot*. 88–99

FARRELL, THOMAS J. The *fyn* of the *Troilus*. 38–53

FOX-GOOD, JACQUELYN A. Ophelia's mad songs: music, gender, power. 217–38

GECKLE, GEORGE L. The 1604 and 1616 versions of *Dr Faustus*: text and performance. 146–61

HALLI, ROBERT W., JR. Cecilia Bulstrode, 'the court pucell'. 295–312

JOHNSON, BRUCE A. The moral landscape of the Pardoner's Tale. 54–61

McFeely, Maureen Connolly. 'This day my sister should the cloister enter': the convent as refuge in *Measure for Measure*. 200–16

Middaugh, Karen L. 'Virtues sphear': court *vs* country in the 1618 masque at Coleorton. 280–94

Mischo, John B. 'That use is not forbidden usury': Shakespeare's procreation sonnets and the problem of usury. 262–79

O'Connell, Michael. God's body: incarnation, physical embodiment, and the fate of biblical theater in the sixteenth century. 62–87

Ornstein, Robert. Shakespeare's art of characterization: an unambiguous perspective. 248–61

Sheppeard, Sallye J. Marlowe's Icarus: culture and myth in *Dr Faustus*. 133–45

Spearing, A. C. The poetic subject from Chaucer to Spenser. 13–37

Wentworth, Michael. 'When first I ended, then I first began': Petrarch's triumph in Michael Drayton's *Idea*. 116–32

Westlund, Joseph. Idealization and the problematic in *The Tempest*. 239–47

Widmayer, Martha. Mistress Overdone's house. 181–99

Technology and the American Imagination

117. De Riz, Francesca Bisutti; Zorzi, Rosella Mamoli; Coslovi, Marina (eds). Technology and the American imagination: an ongoing challenge. Atti del Dodecisimo Convegno Biennale, Università di Venezia, 28–30 ottobre 1993. Venice: Supernova, 1994. pp. xiv, 631. (Rivista di studi anglo-americani annuario dell'AISNA, 8:10.)

Ascari, Maurizio. One-way words: an interpretation of *In the Cage*, by Henry James. 244–54

Balestra, Gianfranca. Edith Wharton, Henry James, and 'the proper vehicle of passion'. 595–604

Bartocci, Clara. From the dynamo to the computer: an ongoing challenge. Nature and technology in John Barth's *Giles Goat-Boy*. 543–5

Benesch, Klaus. Between reproduction and authenticity: the contested status of authorship in Hawthorne's *The Artist of the Beautiful*. 116–23

Bergamini, Oliviero. Technology and power within Edward Bellamy's utopianism. 355–61

Boi, Paola. A train of words: techn-ique and the dis-closure of knowledge in *Jonah's Gourd Vine* by Zora Neale Hurston. 417–27

Cagliero, Roberto. The literature of exhaust. 575–83

Calanchi, Alessandra. *The wandering spectator*: *The Man of the Crowd* di E. A. Poe come esplorazione (pre)tecnologica del tempo e dello spazio. 124–34

CARONIA, ANTONIO. Teorie del corpo e comunicazione interattiva. 527–36

CAROSSO, ANDREA. 'Watson, come here! I want (to see) you!': speech, writing, and interruption from A. G. Bell to the telematic text. 73–83

CARRATELLO, MATTIA. Dal *flipper* alla simulazione: *The Universal Baseball Association* di Robert Coover. 310–13

COVI, GIOVANNA. The post-colonial cyborg: Jessica Hagedorn's *Dogeaters*. 499–508

CRIVELLI, RENZO S. Ashbery and Parmigianino: alchemy *vs* technology. 159–70

DANIELE, DANIELA. Travelogues in a broken landscape: Robert Smithson's mixed-medial tribute to William Carlos Williams. 94–105

DE ANGELIS, VALERIO MASSIMO. L'automobile: le macchine della narrazione di Stephen King. 277–83

FABI, M. GIULIA. 'Utopian melting': technology, homogeneity, and the American dream in *Looking Backward*. 346–54

HENNESSEY, WILLIAM J. The automobile and the American imagination. 605–17

HERMAN, LUC. Enzian's meditation on technology in *Gravity's Rainbow*. 556–62

ISERNHAGEN, HARTWIG. Technology and the body: 'postmodernism' and the voices of John Barth. 563–70

MARÇAIS, DOMINIQUE. Confidence and faith in scientific progress in Melville's *The Confidence-Man*. 237–43

MARIANI, GIORGIO. Technology and storytelling: Leslie Silko's *Ceremony* as world epic. 451–8

MIDOLO, CHIARA. 'Machines come natural to your kind': the machine and the body in Paule Marshall's *The Chosen Place, the Timeless People*. 410–16

MINGANTI, FRANCO. Hypertextually, maybe? Rob Swigart's interactive fiction: *Portal*. 84–93

MULAS, FRANCO. The mechanical world in the Italian-American novel. 395–401

NIEMEYER, MARC. The transatlantic cable in popular poetry. 227–36

ORESTANO, FRANCESCA. Wiring the system: Samuel F. B. Morse between art and science. 214–21

PEDERSEN, E. MARTIN. Dressing the skeleton: the oral-to-written folk process in a jump story. 135–44

PISAPIA, BIANCAMARIA. Kurt Vonnegut, il *computer*, ovvero l'epica tenzone tra il racconto e la cibernetica (in due assalti). 265–8

PORTELLI, ALESSANDRO.   Fornaci: *the fire next time*, ovvero *the power of Blackness*. Gli afroamericani come fonte energetica. 269–76

ROSSI, UMBERTO.   P. K. Dick e la questione della tecnica (o della tecnologia). 473–83

SCACCHI, ANNA.   Il *gadget* e l'androide: dal mito dell'apprendista stregone al simulacro. 289–96

SCANNAVINI, ANNA.   Il *robot* e il 'piano' nel ciclo della Fondazione di Asimov. 297–302

SCARSELLA, ALESSANDRO.   'Una macchina da scrivere ad energia orgonica azionata dal boia' ovvero: paradossi tecnologici di William Burroughs. 320–4

SIMPSON, MARK.   'The amateur! The amateur!': notes on *Apocalypse Now*. 106–15

STASKOWSKI, ANDRÉA.   *Blade Runner*: the future as the past, the postmodern present; or, How to be human in the future. 185–91

STEFANELLI, MARIA ANITA.   Dinosaurs in the badlands: Michael Crichton's *Jurassic Park* and Robert Kroetsch's *Badlands*. 402–9

TATTONI, IGINA.   Il registratore: *autobiography: a self-recorded fiction*. 284–8

TERRANOVA, TIZIANA.   Cyber-catastrophes: the sinful technology of Pat Cadigan. 516–26

TICHI, CECELIA.   The twentieth-century television mentality. 3–15

VALLORANI, NICOLETTA.   La rappresentazione imperfetta: tecnologia, corpo e linguaggio in *The Girl Who Was Plugged In* di James Tiptree Jr. 490–8

VAN DIJCK, JOSÉ.   Imagining reproduction: feminist fictions of new reproductive technologies. 484–9

VINCENT, BERNARD.   Paul Goodman: an Edenic voice in the technological *inferno*. 372–7

VISTARCHI, ANGELA.   Cyberpunk in Gibson's Sprawl Trilogy. 509–15

Textual and Theatrical Shakespeare

118. PECHTER, EDWARD (ed.).   Textual and theatrical Shakespeare: questions of evidence. Iowa City: Iowa UP, 1996. pp. viii, 266. (Studies in theatre history and culture.)

BRISTOL, MICHAEL D.   How good does evidence have to be? 22–43

DESSEN, ALAN C.   Recovering Elizabethan staging: a reconsideration of the evidence. 44–65

HODGDON, BARBARA.   'Here apparent': photography, history, and the theatrical unconscious. 181–209

LIEBLEIN, LEANORE.   Theatre archives at the intersection of production and reception: the example of Québécois Shakespeare. 164–80

McLuskie, Kathleen E.   The shopping complex: materiality and the Renaissance theatre. 86–101

Osborne, Laurie E.   The rhetoric of evidence: the narration and display of Viola and Olivia in the nineteenth century. 124–43

Pechter, Edward.   Textual and theatrical Shakespeare: questions of evidence. 1–21

Ripley, John.   *Coriolanus* as Tory propaganda. 102–23

Shaw, Catherine M.   Edwin Booth's *Richard II* and the divided nation. 144–63

Weimann, Robert.   Performance-game and representation in *Richard III*. 66–85

Worthen, W. B.   Invisible bullets, violet beards: reading actors reading. 210–29

The Theatrical Gamut

119. Brater, Enoch (ed.).   The theatrical gamut: notes for a post-Beckettian stage. Ann Arbor: Michigan UP, 1995. pp. xi, 304. (Theater: theory/text/performance.) Rev. by Malcolm Page in Essays in Theatre (15:1) 1996, 121–2.

Abbott, H. Porter.   Consorting with spirits: the arcane craft of Beckett's later drama. 91–106

Ben-Zvi, Linda.   'Aroun the worl': the signifyin(g) theater of Suzan-Lori Parks. 189–208

Blau, Herbert.   Afterthought from the vanishing point: theater at the end of the real. 279–98

Brown, John Russell.   Back to Bali. 1–19

Coco, Bill.   The dramaturgy of the dream play: monologues by Breuer, Chaikin, Shepard. 159–70

Diamond, Elin.   'The garden is a mess': maternal space in Bowles, Glaspell, Robins. 121–39

Esslin, Martin.   Beckett's German context. 41–50

Locatelli, Carla.   Delogocentering silence: Beckett's ultimate unwording. 67–89

McCarthy, Gerry.   'Codes from a mixed-up machine': the disintegrating actor in Beckett, Shepard, and, surprisingly, Shakespeare. 171–87

Orr, John.   Paranoia and celebrity in American dramatic writing: 1970–90. 141–58

Reinelt, Janelle.   Is the English epic over? 209–22

Rodríguez-Gago, Antonia.   Molly's 'happy nights' and Winnie's 'happy days'. 29–40

Takahashi, Yasunari.   Memory inscribed in the body: *Krapp's Last Tape* and the Noh play *Izutsu*. 51–65

ZEIFMAN, HERSH. All my sons after the Fall: Arthur Miller and the rage for order. 107–20

Theorizing Satire

120. CONNERY, BRIAN A.; COMBE, KIRK (eds). Theorizing satire: essays in literary criticism. Basingstoke: Macmillan; New York: St Martin's Press, 1995. pp. xi, 212.

BOGEL, FREDRIC V. The difference satire makes: reading Swift's poems. 43–53

CLARK, JOHN R. Vapid voices and sleazy styles. 19–42

COMBE, KIRK. The new voice of political dissent: the transition from complaint to satire. 73–94

GUTLEBEN, CHRISTIAN. English academic satire from the Middle Ages to the postmodern: distinguishing the comic from the satiric. 133–47

MACKIE, ERIN. The culture market, the marriage market, and the exchange of language: Swift and the progress of desire. 173–92

NASH, RICHARD. Satyrs and satire in Augustan England. 95–105

ROWLAND, JON. From cheated sight to false light: analogy in Swift and Churchill. 107–32

SIBLEY, GAY. *Satura* from Quintilian to Joe Bob Briggs: a new look at an old word. 57–72

TROOST, LINDA V. Economic discourse in the Savoy Operas of W. S. Gilbert. 193–207

This Is About Vision

121. BALASSI, WILLIAM; CRAWFORD, JOHN F.; EYSTUROY, ANNIE O. (eds). This is about vision: interviews with Southwestern writers. Albuquerque: New Mexico UP, 1990. pp. 204. (New American studies in the American West.) Rev. by Glen Newkirk in RMRLL (45:1/2) 1991, 91–2.

ADAMS, CHARLES. Frank Waters. 14–25

BERNELL, SUE; KARNI, MICHAELA. Tony Hillerman. 40–51

CRAWFORD, JOHN. Rudolfo Anaya. 82–93

CRAWFORD, JOHN; EYSTUROY, ANNIE O. Jimmy Santiago Baca. 180–93

CRAWFORD, JOHN; EYSTUROY, ANNIE O. Luci Tapahonso. 194–202

CRAWFORD, JOHN; SMITH, PATRICIA CLARK. Joy Harjo. 170–9

CRAWFORD, JOHN; SMITH, PATRICIA CLARK. Margaret Randall. 70–81

EYSTUROY, ANNIE O. Denise Chávez. 156–69

EYSTUROY, ANNIE O. Paula Gunn Allen. 94–107

GAGE, NANCY. Mark Medoff. 108–17

JIMERSON, KAY.   Edward Abbey. 52–7

JOHNSON, DAVID.   Frances Gillmor. 26–39

OWENS, LOUIS.   N. Scott Momaday. 58–69

REBOLLEDO, TEY DIANA.   Pat Mora. 128–39

SMITH, PATRICIA CLARK.   Linda Hogan. 140–55

THOMPSON, PHYLLIS.   John Nichols. 118–27

Tradition in Transition

122. RIBEIRO, ALVARO; BASKER, JAMES G. (eds).   Tradition in transition: women writers, marginal texts, and the eighteenth-century canon. Oxford: Clarendon Press; New York: OUP, 1996. pp. xvii, 350.

ARMSTRONG, KATHERINE A.   'I was a kind of an historian': the productions of history in Defoe's *Colonel Jack*. 97–110

BARKER, ANTHONY D.   Poetry from the provinces: amateur poets in the *Gentleman's Magazine* in the 1730s and 1740s. 241–56

BASKER, JAMES G.   Radical affinities: Mary Wollstonecraft and Samuel Johnson. 41–55

BUTLER, MARILYN.   Edgeworth's stern father: escaping Thomas Day, 1795–1801. 75–93

CHAKRABARTI, SHIRSHENDU.   Master and servant: social mobility and the ironic exchange of roles in Swift's *Directions to Servants*. 111–26

FAIRER, DAVID.   'Sweet native stream!': Wordsworth and the school of Warton. 314–38

GERRARD, CHRISTINE.   Parnell, Pope, and pastoral. 221–40

GROOM, NICK.   Celts, Goths, and the nature of the literary source. 275–96

HUDSON, NICHOLAS.   'Oral tradition': the evolution of an eighteenth-century concept. 161–76

LONDON, APRIL.   Jane West and the politics of reading. 56–74

McGOWAN, IAN.   Boswell at work: the revision and publication of the *Journal of a Tour to the Hebrides*. 127–43

REIMANN, K. A.   'Great as he is in his own good opinion': the *Bounty* mutiny and Lieutenant Bligh's construction of self. 198–218

RIBEIRO, ALVARO.   The 'chit-chat way': the letters of Mrs Thrale and Dr Burney. 25–40

SUAREZ, MICHAEL F.   Trafficking in the Muse: Dodsley's *Collection of Poems* and the question of canon. 297–313

TURNER, KATHERINE S. H.   At the boundaries of fiction: Samuel Paterson's *Another Traveller!* 144–60

WENDORF, RICHARD.   Sir Joshua's French Revolution. 177–97

WILLIAMS, CAROLYN D.   Poetry, pudding, and Epictetus: the consistency of Elizabeth Carter. 3–24

WILLIAMSON, PAUL.   William Collins and the idea of liberty. 257–74

Traditions, Voices, and Dreams

123. FRIEDMAN, MELVIN J.; SIEGEL, BEN (eds).   Traditions, voices, and dreams: the American novel since the 1960s. Newark: Delaware UP; London; Toronto: Assoc. UPs, 1995. pp. 335.

BRIENZA, SUSAN.   Writing as witnessing: the many voices of E. L. Doctorow. 168–95

CRONIN, GLORIA L.   Fundamentalist views and feminist dilemmas: Elizabeth Dewberry Vaughn's *Many Things Have Happened Since He Died* and *Break the Heart of Me*. 254–78

GILLESPIE, MICHAEL PATRICK.   Baroque Catholicism in Southern fiction: Flannery O'Connor, Walker Percy, and John Kennedy Toole. 25–47

HENKE, SUZETTE A.   Women's life-writing and the minority voice: Maya Angelou, Maxine Hong Kingston, and Alice Walker. 210–33

KLINKOWITZ, JEROME.   Toward a new American mainstream: John Updike and Kurt Vonnegut. 150–67

KOELB, CLAYTON.   The metamorphosis of the classics: John Barth, Philip Roth, and the European tradition. 108–28

KRUPNICK, MARK.   Jewish Jacobites: Henry James's presence in the fiction of Philip Roth and Cynthia Ozick. 89–107

MELLARD, JAMES M.   Origins, language, and the constitution of reality: Norman Mailer's *Ancient Evenings*. 131–49

NAGEL, JAMES.   Desperate hopes, desperate lives: depression and self-realization in Jamaica Kincaid's *Annie John* and *Lucy*. 237–53

SAFER, ELAINE.   Dreams and nightmares: 'high-tech paranoia' and the Jamesonian sublime – an approach to Thomas Pynchon's postmodernism. 279–97

SCHAUB, THOMAS.   Lingering hopes, faltering dreams: Marilynne Robinson and the politics of contemporary American fiction. 298–321

SIEGEL, BEN.   Simply not a mandarin: Saul Bellow as Jew and Jewish writer. 62–88

WAGNER-MARTIN, LINDA.   Panoramic, unpredictable, and human: Joyce Carol Oates's recent novels. 196–209

WEST, JAMES L. W., III.   Voices interior and exterior: William Styron's narrative personae. 48–61

Travel and Drama in Shakespeare's Time

124. MAQUERLOT, JEAN-PIERRE; WILLEMS, MICHÈLE (eds).   Travel and drama in Shakespeare's time. Cambridge; New York: CUP, 1996. pp. ix, 262.

BATE, JONATHAN. The Elizabethans in Italy. 55–74

EDWARDS, PHILIP. Tragic form and the voyagers. 75–86

GIBBONS, BRIAN. The wrong end of the telescope. 141–59

GURR, ANDREW. Industrious Ariel and idle Caliban. 193–208

HADFIELD, ANDREW. 'The naked and the dead': Elizabethan perceptions of Ireland. 32–54

HATTAWAY, MICHAEL. 'Seeing things': Amazons and cannibals. 179–92

HOLLAND, PETER. 'Travelling hopefully': the dramatic form of journeys in English Renaissance drama. 160–78

MAQUERLOT, JEAN-PIERRE; WILLEMS, MICHÈLE. Introduction. 1–13

MUIR, KENNETH. Lope de Vega and Shakespeare. 239–54

MULRYNE, J. R. Nationality and language in Thomas Kyd's *The Spanish Tragedy*. 87–105

PARR, ANTHONY. Foreign relations in Jacobean England: the Sherley brothers and the 'voyage of Persia'. 14–31

PEYRÉ, YVES. Marlowe's Argonauts. 106–23

POTTER, LOIS. Pirates and 'turning Turk' in Renaissance drama. 124–40

SALINGAR, LEO. The New World in *The Tempest*. 209–22

WALCH, GÜNTER. 'What's past is prologue': metatheatrical memory and transculturation in *The Tempest*. 223–38

Trends in English and American Studies

125. COELSCH-FOISNER, SABINE; GÖRTSCHACHER, WOLFGANG; KLEIN, HOLGER M. (eds). Trends in English and American studies: literature and the imagination: essays in honour of James Lester Hogg. Lewiston, NY; Lampeter: Mellen Press, 1996. pp. v, 459.

BACHINGER, KATRINA. Setting allegory adrift in John Ashbery's *Mountains and Rivers*, James Joyce's *Portrait of the Artist as a Young Man*, and Vincent O'Sullivan's *Let the River Stand*. 285–93

BASKIYAR, DHARNI DHAR. Indian echoes in Shelley: an interpretation. 205–14

COELSCH-FOISNER, SABINE. Sex-maniacs, errant knights and lady professors: romance and satire in Lodge's university novels. 333–49

COSGROVE, BRIAN. 'Between politics and transcendence': history and utopian possibility in the work of Seamus Heaney. 305–18

GIDDEY, ERNEST. Rocks and waves: Virginia Woolf, Leslie Stephen, and Byron. 295–304

GÖRTSCHACHER, WOLFGANG. (Re)writing contemporary literary history: (small) presses, little magazines, university curricula. 319–31

HARWELL, THOMAS MEADE.   The Hispanic owl in South Texas. 37–52

HIGASHIMAKA, ITSUYO.   The early stages of Byron's relationship with Gifford. 161–9

JACK, IAN.   Swinburne's *Ave atque Vale*. 241–53

KELSALL, MALCOLM.   Inventing America: Jefferson seals the Revolution. 365–74

KIRBY, I. J.   *Twelfth Night* I.1.5–7. 71–4

KITZBERGER, INGRID ROSA.   Archetypal images of transformation and the self in Percy Bysshe Shelley's *The Revolt of Islam*. 171–87

KLEIN, HOLGER.   Shakespeare als Buch. 85–110

LETELLIER, ROBERT IGNATIUS.   Some feminine perceptions of freedom in an age of restoration and absolutism: prophetic and realistic voices in the writings of Margaret Cavendish and Madame de Lafayette. 129–44

MALL, G. J. ZAMBARDI.   Literature of the absurd. 397–411

MARTIN, JOHN STEPHEN.   Emerson as a phenomenological philosopher and poet. 227–40

MÜLLER, ULRICH.   Modern morality plays of Broadway: *Jelly's Last Jam* and *Angels in America*. 375–84

O'NEILL, MICHAEL.   Blake and the self-conscious poem. 145–59

PURSGLOVE, GLYN.   William Strode's *Faire Chloris* and her metamorphoses. 111–28

RAIZIS, MARIUS BYRON.   The origin and culmination of Shelley's philhellenism. 189–204

SATZINGER, CHRISTA.   Oscar Wilde – rehabilitated at last. 255–68

STEVENSON, WARREN.   Madeline unhoodwink'd: *The Eve of St Agnes* as self-reflexive romance. 215–26

STROBL, GERWIN.   *Quartet* and *Four Quartets*: the influence of T. S. Eliot on Paul Scott. 269–84

TRUCHLAR, LEO.   Wozu lese und schreibe ich? Notizen aus Anlass meiner Lektüren von Adrienne Rich und Friederike Mayröcker. 3–14

VAN DOMELEN, JOHN E.   Shakespeare's primitive and the dream of perfection. 75–83

WAHL, BILL.   A wondrous novel: *Wheel of Fortune*. 351–64

WHARTON, JANET.   William Bercher's *Dyssputacion off the Nobylytye of Wymen*: text and transmission. 53–69

Victorian Literature and the Victorian Visual Imagination

126. CHRIST, CAROL T.; JORDAN, JOHN O. (eds).   Victorian literature and the Victorian visual imagination. Berkeley; London: California UP, 1995. pp. xxix, 371. Rev. by Roger Ebbatson in TRB (6:5) 1996, 325–7; by Suzanne Ozment in NCS (10) 1996, 138–40; by Robert Douglas-Fairhurst in TLS, 1 Mar. 1996, 3–4.

ADAMS, JAMES ELI.   The hero as spectacle: Carlyle and the persistence of dandyism. 213–32

BAILIN, MIRIAM.   Seeing is believing in *Enoch Arden*. 313–26

CASTERAS, SUSAN P.   Seeing the unseen: pictorial problematics and Victorian images of class, poverty, and urban life. 264–88

CURTIS, GERARD.   Shared lines: pen and pencil as trace. 27–59

FISHER, JUDITH. L.   Image *versus* text in the illustrated novels of William Makepeace Thackeray. 60–87

HANDY, ELLEN.   Dust piles and damp pavements: excrement, repression, and the Victorian city in photography and literature. 111–33

HOMANS, MARGARET.   Victoria's sovereign obedience: portraits of the Queen as wife and mother. 169–97

JAFFE, AUDREY.   Spectacular sympathy: visuality and ideology in Dickens's *A Christmas Carol*. 327–44

SHIRES, LINDA M.   The author as spectacle and commodity: Elizabeth Barrett Browning and Thomas Hardy. 198–212

STEIN, RICHARD L.   Secret figures: Victorian urban iconography. 233–63

STEWART, GARRETT.   Reading figures: the legible image of Victorian textuality. 345–67

THOMAS, RONALD R.   Making darkness visible: capturing the criminal and observing the law in Victorian photography and detective fiction. 134–68

Visions of the Fantastic

127. BECKER, ALLIENNE R. (ed.).   Visions of the fantastic: selected essays from the Fifteenth International Conference of the Fantastic in the Arts. Westport, CT; London: Greenwood Press, 1996. pp. xxi, 205. (Contributions to the study of science fiction and fantasy, 68.)

ALDISS, BRIAN.   If Hamlet's uncle had been a nicer guy. 21–4

DICKENS, DAVID B.   Bürger's ballad *Lenore*: en route to *Dracula*. 131–8

FLANNERY, JAMES W.   Staging the phantasmagorical: the theatrical challenges and rewards of William Butler Yeats. 149–65

FREDERICK, JOAN.   Order from chaos: war, pestilence, and the near-death experience in Katherine Anne Porter's *Pale Horse, Pale Rider*. 25–31

INGERSOLL, EARL G.   The engendering of narrative in Doris Lessing's *Shikasta* and Margaret Atwood's *The Handmaid's Tale*. 39–47

JURKIEWICZ, KENNETH.   Francis Coppola's secret gardens: *Bram Stoker's 'Dracula'* and the *auteur* as decadent visionary. 167–71

MCALLISTER, ROBIN.   Borges' *El Aleph* and Poe's *The Fall of the House of Usher*: two studies in the poetics of gothic romance. 83–8

MCJANNET, TAMMY D.   The emphasis on the European contact situation in the American science-fiction novel's representation of culture. 89–94

MALEKIN, PETER.   Re-membering: time and myth in *Kleinzeit* and *The Medusa Frequency*. 189–95

MERRILL, CATHERINE.   The flesh made word: *Miss Lonelyhearts'* sublime grotesque. 33–8

MILLER, ELIZABETH.   *Frankenstein* and *Dracula*: the question of influence. 123–9

PENNINGTON, JOHN.   Pierre Menard in cyberspace: the Internet as intertext. 181–8

WEBB, JANEEN.   Simmons and Powers: postmodernism to post-romanticism. 139–46

The Wit of Seventeenth-Century Poetry

128. SUMMERS, CLAUDE J.; PEBWORTH, TED-LARRY (eds).   The wit of seventeenth-century poetry. Columbia; London: Missouri UP, 1995. pp. viii, 222. Rev. by Robert Shenk in BJJ (3) 1996, 207–10; by Brian Blackley in JDJ (15) 1996, 219–33; by Michael G. Brennan in NQ (43:3) 1996, 343–4.

ALLEN, M. C.   George Herbert's pastoral wit. 119–34

ELLIS, JIM.   The wit of circumcision, the circumcision of wit. 62–77

EVANS, ROBERT C.   Wit and the power of Jonson's *Epigrammes*. 101–18

KELLY, ERNA.   Women's wit. 42–61

MARTIN, CATHERINE GIMELLI.   Pygmalion's progress in the garden of love; or, The wit's work is never Donne. 78–100

QUINSEY, KATHERINE M.   *Religio Laici?* Dryden's men of wit and the printed word. 199–214

ROBERTS, LORRAINE.   The 'truewit' of Crashaw's poetry. 171–82

ROLLIN, ROGER B.   Witty by design: Robert Herrick's *Hesperides*. 135–50

SEELIG, SHARON CADMAN.   My curious hand or eye: the wit of Richard Lovelace. 151–70

SESSIONS, W. A.   Marvell's Mower: the wit of survival. 183–98

STANWOOD, P. G.; JOHNSON, LEE M.   The structure of wit: 'is all good structure in a winding stair?'. 22–41

WILCOX, HELEN.   'No more wit than a Christian?': the case of devotional poetry. 9–21

Women, the Book and the Worldly

129.   SMITH, LESLEY; TAYLOR, JANE H. M. (eds).   Women, the book and the worldly: selected proceedings of the St Hilda's conference, 1993: vol. II. Cambridge; Rochester, NY: Brewer, 1995. pp. xiv, 193. Rev. by Bella Millett in NQ (43:4) 1996, 470–1.

BOFFEY, JULIA.   Lydgate's lyrics and women readers. 139–49

GOODMAN, JENNIFER R.   *'That wommen holde in ful greet reverence'*: mothers and daughters reading chivalric romances. 25–30

KENNEDY, BEVERLY.   The variant passages in the Wife of Bath's Prologue and the textual transmission of the *Canterbury Tales*: the 'great tradition' revisited. 85–101

STOCKER, MARGARITA.   Apocryphal entries: Judith and the politics of Caxton's *Golden Legend*. 167–81

SUMMIT, JENNIFER.   William Caxton, Margaret Beaufort and the romance of female patronage. 151–65

Women of the Word

130.   BASKIN, JUDITH R. (ed.).   Women of the word: Jewish women and Jewish writing. Detroit, MI: Wayne State UP, 1994. pp. 382.

BURSTEIN, JANET.   Mother at the center: Jewish American women's stories of the 1920s. 182–96

COHEN, SARAH BLACHER.   Cynthia Ozick: prophet for parochialism. 283–98

HOROWITZ, SARA R.   Memory and testimony of women survivors of Nazi genocide. 258–82

KESSNER, CAROLE S.   Matrilineal dissent: the rhetoric of zeal in Emma Lazarus, Marie Syrkin, and Cynthia Ozick. 197–215

WEXLER, LAURA.   Looking at Yezierska. 153–81

The Work of Dissimilitude

131.   ALLEN, DAVID G.; WHITE, ROBERT A. (eds).   The work of dissimilitude: essays from the Sixth Citadel Conference on Medieval and Renaissance Literature. Newark: Delaware UP; London; Toronto: Assoc. UPs, 1992. pp. 292. Rev. by Amanda Piesse in DUJ (55:1) 1994, 141–3.

BRADSHAW, DAVID J.   Bosola: a perspective that shows us tragedy. 243–56

CAMPBELL, MARY A.   The illustrated travel book and the birth of ethnography: part 1 of De Bry's *America*. 177–95

COX, CATHERINE I.   *'Horn-pypes and funeralls'*: suggestions of hope in Shakespeare's tragedies. 216–34

Cox, Catherine S.   *Graelent* and *Sir Gawain*: a new analogue for Bertilak's lady. 57–66

Halio, Jay L.   The promised endings of *King Lear*. 235–42

Hardison, O. B., Jr.   Crosscurrents in English sixteenth-century prosody. 116–30

Harvey, Nancy Lenz.   Chaucer's *Troilus and Criseyde* and the idea of '*pleye*'. 48–56

Hinely, Jan Lawson.   'Freedom through bondage': Wyatt's appropriation of the Penitential Psalms of David. 148–65

Kinney, Arthur F.   Figuring medieval and Renaissance literature. 13–34

Klein, Lisa M.   The Petrarchanism of Sir Thomas Wyatt reconsidered. 131–47

Koch, Mark.   The desanctification of the beggar in rogue pamphlets of the English Renaissance. 91–104

Marx, Michael Steven.   Biblical allusions and intertextual assurances in George Herbert's *Affliction (1)*. 257–65

Peterson, Douglas L.   The origins of Tudor comedy: Plautus, *Jack Jugeler*, and the folk-play as mediating form. 105–15

Read, David.   Ralegh's *Discoverie of Guiana* and the Elizabethan model of empire. 166–76

Sanders, Arnold A.   Ruddymane and Canace, lost and found: Spenser's reception of *Confessio Amantis* 3 and Chaucer's Squire's Tale. 196–215

Shoaf, R. A.   'For there is figures in all things': juxtology in Shakespeare, Spenser, and Milton. 266–85

Vasta, Edward.   Narrative pessimism and textual optimism in Chaucer's *House of Fame*. 35–47

Ward, Laviece C.   Historiography on the eve of the Reformation in an early sixteenth-century English manuscript, e Museo 160. 81–90

Westrem, Scott D.   Two routes to pleasant instruction in late fourteenth-century literature. 67–80

Writing India 1757–1990

132. Moore-Gilbert, Bart (ed.).   Writing India 1757–1990: the literature of British India. Manchester; New York: Manchester UP, 1996. pp. x, 271.

Colwell, Danny.   'I am your Mother and your Father': Paul Scott's Raj Quartet and the dissolution of imperial identity. 213–35

Lane, Christopher.   Volatile desire: ambivalence and distress in Forster's colonial narratives. 188–212

LEASK, NIGEL.   Towards an Anglo-Indian poetry? The colonial muse in the writings of John Leyden, Thomas Medwin and Charles D'Oyly. 52–85

MAJEED, JAVED.   Meadows Taylor's *Confessions of a Thug*: the Anglo-Indian novel as a genre in the making. 86–110

MOORE-GILBERT, BART.   'The Bhabhal of tongues': reading Kipling, reading Bhabha. 111–38

MOORE-GILBERT, BART.   Introduction: writing India, reorienting colonial discourse analysis. 1–29

PARNELL, TIM.   Salman Rushdie: from colonial politics to post-modern poetics. 236–62

PAXTON, NANCY L.   Secrets of the colonial harem: gender, sexuality, and the law in Kipling's novels. 139–62

SAINSBURY, ALISON.   Married to the Empire: the Anglo-Indian domestic novel. 163–87

TELTSCHER, KATE.   'The fearful name of the Black Hole': fashioning an imperial myth. 30–51

BIBLIOGRAPHY

GENERAL

133. APPEL, CHARLOTTE. Bogmarkedets og læsningens historie *ca.* 1500–1700 i nyere europæisk forskning: en introduktion. (Recent European research in the history of books and reading 1500–1700: an introduction.) Fund og forskning i det Kongelige Biblioteks samlinger (32) 1993, 185–234.

134. BARLOW, WM P., JR. Bibliography and bibliophily. PBSA (90:2) 1996, 139–50.

135. BATTESTIN, MARTIN C. Fredson Thayer Bowers: a checklist and chronology. SB (46) 1993, 155–86.

136. BUSCH, CHRISTOPHER S. A historical bibliographical survey of the Steinbeck Monograph Series (1971–91) and the Steinbeck Essay Series (1986–91). SteiQ (26:1/2) 1993, 23–37.

137. DARNTON, ROBERT; DASKALOVA, KRASSIMIRA. Book history, the state of play: an interview with Robert Darnton. SHARP News (3:3) 1994, 2–4.

138. DONALDSON, ROBERT. Fragments of the *Aberdeen Breviary.* Edinburgh Bibliographical Society Transactions (6:3) 1995, 71–86. (Early Scottish imprints.)

139. FATTAHI, RAHMATOLLAH. Super records: an approach towards the description of works appearing in various manifestations. Library Review (45:4) 1996, 19–29.

140. GERRITSEN, JOHAN. Preserved abroad: some notes on *STC*-books in Holland and Germany. *In* (pp. 101–8) **11**.

141. GREETHAM, D. C. Textual scholarship: an introduction. (Bibl. 1995, 72.) Rev. by Bodo Plachta in editio (8) 1994, 229–30; by James Thorpe in Text (Ann Arbor) (7) 1994, 543–6.

142. HOWARD-HILL, T. H. The history of the book in departments of literature. CanRCL (23:1) 1996, 207–15.

143. INGRAM, RANDALL. The writing poet: the descent from song in *The Poems of Mr John Milton, Both English and Latin* (1645). MStud (34) 1996, 179–97.

144. IVES, MAURA. Descriptive bibliography and the Victorian periodical. SB (49) 1996, 61–94.

145. —— Listing periodical contributions in descriptive bibliographies: questions of scope, arrangement, and content. PBSA (90:3) 1996, 321–42.

146. McCORMACK, W. J. Bibliophile's diary: number eight. Long Room (41) 1996, 7–17.

147. McKITTERICK, DAVID. The survival of books. BC (43:1) 1994, 9–26.

148. NEAVILL, GORDON B. From printing history to history of the book. CanRCL (23:1) 1996, 225–37.

149. NEEDHAM, PAUL. Allan H. Stevenson and the bibliographical uses of paper. SB (47) 1994, 23–64.

150. QUARTERMAIN, PETER. Undoing the book. Text (Ann Arbor) (9) 1996, 119–32.

151. RICHARDSON, BRIAN. Dealing with books: naming texts and the logic of entitlement. CanRCL (23:1) 1996, 239–58.

152. ROSE, MARK. Authors and owners: the invention of copyright. (Bibl. 1995, 76.) Rev. by Robert L. Patten in SHARP News (4:2) 1995, 4–5; by Christopher Skelton-Foord in BJECS (19:1) 1996, 87.

153. SMYTHE, COLIN. A. L. Burt's 1898 edition of *Irish Fairy and Folk Tales* 'edited by W. B. Yeats'. Yeats Annual (12) 1996, 248–52.

154. —— W. B. Yeats, Austin Spare and *Eight Poems* (*Wade* 114). Yeats Annual (12) 1996, 253–63.

155. TANSELLE, G. THOMAS. A description of descriptive bibliography. SB (45) 1992, 1–30.

156. —— The life and work of Fredson Bowers. SB (46) 1993, 1–154.

157. —— The life and work of Fredson Bowers. Foreword by David L. Vander Meulen. Checklist and chronology by Martin C. Battestin. (Bibl. 1995, 78.) Rev. by Hugh Amory in Text (Ann Arbor) (9) 1996, 466–74; by Thomas L. Berger in YES (26) 1996, 338–9.

158. WEST, JAMES L. W., III. Book history at Penn State. JSchP (27:3) 1996, 127–34.

159. WINSHIP, MICHAEL. The art preservative: from the history of the book back to printing history. PrH (17:1) 1995, 14–23.

160. WOLPE, BERTHOLD. Caledonian miscellany. Edinburgh Bibliographical Society Transactions (6:2) 1993, 39–54.

BINDING

161. ELLENBERG, KAREN T. The book arts and presentation: an interview with George M. Cunha. KenR (11:3) 1992, 58–68.

162. FOOT, MIRJAM M. A binding by Joshua Eddowes, *c.*1780. BC (43:1) 1994, 92–4. (English and foreign bookbindings, 66.)

163. GOULDEN, R. J. Dorrell and Goulden: a dated commercial binding and a copycat. BC (43:3) 1994, 408–11. (English and foreign bookbindings, 68.)

164. MATTHEWS, JACK. The binding of books and the matter of the spirit. AR (54:4) 1996, 479–87.

165. MORRIS, J. A blocked binding by Alexander Banks, Junior, Edinburgh 1854. Bibliotheck (20) 1995, 24–8. (Scottish bookbindings, 7.)

166. MORRIS, JOHN. A Bible bound at Restalrig in 1709. Edinburgh Bibliographical Society Transactions (6:3) 1995, 87–91.

167. MYNORS, R. A. B.; THOMSON, R. M. Catalogue of the manuscripts of Hereford Cathedral Library. With a contribution on the bindings by Michael Gullick. (Bibl. 1995, 83.) Rev. by Andrew G. Watson in EHR (111:442) 1996, 674–5.

168. PEARSON, DAVID. A binding by Benjamin West, *ca.*1840. BC (45:1) 1996, 83–6. (English and foreign bookbindings, 73.)

169. —— A binding by William Matthews, *ca.*1929. BC (45:4) 1996, 526–8. (English and foreign bookbindings, 76.)

170. —— A Durham binding of 1634. BC (43:4) 1994, 553–6. (English and foreign bookbindings, 67.)

171. RHODES, DENNIS E. (ed.). Bookbindings and other bibliophily: essays in honour of Anthony Hobson. Foreword by Frederick B. Adams. Verona: Valdonega, 1994. pp. 365. Rev. by Steve Miller in Libraries & Culture (31:3/4) 1996, 680–1.

172. WOUDHUYSEN, H. R. The English Grolier. TLS, 26 Apr. 1996, 32.

BOOK ILLUSTRATION

For work on the illustrations, etc., of William Blake, see under
'Eighteenth Century Authors: William Blake'.

173. ALEXANDER, DAVID.   Affecting moments: prints of English literature made in the age of Romantic sensibility, 1775–1800. York: Univ. of
York, 1993. pp. 72. Rev. by Alun David in Shandean (7) 1995, 109–11.

174. ANDERSON, PATRICIA.   The printed image and the transformation of popular culture, 1790–1860. (Bibl. 1995, 85.) Rev. by
Robert L. Patten in AHR (98:2) 1993, 490–2.

175. ANON.   Realms of Tolkien: images of Middle-earth. New York:
HarperPrism, 1996. 1 vol. (unpaged).

176. AYME, CLAUDE.   Des *Bab Ballads* aux Savoy Operas: Gilbert et
la caricature. CVE (43) 1996, 119–37.

177. BADARACCO, CLAIRE HOERTZ.   Trading words: poetry,
typography, and illustrated books in the modern literary economy.
Baltimore, MD; London: Johns Hopkins UP, 1995. pp. xiii, 259. Rev. by
S[ebastian] C[arter] in TLS, 17 May 1996, 32.

178. BARRETT, DEBBIE L.   *Pericles*, social redemption, and the iconography of *Veritas temporis filia*. Shakespeare Yearbook (2) 1991, 77–94.

179. BATH, MICHAEL; MANNING, JOHN; YOUNG, ALAN R. (eds).   The
art of the emblem. Essays in honour of Karl Josef Höltgen. New York:
AMS Press, 1993. pp. xiii, 272. (AMS studies in the emblem, 10.)

180. BECHER, ANNE G.   Barlow's *Aesop* at Oxford. JPHS (25) 1996,
5–20.

181. BENTLEY, G. E., JR.   The journeyman and the genius: James
Parker and his partner William Blake with a list of Parker's engravings.
SB (49) 1996, 208–31.

182. BERONÄ, DAVID A.   Chronicles in black and white: the woodcut
novels of Masereel and Ward. Biblio (1:2) 1996, 38–41.

183. BLEWETT, DAVID.   The illustration of *Robinson Crusoe*, 1719–1920.
Gerrards Cross: Smythe, 1995. pp. 235. Rev. by Ruari McLean in BC
(45:3) 1996, 409–10; by Andrew Varney in NQ (43:4) 1996, 480–1; by
Peter Sabor in ECF (9:1) 1996, 122–4.

184. BROWN, MURRAY L.   *Emblemata rhetorica*: glossing emblematic discourse in Richardson's *Clarissa*. StudN (27:4) 1995, 455–76.

185. BROWN-DAVIDSON, TERRI.   Inside literature's weird, wonderful
night kitchen: the picture books of Maurice Sendak. HC (32:1) 1995,
1–10.

186. BUSBY, KEITH (ed.).   Word and image in Arthurian literature.
New York; London: Garland, 1996. pp. ix, 372.

187. CAMPBELL, MARY A.   The illustrated travel book and the birth
of ethnography: part 1 of De Bry's *America*. In (pp. 177–95) **131**.

188. CAPLIN, ELLIOTT.   Al Capp remembered. Bowling Green, OH:
Bowling Green State Univ. Popular Press, 1994. pp. 148. Rev. by Garyn
Roberts in JPC (29:4) 1996, 233.

189. CORDERY, GARETH.   Furniss, Dickens and illustration. DickQ
(13:1) 1996, 34–41; (13:2) 1996, 98–110.

190. DALY, PETER M., *et al.* (eds).   The English emblem tradition:

vol. 2. Toronto; London: Toronto UP, 1993. pp. xvii, 546. (Index emblematicus.) Rev. by C. W. R. D. Moseley in YES (26) 1996, 266–7.

191. DALZIEL, PAMELA.   Anxieties of representation: the serial illustrations to Hardy's *The Return of the Native*. NineL (51:1) 1996, 84–110.

192. DAY, W. G.   Michael Angelo Rooker's illustrations to *Tristram Shandy*. Shandean (7) 1995, 30–42.

193. DE VOOGD, PETER.   Sterne all the fashion: a sentimental fan. Shandean (8) 1996, 133–6.

194. DILWORTH, THOMAS.   David Jones's *The Deluge*: engraving the structure of the modern long poem. JML (19:1) 1994, 5–30.

195. DÖLVERS, HORST.   Walter Cranes *Aesop* im Kontext seiner Entstehung. Buchkunst und Bilderbuch im viktorianischen England. (Bibl. 1994, 119.) Rev. by Joachim Möller in LWU (29:2) 1996, 121–3; by Armin Geraths in AAA (21:2) 1996, 318–20.

196. DORRELL, LARRY D.; CURTIS, DAN B.; RAMPAL, KULDIP R. Book-worms without books? Students reading comic books in the school house. JPC (29:2) 1995, 223–34.

197. FISHER, JUDITH L.   Image *versus* text in the illustrated novels of William Makepeace Thackeray. *In* (pp. 60–87) **126**.

198. FODEN, PETER.   Fell's forgotten legacy: the intaglio collection of the Oxford University Press museum. JPHS (25) 1996, 21–30.

199. FOX-FRIEDMAN, JEANNE.   Howard Pyle and the chivalric order in America: King Arthur for children. Arthuriana (6:1) 1996, 77–95.

200. FROELICH, JANET.   Cover boy. NYTM, 10 Nov. 1996, 50–1. (Chip Kidd.)

201. GOLDFARB, SHELDON.   New Thackeray drawings. ThN (43) 1996, 3.

202. GOLDMAN, PAUL.   The Dalziel brothers and the British Museum. BC (45:3) 1996, 341–50.

203. —— Victorian illustration: the pre-Raphaelites, the Idyllic School, and the high Victorians. Aldershot: Scolar Press; Brookfield, VT: Ashgate, 1996. pp. xviii, 391.

204. HAMILTON, JAMES.   Wood engraving in Britain, *c*.1890–1990. London: Barrie & Jenkins, 1994. pp. 224. Rev. by Joanna Selborne in BC (43:3) 1994, 441–4.

205. HAMMOND, WAYNE G.; SCULL, CHRISTINA.   J. R. R. Tolkien: artist & illustrator. (Bibl. 1995, 107.) Rev. by Raymond Lister in SEVEN (13) 1996, 110–13.

206. HARTWIG, JOAN.   Marvell's metamorphic *Fleckno*. SELit (36:1) 1996, 171–212.

207. HOLLANDER, JOHN.   The figure on the page: words and images in Wright Morris's *The Home Place*. YJC (9:1) 1996, 93–108.

208. HÖLTGEN, KARL JOSEF.   Catholic pictures *versus* Protestant words? The adaptation of the Protestant sources in Quarles's *Emblemes*. Emblematica (9:1) 1995, 221–38.

209. —— DALY, PETER M.; LOTTES, WOLFGANG (eds).   Word and visual imagination: studies in the interaction of English literature and the visual arts. (Bibl. 1990, 57.) Rev. by Ulrich Weisstein in GRM (42:4) 1992, 473–6.

210. HOOPER, STEPHEN.   Dal Stivens as Australian cultural critic: Australian landscape, folklore and comic strips. Australian Folklore (11) 1996, 46–52.

211. HORNE, ALAN.   The dictionary of 20th-century British book illustrators. Woodbridge, Suffolk: Antique Collectors' Club, 1994. pp. 456. Rev. by Michael Felmingham in BC (45:1) 1996, 132–3.

212. HOUFE, SIMON.   The last of the Dalziels. BC (45:3) 1996, 351–7.

213. KUNZLE, DAVID.   The history of the comic strip: vol. 2, The nineteenth century. (Bibl. 1995, 115.) Rev. by James Smith Allen in AHR (96:5) 1991, 1508–9.

214. LAING, JANE.   Cicely Mary Barker and her art. London: Warne, 1995. pp. 128. Rev. by Andrea Immel in BC (45:2) 1996, 274–5.

215. LASNER, MARK SAMUELS.   A selective checklist of the published work of Aubrey Beardsley. (Bibl. 1995, 116.) Rev. by Joseph H. Gardner in ANQ (9:4) 1996, 51–2; by Linda Gertner Zatlin in NCS (10) 1996, 143–4.

216. LEBAILLY, HUGUES.   Dr Dodgson & Mr Carroll: de la caricature au portrait. CVE (43) 1996, 169–83.

217. LEWIS, DAVID.   Going along with Mr Gumpy: polysystemy & play in the modern picture book. Signal (80) 1996, 105–19.

218. McCONCHIE, R. W.   Some Australian literary illustrators. New Courant (5) 1996, 58–65.

219. McKENNA, MARY LOU.   'Masks of words and painted plots': Swinburne and nineteenth-century emblematics. Emblematica (9:1) 1995, 177–97.

220. MANCOFF, DEBRA N.   Problems with the pattern: William Morris's Arthurian imagery. Arthuriana (6:3) 1996, 55–68.

221. MANN, JESSE D.   A little known incident of plagiarism in the career of Arthur Rackham. BC (45:2) 1996, 214–17. (*Rip Van Winkle.*)

222. MARTIN, RICHARD.   American chronicle: J. C. Leyendecker's icons of time. JAC (19:1) 1996, 57–85.

223. METCALF, GREG.   'If you read it, I wrote it': the anonymous career of comic book writer Paul S. Newman. JPC (29:1) 1995, 147–62.

224. MILES, PETER.   Smollett, Rowlandson, and a problem of identity: decoding names, bodies, and gender in *Humphry Clinker*. ECL (20:1) 1996, 1–23.

225. MÖLLER, HANS; VIRR, RICHARD.   Stephen Leacock and his books. Fontanus (7) 1994, 15–32.

226. MOSER, BARRY.   God, posterity, and well-made objects. PULC (57:2) 1996, 308–31.

227. MOSS, ELAINE.   Clever Bill: William Nicholson, children & picture books. Signal (80) 1996, 98–104.

228. MYER, VALERIE GROSVENOR.   Martha as Magdalen: an illustration in *David Copperfield*. NQ (43:4) 1996, 430.

229. NETICK, ANNE TYLER.   Doré's *The Raven* on display. PoeM (23) 1993, 5–9.

230. O'CONNOR, ROBERT H. (ed.).   Henry William Bunbury's *Tales of the Devil*. Lewiston, NY; Lampeter: Mellen Press, 1994. pp. 89.

231. OPIE, BRIAN.   Illustrating *Paradise Lost*. TLR (29) 1996, 25–46.

232. PATTEN, ROBERT L.   George Cruikshank's life, times, and art: vol. 1, 1792–1835. (Bibl. 1995, 131.) Rev. by John Sutherland in Review (16) 1994, 169–75.

233. PAULSON, RONALD.   Putting out the fire in Her Imperial Majesty's apartment: opposition politics, anticlericalism, and aesthetics. ELH (63:1) 1996, 79–107. (Swift and Hogarth.)

234. PEATTIE, ROGER W.   Frank W. Burgess: bookseller and book cover artist. BC (43:1) 1994, 59–74.

235. PIQUET, MARTINE. Dans les griffes de Svengali: caricature anti-sémite littéraire dans *Trilby* de George Du Maurier (1894). CVE (43) 1996, 73–88.

236. POMEROY, JANE R. On the changes made in wood engravings in the stereotyping process. PrH (17:2) 1995, 35–40.

237. RIACH, ALAN. Nobody's children: orphans and their ancestors in popular Scottish fiction after 1945. *In* (pp. 51–83) **115**.

238. ROBERTS, GARYN G. Dick Tracy and American culture. (Bibl. 1995, 135.) Rev. by Gary Hoppenstand in JPC (29:4) 1996, 248–50.

239. ROGERSON, IAN. Agnes Miller Parker and the Limited Editions Club's *Jude the Obscure*. BJRL (78:1) 1996, 143–53.

240. ROLLOCK, BARBARA. Black authors & illustrators of children's books: a biographical dictionary. (Bibl. 1990, 2304.) New York; London: Garland, 1992. pp. xviii, 234. (Garland reference library of the humanities, 1316.) (Second ed.: first ed. 1988.) Rev. by Stan Evans in AAR (28:4) 1994, 683–5.

241. ROWSON, MARTIN. Hyperboling gravity's ravelin: a comic book version of *Tristram Shandy*. Shandean (7) 1995, 62–86.

242. SCHULTZ, ELIZABETH A. Unpainted to the last: *Moby-Dick* and twentieth-century American art. (Bibl. 1995, 139.) Rev. by Irving Malin and Christopher Sten in MelSE (107) 1996, 23–6.

243. SHANNON, EDWARD A. 'That we may mis-unda-stend each udda': the rhetoric of *Krazy Kat*. JPC (29:2) 1995, 209–22.

244. SILCOX, MARY V. Three (?) editions of Combe's *Theater of Fine Devices*. Emblematica (9:1) 1995, 217–19.

245. SIMONDS, PEGGY MUÑOZ. The iconography of transformed fish in Shakespeare's *Pericles*: a study of the rusty armor *topos* in the English Renaissance. *In* (pp. 121–61) **111**.

246. SNODGRASS, CHRIS. Aubrey Beardsley: dandy of the grotesque. Oxford; New York: OUP, 1995. pp. xix, 338. Rev. by Stanley Weintraub in ELT (39:4) 1996, 474–8; by Linda G. Zatlin in Criticism (38:3) 1996, 482–5.

247. SOUPEL, SERGE. Marold's *Voyage sentimental*. Shandean (8) 1996, 121–8.

248. STANTON, JOSEPH. The dreaming picture books of Chris Van Allsburg. ChildLit (24) 1996, 161–79.

249. STRING, TATIANA C. Henry VIII's illuminated 'Great Bible'. JWCI (59) 1996, 315–24.

250. TABACHNICK, STEPHEN. A course in the graphic novel. RWT (1:2) 1994, 141–55.

251. THOMPSON, HILARY. Enclosure and childhood in the wood engravings of Thomas and John Bewick. ChildLit (24) 1996, 1–22.

252. TRACHTENBERG, ALAN. Wright Morris's 'photo-texts'. YJC (9:1) 1996, 109–19.

253. WALTERS, DOUGLAS. J. S. Le Fanu's *Schalken the Painter*: a portfolio. Ghosts and Scholars (22) 1996, 35–9.

254. WHITAKER, MURIEL. The legends of King Arthur in art. (Bibl. 1994, 147.) Rev. by Debra N. Mancoff in Quondam et Futurus (1:3) 1991, 82–9.

255. WITEK, JOSEPH. The dream of total war: the limits of a genre. JPC (30:2) 1996, 37–45. (Comic books.)

BOOK PRODUCTION, PRINTING, AND TYPOGRAPHY

256. ARGETSINGER, MARK.   Adobe Garamond: a review. PrH (13:2/14:1) 1991/92, 69–86.

257. BADARACCO, CLAIRE HOERTZ.   Trading words: poetry, typography, and illustrated books in the modern literary economy. *See* **177**.

258. BARRETT, TIMOTHY.   Fifteenth-century papermaking. PrH (15:2) 1993, 33–41.

259. BISHOP, EDWARD.   Re:covering Modernism – format and function in the little magazines. *In* (pp. 287–319) **69**.

260. BOEHM, ALAN D.   The 1798 *Lyrical Ballads* and the poetics of late eighteenth-century book production. ELH (63:2) 1996, 453–87.

261. BROWNRIGG, LINDA L. (ed.).   Making the medieval book: techniques of production. Proceedings of the Fourth Conference of the Seminar in the History of the Book to 1500, Oxford, July 1992. (Bibl. 1995, 149.) Rev. by Rosamond McKitterick in TLS, 12 Apr. 1996, 33.

262. CARLSON, DAVID R.   English Humanist books: writers and patrons, manuscript and print, 1475–1525. (Bibl. 1995, 151.) Rev. by Suzanne Trill in EngS (76:5) 1995, 484–5; by Tim William Machan in ChauY (3) 1996, 168–70; by Damian Grace in Parergon (13:2) 1996, 234–5; by Peter Auksi in ESCan (22:4) 1996, 491–3.

263. CARTER, MATTHEW.   Theories of letterform construction: part one. PrH (13:2/14:1) 1991/92, 3–16.

264. COST, PATRICIA A.   Linn Boyd Benton, Morris Fuller Benton, and typemaking at ATF. PrH (16:1/2) 1994, 27–44.

265. CYR, PAUL A.   Joel Munsell, Aldus's disciple in Albany. PrH (15:2) 1993, 13–22.

266. DANE, JOSEPH A.   The curse of the mummy paper. PrH (17:2) 1995, 18–25.

267. —— Perfect order and perfected order: the evidence from press-variants of early seventeenth-century quartos. PBSA (90:3) 1996, 272–320.

268. DIX, ROBIN; DARBY, TRUDI LAURA.   The bibliographical significance of the turned letter. SB (46) 1993, 263–70.

269. DOOLEY, ALLAN C.   Author and printer in Victorian England. (Bibl. 1995, 153.) Rev. by Simon Gatrell in Review (16) 1994, 301–12; by Daniel Karlin in Text (Ann Arbor) (8) 1995, 448–55.

270. DREYFUS, JOHN.   Into print: selected writings on printing history, typography and book production. (Bibl. 1995, 154.) Rev. by W. M. Watson in Library Review (45:3) 1996, 55–6.

271. —— A typographical masterpiece: an account by John Dreyfus of Eric Gill's collaboration with Robert Gibbings in producing the Golden Cockerel Press edition of *The Four Gospels* in 1931. San Francisco: Book Club of California, 1990. pp. xii, 105. (Book Club of California pubs, 194.) Rev. by Peter Van Wingen in PrH (13:2/14:1) 1991/92, 108–9.

272. EDWARDS, GAVIN.   William Hazlitt and the case of the initial letter. Text (Ann Arbor) (9) 1996, 260–79.

273. FRANKLIN, COLIN.   Book collecting as one of the fine arts, and other essays. Aldershot: Scolar Press; Brookfield, VT: Ashgate, 1996. pp. x, 138. Rev. by J.H.C.L. in TLS, 12 July 1996, 32.

274. —— The Kelmscott Press and William Morris. Biblio (1:1) 1996, 22–3.

275. —— Print and design in eighteenth-century editions of Shakespeare. BC (43:4) 1994, 517–28.

276. FRIEDMAN, JOHN B. Northern English books, owners, and makers in the late Middle Ages. (Bibl. 1995, 156.) Rev. by Benjamin G. Kohl in Albion (28:4) 1996, 672–3.

277. GARVEY, M. ELEANOR. Leaves from an album of printing and graphic arts. PrH (13:1) 1991, 23–7.

278. GROSS, ROBERT A. *The Cambridge History of American Literature.* Book (34) 1994, 4–7 (review-article).

279. HALL, DAVID D. Cultures of print: essays in the history of the book. Amherst: Massachusetts UP, 1996. pp. 195. (Studies in print culture and the history of the book.)

280. HANSON, DAVID A. Baron Frederick Wilhelm von Egloffstein: inventor of the first commercial halftone process in America. PrH (15:1) 1993, 12–24.

281. HARRIS, ELIZABETH M. The rail presses. PrH (15:2) 1993, 42–8.

282. HOLTZBERG-CALL, MAGGIE. The lost world of the craft printer. (Bibl. 1992, 237.) Rev. by Scott Hamilton Suter in MidAF (23:1) 1995, 56–7.

283. HUTNER, MARTIN. The making of the Book of Common Prayer of 1928. Southbury, CT: Chiswick Book Shop, 1990. pp. xvi, 75. Rev. by John Bidwell in PrH (13:2/14:1) 1991/92, 107–8.

284. HUTNER, MARTIN W. Daniel Berkeley Updike: humanist, scholar, printer. PrH (15:2) 1993, 23–32.

285. JOHNSTON, ALASTAIR. 'Guard the mysteries! Constantly reveal them!': the history of printing as shown in type specimens. PrH (13:2/14:1) 1991/92, 59–68.

286. —— Reflections on the centenary of the Merrymount Press. PrH (15:1) 1993, 28–32.

287. JOWETT, JOHN. Jonson's authorization of type in *Sejanus* and other early quartos. SB (44) 1991, 254–65.

288. KELLY, JERRY. Adobe Garamond: a new adaptation of a sixteenth-century type. PrH (13:2/14:1) 1991/92, 101–6.

289. KIRBY, KENT; REARDON, TOM. Collotype: prince of the printing processes. PrH (13:1) 1991, 3–18.

290. KORNFELD, HEIKE. Der technische Stand des Buchdrucks im 18. Jahrhundert. JfD (5) 1993, 15–32.

291. LEVARIE, NORMA. The art & history of books. Foreword by Nicolas Barker. (Bibl. 1995, 161.) Rev. by Ian Rogerson in Library Review (45:7) 1996, 71–2.

292. LEWIS, JOHN. Such things happen: the life of a typographer. Stowmarket: Unicorn, 1994. pp. x, 212, (plates) 32. Rev. by Norman Scarfe in BC (43:4) 1994, 593–4.

293. McCORISON, MARCUS A. John Mycall – the ingenious typographer of Newburyport. PrH (17:1) 1995, 24–40.

294. McGANN, JEROME. Black riders: the visible language of Modernism. (Bibl. 1995, 164.) Rev. by Heather Bryant Jordan in Review (16) 1994, 121–34; by George Bornstein in Text (Ann Arbor) (8) 1995, 387–96; by Michael Wutz in StudN (27:2) 1995, 228–32.

295. McLEAN, RUARI (ed.). Typographers on type: an illustrated anthology from William Morris to the present day. (Bibl. 1995, 165.) Rev. by W. Malcolm Watson in Library Review (45:7) 1996, 57–8.

296. McMULLIN, B. J. Signing by the page. SB (48) 1995, 259–68.

297. MARKHAM, SANDRA J.   *Memento mori* on silk and stone: Reuben Manley, printer, 1818–42. PrH (15:1) 1993, 3–11.

298. MATHISON, H.   'Gude black prent': how the Edinburgh book trade dealt with Burns's *Poems*. Bibliotheck (20) 1995, 70–87.

299. MORTIMER, RUTH.   The Bibliographical Society of America: publishing about printing. PrH (13:1) 1991, 30–3.

300. MOSS, M.   The curious case of Duncan Stevenson, printer to Edinburgh University. Bibliotheck (20) 1995, 88–97.

301. NINK, RUDOLF.   Literatur und Typographie. Wort-Bild-Synthesen in der englischen Prosa des 16. bis 20. Jahrhunderts. (Bibl. 1994, 166.) Rev. by Horst Dölvers in Archiv (233:2) 1996, 391–3.

302. O'CONNELL, BONNIE.   The quality of response: Kim Merker and the literary fine press. BkIA (64) 1996, 3–13.

303. PARKER, MIKE.   Starling Burgess, type designer? PrH (16:1/2) 1994, 52–108.

304. PATRICK, KEVIN.   Words made new: book production and collecting in the computer age. Biblio (1:3) 1996, 38–41.

305. PATTEN, ROBERT L.   When is a book not a book? Biblion (4:2) 1996, 35–63.

306. RIDDELL, JAMES A.   The printing of the plays in the Jonson folio of 1616. SB (49) 1996, 149–68.

307. RIDEOUT, TANIA.   The reasoning eye: Alexander Pope's typographic vision in the *Essay on Man*. JWCI (55) 1992, 249–62.

308. ROGERS, SHEF.   How many *T*s had Ezra Pound's printer? SB (49) 1996, 277–83.

309. SAXE, STEPHEN O.   The Goodman common press: the oldest American-made press. PrH (13:1) 1991, 28–9.

310. —— The Gregynog Press Paradiso type. APHA (124) 1996, 3.

311. —— The Landis Valley Museum Ramage press. PrH (15:1) 1993, 26–7.

312. —— On the track of old common presses. APHA (126) 1996, 3.

313. —— 'A small old printing press'. PrH (16:1/2) 1994, 25–6. (Isaiah Thomas's press in Worcester, MA.)

314. SHEP, SYDNEY J.   A new dawning: Wai-te-ata Press and letterpress printing in New Zealand. BC (45:4) 1996, 457–75.

315. SHORTER, ALFRED H.   Studies on the history of papermaking in Britain. Ed. Richard L. Hills. Aldershot; Brookfield, VT: Variorum, 1993. pp. xi, 348. (Collected studies, 425.) Rev. by Richard W. Clement in Libraries & Culture (31:3/4) 1996, 679.

316. SOLOTAROFF, TED.   The paperbacking of publishing. WD (72:3) 1992, 80.

317. TAKAMIYA, TOSHIYUKI.   Chapter divisions and page breaks in Caxton's *Morte Darthur*. PoetT (45) 1996, 63–78.

318. TANSELLE, G. THOMAS.   Printing history and other history. SB (48) 1995, 269–89.

319. TAYLOR, W. THOMAS.   The temper of the present. PrH (17:1) 1995, 41–6.

320. TRACY, WALTER.   Why Egyptian? PrH (16:1/2) 1994, 3–10.

321. TURNER, JOHN R.   Title-pages produced by the Walter Scott Publishing Co. Ltd. SB (44) 1991, 323–31.

322. TWYMAN, MICHAEL.   Early lithographed books: a study of the design and production of improper books in the age of the hand press, with a catalogue. (Bibl. 1991, 172.) Rev. by Hans-Jürgen Imiela in JfD (5) 1993, 36.

323. WALLIS, LAWRENCE W.   Type designs by George W. Jones for the Linotype machine. PrH (16:1/2) 1994, 11–24.

324. WEEDON, ALEXIS.   An analysis of the cost of book production in nineteenth-century Britain. AEB (9:1/2) 1995, 24–48.

325. WEGNER, J. P.   *Festschriften* of the book industries – an international bibliography. JfD (5) 1993, 10–12.

326. WEISS, ADRIAN.   Bibliographical methods for identifying unknown printers in Elizabethan/Jacobean books. SB (44) 1991, 183–228.

327. —— Shared printing, printer's copy, and the text(s) of Gascoigne's *A Hundreth Sundrie Flowres*. SB (45) 1992, 71–104.

328. WINSHIP, MICHAEL.   The art preservative: from the history of the book back to printing history. *See* **159**.

329. YAMADA, AKIHIRO.   Thomas Creede, printer to Shakespeare and his contemporaries. Tokyo: Meisei UP, 1994. pp. xxiv, 287. Rev. by Adrian Weiss in AEB (9:1/2) 1995, 61–8.

MANUSCRIPTS

330. ALEXANDER, JONATHAN J. G.   Medieval illuminators and their methods of work. (Bibl. 1995, 172.) Rev. by Stephen G. Nichols in AHR (99:3) 1994, 879–80.

331. ANON. (comp.).   The British Library catalogue of additions to the manuscripts: new series: 1986–1990. London: British Library, 1993. 3 vols. pp. 1071. Rev. by David McKitterick in TLS, 25 Feb. 1994, 28.

332. —— Chronique. Gazette du livre médiéval (20) 1992, 32–60; (28) 1996, 48–80; (29) 1996, 41–84. (Includes bibliography on MSS.)

333. ARMSTRONG, ALISON (ed.).   *The Herne's Egg*: manuscript materials. (Bibl. 1995, 173.) Rev. by Richard Allen Cave in Yeats Annual (12) 1996, 290–303.

334. ATKINS, A. R.   A bibliographical analysis of the manuscript of D. H. Lawrence's *The White Peacock*. SB (44) 1991, 344–64.

335. BACKHOUSE, JANET.   The Lindisfarne Gospels: a masterpiece of book painting. (Bibl. 1995, 175.) Rev. by Stuart James in Library Review (45:8) 1996, 46–7.

336. BATELY, JANET; BROWN, MICHELLE P.; ROBERTS, JANE (eds). A palaeographer's view: the selected writings of Julian Brown. Preface by Albinia C. de la Mare. (Bibl. 1994, 180.) Rev. by Dáibhí Ó Cróinín in Early Medieval Europe (3:1) 1994, 73–5.

337. BAYLESS, MARTHA.   Medieval manuscript pages: wall trophies or historical treasures? Biblio (1:1) 1996, 44–7.

338. BEAL, P. (ed.).   Index of English literary manuscripts: vol. 2, 1625–1700: part 2, Lee–Wycherley. (Bibl. 1995, 177.) Rev. by F. Korsten in EngS (76:5) 1995, 488–9.

339. BLANCHFIELD, LYNNE S.   Rate revisited: the compilation of the narrative works in MS Ashmole 61. *In* (pp. 208–20) **104**.

340. BOFFEY, JULIA.   Lydgate's lyrics and women readers. *In* (pp. 139–49) **129**.

341. BONESS, NEIL.   Manuscripts in the Antipodes: the origins of the Sydney collections. Parergon (13:2) 1996, 183–94.

342. BRAEKMAN, MARTINA.   *How a Lover Praiseth His Lady*

(Bodl. MS Fairfax 16): a Middle English courtly poem re-appraised. Med (8) 1995, 27–73.

343.   BREWER, CHARLOTTE; RIGG, A. G. (introds).   *Piers Plowman*: a facsimile of the Z-text in Bodleian Library, Oxford, MS Bodley 851. (Bibl. 1995, 182.) Rev. by Lister M. Matheson in NQ (43:1) 1996, 77–8.

344.   CAMILLE, MICHAEL.   The dissenting image: a postcard from Matthew Paris. *In* (pp. 115–50) **17**.

345.   CLARK, DAVID R. (ed.).   *The Winding Stair* (1929): manuscript materials. (Bibl. 1995, 190.) Rev. by Peter McDonald in TLS, 27 Sept. 1996, 10–11.

346.   CROSS, JAMES E.; TUNBERG, JENNIFER MORRISH (eds).   The Copenhagen Wulfstan collection: Copenhagen Kongelige Bibliotek Gl. kgl. sam. 1595. (Bibl. 1995, 197.) Rev. by Johan Gerritsen in EngS (76:2) 1995, 202–4.

347.   DUMVILLE, DAVID N.   English Caroline script and monastic history: studies in Benedictinism, AD 950–1030. (Bibl. 1995, 202.) Rev. by Sarah Foot in Early Medieval Europe (5:2) 1996, 227–8; by Catherine Cubitt in EHR (111:441) 1996, 409–10.

348.   —— English square minuscule script: the mid-century phases. ASE (23) 1994, 133–64.

349.   DUNCAN-JONES, K.   Notable accessions: Western manuscripts. BLR (15:4) 1996, 308–14. (Letter from Essex to Penelope Rich.)

350.   EDWARDS, A. S. G.   The transmission and audience of Osbern Bokenham's *Legendys of Hooly Wummen*. *In* (pp. 157–67) **56**.

351.   —— (gen. ed.).   The index of Middle English prose : handlist 8, A handlist of manuscripts containing Middle English prose in Oxford college libraries, by S. J. Ogilvie-Thomson. (Bibl. 1994, 199.) Rev. by G. A. Lester in EngS (76:1) 1995, 99–100.

352.   —— The index of Middle English prose : handlist 10, Manuscripts in Scandinavian collections. By Irma Taavitsainen. (Bibl. 1995, 205.) Rev. by E. G. Stanley in NQ (43:3) 1996, 310–11; by G. A. Lester in EngS (77:3) 1996, 282–3.

353.   —— The index of Middle English prose : handlist 11, Manuscripts in the Library of Trinity College, Cambridge. By Linne R. Mooney. (Bibl. 1995, 206.) Rev. by E. G. Stanley in NQ (43:3) 1996, 310–11.

354.   FAUSBØLL, ELSE.   More Ælfric fragments. EngS (76:4) 1995, 302–6.

355.   FLETCHER, ALAN J.   A hive of industry or a hornets' nest? MS Sidney Sussex 74 and its scribes. *In* (pp. 131–55) **56**.

356.   FREDELL, JOEL.   Decorated initials in the Lincoln Thornton Manuscript. SB (47) 1994, 78–88.

357.   GAMESON, RICHARD.   The origin of the Exeter Book of Old English poetry. ASE (25) 1996, 135–85.

358.   GARSIDE, P. D.   An annotated checklist of Hogg's literary manuscripts in the Alexander Turnbull Library, Wellington, New Zealand. Bibliotheck (20) 1995, 5–23.

359.   GNEUSS, HELMUT.   Books and libraries in early England. Aldershot; Brookfield, VT: Variorum, 1996. 1 vol. (various pp.) (Variorum reprints: collected studies, 558.)

360.   GOLDBERG, JONATHAN.   Writing matter: from the hands of the English Renaissance. (Bibl. 1993, 166.) Rev. by David Cressy in AHR (96:5) 1991, 1531; by Richard Halpern in Shakespeare Yearbook (2) 1991, 266–9; by D. C. Greetham in Text (Ann Arbor) (9) 1996, 408–29.

361. GOSLEE, NANCY MOORE (ed.).   The *Homeric Hymns* and *Prometheus* drafts notebook: Bodleian MS. Shelley adds.e.12. New York; London: Garland, 1996. pp. lxxxv, 318. (Bodleian Shelley manuscripts, 18.)

362. GRANT, RAYMOND J. S.   A copied 'Tremulous' Worcester gloss at Corpus. NM (97:3) 1996, 279–83.

363. GREETHAM, D. C.   Getting personal/going public. Review (17) 1995, 225–52 (review-article).

364. GRIFFITHS, JEREMY.   New light on the provenance of a copy of the *Canterbury Tales*, John Rylands Library, MS Eng. 113. BJRL (77:2) 1995, 25–30.

365. HAMILTON, CHARLES.   Great forgers and famous fakes: the manuscript forgers of America and how they duped the experts. Lakewood, CO: Glenbridge, 1996. pp. xxiv, 294. (Second ed.: first ed. 1980.)

366. HANNA, RALPH, III.   John Shirley and British Library, MS Additional 16165. SB (49) 1996, 95–105.

367. —— Pursuing history: Middle English manuscripts and their texts. Stanford, CA: Stanford UP, 1996. pp. xii, 362. (Figurae.)

368. —— With an *O* (Yorks.) or an *I* (Salop.)? The Middle English lyrics of British Library Additional 45896. SB (48) 1995, 290–7.

369. HIEATT, CONSTANCE B.   The Middle English culinary recipes in MS Harley 5401: an edition and commentary. MÆ (65:1) 1996, 54–71.

370. HOLDSWORTH, CAROLYN (ed.).   *The Wind among the Reeds*: manuscript materials. (Bibl. 1995, 230.) Rev. by Warwick Gould in Yeats Annual (12) 1996, 304–14.

371. HOUWEN, L. A. J. R.   *The Deidis of Armorie*: an edition of Harley MS 6149, ff. 5–42: a fifteenth-century heraldic manual and bestiary. (Bibl. 1991, 226.) Rev. by A. S. G. Edwards in NQ (43:2) 1996, 205–6.

372. HULSE, LYNN.   *The King's Entertainment* by the Duke of Newcastle. Viator (26) 1995, 355–405.

373. HUWS, DANIEL.   MS Porkington 10 and its scribe. *In* (pp. 188–207) **104**.

374. JONES, STEVEN E. (ed.).   Drafts for *Laon and Cythna*, Cantos V–XII: Bodleian MS Shelley adds.e.10. (Bibl. 1995, 235.) Rev. by William Keach in KSJ (45) 1996, 199–201.

375. JOUKOVSKY, NICHOLAS A.   Thomas Love Peacock's manuscript *Poems* of 1804. SB (47) 1994, 196–211.

376. KEISER, GEORGE R.   A new text of, and new light on, the *Supplement to the Index of Middle English Verse*, 4106.5. NQ (43:1) 1996, 15–18.

377. —— Reconstructing Robert Thornton's herbal. MÆ (65:1) 1996, 35–53. (Lincoln Cathedral MS 91.)

378. KENNEDY, BEVERLY.   Cambridge MS Dd.4.24: a misogynous scribal revision of the Wife of Bath's Prologue? ChauR (30:4) 1996, 343–58.

379. KIERNAN, KEVIN S.   *Beowulf* and the *Beowulf* manuscript. (Bibl. 1984, 316.) Ann Arbor: Michigan UP, 1996. pp. xxx, 328. (Revised ed.: first ed. 1981.)

380. KNOLES, THOMAS.   Notes on research collections: post-1876 manuscript materials for the study of the history of the book at AAS. Book (35) 1995, 1–3.

381. KORNEXL, LUCIA.   The *Regularis concordia* and its Old English gloss. ASE (24) 1995, 95–130.

382. KRYGIER, MARCIN.   Plural markers of the Old English nouns of relationship in the two manuscripts of Laȝamon's *Brut*. *In* (pp. 47–68) **68**.

383.   LE SAUX, FRANÇOISE (ed.).   The text and tradition of Laȝamon's *Brut*. (Bibl. 1994, 221.) Rev. by John Frankis in NQ (43:3) 1996, 312–13.

384.   LOVE, HAROLD.   Scribal publication in seventeenth-century England. (Bibl. 1995, 241.) Rev. by Ted-Larry Pebworth in Review (18) 1996, 165–74.

385.   LUCAS, PETER J.   The *Metrical Epilogue* to the Alfredian *Pastoral Care*: a postscript from Junius. ASE (24) 1995, 43–50.

386.   MCCLELLAN, WILLIAM.   A codicological analysis of the quire structure of MS HM 140 and its implications for a revised *ordinatio*. Text (Ann Arbor) (9) 1996, 187–98.

387.   —— The consequences of *treuth*: reading two versions of the Clerk's Tale. Genre (25:2/3) 1992, 153–78. (MS HM 140, and Ellesmere MS.)

388.   MCKENZIE, D. F.   A new Congreve literary autograph. BLR (15:4) 1996, 292–9.

389.   MAPSTONE, SALLY.   Scots and their books in the Middle Ages and the Renaissance: an exhibition in the Bodleian Library, Oxford. Oxford: Bodleian Library, 1996. pp. 30.

390.   MAROTTI, ARTHUR F.   Manuscript, print, and the English Renaissance lyric. (Bibl. 1995, 245.) Rev. by Katherine Duncan-Jones in TLS, 16 Feb. 1996, 26.

391.   MEALE, CAROL M.   '*Prenes: engre*': an early sixteenth-century presentation copy of *The Erle of Tolous*. *In* (pp. 221–36) **104**.

392.   MINNIS, A. J. (ed.).   Late-medieval religious texts and their transmission: essays in honour of A. I. Doyle. *See* **56**.

393.   MOONEY, LINNE R.   More manuscripts written by a Chaucer scribe. ChauR (30:4) 1996, 401–7.

394.   MUIR, BERNARD J. (ed.).   The Exeter anthology of Old English poetry: an edition of Exeter Dean and Chapter MS 3501. Exeter: Exeter UP, 1994. 2 vols. pp. xiv, 817. (Exeter medieval English texts and studies.) Rev. by Hugh Magennis in EngS (76:5) 1995, 474–7; by Carolyne Larrington in MÆ (65:1) 1996, 128–9.

395.   MURA, KAREN E.   Thomas Wardon: a mid-fifteenth-century reader, 1448–62. FCS (22) 1996, 42–54. (Soc. of Antiquaries of London, MS 101.)

396.   NEWHAUSER, RICHARD.   '*Strong it is to flitte*' – a Middle English poem on death and its pastoral context. *In* (pp. 319–36) **61**.

397.   NOEL, WILLIAM.   The Harley Psalter. Cambridge; New York: CUP, 1995. pp. xvii, 231. (Cambridge studies in palaeography and codicology, 4.) Rev. by Paul Binski in TLS, 16 Aug. 1996, 32.

398.   OBERHAUS, DOROTHY HUFF.   Emily Dickinson's fascicles: method & meaning. (Bibl. 1995, 257.) Rev. by John Gerlach in EDJ (5:1) 1996, 121–3.

399.   OWEN, CHARLES A., JR.   The manuscripts of the *Canterbury Tales*. (Bibl. 1995, 259.) Rev. by Klaus Bitterling in Ang (114:1) 1996, 109–12.

400.   PAGE, R. I.   An Old English fragment from Westminster Abbey. ASE (25) 1996, 201–7.

401.   PARKINSON, THOMAS; BRANNEN, ANNE (eds).   *Michael Robartes and the Dancer*: manuscript materials. (Bibl. 1994, 235.) Rev. by Wayne K. Chapman in Yeats Annual (12) 1996, 320–3; by Peter McDonald in TLS, 27 Sept. 1996, 10–11.

402. Parrish, Stephen (ed.). *The Wild Swans at Coole*: manuscript materials. (Bibl. 1994, 236.) Rev. by Wayne K. Chapman in Yeats Annual (12) 1996, 315–19; by Peter McDonald in TLS, 27 Sept. 1996, 10–11.

403. Pebworth, Ted-Larry. Publication before the triumph of print. Review (18) 1996, 165–74 (review-article).

404. Pezzini, Domenico. Book IV of St Bridget's *Revelations* in an Italian (MS Laurenziano 27.10) and an English translation (MS Harley 4800) of the fifteenth century. Aevum (70:3) 1996, 487–506.

405. —— Un trattato sulla vita contemplativa e attiva dalle *Revelationes* (VI, 65) di Santa Brigida: edizione di *An Informacion of Contemplatif Lyf and Actif* dal MS Oxford, Bodley 423. Aevum (68:2) 1994, 379–406.

406. Phillips, Catherine (ed.). *The Hour-Glass*: manuscript materials. (Bibl. 1994, 239.) Rev. by Richard Allen Cave in Yeats Annual (12) 1996, 279–89.

407. Pinti, Daniel J. Governing the Cook's Tale in Bodley 686. ChauR (30:4) 1996, 379–88.

408. Priestman, Judith. An unpublished letter by W. H. Auden. BLR (15:4) 1996, 325–9.

409. Quinn, Mary A. (ed.). Shelley's 1821–1822 Huntington notebook: a facsimile of Huntington MS HM 2111. New York; London: Garland, 1996. pp. lxxii, 351. (Manuscripts of the younger Romantics: Percy Bysshe Shelley, 7.)

410. Rafferty, Margaret. The Winchester Manuscript of Sir Thomas Malory's *Le Morte Darthur*: palaeographical evidence for the structure of the Arthuriad. Textures (10) 1996, 23–33.

411. Reichl, Karl. 'No more ne willi wiked be': religious poetry in a Franciscan manuscript (Digby 2). *In* (pp. 297–317) **61**.

412. Reiman, Donald H. The study of modern manuscripts: public, confidential, and private. (Bibl. 1995, 266.) Rev. by D. C. Greetham in Review (17) 1995, 225–52.

413. Richards, Mary P. (ed.). Anglo-Saxon manuscripts: basic readings. New York; London: Garland, 1994. pp. xv, 401. (Garland reference library of the humanities, 1434.) (Basic readings in Anglo-Saxon England, 2.)

414. Rumble, Alexander R. The Rylands, the Bible and early English literature: an illustrated note. BJRL (77:3) 1995, 205–17.

415. Rusche, Philip G. Dry-point glosses to Aldhelm's *De laudibus virginitatis* in Beinecke 401. ASE (23) 1994, 195–213.

416. Sanders, Arnold. Hypertext, learning, and memory: some implications from manuscript tradition. Text (Ann Arbor) (8) 1995, 125–43.

417. Sargent, Michael G. (ed.). Nicholas Love's *Mirror of the Blessed Life of Jesus Christ*: a critical edition based on Cambridge University Library Additional MSS 6578 and 6686. (Bibl. 1995, 274.) Rev. by Kantik Ghosh in MÆ (65:1) 1996, 136.

418. Scott, P.; Hansen, J. S. Three newly identified James Hogg manuscript poems at the University of South Carolina. Bibliotheck (21) 1996, 34–8.

419. Shapiro, L. Dennis. Manuscripts and the World Wide Web. MSS (48:3) 1996, 213–28.

420. Shawcross, John T. Notes on an important volume of Donne's poetry and prose. JDJ (9:2) 1990, 137–9.

421. SMITH, MARGARET.   Newly acquired Brontë letters, transcriptions and notes. BST (21:7) 1996, 323–36.

422. SMITH, MARGARET M.; LINDSAY, ALEXANDER (eds).   Index of English literary manuscripts: vol. 3, 1700–1800: part 3, Alexander Pope–Sir Richard Steele, with a first-line index to parts 1–3. With contributions by John Goodridge and Christine Alexander. (Bibl. 1995, 277.) Rev. by James E. May in ECS (28:2) 1994/95, 270–2; by J. P. Vander Motten in EngS (76:1) 1995, 103–4; by Christopher Skelton-Foord in BJECS (19:1) 1996, 87–8.

423. SPROUSE, JAMES R.   Middle English dialect investigation and the Middle English manuscript: the case of the Bodleian Manuscript 6923. SECOLR (15:2) 1991, 87–99.

424. STEVENS, MARTIN; WOODWARD, DANIEL (eds).   The Ellesmere Chaucer: essays in interpretation. (Bibl. 1995, 281.) Rev. by Peter Mack in TLS, 5 Apr. 1996, 23–4.

425. STEVICK, ROBERT D.   The earliest Irish and English bookarts: visual and poetic forms before AD 1000. (Bibl. 1995, 282.) Rev. by Barbara C. Raw in MÆ (65:1) 1996, 125–7; by Carol A. Farr in Albion (28:4) 1996, 657–8; by John Blundell in Early Medieval Europe (5:1) 1996, 119–20.

426. SULLIVAN, ERNEST W., II.   Updating the John Donne listings in Peter Beal's *Index of English Literary Manuscripts*, II. JDJ (9:2) 1990, 141–8.

427. TAYLOR, SEAN.   The F scribe and the R manuscript of *Piers Plowman B*. EngS (77:6) 1996, 530–48.

428. THOMAS, GRAHAM C. G.; HUWS, DANIEL (comps).   Summary catalogue of the manuscripts of South Glamorgan Libraries, Cardiff Central Library, commonly referred to as the 'Cardiff MSS'. Aberystwyth: National Library of Wales, 1994. pp. vii, 456.

429. THOMPSON, JOHN J.   Another look at the religious texts in Lincoln, Cathedral Library, MS 91. *In* (pp. 169–87) **56**.

430. —— Looking behind the book: MS Cotton Caligula A.ii, part 1, and the experience of its texts. *In* (pp. 171–87) **104**.

431. TIEKEN-BOON VAN OSTADE, INGRID.   The two versions of Malory's *Morte d'Arthur*: multiple negation and the editing of the text. (Bibl. 1995, 286.) Rev. by Helen Cooper in MÆ (65:2) 1996, 321–2.

432. TITE, COLIN G. C.   The manuscript library of Sir Robert Cotton. (Bibl. 1995, 287.) Rev. by Chris R. Kyle in BC (45:2) 1996, 273–4.

433. TOSWELL, M. J.   The format of Bibliothèque Nationale MS lat. 8824: the Paris Psalter. NQ (43:2) 1996, 130–3.

434. TREHARNE, E. M.   A unique Old English formula for excommunication from Cambridge, Corpus Christi College 303. ASE (24) 1995, 185–211.

435. VOSS, MANFRED.   Altenglische Glossen aus MS British Library, Cotton Otho E.i. AAA (21:2) 1996, 179–203.

436. WALLNER, BJÖRN.   An interpolated Middle English version of the *Anatomy* of Guy de Chauliac: part 2, Introduction, notes, glossary. Edited from Glasgow Univ. Library, Hunter MS 95. Lund: Lund UP; Bromley: Chartwell-Bratt, 1996. pp. 66. (Pubs of the New Soc. of Letters at Lund, 89.)

437. WARD, LAVIECE C.   Historiography on the eve of the Reformation in an early sixteenth-century English manuscript, e Museo 160. *In* (pp. 81–90) **131**.

438. WEBBER, TERESA. Scribes and scholars at Salisbury Cathedral, 1075–1125. (Bibl. 1995, 294.) Rev. by Robert B. Patterson in AHR (99:3) 1994, 887.

439. WERNER, MARTA L. (ed.). Emily Dickinson's open folios: scenes of reading, surfaces of writing. (Bibl. 1995, 296.) Rev. by Adam Frank in AL (68:4) 1996, 853–4.

COLLECTING AND THE LIBRARY

440. ALBLAS, JACQUES B. H. The Bunyan collection of the Vrije Universiteit, Amsterdam. Bunyan Studies (6) 1995/96, 78–84.

441. ALSTON, R. C. Books with manuscript: a short title catalogue of books with manuscript notes in the British Library: including books with manuscript additions, proofsheets, illustrations, corrections: with indexes of owners and books with authorial annotations. London: British Library, 1994. pp. xiii, 663. Rev. by T. A. Birrell in EngS (76:3) 1995, 284–5; by Robert L. Dawson in Libraries & Culture (31:3/4) 1996, 677–9.

442. ANON. Early imprints in New Zealand libraries: a finding list of books printed before 1801 held in libraries in the Wellington region. Wellington: Alexander Turnbull Library, 1995. pp. xi, 314. Rev. by David McKitterick in BC (45:4) 1996, 573–5.

443. —— (comp.). The British Library catalogue of additions to the manuscripts: new series: 1986–1990. See **331**.

444. —— Chronique. See **332**.

445. —— F. Scott Fitzgerald: centenary exhibition, September 24, 1896 – September 24, 1996: the Matthew J. and Arlyn Bruccoli Collection, the Thomas Cooper Library. Columbia: South Carolina UP for Thomas Cooper Library, 1996. pp. 110, (plates) 16.

446. AYRES, PHILIP. Burlington's library at Chiswick. SB (45) 1992, 113–27.

447. BAKY, JOHN S. Literary resources of the Vietnam War. WLA (5:1) 1993, 15–24.

448. BARROWMAN, RACHEL. The Turnbull: a library and its world. (Bibl. 1995, 313.) Rev. by John Roberts in New Zealand Books (6:1) 1996, 13; by Chris Hilliard in NZJH (30:1) 1996, 92–3; by S. R. Strachan in NZLib (48:7) 1996, 130–2.

449. BASBANES, NICHOLAS A. A gentle madness: bibliophiles, biblio-manes, and the eternal passion for books. (Bibl. 1995, 314.) Rev. by Michael Dirda in BkW, 30 July 1995, 2.

450. —— 'Whoever to steal this volume tries, out with his eyes, out with his eyes.' Biblio (1:1) 1996, 24–8.

451. BAYLESS, MARTHA. Getting in to book collections: mission impossible? Biblio (1:3) 1996, 16–20.

452. —— Medieval manuscript pages: wall trophies or historical treasures? See **337**.

453. BELL, ALLAN. Munificent, wise and thoughtful gifts: Grace and Peter Redpath and the Redpath Tracts. Fontanus (6) 1993, 45–67.

454. BERGER, SIDNEY E. Else fine, and other features of the dealer's catalog. Biblio (1:2) 1996, 42–6; (1:3) 1996, 42–6.

455. BEYER, PRESTON (comp.). Essays on collecting John Steinbeck books. Bradenton, FL: Opuscula, 1989. pp. 38. Rev. by Donald L. Siefker in SteiQ (23:3/4) 1990, 113–14.

456. Billington, James H.   Libraries, the Library of Congress, and the information age. Daedalus (125:4) 1996, 35–54.

457. Birney, Alice L.   Missing Whitman notebooks returned to the Library of Congress. WWQR (12:4) 1995, 217–29.

458. Black, Barbara J.   Fugitive articulation of an all-obliterated tongue: Fitzgerald's *Rubáiyát* and the politics of collecting. In-between (5:2) 1996, 161–86.

459. Blair, Stanley S.   The Gay Wilson Allen papers. WWQR (12:2) 1994, 106–8.

460. Boness, Neil.   Manuscripts in the Antipodes: the origins of the Sydney collections. *See* **341**.

461. Carrigan, Dennis P.   Commercial journal publishers and university libraries: retrospect and prospect. JSchP (27:4) 1996, 208–21.

462. Chamberlain, Kathleen.   The search for Stratemeyer: twenty minutes in the archives. DNR (65:4) 1996, 125–9.

463. Chevrefils, Marlys (comp.); Tener, Jean F.; Steele, Apollonia (eds).   The Clark Blaise papers: first and second accession: an inventory of the archive at the University of Calgary libraries. (Bibl. 1992, 414.) Rev. by Denyse Lynde in ESCan (22:4) 1996, 479–81.

464. Clapinson, Mary.   W. D. Macray (1826–1916) historian of the Bodleian. BLR (15:4) 1996, 300–7.

465. Clarke, Stephen; Gretton, John.   R. W. Ketton-Cremer: an annotated bibliography. Dereham, Norfolk: Dereham Books, 1995. pp. xii, 206. Rev. by David McKitterick in BC (45:2) 1996, 276–7.

466. Cohen, Marilyn; Reid-Walsh, Jacqueline.   Early children's books in the McGill University libraries. Fontanus (4) 1991, 175–9.

467. Cohen, Martin.   The Redpath family and the McGill libraries' collections. Fontanus (6) 1993, 143–7.

468. Coustillas, Pierre.   Thirty letters about Gissing to be rescued from oblivion. GissJ (32:4) 1996, 23–4.

469. Cox, H. Bartholomew.   Replevin: part one, What the king threw out. Biblio (1:2) 1996, 32–6.

470. de la Bédoyère, G.   John Evelyn's library catalogue. BC (43:4) 1994, 529–48.

471. DeWitt, Donald L.   Guides to archives and manuscript collections in the United States: an annotated bibliography. Westport, CT; London: Greenwood Press, 1994. pp. xi, 478. (Bibliographies and indexes in library and information science, 8.) Rev. by Marcia Pankake in AEB (9:1/2) 1995, 55–8.

472. Diefendorf, Elizabeth.   The New York Public Library's books of the century. New York; Oxford: OUP, 1996. pp. 229.

473. Dumville, David N.   Anglo-Saxon books: treasure in Norman hands? Anglo-Norman Studies (16) 1993, 83–99.

474. Duncan-Jones, K.   Notable accessions: Western manuscripts. *See* **349**.

475. Feather, John.   Robert Triphook and Francis Douce: a bookseller and one of his customers. BLR (15:5/6) 1996, 468–79.

476. Feeney, Joseph J.   The Bischoff collection at Gonzaga University: a preliminary account. HopQ (23:3/4) 1996, 71–92.

477. Fowler, Rowena.   Browning's music: the L. L. Bloomfield collection. RES (47:185) 1996, 35–46.

478. Franklin, Colin.   Book collecting as one of the fine arts, and other essays. *See* **273**.

479.   GARSIDE, P. D.   An annotated checklist of Hogg's literary manuscripts in the Alexander Turnbull Library, Wellington, New Zealand.
See **358**.

480.   GNEUSS, HELMUT.   Books and libraries in early England. *See* **359**.

481.   GOEDEKEN, EDWARD A.   The literature of American library history, 1993–1994. Libraries & Culture (31:3/4) 1996, 603–44.

482.   GOLDMAN, PAUL.   The Dalziel brothers and the British Museum.
See **202**.

483.   GRAFFAGNINO, J. KEVIN (comp.).   Only in books: writers, readers
& bibliophiles on their passion. Madison, WI: Madison House, 1996.
pp. xix, 266.

484.   GRIZZARD, FRANK E., JR   Why I have 500 copies of the same
book. Biblio (1:3) 1996, 22–3.

485.   HALAC, DENNIS.   Catheriana at the Bancroft. WCPMN (36:2)
1992, 10–12.

486.   HALKYARD, STELLA K.; McCULLY, C. B.   'Thoughts of inventive
brains and the rich effusions of deep hearts': some of the twentieth-
century literary archives of the John Rylands University Library of
Manchester. BJRL (77:2) 1995, 105–21.

487.   HALL, PETER DOBKIN.   'To make us bold and learn to read – to
be friends to each other, and friends to the world': libraries and the
origins of civil society in the United States. Libraries & Culture (31:1)
1996, 14–35.

488.   HAMMERMAN, HARLEY J.   On collecting O'Neill. EOR (15:1)
1991, 93–6.

489.   HASKELL, MARY B.   Brother, can you spare a dime? The
Rockefeller family and libraries. Libraries & Culture (31:1) 1996, 130–43.

490.   HATCHWELL, RICHARD.   A Francis Davison/William Drummond
conundrum. BLR (15:5/6) 1996, 364–7.

491.   HILLYARD, BRIAN.   Acquisitions of incunables by the Advocates'
Library before 1808. Edinburgh Bibliographical Society Transactions
(6:3) 1995, 92–114.

492.   HUBER, WERNER.   Irish novels in a German court library of the
early 19th century. *In* (pp. 37–44) **49**.

493.   JOHNSON, DEIDRE A.   The search for Stratemeyer: Stratemeyer
Syndicate archives box 7856; or, What the NYPL archives revealed.
DNR (65:4) 1996, 130–9.

494.   JOSEY, E. J.   The Black librarian in America revisited. Metuchen,
NJ; London: Scarecrow Press, 1994. pp. viii, 382. Rev. by John Mark
Tucker in Libraries & Culture (31:3/4) 1996, 645–55.

495.   KIESSLING, NICOLAS K.   The library of Robert Burton: new
discoveries. BC (45:2) 1996, 171–9.

496.   —— The location of two lost volumes of ballads, Wood 399 and
Wood 400. BLR (15:4) 1996, 260–91.

497.   KNOLES, THOMAS.   Notes on research collections: post-1876
manuscript materials for the study of the history of the book at AAS.
See **380**.

498.   LANDON, RICHARD.   Provenance: inscribing significance. Biblio
(1:1) 1996, 48–51.

499.   LEPA, JACK.   Book collecting 101: To buy or not to buy.
Biblio (1:1) 1996, 66–9.

500.   —— Historical mysteries: matters of fact *and* fiction. Biblio (1:3)
1996, 12–15.

501. —— Mysteries – hard boiled. Biblio (1:2) 1996, 16–19.

502. LINDOP, GREVEL.   De Quincey and the Portico Library. BJRL (76:1) 1994, 179–86.

503. LOCKE, IAN.   Old newspapers: the how and why of collecting. Biblio (1:3) 1996, 24–9.

504. McCORMACK, W.J.   Bibliophile's diary: number eight. *See* **146**.

505. McCOWN, ROBERT A.   Iowa authors on Iowa: a sesquicentennial reading list. BkIA (65) 1996, 26–7.

506. McWHORTER, GEORGE T.   Each one as before will chase his favorite phantom. Biblio (1:2) 1996, 20–5.

507. MARCUSON, AGNES BONDURANT.   Board member acquires Poe manuscript. PoeM (24) 1994, 3–5.

508. MATTHEWS, JACK.   Books and beetles. AR (49:3) 1991, 325–35.

509. MAY, JAMES E.   Scribleriana transferred: 1993–1994. Scriblerian (28:1/2) 1995/96, 108–20.

510. MEDLIN, DOROTHY.   André Morellet's library. Libraries & Culture (31:3/4) 1996, 574–602.

511. MEYER, RICHARD W.   The library in scholarly communication. SSQ (77:1) 1996, 210–17.

512. MICHEL, ROBERT.   The Austin 'Dink' Carroll papers in the University Archives. Fontanus (6) 1993, 149–56. (McGill Univ.)

513. MITCHELL, TED.   'Two tons of manuscript': Thomas Wolfe archives. NCLR (2:2) 1995, 214–15.

514. MOORE, EARL.   Auction trends. MSS (47:4) 1995, 308–23.

515. MOORE, GENE M.   Conrad items in the Dent archive in North Carolina. NQ (43:4) 1996, 438–9.

516. —— A 'lost' Conrad letter rediscovered. NQ (43:4) 1996, 437–8.

517. MORRISON, STUART.   Records of a bibliophile: the catalogues of Consul Joseph Smith and some aspects of his collecting. BC (43:1) 1994, 27–58.

518. MORTIMER, ROGER.   The Matthew J. and Arlyn Bruccoli collection of F. Scott Fitzgerald. MSS (48:3) 1996, 185–93.

519. NORTON, DAVID FATE; NORTON, MARY J.   The David Hume library. Edinburgh: Edinburgh Bibliographical Soc.; National Library of Scotland, 1996. pp. 156. (Edinburgh Bibliographical Soc. occasional pubs.)

520. O'NEILL, ROBERT K.   Preserving Ireland's cultural heritage: the Burns Library special Irish collection. Biblio (1:1) 1996, 16–21.

521. PARMER, JEROME F.   Netting books on-line: book collecting enters the twenty-first century. Biblio (1:2) 1996, 12–14.

522. PATRICK, KEVIN.   Words made new: book production and collecting in the computer age. *See* **304**.

523. PEATTIE, ROGER.   Four letters about Whitman in the Angeli-Dennis papers. WWQR (12:4) 1995, 246–52.

524. PENZLER, OTTO.   Collecting mystery fiction: Ian Fleming's James Bond. AD (29:1) 1996, 44–51.

525. —— Collecting mystery fiction: Rex Stout: part 1. AD (29:3) 1996, 302–6; (29:4) 1996, 418–24, 428–9.

526. PITTAS-GIROUX, JUSTIN A.   Auld acquaintance not forgot: Thomas Cooper Library's Burns collection. Biblio (1:2) 1996, 28–31.

527. POTTLE, MARION S.; ABBOTT, CLAUDE COLLEER; POTTLE, FREDERICK A.   Catalogue of the papers of James Boswell at Yale University: for the greater part formerly the collection of Lieut.-Colonel

Ralph Heyward Isham. (Bibl. 1994, 298.) Rev. by David Yerkes in Text (Ann Arbor) (9) 1996, 474–6.

528. PREST, WILFRID R.	Law, learning and religion: gifts to Gray's Inn Library in the 1630s. Parergon (14:1) 1996, 205–22.

529. RAUCHBAUER, OTTO.	The Edith Œnone Somerville Archive in Drishane: a catalogue and an evaluative essay. (Bibl. 1995, 371.) Rev. by John Cronin in Irish Review (17/18) 1995, 182–5; by Maurice Harmon in NQ (43:2) 1996, 237–8; by Brian Donnelly in IUR (26:2) 1996, 385.

530. RAVEN, JAMES.	The representation of philanthropy and reading in the eighteenth-century library. Libraries & Culture (31:2) 1996, 492–510.

531. REICHARDT, PAUL F.	A seventeenth-century acknowledgement of *Sir Gawain and the Green Knight* in an early catalogue of the Cottonian library. SB (49) 1996, 129–33.

532. RHODES, DENNIS E. (ed.).	Bookbindings and other bibliophily: essays in honour of Anthony Hobson. Foreword by Frederick B. Adams. *See* **171**.

533. ROBERTS, RALPH.	Warning: paper enemies at large. Biblio (1:1) 1996, 52–6.

534. RUDE, DONALD W.; CARROLL, CHARLES T.	Unreported Conrad manuscripts and proofs. Conradiana (28:2) 1996, 96–100.

535. RUMBLE, ALEXANDER R.	The Rylands, the Bible and early English literature: an illustrated note. *See* **414**.

536. SALVADOR, MERCEDES; MORA, MARÍA JOSÉ; PORTILLO, RAFAEL. Fondos de interés para los estudios ingleses en la Biblioteca del Arzobispado de Sevilla. Atlantis (17:1/2) 1995, 323–32.

537. SHADDY, ROBERT ALAN.	A world of sentimental attachments: the cult of collecting, 1890–1930. BC (43:2) 1994, 185–200.

538. SHARPE, R., *et al.* (eds).	English Benedictine libraries: the shorter catalogues. London: British Library in assn with British Academy, 1996. pp. xxx, 931, (plates) 16. (Corpus of British medieval library catalogues, 4.)

539. SIBLEY, JOAN M.	The John Fowles papers at the Harry Ransom Humanities Research Center, the University of Texas at Austin. TCL (42:1) 1996, 187–91.

540. SINNETTE, ELINOR DES VERNEY; COATES, W. PAUL; BATTLE, THOMAS C. (eds).	Black bibliophiles and collectors: preservers of Black history. Washington, DC: Howard UP, 1990. pp. xix, 236. Rev. by John Mark Tucker in Libraries & Culture (31:3/4) 1996, 645–55.

541. SMITH, KATHERINE M.	Accessions. PoeM (26) 1996, 37–40.

542. —— New accessions of the Poe Foundation, Inc. PoeM (21) 1991, 22–4; (22) 1992, 25–8; (23) 1993, 25–6; (24) 1994, 27–30; (25) 1995, 27–31.

543. STEINGRAPH, SETH.	Book price guides and references: a review. Biblio (1:3) 1996, 30–7.

544. TAYLOR, MICHAEL; BRADTKE, ELAINE.	Resources in the Vaughan Williams Memorial Library. FMJ (7:2) 1996, 205–15.

545. THOMAS, GRAHAM C. G.; HUWS, DANIEL (comps).	Summary catalogue of the manuscripts of South Glamorgan Libraries, Cardiff Central Library, commonly referred to as the 'Cardiff MSS'. *See* **428**.

546. TUCKER, JOHN MARK.	Let the circle be unbroken: the struggle for continuity in African-American library scholarship 1970–1995. Libraries & Culture (31:3/4) 1996, 645–55 (review-article).

547. TURNER, MICHAEL L.	Who was Walter Harding? Some

preliminary notes on his English antecedents: part one. BLR (15:5/6) 1996, 422–54.

548. VALAUSKAS, EDWARD J.   Copyright and the re-invention of libraries. Libri (46:4) 1996, 196–200.

549. WALTERS, GWYN.   The library of Thomas Burgess (1756–1837). BC (43:3) 1994, 351–75.

550. WATSON, PAULA D.   Carnegie ladies, lady Carnegies: women and the building of libraries. Libraries & Culture (31:1) 1996, 159–96.

551. WEST, ANTHONY JAMES.   In search of missing copies of the Shakespeare first folio. BC (43:3) 1994, 396–407.

552. ——— The number and distribution of Shakespeare first folios 1902 and 1995. AEB (9:1/2) 1995, 1–23.

553. WHITEMAN, BRUCE.   Leacock remains at McGill: some notes on the Stephen Leacock collection. Fontanus (7) 1994, 11–14.

554. ——— Recent additions to the David Hume collection. Fontanus (4) 1991, 181–3. (McGill Dept of Rare Books.)

555. WILSON, ROBERT A.   Marching to a different drummer: collecting 'Beat' poets. Biblio (1:1) 1996, 30–4.

556. WOUDHUYSEN, H. R.   Forster in Park Lane. TLS, 21 June 1996, 29.

TEXTUAL STUDIES

For textual studies of Shakespeare, see under 'William Shakespeare: Editions and Textual Criticism'.

557. ABRAMS, RICHARD.   W[illiam] S[hakespeare]'s *Funeral Elegy* and the turn from the theatrical. SELit (36:2) 1996, 435–60.

558. ADAMS, ROBERT.   Editing *Piers Plowman B*: the imperative of an intermittently critical edition. SB (45) 1992, 31–68.

559. ALEXANDER, CHRISTINE.   Milestones in Brontë textual scholarship. Text (Ann Arbor) (9) 1996, 353–68 (review-article).

560. ANDERSON, KATHRYN MURPHY.   Editing and contextualizing early modern women in England. ColLit (23:1) 1996, 217–25 (review-article).

561. ARN, MARY-JO.   On punctuating medieval literary texts. Text (Ann Arbor) (7) 1994, 161–74.

562. ——— (ed.).   *Fortunes Stabilnes*: Charles of Orleans's English book of love: a critical edition. Binghamton, NY: Medieval & Renaissance Texts & Studies, 1994. pp. xiii, 624. (Medieval & Renaissance texts & studies, 138.) Rev. by Julia Boffey in MÆ (65:2) 1996, 319–20.

563. ATKINS, A. R.   A bibliographical analysis of the manuscript of D. H. Lawrence's *The White Peacock. See* **334**.

564. AYLING, RONALD.   Sean O'Casey's editions: a note on their publishing history. Notes on Modern Irish Literature (4) 1992, 5–10.

565. BAER, JOEL H.   Bold Captain Avery in the Privy Council: early variants of a broadside ballad from the Pepys Collection. FMJ (7:1) 1995, 4–26.

566. BAJETTA, CARLO M.   Unrecorded extracts by Sir Walter Ralegh. NQ (43:2) 1996, 138–40.

567. BAMMESBERGER, ALFRED.   The emendation of *Beowulf*, l. 586. NM (97:4) 1996, 379–82.

568. —— A textual note on *Beowulf* 431–432. EngS (76:4) 1995, 297–301.

569. BARON, HELEN V.   The surviving galley proofs of Lawrence's *Sons and Lovers*. SB (45) 1992, 231–51.

570. BATTESTIN, MARTIN C.   Fredson Thayer Bowers: a checklist and chronology. *See* **135**.

571. BAWCUTT, N. W.   New Jonson documents. RES (47:185) 1996, 50–2.

572. BENZEL, MICHAEL.   Textual variants in *A Note on Jane Austen/ Jane Austen*. EWeltyN (20:2) 1996, 2–7.

573. BEVINGTON, DAVID; RASMUSSEN, ERIC (eds).   Doctor Faustus A- and B-texts (1604, 1616). (Bibl. 1993, 319.) Rev. by Constance Brown Kuriyama in MedRen (8) 1996, 241–8.

574. BISENIEKS, DAINIS.   How not to edit Mervyn Peake. PeakeS (4:4) 1996, 31–8.

575. BITTERLING, KLAUS.   A note on the Scottish *Buik of Alexander*. SLJ (23:2) 1996, 89–90.

576. BLACKMORE, TIM.   Talking with *Strangers*: interrogating the many texts that became Heinlein's *Stranger in a Strange Land*. Extrapolation (36:2) 1995, 136–50.

577. BLANCHFIELD, LYNNE S.   Rate revisited: the compilation of the narrative works in MS Ashmole 61. *In* (pp. 208–20) **104**.

578. BOLES, JOHN B.   Why editing matters. SSQ (77:1) 1996, 198–203.

579. BORCK, JIM SPRINGER.   Composed in tears: the *Clarissa* project. StudN (27:3) 1995, 341–50.

580. BORNSTEIN, GEORGE.   The end(s) of Modernist editing. Review (17) 1995, 185–202 (review-article).

581. BOULTON, JAMES T.   Editing D. H. Lawrence's letters: the editor's creative role. Prose Studies (19:2) 1996, 211–20.

582. BOWDEN, ANN; TODD, WILLIAM B.   Scott's commentary on *The Journal of a Tour to the Hebrides with Samuel Johnson*. SB (48) 1995, 229–48.

583. BRACK, O. M., JR.   Samuel Johnson and the Preface to Abbé Prévost's *Memoirs of a Man of Quality*. SB (47) 1994, 155–64.

584. —— Smollett's *Peregrine Pickle* revisited. StudN (27:3) 1995, 260–72.

585. BRAEKMAN, MARTINA.   *How a Lover Praiseth His Lady* (Bodl. MS Fairfax 16): a Middle English courtly poem re-appraised. *See* **342**.

586. BREWER, CHARLOTTE.   Editing *Piers Plowman*. MÆ (65:2) 1996, 286–93 (review-article).

587. —— Editing *Piers Plowman*: the evolution of the text. Cambridge; New York: CUP, 1996. pp. xv, 459. (Cambridge studies in medieval literature, 28.)

588. BRIGGS, AUSTIN.   The full stop at the end of 'Ithaca': thirteen ways – and then some – of looking at a black dot. JSA (7) 1996, 125–44.

589. BRIGGS, JULIA.   Editing Woolf for the nineties. SoCR (29:1) 1996, 67–77.

590. BROOKE, SEBASTIAN.   Three early Tudor verse texts. NQ (43:4) 1996, 404–17. (Texts on Robert Barnes.)

591. BROOKS, ROGER L.   Matthew Arnold's *Then Comes the Whistling Clown*. BC (43:4) 1994, 549–52.

592. BROUDE, RONALD.   Establishing texts in quasi-improvisatory traditions. Text (Ann Arbor) (7) 1994, 127–44.

593. BRYANT, JOHN.   Politics, imagination, and the fluid text. SLI (29:2) 1996, 89–107.

594. BUSH, RONALD. Changing his mind about how to do a girl in: poetry, narrative, and gender in the revisions of Henry James's *Daisy Miller*. Letterature d'America (55) 1994, 33–52.

595. —— 'Unstill, ever turning': the composition of Ezra Pound's *Drafts & Fragments*. Text (Ann Arbor) (7) 1994, 397–422.

596. BUTLER, MARILYN. Editing women. StudN (27:3) 1995, 273–83.

597. CAMPBELL, IAN. *Peter Lithgow*: new fiction by Thomas Carlyle. SSL (29) 1996, 1–13.

598. CARNEY, MARY. Dickinson's poetic revelations: variants as process. EDJ (5:2) 1996, 134–8.

599. CAUCHI, SIMON. Harington's *Orlando Furioso*: a 'spare leafe' and a stop-press correction. SB (45) 1992, 68–70.

600. CHENGGES, CATHERINE H. Substantive variants in *The Bride of the Innisfallen*. EWeltyN (19:1) 1995, 1–12.

601. CHERNAIK, WARREN; DAVIS, CAROLINE; DEEGAN, MARILYN (eds). The politics of the electronic text. Oxford: Office for Humanities Communication, Oxford Univ.; London: Centre for English Studies, Univ. of London, 1993. pp. vi, 98. (Office for Humanities Communication pubs, 3.) Rev. by Arthur P. Young in AEB (8:3/4) 1994, 212–15.

602. CHRIST, CAROL T. (ed.). The mill on the Floss. (Bibl. 1994, 342.) Rev. by Delia da Sousa Correa in NQ (43:1) 1996, 108–9.

603. COETZEE, PAULETTE; MACKENZIE, CRAIG. Bessie Head: re-discovered early poems. EngA (23:1) 1996, 29–46.

604. COHEN, PHILIP. Is there a text in this discipline? Textual scholarship and American literary studies. AmLH (8:4) 1996, 728–44 (review-article).

605. —— The making and marketing of Huck Finn. Text (Ann Arbor) (8) 1995, 349–75 (review-article).

606. COLANZI, RITA M. Tennessee Williams's revision of *Suddenly Last Summer*. JML (16:4) 1990, 651–2.

607. COLVERT, JAMES B. Fred Holland Day, Louise Imogen Guiney, and the text of Stephen Crane's *The Black Riders*. ALR (28:2) 1996, 18–24.

608. COOK, DON L. The Thoreau edition: an evolving institution. Text (Ann Arbor) (8) 1995, 325–48 (review-article).

609. CRAIK, T. W. 'Politic French', 'politic frenzy', or 'politic study'? A crux in Ford's *The Broken Heart*. NQ (43:2) 1996, 191–2.

610. DANE, JOSEPH A. Bibliographical history *versus* bibliographical evidence: the Plowman's Tale and early Chaucer editions. BJRL (78:1) 1996, 47–61.

611. —— Copy-text and its variants in some recent Chaucer editions. SB (44) 1991, 164–83.

612. —— The lure of oral theory in medieval criticism: from edited 'text' to critical 'work'. Text (Ann Arbor) (7) 1994, 145–60.

613. DAVIES, DAMIAN WALFORD. Wordsworth's 'lamphole' or 'loophole'? A glimmering from *The Prelude*. NQ (43:4) 1996, 424–5.

614. DAVIS, TOM. The epic of bibliography: Alexander Pope and textual criticism. Text (Ann Arbor) (9) 1996, 342–52 (review-article).

615. DE SAILLY, ROSALIND. Problems of life and mind: the George Eliot of the manuscripts. Parergon (13:2) 1996, 137–49.

616. DE TIENNE, ANDRÉ. Selecting alterations for the apparatus of a critical edition. Text (Ann Arbor) (9) 1996, 33–62.

617. DI CESARE, MARIO A. (ed.). George Herbert, *The Temple*:

a diplomatic edition of the Bodleian Manuscript (Tanner 307). Binghamton, NY: Medieval & Renaissance Texts & Studies, 1995. pp. lxxx, 313, 107. (Medieval & Renaissance texts & studies, 54.) (Renaissance English Text Soc., seventh series, 17.) Rev. by Ted-Larry Pebworth in GHJ (19:1/2) 1995/96, 112–15; by H. R. Woudhuysen in TLS, 5 Apr. 1996, 36.

618. DIEKSTRA, F. N. M. *A Good Remedie aȝens Spirituel Temptacions*: a conflated Middle English version of William Flete's *De remediis contra temptationes* and pseudo-Hugh of St Victor's *De pusillanimitate* in London BL MS Royal 18.A.x. EngS (76:4) 1995, 307–54.

619. DIX, ROBIN; DARBY, TRUDI LAURA. The bibliographical significance of the turned letter. *See* **268**.

620. DOBRANSKI, STEPHEN B. Samson and the *omissa*. SELit (36:1) 1996, 149–69.

621. DOCK, JULIE BATES. 'But one expects that': Charlotte Perkins Gilman's *The Yellow Wallpaper* and the shifting light of scholarship. PMLA (111:1) 1996, 52–65.

622. DONALDSON, SANDRA. Notes & queries. NMAS (9) 1992, 16–17. (On errors in the Fawcett Crest ed. of *Surfacing*.)

623. DONOHUE, JOSEPH; BERGGREN, RUTH (eds). Oscar Wilde's *The Importance of Being Earnest*: a reconstructive critical edition of the text of the first production, St James's Theatre, London, 1895. (Bibl. 1995, 440.) Rev. by Karl Beckson in ELT (39:3) 1996, 375–8; by Norman White in NQ (43:4) 1996, 489–90.

624. DOYLE, A. I. '*Lectulus noster floridus*': an allegory of the penitent soul. *In* (pp. 179–90) **61**.

625. DOYNO, VICTOR A. Writing *Huck Finn*: Mark Twain's creative process. (Bibl. 1993, 342.) Rev. by Philip Cohen in Text (Ann Arbor) (8) 1995, 363–73.

626. DUNCAN, THOMAS G. The maid in the moor and the Rawlinson text. RES (47:186) 1996, 151–62.

627. DUNCAN-JONES, KATHERINE. 'Preserved dainties': late Elizabethan poems by Sir Robert Cecil and the Earl of Clanricarde. BLR (14:2) 1992, 136–44.

628. EDWARDS, A. S. G. The transmission and audience of Osbern Bokenham's *Legendys of Hooly Wummen*. *In* (pp. 157–67) **56**.

629. EDWARDS, GAVIN. William Hazlitt and the case of the initial letter. *See* **272**.

630. EGGERT, PAUL. Document and text: the 'life' of the literary work and the capacities of editing. Text (Ann Arbor) (7) 1994, 1–24.

631. —— Document or process as the site of authority: establishing chronology of revision in competing typescripts of Lawrence's *The Boy in the Bush*. SB (44) 1991, 364–76.

632. —— Editing paintings/conserving literature: the nature of the 'work'. SB (47) 1994, 65–78.

633. EMBREE, DAN; URQUHART, ELIZABETH (eds). *The Simonie*: a parallel text edition. Ed. from MSS Advocates 19.2.1, Bodley 48, and Peterhouse College [*sic*] 104. Heidelberg: Winter, 1991. pp. 178. (Middle English texts, 24.) Rev. by Tim William Machan in Text (Ann Arbor) (8) 1995, 401–4.

634. FABI, M. GIULIA. The 'unguarded expressions of the feelings of the Negroes': gender, slave resistance, and William Wells Brown's revisions of *Clotel*. AAR (27:4) 1993, 639–54.

635. FARNSWORTH, JANE.   Voicing female desire in *Poem XLIX*. SELit (36:1) 1996, 57–72. (Poem in Maitland Quarto MS.)

636. FAUSBØLL, ELSE.   More Ælfric fragments. *See* **354**.

637. FEENEY, JOSEPH J.   Four newfound Hopkins letters: an annotated edition, with a fragment of another letter. HopQ (23:1/2) 1996, 3–40.

638. FELLOWS, JENNIFER.   *Bevis redivivus*: the printed editions of *Sir Bevis of Hampton*. *In* (pp. 251–68) **104**.

639. FERRER, DANIEL.   Joyce's notebooks: publicizing the private sphere of writing. *In* (pp. 202–22) **69**.

640. FIELD, P. J. C.   The empire of Lucius Iberius. SB (49) 1996, 106–28. (Alliterative *Morte Arthure* and Malory.)

641. FINKELSTEIN, DAVID.   Breaking the thread: the authorial re-invention of John Hanning Speke in his *Journal of the Discovery of the Source of the Nile*. Text (Ann Arbor) (9) 1996, 280–96.

642. FINNERAN, RICHARD J.   *The Collected Letters of W. B. Yeats*: a project in disarray. Review (18) 1996, 45–58 (review-article).

643. —— 'That word known to all men' in *Ulysses*: a reconsideration. JJQ (33:4) 1996, 569–82.

644. FLANNAGAN, ROY.   Editing Milton's masque. Text (Ann Arbor) (9) 1996, 234–59.

645. FLETCHER, ALAN J.   A hive of industry or a hornets' nest? MS Sidney Sussex 74 and its scribes. *In* (pp. 131–55) **56**.

646. FLETCHER, CHRISTOPHER.   Lord Byron – unrecorded autograph poems. NQ (43:4) 1996, 425–8.

647. FRANZEN, CHRISTINE.   Late copies of Anglo-Saxon charters. *In* (pp. 42–70) **114**.

648. FRONT, DOV.   Which is the first unauthorised edition of the *Religio Medici*? BC (45:3) 1996, 334–40.

649. FROULA, CHRISTINE.   Corpse, monument, *hypocrite lecteur*: text and transference in the reception of *The Waste Land*. Text (Ann Arbor) (9) 1996, 297–314.

650. GABLER, HANS WALTER.   Optionen und Lösungen: zur kritischen und synoptischen Edition von James Joyces *Ulysses*. editio (9) 1995, 179–213.

651. GECKLE, GEORGE L.   The 1604 and 1616 versions of *Dr Faustus*: text and performance. *In* (pp. 146–61) **116**.

652. GOLDFARB, SHELDON.   Discomposure repeated once again: the textual problem in Chapter 17 of *Vanity Fair*. ThN (44) 1996, 1–4.

653. GOSLEE, NANCY MOORE (ed.).   The *Homeric Hymns* and *Prometheus* drafts notebook: Bodleian MS. Shelley adds.e.12. *See* **361**.

654. GOSSETT, SUZANNE.   Why should a woman edit a man? Text (Ann Arbor) (9) 1996, 111–18.

655. GOUIRAND, JACQUELINE.   Star-equilibrium: the evolution of the 'Mino' chapter in *Women in Love*. Études Lawrenciennes (13) 1996, 75–93.

656. GRACE, SHERRILL.   Thoughts towards the archeology of editing: *Caravan of Silence*. MalLR (29/30) 1991/92, 64–77.

657. GREEN, RICHARD FIRTH.   The *Canterbury Tales*, D117: *wrighte* or *wight*? NQ (43:3) 1996, 259–61.

658. GREETHAM, D. C.   Getting personal/going public. *See* **363**.

659. —— If that was then, is this now? StudN (27:3) 1995, 427–50. (Editing fiction.)

660. —— Parallel texts. Text (Ann Arbor) (9) 1996, 408–29 (review-article).

661. —— (Textual) criticism and deconstruction. SB (44) 1991, 1–30.

662. —— Textual forensics. PMLA (111:1) 1996, 32–51.

663. GREETHAM, DAVID. The telephone directory and Dr Seuss: scholarly editing after *Feist versus Rural Telephone*. SLI (29:2) 1996, 53–74.

664. GRIFFITH, M. S. Some difficulties in *Beowulf*, lines 874–902: Sigemund reconsidered. ASE (24) 1995, 11–41.

665. GRIGELY, JOSEPH. Textual criticism and the arts: the problem of textual space. Text (Ann Arbor) (7) 1994, 25–60.

666. GWIN, MINROSE C. *Mosquitoes*' missing bite: the four deletions. FJ (9:1/2) 1993/94, 31–41.

667. HALL, J. R. *Beowulf* 2298A: on þ(ā) *westenne*? NQ (43:3) 1996, 254–7.

668. HAMILTON, A. C. Problems in reconstructing an Elizabethan text: the example of Sir Philip Sidney's *Triumph*. ELR (26:3) 1996, 451–81.

669. HANKS, D. THOMAS, JR; KAMPHAUSEN, ARMINDA; WHEELER, JAMES. Circling back in Chaucer's *Canterbury Tales*: on punctuation, misreading, and reader response. ChauY (3) 1996, 35–53.

670. HANNA, RALPH, III. John Shirley and British Library, MS Additional 16165. *See* **366**.

671. —— Pursuing history: Middle English manuscripts and their texts. *See* **367**.

672. —— Robert the Ruyflare and his companions. *In* (pp. 81–96) **61**.

673. —— With an *O* (Yorks.) or an *I* (Salop.)? The Middle English lyrics of British Library Additional 45896. *See* **368**.

674. HARDMAN, PHILLIPA. Lydgate's *Life of Our Lady*: a text in transition. MÆ (65:2) 1996, 248–68.

675. HART, CLIVE; STEVENSON, KAY GILLILAND. John Armstrong's *The Oeconomy of Love*: a critical edition with commentary. ECL (19:3) 1995, 38–69.

676. HARTUNG, ALBERT E. The Parson's Tale and Chaucer's penance. *In* (pp. 61–80) **61**.

677. HAULE, JAMES M. Virginia Woolf's revisions of *The Voyage Out*: some new evidence. TCL (42:3) 1996, 309–21.

678. HIEATT, CONSTANCE B. The Middle English culinary recipes in MS Harley 5401: an edition and commentary. *See* **369**.

679. HIGDON, DAVID LEON; HARPER, MARK C. Auden 'abandons' a poem: problems with eclectic texts. Text (Ann Arbor) (7) 1994, 423–34.

680. HILL, W. SPEED. Scripture as text, text as Scripture: the case of Richard Hooker. Text (Ann Arbor) (9) 1996, 93–110.

681. —— Where we are and how we got here: editing after post-structuralism. SStud (24) 1996, 38–46.

682. HOLDEMAN, DAVID. Interpreting textual processes: the case of Yeats's *In the Seven Woods*. Text (Ann Arbor) (8) 1995, 249–65.

683. HOLTZ, WILLIAM. Ghost and host in the Little House books. SLI (29:2) 1996, 41–51.

684. HORNE, PHILIP. Henry James and revision: the New York edition. (Bibl. 1994, 375.) Rev. by Hans-Joachim Lang in ZAA (42:4) 1994, 403–4.

685. HULSE, LYNN. *The King's Entertainment* by the Duke of Newcastle. *See* **372**.

686. HUNT, TIM. Double the *Axe*, double the fun: is there a final version of Jeffers's *The Double Axe*? Text (Ann Arbor) (7) 1994, 435–57.

687. HUNT, TONY.   The poetic vein: phlebotomy in Middle English and Anglo-Norman verse. EngS (77:4) 1996, 311–22.

688. HUNTER, J. PAUL.   Editing for the classroom: texts in contexts. StudN (27:3) 1995, 284–94.

689. —— (ed.).   *Frankenstein*: the 1818 text, contexts, nineteenth-century responses, modern criticism. New York; London: Norton, 1996. pp. xii, 339. (Norton critical ed.).

690. HUWS, DANIEL.   MS Porkington 10 and its scribe. *In* (pp. 188–207) **104**.

691. JAMES, STEPHEN.   Revision as redress? Robert Lowell's manuscripts. EC (46:1) 1996, 28–51.

692. JANSOHN, CHRISTA.   Die D. H. Lawrence-Ausgabe der Cambridge University Press. editio (5) 1991, 199–212.

693. JARDINE, MICHAEL; POYNTING, SARAH.   Renaissance drama: excluding Shakespeare: editions and textual scholarship. YWES (75) 1994, 262–7.

694. JONES, LOUISE CONLEY.   A textual analysis of Marlowe's *Doctor Faustus* with director's book: stage action as metaphor. Lewiston, NY; Lampeter: Mellen Press, 1996. pp. 172. (Studies in Renaissance literature, 12.) (Cf. bibl. 1991, 4446.)

695. JONES, STEVEN E.   Material intertextuality: the case of Shelley's rough-draft notebooks. Text (Ann Arbor) (8) 1995, 239–47.

696. JORDAN, HEATHER BRYANT.   *Ara Vos Prec*: a rescued volume. Text (Ann Arbor) (7) 1994, 349–64.

697. JOUKOVSKY, NICHOLAS A.   Thomas Love Peacock's manuscript *Poems* of 1804. *See* **375**.

698. JOWETT, JOHN.   Jonson's authorization of type in *Sejanus* and other early quartos. *See* **287**.

699. KAPPEL, ANDREW J.   Presenting Miss Moore, Modernist: T. S. Eliot's edition of Marianne Moore's *Selected Poems*. JML (19:1) 1994, 129–50.

700. KARRER, WOLFGANG; PUSCHMANN-NALENZ, BARBARA (eds).   The African-American short story 1970 to 1990: a collection of critical essays. (Bibl. 1993, 1.) Rev. by Thomas Huke in ZAA (44:2) 1996, 188–9.

701. KAUVAR, ELAINE M.   Notes toward editing a contemporary writer's letters. StudN (27:3) 1995, 401–12.

702. KEISER, GEORGE R.   A new text of, and new light on, the *Supplement to the Index of Middle English Verse*, 4106.5. *See* **376**.

703. —— Reconstructing Robert Thornton's herbal. *See* **377**.

704. KELLY, LIONEL.   Emily Dickinson: imagining a text. EDJ (5:2) 1996, 155–61.

705. KENNEDY, BEVERLY.   Cambridge MS Dd.4.24: a misogynous scribal revision of the Wife of Bath's Prologue? *See* **378**.

706. —— The variant passages in the Wife of Bath's Prologue and the textual transmission of the *Canterbury Tales*: the 'great tradition' revisited. *In* (pp. 85–101) **129**.

707. KETTERER, DAVID.   (De)Composing *Frankenstein*: the import of altered character names in the last draft. SB (49) 1996, 232–76.

708. KIBLER, JAMES E.   Simms's first published fiction. SB (44) 1991, 376–80.

709. —— The unpublished preface to W. G. Simms's *Collected Poems*. SB (49) 1996, 291–3.

710. KIELY, DECLAN D. 'The termination of this solitaire': a textual error in *Murphy*. JBecS (6:1) 1996, 135–6.

711. KIERNAN, KEVIN S. *Beowulf* and the *Beowulf* manuscript. *See* **379**.

712. KOLB, GWIN J.; DEMARIA, ROBERT, JR. The preliminaries to Dr Johnson's *Dictionary*: authorial revisions and the establishment of the texts. SB (48) 1995, 121–33.

713. KORNEXL, LUCIA. The *Regularis concordia* and its Old English gloss. *See* **381**.

714. KRAMER, DALE. The compositor as copy-text. Text (Ann Arbor) (9) 1996, 369–88 (review-article).

715. LATHAM, DAVID. Literal and literary texts: Morris' 'Story of Dorothea'. VP (34:3) 1996, 329–39.

716. LAU, BETH. Editing Keats's marginalia. Text (Ann Arbor) (7) 1994, 337–48.

717. LAURENCE, DAN H.; PETERS, MARGOT (eds). Unpublished Shaw. Shaw (16) 1996, 1–220.

718. LAVAGNINO, JOHN. Reading, scholarship, and hypertext editions. Text (Ann Arbor) (8) 1995, 109–24.

719. LAVAZZI, TOM. Editing Schwerner: versions of Armand Schwerner's 'design-tablet'. Text (Ann Arbor) (8) 1995, 267–301.

720. LEADER, ZACHARY. Revision and Romantic authorship. Oxford: Clarendon Press; New York: OUP, 1996. pp. ix, 354. Rev. by Frank Kermode in LRB (18:11) 1996, 15–16; by Angela Leighton in TLS, 2 Aug. 1996, 5–6.

721. LERNOUT, GEERT. The real 'scandal' of *Ulysses*. EEM (2:1) 1993, 47.

722. LINDSAY, ALEXANDER. A lost ballad by Thomas Warton the Elder. Scriblerian (28:1/2) 1995/96, 1–5.

723. —— Thomson and the Countess of Hertford yet once more. RES (47:188) 1996, 539–41.

724. LINDSTRÖM, BENGT. Some textual notes on the ME *Genesis and Exodus*. EngS (77:6) 1996, 513–16.

725. LOIZEAUX, ELIZABETH BERGMANN. Yeats's spirits: *Vision* papers, Maud Gonne, and the theatre. Review (18) 1996, 217–33 (review-article).

726. LOOMIS, CATHERINE. Elizabeth Southwell's manuscript account of the death of Queen Elizabeth (with text). ELR (26:3) 1996, 482–509.

727. LOVE, HAROLD. The new 'A' text of *Signior Dildo*. SB (49) 1996, 169–75.

728. LUCAS, PETER J. The *Metrical Epilogue* to the Alfredian *Pastoral Care*: a postscript from Junius. *See* **385**.

729. MCCLELLAN, WILLIAM. A codicological analysis of the quire structure of MS HM 140 and its implications for a revised *ordinatio*. *See* **386**.

730. —— The consequences of *treuth*: reading two versions of the Clerk's Tale. *See* **387**.

731. —— The transcription of the Clerk's Tale in MS HM 140: interpreting textual effects. SB (47) 1994, 89–103.

732. MCDERMOTT, ANNE. Textual transformations: *The Memoirs of Martinus Scriblerus* in Johnson's *Dictionary*. SB (48) 1995, 133–48.

733. MCDONALD, W. U., JR. Textual variants in *Going to Naples*. EWeltyN (19:2) 1995, 1–6.

734. —— Textual variants in *No Place for You, My Love*. EWeltyN (20:1) 1996, 6–8.

735. —— Textual variants in *Spring/Ladies in Spring*. EWeltyN (20:1) 1996, 4–6.

736. McGann, Jerome. The complete writings and pictures of Dante Gabriel Rossetti: a hypermedia research archive. Text (Ann Arbor) (7) 1994, 95–105.

737. —— The rationale of hypertext. EEM (4:2) 1995, 34–40.

738. —— The rationale of hypertext. Text (Ann Arbor) (9) 1996, 11–32.

739. McGann, Jerome J. The textual condition. (Bibl. 1995, 508.) Rev. by George Bornstein in Text (Ann Arbor) (8) 1995, 387–96.

740. McGillivray, Murray. Towards a post-critical edition: theory, hypertext, and the presentation of Middle English works. Text (Ann Arbor) (7) 1994, 175–99.

741. McGovern, Eugene. Notes on a few misprints and such in Lewis's works. CSL (24:9/10) 1993, 12–13.

742. McGowan, Ian. Boswell at work: the revision and publication of the *Journal of a Tour to the Hebrides*. In (pp. 127–43) **122**.

743. Machan, Tim William. Speght's *Works* and the invention of Chaucer. Text (Ann Arbor) (8) 1995, 145–70.

744. —— Textual criticism and Middle English texts. (Bibl. 1994, 393.) Rev. by A. S. G. Edwards in MÆ (65:2) 1996, 313–14; by Bella Millett in SAC (18) 1996, 243–7; by Julia Boffey in NQ (43:1) 1996, 72–3.

745. —— Thomas Berthelette and Gower's *Confessio*. SAC (18) 1996, 143–66.

746. McKenzie, D. F. A new Congreve literary autograph. *See* **388**.

747. McMullin, B. J. Notes on cancellation in Scott's *Life of Napoleon*. SB (45) 1992, 222–31.

748. McVea, Deborah. The Eastwood dialect: an error in the Cambridge edition of D. H. Lawrence's *The White Peacock*. NQ (43:4) 1996, 443–4.

749. Marcus, Leah S. Unediting the Renaissance: Shakespeare, Marlowe, Milton. London; New York: Routledge, 1996. pp. xi, 268.

750. Marsden, Richard. The death of the messenger: the *spelboda* in the Old English *Exodus*. BJRL (77:3) 1995, 141–64.

751. Matsumoto, Hiroyuki. A note on *sothe* in l. 11 in *The Destruction of Troy*. MESN (34) 1996, 11–12.

752. May, James E. Young's corrections to Dodington's *Epistle to Bute*: evidence from the Yale manuscript. SB (46) 1993, 270–82.

753. Mays, J. C. C. Editing Coleridge in the historicized present. Text (Ann Arbor) (8) 1995, 217–37.

754. Meale, Carol M. '*Prenes: engre*': an early sixteenth-century presentation copy of *The Erle of Tolous*. In (pp. 221–36) **104**.

755. Menikoff, Barry. Toward the production of a text: time, space, and *David Balfour*. StudN (27:3) 1995, 351–62.

756. Milder, Robert. Editing Melville's afterlife. Text (Ann Arbor) (9) 1996, 389–407 (review-article).

757. Millett, Bella. *Mouvance* and the medieval author: re-editing *Ancrene Wisse*. In (pp. 9–20) **56**.

758. Minnis, A. J. (ed.). Late-medieval religious texts and their transmission: essays in honour of A. I. Doyle. *See* **56**.

759. Modlin, Charles E.; White, Ray Lewis (eds). *Winesburg, Ohio*: authoritative text, backgrounds and contexts, criticism. New York; London: Norton, 1996. pp. xi 234. (Norton critical eds.)

760. Monsman, Gerald (ed.). *Gaston de Latour*: the revised text, based on the definitive manuscripts & enlarged to incorporate all known fragments. Greensboro, NC: ELT Press, 1995. pp. xlvi, 329. Rev. by S. W. Reid in ELT (39:3) 1996, 345–8.

761. MOONEY, LINNE R.   More manuscripts written by a Chaucer scribe. *See* **393**.

762. MOSER, THOMAS C. (ed.).   *Lord Jim*: an authoritative text, backgrounds, sources, criticism. New York; London: Norton, 1996. pp. xiv, 506. (Norton critical eds.) (Second ed.: first ed. 1968.)

763. MOSSER, DANIEL W.   Reading and editing the *Canterbury Tales*: past, present, and future (?). Text (Ann Arbor) (7) 1994, 201–32.

764. MOTA, MIGUEL; TIESSEN, PAUL (eds).   The cinema of Malcolm Lowry: a scholarly edition of *Tender Is the Night*. Vancouver: British Columbia UP, 1990. pp. xiii, 262. Rev. by William Luhr in JFV (45:1) 1993, 63–6.

765. MUGGLESTONE, L. C.   Alexander Ellis and the virtues of doubt. *In* (pp. 85–98) **114**.

766. MUIR, BERNARD J. (ed.).   The Exeter anthology of Old English poetry: an edition of Exeter Dean and Chapter MS 3501. *See* **394**.

767. MUIR, KENNETH.   Three Marlowe texts. NQ (43:2) 1996, 142–4.

768. MURTAUGH, DANIEL J.   An emotional reflection: sexual realization in Henry James's revisions to *Roderick Hudson*. HJR (17:2) 1996, 182–203.

769. NEWHAUSER, RICHARD.   '*Strong it is to flitte*' – a Middle English poem on death and its pastoral context. *In* (pp. 319–36) **61**.

770. NEWHAUSER, RICHARD G.; ALFORD, JOHN A. (eds).   Literature and religion in the later Middle Ages: philological studies in honor of Siegfried Wenzel. *See* **61**.

771. NEWPORT, KENNETH G. C.   Charles Wesley's interpretation of some biblical prophecies according to a previously unpublished letter dated 25 April, 1754. BJRL (77:2) 1995, 31–52.

772. NICHOL, DONALD W.   From the Bishop of Gloucester to Lord Hailes: the correspondence of William Warburton and David Dalrymple. SB (48) 1995, 169–92.

773. NOVICK, SHELDON M.   Henry James's first published work: *Miss Maggie Mitchell in 'Fanchon the Critic'*. HJR (17:3) 1996, 300–2.

774. OBERHAUS, DOROTHY HUFF.   Emily Dickinson's fascicles: method & meaning. EDJ (5:2) 1996, 148–54.

775. OLDANI, LOUIS J.   Dreiser's *Genius* in the making: composition and revision. SB (47) 1994, 230–52.

776. ORGEL, STEPHEN.   What is an editor? SStud (24) 1996, 23–9.

777. PAGE, R. I.   An Old English fragment from Westminster Abbey. *See* **400**.

778. PAGNINI, MARCELLO.   Knowledge of the text. Textus (1:1) 1988, 5–26.

779. PARKER, HERSHEL.   The *auteur*–author paradox: how critics of the cinema and the novel talk about flawed or even 'mutilated' texts. StudN (27:3) 1995, 413–26.

780. —— The real *Live Oak, with Moss*: straight talk about Whitman's 'gay manifesto'. NineL (51:2) 1996, 145–60.

781. PARRINDER, PATRICK.   On Geert Lernout's *The Real 'Scandal' of 'Ulysses'*. EEM (2:2) 1993, 35–6.

782. PEARSALL, DEREK.   Theory and practice in Middle English editing. Text (Ann Arbor) (7) 1994, 107–26.

783. PEBWORTH, TED-LARRY.   Manuscript transmission and the selection of copy-text in Renaissance coterie poetry. Text (Ann Arbor) (7) 1994, 243–61.

784. —— Publication before the triumph of print. *See* **403**.

785. PERCY, CAROL E.   In the margins: Dr Hawkesworth's editorial emendations to the language of Captain Cook's *Voyages*. EngS (77:6) 1996, 549–78.

786. PETTIT, ALEXANDER.   A few last words, first. StudN (27:3) 1995, 251–9.

787. PEZZINI, DOMENICO.   Book IV of St Bridget's *Revelations* in an Italian (MS Laurenziano 27.10) and an English translation (MS Harley 4800) of the fifteenth century. *See* **404**.

788. —— Un trattato sulla vita contemplativa e attiva dalle *Revelationes* (VI, 65) di Santa Brigida: edizione di *An Informacion of Contemplatif Lyf and Actif* dal MS Oxford, Bodley 423. *See* **405**.

789. PHELPS, C. DEIRDRE.   The edition as art form in textual and interpretive criticism. Text (Ann Arbor) (7) 1994, 61–75.

790. —— Where's the book? The text in the development of literary sociology. Text (Ann Arbor) (9) 1996, 63–92.

791. PINTI, DANIEL J.   Governing the Cook's Tale in Bodley 686. *See* **407**.

792. PITCHER, E. W.   A 'complaint' against *The Petition* of Belinda, an African slave. EAL (31:2) 1996, 200–3.

793. PITCHER, JOHN.   Why editors should write more notes. SStud (24) 1996, 55–62.

794. PORTER, DAVID W.   Ælfric's *Colloquy* and Ælfric Bata. Neophilologus (80:4) 1996, 639–60.

795. PRIESTMAN, JUDITH.   An unpublished letter by W. H. Auden. *See* **408**.

796. PROBYN, CLIVE.   'Travelling west-ward': the lost letter from Jonathan Swift to Charles Ford. SB (44) 1991, 265–70.

797. PULSIANO, PHILLIP.   The originality of the Old English gloss of the Vespasian Psalter and its relation to the gloss of the Junius Psalter. ASE (25) 1996, 37–62.

798. QUARTERMAIN, PETER.   Undoing the book. *See* **150**.

799. QUINN, MARY A. (ed.).   Shelley's 1821–1822 Huntington notebook: a facsimile of Huntington MS HM 2111. *See* **409**.

800. RAFFERTY, MARGARET.   The Winchester Manuscript of Sir Thomas Malory's *Le Morte Darthur*: palaeographical evidence for the structure of the Arthuriad. *See* **410**.

801. RAINEY, LAWRENCE.   The letters and the spirit: Pound's correspondence and the concept of Modernism. Text (Ann Arbor) (7) 1994, 365–96.

802. RASMUSSEN, ERIC.   Rehabilitating the A-text of Marlowe's *Doctor Faustus*. SB (46) 1993, 221–38.

803. —— A textual companion to *Doctor Faustus*. (Bibl. 1993, 426.) Rev. by Hugo Keiper in SJ (132) 1996, 265–7.

804. RAY, MARTIN.   Thomas Hardy's *The Duke's Reappearance*. NQ (43:4) 1996, 435–6.

805. —— Thomas Hardy's *The Son's Veto*: a textual history. RES (47:188) 1996, 542–7.

806. REICHL, KARL.   '*No more ne willi wiked be*': religious poetry in a Franciscan manuscript (Digby 2). *In* (pp. 297–317) **61**.

807. REID, S. W.   Conrad in print and on disk. StudN (27:3) 1995, 375–86.

808. REMLEY, PAUL G.   Questions of subjectivity and ideology in the production of an electronic text of the *Canterbury Tales*. Exemplaria (8:2) 1996, 479–84.

809. REYNOLDS, MARGARET (ed.).   *Aurora Leigh*: authoritative text, backgrounds and contexts, criticism. New York; London: Norton, 1996. pp. xi, 565. (Norton critical eds)

810. RICHARDS, MARY P. (ed.).   Anglo-Saxon manuscripts: basic readings. *See* **413**.

811. RIDDELL, JAMES A.   The concluding pages of the Jonson folio of 1616. SB (47) 1994, 147–54.

812. —— The printing of the plays in the Jonson folio of 1616. *See* **306**.

813. ROBERTS, JOSEPHINE A.   Editing the women writers of early modern England. SStud (24) 1996, 63–70.

814. ROBERTSON, FIONA.   Copied-text: the new Edinburgh Waverleys. RES (47:185) 1996, 59–65 (review-article).

815. ROBINSON, PETER M. W.   Collation, textual criticism, publication, and the computer. Text (Ann Arbor) (7) 1994, 77–94.

816. ROOKSBY, RIKKY.   *Regret*: a Swinburne revision. VP (34:1) 1996, 117–20.

817. ROPER, ALAN.   How much did Farquhar's beaux spend in London? SB (45) 1992, 105–12.

818. ROSOWSKI, SUSAN J.   Willa Cather editing Willa Cather: from Houghton Mifflin to the house of Knopf. SLI (29:2) 1996, 9–25.

819. —— *et al.* Editing Cather. StudN (27:3) 1995, 387–400.

820. ROTHMAN, IRVING N.   Coleridge on the semi-colon in *Robinson Crusoe*: problems in editing Defoe. StudN (27:3) 1995, 320–40.

821. RUDE, DONALD W.; CARROLL, CHARLES T.   Unreported Conrad manuscripts and proofs. *See* **534**.

822. SANDERS, ARNOLD.   Hypertext, learning, and memory: some implications from manuscript tradition. *See* **416**.

823. SANDS, MARGARET.   Re-reading the poems: editing opportunities in variant versions. EDJ (5:2) 1996, 139–47.

824. SCHROEDER, HORST.   A printing error in *The Soul of Man under Socialism*. NQ (43:1) 1996, 49–51.

825. SCHUCHARD, RONALD.   American publishers and the transmission of T. S. Eliot's prose: a sociology of English and American editions. *In* (pp. 171–201) **69**.

826. SCOTT, P.; HANSEN, J. S.   Three newly identified James Hogg manuscript poems at the University of South Carolina. *See* **418**.

827. SCRAGG, D. G.; SZARMACH, PAUL E. (eds).   The editing of Old English: papers from the 1990 Manchester conference. (Bibl. 1994, 423.) Rev. by Fred C. Robinson in NQ (43:4) 1996, 455–7.

828. SHAWCROSS, JOHN T.   Donne's *Aire and Angels*: text and context. JDJ (9:1) 1990, 33–41.

829. —— Notes on an important volume of Donne's poetry and prose. *See* **420**.

830. SHERBO, ARTHUR.   Belated justice to Hilaire Belloc, versifier (1870–1953). SB (45) 1992, 251–64.

831. —— John Nichols's notes in the scholarly commentary of others. SB (44) 1991, 318–22.

832. SHILLINGSBURG, PETER.   Editing Thackeray: a history. StudN (27:3) 1995, 363–74.

833. SHILLINGSBURG, PETER L.   Editions half perceived, half created. SLI (29:2) 1996, 75–88.

834. —— Scholarly editing in the computer age: theory and practice. (Bibl. 1989, 503.) Ann Arbor: Michigan UP, 1996. pp. xvi, 187. (Editorial theory and literary criticism.) (Third ed.: first ed. 1986.)

835. —— Text as matter, concept, and action. SB (44) 1991, 31–82.

836. —— Textual variants, performance variants, and the concept of work. editio (7) 1993, 221–34.

837. SLATER, GRAEME.   Hume's revisions of the *History of England*. SB (45) 1992, 130–57.

838. SMALL, IAN; WALSH, MARCUS (eds).   The theory and practice of text-editing. Essays in honour of James T. Boulton. (Bibl. 1994, 427.) Rev. by D. C. Greetham in Text (Ann Arbor) (7) 1994, 461–77.

839. SMITH, JEREMY J.   A note on constrained linguistic variation in a North-West-Midlands Middle-English scribe. Neophilologus (80:3) 1996, 461–4.

840. SMITH, MARGARET.   Newly acquired Brontë letters, transcriptions and notes. *See* **421**.

841. SMITH, MARTHA NELL.   A hypermedia archive of Dickinson's creative work: part II, Musings on the screen and the book. EDJ (5:2) 1996, 18–25.

842. STANFORTH, SUSAN M.   New light on the text of MacDiarmid's *The Nature of a Bird's World*. SLJ (22:1) 1995, 92–3.

843. STILLINGER, JACK.   Coleridge and textual instability: the multiple versions of the major poems. (Bibl. 1995, 571.) Rev. by A. Banerjee in EngS (77:3) 1996, 289–90.

844. STOVER, LEON (ed.).   *The Island of Doctor Moreau*: a critical text of the 1896 London first edition, with an introduction and appendices. Jefferson, NC; London: McFarland, 1996. pp. xi, 289. (Annotated H. G. Wells, 2.) Rev. by Peter Kemp in TLS, 20 Dec. 1996, 10.

845. —— *The Time Machine: an Invention*: a critical text of the 1895 London first edition, with an introduction and appendices. Jefferson, NC; London: McFarland, 1996. pp. xi, 258. (Annotated H. G. Wells, 1.) Rev. by Peter Kemp in TLS, 20 Dec. 1996, 10.

846. STURMAN, CHRISTOPHER; PURTON, VALERIE.   'Stay near us, Emily': the influence of Emily Sellwood on the Tennyson family in the 1830s. TRB (6:5) 1996, 317–20.

847. SULLIVAN, ERNEST W., II.   1633 vndone. Text (Ann Arbor) (7) 1994, 297–306.

848. —— Updating the John Donne listings in Peter Beal's *Index of English Literary Manuscripts*, II. *See* **426**.

849. TAGUCHI, MAYUMI.   The legend of the Cross before Christ: another prose treatment in English and Anglo-Norman. PoetT (45) 1996, 15–61.

850. TAKAMIYA, TOSHIYUKI.   Chapter divisions and page breaks in Caxton's *Morte Darthur*. *See* **317**.

851. TANSELLE, G. THOMAS.   The Bowen-Merrill issue of *Trilby*. BC (43:3) 1994, 439–40.

852. —— A description of descriptive bibliography. *See* **155**.

853. —— Editing without a copy-text. SB (47) 1994, 1–22.

854. —— The life and work of Fredson Bowers . *See* **156**.

855. —— Textual criticism and literary sociology. SB (44) 1991, 83–143.
856. —— Textual instability and editorial idealism. SB (49) 1996, 1–60.
857. TAYLOR, RICHARD. Towards a textual biography of *The Cantos*. *In* (pp. 223–57) **69**.
858. —— (ed.). Variorum edition of *Three Cantos* by Ezra Pound: a prototype. (Bibl. 1992, 795.) Rev. by Christopher Carr in Text (Ann Arbor) (8) 1995, 477–88.
859. TAYLOR, SEAN. The F scribe and the R manuscript of *Piers Plowman B*. *See* **427**.
860. THOMAS, JOSEPH M. *Roughing It* in style: the 1993 Iowa–California Twain edition. Review (17) 1995, 253–65 (review-article).
861. THOMPSON, JOHN J. Another look at the religious texts in Lincoln, Cathedral Library, MS 91. *In* (pp. 169–87) **56**.
862. —— Looking behind the book: MS Cotton Caligula A.ii, part 1, and the experience of its texts. *In* (pp. 171–87) **104**.
863. THOMSON, LESLIE. A quarto 'marked for performance': evidence of what? MedRen (8) 1996, 176–210. (*The Two Merry Milke-Maids*.)
864. TODD, JANET. 'Pursue that way of fooling, and be damn'd': editing Aphra Behn. StudN (27:3) 1995, 304–19.
865. TREHARNE, E. M. A unique Old English formula for excommunication from Cambridge, Corpus Christi College 303. *See* **434**.
866. TURNER, ELIZABETH A. The Willa Cather scholarly edition: texts for all readers. WCPMN (40:2) 1996, 41–4.
867. TURNER, JAMES GRANTHAM. Elisions and erasures. MQ (30:1) 1996, 27–39.
868. VANDER MEULEN, DAVID L. Fredson Bowers and the editing of *Studies in Bibliography*. Text (Ann Arbor) (8) 1995, 31–6.
869. —— Pope's *Dunciad* of 1728: a history and facsimile. (Bibl. 1994, 440.) Rev. by Tom Davis in Text (Ann Arbor) (9) 1996, 342–52.
870. WALLNER, BJÖRN. An interpolated Middle English version of the *Anatomy* of Guy de Chauliac: part 2, Introduction, notes, glossary. Edited from Glasgow Univ. Library, Hunter MS 95. *See* **436**.
871. WEISS, ADRIAN. Shared printing, printer's copy, and the text(s) of Gascoigne's *A Hundreth Sundrie Flowres*. *See* **327**.
872. WEST, JAMES L. W., III. The scholarly editor as biographer. StudN (27:3) 1995, 295–303.
873. —— (ed.). Dreiser's *Jennie Gerhardt*: new essays on the restored text. Philadelphia: Pennsylvania UP, 1995. pp. ix, 226. Rev. by Stephen C. Brennan in DreiS (27:1) 1996, 35–43.
874. WHARTON, JANET. William Bercher's *Dyssputacion off the Nobylytye of Wymen*: text and transmission. *In* (pp. 53–69) **125**.
875. WHITTAKER, STEPHEN. A Joycean permutation. JJQ (33:3) 1996, 448–9.
876. WIDDOWSON, PETER. Editing readers: the craft of literary studies in the 1990s. Eng (45:182) 1996, 127–44.
877. WILLISON, IAN. Introduction. *In* (pp. xii–xviii) **69**.
878. —— GOULD, WARWICK; CHERNAIK, WARREN (eds). Modernist writers and the marketplace. *See* **69**.
879. WOLFSON, SUSAN J. The gatherings of *Nutting*: reading the Cornell *Lyrical Ballads*. Review (17) 1995, 13–33 (review-article).
880. —— More *Prelude* to ponder; or, Getting your words-worth. Review (16) 1994, 1–20 (review-article).

HISTORY OF PUBLISHING AND BOOKSELLING

881. ABBOTT, CRAIG S.   John Crowe Ransom's ghosts. PBSA (90:2) 1996, 217–21.

882. ALBERTINE, SUSAN (ed.).   A living of words: American women in print culture. (Bibl. 1995, 610.) Rev. by Susan Coultrap-McQuin in TSWL (15:2) 1996, 371–3.

883. ALDERSON, BRIAN.   Some notes on James Burns as a publisher of children's books. BJRL (76:3) 1994, 103–25.

884. ALEXANDER, CHRISTINE.   Milestones in Brontë textual scholarship. *See* **559**.

885. AMORY, HUGH.   Virtual readers: the subscribers to Fielding's *Miscellanies* (1743). SB (48) 1995, 94–112.

886. ANON.   Beadle & Adams. DNR (65:2) 1996, 61–3. (Our popular publishers, 5.)

887. —— Early imprints in New Zealand libraries: a finding list of books printed before 1801 held in libraries in the Wellington region. *See* **442**.

888. —— Norman L. Munro. DNR (65:1) 1996, 17–18. (Our popular publishers, 4.)

889. ARNER, ROBERT D.   Dobson's *Encyclopaedia*: the publisher, text, and publication of America's first *Britannica*, 1789–1803. (Bibl. 1993, 472.) Rev. by Ezra Greenspan in Review (16) 1994, 105–19; by J. A. Leo Lemay in Text (Ann Arbor) (8) 1995, 432–5; by Clorinda Donato in ECS (28:3) 1995, 359–61.

890. ATTON, CHRIS.   Alternative literature: a practical guide for librarians. Aldershot; Brookfield, VT: Gower, 1996. pp. xi, 202.

891. AYLING, RONALD.   Sean O'Casey's editions: a note on their publishing history. *See* **564**.

892. BARKER, NICOLAS.   Pegasus and the publisher. BC (43:4) 1994, 469–83 (review-article).

893. —— The University and the Press at Cambridge. BC (43:2) 1994, 169–84 (review-article).

894. BECHER, ANNE G.   Barlow's *Aesop* at Oxford. *See* **180**.

895. BENTLEY, G. E., JR.   The 'Edwardses of Halifax' as booksellers by catalogue 1749–1835. SB (45) 1992, 187–222.

896. BERTIE, D. M.   David Scott: a Peterhead publisher. Bibliotheck (20) 1995, 98–127.

897. BINNS, J. W.   Printing and paratext in sixteenth-century England: the Oxford and Cambridge presses. CEl (50) 1996, 1–10.

898. BIRRELL, T. A.   The making of a bookseller: the journals of John Petheram (1807–1858). BLR (15:5/6) 1996, 455–67.

899. BLACK, F. A.   Books by express canoe in the Canadian Northwest, 1750–1820. Bibliotheck (21) 1996, 12–33.

900. BLAKE, N. F.   William Caxton and English literary culture. (Bibl. 1993, 474.) Rev. by Ingrid Tieken-Boon van Ostade in EngS (76:1) 1995, 101–2; by Mark Addison Amos in ChauY (3) 1996, 157–61.

901. BLAND, MARK.   'Invisible dangers': censorship and the subversion of authority in early modern England. PBSA (90:2) 1996, 151–93.

902. BOICE, DANIEL.   The Mitchell Kennerley imprint: a descriptive bibliography. Pittsburgh, PA: Pittsburgh UP, 1996. pp. xx, 222. (Pittsburgh series in bibliography.)

903. BONN, THOMAS L. Heavy traffic & high culture: New American Library as literary gatekeeper in the paperback revolution. Carbondale: Southern Illinois UP, 1989. pp. xii, 240. Rev. by Eric J. Sandeen in AmS (34:1) 1993, 165–6.

904. BONNELL, THOMAS F. Patchwork and piracy: John Bell's 'connected system of biography' and the use of Johnson's *Prefaces*. SB (48) 1995, 193–228.

905. BROWN, B. TRAXLER. The northern Grand tour: contemporary Scottish publishing and the Continental tourist, 1760–1810. Bibliotheck (20) 1995, 55–69.

906. BUSCH, CHRISTOPHER S. A historical bibliographical survey of the Steinbeck Monograph Series (1971–91) and the Steinbeck Essay Series (1986–91). *See* **136**.

907. CAIRNS, J. W. Andrew Bell, Jonas Luntley and the London edition of Mackenzie's *Institutions*. Bibliotheck (21) 1996, 7–11.

908. CALDER, J. KENT. Ordeal and renewal: David Laurance Chambers, Hiram Haydn, and *Lie Down in Darkness*. JSchP (27:3) 1996, 171–82.

909. CANNING, PETER. American dreamers: the Wallaces and *Reader's Digest*: an insider's story. New York: Simon & Schuster, 1996. pp. 379.

910. CARACCIOLO, PETER L. The metamorphoses of Wyndham Lewis's *The Human Age*: medium, intertextuality, genre. *In* (pp. 258–86) **69**.

911. CARRIGAN, DENNIS P. Commercial journal publishers and university libraries: retrospect and prospect. *See* **461**.

912. CECIL, MIRABEL. Sebastian Walker, 1942–1991: a kind of Prospero. London; Boston, MA: Walker, 1995. pp. 185. Rev. by Lynn Barker in TLS, 19 Jan. 1996, 34.

913. CLEMENT, RICHARD W. The book in America. Golden, CO: Fulcrum, 1996. pp. x, 150.

914. COLEMAN, JOYCE. Public reading and the reading public in late medieval England and France. Cambridge; New York: CUP, 1996. pp. xiv, 250, (plates) 11. (Cambridge studies in medieval literature, 26.) (Cf. bibl. 1995, 3880.)

915. COLLIN, DOROTHY W. Interventions of the publisher's reader. EngS (77:2) 1996, 133–41.

916. COX, J. RANDOLPH. Fulminations: being further comments and annotations to the episodes in the saga of *Legend*. DNR (65:1) 1996, 19–22.

917. CUMMINS, JULIE. 'Let her sound her trumpet': NYPL children's librarians and their impact on the world of publishing. Biblion (4:1) 1995, 83–114.

918. DARDIS, TOM. Firebrand: the life of Horace Liveright. (Bibl. 1995, 628.) Rev. by Jonathan Yardley in BkW, 2 July 1995, 3.

919. DAVIS, TOM. The epic of bibliography: Alexander Pope and textual criticism. *See* **614**.

920. DE ST JORRE, JOHN. Venus bound: the erotic voyages of the Olympia Press and its writers. (Cf. bibl. 1994, 470.) New York: Random House, 1996. pp. xxii, 358, (plates) 16.

921. DIZER, JOHN T. Researching the *Boys' Own Library*: a Street and Smith experiment. DNR (65:6) 1996, 196–201.

922. DONALDSON, ROBERT. Fragments of the *Aberdeen Breviary*. *See* **138**.

923. DONELSON, KEN.   Adolescent literature and censorship, 1989–1993: a note. ArizEB (36:1) 1993, 71–2.

924. EDDY, D. D.; FLEEMAN, J. D.   A preliminary handlist of books to which Dr Samuel Johnson subscribed. SB (46) 1993, 187–220.

925. ERICKSON, LEE.   The economy of literary form: English literature and the industrialization of publishing, 1800–1850. Baltimore, MD; London: Johns Hopkins UP, 1996. pp. xii, 219. Rev. by John Sutherland in TLS, 31 May 1996, 27.

926. FEATHER, JOHN.   Robert Triphook and Francis Douce: a bookseller and one of his customers. *See* **475**.

927. FELLOWS, JENNIFER.   *Bevis redivivus*: the printed editions of *Sir Bevis of Hampton*. *In* (pp. 251–68) **104**.

928. FERREIRA, PATRICIA.   Ten years of Attic Press. Irish Literary Supplement (12:1) 1993, 14. (Interview with Ailbhe Smith.)

929. FINKELSTEIN, DAVID.   Breaking the thread: the authorial re-invention of John Hanning Speke in his *Journal of the Discovery of the Source of the Nile*. *See* **641**.

930. FOXON, DAVID.   Pope and the early eighteenth-century book trade. Ed. by James McLaverty. (Bibl. 1993, 491.) Rev. by Clive Probyn in Text (Ann Arbor) (8) 1995, 422–7.

931. FRASCA, RALPH.   'The glorious publick virtue so predominant in our rising country': Benjamin Franklin's printing network during the Revolutionary era. AmJ (13:1) 1996, 21–37.

932. FRASER, ANGUS.   A publishing house and its readers, 1841–1880: the Murrays and the Miltons. PBSA (90:1) 1996, 4–47.

933. FRIEDMAN, JEROME.   The battle of the frogs and Fairford's flies: miracles and the pulp press during the English Revolution. New York: St Martin's Press; London: UCL Press, 1993. pp. xv, 304. (Pub. in UK as *Miracles and the Pulp Press during the English Revolution: the Battle of the Frogs and Fairford's Flies*.) Rev. by Eugene R. Cunnar in RMRLL (48:2) 1994, 196–20; by Buchanan Sharp in Albion (26:3) 1994, 507–8; by William G. Bittle in AHR (100:1) 1995, 158; by Martin Ingram in EHR (111:441) 1996, 469–70; by Bernard Capp in Literature and History (5:1) 1996, 108–9.

934. FROST, PETER.   John Lane's Keynote series. BC (45:4) 1996, 485–507.

935. GORDON, DAVID M. (ed.).   Ezra Pound and James Laughlin: selected letters. (Bibl. 1995, 640.) Rev. by William Pratt in WLT (69:2) 1995, 372–3; by Ian F. A. Bell in YES (26) 1996, 328–9.

936. GÖRTSCHACHER, WOLFGANG.   (Re)writing contemporary literary history: (small) presses, little magazines, university curricula. *In* (pp. 319–31) **125**.

937. GOULD, WARWICK.   'Playing at treason with Miss Maud Gonne': Yeats and his publishers in 1900. *In* (pp. 36–80) **69**.

938. GREEN, JAMES N.   'The Cowl knows best what will suit in Virginia': Parson Weems on Southern readers. PrH (17:2) 1995, 26–34.

939. GROSS, ROBERT A.   *The Cambridge History of American Literature*. *See* **278**.

940. HALL, DAVID D.   Cultures of print: essays in the history of the book. *See* **279**.

941. HANNABUSS, S.   Provincial themes in early children's books. Bibliotheck (20) 1995, 31–54.

942. HARDWICK, JOAN.   The Yeats sisters: a biography of Susan and

Elizabeth Yeats. London: Pandora, 1996. pp. viii, 263, (plates) 16. Rev. by Sarah Rigby in LRB (18:14) 1996, 20–1; by Penelope Fitzgerald in TLS, 9 Feb. 1996, 36.

943. HOLBROOK, PAUL EVANS. Thirty-five years of the King Library Press: a dialogue with Carolyn Reading Hammer. KenR (11:3) 1992, 28–43.

944. HORAN, ELIZABETH. To market: the Dickinson copyright wars. EDJ (5:1) 1996, 88–120.

945. HORNE, PHILIP. Henry James and the economy of the short story. *In* (pp. 1–35) **69**.

946. HOWARD-HILL, T. H. The history of the book in departments of literature. *See* **142**.

947. HUTCHISON, ANN M. What the nuns read: literary evidence from the English Bridgettine house, Syon Abbey. MedStud (57) 1995, 205–22.

948. IDE, ARATA. Christopher Marlowe to shosekishou – *Tamburlaine* no shuppan wo chushin ni. (Christopher Marlowe and the stationer: on the publication of *Tamburlaine the Great*.) SEL (73:1) 1996, 1–14.

949. JARVIE, BRENDA (comp.). An Akros thirty, 1965–95: an annotated bibliography of thirty Akros publications selected to mark thirty years of Scottish publishing. Edinburgh: Akros, 1995. pp. 64.

950. JORDAN, HEATHER BRYANT. *Ara Vos Prec*: a rescued volume. *See* **696**.

951. JOYCE, DONALD FRANKLIN. Black book publishers in the United States: a historical dictionary of the presses, 1817–1990. New York; London: Greenwood Press, 1991. pp. xiv, 256. Rev. by John Mark Tucker in Libraries & Culture (31:3/4) 1996, 645–55.

952. KALAIDJIAN, WALTER. Marketing modern poetry and the Southern public sphere. *In* (pp. 297–319) **67**.

953. KEYES, CLARA. Larkspur Press: a bibliography 1975–1990. KenR (11:3) 1992, 69–90.

954. KEYMER, THOMAS. Dying by numbers: *Tristram Shandy* and serial fiction: 1. Shandean (8) 1996, 41–67.

955. KNOLES, THOMAS. Notes on research collections: post-1876 manuscript materials for the study of the history of the book at AAS. *See* **380**.

956. KORNFELD, HEIKE. Der technische Stand des Buchdrucks im 18. Jahrhundert. *See* **290**.

957. KREVANS, NITA. Print and the Tudor poets. *In* (pp. 301–13) **98**.

958. KUENZER, KATHY; DUFOUR, JEANNE. Dufour Editions: a history in bookselling. TransR (44/45) 1994, 14–15.

959. LEDBETTER, KATHRYN. 'BeGemmed and beAmuletted': Tennyson and those 'vapid' gift books. VP (34:2) 1996, 235–45.

960. LEMIRE, EUGENE D. William Morris in America: a publishing history from archives. BC (43:2) 1994, 201–28.

961. LERNOUT, GEERT. The real 'scandal' of *Ulysses*. *See* **721**.

962. LEVINE, JESSICA. Discretion and self-censorship in Wharton's fiction: *The Old Maid* and the politics of publishing. EWR (13:1) 1996, 1–13.

963. LEWIS, GIFFORD. The Yeats sisters and the Cuala. Blackrock, Co. Dublin: Irish Academic Press, 1994. pp. xiv, 199, (plates) 16. Rev. by Richard J. Finneran in ELT (39:2) 1996, 235–6.

964. LOEWENSTEIN, JOSEPH F. Legal proofs and corrected readings: press-agency and the new bibliography. *In* (pp. 93–122) **90**.

965. MCALEER, JOSEPH. Popular reading and publishing in Britain,

1914–1950. (Bibl. 1993, 507.) Rev. by D. L. LeMahieu in AHR (99:2) 1994, 568–9; by John K. Walton in EHR (111:440) 1996, 262–4.

966. McDONALD, PETER D.   Bringing the text to book: John Lane and the making of Arnold Bennett? PBSA (90:1) 1996, 49–68.

967. McGOWAN, IAN.   Boswell at work: the revision and publication of the *Journal of a Tour to the Hebrides*. *In* (pp. 127–43) **122**.

968. McGUINNE, DERMOT.   Colm O Lochlainn and the Sign of the Three Candles: the early decades. Long Room (41) 1996, 43–51.

969. MACHAN, TIM WILLIAM.   Speght's *Works* and the invention of Chaucer. *See* **743**.

970. —— Thomas Berthelette and Gower's *Confessio*. *See* **745**.

971. McKAY, B.   Books in two small market towns: the book trade in Appleby and Penrith. Bibliotheck (20) 1995, 128–43.

972. McKITTERICK, DAVID.   A history of Cambridge University Press: vol. 1, Printing and the book trade in Cambridge, 1534–1698. (Bibl. 1994, 490.) Rev. [by Nicolas Barker] in BC (43:2) 1994, 169–84.

973. McMULLIN, B. J.   Extinguishing the fire at Dod's warehouse in 1762. BC (45:4) 1996, 476–84.

974. —— Signing by the page. *See* **296**.

975. McWHIRTER, DAVID (ed.).   Henry James's New York edition: the construction of authorship. (Bibl. 1995, 662.) Rev. by Philip Horne in TLS, 10 May 1996, 28.

976. MANOGUE, RALPH A.   James Ridgway and America. EAL (31:3) 1996, 264–88.

977. MANSBRIDGE, RONALD.   The Bentham folio Bible. BC (45:1) 1996, 24–8.

978. MARCUS, LAURA.   Virginia Woolf and the Hogarth Press. *In* (pp. 124–50) **69**.

979. MATHISON, H.   'Gude black prent': how the Edinburgh book trade dealt with Burns's *Poems*. *See* **298**.

980. METZGER, BRUCE M.   Some curious Bibles. Text (Ann Arbor) (9) 1996, 1–10. (Presidential address, Soc. for Textual Scholarship, 7 Apr. 1995.)

981. MICHIE, M.   'Mr Wordy' and the Blackwoods: author and publisher in Victorian Scotland. Bibliotheck (21) 1996, 39–54. (Sir Archibald Alison.)

982. MILWARD, BURTON.   The private press tradition in Lexington, Kentucky. KenR (11:3) 1992, 5–27.

983. MOORE, RAYBURN S. (ed.).   The correspondence of Henry James and the House of Macmillan, 1877–1914: 'all the links in the chain'. (Bibl. 1994, 495.) Rev. by Adrian Poole in BC (43:3) 1994, 444–5.

984. MORGAN, EDWIN.   Recycling, mosaic, and collage. Edinburgh Review (93) 1995, 149–66. (Plagiarism and copyright.)

985. MOSS, ANN.   Printed commonplace-books and the structuring of Renaissance thought. Oxford: Clarendon Press; New York: OUP, 1996. pp. ix, 345.

986. MOSS, M.   The curious case of Duncan Stevenson, printer to Edinburgh University. *See* **300**.

987. MYERS, ROBIN; HARRIS, MICHAEL (eds).   A genius for letters: booksellers and bookselling from the 16th to the 20th century. Winchester: St Paul's Bibliographies, 1995. pp. xiv, 188. (Publishing pathways.) Rev. by David Gerard in Library Review (45:7) 1996, 74–6.

988. NEAVILL, GORDON B.   From printing history to history of the book. *See* **148**.

989. NEWCOMB, LORI HUMPHREY.   The romance of service: the simple history of *Pandosto*'s servant readers. *In* (pp. 117–39) **35**.

990. NICHOL, DONALD W.   Arthur Murphy's law: the man who won the first decisive battle in the literary property wars. TLS, 19 Apr. 1996, 15–16.

991. OVENDEN, KEITH.   A fighting withdrawal: the life of Dan Davin, writer, soldier, publisher. Oxford; New York: OUP, 1996. pp. xxii, 469, (plates) 8. Rev. by Ian Richards in NZList, 3 Aug. 1996, 46–7; by Vincent O'Sullivan in New Zealand Books (6:4) 1996, 11–12; by James McNeish in Quote Unquote (38) 1996, 30; by Ian Hamilton in TLS, 27 Dec. 1996, 24.

992. PEATTIE, ROGER W.   Frank W. Burgess: bookseller and book cover artist. *See* **234**.

993. PEBWORTH, TED-LARRY.   The early audiences of Donne's poetic performances. JDJ (15) 1996, 127–39.

994. PETERS, JULIE STONE.   Congreve, the drama, and the printed word. (Bibl. 1994, 503.) Rev. by J. Douglas Canfield in ECS (25:2) 1991/92, 227–31; by Richard B. Wolf in Text (Ann Arbor) (8) 1995, 405–9.

995. RAVEN, JAMES.   Judging new wealth: popular publishing and responses to commerce in England, 1750–1800. (Bibl. 1995, 678.) Rev. by Vera Nünning in ZAA (41:2) 1993, 178–80; by Rocco L. Capraro in AHR (99:2) 1994, 558–9.

996. REGINALD, ROBERT; BURGESS, MARY A.   BP 250: an annotated bibliography of the first 250 publications of the Borgo Press, 1975–1996. San Bernardino, CA: Borgo Press, 1996. pp. 191. (Borgo literary guides, 10.)

997. REID, S. W.   Conrad in print and on disk. *See* **807**.

998. REMER, ROSALIND.   Printers and men of capital: Philadelphia book publishers in the New Republic. Philadelphia: Pennsylvania UP, 1996. pp. xiii, 210. (Early American studies.) Rev. by Robert A. Gross in Book (39) 1996, 2–5.

999. ROSE, JONATHAN.   How historians teach the history of the book. CanRCL (23:1) 1996, 217–24.

1000. ROSOWSKI, SUSAN J.   Willa Cather editing Willa Cather: from Houghton Mifflin to the house of Knopf. *See* **818**.

1001. —— *et al.*   Editing Cather. *See* **819**.

1002. RUBIN, JOAN SHELLEY.   Between culture and consumption: the mediations of the middlebrows. *In* (pp. 163–91) **88**.

1003. SCHUCHARD, RONALD.   American publishers and the transmission of T. S. Eliot's prose: a sociology of English and American editions. *In* (pp. 171–201) **69**.

1004. SEDGWICK, ELLERY.   Horace Scudder and Sarah Orne Jewett: market forces in publishing in the 1890s. AmP (2) 1992, 79–88.

1005. SHARPE, TONY.   T. S. Eliot and ideas of *oeuvre*. *In* (pp. 151–70) **69**.

1006. SHAWCROSS, JOHN T.   'Depth' bibliography: John Milton's bibliographic presence in 1740, as example. Text (Ann Arbor) (9) 1996, 216–33.

1007. SHILLINGSBURG, PETER.   Editing Thackeray: a history. *See* **832**.

1008. SHILLINGSBURG, PETER L.   Pegasus in harness: Victorian publishing and W. M. Thackeray. (Bibl. 1995, 685.) Rev. [by Nicolas Barker] in BC (43:4) 1994, 469–83.

1009. SMITH, MARGARET.   A window on the world: Charlotte Brontë's correspondence with her publishers. An address given at the Brontë Society's Annual Meeting, Haworth, June 1996. BST (21:7) 1996, 339–56.

1010. SOLOMON, HARRY M.   The rise of Robert Dodsley: creating the new age of print. Carbondale: Southern Illinois UP, 1996. pp. ix, 339.

1011. SPADONI, CARL; DONNELLY, JUDY.   A bibliography of McLelland and Stewart imprints, 1909–1985: a publisher's legacy. Toronto: ECW Press, 1994. pp. 862. Rev. by Patricia Fleming in AEB (9:1/2) 1995, 88–90; by Mary Jane Edwards in ESCan (22:2) 1996, 249–51.

1012. STAUFFER, ANDREW M.   The first known publication of Blake's poetry in America. NQ (43:1) 1996, 41–3.

1013. SUAREZ, MICHAEL F.   Trafficking in the Muse: Dodsley's *Collection of Poems* and the question of canon. *In* (pp. 297–313) **122**.

1014. SULLIVAN, LARRY E.; SCHURMAN, LYDIA CUSHMAN (eds). Pioneers, passionate ladies, and private eyes: dime novels, series books, and paperbacks. New York: Haworth Press, 1996. pp. xiv, 306.

1015. SUTHERLAND, JOHN.   Victorian fiction: writers, publishers, readers. (Bibl. 1995, 689.) Rev. by Odin Dekkers in EngS (77:2) 1996, 205–6.

1016. TANSELLE, G. THOMAS.   The Bowen-Merrill issue of *Trilby*. *See* **851**.

1017. ——— Printing history and other history. *See* **318**.

1018. TARVER, J.   Abridged editions of Blair's *Lectures on Rhetoric and Belles Lettres* in America: what nineteenth-century college students really learned about Blair on rhetoric. Bibliotheck (21) 1996, 55–68.

1019. TAYLOR, RICHARD.   Towards a textual biography of *The Cantos*. *In* (pp. 223–57) **69**.

1020. TINKER, NATHAN P.   John Grismond: printer of the unauthorized edition of Katherine Philips's poems (1664). ELN (34:1) 1996, 30–5.

1021. TRENCH, CHALMERS.   The Three Candles Press in the thirties. Long Room (41) 1996, 35–42.

1022. TUCKER, JOHN MARK.   Let the circle be unbroken: the struggle for continuity in African-American library scholarship 1970–1995. *See* **546**.

1023. UNWIN, RAYNER.   Publishing Tolkien. Mythlore (21:2) 1996, 26–9.

1024. VON MALTZAHN, NICHOLAS.   The first reception of *Paradise Lost* (1667). RES (47:188) 1996, 479–99.

1025. WALKER, ERIC C.   The plan to publish *Peter Bell*: a new Wordsworth letter. PBSA (90:1) 1996, 69–93.

1026. WARD, DOUGLAS B.   The reader as consumer: Curtis Publishing Company and its audience, 1910–1930. Journalism History (22:2) 1996, 47–55.

1027. WARNER, MICHAEL.   The letters of the Republic: publication and the public sphere in eighteenth-century America. (Bibl. 1995, 695.) Rev. by Jennifer A. Gehrmann in SHum (18:2) 1991, 200–7.

1028. WATTS, CEDRIC.   Marketing Modernism: how Conrad prospered. *In* (pp. 81–8) **69**.

1029. WEEDON, ALEXIS.   An analysis of the cost of book production in nineteenth-century Britain. *See* **324**.

1030. WEST, JAMES L. W., III.   The Chace Act and Anglo-American literary relations. SB (45) 1992, 303–11.
1031. WEXLER, JOYCE.   Selling sex as art. *In* (pp. 91–108) **67**.
1032. WILLIS, J. H., JR.   Leonard and Virginia Woolf as publishers: the Hogarth Press, 1917–1941. (Bibl. 1995, 697.) Rev. by William M. Harrison in EngS (77:2) 1996, 200–1.
1033. WILLISON, IAN.   Introduction. *In* (pp. xii–xviii) **69**.
1034. —— GOULD, WARWICK; CHERNAIK, WARREN (eds).   Modernist writers and the marketplace. *See* **69**.
1035. WINSHIP, MICHAEL.   American literary publishing in the mid-nineteenth century: the business of Ticknor and Fields. (Bibl. 1995, 699.) Rev. by John William Pye in BC (45:4) 1996, 572–3; by Robert A. Gross in Book (39) 1996, 2–5.
1036. WORTHEN, JOHN.   D. H. Lawrence and the 'expensive edition business'. *In* (pp. 105–23) **69**.
1037. WOUDHUYSEN, H. R.   The Whittington Press. TLS, 10 May 1996, 32.
1038. ZIFF, LARZER.   Writing in the new nation: prose, print, and politics in the early United States. (Bibl. 1995, 702.) Rev. by Jennifer A. Gehrmann in SHum (18:2) 1991, 200–7; by Robert F. Sayre in AHR (98:2) 1993, 558.

CONTEMPORARY PUBLISHING AND BOOKSELLING

1039. ATWOOD, PETER.   Publishing drama in the information age. CanTR (81) 1994, 20–3.
1040. BADARACCO, CLAIRE HOERTZ.   Trading words: poetry, typography, and illustrated books in the modern literary economy. *See* **177**.
1041. BARKER, NICOLAS.   Boydell & Brewer and all that. BC (45:3) 1996, 301–12.
1042. BENNETT, SCOTT.   Re-engineering scholarly communication: thoughts addressed to authors. JSchP (27:4) 1996, 185–96.
1043. BERGER, SIDNEY E.   Else fine, and other features of the dealer's catalog. *See* **454**.
1044. BIRKERTS, SVEN.   The Gutenberg elegies: the fate of reading in an electronic age. (Bibl. 1995, 706.) Rev. by Jonathan Yardley in BkW, 11 Dec. 1994, 3; by David Simpson in ASch (65:1) 1996, 138–42.
1045. BORCK, JIM SPRINGER.   Composed in tears: the *Clarissa* project. *See* **579**.
1046. BOYERS, R., *et al.*   Literary creativity and the publishing industry: a round table. RSAJ (3) 1992, 73–112.
1047. BRUNI, FRANK.   The literary agent as Zelig. NYTM, 11 Aug. 1996, 26–9. (Andrew Wylie.)
1048. BUTLER, MARILYN.   Editing women. *See* **596**.
1049. COETZEE, J. M.   Giving offense: essays on censorship. Chicago; London: Chicago UP, 1996. pp. xi, 289. Rev. by Theodore Ziolkowski in WLT (70:4) 1996, 1038.
1050. D'SOUZA, FRANCES.   A world without censorship? English Today (12:4) 1996, 39–42.
1051. FLOUD, CYNTHIA; FLOUD, SARAH.   Abridgements too far. TLS, 2 Aug. 1996, 24.

1052. FULTZ, JAY.   The Bisons still flourish – in the backlist. JSchP (27:4) 1996, 230–6. (Nebraska UP Bison Book reprints.)

1053. GIRARD, STEPHANIE.   'Standing at the corner of Walk and Don't Walk': Vintage Contemporaries, *Bright Lights, Big City*, and the problems of betweenness. AL (68:1) 1996, 161–85.

1054. GREEFF, RACHELLE.   A quarter-century of prizes. Mail & Guardian (12:47) 1996, 34.

1055. HAYNES, COLIN.   Paperless publishing: the future is now. WD (74:11) 1994, 43–9.

1056. HEIM, MICHAEL HENRY.   Revitalizing the market for literary translation. TransR (48/49) 1995, 16–18.

1057. HULSE, MICHAEL.   Michael Schmidt in conversation. AntR (85/86) 1991, 33–43.

1058. HUNT, NIGEL.   The pre-text of the post-text: thoughts on play publishing by smaller Canadian presses. THC (12:2) 1991, 206–12.

1059. HUNT, RICHARD.   How book publishing *really* works. WD (74:7) 1994, 36–9.

1060. HUNTER, J. PAUL.   Editing for the classroom: texts in contexts. *See* **688**.

1061. JENSEN, MICHAEL.   Digital structure, digital design: issues in designing electronic publications. JSchP (28:1) 1996, 13–22.

1062. JOHNSTON, DILLON.   'My feet on the ground': an interview with Peter Fallon. Irish Literary Supplement (14:2) 1995, 4–5.

1063. KOZLOFF, SARAH.   Audio books in a visual culture. JAC (18:4) 1995, 83–95.

1064. LARGE, PETER J.   Publishing on the Internet. Linguist (35:3) 1996, 86–8.

1065. LAVAGNINO, JOHN.   Reading, scholarship, and hypertext editions. *See* **718**.

1066. LINCECUM, JERRY B.   Peter Fallon: contemporary Irish poet, editor and publisher. Notes on Modern Irish Literature (3) 1991, 52–8.

1067. LINDFORS, BERNTH.   Loaded vehicles: studies in African literary media. Trenton, NJ: Africa World Press, 1996. pp. viii, 216.

1068. LOSS, ARCHIE.   The censor swings: Joyce's work and the new censorship. JJQ (33:3) 1996, 369–76.

1069. MENDLESOHN, FARAH.   Audio books: a new medium for sf? Foundation (64) 1995, 90–6.

1070. MORPHET, TONY.   Ravan: child of a special time. Mail & Guardian (12:44) 1996, 38.

1071. MORRISON, ROBERT.   Revolution and Romanticism: the books of the Woodstock facsimile series. BJRL (77:1) 1995, 189–200.

1072. PEDEN, MARGARET SAYERS.   Knopf, Knopf: who's there? TransR (50) 1996, 27–30.

1073. PEEK, ROBIN P.; NEWBY, GREGORY B. (eds).   Scholarly publishing: the electronic frontier. Cambridge, MA: MIT Press, 1996. pp. xxii, 363.

1074. PERRIN, NOEL.   Glad tidings for readers. BkW, 8 Dec. 1996, 1, 16.

1075. RAINEY, LAWRENCE.   Consuming investments: Joyce's *Ulysses*. JJQ (33:4) 1996, 531–67.

1076. RICHARDSON, BRIAN.   Dealing with books: naming texts and the logic of entitlement. *See* **151**.

1077. RUBIN, LOUIS D., JR.   On the new North Carolina writers. Frank (15) 1996, 54–6.

1078. SAUNDERS, E. STEWART.   Library circulation of university press publications. JSchP (27:3) 1996, 166–70.

1079. SCHULTE, RAINER.   Plays in translation: a profile of *PAJ* Publications/*Performing Arts Journal.* TransR (51/52) 1996, 16–21.

1080. SHIPTON, ROSEMARY.   Value added: professional editors and publishers. JSchP (27:4) 1996, 222–9.

1081. SISLER, WILLIAM P.   Defining the image of the university press. JSchP (28:1) 1996, 55–9.

1082. SOLOTAROFF, TED.   The paperbacking of publishing. *See* **316**.

1083. SPEIRS, LOGAN.   The new poetry. EngS (77:2) 1996, 155–78.

1084. STEINGRAPH, SETH.   Book price guides and references: a review. *See* **543**.

1085. THATCHER, SANFORD G.   Re-engineering scholarly communication: a role for university presses? JSchP (27:4) 1996, 197–207.

1086. TRELOAR, ANDREW.   Electronic scholarly publishing and the World Wide Web. JSchP (27:3) 1996, 135–50.

1087. UNSWORTH, JOHN.   Electronic scholarship; or, Scholarly publishing and the public. JSchP (28:1) 1996, 3–12.

1088. WAKEFIELD, JOHN F.   Portrait of a censor. NIF (38) 1989, 33, 55–7.

1089. WARING, WENDY.   Publishers, fiction, and feminism: riding the 'second wave'. Reader (35/36) 1996, 94–107.

1090. ZAHAROFF, HOWARD G.   Questions and answers about copyright. WD (76:5) 1996, 24–6, 57.

SCHOLARLY METHOD

See also relevant bibliographical sections above and 'Language,
Literature, and the Computer' below.

1091. ALOZIE, NICHOLAS O.   Scholarly writers and the time capsule.
SSQ (77:1) 1996, 218–24.

1092. ANDERSON, DAVID D.   Notes on getting published. SSMLN
(21:2) 1991, 17–20; (21:3) 1991, 6–9.

1093. BAKER, NANCY L.; HULING, NANCY.   A research guide for
undergraduate students: English and American literature. (Bibl. 1989,
491.) New York: Modern Language Assn of America, 1995. pp. viii, 88.
(Fourth ed.: first ed. 1982.)

1094. BATTESTIN, MARTIN C.   The Cusum method: escaping the bog
of subjectivism. ECF (8:4) 1996, 533–8. (Literary attribution.)

1095. CARTER, BONNIE; SKATES, CRAIG.   The Rinehart handbook for
writers. Fort Worth, TX: Harcourt Brace, 1996. pp. xxiii, 620. (Fourth
ed.: first ed. 1988.)

1096. CHARNIGO, RICHARD.   From sources to citation: a concise guide
to the research paper. New York: HarperCollins, 1996. pp. vi, 106.

1097. CHERNAIK, WARREN; DAVIS, CAROLINE; DEEGAN, MARILYN (eds).
The politics of the electronic text. *See* **601**.

1098. COOK, MANUELA.   Translating forms of address. Linguist (35:6)
1996, 174–6.

1099. DAY, ABBY.   How to get research published in journals.
Aldershot; Brookfield, VT: Gower, 1996. pp. xii, 142.

1100. DECONINCK-BROSSARD, FRANÇOISE.   Confessions d'une dix-
huitièmiste 'branchée'. BSEAA (42) 1996, 111–33.

1101. DERRICOURT, ROBIN.   An author's guide to scholarly publishing. Princeton, NJ; Chichester: Princeton UP, 1996. pp. ix, 233.

1102. DRESSKELL, ANNE.   Computer-enhanced copy editing: a survey
report. JSchP (27:3) 1996, 151–65.

1103. EGGERT, PAUL; MORRISON, ELIZABETH (eds).   Manual for
editors. Canberra: Australian Scholarly Editions Centre, English Dept,
University College, Australian Defence Force Academy, 1994. pp. 62.
Rev. by Michael Ackland in English Today (12:1) 1996, 9–10.

1104. FATTAHI, RAHMATOLLAH.   Super records: an approach towards
the description of works appearing in various manifestations. *See* **139**.

1105. FRAZELL, DARYL L.; TUCK, GEORGE.   Principles of editing:
a comprehensive guide for students and journalists. New York:
McGraw-Hill, 1996. pp. xv, 318, (plates) 8.

1106. GALLET-BLANCHARD, LILIANE; MARTINET, MARIE-MADELEINE.
HIDES: Historical Document Expert System. BSEAA (42) 1996, 135–41.

1107. GEBHARDT, RICHARD C., *et al.*   Symposium on peer reviewing
in scholarly journals. RhR (13:2) 1995, 237–54.

1108. HEFFERNAN, JAMES A. W.; LINCOLN, JOHN E.   Writing: a concise
handbook. New York: Norton, 1996. pp. 327.

1109. HEWITT, DAVID; ALEXANDER, J. H.   The Edinburgh edition of
the Waverley novels: a guide for editors. Edinburgh: Edinburgh Edition
of the Waverley Novels, 1996. pp. 158.

1110. HULT, CHRISTINE A.	Researching and writing in the humanities and arts. Boston, MA: Allyn & Bacon, 1996. pp. x, 149.

1111. HUNTER, J. PAUL.	Attribution: some practical issues. ECF (8:4) 1996, 519–22.

1112. IVES, MAURA.	Listing periodical contributions in descriptive bibliographies: questions of scope, arrangement, and content. *See* **145**.

1113. LESTER, JAMES D.	Writing research papers: a complete guide. New York: HarperCollins, 1996. pp. viii, 408. (Eighth ed.: first ed. 1967.)

1114. LI, XIA; CRANE, NANCY B.	Electronic styles: a handbook for citing electronic information. (Bibl. 1993, 572.) Medford, NJ: Information Today, 1996. pp. xviii, 213. (Second ed.: first ed. 1993.)

1115. LIGHT, DEANNA; KRETZSCHMAR, WILLIAM A., JR.	Mapping with numbers. JEL (24:4) 1996, 343–57.

1116. McDONALD, STEPHEN; SALOMONE, WILLIAM.	Reading-based writing. Belmont, CA: Wadsworth, 1996. pp. xxiv, 398.

1117. MANER, MARTIN.	The spiral guide to research writing. Mountain View, CA: Mayfield, 1996. pp. xvi, 425.

1118. MEYER, RICHARD W.	The library in scholarly communication. *See* **511**.

1119. NEWMARK, PETER.	Paragraphs on translation: 41, 42, 43, 44, 46. Linguist (35:1) 1996, 18–21; (35:2) 1996, 60–3; (35:3) 1996, 90–3; (35:4) 1996, 122–5; (35:6) 1996, 184–6.

1120. OSAREH, FARIDEH.	Bibliometrics, citation analysis and co-citation analysis: a review of literature. Libri (46:3) 1996, 149–58; (46:4) 1996, 217–25.

1121. PARKER, FRANK; RILEY, KATHRYN.	Writing for academic publication: a guide to getting started. (Bibl. 1995, 760.) Rev. by Cynthia L. Hallen in NADS (28:2) 1996 (Usage Newsletter insert) 5–7.

1122. PETERS, PAM.	The Cambridge Australian style guide. Cambridge; New York: CUP, 1995. pp. xiii, 848. Rev. by Margery Fee in English Today (12:1) 1996, 7.

1123. —— In search of Australian style. English Today (12:1) 1996, 3–7, 10.

1124. SHILLINGSBURG, PETER L.	Scholarly editing in the computer age: theory and practice. *See* **834**.

1125. SIMON, LINDA.	The pleasures of book reviewing. JSchP (27:4) 1996, 237–41.

1126. SMITH, RON F.; O'CONNELL, LORAINE M.	Editing today. Ames: Iowa State UP, 1996. pp. ix, 227.

1127. STEVENS, BONNIE KLOMP; STEWART, LARRY L.	A guide to literary criticism and research. (Bibl. 1990, 590.) Fort Worth, TX: Harcourt Brace, 1996. pp. xiv, 206. (Third ed.: first ed. 1987.)

1128. TANSELLE, G. THOMAS.	A description of descriptive bibliography. *See* **155**.

1129. WEISS, ADRIAN.	Bibliographical methods for identifying unknown printers in Elizabethan/Jacobean books. *See* **326**.

1130. WELLISCH, HANS.	Indexing from A to Z. New York: Wilson, 1995. pp. xxix, 569. (Second ed.: first ed. 1991.) Rev. by Martin Dowding in JSchP (28:1) 1996, 60–1.

1131. WILLIAMS, JEFFREY.	English in America updated: an interview with Richard Ohmann. MinnR (45/46) 1995/96, 57–75. (*Refers to* bibl. 1976, 800.)

LANGUAGE, LITERATURE, AND THE COMPUTER

1132. AIJMER, KARIN; ALTENBERG, BENGT (eds). English corpus linguistics: studies in honour of Jan Svartvik. (Bibl. 1994, 577.) Rev. by Richard McLain in GL (33:1/2) 1993, 85–9; by John Kirk in JEL (24:3) 1996, 250–8.

1133. ALOZIE, NICHOLAS O. Scholarly writers and the time capsule. *See* **1091**.

1134. BAAYEN, HAARALD; SPROAT, RICHARD. Estimating lexical priorities for low-frequency morphologically ambiguous forms. CompLing (22:2) 1996, 155–66.

1135. BARNBROOK, GEOFF. Language and computers: a practical introduction to the computer analysis of language. Edinburgh: Edinburgh UP, 1996. pp. ix, 209. (Edinburgh textbooks in empirical linguistics.)

1136. BERRESSEM, HANJO. Negotiating the universe of discourse: the topology of hypertext. Amst (41:3) 1996, 397–415.

1137. BILLINGTON, JAMES H. Libraries, the Library of Congress, and the information age. *See* **456**.

1138. BLACK, EZRA, *et al.* (eds). Statistically-driven computer grammars of English: the IBM/Lancaster approach. (Bibl. 1993, 579.) Rev. by Dekai Wu in CompLing (20:3) 1994, 498–500.

1139. BOLTER, JAY DAVID; GRUSIN, RICHARD. Remediation. Configurations (4:3) 1996, 311–58.

1140. CARLETTA, JEAN. Assessing agreement on classification tasks: the kappa statistic. CompLing (22:2) 1996, 249–54.

1141. CARONIA, ANTONIO. Teorie del corpo e comunicazione inter-attiva. *In* (pp. 527–36) **117**.

1142. CHERNAIK, WARREN; DAVIS, CAROLINE; DEEGAN, MARILYN (eds). The politics of the electronic text. *See* **601**.

1143. CLIFFORD, JAMES. Formal semantics and pragmatics for natural language querying. (Bibl. 1990, 604.) Rev. by Alice ter Menlen in CompLing (17:2) 1991, 232–4.

1144. COOK, BRIAN (ed.). The electronic journal: the future of serials-based information. New York: Haworth Press, 1992. pp. xi, 106. Rev. by Walter J. Trybula in Libraries & Culture (31:3/4) 1996, 681–2.

1145. CORRSIN, STEPHEN D. An online database on the bibliography of sword dancing. FMJ (6:5) 1994, 653–7.

1146. CRAWFORD, T. HUGH. *Paterson*, memex, and hypertext. AmLH (8:4) 1996, 665–82.

1147. CUMMING, JOHN D. The Internet and the English language. English Today (11:1) 1995, 3–8.

1148. DERIE, KATE. Mystery on the Internet. AD (29:2) 1996, 152–7.

1149. DIK, SIMON C. Functional grammar in Prolog: an integrated implementation for English, French, and Dutch. Berlin; New York: Mouton de Gruyter, 1992. pp. x, 264. (Natural language processing, 2.) Rev. by Patrick Saint-Dizier in CompLing (19:4) 1993, 695–6.

1150. DOUGLAS, J. YELLOWLEES. What hypertexts can do that print narratives cannot. Reader (28) 1992, 1–22.

1151. DRESSKELL, ANNE.   Computer-enhanced copy editing: a survey report. *See* **1102**.

1152. EVANS, ROGER; GAZDAR, GERALD.   DATR: language for lexical knowledge. CompLing (22:2) 1996, 167–216.

1153. FARRINGDON, JILL M., *et al.*   Analysing for authorship: a guide to the Cusum technique. Cardiff: UP of Wales, 1996. pp. xii, 324.

1154. FEINSTEIN, SANDY.   Hypertextuality and Chaucer; or, Re-ordering the *Canterbury Tales* and other reader prerogatives. RWT (3:2) 1996, 135–48.

1155. FUNKHOUSER, CHRISTOPHER.   Toward a literature moving outside itself: the beginnings of hypermedia poetry. Talisman (16) 1996, 221–7.

1156. GALLET-BLANCHARD, LILIANE; MARTINET, MARIE-MADELEINE.   HIDES: Historical Document Expert System. *See* **1106**.

1157. GILBERT, REID.   Computers and theatre: mimesis, simulation and interconnectivity. CanTR (81) 1994, 10–15.

1158. GREENBAUM, SIDNEY (ed.).   Comparing English worldwide: the International Corpus of English. Oxford: Clarendon Press; New York: OUP, 1996. pp. xvi, 286. Rev. by Manfred Görlach in EWW (17:2) 1996, 301–3.

1159. HARPOLD, TERRY.   The misfortunes of the digital text. RWT (3:2) 1996, 95–114.

1160. HAYNES, COLIN.   Paperless publishing: the future is now. *See* **1055**.

1161. HOLMES, MICHAEL E.   Naming virtual space in computer-mediated conversation. ERGS (52:2) 1995, 212–21.

1162. JACOB, HERBERT.   The future is electronic. SSQ (77:1) 1996, 204–9.

1163. JACOBSON, DAVID.   Contexts and cues in cyberspace: the pragmatics of naming in text-based virtual reality. JAR (52:4) 1996, 461–79.

1164. JENSEN, MICHAEL.   Digital structure, digital design: issues in designing electronic publications. *See* **1061**.

1165. JOHANSSON, STIG; STENSTRÖM, ANNA-BRITA (eds).   English computer corpora: selected papers and research guide. (Bibl. 1992, 1045.) Rev. by Gerhard Leitner in ZAA (41:3) 1993, 263–5; by Katy Emck in CanRCL (20:1/2) 1993, 79–88.

1166. JOYCE, MICHAEL.   Of two minds: hypertext, pedagogy, and poetics. Ann Arbor: Michigan UP, 1995. pp. viii, 277. (Studies in literature and science.) Rev. by James J. Sosnoski in MFS (42:4) 1996, 938–40.

1167. KIRKLAND, WILL.   Computers and translation: language add-on modules for English-language word processors. TransR (44/45) 1994, 48–9.

1168. KNOWLES, GERRY; WILLIAMS, BRIONY; TAYLOR, L. (eds). A corpus of formal British English speech: the Lancaster/IBM Spoken English Corpus. Harlow; New York: Longman, 1996. pp. vii, 269. (Real language.)

1169. KORG, JACOB.   Gissing on the Internet. GissJ (32:4) 1996, 25–6.

1170. KRETZSCHMAR, WILLIAM A., JR; KONOPKA, RAFAL.   Management of linguistic databases. JEL (24:1) 1996, 61–70.

1171. LANDOW, GEORGE P.   Hypertext: the convergence of contemporary critical theory and technology. (Bibl. 1995, 813.) Rev. by Benzi Zhang in CanRCL (20:3/4) 1993, 492–6; by Paul Morgan in Text (Ann Arbor) (7) 1994, 488–92.

1172. —— (ed.).   Hyper/text/theory. (Bibl. 1995, 814.) Rev. by Myron Tuman in SAtlR (61:2) 1996, 173–6.

1173. LANHAM, RICHARD A.   The electronic word: democracy, technology, and the arts. (Bibl. 1995, 815.) Rev. by George P. Landow in CompLing (21:1) 1995, 116–19; by William H. O'Donnell in Text (Ann Arbor) (9) 1996, 446–52.

1174. LARGE, PETER J.   Publishing on the Internet. *See* **1064**.

1175. LAVAGNINO, JOHN.   Reading, scholarship, and hypertext editions. *See* **718**.

1176. LI, XIA; CRANE, NANCY B.   Electronic styles: a handbook for citing electronic information. *See* **1114**.

1177. LIGHT, DEANNA; KRETZSCHMAR, WILLIAM A., JR.   Mapping with numbers. *See* **1115**.

1178. McENERY, TONY; WILSON, ANDREW.   Corpus linguistics. Edinburgh: Edinburgh UP, 1996. pp. 209. (Edinburgh textbooks in empirical linguistics.)

1179. McGANN, JEROME.   The complete writings and pictures of Dante Gabriel Rossetti: a hypermedia research archive. *See* **736**.

1180. —— The rationale of hypertext. *See* **737**.

1181. —— The rationale of hypertext. *See* **738**.

1182. McGILLIVRAY, MURRAY.   Towards a post-critical edition: theory, hypertext, and the presentation of Middle English works. *See* **740**.

1183. McMAHON, JOHN G.; SMITH, FRANCIS J.   Improving statistical language model performance with automatically generated word hierarchies. CompLing (22:2) 1996, 217–47.

1184. MARKLEY, ROBERT (ed.).   Virtual realities and their discontents. Baltimore, MD; London: Johns Hopkins UP, 1996. pp. 162. Rev. by William Lavender in NOR (22:2) 1996, 107–9.

1185. MAYNOR, NATALIE.   A short guide to Internet resources for linguists. SECOLR (18:1) 1994, 80–8.

1186. MEIJS, WILLEM.   Morphology and lexis in a computational setting. Textus (8:2) 1995, 355–70.

1187. MINGANTI, FRANCO.   Hypertextually, maybe? Rob Swigart's interactive fiction: *Portal*. *In* (pp. 84–93) **117**.

1188. —— Updating (electronic) storytelling. Amst (41:3) 1996, 417–30.

1189. MITTON, ROGER.   English spelling and the computer. London; New York: Longman, 1996. pp. x, 207. (Studies in language and linguistics.)

1190. OOSTDIJK, NELLEKE.   Corpus linguistics and the automatic analysis of English. (Bibl. 1993, 593.) Rev. by Ted Briscoe in CompLing (19:1) 1993, 210–13.

1191. PARMER, JEROME F.   Netting books on-line: book collecting enters the twenty-first century. *See* **521**.

1192. PATRICK, KEVIN.   Words made new: book production and collecting in the computer age. *See* **304**.

1193. PEEK, ROBIN P.; NEWBY, GREGORY B. (eds).   Scholarly publishing: the electronic frontier. *See* **1073**.

1194. PENNINGTON, JOHN.   Pierre Menard in cyberspace: the Internet as intertext. *In* (pp. 181–8) **127**.

1195. PRAT ZAGREBELSKY, MARIA TERESA.   Watching English lexis change: from dictionaries of neologisms to computerised corpora. Textus (8:2) 1995, 249–66.

1196. PULMAN, STEPHEN G.   Unification encodings of grammatical notations. CompLing (22:3) 1996, 295–327.

1197. REMLEY, PAUL G.   Questions of subjectivity and ideology in the production of an electronic text of the *Canterbury Tales*. *See* **808**.

1198. RITCHIE, GRAEME D.   Computational morphology: practical mechanisms for the English lexicon. (Bibl. 1993, 595.) Rev. by Evan L. Antworth in CompLing (18:3) 1992, 365–7.

1199. ROBINSON, PETER M. W.   Collation, textual criticism, publication, and the computer. *See* **815**.

1200. RUPP-SERANO, KAREN.   From Gutenberg to gigabytes: the electronic periodical comes of age. AmP (4) 1994, 96–104.

1201. SANDERS, ARNOLD.   Hypertext, learning, and memory: some implications from manuscript tradition. *See* **416**.

1202. SHAPIRO, L. DENNIS.   Manuscripts and the World Wide Web. *See* **419**.

1203. SHILLINGSBURG, PETER L.   Scholarly editing in the computer age: theory and practice. *See* **834**.

1204. SMADJA, FRANK; HATZIVASSILOGLOU, VASILEIOS; McKEOWN, KATHLEEN R.   Translating collocations for bilingual lexicons: a statistical approach. CompLing (22:1) 1996, 1–38.

1205. SMITH, MARTHA NELL.   A hypermedia archive of Dickinson's creative work: part II, Musings on the screen and the book. *See* **841**.

1206. SMITH, RON F.; O'CONNELL, LORAINE M.   Editing today. *See* **1126**.

1207. STEFFENSEN, JAN B.   The mysterious Internet. AD (29:2) 1996, 149–50.

1208. STUBBS, MICHAEL.   Text and corpus analysis: computer-assisted studies of language and institutions. Oxford; Cambridge, MA: Blackwell, 1996. pp. 272. (Language in society, 23.)

1209. THOMPSEN, PHILIP A.   An episode of flaming: a creative narrative. ERGS (51:1) 1994, 51–72.

1210. TRELOAR, ANDREW.   Electronic scholarly publishing and the World Wide Web. *See* **1086**.

1211. TURNER, SCOTT R.   The creative process: a computer model of storytelling and creativity. (Bibl. 1995, 859.) Rev. by Keith Oatley in CompLing (21:4) 1995, 579–81.

1212. UNSWORTH, JOHN.   Electronic scholarship; or, Scholarly publishing and the public. *See* **1087**.

1213. VICKERS, BRIAN.   Whose thumbprints? A more plausible author for *A Funeral Elegy*. TLS, 8 Mar. 1996, 16–18.

1214. WALKER, MARILYN A.   Limited attention and discourse structure. CompLing (22:2) 1996, 255–64.

1215. WATT, R. J. C.   Electronic Hopkins. HopQ (23:1/2) 1996, 41–60.

1216. WITHGOTT, M. MARGARET; CHEN, FRANCINE R.   Computational models of American speech. (Bibl. 1993, 602.) Rev. by Judith Markowitz in CompLing (20:1) 1994, 125–7.

NEWSPAPERS AND OTHER PERIODICALS

1217. ABRAHAMSON, DAVID. Magazine-made America: the cultural transformation of the postwar periodical. Cresskill, NJ: Hampton Press, 1996. pp. ix, 116. (Hampton Press communications.) Rev. by Joseph P. Bernt in AmP (6) 1996, 147–9.

1218. —— (ed.). The American magazine: research perspectives and prospects. (Bibl. 1995, 866.) Rev. by Katherine Ann Bradshaw in AmP (6) 1996, 152–5.

1219. ALEXANDER, J. H. (ed.). Tavern sages: selections from the *Noctes Ambrosianae*. (Bibl. 1993, 605.) Rev. by Michelle Raye Williams in SLJ (supp. 42) 1995, 7–8.

1220. ANDREWS, PETER. The press. AH (45:6) 1994, 36–42, 44–6, 50–2, 56, 58, 60, 62, 64–5.

1221. APPLEFIELD, DAVID. George Plimpton, editor of the *Paris Review*: interviewing the interviewer. Frank (15) 1996, 7–17.

1222. APPLEGATE, EDD. Literary journalism: a biographical dictionary of writers and editors. Westport, CT; London: Greenwood Press, 1996. pp. xxi, 326.

1223. ARNER, ROBERT D. *The Child of Snow*: a misidentified 'early American' short story. EAL (31:1) 1996, 98–100.

1224. ASHTON, SUSANNA. What brings home the Bacon? Shakespeare and turn-of-the-century American authorship. AmP (6) 1996, 1–28.

1225. BARKER, ANTHONY D. Poetry from the provinces: amateur poets in the *Gentleman's Magazine* in the 1730s and 1740s. *In* (pp. 241–56) **122**.

1226. BARZUN, JACQUES. Attitudes and assumptions. ASch (64:3) 1995, 474–6.

1227. —— The press and the prose. ASch (63:4) 1994, 569–76.

1228. BAUER, DALE. The figure of the film critic as virile poet: Delmore Schwartz at the *New Republic* in the 1930s. *In* (pp. 110–19) **19**.

1229. BAUERLEIN, MARK. Emily Dickinson, *Harper's*, and femininity. EDJ (5:2) 1996, 72–7.

1230. BEETHAM, MARGARET. A magazine of her own? Domesticity and desire in the woman's magazine, 1800–1914. London; New York: Routledge, 1996. pp. xii, 242.

1231. BERGMANN, HANS. God in the street: New York writing from the penny press to Melville. Philadelphia, PA: Temple UP, 1995. pp. x, 260. Rev. by Kim Martin Long in AmP (6) 1996, 160–2.

1232. BERKENKOTTER, CAROL. Evolution of a scholarly forum: *Reader*, 1977–1988. Reader (26) 1991, 1–26.

1233. BERMAN, RUTH. Fantasy fiction and fantasy criticism in some nineteenth-century periodicals. Extrapolation (37:1) 1996, 63–95.

1234. BISHOP, EDWARD. Re:covering Modernism – format and function in the little magazines. *In* (pp. 287–319) **69**.

1235. BOUR, ISABELLE. The Clio of the North; or, The image of history. Francis Jeffrey's reviews (1802–1812). Études Écossaises (1) 1992, 181–90.

1236. BRADLEY, PATRICIA. Forerunner of the 'dark ages': Philadelphia's tradition of a partisan press. AmJ (13:2) 1996, 126–40.

1237. BURKHALTER, NANCY. Women's magazines and the suffrage movement: did they help or hinder the cause? JAC (19:2) 1996, 13–24.

1238. BURNS, BEN. Nitty gritty: a White editor in Black journalism. Jackson; London: Mississippi UP, 1996. pp. xiii, 230.

1239. CAMERON, J. M. R. Sir John Barrow as a *Quarterly* reviewer, 1809–1843. NQ (43:1) 1996, 34–7.

1240. CANNING, PETER. American dreamers: the Wallaces and *Reader's Digest*: an insider's story. *See* **909**.

1241. CARR, GRAHAM. Design as content: foreign influences and the identity of English-Canadian intellectual magazines, 1919–39. ARCS (18:2) 1988, 181–93.

1242. CARRIGAN, DENNIS P. Commercial journal publishers and university libraries: retrospect and prospect. *See* **461**.

1243. CAVERLY, ALICE RENÉ. Directory of small magazines and literary journals. NCLR (2:2) 1995, 221–6.

1244. —— WADE, CRYSTAL. A directory of small magazines and literary journals. NCLR (5) 1996, 212–21.

1245. CHRISTIE, WILLIAM. The printer's devil in Coleridge's *Biographia Literaria*. Prose Studies (19:1) 1996, 37–54.

1246. CLIFTON, MERRITT. A flash of light: the evolution of anti-nuclear consciousness in an alternative literary journal (*Samisdat*, 1973–1990). *In* (pp. 27–51) **77**.

1247. COLBERT, ANN. Philanthropy in the newsroom: women's editions of newspapers, 1894–1896. Journalism History (22:2) 1996, 91–9.

1248. COOK, BRIAN (ed.). The electronic journal: the future of serials-based information. *See* **1144**.

1249. COREY, MARY F. Mixed messages: representations of consumption and anti-consumption in the *New Yorker* magazine, 1945–1952. AmP (4) 1994, 78–95.

1250. COX, J. RANDOLPH, *et al.* (comps). The year's work in dime novels, series books, and pulp magazines 1995. DNR (65:supp.) 1996, 1–35.

1251. CRONIN, MARY M. Brother's keeper: the reform journalism of the *New England Magazine*. Journalism History (22:1) 1996, 15–23.

1252. CUOZZO, STEVEN. It's alive! How America's oldest newspaper cheated death and why it matters. New York: Times Books, 1996. pp. viii, 342. (*New York Post.*)

1253. DALZIEL, PAMELA. Anxieties of representation: the serial illustrations to Hardy's *The Return of the Native*. *See* **191**.

1254. DAMON-MOORE, HELEN. Magazines for the millions: gender and commerce in the *Ladies' Home Journal* and the *Saturday Evening Post*, 1880–1910. (Bibl. 1994, 624.) Rev. by Jennifer Scanlon in JAC (18:4) 1995, 109–10; by Martin Green in SHARP News (4:2) 1995, 5–6; by Salme Harju Steinberg in AHR (101:1) 1996, 249–50.

1255. DE MONTLUZIN, EMILY LORRAINE. Attributions of authorship in the *Gentleman's Magazine*, 1731–77: a supplement to Kuist. SB (44) 1991, 271–302.

1256. —— Attributions of authorship in the *Gentleman's Magazine*, 1778–92: a supplement to Kuist. SB (45) 1992, 158–87.

1257. —— Attributions of authorship in the *Gentleman's Magazine*, 1793–1808: a supplement to Kuist. SB (46) 1993, 320–49.

1258. —— Attributions of authorship in the *Gentleman's Magazine*, 1809–26: a supplement to Kuist. SB (47) 1994, 164–95.

1259. —— Attributions of authorship in the *Gentleman's Magazine*, 1827–48: a supplement to Kuist. SB (49) 1996, 176–207.

1260. DIZER, JOHN T.   *Boys' Life*: the real beginnings. DNR (65:2) 1996, 39–49.

1261. DOUGLAS, GEORGE H.   The smart magazines: 50 years of literary revelry and high jinks at *Vanity Fair*, the *New Yorker*, *Life*, *Esquire*, and the *Smart Set*. (Bibl. 1992, 1113.) Rev. by David E. E. Sloane in AmP (3) 1993, 130–1; by Jan Cohn in AmS (34:1) 1993, 168–9.

1262. DOWNIE, J. A.; CORNS, THOMAS N. (eds).   Telling people what to think: early eighteenth-century periodicals from the *Review* to the *Rambler*. (Bibl. 1995, 904.) Rev. by Bertrand A. Goldgar in Scriblerian (28:1/2) 1995/96, 82–4.

1263. DROTNER, KIRSTEN.   English children and their magazines, 1751–1945. (Bibl. 1989, 565.) Rev. by Mitzi Myers in CLAQ (17:1) 1992, 41–5.

1264. FAVRET, MARY A.   War correspondence: reading Romantic war. Prose Studies (19:2) 1996, 173–85.

1265. FINKELSTEIN, DAVID.   An index to *Blackwood's Magazine*, 1901–1980. (Bibl. 1995, 906.) Rev. by John Gillard Watson in NQ (43:3) 1996, 370–1.

1266. FORMAN, MURRAY.   Media form and cultural space: negotiating Rap 'fanzines'. JPC (29:2) 1995, 171–88.

1267. FORTSON, BENJAMIN W., IV.   The press and the prose: an exchange. ASch (64:3) 1995, 471–3.

1268. FOSTER, R. F.   'When the newspapers have forgotten me': Yeats, obituarists, and Irishness. Yeats Annual (12) 1996, 163–79.

1269. FREEMAN, ELIZABETH.   'What factory girls had power to do': the techno-logic of working-class feminine publicity in *The Lowell Offering*. AQ (50:2) 1994, 109–28.

1270. GARVEY, ELLEN GRUBER.   The adman in the parlor: magazines and the gendering of consumer culture, 1880s to 1910s. New York; Oxford: OUP, 1996. pp. viii, 230. (Cf. bibl. 1993, 636.) Rev. by Jan Cohn in JAC (19:3) 1996, 127–8.

1271. GEBHARDT, RICHARD C., *et al.*   Symposium on peer reviewing in scholarly journals. *See* **1107**.

1272. GILDEA, DENNIS.   'Cross counter': the Heenan–Morrissey fight of 1858 and Frank Queen's attack on the 'respectable press'. ColbyQ (32:1) 1996, 11–22.

1273. GILMARTIN, KEVIN.   Print politics: the press and radical opposition in early nineteenth-century England. Cambridge; New York: CUP, 1996. pp. xiv, 274. (Cambridge studies in Romanticism, 21.)

1274. GLAZENER, NANCY.   Regional accents: populism, feminism, and New England women's regionalism. AQ (52:2) 1996, 33–53. (*Arena*, Boston, est. 1889.)

1275. GÖRTSCHACHER, WOLFGANG.   (Re)writing contemporary literary history: (small) presses, little magazines, university curricula. *In* (pp. 319–31) **125**.

1276. GOUGEON, LEN.   Whitman and the *Commonwealth*. WWQR (9:4) 1992, 208–11.

1277. GRANT, THOMAS.   The *American Spectator*'s R. Emmett Tyrrell, Jr: Chicken McMencken. JAC (19:2) 1996, 103–9.

1278. GREENWALD, MARILYN S.   'All brides are not beautiful': the rise of Charlotte Curtis at the *New York Times*. Journalism History (22:3) 1996, 100–9.

1279. HAMILTON, JOHN MAXWELL; KRIMSKY, GEORGE A.   Hold the press: the inside story on newspapers. Baton Rouge; London: Louisiana State UP, 1996. pp. 190.

1280. HAMILTON, STEPHEN.   New Zealand English-language periodicals of literary interest active 1920s–1960s. Unpub. doct. diss., Univ. of Auckland, 1996.

1281. HAMPSON, ROBERT.   Conrad, Curle and the *Blue Peter*. *In* (pp. 89–104) **69**.

1282. HARLING, PHILIP.   Leigh Hunt's *Examiner* and the language of patriotism. EHR (111:444) 1996, 1159–81.

1283. HARRIS, DANIEL.   From *After Dark* to *Out*: the invention of the Teflon magazine. AR (54:2) 1996, 174–93.

1284. HARRIS, ROBERT.   A patriot press: national politics and the London press in the 1740s. (Bibl. 1995, 925.) Rev. by Stephen Taylor in Scriblerian (28:1/2) 1995/96, 84–5.

1285. HASEGAWA, HIROKAZU.   Hemingway to 'dansei taishuushi' to iu shisou – *Esquire*, dokusha, soshite 1930 nendai. (Hemingway and the ideology of the 'magazine for men': *Esquire*, the readers, and the 1930s.) StAL (33) 1996, 35–50.

1286. HEARN, CHARLES R.   F. Scott Fitzgerald and the popular magazine formula story of the twenties. JAC (18:3) 1995, 33–40.

1287. HEIDENRY, JOHN.   Theirs was the kingdom: Lila and DeWitt Wallace and the story of the *Reader's Digest*. New York: Norton, 1993. pp. 701. Rev. by Jonathan Yardley in BkW, 15 Aug. 1993, 3.

1288. HUMPHREY, CAROL SUE.   The press of the young Republic, 1783–1833. Westport, CT; London: Greenwood Press, 1996. pp. xiv, 182. (History of American journalism, 2.)

1289. —— 'This popular engine': New England newspapers during the American Revolution, 1775–1789. (Bibl. 1994, 642.) Rev. by Vera Nünning in ZAA (41:1) 1993, 78–80.

1290. HUTCHINSON, GEORGE.   Mediating 'race' and 'nation': the cultural politics of the *Messenger*. AAR (28:4) 1994, 531–48.

1291. HUTTON, FRANKIE.   The early Black press in America, 1827 to 1860. (Bibl. 1993, 655.) Rev. by Harry Amana in AmP (4) 1994, 106–12.

1292. IVES, MAURA.   Descriptive bibliography and the Victorian periodical. *See* **144**.

1293. JANSSEN, MARIAN.   The *Kenyon Review*, 1939–1970: a critical history. (Bibl. 1991, 809.) Rev. by Sanford Pinsker in Salmagundi (92) 1991, 227–37; by Mary Ellen Zuckerman in AmP (2) 1992, 136–9.

1294. JOHANSEN, PETER.   Where's the meaning and the hope? Trends in employee publications. JPC (29:3) 1995, 129–38.

1295. JONES, ALED.   Powers of the press: newspapers, power and the public in nineteenth-century England. Aldershot: Scolar Press; Brookfield, VT: Ashgate, 1996. pp. xii, 231. (Nineteenth century.)

1296. JONES, MARGARET C.   Heretics & hellraisers: women contributors to *The Masses*, 1911–1917. (Bibl. 1995, 932.) Rev. by Susan Belasco Smith in AmP (4) 1994, 132–3.

1297. KELLER, KATHRYN.   Mothers and work in popular American magazines. Westport, CT; London: Greenwood Press, 1994. pp. 194.

(Contributions in women's studies, 139.) Rev. by Jan Cohn in JAC (18:4) 1995, 103–4.

1298. KNIGHT, MELINDA.   Little magazines and the emergence of Modernism in the *fin de siècle*. AmP (6) 1996, 29–45.

1299. KOIKE, SHIGERU (ed.).   Victorian *Punch* – zuzou shiryou de yomu 19 seiki sekai. (Victorian *Punch*: reading the 19th-century world through iconographic materials.) Tokyo: Kashiwa Shobo, 1996. pp. 432.

1300. KOPLEY, RICHARD.   Edgar Allan Poe and the *Philadelphia Saturday News*. (Bibl. 1992, 1147.) Rev. by Burton R. Pollin in AmP (3) 1993, 131–3; by Agnes Bondurant Marcuson in PoeM (23) 1993, 22–3.

1301. KRIEGER, MILTON.   Building the republic through letters: *Abbia: Cameroon Cultural Review*, 1963–82, and its legacy. RAL (27:2) 1996, 155–77.

1302. KUIST, JAMES M.   A collaboration in learning: the *Gentleman's Magazine* and its ingenious contributors. SB (44) 1991, 302–17.

1303. KUNKEL, THOMAS.   Genius in disguise: Harold Ross of the *New Yorker*. New York: Random House, 1995. pp. 497. Rev. by Judith Yaross Lee in AmP (6) 1996, 157–60.

1304. LEDBETTER, KATHRYN.   Battles for Modernism and *Wheels*. JML (19:2) 1995, 322–8.

1305. LEITZ, ROBERT C., III.   Norris in cyberspace. FNS (22) 1996, 6, 8.

1306. LINDFORS, BERNTH.   Loaded vehicles: studies in African literary media. *See* **1067**.

1307. LINTON, DAVID.   The twentieth-century newspaper press in Britain: an annotated bibliography. Introd. by Ray Boston. (Bibl. 1994, 652.) Rev. by J. O. Baylen in Albion (28:2) 1996, 360–1.

1308. LOCKE, IAN.   Old newspapers: the how and why of collecting. *See* **503**.

1309. LORENZ, LEE.   The art of the *New Yorker*, 1925–1995. New York: Knopf, 1995. pp. viii, 191. Rev. by Judith Yaross Lee in AmP (6) 1996, 157–60.

1310. MCCORMACK, K.   George Eliot's first fiction: targetting *Blackwood's*. Bibliotheck (21) 1996, 69–80.

1311. MCCORMACK, W. J.   'Never put your name to an anonymous letter': serial reading in the *Dublin University Magazine*, 1861 to 1869. YES (26) 1996, 100–15.

1312. MCCRACKEN, ELLEN MARIE.   Decoding women's magazines from *Mademoiselle* to *Ms*. (Bibl. 1995, 946.) Rev. by Frances M. Maplezzi in AmP (4) 1994, 118–21.

1313. MCDERMOTT, PATRICE.   The risks and responsibilities of feminist academic journals. NWSAJ (6:3) 1994, 373–83.

1314. MACHOR, JAMES L.   Poetics as ideological hermeneutics: American fiction and the historicized reader of the early nineteenth century. Reader (25) 1991, 49–64.

1315. MCMAHON, TIMOTHY G.   Cultural nativism and Irish-Ireland: the *Leader* as a source for Joyce's *Ulysses*. JSA (7) 1996, 67–85.

1316. MCVICKER, MARY FRECH.   Courants, messengers, and a plain dealer: how your paper got its name. AH (45:6) 1994, 40–1.

1317. MANOIM, IRWIN.   You have been warned: the first ten years of the *Mail & Guardian*. Johannesburg; London: Penguin, 1996. pp. 217.

1318. MAREK, JAYNE E.   Women editing Modernism: 'little' magazines & literary history. (Bibl. 1995, 948.) Rev. by Carolyn Kitch in JMCQ (73:3) 1996, 773–4.

1319. MARTEN, JAMES.   For the good, the true, and the beautiful: Northern children's magazines and the Civil War. CWH (41:1) 1995, 57–75.

1320. MARTIN, RICHARD.   American chronicle: J. C. Leyendecker's icons of time. *See* **222**.

1321. MELLOWN, ELGIN W.   An annotated checklist of contributions by Bloomsbury and other British avant-garde writers (and of articles relating to them) in *Vogue* magazine during the editorship of Dorothy Todd, 1923–1927. BB (53:3) 1996, 227–34.

1322. MOREL, MICHEL.   Le *Reader's Digest* tel qu'en lui-même les années le changent. RANAM (29) 1996, 89–104.

1323. MORRIS, DANIEL.   Hemingway and *Life*: consuming revolutions. AmP (3) 1993, 62–74.

1324. MORRISON, ROBERT.   *Blackwood's* under William Blackwood. SLJ (22:1) 1995, 61–5.

1325. MORRISSON, MARK.   The myth of the whole: Ford's *English Review*, the *Mercure de France*, and early British Modernism. ELH (63:2) 1996, 513–33.

1326. MULLEN, BILL.   Popular fronts: *Negro Story* magazine and the African-American literary response to World War II. AAR (30:1) 1996, 5–15.

1327. MURPHY, MICHAEL.   'One hundred per cent Bohemia': pop decadence and the aestheticization of commodity in the rise of the slicks. *In* (pp. 61–89) **67**.

1328. MURPHY, PAUL THOMAS.   Toward a working-class canon: literary criticism in British working-class periodicals, 1816–1858. (Bibl. 1995, 959.) Rev. by Kevin Gilmartin in Criticism (38:3) 1996, 475–7.

1329. MYERSON, JOEL.   Willis Gaylord Clark: an autobiographical sketch. AmP (2) 1992, 1–5.

1330. NELSON, CLAUDIA.   Invisible men: fatherhood in Victorian periodicals, 1850–1910. Athens; London: Georgia UP, 1995. pp. viii, 332. Rev. by Katherine V. Snyder in Prose Studies (19:3) 1996, 296–9; by Billie Andrew Inman in Albion (28:1) 1996, 138–41.

1331. NOONAN, JAMES.   The making (and breaking) of a regional theatre critic: Audrey Ashley at the *Ottawa Citizen* 1961–1985. TRC (17:1) 1996, 83–118.

1332. NOURIE, ALAN; NOURIE, BARBARA (eds).   The American mass-market magazine. Westport, CT; London: Greenwood Press, 1990. pp. x, 611. (Historical guides to the world's periodicals and magazines.) Rev. by Joseph P. Bernt in AmP (2) 1992, 139–41.

1333. OEHLSCHLAEGER, FRITZ (ed.).   Old Southwest humor from the *St Louis Reveille* 1844–1850. (Bibl. 1995, 965.) Rev. by P. M. Zall in GateH (11:4) 1990/91, 78–9.

1334. OKKER, PATRICIA.   Our sister editors: Sarah J. Hale and the tradition of nineteenth-century American women editors. Athens; London: Georgia UP, 1995. pp. vii, 264. Rev. by Patricia Larson Kalyjian in AL (68:2) 1996, 465–6.

1335. —— Sarah Josepha Hale, Lydia Sigourney, and the poetic tradition in two nineteenth-century women's magazines. AmP (3) 1993, 32–42.

1336. Osthaus, Carl R.   Partisans of the Southern press: editorial spokesmen of the nineteenth century. (Bibl. 1994, 660.) Rev. by Donald E. Reynolds in CWH (42:1) 1996, 67–8.

1337. Parker, David B.   Alias Bill Arp: Charles Henry Smith and the South's 'goodly heritage'. (Bibl. 1992, 1168.) Rev. by David E. E. Sloane in AmP (2) 1992, 141–2.

1338. Payne, Kenneth.   Cities of paradise, comrade kingdoms, and worlds of light: some versions of the Socialist utopia in the *Comrade* (1901–1905). AmP (6) 1996, 46–60.

1339. Peek, Robin P.; Newby, Gregory B. (eds).   Scholarly publishing: the electronic frontier. *See* **1073**.

1340. Pettengill, Claire C.   Against novels: Fanny Fern's newspaper fiction and the reform of print culture. AmP (6) 1996, 61–91.

1341. Pollin, Burton R.   A posthumous assessment: the 1849–1850 periodical press response to Edgar Allan Poe. AmP (2) 1992, 6–50.

1342. Potter, Vilma.   Idella Purnell's *PALMS* and godfather Witter Bynner. AmP (4) 1994, 47–64.

1343. Potter, Vilma Raskin.   A reference guide to Afro-American publications and editors, 1827–1946. (Bibl. 1993, 680.) Rev. by Harry Amana in AmP (4) 1994, 106–12.

1344. Presley, John W.   *The Owl*: an extended bibliographic note. Gravesiana (1:1) 1996, 33–45.

1345. Radford, Fred.   Anticipating *Finnegans Wake*: the *United Irishman* and La Belle Iseult. JJQ (33:2) 1996, 237–43.

1346. Raymond, Joad.   The invention of the newspaper: English newsbooks, 1641–1649. Oxford: Clarendon Press; New York: OUP, 1996. pp. xii, 379.

1347. Riley, Sam G. (ed.).   American magazine journalists, 1741–1850. Detroit, MI; London: Gale Research, 1988. pp. xv, 430. (Dictionary of literary biography, 73.) Rev. by Andrew Jay Hoffman in AmP (3) 1993, 120–3.

1348. —— American magazine journalists, 1850–1900. Detroit, MI; London: Gale Research, 1988. pp. xvii, 387. (Dictionary of literary biography, 79.) Rev. by Andrew Jay Hoffman in AmP (3) 1993, 120–3.

1349. —— American magazine journalists, 1900–1960: first series. Detroit, MI; London: Gale Research, 1990. pp. xv, 401. (Dictionary of literary biography, 91.) Rev. by Andrew Jay Hoffman in AmP (3) 1993, 120–3.

1350. Rivalain, Odile Boucher.   From 'literary insignificancies' to 'the sacredness of the writer's art': aspects of fiction criticism in the *Westminster Review*, 1824–1857. CVE (44) 1996, 33–46.

1351. Room, Adrian.   Troubled *Times*. English Today (12:3) 1996, 26–7. (Solecisms and misspellings in the *Times*.)

1352. Rupp-Serano, Karen.   From Gutenberg to gigabytes: the electronic periodical comes of age. *See* **1200**.

1353. Schneirov, Matthew.   The dream of a new social order: popular magazines in America, 1893–1914. (Bibl. 1995, 981.) Rev. by Jan Cohn in JAC (19:1) 1996, 105–6.

1354. Scholnick, Joshua David.   Democrats abroad: Continental literature and the American bard in *United States Magazine and Democratic Review*. AmP (3) 1993, 75–99.

1355. Scholnick, Robert J.   'Culture' or democracy: Whitman, Eugene Benson, and the *Galaxy*. WWQR (13:4) 1996, 189–98.

1356. SCHULTE, RAINER.   Plays in translation: a profile of *PAJ* Publications/*Performing Arts Journal. See* **1079**.

1357. SCHULTZ, HEIDI M.   The editor's desk at *Saturn's Magazine* 1849–1851. AmP (6) 1996, 92–134.

1358. SEDGWICK, ELLERY.   The *Atlantic Monthly*, 1857–1909: Yankee humanism at high tide and ebb. (Bibl. 1994, 669.) Rev. by Jack Beatty in BkW, 10 July 1994, 7; by Elizabeth Kolmer in AmS (37:1) 1996, 185–6.

1359. —— Henry James and the *Atlantic Monthly*: editorial perspectives on James' 'friction with the market'. SB (45) 1992, 311–32.

1360. —— Horace Scudder and Sarah Orne Jewett: market forces in publishing in the 1890s. *See* **1004**.

1361. SHANNON, EDWARD A.   'That we may mis-unda-stend each udda': the rhetoric of *Krazy Kat. See* **243**.

1362. SHERBO, ARTHUR.   From *Shenandoah*: overlooked reviews of and poems by Eliot, Faulkner, Stevens, Hemingway, Graves, Spender, and others. NQ (43:4) 1996, 445–7.

1363. —— From the *Bookman* of London. SB (46) 1993, 349–57.

1364. —— From the *London Mercury*. SB (45) 1992, 292–302.

1365. —— Last gleanings from the *Critic*: Clemens, Whitman, Hardy, Thackeray, and others. SB (47) 1994, 212–21.

1366. —— A mixed bag from the *Bookman* of New York. SB (44) 1991, 332–44.

1367. —— More periodical grubbings: Sean O'Faolain's contributions to the *Bell*. NQ (43:1) 1996, 59–60.

1368. —— Pádraic Colum in the *Dublin Magazine*. SB (49) 1996, 284–90.

1369. —— Shaw's forgotten lecture (and other matters Shavian). SB (47) 1994, 221–30.

1370. SHEVELOW, KATHRYN.   Women and print culture: the construction of femininity in the early periodical. (Bibl. 1990, 680.) Rev. by Greg Laugero in ECS (28:4) 1995, 433.

1371. SMITH, ROZ.   The local press: what's in it for *you*? SLang (14/15) 1995/96, 148–57.

1372. SOMMERVILLE, C. JOHN.   The news revolution in England: the cultural dynamics of daily information. New York; Oxford: OUP, 1996. pp. viii, 197.

1373. STERN, MADELEINE B.   Louisa May Alcott and the Boston *Saturday Evening Gazette*. AmP (2) 1992, 64–78.

1374. STREITMATTER, RODGER.   Unspeakable: the rise of the gay and lesbian press in America. London; Boston, MA: Faber & Faber, 1995. pp. xiv, 424. Rev. by Edra Charlotte Bogle in AmP (6) 1996, 149–52; by James Miller in AmJ (13:3) 1996, 380–3.

1375. SUGGS, HENRY LEWIS (ed.).   The Black press in the Middle West, 1865–1985. Westport, CT; London: Greenwood Press, 1996. pp. vi, 410. (Contributions in Afro-American and African studies, 177.)

1376. SUTTON, WALTER (ed.).   Pound, Thayer, Watson, and the *Dial*: a story in letters. (Bibl. 1994, 678.) Rev. by Earl E. Stevens in ELT (39:3) 1996, 396–9.

1377. SZUBERLA, GUY.   The making and breaking of Chicago's *American*. AmP (2) 1992, 100–12.

1378. TAGG, JAMES.   Benjamin Franklin Bache and the Philadelphia *Aurora*. Philadelphia: Pennsylvania UP, 1991. pp. xiv, 431. Rev. by Richard Buel, Jr, in AHR (98:1) 1993, 239–41.

1379. TERES, HARVEY.   Remaking Marxist criticism: *Partisan Review*'s Eliotic Leftism, 1934–1936. *In* (pp. 65–84) **41**.

1380. THOMPSON, JULIUS E.   The Black press in Mississippi, 1865–1985. (Bibl. 1994, 680.) Rev. by James L. Conyers, Jr, in JAC (18:4) 1995, 99–101.

1381. TINKLER, PENNY.   Constructing girlhood: popular magazines for girls growing up in England, 1920–1950. (Bibl. 1995, 998.) Rev. by Amy Beth Aronson in AmP (6) 1996, 144–6.

1382. TURNER, CATHERINE.   The angel of the shelter: American women and the atomic bomb. Krieg und Literatur (1) 1995, 25–40.

1383. VANDEN HEUVEL, JON; LAMAY, CRAIG; FITZSIMON, MARTHA (eds). Untapped sources: America's newspaper archives and histories. (Bibl. 1992, 1188.) Rev. by E. Claire Jerry in AmP (2) 1992, 145–8.

1384. VANDER MEULEN, DAVID L.   Fredson Bowers and the editing of *Studies in Bibliography*. *See* **868**.

1385. VANN, J. DON; VANARSDEL, ROSEMARY T. (eds).   Victorian periodicals and Victorian society. (Bibl. 1995, 999.) Rev. by Joanne Shattock in Albion (28:2) 1996, 335–7.

1386. VIEGENER, MATIAS.   'Kinky escapades, bedroom techniques, unbridled passion, and secret sex codes'. *In* (pp. 234–56) **12**.

1387. WATTS, CEDRIC.   Marketing Modernism: how Conrad prospered. *In* (pp. 81–8) **69**.

1388. WELLS, DANIEL A.   Thoreau's reputation in the major magazines, 1862–1900: a summary and index. AmP (4) 1994, 12–23.

1389. WINKLER, KARL TILMAN.   Handwerk und Markt: Druckerhandwerk, Vertriebswesen und Tagesschrifttum in London 1695–1750. Stuttgart: Steiner, 1993. pp. xvi, 770. Rev. by Johan Gerritsen in Archiv (233:2) 1996, 388–91.

1390. WU, DUNCAN.   Wordsworth and the *Courier*'s review of *The Excursion*. NQ (43:1) 1996, 33–4.

1391. —— Wordsworth and the *Westmorland Advertiser*. NQ (43:4) 1996, 420–1.

1392. YOUNG, STEPHEN FLINN.   *The Kudzu*: sixties generational revolt – even in Mississippi. SoQ (34:3) 1996, 122–36.

THE ENGLISH LANGUAGE

GENERAL STUDIES

THE ENGLISH LANGUAGE

1393. ALGEO, JOHN. The American language and its British dialect. SECOLR (19:2) 1995, 114–25.

1394. ANDO, SADAO. Eigogaku no shiten. (Viewpoints on English linguistics.) Tokyo: Kaitakusha, 1996. pp. xii, 234.

1395. ANON. The American Heritage book of English usage. Boston, MA: Houghton Mifflin, 1996. pp. xii, 290.

1396. —— Summaries of theses. EWW (17:2) 1996, 261–83.

1397. —— (comp.). Schriftenverzeichnis Horst Weinstock. *In* (pp. 363–70) **11**.

1398. —— (ed.). Gengo to bunka no shosou: Okuda Hiryoyuki kyouju taikan kinen ronbunshu. (Aspects of language and culture: essays in commemoration of Professor Hiroyuki Okuda's retirement.) Tokyo: Eihosha, 1996. pp. viii, 340.

1399. BARNBROOK, GEOFF. Language and computers: a practical introduction to the computer analysis of language. *See* **1135**.

1400. BLAKE, N. F.; MOORHEAD, JEAN. Introduction to English language. (Bibl. 1993, 721.) Rev. by Frances Austin in EngS (76:3) 1995, 286–7.

1401. BOLINGER, DWIGHT. Oddments of English. JEL (24:1) 1996, 4–24.

1402. BURCHFIELD, ROBERT. Unlocking the English language. Introd. by Harold Bloom. (Bibl. 1992, 1203.) Rev. by T. C. Holyoke in AR (49:3) 1991, 467–8.

1403. BURGESS, ANTHONY. A mouthful of air: languages, languages – especially English. (Bibl. 1993, 722.) Rev. by Marie Arana-Ward in BkW, 15 Aug. 1996, 3, 7.

1404. CHIBA, SHUJI (ed.). Synchronic and diachronic approaches to language. (Bibl. 1994, 79.) Rev. by Elly van Gelderen in SL (20:3) 1996, 721–4.

1405. COCHRANE, ROBERTSON. The way we word: musing on the meaning of everyday English. Saskatoon, Sask.: Fifth House, 1993. pp. xi, 195. Rev. by J. G. Keogh in AntR (93/94) 1993, 31–8.

1406. CRIVELLI, RENZO S.; SAMPIETRO, LUIGI (eds). Il passaggiere italiano: saggi sulle letterature di lingua inglese in onore di Sergio Rossi. Rome: Bulzoni, 1994. pp. 569. (Biblioteca di anglistica, 4.) Rev. by Maria Scaglione in Filologia e critica (19:3) 1994, 468–73.

1407. CRYSTAL, DAVID. Reithed in gloom. English Today (12:3) 1996, 38–40. (Comments on Jean Aitchison's Reith Lecture on language and linguistics.)

1408. GRAMLEY, STEPHAN; PÄTZOLD, KURT-MICHAEL. A survey of modern English. (Bibl. 1995, 1011.) Rev. by Josef Schmied in ZAA (42:1) 1994, 59–61.

1409. HAFFENDEN, JOHN (ed.).   The strengths of Shakespeare's shrew: essays, memoirs, and reviews. By William Empson. Sheffield: Sheffield Academic Press, 1996. pp. 246. Rev. by David Norbrook in TLS, 10 May 1996, 27.

1410. JASZCZOLT, KATARZYNA.   English language: general. YWES (75) 1994, 1–8.

1411. KRETZSCHMAR, WILLIAM A., JR; KONOPKA, RAFAL.   Management of linguistic databases. *See* **1170**.

1412. MCARTHUR, TOM (ed.); MCARTHUR, ROSHAN (asst ed.).   The Oxford companion to the English language. (Bibl. 1994, 706.) Oxford; New York: OUP, 1996. (Abridged ed.: first ed. 1992.)

1413. —— MCARTHUR, FERI (eds).   The Oxford companion to the English language. (Bibl. 1994, 706.) Rev. by Klaus Hansen in ZAA (42:2) 1994, 174–5.

1414. MCENERY, TONY; WILSON, ANDREW.   Corpus linguistics. *See* **1178**.

1415. MARSHALL, JEREMY; MCDONALD, FRED (eds).   Questions of English. Oxford; New York: OUP, 1995. pp. 192.

1416. O'CONNER, PATRICIA T.   Woe is I: the grammarphobe's guide to better English in plain English. New York: Putnam, 1996. pp. xii, 227.

1417. PENELOPE, JULIA.   Speaking freely: unlearning the lies of the fathers' tongues. (Bibl. 1992, 1222.) Rev. by Delma McLeod-Porter in SECOLR (15:2) 1991, 225–7; by Cheris Kramarae in Signs (17:3) 1992, 666–71.

1418. POLLNER, CLAUSDIRK; ROHLFING, HELMUT; HAUSMANN, FRANK-RUTGER (eds).   *Bright is the ring of words*: Festschrift für Horst Weinstock zum 65. Geburtstag. *See* **11**.

1419. SKOUSEN, ROYAL.   Analogical modeling of language. (Bibl. 1990, 728.) Rev. by Miroslaw Baniko in CompLing (17:2) 1991, 246–8.

1420. TAKESUE, MASATARO.   Eigogaku ronsetsushu. (Essays on English linguistics.) Osaka: Izumiya Shoten, 1996. pp. 448.

1421. TIEKEN-BOON VAN OSTADE, INGRID; FRANKIS, JOHN (eds).   Language usage and description: studies presented to N. E. Osselton on the occasion of his retirement. (Bibl. 1991, 59.) Rev. by John Insley in ZAA (43:1) 1995, 93–5.

1422. TYDEMAN, WILLIAM (ed.).   The Welsh connection: essays by past and present members of the Department of English Language and Literature, University College of North Wales, Bangor. (Bibl. 1986, 792.) Rev. by Jeremy Hooker in PN Review (17:5) 1991, 60.

1423. WALES, KATIE.   Personal pronouns in present-day English. Cambridge; New York: CUP, 1996. pp. xvii, 234. (Studies in English language.)

1424. WEINSTOCK, CAROLA; WEINSTOCK, ALEXANDER; WEINSTOCK, CONSTANZE.   Alphabetum auctoris emeriti. *In* (pp. 333–62) **11**.

HISTORY AND DEVELOPMENT OF ENGLISH

1425. BAILEY, RICHARD W.   Images of English: a cultural history of the language. (Bibl. 1994, 714.) Rev. by Connie Eble in SECOLR (16:2) 1992, 207–8; by Domenico Pezzini in Aevum (68:3) 1994, 774–8; by Lawrence M. Davis in AS (71:3) 1996, 314–20.

1426. —— Nineteenth-century English. Ann Arbor: Michigan UP, 1996. pp. viii, 372.

1427. BARBER, CHARLES. The English language: a historical introduction. (Bibl. 1995, 1020.) Rev. by Frances Austin in EngS (76:3) 1995, 285–6; by Elly van Gelderen in SL (20:3) 1996, 719–20.

1428. BLAKE, N. F. Essays on Shakespeare's language: first series. Misterton, S. Yorks: Language Press, 1996. pp. 172.

1429. —— A history of the English language. Basingstoke: Macmillan; New York: New York UP, 1996. pp. xv, 382.

1430. BLANK, PAULA. Broken English: dialects and the politics of language in Renaissance writings. London; New York: Routledge, 1996. pp. viii, 211. (The politics of language.) (Cf. bibl. 1991, 2042.)

1431. BREEZE, ANDREW. The provenance of the Rushworth Mercian gloss. NQ (43:4) 1996, 394–5.

1432. BRINTON, LAUREL J. Pragmatic markers in English: grammaticalization and discourse functions. Berlin; New York: Mouton de Gruyter, 1996. pp. xvi, 412. (Topics in English linguistics, 19.)

1433. BRITTON, DEREK (ed.). English historical linguistics 1994. Papers from the 8th International Conference on English Historical Linguistics (Edinburgh, 19–23 September 1994.) *See* **27**.

1434. BRYSON, BILL. Made in America. (Bibl. 1994, 722.) New York: Morrow, 1994. Rev. by Barbara Wallraff in BkW, 23 Apr. 1995, 3, 6.

1435. BURROW, J. A.; TURVILLE-PETRE, THORLAC. A book of Middle English. (Bibl. 1995, 1024.) Oxford; Cambridge, MA: Blackwell, 1996. pp. vii, 373. (Second ed.: first ed. 1992.)

1436. CARTLIDGE, NEIL. The date of *The Owl and the Nightingale*. MÆ (65:2) 1996, 230–47.

1437. ČERMÁK, JAN. '*Hie dygel lond warigeað*': spatial imagery in five *Beowulf* compounds. Linguistica Pragensia (6:1) 1996, 24–34.

1438. CONSTABLE, GILES. The language of preaching in the twelfth century. Viator (25) 1994, 131–52.

1439. DÍAZ VERA, JAVIER E. From Domesday Book to Lay Subsidy Rolls: place-names as informants of linguistic change. SAP (30) 1996, 37–43.

1440. DIENSBERG, BERNHARD. French transplanted: a re-evaluation of the importance of Anglo-French in the development of the English language during the Middle English period. *In* (pp. 253–66) **68**.

1441. DILLARD, J. L. A history of American English. (Bibl. 1993, 743.) Rev. by Robert A. Peters in JEL (24:1) 1996, 85.

1442. FISIAK, JACEK (ed.). Middle English miscellany: from vocabulary to linguistic variation. *See* **68**.

1443. FLEMING, JULIET. Dictionary English and the female tongue. *In* (pp. 175–204) **89**.

1444. FRANZEN, CHRISTINE. Late copies of Anglo-Saxon charters. *In* (pp. 42–70) **114**.

1445. GNEUSS, HELMUT. Language and history in early England. Aldershot; Brookfield, VT: Variorum, 1996. 1 vol. (various pp.) (Collected studies, 559.)

1446. GRADDOL, DAVID; LEITH, DICK; SWANN, JOAN (eds). English: history, diversity and change. London; New York: Routledge in assn with Open Univ., 1996. pp. 394. Rev. by Manfred Görlach in EWW (17:2) 1996, 303–4.

1447. GRETSCH, MECHTHILD. The language of the Fonthill Letter. ASE (23) 1994, 57–102.

1448. HANNA, RALPH, III. With an *O* (Yorks.) or an *I* (Salop.)? The Middle English lyrics of British Library Additional 45896. *See* **368**.

1449. HASHIMOTO, ISAO. Seisho no eigo – kyuuyaku genten kara mita. (Biblical English in relation to the original of the Old Testament.) Tokyo: Eichosha, 1996. pp. xx, 274.

1450. HASKETT, TIMOTHY S. '*I have ordeyned and make my testament and last wylle in this forme*': English as a testamentary language, 1387–1450. MedStud (58) 1996, 149–206.

1451. HIGUCHI, MASAYUKI. Studies in Chaucer's English. Tokyo: Eihosha, 1996. pp. viii, 506.

1452. HOGG, RICHARD M. (gen. ed.). The Cambridge history of the English language: vol. 1, The beginnings to 1066. Ed. by Richard M. Hogg. (Bibl. 1995, 1038.) Rev. by Domenico Pezzini in Aevum (68:3) 1994, 771–4; by Josef Schmied in ZAA (44:3) 1996, 270–2.

1453. —— The Cambridge history of the English language: vol. 2, 1066–1476. Ed. by Norman Blake. (Bibl. 1995, 1039.) Rev. by Domenico Pezzini in Aevum (68:3) 1994, 771–4; by Josef Schmied in ZAA (44:3) 1996, 270–2.

1454. —— The Cambridge history of the English language: vol. 5, English in Britain and overseas: origins and development. Ed. by Robert Burchfield. (Bibl. 1995, 1040.) Rev. by Klaus Hansen in ZAA (43:4) 1995, 351–3; by Josef Schmied in ZAA (44:4) 1996, 362–4; by W. Nelson Francis in Language in Society (25:2) 1996, 297–30.

1455. IGLESIAS-RÁBADE, LUIS. The multi-lingual pulpit in England (1100–1500). Neophilologus (80:3) 1996, 479–92.

1456. KATO, KAZUMITSU. Bunka no nagarekara miru eigo – gensen kara gendai no variety made. (English reflecting cultural history: from the origin to modern varieties.) Tokyo: Sanshusha, 1996. pp. 400.

1457. KOERNER, KONRAD (ed.). Language and society in early modern England: selected essays 1981–1994. By Vivian Salmon. Amsterdam; Philadelphia, PA: Benjamins, 1996. pp. viii, 276. (Amsterdam studies in the theory and history of linguistic science, III: Studies in the history of the language sciences, 77.)

1458. KORNEXL, LUCIA. The *Regularis concordia* and its Old English gloss. *See* **381**.

1459. KYTÖ, MERJA. English historical corpora: report on developments in 1995. ICAME Journal (20) 1996, 117–30.

1460. LAING, MARGARET. Catalogue of sources for a linguistic atlas of early medieval English. (Bibl. 1995, 1048.) Rev. by P. R. Kitson in EngS (77:1) 1996, 104–7.

1461. LASS, ROGER. Old English: a historical linguistic companion. (Bibl. 1995, 1049.) Rev. by Bengt Odenstedt in MS (90:1) 1996, 106–8; by Olga Fischer in SL (20:3) 1996, 686–91.

1462. LESTER, G. A. The language of Old and Middle English poetry. Basingstoke: Macmillan; New York: St Martin's Press, 1996. pp. vii, 182.

1463. LEWIS, GILLIAN. The origins of New Zealand English: a report on work in progress. NZEJ (10) 1996, 25–30.

1464. LOTT, ERIC. White kids and no kids at all: languages of race in antebellum US working-class culture. *In* (pp. 175–211) **100**.

1465. McCULLY, C. B.; ANDERSON, J. J. (eds). English historical metrics. Cambridge; New York: CUP, 1996. pp. xi, 257.

1466. McMAHON, APRIL. Understanding language change. Cambridge; New York: CUP, 1994. pp. xi, 361. Rev. by Wim van der Wurff in SL (20:3) 1996, 680–6.

1467. MANABE, KAZUMI. 14 seiki eigo ni okeru shieki koubun no futeishi hyoushiki oyobi shieki doushi *do* to *make* no kyougou kankei. (The marker of the infinitive governed by causative verbs and the rivalry between causative *do* and *make* in fourteenth-century English.) SEL (73:1) 1996, 107–15.

1468. MARGHERITA, GAYLE. The romance of origins: language and sexual difference in Middle English literature. (Bibl. 1995, 1051.) Rev. by Paul Theiner in SAC (18) 1996, 247–51.

1469. MESTHRIE, RAJEND. *Imagint excusations*: missionary English in the nineteenth-century Cape Colony, South Africa. WorldE (15:2) 1996, 139–57.

1470. MILLWARD, C. M. A biography of the English language. (Bibl. 1989, 687.) Fort Worth, TX: Harcourt Brace, 1996. pp. xvi, 441. (Second ed.: first ed. 1989.) Rev. [of first ed.] by Ann W. Sharp in SECOLR (15:1) 1991, 116–17.

1471. MILROY, JAMES. Linguistic variation and change: on the historical sociolinguistics of English. (Bibl. 1995, 1055.) Rev. by Connie Eble in SECOLR (18:1) 1994, 100–1; by William A. Kretzschmar, Jr, in JEL (24:3) 1996, 259–61.

1472. MITCHELL, BRUCE. An invitation to Old English and Anglo-Saxon England. (Bibl. 1995, 1056.) Rev. by Belén Méndez Naya in SELIM (5) 1995, 142–6; by Jan Čermák in MÆ (65:1) 1996, 127–8.

1473. MONTES, CATALINA; FERNÁNDEZ ÁLVAREZ, Mª PILAR; RODRÍGUEZ, GUDELIA. El Inglés Antiguo en el marco de las lenguas germánicas occidentales. Madrid: Consejo Superior de Investigaciones Científicas, 1995. pp. 513. (Textos universitarios, 24.) Rev. by Jorge Luis Bueno Alonso in SELIM (5) 1995, 156–9.

1474. MUGGLESTONE, L. C. Alexander Ellis and the virtues of doubt. *In* (pp. 85–98) **114**.

1475. NEVALAINEN, TERTTU; RAUMOLIN-BRUNBERG, HELENA. Social stratification in Tudor English? *In* (pp. 303–26) **27**.

1476. NEWHAUSER, RICHARD G.; ALFORD, JOHN A. (eds). Literature and religion in the later Middle Ages: philological studies in honor of Siegfried Wenzel. *See* **61**.

1477. PENZL, HERBERT. Englisch: eine Sprachgeschichte nach Texten von 350 bis 1992: vom Nordisch-Westgermanischen zum Neuenglischen. (Bibl. 1995, 1058.) Rev. by Manfred Görlach in Ang (114:2) 1996, 252–4.

1478. POTTER, RUSSELL A. Chaucer and the authority of language: the politics and poetics of the vernacular in late medieval England. Assays (6) 1991, 73–91.

1479. ROBINSON, ORRIN W. Old English and its closest relatives: a survey of the earliest Germanic languages. (Bibl. 1995, 1059.) Rev. by Klaus Faiß in ZAA (41:1) 1993, 74–5.

1480. SCHENDL, HERBERT. Text types and code-switching in medieval and early modern English. VIEWS (5) 1996, 50–62.

1481. SMITH, JEREMY. An historical study of English: function, form and change. London; New York: Routledge, 1996. pp. xvii, 225.

1482. SMITH, JEREMY J.   A note on constrained linguistic variation in a North-West-Midlands Middle-English scribe. *See* **839**.

1483. SPROUSE, JAMES R.   Middle English dialect investigation and the Middle English manuscript: the case of the Bodleian Manuscript 6923. *See* **423**.

1484. STEIN, DIETER; TIEKEN-BOON VAN OSTADE, INGRID (eds). Towards a standard English, 1600–1800. (Bibl. 1994, 763.) Rev. by Klaus Hansen in ZAA (42:4) 1994, 376–8.

1485. SUNDBY, BERTIL; BJØRGE, ANNE KARI; HAUGLAND, KARI E. A dictionary of English normative grammar 1700–1800. (Bibl. 1994, 764.) Rev. by Josef Schmied in ZAA (41:4) 1993, 369–71.

1486. SWIDERSKI, RICHARD M.   The metamorphosis of English: versions of other languages. Westport, CT: Bergin & Garvey, 1996. pp. xii, 143.

1487. TIEKEN-BOON VAN OSTADE, INGRID.   Social network theory and eighteenth-century English: the case of Boswell. *In* (pp. 327–37) **27**.

1488. TORKAR, ROLAND.   Two Latin excerpts (*Sacramentarium Gregorianum*, and Isidore, *Sententiae*) with Old English translation. NQ (43:4) 1996, 389–94.

1489. TOSWELL, M. J.; TYLER, E. M. (eds).   Studies in English language and literature. 'Doubt wisely': papers in honour of E. G. Stanley. *See* **114**.

1490. TSURUSHIMA, H.   Domesday interpreters. Anglo-Norman Studies (18) 1995, 201–22.

1491. VOSS, MANFRED.   Altenglische Glossen aus MS British Library, Cotton Otho E.i. *See* **435**.

1492. WASWO, RICHARD.   Language and meaning in the Renaissance. (Bibl. 1989, 668.) Rev. by Jonathan Hart in CanRCL (18:2/3) 1991, 365–92.

1493. WEŁNA, JERZY.   The Middle English source of a present-day dialectal distinction. *In* (pp. 267–80) **68**.

1494. WRIGHT, LAURA.   About the evolution of Standard English. *In* (pp. 99–115) **114**.

HISTORY OF LINGUISTICS

1495. ANDRESEN, JULIE TETEL.   Linguistics in America, 1769–1924: a critical history. (Bibl. 1990, 807.) Rev. by Connie Eble in SECOLR (16:1) 1992, 107–9.

1496. CANNON, GARLAND; BRINE, KEVIN R. (eds).   Objects of enquiry: the life, contributions, and influences of Sir William Jones (1746–1794). New York; London: New York UP, 1995. pp. x, 185, (plates) 16.

1497. COLEMAN, JULIE.   English language: history of English linguistics. YWES (75) 1994, 8–11.

1498. HORGAN, A. D.   Johnson on language. (Bibl. 1995, 1078.) Rev. by John Wiltshire in ELN (34:1) 1996, 100–1.

1499. HUCK, GEOFFREY J.; GOLDSMITH, JOHN A.   Ideology and linguistic theory: Noam Chomsky and the Deep Structure debates. London; New York: Routledge, 1995. pp. x, 186. (History of linguistic thought.) Rev. by Georges Rebuschi in Bulletin de la Société de Linguistique de Paris (91:1) 1996, 30–4.

1500. ISERMAN, MICHAEL.   John Wallis on adjectives: the discovery of phrase structure in the *Grammatica Linguae Anglicanae* (1653). Historiographia Linguistica (23:1/2) 1996, 47–72.

1501. KNIEZSA, VERONIKA.   'Proper words in proper places': Jonathan Swift on language. *In* (pp. 182–93) **112**.

1502. KOERNER, KONRAD.   Publications by Vivian Salmon (1957–1996). Historiographia Linguistica (23:1/2) 1996, 243–54.

1503. LIUZZA, ROY M.   Orthography and historical linguistics. JEL (24:1) 1996, 25–44.

1504. MUGGLESTONE, L. C.   Alexander Ellis and the virtues of doubt. *In* (pp. 85–98) **114**.

1505. MURRAY, STEPHEN O.   Theory groups and the study of language in North America: a social history. Amsterdam; Philadelphia, PA: Benjamins, 1994. pp. xix, 594. (Amsterdam studies in the theory and history of linguistic science, III: Studies in the history of the language sciences, 69.) Rev. by Regna Darnell in Language in Society (25:3) 1996, 445–9.

1506. NATE, RICHARD.   The interjection as a grammatical category in John Wilkins' philosophical language. Historiographia Linguistica (23:1/2) 1996, 89–109.

1507. PIERINI, PATRIZIA.   Il descrittivismo inglese tra Ottocento e Novecento: Henry Sweet e Otto Jespersen. Annali anglistica (36:1–3) 1993, 155–72.

1508. RITT, NIKOLAUS.   Darwinising historical linguistics: applications of a dangerous idea. VIEWS (5) 1996, 24–47.

1509. SCHENDL, HERBERT.   Who does the copying? Some thoughts on N. Ritt's Darwinian historical linguistics. VIEWS (5) 1996, 47–9.

1510. SCHREYER, RÜDIGER.   The invisible hand in the history of language. *In* (pp. 309–23) **11**.

1511. SUBBIONDO, JOSEPH L.   From pragmatics to semiotics: the influence of John Wilkins' pulpit oratory on his philosophical language. Historiographia Linguistica (23:1/2) 1996, 111–22.

1512. TAYLOR, DENNIS.   Hardy's literary language and Victorian philology. (Bibl. 1995, 1085.) Rev. by Michael Thorpe in EngS (76:6) 1995, 589–90; by N. F. Blake in LangL (4:1) 1995, 67–9; by Phillip Mallett in YES (26) 1996, 301–2.

PHONETICS AND PHONOLOGY

HISTORICAL PHONETICS AND
PHONOLOGY OF ENGLISH

1513. BAMMESBERGER, ALFRED.   Der Kontrast /ae/ ~ /a/ im altenglischen Vokalsystem. Ang (114:2) 1996, 236–49.

1514. BEAL, JOAN.   The Jocks and the Geordies: modified standards in eighteenth-century pronouncing dictionaries. *In* (pp. 363–82) **27**.

1515. BERG, THOMAS.   Word-final voicing in the history of English: a case of unnatural phonology? EngS (76:2) 1995, 185–201.

1516. GREENE, SALLY.   Dissimilation of noncontiguous consonants in English. SECOLR (16:1) 1992, 41–70.

1517. HOGG, RICHARD M.   Tertiary stress in Old English: some reflections on explanatory inadequacy. *In* (pp. 3–12) **27**.

1518. JONES, CHARLES.   A language suppressed: the pronunciation of the Scots language in the 18th century. Edinburgh: Donald, 1995. pp. ix, 278. Rev. by Carol Percy in NQ (43:4) 1996, 492–3.

1519. KAMINASHI, KEIKO.   Stress theory and phonology in Old and Middle English. Tokyo: Liber Shuppan, 1996. pp. 316.

1520. KATAYAMA, YOSHIO, *et al.*   Eigo onseigaku no kiso – onhenka to *prosody* wo chuushin ni. (The essentials of phonetics of the English language: focusing on sound change and prosody.) Tokyo: Kenkyusha Shuppan, 1996. pp. x, 146.

1521. McMAHON, APRIL M. S.   On the use of the past to explain the present: the history of /r/ in English and Scots. *In* (pp. 73–89) **27**.

1522. MINKOVA, DONKA.   Verse structure as evidence for prosodic reconstruction in Old English. *In* (pp. 13–37) **27**.

1523. MUGGLESTONE, LYNDA.   Talking proper: the rise of accent as a social symbol. (Bibl. 1995, 1093.) Rev. by Carol Percy in NQ (43:4) 1996, 491–2.

1524. PETERS, ROBERT A.   Early modern English consonants. JEL (24:1) 1996, 45–51.

1525. PLATZER, HANS.   The temporary merger of OE *scitan* and *scyttan*; or, A case of harmless homophony. SAP (30) 1996, 69–82.

1526. RITT, NIKOLAUS.   Quantity adjustment: vowel lengthening and shortening in early Middle English. (Bibl. 1994, 809.) Rev. by André Crépin in Bulletin de la Société de Linguistique de Paris (91:2) 1996, 325–6.

1527. STOCKWELL, ROBERT P.   Old English short diphthongs and the theory of glide emergence. *In* (pp. 57–72) **27**.

1528. SUZUKI, SEIICHI.   On the syllable weight of -VC# in Old English: a metrical perspective. *In* (pp. 39–55) **27**.

1529. WEINSTOCK, HORST.   The rise of the letter-name *aitch*. EngS (76:4) 1995, 355–66.

PHONETICS AND PHONOLOGY OF
CONTEMPORARY ENGLISH

1530. ARISTIDES.   So to speak. ASch (65:1) 1996, 7–14.

1531. BAILEY, LUCILLE M.   The persistence of /mɪzrɪs/ among young speakers in Kentucky. SECOLR (20:1) 1996, 54–63.

1532. BAUER, LAURIE; HOLMES, JANET.   Getting into a flap! /t/ in New Zealand English. WorldE (15:1) 1996, 115–24.

1533. BAYARD, DONN; BARTLETT, CHRISTOPHER.   'You must be from Gorrre': attitudinal effects of Southland rhotic accents and speaker gender on NZE listeners and the question of NZE regional variation. Te Reo (39) 1996, 25–45.

1534. BERG, THOMAS.   On the relationship between voice and word class in English. ZAA (41:3) 1993, 198–212.

1535. BERKLEY, DEBORAH MILAN.   The OCP and gradient data. StudLS (24:1/2) 1994, 59–72.

1536. BURZIO, LUIGI.   Principles of English stress. (Bibl. 1994, 824.) Rev. by Klaus Hansen in ZAA (44:3) 1996, 268–70.

1537. BYRD, DANI.   Influences on articulatory timing in consonant sequences. JPhon (24:2) 1996, 209–44.

1538. —— TAN, CHENG CHENG.   Saying consonant clusters quickly. JPhon (24:2) 1996, 263–82.

1539. CAMERON, DEBORAH.   The accents of politics. CritQ (38:4) 1996, 93–6.

1540. CAMPBELL, ELIZABETH; GORDON, ELIZABETH.   'What do you fink?' Is New Zealand English losing its *th*? NZEJ (10) 1996, 40–6.

1541. CHING, MARVIN K. L.   GreaZy/greaSy and other /z/–/s/ choices in Southern pronunciation. JEL (24:4) 1996, 295–307.

1542. CHIRREY, DEBORAH.   Phonetic descriptions of Scottish accents: a historical perspective. SLang (14/15) 1995/96, 190–203.

1543. COLLINS, BEVERLEY; MEES, INGER M.   Spreading everywhere? How recent a phenomenon is glottalisation in Received Pronunciation? EWW (17:2) 1996, 175–87.

1544. COUPER-KUHLEN, ELIZABETH; SELTING, MARGARET (eds). Prosody in conversation: interactional studies. Cambridge; New York: CUP, 1996. pp. xii, 471. (Studies in interactional sociolinguistics, 12.)

1545. CRYSTAL, DAVID.   Phonaesthetically speaking. English Today (11:2) 1995, 8–12.

1546. DILLEY, L.; SHATTUCK-HUFNAGEL, S.; OSTENDORF, M.   Glottalization of word-initial vowels as a function of prosodic structure. JPhon (24:4) 1996, 423–44.

1547. FRASER, HELEN.   Guy-dance with pro-nun-see-ay-shon. English Today (12:3) 1996, 28–37.

1548. GAGLIARDI, CESARE.   Per un'analisi fonostilistica del testo inglese. Textus (2:1/2) 1989, 141–60.

1549. GIEGERICH, HEINZ J.   English phonology: an introduction. (Bibl. 1995, 1122.) Rev. by Klaus Hansen in ZAA (42:1) 1994, 65–7.

1550. GLAUSER, BEAT.   The sound /x/ in Scots. Études Écossaises (supp.) 1994, 19–37.

1551. HARRIS, JOHN.   On the trail of short *u*. EWW (17:1) 1996, 1–42.

1552. HAWKINS, OPAL W.   Syllable variation through deletion. SECOLR (18:2) 1994, 103–38.

1553. HINTON, VIRGINIA A.   Interlabial pressure during production of bilabial phones. JPhon (24:3) 1996, 337–49.

1554. HOLMES, JANET.   Losing voice: is final /z/ devoicing a feature of Maori English? WorldE (15:2) 1996, 193–205.

1555. —— Three chairs for New Zealand English: the EAR/AIR merger. English Today (11:3) 1995, 14–18.

1556. HUGHES, ARTHUR; TRUDGILL, PETER.   English accents and dialects: an introduction to social and regional varieties of English in the British Isles. (Bibl. 1992, 1305.) London; New York: Arnold, 1996. pp. 142. (Third ed.: first ed. 1979.)

1557. JOWITT, DAVID.   Queen Elizabeth's English: a response to Katie Wales. English Today (11:2) 1995, 13–15.

1558. JUN, JONGHO.   Gradient assimilation. JELL (42:4) 1996, 941–58.

1559. KINGSTON, JOHN; BECKMAN, MARY E. (eds).   Between the grammar and the physics of speech. (Bibl. 1995, 1140.) Rev. by Scott Meredith in CompLing (18:3) 1992, 357–9.

1560. KOBAYASHI, YASUHIDE.   Eigo kyousei-ron. (Essays on stress in the English language.) Kyoto: Kyoto Shugakusha, 1996. pp. iv, 242.

1561. MACLAGAN, MARGARET; GORDON, ELIZABETH.   The changing sound of New Zealand English. New Zealand Speech-Language Therapists' Journal (50) 1995, 32–40.

1562. —— —— Women's role in sound change: the case of two New Zealand closing diphthongs. NZEJ (10) 1996, 5–9.

1563. MACLAGAN, MARGARET A.; GORDON, ELIZABETH. Out of the AIR and into the EAR: another view of the New Zealand diphthong merger. LVC (8:1) 1996, 125–47.

1564. MORRISON, SHARON R.   A re-examination of cardinal vowels and auditory equidistance. StudLS (23:1) 1993, 117–29.

1565. MORRISSON, MARK.   Performing the pure voice: elocution, verse recitation, and Modernist poetry in prewar London. Modernism/Modernity (3:3) 1996, 25–50.

1566. MOSEY, BRYAN; CHAMONIKOLASOVÁ, JANA.   Nucleus position and tone unit length. Brno Studies in English (22) 1996, 15–22.

1567. MOSSOP, JONATHAN W.   Markedness and fossilization in the interlanguage phonology of Brunei English. WorldE (15:2) 1996, 171–82.

1568. NOLAN, FRANCIS; HOLST, TARA; KÜHNERT, BARBARA. Modelling (s) to (ʃ) accommodation in English. JPhon (24:1) 1996, 113–37.

1569. ONO, SHOICHI.   Eigo onsei no kiso. (The basis of English phonetics.) Tokyo: Liber Shuppan, 1996. pp. x, 174.

1570. PEDERSON, LEE.   A Southern phonology. SECOLR (17:1) 1993, 36–54.

1571. PÖDÖR, DÓRA.   The phonology of Scottish Gaelic loanwords in Lowland Scots. SLang (14/15) 1995/96, 174–89.

1572. RASTALL, PAUL.   Some shifting vowels and stress patterns in English. English Today (12:1) 1996, 56–7.

1573. ROBERTSON, SHELLEY.   Maori English and the bus-driving listener: a study of ethnic identification and phonetic cues. WWPL (8) 1996, 54–69.

1574. RYDLAND, KURT.   The Orton Corpus and Northumbrian phonology: the material from Bamburgh and Bellingham (Northumberland). EngS (76:6) 1995, 547–86.

1575. SABINO, ROBIN; HAAK, NANCY.   Distinguishing questions from statements by prosodic cues alone: 'You didn't hear what I meant.' SECOLR (19:2) 1995, 151–70.

1576. SANTA ANA A., OTTO.   Sonority and syllable structure in Chicano English. LVC (8:1) 1996, 63–89. (Los Angeles Chicano.)

1577. SIMO BOBDA, AUGUSTIN.   Aspects of Cameroon English phonology. New York; Frankfurt; Bern; Paris: Lang, 1994. pp. xxv, 427. (European univ. studies, XIV: Anglo-Saxon language and literature, 272.) Rev. by Manfred Görlach in EWW (17:2) 1996, 314–15.

1578. SMIT, UTE. Who speaks like that? Accent recognition and language attitudes. SA Journal of Linguistics (14:3) 1996, 100–7.

1579. SOUTHARD, BRUCE. An acoustical analysis of Raven I. McDavid, Jr's pronunciation of vowel norms for the *Linguistic Atlas of the United States and Canada*. JEL (24:4) 1996, 332–42.

1580. TAKEBAYASHI, SHIGERU. Eigo onseigaku. (English phonetics.) Tokyo: Kenkyusha, 1996. pp. xvi, 518.

1581. TAYLOR, BEN. Gay men, femininity and /t/ in New Zealand English. WWPL (8) 1996, 70–92.

1582. TAYLOR, DAVID S. Demystifying word stress. English Today (12:4) 1996, 46–52.

1583. TENCH, PAUL. The intonation systems of English. London; New York: Cassell, 1996. pp. ix, 160.

1584. TIEDE, MARK K. An MRI-based study of pharyngeal volume contrasts in Akan and English. JPhon (24:4) 1996, 399–421.

1585. TRASK, R. L. A dictionary of phonetics and phonology. London; New York: Routledge, 1996. pp. x, 424.

1586. VAN LEYDEN, KLASKE; VAN HEUVEN, VINCENT J. Lexical stress and spoken word recognition: Dutch *vs* English. Linguistics in The Netherlands (1996) 159–70.

1587. WALES, KATIE. A response to David Jowitt's response … . English Today (11:2) 1995, 16–17.

1588. YANG, BYUNGGON. A comparative study of American English and Korean vowels produced by male and female speakers. JPhon (24:2) 1996, 245–61.

SPELLING, PUNCTUATION, HANDWRITING

1589. ANON. Merriam-Webster's notebook guide to punctuation. Springfield, MA: Merriam-Webster, 1996. pp. 61.

1590. ARN, MARY-JO. On punctuating medieval literary texts. *See* **561**.

1591. AYAFOR, MIRIAM. An orthography for Kamtok. English Today (12:4) 1996, 53–7.

1592. BERGIEN, ANGELIKA. On the historical background of English punctuation. ZAA (42:3) 1994, 243–50.

1593. CARNEY, EDWARD. A survey of English spelling. (Bibl. 1994, 887.) Rev. by Klaus Hansen in ZAA (44:3) 1996, 266–8.

1594. DANIELS, PETER T.; BRIGHT, WILLIAM (eds). The world's writing systems. Oxford; New York: OUP, 1996. pp. xlv, 920. Rev. by John A. C. Greppin in TLS, 19 Apr. 1996, 13.

1595. DUMVILLE, DAVID N. English square minuscule script: the mid-century phases. *See* **348**.

1596. ERARD, MICHAEL. Colons descending: an interim assessment. English Today (12:4) 1996, 43–5.

1597. GRAUSTEIN, GOTTFRIED. Zu Swifts Schreibvarianten: anstelle einer Fußnote. ZAA (42:4) 1994, 327–31.

1598. GREETHAM, D. C. Parallel texts. *See* **660**.

1599. KENYON, RALPH. On the use of quotation marks. ERGS (51:1) 1994, 47–50.

1600. KNIEZSA, VERONIKA. The orthography of Older Scots: the manuscripts of Barbour's *The Bruce*. In (pp. 167–82) **11**.

1601. LIUZZA, ROY M.   Orthography and historical linguistics. *See* **1503**.

1602. MICHELSEN, MARTINA.   Weg vom Work – zum Gedankenstrich: zur stilistischen Funktion eines Satzzeichens in der englischen Literatur des 17. und 18. Jahrhunderts. Munich: Fink, 1993. pp. 283. (Münchener Studien zur neueren englischen Literatur, 6.) Rev. by Wolfgang Hörner in Shandean (7) 1995, 114–18.

1603. MITTON, ROGER.   English spelling and the computer. *See* **1189**.

1604. PARKES, M. B.   Pause and effect: an introduction to the history of punctuation in the West. (Bibl. 1995, 1185.) Rev. by Anna Lia Gaffuri in Aevum (68:2) 1994, 477–8; by Paul Saenger in AEB (9:1/2) 1995, 49–51; by D. C. Greetham in Text (Ann Arbor) (9) 1996, 408–29.

1605. PRESTON, JEAN F.; YEANDLE, LAETITIA.   English handwriting, 1400–1650: an introductory manual. (Bibl. 1993, 847.) Rev. by D. C. Greetham in Text (Ann Arbor) (9) 1996, 408–29.

1606. ROOM, ADRIAN.   Troubled *Times*. *See* **1351**.

1607. TREIP, MINDELE.   Comments on Milton's punctuation. From a panel devoted to editing at the Fifth International Milton Symposium. MQ (30:4) 1996, 171–3.

GRAMMAR

MORPHOLOGY OF CONTEMPORARY ENGLISH

1608. BAAYEN, HAARALD; SPROAT, RICHARD. Estimating lexical priorities for low-frequency morphologically ambiguous forms. *See* **1134**.

1609. BAUER, LAURIE. Derivational paradigms. Yearbook of Morphology 1996, 243–56.

1610. —— BAUER, INGRID. Word-formation in the playground. AS (71:1) 1996, 111–12. (Diminutives.)

1611. BERG, THOMAS. On the relationship between voice and word class in English. *See* **1534**.

1612. BÖRJARS, KERSTI; VINCENT, NIGEL; CHAPMAN, CAROL. Paradigms, periphrases and pronominal inflection: a feature-based account. Yearbook of Morphology 1996, 155–80.

1613. FISCHER, OLGA; VAN DER WURFF, WIM. English language: morphology. YWES (75) 1994, 31–4.

1614. GRAM-ANDERSEN, KNUD. The ever-whirling wheel: a study in word formation. (Bibl. 1995, 1198.) Rev. by Bent Sunesen in EngS (77:3) 1996, 300–3.

1615. HELM, NELSON, JR. Nouning the verb. ERGS (52:3) 1995, 348–9.

1616. HLADKÝ, JOSEF. Zdvojování jako slovotvorný prostředek v češtině a angličtině. (Reduplication in Czech and English.) ČMF (78:2) 1996, 79–87.

1617. JAMES, FRANCIS. Semantics of the English subjunctive. (Bibl. 1987, 1040.) Rev. by Peter A. Machonis in SECOLR (15:1) 1991, 108–10.

1618. MARSLEN-WILSON, WILLIAM; ZHOU, XIAOLIN; FORD, MIKE. Morphology, modality, and lexical architecture. Yearbook of Morphology 1996, 117–34.

1619. MEIJS, WILLEM. Morphology and lexis in a computational setting. *See* **1186**.

1620. NASH, LÉA. The internal ergative subject hypothesis. NELS (26) 1996, 195–209.

1621. PEARSON, BRUCE L. The neglect of morphology and the lexicon. SECOLR (17:2) 1993, 142–64.

1622. PLAG, INGO. Selectional restrictions in English suffixation revisited: a reply to Fabb (1988). Linguistics (34:4) 1996, 769–98. (*Refers to* bibl. 1988, 595.)

1623. PRAUSE, THOMAS. Zum Problem Wortbildung und Übersetzung: dargestellt an den Modellen *breakout* und *toxic-waste dump*. ZAA (42:4) 1994, 317–26.

1624. STUMP, GREGORY T. Template morphology and inflectional morphology. Yearbook of Morphology 1996, 217–41.

1625. VIERECK, WOLFGANG. Some notes on possessives. *In* (pp. 325–31) **11**.

HISTORICAL MORPHOLOGY OF ENGLISH

1626. ANSHEN, FRANK; ARONOFF, MARK. Morphology in real time. Yearbook of Morphology 1996, 9–12.

1627. COLMAN, FRAN. Morphology: Old and Middle English – derivational and inflectional. *In* (pp. 3–28) **68**.

1628. DALTON-PUFFER, CHRISTIANE. The French influence on Middle English morphology: a corpus-based study of derivation. Berlin; New York: Mouton de Gruyter, 1996. pp. xiii, 284. (Topics in English linguistics, 20.)

1629. GÖRLACH, MANFRED. Morphological standardization: the strong verb in Scots. *In* (pp. 161–81) **27**.

1630. KASTOVSKY, DIETER. Categorial restructuring of the weak verbs in late Old English and Middle English. *In* (pp. 29–45) **68**.

1631. —— Verbal derivation in English: a historical survey; or, Much ado about nothing. *In* (pp. 93–117) **27**.

1632. KRYGIER, MARCIN. Plural markers of the Old English nouns of relationship in the two manuscripts of Laȝamon's *Brut*. *In* (pp. 47–68) **68**.

1633. MAZZON, GABRIELLA. The language of emotions in Shakespeare's poems: an aspect of archaism and innovation in Elizabethan English word-formation. Textus (8:2) 1995, 281–93.

1634. NUÑEZ PERTEJO, PALOMA. On the origin and history of the English prepositional type *a-hunting*: a corpus-based study. RAEI (9) 1996, 105–17.

1635. OGURA, MICHIKO. The interchangeability of Old English verbal prefixes. ASE (24) 1995, 67–93.

1636. SCHENDL, HERBERT. The 3rd-person plural present indicative in early modern English – variation and linguistic contact. *In* (pp. 143–60) **27**.

1637. WEŁNA, JERZY. English historical morphology. Warsaw: Univ. of Warsaw, 1996. pp. 237.

SINGLE MORPHEMES

1638. *-aholic*] GOZZI, RAYMOND, JR. Confessions of a metaphoraholic. ERGS (52:1) 1995, 51–4.

1639. *cyber-*] NAGEL, RAINER. Das Wortbildungsmorphem *cyber*. ZAA (42:2) 1994, 163–70.

1640. *-ie*] NURMI, TARU. *Aussies* and *mozzies*: on the hypocoristic/diminutive suffix *-y/ie* in Australian English. New Courant (5) 1996, 85–97.

1641. *-s*] OGURA, MIEKO; WANG, WILLIAM S.-Y. Snowball effect in lexical diffusion: the development of *-s* in the third-person singular present indicative in English. *In* (pp. 119–41) **27**.

1642. *-s's*] BATTISTELLA, EDWIN. *s's*. (Possessive form for words ending in *s*.) SECOLR (17:2) 1993, 127–41.

1643. *-wif*] MENZER, MELINDA J. *Aglæcwif* (*Beowulf* 1259a): implications for *-wif* compounds, Grendel's mother, and other *aglæcan*. ELN (34:1) 1996, 1–6.

1644. *-y*] NURMI, TARU. *Aussies* and *mozzies*: on the hypocoristic/diminutive suffix *-y/ie* in Australian English. *See* **1640**.

SYNTAX OF CONTEMPORARY ENGLISH

1645. ABNEY, LISA. Pronoun shift in oral folklore, personal experience and literary narratives; or, 'What's up with *you*?' SECOLR (20:2) 1996, 203–26.

1646. ACETO, MICHAEL. Syntactic innovation in a Caribbean creole:

the Bastimentos variety of Panamanian Creole English. EWW (17:1) 1996, 43–61.

1647. AHULU, SAMUEL. Variation in the use of complex verbs in international English. English Today (11:2) 1995, 28–34.

1648. ALLERTON, D. J. 'Headless' noun phrases: how to describe the exceptional findings. EngS (76:1) 1995, 81–90. (Problems of English grammar, 4.)

1649. AZZARO, GABRIELE. Semantic syntax: English phrasal verbs. Textus (5) 1992, 83–110.

1650. BAKIR, MURTADHA J. Notes on passive and pseudo-intransitive constructions in English and Arabic. PSiCL (31) 1996, 39–49.

1651. BALTIN, MARK; POSTAL, PAUL M. More on reanalysis - hypotheses. LI (27:1) 1996, 127–45.

1652. BENNETT-KASTOR, TINA L. Anaphora, nonanaphora, and the generic use of pronouns by children. AS (71:3) 1996, 285–301.

1653. BERG, THOMAS. On the relationship between voice and word class in English. *See* **1534**.

1654. BERGVALL, VICTORIA L. Topic ... comment: Humpty Dumpty does syntax: through the looking-glass, and what Alice found there. Natural Language and Linguistic Theory (14:2) 1996, 433–43.

1655. BHATT, RAKESH M. On the grammar of code-switching. WorldE (15:3) 1996, 369–75.

1656. BITTNER, MARIA; HALE, KEN. The structural determination of case and agreement. LI (27:1) 1996, 1–68.

1657. BÖRJARS, KERSTI; VINCENT, NIGEL; CHAPMAN, CAROL. Paradigms, periphrases and pronominal inflection: a feature-based account. *See* **1612**.

1658. BOŠKOVIĆ, ŽELJKO. Selection and the categorial statue of infinitival complements. Natural Language and Linguistic Theory (14:2) 1996, 269–304.

1659. BRINTON, LAUREL J. Attitudes toward increasing segmentalization: complex and phrasal verbs in English. JEL (24:3) 1996, 186–205.

1660. BROWNING, M. A. CP recursion and *that-t* effects. LI (27:2) 1996, 237–55.

1661. CHALKER, SYLVIA. English grammar: word by word. Walton-on-Thames: Nelson, 1990. pp. 448. Rev. by John Algeo in IJL (8:2) 1995, 126–42.

1662. —— The little Oxford dictionary of English grammar. Oxford; New York: OUP, 1996. pp. x, 266.

1663. COLLINS, PETER C. *Get*-passives in English. WorldE (15:1) 1996, 43–56.

1664. CONRAD, BENT; SCHOUSBOE, STEEN. Meaning and English grammar. Copenhagen: Dept of English, Univ. of Copenhagen, 1992. pp. 119. (Pubs on English themes, 19.) (Second ed.: first ed. 1989.)

1665. COWIE, A. P.; HOWARTH, PETER. Phraseology – a select bibliography. IJL (9:1) 1996, 38–51.

1666. CRAIG, WILLIAM LANE. Tense and the new B-theory of language. Philosophy (71:275) 1996, 5–26.

1667. CRITTENDEN, CHARLOTTE C. 'Broad reference' in pronouns: handbooks *versus* professional writers. PADS (78) 1994, 115–22.

1668. DAVIDSON, GEORGE (comp.). Chambers guide to grammar and usage. Edinburgh: Chambers, 1996. pp. 528.

1669. DECLERCK, RENAAT.   Tense choice in adverbial *when* clauses. Linguistics (34:2) 1996, 225–61.

1670. DEPRAETERE, ILSE.   Foregrounding in English relative clauses. Linguistics (34:4) 1996, 699–731.

1671. DIK, SIMON C.   Functional grammar in Prolog: an integrated implementation for English, French, and Dutch. *See* **1149**.

1672. DOHERTY, MONIKA.   Passive perspectives; different preferences in English and German: a result of parameterized processing. Linguistics (34:3) 1996, 591–643.

1673. ESSER, JÜRGEN.   Zur Terminologie und Analyse von nominalen *ing*-Sätzen ('Gerundien'). ZAA (42:1) 1994, 21–6.

1674. FISCHER, OLGA; VAN DER WURFF, WIM.   English language: syntax. YWES (75) 1994, 34–74.

1675. FLANIGAN, BEVERLY OLSON; INAL, EMEL.   Object relative pronoun use in native and non-native English: a variable rule analysis. LVC (8:2) 1996, 203–26.

1676. FUJITA, KOJI.   Double objects, causatives, and derivational economy. LI (27:1) 1996, 146–73.

1677. GELUYKENS, RONALD.   From discourse process to grammatical construction: on left-dislocation in English. (Bibl. 1995, 1273.) Rev. by Betty J. Birner in SL (20:2) 1996, 455–65.

1678. GHOMESHI, JILA; RITTER, ELIZABETH.   Binding, possessives, and the structure of DP. NELS (26) 1996, 87–100. (English and Persian.)

1679. GÓMEZ GONZÁLEZ, MARÍA.   Theme: topic or discourse framework? Misc (17) 1996, 123–40.

1680. GORRELL, ROBERT.   The future of past tenses. English Today (11:4) 1995, 25–7.

1681. GREENBAUM, SIDNEY.   The Oxford English grammar. Oxford; New York: OUP, 1996. pp. xv, 652. Rev. by Hugh Kenner in LRB (18:14) 1996, 16; by Laurence Urdang in Verbatim (23:1) 1996, 19–22.

1682. —— NELSON, GERALD.   Positions of adverbial clauses in British English. WorldE (15:1) 1996, 69–81.

1683. GRIMSHAW, JANE B.   Argument structure. (Bibl. 1990, 958.) Rev. by Edwin Battistella in SECOLR (16:1) 1992, 104–7.

1684. GROSU, ALEXANDER.   The proper analysis of 'missing-P' free relative constructions. LI (27:2) 1996, 257–93.

1685. HAZEN, KIRK.   Dialect affinity and subject–verb concord: the Appalachian–Outer Banks connection. SECOLR (20:1) 1996, 25–53.

1686. HERBST, THOMAS; ROE, IAN.   How obligatory are obligatory complements? An alternative approach to the categorization of subjects and other complements in valency grammar. EngS (77:2) 1996, 179–99.

1687. HERRIMAN, JENNIFER; SEPPÄNEN, AIMO.   What is an indirect object? EngS (77:5) 1996, 484–500.

1688. HISLOP, LINDSAY.   English relative clauses and the NP accessibility hierarchy. SECOLR (15:2) 1991, 169–82.

1689. HONEY, JOHN.   A new rule for the Queen and I? English Today (11:4) 1995, 3–8.

1690. HORNSTEIN, NORBERT.   As time goes by: tense and universal grammar. (Bibl. 1990, 965.) Rev. by Mary Dalrymple in CompLing (17:3) 1991, 337–9.

1691. HUDSON, RICHARD.   English word grammar. (Bibl. 1995, 1191.) Rev. by Lynne J. Cahill in CompLing (18:1) 1992, 92–4.

1692. ILSON, ROBERT. *A(n)*-dropping. English Today (11:1) 1995, 42–4.

1693. JACOBS, RODERICK A. English syntax: a grammar for English language professionals. (Bibl. 1995, 1291.) Rev. by Joe Trotta in MS (90:1) 1996, 112–13.

1694. JACOBSSON, BENGT. A new look at 'predicative-only' adjectives in English. JEL (24:3) 1996, 206–19.

1695. JUCKER, ANDREAS (ed.). The noun phrase in English: its structure and variability. Heidelberg: Winter, 1993. pp. 180. (Anglistik & Englischunterricht, 49.) Rev. by Isabel Karely León Pérez in Atlantis (17:1/2) 1995, 392–4.

1696. KAPLAN, JEFFREY P. English grammar: principles and facts. Englewood Cliffs, NJ; London: Prentice Hall, 1989. pp. x, 358. Rev. by Alan Manning in American Dialect Society Teaching Newsletter (Sept. 1993) 3–4 (supplement to NADS (25:3) 1993).

1697. KARSTADT, ANGELA. Relative markers in Swedish-American English: evidence for a contact language phenomenon? AS (71:1) 1996, 27–48.

1698. KATHMAN, DAVID. Infinitival complements in a Minimalist theory of grammar. StudLS (24:1/2) 1994, 293–301.

1699. KIM, BYONG-KWON. VP-internal subject hypothesis and ATB gap parallelism. StudLS (24:1/2) 1994, 318–32. (English–Korean.)

1700. KIM, SEONG WOOK. Passivizability: a functional account. JELLC (38:1) 1996, 321–48.

1701. KINOSHITA, HIROTOSHI. Eigo no doushi – katachi to kokoro. (English verbs: their forms and meanings.) (Bibl. 1991, 1052.) Fukuoka: Kyushu UP, 1996. pp. viii, 270. (Revised ed.: first ed. 1991.)

1702. KIRSTEN, HANS. Ein Plädoyer für das Gerundium. ZAA (42:1) 1994, 16–20.

1703. KNOTT, ALISTAIR; MELLISH, CHRIS. A feature-based account of the relations signalled by sentence and clause connectives. Language and Speech (39:2/3) 1996, 143–83.

1704. KUDRNÁČOVÁ, NADĚŽDA. The verbs *fall, sink, sag* and *droop* in body part movement. Brno Studies in English (22) 1996, 55–62.

1705. LEVIN, BETH. English verb classes and alternations: a preliminary investigation. (Bibl. 1995, 1193.) Rev. by Harold Somers in CompLing (20:3) 1994, 495–7.

1706. MAHOOTIAN, SHAHRZAD. Code-switching and universal constraints: evidence from Farsi/English. WorldE (15:3) 1996, 377–84.

1707. MAIR, CHRISTIAN; HUNDT, MARIANNE. Why is the progressive becoming more frequent in English? A corpus-based investigation of language change in progress. ZAA (43:2) 1995, 111–22.

1708. MALONE, JOSEPH L. Referring expressions in bound position: infraction of Principle C of the binding theory. GL (33:1/2) 1993, 1–56.

1709. MEYER, CHARLES F. Coordinate structures in English. WorldE (15:1) 1996, 29–41.

1710. MEYER, MATTHIAS. Das englische Perfekt: grammatischer Status, Semantik und Zusammenspiel mit dem Progressive. (Bibl. 1994, 1019.) Rev. by Peter Lucko in ZAA (41:3) 1993, 265–8.

1711. MINDT, DIETER. Zeitbezug im Englischen: eine didaktische Grammatik des englischen Futurs. (Cf. bibl. 1994, 1022, where ·title misspelt.) Rev. by Hans Kirsten in ZAA (42:2) 1994, 176–8.

1712. MÜLLER, GEREON; STERNEFELD, WOLFGANG. Ā-chain

formation and economy of derivation. LI (27:3) 1996, 480–511. (English and German.)

1713. MURATA, YUZABURO; NARITA, KEIICHI.   Eigo no bunpou. (English grammar.) Tokyo: Taishukan, 1996. pp. xii, 172. (Take-off series of English linguistics, 2.)

1714. MURPHY, M. LYNNE.   Discourse markers and sentential syntax. StudLS (23:1) 1993, 163–7.

1715. NAGLE, STEPHEN J.   Inferential change and syntactic modality in English. New York; Frankfurt; Bern; Paris: Lang, 1989. pp. 135. (Bamberger Beiträge zur englischen Sprachwissenschaft, 23.) (Cf. bibl. 1987, 1154.) Rev. by Thomas Nunnally in SECOLR (15:1) 1991, 114–16.

1716. NAPOLI, DONNA JO.   Predication theory: a case study for indexing theory. (Bibl. 1989, 814.) Rev. by Melita Staurou-Sephake in Glossologia (9/10) 1990/91, 293–309.

1717. NASH, LÉA.   The internal ergative subject hypothesis. *See* **1620**.

1718. OBA, YOKIO.   Yuui kouka to saishou renketsu jouken. (Superiority effects and minimal link condition.) SEL (73:1) 1996, 89–106. (On *wh*-phrases.)

1719. OBERLANDER, JON; DELIN, JUDY.   The function and interpretation of reverse *wh*-clefts in spoken discourse. Language and Speech (39:2/3) 1996, 185–227.

1720. OGIHARA, TOSHIYUKI.   Tense, attitudes, and scope. Dordrecht; London: Kluwer, 1996. pp. xiv, 278. (Studies in linguistics and philosophy, 58.) Rev. by Henriëtte de Swart in Linguistic Analysis (26:3/4) 1996, 252–9.

1721. OJEA LÓPEZ, ANA I.   The distribution of adverbial phrases in English. Atlantis (17:1/2) 1995, 181–206.

1722. OLSEN, MARI BROMAN.   The semantics and pragmatics of lexical aspect features. StudLS (24:1/2) 1994, 361–75.

1723. PALACIOS MARTÍNEZ, IGNACIO MIGUEL.   Notes on the use and meaning of negation in contemporary written English. Atlantis (17:1/2) 1995, 207–27.

1724. PALANCAR, ENRIQUE.   Effectors, more than mere instruments. EIUC (4) 1996, 67–90.

1725. PALMER, F. R. (ed.).   Grammar and meaning: essays in honour of Sir John Lyons. Cambridge; New York: CUP, 1995. pp. xiii, 265.

1726. PAPI, MARCELLA BERTUCCELLI.   Determining the proposition expressed by an utterance: the role of 'domain adverbs'. Textus (5) 1992, 123–40.

1727. PELYVAS, PETER.   Subjectivity in English: generative grammar *versus* the cognitive theory of epistemic grounding. New York; Frankfurt; Bern; Paris: Lang, 1996. pp. 208. (MetaLinguistica, 3.)

1728. PETERS, PAM.   Comparative insights into comparison. WorldE (15:1) 1996, 57–67. (British and Australian English.)

1729. POSTMA, GERTJAN; ROORYCK, JOHAN.   Modality and possession in NPs. NELS (26) 1996, 273–87.

1730. PROGOVAC, LJILJANA.   Negative and positive polarity: a binding approach. Cambridge; New York: CUP, 1994. pp. xii, 168. (Cambridge studies in linguistics, 68.) Rev. by Jack Hoeksema in SL (20:1) 1996, 196–207.

1731. PULMAN, STEPHEN G.   Unification encodings of grammatical notations. *See* **1196**.

1732. RAAB-FISCHER, ROSWITHA.   Löst der Genitiv die *of*-phrase ab?

Eine korpusgestützte Studie zum Sprachwandel im heutigen Englisch. ZAA (43:2) 1995, 123–32.

1733. RASTALL, P. R. A functional view of English grammar. Lewiston, NY; Lampeter: Mellen Press, 1995. pp. 155.

1734. RASTALL, PAUL. Definite article or no definite article? English Today (11:2) 1995, 37–9.

1735. ROHDENBURG, GÜNTER. On the replacement of finite complement clauses by infinitives in English. EngS (76:4) 1995, 367–88.

1736. ROSEN, SARA THOMAS. Events and verb classification. Linguistics (34:2) 1996, 191–223.

1737. RUDANKO, JUHANI. Prepositions and complement clauses: a syntactic and semantic study of verbs governing prepositions and complement clauses in present-day English. Albany: New York State UP, 1996. pp. viii, 211. (SUNY series in linguistics.)

1738. SAFIR, KEN. Derivation, representation, and resumption: the domain of weak crossover. LI (27:2) 1996, 313–39.

1739. SALMI-TOLONEN, TARJA. If X then Y: some observations on conditionals in English legislative discourse. *In* (pp. 265–75) Natalia Baschmakoff, Arja Rosenholm, Hannu Tommola (eds), Aspekteja. Tampere: Univ. of Tampere, 1996. pp. i, 381. (Slavica Tamperensia, 5.)

1740. SEDLEY, DOROTHY. Anatomy of English: an introduction to the structure of Standard American English. New York: St Martin's Press, 1990. pp. xviii, 281. Rev. by Lynn M. Berk in SECOLR (15:2) 1991, 217–18.

1741. SEPPÄNEN, AIMO; BERGH, GUNNAR. Subject extraction in English: some problems of interpretation. SAP (30) 1996, 45–67.

1742. SHELSTAD, LORRAINE. Agrammatism and functional categories. CWPL (14) 1991, 67–83.

1743. SHIMOJI, YOSHIO. Eigogaku no mado – eigo tougoron gaisetsu. (A window on English linguistics: an introduction to the syntax of the English language.) Tokyo: Eihosha, 1996. pp. viii, 246.

1744. SOMMER, ELISABETH. Prepositions in Black English vernacular. SECOLR (15:2) 1991, 183–99.

1745. STALMASZCZYK, PIOTR. Theta roles and the theory of theta-binding. PSiCL (31) 1996, 97–110.

1746. TAJSNER, PRZEMYSŁAW. Some notes on adjunction to VP. PSiCL (31) 1996, 51–63.

1747. TAYLOR, JOHN R. Possessives in English: an exploration in cognitive grammar. Oxford: Clarendon Press; New York: OUP, 1996. pp. xi, 368.

1748. THIEDE, RALF. The 'possessive case' in English: a postmortem. SECOLR (20:1) 1996, 101–16.

1749. THOMAS, LINDA. Beginning syntax. Oxford; Cambridge, MA: Blackwell, 1993. pp. x, 209. Rev. by Bas Aarts in Ang (114:1) 1996, 91–4.

1750. THOMPSON, ELLEN. The syntax and semantics of temporal adjunct clauses. StudLS (24:1/2) 1994, 419–28.

1751. TORSELLO, CAROL TAYLOR. If we were to take lexical structure seriously … : implications for the hypotaxis/embedding distinction. Textus (9:1) 1996, 107–19.

1752. TRACY, ROSEMARY (ed.). Who climbs the grammar-tree? Essays for David Reibel's 60th birthday. (Bibl. 1995, 1346.) Rev. by Elly van Gelderen in EngS (76:3) 1995, 287–8.

1753. URA, HIROYUKI. On the structure of 'double objects' and certain differences between British and American English. SEL (72:2) 1996, 269–85.

1754.   van Gelderen, Elly.   Parameterizing agreement features in Arabic, Bantu languages, and varieties of English. Linguistics (34:4) 1996, 753–67.

1755.   Viereck, Wolfgang.   Some notes on possessives. *In* (pp. 325–31) **11**.

1756.   Virtanen, Tuija.   Discourse functions of adverbial placement in English: clause-initial adverbials of time and place in narratives and procedural place descriptions. (Bibl. 1995, 1354.) Rev. by Monika Fludernik in LangL (4:1) 1995, 64–7.

1757.   von Bergen, Anke; von Bergen, Karl.   Negative Polarität im Englischen. (Bibl. 1993, 981.) Rev. by Jacob Hoeksema in SL (20:2) 1996, 473–76.

1758.   Warner, Anthony R.   English auxiliaries: structure and history. (Bibl. 1995, 1357.) Rev. by André Crépin in Bulletin de la Société de Linguistique de Paris (91:2) 1996, 322–5; by Jeremy J. Smith in Ang (114:2) 1996, 250–2.

1759.   Yang, Yonglin.   The cooperative principle and the functional transition in English verbs. SAP (30) 1996, 97–105.

1760.   Yoon, James Hye Suk.   Nominal gerund phrases in English as phrasal zero derivations. Linguistics (34:2) 1996, 329–56.

1761.   Zhou, Kaixin.   A modest view on the subjunctive mood. EngS (77:1) 1996, 92–6.

HISTORICAL SYNTAX OF ENGLISH

1762.   Arnold, Mark D.   A unified analysis of P-stranding, ECM, and *that*-deletion, and the subsequent loss of verb movement in English. NELS (26) 1996, 1–15.

1763.   Ball, Catherine N.   A diachronic study of relative markers in spoken and written English. LVC (8:2) 1996, 227–58.

1764.   Camiciotti, Gabriella Del Lungo.   The modal system in late Middle English: the case of Capgrave's *Chronicle*. Textus (2:1/2) 1989, 207–16.

1765.   Curzan, Anne.   Third person pronouns in *The Peterborough Chronicle*. NM (97:3) 1996, 301–14.

1766.   de la Cruz, Juan.   Complex locative expressions in Middle English. A study of structural complexity and ambivalence. *In* (pp. 207–32) **68**.

1767.   —— Saameño, Emilio.   The Middle English prepositional passive: analogy and GB. NM (97:2) 1996, 169–86.

1768.   Denison, David.   The case of the unmarked pronoun. *In* (pp. 287–99) **27**.

1769.   Escribano, José Luis G.   On disfunctional [*sic*] syntactic change in early Modern English: the case of the 'group genitive'; or, Why genitives no longer appear with postnominal restrictive adjuncts. Atlantis (17:1/2) 1995, 45–87.

1770.   Fanego, Teresa.   On the historical development of English retrospective verbs. NM (97:1) 1996, 71–9.

1771.   Fischer, Olga.   Verbal complementation in early ME: how do the infinitives fit in? *In* (pp. 247–70) **27**.

1772. FRISCH, STEFAN. Reanalysis precedes syntactic change: evidence from Middle English. StudLS (24:1/2) 1994, 187–201.

1773. IYEIRI, YOKO. Negative contraction and syntactic conditions in Middle English verse. EngS (76:5) 1995, 424–33.

1774. KOHNEN, THOMAS. Ausbreitungsmuster syntaktischer Standardisierung bei der Entwicklung englischer Partizipialkonstruktionen (Partizip Präsens) 1450–1700. Ang (114:2) 1996, 154–201.

1775. KOOPMAN, WILLEM F. Evidence for clitic adverbs in Old English: an evaluation. *In* (pp. 223–45) **27**.

1776. LÓPEZ COUSO, MARÍA JOSÉ. A look at *that/zero* variation in Restoration English. *In* (pp. 271–86) **27**.

1777. —— MÉNDEZ NAYA, BELÉN. On the use of subjunctive and modals in Old and Middle English dependent commands and requests: evidence from the Helsinki Corpus. NM (97:4) 1996, 411–21.

1778. MÉNDEZ NAYA, BELÉN. *Cweðan, secgan* and *cyðan*: on mood selection in Old English dependent statements. Atlantis (17:1/2) 1995, 127–44.

1779. MITCHELL, BRUCE; IRVINE, SUSAN. A critical bibliography of Old English syntax: supplement 1989–1992. NM (97:1) 1996, 1–28; (97:2) 1996, 121–61; (97:3) 1996, 255–78.

1780. MYHILL, JOHN. The development of the strong obligation system in American English. AS (71:4) 1996, 339–88.

1781. NAGUCKA, RUTA. Spatial relations in Chaucer's *Treatise on the Astrolabe*. *In* (pp. 233–44) **68**.

1782. NUNNALLY, THOMAS E. An evaluative taxonomy of diachronic corpora. SECOLR (15:1) 1991, 21–36.

1783. OGURA, MICHIKO. Verbs in medieval English: differences in verb choice in verse and prose. Berlin; New York: Mouton de Gruyter, 1996. pp. xxi, 260. (Topics in English linguistics, 17.)

1784. PERCY, CAROL. Eighteenth-century normative grammar in practice: the case of Captain Cook. *In* (pp. 339–62) **27**.

1785. PÉREZ GUERRA, JAVIER. Syntax and information hand in hand? On extraposition and inversion from late Middle English to contemporary English. SELIM (5) 1995, 91–106.

1786. ROT, SÁNDOR. Periphrastic verbal constructions in Middle English. *In* (pp. 273–82) **11**.

1787. SCHNEIDER, EDGAR W. Towards syntactic isomorphism and semantic dissimilation: the semantics and syntax of prospective verbs in early modern English. *In* (pp. 199–220) **27**.

1788. VAN GELDEREN, ELLY. The case of the object in the history of English. Linguistic Analysis (26:1/2) 1996, 117–33.

1789. YAMAKAWA, KIKUO. Studies in historical English syntax. Tokyo: Kenkyusha, 1996. pp. xii, 232.

SINGLE SYNTACTICAL ITEMS

1790. *both*] BRISSON, CHRISTINE. Distributivity, asymmetry, and *both*. NELS (26) 1996, 17–30.

1791. *con*] IYEIRI, YOKO. The periphrastic use of *con* reconsidered: the authorship of the Cotton Nero A.x poems. SN (68:1) 1996, 3–8.

1792. *down to*] AUSTIN, FRANCES. Points of Modern English usage: LXXII. EngS (77:1) 1996, 97–103.

1793. *do*] MANABE, KAZUMI.   14 seiki eigo ni okeru shieki koubun no futeishi hyoushiki oyobi shieki doushi *do* to *make* no kyougou kankei. *See* **1467**.

1794. *for ... to*] ERDMANN, PETER.   Die *for ... to* Konstruktion nach dem Verb *want*. ZAA (41:2) 1993, 124–32.

1795. *get to*] BEAN, JUDITH MATTSON.   The evolution of inchoatives *go to* and *get to*. SECOLR (15:1) 1991, 69–86.

1796. *go to*] —— The evolution of inchoatives *go to* and *get to*. *See* **1795**.

1797. *habban*] OGURA, MICHIKO.   Old English *habban* + past participle of a verb of motion. *In* (pp. 199–214) **114**.

1798. *had +V-ed*] RICKFORD, JOHN R.; RAFAL, CHRISTINE THÉBERGE. Preterite *had* + V-*ed* in the narratives of African-American preadolescents. AS (71:3) 1996, 227–54.

1799. *I'm*] WOLFRAM, WALT.   Delineation and description in dialectology: the case of perfective *I'm* in Lumbee English. AS (71:1) 1996, 5–26.

1800. *-ing at*] RUDANKO, JUHANI.   *Balking at* and *working at*: on verbs governing *at -ing* in present-day English. EngS (76:3) 1995, 264–81.

1801. *it is*] PORTER, KEVIN J.   Stylistic considerations for *there is* and *it is*. SECOLR (19:2) 1995, 171–83.

1802. *like*] PLAT, JEAN-LUC.   *Like*. ERGS (52:1) 1995, 66–9.

1803. *likely*] AUSTIN, FRANCES.   Points of Modern English usage: LXXII. *See* **1792**.

1804. *make*] MANABE, KAZUMI.   14 seiki eigo ni okeru shieki koubun no futeishi hyoushiki oyobi shieki doushi *do* to *make* no kyougou kankei. *See* **1467**.

1805. *need*] MURRAY, THOMAS E.; FRAZER, TIMOTHY C.; SIMON, BETH LEE.   *Need* + past participle in American English. AS (71:3) 1996, 255–71.

1806. *one(s)*] CAMPBELL, RICHARD.   *One(s)*: the lonely number. NELS (26) 1996, 43–55. (Pronominal *one*.)

1807. *seem*] GRAZIANO-KING, JANINE.   Selection properties of raising verbs. StudLS (24:1/2) 1994, 204–14.

1808. *that*] KUTRYB, CAROL.   The effect of complementizer *that* on extraction from embedded clauses. StudLS (25:1) 1995, 67–73.

1809. *that/zero*] LÓPEZ COUSO, MARÍA JOSÉ.   A look at *that/zero* variation in Restoration English. *In* (pp. 271–86) **27**.

1810. *that's*] SEPPÄNEN, AIMO; KJELLMER, GÖRAN.   The dog that's leg was run over: on the genitive of the relative pronoun. EngS (76:4) 1995, 389–400.

1811. *there is*] PORTER, KEVIN J.   Stylistic considerations for *there is* and *it is*. *See* **1801**.

1812. *up to*] AUSTIN, FRANCES.   Points of Modern English usage: LXXII. *See* **1792**.

1813. *who*] CHING, MARVIN K. L.   The predictability of *who* as relative pronoun for collective nouns. SECOLR (18:2) 1994, 164–84.

1814. *will*] ZIEGLER, DEBRA.   A synchronic perspective on the grammaticalisation of *will* in hypothetical predicates. SL (20:2) 1996, 411–42.

VOCABULARY

VOCABULARY OF CONTEMPORARY ENGLISH

1815. ALDERSON, SIMON J.   The Augustan attack on the pun. ECL (20:3) 1996, 1–19.

1816. ALGEO, JOHN; ALGEO, ADELE.   Among the new words. AS (71:1) 1996, 86–97; (71:2) 1996, 184–97; (71:3) 1996, 302–13; (71:4) 1996, 421–34.

1817. ALLEN, IRVING LEWIS.   Unkind words: ethnic labeling from Redskin to WASP. New York: Bergin & Garvey, 1990. pp. ix, 143. Rev. by Dick Sweterlitsch in MidAF (20:2) 1992, 131–3.

1818. ARCHIBALD, JOHN.   The structure of the colour lexicon. CWPL (15) 1992, 1–11.

1819. ARISTIDES.   Ticked to the min. ASch (65:3) 1996, 327–34.

1820. AYTO, JOHN.   Euphemisms: over 3,000 ways to avoid being rude or giving offence. (Bibl. 1993, 1051.) Rev. by Janet Whitcut in IJL (9:1) 1996, 77.

1821. BARZUN, JACQUES.   The press and the prose. *See* **1227**.

1822. BRUTI, SILVIA.   Lexical anaphoras: the case of epithets. Textus (9:1) 1996, 27–42.

1823. BURRIDGE, KATE.   Political correctness: euphemism with attitude. English Today (12:3) 1996, 42–3.

1824. CARLESS, DAVID R.   Politicised expressions in the *South China Morning Post*. English Today (11:2) 1995, 18–22.

1825. CARRIKER, KITTI.   Neologisms and hypograms in the language of Stephen Dedalus: a Riffaterrean reading of *Portrait*. Notes on Modern Irish Literature (7:2) 1995, 10–15.

1826. COWIE, A. P.; HOWARTH, PETER.   Phraseology – a select bibliography. *See* **1665**.

1827. CRYSTAL, DAVID.   Phonaesthetically speaking. *See* **1545**.

1828. CUTLER, CHARLES L.   O brave new words! Native-American loanwords in current English. (Bibl. 1994, 1133.) Rev. by Tim Fox in GateH (15:3) 1994/95, 67–8; by Janine Scancarelli in ANQ (9:2) 1996, 56–9; by Fiona Robertson in NQ (43:2) 1996, 206–7.

1829. DE PRAP, REED.   New corrupt-speak of the RDP. Mail & Guardian (12:38) 1996, 8.

1830. DE WOLF, GAELAN DODDS.   Word choice: lexical variation in two Canadian surveys. JEL (24:2) 1996, 131–55.

1831. DuBOSE, THOMAS.   Saucers and sightings: the lexicon of UFOlogy. English Today (12:1) 1996, 45–9.

1832. EBLE, CONNIE C.   Slang and sociability: in-group language among college students. Chapel Hill; London: North Carolina UP, 1996. pp. x, 228.

1833. ELSTER, CHARLES HARRINGTON.   There's a word for it! A grandiloquent guide to life. New York: Scribner, 1996. pp. 272.

1834. ENGLISH, MARK.   More crow-scaring jargon. English Today (12:1) 1996, 51–3.

1835. FRANK, THOMAS.   On lexical innovation. Textus (2:1/2) 1989, 113–40.

1836. GACHELIN, JEAN-MARC.   More on scarecrows. English Today (12:1) 1996, 50–1.

1837. GEORGE, WILMA; YAPP, BRUNSDON.   The naming of the beasts: natural history in the medieval bestiary. London: Duckworth, 1991. pp. xiv, 231. Rev. by Karen Reeds in Isis (84:3) 1993, 567–8.

1838. GILLMEISTER, HEINER.   The language of English sports medieval and modern. Archiv (233:2) 1996, 268–85.

1839. GOODSON, F. TODD.   Schoolspeak: breaking the code. ERGS (52:4) 1995/96, 470–5.

1840. GORDON, JOHN.   *Joyce egg* and *claddagh ring*: Joycean artifacts in *Ulysses* and *Finnegans Wake*. Notes on Modern Irish Literature (5) 1993, 43–51.

1841. HART, JOHN FRASER.   On the classification of barns. MatC (26:3) 1994, 37–46.

1842. HAYMES, RICHARD D.   Corporate lingo: a new meaning. ERGS (52:2) 1995, 222–7.

1843. HERBST, THOMAS.   What are collocations: sandy beaches or false teeth? EngS (77:4) 1996, 379–93.

1844. HILLIAM, DAVID.   Do you know English word origins? From *academy* to *zodiac*. Bournemouth: Pocket Reference Books, 1996. pp. 132.

1845. HORTON, ANDREW.   High-flying acronyms. English Today (11:4) 1995, 28–30.

1846. ISAACSON, DAVID.   Power users dump baudy language: the ambivalent nature of computer slang. Verbatim (22:3) 1996, 1–3.

1847. ISIL, OLIVIA A.   When a loose cannon flogs a dead horse there's the devil to pay: seafaring words in everyday speech. Camden, ME: International Marine, 1996. pp. x, 134.

1848. JACOBSSON, BENGT.   A new look at 'predicative-only' adjectives in English. *See* **1694**.

1849. JOHNSON, ELLWOOD.   The pursuit of power: studies in the vocabulary of Puritanism. New York; Frankfurt; Bern; Paris: Lang, 1995. pp. 281. (American univ. studies, VII: Theology and religion, 180.) Rev. by A. N. McLaren in JAStud (30:3) 1996, 480–1.

1850. JOHNSON, STERLING.   English as a second f*cking [*sic*] language. Pacific Grove, CA: ESFL UP, 1996. pp. 88. (Swearing.)

1851. JOHNSTON, PAUL DENNITHORNE.   The joy of words: confessions of a verbaholic. ERGS (53:2) 1996, 131–7.

1852. KRETZSCHMAR, WILLIAM A., JR.   Dimensions of variation in American English vocabulary. EWW (17:2) 1996, 189–211.

1853. LEAP, WILLIAM L.   Word's out: gay men's English. Minneapolis: Minnesota UP, 1996. pp. xxii, 180.

1854. LIU, DILIN; FARHA, BRYAN.   Three strikes and you're out. English Today (12:1) 1996, 36–40. (Sports jargon in US English.)

1855. McARTHUR, ROSHAN.   Taboo words in print. English Today (12:3) 1996, 50–8 (review-article).

1856. MEIJS, WILLEM.   Morphology and lexis in a computational setting. *See* **1186**.

1857. MILES, JACK.   Political correctness and the American newspaper: the case of the *Los Angeles Times* stylebook. English Today (11:1) 1995, 14–18.

1858. MODIANO, MARKO.   A Mid-Atlantic lexical register. MS (90:1) 1996, 10–14.

1859. MORITA, JUNYA.   Lexicalization by way of context-dependent nonce-word formation. EngS (76:5) 1995, 468–73.

1860. MÜHLHAUS, SUSANNE.   Describing medical eponyms. English Today (11:2) 1995, 48–53.

1861. Murray, Thomas E.   The folk argot of Midwestern gangs. MidF (19:2) 1993, 113–48.

1862. Nash, Rose; Fayer, Joan M.   Changing lexical features in Puerto Rican English. WorldE (15:3) 1996, 281–94.

1863. Newmark, Peter.   Paragraphs on translation: 41, 42, 43, 44, 46. *See* **1119**.

1864. Noble, Allen G.; Cleek, Richard K.   Reply to Hart. MatC (27:1) 1995, 25–30.

1865. Ó Muirithe, Diarmaid.   The words we use. Blackrock, Co. Dublin; Portland, OR: Four Courts Press, 1996. pp. 134.

1866. Paikeday, Thomas M.   Lexicon. English Today (11:1) 1995, 19–20; (11:2) 1995, 23–5; (11:3) 1995, 23–5; (11:4) 1995, 23–4. (Neologisms.)

1867. ——— New words and senses. English Today (12:1) 1996, 54–5.

1868. Prat Zagrebelsky, Maria Teresa.   Processes of lexical and semantic innovation in contemporary English: the case of the Gulf War. Textus (5) 1992, 111–22.

1869. Pulcini, Virginia.   Some new English words in Italian. Textus (8:2) 1995, 267–79.

1870. Rastall, Paul.   Metaphor and the names of plants. English Today (12:2) 1996, 30–1.

1871. Roberts, Dale.   Kaleidoscope: the language at large. English Today (11:2) 1995, 35–6; (12:2) 1996, 21–2.

1872. Rodríguez González, Félix (ed.).   Spanish loanwords in the English language: a tendency towards hegemony reversal. Berlin; New York: Mouton de Gruyter, 1996. pp. xii, 301. (Topics in English linguistics, 18.)

1873. St Leon, Mark.   Australian circus language: a report on the nature, origin and circumstances of Aussie argot under the big top. Australian Folklore (11) 1996, 190–8.

1874. Seabrook, Mike.   All gone pear-shaped: opportunities for mis-understanding the police. Verbatim (22:4) 1996, 11–13.

1875. Stanciu, Dumitru.   Particular aspects of synonymy and selection with the proverb. Proverbium (9) 1992, 231–47.

1876. Sylvester, Louise.   Scarecrows and bogeymen in the *OED*. English Today (11:2) 1995, 25–7.

1877. Temianka, Daniel.   The king of wordsmiths. Verbatim (23:1) 1996, 4–6.

1878. Towner, George.   Creating an English anagrammicon. English Today (11:3) 1995, 25–8.

1879. Waldrep, Christopher.   The making of a border state society: James McGready, the Great Revival, and the prosecution of profanity in Kentucky. AHR (99:3) 1994, 767–84.

1880. Waugh, Linda R.   Let's take the con out of iconicity: con-straints on iconicity in the lexicon. AJSem (9:1) 1992, 7–47.

HISTORICAL VOCABULARY OF ENGLISH

1881. Bartelt, Guillermo.   A note on Old English kinship seman-tics. JEL (24:2) 1996, 116–22.

1882. Bately, Janet.   Towards a Middle English thesaurus: some terms relating to fortune, fate and chance. *In* (pp. 69–82) **68**.

1883. BIGGAM, C. P. Sociolinguistic aspects of Old English colour lexemes. ASE (24) 1995, 51–65.

1884. BURNLEY, DAVID. Chaucer's literary terms. Ang (114:2) 1996, 202–35.

1885. CASSIDY, FREDERIC G. The Anglo-Saxon interjection. *In* (pp. 45–8) **11**.

1886. COLEMAN, JULIE. The treatment of sexual vocabulary in Middle English dictionaries. *In* (pp. 183–206) **68**.

1887. DESSEN, ALAN C. Recovering Shakespeare's theatrical vocabulary. (Bibl. 1995, 1475.) Rev. by Stephen J. Phillips in NQ (43:3) 1996, 335–6; by Stevie Simkin in Eng (45:181) 1996, 89–96.

1888. FISCHER, ANDREAS. The vocabulary of very late Old English. *In* (pp. 29–41) **114**.

1889. FLAVELL, LINDA; FLAVELL, ROGER. Dictionary of word origins. London: Cathie, 1995. pp. x, 277.

1890. GILLMEISTER, HEINER. The language of English sports medieval and modern. *See* **1838**.

1891. GRIFFITH, MARK S. Does *wyrd bið ful aræd* mean 'Fate is wholly inexorable'? *In* (pp. 133–56) **114**.

1892. HEALEY, ANTONETTE diPAOLO. Reasonable doubt, reasoned choice: the letter *A* in the *Dictionary of Old English*. *In* (pp. 71–84) **114**.

1893. HLADKÝ, JOSEF. The first Latin words in English. Brno Studies in English (22) 1996, 49–54.

1894. JOHNSON, ELLEN. Lexical change and variation in the southeastern United States, 1930–1990. Tuscaloosa; London: Alabama UP, 1996. pp. xiii, 318. (Cf. bibl. 1993, 1079.) Rev. by Bradley Harris in SECOLR (20:2) 1996, 231–8.

1895. KANNO, MASAHIKO. Studies in Chaucer's words: a contextual and semantic approach. Tokyo: Eihosha, 1996. pp. xiv, 226.

1896. KITSON, PETER. The dialect position of the Old English Orosius. SAP (30) 1996, 3–35.

1897. LEONARD, ROBERT A. Money and language. *In* (pp. 3–13) **71**.

1898. LIBERMAN, ANATOLY. Etymological studies: VI, Some obscure English words (from the files of *An Analytic Dictionary of English Etymology*). GL (33:3) 1993, 163–77.

1899. LOCKWOOD, W. B. An informal introduction to English etymology. Montreux; London: Minerva Press, 1995. pp. vii, 188.

1900. McINTOSH, ANGUS; LAING, MARGARET. Middle English *windown*, 'window': a word-geographical note. NM (97:3) 1996, 295–300.

1901. McNELIS, JAMES I., III. The sword mightier than the pen? Hrothgar's hilt, theory, and philology. *In* (pp. 175–85) **114**.

1902. MOESSNER, LILO. *'Besyde Latyn our langage is imperfite'*: the contribution of Gavin Douglas to the development of the Scots lexicon. Études Écossaises (supp.) 1994, 5–17.

1903. MOSKOWICH, ISABEL; SEOANE, ELENA. Scandinavian loans and processes of word-formation in ME: some preliminary considerations. *In* (pp. 185–98) **27**.

1904. NORRI, JUHANI. On the origins of plant names in fifteenth-century English. *In* (pp. 159–81) **68**.

1905. OKAMURA, TOSHIAKI. Shakespeare no shingo, shingogi no kenkyu. (A study of Shakespeare's neologisms.) Hiroshima: Keisuisha, 1996. pp. 454.

1906. PULSIANO, PHILLIP. The originality of the Old English gloss of the Vespasian Psalter and its relation to the gloss of the Junius Psalter. *See* **797**.

1907. RAMSON, BILL.   More famous Australian etymologies. Verbatim (22:3) 1996, 11–12.

1908. RITTER, ELIZABETH; ROSEN, SARA THOMAS.   The incompatibility of lexical derivation and post-lexical arguments. CWPL (17) 1995, 11–15.

1909. ROBERTS, JANE.   Laȝamon's plain words. *In* (pp. 107–22) **68**.

1910. ROTHWELL, W.   The Anglo-French element in the vulgar register of late Middle English. NM (97:4) 1996, 423–36.

1911. RUSCHE, PHILIP G.   Dry-point glosses to Aldhelm's *De laudibus virginitatis* in Beinecke 401. *See* **415**.

1912. SAUER, HANS.   English plant names in the thirteenth century: the trilingual Harley vocabulary. *In* (pp. 135–58) **68**.

1913. STANLEY, ERIC.   Paradise lost of the Old English dual. *In* (pp. 1–27) **26**.

1914. SYLVESTER, LOUISE.   Procedures in classifying Middle English vocabulary: some preliminary observations. *In* (pp. 123–33) **68**.

1915. TAVORMINA, M. TERESA; YEAGER, R. F. (eds).   The endless knot: essays on Old and Middle English in honor of Marie Borroff. *See* **26**.

SINGLE WORDS AND PHRASES

1916. *aglæcwif*]   MENZER, MELINDA J.   *Aglæcwif* (*Beowulf* 1259a): implications for *-wif* compounds, Grendel's mother, and other *aglæcan*. *See* **1643**.

1917. *aitch*]   WEINSTOCK, HORST.   The rise of the letter-name *aitch*. *See* **1529**.

1918. *any*]   RULLMANN, HOTZE.   Two types of negative polarity items. NELS (26) 1996, 335–50.

1919. *balles*]   KIRBY, IAN J.   First in the field? A 'new-old' word in Laȝamon's *Brut*. *In* (pp. 163–6) **11**.

1920. *billions*]   MACNEAL, EDWARD.   Millions–billions. ERGS (51:1) 1994, 18–22. (Mathsemantics.)

1921. *bold hives*]   CAVENDER, ANTHONY.   A note on the origin and meaning of *bold hives* in the American South. SF (53:1) 1996, 17–24.

1922. *boodle*]   THOMPSON, GEORGE A., JR.   Counterfeiters' jargon of the 1820s. AS (71:3) 1996, 334–5.

1923. *bottom line*]   GOZZI, RAYMOND, JR.   Economic metaphors for education. ERGS (51:4) 1994/95, 417–21.

1924. *burh*]   COX, BARRIE.   The pattern of Old English *burh* in early Lindsey. ASE (23) 1994, 35–56.

1925. *civility*]   TITLESTAD, P. J. H.   The 'pretty young man Civility': Bunyan, Milton & Blake and patterns of Puritan thought. Bunyan Studies (6) 1995/96, 34–43.

1926. *clædur*]   BREEZE, ANDREW.   A Celtic etymology for Old English *clædur* 'clapper'. SELIM (5) 1995, 119–21.

1927. *coinacker*]   THOMPSON, GEORGE A., JR.   Counterfeiters' jargon of the 1820s. *See* **1922**.

1928. *colony*]   BROOKS, CHRISTOPHER K.   Controlling the metaphor:

language and self-definition in Revolutionary America. CLIO (25:3)
1996, 233–54.

1929. *cunning*] PITCHER, E. W.   Cooper's cunning and Heyward as
cunning-man in *The Last of the Mohicans*. ANQ (9:1) 1996, 10–17.

1930. *cutting a deal*] JONES, BRUCE WILLIAM.   Cutting deals and
striking bargains. English Today (12:2) 1996, 35–40.

1931. *cyberspace*] GOZZI, RAYMOND, JR.   The *cyberspace* metaphor.
ERGS (51:2) 1994, 218–23.

1932. *day*] VILPPULA, MATTI.   The sun and the definition of *day*.
IJL (8:1) 1995, 29–38.

1933. *deceiving*] MOÏSE, EDWIN.   An archaism in John Keats's *Ode to
a Nightingale*. NQ (43:4) 1996, 425.

1934. *diary*] TEUBERT, WOLFGANG.   Comparable or parallel
corpora? IJL (9:3) 1996, 238–64. (English and German.)

1935. *discretion*] HILLMAN, DAVID.   Puttenham, Shakespeare, and
the abuse of rhetoric. SELit (36:1) 1996, 73–90.

1936. *disposition*] GINSBERG, WARREN.   Chaucer's disposition. *In* (pp.
129–40) **26**.

1937. *drake*] HOUGH, CAROLE.   An Old English etymon for Modern
English *drake* 'male duck'. Neophilologus (80:4) 1996, 613–15.

1938. *drug*] BERNSTEIN, CYNTHIA.   *Drug* usage among high school
students in Silsbee, Texas: a study of the preterite. PADS (78) 1994,
138–43.

1939. *elvish*] BURROW, J. A.   Elvish Chaucer. *In* (pp. 105–11) **26**.

1940. *estas*] BREEZE, ANDREW.   Old English *estas* 'relishes' in the
Flintshire Domesday. NQ (43:1) 1996, 14–15.

1941. *even*] RULLMANN, HOTZE.   Two types of negative polarity
items. *See* **1918**.

1942. *fair dinkum*] JOHNSTONE, IAN M.   Fair dinkum and good faith
– Aussie and legal honesty compared: a meeting of folklore and lawyer's
law. Australian Folklore (8) 1993, 152–60.

1943. *fan*] SHULMAN, DAVID.   On the early use of *fan* in baseball.
AS (71:3) 1996, 328–31.

1944. *felon*] EISENMAN, RUSSELL.   A reply to Mark S. Cohen. ERGS
(53:1) 1996, 47–51.

1945. *feminism*] LIEPE-LEVINSON, KATHERINE; LEVINSON, MARTIN H.
'Glossing over' feminism? A general semantics critique. ERGS (52:4)
1995/96, 440–54.

1946. *folk*] SOMMERS, LAURIE KAY.   Definitions of *folk* and *lore* in the
Smithsonian Festival of American Folklife. JFR (33:3) 1996, 227–31.

1947. *folklore*] ANON. (comp.).   Definitions of folklore. JFR (33:3)
1996, 255–64.

1948. *folklore*] MAZO, JEFFREY ALAN.   'A good Saxon compound'.
Folklore (107) 1996, 107–8.

1949. *folklore*] MONTENYOHL, ERIC.   Divergent paths: on the evolution of *folklore* and *folkloristics*. JFR (33:3) 1996, 232–5.

1950. *folklore*] TOKOFSKY, PETER.   Folk-lore and *Volks-Kunde*: compounding compounds. JFR (33:3) 1996, 207–11.

1951. *folkloristics*] MONTENYOHL, ERIC. · Divergent paths: on the
evolution of *folklore* and *folkloristics*. *See* **1949**.

1952. *fork*] DORFMAN, TONI.   The fateful crossroads: 'fork' clusters
in Shakespeare's plays. ShB (12:1) 1994, 31–4.

1953. *frætwe, frætwan*] TYLER, ELIZABETH M. How deliberate is deliberate verbal repetition? *In* (pp. 508–30) **114**.

1954. *fragment*] CRAWFORD, ROBERT. Native language. CompCrit (18) 1996, 71–90. (Discusses use of *fragment* in literary titles.)

1955. *fyn*] FARRELL, THOMAS J. The *fyn* of the *Troilus*. *In* (pp. 38–53) **116**.

1956. *gesyfleð*] SCHAFFNER, PAUL. The errant morsel in *Solomon and Saturn* II: liturgy, lore, and lexicon. MedStud (57) 1995, 223–57.

1957. *global village*] GOZZI, RAYMOND, JR. Will the media create a global village? ERGS (53:1) 1996, 65–8.

1958. *goldhordus*] PORTER, DAVID W. Old English *goldhordus*: a privy or just a treasurehouse? NQ (43:3) 1996, 257–8.

1959. *Good heavens!*] OAKS, DALLIN D. 'Good heavens!': an Old English euphemism? GL (33:1/2) 1993, 57–63.

1960. *green room*] BRYAN, GEORGE B. On the theatrical origins of the expression *green room*. Proverbium (9) 1992, 31–6.

1961. *grockle*] BETTS, JEROME. The grockles of Goodrington. Verbatim (23:2) 1996, 5–7.

1962. *hacche-man*] HOUGH, CAROLE. ME *hacche-man*. NQ (43:3) 1996, 268.

1963. *hopefully*] HUNDT, MARIANNE. Beyond hope: on the use of *hopefully* in New Zealand English. NZEJ (10) 1996, 31–4.

1964. *hreol*] BREEZE, ANDREW. Old English *hreol* 'reel': Welsh *rheol* 'rule'. SELIM (5) 1995, 122–6.

1965. *information superhighway*] GOZZI, RAYMOND, JR. The *information superhighway* as metaphor. ERGS (51:3) 1994, 321–7.

1966. *īsig*] LIBERMAN, ANATOLY. The 'icy' ship of Scyld Scefing: *Beowulf* 33. *In* (pp. 183–94) **11**.

1967. *joy*] DILLER, HANS-JÜRGEN. *Joy* and *mirth* in Middle English and a little bit in Old: a plea for the consideration of genre in historical semantics. *In* (pp. 83–105) **68**.

1968. *just*] KISHNER, JEFFREY M. How *just* gets its meanings: polysemy and context in psychological semantics. Language and Speech (39:1) 1996, 19–36.

1969. *kill, kill, kill*] MOORE, PETER. Kill, kill, kill. ER (2:2) 1994, 19–22.

1970. *larges(se)*] FARLEY-HILLS, DAVID. *Largesse* in *Sir Gawain and the Green Knight*. NQ (43:2) 1996, 136–8.

1971. *lenative*] WRIGHT, LOUISE E. Webster's lenative poisons. JEL (24:3) 1996, 182–5.

1972. *lesbian*] SCANLON, JOAN. Bad language *vs* bad prose? *Lady Chatterley* and *The Well*. CritQ (38:3) 1996, 3–13.

1973. *literature*] TERRY, RICHARD. The eighteenth-century invention of English literature: a truism revisited. BJECS (19:1) 1996, 47–62.

1974. *lore*] SOMMERS, LAURIE KAY. Definitions of *folk* and *lore* in the Smithsonian Festival of American Folklife. *See* **1946**.

1975. *mango*] BERGDAHL, DAVID. *Mango*: the pepper puzzlement. AS (71:3) 1996, 335–6.

1976. *map*] GOZZI, RAYMOND, JR. The fable of the electric maps and the mutating territory. ERGS (53:2) 1996, 211–17. (Mapping metaphors in technology.)

1977. *millions*] MACNEAL, EDWARD. Millions–billions. *See* **1920**.

1978. *mirth*] DILLER, HANS-JÜRGEN. *Joy* and *mirth* in Middle English and a little bit in Old: a plea for the consideration of genre in historical semantics. *In* (pp. 83–105) **68**.

1979. *mumbo jumbo*] PITCHER, E. W. *Mumbo jumbo*: idol babble. NQ (43:1) 1996, 27.

1980. *my*] SCHWALM, GISELA. *First person possessive*: Determination als Stilmittel in Walker Percys *Lancelot*. ZAA (41:3) 1993, 213–26.

1981. *nation*] KUUSISTO, PEKKA. Part of being a nation is getting the history wrong? Notes on concepts related to ethnicity. Pragmatics, Ideology and Contacts Bulletin (3) 1996, 10–15.

1982. *nunnery*] DOLOFF, STEVEN. Hamlet's 'nunnery' and Agrippa's 'stewes of harlottes'. NQ (43:2) 1996, 158–9.

1983. *other*] MACKEY, NATHANIEL. *Other*: from noun to verb. Representations (39) 1992, 51–70.

1984. *peintunge*] MILLETT, BELLA. *Peintunge* and *schadewe* in *Ancrene Wisse* Part 4. NQ (43:4) 1996, 399–403.

1985. *pop*] VON SCHNEIDEMESSER, LUANNE. Soda or pop? JEL (24:4) 1996, 270–87.

1986. *projection*] GOZZI, RAYMOND, JR. The *projection* metaphor in psychology. ERGS (52:2) 1995, 197–201.

1987. *pure*] STRAUSS, MICHAEL J. What's pure? ERGS (51:2) 1994, 181–8.

1988. *purpose*] WALZER, ARTHUR E. The meanings of *purpose*. RhR (10:1) 1991, 118–29.

1989. *put on*] RUHL, CHARLES. *Put on* 'pretend, deceive'. SECOLR (20:2) 1996, 135–60.

1990. *race*] HUDSON, NICHOLAS. From 'nation' to 'race': the origin of racial classification in eighteenth-century thought. ECS (29:3) 1996, 247–64.

1991. *reeve*] ROBERTS, JULIAN. An ill-fated irruption of ruffs. BLR (15:5/6) 1996, 416–21. (Birds.)

1992. *rodomontade*] RONNICK, MICHELE VALERIE. A fourth use of the verb *rodomontade* in the eighteenth century. Verbatim (22:3) 1996, 23.

1993. *rōt*] HOUGH, CAROLE. Old English *rōt* in place-names. NQ (43:2) 1996, 128–9.

1994. *ruff*] ROBERTS, JULIAN. An ill-fated irruption of ruffs. *See* **1991**.

1995. *sanction*] KJELLMER, GÖRAN. Multiple meaning and interpretation: the case of *sanction*. ZAA (41:2) 1993, 115–23.

1996. *schadewe*] MILLETT, BELLA. *Peintunge* and *schadewe* in *Ancrene Wisse* Part 4. *See* **1984**.

1997. *scitan*] PLATZER, HANS. The temporary merger of OE *scitan* and *scyttan*; or, A case of harmless homophony. *See* **1525**.

1998. *scyttan*] —— The temporary merger of OE *scitan* and *scyttan*; or, A case of harmless homophony. *See* **1525**.

1999. *sith*] SMITH, MACKLIN. *Sith* and *syn* in Chaucer's *Troilus*. ChauR (26:3) 1992, 266–82.

2000. *sness*] BREEZE, ANDREW. Middle English *sness* 'cluster': Middle Irish *popp* 'shoot, tendril'. SELIM (5) 1995, 132–6.

2001. *soda*] VON SCHNEIDEMESSER, LUANNE. Soda or pop? *See* **1985**.

2002. *sothe*] MATSUMOTO, HIROYUKI. A note on *sothe* in l. 11 in *The Destruction of Troy*. *See* **751**.

2003. *spaceship*] MUIR, STAR A. The web and the spaceship: metaphors of the environment. ERGS (51:2) 1994, 145–52.

2004. *spelboda*] MARSDEN, RICHARD. The death of the messenger: the *spelboda* in the Old English *Exodus*. *See* **750**.

2005. *sterte*] BITTERLING, KLAUS. Margery Kempe, an English *sterte* in Germany. NQ (43:1) 1996, 21–2.

2006. *striking a bargain*] JONES, BRUCE WILLIAM. Cutting deals and striking bargains. *See* **1930**.

2007. *structure*] GOZZI, RAYMOND, JR. *Structure*: the intellectual's metaphor. ERGS (51:1) 1994, 76–9.

2008. *stylometrics*] BINONGO, JOSÉ NILO G.; SMITH, M. W. A. Stylometry. NQ (43:4) 1996, 448–52.

2009. *stylometry*] —————— Stylometry. *See* **2008**.

2010. *suspect*] McMILLAN, JAMES B. *Suspect* in dictionaries. AS (71:1) 1996, 106–9.

2011. *swefn*] HARBUS, ANTONINA. Old English *swefn* and *Genesis B* line 720. *In* (pp. 157–74) **114**.

2012. *syn*] SMITH, MACKLIN. *Sith* and *syn* in Chaucer's *Troilus*. *See* **1999**.

2013. *tagild*] BREEZE, ANDREW. Richard Rolle's *tagild* 'entangled': Welsh *tagu* 'choke', *tagell* 'snare'. SELIM (5) 1995, 127–31.

2014. *territory*] GOZZI, RAYMOND, JR. The fable of the electric maps and the mutating territory. *See* **1976**.

2015. *tharf-cakes*] BIGGAM, CAROLE P. Old English *þeru* and Modern English *tharf-cakes*. SELIM (5) 1995, 109–15.

2016. *þeru*] —— Old English *þeru* and Modern English *tharf-cakes*. *See* **2015**.

2017. *ðin*] STACZEK, JOHN. *Ðin* in late Middle English and its contemporary reflex in instructional settings. *In* (pp. 245–52) **68**.

2018. *to begin with*] LIPKA, LEONHARD; SCHMID, HANS-JÖRG. *To begin with*: degrees of idiomaticity, textual functions and pragmatic exploitations of a fixed expression. ZAA (42:1) 1994, 6–15.

2019. *tolouse*] BREEZE, ANDREW. The *Gawain*-poet and Toulouse. NQ (43:3) 1996, 266–8.

2020. *torres*] —— *Torres* 'towering clouds' in *Pearl* and *Cleanness*. NQ (43:3) 1996, 264–6.

2021. *vipassana*] BISCHOFF, ROGER. Some notes concerning the entry *vipassana* in the *Oxford English Dictionary Additions Series*, Vol. 2 (Clarendon Press, Oxford: 1993). IJL (9:1) 1996, 35–7.

2022. *virtual*] FRICK, THOMAS. Either/or. AR (54:3) 1996, 286–302.

2023. *web*] MUIR, STAR A. The web and the spaceship: metaphors of the environment. *See* **2003**.

2024. *wild geese*] MURPHY, JAMES H. The wild geese. Irish Review (16) 1994, 23–8.

2025. *window*] McINTOSH, ANGUS; LAING, MARGARET. Middle English *window*, 'window': a word-geographical note. *See* **1900**.

2026. *working class*] MAUTNER, THOMAS. 'The working class of people': an early eighteenth-century source. NQ (43:3) 1996, 299–303.

2027. *worry*] LESTER, TOBY. Worries about words. ERGS (52:4) 1995/96, 401–5.

2028. *wriggle*] —— Worries about words. *See* **2027**.

2029. *wring*] —— Worries about words. *See* **2027**.

2030. *wrong*] —— Worries about words. *See* **2027**.

2031. *y'all*] MAYNOR, NATALIE. The pronoun *y'all*: questions and some tentative answers. JEL (24:4) 1996, 288–94.

LEXICOGRAPHY

GENERAL STUDIES

2032. ALLEN, ROBERT.   The year of the dictionaries. English Today (12:2) 1996, 41–7 (review-article).

2033. ANDREASSON, ANNE-MARIE.   *Svenska Akademiens Ordbok* and *Oxford English Dictionary*: a comparison of their microstructure. IJL (9:2) 1996, 83–101.

2034. ATKINS, B. T. S.; LEVIN, BETH.   Building on a corpus: a linguistic and lexicographical look at some near-synonyms. IJL (8:2) 1995, 85–114.

2035. BEAL, JOAN.   The Jocks and the Geordies: modified standards in eighteenth-century pronouncing dictionaries. *In* (pp. 363–82) **27**.

2036. BÉJOINT, HENRI.   Tradition and innovation in modern English dictionaries. (Bibl. 1994, 1236.) Rev. by Adam Kilgarriff in Linguistics (34:6) 1996, 1278–81.

2037. BISCHOFF, ROGER.   Some notes concerning the entry *vipassana* in the *Oxford English Dictionary Additions Series*, Vol. 2 (Clarendon Press, Oxford: 1993). *See* **2021**.

2038. BUTLER, SUSAN.   World English in an Asian context: the *Macquarie Dictionary* project. WorldE (15:3) 1996, 347–57.

2039. CHING, MARVIN K. L.   Examining the trustworthiness of the latest *OED* in reflecting current English. StudLS (23:1) 1993, 73–82.

2040. COLEMAN, JULIE.   English language: lexicography, lexicology and semantics. YWES (75) 1994, 24–30.

2041. —— The treatment of sexual vocabulary in Middle English dictionaries. *In* (pp. 183–206) **68**.

2042. DELBRIDGE, ARTHUR; YALLOP, COLIN.   The *Macquarie Dictionary*. English Today (12:1) 1996, 11–14.

2043. EVANS, ROGER; GAZDAR, GERALD.   DATR: language for lexical knowledge. *See* **1152**.

2044. FLEMING, JULIET.   Dictionary English and the female tongue. *In* (pp. 175–204) **89**.

2045. FRASER, HELEN.   Guy-dance with pro-nun-see-ay-shon. *See* **1547**.

2046. GILLIVER, PETER M.   At the wordface: J. R. R. Tolkien's work on the *Oxford English Dictionary*. Mythlore (21:2) 1996, 173–86.

2047. GÖRLACH, MANFRED; MAŃCZAK-WOHLFELD, ELŻBIETA.   The projected *Usage Dictionary of Anglicisms in Selected European Languages* (*UDASEL*). EEM (3:2) 1994, 65–9.

2048. GREEN, JONATHON.   Chasing the sun: dictionary-makers and the dictionaries they made. London: Cape; New York: Holt, 1996. pp. 423, (plates) 8.

2049. GREENE, DEIRDRE.   Tolkien's dictionary poetics: the influence of the *OED*'s defining style on Tolkien's fiction. Mythlore (21:2) 1996, 195–9.

2050. HEALEY, ANTONETTE DIPAOLO.   Reasonable doubt, reasoned choice: the letter *A* in the *Dictionary of Old English*. *In* (pp. 71–84) **114**.

2051. IAMARTINO, GIOVANNI.   Dyer's and Burke's addenda and corrigenda to Johnson's *Dictionary* as clues to its contemporary reception. Textus (8:2) 1995, 199–248.

2052. McDavid, Virginia G.   A comparison of usage panel judgments in *American Heritage Dictionary* 2 and usage conclusions and recommendations in *Webster's Dictionary of English Usage*. PADS (78) 1994, 123–8.

2053. Milton, Colin.   'Shibboleths o the Scots': Hugh MacDiarmid and Jamieson's *Etymological Dictionary of the Scottish Language*. SLang (14/15) 1995/96, 1–14.

2054. Morton, Herbert C.   The story of Webster's third: Philip Gove's controversial dictionary and its critics. (Bibl. 1995, 1581.) Rev. by Jonathan Yardley in BkW, 4 Sept. 1994, 3; by Jeffery Triggs in SHARP News (4:3) 1995, 7–8; by Robert L. Chapman in IJL (9:4) 1996, 367–71.

2055. Nagashima, Daisuke.   How Johnson read Hale's *Origination* for his dictionary: a linguistic view. AJ (7) 1996, 247–97.

2056. Norri, Juhani.   Regional labels in some British and American dictionaries. IJL (9:1) 1996, 1–29.

2057. Ottenhoff, John.   The perils of prescriptivism: usage notes and *The American Heritage Dictionary*. AS (71:3) 1996, 272–84.

2058. Pauwels, Paul.   Explaining what to whom? English Today (12:2) 1996, 52–5 (review-article).

2059. Pearson, Bruce L.   The neglect of morphology and the lexicon. *See* **1621**.

2060. Prat Zagrebelsky, Maria Teresa.   Watching English lexis change: from dictionaries of neologisms to computerised corpora. *See* **1195**.

2061. Procter, Paul.   The making of a modern dictionary. MS (90:1) 1996, 3–8.

2062. Reddick, Allen.   The making of Johnson's dictionary, 1746–1773. (Bibl. 1994, 1260.) Cambridge; New York: CUP, 1996. pp. xxi, 252, (plates) 8. (Cambridge studies in publishing and printing history.) (Revised ed.: first ed. 1990.)

2063. Schnelle, Helmut.   The logic of Cobuild-type dictionary-semantics. Textus (8:2) 1995, 295–312.

2064. Shepherd, Valerie.   Anne Elizabeth Baker's *Glossary of Northamptonshire Words and Phrases* and John Clare's rustic idiom. JCSJ (15) 1996, 69–75 (review-article).

2065. Sinclair, J. M.   Text corpora: lexicographers' needs. ZAA (41:1) 1993, 5–14.

2066. Sinclair, John.   An international project in multilingual lexicography. IJL (9:3) 1996, 179–96.

2067. Smadja, Frank; Hatzivassiloglou, Vasileios; McKeown, Kathleen R.   Translating collocations for bilingual lexicons: a statistical approach. *See* **1204**.

2068. Starnes, De Witt T.; Noyes, Gertrude E.   The English dictionary from Cawdrey to Johnson, 1604–1755. Introd. by Gabriele Stein. (Bibl. 1993, 1228.) Rev. by Fredric Dolezal in AS (71:2) 1996, 205–10.

2069. Svartvik, Jan.   Lexis in English language corpora. ZAA (41:1) 1993, 15–30.

2070. Taylor, Peter.   Lexical semantics across categories: what prepositions can tell us about the lexical entries of verbs. Textus (8:2) 1995, 333–53.

2071. Teubert, Wolfgang.   Comparable or parallel corpora? *See* **1934**.

2072. URDANG, LAURENCE.   The uncommon use of proper names. IJL (9:1) 1996, 30–4.

2073. VILPPULA, MATTI.   The sun and the definition of *day*. See **1932**.

2074. WILLINSKY, JOHN.   Empire of words: the reign of the *OED*. (Bibl. 1995, 1589.) Rev. by Jeffery Triggs in SHARP News (4:3) 1995, 7–8; by Louis T. Milic in English Today (11:3) 1995, 54; by Diana Postlethwaite in Albion (28:1) 1996, 172–4; by David Yerkes in Review (18) 1996, 103–7; by Wanda Creaser in RMRLL (50:1) 1996, 108–9; by Fred C. Robinson in Modernism/Modernity (3:2) 1996, 125–6; by Ronald H. Fritze in Libraries & Culture (31:3/4) 1996, 669–70.

DICTIONARIES OF ENGLISH

2075. AGNES, MICHAEL (ed.)   Webster's New World dictionary and thesaurus. With principal thesaurus text by Charlton Laird. New York: Macmillan, 1996. pp. xv, 734.

2076. ALLSOPP, RICHARD (ed.).   Dictionary of Caribbean English usage. With a French and Spanish supplement ed. by Jeannette Allsopp. Oxford; New York: OUP, 1996. pp. lxxviii, 697. Rev. by Manfred Görlach in EWW (17:2) 1996, 289–96.

2077. ANON. (ed.).   Cambridge international dictionary of English. (Bibl. 1995, 1593.) Rev. by Arne Olofsson in MS (90:1) 1996, 99–103.

2078. —— Glossary of Northamptonshire words and phrases. By Anne Elizabeth Baker. Thetford, Norfolk: Lark, 1995. 2 vols. pp. xviii, 410; 439. (Facsim. reprint of 1854 ed.) Rev. by Valerie Shepherd in JCSJ (15) 1996, 69–75.

2079. BARKER, F. S.; HOLTZHAUSEN, M. M. E.   South African labour glossary. Cape Town: Juta, 1996. pp. ix, 195.

2080. BATELY, JANET.   Towards a Middle English thesaurus: some terms relating to fortune, fate and chance. *In* (pp. 69–82) **68**.

2081. BERTRAM, ANNE.   NTC's dictionary of folksy, regional, and rural sayings. Ed. by Richard A. Spears. Lincolnwood, IL: NTC, 1996. pp. xi, 381.

2082. BRAHAM, CAROL G. (ed.).   Random House Webster's dictionary. New York: Ballantine, 1996. pp. xv, 816. (Second ed.: first ed. 1993.)

2083. BROOKS, MAUREEN; RITCHIE, JOAN (comps).   Tassie terms: a glossary of Tasmanian words. Melbourne; New York; Oxford: OUP, 1995. pp. xvii, 174.

2084. —— —— (eds).   Words from the West: a glossary of Western Australian terms. (Bibl. 1994, 1271.) Rev. by Manfred Görlach in EWW (17:2) 1996, 316–17.

2085. BURCHFIELD, R. W. (ed.).   The new Fowler's modern English usage. (Bibl. 1967, 710.) Oxford: Clarendon Press; New York: OUP, 1996. pp. xxiii, 864. (Third ed.: first ed. 1926.)

2086. CAVENDER, ANTHONY (ed.).   A folk medical lexicon of South Central Appalachia. Johnson City: East Tennessee State Univ., 1990. pp. xiii, 36. (History of Medicine Soc. of Appalachia misc. papers, 1.) Rev. by Michael Montgomery in SECOLR (16:2) 1992, 201–2.

2087. CHALKER, SYLVIA.   The little Oxford dictionary of English grammar. See **1662**.

2088. CLARK, THOMAS L.   Western lore and language: a dictionary

for enthusiasts of the American West. Salt Lake City: Utah UP, 1996.
pp. xvi, 266.

2089. CULLEN, KAY; SARGEANT, HOWARD (comps).　Chambers dictionary of phrasal verbs. Edinburgh: Chambers, 1996. pp. xi, 436.

2090. DALZELL, TOM.　Flappers 2 rappers: American youth slang. Springfield, MA: Merriam-Webster, 1996. pp. xiii, 256.

2091. DAVIS, J. MADISON; FRANKFORTER, A. DANIEL.　The Shakespeare name dictionary. (Bibl. 1995, 1603.) Rev. by Paul Bertram in ShB (14:2) 1996, 45–6.

2092. FARWELL, HAROLD, JR.; NICHOLAS, J. KARL (eds).　Smoky Mountain voices: a lexicon of Southern Appalachian speech based on the research of Horace Kephart. (Bibl. 1993, 1245.) Rev. by Michael Ellis in SECOLR (19:1) 1995, 164–6.

2093. FLAVELL, LINDA; FLAVELL, ROGER.　Dictionary of word origins. *See* **1889**.

2094. HANDS, PENNY (comp.).　Chambers dictionary of idioms. Edinburgh: Chambers, 1996. pp. viii, 404.

2095. HEIFETZ, JOSEFA.　The word lover's dictionary: unusual, obscure, and preposterous words. Secaucus, NJ: Carol, 1995. pp. 264.

2096. HENDRICKSON, ROBERT.　Whistlin' Dixie: a dictionary of Southern expressions. (Bibl. 1993, 1256.) Rev. by Jesse Earle Bowden in FHQ (72:4) 1994, 511–13.

2097. —— Yankee talk: a dictionary of New England expressions. New York: Facts on File, 1996. pp. xvi, 255. (Facts on File dictionary of American regional expressions, 3.) Rev. by John Algeo in Verbatim (23:2) 1996, 23.

2098. KIRKPATRICK, BETTY.　Chambers dictionary of idioms and catch phrases. Edinburgh: Chambers, 1995. pp. ix, 310.

2099. —— Dictionary of clichés. London: Bloomsbury, 1996. pp. xiv, 207.

2100. LAMB, GREGOR.　Orkney wordbook: a dictionary of the dialect of Orkney. Birsay: Byrgisey, 1995. pp. 144. (Revised ed.: first ed. 1988.)

2101. LIGHTER, J. E. (ed.).　Random House historical dictionary of American slang: vol. 1, A–G. New York; London: Random House, 1994. pp. lxiv, 1006. Rev. by Gerald Leonard Cohen in AS (71:1) 1996, 103–5.

2102. MACAFEE, C. I. (ed.).　A concise Ulster dictionary. Oxford; New York: OUP, 1996. pp. xli, 405. Rev. by Keith Jeffery in TLS, 1 Nov. 1996, 10–11.

2103. McCORMICK, CATHERINE M.　British–American/American–British: Hippocrene dictionary and phrasebook. New York: Hippocrene, 1996. pp. 154.

2104. PEARSALL, JUDY; TRUMBLE, BILL (eds).　The Oxford English reference dictionary. (Bibl. 1995, 1623.) Rev. by Eric Korn in TLS, 1 Nov. 1996, 36.

2105. PFEFFER, J. ALAN; CANNON, GARLAND.　German loanwords in English: an historical dictionary. (Bibl. 1995, 1625.) Rev. by Anja Müller in ZAA (44:1) 1996, 82–4; by Manfred Görlach in IJL (9:1) 1996, 77–9.

2106. PICKERING, DAVID.　Dictionary of abbreviations. London; New York: Cassell, 1996. pp. viii, 340.

2107. POLLINGTON, STEPHEN.　Wordcraft. Pinner: Anglo-Saxon Books, 1993. pp. 233. (English–Old English.)

2108. PROCTER, PAUL (ed.).　Cambridge international dictionary of

English. Cambridge; New York: CUP, 1995. pp. xviii, 1774. Rev. by Robert Allen in English Today (12:2) 1996, 41–7; by Paul Pauwels in English Today (12:2) 1996, 52–5.

2109. PULA, ROBERT P.   A general semantics glossary. ERGS (51:1) 1994, 84–7; (51:2) 1994, 224–6; (51:4) 1994, 440–52; (52:1) 1995, 59–65; (52:2) 1995, 208–11; (52:3) 1995, 344–7; (52:4) 1995/96, 476–81; (53:2) 1996, 221–6; (53:3) 1996, 326–32.

2110. REES, NIGEL.   Dictionary of catchphrases. London: Cassell, 1995. pp. vii, 230.

2111. ROOM, ADRIAN.   The Hutchinson concise dictionary of word origins. Oxford: Helicon, 1995. pp. vii, 195.

2112. SHEWMAKER, EUGENE F.   Shakespeare's language: a glossary of unfamiliar words in Shakespeare's plays and poems. New York: Facts on File, 1996. pp. xii, 515.

2113. SILVA, PENNY, *et al.* (eds).   A dictionary of South African English on historical principles. Oxford; New York: OUP in assn with Dictionary Unit for South African English, 1996. pp. xxix, 825.

2114. SIMS-KIMBREY, JOAN.   Wodds and doggerybaw: a Lincolnshire dialect dictionary. Boston: Kay, 1995. pp. xiii, 370. (Talk of Lincolnshire.)

2115. SINCLAIR, JOHN, *et al.* (eds).   Collins COBUILD English dictionary. (Bibl. 1989, 1147.) London: HarperCollins, 1995. pp. xxxix, 1951. (Second ed.: first ed. 1987.) Rev. by Robert Allen in English Today (12:2) 1996, 41–7; by Paul Pauwels in English Today (12:2) 1996, 52–5.

2116. SPEVACK, MARVIN.   A Shakespeare thesaurus. (Bibl. 1995, 1638.) Rev. by Jay L. Halio in ShB (12:3) 1994, 44; by Christian J. Kay in IJL (9:1) 1996, 71–5.

2117. TRASK, R. L.   A dictionary of phonetics and phonology. *See* **1585**.

2118. VICKERY, ROY.   A dictionary of plant lore. (Bibl. 1995, 1646.) Rev. by Tecwyn Vaughan Jones in Folk Life (34) 1995/96, 106–7.

2119. WELLS, J. C.   Longman pronunciation dictionary. (Bibl. 1991, 1591.) Rev. by Brian M. Sietsema in IJL (8:4) 1995, 357–62.

2120. WILLIAMS, GORDON.   A dictionary of sexual language and imagery in Shakespearean and Stuart literature. (Bibl. 1995, 1650.) Rev. by Douglas Bruster in EMLS (2:2) 1996, 13.1–6.

NAMES

GENERAL STUDIES

2121. ANDREWS, EDNA.   Cultural sensitivity and political correctness: the linguistic problem of naming. AS (71:4) 1996, 389–404.

2122. ASHLEY, LEONARD R. N.   Native-American county names in Iowa. MidF (21:1/2) 1995, 39–43.

2123. —— The placenames of Kansas. MidF (21:1/2) 1995, 19–29.

2124. —— What's in a name? Everything you wanted to know. Baltimore, MD: Genealogical Publishing, 1989. pp. xii, 257. Rev. by Sterling Eisiminger in SECOLR (15:1) 1991, 102–3.

2125. BAKER, RONALD L.   From Needmore to Prosperity: Hoosier place names in folklore and history. Bloomington: Indiana UP, 1995. pp. 371. Rev. by Timothy C. Frazer in MidAF (24:2) 1996, 98–9.

2126. CALLARY, EDWARD.   Names on the air: the call signs of radio stations in Northern Illinois. MidF (21:1/2) 1995, 61–71.

2127. COHEN, GERALD LEONARD.   Some notes on Missouri's wealth of interesting placenames: Tightwad, Peculiar, Whoopup, Old Dishrag. MidF (21:1/2) 1995, 52–60.

2128. COLMAN, FRAN.   Names will never hurt me. *In* (pp. 13–28) **114**.

2129. COX, BARRIE.   The pattern of Old English *burh* in early Lindsey. *See* **1924**.

2130. CRAWFORD, ROBERT.   Native language. *See* **1954**.

2131. CULLETON, CLAIRE A.   Names and naming in Joyce. Madison; London: Wisconsin UP, 1994. pp. xi, 148. Rev. by Fritz Senn in JJQ (33:2) 1996, 293–300.

2132. DAGGETT, ROWAN KEIM.   The Anglicization of Miami and Potawatomi placenames in the Upper Wabash valley. MidF (21:1/2) 1995, 44–51.

2133. DEVOST, NADINE.   Hemingway's girls: unnaming and re-naming Hemingway's female characters. HemR (14:1) 1994, 46–59.

2134. DÍAZ VERA, JAVIER E.   From Domesday Book to Lay Subsidy Rolls: place-names as informants of linguistic change. *See* **1439**.

2135. DICKSON, PAUL.   What's in a name? Reflections of an irrepressible name collector. Springfield, MA: Merriam-Webster, 1996. pp. xv, 268.

2136. DUYFHUIZEN, BERNARD.   Periphrastic naming in Mary Shelley's *Frankenstein*. StudN (27:4) 1995, 477–92.

2137. EMERSON, RALPH H.   Some secrets of English nicknames. Verbatim (22:3) 1996, 12–13.

2138. —— The unpronounceables: difficult literary names 1500–1940. ELN (34:2) 1996, 63–74.

2139. FELLOWS-JENSEN, GILLIAN.   Hastings, Nottingham, Mucking and Donnington: a survey of research into *ing*-formations in England. NoB (84) 1996, 43–60.

2140. FIELD, JOHN.   A history of English field-names. (Bibl. 1995, 1676.) Rev. by Margaret Gelling in Early Medieval Europe (4:2) 1995, 223–4; by J. R. Maddicott in EHR (111:443) 1996, 1039.

2141. FRAZER, TIMOTHY C.   Personal name selection as a geographic variable in Illinois. MidF (21:1/2) 1995, 72–6.

2142. GASQUE, THOMAS J.   Lewis and Clark's onomastic assumptions. MidF (21:1/2) 1995, 30–8.

2143. GRIMSHAW, JAMES A., JR.   Onomastics in Flannery O'Connor's *Parker's Back*. NCL (24:3) 1994, 6–8.

2144. HARDER, KELSIE B.   Some naming procedures in the Midwest. MidF (21:1/2) 1995, 10–18.

2145. HOUGH, CAROLE.   English language: onomastics. YWES (75) 1994, 74–9.

2146. —— Old English *rōt* in place-names. *See* **1993**.

2147. JACOBSON, DAVID.   Contexts and cues in cyberspace: the pragmatics of naming in text-based virtual reality. *See* **1163**.

2148. KRISTENSSON, GILLIS.   Four English place-name etymologies. NOWELE (28/29) 1996, 431–7.

2149. LAWSON, EDWIN D.   More names and naming: an annotated bibliography. Westport, CT; London: Greenwood Press, 1995. pp. xix, 298. (Bibliographies and indexes in anthropology, 9.)

2150. McLAVERTY, JAMES.   Naming and blaming: the poetics of mock epic. Review (16) 1994, 221–36 (review-article).

2151. MILLAR, ROBERT McCOLL.   'Why is *Lebanon* called *the Lebanon?*': some suggestions for the grammatical and socio-political reasonings behind the use or non-use of *the* with the names of nation states in English. NQ (43:1) 1996, 22–7.

2152. MINER, EARL.   Naming properties: nominal reference in travel writings by Bashō and Sora, Johnson and Boswell. Ann Arbor: Michigan UP, 1996. pp. xvi, 318.

2153. MORRIS, ALLEN.   Florida place names. Sarasota, FL: Pineapple Press, 1995. pp. xiii, 291. Rev. by Charles Douglass in FHQ (75:2) 1996, 210–11.

2154. MULLER, ROY.   Names in science fiction and fantasy. Textures (10) 1996, 3–7.

2155. MUSCHELL, DAVID.   What in the word? Origins of words dealing with people and places. Bradenton, FL: McGuinn & McGuire, 1996. pp. viii, 216.

2156. NAGEL, RAINER.   Normenvorgabe in der literarischen Übersetzung: illustriert an den Eigennamen in J. R. R. Tolkiens *The Lord of the Rings*. ZAA (43:1) 1995, 1–10.

2157. NEWQUIST, DAVID L.   The spirit of place: the place of spirit. Midamerica (23) 1996, 47–55.

2158. NICOLAISEN, W. F. H.   In praise of William J. Watson (1865–1948): Celtic place-name scholar. SLang (14/15) 1995/96, 15–30.

2159. —— Onomastic aspects of *Clerk Colvill*. ARV (48) 1992, 31–41.

2160. NOBLE, ALLEN G.; CLEEK, RICHARD K.   Sorting out the nomenclature of English barns. MatC (26:1) 1994, 49–63.

2161. OGBOWEI, G. 'EBINYO; BELL-GAM, IBIERE.   *Sozaboy*: language and a disordered world. ESA (38:1) 1995, 1–17.

2162. POLLIN, BURTON R.   Names used for humor in Poe's fiction. PoeM (22) 1992, 15–19.

2163. RYMES, BETSY.   Naming as social practice: the case of Little Creeper from Diamond Street. Language in Society (25:2) 1996, 237–60.

2164. SANDRED, KARL INGE, *et al.*   The place-names of Norfolk: part II, The hundreds of East and West Flegg, Happing and Tunstead. Nottingham: English Place-Name Soc., 1996. pp. xxvi, 224. (English Place-Name Soc. pubs, 72.)

2165. TAYLOR, BRIAN.   Ocker, Richo and the other Aussie Dunny.

Mucking about with people's names in Australian English: what is the code? Australian Folklore (8) 1993, 112–37.

2166. URDANG, LAURENCE. Naming names. English Today (11:3) 1995, 19–22. (New Zealand place-names.)

2167. —— The uncommon use of proper names. *See* **2072**.

2168. VIZENOR, GERALD. Native-American Indian identities: auto-inscriptions and the cultures of names. Genre (25:4) 1992, 431–40.

2169. WILLIAMS, DAVID. Cyberwriting and the borders of identity: 'what's in a name' in Kroetsch's *The Puppeteer* and Mistry's *Such a Long Journey*? CanL (149) 1996, 55–71.

2170. WINNIFRITH, TOM. A note on some place-names in north-west Derbyshire. BST (21:7) 1996, 337–8. (Names used in *Jane Eyre*.)

SINGLE NAMES

2171. *Bell*] STEPHENSON, WILL; STEPHENSON, MIMOSA. A source in J. G. Lockhart for Charlotte Brontë's pseudonym. SSL (29) 1996, 258–61.

2172. *Boomers*] GOZZI, RAYMOND, JR. The *Generation X* and *Boomers* metaphors. ERGS (52:3) 1995, 331–5.

2173. *Brooklynese*] SHULMAN, DAVID. No *Brooklynese*, please! AS (71:3) 1996, 331–3.

2174. *Cotterstock*] HOUGH, CAROLE. The place-name *Cotterstock*. EngS (77:4) 1996, 375–8.

2175. *Ermonie*] ECKHARDT, CAROLINE D. The meaning of 'Ermonie' in *Sir Tristrem*. SP (93:1) 1996, 21–41.

2176. *Fluellen*] HOPKINS, LISA. Fluellen's name. SStud (24) 1996, 148–55.

2177. *Generation X*] GOZZI, RAYMOND, JR. The *Generation X* and *Boomers* metaphors. *See* **2172**.

2178. *Hoosier*] BAKER, RONALD L. Who's a Hoosier? MidF (21:1/2) 1995, 77–86.

2179. *Iago*] MOORE, PETER R. Shakespeare's Iago and Santiago Matamoros. NQ (43:2) 1996, 162–3.

2180. *Jacob*] —— Jacobus, Jacob, James: historicité et onomastique dans *The Master of Ballantrae* de Robert Louis Stevenson. Études Écossaises (1) 1992, 293–301.

2181. *Jacobus*] NAUGRETTE, JEAN-PIERRE. Jacobus, Jacob, James: historicité et onomastique dans *The Master of Ballantrae* de Robert Louis Stevenson. *See* **2180**.

2182. *James*] —— Jacobus, Jacob, James: historicité et onomastique dans *The Master of Ballantrae* de Robert Louis Stevenson. *See* **2180**.

2183. *Laputa*] ARGENT, JOSEPH E. The etymology of a dystopia: Laputa reconsidered. ELN (34:1) 1996, 36–40.

2184. *New England*] MORSE, JONATHAN. Some of the things we mean when we say 'New England'. EDJ (5:2) 1996, 209–14.

2185. *Pozzo*] BRYDEN, MARY. Pozzo in Samuel Beckett's *Waiting for Godot*. NQ (43:1) 1996, 60–1.

2186. *Thursley*] HOUGH, CAROLE. The place-name *Thursley*. NQ (43:4) 1996, 387–9.

2187. *Utopia*] HÖLSCHER, LUCIAN. Utopie. Utopian Studies (7:2) 1996, 1–65.

2188. *Whitgift*] ROBERTS, DAVID. A new allusion in *Hamlet*? NQ (43:2) 1996, 157–8.

MEANING

SEMANTICS

2189. ANON.   Free speech and the level playing field. GSB (61) 1995, 31–3.

2190. ARMSTRONG, SUSAN.   Thematic roles: a semantic feature analysis. CWPL (17) 1995, 51–6.

2191. AZZARO, GABRIELE.   Semantic syntax: English phrasal verbs. *See* **1649**.

2192. BARRATT, LESLIE B.; KONTRA, MIKLÓS.   Matching Hungarian and English color terms. IJL (9:2) 1996, 102–17.

2193. BARTELT, GUILLERMO.   A note on Old English kinship semantics. *See* **1881**.

2194. BLEYLE, C. D. W.   Semantic prerequisites and options for threats. SECOLR (19:2) 1995, 184–201.

2195. BOURLAND, D. DAVID, JR.   E-Prime: speaking crisply. ERGS (53:1) 1996, 26–38.

2196. BOWLES, GEORGE.   Affirming the consequent. Argumentation (10:3) 1996, 429–44.

2197. CACCIARI, C.; TABOSSI, PATRIZIA (eds).   Idioms: processing, structure, and interpretation. Hillsdale, NJ: Erlbaum, 1993. pp. xviii, 337.

2198. CLIFFORD, JAMES.   Formal semantics and pragmatics for natural language querying. *See* **1143**.

2199. COLEMAN, JULIE.   English language: lexicography, lexicology and semantics. *See* **2040**.

2200. DAVIS, DANIEL R.; EELES, JUDITH A.   Trade mark law: linguistic issues. Language & Communication (16:3) 1996, 255–62.

2201. DILLER, HANS-JÜRGEN.   *Joy* and *mirth* in Middle English and a little bit in Old: a plea for the consideration of genre in historical semantics. *In* (pp. 83–105) **68**.

2202. EATON, TREVOR.   Literary semantics as a science. JLSem (25:1) 1996, 7–65.

2203. FELLBAUM, CHRISTIANE.   Co-occurrence and antonymy. IJL (8:4) 1995, 281–303.

2204. FREEMAN, JAMES B.   Consider the source: one step in assessing premise acceptability. Argumentation (10:3) 1996, 453–60.

2205. GÓMEZ GONZÁLEZ, MARÍA.   Theme: topic or discourse framework? *See* **1679**.

2206. ITANI, REIKO.   What is the literal meaning of a sentence? Links & Letters (3) 1996, 39–48.

2207. JACKENDOFF, RAY.   Semantic structures. (Bibl. 1990, 1350.) Rev. by Yorick Wilks in CompLing (18:1) 1992, 95–7; rejoinder in (18:2) 1992, 240–2.

2208. JOSWIG-MEHNERT, DAGMAR; YULE, GEORGE.   The trouble with graffiti. JEL (24:2) 1996, 123–30.

2209. KISHNER, JEFFREY M.   How *just* gets its meanings: polysemy and context in psychological semantics. *See* **1968**.

2210. KJELLMER, GÖRAN.   Multiple meaning and interpretation: the case of *sanction*. *See* **1995**.

2211. LIEPE-LEVINSON, KATHERINE; LEVINSON, MARTIN H.   'Glossing over' feminism? A general semantics critique. *See* **1945**.

2212. McMahon, John G.; Smith, Francis J. Improving statistical language model performance with automatically generated word hierarchies. *See* **1183**.

2213. MacNeal, Edward. Looking ahead: why the real lesson of Vietnam eludes Robert McNamara. ERGS (52:3) 1995, 255–75.

2214. —— Millions–billions. *See* **1920**.

2215. —— Natural wonders. ERGS (53:1) 1996, 19–25. (Math-semantics.)

2216. —— One more time. ERGS (52:2) 1995, 174–85. (On ambiguity of phrases such as 'three times more'.)

2217. —— Playing the percentages: sex in Connecticut. ERGS (53:3) 1996, 275–84.

2218. Mettinger, Arthur. Aspects of semantic opposition in English. (Bibl. 1994, 1388.) Rev. by D. A. Cruse in IJL (9:2) 1996, 163–9.

2219. —— (Image-)schematic properties of antonymous adjectives. VIEWS (5) 1996, 12–26.

2220. Nagle, Stephen J. Inferential change and syntactic modality in English. *See* **1715**.

2221. Nagucka, Ruta. Spatial relations in Chaucer's *Treatise on the Astrolabe*. *In* (pp. 233–44) **68**.

2222. Ogihara, Toshiyuki. Tense, attitudes, and scope. *See* **1720**.

2223. Olsen, Mari Broman. The semantics and pragmatics of lexical aspect features. *See* **1722**.

2224. Palmer, F. R. (ed.). Grammar and meaning: essays in honour of Sir John Lyons. *See* **1725**.

2225. Papafragou, Anna. Figurative language and the semantics – pragmatics distinction. LangL (5:3) 1996, 179–93.

2226. Papi, Marcella Bertuccelli. Semantic vagueness and degree-of-precision adverbs. Textus (8:2) 1995, 313–31.

2227. Plat, Jean-Luc. *Like. See* **1802**.

2228. Prat Zagrebelsky, Maria Teresa. Processes of lexical and semantic innovation in contemporary English: the case of the Gulf War. *See* **1868**.

2229. Pula, Robert P. A general semantics glossary. *See* **2109**.

2230. —— The tyranny of agreement: a response to a response. ERGS (53:1) 1996, 96–105.

2231. Rauch, Irmengard. Deconstruction, prototype theory, and semiotics. AJSem (9:4) 1992, 131–40.

2232. Raukko, Jarno. 'No more polysemy', says the nationalist language police: the paradoxical battle between semantic flexibility and normativism. Pragmatics, Ideology, and Contacts Bulletin (3) 1996, 36–44.

2233. Rösel, Petr. Valenzsaturierung durch Komposition. Eine korpusbasierte Studie. AAA (21:1) 1996, 3–27.

2234. Rudanko, Juhani. Prepositions and complement clauses: a syntactic and semantic study of verbs governing prepositions and complement clauses in present-day English. *See* **1737**.

2235. Rullmann, Hotze. Two types of negative polarity items. *See* **1918**.

2236. Russell, Charles G.; Many, Paul. How language collectives compromise journalistic accuracy. ERGS (51:1) 1994, 88–94.

2237. Safir, Ken. Semantic atoms of anaphora. Natural Language and Linguistic Theory (14:3) 1996, 545–89.

2238. Schneider, Edgar W.   Towards syntactic isomorphism and semantic dissimilation: the semantics and syntax of prospective verbs in early modern English. *In* (pp. 199–220) **27**.

2239. Schnelle, Helmut.   The logic of Cobuild-type dictionary-semantics. *See* **2063**.

2240. Sinclair, John.   The search for units of meaning. Textus (9:1) 1996, 75–106.

2241. Strauss, Michael J.   What's pure? *See* **1987**.

2242. Taylor, Peter.   Lexical semantics across categories: what prepositions can tell us about the lexical entries of verbs. *See* **2070**.

2243. Thompson, Ellen.   The syntax and semantics of temporal adjunct clauses. *See* **1750**.

2244. Ungerer, Friedrich.   Basic level concepts and parasitic categorization: a cognitive alternative to conventional semantic hierarchies. ZAA (42:2) 1994, 148–62.

2245. Vicente, Begoña.   On the semantics and pragmatics of metaphor: coming full circle. LangL (5:3) 1996, 195–208.

2246. Walzer, Arthur E.   The meanings of *purpose*. *See* **1988**.

2247. Warren, Beatrice.   Sense developments: a contrastive study of the development of slang senses and novel standard senses in English. (Bibl. 1995, 1801.) Rev. by Werner Plehn in ZAA (44:4) 1996, 364–5.

2248. Waugh, Linda R.   Let's take the con out of iconicity: constraints on iconicity in the lexicon. *See* **1880**.

2249. Weatherly, Joan.   Where physics meets metaphysics: the semantic threshold. SECOLR (19:1) 1995, 59–79.

2250. Welte, Werner.   Englische Semantik: ein Lehr- und Arbeitsbuch mit umfassenden Bibliographie. (Bibl. 1995, 1804.) Rev. by Klaus Hansen in ZAA (42:3) 1994, 253–4.

PRAGMATICS

2251. Baker, Russell (ed.).   Russell Baker's book of American humor. New York: Norton, 1993. pp. 598. Rev. by Borling Lowrey in BkW, 5 Dec. 1993, 3, 16.

2252. Berbeira Gardón, José L.   Scope-ambiguity, modal verbs and quantification. EIUC (4) 1996, 53–66.

2253. Berger, Arthur Asa.   No laughing matter: eight scholars in search of a joke. ERGS (51:1) 1994, 29–35.

2254. Bleyle, C. D. W.   Semantic prerequisites and options for threats. *See* **2194**.

2255. Boyd, Christopher. Speaking Rushian. ERGS (51:3) 1994, 251–60. (Analysis of talk-show host Rush Limbaugh's persuasive methods.)

2256. Brinton, Laurel J.   Pragmatic markers in English: grammaticalization and discourse functions. *See* **1432**.

2257. Charles, Joel.   Replies to negative questions in the courtroom. AS (71:1) 1996, 109–11.

2258. Clifford, James.   Formal semantics and pragmatics for natural language querying. *See* **1143**.

2259. Couper-Kuhlen, Elizabeth; Selting, Margaret (eds). Prosody in conversation: interactional studies. *See* **1544**.

2260. Craig, Robert T.   Practical-theoretical argumentation. Argumentation (10:3) 1996, 461–74.

2261. Creswell, Cassandre. Criticizing with a question. StudLS (23:2) 1993, 25–32.

2262. Curell, Hortènsia; Moyer, Melissa G. A selected and annotated bibliography on pragmatics. Links & Letters (3) 1996, 105–23 (review-article).

2263. Dzameshie, Alex K. The use of politeness strategies as solidarity and deference moves in Christian sermonic discourse. SECOLR (17:2) 1993, 113–26.

2264. Esterhammer, Angela. Speech acts and world-creation: the dual function of the performative. CanRCL (20:3/4) 1993, 285–304.

2265. Fludernik, Monika. Linguistic signals and interpretative strategies: linguistic models in performance, with special reference to free indirect discourse. LangL (5:2) 1996, 93–113.

2266. Fuller, Janet M. Deconstructing the defense: irony and style switching as linguistic strategies in the courtroom. SECOLR (18:1) 1994, 31–44.

2267. Galasinski, Dariusz. Pretending to cooperate: how speakers hide evasive actions. Argumentation (10:3) 1996, 375–88.

2268. Geis, Michael L. Speech acts and conversational interaction. Cambridge; New York: CUP, 1995. pp. xiv, 248.

2269. Green, Keith (ed.). New essays in deixis: discourse, narrative, literature. (Bibl. 1995, 35.) Rev. by Roger Fowler in LangL (5:2) 1996, 146–7.

2270. Jackendoff, Ray. The proper treatment of measuring out, telicity, and perhaps even quantification in English. Natural Language and Linguistic Theory (14:2) 1996, 305–54.

2271. Jacobs, Don Trent. The red flags of persuasion. ERGS (52:4) 1995/96, 375–92.

2272. Johnstone, Barbara. Violence and civility in discourse: uses of mitigation by rural Southern White men. SECOLR (16:1) 1992, 1–19.

2273. Knott, Alistair; Mellish, Chris. A feature-based account of the relations signalled by sentence and clause connectives. *See* **1703**.

2274. Komter, Martha. Conflict and cooperation in job interviews: a study of talk, tasks and ideas. (Bibl. 1992, 1873.) Rev. by Nancy Barendse in SECOLR (17:2) 1993, 182–5.

2275. Lakoff, Robin. Many stories, multiple meanings: narrative in the O. J. Simpson case as a cultural discourse event. Links & Letters (3) 1996, 49–60.

2276. Lew, Robert. Exploitation of linguistic ambiguity in English and Polish jokes. PSiCL (31) 1996, 127–33.

2277. Lucy, Niall; McHoul, Alec. The logical status of Searlean discourse. Boundary 2 (23:3) 1996, 219–41. (*Refers to* bibl. 1994, 1447.)

2278. Mathalt, Minna-Liisa. Miscommunication and strategies in interpreted interaction. Teaching & Learning (2) 1996, 15–23.

2279. Moran, Terence P. Public doublespeak and image manipulation. GSB (61) 1995, 39–45.

2280. Nielsen, Anne Ellerup. The argumentative impact of causal relations: an exemplary analysis of the free predicate in the promotional discourse. Argumentation (10:3) 1996, 329–45.

2281. Olsen, Mari Broman. The semantics and pragmatics of lexical aspect features. *See* **1722**.

2282. Palacios Martínez, Ignacio Miguel. Notes on the use and meaning of negation in contemporary written English. *See* **1723**.

2283. PAPAFRAGOU, ANNA.   Figurative language and the semantics–pragmatics distinction. *See* **2225**.

2284. PAPI, MARCELLA BERTUCCELLI.   Determining the proposition expressed by an utterance: the role of 'domain adverbs'. *See* **1726**.

2285. PENZ, HERMINE.   Language and control in American TV talk shows: an analysis of linguistic strategies. Tübingen: Narr, 1996. pp. ix, 192.

2286. ROZIK, ELI.   Categorization of speech acts in play and performance. JDTC (8:1) 1993, 117–32.

2287. RUDANKO, JUHANI.   Pleading with an unreasonable king: on the Kent and Pauline episodes in Shakespeare. EIUC (4) 1996, 11–22.

2288. SCHULZE, RAINER.   How to express 'dislike' in words: an investigation into the metapragmatics of English. ZAA (42:4) 1994, 306–16.

2289. SIFIANOU, MARIA.   Politeness phenomena in England and Greece: a cross-cultural perspective. (Bibl. 1994, 1450.) Rev. by Maro Kakride-Ferrari in Glossologia (9/10) 1990/91, 288–92.

2290. SMELTZER, MARK A.   Lying and intersubjective truth: a communication-based approach to understanding lying. Argumentation (10:3) 1996, 361–73.

2291. STRAUSS, MICHAEL J.   97% fat free: on the art of misinforming. ERGS (52:3) 1995, 284–91.

2292. SULLIVAN, LAURA L.   'Are you there? ... Please pick up ...': the telephone answering machine and social interaction. SECOLR (18:2) 1994, 139–63.

2293. TOMLINSON, BARBARA.   The politics of textual vehemence; or, Go to your room until you learn how to act. Signs (22:1) 1996, 86–114.

2294. URBANOVÁ, LUDMILA.   Modification of the illocutionary force. Brno Studies in English (22) 1996, 63–70.

2295. VALLDUVÍ, ENRIC; ENGDAHL, ELISABET.   The linguistic realization of information packaging. Linguistics (34:3) 1996, 459–519.

2296. VANDERVEKEN, DANIEL.   Meaning and speech acts: vol. 1, Principles of language use; vol. 2, Formal semantics of success and satisfaction. (Bibl. 1993, 1425.) Rev. by Amichai Kronfeld in CompLing (19:2) 1993, 385–9.

2297. VAN EEMEREN, FRANS H., *et al.*   Argumentation illuminated. Amsterdam: SIC SAT, 1992. pp. xiii, 294. (Sic sat, 1.) Rev. by James M. Freeman in Argumentation (10:3) 1996, 409–14.

2298. VICENTE, BEGOÑA.   On the semantics and pragmatics of metaphor: coming full circle. *See* **2245**.

2299. WALKER, MARILYN A.   Inferring acceptance and rejection in dialog by default rules of inference. Language and Speech (39:2/3) 1996, 265–304.

2300. WALTER, BETTYRUTH.   The jury summation as speech genre: an ethnographic study of what it means to those who use it. (Bibl. 1988, 971.) Rev. by Marvin K. L. Ching in SECOLR (15:2) 1991, 228–30.

2301. WALTON, DOUGLAS.   The witch hunt as a structure of argumentation. Argumentation (10:3) 1996, 389–407.

2302. WOOD, LEE ALEXANDRA.   *Voir dire* hardship-case requests and possible consequences from patterns of interaction. SECOLR (20:2) 1996, 182–202.

RHETORIC AND FIGURES OF SPEECH

2303. ALLISTON, APRIL.   Gender and the rhetoric of evidence in early-modern historical narratives. CLS (33:3) 1996, 233–57.

2304. BADENHAUSEN, RICHARD. Representing experience and reasserting identity: the rhetoric of combat in British literature of World War I. Style (30:2) 1996, 268–88.

2305. BAILIN, ALAN. Meaning change: metaphorical and literal. JLSem (24:3) 1995, 211–30.

2306. BATES, CATHERINE. The rhetoric of courtship: courting and courtliness in Elizabethan language and literature. (Bibl. 1995, 1901.) Rev. by Richard C. McCoy in Review (16) 1994, 315–18; by Lois Potter in JBS (34:4) 1995, 536–42; by Jameela Lares in RSQ (26:3) 1996, 61–4.

2307. BENDER, JOHN; WELLBERY, DAVID E. (eds). The ends of rhetoric: history, theory, practice. Stanford, CA: Stanford UP, 1990. pp. xiv, 238. Rev. by John D. Schaeffer in Style (25:4) 1991, 640–4.

2308. BENNETT, ANDREW F. Churchill's speechmaking: a response to Wolfgang Mieder. Folklore (107) 1996, 93. (*Response to* bibl. 1995, 2004.)

2309. BENOIT, WILLIAM L. The genesis of rhetorical action. SCJ (59:4) 1994, 342–55.

2310. BERGMAN, DAVID. Strategic camp: the art of gay rhetoric. *In* (pp. 92–109) **12**.

2311. BETHLEHEM, LOUISE SHABAT. Simile and figurative language. PT (17:2) 1996, 203–40.

2312. BETTINGER, ELFI. Das umkäpfte Bild. Zur Metapher bei Virginia Woolf. (Bibl. 1993, 1443.) Rev. by Götz Schmitz in Archiv (233:1) 1996, 188–9.

2313. BEX, TONY. Parody, genre and literary meaning. JLSem (25:3) 1996, 225–44.

2314. BLACK, EDWIN. Rhetorical questions: studies of public discourse. (Bibl. 1992, 1899.) Rev. by William E. Coleman, Jr, in ERGS (51:2) 1994, 239.

2315. BLAKE, N. F. Lexical links in Shakespeare. PoetT (45) 1996, 79–103.

2316. BLUNCK, PAULA. From a 'rational' structure to a 'sociotechnical' system: a whole-mind metaphor for organizational change. ERGS (51:4) 1994/95, 442–31.

2317. BLYTHE, JOAN HEIGES. Sins of the tongue and rhetorical prudence in *Piers Plowman*. *In* (pp. 119–42) **61**.

2318. BOHLKEN, BOB. The idiom experience. ERGS (53:2) 1996, 218–20.

2319. BRAET, ANTOINE. On the origin of normative argumentation theory: the paradoxical case of the *Rhetoric to Alexander*. Argumentation (10:3) 1996, 347–59.

2320. BROWN, CONSTANCE A. Severed ears: an image of the Vietnam War. WLA (4:1) 1992, 25–42.

2321. BROWN, MURRAY L. *Emblemata rhetorica*: glossing emblematic discourse in Richardson's *Clarissa*. *See* **184**.

2322. BROWN, STUART C. I. A. Richards' new rhetoric: multiplicity, instrument, and metaphor. RhR (10:2) 1992, 218–31.

2323. CALLAGHAN, PATSY; DOBYNS, ANN. Literary conversation: thinking, talking, and writing about literature. Boston, MA; London: Allyn & Bacon, 1996. pp. xi, 260.

2324. CAMARGO, MARTIN. Rhetorical ethos and the Nun's Priest's Tale. CLS (33:2) 1996, 173–86.

2325. —— (ed.). Medieval rhetorics of prose composition: five

English *artes dictandi* and their tradition. (Bibl. 1995, 1914.) Rev. by John O. Ward in Parergon (14:1) 1996, 277–9.

2326.   CAMPBELL, JOANN (ed.).   Toward a feminist rhetoric: the writing of Gertrude Buck. Pittsburgh, PA: Pittsburgh UP, 1996. pp. xliii, 287. (Pitt series in composition, literacy and culture.)

2327.   CAMPBELL, KARLYN KOHRS.   Hearing women's voices. CommEd (40:1) 1991, 33–48.

2328.   —— The rhetorical act. Belmont, CA: Wadsworth, 1996. pp. xvii, 398. (Second ed.: first ed. 1982.)

2329.   —— BURKHOLDER, THOMAS R.   Critiques of contemporary rhetoric. Belmont, CA: Wadsworth, 1996. pp. xiii, 335.

2330.   CARRUTHERS, MARY J.   Invention, mnemonics, and stylistic ornament in *Psychomachia* and *Pearl*. In (pp. 201–13) **26**.

2331.   CARTER, ALBERT HOWARD, III.   Metaphors in the physician–patient relationship. Soundings (72) 1989, 153–64.

2332.   CHAPEL, GEORGE.   Rhetorical synthesis and the discourse of Jack Kemp. SCJ (61:4) 1996, 342–62.

2333.   CIFARELLI, MARIA RITA.   Militanza per la pace e retorica della guerra: le intellettuali inglesi e la Grande Guerra. QLLSM (7) 1995, 69–106.

2334.   CLARK, STEPHEN H.   The 'failing soul': Macpherson's response to Locke. ECL (19:1) 1995, 39–56.

2335.   CLARKE, BRUCE.   Allegories of Victorian thermodynamics. Configurations (4:1) 1996, 67–90.

2336.   CMIEL, KENNETH.   Democratic eloquence: the fight over popular speech in nineteenth-century America. (Bibl. 1995, 1922.) Rev. by David Grimsted in AHR (96:4) 1991, 1268–9.

2337.   COE, RICHARD M.   Beyond diction: using Burke to empower words – and actions. RhR (11:2) 1993, 368–77.

2338.   COLELLA, SILVANA.   Il lungo addio: retorica e militanza nella campagna per il voto. QLLSM (7) 1995, 43–68.

2339.   COMO, JAMES.   The centrality of rhetoric to an understanding of C. S. Lewis. CSL (25:1) 1993, 1–7.

2340.   CONDREN, CONAL.   The language of politics in seventeenth-century England. Basingstoke: Macmillan; New York: St Martin's Press, 1994. pp. xi, 215. (Studies in modern history.) Rev. by Barbara Shapiro in AHR (101:2) 1996, 480–1.

2341.   COUSINS, A. D.   Towards a reconsideration of Shakespeare's Adonis: rhetoric, Narcissus, and the male gaze. SN (68:2) 1996, 195–204.

2342.   COVINO, WILLIAM A.   Grammars of transgression: golems, cyborgs, and mutants. RhR (14:2) 1996, 355–73.

2343.   CRISP, PETER.   Imagism's metaphors – a test case. LangL (5:2) 1996, 79–92.

2344.   CRUSIUS, TIMOTHY.   Neither trust nor suspicion: Kenneth Burke's rhetoric and hermeneutics. SLI (28:2) 1995, 79–90.

2345.   DAGENAIS, JULIA.   Frontier preaching as formulaic poetry. MidAF (19:2) 1991, 118–26.

2346.   D'ANGELO, FRANK.   The four master tropes: analogues of development. RhR (11:1) 1992, 91–106.

2347.   DEAN, SHARON.   Literature and composition theory: Joyce Carol Oates' journal stories. RhR (10:2) 1992, 311–20.

2348.   DIMOCK, WAI CHEE.   Class, gender, and a history of metonymy. In (pp. 57–104) **100**.

2349. DOHERTY, GERALD. The art of appropriation: the rhetoric of sexuality in D. H. Lawrence. Style (30:2) 1996, 289–308.

2350. —— Metaphor and mental disturbance: the case of *Lady Chatterley's Lover*. Style (30:1) 1996, 113–29.

2351. DONAVIN, GEORGIANA. The medieval rhetoric of identification: a Burkean reconception. RSQ (26:2) 1996, 51–66.

2352. DONOVAN, JOSEPHINE. Style and power. *In* (pp. 85–94) **33**.

2353. DORSEY, PETER A. Becoming the other: the mimesis of metaphor in Douglass's *My Bondage and My Freedom*. PMLA (111:3) 1996, 435–50.

2354. DOWLING, PAUL M. Polite wisdom: heathen rhetoric in Milton's *Areopagitica*. Lanham, MD; London: Rowman & Littlefield, 1995. pp. xxxii, 113. Rev. by John Mulryan in Cithara (36:1) 1996, 34–6.

2355. DOWNS-GAMBLE, MARGARET. New pleasures prove: evidence of dialectical *disputatio* in early modern manuscript culture. EMLS (2:2) 1996, 2.1–33.

2356. DUNN, KEVIN. Pretexts of authority: the rhetoric of authorship in the Renaissance preface. (Bibl. 1994, 1487.) Rev. by Raymond D. Tumbleson in Prose Studies (19:1) 1996, 117–19.

2357. ENDERS, JODY. Rhetoric and the origins of medieval drama. (Bibl. 1995, 1939.) Rev. by Scott D. Troyan in ChauY (3) 1996, 178–80.

2358. ENOS, THERESA (ed.). Encyclopedia of rhetoric and composition: communication from ancient times to the information age. New York; London: Garland, 1996. pp. xxiv, 803. (Garland reference library of the humanities, 1389.) Rev. by Glen McClish in RSQ (26:4) 1996, 123–5.

2359. —— Learning from the histories of rhetoric: essays in honor of Winifred Bryan Horner. Carbondale: Southern Illinois UP, 1993. pp. viii, 183. Rev. by James Yawn in RSQ (26:3) 1996, 69–72.

2360. EPSTEIN, JAMES A. Radical expression: political language, ritual, and symbol in England, 1790–1850. (Bibl. 1995, 1940.) Rev. by Marc Baer in AHR (101:1) 1996, 182–3.

2361. ERICKSON, PAUL D. Henry David Thoreau's apotheosis of John Brown: a study of nineteenth-century rhetorical heroism. SCJ (61:4) 1996, 302–11.

2362. ERVIN, ELIZABETH. Interdisciplinarity or 'an elaborate edifice built on sand'? Rethinking rhetoric's place. RhR (12:1) 1993, 84–105.

2363. FARRELL, THOMAS B. Norms of rhetorical culture. (Bibl. 1995, 1941.) Rev. by Richard Leo Enos in RSQ (26:3) 1996, 57–9; by Charles Arthur Willard in Argumentation (10:2) 1996, 317–25.

2364. FAY, ELIZABETH A. Eminent rhetoric: language, gender, and cultural tropes. (Bibl. 1994, 1490.) Rev. by Karen Fitts in ColLit (23:1) 1996, 235–7.

2365. FISCHLIN, DANIEL. Metalepsis and the rhetoric of lyric affect. ESCan (22:3) 1996, 315–35.

2366. FLIEGELMAN, JAY. Declaring independence: Jefferson, natural language, & the culture of performance. (Bibl. 1995, 1947.) Rev. by Stephen E. Lucas in AHR (99:3) 1994, 969–70; by Saul Cornell in AmS (35:2) 1994, 150–2.

2367. GAJDUSEK, ROBERT E. The oxymoronic compound and the ambiguous noun: paradox as paradigm in *A Farewell to Arms*. NDQ (63:3) 1996, 40–9.

2368. GANNETT, CINTHIA. Gender and the journal: diaries and academic discourse. Albany: New York State UP, 1992. pp. xiv, 262. (SUNY series: literacy, culture, and learning.) Rev. by Gloria Bowles in NWSAJ (4:3) 1992, 373–9.

2369. GARDINER, ELLEN.   Peter Elbow's rhetoric of reading. RhR (13:2) 1995, 321–30.

2370. GARDINER, JUDITH KEGAN.   Re-gendering individualism: Margaret Fell Fox and Quaker rhetoric. *In* (pp. 205–24) **89**.

2371. GIDDENS, ELIZABETH.   An epistemic case study: identification and attitude change in John McPhee's *Coming into the Country*. RhR (11:2) 1993, 378–99.

2372. GILLES, ROGER.   Richard Weaver revisited: rhetoric left, right, and middle. RhR (15:1) 1996, 128–41.

2373. GINSBERG, WARREN.   Chaucer's Canterbury poetics: irony, allegory, and the Prologue to the Manciple's Tale. SAC (18) 1996, 55–89.

2374. GLENN, CHERYL.   Remapping rhetorical territory. RhR (13:2) 1995, 287–303.

2375. GOLDFINE, RUTH RODAK; KING, GINA MARIE.   Never at a loss for words: why do clichés live on? ERGS (51:3) 1994, 338–50.

2376. GOZZI, RAYMOND, JR.   Confessions of a metaphoraholic. *See* **1638**.

2377. —— The *cyberspace* metaphor. *See* **1931**.

2378. —— Economic metaphors for education. *See* **1923**.

2379. —— The fable of the electric maps and the mutating territory. *See* **1976**.

2380. —— The *Generation X* and *Boomers* metaphors. *See* **2172**.

2381. —— The *information superhighway* as metaphor. *See* **1965**.

2382. —— The *projection* metaphor in psychology. *See* **1986**.

2383. —— *Structure*: the intellectual's metaphor. *See* **2007**.

2384. —— Will the media create a global village? *See* **1957**.

2385. GRAHAM, KENNETH J. E.   The performance of conviction: plainness and rhetoric in the early English Renaissance. (Bibl. 1995, 1960.) Rev. by M. L. Stapleton in ShB (12:4) 1994, 45.

2386. GREENBERG, MARK L. (ed.).   Speak silence: rhetoric and culture in Blake's *Poetical Sketches*. Detroit, MI: Wayne State UP, 1996. pp. 221.

2387. GWARA, SCOTT.   A metaphor in *Beowulf* 2487a: *gūðhelm tōglād*. SP (93:4) 1996, 333–48.

2388. HAAS, LYNDA.   The daughter's seduction; or, Writing with the rhetors. Pre/Text (15:3/4) 1994, 138–81.

2389. HAAS, MANUEL.   '*I must speak, but what, oh love?*': John Marstons *Antonio*-Stücke als vergebliche Suche nach der angemessenen Dramensprache. ZAA (44:2) 1996, 124–33.

2390. HAGEN, PETER L.   'Pure persuasion' and verbal irony. SCJ (61:1) 1995, 46–58.

2391. HALPER, LOUISE A.   Tropes of anxiety and desire: metaphor and metonymy in the law of takings. YJLH (8:1) 1996, 31–62.

2392. HART, RODERICK P.   Modern rhetorical criticism. Glenview, IL: Scott, Foresman; Little Brown Higher Education, 1990. pp. 542. (Scott, Foresman/Little, Brown rhetoric and society.) Rev. by Nancy R. Dunbar in ComQ (40:1) 1992, 84–5.

2393. HARWOOD, BRITTON J.   Chaucer on '*speche*': *House of Fame*, the Friar's Tale, and the Summoner's Tale. ChauR (26:4) 1992, 343–9.

2394. HAWES, CLEMENT.   Mania and literary style: the rhetoric of enthusiasm from the Ranters to Christopher Smart. Cambridge; New York: CUP, 1996. pp. xii, 243. (Cambridge studies in eighteenth-century English literature and thought, 29.)

2395. HAWES, THOMAS; THOMAS, SARAH. Rhetorical uses of theme in newspaper editorials. WorldE (15:2) 1996, 159–70.

2396. HAYNE, VICTORIA. 'All language then is vile': the theatrical critique of political rhetoric in Nathaniel Lee's *Lucius Junius Brutus*. ELH (63:2) 1996, 337–65.

2397. HILLMAN, DAVID. Puttenham, Shakespeare, and the abuse of rhetoric. *See* **1935**.

2398. HOBSON, CHRISTOPHER Z. Bastard speech: the rhetoric of 'commodity' in *King John*. Shakespeare Yearbook (2) 1991, 95–114.

2399. HOGAN, J. MICHAEL; WILLIAMS, L. GLEN. Defining 'the enemy' in Revolutionary America: from the rhetoric of protest to the rhetoric of war. SCJ (61:4) 1996, 277–88.

2400. HUNTER, JOHN. The Euphuistic memory: Humanist culture and Bacon's *Advancement of Learning*. RenP 1995, 47–63.

2401. HURST, MARY JANE. The road to the White House: a comparison of language in candidate Clinton's acceptance speech and language in President Clinton's inaugural address. SECOLR (19:1) 1995, 80–103.

2402. HUTCHEON, LINDA. Irony's edge: the theory and politics of irony. (Bibl. 1995, 1976.) Rev. by Camille R. La Bossière in ESCan (22:3) 1996, 359–61; by Glenn Willmott in ECanW (58) 1996, 151–7; by Hans H. Rudnick in WLT (70:1) 1996, 245–6.

2403. JACOBUS, LEE A. Milton: the rhetorical gesture of monody. *In* (pp. 447–60) **98**.

2404. JAHN, MANFRED. Windows of focalization: deconstructing and reconstructing a narratological concept. Style (30:2) 1996, 241–67.

2405. KACHRU, YAMUNA. Contrastive rhetoric in world Englishes. English Today (11:1) 1995, 21–31.

2406. —— Kachru revisits contrasts. English Today (12:1) 1996, 41–4.

2407. KAHN, VICTORIA. Machiavellian rhetoric from the Counter-Reformation to Milton. (Bibl. 1995, 1982.) Rev. by William J. Bouwsma in AHR (101:1) 1996, 173.

2408. KATZ, STEVEN B. The epistemic music of rhetoric: toward the temporal dimension of affect in reader-response and writing. Carbondale: Southern Illinois UP, 1996. pp. xiv, 350.

2409. KAUFER, DAVID S.; BUTLER, BRIAN S. Rhetoric and the arts of design. Mahwah, NJ: Erlbaum, 1996. pp. xvii, 322.

2410. KAUL, SUVIR. Colonial figures and postcolonial reading. Diacritics (26:1) 1996, 74–89 (review-article).

2411. KENNEDY, THOMAS C. Rhetoric and meaning in *The House of Fame*. SN (68:1) 1996, 9–23.

2412. KINNEY, ARTHUR F. Figuring medieval and Renaissance literature. *In* (pp. 13–34) **131**.

2413. KLENOTIC, JEFFREY F. The place of rhetoric in 'new' film historiography: the discourse of corrective revisionism. Film History (6:1) 1994, 45–58.

2414. KOSKI, LENA. Sexual metaphors in Emily Dickinson's letters to Susan Gilbert. EDJ (5:2) 1996, 26–31.

2415. KYNDRUP, MORTEN. Framing and fiction: studies in the rhetoric of novel, interpretation, and history: a composition. (Bibl. 1993, 1485.) Rev. by Steven Scott in CanRCL (23:4) 1996, 1255–8.

2416. LANE, BELDEN C.   Prayer without language in the apophatic tradition: knowing God as 'inaccessible mountain' – 'marvelous desert'. SM (ns 2) 1996, 3–29.

2417. LAW, JULES DAVID.   The rhetoric of empiricism: language and perception from Locke to I. A. Richards. (Bibl. 1995, 1990.) Rev. by Adam Potkay in ECL (19:2) 1995, 103–10; by Gary Day in BJECS (19:1) 1996, 88; by Timothy J. Reiss in ECS (29:3) 1996, 337–9; by Gary Wihl in PT (17:2) 1996, 270–3.

2418. LEEMAN, RICHARD W.   Spatial metaphors in African-American discourse. SCJ (60:2) 1995, 165–80.

2419. —— (ed.).   African-American orators: a bio-critical source-book. Westport, CT; London: Greenwood Press, 1996. pp. xxv, 452.

2420. LOWANCE, MASON I., JR; WESTBROOK, ELLEN E.; DE PROSPO, R. C. (eds).   The Stowe debate: rhetorical strategies in *Uncle Tom's Cabin*. (Bibl. 1994, 1511.) Rev. by Beth Maclay Doriani in AL (68:2) 1996, 464–5; by Theodore R. Hovet in AmS (37:2) 1996, 198–9; by Nancy Lusignan Schultz in ColLit (23:3) 1996, 196–8.

2421. LYALL, RODERICK J.   The construction of a rhetorical voice in sixteenth-century Scottish letters. Prose Studies (19:2) 1996, 127–35.

2422. McCONNELL, KATHLEEN.   Textile tropes in *The Afterlife of George Cartwright*. CanL (149) 1996, 91–109.

2423. McPHAIL, MARK LAWRENCE.   Zen in the art of rhetoric: an inquiry into coherence. Albany: New York State UP, 1996. pp. ix, 220. (SUNY series in speech communication.) Rev. by Sum Hum in RhR (15:1) 1996, 228–31.

2424. MAHBOBAH, ALBARAQ.   Hysteria, rhetoric, and the politics of reversal in Henry James's *The Turn of the Screw*. HJR (17:2) 1996, 149–61.

2425. MAILLOUX, STEVEN.   Persuasions good and bad: Bunyan, Iser, and Fish on rhetoric and hermeneutics in literature. SLI (28:2) 1995, 43–61.

2426. MANNING, SUSAN.   Naming of parts; or, The comforts of classification: Thomas Jefferson's construction of America as fact and myth. JAStud (30:3) 1996, 345–64.

2427. MAO, LU MING R.   I conclude not: toward a pragmatic account of metadiscourse. RhR (11:2) 1993, 265–89.

2428. MERRILL, YVONNE DAY.   The social construction of Western women's rhetoric before 1750. Lewiston, NY; Lampeter: Mellen Press, 1996. pp. 276. (Women's studies, 9.) (Cf. bibl. 1994, 1517.)

2429. MIKKONEN, KAI.   Theories of metamorphosis: from metatrope to textual revision. Style (30:2) 1996, 309–40.

2430. MIXON, J. WILSON, JR.   Keeping it on the road: a metaphor for the economy? ERGS (52:3) 1995, 292–8.

2431. MOOIJ, J. J. A.   On metaphor in poetry. CanRCL (19:3) 1992, 313–29.

2432. MORTON, TIMOTHY.   Trade winds. EAS (49) 1996, 19–41.

2433. MUIR, STAR A.   The web and the spaceship: metaphors of the environment. *See* **2003**.

2434. MÜLLER, WOLFGANG G.   Drei Formen des Wortspiels bei Shakespeare: Paronomasie, Paronymie, Polyptoton. *In* (pp. 205–24) **11**.

2435. NEWTON, ALLYSON P.   At 'the very heart of loss': Shakespeare's Enobarbus and the rhetoric of remembering. RenP 1995, 81–91.

2436. NORTON, JANICE. Rhetorical criticism as ethical action: *cherchez la femme*. SCJ (61:1) 1995, 29–45.

2437. O'LEARY, STEPHEN D.; WRIGHT, MARK H. Psychoanalysis and Burkeian rhetorical criticism. SCJ (61:2) 1995, 104–21.

2438. OLSON, GARY A. (ed.). Philosophy, rhetoric, literary criticism: (inter)views. Foreword by Clifford Geertz. Introd. by Patricia Bizzell. Commentary by David Bleich. Carbondale: Southern Illinois UP, 1994. pp. xii, 250. Rev. by Xin Liu Gale in RSQ (26:3) 1996, 65–7.

2439. OMORI, AYAKO. Meaning and metaphor. PoetT (46) 1996, 119–36.

2440. ORIARD, MICHAEL. Sporting with the gods: the rhetoric of play and game in American culture. (Bibl. 1993, 1496.) Rev. by Christian K. Messenger in AHR (98:2) 1993, 581–2.

2441. O'ROURKE, SEAN PATRICK, *et al*. The most significant passage on rhetoric in the works of Francis Bacon. RSQ (26:3) 1996, 31–55.

2442. PAINTER, ANDREW. On metaphor in the early poetry of Robert Graves: anticipating an alternative poetics. Gravesiana (1:1) 1996, 11–20.

2443. PAPAFRAGOU, ANNA. Figurative language and the semantics–pragmatics distinction. *See* **2225**.

2444. PASSALACQUA, GABRIELLA GALLIANO. *Inventio e figurae* nei '*present discontents*': osservazioni sull'aspetto retorico del discorso politico burkeano. QLLSM (2) 1987, 59–86.

2445. PETTIT, ALEXANDER. Lord Bolingbroke's *Remarks on the History of England* and the rhetoric of political controversy. AJ (7) 1996, 365–95.

2446. PHELAN, JAMES. Narrative as rhetoric: technique, audiences, ethics, ideology. Columbus: Ohio State UP, 1996. pp. xiv, 237. (Theory and interpretation of narrative.)

2447. PICCHIONI, PAOLA. Eco come figura retorica e mitologica in *Loin de l'Être* di Stevie Smith. Annali anglistica (36:1–3) 1993, 137–53.

2448. —— Retorica e neoretorica in *Paradise Lost*. Textus (4) 1991, 33–68.

2449. PIZZORNO, PATRIZIA GRIMALDI. Metaphor and *exemplum* in the Nun's Priest's Tale. Assays (9) 1996, 79–99.

2450. PORTER, JAMES E. Audience and rhetoric: an archeological composition of the discourse community. Englewood Cliffs, NJ; London: Prentice Hall, 1992. pp. xv, 185. Rev. by Jack Selzer in RSQ (26:4) 1996, 126–9.

2451. POTKAY, ADAM. The fate of eloquence in the age of Hume. (Bibl. 1994, 1537.) Rev. by Stephen Copley in BJECS (19:2) 1996, 227–8; by Glen McClish in RSQ (26:2) 1996, 96–8; by Michael Prince in Criticism (38:2) 1996, 331–5.

2452. RAJAN, B. From centre to circumference: modern migrations of a Miltonic metaphor. In-between (5:1) 1996, 3–21.

2453. RATCLIFFE, KRISTA. A rhetoric of textual feminism: (re)reading the emotional in Virginia Woolf's *Three Guineas*. RhR (11:2) 1993, 400–17.

2454. RAYMOND, JOAD. The cracking of the republican spokes. Prose Studies (19:3) 1996, 255–74.

2455. RELIHAN, CONSTANCE C. Rhetoric, gender, and audience construction in Thomas Nashe's *The Unfortunate Traveller. In* (pp. 141–52) **35**.

2456. RICHARDS, BERNARD. Apostrophe. ERev (5:3) 1995, 26–8.

2457. ROBERTSON, ANDREW W. The language of democracy:

political rhetoric in the United States and Britain, 1790–1900. (Bibl. 1995, 2021.) Rev. by John Seelye in AL (68:2) 1996, 461–2.

2458. ROOCHNIK, DAVID. Stanley Fish and the old quarrel between rhetoric and philosophy. CritR (5:2) 1991, 225–46.

2459. ROYER, DANIEL J. New challenges to epistemic rhetoric. RhR (9:2) 1991, 282–97.

2460. RUBIN, DONALD L. (ed.). Composing social identity in written language. Hillsdale, NJ: Erlbaum, 1995. pp. viii, 252. Rev. by Robert B. Kaplan in Language in Society (25:4) 1996, 623–6.

2461. SADOSKI, MARK. Imagination, cognition, and persona. RhR (10:2) 1992, 266–78.

2462. SALVADOR, MICHAEL. The rhetorical genesis of Ralph Nader: a functional exploration of narrative and argument in public discourse. SCJ (59:3) 1994, 227–39.

2463. —— The rhetorical subversion of cultural boundaries: the National Consumers' League. SCJ (59:4) 1994, 318–32.

2464. SCANLON, LARRY. Narrative, authority, and power: the medieval exemplum and the Chaucerian tradition. (Bibl. 1995, 2027.) Rev. by A. C. Spearing in SAC (18) 1996, 289–94; by Sally Mapstone in NQ (43:4) 1996, 467–9.

2465. SCHILB, JOHN. 'Traveling theory' and the defining of the new rhetorics. RhR (11:1) 1992, 34–48.

2466. SELLARS, ROY. Milton's wen. Prose Studies (19:3) 1996, 221–37.

2467. SEMINO, ELENA; SWINDLEHURST, KATE. Metaphor and mind style in Ken Kesey's *One Flew over the Cuckoo's Nest*. Style (30:1) 1996, 143–66.

2468. SEVERI, RITA. Shakespearean caterpillars (*Richard II*, III, vv. 164–166). Quaderni di lingue e letterature (18) 1993, 649–53.

2469. SHAPIRO, IRVING DAVID. Fallacies of logic: argumentation cons. ERGS (53:3) 1996, 251–65.

2470. SHORT, BRYAN C. Emily Dickinson and the Scottish New Rhetoric. EDJ (5:2) 1996, 261–6.

2471. SKERPAN, ELIZABETH. The rhetoric of politics in the English Revolution, 1642–1660. (Bibl. 1995, 2035.) Rev. by Gerald M. MacLean in Review (16) 1994, 177–95; by Lois Potter in JBS (34:4) 1995, 536–42; by R. C. Richardson in Literature and History (5:1) 1996, 106–8; by Jameela Lares in RSQ (26:3) 1996, 61–4.

2472. SMITH, NIGEL. The English Revolution and the end of rhetoric: John Toland's *Clito* (1700) and the republican daemon. EAS (49) 1996, 1–18.

2473. SOLOMON, WILLIAM. Politics and rhetoric in the novel in the 1930s. AL (68:4) 1996, 799–818.

2474. SOMERSET, FIONA E. Vernacular argumentation in *The Testimony of William Thorpe*. MedStud (58) 1996, 207–41.

2475. STANWOOD, P. G. Donne's art of preaching and the reconstruction of Tertullian. JDJ (15) 1996, 153–69.

2476. STEEN, GERARD. Understanding metaphor in literature: an empirical approach. (Bibl. 1995, 2039.) Rev. by Denis E. B. Pollard in JLSem (25:1) 1996, 94–5; by Rachel Giora in CanRCL (23:4) 1996, 1244–9.

2477. STEGGLE, MATTHEW. Rhetorical ordering in Moulsworth's *Memorandum*. CritM (10:supp.) 1996, 27–31.

2478. STOVEL, NORA FOSTER. The woman in the moon: metaphor,

myth and marriage in *The Rainbow* and *Women in Love*. Études
Lawrenciennes (13) 1996, 95–122.

2479. SUBBIONDO, JOSEPH L. From pragmatics to semiotics: the
influence of John Wilkins' pulpit oratory on his philosophical language.
See **1511**.

2480. SULERI, SARA. The rhetoric of English India. (Bibl. 1995, 2046.)
Rev. by George Lang in CanRCL (20:3/4) 1993, 552–6; by Suvir Kaul
in Diacritics (26:1) 1996, 74–83.

2481. SULLIVAN, DALE L. The epideictic character of rhetorical criticism. RhR (11:2) 1993, 339–49.

2482. SWARTZ, OMAR. Kenneth Burke's theory of form: rhetoric, art,
and cultural analysis. SCJ (61:4) 1996, 312–21.

2483. SWEARINGEN, C. JAN. Homiletics and hermeneutics: the
rhetorical spaces in between. SLI (28:2) 1995, 27–42.

2484. TARVER, J. Abridged editions of Blair's *Lectures on Rhetoric and
Belles Lettres* in America: what nineteenth-century college students really
learned about Blair on rhetoric. *See* **1018**.

2485. TERRY, RICHARD. 'Metempsychosis': a metaphor for literary
tradition in Dryden and his contemporaries. Bunyan Studies (6)
1995/96, 56–69.

2486. TRITES, ROBERTA SEELINGER. Is flying extraordinary? Patricia
MacLachlan's use of aporia. ChildLit (23) 1995, 202–20.

2487. TROMBOLD, CHRIS B. Alimentary Eliot: digestive references
and metaphors in T. S. Eliot's writings. ELN (34:2) 1996, 45–59.

2488. TURNER, BRIAN. Giving good reasons: environmental appeals
in the non-fiction of John McPhee. RhR (13:1) 1994, 164–82.

2489. ULMAN, H. LEWIS. Things, thoughts, words, and actions: the
problem of language in late eighteenth-century British rhetorical theory.
(Bibl. 1994, 1562.) Rev. by Alison Hickey in Prose Studies (19:1) 1996,
110–13.

2490. VAN EEMMEREN, FRANS H., *et al.* Argumentation illuminated.
See **2297**.

2491. VICENTE, BEGOÑA. On the semantics and pragmatics of
metaphor: coming full circle. *See* **2245**.

2492. WALL, ANTHONY. Developing a taste for metaphors. *In* (pp.
49–72) **62**.

2493. WALLS, KATHRYN. Medieval 'allegorical imagery' in *c*.1630:
Will. Baspoole's revision of *The Pilgrimage of the Lyfe of the Manhode*. *In* (pp.
304–22) **114**.

2494. WILEY, MARK. Reading and writing in an American grain.
RhR (11:1) 1992, 133–46.

2495. WILSON, PAULA. The rhythm of rhetoric: Jesse Jackson at the
1988 Democratic national convention. SCJ (61:3) 1996, 253–64.

2496. WINTEROWD, W. ROSS. I. A. Richards, literary theory, and
Romantic composition. RhR (11:1) 1992, 59–78.

2497. WOLF, MANFRED. The aphorism. ERGS (51:4) 1994/95, 432–9.

2498. YOON, HEE OYCK. Shakespeare heuigeuk e natanan heuigeuk-
jeok susahak gwa se gazi daehwa yangsik. (Comic rhetoric and three
types of dialogue in Shakespeare's comedies.) ShR (29) 1996, 135–54.

MEDIUM AND REGISTER

SPOKEN DISCOURSE

2499. ABNEY, LISA. Pronoun shift in oral folklore, personal experience and literary narratives; or, 'What's up with *you*? *See* **1645**.

2500. AIJMER, KARIN. Conversational routines in English: convention and creativity. London; New York: Longman, 1996. pp. xvi, 251. (Studies in language and linguistics.)

2501. ANDERSON, LAURIE. Relexicalization and instantial equivalence in conjoint therapeutic discourse. Textus (9:1) 1996, 5–25.

2502. —— What's in a name? Vocatives and participant referentials in multiparty conversation. Textus (4) 1991, 171–215.

2503. ANTAKI, CHARLES. Explaining and arguing: the social organization of accounts. London; Thousand Oaks, CA: Sage, 1994. pp. 210. Rev. by Agnès van Rees in Argumentation (10:2) 1996, 301–6.

2504. ARNDT, HORST; JANNEY, RICHARD W. Speech style and interactional strategy: central organizing principles. NS (90:3) 1991, 223–41.

2505. BARENDSE, NANCY. If you can't say something nice, make it short: the use of negative terms by three television evangelists. SECOLR (15:2) 1991, 146–59.

2506. BERMAN, RUTH A.; SLOBIN, DAN ISAAC. Relating events in narrative: a crosslinguistic developmental study. (Bibl. 1995, 2069.) Rev. by Courtney B. Cazden and Nell K. Duke in Language in Society (25:1) 1996, 122–5.

2507. BIRNER, BETTY J. The discourse function of inversion in English. New York; London: Garland, 1996. pp. xvi, 187. (Outstanding dissertations in linguistics.)

2508. ——WARD, GREGORY. A crosslinguistic study of postposing in discourse. Language and Speech (39:2/3) 1996, 113–42.

2509. BLUM-KULKA, SHOSHANA. Cultural patterns in dinner talk. SPELL (9) 1996, 77–107.

2510. BODEN, DEIRDRE. The business of talk: organizations in action. Cambridge: Polity Press, 1994. pp. x, 272. Rev. by Paul ten Have in Language in Society (25:3) 1996, 459–63.

2511. BOHM, DAVID. On dialogue. Ed. by Lee Nichol. London; New York: Routledge, 1996. pp. xviii, 101.

2512. BRINTON, LAUREL J. Pragmatic markers in English: grammaticalization and discourse functions. *See* **1432**.

2513. BROCK, ALEXANDER. Symmetrie und Asymmetrie in einem '*phone-in*'. AAA (21:2) 1996, 155–77.

2514. BROWN, DEVIN. Powerful man gets pretty woman: style switching in *Annie Hall*. SECOLR (16:2) 1992, 115–31.

2515. —— Style shifting by a radio talk show host to assert multiple identities and roles. SECOLR (20:2) 1996, 161–81.

2516. BROWN, GILLIAN. Speakers, listeners and communication: explorations in discourse analysis. Cambridge; New York: CUP, 1995. pp. xiii, 251.

2517. CARLETTA, JEAN. Assessing agreement on classification tasks: the kappa statistic. *See* **1140**.

2518. CAROSSO, ANDREA. 'Watson, come here! I want (to see) you!': speech, writing, and interruption from A. G. Bell to the telematic text. *In* (pp. 73–83) **117**.

2519. CASE, SUSAN SCHICK. Gender, language, and the professions: recognition of verbal-repertoire speech. StudLS (25:2) 1995, 149–92.

2520. CLYNE, MICHAEL. Inter-cultural communication at work: cultural values in discourse. (Bibl. 1995, 2072.) Rev. by Robert B. Kaplan in Language in Society (25:3) 1996, 452–6.

2521. COLWELL, GARY. *Why*-questions, determinism and circular reasoning. Argumentation (10:1) 1996, 1–24.

2522. DAUTERMANN, JENNIE. A case for examining professional voices in institutional settings: nurses in conversation. StudLS (25:2) 1995, 193–216.

2523. DAVIS, HAYLEY. Theorizing women's and men's language. Language & Communication (16:1) 1996, 71–9 (review-article).

2524. DREW, PAUL; HERITAGE, J. (eds). Talk at work: interaction in institutional settings. (Bibl. 1994, 1582.) Rev. by Charles Goodwin in Language in Society (25:4) 1996, 616–20.

2525. EMMISON, MICHAEL; GOLDMAN, LAURENCE. What's that you said Sooty? Puppets, parlance and pretence. Language & Communication (16:1) 1996, 17–35.

2526. FAIRCLOUGH, NORMAN. A reply to Henry Widdowson's *Discourse Analysis: a Critical View*. LangL (5:1) 1996, 49–56.

2527. FIRTH, ALAN (ed.). The discourse of negotiation: studies of language in the workplace. Oxford: Pergamon, 1995. pp. xv, 436. Rev. by Pedro M. Garcez in Language in Society (25:3) 1996, 463–8.

2528. FLOWERDEW, JOHN. Discourse and social change in contemporary Hong Kong. Language in Society (25:4) 1996, 557–86.

2529. FLUDERNIK, MONIKA. Linguistic signals and interpretative strategies: linguistic models in performance, with special reference to free indirect discourse. *See* **2265**.

2530. FORD, CECILIA E. Grammar in interaction: adverbial clauses in American English conversations. (Bibl. 1993, 1531.) Rev. by Betty J. Birner in SL (20:2) 1996, 455–65.

2531. FREED, ALICE F.; GREENWOOD, ALICE. Women, men, and type of talk: what makes the difference? Language in Society (25:1) 1996, 1–26.

2532. GOLDER, CAROLINE; COIRIER, PIERRE. The production and recognition of typological argumentative text markers. Argumentation (10:2) 1996, 271–82.

2533. GOODWIN, MARJORIE HARNESS. He-said-she-said: talk as social organization among Black children. Bloomington: Indiana UP, 1990. pp. x, 371. Rev. by Barrie Thorne in Signs (18:2) 1993, 452–4.

2534. GUNTER, RICHARD. Prediction, relevance, and the obligation to respond. SECOLR (15:1) 1991, 1–20.

2535. HAYASHI, REIKO. Cognition, empathy, and interaction: floor management of English and Japanese conversation. Norwood, NJ: Ablex, 1996. pp. xvi, 252. (Advances in discourse processes, 54.)

2536. HOLMES, JANET. Collecting the Wellington Corpus of Spoken New Zealand English: some methodological challenges. NZEJ (10) 1996, 10–15.

2537. —— AINSWORTH, HELEN. Syllable-timing and Maori English. Te Reo (39) 1996, 75–84.

2538. HOLMES, MICHAEL E. Naming virtual space in computer-mediated conversation. *See* **1161**.

2539. HUGHES, REBECCA. English in speech and writing:

investigating language and literature. New York; London: Routledge, 1996. pp. viii, 178. (Interface.)

2540. JOHNSON, GARY; HOLMES, JANET.   The Wellington Corpus of Spoken New Zealand English: transcription and ethical issues. NZEJ (10) 1996, 16–24.

2541. KNOWLES, GERRY; WILLIAMS, BRIONY; TAYLOR, L. (eds). A corpus of formal British English speech: the Lancaster/IBM Spoken English Corpus. *See* **1168**.

2542. KRAUSE, ANDREA J.; GOERING, ELIZABETH M.   Local talk in the global village: an intercultural comparison of American and German talk shows. JPC (29:2) 1995, 189–207.

2543. LANDON, LANA HARTMAN.   Suffering over time: six varieties of pain. Soundings (72) 1989, 75–82.

2544. LEEMAN, RICHARD W.   Spatial metaphors in African-American discourse. *See* **2418**.

2545. LINDE, CHARLOTTE.   Life stories: the creation of coherence. (Bibl. 1993, 1543.) Rev. by David Herman in Style (30:1) 1996, 175–8; by Amy Shuman in Language in Society (25:4) 1996, 620–3.

2546. LONGACRE, ROBERT E.   The grammar of discourse. (Bibl. 1983, 910.) New York; London: Plenum Press, 1996. pp. xvi, 362. (Topics in language and linguistics.) (Second ed.: first ed. 1983.)

2547. MCILVENNY, PAUL.   Heckling in Hyde Park: verbal audience participation in popular public discourse. Language in Society (25:1) 1996, 27–60.

2548. MEINHOF, ULRIKE H.; RICHARDSON, KAY (eds).   Text, discourse and context: representations of poverty in Britain. London; New York: Longman, 1994. pp. vii, 149. (Real language.) Rev. by Franca Bellarsi in LangL (5:2) 1996, 141–4.

2549. MURPHY, M. LYNNE.   Discourse markers and sentential syntax. *See* **1714**.

2550. NEWKIRK, THOMAS.   Barrett Wendell's theory of discourse. RhR (10:1) 1991, 20–30.

2551. OBERLANDER, JON; DELIN, JUDY.   The function and interpretation of reverse *wh*-clefts in spoken discourse. *See* **1719**.

2552. OHMI, MAKOTO.   Eigo *communication* no riron to jissai. (Theory and practice of English communication.) Tokyo: Kenkyusha Shuppan, 1996. pp. x, 322.

2553. OJAIDE, TANURE.   Orality in recent West African poetry. CLAJ (39:3) 1996, 302–19.

2554. OLTEAN, STEFAN.   Free indirect discourse: some referential aspects. JLSem (24:1) 1995, 21–41.

2555. PASSONNEAU, REBECCA J.   Using centering to relax Gricean informational constraints on discourse anaphoric noun phrases. Language and Speech (39:2/3) 1996, 229–64.

2556. PERSON, RAYMOND F., JR.   Restarts in conversation and literature. Language & Communication (16:1) 1996, 61–70.

2557. QUASTHOFF, UTA M. (ed.).   Aspects of oral communication. Berlin; New York: de Gruyter, 1995. pp. vi, 493. (Research in text theory, 21.) Rev. by Elizabeth G. Weber in Language in Society (25:4) 1996, 613–16.

2558. RAUCH, IRMENGARD.   Deconstruction, prototype theory, and semiotics. *See* **2231**.

2559. Reich, Warren Thomas. Speaking of suffering: a moral account of compassion. Soundings (72) 1989, 83–108.

2560. Rice, William Craig. Public discourse and academic inquiry. New York; London: Garland, 1996. pp. xiv, 211. (Garland studies in American popular history and culture.)

2561. Rundell, Michael. The word on the street. English Today (11:3) 1995, 29–33.

2562. Schiffrin, Deborah. Approaches to discourse. (Bibl. 1995, 2109.) Rev. by Helena Halmari in Language in Society (25:1) 1996, 115–18.

2563. —— Narrative as self-portrait: sociolinguistic constructions of identity. Language in Society (25:2) 1996, 167–203.

2564. Shuy, Roger W. Language crimes: the use and abuse of language evidence in the courtroom. (Bibl. 1993, 1553.) Rev. by Hayley Davis and Nigel Love in Language & Communication (16:3) 1996, 301–13.

2565. Sinclair, John M.; Hoey, Michael; Fox, Gwyneth (eds). Techniques of description: spoken and written discourse: a Festschrift for Malcolm Coulthard. (Bibl. 1994, 1600.) Rev. by Tony Bex in LangL (5:2) 1996, 148–53.

2566. Stoll, Pamela. Sequence and hierarchy in discourse organization. RAEI (9) 1996, 119–31.

2567. Tannen, Deborah. Gender and discourse. (Bibl. 1995, 2115.) Rev. by Elisabeth D. Kuhn in NWSAJ (8:2) 1996, 117–25; by Hayley Davis in Language & Communication (16:1) 1996, 71–9.

2568. —— (ed.). Gender and conversational interaction. (Bibl. 1994, 1603.) Rev. by Elisabeth D. Kuhn in NWSAJ (8:2) 1996, 117–25; by Lynna L. Dunn in Language and Speech (39:1) 1996, 95–7.

2569. Tsui, Amy B. M. English conversation. Oxford; New York: OUP, 1994. pp. xviii, 298. Rev. by Karin Aijmer in MS (90:1) 1996, 108–9.

2570. Walker, Marilyn A. Limited attention and discourse structure. *See* **1214**.

2571. Widdowson, H. G. Reply to Fairclough: discourse and interpretation: conjectures and refutations. LangL (5:1) 1996, 57–69.

STYLISTICS OF LITERARY TEXTS

2572. Abney, Lisa. Pronoun shift in oral folklore, personal experience and literary narratives; or, 'What's up with *you*?' *See* **1645**.

2573. Abrams, Richard. In defence of W.S.: reasons for attributing *A Funeral Elegy* to Shakespeare. TLS, 9 Feb. 1996, 25–6.

2574. Alderson, Simon. Alexander Pope and the nature of language. RES (47:185) 1996, 23–34.

2575. Alonso Rodríguez, Pilar. The role of intersentential connectives in complex narrative discourse: Katherine Mansfield's *The Garden Party*. Misc (17) 1996, 17–38.

2576. Austin, Timothy R. Poetic voices: discourse linguistics and the poetic text. (Bibl. 1994, 1613.) Rev. by Joan Weatherly in AS (71:4) 1996, 435–40.

2577. Barchas, Janine. Sarah Fielding's dashing style and eighteenth-century print culture. ELH (63:3) 1996, 633–56.

2578. BATTESTIN, MARTIN C.   The Cusum method: escaping the bog of subjectivism. *See* **1094**.

2579. BEEKMAN, E. M.   The verbal empires of Simon Vestdijk and James Joyce. (Bibl. 1983, 11847.) Rev. by James Geary in JJQ (33:2) 1996, 305–10.

2580. BELL, MICHAEL.   Lawrence, language and relatedness. Études Lawrenciennes (13) 1996, 11–23.

2581. BENITO SÁNCHEZ, JESÚS.   Narrative voice and Blues expression in James Baldwin's *Sonny's Blues*. EIUC (4) 1996, 175–87.

2582. BENSON, JAMES D.; GREAVES, WILLIAM S.; STILLAR, GLENN. Transitivity and ergativity in *The Lotos-Eaters*. LangL (4:1) 1995, 31–48.

2583. BERNSTEIN, CYNTHIA GOLDIN.   Language and literature in context. SECOLR (18:1) 1994, 45–61.

2584. BINONGO, JOSÉ NILO G.; SMITH, M. W. A.   Stylometry. *See* **2008**.

2585. BISHOP, RYAN.   There's nothing natural about natural conversation: a look at dialogue in fiction and drama. Oral Tradition (6:1) 1991, 58–78. (Hemingway, James, Joyce, Mamet, Pinter.)

2586. BOOTH, ROY J.   'As mad as he': simile, analogy and likeness in *Hamlet*. Q/W/E/R/T/Y (6) 1996, 17–22.

2587. BOURLAND, D. DAVID, JR.   E-Prime: speaking crisply. *See* **2195**.

2588. BRAVO GARCÍA, ANTONIO.   El estilo de la descripción de las batallas en el *Brut* de Layamon y en la épica anglosajona de los siglos X–XI. Atlantis (17:1/2) 1995, 5–26.

2589. BREGAZZI, JOSEPHINE.   Changing roles: gender marking through syntactic distribution in the Jacobean theatre. EIUC (4) 1996, 131–47.

2590. BRIAN, MICHAEL.   'A very fine piece of writing': an etymological, Dantean, and gnostic reading of Joyce's *Ivy Day in the Committee Room*. Style (25:3) 1991, 466–87.

2591. BRUCE, DONALD.   Discourse analysis in cultural theory: '*une discipline transversale*'. CanRCL (22:1) 1995, 63–92.

2592. BUCK, R. A.   Reading Forster's style: face actions and social scripts in *Maurice*. Style (30:1) 1996, 69–94.

2593. ÇALISKAN, SEVDA.   The coded language of *Female Quixotism*. SAH (3:2) 1995, 23–35.

2594. CAMPBELL, IAN.   Glossing (glossing). Études Écossaises (supp.) 1994, 59–77.

2595. CANEDA CABRERA, M. TERESA.   *Ulysses* and heteroglossia: a Bakhtinian reading of the 'Nausicaa' episode. RAEI (9) 1996, 33–40.

2596. CAZÉ, ANTOINE.   Penser la syntaxe de la nouvelle poésie américaine. Études littéraires (28:2) 1995, 9–19.

2597. CHAKRAVORTY, SWAPAN.   'Give her more onion': unriddling the Welsh madman's speech in *The Changeling*. NQ (43:2) 1996, 184–7.

2598. CLARK, BILLY.   Stylistic analysis and relevance theory. LangL (5:3) 1996, 163–78.

2599. CLARK, JOHN R.   Vapid voices and sleazy styles. *In* (pp. 19–42) **120**.

2600. CLARKE, ELIZABETH.   Silent, performative words: the language of God in Valdesso and George Herbert. LitTheol (5:4) 1991, 355–74.

2601. COOK, GUY.   Discourse and literature: the interplay of form and mind. (Bibl. 1995, 2143.) Rev. by Laura Hidalgo in EIUC (4) 1996, 237–51; by Geoff Hall in LangL (5:1) 1996, 74–7.

2602. CORCORAN, MARLENA G. Language, character, and gender in the direct discourse of *Dubliners*. Style (25:3) 1991, 439–52.

2603. COULTHARD, M. (ed.). Advances in written text analysis. London; New York: Routledge, 1994. pp. xii, 320. Rev. by Tony Bex in LangL (5:2) 1996, 148–53.

2604. CREWS, BRIAN. Anti-style and the postmodernist novel. RAEI (9) 1996, 41–52.

2605. CROGHAN, MARTIN J. Maria Edgeworth and the tradition of Irish semiotics. *In* (pp. 340–8) **49**.

2606. CRONIN, RICHARD. Keats and the politics of Cockney style. SELit (36:4) 1996, 785–806.

2607. DREXLER, ROBERT DANIEL. Dunbar's aureate language. SLang (14/15) 1995/96, 204–17.

2608. EATON, TREVOR. Literary semantics as a science. *See* **2202**.

2609. ECHERUO, MICHAEL J. C. Joyce's 'epical equidistance'. ESA (39:1) 1996, 1–12.

2610. ESTERHAMMER, ANGELA. Creating states: studies in the performative language of John Milton and William Blake. (Bibl. 1994, 1639.) Rev. by Jason P. Rosenblatt in Cithara (35:1) 1995, 55–7; by David Gay in ESCan (22:3) 1996, 347–9.

2611. FABB, NIGEL, *et al.* (eds). The linguistics of writing: arguments between language and literature. (Bibl. 1989, 1397.) Rev. by Joan Weatherly in SECOLR (18:1) 1994, 89–90; by Michael R. Brown in JEL (24:1) 1996, 82–4.

2612. FABER, PAMELA; WALLHEAD, CELIA. The lexical field of visual perception in *The French Lieutenant's Woman* by John Fowles. LangL (4:2) 1995, 127–43.

2613. FAIRCLOUGH, NORMAN. A reply to Henry Widdowson's *Discourse Analysis: a Critical View*. *See* **2526**.

2614. FARRINGDON, JILL M., *et al.* Analysing for authorship: a guide to the Cusum technique. *See* **1153**.

2615. FLANNERY, KATHRYN T. The emperor's new clothes: literature, literacy, and the ideology of style. Pittsburgh, PA: Pittsburgh UP, 1995. pp. x, 240. (Pittsburgh series in composition, literacy, and culture.) Rev. by Gary Dohrer in RMRLL (50:1) 1996, 70–2.

2616. FLUDERNIK, MONIKA. The fictions of language and the languages of fiction: the linguistic representation of speech and consciousness. (Bibl. 1995, 2160.) Rev. by Wilhelm Füger in GRM (45:2) 1995, 251–4; by Ansgar Nünning in LWU (29:3) 1996, 224–5.

2617. —— Towards a 'natural' narratology. JLSem (25:2) 1996, 97–141.

2618. —— Towards a 'natural' narratology. London; New York: Routledge, 1996. pp. xvi, 454.

2619. FOSTER, DONALD W. *A Funeral Elegy*: W(illiam) S(hakespeare)'s 'best-speaking witnesses'. PMLA (111:5) 1996, 1080–1105.

2620. FOWLER, ROGER. Linguistic criticism. (Bibl. 1989, 1401.) Oxford; New York: OUP, 1996. pp. vi, 262. (Opus.) (Second ed.: first ed. 1986.)

2621. FREEBORN, DENNIS. Style: text analysis and linguistic criticism. Basingstoke: Macmillan, 1996. pp. xxii, 294. (Studies in English language.)

2622. FURROW, MELISSA M. Latin and affect. *In* (pp. 29–41) **26**.

2623. Gagliardi, Cesare.   Per un'analisi fonostilistica del testo inglese. *See* **1548**.

2624. Gass, William H.   Finding a form. Antaeus (75/76) 1994, 366–83.

2625. Gavioli, Laura.   Discourse forces in conversational stories: entertainment *vs* solidarity. Textus (2:1/2) 1989, 161–92.

2626. Gemme, Paola.   Representing the world in discourse: a socio-stylistic analysis of multivocality in *The Journal of Madam Knight*. QLLSM (6) 1993, 83–100.

2627. Genette, Gérard.   Fiction et diction. Paris: Seuil, 1991. pp. 150. Rev. by Uri Margolin in CanRCL (21:3) 1994, 445–56.

2628. Giaufret, Anna.   Il testo e il suo doppio: la *Salomé* di Oscar Wilde e la *Salome* di Alfred Douglas. Un'analisi comparata linguistico-stilistica. QLLSM (5) 1992, 9–28.

2629. Giltrow, Janet; Stouck, David.   Lyrical measures: cohesion and sentence endings in Cather's prose. WCPMN (35:3) 1991, 11–15.

2630. Gorman, David.   Gérard Genette: an Anglo-French checklist to 1996. Style (30:4) 1996, 539–50.

2631. Gray, Francine Du Plessix.   The seduction of the text. BkW, 13 Feb. 1994, 1, 10.

2632. Gray, Piers.   On linearity. CritQ (38:3) 1996, 122–55.

2633. Gregory, Shelly.   ReWaking the mother tongue in *Finnegans Wake*: a Kristevan interpretation. ELN (34:1) 1996, 63–76.

2634. Grosser, Wolfgang; Hogg, James; Hubmayer, Karl (eds). Style, literary and non-literary: contemporary trends in cultural stylistics. Lewiston, NY; Lampeter: Mellen Press, 1995. pp. 357. (Salzburg Univ. studies: English & American studies, 18.)

2635. Guerra de la Torre, Juana T.   Fractals in Gertrude Stein's 'word-system': natural reality and/or verbal reality. Atlantis (17:1/2) 1995, 89–114.

2636. Gutleben, Christian.   English academic satire from the Middle Ages to the postmodern: distinguishing the comic from the satiric. *In* (pp. 133–47) **120**.

2637. Hanauer, David.   Literary and poetic text categorization judgements. JLSem (24:3) 1995, 187–210.

2638. Hart, David.   The fixed expression and its manipulation: evidence from the modern drama text. Textus (9:1) 1996, 63–74.

2639. Head, Pauline.   Voices of stone: the multifaceted speech of *The Dream of the Rood* and the Ruthwell Cross. Assays (9) 1996, 57–77.

2640. Henry, Richard.   Pretending and meaning: toward a pragmatic theory of fictional discourse. Westport, CT; London: Greenwood Press, 1996. pp. 125. (Contributions in philosophy.) (Cf. bibl. 1995, 3289.)

2641. Herman, David.   Universal grammar and narrative form. Durham, NC; London: Duke UP, 1995. pp. x, 281. (Sound and meaning.) (Cf. bibl. 1993, 1592.) Rev. by Marie-Laure Ryan in Style (30:3) 1996, 514–18.

2642. Herman, Vimala.   Dramatic discourse: dialogue as interaction in plays. (Bibl. 1995, 2174.) Rev. by Bronwen Thomas in LangL (5:3) 1996, 225–7.

2643. Hess, Natalie.   Code-switching and style-shifting as markers of liminality in literature. LangL (5:1) 1996, 5–18.

2644. Heydel, Maren.   The concept of translational equivalence in literary discourse and the role of *progressive aspect* in the English translation of Christa Wolf's novel *Nachdenken über Christa T. (The Quest for Christa T.).* ZAA (44:2) 1996, 101–23.

2645. HILTON, NELSON. Lexis complexes: literary interventions. Athens; London: Georgia UP, 1995. pp. 225.

2646. HOPKINS, CHRIS. Translating Caradoc Evans's Welsh English. Style (30:3) 1996, 433–44.

2647. HOWARD, ROSEMARY. Intimations of wonder in Wittgenstein and Lawrence. Études Lawrenciennes (13) 1996, 25–39.

2648. HUGHES, REBECCA. English in speech and writing: investigating language and literature. *See* **2539**.

2649. HURST, MARY JANE. The voice of the child in American literature: linguistic approaches to fictional child language. (Bibl. 1995, 2179.) Rev. by Janice Jake in SECOLR (16:2) 1992, 210–13; by Joseph Hawes in AmS (34:1) 1993, 180; by Elizabeth N. Goodenough in ChildLit (23) 1995, 261–4.

2650. IYEIRI, YOKO. The periphrastic use of *con* reconsidered: the authorship of the Cotton Nero A.x poems. *See* **1791**.

2651. JAECKLE, DANIEL P. Imaging social languages in Marvell's *The Last Instructions.* Style (30:3) 1996, 371–85.

2652. JAMES, G. INGLI. The holy and the heterodox: William Blake's transformational use of religious language. SM (14:1) 1991, 31–44.

2653. JASPER, DAVID. The death and rebirth of religious language. ReLit (28:1) 1996, 5–19.

2654. JOHNSTON, PAUL DENNITHORNE. The joy of words: confessions of a verbaholic. *See* **1851**.

2655. KARPIŃSKI, EWA C. The rhetoric of liberation in Harriet Jacobs' *Incidents in the Life of a Slave Girl, Written by Herself.* ZRL (38:1/2) 1995, 75–85.

2656. KATZ, DANIEL. 'Alone in the accusative': Beckett's narcissistic echoes. Samuel Beckett Today (5) 1996, 57–71.

2657. KEARNS, MICHAEL. Melville's chaotic style and the use of generative models: an essay in method. Style (30:1) 1996, 50–68.

2658. KIHARA, YOSHIHIKO. 'A patchwork of conceits, borrowings, deceptions': style in William Gaddis's *Carpenter's Gothic.* StAL (33) 1996, 65–81.

2659. KNOWLES, MURRAY; MALMKJÆR, KIRSTEN. Language and control in children's literature. London; New York: Routledge, 1996. pp. xii, 284.

2660. KNUTSON, ELIZABETH. Literary pragmatics and the concept of readability. RWT (3:1) 1995, 89–103.

2661. KONDO, KYOKO KAY. Colours, images and related adjectives in *Women in Love.* Études Lawrenciennes (13) 1996, 59–73.

2662. KROHN, FRANKLIN B.; SUAZO, FRANCES L. Contemporary urban music: controversial messages in hip-hop and rap lyrics. ERGS (52:2) 1995, 139–54.

2663. LANGELAND, AGNES SCOTT. Rushdie's language. English Today (12:1) 1996, 16–22.

2664. LECERCLE, JEAN-JACQUES. The current state of stylistics. EEM (2:1) 1993, 14–18.

2665. LEECH, JAMES. Alexander Pope: the 'sound an eccho to the sense'. ERev (7:2) 1996, 29–31.

2666. LOOBY, CHRISTOPHER. Voicing America: language, literary form, and the origins of the United States. Chicago; London:

Chicago UP, 1996. pp. xi, 287. Rev. by Grantland S. Rice in EAL (31:3) 1996, 312–13.

2667. LUCAS, MICHAEL A.   Stylistic variation in *An Anarchist*. Conradiana (28:2) 1996, 86–95.

2668. MACKAY, RAY.   Mything the point: a critique of objective stylistics. Language & Communication (16:1) 1996, 81–93.

2669. MACMAHON, BARBARA.   Indirectness, rhetoric and interpretative use: communicative strategies in Browning's *My Last Duchess*. LangL (5:3) 1996, 209–23.

2670. MÄKINEN, ANTTI.   On Patrick White's language in general and in *Riders in the Chariot* in particular. New Courant (5) 1996, 75–84.

2671. MARGOLIN, URI.   Telling our story: on 'we' literary narratives. LangL (5:2) 1996, 115–33.

2672. MARTÍNEZ MARTÍNEZ, MARÍA ÁNGELES.   Function and linguistic organization: an analysis of character and setting in Thomas Pynchon's *Under the Rose* rewritten in *V*. EIUC (4) 1996, 105–29.

2673. MAZO, JEFFREY ALAN.   Compound diction and traditional style in *Beowulf* and *Genesis A*. Oral Tradition (6:1) 1991, 79–92.

2674. MAZZON, GABRIELLA.   The language of emotions in Shakespeare's poems: an aspect of archaism and innovation in Elizabethan English word-formation. *See* **1633**.

2675. MIKALACHKI, JODI.   Gender, cant, and cross-talking in *The Roaring Girl*. RenD (25) 1994, 119–43.

2676. MILLER, MIRIAM YOUNGERMAN.   'Thy speech is strange and uncouth': language in the children's historical novel of the Middle Ages. ChildLit (23) 1995, 71–90.

2677. MILWARD, PETER.   The biblical language of *King Lear*. Shakespeare Yearbook (2) 1991, 212–15.

2678. MOORE, MICHAEL.   Pathological communication patterns in Heller's *Catch-22*. ERGS (52:4) 1995/96, 431–9.

2679. MUCCI, CLARA.   In praise of punning; or, Poetic language: women, fools, madness, and literature at the margins. Textus (9:1) 1996, 243–84.

2680. NIERAGDEN, GÖRAN.   Action, speech and thought: (de)constructing gender stereotypes in Katherine Mansfield's *A Birthday* and *The Escape* from a systemic grammar perspective. ZAA (44:1) 1996, 1–10.

2681. —— Comedy and menace: a Gricean look at the dialogue in Joe Orton's *Loot*. GRM (44:1) 1994, 77–86.

2682. NORRICK, NEAL R.; BAKER, WILLIAM.   Metalingual humor in Pinter's early plays. EngS (76:3) 1995, 253–63.

2683. O'KEEFFE, BERNARD.   The language of *Trainspotting*. ERev (7:2) 1996, 6–8.

2684. OLIVA, JUAN IGNACIO.   El lenguaje de las novelas indostanas de Salman Rushdie. RCEI (28) 1994, 23–40.

2685. OLTEAN, STEFAN.   Free indirect discourse: some referential aspects. *See* **2554**.

2686. ONEGA JAÉN, SUSANA; GARCÍA LANDA, JOSÉ ÁNGEL (eds). Narratology: an introduction. London; New York: Longman, 1996. pp. xii, 324. (Longman critical readers.) Rev. by Maria Jesús Martínez in Misc (17) 1996, 241–4.

2687. OSBERG, RICHARD H.   A voice for the Prioress: the context of English devotional prose. SAC (18) 1996, 25–54.

2688. OSTEEN, MARK. The treasure-house of language: managing symbolic economies in Joyce's *Portrait*. StudN (27:2) 1995, 154–68.

2689. PADOL, LISA. Whose English? Language in the modern Arthurian novel. Mythlore (20:4) 1995, 20–4, 29.

2690. PARRINDER, PATRICK. Shakespeare and (non) Standard English. EEM (5:1) 1996, 14–20.

2691. PERCY, CAROL. Eighteenth-century normative grammar in practice: the case of Captain Cook. *In* (pp. 339–62) **27**.

2692. PERSON, RAYMOND F., JR. Restarts in conversation and literature. *See* **2556**.

2693. POMORSKA, KRYSTYNA; RUDY, STEPHEN (eds). Language in literature. By Roman Jakobson. (Bibl. 1992, 2103.) Rev. by Joan Weatherly in SECOLR (18:1) 1994, 92–4.

2694. POTTER, LOIS. The politics of language in early modern England. JBS (34:4) 1995, 536–42 (review-article).

2695. POTTER, RUSSELL A. Chaucer and the authority of language: the politics and poetics of the vernacular in late medieval England. *See* **1478**.

2696. RICKARD, PETER. The transferred epithet in modern English prose. Cambridge: Rickard, 1996. pp. viii, 98.

2697. RICOU, LAURIE. Everyday magic: child languages in Canadian literature. (Bibl. 1992, 2105.) Rev. by Thomas B. Friedman in ARCS (18:1) 1988, 117–18.

2698. ROMINE, SCOTT. Negotiating community in Augustus Baldwin Longstreet's *Georgia Scenes*. Style (30:1) 1996, 1–27.

2699. ROSE, ADAM. Lewis Carroll's *Jabberwocky*: non-sense not nonsense. LangL (4:1) 1995, 1–15.

2700. RUST, MARTHA DANA. Stop the world, I want to get off! Identity and circularity in Gertrude Stein's *The World Is Round*. Style (30:1) 1996, 130–42.

2701. SCHMELING, MAX. Narrative, perspective and cultural otherness. JLS (11:3/4) 1996, 85–96.

2702. SCHWAB, GABRIELE. The mirror and the killer-queen: Otherness in literary language. Bloomington: Indiana UP, 1996. pp. xxii, 212. (Theories of contemporary culture, 18.)

2703. SCHWALM, GISELA. *First person possessive*: Determination als Stilmittel in Walker Percys *Lancelot*. *See* **1980**.

2704. SEMINO, ELENA. Schema theory and the analysis of text worlds in poetry. LangL (4:2) 1995, 79–108.

2705. SHORROCKS, GRAHAM. Language in Percy Janes's novella, *The Picture on the Wall*. JEL (24:3) 1996, 220–33.

2706. SHORT, MICHAEL H. Exploring the language of poems, plays, and prose. Harlow; New York: Longman, 1996. pp. xvi, 399. (Learning about language.)

2707. SIKORSKA, LILIANA. Mapping the problem of sexual desire in *The Book of Margery Kempe*. SAP (30) 1996, 141–8.

2708. SIMPSON, MICHAEL. Who didn't kill Blake's fly: moral law and the rule of grammar in *Songs of Experience*. Style (30:2) 1996, 220–40.

2709. SMEDMAN, LORNA J. 'Cousin to cooning': relation, difference, and racialized language in Stein's nonrepresentational texts. MFS (42:3) 1996, 569–88.

2710. SOMACARRERA, PILAR. Exploring the impenetrability of narrative: a study of linguistic modality in Alice Munro's early fiction. StudCanL (21:1) 1996, 79–91.

2711. SPENCER, LUKE.   A poetics of engagement in E. L. Doctorow's *Ragtime*. LangL (5:1) 1996, 19–30.

2712. STEELE, MEÍLI.   Democratic interpretation and the politics of difference. CL (48:4) 1996, 326–42.

2713. STELLA, MARIA.   Il potere della parola in Emily Brontë. Annali anglistica (36:1–3) 1993, 191–217.

2714. STEWART, FRANK.   A language of the people: an analysis of the use of proverbs and language in Chinua Achebe's novels. SEL (72:2) 1996, 165–80.

2715. STEWART, JACK.   Linguistic incantation and parody in *Women in Love*. Style (30:1) 1996, 95–112.

2716. TALLANT, CAROLE; TRIMBLE, FRANK.   Participating in the poetry playground: staging the nonsense wordplay in children's poetry. CommEd (41:3) 1992, 300–11.

2717. TAN, PETER K. W.   A stylistics of drama: with special focus on Stoppard's *Travesties*. Singapore: Singapore UP, 1993. pp. xi, 248. Rev. by Jonathan Culpeper in LangL (4:1) 1995, 69–72.

2718. TAYLOR, GARY.   Shakespeare and others: the authorship of *Henry the Sixth, Part One*. MedRen (7) 1995, 145–205.

2719. THOMAS, MICHAEL.   *Our Country's Good*: from 'canting slang' to 'refined, literate language'. ERev (7:1) 1996, 18–21.

2720. TIEKEN-BOON VAN OSTADE, INGRID.   Social network theory and eighteenth-century English: the case of Boswell. *In* (pp. 327–37) **27**.

2721. TODD, LORETO.   The language of Irish literature. (Bibl. 1992, 2115.) Rev. by Michael Montgomery in SECOLR (15:2) 1991, 219–22.

2722. TOOLAN, MICHAEL (ed.).   Language, text and context: essays in stylistics. (Bibl. 1994, 1704.) Rev. by Göran Nieragden in EngS (76:1) 1995, 107–8.

2723. TYLER, ELIZABETH M.   How deliberate is deliberate verbal repetition? *In* (pp. 508–30) **114**.

2724. VANDIVERE, JULIE.   Waves and fragments: linguistic construction as subject formation in Virginia Woolf. TCL (42:2) 1996, 221–33.

2725. VICKERS, BRIAN.   Whose thumbprints? A more plausible author for *A Funeral Elegy*. See **1213**.

2726. VISSER, DIRK.   Communicating torture: the dramatic language of Harold Pinter. Neophilologus (80:2) 1996, 327–40.

2727. VON NOLCKEN, CHRISTINA.   A 'certain sameness' and our response to it in English Wycliffite texts. *In* (pp. 191–208) **61**.

2728. WALKER, DAVID.   Language, genre, and revolution. Bunyan Studies (6) 1995/96, 93–100 (review-article).

2729. WEBER, JEAN JACQUES.   English language: stylistics. YWES (75) 1994, 79–84.

2730. WELLS, STANLEY.   In memory of Master William Peter: the difficulties of attributing *A Funeral Elegy* to Shakespeare. TLS, 26 Jan. 1996, 28.

2731. WIDDOWSON, H. G.   Reply to Fairclough: discourse and interpretation: conjectures and refutations. See **2571**.

2732. WILLIAMS, KEMP.   The style of paradox: thematic and linguistic duality in *Cry, the Beloved Country*. ESA (39:2) 1996, 1–15.

2733. WIMSATT, JAMES I.   Rhyme, the icons of sound, and the Middle English *Pearl*. Style (30:2) 1996, 189–219.

2734. WINTER, HELMUT.   Simplicity, complexity, and the essay. CR (40:3) 1996, 573–86.

2735. WORTHINGTON, B. A.   Style and the Oxford school. QLLSM (2) 1987, 219–32.

2736. WORYMA, PIOTR.   A sample contrastive analysis of *The Blue Hotel* by Stephen Crane and *The Nigger of the Narcissus* by Joseph Conrad. SAP (30) 1996, 159–68.

STYLISTICS OF NON-LITERARY TEXTS

2737. ALOZIE, NICHOLAS O.   Scholarly writers and the time capsule. *See* **1091**.

2738. ANDERSON, DOUGLAS.   Contemporary sports reporting. Chicago: Nelson-Hall, 1994. pp. xvi, 327. (Second ed.: first ed. 1985.) Rev. by Gunnar Bergh in MS (90:1) 1996, 110–12.

2739. ANON.   Editorial: escaping from academic prose. JRead (38:1) 1994, 4–5.

2740. ATKINSON, DWIGHT.   The *Philosophical Transactions of the Royal Society of London*, 1675–1975: a sociohistorical discourse analysis. Language in Society (25:3) 1996, 333–71.

2741. AXELSSON, MARGARETA WESTERGREN.   Contracted forms in newspaper language: inter- and intra-textual variation. ICAME Journal (20) 1996, 5–21.

2742. BARZUN, JACQUES.   Attitudes and assumptions. *See* **1226**.

2743. —— The press and the prose. *See* **1227**.

2744. BEX, TONY.   Variety in written English: texts in society; societies in text. London; New York: Routledge, 1996. pp. xii, 221. (Interface.)

2745. BULHOF, ILSE N.   The language of science: a study of the relationship between literature and science in the perspective of a hermeneutical ontology, with a case study of Darwin's *The Origin of Species*. Leiden; New York: Brill, 1992. pp. vi, 207. (Brill's studies in intellectual history, 34.) Rev. by Robert J. Richards in Isis (85:2) 1994, 346–7.

2746. CARRARD, PHILIPPE.   Part of the way with verbal play: the ludic mode in scholarly titling. Style (30:4) 1996, 566–83.

2747. CARTER, JIMMY.   From politics to poetics. BkW, 2 July 1995, 1, 10.

2748. COULTHARD, M. (ed.).   Advances in written text analysis. *See* **2603**.

2749. CRITTENDEN, CHARLOTTE C.   'Broad reference' in pronouns: handbooks *versus* professional writers. *See* **1667**.

2750. CULY, CHRISTOPHER.   Null objects in English recipes. LVC (8:1) 1996, 91–124.

2751. DE BERNADI, BIANCA; ANTOLINI, EMANUELA.   Structural differences in the production of written arguments. Argumentation (10:2) 1996, 175–96.

2752. FAIRCLOUGH, NORMAN.   A reply to Henry Widdowson's *Discourse Analysis: a Critical View*. *See* **2526**.

2753. FERRINGTON, GARY; ANDERSON-INMAN, LYNNE.   Media literacy: upfront and on-line. JAAL (39:8) 1996, 666–70.

2754. FORTSON, BENJAMIN W., IV.   The press and the prose: an exchange. *See* **1267**.

2755. GIBBONS, JOHN (ed.).   Language and the law. London; New York: Longman, 1994. pp. xiv, 476. (Language in social life.) Rev. by R. Coulon in LangL (4:2) 1995, 151–3; by Roger W. Shuy in JEL (24:2) 1996, 165–6; by Hayley Davis and Nigel Love in Language & Communication (16:3) 1996, 301–13.

2756. GLEDHILL, CHRIS.   Collocation and genre analysis: the phraseology of grammatical items in cancer research abstracts and articles. ZAA (43:1) 1995, 11–36.

2757. GREEN, BARBARA.   Advertising feminism: ornamental bodies/docile bodies and the discourse of suffrage. *In* (pp. 191–220) **67**.

2758. GROSSER, WOLFGANG; HOGG, JAMES; HUBMAYER, KARL (eds). Style, literary and non-literary: contemporary trends in cultural stylistics. *See* **2634**.

2759. GUZZETTI, BARBARA J., *et al.*   Improving physics texts: students speak out. JRead (38:8) 1995, 656–63.

2760. HARLING, PHILIP.   Leigh Hunt's *Examiner* and the language of patriotism. *See* **1282**.

2761. HAWES, THOMAS; THOMAS, SARAH.   Actional and relational verbs in newspaper editorials. SAP (30) 1996, 131–9.

2762. —— —— Rhetorical uses of theme in newspaper editorials. *See* **2395**.

2763. HOEY, MICHAEL.   Patterns of lexis in text. (Bibl. 1992, 2142.) Rev. by Christina Schäffner in ZAA (42:3) 1994, 254–7.

2764. HYLAND, KEN.   Getting serious about being tentative: how scientists hedge. NZSAL (1) 1995, 35–50.

2765. KARVONEN, PIRJO.   Hidden norms of language. Pragmatics, Ideology, and Contacts Bulletin (3) 1996, 30–2.

2766. KIDDER, TRACY.   Facts and the nonfiction writer. BkW, 5 Sept. 1993, 1, 10.

2767. LEITNER, GERHARD; HESSELMANN, MARKUS.   'What do you do with a ball in soccer?' – medium, mode, and pluricentricity in soccer reporting. WorldE (15:1) 1996, 83–102. (Indian and Ghanaian English.)

2768. McCONNELL, FRANK.   Desecrating literature: reading the *PMLA*. Cweal (123:7) 1996, 24, 26–7.

2769. McCULLOUGH, LAURENCE B.   The abstract character and transforming power of medical language. Soundings (72) 1989, 111–25.

2770. MACNEAL, EDWARD.   Looking ahead: why the real lesson of Vietnam eludes Robert McNamara. *See* **2213**.

2771. MEINHOF, ULRIKE H.; RICHARDSON, KAY (eds).   Text, discourse and context: representations of poverty in Britain. *See* **2548**.

2772. MILANI, CELESTINA.   Note semiologiche e linguistiche a un corpus pubblicitario inglese e italiano. Quaderni di lingue e letterature (18) 1993, 499–523.

2773. MULVEY, CHRISTOPHER.   Travel literature: the 'Medland' trope in the British holiday brochure. JPC (29:4) 1996, 99–115.

2774. MYERS, GREG.   Words in ads. London; New York: Arnold, 1994. pp. x, 222. Rev. by Gloria Corpas Pastor in LangL (5:2) 1996, 144–6.

2775. —— Writing biology: texts in the social construction of scientific knowledge. Madison; London: Wisconsin UP, 1990. pp. xvi, 304. Rev. by David Banks in LangL (4:2) 1995, 145–7.

2776. PALACIOS MARTÍNEZ, IGNACIO MIGUEL.   Notes on the use and meaning of negation in contemporary written English. *See* **1723**.

2777. PARTINGTON, ALAN. 'An all-American villain': a corpus-based study of relexicalization in newspaper headlines. Textus (9:1) 1996, 43–61.

2778. PERCY, CAROL E. In the margins: Dr Hawkesworth's editorial emendations to the language of Captain Cook's *Voyages*. See **785**.

2779. PFATTEICHER, PHILIP H. The school of the church: worship and Christian formation. Valley Forge, PA: Trinity Press, 1995. pp. ix, 149. Rev. by David Jasper in LitTheol (10:3) 1996, 299.

2780. POLLITT, KATHA; ANDERSON, MARTIN. The language of Left and Right. BkW, 9 Apr. 1995, 1, 10–11.

2781. RICE, WILLIAM CRAIG. Public discourse and academic inquiry. See **2560**.

2782. ROOM, ADRIAN. Troubled *Times. See* **1351**.

2783. RUSSELL, CHARLES G.; MANY, PAUL. How language collectives compromise journalistic accuracy. See **2236**.

2784. SALMI-TOLONEN, TARJA. If X then Y: some observations on conditionals in English legislative discourse. See **1739**.

2785. SCHAFFER, DEBORAH. Shocking secrets revealed! The language of tabloid headlines. ERGS (52:1) 1995, 27–46.

2786. SCHLEY, JIM. News. *In* (pp. 97–105) **77**.

2787. SCHMIED, JOSEF; HUDSON-ETTLE, DIANA. Analyzing the style of East African newspapers in English. WorldE (15:1) 1996, 103–13.

2788. SCHNEUWLY, BERNARD. Content and formulation: writing argumentative texts in pairs. Argumentation (10:2) 1996, 213–26.

2789. SIBLEY, GAY. *Satura* from Quintilian to Joe Bob Briggs: a new look at an old word. *In* (pp. 57–72) **120**.

2790. SMITH, ROZ. The local press: what's in it for *you? See* **1371**.

2791. STEFFEN, THERESE. Linguistic features of cartoon captions in the *New Yorker*. PCR (6:1) 1995, 133–47.

2792. STUBBS, MICHAEL. Text and corpus analysis: computer-assisted studies of language and institutions. See **1208**.

2793. THOMPSEN, PHILIP A. An episode of flaming: a creative narrative. See **1209**.

2794. VLČKOVÁ, JITKA. Text typology of personal advertising. Brno Studies in English (22) 1996, 89–96.

2795. WENDORF, RICHARD. Sir Joshua's French Revolution. *In* (pp. 177–97) **122**.

2796. WIDDOWSON, H. G. Reply to Fairclough: discourse and interpretation: conjectures and refutations. See **2571**.

DIALECTS

GENERAL STUDIES

2797. CARPENTER, LYNETTE; KOLMAR, WENDY K. (eds). Haunting the house of fiction: feminist perspectives on ghost stories by American women. (Bibl. 1993, 23.) Rev. by Timmel Duchamp in Signs (17:4) 1992, 848–52.

2798. CHESHIRE, JENNY (ed.). English around the world: sociolinguistic perspectives. (Bibl. 1993, 1675.) Rev. by Klaus Hansen in ZAA (41:3) 1993, 258–9.

2799. EASINGWOOD, PETER; GROSS, KONRAD; KLOOSS, WOLFGANG (eds). Probing Canadian culture. (Bibl. 1993, 36.) Rev. by Axel Knoenagel in CanRCL (20:1/2) 1993, 277–80.

2800. GÖRLACH, MANFRED. And is it English? EWW (17:2) 1996, 153–74.

2801. —— Englishes: studies in varieties of English 1984–1988. (Bibl. 1994, 1765.) Rev. by Uwe Carls in ZAA (41:3) 1993, 259–61.

2802. —— More Englishes: new studies in varieties of English, 1988–1994. (Bibl. 1995, 2362.) Rev. by John Spencer in EWW (17:1) 1996, 129–32.

2803. HANSEN, KLAUS; CARLS, UWE; LUCKO, PETER. Die Differenzierung des Englischen in nationale Varianten: eine Einführung. Berlin: Schmidt, 1996. pp. 276. Rev. by Christoph Stephan in EWW (17:2) 1996, 285–8.

2804. KLEMOLA, JUHANI; KYTÖ, MERJA; RISSANEN, MATTI (eds). Speech past and present: studies in English dialectology in memory of Ossi Ihalainen. New York; Frankfurt; Bern; Paris: Lang, 1996. pp. 474. (Univ. of Bamberg Studies in English Linguistics, 38.) Rev. by Christoph Stephan in EWW (17:1) 1996, 141–3.

2805. MANCOFF, DEBRA N. (ed.). The Arthurian revival: essays on form, tradition, and transformation. (Bibl. 1993, 3.) Rev. by Norman D. Hinton in Quondam et Futurus (3:2) 1993, 72–6.

2806. UPTON, CLIVE; WIDDOWSON, J. D. A. An atlas of English dialects. Oxford; New York: OUP, 1996. pp. xxiii, 193. Rev. by Manfred Görlach in EWW (17:2) 1996, 309–10.

2807. WHITLOCK, GILLIAN; TIFFIN, HELEN (eds). Re-siting Queen's English. Essays presented to John Pengwerne Matthews. (Bibl. 1995, 47.) Rev. by Jennifer Lawn in CanL (149) 1996, 149–50.

2808. WOODS, NICOLA. English language: dialectology and sociolinguistics (including creolistics). YWES (75) 1994, 11–24.

DIALECTS OF THE BRITISH ISLES

2809. ANON. (ed.). Glossary of Northamptonshire words and phrases. By Anne Elizabeth Baker. *See* **2078**.

2810. BEAL, JOAN. The Jocks and the Geordies: modified standards in eighteenth-century pronouncing dictionaries. *In* (pp. 363–82) **27**.

2811. BÖRJARS, KERSTI; VINCENT, NIGEL; CHAPMAN, CAROL. Paradigms, periphrases and pronominal inflection: a feature-based account. *See* **1612**.

2812. BREEZE, ANDREW. The provenance of the Rushworth Mercian gloss. *See* **1431**.

2813. BROWN, IAN. Problems of defining 'Standard' Scots: some linguistic and theatrical aspects. ZAA (43:4) 1995, 291–302.

2814. CALDER, ANGUS. Language, Empire and the 'home colonies'. Span (42/43) 1996, 1–14.

2815. CHIRREY, DEBORAH. Phonetic descriptions of Scottish accents: a historical perspective. *See* **1542**.

2816. COGGLE, PAUL. Do you speak Estuary? The new Standard English. (Bibl. 1993, 1680.) Rev. by Thomas Herbst in ZAA (43:1) 1995, 95–6.

2817. CORRIGAN, KAREN P. 'Plain life' depicted in 'fiery shorthand': sociolinguistic aspects of the languages and dialects of Scotland and Ulster as portrayed in Scott's *Waverley* and Banim's *The Boyne Water*. SLang (14/15) 1995/96, 218–33.

2818. DOUGLAS, SHEILA. The language of Perthshire travellers. SLang (14/15) 1995/96, 81–9.

2819. GACHELIN, JEAN-MARC. From the permanence of Scots to the revival of diachrony. English Today (11:4) 1995, 51–4.

2820. GERMON, JOHN. 'Zee 'ee dreckly'. Newton Abbot: Orchard, 1995. pp. 38. (Devon dialect.)

2821. GLAUSER, BEAT. The sound /x/ in Scots. *See* **1550**.

2822. GÖRLACH, MANFRED. Morphological standardization: the strong verb in Scots. *In* (pp. 161–81) **27**.

2823. HANNA, RALPH, III. With an *O* (Yorks.) or an *I* (Salop.)? The Middle English lyrics of British Library Additional 45896. *See* **368**.

2824. HARDIE, KIM. Scots: matters of identity and nationalism. SLang (14/15) 1995/96, 141–7.

2825. HENRY, ALISON. Belfast English and Standard English: dialect variation and parameter setting. (Bibl. 1995, 2378.) Rev. by Lesley Milroy in Language in Society (25:3) 1996, 471–6.

2826. HUGHES, ARTHUR; TRUDGILL, PETER. English accents and dialects: an introduction to social and regional varieties of English in the British Isles. *See* **1556**.

2827. INOUE, FUMIO. Subjective dialect division in Great Britain. AS (71:2) 1996, 142–61.

2828. JONES, CHARLES. A language suppressed: the pronunciation of the Scots language in the 18th century. *See* **1518**.

2829. KINGSMORE, RONA K. Ulster Scots speech: a sociolinguistic study. Ed. by Michael B. Montgomery. Foreword by James Milroy and Lesley Milroy. Tuscaloosa; London: Alabama UP, 1995. pp. xxv, 244.

2830. KITSON, PETER. The dialect position of the Old English Orosius. *See* **1896**.

2831. KNIEZSA, VERONIKA. The orthography of Older Scots: the manuscripts of Barbour's *The Bruce. In* (pp. 167–82) **11**.

2832. LAMB, GREGOR. Orkney wordbook: a dictionary of the dialect of Orkney. *See* **2100**.

2833. LINDBERG, CONRAD. The Wyclif Bible in Scots. *In* (pp. 195–203) **11**.

2834. MACAFEE, C. I. (ed.). A concise Ulster dictionary. *See* **2102**.

2835. MACAULAY, RONALD K. S. Remarkably common eloquence: the aesthetics of urban dialect. SLang (14/15) 1995/96, 66–80.

2836. McMahon, April M. S.   On the use of the past to explain the present: the history of /r/ in English and Scots. *In* (pp. 73–89) **27**.

2837. McVea, Deborah.   The Eastwood dialect: an error in the Cambridge edition of D. H. Lawrence's *The White Peacock*. *See* **748**.

2838. Milroy, James; Milroy, Lesley (eds).   Real English: the grammar of English dialects in the British Isles. (Bibl. 1994, 1788.) Rev. by Klaus Hansen in ZAA (44:2) 1996, 172–4.

2839. Milton, Colin.   'Shibboleths o the Scots': Hugh MacDiarmid and Jamieson's *Etymological Dictionary of the Scottish Language*. *See* **2053**.

2840. Moessner, Lilo.   '*Besyde Latyn our langage is imperfite*': the contribution of Gavin Douglas to the development of the Scots lexicon. *See* **1902**.

2841. Ó Muirithe, Diarmaid.   The words we use. *See* **1865**.

2842. Peters, Pam.   Comparative insights into comparison. *See* **1728**.

2843. Pödör, Dóra.   The phonology of Scottish Gaelic loanwords in Lowland Scots. *See* **1571**.

2844. Rydland, Kurt.   The Orton Corpus and Northumbrian phonology: the material from Bamburgh and Bellingham (Northumberland). *See* **1574**.

2845. Shepherd, Valerie.   Anne Elizabeth Baker's *Glossary of Northamptonshire Words and Phrases* and John Clare's rustic idiom. *See* **2064**.

2846. Sims-Kimbrey, Joan.   Wodds and doggerybaw: a Lincolnshire dialect dictionary. *See* **2114**.

2847. Smith, Roz.   The local press: what's in it for *you*? *See* **1371**.

2848. Sprouse, James R.   Middle English dialect investigation and the Middle English manuscript: the case of the Bodleian Manuscript 6923. *See* **423**.

2849. Upton, Clive; Sanderson, Stewart; Widdowson, John.   Word maps: a dialect atlas of England. (Bibl. 1989, 1485.) Rev. by John H. Snow in SECOLR (15:2) 1991, 215–17.

2850. Wełna, Jerzy.   The Middle English source of a present-day dialectal distinction. *In* (pp. 267–80) **68**.

2851. Wilson, William Morrice.   Speak o' the North-East. (Bibl. 1995, 2408.) Rev. by J. Derrick McClure in EWW (17:2) 1996, 311–13.

DIALECTS OF NORTH AMERICA

2852. Algeo, John.   The American language and its British dialect. *See* **1393**.

2853. Anderson, Lisa M.   From blackface to 'genuine Negroes': nineteenth-century minstrelsy and the icon of the 'Negro'. TRI (21:1) 1996, 17–23.

2854. Arndt, Horst; Janney, Richard W.   Speech style and interactional strategy: central organizing principles. *See* **2504**.

2855. Bailey, Guy; Tillery, Jan.   The persistence of Southern American English. JEL (24:4) 1996, 308–21.

2856. Bailey, Lucille M.   The persistence of /mɪzrɪs/ among young speakers in Kentucky. *See* **1531**.

2857. Bernstein, Cynthia.   *Drug* usage among high school students in Silsbee, Texas: a study of the preterite. *See* **1938**.

2858. BERTRAM, ANNE. NTC's dictionary of folksy, regional, and rural sayings. Ed. by Richard A. Spears. *See* **2081**.

2859. BUTLER, TODD. Exploring the antilanguage of gangster rap. SECOLR (19:1) 1995, 1–24.

2860. BUTTERS, RONALD R. The death of Black English: divergence and convergence in Black and White vernaculars. (Bibl. 1994, 1801.) Rev. by Peter Lucko in ZAA (41:3) 1993, 261–3; by Guy Bailey in AS (71:1) 1996, 98–103.

2861. CAVENDER, ANTHONY. A note on the origin and meaning of *bold hives* in the American South. *See* **1921**.

2862. —— (ed.). A folk medical lexicon of South Central Appalachia. *See* **2086**.

2863. CHING, MARVIN K. L. GreaZy/greaSy and other /z/–/s/ choices in Southern pronunciation. *See* **1541**.

2864. CLARK, THOMAS L. Western lore and language: a dictionary for enthusiasts of the American West. *See* **2088**.

2865. COCHRANE, ROBERTSON. The way we word: musing on the meaning of everyday English. *See* **1405**.

2866. DALZELL, TOM. Flappers 2 rappers: American youth slang. *See* **2090**.

2867. DE WOLF, GAELAN DODDS. Word choice: lexical variation in two Canadian surveys. *See* **1830**.

2868. DINGUS, ANNE. More Texas sayings than you can shake a stick at. Houston, TX: Gulf, 1996. pp. vi, 120.

2869. EBLE, CONNIE. Prolegomenon to the study of Cajun English. SECOLR (17:2) 1993, 165–77.

2870. EBLE, CONNIE C. Slang and sociability: in-group language among college students. *See* **1832**.

2871. FALCOFF, MARK. North of the border: origins and fallacies of the 'Hispanic' threat to the United States. TLS, 17 May 1996, 14–15.

2872. FLANIGAN, BEVERLY OLSON; INAL, EMEL. Object relative pronoun use in native and non-native English: a variable rule analysis. *See* **1675**.

2873. FRAZER, TIMOTHY C. Chicano English and Spanish interference in the Midwestern United States. AS (71:1) 1996, 72–85.

2874. —— (ed.). 'Heartland' English: variation and transition in the American Midwest. (Bibl. 1995, 2430.) Rev. by Ellen Johnson in SECOLR (18:2) 1994, 201–6; by Joan H. Hall in JEL (24:4) 1996, 373–80.

2875. GILYARD, KEITH. Let's flip the script: an African-American discourse on language, literature, and learning. Detroit, MI: Wayne State UP, 1996. pp. 141. (African American life.)

2876. GLOWKA, A. WAYNE; LANCE, DONALD M. (eds). Language variation in North American English: research and teaching. (Bibl. 1994, 1817.) Rev. by Michael Aceto in AS (71:2) 1996, 210–14; by Bruce Southard in JEL (24:4) 1996, 369–72.

2877. HAWKINS, OPAL W. Syllable variation through deletion. *See* **1552**.

2878. HAZEN, KIRK. Dialect affinity and subject–verb concord: the Appalachian–Outer Banks connection. *See* **1685**.

2879. HENDRICKSON, ROBERT. Yankee talk: a dictionary of New England expressions. *See* **2097**.

2880. JOHNSON, ELLEN.   Lexical change and variation in the southeastern United States, 1930–1990. *See* **1894**.

2881. JOHNSTONE, BARBARA.   Violence and civility in discourse: uses of mitigation by rural Southern White men. *See* **2272**.

2882. KARSTADT, ANGELA.   Relative markers in Swedish-American English: evidence for a contact language phenomenon? *See* **1697**.

2883. KRETZSCHMAR, WILLIAM A., JR.   Dimensions of variation in American English vocabulary. *See* **1852**.

2884. —— The making of the *LAMSAS Handbook*. SECOLR (19:1) 1995, 48–58. (Handbook of the Linguistic Atlas of the Middle and South Atlantic States.)

2885. —— Quantitative areal analysis of dialect features. LVC (8:1) 1996, 13–39.

2886. —— *et al.* (eds).   Handbook of the linguistic atlas of the Middle and South Atlantic states. (Bibl. 1995, 2436.) Rev. by Erik R. Thomas in SECOLR (19:2) 1995, 205–9.

2887. LIGHT, DEANNA; KRETZSCHMAR, WILLIAM A., JR.   Mapping with numbers. *See* **1115**.

2888. LIGHTER, J. E. (ed.).   Random House historical dictionary of American slang: vol. 1, A–G. *See* **2101**.

2889. LITTLE, GRETA D.; MONTGOMERY, MICHAEL (eds).   Centennial usage studies. (Bibl. 1994, 1828.) Rev. by E. W. Gilman in AS (71:4) 1996, 440–4.

2890. LIU, DILIN; FARHA, BRYAN.   Three strikes and you're out. *See* **1854**.

2891. McMILLAN, JAMES B.; MONTGOMERY, MICHAEL B.   Annotated bibliography of Southern American English. Tuscaloosa; London: Alabama UP, 1989. pp. xvi, 444. (Second ed.: first ed. 1971.) Rev. by Marvin K. L. Ching in SECOLR (15:1) 1991, 118–19.

2892. MAYNOR, NATALIE.   The pronoun *y'all*: questions and some tentative answers. *See* **2031**.

2893. MAZRUI, ALAMIN.   African languages in the African American experience. *In* (pp. 75–90) **55**.

2894. MONTGOMERY, MICHAEL.   Does Tennessee have three 'grand dialects'? Evidence from the *Linguistic Atlas of the Gulf States*. TFSB (57:2) 1995, 68–86.

2895. —— The future of Southern American English. SECOLR (20:1) 1996, 1–24.

2896. MUFWENE, SALIKOKO S.; CONDON, NANCY (eds).   Africanisms in Afro-American language varieties. (Bibl. 1995, 2442.) Rev. by Robin Sabino in SECOLR (20:1) 1996, 127–31.

2897. MURRAY, THOMAS E.; FRAZER, TIMOTHY C.; SIMON, BETH LEE.   *Need* + past participle in American English. *See* **1805**.

2898. MURRAY, THOMAS EDWARD; ROSS-MURRAY, CARMIN D.   Under cover of law: more on the legality of surreptitious recording. Tuscaloosa; London: Alabama UP, 1996. pp. iii, 82. (Pubs of the American Dialect Soc., 79.)

2899. PEARSON, JULIA KNOX.   Linguistic evidence for population movement in North America. SECOLR (20:1) 1996, 88–100.

2900. PEDERSON, LEE.   LAMR/LAWS and the main chance. JEL (24:3) 1996, 234–49. (Linguistic Atlas of the Middle Rockies / Linguistic Atlas of the Western States.)

2901. —— LAWCU Project worksheets. JEL (24:1) 1996, 52–60. (Linguistic Atlas of Wyoming, Colorado and Utah.)

2902. —— A Southern phonology. *See* **1570**.

2903. PRESTON, DENNIS R., *et al.* (eds). American dialect research. (Bibl. 1995, 2445.) Rev. by Josef Schmied in ZAA (42:4) 1994, 387–90.

2904. RAHN, SUZANNE. The changing language of Black child characters in American children's books. *In* (pp. 225–58) **48**.

2905. RICH, JOHN STANLEY; MONTGOMERY, MICHAEL. A century of scholarly commentary on Alabama English. SECOLR (17:1) 1993, 12–35.

2906. RICKFORD, JOHN R.; RAFAL, CHRISTINE THÉBERGE. Preterite *had* + V-*ed* in the narratives of African-American preadolescents. *See* **1798**.

2907. ROBERTS, DALE. Kaleidoscope: the language at large. *See* **1871**.

2908. SANTA ANA A., OTTO. Sonority and syllable structure in Chicano English. *See* **1576**.

2909. SCHMIED, JOSEF. Empirical comparative research in Black English in the United States and in Africa. ZAA (41:4) 1993, 294–304.

2910. SCHNEIDER, EDGAR W. American earlier Black English: morphological and syntactic variables. (Bibl. 1994, 1842.) Rev. by Alexander Hull in SECOLR (16:1) 1992, 112–14.

2911. —— (ed.). Focus on the USA. Amsterdam; Philadelphia, PA: Benjamins, 1996. pp. 368. (Varieties of English around the world, general series, 16.)

2912. SEDLEY, DOROTHY. Anatomy of English: an introduction to the structure of Standard American English. *See* **1740**.

2913. SELLS, PETER; RICKFORD, JOHN; WASOW, THOMAS. An optimality theoretic approach to variation in negative inversion in AAVE. Natural Language and Linguistic Theory (14:3) 1996, 591–627.

2914. SOMMER, ELISABETH. Prepositions in Black English vernacular. *See* **1744**.

2915. SOUTHARD, BRUCE. An acoustical analysis of Raven I. McDavid, Jr's pronunciation of vowel norms for the *Linguistic Atlas of the United States and Canada*. *See* **1579**.

2916. THOMAS, ERIK; BAILEY, GUY. A case of competing mergers and their resolution. SECOLR (16:2) 1992, 179–200.

2917. URA, HIROYUKI. On the structure of 'double objects' and certain differences between British and American English. *See* **1753**.

2918. WALDREP, CHRISTOPHER. The making of a border state society: James McGready, the Great Revival, and the prosecution of profanity in Kentucky. *See* **1879**.

2919. WOLFRAM, WALT. Delineation and description in dialectology: the case of perfective *I'm* in Lumbee English. *See* **1799**.

2920. —— Dialects and American English. (Bibl. 1992, 2267.) Rev. by William A. Kretzschmar, Jr, in JEL (24:2) 1996, 167–8.

2921. YANG, BYUNGGON. A comparative study of American English and Korean vowels produced by male and female speakers. *See* **1588**.

DIALECTS OF THE REST OF THE WORLD

2922. ADAMS, KAREN L. White supremacy or apple pie? The politics of making English the official language of Arizona. ArizEB (34:2) 1992, 23–9.

2923.   AHULU, SAMUEL.   Just how innovative are the 'New Englishes'? English Today (12:2) 1996, 32–4.

2924.   ALLSOPP, RICHARD (ed.).   Dictionary of Caribbean English usage. With a French and Spanish supplement ed. by Jeannette Allsopp. *See* **2076**.

2925.   AMBATCHEW, MICHAEL DANIEL.   English in Ethiopia. English Today (11:3) 1995, 43–4.

2926.   BAILEY, GUY; SMITH, CLYDE.   Southern English in Brazil, no? SECOLR (16:1) 1992, 71–89.

2927.   BANDA, FELIX.   The scope and categorization of African English: some sociolinguistic considerations. EWW (17:1) 1996, 63–75.

2928.   BARKER, F. S.; HOLTZHAUSEN, M. M. E.   South African labour glossary. *See* **2079**.

2929.   BAUER, LAURIE; HOLMES, JANET.   Getting into a flap! /t/ in New Zealand English. *See* **1532**.

2930.   BAUMGARDNER, ROBERT J. (ed.).   South Asian English: structure, use, and users. Urbana: Illinois UP, 1996. pp. xx, 286. (English in the global context.)

2931.   BAYARD, DONN; BARTLETT, CHRISTOPHER.   'You must be from Gorrre': attitudinal effects of Southland rhotic accents and speaker gender on NZE listeners and the question of NZE regional variation. *See* **1533**.

2932.   BOYLE, JOSEPH; TOMLINSON, RUTH.   Job interviews in Hong Kong. English Today (11:3) 1995, 36–9.

2933.   BROOKS, MAUREEN; RITCHIE, JOAN (comps).   Tassie terms: a glossary of Tasmanian words. *See* **2083**.

2934.   BUTLER, SUSAN.   World English in an Asian context: the *Macquarie Dictionary* project. *See* **2038**.

2935.   CAMPBELL, ELIZABETH; GORDON, ELIZABETH.   'What do you fink?' Is New Zealand English losing its *th*? *See* **1540**.

2936.   CARLESS, DAVID R.   Politicised expressions in the *South China Morning Post*. *See* **1824**.

2937.   COURTNEY, NEIL.   The nature of Australian. English Today (12:2) 1996, 23–9.

2938.   CROWLEY, DANIEL J.   'Strine', immigration, and the Australian identity. JFR (32:1) 1995, 49–63.

2939.   DAVIDSON, KEITH.   The Malta experience. English Today (12:4) 1996, 15–23.

2940.   DELBRIDGE, ARTHUR; YALLOP, COLIN.   The *Macquarie Dictionary*. *See* **2042**.

2941.   DE PRAP, REED.   New corrupt-speak of the RDP. *See* **1829**.

2942.   DSEAGU, SAMUEL A.   English in Ghana. ESA (39:1) 1996, 57–66.

2943.   GOUGH, DAVID.   The English of White Eastern Cape farmers in South Africa. WorldE (15:3) 1996, 257–65.

2944.   HARKINS, JEAN.   Bridging two worlds: Aboriginal English and crosscultural understanding. St Lucia: Queensland UP, 1994. pp. x, 228. Rev. by Gerhard Leitner in EWW (17:1) 1996, 135–8.

2945.   HARRIS, JOHN.   On the trail of short *u*. *See* **1551**.

2946.   HOLMES, JANET.   Collecting the Wellington Corpus of Spoken New Zealand English: some methodological challenges. *See* **2536**.

2947.   —— Losing voice: is final /z/ devoicing a feature of Maori English? *See* **1554**.

2948. —— Three chairs for New Zealand English: the EAR/AIR merger. *See* **1555**.

2949. —— AINSWORTH, HELEN.   Syllable-timing and Maori English. *See* **2537**.

2950. HUNDT, MARIANNE.   Beyond hope: on the use of *hopefully* in New Zealand English. *See* **1963**.

2951. JENKINS, ELWYN.   Who calls the tune in language matters? A look at some language services in South Africa. English Academy Review (11) 1996, 5–14.

2952. JOHNSON, GARY; HOLMES, JANET.   The Wellington Corpus of Spoken New Zealand English: transcription and ethical issues. *See* **2540**.

2953. JOHNSTONE, IAN M.   Fair dinkum and good faith – Aussie and legal honesty compared: a meeting of folklore and lawyer's law. *See* **1942**.

2954. KING, JEANETTE.   Maori English as a solidarity marker for *te reo Maori*. NZSAL (1) 1995, 51–9.

2955. LEITNER, GERHARD.   '*Have I your permission to leave, sir?*' – die Herausforderung der neuen Formen des Englisch für die Anglistik. NS (90:1) 1991, 23–38.

2956. —— HESSELMANN, MARKUS.   'What do you do with a ball in soccer?' – medium, mode, and pluricentricity in soccer reporting. *See* **2767**.

2957. LEWIS, GILLIAN.   The origins of New Zealand English: a report on work in progress. *See* **1463**.

2958. LI, DONG.   English in China. English Today (11:1) 1995, 53–6.

2959. MACLAGAN, MARGARET ; GORDON, ELIZABETH.   The changing sound of New Zealand English. *See* **1561**.

2960. —— —— Women's role in sound change: the case of two New Zealand closing diphthongs. *See* **1562**.

2961. MACLAGAN, MARGARET A.; GORDON, ELIZABETH.   Out of the AIR and into the EAR: another view of the New Zealand diphthong merger. *See* **1563**.

2962. MESTHRIE, RAJEND.   *Imagint excusations*: missionary English in the nineteenth-century Cape Colony, South Africa. *See* **1469**.

2963. MODIANO, MARKO.   A Mid-Atlantic lexical register. *See* **1858**.

2964. MOSSOP, JONATHAN W.   Markedness and fossilization in the interlanguage phonology of Brunei English. *See* **1567**.

2965. NASH, ROSE; FAYER, JOAN M.   Changing lexical features in Puerto Rican English. *See* **1862**.

2966. NURMI, TARU.   *Aussies* and *mozzies*: on the hypocoristic/diminutive suffix *-y/ie* in Australian English. *See* **1640**.

2967. PANDEY, ANITA.   The pragmatics of code alteration in Nigerian English. StudLS (25:1) 1995, 75–117.

2968. PETERS, PAM.   The Cambridge Australian style guide. *See* **1122**.

2969. —— Comparative insights into comparison. *See* **1728**.

2970. —— In search of Australian style. *See* **1123**.

2971. RAMSON, BILL.   More famous Australian etymologies. *See* **1907**.

2972. ROBERTSON, SHELLEY.   Maori English and the bus-driving listener: a study of ethnic identification and phonetic cues. *See* **1573**.

2973. —— Wellington busdrivers' attitudes towards speakers of Maori and Pakeha New Zealand English. NZEJ (10) 1996, 35–9.

2974. ST LEON, MARK.   Australian circus language: a report on the nature, origin and circumstances of Aussie argot under the big top. *See* **1873**.

2975. SCHMIED, JOSEF.   Empirical comparative research in Black English in the United States and in Africa. *See* **2909**.

2976. —— HUDSON-ETTLE, DIANA.   Analyzing the style of East African newspapers in English. *See* **2787**.

2977. SILVA, PENNY, *et al.* (eds).   A dictionary of South African English on historical principles. *See* **2113**.

2978. SIMO BOBDA, AUGUSTIN.   Aspects of Cameroon English phonology. *See* **1577**.

2979. SINGH, RAJENDRA; DASGUPTA, PROBAL; LELE, JAYANT (eds). Explorations in Indian sociolinguistics. New Delhi; London; Thousand Oaks, CA: Sage, 1995. pp. 258. (Language and development, 2.)

2980. SMIT, UTE.   A new English for a new South Africa? Language attitudes, language planning and education. Vienna: Braumüller, 1996. pp. vi, 263. (Austrian studies in English, 83.)

2981. —— South African English in the 1990s: a field study on status, roles and attitudes. EWW (17:1) 1996, 77–109.

2982. —— Who speaks like that? Accent recognition and language attitudes. *See* **1578**.

2983. TAYLOR, BEN.   Gay men, femininity and /t/ in New Zealand English. *See* **1581**.

2984. TAYLOR, BRIAN.   Ocker, Richo and the other Aussie Dunny. Mucking about with people's names in Australian English: what is the code? *See* **2165**.

2985. TAYLOR, MONICA E.   Jamaica and the economics of English. English Today (12:4) 1996, 25–31. (Standard English in the Caribbean.)

2986. YAJUN, JIANG.   Chinglish and China English. English Today (11:1) 1995, 51–3.

ENGLISH AS A WORLD LANGUAGE

2987. AL-ABED AL HAQ, FAWWAZ; SMADI, OQLAH.   Spread of English and Westernization in Saudi Arabia. WorldE (15:3) 1996, 307–17.

2988. AHULU, SAMUEL.   Variation in the use of complex verbs in international English. *See* **1647**.

2989. BATTENBURG, JOHN D.   English in the Maghreb. English Today (12:4) 1996, 3–14.

2990. BERNS, MARGIE.   English in the European Union. English Today (11:3) 1995, 3–11.

2991. BLACKFORD, PAUL.   Atmosphere English. Verbatim (23:1) 1996, 12–13.

2992. CALDER, ANGUS.   Language, Empire and the 'home colonies'. *See* **2814**.

2993. CRISMORE, AVON; NGEOW, KAREN YEOK-HWA; SOO, KENG-SOON.   Attitudes toward English in Malaysia. WorldE (15:3) 1996, 319–35.

2994. CUMMING, JOHN D.   The Internet and the English language. *See* **1147**.

2995. DAVIDSON, KEITH.   Is English a Swiss language? English Today (11:2) 1995, 40–4.

2996. DE KLERK, VIVIAN (ed.).   Focus on South Africa. Amsterdam;

Philadelphia, PA: Benjamins, 1996. pp. 325. (Varieties of English around the world: general series, 15.) Rev. by John Spencer in EWW (17:2) 1996, 296–300.

2997. GRAHAM, GORDON. World publishing and the English language. English Today (11:1) 1995, 9–12.

2998. GREENBAUM, SIDNEY (ed.). Comparing English worldwide: the International Corpus of English. *See* **1158**.

2999. GREENBAUM, SIDNEY; NELSON, GERALD. The International Corpus of English (ICE) project. WorldE (15:1) 1996, 3–15.

3000. HANSEN, KLAUS. Zum Englischen in Westafrika. ZAA (41:4) 1993, 305–17.

3001. HARTMANN, REINHARD (ed.). The English language in Europe. Oxford: Intellect, 1996. pp. 60. (Europa, 2:3.)

3002. HILGENDORF, SUZANNE K. The impact of English in Germany. English Today (12:3) 1996, 3–14.

3003. KACHRU, BRAJ B. The paradigms of marginality. WorldE (15:3) 1996, 241–55.

3004. KACHRU, YAMUNA. Contrastive rhetoric in world Englishes. *See* **2405**.

3005. —— Kachru revisits contrasts. *See* **2406**.

3006. LOONEN, PIETER. English in Europe: from timid to tyrannical? English Today (12:2) 1996, 3–9.

3007. LOWENBERG, PETER H. Standards and norms for world Englishes: issues and attitudes. StudLS (20:2) 1990, 123–37.

3008. MODIANO, MARKO. The Americanization of Euro-English. WorldE (15:2) 1996, 207–15.

3009. MUNRO, VICKI R. International graduate students and the spread of English. WorldE (15:3) 1996, 337–45.

3010. NEWMAN, BARRY. Global chatter: the reality of 'business English'. English Today (12:2) 1996, 16–19, 64.

3011. PHILLIPSON, ROBERT. On English in Europe. English Today (12:4) 1996, 58–9.

3012. SMITH, ROSS. Single market, single currency, single language. English Today (12:2) 1996, 10–14.

PIDGINS AND CREOLES

3013. ACETO, MICHAEL. Syntactic innovation in a Caribbean creole: the Bastimentos variety of Panamanian Creole English. *See* **1646**.

3014. ADONE, DANY; PLAG, INGO (eds). Creolization and language change. Tübingen: Niemeyer, 1994. pp. 160. (Linguistische Arbeiten, 317.) Rev. by Suzanne Romaine in Linguistics (34:6) 1996, 1277–8; by John H. McWhorter in Language in Society (25:1) 1996, 156–9.

3015. AHULU, SAMUEL. Hybridized English in Ghana. English Today (11:4) 1995, 31–6.

3016. AYAFOR, MIRIAM. An orthography for Kamtok. *See* **1591**.

3017. BAILEY, GUY; MAYNOR, NATALIE; CUKOR-AVILA, PATRICIA. The emergence of Black English: text and commentary. (Bibl. 1994, 1943.) Rev. by George Dorrill in SECOLR (18:1) 1994, 95–7.

3018. BAKER, PHILIP (ed.). From contact to creole and beyond. London: Westminster UP for Creole Linguistics Research Group, 1995.

pp. 268. (Westminster creolistics, 1.) Rev. by Magnus Huber in EWW (17:1) 1996, 150–2.

3019. CUNNINGHAM, IRMA ALOYCE EWING. A syntactic analysis of Sea Island Creole. (Bibl. 1995, 2522.) Rev. by Katherine Wyly Mille in SECOLR (17:1) 1993, 85–7.

3020. DEVONISH, HUBERT. *Kom groun Jamiekan Daans Haal liricks: memba se a plie wi a plie.* Contextualizing Jamaican 'Dance Hall' music: Jamaican language at play in a speech event. EWW (17:2) 1996, 213–37.

3021. EZENWA-OHAETO. Bridges of orality: Nigerian pidgin poetry. WLT (69:1) 1995, 69–77.

3022. FARACLAS, NICHOLAS G. Nigerian pidgin. London; New York: Routledge, 1996. pp. xv, 297.

3023. FOSTER, ROBERT; MÜHLHÄUSLER, PETER. Native tongue, captive voice: the representation of the Aboriginal 'voice' in colonial South Australia. Language & Communication (16:1) 1996, 1–16.

3024. GIBSON, KEAN. An analogy between the continuums of Guyanese Creole and Guyanese Comfa. JCS (11:1/2) 1995/96, 3–13.

3025. HUBER, MAGNUS; GÖRLACH, MANFRED. Texts: West African Pidgin English. EWW (17:2) 1996, 239–58.

3026. LALLA, BARBARA; D'COSTA, JEAN (eds). Language in exile: three hundred years of Jamaican Creole. (Bibl. 1994, 1960.) Rev. by Salikoko Mufwene in SECOLR (15:2) 1991, 200–4.

3027. MONTGOMERY, MICHAEL (ed.). The crucible of Carolina: essays in the development of Gullah language and culture. Athens; London: Georgia UP, 1994. pp. x, 239. Rev. by Tracey L. Weldon in SECOLR (20:1) 1996, 132–4; by Peter H. Wood in GaHQ (80:2) 1996, 400–2.

3028. MORGAN, MARCYLIENA H. (ed.). Language & the social construction of identity in creole situations. (Bibl. 1994, 1964.) Rev. by Christine Jourdan in Language in Society (25:3) 1996, 487–91.

3029. SABINO, ROBIN. A peak at death: assessing continuity and change in an underdocumented language. LVC (8:1) 1996, 41–61. (English Creole in Danish West Indies.)

3030. SEBBA, MARK. How do you spell *patwa*? CritQ (38:4) 1996, 50–63. (Development of British creole.)

3031. THOMASON, SARAH GREY; KAUFMAN, TERRENCE. Language contact, creolization, and genetic linguistics. (Bibl. 1994, 1977.) Rev. by J. L. Dillard in SECOLR (15:2) 1991, 205–8.

3032. TODD, LORETO. Tracking the homing pidgin: a millennium report. English Today (11:1) 1995, 33–41.

3033. WEKKER, HERMAN. The English-based creoles of Surinam. English Today (12:4) 1996, 33–8.

3034. WOODS, NICOLA. English language: dialectology and sociolinguistics (including creolistics). *See* **2808**.

3035. YARUPAWA, SHEM. Domain dependent code choices and their implications for the future of the Musom language. LLM (27:1) 1996, 83–100.

SOCIOLINGUISTICS

3036. ADAMS, KAREN L. White supremacy or apple pie? The politics of making English the official language of Arizona. *See* **2922**.

3037. ANDREWS, EDNA. Cultural sensitivity and political correctness: the linguistic problem of naming. *See* **2121**.

3038. ANTAKI, CHARLES. Explaining and arguing: the social organization of accounts. *See* **2503**.

3039. BANDA, FELIX. The scope and categorization of African English: some sociolinguistic considerations. *See* **2927**.

3040. BAYARD, DONN; BARTLETT, CHRISTOPHER. 'You must be from Gorrre': attitudinal effects of Southland rhotic accents and speaker gender on NZE listeners and the question of NZE regional variation. *See* **1533**.

3041. BENNETT-KASTOR, TINA L. Anaphora, nonanaphora, and the generic use of pronouns by children. *See* **1652**.

3042. BIBER, DOUGLAS; FINEGAN, EDWARD (eds). Sociolinguistic perspectives on register. Oxford; New York: OUP, 1994. pp. x, 385. (Oxford studies in sociolinguistics.) Rev. by Manfred Görlach in JEL (24:3) 1996, 262–4.

3043. BIGGAM, C. P. Sociolinguistic aspects of Old English colour lexemes. *See* **1883**.

3044. BLUM-KULKA, SHOSHANA. Cultural patterns in dinner talk. *See* **2509**.

3045. BURRIDGE, KATE. Political correctness: euphemism with attitude. *See* **1823**.

3046. CAMERON, DEBORAH. The accents of politics. *See* **1539**.

3047. —— Verbal hygiene. London; New York: Routledge, 1995. pp. xvi, 264. (Politics of language.) Rev. by Anthea Fraser Gupta in English Today (12:4) 1996, 60–1.

3048. CAMPBELL, KARLYN KOHRS. Hearing women's voices. *See* **2327**.

3049. CASE, SUSAN SCHICK. Gender, language, and the professions: recognition of verbal-repertoire speech. *See* **2519**.

3050. COATES, JENNIFER. Women, men, and language: a sociolinguistic account of gender differences in language. (Bibl. 1995, 2540.) Rev. by Elisabeth D. Kuhn in NWSAJ (8:2) 1996, 117–25.

3051. —— CAMERON, DEBORAH (eds). Women in their speech communities: new perspectives on language and sex. London; New York: Longman, 1988. pp. viii, 191. Rev. by Bettie Horne in SECOLR (15:1) 1991, 110–13.

3052. CUTTS, MARTIN. Writing on the wall for law language. English Today (11:3) 1995, 45–53.

3053. DAUTERMANN, JENNIE. A case for examining professional voices in institutional settings: nurses in conversation. *See* **2522**.

3054. DAVIS, HAYLEY. Theorizing women's and men's language. *See* **2523**.

3055. DEFRANCISCO, VICTORIA LETO. Difference or dominance: a critique of two theoretical attempts to explain gender-based communication barriers. StudLS (25:2) 1995, 29–46.

3056. EISENMAN, RUSSELL. The language of criminal justice: an essay in clarification. ERGS (52:1) 1995, 80–6.

3057. —— A reply to Mark S. Cohen. *See* **1944**.

3058. FREED, ALICE F.; GREENWOOD, ALICE. Women, men, and type of talk: what makes the difference? *See* **2531**.

3059. GIBBONS, JOHN (ed.). Language and the law. *See* **2755**.

3060. GONZÁLEZ CRUZ, ISABEL. Sociolingüística británica: introducción a la obra de Peter Trudgill. RCEI (28) 1994, 213–15.

3061. GOODSON, F. TODD.   Schoolspeak: breaking the code. *See* **1839**.

3062. GOODWIN, MARJORIE HARNESS.   He-said-she-said: talk as social organization among Black children. *See* **2533**.

3063. GREENAWALT, KENT.   Fighting words: individuals, communities, and liberties of speech. Princeton, NJ; Chichester: Princeton UP, 1995. pp. xi, 189. Rev. by Donald Meiklejohn in Ethics (106:4) 1996, 871–3.

3064. GUMPERZ, JENNY C.; GUMPERZ, JOHN J.   Treacherous words: gender and power in academic assessment. FL (30:3/4) 1996, 167–88.

3065. HAIMAN, FRANKLYN S.   Sexist speech and the First Amendment. CommEd (40:1) 1991, 1–5.

3066. HARDMAN, M. J.   The sexist circuits of English. Humanist (56:2) 1996, 25–32.

3067. HAYMES, RICHARD D. Corporate lingo: a new meaning. *See* **1842**.

3068. INOUE, FUMIO.   Subjective dialect division in Great Britain. *See* **2827**.

3069. JACOBS, GREG.   Lesbian and gay male language use: a critical review of the literature. AS (71:1) 1996, 49–71.

3070. KAMWANGAMALU, NKONKO M.   Sociolinguistic aspects of siSwati–English bilingualism. WorldE (15:3) 1996, 295–305.

3071. KEHL, D. G.   Higher educanto: doublespeak in academe. ERGS (51:3) 1994, 332–7.

3072. KEY, MARY RITCHIE.   Male/female language: with a comprehensive bibliography. Lanham, MD; London: Scarecrow Press, 1996. pp. xxxv, 324. (Second ed.: first ed. 1975.)

3073. KINGSMORE, RONA K.   Ulster Scots speech: a sociolinguistic study. Ed. by Michael B. Montgomery. Foreword by James Milroy and Lesley Milroy. *See* **2829**.

3074. KUHN, ELISABETH D.   Review essay: gender and language. NWSAJ (8:2) 1996, 117–25.

3075. LANGEVIN, LYSANNE.   Of manpower and words: a study of linguistic markers of inclusion and exclusion in managerial work in the education system. StudLS (25:2) 1995, 217–61.

3076. MACLAGAN, MARGARET ; GORDON, ELIZABETH.   Women's role in sound change: the case of two New Zealand closing diphthongs. *See* **1562**.

3077. MATSUDA, MARI J., *et al.*   Words that wound: critical race theory, assaultive speech, and the First Amendment. Boulder, CO: Westview Press, 1993. pp. viii, 160. (New perspectives on law, culture, and society.) Rev. by Andrew Altman in Ethics (106:1) 1995, 211–13.

3078. MICHARD, CLAIRE; VIOLLET, CATHERINE.   Sex and gender in linguistics: fifteen years of feminist research in the United States and Germany. Trans. by Susan Ellis Wolf. Feminist Issues (11:1) 1991, 53–88.

3079. MILES, JACK.   Political correctness and the American newspaper: the case of the *Los Angeles Times* stylebook. *See* **1857**.

3080. MILROY, LESLEY.   Language and social networks. (Bibl. 1990, 1767.) Rev. by Mary Jane Hurst in SECOLR (15:1) 1991, 100–2.

3081. MÜHLHÄUSLER, PETER.   Linguistic ecology: language change and linguistic imperialism in the Pacific region. London; New York: Routledge, 1996. pp. 396. Rev. by Manfred Görlach in EWW (17:2) 1996, 317–18.

3082. NEVALAINEN, TERTTU; RAUMOLIN-BRUNBERG, HELENA. Social stratification in Tudor English? *In* (pp. 303–26) **27**.

3083. PENZ, HERMINE. Politically correct language and language teaching. Moderne Sprachen (40:1) 1996, 44–60.

3084. ROBERTSON, SHELLEY. Maori English and the bus-driving listener: a study of ethnic identification and phonetic cues. *See* **1573**.

3085. —— Wellington busdrivers' attitudes towards speakers of Maori and Pakeha New Zealand English. *See* **2973**.

3086. RUBIN, DONALD L. (ed.). Composing social identity in written language. *See* **2460**.

3087. SCHIFFMAN, HAROLD F. Linguistic culture and language policy. London; New York: Routledge, 1996. pp. xii, 351. Rev. by Manfred Görlach in EWW (17:1) 1996, 143–4.

3088. SCHIFFRIN, DEBORAH. Narrative as self-portrait: sociolinguistic constructions of identity. *See* **2563**.

3089. SINGH, RAJENDRA; DASGUPTA, PROBAL; LELE, JAYANT (eds). Explorations in Indian sociolinguistics. *See* **2979**.

3090. SMIT, UTE. South African English in the 1990s: a field study on status, roles and attitudes. *See* **2981**.

3091. TAYLOR, ANITA. Language and the construction of gender: clarifying ideas about gender. StudLS (25:2) 1995, 11–27.

3092. TAYLOR, BEN. Gay men, femininity and /t/ in New Zealand English. *See* **1581**.

3093. THOMAS, ERIK; BAILEY, GUY. A case of competing mergers and their resolution. *See* **2916**.

3094. TIEKEN-BOON VAN OSTADE, INGRID. Social network theory and eighteenth-century English: the case of Boswell. *In* (pp. 327–37) **27**.

3095. WAKSLER, RACHELLE. She's a *mensch* and he's a bitch: neutralizing gender in the 90s. English Today (11:2) 1995, 3–6.

3096. WALTON, DOUGLAS. The witch hunt as a structure of argumentation. *See* **2301**.

3097. WOODS, NICOLA. English language: dialectology and sociolinguistics (including creolistics). *See* **2808**.

TRANSLATION AND COMPARATIVE LINGUISTICS

3098. ÁLVAREZ, ROMÁN; VIDAL, M. CARMEN ÁFRICA (eds). Translation, power, subversion. Clevedon; Philadelphia, PA: Multilingual Matters, 1996. pp. vi, 157. (Topics in translation, 8.) Rev. by Víctor Manuel Pina Medina in RAEI (9) 1996, 191–4.

3099. ANDERSON, JOHN L. The receptor culture and the consultant's visit. NTrans (5:4) 1991, 23–30.

3100. AVILA, CARMELA NOCERA. *Il libro del cortegiano* nella traduzione di Sir Thomas Hoby (1561): un problema linguistico e culturale. Textus (3:1/2) 1990, 225–41.

3101. BAIK, MARTIN J.; SHIM, ROSA J. Yes, we have no bananas: English negative tags in cross-linguistic communication. StudLS (23:1) 1993, 43–59.

3102. BAKIR, MURTADHA J. Notes on passive and pseudo-intransitive constructions in English and Arabic. *See* **1650**.

3103. BALL, DAVID. Acclaiming Adair: against a certain tendency in translation theory. TransR (50) 1996, 19–22.

3104. BARNSTONE, WILLIS. The poetics of translation: history, theory, practice. (Bibl. 1995, 2575.) Rev. by Raymond Cormier in Albion (28:4) 1996, 119–23.

3105. BARRATT, LESLIE B.; KONTRA, MIKLÓS. Matching Hungarian and English color terms. *See* **2192**.

3106. BASSNETT, SUSAN; LEFEVERE, ANDRÉ (eds). Translation, history and culture. London: Pinter, 1990. pp. viii, 133. Rev. by Christina Schäffner in ZAA (41:2) 1993, 171–4.

3107. BECKER, A. L. Beyond translation: essays towards a modern philology. (Bibl. 1995, 2577.) Rev. by Barbara Toth in RhR (14:2) 1996, 412–16.

3108. BELITT, BEN. The forged feature: toward a poetics of uncertainty: new and selected essays. New York: Fordham UP, 1995. pp. xii, 279. Rev. by Terence Diggory in Salmagundi (112) 1996, 237–45.

3109. BENNANI, BEN. Ibn Tufayl's *Hayy Ibn Yaqzan* and Daniel Defoe's *Robinson Crusoe*: translation as cross-cultural insemination. SM (15:1) 1992, 18–25.

3110. BHATT, RAKESH M. On the grammar of code-switching. *See* **1655**.

3111. BIRNER, BETTY J.; WARD, GREGORY. A crosslinguistic study of postposing in discourse. *See* **2508**.

3112. BOURHIS, RICHARD Y. (ed.). French–English language issues in Canada. Berlin; New York: Mouton de Gruyter, 1994. pp. iv, 271. (IJSL, 105/106.) Rev. by M.G. in EWW (15:2) 1994, 306–7.

3113. BUDICK, SANFORD; ISER, WOLFGANG (eds). The translatability of cultures: figurations of the space between. Stanford, CA: Stanford UP, 1996. pp. xiv, 348. (Irvine studies in the humanities.) Rev. by Rainer Schulte in WLT (70:4) 1996, 1040.

3114. BUSH, PETER. It doesn't sound like English. TLS, 6 Sept. 1996, 11.

3115. CHEN, SU-CHIAO. Code-switching as a verbal strategy among Chinese in a campus setting in Taiwan. WorldE (15:3) 1996, 267–80.

3116. COLDIRON, A. E. B. Rossetti on Villon, Dowson on Verlaine:

'impossibility' and appropriation in translation. Comparatist (17) 1993, 119–40.

3117. ——— *Translatio*, translation, and Charles d'Orléans's paroled poetics. Exemplaria (8:1) 1996, 169–92.

3118. COOK, MANUELA.   Translating forms of address. *See* **1098**.

3119. COULTHARD, MALCOLM; DE BAUBETA, PATRICIA ANNE ODBER (eds).   The knowledges of the translator: from literary interpretation to machine classification. Lewiston, NY; Lampeter: Mellen Press, 1996. pp. ii, 323.

3120. ——————   Theoretical issues and practical cases in Portguese–English translations. Lewiston, NY; Lampeter: Mellen Press, 1996. pp. ii, 189. (Proceedings of the Birmingham International Conference on Translation Theory and Practice, September 17–19, 1993.)

3121. CRAIG, GEORGE.   By whose hand? The special case of Samuel Beckett. TLS, 6 Sept. 1996, 4–6.

3122. CRAIK, ROGER.   The pioneer translators of Rabelais: Sir Thomas Urquhart and Pierre Motteux. TransR (51/52) 1996, 31–4, 36–42.

3123. CRONIN, MICHAEL.   Translating Ireland: translation, languages, cultures. Cork: Cork UP, 1996. pp. xiv, 229. Rev. by Susan Bassnett in TLS, 6 Sept. 1996, 9–10.

3124. CULY, MARTIN M.   The top-down approach to translation. NTrans (7:3) 1993, 28–51.

3125. DELABASTITA, DIRK.   There's a double tongue: an investigation into the translation of Shakespeare's wordplay, with special reference to *Hamlet*. (Bibl. 1993, 1860.) Rev. by Gerhard Müller-Schwefe in ZAA (43:3) 1995, 271–3; by Klaus Bartenschlager in SJ (132) 1996, 259–60.

3126. ——— D'HULST, LIEVEN (eds).   European Shakespeares: translating Shakespeare in the Romantic age. Amsterdam; Philadelphia, PA: Benjamins, 1993. pp. 256. Rev. by Ute Kauer in CanRCL (21:3) 1994, 528–30; by Raimund Borgmeier in ZAA (42:4) 1994, 391–3.

3127. DÉPRATS, JEAN-MICHEL.   Translating Shakespeare for the theatre. Shakespeare Yearbook (5) 1994, 345–58.

3128. DIENSBERG, BERNHARD.   French transplanted: a re-evaluation of the importance of Anglo-French in the development of the English language during the Middle English period. *In* (pp. 253–66) **68**.

3129. DIK, SIMON C.   Functional grammar in Prolog: an integrated implementation for English, French, and Dutch. *See* **1149**.

3130. DINGWANEY, ANURADHA; MAIER, CAROL (eds).   Between languages and cultures: translation and cross-cultural texts. Pittsburgh, PA: Pittsburgh UP, 1995. pp. xiii, 359. (Pittsburgh series in composition, literacy, and culture.)

3131. DOHERTY, MONIKA.   Passive perspectives; different preferences in English and German: a result of parameterized processing. *See* **1672**.

3132. DUVAL, JOHN.   Proverbs. TransR (50) 1996, 23–4.

3133. EVANS, COLIN.   Intimate exchanges: Resnais' translation/transformation of Ayckbourn in *Smoking/No Smoking*. Franco-British Studies (19) 1995, 39–60.

3134. FARRELL, TIM; HOYLE, RICHARD.   Translating implicit information in the light of Saussurean, relevance, and cognitive theories. NTrans (9:1) 1995, 1–15.

3135. FRAZER, TIMOTHY C. Chicano English and Spanish interference in the Midwestern United States. *See* **2873**.

3136. GARFORTH, JULIAN A. Translating Beckett's translations. JBecS (6:1) 1996, 49–70.

3137. —— A trilingual *Godot*. Samuel Beckett Today (5) 1996, 155–74.

3138. GASS, WILLIAM H. In other words. BkW, 24 Nov. 1996, 1, 10–11.

3139. GEERTSEMA, JOHAN. 'Traductions': J. M. Coetzee and the violent 'invention' of the classic. Current Writing (8:1) 1996, 45–60.

3140. GHOMESHI, JILA; RITTER, ELIZABETH. Binding, possessives, and the structure of DP. *See* **1678**.

3141. GODARD, BARBARA. Translating (as) woman. ECanW (55) 1995, 71–82 (review-article).

3142. GOERLING, FRITZ. Cautions concerning dynamic equivalence. NTrans (10:3) 1996, 41–8.

3143. GROSSMAN, EDITH. Surrealism, realism, and translation. TransR (46) 1994, 3–7.

3144. HARTMANN, REINHARD (ed.). The English language in Europe. *See* **3001**.

3145. HEIM, MICHAEL HENRY. Revitalizing the market for literary translation. *See* **1056**.

3146. HEYDEL, MAREN. The concept of translational equivalence in literary discourse and the role of *progressive aspect* in the English translation of Christa Wolf's novel *Nachdenken über Christa T. (The Quest for Christa T.). See* **2644**.

3147. HEYLEN, ROMY. Translation, poetics, and the stage: six French *Hamlet*s. (Bibl. 1995, 2611.) Rev. by Philip Cranston in Comparatist (19) 1995, 158–60.

3148. HLADKÝ, JOSEF. Zdvojování jako slovotvorný prostředek v češtině a angličtině. (Reduplication in Czech and English.) *See* **1616**.

3149. HOLLO, ANSELM. On translation. Talisman (6) 1991, 86–92.

3150. HOPKINS, CHRIS. Translating Caradoc Evans's Welsh English. *See* **2646**.

3151. HUNG, EVA. When they see red: one approach to translation criticism. TransR (48/49) 1995, 56–60.

3152. JACKSON, THOMAS. 'Get the fresh rain down!' – Thomas Kinsella and translation. Notes on Modern Irish Literature (3) 1991, 22–9.

3153. JOHNSTON, DAVID (ed.). Stages of translation. Bath: Absolute Classics, 1996. pp. 294. Rev. by Michael Meyer in TLS, 8 Nov. 1996, 35.

3154. KAMWANGAMALU, NKONKO M. Sociolinguistic aspects of siSwati–English bilingualism. *See* **3070**.

3155. KARSTADT, ANGELA. Relative markers in Swedish-American English: evidence for a contact language phenomenon? *See* **1697**.

3156. KELLMAN, STEVEN G. J. M. Coetzee and Samuel Beckett: the translingual link. CLS (33:2) 1996, 161–72.

3157. KIM, BYONG-KWON. VP-internal subject hypothesis and ATB gap parallelism. *See* **1699**.

3158. KIRKLAND, WILL. Computers and translation: language add-on modules for English-language word processors. *See* **1167**.

3159. KLÉGR, ALEŠ. The noun in translation: a Czech–English contrastive study. Prague: Charles UP, 1996. pp. 241. (Acta Universitatis Carolinae. Philologica. Monographia, 127.)

3160. KLEIN, HOLGER.   Describing translations. Towards a model. Moderne Sprachen (40:2) 1996, 123–44.

3161. KNÚTSSON, PÉTUR.   Intertextual quanta in formula and translation. LangL (4:2) 1995, 109–25.

3162. LABRUM, MARIAN B.   What everyone should know about translation. NTrans (7:2) 1993, 16–20.

3163. LEADERS, MARLIN.   Eliciting figures of speech. NTrans (5:4) 1991, 31–45.

3164. LEW, ROBERT.   Exploitation of linguistic ambiguity in English and Polish jokes. *See* **2276**.

3165. MAEDA, SHOSAKU.   Nichi-ei gogaku kenkyu: Souseki-cho *Kokoro* no eiyaku ni manabu. (A study of Japanese and English: translating Souseki's *Kokoro* into English.) Kyoto: Yamaguchi Shoten, 1996. pp. xii, 304.

3166. MAHOOTIAN, SHAHRZAD.   Code-switching and universal constraints: evidence from Farsi/English. *See* **1706**.

3167. MANN, WILLIAM.   Cross-language text adaptation: understanding language differences and their consequences. NTrans (9:3) 1995, 1–18.

3168. MERINO ÁLVAREZ, RAQUEL.   *¡Vengan corriendo que les tengo un muerto!* (*Busybody*): prototipo de versión española de una obra de teatro comercial. Atlantis (17:1/2) 1995, 145–64.

3169. MILANI, CELESTINA.   Note semiologiche e linguistiche a un corpus pubblicitario inglese e italiano. *See* **2772**.

3170. MOODY, ANDREW J.   Transmission languages and source languages of Chinese borrowings in English. AS (71:4) 1996, 405–20.

3171. MOSKOWICH, ISABEL; SEOANE, ELENA.   Scandinavian loans and processes of word-formation in ME: some preliminary considerations. *In* (pp. 185–98) **27**.

3172. MÜLLER, GEREON; STERNEFELD, WOLFGANG.   Ā-chain formation and economy of derivation. *See* **1712**.

3173. NAGEL, RAINER.   Normenvorgabe in der literarischen Übersetzung: illustriert an den Eigennamen in J. R. R. Tolkiens *The Lord of the Rings*. *See* **2156**.

3174. NEMET-NEJAT, MURAT.   Translation and style. Talisman (6) 1991, 98–100.

3175. NEWMARK, PETER.   Paragraphs on translation: 41, 42, 43, 44, 46. *See* **1119**.

3176. NIRANJANA, TEJASWINI.   Colonialism and the politics of translation. *In* (pp. 35–52) **80**.

3177. ORCHARD, ANDY.   Poetic inspiration and prosaic translation: the making of *Cædmon's Hymn. In* (pp. 402–22) **114**.

3178. PEDEN, MARGARET SAYERS.   Knopf, Knopf: who's there? *See* **1072**.

3179. PENCE, JEFFREY.   Language, history, and the university: de Man on translation. ColLit (23:2) 1996, 83–99.

3180. PÉREZ HERNÁNDEZ, CHANTAL.   A pilot study on translation equivalence between English and Spanish. IJL (9:3) 1996, 218–37.

3181. PIKE, JULIA A. E.   Cross-cultural awareness. NTrans (5:4) 1991, 14–22.

3182. PINTI, DANIEL J.   Dialogism, heteroglossia, and late medieval translation. TransR (44/45) 1994, 16–23.

3183. PULCINI, VIRGINIA.   Some new English words in Italian. *See* **1869**.

3184. RAFFEL, BURTON.   The art of translating prose. (Bibl. 1995, 2655.) Rev. by James A. Parr in Allegorica (17) 1996, 117–18.

3185. —— Translation and creativity. WHR (50:1) 1996, 54–62.

3186. RAUKKO, JARNO.   'No more polysemy', says the nationalist language police: the paradoxical battle between semantic flexibility and normativism. *See* **2232**.

3187. REID, SCOTT.   Lament for a notion: the life and death of Canada's bilingual dream. Vancouver, B.C.: Arsenal Pulp Press, 1993. pp. 320. Rev. by Ekaterini Nikolarea in CanL (148) 1996, 169–71.

3188. RENER, FREDERICK M.   *Interpretatio*: language and translation from Cicero to Tytler. (Bibl. 1992, 2400.) Rev. by George Lang in CanRCL (19:1/2) 1992, 237–51.

3189. RIDDER, SUSAN.   English in Dutch. English Today (11:4) 1995, 44–50. (English expressions in Dutch; emergence of 'Dutchlish' hybrid.)

3190. ROBINSON, DOUGLAS.   Foreignizing experience. CanRCL (20:3/4) 1993, 417–33.

3191. —— The translator's turn. (Bibl. 1995, 2656.) Rev. by George Lang in CanRCL (19:1/2) 1992, 237–51.

3192. ROBYNS, CLEM.   Translation and discursive identity. PT (15:3) 1994, 405–28.

3193. RODRÍGUEZ GONZÁLEZ, FÉLIX (ed.).   Spanish loanwords in the English language: a tendency towards hegemony reversal. *See* **1872**.

3194. SAWYER-LAUÇANNO, CHRISTOPHER.   Translation and tradition. Talisman (12) 1994, 191–6.

3195. SCHRAG, BRIAN E.   Translating song texts as oral compositions. NTrans (6:1) 1992, 44–62.

3196. SCHULTE, RAINER.   Editorial: a blueprint for translation studies. TransR (51/52) 1996, 1–4.

3197. —— Plays in translation: a profile of *PAJ* Publications/*Performing Arts Journal*. *See* **1079**.

3198. —— BIGUENET, JOHN (eds).   Theories of translation: an anthology of essays from Dryden to Derrida. (Bibl. 1992, 2402.) Rev. by Carmen Toledano Buendía in RCEI (28) 1994, 225.

3199. SHEIKH AL-SHABAB, OMAR.   Interpretation and the language of translation: creativity and conventions in translation. London: Janus, 1996. pp. 118.

3200. SHEUNG, SHING-YUE.   Translatibility revisited. AJSem (9:1) 1992, 105–13.

3201. SINCLAIR, JOHN.   An international project in multilingual lexicography. *See* **2066**.

3202. SMADJA, FRANK; HATZIVASSILOGLOU, VASILEIOS; MCKEOWN, KATHLEEN R.   Translating collocations for bilingual lexicons: a statistical approach. *See* **1204**.

3203. STALMASZCZYK, PIOTR.   Theta roles and the theory of theta-binding. *See* **1745**.

3204. STAVANS, ILAN.   The original language. TransR (48/49) 1995, 33–7.

3205. —— Translation and identity. MichQR (35:2) 1996, 280–95.

3206. TEUBERT, WOLFGANG.   Comparable or parallel corpora? *See* **1934**.

3207. THOMAS, ELAINE.   Making and recording editorial decisions early in translation. NTrans (9:2) 1995, 40–3.

3208. TIEDE, MARK K.   An MRI-based study of pharyngeal volume contrasts in Akan and English. *See* **1584**.

3209. TINKLER-VILLANI, VALERIA.   The poetry of Hell and the poetry of Paradise: food for thought for translators, critics, poets and other readers. BJRL (76:1) 1994, 75–92.

3210. TOGNINI-BONELLI, ELENA.   Towards translation equivalence from a corpus linguistics perspective. IJL (9:3) 1996, 197–217. (English and Italian.)

3211. TSURUSHIMA, H.   Domesday interpreters. *See* **1490**.

3212. UNGER, CHRISTOPH.   Types of implicit information and their roles in translation. NTrans (10:4) 1996, 18–30.

3213. VALERO GARCÉS, CARMEN.   Notas en torno a la traducción de literatura juvenil: el ejemplo de *Moby Dick*. Atlantis (17:1/2) 1995, 245–60.

3214. VAN GELDEREN, ELLY.   Parameterizing agreement features in Arabic, Bantu languages, and varieties of English. *See* **1754**.

3215. VAN LEYDEN, KLASKE; VAN HEUVEN, VINCENT J.   Lexical stress and spoken word recognition: Dutch *vs* English. *See* **1586**.

3216. VENUTI, LAWRENCE.   The translator's invisibility: a history of translation. (Bibl. 1995, 2675.) Rev. by Rainer Schulte in WLT (69:4) 1995, 886; by Steven Rendall in CL (48:4) 1996, 359–64; by Terry Hale in TLS, 6 Sept. 1996, 8; by the same in TransR (50) 1996, 47–9; by Michael Wolf Irmscher in TransR (50) 1996, 49–53.

3217. WATT, MILTON.   Redefining 'dynamic equivalence'. NTrans (10:1) 1996, 7–19.

3218. WILBUR, RICHARD.   On formalism, translation, and beloved books of childhood. BWR (22:2) 1996, 142–58.

3219. WISHNIA, KENNETH.   Pardon my *periaktoi*; or, How to evaluate translations from a language you don't know. TransR (48/49) 1995, 50–5.

3220. YANG, BYUNGGON.   A comparative study of American English and Korean vowels produced by male and female speakers. *See* **1588**.

3221. ZATLIN, PHYLLIS.   Observations on theatrical translation. TransR (46) 1994, 14–18.

TRADITIONAL CULTURE

FOLKLORE AND FOLKLIFE

GENERAL

3222. ANON. (comp.). Definitions of folklore. *See* **1947**.

3223. BARON, ROBERT; SPITZER, NICHOLAS R. (eds). Public folklore. Washington, DC: Smithsonian Inst. Press, 1992. pp. xiv, 370. (Pubs of the American Folklore Soc.: new ser.) Rev. by Elaine Eff in MidAF (23:1) 1995, 52–4.

3224. BENNETT, GILLIAN. The Thomsian heritage in the Folklore Society (London). JFR (33:3) 1996, 212–20.

3225. BRUNVAND, JAN HAROLD (ed.). American folklore: an encyclopedia. New York; London: Garland, 1996. pp. xviii, 794. (Garland reference library of the humanities, 1551.)

3226. BYNUM, MARJORIE C. Thomas Washington Talley: a pathmaker in African-American folklore. TFSB (57:4) 1996, 154–65.

3227. CAIRA, DIANA. Kylie Tennant's ear for the people's voices. Australian Folklore (9) 1994, 146–50.

3228. CANTWELL, ROBERT. Ethnomimesis: folklife and the representation of culture. Chapel Hill; London: North Carolina UP, 1993. pp. xx, 323. Rev. by Karyl Denison Robb in JFR (32:3) 1995, 286–7; by Andrew J. Scheiber in AmLH (8:2) 1996, 367–72; by Peter Rollins in JPC (29:4) 1996, 232.

3229. DAVEY, GWENDA BEED; SEAL, GRAHAM (eds). The Oxford companion to Australian folklore. (Bibl. 1995, 2687.) Rev. by Julia C. Bishop in FMJ (7:1) 1995, 88–90.

3230. DE CARO, FRANK (ed.). The folktale cat. Little Rock, AR: August House, 1993. pp. 183. Rev. by W. K. McNeil in MidAF (23:2) 1995, 113–14.

3231. DÉGH, LINDA. American folklore and the mass media. Bloomington: Indiana UP, 1994. pp. 217. (Folklore today.) Rev. by Wilhelm F. H. Nicolaisen in Fabula (36:3/4) 1995, 327–9.

3232. DILLON MERCIER, EILÍS. Folk memory as history – the Irish tradition. *In* (pp. 1–13) **49**.

3233. DYCK, IAN. William Cobbett and rural popular culture. (Bibl. 1993, 1893.) Rev. by Peter Dunkley in AHR (98:4) 1993, 1253–4.

3234. EDWARDS, VANESSA. Keneally's republican push and the Irish influence. Australian Folklore (9) 1994, 14–17.

3235. FISCHER, DAVID HACKETT. Albion's seed: four British folkways in America. (Bibl. 1995, 2688.) Rev. by Neil R. Stout in VH (59:2) 1991, 124–5; by Peter C. Mancall in AmS (33:1) 1992, 103–11.

3236. HARRIS, NEIL. Cultural excursions: marketing appetites and cultural tastes in modern America. (Bibl. 1992, 2423.) Rev. by Jay Mechling in AmS (35:1) 1994, 159–60.

3237. HOOPER, S.; MURPHY, R.; RYAN, J. S. Towards a Dal Stivens bibliography. Australian Folklore (11) 1996, 25–35.

3238. HOOPER, S.; RAINEY, P. Dal Stivens: a neglected Australian folklorist. Australian Folklore (11) 1996, 17–24.

3239. HOOPER, STEPHEN.   Dal Stivens as Australian cultural critic: Australian landscape, folklore and comic strips. *See* **210**.

3240. HUFFORD, MARY; HUNT, MARJORIE; ZEITLIN, STEVEN.   The grand generation: memory, mastery, legacy. Introd. by Barbara Kirshenblatt-Gimblett. Washington, DC: Smithsonian Inst. Traveling Exhibition Service and Office of Folklife Programs in assn with Washington UP, 1987. pp. 127. Rev. by Patrick B. Mullen in JAF (106:421) 1993, 363–5.

3241. JOHNSON, CHRISTOPHER; LUNG, EVE.   Arthur: the legend unveiled. Chieveley, Berks.: Capall Bann, 1995. pp. ii, 162.

3242. JONES, MICHAEL OWEN (ed.).   Putting folklore to use. Lexington: Kentucky UP, 1994. pp. xi, 264. (Pubs of American Folklore Soc., ns.) Rev. by Jack Shortlidge in JAF (108:428) 1995, 210–11.

3243. KODISH, DEBORA.   Making folklore theory public. NYF (21) 1995, 103–11.

3244. KULLMANN, THOMAS.   Irish mythology, Eastern philosophy and literary Modernism in James Stephens' *The Crock of Gold. In* (pp. 53–61) **60**.

3245. MAZO, JEFFREY ALAN.   'A good Saxon compound'. *See* **1948**.

3246. MONTENYOHL, ERIC.   Divergent paths: on the evolution of *folklore* and *folkloristics. See* **1949**.

3247. OWEN, TREFOR M.   Changing folk directions in Wales since the 18th century. Australian Folklore (9) 1994, 23–30.

3248. POCIUS, GERALD L.   Folklore and national identity: Canadian perspectives. Australian Folklore (9) 1994, 36–43.

3249. RIACH, ALAN.   Scotland and the colonial paradigm. Australian Folklore (9) 1994, 31–5.

3250. ROBERTS, JOHN W.   From trickster to badman: the Black folk hero in slavery and freedom. Philadelphia: Pennsylvania UP, 1989. pp. 233. Rev. by Jeannie Thomas in AAR (28:1) 1994, 151–2.

3251. —— History and regionalism in the work of John Mason Brewer. NYF (21) 1995, 113–26.

3252. SCHEIBER, ANDREW J.   Mirrors and menageries: criticism, ethnography, and multiculturalism in contemporary literary praxis. AmLH (8:2) 1996, 364–87 (review-article).

3253. SCHOEMAKER, GEORGE H. (ed.).   The emergence of folklore in everyday life: a fieldguide and sourcebook. (Bibl. 1991, 2536.) Rev. by Teresa Hollingsworth in MidAF (19:2) 1991, 154–6.

3254. SEGAL, ROBERT A. (ed.).   Anthropology, folklore, and myth. New York; London: Garland, 1996. pp. xi, 412. (Theories of myth, 2.)

3255. SHERMAN, JOSEPHA.   A sampler of Jewish-American folklore. (Bibl. 1992, 2436.) Rev. by Sally Wolff in MidAF (23:1) 1995, 60–1.

3256. SIMPSON, JACQUELINE.   Twenty five years of folklore studies in England. Australian Folklore (9) 1994, 18–22.

3257. SOMMERS, LAURIE KAY.   Definitions of *folk* and *lore* in the Smithsonian Festival of American Folklife. *See* **1946**.

3258. TOKOFSKY, PETER.   Folk-lore and *Volks-Kunde*: compounding compounds. *See* **1950**.

3259. WALLS, ROBERT E.; SCHOEMAKER, GEORGE H. (eds).   The old traditional way of life: essays in honor of Warren E. Roberts. (Bibl. 1991, 2542.) Rev. by Bengt Holbek in Fabula (32:4) 1991, 357–8.

AREA STUDIES AND COLLECTIONS
(MISCELLANEOUS)

3260. ABERNETHY, F. E.   Texas Folklore Society, 1909–1943. Denton: North Texas UP, 1992. pp. viii, 326 (Pubs of the Texas Folklore Soc., 51.)

3261. ALLEN, BARBARA; SCHLERETH, THOMAS J. (eds).   Sense of place: American regional cultures. Lexington: Kentucky UP, 1990. pp. 211. Rev. by Frank De Caro in SF (53:2) 1996, 56–9.

3262. ALLEN, MICHAEL.   Western rivermen, 1763–1861: Ohio and Mississippi boatmen and the myth of the alligator horse. (Bibl. 1992, 2441.) Rev. by Paul Andrew Hutton in GateH (12:4) 1991, 70; by James Kirkland in MidAF (22:2) 1994, 109–11.

3263. ALVEY, R. GERALD.   Kentucky bluegrass country. Jackson; London: Mississippi UP, 1992. pp. xxiv, 322. (Folklife in the South.) Rev. by Linda Anderson in JAF (109:433) 1996, 345–7.

3264. ARCHIBALD, MALCOLM.   Scottish animal and bird folklore. Edinburgh: St Andrew Press, 1996. pp. v, 130.

3265. BAKER, RONALD L.   From Needmore to Prosperity: Hoosier place names in folklore and history. *See* **2125**.

3266. BALLARD, LINDA M.   Out of the abstract: the development of the study of Irish folklore. NYF (20:1/2) 1994, 1–13.

3267. BENES, PETER; BENES, JANE MONTAGUE (eds).   Wonders of the invisible world: 1600–1900. Boston, MA: Boston Univ., 1995. pp. 160. (Dublin Seminar for New England Folklife: annual proceedings, 1992.) Rev. by Eleanor Kokar Ott in VH (64:3) 1996, 186–9.

3268. BLUESTEIN, GENE.   Poplore: folk and pop in American culture. Amherst: Massachusetts UP, 1994. pp. xiii, 167. Rev. by Martha Bayles in BkW, 19 Mar. 1995, 8; by Rosemary Dinnage in TLS, 25 Oct. 1996, 31; by Joseph J. Arpad in JAC (19:3) 1996, 113–15.

3269. BUCUVALAS, TINA; BULGER, PEGGY A.; KENNEDY, STETSON. South Florida folklife. Jackson; London: Mississippi UP, 1994. pp. xvii, 254. (Folklife in the South.) Rev. by Michael Schoenecke in JAC (18:4) 1995, 111.

3270. BYRKIT, JAMES W.   Land, sky, and people: the Southwest defined. Journal of the Southwest (34:3) 1992, 257–387.

3271. CAIRNEY, C. THOMAS.   'That evil fiddling': Scotch-Irish folk religion and ethnic boundary maintenance in Southern Missouri. MFSJ (13/14) 1991/92, 17–30.

3272. CALLAHAN, NANCY.   The Freedom Quilting Bee. Tuscaloosa; London: Alabama UP, 1987. pp. xi, 255. (Alabama organization; civil rights in art.) Rev. by Pat Kuhel in MidAF (22:1) 1994, 39–40.

3273. CHOWNING, LARRY S.   Barcat skipper: tales of a Tangier Island waterman. Centreville, MD: Tidewater, 1983. pp. 155. Rev. by Polly Stewart in MidAF (23:1) 1995, 48–51.

3274. —— Harvesting the Chesapeake: tools and traditions. Centreville, MD: Tidewater, 1990. pp. xii, 284. Rev. by Polly Stewart in MidAF (23:1) 1995, 48–51.

3275. CLARK, THOMAS L.   Western lore and language: a dictionary for enthusiasts of the American West. *See* **2088**.

3276. COOPER, CAROLYN.   Afro-Jamaican folk elements in Brodber's *Jane and Louisa Will Soon Come Home*. In (pp. 279–88) **81**.

3277. CRAWFORD, DEBORAH K. E.   The ghost of criticism past. Folklore (107) 1996, 98–101. (*Reply to* bibl. 1995, 2703.)

3278. DAVEY, GWENDA BEED. Ethnicity isn't the only thing that matters: reflections from the Moe Folklife Project. Australian Folklore (11) 1996, 211–19.

3279. DAVIES, CAROLE BOYCE . 'Woman is a nation …': women in Caribbean oral literature. *In* (pp. 165–93) **81**.

3280. FLEMING, MAURICE. *The Ghost o' Mause*, and other tales and traditions of East Perthshire. Edinburgh: Mercat Press, 1995. pp. xiv, 142.

3281. FOWKE, EDITH (comp.). Legends told in Canada. Toronto: Royal Ontario Museum, 1994. pp. 96. Rev. by Jill Clayton in Folklore (106) 1995, 120.

3282. FRANKLIN, WAYNE; STEINER, MICHAEL (eds). Mapping American culture. *See* **66**.

3283. GRIFFITH, JAMES S. A shared space: folklife in the Arizona–Sonora borderlands. Logan: Utah State UP, 1995. pp. x, 207. (Folklife of the West, 1.) Rev. by Joe S. Graham in MidAF (24:2) 1996, 103–4.

3284. —— Southern Arizona folk arts. (Bibl. 1991, 2901.) Rev. by James C. McNutt in MidAF (19:1) 1991, 87–9.

3285. HALL, THOMAS D. Cowboys: a review essay. Journal of the Southwest (35:1) 1993, 106–14.

3286. HARWELL, THOMAS MEADE. The Hispanic owl in South Texas. *In* (pp. 37–52) **125**.

3287. HEATH-STUBBS, JOHN. The folklore I grew up with. Folklore (107) 1996, 1–3.

3288. HENDERSON, HAMISH. Alias MacAlias: writings on song, folk and literature. (Bibl. 1995, 2705.) Rev. by Edward D. (Sandy) Ives in FMJ (6:5) 1994, 672–4.

3289. HOY, JIM; ISERN, TOM. Plains folk: II, The romance of the landscape. Norman; London: Oklahoma UP, 1990. pp. xiii, 202. Rev. by Rachel R. Vukas in MidAF (19:2) 1991, 173–4.

3290. JONES, MICHAEL OWEN (ed.). Putting folklore to use. *See* **3242**.

3291. JORDAN, ROSAN AUGUSTA; DE CARO, FRANK. 'In this folklore land': race, class, identity, and folklore studies in Louisiana. JAF (109:431) 1996, 31–59.

3292. LOMBARDI, BETTY RITCH. Folklife studies in Oklahoma. MidAF (19:1) 1991, 1–9.

3293. MCCASKILL, BARBARA. The folklore of the coasts in Black women's fiction of the Harlem renaissance. CLAJ (39:3) 1996, 273–301.

3294. MCNEIL, W. K. Appalachian images in folk and popular culture. (Bibl. 1994, 2103.) Rev. by C. W. Sullivan, III, in MidAF (24:2) 1996, 93–4.

3295. —— (ed.). Articles from *Arkansas Folklore*. MidAF (20:2) 1992, 110–26.

3296. —— CLEMENTS, WILLIAM M. (eds). An Arkansas folklore sourcebook. (Bibl. 1995, 2711.) Rev. by H. Jane Parker in MidAF (21:2) 1993, 97–100.

3297. MCOWAN, RENNIE. Magic mountains. Edinburgh: Mainstream, 1996. pp. 160.

3298. PARLER, MARY CELESTIA. Folklore from the campus. MidAF (21:1) 1993, 42–7. (Articles from *Arkansas Folklore*.)

3299. PATTERSON, DANIEL W.; ZUG, CHARLES G., III (eds). Arts in earnest: North Carolina folklife. (Bibl. 1995, 2715.) Rev. by Michael Ann Williams in MidAF (19:2) 1991, 147–9.

3300. RYDEN, KENT C. Mapping the invisible landscape: folklore, writing, and the sense of place. (Bibl. 1995, 2718.) Rev. by James C. Moss in JAF (107:425) 1994, 459–62.

3301. SCHULTZ, APRIL. 'To lose the speakable': folklore and landscape in O. E. Rølvaag's *Giants in the Earth. In* (pp. 89–111) **66**.

3302. THOMAS, CHARLES. English Heritage book of Tintagel: Arthur and archaeology. (Bibl. 1995, 2720.) Rev. by Christopher D. Morris in Early Medieval Europe (4:1) 1995, 119–20; by John Blair in EHR (111:441) 1996, 403.

3303. WILLIAMS, MICHAEL ANN. Homeplace: the social use and meaning of the folk dwelling in southwestern North Carolina. (Bibl. 1992, 2463.) Rev. by John Dorst in JAF (106:421) 1993, 359–61.

3304. WILLIAMSON, J. W. Hillbillyland: what the movies did to the mountains and what the mountains did to the movies. Chapel Hill; London: North Carolina UP, 1995. pp. xii, 325. Rev. by Ray Browne in JAC (19:1) 1996, 111–12; by Margaret Ripley Wolfe in GaHQ (80:1) 1996, 200–1.

3305. WRIGHT, DONALD. The invention of tradition. LRC (5:5) 1996, 14–16 (review-article).

PROVERBS, PROVERBIAL EXPRESSIONS, RIDDLES, RHYMES, AND DITES

3306. ABRAHAMS, ROGER D. For folklorists' Chanticleer, 'no cry for feathers, cry for long life'. Proverbium (11) 1994, 15–26. (Proverbs from Nevis.)

3307. BENNETT, ANDREW F. Churchill's speechmaking: a response to Wolfgang Mieder. *See* **2308**.

3308. BENNETT, GILLIAN (ed.). Spoken in jest. (Bibl. 1991, 2587.) Rev. by Ulrich Marzolph in Fabula (35:1/2) 1994, 136–8.

3309. BERGER, TERRY (ed.). Garden proverbs: if you would be happy all your life – plant a garden. Philadelphia, PA; London: Running Press, 1994. pp. 127.

3310. BOWDEN, BETSY. Fluctuating proverbs in three eighteenth-century modernizations of Chaucer's Miller's Tale. Proverbium (9) 1992, 11–29.

3311. —— A modest proposal, relating four millennia of proverb collections to chemistry within the human brain. JAF (109:434) 1996, 440–9.

3312. BRYAN, GEORGE B. On the theatrical origins of the expression *green room. See* **1960**.

3313. —— The proverbial Sherlock Holmes: an index to the Holmesian canon. Proverbium (13) 1996, 47–68.

3314. —— MIEDER, WOLFGANG. 'As Sam Weller said, when finding himself on the stage': Wellerisms in dramatizations of Charles Dickens' *Pickwick Papers*. Proverbium (11) 1994, 57–76.

3315. —— —— (comps). The proverbial Eugene O'Neill: an index to proverbs in the works of Eugene Gladstone O'Neill. Westport, CT; London: Greenwood Press, 1995. pp. 359. (Bibliographies and indexes in American literature, 21.)

3316. CARNES, PACK. The fable and the proverb: intertexts and reception. Proverbium (8) 1991, 55–76.

3317. CHARTERIS-BLACK, JONATHAN. 'Still waters run deep' – proverbs about speech and silence: a cross-linguistic perspective. De Proverbio (1:2) 1995.

3318. DESKIS, SUSAN E. *Beowulf* and the medieval proverb tradition. Tempe, AZ: Medieval & Renaissance Texts & Studies, 1996. pp. 178. (Medieval & Renaissance texts & studies, 155.) (Cf. bibl. 1992, 3516.)

3319. DOCTOR, RAYMOND. Mutant proverbs; or, The tale of the shaggy dog. Proverbium (12) 1995, 119–39.

3320. DUVAL, JOHN. Proverbs. *See* **3132**.

3321. FOLSOM, STEVEN R. 'It won't be long 'fore my ship comes in': brief origins of an English proverbial expression and its form and function in five recent American country music hits. MidF (22:1) 1996, 16–24.

3322. GOODWIN, JOSEPH P. If ignorance is bliss, 'tis folly to be wise: what we don't know *can* hurt us. JFR (32:2) 1995, 155–64.

3323. GREENHILL, PAULINE. Ben Johnson jokes: flaws in the Canadian mosaic. Fabula (34:1/2) 1993, 78–89.

3324. KRIKMANN, ARVO. The great chain metaphor: an 'open sesame' for proverb semantics? Proverbium (11) 1994, 116–24.

3325. KUHEL, PAT. Lebanese-American proverbs and proverbial lore. MidAF (19:2) 1991, 110–17.

3326. MCKAY, IAN. The quest of the folk: antimodernism and cultural selection in twentieth-century Nova Scotia. Montreal; London: McGill–Queen's UP, 1994. pp. xvii, 371. Rev. by Karyl Denison Robb in JFR (32:3) 1995, 285–7; by Margaret Conrad in AHR (101:2) 1996, 596–7; by Donald Wright in LRC (5:5) 1996, 14–16.

3327. MIEDER, WOLFGANG. American proverbs: a study of texts and contexts. (Bibl. 1992, 2468.) Rev. by Vilmos Voigt in Fabula (34:3/4) 1993, 349–51.

3328. —— The apple doesn't fall far from the tree: a historical and contextual proverb study based on books, archives, and databases. MidF (19:2) 1993, 69–98.

3329. —— Good proverbs make good Vermonters: a study of regional proverbs in the United States. Proverbium (9) 1992, 159–78.

3330. —— International bibliography of new and reprinted proverb collections, 1996. De Proverbio (2:1) 1996.

3331. —— International proverb scholarship: an updated bibliography, 1996. De Proverbio (2:1) 1996.

3332. —— 'Make hell while the sun shines': proverbial rhetoric in Winston Churchill's *The Second World War*. De Proverbio (1:2) 1995.

3333. —— BRYAN, GEORGE B. Proverbs in world literature: a bibliography. New York; Frankfurt; Bern; Paris: Lang, 1996. pp. xiv, 305.

3334. MIEDER, WOLFGANG; KINGSBURY, S. A.; HARDER, K. B. (eds). A dictionary of American proverbs. (Bibl. 1995, 2729.) Rev. by Hermine Penz in GRM (43:3) 1993, 363–6.

3335. MONYE, AMBROSE A. The use of proverbs in Ola Rotimi's *The Gods Are Not to Blame*. Proverbium (12) 1995, 251–61.

3336. MOON, PAUL. Blending popular culture and religious instruction: Herbert's *Outlandish Proverbs*. EMLS (2:1) 1996, 6.1–6.

3337. MYRICK, LESLIE DIANE. The deployment of Irish proverbial phrases in Irish adaptations of Greco-Roman epics. Proverbium (11) 1994, 175–87.

3338. NICOLAISEN, W. F. H. The proverbial Scot. Proverbium (11) 1994, 197–206.

3339. NORRICK, NEAL R.   Conversational joking: humor in everyday talk. (Bibl. 1994, 2112.) Rev. by Warren Shibles in SL (20:2) 1996, 465–72.

3340. ORING, ELLIOTT.   Arbiters of taste: an afterword. JFR (32:2) 1995, 165–74.

3341. ORMEROD, DAVID.   'Ripe' and 'rot': a proverb in *As You Like It* and *King Lear*. Neophilologus (80:4) 1996, 661–6.

3342. SALTZMAN, RACHELLE H.   'This buzz is for you': popular responses to the Ted Bundy execution. JFR (32:2) 1995, 101–19.

3343. SCHORES, DANIEL M.   The use of riddles in the Ozarks and other mountain cultures. MFSJ (15/16) 1993/94, 133–42.

3344. SMITH, J. B.   'Bees up flues' and 'chips in porridge': two proverbial sayings in Thomas Hardy's *The Return of the Native*. Proverbium (12) 1995, 315–22.

3345. SMITH, MOIRA.   Whipping up a storm: the ethics and consequences of joking around. JFR (32:2) 1995, 121–36.

3346. —— SALTZMAN, RACHELLE H.   Introduction to tastelessness. JFR (32:2) 1995, 85–99.

3347. STANCIU, DUMITRU.   Particular aspects of synonymy and selection with the proverb. See **1875**.

3348. STANTON, MICHAEL N.   'Advice is a dangerous gift': (pseudo)proverbs in *The Lord of the Rings*. Proverbium (13) 1996, 331–46.

3349. WEST, JOHN O.   Cowboy folk humor: life and laughter in the American West. (Bibl. 1991, 2602.) Rev. by James Hoy in MidAF (19:1) 1991, 96–8.

3350. WINICK, STEPHEN D.   Proverbial strategy and proverbial wisdom in the *Canterbury Tales*. Proverbium (11) 1994, 259–81.

WRITTEN AND PRINTED MATERIALS, INSCRIPTIONS, EPITAPHS, GRAFFITI

3351. JOHNSTONE, IAN M.   A visit to the Western Front: a pilgrimage tour of World War I cemeteries and memorials in northern France and Belgium August–September 1993. Australian Folklore (9) 1994, 60–81.

3352. JONES, ANDREA.   'Here lies the body': eighteenth-century gravestones in the Alamance Presbyterian Churchyard and their symbolic meanings. NCarF (43:1) 1996, 47–68.

3353. JOSWIG-MEHNERT, DAGMAR; YULE, GEORGE.   The trouble with graffiti. See **2208**.

3354. KRIEGEL, LEONARD.   Graffiti: tunnel notes of a New Yorker. ASch (62:3) 1993, 431–6.

3355. MEYER, RICHARD E. (ed.).   Cemeteries and gravemarkers: voices of American culture. Introd. by James Deetz. (Bibl. 1995, 2737.) Rev. by Marshall Joseph Becker in JAF (107:425) 1994, 462–4.

3356. —— Ethnicity and the American cemetery. Bowling Green, OH: Bowling Green State Univ. Popular Press, 1993. pp. 239. Rev. by Marshall Joseph Becker in JAF (107:425) 1994, 462–4.

3357. MICHAEL, NANCY.   Censure of a photocopylore display. JFR (32:2) 1995, 137–54.

3358. ROBINSON, JENNIFER META.   'If love could have saved you': newspaper obituary poems. MidF (19:2) 1993, 99–112.

3359. ROEMER, DANIELLE M.   Photocopy lore and the naturalization of the corporate body. JAF (107:423) 1994, 121–38.

3360. STOKES, SHERRIE.   Gone but not forgotten: Wakulla County's folk graveyards. FHQ (70:2) 1991, 177–91.

3361. STONE, GAYNELL.   Material evidence of ideological and ethnic choice in Long Island gravestones, 1670–1820. MatC (23:3) 1991, 1–30.

3362. WILSON, ROBERT RAWDON.   Graffiti become terror: the idea of resistance. CanRCL (22:2) 1995, 267–85.

NARRATIVE

3363. ABNEY, LISA.   Gender differences in oral folklore narratives. SECOLR (18:1) 1994, 62–79.

3364. —— Pronoun shift in oral folklore, personal experience and literary narratives; or, 'What's up with *you*?' *See* **1645**.

3365. ANON. (sel.).   Best-loved stories told at the National Storytelling Festival. Jonesboro, TN: National Storytelling Press, 1991. pp. 223. Rev. by Jan Rosenberg in MidAF (22:1) 1994, 50–2.

3366. —— More best-loved stories told at the National Storytelling Festival. Jonesboro, TN: National Storytelling Press, 1992. pp. 223. Rev. by Jan Rosenberg in MidAF (22:1) 1994, 50–2.

3367. BAKER, RONALD L.   Who's a Hoosier? *See* **2178**.

3368. BARDEN, THOMAS E.; PROVO, JOHN.   Legends of the American soldiers in the Vietnam War. Fabula (36:3/4) 1995, 217–29.

3369. BARRICK, MAC E.   Lewis the robber: a Pennsylvania folk hero in life and legend. MidF (20:2) 1994, 73–138.

3370. BIRCH, CAROL L.; HECKLER, MELISSA A. (eds).   Who says? Essays on pivotal issues in contemporary storytelling. Little Rock, AR: August House, 1996. pp. 221.

3371. BLAMIRES, DAVID.   Chapbooks, fairytales and children's books in the writings of John Clare: part 1. JCSJ (15) 1996, 26–53.

3372. BOURKE, ANGELA.   The virtual reality of Irish fairy legend. EI (31:1/2) 1996, 7–25.

3373. BOWDEN, BETSY.   Medieval folklore: oxymoron no more. JFR (33:2) 1996, 165–72 (review-article).

3374. BRIDLE, E. M.   The dead'er and his liver: an Australian instance of an international folktale. Australian Folklore (8) 1993, 84–8.

3375. BRUCHAC, JOSEPH.   Strong stories. Agni (44) 1996, 167–9.

3376. BURNS, RICHARD ALLEN.   Folklore and control at an Arkansas prison farm. MidAF (23:1) 1995, 1–12.

3377. BUSBY, CYLIN.   'This is a true story': roles of women in contemporary legend. MidF (20:1) 1994, 5–62.

3378. CAMPION-VINCENT, VÉRONIQUE; RENARD, JEAN-BRUNO (eds). Légendes urbaines: rumeurs d'aujourd'hui. Paris: Payot, 1992. pp. 349. Rev. by Christine Shojaei Kawan in Fabula (36:3/4) 1995, 323–5.

3379. CANAAN, HOWARD.   All hell into his knapsack: the spirit of play in two fairy tales. Mythlore (19:4) 1993, 41–5.

3380. CHOWNING, LARRY S.   Barcat skipper: tales of a Tangier Island waterman. *See* **3273**.

3381. CLASSEN, ALBRECHT.   Die Weltwirkung des *Fortunatus*. Fabula (35:3/4) 1994, 209–25.

3382. CONWAY, ANGELA.   Dark tales of old Cheshire. Wilmslow: Sigma, 1994. pp. ix, 130.

3383. CUNNINGHAM, KEITH (ed.).   The oral tradition of the American West: adventure, courtship, family, and place in traditional recitation. Introd. by W. K. McNeil. (Bibl. 1991, 2659.) Rev. by Louie W. Attebery in MidAF (19:2) 1991, 152–4.

3384. DeSHANE, KENNETH R.   'Sometimes it takes experts to tell the difference': a believer's perspective on Pentecostal sermons. SF (53:2) 1996, 91–111.

3385. DEVLIN, JOSEPH.   The source of Synge's *Playboy of the Western World*. Notes on Modern Irish Literature (7:2) 1995, 5–9.

3386. DIXON, GEOFFREY M.; GREEN, LYNN.   Folktales and legends of East Anglia. Peterborough: Minimax, 1996. pp. 128.

3387. DIXON-KENNEDY, MIKE.   Arthurian myth and legend: an A–Z of people and places. London: Blandford, 1995. pp. 298.

3388. FERRIS, WILLIAM.   'You live and learn, then you die and forget it all': Ray Lum's tales of horses, mules, and men. With foreword by Eudora Welty. New York: Anchor, 1992. pp. xvii, 251. Rev. by Diane O. Tebbets in MidAF (22:2) 1994, 96–8.

3389. FINE, ELIZABETH C.; SPEER, JEAN HASKELL (eds).   Performance, culture, and identity. Westport, CT; London: Praeger, 1992. pp. xii, 303. Rev. by Danielle M. Roemer in JAF (107:424) 1994, 327–9.

3390. FINE, GARY ALAN.   Manufacturing tales: sex and money in contemporary legends. (Bibl. 1994, 2129.) Rev. by Simon J. Bronner in MidAF (20:2) 1992, 129–31.

3391. FLIEGER, VERLYN.   The language of myth: guest of honor address at Mythopoeic Conference xxv, American University, Washington, DC, 1994. Mythlore (21:3) 1996, 4–6.

3392. FOLEY, JOHN MILES.   Immanent art: from structure to meaning in traditional oral epic. Bloomington: Indiana UP, 1991. pp. xvi, 278. Rev. by William Bernard McCarthy in MidAF (22:1) 1994, 58–9.

3393. FOSS, GEORGE.   From White Hall to Bacon Hollow. MidAF (21:2) 1993, 69–92; (22:1) 1994, 15–38, 73–94; (23:1) 1995, 13–37; (23:2) 1995, 67–90.

3394. FOSS, MICHAEL.   The world of Camelot: King Arthur and the Knights of the Round Table. London: O'Mara, 1995. pp. 217.

3395. FOWKE, EDITH (comp.).   Legends told in Canada. *See* **3281**.

3396. GLUCK, SHERNA BERGER; PATAI, DAPHNE (eds).   Women's words: the feminist practice of oral history. New York; London: Routledge, 1991. pp. vi, 234. Rev. by Rebecca Maksel in JAF (107:424) 1994, 332–5.

3397. GOLDBERG, CHRISTINE.   Turandot's sisters: a study of the folktale AT 851. New York; London: Garland, 1993. pp. xiii, 206. (Garland reference library of the humanities, 1694.) (Garland folklore library, 7.) (Cf. bibl. 1982, 2701.) Rev. by Barbara Gobrecht in Fabula (35:3/4) 1994, 336–7; by Lee-Ellen Marvin in JAF (108:427) 1995, 118–19.

3398. GOODRICH, PETER.   The New Age mage: Merlin as contemporary occult icon. JFA (5:1) 1992, 42–73.

3399. GREENHILL, PAULINE.   True poetry: traditional and popular verse in Ontario. Montreal; Buffalo, NY: McGill–Queen's UP, 1989. pp. xvi, 230. Rev. by Thomas M. F. Gerry in ARCS (20:4) 1990, 525–7.

3400. HAFEZ, AZIZA S.   The use of myth, parable and folk tale in Flann O'Brien's *At Swim-Two-Birds* and Etedal Othman's *The Sun's Tattoo*. In (pp. 62–72) **60**.

3401. HAROUN, MAGDA. Donald O'Nery and Goha in folktales of Ireland and Egypt. *In* (pp. 91–6) **60**.

3402. HARTSFIELD, MARIELLA GLENN. Tall Betsy and Dunce Baby: South Georgia folktales. (Bibl. 1992, 2520.) Rev. by Elizabeth Tucker in MidAF (23:1) 1995, 54–6.

3403. HEARNE, BETSY. *Beauty and the Beast*: visions and revisions of an old tale. (Bibl. 1992, 2524.) Rev. by Detlev Fehling in Fabula (32:4) 1991, 321–3.

3404. HENKEN, ELISSA R. Redeemers and outlaws in Welsh tradition. SF (53:3) 1996, 193–205.

3405. HESS, KATHLEEN. The bittersweet vine: fairy tales and nursery rhymes. Mythlore (19:2) 1993, 54–6, 60.

3406. HODSON, JOEL CLARK. Transatlantic legends: T. E. Lawrence and American culture. (Cf. bibl. 1993, 1955.) Rev. by Stephen E. Tabachnick in ELT (39:3) 1996, 361–2.

3407. HOEBING, PHIL. Snake lore in Mark Twain country. MFSJ (15/16) 1993/94, 97–110.

3408. HOLLOWAY, GARY. Saints, demons, and asses: Southern preacher anecdotes. (Bibl. 1992, 2525.) Rev. by Willliam M. Clements in MidAF (19:1) 1991, 74–7.

3409. HUSAIN, SHAHRUKH. Women who wear the breeches: delicious & dangerous tales. London: Virago Press, 1995. pp. xvii, 267.

3410. HYMES, DELL. Coyote: polymorphous but not always perverse. WebS (12:3) 1995, 79–92.

3411. HYNES, WILLIAM H.; DOTY, WILLIAM G. (eds). Mythical trickster figures: contours, contexts, and criticisms. Tuscaloosa; London: Alabama UP, 1993. pp. x, 265. Rev. by Peter Rollins in JPC (29:4) 1996, 237–8.

3412. JOHNSTONE, BARBARA. Stories, community, and place: narratives from middle America. Bloomington: Indiana UP, 1990. pp. 148. Rev. by Frank De Caro in SF (53:1) 1996, 56–9.

3413. JONES, GAYL. Liberating voices: oral tradition in African-American literature. (Bibl. 1994, 2133.) Rev. by Gay Wilentz in AAR (28:1) 1994, 141–5.

3414. KENNEDY, EDWARD DONALD (ed.). King Arthur: a casebook. New York; London: Garland, 1996. pp. lvi, 311. (Garland reference library of the humanities, 1915.) (Arthurian characters and themes, 1.)

3415. LAYIWOLA, DELE. Irish folktales and Beckett's *Molloy*: a study in tropism. *In* (pp. 78–82) **60**.

3416. LITTLETON, C. SCOTT; MALCOR, LINDA A. From Scythia to Camelot: a radical reassessment of the legends of King Arthur, the Knights of the Round Table, and the Holy Grail. (Bibl. 1995, 2770.) Rev. by Betsy Bowden in JFR (33:2) 1996, 165–72.

3417. LURIE, ALISON (ed.). The Oxford book of modern fairy tales. (Bibl. 1993, 1965.) Rev. by Fred Chappell in BkW, 9 May 1996, 2.

3418. McCARTHY, WILLIAM BERNARD (ed.). Jack in two worlds: contemporary North American tales and their tellers. Chapel Hill; London: North Carolina UP, 1994. pp. xlvi, 290. (Pubs of the American Folklore Soc., ns.) Rev. by Jill Clayton in Folklore (107) 1996, 117; by Richard Walker in English Dance and Song (58:2) 1996, 27.

3419. McCLUNEY-CRISWELL, SAMANTHA; CRISWELL, STEPHEN E. 'All the busy humming of the world outside': the evolution of the Lincoln Academy legend. NCarF (43:2) 1996, 160–76.

3420. McNamara, John.   Legends of Breca and Beowulf. SF (53:3) 1996, 153–69.

3421. McNeil, W. K. (ed.).   Articles from *Arkansas Folklore. See* **3295**.

3422. Manganaro, Marc.   Myth, rhetoric, and the voice of authority: a critique of Frazer, Eliot, Frye, and Campbell. (Bibl. 1995, 2773.) Rev. by Donald Mackenzie in LitTheol (10:4) 1996, 384–7.

3423. Martínez Pizarro, Joaquín.   Kings in adversity: a note on Alfred and the cakes. Neophilologus (80:2) 1996, 319–26.

3424. Mbele, Joseph L.   Jesse James at Northfield: a folkloristic study. DNR (65:5) 1996, 154–66.

3425. Meisenhelder, Susan.   Conflict and resistance in Zora Neale Hurston's *Mules and Men.* JAF (109:433) 1996, 267–88.

3426. Metting, Fred.   Exploring oral traditions through the written text. JRead (38:4) 1994/95, 282–9.

3427. Minton, John.   'Big 'Fraid and Little 'Fraid: an Afro-American folktale. Helsinki: Academia Scientiarum Fennica, 1993. pp. 111. (FF communications, 253.) (Tale type 1676a/Motif K1682.1.) Rev. by Lee Haring in Fabula (36:1/2) 1995, 149–51; by William H. Wiggins, Jr, in JFR (32:3) 1995, 289–95; by Sw. Anand Prahlad in AAR (30:2) 1996, 309–11.

3428. Mobley, Marilyn Sanders.   Folk roots and mythic wings in Sarah Orne Jewett and Toni Morrison: the cultural function of narrative. (Bibl. 1995, 2778.) Rev. by Linda Krumholz in Signs (22:1) 1996, 243–8.

3429. Moravec, Mark L.   Organ kidnap legends. Australian Folklore (8) 1993, 89–99.

3430. Morrow, Lynn.   Silas Turnbo's Ozark voices. MidAF (24:2) 1996, 65–73.

3431. Mullen, Patrick B.   Listening to old voices: folklore, life stories, and the elderly. Urbana: Illinois UP, 1992. pp. xii, 292. (Folklore and society.) Rev. by C. Kurt Dewhurst in MidAF (21:1) 1993, 52–4; by Mark E. Workman in JAF (109:431) 1996, 96–7.

3432. Murphy, Maureen.   Folk narrative motifs in Egyptian, Irish and Native-American folklore and literature. *In* (pp. 39–52) **60**.

3433. Murray, Carol.   The stolen woman: oral narrative, postmodernism and the feminist turn in anthropology. CanRCL (21:3) 1994, 295–309.

3434. Narváez, Peter (ed.).   The good people: new fairylore essays. (Bibl. 1992, 2543.) Rev. by Ulrika Wolf-Knuts in ARV (49) 1993, 182–3; by Wilhelm F. H. Nicolaisen in Fabula (34:3/4) 1993, 356–8; by Leonard Norman Primiano in JAF (109:431) 1996, 105–8.

3435. Neralich, Jon.   'They're gonna come after you': snake stories from the Ozarks. MidAF (24:2) 1996, 55–64.

3436. Nusbaum, Philip.   Jocular conversation and conversational joke telling: a case study. NYF (20:1/2) 1994, 15–38.

3437. Oring, Elliott.   Jokes and their relations. (Bibl. 1992, 2546.) Rev. by Andreas Schmidt in Fabula (35:3/4) 1994, 356–7; by Moira Smith in SF (53:1) 1996, 59–61.

3438. Panttaja, Elisabeth.   The poor girl and the bad man: fairytales of feminine power. KenR (12:1/2) 1993, 29–37.

3439. Parler, Mary Celestia.   Folklore from the campus. *See* **3298**.

3440. Pedersen, E. Martin.   Dressing the skeleton: the oral-to-written folk process in a jump story. *In* (pp. 135–44) **117**.

3441. —— Ending the yarn. RSAJ (7) 1996, 79–89.

3442. Peebles, Curtis. Watch the skies! A chronicle of the flying saucer myth. Washington, DC: Smithsonian Inst. Press, 1994. pp. x, 342. Rev. by Amanda Carson Banks in JAF (109:431) 1996, 103–4; by Ed Hatton in JPC (30:2) 1996, 216–17.

3443. Perry, Evelyn M. The battle to possess Sherwood. JAF (109:434) 1996, 437–40.

3444. Phillips, Graham. The search for the Grail. London: Century, 1995. pp. 182, (plates) 8.

3445. Rosenberg, Bruce A. Folklore and literature: rival siblings. (Bibl. 1993, 1979.) Rev. by Ruth B. Bottigheimer in JAF (106:421) 1993, 361–2; by Michael Patrick in MidAF (22:1) 1994, 52–3.

3446. Ross, Míceál. Androgynous Bloom: forerunners in Irish and Egyptian folk tradition. In (pp. 83–90) **60**.

3447. Rowen, Norma. Reinscribing Cinderella: Jane Austen and the fairy tale. In (pp. 29–36) **36**.

3448. Ryan, J. S. From Bush yarns to urban legends; or, The later folkloric career of Bill Scott. Australian Folklore (11) 1996, 69–78 (review-article).

3449. Sax, Boria. The frog king: on legends, fables, fairy tales and anecdotes of animals. (Bibl. 1990, 1903.) Rev. by Gillian Adams in CLAQ (21:1) 1996, 49.

3450. Schmidt, Gary D.; Hettinga, Donald R. (eds). Sitting at the feet of the past: retelling the North American folktale for children. Westport, CT; London: Greenwood Press, 1992. pp. xiii, 239. (Contributions to the study of world literature, 45.) Rev. by Jon C. Stott in ChildLit (24) 1996, 193–8.

3451. Silver, James L. An oral history of underground coal mining: a tape-recorded interview with a retired miner. MidF (19:1) 1993, 34–47.

3452. Smith, J. B. Towards the demystification of Lawrence Lazy. Folklore (107) 1996, 101–5.

3453. Stahl, Sandra Dolby. Literary folkloristics and the personal narrative. (Bibl. 1995, 2792.) Rev. by Juha Y. Pentikäinen in Fabula (32:4) 1991, 349–52.

3454. Tangherlini, Timothy R. Once upon a time: approaches to popular folktale collections. MidAF (24:2) 1996, 86–92 (review-article).

3455. Tatar, Maria. Is anybody out there listening? Fairy tales and the voice of the child. In (pp. 275–83) **48**.

3456. Thigpen, Kenneth A. Thomas Pynchon e gli alligatori nelle fogne: letteratura e folklore urbano. Àcoma (2) 1994, 43–9.

3457. Turner, Patricia A. I heard it through the grapevine: rumor in African-American culture. (Bibl. 1994, 2146.) Rev. by William H. Wiggins, Jr, in JFR (32:3) 1995, 289–95.

3458. Vest, Jay Hansford C. My mother's brother: *Monacan* narratives of the wolf from the Virginia Blue Ridge. WebS (12:3) 1995, 117–22.

3459. Walker, Richard. 'The Chatsby': jottings from the travels of a journeyman storyteller. English Dance and Song (58:1) 1996, 9; (58:4) 1996, 5

3460. Warner, Marina. From the beast to the blonde: on fairy tales and their tellers. (Bibl. 1995, 2799.) Rev. by Michael Dirda in BkW, 29 Oct. 1995, 5.

3461. Wildridge, Aimee. Performing folklore at a family dinner: transcription of a tape-recorded interview. MidF (19:1) 1993, 48–60.

3462. Yolen, Jane.   Foreword: the Rumpelstiltskin factor. JFA (5:2) 1992, 11–13.

3463. Zipes, Jack.   Recent trends in the contemporary American fairy tale. JFA (5:1) 1992, 13–41.

3464. —— Recent trends in the contemporary American fairy tale. *In* (pp. 1–17) **36**.

3465. —— (ed.).   The trials & tribulations of Little Red Riding Hood. (Bibl. 1995, 2802.) Rev. by Pat Pinsent in CritS (8:1) 1996, 124–6.

SONG AND MUSIC

3466. Allen, Michael.   'Row, boatmen, row!': songs of the early Ohio and Mississippi rivermen. GateH (14:3) 1993/94, 46–59.

3467. Allen, Ray.   Back home: Southern identity and African-American gospel quartet performance. *In* (pp. 112–35) **66**.

3468. Anderson, Hugh.   Virtue in a wilderness: Cecil Sharp's Australian sojourn, 1882–1892. FMJ (6:5) 1994, 617–52.

3469. Arthur, Dave.   *Bold Nelson's Praise.* English Dance and Song (58:4) 1996, 20–1.

3470. Atkinson, David.   English folk song: an introductory bibliography based on the holdings of the Vaughan Williams Memorial Library of the English Folk Dance and Song Society. London: English Folk Dance and Song Soc., 1996. pp. 47. (Vaughan Williams Memorial Library leaflets, 23.) Rev. by Geoff Doel and Fran Doel in English Dance and Song (58:4) 1996, 15.

3471. Baer, Joel H.   Bold Captain Avery in the Privy Council: early variants of a broadside ballad from the Pepys Collection. *See* **565**.

3472. Baker, David; Welsby, Joan.   Hymns and hymn singing: a popular guide. Norwich: Canterbury Press, 1993. pp. 133. (Popular guides.) Rev. by Sally Drage in FMJ (7:1) 1995, 104–5.

3473. Borlase, Tim (ed.).   Songs of Labrador. Fredericton, N.B.: Goose Lane, 1993. pp. 214. Rev. by Julia C. Bishop in FMJ (7:1) 1995, 110–11.

3474. Brown, Mary Ellen.   Historical ballad scholarship. JFR (31:1–3) 1994, 179–222. (Reprints essays by Joseph Addison, William Motherwell, F. J. Child.)

3475. Buchan, David.   The Anglophone comic ballads. ARV (48) 1992, 289–95.

3476. Burkart, Julia.   Introduction: socio-economic background of the Delta Blues. MidAF (24:1) 1996, 1–8.

3477. Carr, Joe; Munde, Alan.   Prairie nights to neon lights: the story of country music in west Texas. Lubbock: Texas Tech UP, 1995. pp. x, 243. Rev. by Rob Weiner in JAC (19:2) 1996, 133.

3478. Cauthen, Joyce H.   With fiddle and well-rosined bow: old-time fiddling in Alabama. (Bibl. 1991, 2776.) Rev. by Augustus Burns in FHQ (69:3) 1991, 390–1.

3479. Cohane, Mary Ellen; Goldstein, Kenneth S.   Folksongs and the ethnography of singing in Patrick Kennedy's *The Banks of the Boro.* JAF (109:434) 1996, 425–36.

3480. Cohen, Norm.   Traditional Anglo-American folk music: an annotated discography of published sound recordings. (Bibl. 1995, 2807.) Rev. by Keith Chandler in FMJ (7:1) 1995, 76–8.

3481. Conway, Cecilia.   African banjo echoes in Appalachia:

a study of folk traditions. Knoxville: Tennessee UP, 1995. pp. xxviii, 394. (Pubs of the American Folklore Soc., ns.) Rev. by Art Rosenbaum in GaHQ (80:2) 1996, 411–13.

3482. COOKSEY, THOMAS L.   Mrs Bond's ducks and Trollope's *Popenjoy*. NQ (43:1) 1996, 48.

3483. COWLEY, JOHN.   Carnival, Canboulay and calypso: traditions in the making. Cambridge; New York: CUP, 1996. pp. xv, 293. Rev. by Donald R. Hill in FMJ (7:2) 1996, 217–18.

3484. DAWNEY, MICHAEL.   Standardised English folk carols. English Dance and Song (58:4) 1996, 22–3.

3485. DUGAW, DIANNE.   Warrior women and popular balladry, 1650–1850. (Bibl. 1993, 1999.) Rev. by Constance A. Sullivan in Signs (17:2) 1992, 458–61.

3486. EVERTS-BOEHM, DANA.   'Oh, don't you remember?': a family portrait of *Babes in the Woods*. MFSJ (17) 1995, 17–31.

3487. FITZWILSON, MARY ANN.   With hammers of their own design: scholarly treatment of the John Henry tradition. MFSJ (17) 1995, 33–54.

3488. FOLSOM, STEVEN R.   'It won't be long 'fore my ship comes in': brief origins of an English proverbial expression and its form and function in five recent American country music hits. *See* **3321**.

3489. FOSS, GEORGE.   From White Hall to Bacon Hollow. *See* **3393**.

3490. FOWKE, EDITH; RAHN, JAY.   A family heritage: the story and songs of LaRena Clark. Calgary, Alta: Calgary UP, 1994. pp. 308. Rev. by Steve Roud in Folklore (107) 1996, 120.

3491. GAGNÉ, RICHARD.   From session to CD: recent influences on Irish traditional dance music in America. FF (27:2) 1996, 79–95.

3492. GARDHAM, STEVE.   *The Wreck of the Industry*: origins of an oral ballad. English Dance and Song (58:3) 1996, 2–3.

3493. GORE, CHARLES (ed.).   The Scottish fiddle music index: tune titles from the 18th- & 19th-century printed instrumental music collections, list of indexed and related collections and where to find them, index to numerical musical theme codes. Musselburgh: Amaising, 1994. 1 vol. (various pp.) Rev. by Peggy Duesenberry in FMJ (7:2) 1996, 221–2.

3494. GREEN, ARCHIE (ed.).   Songs about work: essays in occupational culture for Richard A. Reuss. Bloomington: Folklore Inst., Indiana Univ., 1993. pp. vi, 360. (Special pubs of the Folklore Inst., 3.) Rev. by Patrick Huber in JAF (108:428) 1995, 211–13; by John Ashton in FMJ (7:1) 1995, 102–4.

3495. HANSEN, GREGORY.   The relevance of 'authentic tradition' in studying an oldtime Florida fiddler. SF (53:2) 1996, 67–89.

3496. HARRIS, JOSEPH (ed.).   The ballad and oral literature. (Bibl. 1994, 2167.) Rev. by Julia C. Bishop in FMJ (6:5) 1994, 674–6.

3497. HOUSEWRIGHT, WILEY L.   A history of music and dance in Florida, 1565–1865. (Bibl. 1992, 2595.) Rev. by Patricia C. Griffin in FHQ (70:4) 1992, 495–6.

3498. HOWARD, JESSICA H.   *Hallelujah!*: transformation in film. AAR (30:3) 1996, 441–51.

3499. HOY, JAMES.   F. H. Maynard, author of *The Cowboy's Lament*. MidAF (21:2) 1993, 61–8.

3500. IVES, EDWARD D.   Folk-songs of New Brunswick. (Bibl. 1993, 2003.) Rev. by Jean R. Freedman in FF (27:1) 1996, 81–2.

3501. JOHNSTON, JAMES J.   Will the real Daniel Martin please stand up? MidAF (21:1) 1993, 28–41.

3502. JONES, LEWIS. The sacred harp: American shape note hymns cross the Atlantic. English Dance and Song (58:1) 1996, 2.

3503. JONSSON, BENGT R. (ed.). The Stockholm Ballad Conference 1991: proceedings of the 21st International Ballad Conference, August 19–22, 1991. Stockholm: Svenskt visarkiv, 1993. pp. 288. (Skrifter/ utgivna av Svenskt visarkiv, 12.) Rev. by David Atkinson in FMJ (7:1) 1995, 93–5.

3504. KAPLAN, MAX (ed.). Barbershopping: musical and social harmony. Rutherford, NJ: Fairleigh Dickinson UP; London; Toronto: Assoc. UPs, 1993. pp. 149. Rev. by Christopher Wiltshire in FMJ (7:1) 1995, 107–8.

3505. KEEGAN, BRIDGET. Broadsides, ballads and books: the land-scape of cultural literacy in *The Village Minstrel*. JCSJ (15) 1996, 11–18.

3506. KERRIDGE, ROY. The singing harp. English Dance and Song (58:1) 1996, 5.

3507. KERRIGAN, CATHERINE. Reclaiming history: the ballad as a women's tradition. Études Écossaises (1) 1992, 343–50.

3508. KIESSLING, NICOLAS K. The location of two lost volumes of ballads, Wood 399 and Wood 400. *See* **496**.

3509. LIEBERMAN, ROBBIE. My song is my weapon: People's Songs, American Communism, and the politics of culture, 1930–1950. (Bibl. 1991, 2793.) Rev. by Peter Goldsmith in YTM (23) 1991, 148–50.

3510. LIGHTFOOT, WILLIAM E. Review essay: folksong and the 'new aesthetic'. MidAF (23:1) 1995, 38–47.

3511. LINN, KAREN. That half-barbaric twang: the banjo in American popular culture. (Bibl. 1992, 2598.) Rev. by Dennis Howitt in FMJ (7:2) 1996, 242–4.

3512. LIVINGSTON, CAROLE ROSE. British broadside ballads of the sixteenth century: a catalogue of the extant sheets and an essay. (Bibl. 1992, 2600.) Rev. by Steven W. May in ANQ (9:4) 1996, 49–51.

3513. LOGSDON, GUY. Woody Guthrie and his Oklahoma Hills. MidAF (19:1) 1991, 57–73.

3514. —— (ed.). 'The Whorehouse Bells Were Ringing' and other songs cowboys sing. (Bibl. 1991, 2795.) Rev. by Keith Cunningham in MidAF (19:1) 1991, 80–1.

3515. LOMAX, ALAN. The land where the Blues began. New York: Pantheon, 1993. pp. xv, 539. Rev. by Rob van der Bliek in YTM (27) 1995, 163–5.

3516. LOTT, ERIC. Love and theft: the racial unconscious of Blackface minstrelsy. Representations (39) 1992, 23–50.

3517. LUNDGREN, TIM. The Robin Hood ballads and the English outlaw tradition. SF (53:3) 1996, 225–47.

3518. LYLE, EMILY (ed.). Scottish ballads. Edinburgh: Canongate Press, 1994. pp. 288. (Canongate classics, 55.) Rev. by Kaye McAlpine in Folklore (107) 1996, 126.

3519. MCALPINE, KAYE. 'I'd gie them a': the formula in *Geordie* and other ballads. Folklore (107) 1996, 71–6.

3520. —— *Sir Hugh le Blond*: distinguishing the Scottish strand in Child [59]. SLJ (23:2) 1996, 16–34.

3521. MAC AOIDH, CAOIMHÍN. Between the jigs and reels. Manor-hamilton, Co. Leitrim: Drumlin, 1994. pp. 320. Rev. by Josephine L. Miller in FMJ (7:2) 1996, 245–6.

3522. MCCARTHY, WILLIAM BERNARD. The ballad matrix:

personality, milieu, and the oral tradition. (Bibl. 1993, 2004.) Rev. by
Tim Cooley in MidAF (19:2) 1991, 160–2.

3523. McDONALD, BARRY.   The idea of tradition examined in the
light of two Australian musical studies. YTM (28) 1996, 106–30.

3524. —— Thunderbolt, folksong, and the legend of the 'Noble
Robber'. Australian Folklore (8) 1993, 40–7.

3525. McKENRY, KEITH.   Australian Bush song and recitation.
Australian Folklore (11) 1996, 4–5.

3526. —— Discography of recent items: Allan Scott's contributions to
Australian Bush songs and poems – *The Battler* series. Australian Folklore
(11) 1996, 6–12.

3527. MACKEY, NATHANIEL.   *Other*: from noun to verb. *See* **1983**.

3528. MacKINNON, NIALL.   The British folk scene: musical performance and social identity. Buckingham; Philadelphia, PA: Open UP,
1993. pp. 151. (Popular music in Britain.) Rev. by Roy Bailey in
FMJ (6:5) 1994, 658–60.

3529. McNEIL, W. K. (ed.).   The Stilley collection of Ozark folk
songs. MidAF (20:1) 1992, 3–64; (20:2) 1992, 77–109.

3530. MALONE, BILL C.   Singing cowboys and musical mountaineers:
Southern culture and the roots of country music. Athens; London:
Georgia UP, 1993. pp. viii, 155. (Mercer Univ. Lamar memorial
lectures, 34.) Rev. by Edgar D. McKinney in GateH (14:4) 1993/94, 70;
by Augustus Burns, III, in FHQ (73:3) 1995, 393–5.

3531. MARSHALL, HOWARD WIGHT.   *Marmaduke's Hornpipe*: speculations on the life and times of a historic Missouri fiddle tune.
MFSJ (13/14) 1991/92, 101–22.

3532. MINET, LOUISE.   Jeff Warner interviewed. English Dance and
Song (58:1) 1996, 8.

3533. MONGE, LUIGI.   'Il blues del boia' di Blind Lemon Jefferson.
QLLSM (2) 1987, 197–218.

3534. MRYTZ, BARBARA.   Das Verhältnis von Mündlichkeit und
Schriftlichkeit in Textkonstitution und Tradierung der Balladen des
Child-Korpus: ein Beitrag zur Kompatibilität von Literaturwissenschaft
und Volkskunde. (Bibl. 1994, 2175.) Rev. by Tom Cheesman in Fabula
(34:3/4) 1993, 351–3.

3535. NEWMAN, KATHARINE D.   Never without a song: the years and
songs of Jennie Devlin, 1865–1952. (Bibl. 1995, 2823.) Rev. by W. K.
McNeil in MidAF (24:2) 1996, 95–7.

3536. NEWQUIST, DAVID L.   Tracking *The Rock Island Line*.
Midamerica (18) 1991, 44–58.

3537. NICOLAISEN, W. F. H.   Onomastic aspects of *Clerk Colvill*.
See **2159**.

3538. O'CONNOR, PATRICK JOSEPH.   The Black experience and the
Blues in 1950s Wichita. MidAF (21:1) 1993, 1–17.

3539. OLSON, IAN.   Nationalism or internationalism in folk dance and
song? English Dance and Song (58:3) 1996, 16–18.

3540. PALMER, ROY.   'Veritable dunghills': Professor Child and the
broadside. FMJ (7:2) 1996, 155–66.

3541. PARIS, MICHAEL.   Country Blues on the screen: the Leadbelly
films. JAStud (30:1) 1996, 119–25.

3542. PATTERSON, BEVERLY BUSH.   The sound of the dove: singing in
Appalachian Primitive Baptist churches. Urbana: Illinois UP, 1995.

pp. x, 238. (Music in American life.) Rev. by Ian Russell in FMJ (7:2) 1996, 223–4.

3543. PATTERSON, DANIEL W. (ed.).   Sounds of the South: a report and selected papers from a Conference on the Collecting and Collections of Southern Traditional Music, held in Chapel Hill, April 6–8, 1989, to celebrate the opening of the Southern Folklife Collection. Durham, NC; London: Duke UP, 1991. pp. xiv, 219. (Music/American studies.) (Occasional papers, Southern Folklife Collection, 1.) Rev. by David Sanjek in JAF (109:432) 1996, 216–18.

3544. PEN, RON.   The career of John Jacob Niles: a study in the intersection of elite, traditional, and popular musical performance. KenR (12:1/2) 1993, 3–11.

3545. PORTER, GERALD.   Airs and graces: interpretation based on the musical record. A case study. ARV (48) 1992, 205–14.

3546.   —— Cobblers all: occupation as identity and cultural message. FMJ (7:1) 1995, 43–61.

3547.   —— The English occupational song. Umeå: Umeå Univ.; Stockholm: Almqvist & Wiksell, 1992. pp. 184. (Acta Universitatis Umensis: Umeå studies in the humanities, 105.) Rev. by Svend Nielsen in ARV (49) 1993, 149–50; by A. E. Green in FMJ (6:5) 1994, 671–2.

3548.   —— 'Work the old lady out of the ditch': singing at work by English lacemakers. JFR (31:1–3) 1994, 35–55.

3549. POST, JENNIFER.   Family song traditions: the Pierce-Spaulding family. NF (30) 1995, 57–89.

3550. PROCTOR, DAVID.   Music of the sea. London: HMSO in assn with National Maritime Museum, Greenwich, 1992. pp. x, 149. Rev. by Cyril Tawney in FMJ (6:5) 1994, 678–9.

3551. PURSER, JOHN.   Scotland's music: a history of the traditional and classical music of Scotland from earliest times to the present day. Edinburgh: Mainstream; BBC Scotland, 1992. pp. 311. Rev. by Vic Gammon in FMJ (6:5) 1994, 663–5.

3552. QUIGLEY, COLIN.   Music from the heart: compositions of a folk fiddler. Athens; London: Georgia UP, 1995. pp. xiii, 273. Rev. by Hazel Fairbairn in FMJ (7:2) 1996, 232–4.

3553. RIACH, ALAN.   Scotland and the colonial paradigm. *See* **3249**.

3554. RIEUWERTS, SIGRID.   Field-collecting of English and Scottish ballads: a researcher's point of view. ARV (48) 1992, 237–46.

3555.   —— The folk-ballad: the illegitimate Child of the popular ballad. JFR (33:3) 1996, 221–6.

3556.   —— 'The genuine ballads of the people': F. J. Child and the ballad cause. JFR (31:1–3) 1994, 1–34.

3557. ROSENBERG, NEIL V. (ed.).   Transforming tradition: folk music revivals examined. Foreword by Alan Jabbour. Urbana: Illinois UP, 1993. pp. xiii, 340. (Pubs of the American Folklore Soc., ns.) Rev. by Dave Adamson in FMJ (6:5) 1994, 667–9; by William E. Lightfoot in MidAF (23:1) 1995, 38–47; by Gregory Hansen in FF (27:1) 1996, 89–91.

3558. SANDERS, KAREN J.   Making the babes our own: a search for a song. MFSJ (17) 1995, 1–16.

3559. SARJEANT, WILLIAM A. S.   *Black Is the Colour of My True Love's Heart*: a crime novel with a folk-song theme. English Dance and Song (58:2) 1996, 6–8.

3560. SHIELDS, HUGH.   Narrative singing in Ireland: lays, come-all-yes and other songs. (Bibl. 1994, 2188.) Rev. by Tom Cheesman in

Fabula (35:3/4) 1994, 364–5; by W. F. H. Nicolaisen in FMJ (7:1) 1995, 79–80.

3561. SMITH, STEPHANIE.   The categorization and performance aesthetics of narrative song among Scottish folk revival singers. ARV (48) 1992, 225–36.

3562. SOUTHWORTH, JOHN.   The English medieval minstrel. (Bibl. 1995, 2832.) Rev. by Christopher Smith in Quondam et Futurus (2:2) 1992, 91–2.

3563. STONEBACK, H. R.   Songs of 'anger and survival': John Steinbeck on Woody Guthrie. SteiQ (23:1/2) 1990, 34–41.

3564. TATE, BRAD.   Jock Graham's 'secret' folio of old Left song. Australian Folklore (11) 1996, 53–64.

3565. TAYLOR, MICHAEL; BRADTKE, ELAINE.   Resources in the Vaughan Williams Memorial Library. See **544**.

3566. THOMPSON, ROSELLE.   Passion, people, and politics: a socio-historical analysis of the calypso as orature. JCS (11:1/2) 1995/96, 57–85.

3567. TITON, JEFF TODD (sel.).   Downhome Blues lyrics: an anthology from the post-World War II era. (Bibl. 1991, 2821.) Rev. by John White in JAStud (30:1) 1996, 133–4.

3568. TRIBE, IVAN M.   The Stonemans: an Appalachian family and the music that shaped their lives. (Bibl. 1995, 2835.) Rev. by Mike Yates in FMJ (7:2) 1996, 100–1.

3569. TURNER, MICHAEL L.   Who was Walter Harding? Some preliminary notes on his English antecedents: part one. See **547**.

3570. WEBSTER, JACK.   Gavin Greig and north-east rural life. AUR (56:4) 1996, 473–7.

3571. WÜRZBACH, NATASCHA; SALZ, SIMONE M.   Motif index of the Child corpus: the English and Scottish popular ballad. Trans. by Gayna Walls. (Bibl. 1995, 2838.) Rev. by Fritz Wagner in Fabula (37:3/4) 1996, 317–18; by Tom Cheesman in Fabula (37:3/4) 1996, 366–8.

3572. ZETTSU, TOMOYUKI.   Slavery, song, and the South: Cather's refiguration of Stowe and Foster in *A Lost Lady*. AQ (52:2) 1996, 87–104.

3573. ZILBERG, JONATHAN.   Yes, it's true: Zimbabweans love Dolly Parton. JPC (29:1) 1995, 111–25.

DANCE AND DRAMA

3574. ADSHEAD-LANSDALE, JANET; LAYSON, JUNE (eds).   Dance history: an introduction. London; New York: Routledge, 1994. pp. xii, 289. (Second ed.: first ed. 1983.) Rev. by Chris Metherell in FMJ (7:1) 1995, 95–6.

3575. ANON.   Scotland's dances: a review of the 1994 Conference on the Diversity of the Scottish Tradition of Dance: 25/26 October, Albert Hall, Stirling. Edinburgh: Scottish Arts Council, 1994. pp. 51. Rev. by Joan Flett in FMJ (7:1) 1995, 87–8.

3576. BARTRAM, CHRIS.   The fiddle in southern England. English Dance and Song (58:2) 1996, 2–5.

3577. BUCKLAND, THERESA JILL.   Institutions and ideology in the dissemination of morris dances in the northwest of England. YTM (23) 1991, 53–67.

3578. CHANDLER, KEITH.   'Ribbons, bells, and squeaking fiddles': the social history of morris dancing in the English South Midlands,

1660–1900. (Bibl. 1995, 2839.) Rev. by Alun Howkins in FMJ (7:1) 1995, 78–9.

3579.   COLEMAN, GREGORY D.   'We're Heaven bound': portrait of a Black sacred drama. Athens; London: Georgia UP, 1994. pp. xi, 199. Rev. by Sandy Dwayne Martin in GaHQ (80:1) 1996, 203–4.

3580.   CORRSIN, STEPHEN D.   An online database on the bibliography of sword dancing. *See* **1145**.

3581.   —— Sword dancing in Britain: an annotated bibliography based on the holdings of the Vaughan Williams Memorial Library of EFDSS. London: English Folk Dance and Song Soc., 1993. pp. iv, 34. (Vaughan Williams Memorial Library leaflets, 21.) Rev. by Ivor Allsop in FMJ (6:5) 1994, 687.

3582.   DARLINGTON, WILF.   *Go George, I Can't Endure You*: a country dance and its tune. FMJ (7:1) 1995, 62–70.

3583.   DAVIS, AMY.   *Deep in My Heart*: competition and the function of stepping in an African-American sorority. NCarF (43:2) 1996, 82–95.

3584.   DOBSON, BOB.   Concerning clogs. Blackpool: Landy, 1993. pp. 87, (plates) 8. (Second ed.: first ed. 1979.) Rev. by Sam Sherry in FMJ (6:5) 1994, 685–6.

3585.   DOUGLAS, AUDREY.   'Owre thanssynge day': parish dance and procession in Salisbury. FMJ (6:5) 1994, 600–16.

3586.   FAIRBAIRN, HAZEL.   Changing contexts for traditional dance music in Ireland: the rise of group performance practice. FMJ (6:5) 1994, 566–99.

3587.   FLINN, JULIANA.   American country dancing: a religious experience. JPC (29:1) 1995, 61–9.

3588.   GLASSBERG, DAVID.   American historical pageantry: the uses of tradition in the early twentieth century. (Bibl. 1992, 2628.) Rev. by Florence C. Smith in GateH (12:2) 1991, 78.

3589.   HAYWARD, BRIAN.   *Galoshins*: the Scottish folk play. (Bibl. 1993, 2015.) Rev. by Keith Chandler in FMJ (6:5) 1994, 669–71.

3590.   HEANEY, MIKE.   Introductory bibliography on morris dancing. London: Vaughan Williams Memorial Library; English Folk Dance and Song Soc., 1985. pp. 35. (Vaughan Williams Memorial Library leaflets, 19.) Rev. by Sue Swift in English Dance and Song (57:4) 1995, 25.

3591.   KERRIDGE, ROY.   The singing harp. *See* **3506**.

3592.   MILLINGTON, PETER.   Mrs Ewing and the textual origin of the St Kitts Mummies' play. Folklore (107) 1996, 77–89.

3593.   MOYLAN, TERRY (ed.).   Johnny O'Leary of Sliabh Luachra: dance music from the Cork–Kerry border. Dublin: Lilliput Press, 1994. pp. xvi, 213. Rev. by Alan Ward in FMJ (7:2) 1996, 241–2.

3594.   NICELEY, DAWN L.   The Corn Crib Theatre, a long surviving professional Toby company. MidAF (22:1) 1994, 1–14.

3595.   OLSON, IAN.   Nationalism or internationalism in folk dance and song? *See* **3539**.

3596.   PETERSON, DOUGLAS L.   The origins of Tudor comedy: Plautus, *Jack Jugeler*, and the folk-play as mediating form. *In* (pp. 105–15) **131**.

3597.   PETTITT, TOM.   Customary drama: social and spatial patterning in traditional encounters. FMJ (7:1) 1995, 27–42.

3598.   PILLING, JULIAN.   A Black composer of country dances in the 18th century. English Dance and Song (58:2) 1996, 9. (Ignatius Sancho.)

3599.   SPALDING, SUSAN EIKE; WOODSIDE, JANE HARRIS (eds). Communities in motion: dance, community, and tradition in America's

Southeast and beyond. Westport, CT; London: Greenwood Press, 1995. pp. xii, 273. (Contributions to the study of music and dance, 35.) Rev. by Joyce Cauthen in AlaR (49:4) 1996, 307–9.

3600. TREW, JOHANNE.   Ottawa Valley fiddling: issues of identity and style. BJCS (11:2) 1996, 339–44.

3601. VIDRICKSEN, ROBERTA.   House dances in the Flint Hills; or, Whad'ja do for fun, Granny? MidAF (22:1) 1994, 68–72.

3602. WICKENS, DENYS; WICKENS, JENNIFER.   *Stay and Take Your Petticoat with You.* English Dance and Song (58:3) 1996, 5.

3603. YARGER, LISA J.   'That's ... where stepping came from': Afrocentricity and beliefs about stepping. NCarF (43:2) 1996, 109–19.

CUSTOM AND BELIEF

3604. ABURROW, YVONNE.   The enchanted forest: the magical lore of trees. Chieveley, Berks.: Capall Bann, 1993. pp. iv, 198.

3605. ARTHUR, DAVE.   The fairy tradition. English Dance and Song (58:1) 1996, 18–19.

3606. BAKER, MARGARET.   Discovering the folklore of plants. (Bibl. 1980, 2638.) Princes Risborough: Shire, 1996. pp. 168. (Discovering, 74.) (Third ed.: first ed. 1969.)

3607. BAUMAN, RICHARD; SAWIN, PATRICIA; CARPENTER, INTA GALE. Reflections on the Folklife Festival: an ethnography of participant experience. (Bibl. 1993, 2025.) Rev. by Elaine Eff in MidAF (23:1) 1995, 52–4.

3608. BILLINGTON, SANDRA.   Mock kings in medieval society and Renaissance drama. (Bibl. 1995, 2849.) Rev. by Naomi Conn Liebler in MedRen (7) 1995, 373–8.

3609. BLUESTEIN, GENE.   Poplore: folk and pop in American culture. *See* **3268**.

3610. BOYER, PAUL.   When time shall be no more: prophecy belief in modern American culture. Cambridge, MA: Belknap Press of Harvard UP, 1992. pp. xiv, 468, (plates) 16. Rev. by Bruce Kuklick in AHR (98:3) 1993, 827–8; by Ray B. Browne in JAC (18:1) 1995, 112–13; by Mark Hulsether in AmQ (48:2) 1996, 375–83.

3611. BROWNE, RAY B.; MARSDEN, MICHAEL T. (eds).   The cultures of celebrations. Bowling Green, OH: Bowling Green State Univ. Popular Press, 1994. pp. 244. (Outdoor entertainment.) Rev. by Scott Collison in JAF (109:431) 1996, 101–3.

3612. BUCKLAND, THERESA; WOOD, JULIETTE (eds).   Aspects of British calendar customs. (Bibl. 1994, 2221.) Rev. by Teri Brewer in FMJ (6:5) 1994, 660–1; by Ray Browne in JPC (29:4) 1996, 231–2.

3613. CAMPION-VINCENT, VÉRONIQUE.   Demonologies in contemporary legends and panics. Fabula (34:3/4) 1993, 238–51.

3614. CAVENDER, ANTHONY (ed.).   A folk medical lexicon of South Central Appalachia. *See* **2086**.

3615. CHOWNING, LARRY S.   Barcat skipper: tales of a Tangier Island waterman. *See* **3273**.

3616. —— Harvesting the Chesapeake: tools and traditions. *See* **3274**.

3617. COWLEY, JOHN.   Carnival, Canboulay and calypso: traditions in the making. *See* **3483**.

3618. CURTIS, BRUCE.   The strange birth of Santa Claus: from Artemis the goddess and Nicholas the saint. JAC (18:4) 1995, 17–32.

3619. DAVIES, MARION.   Lore of the sacred horse. Chieveley, Berks.: Capall Bann, 1995. pp. ii, 219.

3620. DAVIES, OWEN.   Healing charms in use in England and Wales 1700–1950. Folklore (107) 1996, 19–32.

3621. DAVIS, DEBORAH R.   Famine ghosts and the 'Féar Gortach': a strand of Irish belief. FF (27:2) 1996, 39–52.

3622. DUNDES, ALAN.   'Jumping the broom': on the origin and meaning of an African-American wedding custom. JAF (109:433) 1996, 324–9.

3623. FERRIS, WILLIAM.   'You live and learn, then you die and forget it all': Ray Lum's tales of horses, mules, and men. With foreword by Eudora Welty. *See* **3388**.

3624. FIELDS, KIERAN.   Witches down under. Australian Folklore (9) 1994, 174–6.

3625. FLOYD, E. RANDALL.   Ghost lights, and other encounters with the unknown. Little Rock, AR: August House, 1993. pp. 191. Rev. by Frank Reuter in MidAF (21:2) 1993, 111–13.

3626. FRESE, PAMELA R. (ed.).   Celebrations of identity: multiple voices in American ritual performance. Westport, CT: Bergin & Garvey, 1993. pp. xxii, 232. Rev. by Diane Sidener Young in JAF (109:432) 1996, 205–7.

3627. FURST, WENDY.   Women and the folklore of housework. MidF (22:1) 1996, 34–41.

3628. GRABILL, JOSEPH L.   Nature and festivals. SHum (19:2) 1992, 126–44.

3629. GREEN, ARCHIE.   Wobblies, pile butts, and other heroes: labor-lore explorations. Urbana: Illinois UP, 1993. pp. xii, 523. (Pubs of the American Folklore Soc., ns.) Rev. by Patrick B. Mullen in MidAF (21:2) 1993, 107–10; by Gerald Porter in FMJ (7:1) 1995, 96–8; by Robert E. Walls in JAF (108:427) 1995, 93–5.

3630. GRIDER, SYLVIA ANN.   Conservatism and dynamism in the contemporary celebration of Halloween: institutionalization, commercialization, gentrification. SF (53:1) 1996, 3–15.

3631. HUNT, ARTHUR J.   Birds-in-lore: an introduction to the folklore and social history of selected European species. Chinnor: Hunt, 1996. pp. viii, 212, (plates) 20.

3632. HUTTON, RONALD.   The rise and fall of Merry England: the ritual year, 1400–1700. (Bibl. 1995, 2861.) Rev. by Roy Judge in FMJ (7:1) 1995, 74–6; by Christopher Haigh in EHR (111:444) 1996, 1274–5.

3633. —— The stations of the sun: a history of the ritual year in Britain. Oxford; New York: OUP, 1996. pp. xx, 542, (plates) 16. Rev. by Roy Judge in FMJ (7:2) 1996, 224–6; by Eamon Duffy in TLS, 11 Oct. 1996, 4.

3634. IVES, EDWARD D.   George Magoon and the down east game war: history, folklore, and the law. Urbana: Illinois UP, 1993. pp. xiv, 335. (Folklore and society.) (Pubs of the American Folklore Soc., ns.) (Hunting in Maine.) Rev. by Jan Gustafson in ARV (50) 1994, 231–3.

3635. JUDGE, ROY.   May Day in England: an introductory bibliography. (Bibl. 1991, 2863.) Rev. by Geoff Doel and Fran Doel in English Dance and Song (58:4) 1996, 15.

3636. KAYSER NIELSEN, NIELS.   Fra Robin Hood til fodbold: en kulturanalytisk studie i arbejderklassens kropskultur i England i 1800-tallet. Odense: Odense UP, 1992. pp. 375. (Odense Univ. studies in history and social sciences, 154.) Rev. by Jens Petter Kollhøj in ARV (52) 1996, 150–1.

3637. KINSER, SAMUEL. Carnival, American style: Mardi Gras at New Orleans and Mobile. (Bibl. 1995, 2862.) Rev. by Robert E. Snyder in FHQ (69:4) 1991, 512–14; by Michael D. Bristol in JRS (6:1) 1992, 184–6; by Frank De Caro in SF (53:3) 1996, 251–3.

3638. LAROQUE, FRANÇOIS. Shakespeare's festive world: Elizabethan seasonal entertainment and the professional stage. Trans. by Janet Lloyd. (Bibl. 1995, 2863.) Rev. by Retha Warnicke in AHR (98:2) 1993, 487.

3639. MacDONALD, JOAN H. The Australian emergence of the Scottish 'wise man' in the fiction of Rolf Boldrewood. Australian Folklore (8) 1993, 55–63.

3640. McMILLAN, DOUGLAS J. Folk belief in some of Ovid Williams Pierce's early short stories. NCL (25:4) 1995, 7–8.

3641. MEYER, RICHARD E. (ed.). Ethnicity and the American cemetery. *See* **3356**.

3642. MORGAN, JACK. Cockfighting: a rural American tradition. MFSJ (15/16) 1993/94, 119–32.

3643. MORRIS, MARK. The tradition of the shivaree. MidF (22:1) 1996, 5–15.

3644. NEUSTADT, KATHY. Clambake: a history and celebration of an American tradition. (Bibl. 1995, 2867.) Rev. by Suzanne Waldenberger in FF (27:1) 1996, 79–80.

3645. PHILPIN, SUE. Woollen yarn healing. Folk Life (34) 1995/96, 80–2.

3646. PICKERING, DAVID. Dictionary of superstitions. London; New York: Cassell, 1996. pp. vi, 294.

3647. REED, DANIEL. The 1993 celebration of Martin Luther King, Jr, Day in Bloomington, Indiana: tradition, interpretation, and conflicts of identity. MidF (22:1) 1996, 25–33.

3648. RIETI, BARBARA. Strange terrain: the fairy world in Newfoundland. St John's, Nfld: Inst. of Social and Economic Research, 1991. pp. xvii, 273. (Social and economic studies, 45.) Rev. by David E. Gay in FF (27:1) 1996, 88–9.

3649. SIMPSON, JACQUELINE. Witches and witchbusters. Folklore (107) 1996, 5–18.

3650. SZCZELKUN, STEFAN. The conspiracy of good taste: William Morris, Cecil Sharp, Clough Williams-Ellis and the repression of working-class culture in the 20th century. London: Working Press, 1993. pp. 128. Rev. by Dave Harker in FMJ (7:1) 1995, 108–9.

3651. THOMPSON, E. P. Customs in common. (Bibl. 1993, 2046.) Rev. by Trefor Owen in Folklore (107) 1996, 116.

3652. WALES, TONY. Customs club. English Dance and Song (58:1) 1996, 11; (58:2) 1996, 18; (58:3) 1996, 4; (58:4) 1996, 3.

3653. WALSH, MARTIN W. November bull-running in Stamford, Lincolnshire. JPC (30:1) 1996, 233–47.

3654. WALTER, TONY. Funeral flowers: a response to Drury. Folklore (107) 1996, 106–7. (*Reply to* bibl. 1994, 2226.)

3655. WATSON, GREER. Magic or make-believe? Acquiring conventions of witches and witchcraft. JFA (6:4) 1993, 341–59.

3656. WHITSITT, JULIA. Peripatetic proselytizing. PTFS (52) 1993, 201–7.

3657. WILLIAMS, CLOVER NOLAN.   The bachelor's transgression: identity and difference in the bachelor party. JAF (107:423) 1994, 106–20.

3658. WILSON, EDWIN.   Paradise lost: plant-lore on the far north coast of New South Wales. Australian Folklore (9) 1994, 104–13.

3659. WOJCIK, DANIEL.   'Polaroids from Heaven': photography, folk religion, and the miraculous image tradition at a Marian apparition site. JAF (109:432) 1996, 129–48.

MATERIAL CULTURE, TECHNIQUES AND OCCUPATIONS, FOLK ARTS AND CRAFTS

3660. ALLMENDINGER, BLAKE.   The cowboy: representations of labor in an American work culture. (Bibl. 1992, 2689.) Rev. by Richard W. Etulain in AHR (99:3) 1994, 987; by David A. Zonderman in AmLH (8:2) 1996, 341–3.

3661. ANON.   Nineteenth-century agricultural journals as a resource for material culture studies. MatC (23:1) 1991, 43–6.

3662. BENBERRY, CUESTA.   Always there: the African-American presence in American quilts. Forewords by Jonathan Holstein and Shelly Zegart. Louisville: Kentucky Quilt Project, 1992. pp. 132. Rev. by Laurel Horton in JAF (106:421) 1993, 355–6.

3663. BREARS, PETER.   'Bygones' in *The Connoisseur*. Folk Life (34) 1995/96, 30–42.

3664. CALLAHAN, NANCY.   The Freedom Quilting Bee. *See* **3272**.

3665. CARNEY, GEORGE O.   Slappin' collars and stabbin' pipe: occupational folklife of old-time pipeliners in the Oklahoma oil patch. MidAF (19:1) 1991, 39–56.

3666. CHOWNING, LARRY S.   Harvesting the Chesapeake: tools and traditions. *See* **3274**.

3667. CLARK, RICKY.   Quilted gardens: floral quilts of the nineteenth century. Nashville, TN: Rutledge Hill Press, 1994. pp. xi, 115. Rev. by Lorre M. Weidlich in JAF (109:432) 1996, 202–3.

3668. DEMELLO, MARGO.   'Not just for bikers anymore': popular representations of American tattooing. JPC (29:3) 1995, 37–52.

3669. DUFFY, KAREN M.   The works of Virgil Boruff, Indiana limestone craftsman. MidF (22:2) 1996, 5–71.

3670. ELSLEY, JUDY.   Quilts as text(iles): the semiotics of quilting. New York; Frankfurt; Bern; Paris: Lang, 1996. pp. 82. (Berkeley insights in linguistics and semiotics, 16.) (Cf. bibl. 1991, 2899.)

3671. FURST, WENDY.   Women and the folklore of housework. *See* **3627**.

3672. GRIFFITH, JAMES S.   Southern Arizona folk arts. *See* **3284**.

3673. HUNT, TERRY.   Akubra; or, The art of felt-making for Australian hats. Australian Folklore (9) 1994, 185–91.

3674. JONES, MICHAEL OWEN.   Craftsman of the Cumberlands: traditions & creativity. (Bibl. 1977, 2163.) Lexington: Kentucky UP, 1989. pp. xiii, 289. (Pubs of the American Folklore Soc., ns.) (Revised ed.: first ed. 1975.) (Kentucky chairmakers.) Rev. by Gerald L. Pocius in JAF (109:432) 1996, 199–200.

3675. MILBAUER, JOHN A.   Folk monuments of Afro-Americans: a perspective on Black culture. MidAF (19:2) 1991, 99–109.

3676. MULHOLLAND, JOAN.   Patchwork: the evolution of a women's genre. JAC (19:4) 1996, 57–69.

3677. Pocius, Gerald L. (ed.).   Living in a material world: Canadian and American approaches to material culture. St John's, Nfld: Inst. of Social and Economic Research, Memorial Univ. of Newfoundland, 1991. pp. xix, 290. Rev. by Dorothy Noyes in JAF (106:421) 1993, 347–9.

3678. Schlereth, Thomas J.   Cultural history and material culture: everyday life, landscapes, museums. (Bibl. 1995, 2888.) Rev. by Philip Nusbaum in MidAF (19:2) 1991, 162–5; by John B. Wolford in JAF (106:421) 1993, 353–5.

3679. Torsney, Cheryl B.; Elsley, Judy (eds).   Quilt culture: tracing the pattern. (Bibl. 1995, 2891.) Rev. by Laurel Horton in MidAF (23:2) 1995, 104–8.

3680. West, Andrew.   A travelling basketmaker – and more: Philla Davis. Folk Life (34) 1995/96, 100–4.

CHILDREN'S TRADITIONS

3681. Bailey, Jay.   Fist fights and flattened pennies: some games and activities of Western Oklahoma children, 1939–1949. MidAF (19:1) 1991, 10–38.

3682. Butler, Francelia.   Skipping around the world: the ritual nature of folk rhymes. Hamden, CT: Shoe String Press, 1989. pp. xiv, 223. Rev. by John Cech in CLAQ (17:1) 1992, 46–7.

3683. Caplan, Theresa, et al. (comps).   Folk, fantasy & play: selections from the Caplan Collection of the Children's Museum of Indianapolis. Indianapolis, IN: Children's Museum of Indianapolis, 1991. pp. 126. Rev. by Justine McGovern in JAF (106:421) 1993, 370–1.

3684. Clark, Cindy Dell.   Flights of fancy, leaps of faith: children's myths in contemporary America. Chicago; London: Chicago UP, 1995. pp. viii, 158, (plates) 8. Rev. by Donna M. Lanclos in JAF (109:433) 1996, 339–41.

3685. Hastings, Scott E.   Miss Mary Mac all dressed in black: tongue twisters, jump rope rhymes and other children's lore from New England. (Bibl. 1991, 2923.) Rev. by Linda A. Hughes in MidAF (23:1) 1995, 51–2.

3686. Hess, Kathleen.   The bittersweet vine: fairy tales and nursery rhymes. *See* **3405**.

3687. Kerridge, Roy.   The singing harp. *See* **3506**.

3688. Kertzer, Adrienne.   Reclaiming her maternal pre-text: Little Red Riding Hood's mother and three young adult novels. CLAQ (21:1) 1996, 20–7.

3689. Opie, Iona.   The people in the playground. Oxford; New York: OUP, 1993. pp. ix, 240. Rev. by Tecwyn Vaughan Jones in FMJ (7:1) 1995, 101–2.

3690. Rollin, Lucy.   Cradle and all: a cultural and psychoanalytic reading of nursery rhymes. (Bibl. 1995, 2898.) Rev. by Harry Eiss in JAC (17:1) 1994, 94.

3691. Zipes, Jack.   Fairy tale as myth: myth as fairy tale. (Bibl. 1995, 2901.) Rev. by Sabine Wienker-Piepho in Fabula (36:1/2) 1995, 179–82.

3692. —— Towards a theory of the fairy-tale film: the case of *Pinocchio*. LU (20:1) 1996, 1–24.

ENGLISH LITERATURE

GENERAL

GENERAL LITERARY STUDIES

3693. ABRAMS, M. H. (gen. ed.). The Norton anthology of English literature. (Bibl. 1995, 2902.) Rev. by Stephen C. Behrendt in CritM (9:1) 1995, 95–105.

3694. ALLUMS, LARRY (ed.). The epic cosmos. Introd. by Louise Cowan. *See* **29**.

3695. ALPERS, PAUL J. What is pastoral? Chicago; London: Chicago UP, 1996. pp. xiii, 429. Rev. by Luc Deitz in arcadia (31:1/2) 1996, 330–3.

3696. ANDERSON, SARAH (ed.). The Virago book of spirituality: of women and angels. London: Virago Press, 1996. pp. x, 336. Rev. by Emma Tristram in TLS, 22 Nov. 1996, 14.

3697. ANDREWS, CLARENCE. Michigan in literature. (Bibl. 1992, 2717.) Rev. by David D. Anderson in SSMLN (23:1) 1993, 10–12.

3698. ANGEL-PEREZ, ELISABETH. Histoire de la littérature anglaise. Paris: Hachette, 1994. pp. 160. (Hachette supérieur, 24.)

3699. ANON. (comp.). Doctoral dissertations in American studies, 1995–1996. AmQ (48:4) 1996, 751–83.

3700. —— Schriftenverzeichnis Horst Weinstock. *In* (pp. 363–70) **11**.

3701. ARISTIDES. A real page-turner. ASch (65:2) 1996, 167–76.

3702. ARMITT, LUCIE. Theorising the fantastic. London: Arnold; New York: St Martin's Press, 1996. pp. viii, 205. (Interrogating texts.)

3703. ASSMANN, ALEIDA. Texts, traces, trash: the changing media of cultural memory. YREAL (12) 1996, 31–44.

3704. ATWOOD, MARGARET. Strange things: the malevolent North in Canadian literature. (Bibl. 1995, 2914.) Rev. by W. J. Keith in LRC (5:4) 1996, 13–14.

3705. AUCHINCLOSS, LOUIS. The man behind the book: literary profiles. Boston, MA: Houghton Mifflin, 1996. pp. xi, 208.

3706. BAILEY, PAUL (ed.). The Oxford book of London. Oxford; New York: OUP, 1995. pp. xviii, 377. Rev. by Oliver Reynolds in TLS, 21 June 1996, 32.

3707. BAILIN, ALAN. Meaning change: metaphorical and literal. *See* **2305**.

3708. BARBOUR, JAMES; QUIRK, TOM (eds). Writing the American classics. (Bibl. 1993, 2081.) Rev. by Christopher S. Busch in SteiQ (24:1/2) 1991, 43–6.

3709. BARKSDALE, RICHARD K. Praisesong of survival: lectures and essays, 1957–89. Introd. by R. Baxter Miller. (Bibl. 1993, 2082.) Rev. by Keneth Kinnamon in LHR (12:2) 1993, 24–6; by Christopher C. De Santis in AAR (28:1) 1994, 147–50.

3710. BARNEY, RICHARD A. Filthy thoughts; or, Cultural criticism and the ordure of things. Genre (27:4) 1994, 275–93.

3711. BARRECA, REGINA. Untamed and unabashed: essays on women and humor in British literature. (Bibl. 1994, 2254. Rev. by June Sochen in Signs (21:3) 1996, 795–8.

3712. BARTON, ANNE. The wild man in the forest. CompCrit (18) 1996, 21–54. (Illustrated.)

3713. BARUCH, ELAINE HOFFMAN. Women, love, and power: literary and psychoanalytic perspectives. (Bibl. 1993, 2084.) Rev. by Natasha Saje in Signs (19:1) 1993, 276–9.

3714. BAUCOM, IAN. Mournful histories: narratives of postimperial melancholy. MFS (42:2) 1996, 259–88.

3715. BEHLER, ERNST. Irony and the discourse of modernity. (Bibl. 1995, 2923.) Rev. by Lilian R. Furst in CanRCL (18:4) 1991, 613–15; by Christian Moser in arcadia (28:1) 1993, 74–9.

3716. BELL, MILLICENT. On Venice. Raritan (13:4) 1994, 124–45 (review-article).

3717. BENJAMIN, MARINA (ed.). A question of identity: women, science, and literature. See **94**.

3718. BENNETT, BRUCE. An Australian compass: essays on place and direction in Australian literature. (Bibl. 1994, 2260.) Rev. by Norbert H. Platz in ZAA (42:4) 1994, 406–9.

3719. BENNETT, DONNA. Conflicted vision: a consideration of canon and genre in English-Canadian literature. *In* (pp. 131–49) **13**.

3720. BERCOVITCH, SACVAN. The rites of assent: transformations in the symbolic construction of America. (Bibl. 1995, 2928.) Rev. by Jude Davies in Literature and History (5:1) 1996, 118–19.

3721. —— (gen. ed.); PATELL, CYRUS R. K. (assoc. ed.). The Cambridge history of American literature: vol. 1, 1590–1820. (Bibl. 1995, 2929.) Rev. by Carla Mulford in AL (68:1) 1996, 227–8.

3722. BESSERMAN, LAWRENCE (ed.). The challenge of periodization: old paradigms and new perspectives. New York; London: Garland, 1996. pp. xxiv, 244. (Garland reference library of the humanities, 1938.)

3723. BEVERLEY, JOHN. Against literature. (Bibl. 1994, 2265.) Rev. by Evan Watkins in MFS (40:2) 1994, 451–3.

3724. BIRKLE, CARMEN; SIEBALD, MANFRED (comps). Deutsche amerikanistische Veröffentlichungen 1995/Publications in American studies from German-speaking countries, 1995. Amst (41:4) 1996, 718–38.

3725. BLAICHER, GÜNTHER. Das Deutschlandbild in der englischen Literatur. (Bibl. 1994, 2268.) Rev. by Peter Edgerly Firchow in GRM (44:2) 1994, 244–7.

3726. BLAMIRES, DAVID. Fortunatus in his many English guises. Lewiston, NY; Lampeter: Mellen Press, 1996. pp. 158. (Studies in comparative literature, 19.)

3727. BLOOM, HAROLD. The Western canon: the books and school of the ages. (Bibl. 1995, 2934.) Rev. by R. W. French in WWQR (12:2) 1994, 117–20; by Michael Dirda in BkW, 25 Sept. 1994, 1, 13; by Karen A. Weisman in Salmagundi (112) 1996, 216–25; by Graham Good in CanL (151) 1996, 152–5; by Warren Hope in ER (4:1) 1996, 47–8; by Stanley Stewart in Cithara (35:2) 1996, 27–33; by John J. Burke, Jr, in SAtlR (61:1) 1996, 129–33; by Mary Ann Frese Witt in Comparatist (20) 1996, 179–82; by William Kerrigan in CLIO (25:2) 1996, 195–206.

3728. Bobo, Jacqueline.   Black women as cultural readers. (Bibl. 1995, 2935.) Rev. by Maria Pramaggiore in NWSAJ (8:2) 1996, 130–1; by Clare Weissenberg in JAStud (30:2) 1996, 318–20.

3729. Boehmer, Elleke.   Colonial and postcolonial literature: migrant metaphors. (Bibl. 1995, 2936.) Rev. by Amal Amireh in WLT (70:3) 1996, 768–9.

3730. Boitani, Piero.   The shadow of Ulysses: figures of a myth. Trans. by Anita Weston. (Bibl. 1995, 2937.) Rev. by Richard Jenkyns in MÆ (65:2) 1996, 298–9.

3731. Bolongaro, Eugenio.   From literariness to genre: establishing the foundations for a theory of literary genres. Genre (25:2/3) 1992, 277–313.

3732. Boose, Lynda E.; Flowers, Betty E. (eds).   Daughters and fathers. (Bibl. 1993, 2095.) Rev. by Bernice W. Kliman in ShB (9:2) 1991, 35–6.

3733. Bowman, Michael S.   Performing literature in an age of textuality. CommEd (45:2) 1996, 96–101.

3734. Bradbury, Malcolm (gen. ed.).   The atlas of literature. London; New York: De Agostini, 1996. pp. 352. Rev. by Paul Dean in TLS, 1 Nov. 1996, 12–13.

3735. Bradford, Richard (ed.).   Introducing literary studies. London; New York: Prentice Hall; Harvester Wheatsheaf, 1996. pp. xiv, 768.

3736. Breuer, Horst.   Historische Literaturpsychologie: von Shakespeare bis Beckett. (Bibl. 1992, 2749.) Rev. by Wilhelm Füger in GRM (42:2) 1992, 250–2.

3737. Brittnacher, Hans Richard.   Erregte Lektüre – der Skandal der phantastischen Literatur. GRM (44:1) 1994, 1–17.

3738. Bronfen, Elisabeth.   Over her dead body: death, femininity and the aesthetic. (Bibl. 1995, 2943.) Rev. by Mary Howard in BJECS (19:1) 1996, 102–3.

3739. Brooke-Rose, Christine.   Exsul. PT (17:3) 1996, 289–303.

3740. —— Stories, theories and things. (Bibl. 1994, 2278.) Rev. by Nicolas Tredell in PN Review (18:1) 1991, 60–3.

3741. Brooks, Cleanth.   Community, religion, and literature: essays. (Bibl. 1995, 2944.) Rev. by Irving Malin in SoQ (34:1) 1995, 155–6; by John N. Duvall in ColLit (23:2) 1996, 192–4; by Donald G. Marshall in ChrisL (46:1) 1996, 81–2.

3742. Brooks, Peter.   Storytelling without fear? Confession in law & literature. YJLH (8:1) 1996, 1–29.

3743. Bruce, Donald; Purdy, Anthony (eds).   Literature and science. *See* **62**.

3744. Bryan, Violet Harrington.   The myth of New Orleans in literature: dialogues of race and gender. (Bibl. 1994, 2280.) Rev. by Herman F. Bostick in CLAJ (40:1) 1996, 112–15.

3745. Budd, Louis J.; Cady, Edwin H. (eds).   On humor. (Bibl. 1992, 2754.) Rev. by Kenneth D. Pimple in MidAF (22:1) 1994, 49–50.

3746. Budick, Sanford; Iser, Wolfgang (eds).   Languages of the unsayable: the play of negativity in literature and literary theory. (Bibl. 1995, 2951.) Rev. by Marius Buning in LitTheol (5:4) 1991, 408–10.

3747. Burgess, Moira.   Reading Glasgow: a Book Trust Scotland literary guide to authors and books associated with the city. Edinburgh: Book Trust Scotland, 1996. pp. 76.

3748. BURKE, SEÁN. Authorship: from Plato to the postmodern: a reader. Edinburgh: Edinburgh UP, 1995. pp. xxx, 349.

3749. CALINESCU, MATEI. Rereading. (Bibl. 1995, 2955.) Rev. by Wallace Martin in MFS (40:2) 1994, 455–6; by Rachel Bouvet in CanRCL (21:3) 1994, 506–12; by Margaret Anne Doody in Comparatist (19) 1995, 140–2; by John Burt Foster, Jr, in PT (17:2) 1996, 253–61.

3750. CAREY, JOHN. The canon. Is there an agreed catalogue of great authors and texts? ERev (7:1) 1996, 15–17.

3751. CARPENTER, DAVID. Writing home: selected essays. Saskatoon, Sask.: Fifth House, 1994. pp. xiii, 177. Rev. by Catherine Hunter in CanL (149) 1996, 146.

3752. CARR, HELEN. Inventing the American primitive: politics, gender, and the representation of Native American literary traditions, 1789–1936. New York: New York UP, 1996. pp. 286.

3753. CHÉNETIER, MARC. L'invention de la tradition; ou, L'art d'accommoder les restes. RANAM (29) 1996, 165–82.

3754. CHOI, KYONG DO. Ganeum eui munhak. (Adultery in literature.) JELL (42:2) 1996, 323–33.

3755. CHRISTENSEN, BRYCE J. The family in utopia. Ren (44:1) 1991, 31–44.

3756. CHURCHILL, WARD. Fantasies of the master race: literature, cinema and the colonization of American Indians. Ed. by M. Annette Jaimes. Monroe, ME: Common Courage Press, 1992. pp. 304. Rev. by James McKenzie in NDQ (60:3) 1992, 114–24.

3757. CLARIDGE, LAURA; LANGLAND, ELIZABETH (eds). Out of bounds: male writers and gender(ed) criticism. (Bibl. 1992, 69.) Rev. by Lesley Ferris in Signs (18:1) 1992, 162–72.

3758. CLARK, JOHN R. Vapid voices and sleazy styles. *In* (pp. 19–42) **120**.

3759. CLUNAS, ALEX. Composing in transit. Raritan (13:4) 1994, 92–101.

3760. COELSCH-FOISNER, SABINE; GÖRTSCHACHER, WOLFGANG; KLEIN, HOLGER M. (eds). Trends in English and American studies: literature and the imagination: essays in honour of James Lester Hogg. *See* **125**.

3761. COETZEE, AMPIE. South African literature and narrating the nation. JLS (10:3/4) 1995, 279–301.

3762. COHEN, JEFFREY JEROME. Monster culture (seven theses). *In* (pp. 3–25) **72**.

3763. —— (ed.). Monster theory: reading culture. *See* **72**.

3764. COHEN, LAURENCE ROBERT. Performative power of the language of utopia. ArizEB (34:2) 1992, 33–6.

3765. COLLEY, ANN C. The search for synthesis in literature and art: the paradox of space. Athens; London: Georgia UP, 1990. pp. x, 175. Rev. by Sherrill E. Grace in CanRCL (19:3) 1992, 426–7.

3766. CONLEY, KATHARINE. Automatic woman: the representation of woman in Surrealism. Lincoln; London: Nebraska UP, 1996. pp. xvi, 179.

3767. CONNERY, BRIAN A.; COMBE, KIRK (eds). Theorizing satire: essays in literary criticism. *See* **120**.

3768. CONNOR, KIMBERLY RAE. Conversions and visions in the writings of African-American women. (Bibl. 1994, 2298.) Rev. by Kimberly N. Brown in TSWL (14:2) 1995, 387–9; by Ngwarsungu Chiwengo in SAtlR (61:4) 1996, 123–4.

3769. Cook, Albert.   Canons and wisdoms. (Bibl. 1995, 2967.) Rev. by Robert Langbaum in Review (17) 1995, 1–12.

3770. Cooper, Helen M.; Munich, Adrienne Auslander; Squier, Susan Merrill (eds).   Arms and the woman: war, gender, and literary representation. (Bibl. 1991, 2977.) Rev. by Constance A. Sullivan in Signs (17:2) 1992, 458–61.

3771. Cottom, Daniel.   Ravishing tradition: cultural forces and literary history. Ithaca, NY; London: Cornell UP, 1996. pp. xi, 220.

3772. Crawford, Robert.   Devolving English literature. (Bibl. 1995, 2971.) Rev. by Christian Moser in Archiv (233:1) 1996, 162–4.

3773. Cro, Stelio.   The noble savage: allegory of freedom. (Bibl. 1992, 2772.) Rev. by Richard A. Young in CanRCL (19:3) 1992, 446–8.

3774. Crump, R. W. (ed.).   Order in variety: essays and poems in honor of Donald E. Stanford. *See* **79**.

3775. Cummins, Walter.   'They fancied themselves free': exploration and individualism. WebS (11:2) 1994, 137–47.

3776. Cunningham, Valentine.   If the cap fits: figuring the space of the human. YREAL (12) 1996, 45–63.

3777. Daiches, David (ed.).   The new companion to Scottish culture. Edinburgh: Polygon, 1993. pp. 385. (Revised and updated ed. of bibl. 1987, 2439.) Rev. by Aileen Christianson in SLJ (supp. 43) 1995, 38–41.

3778. Das, Sisir Kumar.   Popular literature and the reading public. IndL (39:5) 1996, 145–52.

3779. Davidson, Arnold E.   The canonization of Canada's women writers. ARCS (19:2) 1989, 203–10 (review-article).

3780. Davidson, Cathy N.; Wagner-Martin, Linda (eds).   The Oxford companion to women's writing in the United States. (Bibl. 1995, 2973.) Rev. by Nicole Tonkovich in NWSAJ (7:3) 1995, 134–9; by Eva-Marie Kröller in CanL (149) 1996, 146–7; by Catharine F. Seigel in ColLit (23:1) 1996, 233–5.

3781. Davis, Cynthia J.; West, Kathryn.   Women writers in the United States: a timeline of literary, cultural and social history. New York; Oxford: OUP, 1996. pp. xvi, 488.

3782. Davis-Goff, Annabel (comp.).   The literary companion to gambling: an anthology of prose and poetry. London: Sinclair-Stevenson, 1996. pp. xix, 246. Rev. by John Mullan in TLS, 27 Dec. 1996, 36.

3783. Dayal, Samir.   Diaspora and double consciousness. JMMLA (29:1) 1996, 46–62.

3784. Dean, John.   American popular culture / La culture populaire américaine. Nancy: Presses Universitaires de Nancy, 1992. pp. 276. (Univers anglo-américain.) Rev. by André J. M. Prévos in JPC (29:2) 1995, 258–9.

3785. Deane, Seamus (gen. ed.); Carpenter, Andrew; Williams, Jonathan (assoc. eds).   The Field Day anthology of Irish writing: vol. 1. (Bibl. 1995, 2977.) Rev. by Evelyn Toynton in ASch (62:2) 1993, 283–92.

3786. ————— The Field Day anthology of Irish writing: vol. 2. (Bibl. 1995, 2978.) Rev. by Evelyn Toynton in ASch (62:2) 1993, 283–92.

3787. ———————— The Field Day anthology of Irish writing: vol. 3. (Bibl. 1995, 2979.) Rev. by Evelyn Toynton in ASch (62:2) 1993, 283–92.

3788. DE GROOT, H. B.; LEGGATT, ALEXANDER (eds). Craft and tradition: essays in honour of William Blissett. *See* **16**.

3789. DELANY, SAMUEL R. Silent interviews: on language, race, sex, science fiction, and some comics: a collection of written interviews. (Bibl. 1995, 2980.) Rev. by Heather MacLean in Extrapolation (36:2) 1995, 163–5.

3790. DELLAMORA, RICHARD. Apocalyptic overtures: sexual politics and the sense of an ending. (Bibl. 1994, 2311.) Rev. by Eric Savoy in ESCan (22:3) 1996, 361–4.

3791. DENBY, DAVID. Great books: my adventures with Homer, Rousseau, Woolf, and other indestructible writers of the Western world. New York: Simon & Schuster, 1996. pp. 492. Rev. by David Damrosch in BkW, 29 Sept. 1996, 3, 14.

3792. DENHAM, ROBERT D. (ed.). Reading the world: selected writings, 1935–1976. By Northrop Frye. (Bibl. 1995, 2982.) Rev. by Jonathan Hart in CanRCL (20:1/2) 1993, 139–71.

3793. DiGAETANI, JOHN LOUIS (ed.). Money: lure, lore, and literature. *See* **71**.

3794. DIMOCK, WAI-CHEE. Residues of justice: literature, law, philosophy. Berkeley; London: California UP, 1996. pp. xi, 278.

3795. DOCHERTY, THOMAS. Big texts: a critique of literary economy. YES (26) 1996, 249–59.

3796. DOLLIMORE, JONATHAN. Sexual dissidence: Augustine to Wilde, Freud to Foucault. (Bibl. 1994, 2313.) Rev. by Colleen Lamos in Signs (19:3) 1994, 826–30.

3797. DONOGHUE, DENIS. England, their England: commentaries on English language and literature. (Bibl. 1988, 1473.) Rev. by Frederick Pollack in Salmagundi (88/89) 1990/91, 486–509.

3798. DONOVAN, KATIE; JEFFARES, A. NORMAN; KENNELLY, BRENDAN (sels). Ireland's women: writings past and present. London: Kyle Cathie, 1994; New York: Norton, 1995. pp. xxiii, 552. Rev. by P.C. in TLS, 27 Sept. 1996, 32.

3799. DOTTERER, RONALD; BOWERS, SUSAN (eds). Gender, culture, and the arts: women, the arts, and society. *See* **37**.

3800. ———————— Sexuality, the female gaze, and the arts: women, the arts, and society. *See* **109**.

3801. DUBBELD, C. E. Text and reception in Southern Africa: a select bibliography of journal articles & interviews published in Southern Africa, 1995. Current Writing (8:1) 1996, 126–33.

3802. DuPLESSIS, RACHEL BLAU. The pink guitar: writing as feminist practice. (Bibl. 1994, 2316.) Rev. by Jeanne Heuving in ConLit (37:2) 1996, 317–24.

3803. EBERSOLE, GARY L. Captured by texts: Puritan to postmodern images of Indian captivity. Charlottesville; London: Virginia UP, 1995. pp. viii, 322. (Studies in religion and culture.) Rev. by David Murray in JAStud (30:2) 1996, 330–1.

3804. EGGERT, PAUL. Making sense of multiple authorship. Text (Ann Arbor) (8) 1995, 305–23 (review-article).

3805. ELDRIDGE, RICHARD (ed.). Beyond representation: philosophy and poetic imagination. Cambridge; New York: CUP, 1996.

pp. xii, 306. (Cambridge studies in philosophy and the arts.) Rev. by John Kerrigan in TLS, 18 Oct. 1996, 26.

3806.   ELIOT, SIMON.   The Reading Experience Database (RED). SHARP News (2:4) 1993, 1–3.

3807.   ESROCK, ELLEN J.   The reader's eye: visual imaging as reader response. (Bibl. 1994, 2322.) Rev. by Stefan Horlacher in ZAA (44:1) 1996, 94–6.

3808.   FADERMAN, LILLIAN (ed.).   Chloe plus Olivia: an anthology of lesbian literature from the seventeenth century to the present. London: Viking, 1994. pp. xxvii, 812. Rev. by V.C. in TLS, 31 May 1996, 30.

3809.   FARMER, PENELOPE.   Two; or, The book of twins and doubles: an autobiographical anthology. London: Virago Press, 1996. pp. viii, 482. Rev. by Claire Harman in TLS, 28 June 1996, 31.

3810.   FAULKNER, DONALD W. (ed.).   New England writers and writing. By Malcolm Cowley. Hanover, NH; London: UP of New England, 1996. pp. xx, 313. (Library of New England.)

3811.   FAUSETT, DAVID.   Writing the new world: imaginary voyages and utopias of the great southern land. (Bibl. 1995, 2994.) Rev. by James R. Burns in EMLS (2:2) 1996, 11.1–7.

3812.   FEICHTINGER, BARBARA.   Die eine und die vielen: Identität und Variation im literarischen Kleopatra-Bild von der Antike bis zu Shakespeare. LJGG (37) 1996, 89–111.

3813.   FENDER, STEPHEN.   Sea changes: British emigration and American literature. (Bibl. 1995, 2996.) Rev. by Benjamin Goluboff in AmS (34:2) 1993, 118–19; by Moses Rischin in AHR (99:2) 1994, 634.

3814.   FILMER-DAVIES, CATH.   King Arthur in the marketplace, King Arthur in the myth. Mythlore (21:3) 1996, 12–16.

3815.   FINNEY, GAIL.   Unity in difference? An introduction. *In* (pp. 1–13) **64**.

3816.   —— (ed.).   Look who's laughing: gender and comedy. *See* **64**.

3817.   FIORENTINO, DANIELE.   Dai mondo sotterranei alla luce: l'universo nel racconto degli Indiani d'America. Àcoma (2) 1994, 50–6.

3818.   FITZ, EARL E.   Rediscovering the New World: inter-American literature in a comparative context. (Bibl. 1992, 2794.) Rev. by George Lang in CanRCL (20:1/2) 1993, 105–24.

3819.   FOX, RICHARD WIGHTMAN; LEARS, T. J. JACKSON (eds).   The power of culture: critical essays in American history. *See* **88**.

3820.   FRANKLIN, COLIN.   Book collecting as one of the fine arts, and other essays. *See* **273**.

3821.   FREESE, PETER.   Universality *vs* ethnocentricity; or, The literary canon in a multicultural society. ZAA (44:2) 1996, 155–70.

3822.   FRIEDLAND, M. L. (ed.).   Rough justice: essays on crime in literature. *See* **105**.

3823.   FRIEDMAN, BARTON R., *et al.*   Bibliography: relations of literature and science, 1994. Configurations (4:2) 1996, 251–310.

3824.   FRYE, NORTHROP.   Myth and metaphor: selected essays, 1974–1988. Ed. by Robert D. Denham. (Bibl. 1991, 2995.) Rev. by Jonathan Hart in CanRCL (19:1/2) 1992, 119–54.

3825.   FURST, LILIAN R. (ed.).   Realism. London; New York: Longman, 1992. pp. ix, 350. (Modern literatures in perspective.) Rev. by Peter Faulkner in RES (46:182) 1995, 305–6.

3826.   —— GRAHAM, PETER W. (eds).   Disorderly eaters: texts in self-empowerment. *See* **24**.

3827. GALE, STEVEN H. (ed.). Encyclopedia of British humorists: Geoffrey Chaucer to John Cleese. New York; London: Garland, 1996. 2 vols. pp. xxxii, 1307. (Garland reference library of the humanities, 906.)

3828. GASS, WILLIAM H. Finding a form: essays. New York: Knopf, 1996. pp. x, 354.

3829. —— I've got a little list. Salmagundi (109/110) 1996, 20–38. (Lists in literary works.)

3830. GELFANT, BLANCHE H. Cross-cultural reckonings: a triptych of Russian, American, and Canadian texts. (Bibl. 1995, 3002.) Rev. by Ellen Pifer in AL (68:1) 1996, 279–80.

3831. GÉRARD, ALBERT S., *et al.* Comparative literature and African literatures. Ed. by C. F. Swanepoel. Pretoria: Via Afrika, 1993. pp. 273. Rev. by Robert P. Smith, Jr, in WLT (69:2) 1995, 415–16.

3832. GERRARD, CHRISTINE. Parody. ERev (5:4) 1995, 20–4.

3833. GILBERT, SANDRA M.; GUBAR, SUSAN (comps). The Norton anthology of literature by women: the traditions in English. (Bibl. 1988, 1490.) New York; London: Norton, 1996. pp. xxxviii, 2452. (Second ed.: first ed. 1985.)

3834. GILLESPIE, GERALD. The city of wo/man: labyrinth, wilderness, garden. CompCrit (18) 1996, 107–25.

3835. —— The relevance of irrelevance: games and puzzles in the humoristic tradition since the Renaissance. JLS (11:3/4) 1996, 62–81.

3836. —— The spaces of truth and cathedral window light. Literator (17:3) 1996, 93–118.

3837. GILLOOLY, EILEEN. Women and humor. Feminist Studies (17:3) 1991, 473–92 (review-article).

3838. GLADSKY, THOMAS S. Princes, peasants, and other Polish selves: ethnicity in American literature. (Bibl. 1995, 3004.) Rev. by Michael Munley in MFS (40:1) 1994, 145–7.

3839. GLOTFELTY, CHERYLL; FROMM, HAROLD (eds). The ecocriticism reader: landmarks in literary ecology. Athens; London: Georgia UP, 1996. pp. xxxvii, 415. Rev. by Simon Estok in CanRCL (23:4) 1996, 1241–4.

3840. GODZICH, WLAD. The culture of literacy. (Bibl. 1995, 3007.) Rev. by Theodore Ziolkowski in WLT (69:2) 1995, 446–7; by Daniel T. O'Hara in AnnS (11:1/2) 1996, 175–91.

3841. GOETSCH, PAUL. Mündliches Wissen in neuzeitlicher Literatur. *In* (pp. 17–35) **73**.

3842. —— Die Rolle der mündlichen Tradition bei der literarischen Konstruktion sozialer Identität. *In* (pp. 289–302) **73**.

3843. GOLDIE, TERRY. Fear and temptation: the image of the indigene in Canadian, Australian, and New Zealand literatures. (Bibl. 1994, 2342.) Rev. by Robin McGrath in ARCS (20:4) 1990, 523–5.

3844. GOLLNICK, JAMES (ed.). Comparative studies in Merlin from the Vedas to C. G. Jung. *See* **15**.

3845. GOODHART, SANDOR. Sacrificing commentary: reading the end of literature. Baltimore, MD; London: Johns Hopkins UP, 1996. pp. xiv, 362.

3846. GOODRICH, PETER H. The alchemical Merlin. *In* (pp. 91–110) **15**.

3847. GRAY, PAUL H. The thoroughbred and the four-wheeled cab: performance beyond literature. CommEd (45:2) 1996, 102–7.

3848. GREENHILL, PAULINE.   True poetry: traditional and popular verse in Ontario. *See* **3399**.

3849. GRIFFIN, DUSTIN.   Satire: a critical reintroduction. (Bibl. 1995, 3010.) Rev. by J. Douglas Canfield in ECS (29:3) 1996, 330–2.

3850. GRIFFIN, EDWARD M.   Something else in place of all that. AmS (35:2) 1994, 5–19.

3851. GRIFFITHS, BILL.   Meet the dragon: an introduction to Beowulf's adversary. Loughborough: Heart of Albion Press, 1996. pp. 47.

3852. GROSS, ROBERT A.   *The Cambridge History of American Literature.* *See* **278**.

3853. GUILLORY, JOHN.   Cultural capital: the problem of literary canon formation. (Bibl. 1995, 3011.) Rev. by Herbert Lindenberger in Comparatist (18) 1994, 165–9; by Thomas Reinert in MFS (42:1) 1996, 221–4; by Daniel T. O'Hara in AnnS (11:1/2) 1996, 175–91.

3854. GURNAH, ABDULRAZAK (ed.).   Essays on African writing: 1, A re-evaluation. Oxford; Portsmouth, NH: Heinemann, 1993. Rev. by Joseph John in WLT (69:2) 1995, 414–15.

3855. GUTLEBEN, CHRISTIAN.   English academic satire from the Middle Ages to the postmodern: distinguishing the comic from the satiric. *In* (pp. 133–47) **120**.

3856. GUTWIRTH, MARCEL.   Laughing matter: an essay on the comic. (Bibl. 1993, 2149.) Rev. by Stuart M. Tave in CL (48:2) 1996, 181–3.

3857. HADFIELD, ANDREW; McVEAGH, JOHN (eds).   Strangers to that land: British perceptions of Ireland from the Reformation to the Famine. Gerrards Cross: Smythe, 1994. pp. xii, 315. (Ulster editions and monographs, 5.)

3858. HAMMOND, PAUL.   Love between men in English literature. Basingstoke: Macmillan; New York: St Martin's Press, 1996. pp. xv, 255, (plates) 4.

3859. HARLOW, BARBARA.   Barred: women, writing, and political detention. (Bibl. 1993, 2152.) Rev. by Stanlie M. James in Signs (21:2) 1996, 467–71.

3860. HARMON, WILLIAM; HOLMAN, C. HUGH.   A handbook to literature. (Bibl. 1992, 2828.) Upper Saddle River, NJ: Prentice Hall, 1996. pp. ix, 669. (Seventh ed.: first ed. 1936.)

3861. HASCHAK, PAUL G.   Utopian/dystopian literature: a bibliography of literary criticism. (Bibl. 1995, 3019.) Rev. by Toby Widdicombe in AEB (9:1/2) 1995, 58–60; in Scriblerian (28:1/2) 1995/96, 99.

3862. HAWKINS, HARRIETT.   The general dynamics of desire. CritS (8:3) 1996, 233–45.

3863. HAWKINS-DADY, MARK (ed.).   Reader's guide to literature in English. London; Chicago: Fitzroy Dearborn, 1996. pp. xxxix, 970. Rev. by Paul Dean in TLS, 1 Nov. 1996, 12–13.

3864. HAYES, ELIZABETH T. (ed.).   Images of Persephone: feminist readings in Western literature. *See* **46**.

3865. HEDGES, INEZ.   Breaking the frame: film language and the experience of limits. Bloomington: Indiana UP, 1991. pp. xvi, 160. Rev. by Richard W. McCormick in Signs (18:1) 1992, 173–87.

3866. HIDALGO, PILAR.   The New Historicism and its female discontents. *In* (pp. 131–48) **38**.

3867. HIGONNET, MARGARET R.   New cartographies: an introduction. *In* (pp. 1–19) **97**.

3868. —— Templeton, Joan (eds). Reconfigured spheres: feminist explorations of literary space. *See* **97**.

3869. Hodgkinson, Tom; De Abaitua, Matthew (eds). The idler's companion: an anthology of lazy literature. London: Fourth Estate, 1996. pp. 176. Rev. by Giles Foden in TLS, 22 Nov. 1996, 7.

3870. Hogan, Robert, *et al.* (eds). Dictionary of Irish literature. (Bibl. 1984, 2133.) Westport, CT; London: Greenwood Press, 1996. 2 vols. pp. xx, 1413. (Revised and expanded ed.: first ed. 1979.)

3871. Holloway, Karla F. C. Moorings and metaphors: figures of culture and gender in Black women's literature. (Bibl. 1995, 3024.) Rev. by Carolyn Richardson Hodges in Comparatist (17) 1993, 154–7; by Akasha (Gloria) Hull in Signs (19:3) 1994, 762–5.

3872. Hölscher, Lucian. Utopie. *See* **2187**.

3873. Horton, John. Life, literature and ethical theory: Martha Nussbaum on the role of the literary imagination in ethical thought. *In* (pp. 70–97) **63**.

3874. —— Baumeister, Andrea T. Literature, philosophy and political theory. *In* (pp. 1–31) **63**.

3875. —— —— (eds). Literature and the political imagination. *See* **63**.

3876. Howe, Irving. The self in literature. Salmagundi (90/91) 1991, 56–71.

3877. Hunter, J. Paul. Editing for the classroom: texts in contexts. *See* **688**.

3878. Islam, Syed Manzurul. Ethics of travel: from Marco Polo to Kafka. Manchester; New York: Manchester UP, 1996. pp. ix, 240. Rev. by A.H. in TLS, 29 Nov. 1996, 32.

3879. Jackson, Guida M. Traditional epics: a literary companion. Oxford; New York: OUP, 1995. pp. xviii, 732.

3880. Jackson, Laura (Riding). The human being in literature. DQ (31:1) 1996, 37–9.

3881. Jeffares, A. Norman. Images of invention: essays on Irish writing. Gerrards Cross: Smythe, 1996. pp. x, 351. (Irish literary studies, 46.) Rev. by Norman Vance in TLS, 27 Sept. 1996, 13.

3882. Jensen, Ejner J. Comedy and the human community. CR (40:3) 1996, 517–25.

3883. Johnson, Christopher; Lung, Eve. Arthur: the legend unveiled. *See* **3241**.

3884. Jordan, Casper LeRoy. A bibliographical guide to African-American women writers. (Bibl. 1995, 3033.) Rev. by Craig Werner in AAR (29:3) 1995, 509–10.

3885. Kantak, V. Y. In search of a valid response to literature. In-between (1:2) 1992, 125–40.

3886. Kaplan, Caren. Questions of travel: postmodern discourses of displacement. Durham, NC; London: Duke UP, 1996. pp. xv, 238. (Post-contemporary interventions.)

3887. Kaplan, Carey; Rose, Ellen Cronan. The canon and the common reader. (Bibl. 1995, 3036.) Rev. by Paula Marantz Cohen in NWSAJ (4:3) 1992, 379–82.

3888. Kato, Fumihiko. Bungakushi to text. (The history of literature and texts.) Kyoto: Nakanishiya Shuppan, 1996. pp. viii, 260.

3889. Kernan, Alvin. The death of literature. (Bibl. 1995, 3042.) Rev. by Steven G. Kellman in GetR (4:2) 1991, 283–91.

3890. KEROES, JO.   Half someone else's: theories, stories, and the conversation of literature. Reader (25) 1991, 1–15.

3891. KESTER-SHELTON, PAMELA (ed.).   Feminist writers. Foreword by Hortense Spillers. Detroit, MI: St James Press, 1996. pp. xxiii, 641.

3892. KRAJKA, WIESŁAW.   Nationalism and sexuality: crises of identity. ZRL (38:1/2) 1995, 113–20.

3893. KUYKENDALL, SUE.   Reinventing the empowered self: feminine adventures in masculinity. ColLit (23:1) 1996, 193–203 (review-article).

3894. LACY, NORRIS J. (ed.)   The new Arthurian encyclopedia. (Bibl. 1991, 3610.) New York; London: Garland, 1996. pp. xxxviii, 615. (Garland reference library of the humanities, 931.) (Updated ed: first ed. 1986.)

3895. LANDMAN, JANET.   'To break the sea frozen inside': transformative effects of literature. Reader (27) 1992, 1–11.

3896. LANDRY, DONNA.   Mud, blood, and muck: country filth. Genre (27:4) 1994, 315–32.

3897. LANGENHORST, GEORG.   Hiob unser Zeitgenosse: die literarische Hiob-Rezeption im 20. Jahrhundert als theologische Herausforderung. Mainz: Grünewald, 1994. pp. 448. (Theologie und Literatur, 1.) Rev. by Hans Otto Horch in Aschkenas (6:1) 1996, 229–30.

3898. LEADER, ZACHARY.   Writer's block. (Bibl. 1994, 2394.) Rev. by Steven G. Kellman in GetR (4:2) 1991, 283–91.

3899. LECKER, ROBERT.   Canadian canons: essays in literary value. *See* **13**.

3900. —— Introduction. *In* (pp. 3–16) **13**.

3901. LEDWON, LENORA (ed.).   Law and literature: text and theory. New York; London: Garland, 1996. pp. xv, 501. (Garland reference library of the humanities, 1784.) (Cf. bibl. 1993, 7689.)

3902. LEEMING, DAVID ADAMS; DROWNE, KATHLEEN MORGAN. Encyclopedia of allegorical literature. Santa Barbara, CA: ABC-CLIO, 1996. pp. ix, 326. (ABC-CLIO literary companion.)

3903. LEITHAUSER, BRAD.   Penchants & places: essays and criticism. New York: Knopf, 1995. pp. x, 289. Rev. by Catherine Kord in AR (54:1) 1996, 108.

3904. LEVINE, MICHAEL G.   Writing through repression: literature, censorship, psychoanalysis. (Bibl. 1994, 2398.) Rev. by Susan Derwin in MFS (42:1) 1996, 250–2.

3905. LEVITT, MORTON P., *et al.*   1988 annual review. JML (16:2/3) 1988/89, 185–456.

3906. —— 1991–1992 annual review double issue. JML (19:3/4) 1996, 351–554.

3907. LEWES, DARBY.   Utopian sexual landscapes: an annotated checklist of British somatopias. Utopian Studies (7:2) 1996, 167–95.

3908. LICHTMAN, SUSAN A.   The female hero in women's literature and poetry. Lewiston, NY; Lampeter: Mellen Press, 1996. pp. 81. (Women's studies, 10.)

3909. LIMB, PETER; VOLET, JEAN-MARIE.   Bibliography of African literatures. Lanham, MD; London: Scarecrow Press, 1996. pp. xxiii, 433. (Scarecrow area bibliographies, 10.)

3910. LINDENBERGER, HERBERT.   The history in literature: on value, genre, institutions. (Bibl. 1995, 3053.) Rev. by Suzann Bick in AR (49:2) 1991, 300–1.

3911. LLOYD, ROSEMARY. Closer & closer apart: jealousy in literature. (Bibl. 1995, 3056.) Rev. by John Bayley in TLS, 19 Apr. 1996, 3–4.

3912. LOGGIA, MARJORIE; YOUNG, GLENN (eds). The collected work of Harold Clurman: six decades of commentary on theatre, dance, music, film, arts, and letters. New York: Applause, 1994. pp. xiii, 1101. Rev. by Morris Freedman in ASch (64:3) 1995, 444–8.

3913. LUTWACK, LEONARD. Birds in literature. (Bibl. 1995, 3057.) Rev. by Mark Christhilf in ModAge (38:3) 1996, 287–9.

3914. MADSEN, DEBORAH L. Allegory in America: from Puritanism to postmodernism. Basingstoke: Macmillan; New York: St Martin's Press, 1996. pp. ix, 193. (Studies in literature and religion.) Rev. by Val Gough in JAStud (30:3) 1996, 495–6.

3915. MAFFI, MARIO. 'The subway and the cellar': breve viaggio nei sotterranei d'America. Àcoma (2) 1994, 16–21.

3916. MAGES, MICHAEL J. The dark stain: the role of innate depravity in American literature, 1620–1940. Bethesda, MD: Austin & Winfield, 1996. pp. 363.

3917. MALZAHN, MANFRED. Between the kailyard and the world revolution: configurations of Scottish culture. SLJ (23:2) 1996, 54–68.

3918. MANCOFF, DEBRA N. Rex quondam rexque ens. Quondam et Futurus (2:3) 1992, 55–68.

3919. MANLOVE, COLIN. Christian fantasy: from 1200 to the present. (Bibl. 1994, 2410.) Rev. by Nancy-Lou Patterson in Mythlore (19:2) 1993, 38–9.

3920. MARSH, KATE (ed.). Writers and their houses: a guide to the writers' houses of England, Scotland, Wales and Ireland: essays by modern writers. (Bibl. 1994, 2411.) Rev. by Francis Stead Sellers in BkW, 5 Dec. 1996, 6.

3921. MARTIN, TERENCE. Parables of possibility: the American need for beginnings. (Bibl. 1995, 3066.) Rev. by Armida Gilbert in AL (68:1) 1996, 233–5; by Kevin McCarron in CritS (8:3) 1996, 347; by Peter Rawlings in JAStud (30:2) 1996, 292–3.

3922. MELBERG, ARNE. Theories of mimesis. (Bibl. 1995, 3070.) Rev. by Peter Faulkner in NQ (43:3) 1996, 376–7.

3923. MELLARD, JAMES M. Reading 'landscape' in literature. CR (40:3) 1996, 471–90.

3924. METTING, FRED. Exploring oral traditions through the written text. *See* **3426**.

3925. MEYER, WILLIAM E. H., JR. The hypervisual essence of American democracy: a multi-discipline free synthesis. JAC (18:2) 1995, 35–44.

3926. MICHELSON, PETER. Speaking the unspeakable: a poetics of obscenity. (Bibl. 1993, 2194.) Rev. by Kathleen M. Haney in JPC (29:4) 1996, 241–5.

3927. MICHELUCCI, STEFANIA. Cole Street, San Francisco: a conversation with Thom Gunn. QLLSM (8) 1996, 261–88.

3928. MILNER, ANDREW. Literature, culture, and society. New York: New York UP, 1996. pp. vi, 232.

3929. MINER, EARL. Comparative poetics: an intercultural essay on theories of literature. (Bibl. 1990, 2453.) Rev. by Eugene Eoyang in CanRCL (19:4) 1992, 615–20; by Antony Tatlow in CanRCL (20:1/2) 1993, 9–28.

3930. MONTEIRO, GEORGE.   The presence of Camões: influences on the literature of England, America, and Southern Africa. Lexington: Kentucky UP, 1996. pp. 189. (Studies in Romance languages, 40.)

3931. MORRIS, MARY.   Essay on eavesdropping. Agni (43) 1996, 164–70.

3932. MORRIS, PAUL; SAWYER, DEBORAH (eds).   Walk in the Garden: biblical, iconographical and literary images of Eden. Sheffield: JSOT Press, 1992. pp. 327. (Journal for the study of the Old Testament, supp. 136.) Rev. by Hugh S. Pyper in LitTheol (10:4) 1996, 380–1.

3933. MORRISON, TONI.   Playing in the dark: Whiteness and the literary imagination. (Bibl. 1994, 2417.) Rev. by Michele L. Simms-Burton in HemR (13:1) 1993, 98–100; by Thomas Huke in ZAA (42:1) 1994, 81–2; by Donald Klein and Hisham M. Amin in AAR (28:4) 1994, 659–63; by Linda Krumholz in Signs (22:1) 1996, 243–8.

3934. MORSE, RUTH.   Sterile queens and questing orphans. Quondam et Futurus (2:2) 1992, 41–53.

3935. MORSON, GARY SAUL.   Narrative and freedom: the shadows of time. New Haven, CT; London: Yale UP, 1994. pp. xiv, 331. Rev. by Kenneth Womack in Style (30:2) 1996, 361–4.

3936. MULLER, GILBERT H.; WILLIAMS, JOHN A.   The McGraw-Hill introduction to literature. (Bibl. 1985, 2210.) New York; London: McGraw-Hill, 1995. pp. xix, 1148. (Second ed.: first ed. 1985.)

3937. MURPHY, MAUREEN.   Folk narrative motifs in Egyptian, Irish and Native-American folklore and literature. In (pp. 39–52) **60**.

3938. MYRSIADES, LINDA.   Interdisciplinarity, law, language, and literature: a review essay. ColLit (23:1) 1996, 204–16.

3939. NEUMAN, SHIRLEY; KAMBOURELI, SMARO (eds).   A mazing space: writing Canadian women writing. (Bibl. 1989, 40.) Rev. by Arnold E. Davidson in ARCS (19:2) 1989, 205–8.

3940. NEVILLE-SINGTON, PAMELA; SINGTON, DAVID.   Paradise dreamed: how utopian thinkers have changed the modern world. (Bibl. 1994, 2423.) Rev. by Wolfgang Wicht in ZAA (43:3) 1995, 278–80; by Merritt Abrash in Utopian Studies (7:2) 1996, 308–11.

3941. NEWLYN, LUCY.   'Questionable shape': the aesthetics of indeterminacy. In (pp. 209–33) **95**.

3942. NICHOLSON, MERVYN.   Magic food, compulsive eating, and power poetics. In (pp. 43–60) **24**.

3943. NILSEN, DON L. F.   Humor in Irish literature: a reference guide. Westport, CT; London: Greenwood Press, 1996. pp. xvi, 225.

3944. NORDLOH, DAVID J.   General reference works. American Literary Scholarship (1994) 471–7.

3945. NOVY, MARIANNE (ed.).   Cross-cultural performances: differences in women's re-visions of Shakespeare. (Bibl. 1995, 13.) Rev. by Phyllis McBride in ShB (14:1) 1996, 45–6.

3946. NUSSBAUM, MARTHA C.   Poetic justice: the literary imagination and public life. (Bibl. 1995, 3093.) Rev. by David Bromwich in LRB (18:20) 1996, 13–15; by Christopher Hitchens in TLS, 15 Mar. 1996, 9–10; by Thomas Morawetz in YJLH (8:2) 1996, 517–31.

3947. O'DONOGHUE, BERNARD.   Sensibility. ERev (6:4) 1996, 30.

3948. ORODENKER, RICHARD.   The writers' game: baseball writing in America. New York: Twayne; London: Prentice Hall, 1996. pp. xvii, 248. (Twayne's US authors, 663.)

3949. O'SULLIVAN, MAURICE. 'Subtly of herself contemplative': the legends of Lilith. SHum (20:1) 1993, 12–34.

3950. OUEIJAN, NAJI B. The progress of an image: the East in English literature. New York; Frankfurt; Bern; Paris: Lang, 1996. pp. 144. (American univ. studies, IV: English language and literature, 181.)

3951. OZICK, CYNTHIA. Fame & folly: essays. New York: Knopf, 1996. pp. xii, 289.

3952. —— *Portrait of the Artist as a Bad Character* and other essays on writing. London: Pimlico, 1996. pp. 330. Rev. by Bryan Cheyette in TLS, 26 July 1996, 24.

3953. PALMER, FRANK. Literature and moral understanding: a philosophical essay on ethics, aesthetics, education and culture. (Bibl. 1995, 3099.) Rev. by Martin Schiralli in JAE (28:2) 1994, 117–18.

3954. PARKER, PATRICIA. Literary fat ladies: rhetoric, gender, property. (Bibl. 1991, 3060.) Rev. by Patricia Demers in CanRCL (18:2/3) 1991, 327–32.

3955. PATTERSON, JOHN. A dictionary of North Carolina writers: E; F–Gi. NCLR (2:2) 1995, 227–32; (5) 1996, 199–204.

3956. PERKINS, DAVID. Is literary history possible? (Bibl. 1994, 2432.) Rev. by Ethan Bumas in Genre (24:4) 1991, 476–8; by Clément Moisan in PT (14:1) 1993, 228–30; by Robert C. Holub in YCGL (41) 1993, 223–6; by Jeremy Tambling in MLR (90:1) 1995, 120–1.

3957. PERLOFF, MARJORIE. 'Living in the same place': the old mononationalism and the new comparative literature. WLT (69:2) 1995, 249–55.

3958. POLETTO, GIAMPAOLO. Fantastico tra fantasia, soprannaturale e *fantastique*: i contributi dopo Todorov. Quaderni di lingue e letterature (18) 1993, 597–615.

3959. POLLNER, CLAUSDIRK; ROHLFING, HELMUT; HAUSMANN, FRANK-RUTGER (eds). *Bright is the ring of words*: Festschrift für Horst Weinstock zum 65. Geburtstag. *See* **11**.

3960. PORTELLI, ALESSANDRO. '*The power of Blackness*': gli afroamericani, le macchine, e l'energia del sottosuolo. Àcoma (2) 1994, 22–34.

3961. —— *The sky's the limit*: dove comincia e dove finisce l'America. Àcoma (1) 1994, 8–18.

3962. —— The text and the voice: writing, speaking, and democracy in American literature. (Trans. of bibl. 1993, 2220.) (Bibl. 1994, 2438.) Rev. by Harold K. Bush, Jr, in ColLit (23:2) 1996, 181–8.

3963. POWELL, ANTHONY. Miscellaneous verdicts: writings on writers, 1946–1989. (Bibl. 1992, 2920.) Rev. by Alan Rutenberg in ASch (62:4) 1993, 619–22.

3964. PRIESSNITZ, HORST. Neue Nachschlagewerke zur Literatur Australiens. ZAA (41:4) 1993, 357–60.

3965. PRINGLE, DAVID (ed.). St James guide to fantasy writers. New York: St James Press, 1996. pp. xvi, 711. (St James guide to writers.)

3966. PRITCHARD, WILLIAM H. Playing it by ear: literary essays and reviews. (Bibl. 1994, 2440.) Rev. by Anthony G. Medici in Style (30:2) 1996, 357–61.

3967. PRITCHETT, V. S. Complete collected essays. New York: Random House; London: Chatto & Windus, 1991. pp. 1319. (Pub. simultaneously under title *The Complete Essays*.) Rev. by Alan Rutenberg in ASch (62:2) 1993, 296–301.

3968. PURDY, ANTHONY.   Introduction: on science and social discourse. *In* (pp. 5–24) **62**.

3969. QUINONES, RICARDO J.   The changes of Cain: violence and the lost brother in Cain and Abel literature. (Bibl. 1995, 3109.) Rev. by Michael J. Meyer in SteiQ (25:1/2) 1992, 59–61; by Elisheva Schoenfeld in Fabula (34:1/2) 1993, 153–5; by Joel Black in Comparatist (17) 1993, 141–5.

3970. QUIRK, TOM.   Introduction. *In* (pp. 1–10) **7**.

3971. RAGUSSIS, MICHAEL.   Figures of conversion: 'the Jewish Question' and English national identity. Durham, NC; London: Duke UP, 1995. pp. vi, 340. (Post-contemporary interventions.) Rev. by Linda Gertner Zatlin in ANQ (9:4) 1996, 56–8; by Lori Anne Loeb in Albion (28:2) 1996, 307–9.

3972. RICKMAN, H. P.   Philosophy in literature. Madison, NJ: Fairleigh Dickinson UP; London; Toronto: Assoc. UPs, 1996. pp. 197.

3973. RICKS, CHRISTOPHER.   Essays in appreciation. Oxford: Clarendon Press; New York: OUP, 1996. pp. 363. Rev. by Marilyn Butler in LRB (18:15) 1996, 15–16; by Alastair Fowler in TLS, 29 Nov. 1996, 6–7.

3974. RIMMON-KENAN, SHLOMITH.   A glance beyond doubt: narration, representation, subjectivity. Columbus: Ohio State UP, 1996. pp. xi, 160. (Theory and interpretation of narrative.)

3975. ROCKWOOD, BRUCE L.   The good, the bad, and the ironic: two views on law and literature. YJLH (8:2) 1996, 533–58 (review-article).

3976. ROOF, JUDITH.   Come as you are: sexuality and narrative. New York: Columbia UP, 1996. pp. xxxvi, 211.

3977. ROSE, JACQUELINE.   States of fantasy. Oxford: Clarendon Press; New York: OUP, 1996. pp. viii, 188. (Clarendon lectures in English literature, 1994.) Rev. by Edward Said in TLS, 9 Aug. 1996, 7–8.

3978. ROSEN, DAVID.   The changing fictions of masculinity. (Bibl. 1995, 3118.) Rev. by Gavin Schulz in Review (17) 1995, 178–80.

3979. ROSS, MICHAEL L.   Storied cities: literary imaginings of Florence, Venice, and Rome. (Bibl. 1994, 2452.) Rev. by William Blissett in ESCan (22:3) 1996, 368–70.

3980. ROYOT, DANIEL, *et al.*   Foreign scholarship. American Literary Scholarship (1993) 355–407; (1994) 407–69.

3981. —— Scholarship in languages other than English. American Literary Scholarship (1995) 443–508.

3982. RULAND, RICHARD; BRADBURY, MALCOLM.   From Puritanism to postmodernism: a history of American literature. (Bibl. 1994, 2454.) Rev. by Hans-Joachim Lang in ZAA (42:1) 1994, 78–80; by Irena Przemecka in EngS (76:3) 1995, 295–6.

3983. RUSS, JOANNA.   To write like a woman: essays in feminism and science fiction. (Bibl. 1995, 3125.) Rev. by Jeanne Cortiel in MFS (42:4) 1996, 919–21; by Jennifer Johnson in TSWL (15:1) 1996, 170–2; by Lucy Sargisson in Utopian Studies (7:2) 1996, 324–6; by Marleen S. Barr in NWSAJ (8:3) 1996, 181–2; by Heather MacLean in Extrapolation (37:2) 1996, 189–90.

3984. SACHS, VIOLA.   Money and the covenant: the destruction of the American dream. Letterature d'America (50) 1993, 5–17.

3985. SANDERS, JOE (ed.).   Functions of the fantastic: selected essays from the Thirteenth International Conference on the Fantastic in the Arts. *See* **36**.

3986. SCHARNHORST, GARY. General reference works. American Literary Scholarship (1993) 409–13; (1995) 509–13.

3987. SCHEESE, DON. Nature writing: the pastoral impulse in America. New York: Twayne; London: Prentice Hall, 1996. pp. xxi, 227. (Studies in literary themes and genres, 7.)

3988. SCHEIBER, ANDREW J. Mirrors and menageries: criticism, ethnography, and multiculturalism in contemporary literary praxis. *See* **3252**.

3989. SCHENK, LESLIE. The Western canon. WLT (70:2) 1996, 325–8.

3990. SCHOLNICK, ROBERT J. (ed.). American literature and science. (Bibl. 1995, 3133.) Rev. by David W. Noble in AmS (37:1) 1996, 172.

3991. SCHOR, NAOMI. Bad objects: essays popular and unpopular. Durham, NC; London: Duke UP, 1995. pp. xvi, 208.

3992. SCHREIBER, EVELYN JAFFE. Dream visions and stream-of-consciousness: the conscious and unconscious search for meaning. JFA (7:4) 1996, 4–15.

3993. SEABRIGHT, PAUL. The aloofness of liberal politics: can imaginative literature furnish a private space? *In* (pp. 145–69) **63**.

3994. SEALTS, MERTON M. Beyond the classroom: essays on American authors. Columbia; London: Missouri UP, 1996. pp. xvi, 267. Rev. by Thomas Woodson in Cithara (36:1) 1996, 42–3.

3995. SEEBER, HANS ULRICH (ed.). Englische Literaturgeschichte. (Bibl. 1995, 16.) Rev. by Georg Seehase in ZAA (41:2) 1993, 174–7; by Gabriele Helms in CanL (149) 1996, 143–4.

3996. SHARROCK, ROGER. New insights on English authors from Marvell to Larkin: an English variety. (Bibl. 1995, 3138.) Rev. by Roger Pooley in Bunyan Studies (6) 1995/96, 101–3; by Frank McCombie in NQ (43:3) 1996, 371–2.

3997. SHATTOCK, JOANNE. The Oxford guide to British women writers. (Bibl. 1995, 3139.) Rev. by Jacqueline Banerjee in EngS (76:1) 1995, 106–7.

3998. SHATTUCK, ROGER. Forbidden knowledge: from Prometheus to pornography. New York: St Martin's Press, 1996. pp. xiii, 369. Rev. by Robert Alter in TLS, 13 Dec. 1996, 4.

3999. SHAW, HARRY B. The historical pragmatism of Richard K. Barksdale. LHR (13:1) 1994/95, 1–20.

4000. SHAW, JEREMY. The critique of reason in English literature: authoritative seeming and higher rational response. Darmstadt: Dissertations Druck, 1994; Derby: European Inst. Press, 1995. pp. xiii, 301.

4001. SHAWCROSS, JOHN T. The Christ *figura* in some literary texts: image and theme. Cithara (35:2) 1996, 3–17.

4002. SHELL, MARC. Children of the earth: literature, politics, and nationhood. (Bibl. 1995, 3141.) Rev. by Tim Brennan in MFS (40:1) 1994, 201–3; by Danielle Miller in CanRCL (22:2) 1995, 374–7; by Theron Britt in ColLit (23:2) 1996, 171–6.

4003. SHUMWAY, DAVID R. Creating American civilization: a genealogy of American literature as an academic discipline. (Bibl. 1995, 3143.) Rev. by Peter Carafiol in MFS (42:1) 1996, 133–6.

4004. SIMONDS, WENDY; ROTHMAN, BARBARA KATZ. Centuries of solace: expressions of maternal grief in popular literature. Philadelphia, PA: Temple UP, 1992. pp. xiv, 288. (Health, society, and policy.) Rev. by Suzy Beemer in AmP (4) 1994, 114–16.

4005. Simpson-Housley, Paul; Norcliffe, Glen.   A few acres of snow: literary and artistic images of Canada. (Bibl. 1993, 2244.) Rev. by Graeme Wynn in ECanW (55) 1995, 40–50.

4006. Sinclair, Alison.   The deceived husband: a Kleinian approach to the literature of infidelity. (Bibl. 1993, 2245.) Rev. by Bill Overton in Literature and History (5:2) 1996, 92–4.

4007. Sisk, John P.   Last men, mass men, supermen: what is satire good for? Salmagundi (94/95) 1992, 157–68.

4008. Snodgrass, Mary Ellen.   Encyclopedia of satirical literature. Santa Barbara, CA: ABC-CLIO, 1996. pp. xvi, 559. (ABC-CLIO literary companion.)

4009. —— Encyclopedia of utopian literature. (Bibl. 1995, 3149.) Rev. by Kristine J. Anderson in Utopian Studies (7:2) 1996, 341–2.

4010. Spears, André.   Evolution in context: 'deep time', archaeology and the post-Romantic paradigm. CL (48:4) 1996, 343–58.

4011. Spears, Monroe K.   One writer's reality. Columbia; London: Missouri UP, 1996. pp. xi, 129.

4012. Spivack, Charlotte; Staples, Roberta Lynne.   The company of Camelot: Arthurian characters in romance and fantasy. (Bibl. 1995, 3155.) Rev. by Randi Eldevik in JAC (19:2) 1996, 148–9.

4013. Steiner, George.   No passion spent: essays 1978–1995. New Haven, CT: Yale UP; London: Faber & Faber, 1996. pp. xi, 430. Rev. by Andreas Huyssen in LRB (18:15) 1996, 17; by Robert Alter in TLS, 12 Jan. 1996, 23–4.

4014. —— What is comparative literature? CompCrit (18) 1996, 157–71.

4015. Stewart, Stanley.   Canonizing Bloom: a review essay. Cithara (35:2) 1996, 27–33.

4016. Stewart, Susan.   Crimes of writing: problems in the containment of representation. (Bibl. 1995, 3162.) Rev. by Leslie Heywood in MFS (42:4) 1996, 916–17.

4017. Still, Judith; Worton, Michael (eds).   Textuality and sexuality: reading theories and practices. (Bibl. 1994, 81.) Rev. by Catharine Randall in Signs (21:2) 1996, 507–9.

4018. Stillinger, Jack.   Multiple authorship and the myth of solitary genius. (Bibl. 1995, 3163.) Rev. by Paul Eggert in Text (Ann Arbor) (8) 1995, 305–23.

4019. Stock, Robert D.   The flutes of Dionysus: dæmonic enthrallment in literature. (Bibl. 1991, 3095.) Rev. by Nicolas Tredell in PN Review (17:3) 1991, 68–9.

4020. Stonum, Gary Lee.   Themes, topics, criticism. American Literary Scholarship (1993) 341–54; (1994) 393–406; (1995) 429–42.

4021. Storey, Robert F.   Mimesis and the human animal: on the biogenetic foundations of literary representation. Evanston, IL: Northwestern UP, 1996. pp. xxii, 274. (Rethinking theory.)

4022. Stouck, David.   Major Canadian authors: a critical introduction. (Bibl. 1985, 5943.) Lincoln; London: Nebraska UP, 1988. pp. xiv, 330. (Second ed.: first ed. 1984.) Rev. by Vernon R. Lindquist in ARCS (19:4) 1989, 473–4.

4023. Sullivan, C. W., III.   'The Northern thing' reconsidered. JFA (3:3) 1990 (pub. 1994), 21–31.

4024. Sumida, Stephen H.   And the view from the shore: literary traditions of Hawai'i. (Bibl. 1993, 2258.) Rev. by Evelyn Ellerman in CanRCL (19:4) 1992, 668–71.

4025. Summers, Claude J. (ed.).   The gay and lesbian literary heritage: a reader's companion to the writers and their works, from antiquity to the present. (Bibl. 1995, 3164.) Rev. by Jim Marks in BkW, 18 June 1995, 5; by Melinda Kanner in AR (54:1) 1996, 112.

4026. Sundquist, Eric J.   To wake the nations: race in the making of American literature. (Bibl. 1995, 3165.) Rev. by Joy S. Kasson in AHR (99:5) 1994, 1747–8.

4027. Surtees, Angela; Gardner, Steve.   The mechanics of dragons: an introduction to the study of their 'ologies. Mythlore (21:2) 1996, 411–17.

4028. Suzuki, Zenzo.   Igirisu fuushi bungaku no keifu. (The history of satirical literature in Britain.) Tokyo: Kenkyusha Shuppan, 1996. pp. vi, 312.

4029. Teskey, Gordon.   Allegory, materialism, violence. *In* (pp. 293–318) **90**.

4030. —— Allegory and violence. Ithaca, NY; London: Cornell UP, 1996. pp. xiv, 195.

4031. Thacker, Robert.   The Great Prairie fact and literary imagination. (Bibl. 1993, 2266.) Rev. by Frances W. Kaye in ARCS (20:4) 1990, 520–3.

4032. Thomas, Clara.   All my sisters: essays on the work of Canadian women writers. Ottawa: Tecumseh Press, 1994. pp. xv, 380. Rev. by Roxanne Rimstead in ECanW (58) 1996, 60–4.

4033. Toynton, Evelyn.   Themselves. ASch (62:2) 1993, 283–92 (review-article). (Irish writing.)

4034. Trivedi, Harish.   Colonial transactions: English literature and India. (Bibl. 1994, 2486.) Rev. by K. Narayana Chandran in WLT (69:1) 1995, 238; by the same in CamQ (25:2) 1996, 197–200.

4035. Trout, Paul.   Contingencies of canonicity. WebS (13:2) 1996, 86–99.

4036. VanOosting, James.   Acoustic writers and electronic readers: literature through the back door. CommEd (45:2) 1996, 108–11.

4037. van Toorn, Penny.   Early Aboriginal writing and the discipline of literary studies. Meanjin (55:4) 1996, 754–65.

4038. Walker, Nancy; Dresner, Zita (eds).   Redressing the balance: American women's literary humor from colonial times to the 1980s. (Bibl. 1989, 1935.) Rev. by Eileen Gillooly in Feminist Studies (17:3) 1991, 473–92.

4039. Walker, Nancy A.   The disobedient writer: women and narrative tradition. Austin: Texas UP, 1995. pp. viii, 205. Rev. by Cheri Louise Ross in AL (68:2) 1996, 486–7; by Lisa Fry in RMRLL (50:1) 1996, 102–4.

4040. Walker, Steven F.   Landscape as compensation: some multicultural perspectives. SHum (19:2) 1992, 110–25.

4041. Ward, Ian.   Law and literature: possibilities and perspectives. (Bibl. 1995, 3183.) Rev. by Lisa Rodensky in EC (46:4) 1996, 372–81; by Robin Lister in TLS, 19 July 1996, 25; by Bruce L. Rockwood in YJLH (8:2) 1996, 533–58.

4042. WATANABE, TOSHIO.   Yominaosu America bungaku. (Re-reading American literature.) Tokyo: Kenkyusha Shuppan, 1996. pp. viii, 532.

4043. WEINSTOCK, CAROLA; WEINSTOCK, ALEXANDER; WEINSTOCK, CONSTANZE.   Alphabetum auctoris emeriti. *In* (pp. 333–62) **11**.

4044. WEISBERG, RICHARD.   Poethics, and other strategies of law and literature. (Bibl. 1994, 2497.) Rev. by J. U. Anderson, Jr, in SHum (19:1) 1992, 91–4.

4045. WEISSINGER, THOMAS.   Current bibliography. BALF (25:4) 1991, 795–814. (Books about African-Americans).

4046. WELCH, ROBERT (ed.); STEWART, BRUCE (asst ed.).   The Oxford companion to Irish literature. Oxford: Clarendon Press; New York: OUP, 1996. pp. xxv, 614. Rev. by Michael Stephens in BkW, 17 Mar. 1996, 8; by Michael McAteer in Irish Review (19) 1996, 129–32; by Declan Kiberd in TLS, 19 Apr. 1996, 10; by José Lanters in WLT (70:4) 1996, 1006–7; by T. P. Dolan in IUR (26:2) 1996, 385–6.

4047. WHEELER, BONNIE.   The masculinity of King Arthur: from Gildas to the nuclear age. Quondam et Futurus (2:4) 1992, 1–26.

4048. WHITE, EDMUND.   The burning library: writings on art, politics and sexuality, 1969–93. Ed. by David Bergman. (Bibl. 1994, 2499.) Rev. by John Taylor in Salmagundi (111) 1996, 208–12.

4049. WHITE, JAMES BOYD.   Acts of hope: creating authority in litera-ture, law, and politics. Chicago; London: Chicago UP, 1994. pp. xv, 322. Rev. by Linda Myrsiades in ColLit (23:1) 1996, 204–16; by Miller S. Ball in YJLH (8:2) 1996, 465–94.

4050. WHITE, KENNETH.   Scotland, history and the writer. Études Écossaises (1) 1992, 5–20.

4051. WIGET, ANDREW (ed.).   Dictionary of Native American literature. (Bibl. 1994, 2501.) Rev. by Howard Meredith in ChronOkla (74:3) 1996, 338–40.

4052. WILLIAMS, DAVID R.   Critics in the wilderness: literary theory and the spiritual roots of the American wilderness tradition. WebS (11:3) 1994, 120–30.

4053. WIXSON, KELLIE DONOVAN, *et al.*   IASIL bibliography 1995. IUR (26:2) 1996, 356–77. (International Assn for the Study of Irish Literatures.)

4054. WONHAM, HENRY B. (ed.).   Criticism and the color line: de-segregating American literary studies. New Brunswick, NJ: Rutgers UP, 1996. pp. viii, 299. Rev. by Lisa Ruddick in MFS (42:3) 1996, 651–2.

4055. WOTTON, GEORGE.   Knowable communities and communities of readers: reading/writing literature in the new universities. CritS (8:1) 1996, 37–48.

4056. WU, QINGYUN.   Female rule in Chinese and English literary utopias. (Bibl. 1995, 3197.) Rev. by Linda Wong in Utopian Studies (7:2) 1996, 356–8.

4057. WYNNE-DAVIES, MARION.   Women and Arthurian literature: seizing the sword. Basingstoke: Macmillan; New York: St Martin's Press, 1996. pp. viii, 237. Rev. by Marion Shaw in TRB (6:5) 1996, 327–9; by E.A. in TLS, 6 Sept. 1996, 33.

4058. ZILL, NICHOLAS; WINGLEE, MARIANNE.   Who reads literature? The future of the United States as a nation of readers. Cabin John, MD; Washington, DC: Seven Locks Press; National Endowment for the Arts, 1989. pp. 106. Rev. by Catherine Stimpson in JAML (21:2) 1991, 184–6.

4059. ZIOLKOWSKI, THEODORE. Virgil and the Moderns. (Bibl. 1995, 3204.) Rev. by Laurence Lerner in CL (48:2) 1996, 185–8; by W. R. Johnson in CLS (33:1) 1996, 136–40; by Götz Schmitz in Archiv (233:1) 1996, 136–9.

DRAMA AND THE THEATRE

4060. ANON. (ed.). English verse drama: the full-text database. Cambridge: Chadwyck-Healey, 1995. (2 CD-ROMs; 2400 ft 1/2 magnetic tape (1600 bpi).) Rev. by David L. Gants in EMLS (2:1) 1996, 15.1–11.

4061. ASTON, ELAINE. An introduction to feminism and theatre. (Bibl. 1995, 3206.) Rev. by Raimund Schäffner in Forum modernes Theater (11:1) 1996, 112–14.

4062. AUSTIN, GAYLE. Feminist theories for dramatic criticism. (Bibl. 1992, 2986.) Rev. by Steven F. Bloom in EOR (17:1/2) 1993, 198–205.

4063. BAKER, ROGER; BURTON, PETER; SMITH, RICHARD. Drag: a history of female impersonation in the performing arts. (Bibl. 1994, 2507.) Rev. by Thomas Akstens in JDTC (11:1) 1996, 151–3.

4064. BALL, JOHN; PLANT, RICHARD (eds). Bibliography of theatre history in Canada: the beginnings through 1984. Toronto: ECW Press, 1993. pp. xxii, 445. Rev. by Alan Filewod in TRC (15:2) 1994, 207–10.

4065. BARKER, FRANCIS. The culture of violence: tragedy and history. (Bibl. 1995, 3208.) Rev. by Laura Di Michele in Annali anglistica (36:1–3) 1993, 221–7.

4066. BECKERMAN, BERNARD. Theatrical presentation: performer, audience, and act. Ed. by Gloria Brim Beckerman and William Coco. London; New York: Routledge, 1990. pp. xi, 202. Rev. by Harry Keyishian in ShB (11:3) 1993, 46–7.

4067. BENNETT, SUSAN. Theatre audiences: a theory of production and reception. (Bibl. 1994, 2510.) Rev. by Katalin Kürtösi in CanRCL (20:1/2) 1993, 227–9.

4068. BLAU, HERBERT. The audience. Baltimore, MD; London: Johns Hopkins UP, 1990. pp. x, 414. (Parallax: re-visions of culture and society.) Rev. by Scott Cutler Shershow in JDTC (6:2) 1992, 143–7.

4069. BROCKETT, OSCAR. Theatre history, drama, and performance studies: shifting perspectives in the academy. TexPres (15) 1994, 1–10.

4070. BROCKETT, OSCAR G. The essential theatre. (Bibl. 1988, 1573.) Fort Worth, TX: Harcourt Brace, 1996. pp. xi, 495. (Sixth ed.: first ed. 1976.)

4071. BROWN, JOHN RUSSELL (ed.). The Oxford illustrated history of the theatre. (Bibl. 1995, 3212.) Rev. by James Fisher in JDTC (11:1) 1996, 139–40.

4072. BROWNSTEIN, OSCAR LEE. Strategies of drama: the experience of form. New York; London: Greenwood Press, 1991. pp. xxi, 188. (Contributions in drama and theatre studies, 39.) Rev. by Thomas Akstens in JDTC (7:2) 1993, 86–7.

4073. BURKE, SALLY. American feminist playwrights: a critical history. New York: Twayne; London: Prentice Hall, 1996. pp. ix, 270. (Twayne's history of American drama.)

4074. CARLSON, MARVIN.   Theatre semiotics: signs of life. Bloomington: Indiana UP, 1990. pp. xviii, 125. (Advances in semiotics.) Rev. by Katalin Kürtösi in CanRCL (20:1/2) 1993, 225–7.

4075. CASE, SUE-ELLEN (ed.).   Performing feminisms: feminist critical theory and theatre. *See* **84**.

4076. ——— REINELT, JANELLE (eds).   The performance of power: theatrical discourse and politics. *See* **83**.

4077. CLARK, ROBERT.   The new Globe rises. EEM (4:1) 1995, 12–13.

4078. COURTNEY, RICHARD.   Drama and feeling: an aesthetic theory. Montreal; London: McGill–Queen's UP, 1995. pp. xiii, 230. Rev. by Karen Banford in CanTR (86) 1996, 65–6.

4079. DRAKAKIS, JOHN.   Dr Strangelove; or, How I learned to trust in the Globe and set fire to my dreams. EEM (4:1) 1995, 14–16.

4080. ELAM, KEIR.   The wars of the texts. SStud (24) 1996, 81–92 (review-article).

4081. ENGLE, RON; MILLER, TICE L. (eds).   The American stage: social and economic issues from the Colonial period to the present. (Bibl. 1995, 3215.) Rev. by Hans-Joachim Lang in ZAA (42:4) 1994, 401–3; by Alma J. Bennett in JAC (18:1) 1995, 113–14; by Loren Kruger in AmLH (8:4) 1996, 703–5.

4082. FREE, WILLIAM J.   Thinking about theatrical space: place, path, and domain. TexPres (13) 1992, 1–10.

4083. FURTWANGLER, ALBERT.   Assassin on stage: Brutus, Hamlet, and the death of Lincoln. (Bibl. 1993, 2303.) Rev. by Marcia K. Morrison in NETJ (3) 1992, 109–11.

4084. GILBERT, REID.   'My mother wants me to play Romeo before it's too late': framing gender on stage. TRC (14:2) 1993, 123–43.

4085. GURR, ANDREW.   Thinking about the new Globe. EEM (4:1) 1995, 9–11.

4086. HARRIS, MAX.   Theatre and incarnation. (Bibl. 1990, 2195.) Rev. by Richard H. Roberts in LitTheol (5:2) 1991, 248–9.

4087. HAWKINS-DADY, MARK (ed.).   International dictionary of theatre: vol. 2, Playwrights. (Bibl. 1994, 2518.) Rev. by Keith Gore in NQ (43:1) 1996, 94–5.

4088. HAY, SAMUEL A.   African-American theatre: an historical and critical analysis. (Bibl. 1994, 2519.) Rev. by Omofolabo Ajayi in AmS (36:2) 1995, 186–7; by Rena Fraden in AAR (30:3) 1996, 473–6.

4089. HELBO, ANDRE, *et al.*   Approaching theatre. Bloomington: Indiana UP, 1991. pp. ix, 223. (Advances in semiotics.) Rev. by Jerry Dickey in NETJ (3) 1992, 113–14.

4090. HUSTON, HOLLIS.   Flavors of physicality. JDTC (11:1) 1996, 35–54.

4091. HUTCHISON, YVETTE.   Bibliography: articles published in South Africa on theatre and drama in 1994. SATJ (10:1) 1996, 113–14.

4092. JESCHKE, CLAUDIA.   Körper/Bühne/Bewegung: Dramaturgie und Choreographie als theatrale Strategien. Forum modernes Theater (11:2) 1996, 197–213.

4093. JOHNSTON, DAVID (ed.).   Stages of translation. *See* **3153**.

4094. KERR, DAVID.   African popular theatre: from pre-colonial times to the present day. London: Currey; Portsmouth, NH: Heinemann; Nairobi: EAEP; Cape Town: Philip; Harare: Baobab, 1995. pp. x, 278. (Studies in African literature.) Rev. by Harold A. Waters in WLT (70:3) 1996, 745–6.

4095. KERRIGAN, JOHN.   Revenge tragedy: Aeschylus to Armageddon. Oxford: Clarendon Press; New York: OUP, 1996. pp. xv, 404. Rev. by Adam Phillips in LRB (18:18) 1996, 10–11; by Terry Eagleton in TLS, 2 Aug. 1996, 4.

4096. KOBIALKA, MICHAL.   Inbetweenness: spatial folds in theatre historiography. JDTC (5:2) 1991, 85–99.

4097. KRUGER, LOREN.   Our theater? Stages in an American cultural history. AmLH (8:4) 1996, 699–714 (review-article).

4098. LLOYD, DAVID.   Tragedy: a neo-Aristotelian perspective. UES (33:2) 1995, 33–43.

4099. LYÓNS, CHARLES R.   What do we mean when we say character? TexPres (16) 1995, 1–12.

4100. McCALLUM, HEATHER; PINCOE, RUTH (comps).   Directory of Canadian theatre archives. (Bibl. 1993, 2312.) Rev. by John Ball in CanTR (77) 1993, 83–4.

4101. MARTINE, JAMES J.   Drama. American Literary Scholarship (1993) 313–39; (1994) 363–92; (1995) 401–28.

4102. MITCHELL, BEVERLY.   Theater and translation: adaptations across language and space. TexPres (15) 1994, 63–6.

4103. NUTTALL, A. D.   Why does tragedy give pleasure? Oxford: Clarendon Press; New York: OUP, 1996. pp. viii, 110. Rev. by Adam Phillips in LRB (18:18) 1996, 10–11.

4104. OKOCHI, YASUYUKI.   Igirisu engeki shouyou – Shakespeare, Pinter, sonota. (A stroll in the British theatre: Shakespeare, Pinter and others.) Tokyo: Kindai Bungeisha, 1996. pp. 330.

4105. RAYNER, ALICE.   The audience: subjectivity, community, and the ethics of listening. JDTC (7:2) 1993, 3–24.

4106. RICHARDSON, GARY A.   American drama from the Colonial period through World War I: a critical history. (Bibl. 1994, 2531.) Rev. by Daniel J. Watermeier in AmDr (3:2) 1994, 89–93.

4107. ROZIK, ELI.   Categorization of speech acts in play and perform-ance. *See* **2286**.

4108. SCOLNICOV, HANNA.   Woman's theatrical space. (Bibl. 1994, 2533.) Rev. by Beth A. Kattelman in JDTC (10:2) 1996, 121–3.

4109. SHEPHERD, SIMON; WOMACK, PETER.   English drama: a cultural history. Oxford; Cambridge, MA: Blackwell, 1996. pp. xi, 412.

4110. SIDNELL, MICHAEL J. (ed.).   Sources of dramatic theory: 2, Voltaire to Hugo. Cambridge; New York: CUP, 1994. pp. xi, 278. Rev. by David Maskell in NQ (43:2) 1996, 229; by Stevie Simkin in Eng (45:181) 1996, 84–9.

4111. STATES, BERT O.   Tragedy and tragic vision: a Darwinian supplement to Thomas Van Laan. JDTC (6:2) 1992, 5–22.

4112. STOREY, ROBERT.   Comedy, its theorists, and the evolutionary perspective. Criticism (38:3) 1996, 407–41.

4113. STYAN, J. L.   The English stage: a history of drama and performance. Cambridge; New York: CUP, 1996. pp. xvi, 432.

4114. SUCHY, PATRICIA A.   When words collide: the stage direction as utterance. JDTC (6:1) 1991, 69–82.

4115. TAN, PETER K. W.   A stylistics of drama: with special focus on Stoppard's *Travesties*. *See* **2717**.

4116. TRUSSLER, SIMON.   The Cambridge illustrated history of British theatre. (Bibl. 1995, 3238.) Rev. by William Proctor Williams in NQ

(43:2) 1996, 207–8; by Maria DiCenzo in Essays in Theatre (14:2) 1996, 184–6.

4117. Van Laan, Thomas F.   The death-of-tragedy myth. JDTC (5:2) 1991, 5–31.

4118. Wilmeth, Don B.; Miller, Tice L. (eds).   Cambridge guide to American theatre. (Bibl. 1994, 2547.) Rev. by Sam Abel in NETJ (4) 1993, 119–21; by Gary A. Richardson in AmDr (5:1) 1995, 71–7.

4119. Wiszniowska, Marta.   British drama and theatre against contemporary Polish background: a critical reconaissance. PolAS (5) 1994, 73–81.

4120. Wolf, Werner.   Shakespeare und die Entstehung ästhetischer Illusion im englischen Drama. GRM (43:3) 1993, 279–301.

4121. Worthen, W. B.   Of actors and automata: hieroglyphics of modernism. JDTC (9:1) 1994, 3–19.

4122. Zatlin, Phyllis.   Observations on theatrical translation. *See* **3221**.

FICTION

4123. Aldiss, Brian W.   The detached retina: aspects of SF and fantasy. (Bibl. 1995, 3243.) Rev. by Edra Charlotte Bogle in Utopian Studies (7:2) 1996, 213–14.

4124. Alkon, Paul K.   Science fiction before 1900: imagination discovers technology. (Bibl. 1995, 3244.) Rev. by Edward James and Farah Mendlesohn in Extrapolation (36:1) 1995, 83–6; by John Huntington in StudN (28:1) 1996, 114–15.

4125. Almond, Barbara; Almond, Richard.   The therapeutic narrative: fictional relationships and the process of psychological change. Westport, CT; London: Praeger, 1996. pp. xiv, 204.

4126. Anderson, Sarah.   Anderson's travel companion: a guide to the best non-fiction and fiction for travelling. (Bibl. 1995, 3245.) Rev. by Eric Korn in TLS, 26 July 1996, 36.

4127. Anon. (comp.).   Character in fiction. EEM (3:1) 1994, 80. (Mini-checklists, 3.)

4128. —— (ed.).   ECW's biographical guide to Canadian novelists. Toronto: ECW Press, 1993. pp. 252. Rev. by Barbara Pell in ESCan (22:1) 1996, 104–6.

4129. Armitt, Lucie (ed.).   Where no man has gone before: women and science fiction. (Bibl. 1993, 2326.) Rev. by Timmel Duchamp in Signs (17:4) 1992, 848–52; by Ernelle Fife in Extrapolation (36:1) 1995, 67–70.

4130. Armstrong, Nancy.   Desire and domestic fiction: a political history of the novel. (Bibl. 1992, 3032.) Rev. by Greg Laugero in ECS (28:4) 1995, 432–3.

4131. —— Semiotics and family history. AJSem (10:2) 1993, 133–54.

4132. Baldridge, Cates.   The dialogics of dissent in the English novel. (Bibl. 1995, 3247.) Rev. by Daryl S. Ogden in StudN (28:2) 1996, 256–8.

4133. Barnett, Louise K.   Authority and speech: language, society, and self in the American novel. (Bibl. 1995, 3248.) Rev. by Alessandro Portelli in StudN (27:4) 1995, 566–8; by Lionel Kelly in YES (26) 1996, 321–3.

4134. BARNEY, RICHARD A. Subjectivity, the novel, and the *Bildung* blocks of critical theory. Genre (26:4) 1993, 359–75.

4135. BARRON, NEIL (ed.). Anatomy of wonder 4: a critical guide to science fiction. (Bibl. 1995, 3249.) Rev. by Lyman Tower Sargent in Utopian Studies (7:1) 1996, 114–15.

4136. BEAM, JOAN; BRANSTAD, BARBARA. The Native American in long fiction: an annotated bibliography. Lanham, MD; London: Scarecrow Press, 1996. pp. xv, 359. (Native American bibliography, 18.)

4137. BEARE, RHONA. Time travel. Mythlore (21:3) 1996, 33–4.

4138. BEATY, JEROME (ed.). The Norton introduction to fiction. (Sixth ed.: first ed. 1973.) New York; London: Norton, 1996. pp. xvii, 809.

4139. BELL, MICHAEL DAVITT. The problem of American realism: studies in the cultural history of a literary idea. (Bibl. 1995, 3253.) Rev. by Becky Roberts in AmS (35:2) 1994, 146–7; by Daniel H. Borus in ANQ (9:1) 1996, 43–5.

4140. BERMAN, JEFFREY. Narcissism and the novel. (Bibl. 1993, 2333.) Rev. by Catherine Hunter in CanL (149) 1996, 146.

4141. BIRBALSINGH, FRANK. Novels and the nation: essays in Canadian literature. Toronto: TSAR, 1995. pp. xvi, 183. Rev. by Clara Thomas in LRC (5:7) 1996, 25–6.

4142. BOTTING, FRED. The gothic. London; New York: Routledge, 1996. pp. 201. (New critical idiom.) Rev. by R.M. in TLS, 12 Apr. 1996, 32.

4143. BRADBURY, MALCOLM. Dangerous pilgrimages: trans-Atlantic mythologies & the novel. London: Secker & Warburg, 1995; New York: Viking, 1996. pp. x, 514. Rev. by Holly Boren in EC (46:4) 1996, 366–72.

4144. BRANTLINGER, PATRICK. Fictions of state: culture and credit in Britain, 1694–1994. Ithaca, NY; London: Cornell UP, 1996. pp. xii, 291.

4145. BRISTOW, JOSEPH (ed.). The Oxford book of adventure stories. Oxford; New York: OUP, 1995. pp. xxv, 410. Rev. by Richard Phillips in Eng (45:183) 1996, 262–5.

4146. BROSSE, MONIQUE. Le mythe de Robinson. Paris: Lettres modernes, 1993. pp. 151. (Thèmes et mythes.)

4147. BRYANT, MARK (ed.). Sins of the fathers: an anthology of clerical crime. London: Gollancz, 1996. pp. xii, 236.

4148. BUMAS, E. Anthologizing oneself: an extended review of *The Norton Anthology of Short Fiction*, fourth edition, edited by R. V. Cassill. Genre (25:1) 1992, 137–53.

4149. BYATT, A. S.; SODRÉ, IGNÊS. Imagining characters: six conversations about women writers. Ed. by Rebecca Swift. London: Chatto & Windus, 1995. pp. xii, 268. Rev. by Lorna Sage in TLS, 26 Jan. 1996, 25.

4150. CASSILL, R. V. (ed.). The Norton anthology of short fiction. New York: Norton, 1990. pp. xxxii, 1750. (Fourth ed.: first ed. 1978.) Rev. by E. Bumas in Genre (25:1) 1992, 137–53.

4151. CAVALIERO, GLEN. The supernatural and English fiction. (Bibl. 1995, 3264.) Rev. by Kate Behr in NQ (43:1) 1996, 103–5; by Neil Cornwell in EP (21) 1996, 179–81.

4152. CERUTTI, TONI. The reader as artifact: notes from a work in progress. Textus (9:1) 1996, 149–59.

4153. CHOI, JULIE. Fictional objectivity: women novelists 'in' the third person. JELL (42:4) 1996, 855–72.

4154. CLARK, STEPHEN R. L.   How to live forever: science fiction and philosophy. (Bibl. 1995, 3266.) Rev. by Paul Kincaid in Foundation (66) 1996, 119–22; by David Seed in LitTheol (10:3) 1996, 294–5.

4155. CLUTE, JOHN; NICHOLLS, PETER; STABLEFORD, BRIAN (eds).   The encyclopedia of science fiction. (Bibl. 1994, 2562.) Rev. by Nicholas Ruddick in Utopian Studies (7:2) 1996, 241–3.

4156. CORNIS-POPE, MARCEL.   Hermeneutic desire and critical rewriting: narrative interpretation in the wake of poststructuralism. (Bibl. 1995, 3268.) Rev. by Mihai I. Spariosu in CanRCL (22:2) 1995, 361–2.

4157. CORNWELL, NEIL.   Muddle, mystery and alchemy: gothic poetics ride again: a review-article. EP (21) 1996, 174–88.

4158. COX, J. RANDOLPH, *et al.* (comps).   The year's work in dime novels, series books, and pulp magazines 1995. *See* **1250**.

4159. COX, MICHAEL (ed.).   The Oxford book of spy stories. Oxford; New York: OUP, 1996. pp. xix, 356.

4160. ——— ADRIAN, JACK (eds).   The Oxford book of historical stories. Oxford; New York: OUP, 1994. pp. xvii, 441.

4161. CREWS, FREDERICK.   The critics bear it away: American fiction and the academy. (Bibl. 1995, 3269.) Rev. by Margery Sabin in Raritan (13:3) 1994, 132–8.

4162. CURRIE, GREGORY.   The nature of fiction. (Bibl. 1992, 3052.) Rev. by Uri Margolin in CanRCL (19:1/2) 1992, 101–17.

4163. DAVIDSON, ARNOLD E.   Coyote country: fictions of the Canadian West. (Bibl. 1994, 2564.) Rev. by Dick Harrison in MFS (42:1) 1996, 161–4; by Margery Fee in CanL (149) 1996, 128–9.

4164. DE ANGELIS, PALMIRA.   Tra scienza e arte: coincidenze funzionali della storiografia e del romanzo storico. Textus (8:1) 1995, 19–42.

4165. DERWIN, SUSAN.   The ambivalence of form: Lukács, Freud, and the novel. (Bibl. 1995, 3271.) Rev. by David Suchoff in MFS (42:1) 1996, 241–3.

4166. DIYANNI, ROBERT; ROMPF, KRAFT.   The McGraw-Hill book of fiction. New York; London: McGraw-Hill, 1995. pp. xvi, 1236, (plates) 16.

4167. DOLAN, FREDERICK M.   Allegories of America: narratives, metaphysics, politics. Ithaca, NY; London: Cornell UP, 1994. pp. x, 232. (Contestations.) Rev. by Michael Holzman in Criticism (38:2) 1996, 338–42.

4168. DONAWERTH, JANE L.; KOLMERTEN, CAROL A. (eds).   Utopian and science fiction by women: worlds of difference. Foreword by Susan Gubar. (Bibl. 1995, 65.) Rev. by Heather MacLean in Extrapolation (36:3) 1995, 274–7; by Elizabeth Sourbut in Foundation (64) 1995, 114–17; by Maureen T. Reddy in Signs (21:3) 1996, 782–5.

4169. DONOVAN, JOSEPHINE.   Style and power. *In* (pp. 85–94) **33**.

4170. DOODY, MARGARET ANNE.   The true story of the novel. New Brunswick, NJ: Rutgers UP, 1996. pp. xx, 580, (plates) 24. Rev. by Frank Kermode in LRB (18:15) 1996, 14; by Lorna Sage in TLS, 9 Aug. 1996, 5–6.

4171. ELSLEY, JUDY.   Quilts as text(iles): the semiotics of quilting. *See* **3670**.

4172. FEHN, ANN CLARK; HOESTEREY, INGEBORG; TATAR, MARIA M. (eds).   Neverending stories: toward a critical narratology. (Bibl. 1994, 2569.) Rev. by Wilhelm Füger in GRM (44:4) 1994, 481–4; by Wallace Martin in CL (48:1) 1996, 79–81.

4173. FILMER-DAVIES, KATH.   Fantasy fiction and Welsh myth: tales of belonging. Basingstoke: Macmillan; New York: St Martin's Press, 1996. pp. xiii, 177.

4174. FLOCKEMANN, MIKI.   Negotiated readings and emancipatory upheavals: from Fanon's 'colourless literature' to colourful stories by women crisscrossing the Atlantic. English Academy Review (11) 1996, 51–61.

4175. FLOUD, CYNTHIA; FLOUD, SARAH.   Abridgements too far. *See* **1051**.

4176. FRAIMAN, SUSAN.   Unbecoming women: British women writers and the novel of development. (Bibl. 1994, 2573.) Rev. by L. J. Swingle in Review (17) 1995, 109–21; by Mona Scheuermann in StudN (27:1) 1995, 92–3; by Frank G. Nigro in StudN (27:4) 1995, 573–5; by Catherine Maxwell in YES (26) 1996, 295–6.

4177. GABLE, MARIELLA; HYNES, NANCY (ed.).   The literature of spiritual values and Catholic fiction. Lanham, MD; London: UP of America, 1996. pp. xlviii, 277.

4178. GAVIOLI, LAURA.   Discourse forces in conversational stories: entertainment *vs* solidarity. *See* **2625**.

4179. GELDER, KEN.   Reading the vampire. (Bibl. 1994, 2576.) Rev. by Barbara Puschmann-Nalenz in LWU (29:2) 1996, 123–4.

4180. GENETTE, GÉRARD.   Fiction et diction. *See* **2627**.

4181. GILET, P.   Folk tales and science fiction: testing a thesis. Australian Folklore (8) 1993, 142–5.

4182. GILL, PAT.   The conduct of ideology: musings on the origin of the bourgeois self. Genre (26:4) 1993, 461–78. (Conduct books.)

4183. GOODHEART, EUGENE.   Sticks and stones. Agni (43) 1996, 96–104.

4184. GREETHAM, D. C.   If that was then, is this now? *See* **659**.

4185. HAMMOND, BREAN.   The novel also rises. ERev (6:2) 1995, 6–9.

4186. HAROIAN-GUERIN, GIL.   The fatal hero: Diana, deity of the moon, as an archetype of the modern hero in English literature. New York; Frankfurt; Bern; Paris: Lang, 1996. pp. 261. (Writing about women, 21.) (Cf. bibl. 1994, 6783.)

4187. HARTWELL, DAVID G.   Age of wonders: exploring the world of science fiction. (Bibl. 1986, 2838.) New York: Tor, 1996. pp. 319. (Revised ed.: first ed. 1984.)

4188. HENRY, RICHARD.   Pretending and meaning: toward a pragmatic theory of fictional discourse. *See* **2640**.

4189. HILLERMAN, TONY; HERBERT, ROSEMARY (eds).   The Oxford book of American detective stories. New York; Oxford: OUP, 1996. pp. 686. Rev. by Scott Bradfield in TLS, 29 Nov. 1996, 23.

4190. HOFFMAN, MICHAEL J.; MURPHY, PATRICK D. (eds).   Essentials of the theory of fiction. (Bibl. 1990, 9533.) Durham, NC: Duke UP, 1996. pp. xii, 506. (Second ed.: first ed. 1988.)

4191. HOLMAN, DAVID MARION.   A certain slant of light: regionalism and the form of Southern and Midwestern fiction. Introd. by Louis D. Ruvin, Jr. Baton Rouge; London: Louisiana State UP, 1995. pp. 137. (Southern literary studies.)

4192. Ingebretsen, Edward J.   Maps of heaven, maps of hell: religious terror as memory from the Puritans to Stephen King. Armonk, NY; London: Sharpe, 1996. pp. xxxviii, 239. Rev. by Carl Bryan Holmberg in JPC (30:2) 1996, 229–30.

4193. Jacobson, Marcia.   Being a boy again: autobiography and the American boy book. (Bibl. 1995, 3292.) Rev. by Albert E. Stone in AmS (36:2) 1995, 198–200; by James H. Watkins in SAtlR (61:1) 1996, 169–71.

4194. Kadar, Marlene (ed.).   Essays on life writing: from genre to critical practice. Toronto; Buffalo, NY: Toronto UP, 1992. pp. vi, 234. (Theory/culture, 11.) Rev. by Pamela McCallum in CanRCL (21:3) 1994, 516–18.

4195. Kearns, Michael.   Reading novels: toward a cognitive rhetoric. RSQ (26:3) 1996, 17–30.

4196. Keefer, Janice Kulyk.   Under eastern eyes: a critical reading of Maritime fiction. (Bibl. 1989, 2022.) Rev. by Ken MacKinnon in ARCS (18:1) 1988, 115–16.

4197. Kimmel, Lawrence.   Human kind in literature: the ideals of fiction – the fiction of ideals. Analecta Husserliana (49) 1996, 71–8.

4198. Kincaid, Paul.   Very British. Folkestone: British Science Fiction Assn, 1995. pp. 63. Rev. by Andrew M. Butler in Foundation (67) 1996, 124–7.

4199. Korte, Barbara.   Körpersprache in der Literatur: Theorie und Geschichte am Beispiel englischer Erzählprosa. (Bibl. 1993, 2359.) Rev. by Monique Moser-Verrey in Études littéraires (27:1) 1994, 173–5; by Stefanie Köhler in ZAA (43:4) 1995, 363–5; by Gabriele Helms in CanL (149) 1996, 144.

4200. Kundera, Milan.   Testaments betrayed: an essay in nine parts. Trans. from the French by Linda Asher. New York: HarperCollins, 1995. pp. 280. Rev. by Susan Miron in ASch (65:3) 1996, 469–72.

4201. Kuznets, Lois Rostow.   When toys come alive: narratives of animation, metamorphosis, and development. (Bibl. 1994, 2592.) Rev. by Mitzi Myers in ChildLit (24) 1996, 181–7; by Susan R. Gannon in CLAQ (21:1) 1996, 40–2.

4202. Lamarque, Peter; Olsen, Stein Haugom.   Truth, fiction, and literature: a philosophical perspective. (Bibl. 1995, 3296.) Rev. by Denis E. B. Pollard in JLSem (24:3) 1995, 232–6.

4203. Lambert, Ellen Zetzel.   The face of love: feminism and the beauty question. (Bibl. 1995, 3297.) Rev. by Isobel Armstrong in TLS, 31 May 1996, 13.

4204. Langbauer, Laurie.   Women and romance: the consolations of gender in the English novel. (Bibl. 1993, 2362.) Rev. by Natasha Saje in Signs (19:1) 1993, 276–9.

4205. Lanser, Susan S.   Fictions of authority: women writers and narrative voice. (Bibl. 1995, 3298.) Rev. by Ansgar Nünning in ZAA (42:4) 1994, 393–5.

4206. Lodge, David.   After Bakhtin: essays on fiction and criticism. (Bibl. 1995, 3303.) Rev. by Joan Weatherly in SECOLR (18:1) 1994, 90–2.

4207. Lukacher, Ned.   The third wound: Malcolm Bowie, Peter Brooks, and the myth of Actaeon. CL (48:1) 1996, 65–73 (review-article).

4208. McFarlane, Brian.   Novel to film: an introduction to the theory of adaptation. Oxford: Clarendon Press; New York: OUP, 1996. pp. viii, 279.

4209. McLeod, Donald W. (ed.).   Canadian writers and their works: cumulated index: fiction. Toronto: ECW Press, 1993. pp. 102. Rev. by Barbara Pell in ESCan (22:1) 1996, 104–6.

4210. McPherson, Karen S.   Incriminations: guilty women, telling stories. (Bibl. 1994, 2597.) Rev. by Leslie Heywood in MFS (42:4) 1996, 917–19; by Cynthia Hahn in CanL (149) 1996, 139.

4211. Manlove, Colin.   Scottish fantasy literature: a critical survey. (Bibl. 1995, 3305.) Rev. by Lisa Babinec in Edinburgh Review (93) 1995, 214–17.

4212. Marais, Mike.   Colonialism and the epistemological underpinnings of the early English novel. EngA (23:1) 1996, 47–66.

4213. Margolin, Uri.   The nature and functioning of fiction: some recent views. CanRCL (19:1/2) 1992, 101–17 (review-article).

4214. Martin, Graham Dunstan.   How to ruin a novel; or, Modernism, realism and the fantastic. Foundation (66) 1996, 82–92.

4215. Martínez Lorente, Joaquín.   Blurring focalization: psychological expansions of point of view and modality. RAEI (9) 1996, 63–88.

4216. Meaney, Gerardine.   (Un)like subjects: women, theory, fiction. (Bibl. 1994, 2600.) Rev. by Debra Bernardi in MFS (40:2) 1994, 432–4.

4217. Meindl, Dieter.   American fiction and the metaphysics of the grotesque. Columbia; London: Missouri UP, 1996. pp. xi, 234.

4218. Mellard, James M.   Using Lacan, reading fiction. (Bibl. 1994, 2601.) Rev. by Mary S. Gossy in MFS (40:1) 1994, 212–13.

4219. Melling, John Kennedy.   Murder done to death: parody and pastiche in detective fiction. Metuchen, NJ; London: Scarecrow Press, 1996. pp. xiv, 281. Rev. by Patricia Craig in TLS, 11 Oct. 1996, 28.

4220. Mendlesohn, Farah.   Audio books: a new medium for sf? *See* **1069**.

4221. Miller, J. Hillis.   Ariadne's thread: story lines. (Bibl. 1995, 3309.) Rev. by Wallace Martin in CL (48:2) 1996, 180–1.

4222. Mills, Sara; Pearce, Lynne.   Feminist readings/feminists reading. London; New York: Prentice Hall/Harvester Wheatsheaf, 1996. (Second ed.: first ed. 1989.)

4223. Milowicki, Edward J.   The quest for genre: Menippean satire, romance, and the novel. CanRCL (23:4) 1996, 1213–25.

4224. Moglen, Helene.   (Un)gendering the subject: towards a feminist theory of the novel. Genre (25:1) 1992, 65–89.

4225. Moses, Michael Valdez.   The novel and the globalization of culture. (Bibl. 1995, 3311.) Rev. by Michael Gorra in ConLit (37:3) 1996, 501–8.

4226. Muller, Roy.   Names in science fiction and fantasy. *See* **2154**.

4227. Murph, Roxane C.   The Wars of the Roses in fiction: an annotated bibliography, 1440–1994. (Bibl. 1995, 3312.) Rev. by Lorraine Attreed in Albion (28:4) 1996, 679.

4228. Newton, Adam Zachary.   Narrative ethics. (Bibl. 1995, 3313.) Rev. by David Richter in MFS (42:1) 1996, 247–50; by Gary Handwerk in Criticism (38:3) 1996, 485–9.

4229. Nokes, David.   It isn't in the book. TLS, 26 Apr. 1996, 12. (TV adaptations of classic novels.)

4230. NOVAK, MAXIMILLIAN E.   Picturing the thing itself, or not: Defoe, painting, prose fiction, and the arts of describing. ECF (9:1) 1996, 1–20.

4231. NOVY, MARIANNE.   Engaging with Shakespeare: responses of George Eliot and other women novelists. (Bibl. 1995, 3315.) Rev. by Elisabeth Rose Gruner in ANQ (9:1) 1996, 49–51; by Kathryn Walls in AUMLA (85) 1996, 159–60.

4232. O'NEILL, PATRICK.   Points of origin: on focalization in narrative. CanRCL (19:3) 1992, 331–50.

4233. ORR, LEONARD.   Narrative repetition, repetitive narration: a taxonomy. Neohelicon (23:2) 1996, 203–21.

4234. PARKER, HERSHEL.   The *auteur*–author paradox: how critics of the cinema and the novel talk about flawed or even 'mutilated' texts. *See* **779**.

4235. PEDERSEN, E. MARTIN.   Ending the yarn. *See* **3441**.

4236. PERRY, RUTH.   The contribution of gender to the evolution of the novel. MLQ (57:4) 1996, 633–43 (review-article).

4237. PETTIT, ALEXANDER.   A few last words, first. *See* **786**.

4238. PHELAN, JAMES.   Narrative as rhetoric: technique, audiences, ethics, ideology. *See* **2446**.

4239. PIERCE, JOHN J.   Odd genre: a study in imagination and evolution. (Bibl. 1994, 2613.) Rev. by Hank Eidson in Extrapolation (36:1) 1995, 73–6; by Lynn F. Williams in Utopian Studies (7:1) 1996, 141–2.

4240. POLHEMUS, ROBERT M.; HENKLE, ROGER B. (eds).   Critical reconstructions: the relationship of fiction and life. (Bibl. 1995, 12.) Rev. by John M. Lyon in SLJ (supp. 45) 1996, 44–6.

4241. PRINGLE, DAVID.   The ultimate guide to science fiction. (Bibl. 1992, 3105.) Rev. by Roy Shuker in Utopian Studies (7:2) 1996, 320–1.

4242. QUANTIC, DIANE DUFVA.   The nature of the place: a study of Great Plains fiction. (Bibl. 1995, 3330.) Rev. by David Carpenter in AL (68:2) 1996, 489–90; by Liahna Babener in RMRLL (50:1) 1996, 88–91; by Helen M. Dennis in JAStud (30:2) 1996, 286–8; by Mary Ellen Caldwell in NDQ (63:1) 1996, 142–3.

4243. RASHKIN, ESTHER.   Family secrets and the psychoanalysis of narrative. (Bibl. 1995, 3331.) Rev. by Janet Beizer in MFS (40:1) 1994, 206–7.

4244. REED, TONI.   Demon-lovers and their victims in British fiction. (Bibl. 1992, 3110.) Rev. by Pat Kuhel in MidAF (20:2) 1992, 127–9.

4245. REGINALD, ROBERT.   Xenograffiti: essays on fantastic literature. San Bernardino, CA: Borgo Press, 1996. pp. 224. (I. O. Evans studies in the philosophy and criticism of literature, 33.)

4246. REID, IAN.   Narrative exchanges. (Bibl. 1994, 2614.) Rev. by Michael J. Hoffman in MFS (40:1) 1994, 209–10.

4247. RICHETTI, JOHN (ed.).   The Columbia history of the British novel. (Bibl. 1995, 3334.) Rev. by Nicola Bradbury in YES (26) 1996, 304–5.

4248. RICHMOND, E. M.   Annotated bibliography of narrative theory and Renaissance drama. CanRCL (18:2/3) 1991, 393–469.

4249. RICHTER, DAVID H. (ed.).   Narrative/theory. White Plains, NY: Longman, 1996. pp. xii, 330.

4250. RIFELJ, CAROL DE DOBAY. Reading the other: novels and the problem of other minds. (Bibl. 1993, 2385.) Rev. by Irene Kacandes in MFS (40:2) 1994, 453–5; by Kevin McNeilly in CanL (149) 1996, 156–7.

4251. ROBBINS, BRUCE. The servant's hand: English fiction from below. (Bibl. 1995, 3337.) Rev. by James D. Bloom in AnnS (11:1/2) 1996, 193–8.

4252. ROBINSON, FORREST G. Having it both ways: self-subversion in Western popular classics. (Bibl. 1995, 3338.) Rev. by Hugh Egan in AL (68:2) 1996, 492–3.

4253. ROTH, MARTY. Foul & fair play: reading genre in classic detective fiction. (Bibl. 1995, 3341.) Athens: Georgia UP, 1995. pp. 299. Rev. by Kathy DeGrave in MidQ (37:1) 1995, 104–5; by Maureen T. Reddy in ColLit (23:3) 1996, 201–3.

4254. ROWELL, CHARLES H. (ed.). Ancestral house: the Black short story in the Americas and Europe. Boulder, CO; Oxford: Westview Press, 1995. pp. xxxii, 600.

4255. RUESGA, G. ALBERT. Singing and dancing in the baser manner: a plea for the democratization of taste. JPC (29:4) 1996, 117–35.

4256. RUNGE, LAURA L. Gendered strategies in the criticism of early fiction. ECS (28:4) 1995, 363–78.

4257. RUPPERT, PETER. Reader in a strange land: the activity of reading literary utopias. (Bibl. 1989, 2039.) Rev. by Annegret J. Wiemer in CanRCL (18:1) 1991, 86–94.

4258. SADLEK, GREGORY M. Bakhtin, the novel, and Chaucer's *Troilus and Criseyde*. ChauY (3) 1996, 87–101.

4259. SANDERS, JOE (ed.). Science fiction fandom. (Bibl. 1994, 2623.) Rev. by Richard Tuerk in JAC (19:2) 1996, 147.

4260. SCHABERT, INA. In quest of the other person: fiction as biography. (Bibl. 1993, 2396.) Rev. by Wiilie van Peer in CanRCL (20:1/2) 1993, 257–9.

4261. SCHWAB, GABRIELE. The mirror and the killer-queen: Otherness in literary language. *See* **2702**.

4262. SLUSSER, GEORGE; RABKIN, ERIC S. (eds). Styles of creation: aesthetic technique and the creation of fictional worlds. (Bibl. 1994, 2625.) Rev. by Oscar De Los Santos in Extrapolation (36:1) 1995, 79–81.

4263. SMITH, LES W. Confession in the novel: Bakhtin's author revisited. Madison, NJ: Fairleigh Dickinson UP; London; Toronto: Assoc. UPs, 1996. pp. 167.

4264. SMITH, MURRAY. Engaging characters: fiction, emotion, and the cinema. Oxford: Clarendon Press; New York; OUP, 1995. pp. viii, 265.

4265. STATES, BERT O. Dreaming and storytelling. (Bibl. 1995, 3350.) Rev. by Kenneth Gross in CLS (33:2) 1996, 218–21.

4266. STEPHENS, ROBERT O. The family saga in the South: generations and destinies. (Bibl. 1995, 3351.) Rev. by Laurie Champion in AL (68:1) 1996, 265–6; by Jeffrey J. Folks in SAtlR (61:2) 1996, 142–5.

4267. SYMONS, JULIAN (introd.). The art of murder: stories of crime and detection: a select bibliography. London: British Council, 1992. pp. 64.

4268. TABBI, JOSEPH; WUTZ, MICHAEL. Narrative in the new media ecology. Amst (41:3) 1996, 445–64.

4269. TAYLOR, ART. A directory of North Carolina mystery writers. NCLR (2:2) 1995, 232–5.

4270. TURNER, MARTHA A.   Mechanism and the novel: science in the narrative process. (Bibl. 1995, 3358.) Rev. by David Punter in YES (26) 1996, 305–6; by Ansgar Nünning in ZAA (42:4) 1994, 395–7; by Daniel Schenker in StudN (28:1) 1996, 132–5.

4271. WEINSTEIN, ARNOLD.   The fiction of relationship. (Bibl. 1992, 3130.) Rev. by Clayton Koelb in CLS (33:1) 1996, 125–7.

4272. WHITEBROOK, MAUREEN.   Taking the narrative turn: what the novel has to offer political theory. *In* (pp. 32–52) **63**.

4273. WILLIS, CONNIE.   The more and less of writing humorous fiction. WD (76:3) 1996, 32–3.

4274. WILSON, ANNE.   Magical thought in creative writing: the distinctive roles of fantasy and imagination in fiction. (Bibl. 1988, 1570.) Rev. by Mildred Leake Day in Quondam et Futurus (1:4) 1991, 91–4.

4275. WINDER, ROBERT.   The marriage of time & convenience. London: Harvill, 1994. pp. 223. Rev. by Susan Elkin in ERev (5:4) 1995, 36–7.

4276. WOLF, WERNER.   Ästhetische Illusion und Illusionsdurchbrechung in der Erzählkunst: Theorie und Geschichte mit Schwerpunkt auf englischem illusionsstörenden Erzählen. (Bibl. 1995, 3364.) Rev. by Annegret Maack in ZAA (42:3) 1994, 267–70; by Monika Fludernik in PoetA (27:1) 1995, 218–24.

4277. WOODCOCK, GEORGE.   George Woodcock's introduction to Canadian fiction. (Bibl. 1995, 3365.) Rev. by Barbara Pell in ESCan (22:1) 1996, 104–6.

4278. WYATT, JEAN.   Reconstructing desire: the role of the unconscious in women's reading and writing. (Bibl. 1995, 3366.) Rev. by Ellen Cronan Rose in Signs (18:2) 1993, 346–75.

4279. YEAZELL, RUTH BERNARD.   Fictions of modesty: women and courtship in the English novel. (Bibl. 1994, 2637.) Rev. by Robina Barson in Eng (41:169) 1992, 73–7; by Judith Halberstam in Signs (19:1) 1993, 241–4.

4280. ZWINGER, LYNDA.   Daughters, fathers, and the novel: the sentimental romance of heterosexuality. (Bibl. 1995, 3368.) Rev. by Natasha Saje in Signs (19:1) 1993, 276–9.

LITERATURE FOR CHILDREN

4281. ANON.   Who's who of Australian children's writers. Port Melbourne, Vic.: Thorpe in assn with the National Centre for Australian Studies, 1996. pp. xi, 205. (Second ed.: first ed. 1992.)

4282. —— (ed.).   The Arbuthnot Lectures 1980–1989. Chicago: American Library Assn, 1990. pp. viii, 144. Rev. by Susan P. Bloom and Cathryn M. Mercier in ChildLit (24) 1996, 231–4.

4283. ARMSTRONG, FRANCES.   The dollhouse as ludic space, 1690–1920. ChildLit (24) 1996, 23–54.

4284. AVERY, GILLIAN.   Behold the child: American children and their books, 1621–1922. (Bibl. 1995, 3371.) Rev. by Ray Browne in JAC (18:4) 1995, 106; by Julia Wrigley in AHR (101:4) 1996, 1266–7; by Susan R. Gannon in CLAQ (21:3) 1996, 142–4; by Bruce A. Ronda in LU (20:2) 1996, 275–9; by Gillian Adams in Libraries & Culture (31:3/4) 1996, 661–2.

4285. BLAMIRES, DAVID.   Chapbooks, fairytales and children's books in the writings of John Clare: part 1. *See* **3371**.

4286. CLARK, BEVERLY LYON.   Regendering the school story: sassy sissies and tattling tomboys. New York; London: Garland, 1996. pp. viii, 297. (Children's literature and culture, 3.) (Garland reference library of social science, 1060.)

4287. COHEN, MARILYN; REID-WALSH, JACQUELINE.   Early children's books in the McGill University libraries. *See* **466**.

4288. CUMMINS, JULIE.   'Let her sound her trumpet': NYPL children's librarians and their impact on the world of publishing. *See* **917**.

4289. DEMERS, PATRICIA.   Heaven upon earth: the form of moral and religious children's literature to 1850. (Bibl. 1995, 3378.) Rev. by Ruth B. Bottigheimer in ChildLit (24) 1996, 188–92.

4290. DIPPLE, SUE.   Chapbooks: how they be collected by sondrie madde persons, and something of their trew historie, set out for ye delectation of membres of ye Societie for ye Studdy of Children's Bokes. Hodson: Garrett, 1996. pp. 20. (Ye Societie's paunphlettes prynted on Sondrye Occasions, 3.)

4291. DREW, BERNARD A.   The 100 most popular young adult authors: biographical sketches and bibliographies. Englewood, CO: Libraries Unlimited, 1996. pp. xxx, 547.

4292. EDWARDS, KARLENE K.   Fathers and sons in young adult literature. ArizEB (36:1) 1993, 3–8.

4293. FORDYCE, RACHEL (comp.).   Dissertations of note. ChildLit (23) 1995, 271–82; (24) 1996, 241–59.

4294. FOSTER, SHIRLEY; SIMONS, JUDY.   What Katy read: feminist re-readings of 'classic' stories for girls. (Bibl. 1995, 3381.) Rev. by Sherrie A. Inness in NWSAJ (8:3) 1996, 144–53; by M. Daphne Kutzer in LU (20:2) 1996, 288–92; by Laura M. Robinson in ELT (39:3) 1996, 366–9; by Sherrie A. Inness in JPC (30:2) 1996, 204–6.

4295. GOLDTHWAITE, JOHN.   The natural history of make-believe: a guide to the principal works of Britain, Europe, and America. Oxford; New York: OUP, 1996. pp. viii, 386. Rev. by Michele Landsberg in BkW, 5 May 1996, 17.

4296. GOODENOUGH, ELIZABETH; HEBERLE, MARK A.; SOKOLOFF, NAOMI B. (eds.)   Infant tongues: the voice of the child in literature. Foreword by Robert Coles. *See* **48**.

4297. GOODKNIGHT, GLEN.   Is children's literature childish? Mythlore (19:4) 1993, 4–5.

4298. GRISWOLD, JERRY.   Audacious kids: coming of age in America's classic children's books. (Bibl. 1995, 3385.) Rev. by Bruce A. Ronda in CLAQ (20:4) 1995/96, 191–3.

4299. HAMLEY, DENNIS.   Thoughts on narrative, tradition, originality, children, writing, reading … . Signal (79) 1996, 5–16.

4300. HANNABUSS, S.   Provincial themes in early children's books. *See* **941**.

4301. HEARNE, BETSY (ed.).   The Zena Sutherland lectures, 1983–1992. (Bibl. 1993, 2422.) Rev. by Susan P. Bloom and Cathryn M. Mercier in ChildLit (24) 1996, 229–31.

4302. HERZ, SARAH K.; GALLO, DONALD R.   From Hinton to Hamlet: building bridges between young adult literature and the classics. Westport, CT; London: Greenwood Press, 1996. pp. xvi, 127.

4303. HOLLINDALE, PETER; HOWELLS, RHIANON; NEWBY, JACQUI. Re-reading the self: children's books and undergraduate readers. Signal (79) 1996, 62–74.

4304. HUNT, PETER (ed.); RAY, SHEILA (assoc. ed.). International companion encyclopedia of children's literature. London; New York: Routledge, 1996. pp. xv, 923.

4305. KEESHAN, BOB. Books to grow by. Minneapolis, MN: Fairview Press, 1996. pp. 256.

4306. KNOWLES, MURRAY; MALMKJÆR, KIRSTEN. Language and control in children's literature. *See* **2659**.

4307. KOHL, HERBERT R. Should we burn Babar? Essays on children's literature and the power of stories. (Bibl. 1995, 3395.) Rev. by Clare Collins in Cweal (123:7) 1996, 30–1.

4308. LESNIK-OBERSTEIN, KARÍN. Children's literature: criticism and the fictional child. (Bibl. 1995, 3397.) Rev. by Pat Pinsent in CritS (8:1) 1996, 122–4.

4309. LYNN, RUTH NADELMAN. Fantasy literature for children and young adults. (Bibl. 1980, 266.) New Providence, NJ: Bowker, 1995. pp. lxxix, 1092. (Fourth ed.: first ed. 1979.) Rev. by Elaine Ostrey in Utopian Studies (7:1) 1996, 129–31.

4310. MacDONALD, ELEANOR KAY. A window into history: family memory in children's literature. Phoenix, AZ: Oryx, 1996. pp. xiv, 227.

4311. McGILLIS, RODERICK. The nimble reader: literary theory and children's literature. New York: Twayne; London: Prentice Hall, 1996. pp. xi, 230.

4312. MACHET, MYRNA; OLËN, SANDRA; VAN DER WALT, THOMAS (eds). Other worlds, other lives: children's literature experiences: proceedings of the International Conference on Children's Literature, Pretoria, 4–6 April 1995. Pretoria: Unisa Press, 1996. 3 vols. (Univ. of South Africa, Dept of Information Science, Children's Literature Research Unit monographs, 1–3.) Rev. by M. Bester in South African Journal of Library and Information Science (64:4) 1996, 215–16.

4313. MEEK, MARGARET. The constructedness of critics. Signal (81) 1996, 171–88 (review-article).

4314. MONSEAU, VIRGINIA R. Responding to young adult literature. Portsmouth, NH: Boynton/Cook, 1996. pp. xvi, 103. (Young adult literature.)

4315. MYERS, MITZI. The erotics of pedagogy: historical intervention, literary representation, the 'gift of education', and the agency of children. ChildLit (23) 1995, 1–30.

4316. NIKOLAJEVA, MARIA. Children's literature comes of age: toward a new aesthetic. New York; London: Garland, 1996. pp. xii, 239. (Garland reference library of the humanities, 1816.) (Children's literature and culture, 1.) Rev. by Margaret Meek in Signal (81) 1996, 171–88.

4317. NODELMAN, PERRY. The pleasures of children's literature. (Bibl. 1995, 3411.) Harlow; White Plains, NY: Longman, 1996. pp. xvii, 313. (Second ed.: first ed. 1992.)

4318. OLSON, MARILYNN (ed.). Bibliography. CLAQ (21:2) 1996, 54–97.

4319. PERROT, JEAN. Children's literature and the changing status of child readers. Reader (35/36) 1996, 39–54.

4320. PISTOLIS, DONNA REIDY. Hit list: frequently challenged books for children. Chicago: American Library Assn, 1996. pp. ix, 61.

4321. RAY, SHEILA. Books about children's books 1995. Signal (80) 1996, 127–40.

4322. ROLLOCK, BARBARA. Black authors & illustrators of children's books: a biographical dictionary. *See* **240**.

4323. TALLANT, CAROLE; TRIMBLE, FRANK. Participating in the poetry playground: staging the nonsense wordplay in children's poetry. *See* **2716**.

4324. TATAR, MARIA. Is anybody out there listening? Fairy tales and the voice of the child. *In* (pp. 275–83) **48**.

4325. THOMAS, REBECCA L. Connecting cultures: a guide to multi-cultural literature for children. New Providence, NJ: Bowker, 1996. pp. xiii, 676.

4326. TOUPONCE, WILLIAM F. Children's literature and the pleasures of the text. CLAQ (20:4) 1995/96, 175–82.

POETRY

4327. ANON. (ed.). ECW's biographical guide to Canadian poets. Toronto: ECW Press, 1993. pp. 282. Rev. by Cynthia Messenger in ESCan (22:2) 1996, 236–7.

4328. ATTRIDGE, DEREK. Beyond metrics: Richard Cureton's *Rhythmic Phrasing in English Verse*. PT (17:1) 1996, 9–27.

4329. —— A note on Richard Cureton's response. PT (17:1) 1996, 51–4.

4330. —— Poetic rhythm: an introduction. Cambridge; New York: CUP, 1995. pp. xx, 274. Rev. by Tom Barney in LangL (5:3) 1996, 228–30.

4331. AVIRAM, AMITTAI F. Telling rhythm: body and meaning in poetry. (Bibl. 1994, 2659.) Rev. by J. D. Ballam in EC (46:1) 1996, 88–93.

4332. BAHTI, TIMOTHY. Ends of the lyric: direction and consequence in Western poetry. Baltimore, MD; London: Johns Hopkins UP, 1996. pp. viii, 288.

4333. BAKER, DAVID (ed.). Meter in English: a critical engagement. Fayetteville: Arkansas UP, 1996. pp. xxiii, 368.

4334. BAKER, KENNETH (ed.). The Faber book of war poetry. London: Faber & Faber, 1996. pp. xxvi, 598. Rev. by Neil Powell in TLS, 13 Dec. 1996, 24.

4335. —— Unauthorized versions: poems and their parodies. (Bibl. 1990, 2308.) Rev. by C. J. Fox in PN Review (17:3) 1991, 56–7.

4336. BANG, MARY JO (ed.). Whatever you desire: a book of lesbian poetry. (Bibl. 1990, 2309.) Rev. by Patricia Beer in PN Review (17:3) 1991, 56.

4337. BARNEY, TOM. A response to Richard Cureton's *Rhythm and Verse Study*. LangL (4:1) 1995, 49–54. (*Refers to* bibl. 1994, 2665.)

4338. BAXTER, CHARLES. Rhyming action. MichQR (35:4) 1996, 616–30.

4339. BELITT, BEN. The forged feature: toward a poetics of uncertainty: new and selected essays. *See* **3108**.

4340. BERNSTEIN, CHARLES, *et al.* Poetry, community, movement: a conversation. Diacritics (26:3/4) 1996, 196–210.

4341. BLOOM, HAROLD.   Ruin the sacred truths: poetry and belief from the Bible to the present. (Bibl. 1993, 2442.) Rev. by Linda Munk in LitTheol (5:2) 1991, 243–7.

4342. BOWD, GAVIN.   On the Borders: geopoetics, geopolitics. Edinburgh Review (92) 1994, 131–40.

4343. BRADFORD, RICHARD.   The look of it: a theory of visual form in English poetry. Cork: Cork UP, 1993. pp. ix, 197. Rev. by Göran Nieragden in LangL (4:2) 1995, 149–51.

4344. BROGAN, T. V. F. (ed.).   The Princeton handbook of multi-cultural poetries. Princeton, NJ; Chichester: Princeton UP, 1996. pp. xx, 366.

4345. BRYAN, SHARON (ed.).   Where we stand: women poets on literary tradition. (Bibl. 1993, 2445.) Rev. by Catherine Rankovic in JAC (18:1) 1995, 109.

4346. BUDD, MALCOLM.   Values of art: pictures, poetry and music. London; New York: Penguin, 1996. pp. 212. Rev. by John Hyman in TLS, 2 Feb. 1996, 20.

4347. BUGEJA, MICHAEL J.   Truth in poetry. WD (76:6) 1996, 12–14.

4348. CANOVAN, MARGARET.   'Breathes there the man, with soul so dead …': reflections on patriotic poetry and liberal principles. *In* (pp. 170–97) **63**.

4349. CHAPPELL, FRED.   Plow naked: selected writings on poetry. (Bibl. 1993, 2448.) Rev. by Megan Simpson in NCLR (5) 1996, 229–32.

4350. CLARK, S. H.   Sordid images: the poetry of masculine desires. (Bibl. 1994, 2663.) Rev. by Peter Rawlings in EC (46:1) 1996, 63–70.

4351. COOK, ALBERT SPAULDING.   The reach of poetry. West Lafayette, IN: Purdue UP, 1995. pp. xi, 335.

4352. CRAWFORD, ROBERT.   Native language. *See* **1954**.

4353. CRÉPIN, ANDRÉ.   La versification anglaise. Paris: Nathan, 1996. pp. 127. (Collection 128, 140.)

4354. CURETON, RICHARD D.   A response to Derek Attridge. PT (17:1) 1996, 29–50.

4355. —— A response to Tom Barney. LangL (4:1) 1995, 55–9.

4356. CUSHMAN, STEPHEN.   Fictions of form in American poetry. (Bibl. 1995, 3448.) Rev. by Roger Gilbert in AmLH (8:2) 1996, 350–63.

4357. DHARWADKER, VINAY; RAMANUJAN, A. K. (eds).   The Oxford anthology of modern Indian poetry. Delhi; Oxford; New York: OUP, 1994. pp. xx, 265. Rev. by John Oliver Perry in WLT (69:3) 1995, 649–50.

4358. DOBYNS, STEPHEN.   Best words, best order: essays on poetry. New York: St Martin's Press, 1996. pp. xiv, 338.

4359. DOLEZEŬL, LUBOMIR.   Occidental poetics: tradition and progress. Lincoln; London: Nebraska UP, 1990. pp. x, 261. Rev. by Paul Robberecht in CanRCL (21:4) 1994, 735–9.

4360. DUPLESSIS, RACHEL BLAU.   Manifests. Diacritics (26:3/4) 1996, 31–53.

4361. ELDRIDGE, RICHARD (ed.).   Beyond representation: philosophy and poetic imagination. *See* **6**.

4362. ERKKILA, BETSY.   The wicked sisters: women poets, literary history, and discord. (Bibl. 1995, 3455.) Rev. by Katharine Rodier in Review (17) 1995, 131–9; by Corinne E. Blackmer in AmLH (8:1) 1996, 130–53.

4363. FERGUSON, MARGARET; SALTER, MARY JO; STALLWORTHY, JON (eds).   The Norton anthology of poetry. New York; London: Norton, 1996. pp. lxxx, 1998. (Fourth ed.: first ed. 1970)

4364. FITTER, CHRIS.   Poetry, space, landscape: toward a new theory. (Bibl. 1995, 3458.) Rev. by Joanne Woolway in NQ (43:1) 1996, 80; by Stephen Daniels in TLS, 9 Aug. 1996, 8–9.

4365. FRANKOVICH, NICHOLAS (ed.).   The Columbia Granger's index to poetry in collected and selected works. New York: Columbia UP, 1996. pp. xxxviii, 1913.

4366. FRY, PAUL H.   A defense of poetry: reflections on the occasion of writing. (Bibl. 1995, 3460.) Rev. by Christopher J. Knight in ConLit (37:4) 1996, 714–18; by Michael O'Neill in Criticism (38:4) 1996, 642–4.

4367. FULLER, JOHN (ed.).   The Chatto book of love poetry. (Bibl. 1990, 2329.) Rev. by Patricia Beer in PN Review (17:3) 1991, 56.

4368. FURNACE, TOM; BATH, MICHAEL.   Reading poetry: an introduction to skills, theories, and histories. London; New York: Prentice Hall Europe, 1996. pp. xiii, 427.

4369. GARDINIER, SUZANNE.   A world that will hold all the people. Ann Arbor: Michigan UP, 1996. pp. 87. (Poets on poetry.)

4370. GERRARD, CHRISTINE.   Elegy. ERev (5:4) 1995, 29.

4371. GERSON, CAROLE; DAVIES, GWENDOLYN (eds).   Canadian poetry: from the beginnings through the First World War. Toronto: McClelland & Stewart, 1994. pp. xv, 390. (New Canadian library.) Rev. by Bruce Whiteman in JCP (11) 1996, 167–9.

4372. GOLDING, ALAN.   From outlaw to classic: canons in American poetry. (Bibl. 1995, 3461.) Rev. by Kinereth Meyer in AL (68:3) 1996, 652–3.

4373. GRAY, PIERS.   On linearity. *See* **2632**.

4374. HARTMAN, CHARLES O.   Jazz text: voice and improvisation in poetry, jazz, and song. (Bibl. 1994, 2674.) Rev. by Barry Wallenstein in AAR (27:4) 1993, 665–71.

4375. HARVEY, M. L.   Iambic pentameter from Shakespeare to Browning: a study in generative metrics. Lewiston, NY; Lampeter: Mellen Press, 1996. pp. 122. (Studies in comparative literature, 20.)

4376. HEANEY, SEAMUS.   Crediting poetry. In-between (5:2) 1996, 99–114.

4377. —— *Crediting Poetry*: the 1995 Nobel Lecture. WLT (70:2) 1996, 253–9.

4378. —— *Crediting Poetry*: the Nobel lecture. Oldcastle, Co. Meath: Gallery, 1995; New York: Farrar, Straus, & Giroux, 1996. pp. 53.

4379. —— The redress of poetry. (Bibl. 1995, 3474.) Rev. by James Wood in LRB (18:12) 1996, 3, 6; by William Pratt in WLT (70:3) 1996, 698; by William Logan in BkW, 25 Feb. 1996, 4.

4380. HECHT, ANTHONY.   On the laws of the poetic art. (Bibl. 1995, 3475.) Rev. by Mark Ford in TLS, 8 Mar. 1996, 28; by William Logan in BkW, 25 Feb. 1996, 4.

4381. HILL, GEOFFREY.   The enemy's country: words, contexture and other circumstances of language. (Bibl. 1992, 3183.) Rev. by Michael Hamburger in PN Review (18:2) 1991, 54–5; by Andrew Michael Roberts in Eng (41:171) 1992, 261–7.

4382. HOBSBAUM, PHILIP.   Metre, rhythm, and verse form. London; New York: Routledge, 1996. pp. xii, 196. (New critical idiom.) Rev. by Richard Bradford in Eng (45:182) 1996, 186–9.

4383. Hogue, Cynthia.   Scheming women: poetry, privilege, and the politics of subjectivity. (Bibl. 1995, 3477.) Rev. by Timothy Morris in Style (30:1) 1996, 178–80.

4384. Hühn, Peter.   Geschichte der englischen Lyrik: Band 1, Vom 16. Jahrhundert bis zur Romantik; Band 2, Von der viktorianischen Epoche bis zur Gegenwart. (Bibl. 1995, 3479.) Rev. by Adolf Barth in LJGG (37:supp.) 1996, 530–2; by Göran Nieragden in AAA (21:1) 1996, 138–40.

4385. Jackson-Laufer, Guida M.   Encyclopedia of literary epics. Santa Barbara, CA: ABC-CLIO, 1996. pp. xv, 660. (ABC-CLIO literary companions.)

4386. Jones, Jane Anderson; O'Sullivan, Maurice J. (eds).   Florida in poetry: a history of the imagination. Sarasota, FL: Pineapple Press, 1995. pp. xix, 295. Rev. by Kevin M. McCarthy in FHQ (75:1) 1996, 76–8.

4387. Kane, Paul.   Australian poetry: romanticism and negativity. Cambridge; New York: CUP, 1996. pp. viii, 256.

4388. Kane, Stuart A.   Wives with knives: early modern murder ballads and the transgressive commodity. Criticism (38:2) 1996, 219–37.

4389. Kellogg, David.   Perloff's Wittgenstein: w(h)ither poetic theory? Diacritics (26:3/4) 1996, 67–85.

4390. Kermode, Frank.   An appetite for poetry: essays in literary interpretation. (Bibl. 1995, 3482.) Rev. by Donald Mackenzie in LitTheol (5:2) 1991, 247–8; by Gregory Wolfe in ModAge (34:2) 1992, 181–5.

4391. Kinsella, Thomas.   The dual tradition: an essay on poetry and politics in Ireland. Manchester: Carcanet, 1995. pp. vii, 129. (Peppercanister, 18.) Rev. by Patricia Craig in TLS, 26 Jan. 1996, 26; by William Pratt in WLT (70:4) 1996, 967; by M. L. Rosenthal in Ploughshares (22:2/3) 1996, 243–5.

4392. Knight, Christopher J.   Defending poetry – again. ConLit (37:4) 1996, 701–18 (review-article).

4393. Kokotailo, Philip.   Native *and* cosmopolitan: A. J. M. Smith's tradition of English-Canadian poetry. ARCS (20:1) 1990, 31–40.

4394. Krieger, Murray.   Ekphrasis: the illusion of the natural sign. (Bibl. 1993, 2477.) Rev. by Daniel Russell in CanRCL (20:1/2) 1993, 223–5.

4395. Küper, Christoph.   Linguistic givens and metrical codes: five case studies of their linguistic and aesthetic relations. PT (17:1) 1996, 89–126.

4396. Lakoff, George; Turner, Mark.   More than cool reason: a field guide to poetic metaphor. (Bibl. 1991, 3248.) Rev. by John M. Kennedy and John Vervaeke in CanRCL (18:4) 1991, 581–3.

4397. Lauterbach, Ann.   Misquotations from reality. Diacritics (26:3/4) 1996, 143–57.

4398. Lennard, John.   The poetry handbook: a guide to reading poetry in English for pleasure and practical criticism. Oxford; New York: OUP, 1996. pp. xviii, 219.

4399. Lever, Susan (ed.).   The Oxford book of Australian women's verse. Melbourne; Oxford; New York: OUP, 1995. pp. xxii, 259. Rev. by Clive James in TLS, 5 July 1996, 8–10.

4400. McKie, Michael.   Semantic rhyme: a reappraisal. EC (46:4) 1996, 340–58.

4401. McLEOD, DONALD W. (ed.). Canadian writers and their works: cumulated index: poetry. Toronto: ECW Press, 1993. pp. 137. Rev. by Cynthia Messenger in ESCan (22:2) 1996, 236–7.

4402. MOOIJ, J. J. A. On metaphor in poetry. *See* **2431**.

4403. MOON, MICHAEL. Memorial rags. *In* (pp. 233–40) **92**.

4404. MORGAN, EDWIN. Long poems – but how long: W. D. Thomas Memorial Lecture: delivered at the University of Wales Swansea on 27 November 1995. Swansea: Univ. of Wales, Swansea, 1995. pp. 16. (W. D. Thomas Memorial Lecture.)

4405. MORRIS, TIMOTHY. Becoming canonical in American poetry. Champaign: Illinois UP, 1995. pp. xviii, 173. Rev. by Lisa Jadwin in ColLit (23:3) 1996, 171–7.

4406. MPHAHLELE, Es'KIA; MOFFETT, HELEN (eds.). Seasons come to pass: a poetry anthology for Southern African students. Cape Town; Oxford: OUP, 1994. pp. xlv, 290. Rev. by Dirk Klopper in EngA (23:1) 1996, 115–24.

4407. MUSKE, CAROL. Women and poetry. MichQR (35:4) 1996, 586–607.

4408. PACK, ROBERT. The long view: essays on the discipline of hope and poetic craft. (Bibl. 1993, 2487.) Rev. by Harry Marten in GetR (6:2) 1993, 253–61.

4409. PAGE, GEOFF. Loaded canons: Australian poetry anthologies. CritS (6:1) 1994, 20–7.

4410. PARINI, JAY (ed.). The Columbia history of American poetry. (Bibl. 1995, 3500.) Rev. by R. W. French in WWQR (11:4) 1994, 209–12; by Brian A. Bremen in AmS (36:1) 1995, 195–6; by Jonathan Vos Post in Extrapolation (36:2) 1995, 160–3.

4411. PARKER, ALAN MICHAEL; WILLHARDT, MARK (eds). The Routledge anthology of cross-gendered verse. London; New York: Routledge, 1996. pp. 216.

4412. PASTAN, LINDA. Counting the ways. BkW, 11 Feb. 1996, 1–2.

4413. PAULIN, TOM (ed.). The Faber book of vernacular verse. (Bibl. 1990, 2360.) Rev. by C. J. Fox in PN Review (17:4) 1991, 78–9.

4414. PERELMAN, BOB. Poetry in theory. Diacritics (26:3/4) 1996, 158–75.

4415. POWELL, GROSVENOR. The two paradigms for iambic pentameter and twentieth-century metrical experimentation. MLR (91:3) 1996, 561–77.

4416. PRATT, ANNIS. Dancing with goddesses: archetypes, poetry, and empowerment. (Bibl. 1994, 2697.) Rev. by Cynthia Hahn in CanL (149) 1996, 138–9.

4417. PYLKKÖ, PAULI. Game-theoretical aesthetics. AJSem (8:1/2) 1991, 101–11.

4418. QUINN, KENNETH. The sound of verse. *In* (pp. 311–23) **16**.

4419. QUINT, DAVID. Epic and empire: politics and generic form from Virgil to Milton. (Bibl. 1995, 3504.) Rev. by Martin Mueller in CanRCL (21:3) 1994, 491–7; by Annabel Patterson in CLS (33:3) 1996, 300–3.

4420. RAINE, KATHLEEN. The vertical dimension. In-between (2:2) 1993, 131–48.

4421. RICHARDS, BERNARD. Blank verse. ERev (5:3) 1995, 36–41; (7:2) 1996, 22–5.

4422. ROBINSON, PETER.   In the circumstances: about poems and poets. (Bibl. 1995, 3505.) Rev. by Andrew Michael Roberts in Eng (41:171) 1992, 261–7.

4423. SAFIRE, WILLIAM.   On language: poetic allusion watch (PAW). NYTM, 3 Mar. 1996, 34–5.

4424. SCOTT, ROBERT L.   The English hexameter: a short history of a long line. CML (16:2) 1996, 149–74.

4425. SEMINO, ELENA.   Possible worlds in poetry. JLSem (25:3) 1996, 189–224.

4426. SHAW, W. DAVID.   Elegy & paradox: testing the conventions. (Bibl. 1994, 2710.) Rev. by William A. Ulmer in Criticism (38:3) 1996, 473–5.

4427. SLATTERY, DENNIS.   The narrative play of memory in epic. *In* (pp. 331–52) **29**.

4428. SMITH, ROBERT.   Licence. EAS (49) 1996, 140–61.

4429. SPAULDING, JOHN.   The popularity of poetry in America. PCR (7:1) 1996, 145–57.

4430. STEADMAN, JOHN.   Principles of epic: problems of definition, Renaissance and modern. BJJ (3) 1996, 127–44.

4431. STRAUSS, PETER.   Talking poetry: a guide for students, teachers and poets. Cape Town: Philip; Pietermaritzburg: Natal UP, 1993. pp. viii, 205. Rev. by Dirk Klopper in EngA (23:1) 1996, 115–24.

4432. SUVIN, DARKO.   Synchrony as aim and reference. CanRCL (23:2) 1996, 475–83.

4433. SUZUKI, SEIICHI.   In defense of resolution as a metrical principle in the meter of *Beowulf.* EngS (76:1) 1995, 20–33.

4434. TALLANT, CAROLE; TRIMBLE, FRANK.   Participating in the poetry playground: staging the nonsense wordplay in children's poetry. *See* **2716**.

4435. TAMPLIN, RONALD.   Rhythm and rhyme. (Bibl. 1993, 2499.) Rev. by Peter Lewis in CritS (6:2) 1994, 278–9.

4436. TANEJA, G. R.   Leavis, poetry and critical practice. In-between (2:2) 1993, 167–83.

4437. TSUR, REUVEN.   Rhyme and cognitive poetics. PT (17:1) 1996, 55–87.

4438. WATSON, RODERICK (ed.).   The poetry of Scotland: Gaelic, Scots and English, 1380–1980. (Bibl. 1995, 3518.) Rev. by Colin Nicholson in SLJ (supp. 43) 1995, 14–16; by Robert Crawford in LRB (18:3) 1996, 10.

4439. WHITWORTH, JOHN (ed.).   The Faber book of blue verse. (Bibl. 1990, 2375.) Rev. by Patricia Beer in PN Review (17:3) 1991, 55–6.

4440. WILLIAMS, MILLER.   The pleasures of poetic rhyme and meter. WD (76:7) 1996, 33–6, 49.

4441. WOODCOCK, GEORGE.   George Woodcock's introduction to Canadian poetry. (Bibl. 1995, 3521.) Rev. by Cynthia Messenger in ESCan (22:2) 1996, 237–8.

4442. WOODS, GREGORY.   AIDS to remembrance: the uses of elegy. *In* (pp. 155–66) **2**.

PROSE

4443. ATWAN, ROBERT.   Essayism. IowaR (25:2) 1995, 6–14.

4444. BARCLAY, DONALD A.; MAGUIRE, JAMES H.; WILD, PETER (eds). Into the wilderness dream: exploration narratives of the American West,

1500–1805. (Bibl. 1995, 3523.) Rev. by Martin Padget in JAStud (30:1) 1996, 172–4.

4445. CAESAR, TERRY. Forgiving the boundaries: home as abroad in American travel writing. (Bibl. 1995, 3525.) Rev. by Janis P. Stout in AL (68:3) 1996, 659–60; by Peter Carafiol in SAtlR (61:2) 1996, 135–40.

4446. CAREY, JOHN (ed.). The Faber book of science. London; Boston, MA: Faber & Faber, 1995. pp. xxvii, 528. Rev. by George Rousseau in Configurations (4:2) 1996, 233–9.

4447. CASTIGLIA, CHRISTOPHER. Bound and determined: captivity, culture-crossing, and White womanhood from Mary Rowlandson to Patty Hearst. Chicago; London: Chicago UP, 1996. pp. xiv, 254. (Women in culture and society.) (Cf. bibl. 1992, 3042.)

4448. CRAIG, PATRICIA (ed.). The Oxford book of travel stories. Oxford; New York: OUP, 1996. pp. xvi, 441. Rev. by John Bayley in TLS, 26 July 1996, 7–8.

4449. ELDER, JOHN (ed.). American nature writers. New York: Scribner's Sons, 1996. 2 vols. pp. xxiii, 1210.

4450. FLOWER, CELESTE (ed.). Diaries and letters: great writers across the centuries. Harlow; New York: Longman, 1996. pp. viii, 146.

4451. FREDERICK, BONNIE; McLEOD, SUSAN H. (eds). Women and the journey: the female travel experience. Foreword by Catharine R. Stimpson. (Bibl. 1995, 3529.) Rev. by Judith E. Funston in NWSAJ (7:1) 1995, 172–3.

4452. GEORGI-FINDLAY, BRIGITTE. The frontiers of women's writing: women's narratives and the rhetoric of westward expansion. Tucson: Arizona UP 1996. pp. xx, 349.

4453. GILL, PAT. The conduct of ideology: musings on the origin of the bourgeois self. See **4182**.

4454. GROSS, JOHN (ed.). The Oxford book of essays. (Bibl. 1991, 3283.) Rev. by Elizabeth J. Higgins in CLAJ (40:1) 1996, 119–21.

4455. HUBBARD, DOLAN. The sermon and the African-American literary imagination. (Bibl. 1995, 3533.) Rev. by Bruce Rosenberg in Review (18) 1996, 157–63; by Yvonne Chireau in AAR (30:3) 1996, 462–4.

4456. KENYON, OLGA. Women's voices: their lives and loves through two thousand years of letters. Foreword by Gavin Ewart. London: Constable, 1995. pp. 291.

4457. KERMODE, FRANK; KERMODE, ANITA (eds). The Oxford book of letters. (Bibl. 1995, 3536.) Rev. by Sam Schoenbaum in BkW, 10 Sept. 1995, 9.

4458. KORTE, BARBARA. Der Reisebericht aus anglistischer Sicht: Stand, Tendenzen und Desiderate seiner literaturwissenschaftlichen Erforschung. ZAA (42:4) 1994, 364–72.

4459. LAWRENCE, KAREN R. Penelope voyages: women and travel in the British literary tradition. (Bibl. 1995, 3538.) Rev. by Lisa J. Limburg in MFS (42:1) 1996, 183–4; by Johanna M. Smith in TSWL (15:1) 1996, 152–5; by Sue Kuykendall in ColLit (23:1) 1996, 193–203.

4460. MABEY, RICHARD (ed.). The Oxford book of nature writing. (Bibl. 1995, 3540.) Rev. by John Kennedy in AR (54:1) 1996, 106.

4461. METZGER, BRUCE M. Some curious Bibles. See **980**.

4462. MÜLLER, KLAUS PETER. 'The enactment or bringing forth of meaning from a background of understanding' – constructivism, anthropology, and (non-)fictional literature. YREAL (12) 1996, 65–79.

4463. PFISTER, MANFRED (ed.).   The fatal gift of beauty: the Italies of British travellers: an annotated anthology. Amsterdam; Atlanta, GA: Rodopi, 1996. pp. xvi, 554. (Internationale Forschungen zur allgemeinen und vergleichenden Literaturwissenschaft, 15.)

4464. PORTER, DENNIS.   Haunted journeys: desire and transgression in European travel writing. (Bibl. 1995, 3542.) Rev. by Elisabeth Mudimbe-Boyi in CanRCL (20:1/2) 1993, 248–52.

4465. PRATT, MARY LOUISE.   Imperial eyes: travel writing and transculturation. (Bibl. 1995, 3543.) Rev. by Peter Mason in ECL (20:3) 1996, 110–12.

4466. RENNIE, NEIL.   Far-fetched facts: the literature of travel and the idea of the South Seas. (Bibl. 1995, 3544.) Rev. by Greg Dening in LRB (18:21) 1996, 12–13; by Claude Rawson in TLS, 26 July 1996, 3–4.

4467. STEWART, FRANK.   A natural history of nature writing. (Bibl. 1995, 3547.) Rev. by Rick Bass in BkW, 9 Apr. 1995, 3, 12.

4468. WINTER, HELMUT.   Simplicity, complexity, and the essay. *See* **2734**.

BIOGRAPHY AND AUTOBIOGRAPHY

4469. ADAMS, TIMOTHY DOW.   Introduction: life writing and light writing; autobiography and photography. MFS (40:3) 1994, 459–92.

4470. ANDREWS, WILLIAM L. (ed.).   African-American autobiography: a collection of critical essays. *See* **1**.

4471. ASHLEY, KATHLEEN; GILMORE, LEIGH; PETERS, GERALD (eds). Autobiography & postmodernism. (Bibl. 1995, 3549.) Rev. by Kenneth R. Morefield in Style (29:3) 1995, 498–500; by Susanna Egan in CanL (151) 1996, 137–9.

4472. BELL, SUSAN GROAG; YALOM, MARILYN (eds).   Revealing lives: autobiography, biography, and gender. Albany: New York State UP, 1990. pp. xii, 255. (SUNY series in feminist criticism and theory.) Rev. by Sidonie Smith and Camilla Stivers in Signs (18:2) 1993, 392–425.

4473. BENSTOCK, SHARI (ed.).   The private self: theory and practice of women's autobiographical writings. (Bibl. 1992, 3234.) Rev. by Suzanne L. Bunkers in Signs (17:4) 1992, 839–42.

4474. BERRY, J. BILL (ed.).   Located lives: place and idea in Southern autobiography. (Bibl. 1992, 3236.) Rev. by George Hallam in FHQ (70:2) 1991, 231–2.

4475. BLODGETT, HARRIET (ed.).   The Englishwoman's diary: an anthology. (Bibl. 1992, 3237.) Rev. by Gloria Bowles in NWSAJ (4:3) 1992, 373–8.

4476. BRAXTON, JOANNE M.   Black women writing autobiography: a tradition within a tradition. (Bibl. 1995, 3552.) Rev. by Elizabeth Schultz in AmS (33:2) 1992, 134–5; by Sidonie Smith and Camilla Stivers in Signs (18:2) 1993, 392–425.

4477. BRODZKI, BELLA; SCHENCK, CELESTE (eds).   Life/lines: theorizing women's autobiography. Introd. by Germaine Brée. (Bibl. 1992, 53.) Rev. by Suzanne L. Bunkers in Signs (17:4) 1992, 839–42.

4478. BUNKERS, SUZANNE L.; HUFF, CYNTHIA A. (eds).   Inscribing the daily: critical essays on women's diaries. Amherst: Massachusetts UP, 1996. pp. ix, 296.

4479. Buss, Helen M. Mapping our selves: Canadian women's auto-biography in English. (Bibl. 1995, 3554.) Rev. by Christl Verduyn in ESCan (22:1) 1996, 100–2.

4480. Cleto, Fabio. Biografia, ideologia, autor-ità interpretativa (con un caso esemplare). Textus (6) 1993, 179–220.

4481. Connery, Thomas B. Whose lives should be studied? AmJ (13:2) 1996, 217–20.

4482. Eakin, Paul John. Touching the world: reference in auto-biography. (Bibl. 1995, 3557.) Rev. by Ergá Heller in PT (15:3) 1994, 499–500; by Scott Romine in CLS (33:1) 1996, 132–6; by Albert E. Stone in AmS (34:1) 1993, 163–5.

4483. Egan, Susanna. Encounters in camera: autobiography as interaction. MFS (40:3) 1994, 593–618.

4484. Elms, Alan C. Uncovering lives: the uneasy alliance of bio-graphy and psychology. New York; Oxford: Oxford UP, 1994. pp. vi, 315. Rev. by Richard C. S. Trahair in Extrapolation (36:2) 1995, 168–71.

4485. Flower, Celeste (ed.). Diaries and letters: great writers across the centuries. *See* **4450**.

4486. Franklin, V. P. Living our stories, telling our truths: auto-biography and the making of the African-American intellectual tradition. New York: Scribner, 1995. pp. 464. Rev. by Wilson J. Moses in ALH (101:4) 1996, 1270.

4487. Gannett, Cinthia. Gender and the journal: diaries and aca-demic discourse. *See* **2368**.

4488. Gelderman, Carol. Ghostly doubles: biographer and biographee. AR (54:3) 1996, 328–35.

4489. Hamilton, Ian. Keepers of the flame: literary estates and the rise of biography. (Bibl. 1995, 3561.) Rev. by Jonathan Yardley in BkW, 10 Apr. 1994, 3.

4490. Heilbrun, Carolyn G. Feminist biography. NWSAJ (6:1) 1994, 119–23.

4491. Kadar, Marlene (ed.). Essays on life writing: from genre to critical practice. *See* **4194**.

4492. Lionnet, Françoise. Autobiographical voices: race, gender, self-portraiture. (Bibl. 1990, 2406.) Rev. by Suzette A. Henke in CanRCL (18:1) 1991, 109–12; by Sidonie Smith and Camilla Stivers in Signs (18:2) 1993, 392–425.

4493. Meyers, Jeffrey. The spirit of biography. (Bibl. 1990, 2407.) Rev. by John McCormick in CanRCL (18:4) 1991, 617–19.

4494. Miller, Nancy K. Getting personal: feminist occasions and other autobiographical acts. (Bibl. 1995, 3565.) Rev. by Marilyn Yalom in Signs (18:2) 1993, 455–8.

4495. Oldfield, Sybil. The news from the confessional – some reflections on recent autobiographical writing by women and its areas of taboo. CritS (8:3) 1996, 296–305.

4496. Olney, James. The value of autobiography for comparative studies: African *vs* Western autobiography. *In* (pp. 212–23) **1**.

4497. Parke, Catherine N. Biography: writing lives. New York: Twayne; London: Prentice Hall, 1996. pp. xxviii, 175. (Studies in literary themes and genres, 11.)

4498. Rhiel, Mary; Suchoff, David (eds). The seductions of bio-graphy. New York; London: Routledge, 1996. pp. xiii, 219. (Culture work.)

4499. ROBERTSON, MICHAEL.   What have we learned by studying lives? AmJ (13:2) 1996, 212–16.

4500. SCHIWY, MARLENE A.   Taking things personally: women, journal writing, and self-creation. NWSAJ (6:2) 1994, 234–54.

4501. SHORTLAND, MICHAEL; YEO, RICHARD (eds).   Telling lives in science: essays on scientific biography. Cambridge; New York: CUP, 1996. pp. 304.

4502. SMITH, SIDONIE.   A poetics of women's autobiography: marginality and the fictions of self-representation. (Bibl. 1990, 2413.) Rev. by Suzanne L. Bunkers in Signs (17:4) 1992, 839–42.

4503. —— Who's talking/who's talking back: the subject of personal narrative. Signs (18:2) 1993, 392–407 (review-article).

4504. —— WATSON, JULIA (eds).   Getting a life: everyday uses of autobiography. Minneapolis: Minnesota UP, 1996. pp. xii, 415.

4505. STANLEY, LIZ.   The auto/biographical I: the theory and practice of feminist auto/biography. (Bibl. 1993, 2550.) Rev. by Carolyn G. Heilbrun in NWSAJ (6:1) 1994, 119–23.

4506. STEINER, LINDA.   What can be learned? AmJ (13:2) 1996, 206–11.

4507. STICH, K. P. (ed.).   Reflections: autobiography and Canadian literature. Ottawa: Ottawa UP, 1988. pp. xii, 176. (Reappraisals: Canadian writers, 14.) Rev. by D. O. Spettigue in ARCS (19:1) 1989, 125–7.

4508. STREITMATTER, RODGER.   Who should do the studying? AmJ (13:2) 1996, 221–4.

4509. WEST, JAMES L. W., III.   The scholarly editor as biographer. *See* **872**.

4510. WONG, HERTHA DAWN.   Sending my heart back across the years: tradition and innovation in Native American autobiography. (Bibl. 1995, 3572.) Rev. by Sam D. Gill in AHR (98:3) 1993, 942–3; by James W. Parins in AmS (34:1) 1993, 176–7.

4511. WOOD, MARY ELENE.   The writing on the wall: women's autobiography and the asylum. Urbana: Illinois UP, 1994. pp. viii, 202. Rev. by Deborah Barker in AL (68:2) 1996, 466–7; by Susanna Egan in CanL (151) 1996, 137–9.

RELATED STUDIES

4512. BENES, PETER; BENES, JANE MONTAGUE (eds).   Wonders of the invisible world: 1600–1900. *See* **3267**.

4513. BERRY, C. J.   The idea of luxury: a conceptual and historical investigation. Cambridge; New York: CUP, 1994. pp. xiv, 271. (Ideas in context, 30.) Rev. by Malcolm Jack in BJECS (19:2) 1996, 199.

4514. CHARTRAND, HARRY HILLMAN.   Christianity, copyright, and censorship in English-speaking cultures. JAML (22:3) 1992, 253–71.

4515. CRONIN, MICHAEL.   Translating Ireland: translation, languages, cultures. *See* **3123**.

4516. CROUZET, FRANÇOIS; DELOUCHE, FRÉDÉRIC.   Le livre 'anglais' en France. Franco-British Studies (22) 1996, 13–34.

4517. DATHORNE, O. R.   Imagining the world: mythical belief *versus* reality in global encounters. Westport, CT: Bergin & Garvey, 1994. pp. x, 241. Rev. by Roland E. Bush in JCS (11:1/2) 1995/96, 177–83.

4518. DRUXES, HELGA.   The feminization of Dr Faustus: female identity quests from Stendhal to Morgner. University Park: Pennsylvania State UP, 1993. pp. 148. Rev. by Frank G. Nigro in StudN (27:4) 1995, 574–5; by Gail Finney in CLS (33:3) 1996, 297–9.

4519. EISENSTEIN, ÉLIZABETH L.   The end of the book? Some perspectives on media change. ASch (64:4) 1995, 541–55.

4520. EVANS, RICK.   'Masks': literacy, ideology, and hegemony in the academy. RhR (14:1) 1995, 88–103.

4521. GABEL, JOHN B.; WHEELER, CHARLES B.; YORK, ANTHONY D. (eds).   The Bible as literature: an introduction. (Bibl. 1990, 2382.) Oxford; New York: OUP, 1996. pp. xii, 330. (Third ed.; first ed. 1986.)

4522. GRIMSHAW, ANNA; HART, KEITH (eds).   American civilization. By C. L. R. James. (Bibl. 1994, 2756.) Rev. by Edward Margolies in EngS (77:3) 1996, 295–6.

4523. HASKINS, SUSAN.   Mary Magdalen: myth and metaphor. London: HarperCollins, 1993; New York: Harcourt, Brace, 1994. pp. xxii, 518. Rev. by Diane Winston in BkW, 20 Mar. 1994, 4–5.

4524. HUNT, JOHN DIXON.   *Paragone* in paradise: translating the garden. CompCrit (18) 1996, 55–70.

4525. LIFSHITZ, FELICE.   Beyond positivism and genre: 'hagiographical' texts as historical narrative. Viator (25) 1994, 95–113.

4526. MANGUEL, ALBERTO.   A history of reading. London: HarperCollins; New York: Viking, 1996. pp. 372. Rev. by D. J. Enright in TLS, 2 Aug. 1996, 8.

4527. MARTINET, MARIE-MADELEINE.   Le voyage d'Italie dans les littératures européennes. Paris: Presses Universitaires de France, 1996. pp. viii, 341. (Littératures européennes.) Rev. by Paul Denizot in BSEAA (42) 1996, 148–9.

4528. MORVAN, ALAIN; GOURNAY, JEAN-FRANÇOIS; LESSAY, FRANCK. Histoire des idées dans les îles Britanniques. Paris: Presses Universitaires de France, 1996. pp. xii, 354. (Perspectives anglo-saxonnes.) Rev. by Paul Denizot in BSEAA (42) 1996, 149–51.

4529. NAIRN, TOM.   Scottish identity: a cause unwon. Études Écossaises (1) 1992, 21–38.

4530. ORESTANO, FRANCESCA.   Wiring the system: Samuel F. B. Morse between art and science. *In* (pp. 214–21) **117**.

4531. PAGDEN, ANTHONY.   European encounters with the New World: from Renaissance to Romanticism. New Haven, CT; London: Yale UP, 1993. pp. vi, 216. Rev. by Peter Mason in ECL (20:3) 1996, 113–14.

4532. QUARTA, COSIMO.   *Homo utopicus*: on the need for utopia. Trans. by Daniele Procida. Utopian Studies (7:2) 1996, 153–66.

4533. RICHARDS, DAVID.   Masks of difference: cultural representations in literature, anthropology and art. Cambridge; New York: CUP, 1995. pp. xiii, 348. (Cultural margins.) Rev. by Caroline McCracken-Flesher in SLJ (supp. 44) 1996, 20–4.

4534. SCHEPER, GEORGE L.   'Where is our home?': the ambiguity of biblical and Euro-American imaging of wilderness and garden as sacred place. Analecta Husserliana (44) 1995, 321–38.

4535. STAUDER, THOMAS.   Die literarische Travestie: terminologische Systematik und paradigmatische Analyse: Deutschland, England, Frankreich, Italien. (Bibl. 1995, 3611.) Rev. by Martin Brunkhorst in ZAA (44:4) 1996, 369–71.

4536. TAYLOR, GARY.   Cultural selection. New York: BasicBooks, 1996. pp. ix, 325. Rev. by Camille Paglia in BkW, 7 Apr. 1996, 7.

4537. YIP, WAI-LIM.   Diffusion of distances: dialogues between Chinese and Western poetics. Berkeley; London: California UP, 1993. pp. xi, 246. Rev. by Zhang Longxi in CLS (33:1) 1996, 123–5.

LITERARY THEORY

This section is intended to cover general writings **about** literary history, criticism and critical theory. For general works **of** literary history and criticism, see under 'General Literary Studies'.

4538. BATTERSBY, JAMES L.   Reason and the nature of texts. Philadelphia: Pennsylvania UP, 1996. pp. xi, 198.

4539. BONHEIM, HELMUT.   Literary systematics. (Bibl. 1992, 3309.) Rev. by Wilhelm Füger in GRM (41:4) 1991, 461–3.

4540. BOOKER, M. KEITH.   A practical introduction to literary theory and criticism. White Plains, NY: Longman, 1996. pp. xii, 495.

4541. BRANCH, MICHAEL.   Ecocriticism: the nature of nature in literary theory and practice. WebS (11:1) 1994, 41–55.

4542. CALLAGHAN, PATSY; DOBYNS, ANN.   Literary conversation: thinking, talking, and writing about literature. *See* **2323**.

4543. DOCHERTY, THOMAS.   Alterities: criticism, history, representation. Oxford: Clarendon Press; New York: OUP, 1996. pp. ix, 222.

4544. EDMUNDSON, MARK.   Literature against philosophy, Plato to Derrida: a defence of poetry. (Bibl. 1995, 3627.) Rev. by E. B. Greenwood in NQ (43:3) 1996, 377–8; by Christopher J. Knight in ConLit (37:4) 1996, 704–9; by Simon Critchley in TLS, 2 Aug. 1996, 26.

4545. FISHELOV, DAVID.   Metaphors of genre: the role of analogies in genre theory. (Bibl. 1993, 2585.) Rev. by Harry E. Shaw in CLS (33:2) 1996, 221–4; by Paul Smethurst in YES (26) 1996, 341–2.

4546. ——— The strange life and adventures of biological concepts in genre periodization. CanRCL (21:4) 1994, 613–26.

4547. GOODMAN, LIZBETH.   The idea of the canon. *In* (pp. 3–19) **110**.

4548. GORDON, PAUL.   The critical double: figurative meaning in aesthetic discourse. Foreword by J. Hillis Miller. (Bibl. 1995, 3628.) Rev. by Hans H. Rudnick in WLT (69:4) 1995, 885–6.

4549. GRODEN, MICHAEL; KREISWIRTH, MARTIN (eds).   The Johns Hopkins guide to literary theory and criticism. (Bibl. 1995, 3631.) Rev. by W. M. Hagen in WLT (70:1) 1996, 246–7.

4550. HAWKES, DAVID.   Ideology. London; New York: Routledge, 1996. pp. viii, 210. (New critical idiom.)

4551. HERRON, JERRY, *et al.* (eds).   The ends of theory. Introd. by Wallace Martin. Detroit, MI: Wayne State UP, 1996. pp. 326.

4552. HJORT, METTE.   The strategy of letters. (Bibl. 1995, 3633.) Rev. by Willie van Peer in CanRCL (22:2) 1995, 362–5; by Daniel T. O'Hara in AnnS (11:1/2) 1996, 175–91.

4553. KNAPP, STEVEN.   Literary interest: the limits of anti-formalism. (Bibl. 1993, 2594.) Rev. by Robert Langbaum in Review (17) 1995, 1–12; by John Fizer in CLS (33:2) 1996, 214–17.

4554. KRIEGER, MURRAY. The institution of theory. (Bibl. 1995, 3637.) Rev. by David S. Gross in WLT (69:1) 1995, 235.

4555. KROEBER, KARL. Ecological literary criticism: Romantic imagining and the biology of mind. (Bibl. 1994, 2784.) Rev. by Jonathan Bate in ANQ (9:2) 1996, 53–6; by James C. McKusick in KSJ (45) 1996, 213–16; by Timothy Morton in Criticism (38:3) 1996, 478–82.

4556. LU, WEIPING. Learning and self-cultivation in Confucianism *versus* modern Western concepts of originality and individualism. CanRCL (23:4) 1996, 961–82.

4557. McGILLIS, RODERICK. The nimble reader: literary theory and children's literature. *See* **4311**.

4558. MILLER, J. HILLIS. Theory now and then. (Bibl. 1993, 2597.) Rev. by Nicolas Tredell in PN Review (18:1) 1991, 60–3.

4559. NÜNNING, ANSGAR (ed.). Literaturwissenschaftliche Theorien, Modelle und Methoden: eine Einführung. Trier: WVT, 1995. pp. 232. (WVT Handbucher zum Literaturwissenschaftlichen Studium, 1.) Rev. by Stefan Glomb in LJGG (37:supp.) 1996, 536–40; by Göran Nieragden in LWU (29:4) 1996, 305–7.

4560. OLSON, GARY A. (ed.). Philosophy, rhetoric, literary criticism: (inter)views. Foreword by Clifford Geertz. Introd. by Patricia Bizzell. Commentary by David Bleich. *See* **2438**.

4561. RIGHTER, WILLIAM. The myth of theory. (Bibl. 1995, 3646.) Rev. by Colin Nicholson in SLJ (supp. 43) 1995, 29–31.

4562. RONEN, RUTH. Possible worlds in literary theory. (Bibl. 1995, 3647.) Rev. by Denis E. B. Pollard in JLSem (24:3) 1995, 236–8.

4563. RUNGE, LAURA L. Gendered strategies in the criticism of early fiction. *See* **4256**.

4564. SEGAL, ROBERT A. (ed.). Literary criticism and myth. New York; London: Garland, 1996. pp. xi, 373. (Theories of myth, 4.)

4565. SIMPSON, DAVID. Romanticism, nationalism, and the revolt against theory. (Bibl. 1995, 3648.) Rev. by Greg Laugero in ECS (28:4) 1995, 435–7; by Kenneth Cmiel in AmLH (8:1) 1996, 190–1.

4566. SPOLSKY, ELLEN. Gaps in nature: literary interpretation and the modular mind. (Bibl. 1994, 2802.) Rev. by Michael Fischer in PT (17:2) 1996, 262–5; by Jean Boase-Beier in JLSem (25:2) 1996, 185–7.

4567. STEVENS, BONNIE KLOMP; STEWART, LARRY L. A guide to literary criticism and research. *See* **1127**.

4568. VALDÉS, MARIO J. World-making: the literary truth-claim and the interpretation of texts. (Bibl. 1992, 3340.) Rev. by Uri Margolin in CanRCL (21:3) 1994, 445–56.

4569. VENDLER, HELEN. On criticism. IowaR (26:3) 1996, 27–30.

4570. WILSON, R. RAWDON. In Palamedes' shadow: explorations in play, game and narrative theory. (Bibl. 1995, 3649.) Rev. by Ross Chambers in CanRCL (19:1/2) 1992, 95–100.

OLD ENGLISH

GENERAL AND ANONYMOUS

General Literary Studies; Editions and Studies of Anonymous Writings (except *Beowulf*)

4571. ABRAMS, LESLEY, *et al.* Bibliography for 1993; 1994; 1995. ASE (23) 1994, 291–333; (24) 1995, 309–58; (25) 1996, 233–82.

4572. AERTSEN, HENK; BREMMER, ROLF H., JR (eds). Companion to Old English poetry. (Bibl. 1994, 12.) Rev. by María José Mora in Atlantis (17:1/2) 1995, 337–44.

4573. AMODIO, MARK C. Old-English oral-formulaic tradition and Middle-English verse. *In* (pp. 1–20) **22**.

4574. ANDERSON, THEODORE M. The speeches in the *Waldere* fragments. *In* (pp. 21–9) **22**.

4575. BAKER, PETER S. Textual boundaries in Anglo-Saxon works on time (and in some Old English poems). *In* (pp. 445–56) **114**.

4576. BENNETT, HELEN T. Exile and the semiosis of gender in Old English elegies. *In* (pp. 43–58) **14**.

4577. BIGGS, FREDERICK M.; HALL, THOMAS N. Traditions concerning Jamnes and Mambres in Anglo-Saxon England. ASE (25) 1996, 69–89.

4578. BRAGG, LOIS. The modes of the Old English metrical charms. Comparatist (16) 1992, 3–23.

4579. —— *Wulf and Eadwacer, The Wife's Lament,* and women's love lyrics of the Middle Ages. (Bibl. 1989, 2215.) Rev. by Renate Laszlo in GRM (42:3) 1992, 362–4.

4580. BRAVO, ANTONIO. Old and Middle English bibliography 1993–95. SELIM (5) 1995, 166–77.

4581. BRAVO GARCÍA, ANTONIO. El estilo de la descripción de las batallas en el *Brut* de Layamon y en la épica anglosajona de los siglos X–XI. *See* **2588**.

4582. —— GONZALO ABASCAL, PEDRO. Héroes y santos en la literatura anglosajona. Oviedo: Univ. of Oviedo, 1994. pp. 250. Rev. by María Beatriz Hernández Pérez in Atlantis (17:1/2) 1995, 386–7.

4583. CARROLL, BENJAMIN H., JR. Old English prosody. JEL (24:2) 1996, 93–115.

4584. CARRUTHERS, LEO (ed.). Heroes and heroines in medieval English literature: a Festschrift presented to André Crépin on the occasion of his sixty-fifth birthday. (Bibl. 1994, 33.) Rev. by Elizabeth M. Tyler in NQ (43:1) 1996, 69–70.

4585. CAVILL, PAUL. Biblical realignment of a maxim in the Old English *Phoenix*, lines 355b–60. BJRL (77:3) 1995, 193–8.

4586. CLARK, GEORGE. Maldon: history, poetry, and truth. *In* (pp. 66–84) **22**.

4587. CLEMOES, PETER. Interactions of thought and language in Old English poetry. (Bibl. 1995, 3665.) Rev. by E. G. Stanley in NQ (43:2) 1996, 199–203; by Ann Squires in Early Medieval Europe (5:2) 1996, 220–2.

4588. CONDE SILVESTRE, JUAN CAMILO. The spaces of medieval inter-textuality: *Deor* as a palimpsest. SELIM (5) 1995, 63–77.

4589. COOK, PATRICK. *Woriað þa winsalo*: the bonds of exile in *The Wanderer*. Neophilologus (80:1) 1996, 127–37.

4590. COOPER, JANET (ed.). The Battle of Maldon: fiction and fact. (Bibl. 1994, 2828.) Rev. by Eric Christiansen in EHR (111:442) 1996, 665–6.

4591. DAVIS, ADAM. *Agon* and *gnomon*: forms and functions of the Anglo-Saxon riddles. *In* (pp. 110–50) **22**.

4592. DE LACY, PAUL. Aspects of Christianisation and cultural adaptation in the Old English *Judith*. NM (97:4) 1996, 393–410.

4593. DEROLEZ, R. *Genesis*: Old Saxon *and* Old English. EngS (76:5) 1995, 409–23.

4594. DIETRICHSON, JAN W. The making of the couple in Old and Middle English literature. *In* (pp. 113–27) Flemming G. Andersen and Morten Nøjgaard (eds), The making of the couple: the social function of short-form medieval narrative: a symposium. Odense: Odense UP, 1991. pp. 143.

4595. DOANE, A. N. The Saxon Genesis: an edition of the West Saxon *Genesis B* and the Old Saxon Vatican *Genesis*. (Bibl. 1995, 3675.) Rev. by Hans Sauer in Ang (114:2) 1996, 266–8.

4596. ERICKSEN, JANET SCHRUNK. Lands of unlikeness in *Genesis B*. SP (93:1) 1996, 1–20.

4597. EVANS, STEPHEN S. The heroic poetry of Dark-Age Britain: an introduction to its dating, composition, and use as a historical source. Lanham, MD; London: UP of America, 1996. pp. 156.

4598. EXPÓSITO GONZÁLEZ, MARÍA DE LA CRUZ. El propósito de la poesía en la sociedad anglosajona. EIUC (4) 1996, 209–33.

4599. FOLEY, JOHN MILES. Immanent art: from structure to meaning in traditional oral epic. *See* **3392**.

4600. —— (ed.); WOMACK, CHRIS; WOMACK, WHITNEY A. (asst eds). *De gustibus*: essays for Alain Renoir. *See* **22**.

4601. FRANTZEN, ALLEN J. Between the lines: queer theory, the history of homosexuality, and Anglo-Saxon penitentials. JMEMS (26:2) 1996, 255–96.

4602. —— The fragmentation of cultural studies and the fragments of Anglo-Saxon England. Ang (114:3) 1996, 310–39.

4603. FRY, DONALD K. Exeter Riddle 31: feather–pen. *In* (pp. 234–49) **22**.

4604. GAMESON, FIONA; GAMESON, RICHARD. *Wulf and Eadwacer*, *The Wife's Lament*, and the discovery of the individual in Old English verse. *In* (pp. 457–74) **114**.

4605. GAMESON, RICHARD. The origin of the Exeter Book of Old English poetry. *See* **357**.

4606. GEORGE, J.-A. Repentance and retribution: the use of the Book of Daniel in Old and Middle English texts. BJRL (77:3) 1995, 177–92.

4607. GNEUSS, HELMUT. Language and history in early England. *See* **1445**.

4608. GODDEN, M. R. The trouble with Sodom: literary responses to biblical sexuality. BJRL (77:3) 1995, 97–119.

4609. GONZALO ABASCAL, PEDRO; BRAVO, ANTONIO.   Early Christian funeral ceremonies and Germanic funeral rites in Old English epic. SELIM (5) 1995, 46–62.

4610. GRIFFITH, MARK S.   Does *wyrd bið ful aræd* mean 'Fate is wholly inexorable'? *In* (pp. 133–56) **114**.

4611. HARBUS, ANTONINA.   Deceptive dreams in *The Wanderer*. SP (93:2) 1996, 164–79.

4612. —— Old English *swefn* and *Genesis B* line 720. *In* (pp. 157–74) **114**.

4613. HARWOOD, BRITTON J.; OVERING, GILLIAN R. (eds).   Class and gender in early English literature: intersections. *See* **14**.

4614. HEAD, PAULINE.   Voices of stone: the multifaceted speech of *The Dream of the Rood* and the Ruthwell Cross. *See* **2639**.

4615. HEFFERNAN, CAROL FALVO.   The phoenix at the fountain: images of woman and eternity in Lactantius's *Carmen de ave phoenice* and the Old English *Phoenix*. (Bibl. 1989, 2236.) Rev. by Jean H. Jost in Quondam et Futurus (1:4) 1991, 94–9.

4616. HERMANN, JOHN P.   Why Anglo-Saxonists can't read; or, Who took the mead out of medieval studies? Exemplaria (7:1) 1995, 9–26.

4617. HINTON, REBECCA.   *The Dream of the Rood*. Exp (54:2) 1996, 77–9.

4618. HOLLIS, STEPHANIE; WRIGHT, MICHAEL.   Old English prose of secular learning. (Bibl. 1995, 3689.) Rev. by Hugh Magennis in EngS (76:1) 1995, 93–4; by Andy Orchard in Archiv (233:2) 1996, 376–7.

4619. HOUGH, CAROLE.   *The Battle of Maldon* lines 20–21. NM (97:4) 1996, 383–6.

4620. IRVINE, MARTIN.   The making of textual culture: 'grammatica' and literary theory, 350–1100. (Bibl. 1995, 3694.) Rev. by Marcia L. Colish in AHR (101:1) 1996, 162–3; by Nicolette Zeeman in SAC (18) 1996, 222–7; by Suzanne Reynolds in NQ (43:4) 1996, 459–60.

4621. IRVING, EDWARD B., JR.   The advent of poetry: *Christ 1*. ASE (25) 1996, 123–34.

4622. KITSON, PETER.   The dialect position of the Old English Orosius. *See* **1896**.

4623. KORHAMMER, MICHAEL (ed.); REICHL, KARL; SAUER, HANS (asst eds).   Words, texts and manuscripts: studies in Anglo-Saxon culture presented to Helmut Gneuss on the occasion of his sixty-fifth birthday. (Bibl. 1995, 3705.) Rev. by Paul Bibire in Early Medieval Europe (3:1) 1994, 80–1; by Anne Savage in Med (8) 1995, 337–42; by Peter S. Baker in Archiv (233:2) 1996, 378–82.

4624. LERER, SETH.   Literacy and power in Anglo-Saxon literature. (Bibl. 1995, 3708.) Rev. by Elizabeth A. Robertson in Review (17) 1995, 214–23.

4625. LESTER, G. A.   The language of Old and Middle English poetry. *See* **1462**.

4626. LINDSTRÖM, BENGT.   *The Phoenix*, lines 240–2 and 407–9. NQ (43:1) 1996, 13–14.

4627. LOCHRIE, KARMA.   Gender, sexual violence, and the politics of war in the Old English *Judith*. *In* (pp. 1–20) **14**.

4628. MAGENNIS, HUGH.   Images of community in Old English poetry. Cambridge; New York: CUP, 1996. pp. ix, 212. (Cambridge studies in Anglo-Saxon England, 18.)

4629. —— Treatments of treachery and betrayal in Anglo-Saxon texts. EngS (76:1) 1995, 1–19.

4630. MARSDEN, RICHARD. The death of the messenger: the *spelboda* in the Old English *Exodus*. *See* **750**.

4631. —— Old Latin intervention in the Old English *Heptateuch*. ASE (23) 1994, 229–64.

4632. MAZO, JEFFREY ALAN. Compound diction and traditional style in *Beowulf* and *Genesis A*. *See* **2673**.

4633. MEANEY, AUDREY L. Exeter Book Riddle 57 (55) – a double solution? ASE (25) 1996, 187–200.

4634. MÉNDEZ NAYA, BELÉN. *Cweðan, secgan* and *cyðan*: on mood selection in Old English dependent statements. *See* **1778**.

4635. MINKOVA, DONKA. Verse structure as evidence for prosodic reconstruction in Old English. *In* (pp. 13–37) **27**.

4636. MITCHELL, BRUCE. J. R. R. Tolkien and Old English studies: an appreciation. Mythlore (21:2) 1996, 206–12.

4637. MOMMA, H. Metrical stress on alliterating finite verbs in clause-initial *a*-verses: 'some doubts and no conclusions'. *In* (pp. 186–98) **114**.

4638. MORA, MARÍA JOSÉ. The invention of the Old English elegy. EngS (76:2) 1995, 129–39.

4639. MORGAN, EDWIN. The poetry of the city. CompCrit (18) 1996, 91–105.

4640. MORGAN, GWENDOLYN A. Dualism and mirror imagery in Anglo-Saxon riddles. JFA (5:1) 1992, 74–85.

4641. MUIR, BERNARD J. (ed.). The Exeter anthology of Old English poetry: an edition of Exeter Dean and Chapter MS 3501. *See* **394**.

4642. NELSON, MARIE. Structures of opposition in Old English poems. (Bibl. 1992, 3413.) Rev. by Herbert Schendl in Med (9) 1996, 319–20.

4643. NILES, JOHN D. Sign and psyche in Old English poetry. AJSem (9:4) 1992, 11–25.

4644. —— Toward an Anglo-Saxon oral poetics. *In* (pp. 359–77) **22**.

4645. O'KEEFFE, KATHERINE O'BRIEN. Source, method, theory, practice: on reading two Old English verse texts. BJRL (76:1) 1994, 51–73. (*Solomon and Saturn* poems.)

4646. PAGE, R. I. An Old English fragment from Westminster Abbey. *See* **400**.

4647. PASTERNACK, CAROL BRAUN. The textuality of Old English poetry. (Bibl. 1995, 3723.) Rev. by E. G. Stanley in NQ (43:2) 1996, 196–9.

4648. PORTER, JOHN. Anglo-Saxon riddles. Hockwold-cum-Wilton, Norfolk: Anglo-Saxon Books, 1995. pp. 104.

4649. RAUCH, IRMENGARD. Another Old English–Old Saxon isogloss: (REM) activity. *In* (pp. 480–93) **22**.

4650. REMLEY, PAUL G. Old English biblical verse: studies in *Genesis, Exodus* and *Daniel*. Cambridge; New York: CUP, 1996. pp. xvii, 476. (Cambridge studies in Anglo-Saxon England, 16.) (Cf. bibl. 1991, 560.)

4651. RICHARDS, MARY P. (ed.). Anglo-Saxon manuscripts: basic readings. *See* **413**.

4652. ROBERTSON, ELIZABETH A. Historicizing literacy: new directions in Anglo-Saxon criticism. Review (17) 1995, 211–24 (review-article).

4653. ROBINSON, FRED C. *The Tomb of Beowulf* and other essays on Old English. (Bibl. 1995, 3730.) Rev. by David Matthews in EngS (76:5) 1995, 477–8; by Roberta Frank in EHR (111:441) 1996, 406–7.

4654. RODRIGUES, LOUIS J. (trans.).   Anglo-Saxon elegiac verse. Felinfach, Dyfed: Llanerch, 1994. pp. 124.

4655. —— Anglo-Saxon verse charms, maxims & heroic legends. (Bibl. 1993, 2696.) Rev. by Karen Foster in ANQ (9:1) 1996, 56–7.

4656. RUMBLE, ALEXANDER R.   The Rylands, the Bible and early English literature: an illustrated note. *See* **414**.

4657. RUPP, KATRIN.   'Few love to hear the sins they love to act': father–daughter incest in three versions of *Apollonius of Tyre*. SPELL (9) 1996, 225–33.

4658. SAYERS, WILLIAM.   Exeter Book Riddle no. 5: whetstone? NM (97:4) 1996, 387–92.

4659. SCHAEFER, URSULA.   'From an aesthetic point of view …': receptional aspects of Old English poetry. *In* (pp. 494–541) **22**.

4660. SCHAFFNER, PAUL.   The errant morsel in *Solomon and Saturn II* : liturgy, lore, and lexicon. *See* **1956**.

4661. SCHOPF, ALFRED.   Bedas Sterbelied. LJGG (37) 1996, 9–30.

4662. SCHRADER, RICHARD J.   Old English poetry and the genealogy of events. (Bibl. 1995, 3732.) Rev. by Joyce Hill in EngS (76:5) 1995, 478–9; by B. R. Hutcheson in Ang (114:2) 1996, 263–5.

4663. SCRAGG, D. G.   The Bible in *Fontes Anglo-Saxonici*. BJRL (77:3) 1995, 199–203.

4664. SCRAGG, DONALD (ed.).   *The Battle of Maldon* AD 991. (Bibl. 1995, 3734.) Rev. by Judith Jesch in Early Medieval Europe (2:1) 1993, 92–3.

4665. SERRENTINO, ENZA.   Lucano nell'*Exodus* antico inglese. Neophilologus (80:4) 1996, 617–38.

4666. SORRELL, PAUL.   Alcuin's 'comb' riddle. Neophilologus (80:2) 1996, 311–18.

4667. STÉVANOVITCH, COLETTE.   Envelope patterns and the unity of the Old English *Christ and Satan*. Archiv (233:2) 1996, 260–7.

4668. —— Envelope patterns in *Genesis A* and *B*. Neophilologus (80:3) 1996, 465–78.

4669. SWANTON, MICHAEL (ed.).   The dream of the rood. (Bibl. 1987, 2902.) Exeter: Exeter UP, 1996. pp. ix, 150. (Exeter medieval English texts and studies.) (New ed.: first ed. 1987.)

4670. TANKE, JOHN W.   *Wonfeax wale*: ideology and figuration in the sexual riddles of the Exeter Book. *In* (pp. 21–42) **14**.

4671. TASIOULAS, J. A.   The mother's lament: *Wulf and Eadwacer* reconsidered. MÆ (65:1) 1996, 1–18.

4672. TORKAR, ROLAND.   Two Latin excerpts (*Sacramentarium Gregorianum*, and Isidore, *Sententiae*) with Old English translation. *See* **1488**.

4673. TOSWELL, M. J.   Tacitus, Old English heroic poetry, and ethnographic preconceptions. *In* (pp. 493–507) **114**.

4674. ——TYLER, E. M. (eds).   Studies in English language and literature. 'Doubt wisely': papers in honour of E. G. Stanley. *See* **114**.

4675. TOWNSEND, JULIE.   The metre of the *Chronicle*-verse. SN (68:2) 1996, 143–76.

4676. TREHARNE, E. M.   A unique Old English formula for ex-communication from Cambridge, Corpus Christi College 303. *See* **434**.

4677. TREHARNE, ELAINE M.   Old English literature. YWES (75) 1994, 91–123.

4678. TYLER, ELIZABETH M.   How deliberate is deliberate verbal repetition? *In* (pp. 508–30) **114**.

4679. —— Treasure and convention in Old English verse. NQ (43:1) 1996, 2–13.

4680. TYLER, LEE EDGAR.   The heroic oath of Hildebrand. *In* (pp. 551–85) **22**.

4681. WALLACE, CHARLES HARRISON.   The central crux of *The Seafarer*. SN (68:2) 1996, 177–84.

4682. WILCOX, JONATHAN.   Mock-riddle in Old English: Exeter Riddles 86 and 19. SP (93:2) 1996, 180–7.

4683. WRIGHT, CHARLES D.   The blood of Abel and the branches of sin: *Genesis A, Maxims I* and Aldhelm's *Carmen de uirginitate*. ASE (25) 1996, 7–19.

4684. —— The Irish tradition in Old English literature. (Bibl. 1994, 2921.) Rev. by Patrick Sims-Williams in Early Medieval Europe (4:2) 1995, 248–50; by Peter Dendle in ELN (33:3) 1996, 67–9.

Related Studies

4685. BOYNTON, MARK; REYNOLDS, SUSAN.   The author of the Fonthill Letter. ASE (25) 1996, 91–5.

4686. BROWN, GEORGE HARDIN.   The dynamics of literacy in Anglo-Saxon England. BJRL (77:1) 1995, 109–42.

4687. CESSFORD, CRAIG.   A lost Pictish poem? SLJ (23:2) 1996, 7–15.

4688. CLAYTON, MARY; MAGENNIS, HUGH.   The Old English lives of St Margaret. Cambridge; New York: CUP, 1994. pp. xi, 239. (Cambridge studies in Anglo-Saxon England, 9.) Rev. by Peter Dendle in Albion (28:4) 1996, 125–7; by E. G. Stanley in NQ (43:2) 1996, 195–6; by Ann Squires in Early Medieval Europe (5:1) 1996, 88–9; by Donald C. Baker in ELN (34:2) 1996, 75.

4689. DRONKE, URSULA.   Myth and fiction in early Norse lands. Aldershot; Brookfield, VT: Variorum, 1996. 1 vol. (various pagings). (Collected studies, 524.)

4690. DUMVILLE, DAVID N.   Anglo-Saxon books: treasure in Norman hands? *See* **473**.

4691. DÜWEL, KLAUS; NEUMANN, HANNELORE; NOWAK, SEAN (eds). Runische Schriftkultur in kontinental-skandinavischer und -angelsach-sischer Wechselbeziehung: internationales Symposium in der Werner-Reimers-Stiftung vom 24.–27. Juni 1992 in Bad Homburg. Berlin; New York: de Gruyter, 1994. pp. x, 408. (Erganzungsbande zum Reallexikon der germanischen Altertumskunde, 10.) Rev. by Catherine Hills in NQ (43:1) 1996, 65–6.

4692. GRANT, RAYMOND J. S.   Laurence Nowell, William Lambarde, and the laws of the Anglo-Saxons. Amsterdam; Atlanta, GA: Rodopi, 1996. pp. ii, 196. (Costerus, 108.)

4693. GRETSCH, MECHTHILD.   The language of the Fonthill Letter. *See* **1447**.

4694. HIGHAM, N. J.   An English empire: Bede and the early Anglo-Saxon kings. Manchester: Manchester UP, 1995. pp. viii, 269. Rev. by Richard Abels in Albion (28:4) 1996, 658–60.

4695. HILEY, DAVID.   Changes in English chant repertories in the eleventh century as reflected in the Winchester sequences. Anglo-Norman Studies (16) 1993, 137–54.

4696. HOUGH, CAROLE A.   The early Kentish 'divorce laws': a re-consideration of Æthelberht, chs 79 and 80. ASE (23) 1994, 19–34.

4697. JOCHENS, JENNY.   Women in Old Norse society. Ithaca, NY; London: Cornell UP, 1995. pp. xiii, 266.

4698. KENNEDY, ALAN.   Law and litigation in the *Libellus Æthelwoldi episcopi*. ASE (24) 1995, 131–83.

4699. KEYNES, SIMON.   The 'Dunstan B' charters. ASE (23) 1994, 165–93.

4700. LAPIDGE, MICHAEL.   Anglo-Latin literature, 600–899. London; Rio Grande, OH: Hambledon Press, 1996. pp. xvi, 534.

4701. LEIPER, CONRAD.   Cities of the plain: the rhetoric of sodomy in Peter Damian's *Book of Gomorrah*. RR (86:2) 1995, 191–211.

4702. LEYSER, HENRIETTA.   Medieval women: a social history of women in England, 450–1500. London: Weidenfeld & Nicolson, 1995. pp. xi, 337, (plates) 8. Rev. by Marilyn Oliva in Albion (28:3) 1996, 455–6.

4703. McCREADY, WILLIAM D.   Bede and the Isidorian legacy. MedStud (57) 1995, 41–73.

4704. McGURK, PATRICK; ROSENTHAL, JANE.   The Anglo-Saxon gospelbooks of Judith, Countess of Flanders: their text, make-up and function. ASE (24) 1995, 251–308.

4705. ORCHARD, NICHOLAS.   An Anglo-Saxon Mass for St Willibrord and its later liturgical uses. ASE (24) 1995, 1–10.

4706. ——— An eleventh-century Anglo-Saxon missal fragment. ASE (24) 1995, 283–9.

4707. SCHMIDT, GARY D.   The iconography of the Mouth of Hell: eighth-century Britain to the fifteenth century. Selinsgrove, PA: Susquehanna UP; London; Toronto: Assoc. UPs, 1995. pp. 234. Rev. by C. David Benson in MÆ (65:2) 1996, 301.

4708. THOMPSON, PAULINE A.   St Æthelthryth: the making of history from hagiography. *In* (pp. 475–92) **114**.

4709. VAN HOUTS, ELISABETH.   Women and the writing of history in the early Middle Ages: the case of Abbess Matilda of Essen and Aethelweard. Early Medieval Europe (1:1) 1992, 53–68.

4710. WILLIAMS, ANN; SMYTH, ALFRED P.; KIRBY, D. P.   A biographical dictionary of Dark Age Britain. London: Seaby, 1991. pp. xlii, 253. Rev. by David Rollason in Early Medieval Europe (2:1) 1993, 93–4.

AUTHORS

Ælfric

4711. BAKER, PETER S.   Textual boundaries in Anglo-Saxon works on time (and in some Old English poems). *In* (pp. 445–56) **114**.

4712. BRAVO GARCÍA, ANTONIO; GONZALO ABASCAL, PEDRO.   Héroes y santos en la literatura anglosajona. *See* **4582**.

4713. CLAYTON, MARY.   Ælfric's *Judith*: manipulative or manipulated? ASE (23) 1994, 215–27.

4714. FAUSBØLL, ELSE.   More Ælfric fragments. *See* **354**.

4715. GODDEN, M. R.   The trouble with Sodom: literary responses to biblical sexuality. *See* **4608**.

4716. HILL, JOYCE.   Ælfric's sources reconsidered: some case studies from the *Catholic Homilies*. *In* (pp. 362–86) **114**.

4717. LEE, STUART. Ælfric's treatment of source material in his homily on the Books of the Maccabees. BJRL (77:3) 1995, 165–76.

4718. MARSDEN, RICHARD. Old Latin intervention in the Old English *Heptateuch. See* **4631**.

4719. PORTER, DAVID W. Ælfric's *Colloquy* and Ælfric Bata. *See* **794**.

4720. POWELL, TIMOTHY E. The 'three orders' of society in Anglo-Saxon England. ASE (23) 1994, 103–32.

4721. RAW, BARBARA C. Verbal icons in late Old English. BJRL (77:3) 1995, 121–39.

4722. WILCOX, JONATHAN (ed.). Ælfric's prefaces. (Bibl. 1995, 3787.) Rev. by Kevin S. Kiernan in ANQ (9:1) 1996, 31–3.

Æthelwold

4723. PORTER, DAVID W. Æthelwold's bowl and *The Chronicle of Abingdon*. NM (97:2) 1996, 163–7.

Saint Aldhelm

4724. ORCHARD, ANDY. Poetic inspiration and prosaic translation: the making of *Cædmon's Hymn. In* (pp. 402–22) **114**.

4725. RUSCHE, PHILIP G. Dry-point glosses to Aldhelm's *De laudibus virginitatis* in Beinecke 401. *See* **415**.

4726. WRIGHT, CHARLES D. The blood of Abel and the branches of sin: *Genesis A*, *Maxims I* and Aldhelm's *Carmen de uirginitate*. *See* **4683**.

Alfred

4727. IRVINE, SUSAN. Ulysses and Circe in King Alfred's *Boethius*: a Classical myth transformed. *In* (pp. 387–401) **114**.

4728. LUCAS, PETER J. The *Metrical Epilogue* to the Alfredian *Pastoral Care*: a postscript from Junius. *See* **385**.

4729. POWELL, TIMOTHY E. The 'three orders' of society in Anglo-Saxon England. *See* **4720**.

Byrhtferth

4730. BAKER, PETER S. Textual boundaries in Anglo-Saxon works on time (and in some Old English poems). *In* (pp. 445–56) **114**.

4731. GORMAN, MICHAEL. The glosses on Bede's *De temporum ratione* attributed to Byrhtferth of Ramsey. ASE (25) 1996, 209–32.

Cædmon

4732. HERBISON, IVAN. The idea of the 'Christian epic': towards a history of an Old English poetic genre. *In* (pp. 342–61) **114**.

4733. MORLAND, LAURA. Cædmon and the Germanic tradition. *In* (pp. 324–58) **22**.

4734. ORCHARD, ANDY. Poetic inspiration and prosaic translation: the making of *Cædmon's Hymn. In* (pp. 402–22) **114**.

Cynewulf

4735. BJORK, ROBERT E. (ed.). Cynewulf: basic readings. New York; London: Garland, 1996. pp. xxv, 364. (Garland reference library of the humanities, 1869.) (Basic readings in Anglo-Saxon England, 4.)

4736. CHERNISS, MICHAEL D. The oral-tradition opening theme in the poems of Cynewulf. *In* (pp. 40–65) **22**.

4737. GRADON, P. O. E. (ed.).   Cynewulf's *Elene*. (Bibl. 1960, 1568.) Exeter: Exeter UP, 1996. pp. x, 118. (Exeter medieval English texts and studies.) (Revised ed.: first ed. 1958.)

4738. HERBISON, IVAN.   The idea of the 'Christian epic': towards a history of an Old English poetic genre. *In* (pp. 342–61) **114**.

Guthlac

4739. JONES, CHRISTOPHER A.   Envisioning the *cenobium* in the Old English *Guthlac A*. MedStud (57) 1995, 259–91.

Wulfstan

4740. FRANTZEN, ALLEN J.   The fragmentation of cultural studies and the fragments of Anglo-Saxon England. *See* **4602**.

4741. SAUER, HANS.   Die Exkommunikationsriten aus Wulfstans Handbuch und Liebermanns Gesetze. *In* (pp. 283–307) **11**.

BEOWULF

4742. BAMMESBERGER, ALFRED.   Beowulf's last will. EngS (77:4) 1996, 305–10.

4743. —— The emendation of *Beowulf*, l. 586. *See* **567**.

4744. —— A textual note on *Beowulf* 431–432. *See* **568**.

4745. BEACH, SARAH.   Loss and recompense: responsibilities in *Beowulf*. Mythlore (18:2) 1992, 55–65.

4746. BLOOM, HAROLD (ed.).   Beowulf. New York: Chelsea House, 1995. pp. 77. (Bloom's notes.)

4747. BREMMER, ROLF H., JR.   Grendel's arm and the law. *In* (pp. 121–32) **114**.

4748. CARSLEY, CATHERINE A.   Reassessing cultural memory in *Beowulf*. Assays (7) 1992, 31–41.

4749. ČERMÁK, JAN.   '*Hie dygel lond warigeað*': spatial imagery in five *Beowulf* compounds. *See* **1437**.

4750. CREED, ROBERT PAYSON.   Beowulf's fourth act. *In* (pp. 85–109) **22**.

4751. DAVIS, CRAIG.   *Beowulf* and the demise of Germanic legend in England. New York; London: Garland, 1996. pp. xvii, 237. (Garland reference library of the humanities, 1987.) (Albert Bates Lord studies in oral tradition, 17.)

4752. DESKIS, SUSAN E.   *Beowulf* and the medieval proverb tradition. *See* **3318**.

4753. DIETRICHSON, JAN W.   The making of the couple in Old and Middle English literature. *See* **4594**.

4754. EARL, JAMES W.   Thinking about *Beowulf*. (Bibl. 1994, 2970.) Rev. by Carolyne Larrington in MÆ (65:2) 1996, 310–12.

4755. EVANS, STEPHEN S.   The heroic poetry of Dark-Age Britain: an introduction to its dating, composition, and use as a historical source. *See* **4597**.

4756. FEE, CHRISTOPHER.   *Beag & beaghroden*: women, treasure and the language of social structure in *Beowulf*. NM (97:3) 1996, 285–94.

4757. FEENY, SARAH J.   The funeral pyre theme in *Beowulf*. *In* (pp. 185–200) **22**.

4758. FOLEY, JOHN MILES (ed.); WOMACK, CHRIS; WOMACK, WHITNEY A. (asst eds). *De gustibus*: essays for Alain Renoir. *See* **22**.

4759. GONZALO ABASCAL, PEDRO; BRAVO, ANTONIO. Early Christian funeral ceremonies and Germanic funeral rites in Old English epic. *See* **4609**.

4760. GRIFFITH, M. S. Some difficulties in *Beowulf*, lines 874–902: Sigemund reconsidered. *See* **664**.

4761. GRIFFITHS, BILL. Meet the dragon: an introduction to Beowulf's adversary. *See* **3851**.

4762. GWARA, SCOTT. A metaphor in *Beowulf* 2487a: *gūðhelm tōglād*. *See* **2387**.

4763. HALL, J. R. *Beowulf* 2298A: on *þ(ā) westenne*? *See* **667**.

4764. HERBISON, IVAN. The idea of the 'Christian epic': towards a history of an Old English poetic genre. *In* (pp. 342–61) **114**.

4765. HILL, JOHN M. The cultural world in *Beowulf*. (Bibl. 1995, 3827.) Rev. by Carolyne Larrington in MÆ (65:2) 1996, 310–12; by Stephanie Hollis in Parergon (13:2) 1996, 258–60; by Lois Bragg in SAtlR (61:1) 1996, 126–9.

4766. IRVING, EDWARD B., JR. Heroic worlds: the Knight's Tale and *Beowulf*. *In* (pp. 43–59) **61**.

4767. KIERNAN, KEVIN S. *Beowulf* and the *Beowulf* manuscript. *See* **379**.

4768. KNÚTSSON, PÉTUR. Intertextual quanta in formula and translation. *See* **3161**.

4769. LIBERMAN, ANATOLY. The 'icy' ship of Scyld Scefing: *Beowulf* 33. *In* (pp. 183–94) **11**.

4770. LINDAHL, CARL. *Beowulf*, old law, internalized feud. SF (53:3) 1996, 171–91.

4771. LIONARONS, JOYCE TALLY. *Beowulf*: myth and monsters. EngS (77:1) 1996, 1–14.

4772. LORD, ALBERT B. *Beowulf* and the Russian *Byliny*. *In* (pp. 304–23) **22**.

4773. MC HUGH, MÁIRE. The sheaf and the hound: a comparative analysis of the mythic structure of *Beowulf* and *Tain Bo Cúailnge*. QLLSM (1) 1987, 9–43.

4774. MCNAMARA, JOHN. Legends of Breca and Beowulf. *See* **3420**.

4775. MCNELIS, JAMES I., III. The sword mightier than the pen? Hrothgar's hilt, theory, and philology. *In* (pp. 175–85) **114**.

4776. MAGENNIS, HUGH. Images of community in Old English poetry. *See* **4628**.

4777. —— Treatments of treachery and betrayal in Anglo-Saxon texts. *See* **4629**.

4778. MARINO, STEPHEN. *Beowulf*. Exp (54:4) 1996, 195–8.

4779. MAZO, JEFFREY ALAN. Compound diction and traditional style in *Beowulf* and *Genesis A*. *See* **2673**.

4780. MENZER, MELINDA J. *Aglæcwif* (*Beowulf* 1259a): implications for -*wif* compounds, Grendel's mother, and other *aglæcan*. *See* **1643**.

4781. MITCHELL, BRUCE. J. R. R. Tolkien and Old English studies: an appreciation. *See* **4636**.

4782. NEWTON, SAM. The origins of *Beowulf* and the pre-Viking kingdom of East Anglia. (Bibl. 1995, 3836.) Rev. by Ann Squires in Early Medieval Europe (3:1) 1994, 83–4; by R. M. Liuzza in Albion

(28:1) 1996, 73–4; by Carolyne Larrington in Folklore (107) 1996, 118; by Eric Christiansen in EHR (111:440) 1996, 140–1.

4783. NILES, JOHN D.   Sign and psyche in Old English poetry. *See* **4643**.

4784. OSBORN, MARIJANE.   'Verbal sea charts' and Beowulf's approach to Denmark. *In* (pp. 441–55) **22**.

4785. PARKS, WARD.   The traditional narrator in *Beowulf* and Homer. *In* (pp. 456–79) **22**.

4786. RUNDA, TODD.   Beowulf as king in light of the gnomic passages. SELIM (5) 1995, 78–90.

4787. STANLEY, ERIC GERALD.   In the foreground: *Beowulf*. (Bibl. 1995, 3843.) Rev. by Paul Bibire in Early Medieval Europe (5:2) 1996, 249–50; by Rolf H. Bremmer, Jr, in EngS (77:3) 1996, 277–8.

4788. SUZUKI, SEIICHI.   In defense of resolution as a metrical principle in the meter of *Beowulf*. *See* **4433**.

4789. —— Preference conditions for resolution in the meter of *Beowulf*: Kaluza's Law reconsidered. MP (93:3) 1996, 281–306.

4790. THOMPSON, RICKY L.   Tolkien's word-hord *onlēac*. Mythlore (20:1) 1994, 22–34, 36–40.

4791. THORMANN, JANET.   The poetics of absence: 'The Lament of the Sole Survivor' in *Beowulf*. *In* (pp. 542–50) **22**.

4792. TOLLEY, CLIVE.   *Beowulf*'s Scyld Scefing episode: some Norse and Finnish analogues. ARV (52) 1996, 7–48.

4793. WATERHOUSE, RUTH.   *Beowulf* as palimpsest. *In* (pp. 26–39) **72**.

4794. WILSON, ERIC.   The blood wrought peace: a Girardian reading of *Beowulf*. ELN (34:1) 1996, 7–30.

MIDDLE ENGLISH
AND FIFTEENTH CENTURY

GENERAL AND ANONYMOUS

General Literary Studies;
Editions and Studies of Anonymous Writings
(except Drama and the writings of the *Gawain*-Poet)

4795. ALBANO, ROBERT A.   Middle English historiography. (Bibl. 1993, 2784.) Rev. by Ross Mackenzie in SLJ (supp. 44) 1996, 10–12.

4796. ALLEN, DAVID G.; WHITE, ROBERT A. (eds).   Subjects on the world's stage: essays on British literature of the Middle Ages and the Renaissance. *See* **116**.

4797. ——— The work of dissimilitude: essays from the Sixth Citadel Conference on Medieval and Renaissance Literature. *See* **131**.

4798. ALLEN, ROSAMUND.   *The Awntyrs off Arthure*: jests and jousts. *In* (pp. 129–42) **104**.

4799. AMODIO, MARK C.   Introduction: oral poetics in post-Conquest England. *In* (pp. 1–28) **78**.

4800. ——— Old-English oral-formulaic tradition and Middle-English verse. *In* (pp. 1–20) **22**.

4801. ——— (ed.); MILLER, SARAH GRAY (asst ed.).   Oral poetics in Middle English poetry. *See* **78**.

4802. ANDREW, MALCOLM.   The realizing imagination in late medieval English literature. EngS (76:2) 1995, 113–28.

4803. ARCHIBALD, ELIZABETH.   Contextualizing Chaucer's Constance: romance modes and family values. *In* (pp. 161–75) **26**.

4804. ARN, MARY-JO.   On punctuating medieval literary texts. *See* **561**.

4805. BALL, MARTIN.   The knots of narrative: space, time, and focalization in *Morte Arthure*. Exemplaria (8:2) 1996, 355–74.

4806. BARRON, W. R. J.   *The Wars of Alexander*: from reality to romance. *In* (pp. 22–35) **104**.

4807. BARTLETT, ANNE CLARK.   Male authors, female readers: representation and subjectivity in Middle English devotional literature. (Bibl. 1995, 3857.) Rev. by Brendan Biggs in MÆ (65:2) 1996, 314–15; by Denise L. Despres in SAC (18) 1996, 175–8.

4808. BASWELL, CHRISTOPHER.   Virgil in medieval England: figuring the *Aeneid* from the twelfth century to Chaucer. (Bibl. 1995, 3858.) Rev. by Charles Burnett in MÆ (65:2) 1996, 299–300; by Lawrence V. Ryan in Albion (28:2) 1996, 287–8; by Valerie Edden in NQ (43:3) 1996, 310.

4809. BATT, CATHERINE.   Middle English: general and miscellaneous. YWES (75) 1994, 124–34.

4810. ——— Middle English: romances. YWES (75) 1994, 146–51.

4811. BAWCUTT, PRISCILLA.   An early Scottish debate-poem on women. SLJ (23:2) 1996, 35–42.

4812. BECKWITH, SARAH.   Christ's body: identity, culture, and society in late medieval writings. (Bibl. 1995, 3862.) Rev. by David Burr in FCS (22) 1996, 207–8.

4813. Biow, Douglas.   *Mirabile dictu*: representations of the marvelous in medieval and Renaissance epic. Ann Arbor: Michigan UP, 1996. pp. viii, 199. (Stylus.)

4814. Bitterling, Klaus.   Additional bibliographical information for the *Index of Middle English Verse*. NQ (43:1) 1996, 18–19.

4815. —— A note on the Scottish *Buik of Alexander*. *See* **575**.

4816. Blamires, Alcuin.   Women and preaching in medieval orthodoxy, heresy, and saints' lives. Viator (26) 1995, 135–52.

4817. —— Pratt, Karen; Marx, C. W. (eds).   Woman defamed and woman defended: an anthology of medieval texts. (Bibl. 1995, 3864.) Rev. by Evelyn S. Newlyn in NWSAJ (6:1) 1994, 141–4.

4818. Blanchfield, Lynne S.   Rate revisited: the compilation of the narrative works in MS Ashmole 61. *In* (pp. 208–20) **104**.

4819. Blanchot, Jean-Jacques.   Historicité et poésie. Études Écossaises (1) 1992, 59–68.

4820. Bloomfield, Morton W.; Dunn, Charles W.   The role of the poet in early societies. (Bibl. 1992, 3549.) Rev. by Wilhelm F. H. Nicolaisen in Fabula (32:4) 1991, 292–3.

4821. Boenig, Robert.   *The Abbey of the Holy Ghost* and *The Charter of the Abbey of the Holy Ghost*. SM (ns 1) 1995, 133–63. (Commentary and translation.)

4822. —— *The Profits of Tribulation* and *The Remedy against the Troubles of Temptation*: translations from the Middle English. SM (ns 2) 1996, 222–64.

4823. Bose, Mishtooni.   From exegesis to appropriation: the medieval Solomon. MÆ (65:2) 1996, 187–210.

4824. Bradbury, Nancy Mason.   Literacy, orality, and the poetics of Middle English romance. *In* (pp. 39–69) **78**.

4825. —— The *Tale of Gamelyn* as a greenwood outlaw taking. SF (53:3) 1996, 207–23.

4826. Braekman, Martina.   *How a Lover Praiseth His Lady* (Bodl. MS Fairfax 16): a Middle English courtly poem re-appraised. *See* **342**.

4827. Bravo, Antonio.   Old and Middle English bibliography 1993–95. *See* **4580**.

4828. Brewer, Derek (ed.).   Medieval comic tales. (Bibl. 1974, 3874.) Cambridge; Rochester, NY: Brewer, 1996. pp. xxxiv, 190. (Second ed.: first ed. 1973.)

4829. Bryce, Derek.   The mystical way and the Arthurian quest. (Bibl. 1986, 3308.) Felinfach: Llanerch, 1995. pp. 139. (Second ed.: first ed. 1986.)

4830. Bumke, Joachim.   Courtly culture: literature and society in the High Middle Ages. Trans. by Thomas Dunlap. (Bibl. 1992, 3555.) Rev. by Charles T. Wood in AHR (98:4) 1993, 1230–1.

4831. Bunt, G. H. V.   Alexander the Great in the literature of medieval Britain. Groningen, The Netherlands: Forsten, 1994. pp. 109 (Mediaevalia Groningana, 14.)

4832. Calin, William.   The French tradition and the literature of medieval England. (Bibl. 1994, 3018.) Rev. by R. Barton Palmer in SAC (18) 1996, 186–90; by Margaret Harp in BJJ (3) 1996, 200–3; by K. V. Sinclair in Parergon (13:2) 1996, 231–4.

4833. Canfield, J. Douglas.   Word as bond in English literature from the Middle Ages to the Restoration. (Bibl. 1992, 3563.) Rev. by John P. Zomchick in ECS (25:2) 1991/92, 241–4.

4834. CARTLIDGE, NEIL. The date of *The Owl and the Nightingale*. *See* **1436**.

4835. CHAMBERLAIN, DAVID (ed.). New readings of late medieval love poems. *See* **76**.

4836. COHEN, JEFFREY JEROME, *et al.* The armour of an alienating identity. Arthuriana (6:4) 1996, 1–24.

4837. COPELAND, RITA (ed.). Criticism and dissent in the Middle Ages. *See* **17**.

4838. DANE, JOSEPH A. The lure of oral theory in medieval criticism: from edited 'text' to critical 'work'. *See* **612**.

4839. DESKIS, SUSAN E. *Beowulf* and the medieval proverb tradition. *See* **3318**.

4840. DIEKSTRA, F. N. M. *A Good Remedie aȝens Spirituel Temptacions*: a conflated Middle English version of William Flete's *De remediis contra temptationes* and pseudo-Hugh of St Victor's *De pusillanimitate* in London BL MS Royal 18.A.x. *See* **618**.

4841. DIETRICHSON, JAN W. The making of the couple in Old and Middle English literature. *See* **4594**.

4842. DIMARCO, VINCENT. Travels in medieval *femenye*: Alexander the Great and the Amazon queen. LJGG (37) 1996, 47–66.

4843. DIXON-KENNEDY, MIKE. Arthurian myth and legend: an A–Z of people and places. *See* **3387**.

4844. DOYLE, A. I. '*Lectulus noster floridus*': an allegory of the penitent soul. *In* (pp. 179–90) **61**.

4845. DRONKE, PETER. The medieval lyric. (Bibl. 1978, 3052.) Cambridge; Rochester, NY: Brewer, 1996. pp. xxi, 288. (Third ed.: first ed. 1968.)

4846. DUNCAN, THOMAS G. The maid in the moor and the Rawlinson text. *See* **626**.

4847. —— Two Middle English penitential lyrics: sound and scansion. *In* (pp. 55–65) **56**.

4848. —— (ed.). Medieval English lyrics, 1200–1400. London: Penguin, 1995. pp. xlviii, 266. (Penguin classics.) Rev. by Bernard O'Donoghue in TLS, 23 Aug. 1996, 25.

4849. DUNN, VINCENT A. Cattle-raids and courtships: medieval narrative genres in a traditional context. (Bibl. 1990, 2632.) Rev. by Patricia Lysaght in Fabula (32:4) 1991, 305–7.

4850. EBERLY, SUSAN SCHOON. 'Under the schadow of ane hawthorne grene': the hawthorn in medieval love literature. *In* (pp. 15–39) **76**.

4851. ECKHARDT, CAROLINE D. The figure of Merlin in Middle English chronicles. *In* (pp. 21–39) **15**.

4852. —— The meaning of 'Ermonie' in *Sir Tristrem*. *See* **2175**.

4853. EDWARDS, A. S. G. An unrecorded copy of *Index of Middle English Verse* 3724.5. NQ (43:4) 1996, 403.

4854. EDWARDS, ROBERT R. (ed.). Art and context in late medieval English narrative: essays in honour of Robert Worth Frank, Jr. (Bibl. 1995, 3896.) Rev. by Rodney Delasanta in SAC (18) 1996, 209–13; by H. L. Spencer in NQ (43:1) 1996, 76.

4855. EMBREE, DAN; URQUHART, ELIZABETH (eds). *The Simonie*: a parallel text edition. Ed. from MSS Advocates 19.2.1, Bodley 48, and Peterhouse College [*sic*] 104. *See* **633**.

4856. ESSL, MONIKA. Die Rezeption des Artusstoffes in der englischen und amerikanischen Literatur des 20. Jahrhunderts bei Thomas Berger, Marion Zimmer Bradley, E. A. Robinson, Mary Stewart und T. H. White. Lewiston, NY; Lampeter: Mellen Press, 1995. pp. 237. (Salzburg English & American studies, 27.)

4857. FELLOWS, JENNIFER. *Bevis redivivus*: the printed editions of *Sir Bevis of Hampton. In* (pp. 251–68) **104**.

4858. —— *et al.* (eds). Romance reading on the book: essays on medieval narrative presented to Maldwyn Mills. *See* **104**.

4859. FENSTER, THELMA S. (ed.). Arthurian women: a casebook. New York; London: Garland, 1996. pp. lxxvii, 344. (Garland reference library of the humanities, 1499.) (Arthurian characters and themes, 3.)

4860. FERSTER, JUDITH. Fictions of advice: the literature and politics of counsel in late medieval England. Philadelphia: Pennsylvania UP, 1996. pp. xii, 216. (Middle Ages.)

4861. FIELD, P. J. C. The empire of Lucius Iberius. *See* **640**.

4862. FISIAK, JACEK (ed.). Middle English miscellany: from vocabulary to linguistic variation. *See* **68**.

4863. FLETCHER, ALAN J. A hive of industry or a hornets' nest? MS Sidney Sussex 74 and its scribes. *In* (pp. 131–55) **56**.

4864. —— Middle English: other prose. YWES (75) 1994, 160–1.

4865. FLORES, NONA C. (ed.). Animals in the Middle Ages: a book of essays. New York; London: Garland, 1996. pp. xvi, 206. (Garland reference library of the humanities, 1716.) (Garland medieval casebooks, 13.)

4866. FOLEY, JOHN MILES (ed.); WOMACK, CHRIS; WOMACK, WHITNEY A. (asst eds). *De gustibus*: essays for Alain Renoir. *See* **22**.

4867. FOSS, MICHAEL. The world of Camelot: King Arthur and the Knights of the Round Table. *See* **3394**.

4868. FREDELL, JOEL. Decorated initials in the Lincoln Thornton Manuscript. *See* **356**.

4869. FRIEDMAN, BONITA. In love's thrall: *The Court of Love* and its captives. *In* (pp. 173–90) **76**.

4870. FURROW, MELISSA M. Latin and affect. *In* (pp. 29–41) **26**.

4871. GEORGE, J.-A. Repentance and retribution: the use of the Book of Daniel in Old and Middle English texts. *See* **4606**.

4872. GIACCHERINI, ENRICO. The myth of poetry and the poetry of myth in the Middle English *Sir Orfeo*. Textus (6) 1993, 31–41.

4873. GOLDSTEIN, R. JAMES. The matter of Scotland: historical narrative in medieval Scotland. (Bibl. 1994, 3058.) Rev. by Grace G. Wilson in SSL (29) 1996, 327–9; by Daniel J. Pinti in ChauY (3) 1996, 189–91; by Norman MacDougall in EHR (111:440) 1996, 159–60.

4874. GOLLNICK, JAMES. Merlin as psychological symbol: a Jungian view. *In* (pp. 111–31) **15**.

4875. GOODRICH, PETER (ed.). The romance of Merlin: an anthology. (Bibl. 1993, 2853.) Rev. by James Noble in Quondam et Futurus (2:1) 1992, 99–102.

4876. GRANT, RAYMOND J. S. A copied 'Tremulous' Worcester gloss at Corpus. *See* **362**.

4877. GREENSPAN, KATE. Stripped for contemplation. SM (ns 1) 1995, 72–81.

4878. GUERIN, M. VICTORIA. The fall of kings and princes: structure and destruction in Arthurian tragedy. (Bibl. 1995, 3915.) Rev. by Lynn

Ramey in Arthuriana (6:2) 1996, 95–7; by Donald L. Hoffman in Arthuriana (6:2) 1996, 97–8; by Helen Cooper in MÆ (65:1) 1996, 131–3; by Corinne J. Saunders in NQ (43:3) 1996, 324–5; by Laurel Amtower in ELN (34:1) 1996, 92–3.

4879. HAMMOND, GERALD. What was the influence of the medieval English Bible upon the Renaissance Bible? BJRL (77:3) 1995, 87–95.

4880. HANAWALT, BARBARA A. (ed.). Chaucer's England: literature in historical context. (Bibl. 1994, 3064.) Rev. by Jo Ann Hoeppner Moran in AHR (99:5) 1994, 1674–5; by David G. Allen in ChauY (3) 1996, 192–4.

4881. HANNA, RALPH, III. Defining Middle English alliterative poetry. In (pp. 43–64) **26**.

4882. —— Pursuing history: Middle English manuscripts and their texts. See **367**.

4883. —— *Vae octuplex*, Lollard socio-textual ideology, and Ricardian–Lancastrian prose translation. In (pp. 244–63) **17**.

4884. —— With an *O* (Yorks.) or an *I* (Salop.)? The Middle English lyrics of British Library Additional 45896. See **368**.

4885. HARKINS, PATRICIA. The speaking dead in *Sir Amadace and the White Knight*. JFA (3:3) 1990 (pub. 1994), 62–71.

4886. HARLEY, MARTA POWELL (ed.). *The Myrour of Recluses*: a Middle English translation of *Speculum inclusorum*. Madison, NJ: Fairleigh Dickinson UP; London; Toronto: Assoc. UPs, 1995. pp. xxxiii, 90. Rev. by Bella Millett in MÆ (65:2) 1996, 315–16.

4887. HARWOOD, BRITTON J. The alliterative *Morte Arthure* as a witness to epic. In (pp. 241–86) **78**.

4888. ——OVERING, GILLIAN R. (eds). Class and gender in early English literature: intersections. See **14**.

4889. HEFFERNAN, THOMAS J. Sacred biography: saints and their biographers in the Middle Ages. (Bibl. 1990, 2660.) Rev. by Robert Boenig in SM (14:2/3) 1991, 98–100.

4890. HENDERSON, DAVE. Tradition and heroism in the Middle English romances. In (pp. 89–107) **78**.

4891. HIEATT, CONSTANCE B. The Middle English culinary recipes in MS Harley 5401: an edition and commentary. See **369**.

4892. HIGLEY, SARAH LYNN; TAYLOR, PAUL BEEKMAN. In the grasp of the falcon: re-reading the Corpus Christi Carol. Assays (6) 1991, 93–109.

4893. HONEGGER, THOMAS. From Phoenix to Chauntecleer: medieval English animal poetry. Tübingen; Basle: Francke, 1996. pp. x, 288. (Swiss studies in English, 120.)

4894. HUDSON, HARRIET E. Construction of class, family, and gender in some Middle English popular romances. In (pp. 76–94) **14**.

4895. HUNT, TONY. The poetic vein: phlebotomy in Middle English and Anglo-Norman verse. See **687**.

4896. HUWS, DANIEL. MS Porkington 10 and its scribe. In (pp. 188–207) **104**.

4897. HYATTE, REGINALD. The arts of friendship: the idealization of friendship in medieval and early Renaissance literature. Leiden; New York: Brill, 1994. pp. 249. (Brill's studies in intellectual history, 50.) Rev. by Domenico Pezzini in Aevum (69:2) 1995, 457–63; by Peter S. Noble in MÆ (65:1) 1996, 117–18.

4898. IGLESIAS-RÁBADE, LUIS.   The multi-lingual pulpit in England (1100–1500). *See* **1455**.

4899. INGHAM, PATRICIA CLARE.   Masculine military unions: brotherhood and rivalry in *The Avowing of King Arthur*. Arthuriana (6:4) 1996, 25–44.

4900. IYEIRI, YOKO.   Negative contraction and syntactic conditions in Middle English verse. *See* **1773**.

4901. JAGER, ERIC.   Did Eve invent writing? Script and the Fall in 'the Adam Books'. SP (93:3) 1996, 229–50.

4902. —— The tempter's voice: language and the Fall in medieval literature. (Bibl. 1995, 3934.) Rev. by Albrecht Classen in Med (8) 1995, 263–6; by Norm Klassen in MÆ (65:1) 1996, 113–14.

4903. JAMISON, CAROL PARRISH.   A description of the medieval romance based upon *King Horn*. Quondam et Futurus (1:2) 1991, 44–58.

4904. JANKOFSKY, KLAUS P. (ed.).   The *South English Legendary*: a critical assessment. (Bibl. 1995, 3935.) Rev. by Fritz Kemmler in ZAA (42:4) 1994, 390–1.

4905. JUSTICE, STEVEN.   Writing and rebellion: England in 1381. (Bibl. 1995, 3938.) Rev. by David C. Fowler in Review (18) 1996, 1–30; by T. L. Burton in Parergon (14:1) 1996, 292–4.

4906. KEISER, GEORGE R.   A new text of, and new light on, the *Supplement to the Index of Middle English Verse*, 4106.5. *See* **376**.

4907. —— Reconstructing Robert Thornton's herbal. *See* **377**.

4908. KELLY, KATHLEEN COYNE.   With and without illusions: the journey/journal of Alexander the Great. Assays (9) 1996, 101–18.

4909. KENNEDY, EDWARD DONALD (ed.).   King Arthur: a casebook. *See* **3414**.

4910. KIMMELMAN, BURT.   The poetics of authorship in the later Middle Ages: the emergence of the modern literary persona. New York; Frankfurt; Bern; Paris: Lang, 1996. pp. 288. (Studies in the humanities, 21.) (Cf. bibl. 1991, 3913.)

4911. KINNEY, ARTHUR F.   Figuring medieval and Renaissance - literature. *In* (pp. 13–34) **131**.

4912. KLARER, MARIO.   *Topoi* antiker und mittelalterlicher Utopievorstellungen im mittelenglischen *The Isle of Ladies*. GRM (42:2) 1992, 162–77.

4913. KOVACH, CLAUDIA MARIE.   Floating 'Tristan': distortions, indeterminacy, and *différance* within the integrated corpus. Tristania (14) 1993, 31–58.

4914. KRUGER, STEVEN F.   Dreaming in the Middle Ages. (Bibl. 1994, 3090.) Rev. by Marcia L. Colish in AHR (98:4) 1993, 1220–1; by Frank G. Hoffman in Review (16) 1994, 237–49.

4915. KUCZYNSKI, MICHAEL P.   Prophetic song: the Psalms as moral discourse in late medieval England. Philadelphia: Pennsylvania UP, 1995. pp. xxx, 292. Rev. by Ann W. Astell in SAC (18) 1996, 238–40; by James R. Sprouse in SAtlR (61:2) 1996, 167–70.

4916. LACY, NORRIS J. (ed.).   Medieval Arthurian literature: a guide to recent research. New York; London: Garland, 1996. pp. xii, 471. (Garland reference library of the humanities, 1955.)

4917. LANE, BELDEN C.   Prayer without language in the apophatic tradition: knowing God as 'inaccessible mountain' – 'marvelous desert'. *See* **2416**.

4918. LARRINGTON, CAROLYNE.   Women and writing in medieval

Europe: a sourcebook. (Bibl. 1995, 3951.) Rev. by Bella Millett in NQ (43:3) 1996, 308–9; by Diane Watt in Eng (45:182) 1996, 153–7.

4919. LESTER, G. A. The language of Old and Middle English poetry. *See* **1462**.

4920. LINDLEY, ARTHUR. Hyperion and the hobbyhorse: studies in carnivalesque subversion. Newark: Delaware UP; London; Toronto: Assoc. UPs, 1996. pp. 197.

4921. LINDSTRÖM, BENGT. Some textual notes on the ME *Genesis and Exodus. See* **724**.

4922. LUCAS, ANGELA M. (ed.). Anglo-Irish poems of the Middle Ages. Dublin: Columba Press, 1995. pp. 224. (Maynooth bicentenary.) (English poems in British Library MS Harley 913.)

4923. MCALPINE, KAYE. *Sir Hugh le Blond*: distinguishing the Scottish strand in Child [59]. *See* **3520**.

4924. MCCULLY, C. B.; ANDERSON, J. J. (eds). English historical metrics. *See* **1465**.

4925. MCGILLIVRAY, MURRAY. Towards a post-critical edition: theory, hypertext, and the presentation of Middle English works. *See* **740**.

4926. MAPSTONE, SALLY. Scots and their books in the Middle Ages and the Renaissance: an exhibition in the Bodleian Library, Oxford. *See* **389**.

4927. MARTIN, ELLEN. *Sir Orfeo*'s representation as returns [*sic*] to the repressed. Assays (8) 1995, 29–46.

4928. MARX, C. WILLIAM. The Devil's rights and the redemption in the literature of medieval England. (Bibl. 1995, 3964.) Rev. by Carin Ruff in Albion (28:4) 1996, 670–2; by H. L. Spencer in NQ (43:4) 1996, 465–6.

4929. MATSUMOTO, HIROYUKI. A note on *sothe* in l. 11 in *The Destruction of Troy. See* **751**.

4930. MEALE, CAROL M. '*Prenes: engre*': an early sixteenth-century presentation copy of *The Erle of Tolous. In* (pp. 221–36) **104**.

4931. —— (ed.). Readings in medieval English romance. (Bibl. 1995, 3967.) Rev. by Susan Crane in SAC (18) 1996, 251–4.

4932. —— Women and literature in Britain, 1150–1500. (Bibl. 1995, 3968.) Rev. by Judy Quinn in Parergon (13:2) 1996, 276–7.

4933. MEISTER, PETER. Arthurian literature as a distorted model of Christianity. Quondam et Futurus (1:2) 1991, 32–43.

4934. MILLETT, BELLA. *Mouvance* and the medieval author: re-editing *Ancrene Wisse. In* (pp. 9–20) **56**.

4935. —— *Peintunge* and *schadewe* in *Ancrene Wisse* Part 4. *See* **1984**.

4936. —— JACK, GEORGE B.; WADA, YOKO. *Ancrene Wisse*, the Katherine Group, and the Wooing Group. Cambridge; Rochester, NY: Brewer, 1996. pp. xi, 260. (Annotated bibliographies of Old and Middle English literature, 2.)

4937. MILLETT, BELLA; WOGAN-BROWNE, JOCELYN (eds and trans). Medieval English prose for women: selections from the Katherine Group and *Ancrene Wisse*. (Bibl. 1991, 3631.) Rev. by Evelyn S. Newlyn in NWSAJ (6:1) 1994, 141–4.

4938. MINNIS, A. J. (ed.). Late-medieval religious texts and their transmission: essays in honour of A. I. Doyle. *See* **56**.

4939. MITSCH, RUTHMARIE H. The other Isolde. Tristania (15) 1994, 75–85.

4940. MORGAN, GWENDOLYN A. Medieval balladry and the courtly tradition: literature of revolt and assimilation. (Bibl. 1995, 3970.) Rev. by Richard J. Moll in Arthuriana (6:2) 1996, 98–101.

4941. Morse, Ruth.   The medieval Medea. Cambridge; Rochester, NY: Brewer, 1996. pp. xvi, 267.

4942. Mura, Karen E.   Thomas Wardon: a mid-fifteenth-century reader, 1448–62. *See* **395**.

4943. Murdoch, Brian.   The Germanic hero: politics and pragmatism in early medieval poetry. London; Rio Grande, OH: Hambledon Press, 1996. pp. viii, 188.

4944. Newhauser, Richard.   '*Strong it is to flitte*' – a Middle English poem on death and its pastoral context. *In* (pp. 319–36) **61**.

4945. Newhauser, Richard G.; Alford, John A. (eds).   Literature and religion in the later Middle Ages: philological studies in honor of Siegfried Wenzel. *See* **61**.

4946. Noble, James.   The Grail and its guardian: evidence of authorial intent in the Middle English *Joseph of Arimathea*. Quondam et Futurus (1:2) 1991, 1–14.

4947. Nolan, Maura B.   '*With tresone withinn*': *Wynnere and Wastoure*, chivalric self-representation, and the law. JMEMS (26:1) 1996, 1–28.

4948. Norris, Pamela (ed.).   Through the glass window shines the sun: an anthology of medieval poetry and prose. Boston, MA; London: Little, Brown, 1995. pp. 120.

4949. Ogura, Michiko.   Verbs in medieval English: differences in verb choice in verse and prose. *See* **1783**.

4950. Olsen, Alexandra Hennessey.   Oral tradition in the Middle English romance: the case of *Robert of Cisyle. In* (pp. 71–87) **78**.

4951. Osberg, Richard H.   A voice for the Prioress: the context of English devotional prose. *See* **2687**.

4952. Paxson, James J.   The poetics of personification. (Bibl. 1995, 3979.) Rev. by Mark Allen in MÆ (65:1) 1996, 110–11; by Clare R. Kinney in SAC (18) 1996, 266–8.

4953. Pearsall, Derek.   Madness in *Sir Orfeo. In* (pp. 51–63) **104**.

4954. —— Theory and practice in Middle English editing. *See* **782**.

4955. Petroff, Elizabeth Alvilda.   Body and soul: essays on medieval women and mysticism. (Bibl. 1994, 3119.) Rev. by Roberta Davidson in TSWL (14:2) 1995, 376–7; by Margaret R. Miles in JRS (9:2) 1995, 155–6; by David Lawton in MÆ (65:1) 1996, 116–17; by Robert Boenig in SM (ns 2) 1996, 266–8.

4956. Pezzini, Domenico.   Book IV of St Bridget's *Revelations* in an Italian (MS Laurenziano 27.10) and an English translation (MS Harley 4800) of the fifteenth century. *See* **404**.

4957. —— Il sogno della croce e liriche del Duecento inglese sulla Passione. Parma: Pratiche, 1992. pp. 168. (Biblioteca medievale, 25.) Rev. by Paola Tornaghi in Aevum (69:2) 1995, 431–4.

4958. —— Un trattato sulla vita contemplativa e attiva dalle *Revelationes* (VI, 65) di Santa Brigida: edizione di *An Informacion of Contemplatif Lyf and Actif* dal MS Oxford, Bodley 423. *See* **405**.

4959. Pickering, O. S.   The outspoken *South English Legendary* poet. *In* (pp. 21–37) **56**.

4960. —— The *South English Legendary*: teaching or preaching? PoetT (45) 1996, 1–14.

4961. Pinti, Daniel J.   Court, king, and community in *The Taill of Rauf Coilyear*. ChauY (3) 1996, 73–85.

4962. POWELL, SUE. The transmission and circulation of *The Lay Folks' Catechism*. *In* (pp. 67–84) **56**.

4963. RAMBO, ELIZABETH L. Colonial Ireland in medieval English literature. (Bibl. 1994, 3125.) Rev. by Angela M. Lucas in MÆ (65:2) 1996, 303–4; by Robert Easting in SAC (18) 1996, 275–7.

4964. RAND SCHMIDT, KARI ANNE. The authorship of the *Equatorie of the Planetis*. (Bibl. 1995, 3987.) Rev. by Ebbe Klitgård in EngS (77:5) 1996, 503–4.

4965. REAMES, SHERRY L. Artistry, decorum, and purpose in three Middle English retellings of the Cecilia legend. *In* (pp. 177–99) **26**.

4966. REICHL, KARL. '*No more ne willi wiked be*': religious poetry in a Franciscan manuscript (Digby 2). *In* (pp. 297–317) **61**.

4967. RICHMOND, VELMA BOURGEOIS. The legend of Guy of Warwick. New York; London: Garland, 1996. pp. xv, 551. (Garland reference library of the humanities, 1929.) (Garland studies in medieval literature, 14.)

4968. ROGERS, GILLIAN. '*Illuminat vith lawte, and with lufe lasit*': Gawain gives Arthur a lesson in magnanimity. *In* (pp. 94–111) **104**.

4969. RONDOLONE, DONNA LYNNE. *Wyrchipe*: the clash of oral-heroic and literate-Ricardian ideals in the alliterative *Morte Arthure*. *In* (pp. 207–39) **78**.

4970. ROONEY, ANNE. Hunting in Middle English literature. (Bibl. 1995, 3992.) Rev. by Sandra Pierson Prior in SAC (18) 1996, 278–80.

4971. RUDD, GILLIAN. Middle English: alliterative poetry. YWES (75) 1994, 134–40.

4972. —— Middle English: lyrics and miscellaneous verse. YWES (75) 1994, 155–7.

4973. —— Middle English: Middle Scots poetry. YWES (75) 1994, 154–5.

4974. RUMBLE, ALEXANDER R. The Rylands, the Bible and early English literature: an illustrated note. *See* **414**.

4975. SAUNDERS, CORINNE J. The forest of medieval romance: Avernus, Broceliande, Arden. (Bibl. 1995, 3996.) Rev. by J. R. Goodman in SAC (18) 1996, 285–8.

4976. —— '*Symtyme the fende*': questions of rape in *Sir Gowther*. *In* (pp. 286–303) **114**.

4977. SCATTERGOOD, JOHN. Reading the past: essays on medieval and Renaissance literature. Blackrock, Co. Dublin; Portland, OR: Four Courts Press, 1996. pp. 310.

4978. SENIOR, W. A. Medieval literature and modern fantasy: toward a common metaphysic. JFA (3:3) 1990 (pub. 1994), 32–49.

4979. —— *To goon on pilgrimages*: a special issue on modern fantasy and medieval literature. JFA (3:3) 1990 (pub. 1994), 3–5.

4980. SHEPHERD, S. H. A. (ed.). Middle English romances: authoritative texts, sources and backgrounds, criticism. (Bibl. 1995, 3999.) Rev. by Diane Speed in NQ (43:1) 1996, 73.

4981. SHEPHERD, STEPHEN H. A. The Middle English *Pseudo-Turpin Chronicle*. MÆ (65:1) 1996, 19–34.

4982. —— No poet has his travesty alone: *The Weddynge of Sir Gawen and Dame Ragnell*. *In* (pp. 112–28) **104**.

4983. SIGAL, GALE. Erotic dawn-songs of the Middle Ages: voicing the lyric lady. Gainesville: Florida UP, 1996. pp. xii, 241.

4984. SMITH, JEREMY J.   A note on constrained linguistic variation in a North-West-Midlands Middle-English scribe. *See* **839**.

4985. SMITH, LESLEY; TAYLOR, JANE H. M. (eds).   Women, the book and the worldly: selected proceedings of the St Hilda's conference, 1993: vol. II. *See* **129**.

4986. SNYDER, CYNTHIA LOCKARD.   *The Floure and the Leafe*: an alternative approach. *In* (pp. 145–71) **76**.

4987. SOMERSET, FIONA E.   Vernacular argumentation in *The Testimony of William Thorpe*. *See* **2474**.

4988. SPEARING, A. C.   The medieval poet as voyeur: looking and listening in medieval love-narratives. (Bibl. 1995, 4003.) Rev. by Carolynn Van Dyke in ChauY (3) 1996, 219–24.

4989. —— The poetic subject from Chaucer to Spenser. *In* (pp. 13–37) **116**.

4990. SPEED, DIANE.   The pattern of Providence in *Chevelere Assigne*. *In* (pp. 143–54) **104**.

4991. SPROUSE, JAMES R.   Middle English dialect investigation and the Middle English manuscript: the case of the Bodleian Manuscript 6923. *See* **423**.

4992. SQUIRES, ANN.   The treatment of the figure of Judith in the Middle English metrical paraphrase of the Old Testament. NM (97:2) 1996, 187–200.

4993. STEELE, F. J.   Towards a spirituality for lay-folk: the active life in Middle English religious literature from the thirteenth century to the fifteenth. Lewiston, NY; Lampeter: Mellen Press, 1995. pp. 216. (Salzburg studies in English literature, 92: Elizabethan & Renaissance studies, 23.)

4994. STEVICK, ROBERT D. (ed.).   One hundred Middle English lyrics. Introd. by Eric Dahl. Urbana: Illinois UP, 1994. pp. liii, 194. Rev. by David Parker in ChauY (3) 1996, 228–30.

4995. STUART, CHRISTOPHER.   *Havelok the Dane* and Edward I in the 1290s. SP (93:4) 1996, 349–64.

4996. STURGES, ROBERT S.   Medieval interpretation: models of reading in literary narrative, 1100–1500. (Bibl. 1992, 3696.) Rev. by Paul Zumthor in CanRCL (19:4) 1992, 640–2; by Jeanette Beer in ChauY (3) 1996, 231–4.

4997. TAGUCHI, MAYUMI.   The legend of the Cross before Christ: another prose treatment in English and Anglo-Norman. *See* **849**.

4998. TAVORMINA, M. TERESA; YEAGER, R. F. (eds).   The endless knot: essays on Old and Middle English in honor of Marie Borroff. *See* **26**.

4999. THOMPSON, ANNE B.   Audacious fictions: *Anastasia* and the triumph of narrative. Assays (8) 1995, 1–28. (*South English Legendary*.)

5000. THOMPSON, JOHN J.   Another look at the religious texts in Lincoln, Cathedral Library, MS 91. *In* (pp. 169–87) **56**.

5001. —— Looking behind the book: MS Cotton Caligula A.ii, part 1, and the experience of its texts. *In* (pp. 171–87) **104**.

5002. TINKLE, THERESA LYNN.   Medieval Venuses and Cupids: sexuality, hermeneutics, and English poetry. Stanford, CA: Stanford UP, 1996. pp. 294. (Figurae.)

5003. TOSWELL, M. J.; TYLER, E. M. (eds).   Studies in English language and literature. 'Doubt wisely': papers in honour of E. G. Stanley. *See* **114**.

5004. TROYAN, SCOTT D. Textual decorum: a rhetoric of attitudes in medieval literature. (Bibl. 1994, 3150.) Rev. by Alcuin Blamires in MÆ (65:1) 1996, 109–10.

5005. VANDELINDE, HENRY. *Sir Gowther*: saintly knight and knightly saint. Neophilologus (80:1) 1996, 139–47.

5006. VON NOLCKEN, CHRISTINA. A 'certain sameness' and our response to it in English Wycliffite texts. *In* (pp. 191–208) **61**.

5007. WALLNER, BJÖRN. An interpolated Middle English version of the *Anatomy* of Guy de Chauliac: part 2, Introduction, notes, glossary. Edited from Glasgow Univ. Library, Hunter MS 95. *See* **436**.

5008. WALLS, KATHRYN. Medieval 'allegorical imagery' in *c.*1630: Will. Baspoole's revision of *The Pilgrimage of the Lyfe of the Manhode*. *In* (pp. 304–22) **114**.

5009. WEISS, VICTORIA L. Blurring the lines between the play world and the real world in *The Earl of Toulouse*. ChauR (31:1) 1996, 87–98.

5010. WILLIAMS, EDITH WHITEHURST. A woman's struggle for love and independence in the history of Western romantic love. Tristania (17) 1996, 125–55.

5011. WILLIAMS, ELIZABETH. '*A damsell by herselfe alone*': images of magic and femininity from *Lanval* to *Sir Lambewell*. *In* (pp. 155–70) **104**.

5012. WILSON, ANNE. The magical quest: the use of magic in Arthurian romance. (Bibl. 1990, 2758.) Rev. by Mildred Leake Day in Quondam et Futurus (1:4) 1991, 91–4.

5013. WRIGHT, GLENN. '*Other wyse then must we do*': parody and popular narrative in *The Squyr of Lowe Degre*. Comitatus (27) 1996, 14–41.

Drama

5014. BEADLE, RICHARD (ed.). The Cambridge companion to medieval English theatre. (Bibl. 1995, 4024.) Rev. by Arthur Lindley in AUMLA (85) 1996, 148–50.

5015. BECKWITH, SARAH. The present of past things: the York Corpus Christi cycle as a contemporary theatre of memory. JMEMS (26:2) 1996, 355–79.

5016. —— *Sacrum signum*: sacramentality and dissent in York's theatre of Corpus Christi. *In* (pp. 264–88) **17**.

5017. BEIDLER, PETER G., *et al.* Dramatic intertextuality in the Miller's Tale: Chaucer's use of characters from medieval drama as foils for John, Alisoun, Nicholas, and Absolon. ChauY (3) 1996, 1–19.

5018. BENNETT, WILLIAM F. Communication and excommunication in the N-Town *Conception of Mary*. Assays (8) 1995, 119–40.

5019. COUNSELL, COLIN. Traversing the known: spatiality and the gaze in pre- and post-Renaissance theatre. JDTC (11:1) 1996, 19–33.

5020. DAVIDSON, CLIFFORD; STROUPE, JOHN H. (eds). Drama in the Middle Ages: comparative and critical essays: second series. New York: AMS Press, 1991. pp. xi, 389. (AMS studies in the Middle Ages, 18.) Rev. by T. L. Burton in EngS (75:4) 1994, 386–7.

5021. —— —— Iconographic and comparative studies in medieval drama. Introd. by Meg Twycross. Kalamazoo: Medieval Inst., Western Michigan UP, 1991. pp. xii, 215. (Early drama, art, and music monographs, 17.) Rev. by Anne Lancashire in Essays in Theatre (11:2) 1993, 189; by Peter Meredith in YES (25) 1995, 257.

5022. DIETRICHSON, JAN W. The making of the couple in Old and Middle English literature. *See* **4594**.

5023. DILLER, HANS-JÜRGEN. The Middle English Mystery play: a study in dramatic speech and form. Trans. by Frances Wessels. (Bibl. 1995, 4035.) Rev. by Carol M. Meale in Archiv (233:2) 1996, 385–7.

5024. DUBRUCK, EDELGARD E. The current state of research on late-medieval drama, 1993–4: reviews, notes, and bibliography. FCS (22) 1996, 163–91.

5025. FLANIGAN, TOM. Everyman or saint? Doubting Joseph in the Corpus Christi cycles. MedRen (8) 1996, 19–48.

5026. FLETCHER, ALAN J. Middle English: drama. YWES (75) 1994, 161–4.

5027. GIBSON, GAIL MCMURRAY. The theater of devotion: East Anglian drama and society in the late Middle Ages. (Bibl. 1995, 4037.) Rev. by Denise L. Despres in Shakespeare Yearbook (2) 1991, 239–41; by Richard W. Pfaff in AHR (96:4) 1991, 1184–5.

5028. GRENNEN, JOSEPH E. The 'making of works': David Jones and medieval drama. Ren (45:4) 1993, 211–24.

5029. GUSICK, BARBARA I. Time and unredemption: perceptions of Christ's work in the Towneley *Lazarus*. FCS (22) 1996, 19–41.

5030. HIGGINS, ANNE. Work and plays: guild casting in the Corpus Christi drama. MedRen (7) 1995, 76–97.

5031. KLAUSNER, DAVID N. (ed.). Records of early English drama: Herefordshire and Worcestershire. (Bibl. 1993, 2970.) Rev. by John McGavin in MedRen (7) 1995, 370–2.

5032. LEPOW, LAUREN. Enacting the Sacrament: counter-Lollardy in the Towneley Cycle. (Bibl. 1993, 2972.) Rev. by Douglas Sugano in MedRen (7) 1995, 362–5.

5033. MCCUNE, PAT. Order and justice in early Tudor drama. RenD (25) 1994, 171–96.

5034. MACLEAN, SALLY-BETH. Festive liturgy and the dramatic connection: a study of Thames Valley parishes. MedRen (8) 1996, 49–62.

5035. MEAD, STEPHEN X. Four-fold allegory in the Digby *Mary Magdalene*. Ren (43:4) 1991, 269–82.

5036. MEREDITH, PETER. The direct and indirect use of the Bible in medieval English drama. BJRL (77:3) 1995, 61–77.

5037. MULLINI, ROBERTA. The defeat of evil in *The Harrowing of Hell*. Textus (2:1/2) 1989, 193–206.

5038. MURAKAMI, FUMIAKI. Igirisu doutokugeki to sono shuuhen. (English morality plays and related dramas.) Tokyo: Chuo Shoin, 1996. pp. 242.

5039. NORLAND, HOWARD B. Drama in early Tudor Britain, 1485–1558. Lincoln; London: Nebraska UP, 1995. pp. xxix, 394. Rev. by John M. Wasson in Albion (28:2) 1996, 293–4; by David Gowen in NQ (43:3) 1996, 328–9; by Anne Lancashire in Essays in Theatre (15:1) 1996, 110–12; by James C. Cummings in EMLS (2:2) 1996, 14.1–7.

5040. OLSON, GLENDING. Plays as play: a medieval ethical theory of performance and the intellectual context of the *Tretise of Miraclis Pleyinge*. Viator (26) 1995, 195–221.

5041. PETERSEN, ZINA. '*As tuching the beyring of their torchez*': the unwholesome rebellion of York's cordwainers at the rite of Corpus Christi. FCS (22) 1996, 96–108.

5042. RISDEN, EDWARD L. Medieval drama and the sacred experience. SM (14:2/3) 1991, 74–83.

5043. SIKORSKA, LILIANA. *Mankind* and the question of power dynamics: some remarks on the validity of sociolinguistic reading. NM (97:2) 1996, 201–16.

5044. SMITH, JADWIGA S. The concept of space in medieval drama: toward a phenomenological interpretation in medieval studies. Analecta Husserliana (44) 1995, 231–9.

5045. SPECTOR, STEPHEN (ed.). The N-Town Play: Cotton MS Vespasian D.8. (Bibl. 1994, 3210.) Rev. by David Reinheimer in ChauY (3) 1996, 211–14.

5046. STEVENS, MARTIN. Four Middle English Mystery cycles: textual, contextual and critical interpretations. (Bibl. 1989, 2573.) Rev. by George D. Economou in Genre (23:4) 1990, 369–70.

5047. —— CAWLEY, A. C. (eds). The Towneley plays. (Bibl. 1995, 4054.) Rev. by Pamela M. King in MÆ (65:2) 1996, 320–1; by Victor I. Scherb in SAC (18) 1996, 300–2; by George Jack in EngS (77:3) 1996, 278–9.

5048. STICCA, SANDRO. The *Planctus Mariae* in the dramatic tradition of the Middle Ages. Trans. by Joseph R. Berrigan. (Bibl. 1990, 2790.) Rev. by Margaret Monteverde in MedRen (7) 1995, 365–70.

5049. WARD, PATRICIA H. The significance of roses as weapons in *The Castle of Perseverance*. SM (14:2/3) 1991, 84–92.

5050. WICKHAM, GLYNNE. The medieval theatre. (Bibl. 1989, 2581.) Rev. by Domenico Pezzini in Aevum (65:2) 1991, 414–17.

5051. WRIGHT, STEPHEN K. The vengeance of Our Lord: medieval dramatizations of the destruction of Jerusalem. (Bibl. 1993, 2995.) Rev. by Hans-Jürgen Diller in GRM (41:1) 1991, 113–15.

Related Studies

5052. AERS, DAVID; STALEY, LYNN. The powers of the holy: religion, politics, and gender in late medieval English culture. University Park: Pennsylvania State UP, 1996. pp. 310.

5053. BAYLESS, MARTHA. Parody in the Middle Ages: the Latin tradition. Ann Arbor: Michigan UP, 1996. pp. xii, 425. (Recentiores: later Latin texts and contexts.) (Cf. bibl. 1991, 3735.)

5054. BLACKER, JEAN. The faces of time: portrayal of the past in Old French and Latin historical narrative of the Anglo-Norman regnum. Austin: Texas UP, 1994. pp. xv, 263. Rev. by Gabrielle M. Spiegel in AHR (101:3) 1996, 828–9.

5055. —— Where Wace feared to tread: Latin commentaries on Merlin's prophecies in the reign of Henry II. Arthuriana (6:1) 1996, 36–52.

5056. BRAY, DOROTHY ANN. Allegory in the *Navigatio sancti Brendani*. Viator (26) 1995, 1–10.

5057. BROMWICH, RACHEL. Medieval Welsh literature to *c*.1400, including Arthurian studies: a personal guide to University of Wales Press publications. Cardiff: UP of Wales, 1996. pp. 50.

5058. BROWN, MELISSA L. The hope for 'pleasaunce': Richard Ross' translation of Alain Chartier's *La Belle Dame sans Mercy*. In (pp. 119–43) **76**.

5059. BUSBY, KEITH (ed.). Word and image in Arthurian literature. *See* **186**.

5060. CAMILLE, MICHAEL. The dissenting image: a postcard from Matthew Paris. *In* (pp. 115–50) **17**.

5061. Church, Stephen; Harvey, Ruth (eds).   Medieval knighthood: v, Papers from the sixth Strawberry Hill conference 1994. Woodbridge, Suffolk; Rochester, NY: Boydell Press, 1995. pp. xv, 266.

5062. Crawford, Anne (ed.).   Letters of the queens of England, 1100–1547. Stroud: Sutton, 1994. pp. 250. Rev. by Peregrine Horden in EHR (111:443) 1996, 959–60.

5063. Damian-Grint, Peter.   Redating the Royal *Brut* fragment. MÆ (65:2) 1996, 280–5. (The Anglo-Norman *Brut*.)

5064. —— Truth, trust, and evidence in the Anglo-Norman *estoire*. Anglo-Norman Studies (18) 1995, 63–78.

5065. d'Avray, D. L.   Death and the prince: memorial preaching before 1350. Oxford: Clarendon Press; New York: OUP, 1994. pp. xi, 315. Rev. by Alan J. Fletcher in MÆ (65:1) 1996, 122–3.

5066. Dumville, David N.   Anglo-Saxon books: treasure in Norman hands? *See* **473**.

5067. Easting, Robert.   Peter of Bramham's account of a chaplain's vision of Purgatory (*c.*1343?). MÆ (65:2) 1996, 211–29.

5068. Edden, Valerie.   Marian devotion in a Carmelite sermon collection of the late Middle Ages. MedStud (57) 1995, 101–29.

5069. Edwards, Huw M.   Dafydd ap Gwilym: influences and analogues. Oxford: Clarendon Press; New York: OUP, 1996. pp. xiii, 300. (Oxford modern languages and literature monographs.)

5070. Erler, Mary C.   English vowed women at the end of the Middle Ages. MedStud (57) 1995, 155–203.

5071. Freeman, Elizabeth.   Geffrei Gaimar, vernacular historiography, and the assertion of authority. SP (93:2) 1996, 188–206.

5072. Furtado, Antonio L.   Geoffrey of Monmouth: a source of the Grail stories. Quondam et Futurus (1:1) 1991, 1–14.

5073. Gellrich, Jesse M.   Discourse and dominion in the fourteenth century: oral contexts of writing in philosophy, politics, and poetry. Princeton, NJ; Chichester: Princeton UP, 1995. pp. xiv, 304. Rev. by Mary Carruthers in ALH (101:4) 1996, 1194–5; by Andrew Galloway in SAC (18) 1996, 213–22.

5074. George, Wilma; Yapp, Brunsdon.   The naming of the beasts: natural history in the medieval bestiary. *See* **1837**.

5075. Greenway, Diana.   Authority, convention and observation in Henry of Huntingdon's *Historia Anglorvm*. Anglo-Norman Studies (18) 1995, 105–21.

5076. Hahn, Thomas.   Traditional religion, social history, and literary studies. Assays (9) 1996, 25–33.

5077. Herren, Michael W.   Latin letters in early Christian Ireland. Aldershot; Brookfield, VT: Variorum, 1996. 1 vol. (various pagings). (Collected studies, 527.)

5078. Hiley, David.   Changes in English chant repertories in the eleventh century as reflected in the Winchester sequences. *See* **4695**.

5079. Hudson, Anne.   Aspects of the 'publication' of Wyclif's Latin sermons. *In* (pp. 121–9) **56**.

5080. Hunt, Tony.   Early Anglo-Norman receipts for colours. JWCI (58) 1995, 203–9.

5081. Jaeger, C. Stephen.   Courtly love and love at court: public aspects of an aristocratic sensibility. Æstel (4) 1996, 1–27.

5082. Justice, Steven.   Inquisition, speech, and writing: a case from late medieval Norwich. *In* (pp. 289–322) **17**.

5083. KEISER, GEORGE R. Through a fourteenth-century gardener's eyes: Henry Daniel's herbal. ChauR (31:1) 1996, 58–75.

5084. KIECKHEFER, RICHARD. The specific rationality of medieval magic. AHR (99:3) 1994, 813–36.

5085. KNIGHT, ALAN E. Faded pageant: the end of the Mystery plays in Lille. JMMLA (29:1) 1996, 3–14.

5086. LACY, NORRIS J. Medieval French Arthurian literature in English. Quondam et Futurus (1:3) 1991, 55–74.

5087. LEYSER, HENRIETTA. Medieval women: a social history of women in England, 450–1500. *See* **4702**.

5088. LUSCOMBE, D. E. Bec, Christ Church and the correspondence of St Anselm. Anglo-Norman Studies (18) 1995, 1–17. (R. Allen Brown memorial lecture.)

5089. McCAULEY, BARBARA LYNNE. Giraldus 'Silvester' of Wales and his *Prophetic History of Ireland*: Merlin's role in the *Expugnatio Hibernica*. Quondam et Futurus (3:4) 1993, 41–62.

5090. McKENDRICK, SCOT. The *Great History of Troy*: a reassessment of the development of a secular theme in late medieval art. JWCI (54) 1991, 43–82.

5091. MANTELLO, F. A. C.; RIGG, A. G. (eds). Medieval Latin: an introduction and bibliographical guide. Washington, DC: Catholic Univ. of America Press, 1996. pp. xiv, 774.

5092. MASTERS, BERNADETTE. The distribution, destruction, and dedication of authority in medieval literature and its modern derivatives. RR (82:3) 1991, 270–85.

5093. MERTENS, VOLKER; WOLFZETTEL, FRIEDRICH (eds). Fiktionalität im Artusroman: dritte Tagung der Deutschen Sektion der Internationalen Artusgesellschaft in Berlin vom 13.–15. Februar 1992. Tübingen: Niemeyer, 1993. pp. xi, 259. Rev. by Richard J. Utz in Arthuriana (6:2) 1996, 101–3.

5094. MUNDILL, ROBIN R. English medieval Ashkenazim-literature and progress. Aschkenas (1) 1991, 203–10.

5095. NEUENDORF, FIONA TOLHURST. Negotiating feminist and historicist concerns: Guenevere in Geoffrey of Monmouth's *Historia regum Britanniae*. Quondam et Futurus (3:2) 1993, 26–44.

5096. NEWMAN, BARBARA. From virile woman to womanChrist: studies in medieval religion and literature. Philadelphia: Pennsylvania UP, 1995. pp. 355. (Middle Ages.) Rev. by Linda Georgianna in SAC (18) 1996, 260–3.

5097. PEARCY, ROY J. A neglected Anglo-Norman version of *Le Cuvier* (London, British Library Harley 527). MedStud (58) 1996, 243–72.

5098. PINTI, DANIEL J. Dialogism, heteroglossia, and late medieval translation. *See* **3182**.

5099. RAFFINI, CHRISTINE. The passion for place: medieval and Renaissance re-creations of Paradise. Analecta Husserliana (44) 1995, 221–30.

5100. REYNOLDS, SUZANNE. Medieval reading: grammar, rhetoric, and the Classical text. Cambridge; New York: CUP, 1996. pp. xvi, 235. (Cambridge studies in medieval literature, 27.)

5101. RIGG, A. G. Serlo of Wilton: biographical notes. MÆ (65:1) 1996, 96–101.

5102. SALISBURY, JOYCE E. The beast within: animals in the

Middle Ages. London; New York: Routledge, 1994. pp. 238. Rev. by Thomas M. Honegger in SAC (18) 1996, 283–5; by T. L. Burton in Parergon (14:1) 1996, 303–5.

5103. SCHMIDT, GARY D.   The iconography of the Mouth of Hell: eighth-century Britain to the fifteenth century. *See* **4707**.

5104. SHORT, IAN.   *Tam Angli quam Franci*: self-definition in Anglo-Norman England. Anglo-Norman Studies (18) 1995, 153–75.

5105. SLOCUM, KAY.   *Musica coelestis*: a fourteenth-century image of cosmic music. SM (14:2/3) 1991, 3–12.

5106. SMITH, SUSAN L.   The power of women: a *topos* in medieval art and literature. Philadelphia: Pennsylvania UP, 1995. pp. xv, 294. Rev. by Margaret Harp in RMRLL (50:2) 1996, 208–10.

5107. SPONSLER, CLAIRE.   Medieval ethnography: fieldwork in the European past. Assays (7) 1992, 1–30.

5108. SUTTON, ANNE F.; VISSER-FUCHS, LIVIA.   The dark dragon of the Normans: a creation of Geoffrey of Monmouth, Stephen of Rouen, and Merlin Silvester. Quondam et Futurus (2:2) 1992, 1–19.

5109. THOMAS, PATRICK MICHAEL.   Circle as structure: the *Tristan* of Thomas. Quondam et Futurus (1:3) 1991, 41–54.

5110. —— *Tristan* and the avatars of the lunar goddess. Quondam et Futurus (2:3) 1992, 15–20.

5111. THUNDY, ZACHARIAS P.   Merlin in the Indo-European tradition. *In* (pp. 79–90) **15**.

5112. WATKISS, LESLIE; CHIBNALL, MARJORIE (eds and trans).   The Waltham Chronicle: an account of the discovery of our Holy Cross at Montacute and its conveyance to Waltham. Oxford: Clarendon Press; New York: OUP, 1994. pp. liii, 99. (Latin text with parallel English translation.) Rev. by Rosalind Ransford in MÆ (65:1) 1996, 173.

5113. WOGAN-BROWNE, JOCELYN.   The apple's message: some post-Conquest hagiographic accounts of textual transmission. *In* (pp. 39–53) **56**.

AUTHORS
(except Chaucer and the *Gawain* -Poet)

John Barbour

5114. KNIEZSA, VERONIKA.   The orthography of Older Scots: the manuscripts of Barbour's *The Bruce*. *In* (pp. 167–82) **11**.

Osbern Bokenham

5115. DELANY, SHEILA (ed. and trans.).   A legend of holy women: Osbern Bokenham, *Legends of Holy Women*. (Bibl. 1995, 4119.) Rev. by Carol M. Meale in Archiv (233:2) 1996, 383–5.

5116. EDWARDS, A. S. G.   The transmission and audience of Osbern Bokenham's *Legendys of Hooly Wummen*. *In* (pp. 157–67) **56**.

5117. JANKOWSKI, EILEEN S.   Reception of Chaucer's Second Nun's Tale: Osbern Bokenham's *Lyf of S. Cycyle*. ChauR (30:3) 1996, 306–18.

John Capgrave

5118. CAMICIOTTI, GABRIELLA DEL LUNGO.   The modal system in late Middle English: the case of Capgrave's *Chronicle*. *See* **1764**.

5119. WINSTEAD, KAREN A.   Capgrave's Saint Katherine and the perils of gynecocracy. Viator (25) 1994, 361–76.
5120. —— John Capgrave and the Chaucer tradition. ChauR (30:4) 1996, 389–400.

William Caxton

5121. BATT, CATHERINE.   Middle English: Malory and Caxton. YWES (75) 1994, 157–60.
5122. GOODMAN, JENNIFER R.   '*That wommen holde in ful greet reverence*': mothers and daughters reading chivalric romances. *In* (pp. 25–30) **129**.
5123. STOCKER, MARGARITA.   Apocryphal entries: Judith and the politics of Caxton's *Golden Legend*. *In* (pp. 167–81) **129**.
5124. SUMMIT, JENNIFER.   William Caxton, Margaret Beaufort and the romance of female patronage. *In* (pp. 151–65) **129**.
5125. TAKAMIYA, TOSHIYUKI.   Chapter divisions and page breaks in Caxton's *Morte Darthur*. *See* **317**.
5126. WHITAKER, ELAINE E.   A collaboration of readers: categorization of the annotations in copies of Caxton's *Royal Book*. Text (Ann Arbor) (7) 1994, 233–42.

Charles of Orleans

5127. ARN, MARY-JO (ed.).   *Fortunes Stabilnes*: Charles of Orleans's English book of love: a critical edition. *See* **562**.
5128. COLDIRON, A. E. B.   *Translatio*, translation, and Charles d'Orléans's paroled poetics. *See* **3117**.
5129. HODAPP, WILLIAM F.   Minerva's owl in Charles d'Orléans's English poems: a mythographic note on line 4765. ANQ (9:1) 1996, 3–7.

Sir John Clanvowe

5130. CHAMBERLAIN, DAVID.   Clanvowe's cuckoo. *In* (pp. 41–65) **76**.

Gavin Douglas

5131. GHOSH, KANTIK.   '*The fift quheill*': Gavin Douglas's Maffeo Vegio. SLJ (22:1) 1995, 5–21.
5132. MOESSNER, LILO.   '*Besyde Latyn our langage is imperfite*': the contribution of Gavin Douglas to the development of the Scots lexicon. *See* **1902**.

William Dunbar

5133. BAWCUTT, PRISCILLA.   Images of women in the poems of Dunbar. Études Écossaises (1) 1992, 49–58.
5134. —— (ed.).   Selected poems. London; New York: Longman, 1996. pp. xii, 451. (Longman annotated texts.)
5135. DREXLER, ROBERT DANIEL.   Dunbar's aureate language. *See* **2607**.
5136. HABIB, IMTIAZ.   Reading Black women characters of the English Renaissance: colonial inscription and postcolonial recovery. RenP 1996, 67–80.
5137. MORGAN, EDWIN.   The poetry of the city. *See* **4639**.

John Gower

5138. BATT, CATHERINE.   Middle English: Gower, Lydgate, Hoccleve. YWES (75) 1994, 151–3.

5139. Furrow, Melissa M.   Latin and affect. *In* (pp. 29–41) **26**.

5140. Machan, Tim William.   Thomas Berthelette and Gower's *Confessio*. *See* **745**.

5141. Rupp, Katrin.   'Few love to hear the sins they love to act': father–daughter incest in three versions of *Apollonius of Tyre*. *See* **4657**.

5142. Sanders, Arnold A.   Ruddymane and Canace, lost and found: Spenser's reception of *Confessio Amantis* 3 and Chaucer's Squire's Tale. *In* (pp. 196–215) **131**.

5143. Simpson, James.   Sciences and the self in medieval poetry: Alan of Lille's *Anticlaudianus* and John Gower's *Confessio Amantis*. Cambridge; New York: CUP, 1995. pp. xii, 321. (Cambridge studies in medieval literature, 25.) Rev. by Hugh White in MÆ (65:2) 1996, 308–9; by C. Catalini in NQ (43:3) 1996, 322.

5144. Westrem, Scott D.   Two routes to pleasant instruction in late fourteenth-century literature. *In* (pp. 67–80) **131**.

5145. Yeager, R. F.   Ben Jonson's *English Grammar* and John Gower's reception in the seventeenth century. *In* (pp. 227–39) **26**.

Sir Gilbert Hay

5146. Glenn, Jonathan A. (ed.).   The prose works of Sir Gilbert Hay: vol. 3, *The Buke of the Ordre of Knychthede*; and *The Buke of the Gouernaunce of Princis*. (Bibl. 1995, 4148.) Rev. by D. E. van Duin in EngS (76:5) 1995, 483–4; by Elizabeth Ewan in FCS (22) 1996, 221–2.

5147. van Duin, Deborah E.   'Na man micht noumber þe riches': the city of Segar in Sir Gilbert Hay's *Buik of King Alexander*. EngS (77:6) 1996, 517–29.

Robert Henryson

5148. Cox, Catherine S.   Froward language and wanton play: the '*commoun*' text of Henryson's *Testament of Cresseid*. SSL (29) 1996, 58–72.

5149. Greentree, Rosemary.   Reader, teller and teacher: the narrator of Robert Henryson's *Moral Fables*. (Bibl. 1995, 4150.) Rev. by Robert L. Kindrick in SSL (29) 1996, 298–300.

5150. McKenna, Steven R.   Robert Henryson's tragic vision. (Bibl. 1994, 3285.) Rev. by Evelyn S. Newlyn in SSL (29) 1996, 301–4.

5151. Torti, Anna.   Henryson's *Testament of Cresseid*: deconstructing the *auctoritas*. Textus (5) 1992, 3–11.

Walter Hilton

5152. Ross, Ellen M.   Ethical mysticism: Walter Hilton and *The Scale of Perfection*. SM (ns 2) 1996, 160–84.

Thomas Hoccleve

5153. Batt, Catherine.   Middle English: Gower, Lydgate, Hoccleve. *See* **5138**.

5154. Burrow, J. A.   Thomas Hoccleve. (Bibl. 1994, 3293.) Rev. by Christian Zacher in SAC (18) 1996, 294–7.

Peter Idley

5155. Sullivan, Matthew.   More poetry by Peter Idley: transcribed from British Library MS Additional 57335. NM (97:1) 1996, 29–55.

James I, King of Scotland

5156. BLANCHOT, JEAN-JACQUES. Historicité et poésie. *See* **4819**.

5157. JAMES, CLAIR F. *The Kingis Quair*: the plight of the courtly lover. *In* (pp. 95–118) **76**.

Julian of Norwich

5158. BAKER, DENISE NOWAKOWSKI. Julian of Norwich's *Showings*: from vision to book. (Bibl. 1995, 4164.) Rev. by Vincent Gillespie in MÆ (65:2) 1996, 317–18; by Karma Lochrie in AHR (101:2) 1996, 467–8; by Barry Windeatt in SAC (18) 1996, 171–3.

5159. LANE, BELDEN C. Prayer without language in the apophatic tradition: knowing God as 'inaccessible mountain' – 'marvelous desert'. *See* **2416**.

5160. RUUD, JAY. Images of the self and self-image in Julian of Norwich. SM (ns 1) 1995, 82–105.

5161. WATSON, NICHOLAS. '*Yf wommen be double naturelly*': remaking 'woman' in Julian of Norwich's *Revelation of Love*. Exemplaria (8:1) 1996, 1–34.

Margery Kempe

5162. AKEL, CATHERINE S. Familial structure in the religious relationships and visionary experiences of Margery Kempe. SM (ns 1) 1995, 116–32.

5163. BITTERLING, KLAUS. Margery Kempe, an English *sterte* in Germany. *See* **2005**.

5164. FURROW, MELISSA. Unscholarly Latinity and Margery Kempe. *In* (pp. 240–51) **114**.

5165. LUCAS, ELONA K. Poustinia and the 'worldly' spirituality of Margery Kempe. SM (14:2/3) 1991, 61–71.

5166. NEUBURGER, VERENA E. Margery Kempe: a study in early English feminism. New York; Frankfurt; Bern; Paris: Lang, 1994. pp. 219. (European univ. studies, XIV: Anglo-Saxon language and literature, 278.) Rev. by Christa Jansohn in Archiv (233:1) 1996, 232–3.

5167. PIGG, DANIEL F. Medieval theories of textual formation and *The Book of Margery Kempe*. SM (ns 1) 1995, 106–15.

5168. SIKORSKA, LILIANA. Mapping the problem of sexual desire in *The Book of Margery Kempe*. *See* **2707**.

5169. STALEY, LYNN. Margery Kempe's dissenting fictions. (Bibl. 1995, 4181.) Rev. by Nicholas Watson in MÆ (65:1) 1996, 137–8; by Karen A. Winstead in Prose Studies (19:1) 1996, 113–16; by John C. Hirsh in SAC (18) 1996, 297–9; by Deborah S. Ellis in ChauY (3) 1996, 225–7.

William Langland

5170. ADAMS, ROBERT. Editing *Piers Plowman B*: the imperative of an intermittently critical edition. *See* **558**.

5171. AERS, DAVID. Class, gender, medieval criticism and *Piers Plowman*. *In* (pp. 59–75) **14**.

5172. ALFORD, JOHN A. Langland's exegetical drama: the sources of the banquet scene in *Piers Plowman*. *In* (pp. 97–117) **61**.

5173. ANDERSON, J. J. Some aspects of scriptural quotation in *Piers Plowman*: Lady Holy Church. BJRL (77:3) 1995, 19–30.

5174. ASAKA, YOSHIKO. 'Hinkon' to 'yomikaki' no mondai: *Piers*

Plowman to Wycliffe ha. (The problem of poverty and literacy: *Piers Plowman* and the Wycliffites.) StudME (11) 1996, 81–93.

5175. BARNEY, STEPHEN A.   Langland's prosody: the state of study. *In* (pp. 65–85) **26**.

5176. BARR, HELEN.   *Signes and sothe*: language in the *Piers Plowman* tradition. (Bibl. 1994, 3316.) Rev. by Hugh White in MÆ (65:1) 1996, 130–1; by Christina von Nolcken in SAC (18) 1996, 173–5; by S. S. Hussey in NQ (43:1) 1996, 78–9.

5177. BLYTHE, JOAN HEIGES.   Sins of the tongue and rhetorical prudence in *Piers Plowman*. *In* (pp. 119–42) **61**.

5178. BREWER, CHARLOTTE.   Editing *Piers Plowman*. *See* **586**.

5179. —— Editing *Piers Plowman*: the evolution of the text. *See* **587**.

5180. BURROW, J. A.   Langland's fictions. (Bibl. 1995, 4198.) Rev. by Derek Pearsall in Review (17) 1995, 267–70.

5181. DAVLIN, MARY CLEMENTE.   *A game of heuene*: word play and the meaning of *Piers Plowman B*. (Bibl. 1993, 3110.) Rev. by Stanley Hussey in LitTheol (5:3) 1991, 332–7.

5182. DIETRICHSON, JAN W.   The making of the couple in Old and Middle English literature. *See* **4594**.

5183. ECONOMOU, GEORGE (trans.).   William Langland's *Piers Plowman*: the C version: a verse translation. Philadelphia: Pennsylvania UP, 1996. pp. xxxiv, 262. (Middle Ages.)

5184. FOWLER, DAVID C.   Star gazing: *Piers Plowman* and the Peasants' Revolt. Review (18) 1996, 1–30 (review-article).

5185. FURROW, MELISSA M.   Latin and affect. *In* (pp. 29–41) **26**.

5186. GILLESPIE, VINCENT.   Thy will be done: *Piers Plowman* and the *Paternoster*. *In* (pp. 95–119) **56**.

5187. GODDEN, MALCOLM.   The making of *Piers Plowman*. (Bibl. 1993, 3118.) Rev. by Stanley Hussey in LitTheol (5:3) 1991, 332–7.

5188. GRADY, FRANK.   Chaucer reading Langland: *The House of Fame*. SAC (18) 1996, 3–23.

5189. HANNA, RALPH, III.   'Meddling with makings' and Will's work. *In* (pp. 85–94) **56**.

5190. —— Robert the Ruyflare and his companions. *In* (pp. 81–96) **61**.

5191. —— William Langland. (Bibl. 1994, 3331.) Rev. by Christian Zacher in SAC (18) 1996, 294–7.

5192. HARVEY, E. RUTH.   The swallow's nest and the spider's web. *In* (pp. 327–41) **114**.

5193. HUSSEY, STANLEY.   In pursuit of Piers Plowman. LitTheol (5:3) 1991, 332–7 (review-article).

5194. LAWLER, TRAUGOTT.   Conscience's dinner. *In* (pp. 87–103) **26**.

5195. LEES, CLARE A.   Gender and exchange in *Piers Plowman*. *In* (pp. 112–30) **14**.

5196. McRAE, ANDREW.   Fashioning a cultural icon: the ploughman in Renaissance texts. Parergon (14:1) 1996, 187–204.

5197. RUDD, GILLIAN.   Managing language in *Piers Plowman*. (Bibl. 1995, 4220.) Rev. by Helen Barr in MÆ (65:1) 1996, 129–30; by Joseph S. Wittig in SAC (18) 1996, 280–3; by Wendy Scase in NQ (43:1) 1996, 75–6; by Malcolm Andrew in EngS (77:3) 1996, 281–2.

5198. —— Middle English: *Piers Plowman*. YWES (75) 1994, 141–6.

5199. SCASE, WENDY.   *Piers Plowman* and the new anticlericalism.

(Bibl. 1993, 3133.) Rev. by Stanley Hussey in LitTheol (5:3) 1991, 332–7; by Anke Janssen in Med (8) 1995, 489–92.

5200. SCHMIDT, A. V. C. (ed.). *Piers Plowman*: a parallel-text edition of the A, B, C and Z versions: vol. 1, Text. (Bibl. 1995, 4222.) Rev. by Charlotte Brewer in MÆ (65:2) 1996, 286–93; by George Kane in NQ (43:3) 1996, 315–21; by Klaus Bitterling in GRM (46:2) 1996, 246–9.

5201. —— The vision of Piers Plowman: a critical edition of the B-text based on Trinity College Cambridge MS B.15.17. (Bibl. 1981, 3727.) London: Dent; Rutland, VT: Tuttle, 1995. pp. lxxxvi, 550. (Everyman library.) (Second ed.: first ed. 1978.) Rev. by Charlotte Brewer in MÆ (65:2) 1996, 286–93.

5202. —— (trans. and ed.). *Piers Plowman*: a new translation of the B-text. (Bibl. 1994, 3349.) Rev. by Mary Clemente Davlin in ChauY (3) 1996, 204–7.

5203. SHENEMAN, PAUL. Debt and its double in *Piers Plowman*. SN (68:2) 1996, 185–94.

5204. SIMPSON, JAMES. Desire and the scriptural text: Will as reader in *Piers Plowman*. *In* (pp. 215–43) **17**.

5205. —— *Piers Plowman*: an introduction to the B-text. (Bibl. 1994, 3350.) Rev. by Stanley Hussey in LitTheol (5:3) 1991, 332–7.

5206. TAVORMINA, M. TERESA. Kindly similitude: marriage and family in *Piers Plowman*. (Bibl. 1995, 4224.) Rev. by H. L. Spencer in NQ (43:4) 1996, 466–7.

5207. TAYLOR, SEAN. The F scribe and the R manuscript of *Piers Plowman B. See* **427**.

5208. VAUGHAN, MÍCEÁL F. (ed.). *Suche werkis to werche*: essays on *Piers Plowman* in honor of David C. Fowler. (Bibl. 1995, 4225.) Rev. by Malcolm Andrew in EngS (76:5) 1995, 482–3.

5209. WHITE, HUGH. Book's bold speech and the *archana verba* of *Piers Plowman* Passus B xviii. BJRL (77:3) 1995, 31–46.

5210. —— Nature and salvation in *Piers Plowman*. (Bibl. 1991, 3932.) Rev. by Stanley Hussey in LitTheol (5:3) 1991, 332–7.

Laȝamon

5211. ALAMICHEL, MARIE-FRANÇOISE. Doubt and time in Laȝamon's *Brut*. *In* (pp. 219–39) **114**.

5212. AMODIO, MARK C. Introduction: oral poetics in post-Conquest England. *In* (pp. 1–28) **78**.

5213. BARRON, W. R. J.; WEINBERG, S. C. (eds). Brut; or, Hystoria Brutonum. Harlow; New York: Longman, 1995. pp. xxi, 896.

5214. BRAVO GARCÍA, ANTONIO. El estilo de la descripción de las batallas en el *Brut* de Layamon y en la épica anglosajona de los siglos x–xi. *See* **2588**.

5215. BRYAN, ELIZABETH J. Truth and the Round Table in Lawman's *Brut*. Quondam et Futurus (2:4) 1992, 27–35.

5216. HANNA, RALPH, III. Defining Middle English alliterative poetry. *In* (pp. 43–64) **26**.

5217. KIRBY, IAN J. First in the field? A 'new-old' word in Laȝamon's *Brut*. *In* (pp. 163–6) **11**.

5218. KRYGIER, MARCIN. Plural markers of the Old English nouns of relationship in the two manuscripts of Laȝamon's *Brut*. *In* (pp. 47–68) **68**.

5219. LE SAUX, FRANÇOISE H. M. Laȝamon's *Brut*: the poem and its sources. (Bibl. 1992, 3934.) Rev. by Donald L. Hoffman in Quondam et Futurus (1:1) 1991, 91–4.

5220. ROBERTS, JANE.   Laȝamon's plain words. *In* (pp. 107–22) **68**.

Nicholas Love

5221. DOYLE, A. I.   Recusant versions of the *Meditationes Vitae Christi*. BLR (15:5/6) 1996, 411–13.

John Lydgate

5222. BATT, CATHERINE.   Middle English: Gower, Lydgate, Hoccleve. *See* **5138**.

5223. BOFFEY, JULIA.   Lydgate's lyrics and women readers. *In* (pp. 139–49) **129**.

5224. CROCKETT, BRYAN.   Venus unveiled: Lydgate's *Temple of Glas* and the religion of love. *In* (pp. 67–93) **76**.

5225. DEVRIES, DAVID N.   And away go troubles down the drain: late medieval London and the poetics of urban renewal. Exemplaria (8:2) 1996, 401–18.

5226. HANNA, RALPH, III.   John Shirley and British Library, MS Additional 16165. *See* **366**.

5227. HARDMAN, PHILLIPA.   Lydgate's *Life of Our Lady*: a text in transition. *See* **674**.

5228. MCCLELLAN, WILLIAM.   A codicological analysis of the quire structure of MS HM 140 and its implications for a revised *ordinatio*. *See* **386**.

Sir Thomas Malory

5229. ARCHIBALD, ELIZABETH; EDWARDS, A. S. G. (eds).   A companion to Malory. Cambridge; Rochester, NY: Brewer, 1996. pp. xv, 262. (Arthurian studies, 37.)

5230. BATT, CATHERINE.   Middle English: Malory and Caxton. *See* **5121**.

5231. COLE, HARRY E.   Forgiveness as structure: *The Book of Sir Launcelot and Queen Guinevere*. ChauR (31:1) 1996, 36–44.

5232. FEHRENBACHER, RICHARD.   The domestication of *Merlin* in Malory's *Morte Darthur*. Quondam et Futurus (3:4) 1993, 1–16.

5233. FIELD, P. J. C.   The empire of Lucius Iberius. *See* **640**.

5234. —— The life and times of Sir Thomas Malory. (Bibl. 1994, 3368.) Rev. by Dieter Mehl in Med (8) 1995, 498–501; by Kevin T. Grimm in ChauY (3) 1996, 185–8; by Joy Wallace in Parergon (13:2) 1996, 247–8; by John Watts in EHR (111:440) 1996, 162.

5235. —— Malory's Mordred and the *Morte Arthure*. *In* (pp. 77–93) **104**.

5236. FOSS, MICHAEL.   The world of Camelot: King Arthur and the Knights of the Round Table. *See* **3394**.

5237. FRIES, MAUREEN.   The impotent potion: on the minimization of the love theme in the *Tristan en prose* and Malory's *Morte Darthur*. Quondam et Futurus (1:3) 1991, 75–81.

5238. —— What Tennyson really did to Malory's women. Quondam et Futurus (1:1) 1991, 44–55.

5239. GOYNE, JO.   Parataxis and causality in the *Tale of Sir Launcelot du Lake*. Quondam et Futurus (2:4) 1992, 36–48.

5240. GRIMM, KEVIN T.   The reception of Malory's *Morte Darthur* medieval and modern. Quondam et Futurus (2:3) 1992, 1–14.

5241. HANKS, D. THOMAS, JR.   Malory, dialogue, and style. Quondam et Futurus (3:3) 1993, 24–35.

5242. —— Malory's *Book of Sir Tristram*: focusing *Le Morte Darthur*. Quondam et Futurus (3:1) 1993, 14–31.

5243. —— (ed.).   Sir Thomas Malory: views and re-views. (Bibl. 1995, 4254.) Rev. by Stephen Stallcup in Quondam et Futurus (3:1) 1993, 66–9.

5244. HARRIS, E. KAY.   Evidence against Lancelot and Guinevere in Malory's *Morte Darthur*: treason by imagination. Exemplaria (7:1) 1995, 179–208.

5245. HODGES, LAURA F.   Steinbeck's adaptation of Malory's Launcelot: a triumph of realism over supernaturalism. Quondam et Futurus (2:1) 1992, 69–81.

5246. HOFFMAN, DONALD L.   Malory's tragic Merlin. Quondam et Futurus (1:2) 1991, 15–31.

5247. —— Perceval's sister: Malory's 'rejected' masculinities. Arthuriana (6:4) 1996, 72–83.

5248. KELLY, KATHLEEN COYNE.   Malory's body chivalric. Arthuriana (6:4) 1996, 52–71.

5249. KIRCHHOFF, FREDERICK.   'The glory and the freshness of a dream': Arthurian romance as reconstructed childhood. Arthuriana (6:3) 1996, 3–13.

5250. MACBAIN, DANIELLE MORGAN.   Love *versus* politics: competing paradigms of chivalry in Malory's *Morte Darthur*. Quondam et Futurus (2:3) 1992, 21–9.

5251. MILLER, DAVID R.   Sir Thomas Malory's *A Noble Tale of Sir Launcelot du Lake* reconsidered. Quondam et Futurus (1:1) 1991, 25–43.

5252. MORAN, VIRGINIA.   Malory/Guenevere: sexuality as deconstruction. Quondam et Futurus (1:2) 1991, 70–6.

5253. PASTOOR, CHARLES.   Mark and Tristram as parody in Sir Thomas Malory's *Book of Sir Tristram De Lyones*. Tristania (17) 1996, 55–70.

5254. PIGG, DANIEL F.   Language as weapon: the poetics of plot in Malory's *Tale of Sir Gareth*. Quondam et Futurus (2:1) 1992, 16–27.

5255. RAFFERTY, MARGARET.   The Winchester Manuscript of Sir Thomas Malory's *Le Morte Darthur*: palaeographical evidence for the structure of the Arthuriad. *See* **410**.

5256. ROVANG, PAUL R.   Refashioning 'knights and ladies gentle deeds': the intertextuality of Spenser's *Faerie Queene* and Malory's *Morte Darthur*. Madison, NJ: Fairleigh Dickinson UP; London; Toronto: Assoc. UPs, 1996. pp. 160. (Cf. bibl. 1992, 3958.) Rev. by Theodore L. Steinberg in SpenN (27:3) 1996, 7–9.

5257. SIMPSON, ROGER.   William Fulford: an Arthurian reclaimed. Quondam et Futurus (1:1) 1991, 56–72.

5258. TAKAMIYA, TOSHIYUKI.   Chapter divisions and page breaks in Caxton's *Morte Darthur*. *See* **317**.

5259. WILLIAMS, EDITH WHITEHURST.   A woman's struggle for love and independence in the history of Western romantic love. *See* **5010**.

5260. WITHRINGTON, JOHN.   'He telleth the number of the stars; he calleth them all by their names': the lesser knights of Sir Thomas Malory's *Morte Darthur*. Quondam et Futurus (3:4) 1993, 17–27.

'Sir John Mandeville'

5261. DELUZ, CHRISTIANE.   *Le Livre de Jehan de Mandeville*: une 'géographie' au XIVᵉ siècle. Louvain-la-Neuve: Institut d'Études Médiévales, Univ. Catholique de Louvain, 1988. pp. lix, 511, (plates) 16. (Pubs de l'Institut d'Études Médiévales: textes, études, congrès, 8.) Rev. by Klaus Ridder in GRM (41:4) 1991, 46

5262. SEYMOUR, M. C.   Sir John Mandeville. (Bibl. 1995, 4270.) Rev. by Christian Zacher in SAC (18) 1996, 294–7.

5263. WESTREM, SCOTT D.   Two routes to pleasant instruction in late fourteenth-century literature. *In* (pp. 67–80) **131**.

Robert Mannyng

5264. GANIM, JOHN M.   The Devil's writing lessons. *In* (pp. 109–23) **78**.

5265. SULLENS, IDELLE (ed.).   The chronicle. Binghamton, NY: Medieval & Renaissance Texts & Studies, 1996. pp. x, 911. (Medieval & Renaissance Texts & Studies, 153.)

John Metham

5266. PAGE, STEPHEN.   John Metham's *Amoryus and Cleopes*: intertextuality and innovation in a Chaucerian poem. ChauR (31:2) 1996, 201–8.

Orm

5267. SOLOPOVA, ELIZABETH.   The metre of the *Ormulum*. *In* (pp. 423–39) **114**.

John Page

5268. EDWARDS, A. S. G.   *The Siege of Rouen*: a bibliographical note. NQ (43:4) 1996, 403–4.

Richard Rolle

5269. ALFORD, JOHN A.   Rolle's *English Psalter* and *lectio divina*. BJRL (77:3) 1995, 47–59.

5270. BREEZE, ANDREW.   Richard Rolle's *tagild* 'entangled': Welsh *tagu* 'choke', *tagell* 'snare'. *See* **2013**.

5271. FITE, PATRICIA P.   To '*sytt and syng of luf langyng*': the feminine dynamic of Richard Rolle's mysticism. SM (14:2/3) 1991, 13–29.

5272. WATSON, NICHOLAS.   Richard Rolle and the invention of authority. (Bibl. 1994, 3399.) Rev. by Domenico Pezzini in Aevum (68:2) 1994, 458–60.

John Trevisa

5273. FOWLER, DAVID C.   John Trevisa. (Bibl. 1995, 4280.) Rev. by Christian Zacher in SAC (18) 1996, 294–7.

5274. —— The life and times of John Trevisa, medieval scholar. (Bibl. 1995, 4281.) Rev. by Ann M. Hutchinson in TLS, 1 Nov. 1996, 28.

5275. HANNA, RALPH, III.   *Vae octuplex*, Lollard socio-textual ideology, and Ricardian–Lancastrian prose translation. *In* (pp. 244–63) **17**.

5276. SEYMOUR, M. C., *et al.* (eds).   *On the Properties of Things*: John Trevisa's translation of Bartholomaeus Anglicus *De proprietatibus rerum*: a critical text: vol. 3. (Bibl. 1995, 4282.) Rev. by Helgard Ulmschneider in MÆ (65:1) 1996, 124–5.

John Walton

5277. JOHNSON, IAN.   New evidence for the authorship of Walton's Boethius. NQ (43:1) 1996, 19–21.

John Wyclif

5278. LINDBERG, CONRAD.   Literary aspects of the Wyclif Bible. BJRL (77:3) 1995, 79–85.

5279. —— The Wyclif Bible in Scots. *In* (pp. 195–203) **11**.

5280. VON NOLCKEN, CHRISTINA.   A 'certain sameness' and our response to it in English Wycliffite texts. *In* (pp. 191–208) **61**.

GEOFFREY CHAUCER

General Studies, and Works other than *The Canterbury Tales* and *Troilus and Criseyde*

5281. ALLEN, MARK; BOWERS, BEGE K.   An annotated Chaucer bibliography 1994. SAC (18) 1996, 317–96.

5282. ALLEN, VALERIE; AXIOTIS, ARES (eds).   Chaucer. New York: St Martin's Press, 1996. pp. xi, 268. (New casebooks.)

5283. ALLEN, VALERIE; CONNOLLY, MARGARET.   Middle English: Chaucer. YWES (75) 1994, 167–200.

5284. AMBROSINI, RICHARD.   Self-remembrance and the memory of God: Chaucer's *House of Fame* and Augustinian psychology. Textus (2:1/2) 1989, 95–111.

5285. ANDERSON, J. J.   The narrators in the *Book of the Duchess* and the *Parlement of Foules*. ChauR (26:3) 1992, 219–35.

5286. ASTELL, ANN W.   Chaucer and the universe of learning. Ithaca, NY; London: Cornell UP, 1996. pp. xvi, 254.

5287. BENSON, LARRY D.   A glossarial concordance to the *Riverside Chaucer*. (Bibl. 1995, 4290.) Rev. by Paul Schaffner in ChauY (3) 1996, 151–6.

5288. BERTOLET, CRAIG E.   '*My wit is sharp; I love no taryinge*': urban poetry and the *Parlement of Foules*. SP (93:4) 1996, 365–89.

5289. BRADBURY, NANCY MASON.   The *Tale of Gamelyn* as a greenwood outlaw taking. *See* **4825**.

5290. BROSNAHAN, LEGER.   The pendant in the Chaucer portraits. ChauR (26:4) 1992, 424–31.

5291. BURNLEY, DAVID.   Chaucer's literary terms. *See* **1884**.

5292. BURROW, J. A.   Elvish Chaucer. *In* (pp. 105–11) **26**.

5293. CHANCE, JANE.   The mythographic Chaucer: the fabulation of sexual politics. (Bibl. 1995, 4296.) Rev. by John Mulryan in Cithara (34:2) 1995, 43–5; by Mark Allen in SAC (18) 1996, 195–8.

5294. CIGMAN, GLORIA.   Chaucer and the goats of creation. LitTheol (5:2) 1991, 162–80.

5295. COWEN, JANET; KANE, GEORGE (eds).   The legend of good women. (Bibl. 1995, 4298.) Rev. by Joseph A. Dane in SAC (18) 1996, 200–5.

5296. DANE, JOSEPH A.   Copy-text and its variants in some recent Chaucer editions. *See* **611**.

5297. DELANY, SHEILA.   The naked text: Chaucer's *Legend of Good*

Women. (Bibl. 1995, 4299.) Rev. by Dieter Mehl in Ang (114:2) 1996, 269–71.

5298. DELASANTA, RODNEY K.; ROUSSEAU, CONSTANCE M.   Chaucer's *Orygenes upon the Maudeleyne*: a translation. ChauR (30:4) 1996, 319–42.

5299. GALLOWAY, ANDREW.   Chaucer's *Former Age* and the fourteenth-century anthropology of craft: the social logic of a pre-modernist lyric. ELH (63:3) 1996, 535–53.

5300. GANIM, JOHN M.   Chaucerian theatricality. (Bibl. 1993, 3230.) Rev. by Marilynn Desmond in CL (48:4) 1996, 377–81.

5301. GRADY, FRANK.   Chaucer reading Langland: *The House of Fame*. *See* **5188**.

5302. GRAY, DOUGLAS.   Chaucer and the art of digression. StudME (11) 1996, 21–47.

5303. GRUDIN, MICHAELA PAASCHE.   Chaucer and the politics of discourse. Columbia: South Carolina UP, 1996. pp. ix, 200.

5304. HANNA, RALPH, III.   John Shirley and British Library, MS Additional 16165. *See* **366**.

5305. ——— *Vae octuplex*, Lollard socio-textual ideology, and Ricardian–Lancastrian prose translation. *In* (pp. 244–63) **17**.

5306. HANRAHAN, MICHAEL.   Seduction and betrayal: treason in the Prologue to the *Legend of Good Women*. ChauR (30:3) 1996, 229–40.

5307. HARWOOD, BRITTON J.   Building class and gender into Chaucer's *Hous*. *In* (pp. 95–111) **14**.

5308. ——— Chaucer on '*speche*': *House of Fame*, the Friar's Tale, and the Summoner's Tale. *See* **2393**.

5309. HEFFERNAN, CAROL FALVO.   The melancholy muse: Chaucer, Shakespeare, and early medicine. (Bibl. 1995, 4311.) Rev. by Susan Baker in RMRLL (50:2) 1996, 189–90.

5310. HIGGINS, ANNE.   Alceste the washerwoman. *In* (pp. 113–27) **26**.

5311. HIGUCHI, MASAYUKI.   Studies in Chaucer's English. *See* **1451**.

5312. HILL, JOHN M.   Chaucerian belief: the poetics of reverence and delight. (Bibl. 1995, 4314.) Rev. by Marilynn Desmond in CL (48:4) 1996, 377–81.

5313. HONEGGER, THOMAS.   From Phoenix to Chauntecleer: medieval English animal poetry. *See* **4893**.

5314. JOST, JEAN E. (ed.).   Chaucer's humor: critical essays. (Bibl. 1994, 3432.) Rev. by Roy J. Pearcy in SAC (18) 1996, 227–31.

5315. KANNO, MASAHIKO.   Studies in Chaucer's words: a contextual and semantic approach. *See* **1895**.

5316. KENNEDY, THOMAS C.   Rhetoric and meaning in *The House of Fame*. *See* **2411**.

5317. KISER, LISA J.   Truth and textuality in Chaucer's poetry. (Bibl. 1994, 3435.) Rev. by Marilynn Desmond in CL (48:4) 1996, 377–81.

5318. KOVACH, CLAUDIA MARIE.   Floating 'Tristan': distortions, indeterminacy, and *différance* within the integrated corpus. *See* **4913**.

5319. LERER, SETH.   Chaucer and his readers: imagining the author in late medieval England. (Bibl. 1995, 4325.) Rev. by N. F. Blake in EngS (76:1) 1995, 96–8; by Donald C. Baker in ELN (34:1) 1996, 94–6.

5320. LINDEN, STANTON J.   *Darke hierogliphicks*: alchemy in English literature from Chaucer to the Restoration. Lexington: Kentucky UP, 1996. pp. ix, 373. (Studies in the English Renaissance.)

5321. McCLELLAN, WILLIAM.   A codicological analysis of the quire structure of MS HM 140 and its implications for a revised *ordinatio*. *See* **386**.

5322. MACHAN, TIM WILLIAM. Speght's *Works* and the invention of Chaucer. *See* **743**.

5323. MINNIS, A. J. (ed.). Chaucer's *Boece* and the medieval tradition of Boethius. (Bibl. 1994, 3442.) Rev. by N. F. Blake in EngS (76:1) 1995, 98–9.

5324. MINNIS, A. J.; SCATTERGOOD, V. J.; SMITH, J. J. The shorter poems. (Bibl. 1995, 4330.) Rev. by Charlotte C. Morse in NQ (43:3) 1996, 323–4; by Peter Mack in TLS, 5 Apr. 1996, 23–4.

5325. MOONEY, LINNE R. More manuscripts written by a Chaucer scribe. *See* **393**.

5326. MYLES, ROBERT. Chaucerian realism. (Bibl. 1994, 3445.) Rev. by Peter Brown in MÆ (65:1) 1996, 133–4; by William Watts in SAC (18) 1996, 257–60; by N. F. Blake in EngS (77:1) 1996, 110–11.

5327. NAGUCKA, RUTA. Spatial relations in Chaucer's *Treatise on the Astrolabe*. *In* (pp. 233–44) **68**.

5328. NOLAN, BARBARA. Chaucer and the tradition of the *roman antique*. (Bibl. 1995, 4331.) Rev. by Peter Mack in TLS, 5 Apr. 1996, 23–4.

5329. PATTERSON, LEE. Chaucer and the subject of history. (Bibl. 1995, 4333.) Rev. by Joerg O. Fichte in ZAA (41:3) 1993, 272–4.

5330. POTTER, RUSSELL A. Chaucer and the authority of language: the politics and poetics of the vernacular in late medieval England. *See* **1478**.

5331. QUINN, WILLIAM A. Chaucer's *rehersynges*: the performability of the *Legend of Good Women*. (Bibl. 1994, 3450.) Rev. by Donald W. Rowe in SAC (18) 1996, 272–5.

5332. REHYANSKY, KATHERINE HEINRICHS. Wise birds: Chaucer's crow and Machaut's. TPB (29) 1992, 23–33.

5333. RIGBY, S. H. Chaucer in context: society, allegory, and gender. Manchester; New York: Manchester UP, 1996. pp. 205. (Manchester medieval studies.)

5334. ROBINSON, PETER M. W. Collation, textual criticism, publication, and the computer. *See* **815**.

5335. SHIPPEY, T. A. Chaucer's arithmetical mentality and the *Book of the Duchess*. ChauR (31:2) 1996, 184–200.

5336. SHYNNE, GWANGHYUN. Chulhoe eui *allegory* wa *allegory* eui chulhoe. (The allegory of retraction, and the 'retraction' of allegory.) JELL (42:1) 1996, 3–21.

5337. SPEARING, A. C. The poetic subject from Chaucer to Spenser. *In* (pp. 13–37) **116**.

5338. STEMMLER, THEO. Chaucer's ballade *To Rosemounde* – a parody? *In* (pp. 11–23) **61**.

5339. TAYLOR, KARLA. Chaucer reads *The Divine Comedy*. (Bibl. 1991, 4029.) Rev. by Lee Patterson in Comparatist (16) 1992, 141–2.

5340. TAYLOR, PAUL BEEKMAN. Chaucer's chain of love. Madison, NJ: Fairleigh Dickinson UP; London; Toronto: Assoc. UPs, 1996. pp. 215.

5341. VAN DYKE, CAROLYNN. The lyric planet: Chaucer's construction of subjectivity in the *Complaint of Mars*. ChauR (31:2) 1996, 164–72.

5342. VASTA, EDWARD. Narrative pessimism and textual optimism in Chaucer's *House of Fame*. *In* (pp. 35–47) **131**.

5343. WILLIAMS, SEAN D.   Chaucer's *The Complaint of Mars*. Exp (54:3) 1996, 132–4.

5344. WIMSATT, JAMES I.   Chaucer and his French contemporaries: natural music in the fourteenth century. (Bibl. 1995, 4353.) Rev. by Peter Mack in TLS, 5 Apr. 1996, 23–4.

5345. WINSTEAD, KAREN A.   John Capgrave and the Chaucer tradition. *See* **5120**.

The Canterbury Tales

5346. ABRAHAMS, ROGER D.   For folklorists' Chanticleer, 'no cry for feathers, cry for long life'. *See* **3306**.

5347. ADAMS, ROBERT.   Chaucer's 'new Rachel' and the theological roots of medieval anti-Semitism. BJRL (77:3) 1995, 9–18.

5348. ALEXANDER, MICHAEL (ed.).   The *Canterbury Tales*: the first fragment: the General Prologue, the Knight's Tale, the Miller's Tale, the Reeve's Tale, the Cook's Tale: a glossed text. London: Penguin, 1996. pp. xxvi, 293. (Penguin classics.)

5349. AMODIO, MARK C. (ed.); MILLER, SARAH GRAY (asst ed.).   Oral poetics in Middle English poetry. *See* **78**.

5350. AMTOWER, LAUREL.   Mimetic desire and the misappropriation of the ideal in the Knight's Tale. Exemplaria (8:1) 1996, 125–44.

5351. ANDREAS, JAMES R.   Remythologizing the Knight's Tale: *A Midsummer Night's Dream* and *The Two Noble Kinsmen*. Shakespeare Yearbook (2) 1991, 49–67.

5352. ARCHIBALD, ELIZABETH.   Contextualizing Chaucer's Constance: romance modes and family values. *In* (pp. 161–75) **26**.

5353. ARNOVICK, LESLIE K.   Dorigen's promise and scholars' premise: the orality of the speech act in the Franklin's Tale. *In* (pp. 125–47) **78**.

5354. BARR, HELEN.   Laughing at the body in the Miller's Tale. ERev (6:3) 1996, 38–41.

5355. BEIDLER, PETER G.   The price of sex in Chaucer's Shipman's Tale. ChauR (31:1) 1996, 5–17.

5356. —— The Reeve's Tale and its Flemish analogue. ChauR (26:3) 1992, 283–92.

5357. —— (ed.).   The Wife of Bath. Boston, MA: Bedford Books of St Martin's Press; Basingstoke: Macmillan, 1996. pp. xiii, 306. (Case studies in contemporary criticism.)

5358. BEIDLER, PETER G., *et al.*   Dramatic intertextuality in the Miller's Tale: Chaucer's use of characters from medieval drama as foils for John, Alisoun, Nicholas, and Absolon. *See* **5017**.

5359. BIGGS, FREDERICK M.; HOWES, LAURA L.   Theophany in the Miller's Tale. MÆ (65:2) 1996, 269–79.

5360. BOENIG, ROBERT.   Is the Monk's Tale a fragment? NQ (43:3) 1996, 261–4.

5361. BOITANI, PIERO.   'My tale is of a cock'; or, The problems of literal interpretation. *In* (pp. 25–42) **61**.

5362. BOWDEN, BETSY.   Fluctuating proverbs in three eighteenth-century modernizations of Chaucer's Miller's Tale. *See* **3310**.

5363. BRACKEN, CHRISTOPHER.   Constance and the silkweavers: working women and colonial fantasy in Chaucer's the Man of Law's Tale. CritM (8:1) 1994, 13–39.

5364. BREUER, HORST. Die erzählerische Vermittlung in Chaucers *Wife of Bath's Prologue*. GRM (42:1) 1992, 28–47.

5365. BREWER, DEREK. The couple in Chaucer's fabliaux. *In* (pp. 129–43) Flemming G. Andersen and Morten Nøjgaard (eds), The making of the couple: the social function of short-form medieval narrative: a symposium. Odense: Odense UP, 1991. pp. 143.

5366. BRONFMAN, JUDITH. Chaucer's Clerk's Tale: the Griselda story received, rewritten, illustrated. (Bibl. 1994, 3475.) Rev. by Amy W. Goodwin in SAC (18) 1996, 178–81; by Charlotte C. Morse in NQ (43:1) 1996, 79–80.

5367. BROWN, CAROLE KOEPKE. Episodic patterns and the perpetrator: the structure and meaning of Chaucer's Wife of Bath's Tale. ChauR (31:1) 1996, 18–35.

5368. BROWN, PETER. Chaucer at work: the making of the *Canterbury Tales*. (Bibl. 1994, 3476.) Rev. by Lillian M. Bisson in SAC (18) 1996, 181–3.

5369. CAMARGO, MARTIN. Rhetorical ethos and the Nun's Priest's Tale. *See* **2324**.

5370. CHARLES, CASEY. *Adversus* Jerome: liberation theology in the Wife of Bath's Prologue. Assays (6) 1991, 55–72.

5371. COLLETTE, CAROLYN. Seeing and believing in the Franklin's Tale. ChauR (26:4) 1992, 395–410.

5372. CONRAD, PETER. To be continued: four stories and their survival. (Bibl. 1995, 4372.) Rev. by Peter Parker in TLS, 12 Jan. 1996, 25.

5373. COOPER, HELEN. The *Canterbury Tales*. (Bibl. 1994, 3483.) Oxford; New York: OUP, 1996. pp. 439. (Oxford guides to Chaucer.) (Second ed.: first ed. 1991.)

5374. COX, CATHERINE S. '*Grope wel bihynde*': the subversive erotics of Chaucer's Summoner. Exemplaria (7:1) 1995, 145–77.

5375. —— The jangler's '*bourde*': gender, renunciation, and Chaucer's Manciple. SAtlR (61:4) 1996, 1–21.

5376. CRANE, SUSAN. Gender and romance in Chaucer's *Canterbury Tales*. (Bibl. 1995, 4374.) Rev. by T. L. Burton in EngS (77:5) 1996, 504–5.

5377. DANE, JOSEPH A. Bibliographical history *versus* bibliographical evidence: the Plowman's Tale and early Chaucer editions. *See* **610**.

5378. DAWSON, ROBERT B. Custance in context: rethinking the protagonist of the Man of Law's Tale. ChauR (26:3) 1992, 293–308.

5379. DILLON, JANETTE. Chaucer and the 'Marriage Group'. ERev (6:4) 1996, 7–10.

5380. DINSHAW, CAROLYN. Chaucer's queer touches / a queer touches Chaucer. Exemplaria (7:1) 1995, 75–92.

5381. EATON, TREVOR. Literary semantics as a science. *See* **2202**.

5382. EBERLE, PATRICIA J. Crime and justice in the Middle Ages: cases from the *Canterbury Tales* of Geoffrey Chaucer. *In* (pp. 19–51) **105**.

5383. ECKER, RONALD L.; CROOK, EUGENE J. (trans.). The *Canterbury Tales*. Palatka, FL: Hodge & Braddock, 1993. pp. x, 578. Rev. by Malcolm Andrew in EngS (76:5) 1995, 480–1; by John Micheal Crafton in SAC (18) 1996, 198–200.

5384. EDDEN, VALERIE. Sacred and secular in the Clerk's Tale. ChauR (26:4) 1992, 369–76.

5385. EDWARDS, ROBERT R. Source, context, and cultural translation in the Franklin's Tale. MP (94:2) 1996, 141–62.

5386. ERZGRÄBER, WILLI.   The Wife of Bath and Molly Bloom: self-portrait of two women. *In* (pp. 75–82) **11**.

5387. EVANS, ROBERT C.   Nashe's *Choise* and Chaucer's Pardoner. ANQ (9:4) 1996, 21–4.

5388. EVEREST, CAROL A.   Sex and old age in Chaucer's Reeve's Prologue. ChauR (31:2) 1996, 99–114.

5389. FEINSTEIN, SANDY.   Hypertextuality and Chaucer; or, Re-ordering the *Canterbury Tales* and other reader prerogatives. *See* **1154**.

5390. FLAKE, TIMOTHY H.   Love, *trouthe*, and the happy ending of the Franklin's Tale. EngS (77:3) 1996, 209–26.

5391. FLETCHER, ALAN J.   The Summoner and the abominable anatomy of Antichrist. SAC (18) 1996, 91–117.

5392. FRANTZEN, ALLEN J.   The Pardoner's Tale, the pervert, and the price of order in Chaucer's world. *In* (pp. 131–47) **14**.

5393. FRESE, DOLORES WARWICK.   An *ars legendi* for Chaucer's *Canterbury Tales*: a re-constructive reading. (Bibl. 1994, 3505.) Rev. by Sabine Volk-Birke in Med (8) 1995, 493–7; by Marilynn Desmond in CL (48:4) 1996, 377–81.

5394. FRIEDMAN, JOHN B.   Dorigen's '*grisly rokkes blake*' again. ChauR (31:2) 1996, 133–44.

5395. FURROW, MELISSA M.   Latin and affect. *In* (pp. 29–41) **26**.

5396. GANIM, JOHN M.   Double entry in Chaucer's Shipman's Tale: Chaucer and bookkeeping before Pacioli. ChauR (30:3) 1996, 294–305.

5397. GINSBERG, WARREN.   Chaucer's Canterbury poetics: irony, allegory, and the Prologue to the Manciple's Tale. *See* **2373**.

5398. —— Chaucer's disposition. *In* (pp. 129–40) **26**.

5399. GREEN, RICHARD FIRTH.   The *Canterbury Tales*, D117: *wrighte* or *wight*? *See* **657**.

5400. GRIFFITHS, JEREMY.   New light on the provenance of a copy of the *Canterbury Tales*, John Rylands Library, MS Eng. 113. *See* **364**.

5401. GRINNELL, NATALIE.   Griselda speaks: the scriptural challenge to patriarchal authority in the Clerk's Tale. CritM (9:1) 1995, 79–94.

5402. HANKS, D. THOMAS, JR; KAMPHAUSEN, ARMINDA; WHEELER, JAMES.   Circling back in Chaucer's *Canterbury Tales*: on punctuation, misreading, and reader response. *See* **669**.

5403. HARLEY, MARTA POWELL.   Chaucer's use of the Proserpina myth in the Knight's Tale and the Merchant's Tale. *In* (pp. 20–31) **46**.

5404. HARTUNG, ALBERT E.   The Parson's Tale and Chaucer's penance. *In* (pp. 61–80) **61**.

5405. HASENFRATZ, ROBERT.   The science of flatulence: possible sources for the Summoner's Tale. ChauR (30:3) 1996, 241–61.

5406. HEINRICHS, KATHERINE.   Tropological woman in Chaucer: literary elaborations of an exegetical tradition. EngS (76:3) 1995, 209–14.

5407. HIRSH, JOHN C.   Chaucer's Roman tales. ChauR (31:1) 1996, 45–57.

5408. HIRSHFELD, HEATHER.   Martha Moulsworth and Chaucer's Wife of Bath. CritM (10:supp.) 1996, 48–50.

5409. HONEGGER, THOMAS.   From Phoenix to Chauntecleer: medieval English animal poetry. *See* **4893**.

5410. IRVING, EDWARD B., JR.   Heroic worlds: the Knight's Tale and *Beowulf*. *In* (pp. 43–59) **61**.

5411. JANKOWSKI, EILEEN S.   Reception of Chaucer's Second Nun's Tale: Osbern Bokenham's *Lyf of S. Cycyle*. *See* **5117**.

5412. JOHNSON, BRUCE A. The moral landscape of the Pardoner's Tale. *In* (pp. 54–61) **116**.

5413. KELLOGG, A. L. The possible unity of Chaucer's Prioresses. ChauY (3) 1996, 55–71.

5414. KELLY, HENRY ANSGAR. A neo-revisionist look at Chaucer's nuns. ChauR (31:2) 1996, 115–32.

5415. KEMPTON, DANIEL. The Nun's Priest's festive doctrine: '*al that writen is …*'. Assays (8) 1995, 101–18.

5416. KENNEDY, BEVERLY. Cambridge MS Dd.4.24: a misogynous scribal revision of the Wife of Bath's Prologue? *See* **378**.

5417. —— The variant passages in the Wife of Bath's Prologue and the textual transmission of the *Canterbury Tales*: the 'great tradition' revisited. *In* (pp. 85–101) **129**.

5418. KLITGÅRD, EBBE. Chaucer's narrative voice in the Knight's Tale. (Bibl. 1995, 4393.) Rev. by Lois Roney in SAC (18) 1996, 232–4.

5419. LAMBDIN, LAURA C.; LAMBDIN, ROBERT T. (eds). Chaucer's pilgrims: an historical guide to the pilgrims in the *Canterbury Tales*. Westport, CT; London: Greenwood Press, 1996. pp. xiv, 398.

5420. LARES, JAMEELA. Chaucer's Retractions: a '*verray parfit penitence*'. Cithara (34:1) 1994, 18–33.

5421. LÁZARO LAFUENTE, LUIS ALBERTO. Some speculations about Chaucer's Spanish literary sources. SELIM (5) 1995, 18–28.

5422. LEICESTER, H. MARSHALL, JR. Piety and resistance: a note on the representation of religious feeling in the *Canterbury Tales*. *In* (pp. 151–60) **26**.

5423. LERER, SETH. '*Now holde youre mouth*': the romance of orality in the 'Thopas–Melibee' section of the *Canterbury Tales*. *In* (pp. 181–205) **78**.

5424. LOMPERIS, LINDA. Bodies that matter in the court of late medieval England and in Chaucer's Miller's Tale. RR (86:2) 1995, 243–64.

5425. MCCLELLAN, WILLIAM. The consequences of *treuth*: reading two versions of the Clerk's Tale. *See* **387**.

5426. —— The transcription of the Clerk's Tale in MS HM 140: interpreting textual effects. *See* **731**.

5427. MCENTIRE, SANDRA J. Illusions and interpretation in the Franklin's Tale. ChauR (31:2) 1996, 145–63.

5428. MCILHANEY, ANNE E. Sentence and judgment: the role of the fiend in Chaucer's *Canterbury Tales*. ChauR (31:2) 1996, 173–83.

5429. MCKINLEY, KATHRYN L. The silenced knight: questions of power and reciprocity in the Wife of Bath's Tale. ChauR (30:4) 1996, 359–78.

5430. MANDEL, JEROME. Geoffrey Chaucer: building the fragments of the *Canterbury Tales*. (Bibl. 1995, 4400.) Rev. by Joerg O. Fichte in ZAA (41:3) 1993, 270–2; by Charles A. Owen, Jr, in ChauY (3) 1996, 208–10.

5431. MARTINDALE, WIGHT, JR. Chaucer's merchants: a trade-based speculation on their activities. ChauR (26:3) 1992, 309–16.

5432. MARVIN, COREY J. 'I will thee not forsake': the Kristevan maternal space in Chaucer's Prioress's Tale and John of Garland's *Stella maris*. Exemplaria (8:1) 1996, 35–58.

5433. MINNIS, ALASTAIR. Anthropologizing Alisoun: the case of Chaucer's Wife of Bath. YREAL (12) 1996, 203–21.

5434. MORRISON, SUSAN SIGNE.   Don't ask, don't tell: the Wife of Bath and vernacular translations. Exemplaria (8:1) 1996, 97–123.

5435. MOSSER, DANIEL W.   Reading and editing the *Canterbury Tales*: past, present, and future (?). *See* **763**.

5436. OERLEMANS, ONNO.   The seriousness of the Nun's Priest's Tale. ChauR (26:3) 1992, 317–28.

5437. OSBERG, RICHARD H.   A voice for the Prioress: the context of English devotional prose. *See* **2687**.

5438. PARKS, WARD.   Oral tradition and the *Canterbury Tales*. *In* (pp. 149–79) **78**.

5439. PARRY, JOSEPH D.   Dorigen, narration, and coming home in the Franklin's Tale. ChauR (30:3) 1996, 262–93.

5440. PIGG, DANIEL F.   Medieval sign theory and Chaucer's Summoner's Tale: modes of reading and manipulation. TPB (29) 1992, 15–23.

5441. PINTI, DANIEL J.   Governing the Cook's Tale in Bodley 686. *See* **407**.

5442. PIZZORNO, PATRIZIA GRIMALDI.   Metaphor and *exemplum* in the Nun's Priest's Tale. *See* **2449**.

5443. PULHAM, CAROL A.   Promises, promises: Dorigen's dilemma revisited. ChauR (31:1) 1996, 76–86.

5444. REAMES, SHERRY L.   Artistry, decorum, and purpose in three Middle English retellings of the Cecilia legend. *In* (pp. 177–99) **26**.

5445. REMLEY, PAUL G.   Questions of subjectivity and ideology in the production of an electronic text of the *Canterbury Tales*. *See* **808**.

5446. RIDLEY, FLORENCE H.   The *Canterbury Tales*: questions and an answer. *In* (pp. 251–7) **11**.

5447. ROBINSON, PETER (ed.).   Chaucer, The Wife of Bath's Prologue on CD-ROM. Cambridge; New York: CUP, 1996. (1 CD-ROM.)

5448. RUDAT, WOLFGANG E. H.   Chaucer's Merchant and his shrewish wife: the Justinus crux and Augustinian theology. Cithara (35:1) 1995, 24–38.

5449. —— Gender-crossing in the Prioress' Tale: Chaucer's satire on theological anti-Semitism? Cithara (33:2) 1994, 11–18.

5450. —— '*Infernus, et os vulvae*': a second look at Proverbs and Chaucer's Prioress. CEACrit (58:2) 1996, 35–47.

5451. RUGGIERS, PAUL G. (gen. ed.); BAKER, DONALD C. (assoc. ed.). A variorum edition of the works of Geoffrey Chaucer: vol. 2, The *Canterbury Tales*: part 7, The summoner's tale. Ed. by John F. Plummer, III. (Bibl. 1995, 4415.) Rev. by E. G. Stanley in NQ (43:4) 1996, 469–70.

5452. SANDERS, ARNOLD A.   Ruddymane and Canace, lost and found: Spenser's reception of *Confessio Amantis* 3 and Chaucer's Squire's Tale. *In* (pp. 196–215) **131**.

5453. SCHIBANOFF, SUSAN.   Worlds apart: Orientalism, antifeminism, and heresy in Chaucer's Man of Law's Tale. Exemplaria (8:1) 1996, 59–96.

5454. SERRANO REYES, JESÚS L.   Spanish modesty in the *Canterbury Tales*: Chaucer and Don Juan Manuel. SELIM (5) 1995, 29–45.

5455. SHARON-ZISSER, SHIRLEY.   The Squire's Tale and the limits of non-mimetic fiction. ChauR (26:4) 1992, 377–94.

5456. SPILLENGER, PAUL.   '*Oure flessh thou yaf us*': *langour* and Chaucer's consumption of Dante in the *Hugelyn*. ChauY (3) 1996, 103–28.

5457. TAVORMINA, M. TERESA. '*Lo, swilk a complyn*': musical topicality in the Reeve's and Miller's Tales. *In* (pp. 141–50) **26**.

5458. TEJERA LLANO, DIONISIA. The Matter of Israel: the use of little children in the miracles of the Holy Virgin during the Middle Ages. SELIM (5) 1995, 7–17.

5459. THOMPSON, N. S. Chaucer, Boccaccio, and the debate of love: a comparative study of the *Decameron* and the *Canterbury Tales*. Oxford: Clarendon Press; New York: OUP, 1996. pp. 354. (Cf. bibl. 1992, 4140.)

5460. THORMANN, JANET. The circulation of desire in the Shipman's Tale. LitPs (39:3) 1993, 1–15.

5461. TOBIN, LEE ANN. Give the saint her due: hagiographical values for Chaucer's Second Nun's Tale and Graham Greene's *The End of the Affair*. SM (14:2/3) 1991, 48–60.

5462. VOLK-BIRKE, SABINE. Chaucer and medieval preaching: rhetoric for listeners in sermons and poetry. (Bibl. 1994, 3564.) Rev. by Wolfgang Riehle in GRM (43:2) 1993, 248–9; by Rainer Holtei in Med (8) 1995, 497–8.

5463. WALKER, LEWIS. Chaucer in Shakespeare: the case of the Nun's Priest's Tale and *Troilus and Cressida*. UC (15) 1995, 48–60.

5464. WENZEL, SIEGFRIED. Another analogue to the Pardoner's Tale. NQ (43:2) 1996, 134–6. (*Exemplum* in MS Bodley 859.)

5465. WHEATLEY, EDWARD. Commentary displacing text: the Nun's Priest's Tale and the scholastic fable tradition. SAC (18) 1996, 119–41.

5466. WINICK, STEPHEN D. Proverbial strategy and proverbial wisdom in the *Canterbury Tales*. *See* **3350**.

5467. WOODS, WILLIAM F. Society and nature in the Cook's Tale. PLL (32:2) 1996, 189–205.

5468. YESUFU, ABDUL R. The spring motif and the subversion of guaranteed meaning in Chaucer's *The Canterbury Tales*. ESA (38:2) 1995, 1–15.

Troilus and Criseyde

5469. BARNEY, STEPHEN A. Studies in *Troilus*: Chaucer's text, meter, and diction. (Bibl. 1995, 4439.) Rev. by Malcolm Andrew in EngS (76:5) 1995, 479–80; by R. F. Yeager in MÆ (65:1) 1996, 134–5.

5470. BEACH, CHARLES FRANKLYN. C. S. Lewis, courtly love, and Chaucer's *Troilus and Criseyde*. CSL (26:4/5) 1995, 1–10.

5471. BERRY, CRAIG A. The king's business: negotiating chivalry in *Troilus and Criseyde*. ChauR (26:3) 1992, 236–65.

5472. BØRCH, MARIANNE. Poet & persona: writing the reader in *Troilus*. ChauR (30:3) 1996, 215–28.

5473. CALABRESE, MICHAEL A. Chaucer's Ovidian arts of love. (Bibl. 1994, 3578.) Rev. by Peter Brown in MÆ (65:1) 1996, 133–4; by Marilynn Desmond in SAC (18) 1996, 183–6.

5474. COX, CATHERINE S. Froward language and wanton play: the '*commoun*' text of Henryson's *Testament of Cresseid*. *See* **5148**.

5475. FARRELL, THOMAS J. The *fyn* of the *Troilus*. *In* (pp. 38–53) **116**.

5476. FLEMING, JOHN V. Classical imitation and interpretation in Chaucer's *Troilus*. (Bibl. 1993, 3381.) Rev. by Marilynn Desmond in CL (48:4) 1996, 377–81.

5477. HARVEY, NANCY LENZ. Chaucer's *Troilus and Criseyde* and the idea of '*pleye*'. *In* (pp. 48–56) **131**.

5478. Kellogg, Laura D.   Boccaccio's and Chaucer's Cressida. (Bibl. 1995, 4444.) Rev. by Max Staples in Parergon (14:1) 1996, 318.

5479. Oka, Saburo.   Religious sentiments in Chaucer's *Troilus*. StudME (11) 1996, 1–20.

5480. Page, Stephen.   John Metham's *Amoryus and Cleopes*: intertextuality and innovation in a Chaucerian poem. *See* **5266**.

5481. Peyton, Henry Hall, iii.   '*Quod he, I hoppe alwey byhynde!*' TPB (28) 1991, 6–13.

5482. Ross, Valerie A.   Resisting Chaucerian misogyny: reinscribing Criseyde. Æstel (4) 1996, 29–58.

5483. Sadlek, Gregory M.   Bakhtin, the novel, and Chaucer's *Troilus and Criseyde*. *See* **4258**.

5484. —— Love, labor, and sloth in Chaucer's *Troilus and Criseyde*. ChauR (26:4) 1992, 350–68.

5485. Smith, Macklin.   *Sith* and *syn* in Chaucer's *Troilus*. *See* **1999**.

5486. Utz, Richard J.   '*For all that comth, comth by necessitee*': Chaucer's critique of fourteenth-century Boethianism in *Troilus and Criseyde* iv, 957–58. AAA (21:1) 1996, 29–32.

5487. Walker, Lewis.   Chaucer in Shakespeare: the case of the Nun's Priest's Tale and *Troilus and Cressida*. *See* **5463**.

5488. Watts, William.   Translations of Boethius and the making of Chaucer's second *Canticus Troili*. ChauY (3) 1996, 129–41.

THE *GAWAIN*-POET

5489. Amodio, Mark C.   Tradition, modernity, and the emergence of the self in *Sir Gawain and the Green Knight*. Assays (8) 1995, 47–68.

5490. Andrew, Malcolm.   The realizing imagination in late medieval English literature. *See* **4802**.

5491. Benson, C. David.   The lost honor of Sir Gawain. *In* (pp. 30–9) **22**.

5492. Blanch, Robert J.   The current state of *Pearl* criticism. ChauY (3) 1996, 21–33.

5493. ——Wasserman, Julian N.   From *Pearl* to *Gawain*: *forme* to *fynisment*. (Bibl. 1995, 4461.) Rev. by John C. Hirsh in MÆ (65:2) 1996, 316–17; by S. S. Hussey in NQ (43:3) 1996, 314–15.

5494. Breeze, Andrew.   The *Gawain*-poet and Toulouse. *See* **2019**.

5495. —— Sir Gawain's journey and Holywell, Wales. SELIM (5) 1995, 116–18.

5496. —— *Torres* 'towering clouds' in *Pearl* and *Cleanness*. *See* **2020**.

5497. Carruthers, Mary J.   Invention, mnemonics, and stylistic ornament in *Psychomachia* and *Pearl*. *In* (pp. 201–13) **26**.

5498. Christopher, Joe R.   The lady's offer of the red-gold ring. Mythprint (29:8/9) 1992, 5–6, 10.

5499. Clopper, Lawrence M.   The God of the *Gawain*-poet. MP (94:1) 1996, 1–18.

5500. Cox, Catherine S.   *Graelent* and *Sir Gawain*: a new analogue for Bertilak's lady. *In* (pp. 57–66) **131**.

5501. Douglass, Rebecca M.   Missed masses: absence and the function of the liturgical year in *Sir Gawain and the Green Knight*. Quondam et Futurus (2:2) 1992, 20–7.

5502. FARLEY-HILLS, DAVID. *Largesse* in *Sir Gawain and the Green Knight.* See **1970**.

5503. FLETCHER, ALAN J. Middle English: the *Gawain*-poet. YWES (75) 1994, 140–1.

5504. FRANTZEN, ALLEN J. The disclosure of sodomy in *Cleanness.* PMLA (111:3) 1996, 451–64.

5505. GIACCHERINI, ENRICO. The *Gawain*-poet and the language of dreams. Textus (3:1/2) 1990, 3–21.

5506. GODDEN, M. R. The trouble with Sodom: literary responses to biblical sexuality. *See* **4608**.

5507. GODFREY, MARY F. *Sir Gawain and the Green Knight*: the severed head and the body politic. Assays (8) 1995, 69–100.

5508. HANNA, RALPH, III. Defining Middle English alliterative poetry. *In* (pp. 43–64) **26**.

5509. HENDERSON, DAVE. Tradition and heroism in the Middle English romances. *In* (pp. 89–107) **78**.

5510. IYEIRI, YOKO. The periphrastic use of *con* reconsidered: the authorship of the Cotton Nero A.x poems. *See* **1791**.

5511. KIRK, ELIZABETH D. The anatomy of a mourning: reflections on the *Pearl* dreamer. *In* (pp. 215–25) **26**.

5512. KLINE, BARBARA. Duality, reality, and magic in *Sir Gawain and the Green Knight. In* (pp. 107–14) **36**.

5513. MORIYA, YASUYO. The meter of the verse line of the Middle English *Pearl.* StudME (11) 1996, 49–79.

5514. NICKEL, HELMUT. About lace and knot in *Sir Gawayne and the Green Knight.* Quondam et Futurus (1:1) 1991, 15–24.

5515. O'MARA, PHILIP F. Robert Holcot's 'ecumenism' and the Green Knight: part I. ChauR (26:4) 1992, 329–42.

5516. POTKAY, MONICA BRZEZINSKI. *Cleanness* on the question of images. Viator (26) 1995, 181–93.

5517. PRIOR, SANDRA PIERSON. The *Pearl*-poet revisited. (Bibl. 1994, 3620.) Rev. by Jim Rhodes in SAC (18) 1996, 269–71.

5518. PUHVEL, MARTIN. Pride and fall in *Sir Gawain and the Green Knight.* NM (97:1) 1996, 57–70.

5519. PUTTER, AD. An introduction to the *Gawain*-poet. London; New York: Longman, 1996. pp. x, 256.

5520. —— *Sir Gawain and the Green Knight* and French Arthurian romance. (Bibl. 1995, 4488.) Rev. by C. M. Adderley in Arthuriana (6:3) 1996, 83–6; by Helen Cooper in MÆ (65:1) 1996, 131–3; by Corinne J. Saunders in NQ (43:3) 1996, 313–14.

5521. REICHARDT, PAUL F. A seventeenth-century acknowledgement of *Sir Gawain and the Green Knight* in an early catalogue of the Cottonian library. *See* **531**.

5522. ROGERS, GILLIAN. '*Illuminat vith lawte, and with lufe lasit*': Gawain gives Arthur a lesson in magnanimity. *In* (pp. 94–111) **104**.

5523. SADOWSKI, PIOTR. The knight on his quest: symbolic patterns of transition in *Sir Gawain and the Green Knight.* Newark: Delaware UP; London; Toronto: Assoc. UPs, 1996. pp. 289.

5524. SHIPPEY, TOM. Tolkien and the *Gawain*-poet. Mythlore (21:2) 1996, 213–19.

5525. TAYLOR, PAUL BEEKMAN. The failure of family and the demise of dynasty in *Sir Gawain.* SPELL (9) 1996, 207–23.

5526. THOMPSON, RICKY L. Tolkien's word-hord *onlēac. See* **4790**.

5527.   Vantuono, William (ed. and trans.).   *Sir Gawain and the Green Knight*: a dual-language version. (Bibl. 1994, 3630.) Rev. by Dan Embree in Text (Ann Arbor) (7) 1994, 511–16.

5528.   Wimsatt, James I.   Rhyme, the icons of sound, and the Middle English *Pearl*. *See* **2733**.

SIXTEENTH CENTURY

GENERAL

General Literary Studies

5529. ALLEN, DAVID G.; WHITE, ROBERT A. (eds). Subjects on the world's stage: essays on British literature of the Middle Ages and the Renaissance. *See* **116**.

5530. —————— The work of dissimilitude: essays from the Sixth Citadel Conference on Medieval and Renaissance Literature. *See* **131**.

5531. ARMSTRONG, NANCY; TENNENHOUSE, LEONARD. The imaginary Puritan: literature, intellectual labor, and the origins of personal life. (Bibl. 1995, 4495.) Rev. by Kevin Sharpe in AHR (99:1) 1994, 227–8; by Bruce C. Daniels in AmS (35:1) 1994, 171–3; by Malcolm Jack in ECS (28:2) 1994/95, 272–3.

5532. AVERY, GILLIAN. The voice of the child, both godly and unregenerate, in early modern England. *In* (pp. 16–27) **48**.

5533. BATH, MICHAEL; MANNING, JOHN; YOUNG, ALAN R. (eds). The art of the emblem. Essays in honour of Karl Josef Höltgen. *See* **179**.

5534. BENSON, PAMELA JOSEPH. The invention of the Renaissance woman: the challenge of female independence in the literature and thought of Italy and England. (Bibl. 1995, 4497.) Rev. by Katy Emck in CanRCL (20:1/2) 1993, 79–88.

5535. BERNARD, JOHN. Recent studies in Renaissance pastoral. ELR (26:2) 1996, 356–84.

5536. BLANCHARD, W. SCOTT. Scholars' bedlam: Menippean satire in the Renaissance. (Bibl. 1995, 4502.) Rev. by Kirk Combe in NQ (43:3) 1996, 330–1; by Kendrick Prewitt in SAtlR (61:1) 1996, 159–62.

5537. BLANK, PAULA. Broken English: dialects and the politics of language in Renaissance writings. *See* **1430**.

5538. BRACK, O. M., JR; EARLY, MARY. Samuel Johnson's proposals for the *Harleian Miscellany*. SB (45) 1992, 127–30.

5539. BRADSHAW, BRENDAN; HADFIELD, ANDREW; MALEY, WILLY (eds). Representing Ireland: literature and the origins of conflict, 1534–1660. (Bibl. 1995, 4506.) Rev. by Christopher Ivic in CEl (50) 1996, 129–31.

5540. BREDBECK, GREGORY W. Sodomy and interpretation: Marlowe to Milton. (Bibl. 1995, 4509.) Rev. by Theodora A. Jankowski in ShB (10:3) 1992, 44–5.

5541. BREITENBERG, MARK. Anxious masculinity in early modern England. Cambridge; New York: CUP, 1996. pp. x, 225. (Cambridge studies in Renaissance literature and culture, 10.)

5542. —————— Anxious masculinity: sexual jealousy in early modern England. Feminist Studies (19:2) 1993, 377–98.

5543. BRINK, JEAN R. (ed.). Privileging gender in early modern England. *See* **89**.

5544. —————— GENTRUP, WILLIAM F. (eds). Renaissance culture in context: theory and practice. (Bibl. 1993, 41.) Rev. by A. W. Johnson in EMLS (2:1) 1996, 9.1–6.

5545. BURT, RICHARD; ARCHER, JOHN MICHAEL (eds). Enclosure acts: sexuality, property, and culture in early modern England. (Bibl. 1995, 15.) Rev. by Renee Schlueter in RWT (2:1) 1994, 158–61.

5546. CARROLL, WILLIAM C.   Fat king, lean beggar: representations of poverty in the age of Shakespeare. Ithaca, NY; London: Cornell UP, 1996. pp. xiii, 237.

5547. CRANE, MARY THOMAS.   Framing authority: sayings, self, and society in sixteenth-century England. (Bibl. 1995, 4516.) Rev. by Raymond B. Waddington in CL (48:1) 1996, 84–6; by William Zunder in Literature and History (5:2) 1996, 78–9.

5548. CRESSY, DAVID.   Gender trouble and cross-dressing in early modern England. JBS (35:4) 1996, 438–65.

5549. DAVIS, NATALIE ZEMON; FARGE, ARLETTE (eds).   A history of women in the West: vol. III, Renaissance and Enlightenment paradoxes. *See* **42**.

5550. DESAIVE, JEAN-PAUL.   The ambiguities of literature. *In* (pp. 261–94) **42**.

5551. DI CESARE, MARIO A. (ed.).   Reconsidering the Renaissance: papers from the twenty-first annual conference. *See* **98**.

5552. EMCK, KATY.   Strategies of negotiation in English Renaissance literature and criticism. CanRCL (20:1/2) 1993, 79–88 (review-article).

5553. ENGEL, WILLIAM E.   Mapping mortality: the persistence of memory and melancholy in early modern England. Amherst: Massachusetts UP, 1995. pp. xiii, 287. (Massachusetts studies in early modern culture.)

5554. ENTERLINE, LYNN.   The tears of Narcissus: melancholia and masculinity in early modern writing. (Bibl. 1995, 4519.) Rev. by Patricia Demers in CanRCL (23:4) 1996, 1249–52; by Diana E. Henderson in ShB (14:4) 1996, 43.

5555. FALCO, RAPHAEL.   Conceived presences: literary genealogy in Renaissance England. (Bibl. 1994, 3646.) Rev. by Katherine Eggert in SpenN (27:1) 1996, 1–4.

5556. FELPERIN, HOWARD.   The uses of the canon: Elizabethan literature and contemporary theory. (Bibl. 1995, 4521.) Rev. by Robert Rawdon Wilson in CanRCL (20:1/2) 1993, 239–42; by Virginia Mason Vaughan in ShB (11:1) 1993, 43–4.

5557. FERGUSON, MARGARET W.   Moderation and its discontents: recent work on Renaissance women. Feminist Studies (20:2) 1994, 349–66 (review-article).

5558. FINUCCI, VALERIA; SCHWARTZ, REGINA (eds).   Desire in the Renaissance: psychoanalysis and literature. (Bibl. 1995, 14.) Rev. by Thomas H. Luxon in EMLS (2:2) 1996, 5.1–7.

5559. FOWLER, ALASTAIR.   Time's purpled masquers: stars and the afterlife in Renaissance English literature. Oxford: Clarendon Press; New York: OUP, 1996. pp. viii, 171. Rev. by John North in TLS, 13 Dec. 1996, 3–4.

5560. FOX, ALICE.   Virginia Woolf and the literature of the English Renaissance. (Bibl. 1995, 4523.) Rev. by Jane Marcus in Signs (17:4) 1992, 806–19.

5561. FUMERTON, PATRICIA.   Cultural aesthetics: Renaissance literature and the practice of social ornament. (Bibl. 1995, 4524.) Rev. by Richard C. McCoy in Review (16) 1994, 321–6; by Heather Dubrow in CLIO (25:4) 1996, 421–38.

5562. GOLDBERG, JONATHAN.   Sodometries: Renaissance texts, modern sexualities. (Bibl. 1995, 4526.) Rev. by Mario DiGangi in ShB (11:4) 1993, 45–6.

5563. —— (ed.). Queering the Renaissance. *See* **93**.

5564. Greenblatt, Stephen J. Learning to curse: essays in early modern culture. (Bibl. 1995, 4528.) Rev. by Virginia Mason Vaughan in ShB (9:3) 1991, 34; by Paul Stevens in CanRCL (22:2) 1995, 377–80; by Alvin Snider in MedRen (7) 1995, 385–9.

5565. Greene, Thomas M. Ritual and text in the Renaissance. CanRCL (18:2/3) 1991, 179–97.

5566. Habib, Imtiaz. Reading Black women characters of the English Renaissance: colonial inscription and postcolonial recovery. *See* **5136**.

5567. Hadfield, Andrew. Literature, politics, and national identity: Reformation to Renaissance. (Bibl. 1995, 4529.) Rev. by Bernhard Klein in SJ (132) 1996, 235–6.

5568. Hall, Kim F. Things of darkness: economies of race and gender in early modern England. (Bibl. 1995, 4531.) Rev. by Bernadette Andrea in EMLS (2:2) 1996, 9.1–5.

5569. Hart, Jonathan. Narrative, narrative theory, drama: the Renaissance. CanRCL (18:2/3) 1991, 117–65.

5570. Haselkorn, Anne M.; Travitsky, Betty S. (eds). The Renaissance Englishwoman in print: counterbalancing the canon. (Bibl. 1992, 4236.) Rev. by Theodora A. Jankowski in ShB (9:3) 1991, 36–7; by Christy Desmet in Shakespeare Yearbook (2) 1991, 257–60.

5571. Helgerson, Richard. Forms of nationhood: the Elizabethan writing of England. (Bibl. 1995, 4539.) Rev. by F. Smith Fussner in AHR (98:4) 1993, 1243–4; by Bernhard Klein in SJ (132) 1996, 233–5.

5572. Herman, Peter C. Introduction: rethinking the Henrician era. *In* (pp. 1–15) **101**.

5573. —— (ed.). Rethinking the Henrician era: essays on early Tudor texts and contexts. *See* **101**.

5574. Hutson, Lorna. Chivalry for merchants; or, Knights of temperance in the realms of gold. JMEMS (26:1) 1996, 29–59.

5575. Hyatte, Reginald. The arts of friendship: the idealization of friendship in medieval and early Renaissance literature. *See* **4897**.

5576. Jang, Heran. New Historicism and Renaissance text. ShR (28) 1996, 175–94.

5577. Jordan, Constance. Renaissance feminism: literary texts and political models. (Bibl. 1995, 4546.) Rev. by Ruth El Saffar in Signs (17:2) 1992, 494–7.

5578. Kegl, Rosemary. The rhetoric of concealment: figuring gender and class in Renaissance literature. (Bibl. 1994, 3668. Rev. by Karoline Szatek in SNL (46:2) 1996, 43, 45–6.

5579. King, John N. Tudor royal iconography: literature and art in an age of religious crisis. (Bibl. 1990, 3381.) Rev. by Sara Hanna in Shakespeare Yearbook (2) 1991, 236–9.

5580. Kinney, Arthur F. Figuring medieval and Renaissance literature. *In* (pp. 13–34) **131**.

5581. —— (ed.). Poetics and praxis, understanding and imagination: the collected essays of O. B. Hardison, Jr. Athens; London: Georgia UP, 1996. pp. xvi, 457.

5582. Knapp, Jeffrey. An empire nowhere: England, America, and literature from *Utopia* to *The Tempest*. (Bibl. 1994, 3671.) Rev. by Arthur Ferguson in AHR (98:3) 1993, 837–8; by Heather Dubrow in CLIO (25:4) 1996, 421–38.

5583. KNOTT, JOHN R.   Discourses of martyrdom in English literature, 1563–1694. (Bibl. 1995, 4551.) Rev. by John Strachan in Bunyan
Studies (6) 1995/96, 106–8.

5584. KOCH, MARK.   The desanctification of the beggar in rogue
pamphlets of the English Renaissance. *In* (pp. 91–104) **131**.

5585. KRONTIRIS, TINA.   Oppositional voices: women as writers and
translators of literature in the English Renaissance. (Bibl. 1995, 4552.)
Rev. by Margaret W. Ferguson in Feminist Studies (20:2) 1994, 349–66.

5586. LANGE, MARJORY E.   Telling tears in the English Renaissance.
Leiden; New York: Brill, 1996. pp. viii, 279. (Studies in the history of
Christian thought, 70.) (Cf. bibl. 1994, 3805.)

5587. LINDEN, STANTON J.   *Darke hieroglyphicks*: alchemy in English
literature from Chaucer to the Restoration. *See* **5320**.

5588. LOGAN, GEORGE M.; TESKEY, GORDON (eds).   Unfolded tales:
essays on Renaissance romance. (Bibl. 1991, 4204.) Rev. by Jonathan
Hart in CanRCL (18:2/3) 1991, 365–92.

5589. McCOY, RICHARD C.   Poetry at court. Review (16) 1994, 313–27
(review-article).

5590. McEACHERN, CLAIRE.   The poetics of English nationhood,
1590–1612. Cambridge; New York: CUP, 1996. pp. xi, 239. (Cambridge
studies in Renaissance literature and culture, 13.)

5591. McRAE, ANDREW.   God speed the plough: the representation
of agrarian England, 1500–1660. Cambridge; New York: CUP, 1996.
pp. xv, 335. (Past and present.) (Cf. bibl. 1992, 4414.) Rev. by L.H. in
TLS, 10 May 1996, 31.

5592. MANLEY, LAWRENCE.   Literature and culture in early modern
London. (Bibl. 1995, 4554.) Rev. by Arthur B. Ferguson in Albion (28:2)
1996, 294–6; by Andrew McRae in Parergon (13:2) 1996, 269–71.

5593. —— Recent studies in the English Renaissance. SELit (36:1)
1996, 213–58.

5594. MAPSTONE, SALLY.   Scots and their books in the Middle Ages
and the Renaissance: an exhibition in the Bodleian Library, Oxford.
See **389**.

5595. MILLER, DAVID LEE; O'DAIR, SHARON; WEBER, HAROLD.
Introduction: criticism and cultural production. *In* (pp. 1–12) **90**.

5596. —— —— —— (eds).   The production of English Renaissance
culture. *See* **90**.

5597. POTTER, LOIS.   The politics of language in early modern
England. *See* **2694**.

5598. RICHARDSON, DAVID A. (ed.).   Sixteenth-century British non-
dramatic writers: third series. Detroit, MI; London: Gale Research,
1996. pp. xxii, 385. (Dictionary of literary biography, 167.)

5599. SCATTERGOOD, JOHN.   Reading the past: essays on medieval
and Renaissance literature. *See* **4977**.

5600. SCHLEINER, LOUISE.   Tudor and Stuart women writers.
(Bibl. 1995, 4569.) Rev. by Rosemary Kegl in TSWL (15:1) 1996, 149–50;
by Teresa A. Lyle in SAtlR (61:2) 1996, 160–2.

5601. SINFIELD, ALAN.   Faultlines: cultural materialism and the
politics of dissident reading. (Bibl. 1995, 4573.) Rev. by Theodora A.
Jankowski in ShB (11:4) 1993, 46.

5602. SORELIUS, GUNNAR; SRIGLEY, MICHAEL (eds).   Cultural
exchange between European nations during the Renaissance.
Proceedings of the symposium arranged in Uppsala by the Forum for

Renaissance Studies of the English Department of Uppsala University, 5–7 June 1993. (Bibl. 1994, 15.) Rev. by Franco Marenco in SJ (132) 1996, 258–9.

5603. STAUB, SUSAN C. 'Matchlesse monsters of the female sex': murderous women in early modern England. RenP 1995, 109–24.

5604. STEVENS, PAUL. The political ways of paradox: Renaissance literature and modern criticism. ELR (26:2) 1996, 203–24.

5605. STRIER, RICHARD. Resistant structures: particularity, radicalism, and Renaissance texts. (Bibl. 1995, 4578.) Rev. by David Norbrook in GHJ (19:1/2) 1995/96, 110–11; by Andrew McRae in Parergon (14:1) 1996, 312–14; by Mark Robson in EMLS (2:1) 1996, 13.1–5.

5606. SULLIVAN, CERI. The sixteenth century: excluding drama after 1550: general. YWES (75) 1994, 201–12.

5607. SWISS, MARGO; KENT, DAVID A. (eds). Heirs of fame: Milton and writers of the English Renaissance. *See* **40**.

5608. TUDEAU, MARGARET; BERRY, PHILIPPA. Knowledge of/ knowledges in the Renaissance: blindspots in recent re-visions of English Renaissance culture. EEM (3:1) 1994, 75–9.

5609. WARD, LAVIECE C. Historiography on the eve of the Reformation in an early sixteenth-century English manuscript, e Museo 160. *In* (pp. 81–90) **131**.

5610. WATSON, ROBERT N. The rest is silence: death as annihilation in the English Renaissance. (Bibl. 1995, 4588.) Rev. by Christopher Hodgkins in GHJ (19:1/2) 1995/96, 102–9.

5611. WEIMANN, ROBERT. Authority and representation in early modern discourse. Ed. by David Hillman. Baltimore, MD; London: Johns Hopkins UP, 1996. pp. ix, 243. Rev. by Anthony Johnson in EMLS (2:3) 1996, 5.1–8; by A.H. in TLS, 30 Aug. 1996, 32.

5612. WHITE, R. S. Natural law in English Renaissance literature. Cambridge; New York: CUP, 1996. pp. xx, 285.

5613. WILCOX, HELEN; TODD, RICHARD; MACDONALD, ALASDAIR (eds). Sacred and profane: secular and devotional interplay in early modern British literature. *See* **107**.

5614. WILTENBURG, JOY. Disorderly women and female power in the street literature of early modern England and Germany. (Bibl. 1993, 3501.) Rev. by Barbara Corrado Pope in NWSAJ (5:1) 1993, 103–10.

Drama and the Theatre

5615. ANDREWS, MICHAEL CAMERON. This action of our death: the performance of death in English Renaissance drama. (Bibl. 1993, 3504.) Rev. by S. P. Cerasano in ShB (9:2) 1991, 41–2.

5616. AUSTERN, LINDA PHYLLIS. Music in English children's drama of the later Renaissance. Philadelphia, PA; Reading: Gordon & Breach, 1992. pp. xix, 374. (Musicology, 13.) (Cf. bibl. 1985, 2900.) Rev. by Barbara D. Palmer in MedRen (8) 1996, 231–5.

5617. BARASCH, FRANCES K. The Bayeux painting and Shakespearean improvisation. ShB (11:3) 1993, 33–6.

5618. BRADLEY, DAVID. From text to performance in the Elizabethan theatre: preparing the play for the stage. (Bibl. 1995, 4601.) Rev. by William B. Long in Text (Ann Arbor) (8) 1995, 377–80.

5619. BRAUNMULLER, A. R.; HATTAWAY, MICHAEL (eds). The Cambridge companion to English Renaissance drama. (Bibl. 1994, 3703.) Rev. by Michael Shapiro in MedRen (7) 1995, 418–22.

5620. BREIGHT, CURTIS C.   Surveillance, militarism and drama in the Elizabethan era. Basingstoke: Macmillan; New York: St Martin's Press, 1996. pp. xii, 348. (Language, discourse, society.)

5621. BRUSTER, DOUGLAS.   Drama and the market in the age of Shakespeare. (Bibl. 1995, 4603.) Rev. by S. P. Cerasano in Review (17) 1995, 35–43.

5622. BUSHNELL, REBECCA W.   Tragedies of tyrants: political thought and theater in the English Renaissance. (Bibl. 1995, 4604.) Rev. by Theodora A. Jankowski in MedRen (7) 1995, 381–5.

5623. CERASANO, S. P.; WYNNE-DAVIES, MARION (eds).   Renaissance drama by women: texts and documents. London; New York: Routledge, 1996. pp. xii, 237. Rev. by Juliet Fleming in TLS, 23 Aug. 1996, 12–13.

5624. CLARE, JANET.   'Art made tongue-tied by authority': Elizabethan and Jacobean dramatic censorship. (Bibl. 1995, 4605.) Rev. by Richard Burt in MedRen (7) 1995, 404–11.

5625. CLARK, IRA.   Writing and dueling in the English Renaissance. MedRen (7) 1995, 275–304.

5626. COHEN, WALTER.   Drama of a nation: public theater in Renaissance England and Spain. (Bibl. 1993, 3524.) Rev. by Jonathan Hart in CanRCL (18:2/3) 1991, 365–92.

5627. COOK, ALBERT.   Historiography and/or historicism: context and theoretical (de)-integration of Renaissance drama. CR (40:1) 1996, 31–47.

5628. CROCKETT, BRYAN.   The play of paradox: stage and sermon in Renaissance England. Philadelphia: Pennsylvania UP, 1995. pp. x, 213. (Cf. bibl. 1992, 4287.) Rev. by Ceri Sullivan in NQ (43:4) 1996, 476–7.

5629. DESENS, MARLISS C.   The bed-trick in English Renaissance drama: explorations in gender, sexuality, and power. (Bibl. 1995, 4611.) Rev. by Jennifer Richards in NQ (43:3) 1996, 341–2.

5630. DESSEN, ALAN C.   Recovering Elizabethan staging: a re-consideration of the evidence. *In* (pp. 44–65) **118**.

5631. DUTTON, RICHARD.   Mastering the revels: the regulation and censorship of English Renaissance drama. (Bibl. 1995, 4613.) Rev. by David Bevington in AHR (99:1) 1994, 225–6; by T. H. Howard-Hill in Review (16) 1994, 271–80.

5632. EDWARDS, PHILIP.   Tragic form and the voyagers. *In* (pp. 75–86) **124**.

5633. FARLEY-HILLS, DAVID.   The audience implications of some Paul's and Blackfriars' plays. *In* (pp. 205–15) **53**.

5634. FINDLAY, ALISON.   Illegitimate power: bastards in Renaissance drama. (Bibl. 1995, 4618.) Rev. by Peter J. Smith in CEl (50) 1996, 115–18; by Michael G. Brennan in NQ (43:2) 1996, 213–14; by Sandra Clark in SNL (46:1) 1996, 7–8.

5635. FITZPATRICK, TIM.   The Fortune contract and Hollar's original drawing of Southwark: some indications of a smaller first Globe. ShB (14:4) 1996, 5–10.

5636. FORSE, JAMES.   *Arden of Feversham* and *Romeo and Juliet*: two Elizabethan experiments in the genre of 'comedy-suspense'. JPC (29:3) 1995, 85–102.

5637. FORSE, JAMES H.   The play's the thing, wherein to catch the consciousness of the citizen: early modern playscripts as sources for English social/cultural history. PCR (7:2) 1996, 9–19.

5638. FREEDMAN, BARBARA. Elizabethan protest, plague, and plays: rereading the 'documents of control'. ELR (26:1) 1996, 17–45.

5639. FRIEDMAN, DONALD. Bottom, Burbage, and the birth of tragedy. *In* (pp. 315–26) **98**.

5640. FRYE, SUSAN. Elizabeth I: the competition for representation. (Bibl. 1995, 4623.) Rev. by Andrew Smyth in RWT (2:1) 1994, 154–8; by Carole Levin in MedRen (8) 1996, 252–6.

5641. GAMBLE, GILES Y. Power play: Elizabeth I and *The Misfortunes of Arthur*. Quondam et Futurus (1:2) 1991, 59–69.

5642. GIBBONS, BRIAN. The question of place. CEl (50) 1996, 33–43. (Globe Theatre in relation to works by Shakespeare, Jonson, Middleton.)

5643. —— The wrong end of the telescope. *In* (pp. 141–59) **124**.

5644. GOSSETT, SUZANNE. Recent studies in the English masque. ELR (26:3) 1996, 586–627.

5645. GURR, ANDREW. Contraries and hierarchy in the Globe auditorium. ShB (14:4) 1996, 11–13.

5646. —— Playgoing in Shakespeare's London. (Bibl. 1993, 3540.) Cambridge; New York: CUP, 1996. pp. xviii, 307. (Second ed.: first ed. 1987.)

5647. GUTIERREZ, NANCY A. Double standard in the flesh: gender, fasting, and power in English Renaissance drama. *In* (pp. 79–93) **24**.

5648. HAFFENDEN, JOHN (ed.). Essays on Renaissance literature: vol. 2, Drama. By William Empson. (Bibl. 1995, 4629.) Rev. by David Norbrook in TLS, 10 May 1996, 27.

5649. HART, JONATHAN. The crisis in narrative: language, tale, and drama in the Renaissance. CanRCL (18:2/3) 1991, 365–92 (review-article).

5650. —— Narrative, narrative theory, drama: the Renaissance. *See* **5569**.

5651. HATTAWAY, MICHAEL. 'Seeing things': Amazons and cannibals. *In* (pp. 179–92) **124**.

5652. HOENSELAARS, A. J. Broken images of Englishmen and foreigners in English Renaissance drama. GRM (41:2) 1991, 157–73.

5653. —— Images of Englishmen and foreigners in the drama of Shakespeare and his contemporaries: a study of stage characters and national identity in English Renaissance drama, 1558–1642. (Bibl. 1995, 4634.) Rev. by Johan Gerritsen in EngS (76:2) 1995, 204–5.

5654. HOGG, JAMES (ed.). Jacobean drama as social criticism. *See* **53**.

5655. HOSTER, JAY. Tiger's heart: what really happened in the *Groats-worth of Wit* controversy of 1592. Columbus, OH: Ravine, 1993. pp. 96. Rev. by Winifred Frazer in SNL (44:3) 1994, 48, 56.

5656. HOWARD, JEAN E. The stage and social struggle in early modern England. (Bibl. 1995, 4636.) Rev. by Shawn-Marie Garrett in Theater (25:2) 1994, 109–12; by Arthur F. Kinney in MedRen (8) 1996, 256–64; by Richard Helgerson in CL (48:4) 1996, 383–5; by Kathryn Murphy Anderson in ColLit (23:1) 1996, 217–25.

5657. HOWARD, SKILES. 'Ascending the riche mount': performing hierarchy and gender in the Henrician masque. *In* (pp. 16–39) **101**.

5658. HOWARD-HILL, T. H. (ed.). Shakespeare and *Sir Thomas More*: essays on the play and its Shakespearean interest. (Bibl. 1993, 3549.) Rev. by Roslyn L. Knutson in ShB (9:2) 1991, 37–9.

5659. INGRAM, WILLIAM. The business of playing: the beginnings of the adult professional theater in Elizabethan London. (Bibl. 1995, 4637.) Rev. by R. A. Foakes in MedRen (8) 1996, 278–80.

5660. JARDINE, MICHAEL; POYNTING, SARAH.   Renaissance drama: excluding Shakespeare: editions and textual scholarship. *See* **693**.

5661. JONES, NORMAN; WHITE, PAUL WHITFIELD.   *Gorboduc* and royal marriage politics: an Elizabethan playgoer's report of the premiere performance. ELR (26:1) 1996, 3–16.

5662. KIEFER, FREDERICK.   Writing on the Renaissance stage: written words, printed pages, metaphoric books. Newark: Delaware UP; London; Toronto: Assoc. UPs, 1996. pp. 377.

5663. KIRK, ANDREW M.   The mirror of confusion: the representation of French history in English Renaissance drama. New York; London: Garland, 1996. pp. 229. (Garland reference library of the humanities, 1928.) (Garland studies in the Renaissance, 6.)

5664. KNUTSON, ROSLYN L.   Elizabethan documents, captivity narratives, and the market for foreign history plays. ELR (26:1) 1996, 75–110.

5665. KNUTSON, ROSLYN LANDER.   The repertory of Shakespeare's company, 1594–1613. (Bibl. 1995, 4641.) Rev. by Andrew Apter in NETJ (3) 1992, 106–7; by Michael Shapiro in ShB (10:3) 1992, 42.

5666. KURTZ, MARTHA A.   Rethinking gender and genre in the history play. SELit (36:2) 1996, 267–87.

5667. LEVINE, LAURA.   Men in women's clothing: anti-theatricality and effeminization, 1579–1642. (Bibl. 1995, 4642.) Rev. by Thomas Akstens in JDTC (9:2) 1995, 184–6; by Jennifer Richards in NQ (43:3) 1996, 340–1.

5668. LINDLEY, ARTHUR.   Hyperion and the hobbyhorse: studies in carnivalesque subversion. *See* **4920**.

5669. McCUNE, PAT.   Order and justice in early Tudor drama. *See* **5033**.

5670. McDONALD, MARCIA A.   The Elizabethan Poor Laws and the stage in the late 1590s. MedRen (7) 1995, 121–44.

5671. MACINTYRE, JEAN.   Costumes and scripts in the Elizabethan theatres. (Bibl. 1993, 3565.) Rev. by Richard Paul Knowles in CanTR (78) 1994, 61.

5672. McJANNET, LINDA.   Mapping the Ottomans on the Renaissance stage. JTD (2) 1996, 9–34.

5673. MACLEAN, SALLY-BETH.   Festive liturgy and the dramatic connection: a study of Thames Valley parishes. *See* **5034**.

5674. McLUSKIE, KATHLEEN E.   The shopping complex: materiality and the Renaissance theatre. *In* (pp. 86–101) **118**.

5675. MAQUERLOT, JEAN-PIERRE; WILLEMS, MICHÈLE.   Introduction. *In* (pp. 1–13) **124**.

5676. —— —— (eds).   Travel and drama in Shakespeare's time. *See* **24**.

5677. MAUS, KATHARINE EISAMAN.   Inwardness and theater in the English Renaissance. (Bibl. 1995, 4645.) Rev. by Kent Cartwright in Albion (28:4) 1996, 682–4; by Heather Dubrow in CLIO (25:4) 1996, 421–38.

5678. MAZER, CARY M.   The (historical) actor and the text. ShB (10:1) 1992, 18–20.

5679. METZGER, MARY JANELL.   In search of 'the true understanding of the circumstances': making sense of *Arden of Feversham*. Genre (26:2/3) 1993, 155–75.

5680. MULLANEY, STEVEN. The place of the stage: license, play, and power in Renaissance England. (Bibl. 1993, 3572.) Rev. by Nigel Wood in Shakespeare Yearbook (2) 1991, 255–7.

5681. MULRYNE, J. R.; SHEWRING, MARGARET (eds). Theatre of the English and Italian Renaissance. (Bibl. 1993, 3573.) Rev. by Frances K. Barasch in ShB (10:3) 1992, 42–3.

5682. NELSEN, PAUL. An anchored Globe. ShB (10:1) 1992, 5–6.

5683. —— 'We the globe can compass soon': an update on the status of archeology on London's South Bank theatres. ShB (9:2) 1991, 5–6.

5684. NEWMAN, KAREN. Fashioning femininity and English Renaissance drama. (Bibl. 1995, 4652.) Rev. by Betty Travitsky in MedRen (7) 1995, 379–81.

5685. NICHOLSON, ERIC A. The theater. In (pp. 295–314) **42**.

5686. NORLAND, HOWARD B. Drama in early Tudor Britain, 1485–1558. See **5039**.

5687. O'CONNELL, MICHAEL. God's body: incarnation, physical embodiment, and the fate of biblical theater in the sixteenth century. In (pp. 62–87) **116**.

5688. OHTA, KAZUAKI (ed.). Elizabeth-cho engeki to ken'etsu. (Elizabethan drama and censorship.) Tokyo: Eihosha, 1996. pp. iv, 258.

5689. ORGEL, STEPHEN. Impersonations: the performance of gender in Shakespeare's England. Cambridge; New York: CUP, 1996. pp. xv, 179. Rev. by Michael Dobson in LRB (18:21) 1996, 24–5.

5690. ORRELL, JOHN. The accuracy of Hollar's sketch of the Globe. ShB (11:2) 1993, 5–9.

5691. PALMER, BARBARA D. Court and country: the masque as sociopolitical subtext. MedRen (7) 1995, 338–54.

5692. PALMER, DARYL W. Hospitable performances: dramatic genre and cultural practices in early modern England. (Bibl. 1995, 4655.) Rev. by Barry Nass in ShB (12:1) 1994, 49–50.

5693. PARK, WOO-SOO. *Renaissance* youngkukbigeuk eui soerak e gwanhayeo. (A note on the decline of English Renaissance tragedy.) JELLC (38:1) 1996, 195–217.

5694. PAVEL, THOMAS G. The poetics of plot: the case of English Renaissance drama. (Bibl. 1988, 2313.) Rev. by E. Hollis Berry in CanRCL (18:2/3) 1991, 347–52.

5695. PECHTER, EDWARD. What was Shakespeare? Renaissance plays and changing critical practice. (Bibl. 1995, 4658.) Rev. by Peter J. Smith in CEl (50) 1996, 113–15; by Richard Hillman in ESCan (22:3) 1996, 370–3.

5696. PETERSON, DOUGLAS L. The origins of Tudor comedy: Plautus, *Jack Jugeler*, and the folk-play as mediating form. In (pp. 105–15) **131**.

5697. POTTER, LOIS. Pirates and 'turning Turk' in Renaissance drama. In (pp. 124–40) **124**.

5698. RICE, COLIN ESMOND. 'Satan's synagogue': the theatre as antichurch in godly literature of opposition to the Elizabethan public theatre. Textus (1:1) 1988, 81–99.

5699. RICHMOND, E. M. Annotated bibliography of narrative theory and Renaissance drama. See **4248**.

5700. RONAN, CLIFFORD. 'Antike Roman': power symbology and the Roman play in early modern England, 1585–1635. (Bibl. 1995, 4662.) Rev. by Raphael Lyne in TLS, 14 June 1996, 7–8; by Irving Massey in Criticism (38:3) 1996, 490–1.

5701. Rose, Mary Beth.   The expense of spirit: love and sexuality in English Renaissance drama. (Bibl. 1993, 3578.) Rev. by Theodora A. Jankowski in ShB (11:1) 1993, 44–5.

5702. Salkeld, Duncan.   Madness and drama in the age of Shakespeare. (Bibl. 1994, 3765.) Rev. by Alison Findlay in CEl (50) 1996, 122–4; by Roy Porter in Literature and History (5:1) 1996, 101–2.

5703. Sams, Eric (ed.).   Shakespeare's *Edward III*. New Haven, CT; London: Yale UP, 1996. pp. 242. Rev. by John Simon in NewL (79:9) 1996, 32–4.

5704. Schutzman, Julie R.   Alice Arden's freedom and the suspended moment of *Arden of Faversham*. SELit (36:2) 1996, 289–314.

5705. Scott, Michael.   Confrontational comedy. *In* (pp. 167–77) **53**.

5706. Shapiro, James.   Recent studies in Tudor and Stuart drama. SELit (36:2) 1996, 481–525.

5707. Smith, David L.; Strier, Richard; Bevington, David (eds).   The theatrical city: culture, theatre and politics in London, 1576–1649. (Bibl. 1995, 59.) Rev. by George Evans Light in Albion (28:2) 1996, 300–1; by Alexander Leggatt in Essays in Theatre (15:1) 1996, 113–15; by Anne Barton in TLS, 26 Jan. 1996, 18.

5708. Smith, Emma, *et al.*   Renaissance drama: excluding Shakespeare: criticism. YWES (75) 1994, 272–86.

5709. Smith, Peter J.; Hampton-Reeves, Stuart.   Renaissance drama: excluding Shakespeare: theatre history. YWES (75) 1994, 267–72.

5710. Sterling, Eric.   The movement towards subversion: the English history play from Skelton to Shakespeare. Lanham, MD; London: UP of America, 1996. pp. xix, 228. (Cf. bibl. 1992, 4346.)

5711. Taylor, Gary.   Shakespeare and others: the authorship of *Henry the Sixth, Part One*. *See* **2718**.

5712. Traub, Valerie.   The (in)significance of 'lesbian' desire in early modern England. *In* (pp. 62–83) **93**.

5713. Voss, Paul.   The antifraternal tradition in English Renaissance drama. Cithara (33:1) 1993, 3–16.

5714. White, Paul Whitfield.   Theatre and Reformation: Protestantism, patronage, and playing in Tudor England. (Bibl. 1995, 4677.) Rev. by William Zunder in EngS (76:5) 1995, 485–6.

5715. Wilks, John S.   The idea of conscience in Renaissance tragedy. (Bibl. 1992, 4353.) Rev. by Margaret Loftus Ranald in ShB (9:1) 1991, 39–40.

5716. Zimmerman, Susan (ed.).   Erotic politics: desire on the Renaissance stage. (Bibl. 1995, 4679.) Rev. by Mary Bly in ShB (12:1) 1994, 48.

Fiction

5717. Alwes, Derek B.   Elizabethan dreaming: fictional dreams from Gascoigne to Lodge. *In* (pp. 153–67) **35**.

5718. Barbour, Reid.   Deciphering Elizabethan fiction. (Bibl. 1995, 4680.) Rev. by Warren Hope in ER (2:2) 1994, 61–4.

5719. Davis, Walter R.   Silenced women. *In* (pp. 187–209) **35**.

5720. Gondebeaud, Louis.   Récits et romans picaresques en Angleterre (1576–1723). Études littéraires (26:3) 1993/94, 13–27.

5721. Hart, Jonathan.   The crisis in narrative: language, tale, and drama in the Renaissance. *See* **5649**.

5722. RELIHAN, CONSTANCE C.   Fashioning authority: the development of Elizabethan novelistic discourse. (Bibl. 1995, 4684.) Rev. by Jacqueline Vanhoutte in StudN (27:4) 1995, 587–9.
5723. —— Introduction: framing Elizabethan fictions. *In* (pp. 1–15) **35**.
5724. —— (ed.).   Framing Elizabethan fictions: contemporary approaches to early modern narrative prose. *See* **35**.

Poetry

5725. BERETTA, ILVA.   'The world's a garden': garden poetry of the English Renaissance. (Bibl. 1994, 3791.) Rev. by Sukanta Chaudhuri in NQ (43:2) 1996, 208–9.
5726. BIOW, DOUGLAS.   *Mirabile dictu*: representations of the marvelous in medieval and Renaissance epic. *See* **4813**.
5727. BROOKE, SEBASTIAN.   Three early Tudor verse texts. *See* **590**.
5728. DOBIN, HOWARD.   Merlin's disciples: prophecy, poetry, and power in Renaissance England. (Bibl. 1995, 4694.) Rev. by Jill Stephen in MedRen (7) 1995, 411–18.
5729. ERSKINE-HILL, HOWARD.   Poetry and the realm of politics: Shakespeare to Dryden. Oxford: Clarendon Press; New York: OUP, 1996. pp. xiii, 284. Rev. by L.H. in TLS, 30 Aug. 1996, 32.
5730. FARNSWORTH, JANE.   Voicing female desire in *Poem XLIX*. *See* **635**.
5731. FISCHLIN, DANIEL.   Metalepsis and the rhetoric of lyric affect. *See* **2365**.
5732. GRAHAM, VIRGINIA (ed.).   A selection of Metaphysical poets. Oxford: Heinemann Educational, 1996. pp. x, 246. (Heinemann poetry bookshelf.)
5733. HARDISON, O. B., JR.   Crosscurrents in English sixteenth-century prosody. *In* (pp. 116–30) **131**.
5734. KREVANS, NITA.   Print and the Tudor poets. *In* (pp. 301–13) **98**.
5735. LOW, ANTHONY.   The reinvention of love: poetry, politics and culture from Sidney to Milton. (Bibl. 1995, 4703.) Rev. by William Zunder in Literature and History (5:1) 1996, 103–4; by Stefan Mohr in Ang (114:1) 1996, 119–23.
5736. LYALL, RODERICK.   Formalist historicism and older Scots poetry. Études Écossaises (1) 1992, 39–48.
5737. MACDONALD, A. A.   *Contrafacta* and the *Gude and Godlie Ballatis*. *In* (pp. 33–44) **107**.
5738. MCRAE, ANDREW.   Fashioning a cultural icon: the ploughman in Renaissance texts. *See* **5196**.
5739. MAY, STEVEN W.   The Elizabethan courtier poets: the poems and their contexts. (Bibl. 1994, 3808.) Rev. by Richard C. McCoy in Review (16) 1994, 318–21.
5740. PASK, KEVIN.   The emergence of the English author: scripting the life of the poet in early modern England. Cambridge; New York: CUP, 1996. pp. x, 218. (Cambridge studies in Renaissance literature and culture, 12.) (Cf. bibl. 1994, 3828.)
5741. PEBWORTH, TED-LARRY.   Manuscript transmission and the selection of copy-text in Renaissance coterie poetry. *See* **783**.
5742. RAZOVSKY, HELAINE.   Popular hermeneutics: monstrous children in English Renaissance broadside ballads. EMLS (2:3) 1996, 1.1–34.
5743. RØSTVIG, MAREN-SOFIE.   Configurations: a topomorphical approach to Renaissance poetry. (Bibl. 1995, 4710.) Rev. by Christopher

Highley in SpenN (27:1) 1996, 9–13; by A. Kent Hieatt in ELN (34:2) 1996, 79–83.

5744. SCHULER, ROBERT M. (ed.).   Alchemical poetry, 1575–1700: from previously unpublished manuscripts. (Bibl. 1995, 4711.) Rev. by Andrew Hadfield in TLS, 23 Aug. 1996, 25.

5745. SPEARING, A. C.   The poetic subject from Chaucer to Spenser. *In* (pp. 13–37) **116**.

5746. SUMMERS, JOSEPH H.   Collected essays on Renaissance literature. Fairfield, CT: George Herbert Journal, 1993. pp. vi, 269. (*George Herbert Journal* special studies & monographs.) Rev. by John Gouws in NQ (43:1) 1996, 84–5.

5747. TREIP, MINDELE ANNE.   Allegorical poetics and the epic: the Renaissance tradition to *Paradise Lost*. (Bibl. 1995, 4714.) Rev. by Philip Rollinson in Review (18) 1996, 175–9; by John M. Steadman in CLS (33:2) 1996, 198–201.

5748. VAN HEIJNSBERGEN, THEO.   The sixteenth-century Scottish love lyric. *In* (pp. 45–61) **107**.

Prose

5749. AVILA, CARMELA NOCERA.   *Il libro del cortegiano* nella traduzione di Sir Thomas Hoby (1561): un problema linguistico e culturale. *See* **3100**.

5750. BAKER, DAVID WEIL.   Topical utopias: radicalizing Humanism in sixteenth-century England. SELit (36:1) 1996, 1–30.

5751. BERNARD, G. W.   The fall of Wolsey reconsidered. JBS (35:3) 1996, 277–310.

5752. BUICK, STEPHEN.   'A leaden mediocrity': competing views of the Elizabethan Settlement of Religion in *The Stripping of the Altars* and *The Seconde Tome of Homilies*. RenP 1996, 21–31.

5753. CAMPBELL, MARY A.   The illustrated travel book and the birth of ethnography: part 1 of De Bry's *America*. *In* (pp. 177–95) **131**.

5754. CROCKETT, BRYAN.   The play of paradox: stage and sermon in Renaissance England. *See* **5628**.

5755. DAVENPORT, EDWIN.   Elizabethan England's other reformation of manners. ELH (63:2) 1996, 255–78.

5756. DOLAN, FRANCES E.   Dangerous familiars: representations of domestic crime in England, 1550–1700. (Bibl. 1995, 4724.) Rev. by J. A. Sharpe in EHR (111:444) 1996, 1278–9; by Patricia Crawford in JBS (35:3) 1996, 403–8.

5757. DOLOFF, STEVEN.   Hamlet's 'nunnery' and Agrippa's 'stewes of harlottes'. *See* **1982**.

5758. EDWARDS, PHILIP.   Tragic form and the voyagers. *In* (pp. 75–86) **124**.

5759. HADFIELD, ANDREW.   'The naked and the dead': Elizabethan perceptions of Ireland. *In* (pp. 32–54) **124**.

5760. HUNTINGTON, JOHN.   'This ticklish title': Chapman, *Nennio*, and the critique of nobility. ELR (26:2) 1996, 291–312.

5761. KLEIN, BERNHARD.   '*Utterly another people*': Konstruktionen kultureller Differenz im Irland der frühen Neuzeit. ZAA (44:3) 1996, 249–65.

5762. LANCASHIRE, IAN (ed.).   Certaine sermons or homilies appointed to be read in churches, in the time of the late Queene Elizabeth of famous memory. Toronto: Univ. of Toronto Centre for

Computing in the Humanities, 1994. (http://library.utoronto.ca/ www/utel/ret/elizhom.html.) Rev. by Ronald B. Bond in EMLS (2:2) 1996, 15.1–9.

5763. LYALL, RODERICK J. The construction of a rhetorical voice in sixteenth-century Scottish letters. *See* **2421**.

5764. MALEY, WILLY. Spenser's *View* and Stanyhurst's *Description*. NQ (43:2) 1996, 140–2.

5765. NEWMAN, KAREN. Sundry letters, worldly goods: the Lisle letters and Renaissance studies. JMEMS (26:1) 1996, 139–52.

5766. PARKER, DOUGLAS H. *A Proper Dyaloge betwene a Gentillman and a Husbandman*: the question of authorship. BJRL (78:1) 1996, 63–75.

5767. PORIES, KATHLEEN. The intersection of Poor Laws and literature in the sixteenth century: fictional and factual categories. *In* (pp. 17–40) **35**.

5768. PREST, WILFRID. William Lambarde, Elizabethan law reform, and early Stuart politics. JBS (34:4) 1995, 464–80.

5769. RAMAN, SHANKAR. Imaginary islands: staging the East. RenD (26) 1995, 131–61.

5770. ROBERTS, JULIAN. An ill-fated irruption of ruffs. *See* **1991**.

5771. SHEPARD, ALAN CLARKE. William Patten's *Expedition of Somerset into Scotland* (1547) as English imperial discourse. SLJ (22:1) 1995, 22–34.

5772. STRING, TATIANA C. Henry VIII's illuminated 'Great Bible'. *See* **249**.

5773. SUTCLIFFE, CHRIS. The canon of Robert Armin's work: an addition. NQ (43:2) 1996, 171–5. (*A Pil to Purge Melancholie*, 1599.)

Related Studies

5774. AUGHTERSON, KATE (ed.). Renaissance women: a sourcebook: constructions of femininity in England. London; New York: Routledge, 1995. pp. xv, 316, (plates) 8. Rev. by Carrie Hintz in EMLS (2:2) 1996, 6.1–7.

5775. BINNS, J. W. Printing and paratext in sixteenth-century England: the Oxford and Cambridge presses. *See* **897**.

5776. COX, CATHERINE I. From 'the house of the spider' to 'the citadel of God': representations of the plague in early modern England. RenP 1996, 33–42.

5777. DRAUDT, MANFRED. Zum Lokalkolorit in den Shakespeare-Parodien von Perinet, Kringsteiner und Meisl. Nestroyana (16) 1996, 5–23.

5778. EDWARDS, FRANCIS. The division among the English Catholics: 1580–1610. ER (3:2) 1995, 25–34.

5779. ERLER, MARY. The books and lives of three Tudor women. *In* (pp. 5–17) **89**.

5780. HABICHT, WERNER. Texte und Kontexte der englischen Literatur im Jahr 1595. Munich: Bayerische Akademie der Wissenschaften, 1995. pp. 39. (Sitzungsberichte, Jahrgang 1995, 6.) Rev. by Iris Bünsch in LWU (29:4) 1996, 317–18.

5781. HAHN, THOMAS. Traditional religion, social history, and literary studies. *See* **5076**.

5782. HOSINGTON, BRENDA M. England's first female-authored encomium: the Seymour sisters' *Hecatodistichon* (1550) to Marguerite de Navarre. Text, translation, notes, and commentary. SP (93:2) 1996, 117–63.

5783. HULL, SUZANNE W.   Women according to men: the world of Tudor–Stuart women. Walnut Creek, CA; London: AltaMira Press, 1996. pp. 239.

5784. KING, JOHN N.   Henry VIII as David: the king's image and Reformation politics. *In* (pp. 78–92) **101**.

5785. KINTGEN, EUGENE R.   Reading in Tudor England. Pittsburgh, PA: Pittsburgh UP, 1996. pp. x, 242. (Pittsburgh series in composition, literacy, and culture.)

5786. KRAYE, JILL (ed.).   The Cambridge companion to Renaissance Humanism. Cambridge; New York: CUP, 1996. pp. xviii, 320. (Cambridge companions to literature.)

5787. McGEE, TIMOTHY J.   The fall of the noble minstrel: the sixteenth-century minstrel in a musical context. MedRen (7) 1995, 98–120.

5788. ORLIN, LENA COWEN.   'The causes and reasons of all artificial things' in the Elizabethan domestic environment. MedRen (7) 1995, 19–75.

5789. PARRY, GLYN J. R.   The creation and recreation of Puritanism. Parergon (14:1) 1996, 31–55.

5790. RAFFINI, CHRISTINE.   The passion for place: medieval and Renaissance re-creations of Paradise. *See* **5099**.

5791. REID, DAVID.   Hume of Godscroft's *The Origine and Descent of the Most Noble and Jllustre Familie, and Name of Douglas* as Humanist historiography. SLJ (22:1) 1995, 35–45.

5792. WASWO, RICHARD.   Everybody's genealogy: pop history in the Renaissance. SPELL (9) 1996, 53–63.

5793. YAMADA, AKIHIRO.   Thomas Creede, printer to Shakespeare and his contemporaries. *See* **329**.

Literary Theory

This section is intended to contain studies **about** the literary theory, literary historiography, literary criticism, etc., produced *in* the sixteenth century. For modern works **of** literary history and criticism dealing generally with this period, see under 'Sixteenth Century: General Literary Studies'.

5794. FISCHLIN, DANIEL.   Metalepsis and the rhetoric of lyric affect. *See* **2365**.

AUTHORS

Roger Ascham

5795. CUNNINGHAM, KAREN.   'She learns as she lies': work and the exemplary female in English early modern education. Exemplaria (7:1) 1995, 209–35.

John Bale

5796. GORMAN, MICHAEL.   The glosses on Bede's *De temporum ratione* attributed to Byrhtferth of Ramsey. *See* **4731**.

5797. HAPPÉ, PETER.   John Bale. New York: Twayne; London: Prentice Hall, 1996. pp. xvii, 174. (Twayne's English authors, 520.)

5798. KASTAN, DAVID SCOTT. 'Holy wurdes' and 'slypper wit': John Bale's *King Johan* and the poetics of propaganda. *In* (pp. 267–82) **101**.

5799. MAGER, DONALD M. John Bale and early Tudor sodomy discourse. *In* (pp. 140–61) **93**.

William Barker (*fl.*1572)

5800. WHARTON, JANET. William Bercher's *Dyssputacion off the Nobylytye of Wymen*: text and transmission. *In* (pp. 53–69) **125**.

George Buchanan

5801. DURKAN, JOHN; MCKEEMAN, MOIRA J.; CUMMINGS, HELEN. Bibliography of George Buchanan. (Bibl. 1995, 4797.) Rev. by M. A. Screech in Bibliotheck (21) 1996, 81–5.

5802. KELLY, W. A. George Buchanan: addenda to Durkan. Bibliotheck (21) 1996, 1.

William Byrd (1542 or 3–1623)

5803. MOSHER, SALLY E. Was William Byrd's *The Battell* composed for the theater? ER (3:1) 1995, 32–6.

Henry Chettle

5804. BURNETT, MARK THORNTON. Henry Chettle's *Piers Plainness: Seven Years' Prenticeship*: contexts and consumers. *In* (pp. 169–86) **35**.

5805. CARROLL, D. ALLEN. 'For there is an upstart crow'. UC (15) 1995, 150–3.

5806. —— (ed.). Greene's groatsworth of wit: bought with a million of repentance (1592). (Bibl. 1995, 4800.) Rev. by Winifred Frazer in SNL (44:3) 1994, 48, 56; by David Chandler in ER (3:1) 1995, 62–7.

5807. FRAZER, WINIFRED. Two studies of Greene's *Groatsworth*. SNL (44:3) 1994, 48, 56 (review-article).

5808. HESS, W. RON. Robert Greene's *Wit* re-examined. ER (4:2) 1996, 41–8.

5809. HOSTER, JAY. Tiger's heart: what really happened in the *Groats-worth of Wit* controversy of 1592. *See* **5655**.

5810. KAHAN, JEFFREY. Henry Chettle and the unreliable *Romeo*: a reassessment. UC (16) 1996, 92–100.

5811. —— Henry Chettle's *Romeo* Q1 and *The Death of Robert Earl of Huntingdon*. NQ (43:2) 1996, 155–6.

Richard Bourke, Fourth Earl of Clanricarde

5812. DUNCAN-JONES, KATHERINE. 'Preserved dainties': late Elizabethan poems by Sir Robert Cecil and the Earl of Clanricarde. *See* **627**.

Robert Copland

5813. PORIES, KATHLEEN. The intersection of Poor Laws and literature in the sixteenth century: fictional and factual categories. *In* (pp. 17–40) **35**.

Sir John Davies (1569–1626)

5814. HADFIELD, ANDREW. 'The naked and the dead': Elizabethan perceptions of Ireland. *In* (pp. 32–54) **124**.

5815. HOOPER, GLENN.   Writing and landscape in early modern Ireland. Literature and History (5:2) 1996, 1–18.

5816. HOPE, WARREN.   The singing swallow: Sir John Davies and Shakespeare. ER (1:1) 1993, 21–39.

5817. HOWARD, SKILES.   Rival discourses of dancing in early modern England. SELit (36:1) 1996, 31–56.

Thomas Deloney

5818. SUZUKI, MIHOKO.   The London apprentice riots of the 1590s and the fiction of Thomas Deloney. Criticism (38:2) 1996, 181–217.

Queen Elizabeth I

5819. BAKER, ELLIOTT.   The Queen's hand in *The Merchant of Venice*. ER (3:1) 1995, 21–31.

5820. COCH, CHRISTINE.   'Mother of my contreye': Elizabeth I and Tudor constructions of motherhood. ELR (26:3) 1996, 423–50.

5821. SUMMIT, JENNIFER.   'The arte of a ladies penne': Elizabeth I and the poetics of queenship. ELR (26:3) 1996, 395–422.

5822. WALKER, JULIA M.   Reading the tombs of Elizabeth I. *See* **6724**.

Sir Thomas Elyot

5823. HOWARD, SKILES.   Rival discourses of dancing in early modern England. *See* **5817**.

Robert Devereux, Second Earl of Essex

5824. DUNCAN-JONES, K.   Notable accessions: Western manuscripts. *See* **349**.

5825. HAMMER, PAUL E. J.   A reckoning reframed: the 'murder' of Christopher Marlowe revisited. ELR (26:2) 1996, 225–42.

George Gascoigne

5826. BAJETTA, CARLO M.   Ralegh's early poetry and its metrical context. SP (93:4) 1996, 390–411.

5827. SHEIDLEY, WILLIAM E.   George Gascoigne and *The Spoyle of Antwerpe* (1576). WLA (8:1) 1996, 49–64.

5828. STAUB, SUSAN C.   The Lady Frances did watch: Gascoigne's voyeuristic narrative. *In* (pp. 41–54) **35**.

5829. WEISS, ADRIAN.   Shared printing, printer's copy, and the text(s) of Gascoigne's *A Hundreth Sundrie Flowres*. *See* **327**.

Robert Greene

5830. ACKERLEY, CHRIS.   'Do not despair': Samuel Beckett and Robert Greene. JBecS (6:1) 1996, 119–24.

5831. CARROLL, D. ALLEN.   'For there is an upstart crow'. *See* **5805**.

5832. FLEISSNER, ROBERT F.   The 'upstart crow' reclawed: was it Kemp, Wilson, Alleyn, or Shakespeare? UC (15) 1995, 143–9.

5833. FRAZER, WINIFRED.   Two studies of Greene's *Groatsworth*. *See* **5807**.

5834. FRAZER, WINIFRED L.   William Kemp as 'upstart crow'. UC (15) 1995, 140–2.

5835. HESS, W. RON.   Robert Greene's *Wit* re-examined. *See* **5808**.

5836. HOPKINS, LISA. Ford and Greene: two histories of James the Fourth. NQ (43:2) 1996, 193–4.

5837. HOSTER, JAY. Tiger's heart: what really happened in the *Groats-worth of Wit* controversy of 1592. *See* **5655**.

5838. MERRIAM, THOMAS. *Groatsworth*'s added value. NQ (43:2) 1996, 145–9.

5839. MOORE, ANTONY TELFORD. Ford's parody of Edward Alleyn. NQ (43:2) 1996, 190–1.

5840. NEWCOMB, LORI HUMPHREY. The romance of service: the simple history of *Pandosto*'s servant readers. *In* (pp. 117–39) **35**.

5841. PRICE, DIANA. What's in a name? Shakespeare, Shake-scene, and the Clayton loan. ER (4:1) 1996, 3–13.

Bartholomew Griffin

5842. CLITHEROE, FREDERIC (sel. and introd.). Fidessa, more chaste than kind. Newcastle: Lymes Press, 1996. pp. 34.

Richard Hakluyt

5843. BESS, JENNIFER. Hakluyt's *Discourse of Western Planting*. Exp (55:1) 1996, 3–6.

5844. HUTSON, LORNA. Chivalry for merchants; or, Knights of temperance in the realms of gold. *See* **5574**.

Sir John Harington (1561–1612)

5845. CAUCHI, SIMON. Harington's *Orlando Furioso*: a 'spare leafe' and a stop-press correction. *See* **599**.

5846. SCOTT-WARREN, JASON. The privy politics of Sir John Harington's *New Discourse of a Stale Subject, Called the Metamorphosis of Ajax*. SP (93:4) 1996, 412–42.

Raphael Holinshed

5847. HADFIELD, ANDREW. 'The naked and the dead': Elizabethan perceptions of Ireland. *In* (pp. 32–54) **124**.

5848. METZGER, MARY JANELL. In search of 'the true understanding of the circumstances': making sense of *Arden of Feversham*. *See* **5679**.

Richard Hooker

5849. HILL, W. SPEED. Scripture as text, text as Scripture: the case of Richard Hooker. *See* **680**.

5850. LURBE, EVE D. Political power and ecclesiastical power in Richard Hooker's *Laws of Ecclesiastical Polity*. CEl (49) 1996, 15–22.

5851. STANWOOD, P. G. Of prelacy and polity in Milton and Hooker. *In* (pp. 66–84) **40**.

Will Kemp

5852. PALMER, DARYL W. William Kemp's *Nine Daies Wonder* and the transformation of performance culture. JDTC (5:2) 1991, 33–47.

Thomas Kyd

5853. ARDOLINO, FRANK R. Apocalypse and armada in Kyd's *Spanish Tragedy*. Kirksville: Sixteenth Century Journal Publishers, Northeast Missouri State Univ., 1995. pp. viii, 187. (Sixteenth century essays & studies, 29.) Rev. by Barry Nass in ShB (14:4) 1996, 42–3.

5854. BEVINGTON, DAVID (ed.).   The Spanish tragedy. Manchester: Manchester UP; New York: St Martin's Press, 1996. pp. 143. (Revels student eds.)

5855. CUTTS, DAVID.   Writing and revenge: the struggle for authority in Thomas Kyd's *The Spanish Tragedy*. ExRC (22) 1996, 147–59.

5856. MULRYNE, J. R.   Nationality and language in Thomas Kyd's *The Spanish Tragedy*. In (pp. 87–105) **124**.

William Lauder

5857. SONDERGARD, SIDNEY L.   Rediscovering William Lauder's poetic advocacy of the poor. SSL (29) 1996, 158–73.

Thomas Lodge

5858. NELLIST, BRIAN (ed.); BATIN, SIMÔNE (asst ed.).   Rosalynd. Keele: Ryburn, 1995. pp. 127. (Ryburn Renaissance texts and studies.)

Anne Vaughan Lok (Anne Prowse)

5859. HANNAY, MARGARET P.   'Unlock my lipps': the *Miserere mei Deus* of Anne Vaughan Lok and Mary Sidney Herbert, Countess of Pembroke. In (pp. 19–36) **89**.

John Lyly

5860. BEVINGTON, DAVID (ed.).   Endymion. Manchester; New York: Manchester UP, 1996. pp. xvi, 206. (Revels plays.)

5861. GOBBI, STEFANIA.   La metamorfosi annunciata in *Gallathea* di John Lyly. Acme (48:2) 1995, 45–54.

5862. HUNTER, JOHN.   The Euphuistic memory: Humanist culture and Bacon's *Advancement of Learning*. See **2400**.

5863. LINTON, JOAN PONG.   The Humanist in the market: gendering exchange and authorship in Lyly's *Euphues* romances. In (pp. 73–97) **35**.

5864. PINCOMBE, MICHAEL (ed.).   The plays of John Lyly: Eros and Eliza. Manchester; New York: Manchester UP, 1996. pp. xv, 205. (Revels plays companion library.)

5865. VANHOUTTE, JACQUELINE.   Sacrifice, violence, and the Virgin Queen in Lyly's *Gallathea*. CEl (49) 1996, 1–14.

Christopher Marlowe

5866. BARTELS, EMILY C.   Spectacles of strangeness: imperialism, alienation, and Marlowe. (Bibl. 1995, 4844.) Rev. by George L. Geckle in ShB (14:2) 1996, 43–4.

5867. BARTLETT, SALLY A.   Fantasy and mimesis in *Doctor Faustus*. JFA (5:3) 1992, 18–27.

5868. BOERTH, ROBERT.   The Mediterranean and the Mediterranean world on the stage of Marlowe and Shakespeare. JTD (2) 1996, 35–58.

5869. BRAY, ALAN.   Homosexuality and the signs of male friendship in Elizabethan England. In (pp. 40–61) **93**.

5870. BREIGHT, CURTIS C.   Surveillance, militarism and drama in the Elizabethan era. See **5620**.

5871. CHANDLER, DAVID.   Death put off by cunning and forc'd cause. ER (2:1) 1994, 15–20.

5872. COLE, DOUGLAS.   Christopher Marlowe and the renaissance of tragedy. (Bibl. 1995, 4850.) Rev. by David E. Phillips in BJJ (3) 1996, 203–7.

5873.   EDGECOMBE, RODNEY STENNING.   The 'burning chair' in the B-text of *Doctor Faustus*. NQ (43:2) 1996, 144–5.

5874.   FETHERLING, DOUGLAS.   The last word on Marlowe's death. LRC (5:11) 1996, 27.

5875.   GECKLE, GEORGE L.   The 1604 and 1616 versions of *Dr Faustus*: text and performance. *In* (pp. 146–61) **116**.

5876.   GILL, ROMA (ed.).   The complete works of Christopher Marlowe: vol. 2, *Dr Faustus*. (Bibl. 1992, 4487.) Rev. by George L. Geckle in Text (Ann Arbor) (7) 1994, 492–511.

5877.   HAMLIN, WILLIAM M.   'Swolne with cunning of a selfe conceit': Marlowe's Faustus and self-conception. ELN (34:2) 1996, 7–12.

5878.   HAMMER, PAUL E. J.   A reckoning reframed: the 'murder' of Christopher Marlowe revisited. *See* **5825**.

5879.   HAMMILL, GRAHAM.   Faustus's fortunes: commodification, exchange, and the form of literary subjectivity. ELH (63:2) 1996, 309–36.

5880.   HILL, EUGENE D.   Marlowe's 'more Exellent and Admirable methode' of parody in *Tamburlaine* i. RenP 1995, 33–46.

5881.   HOLLAND, PETER.   'Travelling hopefully': the dramatic form of journeys in English Renaissance drama. *In* (pp. 160–78) **124**.

5882.   HOPKINS, LISA.   'And shall I die, and this unconquered?': Marlowe's inverted colonialism. EMLS (2:2) 1996, 1.1–23.

5883.   —— 'Lear, Lear, Lear!': Marlowe, Shakespeare, and the third. UC (16) 1996, 108–23.

5884.   HORGER, J.   Derek Jarman's film adaptation of Marlowe's *Edward II*. ShB (11:4) 1993, 37–40.

5885.   IDE, ARATA.   Christopher Marlowe and the Kentish connection. SEL (English number) 1996, 17–35.

5886.   —— Christopher Marlowe to shosekishou – *Tamburlaine* no shuppan wo chushin ni. (Christopher Marlowe and the stationer: on the publication of *Tamburlaine the Great*.) *See* **948**.

5887.   JONES, LOUISE CONLEY.   A textual analysis of Marlowe's *Doctor Faustus* with director's book: stage action as metaphor. *See* **694**.

5888.   KEEFER, MICHAEL (ed.).   *Doctor Faustus*: a 1604-version edition. (Bibl. 1994, 3915.) Rev. by George L. Geckle in Text (Ann Arbor) (7) 1994, 492–511.

5889.   KEIPER, HUGO.   Marlowe's *Faustus*, Hell, and the editors. AAA (21:2) 1996, 205–38.

5890.   KOTT, JAN.   The Bottom translation: Marlowe and Shakespeare and the carnival tradition. Trans. by Daniela Miedzyrzecka and Lillian Vallee. (Bibl. 1987, 3904.) Rev. by Linda Woodbridge and Robert Rawdon Wilson in CanRCL (18:2/3) 1991, 333–45.

5891.   MCADAM, IAN.   Carnal identity in *The Jew of Malta*. ELR (26:1) 1996, 46–74.

5892.   MCALINDON, T.   *Doctor Faustus*: the predestination theory. EngS (76:3) 1995, 215–20.

5893.   MARCUS, LEAH S.   Unediting the Renaissance: Shakespeare, Marlowe, Milton. *See* **749**.

5894.   MEBANE, JOHN S.   Renaissance magic and the return of the Golden Age: the occult tradition and Marlowe, Jonson, and Shakespeare. (Bibl. 1995, 4864.) Rev. by J. Anthony Burton in ShB (10:2) 1992, 42.

5895. MUIR, KENNETH.   Three Marlowe texts. *See* **767**.

5896. MYERS, BRIAN G.   Terry Hands on *Tamburlaine*: humanity with teeth bared. ShB (11:1) 1993, 21–2.

5897. NICHOLL, CHARLES.   The reckoning: the murder of Christopher Marlowe. (Bibl. 1992, 4493.) New York: Harcourt Brace, 1994. Rev. by Thomas Flanagan in BkW, 6 Mar. 1994, 1, 10; by Gary Goldstein in ER (2:1) 1994, 29–32; by Laurie E. Maguire in MedRen (8) 1996, 276–8.

5898. PEYRÉ, YVES.   Marlowe's Argonauts. *In* (pp. 106–23) **124**.

5899. RASMUSSEN, ERIC.   Rehabilitating the A-text of Marlowe's *Doctor Faustus*. *See* **802**.

5900. SARRATORE, STEVEN T.   Faustus cage(d): a postmodern approach to the scenography for Marlowe's *A Tragical History of Doctor Faustus*. TT (4:2) 1994, 179–88.

5901. SCHOLES, ROBERT.   Devilish bargains. ArsL (6) 1992, 35–40.

5902. SHAPIRO, JAMES.   Rival playwrights: Marlowe, Jonson, Shakespeare. (Bibl. 1994, 3927.) Rev. by Roslyn Lander Knutson in ShB (10:2) 1992, 38–9.

5903. SHEPPEARD, SALLYE J.   Marlowe's Icarus: culture and myth in *Dr Faustus*. *In* (pp. 133–45) **116**.

5904. STOCKHOLDER, KAY.   The aspiring mind of the King's man. UC (11) 1991, 1–23.

5905. SULLIVAN, CERI.   Faustus and the apple. RES (47:185) 1996, 47–50.

5906. SUMMERS, CLAUDE J.   Marlowe and constructions of Renaissance homosexuality. CanRCL (21:1/2) 1994, 27–44.

5907. THOMAS, VIVIEN; TYDEMAN, WILLIAM (eds).   Christopher Marlowe: the plays and their sources. (Bibl. 1994, 3931.) Rev. by Robert A. Logan in ANQ (9:2) 1996, 49–52.

Queen Mary Stuart

5908. DUNNIGAN, SARAH M.   Rewriting the Renaissance language of love and desire: the 'bodily burdein' in the poetry of Mary, Queen of Scots. Gramma (4) 1996, 181–95.

5909. JOHNSON, JACQUELINE F.   Mary Queen of Scots: an annotated bibliography. BB (53:2) 1996, 153–60.

Alexander Montgomerie

5910. LYALL, RODERICK.   Formalist historicism and older Scots poetry. *See* **5736**.

5911. LYALL, RODERICK J.   Montgomerie and Marot: a sixteenth-century translator at work. Études Écossaises (2) 1993, 79–94.

5912. VAN HEIJNSBERGEN, THEO.   The sixteenth-century Scottish love lyric. *In* (pp. 45–61) **107**.

Sir Thomas More

5913. BAKER, DAVID WEIL.   Topical utopias: radicalizing Humanism in sixteenth-century England. *See* **5750**.

5914. BERNARD, G. W.   The fall of Wolsey reconsidered. *See* **5751**.

5915. DETHLOFF, UWE.   Die Rezeption von Thomas Mores *Utopia* in der französischen Renaissance. GRM (43:2) 1993, 209–13.

5916. FORTIER, MARDELLE L.; FORTIER, ROBERT F.   The utopian thought of St Thomas More and its development in literature.

(Bibl. 1993, 3710.) Rev. by Peter V. Sampo in Utopian Studies (7:2) 1996, 261–3.

5917. GIBBONS, BRIAN. The wrong end of the telescope. *In* (pp. 141–59) **124**.

5918. HÖLSCHER, LUCIAN. Utopie. *See* **2187**.

5919. HULSE, CLARK. Dead man's treasure: the cult of Thomas More. *In* (pp. 190–225) **90**.

5920. KUON, PETER. Utopischer Entwurf und fiktionale Vermittlung: Studien zum Gattungswandel der literarischen Utopie zwischen Humanismus und Frühaufklärung. (Bibl. 1986, 4149.) Rev. by Annegret J. Wiemer in CanRCL (18:1) 1991, 86–94.

5921. LOGAN, GEORGE M.; ADAMS, ROBERT M.; MILLER, CLARENCE H. (eds). *Utopia*: Latin text and English translation. Cambridge; New York: CUP, 1994. pp. xlvi, 290. Rev. by Romuald I. Lakowski in EMLS (2:3) 1996, 15.1–7.

5922. MARTZ, LOUIS L. Thomas More: the search for the inner man. (Bibl. 1995, 4899.) Rev. by M. Edmund Hussey in AR (49:1) 1991, 148.

5923. MUELLER, JANEL. 'The whole island like a single family': positioning women in Utopian patriarchy. *In* (pp. 93–122) **101**.

5924. PLETT, HEINRICH F. Utopias Aporien: Ansichten einer prekären Literaturform. *In* (pp. 225–40) **11**.

5925. SELLAR, TOM. A philosophy which knows its stage. Theater (26:1/2) 1995, 82–8.

5926. TAZBIR, JANUSZ. Nowe świadectwa znajomości Morusa w Polsce. (New evidence of knowledge of More in Poland.) PH (40:3) 1996, 29–35.

5927. WEGEMER, GERARD. The *City of God* in Thomas More's *Utopia*. Ren (44:2) 1992, 115–35.

Richard Mulcaster

5928. CUNNINGHAM, KAREN. 'She learns as she lies': work and the exemplary female in English early modern education. *See* **5795**.

Anthony Munday

5929. BERGERON, DAVID M. Thomas Middleton and Anthony Munday: artistic rivalry? SELit (36:2) 1996, 461–79.

Thomas Nashe

5930. BALLESTEROS GONZÁLEZ, ANTONIO. Digression and intertextual parody in Thomas Nashe, Laurence Sterne and James Joyce. *In* (pp. 55–64) **57**.

5931. BATE, JONATHAN. The Elizabethans in Italy. *In* (pp. 55–74) **124**.

5932. CHAKRAVORTY, SWAPAN. 'Give her more onion': unriddling the Welsh madman's speech in *The Changeling*. *See* **2597**.

5933. DUNCAN-JONES, KATHERINE. Nashe in Newgate. TLS, 22 Mar. 1996, 15.

5934. —— 'They say a made a good end': Ben Jonson's epitaph on Thomas Nashe. BJJ (3) 1996, 10–19.

5935. EVANS, ROBERT C. Nashe's *Choise* and Chaucer's Pardoner. *See* **5387**.

5936. KELLER, JAMES R. Thomas Nashe's *The Unfortunate Traveler*: taming the spirit of discontent. ER (1:2) 1993, 7–17.

5937. RELIHAN, CONSTANCE C.   Rhetoric, gender, and audience construction in Thomas Nashe's *The Unfortunate Traveller. In* (pp. 141–52) **35**.

John Northbrooke (*fl.*1568–1579)

5938. HOWARD, SKILES.   Rival discourses of dancing in early modern England. *See* **5817**.

Thomas Norton (1532–1584)

5939. JONES, NORMAN; WHITE, PAUL WHITFIELD.   *Gorboduc* and royal marriage politics: an Elizabethan playgoer's report of the premiere performance. *See* **5661**.

Edward de Vere, Earl of Oxford

5940. BUCKRIDGE, PATRICK.   What did John Marston know about Shakespeare? ER (4:2) 1996, 24–40.

5941. DESPER, C. RICHARD; VEZZOLI, GARY C.   A statistical approach to the Shakespeare authorship question. ER (1:2) 1993, 36–42.

5942. EDWARDS, FRANCIS.   William Shakespeare: why was his true identity concealed? ER (2:2) 1994, 23–48.

5943. HOPE, WARREN.   The singing swallow: Sir John Davies and Shakespeare. *See* **5816**.

5944. MANZO, FRED W.   Who was Joseph Hall's Labeo? ER (3:2) 1995, 53–9.

5945. MOORE, PETER R.   The lame storyteller, poor and despised. ER (3:2) 1995, 4–10.

5946. PRICE, DIANA.   Shakespeare's aristocratic sense of culture. ER (4:2) 1996, 4–23.

5947. STEVENS, JOHN PAUL.   The Shakespeare canon of statutory construction. ER (1:1) 1993, 4–20.

5948. VERE, CHARLES.   Edward de Vere and the psychology of Freudianism. ER (3:2) 1995, 35–52.

5949. —— Sir Philip Sidney satirized in *Merry Wives of Windsor*. ER (2:2) 1994, 3–10.

5950. WHALEN, RICHARD F.   Shakespeare – who was he? The Oxford challenge to the Bard of Avon. (Bibl. 1994, 3953.) Rev. by Roy Sexton in JDTC (10:2) 141–3.

William Painter

5951. DONOVAN, JOSEPHINE.   From avenger to victim: genealogy of a Renaissance novella. TSWL (15:2) 1996, 269–88.

Robert Parry

5952. SIMONS, JOHN.   Robert Parry's *Moderatus*: a study in Elizabethan romance. *In* (pp. 237–50) **104**.

George Peele

5953. JACKSON, MACD. P.   Stage directions and speech headings in Act I of *Titus Andronicus* Q (1594): Shakespeare or Peele? SB (49) 1996, 134–48.

5954. MOFFETT, A. S.   Process and structure shared: similarities between *commedia dell'arte* and *The Old Wives Tale* of George Peele. NETJ (4) 1993, 97–105.

Mary Herbert, Countess of Pembroke

5955. HANNAY, MARGARET P. 'Unlock my lipps': the *Miserere mei Deus* of Anne Vaughan Lok and Mary Sidney Herbert, Countess of Pembroke. *In* (pp. 19–36) **89**.

George Pettie

5956. STOCKTON, SHARON. Making men: visions of social mobility in *A Petite Pallace of Pettie His Pleasure*. *In* (pp. 55–72) **35**.

Sir Walter Ralegh

5957. BAJETTA, CARLO M. Ralegh's early poetry and its metrical context. *See* **5826**.

5958. —— Unrecorded extracts by Sir Walter Ralegh. *See* **566**.

5959. BEDNARZ, JAMES P. The collaborator as thief: Ralegh's (re)vision of the *Faerie Queene*. ELH (63:2) 1996, 279–307.

5960. BEER, ANNA. Textual politics: the execution of Sir Walter Ralegh. MP (94:1) 1996, 19–38.

5961. EDWARDS, PHILIP. Tragic form and the voyagers. *In* (pp. 75–86) **124**.

5962. HAMMER, PAUL E. J. A reckoning reframed: the 'murder' of Christopher Marlowe revisited. *See* **5825**.

5963. READ, DAVID. Ralegh's *Discoverie of Guiana* and the Elizabethan model of empire. *In* (pp. 166–76) **131**.

Thomas Sackville, First Earl of Dorset

5964. JONES, NORMAN; WHITE, PAUL WHITFIELD. *Gorboduc* and royal marriage politics: an Elizabethan playgoer's report of the premiere performance. *See* **5661**.

5965. PORIES, KATHLEEN. The intersection of Poor Laws and literature in the sixteenth century: fictional and factual categories. *In* (pp. 17–40) **35**.

Robert Cecil, Earl of Salisbury

5966. DUNCAN-JONES, KATHERINE. 'Preserved dainties': late Elizabethan poems by Sir Robert Cecil and the Earl of Clanricarde. *See* **627**.

Alexander Scott

5967. LYALL, RODERICK. Formalist historicism and older Scots poetry. *See* **5736**.

Mary Shelton

5968. REMLEY, PAUL G. Mary Shelton and her Tudor literary milieu. *In* (pp. 40–77) **101**.

Sir Philip Sidney

5969. BARBOUR, REID. Recent studies of prose fiction, 1603–1660, including Sidney's *Arcadia*. ELR (26:1) 1996, 167–97.

5970. BAUMLIN, JAMES S. Dialogue and *controversia* in English Renaissance literature: historicizing the reader's response. PMPA (19) 1994, 1–20.

5971. BUCKMAN, TY F. The perils of marriage counselling: John Stubbs, Philip Sidney, and the Virgin Queen. RenP 1995, 125–41.

5972. Camerlingo, Rosanna.   From the courtly world to the infinite universe: Sir Philip Sidney's two *Arcadia*s. Alessandria: dell'Orso, 1993. pp. x, 249. (Confronti letterari, 4.) (Cf. bibl. 1991, 4506.) Rev. by Michael G. Brennan in NQ (43:1) 1996, 83–4.

5973. Craft, William.   Labyrinth of desire: invention and culture in the work of Sir Philip Sidney. (Bibl. 1994, 3968.) Rev. by Michael G. Brennan in NQ (43:1) 1996, 83–4.

5974. Cullen, Patrick Colborn (ed.).   A continuation of Sir Philip Sidney's *Arcadia*. (Bibl. 1995, 4934.) Rev. by Qingyun Wu in Utopian Studies (7:1) 1996, 154–5; by Katherine Duncan-Jones in NQ (43:3) 1996, 345–6.

5975. Doherty, M. J.   Beyond androgyny: Sidney, Milton, and the phoenix. *In* (pp. 34–65) **40**.

5976. Garrett, Martin (ed.).   Philip Sidney: the critical heritage. London; New York: Routledge, 1996. pp. vii, 365. (Critical heritage.)

5977. Hamilton, A. C.   Problems in reconstructing an Elizabethan text: the example of Sir Philip Sidney's *Triumph*. See **668**.

5978. Heninger, S. K., Jr.   Sidney and Spenser: the poet as maker. (Bibl. 1993, 3742.) Rev. by Anthony Esolen in Shakespeare Yearbook (2) 1991, 271–4.

5979. Herman, Peter C.   Squitter-wits and muse-haters: Sidney, Spenser, Milton, and Renaissance antipoetic sentiment. Detroit, MI: Wayne State UP, 1996. pp. 284. (Cf. bibl. 1991, 4313.)

5980. Hopkins, Lisa.   'Lear, Lear, Lear!': Marlowe, Shakespeare, and the third. See **5883**.

5981. Hull, Elizabeth M.   All my deed but copying is: the erotics of identity in *Astrophil and Stella*. TSLL (38:2) 1996, 175–90.

5982. Hunt, Maurice.   *The Countess of Pembroke's Arcadia*, Shakespeare's *A Midsummer Night's Dream*, and the School of the Night: an intertextual nexus. ELit (23:1) 1996, 3–20.

5983. Merrens, Rebecca.   Exchanging cultural capital: troping woman in Sidney and Bacon. Genre (25:2/3) 1992, 179–92.

5984. Minogue, Sally.   A woman's touch: Astrophil, Stella and 'Queen Vertue's Court'. ELH (63:3) 1996, 555–70.

5985. O'Donoghue, Bernard.   Comparisons. ERev (5:3) 1995, 30–1. (Sidney, *With How Sad Steps*; Larkin, *Sad Steps*.)

5986. Phillippy, Patricia Berrahou.   Love's remedies: recantation and Renaissance lyric poetry. (Bibl. 1995, 4946.) Rev. by Andrew Hadfield in NQ (43:3) 1996, 329–30.

5987. Plett, Heinrich F.   Utopias Aporien: Ansichten einer prekären Literaturform. *In* (pp. 225–40) **11**.

5988. Prendergast, Maria Teresa Micaela.   Philoclea parsed: prose, verse, and femininity in Sidney's *Old Arcadia*. *In* (pp. 99–116) **35**.

5989. Rees, Joan.   Sir Philip Sidney and *Arcadia*. (Bibl. 1995, 4947.) Rev. by Navina Hooker in Eng (41:171) 1992, 275–7.

5990. Russell, Henry W.   *Astrophil and Stella*: hell in a very small place. Ren (44:2) 1992, 105–14.

5991. Singer, Daniella E.   Despair and subjectivity in the erotic verse of Sidney and of Donne. Neophilologus (80:3) 1996, 493–500.

5992. Vere, Charles.   Sir Philip Sidney satirized in *Merry Wives of Windsor*. See **5949**.

5993. Wilson, Scott.   Love and the labyrinth: Sir Philip Sidney and the extraordinary forms of desire. Assays (7) 1992, 43–69.

5994. WRIGHT, STEPHANIE J.   The sixteenth century: excluding drama after 1550: Sidney. YWES (75) 1994, 212–14.

John Skelton

5995. BLANCHARD, W. SCOTT.   Skelton: the voice of the mob in sanctuary. *In* (pp. 123–44) **101**.

5996. COINER, NANCY.   Galathea and the interplay of voices in Skelton's *Speke, Parrot. In* (pp. 88–99) **116**.

5997. HERMAN, PETER C.   Leaky ladies and droopy dames: the grotesque realism of Skelton's *The Tunnynge of Elynour Rummynge. In* (pp. 145–67) **101**.

5998. KELLY, JOHN C.   A perfect feast of fools and plenty: carnival in John Skelton's poem *The Tunning of Elinour Rumming.* ESCan (22:2) 1996, 129–48.

5999. KEZAR, DENNIS DEAN.   The fall of a sparrow: Skelton's fictive text and the manufacture of fame. RenP 1995, 15–32.

6000. STERLING, ERIC.   The movement towards subversion: the English history play from Skelton to Shakespeare. *See* **5710**.

6001. TORTI, ANNA.   Reality of allegory or allegory of reality? Skelton's dilemma in *The Bowge of Courte* and *Speke Parott.* Textus (1:1) 1988, 51–80.

Robert Southwell

6002. BROWNLOW, F. W.   Robert Southwell. New York; London: Twayne, 1996. pp. xvi, 156. (Twayne's English authors, 516.)

6003. LOWE-EVANS, MARY.   Southwell's *Christ's Bloody Sweat.* Exp (54:4) 1996, 199–202.

6004. ROBERTS, JOHN R.; ROBERTS, LORRAINE.   'To weave a new webbe in their owne loome': Robert Southwell and Counter-Reformation poetics. *In* (pp. 63–77) **107**.

Edmund Spenser

6005. ABATE, CORINNE S.   Spenser's *The Faerie Queene.* Exp (55:1) 1996, 6–8.

6006. ANDERSON, JUDITH H.; CHENEY, DONALD; RICHARDSON, DAVID A. (eds).   Spenser's life and the subject of biography. Amherst: Massachusetts UP, 1996. pp. xiv, 215. (Massachusetts studies in early modern culture.)

6007. BASEOTTO, PAOLA.   Il selvaggio come incarnazione del male nella *Faerie Queene* di Edmund Spenser. Acme (49:3) 1996, 261–72.

6008. BEDNARZ, JAMES P.   The collaborator as thief: Ralegh's (re)vision of the *Faerie Queene. See* **5959**.

6009. BERGVALL, ÅKE.   Formal and verbal logocentrism in Augustine and Spenser. SP (93:3) 1996, 251–66.

6010. BOHNERT, MICHAEL.   Manly and unmanly masks: the ironies of Britomart's quest in Book v of the *Faerie Queene.* SRASP (19) 1996, 41–9.

6011. BORGSTEDT, THOMAS.   Herz, Altar und Schoß: Nachtrag zu Hoffmannswaldaus Kußgedicht (Pierre de Ronsard, Philippe Desportes, Edmund Spenser). GRM (45:1) 1995, 104–9.

6012. BREEN, JOHN.   The empirical eye: Edmund Spenser's *A View of the Present State of Ireland.* Irish Review (16) 1994, 44–52.

6013. —— The *Faerie Queene* Book I, and the theme of Protestant exile. IUR (26:2) 1996, 226–36.

6014. BROADDUS, JAMES W.   Spenser's allegory of love: social vision in Books III, IV, and V of the *Faerie Queene*. (Bibl. 1995, 4977.) Rev. by Mary Villeponteaux in SpenN (27:3) 1996, 2–4.

6015. BROOKS-DAVIES, DOUGLAS (ed.).   Selected shorter poems. (Bibl. 1995, 4978.) Rev. by Andrew Hadfield in TLS, 16 Feb. 1996, 26.

6016. BROWN, TED.   Pride and pastoral in *The Shepheardes Calendar*. *In* (pp. 101–15) **116**.

6017. BURROW, COLIN.   Epic romance: Homer to Milton. (Bibl. 1995, 4982.) Rev. by Elizabeth J. Bellamy in CL (48:4) 1996, 371–3.

6018. CANNY, NICHOLAS.   Reviewing *A View of the Present State of Ireland*. IUR (26:2) 1996, 252–67.

6019. CARROLL, CLARE.   Spenser and the Irish language: the sons of Milesio in *A View of the Present State of Ireland*, the *Faerie Queene*, Book V, and the *Leabhar Gabhála*. IUR (26:2) 1996, 281–90.

6020. CAVANAGH, SHEILA T.   'Licentious barbarism': Spenser's view of the Irish and the *Faerie Queene*. IUR (26:2) 1996, 268–80.

6021. —— Wanton eyes and chaste desires: female sexuality in the *Faerie Queene*. (Bibl. 1995, 4985.) Rev. by Andrew Hadfield in NQ (43:2) 1996, 209–10.

6022. CHENEY, PATRICK.   Spenser's famous flight: a Renaissance idea of a literary career. (Bibl. 1995, 4986.) Rev. by Mark Vessey in LitTheol (10:4) 1996, 382–4.

6023. COOK, PATRICK J.   Milton, Spenser, and the epic tradition. Aldershot: Scolar Press; Brookfield, VT: Ashgate, 1996. pp. ii, 201. (Cf. bibl. 1991, 4593.)

6024. COUGHLAN, PATRICIA.   The local context of Mutabilitie's plea. IUR (26:2) 1996, 320–41.

6025. CURRAN, JOHN E., JR.   Spenser and the historical revolution: Briton Moniments and the problem of Roman Britain. CLIO (25:3) 1996, 273–92.

6026. DEES, JEROME S., *et al.*   Articles: abstracts and notes. SpenN (27:1) 1996, 13–19; (27:2) 1996, 15–22; (27:3) 1996, 12–19.

6027. DEMPSEY, JOANNE T.   Form and transformation in Ariosto, Tasso, and Spenser. CanRCL (18:2/3) 1991, 323–6.

6028. EGGERT, KATHERINE.   'Changing all that forme of common weale': genre and the repeal of queenship in the *Faerie Queene*, Book 5. ELR (26:2) 1996, 259–90.

6029. ERICKSON, WAYNE.   Mapping the *Faerie Queene*: quest structures and the world of the poem. New York; London: Garland, 1996. pp. 150. (Garland reference library of the humanities, 1835.) (Garland studies in the Renaissance, 3.)

6030. FIKE, MATTHEW A.   Nature as supernature: Donaldson's revision of Spenser. Mythlore (18:2) 1992, 17–20, 22.

6031. FUKUDA, SHOHACHI.   Spenser in Japan 1985–1995. SpenN (27:1) 1996, 19–22.

6032. GLESS, DARRYL J.   Interpretation and theology in Spenser. (Bibl. 1995, 4996.) Rev. by Michael G. Brennan in NQ (43:4) 1996, 473–4; by Mark Vessey in LitTheol (10:4) 1996, 382–4.

6033. GREENE, DEIRDRE.   Higher argument: Tolkien and the tradition of vision, epic and prophecy. Mythlore (21:2) 1996, 45–52.

6034. GREGERSON, LINDA.   The reformation of the subject: Spenser,

Milton, and the English Protestant epic. (Bibl. 1995, 4999.) Rev. by Ronald Bond in SpenN (27:3) 1996, 4–7; by William Zunder in EngS (77:5) 1996, 506–7; by Heather Dubrow in CLIO (25:4) 1996, 421–38.

6035. HADFIELD, ANDREW.   Another look at Serena and Irena. IUR (26:2) 1996, 291–302.

6036. —— 'The naked and the dead': Elizabethan perceptions of Ireland. *In* (pp. 32–54) **124**.

6037. —— (ed.).   Edmund Spenser. London; New York: Longman, 1996. pp. x, 240. (Longman critical readers.)

6038. HAMILTON, A. C.   Closure in Spenser's *The Faerie Queene*. *In* (pp. 23–34) **16**.

6039. HAMLIN, WILLIAM M.   The image of America in Montaigne, Spenser and Shakespeare: Renaissance ethnography and literary reflection. (Bibl. 1995, 5003.) Rev. by Donna C. Woodford in EMLS (2:1) 1996, 11.1–5; by Gesa Mackenthun in JAStud (30:2) 1996, 320–1.

6040. HENDRIX, HOWARD.   'Those wandring eyes of his': watching Guyon watch the naked damsels wrestling. Assays (7) 1992, 71–85.

6041. HENDRIX, LAUREL L.   'A world of glas': the heroine's quest for identity in Spenser's *Faerie Queene* and Stephen R. Donaldson's *Mirror of Her. In* (pp. 91–100) **36**.

6042. HERMAN, PETER C.   Squitter-wits and muse-haters: Sidney, Spenser, Milton, and Renaissance antipoetic sentiment. *See* **5979**.

6043. HOOPER, GLENN.   Writing and landscape in early modern Ireland. *See* **5815**.

6044. INCORVATI, RICK.   Eternal form and timely variations in Spenser's *Epithalamion*. SRASP (19) 1996, 29–39.

6045. KANE, SEAN.   Spenser's broken symmetries. *In* (pp. 13–22) **16**.

6046. KING, JOHN N.   Spenser's poetry and the Reformation tradition. (Bibl. 1995, 5009.) Rev. by Andrew Hadfield in Eng (40:166) 1991, 69–73.

6047. KLEIN, BERNHARD.   The lie of the land: English surveyors, Irish rebels and the *Faerie Queene*. IUR (26:2) 1996, 207–25.

6048. —— '*Utterly another people*': Konstruktionen kultureller Differenz im Irland der frühen Neuzeit. *See* **5761**.

6049. KRAMNICK, JONATHAN BRODY.   The cultural logic of late feudalism: placing Spenser in the eighteenth century. ELH (63:4) 1996, 871–92.

6050. LANE, ROBERT.   Shepheards devises: Edmund Spenser's *Shepheardes Calender* and the institutions of Elizabethan society. (Bibl. 1995, 5011.) Rev. by David Norbrook in EHR (111:441) 1996, 456.

6051. MCDERMOTT, JOHN V.   Spenser's *Faerie Queene*, I.ii.52 and 53. Exp (54:4) 1996, 198–9.

6052. MALEY, WILLY.   Spenser and Ireland: an annotated bibliography, 1986–96. IUR (26:2) 1996, 342–53.

6053. —— Spenser and Scotland: the *View* and the limits of Anglo-Irish identity. Prose Studies (19:1) 1996, 1–18.

6054. —— Spenser's *View* and Stanyhurst's *Description*. *See* **5764**.

6055. —— 'To weet to work *Irenaes* franchisement': Ireland in the *Faerie Queene*. IUR (26:2) 1996, 303–19.

6056. MAZZOLA, ELIZABETH.   Marrying Medusa: Spenser's *Epithalamion* and Renaissance reconstructions of female privacy. Genre (25:2/3) 1992, 193–210.

6057. MELANEY, WILLIAM D.   Spenser's poetic phenomenology:

Humanism and the recovery of place. Analecta Husserliana (44) 1995, 35–44.

6058. Mikics, David.   The limits of moralizing: pathos and subjectivity in Spenser and Milton. (Bibl. 1994, 4045.) Rev. by Andrew Hadfield in NQ (43:2) 1996, 210–11; by Ed Malone in MQ (30:1) 1996, 42–3; by Stephen M. Buhler in SpenN (27:1) 1996, 6–9.

6059. Mulryan, John.   'Is my team ploughing?': the struggle for closure in the *Faerie Queene* 1590 (3.45). BJJ (3) 1996, 145–6.

6060. Murphy, Andrew.   Shakespeare's Irish history. Literature and History (5:1) 1996, 38–59.

6061. Ní Chuilleanáin, Eiléan.   Forged and fabulous chronicles: reading Spenser as an Irish writer. IUR (26:2) 1996, 237–51.

6062. Patterson, Annabel M.   Reading between the lines. (Bibl. 1995, 5032.) Rev. by Lawrence F. Rhu in Review (17) 1995, 149–52.

6063. Pendergast, John S.   Christian allegory and Spenser's 'general intention'. SP (93:3) 1996, 267–87.

6064. Philmus, Maria R. Rohr.   The *Faerie Queene* and Renaissance poetics: another look at Book vi as 'conclusion' to the poem. EngS (76:6) 1995, 497–519.

6065. Radcliffe, David Hill.   Edmund Spenser, a reception history. Columbia, SC: Camden House, 1996. pp. xiii, 239. (Literary criticism in perspective.)

6066. Rambuss, Richard.   Spenser's secret career. (Bibl. 1995, 5034.) Rev. by Lawrence F. Rhu in Review (17) 1995, 147–9.

6067. Reid, Robert L.   The fairy queen: Gloriana or Titania? UC (13) 1993, 16–32.

6068. Riddell, James A.; Stewart, Stanley.   Jonson's Spenser: evidence and historical criticism. (Bibl. 1995, 5035.) Rev. by M. L. Donnelly in SpenN (27:2) 1996, 1–5.

6069. Roche, Thomas P., Jr.   Spenser, Milton, and the representation of evil. *In* (pp. 14–33) **40**.

6070. Rovang, Paul R.   Refashioning 'knights and ladies gentle deeds': the intertextuality of Spenser's *Faerie Queene* and Malory's *Morte Darthur. See* **5256**.

6071. Sanders, Arnold A.   Ruddymane and Canace, lost and found: Spenser's reception of *Confessio Amantis* 3 and Chaucer's Squire's Tale. *In* (pp. 196–215) **131**.

6072. Sawday, Jonathan.   Poison and honey: the politics of the sacred and the profane in Spenser's *Fowre Hymnes* (1596). *In* (pp. 79–92) **107**.

6073. Schleiner, Louise.   Cultural semiotics, Spenser, and the captive woman. (Bibl. 1995, 5039.) Rev. by Raphael Falco in SpenN (27:3) 1996, 9–12.

6074. Shoaf, R. A.   'For there is figures in all things': juxtology in Shakespeare, Spenser, and Milton. *In* (pp. 266–85) **131**.

6075. Steadman, John M.   Moral fiction in Milton and Spenser. (Bibl. 1995, 5047.) Rev. by John Mulryan in Cithara (36:1) 1996, 34–6.

6076. Steppat, Michael.   Chances of mischief: variations of fortune in Spenser. (Bibl. 1993, 3832.) Rev. by J. B. Lethbridge in SpenN (27:2) 1996, 9–12.

6077. Teskey, Gordon.   Allegory , materialism, violence. *In* (pp. 293–318) **90**.

6078. —— Positioning Spenser's *Letter to Raleigh. In* (pp. 35–46) **16**.

6079. UNDERWOOD, VERNE. Who paid for Spenser's funeral? SpenN (27:2) 1996, 22–4.

6080. VOSS, PAUL J. The *Faerie Queene* 1590–1596: the case of Saint George. BJJ (3) 1996, 59–73.

6081. WALLER, GARY. Edmund Spenser: a literary life. (Bibl. 1995, 5053.) Rev. by Jean R. Brink in SpenN (27:2) 1996, 12–15.

6082. WARKENTIN, GERMAINE. Spenser at the still point: a schematic device in *Epithalamion*. *In* (pp. 47–57) **16**.

6083. WEATHERBY, H. L. Dame Nature and the nymph. ELR (26:2) 1996, 243–58.

6084. WEATHERBY, HAROLD L. Mirrors of celestial grace: patristic theology in Spenser's allegory. (Bibl. 1995, 5056.) Rev. by Mark Vessey in LitTheol (10:4) 1996, 382–4.

6085. —— Spenser's legend of *Enkráteia*. SP (93:2) 1996, 207–17.

6086. WOFFORD, SUSANNE LINDGREN. The choice of Achilles: the ideology of figure in the epic. (Bibl. 1995, 5058.) Rev. by Ann W. Astell in Comparatist (18) 1994, 172–4.

6087. WRIGHT, STEPHANIE J. The sixteenth century: excluding drama after 1550: Spenser. YWES (75) 1994, 214–17.

John Stubbs

6088. BUCKMAN, TY F. The perils of marriage counselling: John Stubbs, Philip Sidney, and the Virgin Queen. *See* **5971**.

Henry Howard, Earl of Surrey

6089. SESSIONS, W. A. Surrey's Psalms in the Tower. *In* (pp. 17–31) **107**.

6090. —— Surrey's Wyatt: autumn 1542 and the new poet. *In* (pp. 168–92) **101**.

6091. VAN HEIJNSBERGEN, THEO. The sixteenth-century Scottish love lyric. *In* (pp. 45–61) **107**.

Edmund Tilney

6092. WAYNE, VALERIE (ed.). *The Flower of Friendship*: a Renaissance dialogue contesting marriage. (Bibl. 1995, 5067.) Rev. by R. A. Houlbrooke in EHR (111:440) 1996, 172–3.

William Tyndale

6093. BARNETT, MARY JANE. Tyndale's heretical translation: Lollards, Lutherans, and an economy of circulation. RenP 1996, 1–11.

6094. DANIELL, DAVID. William Tyndale: a biography. (Bibl. 1995, 5069.) Rev. by Michael Dirda in BkW, 25 Dec. 1994, 1, 14; by James Hitchcock in AHR (101:2) 1996, 478; by R. D. Gooder in CamQ (25:1) 1996, 86–102.

6095. DECOURSEY, MATTHEW. Erasmus, Tyndale and popular religion. RenP 1996, 13–20.

6096. DICK, JOHN A. R.; RICHARDSON, ANNE. William Tyndale and the law. (Bibl. 1995, 5070.) Rev. by Robert Willman in Albion (28:4) 1996, 687–9.

6097. GOODER, R. D. William Tyndale. CamQ (25:1) 1996, 86–102 (review-article).

6098. HAMMOND, GERALD. What was the influence of the medieval English Bible upon the Renaissance Bible? *See* **4879**.

14

Nicholas Udall

6099. PITTENGER, ELIZABETH.   'To serve the queere': Nicholas Udall, Master of Revels. *In* (pp. 162–89) **93**.

Henry Wotton (*fl.*1578)

6100. BATE, JONATHAN.   The Elizabethans in Italy. *In* (pp. 55–74) **124**.

Sir Thomas Wyatt

6101. CONCOLATO, MARIA PALERMO.   Il viaggio del testo: i *Salmi penitenziali* dall'Aretino al Wyatt. Filologia e critica (18:3) 1993, 321–33.

6102. COOPER, LOUISE (sel. and introd.).   Poems. Kidderminster: Joe's Press, 1994. pp. 62.

6103. CUNNAR, EUGENE R.   'Break not them then so wrongfully': topical readings of Sir Thomas Wyatt's riddling and bewitched lute and the feminine other. Cithara (32:1) 1992, 3–30.

6104. ESTRIN, BARBARA L.   Laura: uncovering gender and genre in Wyatt, Donne, and Marvell. (Bibl. 1995, 5077.) Rev. by Nathan P. Tinker in EMLS (2:2) 1996, 7.1–5.

6105. —— Wyatt's unlikely likenesses; or, Has the lady read Petrarch? *In* (pp. 219–39) **101**.

6106. GREENE, ROLAND.   The colonial Wyatt: contexts and openings. *In* (pp. 240–66) **101**.

6107. HALASZ, ALEXANDRA.   Wyatt's David. *In* (pp. 193–218) **101**.

6108. HEALE, ELIZABETH.   Lute and harp in Wyatt's poetry. *In* (pp. 3–15) **107**.

6109. HINELY, JAN LAWSON.   'Freedom through bondage': Wyatt's appropriation of the Penitential Psalms of David. *In* (pp. 148–65) **131**.

6110. KLEIN, LISA M.   The Petrarchanism of Sir Thomas Wyatt reconsidered. *In* (pp. 131–47) **131**.

6111. ODABASHIAN, BARBARA.   Thomas Wyatt and the rhetoric of change. *In* (pp. 287–300) **98**.

6112. SCHWARTZ, LOUIS.   'But as for me, Helas, I may no more': Petrarchan imitation and courtly sociability in Wyatt's *Who So List to Hounte*. Comparatist (18) 1994, 1–22.

6113. SCOTT, HARDIMAN (ed.).   Selected poems. Manchester: Fyfield, 1996. pp. 96.

6114. SESSIONS, W. A.   Surrey's Wyatt: autumn 1542 and the new poet. *In* (pp. 168–92) **101**.

6115. VAN HEIJNSBERGEN, THEO.   The sixteenth-century Scottish love lyric. *In* (pp. 45–61) **107**.

WILLIAM SHAKESPEARE

Editions and Textual Criticism

6116. ANDREWS, JOHN F. (ed.).   Othello. Foreword by James Earl Jones. London: Dent; Rutland, VT: Tuttle, 1995. pp. lii, 330. (Everyman Shakespeare.)

6117. —— The winter's tale. Foreword by Adrian Noble. London: Dent; Rutland, VT: Tuttle, 1995. pp. xlix, 310. (Everyman Shakespeare.)

6118. BAIN, ELSPETH; MORRIS, JONATHAN; SMITH, ROB (eds). King Lear. Cambridge; New York: CUP, 1996. pp. 236. (Cambridge school Shakespeare.)

6119. BAKER, JOHN. Found: Shakespeare's manuscript of *Henry IV*. ER (4:1) 1996, 14–46.

6120. BATE, JONATHAN (ed.). Titus Andronicus. (Bibl. 1995, 5087.) Rev. by R. S. White in NQ (43:3) 1996, 332–4; by Dieter Mehl in SJ (132) 1996, 271–2.

6121. BERTRAM, PAUL; KLIMAN, BERNICE W. (eds). The three-text *Hamlet*: parallel texts of the first and second quartos and first folio. (Bibl. 1994, 4086.) Rev. by Maurice Charney in ShB (11:1) 1993, 42.

6122. BIRCH, MADELEINE (ed.). The winter's tale. Harlow; New York: Longman, 1996. pp. xxii, 358. (Longman literature Shakespeare.)

6123. BJELLAND, KAREN T. The cultural value of analytical bibliography and textual criticism: the case of *Troilus and Cressida*. Text (Ann Arbor) (7) 1994, 273–95.

6124. BORIS, EDNA ZWICK. To soliloquize or not to soliloquize. Q/W/E/R/T/Y (6) 1996, 23–8.

6125. BRAUNMULLER, A. R. (ed.). Macbeth. Commentary by David S. Rodes; produced by Michael E. Cohen. New York: Voyager, 1994. 1 CD-ROM (Windows; Macintosh). (Voyager Shakespeare, 1.)

6126. BROWN, JOHN RUSSELL (ed.). King Lear. New York: Applause, 1996. pp. xx, 220. (Applause Shakespeare library.)

6127. —— A midsummer night's dream. With theatre commentary by John Hirsch and Leslie Thomson. New York: Applause, 1996. pp. xxxiii, 137. (Applause Shakespeare library.)

6128. —— The tempest. New York: Applause, 1996. pp. xix, 143. (Applause Shakespeare library.)

6129. CHARNEY, MAURICE; VAUGHAN, STUART (eds). Julius Caesar. New York: Applause, 1996. pp. xxv, 166. (Applause Shakespeare library.)

6130. CLAYTON, THOMAS (ed.). The *Hamlet* first published (Q1, 1603): origins, form, intertextualities. (Bibl. 1995, 5097.) Rev. by Beatrice W. Kliman in ShB (12:2) 1994, 47–9.

6131. CORBIN, PETER. The 'harmless drudgery' of editing Shakespeare: the Arden Shakespeare: third series. Archiv (233:1) 1996, 99–108 (review-article).

6132. CORDNER, MICHAEL. Annotation and performance in Shakespeare. EC (46:4) 1996, 289–301.

6133. CRAIK, T. W. (ed.). King Henry V. (Bibl. 1995, 5099.) Rev. by R. S. White in NQ (43:3) 1996, 332–4; by Dieter Mehl in SJ (132) 1996, 273–4.

6134. DANE, JOSEPH A. Perfect order and perfected order: the evidence from press-variants of early seventeenth-century quartos. *See* **267**.

6135. DAVISON, PETER (ed.). The first quarto of *King Richard III*. Cambridge; New York: CUP, 1996. pp. xiv, 190. (New Cambridge Shakespeare.)

6136. DELL'AVERSANO, CARMEN. Tradizione e innovazione metodologica nella costituzione de testo del *King Lear*. Textus (3:1/2) 1990, 23–73.

6137. DESSEN, ALAN C. Massed entries and theatrical options in *The Winter's Tale*. MedRen (8) 1996, 119–27.

6138. DETOBEL, ROBERT.   On the meaning of 'true copy'. ER (2:2) 1994, 49–54.

6139. DODSWORTH, MARTIN (ed.).   The sonnets and *A Lover's Complaint*. London: Dent; Rutland, VT: Tuttle, 1995. pp. xxv, 194. (Everyman library.)

6140. EGGERT, PAUL.   Document and text: the 'life' of the literary work and the capacities of editing. *See* **630**.

6141. EVANS, G. BLAKEMORE (ed.).   The sonnets. Introd. by Anthony Hecht. Cambridge; New York: CUP, 1996. pp. xvii, 297. (New Cambridge Shakespeare.)

6142. FOAKES, R. A. (ed.).   Macbeth. With a theatre commentary by John Russell Brown. New York: Applause, 1996. pp. xix, 166. (Applause Shakespeare library.)

6143. FOSTER, MAXWELL E.   The play behind the play: *Hamlet* and quarto one. Ed. by Anne Shiras. Pittsburgh, PA: Foster Executors, 1991. pp. 209. Rev. by Kathleen Campbell in ShB (12:1) 1994, 51.

6144. FRANKLIN, COLIN.   Print and design in eighteenth-century editions of Shakespeare. *See* **275**.

6145. GIBSON, JAMES M.   The Philadelphia Shakespeare story: Horace Howard Furness and the Variorum Shakespeare. (Bibl. 1990, 3731.) Rev. by Barbara C. Millard in ShB (10:1) 1992, 44–5.

6146. GOSSETT, SUZANNE.   Why should a woman edit a man? *See* **654**.

6147. GRIFFIN, BENJAMIN.   Shakespeare: editions and textual scholarship. YWES (75) 1994, 221–7.

6148. GRIVELET, MICHEL; MONSARRAT, GILLES (eds).   Œuvres complètes: édition bilingue. Tragédies I et II. Paris: Laffont, 1995. 2 vols. pp. 1110; 1170. (Bouquins.) Rev. by Jean-Marie Maguin in CEI (49) 1996, 103–12.

6149. GURR, ANDREW (ed.).   King Henry V. (Bibl. 1995, 5114.) Rev. by William B. Long in Text (Ann Arbor) (8) 1995, 382–5.

6150. HALIO, JAY L. (ed.).   The first quarto of *King Lear*. (Bibl. 1995, 5116.) Rev. by Martin Coyle in NQ (43:2) 1996, 213; by Howard Mills in ELN (33:3) 1996, 76–7.

6151. —— Shakespeare's *Romeo and Juliet*: texts, contexts, and interpretation. Newark: Delaware UP; London; Toronto: Assoc. UPs, 1995. pp. 155. Rev. by William B. Long in Text (Ann Arbor) (9) 1996, 477–82.

6152. —— The tragedy of King Lear. (Bibl. 1995, 5117.) Rev. by William B. Long in Text (Ann Arbor) (8) 1995, 385–6.

6153. HILL, W. SPEED.   Where we are and how we got here: editing after poststructuralism. *See* **681**.

6154. HILTSCHER, MICHAEL.   Shakespeares Text in Deutschland: Textkritik und Kanonfrage von den Anfängen bis zur Mitte des neunzehnten Jahrhunderts. (Bibl. 1993, 3893.) Rev. by Christa Jansohn in editio (8) 1994, 233–9; by Susanne Scholz in SJ (132) 1996, 268–9.

6155. HINMAN, CHARLTON (ed.).   The first folio of Shakespeare: the Norton facsimile: based on folios in the Folger Shakespeare Library Collection. Introd. by Peter W. M. Blayney. (Bibl. 1970, 3609.) New York; London: Norton, 1996. pp. xxxvii, 928. (Second ed.: first ed. 1968.)

6156. HOLDERNESS, GRAHAM; CARTER, NAOMI.   The king's two bodies: text and genre in *King Lear*. Eng (45:181) 1996, 1–31.

6157. HOLLAND, PETER (ed.).   A midsummer night's dream. (Bibl. 1994, 4106.) Rev. by Christa Jansohn in SJ (132) 1996, 282–3.

6158. HONIGMANN, E. A. J. The texts of *Othello* and Shakespearian revision. London; New York: Routledge, 1996. pp. xix, 187. Rev. by John Jowett in TLS, 23 Aug. 1996, 13–14.

6159. IOPPOLO, GRACE. Revising Shakespeare. (Bibl. 1995, 5126.) Rev. by William B. Long in Text (Ann Arbor) (8) 1995, 380–2; by Werner Brönnimann in Archiv (233:2) 1996, 387–8.

6160. IRACE, KATHLEEN. Reconstruction and adaptation in Q *Henry V*. SB (44) 1991, 228–53.

6161. IRACE, KATHLEEN O. Reforming the 'bad' quartos: performance and provenance of six Shakespearean first editions. (Bibl. 1995, 5127.) Rev. by Eric Sams in NQ (43:2) 1996, 211–12; by Howard Mills in ELN (33:3) 1996, 76–7.

6162. JACKSON, MACD. P. Rhyming in *Pericles*: more evidence of dual authorship. SB (46) 1993, 239–49.

6163. —— Stage directions and speech headings in Act I of *Titus Andronicus* Q (1594): Shakespeare or Peele? See **5953**.

6164. JARVIS, SIMON. Scholars and gentlemen: Shakespearian textual criticism and representations of scholarly labour, 1725–1765. (Bibl. 1995, 5130.) Rev. by R. S. White in NQ (43:3) 1996, 360–1; by Bryan N. S. Gooch in EMLS (2:3) 1996, 9.1–6.

6165. KAHAN, JEFFREY. Henry Chettle and the unreliable *Romeo*: a reassessment. See **5810**.

6166. —— Henry Chettle's *Romeo* Q1 and *The Death of Robert Earl of Huntingdon*. See **5811**.

6167. KASTAN, DAVID SCOTT. The mechanics of culture: editing Shakespeare today. SStud (24) 1996, 30–7.

6168. KLEIN, HOLGER (ed.). *Much Ado About Nothing*: a new critical edition. (Bibl. 1994, 4114.) Rev. by Christa Jansohn in SJ (132) 1996, 285–6.

6169. —— (ed. and trans.). William Shakespeare: *Viel Lärm um Nichts/Much Ado About Nothing*. (Bibl. 1993, 3901.) Rev. by Christa Jansohn in SJ (132) 1996, 286–7.

6170. KNOWLES, RICHARD. *Cum notis variorum*: variorum guides. SNL (44:3) 1994, 53.

6171. MCMULLAN, GORDON. 'Our whole life is like a play': collaboration and the problem of editing. Textus (9:2) 1996, 437–59.

6172. MAGUIN, FRANÇOIS (ed. and trans.). Hamlet. Paris: Flammarion, 1995. pp. 541. (Complete text; bilingual edition.) Rev. by Yves Peyré in CEl (49) 1996, 122.

6173. MAGUIRE, LAURIE E. Shakespearean suspect texts: the 'bad' quartos and their contexts. Cambridge; New York: CUP, 1996. pp. xvii, 427.

6174. MARCUS, LEAH S. Unediting the Renaissance: Shakespeare, Marlowe, Milton. See **749**.

6175. MARTIN, PETER. Edmond Malone, Shakespearean scholar: a literary biography. (Bibl. 1995, 5140.) Rev. by R. S. White in NQ (43:3) 1996, 361–2; by Richard Knowles in ELN (34:2) 1996, 84–5; by Roslyn L. Knutson in ShB (14:4) 1996, 45–6.

6176. MASSAI, SONIA. Tate's critical 'editing' of his source-text(s) for *The History of King Lear*. Textus (9:2) 1996, 501–22.

6177. MEHL, DIETER. Der dritte Arden Shakespeare. SJ (132) 1996, 269–74 (review-article).

6178. MELCHIORI, GIORGIO.   What did Shakespeare write? Textus (9:2) 1996, 339–56.
6179. MEYER, ANN R.   Shakespeare's art and the texts of *King Lear*. SB (47) 1994, 128–46.
6180. MOWAT, BARBARA A.   The problem of Shakespeare's text(s). SJ (132) 1996, 26–43.
6181. ——WERSTEIN, PAUL (eds).   The tragedy of Richard II. New York: Washington Square Press, 1996. pp. lix, 290. (New Folger Library Shakespeare.)
6182. NEILL, MICHAEL (ed.).   The tragedy of Anthony [*sic*] and Cleopatra. (Bibl. 1995, 5144.) Rev. by Dieter Mehl in SJ (132) 1996, 274–7.
6183. ORGEL, STEPHEN (ed.).   The winter's tale. Oxford: Clarendon Press; New York: OUP, 1996. pp. viii, 295. (Oxford Shakespeare.)
6184. —— The winter's tale. Oxford; New York: OUP, 1996. pp. 272. (World's classics.)
6185. OSBORNE, LAURIE E.   The trick of singularity: *Twelfth Night* and the performance editions. Iowa City: Iowa UP, 1996. pp. xvii, 206. (Studies in theatre history and culture.)
6186. OTA, KAZUAKI.   The quarto of *The Second Part of Henry IV* as a revised text. SEL (English number) 1996, 1–16.
6187. PARKER, R. B. (ed.).   The tragedy of Coriolanus. (Bibl. 1995, 5148.) Rev. by Dieter Mehl in SJ (132) 1996, 277–9; by Edward Pechter in ESCan (22:3) 1996, 373–5.
6188. PETERSEN, STEPHEN.   'I do know your tongue': the Shakespeare editions of William Rolfe and H. H. Furness as American cultural signifiers. KenR (13:1/2) 1996, 3–44.
6189. PITCHER, JOHN.   Why editors should write more notes. *See* **793**.
6190. POTTER, LOIS.   Actors and editors, editors as actors. Textus (9:2) 1996, 419–35.
6191. RAMSEY, PAUL.   The literary evidence for Shakespeare as Hand D in the manuscript play *Sir Thomas More*: a re-re-reconsideration. UC (11) 1991, 131–55.
6192. ROBINSON, JOHN V.   A ring of truth: another look at a crux in *Twelfth Night*. ELN (34:2) 1996, 1–6.
6193. RUBIDGE, BRADLEY.   Tristan Tzara edits Sonnet 138: 'When loue of truth sweares that she is my made'. Text (Ann Arbor) (7) 1994, 263–71.
6194. SAMS, ERIC (ed.).   Shakespeare's *Edward III*. *See* **5703**.
6195. SERPIERI, ALESSANDRO.   Is *Hamlet Q1* a generative or a degenerate text? Textus (9:2) 1996, 461–84.
6196. SPEVACK, MARVIN.   James Orchard Halliwell: outlines of a life. Ang (114:1) 1996, 24–56.
6197. TAYLOR, NEIL; THOMPSON, ANN.   Obscenity in *Hamlet* III.ii: 'country matters'. Textus (9:2) 1996, 485–500.
6198. TREADWELL, T. O. (ed.).   A midsommer nights dreame: as it hath been sundry times publikely acted, by the right honourable, the Lord Chamberlaine his servants. London: Harvester Wheatsheaf; Englewood Cliffs, NJ: Prentice Hall, 1996. pp. 128. (Shakespearean originals.)
6199. WARREN, ROGER; WELLS, STANLEY W. (eds).   Twelfth night; or, What you will. (Bibl. 1995, 5158.) Rev. by Christa Jansohn in SJ (132) 1996, 279–82.

6200. WATT, R. J. C. The siege of Orleans and the cursing of Joan: corruptions in the text of *Henry VI Part I*. ELN (33:3) 1996, 1–6.

6201. WELLS, STANLEY. Multiple texts and the Oxford Shakespeare. Textus (9:2) 1996, 375–92.

6202. WERSTINE, PAUL. Editing after the end of editing. SStud (24) 1996, 47–54.

6203. WEST, ANTHONY JAMES. In search of missing copies of the Shakespeare first folio. *See* **551**.

6204. —— The number and distribution of Shakespeare first folios 1902 and 1995. *See* **552**.

6205. WILDERS, JOHN (ed.). Antony and Cleopatra. London; New York: Routledge, 1995. pp. xviii, 331. (Arden Shakespeare.) (Third ed.) Rev. by José Manuel González Fernández de Sevilla in RAEI (8) 1995, 268–70; by Peter Holland in TLS, 28 Apr. 1995, 3–4; by John W. Mahon and Thomas A. Pendleton in SNL (45:3) 1995, 49–53, 59–60, 63; by Howard Mills in Eng (44:180) 1995, 263–7; by John Strachan in CLB (92) 1995, 227–9; by R. S. White in NQ (43:3) 1996, 332–4; by Dieter Mehl in SJ (132) 1996, 272–3.

General Scholarship and Criticism

6206. ABRAMS, RICHARD. In defence of W.S.: reasons for attributing *A Funeral Elegy* to Shakespeare. *See* **2573**.

6207. —— W[illiam] S[hakespeare]'s *Funeral Elegy* and the turn from the theatrical. *See* **557**.

6208. ALBANESE, DENISE. New science, new world. Durham, NC; London: Duke UP, 1996. pp. xi, 244.

6209. ANDERSON, L. M. 'Every good servant does not all commands': Shakespeare's servants and the duty to disobey. UC (12) 1992, 3–15.

6210. ANDERSON, LINDA. Shakespeare's servants. Shakespeare Yearbook (2) 1991, 149–61.

6211. ANON. (ed.). Shakespeare kyouen – eibei bungaku no shiza kara. (A Shakespearean banquet: from the angle of English and American literature.) Tokyo: Eihosha, 1996. pp. xxxii, 620.

6212. ARONSON, ALEX. Shakespeare and the ocular proof. New York: Vantage Press, 1995. pp. vii, 124. Rev. by Michael Yogev in JTD (2) 1996, 201–3.

6213. ASHTON, SUSANNA. What brings home the Bacon? Shakespeare and turn-of-the-century American authorship. *See* **1224**.

6214. ASTINGTON, JOHN H. (ed.). The development of Shakespeare's theatre. (Bibl. 1995, 5171.) Rev. by Alan Somerset in MedRen (8) 1996, 228–31.

6215. BACHE, WILLIAM B.; LOGGINS, VERNON P. Shakespeare's deliberate art. Lanham, MD; London: UP of America, 1996. pp. xviii, 257.

6216. BAKER, ELLIOTT. *The Philosophy of the Plays of Shakespeare Unfolded* – and abridged. ER (2:1) 1994, 6–14.

6217. BALDO, JONATHAN. The unmasking of drama: contested representation in Shakespeare's tragedies. Detroit, MI: Wayne State UP, 1996. pp. 213.

6218. BALLENTINE, ROBERTA. The Shakespeare epitaphs. ShB (14:3) 1996, 25–6.

6219. BARKER, SIMON; HILL, VENETIA. A month in Shakespeare country: Shakespeare, theory and historicism. Literature and History (5:1) 1996, 86–91 (review-article).

6220.   BARROLL, LEEDS.   Politics, plague, and Shakespeare's theater: the Stuart years. (Bibl. 1995, 5173.) Rev. by William B. Long in ShB (12:2) 1994, 50.

6221.   BARTON, ANNE.   Essays, mainly Shakespearean. (Bibl. 1995, 5174.) Rev. by Shawn-Marie Garrett in Theater (25:2) 1994, 109–12; by Richard Jones in JDTC (10:1) 1995, 137–9; by Howard Mills in ELN (33:3) 1996, 75–6; by Ian Donaldson in TLS, 9 Feb. 1996, 27.

6222.   BASNEY, LIONEL.   Is a Christian perspective on Shakespeare productive and/or necessary? *In* (pp. 19–35) **111**.

6223.   BATE, JONATHAN.   Shakespeare and Ovid. (Bibl. 1995, 5175.) Rev. by Simon Barker and Venetia Hill in Literature and History (5:1) 1996, 86–91.

6224.   BATSON, E. BEATRICE (ed.).   Shakespeare and the Christian tradition. *See* **111**.

6225.   BATTENHOUSE, ROY.   Shakespeare's Christianity: the future for scholarship. UC (14) 1994, 4–10.

6226.   BATTENHOUSE, ROY W. (ed.).   Shakespeare's Christian dimension: an anthology of commentary. (Bibl. 1994, 4151.) Rev. by Günther Blaicher in SJ (132) 1996, 240–1.

6227.   BEINER, G.   Shakespeare's agonistic comedy: poetics, analysis, criticism. (Bibl. 1995, 5178.) Rev. by Karl-Heinz Magister in SJ (132) 1996, 248–9.

6228.   BELSEY, CATHERINE.   Postmodern Shakespeare. EIUC (4) 1996, 41–52.

6229.   BERGERON, DAVID M.; DE SOUSA, GERALDO U.   Shakespeare: a study and research guide. (Bibl. 1995, 5181.) Rev. by Frank Occhiogrosso in ShB (14:2) 1996, 46.

6230.   BERNADETE, JOSÉ A.   Metaphysics and poetry: the Quinean approach. PT (17:2) 1996, 129–56.

6231.   BERRY, HERBERT.   Shakespeare, Richard Quiney, and the Cheshire Cheese. ShB (9:1) 1991, 29–30.

6232.   BEVINGTON, DAVID.   Shakespeare and recent criticism: issues for a Christian approach to teaching. *In* (pp. 1–18) **111**.

6233.   BIRCH, ROBERT L.   The Shakespeare authorship question revisited. Romantist (9/10) 1985/86, 43–4.

6234.   BISHOP, T. G.   Shakespeare and the theatre of wonder. Cambridge; New York: CUP, 1996. pp. xii, 222. (Cambridge studies in Renaissance literature and culture, 9.)

6235.   BLAKE, N. F.   Essays on Shakespeare's language: first series. *See* **1428**.

6236.   —— Lexical links in Shakespeare. *See* **2315**.

6237.   BLIGHT, CECILIA.   A Shakespeare bibliography of periodical publications in South Africa in 1993. SSA (7) 1994, 97–9.

6238.   BLOOM, ALLAN.   Love and friendship. (Bibl. 1993, 3955.) Rev. by A. S. Byatt in BkW, 25 July 1996, 1, 14.

6239.   BLYTHE, DAVID-EVERETT.   Shakespeare in Ruskin. Ruskin Gazette (1:9) 1996, 4–8.

6240.   BOYCE, CHARLES.   Shakespeare A to Z: the essential reference to his plays, his poems, his life and times, and more. (Bibl. 1991, 4707.) Rev. by Frank Occhiogrosso in ShB (9:4) 1991, 47.

6241.   BRADSHAW, GRAHAM.   Misrepresentations: Shakespeare and the materialists. (Bibl. 1995, 5188.) Rev. by Larry S. Champion in EngS (76:5) 1995, 487–8; by Christoph Bode in SJ (132) 1996, 231–2.

6242. BRATCHELL, D. F. (ed.). Shakespearean tragedy. (Bibl. 1992, 4729.) Rev. by Thomas Sorge in ZAA (41:2) 1993, 177–8.

6243. BREITENBERG, MARK. Anxious masculinity: sexual jealousy in early modern England. *See* **5542**.

6244. BRINK, ANDRÉ. Destabilising Shakespeare. Grahamstown: Inst. for the Study of English in Africa, Rhodes Univ. for the Shakespeare Soc. of Southern Africa, 1996. pp. ii, 90.

6245. BRISTOL, MICHAEL D. Big-time Shakespeare. London; New York: Routledge, 1996. pp. xvi, 256. Rev. by John D. Sanderson in RAEI (9) 1996, 194–5.

6246. BROOKE, NICHOLAS. Performance structures as social criticism in English classic drama. *In* (pp. 21–6) **53**.

6247. BROWN, JOHN RUSSELL. Back to Bali. *In* (pp. 1–19) **119**.

6248. —— William Shakespeare: writing for performance. Basingstoke: Macmillan; New York: St Martin's Press, 1996. pp. x, 171. Rev. by Peter Hyland in SNL (46:3) 1996, 63–4.

6249. BROWNLOW, F. W. Shakespeare, Harsnett, and the devils of Denham. (Bibl. 1995, 5190.) Rev. by Robin Headlam Wells in YES (26) 1996, 273–4.

6250. BRUSTER, DOUGLAS. New light on the Old Historicism: Shakespeare and the forms of historicist criticism. Literature and History (5:1) 1996, 1–18.

6251. BUCKRIDGE, PATRICK. What did John Marston know about Shakespeare? *See* **5940**.

6252. BUHLER, STEPHEN M. 'Who calls me villain?': blank verse and the black hat. Extrapolation (36:1) 1995, 18–27.

6253. BURELBACH, FREDERICK M. Totemic animals in some Shakespeare plays. *In* (pp. 155–60) **70**.

6254. CAHN, VICTOR L. Shakespeare the playwright: a companion to the complete tragedies, histories, comedies, and romances. (Bibl. 1992, 4735.) Westport, CT; London: Praeger, 1996. pp. xix, 865. (Updated ed.: first ed. 1991.) Rev. by Ralph A. Ranald in ShB (9:3) 1991, 38.

6255. CALLAGHAN, DYMPNA. The castrator's song: female impersonation on the early modern stage. JMEMS (26:2) 1996, 321–53.

6256. CALLAGHAN, DYMPNA C.; HELMS, LORRAINE; SINGH, JYOTSNA. The weyward sisters: Shakespeare and feminist politics. (Bibl. 1995, 5193.) Rev. by John Drakakis in NQ (43:3) 1996, 338–40.

6257. CANTOR, PAUL A. Appropriating Shakespeare. In-between (3:2) 1994, 79–84 (review-article.)

6258. CARROLL, D. ALLEN. 'For there is an upstart crow'. *See* **5805**.

6259. CARROLL, WILLIAM C. Fat king, lean beggar: representations of poverty in the age of Shakespeare. *See* **5546**.

6260. CHANDLER, DAVID. A further reconsideration of Heywood's allusion to Shakespeare. ER (3:2) 1995, 15–24.

6261. CHARNES, LINDA. Notorious identity: materializing the subject in Shakespeare. (Bibl. 1995, 5199.) Rev. by J. Drakakis in NQ (43:1) 1996, 85–7.

6262. CHARNEY, MAURICE. All of Shakespeare. (Bibl. 1993, 3969.) Rev. by Robert F. Willson, Jr, in ShB (12:4) 1994, 43–4.

6263. CHOI, KYUNGHEE. Yeongeuk eui jungchihak: Shakespeare eui hugi sageuk yeongu. (Theatrical politics: a study of Shakespeare's Lancastrian tetralogy.) Unpub. doct. diss., Ewha Woman's Univ., Seoul, 1996.

6264. CLARK, ALICE.   Shakespeare as the French would have him: Voltaire and Nerval. Shakespeare Yearbook (5) 1994, 49–65.

6265. CLARK, IRA.   Writing and dueling in the English Renaissance. *See* **5625**.

6266. COHEN, DEREK.   Shakespeare's culture of violence. (Bibl. 1993, 3973.) Rev. by Laura Di Michele in Annali anglistica (36:1–3) 1993, 221–7.

6267. COLLINS, MICHAEL J.   Where wonder seems familiar: Shakespeare's comedies and the parables of the New Testament. Shakespeare Yearbook (2) 1991, 201–7.

6268. COMBS, JAMES.   Where's Nahum Tate when you need him? Cresset (60:2/3) 1996, 17–19.

6269. COOK, ALBERT.   The transmutation of heroic complexity: Plutarch and Shakespeare. CML (17:1) 1996, 31–43.

6270. COOK, ANN JENNALIE.   Making a match: courtship in Shakespeare and his society. (Bibl. 1995, 5204.) Rev. by William B. Long in ShB (12:4) 1994, 44.

6271. COSTIGAN, EDWARD.   Aspects of narrative in some plays by Shakespeare. EngS (77:4) 1996, 323–42.

6272. COX, CATHERINE I.   'Horn-pypes and funeralls': suggestions of hope in Shakespeare's tragedies. *In* (pp. 216–34) **131**.

6273. COX, JOHN D.   Shakespeare: New Criticism, New Historicism, and the Christian story. *In* (pp. 37–50) **111**.

6274. COX, MURRAY; THEILGAARD, ALICE.   Shakespeare as prompter: the amending imagination and the therapeutic process. London: Kingsley, 1994. pp. xxvi, 454. Rev. by Stephen Longstaffe in CEl (49) 1996, 120–1.

6275. CUVELIER, ELIANE.   Shakespeare, Voltaire, and French taste. Shakespeare Yearbook (5) 1994, 25–47.

6276. DAVIS, PHILIP.   Sudden Shakespeare: the shaping of Shakespeare's creative thought. London: Athlone Press; New York: St Martin's Press, 1996. pp. 259.

6277. DELABASTITA, DIRK; D'HULST, LIEVEN (eds).   European Shakespeares: translating Shakespeare in the Romantic age. *See* **3126**.

6278. DÉPRATS, JEAN-MICHEL.   Translating Shakespeare for the theatre. *See* **3127**.

6279. DESPER, C. RICHARD; VEZZOLI, GARY C.   A statistical approach to the Shakespeare authorship question. *See* **5941**.

6280. DI CESARE, MARIO A. (ed.).   Reconsidering the Renaissance: papers from the twenty-first annual conference. *See* **98**.

6281. DIONNE, CRAIG.   Shakespeare and gender: toward a theory of popular cultural mediation. CritM (8:1) 1994, 81–108.

6282. DOBSON, MICHAEL.   The making of the national poet: Shakespeare, adaptation and authorship, 1660–1769. (Bibl. 1995, 5211.) Rev. by Simon Barker and Venetia Hill in Literature and History (5:1) 1996, 86–91.

6283. DORFMAN, TONI.   The fateful crossroads: 'fork' clusters in Shakespeare's plays. *See* **1952**.

6284. DOTTERER, RICHARD (ed.).   Shakespeare: text, subtext, and context. (Bibl. 1993, 3985.) Rev. by Geraldo U. de Sousa in Shakespeare Yearbook (2) 1991, 261–3.

6285. DOWNS, GERALD E.   A reconsideration of Heywood's allusion to Shakespeare. ER (1:2) 1993, 18–35.

6286. Dubrow, Heather.   Captive victors: Shakespeare's narrative poems and sonnets. (Bibl. 1988, 2650.) Rev. by Camille Wells Slights in CanRCL (18:2/3) 1991, 359–63.

6287. Dusinberre, Juliet.   Shakespeare and the nature of women. (Bibl. 1979, 4386.) Basingstoke: Macmillan; New York: St Martin's Press, 1995. pp. xlix, 329. (Second ed.: first ed. 1975.) Rev. by Rick Waswo in EEM (5:2) 1996, 51–4.

6288. Dutta, Mary Buhl.   'Very bad poetry, captain': Shakespeare in *Star Trek*. Extrapolation (36:1) 1995, 38–45.

6289. Echeruo, Michael J. C.   Shakespeare and the boundaries of kinship. SSA (7) 1994, 1–14.

6290. Edwards, Francis.   William Shakespeare: why was his true identity concealed? *See* **5942**.

6291. Edwards, Philip.   Tragic form and the voyagers. *In* (pp. 75–86) **124**.

6292. Elsom, John (ed.).   Is Shakespeare still our contemporary? (Bibl. 1994, 4187.) Rev. by Patricia L. Carlin in ShB (9:2) 1991, 36–7; by Richard Paul Knowles in CanTR (67) 1991, 110–11.

6293. Engle, Lars.   Shakespearean pragmatism: market of his time. (Bibl. 1995, 5215.) Rev. by Lyell Asher in CLIO (25:2) 1996, 223–8.

6294. Epstein, Norrie.   The friendly Shakespeare: a thoroughly painless guide to the best of the Bard. New York: Viking, 1993. pp. xviii, 550. Rev. by S. Schoenbaum in BkW, 24 Jan. 1993, 7.

6295. Erskine-Hill, Howard.   Poetry and the realm of politics: Shakespeare to Dryden. *See* **5729**.

6296. Farley-Hills, David.   Shakespeare and the rival playwrights 1600–1606. (Bibl. 1994, 4190.) Rev. by Roslyn Lander Knutson in ShB (10:2) 1992, 38–9; by Grace Tiffany in MedRen (7) 1995, 389–93.

6297. Fineman, Joel.   The subjectivity effect in Western literary tradition: essays toward the release of Shakespeare's will. (Bibl. 1993, 4002.) Rev. by James R. Andreas in Comparatist (16) 1992, 142–4.

6298. Fleissner, Robert F.   The likely misascription of *Cardenio* (and thereby *Double Falsehood*) in part to Shakespeare. NM (97:2) 1996, 217–30.

6299. —— The 'upstart crow' reclawed: was it Kemp, Wilson, Alleyn, or Shakespeare? *See* **5832**.

6300. Foakes, R. A. (ed.).   Coleridge's criticism of Shakespeare: a selection. (Bibl. 1990, 3819.) Rev. by Maurice Charney in ShB (11:4) 1993, 44–5.

6301. Foster, Donald W.   *A Funeral Elegy*: W(illiam) S(hakespeare)'s 'best-speaking witnesses'. *See* **2619**.

6302. Frazer, Winifred.   Two studies of Greene's *Groatsworth*. *See* **5807**.

6303. Frazer, Winifred L.   William Kemp as 'upstart crow'. *See* **5834**.

6304. Freedman, Barbara.   Staging the gaze: postmodernism, psychoanalysis, and Shakespearean comedy. (Bibl. 1995, 5217.) Rev. by Margaret Loftus Ranald in ShB (9:3) 1991, 41–2.

6305. Frey, Charles H.   The bias of nature. UC (13) 1993, 2–15.

6306. Gager, Valerie L.   Shakespeare and Dickens: the dynamics of influence. Cambridge; New York: CUP, 1996. pp. xx, 419.

6307. Garner, Shirley Nelson; Sprengnether, Madelon (eds). Shakespearean tragedy and gender. Bloomington: Indiana UP, 1996. pp. viii, 326. Rev. by Maurice Charney in ShB (14:4) 1996, 41–2.

6308. GAY, PENNY. As she likes it: Shakespeare's unruly women. (Bibl. 1995, 5218.) Rev. by Michael Abbot in JDTC (9:2) 1995, 169–70.

6309. GEYER-RYAN, HELGA. Shakespeare after Derrida and Marx: death in Venice and the utopia of the open society. arcadia (31:1/2) 1996, 155–64.

6310. GIBBONS, BRIAN. Shakespeare and multiplicity. (Bibl. 1995, 5219.) Rev. by Klaus Peter Steiger in SJ (132) 1996, 244–5.

6311. —— The wrong end of the telescope. *In* (pp. 141–59) **124**.

6312. GILLIES, JOHN. Shakespeare and the geography of difference. (Bibl. 1995, 5220.) Rev. by Simon Barker and Venetia Hill in Literature and History (5:1) 1996, 86–91.

6313. GOLDBERG, JONATHAN (ed.). Queering the Renaissance. *See* **93**.

6314. GONZÁLEZ, JOSÉ MANUEL. El teatro de Shakespeare hoy: una interpretación radical actualizada. Barcelona: Montesinos, 1993. pp. 118. Rev. by Angel Luis Pujante in Atlantis (17:1/2) 1995, 388–9.

6315. GRADY, HUGH. The modernist Shakespeare: critical texts in a material world. (Bibl. 1995, 5222.) Rev. by Arthur F. Kinney in ELN (33:3) 1996, 77–82.

6316. —— Shakespeare's universal wolf: postmodernist studies in early modern reification. Oxford: Clarendon Press; New York: OUP, 1996. pp. viii, 241.

6317. GRAHAM, ARTHUR. It may be music, but is it Shakespeare? SNL (44:3) 1994, 41, 44, 52.

6318. GRAY, PIERS. On linearity. *See* **2632**.

6319. GREEN, SUSAN. A cultural reading of Charlotte Lennox's *Shakespear Illustrated*. *In* (pp. 228–57) **20**.

6320. GREENBLATT, STEPHEN. Shakespearean negotiations: the circulation of social energy in Renaissance England. (Bibl. 1993, 4016.) Rev. by Pamela McCallum in CanRCL (18:2/3) 1991, 353–8.

6321. GURNEY, LAWRENCE S. Jonson and Shakespeare. SNL (46:3) 1996, 71–2.

6322. GURR, ANDREW. William Shakespeare: the extraordinary life of the most successful writer of all time. London: HarperCollins, 1995. pp. 192.

6323. GUTIERREZ, NANCY A. Double standard in the flesh: gender, fasting, and power in English Renaissance drama. *In* (pp. 79–93) **24**.

6324. HABIB, IMTIAZ. Shakespeare's pluralistic concepts of character: a study in dramatic anamorphism. (Bibl. 1995, 5228.) Rev. by G. B. Shand in ShB (14:3) 1996, 46–7.

6325. HAFFENDEN, JOHN (ed.). The strengths of Shakespeare's shrew: essays, memoirs, and reviews. By William Empson. *See* **1409**.

6326. HAGER, ALAN. Shakespeare's political animal: schema and schemata in the canon. (Bibl. 1993, 4021.) Rev. by Seymour Rudin in ShB (9:3) 1991, 35.

6327. HALLETT, CHARLES A.; HALLETT, ELAINE S. Analyzing Shakespeare's action: scene *versus* sequence. (Cf. bibl. 1995, 5230, where first scholar's middle initial incorrect.) Rev. by Robert Hapgood in ShB (9:4) 1991, 45.

6328. HAMMERSCHMIDT-HUMMEL, HILDEGARD. Ist die Darmstädter Shakespeare-Totenmaske echt? SJ (132) 1996, 58–74.

6329. HAMPTON, TIMOTHY. Mapping the map. SStud (24) 1996, 93–102 (review-article).

6330. HARNER, JAMES L. The *World Shakespeare Bibliography* on CD-ROM 1900–present: its inception and future. Archiv (233:1) 1996, 94–8.

6331. —— (ed.). World Shakespeare bibliography 1995. SQ (47:5) 1996, 498–836.

6332. —— The World Shakespeare Bibliography on CD-ROM: 1990–1993. Cambridge; New York: CUP in assn with Folger Shakespeare Library, 1993. (1 CD-ROM.) Rev. by Hardy Cook in SNL (46:2) 1996, 33–4.

6333. HART, JONATHAN. Theater and world: the problematics of Shakespeare's history. (Bibl. 1994, 4216.) Rev. by Elizabeth M. Richmond-Garza in CanRCL (21:4) 1994, 739–42.

6334. HARTMAN, GEOFFREY H. Shakespeare and the ethical question: Leo Löwenthal *in memoriam*. ELH (63:1) 1996, 1–23.

6335. HARVEY, M. L. Iambic pentameter from Shakespeare to Browning: a study in generative metrics. *See* **4375**.

6336. HAWKES, TERENCE. Meaning by Shakespeare. (Bibl. 1994, 4218.) Rev. by Margaret Loftus Ranald in ShB (14:1) 1996, 46–7.

6337. —— (ed.). Alternative Shakespeares: vol. 2. London; New York: Routledge, 1996. pp. xii, 294. (New accents.)

6338. HILLMAN, DAVID. Puttenham, Shakespeare, and the abuse of rhetoric. *See* **1935**.

6339. HISCOCK, ANDREW. Authority and desire: crises of inter-pretation in Shakespeare and Racine. New York; Frankfurt; Bern; Paris: Lang, 1996. pp. 318. (Studies in Shakespeare, 4.) (Cf. bibl. 1992, 4792.)

6340. HOENIGER, F. DAVID. Medicine and Shakespeare in the English Renaissance. (Bibl. 1995, 5241.) Rev. by Margaret Loftus Ranald in ShB (12:1) 1994, 48–9.

6341. HOGG, JAMES (ed.). Jacobean drama as social criticism. *See* **53**.

6342. HOLDERNESS, GRAHAM. Shakespeare recycled: the making of historical drama. (Bibl. 1995, 5243.) Rev. by Paul N. Siegel in ShB (11:3) 1993, 43–4.

6343. —— LOUGHREY, BRYAN. Shakespeare misconstrued: the true chronicle historie of *Shakespearean Originals*. Textus (9:2) 1996, 393–418.

6344. —— —— MURPHY, ANDREW (eds). Shakespeare: the Roman plays. London; New York: Longman, 1996. pp. vii, 191. (Longman critical readers.)

6345. HOLLAND, NORMAN N.; HOMAN, SIDNEY; PARIS, BERNARD J. (eds). Shakespeare's personality. (Bibl. 1993, 4039.) Rev. by Roger Stritmatter in ER (1:2) 1993, 65–74.

6346. HOLLAND, PETER. 'Travelling hopefully': the dramatic form of journeys in English Renaissance drama. *In* (pp. 160–78) **124**.

6347. HOPE, JONATHAN; WRIGHT, LAURA. Female education in Shakespeare's Stratford and Stratfordian contacts in Shakespeare's London. NQ (43:2) 1996, 149–50.

6348. HOPE, WARREN. The singing swallow: Sir John Davies and Shakespeare. *See* **5816**.

6349. HOSTER, JAY. Tiger's heart: what really happened in the *Groats-worth of Wit* controversy of 1592. *See* **5655**.

6350. HOULAHAN, MARK. Cosmic Hamlets? Contesting Shakespeare in Federation space. Extrapolation (36:1) 1995, 28–37.

6351. HUBERT, JUDD D. Metatheater: the example of Shakespeare. (Bibl. 1993, 4048.) Rev. by Thomas Akstens in JDTC (9:1) 1994, 247–8.

6352. HUGHES, TED. Shakespeare and the goddess of complete being. (Bibl. 1995, 5247.) Rev. by William Kerrigan in Raritan (13:3) 1994, 147–56.

6353. ——— Le Brun, Christopher.   Shakespeare's Ovid. London: Enitharmon Press, 1995. pp. viii, 30, (plates) 2. (Limited ed. of 200 copies.) Rev. by Sarah Annes Brown in CamQ (25:2) 1996, 208–12.

6354. Hyland, Peter.   An introduction to Shakespeare: the dramatist in his context. Basingstoke: Macmillan; New York: St Martin's Press, 1996. pp. vii, 215.

6355. Iser, Wolfgang.   Shakespeares Historien: Genesis und Geltung. (Bibl. 1993, 4054.) Rev. by Wolfgang Riehle in GRM (42:4) 1992, 468–70.

6356. ——— Staging politics: the lasting impact of Shakespeare's histories. Trans. by David Henry Wilson. (Bibl. 1995, 5250.) Rev. by Roger Sales in Literature and History (5:1) 1996, 98–9.

6357. Jardine, Lisa.   Reading Shakespeare historically. London; New York: Routledge, 1996. pp. 207. Rev. by Michael Dobson in LRB (18:21) 1996, 24–5; by Lois Potter in TLS, 14 June 1996, 6.

6358. Jensen, Ejner J.   Shakespeare and the ends of comedy. (Bibl. 1993, 4057.) Rev. by Margaret Loftus Ranald in ShB (12:3) 1994, 47.

6359. Jobson, Susan.   Shakespeare – the cultural weapon. Scrutiny2 (1:1/2) 1996, 112–18.

6360. Johnson, David.   Shakespeare and South Africa. Oxford: Clarendon Press; New York: OUP, 1996. pp. 276.

6361. Johnson, Lemuel A.   Shakespearean imports: whatever happened to Caliban's mother? Or, The problem *with Othello's. RAL (27:1) 1996, 19–63.

6362. Jones, John.   Shakespeare at work. (Bibl. 1995, 5255.) Rev. by Frank Kermode in LRB (18:5) 1996, 6–7; by John Jowett in TLS, 23 Aug. 1996, 13–14.

6363. Kamps, Ivo (ed.).   Shakespeare Left and Right. (Bibl. 1995, 5257.) Rev. by Margaret Loftus Ranald in ShB (12:4) 1994, 45–7.

6364. Kastan, David Scott.   Shakespeare after theory. Textus (9:2) 1996, 357–74.

6365. Kernan, Alvin.   Shakespeare, the king's playwright: theater in the Stuart Court, 1603–1613. (Bibl. 1995, 5264.) Rev. by Jeanie Grant Moore in RMRLL (50:2) 1996, 194–7.

6366. Keyishian, Harry.   The shapes of revenge: victimization, vengeance, and vindictiveness in Shakespeare. (Bibl. 1995, 5266.) Rev. by Laurel L. Hendrix in RMRLL (50:1) 1996, 80–2.

6367. Kiernan, Pauline.   Shakespeare's theory of drama. Cambridge; New York: CUP, 1996. pp. xii, 218. (Cf. bibl. 1992, 4817.)

6368. ——— Bruce, Susan; Cartmell, Deborah.   Shakespeare: criticism. YWES (75) 1994, 231–57.

6369. Kiernan, Victor.   Eight tragedies of Shakespeare: a Marxist study. London; New York: Verso, 1996. pp. 296.

6370. Kiernan, Victor Gordon.   Shakespeare: poet and citizen. (Bibl. 1995, 5267.) Rev. by A. G. R. Smith in Literature and History (5:1) 1996, 97–8.

6371. Kinjo, Seiki.   Shakespeare to hana. (Shakespeare and flowers.) Osaka: Toho Shuppan, 1996. pp. 218.

6372. Kirsch, Arthur.   The passions of Shakespeare's tragic heroes. (Bibl. 1995, 5268.) Rev. by Robert F. Willson, Jr, in ShB (10:1) 1992, 47.

6373. KISHI, TETSUO; PRINGLE, ROGER; WELLS, STANLEY (eds).
Shakespeare and cultural traditions: the selected proceedings of the
International Shakespeare Association World Congress, Tokyo, 1991.
(Bibl. 1995, 5269.) Rev. by Franco Marenco in SJ (132) 1996, 255–8.

6374. KLEIN, HOLGAR [sic]; DAVIDHAZI, PETER; SOKOL, B. J. (eds).
Shakespeare and Hungary. Special theme section: the law and
Shakespeare. Lewiston, NY; Lampeter: Mellen Press, 1996. pp. 452.

6375. KLEIN, HOLGER.   Shakespeare als Buch. In (pp. 85–110) **125**.

6376. KNOPP, DIETHARD.   Bacon and Shakespeare: a comparison of
passages about favourite Renaissance themes. Neohelicon (23:1) 1996,
201–39.

6377. KÖHLER, STEFANIE.   'Shakespeare's mind as the type of the
androgynous': Tendenzen der feministischen Shakespeare-Forschung seit
Mitte der siebziger Jahre. ZAA (43:3) 1995, 201–17.

6378. KOLIN, PHILIP C.   Shakespeare and feminist criticism: an annotated bibliography and commentary. (Bibl. 1995, 5272.) Rev. by Felicia
Hardison Londré in ShB (10:4) 1992, 45–6; by Rhonda Justice-Malloy
in JDTC (7:2) 1993, 84–5; by Annegret Maack in ZAA (41:1) 1993, 85.

6379. KON'NAI, TOKUKO.   Shakespeare no shoki kigeki – sono waku
kouzou to imi. (Shakespeare's early comedies: their framework and
significance.) Tokyo: Kindai Bungeisha, 1996. pp. 202.

6380. KORNSTEIN, DANIEL J.   Kill all the lawyers? Shakespeare's legal
appeal. (Bibl. 1994, 4254.) Rev. by Elfi Bettinger in SJ (132) 1996, 238–9;
by Anthony Julius in TLS, 29 Nov. 1996, 8; by Bruce L. Rockwood in
YJLH (8:2) 1996, 533–58.

6381. KOTT, JAN.   The Bottom translation: Marlowe and
Shakespeare and the carnival tradition. Trans. by Daniela
Miedzyrzecka and Lillian Vallee. See **5890**.

6382. KUJAWINSKA-COURTNEY, KRYSTYNA.   Shakespeare's women
and Polish (male) critics. EEM (4:2) 1995, 53–6.

6383. KULLMANN, THOMAS.   Abschied, Reise und Wiedersehen bei
Shakespeare: zur Gestaltung und Funktion epischer und romanhafter
Motive im Drama. (Bibl. 1993, 4071.) Rev. by Thomas Sorge in
ZAA (41:1) 1993, 83.

6384. KURTZ, MARTHA A.   Rethinking gender and genre in the
history play. See **5666**.

6385. LAY, DARREN EMERSON.   The Taylor of St Paul's: who painted
the Chandos portrait? TLS, 24 May 1996, 17.

6386. LECERCLE, ANN.   Reflections on the feminist approach to
Shakespeare and Lacanian psychoanalysis. Shakespeare Yearbook (5)
1994, 181–90.

6387. LEE, HYANG MI.   Shakespeare malgigeuk e natanan ingan gwa
wooju waeui gwankye yangsang. (Aspects of the relationship between
humankind and the universe in Shakespeare's last plays.) Unpub. doct.
diss., Chungnam National Univ., Korea, 1994.

6388. LEE, HYEON SEOK.   Jayeon eseo jakga ro: 17–18c youngkuk eui
Shakespeare suyong yeongu. (From nature to author: a study of the
appropriation of Shakespeare in England in the seventeenth and
eighteenth centuries.) Unpub. doct. diss., Seoul National Univ., 1996.

6389. LEE, YOUNG CHO.   Shakespeare heuigeuk euo yeosung inmul
yeongu. (A study of female character in Shakespeare's comedies.)
ShR (29) 1996, 155–87.

6390. Levin, Richard.   The new and the old historicizing of Shakespeare. YREAL (11) 1995, 425–48.

6391. Liebler, Naomi Conn.   Shakespeare's festive tragedy: the ritual foundations of genre. (Bibl. 1995, 5282.) Rev. by Jeffrey Kahan in EMLS (2:3) 1996, 12.1–9.

6392. Lombardo, Agostino.   Shakespeare e la forma della tragedia. Textus (1:1) 1988, 27–49.

6393. Long, Charles.   Shakespeare's Merlin. TPB (28) 1991, 14–21.

6394. Lukacher, Ned.   Daemonic figures: Shakespeare and the question of conscience. (Bibl. 1994, 4267.) Rev. by Lyell Asher in CLIO (25) 1996, 223–8; by Chris Stroffolino in SNL (46:3) 1996, 63–4.

6395. McCarthy, Gerry.   'Codes from a mixed-up machine': the disintegrating actor in Beckett, Shepard, and, surprisingly, Shakespeare. *In* (pp. 171–87) **119**.

6396. McDonald, Russ.   The Bedford companion to Shakespeare: an introduction with documents. Boston: Bedford Books of St Martin's Press; Basingstoke: Macmillan, 1996. pp. xix, 373.

6397. Mack, Maynard.   Everybody's Shakespeare: reflections chiefly on the tragedies. (Bibl. 1995, 5288.) Rev. by Tom Treadwell in CritS (8:3) 1996, 343–5.

6398. McMullan, Gordon; Hope, Jonathan (eds).   The politics of tragicomedy: Shakespeare and after. (Bibl. 1995, 5290.) Rev. by Navina Hooker in Eng (41:171) 1992, 271–5; by Verna A. Foster in JDTC (8:1) 1993, 193–5; by Barry Nass in ShB (11:1) 1993, 42–3; by Lawrence Normand in NQ (43:2) 1996, 218; by Jill L. Levenson in MedRen (8) 1996, 264–7.

6399. Maguin, Jean-Marie.   Shakespeare studies in France since 1960. Shakespeare Yearbook (5) 1994, 359–73.

6400. Mahler, Andreas.   A lost world, no new-found land – disorientation and immobility as social criticism in early seventeenth-century tragedy. *In* (pp. 27–43) **53**.

6401. Mahon, John W.   Babe in doublet and hose: Shakespeare's pigs. SNL (46:1) 1996, 15, 23.

6402. Mallin, Eric S.   Inscribing the time: Shakespeare and the end of Elizabethan England. (Bibl. 1995, 5291.) Rev. by Peter C. Herman in Albion (28:4) 1996, 692–4; by Lisa Hopkins in NQ (43:3) 1996, 334–5; by Tony Dawson in EMLS (2:1) 1996, 7.1–9; by Edmund M. Taft in SNL (46:4) 1996, 81, 90.

6403. Mangan, Michael.   A preface to Shakespeare's comedies 1594–1603. London; New York: Longman, 1996. pp. viii, 300. (Preface books.)

6404. Maquerlot, Jean-Pierre; Willems, Michèle.   Introduction. *In* (pp. 1–13) **124**.

6405. —— —— (eds).   Travel and drama in Shakespeare's time. *See* **124**.

6406. Marrapodi, Michele, *et al.* (eds).   Shakespeare's Italy: functions of Italian locations in Renaissance drama. (Bibl. 1994, 4278.) Rev. by Livia Fascia in Annali anglistica (36:1–3) 1993, 234–8; by Stella Fletcher in Literature and History (5:1) 1996, 100.

6407. Martin, Christopher.   Policy in love: lyric and public in Ovid, Petrarch, and Shakespeare. (Bibl. 1994, 4281.) Rev. by Katherine Duncan-Jones in EC (46:2) 1996, 153–8.

6408. MATUS, IRVIN LEIGH. Shakespeare, in fact. (Bibl. 1994, 4282.) Rev. by Thomas O'Brien in CC (45:4) 1995/96, 558–60.

6409. MAZRUI, ALAMIN M. Shakespeare in Africa: between English and Swahili literature. RAL (27:1) 1996, 64–79.

6410. MAZZON, GABRIELLA. The language of emotions in Shakespeare's poems: an aspect of archaism and innovation in Elizabethan English word-formation. *See* **1633**.

6411. MELCHIORI, GIORGIO. Shakespeare's Garter plays: *Edward III* to *Merry Wives of Windsor*. (Bibl. 1995, 5303.) Rev. by Frances K. Barasch in ShB (14:1) 1996, 47; by Michael G. Brennan in NQ (43:4) 1996, 476; by Simon Barker and Venetia Hill in Literature and History (5:1) 1996, 86–91.

6412. MICHELL, JOHN. Who wrote Shakespeare? London; New York: Thames & Hudson, 1996. pp. 272.

6413. MILLER, DAVID LEE; O'DAIR, SHARON; WEBER, HAROLD. Introduction: criticism and cultural production. *In* (pp. 1–12) **90**.

6414. ————— (eds). The production of English Renaissance culture. *See* **90**.

6415. MILLS, HOWARD. Working with Shakespeare. (Bibl. 1995, 5306.) Rev. by Martha Schmoyer LoMonaco in ShB (14:3) 1996, 47.

6416. MIOLA, ROBERT S. Shakespeare and Classical comedy: the influence of Plautus and Terence. (Bibl. 1995, 5309.) Rev. by Anthony Brian Taylor in NQ (43:3) 1996, 331–2.

6417. MIRSKY, MARK JAY. The absent Shakespeare. (Bibl. 1994, 4289.) Rev. by Ronni S. Abramowitz in PLL (32:2) 1996, 206–12.

6418. MOORE, PETER. Kill, kill, kill. *See* **1969**.

6419. MUIR, KENNETH. Lope de Vega and Shakespeare. *In* (pp. 239–54) **124**.

6420. MÜLLER, WOLFGANG G. Drei Formen des Wortspiels bei Shakespeare: Paronomasie, Paronymie, Polyptoton. *In* (pp. 205–24) **11**.

6421. MURRAY, PETER B. Shakespeare's imagined persons: the psychology of role-playing and acting. Basingstoke: Macmillan, 1996. pp. viii, 256.

6422. NEILL, MICHAEL. Bastardy, counterfeiting, and misogyny in *The Revenger's Tragedy*. SELit (36:2) 1996, 397–416.

6423. OKAMURA, TOSHIAKI. Shakespeare no shingo, shingogi no kenkyu. (A study of Shakespeare's neologisms.) *See* **1905**.

6424. ORKIN, MARTIN. Possessing the book and peopling the text. Essays in Theatre (15:1) 1996, 45–57.

6425. ORNSTEIN, ROBERT. Shakespeare's art of characterization: an unambiguous perspective. *In* (pp. 248–61) **116**.

6426. OWENS, W. R. Shakespeare: theatre poet. *In* (pp. 21–33) **110**.

6427. ——— GOODMAN, LIZBETH (eds). Shakespeare, Aphra Behn and the canon. *See* **110**.

6428. PAFFRATH, BERNHARD. 'Die to live'. Das Motiv der Auferstehung in Shakespeares Dramen. (Bibl. 1993, 4111.) Rev. by Günther Blaicher in SJ (132) 1996, 241–2.

6429. PARIS, BERNARD J. Character as a subversive force in Shakespeare: the history and Roman plays. (Bibl. 1995, 5321.) Rev. by Margaret Loftus Ranald in ShB (11:4) 1993, 43–4.

6430. PARKER, PATRICIA. Shakespeare from the margins: language, culture, context. Chicago; London: Chicago UP, 1996. pp. x, 392. Rev. by Michael Dobson in LRB (18:21) 1996, 24–5.

6431. PARRINDER, PATRICK. Shakespeare and (non) Standard English. *See* **2690**.

6432. PENDERGAST, JOHN S. A nation of Hamlets: Shakespeare and cultural politics. Extrapolation (36:1) 1995, 10–17.

6433. PHILLIPS, GRAHAM; KEATMAN, MARTIN. The Shakespeare conspiracy. (Bibl. 1995, 5327.) Rev. by Patrick Buckridge in ER (2:2) 1994, 64–70.

6434. PINCISS, GERALD M.; LOCKYER, ROGER (eds). Shakespeare's world: background readings in the English Renaissance. (Bibl. 1991, 4821.) Rev. by Frank Occhiogrosso in ShB (9:1) 1991, 38–9.

6435. PORTERFIELD, SALLY F. Jung's advice to the players: a Jungian reading of Shakespeare's problem plays. (Bibl. 1994, 4310.) Rev. by Richard L. Homan in NETJ (6) 1995, 120–2.

6436. POTTER, LOIS. Pirates and 'turning Turk' in Renaissance drama. *In* (pp. 124–40) **124**.

6437. PRICE, DIANA. Shakespeare's aristocratic sense of culture. *See* **5946**.

6438. —— What's in a name? Shakespeare, Shake-scene, and the Clayton loan. *See* **5841**.

6439. PROCHÁZKA, MARTIN. Players, puppets, and the ghost: mimesis and simulacrum in Shakespeare, Kleist, and commercial culture. Litteraria Pragensia (6:12) 1996, 26–38.

6440. PUGLIATTI, PAOLA. Shakespeare storico. Rome: Bulzoni, 1993. pp. 79. (Piccola biblioteca shakespeariana, 5.) Rev. by Rossella Ciocca in Annali anglistica (36:1–3) 1993, 238–40.

6441. —— Shakespeare the historian. Basingstoke: Macmillan; New York: St Martin's Press, 1996. pp. xi, 265. Rev. by Lisa Hopkins in NQ (43:4) 1996, 475.

6442. QUENNELL, PETER; JOHNSON, HAMISH. Who's who in Shakespeare. (Bibl. 1995, 5329.) Rev. by Paul Bertram in ShB (14:2) 1996, 45–6.

6443. RACKIN, PHYLLIS. Anti-historians: women's roles in Shakespeare's histories. *In* (pp. 207–22) **84**.

6444. —— Historical difference/sexual difference. *In* (pp. 37–63) **89**.

6445. —— Stages of history: Shakespeare's English chronicles. (Bibl. 1995, 5332.) Rev. by Naomi Conn Liebler in ShB (10:4) 1992, 44–5.

6446. RATCLIFFE, STEPHEN. 'Shakespeare' and 'I'. Exemplaria (8:1) 1996, 259–68.

6447. REINHEIMER, DAVID. Ontological and ethical allusion: Shakespeare in *The Next Generation*. Extrapolation (36:1) 1995, 46–54.

6448. RELIHAN, CONSTANCE C. Community, narrativity, and empowerment in Julia Margaret Cameron's photographic reading of Shakespeare. UC (12) 1992, 41–59.

6449. RICHARDS, BERNARD. Blank verse. *See* **4421**.

6450. RICHMAN, DAVID. Laughter, pain, and wonder: Shakespeare's comedies and the audience in the theater. (Bibl. 1993, 4123.) Rev. by Sam Abel in NETJ (2) 1991, 120–2.

6451. RIEHLE, WOLFGANG. Shakespeare, Plautus and the Humanist tradition. (Bibl. 1995, 5334.) Rev. by Frances K. Barasch in ShB (10:2) 1992, 42–4; by E. A. J. Honigmann in GRM (43:1) 1993, 122–4.

6452. ROBERTS, JEANNE ADDISON. The Shakespearean wild: geography, genus, and gender. (Bibl. 1995, 5335.) Rev. by Thomas Akstens in JDTC (10:2) 1996, 139–41.

6453. —— The universal Shakespeare. UC (16) 1996, 4–12.

6454. ROCKWOOD, BRUCE L.   The good, the bad, and the ironic: two views on law and literature. *See* **3975**.

6455. RYAN, KIERNAN.   Shakespeare. (Bibl. 1995, 5340.) Rev. by Robert Kole in ShB (9:2) 1991, 37; by Nicholas F. Radel in Shakespeare Yearbook (2) 1991, 263–6.

6456. SALTZ, DAVID Z.   Texts in action/action in texts: a case study in critical method. JDTC (6:1) 1991, 29–44.

6457. SAMS, ERIC.   The real Shakespeare: retrieving the early years, 1564–1594. (Bibl. 1995, 5341.) Rev. by Hugh M. Richmond in Albion (28:1) 1996, 95–6; by Bryan S. Gooch in EMLS (2.2) 1996, 13.1–5; by Maurice Hunt in SNL (46:4) 1996, 89–90.

6458. —— The Shakespeare arms: a quatercentenary contribution. TLS, 18 Oct. 1996, 16.

6459. SAMUELS, PEGGY.   Fire not light: Milton's simulacrum of tragicomedy. MQ (30:1) 1996, 1–15.

6460. SCHMIDGALL, GARY.   Shakespeare and the poet's life. (Bibl. 1992, 4895.) Rev. by Harry Keyishian in ShB (9:2) 1991, 39–40.

6461. SCHWALLER, HUGO.   'This sceptred sway': sovereignty in Shakespeare's comedies. (Bibl. 1991, 4834.) Rev. by Thomas Sorge in ZAA (41:1) 1993, 83–4.

6462. SCRAGG, LEAH.   Shakespeare's alternative tales. London; New York: Longman, 1996. pp. 160. (Longman medieval and Renaissance library.)

6463. SHAFFER, PETER.   Brooding in the snow. SJ (132) 1996, 11–25.

6464. SHAHEEN, NASEEB.   Biblical references in Shakespeare's comedies. (Bibl. 1995, 5351.) Rev. by Roger Stritmatter in ER (3:2) 1995, 60–8.

6465. SHAPIRO, JAMES.   Shakespeare and the Jews. (Bibl. 1993, 4136.) Rev. by Douglas Bruster in Albion (28:4) 1996, 691–2; by Bryan Cheyette in TLS, 11 Oct. 1996, 29; by Jacob Korg in CLIO (25:4) 1996, 464–7; by Cheryl Goldstein in Comitatus (27) 1996, 104–8.

6466. SHATRY, ALWI M.   Translations reinterpreted. RAL (27:3) 1996, 73–7.

6467. SHERBO, ARTHUR.   Richard Farmer, Master of Emmanuel College, Cambridge: a forgotten Shakespearean. (Bibl. 1994, 4334.) Rev. by Bernice W. Kliman in ShB (12:3) 1994, 46.

6468. —— Samuel Johnson's critical opinions: a reexamination. Newark: Delaware UP; London; Toronto: Assoc. UPs, 1995. pp. 214.

6469. SHEWMAKER, EUGENE F.   Shakespeare's language: a glossary of unfamiliar words in Shakespeare's plays and poems. *See* **2112**.

6470. SHOAF, R. A.   'For there is figures in all things': juxtology in Shakespeare, Spenser, and Milton. *In* (pp. 266–85) **131**.

6471. SINGH, JYOTSNA.   The influence of feminist criticism/theory on Shakespeare studies 1976–1986. *In* (pp. 381–93) **98**.

6472. SINGH, JYOTSNA G.   Afterword: Shakespeare and the politics of history. Literature and History (5:1) 1996, 78–85.

6473. SLIGHTS, CAMILLE WELLS.   Shakespeare's comic commonwealths. (Bibl. 1995, 5354.) Rev. by Karl-Heinz Magister in SJ (132) 1996, 246–8; by T. G. A. Nelson in Parergon (14:1) 1996, 309–10.

6474. SLIGHTS, WILLIAM W. E.   'Authentic in your place and person': Shakespeare's persons and the problem of reidentification. UC (12) 1992, 16–28.

6475. SMIDT, KRISTIAN. Spirits, ghosts and gods in Shakespeare. EngS (77:5) 1996, 422–38.

6476. —— Unconformities in Shakespeare's later comedies. (Bibl. 1995, 5355.) Rev. by J. M. Blom in EngS (77:1) 1996, 111–12.

6477. SMITH, PETER J. Social Shakespeare: aspects of Renaissance dramaturgy and contemporary society. (Bibl. 1995, 5357.) Rev. by Terence Hawkes in CEl (50) 1996, 120–2.

6478. SORELIUS, GUNNAR. Shakespeare's early comedies: myth, metamorphosis, mannerism. (Bibl. 1993, 4141.) Rev. by Karl-Heinz Magister in SJ (132) 1996, 248.

6479. STENBERG, DAVY. The circle of life and the chain of being: Shakespearean motifs in *The Lion King*. ShB (14:2) 1996, 36–7.

6480. STERLING, ERIC. The movement towards subversion: the English history play from Skelton to Shakespeare. *See* **5710**.

6481. STEVENS, JOHN PAUL. The Shakespeare canon of statutory construction. *See* **5947**.

6482. STOCKTON, SHARON. Aesthetics, politics, and the staging of the world: Wyndham Lewis and the Renaissance. TCL (42:4) 1996, 494–515.

6483. STUDING, RICHARD. Shakespeare in American painting: a catalogue from the late eighteenth century to the present. (Bibl. 1995, 5363.) Rev. by Frances K. Barasch in ShB (12:3) 1994, 44–5.

6484. SUERBAUM, ULRICH. Shakespeares Dramen. Tübingen: Francke, 1996. pp. 340. (UTB, 1907.) Rev. by Iris Bünsch in LWU (29:3) 1996, 235–6.

6485. SUHAMY, HENRI. Shakespeare and the French. Shakespeare Yearbook (5) 1994, 5–23.

6486. TARVIN, WILLIAM L. A 'feeling of reconciliation' and the tragic calm. Comparatist (19) 1995, 46–59.

6487. TASSARA, CARLA. Un drammaturgo al bivio: il *Don Carlos* di Thomas Otway fra Shakespeare e Fletcher. QLLSM (8) 1996, 43–58.

6488. TAVE, STUART M. Lovers, clowns, and fairies: an essay on comedies. (Bibl. 1993, 4145.) Rev. by Robert D. Hume in CL (48:3) 1996, 296–8.

6489. TAYLOR, GARY. Reinventing Shakespeare: a cultural history from the Restoration to the present. (Bibl. 1994, 4353.) Rev. by John Timpane in ShB (12:4) 1994, 42–3.

6490. —— JOWETT, JOHN. Shakespeare reshaped, 1606–1623. (Bibl. 1995, 5365.) Rev. by Leah S. Marcus in Cithara (34:1) 1994, 47–9; by Larry S. Champion in EngS (76:1) 1995, 102–3; by Jay L. Halio in Text (Ann Arbor) (9) 1996, 329–41; by Susanne Scholz in SJ (132) 1996, 268.

6491. THOMAS, VIVIAN. Shakespeare's Roman worlds. (Bibl. 1991, 4856.) Rev. by Harry Keyishian in ShB (9:1) 1991, 38.

6492. THOMSON, PETER. Shakespeare's professional career. (Bibl. 1995, 5367.) Rev. by Harry Keyishian in ShB (12:2) 1994, 49–50.

6493. TOLIVER, HAROLD E. Transported styles in Shakespeare and Milton. (Bibl. 1990, 3945.) Rev. by Stephen X. Mead in Shakespeare Yearbook (2) 1991, 274–6.

6494. TOMPKINS, JOANNE. Re-citing Shakespeare in post-colonial drama. Essays in Theatre (15:1) 1996, 15–22.

6495. TRAUB, VALERIE. Desire and anxiety: circulations of sexuality in Shakespearean drama. (Bibl. 1995, 5369.) Rev. by Theodora A. Jankowski in ShB (11:3) 1993, 44–5.

6496. —— The (in)significance of 'lesbian' desire in early modern England. *In* (pp. 62–83) **93**.

6497. VICKERS, BRIAN. Appropriating Shakespeare: contemporary critical quarrels. (Bibl. 1994, 4358.) Rev. by Christoph Bode in SJ (132) 1996, 226–31; by Richard Fly in CLS (33:2) 1996, 201–5; by Richard Knowles in ELN (33:3) 1996, 70–4; by Willie van Peer in CanRCL (23:4) 1996, 1252–5; by Simon Barker and Venetia Hill in Literature and History (5:1) 1996, 86–91.

6498. —— Returning to Shakespeare. (Bibl. 1993, 4155.) Rev. by Charles R. Forker in Shakespeare Yearbook (2) 1991, 248–50.

6499. —— Whose thumbprints? A more plausible author for *A Funeral Elegy. See* **1213**.

6500. WATERS, D. DOUGLAS. Christian settings in Shakespeare's tragedies. (Bibl. 1994, 4361.) Rev. by Günther Blaicher in SJ (132) 1996, 242–3.

6501. WELLS, CHARLES. The wide arch: Roman values in Shakespeare. (Bibl. 1993, 4161.) Rev. by John S. Mebane in SNL (44:3) 1994, 47.

6502. WELLS, STANLEY. In memory of Master William Peter: the difficulties of attributing *A Funeral Elegy* to Shakespeare. *See* **2730**.

6503. —— Shakespeare's biography and the media. CEI (50) 1996, 45–8.

6504. —— (ed.). Shakespeare: a bibliographical guide. (Bibl. 1993, 4162.) Rev. by Frank Occhiogrosso in ShB (10:4) 1992, 47.

6505. WHITNEY, CHARLES. 'Like Richard the 3ds ghosts': Dorothy Osborne and the uses of Shakespeare. ELN (34:2) 1996, 12–22.

6506. WILSON, RAWDON. Shakespearean narrative. Newark: Delaware UP; London; Toronto: Assoc. UPs, 1995. pp. 313. Rev. by Brian Edwards in AUMLA (85) 1996, 152–3.

6507. WILSON, ROBERT RAWDON. Narrative boundaries in Shakespeare's plays. CanRCL (18:2/3) 1991, 233–61.

6508. WOLF, WERNER. Shakespeare und die Entstehung ästhetischer Illusion im englischen Drama. *See* **4120**.

6509. WOLFENSPERGER, PETER. Shakespeare: impartial and partial: strategies of persuasion in the comedies. Tübingen: Francke, 1994. pp. 255. Rev. by Klaus Peter Steiger in SJ (132) 1996, 245–6; by Norbert Schaffeld in ZAA (44:1) 1996, 84–6.

6510. WOODBRIDGE, LINDA. The scythe of Saturn: Shakespeare and magical thinking. (Bibl. 1995, 5381.) Rev. by Alexander Leggatt in ESCan (22:3) 1996, 364–6; by Margaret Loftus Ranald in ShB (14:3) 1996, 40–2.

6511. —— BERRY, EDWARD (eds). True rites and maimed rites: ritual and anti-ritual in Shakespeare and his age. (Bibl. 1995, 62.) Rev. by Louis Burkhardt in JRS (8:2) 1994, 146–9.

6512. WYMER, ROWLAND. Jacobean pageant or Elizabethan *fin-de-siècle*? The political context of early seventeenth-century tragedy. *In* (pp. 45–58) **53**.

6513. YOON, HEE OYCK. Shakespeare heuigeuk e natanan heuigeuk-jeok susahak gwa se gazi daehwa yangsik. (Comic rhetoric and three types of dialogue in Shakespeare's comedies.) *See* **2498**.

6514. YOUNG, DAVID. The action to the word: structure and style in

Shakespearean tragedy. (Bibl. 1995, 5385.) Rev. by Nathaniel Strout in Shakespeare Yearbook (2) 1991, 253–5.

6515. ZELTER, JOACHIM.   Liebe und Intimität: Shakespeares Welt – unsere Welt. LJGG (37) 1996, 113–36.

Productions

6516. ABEL, DOUGLAS.   Venom in his blood: Edmund Kean's *Othello* contests. NETJ (6) 1995, 69–89.

6517. AGBAW, S. EKEMA.   Africanizing *Macbeth*: 'down-fall'n birthdom'. RAL (27:1) 1996, 102–9.

6518. APPLER, KEITH.   Deconstructing the regional theater with 'performance art' Shakespeare. TT (5:1) 1995, 35–51.

6519. ARMSTRONG, ALAN.   The 1993 Oregon Shakespeare Festival. ShB (12:2) 1994, 31–6.

6520. —— The Oregon Shakespeare Festival. ShB (10:4) 1992, 22–7.

6521. —— The Oregon Shakespeare Festival: 1990. ShB (9:2) 1991, 29–33.

6522. —— Shakespeare in Ashland, 1995: the sixtieth anniversary season. ShB (14:2) 1996, 29–34.

6523. BARROW, CRAIG.   The 1992 Alabama Shakespeare Festival. UC (12) 1992, 146–51.

6524. —— The 1993 Alabama Shakespeare Festival. UC (13) 1993, 143–5.

6525. —— The 1994 Alabama Shakespeare Festival. UC (14) 1994, 139–47.

6526. —— A tale of two Shakespeare Festivals: Stratford's *The Merchant of Venice* and Alabama Shakespeare Festival's *The Winter's Tale*. UC (16) 1996, 146–52.

6527. BASCHIERA, CARLA DENTE.   Kemble: uno Hamlet dell'Ottocento. Textus (3:1/2) 1990, 299–312.

6528. BATE, JONATHAN; JACKSON, RUSSELL (eds).   Shakespeare: an illustrated stage history. Oxford; New York: OUP, 1996. pp. xiii, 253. Rev. by Martin Dodsworth in TLS, 26 Apr. 1996, 16.

6529. BAXTER, MARION.   Titus alone. Shakespeare Society of Southern Africa: Newsletter and Occasional Papers (10/11) 1995, 8–10.

6530. BEARD, MARGARET.   *Macbeth.* Shakespeare Society of Southern Africa: Newsletter and Occasional Papers (10/11) 1995, 7.

6531. BEDFORD, KRISTINA.   *Coriolanus* at the National: 'Th'interpretation of the time'. (Bibl. 1992, 4956.) Rev. by Glenda Frank in ShB (11:1) 1993, 45–6.

6532. BENNETT, SUSAN.   Performing nostalgia: shifting Shakespeare and the contemporary past. London; New York: Routledge, 1996. pp. viii, 199. Rev. by Theresa Smalec in JDTC (11:1) 1996, 135–7; by Robert Grant Williams in EMLS (2:3) 1996, 10.1–4.

6533. BERKOWITZ, GERALD.   The 1995 Edinburgh Festival. ShB (14:1) 1996, 21–2.

6534. BERKOWITZ, GERALD M.   The London and Stratford seasons 1991. ShB (9:4) 1991, 8–11.

6535. BERRY, RALPH.   Shakespeare in performance: castings and metamorphoses. (Bibl. 1995, 5390.) Rev. by Robert F. Willson, Jr, in SNL (46:1) 1996, 10.

6536. BIGGS, MURRAY.   Adapting *Timon of Athens.* ShB (10:2) 1992, 5–10.

6537. Boling, Ronald J. Stage images of Cressida's betrayal. Essays in Theatre (14:2) 1996, 147–58.

6538. Boltz, Ingeborg. Verzeichnis der Shakespeare-Inszenierungen und Bibliographie der Kritiken: Spielzeit 1994/95. SJ (132) 1996, 204–25.

6539. Boquet, Guy. Shakespeare on the French stage: a historical survey. Shakespeare Yearbook (5) 1994, 191–218.

6540. Brailow, David G. *Twelfth Night* across the continents: an interview with Michael Pennington. ShB (14:1) 1996, 29–30.

6541. Bristol, Michael D. How good does evidence have to be? *In* (pp. 22–43) **118**.

6542. Brown, John Russell. Shakespeare's plays in performance. (Bibl. 1969, 3448.) New York: Applause, 1993. pp. x, 235, (plates) 8. (Revised ed.: first ed. 1966.) Rev. by Jay L. Halio in SQ (46:4) 1995, 484.

6543. Browne, Kevin. The nature and personality of Hamlet: Yorick's child. OnS (19) 1996, 120–7.

6544. Brucher, Richard. O'Neill, Othello and Robeson. EOR (18:1/2) 1994, 45–58.

6545. Buchman, Lorne M. Still in movement: Shakespeare on screen. (Bibl. 1994, 4395.) Rev. by James Goodwin in FilmQ (45:4) 1992, 66–7; by Francisco J. Borge-Loquez in ShB (11:4) 1993, 46–7.

6546. Bulman, James C. The merchant of Venice. (Bibl. 1995, 5396.) Rev. by Jay L. Halio in ShB (10:1) 1992, 45–6.

6547. —— On being unfaithful to Shakespeare: Miller, Marowitz, and Wesker. JTD (2) 1996, 59–73.

6548. Cartmell, Deborah. Shakespeare: Shakespeare on screen. YWES (75) 1994, 230–1.

6549. Cavanagh, Dermot. Shakespeare: Shakespeare in the theatre. YWES (75) 1994, 227–9.

6550. Clarke, Kate; Goodman, Lizbeth. Reading *As You Like It*. *In* (pp. 193–250) **110**.

6551. Cohen, Robert. Tears (and acting) in Shakespeare. JDTC (10:1) 1995, 21–30.

6552. Cordner, Michael. Annotation and performance in Shakespeare. *See* **6132**.

6553. Coursen, H. R. The directors and the critics: Stratford-upon-Avon, 1992. ShB (11:2) 1993, 10–14.

6554. —— Reading Shakespeare on stage. (Bibl. 1995, 5403.) Rev. by Mary Bly in ShB (14:1) 1996, 47.

6555. —— Recent *Hamlet*s and the script's larger dimensions. ShB (14:3) 1996, 5–8.

6556. —— Sexual politics in production: England, summer 1990. ShB (9:1) 1991, 9–12.

6557. —— Shakespeare in production: whose history? Athens: Ohio UP, 1996. pp. xiv, 287. Rev. by Samantha Rachel Rabetz in Theater (27:1) 1996, 104–6; by James H. Lake in SNL (46:4) 1996, 91–2.

6558. —— Shakespeare on film and television. UC (15) 1995, 4–16.

6559. —— Shakespearean performance as interpretation. (Bibl. 1995, 5404.) Rev. by Seymour Bernstein in ShB (11:3) 1993, 45–6.

6560. —— Winter of the Scottish play. ShB (10:2) 1992, 10–14.

6561. Cousin, Geraldine. King John. Manchester; New York: Manchester UP, 1994. pp. xi, 152. (Shakespeare in performance.) Rev. by William B. Long in ShB (14:3) 1996, 45–6.

6562. CROWL, SAMUEL.   Hamlet 'most royal': an interview with Kenneth Branagh. ShB (12:4) 1994, 5–8.

6563.   —— Shakespeare observed: studies in performance on stage and screen. (Bibl. 1995, 5406.) Rev. by Marion D. Perret in ShB (12:2) 1994, 49.

6564. DAVIES, ANTHONY; WELLS, STANLEY (eds).   Shakespeare and the moving image: the plays on film and television. (Bibl. 1995, 5408.) Rev. by Stephen J. Phillips in CEl (49) 1996, 115.

6565. DAY, MOIRA.   Shakespeare on the Saskatchewan 1985–1990: 'the Stratford of the West' (NOT). Essays in Theatre (15:1) 1996, 69–90.

6566. DAY, ROGER.   Reading *Othello*. *In* (pp. 89–130) **110**.

6567. DERRICK, PATTY S.   Three Rivers Shakespeare festival. ShB (10:1) 1992, 25–7; (11:4) 1993, 33–4.

6568. DESSEN, ALAN C.   The image and the script: Shakespeare on stage in 1993. ShB (12:1) 1994, 5–8.

6569.   —— Improving the script: staging Shakespeare and others in 1995. ShB (14:1) 1996, 5–8.

6570.   —— Recovering Elizabethan staging: a reconsideration of the evidence. *In* (pp. 44–65) **118**.

6571.   —— Taming the script: *Henry VI*, *Shrew*, and *All's Well* in Ashland and Stratford. ShB (11:1) 1993, 34–7.

6572. DINIA, THAÏS FLORES NOGUEIRA.   *King Lear*'s filmic adaptation: a chaos? CanRCL (23:3) 1996, 775–80.

6573. DUBAR, MONIQUE.   Cleopatra or Hamlet? Sarah between Sardou and Shakespeare. Shakespeare Yearbook (5) 1994, 233–61.

6574. EDGERTON, ELLEN.   'Your answer, sir, is cinematical': Kenneth Branagh's *Much Ado About Nothing*. ShB (12:1) 1994, 42–4.

6575. ELIOT, SIMON.   An English history play: reading and studying *Henry V*. *In* (pp. 35–88) **110**.

6576. FAYARD, NICOLE.   Planchon, Chéreau, and Shakespeare: assuming 'unmasking masks'. Shakespeare Yearbook (5) 1994, 289–305.

6577. FLACHMANN, MICHAEL.   'Swear by your double self': Bassanio's impersonation of Morocco and Aragon in the 1992 Utah Shakespeare Festival. ShB (11:2) 1993, 46–8.

6578. FORTIER, MARK.   Speculations on *2 Henry IV*: theatre historiography, the strait gate of history, and Kenneth Branagh. JDTC (7:1) 1992, 45–69.

6579. FRIEDMAN, DONALD.   Bottom, Burbage, and the birth of tragedy. *In* (pp. 315–26) **98**.

6580. GARDNER, COLIN.   'But seasons come to pass': *The Winter's Tale* in South Africa. SSA (7) 1994, 74–80.

6581. GAUSS, REBECCA.   When is a crowd not a crowd? Challenges of staging *Coriolanus* at the Colorado Shakespeare Festival. OnS (19) 1996, 134–42.

6582. GECKLE, GEORGE L.   Shakespeare in England: the power of desire on stage, Stratford-upon-Avon, fall 1992. ShB (11:2) 1993, 15–19.

6583. GEORGE, DAVID.   Two productions of *Coriolanus*. SNL (46:1) 1996, 9.

6584. GODSALVE, WILLIAM L. H.   Britten's *A Midsummer Night's Dream*: making an opera from Shakespeare's comedy. (Bibl. 1995, 5423.) Rev. by Christian Kelnberger in SJ (132) 1996, 262–4.

6585. GRIFFIN, C. W.   Hippolyta's dress and undress: subtext and scopophilia in *A Midsummer Night's Dream*. ShB (12:2) 1994, 43–4.

6586. GRIFFITHS, TREVOR R. (ed.).   A midsummer night's dream. Cambridge; New York: CUP, 1996. pp. xvi, 234. (Shakespeare in production.)

6587. GURR, ANDREW.   Playgoing in Shakespeare's London. *See* **5646**.

6588. —— The Shakespearian playing companies. Oxford: Clarendon Press; New York: OUP, 1996. pp. viii, 483. Rev. by Peter Holland in TLS, 20 Dec. 1996, 21.

6589. HALIO, JAY L.   Five days, three *King Lear*s. ShB (9:1) 1991, 19–21.

6590. —— A midsummer night's dream. (Bibl. 1994, 4420.) Rev. by Peter J. Smith in CEl (49) 1996, 117–19.

6591. —— Understanding Shakespeare's plays in performance. (Bibl. 1990, 3986.) Rev. by Maurice Charney in ShB (9:3) 1991, 37–8.

6592. HART, JOHN F.   Tygres Heart Shakespeare Company. ShB (10:1) 1992, 31–3.

6593. HELMS, LORRAINE.   Playing the woman's part: feminist criticism and Shakespearean performance. *In* (pp. 196–206) **84**.

6594. HODGDON, BARBARA.   'Here apparent': photography, history, and the theatrical unconscious. *In* (pp. 181–209) **118**.

6595. HOENSELAARS, A. J.   *Macbeth* in the Netherlands. ShB (10:2) 1992, 15–19.

6596. IMPASTATO, DAVID.   Godard's *Lear* ... why is it so bad? ShB (12:3) 1994, 38–41.

6597. —— Orson Welles' *Othello* and the Welles–Smith restoration: definitive version? ShB (10:4) 1992, 38–41.

6598. JACKSON, RUSSELL; SMALLWOOD, ROBERT (eds).   Players of Shakespeare: 3, Further essays in Shakespearian performance. (Bibl. 1995, 5441.) Rev. by Carol Rutter in Essays in Theatre (14:2) 1996, 177–9.

6599. JENSEN, MICHAEL P.   California Shakespeare Festival's twentieth anniversary season. ShB (12:2) 1994, 36–8.

6600. KAHAN, JEFFREY.   *Noh* Shakespeare: an interview with Kuniyoshi Munakata. ShB (14:1) 1996, 26–8.

6601. KEGISHIAN, HARRY.   Performing violence in *King Lear*: Edgar's encounters in 4.6 and 5.3. ShB (14:3) 1996, 36–8.

6602. KEMPER, MARTHA.   Casting imagination into form: Alvina Krause and *A Midsummer Night's Dream*. NETJ (3) 1992, 87–96.

6603. KENNEDY, DENNIS.   Looking at Shakespeare: a visual history of twentieth-century performance. (Bibl. 1995, 5447.) Rev. by James Fisher in JDTC (9:2) 1995, 174–6; by Stephen J. Phillips in CEl (49) 1996, 116–17; by Kay H. Smith in SNL (46:2) 1996, 43, 45–6.

6604. KING, T. J.   Casting Shakespeare's plays: London's actors and their roles, 1590–1642. (Bibl. 1994, 4448.) Rev. by William B. Long in ShB (12:3) 1994, 42–3.

6605. KLEIN, HOLGER.   Ein *Sommernachtstraum*. Spectakel, July/Aug. 1996, 6–9.

6606. KLIMAN, BERNICE W.   *Hamlet*: film, television, and audio performance. (Bibl. 1993, 4219.) Rev. by Patricia B. Worrall in ShB (11:4) 1993, 47.

6607. —— Macbeth. (Bibl. 1995, 5452.) Rev. by Michael P. Jensen in ShB (12:1) 1994, 47.

6608. —— A *Macbeth* for our time. UC (13) 1993, 94–108.

6609. KOLE, ROBERT.   Americans doing Shakespeare: notes of a dramaturg. ShB (12:3) 1994, 21–2.

6610. KUJAWINSKA-COURTNEY, KRYSTYNA.   Shakespeare's women and Polish male critics. ShB (14:1) 1996, 23–5.

6611. LEGGATT, ALEXANDER.   King Lear. (Bibl. 1991, 5070.) Rev. by Ralph A. Ranald in ShB (9:1) 1991, 40–1; by Jay L. Halio in ShB (10:3) 1992, 46–7

6612. LIEBLEIN, LEANORE.   Theatre archives at the intersection of production and reception: the example of Québécois Shakespeare. *In* (pp. 164–80) **118**.

6613. MCKERNAN, LUKE.   Beerbohm Tree's *King John* rediscovered: the first Shakespeare film, September 1899. ShB (11:1) 1993, 35–6; (11:2) 1993, 49–50.

6614. MCROBERTS, J. PAUL.   Shakespearean tragediennes in the early oil days of Pennsylvania. SRASP (19) 1996, 63–76.

6615. MAGNONI, STEFANIA.   Kemble's Shakespeare: the case of *Antony and Cleopatra*. Textus (9:2) 1996, 523–36.

6616. MAHER, MARY Z.   Modern Hamlets and their soliloquies. (Bibl. 1992, 5008.) Rev. by Stephen J. Phillips in NQ (43:3) 1996, 336.

6617. MAHOOD, M. M.   Bit parts in Shakespeare's plays. (Bibl. 1995, 5460.) Rev. by Herbert Weil in ShB (12:3) 1994, 43–4; by Cicely Palser Havely in ERev (5:4) 1995, 24–5.

6618. MAZER, CARY M.   Shakespeare in Philadelphia, 1990–1991. ShB (9:3) 1991, 17–19.

6619. MICHAELS, WENDY.   Playbuilding Shakespeare. Cambridge; New York: CUP, 1996. pp. vii, 167.

6620. MILLER, HAL.   Shakespeare on the Danube. ShB (10:2) 1992, 35–6.

6621. MONTROSE, LOUIS.   The purpose of playing: Shakespeare and the cultural politics of the Elizabethan theatre. Chicago; London: Chicago UP, 1996. pp. xiii, 227. Rev. by Michael Dobson in LRB (18:21) 1996, 24–5.

6622. MOULTON, IAN FREDERICK.   Stratford and Bayreuth: anti-commercialism, nationalism, and the religion of art. Litteraria Pragensia (6:12) 1996, 39–50.

6623. MUKERJI, CHANDRA.   Shakespeare in L.A.: a commentary on *Shakespeare and Modern Commercial Culture*. Litteraria Pragensia (6:12) 1996, 13–25.

6624. MULLIN, MICHAEL.   Theatre at Stratford-upon-Avon: first supplement, a catalogue-index to productions of the Royal Shakespeare Company, 1979–1993. (Bibl. 1995, 5470.) Rev. by Mary Jo Sodd in JDTC (11:1) 1996, 147–9.

6625. MUNOZ, MARIE-CHRISTINE.   Shakespeare, Avignon, Vilar. Shakespeare Yearbook (5) 1994, 273–87.

6626. MYERS, NORMAN J.   Finding 'a heap of jewels' in 'lesser' Shakespeare: *The Wars of the Roses* and *Richard Duke of York*. NETJ (7) 1996, 95–107.

6627. NELSON, PAUL.   Noble thoughts on mighty experiences: an interview with Adrian Noble. ShB (11:3) 1993, 5–10.

6628. NEWELL, ALEX.   The Stratford, Ontario, Festival 1995: a Canadian's overview. ShB (14:1) 1996, 31–4.

6629. ORGEL, STEPHEN.   Impersonations: the performance of gender in Shakespeare's England. *See* **5689**.

6630. OSBORNE, LAURIE E.   The rhetoric of evidence: the narration and display of Viola and Olivia in the nineteenth century. *In* (pp. 124–43) **118**.

6631. PARKER, R. B.   *King Lear*, Sir Donald Wolfit, and *The Dresser*. *In* (pp. 99–109) **16**.

6632. PEARCE, BRIAN.   Directing Shakespeare. Shakespeare Society of Southern Africa: Newsletter and Occasional Papers (9:1/2) 1994, 24–6.

6633. PECHTER, EDWARD.   Textual and theatrical Shakespeare: questions of evidence. *In* (pp. 1–21) **118**.

6634. —— (ed.).   Textual and theatrical Shakespeare: questions of evidence. *See* **118**.

6635. PENDLETON, THOMAS A.   Shakespeare in the golden age of television: Orson Welles' *King Lear*. SNL (44:3) 1994, 58.

6636. PIGEON, RENÉE.   'A garment all of blood': Michael Pennington's Prince Hal. ShB (12:4) 1994, 37–40.

6637. PILKINGTON, ACE G.   Screening Shakespeare from *Richard II* to *Henry V*. (Bibl. 1994, 4475.) Rev. by Jerry L. Crawford in WebS (9:2) 1992, 91–2.

6638. POTTER, LOIS.   Actors and editors, editors as actors. *See* **6190**.

6639. PRICE, DIANA; FOSTER, DONALD W.   SHAXICON and Shakespeare's acting career. SNL (46:2) 1996, 27–8, 46; (46:3) 1996, 57–8.

6640. PUSCHMANN-NALENZ, BARBARA.   Using Shakespeare? The appropriation of *Coriolanus* and *King Henry V* in John Philip Kemble's 1789 productions. Shakespeare Yearbook (5) 1994, 219–32.

6641. QUIGLEY, DANIEL.   'Double exposure': the semiotic ramifications of Mel Gibson in Zeffirelli's *Hamlet*. ShB (11:1) 1993, 38–9.

6642. RAUCHUT, E. A.   The siege oration in Branagh's *Henry V*. ShB (11:1) 1993, 39–40.

6643. REYNOLDS, BRYAN.   The terrorism of Macbeth and Charles Manson: reading cultural construction in Polanski and Shakespeare. UC (13) 1993, 109–29.

6644. RICKS, KATY.   Staging *As You Like It*. ERev (6:3) 1996, 20–4.

6645. SAHEL, PIERRE.   All their yesterdays: a note on the alleged contemporariness of war and violence in Shakespeare. CEl (50) 1996, 49–50.

6646. SAUNDERS, J. G.   'Apparent perversities': text and subtext in the construction of the role of Edgar in Brook's film of *King Lear*. RES (47:187) 1996, 317–30.

6647. SAVIN, JANET.   Shakespeare in Lithuania. ShB (9:1) 1991, 24–5.

6648. SCHLUETER, JUNE.   Tybalt in a bloody sheet, Paris in the tomb: speculations on doubling and staging in *Romeo and Juliet*. Shakespeare Yearbook (2) 1991, 1–22.

6649. SEEMAN, PAM HOLLAND.   Magicians, storytellers and framing devices: *Cymbeline* in production. TexPres (13) 1992, 59–64.

6650. SHALTZ, JUSTIN.   The 1993 Illinois Shakespeare Festival. ShB (12:2) 1994, 20–3.

6651. —— Three *Hamlets* on film. ShB (11:1) 1993, 36–7.

6652. SHAPIRO, MICHAEL.   Gender in play on the Shakespearean stage: boy heroines and female pages. (Bibl. 1995, 5482.) Rev. by Thomas Akstens in JDTC (10:1) 1995, 141–2; by John Drakakis in NQ (43:3) 1996, 338–40; by Anthony B. Dawson in Essays in Theatre (14:2) 1996, 186–8; by Frances K. Barasch and Theodora A. Jankowski in ShB (14:3) 1996, 44–5; by Sandra Clark in SNL (46:1) 1996, 7–8.

6653. Shaughnessy, Robert.   Representing Shakespeare: England, history and the RSC. (Bibl. 1995, 5483.) Rev. by Stephen J. Phillips in CEl (49) 1996, 113–15.

6654. Shaw, Catherine M.   Edwin Booth's *Richard II* and the divided nation. *In* (pp. 144–63) **118**.

6655. Shewring, Margaret.   King Richard II. Manchester; New York: Manchester UP, 1996. pp. xiv, 206. (Shakespeare in performance.)

6656. Shurbanov, Alexander; Sokolova, Boika.   Updating Shakespeare in Bulgaria. EngS (77:5) 1996, 439–44.

6657. Shurgot, Michael.   'Get you a place': staging *The Mousetrap* at the Globe Theatre. ShB (12:3) 1994, 5–9.

6658. Singer, Barry.   All Shakespeare, all the time. NYTM, 16 June 1996, 36–7.

6659. Singleton, Brian.   Mnouchkine and Shakespeare: intercultural theatre practice. Shakespeare Yearbook (5) 1994, 307–26.

6660. Skura, Meredith Anne.   Shakespeare the actor and the purposes of playing. (Bibl. 1995, 5485.) Rev. by Scott McMillin in MedRen (8) 1996, 267–74.

6661. Smith, Emma.   Staging race: *Othello* then and now. ERev (7:2) 1996, 2–5.

6662. Špacek, R.   'I do it more natural': business in Shakespearean playing. ShB (12:4) 1994, 17–22.

6663. Spong, Andy.   Shakespeare's day off. ERev (6:3) 1996, 2–5.

6664. Sprung, Guy; Much, Rita.   Hot ice: Shakespeare in Moscow: a director's diary. Winnipeg, Man.: Blizzard, 1991. pp. xv, 151, (plates) 15. Rev. by Jessica Gardiner in TRC (17:1) 1996, 130–2.

6665. Steele, Kenneth B.   The Stratford, Ontario, Festival 1991: a Canadian's overview. ShB (9:4) 1991, 24–8.

6666. —— The Stratford, Ontario, Festival 1992: a Canadian's overview. ShB (10:4) 1992, 13–17.

6667. —— The Stratford, Ontario, Festival 1993: a Canadian's overview. ShB (12:1) 1994, 26–8.

6668. Suzman, Janet.   Acting with Shakespeare: three comedies. London; New York: Applause, 1996. pp. 153.

6669. Taranow, Gerda.   The Bernhardt *Hamlet*: culture and context. New York; Frankfurt; Bern; Paris: Lang, 1996. pp. xix, 266. (Artists and issues in theatre, 4.)

6670. Taylor, Anthony Brian.   'The Goths protect the Andronici, who go aloft': the implications of a stage direction. NQ (43:2) 1996, 152–5.

6671. Teague, Frances.   Shakespeare's speaking properties. (Bibl. 1993, 4243.) Rev. by Dorothea Kehler in ShB (12:1) 1994, 47–8.

6672. Tempera, Mariangela (ed.).   *Antony and Cleopatra*: dal testo alla scena. Bologna: CLUEB, 1990. pp. 164.

6673. —— *Hamlet*: dal testo alla scena. Bologna: CLUEB, 1990. pp. 183.

6674. —— *The Merchant of Venice*: dal testo alla scena. Bologna: CLUEB, 1994. pp. 290.

6675. Vanrigh, Anny Crunelle.   An account of Terry Hands' production of *Hamlet* (Théâtre Marigny, Paris, 1994). Shakespeare Yearbook (5) 1994, 327–43.

6676. VAUGHAN, VIRGINIA MASON; VAUGHAN, ALDEN T. Tampering with *The Tempest.* ShB (10:1) 1992, 16–17.

6677. VIGUERS, SUSAN. Costuming as interpretation: the Elliott/Olivier and the Brook/Scofield *King Lear.* ShB (12:2) 1994, 44–6.

6678. WALDER, DENNIS. Interim voices: South African theatre today. ERev (6:1) 1995, 8–11.

6679. WARREN, ROGER. Staging Shakespeare's late plays. (Bibl. 1993, 4247.) Rev. by Caldwell Titcomb in ShB (11:1) 1993, 47.

6680. WEIMANN, ROBERT. Performance-game and representation in *Richard III. In* (pp. 66–85) **118**.

6681. WEINSTEIN, CHARLES E. Olivier's *Coriolanus*: the unknown sound recording. ShB (11:4) 1993, 35–6.

6682. WILKINSON, J. NORMAN. Shakespeare in China. NETJ (2) 1991, 39–58.

6683. WILLIAMS, GEORGE WALTON. The staging of Harfleur in *Henry V.* SNL (46:4) 1996, 93, 98.

6684. WILLIAMS, SIMON. Shakespeare on the German stage: vol. 1, 1586–1914. (Bibl. 1990, 4029.) Rev. by Daniel L. Wright in ShB (10:1) 1992, 47.

6685. WILLSON, ROBERT F., JR. Franco Zeffirelli's *Romeo and Juliet* and the uses of cultural translation. UC (16) 1996, 101–7.

6686. —— Recontextualizing Shakespeare on film: *My Own Private Idaho, Men of Respect, Prospero's Books.* ShB (10:3) 1992, 34–7.

6687. —— War and reflection on war: the Olivier and Branagh films of *Henry V.* ShB (9:3) 1991, 27–9.

6688. WILSON, ANN. Staging Shakespeare. CanTR (75) 1993, 19–24.

6689. WORTHEN, W. B. Invisible bullets, violet beards: reading actors reading. *In* (pp. 210–29) **118**.

6690. WRIGHT, LAURENCE. *Much Ado About Nothing*: Linda Louise Swain's production for the Port Elizabeth Shakespearean Festival. SSA (7) 1994, 81.

6691. —— *Othello.* Shakespeare Society of Southern Africa: Newsletter and Occasional Papers (10/11) 1995, 6.

Separate Works

All's Well That Ends Well

6692. BEVINGTON, DAVID. All's well that plays well. *In* (pp. 162–80) **116**.

6693. BLY, MARY. Imagining consummation: women's erotic language in comedies of Dekker and Shakespeare. *In* (pp. 35–52) **64**.

6694. CHO, SUNG WON. Longing for the mother queen: a New Historical reading of *All's Well That Ends Well.* JELL (42:4) 1996, 873–97.

6695. CORDNER, MICHAEL. Annotation and performance in Shakespeare. *See* **6132**.

6696. DESSEN, ALAN C. Taming the script: *Henry VI, Shrew,* and *All's Well* in Ashland and Stratford. *See* **6571**.

6697. KANG, MYUNGHEE. *All's Well That Ends Well*: Helena eui wijangdoen yokmang gwa yeosung jueuijeok sowoe. (*All's Well That Ends Well*: Helena's disguised desires and feminist isolation.) ShR (29) 1996, 1–22.

6698. LEE, MI YOUNG. *All's Well That Ends Well*: kanginhan yeosung eui munjaegeuk. (*All's Well That Ends Well*: a problem play with a strong woman.) EngSt (20) 1996, 145–68.

6699. NAM, HYUN SOOK.   *All's Well That Ends Well*: guijok eui jinjunghan myungye. (*All's Well That Ends Well*: the honour of the aristocracy.) ShR (28) 1996, 73–106.

Antony and Cleopatra

6700. ARCHER, JOHN MICHAEL.   Antiquity and degeneration: the representation of Egypt and Shakespeare's *Antony and Cleopatra*. Genre (27:1/2) 1994, 1–27.

6701. ARP, THOMAS R.   'Where's Seleucus?': Cleopatra's recapitulation. CCTE (61) 1996, 1–8.

6702. BAKER, J. ROBERT.   Absence and subversion: the 'o'erflow' of gender in Shakespeare's *Antony and Cleopatra*. UC (12) 1992, 105–15.

6703. BRINK, JEAN R.   Domesticating the Dark Lady. *In* (pp. 93–108) **89**.

6704. CORBIN, PETER.   The 'harmless drudgery' of editing Shakespeare: the Arden Shakespeare: third series. *See* **6131**.

6705. CURTIS, MARY ANN.   The joining of male and female: the alchemical theme of transmutation in *Antony and Cleopatra*. UC (12) 1992, 116–26.

6706. DUBAR, MONIQUE.   Cleopatra or Hamlet? Sarah between Sardou and Shakespeare. *See* **6573**.

6707. FEICHTINGER, BARBARA.   Die eine und die vielen: Identität und Variation im literarischen Kleopatra-Bild von der Antike bis zu Shakespeare. *See* **3812**.

6708. FRANK, MARCIE.   Fighting women and loving men: Dryden's representation of Shakespeare in *All for Love*. *In* (pp. 310–29) **93**.

6709. GLASSER, MARVIN.   Dramaturgical uses of visual forms in Shakespeare's *Antony and Cleopatra*. UC (14) 1994, 89–104.

6710. HARESNAPE, GEOFFREY.   Sooth to say. Shakespeare Society of Southern Africa: Newsletter and Occasional Papers (9:1/2) 1994, 1–6.

6711. HAWKINS, HARRIETT.   The irregularities of *Antony and Cleopatra*. ERev (6:3) 1996, 15–17.

6712. KOLIN, PHILIP C.   Cleopatra of the Nile and Blanche DuBois of the French Quarter: *Antony and Cleopatra* and *A Streetcar Named Desire*. ShB (11:1) 1993, 25–7.

6713. KUJAWIŃSKA-COURTNEY, KRYSTYNA.   'Th'interpretation of the time': the dramaturgy of Shakespeare's Roman plays. (Bibl. 1993, 4260.) Victoria, BC: Victoria UP, 1993. (English literary studies, 57.) Rev. by John Drakakis in YES (26) 1996, 269–71.

6714. LEE, KYUNG WON.   Domesticating the 'infinite variety': Shakespeare's Cleopatra and the discourse of orientation. ShR (28) 1996, 107–33.

6715. MCDONALD, JOYCE GREEN.   Sex, race, and empire in Shakespeare's *Antony and Cleopatra*. Literature and History (5:1) 1996, 60–77.

6716. MCJANNET, LINDA.   *Gesta Romanorum*: heroic action and stage imagery in *Antony and Cleopatra*. ShB (11:1) 1993, 5–9.

6717. MAGNONI, STEFANIA.   Kemble's Shakespeare: the case of *Antony and Cleopatra*. *See* **6615**.

6718. MEHL, DIETER.   Der dritte Arden Shakespeare. *See* **6177**.

6719. MILES, GEOFFREY.   Shakespeare and the constant Romans.

Oxford: Clarendon Press; New York: OUP, 1996. pp. xii, 231. (Oxford English monographs.) Rev. by Raphael Lyne in TLS, 14 June 1996, 7–8.

6720. NEWTON, ALLYSON P.   At 'the very heart of loss': Shakespeare's Enobarbus and the rhetoric of remembering. *See* **2435**.

6721. SINGH, SUKHBIR.   A Shakespearean source for T. S. Eliot's 'dolphin': *The Waste Land* 2, line 96. ANQ (9:1) 1996, 24–6.

6722. SUJAKU, SHIGEKO.   *Hero* to shiteno Cleopatra, *heroine* to shiteno Antony – *Antony and Cleopatra* ni okeru 'gender' to 'sexuality'. (Cleopatra as 'hero' and Antony as 'heroine': 'gender' and 'sexuality' in *Antony and Cleopatra*.) SEL (73:1) 1996, 15–28.

6723. TEMPERA, MARIANGELA (ed.).   *Antony and Cleopatra*: dal testo alla scena. *See* **6672**.

6724. WALKER, JULIA M.   Reading the tombs of Elizabeth I. ELR (26:3) 1996, 510–30.

6725. WEBER, A. S.   New physics for the nonce: a Stoic and Hermetic reading of Shakespeare's *Antony and Cleopatra*. RenP 1995, 93–107.

6726. WHITNEY, CHARLES.   Charmian's daughter: women, gypsies, and festive ambivalence in *Antony and Cleopatra*. UC (14) 1994, 67–88.

6727. WILDERS, JOHN (ed.).   Antony and Cleopatra. *See* **6205**.

6728. WORTHAM, CHRISTOPHER.   Shakespeare, James I and the Matter of Britain. Eng (45:182) 1996, 97–122.

As You Like It

6729. BARNABY, ANDREW.   The political conscious of Shakespeare's *As You Like It*. SELit (36:2) 1996, 373–95.

6730. BLOOM, DONALD A.   Dwindling into wifehood: the romantic power of the witty heroine in Shakespeare, Dryden, Congreve, and Austen. *In* (pp. 53–79) **64**.

6731. CLARKE, KATE; GOODMAN, LIZBETH.   Reading *As You Like It*. *In* (pp. 193–250) **110**.

6732. DALEY, A. STUART.   Calling and commonwealth in *As You Like It*: a late Elizabethan political play. UC (14) 1994, 28–46.

6733. ELAM, KEIR.   'As they did in the golden world': romantic rapture and semantic rapture in *As You Like It*. CanRCL (18:2/3) 1991, 217–32.

6734. HERMANN, ANNE.   Travesty and transgression: transvestism in Shakespeare, Brecht, and Churchill. *In* (pp. 294–315) **84**.

6735. HUNT, MAURICE.   Words and deeds in *As You Like It*. Shakespeare Yearbook (2) 1991, 23–48.

6736. KOTT, JAN.   The gender of Rosalind: interpretations: Shakespeare, Büchner, Gautier. Trans. by Jadwiga Kosicka and Mark Rosenzweig. (Bibl. 1995, 5531.) Rev. by Andrew Apter in NETJ (4) 1993, 115–17.

6737. LEE, BYUNG EUN.   Shakespeare's class-consciousness in *As You Like It*. ShR (28) 1996, 135–51.

6738. McDONALD, MARCIA A.   The Elizabethan Poor Laws and the stage in the late 1590s. *See* **5670**.

6739. NAUMANN, ANNA C.   Der Witz der Rosalind (Vortrag zu den Shakespeare Tagen im Frühling 1995 in Weimar). SJ (132) 1996, 93–102.

6740. ORMEROD, DAVID.   'Ripe' and 'rot': a proverb in *As You Like It* and *King Lear*. *See* **3341**.

6741. RICKS, KATY.   Staging *As You Like It*. *See* **6644**.

6742. SEATON, DOUGLASS. Shakespeare's *It Was a Lover and His Lass*: the authentic music and its performance. ArsL (8) 1994, 93–104.

The Comedy of Errors
6743. BARROW, CRAIG. The 1992 Alabama Shakespeare Festival. *See* **6523**.
6744. CACIEDO, ALBERTO. 'A formal man again': physiological humours in *The Comedy of Errors*. UC (11) 1991, 24–38.
6745. CHRISTENSEN, ANN C. 'Because their business still lies out a' door': resisting the separation of the spheres in Shakespeare's *The Comedy of Errors*. Literature and History (5:1) 1996, 19–37.
6746. GREEN, DOUGLAS. Mother's word and *The Comedy of Errors*: notes toward a Shakespearean constitution of patriarchy. UC (15) 1995, 17–25.
6747. O'BRIEN, ROBERT VIKING. The madness of Syracusan Antipholus. EMLS (2:1) 1996, 3.1–26.
6748. SLAWSON, RICHARD J. 'Dromio, thou Dromio': the casting of twins in Shakespeare's *Comedy of Errors*. NETJ (2) 1991, 59–71.
6749. YANG, SHARON R. *The Comedy of Errors*: variation on a festive theme. UC (14) 1994, 11–27.

Coriolanus
6750. BLECKI, CATHERINE LA COURREYE. An intertextual study of Volumnia: from legend to character in Shakespeare's *Coriolanus*. *In* (pp. 81–91) **89**.
6751. BLYTHE, DAVID-EVERETT. Lead in *Coriolanus*. SNL (46:1) 1996, 17.
6752. BODY, JACQUES. An explosive transposition: the image of the people in *Coriolanus*, mark 1934. Shakespeare Yearbook (5) 1994, 263–71.
6753. BRINK, JEAN R. Domesticating the Dark Lady. *In* (pp. 93–108) **89**.
6754. DEAN, PAUL. *Coriolanus* – a tragedy of love. Eng (40:167) 1991, 117–34.
6755. GAUSS, REBECCA. When is a crowd not a crowd? Challenges of staging *Coriolanus* at the Colorado Shakespeare Festival. *See* **6581**.
6756. GEORGE, DAVID. Coriolanus' triumphal entry into Rome. NQ (43:2) 1996, 163–5.
6757. —— Two productions of *Coriolanus*. *See* **6583**.
6758. KNOWLES, RONALD. Actions and eloquence: Volumnia's plea in *Coriolanus*. ShB (14:4) 1996, 37–8.
6759. LEGGATT, ALEXANDER. The hidden hero: Shakespeare's *Coriolanus* and Eliot's *Coriolan*. *In* (pp. 89–98) **16**.
6760. LUCKING, DAVID. 'The price of one fair word': negotiating names in *Coriolanus*. EMLS (2:1) 1996, 4.1–22.
6761. MILES, GEOFFREY. Shakespeare and the constant Romans. *See* **6719**.
6762. PLOTZ, JOHN. *Coriolanus* and the failure of performatives. ELH (63:4) 1996, 809–32.
6763. PUSCHMANN-NALENZ, BARBARA. Using Shakespeare? The appropriation of *Coriolanus* and *King Henry V* in John Philip Kemble's 1789 productions. *See* **6640**.
6764. RIPLEY, JOHN. *Coriolanus* as Tory propaganda. *In* (pp. 102–23) **118**.

6765. Shershow, Scott Cutler. Idols of the marketplace: re-thinking the economic determination of Renaissance drama. RenD (26) 1995, 1–27.

6766. Unkefer, Virginia A. The playwright and actor on stage: mothers and sons in *Richard III*, *Coriolanus*, and *Hamlet*. ShB (12:3) 1994, 27–9.

6767. Weinstein, Charles E. Olivier's *Coriolanus*: the unknown sound recording. *See* **6681**.

6768. Yoshioka, Fumio. In the name of the son – identity and self-authorship in *Coriolanus*. SEL (72:2) 1996, 145–63.

Cymbeline

6769. Boe, John. Symbols of transformation in *Cymbeline*. RWT (2:2) 1995, 47–74.

6770. Cunningham, Karen. Female fidelities on trial: proof in the Howard attainder and *Cymbeline*. RenD (25) 1994, 1–31.

6771. Gandhi, Leela. Virtuous monuments: the monumentalizing of women in Shakespeare. In-between (3:1) 1994, 15–39.

6772. Henke, Robert. 'Gentleman-like tears': affective response in Italian tragicomedy and Shakespeare's late plays. CLS (33:4) 1996, 327–49.

6773. Jordan, Constance. Contract and conscience in *Cymbeline*. RenD (25) 1994, 33–58.

6774. Kehler, Dorothea. Shakespeare's *Cymbeline*. Exp (54:2) 1996, 70–2.

6775. Piglionica, Anna Maria. Boccaccio teatrale, Shakespeare narrativo: lo spessore della fiction. Textus (1:2) 1988, 267–90.

6776. Pitcher, John. Why editors should write more notes. *See* **793**.

6777. Revard, Stella P. Myth, masque, and marriage: *Paradise Lost* and Shakespeare's romances. *In* (pp. 114–34) **40**.

6778. Seeman, Pam Holland. Magicians, storytellers and framing devices: *Cymbeline* in production. *See* **6649**.

6779. Shapiro, Michael. Crossgender disguise in *Cymbeline* and its sources. Shakespeare Yearbook (2) 1991, 132–48.

Hamlet

6780. Adair, Vance. Rewriting the (s)crypt: gazing on *Hamlet*'s interiors. Q/W/E/R/T/Y (6) 1996, 5–15.

6781. Aguirre, Manuel. Life, crown, and queen: Gertrude and the theme of sovereignty. RES (47:186) 1996, 163–74.

6782. Aldiss, Brian. If Hamlet's uncle had been a nicer guy. *In* (pp. 21–4) **127**.

6783. Andreas, James R. 'For O, for O, the hobby-horse is forgot': Hamlet and the death of carnival. RenP 1996, 81–91.

6784. Baker, Christopher. Shakespeare's *Hamlet*, I.5.23. Exp (54:2) 1996, 67.

6785. Barker, Walter L. 'The heart of my mystery': emblematic revelation in the *Hamlet* play scene. UC (15) 1995, 75–98.

6786. Baschiera, Carla Dente. Kemble: uno Hamlet dell'Otto-cento. *See* **6527**.

6787. Bernstein, Seymour. Hamlet's rat. ShB (9:4) 1991, 36.

6788. Bigliazzi, Silvia. Fable *versus* fact: Hamlet's ghost in Dylan Thomas's early poetry. Textus (5) 1992, 51–64.

6789. BLOOM, HAROLD (ed.).   William Shakespeare's *Hamlet*. New York: Chelsea House, 1996. pp. 80. (Bloom's notes.)

6790. BONGIORNO, DOMINICK I.   Why did Hamlet enter Ophelia's closet? SNL (46:2) 1996, 32.

6791. BOOTH, ROY J.   'As mad as he': simile, analogy and likeness in *Hamlet. See* **2586**.

6792. BORIS, EDNA ZWICK.   To soliloquize or not to soliloquize. *See* **6124**.

6793. BROWNE, KEVIN.   The nature and personality of Hamlet: Yorick's child. *See* **6543**.

6794. BURTON, J. ANTHONY.   'His quarry cries on hauocke': is it Shakespeare's own judgment on the meaning of *Hamlet?* UC (11) 1991, 62–81.

6795. CANTOR, PAUL.   Shakespeare: *Hamlet*. (Bibl. 1992, 5083.) Rev. by Robert Kole in ShB (9:1) 1991, 41–2.

6796. CHARNEY, MAURICE.   Shakespeare's *Hamlet* in the context of the Hebrew Bible. JTD (2) 1996, 93–100.

6797. CORDNER, MICHAEL.   Annotation and performance in Shakespeare. *See* **6132**.

6798. COURSEN, H. R.   Recent *Hamlet*s and the script's larger dimensions. *See* **6555**.

6799. COURTNEY, RICHARD.   Shakespeare's world of death: the early tragedies, *Romeo and Juliet, Julius Caesar, Hamlet*. Toronto: Simon & Pierre, 1995. pp. 268. (Director's Shakespeare.) Rev. by Karen Bamford in CanTR (86) 1996, 65–6.

6800. COYLE, MARTIN.   Hamlet, Gertrude and the ghost: the punishment of women in Renaissance drama. Q/W/E/R/T/Y (6) 1996, 29–38.

6801. CROWL, SAMUEL.   Hamlet 'most royal': an interview with Kenneth Branagh. *See* **6562**.

6802. DIETRICH, JULIA.   *Hamlet* in the 1960s: an annotated bibliography. (Bibl. 1992, 5093.) Rev. by Linda McJannet in ShB (11:4) 1993, 42.

6803. DOLOFF, STEVEN.   Hamlet's 'nunnery' and Agrippa's 'stewes of harlottes'. *See* **1982**.

6804. DUBAR, MONIQUE.   Cleopatra or Hamlet? Sarah between Sardou and Shakespeare. *See* **6573**.

6805. DUFFY, KEVIN THOMAS, *et al.* (eds).   The Elsinore appeal: People *vs* Hamlet. New York: St Martin's Press, 1996. pp. viii, 183.

6806. FENDT, GENE.   A note on the time scheme in *Hamlet*. NQ (43:2) 1996, 159–60.

6807. FOAKES, R. A.   Hamlet *versus* Lear: cultural politics and Shakespeare's art. (Bibl. 1995, 5572.) Rev. by Ann Thompson in ShB (12:2) 1994, 51; by Jay L. Halio in Archiv (233:1) 1996, 172–4; by Haruo Nakano in SEL (English number) 1996, 81–6.

6808. FOSTER, MAXWELL E.   The play behind the play: *Hamlet* and quarto one. Ed. by Anne Shiras. *See* **6143**.

6809. FOX-GOOD, JACQUELYN A.   Ophelia's mad songs: music, gender, power. *In* (pp. 217–38) **116**.

6810. GILBERT, ANTHONY J.   Shakespearean self-talk, the Gricean maxims and the unconscious. EngS (76:3) 1995, 221–37.

6811. GREEN, DOUGLAS E.   Staging the evidence: Shakespeare's theatrical revengers. UC (12) 1992, 29–40.

6812. HALLETT, CHARLES A.	Structure and performance in *Hamlet*
2.2. ShB (10:4) 1992, 32–7.
6813. HAMADA, SHIHOKO.	*Kōjin* and *Hamlet*: the madness of Hamlet,
Ophelia, and Ichirô. CLS (33:1) 1996, 59–68.
6814. HOPKINS, LISA.	Discovered countries: *Hamlet* and Europe.
Q/W/E/R/T/Y (6) 1996, 39–45.
6815. KEHLER, DOROTHEA.	The outline guide industry and the pro-
cessing of Shakespeare's Gertrude. UC (14) 1994, 47–66.
6816. KELEMEN, ERICK.	*Hamlet* and the Prodigal Son.
Q/W/E/R/T/Y (6) 1996, 47–52.
6817. KELLER, JAMES R.	The knight of the post, Horatio, and King
Hamlet's ghost. ShB (10:1) 1992, 42–3.
6818. LEVIN, RICHARD A.	Fortinbras and the 'conveyance of a
promis'd march'. CEACrit (58:2) 1996, 9–23.
6819. LORANT, ANDRÉ.	D'Amleth à *Hamlet*: de la légende à la
tragédie. Q/W/E/R/T/Y (6) 1996, 53–63.
6820. —— Laforgue's Hamlet. Shakespeare Yearbook (5) 1994,
105–17.
6821. —— Social criticism in *Hamlet* and *The Revenger's Tragedy*. In (pp.
13–19) **53**.
6822. MADELAINE, RICHARD.	Over the nasty sty: sex, death and
Hamlet's alienation. Q/W/E/R/T/Y (6) 1996, 65–71.
6823. MAGUIN, FRANÇOIS (ed. and trans.).	Hamlet. *See* **6172**.
6824. MIKOŁEJKO, ZBIGNIEW.	Byt i niebyt Hamleta. (Existence and
non-existence of Hamlet.) Dialog (1996:4) 176–9.
6825. MORRISON, PAUL.	'Noble deeds and the secret singularity':
Hamlet and *Phèdre*. CanRCL (18:2/3) 1991, 263–88.
6826. NEWMAN, ERIC P.	Shakespeare's fun with a pun on *bunghole*.
ShB (9:2) 1991, 33–4.
6827. NEWSTROM, SCOTT L.	Saying 'goonight' to 'lost' ladies: an
inter-textual interpretation of allusions to *Hamlet*'s Ophelia in Cather's
A Lost Lady and Eliot's *The Waste Land*. WCPMN (39:2/3) 1995, 33–7.
6828. NISCHIK, REINGARD M.	Körpersprache im Drama: ein Beitrag
zur Semiotik des Dramas. GRM (41:3) 1991, 257–69.
6829. NORMAN, JOHN.	Horatio's moist star. ShB (12:3) 1994, 20.
6830. ORGEL, STEPHEN.	What is a character? Text (Ann Arbor) (8)
1995, 101–8.
6831. OWENS, ANNE.	The theatre as a mirror held to the theatre:
Everyman Out of His Humour and *Hamlet*. Q/W/E/R/T/Y (6) 1996,
73–86.
6832. PACCAUD-HUGUET, JOSIANE.	*Under Western Eyes* and *Hamlet*:
where angels fear to tread. Conradiana (28:2) 1996, 83–5. (Correction of
bibl. 1994, 4568.)
6833. PENNINGTON, MICHAEL.	*Hamlet*: a user's guide. London: Hern;
New York: Limelight, 1996. pp. 216. Rev. by R.S. in TLS, 22 Mar. 1996,
32.
6834. QUIGLEY, DANIEL.	'Double exposure': the semiotic
ramifications of Mel Gibson in Zeffirelli's *Hamlet*. *See* **6641**.
6835. RADEMACHER, JÖRG W.	Totalized (auto-)biography as frag-
mented intertextuality: Shakespeare – Sterne – Joyce. *In* (pp. 81–6) **57**.
6836. RAFFEL, BURTON.	*Hamlet* and the tradition of the novel.
ExRC (22) 1996, 31–50.

6837.   REEVES, BILL.   'Mad Max, Larry, and the Bard': *Hamlet* then, and now. PCR (6:1) 1995, 21–7.

6838.   ROBERTS, DAVID.   A new allusion in *Hamlet*? *See* **2188**.

6839.   ROSENBERG, MARVIN.   The masks of Hamlet. (Bibl. 1994, 4575.) Rev. by Frank Occhiogrosso and Cary M. Mazer in ShB (14:4) 1996, 40–1; by Michael Hattaway in YES (26) 1996, 272–3; by Dieter Mehl in Archiv (233:1) 1996, 167–72.

6840.   ROSS, DANIEL W.; HORVATH, BROOKE K.   Inaction in *Othello* and *Hamlet*. UC (11) 1991, 52–61.

6841.   SCHIFFER, JAMES.   Mnemonic cues to passion in *Hamlet*. RenP 1995, 65–79.

6842.   SERPIERI, ALESSANDRO.   Is *Hamlet Q1* a generative or a degenerate text? *See* **6195**.

6843.   SHALTZ, JUSTIN.   Three *Hamlet*s on film. *See* **6651**.

6844.   SHURGOT, MICHAEL.   'Get you a place': staging *The Mousetrap* at the Globe Theatre. *See* **6657**.

6845.   SIMMON, SCOTT.   Concerning the weary legs of Wyatt Earp: the classic Western according to Shakespeare. LitFQ (24:2) 1996, 114–27.

6846.   SMITH, PETER J.; WOOD, NIGEL (eds).   Hamlet. Buckingham; Philadelphia, PA: Open UP, 1996. pp. xii, 161. (Theory in practice.)

6847.   SOHMER, STEVE.   Certain speculations on *Hamlet*, the calendar, and Martin Luther. EMLS (2:1) 1996, 5.1–51.

6848.   STATES, BERT O.   *Hamlet* and the concept of character. (Bibl. 1995, 5603.) Rev. by Thomas Akstens in JDTC (8:2) 1994, 225–7; by Maurice Charney in ShB (14:3) 1996, 40.

6849.   TARANOW, GERDA.   The Bernhardt *Hamlet*: culture and context. *See* **6669**.

6850.   TAYLOR, NEIL; THOMPSON, ANN.   Obscenity in *Hamlet* III.ii: 'country matters'. *See* **6197**.

6851.   TEMPERA, MARIANGELA (ed.).   *Hamlet*: dal testo alla scena. *See* **6673**.

6852.   THATCHER, DAVID.   Shakespeare's *Hamlet*. Exp (54:3) 1996, 134–6.

6853.   —— Sullied flesh, sullied mind: refiguring Hamlet's 'imaginations'. SN (68:1) 1996, 29–38.

6854.   TIFFANY, GRACE.   Anti-theatricalism and revolutionary desire in *Hamlet*; or, The play without the play. UC (15) 1995, 61–74.

6855.   TODA, HITOSHI.   Igirisu bungaku to shinwa. (English literature and myths.) Osaka: Osaka Kyoiku Shuppan, 1996. pp. iv, 254.

6856.   UNKEFER, VIRGINIA A.   The playwright and actor on stage: mothers and sons in *Richard III*, *Coriolanus*, and *Hamlet*. *See* **6766**.

6857.   VANRIGH, ANNY CRUNELLE.   An account of Terry Hands' production of *Hamlet* (Théâtre Marigny, Paris, 1994). *See* **6675**.

6858.   VEST, JAMES M.   The French face of Ophelia from Belleforest to Baudelaire. (Bibl. 1992, 5130.) Rev. by Susan Baker in ShB (10:3) 1992, 45–6.

6859.   VILQUIN, JEAN-PIERRE.   Spectacle et spectaculaire dans *Hamlet*. Q/W/E/R/T/Y (6) 1996, 87–95.

6860.   WARD, PATRICIA H.   The 'witchcraft of his wits': Claudius' manipulation of the arts of rhetoric. ShB (9:3) 1991, 31–3.

6861.   WOOD, ROBERT E.   Some necessary questions of the play: a stage-centered analysis of Shakespeare's *Hamlet*. (Bibl. 1995, 5612.)

Rev. by Bradley S. Berens in ShB (14:3) 1996, 43–4; by Norman L. Lofland in ELN (34:1) 1996, 97.

6862. YIM, SUNG-KYUN. Jungeui wa sarang: *Hamlet* eui munje. (Justice and love: *Hamlet*'s problem.) ShR (28) 1996, 153–74.

6863. YOSHIOKA, FUMIO. Silence, speech, and spectacle in *Hamlet*. SStudT (31) 1993, 1–33.

6864. ZITNER, S. P. Zigzag in *Hamlet* I.v. *In* (pp. 81–8) **16**.

Henry IV

6865. BAKER, CHRISTOPHER. A Prayer Book allusion in *2 Henry IV*. NQ (43:2) 1996, 156–7.

6866. BAKER, JOHN. Found: Shakespeare's manuscript of *Henry IV*. *See* **6119**.

6867. BARROW, CRAIG. The 1993 Alabama Shakespeare Festival. *See* **6524**.

6868. FORTIER, MARK. Speculations on *2 Henry IV*: theatre historiography, the strait gate of history, and Kenneth Branagh. *See* **6578**.

6869. HARRINGTON, GARY. 'A plague of all cowards': *Macomber* and *Henry IV*. HemR (15:2) 1996, 96–103.

6870. HELMBOLD, ANITA. King of the revels or king of the rebels? Sir John Falstaff revisited. UC (16) 1996, 70–91.

6871. HODGDON, BARBARA. Henry IV, part two. (Bibl. 1995, 5619.) Rev. by Cary M. Mazer in ShB (14:4) 1996, 44–5.

6872. HOWARD, JEAN E. Forming the commonwealth: including, excluding, and criminalizing women in Heywood's *Edward IV* and Shakespeare's *Henry IV*. *In* (pp. 109–21) **89**.

6873. KRIMS, MARVIN B. Hotspur's antifeminine prejudice in Shakespeare's *1 Henry IV*. LitPs (40:1/2) 1994, 118–32.

6874. MURPHY, ANDREW. Shakespeare's Irish history. *See* **6060**.

6875. OTA, KAZUAKI. The quarto of *The Second Part of Henry IV* as a revised text. *See* **6186**.

6876. PAYNE, CRAIG. Shakespeare's *Henry IV, Part 2*. Exp (54:2) 1996, 67–70.

6877. PIGEON, RENÉE. 'A garment all of blood': Michael Pennington's Prince Hal. *See* **6636**.

6878. ROMÁN, DAVID. Shakespeare out of Portland: Gus Van Sant's *My Own Private Idaho*, homoneurotics, and boy actors. *In* (pp. 311–33) **30**.

6879. SINGLETON, BRIAN. Mnouchkine and Shakespeare: intercultural theatre practice. *See* **6659**.

6880. WILLSON, ROBERT F., JR. Recontextualizing Shakespeare on film: *My Own Private Idaho, Men of Respect, Prospero's Books*. *See* **6686**.

6881. WOMERSLEY, DAVID. Why is Falstaff fat? RES (47:185) 1996, 1–22.

6882. WOOD, NIGEL (ed.). Henry IV, Parts one and two. (Bibl. 1995, 5634.) Rev. by Edmund M. Taft in SNL (46:3) 1996, 59–60.

Henry V

6883. BARROW, CRAIG. The 1994 Alabama Shakespeare Festival. *See* **6525**.

6884. CORBIN, PETER. The 'harmless drudgery' of editing Shakespeare: the Arden Shakespeare: third series. *See* **6131**.

6885. DAY, MOIRA. Shakespeare on the Saskatchewan 1985–1990: 'the Stratford of the West' (NOT). *See* **6565**.

6886. ELIOT, SIMON.   An English history play: reading and studying *Henry V. In* (pp. 35–88) **110**.

6887. HOPKINS, LISA.   Fluellen's name. *See* **2176**.

6888. IRACE, KATHLEEN.   Reconstruction and adaptation in Q *Henry V. See* **6160**.

6889. McDONALD, MARCIA A.   The Elizabethan Poor Laws and the stage in the late 1590s. *See* **5670**.

6890. MAHON, JOHN W.   Monkey business. SNL (46:1) 1996, 18, 23.

6891. MEHL, DIETER.   Der dritte Arden Shakespeare. *See* **6177**.

6892. MERON, THEODOR.   Henry's wars and Shakespeare's laws: perspectives on the law of war in the later Middle Ages. (Bibl. 1995, 5651.) Rev. by Christopher Allmand in EHR (111:443) 1996, 964–5; by Ian Gentles in JBS (35:4) 1996, 545–6.

6893. MURPHY, ANDREW.   Shakespeare's Irish history. *See* **6060**.

6894. PUSCHMANN-NALENZ, BARBARA.   Using Shakespeare? The appropriation of *Coriolanus* and *King Henry V* in John Philip Kemble's 1789 productions. *See* **6640**.

6895. RAUCHUT, E. A.   The siege oration in Branagh's *Henry V. See* **6642**.

6896. SHEPPARD, PHILIPPA.   Shakespeare recycles again. NQ (43:2) 1996, 157.

6897. WILLIAMS, GEORGE WALTON.   Five-act structure and the choruses in *Henry V*. CEl (50) 1996, 11–17.

6898. —— The staging of Harfleur in *Henry V. See* **6683**.

6899. WILLSON, ROBERT F., JR.   War and reflection on war: the Olivier and Branagh films of *Henry V. See* **6687**.

6900. WOMERSLEY, DAVID.   Why is Falstaff fat? *See* **6881**.

Henry VI

6901. DESSEN, ALAN C.   Taming the script: *Henry VI, Shrew*, and *All's Well* in Ashland and Stratford. *See* **6571**.

6902. LEVINE, NINA.   Lawful symmetry: the politics of treason in *2 Henry VI*. RenD (25) 1994, 197–218.

6903. MAGUIRE, NANCY KLEIN.   Factionary politics: John Crowne's *Henry VI. In* (pp. 70–92) **21**.

6904. MERRIAM, THOMAS.   *Groatsworth*'s added value. *See* **5838**.

6905. MURPHY, ANDREW.   Shakespeare's Irish history. *See* **6060**.

6906. MYERS, NORMAN J.   Finding 'a heap of jewels' in 'lesser' Shakespeare: *The Wars of the Roses* and *Richard Duke of York. See* **6626**.

6907. OWENS, MARGARET E.   The many-headed monster in *Henry VI, Part II*. Criticism (38:3) 1996, 367–82.

6908. SHEPPARD, PHILIPPA.   Shakespeare recycles again. *See* **6896**.

6909. TAYLOR, GARY.   Shakespeare and others: the authorship of *Henry the Sixth, Part One. See* **2718**.

6910. WATT, R. J. C.   The siege of Orleans and the cursing of Joan: corruptions in the text of *Henry VI Part I. See* **6200**.

Henry VIII

6911. BATTENHOUSE, ROY.   Shakespeare's *Henry VIII* reconsidered in the light of Boethian and biblical commonplaces. *In* (pp. 51–82) **111**.

6912. HART, JONATHAN.   *Henry VIII*: the play as history and anti-history. Aevum (65:3) 1991, 561–70.

6913. NOLL, MARK A. The Reformation and Shakespeare: focus on *Henry VIII. In* (pp. 83–101) **111**.

6914. READINGS, BILL. When did the Renaissance begin? The Henrician court and the Shakespearean stage. *In* (pp. 283–302) **101**.

Julius Caesar
6915. BLOOM, HAROLD (ed.). William Shakespeare's *Julius Caesar*. New York: Chelsea House, 1996. pp. 72. (Bloom's notes.)

6916. BUHLER, STEPHEN M. No spectre, no sceptre: the agon of materialist thought in Shakespeare's *Julius Caesar*. ELR (26:2) 1996, 313–32.

6917. CHARNEY, MAURICE; VAUGHAN, STUART (eds). Julius Caesar. *See* **6129**.

6918. COURTNEY, RICHARD. Shakespeare's world of death: the early tragedies, *Romeo and Juliet, Julius Caesar, Hamlet. See* **6799**.

6919. GIRARD, RENÉ. Collective violence and sacrifice in Shakespeare's *Julius Caesar*. Salmagundi (88/89) 1990/91, 399–419.

6920. MILES, GEOFFREY. Shakespeare and the constant Romans. *See* **6719**.

6921. TRICOMI, ALBERT H. Shakespeare, Chapman, and the Julius Caesar play in Renaissance Humanist drama. *In* (pp. 395–412) **98**.

6922. VISSER, NICHOLAS. Plebeian politics in *Julius Caesar*. SSA (7) 1994, 22–31.

6923. WEIER, GARY M. Perspectivism and form in drama: a Burkean analysis of *Julius Caesar*. ComQ (44:2) 1996, 246–59.

6924. WEINIG, EDELBERT. Die kontextuelle Funktion biblischer Anspielungen in Shakespeares *Julius Caesar*. SJ (132) 1996, 130–7.

6925. WILSON, RICHARD. A brute part: *Julius Caesar* and the rites of violence. CEl (50) 1996, 19–32.

King John
6926. CANDIDO, JOSEPH (ed.). King John. London; Atlantic Highlands, NJ: Athlone Press, 1996. pp. xvi, 415. (Shakespeare, the critical tradition.)

6927. COUSIN, GERALDINE. King John. *See* **6561**.

6928. HEBERLE, MARK A. 'Innocent prate': *King John* and Shakespeare's children. *In* (pp. 28–43) **48**.

6929. HOBSON, CHRISTOPHER Z. Bastard speech: the rhetoric of 'commodity' in *King John. See* **2398**.

6930. MCKERNAN, LUKE. Beerbohm Tree's *King John* rediscovered: the first Shakespeare film, September 1899. *See* **6613**.

6931. MARTELLA, GIUSEPPE. Il dialogo nel dramma storico: *King John* di W. Shakespeare. Textus (1:2) 1988, 197–211.

King Lear
6932. ALFAR, CRISTINA LEÓN. King Lear's 'immoral' daughters and the politics of kingship. Exemplaria (8:2) 1996, 375–400.

6933. BAIN, ELSPETH; MORRIS, JONATHAN; SMITH, ROB (eds). King Lear. *See* **6118**.

6934. BARROW, CRAIG. The 1992 Alabama Shakespeare Festival. *See* **6523**.

6935. BLOOM, HAROLD (ed.). William Shakespeare's *King Lear*. Broomall, PA: Chelsea House, 1995. pp. 86. (Bloom's notes.)

6936. BROWN, JOHN RUSSELL (ed.).   King Lear. *See* **6126**.

6937. BUSHNELL, REBECCA W. (ed.).   *King Lear* and *Macbeth*, 1674–1995: an annotated bibliography of Shakespeare studies. Binghamton, NY: Medieval & Renaissance Texts & Studies, 1996. pp. x, 105. (Pegasus Shakespeare bibliographies.)

6938. CALLAGHAN, DYMPNA.   Woman and gender in Renaissance tragedy: a study of *King Lear, Othello, The Duchess of Malfi* and *The White Devil*. (Bibl. 1993, 4400.) Rev. by Cynthia Marshall in Shakespeare Yearbook (2) 1991, 269–71.

6939. CANZANO, MARIA ANTONIETTA.   Tutti pazzi in *Re Lear*. Annali anglistica (36:1–3) 1993, 31–60.

6940. CLARK, S. H.   'Ancestral Englishness' in *King Lear*. SStudT (31) 1993, 35–63.

6941. COUPE, LAURENCE.   *King Lear*: Christian fairy tale. ERev (6:4) 1996, 2–6.

6942. COWAN, S. A.   Eatbugs, Edgar, and Odin: the influence of Shakespeare and Northern mythology on Williams's *Tailchaser's Song*. Extrapolation (37:1) 1996, 5–21.

6943. DELL'AVERSANO, CARMEN.   Tradizione e innovazione metodologica nella costituzione de testo del *King Lear*. *See* **6136**.

6944. DINIA, THAÏS FLORES NOGUEIRA.   *King Lear*'s filmic adaptation: a chaos? *See* **6572**.

6945. DORFMAN, TONI.   The fateful crossroads: 'fork' clusters in Shakespeare's plays. *See* **1952**.

6946. FLEISSNER, ROBERT F.   Lear's 'learnèd Theban' and 'justice(r)': a resonance of Tiresias. Shakespeare Yearbook (2) 1991, 182–6.

6947. HALIO, JAY L.   Five days, three *King Lear*s. *See* **6589**.

6948. —— The promised endings of *King Lear*. In (pp. 235–42) **131**.

6949. —— (ed.).   Critical essays on Shakespeare's *King Lear*. New York: G. K. Hall; London: Prentice Hall, 1996. pp. xi, 236. (Critical essays on British literature.)

6950. HALLETT, CHARLES A.   Staging Shakespeare's dramatic questions: intensifying techniques in Act Two of *King Lear*. ShB (9:3) 1991, 5–12.

6951. HAWKES, TERENCE.   William Shakespeare: *King Lear*. (Bibl. 1995, 5695.) Rev. by Paul A. Cantor in In-between (5:2) 1996, 187–93.

6952. HEROLD, NIELS.   Madness and the medium in *King Lear*. Shakespeare Yearbook (2) 1991, 170–81.

6953. HOLDERNESS, GRAHAM; CARTER, NAOMI.   The king's two bodies: text and genre in *King Lear*. *See* **6156**.

6954. HOPKINS, LISA.   *King Lear* and the numbers game. SSA (7) 1994, 32–9.

6955. —— 'Lear, Lear, Lear!': Marlowe, Shakespeare, and the third. *See* **5883**.

6956. IMPASTATO, DAVID.   Godard's *Lear* ... why is it so bad? *See* **6596**.

6957. KANG, SEOK-CHOO.   *King Lear* e natanan isangjueui. (Idealism in *King Lear*.) ShR (28) 1996, 1–25.

6958. KEGISHIAN, HARRY.   Performing violence in *King Lear*: Edgar's encounters in 4.6 and 5.3. *See* **6601**.

6959. MARKELS, JULIAN.   Melville and the politics of identity: from *King Lear* to *Moby-Dick*. (Bibl. 1993, 4413.) Rev. by Theodore R. Hovet in AmS (36:1) 1995, 192–3; by Linck C. Johnson in AL (68:1) 1996, 243–4; by Eric Fretz in SAF (24:1) 1996, 125–6.

6960. MASSAI, SONIA. Tate's critical 'editing' of his source-text(s) for *The History of King Lear*. See **6176**.

6961. MEYER, ANN R. Shakespeare's art and the texts of *King Lear*. See **6179**.

6962. MILWARD, PETER. The biblical language of *King Lear*. See **2677**.

6963. OGDEN, JAMES. A misattributed speech in *King Lear*? SNL (44:3) 1994, 45, 54.

6964. ORGEL, STEPHEN. What is a character? See **6830**.

6965. ORMEROD, DAVID. 'Ripe' and 'rot': a proverb in *As You Like It* and *King Lear*. See **3341**.

6966. PARKER, R. B. *King Lear*, Sir Donald Wolfit, and *The Dresser*. In (pp. 99–109) **16**.

6967. PENDLETON, THOMAS A. Shakespeare in the golden age of television: Orson Welles' *King Lear*. See **6635**.

6968. REID, ROBERT L. Lear's three shamings: Shakespearean psychology and tragic form. RenP 1996, 93–112.

6969. ROARK, CHRIS. Hurston's Shakespeare: 'something like a king, bigger and better!' CLAJ (40:2) 1996, 197–213.

6970. RUDANKO, JUHANI. Pleading with an unreasonable king: on the Kent and Pauline episodes in Shakespeare. See **2287**.

6971. SAUNDERS, J. G. 'Apparent perversities': text and subtext in the construction of the role of Edgar in Brook's film of *King Lear*. See **6646**.

6972. SPINRAD, PHOEBE S. Dramatic 'pity' and the death of Lear. Ren (43:4) 1991, 231–40.

6973. STEVENSON, MELANIE A. Prospero back home in Milan: Bond's *Lear* as paradigm for post-imperial Britain. Essays in Theatre (15:1) 1996, 23–34.

6974. VAN PELT, TAMISE. Entitled to be king: the subversion of the subject in *King Lear*. LitPs (42:1/2) 1996, 100–12.

6975. VIGUERS, SUSAN. Costuming as interpretation: the Elliott/ Olivier and the Brook/Scofield *King Lear*. See **6677**.

6976. WASSON, JOHN. Cordelia's kind nursery. UC (11) 1991, 82–91.

6977. WELCH, DENNIS M. *Christabel, King Lear*, and the Cinderella folktale. PLL (32:3) 1996, 291–314.

6978. WORTHAM, CHRISTOPHER. Shakespeare, James I and the Matter of Britain. See **6728**.

6979. WRIGHT, NANCY GLASS. Banqueting as symbol in *King Lear* and *Macbeth*. TPB (28) 1991, 22–30.

6980. YORKE, FELICITY. Constitutional crisis and ideological conflict in *King Lear*. Textus (1:2) 1988, 233–66.

A Lover's Complaint

6981. DODSWORTH, MARTIN (ed.). The sonnets and *A Lover's Complaint*. See **6139**.

Love's Labour's Lost

6982. ALVIS, JOHN. Derivative loves are labor lost. Ren (48:4) 1996, 247–58.

6983. CARROLL, D. ALLEN. The 'charge-house on the top of the mountain' (*Love's Labour's Lost* V.i.72). ELN (33:3) 1996, 8–12.

6984. FLEISSNER, ROBERT F.   Love's lost in *Othello*: what 'the base Indian' is founded on. EngS (76:2) 1995, 140–2.

6985. HEHL, URSULA.   Elements of narcissistic personality disorders in *Love's Labour's Lost*. LitPs (40:1/2) 1994, 24–47.

6986. LONDRE, FELICIA.   Elizabethan views of the 'Other': French, Spanish, and Russians in *Love's Labor's Lost*. ER (3:1) 1995, 3–20.

Macbeth

6987. AGBAW, S. EKEMA.   Africanizing *Macbeth*: 'down-fall'n birth-dom'. *See* **6517**.

6988. BALDO, JONATHAN.   The politics of aloofness in *Macbeth*. ELR (26:3) 1996, 531–60.

6989. BEARD, MARGARET.   *Macbeth*. *See* **6530**.

6990. BLAIR, DAVID.   What happens in *Macbeth* Act I Scene vii? RES (47:188) 1996, 534–9.

6991. BLITS, JAN H.   The insufficiency of virtue: *Macbeth* and the natural order. Lanham, MD: Rowman & Littlefield, 1996. pp. ix, 229.

6992. BRAUNMULLER, A. R. (ed.).   Macbeth. Commentary by David S. Rodes; produced by Michael E. Cohen. *See* **6125**.

6993. BUSHNELL, REBECCA.   Tyranny and effeminacy in early modern England. *In* (pp. 339–54) **98**.

6994. BUSHNELL, REBECCA W. (ed.).   *King Lear* and *Macbeth*, 1674–1995: an annotated bibliography of Shakespeare studies. *See* **6937**.

6995. CALLAGHAN, DYMPNA.   Wicked women in *Macbeth*: a study of power, ideology, and the production of motherhood. *In* (pp. 355–69) **98**.

6996. COURSEN, H. R.   Winter of the Scottish play. *See* **6560**.

6997. FOAKES, R. A. (ed.).   Macbeth. With a theatre commentary by John Russell Brown. *See* **6142**.

6998. GILBERT, ANTHONY J.   Shakespearean self-talk, the Gricean maxims and the unconscious. *See* **6810**.

6999. HOENSELAARS, A. J.   *Macbeth* in the Netherlands. *See* **6595**.

7000. KINNEY, ARTHUR F.   Re-historicising *Macbeth*. *In* (pp. 93–103) **107**.

7001. KLIMAN, BERNICE W.   A *Macbeth* for our time. *See* **6608**.

7002. —— Thanes in the folio *Macbeth*. ShB (9:1) 1991, 5–8.

7003. LEE, HWAHN-TAE.   Munhak e natanan jaah silhyun eui muje: *Macbeth* eui kyungwu. (The problem of self-realization in literature: the case of *Macbeth*.) JELL (42:1) 1996, 159–77.

7004. OMBERG, MARGARET.   Macbeth's barren sceptre. SN (68:1) 1996, 39–47.

7005. REYNOLDS, BRYAN.   The terrorism of Macbeth and Charles Manson: reading cultural construction in Polanski and Shakespeare. *See* **6643**.

7006. SCHOENBAUM, SAMUEL (ed.).   *Macbeth*: critical essays. (Bibl. 1991, 5110.) Rev. by Irene G. Dash in ShB (10:4) 1992, 43–4.

7007. SWANDER, HOMER.   No exit for a dead body: what to do with a scripted corpse? JDTC (5:2) 1991, 139–52.

7008. TANNER, JO A.   Classical Black theatre: the Federal Theatre's all-Black *Voodoo Macbeth*. JADT (7:1) 1995, 50–63.

7009. TEMPERA, MARIANGELA.   The art of lying in *Macbeth*. Textus (6) 1993, 57–76.

7010. TURNER, JOHN.   Macbeth. (Bibl. 1992, 5257.) Rev. by Robin Hamilton in CritS (6:2) 1994, 279–81.

7011. WILLS, GARRY.   Witches and Jesuits: Shakespeare's *Macbeth*. (Bibl. 1995, 5755.) Rev. by Barry Edelstein in BkW, 30 Oct. 1994, 2; by Ed Peaco in AR (54:1) 1996, 105; by Michael T. Siconolfi in EMLS (2:3) 1996, 11.1–13; by Thomas Akstens in NETJ (7) 1996, 123–4.

7012. WILLSON, ROBERT F., JR.   Recontextualizing Shakespeare on film: *My Own Private Idaho, Men of Respect, Prospero's Books*. *See* **6686**.

7013. WORTHAM, CHRISTOPHER.   Shakespeare, James I and the Matter of Britain. *See* **6728**.

7014. WRIGHT, NANCY GLASS.   Banqueting as symbol in *King Lear* and *Macbeth*. *See* **6979**.

Measure for Measure
7015. BENNETT, ROBERT.   Redemption and damnation: *Measure for Measure* and *Othello* as contrasting paired visions. SRASP (19) 1996, 13–20.

7016. BROWN, CAROLYN E.   Duke Vincentio of *Measure for Measure* and King James I of England: 'the poorest princes in Christendom'. CLIO (26:1) 1996, 51–78.

7017. DODD, WILLIAM.   Power and performance: *Measure for Measure* in the public theater of 1604–1605. SStud (24) 1996, 211–40.

7018. FRIEDMAN, MICHAEL D.   'Wishing a more strict restraint': feminist performance and the silence of Isabella. SRASP (19) 1996, 1–11.

7019. HALLETT, CHARLES.   Is there 'charity in sin'? Sexual harassment in *Measure for Measure*. ShB (11:4) 1993, 23–6.

7020. LECHTER-SIEGEL, AMY.   Isabella's silence: the consolidation of power in *Measure for Measure*. *In* (pp. 471–80) **98**.

7021. McFEELY, MAUREEN CONNOLLY.   'This day my sister should the cloister enter': the convent as refuge in *Measure for Measure*. *In* (pp. 200–16) **116**.

7022. POWERS, ALAN.   *Measure for Measure* and law reform in 1604. UC (15) 1995, 35–47.

7023. THATCHER, DAVID.   The uncomfortable 'Friar' in *Measure for Measure*. SJ (132) 1996, 114–27.

7024. WIDMAYER, MARTHA.   Mistress Overdone's house. *In* (pp. 181–99) **116**.

The Merchant of Venice
7025. ANON. (comp.).   Do you sympathise with Shylock? ERev (6:4) 1996, 24–7. (Group discussion.)

7026. BAKER, ELLIOTT.   The Queen's hand in *The Merchant of Venice*. *See* **5819**.

7027. BARROW, CRAIG.   A tale of two Shakespeare Festivals: Stratford's *The Merchant of Venice* and Alabama Shakespeare Festival's *The Winter's Tale*. *See* **6526**.

7028. BREITENSTEIN, ROLF.   Warum schweigt Bassanio? Eine Kommunikationslücke im *Kaufmann von Venedig*. SJ (132) 1996, 128–9.

7029. BULMAN, JAMES C.   On being unfaithful to Shakespeare: Miller, Marowitz, and Wesker. *See* **6547**.

7030. FLACHMANN, MICHAEL.   'Swear by your double self': Bassanio's impersonation of Morocco and Aragon in the 1992 Utah Shakespeare Festival. *See* **6577**.

7031. GROSS, JOHN.   Shylock: a legend and its legacy. (Bibl. 1995, 5774.) Rev. by Robert M. Adams in ASch (62:4) 1993, 629–31; by Hans

Otto Horch in Aschkenas (6:1) 1996, 228–9; by Brian Boyd in BkW, 11 Apr. 1996, 1, 14.

7032. HASSEL, R. CHRIS, JR.   Which is the Christian here, and which the Jew? Christian patterns in *The Merchant of Venice. In* (pp. 103–19) **111**.

7033. KACHUCK, RHODA S.   Yiddish journals and Shylock. SNL (46:3) 1996, 61, 72.

7034. LANDIS, JOAN HUTTON.   'By two-headed Janus': double discourse in *The Merchant of Venice.* UC (16) 1996, 13–30.

7035. MCLEAN, SUSAN.   Prodigal sons and daughters: transgression and forgiveness in *The Merchant of Venice.* PLL (32:1) 1996, 45–62.

7036. PICKER, JOHN M.   Shakespeare divided: revision and transformation in Marowitz's *Variations on the 'Merchant of Venice'* and Wesker's *Shylock.* JTD (2) 1996, 75–91.

7037. ROSENHEIM, JUDITH.   Allegorical commentary in *The Merchant of Venice.* SStud (24) 1996, 156–210.

7038. SCHWANITZ, DIETRICH.   Shylock: von Shakespeare bis zum Nürnberger Prozess. Hamburg: Krämer, 1989. pp. 293. Rev. by Richard Chaim Schneider in Aschkenas (1) 1991, 244–5.

7039. TEMPERA, MARIANGELA (ed.).   *The Merchant of Venice*: dal testo alla scena. *See* **6674**.

7040. WHEELER, THOMAS (ed.).   *The Merchant of Venice*: critical essays. (Bibl. 1995, 5786.) Rev. by Margaret Loftus Ranald in ShB (11:4) 1993, 42–3.

The Merry Wives of Windsor

7041. BOOTH, ROY J.   Meddling with awl: reading Dekker's *The Shoemaker's Holiday* (with a note on *The Merry Wives of Windsor*.) Eng (41:171) 1992, 193–211.

7042. MOSS, ROGER.   Falstaff as a woman. JDTC (10:1) 1995, 31–41.

7043. ROSS, CHARLES STANLEY.   Shakespeare's *Merry Wives* and the law of fraudulent conveyance. RenD (25) 1994, 145–69.

7044. VERE, CHARLES.   Sir Philip Sidney satirized in *Merry Wives of Windsor. See* **5949**.

A Midsummer Night's Dream

7045. ANDREAS, JAMES R.   Remythologizing the Knight's Tale: *A Midsummer Night's Dream* and *The Two Noble Kinsmen. See* **5351**.

7046. BARROW, CRAIG.   The 1993 Alabama Shakespeare Festival. *See* **6524**.

7047. BARUZZO, BARBARA.   Le *Metamorfosi* di Ovidio e *A Midsummer Night's Dream* di W. Shakespeare: il linguaggio come gioco di forme. Textus (6) 1993, 77–103.

7048. BAXTER, JOHN.   Growing to a point: mimesis in *A Midsummer Night's Dream.* ESCan (22:1) 1996, 17–33.

7049. BLYTHE, DAVID-EVERETT.   Shakespeare's *A Midsummer Night's Dream.* Exp (55:1) 1996, 8–10.

7050. BOEHRER, BRUCE THOMAS.   Bestial buggery in *A Midsummer Night's Dream. In* (pp. 123–50) **90**.

7051. BROWN, JOHN RUSSELL (ed.).   A midsummer night's dream. With theatre commentary by John Hirsch and Leslie Thomson. *See* **6127**.

7052. DUTTON, RICHARD (ed.).   A midsummer night's dream. Basingstoke: Macmillan, 1996. pp. ix, 270. (New casebooks.)

7053. ELLIS, SYLVIA C.   Seeing straight and seeing too much in *A Midsummer Night's Dream*. ERev (6:2) 1995, 2–5.

7054. FRIEDMAN, DONALD.   Bottom, Burbage, and the birth of tragedy. *In* (pp. 315–26) **98**.

7055. GRIFFIN, C. W.   Hippolyta's dress and undress: subtext and scopophilia in *A Midsummer Night's Dream*. *See* **6585**.

7056. GRIFFITHS, TREVOR R. (ed.).   A midsummer night's dream. *See* **6586**.

7057. HALLIWELL, MICHAEL.   *The Enchanted Wood*: Benjamin Britten's version of *A Midsummer Night's Dream*. SSA (7) 1994, 40–50.

7058. HUNT, MAURICE.   *The Countess of Pembroke's Arcadia*, Shakespeare's *A Midsummer Night's Dream*, and the School of the Night: an intertextual nexus. *See* **5982**.

7059. KEMPER, MARTHA.   Casting imagination into form: Alvina Krause and *A Midsummer Night's Dream*. *See* **6602**.

7060. KLEIN, HOLGER.   Ein *Sommernachtstraum*. *See* **6605**.

7061. MCRAE, JOHN.   Will it please you to hear a Bergomask dance? The mechanicals' dance in *A Midsummer Night's Dream*. Textus (1:2) 1988, 183–96.

7062. REID, ROBERT L.   The fairy queen: Gloriana or Titania? *See* **6067**.

7063. STAVIG, MARK.   The forms of things unknown: Renaissance metaphor in *Romeo and Juliet* and *A Midsummer Night's Dream*. (Bibl. 1995, 5807.) Rev. by Frances K. Barasch in ShB (14:4) 1996, 45.

7064. TAYLOR, MARK.   Female desire in *A Midsummer Night's Dream*. Shakespeare Yearbook (2) 1991, 115–31.

7065. TREADWELL, T. O. (ed.).   A midsommer nights dreame: as it hath been sundry times publikely acted, by the right honourable, the Lord Chamberlaine his servants. *See* **6198**.

Much Ado About Nothing

7066. BATTENHOUSE, ROY.   Toward understanding patriarchy in *Much Ado*. Shakespeare Yearbook (2) 1991, 193–200.

7067. EDGERTON, ELLEN.   'Your answer, sir, is cinematical': Kenneth Branagh's *Much Ado About Nothing*. *See* **6574**.

7068. GANDHI, LEELA.   Virtuous monuments: the monumentalizing of women in Shakespeare. *See* **6771**.

7069. GRAY, FRANCES.   Shakespeare, shrews and screwballs. ERev (5:3) 1995, 2–5.

7070. LANE, ROBERT.   'Foremost in report': social identity and masculinity in *Much Ado About Nothing*. UC (16) 1996, 31–47.

7071. PARTEE, MORRISS HENRY.   The comic equilibrium of *Much Ado About Nothing*. UC (12) 1992, 60–73.

7072. WELLER, PHILIP.   'Kill Claudio': a laugh almost killed by the critics. JDTC (11:1) 1996, 101–10.

7073. WRIGHT, LAURENCE.   *Much Ado About Nothing*: Linda Louise Swain's production for the Port Elizabeth Shakespearean Festival. *See* **6690**.

Othello

7074. ABEL, DOUGLAS.   Venom in his blood: Edmund Kean's *Othello* contests. *See* **6516**.

7075. ALTIERI, CHARLES.   The values of articulation: aesthetics after the aesthetic ideology. *In* (pp. 66–89) **6**.

7076. ANDREWS, JOHN F. (ed.).   Othello. Foreword by James Earl Jones. *See* **6116**.

7077. BARROW, CRAIG.   The 1994 Alabama Shakespeare Festival. *See* **6525**.

7078. BARTELS, EMILY C.   Strategies of submission: Desdemona, the Duchess, and the assertion of desire. SELit (36:2) 1996, 417–33.

7079. BENNETT, ROBERT.   Redemption and damnation: *Measure for Measure* and *Othello* as contrasting paired visions. *See* **7015**.

7080. BLOOM, HAROLD (ed.).   William Shakespeare's *Othello*. New York: Chelsea House, 1996. pp. 88. (Bloom's notes.)

7081. BOERTH, ROBERT.   The Mediterranean and the Mediterranean world on the stage of Marlowe and Shakespeare. *See* **5868**.

7082. BRUCHER, RICHARD.   O'Neill, Othello and Robeson. *See* **6544**.

7083. BURNS, EDWARD.   The sharp spectator. *In* (pp. 193–203) **53**.

7084. CALDERWOOD, JAMES L.   The properties of *Othello*. (Bibl. 1993, 4516.) Rev. by Imtiaz Habib in Shakespeare Yearbook (2) 1991, 241–4.

7085. COLLINS, KRIS.   White-washing the Black-a-Moor: *Othello*, Negro minstrelsy and parodies of Blackness. JAC (19:3) 1996, 87–101.

7086. DAY, ROGER.   Reading *Othello*. *In* (pp. 89–130) **110**.

7087. DIEHL, HUSTON.   Bewhored images and imagined whores: iconophobia and gynophobia in Stuart love tragedies. ELR (26:1) 1996, 111–37.

7088. DOLOFF, STEVEN.   Othello's 'ocular proof' and the skepticism of Sextus Empiricus. ShB (12:4) 1994, 40.

7089. DRAUDT, MANFRED.   Zum Lokalkolorit in den Shakespeare-Parodien von Perinet, Kringsteiner und Meisl. *See* **5777**.

7090. FERGUSON, MARGARET.   News from the New World: miscegenous romance in Aphra Behn's *Oroonoko* and *The Widow Ranter*. *In* (pp. 151–89) **90**.

7091. FLEISSNER, ROBERT F.   Love's lost in *Othello*: what 'the base Indian' is founded on. *See* **6984**.

7092. GANDHI, LEELA.   Virtuous monuments: the monumentalizing of women in Shakespeare. *See* **6771**.

7093. GEORGE, DAVID.   Night, hell, and epilepsy in *Othello*. BJJ (3) 1996, 75–86.

7094. GILBERT, ANTHONY J.   Shakespearean self-talk, the Gricean maxims and the unconscious. *See* **6810**.

7095. GREEN, DOUGLAS E.   Staging the evidence: Shakespeare's theatrical revengers. *See* **6811**.

7096. HIDALGO, PILAR.   The New Historicism and its female discontents. *In* (pp. 131–48) **38**.

7097. HONIGMANN, E. A. J.   Social questioning in Elizabethan and Jacobean plays, with special reference to *Othello*. *In* (pp. 3–11) **53**.

7098. —— The texts of *Othello* and Shakespearian revision. *See* **6158**.

7099. HUSSEY, STANLEY.   Persuasion in *Othello*. *In* (pp. 127–43) **11**.

7100. IMPASTATO, DAVID.   Orson Welles' *Othello* and the Welles–Smith restoration: definitive version? *See* **6597**.

7101. LIM, WALTER S. H.   Representing the other: *Othello*, colonialism, discourse. UC (13) 1993, 57–78.

7102. MANZANAS CALVO, ANA MARÍA.   The making and unmaking of a colonial subject: Othello. Misc (17) 1996, 189–205.

7103. MOORE, PETER R.   Shakespeare's Iago and Santiago Matamoros. *See* **2179**.

7104. OTTEN, CHARLOTTE F.   What's wrong with his feet? SNL (46:4) 1996, 87–8.

7105. ROSS, DANIEL W.; HORVATH, BROOKE K.   Inaction in *Othello* and *Hamlet*. *See* **6840**.

7106. RULON-MILLER, NINA.   *Othello*'s Bianca: climbing out of the bed of patriarchy. UC (15) 1995, 99–114.

7107. SHURGOT, MICHAEL W.   Othello's jealousy and the 'gate of Hell'. UC (12) 1992, 96–104.

7108. SMITH, EMMA.   Staging race: *Othello* then and now. *See* **6661**.

7109. VAUGHAN, VIRGINIA MASON.   *Othello*: a contextual history. (Bibl. 1995, 5837.) Rev. by Helga Quadflieg in SJ (132) 1996, 251–5.

7110. WATTERSON, WILLIAM COLLINS.   'O monstrous world': Shakespeare's beast with two backs. UC (13) 1993, 79–93.

7111. WIDMAYER, MARTHA.   Brabantio and Othello. EngS (77:2) 1996, 113–26.

7112. WILSON, ANDREW.   Bidding goodbye to the plumed troop and the big wars: the presence of *Othello* in *A Farewell to Arms*. HemR (15:2) 1996, 52–66.

7113. WRIGHT, LAURENCE.   *Othello*. *See* **6691**.

Pericles

7114. BARRETT, DEBBIE L.   *Pericles*, social redemption, and the iconography of *Veritas temporis filia*. *See* **178**.

7115. HANNA, SARA.   Christian vision and iconography in *Pericles*. UC (11) 1991, 92–116.

7116. JACKSON, MACD. P.   Rhyming in *Pericles*: more evidence of dual authorship. *See* **6162**.

7117. KIM, HAN.   Endless story, *Pericles*: words and open ending. ShR (29) 1996, 71–104. (Text in Korean.)

7118. PRENDERGAST, MARIA TERESA MICAELA.   Engendering *Pericles*. LitPs (42:4) 1996, 53–75.

7119. RUPP, KATRIN.   'Few love to hear the sins they love to act': father–daughter incest in three versions of *Apollonius of Tyre*. *See* **4657**.

7120. SAMPSON, GRANT.   Comedy as epic action: structural variants in *Pericles*, *Plain-Dealer*, and *Picnic*. TexPres (13) 1992, 53–7.

7121. SIMONDS, PEGGY MUÑOZ.   The iconography of transformed fish in Shakespeare's *Pericles*: a study of the rusty armor *topos* in the English Renaissance. *In* (pp. 121–61) **111**.

7122. SPRADLEY, DANA LLOYD.   *Pericles* and the Jacobean family romance of union. Assays (7) 1992, 87–118.

The Phoenix and the Turtle

7123. FLEISSNER, R. F.   *The Phoenix* re-viewed: name-play, wordplay, and Shakespearean authorship authenticated. UC (12) 1992, 141–5.

7124. McCULLY, ROBERT S.   *The Phoenix and the Turtle*: a Jungian interpretation. Shakespeare Yearbook (2) 1991, 187–92.

The Rape of Lucrece

7125. CAMINO, MERCEDES MAROTO.   'The stage am I?': raping Lucrece in early modern England. Lewiston, NY; Lampeter:

Mellen Press, 1995. pp. 222. (Salzburg Univ. studies: Elizabethan and Renaissance studies, 120.)

7126. FEITELBERG, DOREEN. The theme of love and wooing and the consequences of seduction in Shakespeare's poems *Venus and Adonis* and *The Rape of Lucrece*. SSA (7) 1994, 51–60.

7127. GANDHI, LEELA. Virtuous monuments: the monumentalizing of women in Shakespeare. *See* **6771**.

7128. PLANT, SARAH. Shakespeare's Lucrece as chaste bee. CEl (49) 1996, 51–7.

7129. SCHOLZ, SUSANNE. Textualizing the body politic: national identity and the female body in *The Rape of Lucrece*. SJ (132) 1996, 103–13.

7130. WASHINGTON, EDWARD T. Vanishing villains: the role of Tarquin in Shakespeare's *Lucrece*. UC (14) 1994, 126–38.

Richard II

7131. BARROW, CRAIG. The 1992 Alabama Shakespeare Festival. *See* **6523**.

7132. CORDNER, MICHAEL. Annotation and performance in Shakespeare. *See* **6132**.

7133. GRAYBILL, MARK S. 'Give me the glass, and therein will I read': narcissism and metadrama in *Richard II*. SRASP (19) 1996, 21–8.

7134. HAN, SANG-OK. *Richard II* eui siljonjeok sarlm chugu. (The search for an existential life in *Richard II*.) ShR (29) 1996, 285–321.

7135. KLEIN, HOLGER. Shakespeares *Richard II*: von Schein und Wirklichkeit der Macht. Spectakel, July/Aug. 1996, 58–60.

7136. MOWAT, BARBARA A.; WERSTEIN, PAUL (eds). The tragedy of Richard II. *See* **6181**.

7137. MUNOZ, MARIE-CHRISTINE. Shakespeare, Avignon, Vilar. *See* **6625**.

7138. MURPHY, ANDREW. Shakespeare's Irish history. *See* **6060**.

7139. SEVERI, RITA. Shakespearean caterpillars (*Richard II*, III, vv. 164–166). *See* **2468**.

7140. SHAW, CATHERINE M. Edwin Booth's *Richard II* and the divided nation. *In* (pp. 144–63) **118**.

7141. SHEWRING, MARGARET. King Richard II. *See* **6655**.

7142. SINGLETON, BRIAN. Mnouchkine and Shakespeare: intercultural theatre practice. *See* **6659**.

7143. TIPTON, ALZADA J. *Richard II* and theories of the subaltern magistrate. UC (16) 1996, 48–69.

Richard III

7144. BUSHNELL, REBECCA. Tyranny and effeminacy in early modern England. *In* (pp. 339–54) **98**.

7145. DAVISON, PETER (ed.). The first quarto of *King Richard III*. *See* **6135**.

7146. DERRY, STEPHEN. A horse for Richard III. NQ (43:2) 1996, 150–2.

7147. DILWORTH, THOMAS. Liturgical echoes: David Jones on Shakespeare's *Richard III*, V, iii. ELN (33:3) 1996, 6–8.

7148. LAROCCO, STEVE. Contentious intimations: John Donne, *Richard III*, and the transgressive structures of seduction. Exemplaria (7:1) 1995, 237–67.

7149. LECOURAS, PETER. A note on egomania and sound in *Richard III*. ShB (14:1) 1996, 44.

7150. LEE, B. S. Queen Margaret's curse on Richard of Gloucester. SSA (7) 1994, 15–21.

7151. LEVIN, HARRY. Two tents on Bosworth Field: *Richard III*, V, iii, iv, v. CanRCL (18:2/3) 1991, 199–216.

7152. MYERS, NORMAN J. Finding 'a heap of jewels' in 'lesser' Shakespeare: *The Wars of the Roses* and *Richard Duke of York*. *See* **6626**.

7153. ORR, MARY. Plotting Shakespeare: the undercover structures of historical drama in *Le Palace* by Claude Simon. Shakespeare Yearbook (5) 1994, 169–80.

7154. POLLARD, DAVID. Richard in the 'amorous looking glass'. UC (13) 1993, 47–56.

7155. SANDERS, ÈVE RACHELE. Subtle shining secrecies: writing and male identity in *Richard III*. Assays (9) 1996, 119–51.

7156. TROTTER, JACK E. 'Was ever woman in this humour won?': love and loathing in Shakespeare's *Richard III*. UC (13) 1993, 33–46.

7157. UNKEFER, VIRGINIA A. The playwright and actor on stage: mothers and sons in *Richard III*, *Coriolanus*, and *Hamlet*. *See* **6766**.

7158. WEIMANN, ROBERT. Performance-game and representation in *Richard III*. *In* (pp. 66–85) **118**.

Romeo and Juliet

7159. ANDREWS, MICHAEL CAMERON. 'Cock-a-hoop'. UC (12) 1992, 91–5.

7160. BÖSCHENBRÖKER, RIKA. Repräsentationen der Liebe in *Romeo and Juliet*: das Epithalamium. SJ (132) 1996, 44–57.

7161. BROWN, CAROLYN E. Juliet's taming of Romeo. SELit (36:2) 1996, 333–55.

7162. CAREY, LEO. New Shakespearian influence in Milton. NQ (43:3) 1996, 268–9.

7163. COURTNEY, RICHARD. Shakespeare's world of death: the early tragedies, *Romeo and Juliet*, *Julius Caesar*, *Hamlet*. *See* **6799**.

7164. CRUNELLE-VANRIGH, ANNY. 'O trespass sweetly urged': the sex of space in *Romeo and Juliet*. CEl (49) 1996, 39–49.

7165. DAY, MOIRA. Shakespeare on the Saskatchewan 1985–1990: 'the Stratford of the West' (NOT). *See* **6565**.

7166. FORSE, JAMES. *Arden of Feversham* and *Romeo and Juliet*: two Elizabethan experiments in the genre of 'comedy-suspense'. *See* **5636**.

7167. FRANSON, J. KARL. 'Too soon marr'd': Juliet's age as symbol in *Romeo and Juliet*. PLL (32:3) 1996, 244–62.

7168. GOLDBERG, JONATHAN. *Romeo and Juliet*'s open Rs. *In* (pp. 218–35) **93**.

7169. GOLDSTEIN, MARTIN. The tragedy of old Capulet: a patriarchal reading of *Romeo and Juliet*. EngS (77:3) 1996, 227–39.

7170. HALIO, JAY L. (ed.). Shakespeare's *Romeo and Juliet*: texts, contexts, and interpretation. *See* **6151**.

7171. KAHAN, JEFFREY. Henry Chettle and the unreliable *Romeo*: a reassessment. *See* **5810**.

7172. —— Henry Chettle's *Romeo* Q1 and *The Death of Robert Earl of Huntingdon*. *See* **5811**.

7173. NEWELL, ALEX. Critical interpretation and dramatic performance: the chorus in *Romeo and Juliet*. ShB (10:3) 1992, 20–2.

7174. PORTER, JOSEPH A.   Shakespeare's Mercutio: his history and drama. (Bibl. 1991, 5197.) Rev. by Jill Levenson in ShB (10:3) 1992, 45.

7175. SCHLUETER, JUNE.   Tybalt in a bloody sheet, Paris in the tomb: speculations on doubling and staging in *Romeo and Juliet*. See **6648**.

7176. WATERS, D. DOUGLAS.   Fate and fortune in *Romeo and Juliet*. UC (12) 1992, 74–90.

7177. WILLSON, ROBERT F., JR.   Franco Zeffirelli's *Romeo and Juliet* and the uses of cultural translation. See **6685**.

7178. WITT, ROBERT W.   Montague or Capulet? *Romeo and Juliet*: III. i. 184. UC (15) 1995, 136–9.

Sir Thomas More

7179. RAMSEY, PAUL.   The literary evidence for Shakespeare as Hand D in the manuscript play *Sir Thomas More*: a re-re-reconsideration. See **6191**.

The Sonnets

7180. DINGLEY, R. J.   Time transfixing youth's flourish: a note on Sonnet 60. ShB (12:3) 1994, 41–2.

7181. DODSWORTH, MARTIN (ed.).   The sonnets and *A Lover's Complaint*. See **6139**.

7182. EVANS, G. BLAKEMORE (ed.).   The sonnets. Introd. by Anthony Hecht. See **6141**.

7183. GRAVES, ROY NEIL.   Shakespeare's Sonnet 126. Exp (54:4) 1996, 203–7.

7184. ——   Suppressed design in Shakespeare's sonnets: toward envisioning the lost 'First Folio'. UC (15) 1995, 115–35.

7185. HEGARTY, EMILY.   Some suspect of ill: Shakespeare's sonnets and 'the perfect mate'. Extrapolation (36:1) 1995, 55–64.

7186. HONNEYMAN, DAVID.   Shakespeare's sonnets and the Court of Navarre. Braunton, Devon: Merlin, 1996. pp. viii, 207.

7187. HOPE, WARREN.   What are Shakespeare's sonnets? ER (3:2) 1995, 11–14.

7188. KIM, OK-YUP.   Shakespeare eui sonnets e natanan geukjeok gibeob. (The dramatic technique of Shakespeare's sonnets.) EngSt (20) 1996, 41–65.

7189. LINKE, HARALD.   Ich weiss die Liebe vom Idol zu trennen – Anmerkungen zu meiner Übersetzung der Sonette Shakespeares. SJ (132) 1996, 138–49.

7190. MEHL, DIETER; WEISS, WOLFGANG (eds).   Shakespeares Sonette in europäischen Perspektiven. (Bibl. 1995, 5901.) Rev. by Kurt Tetzeli von Rosador in YES (26) 1996, 274–5.

7191. MISCHO, JOHN B.   'That use is not forbidden usury': Shakespeare's procreation sonnets and the problem of usury. *In* (pp. 262–79) **116**.

7192. OMORI, AYAKO.   Meaning and metaphor. See **2439**.

7193. RUBIDGE, BRADLEY.   Tristan Tzara edits Sonnet 138: 'When loue of truth sweares that she is my made'. See **6193**.

7194. SCHUENKE, CHRISTA.   *Rough winds do shake the darling buds of May*: zu meiner Neuübersetzung sämtlicher Sonette von William Shakespeare, erschienen 1994 im Straelener Manuskripte Verlag. SJ (132) 1996, 150–60.

7195. STANBROUGH, HARVEY. Shakespeare's Sonnet 144. Exp (55:1) 1996, 10–12.

7196. STAPLETON, M. L. Harmful eloquence: Ovid's *Amores* from antiquity to Shakespeare. Ann Arbor: Michigan UP, 1996. pp. xi, 175.

7197. TRIMPI, WESLEY. Whose worth's unknown, although his height be taken. *In* (pp. 79–88) **79**.

7198. VON ROSADOR, KURT TETZELI. Spiel-Räume von Shakespeares Sonetten: zu Rainer Iwersens Übersetzungen. SJ (132) 1996, 161–8.

7199. WEST, WILLIAM N. Nothing as given: economies of the gift in Derrida and Shakespeare. CL (48:1) 1996, 1–18.

7200. WILKINSON, JANE. Shakespeare's 'astronomy': a reading of Sonnets XIV and XV. Textus (1:2) 1988, 213–32.

7201. YOSHINAKA, TAKASHI. 'Thy beauty's form in table of my heart': theories of vision in Shakespeare's sonnets. PoetT (45) 1996, 105–23.

The Taming of the Shrew

7202. BAKER, STUART E. Masks and faces in *The Taming of the Shrew*. NETJ (1) 1990, 45–59.

7203. CHO, SUNG-WON. The world upside-down in *The Taming of the Shrew*. ShR (29) 1996, 245–83. (Text in Korean.)

7204. CHRISTENSEN, ANN C. Of household stuff and homes: the stage and social practice in *The Taming of the Shrew*. ExRC (22) 1996, 127–45.

7205. DESSEN, ALAN C. Taming the script: *Henry VI, Shrew*, and *All's Well* in Ashland and Stratford. *See* **6571**.

7206. DOLAN, FRANCES E. (ed.). *The Taming of the Shrew*: texts and contexts. Boston, MA: Bedford Books of St Martin's Press; Basingstoke: Macmillan, 1996. pp. xv, 347.

7207. DOWNS-GAMBLE, MARGARET. The taming-school: *The Taming of the Shrew* as lesson in Renaissance Humanism. *In* (pp. 65–78) **89**.

7208. GRAY, FRANCES. Shakespeare, shrews and screwballs. *See* **7069**.

7209. KIM, SUN-HEE. *The Taming of the Shrew* eui sahoejeok gochal. (Social and cultural approaches to *The Taming of the Shrew*.) ShR (29) 1996, 41–69.

7210. MAGUIRE, LAURIE E. Cultural control in *The Taming of the Shrew*. RenD (26) 1995, 83–104.

7211. MOISAN, THOMAS. 'What's that to you?'; or, Facing facts: anti-paternalist chords and social discords in *The Taming of the Shrew*. RenD (26) 1995, 105–29.

7212. PRIEST, DALE G. Katherina's conversion in *The Taming of the Shrew*: a theological heuristic. Ren (47:1) 1994, 31–40.

7213. WILSON, LUKE. Promissory performances. RenD (25) 1994, 59–87.

7214. YACHNIN, PAUL. Personations: *The Taming of the Shrew* and the limits of theoretical criticism. EMLS (2:1) 1996, 2.1–31.

The Tempest

7215. BARROW, CRAIG. The 1994 Alabama Shakespeare Festival. *See* **6525**.

7216. BROWN, JOHN RUSSELL (ed.). The tempest. *See* **6128**.

7217. CHOI, YOUNG-JU. Prospero eui geukjang: mangehan yeonheesung. (The exhilarating play-making and pleasure-making activity of Prospero's theatre.) ShR (28) 1996, 195–217.

7218. CHONG, BYONG-IL.   *The Tempest* e natanan isanghyang. ('Shakestopia' in *The Tempest*.) ShR (29) 1996, 189–210.

7219. CUMMINGS, PETER.   The alchemical storm: etymology, wordplay, and new world *kairos* in Shakespeare's *The Tempest*. UC (12) 1992, 127–40.

7220. DI DONNA, ERMINIA.   Il movimento verso l'indifferenziato: *The Tempest* di W. Shakespeare. Annali anglistica (36:1–3) 1993, 61–84.

7221. FORTIER, MARK.   Two-voiced, delicate monster: *The Tempest*, romance, and post-colonialism. Essays in Theatre (15:1) 1996, 91–101.

7222. FOX-GOOD, JACQUELYN.   Other voices: the sweet, dangerous air(s) of Shakespeare's *Tempest*. SStud (24) 1996, 241–74.

7223. FRYE, NORTHROP.   Shakespeare's *The Tempest*. Shen (42:4) 1992, 36–50.

7224. GREENMAN, DAVID J.   Old Montaigne into new Prospero: the metamorphosis of a refashioned self. Shakespeare Yearbook (2) 1991, 162–9.

7225. GURR, ANDREW.   Industrious Ariel and idle Caliban. *In* (pp. 193–208) **124**.

7226. HALPERN, RICHARD.   'The picture of Nobody': White cannibalism in *The Tempest*. *In* (pp. 262–92) **90**.

7227. HARCOURT, JOHN B.   Prospero: the storm within. UC (14) 1994, 110–25.

7228. HART, JONATHAN.   Redeeming *The Tempest*: romance and politics. CEl (49) 1996, 23–38.

7229. HENKE, ROBERT.   'Gentleman-like tears': affective response in Italian tragicomedy and Shakespeare's late plays. *See* **6772**.

7230. HOWARD, THOMAS.   'Peace, Paulina', 'My charms are all o'erthrown': Christian patterns in *The Winter's Tale* and *The Tempest*. *In* (pp. 163–75) **111**.

7231. KNIGHTEN, MERRELL.   The triple paternity of *Forbidden Planet*. ShB (12:3) 1994, 36–7.

7232. NEROZZI, PATRIZIA BELLMAN.   La scacchiera di Ferdinando. Textus (1:2) 1988, 175–82.

7233. REVARD, STELLA P.   Myth, masque, and marriage: *Paradise Lost* and Shakespeare's romances. *In* (pp. 114–34) **40**.

7234. RONK, MARTHA.   Narration as usurpation in *The Tempest*. Assays (7) 1992, 119–36.

7235. SALINGAR, LEO.   The New World in *The Tempest*. *In* (pp. 209–22) **124**.

7236. SALTER, DENIS.   Introduction: the end(s) of Shakespeare. Essays in Theatre (15:1) 1996, 3–14.

7237. STOCKHOLDER, KAY.   The aspiring mind of the King's man. *See* **5904**.

7238. STORHOFF, GARY.   'The only voice is your own': Gloria Naylor's revision of *The Tempest*. AAR (29:1) 1995, 35–45.

7239. SZÖNYI, GYÖRGY E.   'My charms are all o'erthrown': the social and ideological context of the magician in Jacobean drama. *In* (pp. 107–23) **53**.

7240. VAN DOMELEN, JOHN E.   Shakespeare's primitive and the dream of perfection. *In* (pp. 75–83) **125**.

7241. VAUGHAN, ALDEN T.; VAUGHAN, VIRGINIA MASON.   Shakespeare's Caliban: a cultural history. (Bibl. 1994, 4866.) Rev. by Brian Rose in JDTC (7:1) 1992, 193–5; by Michael Dobson in AHR (98:2)

1993, 487–8; by Susan Baker in ShB (11:3) 1993, 42–3; by Helga Quadflieg in SJ (132) 1996, 251–5.

7242. VAUGHAN, VIRGINIA MASON; VAUGHAN, ALDEN T. Tampering with *The Tempest. See* **6676**.

7243. WALCH, GÜNTER. 'What's past is prologue': metatheatrical memory and transculturation in *The Tempest. In* (pp. 223–38) **124**.

7244. WESTLUND, JOSEPH. Idealization and the problematic in *The Tempest. In* (pp. 239–47) **116**.

7245. WILLIAMS, GEORGE WALTON. Exit pursued by a quaint device: the bear in *The Winter's Tale*. UC (14) 1994, 105–9.

7246. WILLSON, ROBERT F., JR. Recontextualizing Shakespeare on film: *My Own Private Idaho, Men of Respect, Prospero's Books. See* **6686**.

7247. WILSON, LUKE. Promissory performances. *See* **7213**.

7248. WYNTER, SYLVIA. Afterword: *Beyond Miranda's Meanings: Un/Silencing the 'Demonic Ground' of Caliban's 'Woman'. In* (pp. 355–72) **81**.

Timon of Athens
7249. BIGGS, MURRAY. Adapting *Timon of Athens. See* **6536**.

7250. CANTOR, PAUL A. *Timon of Athens*: the corrupt city and the origins of philosophy. In-between (4:1) 1995, 25–40.

7251. FISCHER, SANDRA K. 'Cut my heart in sums': Shakespeare's economics and *Timon of Athens. In* (pp. 187–95) **71**.

7252. WILSON, LUKE. Promissory performances. *See* **7213**.

Titus Andronicus
7253. BARKER, FRANCIS. Treasures of culture: *Titus Andronicus* and death by hanging. *In* (pp. 226–61) **90**.

7254. BAXTER, MARION. Titus alone. *See* **6529**.

7255. BRINK, JEAN R. Domesticating the Dark Lady. *In* (pp. 93–108) **89**.

7256. CHARNEY, MAURICE. Titus Andronicus. (Bibl. 1992, 5409.) Rev. by William B. Long in ShB (9:4) 1991, 45–6.

7257. CORBIN, PETER. The 'harmless drudgery' of editing Shakespeare: the Arden Shakespeare: third series. *See* **6131**.

7258. GREEN, DOUGLAS E. Staging the evidence: Shakespeare's theatrical revengers. *See* **6811**.

7259. HARRIS, BERNICE. Sexuality as a signifier for power relations: using Lavinia, of Shakespeare's *Titus Andronicus*. Criticism (38:3) 1996, 383–406.

7260. JACKSON, MACD. P. Stage directions and speech headings in Act I of *Titus Andronicus* Q (1594): Shakespeare or Peele? *See* **5953**.

7261. KOLIN, PHILIP C. (ed.). *Titus Andronicus*: critical essays. (Bibl. 1995, 5963.) Rev. by James Fisher in JDTC (10:2) 1996, 144–6.

7262. MEHL, DIETER. Der dritte Arden Shakespeare. *See* **6177**.

7263. METZ, G. HAROLD. Shakespeare's earliest tragedy: studies in *Titus Andronicus*. Madison, NJ: Fairleigh Dickinson UP; London; Toronto: Assoc. UPs, 1996. pp. 309.

7264. SMITH, MOLLY EASO. Spectacles of torment in *Titus Andronicus*. SELit (36:2) 1996, 315–31.

7265. TAYLOR, ANTHONY BRIAN. 'The Goths protect the Andronici, who go aloft': the implications of a stage direction. *See* **6670**.

7266. WHITE, JEANNETTE S. Shakespeare's *Titus Andronicus*. Exp (54:4) 1996, 207–9.

Troilus and Cressida

7267. BJELLAND, KAREN T. The cultural value of analytical bibliography and textual criticism: the case of *Troilus and Cressida*. See **6123**.

7268. BOLING, RONALD J. Stage images of Cressida's betrayal. See **6537**.

7269. BOYLE, CHARLES. Bitter fruit: *Troilus and Cressida* in Queen Elizabeth's Court. ER (2:2) 1994, 11–18.

7270. BREDBECK, GREGORY W. Constructing Patroclus: the high and low discourses of Renaissance sodomy. In (pp. 77–91) **83**.

7271. COOK, CAROL. Unbodied figures of desire. In (pp. 177–95) **84**.

7272. DODD, MARK ROBERT. The history of *Troilus and Cressida*. UC (11) 1991, 39–51.

7273. HEHL, URSULA. 'This is, and is not, Cressid': narzisstische Persönlichkeitsstörungen als Erklärungsmodell für Shakespeares *Troilus and Cressida*. SJ (132) 1996, 75–92.

7274. HELMS, LORRAINE. Playing the woman's part: feminist criticism and Shakespearean performance. In (pp. 196–206) **84**.

7275. HOPKINS, LISA. *The Broken Heart* and *Troilus and Cressida*. NQ (43:2) 1996, 192–3.

7276. SABBADINI, SILVANO. Il tempo, le rovine e le maschere. Textus (1:2) 1988, 151–73.

7277. SHAHEEN, NASEEB. Biblical echoes in *Troilus and Cressida*. NQ (43:2) 1996, 160–2.

7278. TROISI, FEDERICA. Tersite: da Omero a Shakespeare. Textus (5) 1992, 13–33.

7279. WALKER, LEWIS. Chaucer in Shakespeare: the case of the Nun's Priest's Tale and *Troilus and Cressida*. See **5463**.

Twelfth Night

7280. ANSON, ROBERT D. A lightweight elephant slept here. UC (16) 1996, 141–5.

7281. APPLER, KEITH. Deconstructing the regional theater with 'performance art' Shakespeare. See **6518**.

7282. BRAILOW, DAVID G. *Twelfth Night* across the continents: an interview with Michael Pennington. See **6540**.

7283. BUTLER, COLIN. The case of Malvolio. ERev (5:4) 1995, 2–5.

7284. CAHILL, EDWARD. The problem of Malvolio. ColLit (23:2) 1996, 62–82.

7285. CHARDIN, JEAN-JACQUES (ed.). *Twelfth Night*: le langage en fête. Actes du Colloque Shakespeare de Nancy (17–18 novembre 1995). Paris: Messene, 1996. pp. 174.

7286. DESPER, C. RICHARD. Allusions to Edmund Campion in *Twelfth Night*. ER (3:1) 1995, 37–47.

7287. EDGECOMBE, RODNEY STENNING; BARASCH, FRANCES K. The *Castiliano Vulgo* crux in *Twelfth Night*. SNL (46:2) 1996, 49; (46:4) 1996, 85.

7288. GREEN, DOUGLAS E. Shakespeare's violation: 'One face, one voice, one habit, and two persons'. In (pp. 327–38) **98**.

7289. HUTSON, LORNA. On not being deceived: rhetoric and the body in *Twelfth Night*. TSLL (38:2) 1996, 140–74.

7290. KIRBY, I. J. *Twelfth Night* I.1.5–7. In (pp. 71–4) **125**.

7291. LAKE, JAMES H. The psychology of primacy and recency effects upon audience response in *Twelfth Night*. UC (15) 1995, 26–34.

7292. Mancini, Bianca Concolino. Da Ovidio a Shakespeare: le metamorfosi del travestimento. Filologia e critica (18:1) 1993, 87–99.

7293. Masello, Steven J. Shakespeare's comic revenge in *Twelfth Night*. Shakespeare Yearbook (2) 1991, 68–76.

7294. Monahan, Jerome. *Twelfth Night*: a comedy of misreadings. ERev (7:1) 1996, 2–5.

7295. Orgel, Stephen. What is a character? *See* **6830**.

7296. Osborne, Laurie E. The rhetoric of evidence: the narration and display of Viola and Olivia in the nineteenth century. *In* (pp. 124–43) **118**.

7297. —— The trick of singularity: *Twelfth Night* and the performance editions. *See* **6185**.

7298. Robinson, John V. A ring of truth: another look at a crux in *Twelfth Night. See* **6192**.

7299. Sabbadini, Silvano. Le maschere dell'eros. Textus (3:1/2) 1990, 75–93.

7300. Shurgot, Michael W. Feste's perch. ShB (14:2) 1996, 39–40.

7301. Singleton, Brian. Mnouchkine and Shakespeare: intercultural theatre practice. *See* **6659**.

7302. Stone, James W. The transvestic glove-text of *Twelfth Night*. Assays (9) 1996, 153–76.

7303. Summers, Joseph H. Collected essays on Renaissance literature. *See* **5746**.

7304. White, R. S. (ed.). Twelfth night. Basingstoke: Macmillan; New York: St Martin's Press, 1996. pp. ix, 221. (New casebooks.)

The Two Gentlemen of Verona

7305. Montini, Donatella. La lettera della scena shakespeariana tra oggetto e scrittura: un esempio: *The Two Gentlemen of Verona*. Textus (3:1/2) 1990, 95–124.

7306. Schlueter, June (ed.). *Two Gentlemen of Verona*: critical essays. New York; London: Garland, 1996. pp. xxv, 288. (Garland reference library of the humanities, 1645.) (Shakespeare criticism, 15.)

The Two Noble Kinsmen

7307. Andreas, James R. Remythologizing the Knight's Tale: *A Midsummer Night's Dream* and *The Two Noble Kinsmen. See* **5351**.

7308. Blincoe, Noel R. The analogous qualities of *The Two Noble Kinsmen* and *Masque of the Inner Temple and Grey's Inn*. NQ (43:2) 1996, 168–71.

7309. Bonelli, Elena. The Elizabethan (ma)lady: lovesickness and the medicalization of desire in *The Two Noble Kinsmen*. Textus (6) 1993, 43–55.

7310. Helms, Lorraine. Playing the woman's part: feminist criticism and Shakespearean performance. *In* (pp. 196–206) **84**.

7311. Mallette, Richard. Same-sex erotic friendship in *The Two Noble Kinsmen*. RenD (26) 1995, 29–52.

Venus and Adonis

7312. Cousins, A. D. Towards a reconsideration of Shakespeare's Adonis: rhetoric, Narcissus, and the male gaze. *See* **2341**.

7313. Feitelberg, Doreen. The theme of love and wooing and the consequences of seduction in Shakespeare's poems *Venus and Adonis* and *The Rape of Lucrece. See* **7126**.

7314. MERRIX, ROBERT P.   The 'beste noire': the medieval role of the boar in *Venus and Adonis*. UC (11) 1991, 117–30.

The Winter's Tale

7315. ANDREWS, JOHN F. (ed.).   The winter's tale. Foreword by Adrian Noble. *See* **6117**.

7316. BARROW, CRAIG.   A tale of two Shakespeare Festivals: Stratford's *The Merchant of Venice* and Alabama Shakespeare Festival's *The Winter's Tale. See* **6526**.

7317. BIRCH, MADELEINE (ed.).   The winter's tale. *See* **6122**.

7318. DESSEN, ALAN C.   Massed entries and theatrical options in *The Winter's Tale. See* **6137**.

7319. DIMATTEO, ANTHONY.   *Antiqui dicunt*: myth and its critique in *The Winter's Tale*. NQ (43:2) 1996, 165–8.

7320. DUFFIN, ROSS W.   An encore for Shakespeare's rare Italian master. ER (2:1) 1994, 21–5.

7321. FABISZAK, JACEK.   A portrait of the artist as a Shakespearian character in *The Winter's Tale*. SAP (30) 1996, 149–57.

7322. FORTIER, MARK.   Married with children: *The Winter's Tale* and social history; or, Infacticide in earlier seventeenth-century England. MLQ (57:4) 1996, 579–603.

7323. GARDNER, COLIN.   'But seasons come to pass': *The Winter's Tale* in South Africa. *See* **6580**.

7324. HALE, JOHN K.   Autolycus as 'festive presence' in *The Winter's Tale*. SNL (46:3) 1996, 73.

7325. HENKE, ROBERT.   'Gentleman-like tears': affective response in Italian tragicomedy and Shakespeare's late plays. *See* **6772**.

7326. HOWARD, THOMAS.   'Peace, Paulina', 'My charms are all o'erthrown': Christian patterns in *The Winter's Tale* and *The Tempest. In* (pp. 163–75) **111**.

7327. HUTCHINGS, GEOFFREY.   Justice and reconciliation: *The Winter's Tale*. SSA (7) 1994, 61–73.

7328. KAPLAN, M. LINDSAY; EGGERT, KATHERINE.   'Good queen, my lord, good queen': sexual slander and the trials of female authority in *The Winter's Tale*. RenD (25) 1994, 89–118.

7329. KWON, EUI-MOO.   *The Winter's Tale* eui time gwa euimi. (The meaning of time in *The Winter's Tale*.) ShR (28) 1996, 27–48.

7330. MALONE, MAGGIE.   Tale-telling in *The Winter's Tale*. EP (21) 1996, 136–60.

7331. ORGEL, STEPHEN (ed.).   The winter's tale. *See* **6183**.

7332. —— The winter's tale. *See* **6184**.

7333. PARK, HYO-CHUN.   *The Winter's Tale* e natanan sarlmeui gwanjo. (Meditations on life in *The Winter's Tale*.) ShR (29) 1996, 105–33.

7334. RAHBEK, ULLA.   Tales of love, lust, jealousy and revenge: inter-textuality in Marion Halligan's *Spidercup*. EngS (77:4) 1996, 367–74.

7335. REVARD, STELLA P.   Myth, masque, and marriage: *Paradise Lost* and Shakespeare's romances. *In* (pp. 114–34) **40**.

7336. RONK, MARTHA.   Disjunction and subjectivity in *The Winter's Tale*. UC (16) 1996, 124–40.

7337. RUDANKO, JUHANI.   Pleading with an unreasonable king: on the Kent and Pauline episodes in Shakespeare. *See* **2287**.

7338.   Sokol, B. J.   Art and illusion in *The Winter's Tale*. (Bibl. 1994, 4918.) Rev. by Sukanta Chaudhuri in NQ (43:3) 1996, 337.

7339.   Talvacchia, Bette.   The rare Italian master and the posture of Hermione in *The Winter's Tale*. ER (1:1) 1993, 40–57.

7340.   Thatcher, David.   Antigonus' dream in *The Winter's Tale*. UC (13) 1993, 130–42.

7341.   Williams, George Walton.   Exit pursued by a quaint device: the bear in *The Winter's Tale*. *See* **7245**.

7342.   Wolf, Janet S.   'Like an old tale still': Paulina, 'triple Hecate', and the Persephone myth in *The Winter's Tale*. *In* (pp. 32–44) **46**.

SEVENTEENTH CENTURY

GENERAL

General Literary Studies

7343. ALLEN, DAVID G.; WHITE, ROBERT A. (eds). Subjects on the world's stage: essays on British literature of the Middle Ages and the Renaissance. *See* **116**.

7344. ———— The work of dissimilitude: essays from the Sixth Citadel Conference on Medieval and Renaissance Literature. *See* **131**.

7345. ANDERSON, KATHRYN MURPHY. Editing and contextualizing early modern women in England. *See* **560**.

7346. ANON. Recent articles. Scriblerian (28:1/2) 1995/96, 6–57.

7347. ANSELMENT, RAYMOND A. The realms of Apollo: literature and healing in seventeenth-century England. (Bibl. 1995, 6021.) Rev. by Helen King in Albion (28:3) 1996, 481–2; by Hal Jensen in TLS, 15 Mar. 1996, 10; by Brian H. Childs in LitMed (15:2) 1996, 263–6.

7348. AVERY, GILLIAN. The voice of the child, both godly and unregenerate, in early modern England. *In* (pp. 16–27) **48**.

7349. BATH, MICHAEL; MANNING, JOHN; YOUNG, ALAN R. (eds). The art of the emblem. Essays in honour of Karl Josef Höltgen. *See* **179**.

7350. BENEDICT, BARBARA M. Making the modern reader: cultural mediation in early modern literary anthologies. Princeton, NJ; Chichester: Princeton UP, 1996. pp. 252.

7351. BERNARD, JOHN. Recent studies in Renaissance pastoral. *See* **5535**.

7352. BLANK, PAULA. Broken English: dialects and the politics of language in Renaissance writings. *See* **1430**.

7353. BOWERS, TONI. The politics of motherhood: British writing and culture, 1680–1760. Cambridge; New York: CUP, 1996. pp. xvi, 262.

7354. BRACK, O. M., JR; EARLY, MARY. Samuel Johnson's proposals for the *Harleian Miscellany*. *See* **5538**.

7355. BRAVERMAN, RICHARD. Plots and counterplots: sexual politics and the body politic in English literature, 1660–1730. (Bibl. 1995, 6028.) Rev. by Ian McCormick in BJECS (19:1) 1996, 84–5; by Ronald Knowles in YES (26) 1996, 282–3.

7356. BREITENBERG, MARK. Anxious masculinity in early modern England. *See* **5541**.

7357. ——— Anxious masculinity: sexual jealousy in early modern England. *See* **5542**.

7358. BRINK, JEAN R. (ed.). Privileging gender in early modern England. *See* **89**.

7359. CARROLL, WILLIAM C. Fat king, lean beggar: representations of poverty in the age of Shakespeare. *See* **5546**.

7360. CHAMBERS, D. D. C. The reinvention of the world: English writing, 1650–1750. London; New York: Arnold, 1996. pp. x, 218. (Writing in history.) Rev. by R. E. Foust in NOR (22:3/4) 1996, 186–8.

7361. CHERNAIK, WARREN. Sexual freedom in Restoration literature. (Bibl. 1995, 6035.) Rev. by Kirk Combe in NQ (43:2) 1996, 219.

7362. Clancy, Thomas H.   English Catholic books, 1641–1700: a bibliography. (Bibl. 1977, 125.) Brookfield, VT; Aldershot: Scolar Press, 1996. pp. xviii, 215. (Revised ed.: first ed. 1974.)

7363. Claridge, Henry.   American literature to 1900: American literature to 1830. YWES (75) 1994, 556–62.

7364. —— American literature to 1900: general. YWES (75) 1994, 554–6.

7365. Cohen, Daniel A.   Pillars of salt, monuments of grace: New England crime literature and the origins of American popular culture, 1676–1860. (Bibl. 1995, 6037.) Rev. by Roger Lane in AHR (99:3) 1994, 967; by Gerald McFarland in VH (63:2) 1995, 115–17.

7366. Corns, Thomas N.   Uncloistered virtue: English political literature, 1640–1660. (Bibl. 1995, 6040.) Rev. by Gerald M. MacLean in Review (16) 1994, 177–95; by Lois Potter in JBS (34:4) 1995, 536–42.

7367. Cressy, David.   Gender trouble and cross-dressing in early modern England. *See* **5548**.

7368. Davis, Natalie Zemon; Farge, Arlette (eds).   A history of women in the West: vol. III, Renaissance and Enlightenment paradoxes. *See* **42**.

7369. Desaive, Jean-Paul.   The ambiguities of literature. *In* (pp. 261–94) **42**.

7370. Di Cesare, Mario A. (ed.).   Reconsidering the Renaissance: papers from the twenty-first annual conference. *See* **98**.

7371. Di Florio, Rita.   Il libertinismo come forma embrionale del pensiero illuminista. Annali anglistica (36:1–3) 1993, 85–110.

7372. Donoghue, Emma.   Passions between women: British lesbian culture, 1668–1801. London: Scarlet Press, 1993; New York: HarperCollins, 1995. pp. 314. Rev. by R. L. Widmann in BkW, 24 Sept. 1995, 12; by Betty Rizzo in Scriblerian (28:1/2) 1995/96, 90–1.

7373. Downie, James Alan.   To settle the succession of the state: literature and politics, 1678–1750. (Bibl. 1995, 6044.) Rev. by David Eastwood in NQ (43:4) 1996, 481; by Susan J. Owen in Eng (45:182) 1996, 148–50.

7374. Engel, William E.   Mapping mortality: the persistence of memory and melancholy in early modern England. *See* **5553**.

7375. Felsenstein, Frank.   Anti-Semitic stereotypes: a paradigm of Otherness in English popular culture, 1660–1830. (Bibl. 1995, 6046.) Rev. by Vincent Carretta in Albion (28:1) 1996, 115–16; by Mark Levene in NQ (43:2) 1996, 227–8; by Melvyn New in ECF (8:2) 1996, 293–5.

7376. Ferguson, Margaret W.   Moderation and its discontents: recent work on Renaissance women. *See* **5557**.

7377. Fowler, Alastair.   Time's purpled masquers: stars and the afterlife in Renaissance English literature. *See* **5559**.

7378. Foxton, Rosemary.   'Hear the word of the Lord': a critical and bibliographical study of Quaker women's writing 1650–1700. Melbourne: Bibliographical Soc. of Australia and New Zealand, 1994. pp. 77. (BSANZ occasional pubs, 4.) Rev. by Hilda L. Smith in Albion (28:2) 1996, 305–6.

7379. Gallagher, Catherine.   Nobody's story: the vanishing acts of women writers in the marketplace, 1670–1820. (Bibl. 1995, 6048.) Rev. by George Haggerty in TSWL (14:2) 1995, 381–3; by Gary Kelly in AHR (101:2) 1996, 484–5; by Lennard J. Davis in ECS (29:4) 1996, 443–5; by Sue Kuykendall in ColLit (23:1) 1996, 193–203.

7380. GILLESPIE, STUART; OGDEN, JAMES; POOLEY, ROGER.   The later seventeenth century: general. YWES (75) 1994, 312–19.

7381. —————— The later seventeenth century: other authors. YWES (75) 1994, 322–31.

7382. GOLDBERG, JONATHAN (ed.).   Queering the Renaissance. *See* **93**.

7383. GRIFFIN, DUSTIN.   Literary patronage in England, 1650–1800. Cambridge; New York: CUP, 1996. pp. x, 317.

7384. GRUNDY, ISOBEL; WISEMAN, SUSAN (eds).   Women, writing, history 1640–1740. (Bibl. 1995, 6051.) Rev. by Melinda Alliker Rabb in ECS (28:3) 1995, 349–51.

7385. HABIB, IMTIAZ.   Reading Black women characters of the English Renaissance: colonial inscription and postcolonial recovery. *See* **5136**.

7386. HALLI, ROBERT W., JR.   Cecilia Bulstrode, 'the court pucell'. *In* (pp. 295–312) **116**.

7387. HARRIS, SHARON M. (ed.).   American women writers to 1800. Oxford; New York: OUP, 1996. pp. xii, 452. Rev. by R. C. De Prospo in EAL (31:2) 1996, 189–93.

7388. HART, JONATHAN.   Mediation in the exchange between Europeans and Native Americans in the early modern period. CanRCL (22:2) 1995, 319–43.

7389. HILL, CHRISTOPHER.   Liberty against the law: some seventeenth-century controversies. London: Lane; New York: Penguin, 1996. pp. x, 354. Rev. by Derek Hirst in TLS, 12 July 1996, 6.

7390. HINDS, HILARY.   God's Englishwomen: seventeenth-century radical sectarian writing and feminist criticism. Manchester; New York: Manchester UP, 1996. pp. vii, 264.

7391. HOBBY, ELAINE.   Virtue of necessity: English women's writing, 1649–1688. (Bibl. 1988, 3085.) Rev. by Margaret W. Ferguson in Feminist Studies (20:2) 1994, 349–66.

7392. HUTSON, LORNA.   Chivalry for merchants; or, Knights of temperance in the realms of gold. *See* **5574**.

7393. KINNEY, ARTHUR F.   Figuring medieval and Renaissance literature. *In* (pp. 13–34) **131**.

7394. —— (ed.).   Poetics and praxis, understanding and imagination: the collected essays of O. B. Hardison, Jr. *See* **5581**.

7395. LANGE, MARJORY E.   Telling tears in the English Renaissance. *See* **5586**.

7396. LEE, HYEON SEOK.   Jayeon eseo jakga ro: 17–18c youngkuk eui Shakespeare suyong yeongu. (From nature to author: a study of the appropriation of Shakespeare in England in the seventeenth and eighteenth centuries.) *See* **6388**.

7397. LESLIE, MICHAEL; RAYLOR, TIMOTHY (eds).   Culture and cultivation in early modern England: writing and the land. (Bibl. 1995, 6075.) Rev. by Lois Potter in JBS (34:4) 1995, 536–42.

7398. LEWALSKI, BARBARA KIEFER.   Writing women in Jacobean England. (Bibl. 1995, 6076.) Rev. by Margaret W. Ferguson in Feminist Studies (20:2) 1994, 349–66; by Rosemary Kegl in TSWL (15:1) 1996, 147–9; by Marion Spies in ZAA (44:4) 1996, 371–3; by Susan Dwyer Amussen in JBS (35:1) 1996, 114–18; by Kathryn Murphy Anderson in ColLit (23:1) 1996, 217–25.

7399. LEWIS, JAYNE ELIZABETH.   The English fable: Aesop and literary culture, 1651–1740. Cambridge; New York: CUP, 1996. pp. x, 234.

(Cambridge studies in eighteenth-century English literature and thought, 28.)

7400. LINDEN, STANTON J. *Darke hierogliphicks*: alchemy in English literature from Chaucer to the Restoration. *See* **5320**.

7401. LOVE, HAROLD. The new 'A' text of *Signior Dildo*. *See* **727**.

7402. LUXON, THOMAS H. Literal figures: Puritan allegory and the Reformation crisis in representation. (Bibl. 1995, 6078.) Rev. by David Walker in Bunyan Studies (6) 1995/96, 93–100; by David Gay in EMLS (2:3) 1996, 6.1–5.

7403. McCOY, RICHARD C. Poetry at court. *See* **5589**.

7404. McEACHERN, CLAIRE. The poetics of English nationhood, 1590–1612. *See* **5590**.

7405. MacLEAN, GERALD. Literacy, class, and gender in Restoration England. Text (Ann Arbor) (7) 1994, 307–35.

7406. —— Literature, culture, and society in Restoration England. *In* (pp. 3–27) **21**.

7407. —— (ed.). Culture and society in the Stuart Restoration: literature, drama, history. *See* **21**.

7408. McRAE, ANDREW. God speed the plough: the representation of agrarian England, 1500–1660. *See* **5591**.

7409. MANLEY, LAWRENCE. Recent studies in the English Renaissance. *See* **5593**.

7410. MAY, JAMES E. Scribleriana transferred: 1993–1994. *See* **509**.

7411. MICHELSEN, MARTINA. Weg vom Work – zum Gedankenstrich: zur stilistischen Funktion eines Satzzeichens in der englischen Literatur des 17. und 18. Jahrhunderts. *See* **1602**.

7412. MILLER, DAVID LEE; O'DAIR, SHARON; WEBER, HAROLD. Introduction: criticism and cultural production. *In* (pp. 1–12) **90**.

7413. —— —— —— (eds). The production of English Renaissance culture. *See* **90**.

7414. MULLAN, JOHN. Gendered knowledge, gendered minds: women and Newtonianism, 1690–1760. *In* (pp. 41–56) **94**.

7415. NELSON, DANA D. The word in black and white: reading 'race' in American literature, 1638–1867. (Bibl. 1995, 6085.) Rev. by Michele Birnbaum in ECent (37:1) 1996, 94–6; by Gary Ashwill in AAR (30:2) 1996, 286–9.

7416. OSBORNE, MELANIE. The earlier seventeenth century, excluding drama. YWES (75) 1994, 289–96.

7417. PARKS, LYNN A. Capitalism in early American literature: texts and contexts. New York; Frankfurt; Bern; Paris: Lang, 1996. pp. 183. (Studies on themes and motifs in literature, 27.) (Cf. bibl. 1994, 2427.)

7418. PEBWORTH, TED-LARRY. The early audiences of Donne's poetic performances. *See* **993**.

7419. —— Publication before the triumph of print. *See* **403**.

7420. PORTER, DAVID. Writing China: legitimacy and representation 1606–1773. CLS (33:1) 1996, 98–122.

7421. POTTER, LOIS. The politics of language in early modern England. *See* **2694**.

7422. —— Secret rites and secret writing: Royalist literature, 1641–1660. (Bibl. 1995, 6093.) Rev. by Nancy Klein Maguire in MedRen (7) 1995, 432–6.

7423. PRESCOTT, ANNE LAKE. The odd couple: Gargantua and Tom Thumb. *In* (pp. 75–91) **72**.

7424. PREST, WILFRID R.   Law, learning and religion: gifts to Gray's Inn Library in the 1630s. *See* **528**.

7425. RAWSON, CLAUDE.   Satire and sentiment, 1660–1830. (Bibl. 1995, 6095.) Rev. by Charles A. Knight in ECS (30:1) 1996, 100–1; by Allan Ingram in YES (26) 1996, 284–5; by Martin Brunkhorst in ZAA (44:3) 1996, 273–4.

7426. RITCHIE, DANIEL E.   Reconstructing literature in an ideological age: a biblical poetics and literary studies from Milton to Burke. Grand Rapids, MI: Eerdmans, 1996. pp. ix, 302.

7427. ROBERTS, JOSEPHINE A.   Editing the women writers of early modern England. *See* **813**.

7428. SCHEICK, WILLIAM J.   Literature to 1800. American Literary Scholarship (1993) 145–64; (1994) 187–201; (1995) 193–205.

7429. SERRATORE, MONICA.   Barocco della rivoluzione: ovvero l'allegoria della modernità. Annali anglistica (38:3) 1995, 37–60.

7430. SHERBO, ARTHUR.   John Nichols's notes in the scholarly commentary of others. *See* **831**.

7431. SIMMONS, EVA (ed.).   Bloomsbury guides to English literature: Augustan literature: a guide to Restoration and eighteenth-century literature, 1600–1789. London: Bloomsbury, 1994. pp. 295.

7432. SMITH, NIGEL.   Literature and revolution in England, 1640–1660. (Bibl. 1995, 6107.) Rev. by David Walker in Bunyan Studies (6) 1995/96, 93–100; by Thomas N. Corns in Prose Studies (19:1) 1996, 116–17; by Alastair Fowler in EC (46:1) 1996, 52–60; by Derek Hirst in EHR (111:444) 1996, 1285–6; by R. C. Richardson in Literature and History (5:1) 1996, 106–8.

7433. SPENGEMANN, WILLIAM C.   A new world of words: redefining early American literature. (Bibl. 1995, 6110.) Rev. by Deborah L. Madsen in AmS (36:2) 1995, 189–90.

7434. STAFFORD, FIONA J.   The last of the race: the growth of a modern myth from Milton to Darwin. (Bibl. 1994, 4992.) Rev. by Penny Fielding in SLJ (supp. 42) 1995, 14–17; by Katherine A. Armstrong in BJECS (19:1) 1996, 104; by Karina Williamson in NQ (43:2) 1996, 241–2.

7435. STAUB, SUSAN C.   'Matchlesse monsters of the female sex': murderous women in early modern England. *See* **5603**.

7436. STEVENS, PAUL.   The political ways of paradox: Renaissance literature and modern criticism. *See* **5604**.

7437. SWISS, MARGO; KENT, DAVID A. (eds).   Heirs of fame: Milton and writers of the English Renaissance. *See* **40**.

7438. TELTSCHER, KATE.   India inscribed: European and British writing on India, 1600–1800. (Bibl. 1995, 6113.) Rev. by C. A. Bayly in TLS, 12 July 1996, 29.

7439. THOMPSON, JAMES.   Recent studies in the Restoration and eighteenth century. SELit (36:3) 1996, 693–746.

7440. WALKER, DAVID.   Language, genre, and revolution. *See* **2728**.

7441. WARNER, MICHAEL.   New English Sodom. *In* (pp. 330–58) **93**.

7442. WEINBROT, HOWARD D.   Britannia's issue: the rise of British literature from Dryden to Ossian. (Bibl. 1995, 6118.) Rev. by Julian Ferraro in YES (26) 1996, 285–6; by Vera Nünning in ZAA (44:1) 1996, 86–8.

7443. WHITE, R. S.   Natural law in English Renaissance literature. *See* **5612**.

7444. WILCOX, HELEN; TODD, RICHARD; MACDONALD, ALASDAIR (eds). Sacred and profane: secular and devotional interplay in early modern British literature. *See* **107**.

7445. ZWICKER, STEVEN N. Lines of authority: politics and English literary culture, 1649–1689. (Bibl. 1995, 6126.) Rev. by John Spurr in EHR (111:441) 1996, 473–5; by Christopher Hill in Literature and History (5:2) 1996, 79–80.

Drama and the Theatre

7446. ANON. (ed.). Fushu kigeki no hen'you – ousei fukkoki kara Jane Austen made. (The metamorphosis of the comedy of manners: from the Restoration to Jane Austen.) Tokyo: Chuo UP, 1996. pp. vi, 258.

7447. BACH, REBECCA ANN. 'Ty good shubshects': the Jacobean masque as colonial discourse. MedRen (7) 1995, 206–23.

7448. BACKSCHEIDER, PAULA R. 'Endless aversion rooted in the soul': divorce in the 1690–1730 theater. ECent (37:2) 1996, 99–135.

7449. BAUMANN, UWE. The presentation of the Roman imperial court in Jacobean tragedy. *In* (pp. 73–93) **53**.

7450. BAWCUTT, N. W. New entries from the office-book of Sir Henry Herbert. ELR (26:1) 1996, 155–66.

7451. —— (ed.). The control and censorship of Caroline drama: the records of Sir Henry Herbert, Master of the Revels, 1623–73. Oxford: Clarendon Press; New York: OUP, 1996. pp. viii, 350.

7452. BRAVERMAN, RICHARD. The rake's progress revisited: politics and comedy in the Restoration. *In* (pp. 140–68) **20**.

7453. BREGAZZI, JOSEPHINE. Changing roles: gender marking through syntactic distribution in the Jacobean theatre. *See* **2589**.

7454. BRYAN, GEORGE B. On the theatrical origins of the expression *green room. See* **1960**.

7455. CALLAGHAN, DYMPNA. The castrator's song: female impersonation on the early modern stage. *See* **6255**.

7456. CAMINO, MERCEDES MAROTO. 'The stage am I?': raping Lucrece in early modern England. *See* **7125**.

7457. CANFIELD, J. DOUGLAS. Shifting tropes of ideology in English serious drama, late Stuart to early Georgian. *In* (pp. 195–227) **20**.

7458. —— PAYNE, DEBORAH C. (eds). Cultural readings of Restoration and eighteenth-century English theater. *See* **20**.

7459. CERASANO, S. P.; WYNNE-DAVIES, MARION (eds). Renaissance drama by women: texts and documents. *See* **5623**.

7460. CLARK, IRA. Writing and dueling in the English Renaissance. *See* **5625**.

7461. COOK, ALBERT. Historiography and/or historicism: context and theoretical (de)-integration of Renaissance drama. *See* **5627**.

7462. CORBIN, PETER. 'A dog's obeyed in office': kingship and authority in Jacobean tragedy. *In* (pp. 59–71) **53**.

7463. CROCKETT, BRYAN. The play of paradox: stage and sermon in Renaissance England. *See* **5628**.

7464. DANE, JOSEPH A. Perfect order and perfected order: the evidence from press-variants of early seventeenth-century quartos. *See* **267**.

7465. DESSEN, ALAN C. Recovering Elizabethan staging: a reconsideration of the evidence. *In* (pp. 44–65) **118**.

7466. FARLEY-HILLS, DAVID. The audience implications of some Paul's and Blackfriars' plays. *In* (pp. 205–15) **53**.

7467. FINKE, LAURIE A.   Painting women: images of femininity in Jacobean tragedy. *In* (pp. 223–36) **84**.

7468. FORSE, JAMES H.   The play's the thing, wherein to catch the consciousness of the citizen: early modern playscripts as sources for English social/cultural history. *See* **5637**.

7469. GIBBONS, BRIAN.   The question of place. *See* **5642**.

7470. —— The wrong end of the telescope. *In* (pp. 141–59) **124**.

7471. GILL, PAT.   Interpreting ladies: women, wit, and morality in the Restoration comedy of manners. (Bibl. 1994, 5028.) Rev. by Harold Weber in Criticism (38:1) 1996, 151–3.

7472. GOSSETT, SUZANNE.   Recent studies in the English masque. *See* **5644**.

7473. —— Why should a woman edit a man? *See* **654**.

7474. GURR, ANDREW.   Playgoing in Shakespeare's London. *See* **5646**.

7475. —— The war of 1614–1618: Jacobean absolutism, local authority and a crisis of overproduction. ELR (26:1) 1996, 138–54.

7476. GUTIERREZ, NANCY A.   Double standard in the flesh: gender, fasting, and power in English Renaissance drama. *In* (pp. 79–93) **24**.

7477. HATTAWAY, MICHAEL.   'Seeing things': Amazons and cannibals. *In* (pp. 179–92) **124**.

7478. HILL, ERROL.   The Jamaican stage, 1655–1900: profile of a colonial theatre. (Bibl. 1995, 6154.) Rev. by Eckhard Breitinger in ZAA (41:2) 1993, 187–8; by Michal J. Rozbicki in AHR (99:5) 1994, 1784.

7479. HOENSELAARS, A. J.   Broken images of Englishmen and foreigners in English Renaissance drama. *See* **5652**.

7480. HOGG, JAMES (ed.).   Jacobean drama as social criticism. *See* **53**.

7481. HOLLAND, PETER.   'Travelling hopefully': the dramatic form of journeys in English Renaissance drama. *In* (pp. 160–78) **124**.

7482. HUGHES, DEREK.   English drama, 1660–1700. Oxford: Clarendon Press; New York: OUP, 1996. pp. viii, 503. Rev. by Jonathan Bate in TLS, 28 June 1996, 13.

7483. HUSSEY, STANLEY.   Social stratification by language. *In* (pp. 179–91) **53**.

7484. JARDINE, MICHAEL; POYNTING, SARAH.   Renaissance drama: excluding Shakespeare: editions and textual scholarship. *See* **693**.

7485. KAMPS, IVO.   Historiography and ideology in Stuart drama. Cambridge; New York: CUP, 1996. pp. xiv, 255. (Cf. bibl. 1991, 5375.)

7486. KAVENIK, FRANCES M.   British drama 1660–1779: a critical history. (Bibl. 1995, 6161.) Rev. by Nancy Copeland in Essays in Theatre (14:2) 1996, 188–91.

7487. KIEFER, FREDERICK.   Writing on the Renaissance stage: written words, printed pages, metaphoric books. *See* **5662**.

7488. KIRK, ANDREW M.   The mirror of confusion: the representation of French history in English Renaissance drama. *See* **5663**.

7489. KISS, ATTILA.   Abjection and power: the semiotics of violence in Jacobean tragedy. *In* (pp. 95–105) **53**.

7490. KNUTSON, ROSLYN L.   Elizabethan documents, captivity narratives, and the market for foreign history plays. *See* **5664**.

7491. LEINWAND, THEODORE B.   The city staged: Jacobean comedy, 1603–1613. (Bibl. 1989, 4172.) Rev. by Scott Cutler Shershow in JDTC (6:1) 1991, 144–6.

7492. LINDLEY, DAVID (ed.). Court masques: Jacobean and Caroline entertainments, 1605–1640. (Bibl. 1995, 6166.) Rev. by Richard Luckett in TLS, 29 Nov. 1996, 18–19.

7493. LUSARDI, JAMES P.; GRAS, HENK. Abram Booth's eyewitness account of the 1629 Lord Mayor's Show. ShB (11:3) 1993, 19–23.

7494. McDONALD, MARCIA A. The Elizabethan Poor Laws and the stage in the late 1590s. *See* **5670**.

7495. MacINTYRE, JEAN. Production resources at the Whitefriars Playhouse, 1609–1612. EMLS (2:3) 1996, 2.1–35.

7496. McJANNET, LINDA. Mapping the Ottomans on the Renaissance stage. *See* **5672**.

7497. McLUSKIE, KATHLEEN E. The shopping complex: materiality and the Renaissance theatre. *In* (pp. 86–101) **118**.

7498. MAGUIRE, NANCY KLEIN. Regicide and Restoration: English tragicomedy, 1660–1671. (Bibl. 1995, 6169.) Rev. by Eric Wilson in ShB (12:1) 1994, 50–1; by Paul Seaward in EHR (111:440) 1996, 188–9; by Richard Allen Cave in YES (26) 1996, 283–4.

7499. MAHLER, ANDREAS. A lost world, no new-found land – disorientation and immobility as social criticism in early seventeenth-century tragedy. *In* (pp. 27–43) **53**.

7500. MANN, DAVID D.; MANN, SUSAN GARLAND; GARNIER, CAMILLE. Women playwrights in England, Ireland, and Scotland, 1660–1823. Bloomington: Indiana UP, 1996. pp. xiii, 417.

7501. MAQUERLOT, JEAN-PIERRE; WILLEMS, MICHÈLE. Introduction. *In* (pp. 1–13) **124**.

7502. —— —— (eds). Travel and drama in Shakespeare's time. *See* **124**.

7503. MEERA, MOHAMMED NAGOOR. Naked shingles on the beach of life: the Jacobean age. WLR (1:1) 1996, 48–56.

7504. MIDDAUGH, KAREN L. 'Virtues sphear': court *vs* country in the 1618 masque at Coleorton. *In* (pp. 280–94) **116**.

7505. MONTAÑO, JOHN PATRICK. The quest for consensus: the Lord Mayor's Day shows in the 1670s. *In* (pp. 31–51) **21**.

7506. NEILL, MICHAEL. Bastardy, counterfeiting, and misogyny in *The Revenger's Tragedy*. *See* **6422**.

7507. NICHOLSON, ERIC A. The theater. *In* (pp. 295–314) **42**.

7508. OHTA, KAZUAKI (ed.). Elizabeth-cho engeki to ken'etsu. (Elizabethan drama and censorship.) *See* **5688**.

7509. OWEN, SUSAN J. Restoration theatre and crisis. Oxford: Clarendon Press; New York: OUP, 1996. pp. xii, 343.

7510. PALMER, BARBARA D. Court and country: the masque as sociopolitical subtext. *See* **5691**.

7511. PARK, WOO-SOO. *Renaissance* youngkukbigeuk eui soerak e gwanhayeo. (A note on the decline of English Renaissance tragedy.) *See* **5693**.

7512. PARKER, BRIAN. *A Fair Quarrel* (1617), the duelling code, and Jacobean law. *In* (pp. 52–75) **105**.

7513. PAYNE, DEBORAH C. Comedy, satire, or farce? Or, The generic difficulties of Restoration dramatic satire. TSL (37) 1995, 1–22.

7514. —— Reified object or emergent professional? Retheorizing the Restoration actress. *In* (pp. 24–38) **20**.

7515. PETERS, J. S. The novelty; or, Print, money, fashion, getting, spending, and glut. *In* (pp. 169–94) **20**.

7516. PIAZZA, ANTONELLA. *The Witch of Edmonton*: the space of the witch's body as formation and critique of the enclosed body. Textus (9:1) 1996, 161–72.

7517. POTTER, LOIS. Pirates and 'turning Turk' in Renaissance drama. *In* (pp. 124–40) **124**.

7518. RANDALL, DALE B. J. Winter fruit: English drama, 1642–1660. Lexington: Kentucky UP, 1995. pp. xiv, 454. Rev. by Marliss Desens in RMRLL (50:2) 1996, 205–6.

7519. RICE, COLIN ESMOND. Puritans and the theatre in the reign of James I. QLLSM (3) 1989, 281–307.

7520. —— 'Satan's synagogue': the theatre as antichurch in godly literature of opposition to the Elizabethan public theatre. *See* **5698**.

7521. RICHARDS, JEFFREY H. Theater enough: American culture and the metaphor of the world stage, 1607–1789. (Bibl. 1993, 4815.) Rev. by Jean-Christophe Agnew in AHR (98:2) 1993, 551–2; by David Grimstead in AmS (34:1) 1993, 184–5.

7522. ROSENTHAL, LAURA J. Playwrights and plagiarists in early modern England: gender, authorship, literary property. Ithaca, NY; London: Cornell UP, 1996. pp. x, 257.

7523. SAMUELS, PEGGY. Fire not light: Milton's simulacrum of tragi-comedy. *See* **6459**.

7524. SCOTT, MICHAEL. Confrontational comedy. *In* (pp. 167–77) **53**.

7525. SHAPIRO, JAMES. Recent studies in Tudor and Stuart drama. *See* **5706**.

7526. SMITH, EMMA, *et al.* Renaissance drama: excluding Shakespeare: criticism. *See* **5708**.

7527. SMITH, PETER J.; HAMPTON-REEVES, STUART. Renaissance drama: excluding Shakespeare: theatre history. *See* **5709**.

7528. SPRADLEY, DANA LLOYD. *Pericles* and the Jacobean family romance of union. *See* **7122**.

7529. STRAUB, KRISTINA. Actors and homophobia. *In* (pp. 258–80) **20**.

7530. SZÖNYI, GYÖRGY E. 'My charms are all o'erthrown': the social and ideological context of the magician in Jacobean drama. *In* (pp. 107–23) **53**.

7531. TATE, WILLIAM. King James I and the Queen of Sheba. ELR (26:3) 1996, 561–85.

7532. THOMSON, LESLIE. A quarto 'marked for performance': evidence of what? *See* **863**.

7533. TIPPETTS, NANCY LYN. Sisterhood, brotherhood, and equal-ity of the sexes in the Restoration comedies of manners. (Bibl. 1994, 5083.) Rev. by David Roberts in NQ (43:3) 1996, 353–4.

7534. TRAUB, VALERIE. The (in)significance of 'lesbian' desire in early modern England. *In* (pp. 62–83) **93**.

7535. TRUSSLER, SIMON (ed.). The play of personality in the Restoration theatre. By Anthony Masters. (Bibl. 1992, 5632.) Rev. by Richard Allen Cave in YES (26) 1996, 283–4.

7536. WYMER, ROWLAND. Jacobean pageant or Elizabethan *fin-de-siècle*? The political context of early seventeenth-century tragedy. *In* (pp. 45–58) **53**.

Fiction

7537. BALLASTER, ROS. Seductive forms: women's amatory fiction from 1684–1740. (Bibl. 1995, 6186.) Rev. by Hans Turley in StudN (27:2) 1995, 215–18.

7538. BARBOUR, REID. Recent studies of prose fiction, 1603–1660, including Sidney's *Arcadia. See* **5969**.

7539. GONDEBEAUD, LOUIS. Récits et romans picaresques en Angleterre (1576–1723). *See* **5720**.

7540. McKEON, MICHAEL. The origins of the English novel, 1600–1740. (Bibl. 1990, 4369.) Rev. by Elissa L. Stuchlik in Genre (23:1) 1990, 63–7.

7541. RACAULT, JEAN-MICHEL. L'utopie narrative en France et en Angleterre: 1675–1761. (Bibl. 1993, 4837.) Rev. by Roseann Runte in CanRCL (20:1/2) 1993, 246–8.

7542. SAMUELS, SHIRLEY. Romances of the Republic: women, the family, and violence in the literature of the early American nation. Oxford; New York: OUP, 1996. pp. viii, 198.

7543. TODD, JANET. The sign of Angellica: women, writing and fiction, 1660–1800. (Bibl. 1994, 5091.) Rev. by Mary Poovey in Signs (18:2) 1993, 430–3.

Literature for Children

7544. BOTTIGHEIMER, RUTH B. The child-reader of children's Bibles, 1656–1753. *In* (pp. 44–56) **48**.

Poetry

7545. ABRAMS, RICHARD. W[illiam] S[hakespeare]'s *Funeral Elegy* and the turn from the theatrical. *See* **557**.

7546. BARASH, CAROL. English women's poetry, 1649–1714: politics, community, and linguistic authority. Oxford: Clarendon Press; New York: OUP, 1996. pp. xii, 345.

7547. BELLANY, ALASTAIR. A poem on the archbishop's hearse: Puritanism, libel, and sedition after the Hampton Court conference. JBS (34:2) 1995, 137–64.

7548. BRADY, PATRICK. Rococo poetry in English, French, German, Italian: an introduction. Knoxville, TN: New Paradigm Press, 1992. pp. 109. Rev. by T. M. Pratt in MLR (90:3) 1995, 722.

7549. CARUSO, CARLO. Il sonetto inglese nel sedicesimo secolo. QLLSM (1) 1987, 283–303.

7550. CLEMENTS, ARTHUR L. Poetry of contemplation: John Donne, George Herbert, Henry Vaughan, and the modern period. (Bibl. 1995, 6196.) Rev. by Anthony Low in JDJ (9:2) 1990, 183–7.

7551. COMBE, KIRK. The new voice of political dissent: the transition from complaint to satire. *In* (pp. 73–94) **120**.

7552. DOWNS-GAMBLE, MARGARET. New pleasures prove: evidence of dialectical *disputatio* in early modern manuscript culture. *See* **2355**.

7553. ELLIS, JIM. The wit of circumcision, the circumcision of wit. *In* (pp. 62–77) **128**.

7554. ERSKINE-HILL, HOWARD. Poetry and the realm of politics: Shakespeare to Dryden. *See* **5729**.

7555. —— The poetry of opposition and revolution: Dryden to Wordsworth. Oxford: Clarendon Press; New York: OUP, 1996. pp. 270. Rev. by Matthew Reynolds in TLS, 27 Dec. 1996, 11–12.

7556. EVANS, ROBERT C.; WIEDEMANN, BARBARA (eds). 'My name was Martha': a Renaissance woman's autobiographical poem. (Bibl. 1994, 5102.) Rev. by Vivienne Larminie in EHR (111:442) 1996, 717–18; by Diane Purkiss in YES (26) 1996, 278–9; by Kathryn Murphy Anderson in ColLit (23:1) 1996, 217–25.

7557. FISCHLIN, DANIEL. Metalepsis and the rhetoric of lyric affect. *See* **2365**.

7558. —— 'Sighes and teares make life to last': the purgation of grief and death through trope in the English ayre. Criticism (38:1) 1996, 1–25.

7559. FOSTER, DONALD W. *A Funeral Elegy*: W(illiam) S(hakespeare)'s 'best-speaking witnesses'. *See* **2619**.

7560. GRAHAM, VIRGINIA (ed.). A selection of Metaphysical poets. *See* **5732**.

7561. HAMMOND, GERALD. Fleeting things: English poets and poems, 1616–1660. (Bibl. 1995, 6203.) Rev. by R. E. Pritchard in PN Review (17:3) 1991, 65–6.

7562. KELLY, ERNA. Women's wit. *In* (pp. 42–61) **128**.

7563. KERRIGAN, WILLIAM. A theory of female coyness. TSLL (38:2) 1996, 209–22.

7564. LOW, LISA; HARDING, ANTHONY JOHN (eds). Milton, the Metaphysicals and Romanticism. (Bibl. 1995, 31.) Rev. by Colin Burrow in CamQ (25:1) 1996, 84.

7565. McRAE, ANDREW. Fashioning a cultural icon: the ploughman in Renaissance texts. *See* **5196**.

7566. MARKLEY, ROBERT. 'Credit exhausted': satire and scarcity in the 1690s. TSL (37) 1995, 110–26.

7567. PASK, KEVIN. The emergence of the English author: scripting the life of the poet in early modern England. *See* **5740**.

7568. PEBWORTH, TED-LARRY. Manuscript transmission and the selection of copy-text in Renaissance coterie poetry. *See* **783**.

7569. RAMBUSS, RICHARD. Pleasure and devotion: the body of Jesus and seventeenth-century religious lyric. *In* (pp. 253–79) **93**.

7570. RAZOVSKY, HELAINE. Popular hermeneutics: monstrous children in English Renaissance broadside ballads. *See* **5742**.

7571. SCHUCHARD, RONALD (ed.). The varieties of Metaphysical poetry: the Clark Lectures at Trinity College, Cambridge, 1926, and the Turnbull Lectures at the Johns Hopkins University, 1933, by T. S. Eliot. (Bibl. 1995, 6227.) Rev. by Robert Craft in BkW, 22 May 1994, 4; by William H. Pritchard in ASch (64:3) 1995, 452–6; by James F. Loucks in ANQ (9:1) 1996, 33–7.

7572. SCODEL, JOSHUA. The pleasures of restraint: the mean of coyness in Cavalier poetry. Criticism (38:2) 1996, 239–79.

7573. SIMPSON, ROGER. Merlin and Hull: a seventeenth-century prophecy. Quondam et Futurus (3:1) 1993, 60–5.

7574. SUMMERS, CLAUDE J.; PEBWORTH, TED-LARRY (eds). The wit of seventeenth-century poetry. *See* **128**.

7575. SUMMERS, JOSEPH H. Collected essays on Renaissance literature. *See* **5746**.

7576. TERRY, RICHARD. 'Metempsychosis': a metaphor for literary tradition in Dryden and his contemporaries. *See* **2485**.

7577. WHEELER, ANGELA J. English verse satire from Donne to Dryden: imitation of Classical models. (Bibl. 1994, 5131.) Rev. by Stephan Lieske in ZAA (43:3) 1995, 273–4.

7578. WILCOX, HELEN. 'No more wit than a Christian?': the case of devotional poetry. *In* (pp. 9–21) **128**.

Prose

7579. ANSELMENT, RAYMOND A. The deliverances of Alice Thornton: the re-creation of a seventeenth-century life. Prose Studies (19:1) 1996, 19–36.

7580. APPELBAUM, ROBERT. Utopian Dubrovnik, 1659: an English fantasy. Utopian Studies (7:2) 1996, 66–92.

7581. BEER, ANNA. Textual politics: the execution of Sir Walter Ralegh. *See* **5960**.

7582. BELL, ALLAN. Munificent, wise and thoughtful gifts: Grace and Peter Redpath and the Redpath Tracts. *See* **453**.

7583. BLAND, MARK. 'Invisible dangers': censorship and the subversion of authority in early modern England. *See* **901**.

7584. BOESKY, AMY. Milton's Heaven and the model of the English utopia. SELit (36:1) 1996, 91–110.

7585. BURNS, JAMES. William Lithgow's Dalida: a seventeenth-century traveller's departure from Scotland. SLJ (23:1) 1996, 5–12.

7586. BURNS, JAMES R. William Lithgow and the Englishing of Loreto. NQ (43:2) 1996, 175–8.

7587. CLARK, IRA. Writing and dueling in the English Renaissance. *See* **5625**.

7588. CORNS, THOMAS N.; LOEWENSTEIN, DAVID (eds). The emergence of Quaker writing: Dissenting literature in seventeenth-century England. London: Cass, 1995. pp. 148.

7589. CROCKETT, BRYAN. The play of paradox: stage and sermon in Renaissance England. *See* **5628**.

7590. DANE, JOSEPH A. Perfect order and perfected order: the evidence from press-variants of early seventeenth-century quartos. *See* **267**.

7591. EDWARDS, PHILIP. Tragic form and the voyagers. *In* (pp. 75–86) **124**.

7592. FERGUSON, MOIRA. Seventeenth-century Quaker women: displacement, colonialism, and anti-slavery discourse. *In* (pp. 221–40) **21**.

7593. FRIEDMAN, JEROME. The battle of the frogs and Fairford's flies: miracles and the pulp press during the English Revolution. *See* **933**.

7594. GARDINER, JUDITH KEGAN. Re-gendering individualism: Margaret Fell Fox and Quaker rhetoric. *In* (pp. 205–24) **89**.

7595. HALTUNEN, KAREN. Early American murder narratives: the birth of horror. *In* (pp. 67–101) **88**.

7596. HEBEL, UDO J. Sanctioned images: court orders, legal codes, synodal resolutions, and the cultural contestation of seventeenth-century Puritan New England. YREAL (11) 1995, 43–74.

7597. HOBBY, ELAINE. The politics of women's prophecy in the English Revolution. *In* (pp. 295–306) **107**.

7598. —— A woman's best setting out is silence: the writings of Hannah Wolley. *In* (pp. 179–200) **21**.

7599. ILIFFE, ROBERT. 'Is he like other men?': the meaning of the *Principia Mathematica*, and the author as idol. *In* (pp. 159–76) **21**.

7600. KENNEDY, LAURENCE. Standing armies revisited (1697–1700): authorship, chronology, and public perception. NQ (43:3) 1996, 287–92.

7601. LARES, JAMEELA. *Paradise Lost*, Books XI and XII, and the homiletic tradition. MStud (34) 1996, 99–116.

7602. LOFTIS, JOHN E.   Congreve's *Way of the World* and popular criminal literature. SELit (36:3) 1996, 561–78.

7603. LOOMIS, CATHERINE.   Elizabeth Southwell's manuscript account of the death of Queen Elizabeth (with text). *See* **726**.

7604. MACLEAN, GERALD M.   Literature and politics in Revolutionary England, 1640–1660. Review (16) 1994, 177–95 (review-article).

7605. MARKLEY, ROBERT.   Fallen languages: crises of representation in Newtonian England, 1660–1740. (Bibl. 1995, 6267.) Rev. by Timothy J. Reiss in ECS (29:3) 1996, 337–9.

7606. MARTINAZZI, LAURA.   Tre documenti ufficiali della Virginia Company. Acme (48:3) 1995, 167–75.

7607. MICHEL, ROBERT.   *Pseudochristus*: a religious romance, 1649–1650. Fontanus (6) 1993, 97–118.

7608. MULLIGAN, LOTTE.   Self-scrutiny and the study of nature: Robert Hooke's diary as natural history. JBS (35:3) 1996, 311–42.

7609. PARR, ANTHONY.   Foreign relations in Jacobean England: the Sherley brothers and the 'voyage of Persia'. *In* (pp. 14–31) **124**.

7610. PARRY, GRAHAM.   Milton's *History of Britain* and the seventeenth-century antiquarian scene. Prose Studies (19:3) 1996, 238–46.

7611. RAYMOND, JOAD.   The cracking of the republican spokes. *See* **2454**.

7612. SCHOLZ, BERNHARD F.   Self-fashioning by mail: the letters of a Renaissance misfit. Prose Studies (19:2) 1996, 136–48.

7613. SINGH, JYOTSNA G.   Colonial narratives/cultural dialogues: 'discoveries' of India in the language of colonialism. London; New York: Routledge, 1996. pp. viii, 196.

7614. TROWELL, STEPHEN.   George Keith: post-Restoration Quaker theology and the experience of defeat. BJRL (76:1) 1994, 119–37.

7615. —— Unitarian and/or Anglican: the relationship of Unitarianism to the Church from 1687 to 1698. BJRL (78:1) 1996, 77–101. (*A Brief History of the Unitarians*, 1687.)

7616. WHITWORTH, MICHAEL.   T. E. Hulme's quotations from Milton and Ireton. NQ (43:4) 1996, 441–3.

7617. WILLIAMS, DANIEL E. (comp.).   Pillars of salt: an anthology of early American criminal narratives. (Bibl. 1995, 6287.) Rev. by Dawn Keetley in AmS (37:2) 1996, 190–2.

7618. ZIFF, LARZER.   Conquest and recovery in early writings from America. AL (68:3) 1996, 509–25.

Biography and Autobiography

7619. KEEBLE, N. H. Obedient subjects? The loyal self in some later seventeenth-century Royalist women's memoirs. *In* (pp. 201–18) **21**.

7620. SHERMAN, STUART.   Telling time: clocks, diaries, and English diurnal form, 1660–1785. Chicago; London: Chicago UP, 1996. pp. xv, 323.

Related Studies

7621. ALMOND, PHILIP C.   Heaven and Hell in Enlightenment England. Cambridge; New York: CUP, 1994. pp. xiii, 218. Rev. by R. D. Stock in Scriblerian (28:1/2) 1995/96, 92–3; by Paul Christianson in AHR (101:3) 1996, 846–7.

7622. BECHER, ANNE G.   Barlow's *Aesop* at Oxford. *See* **180**.

7623. BERMINGHAM, ANN; BREWER, JOHN (eds). The consumption of culture, 1600–1800: image, object, text. London; New York: Routledge, 1995. pp. xiv, 548, (plates) 100. (Consumption and culture in 17th and 18th centuries.) Rev. by W. A. Speck in EHR (111:442) 1996, 657–9; by James Raven in TLS, 5 July 1996, 30; by Jeremy Black in HT (46:3) 1996, 56.

7624. CAMPBELL, MARY BAINE. *Anthropometamorphosis*: John Bulwer's monsters of cosmology and the science of culture. *In* (pp. 202–22) **72**.

7625. CARRÉ, JACQUES (ed.). The crisis of courtesy: studies in the conduct-book in Britain, 1600–1900. Leiden; New York: Brill, 1994. pp. vi, 201, (plates) 16. (Brill's studies in intellectual history, 51.) Rev. by Alan T. McKenzie in Scriblerian (28:1/2) 1995/96, 104–5; by Peter Borsay in BJECS (19:2) 1996, 203–4.

7626. COPE, ESTHER S. Handmaid of the Holy Spirit: Dame Eleanor Davies, never soe mad a ladie. Ann Arbor: Michigan UP, 1992. pp. xvii, 247. Rev. by Teresa Feroli in TSWL (14:2) 1995, 377–81; by Susan Dwyer Amussen in JBS (35:1) 1996, 114–18.

7627. COX, CATHERINE I. From 'the house of the spider' to 'the citadel of God': representations of the plague in early modern England. *See* **5776**.

7628. DANIELS, BRUCE C. Sober mirth and pleasant poisons: Puritan ambivalence toward leisure and recreation in Colonial New England. AmS (34:1) 1993, 121–37.

7629. EDWARDS, FRANCIS. The division among the English Catholics: 1580–1610. *See* **5778**.

7630. ELDRIDGE, LARRY D. A distant heritage: the growth of free speech in early America. New York: New York UP, 1994. pp. xv, 198. Rev. by Ray B. Browne in JAC (18:4) 1995, 97.

7631. GOLDGAR, ANNE, Impolite learning: conduct and community in the republic of letters, 1680–1750. New Haven, CT; London: Yale UP, 1995. pp. xiii, 395. Rev. by Roger Chartier in TLS, 16 Aug. 1996, 12.

7632. GREENGRASS, MARK; LESLIE, MICHAEL; RAYLOR, TIMOTHY (eds). Samuel Hartlib and universal reformation: studies in intellectual communication. Cambridge; New York: CUP, 1994. pp. xi, 372. (Hartlib Papers Project of the Univ. of Sheffield.) Rev. by Douglas Chambers in Albion (28:3) 1996, 491–3.

7633. HANRATTY, GERALD. Philosophers of the Enlightenment: Locke, Hume and Berkeley revisited. Blackrock, Co. Dublin; Portland, OR: Four Courts Press, 1995. pp. 93.

7634. HART, CLIVE; STEVENSON, KAY GILLILAND. Heaven and the flesh: imagery of desire from the Renaissance to the Rococo. Cambridge; New York: CUP, 1995. pp. xiv, 237. Rev. by Peter J. Smith in CEl (50) 1996, 118–20.

7635. HULL, SUZANNE W. Women according to men: the world of Tudor–Stuart women. *See* **5783**.

7636. HUNTER, MICHAEL. Science and the shape of orthodoxy: intellectual change in late seventeenth-century Britain. Woodbridge, Suffolk; Rochester, NY: Boydell Press, 1995. pp. xii, 345. Rev. by Margaret J. Osler in Albion (28:3) 1996, 489–90; by Justin Champion in HT (46:12) 1996, 52–3.

7637. KRIKMANN, ARVO. The great chain metaphor: an 'open sesame' for proverb semantics? *See* **3324**.

7638.   Loewenstein, Joseph F.   Legal proofs and corrected readings: press-agency and the new bibliography. *In* (pp. 93–122) **90**.

7639.   Mack, Phyllis.   Visionary women: ecstatic prophecy in seventeenth-century England. (Bibl. 1995, 6312.) Rev. by Teresa Feroli in TSWL (14:2) 1995, 377–81; by Susan Dwyer Amussen in JBS (35:1) 1996, 114–18.

7640.   McKeon, Michael.   Historicizing patriarchy: the emergence of gender difference in England, 1660–1760. ECS (28:3) 1995, 295–322.

7641.   Pahl, Jon.   Paradox lost: free will and political liberty in American culture, 1630–1760. Baltimore, MD; London: Johns Hopkins UP, 1992. pp. xvi, 234. (New studies in American intellectual and cultural history.) Rev. by Jonathan M. Chu in AHR (98:5) 1993, 1675–6.

7642.   Parry, Glyn J. R.   The creation and recreation of Puritanism. *See* **5789**.

7643.   Pender, Stephen.   'No monsters in the resurrection': inside some conjoined twins. *In* (pp. 143–67) **72**.

7644.   Schmitz, Götz.   Satirical elements in Latin comedies acted on the occasion of royal visits to Cambridge University. *In* (pp. 217–30) **53**.

7645.   Sharpe, Kevin; Lake, Peter (eds).   Culture and politics in early Stuart England. Basingstoke: Macmillan, 1994. pp. x, 382. (Problems in focus.) Rev. by Richard Cust in EHR (111:442) 1996, 713–14; by Elizabeth Heale in YES (26) 1996, 280–1; by John Kenyon in JBS (35:2) 1996, 266–9.

7646.   Warnicke, Retha.   Private and public: the boundaries of women's lives in early Stuart England. *In* (pp. 123–40) **89**.

Literary Theory

This section is intended to contain studies **about** the literary theory, literary historiography, literary criticism, etc., produced *in* the seventeenth century. For modern works **of** literary history and criticism dealing generally with this period, see under 'Seventeenth Century: General Literary Studies'.

7647.   Anon. (ed.).   Women critics 1660–1820: an anthology. By the Folger Collective on Early Women Critics. (Bibl. 1995, 6323.) Rev. by E.B. in TLS, 31 May 1996, 30.

AUTHORS

Lancelot Andrewes

7648.   Hewison, P. E. (ed.).   Selected writings. Manchester: Carcanet, 1995. pp. xvi, 158. (Fyfield books.) Rev. by M.I. in TLS, 23 Feb. 1996, 32.

7649.   Rudrum, Alan.   T. S. Eliot on Lancelot Andrewes's 'word within a word'. ANQ (9:4) 1996, 43–4.

Robert Armin

7650.   Sutcliffe, Chris.   The canon of Robert Armin's work: an addition. *See* **5773**.

Mary Astell

7651. JOHNS, ALESSA. Mary Astell's 'excited needles': theorizing feminist utopia in seventeenth-century England. Utopian Studies (7:1) 1996, 60–74.

7652. ROSE, MARY BETH. 'Vigorous most / When most unactive deem'd': gender and the heroics of endurance in Milton's *Samson Agonistes*, Aphra Behn's *Oroonoko*, and Mary Astell's *Some Reflections upon Marriage*. MStud (33) 1996, 83–109.

7653. ZANDER, HORST. Die verheiratete Frau als Dienerin und Sklavin: zur Eheproblematik bei Mary Astell und Daniel Defoe. AAA (21:2) 1996, 239–53.

Francis Bacon

7654. ALBANESE, DENISE. New science, new world. *See* **6208**.

7655. ARCHER, JOHN MICHAEL. Surveillance and enlightenment in Bacon's *New Atlantis*. Assays (6) 1991, 111–27.

7656. ASHTON, SUSANNA. What brings home the Bacon? Shakespeare and turn-of-the-century American authorship. *See* **1224**.

7657. BAKER, ELLIOTT. *The Philosophy of the Plays of Shakespeare Unfolded* – and abridged. *See* **6216**.

7658. HAMMILL, GRAHAM. The epistemology of expuragtion: Bacon and *The Masculine Birth*. *In* (pp. 236–52) **93**.

7659. HUNTER, JOHN. The Euphuistic memory: Humanist culture and Bacon's *Advancement of Learning*. *See* **2400**.

7660. KNOPP, DIETHARD. Bacon and Shakespeare: a comparison of passages about favourite Renaissance themes. *See* **6376**.

7661. LEVAO, RONALD. Francis Bacon and the mobility of science. Representations (40) 1992, 1–32.

7662. MERRENS, REBECCA. Exchanging cultural capital: troping woman in Sidney and Bacon. *See* **5983**.

7663. O'ROURKE, SEAN PATRICK, *et al.* The most significant passage on rhetoric in the works of Francis Bacon. *See* **2441**.

7664. PELTONEN, MARKKU (ed.). The Cambridge companion to Bacon. Cambridge; New York: CUP, 1996. pp. xv, 372. Rev. by John Bossy in TLS, 11 Oct. 1996, 3–4.

7665. PLETT, HEINRICH F. Utopias Aporien: Ansichten einer prekären Literaturform. *In* (pp. 225–40) **11**.

7666. RODRÍGUEZ GARCÍA, JOSÉ MARÍA. Bacon, Essex, and discipline. Misc (17) 1996, 227–39.

7667. ROSE, DAN. The repatriation of anthropology. AmLH (8:1) 1996, 170–83.

7668. SESSIONS, W. A. Francis Bacon revisited. New York: Twayne; London: Prentice Hall, 1996. pp. xx, 180. (Twayne's English authors, 523.)

7669. TATE, WILLIAM. King James I and the Queen of Sheba. *See* **7531**.

7670. VICKERS, ILSE. Defoe and the new sciences. Cambridge; New York: CUP, 1996. pp. xvi, 196. (Cambridge studies in eighteenth-century English literature and thought, 32.) (Cf. bibl. 1988, 3914.)

7671. WALZER, ARTHUR E. The meanings of *purpose*. *See* **1988**.

Jane Barker

7672. KING, KATHRYN R.   Jane Barker, Mary Leapor and a chain of very odd contingencies. ELN (33:3) 1996, 14–27.

Beaumont and Fletcher

7673. BOWERS, FREDSON (gen. ed.).   The dramatic works in the Beaumont and Fletcher canon: vol. 10, *Honest Man's Fortune, Rollo, Duke of Normandy, The Spanish Curate, The Lovers' Progress, The Fair Maid of the Inn, The Laws of Candy*. Cambridge; New York: CUP, 1996. pp. vi, 752.

7674. DORANGEON, SIMONE.   Beaumont and Fletcher, or a self-subverting praise of virtue in an impure society. *In* (pp. 275–84) **53**.

7675. FINKELPEARL, PHILIP J.   Court and country politics in the plays of Beaumont and Fletcher. (Bibl. 1992, 5781.) Rev. by Eugene M. Waith in Shakespeare Yearbook (2) 1991, 229–31; by Eric Rasmussen in MedRen (7) 1995, 426–32.

7676. MASTEN, JEFF.   My two dads: collaboration and the reproduction of Beaumont and Fletcher. *In* (pp. 280–309) **93**.

7677. TASSARA, CARLA.   Un drammaturgo al bivio: il *Don Carlos* di Thomas Otway fra Shakespeare e Fletcher. *See* **6487**.

Francis Beaumont

7678. BLINCOE, NOEL R.   The analogous qualities of *The Two Noble Kinsmen* and *Masque of the Inner Temple and Grey's Inn*. *See* **7308**.

7679. WHITWORTH, CHARLES.   'The knight of the calf-skin': a note on *The Knight of the Burning Pestle*, II.306. CEI (49) 1996, 59–60.

Aphra Behn

7680. ALLISTON, APRIL.   Gender and the rhetoric of evidence in early-modern historical narratives. *See* **2303**.

7681. BURNS, EDWARD.   Rochester, Behn and the martyrdom of lust. *In* (pp. 329–36) **107**.

7682. CARLSON, SUSAN.   Aphra Behn's *The Emperor of the Moon*: staging seventeenth-century farce for twentieth-century tastes. Essays in Theatre (14:2) 1996, 117–30.

7683. COPELAND, NANCY.   Imagining Aphra: reinventing a female subject. TT (4:2) 1994, 135–44.

7684. DAVIS, LENNARD J.   The dreadful gulph and the glass cadaver: decomposing women in early modern literature. Genre (23:2/3) 1990, 121–33.

7685. DEAR, JEANNIE.   Nobodies and somebodies in eighteenth-century women's writing. ECent (37:2) 1996, 184–90 (review-article).

7686. FERGUSON, MARGARET.   News from the New World: miscegenous romance in Aphra Behn's *Oroonoko* and *The Widow Ranter*. *In* (pp. 151–89) **90**.

7687. FITZMAURICE, JAMES.   The narrator in Aphra Behn's *The Fair Jilt*. ZAA (42:2) 1994, 131–8.

7688. FROHOCK, RICHARD.   Violence and awe: the foundations of government in Aphra Behn's New World settings. ECF (8:4) 1996, 437–52.

7689. GOODFELLOW, SARAH.   'Such masculine strokes': Aphra Behn as translator of *A Discovery of New Worlds*. Albion (28:2) 1996, 229–50.

7690. HICKS, MALCOLM (ed.).   Selected poems. (Bibl. 1993, 4936.) Rev. in Scriblerian (28:1/2) 1995/96, 88–9.

7691. HUTNER, HEIDI (ed.). Rereading Aphra Behn: history, theory, and criticism. (Bibl. 1995, 6369.) Rev. by Lori Snook in Genre (26:2/3) 1993, 353–5.

7692. KELLY, ERNA. Women's wit. *In* (pp. 42–61) **128**.

7693. KINNEY, SUZ-ANNE. Confinement sharpens the invention: Aphra Behn's *The Rover* and Susanna Centlivre's *The Busie Body*. *In* (pp. 81–98) **64**.

7694. LOMAX, MARION (ed.). The rover. London: Black, 1994. pp. xxxiv, 126. (New mermaids.)

7695. LUSSIER, MARK S. 'Marrying that hated object': the carnival of desire in Behn's *The Rover*. *In* (pp. 225–39) **89**.

7696. MARKLEY, ROBERT. 'Be impudent, be saucy, forward, bold, touzing, and leud': the politics of masculine sexuality and feminine desire in Behn's Tory comedies. *In* (pp. 114–40) **20**.

7697. OWEN, SUSAN J. Restoration theatre and crisis. *See* **7509**.

7698. OWENS, W. R.; GOODMAN, LIZBETH. Remaking the canon: Aphra Behn's *The Rover*. *In* (pp. 131–91) **110**.

7699. —— —— (eds). Shakespeare, Aphra Behn and the canon. *See* **110**.

7700. PLASA, CARL; RING, BETTY J. (eds). The discourse of slavery: Aphra Behn to Toni Morrison. (Bibl. 1995, 6377.) Rev. by A. Robert Lee in NQ (43:2) 1996, 244–5.

7701. ROACH, JOSEPH. The artificial eye: Augustan theater and the empire of the visible. *In* (pp. 131–45) **83**.

7702. ROSE, MARY BETH. 'Vigorous most / When most unactive deem'd': gender and the heroics of endurance in Milton's *Samson Agonistes*, Aphra Behn's *Oroonoko*, and Mary Astell's *Some Reflections upon Marriage*. *See* **7652**.

7703. TODD, JANET. 'Pursue that way of fooling, and be damn'd': editing Aphra Behn. *See* **864**.

7704. —— (ed.). Aphra Behn studies. Cambridge; New York: CUP, 1996. pp. viii, 334.

7705. —— *Oroonoko, The Rover*, and other works. (Bibl. 1995, 6383.) Rev. in Scriblerian (28:1/2) 1995/96, 88–9.

7706. —— The works of Aphra Behn: vol. 2, Love letters between a nobleman and his sister (1684–7). London: Pickering, 1993. pp. xiv, 473. (Pickering masters.)

7707. —— The works of Aphra Behn: vol. 5, The plays 1671–1677. London: Pickering, 1996. pp. xvi, 583. (Pickering masters.) Rev. by Ros Ballaster in TLS, 6 Dec. 1996, 18.

7708. —— The works of Aphra Behn: vol. 6, The plays 1678–1682. London: Pickering, 1996. pp. vii, 486. (Pickering masters.) Rev. by Ros Ballaster in TLS, 6 Dec. 1996, 18.

7709. —— The works of Aphra Behn: vol. 7, The plays 1682–1696. London: Pickering, 1996. pp. vii, 474. (Pickering masters.) Rev. by Ros Ballaster in TLS, 6 Dec. 1996, 18.

William Bradford

7710. BROWN, THOMAS H. Predetermining interpretation: William Bradford's *Of Plymouth Plantation*. WebS (12:2) 1995, 111–16.

Anne Bradstreet

7711. KELLY, ERNA. Women's wit. *In* (pp. 42–61) **128**.

7712. WRIGHT, NANCY E.   Epitaphic conventions and the reception of Anne Bradstreet's public voice. EAL (31:3) 1996, 243–63.

Richard Brome

7713. CLARK, IRA.   Professional playwrights: Massinger, Ford, Shirley, and Brome. (Bibl. 1995, 6397.) Rev. by Martin Butler in YES (26) 1996, 277–8.

7714. KEWES, PAULINA.   The politics of the stage and the page: source plays for George Powell's *A Very Good Wife* (1693) in their production and publication contexts. ZRL (37:1/2) 1994, 41–52.

7715. PARR, ANTHONY (ed.).   Three Renaissance travel plays. Manchester: Manchester UP; New York: St Martin's Press, 1995. pp. xii, 330. (Revels plays companion library.) (*Antipodes, The Travels of the Three English Brothers, The Sea Voyage.*) Rev. by Eric Wilson in EMLS (2:2) 1996, 10.1–6.

Sir Thomas Browne

7716. FRONT, DOV.   Which is the first unauthorised edition of the *Religio Medici*? *See* **648**.

7717. ROEBUCK, GRAHAM.   Elegies for Donne: Great Tew and the poets. JDJ (9:2) 1990, 125–35.

7718. SEELIG, SHARON CADMAN.   Generating texts: the progeny of seventeenth-century prose. Charlottesville; London: Virginia UP, 1996. pp. x, 202.

John Bunyan

7719. ALBLAS, JACQUES B. H.   The Bunyan collection of the Vrije Universiteit, Amsterdam. *See* **440**.

7720. DANIELSON, DENNIS.   Milton, Bunyan, and the clothing of Truth and Righteousness. *In* (pp. 247–69) **40**.

7721. FRANSON, J. KARL.   From Vanity Fair to Emerald City: Baum's debt to Bunyan. ChildLit (23) 1995, 91–114.

7722. GRAHAM, ELSPETH.   'Lewd, profane swaggerers' and charismatic preachers: John Bunyan and George Fox. *In* (pp. 307–18) **107**.

7723. GREAVES, RICHARD L.   'Let truth be free': John Bunyan and the Restoration crisis of 1667–1673. Albion (28:4) 1996, 587–605.

7724. KEEBLE, N. H.   'Till one greater man / Restore us …': restoration images in Milton and Bunyan. Bunyan Studies (6) 1995/96, 6–33.

7725. MAILLOUX, STEVEN.   Persuasions good and bad: Bunyan, Iser, and Fish on rhetoric and hermeneutics in literature. *See* **2425**.

7726. MANNING, ROBERT.   *The Pilgrim's Progress*: a vindication and celebration of Vaughan Williams's neglected masterpiece. Bunyan Studies (6) 1995/96, 70–7.

7727. MARTIN, W. TODD.   *The Enormous Room*: cummings' re-interpretation of John Bunyan's Doubting Castle. Spring (5) 1996, 112–19.

7728. RANDALL, JAMES GREGORY.   'The primrose way': John Bunyan's *The Life and Death of Mr Badman* and the picaresque. 1650–1850 (2) 1996, 167–84.

7729. SWAIM, KATHLEEN M.   *Pilgrim's Progress*, Puritan progress: discourses and contexts. (Bibl. 1995, 6438.) Rev. by William Lamont in Literature and History (5:1) 1996, 109–10.

7730. TITLESTAD, P. J. H. The 'pretty young man Civility': Bunyan, Milton & Blake and patterns of Puritan thought. *See* **1925**.

7731. WALKER, DAVID. Language, genre, and revolution. *See* **2728**.

7732. ZINCK, ARLETTE M. 'Doctrine by ensample': sanctification through literature in Milton and Bunyan. Bunyan Studies (6) 1995/96, 44–55.

Robert Burton

7733. FAULKNER, THOMAS C.; KIESSLING, NICOLAS K.; BLAIR, RHONDA L. (eds). The anatomy of melancholy: vol. I, Text, the first partition. (Bibl. 1993, 4965.) Rev. by Ernest W. Sullivan, II, in Text (Ann Arbor) (7) 1994, 521–9.

7734. GOODSON, A. C. Frankenstein in the age of Prozac. LitMed (15:1) 1996, 17–32.

7735. KIESSLING, NICOLAS K. The library of Robert Burton: new discoveries. *See* **495**.

7736. SEELIG, SHARON CADMAN. Generating texts: the progeny of seventeenth-century prose. *See* **7718**.

Samuel Butler (1612–1680)

7737. BRAVERMAN, RICHARD. Satiric embodiments: Butler, Swift, Sterne. TSL (37) 1995, 76–93.

Thomas Campion

7738. LOUGHLIN, MARIE H. 'Love's friend and stranger to virginitie': the politics of the virginal body in Ben Jonson's *Hymenaei* and Thomas Campion's *The Lord Hay's Masque*. ELH (63:4) 1996, 833–49.

Thomas Carew

7739. ROEBUCK, GRAHAM. Elegies for Donne: Great Tew and the poets. *See* **7717**.

7740. SWANN, MARJORIE. Cavalier love: fetishism and its discontents. LitPs (42:3) 1996, 15–35.

Elizabeth Cary, Viscountess Falkland

7741. BERRY, BOYD M. Feminine construction of patriarchy; or, What's comic in *The Tragedy of Mariam*. MedRen (7) 1995, 257–74.

7742. BRACKETT, GINGER ROBERTS. Elizabeth Cary: writer of conscience. Greensboro, NC: Morgan Reynolds, 1996. pp. 94. (World writers.)

7743. FOSTER, DONALD W. Resurrecting the author: Elizabeth Tanfield Cary. *In* (pp. 141–73) **89**.

George Chapman

7744. HUNTINGTON, JOHN. 'This ticklish title': Chapman, *Nennio*, and the critique of nobility. *See* **5760**.

7745. MARGESON, JOHN. Individualism and order in the *Byron* plays of Chapman and Jonson's *Catiline*. *In* (pp. 111–21) **16**.

7746. TRICOMI, ALBERT H. Shakespeare, Chapman, and the Julius Caesar play in Renaissance Humanist drama. *In* (pp. 395–412) **98**.

Edward Hyde, Earl of Clarendon

7747. ROEBUCK, GRAHAM.   Elegies for Donne: Great Tew and the poets. *See* **7717**.

John Clavel

7748. PAFFORD, J. H. P.   John Clavell 1601–43: highwayman, author, lawyer, doctor. With a reprint of his poem *A Recantation of an Ill Led Life*, 1634. (Bibl. 1994, 5290.) Rev. by David Underdown in EHR (111:444) 1996, 1277–8.

William Congreve

7749. BARTLETT, LAURENCE.   William Congreve, an annotated bibliography, 1978–1994. Lanham, MD; London: Scarecrow Press, 1996. pp. xii, 109. (Scarecrow author bibliographies, 97.)

7750. BLOOM, DONALD A.   Dwindling into wifehood: the romantic power of the witty heroine in Shakespeare, Dryden, Congreve, and Austen. *In* (pp. 53–79) **64**.

7751. COUNSELL, COLIN.   Traversing the known: spatiality and the gaze in pre- and post-Renaissance theatre. *See* **5019**.

7752. DI FLORIO, RITA.   Il libertinismo come forma embrionale del pensiero illuminista. *See* **7371**.

7753. GRIFFITHS, TREVOR R. (ed.).   The way of the world. London: Hern, 1995. pp. xx, 106. (Drama classics.)

7754. LOFTIS, JOHN E.   Congreve's *Way of the World* and popular criminal literature. *See* **7602**.

7755. MCKENZIE, D. F.   A new Congreve literary autograph. *See* **388**.

7756. SIEBER, ANITA.   Character portrayal in Congreve's comedies *The Old Batchelour*, *Love for Love*, and *The Way of the World*. Lewiston, NY; Lampeter: Mellen Press, 1996. pp. v, 151. (Salzburg studies in English literature. Poetic drama & poetic theory, 183.)

Thomas Coryate

7757. BATE, JONATHAN.   The Elizabethans in Italy. *In* (pp. 55–74) **124**.

7758. ROEBUCK, GRAHAM.   *Johannes Factus* and the anvil of the wits. JDJ (15) 1996, 141–52.

Abraham Cowley

7759. AUSTIN, MICHAEL.   Saul and the social contract: constructions of 1 Samuel 8–11 in Cowley's *Davideis* and Defoe's *Jure Divino*. PLL (32:4) 1996, 410–36.

Richard Crashaw

7760. BECK, JOYCE LORRAINE.   Negative subjectivity in Luce Irigaray's *La Mystérique*, Donne's *A Nocturnall Upon S. Lucies Day*, and Crashaw's *Glorious Epiphanie*. SM (15:1) 1992, 3–17.

7761. ELLIS, JIM.   The wit of circumcision, the circumcision of wit. *In* (pp. 62–77) **128**.

7762. FORKER, CHARLES.   The religious sensibility of Richard Crashaw. In-between (1:1) 1992, 57–76.

7763. HEALY, THOMAS F.   Richard Crashaw. (Bibl. 1989, 4375.) Rev. by Maureen Sabine in JDJ (9:2) 1990, 173–82.

7764. JOHNSON, JEFFREY.   'Til we mix wounds': liturgical paradox and Crashaw's Classicism. *In* (pp. 251–8) **107**.

7765. PARRISH, PAUL A. Milton and Crashaw: the Cambridge and Italian years. *In* (pp. 208–29) **40**.

7766. ROBERTS, JOHN R. (ed.). New perspectives on the life and art of Richard Crashaw. (Bibl. 1993, 4994.) Rev. by Maureen Sabine in JDJ (9:2) 1990, 173–82.

7767. ROBERTS, LORRAINE. The 'truewit' of Crashaw's poetry. *In* (pp. 171–82) **128**.

7768. SABINE, MAUREEN. 'My souls country-man': the critical recovery of Crashaw. JDJ (9:2) 1990, 173–82 (review-article).

7769. WARWICK, CLAIRE. 'Love thou art absolute': Richard Crashaw and the discourse of human and divine love. *In* (pp. 237–50) **107**.

John Crowne

7770. MAGUIRE, NANCY KLEIN. Factionary politics: John Crowne's *Henry VI. In* (pp. 70–92) **21**.

Samuel Danforth, I

7771. RONNICK, MICHELE VALERIE. A Horatian influence on the verse of Samuel Danforth (1626–1674). ELN (32:1) 1994, 37–9.

Samuel Daniel

7772. DONNO, ELIZABETH S. (ed.). Three Renaissance pastorals: Tasso, Guarini, Daniel. (Bibl. 1994, 5298.) Rev. by Chris Wortham in Parergon (14:1) 1996, 283–4.

7773. JONES, STANLEY. Further quotations and reminiscences in Hazlitt: Daniel, the Bible, Milton, Paine, Dorset. NQ (43:1) 1996, 37–8.

7774. WORTHAM, SIMON. *The glasse of majesty*: reflections on New Historicism and cultural materialism. Angelaki (2:2) 1996, 47–57.

Francis Davison

7775. HATCHWELL, RICHARD. A Francis Davison/William Drummond conundrum. *See* **490**.

John Day

7776. PARR, ANTHONY (ed.). Three Renaissance travel plays. *See* **7715**.

Thomas Dekker

7777. BLY, MARY. Imagining consummation: women's erotic language in comedies of Dekker and Shakespeare. *In* (pp. 35–52) **64**.

7778. BOOTH, ROY J. Meddling with awl: reading Dekker's *The Shoemaker's Holiday* (with a note on *The Merry Wives of Windsor*.) *See* **7041**.

7779. BORN-LECHLEITNER, ILSE. Implicit social criticism in *The Witch of Edmonton. In* (pp. 261–74) **53**.

7780. CHAKRAVORTY, SWAPAN. 'Give her more onion': unriddling the Welsh madman's speech in *The Changeling. See* **2597**.

7781. CLASSEN, ALBRECHT. Die Weltwirkung des *Fortunatus. See* **3381**.

7782. DAALDER, JOOST. Madness in parts 1 and 2 of *The Honest Whore*: a case for close reading. AUMLA (86) 1996, 63–79.

7783. HONIGMANN, E. A. J. Social questioning in Elizabethan and Jacobean plays, with special reference to *Othello. In* (pp. 3–11) **53**.

7784. JACOBS, DEBORAH. Critical imperialism and Renaissance drama: the case of *The Roaring Girl. In* (pp. 73–84) **33**.

7785. McLUSKIE, KATHLEEN E.   Dekker and Heywood: professional dramatists. (Bibl. 1994, 5307.) Rev. by Simon Morgan-Russell in SNL (44:3) 1994, 55; by Susan Baker in ShB (14:3) 1996, 42–3.

7786. OLIVIA, LEANORA.   The erotic goals of defiant virgins: a comparative study of late antique poetry and early modern drama. TexPres (17) 1996, 39–45.

7787. PIAZZA, ANTONELLA.   *The Witch of Edmonton*: the space of the witch's body as formation and critique of the enclosed body. See **7516**.

7788. STRAZNICKY, MARTA.   The end(s) of discord in *The Shoemaker's Holiday*. SELit (36:2) 1996, 357–72.

7789. WORTHAM, SIMON.   *The glasse of majesty*: reflections on New Historicism and cultural materialism. See **7774**.

John Donne

7790. ALBANESE, DENISE.   New science, new world. See **6208**.

7791. BAKER-SMITH, DOMINIC.   John Donne as medievalist. In (pp. 185–93) **107**.

7792. BAUMLIN, JAMES S.   Dialogue and *controversia* in English Renaissance literature: historicizing the reader's response. See **5970**.

7793. BECK, JOYCE LORRAINE.   Negative subjectivity in Luce Irigaray's *La Mystérique*, Donne's *A Nocturnall Upon S. Lucies Day*, and Crashaw's *Glorious Epiphanie*. See **7760**.

7794. BLANK, PAULA.   Comparing Sappho to Philaenis: John Donne's 'homopoetics'. PMLA (110:3) 1995, 358–68.

7795. BOOTY, JOHN (ed.).   John Donne: selections from *Divine Poems, Sermons, Devotions*, and *Prayers*. Preface by P. G. Stanwood. New York: Paulist Press, 1990. pp. vii, 309. (Classics of Western spirituality.) Rev. by Arthur L. Clements in SM (14:4) 1991, 77–9.

7796. BROWN, MEG LOTA.   Donne and the politics of conscience in early modern England. (Bibl. 1995, 6505.) Rev. by Jeanne Shami in JDJ (15) 1996, 213–17.

7797. BURKE, VICTORIA.   John Donne and the true Church. ERev (5:3) 1995, 32–5.

7798. BUTLER, GEORGE F.   Donne's *Biathanatos* and *Samson Agonistes*: ambivalence and ambiguity. MStud (34) 1996, 199–219.

7799. CAREY, JOHN (ed.).   Selected poetry. Oxford; New York: OUP, 1996. pp. xxvi, 265. (World's classics.)

7800. CREASER, JOHN.   Milton: the truest of the sons of Ben. In (pp. 158–83) **40**.

7801. DAVIES, DAMIAN WALFORD.   Blake, Donne, and death. NQ (43:1) 1996, 40–1.

7802. DAVIES, STEVIE.   John Donne. (Bibl. 1995, 6511.) Rev. by Graham Parry in In-between (5:2) 1996, 195–8.

7803. EDGECOMBE, RODNEY STENNING.   Eschatological elements in Donne's *Anniversarie*. JDJ (15) 1996, 63–73.

7804. ELLIS, JIM.   The wit of circumcision, the circumcision of wit. In (pp. 62–77) **128**.

7805. FLYNN, DENNIS.   John Donne and the ancient Catholic nobility. (Bibl. 1995, 6516.) Rev. by Maureen Sabine in JDJ (15) 1996, 203–11; by Elizabeth Hodgson in EMLS (2:1) 1996, 10.4–7.

7806. FRANSSEN, PAUL J. C. M.   Donne's jealous God and the concept of sacred parody. In (pp. 151–62) **107**.

7807. FREER, COBURN. John Donne and Elizabethan economic theory. Criticism (38:4) 1996, 497–520.

7808. FRIEDMAN, DONALD M. Christ's image and likeness in Donne. JDJ (15) 1996, 75–94.

7809. FRONTAIN, RAYMOND-JEAN. Translating heavenwards: *Upon the Translation of the Psalmes* and John Donne's poetics of praise. ExRC (22) 1996, 103–25.

7810. FROST, KATE GARTNER. The Lothian portrait: a prolegomenon. JDJ (15) 1996, 95–125.

7811. GARDINER, ANNE BARBEAU. Donne and the Real Presence of the absent lover. JDJ (9:2) 1990, 113–24.

7812. GOOCH, BRYAN N. S. Music for Donne. JDJ (15) 1996, 171–88.

7813. GRAZIANI, RENÉ. Donne's *Anniversaries* and the beatification of Elizabeth Drury by poetic licence. *In* (pp. 59–80) **16**.

7814. GUIBBORY, ACHSAH. Donne, the idea of woman, and the experience of love. JDJ (9:1) 1990, 105–12.

7815. —— *The Relique*, the Song of Songs, and Donne's *Songs and Sonets*. JDJ (15) 1996, 23–44.

7816. HALEWOOD, WILLIAM H. The predicament of the westward rider. SP (93:2) 1996, 218–28.

7817. HANSHAW, LARRY. The literary influence of alchemy: an explication of selected works. PCR (6:1) 1995, 61–73.

7818. HERZ, JUDITH SCHERER. Resisting mutuality. JDJ (9:1) 1990, 27–31. (*Aire and Angels*.)

7819. HESTER, M. THOMAS. 'Let me love': reading the sacred 'currant' of Donne's profane lyrics. *In* (pp. 129–50) **107**.

7820. —— (ed.). John Donne's 'desire of more': the subject of Anne More Donne in his poetry. Newark: Delaware UP; London; Toronto: Assoc. UPs, 1996. pp. 265.

7821. JANG, YOUNG-GIL. John Donne ongho reul wihan gujo balsangronjeok jeopgeun. (A defence of John Donne in the light of genetic structuralism.) JELL (42:3) 1996, 497–521.

7822. JOHNSON, JEFFREY. Gold in the washes: Donne's last going into Germany. Ren (46:3) 1994, 199–207.

7823. KLEIMAN, ED. Adamant in grace: the subtlety of Donne's most subtle craftsman. EngS (77:4) 1996, 343–50.

7824. LABRIOLA, ALBERT C. Painting and poetry of the cult of Elizabeth I: the Ditchley portrait and Donne's *Elegie: Going to Bed*. SP (93:1) 1996, 42–63.

7825. —— 'This dialogue of one': rational argument and affective discourse in Donne's *Aire and Angels*. JDJ (9:1) 1990, 77–83.

7826. LAROCCO, STEVE. Contentious intimations: John Donne, *Richard III*, and the transgressive structures of seduction. *See* **7148**.

7827. LAZO, RODRIGO. In search of El Dorado: desire and history in Donne's language of colonization. Exemplaria (8:1) 1996, 269–86.

7828. MARTIN, CATHERINE GIMELLI. Pygmalion's progress in the garden of love; or, The wit's work is never Donne. *In* (pp. 78–100) **128**.

7829. MAULE, JEREMY. Donne and the past. *In* (pp. 203–21) **107**.

7830. MUELLER, JANEL. The play of difference in Donne's *Aire and Angels*. JDJ (9:1) 1990, 85–94.

7831. PAYNE, CRAIG. Donne's *Holy Sonnet XIV*. Exp (54:4) 1996, 209–13.

7832. Pebworth, Ted-Larry.   The early audiences of Donne's poetic performances. *See* **993**.

7833. —— Manuscript transmission and the selection of copy-text in Renaissance coterie poetry. *See* **783**.

7834. Price, Michael W.   'Offending without witnes': recusancy, equivocation, and face-painting in Donne's early life and writings. ExRC (22) 1996, 51–81.

7835. Raspa, Anthony (ed.).   Pseudo-martyr. (Bibl. 1995, 6549.) Rev. by Elizabeth Hodgson in EMLS (2:1) 1996, 10.1–3.

7836. Revard, Stella P.   The angelic messenger in *Aire and Angels*. JDJ (9:1) 1990, 15–17.

7837. Roberts, John R.   'Just such disparitie': the critical debate about *Aire and Angels*. JDJ (9:1) 1990, 43–64.

7838. Roebuck, Graham.   Elegies for Donne: Great Tew and the poets. *See* **7717**.

7839. —— *Johannes Factus* and the anvil of the wits. *See* **7758**.

7840. Sabine, Maureen.   'A place of honor': Dennis Flynn's biography of Donne. JDJ (15) 1996, 203–11 (review-article).

7841. Schoenfeldt, Michael C.   Patriarchal assumptions and egalitarian designs. JDJ (9:1) 1990, 23–6. (*Aire and Angels*.)

7842. Seelig, Sharon Cadman.   Generating texts: the progeny of seventeenth-century prose. *See* **7718**.

7843. Sellin, Paul R.   The mimetic poetry of Jack and John Donne: a field theory for the amorous and the divine. *In* (pp. 163–72) **107**.

7844. Shawcross, John T.   Donne's *Aire and Angels*: text and context. *See* **828**.

7845. —— Notes on an important volume of Donne's poetry and prose. *See* **420**.

7846. —— Some rereadings of John Donne's poems. JDJ (15) 1996, 45–61.

7847. Shell, Cheryl A.   The foe in sight: discovering the enemy in Donne's *Elegie XIX*. WLA (4:2) 1992, 1–18.

7848. Singer, Daniella E.   Despair and subjectivity in the erotic verse of Sidney and of Donne. *See* **5991**.

7849. Slights, Camille Wells.   Air, angels, and the progress of love. JDJ (9:1) 1990, 95–104.

7850. Smith, A. J.; Phillips, Catherine (eds).   John Donne: the critical heritage: vol. II. London; New York: Routledge, 1996. pp. xlii, 504. (Critical heritage.)

7851. Spinrad, Phoebe S.   *Aire and Angels* and questionable shapes. JDJ (9:1) 1990, 19–22.

7852. Spurr, Barry.   The John Donne papers of Wesley Milgate. JDJ (15) 1996, 189–201.

7853. Stanwood, P. G.   Donne's art of preaching and the reconstruction of Tertullian. *See* **2475**.

7854. —— Donne's reinvention of the Fathers: sacred truths suitably expressed. *In* (pp. 195–201) **107**.

7855. Stapleton, M. L.   'Why should they not alike in all parts touch?': Donne and the elegiac tradition. JDJ (15) 1996, 1–22.

7856. Stein, Arnold.   Interpretation: *Aire and Angels*. JDJ (9:1) 1990, 65–75.

7857. Stringer, Gary A.   Some sacred and profane con-texts of John Donne's *Batter My Hart*. *In* (pp. 173–83) **107**.

7858. STROMMER, JEAN THERESA; STROMMER, JOAN ELIZABETH. Transcendence in poetry, music and film: *La Corona* (John Donne, Ernst Krenek, Joan & Jean Strommer, 1609/1941/1987): iconic implications of circular structures. Analecta Husserliana (49) 1996, 107–13.

7859. SULLIVAN, CERI. Seventeenth-century wreath poems. GHJ (19:1/2) 1995/96, 95–101.

7860. SULLIVAN, ERNEST W., II. 1633 vndone. *See* **847**.

7861. —— Updating the John Donne listings in Peter Beal's *Index of English Literary Manuscripts*, II. *See* **426**.

7862. SWISS, MARGO. *Lachrymae Christi*: the theology of tears in Milton's *Lycidas* and Donne's sermon *Jesus Wept*. *In* (pp. 135–57) **40**.

7863. TAYLER, EDWARD W. Donne's idea of a woman: structure and meaning in *The Anniversaries*. (Bibl. 1995, 6563.) Rev. by John Mulryan in Cithara (36:1) 1996, 34–6.

7864. TEBEAUX, ELIZABETH. Memory, reason, and the quest for certainty in the *Sermons* of John Donne. Ren (43:3) 1991, 195–213.

7865. VANDER PLOEG, SCOTT D. Donne's 'witchcraft by a picture' as evidence of a performative aesthetic. SRASP (19) 1996, 51–61.

7866. WILTENBURG, ROBERT. Donne's dialogue of one: the self and the soul. *In* (pp. 413–27) **98**.

7867. YOUNG, R. V. Angels in *Aire and Angels*. JDJ (9:1) 1990, 1–14.

Michael Drayton

7868. BLAINE, MARLIN E. Drayton's Agincourt in 1606: history, genre, and national consciousness. RenP 1996, 53–65.

7869. WENTWORTH, MICHAEL. 'When first I ended, then I first began': Petrarch's triumph in Michael Drayton's *Idea*. *In* (pp. 116–32) **116**.

William Drummond of Hawthornden

7870. HATCHWELL, RICHARD. A Francis Davison/William Drummond conundrum. *See* **490**.

John Dryden

7871. BLOOM, DONALD A. Dwindling into wifehood: the romantic power of the witty heroine in Shakespeare, Dryden, Congreve, and Austen. *In* (pp. 53–79) **64**.

7872. CALDWELL, TANYA. Honey and venom: Dryden's third *Georgic*. ECL (20:3) 1996, 20–36.

7873. CORDNER, MICHAEL; CLAYTON, RONALD (eds). Four Restoration marriage plays. Oxford; New York: OUP, 1995. pp. lx, 439. (Oxford drama library.) (John Dryden, *Amphitryon; or, The Two Sosias*; Nathaniel Lee, *The Princess of Cleves*; Thomas Otway, *The Soldiers' Fortune*; Thomas Southerne, *The Wives' Excuse; or, Cuckolds Make Themselves*.)

7874. DEARING, VINTON A. (ed.). The works of John Dryden: vol. 12, Plays: *Amboyna, The State of Innocence, Aureng-Zebe*. (Bibl. 1995, 6578.) Rev. by David Hopkins in NQ (43:3) 1996, 350–2.

7875. FRANK, MARCIE. Fighting women and lovng men: Dryden's representation of Shakespeare in *All for Love*. *In* (pp. 310–29) **93**.

7876. GILLESPIE, STUART; OGDEN, JAMES. The later seventeenth century: Dryden. YWES (75) 1994, 319–22.

7877. HAMMOND, PAUL (ed.). The poems of John Dryden: vol. 1,

1649–1681. (Bibl. 1995, 6583.) Rev. by David Womersley in NQ (43:3) 1996, 352–3.

7878. —— The poems of John Dryden: vol. 2, 1682–1685. (Bibl. 1995, 6584.) Rev. by David Womersley in NQ (43:3) 1996, 352–3.

7879. HARTH, PHILLIP.   Pen for a party: Dryden's Tory propaganda in its contexts. (Bibl. 1995, 6585.) Rev. by K. J. H. Berland in Scriblerian (28:1/2) 1995/96, 59–61; by Colin Nicholson in BJECS (19:1) 1996, 90–1; by John Spurr in EHR (111:441) 1996, 473–5; by Ivan Roots in Literature and History (5:1) 1996, 110–12; by Helmut Castrop in Archiv (233:1) 1996, 174–6.

7880. HINNANT, CHARLES H.   Augustan semiosis. TSL (37) 1995, 256–74.

7881. KAMINSKI, THOMAS.   Rehabilitating 'Augustanism': on the roots of 'polite letters' in England. ECL (20:3) 1996, 49–65.

7882. KINGSLEY, MARGERY A.   'High on a throne of his own labours rear'd': *Mac Flecknoe*, Jeremiad and cultural myth. MP (93:3) 1996, 327–51.

7883. KRAMER, DAVID BRUCE.   The imperial Dryden: the poetics of appropriation in seventeenth-century England. (Bibl. 1995, 6592.) Rev. by Denise Cuthbert in AUMLA (85) 1996, 157–8.

7884. KROLL, RICHARD.   Instituting imperialism: Hobbes's *Leviathan* and Dryden's *Marriage à la Mode*. *In* (pp. 39–66) **20**.

7885. LEE, KYUNG-WON.   John Dryden eui sikmingeuk gwa gidokkyo jekukjueui eui shinhwa. (John Dryden's colonial plays and the myth of Christian imperialism.) JELL (42:2) 1996, 439–62.

7886. McHENRY, ROBERT W., JR (ed.).   The temper of John Dryden. By Thomas H. Fujimura. (Bibl. 1995, 6596.) Rev. by Wendy Jones Nakanishi in EngS (76:5) 1995, 491–2; by Colin Nicholson in BJECS (19:1) 1996, 89.

7887. MINER, EARL; BRADY, JENNIFER (eds).   Literary transmission and authority: Dryden and other writers. (Bibl. 1995, 6599.) Rev. by Colin Nicholson in BJECS (19:1) 1996, 89–90; by John Dolan in AUMLA (86) 1996, 117–18; by David F. Venturo in CLS (33:3) 1996, 322–6.

7888. MORTON, TIMOTHY.   Trade winds. *See* **2432**.

7889. OWEN, SUSAN J.   Restoration theatre and crisis. *See* **7509**.

7890. PAIGE, LINDA ROHRER.   'A stranger in a strange land': biblical typology of the Exodus in Dryden's *The Spanish Friar; or, The Double Discovery*. PLL (32:3) 1996, 263–76.

7891. QUINSEY, KATHERINE M.   *Religio Laici*? Dryden's men of wit and the printed word. *In* (pp. 199–214) **128**.

7892. ROACH, JOSEPH.   The artificial eye: Augustan theater and the empire of the visible. *In* (pp. 131–45) **83**.

7893. SCHILLE, CANDY B. K.   Self-assessment in Dryden's *Amphitryon*. SELit (36:3) 1996, 545–60.

7894. STAFFEL, PETER L.   Dryden's heroic epic theory. Comparatist (15) 1991, 22–40.

7895. TERRY, RICHARD.   'Metempsychosis': a metaphor for literary tradition in Dryden and his contemporaries. *See* **2485**.

7896. WALTON, BRAD.   Merlin and the divine machinery of Dryden's *King Arthur. In* (pp. 41–52) **15**.

7897. ZWICKER, STEVEN.   Milton, Dryden, and the politics of literary controversy. *In* (pp. 270–89) **40**.

7898. ZWICKER, STEVEN N.   Milton, Dryden, and the politics of literary controversy. *In* (pp. 137–58) **21**.

7899. —— The paradoxes of tender conscience. ELH (63:4) 1996, 851–69. (*The Hind and the Panther.*)

Thomas D'Urfey

7900. SHERBERT, GARRY.   Menippean satire and the poetics of wit: ideologies of self-consciousness in Dunton, D'Urfey, and Sterne. New York; Frankfurt; Bern; Paris: Lang, 1996. pp. xvii, 225. (Comparative cultures and literatures, 8.) (Cf. bibl. 1993, 6343.)

John Eliot

7901. BAUER, RALPH.   John Eliot, the Praying Indian, and the rhetoric of a New England errand. ZAA (44:4) 1996, 331–45.

Ephelia

7902. MULVIHILL, MAUREEN E.   'Butterfly' of the Restoration court: a preview of Lady Mary Villiers, the new 'Ephelia' candidate. ANQ (9:4) 1996, 25–39.

John Evelyn

7903. DE LA BÉDOYÈRE, G.   John Evelyn's library catalogue. *See* **470**.

John Fletcher

7904. BERGERON, DAVID M.   Fletcher's *The Woman's Prize*, transgression, and *querelle des femmes*. MedRen (8) 1996, 146–64.

7905. CALDER, ALISON.   'I am unacquainted with that language, Roman': male and female experiences of war in Fletcher's *Bonduca*. MedRen (8) 1996, 211–26.

7906. FLEISSNER, ROBERT F.   The likely misascription of *Cardenio* (and thereby *Double Falsehood*) in part to Shakespeare. *See* **6298**.

7907. HATTAWAY, MICHAEL.   'Seeing things': Amazons and cannibals. *In* (pp. 179–92) **124**.

7908. McMULLAN, GORDON.   The politics of unease in the plays of John Fletcher. (Bibl. 1995, 6620.) Rev. by Julia Briggs in EC (46:1) 1996, 60–3.

7909. PARR, ANTHONY (ed.).   Three Renaissance travel plays. *See* **7715**.

7910. RADEL, NICHOLAS F.   Fletcherian tragicomedy, cross-dressing, and the constriction of homoerotic desire in early modern England. RenD (26) 1995, 53–82.

7911. RAMAN, SHANKAR.   Imaginary islands: staging the East. *See* **5769**.

Phineas Fletcher

7912. QUINT, DAVID.   Milton, Fletcher and the Gunpowder Plot. JWCI (54) 1991, 261–8.

John Ford

7913. BORN-LECHLEITNER, ILSE.   Implicit social criticism in *The Witch of Edmonton*. *In* (pp. 261–74) **53**.

7914. COYLE, MARTIN.   Hamlet, Gertrude and the ghost: the punishment of women in Renaissance drama. *See* **6800**.

7915. CRAIK, T. W. 'Politic French', 'politic frenzy', or 'politic study'? A crux in Ford's *The Broken Heart*. *See* **609**.

7916. DAPHINOFF, DIMITER. How conservative was John Ford? *In* (pp. 231–8) **53**.

7917. DIEHL, HUSTON. Bewhored images and imagined whores: iconophobia and gynophobia in Stuart love tragedies. *See* **7087**.

7918. HOPKINS, LISA. *The Broken Heart* and *Troilus and Cressida*. *See* **7275**.

7919. —— Ford and Greene: two histories of James the Fourth. *See* **5836**.

7920. MOORE, ANTONY TELFORD. Ford's parody of Edward Alleyn. *See* **5839**.

7921. PIAZZA, ANTONELLA. *The Witch of Edmonton*: the space of the witch's body as formation and critique of the enclosed body. *See* **7516**.

7922. SORGE, THOMAS. Baroque theatricality and anxiety in the drama of John Ford. *In* (pp. 125–45) **53**.

7923. STOCK, L. E., *et al.* (eds). The nondramatic works of John Ford. Binghamton, NY: Medieval & Renaissance Texts & Studies, 1991. pp. xix, 460. (Medieval & Renaissance texts & studies, 85.) (Renaissance English Text Soc., 7:15.) Rev. by Thomas C. Faulkner in Text (Ann Arbor) (7) 1994, 516–21.

Francis Godwin ('Domingo Gonzales')

7924. ADAMS, JOHN. Outer space and the New World in the imagination of eighteenth-century Europeans. ECL (19:1) 1995, 70–83.

Joseph Hall

7925. AGGELER, GEOFFREY. Ben Jonson's Justice Overdo and Joseph Hall's Good Magistrate. EngS (76:5) 1995, 434–42.

7926. FINCHAM, KENNETH; LAKE, PETER. Popularity, prelacy and Puritanism in the 1630s: Joseph Hall explains himself. EHR (111:443) 1996, 856–81.

7927. LACASSAGNE, CLAUDE. Joseph Hall (1574–1656): l'invention de la tradition classique en Angleterre. RANAM (29) 1996, 119–30.

7928. MANZO, FRED W. Who was Joseph Hall's Labeo? *See* **5944**.

George Herbert

7929. ALLEN, M. C. George Herbert's pastoral wit. *In* (pp. 119–34) **128**.

7930. APPELBAUM, ROBERT. Tip-toeing to the apocalypse: Herbert, Milton, and the modern sense of time. GHJ (19:1/2) 1995/96, 27–54.

7931. AYCOCK, ROY E. Music as metaphor in Herbert's poetry. ArsL (7) 1993, 82–92.

7932. CLARKE, ELIZABETH. Herbert's house of pleasure? Ejaculations sacred and profane. GHJ (19:1/2) 1995/96, 55–71.

7933. —— Silent, performative words: the language of God in Valdesso and George Herbert. *See* **2600**.

7934. COOLEY, RONALD W. George Herbert's *Country Parson* and the enclosure of professional fields. GHJ (19:1/2) 1995/96, 1–25.

7935. DI CESARE, MARIO A. (ed.). George Herbert, *The Temple*: a diplomatic edition of the Bodleian Manuscript (Tanner 307). *See* **617**.

7936. GRAVES, ROY NEIL. Herbert's *The Collar*. Exp (54:2) 1996, 73–7.

7937. HABIB, IMTIAZ. Reading Black women characters of the

English Renaissance: colonial inscription and postcolonial recovery. *See* **5136**.

7938. HILL, DARCI N. 'The Church Militant' resurrected: mythic elements in George Herbert's *The Temple*. Mythlore (21:1) 1995, 29–32.

7939. HODGKINS, CHRISTOPHER. Authority, church, and society in George Herbert: return to the middle way. (Bibl. 1995, 6655.) Rev. by Sidney Gottlieb in Literature and History (5:2) 1996, 81–3.

7940. JOHNSON, BRUCE A. 'To love the strife': George Herbert's struggle for his poetry. Ren (46:2) 1994, 105–16.

7941. LOGGINS, VERNON P. Herbert's architectural temple: a reconsideration. CLAJ (40:1) 1996, 82–9.

7942. LOW, ANTHONY. George Herbert: 'the best love'. Ren (45:3) 1993, 159–78.

7943. MARTIN, ANTHONY. George Herbert and sacred 'parodie'. SP (93:4) 1996, 443–70.

7944. MARX, MICHAEL STEVEN. Biblical allusions and intertextual assurances in George Herbert's *Affliction (1)*. *In* (pp. 257–65) **131**.

7945. MOON, PAUL. Blending popular culture and religious instruction: Herbert's *Outlandish Proverbs*. *See* **3336**.

7946. POWERS-BECK, JEFFREY. The fusion of 'social eminence with divine eminence': George Herbert and the king's stamp. *In* (pp. 197–207) **71**.

7947. —— 'Slack time' and the 'uncessant minutes': time in *The Two Herberts*. RenP 1996, 113–24.

7948. PRITCHARD, R. E. George Herbert and Lady Mary Wroth: a root for *The Flower*? RES (47:187) 1996, 386–9.

7949. RAY, ROBERT H. A George Herbert companion. (Bibl. 1995, 6664.) Rev. by Elizabeth Clarke in NQ (43:4) 1996, 477–8.

7950. RICHEY, ESTHER GILMAN. 'Wrapt in nights mantle': George Herbert's parabolic art. JDJ (9:2) 1990, 157–71.

7951. ROBERTS, JOHN R. 'Me thoughts I heard one calling, *Child!*': Herbert's *The Collar*. Ren (45:3) 1993, 197–204.

7952. RUBIN, DEBORAH. 'Let your death be my *Iliad*': Classical allusion and Latin in George Herbert's *Memoriae Matris Sacrum*. *In* (pp. 429–45) **98**.

7953. SIEGFRIED, BRANDIE R. Gambling on the divine: the culture of card games in Herbert's *Temple*. GHJ (19:1/2) 1995/96, 72–94.

7954. STANWOOD, P. G.; JOHNSON, LEE M. The structure of wit: 'is all good structure in a winding stair?'. *In* (pp. 22–41) **128**.

7955. STEWART, STANLEY. Investigating Herbert criticism. Ren (45:3) 1993, 131–58.

7956. SULLIVAN, CERI. Seventeenth-century wreath poems. *See* **7859**.

7957. TOLIVER, HAROLD. George Herbert's Christian narrative. (Bibl. 1994, 5449.) Rev. by Richard Todd in YES (26) 1996, 279–80.

7958. TOWNSEND, ANN. The problem of sincerity: the lyric plain style of George Herbert and Louise Glück. Shen (46:4) 1996, 43–61.

7959. VAN NUIS, HERMINE J. 'The heart in pilgrimage': a Jungian reading of George Herbert's *The Altar* and *Iesu*. RWT (4:1) 1996, 135–46.

7960. WHITE, JAMES BOYD. 'This book of starres': learning to read George Herbert. (Bibl. 1995, 6676.) Rev. by Wayne Booth in MichQR (35:2) 1996, 379–86; by David Jasper in LitTheol (10:2) 1996, 194–6.

7961. WILCOX, HELEN.   'No more wit than a Christian?': the case of devotional poetry. *In* (pp. 9–21) **128**.

7962. YOUNG, R. V.   Herbert and the Real Presence. Ren (45:3) 1993, 179–95.

Edward, Lord Herbert of Cherbury

7963. POWERS-BECK, JEFFREY.   'Slack time' and the 'uncessant minutes': time in *The Two Herberts*. *See* **7947**.

Robert Herrick (1591–1674)

7964. ELLIS, JIM.   The wit of circumcision, the circumcision of wit. *In* (pp. 62–77) **128**.

7965. ROLLIN, ROGER B.   Witty by design: Robert Herrick's *Hesperides*. *In* (pp. 135–50) **128**.

7966. SCHANFIELD, LILLIAN.   'Tickled with desire': a view of eroticism in Herrick's poetry. LitPs (39:1/2) 1993, 63–83.

7967. SWANN, MARJORIE.   Cavalier love: fetishism and its discontents. *See* **7740**.

Thomas Heywood

7968. CHANDLER, DAVID.   A further reconsideration of Heywood's allusion to Shakespeare. *See* **6260**.

7969. COYLE, MARTIN.   Hamlet, Gertrude and the ghost: the punishment of women in Renaissance drama. *See* **6800**.

7970. CRUPI, CHARLES W.   Ideological contradiction in Part 1 of Heywood's *Edward IV*: 'Our musicke runs ... much upon discords'. MedRen (7) 1995, 224–56.

7971. DOWNS, GERALD E.   A reconsideration of Heywood's allusion to Shakespeare. *See* **6285**.

7972. HONIGMANN, E. A. J.   Social questioning in Elizabethan and Jacobean plays, with special reference to *Othello*. *In* (pp. 3–11) **53**.

7973. HOWARD, JEAN E.   Forming the commonwealth: including, excluding, and criminalizing women in Heywood's *Edward IV* and Shakespeare's *Henry IV*. *In* (pp. 109–21) **89**.

7974. JANKOWSKI, THEODORA A.   Historicizing and legitimating capitalism: Thomas Heywood's *Edward IV* and *If You Know Not Me, You Know Nobody*. MedRen (7) 1995, 305–37.

7975. RAMSEY, PAUL.   The literary evidence for Shakespeare as Hand D in the manuscript play *Sir Thomas More*: a re-re-reconsideration. *See* **6191**.

7976. YOUNG, ALAN R.   His Majesty's royal ship: a critical edition of Thomas Heywood's *A True Description of His Majesties Royall Ship*. (Bibl. 1991, 5736.) Rev. by Ralph A. Ranald in ShB (10:1) 1992, 46–7.

Thomas Hobbes

7977. CANTALUPO, CHARLES.   'By art is created that great ... state': Milton's *Paradise Lost* and Hobbes's *Leviathan*. *In* (pp. 184–207) **40**.

7978. HOULAHAN, MARK.   *Leviathan* (1651): Thomas Hobbes and Protestant apocalypse. 1650–1850 (2) 1996, 95–110.

7979. KROLL, RICHARD.   Instituting imperialism: Hobbes's *Leviathan* and Dryden's *Marriage à la Mode*. *In* (pp. 39–66) **20**.

7980. VENTER, J. J.   World-picture, individual, society. Neohelicon (23:1) 1996, 175–99.

7981. ZIMBARDO, ROSE. The semiotics of Restoration satire. TSL (37) 1995, 23–42.

Lucy Hutchinson
7982. DE QUEHEN, HUGH. Ease and flow in Lucy Hutchinson's Lucretius. SP (93:3) 1996, 288–303.

James I and VI, King of England and Scotland
7983. BERGERON, DAVID M. King James, his *Phoenix*, and desire. RenP 1996, 43–51.
7984. POLLNER, CLAUSDIRK. A royal gift – the *Basilikon Doron* of James VI. *In* (pp. 241–9) **11**.
7985. SPRADLEY, DANA LLOYD. *Pericles* and the Jacobean family romance of union. *See* **7122**.
7986. TATE, WILLIAM. King James I and the Queen of Sheba. *See* **7531**.
7987. WALKER, JULIA M. Reading the tombs of Elizabeth I. *See* **6724**.
7988. WORTHAM, CHRISTOPHER. Shakespeare, James I and the Matter of Britain. *See* **6728**.

Ben Jonson
7989. AGGELER, GEOFFREY. Ben Jonson's Justice Overdo and Joseph Hall's Good Magistrate. *See* **7925**.
7990. ANDREW, MARTIN. 'Cut so like (her) character': preconstructing Celia in *Volpone*. MedRen (8) 1996, 94–118.
7991. AYRES, PHILIP J. (ed.). Sejanus his fall. (Bibl. 1991, 5747.) Rev. by Maurice Charney in ShB (10:2) 1992, 44; by Jennifer Brady in MedRen (7) 1995, 393–401.
7992. BACH, REBECCA ANN. 'Ty good shubshects': the Jacobean masque as colonial discourse. *See* **7447**.
7993. BARBOUR, RICHMOND. 'When I acted young Antinous': boy actors and the erotics of Jonsonian theater. PMLA (110:5) 1995, 1006–22.
7994. BATE, JONATHAN. The Elizabethans in Italy. *In* (pp. 55–74) **124**.
7995. BAWCUTT, N. W. New Jonson documents. *See* **571**.
7996. BEHUNIN, ROBERT. Classical wonder in Jonson's masques. BJJ (3) 1996, 39–57.
7997. BOEHRER, BRUCE. Ben Jonson and the *traditio basiorum*: Catullan imitation in *The Forrest* 5 and 6. PLL (32:1) 1996, 63–84.
7998. BRADY, JENNIFER; HERENDEEN, W. H. (eds). Ben Jonson's 1616 folio. (Bibl. 1995, 6710.) Rev. by Stuart M. Kurland in MedRen (7) 1995, 401–4.
7999. BROOKE, NICHOLAS. Performance structures as social criticism in English classic drama. *In* (pp. 21–6) **53**.
8000. BRYAN, LYNN; EVANS, ROBERT C. Jonson's response to Lipsius on the happy life. NQ (43:2) 1996, 181–2.
8001. CREASER, JOHN. Milton: the truest of the sons of Ben. *In* (pp. 158–83) **40**.
8002. DE QUEHEN, A. H. *The Silent Woman* in the Restoration. *In* (pp. 137–46) **16**.
8003. DONALDSON, IAN. Jonson's walk to Scotland. (Bibl. 1995, 6719.) Rev. by Donald Mackenzie in SLJ (supp. 42) 1995, 17–18.
8004. DUNCAN-JONES, E. E. Jonson's Queen Cis. BJJ (3) 1996, 147–51.

8005. DUNCAN-JONES, KATHERINE. 'They say a made a good end': Ben Jonson's epitaph on Thomas Nashe. *See* **5934**.

8006. DUTTON, RICHARD.   Ben Jonson: authority, criticism. Basingstoke: Macmillan; New York: St Martin's Press, 1996. pp. xxiii, 249. Rev. by K[atherine] D[uncan]-J[ones] in TLS, 2 Aug. 1996, 32.

8007. EVANS, ROBERT C.   Ben Jonson and the poetics of patronage. (Bibl. 1993, 5163.) Rev. by Daniel J. Vitkus in ShB (9:2) 1991, 40–1.

8008.   —— Jonson and the contexts of his time. (Bibl. 1995, 6726.) Rev. by Julie Sanders in NQ (43:2) 1996, 216–17.

8009.   —— Wit and the power of Jonson's *Epigrammes*. *In* (pp. 101–18) **128**.

8010. GURNEY, LAWRENCE S.   Jonson and Shakespeare. *See* **6321**.

8011. HALL, KIM F.   Sexual politics and cultural identity in *The Masque of Blackness*. *In* (pp. 3–18) **83**.

8012. HANSHAW, LARRY.   The literary influence of alchemy: an explication of selected works. *See* **7817**.

8013. HARP, RICHARD.   Ben Jonson's comic apocalypse. Cithara (34:1) 1994, 34–43.

8014. HERENDEEN, WYMAN H.   Ben Jonson and the play of words. *In* (pp. 123–36) **16**.

8015. HOPKINS, LISA.   An echo of *Hymenaei* in *The Changeling*. NQ (43:2) 1996, 184.

8016. JENKINS, HUGH.   From common wealth to commonwealth: the alchemy of *To Penshurst*. CLIO (25:2) 1996, 165–80.

8017. JOHNSON, A. W.   Ben Jonson: poetry and architecture. (Bibl. 1995, 6742.) Rev. by Timothy Erwin in BJJ (3) 1996, 187–91; by Martin Butler in NQ (43:2) 1996, 214–15.

8018. JOWETT, JOHN.   Jonson's authorization of type in *Sejanus* and other early quartos. *See* **287**.

8019. KAY, W. DAVID.   Ben Jonson: a literary life. (Bibl. 1995, 6743.) Rev. by David McPherson in BJJ (3) 1996, 191–4.

8020. KENDRICK, CHRISTOPHER.   Agons of the manor: *Upon Appleton House* and agrarian capitalism. *In* (pp. 13–55) **90**.

8021. LEVIN, RICHARD A.   A link between two Jonson poems. ANQ (9:1) 1996, 8–10.

8022. LOUGHLIN, MARIE H.   'Love's friend and stranger to virginitie': the politics of the virginal body in Ben Jonson's *Hymenaei* and Thomas Campion's *The Lord Hay's Masque*. *See* **7738**.

8023. LYNCH, KATHLEEN.   The dramatic festivity of *Bartholomew Fair*. MedRen (8) 1996, 128–45.

8024. McDONALD, MARCIA A.   The Elizabethan Poor Laws and the stage in the late 1590s. *See* **5670**.

8025. MARGESON, JOHN.   Individualism and order in the *Byron* plays of Chapman and Jonson's *Catiline*. *In* (pp. 111–21) **16**.

8026. MILLER, SHANNON.   Consuming mothers/consuming merchants: the carnivalesque economy of Jacobean city comedy. MLS (26:2/3) 1996, 73–97.

8027. NEILL, MICHAEL.   Bastardy, counterfeiting, and misogyny in *The Revenger's Tragedy*. *See* **6422**.

8028. NELLHAUS, TOBIN.   Self-possessed Jonson: reason, will, ownership, power. JDTC (8:1) 1993, 5–17.

8029. OWENS, ANNE.   The theatre as a mirror held to the theatre: *Everyman Out of His Humour* and *Hamlet*. *See* **6831**.

8030. PEACOCK, JOHN. The Stuart court masque and the theatre of the Greeks. JWCI (56) 1993, 183–208.

8031. PREUSSNER, ARNOLD. Re-staging Jonson's *The New Inn*. PMPA (18) 1993, 1–7.

8032. PROBST, NEIL P. A topical index to Jonson's *Discoveries*. BJJ (3) 1996, 153–77.

8033. RIDDELL, JAMES A. The concluding pages of the Jonson folio of 1616. *See* **811**.

8034. —— The printing of the plays in the Jonson folio of 1616. *See* **306**.

8035. RIGGS, DAVID. Ben Jonson: a life. (Bibl. 1993, 5183.) Rev. by Robert N. Watson in Shakespeare Yearbook (2) 1991, 231–6.

8036. SANDERS, JULIE. 'The day's sports devised in the inn': Jonson's *The New Inn* and theatrical politics. MLR (91:3) 1996, 545–60.

8037. SHERSHOW, SCOTT CUTLER. Idols of the marketplace: rethinking the economic determination of Renaissance drama. *See* **6765**.

8038. SILBERMAN, LAUREN. To write sorrow in Jonson's *On My First Sonne*. JDJ (9:2) 1990, 149–55.

8039. SLIGHTS, WILLIAM W. E. Ben Jonson and the art of secrecy. (Bibl. 1994, 5517.) Rev. by John Ross in AUMLA (85) 1996, 150–1; by Tom Hoenselaars in BJJ (3) 1996, 194–7; by Andrew McRae in Parergon (14:1) 1996, 310–12; by Bruce Boehrer in SAtlR (61:1) 1996, 122–4.

8040. SMITH, BARBARA. The women of Ben Jonson's poetry: female representations in the non-dramatic verse. (Bibl. 1995, 6769.) Rev. by Caroline McManus in BJJ (3) 1996, 197–200.

8041. STERLING, ERIC; EVANS, ROBERT C. Erasmus's 'beggar talk' and Jonson's *Alchemist*. NQ (43:2) 1996, 178–81.

8042. SZÖNYI, GYÖRGY E. 'My charms are all o'erthrown': the social and ideological context of the magician in Jacobean drama. *In* (pp. 107–23) **53**.

8043. WOLLMAN, RICHARD B. 'Speak that I may see thee': aurality in Ben Jonson's print poetry. BJJ (3) 1996, 21–38.

8044. WORTHAM, SIMON. *The glasse of majesty*: reflections on New Historicism and cultural materialism. *See* **7774**.

8045. YEAGER, R. F. Ben Jonson's *English Grammar* and John Gower's reception in the seventeenth century. *In* (pp. 227–39) **26**.

Thomas Jordan

8046. MONTAÑO, JOHN PATRICK. The quest for consensus: the Lord Mayor's Day shows in the 1670s. *In* (pp. 31–51) **21**.

Henry King

8047. ROEBUCK, GRAHAM. Elegies for Donne: Great Tew and the poets. *See* **7717**.

Aemilia Lanyer

8048. CAMPBELL, W. GARDNER. The figure of Pilate's wife in Aemilia Lanyer's *Salve Deus Rex Judæorum*. RenP 1995, 1–13.

8049. GUIBBORY, ACHSAH. The Gospel according to Aemilia: women and the sacred in Aemilia Lanyer's *Salve Deus Rex Judaeorum*. *In* (pp. 105–26) **107**.

8050. SCHNELL, LISA. 'So great a difference is there in degree':

Aemilia Lanyer and the aims of feminist criticism. MLQ (57:1) 1996, 23–35.

8051. Woods, Susanne (ed.). The poems of Aemilia Lanyer: *Salve Deus Rex Judaeorum*. (Bibl. 1995, 6785.) Rev. by Victoria Burke in NQ (43:2) 1996, 217.

Nathaniel Lee

8052. Cordner, Michael; Clayton, Ronald (eds). Four Restoration marriage plays. *See* **7873**.

8053. Hayne, Victoria. 'All language then is vile': the theatrical critique of political rhetoric in Nathaniel Lee's *Lucius Junius Brutus*. *See* **2396**.

John Locke

8054. Caruth, Cathy. Empirical truths and critical fictions: Locke, Wordsworth, Kant, Freud. (Bibl. 1994, 5522.) Rev. by Robert Wilcocks in CanRCL (18:4) 1991, 590–7; by Adam Potkay in ECL (19:2) 1995, 103–10.

8055. Clark, Stephen H. The 'failing soul': Macpherson's response to Locke. *See* **2334**.

8056. Patterson, Annabel. Locke and keys: Locke studies after Richard Ashcraft. Review (18) 1996, 235–48 (review-article).

8057. Walker, William. Locke, literary criticism, and philosophy. (Bibl. 1994, 5525.) Rev. by Adam Potkay in ECL (19:2) 1995, 103–10; by Annabel Patterson in Review (18) 1996, 240–5.

8058. Walmsley, Peter. Prince Maurice's rational parrot: civil discourse in Locke's *Essay*. ECS (28:4) 1995, 413–25.

Richard Lovelace

8059. Seelig, Sharon Cadman. My curious hand or eye: the wit of Richard Lovelace. *In* (pp. 151–70) **128**.

8060. Semler, L. E. Richard Lovelace and the Mannerist grotesque. AUMLA (85) 1996, 69–82.

John Marston

8061. Buckridge, Patrick. What did John Marston know about Shakespeare? *See* **5940**.

8062. Haas, Manuel. '*I must speak, but what, oh love?*': John Marstons *Antonio*-Stücke als vergebliche Suche nach der angemessenen Dramensprache. *See* **2389**.

8063. Howard, Jean E. Mastering difference in *The Dutch Courtesan*. SStud (24) 1996, 105–17.

8064. Kahan, Jeffrey. Reassessing the use of doubling in Marston's *Antonio and Mellida*. EMLS (2:2) 1996, 4.1–12.

8065. Wharton, T. F. The critical fall and rise of John Marston. (Bibl. 1994, 5530.) Rev. by Peter Hyland in NQ (43:1) 1996, 88.

Andrew Marvell

8066. Benet, Diana Treviño. The genius of the wood and the prelate of the grove: Milton and Marvell. *In* (pp. 230–46) **40**.

8067. Hartwig, Joan. Marvell's metamorphic *Fleckno*. *See* **206**.

8068. Jaeckle, Daniel P. The dialogization of genres in Marvell's *Upon Appleton House*. Genre (23:4) 1990, 257–78.

8069. —— Imaging social languages in Marvell's *The Last Instructions*. *See* **2651**.

8070. KENDRICK, CHRISTOPHER. Agons of the manor: *Upon Appleton House* and agrarian capitalism. *In* (pp. 13–55) **90**.

8071. POWELL, MICHAEL. Andrew Marvell, Sir Thomas Widdrington, and Appleton House. NQ (43:3) 1996, 281–4.

8072. ROGERS, JOHN. The matter of revolution: science, poetry, and politics in the age of Milton. Ithaca, NY; London: Cornell UP, 1996. pp. xvi, 257.

8073. SESSIONS, W. A. Marvell's Mower: the wit of survival. *In* (pp. 183–98) **128**.

8074. SRIGLEY, MICHAEL. Stanza 72 of Marvell's *Upon Appleton House*. NQ (43:3) 1996, 284–7.

8075. SULLIVAN, CERI. Seventeenth-century wreath poems. *See* **7859**.

8076. SWANN, CHARLES. A Christina Rossetti debt to Marvell? NQ (43:4) 1996, 432.

Philip Massinger

8077. CLARK, IRA. The moral art of Philip Massinger. (Bibl. 1995, 6827.) Rev. by Peter Hyland in NQ (43:1) 1996, 89.

8078. DE SILVA, D. M. Society, politics, and the aesthetic life of Massinger's plays. *In* (pp. 239–59) **53**.

8079. HATTAWAY, MICHAEL. 'Seeing things': Amazons and cannibals. *In* (pp. 179–92) **124**.

8080. OLIVIA, LEANORA. The erotic goals of defiant virgins: a comparative study of late antique poetry and early modern drama. *See* **7786**.

Cotton Mather

8081. BAUER, RALPH. John Eliot, the Praying Indian, and the rhetoric of a New England errand. *See* **7901**.

8082. BRUMM, URSULA. Consensus and conspiracy in American literature. YREAL (11) 1995, 29–41.

8083. CARROLL, LORRAYNE. 'My outward man': the curious case of Hannah Swarton. EAL (31:1) 1996, 45–73.

8084. SWEARINGEN, C. JAN. Homiletics and hermeneutics: the rhetorical spaces in between. *See* **2483**.

Increase Mather

8085. CARROLL, LORRAYNE. 'My outward man': the curious case of Hannah Swarton. *See* **8083**.

Sir John Mennes

8086. RAYLOR, TIMOTHY. Cavaliers, clubs, and literary culture: Sir John Mennes, James Smith, and the Order of the Fancy. (Bibl. 1995, 6838.) Rev. by Kirk Combe in NQ (43:1) 1996, 90; by William Zunder in EngS (77:3) 1996, 284–5.

Middleton and Rowley

8087. BROMHAM, A. A. A suggestive source for a scene in *The Old Law*. NQ (43:2) 1996, 182–3.

8088. CHAKRAVORTY, SWAPAN. 'Give her more onion': unriddling the Welsh madman's speech in *The Changeling*. *See* **2597**.

8089. EATON, SARA.   Beatrice-Joanna and the rhetoric of love in *The Changeling. In* (pp. 237–48) **84**.

8090. HOGG, JAMES.   William Hayley's *Marcella* and Thomas Middleton and William Rowley's *The Changeling*: a watered-down Jacobean masterpiece. *In* (pp. 319–61) **53**.

8091. HOPKINS, LISA.   An echo of *Hymenaei* in *The Changeling. See* **8015**.

Thomas Middleton

8092. BERGERON, DAVID M.   Thomas Middleton and Anthony Munday: artistic rivalry? *See* **5929**.

8093. BROMHAM, A. A.   'Have you read Lipsius?': Thomas Middleton and Stoicism. EngS (77:5) 1996, 401–21.

8094. BROOKE, NICHOLAS.   Performance structures as social criticism in English classic drama. *In* (pp. 21–6) **53**.

8095. CHAKRAVORTY, SWAPAN.   Society and politics in the plays of Thomas Middleton. Oxford: Clarendon Press; New York: OUP, 1996. pp. xii, 230. (Oxford English monographs.) (Cf. bibl. 1992, 6074.) Rev. by A.H. in TLS, 30 Aug. 1996, 32.

8096. COYLE, MARTIN.   Hamlet, Gertrude and the ghost: the punishment of women in Renaissance drama. *See* **6800**.

8097. DIEHL, HUSTON.   Bewhored images and imagined whores: iconophobia and gynophobia in Stuart love tragedies. *See* **7087**.

8098. FOAKES, R. A. (ed.).   The revenger's tragedy. Manchester: Manchester UP; New York: St Martin's Press, 1996. pp. 137. (Revels student eds.)

8099. HOGG, JAMES.   An ephemeral hit: Thomas Middleton's *A Game at Chess. In* (pp. 285–318) **53**.

8100. IOPPOLO, GRACE.   Sexual treason, treasonous sexuality, and the eventful politics of James I in Middleton's *Hengist, King of Kent*. BJJ (3) 1996, 87–107.

8101. JACOBS, DEBORAH.   Critical imperialism and Renaissance drama: the case of *The Roaring Girl. In* (pp. 73–84) **33**.

8102. KEWES, PAULINA.   The politics of the stage and the page: source plays for George Powell's *A Very Good Wife* (1693) in their production and publication contexts. *See* **7714**.

8103. MIKALACHKI, JODI.   Gender, cant, and cross-talking in *The Roaring Girl. See* **2675**.

8104. MILLER, SHANNON.   Consuming mothers/consuming merchants: the carnivalesque economy of Jacobean city comedy. *See* **8026**.

8105. NEILL, MICHAEL.   Bastardy, counterfeiting, and misogyny in *The Revenger's Tragedy. See* **6422**.

8106. RIZZOLI, RENATO.   La peripezia ironica: vendetta e ideologia di corte in *The Revenger's Tragedy*. Textus (6) 1993, 105–33.

8107. SCHAFER, ELIZABETH.   Thomas Holmes of Salisbury and Winchester and the dedicatory letter of Thomas Middleton's *The Witch*. NQ (43:2) 1996, 188–90.

8108. STEEN, SARA JAYNE.   Ambrosia in an earthern vessel: three centuries of audience and reader response to the works of Thomas Middleton. (Bibl. 1994, 5571.) Rev. by Diane Purkiss in YES (26) 1996, 275–6.

8109. TAYLOR, MICHAEL (ed.).   A mad world, my masters; Michaelmas term; A trick to catch the old one; No wit, no help like a woman's. Oxford; New York: OUP, 1995. pp. xxvi, 389. (World's classics.)

8110. WORTHAM, SIMON. *The glasse of majesty*: reflections on New Historicism and cultural materialism. *See* **7774**.

John Milton

8111. ACHINSTEIN, SHARON. Milton and the revolutionary reader. (Bibl. 1995, 6858.) Rev. by Thomas G. Olsen in Prose Studies (19:3) 1996, 299–302; by Robert T. Fallon in AHR (101:4) 1996, 1204; by Colin Burrow in CamQ (25:1) 1996, 85; by N. H. Keeble in NQ (43:3) 1996, 346–7; by Cheryl Thrash in MQ (30:1) 1996, 39–41.

8112. —— *Samson Agonistes* and the drama of dissent. MStud (33) 1996, 133–58.

8113. ALBANESE, DENISE. New science, new world. *See* **6208**.

8114. APPELBAUM, ROBERT. Tip-toeing to the apocalypse: Herbert, Milton, and the modern sense of time. *See* **7930**.

8115. ARMITAGE, DAVID; HIMY, ARMAND; SKINNER, QUENTIN (eds). Milton and republicanism. (Bibl. 1995, 6862.) Rev. by David Norbrook in TLS, 2 Feb. 1996, 4–6.

8116. BAUMLIN, JAMES S. The Aristotelian ethic of Milton's *Paradise Regained*. Ren (47:1) 1994, 41–57.

8117. BEDFORD, R. D. Jodocus Crull and Milton's *A Brief History of Moscovia*. RES (47:186) 1996, 207–11.

8118. BELLAMY, ELIZABETH J. Milton's Freud: the law of psycho-analysis in Eve's dream. LitPs (42:3) 1996, 36–47.

8119. BENET, DIANA TREVIÑO. The genius of the wood and the prelate of the grove: Milton and Marvell. *In* (pp. 230–46) **40**.

8120. —— LIEB, MICHAEL (eds). Literary Milton: text, pretext, context. (Bibl. 1994, 5580.) Rev. by Colin Burrow in CamQ (25:1) 1996, 82.

8121. BENNETT, JOAN S. Reviving liberty: radical Christian Humanism in Milton's great poems. (Bibl. 1993, 5272.) Rev. by William Myers in LitTheol (5:2) 1991, 234–9.

8122. BERGE, MARK. Milton's Orphic harmony: Ovidian imitation and Christian revelation in *The Nativity Ode* and *The Passion*. *In* (pp. 259–74) **107**.

8123. BERNADETE, JOSÉ A. Metaphysics and poetry: the Quinean approach. *See* **6230**.

8124. BLYTHE, DAVID-EVERETT. Milton's bird charm. MQ (30:4) 1996, 170–1.

8125. BOEHRER, BRUCE. 'Female for race': euhemerism and the Augustinian doctrine of marriage in *Paradise Lost*. SAtlR (61:4) 1996, 23–37.

8126. BOESKY, AMY. Milton, Galileo, and sunspots: optics and certainty in *Paradise Lost*. MStud (34) 1996, 23–43.

8127. —— Milton's Heaven and the model of the English utopia. *See* **7584**.

8128. BOSSI, EMANUELA. '*The spirits of freedom they tried hard to quell*': John Milton e *The Beaux' Stratagem* di George Farquhar. Acme (48:2) 1995, 55–71.

8129. BURNS, NORMAN T. 'Then stood up Phinehas': Milton's anti-nomianism, and Samson's. MStud (33) 1996, 27–46.

8130. BUTLER, GEORGE F. Donne's *Biathanatos* and *Samson Agonistes*: ambivalence and ambiguity. *See* **7798**.

8131. —— Statius and Milton's 'adamantine chains': the *Thebaid* and *Paradise Lost* 1.48. MQ (30:4) 1996, 167–70.

8132. CABLE, LANA. Carnal rhetoric: Milton's iconoclasm and the poetics of desire. (Bibl. 1995, 6872.) Rev. by Colin Burrow in CamQ (25:1) 1996, 83–4; by David Norbrook in TLS, 2 Feb. 1996, 4–6; by Glenn A. Steinberg in ColLit (23:3) 1996, 193–6.

8133. CACICEDO, AL. 'Conversing, looking, loving': the discourse of reason in *Paradise Lost*. Cithara (32:2) 1993, 13–38.

8134. CAMPBELL, GORDON. Milton's Spanish. MQ (30:3) 1996, 127–32.

8135. —— Popular traditions of God in the Renaissance. *In* (pp. 501–20) **98**.

8136. —— (ed.). Milton: a biography: vol. 1, The life; vol. 2, A biographical commentary. By William Riley Parker. (Bibl. 1972, 5139.) Oxford: Clarendon Press; New York: OUP, 1996. pp. 1539. (Second ed.: first ed. 1968.)

8137. CANTALUPO, CHARLES. 'By art is created that great ... state': Milton's *Paradise Lost* and Hobbes's *Leviathan*. *In* (pp. 184–207) **40**.

8138. CAREY, LEO. New Shakespearian influence in Milton. *See* **7162**.

8139. CARRITHERS, GALE H., JR; HARDY, JAMES D., JR. Milton and the hermeneutic journey. (Bibl. 1994, 5590.) Rev. by Colin Burrow in CamQ (25:1) 1996, 83.

8140. COOK, PATRICK J. Intuition, discourse, and the human face divine in *Paradise Lost*. ELit (23:2) 1996, 147–64.

8141. —— Milton, Spenser, and the epic tradition. *See* **6023**.

8142. COOKSON, SANDRA. 'Linkèd sweetness': Milton, Handel and the companion poems. MQ (30:3) 1996, 132–42.

8143. CORNS, THOMAS N. Regaining *Paradise Lost*. (Bibl. 1995, 6880.) Rev. by David Norbrook in TLS, 2 Feb. 1996, 4–6.

8144. —— 'Varnish on a harlot's cheek': John Milton and the hierarchies of secular and divine literature. *In* (pp. 275–81) **107**.

8145. CORTHELL, RONALD J. Milton and the possibilities of theory. *In* (pp. 489–99) **98**.

8146. DANIELSON, DENNIS. Milton, Bunyan, and the clothing of Truth and Righteousness. *In* (pp. 247–69) **40**.

8147. DAVIES, J. M. Q. Blake's *Paradise Lost* designs reconsidered. *In* (pp. 143–81) **47**.

8148. DOBRANSKI, STEPHEN B. Samson and the *omissa*. *See* **620**.

8149. DOHERTY, M. J. Beyond androgyny: Sidney, Milton, and the phoenix. *In* (pp. 34–65) **40**.

8150. DOWLING, PAUL M. Polite wisdom: heathen rhetoric in Milton's *Areopagitica*. *See* **2354**.

8151. DRISCOLL, JAMES P. The unfolding God of Jung and Milton. (Bibl. 1995, 6887.) Rev. by Julia A. Bowen in In-between (5:2) 1996, 199–202.

8152. DUGAS, DON-JOHN. 'Such Heav'n-taught numbers should be more than read': *Comus* and Milton's reputation in mid-eighteenth-century England. MStud (34) 1996, 137–57.

8153. DUROCHER, RICHARD J. The wounded earth in *Paradise Lost*. SP (93:1) 1996, 93–115.

8154. DUST, PHILIP. Milton's *Paradise Lost* and Grotius' *De jure belli ac pacis* (*The Law of War and Peace*). Cithara (33:1) 1993, 17–26.

8155. ENGLE, LARS. Milton, Bakhtin, and the unit of analysis. *In* (pp. 476–88) **98**.

8156. EVANS, J. MARTIN. Milton's imperial epic: *Paradise Lost* and the discourse of colonialism. Ithaca, NY; London: Cornell UP, 1996. pp. xi, 194.

8157. FALCONER, RACHEL. Orpheus dis(re)membered: Milton and the myth of the poet-hero. Sheffield: Sheffield Academic Press, 1996. pp. 227. (Cf. bibl. 1991, 5848.)

8158. FALLON, ROBERT THOMAS. Milton in government. (Bibl. 1995, 6893.) Rev. by Perez Zagorin in AHR (99:5) 1994, 1686–7; by Christopher Hill in EHR (111:441) 1996, 467–8.

8159. FLANNAGAN, ROY. Editing Milton's masque. *See* **644**.

8160. —— Reflections on Milton and Ariosto. EMLS (2:3) 1996, 4.1–16.

8161. FOREY, MARGARET. Milton's Satan: wisdom reversed. EC (46:4) 1996, 302–18.

8162. FORSYTH, NEIL. Rebellion in *Paradise Lost*: impossible original. MQ (30:4) 1996, 151–62.

8163. FRANSON, J. KARL. 'His volant touch': Milton and the golden section. MStud (34) 1996, 117–35.

8164. FREED, EUGENIE R. The transmutation of Satan in Milton's *Paradise Regained*. SAJMRS (5:1) 1995, 119–35.

8165. FRY, CARROL; KEMP, CHRISTOPHER. Rambo agonistes. LitFQ (24:4) 1996, 367–75.

8166. GRAHAM, JEAN E. 'Ay me': selfishness and empathy in *Lycidas*. EMLS (2:3) 1996, 3.1–21.

8167. GREEN, MANDY. 'The vine and her elm': Milton's Eve and the transformation of an Ovidian motif. MLR (91:2) 1996, 301–16.

8168. GREENE, DEIRDRE. Higher argument: Tolkien and the tradition of vision, epic and prophecy. *See* **6033**.

8169. GREGERSON, LINDA. A colonial writes the Commonwealth: Milton's *History of Britain*. Prose Studies (19:3) 1996, 247–54.

8170. GREGORY, E. R. Milton's Protestant sonnet lady: revisions in the *donna angelicata* tradition. CLS (33:3) 1996, 258–79.

8171. GROSE, CHRISTOPHER. Milton and the sense of tradition. (Bibl. 1990, 4720.) Rev. by William Myers in LitTheol (5:2) 1991, 234–9.

8172. HALE, JOHN K. England as Israel in Milton's writings. EMLS (2:2) 1996, 3.1–54.

8173. —— Milton meditates the ode. CML (16:4) 1996, 341–58.

8174. HART, D. BENTLEY. Matter, monism, and narrative: an essay on the metaphysics of *Paradise Lost*. MQ (30:1) 1996, 16–27.

8175. HAWKINS, HARRIETT. The seductions of Comus. ERev (6:2) 1995, 17–19.

8176. HERMAN, PETER C. Squitter-wits and muse-haters: Sidney, Spenser, Milton, and Renaissance antipoetic sentiment. *See* **5979**.

8177. HILL, CHRISTOPHER. Milton, monsters and maypoles. ERev (6:2) 1995, 20–3.

8178. HOLLIS, HILDA. Without charity: an intertextual study of Milton's *Comus*. MStud (34) 1996, 159–78.

8179. HONEYGOSKY, STEPHEN R. Milton's claim to inspiration: fact or fiction? In-between (5:2) 1996, 139–59.

8180. —— Milton's house of God: the invisible and visible church. (Bibl. 1994, 5639.) Rev. by Stanley Archer in SM (ns 2) 1996, 270–1; by

Robert L. Entzminger in Literature and History (5:1) 1996, 92–4; by Christopher Hill in Literature and History (5:1) 1996, 94–5.

8181. —— The mystical in Milton: a radical Protestant view. SM (14:1) 1991, 45–59.

8182. HUCKABAY, CALVIN. John Milton: an annotated bibliography, 1968–1988. Ed. by Paul J. Klemp. Pittsburgh, PA: Duquesne UP, 1996. pp. xxiv, 535.

8183. INGRAM, RANDALL. The writing poet: the descent from song in *The Poems of Mr John Milton, Both English and Latin* (1645). *See* **143**.

8184. JACOBUS, LEE A. Milton: the rhetorical gesture of monody. *In* (pp. 447–60) **98**.

8185. JONES, EDWARD. Milton's sonnets: an annotated bibliography, 1900–1992. (Bibl. 1994, 5647.) Rev. by Anna K. Nardo in MQ (30:3) 1996, 145–6.

8186. JONES, STANLEY. Further quotations and reminiscences in Hazlitt: Daniel, the Bible, Milton, Paine, Dorset. *See* **7773**.

8187. JOOMA, MINAZ. The alimentary structures of incest in *Paradise Lost.* ELH (63:1) 1996, 25–43.

8188. JUSTUS, JOHN A. Milton's dichotomous God. WLR (1:1) 1996, 65–79

8189. KASTOR, FRANK S. C. S. Lewis's John Milton: influence, presence, and beyond. CSL (24:9/10) 1993, 1–12.

8190. KEEBLE, N. H. 'Till one greater man / Restore us …': restoration images in Milton and Bunyan. *See* **7724**.

8191. KELLER, JAMES R. Rage against order: O'Neill's Yank and Milton's Satan. EOR (17:1/2) 1993, 45–52.

8192. KEZAR, DENNIS. The 'careful ploughman' of *Paradise Lost*, IV.983. NQ (43:3) 1996, 274–6.

8193. KLEMP, P. J. *Paradise Lost*: an annotated bibliography. Lanham, MD; London: Scarecrow Press, 1996. pp. xii, 249. (Magill bibliographies.)

8194. KNOPPERS, LAURA LUNGER. Historicizing Milton: spectacle, power, and poetry in Restoration England. (Bibl. 1995, 6930.) Rev. by N. H. Keeble in NQ (43:3) 1996, 348; by David Norbrook in TLS, 2 Feb. 1996, 4–6.

8195. KRANIDAS, THOMAS. The *Colasterion*: Milton's plural adversary. Prose Studies (19:3) 1996, 275–81.

8196. KROOK, ANNE K. The hermeneutics of opposition in *Paradise Regained* and *Samson Agonistes*. SELit (36:1) 1996, 129–47.

8197. LARES, JAMEELA. Milton and the 'Office of a Pulpit'. BJJ (3) 1996, 109–26.

8198. —— *Paradise Lost*, Books XI and XII, and the homiletic tradition. *See* **7601**.

8199. LEONARD, JOHN. 'Good things': a reply to William Kerrigan. MQ (30:3) 1996, 117–27. (*Reply to* bibl. 1994, 5650.)

8200. —— Naming in Paradise: Milton and the language of Adam and Eve. (Bibl. 1994, 5660.) Rev. by William Myers in LitTheol (5:2) 1991, 234–9.

8201. —— Revolting as backsliding in Milton's Sonnet XII. NQ (43:3) 1996, 269–73.

8202. LEVI, PETER. Eden renewed: the public and private life of John Milton. Basingstoke: Macmillan; New York: St Martin's Press, 1996. pp. xx, 332.

8203. LIEB, MICHAEL. Milton and the culture of violence. (Bibl. 1995, 6938.) Rev. by David Norbrook in TLS, 2 Feb. 1996, 4–6.

8204. —— 'Our living dread': the God of *Samson Agonistes*. MStud (33) 1996, 3–25.

8205. LIPKING, LAWRENCE. The genius of the shore: Lycidas, Adamastor, and the poetics of nationalism. PMLA (111:2) 1996, 205–21.

8206. LOEWENSTEIN, DAVID. The revenge of the saint: radical religion and politics in *Samson Agonistes*. MStud (33) 1996, 159–80.

8207. LOUDEN, BRUCE. Milton and the appropriation of a Homeric technique. CML (16:4) 1996, 325–40.

8208. LUXON, THOMAS H. Rough trade: Milton as Ajax in 'the place of punishment'. Prose Studies (19:3) 1996, 282–91.

8209. McHENRY, JAMES PATRICK. A Milton herbal. MQ (30:2) 1996, 45–115.

8210. McINNIS, JUDY B. Communal rites: tea, wine and Milton in Barbara Pym's novels. Ren (48:4) 1996, 279–95.

8211. MacLEAN, GERALD M. Literature and politics in Revolutionary England, 1640–1660. *See* **7604**.

8212. MARCUS, LEAH S. Unediting the Renaissance: Shakespeare, Marlowe, Milton. *See* **749**.

8213. MARTIN, CATHERINE GIMELLI. 'Boundless the deep': Milton, Pascal, and the theology of relative space. ELH (63:1) 1996, 45–78.

8214. MELBOURNE, JANE. Biblical intertextuality in *Samson Agonistes*. SELit (36:1) 1996, 111–27.

8215. MONNICKENDAM, ANDREW. Epic ends and novel beginnings in *Paradise Lost. In* (pp. 283–94) **107**.

8216. MORTON, TIMOTHY. Trade winds. *See* **2432**.

8217. MUELLER, JANEL. Just measures? Versification in *Samson Agonistes*. MStud (33) 1996, 47–82.

8218. MULRYAN, JOHN. 'Through a glass darkly': Milton's re-invention of the mythological tradition. Pittsburgh, PA: Duquesne UP, 1996. pp. xii, 345. (Duquesne studies: Language & literature, 21.)

8219. MYERS, WILLIAM. Miltonic reflections. LitTheol (5:2) 1991, 234–9 (review-article).

8220. NEWLYN, LUCY. *Paradise Lost* and the Romantic reader. (Bibl. 1995, 6961.) Rev. by David Walker in Bunyan Studies (6) 1995/96, 93–100.

8221. OPIE, BRIAN. Illustrating *Paradise Lost. See* **231**.

8222. PARRISH, PAUL A. Milton and Crashaw: the Cambridge and Italian years. *In* (pp. 208–29) **40**.

8223. PARRY, GRAHAM. Milton's *History of Britain* and the seventeenth-century antiquarian scene. *See* **7610**.

8224. PICCHIONI, PAOLA. Retorica e neoretorica in *Paradise Lost. See* **2448**.

8225. POLLOCK, JOHN. 'Cambridge ladies': comments on Milton and cummings. NCL (22:5) 1992, 2.

8226. QUINT, DAVID. Milton, Fletcher and the Gunpowder Plot. *See* **7912**.

8227. RAJAN, B. From centre to circumference: modern migrations of a Miltonic metaphor. *See* **2452**.

8228. RAYMOND, JOAD. Milton. YWES (75) 1994, 297–311.

8229. REEVES, CHARLES ERIC. 'Lest wilfully transgressing': Raphael's narration and knowledge in *Paradise Lost*. MStud (34) 1996, 83–98.

8230. REID, DAVID.   The humanism of Milton's *Paradise Lost*. (Bibl. 1995, 6980.) Rev. by N. H. Keeble in NQ (43:3) 1996, 347.

8231. REVARD, STELLA P.   Myth, masque, and marriage: *Paradise Lost* and Shakespeare's romances. *In* (pp. 114–34) **40**.

8232. RICHARDS, BERNARD.   Blank verse. *See* **4421**.

8233. ROCHE, THOMAS P., JR.   Spenser, Milton, and the representation of evil. *In* (pp. 14–33) **40**.

8234. ROGERS, JOHN.   The matter of revolution: science, poetry, and politics in the age of Milton. *See* **8072**.

8235. —— The secret of *Samson Agonistes*. MStud (33) 1996, 111–32.

8236. ROSE, MARY BETH.   'Vigorous most / When most unactive deem'd': gender and the heroics of endurance in Milton's *Samson Agonistes*, Aphra Behn's *Oroonoko*, and Mary Astell's *Some Reflections upon Marriage*. *See* **7652**.

8237. RØSTVIG, MAREN-SOFIE.   The craftsmanship of God: some structural contexts for the *Poems of Mr John Milton* (1645). *In* (pp. 85–113) **40**.

8238. RUMRICH, JOHN.   Milton's God and the matter of Chaos. PMLA (110:5) 1995, 1035–46.

8239. —— Milton's poetics of generation. TSLL (38:2) 1996, 191–208.

8240. RUMRICH, JOHN P.   Milton unbound: controversy and re-interpretation. Cambridge; New York: CUP, 1996. pp. xv, 186.

8241. SAMUELS, PEGGY.   Fire not light: Milton's simulacrum of tragicomedy. *See* **6459**.

8242. SCHÄFFNER, RAIMUND.   '*for orders and degrees / Jar not with liberty, but well consist*': Freiheit und Herrschaft bei John Milton und Gerrard Winstanley. ZAA (44:4) 1996, 317–30.

8243. SCHULMAN, LYDIA DITTLER.   *Paradise Lost* and the rise of the American Republic. (Bibl. 1993, 5353.) Rev. by John Canup in AHR (99:2) 1994, 641.

8244. SCHWARTZ, REGINA M.   Remembering and repeating: biblical creation in *Paradise Lost*. (Bibl. 1995, 6999.) Rev. by William Myers in LitTheol (5:2) 1991, 234–9.

8245. SCODEL, JOSHUA.   *Paradise Lost* and Classical ideals of pleasurable restraint. CL (48:3) 1996, 189–236.

8246. SELLARS, ROY.   Milton's wen. *See* **2466**.

8247. SELLIN, PAUL R.   John Milton's *Paradise Lost* and *De doctrina Christiana* on predestination. MStud (34) 1996, 45–60.

8248. SHAWCROSS, JOHN T.   'Depth' bibliography: John Milton's bibliographic presence in 1740, as example. *See* **1006**.

8249. —— Misreading Milton. MStud (33) 1996, 181–203. (*Samson Agonistes*.)

8250. SHITAKA, HIDEYUKI.   Milton's idea of the Son in the shaping of *Paradise Lost* as a Christocentric epic. Tokyo: Eihosha, 1996. pp. xiv, 316.

8251. SHOAF, R. A.   'For there is figures in all things': juxtology in Shakespeare, Spenser, and Milton. *In* (pp. 266–85) **131**.

8252. —— 'Our names are debts': Messiah's account of himself. *In* (pp. 461–73) **98**.

8253. SMITH, GREG.   Binary opposition and sexual power in *Paradise Lost*. MidQ (37:4) 1996, 383–99.

8254. STANWOOD, P. G.   Of prelacy and polity in Milton and Hooker. *In* (pp. 66–84) **40**.

8255. —— (ed.). Of poetry and politics: new essays on Milton and his world. (Bibl. 1995, 7007.) Rev. by Beverley Sherry in AUMLA (86) 1996, 119–20.

8256. STANWOOD, P. G.; JOHNSON, LEE M. The structure of wit: 'is all good structure in a winding stair?' *In* (pp. 22–41) **128**.

8257. STEADMAN, JOHN M. Two theological epics: reconsiderations of the Dante–Milton parallel. Cithara (35:1) 1995, 5–23.

8258. STEIN, ARNOLD. Imagining death: the ways of Milton. JAE (30:2) 1996, 77–91.

8259. STEVENS, PAUL. *Paradise Lost* and the colonial imperative. MStud (34) 1996, 3–21.

8260. STEWART, MARILYN. Human dreams and angelic visions: world-making in *Paradise Lost*. *In* (pp. 185–215) **29**.

8261. SWEARINGEN, C. JAN. Homiletics and hermeneutics: the rhetorical spaces in between. *See* **2483**.

8262. SWISS, MARGO. *Lachrymae Christi*: the theology of tears in Milton's *Lycidas* and Donne's sermon *Jesus Wept*. *In* (pp. 135–57) **40**.

8263. —— KENT, DAVID A. (eds). Heirs of fame: Milton and writers of the English Renaissance. *See* **40**.

8264. TANNER, JOHN S. Anxiety in Eden: a Kierkegaardian reading of *Paradise Lost*. (Bibl. 1995, 7011.) Rev. by Neal W. Kramer in BYUS (35:3) 1995/96, 181–7.

8265. THEIS, JEFFREY S. The environmental ethics of *Paradise Lost*: Milton's exegesis of Genesis i–iii. MStud (34) 1996, 61–81.

8266. THOMSEN, KERRI LYNNE. Ceres in *Paradise Lost*. MQ (30:3) 1996, 142–5.

8267. TITLESTAD, P. J. H. The 'pretty young man Civility': Bunyan, Milton & Blake and patterns of Puritan thought. *See* **1925**.

8268. TREIP, MINDELE. Comments on Milton's punctuation. From a panel devoted to editing at the Fifth International Milton Symposium. *See* **1607**.

8269. TURNER, JAMES GRANTHAM. Elisions and erasures. *See* **867**.

8270. VAN ANGLEN, K. P. The New England Milton: literary reception and cultural authority in the Early Republic. (Bibl. 1995, 7014.) Rev. by Deborah L. Madsen in AmS (35:2) 1994, 141–2.

8271. VON MALTZAHN, NICHOLAS. The first reception of *Paradise Lost* (1667). *See* **1024**.

8272. —— Milton's *History of Britain*: republican historiography in the English Revolution. (Bibl. 1994, 5728.) Rev. by Stephan Lieske in ZAA (43:2) 1995, 179–81.

8273. —— The Royal Society and the provenance of Milton's *History of Britain* (1670). MQ (30:4) 1996, 162–7.

8274. WALKER, DAVID. Language, genre, and revolution. *See* **2728**.

8275. WHITWORTH, MICHAEL. T. E. Hulme's quotations from Milton and Ireton. *See* **7616**.

8276. WORDEN, BLAIR. Milton, *Samson Agonistes*, and the Restoration. *In* (pp. 111–36) **21**.

8277. ZAGORIN, PEREZ. Milton: aristocrat & rebel: the poet and his politics. (Bibl. 1995, 7023.) Rev. by Barbara K. Lewalski in AHR (99:2) 1994, 552–3; by Christopher Hill in EHR (111:440) 1996, 184–5.

8278. ZIMMERMAN, SHARI A. From insufficiency to imaginary mastery: the illusory resolve of the Miltonic subject. ELit (23:1) 1996, 21–41.

8279. ZINCK, ARLETTE M.   'Doctrine by ensample': sanctification through literature in Milton and Bunyan. *See* **7732**.

8280. ZWICKER, STEVEN.   Milton, Dryden, and the politics of literary controversy. *In* (pp. 270–89) **40**.

8281. ZWICKER, STEVEN N.   Milton, Dryden, and the politics of literary controversy. *In* (pp. 137–58) **21**.

Martha Moulsworth

8282. ANDERSON, KATHRYN MURPHY.   Editing and contextualizing early modern women in England. *See* **560**.

8283. BAREFOOT, BEBE.   Martha Moulsworth/poet. CritM (10:supp.) 1996, 75–7.

8284. BOWDEN, KEVIN.   An archetypal approach to the *Memorandum* by Martha Moulsworth. CritM (10:supp.) 1996, 68–74.

8285. CROCKER, MICHAEL W.   Moulsworth's *Memorandum*: a critical concordance. CritM (10:supp.) 1996, 119–21.

8286. DEPAS-ORANGE, ANN.   Moulsworth's life and times. CritM (10:supp.) 1996, 7–10.

8287. —— (ed.).   The *Memorandum* of Martha Moulsworth: a modernized text. CritM (10:supp.) 1996, 11–25.

8288. GAUDIO, JOANNE M.   Genealogy in support of unconventionality in Martha Moulsworth's *Memorandum*. CritM (10:supp.) 1996, 39–43.

8289. HIRSHFELD, HEATHER.   Martha Moulsworth and Chaucer's Wife of Bath. *See* **5408**.

8290. HUMPHREY, MARY JANE.   Saving a life. CritM (10:supp.) 1996, 62–7.

8291. LIAS, RONI.   Biblical allusions and biblical versions in Moulsworth's *Memorandum*. CritM (10:supp.) 1996, 51–6.

8292. NILAND, KURT R.   Moulsworth and recent feminist theory: the example of Adrienne Rich. CritM (10:supp.) 1996, 78–83.

8293. PIRNIE, KAREN WORLEY.   Moulsworth, Freud, and Lacan. CritM (10:supp.) 1996, 84–92.

8294. ROBSON, MARK.   Day of the dead. CritM (10:supp.) 1996, 93–7.

8295. STEGGLE, MATTHEW.   Rhetorical ordering in Moulsworth's *Memorandum*. *See* **2477**.

8296. STUART, ELAINE POTTS.   Poetically apropos: poetic form and Martha Moulsworth's portrayal of her father. CritM (10:supp.) 1996, 36–8.

8297. WRIGHT, JONATHAN.   Moulsworth and the fathers. CritM (10:supp.) 1996, 57–61.

Margaret Cavendish, Duchess of Newcastle

8298. BATTIGELLI, ANNA.   Between the glass and the hand: the eye in Margaret Cavendish's *Blazing World*. 1650–1850 (2) 1996, 25–38.

8299. BROWN, SYLVIA.   Margaret Cavendish: strategies rhetorical and philosophical against the charge of wantonness; or, Her excuses for writing so much. CritM (6:1) 1991, 20–45.

8300. FOWLER, ELLAYNE.   Margaret Cavendish and the ideal commonwealth. Utopian Studies (7:1) 1996, 38–48.

8301. HINTZ, CARRIE.   'But one opinion': fear of dissent in Cavendish's *New Blazing World*. Utopian Studies (7:1) 1996, 25–37.

8302. KEEBLE, N. H. Obedient subjects? The loyal self in some later seventeenth-century Royalist women's memoirs. *In* (pp. 201–18) **21**.

8303. KELLY, ERNA. Women's wit. *In* (pp. 42–61) **128**.

8304. LESLIE, MARINA. Gender, genre and the utopian body in Margaret Cavendish's *Blazing World*. Utopian Studies (7:1) 1996, 6–24.

8305. LETELLIER, ROBERT IGNATIUS. Some feminine perceptions of freedom in an age of restoration and absolutism: prophetic and realistic voices in the writings of Margaret Cavendish and Madame de Lafayette. *In* (pp. 129–44) **125**.

8306. MERRENS, REBECCA. A nature of 'infinite sense and reason': Margaret Cavendish's natural philosophy and the 'noise' of a feminized nature. WS (25:5) 1996, 421–38.

8307. PLETT, HEINRICH F. Utopias Aporien: Ansichten einer prekären Literaturform. *In* (pp. 225–40) **11**.

8308. ROGERS, JOHN. The matter of revolution: science, poetry, and politics in the age of Milton. *See* **8072**.

8309. ROWSELL, JENNIFER (ed.). The Convent of Pleasure: a comedy. Oxford: Seventeenth Century Press, 1995. pp. 41.

8310. STEVENSON, JAY. The mechanist-vitalist soul of Margaret Cavendish. SELit (36:3) 1996, 527–43.

William Cavendish, Duke of Newcastle

8311. HULSE, LYNN. *The King's Entertainment* by the Duke of Newcastle. *See* **372**.

John Norris

8312. KORSTEN, FRANS. The Restoration poetry of John Norris. *In* (pp. 319–28) **107**.

'Orinda' (Katherine Philips)

8313. McDOWELL, PAULA. Consuming women: the life of the 'literary lady' as popular culture in eighteenth-century England. Genre (26:2/3) 1993, 219–52.

8314. TINKER, NATHAN P. John Grismond: printer of the unauthorized edition of Katherine Philips's poems (1664). *See* **1020**.

Roger Boyle, First Earl of Orrery

8315. FLORES, STEPHAN P. Orrery's *The Generall* and *Henry the Fifth*: sexual politics and the desire for friendship. ECent (37:1) 1996, 56–74.

Dorothy Osborne

8316. OTTWAY, SHEILA. Dorothy Osborne's love letters: novelistic glimmerings and the Ovidian self. Prose Studies (19:2) 1996, 149–59.

8317. WHITNEY, CHARLES. 'Like Richard the 3ds ghosts': Dorothy Osborne and the uses of Shakespeare. *See* **6505**.

Thomas Otway

8318. CORDNER, MICHAEL; CLAYTON, RONALD (eds). Four Restoration marriage plays. *See* **7873**.

8319. MUNNS, JESSICA. 'The monster libell': power, politics, and the press in Thomas Otway's *The Poet's Complaint of His Muse*. TSL (37) 1995, 59–75.

8320. Tassara, Carla.   Un drammaturgo al bivio: il *Don Carlos* di Thomas Otway fra Shakespeare e Fletcher. *See* **6487**.
8321. —— 'Venezia salva': storia di un tema tragico. Da Thomas Otway a Simone Weil. QLLSM (6) 1993, 263–320.

Samuel Pepys

8322. Turner, James Grantham.   Pepys and the private parts of monarchy. *In* (pp. 95–110) **21**.

George Powell

8323. Kewes, Paulina.   The politics of the stage and the page: source plays for George Powell's *A Very Good Wife* (1693) in their production and publication contexts. *See* **7714**.

Samuel Purchas

8324. Parr, Anthony.   Foreign relations in Jacobean England: the Sherley brothers and the 'voyage of Persia'. *In* (pp. 14–31) **124**.

Francis Quarles

8325. Ellis, Jim.   The wit of circumcision, the circumcision of wit. *In* (pp. 62–77) **128**.
8326. Höltgen, Karl Josef.   Catholic pictures *versus* Protestant words? The adaptation of the Protestant sources in Quarles's *Emblemes*. *See* **208**.

Eldred Revett

8327. Wilcox, Helen.   'No more wit than a Christian?': the case of devotional poetry. *In* (pp. 9–21) **128**.

John Wilmot, Earl of Rochester

8328. Burns, Edward.   Rochester, Behn and the martyrdom of lust. *In* (pp. 329–36) **107**.
8329. Dunn, Allen.   The mechanics of transport: sublimity and the imagery of abjection in Rochester, Swift, and Burke. TSL (37) 1995, 94–109.
8330. Gill, Pat.   'Filth of all hues and odors': public parks, city showers, and promiscuous acquaintance in Rochester and Swift. Genre (27:4) 1994, 333–50.
8331. Love, Harold.   The new 'A' text of *Signior Dildo*. *See* **727**.
8332. Thormählen, Marianne.   Rochester: the poems in context. (Bibl. 1995, 7063.) Rev. by Larry Carver in Scriblerian (28:1/2) 1995/96, 69–70; by Barry Coward in Literature and History (5:2) 1996, 83–4.
8333. Weber, Harold.   Carolinean sexuality and the Restoration stage: reconstructing the royal phallus in *Sodom*. *In* (pp. 67–88) **20**.
8334. Zimbardo, Rose.   The semiotics of Restoration satire. *See* **7981**.

Mary Rowlandson

8335. Carroll, Lorrayne.   'My outward man': the curious case of Hannah Swarton. *See* **8083**.
8336. Howe, Susan.   The birth-mark: unsettling the wilderness in American literary history. Hanover, NH; London: UP of New England,

1993. pp. xiii, 189. Rev. by Merle Lyn Bachman in Talisman (12) 1994, 103–5.

8337. McQuillan, Gene. 'Extarminate the varlets!': the reconstruction of captivity narratives in *Dances with Wolves*. PCR (6:2) 1995, 71–82.

8338. Wesley, Marilyn C. Moving targets: the travel text in *A Narrative of the Captivity and Restauration of Mrs Mary Rowlandson*. ELit (23:1) 1996, 42–57.

8339. Woodard, Maureen L. Female captivity and the deployment of race in three early American texts. PLL (32:2) 1996, 115–46.

Samuel Rowley

8340. Diehl, Huston. Bewhored images and imagined whores: iconophobia and gynophobia in Stuart love tragedies. *See* **7087**.

8341. Piazza, Antonella. *The Witch of Edmonton*: the space of the witch's body as formation and critique of the enclosed body. *See* **7516**.

William Rowley

8342. Born-Lechleitner, Ilse. Implicit social criticism in *The Witch of Edmonton*. *In* (pp. 261–74) **53**.

8343. Dix, Robin; Darby, Trudi Laura. The bibliographical significance of the turned letter. *See* **268**.

Charles Sackville, Sixth Earl of Dorset

8344. Jones, Stanley. Further quotations and reminiscences in Hazlitt: Daniel, the Bible, Milton, Paine, Dorset. *See* **7773**.

George Savile, First Marquis of Halifax

8345. Brown, Mark N. (ed.). The works of George Savile Marquis of Halifax. (Bibl. 1993, 5415.) Rev. by Harold Love in Text (Ann Arbor) (7) 1994, 530–2.

Thomas Shadwell

8346. Hulse, Lynn. *The King's Entertainment* by the Duke of Newcastle. *See* **372**.

8347. Marsden, Jean I. Ideology, sex, and satire: the case of Thomas Shadwell. TSL (37) 1995, 43–58.

James Shirley

8348. Burks, Deborah G. 'This sight doth shake all that is man within me': sexual violence and the rhetoric of dissent in *The Cardinal*. JMEMS (26:1) 1996, 153–90.

8349. Cameron, Joanna M. Centlivre, not Shirley: correcting an error in Joseph Wood Krutch's *Comedy and Conscience after the Restoration*. NQ (43:3) 1996, 292–6.

8350. Kewes, Paulina. The politics of the stage and the page: source plays for George Powell's *A Very Good Wife* (1693) in their production and publication contexts. *See* **7714**.

8351. Kong, Sung-Uk. *Renaissance* bigeuk sokeui 'Cardinal': James Shirley eui *The Cardinal* eul jungsim euro. (The dramatic role of the Cardinal in James Shirley's *The Cardinal*.) ShR (29) 1996, 23–39.

8352. Robins, Nicholas. 'Thou flattering world, farewell!'

A Caroline connoisseur: the sly proprieties of James Shirley, metropolitan play-maker. TLS, 11 Oct. 1996, 20–1.

Thomas Southerne

8353. CORDNER, MICHAEL; CLAYTON, RONALD (eds).   Four Restoration marriage plays. *See* **7873**.

Rachel Speght

8354. LEWALSKI, BARBARA KIEFER (ed.).   The polemics and poems of Rachel Speght. New York; Oxford: OUP, 1996. pp. 107. (Women writers in English 1350–1850.)

Thomas Sprat

8355. ANSELMENT, RAYMOND A.   Thomas Sprat's *The Plague of Athens*: Thucydides, Lucretius, and the 'Pindaric way'. BJRL (78:1) 1996, 3–20.

Peter Sterry

8356. MATAR, N. I. (ed.).   Peter Sterry: select writings. (Bibl. 1994, 5780.) Rev. by Ceri Sullivan in NQ (43:3) 1996, 348–9.

William Strode

8357. PURSGLOVE, GLYN.   William Strode's *Faire Chloris* and her metamorphoses. *In* (pp. 111–28) **125**.

Sir John Suckling

8358. SWANN, MARJORIE.   Cavalier love: fetishism and its discontents. *See* **7740**.
8359. VAN STRIEN, KEES.   Sir John Suckling in Holland. EngS (76:5) 1995, 443–54.

Nahum Tate

8360. COMBS, JAMES.   Where's Nahum Tate when you need him? *See* **6268**.
8361. HOLDERNESS, GRAHAM; CARTER, NAOMI.   The king's two bodies: text and genre in *King Lear*. *See* **6156**.
8362. MASSAI, SONIA.   Tate's critical 'editing' of his source-text(s) for *The History of King Lear*. *See* **6176**.
8363. RIPLEY, JOHN.   *Coriolanus* as Tory propaganda. *In* (pp. 102–23) **118**.
8364. WALKLING, ANDREW R.   Politics and the Restoration masque: the case of *Dido and Aeneas*. *In* (pp. 52–69) **21**.

Edward Taylor

8365. ADAMS, PERCY G.   Edward Taylor's love affair with sounding language. *In* (pp. 12–31) **79**.
8366. MILLER, DAVID G.   The Word made flesh made word: the failure and redemption of metaphor in Edward Taylor's *Christographia*. Selinsgrove, PA: Susquehanna UP; London; Toronto: Assoc. UPs, 1995. pp. 149. (Cf. bibl. 1992, 6274.) Rev. by J. Daniel Patterson in EAL (31:2) 1996, 195–6.
8367. SCHEICK, WILLIAM J.   Taylor's *Prologue*. Exp (55:1) 1996, 12–14.

Sir William Temple

8368. MURRAY, CIARAN. The Japanese garden and the mystery of Swift. *In* (pp. 159–68) **49**.

Cyril Tourneur

8369. CORBIN, PETER. 'A dog's obeyed in office': kingship and authority in Jacobean tragedy. *In* (pp. 59–71) **53**.

8370. COYLE, MARTIN. Hamlet, Gertrude and the ghost: the punishment of women in Renaissance drama. *See* **6800**.

8371. FOAKES, R. A. (ed.). The revenger's tragedy. *See* **8098**.

8372. LORANT, ANDRÉ. Social criticism in *Hamlet* and *The Revenger's Tragedy*. *In* (pp. 13–19) **53**.

8373. NEILL, MICHAEL. Bastardy, counterfeiting, and misogyny in *The Revenger's Tragedy*. *See* **6422**.

8374. PREUSSNER, ARNOLD. Tourneur's *The Atheist's Tragedy* in performance. PMPA (21) 1996, 69–76.

8375. RIZZOLI, RENATO. La peripezia ironica: vendetta e ideologia di corte in *The Revenger's Tragedy*. *See* **8106**.

Thomas Traherne

8376. BALAKIER, JAMES J. 'It doth not by another engine work': the self-referral dynamics of Thomas Traherne's *My Spirit*. SM (ns 2) 1996, 135–59.

8377. McKEE, SHIRLEY. Traherne's *The Circulation*. Exp (54:3) 1996, 136–9.

Sir Thomas Urquhart

8378. CRAIK, ROGER. The pioneer translators of Rabelais: Sir Thomas Urquhart and Pierre Motteux. *See* **3122**.

Sir John Vanbrugh

8379. McCORMICK, FRANK. Sir John Vanbrugh: a reference guide. New York: G. K. Hall; Toronto; Oxford: Maxwell Macmillan, 1992. pp. xxiv, 228. Rev. by Brian Corman in Scriblerian (28:1/2) 1995/96, 97–9.

Henry Vaughan

8380. FARNELL, SILVINE MARBURY. Henry Vaughan's *The Morning-Watch*: an experience of a higher state of consciousness. SM (15:4) 1992, 44–64.

8381. FLEISSNER, ROBERT F. 'Spot of time' in Frost: Beddoes, Vaughan – or Wordsworth in *Stopping by the Woods*? RFR (1993) 24–8.

8382. GICHARD, HELEN (comp.). A selection of the poems of Henry Vaughan. Abertillery, Gwent: Old Bakehouse, 1995. pp. 48.

8383. PRINEAS, MATTHEW. The dream of the book and the poetry of failure in Henry Vaughan's *Silex Scintillans*. ELR (26:2) 1996, 333–55.

8384. RUDRUM, ALAN. A nautical metaphor in Henry Vaughan's *Cock-Crowing*. ELN (33:3) 1996, 12–14.

8385. SULLIVAN, CERI. Seventeenth-century wreath poems. *See* **7859**.

Edmund Waller

8386. ZIMBARDO, ROSE.   The semiotics of Restoration satire.
See **7981**.

Simon Wastell

8387. VICKERS, BRIAN.   Whose thumbprints? A more plausible
author for *A Funeral Elegy. See* **1213**.

John Webster

8388. BARTELS, EMILY C.   Strategies of submission: Desdemona, the
Duchess, and the assertion of desire. *See* **7078**.
8389. BOOTH, ROY.   John Webster's heart of glass. Eng (40:167) 1991,
97–113.
8390. ——— 'Never in mine own shape': Webster's tragic disguisings.
ERev (5:3) 1995, 14–17.
8391. BRADSHAW, DAVID J.   Bosola: a perspective that shows us
tragedy. *In* (pp. 243–56) **131**.
8392. BROWN, JOHN RUSSELL (ed.).   The white devil. Manchester:
Manchester UP; New York: St Martin's Press, 1996. pp. 168. (Revels
student eds.) (Based on bibl. 1960, 3080.)
8393. CRAIG, SHERYL.   'She and I were twins': double identity in
The Duchess of Malfi. PMPA (19) 1994, 21–7.
8394. DIEHL, HUSTON.   Bewhored images and imagined whores:
iconophobia and gynophobia in Stuart love tragedies. *See* **7087**.
8395. FININ-FARBER, KATHRYN R.   Framing (the) woman: *The White
Devil* and the deployment of law. RenD (25) 1994, 219–45.
8396. FLECHE, BETSY.   Cryptonomy: the theater of madness and
mysticism of Webster's *The Duchess of Malfi.* SM (14:4) 1991, 43–69.
8397. GONZÁLEZ FERNÁNDEZ DE SEVILLA, JOSÉ MANUEL.   The
Jacobean radical picture of *The White Devil.* RAEI (9) 1996, 53–61.
8398. GUNBY, DAVID.   Webster's *The Devil's Law-Case.* Exp (54:4)
1996, 213–15.
8399. HOGG, JAMES.   Court satire in John Webster's *The White Devil.*
In (pp. 147–65) **53**.
8400. KISTNER, A. L.; KISTNER, M. K.   Man's will and its futility in
The Duchess of Malfi. SN (68:1) 1996, 49–60.
8401. LUCKYJ, CHRISTINA (ed.).   The white devil. London: Black,
1996. pp. xxxii, 152. (New mermaids.) (Second ed.: first ed. 1966.)
8402. MAHLER, ANDREAS.   A lost world, no new-found land –
disorientation and immobility as social criticism in early seventeenth-
century tragedy. *In* (pp. 27–43) **53**.
8403. PETERSON, JEAN.   Space, signs, and voyeurism in *The Duchess of
Malfi*: an interview with Cary M. Mazer. ShB (12:2) 1994, 28–9.
8404. RIZZOLI, RENATO.   La vendetta come potere: materialismo e
disseminazione della peripezia in *The White Devil.* QLLSM (8) 1996,
9–42.
8405. SCHLUETER, JUNE.   Who was John Wobster [*sic*]? New evidence
concerning the playwright/minstrel in Germany. MedRen (8) 1996,
165–75.
8406. TOSI, LAURA.   Convenzioni metadrammatiche/metateatrali
nel teatro tragico di Webster. Textus (4) 1991, 3–32.
8407. WIGGINS, LYDIA.   Ferdinand's psychopathology in John
Webster's *The Duchess of Malfi.* TPB (28) 1991, 31–9.

8408. WRIGHT, LOUISE E.   Webster's lenative poisons. *See* **1971**.

John Wilkins

8409. ADAMS, JOHN.   Outer space and the New World in the imagination of eighteenth-century Europeans. *See* **7924**.

Roger Williams

8410. WERTHEIMER, ERIC.   'To spell out each other': Roger Williams, Perry Miller, and the Indian. AQ (50:2) 1994, 1–18.

Gerrard Winstanley

8411. BOESKY, AMY.   Milton's Heaven and the model of the English utopia. *See* **7584**.

8412. ROGERS, JOHN.   The matter of revolution: science, poetry, and politics in the age of Milton. *See* **8072**.

8413. SCHÄFFNER, RAIMUND.   '*for orders and degrees / Jar not with liberty, but well consist*': Freiheit und Herrschaft bei John Milton und Gerrard Winstanley. *See* **8242**.

George Wither

8414. HARTWIG, JOAN.   Marvell's metamorphic *Fleckno*. *See* **206**.

8415. NORBROOK, DAVID.   Some notes on the canon of George Wither. NQ (43:3) 1996, 276–81.

Anthony Wood

8416. KIESSLING, NICOLAS K.   The location of two lost volumes of ballads, Wood 399 and Wood 400. *See* **496**.

Lady Mary Wroth

8417. BUGEJA, MICHAEL.   The female masters: a look at three underrated women poets offers fresh lessons in craft. WD (75:4) 1995, 16–19.

8418. MILLER, NAOMI J.   Changing the subject: Mary Wroth and figurations of gender in early modern England. Lexington: Kentucky UP, 1996. pp. xi, 279. (Studies in the English Renaissance.) Rev. by Curtis Perry in TSWL (15:2) 1996, 361–2.

8419. PRITCHARD, R. E.   George Herbert and Lady Mary Wroth: a root for *The Flower*? *See* **7948**.

William Wycherley

8420. BURKE, HELEN.   'Law-suits', 'love-suits', and the family property in Wycherley's *The Plain Dealer*. *In* (pp. 89–113) **20**.

8421. DI FLORIO, RITA.   Il libertinismo come forma embrionale del pensiero illuminista. *See* **7371**.

8422. HYNES, PETER.   Against theory? Knowledge and action in Wycherley's plays. MP (94:2) 1996, 163–89.

8423. NELSON, T. G. A.   Stooping to conquer in Goldsmith, Haywood, and Wycherley. EC (46:4) 1996, 319–39.

8424. SAMPSON, GRANT.   Comedy as epic action: structural variants in *Pericles*, *Plain-Dealer*, and *Picnic*. *See* **7120**.

EIGHTEENTH CENTURY

GENERAL

General Literary Studies

8425. AHEARN, EDWARD J.   Visionary fictions: apocalyptic writing from Blake to the modern age. New Haven, CT; London: Yale UP, 1996. pp. x, 198.

8426. ALDERSON, SIMON J.   The Augustan attack on the pun. *See* **1815**.

8427. ALEXANDER, DAVID.   Affecting moments: prints of English literature made in the age of Romantic sensibility, 1775–1800. *See* **173**.

8428. ANON.   Recent articles. *See* **7346**.

8429. BADER, RUDOLF.   The visitable past. Images of Europe in Anglo-Australian literature. (Bibl. 1993, 5482.) Rev. by Michael Wilding in ZAA (41:4) 1993, 375–7.

8430. BASSARD, KATHERINE CLAY.   The daughters' arrival: the earliest Black women's writing community. Callaloo (19:2) 1996, 508–18.

8431. BAYM, NINA.   American women writers and the work of history, 1790–1860. (Bibl. 1995, 7148.) Rev. by Joyce W. Warren in AHR (101:5) 1996, 1614–15; by Sharon M. Harris in AL (68:1) 1996, 231–2; by Marcia Robertson in NCS (10) 1996, 146–8; by Anne C. Rose in Legacy (13:2) 1996, 156–7.

8432. BELL, IAN A.   Literature and crime in Augustan England. (Bibl. 1995, 7150.) Rev. by William Jewett in ECS (25:2) 1991/92, 231–5.

8433. BENDER, JOHN.   A new history of the Enlightenment? *In* (pp. 62–83) **91**.

8434. BENEDICT, BARBARA M.   Making the modern reader: cultural mediation in early modern literary anthologies. *See* **7350**.

8435. BOWDEN, BETSY.   Fluctuating proverbs in three eighteenth-century modernizations of Chaucer's Miller's Tale. *See* **3310**.

8436. BOWERS, TONI.   The politics of motherhood: British writing and culture, 1680–1760. *See* **7353**.

8437. BRAUDY, LEO.   Varieties of literary affection. *In* (pp. 26–41) **91**.

8438. BROWN, MARSHALL.   Commentary. *In* (pp. 211–20) **91**.

8439. —— Preromanticism. (Bibl. 1995, 7155.) Rev. by Lilian R. Furst in Comparatist (17) 1993, 152–4.

8440. BURT, E. S.; NEWMARK, KEVIN; WARMINSKI, ANDRZEJ (eds). Romanticism and contemporary criticism: the Gauss Seminar and other papers. By Paul de Man. (Bibl. 1995, 7159.) Rev. by Luiza Lobo in CanRCL (21:4) 1994, 742–4.

8441. BYGRAVE, STEPHEN (ed.).   Romantic writings. London; New York: Routledge in assn with Open Univ., 1996. pp. x, 352. (Approaching literature.)

8442. CASTLE, TERRY.   The female thermometer: eighteenth-century culture and the invention of the uncanny. (Bibl. 1995, 7160.) Rev. by Cynthia Lowenthal in ColLit (23:3) 1996, 199–201.

8443. CHAMBERS, D. D. C.   The reinvention of the world: English writing, 1650–1750. *See* **7360**.

8444. CHASE, CYNTHIA (ed.).   Romanticism. (Bibl. 1995, 7161.) Rev. by Rolf P. Lessenich in Archiv (233:1) 1996, 176–9.

8445. CLARIDGE, HENRY.   American literature to 1900: American literature to 1830. *See* **7363**.

8446. —— American literature to 1900: general. *See* **7364**.

8447. COHEN, MICHÈLE.   Fashioning masculinity: national identity and language in the eighteenth century. London; New York: Routledge, 1996. pp. xii, 177.

8448. COLTHARP, DUANE.   History and the primitive: Homer, Blackwell, and the Scottish Enlightenment. ECL (19:1) 1995, 57–69.

8449. CRANSTON, MAURICE.   The Romantic movement. (Bibl. 1995, 7165.) Rev. by Andrew Elfenbein in ERR (7:1) 1996, 107–10.

8450. DAME, FREDERICK WILLIAM.   Jean-Jacques Rousseau in American literature: traces, influence, transformation, 1760–1860: a paradigm of French–German culture emanation in America. New York; Frankfurt; Bern; Paris: Lang, 1996. pp. 428. (European univ. studies, XIV: Anglo-Saxon language and literature, 310.)

8451. DAMROSCH, LEO.   Reaching mid-career in 'the eighteenth century': some personal reflections. *In* (pp. 200–10) **91**.

8452. —— (ed.).   The profession of eighteenth-century literature: reflections on an institution. *See* **91**.

8453. DAUBER, KENNETH.   The idea of authorship in America: democratic poetics from Franklin to Melville. (Bibl. 1993, 5504.) Rev. by Jennifer A. Gehrmann in SHum (18:2) 1991, 200–7.

8454. DAVIS, NATALIE ZEMON; FARGE, ARLETTE (eds).   A history of women in the West: vol. III, Renaissance and Enlightenment paradoxes. *See* **42**.

8455. DAY, AIDAN.   Romanticism. London; New York: Routledge, 1996. pp. xii, 217. (New critical idiom.)

8456. DECONINCK-BROSSARD, FRANÇOISE.   Confessions d'une dix-huitièmiste 'branchée'. *See* **1100**.

8457. DE MONTLUZIN, EMILY LORRAINE.   Attributions of authorship in the *Gentleman's Magazine*, 1731–77: a supplement to Kuist. *See* **1255**.

8458. —— Attributions of authorship in the *Gentleman's Magazine*, 1778–92: a supplement to Kuist. *See* **1256**.

8459. —— Attributions of authorship in the *Gentleman's Magazine*, 1793–1808: a supplement to Kuist. *See* **1257**.

8460. DERINGER, LUDWIG.   Das Bild des Pazifischen Nordwestens: von den Anfängen bis zur Gegenwart. Vergleichende Studien zur kanadischen und amerikanischen Literatur zwischen Regionalismus und Universalismus. Tübingen: Stauffenburg, 1996. pp. xiv, 395. (Transatlantic perspectives, 5.)

8461. DERITTER, JONES.   The embodiment of characters: the representation of physical experience on stage and in print, 1728–1749. (Bibl. 1995, 7169.) Rev. by Alan T. McKenzie in Scriblerian (28:1/2) 1995/96, 85–6; by John Richetti in ECS (30:1) 1996, 99–100.

8462. DONOGHUE, EMMA.   Passions between women: British lesbian culture, 1668–1801. *See* **7372**.

8463. DONOGHUE, FRANK.   The fame machine: book reviewing and eighteenth-century literary careers. Stanford, CA: Stanford UP, 1996. pp. viii, 213. Rev. by David Womersley in TLS, 18 Oct. 1996, 27.

8464. DUGAS, DON-JOHN.   'Such Heav'n-taught numbers should be more than read': *Comus* and Milton's reputation in mid-eighteenth-century England. *See* **8152**.

8465. DULONG, CLAUDE.   From conversation to creation. *In* (pp. 395–419) **42**.

8466. EPSTEIN, WILLIAM H.   Professing Gray: the resumption of authority in eighteenth-century studies. *In* (pp. 84–94) **91**.

8467. FABI, M. GIULIA.   La tradizione invisibile: le radici ottocentesche della narrativa femminile afroamericana. Àcoma (3) 1995, 29–37.

8468. FAUSETT, DAVID.   Images of the Antipodes in the eighteenth century: a study in stereotyping. (Bibl. 1995, 7172.) Rev. by J. C. Davis in Utopian Studies (7:2) 1996, 253–4.

8469. FERGUSON, FRANCES.   Solitude and the sublime: Romanticism and the aesthetics of individuation. (Bibl. 1995, 7174.) Rev. by Francesco Minetti in Annali anglistica (36:1–3) 1993, 228–33.

8470. FOSTER, FRANCES SMITH.   Written by herself: literary production by African-American women, 1746–1892. (Bibl. 1995, 7176.) Rev. by Maryemma Graham and Gina Rossetti in TSWL (14:2) 1995, 384–7; by Jean Fagan Yellin in AAR (30:2) 1996, 281–3; by Sandra Gunning in Signs (21:2) 1996, 455–9.

8471. GALLET-BLANCHARD, LILIANE; MARTINET, MARIE-MADELEINE. HIDES: Historical Document Expert System. *See* **1106**.

8472. GALPERIN, WILLIAM H.   The return of the visible in British Romanticism. (Bibl. 1995, 7178.) Rev. by Steven Goldsmith in ERR (7:1) 1996, 90–7.

8473. GRIFFIN, DUSTIN.   Literary patronage in England, 1650–1800. *See* **7383**.

8474. GRUNDY, ISOBEL.   Attribution to women. ECF (8:4) 1996, 522–5.

8475. GUTHRIE, NEIL.   'No truth or very little in the whole story'? A reassessment of the Mohock scare of 1712. ECL (20:2) 1996, 33–56.

8476. HARRIES, ELIZABETH WANNING.   The unfinished manner: essays on the fragment in the later eighteenth century. (Bibl. 1994, 5857.) Rev. by Alistair M. Duckworth in ECF (9:1) 1996, 103–6.

8477. HARRIS, SHARON M. (ed.).   American women writers to 1800. *See* **7387**.

8478. HAWES, CLEMENT.   Mania and literary style: the rhetoric of enthusiasm from the Ranters to Christopher Smart. *See* **2394**.

8479. HEANEY, PETER (ed.).   An anthology of eighteenth-century satire: Grub-Street. (Bibl. 1995, 7187.) Rev. by David Hopkins in NQ (43:2) 1996, 219–20.

8480. HENDERSON, ANDREA K.   Romantic identities: varieties of subjectivity, 1774–1830. Cambridge; New York: CUP, 1996. pp. xii, 198. (Cambridge studies in Romanticism, 20.) (Cf. bibl. 1992, 6354.)

8481. HOCHBRUCK, W.   'Native American literature': developments, contexts and problems. AntR (93/94) 1993, 265–76.

8482. HUDSON, NICHOLAS.   'Oral tradition': the evolution of an eighteenth-century concept. *In* (pp. 161–76) **122**.

8483. JONES, CHRIS.   Radical sensibility: literature and ideas in the 1790s. (Bibl. 1995, 7194.) Rev. by Robert Miles in BJECS (19:2) 1996, 224–5; by Jane Spencer in YES (26) 1996, 287–8.

8484. KAMINSKI, THOMAS.   Rehabilitating 'Augustanism': on the roots of 'polite letters' in England. *See* **7881**.

8485. KELLY, GARY. Women, writing, and revolution, 1790–1827. (Bibl. 1995, 7196.) Rev. by Claudia Johnson in ECS (29:4) 1996, 440–1.

8486. KELLY, VERONICA; VON MÜCKE, DOROTHEA (eds). Body & text in the eighteenth century. *See* **10**.

8487. KUIST, JAMES M. A collaboration in learning: the *Gentleman's Magazine* and its ingenious contributors. *See* **1302**.

8488. LAUGERO, GREG. Publicity, gender, and genre: a review essay. ECS (28:4) 1995, 429–38.

8489. LEE, HYEON SEOK. Jayeon eseo jakga ro: 17–18c youngkuk eui Shakespeare suyong yeongu. (From nature to author: a study of the appropriation of Shakespeare in England in the seventeenth and eighteenth centuries.) *See* **6388**.

8490. LEVINE, JOSEPH M. The battle of the books: history and literature in the Augustan age. (Bibl. 1995, 7205.) Rev. by Robert A. McCaughey in AHR (98:1) 1993, 118–19.

8491. LEWIS, JAYNE ELIZABETH. The English fable: Aesop and literary culture, 1651–1740. *See* **7399**.

8492. LIPKING, LAWRENCE. Inventing the eighteenth centuries: a long view. *In* (pp. 7–25) **91**.

8493. LOOBY, CHRISTOPHER. Voicing America: language, literary form, and the origins of the United States. *See* **2666**.

8494. LUBBERS, KLAUS. Born for the shade: stereotypes of the Native American in United States literature and the visual arts 1776–1894. (Bibl. 1995, 7207.) Rev. by Hartmut Lutz in ZAA (44:3) 1996, 277–8.

8495. MCCORMACK, W. J. From Burke to Beckett: ascendancy, tradition and betrayal in literary history. (Bibl. 1990, 4895.) Cork: Cork UP, 1994. pp. 470. (Revised ed.: first ed. 1985.) Rev. by John Cronin in Irish Review (17/18) 1995, 180–2.

8496. MCDERMOTT, ANNE. Textual transformations: *The Memoirs of Martinus Scriblerus* in Johnson's *Dictionary*. *See* **732**.

8497. MCDOWELL, PAULA. Consuming women: the life of the 'literary lady' as popular culture in eighteenth-century England. *See* **8313**.

8498. MCKEON, MICHAEL. Cultural crisis and dialectical method: destabilizing Augustan literature. *In* (pp. 42–61) **91**.

8499. MCWILLIAMS, JOHN P., JR. The American epic: transforming a genre, 1770–1860. (Bibl. 1995, 7209.) Rev. by Philip Barnard in AmS (33:2) 1992, 129; by Hans-Joachim Lang in ZAA (42:3) 1994, 280–2.

8500. MASSOUD, MARY M. F. Literary parallels: eighteenth-century Anglo-Irish literature and twentieth-century Egyptian literature. *In* (pp. 3–22) **60**.

8501. MAY, JAMES E. Scribleriana transferred: 1993–1994. *See* **509**.

8502. MEYER, WILLIAM E. H., JR. The hypervisual standard of American popular culture. PCR (5:1) 1994, 5–22.

8503. MICHELSEN, MARTINA. Weg vom Work – zum Gedankenstrich: zur stilistischen Funktion eines Satzzeichens in der englischen Literatur des 17. und 18. Jahrhunderts. *See* **1602**.

8504. MOGEN, DAVID; SANDERS, SCOTT P.; KARPINSKI, JOANNE B. (eds). Frontier gothic: terror and wonder at the frontier in American literature. (Bibl. 1995, 7214.) Rev. by Hans-Joachim Lang in ZAA (43:1) 1995, 103–4.

8505. MOORE-GILBERT, BART. Introduction: writing India, re-orienting colonial discourse analysis. *In* (pp. 1–29) **132**.

8506. —— (ed.).   Writing India 1757–1990: the literature of British India. *See* **132**.

8507.   MULLAN, JOHN.   Gendered knowledge, gendered minds: women and Newtonianism, 1690–1760. *In* (pp. 41–56) **94**.

8508.   NASH, RICHARD.   Satyrs and satire in Augustan England. *In* (pp. 95–105) **120**.

8509.   NEWEY, VINCENT (ed.).   Centring the self: subjectivity, society, and reading from Thomas Gray to Thomas Hardy. (Bibl. 1995, 7218.) Rev. by Greg Crossan in NQ (43:2) 1996, 243–4.

8510.   NICHOL, DONALD W.   Arthur Murphy's law: the man who won the first decisive battle in the literary property wars. *See* **990**.

8511.   NICHOLSON, COLIN.   Writing and the rise of finance: capital satires of the early eighteenth century. (Bibl. 1995, 7219.) Rev. by Siyeon Lee in SLJ (supp. 42) 1995, 6–7; by J. A. Downie in Albion (28:3) 1996, 490–1; by Stephen Copley in BJECS (19:1) 1996, 109; by Gerald M. MacLean in Review (18) 1996, 81–102.

8512.   NICKELS, CAMERON C.   New England humor: from the Revolutionary War to the Civil War. (Bibl. 1995, 7220.) Rev. by Henry B. Wonham in SAH (3:1) 1994, 124–7.

8513.   OHI, KOUJI.   Tegami no naka no America – 'atarashii kyouwakoku' no shinwa to ideology. (America in letters: the myth and ideology of a 'New Republic'.) Tokyo: Eihosha, 1996. pp. 278.

8514.   PAGEARD, ROBERT.   Le tableau de mœurs: esprit et histoire d'un genre littéraire. GRM (45:3) 1995, 257–67.

8515.   PARKS, LYNN A.   Capitalism in early American literature: texts and contexts. *See* **7417**.

8516.   PORTER, DAVID.   Writing China: legitimacy and representation 1606–1773. *See* **7420**.

8517.   RIASANOVSKY, NICHOLAS V.   The emergence of Romanticism. (Bibl. 1994, 5892.) Rev. by Irena Grudzinska Gross in AHR (99:2) 1994, 536.

8518.   RIBEIRO, ALVARO; BASKER, JAMES G. (eds).   Tradition in transition: women writers, marginal texts, and the eighteenth-century canon. *See* **122**.

8519.   RICHARDSON, ALAN.   Literature, education, and Romanticism: reading as social practice, 1780–1832. (Bibl. 1995, 7226.) Rev. by John W. Osborne in Albion (28:1) 1996, 124–5; by Paul Keen in BJECS (19:2) 1996, 226–7; by Scott B. Harshbarger in KSJ (45) 1996, 218–20.

8520.   RITCHIE, DANIEL E.   Reconstructing literature in an ideological age: a biblical poetics and literary studies from Milton to Burke. *See* **7426**.

8521.   ROSS, TREVOR.   The emergence of 'literature': making and reading the English canon in the eighteenth century. ELH (63:2) 1996, 397–422.

8522.   SCHEICK, WILLIAM J.   Literature to 1800. *See* **7428**.

8523.   SCHOR, ESTHER.   Bearing the dead: the British culture of mourning from the Enlightenment to Victoria. Princeton, NJ; Chichester: Princeton UP, 1994. pp. x, 290. (Literature in history.) Rev. by Richard C. Sha in Prose Studies (19:3) 1996, 305–7; by Robert Inglesfield in Albion (28:2) 1996, 330–1.

8524.   SHERBO, ARTHUR.   John Nichols's notes in the scholarly commentary of others. *See* **831**.

8525.   SIMMONS, EVA (ed.).   Bloomsbury guides to English literature:

Augustan literature: a guide to Restoration and eighteenth-century literature, 1600–1789. *See* **7431**.

8526.   SMITH, ALLAN LLOYD; SAGE, VICTOR (eds).   Gothick origins and innovations: papers from the First International Gothic Conference, held at the University of East Anglia, Norwich, June 1991. (Bibl. 1994, 32.) Rev. by Randi Gunzenhäuser in Amst (41:2) 1996, 319–20; by Neil Cornwell in EP (21) 1996, 181.

8527.   TERRY, RICHARD.   The eighteenth-century invention of English literature: a truism revisited. *See* **1973**.

8528.   THOMPSON, JAMES.   Recent studies in the Restoration and eighteenth century. *See* **7439**.

8529.   TODD, DENNIS.   Imagining monsters: miscreations of the self in eighteenth-century England. (Bibl. 1995, 7240.) Rev. by Bridget Orr in Albion (28:4) 1996, 702–3.

8530.   TURNER, CHERYL.   Living by the pen: women writers in the eighteenth century. (Bibl. 1995, 7241.) Rev. by Kathryn R. King in StudN (27:1) 1995, 105–7; by Ann Messenger in ANQ (9:1) 1996, 47–8; by Mona Scheuermann in ECF (8:4) 1996, 545–7.

8531.   VON MÜCKE, DOROTHEA E.   Virtue and the veil of illusion: generic innovation and the pedagogical project in eighteenth-century literature. (Bibl. 1995, 7245.) Rev. by Richard A. Barney in ECent (37:2) 1996, 174–83.

8532.   WAGNER, PETER.   Reading iconotexts: from Swift to the French Revolution. (Bibl. 1995, 7247.) Rev. by A.H. in TLS, 9 Feb. 1996, 28.

8533.   WILLIAMS, ANNE.   Art of darkness: a poetics of gothic. (Bibl. 1995, 7251.) Rev. by Kim Ian Michasiw in ECF (8:2) 1996, 308–9; by Neil Cornwell in EP (21) 1996, 182–3; by Kari J. Winter in SAtlR (61:1) 1996, 171–3; by Susan Wolstenholme in Criticism (38:4) 1996, 633–5.

8534.   WILSON, CAROL SHINER; HAEFNER, JOEL (eds).   Re-visioning Romanticism: British women writers, 1776–1837. *See* **103**.

8535.   WOLPE, BERTHOLD.   Caledonian miscellany. *See* **160**.

8536.   WOOD, MARCUS.   Radical satire and print culture, 1790–1822. (Bibl. 1995, 7253.) Rev. by James Epstein in AHR (101:2) 1996, 486–7; by Charles A. Knight in ECS (30:1) 1996, 101–2.

8537.   WOOD, NIGEL.   The eighteenth century: general. YWES (75) 1994, 334–49.

8538.   WU, DUNCAN (ed.).   Romanticism: a critical reader. (Bibl. 1995, 7256.) Rev. by Philip Cox in NQ (43:1) 1996, 98–9.

8539.   —— Romanticism: an anthology. (Bibl. 1995, 7257.) Rev. by Stephen C. Behrendt in CritM (9:1) 1995, 95–105; by E. D. Mackerness in NQ (43:1) 1996, 97–8.

8540.   YOON, HYONYUNG.   France hyeokmyoung eui nangman jueuijeok hyeongsangwha. (The Romantic configuration of the French Revolution.) JELL (42:2) 1996, 333–44.

Drama and the Theatre

8541.   ANON. (ed.).   Fushu kigeki no hen'you – ousei fukkoki kara Jane Austen made. (The metamorphosis of the comedy of manners: from the Restoration to Jane Austen.) *See* **7446**.

8542.   ANTHONY, M. SUSAN.   'This sort of thing … ': productions of gothic plays in America, 1790–1830. JADT (6:2/3) 1994, 81–92.

8543. BACKSCHEIDER, PAULA R.   'Endless aversion rooted in the soul': divorce in the 1690–1730 theater. *See* **7448**.

8544. BROWN, JARED.   The theatre in America during the Revolution. Cambridge; New York: CUP, 1995. pp. ix, 229. (Cambridge studies in American theatre and drama.)

8545. BURROUGHS, CATHERINE B.   English Romantic women writers and theatre theory: Joanna Baillie's Prefaces to the *Plays on the Passions*. *In* (pp. 274–96) **103**.

8546. CAMPBELL, DONALD.   Playing for Scotland: a history of the Scottish stage, 1715–1965. Edinburgh: Mercat, 1996. pp. xii, 154. Rev. by Peter Thomson in TLS, 13 Dec. 1996, 20.

8547. CANFIELD, J. DOUGLAS.   Shifting tropes of ideology in English serious drama, late Stuart to early Georgian. *In* (pp. 195–227) **20**.

8548. —— PAYNE, DEBORAH C. (eds).   Cultural readings of Restoration and eighteenth-century English theater. *See* **20**.

8549. CARLYON, DAVID.   'Blow your nose with your fingers': the rube story as crowd control. NETJ (7) 1996, 1–22.

8550. COX, JEFFREY; COX, NANCY (eds).   Seven gothic dramas, 1789–1825. Athens: Ohio UP, 1992. pp. 425. (Francis North, *The Kentish Barons*; J. C. Cross, *Julia of Louvain; or, Monkish Cruelty*; M. G. Lewis, *The Castle Spectre, The Captive*; Joanna Baillie, *De Monfort*; C. R. Maturin, *The Castle of Aldobrand*; R. B. Peake, *Presumption; or, The Fate of Frankenstein*.) Rev. by Janice E. Patten in TJ (45:4) 1993, 562–4.

8551. DONKIN, ELLEN.   Getting into the act: women playwrights in London, 1776–1829. (Bibl. 1995, 7260.) Rev. by Jane Montgomery in TLS, 1 Mar. 1996, 27.

8552. DUDDEN, FAYE E.   Women in the American theatre: actresses and audiences, 1790–1870. (Bibl. 1995, 7261.) Rev. by Dawn E. Keetley in NWSAJ (7:1) 1995, 164–7; by Ellen Donkin in Signs (21:3) 1996, 774–7; by Kay M. Robinson in JAC (19:1) 1996, 99.

8553. FLETCHER, JILL.   The story of theatre in South Africa: a guide to its history from 1780–1930. Cape Town: Vlaeberg, 1994. pp. 160. Rev. by Edwin Hees in SATJ (9:1) 1995, 113–18.

8554. HENDERSON, MARY C.   Theater in America: 250 years of plays, players, and productions. New York: Abrams, 1996. pp. 352. (New, updated ed.: first ed. 1986.)

8555. MANN, DAVID D.; MANN, SUSAN GARLAND; GARNIER, CAMILLE.   Women playwrights in England, Ireland, and Scotland, 1660–1823. *See* **7500**.

8556. PORTER, SUSAN L.   With an air debonair: musical theatre in America, 1785–1815. (Bibl. 1995, 7275.) Rev. by Francis Hodge in AHR (98:1) 1993, 241.

8557. ROSENTHAL, LAURA J.   Playwrights and plagiarists in early modern England: gender, authorship, literary property. *See* **7522**.

8558. STRAUB, KRISTINA.   Actors and homophobia. *In* (pp. 258–80) **20**.

8559. —— Sexual suspects: eighteenth-century players and sexual ideology. (Bibl. 1994, 5927.) Rev. by Colleen Lamos in Signs (19:3) 1994, 826–30.

8560. TAYLOR, RICHARD C.   John Gay's theatrical career: *The Beggar* and his 'other' productions. Review (17) 1995, 123–9 (review-article).

8561. THOMPSON, JAMES.   'Sure I have seen that face before': representation and value in eighteenth-century drama. *In* (pp. 281–308) **20**.

8562. WINTON, CALHOUN. John Gay and the London theatre. (Bibl. 1995, 7278.) Rev. by Laura H.-B. Miller in JDTC (8:2) 1994, 238; by Richard C. Taylor in Review (17) 1995, 123–9.

8563. WOOD, NIGEL. The eighteenth century: drama. YWES (75) 1994, 376–81.

Fiction

8564. ALLISTON, APRIL. Virtue's faults: correspondences in eighteenth-century British and French women's fiction. Stanford, CA: Stanford UP, 1996. pp. xiv, 318.

8565. BANERJEE, JACQUELINE P. Through the northern gate: childhood and growing up in British fiction, 1719–1901. New York; Frankfurt; Bern; Paris: Lang, 1996. pp. xxix, 244. (Studies in nineteenth-century British literature, 6.)

8566. BARTOLOMEO, JOSEPH F. A new species of criticism: eighteenth-century discourse on the novel. (Bibl. 1995, 7282.) Rev. by Aileen Douglas in BJECS (19:2) 1996, 229.

8567. BATOR, PAUL. The University of Edinburgh Belles Lettres Society (1759–64) and the rhetoric of the novel. RhR (14:2) 1996, 280–98.

8568. BOUR, ISABELLE. Le roman dans l'histoire: l'année 1796 en Angleterre. BSEAA (42) 1996, 83–98.

8569. BOWER, ALAN. The eighteenth century: novel. YWES (75) 1994, 367–76.

8570. BRUHM, STEVEN. Gothic bodies: the politics of pain in Romantic fiction. (Bibl. 1994, 5941.) Rev. by Kate Behr in NQ (43:2) 1996, 242–3; by Jerrold E. Hogle in KSJ (45) 1996, 216–18.

8571. CLERY, E. J. The rise of supernatural fiction, 1762–1800. (Bibl. 1995, 7287.) Rev. by Kate Behr in NQ (43:1) 1996, 103–5; by D. L. Macdonald in ECF (8:4) 1996, 553–4; by Neil Cornwell in EP (21) 1996, 178.

8572. COPELAND, EDWARD. Women writing about money: women's fiction in England, 1790–1820. (Bibl. 1995, 7288.) Rev. by Janice Farrar Thaddeus in ECS (29:2) 1995/96, 235–7; by Roger Sales in Albion (28:1) 1996, 141–4; by Tess Cosslett in NQ (43:2) 1996, 230; by Thomas K. Meier in ECF (8:4) 1996, 547–8.

8573. DEAR, JEANNIE. Fires in the brain: the chiliastic traits of eighteenth-century Sentimental fiction. RWT (4:1) 1996, 119–33.

8574. DUNCAN, IAN. Modern romance and transformations of the novel: the gothic, Scott, Dickens. (Bibl. 1995, 7297.) Rev. by Kim Ian Michasiw in SSL (29) 1996, 308–13.

8575. ELLIS, MARKMAN. The politics of sensibility: race, gender and commerce in the Sentimental novel. Cambridge; New York: CUP, 1996. pp. xi 264. (Cambridge studies in Romanticism, 18.) (Cf. bibl. 1993, 5635.)

8576. FAVRET, MARY A. Romantic correspondence: women, politics, and the fiction of letters. (Bibl. 1995, 7298.) Rev. by Greg Laugero in ECS (28:4) 1995, 433–5.

8577. FITZGERALD, LAURIE. Shifting genres, changing realities: reading the late eighteenth-century novel. (Bibl. 1995, 7299.) Rev. by Eleanor Ty in ECF (8:3) 1996, 431–3.

8578. FOLKENFLIK, ROBERT. The heirs of Ian Watt. ECS (25:2) 1991/92, 203–17.

8579. García Landa, José Ángel.   Nivel narrativo, status, persona y typología de las narraciones. Misc (17) 1996, 91–121.

8580. Gessner-Utsch, Bettina.   Subjektiver Roman: Studien zum Verhältnis von fiktionalen Subjektivitäts- und Wirklichkeits-konzeptionen in England vom 18. Jahrhundert bis zum Modernismus. Frankfurt; New York: Lang, 1994. pp. 323. (Aspekte der englischen Gesites- und Kulturgeschichte / Aspects of English intellectual, cultural, and literary history, 26.) Rev. by Ansgar Nünning in ZAA (43:2) 1995, 187–9.

8581. Gonda, Caroline.   Reading daughters' fictions, 1709–1834: novels and society from Manley to Edgeworth. Cambridge; New York: CUP, 1996. pp. xx, 287. (Cambridge studies in Romanticism, 19.) (Cf. bibl. 1992, 6449.)

8582. Gondebeaud, Louis.   Récits et romans picaresques en Angleterre (1576–1723). See **5720**.

8583. Green, Katherine Sobba.   The courtship novel 1740–1820: a feminized genre. (Bibl. 1993, 5640.) Rev. by Judith Halberstam in Signs (19:1) 1993, 241–4.

8584. Halberstam, Judith.   Skin shows: gothic horror and the technology of monsters. Durham, NC; London: Duke UP, 1995. pp. x, 215. (Cf. bibl. 1991, 7084.) Rev. by F.B. in TLS, 24 May 1996, 36; by Steffen Hantke in JAC (19:2) 1996, 139–40.

8585. Haltunen, Karen.   Early American murder narratives: the birth of horror. *In* (pp. 67–101) **88**.

8586. Harris, Sharon M. (ed.).   Redefining the political novel: American women writers, 1797–1901. See **99**.

8587. Hopes, Jeffrey.   De l'histoire aux histoires: le récit historique romancé au début du dix-huitième siècle. BSEAA (42) 1996, 73–81.

8588. Howard, Jacqueline.   Reading gothic fiction: a Bakhtinian approach. (Bibl. 1994, 5956.) Rev. by John Strachan in BJECS (19:1) 1996, 97–8; by April London in ECF (8:4) 1996, 551–2.

8589. Huber, Werner.   Irish novels in a German court library of the early 19th century. *In* (pp. 37–44) **49**.

8590. Kaufmann, David.   The business of common life: novels and classical economics between revolution and reform. (Bibl. 1995, 7307.) Rev. by John E. Loftis in RMRLL (50:1) 1996, 78–80; by Deidre Lynch in ECF (8:4) 1996, 548–9.

8591. Kilgour, Maggie.   The rise of the gothic novel. (Bibl. 1995, 7308.) Rev. by Kate Behr in NQ (43:3) 1996, 362–3; by Victor Sage in ECF (8:4) 1996, 549–51; by Neil Cornwell in EP (21) 1996, 181–2.

8592. Kullmann, Thomas.   Vermenschlichte Natur: zur Bedeutung von Landschaft und Wetter im englischen Roman von Ann Radcliffe bis Thomas Hardy. Tübingen: Niemeyer, 1995. pp. 510. (Buchreihe der Anglia, 33.) Rev. by Elmar Schenkel in LJGG (37:supp.) 1996, 519–22.

8593. Lyall, Francis.   To the moon – in 1798: an Aberdeen curiosity. AUR (56:3) 1996, 360–6.

8594. McNeil, David.   The grotesque depiction of war and the military in eighteenth-century English fiction. Newark: Delaware UP; London; Toronto: Assoc. UPs, 1990. pp. 229.

8595. Merrett, Robert James.   Natural history and the eighteenth-century English novel. ECS (25:2) 1991/92, 145–70.

8596. Miles, Robert.   Gothic writing, 1750–1820: a genealogy. (Bibl. 1995, 7312.) Rev. by Emma McEvoy in BJECS (19:1) 1996, 96–7.

8597. Mishra, Vijay. The gothic sublime. (Bibl. 1995, 7313.) Rev. by Stephen Bernstein in CLIO (25:3) 1996, 333–8.

8598. Nelson, T. G. A. Children, parents, and the rise of the novel. (Bibl. 1995, 7314.) Rev. by Ruth Perry in ECF (9:1) 1996, 107–9.

8599. Nussbaum, Felicity A. Torrid zones: maternity, sexuality, and empire in eighteenth-century English narratives. (Bibl. 1995, 7316.) Rev. by George Haggerty in TSWL (15:2) 1996, 363–5; by Claire Harman in TLS, 12 July 1996, 28–9.

8600. Paulson, Ronald. The beautiful, novel, and strange: aesthetics and heterodoxy. Baltimore, MD; London: Johns Hopkins UP, 1996. pp. xix, 369.

8601. Pitcher, E. W. Eighteenth-century gothic fragments and the paradigm of violation and repair. SSF (33:1) 1996, 35–42.

8602. Prince, Michael. Philosophical dialogue in the British Enlightenment: theology, aesthetics and the novel. Cambridge; New York: CUP, 1996. pp. xiv, 282. (Cambridge studies in eighteenth-century English literature and thought, 31.)

8603. Pringle, David. Imaginary people: a who's who of fictional characters from the eighteenth century to the present day. (Bibl. 1988, 6336.) Aldershot; Brookfield, VT: Scolar Press, 1996. pp. x, 296. (Second ed.: first ed. 1987.)

8604. Rees, Christine. Utopian imagination and eighteenth-century fiction. London; New York: Longman, 1996. pp. vi, 296. (Studies in eighteenth- and nineteenth-century literature.) Rev. by Gregory Claeys in Utopian Studies (7:2) 1996, 322–3.

8605. Richetti, John (ed.). The Cambridge companion to the eighteenth-century novel. Cambridge; New York: CUP, 1996. pp. xiii, 283. (Cambridge companions to literature.)

8606. Richter, David H. The progress of romance: literary historiography and the gothic novel. Columbus: Ohio State UP, 1996. pp. xi, 242. (Theory and interpretation of narrative.)

8607. Saar, Doreen Alvarez; Schofield, Mary Anne (comps). Eighteenth-century Anglo-American women novelists: a critical reference guide. New York: G. K. Hall; London: Prentice Hall, 1996. pp. xxii, 664. (Critical reference guides.)

8608. Samuels, Shirley. Romances of the Republic: women, the family, and violence in the literature of the early American nation. *See* **7542**.

8609. Schellenberg, Betty A. The conversational circle: re-reading the English novel, 1740–1775. Lexington: Kentucky UP, 1996. pp. 165. (Cf. bibl. 1992, 6480.)

8610. Scheuermann, Mona. Her bread to earn: women, money, and society from Defoe to Austen. (Bibl. 1995, 7321.) Rev. by Kevin L. Cope in StudN (27:1) 1995, 99–103; by Nick Groom in BJECS (19:1) 1996, 112–13.

8611. Schofield, Mary Anne. Romance subversion: eighteenth-century feminine fiction. *In* (pp. 75–86) **109**.

8612. Shaffer, Julie. Non-canonical women's novels of the Romantic era: Romantic ideologies and the problematics of gender and genre. StudN (28:4) 1996, 469–92.

8613. Slocum, Robert B. New England in fiction 1787–1990: an annotated bibliography. (Bibl. 1994, 5978.) Rev. by Kyle Donaldson in BB (53:2) 1996, 175–6.

8614. SPACKS, PATRICIA MEYER.   Desire and truth: functions of plot in eighteenth-century English novels. (Bibl. 1995, 7324.) Rev. by Dieter Kranz in ZAA (41:3) 1993, 274–6.

8615. THOMPSON, JAMES.   Models of value: eighteenth-century political economy and the novel. Durham, NC; London: Duke UP, 1996. pp. viii, 271.

8616. VAN GORP, HENDRIK.   Problems of comparative reception studies: the case of the gothic novel (1790–1825). JLS (11:3/4) 1996, 100–11.

8617. WATSON, NICOLA J.   Revolution and the form of the British novel, 1790–1825: intercepted letters, interrupted seductions. (Bibl. 1995, 7332.) Rev. by Claudia Johnson in ECS (29:4) 1996, 441–2; by Sarah R. Marino in SAtlR (61:3) 1996, 146–8.

8618. WEYLER, KAREN A.   'A speculating spirit': trade, speculation, and gambling in early American fiction. EAL (31:3) 1996, 207–42.

8619. WIEHAHN, RIALETTE.   Comparative reception studies of the gothic novel. JLS (11:3/4) 1996, 112–15.

8620. WILLIAMS, ANNE PATRICIA.   Description and tableau in the eighteenth-century British Sentimental novel. ECF (8:4) 1996, 465–84.

8621. WINTER, KARI J.   Subjects of slavery, agents of change: women and power in gothic novels and slave narratives, 1790–1865. (Bibl. 1995, 7334.) Rev. by Winifred Morgan in AmS (35:1) 1994, 155.

8622. WOLF, WERNER.   Angst und Schrecken als Attraktion: zu einer gender-orientierten Funktionsgeschichte des englischen Schauerromans im 18. und frühen 19. Jahrhundert. ZAA (43:1) 1995, 37–59.

8623. WOODWARD, CAROLYN.   'My heart so wrapt': lesbian disruptions in eighteenth-century British fiction. Signs (18:4) 1993, 838–65.

8624. —— Who wrote *The Cry*? A fable for our times. ECF (9:1) 1996, 91–7.

8625. ZOMCHICK, JOHN P.   Family and the law in eighteenth-century fiction: the public conscience in the private sphere. (Bibl. 1995, 7336.) Rev. by George E. Haggerty in CLIO (25:1) 1995, 119–21; by Murray L. Brown in StudN (27:2) 1995, 248–50.

Literature for Children

8626. ABBOTT, MARY.   Easy as A, B, C. Signal (80) 1996, 120–6.

8627. BOTTIGHEIMER, RUTH B.   The child-reader of children's Bibles, 1656–1753. *In* (pp. 44–56) **48**.

8628. DROTNER, KIRSTEN.   English children and their magazines, 1751–1945. *See* **1263**.

8629. THOMPSON, HILARY.   Enclosure and childhood in the wood engravings of Thomas and John Bewick. *See* **251**.

Poetry

8630. ARMSTRONG, ISOBEL.   Caterpillar on the skin. TLS, 12 July 1996, 28.

8631. ASHFIELD, ANDREW (ed.).   Romantic women poets, 1770–1838: an anthology. (Bibl. 1995, 7343.) Rev. by Stephen C. Behrendt in CritM (9:1) 1995, 95–105; by Jacqueline Banerjee in EngS (77:6) 1996, 597–8.

8632. BARASH, CAROL.   English women's poetry, 1649–1714: politics, community, and linguistic authority. *See* **7546**.

8633. BARKER, ANTHONY D.   Poetry from the provinces: amateur poets in the *Gentleman's Magazine* in the 1730s and 1740s. *In* (pp. 241–56) **122**.

8634. BEALE, DONALD A.   Shelley, the 'nation', and the National Anthem. Pretexts (5:1/2) 1995, 32–45.

8635. BOWER, ALAN.   The eighteenth century: poetry. YWES (75) 1994, 349–57.

8636. BRADY, PATRICK.   Rococo poetry in English, French, German, Italian: an introduction. *See* **7548**.

8637. BREEN, JENNIFER (ed.).   Women Romantic poets, 1785–1832: an anthology. (Bibl. 1994, 6000.) Rev. by Stephen C. Behrendt in CritM (9:1) 1995, 95–105.

8638. BURWICK, FREDERICK.   Poetic madness and the Romantic imagination. University Park: Pennsylvania State UP, 1996. pp. 307.

8639. COLOMB, GREGORY G.   Designs on truth: the poetics of the Augustan mock-epic. (Bibl. 1995, 7351.) Rev. by James McLaverty in Review (16) 1994, 221–36.

8640. COX, PHILIP.   Gender, genre, and the Romantic poets: an introduction. Manchester; New York: Manchester UP, 1996. pp. 170.

8641. DAVIE, DONALD.   The eighteenth-century hymn in England. (Bibl. 1995, 7352.) Rev. by Colin Haydon in Literature and History (5:1) 1996, 112–13; by Alan Shelston in LitTheol (10:4) 1996, 378–9.

8642. DOWLING, WILLIAM C.   Ideology and the flight from history in eighteenth-century poetry. *In* (pp. 135–53) **91**.

8643. ELDRIDGE, RICHARD (ed.).   Beyond representation: philosophy and poetic imagination. *See* **3805**.

8644. ERSKINE-HILL, HOWARD.   The poetry of opposition and revolution: Dryden to Wordsworth. *See* **7555**.

8645. FULFORD, TIM.   Landscape, liberty and authority: poetry, criticism and politics from Thomson to Wordsworth. Cambridge; New York: CUP, 1996. pp. xiii, 251. (Cambridge studies in eighteenth-century English literature and thought, 30.)

8646. GERRARD, CHRISTINE.   Parnell, Pope, and pastoral. *In* (pp. 221–40) **122**.

8647. —— The patriot opposition to Walpole: politics, poetry, and myth, 1725–1742. (Bibl. 1995, 7356.) Rev. by Karen O'Brien in BJECS (19:2) 1996, 208–9.

8648. GOODRIDGE, JOHN.   Rural life in eighteenth-century English poetry. Cambridge; New York: CUP, 1995. pp. xiv, 227. (Cambridge studies in eighteenth-century English literature and thought, 27.)

8649. —— (ed.).   The independent spirit: John Clare and the self-taught tradition. (Bibl. 1994, 44.) Rev. by Brian Maidment in JCSJ (15) 1996, 88–91; by Robert Heyes in Eng (45:181) 1996, 79–84.

8650. HAEFNER, JOEL.   The Romantic scene(s) of writing. *In* (pp. 256–73) **103**.

8651. HOAGLAND, TONY.   Body and soul. GetR (8:3) 1995, 505–22 (review-article).

8652. JAIN, NALINI; RICHARDSON, JOHN (eds).   Eighteenth-century English poetry: the annotated anthology. (Bibl. 1994, 6010.) Rev. by Thomas J. Regan in Scriblerian (28:1/2) 1995/96, 81–2.

8653. JOHNSON, C. R.   Provincial poetry 1789–1839: British verse printed in the provinces: the Romantic background. Introd. by Robert Woof. (Bibl. 1993, 5707.) Rev. by William St Clair in BC (43:2) 1994, 302–3.

8654. JONES, RACHEL. 'All that fame hath cost …': the response to fame of British women poets from 1770 to 1835. Unpub. doct. diss., Massey Univ., 1996.

8655. KORTE, BARBARA. Sehweisen literarischer Landschaft – ein Literaturbericht. GRM (44:3) 1994, 255–65.

8656. LEONARD, TOM (ed.). Radical Renfrew: poetry from the French Revolution to the First World War by poets born, or sometime resident in, the County of Renfrewshire. (Bibl. 1990, 5008.) Rev. by C. J. Fox in PN Review (17:4) 1991, 79.

8657. MCGANN, JEROME J. (ed.). The new Oxford book of Romantic period verse. (Bibl. 1995, 7362.) Rev. by Stephen C. Behrendt in CritM (9:1) 1995, 95–105.

8658. PITTOCK, MURRAY G. H. Poetry and Jacobite politics in eighteenth-century Britain and Ireland. (Bibl. 1995, 7368.) Rev. by Jeremy Black in SLJ (supp. 42) 1995, 4–5; by Daniel Szechi in Albion (28:2) 1996, 312–13; by John Wiltshire in ELN (34:1) 1996, 101.

8659. PRIVATEER, PAUL MICHAEL. Romantic voices: identity and ideology in British poetry, 1789–1850. (Bibl. 1994, 6021.) Rev. by A. Banerjee in EngS (76:3) 1995, 282.

8660. ROY, G. ROSS. Poems and songs spuriously attributed to Robert Burns. Études Écossaises (3) 1996, 11–24.

8661. SUAREZ, MICHAEL F. Trafficking in the Muse: Dodsley's *Collection of Poems* and the question of canon. *In* (pp. 297–313) **122**.

8662. YARRINGTON, ALISON; EVEREST, KELVIN (eds). Reflections of Revolution: images of Romanticism. (Bibl. 1995, 7372.) Rev. by Robert Miles in BJECS (19:2) 1996, 211–12.

Prose

8663. ANSELMENT, RAYMOND A. 'The wantt of health': an early eighteenth-century self-portrait of sickness. LitMed (15:2) 1996, 225–43. (Elizabeth Freke.)

8664. BELL, ALLAN. Munificent, wise and thoughtful gifts: Grace and Peter Redpath and the Redpath Tracts. *See* **453**.

8665. BLAKEMORE, STEVEN. Revolution and the French disease: Laetitia Matilda Hawkins's *Letters* to Helen Maria Williams. SELit (36:3) 1996, 673–91.

8666. BOHLS, ELIZABETH A. Women travel writers and the language of aesthetics, 1716–1818. Cambridge; New York: CUP, 1995. pp. x, 309. (Cambridge studies in Romanticism, 13.) Rev. by Katherine Turner in TLS, 1 Mar. 1996, 27.

8667. BRANT, CLARE. Dueling by sword and pen: *The Vauxhall Affray* of 1773. Prose Studies (19:2) 1996, 160–72.

8668. BROOKS, MARILYN. Priestley's plan for a 'continually improving' translation of the Bible. Enlightenment and Dissent (15) 1996, 89–106.

8669. CHRISMAN, KIMBERLY. *Unhoop* the fair sex: the campaign against the hoop petticoat in eighteenth-century England. ECS (30:1) 1996, 5–23.

8670. COLOMBO, CLAIRE MILLER. 'This pen of mine will say too much': public performance in the journals of Anna Larpent. TSLL (38:3/4) 1996, 285–301.

8671. DEMOS, JOHN. The unredeemed captive: a family story from early America. New York: Knopf, 1994. pp. xiii, 315. Rev. by

Colin G. Calloway in VH (63:1) 1995, 48–50; by Alan Taylor in WMQ (52:3) 1995, 517–19.

8672. DICKINSON, PETER. Documenting 'North' in Canadian poetry and music. ECanW (59) 1996, 105–22. (Samuel Hearne's *Journey ... to the Northern Ocean*, 1795; Don Gutteridge.)

8673. EDWARDS, PHILIP. The story of the voyage: sea-narratives in eighteenth-century England. (Bibl. 1995, 7380.) Rev. by Barry Gough in Albion (28:1) 1996, 111–12; by Katherine Turner in BJECS (19:2) 1996, 228.

8674. FAVRET, MARY A. War correspondence: reading Romantic war. *See* **1264**.

8675. FLYNN, PHILIP. Enlightened Scotland: a study and selection of Scottish philosophical prose from the eighteenth and early nineteenth centuries. Edinburgh: Scottish Academic Press, 1992. pp. xxii, 356. Rev. by Karen O'Brien in RES (46:182) 1995, 302–3.

8676. FREESE, PETER. 'Westward the Course of Empire takes its Way': the *translatio*-concept in popular American writing and painting. Amst (41:2) 1996, 265–95.

8677. GELBART, NINA RATTNER. Female journalists. *In* (pp. 420–43) **42**.

8678. GEMME, PAOLA. Representing the world in discourse: a socio-stylistic analysis of multivocality in *The Journal of Madam Knight*. *See* **2626**.

8679. HALTUNEN, KAREN. Early American murder narratives: the birth of horror. *In* (pp. 67–101) **88**.

8680. HARRISON, KEITH. Samuel Hearne, Matonabbee, and the 'esquimaux girl': cultural subjects, cultural objects. CanRCL (22:3/4) 1995, 647–57.

8681. HOPES, JEFFREY. De l'histoire aux histoires: le récit historique romancé au début du dix-huitième siècle. *See* **8587**.

8682. LAMB, JONATHAN. Minute particulars and the representation of South Pacific discovery. ECS (28:3) 1995, 281–94.

8683. LOFTIS, JOHN E. Congreve's *Way of the World* and popular criminal literature. *See* **7602**.

8684. McGINTY, J. WALTER. John Goldie and Robert Burns. SSL (29) 1996, 238–44.

8685. MACLEOD, EMMA VINCENT. Women at war: British women and the debate on the wars against Revolutionary France in the 1790s. Enlightenment and Dissent (15) 1996, 3–32.

8686. MAUTNER, THOMAS. 'The working class of people': an early eighteenth-century source. *See* **2026**.

8687. MAYER, ROBERT. *The History of Myddle*: memory, history, and power. SP (93:1) 1996, 64–92.

8688. MELMAN, BILLIE. Women's Orients: English women and the Middle East, 1718–1918: sexuality, religion and work. (Bibl. 1995, 7395.) Rev. by Dorothy O. Helly in AHR (99:2) 1994, 556–7.

8689. MORÈRE, PIERRE. *The Travels of Mungo Park*: récit et signification. Études Écossaises (2) 1993, 143–53.

8690. NEVERS, KEVIN L. Immovable objects, irresistible forces: the sublime and the technological in the eighteenth century. ECL (19:1) 1995, 18–38.

8691. NEWPORT, KENNETH G. C. Methodists and the Millennium: eschatological expectation and the interpretation of biblical prophecy in early British Methodism. BJRL (78:1) 1996, 103–22.

8692. NICHOL, DONALD W.   Warburton (not!) on copyright: clearing up the misattribution of *An Enquiry into the Nature and Origin of Literary Property* (1762). BJECS (19:2) 1996, 171–82.

8693. NÜNNING, VERA.   *'The slaves of our pleasures'* oder *'our companions and equals'*? Die Konstruktion von Weiblichkeit im England des 18. Jahrhunderts aus kulturwissenschaftlicher Sicht. ZAA (44:3) 1996, 199–219.

8694. PERCY, CAROL.   Eighteenth-century normative grammar in practice: the case of Captain Cook. *In* (pp. 339–62) **27**.

8695. PERCY, CAROL E.   In the margins: Dr Hawkesworth's editorial emendations to the language of Captain Cook's *Voyages*. *See* **785**.

8696. PITCHER, E. W.   A 'complaint' against *The Petition* of Belinda, an African slave. *See* **792**.

8697. —— An eighteenth-century journey to the *mundum subterraneum*: a utopian satire in the age of revolution. ANQ (9:2) 1996, 9–14.

8698. PORTER, CHARLOTTE M.   William Bartram's travels in the Indian nations. FHQ (70:4) 1992, 434–50.

8699. REGIS, PAMELA (ed.).   Describing early America: Bartram, Jefferson, Crèvecœur, and the rhetoric of natural history. (Bibl. 1993, 5746.) Rev. by Charlotte M. Porter in AHR (99:1) 1994, 295.

8700. REIMANN, K. A.   'Great as he is in his own good opinion': the *Bounty* mutiny and Lieutenant Bligh's construction of self. *In* (pp. 198–218) **122**.

8701. RIBEIRO, ALVARO.   The 'chit-chat way': the letters of Mrs Thrale and Dr Burney. *In* (pp. 25–40) **122**.

8702. RILEY, SAM G. (ed.).   American magazine journalists, 1741–1850. *See* **1347**.

8703. SCHEICK, WILLIAM J.   Logonomic conflict in Hanson's captivity narrative and Ashbridge's autobiography. ECent (37:1) 1996, 3–21.

8704. SHERMAN, SANDRA.   Credit, simulation, and the ideology of contract in the early eighteenth century. ECL (19:3) 1995, 86–102.

8705. SHUTTLETON, DAVID.   Jacobitism and millennial enlightenment: Alexander, Lord Forbes of Pitsligo's 'remarks' on the mystics. Enlightenment and Dissent (15) 1996, 33–56.

8706. SINGH, JYOTSNA G.   Colonial narratives/cultural dialogues: 'discoveries' of India in the language of colonialism. *See* **7613**.

8707. TELTSCHER, KATE.   'The fearful name of the Black Hole': fashioning an imperial myth. *In* (pp. 30–51) **132**.

8708. THÉVENOT, MARIE-HÉLÈNE.   Des côtes d'Écosse aux côtes d'Amérique du Nord: l'odyssée des émigrants écossais aux XVIIIe et XIXe siècles. Études Écossaises (2) 1993, 165–78.

8709. THOMAS, D. O.   Benjamin Hoadly: the ethics of sincerity. Enlightenment and Dissent (15) 1996, 71–88.

8710. TURNER, KATHERINE S. H.   At the boundaries of fiction: Samuel Paterson's *Another Traveller!* *In* (pp. 144–60) **122**.

8711. WENDORF, RICHARD.   Sir Joshua's French Revolution. *In* (pp. 177–97) **122**.

8712. WOOD, NIGEL.   The eighteenth century: prose. YWES (75) 1994, 357–67.

8713. WOOD, VIRGINIA STEELE; BULLARD, MARY R. (eds).   Journal of a visit to the Georgia Islands of St Catharines, Green, Ossabaw, Sapelo, St Simons, Jekyll, and Cumberland, with comments on the Florida islands of Amelia, Talbot, and St George, in 1753. Macon, GA: Mercer UP, 1996. pp. xvii, 103. Rev. by Martha L. Keber in GaHQ (80:4) 1996, 892–3.

Biography and Autobiography

8714. CRANE, ELAINE FORMAN (ed.).   The diary of Elizabeth Drinker: vol. 1, 1758–1795; vol. 2, 1796–1802; vol. 3, 1803–1807. Boston, MA: Northeastern UP, 1991. pp. lxxv, 2398. Rev. by Richard D. Brown in AHR (98:1) 1993, 237–8.

8715. FERGUSON, SALLYANN H.   Christian violence and the slave narrative. AL (68:2) 1996, 297–320.

8716. GATES, HENRY LOUIS, JR.   James Gronniosaw and the trope of the talking book. *In* (pp. 8–25) **1**.

8717. KING, EVERARD H.   James Beattie's *The Minstrel* and the origins of Romantic autobiography. (Bibl. 1995, 7415.) Rev. by Nick Groom in BJECS (19:1) 1996, 111–12.

8718. RAWLINGS, PHILIP (ed.).   Drunks, whores and idle apprentices: criminal biographies of the eighteenth century. (Bibl. 1995, 7417.) Rev. by Peter Wagner in Ang (114:2) 1996, 287–90.

8719. SHERMAN, STUART.   Telling time: clocks, diaries, and English diurnal form, 1660–1785. *See* **7620**.

8720. SIMONS, JUDY.   Diaries and journals of literary women from Fanny Burney to Virginia Woolf. (Bibl. 1992, 6548.) Rev. by Gloria Bowles in NWSAJ (4:3) 1992, 373–9.

Related Studies

8721. ALMOND, PHILIP C.   Heaven and Hell in Enlightenment England. *See* **7621**.

8722. BARKER-BENFIELD, G. J.   The culture of sensibility: sex and society in eighteenth-century Britain. (Bibl. 1995, 7423.) Rev. by Barbara Taylor in JBS (34:2) 1995, 285–6; by Vera Nünning in ZAA (43:2) 1995, 181–2.

8723. BARNEY, RICHARD A.   Re-veiling paradigms: education, psychoanalysis, and the disciplining of eighteenth-century culture. ECent (37:2) 1996, 174–83 (review-article).

8724. BERMINGHAM, ANN; BREWER, JOHN (eds).   The consumption of culture, 1600–1800: image, object, text. *See* **7623**.

8725. BLACK, JEREMY.   Cultural history and the eighteenth century. BSEAA (42) 1996, 7–20.

8726. BROWN, RICHARD D.   Knowledge is power: the diffusion of information in early America, 1700–1865. Oxford; New York: OUP, 1991. pp. xii, 372. Rev. by Peter C. Mancall in AmS (32:2) 1992, 118–20.

8727. BUICKEROOD, JAMES G.   Pursuing the science of man: some difficulties in understanding eighteenth-century maps of the mind. ECL (19:2) 1995, 1–17.

8728. CARBONI, PIERRE.   *Belles lettres*: la fortune d'une expression française dans l'Écosse des Lumières. Études Écossaises (2) 1993, 95–103.

8729. CARRÉ, JACQUES (ed.).   The crisis of courtesy: studies in the conduct-book in Britain, 1600–1900. *See* **7625**.

8730. CLAEYS, GREGORY (ed.).   The political writings of the 1790s: the French Revolution debate in Britain. London; Brookfield, VT: Pickering & Chatto, 1995. 8 vols. Rev. by Rosemary Ashton in TLS, 5 Jan. 1996, 8–9.

8731. CLARKE, TRISTRAM. Politics and prayer books: the Book of Common Prayer in Scotland *c.*1705–1714. Edinburgh Bibliographical Society Transactions (6:2) 1993, 57–70.

8732. CLEVE, GUNNEL. A query about William Law's mysticism. SSp (6) 1996, 220–38.

8733. COL, NORBERT. Le procès Sacheverell (1710): les débuts d'un whiggisme conservateur? BSEAA (42) 1996, 45–59.

8734. DE BOLLA, PETER. The charm'd eye. *In* (pp. 89–111) **10**.

8735. DONALD, DIANA. The age of caricature: satirical prints in the reign of George III. New Haven, CT; London: Yale UP, for Paul Mellon Centre for Studies in British Art, 1996. pp. viii, 248. Rev. by Richard D. Altick in TLS, 20 Sept. 1996, 18–19.

8736. GAVIN, J. Westmorland literary institutions to 1850. Bibliotheck (20) 1995, 144–54.

8737. GOLDGAR, ANNE, Impolite learning: conduct and community in the republic of letters, 1680–1750. *See* **7631**.

8738. HANRATTY, GERALD. Philosophers of the Enlightenment: Locke, Hume and Berkeley revisited. *See* **7633**.

8739. HART, CLIVE; STEVENSON, KAY GILLILAND. Heaven and the flesh: imagery of desire from the Renaissance to the Rococo. *See* **7634**.

8740. HOWARD, SEYMOUR. Some eighteenth-century 'restored' boxers. JWCI (56) 1993, 238–55.

8741. HUDSON, NICHOLAS. From 'nation' to 'race': the origin of racial classification in eighteenth-century thought. *See* **1990**.

8742. LAFON, SYLVIE. La coutume et la mode dans les théories du jugement esthétique chez Adam Smith. Études Écossaises (3) 1996, 77–87.

8743. LOUSSOUARN, SOPHIE. L'évolution de la sociabilité à Londres au dix-huitième siècle: des *coffee-houses* aux *clubs*. BSEAA (42) 1996, 21–44.

8744. LYNCH, DEIRDRE. Overloaded portraits: the excesses of character and countenance. *In* (pp. 112–43) **10**.

8745. MCKEON, MICHAEL. Historicizing patriarchy: the emergence of gender difference in England, 1660–1760. *See* **7640**.

8746. MARKLEY, ROBERT. The rise of nothing: revisionist historiography and the narrative structure of eighteenth-century studies. Genre (23:2/3) 1990, 77–101.

8747. MENNETEAU, PATRICK. Raison, croyance, foi et savoir selon David Hume: débat autour de la définition de la nature humaine au XVIIIe siècle. Études Écossaises (2) 1993, 113–21.

8748. PAHL, JON. Paradox lost: free will and political liberty in American culture, 1630–1760. *See* **7641**.

8749. PERKINS, MAUREEN. Visions of the future: almanacs, time, and cultural change, 1775–1870. Oxford: Clarendon Press; New York: OUP, 1996. pp. viii, 270.

8750. PORTER, ROY; ROBERTS, MARIE MULVEY (eds). Pleasure in the eighteenth century. Washington Square: New York UP; Basingstoke: Macmillan, 1996. pp. xv, 273. (Themes in focus.)

8751. RAVEN, JAMES. The representation of philanthropy and reading in the eighteenth-century library. *See* **530**.

8752. SOMMEREUX, ANN. Francis Hutcheson and the internal sense: a genesis of aesthetics? Études Écossaises (3) 1996, 67–76.

8753. —— Hutcheson et le sentiment du bonheur. Études Écossaises (2) 1993, 105–11.
8754. TAUSCH, HARALD. Vom Bild der Natur zum imaginären Bilderbogen der Vergangenheit: Hermann von Pückler-Muskaus *Andeutungen über Landschaftsgärtnerei* und die Literarisierung des englischen Landschaftsgartens. Archiv (233:1) 1996, 1–19.
8755. THÉVENOT-TOTEMS, MARIE-HÉLÈNE. Flora MacDonald (1722–1790), la Jeanne d'Arc écossaise: mythe et réalité. Études Écossaises (3) 1996, 89–101.
8756. UTZ, HANS. Schotten und Schweizer: *brother mountaineers*: Europa entdeckt die beiden Völker im 18. Jahrhundert. New York; Frankfurt; Bern; Paris: Lang, 1995. pp. 169. (Scottish studies, 17.) Rev. by Hans R. Guggisberg in SSL (29) 1996, 333–5; by Michael Maurer in GRM (46:2) 1996, 236–8.
8757. VALLONE, LYNNE. Disciplines of virtue: girls' culture in the eighteenth and nineteenth centuries. New Haven, CT; London: Yale UP, 1995. pp. x, 230. (Cf. bibl. 1991, 6137.) Rev. by Randi L. Davenport in Albion (28:2) 1996, 320–1; by Lori D. Ginzberg in ALH (101:5) 1996, 1520; by Judith Burdan in SAtlR (61:2) 1996, 131–3.
8758. WEBSTER, ALISON. Francis Hutcheson: political ideals. Analecta Husserliana (49) 1996, 61–70.

Literary Theory

This section is intended to contain studies **about** the literary theory, literary historiography, literary criticsm, etc., produced *in* the eighteenth century. For modern works **of** literary history and criticism dealing generally with this period, see under 'Eighteenth Century: General Literary Studies'.

8759. COURT, FRANKLIN E. Institutionalizing English literature: the culture and politics of literary study, 1750–1900. (Bibl. 1995, 7463.) Rev. by Herbert Lindenberger in Comparatist (18) 1994, 165–9; by Pamela K. Gilbert in Review (17) 1995, 74–5.
8760. HINNANT, CHARLES H. 'Steel for the mind': Samuel Johnson and critical discourse. (Bibl. 1995, 7464.) Rev. by Edward Tomarken in PLL (32:2) 1996, 217–23.
8761. KRAMNICK, JONATHAN BRODY. The cultural logic of late feudalism: placing Spenser in the eighteenth century. *See* **6049**.
8762. ROSS, TREVOR. The emergence of 'literature': making and reading the English canon in the eighteenth century. *See* **8521**.
8763. SHERBO, ARTHUR. Samuel Johnson's critical opinions: a re-examination. *See* **6468**.
8764. TERRY, RICHARD. The eighteenth-century invention of English literature: a truism revisited. *See* **1973**.
8765. WEINSHEIMER, JOEL C. Eighteenth-century hermeneutics: philosophy of interpretation in England from Locke to Burke. (Bibl. 1995, 7466.) Rev. by Alan P. F. Sell in BJECS (19:1) 1996, 93.

AUTHORS

John Adams

8766. BLAKE, DAVID HAVEN, JR.   'Posterity must judge': private and public discourse in Adams–Jefferson letters. AQ (50:4) 1994, 1–30.

Joseph Addison

8767. BROWN, MARY ELLEN.   Historical ballad scholarship. *See* **3474**.

8768. ELLISON, JULIE.   Cato's tears. ELH (63:3) 1996, 571–601. (Addison's *Cato*; Thomson's *Sophonisba*.)

8769. HINNANT, CHARLES H.   Augustan semiosis. *See* **7880**.

8770. KOWALESKI-WALLACE, BETH.   Women, china, and consumer culture in eighteenth-century England. ECS (29:2) 1995/96, 153–67.

8771. SACCAMANO, NEIL.   Wit's breaks. *In* (pp. 45–67) **10**.

8772. WIDMAYER, ANNE F.   Mapping the landscape in Addison's *Pleasures of the Imagination*. RMRLL (50:1) 1996, 19–29.

Mark Akenside

8773. DIX, ROBIN.   The literary relationship of Mark Akenside and David Fordyce. SLJ (23:1) 1996, 13–20.

8774. —— (ed.).   The poetical works of Mark Akenside. Madison, NJ; Fairleigh Dickinson UP; London; Toronto: Assoc. UPs, 1996. pp. 594. Rev. by Steve Clark in TLS, 27 Dec. 1996, 13.

8775. WHITELEY, PAUL.   'A manly and rational spirit of thinking': Akenside's *The Pleasures of Imagination* (1744). Eng (45:183) 1996, 193–211.

Henry Alline

8776. GERRY, THOMAS M. F.   'Green yet free of seasons': Gwendolyn MacEwen and the mystical tradition of Canadian poetry. StudCanL (16:2) 1991/92, 147–61.

John Armstrong

8777. HART, CLIVE; STEVENSON, KAY GILLILAND.   John Armstrong's *The Oeconomy of Love*: a critical edition with commentary. *See* **675**.

Mrs Barbauld

8778. DAVIES, DAMIAN WALFORD.   'A tongue in every star': Wordsworth and Mrs Barbauld's *A Summer Evening's Meditation*. NQ (43:1) 1996, 29–30.

8779. ELLISON, JULIE.   The politics of fancy in the age of sensibility. *In* (pp. 228–55) **103**.

8780. ROSS, MARLON B.   Configurations of feminist reform: the woman writer and the tradition of dissent. *In* (pp. 91–110) **103**.

8781. WILSON, CAROL SHINER.   Lost needles, tangled threads: stitchery, domesticity, and the artistic enterprise in Barbauld, Edgeworth, Taylor, and Lamb. *In* (pp. 167–90) **103**.

Joel Barlow

8782. ZAFAR, RAFIA.   The proof of the pudding: of haggis, hasty pudding, and Transatlantic influence. EAL (31:2) 1996, 133–49.

Lady Anne Barnard

8783. DRIVER, DOROTHY. Lady Anne Barnard's *Cape Journals* and the concept of self-othering. Pretexts (5:1/2) 1995, 46–65.

James Beattie

8784. ROBINSON, ROGER. The madness of Mrs Beattie's family: the strange case of the 'assassin' of John Wilkes. BJECS (19:2) 1996, 183–97.

William Beckford

8785. ALAMOUDI, CARMEN. Un sourire déchiré: l'ironie dans le *Vathek* de Beckford. ECF (8:3) 1996, 401–14.

8786. BOTTING, FRED. Power in the darkness: heterotopias, literature and gothic labyrinths. Genre (26:2/3) 1993, 253–82.

8787. ROBERTS, ADAM; ROBERTSON, ÉRIC. The Giaour's sabre: a reading of Beckford's *Vathek*. SR (35:2) 1996, 199–211.

Henry Ward Beecher

8788. FOX, RICHARD WIGHTMAN. Intimacy on trial: cultural meanings of the Beecher–Tilton affair. *In* (pp. 103–32) **88**.

8789. KOROBKIN, LAURA HANFT. Silent woman, speaking fiction: Charles Reade's *Griffith Gaunt* (1866) at the adultery trial of Henry Ward Beecher. *In* (pp. 45–62) **75**.

George Berkeley

8790. FREESE, PETER. 'Westward the Course of Empire takes its Way': the *translatio*-concept in popular American writing and painting. *See* **8676**.

William Blake

8791. ACKROYD, PETER. Blake. New York: Knopf, 1996. pp. 399. (Cf. bibl. 1995, 7491.) Rev. by Johanna Keller in AR (54:4) 1996, 487–8; by Susanne Schmid in GRM (46:4) 1996, 476–7; by Iain Sinclair in LRB (18:4) 1996, 16–19; by Michael Dirda in BkW, 12 May 1996, 1, 11; by Phoebe Pettingell in NewL (79:3) 1996, 15–16.

8792. BENTLEY, G. E., JR. The foundations move. AEB (9:1/2) 1995, 68–79 (review-article).

8793. —— The journeyman and the genius: James Parker and his partner William Blake with a list of Parker's engravings. *See* **181**.

8794. BULL, MALCOLM. Blake and Watts in *Songs of Experience*. NQ (43:1) 1996, 27–9.

8795. CHONG, CUE-HWAN. Blake's *Milton, a Poem*: jaah haebang eui sihak. (Blake's *Milton, a Poem*: the poetics of self-liberation.) Unpub. doct. diss., Hanyang Univ., Seoul, 1996.

8796. DAVIES, DAMIAN WALFORD. Blake, Donne, and death. *See* **7801**.

8797. DAVIES, J. M. Q. Blake's *Paradise Lost* designs reconsidered. *In* (pp. 143–81) **47**.

8798. DAVIS, MIKE; POUND, ALAN (eds). Selected poems. Oxford; New York: Heinemann, 1996. pp. viii, 168. (Heinemann poetry bookshelf.)

8799. DÖRRBECKER, D. W. (ed.). The continental prophecies. (Bibl. 1995, 7510.) Rev. by Iain Sinclair in LRB (18:4) 1996, 16–19.

8800. EAVES, MORRIS. The counter-arts conspiracy: art and industry in the age of Blake. (Bibl. 1995, 7511.) Rev. by Patricia Anderson in AHR (99:3) 1994, 898–9; by Ralph Pite in Eng (45:182) 1996, 179–81.

8801. —— Essick, Robert N.; Viscomi, Joseph (eds).   The early illuminated books. (Bibl. 1994, 6138.) Rev. by Iain Sinclair in LRB (18:4) 1996, 16–19.

8802. Essick, Robert N.; Viscomi, Joseph (eds).   *Milton, a Poem,* and the final illuminated works, *The Ghost of Abel, On Homer's Poetry, On Virgil's Laocoön.* (Bibl. 1994, 6140.) Rev. by Iain Sinclair in LRB (18:4) 1996, 16–19.

8803. Greenberg, Mark L. (ed.).   Speak silence: rhetoric and culture in Blake's *Poetical Sketches. See* **2386**.

8804. Hallab, Mary Y.   Carter and Blake: the dangers of innocence. *In* (pp. 177–83) **36**.

8805. Hoerner, Fred.   Prolific reflections: Blake's contortion of surveillance in *Visions of the Daughters of Albion.* SR (35:1) 1996, 119–50.

8806. Hur, Yoon-Deok.   Jeontong gwa byeonyong – William Blake eui si e natanan yeyeonjeok *vision* gwa susahak yeongu. (Tradition and transfiguring use: a study of prophetic vision and rhetoric in the poetry of William Blake.) Unpub. doct. diss., Dankook Univ., Korea, 1996.

8807. James, G. Ingli.   The holy and the heterodox: William Blake's transformational use of religious language. *See* **2652**.

8808. Kaplan, Nancy.   Blake's problem and ours: some reflections on the image and the word. RWT (3:2) 1996, 115–33.

8809. Kim, Hee-Sun.   The paradoxical task of Blake/Los in *Jerusalem*: system-building and system-breaking. JELL (42:4) 1996, 761–76.

8810. Kim, Ok-Yeop.   A 'sublime allegory': William Blake eui sangsangryeok gwa sihak. (A 'sublime allegory': William Blake's imagination and poetics.) Unpub. doct. diss., Seoul National Univ., 1995.

8811. Lincoln, Andrew (ed.).   Songs of innocence and of experience. (Bibl. 1993, 5845.) Rev. by Iain Sinclair in LRB (18:4) 1996, 16–19.

8812. Lindop, Grevel.   Newton, Raymond Tallis and the three cultures. PN Review (18:1) 1991, 36–42.

8813. Lussier, Mark S.   Blake's deep ecology. SR (35:3) 1996, 393–408.

8814. —— Eternal dictates: the 'other' of Blakean inspiration. 1650–1850 (2) 1996, 61–74.

8815. Macdonald, Murdo.   The torrent shrieks. Edinburgh Review (96) 1996, 99–108.

8816. Marshall, Peter.   William Blake: visionary anarchist. (Cf. bibl. 1990, 5119, where subtitle omitted.) London: Freedom Press, 1994. pp. 64. (Second ed.: first ed. 1988.)

8817. Mee, Jon.   William Blake and John Wright: two ex-Swedenborgians. *In* (pp. 73–84) **47**.

8818. Noad, Charles E.   Frodo and his spectre: Blakean resonances in Tolkien. Mythlore (21:2) 1996, 58–62.

8819. O'Keefe, Vincent.   Debunking the Romantic ideology: a review of Blake's *Jerusalem.* ERR (7:1) 1996, 40–8.

8820. O'Neill, Michael.   Blake and the self-conscious poem. *In* (pp. 145–59) **125**.

8821. Paananen, Victor N.   William Blake: updated edition. (Bibl. 1978, 5489.) New York: Twayne; London: Prentice Hall, 1996. pp. xxi, 185. (Twayne's English authors, 202.) (Revised ed.: first ed. 1977.)

8822. Paley, Morton D. (ed.).   Jerusalem: the emanation of the giant Albion. (Bibl. 1993, 5851.) Rev. by Iain Sinclair in LRB (18:4) 1996, 16–19.

8823. Porée, Marc. '*Ruinous fragments of life*'; ou, *Le Livre d'Urizen* de A à Z (ou presque). Q/W/E/R/T/Y (6) 1996, 97–106.

8824. Punter, David (ed.). William Blake. Basingstoke: Macmillan; New York: St Martin's Press, 1996. pp. x, 221. (New casebooks.)

8825. Quadri, Marcella. *The Tyger* di William Blake: la creazione del testo poetico. Textus (7) 1994, 7–21.

8826. Richey, William. Blake's altering aesthetic. Columbia; London: Missouri UP, 1996. pp. xii, 197.

8827. —— 'Not Angles, but angels': Blake's pictorial defense of English art. ERR (7:1) 1996, 49–60.

8828. Romero, Milena. The fourfold circle of *Jerusalem*. Textus (7) 1994, 23–39.

8829. Rosso, George Anthony, Jr. Blake's prophetic workshop: a study of *The Four Zoas*. (Bibl. 1993, 5861.) Rev. by Margaret Storch in YES (26) 1996, 292.

8830. Rothenberg, Molly Anne. *Jerusalem*'s 'forgotten remembrances': a Blakean analytics of narrativity and ideology. Genre (23:2/3) 1990, 205–26.

8831. —— Rethinking Blake's textuality. (Bibl. 1994, 6161.) Rev. by Kathryn S. Freeman in ERR (7:1) 1996, 87–90; by Margaret Storch in YES (26) 1996, 292–3.

8832. Schwenger, Peter. Blake's boxes, Coleridge's circles, and the frame of Romantic vision. SR (35:1) 1996, 99–117.

8833. Scott, Peter Dale. Alone on Ararat: Scott, Blake, Yeats, and apocalyptic. ECanW (55) 1995, 288–302.

8834. Shabetai, Karen. The question of Blake's hostility toward the Jews. ELH (63:1) 1996, 139–52.

8835. Simpson, Michael. Who didn't kill Blake's fly: moral law and the rule of grammar in *Songs of Experience*. *See* **2708**.

8836. Sławek, Tadeusz. William Blake i piekielna po-etyka lektury. (William Blake and hellish poet(h)ics of reading.) ZRL (39:1/2) 1996, 81–111.

8837. Sorensen, Peter J. William Blake's recreation of gnostic myth: resolving the apparent incongruities. Lewiston, NY; Lampeter: Mellen Press, 1995. pp. 155. (Salzburg studies in English literature: Romantic reassessment, 118.)

8838. Stauffer, Andrew M. Elizabeth Barrett Browning reads William Blake? VP (34:1) 1996, 114–17.

8839. —— The first known publication of Blake's poetry in America. *See* **1012**.

8840. Storch, Margaret. Sons and adversaries: women in William Blake and D. H. Lawrence. (Bibl. 1993, 5865.) Rev. by Adela Pinch in Signs (19:1) 1993, 264–8.

8841. Tallis, Raymond. Newton's sleep: 1, Poets, scientists and rainbows. PN Review (17:3) 1991, 47–52.

8842. —— Newton's sleep: a reply to Grevel Lindop. PN Review (18:1) 1991, 42–5.

8843. Thompson, E. P. Witness against the beast: William Blake and the moral law. (Bibl. 1994, 6167.) Rev. by Irving Weinman in Agenda (31:4/32:1) 1993/94, 312–16; by Morton D. Paley in Blake (28:2) 1994, 65–6; by Brian Wilkie in MLR (90:2) 1995, 416–17; by François Piquet in EA (48:4) 1995, 496–8; by Michael Scrivener in Criticism (37:1) 1995, 166–71; by John T. Netland in ChrisL (44:2) 1995, 232–4; by Ralph Pite in Eng (45:182) 1996, 176–9; by Roy Porter in EHR (111:442) 1996, 743–4.

8844. TITLESTAD, P. J. H.   The 'pretty young man Civility': Bunyan, Milton & Blake and patterns of Puritan thought. *See* **1925**.

8845. TOLLEY, MICHAEL J.   'Words standing in chariots': the literalism of Blake's imagination. *In* (pp. 125–42) **47**.

8846. TROWBRIDGE, KATELIN E.   Blake's *A Little Girl Lost.* Exp (54:3) 1996, 139–42.

8847. VISCOMI, JOSEPH.   Blake and the idea of the book. (Bibl. 1995, 7554.) Rev. by George Mackie in BC (43:4) 1994, 590–2; by G. E. Bentley, Jr, in AEB (9:1/2) 1995, 68–79; by David Worrall in BJECS (19:1) 1996, 117.

8848. WELCH, DENNIS M.   Blake's *Songs of Experience*: the Word lost and found. EngS (76:3) 1995, 238–52.

8849. WORRALL, DAVID (ed.).   The Urizen books. (Bibl. 1995, 7559.) Rev. by Iain Sinclair in LRB (18:4) 1996, 16–19.

8850. WRIGHT, JULIA M.   'And none shall gather the leaves': unbinding the voice in Blake's *America* and *Europe.* ERR (7:1) 1996, 61–84.

8851. WU, DUNCAN; WORRALL, DAVID.   The nineteenth century: Romantic period: poetry and drama. YWES (75) 1994, 382–402.

Henry St John, Viscount Bolingbroke

8852. PETTIT, ALEXANDER.   Lord Bolingbroke's *Remarks on the History of England* and the rhetoric of political controversy. *See* **2445**.

James Boswell

8853. BOWDEN, ANN; TODD, WILLIAM B.   Scott's commentary on *The Journal of a Tour to the Hebrides with Samuel Johnson. See* **582**.

8854. BROWN, ANTHONY E.   Boswellian studies: a bibliography. (Bibl. 1994, 6173.) Rev. by Anne McDermott in BJECS (19:1) 1996, 92.

8855. COLE, RICHARD D.; BAKER, PETER S.; McCLELLAN, RACHEL (eds).   The general correspondence of James Boswell, 1766–1769: vol. 1, 1766–1767. (Bibl. 1995, 7564.) Rev. by Anne McDermott in BJECS (19:1) 1996, 91–2.

8856. GREENE, DONALD.   The world's worst biography. ASch (62:3) 1993, 365–82.

8857. LUSTIG, IRMA S. (ed.).   Boswell: citizen of the world, man of letters. (Bibl. 1995, 7569.) Rev. by Colby H. Kullman in Albion (28:4) 1996, 698–700.

8858. McGOWAN, IAN.   Boswell at work: the revision and publication of the *Journal of a Tour to the Hebrides. In* (pp. 127–43) **122**.

8859. MINER, EARL.   Naming properties: nominal reference in travel writings by Bashō and Sora, Johnson and Boswell. *See* **2152**.

8860. NEWMAN, DONALD J. (ed.).   James Boswell, psychological interpretations. (Bibl. 1995, 7572.) Rev. by Richard B. Sher in Albion (28:3) 1996, 496–7.

8861. RADNER, JOHN B.   'A very exact picture of his life': Johnson's role in writing the *Life of Johnson.* AJ (7) 1996, 299–342.

8862. ROGERS, PAT.   Johnson and Boswell: the transit of Caledonia. (Bibl. 1995, 7573.) Rev. by W. B. Carnochan in Albion (28:3) 1996,

495–6; by A. F. T. Lurcock in NQ (43:2) 1996, 224; by John Wiltshire in ELN (34:1) 1996, 103–4; by Lars Hartveit in EngS (77:3) 1996, 288–9.

8863. SHER, RICHARD.   Between Johnson and Auchinleck: Boswell's Lord Kames. Études Écossaises (1) 1992, 93–103.

8864. TIEKEN-BOON VAN OSTADE, INGRID.   Social network theory and eighteenth-century English: the case of Boswell. *In* (pp. 327–37) **27**.

8865. VIVIÈS, JEAN.   Boswell et l'histoire: du récit au discours dans *An Account of Corsica*. Études Écossaises (1) 1992, 173–80.

Frances Brooke

8866. HOWELLS, ROBIN.   Dialogism in Canada's first novel: *The History of Emily Montague*. CanRCL (20:3/4) 1993, 437–50.

John Brown

8867. ROBERTS, WILLIAM.   A dawn of imaginative feeling: the contribution of John Brown (1715–66) to eighteenth-century thought and literature. Carlisle: Northern Academic Press, 1996. pp. 259.

William Hill Brown

8868. BARNES, ELIZABETH.   Affecting relations: pedagogy, patriarchy, and the politics of sympathy. AmLH (8:4) 1996, 597–614.

Edmund Burke

8869. DE BRUYN, FRANS.   The literary genres of Edmund Burke: the political uses of literary form. Oxford: Clarendon Press; New York: OUP, 1996. pp. ix, 318.

8870. DUNN, ALLEN.   The mechanics of transport: sublimity and the imagery of abjection in Rochester, Swift, and Burke. *See* **8329**.

8871. EAGLETON, TERRY.   Violence and hegemony in Edmund Burke. Pretexts (5:1/2) 1995, 3–13.

8872. FRIEDMAN, GERALDINE.   The insistence of history: revolution in Burke, Wordsworth, Keats, and Baudelaire. Stanford, CA: Stanford UP, 1996. pp. xii, 270.

8873. FURNISS, TOM.   Edmund Burke's aesthetic ideology: language, gender, and political economy in revolution. (Bibl. 1995, 7582.) (Cambridge studies in Romanticism, 4.) Rev. by Allan Ingram in YES (26) 1996, 286–7.

8874. HART, JEFFREY.   Edmund Burke and the English Revolution. ModAge (39:1) 1996, 11–20.

8875. HINNANT, CHARLES.   'The late unfortunate regicide in France': Burke and the political sublime. 1650–1850 (2) 1996, 111–36.

8876. LANGFORD, PAUL (gen. ed.).   The writings and speeches of Edmund Burke: vol. 6, India: the launching of the Hastings impeachment, 1786–1788. Ed. by Paul Marshall and William B. Todd. (Bibl. 1992, 6700.) Rev. by Regina Janes in Salmagundi (100) 1993, 186–96.

8877. LEDDEN, MARK B.   Revolutionary plots: Helen Maria Williams's *Letters from France*. Prism(s) (3) 1995, 1–13.

8878. McCALMAN, IAIN.   Mad Lord George and Madame La Motte: riot and sexuality in the genesis of Burke's *Reflections on the Revolution in France*. JBS (35:3) 1996, 343–67.

8879. O'BRIEN, CONOR CRUISE.   The great melody: a thematic biography and commented anthology of Edmund Burke. (Bibl. 1995, 7587.)

Rev. by Maurice Cranston in BkW, 17 Jan. 1996, 6, 8; by Regina Janes in Salmagundi (100) 1993, 186–96.

8880. O'NEIL, DANIEL J.   Edmund Burke, Karl Marx, and the contemporary Third World. ModAge (34:4) 1992, 349–58.

8881. PAPPIN, JOSEPH, III.   The case for Edmund Burke's metaphysics. ModAge (34:4) 1992, 325–43.

8882. WENDORF, RICHARD.   Sir Joshua's French Revolution. *In* (pp. 177–97) **122**.

Fanny Burney (Mme D'Arblay)

8883. AUSTIN, ANDREA.   Between women: Frances Burney's *The Wanderer*. ESCan (22:3) 1996, 253–66.

8884. DEAR, JEANNIE.   Nobodies and somebodies in eighteenth-century women's writing. *See* **7685**.

8885. GALPERIN, WILLIAM.   The radical work of Frances Burney's London. ECL (20:3) 1996, 37–48.

8886. HUTNER, HEIDI.   *Evelina* and the problem of the female grotesque. Genre (23:2/3) 1990, 191–203.

8887. JOHNSON, CLAUDIA L.   Equivocal beings: politics, gender, and Sentimentality in the 1790s: Wollstonecraft, Radcliffe, Burney, Austen. (Bibl. 1995, 7603.) Rev. by Janice Farrar Thaddeus in ECS (29:2) 1995/96, 235–7; by Julia Epstein in TSWL (15:1) 1996, 150–2; by Terence Brunk in Albion (28:2) 1996, 313–15; by Margaret Anne Doody in ECF (8:3) 1996, 434–6;

8888. KOWALESKI-WALLACE, BETH.   Women, china, and consumer culture in eighteenth-century England. *See* **8770**.

8889. PERKINS, PAM.   Private men and public women: social criticism in Fanny Burney's *The Wanderer*. ELit (23:1) 1996, 69–83.

8890. ROGERS, PAT.   *Sposi* in Surrey: links between Jane Austen and Fanny Burney. TLS, 23 Aug. 1996, 14–15.

8891. SABOR, PETER (ed.).   The complete plays of Frances Burney: vol. 1, Comedies. (Bibl. 1995, 7607.) Rev. by David Womersley in TLS, 16 Feb. 1996, 27.

8892. SHERMAN, SANDRA.   'Does your ladyship mean an extempore?': wit, leisure, and the mode of production in Frances Burney's *The Witlings*. CR (40:2) 1996, 401–28.

8893. TROIDE, LARS E.; COOKE, STEWART J. (eds).   The early journals and letters of Fanny Burney: vol. 3, The Streatham years: part 1, 1778–1779. Oxford: Clarendon Press; New York: OUP, 1994. pp. xxi, 477. Rev. by Lorna J. Clark in NQ (43:2) 1996, 226–7; by Ingrid Tieken-Boon van Ostade in EngS (77:6) 1996, 594–6.

8894. ZOMCHICK, JOHN.   Satire and the bourgeois subject in Frances Burney's *Evelina*. TSL (37) 1995, 347–66.

Robert Burns

8895. ASSELINEAU, ROGER.   Whitman on Robert Burns: a footnote. WWQR (14:1) 1996, 39.

8896. BAILLIE, SHIRLEY (comp.).   Robert Burns, the ruined farmer: a short biography of the famous Scots poet with some extracts from his works. Morrinsville, New Zealand: McDougall Press, 1996. pp. 53.

8897. DOUGLAS, HUGH.   Robert Burns, the tinder heart. Stroud; Wolfeboro Falls, NH: Sutton, 1996. pp. xviii, 299, (plates) 32.

8898. FINLAY, ALEC, *et al.* A Robert Burns rhapsody. Edinburgh Review (96) 1996, 111–50.

8899. HOGG, PATRICK SCOTT. The lost works of Robert Burns. Edinburgh Review (96) 1996, 57–83.

8900. JAMIESON, R. A. (introd.). Oisin Oisian Ossin Suibne Subney Sweeney Osuine Oswine Ossian Ocean: a (mock?) heroic miscellany. Edinburgh Review (93) 1995, 91–120.

8901. LOW, DONALD (ed.). Poems in Scots and English. London: Dent; Rutland, VT: Tuttle, 1993. pp. xxxvi, 206. (Everyman's library.) Rev. by Kenneth Simpson in SSL (29) 1996, 294–5.

8902. MCCARTHY, THOMAS J. 'Epistolary intercourse': sympathy and the English Romantic letter. ERR (6:2) 1996, 162–82.

8903. MCGINTY, J. WALTER. John Goldie and Robert Burns. *See* **8684**.

8904. MCGUIRK, CAROL (ed.). Selected poems. (Bibl. 1994, 6212.) Rev. by Kenneth Simpson in SSL (29) 1996, 292–4.

8905. MCILVANNEY, LIAM. 'Why shouldna poor folk mowe': Bakhtinian folk humour in Burns's bawdry. SLJ (23:2) 1996, 43–53.

8906. MCINTYRE, IAN. Dirt & deity: a life of Robert Burns. (Bibl. 1995, 7619.) Rev. by Marilyn Butler in LRB (18:3) 1996, 9–10.

8907. MACKAY, JAMES A. RB: a biography of Robert Burns. (Bibl. 1993, 5923.) Rev. by Carol McGuirk in SSL (29) 1996, 295–8.

8908. MACNEACAIL, AONGHAS. Singing across the languages: a speculative excursion. Edinburgh Review (96) 1996, 88–96.

8909. MATHISON, H. 'Gude black prent': how the Edinburgh book trade dealt with Burns's *Poems*. *See* **298**.

8910. PINTARIČ, MIHA. A Slovenian translation of Burns. SLJ (22:1) 1995, 84–91.

8911. PITTAS-GIROUX, JUSTIN A. Auld acquaintance not forgot: Thomas Cooper Library's Burns collection. *See* **526**.

8912. ROY, G. ROSS. Poems and songs spuriously attributed to Robert Burns. *See* **8660**.

8913. —— Scottish poets and the French Revolution. Études Écossaises (1) 1992, 69–79.

8914. SCHARNHORST, GARY. Whitman on Robert Burns: an early essay recovered. WWQR (13:4) 1996, 217–20.

8915. SIMPSON, KENNETH (ed.). Burns now. (Bibl. 1994, 6213.) Rev. by Douglas Mack in SLJ (supp. 43) 1995, 16–20; by James A. Mackay in SSL (29) 1996, 286–92.

8916. SPROTT, GAVIN. Robert Burns: pride and passion: the life, times and legacy. Edinburgh: HMSO, 1996. pp. 191.

8917. WAITE, LORNA J. The most radiant lens: Robert Burns: a place for myth and memory. Edinburgh Review (96) 1996, 45–51.

8918. WHYTE, CHRISTOPHER. Bakhtin at Christ's Kirk: part II, Carnival and the vernacular revival. SSL (29) 1996, 133–57.

William Byrd

8919. LOCKRIDGE, KENNETH A. On the sources of patriarchal rage: the commonplace books of William Byrd and Thomas Jefferson and the gendering of power in the eighteenth century. (Bibl. 1995, 7631.) Rev. by Sheila L. Skemp in AHR (99:1) 1994, 294–5; by Nancy Isenberg in AmQ (48:2) 1996, 367–74.

8920. Pastore, Patrizia. Power and submission: gender roles in William Byrd's *Secret Diary*. RSAJ (6) 1995, 83–92.

Elizabeth Carter

8921. Williams, Carolyn D. Poetry, pudding, and Epictetus: the consistency of Elizabeth Carter. *In* (pp. 3–24) **122**.

Jane Cave

8922. Aaron, Jane. The way above the world: religion in Welsh and Anglo-Welsh women's writing, 1780–1830. *In* (pp. 111–27) **103**.

Susannah Centlivre (Susannah Carroll)

8923. Cameron, Joanna M. Centlivre, not Shirley: correcting an error in Joseph Wood Krutch's *Comedy and Conscience after the Restoration*. *See* **8349**.

8924. Copeland, Nancy (ed.). A bold stroke for a wife. Peterborough, Ont.; Orchard Park, NY; Cardiff: Broadview Press, 1995. pp. 158.

8925. Kinney, Suz-Anne. Confinement sharpens the invention: Aphra Behn's *The Rover* and Susanna Centlivre's *The Busie Body*. *In* (pp. 81–98) **64**.

William Chaigneau

8926. Escarbelt, Bernard. William Chaigneau's Jack Connor: a literary image of the Irish peasant. *In* (pp. 51–7) **106**.

Thomas Chatterton

8927. Goldberg, Brian. Romantic professionalism in 1800: Robert Southey, Herbert Croft, and the letters and legacy of Thomas Chatterton. ELH (63:3) 1996, 681–706.

Mary, Lady Chudleigh

8928. Ezell, Margaret J. M. (ed.). The poems and prose of Mary, Lady Chudleigh. (Bibl. 1995, 7643.) Rev. by Victoria Burke in NQ (43:4) 1996, 479–80.

Charles Churchill

8929. Rowland, Jon. From cheated sight to false light: analogy in Swift and Churchill. *In* (pp. 107–32) **120**.

8930. Sainsbury, John. John Wilkes, debt, and patriotism. JBS (34:2) 1995, 165–95.

Colley Cibber

8931. Straub, Kristina. Colley Cibber's butt: class, race, gender, and the construction of sexual identity. Genre (23:2/3) 1990, 135–59.

Jane Collier

8932. Woodward, Carolyn. Who wrote *The Cry*? A fable for our times. *See* **8624**.

William Collins

8933. Williamson, Paul. William Collins and the idea of liberty. *In* (pp. 257–74) **122**.

Ebenezer Cooke (*c.*1667–*c.*1732)

8934. CAREY, GREGORY A. The poem as con game: dual satire and the three levels of narrative in Ebenezer Cooke's *The Sot-Weed Factor*. SoLJ (23:1) 1990, 9–19.

Hannah Cowley

8935. ISIKOFF, ERIN. Masquerade, modesty, and comedy in Hannah Cowley's *The Belle's Stratagem*. In (pp. 99–117) **64**.

William Cowper

8936. BAIRD, JOHN D.; RYSKAMP, CHARLES (eds). The poems of William Cowper: vol. 2, 1782–1785. Oxford: Clarendon Press; New York: OUP, 1995. pp. xxix, 454. Rev. by Robert Wells in TLS, 5 July 1996, 3–4.

8937. ——— The poems of William Cowper: vol. 3, 1785–1800. Oxford: Clarendon Press; New York: OUP, 1995. pp. lii, 413.

8938. BARZILAI, SHULI. The politics of quotation in *To the Lighthouse*: Mrs Woolf resites Mr Tennyson and Mr Cowper. LitPs (41:3) 1995, 22–43.

8939. CHANDRAN, K. NARAYANA. Walt Whitman and William Cowper: a borrowing. WWQR (9:4) 1992, 211–14.

8940. PEARSON, DAVID. A binding by Benjamin West, *ca.*1840. *See* **168**.

8941. PERKINS, DAVID. Cowper's hares. ECL (20:2) 1996, 57–69.

8942. SAMBROOK, JAMES (ed.). *The Task* and selected other poems. (Bibl. 1995, 7651.) Rev. by David Groves in NQ (43:2) 1996, 226.

George Crabbe

8943. WHITEHEAD, FRANK. George Crabbe: a reappraisal. (Bibl. 1995, 7657.) Rev. by Neil Powell in TLS, 16 Aug. 1996, 11–12.

'J. Hector St John de Crèvecœur' (Michel-Guillaume Jean de Crèvecœur)

8944. MOORE, DENNIS D. 'A family truly divided indeed': domesticity and the Golden Age in Crèvecœur's unpublished manuscripts. SHum (18:2) 1991, 110–23.

Sir Herbert Croft

8945. GOLDBERG, BRIAN. Romantic professionalism in 1800: Robert Southey, Herbert Croft, and the letters and legacy of Thomas Chatterton. *See* **8927**.

Richard Cumberland

8946. DIRCKS, RICHARD (ed.). The unpublished plays of Richard Cumberland. (Bibl. 1994, 6235.) Rev. by Peter Thomson in BJECS (19:1) 1996, 115–16.

8947. STEWART, MAAJA A. Inexhaustible generosity: the fictions of eighteenth-century British imperialism in Richard Cumberland's *The West Indian*. ECent (37:1) 1996, 42–55.

John Dalton

8948. DUGAS, DON-JOHN. 'Such Heav'n-taught numbers should be more than read': *Comus* and Milton's reputation in mid-eighteenth-century England. *See* **8152**.

Mary Davys

8949. RILEY, LINDY.   Mary Davys's satiric novel *Familiar Letters*: refusing patriarchal inscription of women. TSL (37) 1995, 206–21.

8950. SAJÉ, NATASHA.   'The assurance to write, the vanity of expecting to be read': deception and reform in Mary Davys's *The Reform'd Coquet*. ELit (23:2) 1996, 165–77.

Thomas Day

8951. ROWLAND, PETER.   The life and times of Thomas Day, 1748–1789: English philanthropist and author: virtue almost personified. Lewiston, NY; Lampeter: Mellen Press, 1996. pp. xiv, 454. (Studies in British history, 39.)

Daniel Defoe

8952. ANDRIES, LISE (ed.).   Robinson. Paris: Autrement, 1996. pp. 159. (Figures mythiques.)

8953. ARMSTRONG, KATHERINE A.   'I was a kind of an historian': the productions of history in Defoe's *Colonel Jack. In* (pp. 97–110) **122**.

8954. AUSTIN, MICHAEL.   Saul and the social contract: constructions of 1 Samuel 8–11 in Cowley's *Davideis* and Defoe's *Jure Divino. See* **7759**.

8955. BENNANI, BEN.   Ibn Tufayl's *Hayy Ibn Yaqzan* and Daniel Defoe's *Robinson Crusoe*: translation as cross-cultural insemination. *See* **3109**.

8956. BLEWETT, DAVID.   The illustration of *Robinson Crusoe*, 1719–1920. *See* **183**.

8957. BRANTLINGER, PATRICK.   Cashing in on the real: money and the failure of mimesis in Defoe and Trollope. SLI (29:1) 1996, 9–21.

8958. BRODSLEY, LAUREL.   Defoe's *The Journal of the Plague Year*: a model for stories of plagues. *In* (pp. 11–22) **2**.

8959. BROSSE, MONIQUE.   Le mythe de Robinson. *See* **4146**.

8960. BURKE, HELEN.   *Roxana*, corruption, and the progressive myth. Genre (23:2/3) 1990, 103–20.

8961. DAVIS, LENNARD J.   The dreadful gulph and the glass cadaver: decomposing women in early modern literature. *See* **7684**.

8962. DI GIUSEPPE, RITA.   The ghost in the machine: *Moll Flanders* and the body politic. Quaderni di lingue e letterature (18) 1993, 311–26.

8963. DONOGHUE, FRANK.   Inevitable politics: rulership and identity in *Robinson Crusoe*. StudN (27:1) 1995, 1–11.

8964. FALLER, LINCOLN B.   Crime and Defoe: a new kind of writing. (Bibl. 1995, 7673.) Rev. by David Mazella in StudN (27:2) 1995, 220–3; by Christopher Hill in Literature and History (5:2) 1996, 85–6.

8965. FAUSETT, DAVID.   The strange surprizing sources of *Robinson Crusoe*. (Bibl. 1995, 7674.) Rev. by Artur Blaim in Utopian Studies (7:2) 1996, 254–7; by Geoffrey Sill in ECF (8:4) 1996, 539–40.

8966. FURBANK, P. N.; OWENS, W. R.   Defoe de-attributions: a critique of J. R. Moore's *Checklist*. (Bibl. 1995, 7676.) Rev. by J. Paul Hunter in ECF (8:2) 1996, 310–12.

8967. GLISERMAN, MARTIN.   Psychoanalysis, language, and the body of the text. Gainesville: Florida UP, 1996. pp. xii, 196.

8968. HAMMOND, J. R. A Defoe companion. (Bibl. 1993, 5959.) Rev. by Katherine A. Armstrong in BJECS (19:1) 1996, 99–100.

8969. HOPES, JEFFREY. Real and imaginary stories: *Robinson Crusoe* and the *Serious Reflections*. ECF (8:3) 1996, 313–28.

8970. KEANE, PATRICK J. Coleridge's submerged politics: *The Ancient Mariner* and *Robinson Crusoe*. (Bibl. 1995, 7679.) Rev. by Irving N. Rothman in StudN (28:2) 1996, 260–2.

8971. KIBBIE, ANN LOUISE. Monstrous generation: the birth of capital in Defoe's *Moll Flanders* and *Roxana*. PMLA (110:5) 1995, 1023–34.

8972. MAN, JOHN (ed.). A journal of the plague year: being observations of memorials of the most remarkable occurrences, as well publick as private, which happened in London during the last great visitation in 1665, written by a citizen who continued all the while in London. London: Dent; Rutland, VT: Tuttle, 1994. pp. xxiv, 240. (Everyman's library.)

8973. MARAIS, MIKE. Colonialism and the epistemological underpinnings of the early English novel. *See* **4212**.

8974. —— 'One of those islands without an owner': the aesthetics of space in *Robinson Crusoe* and J. M. Coetzee's *Life and Times of Michael K*. Current Writing (8:1) 1996, 19–32.

8975. MICHAEL, STEVEN C. Thinking parables: what *Moll Flanders* does not say. ELH (63:2) 1996, 367–95.

8976. MORRISSEY, LEE. *Robinson Crusoe* and South Sea trade, 1710–1720. *In* (pp. 209–15) **71**.

8977. NEW, PETER. Why Roxana can never find herself. MLR (91:2) 1996, 317–29.

8978. NOVAK, MAXIMILLIAN E. Picturing the thing itself, or not: Defoe, painting, prose fiction, and the arts of describing. *See* **4230**.

8979. —— Whither the Defoe canon? ECF (9:1) 1996, 89–91.

8980. NOWAK, HELGE. '*Completeness is all*': Fortsetzungen und andere Weiterführungen britischer Romane als Beispiel zeitübergreifender und interkultureller Rezeption. (Bibl. 1994, 6268.) Rev. by Dieter Mehl in Archiv (233:1) 1996, 234–5; by Heidi Ganner in AAA (21:1) 1996, 129–33.

8981. O'BRIEN, JOHN F. The character of credit: Defoe's 'Lady Credit', *The Fortunate Mistress*, and the resources of inconsistency in early eighteenth-century Britain. ELH (63:3) 1996, 603–31.

8982. ROTHMAN, IRVING N. Coleridge on the semi-colon in *Robinson Crusoe*: problems in editing Defoe. *See* **820**.

8983. SCOTT, PAUL H. *Defoe in Edinburgh* and other papers. East Linton, East Lothian: Tuckwell Press, 1995. pp. 252. Rev. by Grant G. Simpson in AUR (56:4) 1996, 484–5; by J. H. Alexander in SLJ (supp. 44) 1996, 32–5.

8984. SHERMAN, SANDRA. Credit, simulation, and the ideology of contract in the early eighteenth century. *See* **8704**.

8985. —— Finance and fictionality in the early eighteenth century: accounting for Defoe. Cambridge; New York: CUP, 1996. pp. xii, 222. (Cf. bibl. 1993, 5568.)

8986. SPAAS, LIEVE; STIMPSON, BRIAN (eds). Robinson Crusoe: myths and metamorphoses. Basingstoke: Macmillan; New York: St Martin's Press, 1996. pp. xvii, 328.

8987. STADLER, EVA MARIA. Addressing social boundaries: dressing the female body in early realist fiction. *In* (pp. 20–36) **97**.

8988. STOLER, JOHN A. Daniel Defoe: a partly annotated

bibliography of criticism, 1981–1994: parts I and II. BB (53:1) 1996, 11–22; (53:2) 1996, 125–37.

8989. SVILPIS, JĀNIS.   Bourgeois solitude in *Robinson Crusoe*. ESCan (22:1) 1996, 35–43.

8990. VAUTIER, MARIE.   Les métarécits, le postmodernisme et le mythe postcolonial au Québec: un point de vue de la 'marge'. Études littéraires (27:1) 1994, 43–61.

8991. VICKERS, ILSE.   Defoe and the new sciences. *See* **7670**.

8992. WARNER, JOHN M.   Joyce's grandfathers: myth and history in Defoe, Smollett, Sterne, and Joyce. (Bibl. 1995, 7708.) Rev. by Stephen Soud in StudN (27:1) 1995, 107–9.

8993. WATT, IAN.   Myths of modern individualism: Faust, Don Quixote, Don Juan, Robinson Crusoe. Cambridge; New York: CUP, 1996. pp. xii, 293. Rev. by Frank McConnell in RMRLL (50:2) 1996, 210–12.

8994. ZANDER, HORST.   Die verheiratete Frau als Dienerin und Sklavin: zur Eheproblematik bei Mary Astell und Daniel Defoe. *See* **7653**.

Mary Delany

8995. DEAR, JEANNIE.   Nobodies and somebodies in eighteenth-century women's writing. *See* **7685**.

George Bubb Dodington

8996. MAY, JAMES E.   Young's corrections to Dodington's *Epistle to Bute*: evidence from the Yale manuscript. *See* **752**.

Robert Dodsley

8997. SOLOMON, HARRY M.   The rise of Robert Dodsley: creating the new age of print. *See* **1010**.

8998. SUAREZ, MICHAEL F.   Trafficking in the Muse: Dodsley's *Collection of Poems* and the question of canon. *In* (pp. 297–313) **122**.

8999. TIERNEY, JAMES E.   Eighteenth-century authors and the abuse of the franking system. SB (48) 1995, 112–20.

John Dunton

9000. SHERBERT, GARRY.   Menippean satire and the poetics of wit: ideologies of self-consciousness in Dunton, D'Urfey, and Sterne. *See* **7900**.

Jonathan Edwards

9001. ANDERSON, WALLACE E.; LOWANCE, MASON I., JR; WATTERS, DAVID H. (eds).   Typological writings. (Bibl. 1994, 6281.) Rev. by Christopher Grasso in AmLH (8:4) 1996, 684–5.

9002. CONFORTI, JOSEPH A.   Jonathan Edwards, religious tradition, and American culture. Chapel Hill; London: North Carolina UP, 1995. pp. xiv, 267. Rev. by Philip Gould in AL (68:4) 1996, 849–50; by Donald Weber in EAL (31:3) 1996, 316–18.

9003. GRASSO, CHRISTOPHER.   Images and shadows of Jonathan Edwards. AmLH (8:4) 1996, 683–98 (review-article).

9004. LESSER, M. X.   Jonathan Edwards: an annotated bibliography, 1979–1993. (Bibl. 1994, 6285.) Rev. by Sargent Bush, Jr, in AEB (9:1/2) 1995, 91–3.

9005. MILLER, GORDON. Jonathan Edwards' sublime book of nature. HT (46:7) 1996, 29–35.

9006. OBERG, BARBARA B.; STOUT, HARRY S. (eds). Benjamin Franklin, Jonathan Edwards, and the representation of American culture. (Bibl. 1995, 7716.) Rev. by Mark Valeri in AmS (36:1) 1995, 145–6; by Christopher Grasso in AmLH (8:4) 1996, 685–7.

9007. STEIN, STEPHEN J. (ed.). Jonathan Edwards's writings: text, context, interpretation. Bloomington: Indiana UP, 1996. pp. xix, 219.

9008. YARBROUGH, STEPHEN R.; ADAMS, JOHN C. Delightful conviction: Jonathan Edwards and the rhetoric of conversion. (Bibl. 1993, 5985.) Rev. by Christopher Grasso in AmLH (8:4) 1996, 687–9.

Elizabeth Elstob

9009. ROBINSON, FRED C. Eight letters from Elizabeth Elstob. In (pp. 241–52) **26**.

Olaudah Equiano

9010. MULLEN, HARRYETTE. African signs and spirit writing. Callaloo (19:3) 1996, 670–89.

9011. ORBAN, KATALIN. Dominant and submerged discourses in *The Life of Olaudah Equiano* (or Gustavus Vassa?). AAR (27:4) 1993, 655–64.

9012. RUST, MARION. The subaltern as imperialist: speaking of Olaudah Equiano. In (pp. 21–36) **82**.

George Farquhar

9013. BOSSI, EMANUELA. '*The spirits of freedom they tried hard to quell*': John Milton e *The Beaux' Stratagem* di George Farquhar. See **8128**.

9014. MYERS, WILLIAM (ed.). The constant couple; The twin rivals; The recruiting officer; The beaux' stratagem. Oxford; New York: OUP, 1995. pp. xxix, 399. (World's classics.)

9015. ROPER, ALAN. How much did Farquhar's beaux spend in London? See **817**.

Robert Fergusson

9016. MENNETEAU, PATRICK. Le caractère historique des poèmes de Robert Fergusson. Études Écossaises (1) 1992, 123–41.

9017. —— Robert Fergusson's contribution to the definition of a Scottish cultural identity. Études Écossaises (supp.) 1994, 39–58.

9018. WHYTE, CHRISTOPHER. Bakhtin at Christ's Kirk: part II, Carnival and the vernacular revival. See **8918**.

Henry Fielding

9019. AMORY, HUGH. 'It is very probable I am Lord B– – – –ke': reflections on Fielding's canon. ECF (8:4) 1996, 529–33.

9020. —— Virtual readers: the subscribers to Fielding's *Miscellanies* (1743). See **885**.

9021. BAIRD, JOHN D. Criminal elements: Fielding's *Jonathan Wild*. In (pp. 76–94) **105**.

9022. BATTESTIN, MARTIN C.; PROBYN, CLIVE T. (eds). The correspondence of Henry and Sarah Fielding. (Bibl. 1995, 7729.) Rev. by Wendy Jones Nakanishi in EngS (76:3) 1995, 289.

9023. BELL, IAN A. Henry Fielding: authorship and authority. (Bibl. 1995, 7730.) Rev. by Angela J. Smallwood in NQ (43:2) 1996, 221–2.

9024. BENDER, JOHN; STERN, SIMON (eds).   Tom Jones. Oxford; New York: OUP, 1996. pp. xliii, 916. (World's classics.)

9025. BUTLER, GERALD J.   Making Fielding's novels speak for law and order. ECent (37:3) 1996, 232–43.

9026. CAMPBELL, JILL.   Natural masques: gender and identity in Fielding's plays and novels. (Bibl. 1995, 7735.) Rev. by Kristina Straub in ECS (29:4) 1996, 435–6; by Robert D. Hume in ECF (8:4) 1996, 541–2; by Robert W. Jones in Eng (45:183) 1996, 265–9; by William J. Burling in SAtlR (61:1) 1996, 133–5.

9027. ―――― Tom Jones, Jacobitism, and gender: history and fiction at the ghosting hour. Genre (23:2/3) 1990, 161–90.

9028. CANFIELD, J. DOUGLAS.   The critique of capitalism and the retreat into art in Gay's *Beggar's Opera* and Fielding's *Author's Farce*. TSL (37) 1995, 320–34.

9029. FLYNN, CAROL HOULIHAN.   Closing down the theater; and other critical abuses. ECent (37:3) 1996, 244–56.

9030. GAUTIER, GARY.   Marriage and family in Fielding's fiction. StudN (27:2) 1995, 111–28.

9031. GOLDGAR, BERTRAND A. (introd. and commentary); AMORY, HUGH (textual ed.).   Miscellanies: vol. 2. (Bibl. 1994, 6298.) Rev. by Nick Groom in BJECS (19:1) 1996, 109–11.

9032. HAGGERTY, GEORGE E.   Fielding's novel of atonement: confessional form in *Amelia*. ECF (8:3) 1996, 383–400.

9033. JOHNSON, CHRISTOPHER.   'British championism': early pugilism and the works of Fielding. RES (47:187) 1996, 331–51.

9034. KEEL, GILCHRIST WHITE.   'The author's farce'; or, Henry Fielding's drama as persuasive rhetoric. CCTE (61) 1996, 85–92.

9035. KEYMER, TOM.   Fielding's amanuensis. NQ (43:3) 1996, 303–4.

9036. ―――― (ed.).   The journal of a voyage to Lisbon. London: Penguin, 1996. pp. xxxviii, 142. (Penguin classics.) Rev. by John Mullan in TLS, 28 June 1996, 36.

9037. MACE, NANCY A.   Henry Fielding's novels and the Classical tradition. Newark: Delaware UP; London; Toronto: Assoc. UPs, 1996. pp. 198.

9038. POTTER, TIFFANY.   Honest sins: Henry Fielding's *The Old Debauchees* as libertine moralist drama. TexPres (14) 1993, 75–80.

9039. RICHETTI, JOHN.   Reply to David Richter: ideology and literary form in Fielding's *Tom Jones*. ECent (37:3) 1996, 205–17.

9040. RICHTER, DAVID.   The closing of masterpiece theater: Henry Fielding and the valorization of incoherence. ECent (37:3) 1996, 195–204.

9041. ―――― Ideology and form revisited. ECent (37:3) 1996, 285–6.

9042. SCHNACKERTZ, HERMANN JOSEF.   Hogarth und Fielding: der Innovationsanspruch von Bilderzählung und Roman im 18. Jahrhundert. AAA (21:1) 1996, 63–83.

9043. SMITH, J. F.   An inquiry into narrative deception and its uses in Fielding's *Tom Jones*. (Bibl. 1995, 7750.) Rev. by Connie Capers Thorson in StudN (27:2) 1995, 234–6.

9044. SPACKS, PATRICIA MEYER.   Reply to David Richter: form and ideology: novels at work. ECent (37:3) 1996, 218–31. (*Amelia, Persuasion*.)

9045. STEVENSON, JOHN ALLEN.   Black George and the Black Act. ECF (8:3) 1996, 355–82.

9046. STOCKER, SUSAN. The commercialization of *Tom Jones*. RecL (19) 1993, 49–52.

9047. TOISE, DAVID W. 'A more culpable passion': *Pamela, Joseph Andrews*, and the history of desire. CLIO (25:4) 1996, 393–419.

9048. TUMBLESON, RAYMOND D. The novel's progress: faction, fiction, and Fielding. StudN (27:1) 1995, 12–25.

9049. UGLOW, JENNY. Henry Fielding. Plymouth: Northcote House; London: British Council, 1995. pp. x, 102. (Writers and their work.) Rev. by Robert W. Jones in Eng (45:183) 1996, 269–71.

9050. WALKER, WILLIAM. The determination of Locke, Hume, and Fielding. ECL (20:2) 1996, 70–93.

Sarah Fielding

9051. BARCHAS, JANINE. Sarah Fielding's dashing style and eighteenth-century print culture. *See* **2577**.

9052. BREE, LINDA. Sarah Fielding. New York: Twayne; London: Prentice Hall, 1996. pp. xiii, 176. (Twayne's English authors, 522.)

9053. WOODWARD, CAROLYN. Who wrote *The Cry*? A fable for our times. *See* **8624**.

Hannah Webster Foster

9054. BAKER, DOROTHY Z. 'Detested by the epithet!': definition, maxim, and the language of social *dicta* in Hannah Webster Foster's *The Coquette*. ELit (23:1) 1996, 58–68.

9055. FABI, MARIA GIULIA. *The Coquette*; or, The ambiguities: on the fiction and the reality of independence in the new Republic. RSAJ (1) 1990, 7–26.

9056. HARRIS, SHARON M. Hannah Webster Foster's *The Coquette*: critiquing Franklin's America. *In* (pp. 1–22) **99**.

9057. SIELKE, SABINE. Seduced and enslaved: sexual violence in ante-bellum American literature and contemporary feminist discourse. YREAL (11) 1995, 299–324.

Benjamin Franklin

9058. FRASCA, RALPH. 'The glorious publick virtue so predominant in our rising country': Benjamin Franklin's printing network during the Revolutionary era. *See* **931**.

9059. HUANG, NIAN-SHENG. Benjamin Franklin in American thought and culture, 1790–1990. (Bibl. 1995, 7767.) Rev. by Cecil B. Currey in AHR (101:1) 1996, 232.

9060. SKINFILL, MAURI. Faulkner, Franklin, and the sons of the father. FJ (10:1) 1994, 29–56.

Philip Freneau

9061. ROUND, PHILLIP. 'The posture that we give the dead': Freneau's *Indian Burying Ground* in ethnohistorical context. AQ (50:3) 1994, 1–30.

David Garrick

9062. SECHELSKI, DENISE S. Garrick's body and the labor of art in eighteenth-century theater. ECS (29:4) 1996, 369–89.

John Gay

9063. Canfield, J. Douglas. The critique of capitalism and the retreat into art in Gay's *Beggar's Opera* and Fielding's *Author's Farce*. *See* **9028**.

9064. Dugaw, Dianne. Parody, gender, and transformation in Gay and Handel's *Acis and Galatea*. ECS (29:4) 1996, 345–67.

9065. Gregori, Flavio. Tra Augusta e Dultown: intenzione georgica e visione urbana nei *Trivia* di John Gay. Textus (3:1/2) 1990, 243–71.

9066. MacLean, Gerald M. The anxiety of speculation: satire in an age of imaginary wealth. Review (18) 1996, 81–102 (review-article).

9067. Nokes, David. John Gay, a profession of friendship. (Bibl. 1995, 7781.) Rev. by Arthur J. Weitzman in ASch (65:2) 1996, 304–6; by Paul Ranger in NQ (43:2) 1996, 220–1; by Christopher Baugh in TRI (21:1) 1996, 82–3.

9068. Taylor, Richard C. John Gay's theatrical career: *The Beggar* and his 'other' productions. *See* **8560**.

Edward Gibbon

9069. Baridon, Michel. Historicisme et théorie de la connaissance dans la pensée des Lumières écossaises. Études Écossaises (1) 1992, 81–92.

9070. Cosgrove, Peter. The circulation of genres in Gibbon's *Decline and Fall of the Roman Empire*. ELH (63:1) 1996, 109–38.

9071. Fetherling, Douglas. Revisiting Edward Gibbon. LRC (5:10) 1996, 23.

9072. Palmeri, Frank. Satire in narrative: Petronius, Swift, Gibbon, Melville, and Pynchon. (Bibl. 1991, 6475.) Rev. in Scriblerian (28:1/2) 1995/96, 105–6.

9073. Womersley, David. Gibbon and Classical example: the age of Justinian in *The Decline and Fall*. BJECS (19:1) 1996, 17–31.

9074. —— The secret of South Molton: Gibbon's clemency over the scandal of the Bampton Lectures. TLS, 16 Aug. 1996, 14–15.

William Gilpin

9075. Michasiw, Kim Ian. Nine revisionist theses on the picturesque. Representations (38) 1992, 76–100.

9076. Rogner, David W. Diagramming Coleridge: picturesque aesthetics in *The Nightingale*. PMPA (17) 1992, 10–15.

William Godwin (1756–1836) ('Edward Baldwin')

9077. Bahar, Saba. *Frankenstein*, family politics and population politics. SPELL (9) 1996, 129–41.

9078. Hill-Miller, Katherine C. 'My hideous progeny': Mary Shelley, William Godwin, and the father–daughter relationship. (Bibl. 1995, 7799.) Rev. by Caroline Gonda in CamQ (25:2) 1996, 205–8; by Kate Behr in NQ (43:3) 1996, 363–4; by Dianne F. Sadoff in KSJ (45) 1996, 209–11.

9079. Juengel, Scott J. Godwin, Lavater, and the pleasures of surface. SR (35:1) 1996, 73–97.

9080. Sunstein, Emily W. A William Godwin letter, and young Mary Godwin's part in *Mounseer Nongtongpaw*. KSJ (45) 1996, 19–22.

Oliver Goldsmith

9081. DIXON, PETER. Oliver Goldsmith revisited. Boston, MA: Twayne, 1991. pp. xi, 157. (Twayne's English authors, 487.) Rev. by A. F. T. Lurcock in NQ (43:4) 1996, 482.

9082. DONOGHUE, FRANK. The fame machine: book reviewing and eighteenth-century literary careers. *See* **8463**.

9083. FLINT, CHRISTOPHER. 'The family piece': Oliver Goldsmith and the politics of the everyday in eighteenth-century domestic portraiture. ECS (29:2) 1995/96, 127–52.

9084. MIKHAIL, E. H. (ed.). Goldsmith: interviews and recollections. (Bibl. 1993, 6062.) Rev. by Katherine A. Armstrong in BJECS (19:1) 1996, 120–1.

9085. NELSON, T. G. A. Stooping to conquer in Goldsmith, Haywood, and Wycherley. *See* **8423**.

9086. ZHIJIAN, TAO. Citizen of whose world? Goldsmith's Orientalism. CLS (33:1) 1996, 15–34.

Thomas Gray

9087. GALIGANI, GIUSEPPE. Tra poesia e pittura: *Il Bardo* di Thomas Gray e le arti figurative. Parma: Pratiche, 1995. pp. 127. (Nuovi saggi, 126.) Rev. by C. Maria Laudando in Annali anglistica (38:1/2) 1995, 219–22.

9088. HAGGERTY, GEORGE E. *O lachrymarum fons*: tears, poetry, and desire in Gray. ECS (30:1) 1996, 81–95.

9089. KRAHÉ, PETER. '*Approach and read*': Grays *Elegy* aus sozial- und mentalitätsgeschichtlicher Sicht. GRM (45:4) 1995, 388–404.

Elizabeth Griffith

9090. SKINNER, GILLIAN. 'Above œconomy': Elizabeth Griffith's *The History of Lady Barton* and Henry Mackenzie's *The Man of Feeling*. ECL (19:1) 1995, 1–17.

Elizabeth Gunning

9091. PERKINS, PAM. The fictional identities of Elizabeth Gunning. TSWL (15:1) 1996, 83–98.

Elizabeth Hamilton

9092. THADDEUS, JANICE. Elizabeth Hamilton's *Modern Philosophers* and the uncertainties of satire. TSL (37) 1995, 395–418.

Jupiter Hammon

9093. JOHNSON, LONNELL E. Dilemma of the dutiful servant: the poetry of Jupiter Hammon. *In* (pp. 105–17) **55**.

William Hayley

9094. HOGG, JAMES. William Hayley's *Marcella* and Thomas Middleton and William Rowley's *The Changeling*: a watered-down Jacobean masterpiece. *In* (pp. 319–61) **53**.

Mary Hays

9095. TY, ELEANOR (ed.). The victim of prejudice. Peterborough, Ont.: Broadview Press, 1994. pp. xxxviii, 197. (Broadview literary texts.) Rev. by Rhoda J. Zuk in ESCan (22:4) 1996, 488–91.

Eliza Haywood

9096. Donovan, Josephine.   From avenger to victim: genealogy of a Renaissance novella. *See* **5951**.

9097. Nelson, T. G. A.   Stooping to conquer in Goldsmith, Haywood, and Wycherley. *See* **8423**.

9098. Oakleaf, David (ed.).   Love in excess; or, The fatal enquiry. Peterborough, Ont.: Broadview Press, 1994. pp. 273. (Broadview literary texts.) Rev. by Mary Anne Schofield in ECF (8:2) 1996, 299–300; by Rhoda J. Zuk in ESCan (22:4) 1996, 488–91.

John Hoadly

9099. Maslen, Keith.   Dr Hoadly's *Poems Set to Music by Dr Greene.* SB (48) 1995, 85–94.

Thomas Holcroft

9100. Rosenblum, Joseph.   Thomas Holcroft: literature and politics in England in the age of the French Revolution. Lewiston, NY; Lampeter: Mellen Press, 1995. pp. iv, 143. (Poetic drama & poetic theory, 122.)

David Hume

9101. Baridon, Michel.   Historicisme et théorie de la connaissance dans la pensée des Lumières écossaises. *See* **9069**.

9102. Chézaud, Patrick.   Hume et le sens (commun) de l'histoire. BSEAA (42) 1996, 61–71.

9103. Craig, Cairns.   Out of history. Études Écossaises (1) 1992, 209–28.

9104. Goodman, Dena.   The Hume–Rousseau affair: from private *querelle* to public *procès.* ECS (25:2) 1991/92, 171–201.

9105. Kugler, Michael.   Provincial intellectuals: identity, patriotism, and enlightened peripheries. ECent (37:2) 1996, 156–73.

9106. Lewis, Jayne Elizabeth.   Mary Stuart's 'fatal box': sentimental history and the revival of the casket letters controversy. AJ (7) 1996, 427–73.

9107. Marshall, David.   Arguing by analogy: Hume's standard of taste. ECS (28:3) 1995, 323–43.

9108. Morère, Pierre.   History and historicity in Hume's *Essays.* Études Écossaises (1) 1992, 155–62.

9109. Norton, David Fate; Norton, Mary J.   The David Hume library. *See* **519**.

9110. Price, John Valdimir.   Historicity and narratology in David Hume's *History of England.* Études Écossaises (1) 1992, 143–53.

9111. Slater, Graeme.   Hume's revisions of the *History of England. See* **837**.

9112. Whiteman, Bruce.   Recent additions to the David Hume collection. *See* **554**.

Elizabeth Inchbald

9113. Boardman, Michael.   Inchbald's *A Simple Story*: an anti-ideological reading. ECent (37:3) 1996, 271–84.

9114. Ford, Susan Allen.   'A name more dear': daughters, fathers, and desire in *A Simple Story, The False Friend,* and *Mathilda. In* (pp. 51–71) **103**.

9115. HAGGERTY, GEORGE E.   Female abjection in Inchbald's *A Simple Story*. SELit (36:3) 1996, 655–71.

Thomas Jefferson

9116. BLAKE, DAVID HAVEN, JR.   'Posterity must judge': private and public discourse in Adams–Jefferson letters. *See* **8766**.

9117. KELSALL, MALCOLM.   Inventing America: Jefferson seals the Revolution. *In* (pp. 365–74) **125**.

9118. MANNING, SUSAN.   Naming of parts; or, The comforts of classification: Thomas Jefferson's construction of America as fact and myth. *See* **2426**.

Dr Samuel Johnson

9119. BALDWIN, BARRY.   Plautus in Johnson: an unnoticed quotation. NQ (43:3) 1996, 305–6.

9120. —— (ed. and trans.).   The Latin & Greek poems of Johnson: text, translation, and commentary. London: Duckworth, 1995. pp. ix, 299. Rev. by James McLaverty in NQ (43:2) 1996, 222–4.

9121. BASKER, JAMES G.   Radical affinities: Mary Wollstonecraft and Samuel Johnson. *In* (pp. 41–55) **122**.

9122. BONNELL, THOMAS F.   Patchwork and piracy: John Bell's 'connected system of biography' and the use of Johnson's *Prefaces*. *See* **904**.

9123. BRACK, O. M., JR.   Samuel Johnson and the Preface to Abbé Prévost's *Memoirs of a Man of Quality*. *See* **583**.

9124. —— Samuel Johnson and the translations of Jean Pierre de Crousaz's *Examen* and *Commentaire*. SB (48) 1995, 60–84.

9125. —— EARLY, MARY.   Samuel Johnson's proposals for the *Harleian Miscellany*. *See* **5538**.

9126. BRISTOW, ADRIAN (ed.).   Dr Johnson and Mrs Thrale's tour in North Wales, 1774. Wrexham: Bridge Books, 1995. pp. 147. Rev. by M.F.S. in TLS, 15 Mar. 1996, 33.

9127. CANNON, JOHN.   Samuel Johnson and the politics of Hanoverian England. (Bibl. 1995, 7861.) Rev. by John Phillips in Albion (28:1) 1996, 109–11; by James J. Sack in AHR (101:3) 1996, 847–8; by H. T. Dickinson in BJECS (19:2) 1996, 220; by John Wiltshire in ELN (34:1) 1996, 101–2;

9128. CHAPIN, CHESTER.   Samuel Johnson, anthropologist. ECL (19:3) 1995, 22–37.

9129. CLARK, J. C. D.   The politics of Samuel Johnson. AJ (7) 1996, 27–56.

9130. —— Samuel Johnson: literature, religion, and English cultural politics from the Restoration to Romanticism. (Bibl. 1995, 7863.) Rev. by John Wiltshire in ELN (34:1) 1996, 98–101; by Martin Fitzpatrick in HT (46:5) 1996, 60.

9131. CURLEY, THOMAS M.   Johnson no Jacobite; or, Treason not yet unmasked. AJ (7) 1996, 137–62.

9132. DEMARIA, ROBERT, JR.   The life of Samuel Johnson: a critical biography. (Bibl. 1993, 6107.) Rev. by Allan Ingram in YES (25) 1995, 296–7; by O. M. Brack, Jr, in RMRLL (49:2) 1995, 169–74; by A. F. T. Lurcock in NQ (42:1) 1995, 98–9; by Nicholas Hudson in MP (93:2) 1995, 263–7; by Paul J. Korshin in MP (93:2) 1995, 267–71; by Michael F. Suarez in RES (46:183) 1995, 415–17.

9133. EDDY, D. D.; FLEEMAN, J. D.   A preliminary handlist of books to which Dr Samuel Johnson subscribed. *See* **924**.

9134. ERSKINE-HILL, HOWARD.   Johnson the Jacobite? A response to the new introduction to Donald Greene's *The Politics of Samuel Johnson.* AJ (7) 1996, 3–26.

9135. FAIRER, DAVID.   The publications of J. D. Fleeman. SB (48) 1995, 25–33.

9136. FLECK, RICHARD F.   Samuel Johnson's *Rasselas*: a perspective on Islam. WebS (10:1) 1993, 50–7.

9137. FLEEMAN, J. D.   Dr Johnson and Revd William Dodd. Edinburgh Bibliographical Society Transactions (6:2) 1993, 55–6.

9138. FLEMING, JULIET.   Dictionary English and the female tongue. *In* (pp. 175–204) **89**.

9139. GRAY, JAMES; MURRAY, T. J.   Dr Johnson and Dr James. AJ (7) 1996, 213–45.

9140. GRAY, PIERS.   On linearity. *See* **2632**.

9141. GREENE, DONALD.   Johnson: the Jacobite legend exhumed. A rejoinder to Howard Erskine-Hill and J. C. D. Clark. AJ (7) 1996, 57–135.

9142. —— The world's worst biography. *See* **8856**.

9143. GROSS, GLORIA SYBIL.   This invisible riot of the mind: Samuel Johnson's psychological theory. (Bibl. 1995, 7871.) Rev. by A. F. T. Lurcock in NQ (43:2) 1996, 225.

9144. HOLMES, RICHARD.   Dr Johnson & Mr Savage. (Bibl. 1995, 7872.) Rev. by Michael Dirda in BkW, 4 Sept. 1994, 3, 8; by Peter Schwendener in ASch (64:3) 1995, 467–70.

9145. IAMARTINO, GIOVANNI.   Dyer's and Burke's addenda and corrigenda to Johnson's *Dictionary* as clues to its contemporary reception. *See* **2051**.

9146. JOECKEL, SAMUEL.   Lewis and Samuel Johnson's *Rasselas*: hearing the call of the *Sehnsucht*. CSL (27:4) 1996, 1–6.

9147. KASS, THOMAS G.   The mixed blessings of the imagination in Johnson's *Sermons*. Ren (47:2) 1995, 89–101.

9148. KATRITZKY, LINDE.   Johnson and *The Letters of Junius*: new perspectives on an old enigma. New York; Frankfurt; Bern; Paris: Lang, 1996. pp. 167. (Ars interpretandi, 5.)

9149. KELLY, VERONICA.   Locke's eyes, Swift's spectacles. *In* (pp. 68–85) **10**.

9150. KOLB, GWIN J.; DeMARIA, ROBERT, JR.   The preliminaries to Dr Johnson's *Dictionary*: authorial revisions and the establishment of the texts. *See* **712**.

9151. LAMB, JONATHAN.   Blocked observation: tautology and paradox in *The Vanity of Human Wishes*. TSL (37) 1995, 335–46.

9152. McDERMOTT, ANNE.   Textual transformations: *The Memoirs of Martinus Scriblerus* in Johnson's *Dictionary*. *See* **732**.

9153. MACDONALD, MURDO.   The torrent shrieks. *See* **8815**.

9154. MINER, EARL.   Naming properties: nominal reference in travel writings by Bashō and Sora, Johnson and Boswell. *See* **2152**.

9155. MONTANDON, ALAIN (ed. and trans.)   Histoire de Rasselas, Prince d'Abyssinie. Clermont-Ferrand: Adosa, 1993. pp. 191.

9156. NAGASHIMA, DAISUKE.   How Johnson read Hale's *Origination* for his dictionary: a linguistic view. *See* **2055**.

9157. PEDREIRA, MARK A.   Johnsonian figures: a cornucopia of vanity, idleness, and death in Samuel Johnson's prose writings. 1650–1850 (2) 1996, 241–74.

9158. RADNER, JOHN B. 'A very exact picture of his life': Johnson's role in writing the *Life of Johnson*. *See* **8861**.

9159. RAYAN, KRISHNA. Resistance in reading. Eng (41:171) 1992, 249–53.

9160. REDDICK, ALLEN. The making of Johnson's dictionary, 1746–1773. *See* **2062**.

9161. REDFORD, BRUCE (ed.). The letters of Samuel Johnson: vol. 1, 1731–1772. (Bibl. 1995, 7883.) Rev. by David Yerkes in Text (Ann Arbor) (7) 1994, 478–87.

9162. —— The letters of Samuel Johnson: vol. 2, 1773–1776. (Bibl. 1995, 7884.) Rev. by David Yerkes in Text (Ann Arbor) (7) 1994, 478–87.

9163. —— The letters of Samuel Johnson: vol. 3, 1777–1781. (Bibl. 1995, 7885.) Rev. by David Yerkes in Text (Ann Arbor) (7) 1994, 478–87.

9164. —— The letters of Samuel Johnson: vol. 4, 1782–1784. (Bibl. 1994, 6408.) Rev. by Thomas Woodman in BJECS (19:1) 1996, 113; by David Yerkes in Text (Ann Arbor) (7) 1994, 478–87; by Wendy Jones Nakanishi in EngS (77:6) 1996, 592–4.

9165. —— The letters of Samuel Johnson: vol. 5, Appendices and comprehensive index. (Bibl. 1994, 6409.) Rev. by Thomas Woodman in BJECS (19:1) 1996, 113; by David Yerkes in Text (Ann Arbor) (7) 1994, 478–87; by Wendy Jones Nakanishi in EngS (77:6) 1996, 592–4.

9166. REINERT, THOMAS. Regulating confusion: Samuel Johnson and the crowd. Durham, NC; London: Duke UP, 1996. pp. vii, 195.

9167. ROGERS, PAT. The Samuel Johnson encyclopedia. Westport, CT; London: Greenwood Press, 1996. pp. xxxi, 483.

9168. ROSENBERG, BETH CAROLE. Virginia Woolf and Samuel Johnson: common readers. (Bibl. 1995, 7888.) Rev. by Diane Gillespie in RMRLL (50:2) 1996, 169–78; by Patricia Laurence in ELT (39:3) 1996, 380–3.

9169. SHERBO, ARTHUR. Samuel Johnson's critical opinions: a re-examination. *See* **6468**.

9170. SMITH, DUANE H. Repetitive patterns in Samuel Johnson's *Rasselas*. SELit (36:3) 1996, 623–39.

9171. TOMARKEN, EDWARD. A history of the commentary on selected writings of Samuel Johnson. (Bibl. 1995, 7892.) Rev. by A. F. T. Lurcock in NQ (43:1) 1996, 92–3; by Wendy Jones Nakanishi in EngS (77:3) 1996, 286–7.

9172. VARHUS, SARA B. The 'solitary philosopher' and 'nature's favourite': gender and identity in the *Rambler*. *In* (pp. 61–73) **37**.

9173. WECHSELBLATT, MARTIN. The pathos of example: professionalism and colonialization in Johnson's Preface to the *Dictionary*. YJC (9:2) 1996, 381–403.

9174. WEINBROT, HOWARD D. Johnson, Jacobitism, and the historiography of nostalgia. AJ (7) 1996, 163–211.

Sir William Jones

9175. KNOX-SHAW, P. H. The Eastern *Ancient Mariner*. EC (46:2) 1996, 115–35.

'Junius'

9176. KATRITZKY, LINDE.   Johnson and *The Letters of Junius*: new perspectives on an old enigma. *See* **9148**.

Mary Leapor

9177. GREENE, RICHARD.   Mary Leapor: a study in eighteenth-century women's poetry. (Bibl. 1995, 7897.) Rev. by Wendy Jones Nakanishi in EngS (76:3) 1995, 290; by Bridget Hill in Literature and History (5:2) 1996, 87.

9178. KING, KATHRYN R.   Jane Barker, Mary Leapor and a chain of very odd contingencies. *See* **7672**.

9179. MANDELL, LAURA.   Demystifying (with) the repugnant female body: Mary Leapor and feminist literary history. Criticism (38:4) 1996, 551–82.

9180. RUMBOLD, VALERIE.   The alienated insider: Mary Leapor in *Crumble Hall*. BJECS (19:1) 1996, 63–76.

Sophia Lee

9181. ISAAC, MEGAN LYNN.   Sophia Lee and the gothic of female community. StudN (28:2) 1996, 200–18.

Charlotte Lennox

9182. BERG, TEMMA F.   Getting the mother's story right: Charlotte Lennox and the New World. PLL (32:4) 1996, 369–98.

9183. GARDINER, ELLEN.   Writing men reading in Charlotte Lennox's *The Female Quixote*. StudN (28:1) 1996, 1–11.

9184. GREEN, SUSAN.   A cultural reading of Charlotte Lennox's *Shakespear Illustrated*. *In* (pp. 228–57) **20**.

9185. GRUNDY, ISOBEL.   Attribution to women. *See* **8474**.

9186. HOWARD, SUSAN KUBICA (ed.).   The life of Harriot Stuart, written by herself. Madison, NJ: Fairleigh Dickinson UP; London; Toronto: Assoc. UPs, 1995. pp. 324. (Cf. bibl. 1992, 6948.) Rev. by Danielle Clarke in NQ (43:4) 1996, 483–4; by Jocelyn Coates in ECF (8:2) 1996, 298–9.

9187. MALINA, DEBRA.   Rereading the patriarchal text: *The Female Quixote, Northanger Abbey*, and the trace of the absent mother. ECF (8:2) 1996, 271–92.

9188. MOTOOKA, WENDY.   Coming to a bad end: Sentimentalism, hermeneutics, and *The Female Quixote*. ECF (8:2) 1996, 251–70.

M. G. Lewis

9189. EURIDGE, GARETH M.   The company we keep: comic function in M. G. Lewis's *The Monk*. *In* (pp. 83–90) **36**.

9190. SANDIFORD, KEITH A.   'Monk' Lewis and the slavery sublime: the *agon* of romantic desire in the *Journal*. ELit (23:1) 1996, 84–98.

George Lillo

9191. ROACH, JOSEPH.   The artificial eye: Augustan theater and the empire of the visible. *In* (pp. 131–45) **83**.

9192. STEFFENSEN, JAMES L. (ed.).   The dramatic works of George Lillo; including *Silvia* ed. by Richard Noble. (Bibl. 1995, 7907.) Rev. in Scriblerian (28:1/2) 1995/96, 86–7; by Peter Thomson in BJECS (19:1) 1996, 114–15.

9193. WALLACE, DAVID. Bourgeois tragedy or sentimental melodrama? The significance of George Lillo's *The London Merchant*. ECS (25:2) 1991/92, 123–43.

Henry Mackenzie

9194. DYKSTAL, TIMOTHY. The Sentimental novel as moral philosophy: the case of Henry Mackenzie. Genre (27:1/2) 1994, 59–81.
9195. SKINNER, GILLIAN. 'Above œconomy': Elizabeth Griffith's *The History of Lady Barton* and Henry Mackenzie's *The Man of Feeling*. See **9090**.

James Macpherson

9196. CLARK, STEPHEN H. The 'failing soul': Macpherson's response to Locke. See **2334**.
9197. GASKILL, HOWARD. Ossian in Europe. CanRCL (21:4) 1994, 643–78.
9198. —— (ed.). The poems of Ossian and related works. Introd. by Fiona Stafford. Edinburgh: Edinburgh UP, 1996. pp. xxvi, 573. Rev. by Robert Crawford in LRB (18:19) 1996, 18; by Patrick Crotty in TLS, 29 Mar. 1996, 25.
9199. GROOM, NICK. Celts, Goths, and the nature of the literary source. *In* (pp. 275–96) **122**.
9200. HUDSON, NICHOLAS. 'Oral tradition': the evolution of an eighteenth-century concept. *In* (pp. 161–76) **122**.
9201. JAMIESON, R. A. (introd.). Oisin Oisian Ossn Suibne Subney Sweeney Osuine Oswine Ossian Ocean: a (mock?) heroic miscellany. See **8900**.
9202. MACDONALD, MURDO. The torrent shrieks. See **8815**.
9203. MATTEO, SANTE. Ossian and *Risorgimento*: the poetics of nationalism. Prism(s) (3) 1995, 15–34.
9204. PITTOCK, MURRAY. Forging North Britain in the age of Macpherson. Edinburgh Review (93) 1995, 125–39.

Bernard Mandeville

9205. GORAK, IRENE E. The satirist as producer: Mandeville's *The Fable of the Bees Part Two*. Genre (23:1) 1990, 1–14.
9206. HUNDERT, E. J. The Enlightenment's fable: Bernard Mandeville and the discovery of society. Cambridge; New York: CUP, 1994. pp. xii, 284. (Ideas in context.) Rev. by Andrew Fix in AHR (101:3) 1996, 833–4; by Malcolm Jack in BJECS (19:1) 1996, 116–17; by Jack Fruchtman, Jr, in ECL (20:2) 1996, 100–1.

Mary de la Rivière Manley

9207. DONOVAN, JOSEPHINE. From avenger to victim: genealogy of a Renaissance novella. See **5951**.
9208. RABB, MELINDA ALLIKER. Angry beauties: (wo)Manley satire and the stage. TSL (37) 1995, 127–58.
9209. RUBIK, MARGARETE. 'My life, my soul, my all is fixed upon enjoyment': the unabashed expression of female desire in *The Royal Mischief*. Gramma (4) 1996, 165–79.

James Maxwell ('Poet in Paisley')

9210. Roy, G. Ross.   Scottish poets and the French Revolution. *See* **8913**.

William Julius Mickle

9211.   Bosch, René.   Sterne and Voltaire in Purgatory: a prophecy by W. J. Mickle. Shandean (8) 1996, 98–112.

Lady Mary Wortley Montagu

9212.   Grundy, Isobel (ed.).   Indamora to Lindamira. (Bibl. 1995, 7926.) Rev. by Monica Letzring in Scriblerian (28:1/2) 1995/96, 89–90.
9213.   ——— Romance writings. Oxford: Clarendon Press; New York: OUP, 1996. pp. xxviii, 276. Rev. by Margaret Anne Doody in LRB (18:21) 1996, 14–15; by David Womersley in TLS, 9 Aug. 1996, 23.

Hannah More ('Z')

9214.   Demers, Patricia.   The world of Hannah More. Lexington: Kentucky UP, 1996. pp. 178.
9215.   Ford, Charles Howard.   Hannah More: a critical biography. New York; Frankfurt; Bern; Paris: Lang, 1996. pp. xiv, 309. (Studies in nineteenth-century British literature, 4.) (Cf. bibl. 1992, 6973.)
9216.   Hole, Robert (ed.).   Selected writings of Hannah More. London: Pickering; Brookfield, VT: Pickering & Chatto, 1996. pp. xlviii, 256. (Pickering women's classics.)
9217.   Ross, Marlon B.   Configurations of feminist reform: the woman writer and the tradition of dissent. *In* (pp. 91–110) **103**.

Ralph Morris

9218.   Adams, John.   Outer space and the New World in the imagination of eighteenth-century Europeans. *See* **7924**.

Judith Sargent Murray

9219.   Harris, Sharon M. (ed.).   Selected writings of Judith Sargent Murray. Oxford; New York: OUP, 1995. pp. xliv, 272. (Women writers in English, 1350–1850.)
9220.   Jacoba, Madelon.   The early novella as political message: *The Margaretta Story* by Judith Sargent Murray. SHum (18:2) 1991, 146–64.
9221.   Kritzer, Amelia Howe.   Playing with Republican motherhood: self-representation in plays by Susanna Haswell Rowson and Judith Sargent Murray. EAL (31:2) 1996, 150–66.

Thomas Paine

9222.   Davidson, Edward H.; Scheick, William J.   Authority in Paine's *Common Sense* and *Crisis Papers*. SHum (18:2) 1991, 124–34.
9223.   Fruchtman, Jack, Jr.   Thomas Paine and the religion of nature. (Bibl. 1995, 7933.) Rev. by H. T. Dickinson in BJECS (19:2) 1996, 243–4.
9224.   Hogan, J. Michael; Williams, L. Glen.   Defining 'the enemy' in Revolutionary America: from the rhetoric of protest to the rhetoric of war. *See* **2399**.
9225.   Jones, Stanley.   Further quotations and reminiscences in Hazlitt: Daniel, the Bible, Milton, Paine, Dorset. *See* **7773**.

9226. Mock, Sanford J.   The times that try men's souls. MSS (48:1) 1996, 93–105; (48:3) 1996, 195–206.

Robert Paltock

9227. Merchant, Peter.   Robert Paltock and the refashioning of *Inkle and Yarico*. ECF (9:1) 1996, 37–50.

Thomas Parnell

9228. Gerrard, Christine.   Parnell, Pope, and pastoral. *In* (pp. 221–40) **122**.

Thomas Percy

9229. Groom, Nick.   Celts, Goths, and the nature of the literary source. *In* (pp. 275–96) **122**.

Hester Lynch Piozzi (Mrs Thrale)

9230. Bloom, Edward A.; Bloom, Lillian D. (eds).   The Piozzi letters: correspondence of Hester Lynch Piozzi, 1784–1821 (formerly Mrs Thrale): vol. 4, 1805–1810. Newark: Delaware UP; London; Toronto: Assoc. UPs, 1993. pp. 358. Rev. by Allan Ingram in YES (25) 1995, 298–9.

9231. Bristow, Adrian (ed.).   Dr Johnson and Mrs Thrale's tour in North Wales, 1774. *See* **9126**.

9232. Ribeiro, Alvaro.   The 'chit-chat way': the letters of Mrs Thrale and Dr Burney. *In* (pp. 25–40) **122**.

Alexander Pope

9233. Alderson, Simon.   Alexander Pope and the nature of language. *See* **2574**.

9234. Chandler, Eric V.   Pope's emetic: bodies, books, and filth. Genre (27:4) 1994, 351–76.

9235. Crehan, Stewart.   The economy of 'trivial things'. UES (33:2) 1995, 17–26.

9236. Daniel, Clay.   Pope's *Dunciad* lines 135–42 (1728/29) and lines 157–62 (1743). ANQ (9:1) 1996, 7–8.

9237. Davis, Tom.   The epic of bibliography: Alexander Pope and textual criticism. *See* **614**.

9238. Deutsch, Helen.   Resemblance and disgrace: Alexander Pope and the deformation of culture. Cambridge, MA; London: Harvard UP, 1996. pp. xiii, 273. (Cf. bibl. 1991, 6522.)

9239. Draesner, Ulrike.   'Truth angular and splintered' – die Subversion der Rede in der Reflexion über den Menschen: Bemerkungen zu Alexander Popes *Essay on Man*. GRM (42:3) 1992, 275–303.

9240. Ferraro, Julian.   Taste and use: Pope's *Epistle to Burlington*. BJECS (19:2) 1996, 141–59.

9241. Gerrard, Christine.   Parnell, Pope, and pastoral. *In* (pp. 221–40) **122**.

9242. Griffin, Robert J.   Wordsworth's Pope: a study in literary historiography. Cambridge; New York: CUP, 1995. pp. xii, 190. (Cambridge studies in Romanticism, 17.) Rev. by Duncan Wu in NQ (43:4) 1996, 485; by Michael Baron in Eng (45:183) 1996, 255–9; by J.F. in TLS, 9 Feb. 1996, 28.

9243. HAMMOND, BREAN (ed.).   Pope. London; New York: Longman, 1996. pp. ix, 253. (Longman critical readers.)

9244. HINNANT, CHARLES H.   Augustan semiosis. *See* **7880**.

9245. HUNTER, J. PAUL.   Form as meaning: Pope and the ideology of the couplet. ECent (37:3) 1996, 257–70.

9246. JACKSON, WALLACE; YODER, R. PAUL (eds).   Approaches to teaching Pope's poetry. (Bibl. 1995, 7956.) Rev. by Steven Shankman in Scriblerian (28:1/2) 1995/96, 79–81; by Wendy Jones Nakanishi in EngS (77:3) 1996, 285–6.

9247. KOWALESKI-WALLACE, BETH.   Women, china, and consumer culture in eighteenth-century England. *See* **8770**.

9248. LANDRY, DONNA.   The invention of the countryside: Pope, the 'idiocy of rural life', and the intellectual view from the suburbs. TSL (37) 1995, 301–19.

9249. LEECH, JAMES.   Alexander Pope: the 'sound an eccho to the sense'. *See* **2665**.

9250. LOCKLEAR, GLORIANNA.   Delicious poison: Heloise and Abelard out of time. PCR (4:1) 1993, 39–47.

9251. McLAVERTY, JAMES.   Naming and blaming: the poetics of mock epic. *See* **2150**.

9252. —— Pope in the private and public spheres: annotations in the Second Earl of Oxford's volume of folio poems, 1731–1736. SB (48) 1995, 33–59.

9253. MacLEAN, GERALD M.   The anxiety of speculation: satire in an age of imaginary wealth. *See* **9066**.

9254. MORILLO, JOHN.   Seditious anger: Achilles, James Stuart, and Jacobite politics in Pope's *Iliad* translation. ECL (19:2) 1995, 38–58.

9255. NOGGLE, JAMES.   Skepticism and the sublime advent of modernity in the 1742 *Dunciad*. ECent (37:1) 1996, 22–41.

9256. PARK, WILLIAM; PARKER, LISA M.   Pope in Yonkers. Scriblerian (28:1/2) 1995/96, 71–6.

9257. PAYNE, DEBORAH C.   Comedy, satire, or farce? Or, The generic difficulties of Restoration dramatic satire. *See* **7513**.

9258. PHIDDIAN, ROBERT.   A name for mock-epic: Pope, Bakhtin, and stylization. ECent (37:2) 1996, 136–55.

9259. RIDEOUT, TANIA.   The reasoning eye: Alexander Pope's typographic vision in the *Essay on Man*. *See* **307**.

9260. ROGERS, PAT.   Essays on Pope. (Bibl. 1995, 7974.) Rev. by Wendy Jones Nakanishi in EngS (76:5) 1995, 490–1; by James McLaverty in NQ (43:1) 1996, 91.

9261. —— (ed.).   Alexander Pope. (Bibl. 1993, 6223.) Rev. by Wendy Jones Nakanishi in EngS (76:5) 1995, 489–90; by Charles E. Gobin in Scriblerian (28:1/2) 1995/96, 78–9.

9262. SHEPARD, ALAN.   The literature of a medical hoax: the case of Mary Toft, 'the pretended rabbet-breeder'. ECL (19:2) 1995, 59–77.

9263. SHIN, YANG-SOOK.   *Meorichae Ganggan*: hystery gujo? (*The Rape of the Lock*: hysterical structure?) JELL (42:3) 1996, 523–47.

9264. SMITH, MEL.   Ten letters on death, dying, and condolences. MSS (47:1) 1995, 5–16.

9265. THOMAS, CLAUDIA.   Pope and his *Dunciad* adversaries: skirmishes on the borders of gentility. TSL (37) 1995, 275–300.

9266. THOMAS, CLAUDIA N.   Alexander Pope and his eighteenth-century women readers. (Bibl. 1995, 7981.) Rev. by Valerie Rumbold in

Scriblerian (28:1/2) 1995/96, 58–9; by J. Karen Ray in RMRLL (50:1) 1996, 99–102.

9267. WHEELER, DAVID. Event as text, text as event: reading *The Rape of the Lock*. TSL (37) 1995, 222–32.

9268. WILLIAMS, CAROLYN D. Pope, Homer, and manliness: some aspects of eighteenth-century Classical learning. (Bibl. 1995, 7983.) Rev. by Wendy Jones Nakanishi in EngS (76:1) 1995, 104–5.

9269. WOOD, NIGEL. Mocking the heroic? A context for *The Rape of the Lock*. TSL (37) 1995, 233–55.

Ann Radcliffe

9270. BERGLUND, BIRGITTA. Mrs Radcliffe and *Rebecca*. SN (68:1) 1996, 73–81.

9271. —— Woman's whole existence: the house as an image in the novels of Ann Radcliffe, Mary Wollstonecraft, and Jane Austen. (Bibl. 1995, 7987.) Rev. by Hans-Ulrich Mohr in ZAA (44:4) 1996, 373–5.

9272. BOTTING, FRED. Power in the darkness: heterotopias, literature and gothic labyrinths. *See* **8786**.

9273. HENDERSHOT, CYNDY. The possession of the male body: masculinity in *The Italian*, *Psycho*, and *Dressed to Kill*. RWT (2:2) 1995, 75–112.

9274. MILES, ROBERT. Ann Radcliffe: the great enchantress. (Bibl. 1995, 7997.) Rev. by Neil Cornwell in EP (21) 1996, 175–7.

9275. OSTROWSKI, WITOLD. *The Mysteries of Udolpho*: a gothic novel and much more. AUNC (7) 1996, 161–74.

9276. ROGERS, DEBORAH D. Ann Radcliffe: a bio-bibliography. Westport, CT; London: Greenwood Press, 1996. pp. xii, 209. (Bio-bibliographies in world literature, 4.)

9277. SAGE, VICTOR. The epistemology of error: reading and isolation in *The Mysteries of Udolpho*. Q/W/E/R/T/Y (6) 1996, 107–13.

9278. SAGLIA, DIEGO. Looking at the other: cultural difference and the traveller's gaze in *The Italian*. StudN (28:1) 1996, 12–37.

9279. WHITING, PATRICIA. Literal and literary representations of the family in *The Mysteries of Udolpho*. ECF (8:4) 1996, 485–501.

Allan Ramsay (1686–1758)

9280. MURPHY, MICHAEL. Allan Ramsay as imitator of Horace. Études Écossaises (2) 1993, 123–9.

William Hamilton Reid

9281. SHERBO, ARTHUR. William Hamilton Reid (*fl.*1786–1824): a forgotten poet. SSL (29) 1996, 245–57.

Samuel Richardson

9282. BARCHAS, JANINE. The engraved score in *Clarissa*: an intersection of music, narrative, and graphic design. ECL (20:2) 1996, 1–20.

9283. BEEBEE, THOMAS O. Clarissa on the Continent: translation and seduction. (Bibl. 1993, 6247.) Rev. by Roseann Runte in CanRCL (18:4) 1991, 612–13.

9284. BELLAMY, LIZ. Private virtues, public vices: commercial morality in the novels of Samuel Richardson. Literature and History (5:2) 1996, 19–36.

9285. BORCK, JIM SPRINGER. Composed in tears: the *Clarissa* project. *See* **579**.

9286. BOWDEN, MARTHA.   Composing herself: music, solitude, and St Cecilia in *Clarissa*. 1650–1850 (2) 1996, 185–202.

9287. BROWN, MURRAY L.   Conflicting dreams: Lovelace and the oneirocritical reader. ECL (19:3) 1995, 1–21.

9288. —— *Emblemata rhetorica*: glossing emblematic discourse in Richardson's *Clarissa*. *See* **184**.

9289. BUELER, LOIS E.   Clarissa's plots. (Bibl. 1994, 6510.) Rev. by Murray L. Brown in StudN (28:1) 1996, 118–20.

9290. CHABER, LOIS A.   'This affecting subject': an 'interested' reading of childbearing in two novels by Samuel Richardson. ECF (8:2) 1996, 193–250.

9291. CHOI, INHWAN.   Wejang gwa pyeongi hyungsik: Richardson eui *Clarissa* yeongu. (Disguise and epistolary form: a study of Richardson's *Clarissa*.) JELL (42:2) 1996, 249–72.

9292. CHUNG, EWHA.   Samuel Richardson's *Clarissa*: defining the 'sacred' community and defending religious education. JELL (42:4) 1996, 813–26.

9293. COHEN, PAULA MARANTZ.   The anorexic syndrome and the nineteenth-century domestic novel. *In* (pp. 125–39) **24**.

9294. COOK, ELIZABETH HECKENDORN.   Epistolary bodies: gender and genre in the eighteenth-century republic of letters. Stanford, CA: Stanford UP, 1996. pp. xi, 237. (Cf. bibl. 1991, 6632.)

9295. CUMMINGS, KATHERINE.   Telling tales: the hysteric's seduction in fiction and theory. (Bibl. 1992, 7036.) Rev. by Kevin McNeilly in CanL (149) 1996, 155–6.

9296. DAVIS, LENNARD J.   The dreadful gulph and the glass cadaver: decomposing women in early modern literature. *See* **7684**.

9297. FULTON, GORDON D.   Why look at Clarissa? ECL (20:2) 1996, 21–32.

9298. GLASER, BRIGITTE.   The body in Samuel Richardson's *Clarissa*. Contexts of and contradictions in the development of character. (Bibl. 1994, 6514.) Rev. by Jocelyn Harris in ECF (8:2) 1996, 300–1.

9299. GWILLIAM, TASSIE.   Samuel Richardson's fictions of gender. (Bibl. 1995, 8019.) Rev. by Bridget Hill in Literature and History (5:2) 1996, 87–8.

9300. HOPKINS, LISA.   The transference of *Clarissa*: psychoanalysis and the realm of the feminine. CritS (6:2) 1994, 218–25.

9301. KEYMER, TOM.   Richardson's *Clarissa* and the eighteenth-century reader. (Bibl. 1994, 6519.) Rev. by David C. Hensley in Scriblerian (28:1/2) 1995/96, 64–7.

9302. MAUTNER, THOMAS.   'The working class of people': an early eighteenth-century source. *See* **2026**.

9303. MORAVETZ, MONIKA.   Formen der Rezeptionslenkung im Briefroman des 18. Jahrhunderts: Richardsons *Clarissa*, Rousseaus *Nouvelle Héloïse* und Laclos' *Liaisons dangereuses*. Tübingen: Narr, 1990. pp. ix, 291. (Romanica Monacensia, 34.) Rev. by Sabine Volk-Birke in GRM (44:1) 1994, 113–16.

9304. OGDEN, DARYL S.   Richardson's narrative space-off: Freud, vision and the (heterosexual) problem of reading *Clarissa*. LitPs (42:4) 1996, 37–52.

9305. PETTER, HENRI.   Clarissa's family: false friends, fair friends. SPELL (9) 1996, 65–76.

9306. PRICE, LEAH. *Sir Charles Grandison* and the executor's hand. ECF (8:3) 1996, 329–42.

9307. RAIN, D. C. Deconstructing Richardson: Terry Castle and *Clarissa's Ciphers*. EngS (76:6) 1995, 520–31.

9308. RIVERO, ALBERT J. (ed.). New essays on Samuel Richardson. Basingstoke: Macmillan; New York: St Martin's Press, 1996. pp. viii, 232.

9309. SOUTHAM, BRIAN. *Sir Charles Grandison* and Jane Austen's men. Persuasions (18) 1996, 74–87.

9310. STADLER, EVA MARIA. Addressing social boundaries: dressing the female body in early realist fiction. *In* (pp. 20–36) **97**.

9311. TOISE, DAVID W. 'A more culpable passion': *Pamela, Joseph Andrews*, and the history of desire. *See* **9047**.

Mary Robinson

9312. CULLENS, CHRIS. Mrs Robinson and the masquerade of womanliness. *In* (pp. 266–89) **10**.

9313. CURRAN, STUART. Mary Robinson's *Lyrical Tales* in context. *In* (pp. 17–35) **103**.

9314. FORD, SUSAN ALLEN. 'A name more dear': daughters, fathers, and desire in *A Simple Story, The False Friend*, and *Mathilda*. *In* (pp. 51–71) **103**.

9315. PETERSON, LINDA H. Becoming an author: Mary Robinson's *Memoirs* and the origin of woman artist's autobiography. *In* (pp. 36–50) **103**.

Elizabeth Singer Rowe

9316. HANSEN, MARLENE R. The pious Mrs Rowe. EngS (76:1) 1995, 34–51.

9317. LINDSAY, ALEXANDER. Thomson and the Countess of Hertford yet once more. *See* **723**.

Susanna Rowson

9318. BARONE, DENNIS. 'My vile arts': male and female discourse in *Charlotte Temple*. SHum (18:2) 1991, 135–45.

9319. CASTIGLIA, CHRISTOPHER. Susanna Rowson's *Reuben and Rachel*: captivity, colonization, and the domestication of Columbus. *In* (pp. 23–42) **99**.

9320. FUDGE, KEITH. Sisterhood born from seduction: Susanna Rowson's *Charlotte Temple*, and Stephen Crane's *Maggie Johnson*. JAC (19:1) 1996, 43–50.

9321. KRITZER, AMELIA HOWE. Playing with Republican motherhood: self-representation in plays by Susanna Haswell Rowson and Judith Sargent Murray. *See* **9221**.

9322. SIELKE, SABINE. Seduced and enslaved: sexual violence in antebellum American literature and contemporary feminist discourse. *See* **9057**.

9323. WOODARD, MAUREEN L. Female captivity and the deployment of race in three early American texts. *See* **8339**.

Ignatius Sancho

9324. PILLING, JULIAN. A Black composer of country dances in the 18th century. *See* **3598**.

Richard Savage

9325. O'HARA, J. D.   Savagely damned to fame. JBecS (6:1) 1996, 137–43.

Sarah Scott

9326. DAVIS, LENNARD J.   The dreadful gulph and the glass cadaver: decomposing women in early modern literature. *See* **7684**.

9327. POHL, NICOLE.   'Sweet place, where virtue then did rest': the appropriation of the country-house ethos in Sarah Scott's *Millenium Hall*. Utopian Studies (7:1) 1996, 49–59.

9328. STODDARD, EVE W.   A serious proposal for slavery reform: Sarah Scott's *Sir George Ellison*. ECS (28:4) 1995, 379–96.

Frances Seymour, Countess of Hertford

9329. SIMMS, NORMAN.   A silent love affair: Frances Seymour's *Inkle and Yarico* (1726). AUMLA (85) 1996, 93–101.

Anthony Ashley Cooper, Third Earl of Shaftesbury

9330. ALDRIGE, A. OWEN.   Shaftesbury, Rosicrucianism and links with Voltaire. CanRCL (23:2) 1996, 394–411.

9331. JORDAN, LOTHAR.   Shaftesbury und die deutsche Literatur und Ästhetik des 18. Jahrhunderts: ein Prolegomenon zur Linie Gottsched–Wieland. GRM (44:4) 1994, 410–24.

9332. KLEIN, LAWRENCE E.   Shaftesbury and the culture of politeness: moral discourse and cultural politics in early eighteenth-century England. (Bibl. 1995, 8054.) Rev. by W. A. Speck in EHR (111:442) 1996, 729–30.

Frances Sheridan

9333. DERRY, STEPHEN.   *Emma*, the Earthly Paradise, and *The History of Nourjahad*. NQ (43:4) 1996, 417–18.

Richard Brinsley Sheridan

9334. CARLSON, JULIE A.   Trying Sheridan's *Pizarro*. TSLL (38:3/4) 1996, 359–78.

9335. MACCUBBIN, ROBERT PURKS.   Enacting the tyranny of social forms in Sheridan's *The Rivals*. 1650–1850 (2) 1996, 3–24.

9336. ROSS, CIARAN.   R. B. Sheridan's *The Critic*: handing down, handing on, handing back the burlesque tradition. RANAM (29) 1996, 131–43.

9337. SAINSBURY, JOHN.   John Wilkes, debt, and patriotism. *See* **8930**.

9338. WOOLLEY, JAMES (ed.).   The intelligencer. (Bibl. 1995, 8068.) Rev. by James McLaverty in Text (Ann Arbor) (8) 1995, 409–22.

John Skinner (1721–1807)

9339. WHYTE, CHRISTOPHER.   Bakhtin at Christ's Kirk: part II, Carnival and the vernacular revival. *See* **8918**.

Christopher Smart

9340. BREWSTER, GLEN.   Christopher Smart's cat Jeoffry: 'for he is good to think on'. NCLR (5) 1996, 117–19.

9341. HAWES, CLEMENT.   Mania and literary style: the rhetoric of enthusiasm from the Ranters to Christopher Smart. *See* **2394**.

9342. —— Smart's poetics of place: myth *versus* utopia in *Jubilate Agno*. Genre (27:1/2) 1994, 29–57.

9343. JACOBS, ALAN. Diagnosing Christopher's case: Smart's readers and the authority of Pentecost. Ren (46:2) 1994, 83–103.

Adam Smith

9344. VENTER, J. J. World-picture, individual, society. *See* **7980**.

Charlotte Smith

9345. FRY, CARROLL L. Charlotte Smith. New York: Twayne; London: Prentice Hall, 1996. pp. xii, 170. (Twayne's English authors, 528.)

9346. PASCOE, JUDITH. Female botanists and the poetry of Charlotte Smith. *In* (pp. 193–209) **103**.

9347. ROGERS, KATHARINE M. Romantic aspirations, restricted possibilities: the novels of Charlotte Smith. *In* (pp. 72–88) **103**.

Tobias Smollett

9348. BEASLEY, JERRY C. Tobias Smollett: the Scot in England. SSL (29) 1996, 14–28.

9349. BRACK, O. M., JR. Smollett's *Peregrine Pickle* revisited. *See* **584**.

9350. —— (ed.); CHILTON, LESLIE (asst ed.); GASSMAN, BYRON (introd. and notes). Poems, plays, and *The Briton*. (Bibl. 1993, 6310.) Rev. by John P. Zomchick in Scriblerian (28:1/2) 1995/96, 67–9.

9351. BULCKAEN, DENISE. Les Celtes et la Celtie dans les romans de Tobias Smollett. Études Écossaises (3) 1996, 35–47.

9352. DENIZOT, PAUL. Les Bramble en Écosse; ou, Le Paradis retrouvé. Études Écossaises (3) 1996, 49–59.

9353. DONOGHUE, FRANK. The fame machine: book reviewing and eighteenth-century literary careers. *See* **8463**.

9354. DOUGLAS, AILEEN. Uneasy sensations: Smollett and the body. (Bibl. 1995, 8086.) Rev. by Martin C. Battestin in Albion (28:3) 1996, 493–4; by Karina Williamson in SLJ (supp. 45) 1996, 13–16; by J.M. in TLS, 9 Feb. 1996, 28.

9355. FITZPATRICK, BARBARA LANING. 'Some Pieces in the British Magazine' and 'A small part of the Translation of Voltaire's works': Smollett attributions. ECF (9:1) 1996, 97–100.

9356. JACOBSEN, SUSAN L. 'The tinsel of the times': Smollett's argument against conspicuous consumption in *Humphry Clinker*. ECF (9:1) 1996, 71–88.

9357. LAFON, SYLVIE. Notions d'esthétique dans *Humphry Clinker* de Tobias Smollett. Études Écossaises (2) 1993, 131–41.

9358. MILES, PETER. Smollett, Rowlandson, and a problem of identity: decoding names, bodies, and gender in *Humphry Clinker*. *See* **224**.

9359. MORÈRE, PIERRE. Scotland in Smollett's *The Expedition of Humphry Clinker*. Études Écossaises (supp.) 1994, 151–9.

9360. MURPHY, MICHAEL. Marriage as a metaphor for the Anglo-Scottish parliamentary union of 1707: the example of *Humphry Clinker*. Études Écossaises (3) 1996, 61–5.

9361. SKINNER, JOHN. Constructions of Smollett: a study of genre and gender. Newark: Delaware UP; London; Toronto: Assoc. UPs, 1996. pp. 267.

Laurence Sterne

9362. BAILEY, ANNE HALL. When worlds collide: tracing the line of descent in Laurence Sterne's *Tristram Shandy*. TPB (33) 1996, 53–62.

9363. BALLESTEROS GONZÁLEZ, ANTONIO. Digression and intertextual parody in Thomas Nashe, Laurence Sterne and James Joyce. *In* (pp. 55–64) **57**.

9364. BARBOSA, MARIA JOSÉ SOMERLATE. Sterne and Machado: parodic and intertextual play in *Tristram Shandy* and *Memórias*. Comparatist (16) 1992, 24–48.

9365. BELL, MICHAEL. Laurence Sterne and the twentieth century. *In* (pp. 39–54) **57**.

9366. BOSCH, RENÉ. Sterne and Voltaire in Purgatory: a prophecy by W. J. Mickle. *See* **9211**.

9367. BOWDEN, MARTHA F. The liturgical shape of life at Shandy Hall. Shandean (7) 1995, 43–60.

9368. BRAVERMAN, RICHARD. Satiric embodiments: Butler, Swift, Sterne. *See* **7737**.

9369. CLARKE, STEPHEN. Sterne in Norfolk. Shandean (8) 1996, 69–76.

9370. DAY, W. G. Michael Angelo Rooker's illustrations to *Tristram Shandy*. *See* **192**.

9371. DESCARGUES, MADELEINE. Sterne, Nabokov and the happy (non)ending of biography. *In* (pp. 167–78) **57**.

9372. DE VOOGD, PETER. Sterne all the fashion: a sentimental fan. *See* **193**.

9373. DONOGHUE, FRANK. The fame machine: book reviewing and eighteenth-century literary careers. *See* **8463**.

9374. DUPAS, JEAN-CLAUDE. A sun-dial in a grave: the founding gesture. *In* (pp. 99–108) **57**.

9375. GILLESPIE, GERALD. The relevance of irrelevance: games and puzzles in the humoristic tradition since the Renaissance. *See* **3835**.

9376. GÖBEL, WALTER; GRINT, DAMIAN. Salman Rushdie's silver medal. *In* (pp. 87–98) **57**.

9377. GOULD, REBECCA. Sterne's sentimental Yorick as male hysteric. SELit (36:3) 1996, 641–53.

9378. HART, MICHAEL. 'Many planes of narrative': a comparative perspective on Sterne and Joyce. *In* (pp. 65–80) **57**.

9379. ISHI, SHIGEMITSU. Rorensu Sutahn: Sterne in Japan. Shandean (8) 1996, 9–40.

9380. KEYMER, THOMAS. Dying by numbers: *Tristram Shandy* and serial fiction: 1. *See* **954**.

9381. KING, JERI D. Balzac's *Tristram Shandy*, 322: Sterne and *La Peau de chagrin*. Comparatist (16) 1992, 49–61.

9382. KLEIN, HERBERT. Identity reclaimed: the art of being Tristram. *In* (pp. 123–32) **57**.

9383. KLEIN, HERBERT G. Wer ist Tristrams Vater? – Paternität und Identität in Laurence Sternes *Tristram Shandy*. GRM (42:4) 1992, 415–27.

9384. KRAFT, ELIZABETH. Laurence Sterne revisited. New York: Twayne; London: Prentice Hall, 1996. pp. xviii, 163. (Twayne's English authors, 532.)

9385. LARGE, DUNCAN. 'The freest writer': Nietzsche on Sterne. Shandean (7) 1995, 9–29.

9386. LAUDANDO, CARLA MARIA. Deluge of fragments: Rabelais's *Fourth Book*, Sterne's *Fragment* and Beckett's *Fizzles*. *In* (pp. 157–65) **57**.

9387. MILESI, LAURENT. Have you not forgot to wind up the clock? Tristram Shandy and Jacques *le fataliste* on the (post?)modern psychoanalytic couch. *In* (pp. 179–95) **57**.

9388. MOGLEN, HELENE. (W)holes and noses: the indeterminacies of *Tristram Shandy*. LitPs (41:3) 1995, 44–79.

9389. MONKMAN, KENNETH. Towards a bibliography of Sterne's sermons: some corrections and slight additions. Shandean (7) 1995, 101–3.

9390. NEW, MELVYN. Attribution and sponsorship: the delicate case of Sterne. ECF (8:4) 1996, 525–8.

9391. —— *Tristram Shandy*: a book for free spirits. (Bibl. 1994, 6596.) Rev. by Helen Ostovich in ECF (9:1) 1996, 114–16.

9392. PARNELL, TIM. Sterne and Kundera: the novel of variations and the 'noisy foolishness of human certainty'. *In* (pp. 147–55) **57**.

9393. PEGENAUTE, LOUIS. Three trapped tigers in Shandy Hall. *In* (pp. 133–45) **57**.

9394. PIERCE, DAVID. Introduction. *In* (pp. 7–17) **57**.

9395. —— DE VOOGD, PETER (eds). Laurence Sterne in Modernism and postmodernism. *See* **57**.

9396. PINNEGAR, FRED C. The groin wounds of Tristram and Uncle Toby. Shandean (7) 1995, 87–100.

9397. RADEMACHER, JÖRG W. Totalized (auto-)biography as fragmented intertextuality: Shakespeare – Sterne – Joyce. *In* (pp. 81–6) **57**.

9398. ROWSON, MARTIN. Hyperboling gravity's ravelin: a comic book version of *Tristram Shandy*. *See* **241**.

9399. SANTOVETTI, OLIVIA. The adventurous journey of Lorenzo Sterne in Italy. Shandean (8) 1996, 78–97.

9400. SHERBERT, GARRY. Menippean satire and the poetics of wit: ideologies of self-consciousness in Dunton, D'Urfey, and Sterne. *See* **7900**.

9401. SIM, STUART. 'All that exist are "islands of determinism"': Shandean sentiment and the dilemma of postmodern physics. *In* (pp. 109–21) **57**.

9402. SIMMS, NORMAN. Stuffing sausages as *satura* and foreplay: Apuleius's Lucius and Trim's brother Tom. Shandean (8) 1996, 113–19.

9403. SOUD, STEPHEN. 'Weavers, gardeners, and gladiators': labyrinths in *Tristram Shandy*. ECS (28:4) 1995, 397–411.

9404. SOUPEL, SERGE. Marold's *Voyage sentimental*. *See* **247**.

9405. WATTS, CAROL. The modernity of Sterne. *In* (pp. 19–38) **57**.

9406. ZANDER, HORST. '*Non enim adiectio haec ejus, sed opus ipsum est*': Überlegungen zum Paratext in *Tristram Shandy*. PoetA (28:1/2) 1996, 132–53.

9407. ZWANEVELD, AGNES M. A bookseller's hobby-horse, and the rhetoric of translation: Anthony Ernst Munnikhuisen and Bernardus Brunius, and the first Dutch edition of *Tristram Shandy* (1776–1779). Amsterdam; Atlanta, GA: Rodopi, 1996. pp. xii, 237. (Approaches to translation studies, 13.) Rev. by Peter de Voogd in Shandean (7) 1995, 111–12.

Annis Boudinot Stockton

9408. MULFORD, CARLA (ed.). Only for the eye of a friend: the poems

19

of Annis Boudinot Stockton. Charlottesville; London: Virginia UP, 1995. pp. xxi, 336. Rev. by Dennis D. Moore in EAL (31:3) 1996, 314–16.

Jonathan Swift

9409. ARGENT, JOSEPH E.   The etymology of a dystopia: Laputa reconsidered. *See* **2183**.

9410. BENNETT, SUE.   The act of reading *Gulliver's Travels*. RWT (2:1) 1994, 69–81.

9411. BEX, TONY.   Parody, genre and literary meaning. *See* **2313**.

9412. BLOOM, HAROLD (ed.).   Jonathan Swift's *Gulliver's Travels*. New York: Chelsea House, 1996. pp. 77. (Bloom's notes.)

9413. BOGEL, FREDRIC V.   The difference satire makes: reading Swift's poems. *In* (pp. 43–53) **120**.

9414. BRAVERMAN, RICHARD.   Satiric embodiments: Butler, Swift, Sterne. *See* **7737**.

9415. BYWATERS, DAVID.   Anticlericism in Swift's *Tale of a Tub*. SELit (36:3) 1996, 579–602.

9416. CHAKRABARTI, SHIRSHENDU.   Master and servant: social mobility and the ironic exchange of roles in Swift's *Directions to Servants*. *In* (pp. 111–26) **122**.

9417. CHALMERS, ALAN D.   Jonathan Swift and the burden of the future. (Bibl. 1995, 8124.) Rev. by Norman Vance in TLS, 2 Feb. 1996, 6–7.

9418. CONNERY, BRIAN A.   The *persona* as pretender and the reader as constitutional subject in Swift's *Tale*. TSL (37) 1995, 159–80.

9419. CROGHAN, MARTIN J.   Swift & Conrad: gamekeepers make great poachers. *In* (pp. 208–21) **60**.

9420. CURRY, JUDSON B.   Arguing about the project: approaches to Swift's *An Argument against Abolishing Christianity* and *A Project for the Advancement of Religion*. ECL (20:1) 1996, 67–79.

9421. DIGAETANI, JOHN LOUIS.   Metrical experimentation in Swift's *Wood's Halfpence Poems*. *In* (pp. 217–25) **71**.

9422. DUNN, ALLEN.   The mechanics of transport: sublimity and the imagery of abjection in Rochester, Swift, and Burke. *See* **8329**.

9423. ERSKINE-HILL, HOWARD.   Jonathan Swift, *Gulliver's Travels*. (Bibl. 1993, 6357.) Rev. by Dan Doll in Scriblerian (28:1/2) 1995/96, 76–8.

9424. FABRICANT, CAROLE.   Swift in his own time and ours: some reflections on theory and practice in the profession. *In* (pp. 113–34) **91**.

9425. GILL, JAMES E.   *Pharmakon, pharmakos*, and aporetic structure in Gulliver's 'Voyage to … the Houyhnhnms'. TSL (37) 1995, 181–205.

9426. GILL, PAT.   'Filth of all hues and odors': public parks, city showers, and promiscuous acquaintance in Rochester and Swift. *See* **8330**.

9427. GRAUSTEIN, GOTTFRIED.   Zu Swifts Schreibvarianten: anstelle einer Fußnote. *See* **1597**.

9428. GRAZIANO, ALBA.   Stampa e giornalismo nel primo Swift. Textus (2:1/2) 1989, 73–94.

9429. HIGGINS, IAN.   Swift's politics: a study in disaffection. (Bibl. 1995, 8135.) Rev. by Patrick Reilly in Scriblerian (28:1/2) 1995/96, 61–3; by Carole Fabricant in Criticism (38:1) 1996, 153–8.

9430. HUDSON, NICHOLAS.   '*O divinum scripturae beneficium!*': Swift's satire of writing and its intellectual context. AJ (7) 1996, 343–63.

9431. KELLY, VERONICA. Locke's eyes, Swift's spectacles. *In* (pp. 68–85) **10**.

9432. KNIEZSA, VERONIKA. 'Proper words in proper places': Jonathan Swift on language. *In* (pp. 182–93) **112**.

9433. KNOWLES, RONALD. *Gulliver's Travels*: the politics of satire. New York: Twayne; London: Prentice Hall, 1996. pp. xiii, 169. (Masterwork studies, 158.)

9434. MACKIE, ERIN. 'The anguish, toil, and pain of gathering up herself again': the fabrication of Swift's women. CritM (6:1) 1991, 1–19.

9435. —— The culture market, the marriage market, and the exchange of language: Swift and the progress of desire. *In* (pp. 173–92) **120**.

9436. MACLEAN, GERALD M. The anxiety of speculation: satire in an age of imaginary wealth. *See* **9066**.

9437. McMINN, JOSEPH. Jonathan's travels: Swift and Ireland. Foreword by Michael Foot. (Bibl. 1995, 8145.) Rev. by Oliver W. Ferguson in Scriblerian (28:1/2) 1995/96, 63–4.

9438. MAHONY, ROBERT. Jonathan Swift's Irish identity. (Bibl. 1995, 8146.) Rev. by Norman Vance in TLS, 2 Feb. 1996, 6–7.

9439. MONTAG, WARREN. The unthinkable Swift: the spontaneous philosophy of a Church of England man. (Bibl. 1995, 8149.) Rev. by Anthony T. Vaver in MinnR (45/46) 1995/96, 321–6; by Vaughan Hart in Utopian Studies (7:2) 1996, 307–8; by J. T. Parnell in Albion (28:1) 1996, 106–7; by Carole Fabricant in ECF (8:3) 1996, 417–21.

9440. MURRAY, CIARAN. The Japanese garden and the mystery of Swift. *In* (pp. 159–68) **49**.

9441. PALMERI, FRANK. The metamorphoses of satire in eighteenth-century narrative. CL (48:3) 1996, 237–64.

9442. PATTERSON, FRANK M. Swift's self-portrayals in poetry. PMPA (16) 1991, 51–5.

9443. PAULSON, RONALD. Putting out the fire in Her Imperial Majesty's apartment: opposition politics, anticlericalism, and aesthetics. *See* **233**.

9444. PAYNE, DEBORAH C. Comedy, satire, or farce? Or, The generic difficulties of Restoration dramatic satire. *See* **7513**.

9445. PHIDDIAN, ROBERT. Have you eaten yet? The reader in *A Modest Proposal*. SELit (36:3) 1996, 603–21.

9446. —— Swift's parody. (Bibl. 1995, 8152.) Rev. by Brean S. Hammond in ECF (9:1) 1996, 113–14; by Norman Vance in TLS, 2 Feb. 1996, 6–7.

9447. PROBYN, CLIVE. 'Travelling west-ward': the lost letter from Jonathan Swift to Charles Ford. *See* **796**.

9448. RAWSON, CLAUDE (introd.). Directions to servants. London: Penguin, 1995. pp. xiv, 81. (Syrens.)

9449. ROWLAND, JON. From cheated sight to false light: analogy in Swift and Churchill. *In* (pp. 107–32) **120**.

9450. SHEPARD, ALAN. The literature of a medical hoax: the case of Mary Toft, 'the pretended rabbet-breeder'. *See* **9262**.

9451. SPENCE, JOSEPH (ed.). The sayings of Swift. London: Duckworth, 1994. pp. 64. Rev. by Joseph McMinn in Scriblerian (28:1/2) 1995/96, 78.

9452. STANNARD, MICHAEL. The 'south-east point of New-Holland' as no-place: a possible solution to a textual problem in the fourth voyage of *Gulliver's Travels*. NQ (43:3) 1996, 297–9.

9453. WARNER, MARTIN.   Modes of political imagining. *In* (pp. 98–128) **63**.

9454. WILDING, MICHAEL.   Social visions. (Bibl. 1995, 8171.) Rev. by Tim Youngs in CritS (6:2) 1994, 291–3; by John T. Shawcross in ANQ (9:1) 1996, 41–3.

9455. YOMOTA, INUHIKO.   Kuusou ryokou no shuujigaku – *Gulliver Ryokouki* ron. (Rhetoric of imaginary travels: an essay on *Gulliver's Travels*.) Tokyo: Shichigatsudo, 1996. pp. 454.

John Thelwall

9456. CLAEYS, GREGORY (ed.).   The politics of English Jacobinism: writings of John Thelwall. University Park: Pennsylvania State UP, 1995. pp. lxii, 532. Rev. by Judith Thompson in Criticism (38:4) 1996, 635–41.

James Thomson

9457. BARIDON, MICHEL.   Historicisme et théorie de la connaissance dans la pensée des Lumières écossaises. *See* **9069**.

9458. ELLISON, JULIE.   Cato's tears. *See* **8768**.

9459. KEITH, JENNIFER.   Personification and the limits of the person in Thomson's *The Seasons*. Études Écossaises (3) 1996, 25–34.

9460. LINDSAY, ALEXANDER.   Thomson and the Countess of Hertford yet once more. *See* **723**.

John Toland

9461. McGUINNESS, PHILIP.   Tolerant sectarian: the peculiar contradictions of John Toland. TLS, 27 Sept. 1996, 14–15.

9462. SMITH, NIGEL.   The English Revolution and the end of rhetoric: John Toland's *Clito* (1700) and the republican daemon. *See* **2472**.

Royall Tyler

9463. EVELEV, JOHN.   *The Contrast*: the problem of theatricality and political and social crisis in postrevolutionary America. EAL (31:1) 1996, 74–97.

9464. RINEHART, LUCY.   A nation's 'noble spectacle': Royall Tyler's *The Contrast* as metatheatrical commentary. AmDr (3:2) 1994, 29–52.

Horace Walpole

9465. BENDING, STEPHEN.   Horace Walpole and eighteenth-century garden history. JWCI (57) 1994, 209–26.

9466. BOTTING, FRED.   Power in the darkness: heterotopias, literature and gothic labyrinths. *See* **8786**.

9467. LEWIS, W. S. (ed.).   The Castle of Otranto: a gothic story. With a new introd. and notes by E. J. Clery. Oxford; New York: OUP, 1996. pp. xxxviii, 125. (World's classics.)

William Warburton

9468. NICHOL, DONALD W.   From the Bishop of Gloucester to Lord Hailes: the correspondence of William Warburton and David Dalrymple. *See* **772**.

9469. —— Warburton (not!) on copyright: clearing up the mis-attribution of *An Enquiry into the Nature and Origin of Literary Property* (1762). *See* **8692**.

Mercy Otis Warren

9470. OREOVICZ, CHERYL Z.   *Legacy* profile: Mercy Otis Warren (1728–1814). Legacy (13:1) 1996, 54–63.

9471. RICHARDS, JEFFREY H.   Mercy Otis Warren. (Bibl. 1995, 8193.) Rev. by Sharon M. Harris in EAL (31:2) 1996, 193–5.

Joseph Warton

9472. KRAMNICK, JONATHAN BRODY.   The cultural logic of late feudalism: placing Spenser in the eighteenth century. *See* **6049**.

Thomas Warton the Elder

9473. LINDSAY, ALEXANDER.   A lost ballad by Thomas Warton the Elder. *See* **722**.

Thomas Warton the Younger

9474. FAIRER, DAVID.   'Sweet native stream!': Wordsworth and the school of Warton. *In* (pp. 314–38) **122**.

9475. —— (ed.).   The correspondence of Thomas Warton. (Bibl. 1995, 8194.) Rev. by John Mullan in LRB (18:18) 1996, 19; by David Womersley in TLS, 15 Mar. 1996, 7–8.

Isaac Watts

9476. BULL, MALCOLM.   Blake and Watts in *Songs of Experience*. *See* **8794**.

9477. DAVIE, DONALD.   The 'ending up' of Isaac Watts. PN Review (17:6) 1991, 27–9.

Charles Wesley

9478. DAVIE, DONALD.   The carnality of Charles Wesley. PN Review (18:1) 1991, 10–15.

9479. GIBSON, COLIN.   Popular theology in the hymns of Charles Wesley. Music in the Air, Summer 1996, 2–6.

9480. NEWPORT, KENNETH G. C.   Charles Wesley's interpretation of some biblical prophecies according to a previously unpublished letter dated 25 April, 1754. *See* **771**.

John Wesley

9481. ABELOVE, HENRY.   The evangelist of desire: John Wesley and the Methodists. (Bibl. 1993, 6407.) Rev. by Richard E. Brantley in ECS (25:2) 1991/92, 250–4.

9482. NEWPORT, KENNETH G. C.   Methodists and the Millennium: eschatological expectation and the interpretation of biblical prophecy in early British Methodism. *See* **8691**.

Phillis Wheatley

9483. ELLISON, JULIE.   The politics of fancy in the age of sensibility. *In* (pp. 228–55) **103**.

9484. KENDRICK, ROBERT.   Re-membering America: Phillis Wheatley's intertextual epic. AAR (30:1) 1996, 71–88.

9485. Levernier, James A.   *Legacy* profile: Phillis Wheatley (*ca*.1753–1784). Legacy (13:1) 1996, 65–75.

9486. Watson, Marsha.   A classic case: Phillis Wheatley and her poetry. EAL (31:2) 1996, 103–32.

Gilbert White

9487. Merrett, Robert James.   Natural history and the eighteenth-century English novel. *See* **8595**.

John Wilkes

9488. Cash, Arthur H.   Wilkes, Baxter, and d'Holbach at Leiden and Utrecht: an answer to G. S. Rousseau. AJ (7) 1996, 397–426.

9489. Katritzky, Linde.   Johnson and *The Letters of Junius*: new perspectives on an old enigma. *See* **9148**.

9490. Robinson, Roger.   The madness of Mrs Beattie's family: the strange case of the 'assassin' of John Wilkes. *See* **8784**.

Helen Maria Williams

9491. Blakemore, Steven.   Revolution and the French disease: Laetitia Matilda Hawkins's *Letters* to Helen Maria Williams. *See* **8665**.

9492. Ledden, Mark B.   Revolutionary plots: Helen Maria Williams's *Letters from France*. *See* **8877**.

Anne Finch, Countess of Winchilsea

9493. Hellegers, Desiree.   'The threatening Angel and the speaking Ass': the masculine mismeasure of madness in Anne Finch's *The Spleen*. Genre (26:2/3) 1993, 199–217.

9494. Kowaleski-Wallace, Beth.   Women, china, and consumer culture in eighteenth-century England. *See* **8770**.

Mary Wollstonecraft

9495. Bahar, Saba.   *Frankenstein*, family politics and population politics. *See* **9077**.

9496. Basker, James G.   Radical affinities: Mary Wollstonecraft and Samuel Johnson. *In* (pp. 41–55) **122**.

9497. Gubar, Susan.   Feminist misogyny: Mary Wollstonecraft and the paradox of 'it takes one to know one'. Feminist Studies (20:3) 1994, 453–73.

9498. Hust, Karen.   In suspect terrain: Mary Wollstonecraft confronts Mother Nature in *Letters Written during a Short Residence in Sweden, Norway, and Denmark*. WS (25:5) 1996, 483–505.

9499. Huxman, Susan Schultz.   Mary Wollstonecraft, Margaret Fuller, and Angelina Grimké: symbolic convergence and a nascent rhetorical vision. ComQ (44:1) 1996, 16–28.

9500. Kelly, Gary.   Revolutionary feminism: the mind and career of Mary Wollstonecraft. (Bibl. 1995, 8224.) Rev. by Barbara Penny Kanner in AHR (99:1) 1994, 229–30.

9501. Labbe, Jacqueline.   A family romance: Mary Wollstonecraft, Mary Godwin, and travel. Genre (25:2/3) 1992, 211–28.

9502. Lorch, Jennifer.   Mary Wollstonecraft: the making of a radical feminist. Oxford: Berg; New York: St Martin's Press, 1990. pp. x, 127. (Berg women's series.) Rev. by Catherine N. Parke in ECS (25:2) 1991/92, 260–3.

9503. WILLIAMS, LEIGH; JOHNSTONE, ROSEMARIE. Updating Mary Wollstonecraft: a bibliography of criticism, 1976–1989. BB (48:2) 1991, 103–7.

John Woolman

9504. OEHLSCHLAEGER, FRITZ. Taking John Woolman's Christianity seriously. Ren (48:3) 1996, 191–207.

Edward Young

9505. FISCHER, BERNHARD. Authentizität und ästhetische Objektivität: Youngs *Gedanken über die Original-Werke* (1759) und Goethes *Von Deutscher Baukunst* (1771). GRM (42:2) 1992, 178–94.

9506. MAY, JAMES E. Young's corrections to Dodington's *Epistle to Bute*: evidence from the Yale manuscript. *See* **752**.

9507. TYSDAHL, BJØRN. Edward Young and Wordsworth's *Intimations* ode: originality and imitation. EngS (77:2) 1996, 127–32.

NINETEENTH CENTURY

GENERAL

General Literary Studies

9508. ADAMS, JAMES ELI.   Dandies and desert saints: styles of Victorian masculinity. (Bibl. 1995, 8237.) Rev. by Andrew Elfenbein in Prose Studies (19:3) 1996, 292–6.

9509. AHEARN, EDWARD J.   Visionary fictions: apocalyptic writing from Blake to the modern age. *See* **8425**.

9510. ALTER, ROBERT.   The pleasures of reading in an ideological age. (Bibl. 1989, 5598.) Rev. by Frederick Pollack in Salmagundi (88/89) 1990/91, 486–509.

9511. BAKER, RUSSELL (ed.).   Russell Baker's book of American humor. *See* **2251**.

9512. BALZANO, WANDA.   Il *patchwork* post-coloniale irlandese. Annali anglistica (38:3) 1995, 105–40. (Includes interview with Declan Kiberd, author of *Inventing Ireland*.)

9513. BARBOUR, JAMES; QUIRK, TOM (eds).   Biographies of books: the compositional histories of notable American writings. *See* **7**.

9514. BEASECKER, ROBERT (ed.).   Annual bibliography of Midwestern literature 1991; 1993; 1994. Midamerica (20) 1993, 127–44; (22) 1995, 139–60; (23) 1996, 136–55.

9515. —— PADY, DONALD (eds).   Annual bibliography of Midwestern literature 1989; 1990. Midamerica (18) 1991, 174–96; (19) 1992, 145–66.

9516. BEER, GILLIAN.   Open fields: science in cultural encounter. Oxford; New York: OUP, 1996. pp. viii, 341. Rev. by Jenny Uglow in TLS, 13 Dec. 1996, 5–6.

9517. BEER, JANET.   American literature to 1900: American literature 1865 to 1900. YWES (75) 1994, 572–83.

9518. BEER, JOHN.   Is the Romantic imagination our imagination? *In* (pp. 25–48) **47**.

9519. BENESCH, KLAUS.   Romantic cyborgs: technology, authorship, and the politics of reproduction in nineteenth-century American literature. Amst (41:3) 1996, 339–59.

9520. BERCOVITCH, SACVAN (gen. ed.); PATELL, CYRUS R. K. (assoc. ed.).   The Cambridge history of American literature: vol. 2, 1820–1865. Cambridge; New York: CUP, 1995. pp. xviii, 887. Rev. by Hugh Kenner in TLS, 24 Nov. 1995, 8; by Jens P. Becker in LWU (29:1) 1996, 64–5.

9521. BERGMANN, LINDA S.   Epic, parody, and national identity: George Washington in nineteenth-century American humor. SAH (3:2) 1995, 1–22.

9522. BERKOVE, LAWRENCE I.   19th-century literature. American Literary Scholarship (1993) 165–94.

9523. BERTOLINI, VINCENT J.   Fireside chastity: the erotics of sentimental bachelorhood in the 1850s. AL (68:4) 1996, 707–37.

9524. BEVAN, DAVID (ed.).   Literature and sickness. Amsterdam; Atlanta, GA: Rodopi, 1993. pp. 116. (Rodopi perspectives on modern literature, 8.) Rev. by Robert Wilcocks in CanRCL (23:4) 1996, 1238–40.

9525. Bishop, T. G.   Ceremonies of separation in Australian literature. KenR (12:3) 1995, 119–39.

9526. Brand, Dana.   The spectator and the city in nineteenth-century American literature. (Bibl. 1995, 8255.) Rev. by Benjamin Goluboff in AmS (35:2) 1994, 144–5.

9527. Bromell, Nicholas K.   By the sweat of the brow: literature and labor in antebellum America. (Bibl. 1995, 8259.) Rev. by Ray B. Browne in JAC (18:3) 1995, 103; by David A. Zonderman in AmLH (8:2) 1996, 345–9; by R. W. (Herbie) Butterfield in YES (26) 1996, 323–4.

9528. Brown, Dorothy H.   Louisiana women writers: a bibliography. *In* (pp. 213–334) **65**.

9529. —— Ewell, Barbara C. (eds).   Louisiana women writers: new essays and a comprehensive bibliography. *See* **65**.

9530. Bryant, John.   Melville and repose: the rhetoric of humor in the American renaissance. (Bibl. 1995, 8264.) Rev. by Elizabeth Huyck in AL (68:1) 1996, 240–1; by Dennis Berthold in StudN (28:1) 1996, 115–18.

9531. Bullen, J. B.   The myth of the Renaissance in nineteenth-century writing. (Bibl. 1995, 8266.) Rev. by Jacob Korg in CLIO (25:1) 1995, 101–4.

9532. Buonomo, Leonardo.   Backward glances: exploring Italy, re-interpreting America: 1831–1866. Madison, NJ: Fairleigh Dickinson UP; London; Toronto: Assoc. UPs, 1996. pp. 115.

9533. Burbick, Joan.   Healing the republic: the language of health and the culture of nationalism in nineteenth-century America. (Bibl. 1995, 8267.) Rev. by Hans-Joachim Lang in ZAA (43:4) 1995, 371–3; by Sylvia D. Hoffert in AmS (37:2) 1996, 197–8.

9534. Burkholder, Robert E.   Early 19th-century American literature. American Literary Scholarship (1995) 207–33.

9535. ——   Early 19th-century literature. American Literary Scholarship (1994) 203–22.

9536. Bygrave, Stephen (ed.).   Romantic writings. *See* **8441**.

9537. Cagidemetrio, Alide.   The vanishing of Indian princesses; or, The sentimental transformation of the Pocahontas myth. RSAJ (7) 1996, 5–26.

9538. Carosso, Andrea.   Economy of logic: the emergence of monetary form in Anglo-American pragmatist and idealist discourse. RSAJ (4) 1993, 17–30.

9539. Castronovo, Russ.   Fathering the nation: American geneal-ogies of slavery and freedom. (Bibl. 1995, 8274.) Rev. by Bertram Wyatt-Brown in GaHQ (80:3) 1996, 650–2.

9540. Cavell, Richard.   White technologies. ECanW (59) 1996, 199–210. (Canadian writing on the Arctic.)

9541. Caws, Mary Ann (ed.).   City images: perspectives from litera-ture, philosophy, and film. New York; London: Gordon & Breach, 1991. pp. vi, 278. Rev. by Norbert Reichel in CanRCL (20:3/4) 1993, 526–8.

9542. Chapman, Mary.   'Living pictures': women and *tableaux vivants* in nineteenth-century American fiction and culture. Wide Angle (18:3) 1996, 23–52.

9543. Chapman, Michael.   Southern African literatures. London; New York: Longman, 1996. pp. xxix, 533. (Longman literature in English.)

9544. Cherniavsky, Eva.   That pale mother rising: sentimental discourses and the imitation of motherhood in 19th-century America. Bloomington: Indiana UP, 1995. pp. xiii, 156. Rev. by Michelle Burnham in AL (68:1) 1996, 232–3.

9545. CHEYETTE, BRYAN. Constructions of 'the Jew' in English literature and society: racial representations, 1875–1945. (Bibl. 1995, 8275.) Rev. by Edward A. Abramson in YES (26) 1996, 300–1.

9546. —— (ed.). Between 'race' and culture: representations of 'the Jew' in English and American literature. *See* **5**.

9547. CHISHOLM, SCOTT. Centennial blues: reflections on creativity and literature in Utah. WHR (50:3) 1996, 257–70.

9548. CHRIST, CAROL T.; JORDAN, JOHN O. (eds). Victorian literature and the Victorian visual imagination. *See* **126**.

9549. CIANCI, GIOVANNI. Epilogo con qualche riflessione. QLLSM (4) 1990, 341–53.

9550. CLARIDGE, HENRY. American literature to 1900: American literature to 1830. *See* **7363**.

9551. —— American literature to 1900: general. *See* **7364**.

9552. COLEMAN, DEIRDRE; OTTO, PETER (eds). Imagining Romanticism: essays on English and Australian Romanticisms. *See* **47**.

9553. CORBALLIS, RICHARD. Some echoes of Ireland in New Zealand literature, 1890–1990. *In* (pp. 45–58) **49**.

9554. COSSLETT, TESS. The aseptic male obstetrician and the filthy peasant crone: contemporary women writers' accounts of birth. *In* (pp. 74–96) **94**.

9555. CURTIS, GERARD. Shared lines: pen and pencil as trace. *In* (pp. 27–59) **126**.

9556. DALE, PETER ALLAN. In pursuit of a scientific culture: science, art, and society in the Victorian age. (Bibl. 1992, 7250.) Rev. by Paul A. Robberecht in CanRCL (19:4) 1992, 629–32.

9557. DAME, FREDERICK WILLIAM. Jean-Jacques Rousseau in American literature: traces, influence, transformation, 1760–1860: a paradigm of French–German culture emanation in America. *See* **8450**.

9558. DAVIS, THADIOUS M. Women's art and authorship in the Southern region: connections. *In* (pp. 15–36) **32**.

9559. DAY, AIDAN. Romanticism. *See* **8455**.

9560. DEGUCHI, YASUO (ed.). Seikimatsu no igirisu. (*Fin de siècle* in Britain.) Tokyo: Kenkyusha Shuppan, 1996. pp. vi, 176.

9561. DE MONTLUZIN, EMILY LORRAINE. Attributions of authorship in the *Gentleman's Magazine*, 1793–1808: a supplement to Kuist. *See* **1257**.

9562. —— Attributions of authorship in the *Gentleman's Magazine*, 1809–26: a supplement to Kuist. *See* **1258**.

9563. —— Attributions of authorship in the *Gentleman's Magazine*, 1827–48: a supplement to Kuist. *See* **1259**.

9564. DERIE, KATE. Mystery on the Internet. *See* **1148**.

9565. DERINGER, LUDWIG. Das Bild des Pazifischen Nordwestens: von den Anfängen bis zur Gegenwart. Vergleichende Studien zur kanadischen und amerikanischen Literatur zwischen Regionalismus und Universalismus. *See* **8460**.

9566. DE RIZ, FRANCESCA BISUTTI; ZORZI, ROSELLA MAMOLI; COSLOVI, MARINA (eds). Technology and the American imagination: an ongoing challenge. Atti del Dodecisimo Convegno Biennale, Università di Venezia, 28–30 ottobre 1993. *See* **117**.

9567. DIBATTISTA, MARIA. Introduction. *In* (pp. 3–19) **41**.

9568. —— McDiarmid, Lucy (eds). High and low moderns: literature and culture, 1889–1939. *See* **41**.

9569. Dickerson, Vanessa D. Feminine transactions: money and nineteenth-century British women writers. *In* (pp. 227–43) **71**.

9570. Diffley, Kathleen. Where my heart is turning ever: Civil War stories and constitutional reform, 1861–1875. (Bibl. 1995, 8287.) Rev. by Stuart McConnell in AHR (99:2) 1994, 660.

9571. Dimock, Wai Chee; Gilmore, Michael T. (eds). Rethinking class: literary studies and social formations. *See* **100**.

9572. Dotterer, Ronald; Bowers, Susan (eds). Politics, gender, and the arts: women, the arts, and society. *See* **87**.

9573. Dowling, Linda. The vulgarization of art: the Victorians and aesthetic democracy. Charlottesville; London: Virginia UP, 1996. pp. xiv, 133. (Victorian literature and culture.) Rev. by William C. Engels in RWT (4:1) 1996, 224–9.

9574. Dowling, Linda C. Hellenism and homosexuality in Victorian Oxford. (Bibl. 1995, 8290.) Rev. by David Wayne Thomas in Style (30:3) 1996, 524–30; by William C. Lubenow in Albion (28:1) 1996, 133–4; by J. B. Bullen in YES (26) 1996, 299–300.

9575. Dunne, Robert. Not for White men only: the methodology behind the *Dictionary of Midwestern Literature*. Midamerica (20) 1993, 40–7.

9576. Eagleton, Terry. The flight to the real. *In* (pp. 11–21) **18**.

9577. —— Heathcliff and the Great Hunger: studies in Irish culture. (Bibl. 1995, 8291.) Rev. by Joep Leerssen in Irish Review (17/18) 1995, 167–75; by Joyce Flynn in EI (31:3/4) 1996, 255–60; by Patrick Colm Hogan in ColLit (23:3) 1996, 178–88.

9578. Eiselein, Gregory. Literature and humanitarian reform in the Civil War era. Bloomington: Indiana UP, 1996. pp. xi, 215. (Philanthropic studies.)

9579. Eldridge, C. C. The imperial experience: from Carlyle to Forster. Basingstoke: Macmillan; New York: St Martin's Press, 1996. pp. xv, 212, (plates) 8. (Context and commentary.)

9580. Elfenbein, Andrew. Byron and the Victorians. (Bibl. 1995, 8294.) Rev. by Francis Berry in NQ (43:2) 1996, 235–6; by M. J. Flay in EngS (77:6) 1996, 598–9; by Atara Stein in ERR (7:1) 1996, 101–7.

9581. Epstein, Joseph. Partial payments: essays on writers and their lives. (Bibl. 1989, 5646.) Rev. by Mark Shechner in Salmagundi (90/91) 1991, 263–76.

9582. Erickson, Lee. The economy of literary form: English literature and the industrialization of publishing, 1800–1850. *See* **925**.

9583. Firchow, Peter Edgerly. The death of the German cousin: variations on a literary stereotype, 1890–1920. (Bibl. 1991, 6842.) Rev. by Richard Humphrey in GRM (42:4) 1992, 470–3.

9584. Flint, Kate. Glaciers, science, and the imagination. Textus (8:1) 1995, 43–63.

9585. —— The woman reader, 1837–1914. (Bibl. 1995, 8302.) Rev. by Siv Jansson in YES (26) 1996, 294–5.

9586. Franklin, Wayne; Steiner, Michael (eds). Mapping American culture. *See* **66**.

9587. Fraser, Angus. A publishing house and its readers, 1841–1880: the Murrays and the Miltons. *See* **932**.

9588. Fraser, Wayne. The dominion of women: the personal and the political in Canadian women's literature. (Bibl. 1995, 8306.) Rev. by Barbara Godard in Signs (19:3) 1994, 835–9.

9589. FREEDMAN, JONATHAN. Professions of taste: Henry James, British aestheticism, and commodity culture. (Bibl. 1995, 8307.) Rev. by Millicent Bell in Raritan (13:4) 1994, 124–45.

9590. FUCHS, STEFAN F.-J. Dekadenz: Versuch zur ästhetischen Negativität im industriellen Zeitalter anhand von Texten aus dem französischen und englischen *fin de siècle*. Heidelberg: Winter, 1992. pp. 478. (Beiträge zur neueren Literaturgeschichte, 3:116.) Rev. by Heide Eilert in arcadia (28:1) 1993, 100–2.

9591. FUROMOTO, TOSHI, *et al.* (eds). International aspects of Irish literature. See **49**.

9592. GALCHINSKY, MICHAEL. The origin of the modern Jewish woman writer: romance and reform in Victorian England. Detroit, MI: Wayne State UP, 1996. pp. 275. (Cf. bibl. 1995, 8309.) Rev. by Bryan Cheyette in TLS, 11 Oct. 1996, 29.

9593. GALLET, RENÉ. Romantisme et postromantisme de Coleridge à Hardy: nature et surnature. Paris: L'Harmattan, 1996. pp. 188. (Critiques littéraires.)

9594. GENET, JACQUELINE. Introduction. *In* (pp. 9–17) **106**.

9595. —— (ed.). Rural Ireland, real Ireland? *See* **106**.

9596. GILMARTIN, KEVIN. Print politics: the press and radical opposition in early nineteenth-century England. *See* **1273**.

9597. GINSBERG, ELAINE K. (ed.). Passing and the fictions of identity. *See* **82**.

9598. GOETSCH, PAUL (ed.). Mündliches Wissen in neuzeitlicher Literatur. *See* **73**.

9599. GOLDMAN, PAUL. Victorian illustration: the pre-Raphaelites, the Idyllic School, and the high Victorians. *See* **203**.

9600. GRABES, HERBERT. Writing against time: the paradox of temporality in Modernist and postmodern aesthetics. PoetA (28:3/4) 1996, 368–85.

9601. GUNNING, SANDRA. Race, rape, and lynching: the red record of American literature, 1890–1912. New York; Oxford: OUP, 1996. pp. x, 195. (Race and American culture.)

9602. HAGGERTY, GEORGE E.; ZIMMERMAN, BONNIE (eds). Professions of desire: lesbian and gay studies in literature. *See* **92**.

9603. HALL, DONALD E. (ed.). Muscular Christianity: embodying the Victorian age. *See* **74**.

9604. HAMILTON, KRISTIE. Toward a cultural theory of the antebellum literary sketch. Genre (23:4) 1990, 297–323.

9605. HANDY, ELLEN. Dust piles and damp pavements: excrement, repression, and the Victorian city in photography and literature. *In* (pp. 111–33) **126**.

9606. HASSAN, IHAB. In the mirror of the sun: reflections on Japanese and American literature, Bashō to Cage. WLT (69:2) 1995, 304–11.

9607. HEDGES, ELAINE; FISHKIN, SHELLEY FISHER (eds). Listening to silences: new essays in feminist criticism. *See* **59**.

9608. HENDERSON, ANDREA K. Romantic identities: varieties of subjectivity, 1774–1830. *See* **8480**.

9609. HIRABAYASHI, MITOKO. Matasareta nemuri hime – 19 seiki no josei no hyoushou. (The waiting Sleeping Beauty: a symbol of the nineteenth-century woman.) Kyoto: Kyoto Shugakusha, 1996. pp. x, 172.

9610. HOAGWOOD, TERENCE ALLAN. Politics, philosophy, and the production of Romantic texts. DeKalb: Northern Illinois UP, 1996. pp. 222. Rev. by S.J. in TLS, 6 Dec. 1996, 24.

9611. HOCHBRUCK, W. 'Native American literature': developments, contexts and problems. *See* **8481**.

9612. HORWITZ, HOWARD. By the law of nature: form and value in nineteenth-century America. (Bibl. 1994, 6786.) Rev. by Tamara Plakins Thornton in AmS (34:2) 1993, 142–4.

9613. IVES, MAURA. Descriptive bibliography and the Victorian periodical. *See* **144**.

9614. JANOWITZ, ANNE. Class and literature: the case of Romantic Chartism. *In* (pp. 239–66) **100**.

9615. KABITOGLOU, E. DOUKA. Romanticism and its 'other': an overview/oversight. EEM (5:1) 1996, 21–4.

9616. KARRER, WOLFGANG; KREUTZER, EBERHARD. Werke der englischen und amerikanischen Literatur von 1890 bis zur Gegenwart. Munich: Deutscher Taschenbuch, 1989. pp. 433. (Fourth ed.) Rev. by Gerhard Dohna in NS (90:5) 1991, 570–1.

9617. KENNER, HUGH (introd.). Axel's castle: a study of the imaginative literature of 1870–1930. New York: Modern Library, 1996. pp. xxxvii, 362.

9618. KERN, STEPHEN. The culture of love: Victorians to moderns. (Bibl. 1995, 8336.) Rev. by Peter Bailey in AHR (99:3) 1994, 861–2.

9619. KIERNAN, BRIAN. New literatures in English: Australia. YWES (75) 1994, 704–22.

9620. KINCAID, JAMES R. Annoying the Victorians. (Bibl. 1995, 8337.) Rev. by Anthony H. Harrison in Criticism (38:1) 1996, 166–9.

9621. —— Child-loving: the erotic child and Victorian culture. (Bibl. 1995, 8338.) Rev. by Judith S. Lewis in AHR (99:2) 1994, 565–6; by Naomi J. Wood in ChildLit (23) 1995, 254–60.

9622. KLOOSS, WOLFGANG. Geschichte und Mythos in der Literatur Kanadas: die englischsprachige Métis- und Riel-Rezeption. Heidelberg: Winter, 1989. pp. 384. (Reihe Siegen, 82. Anglistische Abteilung.) Rev. by Paul Goetsch in GRM (41:1) 1991, 116–17.

9623. KOPELSON, KEVIN. Love's litany: the writing of modern homoerotics. (Bibl. 1995, 8341.) Rev. by John Maynard in StudN (28:4) 1996, 597–9.

9624. KUIST, JAMES M. A collaboration in learning: the *Gentleman's Magazine* and its ingenious contributors. *See* **1302**.

9625. LANE, CHRISTOPHER. The ruling passion: British colonial allegory and the paradox of homosexual desire. (Bibl. 1995, 8348.) Rev. by Andrew Elfenbein in Prose Studies (19:3) 1996, 292–6; by Roberto C. Ferrari in ELT (39:4) 1996, 497–500.

9626. LANGLAND, ELIZABETH. Nobody's angels: middle-class women and domestic ideology in Victorian culture. Ithaca, NY; London: Cornell UP, 1995. pp. x, 268. (Reading women writing.) Rev. by Elisabeth Rose Gruner in TSWL (15:2) 1996, 365–8; by John R. Reed in StudN (28:4) 1996, 599–601.

9627. LARMORE, CHARLES. The Romantic legacy. New York: Columbia UP, 1996. pp. xvi, 100.

9628. LASKIN, DAVID. A common life: four generations of American literary friendship and influence. (Bibl. 1994, 6805.) Rev. by Dennis Drabelle in BkW, 14 Aug. 1994, 3, 11.

9629. LAUGERO, GREG.   Publicity, gender, and genre: a review essay. *See* **8488**.

9630. LAUTER, PAUL.   Canons and contexts. (Bibl. 1995, 8350.) Rev. by Paula Marantz Cohen in NWSAJ (4:3) 1992, 379–82.

9631. LEADER, ZACHARY.   Revision and Romantic authorship. *See* **720**.

9632. LEDGER, SALLY.   The New Woman and the crisis of Victorianism. *In* (pp. 22–44) **18**.

9633. —— McCRACKEN, SCOTT.   Introduction. *In* (pp. 1–10) **18**.

9634. —— —— (eds).   Cultural politics at the *fin de siècle*. *See* **18**.

9635. LEVY, ANITA.   Other women: the writing of class, race, and gender, 1832–1898. (Bibl. 1993, 6546.) Rev. by Nancy Armstrong in Signs (18:2) 1993, 433–8; by Maureen Ryan in CanL (148) 1996, 177–9.

9636. LICHTENSTEIN, DIANE.   Writing their nations: the tradition of nineteenth-century American Jewish women writers. (Bibl. 1994, 6810.) Rev. by Paula E. Hyman in AHR (99:1) 1994, 303–4; by Ann R. Shapiro in Signs (22:1) 1996, 234–6.

9637. LITTLEFIELD, DANIEL F., JR; PARINS, JAMES W. (eds).   Native American writing in the Southeast: an anthology, 1875–1935. Jackson; London: Mississippi UP, 1995. pp. xxiv, 248. Rev. by Sharlotte Neely in GaHQ (80:2) 1996, 426–7.

9638. LOOBY, CHRISTOPHER.   Voicing America: language, literary form, and the origins of the United States. *See* **2666**.

9639. LOOTENS, TRICIA.   Lost saints: silence, gender, and Victorian literary canonization. Charlottesville; London: Virginia UP, 1996. pp. xi, 243. (Victorian literature and culture.)

9640. LOVING, JEROME.   Lost in the customhouse: authorship in the American renaissance. (Bibl. 1995, 8362.) Rev. by Albert E. Stone in AmS (34:2) 1993, 150–2.

9641. LOW, GAIL CHING-LIANG.   White skins/Black masks: representation and colonialism. New York; London: Routledge, 1996. pp. xi, 299.

9642. LUFTIG, VICTOR.   Seeing together: friendship between the sexes in English writing from Mill to Woolf. (Bibl. 1995, 8363.) Rev. by Angela Smith in YES (26) 1996, 307–8; by Kelly Hager in StudN (28:1) 1996, 123–5.

9643. McCARRON, KEVIN.   American literature to 1900: American literature 1830 to 1865. YWES (75) 1994, 562–72.

9644. McCONCHIE, R. W.   Some Australian literary illustrators. *See* **218**.

9645. MACDONALD, ROBERT H.   The language of Empire: myths and metaphors of popular imperialism, 1880–1918. (Bibl. 1995, 8366.) Rev. by Martin Lynn in EHR (111:444) 1996, 1333–4.

9646. MACOVSKI, MICHAEL.   Dialogue and literature: apostrophe, auditors, and the collapse of Romantic discourse. (Bibl. 1994, 6824.) Rev. by Megan B. O'Neill in RWT (1:2) 1994, 208–11; by Adrienne Donald in KSJ (45) 1996, 220–2.

9647. MANNING, CAROL S.   Introduction: on defining themes and (mis)placing women writers. *In* (pp. 1–12) **32**.

9648. —— The real beginning of the Southern renaissance. *In* (pp. 37–56) **32**.

9649. —— (ed.).   The female tradition in Southern literature. *See* **32**.

9650. MARR, DAVID. American worlds since Emerson. (Bibl. 1989, 5683.) Rev. by Evan Carton in Raritan (11:2) 1991, 115–27.

9651. MASSEY, IRVING. Identity and community: reflections on English, Yiddish, and French literature in Canada. (Bibl. 1994, 6826.) Rev. by Margaret Michele Cook in ColLit (23:2) 1996, 199–201.

9652. MASSOUD, MARY (ed.). Literary inter-relations: Ireland, Egypt, and the Far East. *See* **60**.

9653. MEIHUIZEN, NICHOLAS. Thomas Taylor: high Romanticism and cultural subversion. ESA (38:2) 1995, 17–25. (Reactions to Taylor's translation and annotation of Plato.)

9654. MEYER, WILLIAM E. H., JR. From *The Sun Also Rises* to *High Noon*: the hypervisual great awakening in American literature and film. Cithara (32:1) 1992, 39–59.

9655. —— From *The Sun Also Rises* to *High Noon*: the hypervisual great awakening in American literature and film. JAC (19:3) 1996, 25–37.

9656. —— The hypervisual standard of American popular culture. *See* **8502**.

9657. MICHIE, ELSIE B. Outside the pale: cultural exclusion, gender difference, and the Victorian woman writer. (Bibl. 1995, 8382.) Rev. by Kathy Alexis Psomiades in Signs (21:2) 1996, 463–6; by Deborah Blenkhorn in CanL (150) 1996, 121–2.

9658. MIGLIORINO, ELLEN GINZBURG. The image of the Revolution in Abolitionist patriotism. RSAJ (6) 1995, 65–82.

9659. MITCHELL, SALLY. The new girl: girls' culture in England, 1880–1915. (Bibl. 1995, 8388.) Rev. by Amy Beth Aronson in AmP (6) 1996, 144–6; by P.C. in TLS, 31 May 1996, 30; by Sherrie A. Inness in NWSAJ (8:3) 1996, 144–53.

9660. MOORE-GILBERT, BART. Introduction: writing India, re-orienting colonial discourse analysis. *In* (pp. 1–29) **132**.

9661. —— (ed.). Writing India 1757–1990: the literature of British India. *See* **132**.

9662. MORRISON, ROBERT. *Blackwood's* under William Blackwood. *See* **1324**.

9663. MORSE, DONALD E.; BERTHA, CSILLA; PÁLFFY, ISTVÁN (eds). A small nation's contribution to the world: essays on Anglo-Irish literature and language. *See* **112**.

9664. MOTT, WESLEY T. (ed.). Biographical dictionary of Transcendentalism. Westport, CT; London: Greenwood Press, 1996. pp. xvi, 315.

9665. —— Encyclopedia of Transcendentalism. Westport, CT; London: Greenwood Press, 1996. pp. xxxiii, 280.

9666. MOYNAHAN, JULIAN. Anglo-Irish: the literary imagination in a hyphenated culture. (Bibl. 1995, 8395.) Rev. by Joyce Flynn in EI (31:3/4) 1996, 255–60.

9667. NEUBAUER, JOHN. The *fin-de-siècle* culture of adolescence. (Bibl. 1995, 8397.) Rev. by Elaine Martin in Comparatist (19) 1995, 144–6.

9668. OHI, KOUJI. Tegami no naka no America – 'atarashii kyouwakoku' no shinwa to ideology. (America in letters: the myth and ideology of a 'New Republic'.) *See* **8513**.

9669. OKKER, PATRICIA. Our sister editors: Sarah J. Hale and the tradition of nineteenth-century American women editors. *See* **1334**.

9670. OLIVER, LAWRENCE J.   Late 19th-century literature. American Literary Scholarship (1995) 235–57.

9671. OPFERMANN, SUSANNE.   Literatur und Geschlecht im 19. Jahrhundert: zur diskursiven Konstruktion von 'Frauenliteratur' in den USA. ZAA (41:2) 1993, 133–46.

9672. PAGEARD, ROBERT.   Le tableau de mœurs: esprit et histoire d'un genre littéraire. *See* **8514**.

9673. PAGETTI, CARLO.   Imperial geography and Victorian imagination: the ghosts of Tasmania. Textus (8:1) 1995, 89–107.

9674. PESMAN, R. L.   The Italian Renaissance in Australia. Parergon (14:1) 1996, 223–39.

9675. RAUBICHECK, WALTER.   Jacques Maritain, T. S. Eliot, and the Romantics. Ren (46:1) 1993, 71–9.

9676. RAVEENDRAN, P. P.   Nationalism, colonialism and Indian English literature. IndL (39:5) 1996, 153–9.

9677. REYNOLDS, KIMBERLEY; HUMBLE, NICOLA.   Victorian heroines: representations of femininity in nineteenth-century literature and art. (Bibl. 1995, 8417.) Rev. by Kathy Alexis Psomiades in Signs (21:2) 1996, 463–6.

9678. ROEDIGER, DAVID.   White looks: hairy apes, true stories and Limbaugh's laughs. MinnR (47) 1996, 37–47.

9679. ROOM, ADRIAN.   Literally entitled: a dictionary of the origins of the titles of over 1300 major literary works of the nineteenth and twentieth centuries. Jefferson, NC; London: McFarland, 1996. pp. v, 249. Rev. by J.H.C.L. in TLS, 28 June 1996, 32.

9680. ROSTON, MURRAY.   Victorian contexts: literature and the visual arts. Basingstoke: Macmillan; New York: New York UP, 1996. pp. ix, 246. Rev. by S.J. in TLS, 6 Dec. 1996, 24.

9681. RUOFF, A. LAVONNE BROWN; WARD, JERRY W., JR (eds).   Redefining American literary history. (Bibl. 1992, 7381.) Rev. by Jake Jakaitis in AAR (27:4) 1993, 673–7.

9682. RYALS, CLYDE DE L.   Recent studies in the nineteenth century. SELit (36:4) 1996, 935–80.

9683. SCHAFFER, KAY.   In the wake of first contact: the Eliza Fraser stories. Cambridge; New York: CUP, 1995. pp. xvi, 320. Rev. by Julian Ferraro in TLS, 19 July 1996, 22.

9684. SCHMIDT, KLAUS H.; SAWYER, DAVID (eds).   Blurred boundaries: critical essays on American literature, language and culture. *See* **8**.

9685. SCHNACKERTZ, HERMANN JOSEF.   Darwinismus und literarischer Diskurs: der Dialog mit der Evolutionsbiologie in der englischen und amerikanischen Literatur. (Bibl. 1994, 6856.) Rev. by Marion Spies in ZAA (41:2) 1993, 182–4; by Bruno Schultze in GRM (44:3) 1994, 345–50.

9686. SCHOR, ESTHER.   Bearing the dead: the British culture of mourning from the Enlightenment to Victoria. *See* **8523**.

9687. SCHULTZE, BRUNO.   Darwin und die literarischen Folgen. GRM (44:3) 1994, 345–50 (review-article).

9688. SHAW, PETER.   Recovering American literature. (Bibl. 1994, 6857.) Rev. by John P. Sisk in ASch (64:2) 1995, 311–12.

9689. SHERBO, ARTHUR.   From the *Bookman* of London. *See* **1363**.

9690. —— From the *London Mercury*. *See* **1364**.

9691. —— Last gleanings from the *Critic*: Clemens, Whitman, Hardy, Thackeray, and others. *See* **1365**.

9692. —— A mixed bag from the *Bookman* of New York. *See* **1366**.

9693. SHERRY, PEGGY MEYER. Telling her story: British women of letters of the Victorian era. PULC (57:1) 1995, 147–62.

9694. SHRIMPTON, NICHOLAS. Pater and the 'aesthetical sect'. CompCrit (17) 1995, 61–84.

9695. SIEGEL, CAROL; KIBBEY, ANN (eds). Eroticism and containment: notes from the flood plain. *See* **30**.

9696. SIMPSON, ROGER. Camelot regained: the Arthurian revival and Tennyson, 1800–1849. (Bibl. 1993, 6617.) Rev. by Rebecca Cochran in Quondam et Futurus (1:4) 1991, 88–91.

9697. SKANDERA-TROMBLEY, LAURA E. Late 19th-century literature. American Literary Scholarship (1994) 223–39.

9698. SLOVIC, SCOTT; NODA, KEN'ICH (eds). America bungaku no 'shizen' wo yomu – *nature writing* no sekai e. (Reading 'nature' in American literature: an introduction to the world of nature writing.) Kyoto: Minerva Shobo, 1996. pp. 456. (Minerva eibei bungaku library, 2.) (Minerva library of English and American literature, 2.)

9699. SMALL, IAN. The economies of taste: literary markets and literary value in the late nineteenth century. ELT (39:1) 1996, 7–18.

9700. SMITH, JONATHAN. Fact and feeling: Baconian science and the nineteenth-century literary imagination. (Bibl. 1995, 8430.) Rev. by Thomas L. Cooksey in NCS (10) 1996, 136–8.

9701. SMITH, STEPHANIE A. Conceived by liberty: maternal figures and nineteenth-century American literature. (Bibl. 1994, 6866.) Rev. by Margit Stange in AL (68:2) 1996, 463–4.

9702. SOLLORS, WERNER; DIEDRICH, MARIA (eds). The Black Columbiad: defining moments in African-American literature and culture. (Bibl. 1995, 7.) Rev. by Malin Walther Pereira in MFS (42:4) 1996, 831–3; by David G. Nicholls in Modernism/Modernity (3:1) 1996, 160–2; by Wolfgang Karrer in AAR (30:4) 1996, 382–4.

9703. SUSSMAN, HERBERT. Victorian masculinities: manhood and masculine poetics in early Victorian literature and art. (Bibl. 1995, 8436.) Rev. by Billie Andrew Inman in Albion (28:1) 1996, 138–41; by Richard Cronin in NQ (43:1) 1996, 106–7; by Daniel Karlin in TLS, 5 Jan. 1996, 23.

9704. SWEETING, ADAM W. Reading houses and building books: Andrew Jackson Downing and the architecture of popular antebellum literature 1835–1855. Hanover, NH; London: New England UP, 1996. pp. x, 230. (Cf. bibl. 1995, 8437.)

9705. TANNER, TONY. Venice desired. (Bibl. 1995, 8439.) Rev. by Millicent Bell in Raritan (13:4) 1994, 124–45.

9706. TATSUMI, TAKAYUKI. New York no seikimatsu. (*Fin de siècle* in New York.) Tokyo: Chikuma Shobo, 1996. pp. 210.

9707. TILTON, ROBERT S. Pocahontas: the evolution of an American narrative. (Bibl. 1994, 6879.) Rev. by Karen Ordahl Kupperman in ALH (101:4) 1996, 1265–6; by Virginia Bernhard in GaHQ (80:2) 1996, 390–1.

9708. TOMIYAMA, TAKAO. Popeye no kageni – Souseki/ Faulkner/ bunkashi. (Behind Popeye: Souseki/Faulkner/cultural history.) Tokyo: Misuzu Shobo, 1996. pp. iv, 334.

9709. TSUBOI, KIYOHIKO; NISHIMAE, TAKASHI. America sakka to Europe. (American writers and Europe.) Tokyo: Eihosha, 1996. pp. 446.

9710. Van Wyk, Johan.   Identity and difference: some nineteenth-
and early twentieth-century South African texts. JLS (10:3/4) 1995,
302–17.

9711. Viswanathan, Gauri.   Masks of conquest: literary studies and
British rule in India. (Bibl. 1995, 8446.) Rev. by George Lang in
CanRCL (20:3/4) 1993, 552–6.

9712. Volk-Birke, Sabine.   *Cliffs of fall frightful*: Selbsterkenntnis und
Weltbild von Thomas Hardy bis Gerard Manley Hopkins. LJGG (37)
1996, 171–91.

9713. Wald, Priscilla.   Constituting Americans: cultural anxiety
and narrative form. Durham, NC; London: Duke UP, 1995. pp. xiv,
390. (New Americanists.) Rev. by Susan S. Williams in Prose Studies
(19:1) 1996, 119–21; by Lisa Ruddick in MFS (42:3) 1996, 652–6; by
Maggie Sale in AL (68:4) 1996, 855–6; by Kevin McCarron in
CritS (8:3) 1996, 346–7; by David Rogers in JAStud (30:1) 1996, 170.

9714. Walker, Nancy A.   A very serious thing: women's humor and
American culture. (Bibl. 1989, 5729.) Rev. by Eileen Gillooly in Feminist
Studies (17:3) 1991, 473–92.

9715. Wallace, Anne D.   Walking, literature, and English culture:
the origins and uses of peripatetic in the nineteenth century. (Bibl. 1995,
8448.) Rev. by Robin Jarvis in Literature and History (5:1) 1996, 113–14.

9716. Warren, Joyce W. (ed.).   The (other) American traditions:
nineteenth-century women writers. (Bibl. 1995, 38.) Rev. by Nancy A.
Walker in AmS (35:1) 1994, 170–1; by Janice Fiamengo in CanL (149)
1996, 130.

9717. Wasserman, Renata R. Mautner.   Exotic nations: literature
and cultural identity in the United States and Brazil, 1830–1930.
(Bibl. 1994, 6886.) Rev. by Earl E. Fitz in CLS (33:4) 1996, 423–7; by
Wayne Franklin in SAF (24:2) 1996, 237–8; by Luiz Fernando Valente
in ColLit (23:2) 1996, 197–9.

9718. Welch, Robert.   Changing states: transformation in modern
Irish writing. (Bibl. 1994, 6888.) Rev. by Jonathan Allison in YES (26)
1996, 316–17.

9719. West, James L. W., III.   The Chace Act and Anglo-American
literary relations. *See* **1030**.

9720. Wheeler, Michael.   Heaven, Hell, and the Victorians.
Cambridge; New York: CUP, 1994. pp. xv, 279, (plates) 14. (Abridged
ed. of bibl. 1995, 8454.) Rev. by Delia da Sousa Correa in NQ (43:1)
1996, 105–6.

9721. Whittemore, Reed.   Six literary lives: the shared impiety of
Adams, London, Sinclair, Williams, Dos Passos, and Tate. (Bibl. 1993,
6645.) Rev. by Susan M. Nuernberg in MFS (40:1) 1994, 152–3.

9722. Wilson, Carol Shiner; Haefner, Joel (eds).   Re-visioning
Romanticism: British women writers, 1776–1837. *See* **103**.

9723. Winterowd, W. Ross.   I. A. Richards, literary theory, and
Romantic composition. *See* **2496**.

9724. Yellin, Jean Fagan.   Women and sisters: the antislavery
feminists in American culture. (Bibl. 1993, 6650.) Rev. by Todd S.
Gernes in AAR (26:1) 1992, 189–92.

9725. Yoon, Hyonyung.   France hyeokmyoung eui nangman
jueuijeok hyeongsangwha. (The Romantic configuration of the
French Revolution.) *See* **8540**.

9726. YOUNG, ELIZABETH. Confederate counterfeit: the case of the cross-dressed Civil War soldier. *In* (pp. 181–216) **82**.

9727. YOUNGQUIST, PAUL. Romanticism, criticism, organicity. Genre (27:3) 1994, 183–208.

9728. ZONDERMAN, DAVID A. Labor history and the language of work. AmLH (8:2) 1996, 341–9 (review-article).

Drama and the Theatre

9729. ANDERSON, LISA M. From blackface to 'genuine Negroes': nineteenth-century minstrelsy and the icon of the 'Negro'. *See* **2853**.

9730. ANON. (ed.). Fushu kigeki no hen'you – ousei fukkoki kara Jane Austen made. (The metamorphosis of the comedy of manners: from the Restoration to Jane Austen.) *See* **7446**.

9731. ANTHONY, M. SUSAN. 'This sort of thing ... ': productions of gothic plays in America, 1790–1830. *See* **8542**.

9732. BAER, MARC. Theatre and disorder in late Georgian London. (Bibl. 1995, 8466.) Rev. by John Bohstedt in AHR (98:1) 1993, 162.

9733. BAKER, WILLIAM M. Captain R. Burton Deane and theatre on the Prairies, 1883–1901. TRC (14:1) 1993, 31–59.

9734. BANK, ROSEMARIE. Time, space, timespace, spacetime: theatre history in simultaneous universes. JDTC (5:2) 1991, 65–84.

9735. BIRD, KYM. Performing politics: propaganda, parody and a women's parliament. TRC (13:1/2) 1992, 168–93.

9736. BRYAN, GEORGE B.; MIEDER, WOLFGANG. 'As Sam Weller said, when finding himself on the stage': Wellerisms in dramatizations of Charles Dickens' *Pickwick Papers*. *See* **3314**.

9737. BURROUGHS, CATHERINE B. English Romantic women writers and theatre theory: Joanna Baillie's Prefaces to the *Plays on the Passions*. *In* (pp. 274–96) **103**.

9738. CAFARELLI, ANNETTE WHEELER. What will Mrs Grundy say? Women and comedy. Criticism (38:1) 1996, 69–83.

9739. CALIMANI, DARIO. Fuori dall'Eden: teatro inglese moderno. Venice: Cafoscarina, 1992. pp. 194. Rev. by Margaret Rose in YES (25) 320–1.

9740. CAMPBELL, DONALD. Playing for Scotland: a history of the Scottish stage, 1715–1965. *See* **8546**.

9741. CARLYON, DAVID. 'Blow your nose with your fingers': the rube story as crowd control. *See* **8549**.

9742. CASTO, MARILYN. Kentucky's Victorian theatres. KenR (13:1/2) 1996, 45–56.

9743. CHAUDHURI, UNA. Staging place: the geography of modern drama. (Bibl. 1995, 8472.) Rev. by Ginger Strand in JDTC (11:1) 1996, 144–7; by Stanton B. Garner, Jr, in Essays in Theatre (14:2) 1996, 175–7; by Cynthia Allan in NETJ (7) 1996, 109–11.

9744. CHOTHIA, JEAN. English drama of the early modern period, 1890–1940. London; New York: Longman, 1996. pp. xii, 336. (Longman literature in English.)

9745. COLLINS, KRIS. White-washing the Black-a-Moor: *Othello*, Negro minstrelsy and parodies of Blackness. *See* **7085**.

9746. COX, JEFFREY; COX, NANCY (eds). Seven gothic dramas, 1789–1825. *See* **8550**.

9747. COX, JEFFREY N. Staging hope: genre, myth, and ideology in the dramas of the Hunt circle. TSLL (38:3/4) 1996, 245–64.

9748. CURRY, J. K.   Petticoat governments: early women theatre managers in the United States. JADT (6:1) 1994, 13–39.

9749. CURRY, JANE KATHLEEN.   Nineteenth-century American women theatre managers. (Bibl. 1994, 6902.) Rev. by Kevin Neuharth in NETJ (6) 1995, 128–30.

9750. DAVIS, TRACY C.   Actresses as working women: their social identity in Victorian culture. (Bibl. 1993, 6664.) Rev. by Lesley Ferris in Signs (18:1) 1992, 162–72.

9751. EMELJANOW, VICTOR.   The nineteenth century: Victorian period: Victorian drama and theatre. YWES (75) 1994, 469–82.

9752. FINKEL, ALICIA.   Romantic stages: set and costume design in Victorian England. Jefferson, NC; London: McFarland, 1996. pp. viii, 207.

9753. FLETCHER, JILL.   The story of theatre in South Africa: a guide to its history from 1780–1930. *See* **8553**.

9754. FORT, TIM.   Three voyages of discovery: the Columbus productions of Imre Kiralfy, E. E. Rice, and Steele MacKaye. JADT (5:2) 1993, 5–30.

9755. GENTILE, JOHN S.   Cast of one: one-person shows from the Chautauqua platform to the Broadway stage. (Bibl. 1990, 5765.) Rev. by Stuart Lenig in JDTC (5:2) 1991, 228–32.

9756. HADLEY, ELAINE.   Melodramatic tactics: theatricalized dissent in the English marketplace, 1800–1885. (Bibl. 1995, 8482.) Rev. by Mark M. Hennelly, Jr, in DickQ (13:3) 1996, 178–82.

9757. HALL, ROGER (ed.).   Reminiscences. By Nate Salsbury. JADT (5:1) 1993, 3–99.

9758. HAMILTON, PAULA; DAICOFF, MARY JANE.   Late-Victorian ladies. TexPres (12) 1991, 35–48.

9759. HENDERSON, MARY C.   Theater in America: 250 years of plays, players, and productions. *See* **8554**.

9760. HIRSHFIELD, CLAIRE.   The actress as social activist: the case of Lena Ashwell. *In* (pp. 72–86) **87**.

9761. JENKINS, ANTHONY.   The making of Victorian drama. (Bibl. 1994, 6920.) Rev. by Dina M. Copelman in JBS (34:3) 1995, 420–1.

9762. JOHNSON, STEPHEN.   'Getting to' Canadian theatre history: on the tension between the new history and the nation state. TRC (13:1/2) 1992, 63–80.

9763. KAPLAN, JOEL H.; STOWELL, SHEILA.   Theatre and fashion: Oscar Wilde to the suffragettes. (Bibl. 1995, 8486.) Rev. by Ann Marie McEntee in JDTC (10:2) 1996, 152–4; by John Stokes in YES (26) 1996, 302–3.

9764. KING, W. D.   Henry Irving's Waterloo: theatrical engagements with Arthur Conan Doyle, George Bernard Shaw, Ellen Terry, Edward Gordon Craig: late Victorian culture, assorted ghosts, old men, war, and history. (Bibl. 1995, 8488.) Rev. by James Fisher in JDTC (9:2) 1995, 178–81; by Alan Filewod in Essays in Theatre (14:2) 1996, 179–81; by John Stokes in YES (26) 1996, 303–4.

9765. LARABEE, ANN.   Going through Harriet: ritual and theatre in the women's colleges. NETJ (3) 1992, 39–59.

9766. LAUTENBACH, CHARLES E.   Della Pringle: Western actress on Eastern stages. ATQ (10:3) 1996, 245–64.

9767. LeVay, John. Margaret Anglin: a stage life. Toronto: Simon & Pierre, 1989. pp. 326. Rev. by Herbert Whitaker in THC (11:1) 1990, 103–53.

9768. Lott, Eric. White kids and no kids at all: languages of race in antebellum US working-class culture. *In* (pp. 175–211) **100**.

9769. McConachie, Bruce A. Historicizing the production of meaning in the theatre. NETJ (4) 1993, 1–17.

9770. —— Melodramatic formations: American theatre and society, 1820–1870. (Bibl. 1995, 8493.) Rev. by David Grimsted in AHR (98:5) 1993, 1683–4; by Stephen M. Archer in AmDr (2:2) 1993, 104–7; by Loren Kruger in AmLH (8:4) 1996, 705–7.

9771. Mallett, Mark E. 'The game of politics': Edwin Forrest and the Jackson democrats. JADT (5:2) 1993, 31–46.

9772. Mann, David D.; Mann, Susan Garland; Garnier, Camille. Women playwrights in England, Ireland, and Scotland, 1660–1823. *See* **7500**.

9773. Mann, George. Theatre Lethbridge: a history of theatrical production in Lethbridge, Alberta (1885–1988). Calgary, Alta: Detselig, 1993. pp. 434. Rev. by Patrick B. O'Neill in TRC (16:1/2) 1995, 129–31.

9774. Marra, Kim. The 'sisterhood of sweetness and light': gender production in American acting styles and theatre historiography. JDTC (7:2) 1993, 193–201.

9775. Mason, Jeffrey D. Melodrama and the myth of America. (Bibl. 1995, 8495.) Rev. by David Grimstead in AmS (36:1) 1995, 180–1; by Loren Kruger in AmLH (8:4) 1996, 707–10; by Ray B. Browne in JAC (19:3) 1996, 130.

9776. Meserve, Walter J. Occupational hazards of the playwright during the age of Jackson. JADT (6:1) 1994, 5–12.

9777. Moody, Jane. 'Fine word, legitimate!': toward a theatrical history of Romanticism. TSLL (38:3/4) 1996, 223–44.

9778. Moylan, Christopher. The idea of therapeutic theater in English and German Romanticism. TexPres (14) 1993, 63–9.

9779. Noonan, James. Lord Lorne goes to the theatre, 1878–1883. THC (11:1) 1990, 29–47.

9780. O'Neill, Patrick B. Thomas Pope Besnard: less than enshrinement. TRC (14:2) 1993, 144–64.

9781. Saddlemyer, Ann (ed.). Early stages: theatre in Ontario 1800–1914. (Bibl. 1993, 6690.) Rev. by John Ripley in CanTR (72) 1992, 82–3.

9782. Shalom, Jack. The Ira Aldridge Troupe: early Black minstrelsy in Philadelphia. AAR (28:4) 1994, 653–8.

9783. Slout, William L. (ed.). Life upon the wicked stage: a visit to the American theatre of the 1860s, 1870s, and 1880s as seen in the pages of the *New York Clipper*. San Bernardino, CA: Borgo Press, 1996. pp. ix, 169. (Clipper studies in the theatre, 14.)

9784. Stephens, John Russell. The profession of the playwright: British theatre 1800–1900. (Bibl. 1994, 6946.) Rev. by Michael R. Booth in AHR (98:2) 1993, 492.

9785. Stephens, Judith L. Gender ideology and dramatic convention in Progressive Era plays, 1890–1920. *In* (pp. 283–93) **84**.

9786. Tanner, Jo A. Dusky maidens: the odyssey of the early Black dramatic actress. Westport, CT; London: Greenwood Press, 1992.

pp. xiii, 171. (Contributions in African-American and African studies, 156.) Rev. by Mary Jo Sodd in JDTC (8:2) 1994, 233–5.

9787. Wu, Duncan; Worrall, David.   The nineteenth century: Romantic period: poetry and drama. *See* **8851**.

Fiction

9788. Alexander, Lynn M.   Loss of the domestic idyll: shop workers in Victorian fiction. *In* (pp. 291–311) **54**.

9789. Allen, Dennis W.   Sexuality in Victorian fiction. (Bibl. 1995, 8509.) Rev. by Pamela K. Gilbert in StudN (27:2) 1995, 214–15.

9790. Ammons, Elizabeth.   Conflicting stories: American women writers at the turn into the twentieth century. (Bibl. 1994, 6953.) Rev. by Josephine Donovan in Signs (19:1) 1993, 232–5.

9791. —— White-Parks, Annette (eds).   Tricksterism in turn-of-the-century American literature: a multicultural perspective. Hanover, NH; London: UP of New England, 1994. pp. xiii, 201. Rev. by Barbara C. Rhodes in CLAJ (40:1) 1996, 116–18.

9792. Arata, Stephen.   Fictions of loss in the Victorian *fin de siècle*. Cambridge; New York: CUP, 1996. pp. xii, 235.

9793. Ardis, Ann L.   New women, new novels: feminism and early Modernism. (Bibl. 1995, 8512.) Rev. by Anne Herrmann in Signs (18:3) 1993, 727–31.

9794. Asker, D. B. D.   The modern bestiary: animals in English fiction, 1880–1945. Lewiston, NY; Lampeter: Mellen Press, 1996. pp. 202. (Studies in British literature, 24.)

9795. Atwood, Margaret; Weaver, Robert (eds).   The new Oxford book of Canadian short stories in English. Toronto; Oxford; New York: OUP, 1996. pp. xv, 462. Rev. by Joyce Carol Oates in TLS, 23 Feb. 1996, 24.

9796. Azim, Firdous.   The colonial rise of the novel. (Bibl. 1994, 6957.) Rev. by Sara Mills in LangL (4:2) 1995, 147–9.

9797. Baker, William; Womack, Kenneth.   The nineteenth century: Victorian period: the novel. YWES (75) 1994, 433–60.

9798. Banerjee, Jacqueline P.   Through the northern gate: childhood and growing up in British fiction, 1719–1901. *See* **8565**.

9799. Bardes, Barbara; Gossett, Suzanne.   Declarations of independence: women and political power in nineteenth-century American fiction. (Bibl. 1993, 6713.) Rev. by Nancy A. Walker in AmS (34:1) 1993, 169–70.

9800. Becker, Allienne R. (ed.).   Visions of the fantastic: selected essays from the Fifteenth International Conference of the Fantastic in the Arts. *See* **127**.

9801. Beene, LynnDianne.   Guide to British prose fiction explication: nineteenth and twentieth century. New York: G. K. Hall; London: Prentice Hall, 1996. pp. xlviii, 697. (Reference pubs in literature.)

9802. Beetz, Kirk H. (ed.).   Beacham's encyclopedia of popular fiction. Osprey, FL: Beacham, 1996. 11 vols. pp. xlvi, 7117.

9803. Bender, Bert.   The descent of love: Darwin and the theory of sexual selection in American fiction, 1871–1926. Philadelphia: Pennsylvania UP, 1996. pp. xvi, 440.

9804. Berman, Ruth.   Fantasy fiction and fantasy criticism in some nineteenth-century periodicals. *See* **1233**.

9805. Bloom, Harold (ed.).   Classic science fiction writers.

New York: Chelsea House, 1995. pp. xii, 186. (Writers of English.) Rev. by James Gunn in Utopian Studies (7:2) 1996, 219–21.

9806. Booth, Alison (ed.). Famous last words: changes in gender and narrative closure. Afterword by U. C. Knoepflmacher. *See* **31**.

9807. Bowers, Bege K.; Brothers, Barbara (eds). Reading and writing women's lives: a study of the novel of manners. *See* **96**.

9808. Brink, André. Reinventing a continent (revisiting history in the literature of the new South Africa: a personal testimony). WLT (70:1) 1996, 17–23.

9809. Brodhead, Richard H. Regionalism and the upper class. *In* (pp. 150–74) **100**.

9810. Brown, Julie (ed.). American women short-story writers: a collection of critical essays. *See* **3**.

9811. Budick, Emily Miller. Engendering romance: women writers and the Hawthorne tradition, 1850–1990. (Bibl. 1994, 6973.) Rev. by Ellen Weinauer in SoQ (34:1) 1995, 150–1.

9812. —— Nineteenth-century American romance: genre and the construction of democratic culture. New York: Twayne; London: Prentice Hall, 1996. pp. xiii, 186. (Twayne's studies in literary themes and genres, 8.)

9813. Butler, Marilyn. Editing women. *See* **596**.

9814. Campbell, Ian. Glossing (glossing). *See* **2594**.

9815. Champagne, Rosaria. The politics of survivorship: incest, women's literature, and feminist theory. New York: New York UP, 1996. pp. x, 246.

9816. Childers, Joseph W. Novel possibilities: fiction and the formation of early Victorian culture. Philadelphia: Pennsylvania UP, 1995. pp. 218. (New cultural studies.) Rev. by F.S. in TLS, 10 May 1996, 31.

9817. Clarke, I. F. (ed.). The tale of the next Great War, 1871–1914: fictions of future warfare and of battles still-to-come. Liverpool: Liverpool UP, 1995. pp. xiv, 382. (Liverpool science fiction texts and studies, 7.) Rev. by Chris N. Gilmore in Foundation (66) 1996, 114–19.

9818. Cohen, William A. Sex scandal: the private parts of Victorian fiction. Durham, NC; London: Duke UP, 1996. pp. x, 256. (Q.) (Cf. bibl. 1994, 6982.)

9819. Cohen-Steiner, Olivier. Le regard de l'autre: le juif dans le roman anglais 1800–1900. Nancy: Presses Universitaires de Nancy, 1994. pp. 288.

9820. Connor, Steven. Reading: the *contretemps*. YES (26) 1996, 232–48.

9821. Cunningham, Valentine. In the reading gaol: postmodernity, texts, and history. (Bibl. 1994, 6986.) Rev. by Edward Neill in EC (46:2) 1996, 186–93.

9822. Davis, Robert Murray. Playing cowboys: low culture and high art in the Western. (Bibl. 1995, 8536.) Rev. by Jim Healey in MidAF (23:1) 1995, 62–3.

9823. DeCicco, Lynne Marie. Women and lawyers in the mid-nineteenth century English novel: uneasy alliances and narrative misrepresentation. Lewiston, NY; Lampeter: Mellen Press, 1996. pp. 334. (Studies in British literature, 25.) (Cf. bibl. 1992, 8406.)

9824. DeLamotte, Eugenia C. Perils of the night: a feminist study of nineteenth-century gothic. (Bibl. 1994, 6992.) Rev. by Timmel

Duchamp in Signs (17:4) 1992, 848–52; by Laurie Aikman in CanL (150) 1996, 107–9.

9825. DEN TANDT, CHRISTOPHE.   Amazons and androgynes: over-civilization and the redefinition of gender roles at the turn of the century. AmLH (8:4) 1996, 639–64.

9826. DiBATTISTA, MARIA.   The lowly art of murder: Modernism and the case of the free woman. *In* (pp. 176–93) **41**.

9827. DICKERSON, VANESSA D.   Angels, money, and ghosts: Victorian female writers of the supernatural. *In* (pp. 87–98) **37**.

9828. ——— Victorian ghosts in the noontide: women writers and the supernatural. Columbia; London: Missouri UP, 1996. pp. ix, 166.

9829. ——— (ed.).   Keeping the Victorian house: a collection of essays. *See* **54**.

9830. DIEDRICH, MARIA.   Aufschrei der Frauen – Diskurs der Männer: der frühviktorianische Industrieroman. (Bibl. 1992, 7521.) Rev. by H. Gustav Klaus in ZAA (41:2) 1993, 180–2.

9831. DIXON, ROBERT.   Writing the colonial adventure: race, gender, and nation in Anglo-Australian popular fiction, 1875–1914. (Bibl. 1995, 8542.) Rev. by Richard Phillips in Eng (45:183) 1996, 259–62; by V.S. in TLS, 15 Mar. 1996, 33.

9832. EAGLETON, TERRY.   Form and ideology in the Anglo-Irish novel. *In* (pp. 135–46) **60**.

9833. ENGLER, BERND; MÜLLER, KURT (eds).   Historiographic meta-fiction in modern American and Canadian literature. (Bibl. 1994, 38.) Rev. by Gabriele Helms in CanL (151) 1996, 161–3; by Thomas Irmer in ZAA (44:3) 1996, 281–3; by Ewald Mengel in PoetA (28:1/2) 1996, 243–53.

9834. ENSOR, ALLISON R.   In search of nineteenth-century Tennessee fiction: beyond Mary Noailles Murfree. TPB (32) 1995, 38–47.

9835. FASICK, LAURA.   God's house, women's place. *In* (pp. 75–103) **54**.

9836. FELTES, N. N.   Literary capital and the late Victorian novel. (Bibl. 1995, 8550.) Rev. by John L. Kijinski in CLIO (25:1) 1995, 106–10.

9837. FIELDING, PENNY.   Writing and orality: nationality, culture, and nineteenth-century Scottish fiction. Oxford: Clarendon Press; New York: OUP, 1996. pp. xii, 251. Rev. by Ina Ferris in SLJ (supp. 45) 1996, 26–30.

9838. FINE, DAVID; SKENAZY, PAUL (eds).   San Francisco in fiction: essays in a regional literature. *See* **108**.

9839. FLINT, KATE (ed.).   Victorian love stories: an Oxford anthology. Oxford; New York: OUP, 1996. pp. xiv, 501. Rev. by Lindsay Duguid in TLS, 13 Dec. 1996, 25.

9840. FOX, PAMELA.   Class fictions: shame and resistance in the British working-class novel, 1890–1945. (Bibl. 1994, 7003.) Rev. by Peter Hitchcock in MFS (42:4) 1996, 867–70; by Pat Wheeler in CritS (8:1) 1996, 120–1.

9841. FURST, LILIAN R.   All is true: the claims and strategies of Realist fiction. (Bibl. 1995, 8557.) Rev. by Henry B. Wonham in AL (68:4) 1996, 860–1.

9842. GARCÍA LANDA, JOSÉ ÁNGEL.   Nivel narrativo, status, persona y typología de las narraciones. *See* **8579**.

9843. GARVEY, ELLEN GRUBER.   The adman in the parlor: magazines and the gendering of consumer culture, 1880s to 1910s. *See* **1270**.

9844. —— Representations of female authorship in turn-of-the-century American magazine fiction. *In* (pp. 85–98) **3**.

9845. GEPPERT, HANS VILMAR. Der realistische Weg: Formen pragmatischen Erzählens bei Balzac, Dickens, Hardy, Keller, Raabe und anderen Autoren des 19. Jahrhunderts. Tübingen: Niemeyer, 1994. pp. xi, 712. (Communicatio, 5.) Rev. by Markus Heilmann in arcadia (30:1) 1995, 72–6.

9846. GESSNER-UTSCH, BETTINA. Subjektiver Roman: Studien zum Verhältnis von fiktionalen Subjektivitäts- und Wirklichkeits-konzeptionen in England vom 18. Jahrhundert bis zum Modernismus. *See* **8580**.

9847. GINSBURG, MICHAL PELED. Economies of change: form and transformation in the nineteenth-century novel. Stanford, CA: Stanford UP, 1996. pp. xii, 251.

9848. GOLDEN, KENNETH L. Science fiction, myth, and Jungian psychology. Lewiston, NY; Lampeter: Mellen Press, 1995. pp. iii, 251.

9849. GONDA, CAROLINE. Reading daughters' fictions, 1709–1834: novels and society from Manley to Edgeworth. *See* **8581**.

9850. GORDON, JAN B. Gossip and subversion in nineteenth-century British fiction: Echo's economies. Basingstoke: Macmillan; New York: St Martin's Press, 1996. pp. xiv, 444.

9851. GORDON, SARAH BARRINGER. 'Our national hearthstone': anti-polygamy fiction and the sentimental campaign against moral diversity in antebellum America. YJLH (8:2) 1996, 295–350.

9852. GREENE, J. LEE. Blacks in Eden: the African-American novel's first century. Charlottesville; London: Virginia UP, 1996. pp. x, 306.

9853. GREENFIELD, JOHN R. (ed.). British short-fiction writers, 1800–1880. Detroit, MI; London: Gale Research, 1996. pp. xv, 402. (Dictionary of literary biography, 159.)

9854. GREENSLADE, WILLIAM. Degeneration, culture, and the novel, 1880–1940. (Bibl. 1995, 8563.) Rev. by Pierre Coustillas in GissJ (32:1) 1996, 32–5; by Nicola Bradbury in YES (26) 1996, 297–8.

9855. GRIFFIN, SUSAN M. Awful disclosures: women's evidence in the escaped nun's tale. PMLA (111:1) 1996, 93–107.

9856. GRIXTI, JOSEPH. Terrors of uncertainty: the cultural contexts of horror fiction. (Bibl. 1993, 6763.) Rev. by Stan Beeler in CanRCL (19:3) 1992, 449–53.

9857. GROSH, RONALD M. Provincialism and cosmopolitanism: a re-assessment of early Midwestern realism. MidM (21) 1993, 9–18.

9858. GUNN, JAMES. The worldview of science fiction. Extrapolation (36:2) 1995, 91–5.

9859. GUY, JOSEPHINE M. The Victorian social-problem novel: the market, the individual and communal life. Basingstoke: Macmillan; New York: St Martin's Press, 1996. pp. x, 238.

9860. HAGGERTY, GEORGE E. Gothic fiction/gothic form. (Bibl. 1994, 7020.) Rev. by Elizabeth Jane Wall Hinds in Genre (23:1) 1990, 71–2.

9861. HALBERSTAM, JUDITH. Skin shows: gothic horror and the technology of monsters. *See* **8584**.

9862. HALL, DONALD E. Fixing patriarchy: feminism and mid-Victorian male novelists. Basingstoke: Macmillan; New York: New York UP, 1996. pp. ix, 236.

9863. HALTUNEN, KAREN. Early American murder narratives: the birth of horror. *In* (pp. 67–101) **88**.

9864. HANSON, CLARE. The lifted veil: women and short fiction in the 1880s and 1890s. YES (26) 1996, 135–42.

9865. HAPGOOD, LYNNE. 'The reconceiving of Christianity': secularisation, realism and the religious novel, 1888–1900. LitTheol (10:4) 1996, 329–50.

9866. HAPKE, LAURA. Tales of the working girl: wage-earning women in American literature, 1890–1925. (Bibl. 1995, 8565.) Rev. by David A. Zonderman in AmLH (8:2) 1996, 343–5.

9867. HARMAN, BARBARA LEAH; MEYER, SUSAN (eds). The new nineteenth century: feminist readings of underread Victorian fiction. *See* **75**.

9868. HARPER, MARJORY. Adventure or exile? The Scottish emigrant in fiction. SLJ (23:1) 1996, 21–32.

9869. HARRIS, SHARON M. (ed.). Redefining the political novel: American women writers, 1797–1901. *See* **99**.

9870. HARRIS, SUSAN K. 19th-century American women's novels: interpretative strategies. (Bibl. 1993, 6768.) Rev. by Nancy A. Walker in AmS (34:1) 1993, 169–70.

9871. HAYWOOD, IAN (ed.). The literature of struggle: an anthology of Chartist fiction. Aldershot: Scolar Press; Brookfield, VT: Ashgate, 1995. pp. vi, 212. (Nineteenth century.) Rev. by Gregory Claeys in Utopian Studies (7:2) 1996, 268–9.

9872. HENNING, MARTHA L. Beyond understanding: appeals to the imagination, passions, and will in mid-nineteenth-century American women's fiction. New York; Frankfurt; Bern; Paris: Lang, 1996. pp. 205. (American univ. studies, XXIV: American literature, 65.) (Cf. bibl. 1994, 9172.)

9873. HEYNS, MICHIEL. Expulsion and the nineteenth-century novel: the scapegoat in English realist fiction. (Bibl. 1995, 8572.) Rev. by Frank McCombie in NQ (43:1) 1996, 109–10.

9874. HIRONO, YUMIKO. 19 seiki igirisu shousetsu no gihou. (Techniques in nineteenth-century English fiction.) Tokyo: Eihosha, 1996. pp. 432.

9875. HOLMES, JOHN. Inheritance and marriage in the nineteenth-century novel. ERev (6:4) 1996, 38–41.

9876. HOLMSTRÖM, LAKSHMI. A note on Indian short stories. JSSE (24) 1995, 13–22.

9877. HORSMAN, ALAN. The Victorian novel. (Bibl. 1993, 6776.) Rev. by Andrew Sanders in Eng (40:167) 1991, 168–74.

9878. HUBEL, TERESA. Whose India? The independence struggle in British and Indian fiction and history. London: Leicester UP; Durham, NC: Duke UP, 1996. pp. x, 234. (Cf. bibl. 1993, 10499.)

9879. HUBER, WERNER. Irish novels in a German court library of the early 19th century. *In* (pp. 37–44) **49**.

9880. INGHAM, PATRICIA. Language of gender and class: transformation in the Victorian novel. London; New York: Routledge, 1996. pp. ix, 197.

9881. INNESS, SHERRIE. Girls will be boys and boys will be girls: cross-dressing in popular turn-of-the-century college fiction. JAC (18:2) 1995, 15–23.

9882. IWASE, SHITSU; KAMOGAWA, TAKAHIRO; SUGA, YUKAKO (eds). Kakusareta ishou – eibeisakka no motif to souzou. (Concealed designs:

motifs and creation of English and American writers.) Tokyo:
Nan'undo, 1996. pp. 346.

9883. JENKINS, RUTH Y. Reclaiming myths of power: women writers
and the Victorian spiritual crisis. (Bibl. 1995, 8579.) Rev. by Charlotte
Crofts in Gaskell Society Journal (10) 1996, 108–10.

9884. JONES, ROGER WALTON. Larry McMurtry and the Victorian
novel. (Bibl. 1994, 7041.) Rev. by Roger C. Lewis in ANQ (9:3) 1996,
61–4.

9885. KANE, PENNY. Victorian families in fact and fiction. (Bibl. 1995,
8587.) Rev. by S.Z. in TLS, 5 Jan. 1996, 28.

9886. KAUL, SUVIR. Colonial figures and postcolonial reading.
See **2410**.

9887. KEARNS, KATHERINE. Nineteenth-century literary Realism:
through the looking-glass. Cambridge; New York: CUP, 1996. pp. x,
308.

9888. KENNEDY, ANDREW; ØVERLAND, ORM (eds). Excursions in
fiction: essays in honour of Professor Lars Hartveit on his 70th birthday. (Bibl. 1994, 27.) Rev. by T. A. Birrell in EngS (76:2) 1995, 206–8.

9889. KESSLER, CAROL FARLEY (ed.). Daring to dream: utopian
fiction by United States women before 1950. Syracuse, NY:
Syracuse UP, 1995. pp. xxviii, 326. (Utopianism and communitarian-
ism.) Rev. by Naomi Jacobs in Utopian Studies (7:2) 1996, 276–8.

9890. KETTERER, DAVID. Canadian science fiction and fantasy.
(Bibl. 1995, 8591.) Rev. by Stan Beeler in CanRCL (20:1/2) 1993, 271–4.

9891. KEYMER, THOMAS. Dying by numbers: *Tristram Shandy* and
serial fiction: 1. *See* **954**.

9892. KIELY, ROBERT. Reverse tradition: postmodern fictions and
the nineteenth-century novel. (Bibl. 1995, 8593.) Rev. by Gabriele
Helms in CanL (148) 1996, 155; by Clara Tuite in AUMLA (86) 1996,
121–2.

9893. KRANIDIS, RITA S. Subversive discourse: the cultural produc-
tion of late Victorian feminist novels. (Bibl. 1995, 8601.) Rev. by Claudia
Nelson in Albion (28:1) 1996, 144–5; by LuAnn McCracken Fletcher in
ELT (39:3) 1996, 363–6.

9894. KRASNER, JAMES. The entangled eye: visual perception and the
representation of nature in post-Darwinian narrative. (Bibl. 1995, 8602.)
Rev. by Gary Willingham-McLain in MFS (40:1) 1994, 203–4.

9895. KUCICH, JOHN. The power of lies: transgression in Victorian
fiction. (Bibl. 1995, 8603.) Rev. by Deirdre Coleman in AUMLA (85)
1996, 161–2; by Christine L. Krueger in Criticism (38:2) 1996, 335–8.

9896. KULLMANN, THOMAS. Vermenschlichte Natur: zur Bedeutung
von Landschaft und Wetter im englischen Roman von Ann Radcliffe
bis Thomas Hardy. *See* **8592**.

9897. LATHAM, ROBERT A.; COLLINS, ROBERT A. (eds). Modes of the
fantastic: selected essays from the Twelfth International Conference on
the Fantastic in the Arts. *See* **70**.

9898. LEE, HERMIONE (introd.). The secret self: a century of
short stories by women. (Bibl. 1995, 8604.) Rev. by Katy Emck in
TLS, 5 Jan. 1996, 20.

9899. LEE, HSIAO-HUNG. Possibilities of hidden things: narrative
transgression in Victorian fictional autobiographies. New York;
Frankfurt; Bern; Paris: Lang, 1996. pp. xiii, 178. (Studies in nineteenth-
century British literature, 5.)

9900. Leveson, Marcia.   People of the book: images of the Jew in South African English fiction 1880–1992. Johannesburg: Witwatersrand UP, 1996. pp. xiii, 277.

9901. Levy, Andrew.   The culture and commerce of the American short story. (Bibl. 1995, 8605.) Rev. by Donald D. Kummings in AL (68:1) 1996, 281–2; by Edward Margolies in EngS (77:3) 1996, 296–7; by Janet Beer Goodwyn in YES (26) 1996, 325–6.

9902. Levy, Helen Fiddyment.   Fiction of the home-place: Jewett, Cather, Glasgow, Porter, Welty, and Naylor. (Bibl. 1995, 8606.) Rev. by M. J. McLendon in AmS (34:1) 1993, 170–1.

9903. Lewes, Darby.   Dream revisionaries: gender and genre in women's utopian fiction, 1870–1920. (Bibl. 1995, 8608.) Rev. by Duangrudi Suksang in Utopian Studies (7:2) 1996, 292–6.

9904. Lund, Michael.   America's continuing story: an introduction to serial fiction, 1850–1900. (Bibl. 1994, 7063.) Rev. by Scott Peeples in AmP (3) 1993, 114–15.

9905. McClain, Larry.   The rhetoric of regional representation: American fiction and the politics of cultural dissent. Genre (27:3) 1994, 227–53.

9906. McCormack, W. J.   'Never put your name to an anonymous letter': serial reading in the *Dublin University Magazine*, 1861 to 1869. *See* **1311**.

9907. Machor, James L.   Poetics as ideological hermeneutics: American fiction and the historicized reader of the early nineteenth century. *See* **1314**.

9908. MacKethan, Lucinda H.   Daughters of time: creating woman's voice in Southern story. (Bibl. 1995, 8612.) Rev. by Rebecca Mark in Signs (18:2) 1993, 443–7.

9909. McMullen, Lorraine; Campbell, Sandra (eds).   Aspiring women: short stories by Canadian women, 1880–1900. (Bibl. 1995, 8613.) Rev. by Janice Fiamengo in CanL (149) 1996, 129–30.

9910. Malchow, H. L.   Gothic images of race in nineteenth-century Britain. Stanford, CA: Stanford UP, 1996. pp. xii, 335.

9911. Melnick, Daniel C.   Fullness of dissonance: modern fiction and the aesthetics of music. (Bibl. 1994, 7072.) Rev. by Judith Barban in Comparatist (20) 1996, 190–2.

9912. Mendes, Peter.   Clandestine erotic fiction in English, 1800–1930: a bibliographic study. (Bibl. 1994, 7073.) Rev. by A. S. G. Edwards in BC (43:3) 1994, 446–7.

9913. Meyer, Susan.   Imperialism at home: race and Victorian women's fiction. Ithaca, NY; London: Cornell UP, 1996. pp. x, 220. (Reading women writing.)

9914. Miles, Robert.   The nineteenth century: Romantic period: fictional prose. YWES (75) 1994, 407–20.

9915. Minter, David.   A cultural history of the American novel: Henry James to William Faulkner. (Bibl. 1995, 8628.) Rev. by Michael Kreyling in ColLit (23:2) 1996, 195–7.

9916. Monk, Leland.   Standard deviations: chance and the modern British novel. (Bibl. 1995, 8630.) Rev. by Brian Richardson in MFS (40:2) 1994, 397–9; by Timothy Morris in StudN (27:4) 1995, 584–6.

9917. Morris, Virginia B.   Double jeopardy: women who kill in Victorian fiction. (Bibl. 1993, 6830.) Rev. by Nicole H. Rafter in Signs (18:2) 1993, 469–71.

9918. Moss, Elizabeth.   Domestic novelists in the Old South: defenders of Southern culture. (Bibl. 1995, 8635.) Rev. by Jan Lewis in AHR (99:1) 1994, 300; by Shirley A. Leckie in FHQ (72:4) 1994, 500–1.

9919. Mullen, Bill.   'A revolutionary tale': in search of African-American women's short-story writing. *In* (pp. 191–207) **3**.

9920. Munk, Erika.   Exiled from nowhere. Theater (26:1/2) 1995, 101–11.

9921. Murphy, Martin.   The Spanish *Waverley*: Blanco White and *Vargas*. Atlantis (17:1/2) 1995, 165–80.

9922. Natoli, Joseph.   Meditating on a postmodern strategy of reading. YES (26) 1996, 260–6.

9923. Nelson, Carolyn Christensen.   British women fiction writers of the 1890s. New York: Twayne; London: Prentice Hall, 1996. pp. xii, 115. (Twayne's English authors, 533.)

9924. Nord, Deborah Epstein.   Walking the Victorian streets: women, representation, and the city. Ithaca, NY; London: Cornell UP, 1995. pp. xiii, 270.

9925. Nunokawa, Jeff.   The afterlife of property: domestic security and the Victorian novel. (Bibl. 1995, 8641.) Rev. by Kathy Alexis Psomiades in Signs (21:2) 1996, 463–6; by Kathleen Sell in WS (25:6) 1996, 637–9.

9926. Orel, Harold.   The historical novel from Scott to Sabatini: changing attitudes toward a literary genre, 1814–1920. (Bibl. 1995, 8644.) Rev. by Bob Irvine in SLJ (supp. 45) 1996, 30–2.

9927. Parker, David.   Ethics, theory and the novel. (Bibl. 1994, 7087.) Rev. by Elizabeth Patnoe in MFS (42:1) 1996, 243–7; by Rikky Rooksby in NQ (43:1) 1996, 117–18; by Steven Connor in TLS, 5 Jan. 1996, 24–5; by Christian Moraru in StudN (28:4) 1996, 607–10.

9928. Pettengill, Claire C.   Against novels: Fanny Fern's newspaper fiction and the reform of print culture. *See* **1340**.

9929. Presley, John Woodrow.   *Finnegans Wake, Lady Pokingham,* and Victorian erotic fantasy. JPC (30:3) 1996, 67–80. (Joyce and the *Pearl*.)

9930. Price Herndl, Diane.   Invalid women: figuring feminine illness in American fiction and culture, 1840–1940. (Bibl. 1995, 8654.) Rev. by Jane E. Przybysz in JAF (109:431) 1996, 97–9.

9931. Pringle, David.   Imaginary people: a who's who of fictional characters from the eighteenth century to the present day. *See* **8603**.

9932. Pykett, Lyn (ed.).   Reading *fin de siècle* fictions. London; New York: Longman, 1996. pp. x, 241. (Longman critical readers.)

9933. Rehberger, Dean.   Vulgar fiction, impure history: the neglect of historical fiction. JAC (18:4) 1995, 59–65.

9934. Richter, David H.   The progress of romance: literary historiography and the gothic novel. *See* **8606**.

9935. Riffaterre, Michael.   Fictional truth. (Bibl. 1994, 7104.) Rev. by Uri Margolin in CanRCL (19:1/2) 1992, 101–17.

9936. Rivalain, Odile Boucher.   From 'literary insignificancies' to 'the sacredness of the writer's art': aspects of fiction criticism in the *Westminster Review*, 1824–1857. *See* **1350**.

9937. Robillard, Douglas (ed.).   American supernatural fiction: from Edith Wharton to the weird tales writers. New York; London; Garland, 1996. pp. xi, 263. (Garland reference library of the humanities, 1855.) (Garland studies in nineteenth-century American literature, 6.)

9938. Rowbotham, Judith.   Good girls make good wives: guidance for girls in Victorian fiction. (Bibl. 1991, 7165.) Rev. by Anne Chandler and Deborah K. Chappel in Signs (18:3) 1993, 674–8.

9939. SAINSBURY, ALISON.   Married to the Empire: the Anglo-Indian domestic novel. *In* (pp. 163–87) **132**.

9940. SAMUELS, SHIRLEY.   Romances of the Republic: women, the family, and violence in the literature of the early American nation. *See* **7542**.

9941. SANDERS, VALERIE.   Eve's renegades: Victorian anti-feminist women novelists. Basingstoke: Macmillan; New York: St Martin's Press, 1996. pp. ix, 249.

9942. SCHEICK, WILLIAM J.   Fictional structure and ethics: the turn-of-the-century English novel. (Bibl. 1991, 7169.) Rev. by Dwight H. Purdy in Conradiana (28:3) 1996, 230–3.

9943. SCHENKEL, ELMAR.   Cyclomanie: Fahrrad und Literatur um 1900. LJGG (37) 1996, 211–28.

9944. SCHOLNICK, JOSHUA DAVID.   Democrats abroad: Continental literature and the American bard in *United States Magazine and Democratic Review*. *See* **1354**.

9945. SCHWARZ, DANIEL R.   The transformation of the English novel, 1890–1930. (Bibl. 1993, 6859.) Rev. by Mark A. Wollaeger in Conradiana (28:2) 1996, 153–7.

9946. SEDGWICK, EVE KOSOFSKY.   Epistemology of the closet. (Bibl. 1993, 6860.) Rev. by John L. Kijinski in Review (16) 1994, 41–61.

9947. SEED, DAVID (ed.).   Anticipations: essays on early science fiction and its precursors. (Bibl. 1995, 5.) Rev. by Arthur B. Evans in Utopian Studies (7:1) 1996, 144–5.

9948. SHARPE, JENNY.   Allegories of empire: the figure of woman in the colonial text. (Bibl. 1995, 8667.) Rev. by Moira Ferguson in MFS (40:2) 1994, 443–4; by Glenda A. Hudson in StudN (27:4) 1995, 591–3; by Suvir Kaul in Diacritics (26:1) 1996, 83–7.

9949. SHUTTLEWORTH, SALLY.   'Preaching to the nerves': psychological disorder in sensation fiction. *In* (pp. 192–222) **94**.

9950. SINGH, G. (ed.).   Collected essays by Q. D. Leavis: vol. 3, The novel of religious controversy. (Bibl. 1995, 8674.) Rev. by M. B. Kinch in ModAge (34:3) 1992, 266–70.

9951. SMALL, HELEN.   Love's madness: medicine, the novel, and female insanity, 1800–1865. Oxford: Clarendon Press; New York: OUP, 1996. pp. x, 260. (Cf. bibl. 1992, 7644.) Rev. by Fiona Stafford in TLS, 9 Aug. 1996, 23.

9952. STERNE, RICHARD CLARK.   Dark mirror: the sense of injustice in modern European and American literature. (Bibl. 1994, 7124.) Rev. by Linda Myrsiades in ColLit (23:1) 1996, 204–16.

9953. STEWART, GARRETT.   Dear reader: the conscripted audience in nineteenth-century British fiction. Baltimore, MD; London: Johns Hopkins UP, 1996. pp. viii, 454.

9954. —— Reading figures: the legible image of Victorian textuality. *In* (pp. 345–67) **126**.

9955. SULLIVAN, LARRY E.; SCHURMAN, LYDIA CUSHMAN (eds). Pioneers, passionate ladies, and private eyes: dime novels, series books, and paperbacks. *See* **1014**.

9956. SUTHERLAND, JOHN.   Is Heathcliff a murderer? Great puzzles in nineteenth-century literature. Oxford; New York: OUP, 1996. pp. x, 258. (World's classics.) Rev. by John Bayley in LRB (18:18) 1996,

20–1; by Simon Jarvis in TLS, 19 July 1996, 25.

9957. Swingle, L. J. Dismantling the master's house. Review (17) 1995, 109–21 (review-article).

9958. Sypher, Eileen. Wisps of violence: producing public and private politics in the turn-of-the-century British novel. (Bibl. 1995, 8685.) Rev. by Marianne DeKoven in MFS (40:2) 1994, 399–400; by Michael Tratner in StudN (28:2) 1996, 244–53.

9959. Tallack, Douglas. The nineteenth-century American short story: language, form, and ideology. (Bibl. 1995, 8686.) Rev. by Aribert Schroeder in Amst (41:3) 1996, 520; by Janet Beer Goodwyn in CritS (8:1) 1996, 137–8; by Kevin McCarron in YES (26) 1996, 324–5.

9960. Tate, Claudia. Domestic allegories of political desire: the Black heroine's text at the turn of the century. (Bibl. 1995, 8687.) Rev. by Frances Richardson Keller in AHR (99:2) 1994, 667; by Michele Birnbaum in StudN (27:2) 1995, 236–8; by Sandra Gunning in AAR (29:1) 1995, 126–9; by the same in Signs (21:2) 1996, 455–9.

9961. Thompson, Jon. Fiction, crime, and empire: clues to modernity and postmodernism. (Bibl. 1995, 8689.) Rev. by Paul Matthew St Pierre in CanL (148) 1996, 185.

9962. Thompson, Nicola Diane. Reviewing sex: gender and the reception of Victorian novels. Basingstoke: Macmillan; Washington Square, NY: New York UP, 1996. pp. ix, 164. (Cf. bibl. 1992, 8152.)

9963. Tibbetts, John C. Phantom fighters: 150 years of occult detection. AD (29:3) 1996, 340–5.

9964. Toda, Hitoshi. Igirisu bungaku to shinwa. (English literature and myths.) *See* **6855**.

9965. Tompkins, Jane. West of everything: the inner life of Westerns. (Bibl. 1995, 8691.) Rev. by Sarah Markgraf in Genre (25:2/3) 1992, 315–19; by Edward Buscombe in JFV (47:1/3) 1995, 124–30.

9966. Tötösy de Zepetnek, Steven. The social dimensions of fiction: on the rhetoric and function of prefacing novels in the nineteenth-century Canadas. Brunswick: Vieweg, 1993. pp. xi, 188. (Systemic and empirical approach to literature, 15.) Rev. by Mary Lu MacDonald in CanL (148) 1996, 164–5; by James Steele in ESCan (22:1) 1996, 117–19.

9967. Trotter, David. The English novel in history, 1895–1920. (Bibl. 1995, 8692.) Rev. by Ian Haywood in CritS (8:3) 1996, 340–2; by Kate Flint in YES (26) 1996, 306–7; by Paul Goetsch in Archiv (233:2) 1996, 411–12.

9968. Van Gorp, Hendrik. Problems of comparative reception studies: the case of the gothic novel (1790–1825). *See* **8616**.

9969. van Wyk Smith, Malvern. Grounds of contest: a survey of South African English literature. (Bibl. 1991, 7199.) Rev. by David van Wyk in JLS (10:3/4) 1994, 437–49.

9970. Villa, Luisa. La forma del nuovo: donne, decadenza, modernità, e la *short story* inglese di fine secolo. QLLSM (7) 1995, 107–32.

9971. Volkmann, Laurenz. Wildnis und Zivilisation: britische Romanschriftsteller des späten 19. und des 20. Jahrhunderts und das internationale Thema. (Bibl. 1994, 7142.) Rev. by Klaus Börner in ZAA (41:3) 1993, 276–8.

9972. Vrettos, Athena. Somatic fictions: imagining illness in Victorian culture. (Bibl. 1995, 8696.) Rev. by John Maynard in Albion (28:3) 1996, 514–15; by Sally Shuttleworth in Isis (87:4) 1996, 740–1.

9973. WAGENKNECHT, EDWARD.   Seven masters of supernatural fiction. Westport, CT; London: Greenwood Press, 1991. pp. vii, 210. (Contributions to the study of science fiction and fantasy, 46.) (Algernon Blackwood, Marjorie Bowen, Walter de la Mare, Henry James, M. R. James, Sheridan Le Fanu, Arthur Machen.)

9974. WARD, MARYANNE C.   Romancing the ending: adaptations in nineteenth-century closure. JMMLA (29:1) 1996, 15–31.

9975. WARWICK, ALEXANDRA.   Vampires and the Empire: fears and fictions of the 1890s. In (pp. 202–20) **18**.

9976. WATSON, RITCHIE DEVON, JR.   Yeoman *versus* cavalier: the Old Southwest's fictional road to rebellion. (Bibl. 1995, 8702.) Rev. by Philip Dubuisson Castille in StudN (28:1) 1996, 135–7.

9977. WEEKES, ANN OWENS.   Irish women writers: an uncharted tradition. (Bibl. 1995, 8703.) Rev. by Suzann Bick in AR (49:3) 1991, 467.

9978. WEINSTEIN, ARNOLD.   Nobody's home: speech, self, and place in American fiction from Hawthorne to DeLillo. (Bibl. 1995, 8705.) Rev. by Irving Malin in MFS (40:3) 1994, 385–6; by Rosemarie A. Battaglia in StudN (27:2) 1995, 240–3.

9979. WEINSTEIN, CINDY.   The literature of labor and the labors of literature: allegory in nineteenth-century American fiction. (Bibl. 1995, 8706.) Rev. by Larry J. Reynolds in AL (68:4) 1996, 856–7; by Kevin McCarron in CritS (8:3) 1996, 345–6; by Val Gough in JAStud (30:1) 1996, 161–2.

9980. WEYLER, KAREN A.   'A speculating spirit': trade, speculation, and gambling in early American fiction. *See* **8618**.

9981. WIEHAHN, RIALETTE.   Comparative reception studies of the gothic novel. *See* **8619**.

9982. WILLIAMS, MADAWC.   Tales of wonder: science fiction and fantasy in the age of Jane Austen. Mythlore (21:2) 1996, 419–30.

9983. WILSON, CHRISTOPHER PIERCE.   White-collar fictions: class and social representation in American literature, 1885–1925. (Bibl. 1995, 8709.) Rev. by Gerald Hong in AmS (35:2) 1994, 143.

9984. WINNIFRITH, TOM.   Fallen women in the nineteenth-century novel. (Bibl. 1995, 8711.) Rev. by Pamela K. Gilbert in StudN (27:4) 1995, 595–6.

9985. WOLF, WERNER.   Angst und Schrecken als Attraktion: zu einer gender-orientierten Funktionsgeschichte des englischen Schauerromans im 18. und frühen 19. Jahrhundert. *See* **8622**.

Literature for Children

9986. ALDERSON, BRIAN.   Some notes on James Burns as a publisher of children's books. *See* **883**.

9987. ALLEN, MARJORIE N.   One hundred years of children's books in America: decade by decade. Foreword by Jane Yolen. New York: Facts on File, 1996. pp. xxvi, 420.

9988. CASTLE, KATHRYN.   Britannia's children: reading colonialism through children's books and magazines. Manchester: Manchester UP; New York: St Martin's Press, 1996. pp. viii, 198. (Studies in imperialism.)

9989. DROTNER, KIRSTEN.   English children and their magazines, 1751–1945. *See* **1263**.

9990. Keller, Holly. Juvenile antislavery narrative and notions of childhood. ChildLit (24) 1996, 86–100.

9991. Khorana, Meena (ed.). British children's writers, 1800–1880. Detroit, MI; London: Gale Research, 1996. pp. xx, 428. (Dictionary of literary biography, 163.)

9992. Kidd, Kenneth. Farming for boys: boyology and the professionalization of boy work. CLAQ (20:4) 1995/96, 148–54.

9993. MacLeod, Anne Scott. American childhood: essays on children's literature of the nineteenth and twentieth centuries. (Bibl. 1995, 8719.) Rev. by Susan R. Gannon in CLAQ (21:3) 1996, 142–4.

9994. Marten, James. For the good, the true, and the beautiful: Northern children's magazines and the Civil War. *See* **1319**.

9995. Miller, Miriam Youngerman. 'Thy speech is strange and uncouth': language in the children's historical novel of the Middle Ages. *See* **2676**.

9996. Rahn, Suzanne. The changing language of Black child characters in American children's books. *In* (pp. 225–58) **48**.

9997. Reynolds, Kimberley. Children's literature in the 1890s and the 1990s. (Bibl. 1995, 8733.) Rev. by Adam Piette in EEM (4:2) 1995, 70–1.

9998. —— Girls only? Gender and popular children's fiction in Britain, 1880–1910. (Bibl. 1990, 6017.) Rev. by Anne Chandler and Deborah K. Chappel in Signs (18:3) 1993, 674–8.

9999. Sandner, David. The fantastic sublime: Romanticism and transcendence in nineteenth-century children's fantasy literature. Westport, CT; London: Greenwood Press, 1996. pp. vi, 160. (Contributions to the study of science fiction and fantasy, 69.)

10000. Thompson, Hilary. Enclosure and childhood in the wood engravings of Thomas and John Bewick. *See* **251**.

10001. West, Máire. Kings, heroes and warriors: aspects of children's literature in Ireland in the era of emergent nationalism. BJRL (76:3) 1994, 165–84.

Poetry

10002. Armstrong, Isobel. Caterpillar on the skin. *See* **8630**.

10003. —— Victorian poetry: poetry, poetics, and politics. (Bibl. 1995, 8738.) Rev. by Julian Wolfreys in AEB (9:1/2) 1995, 79–82; by Jennifer A. Wagner in ANQ (9:1) 1996, 51–4.

10004. Bain, Robert (ed.). Whitman's & Dickinson's contemporaries: an anthology of their verse. Carbondale: Southern Illinois UP, 1996. pp. xxxiv, 555. Rev. by Ed Folsom in WWQR (13:4) 1996, 226–8.

10005. Beer, John. Fragmentations and ironies. *In* (pp. 234–64) **95**.

10006. —— (ed.). Questioning Romanticism. *See* **95**.

10007. Behrendt, Stephen C. Anthologizing British women poets of the Romantic period: the scene today. CritM (9:1) 1995, 94–105 (review-article).

10008. Bennett, Paula. Lesbian poetry in the United States, 1890–1990: a brief overview. *In* (pp. 98–110) **92**.

10009. Bentley, D. M. R. Mimic fires: accounts of early long poems on Canada. (Bibl. 1994, 7175.) Rev. by Tim Heath in CanL (149) 1996, 141–2.

10010. Berger, Dieter A. Die Parodie in der Dichtung der englischen Romantik. (Bibl. 1992, 7703.) Rev. by Sabine Volk-Birke in GRM (44:1) 1994, 116–18.

10011. BLACKMER, CORINNE E.   Writing poetry like a 'woman'. AmLH (8:1) 1996, 130–53 (review-article).

10012. Boos, FLORENCE S.   William Morris, Robert Bulwer-Lytton, and the Arthurian poetry of the 1850s. Arthuriana (6:3) 1996, 31–53.

10013. BRADY, PATRICK.   Rococo poetry in English, French, German, Italian: an introduction. *See* **7548**.

10014. BURWICK, FREDERICK.   Poetic madness and the Romantic imagination. *See* **8638**.

10015. CARUTH, CATHY.   An interview with Geoffrey Hartman. SR (35:4) 1996, 631–52.

10016. COELSCH-FOISNER, SABINE.   Fidelity (and infidelity) in the work of the Pre-Raphaelites. Imaginaires (Reims, France) (1) 1996, 91–107.

10017. COOPER, ALLENE.   Science and the reception of poetry in postbellum American journals. AmP (4) 1994, 24–46.

10018. COSSLETT, TESS (ed.).   Victorian women poets. London; New York: Longman, 1996. pp. x, 286. (Longman critical readers.)

10019. Cox, PHILIP.   Gender, genre, and the Romantic poets: an introduction. *See* **8640**.

10020. D'AVANZO, MARIO L.   A cloud of other poets: Robert Frost and the Romantics. (Bibl. 1992, 7716.) Rev. by Stephen Hahn in RFR (1994) 112–15.

10021. DIEHL, JOANNE FEIT.   Women poets and the American sublime. (Bibl. 1993, 6934.) Rev. by Bonnie Kime Scott in Signs (18:2) 1993, 485–9.

10022. EGAN, KEN, JR.   The machine in the poem: nineteenth-century American poetry and technology. WebS (12:1) 1995, 70–81.

10023. ELAM, HELEN REGUEIRO.   Introduction. SR (35:4) 1996, 491–507. (Geoffrey Hartman's criticism.)

10024. ELDRIDGE, RICHARD (ed.).   Beyond representation: philosophy and poetic imagination. *See* **3805**.

10025. ENGEL, BERNARD F.   A splendid little imperialist war. Midamerica (19) 1992, 48–60.

10026. ERSKINE-HILL, HOWARD.   The poetry of opposition and revolution: Dryden to Wordsworth. *See* **7555**.

10027. FINKELSTEIN, NORMAN.   Statement and commentary. DQ (30:4) 1996, 84–104.

10028. FRANCIS, EMMA.   The nineteenth century: Victorian period: poetry. YWES (75) 1994, 460–9.

10029. FREDMAN, STEPHEN.   The grounding of American poetry: Charles Olson and the Emersonian tradition. (Bibl. 1995, 8756.) Rev. by Roger Gilbert in AmLH (8:2) 1996, 350–63.

10030. FULFORD, TIM.   Landscape, liberty and authority: poetry, criticism and politics from Thomson to Wordsworth. *See* **8645**.

10031. GILBERT, ROGER.   The dream of a common poetry. AmLH (8:2) 1996, 350–63 (review-article).

10032. GLAZER, LEE; KEY, SUSAN.   Carry me back: nostalgia for the Old South in nineteenth-century popular culture. JAStud (30:1) 1996, 1–24. (Popular ballads.)

10033. GOODSON, A. C.   Romantic theory and the critique of language. *In* (pp. 3–28) **95**.

10034. HAEFNER, JOEL. The Romantic scene(s) of writing. *In* (pp. 256–73) **103**.

10035. HOLLANDER, JOHN (ed.). American poetry: the nineteenth century: vol. 1, Freneau to Whitman; vol. 2, Melville to Stickney, American Indian poetry, folk songs and spirituals. (Bibl. 1994, 7202.) Rev. by William H. Pritchard in ASch (63:2) 1994, 302–6; by David Lehman in BkW, 26 Dec. 1996, 1, 11.

10036. JONES, RACHEL. 'All that fame hath cost …': the response to fame of British women poets from 1770 to 1835. *See* **8654**.

10037. KANE, PAUL (ed.). Poetry of the American renaissance: a diverse anthology from the Romantic period. New York: Braziller, 1995. pp. 383. Rev. by Ed Folsom in WWQR (13:4) 1996, 226–8.

10038. KORTE, BARBARA. Sehweisen literarischer Landschaft – ein Literaturbericht. *See* **8655**.

10039. KURTZ, RICHARD L. Occasional verse as history. NCLR (5) 1996, 187.

10040. LEIGHTON, ANGELA; REYNOLDS, MARGARET (eds). Victorian women poets: an anthology. Oxford; Cambridge, MA: Blackwell, 1995. pp. xl, 691. (Blackwell anthologies.) Rev. by Peter Keating in TLS, 26 Jan. 1996, 27.

10041. MCGANN, JEROME. The poetics of sensibility: a revolution in literary style. Oxford: Clarendon Press; New York: OUP, 1996. pp. x, 217. Rev. by Matthew Reynolds in TLS, 27 Dec. 1996, 11–12.

10042. MANNING, PETER J. Reading Romantics: texts and contexts. (Bibl. 1993, 6964.) Rev. by Mark Hollis Parker in Text (Ann Arbor) (8) 1995, 427–32.

10043. METZGER, LORE. One foot in Eden: modes of pastoral in Romantic poetry. (Bibl. 1989, 5981.) Rev. by John Jay Baker in Genre (23:1) 1990, 73–5.

10044. MORASH, CHRIS. Spectres of the Famine. Irish Review (17/18) 1995, 74–9.

10045. NEWLYN, LUCY. 'Reading after': the anxiety of the writing subject. SR (35:4) 1996, 609–30.

10046. NIEMEYER, MARC. The transatlantic cable in popular poetry. *In* (pp. 227–36) **117**.

10047. OKKER, PATRICIA. Sarah Josepha Hale, Lydia Sigourney, and the poetic tradition in two nineteenth-century women's magazines. *See* **1335**.

10048. PITE, RALPH. The circle of our vision: Dante's presence in English Romantic poetry. (Bibl. 1995, 8778.) Rev. by Esther Schor in KSJ (45) 1996, 222–4.

10049. PROCHÁZKA, MARTIN. Romantismus a osobnost: subjektivita v anglické romantické poezii a estetice. (Romanticism and personality: subjectivity in English Romantic poetry and aesthetics.) Pardubice: Mlejnková, 1996. pp. 278.

10050. REID, IAN. The instructive imagination: English with tears. *In* (pp. 241–64) **47**.

10051. REILLY, CATHERINE W. Late Victorian poetry, 1880–1899: an annotated biobibliography. (Bibl. 1994, 7224.) Rev. by Edwin Gilcher in ELT (39:2) 1996, 270–2.

10052. RIEDE, DAVID G., *et al.* Guide to the year's work in Victorian poetry: 1995 and 1996. VP (34:4) 1996, 559–621.

10053. ROWLAND, WILLIAM G., JR. Literature and the marketplace:

Romantic writers and their audiences in Great Britain and the United States. Lincoln; London: Nebraska UP, 1996. pp. xiii, 230.

10054. Roy, G. Ross.   Poems and songs spuriously attributed to Robert Burns. *See* **8660**.

10055. Scholnick, Joshua David.   Democrats abroad: Continental literature and the American bard in *United States Magazine and Democratic Review*. *See* **1354**.

10056. Schwab, Ulrike.   The poetry of the Chartist Movement: a literary and historical study. (Bibl. 1994, 7228.) Rev. by John Belchem in EHR (111:441) 1996, 503–4.

10057. Spiegelman, Willard.   Majestic indolence: English Romantic poetry and the work of art. (Bibl. 1995, 8785.) Rev. by J. Douglas Kneale in Criticism (38:4) 1996, 648–50.

10058. Stevenson, Warren.   Romanticism and the androgynous sublime. Madison, NJ: Fairleigh Dickinson UP; London; Toronto: Assoc. UPs, 1996. pp. 153.

10059. Tamura, Einosuke.   Genjitsu no shigaku – roman-ha to gendaishi. (Poetics of illusion and reality: Romantic and modern poetry.) Tokyo: Fumikura Shobo, 1996. pp. 314.

10060. Taylor, Andrew.   A case of Romantic disinheritance. *In* (pp. 185–201) **47**.

10061. Wagner, Jennifer Ann.   A moment's monument: revisionary poetics and the nineteenth-century English sonnet. Madison, NJ: Fairleigh Dickinson UP; London; Toronto: Assoc. UPs, 1996. pp. 254. (Cf. bibl. 1991, 7302.) Rev. by Earl J. Wilcox in RFR (1996) 99–100.

10062. Walker, Jeffrey.   Bardic ethos and the American epic poem: Whitman, Pound, Crane, Williams, Olson. (Bibl. 1995, 8792.) Rev. by M. Wynn Thomas in WWQR (9:1) 1991, 30–2; by James E. Miller, Jr, in WWQR (9:1) 1991, 36–44; by Daniel Wright in AmS (32:1) 1991, 122.

10063. Wolfson, Susan J.   Romanticism and the question of poetic form. *In* (pp. 133–54) **95**.

10064. Wu, Duncan; Worrall, David.   The nineteenth century: Romantic period: poetry and drama. *See* **8851**.

Prose

10065. Allen, Beverly Bishop.   'The writingest explorers': manuscripts of the Lewis and Clark Expedition. GateH (16:1) 1995/96, 32–9.

10066. Bach, Evelyn.   A traveller in skirts: quest and conquest in the travel narratives of Isabella Bird. CanRCL (22:3/4) 1995, 587–600.

10067. Bell, Allan.   Munificent, wise and thoughtful gifts: Grace and Peter Redpath and the Redpath Tracts. *See* **453**.

10068. Bergmann, Linda S.   A troubled marriage of discourses: science writing and travel narrative in Louis and Elizabeth Agassiz's *A Journey in Brazil*. JAC (18:2) 1995, 83–8.

10069. Blake, Dale.   Women of Labrador: realigning North from the site(s) of *métissage*. ECanW (59) 1996, 164–81. (Accounts of Labrador by Lydia Campbell, Margaret Baikie, Elizabeth Goudie.)

10070. Bohls, Elizabeth A.   Women travel writers and the language of aesthetics, 1716–1818. *See* **8666**.

10071. Bonta, Marcia Myers (ed.).   American women afield: writings by pioneering women naturalists. College Station: Texas A&M

Univ., 1995. pp. xvi, 248. (Louise Lindsey Merrick natural environment series, 20.) Rev. by Sally Gregory Kohlstedt in Isis (87:2) 1996, 376–7.

10072. BROOMFIELD, ANDREA; MITCHELL, SALLY (eds).   Prose by Victorian women: an anthology. New York; London: Garland, 1996. pp. xv, 729. (Garland reference library of the humanities, 1893.)

10073. BROTHERS, BARBARA; GERGITS, JULIA (eds).   British travel writers, 1837–1875. Detroit, MI; London: Gale Research, 1996. pp. xix, 437. (Dictionary of literary biography, 166.)

10074. BROWN, SUSAN.   Alternatives to the missionary position: Anna Leonowens as Victorian travel writer. Feminist Studies (21:3) 1995, 587–614.

10075. BRYDEN, INGA.   The nineteenth century: Victorian period: cultural studies and prose. YWES (75) 1994, 424–33.

10076. CHRISTOPHER, ROBERT.   Narrators of the Arctic: images and movements in Northland narratives. ARCS (18:3) 1988, 259–69.

10077. CLAUSEN, CHRISTOPHER.   How to join the middle classes, with the help of Dr Smiles and Mrs Beeton. ASch (62:3) 1993, 403–18.

10078. COLLIS, CHRISTY.   The voyage of the episteme: narrating the North. ECanW (59) 1996, 26–45. (Sir John Franklin and Arctic exploration writing.)

10079. CONNOR, KIMBERLY RAE.   *To Disembark*: the slave narrative tradition. AAR (30:1) 1996, 35–57.

10080. DAGENAIS, JULIA.   Frontier preaching as formulaic poetry. *See* **2345**.

10081. DAVIS, R.   History or his/story? The explorer cum author. StudCanL (16:2) 1991/92, 93–111.

10082. FAVRET, MARY A.   War correspondence: reading Romantic war. *See* **1264**.

10083. FINKELSTEIN, DAVID.   Breaking the thread: the authorial re-invention of John Hanning Speke in his *Journal of the Discovery of the Source of the Nile*. *See* **641**.

10084. FLYNN, PHILIP.   Enlightened Scotland: a study and selection of Scottish philosophical prose from the eighteenth and early nineteenth centuries. *See* **8675**.

10085. FRAWLEY, MARIA H.   A wider range: travel writing by women in Victorian England. (Bibl. 1994, 7246.) Rev. by Johanna M. Smith in TSWL (15:1) 1996, 152–5.

10086. FREESE, PETER.   'Westward the Course of Empire takes its Way': the *translatio*-concept in popular American writing and painting. *See* **8676**.

10087. GRAHAM, LESLEY.   Belittling Scotland: Scottish travellers in France in the nineteenth century. Études Écossaises (supp.) 1994, 137–49.

10088. —— Écossais, Anglais ou Britanniques? Les voyageurs écossais en France au XIXe siècle et la nationalité écossaise. Études Écossaises (2) 1993, 155–64.

10089. GREENFIELD, BRUCE.   Two nineteenth-century exploration accounts: what are we discovering in 1990? ARCS (20:4) 1990, 473–81 (review-article).

10090. GREWAL, INDERPAL.   Home and harem: nation, gender, empire, and the cultures of travel. London: Leicester UP; Durham, NC: Duke UP, 1996. pp. 286.

10091. HALDANE, KATHERINE J.   'No human foot comes here': Victorian tourists and the Isle of Skye. NCS (10) 1996, 69–91.

10092. HAPGOOD, LYNNE.   Urban utopias: socialism, religion and the city, 1880 to 1900. *In* (pp. 184–201) **18**.

10093. HULAN, RENÉE.   Literary field notes: the influence of ethnography on representations of the North. ECanW (59) 1996, 147–63.

10094. JACOBSON, DAN.   Dr Livingstone, he presumed. ASch (63:1) 1994, 96–101.

10095. JASKOSKI, HELEN.   Andrew Blackbird's smallpox story. Genre (25:4) 1992, 339–49.

10096. JONES, ALED.   Powers of the press: newspapers, power and the public in nineteenth-century England. *See* **1295**.

10097. McCASKILL, BARBARA.   'Yours very truly': Ellen Craft – the fugitive as text and artifact. AAR (28:4) 1994, 509–29.

10098. MAYNARD, JOHN.   Victorian discourses on sexuality and religion. (Bibl. 1995, 8815.) Rev. by John Schad in LitTheol (10:2) 1996, 196–7.

10099. MICHEL, ROBERT.   Diaries from the McGill University Archives – a sampling. Fontanus (5) 1992, 33–53.

10100. MORGAN, SUSAN.   Place matters: gendered geography in Victorian women's travel books about Southeast Asia. New Brunswick, NJ: Rutgers UP, 1996. pp. xi, 345. Rev. by Joyce Zonana in TSWL (15:2) 1996, 369–71.

10101. Moss, CAROLYN J. (ed.).   Kate Field: selected letters. Carbondale: Southern Illinois UP, 1996. pp. xxxii, 255.

10102. PAQUET, SANDRA POUCHET.   The heartbeat of a West Indian slave: *The History of Mary Prince*. AAR (26:1) 1992, 131–46.

10103. PETERSON, CARLA L.   'Doers of the word': African-American women speakers and writers in the North (1830–1880). (Cf. bibl. 1995, 8823, where title incorrect.) Rev. by Adrienne Lash Jones in NWSAJ (8:3) 1996, 172–4; by Joycelyn K. Moody in TSWL (15:2) 1996, 352–5; by Sarah Robbins in SAF (24:2) 1996, 238–40; by Angelo Costanzo in AL (68:2) 1996, 474–5.

10104. RILEY, SAM G. (ed.).   American magazine journalists, 1741–1850. *See* **1347**.

10105. ——   American magazine journalists, 1850–1900. *See* **1348**.

10106. ROBINSON, AMY.   Authority and the public display of identity: *Wonderful Adventures of Mrs Seacole in Many Lands*. Feminist Studies (20:3) 1994, 537–57.

10107. ROSENBERG, BRUCE.   The African-American sermon and literary tradition. Review (18) 1996, 157–63 (review-article).

10108. ROY, PARAMA.   Discovering India, imagining *thuggee*. YJC (9:1) 1996, 121–45.

10109. SCHRIBER, MARY SUZANNE (ed.).   Telling travels: selected writings by nineteenth-century American women abroad. (Bibl. 1995, 8827.) Rev. by Paola Gemme in Legacy (13:2) 1996, 161–2.

10110. STOWE, STEVEN M.   Seeing themselves at work: physicians and the case narrative in the mid-nineteenth-century American South. AHR (101:1) 1996, 41–79.

10111. STOWE, WILLIAM W.   Going abroad: European travel in nineteenth-century American culture. (Bibl. 1995, 8831.) Rev. by Waldemar Zacharasiewicz in Amst (41:4) 1996, 711–14; by M. H. Dunlop in ALH (101:4) 1996, 1276–7; by Peter Carafiol in SAtlR (61:2) 1996, 135–40.

10112. Thévenot, Marie-Hélène. Des côtes d'Écosse aux côtes d'Amérique du Nord: l'odyssée des émigrants écossais aux xviiie et xixe siècles. *See* **8708**.

10113. Tingley, Stephanie A. 'A letter is a joy of earth': Emily Dickinson's letters and Victorian epistolary conventions. EDJ (5:2) 1996, 202–8.

10114. Tiro, Karim M. Denominated *'SAVAGE'*: Methodism, writing, and identity in the works of William Apess, a Pequot. AmQ (48:4) 1996, 653–79.

10115. Vallorani, Nicoletta. Thomas Huxley e lo sguardo del testimone: ossessione visiva, scienza e racconto alla fine dell'800. Textus (8:1) 1995, 109–25.

10116. Weinauer, Ellen M. 'A most respectable looking gentleman': passing, possession, and transgression in *Running a Thousand Miles for Freedom*. *In* (pp. 37–56) **82**.

10117. Whale, John. The nineteenth century: Romantic period: non-fictional prose. YWES (75) 1994, 402–7.

10118. Wolf, James. A woman passing through: Helen Caddick and the maturation of the Empire in British Central Africa. JPC (30:3) 1996, 35–55.

10119. Youngs, Tim. Travellers in Africa: British travelogues, 1850–1900. (Bibl. 1995, 8840.) Rev. by Patrick Brantlinger in ELT (39:2) 1996, 247–50; by David Finkelstein in SLJ (supp. 45) 1996, 33–5.

10120. Zlotnick, Susan. Domesticating imperialism: curry and cookbooks in Victorian England. Frontiers (16:2) 1996, 51–68.

Biography and Autobiography

10121. Accardo, Annalucia. Resistenza, autorità e autorappresentazione nel'autobiografia delle donne nere prima della guerre civile. Àcoma (3) 1995, 14–23.

10122. Andrews, William L. Booker T. Washington, Belle Kearney, and the Southern patriarchy. *In* (pp. 85–97) **43**.

10123. —— The representation of slavery and the rise of Afro-American literary realism 1865–1920. *In* (pp. 77–89) **1**.

10124. Babener, Liahna. The romance of suffering: Midwesterners remember the homestead. Midamerica (22) 1995, 25–34.

10125. Bassard, Katherine Clay. Gender and genre: Black women's autobiography and the ideology of literacy. AAR (26:1) 1992, 119–29.

10126. Bell, Peter (comp.). Victorian biography: a checklist of contemporary biographies of British men and women dying between 1851 and 1901. Introd. by Colin Matthew. Edinburgh: Bell, 1993. pp. 193. Rev. by J. O. Baylen in ELT (39:4) 1996, 523–5.

10127. Bellamy, Joan. Mary Taylor, Ellen Nussey and Brontë biography. BST (21:7) 1996, 275–83.

10128. Bigham, Shauna. What the slaves were really saying: race, signification, and the deconstruction of WPA slave narratives. Griot (15:2) 1996, 22–9.

10129. Bonta, Marcia Myers (ed.). American women afield: writings by pioneering women naturalists. *See* **10071**.

10130. Carby, Hazel V. 'Hear my voice, careless daughters': narratives of slave and free women before Emancipation. *In* (pp. 59–76) **1**.

10131. CLARKE, PATRICIA. Life lines: 19th-century women's letters and diaries. Australian Folklore (11) 1996, 152–8.

10132. CRANE, ELAINE FORMAN (ed.). The diary of Elizabeth Drinker: vol. 1, 1758–1795; vol. 2, 1796–1802; vol. 3, 1803–1807. *See* **8714**.

10133. DUDLEY, DAVID L. My father's shadow: intergenerational conflict in African-American men's autobiography. (Bibl. 1994, 7275.) Rev. by John Sekora in AAR (28:3) 1994, 473–9.

10134. FERGUSON, SALLYANN H. Christian violence and the slave narrative. *See* **8715**.

10135. FITZPATRICK, DAVID. Oceans of consolation: personal accounts of Irish migration to Australia. (Bibl. 1995, 8853.) Rev. by D. George Boyce in Irish Review (19) 1996, 136–8.

10136. GAGNIER, REGENIA. Subjectivities: a history of self-representation in Britain, 1832–1920. (Bibl. 1994, 7277.) Rev. by Dina M. Copelman in JBS (34:3) 1995, 413–15.

10137. GITTER, ELISABETH G. The rhetoric of reticence in John Forster's *Life of Charles Dickens*. DSA (25) 1996, 127–39.

10138. HAMILTON, CYNTHIA S. Revisions, rememories and exorcisms: Toni Morrison and the slave narrative. JAStud (30:3) 1996, 429–45.

10139. HASSAM, ANDREW. Sailing to Australia: shipboard diaries by nineteenth-century British emigrants. (Bibl. 1995, 8860.) Rev. by William R. Jones in Eng (45:182) 1996, 163–6.

10140. HAYNES, CAROLYN. 'A mark for them all to ... hiss at': the formation of Methodist and Pequot identity in the conversion narrative of William Apess. EAL (31:1) 1996, 25–44.

10141. HOLMES, KENNETH L. (ed.). Covered wagon women: diaries and letters from the Western trails: vol. 1, 1840–1849. Lincoln; London: Nebraska UP, 1995. pp. 280. (Orig. pub. 1983.) Rev. by Peter Blake in TLS, 31 May 1996, 11.

10142. HUMEZ, JEAN M. In search of Harriet Tubman's spiritual autobiography. NWSAJ (5:2) 1993, 162–82.

10143. —— Reading *The Narrative of Sojourner Truth* as a collaborative text. Frontiers (16:1) 1996, 29–52.

10144. JUNCKER, CLARA. Behind Confederate lines: Sarah Morgan Dawson. *In* (pp. 16–30) **65**.

10145. NEUMAN, SHIRLEY. Introduction: reading Canadian auto-biography. ECanW (60) 1996, 1–13.

10146. PAQUET, SANDRA POUCHET. West Indian autobiography. *In* (pp. 196–211) **1**.

10147. PARKER, PAMELA CORPRON. Good women, good works: Victorian philanthropy and women's biography. Cresset (59:6) 1996, 17–21.

10148. PETERSON, CARLA L. Secular and sacred space in the spiritual autobiographies of Jarena Lee. *In* (pp. 37–59) **97**.

10149. SABIN, MARGERY. The suttee romance. Raritan (11:2) 1991, 1–24. (Sir William Henry Sleeman's memoirs.)

10150. SIRRIDGE, MARJORIE S.; PFANNENSTIEL, BRENDA R. Daughters of Æsculapius: a selected bibliography of autobiographies of women medical school graduates 1849–1920. LitMed (15:2) 1996, 200–16.

Related Studies

10151. BARBLAN, PAOLO. Les avatars de l'art et du discours sur l'art: de Poe aux nouvelles avant-gardes. New York; Frankfurt; Bern; Paris:

Lang, 1995. pp. 264. (European univ. studies, xx: Philosophy, 464.)
Rev. by Claudia Becker in arcadia (31:1/2) 1996, 333–5.

10152. BOURKE, ANGELA. Reading a woman's death: colonial text and oral tradition in nineteenth-century Ireland. Feminist Studies (21:3) 1995, 553–86.

10153. CARRÉ, JACQUES (ed.). The crisis of courtesy: studies in the conduct-book in Britain, 1600–1900. *See* **7625**.

10154. CASTERAS, SUSAN P. James Smetham: artist, author, Pre-Raphaelite associate. Aldershot: Scolar Press; Brookfield, VT: Ashgate, 1995. pp. xi, 193. Rev. by Christopher Kent in Albion (28:2) 1996, 337–8.

10155. —— Seeing the unseen: pictorial problematics and Victorian images of class, poverty, and urban life. *In* (pp. 264–88) **126**.

10156. CIVARDI, CHRISTIAN. L'histoire et la littérature revisitées par la contre-culture du mouvement ouvrier. Études Écossaises (1) 1992, 283–91.

10157. CLINTON, CATHERINE. Tara revisited: women, war & the plantation legend. New York: Abbeville Press, 1995. pp. 240. Rev. by Steven M. Stowe in GaHQ (80:1) 1996, 191–2.

10158. CORNICK, MARTYN. The impact of the Dreyfus Affair in late-Victorian Britain. Franco-British Studies (22) 1996, 57–82.

10159. DONALD, DIANA. The age of caricature: satirical prints in the reign of George III. *See* **8735**.

10160. FULCHER, JONATHAN. The loyalist response to the Queen Caroline agitations. JBS (34:4) 1995, 481–502.

10161. GAVIN, J. Westmorland literary institutions to 1850. *See* **8736**.

10162. GERARD, JESSICA. The chatelaine: women of the Victorian landed classes and the country house. *In* (pp. 175–206) **54**.

10163. HABEGGER, ALFRED. The father: a life of Henry James, Sr. New York: Farrar, Straus, & Giroux, 1994. pp. viii, 578. Rev. by Linda Simon in ASch (64:3) 1995, 459–61.

10164. HOBBS, CATHERINE (ed.). Nineteenth-century women learn to write. Charlottesville; London: Virginia UP, 1995. pp. xv, 343. (Feminist issues.) Rev. by Lisa Hammond Rashley in SAtlR (61:3) 1996, 156–9.

10165. HOMANS, MARGARET. Victoria's sovereign obedience: portraits of the Queen as wife and mother. *In* (pp. 169–97) **126**.

10166. JENKINS, RUTH Y. Rewriting female subjection: Florence Nightingale's revisionist myth of *Cassandra*. WebS (11:1) 1994, 16–26.

10167. JONES, W. GARETH (ed.). Tolstoi and Britain. Oxford; Washington, DC: Berg, 1995. pp. xii, 303. (Anglo-Russian affinities.) Rev. by Rachel Polonsky in TLS, 4 Oct. 1996, 13.

10168. KIFT, DAGMAR. The Victorian music hall: culture, class, and conflict. Trans. by Roy Kift. Cambridge; New York: CUP, 1996. pp. x, 244. (Updated and revised trans. of *Arbeiterkultur im gesellschaftlichen Konflikt*, Essen: Klartext, 1991.)

10169. LEMAY, J. A. LEO. The origins of the humor of the Old South. SoLJ (23:2) 1991, 3–13.

10170. LINK-HEER, URSULA. Doppelgänger und multiple Persönlich-keiten: eine Faszination der Jahrhundertwende. arcadia (31:1/2) 1996, 273–96.

10171. MATSUMURA, MASAIE, *et al.* (eds). Jouo heika no jidai. (The days of the queen.) Tokyo: Kenkyusha Shuppan, 1996. pp. viii, 240. (Eikoku bunka no seiki, 3.) (Century of British culture, 3.)

10172. —— Minshuu no bunkashi. (Records of popular culture.) Tokyo: Kenkyusha Shuppan, 1996. pp. viii, 240. (Eikoku bunka no seiki, 4.) (Century of British culture, 4.)

10173. —— Teikoku shakai no shoshou. (Aspects of imperial society.) Tokyo: Kenkyusha Shuppan, 1996. pp. viii, 242. (Eikoku bunka no seiki, 2.) (Century of British culture, 2.)

10174. OPPENHEIM, JANET. A mother's role, a daughter's duty: Lady Blanche Balfour, Eleanor Sidgwick, and feminist perspectives. JBS (34:2) 1995, 196–232.

10175. PERKINS, MAUREEN. Visions of the future: almanacs, time, and cultural change, 1775–1870. *See* **8749**.

10176. PINGREE, ALLISON. America's 'United Siamese Brothers': Chang and Eng and nineteenth-century ideologies of democracy and domesticity. *In* (pp. 92–114) **72**.

10177. SÁNCHEZ-EPPLER, KAREN. Raising empires like children: race, nation, and religious education. AmLH (8:3) 1996, 399–425.

10178. SAPPOL, MICHAEL. Sammy Tubbs and Dr Hubbs: anatomical dissection, minstrelsy, and the technology of self-making in post-bellum America. Configurations (4:2) 1996, 131–83.

10179. SEGAL, HOWARD P. Future imperfect: the mixed blessings of technology in America. Amherst: Massachusetts UP, 1994. pp. xviii, 245. Rev. by Philip Abbott in Utopian Studies (7:2) 1996, 330–1.

10180. STEIN, RICHARD L. Secret figures: Victorian urban iconography. *In* (pp. 233–63) **126**.

10181. SZASZ, FERENC M. Homer and the myth of the American West. JWest (35:3) 1996, 3–6.

10182. TARVER, J. Abridged editions of Blair's *Lectures on Rhetoric and Belles Lettres* in America: what nineteenth-century college students really learned about Blair on rhetoric. *See* **1018**.

10183. TAUSCH, HARALD. Vom Bild der Natur zum imaginären Bilderbogen der Vergangenheit: Hermann von Pückler-Muskaus *Andeutungen über Landschaftsgärtnerei* und die Literarisierung des englischen Landschaftsgartens. *See* **8754**.

10184. TORRES, LUIS A. Bilingualism as satire in nineteenth-century Chicano poetry. *In* (pp. 247–62) **80**.

10185. VALLONE, LYNNE. Disciplines of virtue: girls' culture in the eighteenth and nineteenth centuries. *See* **8757**.

10186. ZBORAY, RONALD J.; ZBORAY, MARY SARACINO. Books, reading, and the world of goods in antebellum New England. AmQ (48:4) 1996, 587–622.

Literary Theory

This section is intended to contain studies **about** the literary theory, literary historiography, literary criticism, etc., produced *in* the nineteenth century. For modern works **of** literary history and criticism dealing generally with this period, see under 'Nineteenth Century: General Literary Studies'.

10187. ALCARO, MARION WALKER. Walt Whitman's Mrs G.: a biography of Anne Gilchrist. (Bibl. 1992, 7880.) Rev. by Sherry Ceniza in WWQR (9:4) 1992, 217–20.

10188. ASKE, MARTIN. Critical disfigurings: the 'jealous leer malign' in Romantic criticism. *In* (pp. 49–70) **95**.

10189. BALDICK, CHRIS. Criticism and literary theory 1890 to the present. Harlow; New York: Longman, 1996. pp. xv, 294. (Longman literature in English.)

10190. BARRET-DUCROCQ, FRANÇOISE. *Culture and Anarchy* de Matthew Arnold. Paris: Didier Erudition, 1995. pp. 139.

10191. BEER, JOHN (ed.). Questioning Romanticism. *See* **95**.

10192. BERMAN, RUTH. Fantasy fiction and fantasy criticism in some nineteenth-century periodicals. *See* **1233**.

10193. BONE, DRUMMOND. The question of a European Romanticism. *In* (pp. 121–32) **95**.

10194. BOUR, ISABELLE. The Clio of the North; or, The image of history. Francis Jeffrey's reviews (1802–1812). *See* **1235**.

10195. BROWN, MARY JANE. The last Victorian: a fresh evaluation of George Saintsbury's criticism. Review (16) 1994, 79–91 (review-article).

10196. BURWICK, FREDERICK. The Romantic concept of mimesis: *idem et alter*. *In* (pp. 179–208) **95**.

10197. GOODSON, A. C. Romantic theory and the critique of language. *In* (pp. 3–28) **95**.

10198. JONES, DOROTHY RICHARDSON. 'King of critics': George Saintsbury, 1845–1933, critic, journalist, historian, professor. (Bibl. 1994, 7350.) Rev. by William H. Pritchard in ASch (62:4) 1993, 611–14; by Mary Jane Brown in Review (16) 1994, 79–91.

10199. LANG, BERND-PETER. Gespaltene Modernität, verfehlte Moderne: Matthew Arnolds Kulturkritik. ZAA (43:2) 1995, 133–44.

10200. LEW, LAURIE KANE. Cultural anxiety in Anna Jameson's art criticism. SELit (36:4) 1996, 829–56.

10201. LIPMAN, SAMUEL (ed.). Culture and anarchy. Commentary by Maurice Cowling *et al.* (Bibl. 1995, 8943.) Rev. by Ruth apRoberts in ASch (64:1) 1995, 144–8.

10202. MCCARTHY, DERMOT. Early Canadian literary histories and the function of a canon. *In* (pp. 30–45) **13**.

10203. MCMILLAN, PETER. The literary criticism of Lafcadio Hearn. *In* (pp. 201–10) **49**.

10204. MELLOR, ANNE K. A criticism of their own: Romantic women literary critics. *In* (pp. 29–48) **95**.

10205. MICHALSKI, ROBERT. Towards a popular culture: Andrew Lang's anthropological and literary criticism. JAC (18:3) 1995, 13–17.

10206. RAJAN, TILOTTAMA. Phenomenology and Romantic theory: Hegel and the subversion of aesthetics. *In* (pp. 155–78) **95**.

10207. RIVALAIN, ODILE BOUCHER. From 'literary insignificancies' to 'the sacredness of the writer's art': aspects of fiction criticism in the *Westminster Review*, 1824–1857. *See* **1350**.

10208. SPEVACK, MARVIN. James Orchard Halliwell: outlines of a life. *See* **6196**.

10209. ZUCCATO, EDOARDO. Italian Petrarchism in S. T. Coleridge's theory of poetry. Textus (7) 1994, 95–112.

AUTHORS

Francis Adams

10210. TASKER, MEG.   Francis Adams (1862–1893): a bibliography. St Lucia: Dept of English, Univ. of Queensland, 1996. pp. iv, 51. (Victorian fiction research guides, 24.)

Henry Adams

10211. ACCARDI, BERNARD.   Empiricism and the epistemological rhetoric of *The Education of Henry Adams*. ELit (23:2) 1996, 251–76.

10212. BOVÉ, PAUL A.   Giving thought to America: intellect and *The Education of Henry Adams*. CI (23:1) 1996, 80–108.

10213. DAWIDOFF, ROBERT.   The genteel tradition and the sacred rage: high culture *vs* democracy in Adams, James, and Santayana. (Bibl. 1994, 7370.) Rev. by George Cotkin in AHR (98:1) 1993, 250–1.

10214. JACOBSON, JOANNE.   Authority and alliance in the letters of Henry Adams. (Bibl. 1993, 7114.) Rev. by Keith R. Burich in AmS (34:2) 1993, 146.

10215. MAYER, KURT ALBERT.   Henry Adams and the race for race. Amst (41:1) 1996, 83–111.

10216. MORELAND, KIM.   The medievalist impulse in American literature: Twain, Adams, Fitzgerald, and Hemingway. Charlottesville; London: Virginia UP, 1996. pp. xii, 264.

10217. MURPHY, BRENDA.   Fetishizing the dynamo: Henry Adams and Eugene O'Neill. EOR (16:1) 1992, 85–90.

10218. OWENS, PATRICIA ANN.   The friendship of Henry Adams and John Hay. LH (97:4) 1995, 143–53.

10219. WINNER, VIOLA HOPKINS.   The virgin and the carburetor. AH (46:4) 1995, 88–93.

Jane Addams

10220. BLOOD, MELANIE N.   Ideology and theatre at Hull House under Jane Addams. JADT (5:2) 1993, 71–85.

10221. RUDNICK, LOIS.   Feminist utopian visions and the 'New Woman': Jane Addams and Charlotte Perkins Gilman. *In* (pp. 181–93) **38**.

J. G. Adderley (James Granville) (1861–1942)

10222. HAPGOOD, LYNNE.   'The reconceiving of Christianity': secularisation, realism and the religious novel, 1888–1900. *See* **9865**.

'Max Adeler' (Charles Heber Clark)

10223. KETTERER, DAVID (ed.).   Charles Heber Clark, a family memoir: the autobiography of the American humorist 'Max Adeler'. New York; Frankfurt; Bern; Paris: Lang, 1995. pp. lxi, 417. (American univ. studies, XXIV: American literature, 15.) Rev. by David E. E. Sloane in SAH (3:3) 1996, 119–22.

Louisa M. Alcott

10224. BICKNELL, KENT (ed.).   A long fatal love chase. New York: Random House, 1995. pp. 242. Rev. by Maureen Corrigan in BkW, 3 Sept. 1995, 5.

10225. CAPPELLO, MARY.   'Looking about me with all my eyes':

censored viewing, carnival, and Louisa May Alcott's *Hospital Sketches*. AQ (50:3) 1994, 59–88.

10226. CHAPMAN, MARY. Gender and influence in Louisa May Alcott's *A Modern Mephistopheles*. Legacy (13:1) 1996, 19–37.

10227. —— 'Living pictures': women and *tableaux vivants* in nineteenth-century American fiction and culture. *See* **9542**.

10228. DANIELE, DANIELA. The 'moods' of Louisa May Alcott: growing up a little woman writer in Concord. Letterature d'America (55) 1994, 5–32.

10229. DIGGS, MARYLYNNE. Romantic friends or a 'different race of creatures'? The representation of lesbian pathology in nineteenth-century America. Feminist Studies (21:2) 1995, 317–40.

10230. ELBERT, SARAH (ed.). Moods. (Bibl. 1991, 7481.) Rev. by T. C. Holyoke in AR (49:3) 1991, 469.

10231. FITZPATRICK, TARA. Love's labor's reward: the sentimental economy of Louisa May Alcott's *Work*. NWSAJ (5:1) 1993, 28–44.

10232. KEETLY, DAWN. The power of 'personation': actress Anna Cora Mowatt and the literature of women's public performance in nineteenth-century America. ATQ (10:3) 1996, 187–200.

10233. KEYSER, ELIZABETH LENNOX. Whispers in the dark: the fiction of Louisa May Alcott. (Bibl. 1995, 8974.) Rev. by Mary Wilson Carpenter in AL (68:3) 1996, 646–7; by Jean Perrot in ChildLit (24) 1996, 199–204; by Clare Cotugno in SAF (24:2) 1996, 240–1; by Roberta Seelinger Trites in Legacy (13:1) 1996, 77–8; by Mary Bortnyk Rigsby in TSWL (15:1) 1996, 157–9.

10234. MARCHALONIS, SHIRLEY. Filming the nineteenth century: *The Secret Garden* and *Little Women*. ATQ (10:4) 1996, 273–92.

10235. REARDON, COLLEEN. Music as leitmotif in Louisa May Alcott's *Little Women*. ChildLit (24) 1996, 74–85.

10236. RIGSBY, MARY. 'So like women!': Louisa May Alcott's *Work* and the ideology of relations. *In* (pp. 109–27) **99**.

10237. SHEALY, DANIEL (ed.). Louisa May Alcott's fairy tales and fantasy stories. (Bibl. 1994, 7397.) Rev. by Elizabeth Lennox Keyser in ChildLit (24) 1996, 205–12.

10238. —— STERN, MADELEINE B.; MYERSON, JOEL (eds). Freaks of genius: unknown thrillers of Louisa May Alcott. (Bibl. 1994, 7398.) Rev. by Benjamin Franklin Fisher, IV, in AmP (2) 1992, 124–6; by Elizabeth Lennox Keyser in ChildLit (24) 1996, 205–12.

10239. SHOWALTER, ELAINE. Sister's choice: tradition and change in American women's writing. (Bibl. 1994, 7399.) Rev. by Nancy A. Walker in AmS (34:1) 1993, 169–70; by Birgit Fromkorth in ZAA (41:4) 1993, 80–1; by Melody Graulich in NWSAJ (5:2) 1993, 280–3; by Nancy A. Walker in AmS (34:1) 1993, 169–70; by Elaine Hedges in Signs (19:2) 1994, 507–11.

10240. SMITH, GAIL K. Who was that masked woman? Gender and form in Louisa May Alcott's confidence stories. *In* (pp. 45–59) **3**.

10241. STERN, MADELEINE B. Louisa May Alcott and the Boston *Saturday Evening Gazette*. *See* **1373**.

10242. ——SHEALY, DANIEL (eds). From Jo March's attic: stories of intrigue and suspense. (Bibl. 1994, 7400.) Rev. by Elizabeth Lennox Keyser in ChildLit (24) 1996, 205–12.

10243. YOUNG, ELIZABETH. A wound of one's own: Louisa May Alcott's Civil War fiction. AmQ (48:3) 1996, 439–74.

William Alexander

10244. DONALDSON, WILLIAM (ed.).   Johnny Gibb of Gushetneuk in the Parish of Pyketillim. East Linton, East Lothian: Tuckwell Press, 1995. pp. xxiii, 312. Rev. by Alexander Fenton in AUR (56:3) 1996, 367–8.

10245. —— My uncle the baillie. East Linton, East Lothian: Tuckwell Press, 1995. pp. vi, 217. Rev. by Alexander Fenton in AUR (56:3) 1996, 367–8.

Henry Alford

10246. CRONIN, RICHARD.   Shelleyan incest and the Romantic legacy. KSJ (45) 1996, 61–76.

Horatio Alger, Jr

10247. HENDLER, GLENN.   Pandering in the public sphere: masculinity and the market in Horatio Alger. AmQ (48:3) 1996, 415–38.

10248. NACKENOFF, CAROL.   The fictional republic: Horatio Alger and American political discourse. (Bibl. 1994, 7403.) Rev. by Ray B. Browne in JAC (18:3) 1995, 110–11; by Charles L. Crow in AL (68:1) 1996, 246–7.

Joseph A. Altsheler (Joseph Alexander) (1862–1919)

10249. ANDERSON, DAVID D.   Joseph A. Altsheler, *The Young Trailers*, and I on the Ohio frontier. SSMLN (26:2) 1996, 2–6.

William Archer

10250. ANON. (introd.).   A conversation between Thomas Hardy and William Archer. ERev (5:3) 1995, 6–10.

Sir Edwin Arnold

10251. MENVILLE, DOUGLAS.   The wonderful adventures of Edwin Lester Arnold. Romantist (9/10) 1985/86, 51–4.

Matthew Arnold

10252. ABJADIAN, AMROLLAH.   Arnold's *Tristram and Iseult*; or, The world well lost. Tristania (15) 1994, 113–21.

10253. BARRET-DUCROCQ, FRANÇOISE.   *Culture and Anarchy* de Matthew Arnold. *See* **10190**.

10254. BROOKS, ROGER L.   Matthew Arnold's *Then Comes the Whistling Clown. See* **591**.

10255. GOSLEE, DAVID.   Arnold and the hero-worship of Jesus. ReLit (28:1) 1996, 21–48.

10256. GROB, ALAN.   Arnold's *The Scholar-Gipsy*: the use and abuse of history. VP (34:2) 1996, 149–74.

10257. HARVIE, CHRISTOPHER.   Garron Top to Caer Gybi: images of the inland sea. Irish Review (19) 1996, 44–61.

10258. LANG, BERND-PETER.   Gespaltene Modernität, verfehlte Moderne: Matthew Arnolds Kulturkritik. *See* **10199**.

10259. MITSCH, RUTHMARIE H.   The other Isolde. *See* **4939**.

10260. MURRAY, NICHOLAS.   A life of Matthew Arnold. London: Hodder & Stoughton, 1996. pp. xiii, 400, (plates) 16. Rev. by Nicholas Shrimpton in TLS, 14 June 1996, 4–5.

Jane Austen

10261. AGORNI, MIRELLA. '*I hope somebody cares for these minutiae ...*': le lettere di Jane Austen. Quaderni di lingue e letterature (18) 1993, 17–27.

10262. ARMSTRONG, NANCY. The nineteenth-century Jane Austen: a turning point in the history of fear. Genre (23:2/3) 1990, 227–46.

10263. AUSTEN-LEIGH, JOAN. Jane Austen's favourite nephew. Persuasions (18) 1996, 144–53.

10264. —— Two queries concerning *Emma*. Did Jane Austen forget Mr Knightley? Who wrote Frank Churchill's 'handsome letter'? Persuasions (18) 1996, 54–7.

10265. BALLASTER, Ros. Adapting Jane Austen. ERev (7:1) 1996, 10–13.

10266. BLOOM, DONALD A. Dwindling into wifehood: the romantic power of the witty heroine in Shakespeare, Dryden, Congreve, and Austen. *In* (pp. 53–79) **64**.

10267. BRIGANTI, CHIARA. Austen's shackles and feminine filiation. *In* (pp. 130–49) **87**.

10268. CAPLAN, CLIVE. Jane Austen's soldier brother: the military career of Captain Henry Thomas Austen of the Oxfordshire Regiment of Militia, 1793–1801. Persuasions (18) 1996, 122–43.

10269. CHONG, KYUNG-WOOK. Austen eul ikneun jaemi e geiphaneun yeoksa eui moseup. (A topographical approach to Austen's later works.) EngSt (20) 1996, 169–212.

10270. CLARK, LORNA J. A contemporary's view of Jane Austen. NQ (43:4) 1996, 418–20.

10271. CLARK, ROBERT (ed.). *Sense and Sensibility* and *Pride and Prejudice*. (Bibl. 1995, 9021.) Rev. by Anne Pilgrim in ECF (8:3) 1996, 425–7.

10272. COHEN, PAULA MARANTZ. The anorexic syndrome and the nineteenth-century domestic novel. *In* (pp. 125–39) **24**.

10273. COLLINS, IRENE. Displeasing pictures of clergymen. Persuasions (18) 1996, 109–19.

10274. CROFT, SARAH. Lady Catherine de Bourgh and Mrs Elton in the character of Emma Woodhouse. Persuasions (18) 1996, 33–41.

10275. DERRY, STEPHEN. *Emma*, the Earthly Paradise, and *The History of Nourjahad*. *See* **9333**.

10276. —— Freud, the gothic, and coat symbolism in *Northanger Abbey*. Persuasions (18) 1996, 49–53.

10277. EIFRIG, GAIL McGREW. Pride and prejudice. Cresset (59:7) 1996, 3–4.

10278. EVERETT, BARBARA. Hard romance. LRB (18:3) 1996, 12–14.

10279. FERGUS, JAN. Male whiners in Austen's novels. Persuasions (18) 1996, 98–108.

10280. GARD, ROGER. Jane Austen's novels: the art of clarity. (Bibl. 1995, 9032.) Rev. by Peter L. De Rose in Review (16) 1994, 31–9.

10281. GOLDSTEIN, PHILIP. Criticism and institutions: the conflicted reception of Jane Austen's fiction. SHum (18:1) 1991, 35–55.

10282. GROSS, GLORIA SYBIL. Jane Austen and psychological realism: 'What does a woman want?' *In* (pp. 19–33) **96**.

10283. HALL, LYNDA A. Jane Austen's attractive rogues: Willoughby, Wickham, and Frank Churchill. Persuasions (18) 1996, 186–90.

10284. HANNON, PATRICE.   Austen novels and Austen films: incompatible worlds? Persuasions (18) 1996, 24–32.

10285. HATANO, YOKO.   Fanny Price and Molly Gibson: bearers of the country house tradition. Gaskell Society Journal (10) 1996, 92–101.

10286. HUDSON, GLENDA A.   Sibling love and incest in Jane Austen's fiction. (Bibl. 1993, 7190.) Rev. by Peter L. De Rose in Review (16) 1994, 31–9.

10287. INNOCENTI, LORETTA.   La commedia degli equivoci: *Emma* di Jane Austen. Textus (4) 1991, 69–95.

10288. JOHNSON, CLAUDIA L.   The divine Miss Jane: Jane Austen, Janeites, and the discipline of novel studies. Boundary 2 (23:3) 1996, 143–63.

10289. KAPLAN, DEBORAH.   Mass marketing Jane Austen: men, women, and courtship in two of the recent films. Persuasions (18) 1996, 171–81. (*Emma, Sense and Sensibility*.)

10290. KNOX-SHAW, PETER.   Fanny Price refuses to kowtow. RES (47:186) 1996, 212–17.

10291. LANE, MAGGIE.   Jane Austen and food. (Bibl. 1995, 9054.) Rev. by Roger Sales in Albion (28:1) 1996, 141–4; by F. J. M. Blom in EngS (77:2) 1996, 203–5.

10292. LAURENCE, PATRICIA.   Women's silence as a ritual of truth: a study of literary expressions in Austen, Brontë, and Woolf. *In* (pp. 156–67) **59**.

10293. LAWSON-PEEBLES, ROBERT.   European conflict and Hollywood's reconstruction of English fiction. YES (26) 1996, 1–13.

10294. LE FAYE, DEIRDRE.   A literary portrait re-examined: Jane Austen and Mary Anne Campion. BC (45:4) 1996, 508–25.

10295. LOOSER, DEVONEY.   Jane Austen 'responds' to the Men's Movement. Persuasions (18) 1996, 159–70.

10296. —— (ed.)   Jane Austen and discourses of feminism. (Bibl. 1995, 9057.) Rev. by Laura Dabundo in Criticism (38:4) 1996, 644–8.

10297. LYONS, DONALD.   Passionate precision: *Sense and Sensibility*. FilCo (32:1) 1996, 36–41.

10298. MACDONAGH, OLIVER.   Jane Austen: real and imagined worlds. (Bibl. 1995, 9059.) Rev. by James Fanning in ZAA (42:1) 1994, 71–3.

10299. MACLEOD, EMMA VINCENT.   Women at war: British women and the debate on the wars against Revolutionary France in the 1790s. *See* **8685**.

10300. MCMASTER, JULIET.   Jane Austen, the novelist: essays past and present. Basingstoke: Macmillan; New York: St Martin's Press, 1996. pp. xiv, 203.

10301. —— STOVEL, BRUCE (eds).   Jane Austen's business: her world and her profession. Basingstoke: Macmillan; New York: St Martin's Press, 1996. pp. xx, 237, (plates) 4.

10302. MALINA, DEBRA.   Rereading the patriarchal text: *The Female Quixote, Northanger Abbey*, and the trace of the absent mother. *See* **9187**.

10303. MARTIN, CAROL A.   'These would have been all my friends': Lyme Regis and Jane Austen's Anne Elliot. WebS (11:2) 1994, 127–32.

10304. MATHER, RACHEL R.   The heirs of Jane Austen: twentieth-century writers of the comedy of manners. New York; Frankfurt; Bern;

Paris: Lang, 1996. pp. xii, 142. (American univ. studies, IV: English language and literature, 180.) (Cf. bibl. 1993, 7210.)

10305. MEYERSOHN, MARYLEA. Jane Austen's garrulous speakers: social criticism in *Sense and Sensibility*, *Emma*, and *Persuasion*. In (pp. 35–48) **96**.

10306. MICHASIW, KIM IAN. Nine revisionist theses on the picturesque. *See* **9075**.

10307. MIDDLETON, LINDA C. Anxious spectators and voluntary spies: the novel hauntings of *Northanger Abbey*. Genre (27:1/2) 1994, 105–19.

10308. MINMA, SHINOBU. General Tilney and tyranny: *Northanger Abbey*. ECF (8:4) 1996, 503–18.

10309. MORGAN, SUSAN. Captain Wentworth, British imperialism and personal romance. Persuasions (18) 1996, 88–97.

10310. MYER, MICHAEL GROSVENOR. Talking of the weather: a note on manners in Jane Austen. NQ (43:4) 1996, 418.

10311. NOKES, DAVID. The wild beast uncaged: how Steventon sharpened Jane Austen's pen and instinct for running mad. TLS, 31 May 1996, 14–15.

10312. RAY, JOAN KLINGEL. Austen's *Northanger Abbey*. Exp (54:3) 1996, 142–4.

10313. ROGERS, PAT. *Sposi* in Surrey: links between Jane Austen and Fanny Burney. *See* **8890**.

10314. ROTH, BARRY. An annotated bibliography of Jane Austen studies 1984–94. Athens: Ohio UP, 1996. pp. xxiv, 438.

10315. —— LATKIN, PATRICIA. Jane Austen works and studies: 1996. Persuasions (18) 1996, 59–72.

10316. ROWEN, NORMA. Reinscribing Cinderella: Jane Austen and the fairy tale. *In* (pp. 29–36) **36**.

10317. SALES, ROGER. Jane Austen and representations of Regency England. (Bibl. 1995, 9081.) Rev. by Alice Chandler in ANQ (9:2) 1996, 59–61; by Irene Collins in Literature and History (5:2) 1996, 94.

10318. SEGAL, LORE. The uses of story: Jane Austen on our unwillingness to be parted from our money. AR (54:2) 1996, 133–9.

10319. SHIELDS, CAROL; GIARDINI, ANNE. Martians in Jane Austen? Persuasions (18) 1996, 191–203.

10320. SOUTHAM, BRIAN. Lady Knatchbull's letter: was Jane Austen 'very much below par'? TLS, 29 Mar. 1996, 16.

10321. —— *Sir Charles Grandison* and Jane Austen's men. *See* **9309**.

10322. SOUTHWARD, DAVID. Jane Austen and the riches of embarrassment. SELit (36:4) 1996, 763–84.

10323. SPACKS, PATRICIA MEYER. Reply to David Richter: form and ideology: novels at work. *See* **9044**.

10324. STEFFES, MICHAEL. Slavery and *Mansfield Park*: the historical and biographical context. ELN (34:2) 1996, 23–41.

10325. STEWART, MAAJA A. Domestic realities and imperial fictions: Jane Austen's novels in eighteenth-century contexts. (Bibl. 1995, 9089.) Rev. by Heidi Van de Veire in AUMLA (85) 1996, 162–3.

10326. SUTHERLAND, EILEEN. That infamous flannel waistcoat. Persuasions (18) 1996, 58.

10327. THOMPSON, EMMA. Jane Austen's *Sense and Sensibility*: the screenplay and diaries. London: Bloomsbury; New York: Newmarket

Press, 1995. pp. 288, (plates) 32. Rev. by Jim Welsh in LitFQ (24:1) 1996, 111–12.

10328. TRACY, LAURA.   Relational competence: Jane Austen's *Persuasion*. Persuasions (18) 1996, 154–8.

10329. TUCKER, GEORGE HOLBERT.   Jane Austen's Virginia connections. Persuasions (18) 1996, 120–1.

10330. VLASOPOLOS, ANCA.   Staking claims for no territory: the sea as woman's space. *In* (pp. 72–88) **97**.

10331. VREDENBURGH, JOAN R.   General Tilney and the Milsom Street merchants – brothers under the skin? Persuasions (18) 1996, 42–5.

10332. WALDRON, MARY.   Men of sense and silly wives: the confusions of Mr Knightley. StudN (28:2) 1996, 141–57.

10333. WIESENFARTH, JOSEPH.   The civility of *Emma*. Persuasions (18) 1996, 8–23.

10334. WILKES, JOANNE.   'Song of the dying swan'?: the nineteenth-century response to *Persuasion*. StudN (28:1) 1996, 38–56.

10335. WILLIAMS, MADAWC.   Tales of wonder: science fiction and fantasy in the age of Jane Austen. *See* **9982**.

10336. WILSON, MARGARET MADRIGAL.   The hero and the other man in Jane Austen's novels. Persuasions (18) 1996, 182–5.

10337. WILTSHIRE, JOHN.   Jane Austen and the body: 'the picture of health'. (Bibl. 1992, 8027.) Rev. by Helena Michie in LitMed (12:2) 1993, 273–6; by Frank McCombie in NQ (41:2) 1994, 253–5; by Karina Williamson in EC (44:1) 1994, 52–60; by Juliet McMaster in ECF (6:2) 1994, 189–90; by Claudia L. Johnson in NineL (48:4) 1994, 531–4; by Judith Hattaway in ELN (32:3) 1995, 81–4; by Heidi Van de Veire in AUMLA (84) 1995, 137–8; by Deirdre Le Faye in RES (46:182) 1995, 284–5.

Joanna Baillie

10338. BURROUGHS, CATHERINE B.   English Romantic women writers and theatre theory: Joanna Baillie's Prefaces to the *Plays on the Passions*. *In* (pp. 274–96) **103**.

10339. —— 'A reasonable woman's desire': the private theatrical and Joanna Baillie's *The Tryal*. TSLL (38:3/4) 1996, 265–84.

10340. PURINTON, MARJEAN D.   Romantic ideology unmasked: the mentally constructed tyrannies in dramas of William Wordsworth, Lord Byron, Percy Shelley, and Joanna Baillie. (Bibl. 1995, 9102.) Rev. by Catherine Burroughs in KSJ (45) 1996, 206–8.

R. M. Ballantyne

10341. HANNABUSS, STUART.   Moral islands: a study of Robert Michael Ballantyne, writer for children. SLJ (22:2) 1995, 29–40.

10342. PHILLIPS, R. S.   Space for boyish men and manly boys: the Canadian Northwest in Robert Ballantyne's adventure stories. ECanW (59) 1996, 46–64.

John Banim

10343. CORRIGAN, KAREN P.   'Plain life' depicted in 'fiery shorthand': sociolinguistic aspects of the languages and dialects of Scotland and Ulster as portrayed in Scott's *Waverley* and Banim's *The Boyne Water*. *See* **2817**.

Anne Bannerman

10344. ELFENBEIN, ANDREW. Lesbianism and Romantic genius: the poetry of Anne Bannerman. ELH (63:4) 1996, 929–57.

James Nelson Barker

10345. SARGENT, MARK L. The witches of Salem, the angel of Hadley, and the friends of Philadelphia. AmS (34:1) 1993, 105–20.

10346. SCHECKEL, SUSAN. Domesticating the drama of conquest: Barker's *Pocahontas* on the popular stage. ATQ (10:3) 1996, 231–43.

Thomas Lovell Beddoes

10347. FLEISSNER, ROBERT F. 'Spot of time' in Frost: Beddoes, Vaughan – or Wordsworth in *Stopping by the Woods*? *See* **8381**.

'Cuthbert Bede' (Rev. Edward Bradley)

10348. ANTOR, HEINZ. Ein früher Klassiker des Universitätsromans: Edward Bradleys *The Adventures of Mr Verdant Green, an Oxford Undergraduate, by Cuthbert Bede*. GRM (41:2) 1991, 174–88.

Edward Bellamy

10349. BERGAMINI, OLIVIERO. Technology and power within Edward Bellamy's utopianism. *In* (pp. 355–61) **117**.

10350. BORUS, DANIEL H. (ed.). Looking backward: 2000–1887. (Bibl. 1995, 9107.) Rev. by James J. Kopp in Utopian Studies (7:1) 1996, 115–16.

10351. DERRY, STEPHEN. The Time Traveller's utopian books and his reading of the future. Foundation (65) 1995, 16–24.

10352. FABI, M. GIULIA. 'Utopian melting': technology, homogeneity, and the American dream in *Looking Backward. In* (pp. 346–54) **117**.

Walter Besant

10353. NEETENS, WIM. Problems of a 'democratic text': Walter Besant's impossible story in *All Sorts and Conditions of Men* (1882). *In* (pp. 135–57) **75**.

Ambrose Bierce ('Dod Grile')

10354. CHANDRAN, K. NARAYANA. T. S. Eliot and Ambrose Bierce: another source for the witty rhyme in *A Cooking Egg*. NQ (43:1) 1996, 59.

10355. DE ANGELIS, VALERIO MASSIMO. Ambrose Bierce e le meraviglie della guerra. Letterature d'America (52/53) 1993, 43–78.

10356. FURQUERON, JAMES R.; MARCUSON, AGNES BONDURANT. Poe and two minor writers. PoeM (25) 1995, 7–9.

10357. GRENANDER, M. E. (ed.). Poems of Ambrose Bierce. (Bibl. 1995, 9112.) Rev. by Peter Kratzke in ANQ (9:1) 1996, 39–41.

10358. MORRIS, ROY. Ambrose Bierce: alone in bad company. (Bibl. 1995, 9113.) Rev. by Dennis Drabelle in BkW, 28 Jan. 1996, 4.

10359. OLIVER, LAWRENCE J.; SCHARNHORST, GARY. Charlotte Perkins Gilman *v.* Ambrose Bierce: the literary politics of gender in *fin-de-siècle* California. JWest (32:3) 1993, 52–60.

10360. SCHAEFER, MICHAEL W. Ambrose Bierce on the construction of military history. WLA (7:1) 1995, 1–13.

10361. SMITH, MEL.   Ten letters on death, dying, and condolences. *See* **9264**.

10362. WOLOTKIEWICZ, DIANA A.   Ambrose Bierce's use of the grotesque mode: the pathology of society. JSSE (16) 1991, 81–92.

Clementina Black (1853–1922)

10363. HAPGOOD, LYNNE.   The novel and political agency: Socialism and the work of Margaret Harkness, Constance Howell and Clementina Black, 1888–1896. Literature and History (5:2) 1996, 37–52.

George Henry Boker

10364. KITTS, THOMAS M.   An argument for Boker's *Francesca da Rimini*. AmDr (3:2) 1994, 53–70.

'Rolf Boldrewood' (Thomas Alexander Browne)

10365. MACDONALD, JOAN H.   The Australian emergence of the Scottish 'wise man' in the fiction of Rolf Boldrewood. *See* **3639**.

George Borrow

10366. NEMETH, DAVID J.   Irving Brown: the American Borrow? JGLS (4:1) 1994, 7–31.

Dion Boucicault

10367. RICHARDSON, GARY A.   The Greening of America: the cultural business of Dion Boucicault's *The Shaughraun*. AmDr (3:2) 1994, 1–28.

Mary Elizabeth Braddon (Mrs Maxwell)

10368. EDWARDS, P. D. (ed.).   Aurora Floyd. Oxford; New York: OUP, 1996. pp. xxiv, 416. (World's classics.)

10369. GILBERT, PAMELA K.   Madness and civilization: generic opposition in Mary Elizabeth Braddon's *Lady Audley's Secret*. ELit (23:2) 1996, 218–33.

10370. NEMESVARI, RICHARD.   Robert Audley's secret: male homo-social desire in *Lady Audley's Secret*. StudN (27:4) 1995, 515–28.

The Brontës

10371. ALEXANDER, CHRISTINE.   Milestones in Brontë textual scholarship. *See* **559**.

10372. —— SELLARS, JANE.   The art of the Brontës. (Bibl. 1995, 9136.) Rev. by Peter Funnell in BST (21:7) 1996, 365–7; by Gillian Cumiskey in Gaskell Society Journal (10) 1996, 110–13.

10373. BARKER, JULIET.   The Brontës. (Bibl. 1995, 9138.) Rev. by Beverly Taylor in VIJ (24) 1996, 252–60.

10374. BELLAMY, JOAN.   Mary Taylor, Ellen Nussey and Brontë biography. *See* **10127**.

10375. FERMI, SARAH.   The Brontës at the Clergy Daughters' School: when did they leave? BST (21:6) 1996, 219–31.

10376. HARRIS, MORAG.   Representations of the male in the female imagination: the Brontës and Dickinson. Gramma (4) 1996, 129–51.

10377. IUORIO, LAURA.   Una scrittrice in ascolto: Daphne Du Maurier e la famiglia Brontë. Acme (48:3) 1995, 111–27.

10378. KINGSTON, VICTORIA. A conversation between Victoria Kingston and Juliet Barker, author of *The Brontës*. ERev (6:3) 1996, 11–14.
10379. LEMON, CHARLES (ed.). Early visitors to Haworth: from Ellen Nussey to Virginia Woolf. Haworth: Brontë Soc., 1996. pp. xv, 127. Rev. by Elvira Willmott in BST (21:7) 1996, 369–70; by L.D. in TLS, 2 Aug. 1996, 32.
10380. SMITH, MARGARET. Newly acquired Brontë letters, transcriptions and notes. *See* **421**.

Anne Brontë

10381. BERRY, ELIZABETH HOLLIS. Anne Brontë's radical vision: structures of consciousness. (Bibl. 1995, 9147.) Rev. by Maggie Berg in ESCan (22:4) 1996, 483–5.
10382. CHITHAM, EDWARD. A life of Anne Brontë. (Bibl. 1995, 9149.) Rev. by Deirdre Coleman in AUMLA (85) 1996, 160–1.
10383. DAVIES, STEVIE (ed.). The tenant of Wildfell Hall. London; New York: Penguin, 1996. pp. xxxiv, 535. (Penguin classics.)
10384. FRAWLEY, MARIA H. Anne Brontë. New York: Twayne; London: Prentice Hall, 1996. pp. xiv, 171. (Twayne's English authors, 518.)
10385. GERGITS, JULIA M. Women artists at home. *In* (pp. 105–29) **54**.
10386. JACKSON, REBECCA L. Women as wares: reading the rhetoric of economy in Anne Brontë's *The Tenant of Wildfell Hall*. CCTE (61) 1996, 57–64.
10387. MEYER, SUSAN. Words on 'great vulgar sheets': writing and social resistance in Anne Brontë's *Agnes Grey* (1847). *In* (pp. 3–16) **75**.
10388. NEWMAN, HILARY. Animals in *Agnes Grey*. BST (21:6) 1996, 237–42.
10389. ROSENGARTEN, HERBERT (ed.). The tenant of Wildfell Hall. Introd. by Margaret Smith. (Bibl. 1995, 9150.) Rev. by Christine Alexander in Text (Ann Arbor) (9) 1996, 354–61.
10390. WOELFEL, JAMES. The Christian humanism of Anne Brontë. 1650–1850 (2) 1996, 295–317.

Branwell Brontë

10391. CHENEY, PHYLLIS. Another Branwell liaison? BST (21:7) 1996, 303–11.
10392. COLLINS, ROBERT G. Bringing Branwell in from the cold: retrieving the prose chronicles. BST (21:6) 1996, 253–9.
10393. DINSDALE, ANN. Branwell Brontë and the landlord of the Black Bull. BST (21:7) 1996, 357–9.
10394. NEUFELDT, VICTOR A. (ed.). The poems of Patrick Branwell Brontë: a new text and commentary. (Bibl. 1991, 7622.) Rev. by Christine Alexander in Text (Ann Arbor) (9) 1996, 361–8.

Charlotte Brontë

10395. ALEXANDER, CHRISTINE (ed.). Charlotte Bronte's *High Life in Verdopolis*: a story from the Glass Town saga. London: British Library, 1995. pp. xxiii, 103. Rev. by G.B. in TLS, 10 May 1996, 31.
10396. ALTON, ANNE HIEBERT. Books in the novels of Charlotte Brontë. BST (21:7) 1996, 265–74.

10397. AUERBACH, NINA.   Victorian players and sages. *In* (pp. 183–98) **83**.

10398. BARKER, JULIET.   Miles off the target. TLS, 31 May 1996, 16.

10399. BEATTIE, VALERIE.   The mystery at Thornfield: representations of madness in *Jane Eyre*. StudN (28:4) 1996, 493–505.

10400. BEATY, JEROME.   Misreading *Jane Eyre*: a postformalist paradigm. Columbus: Ohio State UP, 1996. pp. xvi, 259. (Theory and interpretation of narrative.)

10401. BELL, MILLICENT.   *Jane Eyre*: the tale of the governess. ASch (65:2) 1996, 263–9.

10402. BETSINGER, SUE ANN.   *Jane Eyre*: the ascent of woman. *In* (pp. 74–86) **37**.

10403. BEWELL, ALAN.   *Jane Eyre* and Victorian medical geography. ELH (63:3) 1996, 773–808.

10404. BUGEJA, MICHAEL.   The female masters: a look at three underrated women poets offers fresh lessons in craft. *See* **8417**.

10405. COCKCROFT, SUSAN (ed.).   Jane Eyre. Cambridge; New York: CUP, 1996. pp. 528. (Cambridge literature.)

10406. COLELLA, SILVANA.   La casa riformata: ideologia domestica e consenso narrativo in *Mary Barton* e *Shirley*. Textus (6) 1993, 135–78.

10407. D'ALBERTIS, DEIRDRE.   Make-believes in Bayswater and Belgravia: Brontë, Linton, and the Victorian 'flirt'. VIJ (24) 1996, 1–25.

10408. FENNELL, FRANCIS L.; FENNELL, MONICA A.   'Ladies – loaf givers': food, women, and society in the novels of Charlotte Brontë and George Eliot. *In* (pp. 235–58) **54**.

10409. FIMLAND, MARIT.   On the margins of the acceptable: Charlotte Brontë's *Villette*. LitTheol (10:2) 1996, 148–59.

10410. GERGITS, JULIA M.   Women artists at home. *In* (pp. 105–29) **54**.

10411. GLISERMAN, MARTIN.   Psychoanalysis, language, and the body of the text. *See* **8967**.

10412. HALL, AUDREY.   Two possible photographs of Charlotte Brontë. BST (21:7) 1996, 293–302.

10413. HESS, NATALIE.   Code-switching and style-shifting as markers of liminality in literature. *See* **2643**.

10414. HIRSCH, PAM.   Charlotte Brontë and George Sand: the influence of female Romanticism. BST (21:6) 1996, 209–18.

10415. IVES, MAURA.   Housework, mill work, women's work: the functions of cloth in Charlotte Brontë's *Shirley*. *In* (pp. 259–89) **54**.

10416. JADWIN, LISA.   'Caricatured, not faithfully rendered': *Bleak House* as a revision of *Jane Eyre*. MLS (26:2/3) 1996, 111–33.

10417. JORDAN, JOHN O.   Partings welded together: self-fashioning in *Great Expectations* and *Jane Eyre*. DickQ (13:1) 1996, 19–33.

10418. KAPLAN, CARLA.   The erotics of talk: women's writing and feminist paradigms. New York; Oxford: OUP, 1996. pp. x, 240.

10419. KINCAID, JAMES.   Pip and Jane and recovered memories. DSA (25) 1996, 211–25.

10420. KLAVER, CLAUDIA.   Homely aesthetics: *Villette*'s canny narrator. Genre (26:4) 1993, 409–29.

10421. KNEZEVIC, BORISLAV.   The impossible things: quest for knowledge in Charlotte Brontë's *Villette*. LitPs (42:1/2) 1996, 65–99.

10422. KNOEPFLMACHER, U. C.   Afterword: endings as beginnings. *In* (pp. 347–68) **31**.

10423. LASHGARI, DEIRDRE. What some women can't swallow: hunger as protest in Charlotte Brontë's *Shirley*. *In* (pp. 141–52) **24**.

10424. LAURENCE, PATRICIA. Women's silence as a ritual of truth: a study of literary expressions in Austen, Brontë, and Woolf. *In* (pp. 156–67) **59**.

10425. LEE, HSIAO-HUNG. Possibilities of hidden things: narrative transgression in Victorian fictional autobiographies. *See* **9899**.

10426. LONAC, SUSAN. The doll and the double: Charlotte Brontë and the representation of the female self. BST (21:7) 1996, 285–92.

10427. MALONE, CATHERINE. 'We have learnt to love her more than her books': the critical reception of Brontë's *Professor*. RES (47:186) 1996, 175–87.

10428. MARCUS, SHARON. The profession of the author: abstraction, advertising, and *Jane Eyre*. PMLA (110:2) 1995, 206–19.

10429. MASON, MICHAEL (ed.). Jane Eyre. London: Penguin, 1996. pp. xxxvi, 532. (Penguin classics.)

10430. MITCHELL, JUDITH. The stone and the scorpion: the female subject of desire in the novels of Charlotte Brontë, George Eliot, and Thomas Hardy. (Bibl. 1995, 9191.) Rev. by Mary Wilson Carpenter in ESCan (22:2) 1996, 231–3.

10431. NEWMAN, BETH (ed.). *Jane Eyre*: complete, authoritative text with biographical and historical contexts, critical history, and essays from five contemporary critical perspectives. Boston, MA: Bedford Books of St Martin's Press; Basingstoke: Macmillan, 1996. pp. x, 646. (Case studies in contemporary criticism.) Rev. by Bob Duckett in BST (21:7) 1996, 367–8.

10432. PARKIN-GOUNELAS, RUTH. Learning what we have forgotten: repetition as remembrance in early nineteenth-century gothic. ERR (6:2) 1996, 213–26.

10433. PETERS, JOHN G. Inside and outside: *Jane Eyre* and marginalization through labeling. StudN (28:1) 1996, 57–75.

10434. PRESTON, ELIZABETH. Relational reconsiderations: reliability, heterosexuality, and narrative authority in *Villette*. Style (30:3) 1996, 386–408.

10435. SHUTTLEWORTH, SALLY. Charlotte Brontë and Victorian psychology. Cambridge; New York: CUP, 1996. pp. xiv, 289. (Cambridge studies in nineteenth-century literature and culture, 7.) Rev. by Mary Ellis Gibson in VIJ (24) 1996, 260–5.

10436. SMITH, M. (ed.). The letters of Charlotte Brontë: with a selection of letters by family and friends: vol. 1, 1829–1847. (Bibl. 1995, 9198.) Rev. by Edward Chitham in BST (21:6) 1996, 262–3; by Janet Gezari in EC (46:2) 1996, 164–74; by Cynthia E. Huggins in VIJ (24) 1996, 265–9.

10437. SMITH, MARGARET. A window on the world: Charlotte Brontë's correspondence with her publishers. An address given at the Brontë Society's Annual Meeting, Haworth, June 1996. *See* **1009**.

10438. STEPHENSON, WILL; STEPHENSON, MIMOSA. A source in J. G. Lockhart for Charlotte Brontë's pseudonym. *See* **2171**.

10439. STONEMAN, PATSY. Brontë transformations: the cultural dissemination of *Jane Eyre* and *Wuthering Heights*. New York; London: Prentice Hall/Harvester Wheatsheaf, 1995. pp. xiii, 352. Rev. by Bob Duckett in BST (21:7) 1996, 312; by J.H. in TLS, 9 Feb. 1996, 28.

10440. STOWELL, ROBERT. Brontë borrowings: Charlotte Brontë and

Ivanhoe, Emily Brontë and *The Count of Monte Cristo*. BST (21:6) 1996, 243–51.

10441. TAKAHASHI, HISAO.   Brontë shimai to tomoni – *Wuthering Heights* to *Jane Eyre*. (With the Brontës: *Wuthering Heights* and *Jane Eyre*.) Tokyo: Soeisha, 1996. pp. 246.

10442. TAYLER, IRENE.   Holy ghosts: the male muses of Emily and Charlotte Brontë. (Bibl. 1995, 9202.) Rev. by Sandra M. Adams in ELN (33:3) 1996, 82–4.

10443. VANSKIKE, ELLIOTT.   Consistent inconsistencies: the transvestite actress Madame Vestris and Charlotte Brontë's *Shirley*. NineL (50:4) 1996, 464–88.

10444. WARHOL, ROBYN R.   Double gender, double genre in *Jane Eyre* and *Villette*. SELit (36:4) 1996, 857–75.

10445. WINNIFRITH, TOM.   Charlotte and Emily Brontë: a study in the rise and fall of literary reputations. YES (26) 1996, 14–24.

10446. —— A note on some place-names in north-west Derbyshire. *See* **2170**.

10447. ZLOTNICK, SUSAN.   Jane Eyre, Anna Leonowens, and the White woman's burden: governesses, missionaries, and maternal imperialists in mid-Victorian Britain. VIJ (24) 1996, 27–56.

10448. ZONANA, JOYCE.   The sultan and the slave: feminist Orientalism and the structure of *Jane Eyre*. Signs (18:3) 1993, 592–617.

Emily Brontë

10449. BAINES, LAWRENCE.   From page to screen: when a novel is interpreted for film, what gets lost in the translation? JAAL (39:8) 1996, 612–22.

10450. BERG, MAGGIE.   *Wuthering Heights*: the writing in the margin. New York: Twayne; London: Prentice Hall, 1996. pp. xiii, 136. (Twayne's masterworks studies, 163.)

10451. BLOOM, HAROLD (ed.).   Emily Brontë's *Wuthering Heights*. New York: Chelsea House, 1996. pp. 80. (Bloom's notes.)

10452. BOWEN, JOHN.   Literature and ghosts. ERev (6:4) 1996, 12–16.

10453. BRISTOW, JOSEPH (ed.).   Victorian women poets: Emily Brontë, Elizabeth Barrett Browning, Christina Rossetti. Basingstoke: Macmillan; New York: St Martin's Press, 1995. pp. ix, 256. (New casebooks.) Rev. by Tess Cosslett in NQ (43:4) 1996, 486–7.

10454. CHITHAM, EDWARD.   Emily Brontë's Latin. BST (21:6) 1996, 233–6.

10455. COLELLA, SILVANA.   '*Lost vision*': le poesie di Emily Brontë e l'esperienza romantica. QLLSM (3) 1989, 37–65.

10456. CORI, ELISABETTA.   '*I hardly know what to hide and what to reveal*': ellissi e implicatura in *Wuthering Heights* di Emily Brontë. Textus (3:1/2) 1990, 125–37.

10457. DAVIS, DAVIE S.   Heathcliff, Lucifer, and the failure of the Christian myth. PMPA (16) 1991, 56–61.

10458. DONGHI, BEATRICE SOLINAS.   Il lieto fine di *Wuthering Heights*. QLLSM (2) 1987, 111–28.

10459. FRANK, KATHERINE.   Emily Brontë: a chainless soul. (Bibl. 1995, 9219.) Rev. by Suzann Bick in AR (49:3) 1991, 464.

10460. GOODLETT, DEBRA.   Love and addiction in *Wuthering Heights*. MidQ (37:3) 1996, 316–27.

10461. KENNARD, JEAN E.   Lesbianism and the censoring of *Wuthering Heights*. NWSAJ (8:2) 1996, 17–36.

10462. LAWSON-PEEBLES, ROBERT.   European conflict and Hollywood's reconstruction of English fiction. *See* **10293**.

10463. LEVY, ERIC P.   The psychology of loneliness in *Wuthering Heights*. StudN (28:2) 1996, 158–77.

10464. MEDORO, DANA.   'This thing of darkness I / Acknowledge mine': Heathcliff as fetish in *Wuthering Heights*. ESCan (22:3) 1996, 267–81.

10465. MILLS, PAMELA.   Wyler's version of Brontë's storms in *Wuthering Heights*. LitFQ (24:4) 1996, 414–22.

10466. PINION, F. B.   Scott and *Wuthering Heights*. BST (21:7) 1996, 313–22.

10467. ROPER, DEREK; CHITHAM, EDWARD (eds).   The poems of Emily Brontë. Oxford: Clarendon Press; New York: OUP, 1995. pp. xviii, 307. Rev. by Tom Winnifrith in BST (21:7) 1996, 370–1.

10468. RULEWICZ, WANDA.   Niebezpieczne ścięki Emily Brontë. (Emily Brontë's dangerous paths.) AP (23) 1996, 15–22.

10469. STELLA, MARIA.   Il potere della parola in Emily Brontë. *See* **2713**.

10470. STONEMAN, PATSY.   Brontë transformations: the cultural dissemination of *Jane Eyre* and *Wuthering Heights*. *See* **10439**.

10471. —— Catherine Earnshaw's journey to her home among the dead: fresh thoughts on *Wuthering Heights* and *Epipsychidion*. RES (47:188) 1996, 521–33.

10472. STOWELL, ROBERT.   Brontë borrowings: Charlotte Brontë and *Ivanhoe*, Emily Brontë and *The Count of Monte Cristo*. *See* **10440**.

10473. TAKAHASHI, HISAO.   Brontë shimai to tomoni – *Wuthering Heights* to *Jane Eyre*. (With the Brontës: *Wuthering Heights* and *Jane Eyre*.) *See* **10441**.

10474. WALLACE, ROBERT K.   Emily Brontë and Beethoven: Romantic equilibrium in fiction and music. (Bibl. 1990, 6376.) Rev. by James Conely in ArsL (7) 1993, 30–2.

10475. WINNIFRITH, TOM.   Charlotte and Emily Brontë: a study in the rise and fall of literary reputations. *See* **10445**.

Charles Brockden Brown

10476. BAUER, RALPH.   Between repression and transgression: Rousseau's *Confessions* and Charles Brockden Brown's *Wieland*. ATQ (10:4) 1996, 311–29.

10477. BOTTALICO, MICHELE.   The American Frontier and the initiation rite to a national literature: the example of *Edgar Huntly* by Charles Brockden Brown. RSAJ (4) 1993, 3–16.

10478. BURGETT, BRUCE.   Masochism and male sentimentalism: Charles Brockden Brown's *Clara Howard*. AQ (52:1) 1996, 1–25.

10479. CHRISTOPHERSEN, BILL.   The apparition in the glass: Charles Brockden Brown's American gothic. (Bibl. 1995, 9244.) Rev. by Nicholas Rombes in AmS (36:1) 1995, 137–9; by Pamela Clemit in ECF (8:2) 1996, 306–7.

10480. DECKER, JAMES M.   Reassessing Charles Brockden Brown's *Clara Howard*. PMPA (19) 1994, 28–36.

10481. DOWNES, PAUL.   Sleep-walking out of the Revolution: Brown's *Edgar Huntly*. ECS (29:4) 1996, 413–31.

10482. HINDS, ELIZABETH JANE WALL.   Private property: Charles Brockden Brown's economics of virtue. SHum (18:2) 1991, 165–79.

10483. KEITEL, EVELYNE.   Das eigene Fremde, das fremde Eigene: Charles Brockden Browns Romane im kulturellen Spannungsfeld zwischen England und Amerika. Amst (41:4) 1996, 533–55.

10484. LEWIS, PAUL.   Charles Brockden Brown and the gendered canon of early American fiction. EAL (31:2) 1996, 167–88.

10485. WATTS, STEVEN.   The romance of real life: Charles Brockden Brown and the origins of American culture. (Bibl. 1995, 9254.) Rev. by Nicholas Rombes in AmS (36:1) 1995, 137–9; by Mark Wahlgren Summers in ANQ (9:1) 1996, 54–6; by Elizabeth Jane Wall Hinds in StudN (28:1) 1996, 138–9.

10486. WOODARD, MAUREEN L.   Female captivity and the deployment of race in three early American texts. *See* **8339**.

David Paul Brown (1795–1872)

10487. RONNICK, MICHELE VALERIE.   David Paul Brown's *Sertorius; or, The Roman Patriot* (1830): another influence on John Wilkes Booth. JAC (19:1) 1996, 87–92.

George Douglas Brown ('George Douglas', 'Kennedy King')

10488. CAMPBELL, IAN.   *The House with the Green Shutters* and history. Études Écossaises (1) 1992, 303–13.

10489. CRAIG, CAIRNS (ed.).   The house with the green shutters. Edinburgh: Canongate, 1996. pp. xiii, 252. (Canongate classics, 63.)

10490. DECAP, ROGER.   George Douglas et roman dramatique: *The House with the Green Shutters*. Toulouse: Éditions Universitaires du Sud, 1995. pp. 404. (Études littéraires.) Rev. by Pierre Morère in Études Écossaises (3) 1996, 223–7.

10491. SELLIN, BERNARD.   Poétique de la maison dans *The House with the Green Shutters* de George Douglas Brown. Études Écossaises (2) 1993, 187–94.

William Wells Brown

10492. CASHIN, JOAN E. (ed.).   Clotel; or, The president's daughter. Armonk, NY; London: Sharpe, 1996. pp. xxiv, 191. (American history through literature.)

10493. FABI, M. GIULIA.   The 'unguarded expressions of the feelings of the Negroes': gender, slave resistance, and William Wells Brown's revisions of *Clotel*. *See* **634**.

10494. RUFF, LOREN K.   William Wells Brown: dramatic apostle for Abolition. NETJ (2) 1991, 73–83.

The Brownings

10495. KELLEY, PHILIP; LEWIS, SCOTT (eds).   The Brownings' correspondence: vol. 11, July 1845–January 1846, letters 1982–2177. (Bibl. 1993, 7366.) Rev. by Alethea Hayter in TLS, 23 Feb. 1996, 3–4.

10496. MARKUS, JULIA.   Dared and done: the marriage of Elizabeth Barrett and Robert Browning. (Bibl. 1995, 9264.) Rev. by Isabella de Courtivron in BkW, 5 Feb. 1995, 1, 11; by Alethea Hayter in TLS, 23 Feb. 1996, 3–4; by Susan Carlson in MidQ (37:2) 1996, 229–30.

Elizabeth Barrett Browning

10497. Bristow, Joseph (ed.).   Victorian women poets: Emily Brontë, Elizabeth Barrett Browning, Christina Rossetti. *See* **10453**.

10498. Dennis, Barbara.   Elizabeth Barrett Browning: the Hope End years. Bridgend, Mid-Glamorgan: Seren, 1996. pp. 141, (plates) 8. (Border lines.)

10499. Gottlieb, Stacey.   'And God will teach her': consciousness and character in *Ruth* and *Aurora Leigh*. VIJ (24) 1996, 57–86.

10500. Groth, Helen.   Island queens: nationalism, queenliness and women's poetry 1837–1861. EAS (49) 1996, 42–61.

10501. Hudd, Louise.   The politics of a feminist poetics: *Armgart* and George Eliot's critical response to *Aurora Leigh*. EAS (49) 1996, 62–83.

10502. Jukić, Tatjana.   Sound of silence: a reading of Elizabeth Barrett Browning's Sonnet xxxviii. Gramma (4) 1996, 153–63.

10503. Morlier, Margaret M.   She for God in her: Elizabeth Barrett Browning's new Eve. *In* (pp. 127–44) **109**.

10504. Pollock, Mary S.   The anti-canonical realism of Elizabeth Barrett Browning's *Lord Walter's Wife*. SLI (29:1) 1996, 43–53.

10505. Reynolds, Margaret (ed.).   *Aurora Leigh*: authoritative text, backgrounds and contexts, criticism. *See* **809**.

10506. Rundle, Vivienne.   'The inscription of these volumes': the prefatory writings of Elizabeth Barrett Browning. VP (34:2) 1996, 247–78.

10507. Shires, Linda M.   The author as spectacle and commodity: Elizabeth Barrett Browning and Thomas Hardy. *In* (pp. 198–212) **126**.

10508. Stauffer, Andrew M.   Elizabeth Barrett Browning reads William Blake? *See* **8838**.

10509. Tucker, Herbert F.   *Aurora Leigh*: epic solutions to novel ends. *In* (pp. 63–85) **31**.

Robert Browning

10510. Bright, Michael.   Robert Browning's rondures brave. Athens: Ohio UP, 1996. pp. xxiv, 255.

10511. Brown, Susan.   'Pompilia': the woman (in) question. VP (34:1) 1996, 15–37.

10512. Case, Alison.   Browning's *Count Gismond*: a canvas for projection. VP (34:2) 1996, 213–22.

10513. Cervo, Nathan.   Browning's *Johannes Agricola in Meditation*. Exp (54:3) 1996, 148–50.

10514. Dupras, Joseph A.   Browning's *My Last Duchess*: paragon and parergon. PLL (32:1) 1996, 3–20.

10515. Fowler, Rowena.   Browning's music: the L. L. Bloomfield collection. *See* **477**.

10516. Gunn, Thom.   Adventurous song: Robert Duncan as Romantic Modernist. PN Review (17:4) 1991, 14–23.

10517. Harvey, M. L.   Iambic pentameter from Shakespeare to Browning: a study in generative metrics. *See* **4375**.

10518. Hawthorne, Mark D.   Allusions to Robert Browning in Jerzy Kosinski's *The Hermit of 69th Street*. NCL (23:4) 1993, 3–5.

10519. Howe, Elisabeth A.   The dramatic monologue. New York: Twayne; London: Prentice Hall, 1996. pp. xix, 166. (Studies in literary themes and genres, 10.)

10520. Jack, Ian; Inglesfield, Robert (eds).   The poetical works of

Robert Browning: vol. 5, Men and women. Oxford: Clarendon Press; New York: OUP, 1995. pp. lvi, 499.

10521. KARLIN, DANIEL.   Browning's hatreds. (Bibl. 1995, 9303.) Rev. by John Maynard in Review (17) 1995, 53–60.

10522. KIM, HAE-RI.   Robert Browning eui si e natanan hwaja wa chungja eui yeokdongjeok gwankye. (The dynamic relationship between speaker and listener in Robert Browning's dramatic monologues.) Unpub. doct. diss., Kyung Pook National Univ., Korea, 1996.

10523. KIM, SUNG RYOL.   Browning's vision of Keats: *Cleon* and the 'mansion of many apartments' letter. VP (34:2) 1996, 223–33.

10524. LACKEY, MICHAEL.   The Victorian sublime. Litteraria Pragensia (6:11) 1996, 68–84.

10525. MACMAHON, BARBARA.   Indirectness, rhetoric and interpretative use: communicative strategies in Browning's *My Last Duchess*. *See* **2669**.

10526. MAXWELL, CATHERINE.   The poetic context of Christina Rossetti's *After Death*. EngS (76:2) 1995, 143–55.

10527. MAYNARD, JOHN.   Browning: living, hating, loving; or, Uneven developments: theory in the Browning boondocks. Review (17) 1995, 45–64 (review-article).

10528. MILLGATE, MICHAEL.   Testamentary acts: Browning, Tennyson, James, Hardy. (Bibl. 1995, 9308.) Rev. by Simon Gatrell in Text (Ann Arbor) (9) 1996, 452–9.

10529. PATHAK, PRATUL.   The infinite passion of finite hearts: Robert Browning and failure in love. (Bibl. 1992, 8187.) Rev. by John Maynard in Review (17) 1995, 60–4.

10530. ROBERTS, ADAM.   Robert Browning revisited. New York: Twayne; London: Prentice Hall, 1996. pp. xi, 177. (Twayne's English authors, 530.)

10531. RYALS, CLYDE DE L.   The life of Robert Browning: a critical biography. (Bibl. 1995, 9312.) Rev. by John Maynard in Review (17) 1995, 46–52.

10532. WARD, CANDACE.   Damning herself praiseworthily: nullifying women in *The Ring and the Book*. VP (34:1) 1996, 1–14.

10533. WEIKERT, HEIDRUN-EDDA.   Robert Brownings kunstthematische Dichtung: ihr Epochenkontext zwischen Spätgotik und Viktorianismus. (Bibl. 1993, 7417.) Rev. by Ulrich Weisstein in GRM (44:3) 1994, 364–9.

10534. WOOLFORD, JOHN; KARLIN, DANIEL (eds).   The poems of Browning: vol. 1, 1826–1840; vol. 2, 1841–1846. (Bibl. 1993, 7419.) Rev. by Clyde de L. Ryals in Text (Ann Arbor) (8) 1995, 456–62.

William Cullen Bryant

10535. EBERWEIN, JANE DONAHUE.   'Siren Alps': the lure of Europe for American writers. EDJ (5:2) 1996, 176–82.

10536. REEVE, CLAYTON C.   Kindred spirits: William Cullen Bryant, Thomas Cole, and Asher Durand. TPB (32) 1995, 6–17.

Shan F. Bullock

10537. YAHATA, MASAHIKO.   Shan F. Bullock: Gissing's admirer and an ingenious short story writer. GissJ (32:2) 1996, 14–19.

Edward Bulwer-Lytton (Lord Lytton)

10538. DERRY, STEPHEN. The Time Traveller's utopian books and his reading of the future. *See* **10351**.

10539. ROBERTS, ADAM. Dickens's Jarndyce and Lytton's Gawtrey. NQ (43:1) 1996, 45–6.

10540. SNYDER, CHARLES W. Liberty and morality: a political biography of Edward Bulwer-Lytton. (Bibl. 1995, 9324.) Rev. by C. R. Perry in Albion (28:3) 1996, 509–11.

Frances Hodgson Burnett

10541. BIXLER, PHYLLIS. *The Secret Garden*: nature's magic. New York: Twayne; London: Prentice Hall, 1996. pp. xv, 108. (Twayne's masterwork studies, 161.)

10542. CONNELL, EILEEN. Playing house: Frances Hodgson Burnett's Victorian fairy tale. *In* (pp. 149–71) **54**.

10543. GILLISPIE, JULAINE. American film adaptations of *The Secret Garden*: reflections of sociological and historical change. LU (20:1) 1996, 132–52.

10544. McGILLIS, RODERICK. *A Little Princess*: gender and empire. New York: Twayne; London: Prentice Hall, 1996. pp. x, 116. (Twayne's masterwork studies, 159.)

10545. MARCHALONIS, SHIRLEY. Filming the nineteenth century: *The Secret Garden* and *Little Women*. *See* **10234**.

10546. STOLZENBACH, MARY M. Braid Yorkshire: the language of myth? An appreciation of *The Secret Garden* by Frances Hodgson Burnett. Mythlore (20:4) 1995, 25–9.

10547. WILSON, ANNA. Little Lord Fauntleroy: the darling of mothers and the abomination of a generation. AmLH (8:2) 1996, 232–58.

Sarah Harriet Burney

10548. CLARK, LORNA J. A contemporary's view of Jane Austen. *See* **10270**.

George Gordon Noel, Lord Byron

10549. BATE, JONATHAN. Living with the weather. SR (35:3) 1996, 431–47.

10550. BOKER, PAMELA A. Byron's psychic Prometheus: narcissism and self-transformation in the dramatic poem *Manfred*. LitPs (38:1/2) 1992, 1–37.

10551. BREWER, WILLIAM D. The Shelley–Byron conversation. (Bibl. 1995, 9339.) Rev. by Michael J. Neth in ANQ (9:2) 1996, 61–4; by Laura Quinney in KSJ (45) 1996, 202–4.

10552. BRUNNER, LARRY. Dramatic speculation and the quest for faith in Lord Byron's *Cain*. Lewiston, NY; Lampeter: Mellen Press, 1995. pp. ix, 130. (Salzburg Univ. studies: Romantic reassessment, 121.)

10553. CHRISTENSEN, JEROME. Lord Byron's strength: Romantic writing and commercial society. (Bibl. 1995, 9341.) Rev. by John Axcelson in ERR (6:2) 1996, 281–8.

10554. FLETCHER, CHRISTOPHER. Lord Byron – unrecorded autograph poems. *See* **646**.

10555. FRANKLIN, CAROLINE. Byron's heroines. (Bibl. 1992, 8233.) Rev. by L. J. Swingle in Review (17) 1995, 109–21.

10556. GALPERIN, WILLIAM.   Romanticism and/or anti-Semitism. *In* (pp. 16–26) **5**.

10557. GIDDEY, ERNEST.   Rocks and waves: Virginia Woolf, Leslie Stephen, and Byron. *In* (pp. 295–304) **125**.

10558. GRAHAM, PETER W.   The order and disorder of eating in Byron's *Don Juan. In* (pp. 113–23) **24**.

10559. HART, CHRIS (ed.).   Lives of the great Romantics by their contemporaries: vol. 2, Byron. London; Brookfield, VT: Pickering & Chatto, 1996. pp. xxx, 457.

10560. HIGASHIMAKA, ITSUYO.   The early stages of Byron's relationship with Gifford. *In* (pp. 161–9) **125**.

10561. JEWETT, WILLIAM.   Hawthorne's Romanticism: from canon to corpus. MLQ (57:1) 1996, 51–76.

10562. LACHANCE, CHARLES.   Naive and knowledgeable nihilism in Byron's gothic verse. PLL (32:4) 1996, 339–68.

10563. LAZANAS, VASSILIOS I. (ed.).   To epos *He Poliorkia tes Korinthou.* Ektene prolegomena yia te zoe, to ergo kai ten prosopikoteta tou agglou poiete kai megalou philhellena. Emmetre metaphrase tou epous. (Lord Byron, *The Siege of Corinth.* Extended prologue about the life work, and personality of the English poet and great philhellene. Verse translation of the epic.) Athens: Privately published, 1995. pp. 202.

10564. MACDONALD, D. L.   Childhood abuse as Romantic reality: the case of Byron. LitPs (40:1/2) 1994, 10–23.

10565. MARCHAND, LESLIE A. (ed.).   Byron's letters and journals: what comes uppermost. (Bibl. 1995, 9365.) Rev. by Andrew Nicholson in KSJ (45) 1996, 204–6.

10566. MARTIN, PHILIP.   Authorial identity and the critical act: John Clare and Lord Byron. *In* (pp. 71–91) **95**.

10567. PROCHÁZKA, MARTIN.   Byron and Romantic nationalism in Central Europe: the case of Czechs and Slovaks. Litteraria Pragensia (6:11) 1996, 36–52.

10568. RESTIVO, GIUSEPPINA.   Intelletto d'amore e assurdo nella soggettivazione romantica: Prometeo in Byron e Shelley. Textus (7) 1994, 163–86.

10569. ROSEN, F.   Bentham, Byron and Greece: constitutionalism, nationalism, and early Liberal political thought. (Bibl. 1992, 8258.) Rev. by D. L. LeMahieu in AHR (98:5) 1993, 1607–8.

10570. SAGLIA, DIEGO.   Byron and Spain: itinerary in the writing of place. Lewiston, NY; Lampeter: Mellen Press, 1996. pp. 224. (Romantic reassessment, 120.)

10571. —— '*I recur from fiction to truth*': Beppo e il mondo carnevalizzato. Textus (7) 1994, 113–32.

10572. SIMPSON, MICHAEL.   Ancestral voices prophesying what? The moving text in Byron's *Marino Faliero* and *Sardanapalus.* TSLL (38:3/4) 1996, 302–20.

10573. SODERHOLM, JAMES.   Fantasy, forgery, and the Byron legend. Lexington: Kentucky UP, 1996. pp. 195. (Cf. bibl. 1991, 7824.) Rev. by J.F. in TLS, 6 Dec. 1996, 24.

10574. SWINGLE, L. J.   Dismantling the master's house. *See* **9957**.

10575. THOMAS, GORDON K.   Finest Orientalism, Western Sentimentalism, proto-Zionism: the muses of Byron's *Hebrew Melodies.* Prism(s) (1) 1993, 51–66.

George Washington Cable

10576. CLEMAN, JOHN. George Washington Cable revisited. New York: Twayne; London: Prentice Hall, 1996. pp. xv, 214. (Twayne's US authors, 655.)

10577. LADD, BARBARA. Nationalism and the color line in George W. Cable, Mark Twain, and William Faulkner. Baton Rouge; London: Louisiana State UP, 1996. pp. xix, 197. (Southern literary studies.)

10578. MAYER, RUTH. 'Ther's somethin' in blood, after all': late nineteenth-century fiction and the rhetoric of race. YREAL (11) 1995, 119–37.

Thomas Campbell

10579. ROY, G. ROSS. Scottish poets and the French Revolution. *See* **8913**.

William Carleton

10580. KING, SOPHIA HILLAN. 'Pictures drawn from memory': William Carleton's experience of famine. Irish Review (17/18) 1995, 80–9.

10581. KRAUSE, DAVID. A tragic and comic world of compassion. Irish Literary Supplement (13:1) 1994, 32–4.

10582. MEIR, COLIN. Status and style in Carleton's *Traits and Stories of the Irish Peasantry*. *In* (pp. 83–91) **106**.

The Carlyles

10583. RYALS, CLYDE DE L.; FIELDING, KENNETH J. (eds). The collected letters of Thomas and Jane Welsh Carlyle: vol. 19, January – September 1845. (Bibl. 1995, 9391.) Rev. by Michael Timko in SSL (29) 1996, 262–70.

10584. —— —— The collected letters of Thomas and Jane Welsh Carlyle: vol. 20, October 1845 – July 1846. (Bibl. 1995, 9392.) Rev. by Michael Timko in SSL (29) 1996, 262–70.

10585. —— —— The collected letters of Thomas and Jane Welsh Carlyle: vol. 21, August 1846 – June 1847. (Bibl. 1995, 9393.) Rev. by Michael Timko in SSL (29) 1996, 262–70.

Thomas Carlyle

10586. ADAMS, JAMES ELI. The hero as spectacle: Carlyle and the persistence of dandyism. *In* (pp. 213–32) **126**.

10587. CAMPBELL, IAN. *Peter Lithgow*: new fiction by Thomas Carlyle. *See* **597**.

10588. DUPAS, JEAN-CLAUDE. Carlyle, histoires et Histoire. Études Écossaises (1) 1992, 191–200.

10589. ERICKSON, PAUL D. Henry David Thoreau's apotheosis of John Brown: a study of nineteenth-century rhetorical heroism. *See* **2361**.

10590. HALL, DONALD E. On the making and unmaking of monsters: Christian Socialism, muscular Christianity, and the metaphorization of class conflict. *In* (pp. 45–65) **74**.

10591. JESSOP, RALPH. 'A strange apartment': the watch-tower in Carlyle's *Sartor Resartus*. SSL (29) 1996, 118–32.

10592. MAERTZ, GREGORY. Carlyle's critique of Goethe: literature and the cult of personality. SSL (29) 1996, 205–26.

10593. O'GORMAN, FRANCIS.   Ruskin's *Fors Clavigera* of October 1873: an unpublished letter from Carlyle to Tyndall. NQ (43:4) 1996, 430–2.
10594. ROSEN, DAVID.   The volcano and the cathedral: muscular Christianity and the origins of primal manliness. *In* (pp. 17–44) **74**.
10595. SWANN, CHARLES.   Mark Rutherford's *The Revolution in Tanner's Lane* and Carlyle's *French Revolution*. NQ (43:1) 1996, 48–9.

Joseph Comyns Carr

10596. DALZIEL, PAMELA.   Whose *Mistress*? Thomas Hardy's theatrical collaboration. SB (48) 1995, 248–59.

'Lewis Carroll' (Charles Lutwidge Dodgson)

10597. BAKEWELL, MICHAEL.   Lewis Carroll: a biography. London: Heinemann; New York: Norton, 1996. pp. vii, 381.
10598. COHEN, MORTON N.   Lewis Carroll: a biography. (Bibl. 1995, 9416.) Basingstoke: Macmillan, 1995. pp. xxiii, 577. Rev. by Michael Dirda in BkW, 3 Dec. 1995, 1, 8–9; by John Kennedy in AR (54:3) 1996, 368–9; by Marina Warner in LRB (18:1) 1996, 9–10; by Robert Murray Davis in Cweal (123:8) 1996, 24–5.
10599. DOCHERTY, JOHN.   The literary products of the Lewis Carroll–George MacDonald friendship. (Bibl. 1995, 9419.) Rev. by Marina Warner in LRB (18:1) 1996, 9–10.
10600. FORDYCE, RACHEL.   Lewis Carroll: a reference guide. Boston, MA: G. K. Hall, 1988. pp. xxxiv, 160. (Reference guides to literature.) Rev. by Beverly Lyon Clark in CLAQ (16:2) 1991, 91–2.
10601. JONES, JO ELWYN; GLADSTONE, J. FRANCIS.   The Red King's dream; or, Lewis Carroll in Wonderland. (Bibl. 1995, 9421.) Rev. by R. Carroll in TRB (6:5) 1996, 331–2.
10602. LEACH, KAROLINE.   Ina in Wonderland. TLS, 3 May 1996, 15.
10603. LEBAILLY, HUGUES.   Dr Dodgson & Mr Carroll: de la caricature au portrait. *See* **216**.
10604. PENNINGTON, JOHN.   Reader response and fantasy literature: the uses and abuses of interpretation in *Queen Victoria's Alice in Wonderland*. *In* (pp. 55–65) **36**.
10605. POLETTO, GIAMPAOLO.   Fantastico tra fantasia, soprannaturale e *fantastique*: i contributi dopo Todorov. *See* **3958**.
10606. ROSE, ADAM.   Lewis Carroll's *Jabberwocky*: non-sense not nonsense. *See* **2699**.
10607. RUSSELL, W. M. S.   Time before and after *The Time Machine*. Foundation (65) 1995, 24–40.
10608. THOMAS, DONALD.   Lewis Carroll: a portrait with background. London: Murray, 1996. pp. xii, 404.

Charles W. Chesnutt

10609. BLOOMFIELD, MAXWELL.   Constitutional ideology and progressive fiction. JAC (18:1) 1995, 77–85.
10610. BOECKMANN, CATHERINE.   The invisible color: physical description and racial liminality in the novel of passing. YREAL (11) 1995, 255–81.
10611. BRODHEAD, RICHARD H. (ed.).   *The Conjure Woman* and other conjure tales. (Bibl. 1995, 9437.) Rev. by Peter Caccavari in ALR (28:2) 1996, 89–90.

10612. —— The journals of Charles W. Chesnutt. (Bibl. 1995, 9438.) Rev. by Frances Richardson Keller in AAR (29:3) 1995, 519–21; by Peter Caccavari in ALR (28:2) 1996, 89–90.

10613. KNADLER, STEPHEN P. Untragic mulatto: Charles Chesnutt and the discourse of Whiteness. AmLH (8:3) 1996, 426–48.

10614. MAYER, RUTH. 'Ther's somethin' in blood, after all': late nineteenth-century fiction and the rhetoric of race. *See* **10578**.

10615. SELINGER, ERIC. Aunts, uncles, audience: gender and genre in Charles Chesnutt's *The Conjure Woman*. BALF (25:4) 1991, 665–88.

10616. WILSON, CHARLES E., JR. Chesnutt's *Baxter's 'Procrustes'*: cultural fraud as link to cultural identity. *In* (pp. 120–8) **19**.

Lydia Maria Child

10617. CLIFFORD, DEBORAH PICKMAN. Crusader for freedom: a life of Lydia Maria Child. (Bibl. 1992, 8308.) Rev. by Constance M. McGovern in VH (60:4) 1992, 240–1; by Amy Beth Winn in AmP (3) 1993, 117–20; by Jane H. Pease in AHR (98:2) 1993, 562–3; by Rachel Filene Seidman in NWSAJ (5:2) 1993, 253–61.

10618. GOULD, PHILIP. Covenant and republic: historical romance and the politics of Puritanism. Cambridge; New York: CUP, 1996. pp. x, 273. (Cambridge studies in American literature and culture, 103.) (Cf. bibl. 1994, 7014.)

10619. KARCHER, CAROLYN L. The first woman in the Republic: a cultural biography of Lydia Maria Child. (Bibl. 1995, 9448.) Rev. by Andrea M. Atkin in TSWL (15:1) 1996, 155–7; by Dana D. Nelson in AL (68:1) 1996, 235–6; by James Brewer Stewart in AHR (101:3) 1996, 914–15; by Virginia W. Jackson in SAF (24:1) 1996, 127–8; by Judith A. Hunter in CWH (42:3) 1996, 256–8; by Nancy A. Walker in AmS (37:1) 1996, 196; by Elaine Hedges in Legacy (13:2) 1996, 152–3; by Margaret McFadden in NWSAJ (8:2) 1996, 157–8.

10620. MILLS, BRUCE. Cultural reformations: Lydia Maria Child and the literature of reform. (Bibl. 1994, 7757.) Rev. by Andrea M. Atkin in TSWL (15:1) 1996, 155–7; by Marilyn M. Wilton in AL (68:1) 1996, 236–7.

10621. —— Literary excellence and social reform: Lydia Maria Child's ultraisms for the 1840s. *In* (pp. 3–16) **3**.

10622. PATTERSON, MARK R. Surrogacy and slavery: the problematics of consent in 'Baby M.', *Romance of the Republic*, and *Pudd'nhead Wilson*. AmLH (8:3) 1996, 449–70.

Kate Chopin

10623. ANASTASOPOULOU, MARIA. Rites of passage in Kate Chopin's *The Awakening*. SoLJ (23:2) 1991, 19–30.

10624. BAXTER, JUDITH (ed.). *The Awakening* and other stories. Cambridge; New York: CUP, 1996. pp. 256. (Cambridge literature.)

10625. KOLOSKI, BERNARD. Kate Chopin: a study of the short fiction. New York: Twayne; London: Prentice Hall, 1996. pp. xvi, 165. (Twayne's studies in short fiction, 65.)

10626. LeBLANC, ELIZABETH. The metaphorical lesbian: Edna Pontellier in *The Awakening*. TSWL (15:2) 1996, 289–307.

10627. MALZAHN, MANFRED. The strange demise of Edna Pontellier. SoLJ (23:2) 1991, 31–9.

10628. Patterson, Katherine.   Out of a convention of awakening: defining a space beyond awareness. Feminist Issues (11:2) 1991, 101–12.

10629. Peel, Ellen.   Semiotic subversion in *Désirée's Baby*. *In* (pp. 56–73) **65**.

10630. Petry, Alice Hall (ed.).   Critical essays on Kate Chopin. New York: G. K. Hall; London: Prentice Hall, 1996. pp. xiii, 257. (Critical essays on American literature.)

10631. Semi, Leena.   Towards an understanding of the female subject: Kate Chopin's *The Awakening*. Teaching & Learning (2) 1996, 61–71.

10632. Thomas, Heather Kirk.   Kate Chopin: a primary bibliography, alphabetically arranged. ALR (28:2) 1996, 71–88.

10633. Toth, Emily.   Kate Chopin. (Bibl. 1991, 7905.) Rev. by Marcia A. Dalbey in GateH (12:1) 1991, 74–5; by Sidonie Smith and Camilla Stivers in Signs (18:2) 1993, 392–425.

10634. Vlasopolos, Anca.   Staking claims for no territory: the sea as woman's space. *In* (pp. 72–88) **97**.

10635. Weatherford, Kathleen Jeannette.   Kate Chopin's women writers and the anxiety of ambition. JSSE (25) 1995, 61–70.

10636. Wolff, Cynthia Griffin.   Un-utterable longing: the discourse of feminine sexuality in *The Awakening*. SAF (24:1) 1996, 3–22.

John Clare

10637. Blamires, David.   Chapbooks, fairytales and children's books in the writings of John Clare: part 1. *See* **3371**.

10638. Engels, William C.   Clare's mocking tone in *An Invite to Eternity*. JCSJ (15) 1996, 57–67.

10639. Foulkes, Richard (ed.).   John Clare: a bicentenary celebration. (Bibl. 1995, 9479.) Rev. by Simon Kövesi in JCSJ (15) 1996, 86–8.

10640. Haughton, Hugh; Phillips, Adam; Summerfield, Geoffrey (eds).   John Clare in context. (Bibl. 1995, 9482.) Rev. by Roger Sales in Literature and History (5:2) 1996, 68–72.

10641. Keegan, Bridget.   Broadsides, ballads and books: the landscape of cultural literacy in *The Village Minstrel*. *See* **3505**.

10642. Lucas, John.   John Clare. (Bibl. 1995, 9483.) Rev. by Adam Piette in EEM (4:2) 1995, 70–1; by Bob Heyes in JCSJ (15) 1996, 91–3; by Roger Sales in Literature and History (5:2) 1996, 68–72.

10643. Martin, Philip.   Authorial identity and the critical act: John Clare and Lord Byron. *In* (pp. 71–91) **95**.

10644. Paulin, Tom.   John Clare: a Northamptonshire visionary. ERev (5:4) 1995, 6–8.

10645. Robinson, Eric (gen. ed.).   Poems of the middle period, 1822–1837: vol. 1, *The Shepherd's Calendar, Village Stories*, and other poems. Ed. by Eric Robinson, David Powell, and P. M. S. Dawson. Oxford: Clarendon Press; New York: OUP, 1996. pp. xxviii, 376.

10646. —— Poems of the middle period, 1822–1837: vol. 2, Poems in order of manuscript. Ed. by Eric Robinson, David Powell, and P. M. S. Dawson. Oxford: Clarendon Press; New York: OUP, 1996. pp. xiv, 402.

10647. Robinson, Eric; Powell, David (eds).   John Clare by himself. Ashington: Mid-Northumberland Arts Group; Manchester: Carcanet Press, 1996. pp. xxiv, 364.

10648. —— —— Dawson, P. M. S. (eds).   Northborough sonnets. Ashington: Mid-Northumberland Arts Group; Manchester: Carcanet

Press, 1995. pp. xxii, 136. (Carcanet John Clare programme.) Rev. by John Lucas in JCSJ (15) 1996, 83–6.

10649. SALES, ROGER. The John Clare revival. Literature and History (5:2) 1996, 68–72 (review-article).

10650. SHEPHERD, VALERIE. Anne Elizabeth Baker's *Glossary of Northamptonshire Words and Phrases* and John Clare's rustic idiom. *See* **2064**.

10651. SMITH, MATTHEW. The 'peasant poet' replies: *Sketches in the Life of John Clare* as a response to Taylor's Introduction to *Poems Descriptive*. JCSJ (15) 1996, 21–5.

10652. WAREHAM, JOHN. Clare's *Mouse's Nest*. Exp (55:1) 1996, 17–19.

Josephine Clifford

10653. HOILMAN, DENNIS. The ironic rhetoric of abuse: self-justification and self-rejection in the autobiographical stories of Josephine Clifford. Journal of the Southwest (37:3) 1995, 470–81.

Arthur Hugh Clough

10654. HARVIE, CHRISTOPHER. Garron Top to Caer Gybi: images of the inland sea. *See* **10257**.

10655. TASKER, MEG. Time, tense, and genre: a Bakhtinian analysis of Clough's *Bothie*. VP (34:2) 1996, 193–211.

William Cobbett

10656. NATTRASS, LEONORA. William Cobbett: the politics of style. (Bibl. 1995, 9497.) Rev. by E. D. Mackerness in Prose Studies (19:1) 1996, 121–3; by John Stevenson in NQ (43:2) 1996, 232–3.

Derwent Coleridge

10657. HAINTON, RAYMONDE. The unknown Coleridge: the life and times of Derwent Coleridge, 1800–1883. London: Janus, 1996. pp. ix, 313.

Mary Elizabeth Coleridge

10658. BATTERSBY, CHRISTINE. Her blood and his mirror: Mary Coleridge, Luce Irigaray, and the female self. *In* (pp. 249–72) **6**.

10659. JACKSON, VANESSA FURSE. Breaking the quiet surface: the shorter poems of Mary Coleridge. ELT (39:1) 1996, 41–62.

Samuel Taylor Coleridge

10660. ALEXANDER, CAROLINE. The way to Xanadu. (Bibl. 1994, 7816.) Rev. by Michael Upchurch in BkW, 17 July 1994, 4.

10661. ALLEN, RICHARD C. Charles Lloyd, Coleridge, and *Edmund Oliver*. SR (35:2) 1996, 245–94.

10662. ASHTON, ROSEMARY. The life of Samuel Taylor Coleridge: a critical biography. Oxford; Cambridge, MA: Blackwell, 1996. pp. 480. (Blackwell critical biographies, 7.) Rev. by Seamus Perry in TLS, 15 Mar. 1996, 36.

10663. BATE, JONATHAN. Living with the weather. *See* **10549**.

10664. BOEHM, ALAN D. The 1798 *Lyrical Ballads* and the poetics of late eighteenth-century book production. *See* **260**.

10665. BUTLER, JAMES; GREEN, KAREN (eds). *Lyrical Ballads* and other poems, 1797–1800. (Bibl. 1995, 9508.) Rev. by Susan J. Wolfson in

Review (17) 1995, 13–33; by Mark Parker in Text (Ann Arbor) (9) 1996, 434–8.

10666. CARLSON, JULIE A.   In the theatre of Romanticism: Coleridge, nationalism, women. (Bibl. 1995, 9509.) Rev. by Harriet Kramer Linkin in CLIO (25:2) 1996, 207–12.

10667. CHANDLER, DAVID.   Coleridge's 'suspension of disbelief' and Jacob Brucker's *assensus suspensione*. NQ (43:1) 1996, 39–40.

10668. CHRISTIE, WILLIAM.   The printer's devil in Coleridge's *Biographia Literaria. See* **1245**.

10669. COLAIACOMO, PAOLA.   Coleridge e l'imitazione. Textus (7) 1994, 55–65.

10670. COLOMBO, CLAIRE MILLER.   Reading Scripture, writing self: Coleridge's animation of the 'dead letter'. SR (35:1) 1996, 27–53.

10671. CRAWFORD, RACHEL.   Thieves of language: Coleridge, Wordsworth, Scott, and the contexts of *Alice du Clos*. ERR (7:1) 1996, 1–25.

10672. DUNCAN, ERIKA.   Some musings on artistic symbiosis: the demonic and angelic sides of the Coleridge–Wordsworth relationship. LitPs (40:3) 1994, 43–64.

10673. ENGELL, JAMES (ed.).   Coleridge: the early family letters. (Bibl. 1995, 9518.) Rev. by Donald Sultana in NQ (43:1) 1996, 99–101.

10674. FOAKES, R. A. (ed.).   Coleridge's criticism of Shakespeare: a selection. *See* **6300**.

10675. FULFORD, TIM.   The politics of the sublime: Coleridge and Wordsworth in Germany. MLR (91:4) 1996, 817–32.

10676. HARDING, ANTHONY JOHN.   Imagination, patriarchy, and evil in Coleridge and Heidegger. SR (35:1) 1996, 3–26.

10677. HICKEY, ALISON.   Double bonds: Charles Lamb's Romantic collaborations. ELH (63:3) 1996, 735–71.

10678. HUGHES, TED (sel. and introd.).   A choice of Coleridge's verse. London; Boston, MA: Faber & Faber, 1996. pp. viii, 232.

10679. JASPER, DAVID.   The death and rebirth of religious language. *See* **2653**.

10680. JEWETT, WILLIAM.   *The Fall of Robespierre* and the sublime machine of agency. ELH (63:2) 1996, 423–52.

10681. JOHNSTON, KENNETH R.   Self-consciousness, social guilt, and Romantic poetry: Coleridge's Ancient Mariner and Wordsworth's Old Pedlar. *In* (pp. 216–48) **6**.

10682. KESTING, MARIANNE.   Ich-Figuration und Erzähler-schachtelung: zur Selbstreflexion der dichterischen Imagination. GRM (41:1) 1991, 27–45.

10683. KIM, CHUNG-GUN.   Coleridge eui meta-yoonri: Hartley, Paley geurigo Kant eui dodeokron bipan reul jungsimeuro. (Coleridge's meta-ethics: mainly concerned with the morality of Hartley, Paley and Kant.) JELL (42:3) 1996, 653–76.

10684. KITSON, PETER J. (ed.).   Coleridge, Keats and Shelley. Basingstoke: Macmillan; New York: St Martin's Press, 1996. pp. ix, 241. (New casebooks.)

10685. KNOX-SHAW, P. H.   The Eastern *Ancient Mariner. See* **9175**.

10686. LINDOP, GREVEL.   Newton, Raymond Tallis and the three cultures. *See* **8812**.

10687. MCCARTHY, THOMAS J.   'Epistolary intercourse': sympathy and the English Romantic letter. *See* **8902**.

10688. McCusick, James C.   Coleridge and the economy of nature. SR (35:3) 1996, 375–92.

10689. McGavran, James Holt.   Defusing the discharged soldier: Wordsworth, Coleridge, and homosexual panic. PLL (32:2) 1996, 147–65.

10690. Mays, J. C. C.   Editing Coleridge in the historicized present. *See* **753**.

10691. Miyamoto, Nahoko.   'That silent sea': *The Ancient Mariner* as a Romantic world map. SEL (English number) 1996, 37–51.

10692. Naccarato, Peter.   History, technology and the emergence of the Romantic subject. Prism(s) (2) 1994, 1–12.

10693. Nasi, Franco.   In margine a *The Theory of Life* di Samuel Taylor Coleridge. Textus (7) 1994, 67–88.

10694. Paley, Morton D.   Coleridge's later poetry. Oxford: Clarendon Press; New York: OUP, 1996. pp. xii, 147.

10695. Perkins, David.   The *Ancient Mariner* and its interpreters: some versions of Coleridge. MLQ (57:3) 1996, 425–48.

10696. Prickett, Stephen.   *Biographia Literaria*: Chapter Thirteen. *In* (pp. 3–23) **47**.

10697. Roberts, Andrew.   Omnipotence and the Romantic imagination. Eng (40:166) 1991, 1–21.

10698. Roe, Nicholas.   Wordsworth and Coleridge: the radical years. (Bibl. 1992, 8386.) Rev. by Christoph Bode in ZAA (42:3) 1994, 261–5.

10699. Rogner, David W.   Diagramming Coleridge: picturesque aesthetics in *The Nightingale. See* **9076**.

10700. Rothman, Irving N.   Coleridge on the semi-colon in *Robinson Crusoe*: problems in editing Defoe. *See* **820**.

10701. Rowe, M. W.   *Kubla Khan* and the structure of the psyche. Eng (40:167) 1991, 145–54.

10702. Sachithanandan, V. (ed.).   The rime of the ancient mariner. London: Sangam, 1996. pp. 92. (Second ed.: first ed. 1979.)

10703. Schofield, Robin.   Comparisons. ERev (5:4) 1995, 9–13. (Coleridge, *To the River Otter*; Wordsworth, *There Is a Little Unpretending Rill*.)

10704. Schwenger, Peter.   Blake's boxes, Coleridge's circles, and the frame of Romantic vision. *See* **8832**.

10705. Seeman, Chris.   Tolkien's revision of the Romantic tradition. Mythlore (21:2) 1996, 73–83.

10706. Söring, Jürgen.   Provozierte 'Gewalt' – zur Poetologie des Drogenrauschs. arcadia (28:2) 1993, 142–57.

10707. Stead, C. K.   The sad ghost of Coleridge. Textus (7) 1994, 89–94.

10708. Vallins, David.   Coleridge, transcendental idealism, and the ascent of intelligence. Prose Studies (19:1) 1996, 55–75.

10709. —— The letter and the spirit: Coleridge and the metaphysics of prose. MP (94:1) 1996, 39–59.

10710. Welch, Dennis M.   *Christabel, King Lear*, and the Cinderella folktale. *See* **6977**.

10711. Zuccato, Edoardo.   Italian Petrarchism in S. T. Coleridge's theory of poetry. *See* **10209**.

10712. —— S. T. Coleridge, Italy, and the fine arts. Textus (3:1/2) 1990, 273–97.

Sara Coleridge

10713. MEINERS, KATHERINE T.   Imagining cancer: Sara Coleridge and the environment of illness. LitMed (15:1) 1996, 48–63.

Wilkie Collins

10714. BURY, LAURENT.   *Shutting in, shutting out, shutting up*: variations sur l'enfermement dans *The Woman in White* de Wilkie Collins. CVE (43) 1996, 31–46.

10715. CHATTMAN, LAUREN.   Diagnosing the domestic woman in *The Woman in White* and *Dora*. In (pp. 123–53) **30**.

10716. DAVID, DEIRDRE.   Rewriting the male plot in Wilkie Collins's *No Name* (1862): Captain Wragge orders an omelette and Mrs Wragge goes into custody. In (pp. 33–44) **75**.

10717. FURQUERON, JAMES R.; MARCUSON, AGNES BONDURANT.   Poe and two minor writers. *See* **10356**.

10718. HOWE, WINONA.   Charles Dickens and the 'last resource': Arctic cannibalism and *The Frozen Deep*. CVE (44) 1996, 61–83.

10719. NAKAJIMA, TSUYOSHI.   All's fair in love and war: the sexual codes for Victorian women in Wilkie Collins' *No Name*. SEL (73:1) 1996, 29–45.

10720. PETERS, CATHERINE.   The king of inventors: a life of Wilkie Collins. (Bibl. 1995, 9604.) Princeton, NJ: Princeton UP, 1993. Rev. by Dennis Drabelle in BkW, 9 Jan. 1994, 3.

10721. SCHMITT, CANNON.   Alien nation: gender, genre, and English nationality in Wilkie Collins's *The Woman in White*. Genre (26:2/3) 1993, 283–310.

10722. STAVE, SHIRLEY A.   The perfect murder: patterns of repetition and doubling in Wilkie Collins's *The Woman in White*. DSA (25) 1996, 287–303.

10723. ZANDER, ANDELA.   '*Spot the source*': Wilkie Collins' *The Moonstone* und John Fowles' *The French Lieutenant's Woman*. ZAA (41:4) 1993, 341–8.

Rose Terry Cooke

10724. ELROD, EILEEN RAZZARI.   Truth is stranger than non-fiction: gender, religion, and contradiction in Rose Terry Cooke. Legacy (13:2) 1996, 113–29.

10725. LINKON, SHERRY LEE.   Fiction as political discourse: Rose Terry Cooke's antisuffrage short stories. In (pp. 17–31) **3**.

J. Fenimore Cooper

10726. BARKER, MARTIN; SABIN, ROGER.   The lasting of the Mohicans: history of an American myth. Jackson; London: Mississippi UP, 1995. pp. x, 248. (Studies in popular culture.)

10727. BOURASSA, ALAN.   Tracking the dialectic: Theodor Adorno and Michael Mann's *The Last of the Mohicans*. CanRCL (23:3) 1996, 725–37.

10728. DARNELL, DONALD.   James Fenimore Cooper: novelist of manners. (Bibl. 1994, 7885.) Rev. by John Engell in StudN (28:1) 1996, 120–2.

10729. DEAN, JANET E.   The marriage and national myth in *The Pioneers*. AQ (52:4) 1996, 1–29.

10730. DUDENSING, BEATRIX.   Die Symbolik von Mündlichkeit und

Schriftlichkeit in James Fenimore Coopers *Leatherstocking Tales*. New York; Frankfurt; Bern; Paris: Lang, 1993. pp. 179. (Neue Studien zur Anglistik und Amerikanistik, 61.) Rev. by Dieter Schulz in Amst (41:2) 1996, 320–1.

10731.   GOULD, PHILIP.   Covenant and republic: historical romance and the politics of Puritanism. *See* **10618**.

10732.   LAMBERT, STEPHEN.   Cooper's *The Wept of Wish-Ton-Wish*. Exp (54:2) 1996, 80–2.

10733.   LIU, CELESTINE W.   Judith Hutter's stunted growth in James Fenimore Cooper's *The Deerslayer*. MidQ (37:4) 1996, 422–33.

10734.   MCQUILLAN, GENE.   'Extarminate the varlets!': the reconstruction of captivity narratives in *Dances with Wolves*. *See* **8337**.

10735.   MAYER, MAGDALEN.   Racial perceptions in James Fenimore Cooper's *The Last of the Mohicans*. *In* (pp. 41–53) **8**.

10736.   MITCHELL, LEE CLARK.   Leatherstocking, conduct books, and a moral code. YREAL (11) 1995, 75–102.

10737.   NEMOIANU, VIRGIL.   The dialectics of diversity: from Eastern Europe to J. F. Cooper. arcadia (31:1/2) 1996, 127–45.

10738.   —— J. F. Cooper, East European and Afro-American intellectuals: relativising cultural relativism. JLS (11:2) 1996, 15–42.

10739.   PITCHER, E. W.   Cooper's cunning and Heyward as cunning-man in *The Last of the Mohicans*. *See* **1929**.

10740.   RANS, GEOFFREY.   Cooper's Leatherstocking novels: a secular reading. (Bibl. 1994, 7894.) Rev. by Hugh Egan in AmS (34:2) 1993, 115–16.

10741.   SCHACHTERLE, LANCE.   Cooper's *Spy* and the possibility of American fiction. SHum (18:2) 1991, 180–99.

10742.   SCHNELL, MICHAEL.   The for(e)gone conclusion: *The Leatherstocking Tales* as antebellum history. ATQ (10:4) 1996, 331–48.

10743.   SCHULZ, DIETER.   Cooper's knight of Columbus: *Mercedes of Castile* as chivalric romance. Letteratura d'America (44) 1992, 31–46.

10744.   TAYLOR, ALAN.   Fenimore Cooper's America. HT (46:2) 1996, 21–7.

James D. Corrothers

10745.   BRUCE, DICKSON D., JR.   James Corrothers reads a book; or, The lives of Sandy Jenkins. AAR (26:4) 1992, 665–73.

Joseph Stirling Coyne

10746.   BOOTH, MICHAEL R. (ed.).   *The Lights o' London* and other Victorian plays. Oxford; New York: OUP, 1995. pp. xxxiii, 251. (Oxford drama library.)

Pearl Craigie ('John Oliver Hobbes')

10747.   HARDING, MILDRED DAVIS.   Air-bird in the water: the life and works of Pearl Craigie (John Oliver Hobbes). Madison, NJ: Fairleigh Dickinson UP; London; Toronto: Assoc. UPs, 1996. pp. 535.

Mrs Craik (Dinah Maria Mulock)

10748.   DIGGS, MARYLYNNE.   Romantic friends or a 'different race of creatures'? The representation of lesbian pathology in nineteenth-century America. *See* **10229**.

10749. GERGITS, JULIA M.   Women artists at home. *In* (pp. 105–29) **54**.

10750. KAPLAN, CORA (introd.).   *Olive* and *The Half-Caste*. Oxford; New York: OUP, 1996. pp. xxv, 372. (Oxford popular fiction.)

10751. PHILIPOSE, LILY.   The politics of the hearth in Victorian children's fantasy: Dinah Mulock Craik's *The Little Lame Prince*. CLAQ (21:3) 1996, 133–9.

10752. SEELEY, TRACY.   Victorian women's essays and Dinah Mulock's *Thoughts*: creating an *ethos* for argument. Prose Studies (19:1) 1996, 93–109.

Stephen Crane

10753. BASSAN, MAURICE.   The 'true West' of Sam Shepard and Stephen Crane. ALR (28:2) 1996, 11–17.

10754. BROWN, BILL.   The material unconscious: American amusement, Stephen Crane, & the economies of play. Cambridge, MA; London: Harvard UP, 1996. pp. xiii, 335.

10755. COLVERT, JAMES B.   Fred Holland Day, Louise Imogen Guiney, and the text of Stephen Crane's *The Black Riders*. *See* **607**.

10756. DAVIS, LINDA H.   The red room: Stephen Crane and me. ASch (64:2) 1995, 207–20.

10757. DOOLEY, PATRICK K.   The humanism of Stephen Crane. Humanist (56:1) 1996, 14–17.

10758. —— The pluralistic philosophy of Stephen Crane. Foreword by John J. McDermott. (Bibl. 1995, 9648.) Rev. by George Cotkin in AmS (34:2) 1993, 141–2; by David Watson in Literature and History (5:1) 1996, 119–20; by Paul Sorrentino in ALR (29:1) 1996, 90–2.

10759. FUDGE, KEITH.   Sisterhood born from seduction: Susanna Rowson's *Charlotte Temple*, and Stephen Crane's *Maggie Johnson*. *See* **9320**.

10760. GREEN, FRANK (ed.).   The red badge of courage. Cheltenham: Thornes, 1996. pp. 194. (Thornes classic novels.)

10761. MARIANI, GIORGIO.   Ideologia come spettacolo dell'ideologia in *The Red Badge of Courage* di Stephen Crane. Àcoma (1) 1994, 78–89.

10762. MARSHALL, ELAINE.   Crane's *The Monster* seen in the light of Robert Lewis's lynching. NineL (51:2) 1996, 205–24.

10763. MITCHELL, VERNER D.   Reading 'race' and 'gender' in Crane's *The Red Badge of Courage*. CLAJ (40:1) 1996, 60–71.

10764. PIZER, DONALD.   From a home to the world: Stephen Crane's *George's Mother*. PLL (32:3) 1996, 277–90.

10765. ROBERTSON, MICHAEL.   The cultural work of *Active Service*. ALR (28:2) 1996, 1–10.

10766. SCHAEFER, MICHAEL W.   A reader's guide to the short stories of Stephen Crane. New York: G. K. Hall; London: Prentice Hall, 1996. pp. xiii, 468. (Reference pubs in literature.)

10767. SCOTT, GRANT F.   *Going after Cacciato* and the problem of teleology. Greyfriar (31) 1991, 30–6.

10768. SHANAHAN, DANIEL.   The army motif in *The Red Badge of Courage* as a response to industrial capitalism. PLL (32:4) 1996, 399–409.

10769. WILSON, CHRISTOPHER P.   Stephen Crane and the police. AmQ (48:2) 1996, 273–315.

10770. WORYMA, PIOTR.   A sample contrastive analysis of *The Blue Hotel* by Stephen Crane and *The Nigger of the Narcissus* by Joseph Conrad. *See* **2736**.

Francis Marion Crawford

10771. ENG, STEVE.   Reasons for the critical and academic neglect of F. Marion Crawford. Romantist (9/10) 1985/86, 33–5.

Isabella Valancy Crawford

10772. GALVIN, ELIZABETH MCNEILL.   Isabella Valancy Crawford: we scarcely knew her. Toronto: Natural Heritage/Natural History, 1994. pp. xviii, 135. Rev. by Kathleen O'Donnell in CanL (150) 1996, 171; by D. M. R. Bentley in JCP (11) 1996, 185–7.

Bithia Mary (Sheppard) Croker (d.1920)

10773. SAINSBURY, ALISON.   Married to the Empire: the Anglo-Indian domestic novel. *In* (pp. 163–87) **132**.

Catherine Crowe

10774. GEARY, ROBERT F.   The corpse in the dung cart: *The Night-Side of Nature* and the Victorian supernatural tale. *In* (pp. 47–53) **36**.

Mary Anne Cruse

10775. HUNT, ROBERT.   Domesticity, paternalism and isolation: Mary Anne Cruse and the search for moral asylum. SoQ (34:4) 1996, 15–24.

Sarah Anne Curzon (1833–1898)

10776. DERKSEN, CÉLESTE.   Out of the closet: dramatic works by Sarah Anne Curzon. TRC (15:1) 1994, 3–20; (15:2) 1994, 123–35.

Rollin Mallory Daggett (1831–1901)

10777. BERKOVE, LAWRENCE I.   Rollin Mallory Daggett's *My French Friend*: a precursor of *Paul's Case*? WCPMN (38:2) 1994, 31–4.

Ella D'Arcy

10778. FISHER, BENJAMIN FRANKLIN, IV.   Ella D'Arcy: a commentary with a primary and annotated secondary bibliography. ELT (35:2) 1992, 179–211.

Charles Darwin

10779. BEER, GILLIAN.   Darwin and the idea of England. Textus (8:1) 1995, 9–18.

10780. BULHOF, ILSE N.   The language of science: a study of the relationship between literature and science in the perspective of a hermeneutical ontology, with a case study of Darwin's *The Origin of Species*. *See* **2745**.

10781. RAILSBACK, BRIAN E.   Parallel expeditions: Charles Darwin and the art of John Steinbeck. (Bibl. 1995, 9671.) Rev. by Bert Bender in AL (68:4) 1996, 869–70; by Kevin Hearle in TexR (17:1/2) 1996, 112–15.

John Davidson

10782. SLOAN, JOHN. John Davidson, first of the Moderns: a literary biography. (Bibl. 1995, 9672.) Rev. by Pierre Coustillas in GissJ (32:3) 1996, 33–4; by Patrick Crotty in TLS, 2 Feb. 1996, 3–4.

10783. —— (ed.). Selected poems and prose. (Bibl. 1995, 9673.) Rev. by Patrick Crotty in TLS, 2 Feb. 1996, 3–4.

M. E. M. Davis (Mollie Evelyn Moore) (1852–1909)

10784. BRADY, PATRICIA. Mollie Moore Davis: a literary life. *In* (pp. 98–118) **65**.

Rebecca Harding Davis

10785. HARRIS, SHARON M. Rebecca Harding Davis and American Realism. (Bibl. 1994, 7923.) Rev. by Josephine Donovan in Signs (19:1) 1993, 232–5.

10786. MAYER, RUTH. 'Ther's somethin' in blood, after all': late nineteenth-century fiction and the rhetoric of race. *See* **10578**.

10787. PFAELZER, JEAN. Parlor radical: Rebecca Harding Davis and the origins of American social realism. Pittsburgh, PA: Pittsburgh UP, 1996. pp. xi, 282.

10788. —— (ed.). A Rebecca Harding Davis reader: *Life in the Iron-Mills*, selected fiction & essays. Pittsburgh, PA: Pittsburgh UP, 1995. pp. li, 483. Rev. by Carol Farley Kessler in Utopian Studies (7:2) 1996, 316–18.

10789. THOMSON, ROSEMARIE GARLAND. Benevolent maternalism and physically disabled figures: dilemmas of female embodiment in Stowe, Davis, and Phelps. AL (68:3) 1996, 555–86.

William James Dawson (1854–1928)

10790. HAPGOOD, LYNNE. 'The reconceiving of Christianity': secularisation, realism and the religious novel, 1888–1900. *See* **9865**.

10791. —— Urban utopias: socialism, religion and the city, 1880 to 1900. *In* (pp. 184–201) **18**.

Martin R. Delany

10792. CRANE, GREGG D. The lexicon of rights, power, and community in *Blake*: Martin R. Delany's dissent from 'Dred Scott'. AL (68:3) 1996, 527–53.

Thomas De Quincey

10793. BAXTER, EDMUND. De Quincey's art of autobiography. (Bibl. 1995, 9686.) Rev. by Zachary Leader in Eng (40:167) 1991, 162–8.

10794. KESTING, MARIANNE. Ich-Figuration und Erzähler-schachtelung: zur Selbstreflexion der dichterischen Imagination. *See* **10682**.

10795. LEASK, NIGEL. Toward a universal aesthetic: De Quincey on murder as carnival and tragedy. *In* (pp. 92–120) **95**.

10796. LINDOP, GREVEL. De Quincey and the Portico Library. *See* **502**.

10797. —— Newton, Raymond Tallis and the three cultures. *See* **8812**.

10798. PIGLIONICA, ANNA MARIA. The paradoxes of De Quincey's 'impassioned prose'. Textus (5) 1992, 35–50.

10799. ROMAN, L. E. De Quincey's *Suspiria de Profundis*: the reason for incompletion. NQ (43:1) 1996, 43–4.

10800. SÖRING, JÜRGEN. Provozierte 'Gewalt' – zur Poetologie des Drogenrauschs. *See* **10706**.

10801. SUDAN, RAJANI. Englishness 'a'muck': De Quincey's *Confessions*. Genre (27:4) 1994, 377–94.

Charles Dickens

10802. ANDREWS, MALCOLM. Dickens and the grown-up child. (Bibl. 1995, 9707.) Rev. by D.W. in TLS, 30 Aug. 1996, 32.

10803. ARMS, G. D. Reassembling *Bleak House*: 'Is there *three* of 'em then?' LitPs (39:1/2) 1993, 84–96.

10804. ARMSTRONG, MARY. Pursuing perfection: *Dombey and Son*, female homoerotic desire, and the sentimental heroine. StudN (28:3) 1996, 281–302.

10805. BANETH-NOUAILHETAS, ÉMILIENNE. Textiles et texte: la parole vestimentaire dans *David Copperfield*. Q/W/E/R/T/Y (6) 1996, 115–22.

10806. BASTON, JANE. Word and image: the articulation and visualization of power in *Great Expectations*. LitFQ (24:3) 1996, 322–31.

10807. BAUBLES, RAYMOND L., JR. Displaced persons: the cost of speculation in Charles Dickens' *Martin Chuzzlewit. In* (pp. 245–52) **71**.

10808. BAUER, MATTHIAS. Das Leben als Geschichte: poetische Reflexion in Dickens' *David Copperfield*. (Bibl. 1992, 8485.) Rev. by Wilhelm Füger in GRM (44:1) 1994, 118–20.

10809. BAUMGARTEN, MURRAY. Seeing double: Jews in the fiction of F. Scott Fitzgerald, Charles Dickens, Anthony Trollope, and George Eliot. *In* (pp. 44–61) **5**.

10810. BELLETTO, RENÉ. *Les Grandes Espérances* de Charles Dickens. Paris: POL, 1994. pp. 655.

10811. BERRY, LAURA C. In the bosom of the family: the wet-nurse, the railroad, and *Dombey and Son*. DSA (25) 1996, 1–28.

10812. BLOOM, HAROLD (ed.). Charles Dickens' *Great Expectations*. New York: Chelsea House, 1996. pp. 80. (Bloom's notes.)

10813. BOWEN, JOHN. Performing business, training ghosts: transcoding *Nickleby*. ELH (63:1) 1996, 153–75.

10814. BRATTIN, JOEL J. Recent Dickens studies: 1994. DSA (25) 1996, 327–72.

10815. BRILL, OLAF. Horror-Rätsel – Erhebungen zu einer neuen Erzählgattung. Fabula (37:1/2) 1996, 28–70.

10816. BRYAN, GEORGE B.; MIEDER, WOLFGANG. 'As Sam Weller said, when finding himself on the stage': Wellerisms in dramatizations of Charles Dickens' *Pickwick Papers*. *See* **3314**.

10817. BURY, LAURENT. L'écriteau et l'ornement: la prolifération des signes dans *David Copperfield*. Q/W/E/R/T/Y (6) 1996, 123–7.

10818. BUSCH, FREDERICK. Suitors by Boz. GetR (6:4) 1993, 561–78.

10819. BUTLER, COLIN. *Hard Times*: a tale for yesterday and today. ERev (6:2) 1995, 36–8.

10820. CAPONI-DOHERTY, M. GABRIELLA. Charles Dickens and the Italian Risorgimento. DickQ (13:3) 1996, 151–63.

10821. CARDWELL, MARGARET (ed.). Great expectations. (Bibl. 1995, 9721.) Rev. by Marysa Demoor in EngS (76:3) 1995, 294–5; by Dieter Mehl in Archiv (233:1) 1996, 180–1.

10822. CARLISLE, JANICE.   Spectacle as government: Dickens and the working-class audience. *In* (pp. 163–80) **83**.

10823. —— (ed.).   *Great Expectations*: complete, authoritative text with biographical and historical contexts, critical history, and essays from five contemporary critical perspectives. Boston, MA: Bedford Books of St Martin's Press; Basingstoke: Macmillan, 1996. pp. xii, 641. (Case studies in contemporary criticism.) Rev. by Joel J. Brattin in DickQ (13:1) 1996, 47–51.

10824. CHEADLE, BRIAN.   Mystification and the mystery of origins in *Bleak House*. DSA (25) 1996, 29–47.

10825. CHILDERS, JOSEPH W.   *Nicholas Nickleby*'s problem of *doux commerce*. DSA (25) 1996, 49–65.

10826. CHITTICK, KATHRYN.   Dickens and the 1830s. (Bibl. 1994, 7961.) Rev. by Michael Slater in Eng (41:169) 1992, 83–7.

10827. CONNOR, STEVEN (ed.).   Charles Dickens. London; New York: Longman, 1996. pp. 238. (Longman critical readers.)

10828. CORDERY, GARETH.   Furniss, Dickens and illustration. *See* **189**.

10829. CRIBB, TIM.   Travelling through time: transformations of narrative from early to late Dickens. YES (26) 1996, 73–88.

10830. CROWLEY, JAMES P.   Pip's spiritual exercise: the meditative mode in Dickens' *Great Expectations*. Ren (46:2) 1994, 133–43.

10831. CUSUMANO, JOSEPH D.   Transforming Scrooge: Dickens' blueprint for a spiritual awakening. St Paul, MN: Llewellyn, 1996. pp. xii, 170.

10832. DANAHAY, MARTIN A.   Housekeeping and hegemony in Dickens's *Bleak House*. *In* (pp. 3–25) **54**.

10833. DAVIS, PAUL.   The lives and times of Ebenezer Scrooge. (Bibl. 1993, 7796.) Rev. by Brian Rose in JDTC (6:2) 1992, 139–41.

10834. DEVER, CAROLYN M.   Broken mirror, broken words: auto-biography, prosopopeia, and the dead mother in *Bleak House*. StudN (27:1) 1995, 42–62.

10835. DICKENS, CEDRIC.   The George and Vulture in *Pickwick Papers*. London: Dickens, 1995. pp. 12.

10836. DREW, JOHN M. L.   *Voyages extraordinaires*: Dickens's 'travelling essays' and *The Uncommercial Traveller*. DickQ (13:2) 1996, 76–96; (13:3) 1996, 127–50.

10837. DUNN, RICHARD J.   *Oliver Twist*: whole heart and soul. (Bibl. 1994, 7976.) Rev. by Ivan Melada in StudN (27:2) 1995, 218–20.

10838. DUTHEIL, MARTINE HENNARD.   *Great Expectations* as reading lesson. DickQ (13:3) 1996, 164–74.

10839. EDGECOMBE, RODNEY STENNING.   Patrick White and Dickens: two points of contact. JCL (31:1) 1996, 111–14.

10840. —— Reading through the past: 'archaeological' conceits and procedures in *Little Dorrit*. YES (26) 1996, 65–72.

10841. EIGNER, EDWIN M.   The Dickens pantomime. (Bibl. 1993, 7805.) Rev. by Judith Pascoe in Genre (23:4) 1990, 371–2.

10842. FAULKNER, DAVID.   The confidence man: empire and the deconstruction of muscular Christianity in *The Mystery of Edwin Drood*. *In* (pp. 175–93) **74**.

10843. FIELDING, K. J.   Dickens and science? DickQ (13:4) 1996, 200–16.

10844. FLETCHER, LuAnn McCracken. A recipe for perversion: the feminine narrative challenge in *Bleak House*. DSA (25) 1996, 67–89.

10845. GAGER, VALERIE L. Shakespeare and Dickens: the dynamics of influence. *See* **6306**.

10846. GALBRAITH, MARY. Pip as 'infant tongue' and as adult narrator in Chapter One of *Great Expectations*. *In* (pp. 123–41) **48**.

10847. GANE, GILLIAN. The hat, the hook, the eyes, the teeth: Captain Cuttle, Mr Carker, and literacy. DSA (25) 1996, 91–126.

10848. GEPPERT, HANS VILMAR. Der realistische Weg: Formen pragmatischen Erzählens bei Balzac, Dickens, Hardy, Keller, Raabe und anderen Autoren des 19. Jahrhunderts. *See* **9845**.

10849. GITTER, ELISABETH G. The rhetoric of reticence in John Forster's *Life of Charles Dickens*. *See* **10137**.

10850. GREEN, PAUL. Two venal girls: a study in Dickens and Zola. RecL (19) 1993, 21–35.

10851. HAGER, KELLY. Estranging *David Copperfield*: reading the novel of divorce. ELH (63:4) 1996, 989–1019.

10852. HAINING, PETER (ed.). Hunted down: the detective stories of Charles Dickens. London: Owen, 1996; Chester Springs, PA: Dufour, 1996. pp. 223. Rev. by John Whitworth in TLS, 16 Aug. 1996, 10.

10853. HÉBERT, DIANE. The Dickens checklist. DickQ (13:1) 1996, 55–8; (13:2) 1996, 118–20.

10854. ——— The *Dickens Quarterly* checklist. DickQ (13:3) 1996, 185–8; (13:4) 1996, 237–9.

10855. HOLLINGTON, MICHAEL. *David Copperfield* and *Wilhelm Meister*: a preliminary *rapprochement*. Q/W/E/R/T/Y (6) 1996, 129–38.

10856. ——— SADRIN, ANNY. Charles Dickens: *David Copperfield*. Bibliographie établie avec système d'étoiles style Guides Michelin. CVE (44) 1996, 185–201.

10857. HOUSTON, GAIL TURLEY. Consuming fictions: gender, class, and hunger in Dickens's novels. (Bibl. 1994, 8006.) Rev. by Ella Westland in DickQ (13:2) 1996, 111–13.

10858. HOWE, WINONA. Charles Dickens and the 'last resource': Arctic cannibalism and *The Frozen Deep*. *See* **10718**.

10859. HUMPHERYS, ANNE. Louisa Gradgrind's secret: marriage and divorce in *Hard Times*. DSA (25) 1996, 177–95.

10860. HWANG, GYU-HO. Charles Dickens eui saheo soseol yeongu. (A study of Charles Dickens's social novels.) Unpub. doct. diss., Soong Sil Univ., Seoul, 1996.

10861. INGHAM, PATRICIA. Dickens, women, and language. (Bibl. 1995, 9775.) Rev. by Anny Sadrin in CanRCL (20:3/4) 1993, 522–4.

10862. JACOBSON, WENDY S. The genesis of the last novel: *The Mystery of Edwin Drood*. DSA (25) 1996, 197–210.

10863. JADWIN, LISA. 'Caricatured, not faithfully rendered': *Bleak House* as a revision of *Jane Eyre*. *See* **10416**.

10864. JAFFE, AUDREY. Spectacular sympathy: visuality and ideology in Dickens's *A Christmas Carol*. *In* (pp. 327–44) **126**.

10865. JORDAN, JOHN O. Partings welded together: self-fashioning in *Great Expectations* and *Jane Eyre*. *See* **10417**.

10866. JOSE, GWEN (ed.). Hard times. Cambridge; New York: CUP, 1996. pp. 333. (Cambridge literature.)

10867. Joseph, Gerhard.   Who cares who killed Edwin Drood? Or, On the whole, I'd rather be in Philadelphia. NineL (51:2) 1996, 161–75.

10868. Kincaid, James.   Pip and Jane and recovered memories. *See* **10419**.

10869. Lamb, John B.   Domesticating history: revolution and moral management in *A Tale of Two Cities*. DSA (25) 1996, 227–43.

10870. Lanone, Catherine.   Ruptures mnémoniques et tissage narratif dans *David Copperfield*. Q/W/E/R/T/Y (6) 1996, 139–45.

10871. Lee, Hsiao-Hung.   Possibilities of hidden things: narrative transgression in Victorian fictional autobiographies. *See* **9899**.

10872. Lee, Ok.   *Geodaehan Yousan*: Dickens eui haehak gwa geu teukzing. (*Great Expectations*: the characteristics of Dickens's humour.) JELLC (38:2) 1996, 101–29.

10873. Lew, Laurie Kane.   Writing modern pictures: illustrating the real in Ruskin and Dickens. SLI (29:1) 1996, 55–72.

10874. Logan, Thad.   Decorating domestic space: middle-class women and Victorian interiors. *In* (pp. 207–34) **54**.

10875. Lubitz, Rita.   Marital power in Dickens' fiction. New York; Frankfurt; Bern; Paris: Lang, 1996. pp. 146. (Dickens' universe, 3.)

10876. McCuskey, Brian W.   'Your love-sick Pickwick': the erotics of service. DSA (25) 1996, 245–66.

10877. McGuire, Matthew J.   The role of women in the novels of Charles Dickens. London; Washington, DC: Minerva Press, 1995. pp. 78.

10878. Marlow, James E.   Charles Dickens: the uses of time. (Bibl. 1995, 9790.) Rev. by Audrey Jaffe in Review (18) 1996, 109–15.

10879. Monod, Sylvère.   Dickens et l'obsession des prisons. CVE (43) 1996, 65–71.

10880. Moss, Sidney P.; Moss, Carolyn J.   Charles Dickens and his Chicago relatives. (Bibl. 1995, 9796.) Rev. by Paul Schlicke in YES (26) 1996, 293–4.

10881. Mota, Miguel M.   The construction of the Christian community in Charles Dickens' *Bleak House*. Ren (46:3) 1994, 187–98.

10882. Mourby, Adrian.   How Millais burst his own bubble. Ruskin Gazette (1:9) 1996, 19–22.

10883. Myer, Valerie Grosvenor.   Martha as Magdalen: an illustration in *David Copperfield*. *See* **228**.

10884. Netto, Jeffrey A.   Dickens with Kant and Sade. Style (29:3) 1995, 441–58.

10885. Newlin, George.   Every thing in Dickens: ideas and subjects discussed by Charles Dickens in his complete works: a topicon. Westport, CT; London: Greenwood Press, 1996. pp. lviii, 1102.

10886. Nygaard, Susan.   Redecorating Dombey: the power of 'a woman's anger' *versus* upholstery in *Dombey and Son*. CritM (8:1) 1994, 41–80.

10887. Parker, David.   Dickens and the death of Mary Hogarth. DickQ (13:2) 1996, 67–75.

10888. Patten, Robert L.   When is a book not a book? *See* **305**.

10889. Peck, John (ed.).   *David Copperfield* and *Hard Times*: Charles Dickens. (Bibl. 1995, 9804.) Rev. by Richard J. Dunn in DickQ (13:1) 1996, 44–7.

10890. Pointer, Michael.   Charles Dickens on the screen: the film, television, and video adaptations. Lanham, MD; London: Scarecrow Press, 1996. pp. vi, 207.

10891. POPE, NORRIS. The Old Curiosity Shop and the new: Dickens and the age of machinery. DickQ (13:1) 1996, 3–18.

10892. PUSTIANAZ, MARCO. L'ultimo Dickens e la città come soggetto collettivo. QLLSM (4) 1990, 61–76.

10893. REED, JOHN R. Dickens and Thackeray: punishment and forgiveness. (Bibl. 1995, 9811.) Rev. by Valerie Grosvenor Myer in NQ (43:1) 1996, 107–8; by Deborah A. Thomas in DickQ (13:4) 1996, 229–31; by Frederick Kirchhoff in CLIO (25:4) 1996, 459–63; by Todd Pickett in ChrisL (46:1) 1996, 85–7.

10894. REM, TORE. Melodrama *and* parody: a reading that *Nicholas Nickleby* requires? EngS (77:3) 1996, 240–54.

10895. —— Playing around with melodrama: the Crummles episodes in *Nicholas Nickleby*. DSA (25) 1996, 267–85.

10896. ROBERTS, ADAM. Dickens's Jarndyce and Lytton's Gawtrey. *See* **10539**.

10897. ROBSON, JOHN M. Crime in *Our Mutual Friend. In* (pp. 114–40) **105**.

10898. ROSENBERG, BRIAN. Little Dorrit's shadows: character and contradiction in Dickens. Columbia; London: Missouri UP, 1996. pp. xi, 165.

10899. ROWLINSON, MATTHEW. Reading capital with Little Nell. YJC (9:2) 1996, 347–80.

10900. SADRIN, ANNY. Dickens; ou, Le roman-théâtre. (Bibl. 1993, 7889.) Rev. by Nicole Mallet in CanRCL (19:4) 1992, 656–9.

10901. —— Parentage and inheritance in the novels of Charles Dickens. (Bibl. 1995, 9814.) Rev. by Michael Hollington in CVE (44) 1996, 203–7.

10902. SCHAD, JOHN (ed.). Dickens refigured: bodies, desires, and other histories. Manchester; New York: Manchester UP, 1996. pp. xiii, 240.

10903. SELL, ROGER D (ed.). *Great Expectations*, Charles Dickens. (Bibl. 1995, 9820.) Rev. by Joel J. Brattin in DickQ (13:1) 1996, 47–51.

10904. SESTITO, MARISA. Divided Dickens. YES (26) 1996, 34–42.

10905. SEWARD, TIM (ed.). Great expectations. Cambridge; New York: CUP, 1995. pp. 512. (Cambridge literature.)

10906. SIRABIAN, ROBERT. Dickens's *Little Dorrit*. Exp (54:4) 1996, 216–20.

10907. SLATER, MICHAEL (ed.). *The Amusements of the People* and other papers: reports, essays, and reviews, 1834–51. London: Dent; Columbus: Ohio State UP, 1996. pp. xxxviii, 408. (Dent uniform edition of Dickens' journalism, 2.)

10908. —— *Sketches by Boz* and other early papers, 1833–39. (Bibl. 1995, 9826.) Rev. by Robert L. Patten in ANQ (9:4) 1996, 52–6; by John Gross in TLS, 23 Feb. 1996, 12.

10909. SMITH, GRAHAME. Charles Dickens: a literary life. Basingstoke: Macmillan; New York: St Martin's Press, 1996. pp. xiv, 190. (Literary lives.)

10910. STONE, HARRY. The night side of Dickens: cannibalism, passion, necessity. (Bibl. 1995, 9830.) Rev. by Audrey Jaffe in Review (18) 1996, 109–15; by Iain Crawford in SAtlR (61:4) 1996, 125–7.

10911. STOREY, GRAHAM; TILLOTSON, KATHLEEN; EASSON, ANGUS (eds). The letters of Charles Dickens: vol. 7, 1853–1855. (Bibl. 1995, 9831.) Rev. by Marysa Demoor in EngS (76:3) 1995, 293–4.

10912. SUNG, EUN-AE. *Bleak House* eui ijung seosul gwa ijung eui sigak. (Double narrative and double vision in *Bleak House*.) JELL (42:3) 1996, 611–27.

10913. —— Gissing eui Dickens ron. (Gissing on Dickens.) EngSt (20) 1996, 95–122.

10914. TAMBLING, JEREMY. Dangerous crossings: Dickens, digression, and montage. YES (26) 1996, 43–53.

10915. —— Dickens, violence and the modern state: dreams of the scaffold. (Bibl. 1995, 9833.) Rev. by Trey Philpotts in DickQ (13:3) 1996, 176–8; by Matthew Reynolds in TLS, 12 Jan. 1996, 24.

10916. TANABE, YOKO. *Our Mutual Friend* no hyoudai saikou. (Reevaluation of the title of *Our Mutual Friend*.) SEL (73:1) 1996, 47–59.

10917. TERAUCHI, TAKASHI. *Hard Times* kenkyu. (A study of *Hard Times*.) Kyoto: Apollonsha, 1996. pp. iv, 164.

10918. THOMAS, RONALD R. Making darkness visible: capturing the criminal and observing the law in Victorian photography and detective fiction. *In* (pp. 134–68) **126**.

10919. TIFFANY, GRACE. *Our Mutual Friend* in 'Eumaeus': Joyce appropriates Dickens. JML (16:4) 1990, 643–6.

10920. TUCKER, EDWARD L. James and Charles Dickens. HJR (17:2) 1996, 208–9.

10921. WILEY, MARGARET. Mother's milk and Dombey's son. DickQ (13:4) 1996, 217–28.

10922. ZANDER, HORST. '*A jaundiced jail*'; oder, 'Die Familie als Zelle der Gesellschaft'. Die Darstellung der Familie im früh- und mittviktorianischen Roman. ZAA (43:4) 1995, 325–35.

Emily Dickinson

10923. ACKMANN, MARTHA. 'I'm glad I finally surfaced': a Norcross descendent remembers Emily Dickinson. EDJ (5:2) 1996, 120–6.

10924. ALTIERI, CHARLES. Dickinson's dialectic. EDJ (5:2) 1996, 66–71.

10925. ANDŌ, MIDORI. Emily Dickinson's vision of 'circumference' and death from a Japanese perspective. EDJ (5:2) 1996, 221–5.

10926. ARDANAZ, MARGARITA. Emily Dickinson's poetry: on translating silence. EDJ (5:2) 1996, 255–60.

10927. BAIN, ROBERT (ed.). Whitman's & Dickinson's contemporaries: an anthology of their verse. *See* **10004**.

10928. BARRETT, FAITH. Inclusion and exclusion: fictions of self and nation in Whitman and Dickinson. EDJ (5:2) 1996, 240–6.

10929. BAUERLEIN, MARK. Emily Dickinson, *Harper's*, and femininity. *See* **1229**.

10930. BIRDEN, LORENE M. Dickinson's *Dare You See a Soul at the White Heat*. Exp (54:2) 1996, 87–90.

10931. —— Dickinson's *I Send Two Sunsets*. Exp (54:3) 1996, 150–4.

10932. BROGUNIER, JOSEPH. Walking my dog in *Sand Dunes*. JML (16:4) 1990, 648–50.

10933. CAMERON, SHARON. Choosing not choosing: Dickinson's fascicles. (Bibl. 1995, 9854.) Rev. by Lionel Kelly in YES (26) 1996, 331–3.

10934. CARNEY, MARY. Dickinson's poetic revelations: variants as process. *See* **598**.

10935. CHAICHIT, CHANTHANA. Emily Dickinson abroad: the paradox of seclusion. EDJ (5:2) 1996, 162–8.

10936. COLLINS, MARTHA. The outer from the inner. Field (55) 1996, 28–30.

10937. COSTA, CATHERINE. 'My George Eliot': *Deutera* Dickinson/ *Mutter* Eliot. EDJ (5:2) 1996, 59–65.

10938. CRUMBLEY, PAUL. Art's haunted house: Dickinson's sense of self. EDJ (5:2) 1996, 78–84.

10939. DELANY, KATHLEEN. Seeing New Englandly: some notes on Emily Dickinson. Textures (9) 1995, 1–4.

10940. DIEHL, JOANNE FEIT. Selfish desires: Dickinson's poetic ego and the rites of subjectivity. EDJ (5:2) 1996, 100–6.

10941. DOW, WILLIAM. *Elle signe souvent 'Emilie'*: Emily Dickinson and the French critical response. EDJ (5:2) 1996, 226–31.

10942. DUCHAC, JOSEPH. The poems of Emily Dickinson: an annotated guide to commentary in English, 1978–1989. (Bibl. 1995, 9859.) Rev. by Linda K. Robertson in AEB (9:1/2) 1995, 93–4.

10943. EBERWEIN, JANE DONAHUE. 'Siren Alps': the lure of Europe for American writers. *See* **10535**.

10944. ERICKSON, MARIANNE. The scientific education and technological imagination of Emily Dickinson. EDJ (5:2) 1996, 45–52.

10945. FARR, JUDITH (ed.). Emily Dickinson: a collection of critical essays. Upper Saddle River, NJ; London: Prentice Hall, 1996. pp. iv, 268. (New century views, 12.)

10946. FRANCIS, DAVID. The giant at the other side: Emily Dickinson and the inhuman. EDJ (5:2) 1996, 267–72.

10947. GIFFEN, ALLISON. That white sustenance despair: Emily Dickinson and the convention of loss. EDJ (5:2) 1996, 273–9.

10948. GRABHER, GUDRUN M. Emily Dickinson and the Austrian mind. EDJ (5:2) 1996, 10–17.

10949. GRÜNZWEIG, WALTER. Cries of distress: Emily Dickinson's initial German reception from an intercultural perspective. EDJ (5:2) 1996, 232–9.

10950. GUTHRIE, JAMES. Dickinson's *The Parasol Is the Umbrella's Daughter*. Exp (54:2) 1996, 84–7.

10951. —— Law, property, and provincialism in Dickinson's poems and letters to Judge Otis Phillips Lord. EDJ (5:1) 1996, 27–44.

10952. GUTHRIE, JAMES R. 'A revolution in locality': astronomical tropes in Emily Dickinson's poetry. MidQ (37:4) 1996, 365–82.

10953. HAGENBÜCHLE, ROLAND. 'Sumptuous – despair': the function of desire in Emily Dickinson's poetry. EDJ (5:2) 1996, 1–9.

10954. —— 'Sumptuous – despair': the function of desire in Emily Dickinson's poetry. Amst (41:4) 1996, 603–21.

10955. HALLEN, CYNTHIA L. Brave Columbus, brave Columba: Emily Dickinson's search for land. EDJ (5:2) 1996, 169–75.

10956. HARRIS, MORAG. Representations of the male in the female imagination: the Brontës and Dickinson. *See* **10376**.

10957. HEGINBOTHAM, ELEANOR. Dickinson's *What If I Say I Shall Not Wait!* Exp (54:3) 1996, 154–60.

10958. HERNDON, JERRY A. Dickinson's *Some Things That Fly There Be*. Exp (54:2) 1996, 82–3.

10959. HEWITT, ELIZABETH.   Dickinson's lyrical letters and the poetics of correspondence. AQ (52:1) 1996, 27–58.

10960. HOLLOWAY-ATTAWAY, LISSA.   The business of circumference: circularity and dangerous female power in the work of Emily Dickinson. EDJ (5:2) 1996, 183–9.

10961. HORAN, ELIZABETH.   To market: the Dickinson copyright wars. *See* **944**.

10962. HOWE, SUSAN.   The birth-mark: unsettling the wilderness in American literary history. *See* **8336**.

10963. INGOLD, BARBARA SEIB.   Dickinson's *A Narrow Fellow in the Grass*. Exp (54:4) 1996, 220–3.

10964. JUHASZ, SUZANNE; MILLER, CRISTANNE; SMITH, MARTHA NELL. Comic power in Emily Dickinson. (Bibl. 1995, 9876.) Rev. by June Sochen in Signs (21:3) 1996, 795–8.

10965. KELLY, LIONEL.   Emily Dickinson: imagining a text. *See* **704**.

10966. KIRKBY, JOAN.   Dickinson reading. EDJ (5:2) 1996, 247–54.

10967. KOGUCHI, HIROYUKI.   'With gay apostasy': Emily Dickinson's pagan world. SEL (English number) 1996, 53–66.

10968. KOSKI, LENA.   Sexual metaphors in Emily Dickinson's letters to Susan Gilbert. *See* **2414**.

10969. LAMBERT, ROBERT GRAHAM, JR.   A critical study of Emily Dickinson's letters: the prose of a poet. Lewiston, NY; Lampeter: Mellen Press, 1996. pp. xxi, 223.

10970. LANGDELL, CHERI DAVIS.   Pain of silence: Emily Dickinson's silences, poetic *persona* and Ada's selfhood in *The Piano*. EDJ (5:2) 1996, 197–201.

10971. LIM, HEON-KYUNG.   Emily Dickinson si e natanan *parody*. (Parody in Emily Dickinson's poetry.) Unpub. doct. diss., Dongeui Univ., Korea, 1995.

10972. LOEFFELHOLZ, MARY.   Dickinson and the boundaries of feminist theory. (Bibl. 1992, 8652.) Rev. by Hannah Möckel-Rieke in Signs (19:2) 1994, 519–23.

10973. —— Etruscan invitations: Dickinson and the anxiety of the aesthetic in feminist criticism. EDJ (5:1) 1996, 1–26.

10974. LOEHNDORF, ESTHER.   Emily Dickinson: reading a spinster. EDJ (5:2) 1996, 113–19.

10975. LOWENBERG, CARLTON.   Musicians wrestle everywhere: Emily Dickinson & music. (Bibl. 1994, 8119.) Rev. by Laura Feitzinger in ArsL (7) 1993, 140–4.

10976. LYNCH, EDWARD.   Le trasformazioni (traduzioni, tradizioni e tradimenti) di Walt Whitman, Emily Dickinson (e altri) in John Ashbery. Àcoma (8) 1996, 74–80.

10977. MARCELLIN, LEIGH-ANNE URBANOWICZ.   Emily Dickinson's Civil War poetry. EDJ (5:2) 1996, 107–12.

10978. MARIANI, ANDREA.   The system of colors in Emily Dickinson's poetry: preliminary observations. EDJ (5:2) 1996, 39–44.

10979. MESSMER, MARIETTA.   Emily Dickinson and the limits of logic: the example of her Puritan heritage. EDJ (5:2) 1996, 127–33.

10980. MEYER, WILLIAM E. H., JR.   Emily Dickinson's 'final decision': masculine voyeurism or feminine exhibitionism? WebS (10:1) 1993, 100–15.

10981. MORSE, JONATHAN.   Some of the things we mean when we say 'New England'. *See* **2184**.

10982. Mulvihill, John. Why Dickinson didn't title. EDJ (5:1) 1996, 71–87.

10983. Murray, Aífe. Kitchen table poetics: maid Margaret Maher and her poet Emily Dickinson. EDJ (5:2) 1996, 285–92.

10984. Noble, Marianne. Dickinson's sentimental explorations of 'the ecstasy of parting'. EDJ (5:2) 1996, 280–4.

10985. Oberhaus, Dorothy Huff. Emily Dickinson's fascicles: method & meaning. *See* **774**.

10986. Olney, James. The language(s) of poetry: Walt Whitman, Emily Dickinson, Gerard Manley Hopkins. (Bibl. 1994, 8124.) Rev. by Marta L. Werner in Review (17) 1995, 203–9; by Lionel Kelly in YES (26) 1996, 331–3.

10987. Orzeck, Martin; Weisbuch, Robert (eds). Dickinson and audience. Ann Arbor: Michigan UP, 1996. pp. viii, 280.

10988. Pagnattaro, Marisa Anne. Emily Dickinson's erotic *persona*: unfettered by convention. EDJ (5:2) 1996, 32–8.

10989. Plumly, Stanley. Doors ajar. Field (55) 1996, 21–6.

10990. Porter, J. S. Notes on Emily Dickinson's 'terrible simplicity'. AntR (105) 1996, 43–51.

10991. Price, Kenneth M. Whitman and Dickinson. American Literary Scholarship (1995) 61–78.

10992. Runzo, Sandra. Dickinson, performance, and the homo-erotic lyric. AL (68:2) 1996, 347–63.

10993. Salska, Agnieszka. Emily Dickinson in Polish: recent translations. EDJ (5:2) 1996, 215–20.

10994. Sánchez-Eppler, Karen. Touching liberty: abolition, feminism, and the politics of the body. (Bibl. 1994, 8132.) Rev. by Jennifer von Ammon in Legacy (13:2) 1996, 158–9.

10995. Sands, Margaret. Re-reading the poems: editing opportunities in variant versions. *See* **823**.

10996. Schäfer, Heike. The poet's poet: Adrienne Rich and Emily Dickinson. ZAA (43:3) 1995, 244–52.

10997. Short, Bryan C. Emily Dickinson and the Scottish New Rhetoric. *See* **2470**.

10998. Shurr, William H.; Dunlap, Anna; Shurr, Emily Grey (eds). New poems of Emily Dickinson. (Bibl. 1995, 9897.) Rev. by Lionel Kelly in YES (26) 1996, 331–3.

10999. Sielke, Sabine. Dickinson's threshold glances; or, Putting the subject on edge. EDJ (5:2) 1996, 93–9.

11000. Smith, Martha Nell. A hypermedia archive of Dickinson's creative work: part II, Musings on the screen and the book. *See* **841**.

11001. —— Rowing in Eden: rereading Emily Dickinson. (Bibl. 1994, 8139.) Rev. by Lionel Kelly in YES (26) 1996, 331–3.

11002. —— Whitman and Dickinson. American Literary Scholarship (1994) 63–92.

11003. Smith, Robert McClure. The seductions of Emily Dickinson. Tuscaloosa; London: Alabama UP, 1996. pp. x, 222. (Cf. bibl. 1992, 8669.)

11004. Strand, Mark. Views of the mysterious hill: the appearance of Parnassus in American poetry. GetR (4:4) 1991, 669–79.

11005. Sullivan, David. Inter-view: Emily Dickinson and the displaced place of passion. Analecta Husserliana (44) 1995, 101–18.

11006. —— Running the 'double risk': Emily Dickinson fleeing the worm's secretions. EDJ (5:2) 1996, 190–6.

11007. —— Suing Sue: Emily Dickinson addressing Susan Gilbert. EDJ (5:1) 1996, 45–70.

11008. TAPPMEYER, LINDA D.   Theatricality in Emily Dickinson. PMPA (17) 1992, 16–21.

11009. TINGLEY, STEPHANIE A.   'A letter is a joy of earth': Emily Dickinson's letters and Victorian epistolary conventions. *See* **10113**.

11010. WALKER, DAVID.   Stinging work. Field (55) 1996, 14–18.

11011. WARDROP, DANEEN.   Emily Dickinson's gothic wedding: dowered bride and absent groom. ATQ (10:2) 1996, 91–110.

11012. WHITE, FRED D.   'The sun proceeds unmoved': Dickinson's circumference as a context of Jeffers' inhumanism. SDR (34:3) 1996, 49–57.

11013. WILLARD, NANCY.   Questioning the pilgrim. Field (55) 1996, 9–11.

11014. WRIGHT, FRANZ.   Homages: Emily Dickinson. Field (55) 1996, 32–8.

11015. YIN, JOANNA.   Wild nights and white nights: Dickinson's vision of the poet in Anna Akhmatova. EDJ (5:2) 1996, 53–8.

11016. YOUNG, DAVID.   Electric moccasins. Field (55) 1996, 40–7.

Benjamin Disraeli

11017. DINGLEY, ROBERT.   Playing the game: the Continental casinos and the Victorian imagination. CVE (44) 1996, 17–31.

11018. ROBERTSON, LINDA K.   Food and hospitality in Disraeli's *Two Nations*. PMPA (16) 1991, 62–8.

11019. WEINTRAUB, STANLEY.   Disraeli: a biography. (Bibl. 1995, 9915.) Rev. by Jacob A. Stein in ASch (63:2) 1994, 295–302.

11020. WIEBE, M. G., *et al.* (eds).   Benjamin Disraeli letters: vol. 5, 1848–1851. (Bibl. 1995, 9916.) Rev. by Christopher Kent in ESCan (22:1) 1996, 89–92.

11021. WOHL, ANTHONY S.   'Dizzi-Ben-Dizzi': Disraeli as alien. JBS (34:3) 1995, 375–411.

Sarah Disraeli

11022. POLOWETZKY, MICHAEL.   Prominent sisters: Mary Lamb, Dorothy Wordsworth, and Sarah Disraeli. Westport, CT; London: Praeger, 1996. pp. xi, 151.

Mary Mapes Dodge

11023. GANNON, SUSAN R.; THOMPSON, RUTH ANNE.   Mr Scudder and Mrs Dodge: an editorial correspondence and what it tells us. AmP (2) 1992, 89–99.

Frederick Douglass

11024. ANDREWS, WILLIAM L. (ed.).   Critical essays on Frederick Douglass. (Bibl. 1993, 7977.) Rev. by John Sekora in AAR (28:3) 1994, 473–9.

11025. BODZIOCK, JOSEPH.   The big story of Frederick Douglass. Proteus (12:1) 1995, 5–9.

11026. CHAMBLEE, ANGELA E.   Frederick Douglass in the painting of

Jacob Lawrence and the poetry of Robert Hayden. Proteus (12:1) 1995, 19–23.

11027. DORSEY, PETER A. Becoming the other: the mimesis of metaphor in Douglass's *My Bondage and My Freedom. See* **2353**.

11028. GATES, HENRY LOUIS, JR (ed.). Autobiographies. (Bibl. 1995, 9925.) Rev. by Wilson J. Moses in AAR (30:2) 1996, 299–302.

11029. GATEWOOD, WILLARD B. An 'African prince, majestic in his wrath': William S. McFeely's biography of Frederick Douglass. FHQ (70:2) 1991, 192–202 (review-article).

11030. GIBSON, DONALD B. Christianity and individualism: (re-) creation and reality in Frederick Douglass's representation of self. AAR (26:4) 1992, 591–603.

11031. MCDOWELL, DEBORAH E. In the first place: making Frederick Douglass and the Afro-American narrative tradition. *In* (pp. 36–58) **1**.

11032. MCFEELY, WILLIAM S. Frederick Douglass. (Bibl. 1995, 9927.) Rev. by Willard B. Gatewood in FHQ (70:2) 1991, 192–202; by Waldo E. Martin, Jr, in AHR (98:2) 1993, 565–6; by John Sekora in AAR (28:3) 1994, 473–9.

11033. MARTIN, TERRY J. 'A slave in form … [but not] in fact': Frederick Douglass and the paradox of transcendence. Proteus (12:1) 1995, 1–4.

11034. MATHENY, DAVID L. Frederick Douglass: abolition orator. Proteus (12:1) 1995, 35–8.

11035. MORGAN, WINIFRED. Gender-related difference in the slave narratives of Harriet Jacobs and Frederick Douglass. AmS (35:2) 1994, 73–94.

11036. MULLEN, HARRYETTE. African signs and spirit writing. *See* **9010**.

11037. ROYER, DANIEL J. The process of literacy as communal involvement in the narratives of Frederick Douglass. AAR (28:3) 1994, 363–74.

11038. SEKORA, JOHN. The legacy of Frederick Douglass. AAR (28:3) 1994, 473–9 (review-article).

11039. STEPTO, ROBERT B. Narration, authentication, and authorial control in Frederick Douglass' *Narrative* of 1845. *In* (pp. 26–35) **1**.

11040. SUNDQUIST, ERIC J. (ed.). Frederick Douglass: new literary and historical essays. (Bibl. 1994, 8153.) Rev. by John Sekora in AAR (28:3) 1994, 473–9.

Edward Dowden

11041. PATTEN, EVE. A 'general crowd of small singers': Yeats and Dowden reassessed. Yeats Annual (12) 1996, 29–44.

Ménie Muriel Dowie (1867–1945)

11042. SMALL, HELEN (ed.). Gallia. London: Everyman, 1995. pp. xlii, 222. (Everyman library.)

Ernest Dowson

11043. ALKALAY-GUT, KAREN. Overcoming time and despair: Ernest Dowson's *Villanelle*. VP (34:1) 1996, 101–7.

11044. CHARDIN, JEAN-JACQUES. Ernest Dowson (1867–1900) et la crise fin-de-siècle anglaise. (Bibl. 1995, 9942.) Rev. by Rod Boroughs in ELT (39:3) 1996, 369–73.

11045.   COLDIRON, A. E. B.   Rossetti on Villon, Dowson on Verlaine: 'impossibility' and appropriation in translation. *See* **3116**.

11046.   NASSAAR, CHRISTOPHER S.   Dowson's *Cynara*. Exp (54:3) 1996, 168–70.

Sir Arthur Conan Doyle

11047.   ATKINSON, MICHAEL.   The secret marriage of Sherlock Holmes, and other eccentric readings. Ann Arbor: Michigan UP, 1996. pp. x, 198.

11048.   —— Staging the disappearance of Sherlock Holmes: the aesthetics of absence in *The Final Problem*. GetR (4:2) 1991, 206–14.

11049.   BOND, SHERRY ROSE; BOND, SCOTT.   Report from 221B Baker Street. AD (29:1) 1996, 74–8; (29:2) 1996, 203–5; (29:3) 1996, 334–6.

11050.   —— —— Report from 221B Baker Street: Orson Welles meets Sherlock Holmes. AD (29:4) 1996, 461–3.

11051.   BRADWAY, JEFFRY ALAN.   Upon the true provenance of Sherlock Holmes's Stradivarius. BSJ (46:3) 1996, 30–3.

11052.   BRILL, OLAF.   Horror-Rätsel – Erhebungen zu einer neuen Erzählgattung. *See* **10815**.

11053.   BRYAN, GEORGE B.   The proverbial Sherlock Holmes: an index to the Holmesian canon. *See* **3313**.

11054.   DIBATTISTA, MARIA.   The lowly art of murder: Modernism and the case of the free woman. *In* (pp. 176–93) **41**.

11055.   DOYLE, STEVEN T.   Sherlock Holmes: capitalist enemy. BSJ (46:3) 1996, 19–21.

11056.   FETHERSTON, SONIA.   The solitary omission. BSJ (46:4) 1996, 33–7.

11057.   FRANK, LAWRENCE.   Dreaming the Medusa: imperialism, primitivism, and sexuality in Arthur Conan Doyle's *The Sign of Four*. Signs (22:1) 1996, 52–85.

11058.   FRY, SAMUEL EDWIN.   The influence of Mr Sherlock Holmes on 20th-century Arctic exploration. BSJ (46:3) 1996, 22–9.

11059.   FURQUERON, JAMES R.   Elementary Holmes. PoeM (24) 1994, 14–16.

11060.   GILL, CATHY M.   Plumbing the mystery of Sherlock Holmes. BSJ (46:4) 1996, 30–2.

11061.   HALL, CHARLES; BLYTHE, PETER.   Sherlock Holmes and Sir Arthur Conan Doyle in Edinburgh. Edinburgh: Hall, 1995. pp. 48.

11062.   HALL, JOHN.   The dynamics of a falling star: some notes on the late Professor Moriarty. Leeds: Tai Xu, 1996. pp. 32.

11063.   —— YUICHI, HIRAYAMA.   The sporting achievements of Mr Sherlock Holmes. BSJ (46:1) 1996, 43–51.

11064.   HENDERSHOT, CYNDY.   The animal without: masculinity and imperialism in *The Island of Doctor Moreau* and *The Adventure of the Speckled Band*. NCS (10) 1996, 1–32.

11065.   HODGSON, J. A. (ed.).   Sherlock Holmes: the major stories with contemporary critical essays. (Bibl. 1995, 9951.) Rev. by John Gillard Watson in NQ (43:2) 1996, 238–9.

11066.   HODGSON, JOHN A.   An allusion to Arthur Conan Doyle's *A Study in Scarlet* in *The Picture of Dorian Gray*. ELN (34:2) 1996, 41–5.

11067. HYDER, WILLIAM. 'Consulting detective': consulting the canon. BSJ (46:4) 1996, 40–9.

11068. JANN, ROSEMARY. The adventures of Sherlock Holmes: detecting social order. (Bibl. 1995, 9953.) Rev. by Neal Baker in Extrapolation (37:1) 1996, 97–100.

11069. JOFFE, ANDREW; PEARSON, ROBERTA E. The best and wisest *Mensch*. BSJ (46:2) 1996, 27–33.

11070. KESTNER, JOSEPH A. 'Real' men: construction of masculinity in the Sherlock Holmes narratives. SLI (29:1) 1996, 73–88.

11071. KINSLEY, JOSEPH. Professor Moriarty: the French connection. BSJ (46:3) 1996, 13–15.

11072. KRUMM, PASCALE. *A Scandal in Bohemia* and Sherlock Holmes's ultimate mystery solved. ELT (39:2) 1996, 193–203.

11073. McLAUGHLIN, JOSEPH. Holmes and the range: frontiers old and new in *A Study in Scarlet*. Genre (25:1) 1992, 113–35.

11074. MERRILL, EDWARD. Knowledge of construction – nil. BSJ (46:3) 1996, 41–6.

11075. NOLLEN, SCOTT ALLEN. Sir Arthur Conan Doyle at the cinema. Foreword by Nicholas Meyer. Jefferson, NC; London: McFarland, 1996. pp. x, 317.

11076. OSTROWSKI, WITOLD. The composition of the detective novels of Arthur Conan Doyle. Acta Universitatis Lodziensis: Folia Litteraria Anglica (5) 1996, 155–74.

11077. ROSE-BOND, SHERRY. Mary Morstan, madonna: virgin or material girl. BSJ (46:2) 1996, 44–9.

11078. SEBEOK, THOMAS A. Give me another horse. AJSem (8:4) 1991, 41–52.

11079. SHAPIRO, JEFFREY G. The inside man. BSJ (46:2) 1996, 50–3.

11080. SOLBERG, ANDREW L. The funny John H. Watson. BSJ (46:1) 1996, 35–42.

11081. STASHOWER, DANIEL. 'And here there are genuine tears': Jeremy Brett, 1935–1995. AD (29:1) 1996, 86–90.

11082. THOMAS, RONALD R. Making darkness visible: capturing the criminal and observing the law in Victorian photography and detective fiction. *In* (pp. 134–68) **126**.

11083. VAIL, WILLIAM A. Premature burial: new in the annals of crime. BSJ (46:3) 1996, 7–12.

11084. WATER, BILL VANDE. I fancy you have been misdirected. BSJ (46:3) 1996, 34–40.

11085. WILSON, FRANCES. A case of identity: tracking down Sherlock Holmes. WebS (12:2) 1995, 29–46.

Sir Charles D'Oyly, 7th bart (1781–1845)

11086. LEASK, NIGEL. Towards an Anglo-Indian poetry? The colonial muse in the writings of John Leyden, Thomas Medwin and Charles D'Oyly. *In* (pp. 52–85) **132**.

George Du Maurier

11087. GROSSMAN, JONATHAN H. The mythic Svengali: anti-aestheticism in *Trilby*. StudN (28:4) 1996, 525–42.

11088. PIQUET, MARTINE. Dans les griffes de Svengali: caricature antisémite littéraire dans *Trilby* de George Du Maurier (1894). *See* **235**.

11089. TANSELLE, G. THOMAS.   The Bowen-Merrill issue of *Trilby*. *See* **851**.

Paul Laurence Dunbar

11090. ALLEN, CAFFILENE.   The caged bird sings: the Ellison–Dunbar connection. CLAJ (40:2) 1996, 178–90.
11091. BEST, FELTON O.   Crossing the color line: a biography of Paul Laurence Dunbar, 1872–1906. Dubuque, IA: Kendall/Hunt, 1996. pp. vi, 188. (Cf. bibl. 1992, 8713.)

Alice Dunbar-Nelson

11092. BRYAN, VIOLET HARRINGTON.   Race and gender in the early works of Alice Dunbar-Nelson. *In* (pp. 120–38) **65**.

Sara Jeannette Duncan

11093. DEAN, MISAO.   A different point of view: Sara Jeannette Duncan. (Bibl. 1994, 8174.) Rev. by Barbara Godard in Signs (19:3) 1994, 835–9.
11094. TAUSKY, THOMAS E.   An ordered Olympus viewed from a cane chair: Sara Jeannette Duncan's *The Crow's Nest*. ECanW (60) 1996, 100–18.

Theodore Dwight

11095. TOPITZER, DAVID LYNCH.   'Clarinda has ravished my heart': Theodore Dwight, love, and letters. ConnHSB (57:3/4) 1992, 199–211.

George Dyer

11096. DAVIES, DAMIAN WALFORD.   'G.D.' *is* George Dyer. NQ (43:1) 1996, 31.

Edith Eaton ('Sui Sin Far')

11097. PRATHER, WILLIAM N.   Sui Sin Far's railroad baron: a Chinese of the future. ALR (29:1) 1996, 54–61.

Maria Edgeworth

11098. BOUR, ISABELLE.   La construction de l'image de l'Irlande et de l'Écosse dans le roman de langue anglaise: Maria Edgeworth et Walter Scott (1800–1814). Études Écossaises (3) 1996, 159–69.
11099. BUTLER, MARILYN.   Edgeworth's stern father: escaping Thomas Day, 1795–1801. *In* (pp. 75–93) **122**.
11100. CROGHAN, MARTIN J.   Maria Edgeworth and the tradition of Irish semiotics. *In* (pp. 194–206) **112**.
11101. —— Maria Edgeworth and the tradition of Irish semiotics. *In* (pp. 340–8) **49**.
11102. DUNLEAVY, JANET EGLESON.   Maria Edgeworth and the novel of manners. *In* (pp. 49–65) **96**.
11103. FIEROBE, CLAUDE.   The peasantry in the Irish novels of Maria Edgeworth. *In* (pp. 59–69) **106**.
11104. KIRKPATRICK, KATHRYN.   'Going to law about that jointure': women and property in *Castle Rackrent*. CJIS (22:1) 1996, 21–9.
11105. MYERS, MITZI.   Goring John Bull: Maria Edgeworth's Hibernian high jinks *versus* the imperialist imaginary. TSL (37) 1995, 367–94.

11106. —— Of mimicry and (wo)man: *infans* or forked tongue? ChildLit (23) 1995, 66–70.

11107. —— Portrait of the female artist as a young robin: Maria Edgeworth's telltale tailpiece. LU (20:2) 1996, 230–63.

11108. —— Reading Rosamond reading: Maria Edgeworth's 'Wee-Wee Stories' interrogate the canon. *In* (pp. 57–79) **48**.

11109. Skolnik, Christine Maria.   Maria Edgeworth's appeal to the Archbishop of Armagh. NQ (43:1) 1996, 40.

11110. Tamkivi, Külli.   An Estonian quotation in *Castle Rackrent*. NQ (43:1) 1996, 31–2.

11111. Wilson, Carol Shiner.   Lost needles, tangled threads: stitchery, domesticity, and the artistic enterprise in Barbauld, Edgeworth, Taylor, and Lamb. *In* (pp. 167–90) **103**.

'George Egerton' (Mary Chavelita Dunne Bright)

11112. Chrisman, Laura.   Empire, 'race' and feminism at the *fin de siècle*: the work of George Egerton and Olive Schreiner. *In* (pp. 45–65) **18**.

11113. Herrero Granado, María Dolores.   George Egerton's *Wedlock*: unlocking closed doors, searching for a key of one's own. *In* (pp. 165–80) **38**.

11114. McCullough, Kate.   Mapping the *'terra incognita'* of woman: George Egerton's *Keynotes* (1893) and New Woman fiction. *In* (pp. 205–23) **75**.

'George Eliot' (Mary Ann Evans)

11115. Andres, Sophia.   Fortune's wheel in *Daniel Deronda*: sociopolitical turns of the British Empire. VIJ (24) 1996, 87–111.

11116. —— The unhistoric in history: George Eliot's challenge to Victorian historiography. CLIO (26:1) 1996, 79–95.

11117. Ashton, Rosemary.   George Eliot: a life. London: Hamilton, 1996. pp. xiv, 465. Rev. by Isobel Armstrong in TLS, 22 Nov. 1996, 25.

11118. Baker, William.   George Eliot as serial novelist. Review (18) 1996, 147–55 (review-article).

11119. Barrett, Dorothea (ed.).   Romola. London; New York: Penguin, 1996. pp. xxxiv, 640. (Penguin classics.)

11120. Baumgarten, Murray.   Seeing double: Jews in the fiction of F. Scott Fitzgerald, Charles Dickens, Anthony Trollope, and George Eliot. *In* (pp. 44–61) **5**.

11121. Bloom, Harold (ed.).   George Eliot's *Silas Marner*. New York: Chelsea House, 1996. pp. 80. (Bloom's notes.)

11122. Bodenheimer, Rosemarie.   The real life of Mary Ann Evans: George Eliot, her letters and fiction. (Bibl. 1995, 9988.) Rev. by Christine L. Krueger in TSWL (14:2) 1995, 389–90.

11123. Booth, Alison.   Greatness engendered: George Eliot and Virginia Woolf. (Bibl. 1994, 8196.) Rev. by Pamela L. Caughie in MFS (40:2) 1994, 435–41.

11124. —— The silence of great men: statuesque femininity and the ending of *Romola*. *In* (pp. 110–34) **31**.

11125. Bowers, Bege K.   George Eliot's *Middlemarch* and the 'text' of the novel of manners. *In* (pp. 105–17) **96**.

11126. Brown, Andrew (ed.).   Romola. (Bibl. 1994, 8199.) Rev. by

Dale Kramer in Text (Ann Arbor) (9) 1996, 369–88; by Dieter Mehl in Archiv (233:1) 1996, 181–3.

11127. ——— Romola. (Bibl. 1995, 9992.) Rev. by Dieter Mehl in Archiv (233:1) 1996, 181–3.

11128. CARROLL, DAVID.   George Eliot and the conflict of interpretations: a reading of the novels. (Bibl. 1995, 9995.) Rev. by Joseph Wiesenfarth in Review (16) 1994, 289–99.

11129. CAVE, TERENCE (ed.).   Daniel Deronda. London: Penguin, 1995. pp. xl, 849. (Penguin classics.)

11130. ——— Silas Marner: the weaver of Raveloe. Oxford; New York: OUP, 1996. pp. xl, 190. (World's classics.)

11131. COSTA, CATHERINE.   'My George Eliot': *Deutera* Dickinson/ *Mutter* Eliot. *See* **10937**.

11132. CUNNINGHAM, VALENTINE (ed.).   Adam Bede. Oxford; New York: OUP, 1996. pp. xlviii, 598. (World's classics.)

11133. DE SAILLY, ROSALIND.   Problems of life and mind: the George Eliot of the manuscripts. *See* **615**.

11134. DINGLEY, ROBERT.   Playing the game: the Continental casinos and the Victorian imagination. *See* **11017**.

11135. DUPEYRON-LAFAY, FRANÇOISE.   Savoir ancien, savoir nouveau dans *Daniel Deronda*. CVE (43) 1996, 197–209.

11136. FENNELL, FRANCIS L.; FENNELL, MONICA A.   'Ladies – loaf givers': food, women, and society in the novels of Charlotte Brontë and George Eliot. *In* (pp. 235–58) **54**.

11137. FUJISAWA, MATOSHI.   Yasushi Inoue's *Aru onna no shi* and George Eliot's *Silas Marner*: some notes on influence. CLS (33:1) 1996, 69–74.

11138. GREINER, WALTER.   '*Shapen after the average*': zur Macht der Mediokrität in George Eliots *Middlemarch*. ZAA (41:1) 1993, 40–53.

11139. HAIGHT, GORDON S. (ed.).   The mill on the Floss. Introd. by Dinah Birch. Oxford; New York: OUP, 1996. pp. xxxvii, 529. (World's classics.)

11140. HAN, AE-KYUNG.   *Geupjin jueuija Felix Holt* e daehan yeosungronjeok yeongu. (A feminist reading of *Felix Holt, the Radical*.) JELL (42:2) 1996, 273–97.

11141. HENRY, NANCY (ed.).   Impressions of Theophrastus Such. London: Pickering; Iowa City: Iowa UP, 1994. pp. xli, 187. Rev. by John R. Reed in Criticism (38:1) 1996, 169–71.

11142. HIMMELFARB, GERTRUDE.   George Eliot for grown-ups. ASch (63:4) 1994, 577–81.

11143. HOUSTON, NATALIE M.   George Eliot's material history: clothing and realist narrative. SLI (29:1) 1996, 23–33.

11144. HUDD, LOUISE.   The politics of a feminist poetics: *Armgart* and George Eliot's critical response to *Aurora Leigh*. *See* **10501**.

11145. IRWIN, JANE (ed.).   George Eliot's *Daniel Deronda* notebooks. Cambridge; New York: CUP, 1996. pp. xlii, 524.

11146. JACKSON, TONY E.   George Eliot's 'new evangel': *Daniel Deronda* and the ends of realism. Genre (25:2/3) 1992, 229–48.

11147. KRAMER, DALE.   The compositor as copy-text. *See* **714**.

11148. LEE, SE-GYU.   Text eui yeokap – *Silas Marner*. (Textual repression: *Silas Marner*.) JELL (42:3) 1996, 629–51.

11149. LOGAN, THAD.   Decorating domestic space: middle-class women and Victorian interiors. *In* (pp. 207–34) **54**.

11150. McCormack, K. George Eliot's first fiction: targetting *Blackwood's*. *See* **1310**.

11151. Manzer, Patricia K. 'In some old book, somebody just like me': Eliot's Tessa and Hardy's Tess. ELN (33:3) 1996, 33–8.

11152. Martin, Carol A. George Eliot's serial fiction. (Bibl. 1995, 10035.) Rev. by William Baker in Review (18) 1996, 147–55; by Joel J. Brattin in DickQ (13:4) 1996, 232–4.

11153. Maxwell, Catherine. The brooking of desire: Dorothea and deferment in *Middlemarch*. YES (26) 1996, 116–26.

11154. Ogden, Daryl. Double visions: Sarah Stickney Ellis, George Eliot and the politics of domesticity. WS (25:6) 1996, 585–602.

11155. Paxton, Nancy L. George Eliot and Herbert Spencer: feminism, evolutionism, and the reconstruction of gender. (Bibl. 1995, 10044.) Rev. by Adela Pinch in Signs (19:1) 1993, 264–8.

11156. Rischin, Abigail S. Beside the reclining statue: ekphrasis, narrative, and desire in *Middlemarch*. PMLA (111:5) 1996, 1121–32.

11157. Sabin, Margery. The suttee romance. *See* **10149**.

11158. Semmel, Bernard. George Eliot and the politics of national inheritance. (Bibl. 1994, 8240.) Rev. by Nancy W. Ellenberger in JBS (35:4) 1996, 536–41.

11159. Spittles, Brian. George Eliot: godless woman. (Bibl. 1994, 8242.) Rev. by Donald Hawes in AEB (9:1/2) 1995, 86–7.

11160. —— *Middlemarch*: TV *versus* text? ERev (7:1) 1996, 22–5.

11161. Swann, Charles. A George Eliot debt to George Meredith: from *Rhoda Fleming* to *Daniel Deronda*. NQ (43:1) 1996, 46–7.

11162. —— Miss Harleth, Miss Mackenzie: mirror images? NQ (43:1) 1996, 47–8.

11163. Sypher, Eileen. Resisting Gwendolen's 'subjection': *Daniel Deronda*'s proto-feminism. StudN (28:4) 1996, 506–24.

11164. Szirotny, June Skye. Maggie Tulliver's sad sacrifice: confusing but not confused. StudN (28:2) 1996, 178–99.

11165. Thompson, Andrew. Giuseppe Mazzini and George Eliot's *Daniel Deronda*. QLLSM (6) 1993, 101–11.

11166. —— Personal and political: George Eliot's *Felix Holt* reconsidered. QLLSM (5) 1992, 71–98.

11167. Villa, Luisa. Sul genere e la mediazione: la questione del realismo eliotiano in *Daniel Deronda*. Textus (3:1/2) 1990, 139–91.

11168. Winkgens, Meinhard. Mündlichkeit zwischen sozialer Traditionsstiftung und '*gossip*': zur Ambivalenz der Bewertung mündlichen Wissens in George Eliots frühen Regionalromanen. *In* (pp. 105–19) **73**.

11169. Wormald, Mark. Microscopy and semiotic in *Middlemarch*. NineL (50:4) 1996, 501–24.

11170. Yelland, Cris. Hardy's allusions and the problem of 'pedantry'. LangL (4:1) 1995, 17–30.

11171. Zimmerman, Bonnie. George Eliot's sacred chest of language. *In* (pp. 154–76) **31**.

Ebenezer Elliott

11172. Jackson-Houlston, C. M. Elizabeth Gaskell, Manchester song and its contexts. Gaskell Society Journal (10) 1996, 27–41.

Sarah Stickney Ellis

11173. OGDEN, DARYL.   Double visions: Sarah Stickney Ellis, George Eliot and the politics of domesticity. *See* **11154**.

Ralph Waldo Emerson

11174. BAKER, CARLOS.   Emerson among the eccentrics: a group portrait. Introd. and epilogue by James R. Mellow. London; New York: Viking, 1996. pp. xv, 608. Rev. by David Laskin in BkW, 31 Mar. 1996, 4.

11175. BOUGHN, MICHAEL.   Exody and some mechanics of splendor in Blaser and Emerson. Talisman (15) 1995/96, 158–61.

11176. BROWN, LEE RUST.   The Emerson museum. Representations (40) 1992, 57–80.

11177. DEESE, HELEN R.   Transcendental gen(d)erations: Caroline Healey Dall and Ralph Waldo Emerson. TPB (31) 1994, 6–21.

11178. GOUGEON, LEN.   Virtue's hero: Emerson, antislavery and reform. (Bibl. 1992, 8807.) Rev. by Mary Kupiec Cayton in AHR (96:4) 1991, 1267–8; by Barbara L. Green in AR (49:1) 1991, 144; by Theodore R. Hovet in AmS (34:1) 1993, 187.

11179. —— MYERSON, JOEL (eds).   Emerson's antislavery writings. (Bibl. 1995, 10084.) Rev. by Martin Halliwell in JAStud (30:1) 1996, 164.

11180. HUDNUT, ROBERT K.   The aesthetics of Ralph Waldo Emerson: the materials and methods of his poetry. Lewiston, NY; Lampeter: Mellen Press, 1996. pp. iii, 102. (Studies in American religion, 64.)

11181. LOPEZ, MICHAEL.   Emerson and power: creative antagonism in the nineteenth century. DeKalb: Northern Illinois UP, 1996. pp. xii, 257.

11182. McMILLIN, T. S.   Consuming text: transubstantiation and ingestion in the interpretation of Emerson. Criticism (38:1) 1996, 85–114.

11183. MAROVITZ, SANFORD E.   The Emersonian lesson of *Humboldt's Gift*. SBJ (14:1) 1996, 84–95.

11184. MARTIN, JOHN STEPHEN.   Emerson as a phenomenological philosopher and poet. *In* (pp. 227–40) **125**.

11185. MOTT, WESLEY T.   'The strains of eloquence': Emerson and his sermons. (Bibl. 1991, 8513.) Rev. by Linda Munk in LitTheol (5:1) 1991, 125.

11186. NADENICEK, DANIEL JOSEPH.   Civilization by design: Emerson and landscape architecture. NCS (10) 1996, 33–47.

11187. NEWFIELD, CHRISTOPHER.   The Emerson effect: individualism and submission in America. Chicago; London: Chicago UP, 1996. pp. vii, 278.

11188. O'KEEFE, RICHARD R.   Emerson's *Montaigne; or, The Skeptic*: biography as autobiography. ELit (23:2) 1996, 206–17.

11189. —— The rats in the wall: animals in Emerson's *History*. ATQ (10:2) 1996, 111–21.

11190. POIRIER, RICHARD.   Poetry and pragmatism. (Bibl. 1995, 10103.) Rev. by Robin Gail Schulze in Review (16) 1994, 281–7.

11191. QUAYUM, M. A.   Emerson's *Humboldt*: a probable source for Bellow's Von Humboldt Fleisher in *Humboldt's Gift*. NCL (22:4) 1992, 7–8.

11192. —— Quest for equilibrium: Transcendental ideas in Bellow's *Herzog*. SBJ (14:2) 1996, 43–69.

11193. RICHARDSON, ROBERT D., JR. Emerson: the mind on fire: a biography. Frontispiece by Barry Moser. (Bibl. 1995, 10106.) Rev. by Michael Dirda in BkW, 9 Apr. 1995, 6; by John P. Sisk in ASch (65:1) 1996, 132–4; by Albert J. von Frank in AL (68:3) 1996, 642–3; by Theodore Haddin in SAtlR (61:2) 1996, 145–50.

11194. ROBERSON, SUSAN L. 'Degenerate effeminacy' and the making of a masculine spirituality in the sermons of Ralph Waldo Emerson. *In* (pp. 150–72) **74**.

11195. —— Emerson in his sermons: a man-made self. Columbia; London: Missouri UP, 1995. pp. xii, 223. Rev. by Maurice Gonnaud in AL (68:4) 1996, 850–1; by Glen M. Johnson in ALH (101:4) 1996, 1275–6; by Theodore Haddin in SAtlR (61:2) 1996, 145–50.

11196. ROBINSON, DAVID M. Emerson and the conduct of life: pragmatism and ethical purpose in the later work. (Bibl. 1995, 10108.) Rev. by Mary Kupiec Cayton in AmS (36:2) 1995, 195–6; by R. W. (Herbie) Butterfield in YES (26) 1996, 326–7; by Herwig Friedl in ZAA (44:2) 1996, 186–7.

11197. —— Emerson, Thoreau, Fuller, and Transcendentalism. American Literary Scholarship (1993) 3–21; (1994) 3–23; (1995) 3–23.

11198. SLOAN, BENJAMIN. *Houseboat Days* and *Houses Founded on the Sea*: an example of Emerson as source for Ashbery. NCL (23:3) 1993, 5–6.

11199. SLOAN, GARY. Emerson's *Self-Reliance*. Exp (55:1) 1996, 19–22.

11200. SUAREZ, ERNEST. Emerson on Vietnam: Dickey, Bly and the New Left. SoLJ (23:2) 1991, 77–97.

11201. TEICHGRAEBER, RICHARD F., III. Sublime thoughts/penny wisdom: situating Emerson and Thoreau in the American market. (Bibl. 1995, 10115.) Rev. by Kenneth Dauber in AL (68:3) 1996, 641–2; by Daniel J. McInerney in ALH (101:5) 1996, 1622; by Steven Fink in Cithara (35:2) 1996, 38–9.

11202. VON FRANK, ALBERT. The composition of *Nature*: writing and the self in the launching of a career. *In* (pp. 11–40) **7**.

11203. WILEY, MARK. Reading and writing in an American grain. *See* **2494**.

11204. WILSON, ERIC. Weaving, breathing, thinking: the poetics of Emerson's *Nature*. ATQ (10:1) 1996, 5–24.

11205. WOLFE, CARY. The limits of American literary ideology in Pound and Emerson. (Bibl. 1995, 10121.) Rev. by Ian F. A. Bell in YES (26) 1996, 330–1.

11206. ZWARG, CHRISTINA. Feminist conversations: Fuller, Emerson, and the play of reading. (Bibl. 1995, 10122.) Rev. by Malini Johar Schueller in AL (68:4) 1996, 851–3.

Mrs Ewing

11207. MILLINGTON, PETER. Mrs Ewing and the textual origin of the St Kitts Mummies' play. *See* **3592**.

John Meade Falkner

11208. WILSON, EDWARD. A fictional source for the falling tower in John Meade Falkner's *The Nebuly Coat*. NQ (43:4) 1996, 439–40.

Eliza Fenwick

11209. GRUNDY, ISOBEL (ed.). Secresy; or, The ruin on the rock. Peterborough, Ont.: Broadview Press, 1994. pp. 359. (Broadview literary texts.) Rev. by Martha F. Bowden in ECF (7:3) 1995, 323–4; by Rhoda J. Zuk in ESCan (22:4) 1996, 488–91.

'Fanny Fern' (Sara Payson (Willis) Parton)

11210. HAMILTON, KRISTIE. The politics of survival: Sara Parton's *Ruth Hall* and the literature of labor. *In* (pp. 86–108) **99**.

11211. KITCH, CAROLYN L. 'The courage to call things by their right names': Fanny Fern, feminine sympathy, and feminist issues in nineteenth-century American journalism. AmJ (13:3) 1996, 286–303.

11212. PETTENGILL, CLAIRE C. Against novels: Fanny Fern's newspaper fiction and the reform of print culture. *See* **1340**.

11213. WARREN, JOYCE W. Fanny Fern: an independent woman. (Bibl. 1994, 8296.) Rev. by Philip F. Gura in GetR (6:1) 1993, 38–45; by Frances B. Cogan in AHR (98:2) 1993, 571; by Sherry Ceniza in WWQR (11:2) 1993, 89–95.

11214. —— The gender of American individualism: Fanny Fern, the novel, and the American dream. *In* (pp. 150–7) **87**.

Susan Ferrier

11215. KOWALESKI-WALLACE, BETH. Women, china, and consumer culture in eighteenth-century England. *See* **8770**.

Clyde Fitch

11216. HOUCHIN, JOHN H. Depraved women and wicked plays: Olga Nethersole's production of *Sapho*. JADT (6:1) 1994, 40–60.

11217. JOHNSON, KATIE N. Censoring *Sapho*: regulating the fallen woman and the prostitute on the New York stage. ATQ (10:3) 1996, 167–86.

11218. MARRA, KIM. Clyde Fitch: transvestite *metteur-en-scène* of the feminine. NETJ (3) 1992, 15–37.

Edward Fitzball

11219. BOOTH, MICHAEL R. (ed.). *The Lights o' London* and other Victorian plays. *See* **10746**.

Edward Fitzgerald

11220. ALEXANDER, DORIS. Creating literature out of life: the making of four masterpieces. University Park: Pennsylvania State UP, 1996. pp. 253.

11221. BLACK, BARBARA J. Fugitive articulation of an all-obliterated tongue: Fitzgerald's *Rubáiyát* and the politics of collecting. *See* **458**.

11222. QUAGLIA, FABRIZIO. Il giardino del perfetto edonista: le *Rubáiyát* di Edward Fitzgerald. QLLSM (8) 1996, 155–91.

Marjorie Fleming

11223. JOHNSON, ALEXANDRA. The drama of imagination: Marjory Fleming and her diaries. *In* (pp. 80–109) **48**.

11224. MYERS, MITZI. Of mimicry and (wo)man: *infans* or forked tongue? *See* **11106**.

Mary Hallock Foote

11225. MAGUIRE, JAMES H. *Cœur d'Alene* and *Angle of Repose*: justice and the quality of mercy. WebS (8:1) 1991, 39–48.

Mary E. Wilkins Freeman

11226. Berkson, Dorothy. 'A goddess behind a sordid veil': the domestic heroine meets the labor novel in Mary E. Wilkins Freeman's *The Portion of Labor. In* (pp. 149–68) **99**.

11227. Diggs, Marylynne. Romantic friends or a 'different race of creatures'? The representation of lesbian pathology in nineteenth-century America. *See* **10229**.

11228. Getz, John. Mary Wilkins Freeman and Sherwood Anderson: confluence or influence? Midamerica (19) 1992, 74–86.

11229. Glasser, Leah Blatt. In a closet hidden: the life and work of Mary E. Wilkins Freeman. Amherst: Massachusetts UP, 1996. pp. xx, 266.

11230. Nettels, Elsa. New England indigestion and its victims. *In* (pp. 167–84) **24**.

11231. Patrick, Barbara. Lady terrorists: nineteenth-century American women writers and the ghost story. *In* (pp. 73–84) **3**.

Margaret Fuller

11232. Adams, Kimberly Vanesveld. The Madonna and Margaret Fuller. WS (25:4) 1996, 385–405.

11233. Brause, Sharon Stout. Wit in Margaret Fuller's *Summer on the Lake.* PMPA (18) 1993, 18–25.

11234. Capper, Charles. Margaret Fuller: an American romantic life: vol. 1, The private years. (Bibl. 1995, 10153.) Rev. by Jane H. Pease in AHR (99:2) 1994, 651–2; by Cheryl Rose Jacobsen in AmS (35:2) 1994, 159–61; by Patrocinio Schweickart in NWSAJ (7:3) 1995, 116–24.

11235. Chevigny, Bell Gale. The woman and the myth: Margaret Fuller's life and writings. (Bibl. 1982, 7771.) Boston, MA: Northeastern UP, 1994. pp. xlv, 574. (Revised and expanded ed.: first ed. 1976.) Rev. by Joel Myerson in Review (18) 1996, 31–43.

11236. Dickenson, Donna. Margaret Fuller: writing a woman's life. (Bibl. 1995, 10154.) Rev. by Patrocinio Schweickart in NWSAJ (7:3) 1995, 116–24.

11237. —— (ed.). *Woman in the Nineteenth Century* and other writings. Oxford; New York: OUP, 1994. pp. xxxvii, 261. (World's classics.) Rev. by Patrocinio Schweickart in NWSAJ (7:3) 1995, 116–24; by Joel Myerson in Review (18) 1996, 31–43.

11238. Huxman, Susan Schultz. Mary Wollstonecraft, Margaret Fuller, and Angelina Grimké: symbolic convergence and a nascent rhetorical vision. *See* **9499**.

11239. Kelley, Mary (ed.). The portable Margaret Fuller. (Bibl. 1995, 10158.) Rev. by Joel Myerson in Review (18) 1996, 31–43.

11240. Lewis, Tess. Margaret Fuller: the American mind writ large. ASch (65:2) 1996, 284–92.

11241. Myerson, Joel. The canonization of Margaret Fuller. Review (18) 1996, 31–43 (review-article).

11242. —— Supplement to *Margaret Fuller: a Descriptive Bibliography.* StudAR (1996) 187–240. (*Adds to* bibl. 1978, 7232.)

11243. Powers-Beck, Jeffrey. 'Slack time' and the 'uncessant minutes': time in *The Two Herberts. See* **7947**.

11244. Robinson, David M. Emerson, Thoreau, Fuller, and Transcendentalism. *See* **11197**.

11245. Schweickart, Patrocinio.   Margaret Fuller. NWSAJ (7:3) 1995, 116–24 (review-article).

11246. Shealy, Daniel.   Margaret Fuller and her 'maiden': Evelina Metcalf's 1838 school journal. StudAR (1996) 41–65.

11247. Steele, Jeffrey (ed.).   The essential Margaret Fuller. (Bibl. 1992, 8862.) Rev. by Joel Myerson in Review (18) 1996, 31–43.

11248. von Mehren, Joan.   Minerva and the muse: a life of Margaret Fuller. (Bibl. 1995, 10162.) Rev. by Eve Kornfeld in ALH (101:4) 1996, 1276.

John Galt

11249. Campbell, Ian (introd.).   *Annals of the Parish*; and, *The Ayrshire Legatees*. Edinburgh: Mercat Press, 1994. pp. xxviii, 187; viii, 140. (Mercat classics.)

11250. Gray, Alasdair.   Galt. Southfields 1996, 37–9.

11251. Price, Richard.   A tailnote on *The Entail*. Southfields 1996, 40–2.

11252. —— (introd.).   From *[A] Biographical Sketch of John Wilson* by John Galt. Southfields 1996, 27–36.

Mrs Gaskell

11253. Bellamy, Joan.   Mary Taylor, Ellen Nussey and Brontë biography. *See* **10127**.

11254. Colella, Silvana.   La casa riformata: ideologia domestica e consenso narrativo in *Mary Barton* e *Shirley*. *See* **10406**.

11255. Davis, Deanna L.   Feminist critics and literary mothers: daughters reading Elizabeth Gaskell. Signs (17:3) 1992, 507–32.

11256. Edgecombe, R. S.   Two female saviours in nineteenth-century fiction: Jeanie Deans and Mary Barton. EngS (77:1) 1996, 45–58.

11257. Flint, Kate.   Elizabeth Gaskell. Plymouth: Northcote House; London: British Council, 1995. pp. xii, 74. (Writers and their work.) Rev. by Alan Shelston in Gaskell Society Journal (10) 1996, 107.

11258. Gottlieb, Stacey.   'And God will teach her': consciousness and character in *Ruth* and *Aurora Leigh*. *See* **10499**.

11259. Hatano, Yoko.   Fanny Price and Molly Gibson: bearers of the country house tradition. *See* **10285**.

11260. Ingham, Patricia (ed.).   North and south. London: Penguin, 1995. pp. xxviii, 450. (Penguin classics.)

11261. Jackson-Houlston, C. M.   Elizabeth Gaskell, Manchester song and its contexts. *See* **11172**.

11262. Jansson, Siv.   Elizabeth Gaskell: writing against the angel in the house. Gaskell Society Journal (10) 1996, 65–76.

11263. Krueger, Christine L.   'Speaking like a woman': how to have the last word on *Sylvia's Lovers*. *In* (pp. 135–53) **31**.

11264. Kuhlman, Mary H.   Education through experience in *North and South*. Gaskell Society Journal (10) 1996, 14–26.

11265. Leaver, Elizabeth.   What will this world come to? Old ways and education in Elizabeth Gaskell's *My Lady Ludlow*. Gaskell Society Journal (10) 1996, 53–64.

11266. McCausland, Elizabeth D.   Dirty little secrets: Realism and the real in Victorian industrial novels. AJSem (9:3) 1992, 149–65.

11267. Marroni, Francesco.   The shadow of Dante: Elizabeth Gaskell and *The Divine Comedy*. Gaskell Society Journal (10) 1996, 1–13.

11268. MILLER, ANDREW HORTON.   The fragments and small opportunities of *Cranford*. Genre (25:1) 1992, 91–111.
11269. MORSE, DEBORAH DENENHOLZ.   Stitching repentance, sewing
rebellion: seamstress and fallen woman in Elizabeth Gaskell's fiction.
In (pp. 27–73) **54**.
11270. PLATIZKY, ROGER S.   *Mary Barton* and *Frankenstein*. Gaskell
Society Journal (10) 1996, 83–91.
11271. RECCHIO, THOMAS E.   A monstrous reading of *Mary Barton*:
fiction as *communitas*. ColLit (23:3) 1996, 2–22.
11272. REDDY, MAUREEN T.   Men, women, and manners in *Wives
and Daughters*. *In* (pp. 67–83) **96**.
11273. SANDERS, ANDREW.   A crisis of liberalism in *North and South*.
Gaskell Society Journal (10) 1996, 42–52.
11274. UNSWORTH, ANNA.   Ruskin and *Cousin Phillis*. Gaskell Society
Journal (10) 1996, 77–82.
11275. WATSON, J. R.   'Round the sofa': Elizabeth Gaskell tells
stories. YES (26) 1996, 89–99.
11276. WRIGHT, TERENCE.   Elizabeth Gaskell, 'We are not angels':
realism, gender, values. (Bibl. 1995, 10225.) Rev. by Alan Shelston in
Gaskell Society Journal (10) 1996, 105–7; by F.S. in TLS, 9 Feb. 1996, 28.

William Gifford

11277. HIGASHIMAKA, ITSUYO.   The early stages of Byron's relationship with Gifford. *In* (pp. 161–9) **125**.

W. S. Gilbert

11278. AYME, CLAUDE.   Des *Bab Ballads* aux Savoy Operas: Gilbert
et la caricature. *See* **176**.
11279. BRADLEY, IAN (ed.).   The complete annotated Gilbert and
Sullivan. Oxford; New York: OUP, 1996. pp. xiii, 1197.
11280. FISCHLER, ALAN.   From Weydon-Priors to Tower Green:
the sources of *The Yeomen of the Guard*. ELH (63:1) 1996, 203–25.
11281. STEDMAN, JANE W.   W. S. Gilbert: a classic Victorian and his
theatre. Oxford; New York: OUP, 1996. pp. xviii, 374, (plates) 16.
Rev. by Judith Weir in TLS, 26 Apr. 1996, 23–4.
11282. TROOST, LINDA V.   Economic discourse in the Savoy Operas
of W. S. Gilbert. *In* (pp. 193–207) **120**.
11283. WILLIAMS, CAROLYN.   *Utopia, Limited*: nationalism, empire and
parody in the comic operas of Gilbert and Sullivan. *In* (pp. 221–47) **18**.

Algernon Gissing

11284. COUSTILLAS, PIERRE.   Walter Leonard Gissing (1891–1916):
an anniversary. GissJ (32:3) 1996, 13–23. (George Gissing's son.)

George Gissing

11285. COMITINI, PATRICIA.   A feminist fantasy: conflicting ideologies
in *The Odd Women*. StudN (27:4) 1995, 529–43.
11286. COUSTILLAS, PIERRE.   A distinguished acquaintance of
Gissing's at Ciboure: Arthur Brownlow Fforde. GissJ (32:2) 1996, 1–9.
11287. —— Gissing in the *Boston Evening Transcript*: his interview by
Joseph Anderson. GissJ (32:2) 1996, 23–9.
11288. —— A letter from the Western Avernus: Morley Roberts to
his sister Ida. GissJ (32:4) 1996, 13–20.

11289. —— *The Paying Guest* and the praise it won in 1896. GissJ (32:4) 1996, 20–3.

11290. —— Thirty letters about Gissing to be rescued from oblivion. *See* **468**.

11291. —— Walter Leonard Gissing (1891–1916): an anniversary. *See* **11284**.

11292. —— (introd.). A forgotten assessment of *Veranilda*. GissJ (32:2) 1996, 19–23. (By Randolph Faries.)

11293. COUSTILLAS, PIERRE; RANDOLL, GARY. Gissing's 1897 stay at Budleigh Salterton: a topographical enquiry. GissJ (32:1) 1996, 22–8.

11294. DELANY, PAUL. Gissing in prison. GissJ (32:4) 1996, 11–13.

11295. HARMAN, BARBARA LEAH. Joy behind the screen: the problem of 'presentability' in George Gissing's *The Nether World* (1889). *In* (pp. 181–94) **75**.

11296. KORG, JACOB. Gissing on the Internet. *See* **1169**.

11297. POSTMUS, BOUWE. Clara Collet's clairvoyance. GissJ (31:4) 1995, 1–32.

11298. —— (ed.). The poetry of George Gissing. Lewiston, NY; Lampeter: Mellen Press, 1995. pp. xiv, 185. (Studies in British literature, 17.) Rev. by John Sloan in GissJ (32:2) 1996, 29–32.

11299. SELIG, ROBERT. Gissing's *Born in Exile* and Théodule-Armand Ribot's *L'Hérédité psychologique*. GissJ (32:4) 1996, 1–10.

11300. SELIG, ROBERT L. George Gissing. (Bibl. 1995, 10246.) Rev. by Annette R. Federico in ELT (39:2) 1996, 228–31; by Pierre Coustillas in GissJ (32:3) 1996, 35–6.

11301. SUNG, EUN-AE. Gissing eui Dickens ron. (Gissing on Dickens.) *See* **10913**.

11302. TAKEDA, MIHOKO. Between emancipation and restraint: reading the body in *The Odd Women*. GissJ (32:2) 1996, 10–13.

11303. YAHATA, MASAHIKO. Shan F. Bullock: Gissing's admirer and an ingenious short story writer. *See* **10537**.

Parke Godwin

11304. FALSANI, TERESA BOYLE. Parke Godwin's Guenevere: an archetypal transformation. Quondam et Futurus (3:3) 1993, 55–65.

Mrs Gore

11305. HUGHES, WINIFRED. Mindless millinery: Catherine Gore and the silver fork heroine. DSA (25) 1996, 159–76.

'Sarah Grand' (Frances Elizabeth Clarke)

11306. KUCICH, JOHN. Curious dualities: *The Heavenly Twins* (1893) and Sarah Grand's belated Modernist aesthetics. *In* (pp. 195–204) **75**.

John Gray (1866–1934)

11307. INMAN, BILLIE ANDREW. John 'Dorian' Gray and the theme of subservient love in Walter Pater's works of the 1890s. CompCrit (17) 1995, 85–107.

Kate Greenaway

11308. LUNDIN, ANNE. Kate Greenaway's critical and commercial reception. PULC (57:1) 1995, 127–46.

Dora Greenwell

11309. GRAY, JANET. Dora Greenwell's commonplace book. PULC (57:1) 1995, 47–74.

Louise Imogen Guiney

11310. COLVERT, JAMES B. Fred Holland Day, Louise Imogen Guiney, and the text of Stephen Crane's *The Black Riders*. *See* **607**.

Sir Henry Rider Haggard

11311. JOHNSON, HEIDI H. Agricultural anxiety, African erasure: H. Rider Haggard's *Rural England* and *Benita: an African Romance*. VIJ (24) 1996, 113–37.
11312. LOW, GAIL CHING-LIANG. White skins/Black masks: representation and colonialism. *See* **9641**.
11313. RICKELS, LAURENCE A. Mummy's curse. AJSem (9:4) 1992, 47–58.

Edward Everett Hale

11314. BRUMM, URSULA. Consensus and conspiracy in American literature. *See* **8082**.

Sarah Josepha Hale

11315. OKKER, PATRICIA. Sarah Josepha Hale, Lydia Sigourney, and the poetic tradition in two nineteenth-century women's magazines. *See* **1335**.

Thomas Chandler Haliburton

11316. DAVIES, RICHARD A. (ed.). The letters of Thomas Chandler Haliburton. (Bibl. 1989, 6866.) Rev. by Vernon R. Lindquist in ARCS (18:3) 1988, 398–9.

James Hall (1793–1868)

11317. ATHERTON, ERIC. *The Harpe's Head: a Legend of Kentucky*: James Hall's passionate innovation. KenR (12:1/2) 1993, 12–28.

Thomas Hardy

11318. ANON. (introd.). A conversation between Thomas Hardy and William Archer. *See* **10250**.
11319. BAEK, WON-GI. Thomas Hardy eui si e natanan sarlm gwa jukeum eui yeoksuljeok tonghap. (The paradoxical unification of life and death in Thomas Hardy's poetry.) Unpub. doct. diss., Dongguk Univ., Seoul, 1996.
11320. DALZIEL, PAMELA. Anxieties of representation: the serial illustrations to Hardy's *The Return of the Native*. *See* **191**.
11321. —— Whose *Mistress*? Thomas Hardy's theatrical collaboration. *See* **10596**.
11322. —— MILLGATE, MICHAEL (eds). Thomas Hardy's 'Studies, specimens &c.' notebook. (Bibl. 1995, 10288.) Rev. by Michael Thorpe in EngS (76:6) 1995, 590.
11323. DAVIS, W. EUGENE. Phantasmal orchestras: incidental music in *Under the Greenwood Tree* and *Far from the Madding Crowd*. ArsL (8) 1994, 123–34.
11324. DIAMOND, SUZANNE. Mothers in the margins: Thomas

Hardy, D. H. Lawrence, and suffragism's discontents. ColbyQ (32:2) 1996, 100–12.

11325. EBBATSON, ROGER.   Hardy: the margin of the unexpressed. (Bibl. 1995, 10297.) Rev. by Peter Widdowson in Literature and History (5:1) 1996, 114–17.

11326. ——— Thomas Hardy, *The Mayor of Casterbridge*. London; New York: Penguin, 1994. pp. 127. (Penguin critical studies.) Rev. by Patrick Swinden in THJ (10:3) 1994, 89–90.

11327. FISCHLER, ALAN.   From Weydon-Priors to Tower Green: the sources of *The Yeomen of the Guard. See* **11280**.

11328. FUNAYAMA, RYOICHI.   Bungaku no reality to wa nanika – Thomas Hardy kouki shousetsu no sekai. (Literary reality: the world of Thomas Hardy's later novels.) Kyoto: Kamogawa Shuppan, 1996. pp. 300.

11329. GATRELL, SIMON.   Thomas Hardy and the proper study of mankind. (Bibl. 1995, 10305.) Rev. by William W. Morgan in StudN (27:1) 1995, 93–6.

11330. GEORGE, PATRICIA (ed.).   Far from the madding crowd. Cambridge; New York: CUP, 1996. pp. 430. (Cambridge literature.)

11331. GEPPERT, HANS VILMAR.   Der realistische Weg: Formen pragmatischen Erzählens bei Balzac, Dickens, Hardy, Keller, Raabe und anderen Autoren des 19. Jahrhunderts. *See* **9845**.

11332. GIBSON, JAMES.   Thomas Hardy: a literary life. Basingstoke: Macmillan; New York: St Martin's Press, 1996. pp. xi, 206. (Literary lives.)

11333. GIBSON, REX (ed.).   Tess of the d'Urbervilles: a pure woman. Cambridge; New York: CUP, 1996. pp. 448. (Cambridge literature.)

11334. GOETSCH, PAUL.   Hardys Wessex-Romane: Mundlichkeit, Schriftlichkeit, kultureller Wandel. Tübingen: Narr, 1994. pp. 316. (ScriptOralia, 60.) Rev. by Annette Simonis in ZAA (43:2) 1995, 190–1.

11335. GREEN, BRIAN.   Hardy's lyrics: pearls of pity. Basingstoke: Macmillan; New York: St Martin's Press, 1996. pp. x, 243.

11336. HAMMOND, BREAN.   Just a coincidence? Hardy's *Tess* and Fortgibu's plum pudding. ERev (7:2) 1996, 12–15.

11337. HANDS, TIMOTHY.   Thomas Hardy. (Bibl. 1995, 10315.) Rev. by Robert Schweik in ELT (39:3) 1996, 353–7.

11338. ——— (ed.).   Jude the obscure. London: Everyman, 1995. pp. xxxvi, 423. (Everyman library.)

11339. HIGONNET, MARGARET R. (ed.).   The sense of sex: feminist perspectives on Hardy. (Bibl. 1995, 10319.) Rev. by Suzanne R. Johnson in StudN (27:1) 1995, 96–9; by Peter Widdowson in Literature and History (5:1) 1996, 114–17.

11340. HYNES, SAMUEL (ed.).   The dynasts, part third; The famous tragedy of the Queen of Cornwall; The play of 'Saint George'; 'O Jan, O Jan, O Jan'. (Bibl. 1995, 10322.) Rev. by Keith Wilson in ELT (39:3) 1996, 333–44; by Merryn Williams in NQ (43:1) 1996, 111–12; by Michael Thorpe in EngS (77:3) 1996, 291–2.

11341. ——— The dynasts, parts first and second. (Bibl. 1995, 10323.) Rev. by Keith Wilson in ELT (39:3) 1996, 333–44; by Merryn Williams in NQ (43:1) 1996, 111–12; by Michael Thorpe in EngS (77:3) 1996, 291–2.

11342. JACOBSON, DAN.   Thomas Hardy: the poet as philosopher. ASch (65:1) 1996, 114–18.

11343. JEDRZEJEWSKI, JAN. Thomas Hardy and the Church. Basingstoke: Macmillan; New York: St Martin's Press, 1996. pp. ix, 243. (Cf. bibl. 1993, 8289.)

11344. —— (ed.). Outside the gates of the world: selected short stories. London: Dent; Rutland, VT: Tuttle, 1996. pp. xxx, 428. (Everyman library.)

11345. JOHNSON, TREVOR (introd.). *Wessex Poems* and other verses. Keele: Ryburn, 1995. pp. xi, 233. (Poems of Thomas Hardy, 2.) Rev. by Michael Thorpe in EngS (77:3) 1996, 292.

11346. KAMIYAMA, YASUSHI. Thomas Hardy to sakkatachi – hikaku bungakuteki kenkyu. (Thomas Hardy and other writers: a comparative literary study.) Osaka: Sogensha, 1996. pp. 204.

11347. LEAVIS, L. R. Marriage, murder, and morality: *The Secret Agent* and *Tess*. Neophilologus (80:1) 1996, 161–9.

11348. MALLETT, PHILLIP V.; DRAPER, RONALD P. (eds). A spacious vision: essays on Hardy. (Bibl. 1995, 10342.) Rev. by Peter Casagrande in ELT (39:2) 1996, 241–4; by Michael Thorpe in EngS (77:6) 1996, 599–600.

11349. MANFORD, ALAN (ed.). Life's little ironies. Introd. by Norman Page. Oxford; New York: OUP, 1996. pp. 251. (World's classics.)

11350. MANZER, PATRICIA K. 'In some old book, somebody just like me': Eliot's Tessa and Hardy's Tess. *See* **11151**.

11351. MARKS, JOHN. *Beeny Cliff March 1870 – March 1913* by Thomas Hardy. ERev (6:2) 1995, 34–5.

11352. —— Hardy's *In a Museum*. ERev (6:4) 1996, 28–9.

11353. MILLS, SARA; PEARCE, LYNNE. Feminist readings/feminists reading. *See* **4222**.

11354. MISTICHELLI, WILLIAM J. 'This pageantry of fear': the sublime in Thomas Hardy. CVE (44) 1996, 85–109.

11355. MITSCH, RUTHMARIE H. The other Isolde. *See* **4939**.

11356. MORGAN, ROSEMARIE. Cancelled words: rediscovering Thomas Hardy. (Bibl. 1994, 8412.) Rev. by Dieter Zeh in ZAA (42:4) 1994, 397–9.

11357. PETTIT, CHARLES P. C. (ed.). Celebrating Thomas Hardy: insights and appreciations. Basingstoke: Macmillan; New York: St Martin's Press, 1996. pp. xv, 200.

11358. RAY, MARTIN. Thomas Hardy's *The Duke's Reappearance*. *See* **804**.

11359. —— Thomas Hardy's *The Sailor's Mother*. NQ (43:4) 1996, 436–7.

11360. —— Thomas Hardy's *The Son's Veto*: a textual history. *See* **805**.

11361. REISNER, THOMAS A. The narrative time-scheme of *The Woodlanders*. NQ (43:4) 1996, 434–5.

11362. ROGERSON, IAN. Agnes Miller Parker and the Limited Editions Club's *Jude the Obscure*. *See* **239**.

11363. ROSE, STEVEN; O'DONOGHUE, BERNARD. Thomas Hardy's *He Abjures Love*. ERev (7:2) 1996, 32–6.

11364. SEYMOUR-SMITH, MARTIN. Hardy. (Bibl. 1995, 10368.) Rev. by Michael Thorpe in EngS (76:6) 1995, 587–8.

11365. SHELSTON, ALAN (introd.). *Moments of Vision* and miscellaneous verses. (Bibl. 1995, 10369.) Rev. by Michael Thorpe in EngS (77:3) 1996, 292.

11366. SHIRES, LINDA M. The author as spectacle and commodity: Elizabeth Barrett Browning and Thomas Hardy. *In* (pp. 198–212) **126**.

11367. SMITH, J. B. 'Bees up flues' and 'chips in porridge': two proverbial sayings in Thomas Hardy's *The Return of the Native. See* **3344**.

11368. STAVE, SHIRLEY A. The decline of the goddess: nature, culture, and women in Thomas Hardy's fiction. (Bibl. 1995, 10374.) Rev. by Christine Bucher in ELT (39:3) 1996, 357–60.

11369. VOLK-BIRKE, SABINE. *Cliffs of fall frightful*: Selbsterkenntnis und Weltbild von Thomas Hardy bis Gerard Manley Hopkins. *See* **9712**.

11370. WILLIAMS, EDITH WHITEHURST. A woman's struggle for love and independence in the history of Western romantic love. *See* **5010**.

11371. WILSON, KEITH. Revisiting Hardy's verse dramas: a review essay. ELT (39:3) 1996, 333–44.

11372. —— Thomas Hardy on stage. (Bibl. 1995, 10382.) Rev. by John J. Conlon in ELT (39:2) 1996, 221–5; by Merryn Williams in NQ (43:1) 1996, 111–12.

11373. YELLAND, CRIS. Hardy's allusions and the problem of 'pedantry'. *See* **11170**.

Frances Ellen Watkins Harper

11374. BOYD, MELBA JOYCE. Discarded legacy: politics and poetics in the life of Frances E. W. Harper, 1825–1911. (Bibl. 1994, 8435.) Rev. by Margaret Hope Bacon in AAR (30:3) 1996, 485–6; by Catharine F. Seigel in Legacy (13:1) 1996, 81–2.

11375. FOSTER, FRANCES SMITH (ed.). *Minnie's sacrifice*; *Sowing and Reaping*; *Trial and Triumph*: three rediscovered novels. Boston, MA: Beacon Press, 1994. pp. xliii, 286. (Black women writers.) Rev. by Maryemma Graham and Gina Rossetti in TSWL (14:2) 1995, 384–7; by Debra Rosenthal in ALR (29:1) 1996, 89–90.

11376. PETERSON, CARLA L. 'Further liftings of the veil': gender, class, and labor in Frances E. W. Harper's *Iola Leroy*. *In* (pp. 97–112) **59**.

11377. SCHEICK, WILLIAM J. Strategic ellipsis in Harper's *The Two Offers*. SoLJ (23:2) 1991, 14–18.

Charles Harpur

11378. MEAD, PHILIP. Charles Harpur's disfiguring origins: allegory in colonial poetry. *In* (pp. 217–40) **47**.

George Washington Harris

11379. CARON, JAMES E. An allegory of North and South: reading the preface to *Sut Lovingood: Yarns Spun by a 'Nat'ral Born Durn'd Fool'.* SAH (3:2) 1995, 49–61.

11380. ——INGE, M. THOMAS (eds). Sut Lovingood's nat'ral born yarnspinner: essays on George Washington Harris. Tuscaloosa; London: Alabama UP, 1996. pp. xii, 330.

Bret Harte

11381. SCHARNHORST, GARY. Bret Harte: a bibliography. Lanham, MD; London: Scarecrow Press, 1995. pp. xiii, 252. (Scarecrow author bibliographies, 95.)

11382. —— Mark Twain, Bret Harte, and the literary construction of San Francisco. *In* (pp. 21–34) **108**.

11383. —— 'Ways that are dark': appropriations of Bret Harte's *Plain Language from Truthful James*. NineL (51:3) 1996, 377–99.
11384. STONELEY, PETER. Rewriting the Gold Rush: Twain, Harte and homosociality. JAStud (30:2) 1996, 189–209.

Nathaniel Hawthorne

11385. ATTEBERY, BRIAN. American studies: a not so unscientific method. AmQ (48:2) 1996, 316–43.
11386. BAYM, NINA. Hawthorne's *Scarlet Letter*: producing and maintaining an American literary classic. JAE (30:2) 1996, 61–75.
11387. BEN-BASSAT, HEDDA. Marginal existence and communal consensus in *The Scarlet Letter* & *A Fringe of Leaves*. Comparatist (18) 1994, 52–70.
11388. BENESCH, KLAUS. Between reproduction and authenticity: the contested status of authorship in Hawthorne's *The Artist of the Beautiful*. In (pp. 116–23) **117**.
11389. BENTLEY, NANCY. The ethnography of manners: Hawthorne, James, Wharton. (Bibl. 1995, 10403.) Rev. by Holly Boren in JAStud (30:3) 1996, 490–1; by Laura Dluzynski Quinn in SAF (24:2) 1996, 246–7; by Peter Okun in ColLit (23:3) 1996, 203–4.
11390. BERCOVITCH, SACVAN. The office of *The Scarlet Letter*. (Bibl. 1995, 10404.) Rev. by Nancy A. Walker in AmS (35:1) 1994, 174–5.
11391. BERLANT, LAUREN. The anatomy of national fantasy: Hawthorne, utopia, and everyday life. (Bibl. 1995, 10405.) Rev. by Lucy M. Freibert in Signs (18:3) 1993, 684–8.
11392. BLOOM, HAROLD (ed.). Hester Prynne. New York: Chelsea House, 1990. pp. xvi, 200. (Major literary characters.) Rev. by Rita K. Gollin in NHR (17:1) 1991, 24–5.
11393. —— Nathaniel Hawthorne's *The Scarlet Letter*. New York: Chelsea House, 1996. pp. 80. (Bloom's notes.)
11394. BRADBURY, MALCOLM (ed.). The marble faun. Additional apparatus by Stephen Pain. London: Dent; Rutland, VT: Tuttle, 1995. pp. xlvii, 399. (Everyman library.)
11395. BRITT, BRIAN M. The veil of allegory in Hawthorne's *The Blithedale Romance*. LitTheol (10:1) 1996, 44–57.
11396. BROWN, GILLIAN. Domestic individualism: imagining self in nineteenth-century America. (Bibl. 1995, 10409.) Rev. by Nancy Armstrong in Signs (18:2) 1993, 433–8.
11397. CAIN, WILLIAM E. (ed.). The Blithedale romance. Boston, MA: Bedford Books of St Martin's Press; Basingstoke: Macmillan, 1996. pp. xvi, 512. (Bedford cultural eds.)
11398. CALINESCU, MATEI. Secrecy in fiction: textual and intertextual secrets in Hawthorne and Updike. PT (15:3) 1994, 443–65.
11399. CLASBY, NANCY TENFELDE. Being true: *logos* in *The Scarlet Letter*. Ren (45:4) 1993, 247–56.
11400. COLACURCIO, MICHAEL J. The province of piety: moral history in Hawthorne's early tales. Durham, NC; London: Duke UP, 1995. pp. xi, 669. (Second ed.: first ed. 1984.) Rev. by A. James Wohlpart in SAtlR (61:3) 1996, 176–8.
11401. DE ANGELIS, VALERIO MASSIMO. Voci del palco: George Bancroft, Nathaniel Hawthorne, e la scrittura dell'oralità. Àcoma (6) 1996, 35–43.

11402. Di Loreto, Sonia.   Dogane: *The Custom House* e *Beloved*. Àcoma (6) 1996, 27–34.

11403. Draxelbauer, Michael.   'Visible obscurity': a reappraisal of Nathaniel Hawthorne's *The Blithedale Romance*. LWU (29:3) 1996, 183–205.

11404. Dunne, Michael.   Hawthorne's narrative strategies. (Bibl. 1995, 10424.) Rev. by Dennis Berthold in NHR (22:1) 1996, 56–9.

11405. —— The narrative authority of history in Hawthorne's *The House of the Seven Gables*. TPB (29) 1992, 6–14.

11406. Easton, Alison.   The making of the Hawthorne subject. Columbia; London: Missouri UP, 1996. pp. xiii, 311.

11407. Egan, Ken, Jr.   The adulteress in the market-place: Hawthorne and *The Scarlet Letter*. StudN (27:1) 1995, 26–41.

11408. Felker, Christopher D.   Reinventing Cotton Mather in the American renaissance: *Magnalia Christi Americana* in Hawthorne, Stowe, and Stoddard. (Bibl. 1995, 10427.) Rev. by Reiner Smolinski in Amst (41:1) 1996, 131–5; by Kevin McCarron in CritS (8:3) 1996, 347–8.

11409. Gilmore, Michael T.   Hawthorne and the making of the middle class. *In* (pp. 215–38) **100**.

11410. Goodman, Margaret.   Posthumous journeys: *The Great Divorce* and other travels to eternity. CSL (27:1/2) 1996, 1–8.

11411. Hayford, Harrison.   Melville's *Monody*: really for Hawthorne? Evanston, IL: Northwestern UP, 1990. pp. 40. Rev. by Robert Milder in Text (Ann Arbor) (9) 1996, 389–407.

11412. Herbert, T. Walter.   Dearest beloved: the Hawthornes and the making of the middle-class family. (Bibl. 1995, 10439.) Rev. by Carolyn Johnston in AHR (99:2) 1994, 650–1.

11413. Idol, John L., Jr; Jones, Buford (eds).   Nathaniel Hawthorne: the contemporary reviews. (Bibl. 1995, 10447.) Rev. by Hans-Joachim Lang in ZAA (43:4) 1995, 368–70.

11414. Jewett, William.   Háwthorne's Romanticism: from canon to corpus. *See* **10561**.

11415. Kim, Ji-Won.   Text eui dokja hyungsung: N. Hawthorne eui *Jeoleun Goodman Brown* geul ilgi. (Text edifies its reader: a reading of N. Hawthorne's *Young Goodman Brown*.) JELL (42:1) 1996, 141–58.

11416. Laffrado, Laura.   The Persephone myth in Hawthorne's *Tanglewood Tales*. *In* (pp. 75–83) **46**.

11417. Lang, Hans-Joachim.   Auf der Suche nach Hawthorne: die Buchproduktion: Teil ii, 1989–1994. Amst (41:4) 1996, 657–701.

11418. McDermott, John V.   Hawthorne's *The Wives of the Dead*. Exp (54:3) 1996, 145–7.

11419. Miller, Edwin Haviland.   Salem is my dwelling-place: a life of Nathaniel Hawthorne. (Bibl. 1995, 10471.) Rev. by Joy S. Kasson in AHR (98:3) 1993, 948–9; by William E. Lenz in AmS (34:2) 1993, 139–41; by Philip F. Gura in GetR (6:1) 1993, 38–45.

11420. Mueller, Monika.   This infinite fraternity of feeling: gender, genre, and homoerotic crisis in Hawthorne's *The Blithedale Romance* and Melville's *Pierre*. Madison, NJ: Fairleigh Dickinson UP; London; Toronto: Assoc. UPs, 1996. pp. 229. (Cf. bibl. 1992, 9075.)

11421. Okada, Ryoichi.   Hawthorne no tanpen shousetsu. (Hawthorne's short stories.) Tokyo: Hokuseido Shoten, 1996. pp. 284.

11422. Packard, Christopher F.   Who's laughing now?

Sentimental readers and authorial revenge in *Alice Doane's Appeal*. AQ (52:3) 1996, 1–20.

11423. PARNELL, DAVID.   A Hawthornian analysis of Hemingway's *For Whom the Bell Tolls*. REAL (18) 1992, 5–13.

11424. PERSON, LELAND S., JR.   Hawthorne. American Literary Scholarship (1993) 23–37; (1994) 25–38; (1995) 25–36.

11425. PISAPIA, BIANCAMARIA.   *Il fauno di marmo: romance*: metaromanzo, teleromanzo. Àcoma (6) 1996, 44–51.

11426. POLK, NOEL.   Welty, Hawthorne, and Poe: men of the crowd and the landscape of alienation. LWU (29:4) 1996, 261–70.

11427. PORTELLI, ALESSANDRO.   'Tu non andrai da solo', ovvero, 'E va bene, andrò all'inferno'. La dannazione volontaria di Hester Prynne. Àcoma (6) 1996, 18–26.

11428. SCHIFF, JAMES A.   Updike's version: rewriting *The Scarlet Letter*. (Bibl. 1995, 10501.) Rev. by George J. Searles in MFS (40:2) 1994, 381–2.

11429. SMITH, LISA HERB.   'Some perilous stuff': what the religious reviewers really said about *The Scarlet Letter*. AmP (6) 1996, 135–43.

11430. STREEBY, SHELLEY.   Haunted houses: George Lippard, Nathaniel Hawthorne, and middle-class America. Criticism (38:3) 1996, 443–72.

11431. SWISHER, CLARICE (ed.).   Readings on Nathaniel Hawthorne. San Diego, CA: Greenhaven Press, 1996. pp. 191. (Greenhaven Press literary companion to American authors.)

11432. VALENTI, PATRICIA DUNLAVY.   Sophia Peabody Hawthorne's *American Notebooks*. StudAR (1996) 115–85.

11433. VANDERSEE, CHARLES.   Regarding a classic: effusions of the ineffable. Cresset (60:2/3) 1996, 5–8.

11434. VENTURA, MARY K.   'Alice Doane's appeal': the seducer revealed. ATQ (10:1) 1996, 25–39.

11435. WEBER, ALFRED; LUECK, BETH; BERTHOLD, DENNIS.   Hawthorne's American travel sketches. (Bibl. 1992, 9106.) Rev. by Benjamin Goluboff in AmS (34:1) 1993, 187.

11436. WELSH, JIM.   Classic folly: *The Scarlet Letter*. LitFQ (23:4) 1995, 299–300.

11437. YAHAGI, SANZO.   America renaissance no pessimism: Hawthorne and Melville kenkyu. (Pessimism in the American renaissance: a study of Hawthorne and Melville.) Tokyo: Kaibunsha Shuppan, 1996. pp. 370.

John Hay

11438. OWENS, PATRICIA ANN.   The friendship of Henry Adams and John Hay. *See* **10218**.

William Hazlitt

11439. EDWARDS, GAVIN.   William Hazlitt and the case of the initial letter. *See* **272**.

11440. GELPI, BARBARA CHARLESWORTH.   King Cophetua and Coventry Patmore. VP (34:4) 1996, 477–92.

11441. JONES, STANLEY.   Further quotations and reminiscences in Hazlitt: Daniel, the Bible, Milton, Paine, Dorset. *See* **7773**.

11442. ROOT, CHRISTINA.   Jacobin poetics and Napoleonic politics: Hazlitt's critique of Wordsworth. ERR (6:2) 1996, 227–45.

11443. SCHROEDER, HORST. An unacknowledged quotation in *Pen, Pencil and Poison*. NQ (43:1) 1996, 51–2.

Lafcadio Hearn (Koizumi Yakumo)

11444. DAWSON, CARL. Lafcadio Hearn and the vision of Japan. (Bibl. 1995, 10536.) Rev. by Joseph W. Slade in AmP (3) 1993, 123–4; by David Strauss in AmLH (8:3) 1996, 584–6.

11445. HIRAKAWA, SUKEHIRO. Orientalna yume – Koizumi Yakumo to rei no sekai. (Oriental dreams: Yakumo Koizumi and the world of spirits.) Tokyo: Chikuma Shobo, 1996. pp. 330.

11446. HUGHES, GEORGE. An Irish version of Lafcadio Hearn. CLS (33:1) 1996, 82–97.

11447. MCMILLAN, PETER. The literary criticism of Lafcadio Hearn. *In* (pp. 201–10) **49**.

11448. RONAN, SEAN G. Hearn's Irish background. *In* (pp. 196–200) **49**.

11449. SENBOKUYA, KOICHI. Jinsei no kyoushi Lafcadio Hearn. (Lafcadio Hearn: a teacher of the way of life.) Tokyo: Kobunsha, 1996. pp. 382.

11450. WATARAI, YOSHIICHI. Lafcadio Hearn's *kwaidan* and Japanese mythologies of the dead. *In* (pp. 73–7) **60**.

Felicia Dorothea Hemans

11451. AARON, JANE. The way above the world: religion in Welsh and Anglo-Welsh women's writing, 1780–1830. *In* (pp. 111–27) **103**.

11452. LINLEY, MARGARET. Sappho's conversions in Felicia Hemans, Letitia Landon, and Christina Rossetti. Prism(s) (4) 1996, 15–42.

11453. MCGANN, JEROME J. Literary history, Romanticism, and Felicia Hemans. *In* (pp. 210–27) **103**.

11454. WOLFSON, SUSAN J. 'Domestic affections' and 'the spear of Minerva': Felicia Hemans and the dilemma of gender. *In* (pp. 128–66) **103**.

G. A. Henty

11455. NEWBOLT, PETER. G. A. Henty, 1832–1902: a bibliographical study of his British editions, with short accounts of his publishers, illustrators and designers, and notes on production methods used for his books. Aldershot: Scolar Press; Brookfield, VT: Ashgate, 1996. pp. xv, 710.

Caroline Lee Hentz

11456. HUNT, ROBERT. A domesticated slavery: political economy in Caroline Hentz's fiction. SoQ (34:4) 1996, 25–35.

11457. STANESA, JAMIE. Legacy profile: Caroline Lee Whiting Hentz (1800–1856). Legacy (13:2) 1996, 130–41.

James A. Herne

11458. WEGNER, PAMELA S. *Margaret Fleming*: James A. Herne's contributions to American realism. NETJ (1) 1990, 19–29.

Thomas Wentworth Higginson

11459. PICKER, JOHN M. The union of music and text in Whitman's

Drum-Taps and Higginson's *Army Life in a Black Regiment.* WWQR (12:4) 1995, 230–45.

James Hogg

11460. CRAIG, CAIRNS. Out of history. *See* **9103**.

11461. FERGUSON, FRANCES. Romantic memory. SR (35:4) 1996, 509–33.

11462. GARSIDE, P. D. An annotated checklist of Hogg's literary manuscripts in the Alexander Turnbull Library, Wellington, New Zealand. *See* **358**.

11463. —— (ed.). A queer book. (Bibl. 1995, 10555.) Rev. by Iain Crichton Smith in SSL (29) 1996, 281–6; by Edwin Morgan in SLJ (supp. 44) 1996, 5–6; by John Barrell in LRB (18:4) 1996, 14–15; by James Kidd in Library Review (45:7) 1996, 62–4.

11464. GROVES, DAVID; HASLER, ANTONY; MACK, DOUGLAS S. (eds). The three perils of woman; or, Love, leasing, and jealousy: a series of domestic Scottish tales. (Bibl. 1995, 10556.) Rev. by Iain Crichton Smith in SSL (29) 1996, 281–6; by Douglas S. Mack in ECL (20:3) 1996, 92–106; by Edwin Morgan in SLJ (supp. 44) 1996, 3–5; by John Barrell in LRB (18:4) 1996, 14–15; by James Kidd in Library Review (45:7) 1996, 62–4.

11465. HUGHES, GILLIAN (ed.). Tales of the wars of Montrose. Edinburgh: Edinburgh UP, 1996. pp. xxxv, 311. (Stirling/South Carolina research ed. of the collected works of James Hogg, 4.) Rev. by Christopher MacLachlan in SHogg (6) 1995, 89–91; by Iain Crichton Smith in SSL (29) 1996, 336–7; by Ian Campbell in NQ (43:4) 1996, 488–9.

11466. MACK, DOUGLAS S. Culloden and after: Scottish Jacobite novels. ECL (20:3) 1996, 92–106 (review-article).

11467. —— (ed.). The shepherd's calendar. (Bibl. 1995, 10561.) Rev. by Iain Crichton Smith in SSL (29) 1996, 281–6; by Edwin Morgan in SLJ (supp. 44) 1996, 2–3; by John Barrell in LRB (18:4) 1996, 14–15; by James Kidd in Library Review (45:7) 1996, 62–4.

11468. MONNICKENDAM, ANDREW. Historicity and representation in the Scottish novel. Études Écossaises (1) 1992, 229–42.

11469. SCOTT, P.; HANSEN, J. S. Three newly identified James Hogg manuscript poems at the University of South Carolina. *See* **418**.

Marietta Holley

11470. CURRY, JANE. Marietta Holley. New York: Twayne; London: Prentice Hall, 1996. pp. xviii, 114. (Twayne's US authors, 658.)

11471. GWATHMY, GWENDOLYN B. 'Who will read the book, Samantha?': Marietta Holley and the 19th-century reading public. SAH (3:1) 1994, 28–50.

11472. MORRIS, LINDA A. Women vernacular humorists in nineteenth-century America: Ann Stephens, Francis [*sic*] Whitcher, and Marietta Holley. (Bibl. 1991, 8892.) Rev. by Eileen Gillooly in Feminist Studies (17:3) 1991, 473–92.

Oliver Wendell Holmes

11473. DIGGS, MARYLYNNE. Romantic friends or a 'different race of creatures'? The representation of lesbian pathology in nineteenth-century America. *See* **10229**.

Thomas Hood

11474. Thorogood, Peter (sel. and introd.).   Thomas Hood, poems comic and serious. Bramber, W. Sussex: Bramber Press, 1995. pp. 119.

Johnson Jones Hooper

11475. O'Brien, Sheila Ruzycki.   Writing with a forked pen: racial dynamics and Johnson Jones Hooper's twin tale of swindling Indians. AmS (35:2) 1994, 95–113.

Gerard Manley Hopkins

11476. Barth, J. Robert.   Wordsworth and Hopkins: in pursuit of transcendence. Ren (48:3) 1996, 175–89.
11477. Belitt, Ben.   Hopkins observing 'rehearsals'. Salmagundi (98/99) 1993, 141–68.
11478. Bizup, Joseph.   Hopkins' influence on Percy's *Love in the Ruins*. Ren (46:4) 1994, 247–59.
11479. Boggs, Rebecca M. C.   Hopkins's *As Kingfishers Catch Fire*. Exp (54:4) 1996, 223–6.
11480. Bronzwaer, W.   Hopkins' pleromatische volheid. (Hopkins' pleromatic completeness.) De Gids (159:1) 1996, 11–16.
11481. Carriere, Peter M.   Hopkins's *Spring*. Exp (54:3) 1996, 160–2.
11482. Carson, Ricks.   Hopkins's *Binsey Poplars*. Exp (54:3) 1996, 162–4.
11483. Downes, David Anthony.   Hopkins' achieved self. Lanham, MD; London: UP of America, 1996. pp. xiii, 205. Rev. by Michael E. Allsopp in ChrisL (46:1) 1996, 88–90.
11484. Emig, Rainer.   Modernism in poetry: motivations, structures and limits. London; New York: Longman, 1995. pp. xii, 270. (Studies in twentieth-century literature.) (Cf. bibl. 1993, 8489.)
11485. Feeney, Joseph J.   The Bischoff collection at Gonzaga University: a preliminary account. *See* **476**.
11486. —— Four newfound Hopkins letters: an annotated edition, with a fragment of another letter. *See* **637**.
11487. Fitzhugh, Mike.   Hopkins's mystic line: *The Wreck of the Deutschland* as a revelatory path. SM (ns 2) 1996, 78–91.
11488. Fontana, Ernest.   Wordsworth and Hopkins' *To What Serves Mortal Beauty?* HopQ (23:1/2) 1996, 61–7.
11489. Hollahan, Eugene.   Himmelfarb's culture of poverty and Hopkins's 'poor Jackself'. CLIO (25:1) 1995, 43–62.
11490. Koh, Jungja.   Hopkins eui *Gotong eui Sonnets*: siin euroseoeui wigi. (Hopkins's 'Terrible Sonnets': his crisis as a poet.) JELL (42:3) 1996, 549–70.
11491. Kutash, Emilie F.   Gerard Manley Hopkins: aerial tropics/ divine objects. LitPs (38:4) 1992, 44–62.
11492. Mortimer, Anthony (ed.).   The authentic cadence: centennial essays on Gerard Manley Hopkins. Fribourg, Switzerland: Fribourg UP, 1992. pp. ix, 208. (Seges, ns 10.) Rev. by Gudrun M. Grabher in GRM (44:1) 1994, 120–3; by Hans-Werner Ludwig in ZAA (42:2) 1994, 184–7.
11493. Nixon, Jude V.   Portrait of a friendship: the unpublished letters of the Hopkins family to Robert Bridges. Ren (44:4) 1992, 265–302.

11494. PALMER, PAMELA. A Hopkins bibliography 1991. HopQ (23:3/4) 1996, 120–38.

11495. SLAKEY, ROGER L. *God's Grandeur* and divine impersoning. VP (34:1) 1996, 73–85.

11496. STANFORD, DONALD E. The harried life of Gerard Manley Hopkins. Review (16) 1994, 209–19 (review-article).

11497. VENDLER, HELEN. The breaking of style: Hopkins, Heaney, Graham. (Bibl. 1995, 10590.) Rev. by James Wood in LRB (18:6) 1996, 22–3; by Mary Kaiser in WLT (70:3) 1996, 699–700; by William Logan in BkW, 25 Feb. 1996, 4; by William T. Cotton in NOR (22:1) 1996, 114–25.

11498. VOLK-BIRKE, SABINE. *Cliffs of fall frightful*: Selbsterkenntnis und Weltbild von Thomas Hardy bis Gerard Manley Hopkins. *See* **9712**.

11499. WARD, BERNADETTE. Newman's *Grammar of Assent* and the poetry of Gerard Manley Hopkins. Ren (43:1/2) 1990/91, 105–20.

11500. WATT, R. J. C. Electronic Hopkins. *See* **1215**.

11501. WHITE, NORMAN. Hopkins: a literary biography. (Bibl. 1995, 10592.) Rev. by Donald E. Stanford in Review (16) 1994, 209–19.

11502. —— Hopkins as the crow of Maenefa. HopQ (23:3/4) 1996, 113–20.

11503. ZONNEVELD, SJAAK. The random grim forge: a study of social ideas in the work of Gerard Manley Hopkins. (Bibl. 1995, 10593.) Rev. by Norman White in NQ (43:2) 1996, 236–7.

Pauline Elizabeth Hopkins

11504. BERG, ALLISON. Reconstructing motherhood: Pauline Hopkins' *Contending Forces*. SAF (24:2) 1996, 131–50.

11505. BROOKS, KRISTINA. New Woman, fallen woman: the crisis of reputation in turn-of-the-century novels by Pauline Hopkins and Edith Wharton. Legacy (13:2) 1996, 91–112.

11506. GILLMAN, SUSAN. Pauline Hopkins and the occult: African-American revisions of nineteenth-century sciences. AmLH (8:1) 1996, 57–82.

11507. GRUESSER, JOHN. Pauline Hopkins' *Of One Blood*: creating an Afrocentric fantasy for a Black middle class audience. *In* (pp. 74–83) **70**.

11508. GRUESSER, JOHN CULLEN (ed.). The unruly voice: rediscovering Pauline Elizabeth Hopkins. Introd. by Nellie Y. McKay. Afterword by Elizabeth Ammons. Urbana: Illinois UP, 1996. pp. xii, 240.

11509. PAMPLIN, CLAIRE. 'Race' and identity in Pauline Hopkins's *Hagar's Daughter*. *In* (pp. 169–83) **99**.

11510. PETERSON, CARLA L. Unsettled frontiers: race, history, and romance in Pauline Hopkins's *Contending Forces*. *In* (pp. 177–96) **31**.

Richard Hengist Horne

11511. COLLIN, DOROTHY W. Interventions of the publisher's reader. *See* **915**.

Julia Ward Howe

11512. DETSI, ZOE. Seduction, revenge, and suicide in Julia Ward Howe's *Leonora; or, The World's Own*. NETJ (7) 1996, 57–75.

Constance Howell

11513. HAPGOOD, LYNNE.   The novel and political agency: Socialism and the work of Margaret Harkness, Constance Howell and Clementina Black, 1888–1896. *See* **10363**.

W. D. Howells

11514. BOECKMANN, CATHERINE.   The invisible color: physical description and racial liminality in the novel of passing. *See* **10610**.

11515. BORUS, DANIEL H.   Writing Realism: Howells, James, and Norris in the mass market. (Bibl. 1993, 8527.) Rev. by George Cotkin in AmS (34:1) 1993, 166–7.

11516. CROWLEY, JOHN W.   The unsmiling aspects of life: *A Hazard of New Fortunes. In* (pp. 78–109) **7**.

11517. —— (ed.).   The rise of Silas Lapham. Oxford; New York: OUP, 1996. pp. xliii, 390. (World's classics.)

11518. DAUGHERTY, SARAH B.   William Dean Howells and Mark Twain: the Realism war as a campaign that failed. ALR (29:1) 1996, 12–28.

11519. DIMOCK, WAI CHEE.   Uneven development: American Realism and cultural history. YREAL (11) 1995, 103–17.

11520. GULDAGER, CARL.   William Dean Howells: the lookout on the watchtower. ModAge (38:3) 1996, 237–44.

11521. HEDGES, WARREN.   Howells's 'wretched fetishes': character, Realism, and other modern instances. TSLL (38:1) 1996, 26–50.

11522. LI, HSIN-YING.   For love or money: courtship and class conflict in Howells' *The Rise of Silas Lapham.* SAF (24:1) 1996, 101–21.

11523. MCWILLIAMS, JIM.   An 1890 interview with W. D. Howells. ANQ (9:1) 1996, 21–4.

11524. MADIGAN, ANDREW J.   Fathers and sons in *Silas Lapham*: the rise of the business man and the decline of social syntax. PMPA (20) 1995, 13–22.

11525. NETTELS, ELSA.   New England indigestion and its victims. *In* (pp. 167–84) **24**.

11526. PATTISON, EUGENE H.   The landscape and the sense of the past: William Dean Howells's *The Kentons.* Midamerica (20) 1993, 48–58.

11527. THOMAS, BROOK.   The risky business of accessing the economy of Howells's realism in *The Rise of Silas Lapham.* YREAL (11) 1995, 229–53.

Elbert Hubbard

11528. WHITE, BRUCE.   Jack London on Elbert Hubbard: from 'splendid character' to cad. JLJ (3) 1996, 57–66.

Thomas Hughes (1822–1896)

11529. ALLEN, DENNIS W.   Young England: muscular Christianity and the politics of the body in *Tom Brown's Schooldays. In* (pp. 114–32) **74**.

11530. ROSEN, DAVID.   The volcano and the cathedral: muscular Christianity and the origins of primal manliness. *In* (pp. 17–44) **74**.

Fergus Hume

11531. RYAN, J. S.   A Fergus Hume novel's occult folklore and the ancient continent of Lemuria. Australian Folklore (9) 1994, 132–4.

Leigh Hunt

11532. Cox, Jeffrey N. Staging hope: genre, myth, and ideology in the dramas of the Hunt circle. *See* **9747**.

11533. Edgecombe, Rodney Stenning. Leigh Hunt and the poetry of fancy. (Bibl. 1995, 10620.) Rev. by Dave Williams in NQ (43:1) 1996, 96–7; by Nicholas Roe in KSJ (45) 1996, 212–13.

11534. Harling, Philip. Leigh Hunt's *Examiner* and the language of patriotism. *See* **1282**.

11535. Kidwai, A. R.; Newey, Vincent. Leigh Hunt's *Abraham and the Fire-Worshipper*: a possible source. NQ (43:1) 1996, 44–5.

Jean Ingelow

11536. Knoepflmacher, U. C. Male patronage and female authorship: the case of John Ruskin and Jean Ingelow. PULC (57:1) 1995, 13–46.

Washington Irving

11537. Abdoo, Sherlyn. 'Before daybreak': the unfinished quest of Washington Irving's headless horseman of Sleepy Hollow. Analecta Husserliana (44) 1995, 145–60.

11538. Benoit, Raymond. Archetypes and ecotones: the tree in Faulkner's *The Bear* and Irving's *Rip Van Winkle*. NCL (22:1) 1992, 4–5.

11539. —— Irving's *The Legend of Sleepy Hollow*. Exp (55:1) 1996, 15–17.

11540. Eberwein, Jane Donahue. 'Siren Alps': the lure of Europe for American writers. *See* **10535**.

11541. Giorcelli, Cristina. Voyage among the vanquished: Washington Irving's *Companions of Columbus*. Letteratura d'America (44) 1992, 5–30.

11542. Greenfield, Bruce. The politics of the romantic traveller in Washington Irving's *Astoria* and *The Adventures of Captain Bonneville*. Letteratura d'America (39) 1990, 113–41.

11543. Mann, Jesse D. A little known incident of plagiarism in the career of Arthur Rackham. *See* **221**.

11544. Manning, Susan (ed.). The sketch-book of Geoffrey Crayon, Gent. Oxford; New York: OUP, 1996. pp. xxxvii, 353. (World's classics.)

11545. Murray, Laura J. The aesthetic of dispossession: Washington Irving and ideologies of (de)colonization in the early Republic. AmLH (8:2) 1996, 205–31.

11546. Shurr, William H. Walt Whitman's apocalypticism and Washington Irving's *Columbus*. Letteratura d'America (44) 1992, 57–67.

Harriet Jacobs

11547. Braxton, Joanne M.; Zuber, Sharon. Silences in Harriet 'Linda Brent' Jacobs's *Incidents in the Life of a Slave Girl*. In (pp. 146–55) **59**.

11548. Cutter, Martha J. Dismantling 'the master's house': critical literacy in Harriet Jacobs' *Incidents in the Life of a Slave Girl*. Callaloo (19:1) 1996, 209–25.

11549. Davie, Sharon. 'Reader, my story ends with freedom': Harriet Jacobs's *Incidents in the Life of a Slave Girl*. In (pp. 86–109) **31**.

11550. Foster, Frances Smith. Parents and children in autobiography by Southern Afro-American writers. In (pp. 98–109) **43**.

11551. GARFIELD, DEBORAH M.   Speech, listening, and female sexuality in *Incidents in the Life of a Slave Girl.* AQ (50:2) 1994, 19–49.

11552. KAPLAN, CARLA.   The erotics of talk: women's writing and feminist paradigms. *See* **10418**.

11553. KARPIŃSKI, EWA C.   The rhetoric of liberation in Harriet Jacobs' *Incidents in the Life of a Slave Girl, Written by Herself. See* **2655**.

11554. LOVELL, THOMAS B.   By dint of labor and economy: Harriet Jacobs, Harriet Wilson, and the salutary view of wage labor. AQ (52:2) 1996, 1–32.

11555. MORGAN, WINIFRED.   Gender-related difference in the slave narratives of Harriet Jacobs and Frederick Douglass. *See* **11035**.

11556. NÜSSLER, ULRIKE.   'Across the Black's body': Herman Melville's *Benito Cereno* and Harriet Jacobs's *Incidents in the Life of a Slave Girl* – a critical collage. *In* (pp. 55–79) **8**.

11557. SIELKE, SABINE.   Seduced and enslaved: sexual violence in antebellum American literature and contemporary feminist discourse. *See* **9057**.

11558. SOROSIO, CAROLYN.   'There is Might in Each': conceptions of self in Harriet Jacobs's *Incidents in the Life of a Slave Girl, Written by Herself.* Legacy (13:1) 1996, 1–18.

Alice James

11559. ANDERSON, LINDA (ed.).   Her life in letters. Bristol: Thoemmes Press, 1996. pp. xxviii, 271. (Her write, his name.)

Henry James

11560. AKIYAMA, MASAYUKI.   A comparative study of Henry James and major Japanese writers. (Bibl. 1993, 8562.) Rev. by Meera Viswanathan in CanRCL (20:3/4) 1993, 528–30.

11561. —— Henry James no sekai – America, Europe, touyou. (The world of Henry James: America, Europe and the East.) Tokyo: Nan'undo, 1996. pp. 206.

11562. ALLIATA, MICHELA VANON.   A caravan of gypsies: James, Sargent, and the American symptom. RSAJ (5) 1994, 29–49.

11563. ARATA, STEPHEN D.   Object lessons: reading the museum in *The Golden Bowl. In* (pp. 199–229) **31**.

11564. ARMSTRONG, PAUL B.   Art and the construction of community in *The Death of the Lion.* HJR (17:2) 1996, 99–108.

11565. —— Cultural differences in Conrad and James: *Under Western Eyes* and *The Ambassadors.* YREAL (12) 1996, 143–62.

11566. ASCARI, MAURIZIO.   One-way words: an interpretation of *In the Cage*, by Henry James. *In* (pp. 244–54) **117**.

11567. —— Three aesthetes in profile: Gilbert Osmond, Mark Ambient, and Gabriel Nash. RSAJ (7) 1996, 39–62.

11568. AUCHARD, JOHN (ed.).   Italian hours. (Bibl. 1993, 8565.) Rev. by Millicent Bell in Raritan (13:4) 1994, 124–45.

11569. BAKER, WILLIAM D.   Henry James in Ohio – eight reviews of his work. SSMLN (26:3) 1996, 6–8.

11570. BALESTRA, GIANFRANCA.   Edith Wharton, Henry James, and 'the proper vehicle of passion'. *In* (pp. 595–604) **117**.

11571. BALSAMO, GIAN.   Henry James and Emma Bovary. CanRCL (18:4) 1991, 547–56.

11572. BAMBERG, ROBERT D. (ed.).   *The Portrait of a Lady*: an authoritative text, Henry James and the novel, reviews and criticism. (Bibl. 1995, 10654.) Rev. by Bernard Richards in NQ (43:3) 1996, 365.

11573. BELL, MILLICENT. Meaning in Henry James. (Bibl. 1995, 10658.) Rev. by Daniel T. O'Hara in Review (16) 1994, 251–69; by Rayburn S. Moore in StudN (27:1) 1995, 88–9.

11574. —— On Venice. *See* **3716**.

11575. BEN-JOSEPH, ELI. Aesthetic persuasion: Henry James, the Jews and race. Lanham, MD; London: UP of America, 1996. pp. xi, 252.

11576. BISHOP, RYAN. There's nothing natural about natural conversation: a look at dialogue in fiction and drama. *See* **2585**.

11577. BLAIR, SARA. Henry James, Jack the Ripper, and the cosmopolitan Jew: staging authorship in *The Tragic Muse*. ELH (63:2) 1996, 489–512.

11578. —— Henry James and the writing of race and nation. Cambridge; New York: CUP, 1996. pp. x, 259.

11579. BRADBURY, NICOLA (ed.). The portrait of a lady. Oxford; New York: OUP, 1995. pp. xxxiii, 634. (World's classics.)

11580. BUSH, RONALD. Changing his mind about how to do a girl in: poetry, narrative, and gender in the revisions of Henry James's *Daisy Miller*. *See* **594**.

11581. CARAMELLO, CHARLES. Henry James, Gertrude Stein, and the biographical act. Chapel Hill; London: North Carolina UP, 1996. pp. xii, 275.

11582. FOLLINI, TAMARA. Pandora's box: the family correspondence in *Notes of a Son and Brother*. CamQ (25:1) 1996, 26–40.

11583. FREEDMAN, JONATHAN. Henry James and the discourses of anti-Semitism. *In* (pp. 62–83) **5**.

11584. GALE, ROBERT L. Henry James. American Literary Scholarship (1993) 85–100.

11585. GEOFFROY-MENOUX, SOPHIE. Miroirs d'outre-monde: Henry James et la création fantastique. Paris: L'Harmattan; Saint-Denis: Univ. de la Réunion, 1996. pp. 302 ('Americana'.)

11586. GIORCELLI, CRISTINA. An hermetic reading of money in Henry James's *The Coxon Fund*. Letteratura d'America (50) 1993, 51–69.

11587. GOODMAN, SUSAN. Edith Wharton's inner circle. (Bibl. 1995, 10691.) Rev. by Daniel Mark Fogel in BkW, 31 July 1994, 3.

11588. GRAHAM, KENNETH. Henry James: a literary life. (Bibl. 1995, 10692.) Rev. by Bernard Richards in NQ (43:3) 1996, 367–8.

11589. GRAHAM, WENDY. Henry James's subterranean blues: a rereading of *The Princess Casamassima*. MFS (40:1) 1994, 51–84.

11590. —— Henry James's thwarted love. *In* (pp. 66–95) **30**.

11591. HABEGGER, ALFRED. Henry James and the 'woman business'. (Bibl. 1992, 9263.) Rev. by Christine Richards in Eng (40:166) 1991, 79–85.

11592. HAYES, KEVIN J. (ed.). Henry James: the contemporary reviews. Cambridge; New York: CUP, 1996. pp. xxiii, 477. (American critical archives, 7.)

11593. HIRAIDE, SHOJI. Isabel no *maternal strain* ni tsuite – Henry James no *The Portrait of a Lady*. (Isabel's 'maternal strain' – Henry James's *The Portrait of a Lady*.) SEL (73:1) 1996, 61–73.

11594. HOCHMAN, BARBARA. Disappearing authors and resentful readers in late nineteenth-century American fiction: the case of Henry James. ELH (63:1) 1996, 177–201.

11595. Hocks, Richard A.   'Quite the best, "all round", of all my productions': the multiple versions of the Jamesian germ for *The Ambassadors*. *In* (pp. 110–30) **7**.

11596. Holly, Carol.   Intensely family: the inheritance of family shame and the autobiographies of Henry James. (Bibl. 1995, 10703.) Rev. by Allan Hepburn in AL (68:4) 1996, 859–60; by Scott S. Derrick in SAF (24:2) 1996, 248–9.

11597. Honour, Hugh; Fleming, John.   The Venetian hours of Henry James, Whistler and Sargent. (Bibl. 1992, 9268.) Rev. by Millicent Bell in Raritan (13:4) 1994, 124–45.

11598. Horne, Philip.   Henry James and the economy of the short story. *In* (pp. 1–35) **69**.

11599. —— The lessons of Flaubert: James and *L'Éducation sentimentale*. YES (26) 1996, 154–62.

11600. Ian, Marcia.   Henry James and the spectacle of loss: psycho-analytic metaphysics. *In* (pp. 115–36) **18**.

11601. Intonti, Vittoria.   *The Figure in the Carpet* as an allegory of reading. RSAJ (7) 1996, 27–37.

11602. Izzo, Donatella.   *Daisy Miller* e il discorso dell'ideologia. RSAJ (1) 1990, 45–68.

11603. —— Women, portraits, and painters: *The Madonna of the Future* and *The Sweetheart of M. Briseux*. RSAJ (5) 1994, 5–28.

11604. Jackson, Timothy P.   Waiting in *The Wings of the Dove*: patience as a Jamesian virtue. Ren (44:4) 1992, 227–47.

11605. Jahn, Manfred.   Windows of focalization: deconstructing and reconstructing a narratological concept. *See* **2404**.

11606. Jin, Myung-Hee.   *The American* gwa *The Spoils of Poynton* yeongu. (A study of *The American* and *The Spoils of Poynton*.) JELLC (38:1) 1996, 151–73.

11607. Jolly, Roslyn.   Henry James: history, narrative, fiction. (Bibl. 1995, 10711.) Rev. by Bernard Richards in NQ (43:3) 1996, 366–7.

11608. Joseph, Mary J.   Suicide in Henry James's fiction. (Bibl. 1995, 10713.) Rev. by Arthrell D. Sanders in CLAJ (39:4) 1996, 504–9.

11609. Kabel, Hanno.   Money, alienation, and the leisure class: Henry James, Edith Wharton, Thorstein Veblen. ZAA (44:4) 1996, 346–57.

11610. Kaplan, Fred.   Henry James: the imagination of a genius: a biography. (Bibl. 1993, 8606.) Rev. by Juan J. Lanero in Atlantis (17:1/2) 1995, 394–6.

11611. Katayama, Etsuo.   Shiten no gihou no shintenkai – *The Spoils of Poynton* saikou. (A new phase of point of view – *The Spoils of Poynton* reconsidered.) SEL (73:1) 1996, 75–87.

11612. Kearns, Michael.   Narrative discourse and the imperative of sympathy in *The Bostonians*. HJR (17:2) 1996, 162–81.

11613. Kehde, Suzanne.   Voices from the margin: bag ladies and others. *In* (pp. 25–38) **33**.

11614. Kim, Hong-Sook.   'Hwansang' gwa 'shilje' eui byunjeung-beob: Henry James eui yuryung soseol yeongu. (The dialectics of 'fantasy' and 'reality': a study of Henry James's ghost stories.) Unpub. doct. diss., Korea Univ., Seoul, 1996.

11615. KLARER, MARIO. '*This is not a real thing*': Repräsentation, Illustration und Simulation bei Henry James. ZAA (42:4) 1994, 340–51.

11616. KLEVAN, EDWARD. Smiling and hiding: the earlier novels and tales of Henry James. CamQ (25:2) 1996, 152–69. (*Cambridge Quarterly* prize essay.)

11617. KOO, EUNSOOK. Ideology as a shadow in the text: Henry James's *The Turn of the Screw.* JELLC (38:1) 1996, 35–55.

11618. KOPRINCE, SUSAN. Edith Wharton, Henry James, and *Roman Fever.* JSSE (25) 1995, 21–31.

11619. KRAMER, LAWRENCE. *Revenants*: masculine thresholds in Schubert, James, and Freud. MLQ (57:3) 1996, 449–77.

11620. KRIEG, JOANN P. Health capital: Henry James' *The Wings of the Dove. In* (pp. 111–20) **71**.

11621. KRUPNICK, MARK. Jewish Jacobites: Henry James's presence in the fiction of Philip Roth and Cynthia Ozick. *In* (pp. 89–107) **123**.

11622. LANDAU, JOHN. A thing divided: representation in the late novels of Henry James. Madison, NJ: Fairleigh Dickinson UP; London; Toronto: Assoc. UPs, 1996. pp. 187.

11623. LANE, CHRISTOPHER. The impossibility of seduction in James's *Roderick Hudson* and *The Tragic Muse.* AL (68:4) 1996, 739–64.

11624. LOGAN, THAD. Decorating domestic space: middle-class women and Victorian interiors. *In* (pp. 207–34) **54**.

11625. LUSTIG, T. J. Henry James and the ghostly. (Bibl. 1995, 10723.) Rev. by Greg W. Zacharias in HJR (17:3) 1996, 306–8; by Neil Cornwell in EP (21) 1996, 183–4.

11626. MACCOMB, DEBRA. Divorce of a nation; or, Can Isabel Archer resist history? HJR (17:2) 1996, 129–48.

11627. MAHBOBAH, ALBARAQ. Hysteria, rhetoric, and the politics of reversal in Henry James's *The Turn of the Screw. See* **2424**.

11628. MARTIN, W. R.; OBER, WARREN U. Henry James's apprenticeship: the tales, 1864–1882. (Bibl. 1995, 10728.) Rev. by Ed Kleiman in ESCan (22:3) 1996, 349–51.

11629. MIZRUCHI, SUSAN L. Reproducing women in *The Awkward Age.* Representations (38) 1992, 101–30.

11630. MONK, LELAND. A terrible beauty is born: Henry James, aestheticism, and homosexual panic. *In* (pp. 247–65) **9**.

11631. MONTEIRO, GEORGE. 'There *is* a figure in the carpet': James, Hueffer, and Garnett. NineL (51:2) 1996, 225–32.

11632. MURPHY, KATHLEEN. Jane Campion's shining: portrait of a director. FilCo (32:6) 1996, 28–31, 33.

11633. MURTAUGH, DANIEL J. An emotional reflection: sexual realization in Henry James's revisions to *Roderick Hudson. See* **768**.

11634. NELSON, MICHELLE D. *Watch and Ward*: James's fantasy of omnipotence. Style (29:3) 1995, 375–88.

11635. NETTELS, ELSA. Tradition and the woman artist: James's *The Tragic Muse* and Cather's *The Song of the Lark.* WCPMN (36:3) 1992, 27–31.

11636. NOVICK, SHELDON M. Henry James: the young master. New York: Random House, 1996. pp. xx, 550, (plates) 16. Rev. by Millicent Bell in TLS, 6 Dec. 1996, 3–4.

11637. —— Henry James's first published work: *Miss Maggie Mitchell in 'Fanchon the Critic'. See* **773**.

11638. ORLICH, ILEANA ALEXANDRA. Henry James and the politics of authorship: (re)constructing the portrait of the artist-critic. CR (40:3) 1996, 537–60.

11639. —— Tracking the missing link: Maupassant's *Promenade* and James's *The Beast in the Jungle*. Comparatist (18) 1994, 71–89.

11640. PARK, YONG-SOO. Sijeom inmul eui shinroesung: Henry James eui *Poynton eui Sujangpum* yeongu. (Reliability of the reflector: a study of Henry James's *The Spoils of Poynton*.) JELLC (38:1) 1996, 57–100.

11641. POOLE, ADRIAN. Dying before the end: the reader in *The Portrait of a Lady*. YES (26) 1996, 143–53.

11642. —— (ed.). What Maisie knew. Oxford; New York: OUP, 1996. pp. xxxvi, 294. (World's classics.)

11643. POSNOCK, ROSS. The trial of curiosity: Henry James, William James, and the challenge of modernity. (Bibl. 1995, 10742.) Rev. by David Marr in AHR (98:2) 1993, 582–3; by Daniel T. O'Hara in Review (16) 1994, 251–69.

11644. RAWLINGS, PETER (ed.). Henry James: essays on art and drama. Aldershot: Scolar Press; Brookfield, VT: Ashgate, 1996. pp. ix, 537.

11645. RIVKIN, JULIE. False positions: the representational logics of Henry James's fiction. Stanford, CA: Stanford UP, 1996. pp. viii, 225.

11646. SARRIS, FOTIOS. Fetishism in *The Spoils of Poynton*. NineL (51:1) 1996, 53–83.

11647. SCHAFFER, TALIA. Some chapter of some other story: Henry James, Lucas Malet, and the real past of *The Sense of the Past*. HJR (17:2) 1996, 109–28.

11648. SCHEIBER, ANDREW J. The doctor's order: eugenic anxiety in Henry James's *Washington Square*. LitMed (15:2) 1996, 244–62.

11649. SCHILLER, EMILY. Melodrama redeemed; or, The death of innocence: Milly or mortality in *The Wings of the Dove*. SAF (24:2) 1996, 193–214.

11650. SCHMELING, MAX. Narrative, perspective and cultural otherness. *See* **2701**.

11651. SCHWARZSCHILD, EDWARD L. Revising vulnerability: Henry James's confrontation with photography. TSLL (38:1) 1996, 51–78.

11652. SEDGWICK, ELLERY. Henry James and the *Atlantic Monthly*: editorial perspectives on James' 'friction with the market'. *See* **1359**.

11653. SMIDT, KRISTIAN. T. S. Eliot's criticism of modern prose fiction. EngS (76:1) 1995, 64–80.

11654. SOLOMON, MELISSA. The female world of exorcism and displacement (or, relations between women in Henry James's nineteenth-century *The Portrait of a Lady*). StudN (28:3) 1996, 395–413.

11655. STANLEY, SANDRA KUMAMOTO. Female acquisition in *The Spoils of Poynton. In* (pp. 131–48) **54**.

11656. STRYCHACZ, THOMAS. Modernism, mass culture, and professionalism. (Bibl. 1995, 10762.) Rev. by David Punter in YES (26) 1996, 340–1; by Michael Tratner in StudN (28:2) 1996, 244–53.

11657. TANNER, TONY. Henry James and the art of nonfiction. (Bibl. 1995, 10764.) Rev. by Adeline R. Tintner in ELT (39:4) 1996, 518–22.

11658. TEAHAN, SHEILA. The rhetorical logic of Henry James. (Bibl. 1995, 10766.) Rev. by Gustavus Stadler in AL (68:4) 1996, 858–9; by Craig Monk in JAStud (30:3) 1996, 492–3.

11659. TERRAMORSI, BERNARD. Henry James; ou, Le sens des profondeurs: essai sur les nouvelles fantastiques. Saint-Denis: Univ. de La Réunion; Paris: L'Harmattan, 1996. pp. 326. (Americana.)

11660. THORMANN, JANET. The unconscious and the construction of the child. LitPs (42:4) 1996, 16–36.

11661. TINTNER, ADELINE R. A bibliographical and biographical note: Henry James's markings in Zola's *La Débâcle*. HJR (17:2) 1996, 204–7.

11662. —— The cosmopolitan world of Henry James: an intertextual study. (Bibl. 1995, 10767.) Rev. by Priscilla L. Walton in CanRCL (20:1/2) 1993, 255–7.

11663. TREITEL, ILONA. The dangers of interpretation: art and artists in Henry James and Thomas Mann. New York; London: Garland, 1996. pp. xi, 316. (Garland reference library of the humanities, 1959.) (Origins of Modernism.)

11664. TUCKER, EDWARD L. James and Charles Dickens. *See* **10920**.

11665. VILLA, LUISA. Henry James: la metropoli e il suo soggetto. QLLSM (4) 1990, 107–22.

11666. VOPAT, CAROLE. Becoming a lady: the origins and development of 'Isabel Archer's ideal self'. LitPs (38:1/2) 1992, 38–56.

11667. WALKER, PIERRE A. Reading Henry James in French cultural contexts. (Bibl. 1995, 10773.) Rev. by Mary Cross in ELT (39:1) 1996, 85–8.

11668. WEGENER, FREDERICK. Henry James on James Payn: a forgotten critical text. NEQ (67:1) 1994, 115–31.

11669. WIESENFARTH, JOSEPH. *The Portrait of a Lady*: gothic manners in Europe. *In* (pp. 119–39) **96**.

11670. ZACHARIAS, GREG W. Henry James. American Literary Scholarship (1994) 111–26; (1995) 97–115.

William James

11671. COTKIN, GEORGE. William James: public philosopher. (Bibl. 1993, 8677.) Rev. by Robert C. Bannister in AHR (96:4) 1991, 1268.

11672. CRUZ HERNÁNDEZ, JUAN JOSÉ. *The Genteel Tradition in American Philosophy* as a valedictory indictment of the United States. Misc (17) 1996, 71–90.

11673. FOLLINI, TAMARA. Pandora's box: the family correspondence in *Notes of a Son and Brother*. *See* **11582**.

11674. HORN, JASON G. Figuring freedom as religious experience: Mark Twain, William James, and *No. 44, The Mysterious Stranger*. AQ (52:1) 1996, 95–123.

11675. HORN, JASON GARY. Mark Twain and William James: crafting a free self. Columbia; London: Missouri UP, 1996. pp. xiii, 189. (Cf. bibl. 1995, 10794.)

11676. LANE, CHRISTOPHER. *Thoughts for the Times on War and Death*: militarism and its discontents. LitPs (41:3) 1995, 1–12.

11677. RAMSEY, BENNETT. Submitting to freedom: the religious vision of William James. (Bibl. 1993, 8680.) Rev. by Thomas D. Hamm in AHR (99:3) 1994, 980–1.

11678. SKRUPSKELIS, IGNAS K.; BERKELEY, ELIZABETH M. (eds). The correspondence of William James: vol. 4, 1856–1877. Charlottesville; London: Virginia UP, 1995. pp. lxvi, 714.

Richard Jefferies

11679.   KEITH, W. J.   The Jefferies canon: notes on essays attributed to Richard Jefferies without full documentary evidence. Oxford: Petton, 1995. pp. 40.

Sarah Orne Jewett

11680.   CHURCH, JOSEPH.   Transcendent daughters in Jewett's *Country of the Pointed Firs*. (Bibl. 1994, 8703.) Rev. by Victoria Brehm in AL (68:1) 1996, 247–8.

11681.   —— A woman's psychological journey in Jewett's *The King of Folly Island*. ELit (23:2) 1996, 234–50.

11682.   FOOTE, STEPHANIE.   'I feared to find myself a foreigner': revisiting regionalism in Sarah Orne Jewett's *The Country of the Pointed Firs*. AQ (52:3) 1996, 37–61.

11683.   HELLER, TERRY (ed.).   *The Country of the Pointed Firs* and other fiction. Oxford; New York: OUP, 1996. pp. xxx, 355. (World's classics.)

11684.   HOWARD, JUNE.   Unraveling regions, unsettling periods: Sarah Orne Jewett and American literary history. AL (68:2) 1996, 365–84.

11685.   —— (ed.).   New essays on *The Country of the Pointed Firs*. (Bibl. 1994, 8705.) Rev. by Kurt Müller in Amst (41:4) 1996, 710–11; by Susanne Opfermann in ZAA (44:2) 1996, 184–5.

11686.   ROMINES, ANN.   The hermit's parish: Jeanne Le Ber and Cather's legacy from Jewett. CathS (1) 1990, 147–58.

11687.   SEDGWICK, ELLERY.   Horace Scudder and Sarah Orne Jewett: market forces in publishing in the 1890s. *See* **1004**.

Geraldine Jewsbury

11688.   ROSEN, JUDITH.   At home upon a stage: domesticity and genius in Geraldine Jewsbury's *The Half Sisters* (1848). *In* (pp. 17–32) **75**.

Ellen Johnston

11689.   KLAUS, GUSTAV.   Working women writing verse: the case of Ellen Johnston 'the factory girl'. Études Écossaises (1) 1992, 351–9.

Henry Arthur Jones

11690.   BOOTH, MICHAEL R. (ed.).   *The Lights o' London* and other Victorian plays. *See* **10746**.

John Keats

11691.   AAMODT, TERRIE.   Escape from 'slow-time': sculpture and tactile temporality in Keats's later poems. Topic (46) 1996, 45–56.

11692.   BARNARD, JOHN.   Keats echoes Kirke White. RES (47:187) 1996, 389–92.

11693.   BATE, JONATHAN.   Living with the weather. *See* **10549**.

11694.   BECKER, MICHAEL G.   Keats's fantasia: the *Ode on Melancholy*, sonata form and Mozart's *Fantasia in C Minor* for piano, K. 475. Comparatist (17) 1993, 18–37.

11695.   BRANSCOMB, JACK.   Edwin Arlington Robinson's wretched wight: *Miniver Cheevy* and *La Belle Dame sans Merci*. ANQ (9:1) 1996, 17–21.

11696.   BROMWICH, DAVID.   John Keats at 200. SRev (81:4) 1996, 533–7.

11697. CHALK, MIRIAM (sel. and introd.). Selected poems. Kidderminster: Joe's Press, 1994. pp. 50.

11698. COLBURN, DON. A feeling for light and shade: John Keats and his *Ode to a Nightingale*. GetR (5:2) 1992, 216–38.

11699. COOK, ELIZABETH (ed.). Selected poetry. Oxford; New York: OUP, 1994. pp. xxii, 260. (World's classics.)

11700. CRONIN, RICHARD. Keats and the politics of Cockney style. *See* **2606**.

11701. FRIEDMAN, GERALDINE. The insistence of history: revolution in Burke, Wordsworth, Keats, and Baudelaire. *See* **8872**.

11702. HALPERN, NICK. Mist and crag: the poetry of Keats's walking tour. Topic (46) 1996, 12–24.

11703. HAVERKAMP, ANSELM. Leaves of mourning: Hölderlin's late work, with an essay on Keats and melancholy. Trans. by Vernon Chadwick. Albany: New York State UP, 1996. pp. xii, 163. (Intersections: philosophy and critical theory.)

11704. HILTON, NELSON. Keats, teats, and the fane of poesy. *In* (pp. 49–72) **47**.

11705. HÖFELE, ANDREAS. Jetzt-Theater: zur Inszenierung der emphatischen Präsenz. Forum modernes Theater (11:1) 1996, 45–55.

11706. JEWETT, WILLIAM. Hawthorne's Romanticism: from canon to corpus. *See* **10561**.

11707. JOHNSTON, EILEEN TESS. 'Beautiful things made new': transformations of Keats's *Hyperion* in Tennyson's *Morte d'Arthur* and *The Passing of Arthur*. TRB (6:5) 1996, 289–301.

11708. JONES, ANDREW O. 'At a house in Hampstead': a personal account of Keats's place in American popular culture. Topic (46) 1996, 1–6.

11709. JONES, ELIZABETH. Keats in the suburbs. KSJ (45) 1996, 23–43.

11710. KERCSMAR, RHONDA RAY. Keats's violation of romance: transgression in *The Eve of St Agnes*. Topic (46) 1996, 25–35.

11711. KIM, SUNG RYOL. Browning's vision of Keats: *Cleon* and the 'mansion of many apartments' letter. *See* **10523**.

11712. KITSON, PETER J. (ed.). Coleridge, Keats and Shelley. *See* **10684**.

11713. LAU, BETH. Editing Keats's marginalia. *See* **716**.

11714. MASON, KENNETH M., JR. Keats and the act of translation: the discovery of voice in *On First Looking into Chapman's Homer*. Topic (46) 1996, 7–11.

11715. MOÏSE, EDWIN. An archaism in John Keats's *Ode to a Nightingale*. *See* **1933**.

11716. O'HEARN, DANIEL. Black border: Keats's urn and the displacement of fear. Topic (46) 1996, 38–44.

11717. PAPETTI, VIOLA. Keats e la morte, il sonno, il sogno, la visione. Textus (7) 1994, 187–92.

11718. PEREIRA, ERNEST. Keats and self-criticism. UES (33:2) 1995, 2–16.

11719. RAHBEK, ULLA. Tales of love, lust, jealousy and revenge: intertextuality in Marion Halligan's *Spidercup*. *See* **7334**.

11720. RAYAN, KRISHNA. Resistance in reading. *See* **9159**.

11721. ROE, NICHOLAS (ed.). Keats and history. (Bibl. 1995, 10851.)

Rev. by Miriam Allott in NQ (43:2) 1996, 234–5; by Geoff Finch in Eng (45:182) 1996, 170–5.

11722. Scott, Grant F.   The sculpted word: Keats, ekphrasis, and the visual arts. (Bibl. 1994, 8751.) Rev. by Nancy Moore Goslee in ERR (6:2) 1996, 277–81; by Nigel Spivey in TLS, 12 Jan. 1996, 24.

11723. Smith, Hillas.   Keats and medicine. Newport, Isle of Wight: Cross, 1995. pp. 127.

11724. Stephenson, Will; Stephenson, Mimosa.   A Keats allusion in Walker Percy's *The Last Gentleman*. NCL (22:3) 1992, 3–4.

11725. Stevenson, Warren.   Madeline unhoodwink'd: *The Eve of St Agnes* as self-reflexive romance. *In* (pp. 215–26) **125**.

11726. Stillinger, Jack.   Poets who revise, poets who don't, and critics who should. JAE (30:2) 1996, 119–33.

11727. Tallis, Raymond.   Newton's sleep: 1, Poets, scientists and rainbows. *See* **8841**.

11728. White, Keith D.   John Keats and the loss of Romantic innocence. Amsterdam; Atlanta, GA: Rodopi, 1996. pp. xv, 194, (plates) 2. (Costerus, 107.)

Elizabeth Keckley

11729. Sielke, Sabine.   Seduced and enslaved: sexual violence in antebellum American literature and contemporary feminist discourse. *See* **9057**.

Henry F. Keenan

11730. Dunne, Robert.   Dueling ideologies of America in *The Bread-Winners* and *The Money-Makers*. ALR (28:3) 1996, 30–7.

Patrick Kennedy (1801–1873)

11731. Cohane, Mary Ellen; Goldstein, Kenneth S.   Folksongs and the ethnography of singing in Patrick Kennedy's *The Banks of the Boro*. *See* **3479**.

Charles J. Kickham

11732. Carpentier, Godeleine.   The peasantry in Kickham's tales and novels: an epitome of the writer's realism, idealism and ideology. *In* (pp. 93–107) **106**.

11733. Dalsimer, Adele M.   'Knocknagow is no more', but when was it? *In* (pp. 189–95) **49**.

'Clover King' (Clara Collet)

11734. Postmus, Bouwe.   Clara Collet's clairvoyance. *See* **11297**.

Grace King

11735. Coleman, Linda S.   At odds: race and gender in Grace King's short fiction. *In* (pp. 32–55) **65**.

Charles Kingsley

11736. Fasick, Laura.   Charles Kingsley's scientific treatment of gender. *In* (pp. 91–113) **74**.

11737. Hall, Donald E.   On the making and unmaking of monsters: Christian Socialism, muscular Christianity, and the metaphorization of class conflict. *In* (pp. 45–65) **74**.

11738. McCausland, Elizabeth D.   Dirty little secrets: Realism and the real in Victorian industrial novels. *See* **11266**.

11739. Rosen, David.   The volcano and the cathedral: muscular Christianity and the origins of primal manliness. *In* (pp. 17–44) **74**.

11740. Srebrnik, Patricia.   The re-subjection of 'Lucas Malet': Charles Kingsley's daughter and the response to muscular Christianity. *In* (pp. 194–214) **74**.

11741. Wee, C. J. W.-L.   Christian manliness and national identity: the problematic construction of a racially 'pure' nation. *In* (pp. 66–88) **74**.

Caroline M. Kirkland ('Mrs Mary Cleavers')

11742. Larson, Kelli A.   Kirkland's myth of the American Eve: re-visioning the frontier experience. MidM (20) 1992, 9–14.

Charles Lamb

11743. Hickey, Alison.   Double bonds: Charles Lamb's Romantic collaborations. *See* **10677**.

11744. McCarthy, Thomas J.   'Epistolary intercourse': sympathy and the English Romantic letter. *See* **8902**.

Mary Lamb

11745. Hickey, Alison.   Double bonds: Charles Lamb's Romantic collaborations. *See* **10677**.

11746. Marsden, Jean I.   Letters on a tombstone: mothers and literacy in Mary Lamb's *Mrs Leicester's School*. ChildLit (23) 1995, 31–44.

11747. Polowetzky, Michael.   Prominent sisters: Mary Lamb, Dorothy Wordsworth, and Sarah Disraeli. *See* **11022**.

11748. Wilson, Carol Shiner.   Lost needles, tangled threads: stitchery, domesticity, and the artistic enterprise in Barbauld, Edgeworth, Taylor, and Lamb. *In* (pp. 167–90) **103**.

Archibald Lampman

11749. Campbell, Wanda.   Educating Adam: Lampman's *The Story of an Affinity*. ECanW (58) 1996, 158–75.

Letitia Elizabeth Landon (L.E.L.)

11750. Linley, Margaret.   Sappho's conversions in Felicia Hemans, Letitia Landon, and Christina Rossetti. *See* **11452**.

11751. Riess, Daniel.   Laetitia Landon and the dawn of English post-Romanticism. SELit (36:4) 1996, 807–27.

11752. Sypher, F. J. (ed.).   Critical writings. Delmar, NY: Scholars' Facsimiles & Reprints, 1996. pp. 206. (Scholars' facsimiles & reprints, 500.)

Walter Savage Landor

11753. Roberts, Adam.   'Geborish': a reading of Landor's *Gebir*. Eng (45:181) 1996, 32–43.

Mary E. Bradley Lane

11754. Suksang, Duangrudi.   A world of their own: the separatist utopian vision of Mary E. Bradley Lane's *Mizora*. *In* (pp. 128–48) **99**.

Andrew Lang

11755. MICHALSKI, ROBERT. Towards a popular culture: Andrew Lang's anthropological and literary criticism. *See* **10205**.

11756. SCOTT, MARK. Andrew Lang's *Scythe Song* becomes Robert Frost's *Mowing*: Frost's practice of poetry. RFR (1991) 30–8.

'John Law' (Margaret Harkness)

11757. HAPGOOD, LYNNE. The novel and political agency: Socialism and the work of Margaret Harkness, Constance Howell and Clementina Black, 1888–1896. *See* **10363**.

Emma Lazarus

11758. KESSNER, CAROLE S. Matrilineal dissent: the rhetoric of zeal in Emma Lazarus, Marie Syrkin, and Cynthia Ozick. *In* (pp. 197–215) **130**.

11759. YOUNG, BETTE ROTH. Emma Lazarus and her Jewish problem. AJH (84:4) 1996, 291–313.

Edward Lear

11760. LEVI, PETER. Edward Lear: a biography. (Bibl. 1995, 10937.) Rev. by Karl Beckson in BkW, 23 July 1995, 4–5.

11761. UPTON, LEE. Through the lens of Edward Lear: contesting sense in the poetry of Elizabeth Bishop. SHum (19:1) 1992, 68–79.

'Vernon Lee' (Violet Paget)

11762. VITA-FINZI, PENELOPE. Italian background: Edith Wharton's debt to Vernon Lee. EWR (13:1) 1996, 14–18.

Sheridan Le Fanu

11763. ACHILLES, JOCHEN. Sheridan Le Fanu und die schauer-romantische Tradition. (Bibl. 1994, 8770.) Rev. by Armin Arnold in CanRCL (19:4) 1992, 655–7.

11764. CRAWFORD, GARY WILLIAM. J. Sheridan Le Fanu: a bio-bibliography. (Bibl. 1995, 10941.) Rev. by Jared C. Lobdell in Extrapolation (37:3) 1996, 277–9.

11765. HELLER, TAMAR. The vampire in the house: hysteria, female sexuality, and female knowledge in Le Fanu's *Carmilla* (1872). *In* (pp. 77–95) **75**.

11766. SIGNOROTTI, ELIZABETH. Repossessing the body: transgressive desire in *Carmilla* and *Dracula*. Criticism (38:4) 1996, 607–32.

11767. WALTERS, DOUGLAS. J. S. Le Fanu's *Schalken the Painter*: a portfolio. *See* **253**.

Amy Levy

11768. ROCHELSON, MERI-JANE. Jews, gender, and genre in late Victorian England: Amy Levy's *Reuben Sachs*. WS (25:4) 1996, 311–28.

G. H. Lewes

11769. ASHTON, ROSEMARY. G. H. Lewes: a life. (Bibl. 1995, 10946.) Rev. by Richard Jones in ASch (62:3) 1993, 470–4; by Robert Barnard in BST (21:7) 1996, 283–4.

11770. BAKER, WILLIAM (ed.). The letters of George Henry Lewes. (Bibl. 1995, 10947.) Rev. by Carol A. Martin in RMRLL (50:2) 1996,

179–81; by Mara Kalnins in NQ (43:4) 1996, 485–6; by Rosemary Ashton in TLS, 26 July 1996, 23.

11771. BOOTH, MICHAEL R. (ed.). *The Lights o' London* and other Victorian plays. *See* **10746**.

John Leyden

11772. LEASK, NIGEL. Towards an Anglo-Indian poetry? The colonial muse in the writings of John Leyden, Thomas Medwin and Charles D'Oyly. *In* (pp. 52–85) **132**.

Elizabeth Lynn Linton

11773. ANDERSON, NANCY FIX. Eliza Lynn Linton: *The Rebel of the Family* (1880) and other novels. *In* (pp. 117–33) **75**.

11774. D'ALBERTIS, DEIRDRE. Make-believes in Bayswater and Belgravia: Brontë, Linton, and the Victorian 'flirt'. *See* **10407**.

George Lippard

11775. STREEBY, SHELLEY. Haunted houses: George Lippard, Nathaniel Hawthorne, and middle-class America. *See* **11430**.

Charles Lloyd

11776. ALLEN, RICHARD C. Charles Lloyd, Coleridge, and *Edmund Oliver*. *See* **10661**.

11777. HICKEY, ALISON. Double bonds: Charles Lamb's Romantic collaborations. *See* **10677**.

J. G. Lockhart

11778. BOUR, ISABELLE. John Gibson Lockhart's *Memoirs of the Life of Sir Walter Scott, Bart*; or, The absent author. SSL (29) 1996, 37–44.

11779. STEPHENSON, WILL; STEPHENSON, MIMOSA. A source in J. G. Lockhart for Charlotte Brontë's pseudonym. *See* **2171**.

Henry Wadsworth Longfellow

11780. HARALSON, ERIC L. Mars in petticoats: Longfellow and sentimental masculinity. NineL (51:3) 1996, 327–55.

11781. MOORE, EARL. Auction trends. *See* **514**.

Augustus Baldwin Longstreet

11782. ROMINE, SCOTT. Negotiating community in Augustus Baldwin Longstreet's *Georgia Scenes*. *See* **2698**.

Thomas Babington, Lord Macaulay

11783. CIVARDI, CHRISTIAN. L'invention du kilt: de l'appropriation symbolique à l'expropriation physique. RANAM (29) 1996, 63–87.

11784. HAWES, DONALD (introd.). The works of Lord Macaulay. Ware: Wordsworth, 1995. pp. x, 128. (Wordsworth poetry library.)

Louisa S. McCord

11785. LOUNSBURY, RICHARD C. (ed.). Louisa S. McCord: poems, drama, biography, letters. Charlottesville; London: Virginia UP, 1996. pp. xii, 487. (Pubs of the Southern Texts Soc.)

George MacDonald

11786. ALEXANDER, JONATHAN.   Those infinite lands of uncertainty: George MacDonald and the fantastic imagination. CSL (25:7/8) 1994, 5–12.

11787. ANKENY, REBECCA THOMAS.   Teacher and pupil: reading, ethics, and human dignity in George MacDonald's *Mary Marston*. SSL (29) 1996, 227–37.

11788. AUSTER, MARTIN.   The Celtic imagination in exile. Australian Folklore (11) 1996, 112–20.

11789. CARNELL, CORBIN SCOTT.   Echoes of George MacDonald's *Lilith* in the works of C. S. Lewis. CSL (24:7/8) 1993, 15.

11790. GRAY, WILLIAM N.   George MacDonald, Julia Kristeva, and the black sun. SELit (36:4) 1996, 877–93.

11791. GUNTHER, ADRIAN.   *The Day Boy and the Night Girl*. SEVEN (13) 1996, 25–44.

11792. —— The multiple realms of George MacDonald's *Phantastes*. SSL (29) 1996, 174–90.

11793. MCLAUGHLIN, SARA PARK.   A legacy of truth: the influence of George MacDonald's *Unspoken Sermons* on C. S. Lewis's *Mere Christianity*. CSL (24:4) 1993, 1–6.

11794. MARSHALL, CYNTHIA.   Essays on C. S. Lewis and George MacDonald: truth, fiction, and the power of imagination. (Bibl. 1995, 10967.) Rev. by Nancy-Lou Patterson in Mythlore (21:1) 1995, 59–60.

11795. PENNINGTON, JOHN.   Muscular spirituality in George MacDonald's Curdie books. *In* (pp. 133–49) **74**.

11796. RISO, MARY.   Awakening in fairyland: the journey of a soul in George MacDonald's *The Golden Key*. Mythlore (20:4) 1995, 46–51.

James McHenry

11797. SARGENT, MARK L.   The witches of Salem, the angel of Hadley, and the friends of Philadelphia. *See* **10345**.

Sarah Pratt McLean (Sarah P. McLean Greene)

11798. OAKES, KAREN KILCUP.   'I like a woman to be a woman': theorizing gender in the humor of Stowe and Greene. SAH (3:3) 1996, 14–38.

James Clarence Mangan

11799. CHUTO, JACQUES (ed.).   Poems, 1818–1837. Blackrock, Co. Dublin: Irish Academic Press, 1996. pp. xvii, 420. (Collected works of James Clarence Mangan.)

11800. MURPHY, JAMES H.   The wild geese. *See* **2024**.

11801. SHANNON-MANGAN, ELLEN.   James Clarence Mangan: a biography. Blackrock, Co. Dublin; Portland, OR: Irish Academic Press, 1996. pp. xix, 493,

Harriet Martineau

11802. HASSETT, CONSTANCE W.   Siblings and antislavery: the literary and political relations of Harriet Martineau, James Martineau, and Maria Weston Chapman. Signs (21:2) 1996, 374–409.

11803. HUNTER, SHELAGH.   Harriet Martineau: the poetics of moralism. (Bibl. 1995, 10980.) Rev. by Sally Shuttleworth in TLS, 16 Aug. 1996, 10.

11804. Littcon, Alfred G.   Miss Thoreau's trumpet. TSB (216) 1996, 5–6.

Brander Matthews

11805. Oliver, Laurence J.   Brander Matthews, Theodore Roosevelt, and the politics of American literature, 1880–1920. (Bibl. 1993, 8782.) Rev. by George Cotkin in AHR (98:3) 1993, 958; by Robert M. Crunden in AmS (36:1) 1995, 193–4.

C. R. Maturin

11806. Kosok, Heinz.   Charles Robert Maturin and colonialism. *In* (pp. 228–34) **60**.
11807. Williams, Madawc.   Tales of wonder: science fiction and fantasy in the age of Jane Austen. *See* **9982**.

F. D. Maurice

11808. Hall, Donald E.   On the making and unmaking of monsters: Christian Socialism, muscular Christianity, and the metaphorization of class conflict. *In* (pp. 45–65) **74**.
11809. Walsh, Cheryl.   The Incarnation and the Christian Socialist conscience in the Victorian Church of England. JBS (34:3) 1995, 351–74.

Thomas Medwin

11810. Leask, Nigel.   Towards an Anglo-Indian poetry? The colonial muse in the writings of John Leyden, Thomas Medwin and Charles D'Oyly. *In* (pp. 52–85) **132**.

Herman Melville

11811. Andriano, Joseph.   Brother to dragons: race and evolution in *Moby-Dick*. ATQ (10:2) 1996, 141–53.
11812. Arnold, David Scott.   Liminal readings: forms of otherness in Melville, Joyce, and Murdoch. (Bibl. 1993, 8785.) Rev. by Hugh S. Pyper in LitTheol (10:3) 1996, 297–8.
11813. Attebery, Brian.   American studies: a not so unscientific method. *See* **11385**.
11814. Baldwin, Marc D.   Herman Melville's *The Lightning-Rod Man*: discourse of the deal. JSSE (21) 1993, 9–18.
11815. Bartley, William.   'The creature of his own tasteful hands': Herman Melville's *Benito Cereno* and the 'empire of might'. MP (93:4) 1996, 445–67.
11816. Baumgarten, Matthew R.   Melville, Gauguin, and their angel art. MelSE (105) 1996, 11–12.
11817. Bellis, Peter J.   No mysteries out of ourselves: identity and textual form in the novels of Herman Melville. (Bibl. 1993, 8786.) Rev. by Thomas Huke in ZAA (43:2) 1995, 193–4.
11818. Bergmann, Hans.   God in the street: New York writing from the penny press to Melville. *See* **1231**.
11819. Birk, John F.   Herman Melville's *Billy Budd* and the cybernetic imagination. Lewiston, NY; Lampeter: Mellen Press, 1995. pp. 255. (Studies in American literature, 20.)
11820. Boker, Pamela A.   The grief taboo in American literature: loss and prolonged adolescence in Twain, Melville, and Hemingway.

New York: New York UP, 1996. pp. xiii, 357. (Literature and psycho-analysis, 8.) (Cf. bibl. 1995, 10990.)

11821. BRYANT, JOHN. Melville, Twain and Quixote: variations on the comic debate. SAH (3:1) 1994, 1–27.

11822. ——— Melville's rose poems: as they fell. AQ (52:4) 1996, 49–84.

11823. ——— Poe's Ape of unReason: humor, ritual, and culture. NineL (51:1) 1996, 16–52.

11824. BUCKLEY, J. F.   Skirting the phallus, circumscribing the community: Steelkilt as transvestic rebel. MelSE (104) 1996, 14–19.

11825. CARTER, STEVEN.   Avatars of the third other. PCR (4:1) 1993, 25–37.

11826. ——— Estragon's ancient wound: a note on *Waiting for Godot*. JBecS (6:1) 1996, 125–33.

11827. CASSA, MARIO.   Osservazioni su Bartleby. Quaderni di lingue e letterature (19) 1994, 253–6.

11828. COOK, JONATHAN A.   Satirical apocalypse: an anatomy of Melville's *The Confidence-Man*. Westport, CT; London: Greenwood Press, 1996. pp. xiv, 280. (Contributions to the study of world literature, 67.) (Cf. bibl. 1995, 10997.)

11829. COUSER, G. THOMAS.   The hunt for 'Big Red': *The Bedford Incident*, Melville, and the Cold War. LitFQ (24:1) 1996, 32–8.

11830. COWAN, BAINARD.   America between two myths: *Moby-Dick* as epic. *In* (pp. 217–46) **29**.

11831. CREECH, JAMES.   Closet writing/gay reading: the case of Melville's *Pierre*. (Bibl. 1995, 10998.) Rev. by R. W. (Herbie) Butterfield in YES (26) 1996, 323–4.

11832. CURNUTT, KIRK.   The rumor about Bartleby: orality, chancery, narrative authority. JSSE (19) 1992, 9–24.

11833. DAVIS, CLARK.   After the whale: Melville in the wake of *Moby-Dick*. (Bibl. 1995, 11001.) Rev. by Kenneth Dauber in SAtlR (61:4) 1996, 127–30.

11834. DESAI, R. W.   Truth's 'ragged edges': a phenomenological inquiry into the Captain Vere–Billy relationship in Melville's *Billy Budd, Sailor*. SHum (19:1) 1992, 11–26.

11835. DILLINGHAM, WILLIAM B.   Melville & his circle: the last years. Athens; London: Georgia UP, 1996. pp. xiii, 213.

11836. DOVE-RUMÉ, JANINE.   *The Encantadas*: two sides to Melville's natural history. Letteratura d'America (39) 1990, 91–112.

11837. DUNCAN, L. FALLON.   Herman Melville's *Bartleby* and Franz Kafka's *Metamorphosis*: a study in thematic affinities and narrative technique. Comparatist (15) 1991, 116–28.

11838. FLUCK, WINFRIED.   Cultures of criticism: Herman Melville's *Moby-Dick*, expressive individualism, and the New Historicism. YREAL (11) 1995, 207–28.

11839. FREDRICKS, NANCY.   Melville's art of democracy. (Bibl. 1995, 11008.) Rev. by Bruce L. Grenberg in AL (68:1) 1996, 241–2.

11840. GALE, ROBERT L.   A Herman Melville encyclopedia. (Bibl. 1995, 11010.) Rev. by Clark Davis in SAtlR (61:1) 1996, 135–6.

11841. GARNER, STANTON.   The Civil War world of Herman Melville. (Bibl. 1995, 11011.) Rev. by Sanford E. Marovitz in CWH (41:1) 1995, 81–3; by Haskell Springer in AmS (36:1) 1995, 190–2; by Robert Milder in AL (68:1) 1996, 239–40; by Robert H. Byer in EC (46:2) 1996, 175–86.

11842. Gretchko, John M. J.   Fiddling with Melville's *Fiddler*. MelSE (104) 1996, 20–3.

11843. Habermeier, Steffi.   On interpreting Bartleby. ZAA (42:4) 1994, 352–63.

11844. Haydock, John S.   Melville's *Séraphita*: *Billy Budd, Sailor*. MelSE (104) 1996, 2–13.

11845. Hayford, Harrison.   Melville's *Monody*: really for Hawthorne? *See* **11411**.

11846. —— *et al.* (eds).   Clarel: a poem and pilgrimage in the Holy Land. (Bibl. 1993, 8810.) Rev. by Robert Milder in Text (Ann Arbor) (9) 1996, 389–407.

11847. Higgins, Brian; Parker, Hershel (eds).   Herman Melville: the contemporary reviews. (Bibl. 1995, 11020.) Rev. by Steven Olsen-Smith in MelSE (106) 1996, 19–20.

11848. Horsford, Howard C.; Horth, Lynn (eds).   Journals. (Bibl. 1995, 11021.) Rev. by Robert Milder in Text (Ann Arbor) (9) 1996, 389–407.

11849. Husni, Khalil.   The metaphysics of light, colors, and darkness in Melville's *Pierre*: narrator *versus* hero. CLAJ (39:4) 1996, 468–88.

11850. Imbert, Michel.   Coins as icons and the fetishism of money in *Moby-Dick; or, The Whale*. Letterature d'America (50) 1993, 33–49.

11851. Kearns, Michael.   Melville's chaotic style and the use of generative models: an essay in method. *See* **2657**.

11852. Kelley, Wyn.   Melville's city: literary and urban form in nineteenth-century New York. Cambridge; New York: CUP, 1996. pp. xiv, 312. (Cambridge studies in American literature and culture, 100.)

11853. Kim, Jin-Kyung.   *Bartleby the Scrivener* sege eui galdeung. (A reading of *Bartleby the Scrivener*.) EngSt (20) 1996, 67–94.

11854. Kim, Sang-Ok.   Melville soseol e isseoseoeui ak eui yangsang. (Aspects of evil in Melville's novels.) Unpub. doct. diss., Keimyung Univ., Korea, 1996.

11855. Kirby, David.   Herman Melville. (Bibl. 1993, 8817.) Rev. by Theodore R. Hovet in AmS (36:1) 1995, 192–3.

11856. Lawson, Benjamin Sherwood.   Federated fancies: Balzac's *Lost Illusions* and Melville's *Pierre*. *In* (pp. 37–47) **51**.

11857. López Liquete, María Felisa.   The presence–absence of women in the work of Herman Melville. Atlantis (17:1/2) 1995, 115–26.

11858. McQuillan, Gene.   'Extarminate the varlets!': the reconstruction of captivity narratives in *Dances with Wolves*. *See* **8337**.

11859. Marçais, Dominique.   Confidence and faith in scientific progress in Melville's *The Confidence-Man*. *In* (pp. 237–43) **117**.

11860. —— The Spanish language: its significance in Melville's *Benito Cereno*. Letterature d'America (44) 1992, 47–56.

11861. Matterson, Stephen.   Indian-hater, wild man: Melville's *Confidence-Man*. AQ (52:3) 1996, 21–35.

11862. Maufort, Marc.   Songs of American experience: the vision of O'Neill and Melville. New York; Frankfurt; Bern; Paris: Lang, 1990. pp. xiv, 224. Rev. by James J. Martine in EOR (15:1) 1991, 109–12.

11863. Milder, Robert.   Editing Melville's afterlife. *See* **756**.

11864. Monteiro, George.   Melville in *The Author*: an obituary and three literary notes. MelSE (105) 1996, 10–11.

11865. —— *Moby-Dick* and *The Naked and the Dead* reviewed in the *Fourth International*. MelSE (106) 1996, 15–16.

11866. MORGAN, JOHN.   Herman Melville and the 'savior of Missouri' – *Lyon* and its historical background. PMPA (16) 1991, 69–77.

11867. MORGAN, WINIFRED.   *Bartleby* and the failure of conventional virtue. Ren (45:4) 1993, 257–71.

11868. MUELLER, MONIKA.   This infinite fraternity of feeling: gender, genre, and homoerotic crisis in Hawthorne's *The Blithedale Romance* and Melville's *Pierre. See* **11420**.

11869. NÜSSLER, ULRIKE.   'Across the Black's body': Herman Melville's *Benito Cereno* and Harriet Jacobs's *Incidents in the Life of a Slave Girl* – a critical collage. *In* (pp. 55–79) **8**.

11870. OBUCHOWSKI, PETER A.   Melville's *Pierre*: Plinlimmon as satirist satirized. CLAJ (39:4) 1996, 489–97.

11871. OLSEN-SMITH, STEVE.   Herman Melville's planned work on remorse. NineL (50:4) 1996, 489–500.

11872. OSCHMANN, DIRK.   Reading (in) the 'doubloon'-chapter in Melville's *Moby-Dick; or, The Whale*. ZAA (44:2) 1996, 142–54.

11873. PARKER, HERSHEL (ed.).   Pierre, or, The ambiguities. New York; London: HarperCollins, 1995. pp. xlvi, 449. Rev. by Richard Poirier in LRB (18:19) 1996, 19–22.

11874. PHILBRICK, NATHANIEL.   A window on the prey: the hunter sees a human face in Hemingway's *After the Storm* and Melville's *The Grand Armada*. HemR (14:1) 1994, 25–35.

11875. PINNEGAR, FRED C.   The 'hacknied subject' of whaling: Melville's research in *McCulloch's Dictionary*. MelSE (105) 1996, 1–7

11876. POOLE, GORDON.   Naples in the time of Melville: Italian politics 1857. MelSE (105) 1996, 8–9.

11877. POST-LAURIA, SHEILA.   Correspondent colorings: Melville in the marketplace. Amherst: Massachusetts UP, 1996. pp. xv, 276.

11878. RADLOFF, BERNHARD.   Cosmopolis and truth: Melville's critique of modernity. New York; Frankfurt; Bern; Paris: Lang, 1996. pp. x, 253. (Studies on themes and motifs in literature, 16.) Rev. by Allison Chestnut in ChrisL (46:1) 1996, 90–1.

11879. —— Will and representation: the philosophical foundations of Melville's *theatrum mundi*. New York; Frankfurt; Bern; Paris: Lang, 1996. pp. xiii, 347. (Studies on themes and motifs in literature, 17.)

11880. REDDICK, MARCIA.   'Something, somehow like original sin': striking the uneven balance in 'The Town-Ho's Story' and *Moby-Dick*. ATQ (10:2) 1996, 81–9.

11881. REISS, BENJAMIN.   Madness and mastery in Melville's *Benito Cereno*. Criticism (38:1) 1996, 115–50.

11882. RENKER, ELIZABETH.   Strike through the mask: Herman Melville and the scene of writing. Baltimore, MD; London: Johns Hopkins UP, 1996. pp. xxiii, 182. (Cf. bibl. 1992, 9516.)

11883. ROBERTSON-LORANT, LAURIE.   Melville: a biography. New York: Clarkson Potter, 1996. pp. xxv, 710.

11884. ROSENBERRY, EDWARD H.   *Moby-Dick*, American icon. QLLSM (8) 1996, 193–204.

11885. RUSSO, PAOLA.   *Mardi*: cinque partenze senza ritorno. RSAJ (2) 1991, 3–19.

11886. SAMSON, JOHN.   Melville. American Literary Scholarship (1995) 49–59.

11887. SANBORN, GEOFFREY.   Where's the rest of me? The melancholy death of Benito Cereno. AQ (52:1) 1996, 59–93.

11888. SCHARNHORST, GARY. More uncollected Melville reviews and notices. MelSE (106) 1996, 12–14.

11889. SHAW, PETER. The fate of a story. ASch (62:4) 1993, 591–600. (*Billy Budd.*)

11890. SHORT, BRYAN C. Cast by means of figures: Herman Melville's rhetorical development. (Bibl. 1995, 11048.) Rev. by Stan Goldman in StudN (27:1) 1995, 103–5.

11891. SPANOS, WILLIAM V. The errant art of *Moby-Dick*: the canon, the Cold War, and the struggle for American studies. (Bibl. 1995, 11050.) Rev. by T. Hugh Crawford in AL (68:3) 1996, 644–5; by Val Gough in JAStud (30:2) 1996, 303–5.

11892. STEN, CHRISTOPHER. Sounding the whale: *Moby-Dick* as epic novel. Kent, OH; London: Kent State UP, 1996. pp. ix, 91. (Previously pub. as Chapter 6 of **11893**.)

11893. —— The weaver-god, he weaves: Melville and the poetics of the novel. Kent, OH; London: Kent State UP, 1996. pp. xii, 361.

11894. —— (ed.). Savage eye: Melville and the visual arts. (Bibl. 1995, 11051.) Rev. by Willie van Peer in CanRCL (20:3/4) 1993, 524–6.

11895. TIESSEN, PAUL (introd.). *Moby-Dick* adapted (1945). MalLR (36/37) 1995, 96–153.

11896. VALERO GARCÉS, CARMEN. Notas en torno a la traducción de literatura juvenil: el ejemplo de *Moby Dick*. *See* **3213**.

11897. VERSTER, FRANÇOIS. Reading the whale: Ahab's apocalyptic quest. ESA (38:1) 1995, 45–56.

11898. WALLACE, ROBERT K. Melville & Turner: spheres of love and fright. (Bibl. 1995, 11054.) Rev. by Hans Bergmann in Comparatist (18) 1994, 190–2.

11899. —— Sounding out Stella: an interview with the artist. MelSE (107) 1996, 3–19.

11900. WEISS, PHILLIP. Herman-neutics. NYTM, 15 Dec. 1996, 60–5, 70, 72.

11901. WENKE, JOHN. Melville. American Literary Scholarship (1993) 49–64; (1994) 49–62.

11902. —— Melville's muse: literary creation and the forms of philosophical fiction. (Bibl. 1995, 11057.) Rev. by Kenneth Dauber in SAtlR (61:4) 1996, 127–30; by Merton M. Sealts, Jr, in MelSE (106) 1996, 20–2.

11903. WEST, ROBIN. Invisible victims: a comparison of Susan Glaspell's *Jury of Her Peers*, and Herman Melville's *Bartleby the Scrivener*. CSLL (8:1) 1996, 203–49.

11904. WINSLOW, RICHARD E., III. Contemporary notice of Melville at home and abroad. MelSE (106) 1996, 1–11.

11905. YAHAGI, SANZO. America renaissance no pessimism: Hawthorne and Melville kenkyu. (Pessimism in the American renaissance: a study of Hawthorne and Melville.) *See* **11437**.

11906. YANG, SEOKWON. *Moby-Dick* gwa soonggosung eui jeongchi. (*Moby-Dick* and the politics of the sublime.) JELL (42:2) 1996, 299–322.

11907. YOUNG, PHILIP. The private Melville. (Bibl. 1995, 11061.) Rev. by Theodore R. Hovet in AmS (36:1) 1995, 192–3.

11908. ZETTSU, TOMOYUKI. In quest of the 'beautiful thing': *Paterson* and *Moby-Dick*. StAL (33) 1996, 1–17.

George Meredith

11909. BROSCH, RENATE. Der Anfang von *One of Our Conquerors*: Funktionalisierte Obsksurität im Roman. LWU (29:3) 1996, 161–70.

11910. DINGLEY, ROBERT. Playing the game: the Continental casinos and the Victorian imagination. *See* **11017**.

11911. FLETCHER, PAULINE. 'Trifles light as air' in Meredith's *Modern Love*. VP (34:1) 1996, 87–99.

11912. GINDELE, KAREN C. When women laugh wildly and (gentle) men roar: Victorian embodiments of laughter. *In* (pp. 139–60) **64**.

11913. LANG, CLAIRE. Le mariage-prison dans l'œuvre de George Meredith. CVE (43) 1996, 55–64.

11914. McWHIRTER, DAVID. Feminism/gender/comedy: Meredith, Woolf, and the reconfiguration of comic distance. *In* (pp. 189–204) **64**.

11915. SWANN, CHARLES. A George Eliot debt to George Meredith: from *Rhoda Fleming* to *Daniel Deronda*. *See* **11161**.

'Owen Meredith' (Edward Robert Bulwer Lytton, First Earl of Lytton)

11916. BOOS, FLORENCE S. William Morris, Robert Bulwer-Lytton, and the Arthurian poetry of the 1850s. *See* **10012**.

Alice Meynell

11917. MOEYES, PAUL. The eye of the whirlwind – the poetry of Alice Meynell. Neophilologus (80:1) 1996, 149–59.

John Stuart Mill

11918. BAUCOM, IAN. Mournful histories: narratives of postimperial melancholy. *See* **3714**.

11919. CHRÉTIEN, MAURICE, *et al.* *On Liberty* by John Stuart Mill. Paris: Didier Erudition, 1996. pp. 144.

11920. GAGNIER, REGENIA. Is market society the *fin* of history? *In* (pp. 290–310) **18**.

11921. PRUM, MICHEL. John Stuart Mill, critique de William Thompson. Q/W/E/R/T/Y (6) 1996, 235–9.

11922. RILEY, JONATHAN. *On Liberty* and the Periclean ideal. Q/W/E/R/T/Y (6) 1996, 241–8.

11923. SABIN, MARGERY. The suttee romance. *See* **10149**.

11924. WOLFF, JONATHAN. John Stuart Mill, liberalism and offence. Q/W/E/R/T/Y (6) 1996, 249–54.

Hugh Miller

11925. ROBB, DAVID S. Miller and Edinburgh: *My Schools and Schoolmasters*. SLJ (22:2) 1995, 14–28.

'Joaquin Miller' (Cincinnatus Hiner Miller)

11926. SULLIVAN, WILLIAM L. Wild West poet in London: Joaquin Miller. Biblio (1:1) 1996, 40–3.

Susanna Moodie

11927. THOMPSON, ELIZABETH. An early review of *Roughing It in the Bush*. CanL (151) 1996, 202–4.

George Moore

11928. Monès, Mona H.   George Moore's *Muslin* and Abdel Rahman Al-Sharqawi's *The Earth*: novels of social protest. *In* (pp. 252–65) **60**.

Thomas Moore (1779–1852)

11929. Basta, Samira.   The factual and the imaginary in Thomas Moore's Egyptian tale, *The Epicurean*. *In* (pp. 125–32) **60**.

Lady Morgan (Sydney Owenson)

11930. Brihault, Jean.   Lady Morgan: deep furrows. *In* (pp. 71–81) **106**.

11931. Ferris, Ina.   Narrating cultural encounter: Lady Morgan and the Irish national tale. NineL (51:3) 1996, 287–303.

William Morris

11932. Beatty, C. J. P.   A previously unpublished letter of Jane Morris. NQ (43:4) 1996, 432–3.

11933. Boos, Florence.   The design of William Morris' *The Earthly Paradise*. Lewiston, NY; Lampeter: Mellen Press, 1990. pp. 530. (Studies in British literature, 6.) Rev. by Carole Silver in VS (38:2) 1995, 311–12.

11934. Boos, Florence S.   1896–1996: Morris' poetry at the *fin de millénaire*. VP (34:3) 1996, 285–98.

11935. —— William Morris, Robert Bulwer-Lytton, and the Arthurian poetry of the 1850s. *See* **10012**.

11936. Derry, Stephen.   The Time Traveller's utopian books and his reading of the future. *See* **10351**.

11937. Faulkner, Peter.   The male as lover, fool, and hero: *Goldilocks* and the late prose romances. VP (34:3) 1996, 413–24.

11938. Franklin, Colin.   The Kelmscott Press and William Morris. *See* **274**.

11939. Goodwin, Ken.   The summation of a poetic career: *Poems by the Way*. VP (34:3) 1996, 397–410.

11940. Harvey, Charles; Press, Jon.   William Morris: art and idealism. HT (46:5) 1996, 15–21.

11941. Herbert, Karen.   Dissident language in *The Defence of Guenevere*. VP (34:3) 1996, 313–27.

11942. Hodgson, Amanda.   'The highest poetry': epic narrative in *The Earthly Paradise* and *Idylls of the King*. VP (34:3) 1996, 341–54.

11943. Janowitz, Anne.   *The Pilgrims of Hope*: William Morris and the dialectic of Romanticism. *In* (pp. 160–83) **18**.

11944. Julian, Linda.   *Laxdœla saga* and 'The Lovers of Gudrun': Morris' poetic vision. VP (34:3) 1996, 355–71.

11945. Kelvin, Norman.   Morris, the 1890s, and the problematic autonomy of art. VP (34:3) 1996, 425–32.

11946. —— (ed.).   The collected letters of William Morris: vol. 3, 1889–1892. Princeton, NJ; Chichester: Princeton UP, 1996. pp. lxv, 537. Rev. by Fiona MacCarthy in TLS, 31 May 1996, 18–19; by Peter Stansky in ELT (39:4) 1996, 463–7; by Frederick Kirchoff in VP (34:4) 1996, 623–6.

11947. Kirchhoff, Frederick.   'The glory and the freshness of a dream': Arthurian romance as reconstructed childhood. *See* **5249**.

11948. Kumar, Krishan (ed.).   News from nowhere; or, An epoch of rest: being some chapters from a utopian romance. Cambridge; New York: CUP, 1995. pp. xxxii, 229. (Cambridge texts in the history of political thought.) Rev. by Adriana Corrado in Utopian Studies (7:2) 1996, 280–2.

11949. LATHAM, DAVID.   Literal and literary texts: Morris' 'Story of Dorothea'. *See* **715**.

11950. LEMIRE, EUGENE D.   William Morris in America: a publishing history from archives. *See* **960**.

11951. LINDSAY, JACK.   William Morris, dreamer of dreams. Revised and ed. by David Gerard. London: Nine Elms, 1991. pp. 16. Rev. by Kenneth Payne in Utopian Studies (7:1) 1996, 128–9.

11952. LONDRAVILLE, JANIS; LONDRAVILLE, RICHARD.   No idle singers of empty days: the unpublished correspondence of John Quinn and May Morris. JML (19:1) 1994, 89–114.

11953. McCARTHY, FIONA.   Our debt to Morris. Ruskin Gazette (1:9) 1996, 23–5.

11954. MacCARTHY, FIONA.   William Morris: a life for our time. (Bibl. 1995, 11104.) Rev. by Michael Dirda in BkW, 24 Sept. 1995, 6; by Bonnie J. Robinson in ELT (39:4) 1996, 468–70; by Norman Kelvin in VP (34:1) 1996, 121–4.

11955. MANCOFF, DEBRA N.   Problems with the pattern: William Morris's Arthurian imagery. *See* **220**.

11956. SHAW, W. DAVID.   Arthurian ghosts: the phantom art of *The Defence of Guenevere*. VP (34:3) 1996, 299–312.

11957. SMITH, LINDSAY.   Victorian photography, painting and poetry: the enigma of visibility in Ruskin, Morris and the Pre-Raphaelites. (Bibl. 1995, 11109.) Rev. by Robert Douglas-Fairhurst in TLS, 1 Mar. 1996, 3–4; by Jens P. Becker in LWU (29:4) 1996, 318.

11958. STRUVE, LAURA.   The public life and private desires of women in William Morris's *Defence of Guenevere*. Arthuriana (6:3) 1996, 15–28.

11959. TUCKER, HERBERT F.   All for the tale: the epic macropoetics of Morris' *Sigurd the Volsung*. VP (34:3) 1996, 373–94.

Arthur Morrison

11960. GREENFIELD, JOHN.   Ideological naturalism and representation of class in Arthur Morrison's *A Child of the Jago*. SLI (29:1) 1996, 89–102.

11961. KIJINSKI, JOHN L.   Ethnography in the East End: native customs and colonial solutions in *A Child of the Jago*. ELT (37:4) 1994, 490–501.

Anna Cora Mowatt

11962. RICHARDS, JEFFREY H.   Chastity and the stage in Mowatt's *Stella*. SAF (24:1) 1996, 87–100.

John Henry Newman

11963. BLOCK, ED, JR.   Venture and response: the dialogic strategy of John Henry Newman's *Loss and Gain*. Ren (43:1/2) 1990/91, 45–60.

11964. CROWLEY, ALAN J.   The performance of the *Grammar*: reading and writing Newman's narrative of assent. Ren (43:1/2) 1990/91, 137–58.

11965. DELAURA, DAVID J.   'O unforgotten voice': the memory of Newman in the nineteenth century. Ren (43:1/2) 1990/91, 81–104.

11966. EDGECOMBE, RODNEY STENNING. Muriel Spark, Cardinal Newman and an aphorism in *Memento Mori*. NCL (24:1) 1994, 12.

11967. KER, IAN. Newman's conversion to the Catholic Church: another perspective. Ren (43:1/2) 1990/91, 17–27.

11968. MORAN, COLIN. Cardinal Newman and jury verdicts: reason, belief, and certitude. YJLH (8:1) 1996, 63–91.

11969. MULLER, JILL. John Henry Newman and the education of Stephen Dedalus. JJQ (33:4) 1996, 593–603.

11970. PELIKAN, JAROSLAV. The idea of the university: a re-examination. (Bibl. 1995, 11128.) Rev. by Robert A. McCaughey in AHR (98:1) 1993, 118–19.

11971. REIDY, JAMES. Newman and Christian humanism. Ren (44:4) 1992, 249–64.

11972. STASNY, JOHN; NELSON, BYRON. From dream to drama: *The Dream of Gerontius* by John Henry Newman and Edward Elgar. Ren (43:1/2) 1990/91, 121–35.

11973. TENNYSON, G. B. Removing the veil: Newman as a literary artist. Ren (43:1/2) 1990/91, 29–44.

11974. TRUMALESH, K. V. Autobiography's search for truth: Newman and Gandhi. CR (40:1) 1996, 99–123.

11975. WARD, BERNADETTE. Newman's *Grammar of Assent* and the poetry of Gerard Manley Hopkins. *See* **11499**.

11976. WOODFIELD, MALCOLM. Knowing without telling: Newman and the resistance to narrative. Ren (43:1/2) 1990/91, 61–80.

11977. WRIGHT, T. R. Newman on literature: 'thinking out into language'. LitTheol (5:2) 1991, 181–97.

Mordecai M. Noah

11978. KLEINMAN, CRAIG. Pigging the nation: staging the Jew in M. M. Noah's *She Would Be a Soldier*. ATQ (10:3) 1996, 201–17.

Caroline Norton

11979. GROTH, HELEN. Island queens: nationalism, queenliness and women's poetry 1837–1861. *See* **10500**.

Mrs Oliphant

11980. CALDER, JENNI. Science and the supernatural in the stories of Margaret Oliphant. *In* (pp. 173–91) **94**.

11981. FINKELSTEIN, DAVID. Reassessing Margaret Oliphant. SLJ (supp. 45) 1996, 1–5 (review-article).

11982. GINDELE, KAREN C. When women laugh wildly and (gentle) men roar: Victorian embodiments of laughter. *In* (pp. 139–60) **64**.

11983. HELMS, GABRIELE. 'A little try at the autobiography': conflict and contradiction in Margaret Oliphant's writing. Prose Studies (19:1) 1996, 76–92.

11984. JAY, ELISABETH. Mrs Oliphant, 'a fiction to herself': a literary life. (Bibl. 1995, 11136.) Rev. by Sonya Rudikoff in ASch (65:2) 1996, 292–6; by Barbara Thaden in ELT (39:1) 1996, 133–4; by David Finkelstein in SLJ (supp. 45) 1996, 3–4.

11985. O'MEALY, JOSEPH H. Mrs Oliphant, *Miss Marjoribanks* (1866), and the Victorian canon. *In* (pp. 63–76) **75**.

11986. RUBIK, MARGARETE. The novels of Mrs Oliphant: a subversive view of traditional themes. (Bibl. 1994, 8912.) Rev. by D. J. Trela in AEB (9:1/2) 1995, 83–5; by Margaret Elphinstone in SSL (29) 1996, 321–4; by David Finkelstein in SLJ (supp. 45) 1996, 4–5.

11987.   TRELA, D. J. (ed.).   Margaret Oliphant: critical essays on a gentle subversive. (Bibl. 1995, 11138.) Rev. by Barbara Thaden in ELT (39:1) 1996, 130–3.

Lloyd Osbourne

11988.   PASCOE, DAVID (introd.).   The wrong box. Oxford; New York: OUP, 1995. pp. 152. (Oxford popular fiction.)

'Ouida' (Marie Louise de la Ramée)

11989.   JORDAN, JANE.   Ouida: the enigma of a literary identity. PULC (57:1) 1995, 75–105.
11990.   RUSSO, JOHN PAUL.   Ouida's family romance: *In Maremma*. PCR (4:2) 1993, 37–49.

'Our Nig' (Harriet Wilson)

11991.   DAVIS, CYNTHIA J.   Speaking the body's pain: Harriet Wilson's *Our Nig*. AAR (27:3) 1993, 391–404.
11992.   JONES, JILL.   The disappearing 'I' in *Our Nig*. Legacy (13:1) 1996, 38–53.
11993.   LOVELL, THOMAS B.   By dint of labor and economy: Harriet Jacobs, Harriet Wilson, and the salutary view of wage labor. *See* **11554**.

Francis Edward Paget

11994.   WILSON, EDWARD.   A fictional source for the falling tower in John Meade Falkner's *The Nebuly Coat*. *See* **11208**.

Francis Parkman

11995.   SKAGGS, MERRILL MAGUIRE.   Cather's use of Parkman's histories in *Shadows on the Rock*. CathS (2) 1993, 140–55.

Walter Pater

11996.   ADAMS, JAMES ELI.   Pater's muscular aestheticism. *In* (pp. 215–38) **74**.
11997.   BANN, STEPHEN.   Epilogue: on the homelessness of the image. CompCrit (17) 1995, 123–8.
11998.   BIZZOTTO, ELISA; MARUCCI, FRANCO (eds).   Walter Pater (1839–1894): le forme della modernità = the forms of modernity. Atti del convegno – Venezia Ca'Foscari 1 e 2 dicembre 1994. Bologna; Cisalpino, 1996. pp. 319.
11999.   BRAKE, LAUREL.   Walter Pater. (Bibl. 1995, 11151.) Rev. by Adam Piette in EEM (4:2) 1995, 70–1.
12000.   CARRIER, DAVID.   Baudelaire, Pater and the origins of Modernism. CompCrit (17) 1995, 109–21.
12001.   DONOGHUE, DENIS.   The antinomian Pater: 1894–1994. CompCrit (17) 1995, 3–19.
12002.   —— Walter Pater: lover of strange souls. (Bibl. 1995, 11153.) Rev. by Michael Dirda in BkW, 11 June 1995, 4; by James Eli Adams in RMRLL (50:2) 1996, 185–7; by Gerald Monsman in ELT (39:4) 1996, 470–4.
12003.   FONTANA, ERNEST.   Whitman, Pater, and *An English Poet*. WWQR (14:1) 1996, 12–20.

12004. GAGNIER, REGENIA. Is market society the *fin* of history? *In* (pp. 290–310) **18**.

12005. INMAN, BILLIE ANDREW. John 'Dorian' Gray and the theme of subservient love in Walter Pater's works of the 1890s. *See* **11307**.

12006. ISER, WOLFGANG. Enfoldings in Paterian discourse: modes of translatability. CompCrit (17) 1995, 41–60.

12007. MAEKAWA, YUICHI. Walter Pater – seishin no dandism. (Walter Pater: mental dandyism.) Tokyo: Kenkyusha Shuppan, 1996. pp. 304.

12008. MONSMAN, GERALD (ed.). *Gaston de Latour*: the revised text, based on the definitive manuscripts & enlarged to incorporate all known fragments. *See* **760**.

12009. READ, RICHARD. Art criticism *versus* poetry: an introduction to Adrian Stokes's *Pisanello*. CompCrit (17) 1995, 133–60.

12010. SHRIMPTON, NICHOLAS. Pater and the 'aesthetical sect'. *See* **9694**.

12011. VILLA, LUISA. Verso/attraverso *The Hill of Dreams*: Walter Pater, Arthur Machen, l'oggetto estetico e la decadenza. Textus (1:1) 1988, 101–45.

12012. WOLLHEIM, RICHARD. Walter Pater: from philosophy to art. CompCrit (17) 1995, 21–40.

Coventry Patmore

12013. CROOK, J. MORDAUNT. Coventry Patmore and the aesthetics of architecture. VP (34:4) 1996, 519–43.

12014. FISHER, BENJAMIN F. Introduction. Patmore: 'teacups and muffins' or pertinacious Victorian poet? VP (34:4) 1996, 439–55.

12015. —— The supernatural in Patmore's poetry. VP (34:4) 1996, 544–57.

12016. GELPI, BARBARA CHARLESWORTH. King Cophetua and Coventry Patmore. *See* **11440**.

12017. HARTNELL, ELAINE. 'Nothing but sweet and womanly': a hagiography of Patmore's angel. VP (34:4) 1996, 457–76.

12018. PIERSON, ROBERT M. Coventry Patmore's ideas concerning English prosody and *The Unknown Eros* read accordingly. VP (34:4) 1996, 493–518.

James Kirke Paulding

12019. ADERMAN, RALPH M. Paulding's anonymous writings: new attributions and speculations. SB (46) 1993, 370–81.

James Payn

12020. WEGENER, FREDERICK. Henry James on James Payn: a forgotten critical text. *See* **11668**.

Thomas Love Peacock

12021. JOUKOVSKY, NICHOLAS A. Peacock and his 'pet politician': an unpublished Latin squib on the coalition against Palmerston. MLR (91:4) 1996, 833–9.

12022. —— Thomas Love Peacock's manuscript *Poems* of 1804. *See* **375**.

Elia Peattie

12023. Szuberla, Guy.   Peattie's *Precipice* and the 'settlement house' novel. Midamerica (20) 1993, 59–75.

Elizabeth Stuart Phelps ('H. Trusta')

12024. Lang, Amy Schrager.   The syntax of class in Elizabeth Stuart Phelps's *The Silent Partner*. In (pp. 267–85) **100**.

12025. Patrick, Barbara.   Lady terrorists: nineteenth-century American women writers and the ghost story. In (pp. 73–84) **3**.

12026. Thomson, Rosemarie Garland.   Benevolent maternalism and physically disabled figures: dilemmas of female embodiment in Stowe, Davis, and Phelps. See **10789**.

Sir Arthur Wing Pinero

12027. Bratton, Jacqueline S. (ed.).   The magistrate; The schoolmistress; The second Mrs Tanqueray; Trelawny of the 'Wells'. (Bibl. 1995, 11174.) Rev. by J. P. Wearing in ELT (39:1) 1996, 116–19.

Edgar Allan Poe

12028. Anon. (ed.).   E. A. Poe no meikyu tansaku. (A quest for the labyrinth of E. A. Poe.) Tokyo: E. A. Poe Soc., Inst. of Language and Culture, Tsuda Women's College, 1996. pp. iv, 188.

12029. Blevins, Michael S.   A few words on Poe's secret writing. PoeM (24) 1994, 21–3.

12030. Brill, Olaf.   Horror-Rätsel – Erhebungen zu einer neuen Erzählgattung. See **10815**.

12031. Brown, Arthur A.   Literature and the impossibility of death: Poe's *Berenice*. NineL (50:4) 1996, 448–63.

12032. Bryant, John.   Poe's Ape of unReason: humor, ritual, and culture. See **11823**.

12033. Cagliero, Roberto.   'L'uomo della folla': Poe e la città. QLLSM (4) 1990, 23–39.

12034. Calanchi, Alessandra.   *The wandering spectator*: *The Man of the Crowd* di E. A. Poe come esplorazione (pre)tecnologica del tempo e dello spazio. In (pp. 124–34) **117**.

12035. Carlson, Eric W. (ed.).   A companion to Poe studies. Westport, CT; London: Greenwood Press, 1996. pp. xiv, 604.

12036. Dickey, James.   Floating on the floor. PoeM (24) 1994, 11–13.

12037. Fisher, Benjamin F.   Poe. American Literary Scholarship (1993) 39–48; (1994) 39–47.

12038. Freeland, Natalka.   'One of an infinite series of mistakes': mystery, influence, and Edgar Allan Poe. ATQ (10:2) 1996, 123–39.

12039. Frey, Matthew.   Poe's *The Fall of the House of Usher*. Exp (54:4) 1996, 215–16.

12040. Furqueron, James R.   Elementary Holmes. See **11059**.

12041. ——Marcuson, Agnes Bondurant.   Poe and two minor writers. See **10356**.

12042. Garrett, Peter K.   The force of a frame: Poe and the control of reading. YES (26) 1996, 54–64.

12043. Giartosio, Tommaso.   '*Imitative propensities*': mimesi e schiavitù negli scritti di Poe. Acoma (8) 1996, 81–94.

12044. Hutchisson, James M.   Poe, hoaxing, and the 'digressions' in *Arthur Gordon Pym*. CEACrit (58:2) 1996, 24–34.

12045. ILLO, JOHN. Poe & Nodier: another French connection. PoeM (24) 1994, 6–10.

12046. IRWIN, JOHN T. The mystery to a solution: Poe, Borges, and the analytic detective story. (Bibl. 1995, 11197.) Rev. by Fred See in MFS (40:2) 1994, 343–53; by Agnes Bondurant Marcuson in PoeM (24) 1994, 20; by J. Gerald Kennedy in AmLH (8:3) 1996, 545–6; by Edgardo Krebs in ASch (65:3) 1996, 467–9; by Robert Lima in CLS (33:1) 1996, 129–32.

12047. JUSTIN, HENRI; GRESSET, MICHEL; JAWORSKI, PHILIPPE (eds). Edgar Allan Poe: écrivain. By Claude Richard. Montpellier: Univ. Paul Valéry, 1990. pp. 312. (Delta.) Rev. by Agnes Bondurant Marcuson in PoeM (21) 1991, 20–1.

12048. KENNEDY, J. GERALD. The violence of melancholy: Poe against himself. AmLH (8:3) 1996, 533–51 (review-article).

12049. KESTING, MARIANNE. Ich-Figuration und Erzähler-schachtelung: zur Selbstreflexion der dichterischen Imagination. *See* **10682**.

12050. KOPLEY, RICHARD (ed.). Poe's Pym: critical explorations. (Bibl. 1995, 11201.) Rev. by Agnes Bondurant Marcuson in PoeM (23) 1993, 20–2.

12051. KULP, NANCY. The spotlight of symbolism on Swedenborg and Poe. PoeM (21) 1991, 1–3.

12052. LANIER, DORIS. Poe, Sartain, and *The Bells*. PoeM (23) 1993, 16–17.

12053. LJUNGQUIST, KENT P. Poe. American Literary Scholarship (1995) 37–48.

12054. —— Poe's *Autobiography*: a new exchange of reviews. AmP (2) 1992, 51–63.

12055. MCALLISTER, ROBIN. Borges' *El Aleph* and Poe's *The Fall of the House of Usher*: two studies in the poetics of gothic romance. *In* (pp. 83–8) **127**.

12056. MADDEN, FRED. Poe's *The Black Cat* and Freud's *The Uncanny*. LitPs (39:1/2) 1993, 52–62.

12057. MARCUSON, AGNES BONDURANT. Board member acquires Poe manuscript. *See* **507**.

12058. —— Silverman evokes memory of Henry Poe. PoeM (22) 1992, 10–12.

12059. MEYERS, JEFFREY. Edgar Allan Poe: his life and legacy. (Bibl. 1993, 8981.) Rev. by Mark C. Carnes in AHR (98:5) 1993, 1682; by J. Gerald Kennedy in AmLH (8:3) 1996, 538–40.

12060. NADAL BLASCO, MARITA. 'The death of a beautiful woman is, unquestionably, the most poetical topic in the world': poetic and parodic treatment of women in Poe's tales. *In* (pp. 151–63) **38**.

12061. NETICK, ANNE TYLER. Doré's *The Raven* on display. *See* **229**.

12062. —— A new Poe publication: Poe's Russian connection. PoeM (26) 1996, 2–6, 41–2.

12063. —— Poe & poetry's progress. PoeM (25) 1995, 20–2.

12064. PAHL, DENNIS. De-composing Poe's *Philosophy*. TSLL (38:1) 1996, 1–25.

12065. —— Framing Poe: fictions of self and self-containment. SHum (20:1) 1993, 1–11.

12066. PERRY, DENNIS R. Imps of the perverse: discovering the Poe/Hitchcock connection. LitFQ (24:4) 1996, 393–9.

12067. PIASECKA, EWA.   Edgar Allan Poe w Młodej Polsce: dopełnienia i sprostowania. (Edgar Allan Poe in Young Poland: additions and corrections.) Ruch Literacki (37:5) 1996, 603–13.

12068. POLK, NOEL.   Welty, Hawthorne, and Poe: men of the crowd and the landscape of alienation. *See* **11426**.

12069. POLLIN, BURTON.   A New Englander's obituary eulogy of Poe. AmP (4) 1994, 1–11.

12070. POLLIN, BURTON R.   Names used for humor in Poe's fiction. *See* **2162**.

12071. —— Poe: the 'virtual' inventor, practitioner, and inspirer of modern science fiction. PoeM (26) 1996, 18–28, 42–4.

12072. —— A posthumous assessment: the 1849–1850 periodical press response to Edgar Allan Poe. *See* **1341**.

12073. —— Stephen King's fiction and the legacy of Poe. JFA (5:4) 1992, 2–25.

12074. QUIRK, TOM.   What if Poe's humorous tales were funny? Poe's *X-ing a Paragrab* and Twain's *Journalism in Tennessee*. SAH (3:2) 1995, 36–48.

12075. RIPPL, GABRIELE.   E. A. Poe and the anthropological turn in literary studies. YREAL (12) 1996, 223–42.

12076. SEE, FRED.   Mapping amazement: John Irwin and the calculus of speculation. MFS (40:2) 1994, 343–53 (review-article).

12077. SILVERMAN, KENNETH.   Edgar A. Poe: mournful and never-ending remembrance. (Bibl. 1995, 11228.) Rev. by Welford D. Taylor in PoeM (22) 1992, 8–9; by Philip F. Gura in GetR (6:1) 1993, 38–45; by J. Gerald Kennedy in AmLH (8:3) 1996, 538–40.

12078. SMITH, KATHERINE M.   Accessions. *See* **541**.

12079. —— John Wooster Robertson, M.D., benefactor. PoeM (22) 1992, 4–7.

12080. —— New accessions of the Poe Foundation, Inc. *See* **542**.

12081. SPENTZOU, EFFIE.   Helen of Troy and the poetics of innocence: from ancient fiction to modern metafiction. CML (16:4) 1996, 301–24.

12082. TANZMAN, LEA.   Poe's *A Tale of the Ragged Mountains* as a source for Golding's post-mortem consciousness technique in *Pincher Martin*. NCL (25:4) 1995, 6–7.

12083. VAIL, WILLIAM A.   Premature burial: new in the annals of crime. *See* **11083**.

12084. ZACCARIA, PAOLA.   *Silence – a Fable* di Edgar Allan Poe: la lotta fra scrittura del visibile e scrittura dell'udibile. RSAJ (1) 1990, 27–43.

John Polidori

12085. BARBOUR, JUDITH.   Dr John William Polidori: author of *The Vampyre*. In (pp. 85–110) **47**.

12086. MACDONALD, D. L.; SCHERF, KATHLEEN (eds).   *The Vampyre* and *Ernestus Berchtold; or, The Modern Oedipus*: collected fiction of John William Polidori. (Bibl. 1995, 11238.) Rev. by Ghislaine McDayter in KSJ (45) 1996, 208–9.

Thomas Powell

12087. OLSEN-SMITH, STEVE.   Herman Melville's planned work on remorse. *See* **11871**.

Howard Pyle

12088.   Fox-Friedman, Jeanne.   Howard Pyle and the chivalric order in America: King Arthur for children. *See* **199**.

Charles Reade

12089.   Grigsby, Ann.   Charles Reade's *Hard Cash*: lunacy reform through sensationalism. DSA (25) 1996, 141–58.
12090.   Korobkin, Laura Hanft.   Silent woman, speaking fiction: Charles Reade's *Griffith Gaunt* (1866) at the adultery trial of Henry Ward Beecher. *In* (pp. 45–62) **75**.

Thomas Mayne Reid

12091.   Maher, Susan Naramore.   Westering Crusoes: Mayne Reid's *The Desert Home* and the plotting of the American West. Journal of the Southwest (35:1) 1993, 93–105.

George W. M. Reynolds

12092.   Grose, Janet L.   G. W. M. Reynolds's *The Rattlesnake's History*: social reform through sensationalized realism. SLI (29:1) 1996, 35–42.

Anna M. Richards

12093.   Sigler, Carolyn.   Brave new Alice: Anna Matlack Richards's maternal wonderland. ChildLit (24) 1996, 55–73.

John Richardson

12094.   Beasley, David.   Rereading Richardson's *Wacousta*. ARCS (18:3) 1988, 381–6 (review-article).
12095.   Cronk, Douglas R. (ed.).   Wacousta; or, The prophecy: a tale of the Canadas. (Bibl. 1993, 9001.) Rev. by David Beasley in ARCS (18:3) 1988, 381–6.

Sir Charles G. D. Roberts

12096.   Adams, John Coldwell.   More letters for the Roberts collection. StudCanL (16:1) 1991, 54–62.
12097.   Dean, Misao.   Political science: realism in Roberts's animal stories. StudCanL (21:1) 1996, 1–16.
12098.   Ware, Tracy.   A Canadian source for Frost's *Design*? JML (16:4) 1990, 646–8.

'Rosa Matilda' (Charlotte Dacre)

12099.   Botting, Fred.   Power in the darkness: heterotopias, literature and gothic labyrinths. *See* **8786**.

'John Ross' (Charles Rawdon Maclean)

12100.   Gray, Stephen (ed.).   The Natal papers of 'John Ross': *Loss of the Brig Mary at Natal, with Early Recollections of That Settlement*, and *Among the Caffres*. (Bibl. 1992, 9682.) Rev. by Tony Voss in SARB (41) 1996, 10–12.

Christina Rossetti

12101.   Bristow, Joseph (ed.).   Victorian women poets: Emily Brontë, Elizabeth Barrett Browning, Christina Rossetti. *See* **10453**.

12102. CORNER, MARTIN (introd.).   The works of Christina Rossetti. Ware: Wordsworth, 1995. pp. xx, 450. (Wordsworth poetry library.)

12103. GILBERT, PAMELA K.   'A horrid game': woman as social entity in Christina Rossetti's prose. Eng (41:169) 1992, 1–23.

12104. GRASS, SEAN C.   Nature's perilous variety in Rossetti's *Goblin Market*. NineL (51:3) 1996, 356–76.

12105. GROTH, HELEN.   Island queens: nationalism, queenliness and women's poetry 1837–1861. *See* **10500**.

12106. LINLEY, MARGARET.   Sappho's conversions in Felicia Hemans, Letitia Landon, and Christina Rossetti. *See* **11452**.

12107. MARSH, JAN (ed.).   Poems and prose. London: Dent; Rutland, VT: Tuttle, 1994. pp. xxxiii, 488. (Everyman's library.)

12108. MAXWELL, CATHERINE.   The poetic context of Christina Rossetti's *After Death*. *See* **10526**.

12109. O'REILLY, SHELLEY.   Absinthe makes the tart grow fonder: a note on 'wormwood' in Christina Rossetti's *Goblin Market*. VP (34:1) 1996, 108–14.

12110. SMULDERS, SHARON.   Christina Rossetti revisited. New York: Twayne; London: Prentice Hall, 1996. pp. xiii, 183. (Twayne's English authors, 517.)

12111. SULLIVAN, BRAD.   'Grown sick with hope deferred': Christina Rossetti's darker musings. PLL (32:3) 1996, 227–43.

12112. SWANN, CHARLES.   A Christina Rossetti debt to Marvell? *See* **8076**.

Dante Gabriel Rossetti

12113. COLDIRON, A. E. B.   Rossetti on Villon, Dowson on Verlaine: 'impossibility' and appropriation in translation. *See* **3116**.

12114. JULIAN-AMALRIC, MAGALI.   Les thèmes bibliques dans les tableaux Pré-Raphaélites. CVE (44) 1996, 47–60.

12115. MCGANN, JEROME.   The complete writings and pictures of Dante Gabriel Rossetti: a hypermedia research archive. *See* **736**.

12116. MOURBY, ADRIAN.   How Millais burst his own bubble. *See* **10882**.

12117. PEATTIE, ROGER W.   Frank W. Burgess: bookseller and book cover artist. *See* **234**.

12118. RAHBEK, ULLA.   Tales of love, lust, jealousy and revenge: intertextuality in Marion Halligan's *Spidercup*. *See* **7334**.

12119. RICHARDS, BERNARD.   Epiphany. ERev (7:1) 1996, 31–3.

12120. YAMAGUCHI, ERIKO.   The perfect hero: cruel masculinity in D. G. Rossetti's *The Death of Breuse sans Pitié*. Arthuriana (6:4) 1996, 85–101.

Giovanni Ruffini

12121. CHRISTENSEN, ALLAN CONRAD.   A European version of Victorian fiction: the novels of Giovanni Ruffini. Amsterdam; Atlanta, GA: Rodopi, 1996. pp. 177. (Text, 7.)

John Ruskin

12122. BLYTHE, DAVID-EVERETT.   Shakespeare in Ruskin. *See* **6239**.

12123. EMERSON, SHEILA.   Ruskin: the genesis of invention. (Bibl. 1995, 11283.) Rev. by Laurie Kane Lew in EC (46:1) 1996, 70–8.

12124. GAGNIER, REGENIA. Is market society the *fin* of history? *In* (pp. 290–310) **18**.

12125. HEWISON, ROBERT. Ruskin and Oxford: the art of education. Oxford: Clarendon Press; New York: OUP, 1996. pp. xvi, 155.

12126. JULIAN-AMALRIC, MAGALI. Les thèmes bibliques dans les tableaux Pré-Raphaélites. *See* **12114**.

12127. KNOEPFLMACHER, U. C. Male patronage and female authorship: the case of John Ruskin and Jean Ingelow. *See* **11536**.

12128. LEW, LAURIE KANE. Writing modern pictures: illustrating the real in Ruskin and Dickens. *See* **10873**.

12129. LLOYD, JENNIFER M. Raising lilies: Ruskin and women. JBS (34:3) 1995, 325–50.

12130. MOURBY, ADRIAN. How Millais burst his own bubble. *See* **10882**.

12131. O'GORMAN, FRANCIS. Ruskin and the scientists: John Lubbock and Oliver Lodge. Ruskin Gazette (1:9) 1996, 9–18.

12132. —— Ruskin's *Fors Clavigera* of October 1873: an unpublished letter from Carlyle to Tyndall. *See* **10593**.

12133. SEWELL, BRIAN. Ruskin and the history of art. Ruskin Gazette (1:9) 1996, 2–3.

12134. UNSWORTH, ANNA. Ruskin and *Cousin Phillis*. *See* **11274**.

12135. WEIKERT, HEIDRUN-EDDA. Zur Einschätzung von Mittelalter und Renaissance: früh- und spätviktorianische Perspektiven. ZAA (43:4) 1995, 303–24.

12136. WHEELER, MICHAEL (ed.). Ruskin and the environment: the storm-cloud of the nineteenth century. (Bibl. 1995, 11301.) Rev. by Gary Wihl in Albion (28:3) 1996, 521–3.

Epes Sargent

12137. ALLIATA, MICHELA VANON. A caravan of gypsies: James, Sargent, and the American symptom. *See* **11562**.

Sarah Savage

12138. LOVELL, THOMAS B. Separate spheres and extensive circles: Sarah Savage's *The Factory Girl* and the celebration of industry in early nineteenth-century America. EAL (31:1) 1996, 1–24.

Olive Schreiner

12139. ANON. All about Olive. NELM News (27) 1996, 3.

12140. BERKMAN, JOYCE AVRECH. The healing imagination of Olive Schreiner: beyond South African colonialism. (Bibl. 1994, 9023.) Rev. by Margaret Strobel in AHR (96:4) 1991, 1256.

12141. CHRISMAN, LAURA. Empire, 'race' and feminism at the *fin de siècle*: the work of George Egerton and Olive Schreiner. *In* (pp. 45–65) **18**.

12142. GAGNIER, REGENIA. Is market society the *fin* of history? *In* (pp. 290–310) **18**.

12143. LAWSON, ELIZABETH. Of lies and memory: *The Story of an African Farm*, book of the white feather. CVE (44) 1996, 111–25.

12144. SANDWITH, CORINNE. Schreiner *versus* Schreiner: a contest of value. JLS (10:3/4) 1995, 359–72.

12145. VILLA, LUISA. Scienza e allegoria negli anni Ottanta: appunti sul caso Schreiner. Textus (8:1) 1995, 65–87.

Sir Walter Scott

12146. ALEXANDER, J. H. (ed.).   The bride of Lammermoor. Edinburgh: Edinburgh UP; New York: Columbia UP, 1995. pp. xvi, 398. (Edinburgh ed. of the Waverley novels, 7a.) Rev. by Fiona Robertson in SLJ (supp. 45) 1996, 21–6.

12147. —— A legend of the wars of Montrose. Edinburgh: Edinburgh UP; New York: Columbia UP, 1995. pp. xvi, 271. (Edinburgh ed. of the Waverley novels, 7b.) Rev. by Fiona Robertson in SLJ (supp. 45) 1996, 21–6.

12148. —— HEWITT, DAVID (eds).   Scott in carnival. (Bibl. 1994, 9034.) Rev. by James Anderson in SSL (29) 1996, 316–18.

12149. BOUR, ISABELLE.   La construction de l'image de l'Irlande et de l'Écosse dans le roman de langue anglaise: Maria Edgeworth et Walter Scott (1800–1814). *See* **11098**.

12150. ——John Gibson Lockhart's *Memoirs of the Life of Sir Walter Scott, Bart*; or, The absent author. *See* **11778**.

12151. BOWDEN, ANN; TODD, WILLIAM B.   Scott's commentary on *The Journal of a Tour to the Hebrides with Samuel Johnson. See* **582**.

12152. CHIELI, MARIATERESA.   *Grannie's Spindle*: le età del *romance* in Scott. Textus (9:1) 1996, 173–222.

12153. CIVARDI, CHRISTIAN.   L'invention du kilt: de l'appropriation symbolique à l'expropriation physique. *See* **11783**.

12154. CORRIGAN, KAREN P.   'Plain life' depicted in 'fiery shorthand': sociolinguistic aspects of the languages and dialects of Scotland and Ulster as portrayed in Scott's *Waverley* and Banim's *The Boyne Water. See* **2817**.

12155. CRAIG, CAIRNS.   Out of history. *See* **9103**.

12156. CRAWFORD, RACHEL.   Thieves of language: Coleridge, Wordsworth, Scott, and the contexts of *Alice du Clos. See* **10671**.

12157. DRESCHER, HORST W.   Sir Walter Scott: Geschichte, Über-lieferung und die Erfahrung nationaler Identität. *In* (pp. 95–104) **73**.

12158. —— Sir Walter Scott: history, tradition and the experience of national identity. Études Écossaises (1) 1992, 163–71.

12159. DUNCAN, IAN (ed.).   Ivanhoe. Oxford; New York: OUP, 1996. pp. xxxvii, 581. (World's classics.)

12160. EDGECOMBE, R. S.   Two female saviours in nineteenth-century fiction: Jeanie Deans and Mary Barton. *See* **11256**.

12161. FERNS, CHRIS.   That obscure object of desire: Sir Walter Scott and the borders of gender. ESCan (22:2) 1996, 149–66.

12162. FREEMAN, BRIAN GILBERT.   Hegel, Walter Scott, and 'honest language': the case of *Rob Roy*. Prism(s) (2) 1994, 13–24.

12163. HALDANE, KATHERINE J.   'No human foot comes here': Victorian tourists and the Isle of Skye. *See* **10091**.

12164. HARTVEIT, LARS.   'Silent intercourse': the impact of the 18th-century conceptual heritage on *The Antiquary* and *St Ronan's Well*. EngS (77:1) 1996, 32–44.

12165. HEWITT, DAVID; ALEXANDER, J. H.   The Edinburgh edition of the Waverley novels: a guide for editors. *See* **1109**.

12166. INGLIS, TONY (ed.).   The heart of Midlothian. (Bibl. 1994, 9052.) Rev. by Lionel Lackey in SSL (29) 1996, 338–9.

12167. JOHNSON, CHRISTOPHER.   Anti-pugilism: violence and justice in Scott's *The Two Drovers*. SLJ (22:1) 1995, 46–60.

12168. ——— Scott and the German historical drama. Archiv (233:1) 1996, 20–36.

12169. KERRIGAN, CATHERINE.   Nationalism and gender: Scottish myths of the female. Études Écossaises (supp.) 1994, 105–11.

12170. KROPF, DAVID GLENN.   Authorship as alchemy: subversive writing in Pushkin, Scott, and Hoffmann. (Bibl. 1994, 9054.) Rev. by J. H. Alexander in SLJ (supp. 42) 1995, 12–14.

12171. McCRACKEN-FLESHER, CAROLINE.   Speaking the colonized subject in Walter Scott's *Malachi Malagrowther* letters. SSL (29) 1996, 73–84.

12172. MACK, DOUGLAS S.   Culloden and after: Scottish Jacobite novels. *See* **11466**.

12173. McMULLIN, B. J.   Notes on cancellation in Scott's *Life of Napoleon*. *See* **747**.

12174. MILLGATE, JANE.   Scott and the law: *The Heart of Midlothian. In* (pp. 95–113) **105**.

12175. MITCHELL, JEROME.   More Scott operas: further analyses of operas based on the works of Sir Walter Scott. Lanham, MD; London: UP of America, 1996. pp. 328.

12176. MONNICKENDAM, ANDREW.   Lost causes: national identity and postmodernism. Études Écossaises (3) 1996, 105–15.

12177. ORR, MARILYN.   Public and private I: Walter Scott and the anxiety of authorship. ESCan (22:1) 1996, 45–58.

12178. PINION, F. B.   Scott and *Wuthering Heights. See* **10466**.

12179. RITVO, HARRIET.   Race, breed, and myths of origin: Chillingham cattle as Ancient Britons. Representations (39) 1992, 1–22.

12180. ROBB, DAVID S.   Miller and Edinburgh: *My Schools and Schoolmasters. See* **11925**.

12181. ROBERTSON, FIONA.   Copied-text: the new Edinburgh Waverleys. *See* **814**.

12182. ——— Legitimate histories: Scott, gothic, and the authorities of fiction. (Bibl. 1995, 11338.) Rev. by J. H. Alexander in SLJ (supp. 42) 1995, 9–12; by Jerome Mitchell in SSL (29) 1996, 314–15.

12183. SARGENT, MARK L.   The witches of Salem, the angel of Hadley, and the friends of Philadelphia. *See* **10345**.

12184. SCOTT, PETER DALE.   Alone on Ararat: Scott, Blake, Yeats, and apocalyptic. *See* **8833**.

12185. SHAW, HARRY E. (ed.).   Critical essays on Sir Walter Scott: the Waverley novels. New York: G. K. Hall; London: Prentice Hall, 1996. pp. xi, 222. (Critical essays on British literature.)

12186. SINGER, DANIELLA E.   Scott's analysis of justice, law, and equity in *Peveril of the Peak*: the significance of Martindale. SN (68:1) 1996, 61–71.

12187. STEWART, RALPH.   The enchanted world of the Lady of the Lake. SLJ (22:2) 1995, 5–13.

12188. STOWELL, ROBERT.   Brontë borrowings: Charlotte Brontë and *Ivanhoe*, Emily Brontë and *The Count of Monte Cristo. See* **10440**.

12189. SUHAMY, HENRI.   *Waverley*; ou, Le voyage dans le passé. BSEAA (42) 1996, 99–110.

12190. SUTHERLAND, JOHN.   The life of Walter Scott. (Bibl. 1995, 11344.) Rev. by Tony Inglis in SLJ (supp. 43) 1995, 20–5; by Fiona Robertson in NQ (43:2) 1996, 230–2; by D. S. Carne-Ross in EC (46:4) 1996, 359–66; by Ina Ferris in Criticism (38:1) 1996, 158–60.

Mary Seacole (1805–1881)

12191. PAQUET, SANDRA POUCHET. The enigma of arrival: *The Wonderful Adventures of Mrs Seacole in Many Lands*. AAR (26:4) 1992, 651–63.

'Charles Sealsfield' (Karl Postl)

12192. ARNDT, KARL J. R. (ed.). Journalistik und vermischte Schriften. Hildesheim; New York: Olms, 1991. pp. iv, 476. (Sämtliche Werke, 24.) Rev. by Franz Schüppen in Amst (38:2) 1993, 314–16.
12193. SCHÖPP, JOSEPH C. Charles Sealsfield: der aufgeklärte europäische Reisende als amerikanischer Mythenbildner. ZAA (42:3) 1994, 216–24.

Catharine Maria Sedgwick

12194. GEE, KAREN RICHARDSON. Women, wilderness, and liberty in Sedgwick's *Hope Leslie*. SHum (19:2) 1992, 161–70.
12195. GOULD, PHILIP. Covenant and republic: historical romance and the politics of Puritanism. *See* **10618**.
12196. KALAYJIAN, PATRICIA LARSON. Revisioning America's (literary) past: Sedgwick's *Hope Leslie*. NWSAJ (8:3) 1996, 63–76.
12197. ROSS, CHERI LOUISE. (Re)writing the frontier romance: Catharine Maria Sedgwick's *Hope Leslie*. CLAJ (39:3) 1996, 320–40.
12198. SCHEIBER, ANDREW J. Mastery and majesty: subject, object, and the power of authorship in Catharine Sedgwick's *Cacoethes Scribendi*. ATQ (10:1) 1996, 41–58.
12199. ZAGARELL, SANDRA A. Expanding 'America': Lydia Sigourney's *Sketch of Connecticut*, Catharine Sedgwick's *Hope Leslie*. *In* (pp. 43–65) **99**.

Canon Sheehan (Patrick Augustine Sheehan)

12200. FLEISCHMANN, RUTH. Knowledge of the world as the forbidden fruit: Canon Sheehan and Joyce on the *sacrificium intellectus*. *In* (pp. 127–37) **112**.

Mary Shelley

12201. BAHAR, SABA. *Frankenstein*, family politics and population politics. *See* **9077**.
12202. —— Monstrosity, historicity and *Frankenstein*. EEM (4:2) 1995, 12–15.
12203. BALLESTEROS GONZÁLEZ, ANTONIO. A Romantic vision of millenarian disease: placing and displacing death in Mary Shelley's *The Last Man*. Misc (17) 1996, 51–61.
12204. BENNETT, BETTY T. (ed.). The letters of Mary Wollstonecraft Shelley: vol. 3, 'What years I have spent!' (Bibl. 1990, 7908.) Rev. by L. J. Clark in Text (Ann Arbor) (8) 1995, 435–44; by Charles E. Robinson in Text (Ann Arbor) (8) 1995, 444–7.
12205. —— Selected letters of Mary Wollstonecraft Shelley. (Bibl. 1995, 11359.) Rev. by Sarah Booth Conroy in BkW, 16 July 1995, 1, 10.
12206. BLOOM, HAROLD (ed.). Mary Shelley's *Frankenstein*. New York: Chelsea House, 1996. pp. 72. (Bloom's notes.)
12207. BOWEN, ARLENE. Mary Shelley's rose-eating cat, Lucian, and *Frankenstein*. KSJ (45) 1996, 16–19.
12208. BUTLER, MARILYN (ed.). Frankenstein; or, The modern

Prometheus. (Bibl. 1994, 9088.) Rev. by Emma McEvoy in BJECS (19:1) 1996, 97.

12209. CHANDLER, WAYNE A. *Frankenstein's* many readers. Extrapolation (37:1) 1996, 37–45.

12210. CLEMIT, PAMELA (ed.). *Matilda*, dramas, reviews & essays, prefaces & notes. London; Brookfield, VT: Pickering, 1996. pp. viii, 449. (Novels and selected works of Mary Shelley, 2.) (Pickering masters.)

12211. CORDARO, JOSEPH. Long day's journey into *Frankenstein*. EOR (18:1/2) 1994, 116–28.

12212. COVI, GIOVANNA. The matrushka monster of feminist criticism. Textus (2:1/2) 1989, 217–36.

12213. COX, JEFFREY N. Staging hope: genre, myth, and ideology in the dramas of the Hunt circle. *See* **9747**.

12214. CRAWLEY, FRANCIS P. The human face of Mary Shelley's *Frankenstein*. Analecta Husserliana (49) 1996, 195–202.

12215. CROOK, NORA; CLEMIT, PAMELA (gen. eds). The novels and selected works of Mary Shelley. London; Brookfield, VT: Pickering, 1996. 8 vols. (Pickering masters.) Rev. by Claire Tomalin in TLS, 29 Nov. 1996, 9.

12216. DAVIS, LENNARD J. The dreadful gulph and the glass cadaver: decomposing women in early modern literature. *See* **7684**.

12217. DUYFHUIZEN, BERNARD. Periphrastic naming in Mary Shelley's *Frankenstein*. *See* **2136**.

12218. FISCH, AUDREY A.; MELLOR, ANNE K.; SCHOR, ESTHER H. (eds). The other Mary Shelley: beyond *Frankenstein*. (Bibl. 1995, 11371.) Rev. by L. J. Swingle in Review (17) 1995, 109–21.

12219. FORD, SUSAN ALLEN. 'A name more dear': daughters, fathers, and desire in *A Simple Story*, *The False Friend*, and *Mathilda*. *In* (pp. 51–71) **103**.

12220. FORRY, STEVEN EARL. Hideous progenies: dramatizations of *Frankenstein* from Mary Shelley to the present. (Bibl. 1990, 7912.) Rev. by Brian Rose in JDTC (6:2) 1992, 139–41.

12221. FREDRICKS, NANCY. On the sublime and beautiful in Shelley's *Frankenstein*. ELit (23:2) 1996, 178–89.

12222. FROST, R. J. 'It's alive!' *Frankenstein*: the film, the feminist novel and science fiction. Foundation (67) 1996, 75–94.

12223. GARRETT, MARGARET DAVENPORT. Writing and re-writing incest in Mary Shelley's *Mathilda*. KSJ (45) 1996, 44–60.

12224. GLANCE, JONATHAN C. Beyond the bounds of reverie? Another look at the dreams in *Frankenstein*. JFA (7:4) 1996, 30–47.

12225. GOODSON, A. C. Frankenstein in the age of Prozac. *See* **7734**.

12226. HIRSCH, DAVID A. HEDRICH. Liberty, equality, monstrosity: revolutionizing Mary Shelley's *Frankenstein*. *In* (pp. 115–40) **72**.

12227. HONIGSBERG, DAVID M. Rava's golem. JFA (7:2/3) 1996, 137–45.

12228. HUNTER, J. PAUL (ed.). *Frankenstein*: the 1818 text, contexts, nineteenth-century responses, modern criticism. *See* **689**.

12229. KETTERER, DAVID. (De)Composing *Frankenstein*: the import of altered character names in the last draft. *See* **707**.

12230. LABBE, JACQUELINE. A family romance: Mary Wollstonecraft, Mary Godwin, and travel. *See* **9501**.

12231. MACDONALD, D. L.; SCHERF, KATHLEEN (eds).   Frankenstein; or, The modern Prometheus. (Bibl. 1995, 11385.) Rev. by Rhoda J. Zuk in ESCan (22:4) 1996, 488–91.

12232. McKEEVER, KERRY.   Naming the daughter's suffering: melancholia in Mary Shelley's *Mathilda*. ELit (23:2) 1996, 190–205.

12233. McLANE, MAUREEN NOELLE.   Literate species: populations, 'humanities', and *Frankenstein*. ELH (63:4) 1996, 959–88.

12234. MELCHIORI, BARBARA ARNETT.   The Tree of Life. Textus (8:1) 1995, 173–85.

12235. MILLER, CALVIN CRAIG.   Spirit like a storm: the story of Mary Shelley. Greensboro, NC: Reynolds, 1996. pp. 122. (World writers.)

12236. MILLER, ELIZABETH.   *Frankenstein* and *Dracula*: the question of influence. *In* (pp. 123–9) **127**.

12237. MOSKAL, JEANNE (ed.).   Travel writing. London; Brookfield, VT: Pickering & Chatto, 1996. pp. xii, 454. (Novels and selected works of Mary Shelley, 8.) (Pickering masters.)

12238. NEGRA, DIANE.   Coveting the feminine: Victor Frankenstein, Norman Bates, and Buffalo Bill. LitFQ (24:2) 1996, 193–200.

12239. PARKIN-GOUNELAS, RUTH.   Learning what we have forgotten: repetition as remembrance in early nineteenth-century gothic. *See* **10432**.

12240. PERKINS, MARGO V.   The nature of otherness: class and difference in Mary Shelley's *Frankenstein*. SHum (19:1) 1992, 27–42.

12241. PLATIZKY, ROGER S.   *Mary Barton* and *Frankenstein*. *See* **11270**.

12242. ROBERTS, MARIE MULVEY.   The male scientist, man-midwife, and female monster: appropriation and transmutation in *Frankenstein*. *In* (pp. 59–73) **94**.

12243. SARVER, STEPHANIE.   Homer Simpson meets Frankenstein: cinematic influence in Nathanael West's *The Day of the Locust*. LitFQ (24:2) 1996, 217–22.

12244. SMITH, JOHANNA M.   Mary Shelley. New York: Twayne; London: Prentice Hall, 1996. pp. xv, 197. (Twayne's English authors, 526.)

12245. SUNSTEIN, EMILY W.   A William Godwin letter, and young Mary Godwin's part in *Mounseer Nongtongpaw*. *See* **9080**.

12246. SWINGLE, L. J.   Dismantling the master's house. *See* **9957**.

12247. THOMPSON, TERRY W.   Wrapped in darkness: Hecate in Chapter Sixteen of *Frankenstein*. ELN (33:3) 1996, 28–32.

12248. VINE, STEVEN.   Filthy types: *Frankenstein*, figuration, femininity. CritS (8:3) 1996, 246–58.

12249. WILLIAMS, MADAWC.   Tales of wonder: science fiction and fantasy in the age of Jane Austen. *See* **9982**.

12250. ZAKHARIEVA, BOURIANA.   Frankenstein of the nineties: the composite body. CanRCL (23:3) 1996, 739–52.

Percy Bysshe Shelley

12251. BASKIYAR, DHARNI DHAR.   Indian echoes in Shelley: an interpretation. *In* (pp. 205–14) **125**.

12252. BEALE, DONALD A.   Shelley, the 'nation', and the National Anthem. *See* **8634**.

12253. BENNETT, BETTY T.; CURRAN, STUART.   Shelley: poet and legislator of the world. Baltimore, MD; London: Johns Hopkins UP, 1996. pp. xix, 310.

12254. BODE, CHRISTOPH. *'And what were thou —?'*: Essay über Shelley und das Erhabene. (Bibl. 1993, 9161.) Rev. by Horst Höhne in ZAA (43:2) 1995, 185–7.

12255. BOWEN, ARLENE. Mary Shelley's rose-eating cat, Lucian, and *Frankenstein*. See **12207**.

12256. BRIGHAM, LINDA C. Count Cenci's abysmal credit. TSLL (38:3/4) 1996, 340–58.

12257. CHICHESTER, TEDDI LYNN. Shelley's imaginative transsexualism in *Laon and Cythna*. KSJ (45) 1996, 77–101.

12258. COLWELL, FREDERIC S. Figures in a Promethean landscape. KSJ (45) 1996, 118–31.

12259. COX, JEFFREY N. Staging hope: genre, myth, and ideology in the dramas of the Hunt circle. See **9747**.

12260. CRONIN, RICHARD. Shelleyan incest and the Romantic legacy. See **10246**.

12261. DUFF, DAVID. Romance and revolution: Shelley and the politics of a genre. (Bibl. 1995, 11411.) Rev. by Stephen C. Behrendt in KSJ (45) 1996, 197–9.

12262. ENDO, PAUL. *The Cenci*: recognizing the Shelleyan sublime. TSLL (38:3/4) 1996, 379–97.

12263. ERKELENZ, MICHAEL. The genre and politics of Shelley's *Swellfoot the Tyrant*. RES (47:188) 1996, 500–20.

12264. FINN, MARY E. The ethics and aesthetics of Shelley's *The Cenci*. SR (35:2) 1996, 177–97.

12265. FREEMAN, JOHN. The spirit of poetry and the importance of joy: Shelley's revolutionary animism. 1650–1850 (2) 1996, 275–94.

12266. FROSCH, THOMAS. Psychological dialectic in Shelley's *Song of Apollo* and *Song of Pan*. KSJ (45) 1996, 102–17.

12267. GARRARD, GREG. Radical pastoral? SR (35:3) 1996, 449–65.

12268. GOSLEE, NANCY MOORE (ed.). The *Homeric Hymns* and *Prometheus* drafts notebook: Bodleian MS. Shelley adds.e.12. See **361**.

12269. HALSEY, ALAN. The text of Shelley's death. Leominster: Five Seasons Press, 1995. pp. 82. (Limited ed. of 200 signed and numbered copies.)

12270. JEWETT, WILLIAM. Hawthorne's Romanticism: from canon to corpus. See **10561**.

12271. —— Strange flesh: Shelley and the performance of skepticism. TSLL (38:3/4) 1996, 321–39.

12272. JOHNSON, ANTHONY L. A study in Romantic form: Shelley's *Ozymandias*. Textus (7) 1994, 133–62.

12273. JONES, STEVEN E. Material intertextuality: the case of Shelley's rough-draft notebooks. See **695**.

12274. KAUFMAN, ROBERT. Legislators of the post-everything world: Shelley's *Defence* of Adorno. ELH (63:3) 1996, 707–33.

12275. KIM, UI-RAK. The poetic form of Shelley's lyrics. JELL (42:4) 1996, 777–89.

12276. KITSON, PETER J. (ed.). Coleridge, Keats and Shelley. See **10684**.

12277. KITZBERGER, INGRID ROSA. Archetypal images of transformation and the self in Percy Bysshe Shelley's *The Revolt of Islam*. *In* (pp. 171–87) **125**.

12278. McCARTHY, THOMAS J. 'Epistolary intercourse': sympathy and the English Romantic letter. See **8902**.

12279. McQuillan, Gene.   Mont Blanc, Romantic tourism, and the legacy of travel writing. Prism(s) (3) 1995, 35–53.

12280. Morton, Timothy.   Shelley and the revolution in taste: the body and the natural world. (Bibl. 1995, 11423.) Rev. by Chris Jones in NQ (43:1) 1996, 102–3; by Jonathan Bate in KSJ (45) 1996, 195–7.

12281.   —— Shelley's green desert. SR (35:3) 1996, 409–30.

12282.   —— Trade winds. *See* **2432**.

12283. Murphy, John F.   Time's tale: the temporal poetics of Shelley's *Alastor*. KSJ (45) 1996, 132–55.

12284. Murray, E. B. (ed.).   The prose works of Percy Bysshe Shelley: vol. 1. (Bibl. 1995, 11425.) Rev. by G. Kim Blank in EngS (76:3) 1995, 291–2; by Pamela Clemit in NQ (43:2) 1996, 233–4; by Christoph Bode in ZAA (44:4) 1996, 375–6.

12285. O'Donnell, Brennan.   *The Cenci* writ small: a production of Shelley's play in Baltimore. ERR (6:2) 1996, 269–76.

12286. O'Neill, Michael.   The human mind's imaginings: conflict and achievement in Shelley's poetry. (Bibl. 1993, 9211.) Rev. by Ralph Pite in Eng (40:166) 1991, 73–9.

12287.   —— Percy Bysshe Shelley: a literary life. (Bibl. 1993, 9213.) Rev. by Ralph Pite in Eng (40:166) 1991, 73–9.

12288.   —— The sensitive-plant. CamQ (25:2) 1996, 103–23.

12289.   —— (ed.).   Shelley. (Bibl. 1995, 11426.) Rev. by Christoph Bode in ZAA (44:4) 1996, 376–8.

12290. Orel, Harold.   Shelley and the Irish question. CJIS (22:1) 1996, 87–95.

12291. Pite, Ralph.   How Green were the Romantics? SR (35:3) 1996, 357–73.

12292. Quinn, Mary A. (ed.).   Shelley's 1821–1822 Huntington notebook: a facsimile of Huntington MS HM 2111. *See* **409**.

12293. Raizis, Marius Byron.   The origin and culmination of Shelley's philhellenism. *In* (pp. 189–204) **125**.

12294. Restivo, Giuseppina.   Intelletto d'amore e assurdo nella soggettivazione romantica: Prometeo in Byron e Shelley. *See* **10568**.

12295. Roberts, Hugh.   Chaos and evolution: a quantum leap in Shelley's process. KSJ (45) 1996, 156–94.

12296.   —— Shelley among the post-Kantians. SR (35:2) 1996, 295–329.

12297. Shelley, Bryan.   Shelley and Scripture: the interpreting angel. (Bibl. 1995, 11431.) Rev. by William A. Ulmer in SAtlR (61:2) 1996, 176–8.

12298. Stelzig, Eugene.   'The happy few': notes on Romanticism and the aristocracy of consciousness. Prism(s) (4) 1996, 43–53.

12299. Stoneman, Patsy.   Catherine Earnshaw's journey to her home among the dead: fresh thoughts on *Wuthering Heights* and *Epipsychidion*. *See* **10471**.

12300. Strand, Ginger; Zimmerman, Sarah.   Finding an audience: Beatrice Cenci, Percy Shelley, and the stage. ERR (6:2) 1996, 246–68.

12301. Weisman, Karen A.   Imageless truths: Shelley's poetic fictions. (Bibl. 1995, 11439.) Rev. by Lisa Vargo in ESCan (22:3) 1996, 366–8; by Mark Kipperman in Criticism (38:1) 1996, 160–6.

12302. Wilkinson, Jane.   Re-meditated art: *To a Skylark* across cultures. Textus (5) 1992, 65–81.

12303. Yamada, Chiyoshi.   Chi to ten wa sakete – Shelley sakuhin kenkyu. (A crack between Heaven and Earth: a study of Shelley's works.) Tokyo: Eihosha, 1996. pp. 244.

12304. YOUNG-OK, AN.   Beatrice's gaze revisited: anatomizing *The Cenci*. Criticism (38:1) 1996, 27–68.

12305. ZBIERSKI, HENRYK.   P. B. Shelley in Poland: a survey. PolAS (5) 1994, 25–32.

Lydia Huntley Sigourney

12306. BAYM, LINDA.   Reinventing Sigourney. *In* (pp. 66–85) **99**.

12307. OKKER, PATRICIA.   Sarah Josepha Hale, Lydia Sigourney, and the poetic tradition in two nineteenth-century women's magazines. *See* **1335**.

12308. WAIT, GARY E.; FOX, ELIZABETH PRATT; WILKIE, EVERETT C., JR.   'Good thoughts in good dress': Lydia Sigourney, Hartford poet. ConnHSB (57:1/2) 1992, 5–127.

12309. ZAGARELL, SANDRA A.   Expanding 'America': Lydia Sigourney's *Sketch of Connecticut*, Catharine Sedgwick's *Hope Leslie*. *In* (pp. 43–65) **99**.

William Gilmore Simms ('Frank Cooper')

12310. GUILDS, JOHN CALDWELL.   Simms: a literary life. (Bibl. 1992, 9875.) Rev. by Jon L. Wakelyn in AHR (99:2) 1994, 653–4.

12311. KIBLER, JAMES E.   Simms's first published fiction. *See* **708**.

12312. —— The unpublished preface to W. G. Simms's *Collected Poems*. *See* **709**.

12313. KIBLER, JAMES EVERETT, JR (ed.).   Poetry and the practical. Fayetteville: Arkansas UP, 1996. pp. xlvii, 124. (Simms.)

12314. WATSON, CHARLES S.   From nationalism to secessionism: the changing fiction of William Gilmore Simms. (Bibl. 1994, 9163.) Rev. by Roger West in AlaR (49:4) 1996, 293–5.

George R. Sims

12315. BOOTH, MICHAEL R. (ed.).   *The Lights o' London* and other Victorian plays. *See* **10746**.

Horace Smith

12316. COX, JEFFREY N.   Staging hope: genre, myth, and ideology in the dramas of the Hunt circle. *See* **9747**.

Samuel Francis Smith

12317. BRANHAM, ROBERT JAMES.   'Of thee I sing': contesting *America*. AmQ (48:4) 1996, 623–52.

Robert Southey

12318. GOLDBERG, BRIAN.   Romantic professionalism in 1800: Robert Southey, Herbert Croft, and the letters and legacy of Thomas Chatterton. *See* **8927**.

12319. JEWETT, WILLIAM.   *The Fall of Robespierre* and the sublime machine of agency. *See* **10680**.

12320. SIMMONS, CLARE A.   'Useful and wasteful both': Southey's *Thalaba the Destroyer* and the function of annotation in the Romantic Oriental poem. Genre (27:1/2) 1994, 83–104.

12321. SMITH, MARGARET. Newly acquired Brontë letters, transcriptions and notes. *See* **421**.

E. D. E. N. Southworth

12322. INGS, KATHARINE NICHOLSON. Blackness and the literary imagination: uncovering *The Hidden Hand. In* (pp. 131–50) **82**.

Sir Leslie Stephen

12323. BICKNELL, JOHN W. (ed.). Selected letters of Leslie Stephen: vol. 2, 1882–1904. Basingstoke: Macmillan; Columbus: Ohio State UP, 1996. pp. 283.

12324. ——— REGER, MARK A. (eds). Selected letters of Leslie Stephen: vol. 1, 1864–1882. Basingstoke: Macmillan; Columbus: Ohio State UP, 1996. pp. xix, 286.

12325. GIDDEY, ERNEST. Rocks and waves: Virginia Woolf, Leslie Stephen, and Byron. *In* (pp. 295–304) **125**.

12326. STENFORS, BRIAN D. Signs of the times: Leslie Stephen's letters to the *Nation* from 1866–1873. New York; Frankfurt; Bern; Paris: Lang, 1996. pp. xiii, 267. (American univ. studies, IV: English language and literature, 147.)

Robert Louis Stevenson

12327. ALEXANDER, DORIS. Creating literature out of life: the making of four masterpieces. *See* **11220**.

12328. BELL, IAN. Robert Louis Stevenson: dreams of exile: a biography. (Bibl. 1995, 11475.) Rev. by Karl Beckson in BkW, 9 Jan. 1994, 3–4; by Owen Dudley Edwards in ChesR (20:2/3) 1994, 317–30; by Alexander B. Clunas in SSL (29) 1996, 329–32.

12329. BOOTH, BRADFORD A.; MEHEW, ERNEST (eds). The letters of Robert Louis Stevenson: vol. 1, 1854 – April 1874. (Bibl. 1995, 11476.) Rev. by Catherine Kerrigan in SSL (29) 1996, 270–81.

12330. ——— The letters of Robert Louis Stevenson: vol. 2, April 1874 – July 1879. (Bibl. 1995, 11477.) Rev. by Catherine Kerrigan in SSL (29) 1996, 270–81.

12331. ——— The letters of Robert Louis Stevenson: vol. 3, August 1879 – September 1882. (Bibl. 1995, 11478.) Rev. by Catherine Kerrigan in SSL (29) 1996, 270–81.

12332. ——— The letters of Robert Louis Stevenson: vol. 4, October 1882 – June 1884. (Bibl. 1995, 11479.) Rev. by Catherine Kerrigan in SSL (29) 1996, 270–81.

12333. DERRY, STEPHEN. *The Island of Doctor Moreau* and Stevenson's *The Ebb-Tide.* NQ (43:4) 1996, 437.

12334. HARDESTY, WILLIAM H., III; MANN, DAVID D. Odds on *Treasure Island.* SSL (29) 1996, 29–36.

12335. HUBBARD, TOM. Ordered south? Scottish artists in the Mediterranean, 1864–1927. Études Écossaises (2) 1993, 179–86.

12336. JOLLY, ROSLYN (ed.). South Sea tales. Oxford; New York: OUP, 1996. pp. xliii, 289. (World's classics.)

12337. KERRIGAN, CATHERINE (ed.). Weir of Hermiston. Edinburgh: Edinburgh UP, 1995. pp. xxxvi, 178. (Collected works of Robert Louis Stevenson: centenary ed.) Rev. by J.C. in TLS, 12 Apr. 1996, 32; by Burkhard Niederhoff in AAA (21:2) 1996, 321–3.

12338. McGuinn, Nicholas (ed.). Treasure Island. Cambridge; New York: CUP, 1995. pp. 256. (Cambridge literature.).

12339. Mack, Douglas S. Culloden and after: Scottish Jacobite novels. *See* **11466**.

12340. McLynn, Frank. Robert Louis Stevenson: a biography. (Bibl. 1995, 11502.) Rev. by J. C. Furnas in ASch (63:4) 1994, 619–22; by Alexander B. Clunas in SSL (29) 1996, 329–32.

12341. Maxwell, Richard. Going after Stevenson's treasure. Cresset (60:2/3) 1996, 10–12.

12342. Melchiori, Barbara Arnett. The Tree of Life. *See* **12234**.

12343. Menikoff, Barry. Toward the production of a text: time, space, and *David Balfour*. *See* **755**.

12344. —— (ed.). Tales from the prince of storytellers. (Bibl. 1994, 9201.) Rev. by Katherine Linehan in StudN (28:1) 1996, 129–30.

12345. Menneteau, Patrick. *Dr Jekyll and Mr Hyde*: savoirs anciens et savoirs nouveaux. Études Écossaises (3) 1996, 171–7.

12346. Naugrette, Jean-Pierre. Jacobus, Jacob, James: historicité et onomastique dans *The Master of Ballantrae* de Robert Louis Stevenson. *See* **2181**.

12347. Niederhoff, Burkhard. The double devil's advocate. A reading of Robert Louis Stevenson's short story *Markheim*. LWU (29:2) 1996, 83–95.

12348. —— Erzähler und Perspektive bei Robert Louis Stevenson. (Bibl. 1995, 11507.) Rev. by Klaus H. Börner in ZAA (44:2) 1996, 175–7; by Horst Dölvers in AAA (21:1) 1996, 117–20.

12349. Pascoe, David (introd.). The wrong box. *See* **11988**.

12350. Pennington, John. Textual doubling and divided selves: the strange case of Dr Jekyll and Mary Reilly. JFA (6:2/3) 1993, 203–16.

12351. Petersen, Per Serritslev. The Dr Jekyll and Mr Hyde motif in Jack London's science fiction: formula and intertextuality in *When the World Was Young*. JLJ (3) 1996, 105–16.

12352. Poole, Adrian (ed.). The Master of Ballantrae: a winter's tale. London; New York: Penguin, 1996. pp. xxx, 249. (Penguin classics.)

12353. Rose, Brian. Transformations of terror: reading changes in social attitudes through film and television adaptations of Stevenson's *Dr Jekyll and Mr Hyde*. In (pp. 37–52) **113**.

12354. Rose, Brian A. Jekyll and Hyde adapted: dramatizations of cultural anxiety. Westport, CT; London: Greenwood Press, 1996. pp. xi, 176. (Contributions in drama and theatre studies, 66.) (Cf. bibl. 1994, 6942.)

12355. Sandison, Alan. Robert Louis Stevenson and the appearance of Modernism: a future feeling. Basingstoke: Macmillan; New York: St Martin's Press, 1996. pp. ix, 424.

12356. —— 'Two-fold and multiple natures': modernism and dandyism in R. L. Stevenson's *New Arabian Nights*. AUMLA (86) 1996, 17–31.

12357. Sellin, Bernard. Narrator and narrative voices in *The Master of Ballantrae*. Études Écossaises (supp.) 1994, 113–23.

12358. Terry, R. C. (ed.). Robert Louis Stevenson: interviews and recollections. Basingstoke: Macmillan; Iowa City: Iowa UP, 1996. pp. xxxi, 216, (plates) 8. (Interviews and recollections.)

12359. Watts, Cedric. *The Ebb-Tide* and *Victory*. Conradiana (28:2) 1996, 133–7.

12360. Williams, M. Kellen. 'Down with the door, Poole':

designating deviance in Stevenson's *Strange Case of Dr Jekyll and Mr Hyde*. ELT (39:4) 1996, 412–29.

Elizabeth Drew Barstow Stoddard

12361. MATTER-SEIBEL, SABINA. 'Untranslated signs': narrative anxiety in first-person fiction written by nineteenth-century women. *In* (pp. 81–98) **8**.

12362. MORRIS, TIMOTHY. Elizabeth Stoddard: an examination of her work as pivot between exploratory fiction and the modern short story. *In* (pp. 33–44) **3**.

12363. NETTELS, ELSA. New England indigestion and its victims. *In* (pp. 167–84) **24**.

Bram Stoker

12364. APPLEBY, ROBIN S. *Dracula* and *Dora*: the diagnosis and treatment of alternative narratives. LitPs (39:3) 1993, 16–37.

12365. BELFORD, BARBARA. Bram Stoker: a biography of the author of *Dracula*. New York: Knopf, 1996. pp. xv, 381. Rev. by Karl Beckson in BkW, 21 Apr. 1996, 4–5.

12366. BRANSON, STEPHANIE R. The 'curse of immortality': some philosophical implications of Bram Stoker's *Dracula* and Anne Rice's *Interview with the Vampire*. PCR (5:2) 1994, 33–41.

12367. BRENNAN, MATTHEW C. The novel as nightmare: decentering of the self in Bram Stoker's *Dracula*. JFA (7:4) 1996, 48–59.

12368. —— Repression, knowledge, and saving souls: the role of the 'New Woman' in Stoker's *Dracula* and Murnau's *Nosferatu*. SHum (19:1) 1992, 1–10.

12369. DICKENS, DAVID B. Bürger's ballad *Lenore*: en route to *Dracula*. *In* (pp. 131–8) **127**.

12370. ELLMANN, MAUD (ed.). Dracula. Oxford; New York: OUP, 1996. pp. xxxiii, 389. (World's classics.)

12371. GLOVER, DAVID. Vampires, mummies, and liberals: Bram Stoker and the politics of popular fiction. Durham, NC; London: Duke UP, 1996. pp. x, 212.

12372. HALBERSTAM, JUDITH. Technologies of monstrosity: Bram Stoker's *Dracula*. *In* (pp. 248–66) **18**.

12373. HALL, JASMINE YONG. Solicitors soliciting: the dangerous circulation of professionalism in *Dracula* (1897). *In* (pp. 97–116) **75**.

12374. HANSEN, TOM. Unholy matrimony: the kiss of the vampire. TexR (17:1/2) 1996, 51–63.

12375. HOLLINGER, VERONICA. The vampire and/as the alien. JFA (5:3) 1992, 5–17.

12376. HOMAN, RICHARD L. Freud's 'seduction theory' on stage: Deane's and Balderston's *Dracula*. LitPs (38:1/2) 1992, 57–70.

12377. JURKIEWICZ, KENNETH. Francis Coppola's secret gardens: *Bram Stoker's 'Dracula'* and the *auteur* as decadent visionary. *In* (pp. 167–71) **127**.

12378. MILLER, ELIZABETH. *Frankenstein* and *Dracula*: the question of influence. *In* (pp. 123–9) **127**.

12379. NICHOLSON, MERVYN. Bram Stoker and C. S. Lewis: *Dracula* as a source for *That Hideous Strength*. Mythlore (19:3) 1993, 16–22.

12380. RICKELS, LAURENCE A. Mummy's curse. *See* **11313**.

12381. SIGNOROTTI, ELIZABETH. Repossessing the body: transgressive desire in *Carmilla* and *Dracula*. *See* **11766**.

12382. SMART, ROBERT A. Blood and money in Bram Stoker's *Dracula*: the struggle against monopoly. *In* (pp. 253–60) **71**.

12383. TAYLOR, SUSAN B. Stoker's *Dracula*. Exp (55:1) 1996, 29–31.

12384. WINTHROP-YOUNG, GEOFFREY. Undead networks: information processing and media boundary conflicts in *Dracula*. *In* (pp. 107–29) **62**.

John Augustus Stone

12385. MASON, JEFFREY D. The politics of *Metamora*. *In* (pp. 92–110) **83**.

Harriet Beecher Stowe

12386. BENDER, EILEEN T. Repossessing *Uncle Tom's Cabin*: Toni Morrison's *Beloved*. *In* (pp. 129–42) **19**.

12387. BLOOM, HAROLD (ed.). Harriet Beecher Stowe's *Uncle Tom's Cabin*. New York: Chelsea House, 1996. pp. 72. (Bloom's notes.)

12388. BOYD, RICHARD. Violence and sacrificial displacement in Harriet Beecher Stowe's *Dred*. AQ (50:2) 1994, 51–72.

12389. CRANE, GREGG D. Dangerous sentiments: sympathy, rights, and revolution in Stowe's antislavery novels. NineL (51:2) 1996, 176–204.

12390. DONOVAN, JOSEPHINE. A source for Stowe's ideas on race in *Uncle Tom's Cabin*. NWSAJ (7:3) 1995, 24–34.

12391. HEDRICK, JOAN D. Harriet Beecher Stowe: a life. (Bibl. 1995, 11540.) Rev. by James R. Mellow in BkW, 27 Feb. 1994, 3, 7; by Sarah Whitmer Foster and John T. Foster, Jr, in FHQ (74:1) 1995, 75–7; by Joyce Warren in SAF (24:1) 1996, 123–5; by Theodore R. Hovet in AmS (37:1) 1996, 178–9.

12392. —— Parlor literature: Harriet Beecher Stowe and the question of 'great women artists'. Signs (17:2) 1992, 275–303.

12393. HOVET, THEODORE R. Rummaging through the past: the cultural work of nostalgia in Harriet Beecher Stowe's *My Wife and I*. ColbyQ (32:2) 1996, 113–24.

12394. JOHNSTON, NORMA. Harriet: the life and world of Harriet Beecher Stowe. New York: Four Winds Press; Toronto: Maxwell Macmillan, 1994. pp. xiii, 242.

12395. LEWIS, GLADYS SHERMAN. Message, messenger, and response: Puritan forms and cultural reformation in Harriet Beecher Stowe's *Uncle Tom's Cabin*. (Bibl. 1994, 9239.) Rev. by Theodore R. Hovet in AmS (36:2) 1996, 199–200.

12396. MERISH, LORI. Sentimental consumption: Harriet Beecher Stowe and the aesthetics of middle-class ownership. AmLH (8:1) 1996, 1–33.

12397. OAKES, KAREN KILCUP. 'I like a woman to be a woman': theorizing gender in the humor of Stowe and Greene. *See* **11798**.

12398. PATRICK, BARBARA. Lady terrorists: nineteenth-century American women writers and the ghost story. *In* (pp. 73–84) **3**.

12399. SHEA, MAURA E. Spinning toward salvation: the ministry of spinsters in Harriet Beecher Stowe. ATQ (10:4) 1996, 293–310.

12400. SMITH, KAREN R. *Resurrection, Uncle Tom's Cabin*, and the reader in crisis. CLS (33:4) 1996, 350–71.

12401. Stern, Julia.   Spanish masquerade and the drama of racial identity in *Uncle Tom's Cabin*. *In* (pp. 103–30) **82**.

12402. Szczesiul, Anthony E.   The canonization of Tom and Eva: Catholic hagiography and *Uncle Tom's Cabin*. ATQ (10:1) 1996, 59–71.

12403. Thomson, Rosemarie Garland.   Benevolent maternalism and physically disabled figures: dilemmas of female embodiment in Stowe, Davis, and Phelps. *See* **10789**.

12404. Zettsu, Tomoyuki.   Slavery, song, and the South: Cather's refiguration of Stowe and Foster in *A Lost Lady*. *See* **3572**.

Idah Strobridge

12405. Ronald, Ann.   Idah Meacham Strobridge: the second Mary Austin? WebS (11:2) 1994, 97–103.

R. S. Surtees

12406. Gash, Norman.   Robert Surtees and early Victorian society. (Bibl. 1995, 11559.) Rev. by R. J. Olney in EHR (111:441) 1996, 506–7; by Michael Hurst in Literature and History (5:2) 1996, 91.

Margaret J. M. Sweat

12407. Diggs, Marylynne.   Romantic friends or a 'different race of creatures'? The representation of lesbian pathology in nineteenth-century America. *See* **10229**.

Algernon Charles Swinburne

12408. Alkalay-Gut, Karen.   Swinburne's twisted circle: the logic of *A Match*. VIJ (24) 1996, 139–60.

12409. Jack, Ian.   Swinburne's *Ave atque Vale*. *In* (pp. 241–53) **125**.

12410. Lambdin, Laura.   Swinburne's early Arthurian poems: shadows of his mature vision. Quondam et Futurus (3:4) 1993, 63–76.

12411. McKenna, Mary Lou.   'Masks of words and painted plots': Swinburne and nineteenth-century emblematics. *See* **219**.

12412. Meyers, Terry L.   Swinburne and Whitman: further evidence. WWQR (14:1) 1996, 1–11.

12413. Rooksby, Rikky.   *Regret*: a Swinburne revision. *See* **816**.

12414. Wagner-Lawlor, Jennifer.   Metaphorical 'indiscretion' and literary survival in Swinburne's *Anactoria*. SELit (36:4) 1996, 917–34.

John Addington Symonds

12415. Cohen, Ed.   The double lives of man: narration and identification in late nineteenth-century representations of ec-centric masculinities. *In* (pp. 85–114) **18**.

Arthur Symons

12416. Mitsch, Ruthmarie H.   The other Isolde. *See* **4939**.

Jane Taylor

12417. Wilson, Carol Shiner.   Lost needles, tangled threads: stitchery, domesticity, and the artistic enterprise in Barbauld, Edgeworth, Taylor, and Lamb. *In* (pp. 167–90) **103**.

Philip Meadows Taylor

12418. MAJEED, JAVED. Meadows Taylor's *Confessions of a Thug*: the Anglo-Indian novel as a genre in the making. *In* (pp. 86–110) **132**.

Tabitha Tenney

12419. ÇALISKAN, SEVDA. The coded language of *Female Quixotism*. *See* **2593**.

Alfred, Lord Tennyson

12420. BAILIN, MIRIAM. Seeing is believing in *Enoch Arden*. *In* (pp. 313–26) **126**.

12421. BARZILAI, SHULI. The politics of quotation in *To the Lighthouse*: Mrs Woolf resites Mr Tennyson and Mr Cowper. *See* **8938**.

12422. BENSON, JAMES D.; GREAVES, WILLIAM S.; STILLAR, GLENN. Transitivity and ergativity in *The Lotos-Eaters*. *See* **2582**.

12423. BOYCE, DOUGLAS. The Haddesley connection. TRB (6:5) 1996, 302–10.

12424. BRUCKMULLER-GENLOT, DANIELLE. Une nouvelle venue à Camelot ... la Dame de Shalott: prises, reprises, sur-prises, méprises. RANAM (29) 1996, 29–61.

12425. BUCKLEY, JEROME H. Tennyson's landscapes. TRB (6:5) 1996, 278–88.

12426. CAMPBELL, MATTHEW. Tennyson's epic procrastination. Eng (45:181) 1996, 44–61.

12427. CRONIN, RICHARD. Shelleyan incest and the Romantic legacy. *See* **10246**.

12428. DANIEL, LANELLE. Mirrors and curses: Blanche DuBois and the Lady of Shalott. NCL (23:1) 1993, 2–3.

12429. EDMUNDS, PAUL. The inward eye: visionary apprehensions in Wordsworth and Tennyson. ESA (38:2) 1995, 27–35.

12430. FRIES, MAUREEN. What Tennyson really did to Malory's women. *See* **5238**.

12431. HAIR, DONALD S. Soul and spirit in *In Memoriam*. VP (34:2) 1996, 175–91.

12432. HILL, ALAN G. Tennyson and F. A. Inderwick: a new correspondence. TRB (6:5) 1996, 311–16.

12433. HODGSON, AMANDA. 'The highest poetry': epic narrative in *The Earthly Paradise* and *Idylls of the King*. *See* **11942**.

12434. HOWE, ELISABETH A. The dramatic monologue. *See* **10519**.

12435. JOHNSON, CHRISTOPHER D. Poisoned dreams and blasted speculations: Tennyson's *Lucretius* and Auguste Comte. PMPA (18) 1993, 8–17.

12436. JOHNSTON, EILEEN TESS. 'Beautiful things made new': transformations of Keats's *Hyperion* in Tennyson's *Morte d'Arthur* and *The Passing of Arthur*. *See* **11707**.

12437. JOSEPH, GERHARD. Commodifying Tennyson: the historical transformation of 'brand loyalty'. VP (34:2) 1996, 133–47.

12438. KOVACH, CLAUDIA MARIE. Floating 'Tristan': distortions, indeterminacy, and *différance* within the integrated corpus. *See* **4913**.

12439. LACKEY, MICHAEL. The Victorian sublime. *See* **10524**.

12440. LEDBETTER, KATHRYN. 'BeGemmed and beAmuletted': Tennyson and those 'vapid' gift books. *See* **959**.

12441. LEVI, PETER.   Tennyson. (Bibl. 1995, 11585.) Rev. by Evelyn Toynton in ASch (64:1) 1995, 151–3.

12442. McSWEENEY, KERRY.   Performing *The Solitary Reaper* and *Tears, Idle Tears*. Criticism (38:2) 1996, 281–302.

12443. MAXWELL, CATHERINE.   The poetic context of Christina Rossetti's *After Death. See* **10526**.

12444. PICKERING, OUTI.   Tennyson's *Mariana* and Larkin's *The Whitsun Weddings*. NQ (43:4) 1996, 447–8.

12445. RAIZIS, MARIOS BYRON.   Heroismos kai poiese. (Heroism and poetry.) Philologike Protochronia (53) 1996, 55–8.

12446. RICKS, DAVID.   *In Memoriam* v: a note. NQ (43:4) 1996, 428–9.

12447. ROWLINSON, MATTHEW.   Tennyson's fixations: psychoanalysis and the topics of the early poetry. (Bibl. 1995, 11592.) Rev. by G. Kim Blank in YES (26) 1996, 296–7; by John Maynard in VP (34:1) 1996, 124–30.

12448. SCOTT, PATRICK.   Tennyson, Lincolnshire, and provinciality: the topographical narrative of *In Memoriam*. VP (34:1) 1996, 39–51.

12449. SHERBO, ARTHUR.   Tennyson and John Bright. NQ (43:1) 1996, 52–3.

12450. SIMPSON, ROGER.   William Fulford: an Arthurian reclaimed. *See* **5257**.

12451. SPENTZOU, EFFIE.   Helen of Troy and the poetics of innocence: from ancient fiction to modern metafiction. *See* **12081**.

12452. STEPHENSON, WILL; STEPHENSON, MIMOSA.   Proto-modernism in Tennyson's *The Holy Grail*. Quondam et Futurus (2:4) 1992, 49–55.

12453. STOTT, REBECCA (ed.).   Tennyson. London; New York: Longman, 1996. pp. viii, 223. (Longman critical readers.) Rev. by Matthew Campbell in TRB (6:5) 1996, 329–31.

12454. THWAITE, ANN.   Emily Tennyson: the poet's wife. London; Boston, MA: Faber & Faber, 1996. pp. xix, 716, (plates) 16. Rev. by Roger Evans in TRB (6:5) 1996, 321–4; by Penelope Fitzgerald in TLS, 4 Oct. 1996, 32.

12455. TIGGES, WIM.   Leaves or letters? A crux in Tennyson's *In Memoriam*. VP (34:2) 1996, 279–82.

Charles Tennyson (Charles Tennyson Turner)

12456. BOYCE, DOUGLAS.   The Haddesley connection. *See* **12423**.

12457. STURMAN, CHRISTOPHER; PURTON, VALERIE.   'Stay near us, Emily': the influence of Emily Sellwood on the Tennyson family in the 1830s. *See* **846**.

William Makepeace Thackeray

12458. BARKER, NICOLAS.   Pegasus and the publisher. *See* **892**.

12459. CLARKE, MICAEL M.   Thackeray and women. (Bibl. 1995, 11604.) Rev. by Frederick Kirchhoff in CLIO (25:4) 1996, 459–63.

12460. COLBY, ROBERT A.   Thackeray and Russia. ThN (43) 1996, 1–3.

12461. COSSA, FRANK.   Images of perfection: life imitates art in Kubrick's *Barry Lyndon*. ECL (19:2) 1995, 79–82.

12462. ENGELL, JOHN.   *Barry Lyndon*, a picture of irony. ECL (19:2) 1995, 83–8.

12463. FISHER, JUDITH L.   Image *versus* text in the illustrated novels of William Makepeace Thackeray. *In* (pp. 60–87) **126**.

12464. FLETCHER, ROBERT P. 'Proving a thing even while you contradict it': fictions, beliefs, and legitimation in *The Memoirs of Barry Lyndon, Esq.* StudN (27:4) 1995, 493–514.

12465. GINDELE, KAREN C. When women laugh wildly and (gentle)men roar: Victorian embodiments of laughter. *In* (pp. 139–60) **64**.

12466. GOLDFARB, SHELDON. Discomposure repeated once again: the textual problem in Chapter 17 of *Vanity Fair. See* **652**.

12467. —— New Thackeray drawings. *See* **201**.

12468. HARDEN, EDGAR F. (ed.). Selected letters of William Makepeace Thackeray. Washington Square: New York UP, 1996. pp. xxxv, 416.

12469. HARRIS, KURT W. Narrators and narratees in W. M. Thackeray's *The Virginians.* ThN (44) 1996, 5–7.

12470. HORTON, MERRILL. Thackeray in Faulkner. ThN (43) 1996, 3–4.

12471. JADWIN, LISA. Clytemnestra rewarded: the double conclusion of *Vanity Fair. In* (pp. 35–61) **31**.

12472. JOHNSON, JEFFREY L. L. The eighteenth-century ape: *Barry Lyndon* and the Darwinian pessimism of Stanley Kubrick. ECL (19:2) 1995, 89–91.

12473. LOGAN, THAD. Decorating domestic space: middle-class women and Victorian interiors. *In* (pp. 207–34) **54**.

12474. MARKS, PATRICIA. '*Mon pauvre prisonnier*': Becky Sharp and the triumph of Napoleon. StudN (28:1) 1996, 76–92.

12475. PASCOE, DAVID (ed.). The Newcomes. London; New York: Penguin, 1996. pp. xxxi, 847. (Penguin classics.)

12476. SCHAD, JOHN. Reading the long way round: Thackeray's *Vanity Fair.* YES (26) 1996, 25–33.

12477. SHILLINGSBURG, PETER. Editing Thackeray: a history. *See* **832**.

12478. —— (ed.). *Vanity Fair*: an authoritative text, backgrounds and contents, criticism. (Bibl. 1995, 11616.) Rev. by Thomas L. McHaney in Text (Ann Arbor) (7) 1994, 532–8.

12479. SHILLINGSBURG, PETER L. (ed.). *Flore et Zéphyr*; *The Yellowplush Correspondence*; *The Tremendous Adventures of Major Gahagan*. With commentary by S. A. Muresianu and Nicholas Pickwoad. (Bibl. 1992, 10025.) Rev. by Thomas L. McHaney in Text (Ann Arbor) (7) 1994, 532–8.

12480. —— *The History of Pendennis*. With commentary by Nicholas Pickwoad. (Bibl. 1992, 10026.) Rev. by Thomas L. McHaney in Text (Ann Arbor) (7) 1994, 532–8.

12481. —— (gen. ed.). The history of Henry Esmond. Ed. by Edgar F. Harden. (Bibl. 1993, 9387.) Rev. by Thomas L. McHaney in Text (Ann Arbor) (7) 1994, 532–8.

12482. SUZUKI, SACHIKO. Thackeray wo yomu – zoku fuanna Victorian. (Reading Thackeray: apprehension of another Victorian.) Tokyo: Shinozaki Shorin, 1996. pp. iv, 206.

12483. THOMAS, DEBORAH A. Thackeray and slavery. (Bibl. 1995, 11618.) Rev. by Judith L. Fisher in StudN (27:2) 1995, 238–40.

12484. WATSON, JOHN. Thackeray and Becky Sharp: creating women. DSA (25) 1996, 305–25.

James Thomson ('B.V.')

12485. MORGAN, EDWIN. The poetry of the city. *See* **4639**.

Henry David Thoreau

12486. Borst, Raymond R. (comp.).   The Thoreau log: a documentary life of Henry David Thoreau, 1817–1862. (Bibl. 1992, 10037.) Rev. by Philip F. Gura in GetR (7:2) 1994, 325–32.

12487. Branch, Michael P.; Pierce, Jessica.   'Another name for health': Thoreau and modern medicine. LitMed (15:1) 1996, 129–45.

12488. Buell, Lawrence.   The environmental imagination: Thoreau, nature writing, and the formation of American culture. (Bibl. 1995, 11628.) Rev. by Jonathan Bate in ANQ (9:2) 1996, 53–6; by Marco Portales in AL (68:3) 1996, 640–1; by Heather Kirk Thomas in NCS (10) 1996, 141–2.

12489. Clippinger, David.   Luminosity, transcendence, and the certainty of not knowing. Talisman (14) 1995, 9–30.

12490. Cook, Don L.   The Thoreau edition: an evolving institution. *See* **608**.

12491. Dean, Bradley P.; Hoag, Ronald Wesley.   Thoreau's lectures after *Walden*: an annotated calendar. StudAR (1996) 241–362.

12492. Dove-Rumé, Janine.   Money, body, and language in Thoreau's *Walden*. Letterature d'America (50) 1993, 19–32.

12493. Erickson, Paul D.   Henry David Thoreau's apotheosis of John Brown: a study of nineteenth-century rhetorical heroism. *See* **2361**.

12494. Fanuzzi, Robert.   Thoreau's urban imagination. AL (68:2) 1996, 321–46.

12495. Fink, Steven.   Prophet in the marketplace: Thoreau's development as a professional writer. (Bibl. 1995, 11634.) Rev. by Ezra Greenspan in Review (16) 1994, 105–19.

12496. Harding, Walter.   Additions to the Thoreau bibliography. TSB (214) 1996, 4–7; (215) 1996, 7–8; (217) 1996, 7.

12497. ——— (ed.).   Selections from the journals. New York: Dover; London: Constable, 1995. pp. v, 55.

12498. ——— (foreword and notes).   *Walden*: an annotated edition. (Bibl. 1995, 11647.) Rev. by Joel Myerson in TSB (217) 1996, 7–8.

12499. Harris, Thomas S.   Additions to the Thoreau bibliography. TSB (216) 1996, 7.

12500. Kamioka, Katsumi.   Mori no seikatsu – kansona seikatsu, takaki omoi. (Life in the woods: simple life and noble mind.) Tokyo: Oshisha, 1996. pp. 302.

12501. Littcon, Alfred G.   Miss Thoreau's trumpet. *See* **11804**.

12502. Myerson, Joel (ed.).   The Cambridge companion to Henry David Thoreau. (Bibl. 1995, 11659.) Rev. by Dieter Schulz in Amst (41:3) 1996, 519–20; by Tjebbe A. Westendorp in JAStud (30:3) 1996, 469–71.

12503. Nocera, Gigliola.   Henry David Thoreau's *de-genera* description. RSAJ (6) 1995, 51–63.

12504. Raatz, Volker.   'My own use': Henry David Thoreau and technological progress. *In* (pp. 27–40) **8**.

12505. Robinson, David M.   Emerson, Thoreau, Fuller, and Transcendentalism. *See* **11197**.

12506. Rosenblum, Nancy L. (ed.).   Political writings. Cambridge; New York: CUP, 1996. pp. xxxv, 175. (Cambridge texts in the history of political thought.)

12507. Scheese, Don.   Thoreau's *Journal*: the creation of a sacred place. *In* (pp. 139–51) **66**.

12508. SEELIG, SHARON CADMAN. Generating texts: the progeny of seventeenth-century prose. *See* **7718**.

12509. SHANLEY, J. LYNDON (ed.). Walden. Introd. by Joyce Carol Oates. Princeton, NJ; Oxford: Princeton UP, 1989. pp. xviii, 352. Rev. by Don L. Cook in Text (Ann Arbor) (8) 1995, 333–4.

12510. SLOVIC, SCOTT. Marginality, midnight optimism, and the natural cipher: an approach to Thoreau and Eiseley. WebS (9:1) 1992, 25–43.

12511. WATTERSON, WILLIAM COLLINS. Gerontion as jokester: humor and anxiety in Robert Frost's *Directive*. RFR (1992) 59–67.

12512. WELLS, DANIEL A. Thoreau's reputation in the major magazines, 1862–1900: a summary and index. *See* **1388**.

12513. YU, NING. Thoreau's critique of the American pastoral in *A Week*. NineL (51:3) 1996, 304–26.

Mary Tighe

12514. LINKIN, HARRIET KRAMER. Romanticism and Mary Tighe's *Psyche*: peering at the hem of her blue stockings. SR (35:1) 1996, 55–72.

Albion W. Tourgée

12515. BOECKMANN, CATHERINE. The invisible color: physical description and racial liminality in the novel of passing. *See* **10610**.

George Alfred Townsend (1841–1914)

12516. SHIELDS, JERRY (ed.). Gath's literary work and folk: and other selected writings of George Alfred Townsend. Wilmington: Delaware Heritage Press, 1996. pp. 378.

Catharine Parr Traill

12517. PETERMAN, MICHAEL A.; BALLSTADT, CARL (eds). Forest and other gleanings: the fugitive writings of Catharine Parr Traill. Ottawa: Ottawa UP, 1994. pp. 250. (Canadian short story library, 18.) Rev. by Kathleen O'Donnell in CanL (150) 1996, 170.

Sarah Trimmer

12518. FERGUSON, MOIRA. Sarah Trimmer's warring worlds. CLAQ (21:3) 1996, 105–10.

12519. KEUTSCH, WILFRIED. Teaching the poor: Sarah Trimmer, God's own handmaid. BJRL (76:3) 1994, 43–57.

Anthony Trollope

12520. BAUMGARTEN, MURRAY. Seeing double: Jews in the fiction of F. Scott Fitzgerald, Charles Dickens, Anthony Trollope, and George Eliot. *In* (pp. 44–61) **5**.

12521. BRANTLINGER, PATRICK. Cashing in on the real: money and the failure of mimesis in Defoe and Trollope. *See* **8957**.

12522. COOKSEY, THOMAS L. Mrs Bond's ducks and Trollope's *Popenjoy*. *See* **3482**.

12523. CRAIG, SHERYL. Trollope and the language of flowers. PMPA (20) 1995, 9–12.

12524. DELANEY, FRANK (introd.). The landleaguers. London: Trollope Soc., 1995. pp. xix, 357.

12525. FRASER, ANTONIA (introd.).   Framley Parsonage. London: Trollope Soc., 1996. pp. xviii, 496.

12526. GLENDINNING, VICTORIA.   Trollope. (Bibl. 1995, 11694.) Rev. by Richard D. Altick in BkW, 7 Feb. 1996, 9.

12527. JAMES, P. D. (introd.).   Doctor Thorne. London: Trollope Soc., 1996. pp. xiii, 524.

12528. KINCAID, JAMES R.   Anthony Trollope and the unmannerly novel. *In* (pp. 87–104) **96**.

12529. NARDIN, JANE.   Trollope & Victorian moral philosophy. Athens: Ohio UP, 1996. pp. 172.

12530. SADLEIR, MICHAEL; PAGE, FREDERICK (eds).   Barchester Towers. Introd. and notes by John Sutherland. Oxford; New York: OUP, 1996. pp. xliii, 328. (World's classics.)

12531. SHIFRIN, MALCOLM.   Two Turkish baths in Jermyn Street. NQ (43:4) 1996, 430.

12532. SKILTON, DAVID.   An autobiography. London; New York: Penguin, 1996. pp. xxvi, 285. (Penguin classics.)

12533. SWANN, CHARLES.   Miss Harleth, Miss Mackenzie: mirror images? *See* **11162**.

12534. THIRLWELL, ANGELA (introd.).   Nina Balatka: the story of a maiden of Prague. London: Trollope Soc., 1996. pp. xvii, 186.

12535. WEINBERG, LOUISE.   Is it all right to read Trollope? ASch (62:3) 1993, 447–51.

Frances Trollope

12536. BANK, ROSEMARIE.   Mrs Trollope visits the theatre: cultural diplomacy and historical appropriation. JADT (5:3) 1993, 16–27.

Sojourner Truth

12537. HUMEZ, JEAN M.   Reading *The Narrative of Sojourner Truth* as a collaborative text. *See* **10143**.

12538. MABEE, CARLETON; NEWHOUSE, SUSAN MABEE.   Sojourner Truth: slave, prophet, legend. (Bibl. 1995, 11726.) Rev. by Adrienne Lash Jones in NWSAJ (8:3) 1996, 172–4; by Kimberly Rae Connor in AAR (30:2) 1996, 294–7.

Martin Farquhar Tupper

12539. COULOMBE, JOSEPH L.   'To destroy the teacher': Whitman and Martin Farquhar Tupper's 1851 trip to America. WWQR (13:4) 1996, 199–209.

'Mark Twain' (Samuel L. Clemens)

12540. ANDERSON, DAVID D.   Mark Twain in England. SSMLN (23:2) 1993, 5–11.

12541. ARAC, JONATHAN.   Putting the river on new maps: nation, race, and beyond in reading *Huckleberry Finn*. AmLH (8:1) 1996, 110–29.

12542. ASPIZ, HAROLD.   Tom Sawyer's games of death. StudN (27:2) 1995, 141–53.

12543. ATTEBERY, BRIAN.   American studies: a not so unscientific method. *See* **11385**.

12544. BAETZHOLD, HOWARD G.   'Well, my book is written – let it go ... .' *In* (pp. 41–77) **7**.

12545. BEAUCHAMP, GORMAN. The American vandal in Italy. CR (40:1) 1996, 69–79.

12546. BOKER, PAMELA A. The grief taboo in American literature: loss and prolonged adolescence in Twain, Melville, and Hemingway. *See* **11820**.

12547. BOUGHN, MICHAEL. Rethinking Mark Twain's skepticism: ways of knowing and forms of freedom in the *Adventures of Huckleberry Finn*. AQ (52:4) 1996, 31–48.

12548. BREINIG, HELMBRECHT. Macht und Gegenmacht: mündliches Wissen und Schriftlichkeit in Mark Twains *A Connecticut Yankee in King Arthur's Court*. *In* (pp. 121–35) **73**.

12549. BRIDEN, EARL F. Playing the live stock market: topical humor in *Huckleberry Finn*. ANQ (9:2) 1996, 14–16.

12550. BRITTON, WESLEY. Two visions of medievalism and determinism: Mark Twain and John Kennedy Toole's *A Confederacy of Dunces*. SoQ (34:1) 1995, 17–23.

12551. BRYANT, JOHN. Melville, Twain and Quixote: variations on the comic debate. *See* **11822**.

12552. BUDD, LOUIS J. Listing of and selections from newspaper and magazine interviews with Samuel L. Clemens: a supplement. ALR (28:3) 1996, 63–90.

12553. CAGIDEMETRIO, ALIDE. La meraviglia senza meraviglia di Hank Morgan, l'americano alla corte di Re Artù. Letterature d'America (52/53) 1993, 5–42.

12554. CAMFIELD, GREGG. Sentimental Twain: Samuel Clemens in the maze of moral philosophy. (Bibl. 1995, 11741.) Rev. by Gwendolyn B. Gwathmey in SAH (3:2) 1995, 108–12; by Jason G. Horn in SAF (24:2) 1996, 242–6.

12555. CARDWELL, GUY. The man who was Mark Twain. (Bibl. 1995, 11742.) Rev. by William D. Baker in AR (49:3) 1991, 616; by Richard Francis in PN Review (18:1) 1991, 63–4; by Theodore R. Hovet in AmS (34:2) 1993, 116–17.

12556. CASH, ROBERT D. The problem of Jim in Mark Twain's *Adventures of Huckleberry Finn*. ArizEB (34:2) 1992, 12–13.

12557. COHEN, PHILIP. The making and marketing of Huck Finn. *See* **605**.

12558. COLLINS, BRIAN. Presidential reconstructions: Mark Twain's *Letters from Hawaii* and the integration of civil society. AmS (37:1) 1996, 51–62.

12559. COOLEY, JOHN (ed.). Mark Twain's aquarium: the Samuel Clemens angelfish correspondence, 1905–1910. (Bibl. 1995, 11744.) Rev. by Bill Baker in AR (49:3) 1991, 466.

12560. DALRYMPLE, SCOTT. Just war, pure and simple: *A Connecticut Yankee in King Arthur's Court* and the American Civil War. ALR (29:1) 1996, 1–11.

12561. DAUGHERTY, SARAH B. William Dean Howells and Mark Twain: the Realism war as a campaign that failed. *See* **11518**.

12562. DAVIS, CHESTER L., SR. Russia reprinted *The Czar's Soliloquy*. Twainian (52:4) 1996, 2–4.

12563. DE KOSTER, KATIE (ed.). Readings on Mark Twain. San Diego, CA: Greenhaven Press, 1996. pp. 215. (Greenhaven Press literary companion to American authors.)

12564. EDDINGS, DENNIS W.   The frog and the ram *redux*: a response to John Bryant. SAH (3:2) 1995, 98–101.

12565. EMERSON, EVERETT.   Mark Twain's quarrel with God. *In* (pp. 32–48) **79**.

12566. FISCHER, VICTOR; FRANK, MICHAEL B. (eds); SALAMO, LIN (assoc. ed.).   Mark Twain's letters: vol. 4, 1870–1871. Berkeley; London: California UP, 1995. pp. xxxiii, 792. (Mark Twain papers, 1835–1910.) Rev. by William Baker in AR (54:2) 1996, 244–5.

12567. FISHKIN, SHELLEY FISHER.   Was Huck Black? Mark Twain and African-American voices. (Bibl. 1995, 11753.) Rev. by Karen Lystra in AHR (98:5) 1993, 1559–61; by Mary Jane Hurst in SECOLR (17:2) 1993, 185–7; by Albert E. Stone in AmS (34:2) 1993, 109–11; by Pascal Covici, Jr, in AAR (29:1) 1995, 129–31; by Alan Gribben in StudN (27:2) 1995, 243–7.

12568. —— (foreword).   Speeches. Introd. by Hal Holbrook. Afterword by David Barrow. New York; Oxford: OUP, 1996. pp. xlii, 434, 27. (Oxford Mark Twain.) (Facsim. of ed. pub. New York: Harper, 1910.)

12569. FLORENCE, DON.   Persona and humor in Mark Twain's early writings. (Bibl. 1995, 11754.) Rev. by John Wegner in TexR (17:1/2) 1996, 136–7.

12570. GIBIAN, PETER.   Levity and gravity in Twain: the bipolar dynamics of the early tales. SAH (3:1) 1994, 80–94.

12571. GILMAN, SANDER L.   Mark Twain and the diseases of the Jews. *In* (pp. 27–43) **5**.

12572. GRAFF, GERALD; PHELAN, JAMES (eds).   *Adventures of Huckleberry Finn*: a case study in critical controversy. (Bibl. 1995, 11759.) Rev. by Douglas Hewitt in NQ (43:1) 1996, 114–15; by Peter Messent in JAStud (30:3) 1996, 499–500.

12573. GREENBAUM, ANDREA.   'A number-one trouble maker': Mark Twain's anti-Semitic discourse in *Concerning the Jews*. StudAJL (15) 1996, 73–7.

12574. GRIBBEN, ALAN.   Mark Twain. American Literary Scholarship (1995) 79–95.

12575. HARRIS, MARK.   Theodor's imperfection creation: a new reading of Mark Twain's *The Mysterious Stranger*. Cithara (31:2) 1992, 30–7.

12576. HARRIS, SUSAN K.   The courtship of Olivia Langdon and Mark Twain. Cambridge; New York: CUP, 1996. pp. xiii, 202. (Cambridge studies in American literature and culture, 101.)

12577. HAYES, KEVIN.   Mark Twain's earliest London lecture: three known reports. SAH (3:1) 1994, 116–19.

12578. HENNINGER, FRANCIS J.   The tragic Mr Clemens. UDR (23:3) 1996, 39–45.

12579. HOEBING, PHIL.   Snake lore in Mark Twain country. *See* **3407**.

12580. HOLMES, RICHARD.   If I could I would: Mark Twain's druthers. Twainian (52:1) 1996, 2–4.

12581. HORN, JASON G.   Figuring freedom as religious experience: Mark Twain, William James, and *No. 44, The Mysterious Stranger*. *See* **11674**.

12582. HORN, JASON GARY.   Mark Twain and William James: crafting a free self. *See* **11675**.

12583. JOHNSON, CLAUDIA DURST. Understanding *Adventures of Huckleberry Finn*: a student casebook to issues, sources, and historical documents. Westport, CT; London: Greenwood Press, 1996. pp. xv, 246. (Literature in context.)

12584. KAPLAN, JUSTIN (introd.). Adventures of Huckleberry Finn. Foreword and addendum by Victor Doyno. London: Bloomsbury; New York: Random House, 1996. pp. xxviii, 418.

12585. KISKIS, MICHAEL J. Mark Twain and collaborative autobiography. SLI (29:2) 1996, 27–40.

12586. KNOPER, RANDALL. Acting naturally: Mark Twain in the culture of performance. (Bibl. 1995, 11780.) Rev. by Gregg Camfield in AL (68:1) 1996, 245–6.

12587. LADD, BARBARA. Nationalism and the color line in George W. Cable, Mark Twain, and William Faulkner. *See* **10577**.

12588. LOWRY, RICHARD S. 'Littery man': Mark Twain and modern authorship. Oxford; New York: OUP, 1996. pp. x, 177. (Commonwealth Center studies in American culture.)

12589. MACLEOD, CHRISTINE. Telling the truth in a tight place: *Huckleberry Finn* and the Reconstruction era. SoQ (34:1) 1995, 5–16.

12590. AL-MADANI, YUSUR. Navigation as exploration: the fantastic education of Sindbad the Sailor in the *Arabian Nights* and Twain's *Huckleberry Finn*. CanRCL (23:4) 1996, 901–12.

12591. MALCOLM, DONALD. Mark Twain's gnostic old age: annihilation and transcendence in *No. 44, the Mysterious Stranger*. ALR (28:2) 1996, 41–58.

12592. MATCHIE, THOMAS. Literary continuity in Sandra Cisneros's *The House on Mango Street*. MidQ (37:1) 1995, 67–79.

12593. MESSENT, PETER. Keeping both eyes open: *The Stolen White Elephant* and Mark Twain's humor. SAH (3:2) 1995, 62–84.

12594. MICHAELSEN, SCOTT. Twain's *The American Claimant* and the figure of Frankenstein: a reading in rhetorical hermeneutics. *In* (pp. 195–203) **70**.

12595. MICHELSON, BRUCE. Mark Twain on the loose: a comic writer and the American self. (Bibl. 1995, 11793.) Rev. by Louis J. Budd in AL (68:1) 1996, 244–5; by Jason G. Horn in SAF (24:2) 1996, 242–6.

12596. MORELAND, KIM. The medievalist impulse in American literature: Twain, Adams, Fitzgerald, and Hemingway. *See* **10216**.

12597. MORRIS, WILLIE. Going home with Mark Twain. With photographs by Allen Hess. AH (47:6) 1996, 64–74, 76.

12598. —— (introd.). Life on the Mississippi. Foreword by Shelley Fisher Fishkin. Afterword by Lawrence Howe. New York; Oxford: OUP, 1996. pp. lii, 624, 39. (Oxford Mark Twain.) (Facsim. of ed. pub. Boston, MA: Osgood, 1883.)

12599. MÜLLER, KURT. Wider die Macht der (Vor-)Schriften: Spielformen intertextueller Enthierarchisierung in Mark Twains *Huckleberry Finn*. PoetA (28:1/2) 1996, 181–99.

12600. PATTERSON, MARK R. Surrogacy and slavery: the problematics of consent in 'Baby M.', *Romance of the Republic*, and *Pudd'nhead Wilson*. *See* **10622**.

12601. PUGHE, THOMAS. Reading the picaresque: Mark Twain's *The Adventures of Huckleberry Finn*, Saul Bellow's *The Adventures of Augie March*, and more recent adventures. EngS (77:1) 1996, 59–70.

12602. QUIRK, TOM. Coming to grips with *Huckleberry Finn*: essays on a book, a boy, and a man. (Bibl. 1995, 11797.) Rev. by Abby H. P. Werlock in SAH (3:1) 1994, 127–32; by David E. E. Sloane in StudN (27:2) 1995, 232–4.

12603. —— Mark Twain. American Literary Scholarship (1993) 65–83; (1994) 93–109.

12604. —— What if Poe's humorous tales were funny? Poe's *X-ing a Paragrab* and Twain's *Journalism in Tennessee. See* **12074**.

12605. RASMUSSEN, R. KENT.   Mark Twain A to Z: the essential reference to his life and writings. Foreword by Thomas A. Tenney. New York: Facts on File, 1996. pp. xxiv, 552.

12606. ROBINSON, FORREST G. (ed.).   The Cambridge companion to Mark Twain. (Bibl. 1995, 11802.) Rev. by Laura Skandera-Trombley in SoQ (34:3) 1996, 155–6.

12607. ROLLIN, LUCY (ed.).   The prince and the pauper. Oxford; New York: OUP, 1996. pp. xxxiii, 240. (World's classics.)

12608. RUSSELL, W. M. S.   Time before and after *The Time Machine. See* **10607**.

12609. RYAN, FRANCIS J.   Educational perspectives in Mark Twain's *Life on the Mississippi*. SHum (18:1) 1991, 56–68.

12610. SCHARNHORST, GARY.   Mark Twain, Bret Harte, and the literary construction of San Francisco. *In* (pp. 21–34) **108**.

12611. SKANDERA-TROMBLEY, LAURA E.   Mark Twain in the company of women. (Bibl. 1995, 11806.) Rev. by Joseph B. McCullough in SAH (3:2) 1995, 112–16; by Linda A. Morris in AHR (101:3) 1996, 915–16; by Lawrence Howe in AL (68:2) 1996, 468–70; by Kenneth S. Lynn in TLS, 17 May 1996, 3–4; by Ray B. Browne in JAC (19:3) 1996, 132; by Henry B. Wonham in ALR (28:3) 1996, 91–2.

12612. SMITH, HARRIET ELINOR; BRANCH, EDGAR MARQUESS (eds). Roughing it. (Bibl. 1994, 9425.) Rev. by Joseph M. Thomas in Review (17) 1995, 253–65; by Pascal Covici in SAH (3:2) 1995, 102–8.

12613. STAHL, J. D.   Mark Twain, culture and gender: envisioning America through Europe. (Bibl. 1995, 11809.) Rev. by Charles L. Crow in JAC (18:1) 1995, 120–1; by Achim Hescher in Amst (41:4) 1996, 714–15; by Carolyn Leutzinger Richey in ChildLit (24) 1996, 213–16; by Jason G. Horn in SAF (24:2) 1996, 242–6; by David Leverenz in StudN (28:2) 1996, 274–6.

12614. —— Mark Twain's 'Slovenly Peter' in the context of Twain and German culture. LU (20:2) 1996, 166–80.

12615. STEINBRINK, JEFFREY.   Getting to be Mark Twain. (Bibl. 1995, 11810.) Rev. by Linda L. Kick in GateH (13:1) 1991/92, 71.

12616. STONELEY, PETER.   Rewriting the Gold Rush: Twain, Harte and homosociality. *See* **11384**.

12617. TAKAKO, TAKEDA.   Twinship: *Pudd'nhead Wilson* to *Those Extraordinary Twins* no kankei. (Twinship: the relationship between *Pudd'nhead Wilson* and *Those Extraordinary Twins*.) SEL (72:2) 1996, 197–208.

12618. TANNER, STEPHEN L.   The art of self-deprecation in American literary humor. SAH (3:3) 1996, 54–65.

12619. THOMAS, JOSEPH M.   *Roughing It* in style: the 1993 Iowa–California Twain edition. *See* **860**.

12620. WONHAM, HENRY B.   Getting to the bottom of *Pudd'nhead Wilson*: or, A critical vision focused (too well?) for irony. AQ (50:3) 1994, 111–26.

12621. —— Mark Twain and the art of the tall tale. (Bibl. 1995, 11817.) Rev. by Laura Skandera-Trombley in SAH (3:1) 1994, 132–3; by Alan Gribben in StudN (27:2) 1995, 243–7.

12622. WRIGHT, DANIEL L. Flawed communities and the problem of moral choice in the fiction of Mark Twain. SoLJ (24:1) 1991, 88–97.

John Veitch (1829–1894)

12623. COWLEY, STEPHEN. John Veitch, Scottish philosopher, poet and literary critic. Edinburgh Review (92) 1994, 141–7.

Mrs Humphry Ward (Mary Augusta Arnold)

12624. HAPGOOD, LYNNE. 'The reconceiving of Christianity': secularisation, realism and the religious novel, 1888–1900. *See* **9865**.

12625. SUTHERLAND, JOHN. Mrs Humphry Ward: eminent Victorian, pre-eminent Edwardian. (Bibl. 1993, 9518.) Rev. by Frances MacDonald in AntR (93/94) 1993, 141–6.

12626. TYLEE, CLAIRE M. 'Munitions of the mind': travel writing, imperial discourse and Great War propaganda by Mrs Humphry Ward. ELT (39:2) 1996, 171–92.

12627. WILT, JUDITH. The romance of faith: Mary Ward's Robert Elsmere and Richard Meynell. LitTheol (10:1) 1996, 33–43.

12628. —— 'Transition time': the political romances of Mrs Humphry Ward's *Marcella* (1894) and *Sir George Tressady* (1896). *In* (pp. 225–46) **75**.

Jane West

12629. LONDON, APRIL. Jane West and the politics of reading. *In* (pp. 56–74) **122**.

Frances M. Whitcher

12630. MORRIS, LINDA A. Women's humor in the age of gentility: the life and works of Frances Miriam Whitcher. (Bibl. 1992, 10171.) Rev. by Frances B. Cogan in AHR (99:2) 1994, 646–7.

Henry Kirke White

12631. BARNARD, JOHN. Keats echoes Kirke White. *See* **11692**.

Joseph Blanco White

12632. MURPHY, MARTIN. The Spanish *Waverley*: Blanco White and *Vargas*. *See* **9921**.

William Hale White ('Mark Rutherford')

12633. SWANN, CHARLES. Mark Rutherford's *The Revolution in Tanner's Lane* and Carlyle's *French Revolution*. *See* **10595**.

Walt Whitman

12634. ABRAMS, SAM. 'What is this you bring, my America' – the Library of America Whitman. MLS (26:2/3) 1996, 19–52.

12635. —— (ed.). The neglected Walt Whitman: vital texts. New York: Four Walls Eight Windows, 1993. pp. viii, 200. Rev. by Roberts W. French in WWQR (11:2) 1993, 84–6.

12636. AKERS, PHILIP. The principle of life: a new concept of reality based on Walt Whitman's *Leaves of Grass*. New York: Vantage Press,

1991. pp. vi, 186. Rev. by M. James Killingsworth in WWQR (10:3) 1993, 162–4.

12637. ALEGRIA, FERNANDO, *et al.*   Whitman in translation: a seminar. WWQR (13:1/2) 1995, 1–58.

12638. ALLEN, GAY WILSON.   History of my Whitman studies. WWQR (9:2) 1991, 91–100.

12639. —— FOLSOM, ED (eds).   Walt Whitman and the world. (Bibl. 1995, 11841.) Rev. by Joe Moran in JAStud (30:3) 1996, 493.

12640. ASPIZ, HAROLD.   Whitman's *Poem of the Road*. WWQR (12:3) 1995, 170–85.

12641. ASSELINEAU, ROGER.   My discovery and exploration of the Whitman continent, 1941–1991. WWQR (9:1) 1991, 15–23.

12642. —— Whitman on Robert Burns: a footnote. *See* **8895**.

12643. BAIN, ROBERT (ed.).   Whitman's & Dickinson's contemporaries: an anthology of their verse. *See* **10004**.

12644. BARRETT, FAITH.   Inclusion and exclusion: fictions of self and nation in Whitman and Dickinson. *See* **10928**.

12645. BAUERLEIN, MARK.   Whitman and the American idiom. (Bibl. 1994, 9455.) Rev. by Ezra Greenspan in WWQR (9:4) 1992, 220–3.

12646. —— Whitman's analogues. Review (18) 1996, 135–46 (review-article).

12647. BEACH, CHRISTOPHER.   Walt Whitman, literary culture, and the discourse of distinction. WWQR (12:2) 1994, 73–85.

12648. BETHEL, DENISE B.   Notes on an early daguerreotype of Walt Whitman. WWQR (9:3) 1992, 148–53.

12649. BIRNEY, ALICE L.   Missing Whitman notebooks returned to the Library of Congress. *See* **457**.

12650. BIRNEY, ALICE LOTVIN.   Whitman to C. W. Post: a lost letter located. WWQR (11:1) 1993, 30–1.

12651. BLAIR, STANLEY S.   The Gay Wilson Allen papers. *See* **459**.

12652. BLOOD, MELANIE N.   The Neighborhood Playhouse's *Salut au Monde*: a theatrical vision of 1920s America. JADT (7:2) 1995, 41–56.

12653. BROWN, SUSAN MARGARET.   The Whitman/Pessoa connection. WWQR (9:1) 1991, 1–14.

12654. BYERS, THOMAS B.   What I cannot say: self, word, and world in Whitman, Stevens, and Merwin. (Bibl. 1992, 10183.) Rev. by James E. Miller, Jr, in WWQR (9:1) 1991, 36–44.

12655. CALLOW, PHILIP.   From noon to starry night: a life of Walt Whitman. (Bibl. 1993, 9526.) Rev. by Susan Dean in WWQR (10:4) 1993, 213–17; by Betsy Erkkila in AL (68:4) 1996, 854–5.

12656. CAMBONI, MARINA.   Columbus on stage: the representation of Whitman's personal and American drama. Letterature d'America (44) 1992, 90–109.

12657. CANTONI, LOUIS J.   Walt Whitman, secular mystic. SSMLN (26:3) 1996, 16–17.

12658. CAVELL, RICHARD; DICKINSON, PETER.   Bucke, Whitman, and the cross-border homosocial. ARCS (26:3) 1996, 425–48.

12659. CENIZA, SHERRY.   Women's letters to Walt Whitman: some corrections. WWQR (9:3) 1992, 142–7.

12660. CHANDRAN, K. NARAYANA.   Walt Whitman and William Cowper: a borrowing. *See* **8939**.

12661. CHAPMAN, JEANNE; MACISAAC, ROBERT (eds). With Walt Whitman in Camden: vol. 7, July 7, 1890–February 10, 1891. (Bibl. 1995, 11849.) Rev. by Jerome Loving in WWQR (10:1) 1992, 40–1.

12662. CHISTOVA, I. Turgenev and Whitman. WWQR (13:1/2) 1995, 68–72.

12663. CLANCY, BARBARA M. 'If he be not himself the age transfigured': the poet, the 'cultivating class', and Whitman's 1855 *Song of Myself*. WWQR (14:1) 1996, 21–38.

12664. CLARK, WILLIAM BEDFORD. Whitman, Warren, and the literature of discovery. WWQR (10:1) 1992, 10–15.

12665. CLARKE, GRAHAM. Walt Whitman: the poem as private history. (Bibl. 1995, 11850.) Rev. by Kenneth M. Price in WWQR (9:1) 1991, 28–30.

12666. —— (ed.). Walt Whitman: critical assessments: vol. 1, The man and the myth: biographical studies; vol. 2, The response to the writing; vol. 3, Writers on Whitman's writing; vol. 4, Walt Whitman in the twentieth century: a chronological overview. Robertsbridge, Sussex: Helm Information, 1995. pp. xviii, 2045. (Helm Information critical assessments of writers in English.)

12667. COMER, KEITH V. Strange meetings: Walt Whitman, Wilfred Owen and poetry of war. Lund: Lund UP, 1996. pp. 205. (Lund studies in English, 91.) (Cf. bibl. 1993, 9527.)

12668. COSTA, ALESSANDRA FANTONI. Walt Whitman e la città. QLLSM (4) 1990, 41–59.

12669. COULOMBE, JOSEPH L. 'To destroy the teacher': Whitman and Martin Farquhar Tupper's 1851 trip to America. *See* **12539**.

12670. DOUGHERTY, JAMES. Walt Whitman and the citizen's eye. (Bibl. 1995, 11852.) Rev. by M. Jimmie Killingsworth in WWQR (11:4) 1994, 203–6; by Robert Scholnick in AmS (36:1) 1995, 127–9.

12671. ERKKILA, BETSY; GROSSMAN, JAY (eds). Breaking bounds: Whitman and American cultural studies. Oxford; New York: OUP, 1996. pp. x, 292. Rev. by Gregory Eiselein in WWQR (13:3) 1996, 162–6; by Tyler Hoffman in SAtlR (61:4) 1996, 137–41.

12672. FINNERAN, RICHARD J. 'That word known to all men' in *Ulysses*: a reconsideration. *See* **643**.

12673. FOLSOM, ED. Walt Whitman: a current bibliography. WWQR (14:1) 1996, 42–4.

12674. —— Walt Whitman's native representations. (Bibl. 1995, 11854.) Rev. by M. Jimmie Killingsworth in WWQR (12:1) 1994, 52–6; by Mark Bauerlein in Review (18) 1996, 135–46; by Martin Klammer in AmS (37:1) 1996, 182–3.

12675. —— Whitman: a current bibliography. WWQR (9:1) 1991, 45–53; (9:2) 1991, 111–14; (9:3) 1992, 162–9; (9:4) 1992, 224–31; (10:1) 1992, 42–58; (10:2) 1992, 91–8; (10:3) 1993, 165–70; (10:4) 1993, 221–5; (11:1) 1993, 41–9; (11:2) 1993, 96–100; (11:3) 1994, 148–53; (11:4) 1994, 213–20; (12:1) 1994, 59–62; (12:2) 1994, 121–6; (12:3) 1995, 192–6; (12:4) 1995, 268–73.

12676. —— Whitman naked? WWQR (11:4) 1994, 200–2.

12677. —— The Whitman recording. WWQR (9:4) 1992, 214–16.

12678. —— (ed.). Walt Whitman: the centennial essays. (Bibl. 1995, 11855.) Rev. by David S. Reynolds in WWQR (12:1) 1994, 57–8.

12679. FONE, BYRNE R. S. Masculine landscapes: Walt Whitman and the homoerotic text. (Bibl. 1995, 11856.) Rev. by Charley Shively in WWQR (10:2) 1992, 84–6.

12680. FONTANA, ERNEST.   Whitman, Pater, and *An English Poet. See* **12003**.

12681. GARDNER, THOMAS.   Discovering ourselves in Whitman: the contemporary American long poem. (Bibl. 1993, 9534.) Rev. by James E. Miller, Jr, in WWQR (9:1) 1991, 36–44.

12682. GOODMAN, SUSAN.   Edith Wharton's *Sketch of an Essay on Walt Whitman*. WWQR (10:1) 1992, 3–9.

12683. GOUGEON, LEN.   Whitman and the *Commonwealth. See* **1276**.

12684. GRAVES, ROY NEIL.   Whitman's *A Riddle Song*. Exp (55:1) 1996, 22–5.

12685. GREENLAND, CYRIL; COLOMBO, JOHN ROBERT (eds).   Walt Whitman's Canada. Willowdale, Ont.: Hounslow Press, 1992. pp. xvi, 245. (Limited ed. of 125 signed and numbered copies.) Rev. by Ed Folsom in WWQR (10:4) 1993, 218–20.

12686. GREENSPAN, EZRA.   Walt Whitman and the American reader. (Bibl. 1993, 9536.) Rev. by Harold Aspiz in WWQR (9:2) 1991, 101–4; by Robert J. Scholnick in AmP (2) 1992, 134–6.

12687. —— (ed.).   The Cambridge companion to Walt Whitman. (Bibl. 1995, 11858.) Rev. by Martin Klammer in WWQR (13:3) 1996, 166–8; by Tjebbe A. Westendorp in JAStud (30:2) 1996, 340–1.

12688. GRIFFIN, LARRY D.   Walt Whitman's voice. WWQR (9:3) 1992, 125–33.

12689. GRÜNZWEIG, WALTER.   Walt Whitman: die deutschsprachige Rezeption als interkulturelles Phänomen. (Bibl. 1992, 10196.) Rev. by Robert K. Martin in WWQR (11:2) 1993, 82–4.

12690. HAIGNEY, JESSICA.   Walt Whitman and the French Impressionists: a study of analogies. (Bibl. 1991, 9887.) Rev. by Ruth L. Bowan in WWQR (9:2) 1991, 108–10.

12691. HEFFERNAN, THOMAS FAREL.   Walt Whitman in Trimming Square. WWQR (11:1) 1993, 32–4.

12692. KELLER, KARL.   Walt Whitman camping. *In* (pp. 113–20) **12**.

12693. KESSLER, MILTON.   Notes to accompany Whitman's letter of July 28, 1891. WWQR (11:3) 1994, 137–41.

12694. KILLINGSWORTH, M. JIMMIE.   The growth of *Leaves of Grass*: the organic tradition in Whitman studies. (Bibl. 1993, 9540.) Rev. by Ed Folsom in WWQR (11:1) 1993, 37–40.

12695. KIRCHDORFER, ULF.   Whitman's debt to the muse. WWQR (10:3) 1993, 149–53.

12696. KLAMMER, MARTIN.   Whitman, slavery, and the emergence of *Leaves of Grass*. (Bibl. 1995, 11864.) Rev. by Larry D. Griffin in WWQR (12:4) 1995, 261–3; by Kenneth M. Price in AL (68:3) 1996, 645–6; by Ezra Greenspan in ALH (101:4) 1996, 1283–4; by Jerome Loving in ALR (28:2) 1996, 93–4.

12697. KNAPP, BETTINA L.   Walt Whitman. (Bibl. 1993, 9541.) Rev. by Ed Folsom in WWQR (11:3) 1994, 144–5.

12698. KNIGHT, DENISE D.   'With the first grass-blade': Whitman's influence on the poetry of Charlotte Perkins Gilman. WWQR (11:1) 1993, 18–29.

12699. KOUYMJIAN, DICKRAN.   Whitman and Saroyan: singing the song of America. WWQR (10:1) 1992, 16–24.

12700. KRIEG, JOANN P.   Democracy in action: naming the bridge for Walt Whitman. WWQR (12:2) 1994, 108–14.

12701. —— Emory Holloway's final word on Whitman's son. WWQR (10:2) 1992, 74–80.

12702. —— Grace Ellery Channing and the Whitman calendar. WWQR (12:4) 1995, 252–6.

12703. —— Letters from Warry. WWQR (11:4) 1994, 163–73.

12704. LI, XILAO.   Walt Whitman and Asian-American writers. WWQR (10:4) 1993, 179–94.

12705. LOVING, JEROME.   *Broadway the Magnificent!*: a newly discovered Whitman essay. WWQR (12:4) 1995, 209–16.

12706. —— Emory Holloway and the quest for Whitman's 'manhood'. WWQR (11:1) 1993, 1–17.

12707. —— A newly discovered Whitman poem. WWQR (11:3) 1994, 117–22.

12708. —— 'A young woman meets Walt Whitman': Anne Montgomerie Traubel's first impression of the poet. WWQR (12:2) 1994, 104–5.

12709. LYNCH, EDWARD.   Le trasformazioni (traduzioni, tradizioni e tradimenti) di Walt Whitman, Emily Dickinson (e altri) in John Ashbery. *See* **10976**.

12710. MCCULLOUGH, KEN.   An interview with U Sam Oeur. WWQR (13:1/2) 1995, 64–7. (On translating Whitman into Khmer.)

12711. MCWILLIAMS, JIM.   An unknown 1879 profile of Whitman. WWQR (11:3) 1994, 141–3.

12712. MARCUS, MORDECAI.   *Crossing Brooklyn Ferry*: Whitman's sexual dying into eternity. LitPs (39:1/2) 1993, 121–34.

12713. MARTIN, ROBERT K. (ed.).   The continuing presence of Walt Whitman: the life after the life. (Bibl. 1995, 11869.) Rev. by Jay Grossman in WWQR (10:3) 1993, 154–60.

12714. MAYHAN, WILLIAM F.   The idea of music in *Out of the Cradle Endlessly Rocking*. WWQR (13:3) 1996, 113–28.

12715. MEYERS, TERRY L.   Swinburne and Whitman: further evidence. *See* **12412**.

12716. MILLER, EDWIN HAVILAND (introd.).   Whitman correspondence. WWQR (8:3/4) 1991, 1–106.

12717. MILLER, JAMES E., JR.   *Leaves of Grass*: America's lyric-epic of self-discovery. (Bibl. 1993, 9547.) Rev. by Robert Scholnick in AmS (36:1) 1995, 127–9.

12718. MITCHELL, STEPHEN (ed.).   Song of myself. Boston, MA: Shambhala, 1993. pp. xv, 155. Rev. by Ed Folsom in WWQR (11:3) 1994, 145–7.

12719. MOLLOY, SYLVIA.   His America, our America: José Martí reads Whitman. MLQ (57:2) 1996, 369–79.

12720. MOON, MICHAEL.   Disseminating Whitman: revision and corporeality in *Leaves of Grass*. (Bibl. 1995, 11871.) Rev. by Jerome Loving in WWQR (9:2) 1991, 104–7.

12721. MORGAN, EDWIN.   The poetry of the city. *See* **4639**.

12722. MULLIN, JOSEPH EUGENE.   The Whitman of *Specimen Days*. IowaR (24:1) 1994, 148–61.

12723. MULLINS, MAIRE.   *Leaves of Grass* as a 'woman's book'. WWQR (10:4) 1993, 195–208.

12724. Murray, Martin G.   A brother's love. WWQR (10:4) 1993, 209–12.

12725. —— Bunkum *did* go sogering. WWQR (10:3) 1993, 142–8.

12726. —— 'I knew Reuben Farwell as a first-class soldier': an unpublished Whitman letter. WWQR (13:3) 1996, 159–61.

12727. —— 'Peter the Great': a biography of Peter Doyle. WWQR (12:1) 1994, 1–51.

12728. Myerson, Joel.   Walt Whitman: a descriptive bibliography. (Bibl. 1995, 11873.) Rev. by Jerome Loving in WWQR (11:4) 1994, 206–9; by James E. Miller, Jr, in BB (53:3) 1996, 265–7.

12729. —— (ed.).   Whitman in his own time: a biographical chronicle of his life, drawn from recollections, memoirs, and interviews by friends and associates. (Bibl. 1994, 9477.) Rev. by M. Wynn Thomas in WWQR (10:2) 1992, 81–4.

12730. Nathanson, Tenney.   Whitman's presence: body, voice, and writing in *Leaves of Grass*. (Bibl. 1995, 11875.) Rev. by James Perrin Warren in WWQR (11:1) 1993, 35–7.

12731. Oerlemans, Onno.   Representing the kosmos: the 'lyric turn' in Whitman. WWQR (12:3) 1995, 150–69.

12732. Olsen-Smith, Stephen.   Two views of Whitman in 1856: uncollected reviews of *Leaves of Grass* from the New York *Daily News* and *Frank Leslie's Illustrated Newspaper*. WWQR (13:4) 1996, 210–16.

12733. Orvell, Miles.   The artist looks at the machine: Whitman, Sheeler, and American Modernism. Amst (41:3) 1996, 361–79.

12734. Pack, Tae-hyo.   W. Whitman si eui byunjeungbeobjeok jukeum euishik. (The dialectic of death-consciousness in W. Whitman's poetry.) Unpub. doct. diss., Hyosung Catholic Univ., Korea, 1996.

12735. Parker, Hershel.   The real *Live Oak, with Moss*: straight talk about Whitman's 'gay manifesto'. *See* **780**.

12736. Paro, Maria Clara Bonetti.   Walt Whitman and Brazil. WWQR (11:2) 1993, 57–66.

12737. Peattie, Roger.   Four letters about Whitman in the Angeli-Dennis papers. *See* **523**.

12738. Phillips, Dana.   Whitman and genre: the dialogic in *Song of Myself*. AQ (50:3) 1994, 31–58.

12739. Picker, John M.   The union of music and text in Whitman's *Drum-Taps* and Higginson's *Army Life in a Black Regiment*. *See* **11459**.

12740. Price, Kenneth M.   An interview with Zhao Luorui. WWQR (13:1/2) 1995, 59–63. (On translating Whitman into Chinese.)

12741. —— Whitman and Dickinson. *See* **10991**.

12742. —— Whitman and tradition: the poet in his century. (Bibl. 1993, 9557.) Rev. by Robert Scholnick in AmS (36:1) 1995, 127–9.

12743. —— (ed.).   Walt Whitman: the contemporary reviews. Cambridge; New York: CUP, 1996. pp. xxiv, 356. (American critical archives, 9.)

12744. Reynolds, David S.   Walt Whitman's America: a cultural biography. (Bibl. 1995, 11881.) Rev. by Jerome Loving in WWQR (12:4) 1995, 257–61; by Wendy Smith in BkW, 9 Apr. 1995, 7; by Melvin Landsberg in AmS (37:1) 1996, 180–2.

12745. Rietz, John.   Another Whitman photograph: the Gurney and Rockwood sessions reconsidered. WWQR (9:1) 1991, 24–5.

12746. Salska, Agnieszka.   Whitman's *Columbus*: from myth to consolation. Letteratura d'America (44) 1992, 69–89.

12747. SCHARNHORST, GARY.   Whitman on Robert Burns: an early essay recovered. *See* **8914**.

12748. SCHEICK, WILLIAM J.   The parenthetical mode of Whitman's *When I Read the Book*. WWQR (13:4) 1996, 221–4.

12749. SCHOLNICK, ROBERT J.   'Culture' or democracy: Whitman, Eugene Benson, and the *Galaxy*. *See* **1355**.

12750. —— 'The original eye': Whitman, Schelling and the return to origins. WWQR (11:4) 1994, 174–99.

12751. SCHWIEBERT, JOHN E.   The frailest leaves: Whitman's poetic technique and style in the short poem. (Bibl. 1993, 9562.) Rev. by Michael Tavel Clarke in WWQR (12:4) 1995, 263–7.

12752. SHURR, WILLIAM H.   Walt Whitman's apocalypticism and Washington Irving's *Columbus*. *See* **11546**.

12753. SILL, GEOFFREY M. (ed.).   Walt Whitman of Mickle Street: a centennial collection. (Bibl. 1994, 9485.) Rev. by Ezra Greenspan in WWQR (12:3) 1995, 186–91.

12754. —— TARBELL, ROBERTA K. (eds).   Walt Whitman and the visual arts. Introd. by David Reynolds. (Bibl. 1994, 9486.) Rev. by David Lubi in AmS (35:2) 1994, 138–9; by Robert K. Martin in WWQR (13:3) 1996, 169–70.

12755. SMITH, MARTHA NELL.   Whitman and Dickinson. *See* **11002**.

12756. STANSELL, CHRISTINE.   Whitman at Pfaff's: commercial culture, literary life, and New York bohemia at mid-century. WWQR (10:3) 1993, 107–26.

12757. SZCZESIUL, ANTHONY.   The maturing vision of Walt Whitman's 1871 version of *Drum-Taps*. WWQR (10:3) 1993, 127–41.

12758. THOMAS, M. WYNN.   From Walt to Waldo: Whitman's Welsh admirers. WWQR (10:2) 1992, 61–73.

12759. THURIN, ERIK INGVAR.   Whitman between impressionism and expressionism: language of the body, language of the soul. (Bibl. 1995, 11884.) Rev. by James Perrin Warren in WWQR (13:4) 1996, 225–6.

12760. TOLIVER, BROOKS.   *Leaves of Grass* in Debussy's prose. WWQR (11:2) 1993, 67–81.

12761. TSUNEDA, SHIRO.   Musou no tensai no hikari to kage, II – Whitman *Kusano ha* no sekai. (Light and shade of an imaginative genius: II, The world of Whitman's *Leaves of Grass*.) Tokyo: Aratake Shuppan, 1996. pp. xiv, 426.

12762. TUTEN, NANCY LEWIS.   The language of sexuality: Walt Whitman and Galway Kinnell. WWQR (9:3) 1992, 134–41.

12763. VERDINO-SÜLLWOLD, CARLA MARIA; HAMPSON, THOMAS.   'The frailest leaves of me': a study of the text and music for Whitman's *To What You Said*. WWQR (12:3) 1995, 133–49.

12764. WACKER, JILL.   Sacred panoramas: Walt Whitman and New York City parks. WWQR (12:2) 1994, 86–103.

12765. WALKINGTON, J. W.   Mystical experience in H.D. and Walt Whitman: an intertextual reading of *Tribute to the Angels* and *Song of Myself*. WWQR (11:3) 1994, 123–36.

12766. WARREN, JAMES PERRIN.   Walt Whitman's language experiment. (Bibl. 1992, 10226.) Rev. by Kenneth M. Price in WWQR (9:1) 1991, 28–30.

12767. WARTOFSKY, STEVEN A.   Whitman's impossible mother. WWQR (9:4) 1992, 196–207.

12768. Weltzian, O. Alan.   Walt Whitman and Frederick Delius, endlessly rocking. WWQR (13:3) 1996, 129–47.

12769. Whelan, Carol Zapata.   'Do I contradict myself?': progression through contraries in Walt Whitman's *The Sleepers*. WWQR (10:1) 1992, 25–39.

12770. Wohlpart, A. James.   From outsetting bard to mature poet: Whitman's *Out of the Cradle* and the 'Sea-Drift' cluster. WWQR (9:2) 1991, 77–90.

12771. —— From the material to the spiritual in the 'Sea-Drift' cluster: transcendence in *On the Beach at Night, The World below the Brine*, and *On the Beach at Night Alone*. WWQR (13:3) 1996, 149–58.

12772. Yatchisin, George.   A listening to Walt Whitman and James Wright. WWQR (9:4) 1992, 175–95.

A. D. T. Whitney

12773. Matter-Seibel, Sabina.   'Untranslated signs': narrative anxiety in first-person fiction written by nineteenth-century women. *In* (pp. 81–98) **8**.

John Greenleaf Whittier

12774. Grant, David.   'The unequal sovereigns of a slaveholding land': the North as subject in Whittier's *The Panorama*. Criticism (38:4) 1996, 521–49.

Ella Wheeler Wilcox

12775. Romine, Scott.   Ella Wheeler Wilcox as a source for W. B. Yeats's *The Choice*. Notes on Modern Irish Literature (4) 1992, 17–21.

Oscar Wilde

12776. Badinter, Robert.   Oscar Wilde o niesprawiedliwości. (Oscar Wilde; or, On injustice.) Trans. by Anna Wasilewska. Dialog (1996:7) 99–109.

12777. Ball, David.   Oscar Wilde and the practice of transformation. Eng (40:166) 1991, 23–35.

12778. Behrendt, Patricia Flanagan.   Oscar Wilde: eros and aesthetics. (Bibl. 1995, 11896.) Rev. by John L. Kijinski in Review (16) 1994, 41–61.

12779. Bush, Ronald.   James Joyce and Oscar Wilde. In-between (4:2) 1995, 115–26.

12780. Chamberlin, J. E.   Oscar Wilde. *In* (pp. 141–56) **105**.

12781. Clayworth, Anya; Small, Ian (introds).   *Amiel and Lord Beaconsfield*: an unpublished review by Oscar Wilde. ELT (39:3) 1996, 284–97.

12782. Eltis, Sos.   Revising Wilde: society and subversion in the plays of Oscar Wilde. Oxford: Clarendon Press; New York: OUP, 1996. pp. viii, 226. (Oxford English monographs.)

12783. Gagnier, Regenia.   Is market society the *fin* of history? *In* (pp. 290–310) **18**.

12784. Giaufret, Anna.   Il testo e il suo doppio: la *Salomé* di Oscar Wilde e la *Salome* di Alfred Douglas. Un'analisi comparata linguistico-stilistica. *See* **2628**.

12785. Gillespie, Michael Patrick.   Oscar Wilde and the poetics of ambiguity. Gainesville: Florida UP, 1996. pp. xi, 204.

12786. —— *The Picture of Dorian Gray*: 'what the world thinks me'. (Bibl. 1995, 11915.) Rev. by Karl Beckson in ELT (39:3) 1996, 373–5.

12787. GOODMAN, JONATHAN (comp.). The Oscar Wilde file. (Bibl. 1988, 5807.) Rev. by B.K. in TLS, 21 Apr. 1995, 28.

12788. HODGSON, JOHN A. An allusion to Arthur Conan Doyle's *A Study in Scarlet* in *The Picture of Dorian Gray*. See **11066**.

12789. INMAN, BILLIE ANDREW. John 'Dorian' Gray and the theme of subservient love in Walter Pater's works of the 1890s. See **11307**.

12790. KIRCHHOFER, ANTON. The text in the closet: concealment and disclosure in James Joyce's *Ulysses*. ZAA (44:1) 1996, 27–43.

12791. KNOX, MELISSA. Oscar Wilde: a long and lovely suicide. (Bibl. 1995, 11927.) Rev. by Gary Schmidgall in Review (17) 1995, 319–27; by William Green in TRI (21:1) 1996, 84–5.

12792. ŁETOWSKA, EWA. Od Condorceta do Oscar Wilde'a. (From Condorcet to Oscar Wilde.) Dialog (1996:7) 110–16.

12793. MARTÍNEZ VICTORIO, LUIS JAVIER. Transgresión estética y perversión racionalista en *The Picture of Dorian Gray*. EIUC (4) 1996, 161–74.

12794. MELVILLE, JOY. Mother of Oscar: the life of Jane Francesca Wilde. (Bibl. 1995, 11935.) Rev. by Gary Schmidgall in Review (17) 1995, 327–30.

12795. MONTESPERELLI, FRANCESCA. I segni dell'indicibile: emergenze del'inconscio nelle fiabe di Oscar Wilde. Textus (2:1/2) 1989, 41–72.

12796. NUNOKAWA, JEFF. The importance of being bored: the dividends of *ennui* in *The Picture of Dorian Gray*. StudN (28:3) 1996, 357–71.

12797. NUNOKAWA, JEFFREY. The disappearance of the homosexual in *The Picture of Dorian Gray*. In (pp. 183–90) **92**.

12798. ONO, MOTOKO. Portraits of a mask: Wilde, Joyce and Mishima. In (pp. 112–16) **60**.

12799. PATERSON, GARY H. Oscar and the Scarlet Woman. AntR (85/86) 1991, 241–54.

12800. PILLONCA, GIOVANNI. Wilde in *Ulysses*: il valore di una presenza. Textus (3:1/2) 1990, 313–28.

12801. PINE, RICHARD. The thief of reason: Oscar Wilde and modern Ireland. Dublin: Gill & Macmillan; New York: St Martin's Press, 1995. pp. xiii, 478. (Gill's studies in Irish literature.)

12802. PRICE, JODY. A map with utopia: Oscar Wilde's theory for social transformation. New York; Frankfurt; Bern; Paris: Lang, 1996. pp. 249. (American univ. studies, IV: English language and literature, 162.)

12803. RABY, PETER. *The Importance of Being Earnest*: a reader's companion. (Bibl. 1995, 11950.) Rev. by G. A. Cevasco in ELT (39:1) 1996, 113–15; by Michael Patrick Gillespie in ELT (39:2) 1996, 263–6.

12804. ROBBINS, RUTH. 'A very curious construction': masculinity and the poetry of A. E. Housman and Oscar Wilde. In (pp. 137–59) **18**.

12805. ROHSE, CORINNA SUNDARARAJAN. The sphinx goes wild(e): Ada Leverson, Oscar Wilde, and the gender equipollence of parody. In (pp. 119–36) **64**.

12806. SATZINGER, CHRISTA. Oscar Wilde – rehabilitated at last. In (pp. 255–68) **125**.

12807. SCHROEDER, HORST. A printing error in *The Soul of Man under Socialism*. See **824**.

12808. —— An unacknowledged quotation in *Pen, Pencil and Poison*. *See* **11443**.

12809. —— Wilde, Wainewright, and Fuseli. NQ (43:4) 1996, 433–4.

12810. SEDGWICK, EVE KOSOFSKY. Tales of the avunculate: queer tutelage in *The Importance of Being Earnest*. *In* (pp. 191–209) **92**.

12811. SINFIELD, ALAN. The Wilde century: effeminacy, Oscar Wilde and the queer moment. (Bibl. 1995, 11957.) Rev. by Ellis Hanson in MFS (42:1) 1996, 178–80.

12812. SMALL, IAN. The economies of taste: literary markets and literary value in the late nineteenth century. *See* **9699**.

12813. STOKES, JOHN. Oscar Wilde: myths, miracles and imitations. Cambridge; New York: CUP, 1996. pp. xiv, 216. Rev. by David Trotter in TLS, 28 June 1996, 15.

12814. VANHOUTTE, JACQUELINE. *Salome*'s earnestness. TexPres (13) 1992, 83–7.

12815. WALDREP, SHELTON. The aesthetic realism of Oscar Wilde's *Dorian Gray*. SLI (29:1) 1996, 103–12.

12816. WEINTRAUB, STANLEY. 'The Hibernian School': Oscar Wilde and Bernard Shaw. *In* (pp. 169–79) **49**.

12817. ZELTER, JOACHIM. Critical fallibilism in Oscar Wilde: Karl Popper anticipated? ZAA (43:3) 1995, 218–33.

12818. —— Sinnhafte Fiktion und Wahrheit. Untersuchungen zur ästhetischen und epistemologischen Problematik des Fiktionsbegriffs im Kontext europäischer Ideen- und englischer Literaturgeschichte. (Bibl. 1995, 11972.) Rev. by Wolfgang Iser in GRM (46:3) 1996, 362–5; by Stephan Lieske in ZAA (44:1) 1996, 88–9.

David Willson

12819. GERRY, THOMAS M. F. 'Green yet free of seasons': Gwendolyn MacEwen and the mystical tradition of Canadian poetry. *See* **8776**.

Alexander Wilson

12820. ROY, G. ROSS. Scottish poets and the French Revolution. *See* **8913**.

Dorothy Wordsworth

12821. HILL, ALAN G. (ed.). The letters of William and Dorothy Wordsworth: vol. 8, A supplement of new letters. (Bibl. 1995, 11979.) Rev. by G. Kim Blank in EngS (76:5) 1995, 492–4.

12822. POLOWETZKY, MICHAEL. Prominent sisters: Mary Lamb, Dorothy Wordsworth, and Sarah Disraeli. *See* **11022**.

12823. YUNGBLUT, LAURA H. Dorothy Wordsworth: a natural life. UDR (24:2) 1996, 31–8.

William Wordsworth

12824. BACIGALUPO, MASSIMO. Esperienza e coscienza in Wordsworth. Textus (7) 1994, 41–53.

12825. BAKER, JEFFREY. The deaf man and the blind man. CritS (8:3) 1996, 259–69.

12826. BARNES, MARGARET G. Twentieth-century Wordsworth: a study of twentieth-century ideas in Wordsworth's philosophy. London: Janus, 1996. pp. 61.

12827. Baron, Michael. Language and relationship in Wordsworth's writing. (Bibl. 1995, 11985.) Rev. by Kelly Grover in EC (46:2) 1996, 158–64.

12828. Barth, J. Robert. Wordsworth and Hopkins: in pursuit of transcendence. *See* **11476**.

12829. Bate, Jonathan. Romantic ecology: Wordsworth and the environmental tradition. (Bibl. 1995, 11986.) Rev. by Michael Baron in Eng (41:169) 1992, 78–83; by A. Banerjee in EngS (76:3) 1995, 282–3.

12830. Boehm, Alan D. The 1798 *Lyrical Ballads* and the poetics of late eighteenth-century book production. *See* **260**.

12831. Bradley, Jerry. Romanticism in the 1950s: the Movement's debt to Wordsworth. CCTE (61) 1996, 115–21.

12832. Bromwich, David. Revolutionary justice and Wordsworth's *Borderers*. Raritan (13:3) 1994, 1–24.

12833. Butler, James A. The duty to withhold the facts: family and scholars on Wordsworth's French daughter. PULC (57:2) 1996, 287–307.

12834. —— Tourist or native son: Wordsworth's homecomings of 1799–1800. NineL (51:1) 1996, 1–15.

12835. Chandler, David. Wordsworth's 'dispossessed' cuckoo anticipated. NQ (43:4) 1996, 421–2.

12836. Collings, David. Wordsworthian errancies: the poetics of cultural dismemberment. (Bibl. 1995, 11994.) Rev. by John Rieder in ERR (7:1) 1996, 97–101.

12837. Crawford, Rachel. Thieves of language: Coleridge, Wordsworth, Scott, and the contexts of *Alice du Clos*. *See* **10671**.

12838. Davies, Damian Walford. 'G.D.' *is* George Dyer. *See* **11096**.

12839. —— 'Some uncertain notice': the hermit of *Tintern Abbey*. NQ (43:4) 1996, 422–4.

12840. —— 'A tongue in every star': Wordsworth and Mrs Barbauld's *A Summer Evening's Meditation*. *See* **8778**.

12841. —— Wordsworth's 'lamphole' or 'loophole'? A glimmering from *The Prelude*. *See* **613**.

12842. Duncan, Erika. Some musings on artistic symbiosis: the demonic and angelic sides of the Coleridge–Wordsworth relationship. *See* **10672**.

12843. Dykstra, Scott. Wordsworth's 'solitaries' and the problem of literary reference. ELH (63:4) 1996, 893–928.

12844. Easterlin, Nancy. Wordsworth and the question of 'Romantic religion'. Lewisburg, PA: Bucknell UP; London; Toronto: Assoc. UPs, 1996. pp. 182. (Cf. bibl. 1992, 10295.)

12845. Edmunds, Paul. The inward eye: visionary apprehensions in Wordsworth and Tennyson. *See* **12429**.

12846. Fairer, David. 'Sweet native stream!': Wordsworth and the school of Warton. *In* (pp. 314–38) **122**.

12847. Ferguson, Frances. Romantic memory. *See* **11461**.

12848. Fischer, Michael. Wordsworth and the reception of poetry. *In* (pp. 197–215) **6**.

12849. Fleissner, Robert F. The road elected: a Wordsworthian–Frost synthesis by Grace Noll Crowell. RFR (1991) 18–23.

12850. —— 'Spot of time' in Frost: Beddoes, Vaughan – or Wordsworth in *Stopping by the Woods*? *See* **8381**.

12851. FONTANA, ERNEST.   Wordsworth and Hopkins' *To What Serves Mortal Beauty? See* **11488**.

12852. FRIEDMAN, GERALDINE.   The insistence of history: revolution in Burke, Wordsworth, Keats, and Baudelaire. *See* **8872**.

12853. FRY, PAUL H.   Green to the very door? The natural Wordsworth. SR (35:4) 1996, 535–51.

12854. FULFORD, TIM.   The politics of the sublime: Coleridge and Wordsworth in Germany. *See* **10675**.

12855. GALPERIN, WILLIAM.   Romanticism and/or anti-Semitism. *In* (pp. 16–26) **5**.

12856. GARRARD, GREG.   Radical pastoral? *See* **12267**.

12857. GOODMAN, KEVIS BEA.   Making time for history: Wordsworth, the New Historicism, and the apocalyptic fallacy. SR (35:4) 1996, 563–77.

12858. GRIFFIN, ROBERT J.   Wordsworth's Pope: a study in literary historiography. *See* **9242**.

12859. HALE, ROBERT C.   Revolution and the 'low-down folk': poetic strategies for the masses in William Wordsworth's *Lyrical Ballads* and Langston Hughes' *Fine Clothes to the Jew*. LHR (13:2) 1995, 54–67.

12860. HALLAM, N.   Wordsworth alone. CamQ (25:1) 1996, 41–60. (*Cambridge Quarterly* prize essay.)

12861. HANEY, DAVID P.   William Wordsworth and the hermeneutics of incarnation. (Bibl. 1995, 12013.) Rev. by Jonathan Bate in YES (26) 1996, 290–1.

12862. HANLEY, KEITH; BARRON, DAVID.   An annotated critical bibliography of William Wordsworth. London: Prentice Hall; New York: Harvester Wheatsheaf, 1995. pp. xiii, 329.

12863. HOFMANN, RUTH.   Making sense of the senses: nature as imagination's scene in William Wordsworth's *Prelude*. Litteraria Pragensia (6:11) 1996, 53–67.

12864. JACOBUS, MARY.   Romanticism, writing and sexual difference: essays on *The Prelude*. (Bibl. 1993, 9661.) Rev. by Adela Pinch in Signs (19:1) 1993, 264–8.

12865. JOHNSTON, KENNETH R.   Self-consciousness, social guilt, and Romantic poetry: Coleridge's Ancient Mariner and Wordsworth's Old Pedlar. *In* (pp. 216–48) **6**.

12866. JONES, GREGORY.   'Rude intercourse': uncensoring Wordsworth's *Nutting*. SR (35:2) 1996, 213–43.

12867. JONES, MARK.   The Lucy poems: a case study in literary knowledge. (Bibl. 1995, 12016.) Rev. by S.J. in TLS, 9 Feb. 1996, 28.

12868. KHAN, JALAL UDDIN.   The theme of duty in Wordsworth's *Addressed to —— on the Longest Day*. ELN (34:1) 1996, 40–7.

12869. KIM, JONG-GAB.   Hyeokmyung gwa siin: Wordsworth eui *Seogok* eul jungsim euro. (Politics and poetics in Wordsworth's *The Prelude*.) JELL (42:1) 1996, 24–42.

12870. KING, FRANCIS.   Wordsworth's Italian Alps. *In* (pp. 111–24) **47**.

12871. KNEALE, J. DOUGLAS.   Gentle hearts and hands: reading Wordsworth after Geoffrey Hartman. SR (35:4) 1996, 579–607.

12872. LANGAN, CELESTE.   Romantic vagrancy: Wordsworth and the simulation of freedom. (Bibl. 1995, 12019.) Rev. by Simon Jarvis in TLS, 24 May 1996, 7.

12873. LINDOP, GREVEL.   Newton, Raymond Tallis and the three cultures. *See* **8812**.

12874. LISCIO, LORRAINE.   Marilynne Robinson's *Housekeeping*: misreading *The Prelude*. *In* (pp. 139–62) **28**.

12875. LIU, ALAN.   The New Historicism and the work of mourning. SR (35:4) 1996, 553–62.

12876. LIU, YU.   Revaluating revolution and radicalness in the *Lyrical Ballads*. SELit (36:4) 1996, 747–61.

12877. McGAVRAN, JAMES HOLT.   Defusing the discharged soldier: Wordsworth, Coleridge, and homosexual panic. *See* **10689**.

12878. McSWEENEY, KERRY.   Performing *The Solitary Reaper* and *Tears, Idle Tears. See* **12442**.

12879. MASSEY, LANCE.   *Tintern Abbey's* 'tranquil restoration': toward a methodology of healing in an age of anxiety. PMPA (21) 1996, 45–61.

12880. MATSUSHITA, SENKICHI.   Wordsworth-kou – hito, shizen, yuiitsusha – fugue no youni. (A study of Wordsworth: humanity, nature and a solitary person – in the form of the fugue.) Kyoto: Kyoto Shugakusha, 1996. pp. iv, 618.

12881. MORGAN, EDWIN.   The poetry of the city. *See* **4639**.

12882. NACCARATO, PETER.   History, technology and the emergence of the Romantic subject. *See* **10692**.

12883. NEVELDINE, ROBERT BURNS.   Wordsworth's *Nutting* and the violent end of reading. ELH (63:3) 1996, 657–80.

12884. O'DONNELL, BRENNAN.   The passion of meter: a study of Wordsworth's metrical art. (Bibl. 1995, 12031.) Rev. by Kyle Grimes in SAtlR (61:3) 1996, 134–6.

12885. OMORI, AYAKO.   Meaning and metaphor. *See* **2439**.

12886. PETERFREUND, STUART.   Dying into Newtonian time: Wordsworth and the elegiac task. Genre (23:4) 1990, 279–96.

12887. PITE, RALPH.   How Green were the Romantics? *See* **12291**.

12888. REED, MARK L. (ed.).   The thirteen-book *Prelude*. (Bibl. 1994, 9612.) Rev. by Susan J. Wolfson in Review (16) 1994, 1–20; by Theresa M. Kelley in Text (Ann Arbor) (9) 1996, 430–4.

12889. RICHARDS, BERNARD.   Epiphany. *See* **12119**.

12890. ROBERTS, ANDREW.   Omnipotence and the Romantic imagination. *See* **10697**.

12891. ROBERTS, W. G.   Wordsworth and the technology of skating. BJECS (19:2) 1996, 161–70.

12892. ROOT, CHRISTINA.   Jacobin poetics and Napoleonic politics: Hazlitt's critique of Wordsworth. *See* **11442**.

12893. RUDY, JOHN G.   Wordsworth and the Zen mind: the poetry of self-emptying. Albany: New York State UP, 1996. pp. xv, 268.

12894. SCHOENFIELD, MARK.   The professional Wordsworth: law, labor, & the poet's contract. Athens; London: Georgia UP, 1996. pp. xiv, 360.

12895. SCHOFIELD, ROBIN.   Comparisons. *See* **10703**.

12896. SCOFIELD, MARTIN.   Desire, relationship and perception in Wordsworth's poetry. EngS (77:4) 1996, 351–66.

12897. SETZER, SHARON M.   Precedent and perversity in Wordsworth's *Sonnets upon the Punishment of Death*. NineL (50:4) 1996, 427–47.

12898. SIMPKINS, SCOTT.   Telling the reader what to do: Wordsworth and the Fenwick notes. Reader (26) 1991, 39–64.

12899. SMITH, WILLIAM S.   Medieval ruins and Wordsworth's *The Tuft of Primroses*: 'a universe of analogies'. Analecta Husserliana (44) 1995, 243–9.

12900. STELZIG, EUGENE.   'The happy few': notes on Romanticism and the aristocracy of consciousness. *See* **12298**.

12901. TALLIS, RAYMOND.   Newton's sleep: 1, Poets, scientists and rainbows. *See* **8841**.

12902. —— Newton's sleep: a reply to Grevel Lindop. *See* **8842**.

12903. THORMANN, JANET.   The unconscious and the construction of the child. *See* **11660**.

12904. TYSDAHL, BJØRN.   Edward Young and Wordsworth's *Intimations* ode: originality and imitation. *See* **9507**.

12905. ULMER, WILLIAM A.   Wordsworth, the one life, and *The Ruined Cottage*. SP (93:3) 1996, 304–31.

12906. WALKER, ERIC C.   The plan to publish *Peter Bell*: a new Wordsworth letter. *See* **1025**.

12907. WILSON, DOUGLAS B.   The Romantic dream: Wordsworth and the poetics of the unconscious. (Bibl. 1994, 9626.) Rev. by William Galperin in YES (26) 1996, 288–90.

12908. WOLFSON, SUSAN J.   The gatherings of *Nutting*: reading the Cornell *Lyrical Ballads*. *See* **879**.

12909. —— More *Prelude* to ponder; or, Getting your words-worth. *See* **880**.

12910. WU, DUNCAN.   Wordsworth and the *Courier*'s review of *The Excursion*. *See* **1390**.

12911. ——Wordsworth and the *Westmorland Advertiser*. *See* **1391**.

12912. —— Wordsworth's Fisher King. In-between (5:2) 1996, 123–37.

12913. —— Wordsworth's reading, 1800–1815. (Bibl. 1995, 12077.) Rev. by Michael Baron in Eng (45:183) 1996, 252–5; by D[avid] McK[itterick] in TLS, 6 Sept. 1996, 33.

Charlotte M. Yonge

12914. WHEATLEY, KIM.   Death and domestication in Charlotte M. Yonge's *The Clever Woman of the Family*. SELit (36:4) 1996, 895–915.

Israel Zangwill

12915. UDELSON, JOSEPH H.   Dreamer of the ghetto: the life and works of Israel Zangwill. (Bibl. 1992, 10378.) Rev. by Horst Weinstock in Aschkenas (3) 1993, 384–5.

TWENTIETH CENTURY

GENERAL

General Literary Studies

12916. ABODUNRIN, FEMI.   New literatures in English: Africa. YWES (75) 1994, 692–704.

12917. ADELL, SANDRA.   Double-consciousness/double bind: theoretical issues in twentieth-century Black literature. (Bibl. 1994, 9646.) Rev. by Malin Lavon Walther in MFS (42:1) 1996, 136–8; by Lindon Barrett in AL (68:2) 1996, 476–7.

12918. AGUILAR-SAN JUAN, KARIN.   Landmarks in literature by Asian-American lesbians. Signs (18:4) 1993, 936–43.

12919. AHEARN, EDWARD J.   Visionary fictions: apocalyptic writing from Blake to the modern age. *See* **8425**.

12920. AHMAD, AIJAZ.   In theory: classes, nations, literatures. (Bibl. 1994, 9648.) Rev. by George Lang in CanRCL (20:3/4) 1993, 552–6; by Neil Larsen in MinnR (45/46) 1995/96, 285–90.

12921. AJAYI, OMOFOLABO.   From his symbol to her icon: an analysis of the presentation of women in African contemporary literary works. AJSem (8:3) 1991, 31–52.

12922. ALEXANDER, NEVILLE.   Mainstreaming by confluence: the multilingual context of literature in South Africa. WLT (70:1) 1996, 9–11.

12923. ALLISON, DOROTHY.   Skin: talking about sex, class, & literature. Ithaca, NY: Firebrand, 1994; London: HarperCollins, 1995. pp. 261. Rev. by John Alexander Williams in AppalJ (23:3) 1996, 304–11.

12924. ALS, HILTON.   The women. New York: Farrar, Straus, & Giroux, 1996. pp. 145. (Afro-American women authors.)

12925. ALTER, ROBERT.   Scholem and Modernism. PT (15:3) 1994, 429–42.

12926. ALTOBELLO, PATRICIA; PIERCE, DEIRDRE.   The literary sands of Key West. Washington, DC: Starrhill Press, 1996. pp. 71.

12927. ANANTHAMURTHY, U. R.   On being a writer in India. In-between (3:2) 1994, 85–100.

12928. ANISFIELD, NANCY (ed.).   The nightmare considered: critical essays on nuclear war literature. *See* **77**.

12929. APPLEGATE, NANCY; APPLEGATE, JOE.   'Ted Bundy as one-night stand': black humor and the serial killer. NCL (25:1) 1995, 13–14.

12930. ARMSTRONG, JEANNETTE (ed.).   Looking at the words of our people: First Nations analysis of literature. Penticton, B.C.: Theytus, 1993. pp. 214. Rev. by Margery Fee in CanL (149) 1996, 127–8.

12931. ARTEAGA, ALFRED (ed.).   An other tongue: nation and ethnicity in the linguistic borderlands. *See* **80**.

12932. ASHCROFT, BILL; GRIFFITHS, GARETH; TIFFIN, HELEN (eds). The post-colonial studies reader. (Bibl. 1995, 12091.) Rev. by Johannes Fischer in ZAA (44:1) 1996, 93–4; by Brinda Bose in WLT (70:2) 1996, 483.

12933. ATTON, CHRIS.   Alternative literature: a practical guide for librarians. *See* **890**.

12934. BACKUS, MARGOT GAYLE.   Homophobia and the imperial demon lover: gothic narrativity in Irish representations of the Great War. CanRCL (21:1/2) 1994, 45–63.

12935. BAIN, DAVID HAWARD; DUFFY, MARY SMYTH (eds). Whose woods these are: a history of the Bread Loaf Writers' Conference, 1926–1992. Preface by Marvin Bell. (Bibl. 1993, 9754.) Rev. by Elaine Keen Harrington in VH (62:4) 1994, 235–7.

12936. BAIN, ROBERT; FLORA, JOSEPH M. (eds). Contemporary poets, dramatists, essayists, and novelists of the South: a bio-bibliographical sourcebook. (Bibl. 1995, 12094.) Rev. by Michael Kreyling in AEB (9:1/2) 1995, 94–6.

12937. BAK, HANS, *et al.* (eds). Post-war literatures in English: a lexicon of contemporary authors. Groningen, The Netherlands: Nijhoff, 1995. (Various pagings.) (Additions to bibl. 1994, 9665.) (Individual bibliographies of Kingsley Amis, J. G. Ballard, Paul Bowles, Ed Bullins, Bruce Chatwin, Douglas Coupland, Philip K. Dick, Joan Didion, Jenny Diski, Joseph Heller, Charles Johnson, Andrew Motion, Louis Nowra, Flannery O'Connor, Chaim Potok, Richard Powers, Wallace Stegner, Mark Strand, Graham Swift, Lanford Wilson, David Wright.)

12938. BAKER, RUSSELL (ed.). Russell Baker's book of American humor. *See* **2251**.

12939. BAKY, JOHN S. Literary resources of the Vietnam War. *See* **447**.

12940. BALASSI, WILLIAM; CRAWFORD, JOHN F.; EYSTUROY, ANNIE O. (eds). This is about vision: interviews with Southwestern writers. *See* **121**.

12941. BALLARD, J. G. A user's guide to the millennium: essays and reviews. New York: Picador USA; London: HarperCollins, 1996. pp. 304. Rev. by E.J. in TLS, 12 Apr. 1996, 32.

12942. BALZANO, WANDA. Il *patchwork* post-coloniale irlandese. *See* **9512**.

12943. BARAKA, IMAMU AMIRI. Eulogies. New York: Marsilio, 1996. pp. x, 225.

12944. BARBOUR, JAMES; QUIRK, TOM (eds). Biographies of books: the compositional histories of notable American writings. *See* **7**.

12945. BARNES, KIM; BLEW, MARY CLEARMAN (eds). Circle of women: an anthology of contemporary Western women writers. New York; London: Penguin, 1994. pp. xiv, 400.

12946. BARNES, THOMAS G. 'Canada, true north': a 'here there' or a Boreal myth? ARCS (19:4) 1989, 369–79.

12947. BASKIN, JUDITH R. (ed.). Women of the word: Jewish women and Jewish writing. *See* **130**.

12948. BATES, MILTON J. The wars we took to Vietnam: cultural conflict and storytelling. Berkeley; London: California UP, 1996. pp. x, 328.

12949. BAUER, DALE M.; McKINSTRY, SUSAN JARET (eds). Feminism, Bakhtin, and the dialogic. *See* **33**.

12950. BEASECKER, ROBERT (ed.). Annual bibliography of Midwestern literature 1991; 1993; 1994. *See* **9514**.

12951. BEASECKER, ROBERT; PADY, DONALD (eds). Annual bibliography of Midwestern literature 1989; 1990. *See* **9515**.

12952. BEATTIE, L. ELISABETH (ed.). Conversations with Kentucky writers. Foreword by Wade Hall. Lexington: Kentucky UP, 1996. pp. xiv, 390. (Kentucky remembered.)

12953. BEIDLER, PHILIP D. Scriptures for a generation: what we were reading in the 60s. (Bibl. 1995, 12102.) Rev. by Gaile McGregor in AmS (37:1) 1996, 159–64.

12954. BELL, QUENTIN. Bloomsbury recalled. New York: Columbia UP, 1995. pp. 234. (Cf. bibl. 1995, 12104.) Rev. by Gerda Oldham in AR (54:3) 1996, 358–9; by Susan Davidson in BkW, 21 Apr. 1996, 4.

12955. BENNETT, JAMES R.; LOMBARI, VICTORIA-SUE. Persecuted writers in the twentieth century. BB (53:3) 1996, 235–64.

12956. BENNETT, JUDA. The passing figure: racial confusion in modern American literature. New York; Frankfurt; Bern; Paris: Lang, 1996. pp. viii, 142. (Modern American literature, 6.) (Cf. bibl. 1995, 16070.)

12957. BENSON, EUGENE; CONOLLY, L. W. (eds). Encyclopedia of post-colonial literatures in English. (Bibl. 1995, 12108.) Rev. by William Riggan in WLT (70:1) 1996, 245.

12958. BERGMAN, DAVID. Strategic camp: the art of gay rhetoric. *In* (pp. 92–109) **12**.

12959. —— (ed.). Camp grounds: style and homosexuality. *See* **12**.

12960. BERGONZI, BERNARD. Heroes' twilight: a study of the literature of the Great War. (Bibl. 1980, 10122.) Manchester: Carcanet, 1996. pp. 248. (Third ed.: first ed. 1965.)

12961. —— Wartime and aftermath: English literature and its background, 1939–60. (Bibl. 1995, 12109.) Rev. by Heather Bryant Jordan in Review (16) 1994, 121–34.

12962. BERRY, DIANA; MACKENZIE, CAMPBELL (comps). The legacy of war: poetry, prose, painting and physic. London: Royal Soc. of Medicine Press, 1995. pp. ix, 52.

12963. BEVAN, DAVID (ed.). Literature and sickness. *See* **9524**.

12964. BIRIOTTI, MAURICE; MILLER, NICOLA (eds). What is an author? (Bibl. 1994, 89.) Rev. by Simon Dentith in Literature and History (5:2) 1996, 73–4.

12965. BISHOP, RYAN. There's nothing natural about natural conversation: a look at dialogue in fiction and drama. *See* **2585**.

12966. BISHOP, T. G. Ceremonies of separation in Australian literature. *See* **9525**.

12967. BLACKSHIRE-BELAY, CAROL AISHA (ed.). Language and literature in the African-American imagination. *See* **55**.

12968. BLAESER, KIMBERLY M. The new 'frontier' of Native American literature: dis-arming history with tribal humor. Genre (25:4) 1992, 351–64.

12969. BLOOM, CLIVE (ed.). Creepers: British horror and fantasy in the twentieth century. (Bibl. 1995, 12114.) Rev. by Garyn G. Roberts in JPC (29:2) 1995, 256.

12970. BLY, CAROL. Kidding in the family room: literature and America's psychological class system. IowaR (22:3) 1992, 18–42.

12971. BOGUMIL, MARY L. Voice, dialogue, and community: in search of the 'Other' in African-American texts. AJSem (11:1/2) 1994, 181–96.

12972. BOOTH, ALLYSON. Postcards from the trenches: negotiating the space between Modernism and the First World War. New York; Oxford: OUP, 1996. pp. x, 186. (Cf. bibl. 1991, 10176.)

12973. BOWERBANK, SYLVIA; WAWIA, DOLORES NAWAGESIC. Literature and criticism by Native and Métis women in Canada. Feminist Studies (20:3) 1994, 565–81 (review-article).

12974. BOYERS, R., *et al.*   Literary creativity and the publishing industry: a round table. *See* **1046**.

12975. BRAENDLIN, BONNIE (ed.).   Cultural power/cultural literacy: selected papers from the Fourteenth Annual Florida State University Conference on Literature and Film. *See* **19**.

12976. BRANT, BETH.   Giveaway: Native lesbian writers. Signs (18:4) 1993, 944–7.

12977. BRAXTON, JOANNE M.; McLAUGHLIN, ANDRÉE NICOLA (eds). Wild women in the whirlwind: Afro-American culture and the contemporary literary renaissance. (Bibl. 1990, 8377.) Rev. by Gay Wilentz in NWSAJ (3:2) 1991, 316–20; by Dorothy L. Pennington in AmS (32:1) 1991, 119–20.

12978. BREDESON, CARMEN.   American writers of the 20th century. Springfield, NJ: Enslow, 1996. pp. 104. (Collective biographies.)

12979. BREITINGER, ECKHARD.   *Mongrelization* versus *the absolutism of the pure*: die Internationalisierung der kulturellen Szenerie und die nationalliterarische Fachkonzeption. ZAA (42:4) 1994, 295–305.

12980. BRITT, THERON.   Literature and politics: same difference? ColLit (23:2) 1996, 171–6 (review-article).

12981. BROOKS, PETER.   Body work: objects of desire in modern narrative. (Bibl. 1995, 12123.) Rev. by Garrett Stewart in MFS (40:2) 1994, 423–8; by Pamela K. Gilbert in Review (17) 1995, 77–80; by C. Jodey Castricano in CanL (150) 1996, 127–8; by Ned Lukacher in CL (48:1) 1996, 65–73; by Siv Jansson in YES (26) 1996, 308–9; by Catherine Nesci in CLS (33:4) 1996, 427–31.

12982. BROWN, ANNE E.; GOOZÉ, MARJANNE E. (eds).   International women's writing: new landscapes of identity. *See* **50**.

12983. BROWN, CONSTANCE A.   Severed ears: an image of the Vietnam War. *See* **2320**.

12984. BROWN, DOROTHY H.   Louisiana women writers: a bibliography. *In* (pp. 213–334) **65**.

12985. ——EWELL, BARBARA C. (eds).   Louisiana women writers: new essays and a comprehensive bibliography. *See* **65**.

12986. BRUCCOLI, MATTHEW J.; LAYMAN, RICHARD; ROOD, KAREN L. (eds).   Concise dictionary of British literary biography: vol. 7, Writers after World War II, 1945–1960. Detroit, MI; London: Gale Research, 1991. pp. xv, 420.

12987. BRUCHAC, JOSEPH (ed.).   Returning the gift: poetry and prose from the First North American Native Writers' Festival. Tucson: Arizona UP, 1994. pp. xxix, 369. (Sun tracks, 29.) Rev. by Howard Meredith in WLT (69:2) 1995, 410.

12988. BRYER, JACKSON R. (ed.).   Sixteen modern American authors: vol. 2, A survey of research and criticism since 1972. (Bibl. 1995, 12128.) Rev. by Barbara Heavilin in SteiQ (24:3/4) 1991, 115–18.

12989. BURNETT, PAULA.   New literatures in English: the Caribbean. YWES (75) 1994, 730–46.

12990. BURNS, WAYNE.   The vanishing individual: a voice from the dustheap of history; or, How to be happy without being hopeful. RecL (21) 1995, 1–207.

12991. BURSTEIN, JANET HANDLER.   Writing mothers, writing daughters: tracing the maternal in stories by American Jewish women. Urbana: Illinois UP, 1996. pp. 205.

12992. CAESAR, TERRY. Literature and criticism: in and out of parody in the 30s. Genre (23:1) 1990, 47–62.

12993. CAGIDEMETRIO, ALIDE. The vanishing of Indian princesses; or, The sentimental transformation of the Pocahontas myth. *See* **9537**.

12994. CAGLIERO, ROBERTO. The literature of exhaust. *In* (pp. 575–83) **117**.

12995. CAMERON, ELSPETH. Sweet sub/versions: the feminizing effect of postmodernism on Canadian literature. CanRCL (20:3/4) 1993, 479–89.

12996. CANCALON, ELAINE DAVIS; SPACAGNA, ANTOINE (eds). Intertextuality in literature and film: selected papers from the Thirteenth Annual Florida State University Conference on Literature and Film. *See* **51**.

12997. CANTOR, NORMAN F. Twentieth-century culture: Modernism to deconstruction. (Bibl. 1991, 10195.) Rev. by Carl Landauer in Salmagundi (90/91) 1991, 254–62.

12998. CARUTH, CATHY. Unclaimed experience: trauma, narrative, and history. Baltimore, MD; London: Johns Hopkins UP, 1996. pp. x, 154.

12999. CASTLE, TERRY. The apparitional lesbian: female homosexuality and modern culture. (Bibl. 1995, 12139.) Rev. by Sharon Marcus in TSWL (14:2) 1995, 392–5; by Sue-Ellen Case in AmQ (48:1) 1996, 161–6; by Janet Retseck in WS (25:4) 1996, 411–13; by Linda Lopez McAlister in Signs (21:3) 1996, 743–51.

13000. CAVELL, RICHARD. White technologies. *See* **9540**.

13001. CAWS, MARY ANN (ed.). City images: perspectives from literature, philosophy, and film. *See* **9541**.

13002. CECELSKI, DAVID. A world of fisher folks. NCLR (2:2) 1995, 183–98.

13003. CHAMPAGNE, ROSARIA. The politics of survivorship: incest, women's literature, and feminist theory. *See* **9815**.

13004. CHAPMAN, MICHAEL. Southern African literatures. *See* **9543**.

13005. CHAPPLE, RICHARD (ed.). Social and political change in literature and film: selected papers from the Sixteenth Annual Florida State University Conference on Literature and Film. *See* **113**.

13006. CHERNAIK, LAURA. 'Skulking amongst the gantries': gender difference, species difference and transnational accumulation. Letterature d'America (55) 1994, 113–29.

13007. CHEYETTE, BRYAN (ed.). Between 'race' and culture: representations of 'the Jew' in English and American literature. *See* **5**.

13008. CHILD, LEE HARRISON (ed.). Close to home: revelations and reminiscences by North Carolina authors. Winston-Salem, NC: Blair, 1996. pp. xv, 178.

13009. CHISHOLM, SCOTT. Centennial blues: reflections on creativity and literature in Utah. *See* **9547**.

13010. CHIU, CHRISTINA. Notable Asian Americans: literature and education. New York: Chelsea House, 1995. pp. 125. (Asian-American experience.)

13011. CIANCI, GIOVANNI. Epilogo con qualche riflessione. *See* **9549**.

13012. CLARK, SUZANNE. Sentimental modernism: women writers and the revolution of the word. (Bibl. 1995, 12145.) Rev. by Josephine Donovan in Signs (19:1) 1993, 232–5.

13013. CLAYTON, JAY. The pleasures of Babel: contemporary

American literature and theory. (Bibl. 1995, 12148.) Rev. by Alan Nadel in MFS (40:2) 1994, 371–3; by Russell Reising in AmS (36:1) 1995, 196–8; by Gregory Jay in StudN (27:2) 1995, 197–211; by Walter Kalaidjian in ConLit (37:3) 1996, 492–6.

13014. CLUNE, ANNE.   Mythologising Sweeney. IUR (26:1) 1996, 48–60. (Irish treatments of Suibhne Geilt.)

13015. COATES, K. S.; MORRISON, W. R.   Writing the North: a survey of contemporary Canadian writing on northern regions. ECanW (59) 1996, 5–25.

13016. COBLEY, EVELYN.   Representing war: form and ideology in First World War narratives. (Bibl. 1995, 12150.) Rev. by Bernd Hüppauf in Modernism/Modernity (3:1) 1996, 153–5; by Robert H. Macdonald in ESCan (22:1) 1996, 102–4.

13017. COETZEE, J. M.   Emerging from censorship. Salmagundi (100) 1993, 36–50.

13018. COLEMAN, DEIRDRE; OTTO, PETER (eds).   Imagining Romanticism: essays on English and Australian Romanticisms. *See* **47**.

13019. COLTELLI, LAURA.   Winged words: American-Indian writers speak. (Bibl. 1995, 12152.) Rev. by Sidonie Smith and Camilla Stivers in Signs (18:2) 1993, 392–425.

13020. CONNOLLY, DONNA.   Sisters in arms. WLA (4:2) 1992, 19–29.

13021. CORBALLIS, RICHARD.   Some echoes of Ireland in New Zealand literature, 1890–1990. *In* (pp. 45–58) **49**.

13022. CORN, ALFRED (ed.).   Incarnation: contemporary writers on the New Testament. New York: Viking, 1990. pp. xiv, 361. Rev. by Bernetta Quinn in AntR (85/86) 1991, 89–93.

13023. COSTA, RICHARD HAUER.   An appointment with Somerset Maugham and other literary encounters. (Bibl. 1994, 9707.) Rev. by Steven H. Gale in ELT (39:1) 1996, 134–7.

13024. CROWE, THOMAS RAIN.   Tracking the Asheville literary renaissance. NCLR (2:2) 1995, 153–61.

13025. CUDJOE, SELWYN R. (ed.).   Caribbean women writers: essays from the first International Conference. (Bibl. 1991, 11.) Rev. by Maria Helena Lima in Feminist Studies (21:1) 1995, 115–28.

13026. DAVEY, FRANK.   Reading Canadian literature. (Bibl. 1989, 7820.) Rev. by Neil Besner in ARCS (19:2) 1989, 230–2.

13027. DAVIES, CAROLE BOYCE (ed.).   Moving beyond the boundaries. London: Pluto, 1995. 2 vols. pp. xix, 252; ix, 333. (Black women's writing.) Rev. by Charlotte H. Bruner in WLT (70:2) 1996, 481–2.

13028. DAVIES, CAROLE BOYCE; FIDO, ELAINE SAVORY.   Introduction: women and literature in the Caribbean: an overview. *In* (pp. 1–24) **81**.

13029. —— —— (eds).   Out of the Kumbla: Caribbean women and literature. *See* **81**.

13030. DAVIS, THADIOUS M.   Women's art and authorship in the Southern region: connections. *In* (pp. 15–36) **32**.

13031. DAYMOND, M. J. (ed.).   South African feminisms: writing, theory, and criticism, 1990–1994. New York; London: Garland, 1996. pp. xlix, 343. (Garland reference library of the humanities, 1827.) (Gender and genre in literature, 5.)

13032. DEENA, SIODIAL.   Colonial and canonical marginalization and oppression on the basis of gender. CLAJ (40:1) 1996, 46–59.

13033. DE JONGH, JAMES.   Vicious Modernism: Black Harlem and the literary imagination. (Bibl. 1991, 10224.) Rev. by Linda Hamalian in AAR (26:4) 1992, 687–9.

13034. DE LAURETIS, TERESA.   Sexual indifference and lesbian representation. *In* (pp. 17–39) **84**.

13035. DERIE, KATE.   Mystery on the Internet. *See* **1148**.

13036. DERINGER, LUDWIG.   Das Bild des Pazifischen Nordwestens: von den Anfängen bis zur Gegenwart. Vergleichende Studien zur kanadischen und amerikanischen Literatur zwischen Regionalismus und Universalismus. *See* **8460**.

13037. DE RIZ, FRANCESCA BISUTTI; ZORZI, ROSELLA MAMOLI; COSLOVI, MARINA (eds).   Technology and the American imagination: an ongoing challenge. Atti del Dodecisimo Convegno Biennale, Università di Venezia, 28–30 ottobre 1993. *See* **117**.

13038. DETTMAR, KEVIN J. H. (ed.).   Re-reading the new: a backward glance at Modernism. (Bibl. 1992, 10455.) Rev. by Michael Patrick Gillespie in CLIO (25:1) 1995, 83–94.

13039. —— WATT, STEPHEN (eds).   Marketing Modernisms: self-promotion, canonization, rereading. *See* **67**.

13040. DiBATTISTA, MARIA.   Introduction. *In* (pp. 3–19) **41**.

13041. —— McDIARMID, LUCY (eds).   High and low moderns: literature and culture, 1889–1939. *See* **41**.

13042. DICKSON, JAY.   Surviving Victoria. *In* (pp. 23–46) **41**.

13043. DIETRICH, JULIA.   The old Left in history and literature. New York: Twayne; London: Prentice Hall, 1996. pp. xiii, 217. (Twayne's literature & society, 8.) Rev. by Harvey Teres in AL (68:4) 1996, 867–8.

13044. DIXON, KEITH.   Notes from the Underground: a discussion of cultural politics in contemporary Scotland. Études Écossaises (3) 1996, 117–28.

13045. —— Writers into battle: political dissent among contemporary Scottish writers. Études Écossaises (supp.) 1994, 161–71.

13046. DONNELL, ALISON; WELSH, SARAH LAWSON (eds).   The Routledge reader in Caribbean literature. London; New York: Routledge, 1996. pp. xix, 540.

13047. DONOGHUE, DENIS.   The old moderns: essays on literature and theory. (Bibl. 1994, 9727.) Rev. by Charles Cagle in MidQ (37:2) 1996, 228.

13048. DOTTERER, RONALD; BOWERS, SUSAN (eds).   Politics, gender, and the arts: women, the arts, and society. *See* **87**.

13049. DOWNING, DAVID B.; BAZARGAN, SUSAN (eds).   Image and ideology in modern/postmodern discourse. *See* **44**.

13050. DOYLE, JAMES.   Red letters: notes toward a literary history of Canadian Communism. ECanW (55) 1995, 22–39.

13051. DRIVER, DOROTHY.   Annual bibliography of Commonwealth literature 1994; 1995: South Africa. JCL (30:3) 1995, 151–217; (31:3) 1996, 123–60.

13052. —— Modern South African literature in English: a reader's guide to some recent critical and bibliographic resources. WLT (70:1) 1996, 99–106.

13053. DUCKWORTH, MARILYN (ed.).   Cherries on a plate: New Zealand writers talk about their sisters. Auckland: Random House, 1996. pp. vii, 270.

13054. DUDEK, LOUIS.   In defence of art: critical essays and reviews. (Bibl. 1989, 7813.) Rev. by Philip Kokotailo in ARCS (19:4) 1989, 470–2.

13055. DUNNE, ROBERT.   Not for White men only: the methodology behind the *Dictionary of Midwestern Literature. See* **9575**.

13056. DURIX, CAROLE.   New literatures in English: New Zealand and the South Pacific. YWES (75) 1994, 751–62.

13057. ECHERUO, MICHAEL J. C.   Modernism, Blackface, and the postcolonial condition. RAL (27:1) 1996, 172–87 (review-article).

13058. ELDRIDGE, C. C.   The imperial experience: from Carlyle to Forster. *See* **9579**.

13059. ELLIOTT, BRIDGET; WALLACE, JO-ANN.   Women artists and writers: modernist (im)positionings. London; New York: Routledge, 1994. pp. xiv, 204. Rev. by Sherrill Grace in AL (68:1) 1996, 274–5.

13060. ENGLISH, JAMES F.   Comic transactions: literature, humor, and the politics of community in 20th-century Britain. (Bibl. 1994, 9733.) Rev. by Daniel Schwarz in MFS (42:1) 1996, 185–9.

13061. EPSTEIN, JOSEPH.   Partial payments: essays on writers and their lives. *See* **9581**.

13062. ERZGRÄBER, WILLI.   Von Thomas Hardy bis Ted Hughes: Studien zur modernen englischen und anglo-irischen Literatur. Freiburg im Breisgau: Rombach, 1995. pp. 486. (Rombach Wissenschaft: Reihe Litterae, 27.) Rev. by Ansgar Nünning in GRM (45:4) 1995, 479–82; by Rüdiger Imhof in ZAA (44:2) 1996, 182–4.

13063. ESTES-HICKS, ONITA.   The way we were: precious memories of the Black segregated South. AAR (27:1) 1993, 9–18.

13064. ETULAIN, RICHARD W.   Re-imagining the modern American West: a century of fiction, history, and art. Tucson: Arizona UP, 1996. pp. xxviii, 241. (The modern American West.) Rev. by Benjamin Y. Dixon in JCG (16:1) 1996, 126–9.

13065. EVANS, GARETH.   British working-class and Socialist writing: a bibliography of critical material. RT (48) 1996, 17–20.

13066. EVANS, PATRICK D.   The future of the past: making history out of New Zealand literature. ZAA (42:2) 1994, 122–30.

13067. FADERMAN, LILLIAN.   What is lesbian literature? Forming a historical canon. *In* (pp. 49–59) **92**.

13068. FARWELL, MARILYN R.   The lesbian narrative: 'the pursuit of the inedible by the unspeakable'. *In* (pp. 156–80) **92**.

13069. FIFFER, SHARON SLOAN; FIFFER, STEVE (eds).   Family: American writers remember their own. Afterword by Jane Smiley. New York: Pantheon, 1996. pp. xv, 253.

13070. FISHLIN, DANIEL.   Nuclear pathologies; or, No aporias, not now. CanRCL (23:4) 1996, 1226–32.

13071. FITZ, EARL E.   Whither inter-American literature? CanRCL (18:1) 1991, 1–13.

13072. FLOWERS, SANDRA HOLLIN.   African American nationalist literature of the 1960s: pens of fire. New York; London: Garland, 1996. pp. xxix, 183. (Garland studies in American popular history and culture.)

13073. FLYNN, JOYCE.   From colony to canon: mapping modern Irish literature. EI (31:3/4) 1996, 255–60 (review-article).

13074. FOLKS, JEFFREY J.   Southern writers and the machine: Faulkner to Percy. (Bibl. 1994, 9740.) Rev. by Jens P. Becker in LWU (29:2) 1996, 131–2.

13075. FOSTER, THOMAS C.; SIEGEL, CAROL; BERRY, ELLEN E. (eds). Bodies of writing, bodies in performance. *See* **9**.

13076. FRANKLIN, WAYNE; STEINER, MICHAEL (eds). Mapping American culture. *See* **66**.

13077. FREGA, DONNALEE. Questioning history and revision: contemporary Southern literature and the canon. SoQ (34:2) 1996, 9–21.

13078. FRIEL, RAYMOND. Furth of Scotia. Southfields 1996, xi–xiv.

13079. FUROMOTO, TOSHI, *et al.* (eds). International aspects of Irish literature. *See* **49**.

13080. FUSSELL, PAUL. Wartime: understanding and behavior in the Second World War. (Bibl. 1990, 8430.) Rev. by John P. Sisk in Salmagundi (90/91) 1991, 242–53.

13081. GARDAPHÉ, FRED L. Italian signs, American streets: the evolution of Italian American narrative. Durham, NC; London: Duke UP, 1996. pp. 241. (New Americanists.) (Cf. bibl. 1994, 10436.)

13082. GENET, JACQUELINE. Introduction. *In* (pp. 9–17) **106**.

13083. —— (ed.). Rural Ireland, real Ireland? *See* **106**.

13084. —— HELLEGOUARC'H, WYNNE (eds). Irish writers and their creative process. *See* **52**.

13085. GERVAIS, DAVID. Literary Englands: versions of 'Englishness' in modern writing. (Bibl. 1995, 12191.) Rev. by Pamela K. Gilbert in Review (17) 1995, 74–5; by Günther Blaicher in Ang (114:1) 1996, 114–19.

13086. GILBERT, PAUL. The idea of a national literature. *In* (pp. 198–217) **63**.

13087. GILBERT, SANDRA M.; GUBAR, SUSAN. No man's land: the place of the woman writer in the twentieth century: vol. 3, Letters from the front. New Haven, CT; London: Yale UP, 1994. pp. 496. Rev. by Ann Ardis in TSWL (14:2) 1995, 363–9; by Sandra P. Cookson in WLT (69:3) 1995, 590.

13088. GINSBERG, ELAINE K. (ed.). Passing and the fictions of identity. *See* **82**.

13089. GISH, ROBERT FRANKLIN. Beyond bounds: cross-cultural essays on Anglo, American Indian, and Chicano literature. Albuquerque: New Mexico UP, 1996. pp. xiv, 170.

13090. GODINA, HERIBERTO. The canonical debate – implementing multicultural literature and perspectives. JAAL (39:7) 1996, 544–9.

13091. GOETSCH, PAUL (ed.). Mündliches Wissen in neuzeitlicher Literatur. *See* **73**.

13092. GOMBAR, CHRISTINA. Great women writers, 1900–1950. New York: Facts on File, 1996. pp. viii, 168. (American profiles.)

13093. GORDON-WISE, BARBARA ANN. The reclamation of a queen: Guinevere in modern fantasy. (Bibl. 1991, 10251.) Rev. by Charlotte Wulf in Quondam et Futurus (1:4) 1991, 99–102.

13094. GOSSELIN, ADRIENNE JOHNSON. Beyond the Harlem renaissance: the case of the Black Modernist writers. MLS (26:4) 1996, 37–45.

13095. GRABES, HERBERT. Writing against time: the paradox of temporality in Modernist and postmodern aesthetics. *See* **9600**.

13096. GRAHAM, BRIAN. Panzaic shoes? Notes for Wayne Burns. RecL (22) 1995, 22–34.

13097. GREETHAM, D. C. Getting personal/going public. *See* **363**.

13098. GRIFFIN, FARAH JASMINE. 'Who set you flowin'?': the African-American migration narrative. (Bibl. 1995, 12206.) Rev. by Elizabeth B. House in AL (68:1) 1996, 271–2; by Sam Worley in SoQ (34:2) 1996, 142–3.

13099. GRIFFIN, GABRIELE. Heavenly love? Lesbian images in twentieth-century women's writing. (Bibl. 1993, 9830.) Rev. by Loralee MacPike in NWSAJ (6:3) 1994, 484–8; by Linda Lopez McAlister in Signs (21:3) 1996, 743–51.

13100. —— (ed.).   Outwrite: lesbianism and popular culture. (Bibl. 1994, 9760.) Rev. by Loralee MacPike in NWSAJ (6:3) 1994, 484–8; by Linda Lopez McAlister in Signs (21:3) 1996, 743–51.

13101. GRUESSER, JOHN CULLEN.   White on Black: contemporary literature about Africa. (Bibl. 1995, 12207.) Rev. by Oyekan Owomoyela in AAR (29:1) 1995, 137–40.

13102. GUINNESS, LOUISE (ed.).   Fathers: an anthology. London: Chatto & Windus, 1996. pp. xii, 354. Rev. by Claire Harman in TLS, 22 Nov. 1996, 36.

13103. GUNNING, SANDRA.   Race, rape, and lynching: the red record of American literature, 1890–1912. *See* **9601**.

13104. GUY, TALMADGE C.   Adult education and propaganda: Alain Locke's views on culture, propaganda, and race progress. LHR (13:2) 1995, 68–76.

13105. HACKER, JAMI HUNTSINGER.   Traditional voices speak: story-tellers in contemporary Native-American texts. WebS (12:3) 1995, 131–8.

13106. HAGEMANN, SUSANNE.   A feminist interpretation of Scottish identity. Études Écossaises (supp.) 1994, 79–91.

13107. —— Die schottische Renaissance: Literatur und Nation im 20. Jahrhundert. (Bibl. 1994, 9765.) Rev. by Ian Campbell in SLJ (supp. 44) 1996, 24–5.

13108. HAGGERTY, GEORGE E.; ZIMMERMAN, BONNIE (eds). Professions of desire: lesbian and gay studies in literature. *See* **92**.

13109. HALKYARD, STELLA K.; MCCULLY, C. B.   'Thoughts of inventive brains and the rich effusions of deep hearts': some of the twentieth-century literary archives of the John Rylands University Library of Manchester. *See* **486**.

13110. HAMALIAN, LEO.   D. H. Lawrence and nine women writers. Madison, NJ: Fairleigh Dickinson UP; London; Toronto: Assoc. UPs, 1996. pp. 182.

13111. HARNEY, STEFANO.   Nationalism and identity: culture and the imagination in a Caribbean diaspora. Kingston: Univ. of West Indies; London; Atlantic Highlands, NJ: Zed, 1996. pp. 216. (Cf. bibl. 1993, 9836.)

13112. HARPER, PHILLIP BRIAN.   Framing the margins: the social logic of postmodern culture. (Bibl. 1995, 12212.) Rev. by Philip Heldrich in Style (30:2) 1996, 354–7.

13113. HARRIS, JOSEPH.   Reading the right thing. Reader (27) 1992, 29–47.

13114. HARRIS, TRUDIER.   Greeting the new century with a different kind of magic: an introduction to emerging women writers. Callaloo (19:2) 1996, 232–8.

13115. HARROW, KENNETH W.   Thresholds of change in African literature: the emergence of a tradition. (Bibl. 1994, 9772.) Rev. by Chantal Zabus in WLT (69:1) 1995, 203.

13116. HARTMAN, GEOFFREY.   Public memory and its discontents. Raritan (13:4) 1994, 24–40.

13117. HASHMI, ALAMGIR.   Annual bibliography of Commonwealth literature 1994; 1995: Pakistan. JCL (30:3) 1995, 133–49; (31:3) 1996, 109–21.

13118. HASSAN, IHAB. In the mirror of the sun: reflections on Japanese and American literature, Bashō to Cage. *See* **9606**.

13119. —— Rumors of change: essays of five decades. Tuscaloosa; London: Alabama UP, 1995. pp. xix, 261. Rev. by Bernard F. Dick in WLT (70:3) 1996, 697–8.

13120. HEDGES, ELAINE; FISHKIN, SHELLEY FISHER (eds). Listening to silences: new essays in feminist criticism. *See* **59**.

13121. HENNESSEY, WILLIAM J. The automobile and the American imagination. *In* (pp. 605–17) **117**.

13122. HERMAN, LUC. Concepts of realism. Columbia, SC: Camden House, 1996. pp. 246. (Literary criticism in perspective.)

13123. HEWITT, ANDREW. Political inversions: homosexuality, fascism, & the Modernist imaginary. Stanford, CA: Stanford UP, 1996. pp. 333.

13124. HEYWOOD, LESLIE. Dedication to hunger: the anorexic aesthetic in modern culture. Berkeley; London: California UP, 1996. pp. xvi, 243. (Cf. bibl. 1993, 12107.)

13125. HILLIS, DORIS. Plainspeaking: interviews with Saskatchewan writers. Regina, Sask.: Coteau, 1988. pp. ii, 304. Rev. by Carol L. Beran in ARCS (19:2) 1989, 232–4.

13126. HOCHBRUCK, W. 'Native American literature': developments, contexts and problems. *See* **8481**.

13127. HOCHBRUCK, WOLFGANG. *I have spoken*: die Darstellung und ideologische Funktion indianischer Mündlichkeit in der nordamerikanischen Literatur. Tübingen: Narr, 1991. pp. x, 293. (ScriptOralia, 32.) Rev. by Brigitte Georgi-Findlay in Amst (41:2) 1996, 307–9.

13128. HOGAN, PATRICK COLM. Colonialism and the problem of identity in Irish literature. ColLit (23:3) 1996, 163–70 (review-article).

13129. HOGUE, W. LAWRENCE. Race, modernity, postmodernity: a look at the history and the literatures of people of color since the 1960s. Albany: New York State UP, 1996. pp. xii, 209.

13130. HONG, MARIA (ed.). Growing up Asian American: an anthology. Afterword by Stephen H. Sumida. New York: Morrow, 1993. pp. 416. Rev. by Lisa See in BkW, 30 Jan. 1994, 4.

13131. HORGAN, PAUL. Tracings: a book of partial portraits. (Bibl. 1993, 9853.) Rev. by Jonathan Yardley in BkW, 19 Sept. 1996, 3.

13132. HORSLEY, LEE. Fictions of power in English literature, 1900–1950. London; New York: Longman, 1995. pp. x, 300. (Studies in twentieth-century literature.)

13133. HOWARD, BEN. The pressed melodeon: essays on modern Irish writing. Brownsville, OR: Story Line Press, 1996. pp. xiii, 178.

13134. HURLEY, MICHAEL. A guide to gay and lesbian writing in Australia. St Leonards, N.S.W.: Allen & Unwin, 1996. pp. xix, 298.

13135. HUTCHINSON, GEORGE. Mediating 'race' and 'nation': the cultural politics of the *Messenger*. *See* **1290**.

13136. IKIN, VAN; DOLIN, KIERAN. Annual bibliography of Commonwealth literature 1994; 1995: Australia (including Papua New Guinea). JCL (30:3) 1995, 3–34; (31:3) 1996, 3–43.

13137. IMBERT, PATRICK. L'origine et la fin. CanRCL (18:1) 1991, 15–27.

13138. INGE, TONETTE BOND (ed.). Southern women writers: the new generation. (Bibl. 1993, 9857.) Rev. by Rebecca Mark in Signs (18:2) 1993, 443–7.

13139. JACQUES, GEOFFREY.   Free within ourselves: the Harlem renaissance. New York: Watts, 1996. pp. 128. (African-American experience.)

13140. JADWIN, LISA.   Critiquing the new canon. ColLit (23:3) 1996, 171–7 (review-article).

13141. JARVIE, BRENDA (comp.).   An Akros thirty, 1965–95: an annotated bibliography of thirty Akros publications selected to mark thirty years of Scottish publishing. See **949**.

13142. JASON, PHILIP K.   'The noise is always in my head': auditory images in the literature of the Vietnam War. MidQ (37:3) 1996, 243–55.

13143. JAY, KARLA.   Lesbian Modernism: (trans)forming the (c)anon. In (pp. 72–83) **92**.

13144. JENSEN, JOAN M.   One foot on the Rockies: women and creativity in the modern American West. Albuquerque: New Mexico UP, 1995. pp. ix, 178. (Calvin P. Horn lectures in Western history and culture.) Rev. by Allison B. Wallace in RMRLL (50:1) 1996, 76–8.

13145. JENSEN, KAI.   Whole men: the masculine tradition in New Zealand literature. Auckland: Auckland UP, 1996. pp. vi, 202. (Cf. bibl. 1995, 12227.) Rev. by Heather Murray in NZList, 4 May 1996, 44–5; by Lauris Edmond in New Zealand Books (6:2) 1996, 13; by Michael Morrissey in Quote Unquote (36) 1996, 31–2.

13146. JOHNSON, LEMUEL A.   A-beng: (re)calling the body in(to) question. In (pp. 111–42) **81**.

13147. —— Shakespearean imports: whatever happened to Caliban's mother? Or, The problem with Othello's. See **6361**.

13148. JORDAN, DAVID M.   New World regionalism: literature in the Americas. (Bibl. 1995, 12233.) Rev. by Amaryll Chanady in CanL (150) 1996, 128–30.

13149. KAPLAN, ALICE.   The Céline effect: a 1992 survey of contemporary American writers. Modernism/Modernity (3:1) 1996, 117–36.

13150. KENNEDY, J. GERALD.   Imagining Paris: exile, writing, and American identity. (Bibl. 1995, 12235.) Rev. by James R. Mellow in HemR (13:1) 1993, 95–7; by Michael J. Hoffman in MFS (40:2) 1994, 360–2.

13151. KENNER, HUGH (introd.).   Axel's castle: a study of the imaginative literature of 1870–1930. See **9617**.

13152. KIBERD, DECLAN.   Inventing Ireland. (Bibl. 1995, 12237.) Cambridge, MA: Harvard UP, 1996. Rev. by W. J. Mc Cormack in Yeats Annual (12) 1996, 365–76; by Colm Toibin in LRB (18:8) 1996, 14–16; by Bernard O'Donoghue in TLS, 31 May 1996, 32; by Joyce Flynn in EI (31:3/4) 1996, 255–60; by Michael Stephens in BkW, 17 Mar. 1996, 8.

13153. KIERNAN, BRIAN.   New literatures in English: Australia. See **9619**.

13154. KIRKLAND, RICHARD.   Literature and culture in Northern Ireland since 1965: moments of danger. Harlow; New York: Longman, 1996. pp. viii, 186. (Studies in twentieth-century literature.) (Cf. bibl. 1995, 12240.)

13155. KLOOSS, WOLFGANG.   Geschichte und Mythos in der Literatur Kanadas: die englischsprachige Métis- und Riel-Rezeption. See **9622**.

13156. KNIGHT, CHRISTOPHER J.   The patient particulars: American

Modernism and the technique of originality. (Bibl. 1995, 12241.)
Rev. by Anita Helle in AL (68:2) 1996, 471–2.

13157. KNIPPLING, ALPANA SHARMA (ed.). New immigrant literatures
in the United States: a sourcebook to our multicultural literary heritage.
Westport, CT; London: Greenwood Press, 1996. pp. xix, 386.

13158. KOH, TAI ANN. Annual bibliography of Commonwealth
literature 1990–1993: Malaysia and Singapore. JCL (30:3) 1995, 71–107.

13159. KORTE, BARBARA. Sehweisen literarischer Landschaft – ein
Literaturbericht. *See* **8655**.

13160. KOSHY, SUSAN. The fiction of Asian-American literature.
YJC (9:2) 1996, 315–46.

13161. KRÖLLER, EVA-MARIE. New literatures in English: Canada.
YWES (75) 1994, 722–30.

13162. KRUGER, STEVEN F. AIDS narratives: gender and sexuality,
fiction and science. New York; London: Garland, 1996. pp. xvi, 404.
(Garland reference library of the humanities, 1628.) (Gender and genre
in literature, 7.)

13163. KRUPAT, ARNOLD. Ethnocriticism: ethnography, history,
literature. (Bibl. 1995, 12244.) Rev. by Andrew J. Scheiber in AmLH
(8:2) 1996, 372–5.

13164. —— Scholarship and Native-American studies: a response to
Daniel Littlefield, Jr. AmS (34:2) 1993, 81–100.

13165. KUNENE, MAZISI. Some aspects of South African literature.
WLT (70:1) 1996, 13–16.

13166. LACEY, R. KEVIN; POOLE, FRANCIS (eds). Mirrors on the
Maghrib: critical reflections on Paul and Jane Bowles and other
American writers in Morocco. Delmar, NY: Caravan, 1996. pp. 225.

13167. LALLI, BIANCAMARIA TEDESCHINI. Revolution in the back-
yard. Letterature d'America (41/42) 1990, 61–105. (Americans in
Mexico.)

13168. LANGRAN, PHILIP. New literatures in English: India.
YWES (75) 1994, 746–51.

13169. LEE, A. ROBERT. Introduction. *In* (pp. 1–9) **4**.

13170. —— (ed.). The Beat Generation writers. *See* **4**.

13171. LEGLER, GRETCHEN. (Re)eroticizing human relationships
with the natural world: Native-American and Anglo women writers'
(re)visions. SHum (19:2) 1992, 183–94.

13172. LEVER, RICHARD; WIELAND, JAMES; FINDLAY, SCOTT. Post-
colonial literatures in English: Australia, 1970–1992. New York:
G. K. Hall; London: Prentice Hall, 1996. pp. xxx, 361. (Reference pubs
in literature.)

13173. LHAMON, W. T., JR. Deliberate speed: the origins of a cultural
style in the American 1950s. (Bibl. 1991, 10301.) Rev, by Barry Shank in
AmS (34:1) 1993, 178–9.

13174. LI, XILAO. Walt Whitman and Asian-American writers.
See **12704**.

13175. LIM, SHIRLEY GEOK-LIN. Writing S.E./Asia in English:
against the grain, focus on Asian English-language literature. (Bibl. 1995,
12259.) Rev. by Brinda Bose in WLT (70:4) 1996, 1030.

13176. LIMA, MARIA HELENA. 'Beyond Miranda's meanings':
contemporary critical perspectives on Caribbean women's literatures.
Feminist Studies (21:1) 1995, 115–28 (review-article).

13177. LINCOLN, KENNETH. Indi'n humor: bicultural play in Native

America. (Bibl. 1995, 12260.) Rev. by Joseph Boskin in AmS (35:2) 1994, 130–1.

13178. LINDBERG-SEYERSTED, BRITA.   Black and female: essays on writings by Black women in the diaspora. (Bibl. 1995, 12261.) Rev. by Orm Øverland in EngS (77:3) 1996, 298–300; by Jana Gohrisch in ZAA (44:2) 1996, 192–4; by Justine Tally in AAA (21:2) 1996, 311–14.

13179. LINDFORS, BERNTH.   Comparative approaches to African literatures. (Bibl. 1995, 12263.) Rev. by Joseph John in WLT (69:4) 1995, 849–50.

13180. —— Future returns. *In* (pp. 153–62) **102**.

13181. —— Loaded vehicles: studies in African literary media. *See* **1067**.

13182. LIONNET, FRANÇOISE.   Postcolonial representations: women, literature, identity. (Bibl. 1995, 12266.) Rev. by Debjani Banerjee in RMRLL (50:1) 1996, 55–61; by Chantal Zabus in WLT (70:2) 1996, 480–1; by Michael Strysick in SAtlR (61:3) 1996, 166–9.

13183. LIPSITZ, GEORGE.   Time passages: collective memory and American popular culture. (Bibl. 1995, 12267.) Rev. by Brian Rose in JDTC (6:2) 1992, 157–9; by William Graebner in AmS (33:2) 1992, 121–4.

13184. LITTLEFIELD, DANIEL F., JR; PARINS, JAMES W. (eds).   Native American writing in the Southeast: an anthology, 1875–1935. *See* **9637**.

13185. LLOYD, DAVID.   Adulteration and the nation: monologic nationalism and the colonial hybrid. *In* (pp. 53–92) **80**.

13186. —— Anomalous states: Irish writing and the post-colonial moment. (Bibl. 1994, 9816.) Rev. by C. L. Innes in MFS (40:1) 1994, 182–3; by Heather Zwicker in CanRCL (23:2) 1996, 609–11; by Manfred Mackenzie in CL (48:1) 1996, 90–2.

13187. LOEFFELHOLZ, MARY.   Experimental lives: women and literature, 1900–1945. (Bibl. 1994, 9818.) Rev. by Nancy A. Walker in AmS (34:1) 1993, 171.

13188. LOMBARDO, AGOSTINO (ed.).   Le orme di Prospero: le nuove letterature di lingua inglese: Africa, Caraibi, Canada. Rome: La Nuova Italia Scientifica, 1995. pp. 290. (Studi superiori NIS, 244: Storia delle letterature di lingua inglese.) Rev. by Marina De Chiara in Annali anglistica (38:3) 1995, 146–8.

13189. LONG, SCOTT.   The loneliness of camp. *In* (pp. 78–91) **12**.

13190. LONGLEY, EDNA.   The living stream: literature & revisionism in Ireland. (Bibl. 1995, 12268.) Rev. by Bernard O'Donoghue in Yeats Annual (12) 1996, 328–31.

13191. LOVELOCK, YANN.   Of demotic and synthetic: some thoughts on recent literary awards and recommendations. Southfields 1996, 157–60.

13192. LOWE, LISA.   Immigrant acts: on Asian-American cultural politics. Durham, NC; London: Duke UP, 1996. pp. xii, 252.

13193. LUTZ, HARTMUT.   'Is the canon colorblind?': on the status of authors of color in Canadian literature in English. ZAA (44:1) 1996, 51–81.

13194. LUTZ, TOM.   'Sweat or die': the hedonization of the work ethic in the 1920s. AmLH (8:2) 1996, 259–83.

13195. MCCARTHY, KEVIN M.   Twentieth-century Florida authors. Lewiston, NY; Lampeter: Mellen Press, 1996. pp. iii, 248. (Studies in American literature, 17.)

13196. McConchie, R. W.　　Some Australian literary illustrators. *See* **218**.

13197. McDonogh, Gary W. (ed.).　　The *Florida Negro*: a Federal Writers' Project legacy. Jackson; London: Mississippi UP, 1993. pp. xxxv, 177. Rev. by Robert L. Hall in FHQ (73:3) 1995, 371–2.

13198. McDowell, Deborah E.　　'The changing same': Black women's literature, criticism, and theory. (Bibl. 1995, 12270.) Rev. by Madhu Dubey in MFS (42:4) 1996, 833–6; by Kimberly W. Benston in TSWL (15:2) 1996, 349–52; by Judy Massey Dozier in RMRLL (50:2) 1996, 197–8.

13199. Mackey, Nathaniel.　　Discrepant engagement: dissonance, cross-culturality, and experimental writing. (Bibl. 1995, 12276.) Rev. by Heather Hathaway in AAR (30:1) 1996, 133–5.

13200. McMullen, Kim.　　Decolonizing Rosaleen: some feminist, nationalist, and postcolonialist discourses in Irish studies. JMMLA (29:1) 1996, 32–45.

13201. McNeil, Helen.　　The archaeology of gender in the Beat Movement. *In* (pp. 178–99) **4**.

13202. Maffi, Mario.　　Scritture dei *Latinos* e degli *Asian Americans*. Àcoma (1) 1994, 62–7.

13203. Mall, G. J. Zambardi.　　Literature of the absurd. *In* (pp. 397–411) **125**.

13204. Mallinson, Ann.　　Recollections of five festivals: Writers and Readers Week 1984–1994. Wellington: Brasell; Canterbury, New Zealand: Lincoln UP, 1996. pp. ix, 70.

13205. Manning, Carol S.　　Introduction: on defining themes and (mis)placing women writers. *In* (pp. 1–12) **32**.

13206. —— The real beginning of the Southern renaissance. *In* (pp. 37–56) **32**.

13207. —— (ed.).　　The female tradition in Southern literature. *See* **32**.

13208. Martin, Andrew.　　Receptions of war: Vietnam in American culture. Norman; London: Oklahoma UP, 1993. pp. xxiii, 192. (Oklahoma project for discourse and theory.) Rev. by Matthew C. Stewart in WLA (6:2) 1994, 83–6.

13209. Marx, Edward.　　Forgotten jungle songs: primitivist strategies of the Harlem renaissance. LHR (14:1/2) 1996, 79–93.

13210. Massa, Ann; Stead, Alistair (eds).　　Forked tongues? Comparing twentieth-century British and American literature. *See* **34**.

13211. Massoud, Mary (ed.).　　Literary inter-relations: Ireland, Egypt, and the Far East. *See* **60**.

13212. Mellown, Elgin W.　　An annotated checklist of contributions by Bloomsbury and other British avant-garde writers (and of articles relating to them) in *Vogue* magazine during the editorship of Dorothy Todd, 1923–1927. *See* **1321**.

13213. Metcalf, John.　　Freedom from culture: selected essays 1982–92. Toronto: ECW Press, 1994. pp. 264. Rev. by Catherine Hunter in CanL (149) 1996, 145–6.

13214. Mettke, Edith (ed.).　　Tensions between North and South: studies in modern Commonwealth literature and culture: proceedings of the 8th Commonwealth Literature Conference, Berlin, 14–18 June 1985. (Bibl. 1994, 9837.) Rev. by Erhard Reckwitz in ZAA (42:1) 1994, 84–6.

13215.   MEYER, WILLIAM E. H., JR.   From *The Sun Also Rises* to *High Noon*: the hypervisual great awakening in American literature and film. *See* **9654**.

13216.   —— From *The Sun Also Rises* to *High Noon*: the hypervisual great awakening in American literature and film. *See* **9655**.

13217.   —— The hypervisual standard of American popular culture. *See* **8502**.

13218.   MEYN, ROLF; SCHEIDING, OLIVER.   Treason, treachery, betrayal: politics, ideology, and the process of disillusionment in the literature of the Spanish Civil War. ZAA (42:1) 1994, 27–37.

13219.   MICHAELS, WALTER BENN.   Our America: nativism, modernism, and pluralism. Durham, NC; London: Duke UP, 1995. pp. 186. (Post-contemporary interventions.) Rev. by Marjorie Perloff, Charles Altieri, and Robert von Hallberg, and with a response by Walter Benn Michaels in Modernism/Modernity (3:3) 1996, 99–126; by Robert Merrill in RMRLL (50:2) 1996, 199–200; by Loren Glass in MLS (26:2/3) 1996, 1–17.

13220.   MIHAILOVICH-DICKMAN, VERA.   'Return' in post-colonial writing: a cultural labyrinth. *See* **102**.

13221.   MOLINO, MICHAEL R.   Charting an uncertain flight path: Irish writers and the question of nation, identity, and literature. Comparatist (20) 1996, 41–9.

13222.   MONTEFIORE, JANET.   Men and women writers of the 1930s: the dangerous flood of history. London; New York: Routledge, 1996. pp. xiii, 263.

13223.   MOORE, OPAL.   The problem of (Black) art. *In* (pp. 177–93) **8**.

13224.   MOORE, OPAL J.   Enter, the tribe of woman. Callaloo (19:2) 1996, 340–7.

13225.   MOORE-GILBERT, BART.   Introduction: writing India, re-orienting colonial discourse analysis. *In* (pp. 1–29) **132**.

13226.   —— (ed.).   Writing India 1757–1990: the literature of British India. *See* **132**.

13227.   MORGAN, NINA Y.   The Chinatown aesthetic and the architecture of radical identity. *In* (pp. 217–37) **108**.

13228.   MORRISSON, MARK.   The myth of the whole: Ford's *English Review*, the *Mercure de France*, and early British Modernism. *See* **1325**.

13229.   MORSE, DONALD E.; BERTHA, CSILLA; PÁLFFY, ISTVÁN (eds). A small nation's contribution to the world: essays on Anglo-Irish literature and language. *See* **112**.

13230.   MOTE, DAVE (ed.).   Contemporary popular writers. Detroit, MI: St James Press, 1996. pp. xix, 528.

13231.   MOTT, CHRISTOPHER M.   The art of self-promotion; or, Which self to sell? The proliferation and disintegration of the Harlem renaissance. *In* (pp. 253–74) **67**.

13232.   MOTTE, WARREN.   Playtexts: ludics in contemporary literature. (Bibl. 1995, 12301.) Rev. by Jerome Klinkowitz in MFS (42:4) 1996, 940–2; by Ian Pindar in TLS, 26 July 1996, 25; by Michael Harper in WLT (70:2) 1996, 481; by Steven Scott in CanRCL (23:2) 1996, 374–92.

13233.   MPHANDE, LUPENGA.   Dr Hastings Kamuzu Banda and the Malawi Writers Group: the (un)making of a cultural tradition. RAL (27:1) 1996, 80–101.

13234.   MULDER, WILLIAM.   'Essential gestures': craft and calling in contemporary Mormon letters. WebS (10:3) 1993, 7–25.

13235. Mullen, Bill. Popular fronts: *Negro Story* magazine and the African-American literary response to World War II. *See* **1326**.

13236. Nadel, Alan. Containment culture: American narrative, postmodernism, and the atomic age. Durham, NC; London: Duke UP, 1995. pp. xii, 332. (New Americanists.) Rev. by Jerome Klinkowitz in AL (68:4) 1996, 875–6; by Ben Andrews in JAStud (30:3) 1996, 494–5; by Stephen J. Whitfield in AmS (36:2) 1996, 207–8.

13237. Nair, Supriya. Expressive countercultures and postmodern utopia: a Caribbean context. RAL (27:4) 1996, 71–87.

13238. Narayan, Shyamala A. Annual bibliography of Commonwealth literature 1994; 1995: India. JCL (30:3) 1995, 35–70; (31:3) 1996, 45–85.

13239. Natarajan, Nalini (ed.). Handbook of twentieth-century literatures of India. Westport, CT; London: Greenwood Press, 1996. pp. viii, 440.

13240. Natoli, Joseph; Hutcheon, Linda (eds). A postmodern reader. (Bibl. 1994, 9850.) Rev. by Randall Stevenson in ESCan (22:1) 1996, 119–22.

13241. Ndebele, Njabulo S. South African literature and culture: rediscovery of the ordinary. (Bibl. 1995, 12305.) Rev. by Jan Gorak in DQ (31:1) 1996, 19–25.

13242. Nealon, Jeffrey T. Double reading: postmodernism after deconstruction. (Bibl. 1993, 9926.) Rev. by Michael Zeitlin in CanL (150) 1996, 201–2; by Oliver Scheiding in ZAA (44:1) 1996, 91–3.

13243. Nelson, Emmanuel S. (ed.). AIDS: the literary response. *See* **2**.

13244. Nethersole, Reingard. Im Schatten des Adamastor: Kulturkonflikt am Kap. arcadia (31:1/2) 1996, 179–96.

13245. Newby, Rick; Hunger, Suzanne (eds). Writing Montana literature under the big sky. Helena: Montana Center for the Book, 1996. pp. xii, 348.

13246. Newell, Stephanie. From the brink of oblivion: the anxious masculinism of Nigerian market literatures. RAL (27:3) 1996, 50–67.

13247. Newman, John, *et al.* Vietnam War literature: an annotated bibliography of imaginative works about Americans fighting in Vietnam. (Bibl. 1982, 285.) Lanham, MD: Scarecrow Press, 1996. pp. xi, 667. (Third ed.: first ed. 1982.)

13248. Newquist, David L. The spirit of place: the place of spirit. *See* **2157**.

13249. Nicholls, Peter. Modernisms: a literary guide. (Bibl. 1995, 12309.) Rev. by Peter Rawlings in JAStud (30:3) 1996, 482–3; by Nat Chase in MS (90:1) 1996, 105–6.

13250. Nielsen, Aldon Lynn. Writing between the lines: race and intertextuality. (Bibl. 1994, 9854.) Rev. by Walter Kalaidjian in ConLit (37:3) 1996, 496–500; by William Doreski in AAR (30:4) 1996, 677–8.

13251. North, Michael. The dialect of Modernism: race, language, and twentieth-century literature. (Bibl. 1995, 12311.) Rev. by Ann Ardis in TSWL (14:2) 1995, 363–9; by William J. Maxwell in MinnR (47) 1996, 205–14; by Lisa Ruddick in MFS (42:3) 1996, 648–51.

13252. O'Brien, Sharon. Write now: American literature in the 1980s and 1990s. AL (68:1) 1996, 1–8.

13253. Oliva, Juan Ignacio. La visión radical de la artista: nuevas adquisiciones en el estudio de la literatura postcolonial. RCEI (28) 1994, 217–19 (review-article).

13254. OUDITT, SHARON. Fighting forces, writing women: identity and ideology in the First World War. (Bibl. 1995, 12315.) Rev. by Jean Bethke Elshtain in Modernism/Modernity (3:1) 1996, 152–3.

13255. OWENS, LOUIS. 'The song is very short': Native-American literature and literary theory. WebS (12:3) 1995, 51–62.

13256. OWOMOYELA, OYEKAN (ed.). A history of twentieth-century African literatures. (Bibl. 1993, 9934.) Rev. by Bernard Nganga in AAR (30:1) 1996, 136–8.

13257. PACK, ROBERT; PARINI, JAY (eds). American identities: contemporary multicultural voices. Hanover, NH; London: Middlebury College Press, 1994. pp. xiii, 373. (Bread loaf anthologies.)

13258. PARKER, PETER (ed.). The reader's companion to twentieth-century writers. Consultant ed. Frank Kermode. London: Fourth Estate; Oxford: Helicon, 1995. pp. xxx, 748.

13259. PARR, TONY. Saving literature. Scrutiny2 (1:1/2) 1996, 70–7.

13260. PECK, DAVID. 'The morning that is yours': American and British literary cultures in the thirties. *In* (pp. 214–31) **34**.

13261. PELAN, REBECCA. Contemporary Irish women's literary work. Takahe (26) 1996, 46–8.

13262. PERERA, S. W. Annual bibliography of Commonwealth literature 1994; 1995: Sri Lanka. JCL (30:3) 1995, 219–35; (31:3) 1996, 161–76.

13263. PERREAULT, JEANNE; VANCE, SYLVIA (eds). Writing the circle: Native women of Western Canada: an anthology. (Bibl. 1993, 9943.) Rev. by Sylvia Bowerbank and Dolores Nawagesic Wawia in Feminist Studies (20:3) 1994, 571–7.

13264. PESMAN, R. L. The Italian Renaissance in Australia. *See* **9674**.

13265. PIERCE, DAVID; DE VOOGD, PETER (eds). Laurence Sterne in Modernism and postmodernism. *See* **57**.

13266. PIVATO, JOSEPH. Echo: essays on other literatures. Toronto: Guernica, 1994. pp. 277. (Essay series, 17.) Rev. by Donna Palmateer Pennee in CanL (151) 1996, 186–7; by Clara Thomas in LRC (5:7) 1996, 25–6.

13267. PIZER, DONALD. American expatriate writing and the Paris moment: Modernism and place. Baton Rouge; London: Louisiana State UP, 1996. pp. xv, 149. (Modernist studies.)

13268. PORTELLI, ALESSANDRO. Fornaci: *the fire next time*, ovvero *the power of Blackness*. Gli afroamericani come fonte energetica. *In* (pp. 269–76) **117**.

13269. POWELL, DANNYE ROMINE. Parting the curtains: interviews with Southern writers. (Bibl. 1994, 9866.) Rev. by Robert L. Phillips in SoQ (34:2) 1996, 141–2.

13270. PRIMEAU, RONALD. Romance of the road: the literature of the American highway. Bowling Green, OH: Bowling Green State Univ. Popular Press, 1996. pp. xi, 170.

13271. PROBERT, KENNETH G. (ed.). Writing Saskatchewan: 20 critical essays. Regina, Sask.: Canadian Plains Research Center, Univ. of Regina, 1989. pp. xiv, 183. Rev. by Frances W. Kaye in ARCS (20:2) 1990, 254–5.

13272. PÜTZ, MANFRED (ed.). Nietzsche in American literature and thought. (Bibl. 1995, 12326.) Rev. by Herwig Friedl in Amst (41:1) 1996, 140–7; by Joe Moran in JAStud (30:2) 1996, 303–4; by Eric Levin in EOR (20:1/2) 1996, 155–8; by Franz Link in LJGG (37:supp.) 1996, 524–7.

13273. RAISKIN, JUDITH L.   Snow on the cane fields: women's writing and creole subjectivity. Minneapolis: Minnesota UP, 1996. pp. x, 305.

13274. RAJAN, B.   From centre to circumference: modern migrations of a Miltonic metaphor. See **2452**.

13275. RAVEENDRAN, P. P.   Nationalism, colonialism and Indian English literature. See **9676**.

13276. RAWLINSON, MARK.   This other war: British culture and the Holocaust. CamQ (25:1) 1996, 1–25.

13277. REDIGER, PAT.   Great African Americans in literature. New York: Crabtree, 1996. pp. 64. (Great African Americans.)

13278. REDMOND, LOIS.   Women in waiting. NCLR (2:2) 1995, 95–7.

13279. REED, T. V.   Fifteen jugglers, five believers: literary politics and the poetics of American social movements. (Bibl. 1995, 12330.) Rev. by Theron Britt in ColLit (23:2) 1996, 171–6.

13280. REMAEL, ALINE.   Censorship: cross-media cutting in 1950s–60s Britain. CanRCL (23:2) 1996, 547–60.

13281. RINGNALDA, DON.   Fighting and writing the Vietnam War. (Bibl. 1994, 9872.) Rev. by Philip K. Jason in WLA (7:2) 1995, 130–3; by John Hellmann in AL (68:2) 1996, 493–4.

13282. ROEDIGER, DAVID.   White looks: hairy apes, true stories and Limbaugh's laughs. See **9678**.

13283. ROOM, ADRIAN.   Literally entitled: a dictionary of the origins of the titles of over 1300 major literary works of the nineteenth and twentieth centuries. See **9679**.

13284. ROSS, MARLON B.   Some glances at the Black fag: race, same-sex desire, and cultural belonging. CanRCL (21:1/2) 1994, 193–219.

13285. ROSSO, STEFANO.   Narrativa statunitense e guerra del Vietnam: un canone in formazione. Àcoma (4) 1995, 66–75.

13286. RUBIN, JOAN SHELLEY.   Between culture and consumption: the mediations of the middlebrows. In (pp. 163–91) **88**.

13287. RUBIN, LOUIS D., JR.   Babe Ruth's ghost and other historical and literary speculations. Seattle: Washington UP, 1996. pp. 214.

13288. RUOFF, A. LAVONNE BROWN.   American Indian literatures: an introduction, bibliographic review, and selected bibliography. New York: Modern Language Assn of America, 1990. pp. viii, 200. Rev. by Haining Fang in BB (48:2) 1991, 119–20.

13289. RUPPERT, JAMES.   Theory, discourse, and the Native American literature class. MLS (26:4) 1996, 109–17.

13290. RYAN, JUDITH.   The vanishing subject: early psychology and literary Modernism. (Bibl. 1995, 12341.) Rev. by Eva-Marie Kröller in CanRCL (22:2) 1995, 380–1.

13291. SAN JUAN, E., JR.   The Philippine temptation: dialectics of Philippines–US literary relations. Philadelphia, PA: Temple UP, 1996. pp. x, 305. (Asian-American history and culture.)

13292. SCANNAVINI, ANNA.   Le frontiere della lingua. La commutazione di codice nella letteratura portoricano in inglese. Àcoma (1) 1994, 49–57.

13293. SCHAFFER, KAY.   In the wake of first contact: the Eliza Fraser stories. See **9683**.

13294. Schipper, Mineke. Beyond the boundaries: African literature and literary theory. (Bibl. 1992, 10675.) Rev. by Françoise Lionnet in CanRCL (20:1/2) 1993, 266–9.

13295. Schmidt, Klaus H.; Sawyer, David (eds). Blurred boundaries: critical essays on American literature, language and culture. *See* **8**.

13296. Schultze, Bruno. Darwin und die literarischen Folgen. *See* **9687**.

13297. Schwenger, Peter. Letter bomb: nuclear holocaust and the exploding word. (Bibl. 1994, 9893.) Rev. by David Seed in JAStud (30:2) 1996, 329–30.

13298. Schwiebert, John E. The right to be chaos: writers and other artists on the creative process. WebS (8:2) 1991, 68–80.

13299. Seiler, Tamara. Multi-vocality and national literature: toward a post-colonial and multicultural aesthetic. JCanStud (31:3) 1996, 148–65.

13300. Seltzer, Mark. Bodies and machines. (Bibl. 1994, 9895.) Rev. by Robert E. Streeter in Review (16) 1994, 145–52; by Randi Gunzenhäuser in Amst (41:3) 1996, 515–16.

13301. Sheckels, Theodore F., Jr. The lion on the freeway: a thematic introduction to contemporary South African literature in English. New York; Frankfurt; Bern; Paris: Lang, 1996. pp. xxi, 250. (Studies in world literature in English, 5.)

13302. Shephard, Ben. Digging up the past. TLS, 22 Mar. 1996, 12–13.

13303. Sherbo, Arthur. From the *Bookman* of London. *See* **1363**.

13304. —— From the *London Mercury*. *See* **1364**.

13305. —— Last gleanings from the *Critic*: Clemens, Whitman, Hardy, Thackeray, and others. *See* **1365**.

13306. —— A mixed bag from the *Bookman* of New York. *See* **1366**.

13307. Siegel, Carol; Kibbey, Ann (eds). Eroticism and containment: notes from the flood plain. *See* **30**.

13308. Simpson, Lewis P. The fable of the Southern writer. (Bibl. 1994, 9899.) Rev. by Andrea Dimino in AL (68:2) 1996, 491–2; by Fred Hobson in AlaR (49:2) 1996, 130–2.

13309. Slethaug, Gordon A. Doubles and doubling in the arts. JFA (6:2/3) 1993, 100–6.

13310. Slovic, Scott; Noda, Ken'ich (eds). America bungaku no 'shizen' wo yomu – *nature writing* no sekai e. (Reading 'nature' in American literature: an introduction to the world of nature writing.) *See* **9698**.

13311. Smith, Evans Lansing. *Ricorso* and revelation: an archetypal poetics of Modernism. (Bibl. 1995, 12365.) Rev. by Susan Von Rohr Scaff in RMRLL (50:1) 1996, 95–7.

13312. Smyth, Gerry. Being difficult: the Irish writer in Britain. EI (31:3/4) 1996, 41–57.

13313. Sobolewska, Anna. The mysticism of the everyday. Ren (48:3) 1996, 225–41.

13314. Sojka, Eugenia. Language and subjectivity in the postmodern texts of Anglo-Canadian and Anglo-Québecois writers. CanRCL (21:3) 1994, 355–69.

13315. Sokoloff, Naomi. Childhood lost: children's voices in Holocaust literature. *In* (pp. 259–74) **48**.

13316. SPEARS, TIMOTHY B. 100 years on the road: the traveling salesman in American culture. New Haven, CT; London: Yale UP, 1995. pp. xx, 300. Rev. by Thomas C. Dicke in ALH (101:4) 1996, 1290.

13317. STANFORD, ANN FOLWELL. Mechanisms of disease: African-American women writers, social pathologies, and the limits of medicine. NWSAJ (6:1) 1994, 28–47.

13318. STANSKY, PETER. On or about December 1910: early Bloomsbury and its intimate world. Cambridge, MA; London: Harvard UP, 1996. pp. viii, 289. (Studies in cultural history.)

13319. STANZEL, FRANZ KARL; LÖSCHNIGG, MARTIN (eds). Intimate enemies: English and German literary reactions to the Great War 1914–1918. (Bibl. 1995, 12374.) Rev. by Esther Fritsch in EEM (3:2) 1994, 82–3; by Brian Murdoch in Ang (114:1) 1996, 125–32.

13320. STEFFENSEN, JAN B. The mysterious Internet. *See* **1207**.

13321. STIMPSON, CATHARINE R. The postmodern element in the postmodern humanities. WebS (10:2) 1993, 41–56.

13322. STONE, ALBERT E. Literary aftershocks: American writers, readers, and the bomb. (Bibl. 1994, 9911.) Rev. by Paul Boyer in AmS (36:1) 1995, 199–200; by Alison M. Scott in JAC (19:2) 1996, 152–4.

13323. —— The return of Nat Turner: history, literature, and cultural politics in sixties America. (Bibl. 1994, 9912.) Rev. by Jonathan Little in AmS (34:1) 1993, 175–6.

13324. STRINGER, JENNY (ed.). The Oxford companion to twentieth-century literature in English. Introd. by John Sutherland. Oxford; New York: OUP, 1996. pp. xxi, 751. Rev. by Paul Dean in TLS, 1 Nov. 1996, 12–13.

13325. STURROCK, JOHN (ed.). The Oxford guide to contemporary writing. Oxford; New York: OUP, 1996. pp. 520. Rev. by Paul Dean in TLS, 1 Nov. 1996, 12–13.

13326. SUGARS, CYNTHIA. *Prochain épisode*; or, Charting canonical time. CanRCL (23:4) 1996, 1125–43.

13327. SYMONS, JULIAN. The thirties and the nineties. (Bibl. 1991, 10405.) Rev. by Stephan Lieske in ZAA (41:1) 1993, 88–9.

13328. SYTEK, WIOLETTA. The reception of American literature in Poland in the years 1945–1990. PolAS (5) 1994, 63–72.

13329. TABBI, JOSEPH. Postmodern sublime: technology and American writing from Mailer to cyberpunk. (Bibl. 1995, 12386.) Rev. by M. Keith Booker in Pynchon Notes (34/35) 1994, 199–204; by Marc Redfield in MFS (42:4) 1996, 852–4; by Michael Wutz in AL (68:1) 1996, 278–9; by Hanjo Berressem in Amst (41:3) 1996, 508–11.

13330. TAL, KALÍ. Worlds of hurt: reading the literatures of trauma. Cambridge; New York: CUP, 1996. pp. x, 296. (Cambridge studies in American literature and culture, 95.) (Cf. bibl. 1992, 10708.) Rev. by Maggie Jaffe in WLA (8:2) 1996, 159–66; by Edward F. Palm in SAtlR (61:3) 1996, 154–6.

13331. TATUM, STEPHEN. The solace of animal faces. AQ (50:4) 1994, 133–56.

13332. TERES, HARVEY M. Renewing the Left: politics, imagination and the New York intellectuals. New York; Oxford: OUP, 1996. pp. viii, 326.

13333. THODY, PHILIP. Twentieth-century literature: critical issues and themes. Basingstoke: Macmillan, 1996. pp. xi, 301.

13334. Thomas, Lorenzo.   Alea's children: the avant-garde on the Lower East Side, 1960–1970. AAR (27:4) 1993, 573–8.

13335. Thomson, John.   Annual bibliography of Commonwealth literature 1994; 1995: New Zealand (with the South Pacific islands). JCL (30:3) 1995, 109–31; (31:3) 1996, 87–108.

13336. Tiffin, Chris; Lawson, Alan (eds).   De-scribing empire: post-colonialism and textuality. (Bibl. 1994, 17.) Rev. by Brinda Bose in WLT (69:3) 1995, 656–7.

13337. Tomiyama, Takao.   Popeye no kageni – Souseki/Faulkner/ bunkashi. (Behind Popeye: Souseki/Faulkner/cultural history.) *See* **9708**.

13338. Torgovnick, Marianna.   Gone primitive: savage intellects, modern lives. (Bibl. 1995, 12390.) Rev. by Thomas Haeusster in JCS (9:3) 1993/94, 297–300.

13339. Tötösy de Zepetnek, Steven; Gunew, Sneja.   Postcolonial literatures: a selected bibliography of theory and criticism. CanRCL (22:3/4) 1995, 893–923.

13340. Truchlar, Leo.   Erinnerungslandschaften: Essays zur anglo- amerikanischen Literatur und andere Prosa. (Bibl. 1995, 12392.) Rev. by Paul Neubauer in ZAA (44:4) 1996, 382–4.

13341. —— Unwägbarkeiten. Ausgewählte Aufsätze zur englisch- sprachigen Literatur des 20. Jahrhunderts. Vienna: Böhlau, 1996. pp. 236.

13342. Tsuboi, Kiyohiko; Nishimae, Takashi.   America sakka to Europe. (American writers and Europe.) *See* **9709**.

13343. Turow, Scott.   The burden of race. BkW, 15 Sept. 1996, 1, 8.

13344. TuSmith, Bonnie.   All my relatives: community in contem- porary ethnic American literatures. (Bibl. 1994, 9929.) Rev. by Shirley Geok-lin Lim in Signs (21:2) 1996, 494–8.

13345. Tyner, Erika.   State of American humor 1993. SAH (3:1) 1994, 104–15.

13346. Usmiani, Renate (ed.).   *Kelusultiek*: original women's voices of Atlantic Canada. Halifax, N.S.: Inst. for the Study of Women, Mount Saint Vincent Univ., 1994. pp. 227. Rev. by Claire Wilkshire in CanL (149) 1996, 194–5.

13347. Van Wyk, Johan.   Identity and difference: some nineteenth- and early twentieth-century South African texts. *See* **9710**.

13348. Veldman, Meredith.   Fantasy, the bomb, and the Greening of Britain: romantic protest, 1945–1980. (Bibl. 1994, 9933.) Rev. by Edward James in Foundation (63) 1995, 123–7.

13349. Vizenor, Gerald.   The ruins of representation: shadow survivance and the literature of dominance. *In* (pp. 139–67) **80**.

13350. Wald, Priscilla.   Constituting Americans: cultural anxiety and narrative form. *See* **9713**.

13351. Wall, Cheryl A.   Women of the Harlem renaissance. (Bibl. 1995, 12398.) Rev. by Anne Stavney in TSWL (15:1) 1996, 159–61.

13352. —— (ed.).   Changing our own words: essays on criticism, theory, and writing by Black women. (Bibl. 1992, 10725.) Rev. by Dorothy L. Pennington in AmS (34:1) 1993, 171–3.

13353. Wall, Eamonn.   Exile, attitude, and the Sin-É Café: notes on the 'new Irish'. EI (30:4) 1995, 7–17.

13354. WALSHE, EIBHEAR. Sexing the shamrock. CritS (8:2) 1996, 159–67.

13355. WARD, JERRY W., JR. Black South literature: before day annotations (for Blyden Jackson). AAR (27:2) 1993, 315–26.

13356. WATSON, RODERICK. Visions of Alba: the construction of Celtic roots in modern Scottish literature. Études Écossaises (1) 1992, 253–64.

13357. WATSON, STEPHEN (ed.). Guy Butler: essays and lectures 1949–1991. Cape Town: Philip, 1994. pp. 236.

13358. WEBER, HORST. Cézanne and literature: an essay in cultural history. Heidelberg: Winter, 1991. pp. 73. (Beiträge zur neueren Literaturgeschichte, 3:113.) Rev. by Marianne Kesting in arcadia (28:1) 1993, 93–5.

13359. WELSH, SARAH LAWSON. Annual bibliography of Commonwealth literature 1995: The West Indies. JCL (31:3) 1996, 177–86.

13360. WENDT, ALBERT (ed.). Nuanua: Pacific writing in English since 1980. (Bibl. 1995, 12410.) Rev. by Nigel Rigby in WLT (70:1) 1996, 237–8.

13361. WERNER, CRAIG HANSEN. Playing the changes: from Afro-modernism to the jazz impulse. (Bibl. 1994, 9943.) Rev. by Christopher C. De Santis in SoQ (34:1) 1995, 125–8; by Charles Scruggs in MFS (42:1) 1996, 142–5; by Berndt Ostendorf in Amst (41:3) 1996, 517–19; by John Lowe in AAR (30:4) 1996, 378–81; by Malin LaVon Walther in CLAJ (39:3) 1996, 394–8.

13362. WEST, JAMES L. W., III. The Chace Act and Anglo-American literary relations. *See* **1030**.

13363. WEXLER, JOYCE. The uncommon language of Modernist women writers. WS (25:6) 1996, 571–84.

13364. WHYTE, CHRISTOPHER (ed.). Gendering the nation: studies in modern Scottish literature. (Bibl. 1995, 24.) Rev. by David Stenhouse in SLJ (supp. 43) 1995, 32–7.

13365. WICOMB, ZOË. Reading, writing, and visual production in the new South Africa. JCL (30:2) 1995, 1–15. (Text of the Arthur Ravenscroft Memorial Lecture, delivered at Univ. of Leeds, 26 Jan. 1995.)

13366. WILENTZ, GAY. Binding cultures: Black women writers in Africa and the diaspora. (Bibl. 1995, 12418.) Rev. by Sandra Adell in NWSAJ (5:3) 1993, 433–4; by Linda Krumholz in Signs (22:1) 1996, 243–8.

13367. —— Gayl Jones's oraliterary explorations. AAR (28:1) 1994, 141–5 (review-article).

13368. WILLIAMSON, JANICE. Sounding differences: conversations with seventeen Canadian women writers. (Bibl. 1995, 12423.) Rev. by Max Walkley in AUMLA (85) 1996, 174–5.

13369. WILLISON, IAN. Introduction. *In* (pp. xii–xviii) **69**.

13370. —— GOULD, WARWICK; CHERNAIK, WARREN (eds). Modernist writers and the marketplace. *See* **69**.

13371. WOODS, GREGORY. AIDS to remembrance: the uses of elegy. *In* (pp. 155–66) **2**.

13372. WYATT, DAVID. Out of the sixties: storytelling and the Vietnam generation. (Bibl. 1995, 12428.) Rev. by Bryant Simon in AmS (36:1) 1995, 160–1.

13373. YOUNG, MARY E.   Mules and dragons: popular culture images in the selected writings of African-American and Chinese-American women writers. (Bibl. 1993, 10014.) Rev. by Shirley Geok-lin Lim in Signs (21:2) 1996, 494–8.

13374. ZABOROWSKA, MAGDALENA J.   How we found America: reading gender through East-European immigrant narratives. (Bibl. 1995, 12432.) Rev. by Katherine Stubbs in AL (68:2) 1996, 467–8.

13375. ZACHARASIEWICZ, W.   Southern writers and their readers in France and in the German-speaking countries of Europe. SoQ (34:4) 1996, 81–97.

13376. ZONDERMAN, DAVID A.   Labor history and the language of work. *See* **9728**.

Drama, the Theatre, Cinema, and Radio and Television Drama

13377. ABEL, SAM.   The rabbit in drag: camp and gender construction in the American animated cartoon. JPC (29:3) 1995, 183–202.

13378. ACKER, ALLY.   Reel women: pioneers of the cinema, 1869 to the present. London: Batsford; New York: Continuum, 1991. pp. xxvi, 374. Rev. by Janis L. Pallister in JPFT (20:3) 1992, 82–3; by Harriet Margolis in FilmQ (46:1) 1992, 45–6.

13379. ACKER, BARBARA F.   'I charge thee speak': John Barrymore and his voice coach, Margaret Carrington. JADT (7:3) 1995, 43–57.

13380. ACKERLEY, CHRIS.   Notes towards Lowry's screenplay of *Tender Is the Night*. MalLR (29/30) 1991/92, 31–50.

13381. ACKERMAN, JOHN (ed.).   Dylan Thomas: the filmscripts. London: Dent; Rutland, VT: Tuttle, 1995. pp. xxvii, 414. Rev. by Barbara Hardy in Eng (45:183) 1996, 247–51; by Glyn Maxwell in TLS, 9 Aug. 1996, 36.

13382. ADAMS, JOHN.   Setting as chorus: an iconology of *Dallas*. CritS (6:2) 1994, 180–7.

13383. ADLER, THOMAS P.   American drama, 1940–1960. (Bibl. 1994, 9959.) Rev. by Steven F. Bloom in EOR (17:1/2) 1993, 198–205.

13384. AFFRON, CHARLES; AFFRON, MIRELLA JONA.   Sets in motion: art direction and film narrative. New Brunswick, NJ: Rutgers UP, 1995. pp. xiv, 252. Rev. by Linda C. Ehrlich in FilmQ (50:1) 1996, 62.

13385. AHRENDS, GÜNTER.   Von der Kollusion zur Partizipation? Beispiele der Ritualisierung im experimentellen amerikanischen Theater. Forum modernes Theater (11:1) 1996, 56–69.

13386. AJAYI-SOYINKA, OMOFOLABO.   Black feminist criticism and drama: thoughts on double patriarchy. JDTC (7:2) 1993, 161–76.

13387. ALDGATE, ANTHONY.   Censorship and the permissive society: British cinema and theatre, 1955–1965. (Bibl. 1995, 12439.) Rev. by Richard Weight in HT (46:6) 1996, 58–9; by Alan Rosenthal in FilmQ (50:1) 1996, 40–2.

13388. ALDGATE, TONY.   *Alfie*: Tony Aldgate looks at how a 60s film about a Cockney Lothario dealt with sex, censorship and angry/cynical young men. HT (46:10) 1996, 50–4.

13389. ALEISS, ANGELA.   Prelude to World War II: racial unity and the Hollywood Indian. JAC (18:2) 1995, 25–34.

13390. ALFORD, HENRY.   Taking a page from their book. NYTM, 15 Sept. 1996, 46–7. (Merchant and Ivory.)

13391. ALLEN, CHADWICK. Hero with two faces: the Lone Ranger as treaty discourse. AL (68:3) 1996, 609–38.

13392. ALTER, NORA M. Vietnam protest theatre: the television war on stage. Bloomington: Indiana UP, 1996. pp. xxiv, 225. (Drama and performance studies.) (Cf. bibl. 1991, 10442.)

13393. ANDEREGG, MICHAEL. Cameos, guest stars, and real people, with a special appearance by Orson Welles. MichQR (35:1) 1996, 43–60.

13394. —— (ed.). Inventing Vietnam: the war in film and television. Philadelphia, PA: Temple UP, 1991. pp. ix, 315. (Culture and the moving image.) Rev. by Pat Aufderheide in FilmQ (46:1) 1992, 42–3.

13395. ANDERSON, JOSEPH. Between veridicality and illusion. JDTC (6:2) 1992, 173–82.

13396. ANDOLFI, ANGELA. I misteri di Peter Greenaway. Annali anglistica (36:1–3) 1993, 1–29.

13397. ANDREW, GEOFF. The films of Nicholas Ray: the poet of nightfall. London: Letts, 1991. pp. vii, 226. Rev. by Gregg Rickman in FilmQ (46:1) 1992, 34–5.

13398. ANON. (ed.). How do I look? Queer film and video. Ed. by Bad Object-Choices. Seattle, WA: Bay Press, 1991. pp. 295. Rev. by Alexander Doty in FilmQ (46:1) 1992, 36–7; by Jennifer A. Machiorlatti in JFV (45:2/3) 1993, 106–10.

13399. ARIZTI MARTÍN, BÁRBARA. Female spectatorship in *The Purple Rose of Cairo*. *In* (pp. 387–97) **38**.

13400. ARMSTRONG, GORDON. Unintentional fallacies. JDTC (7:1) 1992, 7–26.

13401. ARORA, POONAM; IRVING, KATRINA. Culturally specific texts, culturally bound audiences: ethnography in the place of its reception. JFV (43:1/2) 1991, 111–22.

13402. ASTON, ELAINE; CLARKE, IAN. Feminist theory and the matriarchal soap: *EastEnders*. CritS (6:2) 1994, 211–17.

13403. ATLAS, MARILYN J. The roles of Chicago in the careers of Ellen Van Volkenburg and Maurice Browne. Midamerica (23) 1996, 64–73.

13404. ATWOOD, PETER. Publishing drama in the information age. *See* **1039**.

13405. AUSLANDER, PHILIP. Presence and resistance: postmodernism and cultural politics in contemporary American performance. (Bibl. 1992, 10756.) Rev. by Paul Matthew St Pierre in CanL (148) 1996, 184–5.

13406. AVISAR, ILAN. Screening the Holocaust: cinema's images of the unimaginable. Bloomington: Indiana UP, 1988. pp. xi, 212, (plates) 6. Rev. by Dan Greenberg in FilmQ (44:4) 1991, 56–7.

13407. AXELROD, MARK. Once upon a time in Hollywood; or, The commodification of form in the adaptation of fictional texts to the Hollywood cinema. LitFQ (24:2) 1996, 201–8.

13408. AZOULAY, KATYA GIBEL. Outside our parents' house: race, culture, and identity. RAL (27:1) 1996, 129–42.

13409. BABUSCIO, JACK. Camp and gay sensibility. *In* (pp. 19–38) **12**.

13410. BADEROON, GABEBA. Postmodernism, television, genre and narrative: extreme visibility. Bracket (1) 1995, 12–37.

13411. BADIR, PATRICIA. Playing solitaire: spectatorship and representation in Canadian women's monodrama. TRC (13:1/2) 1992, 120–33.

13412. BADLEY, LINDA. Film, horror, and the body fantastic.

Westport, CT; London: Greenwood Press, 1995. pp. 199. (Contributions to the study of popular culture, 48.)

13413. BAINES, LAWRENCE.   From page to screen: when a novel is interpreted for film, what gets lost in the translation? *See* **10449**.

13414. BAKER, WILLIAM M.   Captain R. Burton Deane and theatre on the Prairies, 1883–1901. *See* **9733**.

13415. BALIO, TINO (ed.).   Hollywood in the age of television. Boston, MA; London: Unwin Hyman, 1990. pp. 352. Rev. by Richard B. Jewell in FilmQ (45:4) 1992, 48–9.

13416. BALLASTER, ROS.   Adapting Jane Austen. *See* **10265**.

13417. BANHAM, MARTIN; HILL, ERROL; WOODYARD, GEORGE (eds). The Cambridge guide to African and Caribbean theatre. (Bibl. 1995, 12454.) Rev. by Eckhard Breitinger in Forum modernes Theater (11:1) 1996, 103–5; by Tejumola Olaniyan in AAR (30:4) 1996, 686–8.

13418. BARER, BURL.   The Saint: a complete history in print, radio, film, and television of Leslie Charteris' Robin Hood of modern crime, Simon Templar, 1928–1992. Jefferson, NC; London: McFarland, 1993. pp. xii, 419. Rev. by Garyn Roberts in JPC (29:4) 1996, 230–1.

13419. BARKER, SIMON.   'Period' detective drama and the limits of contemporary nostalgia: *Inspector Morse* and the strange case of a lost England. CritS (6:2) 1994, 234–42.

13420. BARLOW, JUDITH E. (ed.).   Plays by American women, 1930–1960. New York; London: Applause, 1994. pp. xxxiv, 542.

13421. BARNES, JOHN.   Filming the Boer War. London: Bishopgate, 1992. pp. 340. (Beginnings of the cinema in England, 1894–1901, 4.) Rev. by Charles Mersser in FilmQ (46:3) 1993, 62.

13422. BARR, TERRY.   Eating kosher, staying closer: families and meals in contemporary Jewish American cinema. JPFT (24:3) 1996, 134–44.

13423. BARRIOS, OLGA.   Formulating the aesthetics of African-American women playwrights: the resonance of the Black Liberation and the Black Theatre movements. *In* (pp. 121–30) **38**.

13424. BASINGER, JEANINE.   A woman's view: how Hollywood spoke to women 1930–1960. New York: Knopf, 1993. pp. viii, 528. Rev. by Carole Zucker in FilmQ (47:4) 1994, 58–9.

13425. BASTON, JANE.   Word and image: the articulation and visualization of power in *Great Expectations*. *See* **10806**.

13426. BAUER, DALE.   The figure of the film critic as virile poet: Delmore Schwartz at the *New Republic* in the 1930s. *In* (pp. 110–19) **19**.

13427. BEARD, WILLIAM.   Insect poetics: Cronenberg's *Naked Lunch*. CanRCL (23:3) 1996, 823–52.

13428. BEAVER, FRANK.   Oliver Stone: wakeup cinema. New York: Twayne; Toronto; Oxford: Maxwell Macmillan, 1994. pp. xvi, 243. (Twayne's filmmakers.) Rev. by Don Kunz in LitFQ (23:4) 1995, 295–6.

13429. BEDARD, ROGER L.; TOLCH, C. JOHN (eds).   Spotlight on the child: studies in the history of American children's theatre. Westport, CT; London: Greenwood Press, 1989. pp. viii, 203. (Contributions in drama and theatre studies, 28.) Rev. by Anthony L. Manna in CLAQ (17:4) 1992/93, 39–41.

13430. BEESON, MARK.   The particulars of acting. TLS, 26 Apr. 1996, 18.

13431. BELL, ELIZABETH; HAAS, LYNDA; SELLS, LAURA (eds).   From mouse to mermaid: the politics of film, gender, and culture.

Bloomington: Indiana UP, 1995. pp. xi, 264. Rev. by Lucy Rollin in LU (20:2) 1996, 296–8.

13432. BENDIX, REGINA.   Seashell bra and happy end: Disney's transformations of *The Little Mermaid*. Fabula (34:3/4) 1993, 280–90.

13433. BENNETT, SUSAN.   Feminist (theatre) historiography Canadian (feminist) theatre: a reading of some practices and theories. TRC (13:1/2) 1992, 144–51.

13434. BENSON, THOMAS W.; ANDERSON, CAROLYN.   Reality fictions: the films of Frederick Wiseman. Carbondale: Southern Illinois UP, 1989. pp. xiii, 404. Rev. by Charles Musser in FilmQ (45:4) 1992, 59.

13435. BERENSTEIN, RHONA J.   White heroines and hearts of darkness: race, gender and disguise in 1930s jungle films. Film History (6:3) 1994, 314–39.

13436. BERGMAN, DAVID (ed.).   Camp grounds: style and homosexuality. *See* **12**.

13437. BERMEL, ALBERT.   Comic agony: mixed impressions in the modern theatre. (Bibl. 1993, 10043.) Rev. by Richard Jones in NETJ (5) 1994, 128–30.

13438. BERNSTEIN, MATTHEW.   Nostalgia, ambivalence, irony: *Song of the South* and race relations in 1946 Atlanta. Film History (8:2) 1996, 219–36.

13439. ——— *Roger and Me*: documentaphobia and mixed modes. JFV (46:1) 1994, 3–18.

13440. ——— Walter Wanger, Hollywood independent. Berkeley; London: California UP, 1994. pp. xx, 464. Rev. by Thomas Doherty in FilmQ (49:4) 1996, 61–2.

13441. BERNSTEIN, MICHAEL ANDRÉ.   The *Schindler's List* effect. ASch (63:3) 1994, 429–32.

13442. BERRY, VENISE T.; MANNING-MILLER, CARMEN L. (eds). Mediated messages and African-American culture: contemporary issues. Thousand Oaks, CA; London: Sage, 1996. pp. xviii, 300.

13443. BERTHA, CSILLA.   'The harmony of reality and fantasy': the fantastic in Irish drama. *In* (pp. 28–42) **112**.

13444. BESSAI, DIANE.   Playwrights of collective creation. (Bibl. 1994, 9985.) Rev. by Chris Johnson in TRC (16:1/2) 1995, 151–3; by Jennifer Harvie in BJCS (11:2) 1996, 367–8.

13445. BICK, ILSA J.   Boys in space: *Star Trek*, latency, and the never-ending story. CinJ (35:2) 1996, 43–60.

13446. ——— 'That hurts!': humor and sadomasochism in *Lolita*. JFV (46:2) 1994, 3–18.

13447. BILLINGTON, MICHAEL.   One night stands: a critic's view of British theatre from 1971–1991. (Bibl. 1994, 9988.) Portsmouth, NH: Heinemann, 1995. Rev. by Ginger Strand in JDTC (11:1) 1996, 141–4.

13448. BLACK, BRIAN.   Authority in the valley: TVA in *Wild River* and the popular media, 1930–1940. JAC (18:2) 1995, 1–14.

13449. BLACK, CHERYL.   Ida Rauh: power player at Provincetown. JADT (6:2/3) 1994, 63–80.

13450. BLACK, GREGORY D.   Censorship: an historical interpretation. JDTC (6:1) 1991, 167–85.

13451. ——— Hollywood censored: morality codes, Catholics, and the movies. (Bibl. 1994, 9990.) Rev. by James M. Skinner in AHR (101:1) 1996, 252; by Stephen Vaughn in FilmQ (49:2) 1995/96, 58–9.

13452. BLACKMORE, TIM.   'Is this going to be another bug-hunt?':

S-F tradition *versus* biology-as-destiny in James Cameron's *Aliens*. JPC (29:4) 1996, 211–26.

13453. BLAIR, JOHN G.   Representations of the family in modern American drama: media implications for the theatre, film and television. SPELL (9) 1996, 117–28.

13454. BLAKE, RICHARD A.   Redeemed in blood: the sacramental universe of Martin Scorsese. JPFT (24:1) 1996, 2–9.

13455. BLANCH, ROBERT J.   George Romero's *Knightriders*: a contemporary Arthurian romance. Quondam et Futurus (1:4) 1991, 61–9.

13456. BLAU, HERBERT.   Afterthought from the vanishing point: theater at the end of the real. *In* (pp. 279–98) **119**.

13457. BLOOM, CLAIRE.   Leaving a doll's house: a memoir. London: Virago Press; Boston, MA: Little, Brown, 1996. pp. x, 251. Rev. by Jonathan Yardley in BkW, 20 Oct. 1996, 3; by Rosemary Dinnage in TLS, 25 Oct. 1996, 31.

13458. BLOOM, CLIVE (ed.).   American drama. (Bibl. 1995, 2.) Rev. by Holger Helbig in LWU (29:1) 1996, 65–6.

13459. BLOOM, THOMAS ALAN.   Kenneth Macgowan and the aesthetic paradigm for the new stagecraft in America. New York; Frankfurt; Bern; Paris: Lang, 1996. pp. xii, 184. (New studies in aesthetics, 20.)

13460. BLUMBERG, MARCIA.   Re-evaluating otherness, building for difference: South African theatre beyond the interregnum. SATJ (9:2) 1995, 27–37.

13461. BLY, MARK (ed.).   The production notebooks. New York: Theatre Communications Group, 1996. pp. xxvi, 238. (Theatre in process, 1.)

13462. BLYTHE, MARTIN.   Naming the other: images of the Maori in New Zealand film and television. Metuchen, NJ; London: Scarecrow Press, 1994. pp. v, 335. Rev. by Gregory A. Waller in FilmQ (49:3) 1996, 57–8.

13463. BODDY, WILLIAM.   Approaching *The Untouchables*: social science and moral panics in early sixties television. CinJ (35:4) 1996, 70–87.

13464. BOESING, MARTHA.   Rushing headlong into the fire at the foot of the mountain. Signs (21:4) 1996, 1011–23.

13465. BOGART, STEPHEN HUMPHREY; PROVOST, GARY.   Bogart: in search of my father. London: Sidgwick & Jackson, 1995. pp. 286. Rev. by Pat Dowell in BkW, 1 Oct. 1995, 10–11.

13466. BOND, SHERRY ROSE; BOND, SCOTT.   Report from 221B Baker Street: Orson Welles meets Sherlock Holmes. *See* **11050**.

13467. BOOZER, JACK.   Seduction and betrayal in the heartland: *Thelma & Louise*. LitFQ (23:3) 1995, 188–96.

13468. —— *Wall Street*: the commodification of perception. *In* (pp. 76–95) **19**.

13469. BORDMAN, GERALD.   American theatre: a chronicle of comedy and drama, 1914–1930. New York; Oxford: OUP, 1995. pp. 446. Rev. by Alma J. Bennett in JAC (19:2) 1996, 157–8.

13470. —— American theatre: a chronicle of comedy and drama, 1930–1969. New York; Oxford: OUP, 1996. pp. 472.

13471. BORDWELL, DAVID.   Cognition and comprehension: viewing and forgetting in *Mildred Pierce*. JDTC (6:2) 1992, 183–98.

13472. —— The power of a research tradition: prospects for progress in the study of film style. Film History (6:1) 1994, 59–79.

13473. BOTTOMORE, STEPHEN. Out of this world: theory, fact and film history. Film History (6:1) 1994, 7–25.

13474. BOUNDS, J. DENNIS. Perry Mason: the authorship and reproduction of a popular hero. Westport, CT; London: Greenwood Press, 1996. pp. xiv, 213, (plates) 11. (Contributions to the study of popular culture, 56.) (Cf. bibl. 1994, 9994.)

13475. BOURASSA, ALAN. Tracking the dialectic: Theodor Adorno and Michael Mann's *The Last of the Mohicans*. See **10727**.

13476. BOURNE, STEPHEN. Brief encounters: lesbians and gays in British cinema, 1930–1971. London; New York: Cassell, 1996. pp. xix, 268.

13477. BOYD, KELLY. Moving pictures? Cinema and society in Britain. JBS (34:1) 1995, 130–5 (review-article).

13478. BOYER, JAY. Sidney Lumet. New York: Twayne; Toronto; Oxford: Maxwell Macmillan, 1993. pp. xvi, 213. Rev. by Susan D. Snyder in JPFT (23:2) 1995, 95.

13479. BOYERS, ROBERT. Writing about movies: an interview with Stanley Kauffmann. Salmagundi (98/99) 1993, 113–27.

13480. BOYLE, DEIRDRE. From portapak to camcorder: a brief history of guerilla television. JFV (44:1/2) 1992, 67–79.

13481. BRADLEY, ANTHONY. The politics of Irishness. ConLit (37:3) 1996, 481–91 (review-article).

13482. BRAENDLIN, BONNIE (ed.). Cultural power/cultural literacy: selected papers from the Fourteenth Annual Florida State University Conference on Literature and Film. See **19**.

13483. BRASK, PER (ed.). Contemporary issues in Canadian drama. Winnipeg, Man.: Blizzard, 1995. pp. 249. Rev. by Maria DiCenzo in CanTR (87) 1996, 75–6.

13484. BRATER, ENOCH (ed.). The theatrical gamut: notes for a post-Beckettian stage. See **119**.

13485. —— COHN, RUBY (eds). Around the Absurd: essays on modern and postmodern drama. (Bibl. 1993, 10056.) Rev. by Steven F. Bloom in EOR (17:1/2) 1993, 198–205.

13486. BRATTON, JACKY; COOK, JIM; GLEDHILL, CHRISTINE (eds). Melodrama: stage, picture, screen. Bloomington: Indiana UP; London: BFI, 1994. pp. xiii, 250. Rev. by Walter Metz in FilmQ (49:4) 1996, 48–51.

13487. BRAUDY, LEO. Ceremonies of innocence. Raritan (13:4) 1994, 71–91. (Nature in film.)

13488. —— 'No body's perfect': method acting and 50s culture. MichQR (35:1) 1996, 191–215.

13489. BREWER, GAY. Raymond Chandler without his knight: contracting worlds in *The Blue Dahlia* and *Playback*. LitFQ (23:4) 1995, 273–8.

13490. BRIANS, PAUL. Nuclear family/nuclear war. *In* (pp. 151–8) **77**.

13491. BRILEY, RON. The Hollywood feature film as historical artifact. FilmH (26:1/4) 1996, 82–4.

13492. BROCKETT, OSCAR G. Power, censorship, and validation. TT (4:1) 1994, 1–13.

13493. BROOKE, STEPHEN; CAMERON, LOUISE. Anarchy in the UK? Ideas of the city and the *fin de siècle* in contemporary English film and literature. Albion (28:4) 1996, 635–56.

13494. BROUWER, JOEL R.   Repositioning: center and margin in Julie Dash's *Daughters of the Dust*. AAR (29:1) 1995, 5–16.

13495. BROWN, DEVIN.   Powerful man gets pretty woman: style switching in *Annie Hall*. *See* **2514**.

13496. BROWN, IAN.   Problems of defining 'Standard' Scots: some linguistic and theatrical aspects. *See* **2813**.

13497. BROWN, JEFFREY.   Gender and the action heroine: hardbodies and the *Point of No Return*. CinJ (35:3) 1996, 52–71.

13498. BROWNLOW, KEVIN.   Behind the mask of innocence. (Bibl. 1992, 10782.) Rev. by Benjamin K. Urish in JPFT (20:3) 1992, 83.

13499. BRUCE-NOVOA, JUAN.   There's many a slip between good intentions and script: *The Milagro Beanfield War*. PS (16:1) 1996, 53–63.

13500. BRUNETTE, PETER; WILLS, DAVID.   Screen/play: Derrida and film theory. Princeton, NJ; Oxford: Princeton UP, 1989. pp. xi, 210. Rev. by Marizio Viano in FilmQ (45:4) 1992, 60–1.

13501. BRUSTEIN, ROBERT.   Harold Clurman and the Group Theatre. JADT (6:1) 1994, 1–4.

13502. BRYER, JACKSON R. (ed.).   The playwright's art: conversations with contemporary American dramatists. *See* **85**.

13503. BUFFINGTON, NANCY.   What about Bob? Doubles and demons in *Twin Peaks*. *In* (pp. 101–6) **36**.

13504. BUHLER, STEPHEN M.   'Who calls me villain?': blank verse and the black hat. *See* **6252**.

13505. BUKATMAN, SCOTT.   Terminal identity: the virtual subject in postmodern science fiction. (Bibl. 1995, 12504.) Rev. by Gregg Rickman in FilmQ (49:1) 1995, 60–1; by David Porush in MFS (42:1) 1996, 224–7.

13506. BURGER, GERD.   Agitation und Argumentation im politischen Theater: die San Francisco Mime Troupe und Peter Schumanns Bread and Puppet Theater als komplementare Modelle aufklarerischen Theaters. Berlin: Verlag für Wissenschaft und Bildung, 1993. pp. 212. Rev. by Bernhard Reitz in ZAA (44:1) 1996, 90–1.

13507. BURK, JULI THOMPSON.   In the *I* of the storm: the problem with pluralism. JDTC (7:2) 1993, 118–32.

13508. BURNETT, RON (ed.).   Explorations in film theory: selected essays from *Ciné-tracts*. Bloomington: Indiana UP, 1991. pp. xxvii, 289. Rev. by Richard W. McCormick in Signs (18:1) 1992, 173–87.

13509. BUTLER, JEREMY G.   Redesigning discourse: feminism, the sitcom, and *Designing Women*. JFV (45:1) 1993, 13–26.

13510. —— (ed.).   Star texts: image and performance in film and television. Detroit, MI: Wayne State UP, 1991. pp. 382. (Contemporary film and television.) Rev. by Carole Zucker in FilmQ (45:4) 1992, 65–6.

13511. BUTLER, JUDITH.   Performative acts and gender constitution: an essay in phenomenology and feminist theory. *In* (pp. 270–82) **84**.

13512. BUXTON, DAVID.   The care of time: the rise and fall of the action series. CritS (6:2) 1994, 202–10.

13513. BYARS, JACKIE.   All that Hollywood allows: re-reading gender in the 1950s melodrama. (Bibl. 1995, 12509.) Rev. by E. Ann Kaplan in Signs (19:2) 1994, 550–5.

13514. BYERS, THOMAS B.   History re-membered: *Forrest Gump*, post-feminist masculinity, and the burial of the counterculture. MFS (42:2) 1996, 419–44.

13515. BYRNSIDE, RON.   *Guys and Dolls*: a musical fable of Broadway. JAC (19:2) 1996, 25–33.

13516. BZOWSKI, FRANCES DIODATO. 'Torchbearers of the earth': women and pageantry between the world wars. JADT (7:3) 1995, 58–78.

13517. —— 'Torchbearers of the earth': women and pageantry, and World War I. JADT (7:2) 1995, 88–111.

13518. —— (comp.). American women playwrights, 1900–1930: a checklist. (Bibl. 1992, 10788.) Rev. by Yvonne Shafer in JDTC (8:2) 1994, 230–3.

13519. CALIMANI, DARIO. Fuori dall'Eden: teatro inglese moderno. See **9739**.

13520. CALLAHAN, TIM. Censoring the world riddle. Mythlore (20:1) 1994, 15–20. (Fantasy film.)

13521. CAMERON, EVAN WILLIAM. Filmmaking, technology, and the colonial experience: an immigrant's account from 'English' Canada of a story of American success. JFV (44:1/2) 1992, 102–13.

13522. CAMPBELL, DONALD. Playing for Scotland: a history of the Scottish stage, 1715–1965. See **8546**.

13523. CAMPION-VINCENT, VÉRONIQUE. Demonologies in contemporary legends and panics. See **3613**.

13524. CANCALON, ELAINE DAVIS; SPACAGNA, ANTOINE (eds). Intertextuality in literature and film: selected papers from the Thirteenth Annual Florida State University Conference on Literature and Film. See **51**.

13525. CANNING, CHARLOTTE. Feminist theaters in the USA: staging women's experience. London; New York: Routledge, 1996. pp. x, 271. (Gender in performance.)

13526. CAPUTI, JANE. Psychic numbing, radical futurelessness, and sexual violence in the nuclear film. In (pp. 58–70) **77**.

13527. CARLSON, MARVIN. Deathtraps: the postmodern comedy thriller. (Bibl. 1995, 12527.) Rev. by Alma J. Bennett in JPC (29:2) 1995, 256–7.

13528. CARLYON, DAVID. 'Blow your nose with your fingers': the rube story as crowd control. See **8549**.

13529. CARNEY, RAY. The films of John Cassavetes: pragmatism, modernism, and the movies. (Bibl. 1994, 10013.) Rev. by Carole Zucker in FilmQ (48:4) 1995, 45–7; by Wheeler Winston Dixon in JFV (48:1/2) 1996, 88–94.

13530. CARPENTER, CHARLES A. American dramatic reactions to the birth of the atomic age. JADT (7:3) 1995, 13–29.

13531. CARROLL, NOËL. Cognitivism, contemporary film theory, and method: response to Warren Buckland. JDTC (6:2) 1992, 199–219.

13532. —— Mystifying movies: fads and fallacies in contemporary film theory. New York: Columbia UP, 1988. pp. x, 262. Rev. by Stephen Prince in FilmQ (45:2) 1991/92, 49–51.

13533. —— Theorizing the moving image. Cambridge; New York: CUP, 1996. pp. xix, 426. (Cambridge studies in film.)

13534. CARSON, DIANE; DITTMAR, LINDA; WELSCH, JANICE R. (eds). Multiple voices in feminist film criticism. (Bibl. 1994, 10016.) Rev. by Ilene S. Goldman in JFV (48:1/2) 1996, 80–7.

13535. CARSON, NEIL. Harlequin in Hogtown: George Luscombe and Toronto Workshop Productions. (Bibl. 1995, 12531.) Rev. by Denis Johnston in CanTR (87) 1996, 65–8.

13536. CARTOSIO, BRUNO. Modi di produzione: Hemingway e Hawks. Àcoma (3) 1995, 84–95.

13537. CASTILLE, PHILIP DUBUISSON.   Compson and Sternwood: William Faulkner's 'Appendix' and *The Big Sleep*. PS (13:3) 1994, 54–61.

13538. CAUGHIE, JOHN; ROCKETT, KEVIN.   The companion to British and Irish cinema. London: Cassell; British Film Inst., 1996. pp. xi, 204, (plates) 24.

13539. CAUTE, DAVID.   Joseph Losey: a revenge on life. Oxford; New York: OUP, 1994. pp. xv, 591. Rev. by Joel E. Siegel in BkW, 9 Oct. 1994, 12, 15.

13540. CAVE, RICHARD ALLEN.   The city *versus* the village. *In* (pp. 281–96) **60**.

13541. CAWELTI, JOHN G.   What rough beast – new Westerns? ANQ (9:3) 1996, 4–15.

13542. CHAM, MBYE B.; ANDRADE-WATKINS, CLAIRE (eds).   Black-frames: critical perspectives on Black independent cinema. (Bibl. 1989, 7996.) Rev. by Frank Ukadike in JFV (44:1/2) 1992, 121–7.

13543. CHAPPLE, RICHARD (ed.).   Social and political change in literature and film: selected papers from the Sixteenth Annual Florida State University Conference on Literature and Film. *See* **113**.

13544. CHÂTEAUVERT, JEAN.   Focalisation et structure du texte scénarique. Études littéraires (26:2) 1993, 19–26.

13545. CHION, MICHEL.   David Lynch. Trans. by Robert Julian. Bloomington: Indiana UP; London: BFI, 1995. pp. xii, 210. (Orig. pub. in French: Paris: Etoile, 1992.) Rev. by Justin Wyatt in FilmQ (50:1) 1996, 43–4.

13546. CHOTHIA, JEAN.   English drama of the early modern period, 1890–1940. *See* **9744**.

13547. CHUMO, PETER N., II.   *The Crying Game*, Hitchcockian romance, and the quest for identity. LitFQ (23:4) 1995, 247–53.

13548. —— Dance, flexibility, and the renewal of genre in *Singin' in the Rain*. CinJ (36:1) 1996, 39–54.

13549. CHURCHILL, WARD.   Fantasies of the master race: literature, cinema and the colonization of American Indians. Ed. by M. Annette Jaimes. *See* **3756**.

13550. CIHA, KAREN; JOSEPH, JANET; MARTIN, TERRY J.   Racism in Walt Disney's *The Jungle Book*. PCR (5:1) 1994, 23–35.

13551. CIMA, GAY GIBSON.   Performing women: female characters, male playwrights, and the modern stage. (Bibl. 1994, 10020.) Rev. by Rena Cook in JDTC (9:1) 1994, 235–8.

13552. CLARKSON, WENSLEY.   Quentin Tarantino: shooting from the hip. London: Piatkus, 1995; Woodstock, NY: Overlook Press, 1996. pp. xxi, 312. Rev. by James M. Welsh in JPFT (24:1) 1996, 46–7.

13553. CLOVER, CAROL J.   Men, women, and chain saws: gender in the modern horror film. London: BFI; Princeton, NJ: Princeton UP, 1992. pp. 260. Rev. by Linda Williams in FilmQ (46:2) 1992/93, 58–60; by Jon Lewis in JFV (45:4) 1993, 71–3; by Lynn Dahlgren in JPFT (22:3) 1994, 135.

13554. CLUM, JOHN M.   Acting gay: male homosexuality in modern drama. (Bibl. 1994, 10022.) Rev. by Jack Watson in NETJ (6) 1995, 119–20.

13555. COATES, PAUL.   Film at the intersection of high and mass culture. (Bibl. 1994, 10023.) Rev. by David Laderman in FilmQ (49:1) 1995, 44–5.

13556. COHAN, STEVEN; HARK, INA RAE (eds).   Screening the male:

exploring masculinities in Hollywood cinema. (Bibl. 1993, 10079.) Rev. by John P. McCarthy in FilmQ (48:1) 1994, 56–7.

13557. COHEN, PAULA MARANTZ. Alfred Hitchcock: the legacy of Victorianism. Lexington: Kentucky UP, 1995. pp. 198. Rev. by Leonard J. Leff in JPC (30:3) 1996, 242–3.

13558. COHN, RUBY. Anglo-American interplay in recent drama. (Bibl. 1995, 12542.) Rev. by Martha Gilman Bower in AL (68:2) 1996, 482–3; by Christopher Perricone in CLIO (25:4) 1996, 472–6.

13559. COLEMAN, GREGORY D. 'We're Heaven bound': portrait of a Black sacred drama. See **3579**.

13560. COLLERAN, JEANNE. Re-situating Fugard, re-thinking revolutionary theatre. SATJ (9:2) 1995, 39–49.

13561. COLLINS, KRIS. White-washing the Black-a-Moor: *Othello*, Negro minstrelsy and parodies of Blackness. See **7085**.

13562. COLLINS, MICHAEL J. The body of the work of the body: physio-textuality in contemporary horror. JFA (5:3) 1992, 28–35.

13563. COMO, JAMES. *Shadowlands* IV. CSL (24:6) 1993, 1–7.

13564. CONDEE, WILLIAM F. Madame Pace's hats: architecture and the creation of drama. JADT (5:3) 1993, 55–64.

13565. CONDEE, WILLIAM FARICY. The search for American national theatre at the Vivian Beaumont. JADT (6:2/3) 1994, 49–62.

13566. CONLEY, TOM. Film hieroglyphs: ruptures in classical cinema. Minneapolis: Minnesota UP, 1991. pp. xxxi, 250. Rev. by Dana Polan in FilmQ (46:1) 1992, 32–4.

13567. CONRADIE, P. J. Debates surrounding an approach to African tragedy. SATJ (10:1) 1996, 25–34.

13568. COOK, DAVID A. A history of narrative film. London; New York: Norton, 1990. pp. xxvi, 1087, (plates) 8. (Third ed.: first ed. 1981.)

13569. COOPER, CAROLINE M. *Field of Dreams*: a favorite of President Clinton – but a typical Reaganite film. LitFQ (23:3) 1995, 163–8.

13570. COPJEC, JOAN (ed.). Shades of *noir*: a reader. (Bibl. 1994, 10028.) Rev. by Lowell Harris in FilmQ (48:1) 1994, 57–8.

13571. CORKIN, STANLEY. Realism and the birth of the modern United States: cinema, literature, and culture. Athens; London: Georgia UP, 1996. pp. x, 240.

13572. CORMACK, MIKE. Ideology and cinematography in Hollywood, 1930–39. New York: St Martin's Press, 1994. pp. viii, 170. (Cf. bibl. 1991, 10497.) Rev. by J. W. Newcomb in LitFQ (23:4) 1995, 297–8.

13573. CORNER, JOHN (ed.). Popular television in Britain: studies in cultural history. (Bibl. 1994, 10030.) Rev. by Kelly Boyd in JBS (34:1) 1995, 130–5.

13574. CORNUT-GENTILLE D'ARCY, CHANTAL. Who's afraid of the *femme fatale* in *Breakfast at Tiffany's*? Exposure and implications of a myth. *In* (pp. 371–85) **38**.

13575. —— —— GARCÍA LANDA, JOSÉ ÁNGEL (eds). Gender, I-deology: essays on theory, fiction and film. See **38**.

13576. CORRIGAN, TIMOTHY. A cinema without walls: movies and culture after Vietnam. (Bibl. 1992, 10814.) Rev. by Christopher Sharrett in FilmQ (45:4) 1992, 25–7.

13577. COSSA, FRANK. Images of perfection: life imitates art in Kubrick's *Barry Lyndon*. See **12461**.

13578. COUNSELL, COLIN. Signs of performance: an introduction to twentieth-century theatre. London; New York: Routledge, 1996. pp. vii, 242.

13579.   COUSER, G. THOMAS.   The hunt for 'Big Red': *The Bedford Incident*, Melville, and the Cold War. *See* **11829**.

13580.   COUSIN, GERALDINE.   Women in dramatic place and time: contemporary female characters on stage. London; New York: Routledge, 1996. pp. vii, 211.

13581.   COVENEY, MICHAEL.   The world according to Mike Leigh. London: HarperCollins, 1996. pp. xv, 255. Rev. by Randall Stevenson in TLS, 26 Apr. 1996, 16.

13582.   CRIPPS, THOMAS.   Making movies Black: the Hollywood message movie from World War II to the Civil Rights era. (Bibl. 1993, 10088.) Rev. by Randall M. Miller in AHR (99:3) 1994, 997–8; by Phyllis R. Klottman in FilmQ (48:1) 1994, 53.

13583.   CROOKS, ROBERT.   Double suture: a semiotic approach to film reception. AJSem (10:3) 1993, 109–33.

13584.   CROW, BRIAN; BANFIELD, CHRIS.   An introduction to post-colonial theatre. Cambridge; New York: CUP, 1996. pp. xiv, 186. (Cambridge studies in modern theatre.)

13585.   CUNNINGHAM, FRANK R.   Sidney Lumet: film and literary vision. (Bibl. 1992, 10819.) Rev. by David Desser in FilmQ (46:1) 1992, 49–50; by Robert K. Johnson in EOR (16:1) 1992, 124–6.

13586.   CURRY, RENÉE R.   *Hairspray*: the revolutionary way to restructure and hold your history. LitFQ (24:2) 1996, 165–8.

13587.   —— To star is to mean: the casting of John Waters's *Hairspray*. *In* (pp. 167–78) **19**.

13588.   —— (ed.).   Perspectives on Woody Allen. New York: G. K. Hall; London: Prentice Hall, 1996. pp. xvi, 256. (Perspectives on film.)

13589.   CZEKAY, ANGELIKA.   Distance and empathy: constructing the spectator of Annie Sprinkle's *post-POST PORN MODERNIST – Still in Search of the Ultimate Sexual Experience*. JDTC (7:2) 1993, 177–92.

13590.   DANIEL, DOUGLASS K.   *Lou Grant*: the making of TV's top newspaper drama. Syracuse, NY: Syracuse UP, 1996. pp. xviii, 269. (Television.) Rev. by Matthew C. Ehrlich in JMCQ (73:3) 1996, 759–60.

13591.   DARBY, WILLIAM.   John Ford's Westerns: a thematic analysis, with a filmography. Jefferson, NC; London: McFarland, 1996. pp. ix, 307.

13592.   DAVIDSON, JANE P.   Golem – Frankenstein – golem of your own. JFA (7:2/3) 1996, 228–43.

13593.   DAVIS, GEOFFREY V.   Theatre for a post-apartheid society. JCL (30:1) 1995, 5–21.

13594.   DAY, MOIRA.   The country mouse at play: theatre in the Peace River District, 1914–1945. THC (12:2) 1991, 115–30.

13595.   DAY, PATRICK.   American popular culture and New Zealand broadcasting: the reception of early radio serials. JPC (30:1) 1996, 203–14.

13596.   DEBELLIS, JACK.   'It captivates … it hypnotizes': Updike goes to the movies. LitFQ (23:3) 1995, 169–87.

13597.   DE CAMP, L. SPRAGUE.   Rubber dinosaurs and wooden elephants: essays on literature, film, and history. San Bernardino, CA: Borgo Press, 1996. pp. 144. (I. O. Evans studies in the philosophy and criticism of literature, 26.)

13598. DeCroix, Rick.   Disney animated classics on video. JPFT (24:2) 1996, 99–104.

13599. —— 'Once upon a time in idealized America ...': simulated utopia and the Hardy Family series. *In* (pp. 152–66) **19**.

13600. Degli-Esposti, Cristina.   Sally Potter's *Orlando* and the neo-baroque scopic regime. CinJ (36:1) 1996, 75–93.

13601. de Grazia, Edward.   How Justice Brennan freed novels and movies during the sixties. CSLL (8:2) 1996, 259–65.

13602. de Jongh, Nicholas.   Not in front of the audience: homo-sexuality on stage. (Bibl. 1995, 12569.) Rev. by Thomas Akstens in JDTC (7:2) 1993, 87–9.

13603. Delamater, Jerome.   Warner Bros' Yellowstone Kelly: a case study of the interaction of film and television in the 1950s. Film History (8:2) 1996, 176–85.

13604. Deleyto Alcala, Celestino.   Regulating desire: castration and fantasy in Blake Edwards' *Switch*. *In* (pp. 419–37) **38**.

13605. Deltcheva, Roumiana.   Destination classified: on the trans-formation of spatial forms in applying the narrative text to film: the case of *Heart of Darkness* and *Apocalypse Now*. CanRCL (23:3) 1996, 753–64.

13606. —— Literature–film relations: selected bibliography (1985–1996). CanRCL (23:3) 1996, 853–71.

13607. Demastes, William W. (ed.).   British playwrights, 1956–1995: a research and production sourcebook. Westport, CT; London: Greenwood Press, 1996. pp. xi, 502.

13608. Denzin, Norman K.   Images of postmodern society: social theory and contemporary cinema. London; Newbury Park, CA: Sage, 1991. pp. xii, 179. (Theory, culture and society.) Rev. by Christopher Sharrett in FilmQ (46:1) 1992, 38.

13609. Desjardins, Mary.   *Meeting Two Queens*: feminist film-making, identity politics, and the melodramatic fantasy. FilmQ (48:3) 1995, 26–33.

13610. Desser, David.   'Consumerist realism': American Jewish life and the classical Hollywood cinema. Film History (8:3) 1996, 261–80.

13611. de Toro, Fernando.   Post-modern fiction and theatricality: simulation, deconstruction, and rhizomatic writing. CanRCL (21:3) 1994, 417–43.

13612. Devereaux, Leslie; Hillman, Roger (eds).   Fields of vision: essays in film studies, visual anthropology, and photography. Berkeley; London: California UP, 1995. pp. xiv, 362. Rev. by Paul Stoller in FilmQ (50:1) 1996, 47–8.

13613. DeVine, Kelly M.   *The Silence of the Lambs*: a sheep in wolf's clothing? PCR (2:2) 1991, 37–45.

13614. DeVinney, Karen.   Transmitting the *Bildungsroman* to the small screen: David Hare's *Dreams of Leaving* and *Heading Home*. LitFQ (24:1) 1996, 92–8.

13615. Diamond, Suzanne.   Who's afraid of George and Martha's parlour? Domestic f(r)ictions and the stir-crazy gaze of Hollywood. LitFQ (24:4) 1996, 407–13.

13616. Diawara, Manthia.   Black American cinema. (Bibl. 1993, 10098.) Rev. by Matthew Bernstein in FilmQ (48:4) 1995, 42–4.

13617. DiCenzo, Maria.   The politics of alternative theatre in Britain, 1968–1990: the case of 7:84 (Scotland). Cambridge; New York: CUP, 1996. pp. xiv, 247. (Cambridge studies in modern theatre.)

13618. DICK, BERNARD F. Columbia's dark ladies and the *femmes fatales* of *film noir*. LitFQ (23:3) 1995, 155–62.

13619. DICKERSON, GLENDA. The cult of true womanhood: toward a womanist attitude in African-American theatre. *In* (pp. 109–18) **84**.

13620. DIENST, RICHARD. Still life in real time: theory after television. Durham, NC; London: Duke UP, 1994. pp. xvi, 207. (Post-contemporary interventions.) Rev. by John P. McCarthy in FilmQ (48:4) 1995, 57–9; by Allen Meek in MFS (42:1) 1996, 252–4.

13621. DITTMAR, LINDA. Feminist film scholarship. NWSAJ (4:3) 1992, 359–65 (review-article).

13622. DIXON, WHEELER WINSTON (ed.). Re-viewing British cinema, 1900–92: essays and interviews. Albany: New York State UP, 1994. pp. xi, 288. Rev. by Gene Phillips in LitFQ (24:3) 1996, 332–3.

13623. DOANE, MARY ANN. *Femmes fatales*: feminism, film theory, psychoanalysis. (Bibl. 1995, 12575.) Rev. by Caryl Flinn in Signs (19:3) 1994, 786–91.

13624. DOHERTY, THOMAS. Projections of war: Hollywood, American culture, and World War II. (Bibl. 1993, 10100.) Rev. by Richard Maltby in FilmQ (48:4) 1995, 53–4; by William J. Palmer in MFS (42:1) 1996, 140–2; by Dickran Tashjian in AmLH (8:4) 1996, 722–5.

13625. DOLAN, JILL. 'Lesbian' subjectivity in realism: dragging at the margins of structure and ideology. *In* (pp. 40–53) **84**.

13626. —— Presence and desire: essays on gender, sexuality, performance. (Bibl. 1993, 10102.) Rev. by Lynda Hall in WS (25:1) 1995, 109–12; by David-Michael Allen in JDTC (10:2) 1996, 131–3.

13627. —— PATRAKA, VIVIAN (VICKI). Pain, passion, and parody: a dialogue. JDTC (8:1) 1993, 83–99.

13628. DOLE, CAROL M. The return of the father in Spielberg's *The Color Purple*. LitFQ (24:1) 1996, 12–16.

13629. DOWN, RICHARD; PERRY, CHRISTOPHER (eds). British television drama research guide 1950–1995: including archive holdings. Dudley: Kaleidoscope, 1995. pp. 311. (Second ed.: first ed. 1994.)

13630. DRENNAN, BARBARA. Theatre history-telling: new historiography, logic and the other Canadian tradition. TRC (13:1/2) 1992, 46–62.

13631. DUFFY, SUSAN. American labor on stage: dramatic interpretations of the steel and textile industries in the 1930s. Westport, CT; London: Greenwood Press, 1996. pp. xii, 156. (Contributions in drama and theatre studies, 72.)

13632. DUNTON, CHRIS. Supplementary listing of Nigerian plays in English. JCL (30:1) 1995, 105–6. (*Adds to* bibl. 1994, 10051.)

13633. DURITZ, CLINTON, JR. A conversation with writer and director Kevin Smith. Film History (8:2) 1996, 237–48.

13634. DUTTA, MARY BUHL. 'Very bad poetry, captain': Shakespeare in *Star Trek*. *See* **6288**.

13635. DYER, RICHARD. Now you see it: studies on lesbian and gay film. (Bibl. 1990, 8655.) Rev. by Chris Straayer in FilmQ (45:4) 1992, 54–6; by Linda Dittmar in NWSAJ (4:3) 1992, 359–65.

13636. EDGERTON, GARY; JACKSON, KATHY MERLOCK. Redesigning Pocahontas: Disney, the 'White man's Indian', and the marketing of dreams. JPFT (24:2) 1996, 90–8.

13637. EDMOND, MURRAY. Old comrades of the future: a history of experimental theatre in New Zealand, 1962–1982. Unpub. doct. diss., Univ. of Auckland, 1996.

13638. EGAN, LEONA RUST. Provincetown as a stage: Provincetown, the Provincetown Players, and the discovery of Eugene O'Neill. (Bibl. 1994, 10057.) Rev. by Frederick C. Wilkins in EOR (17:1/2) 1993, 207–8.

13639. EHRENSTEIN, DAVID. Film in the age of video: 'Oh, we don't know where we're going but we're on our way'. FilmQ (49:3) 1996, 38–42.

13640. EIFRIG, GAIL McGREW. Pride and prejudice. *See* **10277**.

13641. ELIOT, MARC. Walt Disney: Hollywood's dark prince: a biography. Secaucus, NJ: Carol, 1993. pp. xxii, 305. Rev. by Pat Dowell in BkW, 18 July 1993, 5.

13642. ELLIS, R. J. 'Are you a fucking mutant?': *Total Recall*'s fantastic hesitations. Foundation (65) 1995, 81–97.

13643. ENGEL, CHARLENE. Language and the music of the spheres: Steven Spielberg's *Close Encounters of the Third Kind*. LitFQ (24:4) 1996, 376–82.

13644. ENGELL, JOHN. *Barry Lyndon*, a picture of irony. *See* **12462**.

13645. ERENS, PATRICIA (ed.). Issues in feminist film criticism. Bloomington: Indiana UP, 1990. pp. xxvi, 450. Rev. by Linda Dittmar in NWSAJ (4:3) 1992, 359–65; by Cynthia Erb in FilmQ (45:3) 1992, 58–9; by Ilene S. Goldman in JFV (48:1/2) 1996, 80–7.

13646. EVCES, MIKE. *Touch of Evil* and ecological optics: toward a demystification of conventional film editing practice. JDTC (8:2) 1994, 103–9.

13647. EYMAN, SCOTT. Ernst Lubitsch: laughter in paradise. New York; London: Simon & Schuster, 1993. pp. 414. Rev. by Joel E. Siegel in BkW, 2 Jan. 1994, 3.

13648. FABE, MARILYN. Maya Deren's fatal attraction: a psycho-analytic reading of *Meshes of the Afternoon* with a psycho-biographical afterword. WS (25:2) 1996, 137–52.

13649. FALWELL, JOHN. The art of digression: Blake Edwards' *Skin Deep*. LitFQ (24:2) 1996, 177–82.

13650. FARNSWORTH, RODNEY. An Australian cultural synthesis: *Wayang*, the Hollywood romance, and *The Year of Living Dangerously*. LitFQ (24:4) 1996, 348–59.

13651. FARR, CECILIA KONCHAR. 'I too am untranslatable': failings of filming *O Pioneers!* WCPMN (36:3) 1992, 43–4.

13652. FARRED, GRANT. *Menace II Society*: no way out for the boys in the hood. MichQR (35:3) 1996, 475–92.

13653. FARRELL, KIRBY. The economies of *Schindler's List*. AQ (52:1) 1996, 163–88.

13654. FEARNOW, MARK. The meaning of pictures: myth and American history plays of the Great Depression; or, Lincoln died (so you and I might live). JADT (5:3) 1993, 1–15.

13655. FEASTER, FELICIA. The woman on the table: moral and medical discourse in the exploitation cinema. Film History (6:3) 1994, 340–54.

13656. FELLEMAN, SUSAN. How high was his brow? Albert Lewin, his critics and the problem of pretension. Film History (7:4) 1995, 386–400.

13657. FENG, PETER. Being Chinese American, becoming Asian American: *Chan Is Missing*. CinJ (35:4) 1996, 88–118.

13658. FERRELL, JEFF; SANDERS, CLINTON R. (eds).   Cultural criminology. Boston, MA: Northeastern UP, 1995. pp. x, 365.

13659. FERRIS, LESLEY.   Absent bodies, dancing bodies, broken dishes: feminist theory, postmodernism, and the performing arts. Signs (18:1) 1992, 162–72 (review-article).

13660. FERRISS, SUZANNE.   The other in Woody Allen's *Another Woman*. LitFQ (24:4) 1996, 432–8.

13661. FIDO, ELAINE SAVORY .   Finding a way to tell it: methodology and commitment in theatre about women in Barbados and Jamaica. *In* (pp. 331–43) **81**.

13662. FIELDS, L. MARC.   'Masters of our business': the Shuberts and Lew Fields. JADT (7:1) 1995, 1–27.

13663. FILEWOD, ALAN.   Theatre, navy, and the narrative of 'true Canadianism'. TRC (13:1/2) 1992, 94–106.

13664. —— Viewing Canadian theatre/Canadian theatre re-viewing. CanTR (79/80) 1994, 14–17.

13665. —— (ed.).   The *CTR* anthology: fifteen plays from *Canadian Theatre Review*. Toronto; Buffalo, NY; London: Toronto UP, 1993. pp. xx, 683. Rev. by Richard Plant in CanTR (79/80) 1994, 154–7; by Anne Nothof in TRC (15:2) 1994, 214–16; by Jennifer Harvie in BJCS (11:2) 1996, 368–9.

13666. FINE, MARSHALL.   Bloody Sam: the life and films of Sam Peckinpah. New York: Fine, 1991. pp. xvii, 426. Rev. by Stephen Prince in FilmQ (46:1) 1992, 28.

13667. FINNEY, GAIL.   Women in modern drama: Freud, feminism, and European theatre at the turn of the century. (Bibl. 1990, 8669.) Rev. by Lilian R. Furst in GR (66:3) 1991, 149–50; by Joan Templeton in CanRCL (19:3) 1992, 453–5.

13668. FINTER, HELGA.   Der Körper und seine Doubles: zur (De-)Konstruktion von Weiblichkeit auf der Bühne. Forum modernes Theater (11:1) 1996, 15–32.

13669. FISCHER, BARBARA.   A Cyclopean, evil eye: on performance, gender, and photography. CanTR (86) 1996, 9–14.

13670. FISCHOFF, STUART.   Villains in film: anemic renderings. PCR (6:1) 1995, 45–52.

13671. FISHER, JAMES.   *The Show Booth*: *commedia dell'arte* on the twentieth-century American stage. NETJ (1) 1990, 61–78.

13672. FISTER, BARBARA.   Mugging for the camera: narrative strategies in *Brazil*. LitFQ (24:3) 1996, 288–92.

13673. FLETCHER, JILL.   The story of theatre in South Africa: a guide to its history from 1780–1930. *See* **8553**.

13674. FLOCKEMANN, MIKI.   *Medeas* from Corinth and Cape Town: cross-cultural encounters, theatre, and the teaching context. Alternation (3:1) 1996, 83–93.

13675. FLORA, JOSEPH M.   *Shane* (novel and film) at century's end. JAC (19:1) 1996, 51–5.

13676. FLYNN, RICHARD.   Imitation Oz: the sequel as commodity. LU (20:1) 1996, 121–31.

13677. FORSHEY, GERALD E.   American religious and biblical spectaculars. Westport, CT; London: Praeger, 1992. pp. xii, 202. (Media and society.) Rev. by Jeffrey H. Mahan in JAC (17:1) 1994, 100.

13678. FORTE, JEANIE.   Women's performance art: feminism and postmodernism. *In* (pp. 251–69) **84**.

13679. FRADEN, RENA. Blueprints for a Black Federal Theatre, 1935–1939. (Bibl. 1994, 10080.) Rev. by Paul Nadler in AAR (30:3) 1996, 476–8.

13680. FRAIMAN, SUSAN. Geometries of race and gender: Eve Sedgwick, Spike Lee, Charlayne Hunter-Gault. Feminist Studies (20:1) 1994, 67–84.

13681. FRAZIER, ADRIAN. Behind the scenes: Yeats, Horniman, and the struggle for the Abbey Theatre. (Bibl. 1993, 10120.) Rev. by David Krause in Irish Literary Supplement (10:1) 1991, 25–7.

13682. FREEDMAN, BARBARA. Frame-up: feminism, psychoanalysis, theatre. *In* (pp. 54–76) **84**.

13683. FRENCH, WILLIAM W.; WORTHINGTON, JANET. Murder mystery events: playing myth-making, and smashing the fourth wall, all at once. JDTC (8:2) 1994, 111–27.

13684. FRICK, JOHN W. Staging Scottsboro: the violence of representation and class–race 'negotiations' in the 1930s. NETJ (6) 1995, 1–17.

13685. FRIEDBERG, ANNE. Window shopping: cinema and the postmodern. (Bibl. 1993, 10123.) Rev. by Peter Brunette in FilmQ (47:4) 1994, 56–8.

13686. FRIEDMAN, BONNIE. Relinquishing Oz: every girl's anti-adventure story. MichQR (35:1) 1996, 9–28.

13687. FROST, R. J. 'It's alive!' *Frankenstein*: the film, the feminist novel and science fiction. *See* **12222**.

13688. FRUTH, BRYAN, *et al.* The Atomic Age: facts and films from 1945–1965. JPFT (23:4) 1996, 154–60.

13689. FRY, CARROL; KEMP, CHRISTOPHER. Rambo agonistes. *See* **8165**.

13690. FUCHS, CYNTHIA J. Desperately seeking a subject: postmodern sexuality, Seidelman, and Madonna. *In* (pp. 37–52) **109**.

13691. FUCHS, ELINOR. The death of character: perspectives on theater after Modernism. Bloomington: Indiana UP, 1996. (Drama and performance studies.)

13692. —— Play as landscape: another version of pastoral. Theater (25:1) 1994, 44–51.

13693. FULTON, ELIZABETH. On the eve of destruction: technology, nostalgia, and the fetishized maternal body. CritM (10:1) 1996, 90–105.

13694. FULWILER, LAVON. *Babe*: a twentieth-century Nun's Priest's Tale. CCTE (61) 1996, 93–101.

13695. GABBARD, KRIN. The circulation of sadomasochistic desire in the *Lolita* texts. JFV (46:2) 1994, 19–30.

13696. GALE, MAGGIE B. West End women: women on the London stage, 1918–1962. London; New York: Routledge, 1996. pp. x, 262. (Gender in performance.)

13697. GALE, STEVEN H. *The Maltese Falcon*: melodrama or *film noir*? LitFQ (24:2) 1996, 145–7.

13698. GARCÍA LANDA, JOSÉ ÁNGEL. Introduction: gender, I-deology and addictive representation: the film of familiarity. *In* (pp. 13–54) **38**.

13699. GARNER, STANTON B., JR. Bodied spaces: phenomenology and performance in contemporary drama. Ithaca, NY; London: Cornell UP, 1994. pp. x, 260. Rev. by Robert Baker-White in Essays in Theatre (14:2) 1996, 182–4.

13700. GARRETT, GREG. John Huston's *The Battle of San Pietro*. WLA (5:1) 1993, 1–12.

13701. —— The many faces of *Mildred Pierce*: a case study of adaptation and the studio system. LitFQ (23:4) 1995, 287–92.

13702. GEHRING, WES D.   American dark comedy: beyond satire. Foreword by R. Karl Largent. Westport, CT; London: Greenwood Press. pp. xx, 194. (Contributions to the study of popular culture, 55.).

13703. GEIS, DEBORAH R.   Postmodern theatric(k)s: monologue in contemporary American drama. (Bibl. 1993, 10131.) Rev. by Jennifer Harvie in Essays in Theatre (15:1) 1996, 107–8.

13704. GENTRY, RIC.   An interview with Dede Allen. FilmQ (46:1) 1992, 12–22.

13705. GEORGE, DIANA.   Semi-documentary/semi-fiction: an examination of genre in *Strangers in Good Company*. JFV (46:4) 1995, 24–30.

13706. GEORGE, NELSON.   Blackface: reflections on African-Americans and the movies. NY: HarperCollins, 1994. pp. xv, 224. Rev. by Charles Johnson in BkW, 23 Oct. 1994, 4.

13707. GERAGHTY, CHRISTINE.   Women and soap opera: a study of prime time soaps. Cambridge: Polity Press, 1991. pp. 211. Rev. by Caryl Flinn in Signs (19:3) 1994, 786–91.

13708. GERMANOU, MARIA.   Remembrance of things past: the Second World War in the British alternative theatre. Athens: Parousia, 1996. pp. 196. (Parousia, 36.)

13709. GEVER, MARTHA; PARMAR, PRATIBHA; GREYSON, JOHN (eds). Queer looks: perspectives on lesbian and gay film and video. London; New York: Routledge, 1993. pp. xv, 413. Rev. by Jerry White in JFV (47:4) 1995/96, 48–52; by Corey K. Creekmur in FilmQ (49:4) 1996, 56–8.

13710. GEVISSER, MARK.   Truth and consequences in post-apartheid theater. Theater (25:3) 1995, 8–18.

13711. GIANAKARIS, C. J.   Peter Shaffer and the dilemma of adapting for film. TexPres (13) 1992, 17–23.

13712. GIANNETTI, LOUIS.   Understanding movies. Englewood Cliffs, NJ; London: Prentice Hall, 1996. pp. xx, 527. (Seventh ed.: first ed. 1972.)

13713. —— EYMAN, SCOTT.   Flashback: a brief history of film. (Bibl. 1991, 10538.) Englewood Cliffs, NJ; London: Prentice Hall, 1996. pp. xii, 564. (Third ed.: first ed. 1986.)

13714. GIBSON, PAMELA CHURCH; GIBSON, ROMA (eds).   Dirty looks: women, pornography, power. London: BFI; Bloomington: Indiana UP, 1993. pp. x, 238. Rev. by Diane Waldman in FilmQ (48:1) 1994, 45–7.

13715. GILBERT, HELEN; TOMPKINS, JOANNE.   Post-colonial drama: theory, practice, politics. London; New York: Routledge, 1996. pp. ix, 344.

13716. GILBERT, REID.   Chocolate and lipstick: gender (re)construction in dancing docs and dandies. StudCanL (20:2) 1995, 10–21.

13717. —— Computers and theatre: mimesis, simulation and interconnectivity. *See* **1157**.

13718. —— 'Disattending the play': framing and frame breaking. CanTR (70) 1992, 5–9.

13719. GILBERT, SANDRA M.; GUBAR, SUSAN.   Masterpiece theatre: an academic melodrama. (Bibl. 1995, 12619.) Rev. by Elaine Showalter in TLS, 14 June 1996, 9.

13720. GILDZEN, ALEX; KARAGEORGIOU, DIMITRIS.   Joseph Chaikin: a bio-bibliography. Westport, CT; London: Greenwood Press, 1992.

pp. xii, 285. (Bio-bibliographies in the performing arts, 29.) Rev. by Michael J. Noble in BB (53:2) 1996, 174–5.

13721. GILES, FREDA SCOTT. Disparate voices: African-American theatre critics of the 1920s. JADT (7:1) 1995, 28–39.

13722. GILLISPIE, JULAINE. American film adaptations of *The Secret Garden*: reflections of sociological and historical change. *See* **10543**.

13723. GODARD, BARBARA. Between repetition and rehearsal: conditions of (women's) theatre in Canada in a space of reproduction. TRC (13:1/2) 1992, 19–33.

13724. GODIN, SETH (comp.). The encyclopedia of fictional people: the most important characters of the 20th century. New York: Boulevard, 1996. pp. 315.

13725. GOLDSTEIN, LAURENCE. Film as family history. MichQR (32:2) 1993, 285–95 (review-article).

13726. GOLUB, SPENCER. Charlie Chaplin, Soviet icon. *In* (pp. 199–220) **83**.

13727. GOODMAN, LIZBETH. Contemporary feminist theatres: to each her own. (Bibl. 1994, 10107.) Rev. by E. D. Huntley in NWSAJ (6:3) 1994, 503–6.

13728. GOODSON, A. C. Frankenstein in the age of Prozac. *See* **7734**.

13729. GOODWIN, JILL TOMASSON. A career in progress: part 2, Donald Davis, Canadian actor and director, 1959–1990. THC (12:1) 1991, 56–78.

13730. GORDON, JOHN STEELE. *Oklahoma!* AH (44:1) 1993, 58–66, 68, 70–1.

13731. GOTTLIEB, SIDNEY (ed.). Hitchcock on Hitchcock: selected writings and interviews. (Bibl. 1995, 12631.) Rev. by Matthew Bernstein in FilmQ (50:1) 1996, 53–5.

13732. GRACE, SHERRILL. Exploration as construction: Robert Flaherty and *Nanook of the North*. ECanW (59) 1996, 123–46.

13733. GRAHAM, BILL. Sir John Martin-Harvey: the last imperial envoy. TRC (14:1) 1993, 91–103.

13734. GRANT, BARRY KEITH. Rich and strange: the yuppie horror film. JFV (48:1/2) 1996, 4–16.

13735. GRAY, FRANCES. Shakespeare, shrews and screwballs. *See* **7069**.

13736. GRAY, STEPHEN (ed.). South Africa plays. London: Hern; Houghton, South Africa: Heinemann–Centaur, 1993. pp. xiv, 241. Rev. by Chris Dunton in RAL (26:2) 1995, 235–7.

13737. GREENBERG, HARVEY ROY. Screen memories: Hollywood cinema on the psychoanalytic couch. (Bibl. 1994, 10113.) Rev. by Kendall D'Andrade in FilmQ (47:4) 1994, 55–6.

13738. GRIFFITHS, TREVOR R. The twentieth century: drama. YWES (75) 1994, 542–7.

13739. GRINDON, LEGER. Body and soul: the structure of meaning in the boxing film genre. CinJ (35:4) 1996, 54–69.

13740. —— Shadows on the past: studies in the historical fiction film. Philadelphia, PA: Temple UP, 1994. pp. xii, 250. (Culture and the moving image.) Rev. by Virginia Wright Wexman in FilmQ (49:1) 1995, 59–60; by Gregory A. Waller in AHR (101:3) 1996, 813–14.

13741. —— Witness to Hollywood: oral testimony and historical interpretation in Warren Beatty's *Reds*. Film History (5:1) 1993, 85–95.

13742. GRIPSRUD, JOSTEIN. The *Dynasty* years: Hollywood television and critical media studies. London; New York: Routledge, 1995. pp. xii, 316. (Comedia.) Rev. by Charles Maland in FilmQ (50:1) 1996, 40–7.

13743. GRONBECK-TEDESCO, JOHN L.   Absence and the actor's body: Marlon Brando's performance in *A Streetcar Named Desire* on stage and film. StAD (8:2) 1993, 115–26.

13744. GRUNDY, KENNETH W.   Quasi-state censorship in South Africa: the Performing Arts Councils and politicized theater. JAML (24:3) 1994, 241–57.

13745. GUE, RANDY.   'It seems that everything looks good nowadays, as long as it is in the flesh & brownskin': the assertion of cultural difference at Atlanta's 81 Theatre, 1934–1937. Film History (8:2) 1996, 209–18.

13746. HAAS, ROBERT.   The Cronenberg monster: literature, science, and psychology in the cinema of horror. PS (15:2) 1996, 3–10.

13747. HAGEN, BILL.   Malcolm Lowry's 'adjustable blueprint': the screenplay of *Tender Is the Night*. MalLR (29/30) 1991/92, 51–63.

13748. HAILL, LYN (ed.).   Olivier at work: the National years: an illustrated memoir. (Bibl. 1990, 8687.) Rev. by Richard L. Nochimson in ShB (9:2) 1991, 39.

13749. HALBERSTAM, JUDITH.   Skin shows: gothic horror and the technology of monsters. *See* **8584**.

13750. HALSTEAD, JACK.   Re-reviewing Richard Foreman (and theater of images). JDTC (6:2) 1992, 61–79.

13751. HALTOF, MAREK.   The spirit of Australia in *Picnic at Hanging Rock*: a case study in film adaptation. CanRCL (23:3) 1996, 809–22.

13752. HAMALIAN, LEO.   God's angry man. BALF (25:2) 1991, 417–20.

13753. HAMAMOTO, DARRELL Y.   Monitored peril: Asian Americans and the politics of TV representation. Minneapolis: Minnesota UP, 1994. pp. xiii, 311. Rev. by Brooks Robards in JPFT (24:1) 1996, 47–8.

13754. HAMILTON, MARYBETH.   The queen of camp: Mae West, sex and popular culture. London; New York: HarperCollins, 1995; London: Pandora, 1996. pp. x, 278. Rev. by Aisling Foster in TLS, 31 May 1996, 36.

13755. HAMMOND, JOYCE.   Drag queen as angel: transformation and transcendence in *To Wong Foo, Thanks for Everything, Julie Newmar*. JPFT (24:3) 1996, 106–14.

13756. HAMPTON, HOWARD.   Return of the body snatchers. FilCo (32:6) 1996, 82–5.

13757. HANNON, PATRICE.   Austen novels and Austen films: incompatible worlds? *See* **10284**.

13758. HANSEN, MIRIAM.   Babel and Babylon: spectatorship in American silent film. (Bibl. 1992, 10868.) Rev. by Constance Balides in Signs (22:1) 1996, 248–54.

13759. HAPGOOD, ROBERT.   The rights of playwrights: performance theory and American law. JDTC (6:2) 1992, 41–59.

13760. HARALOVICH, MARY BETH.   'Champagne taste on a beer budget': series design and popular appeal of *Magnum, P.I.* JFV (43:1/2) 1991, 123–34.

13761. HARCOURT, PETER.   Imaginary images: an examination of Atom Egoyan's films. FilmQ (48:3) 1995, 2–14.

13762. HARPER, SUE.   Picturing the past: the rise and fall of the British costume film. London: BFI, 1994. pp. x, 239. Rev. by Andrew Higson in Albion (28:1) 1996, 169–71; by Marcia Landy in FilmQ (49:4) 1996, 54–6.

13763. HARRIS, DANIEL.   The death of camp: gay men and Hollywood diva worship: from reverence to ridicule. Salmagundi (112) 1996, 166–91.

13764. HARRIS, ERICH LEON.   African-American screenwriters now: conversations with Hollywood's Black pack. Los Angeles, CA: Silman-James Press, 1996. pp. xiii, 277.

13765. HARRIS, WILL.   Early Black women playwrights and the dual liberation motif. AAR (28:2) 1994, 205–21.

13766. HARRISON, PAUL CARTER; EDWARDS, GUS (eds).   Classic plays from the Negro Ensemble Company. Pittsburgh, PA: Pittsburgh UP, 1995. pp. xxiv, 594. Rev. by Helen Taylor in TLS, 12 July 1996, 21.

13767. HART, DAVID.   The fixed expression and its manipulation: evidence from the modern drama text. *See* **2638**.

13768. HART, LYNDA; PHELAN, PEGGY (eds).   Acting out: feminist performances. Ann Arbor: Michigan UP, 1993. pp. vi, 406. Rev. by Lynda Hall in JDTC (8:2) 1994, 227–30.

13769. HARTMANN, JON.   The trope of Blaxploitation in critical responses to *Sweetback*. Film History (6:3) 1994, 382–404.

13770. HARTY, KEVIN J.   'All the elements of a good movie': cinematic responses to the AIDS pandemic. *In* (pp. 114–30) **2**.

13771. —— Television's *The Adventures of Sir Lancelot*. Quondam et Futurus (1:4) 1991, 71–9.

13772. —— (ed.).   Cinema Arthuriana: essays on Arthurian film. (Bibl. 1993, 10145.) Rev. by Samuel J. Umland and Rebecca A. Umland in Quondam et Futurus (3:1) 1993, 69–72; by Michael N. Salda in ChauY (3) 1996, 198–203.

13773. HARVIE, JENNIFER; KNOWLES, RICHARD PAUL.   Dialogic monologue: a dialogue. TRC (15:2) 1994, 136–63.

13774. HASKIN, PAMELA.   'Saul, can you make me a title?' Interview with Saul Bass. FilmQ (50:1) 1996, 10–17.

13775. HASTINGS, A. WALLER.   *Bambi* and the hunting ethos. JPFT (24:2) 1996, 53–9.

13776. HAUG, KATE.   An interview with Kenneth Anger. Wide Angle (18:4) 1996, 75–92.

13777. HAYWARD, SUSAN.   Key concepts in cinema studies. London; New York: Routledge, 1996. pp. xviii, 467.

13778. HAYWOOD, IAN.   Fathers and sons: locating the absent mother in 1960s children's television series. CritS (6:2) 1994, 195–201.

13779. HEALEY, JIM.   'All this for us': the songs in *Thelma & Louise*. JPC (29:3) 1995, 103–19.

13780. HEBEL, UDO J.   Early African-American women playwrights (1916–1930) and the remapping of twentieth-century American drama. AAA (21:2) 1996, 267–86.

13781. HEDGES, INEZ.   Breaking the frame: film language and the experience of limits. *See* **3865**.

13782. HEDRICK, DONALD K.   Teen Shakespeare: modern commercial culture and collectivity in *Porky's II*. Litteraria Pragensia (6:12) 1996, 76–89.

13783. HEES, EDWIN.   Foreground in the background: landscape and ideology in South African films. SATJ (10:2) 1996, 63–84.

13784. HEGARTY, EMILY.   Some suspect of ill: Shakespeare's sonnets and 'the perfect mate'. *See* **7185**.

13785. Heil, Douglas.   The construction of racism through narrative and cinematography in *The Letter*. LitFQ (24:1) 1996, 17–25.

13786. Helford, Elyce Rae.   Reading masculinities in the 'postpatriarchal' space of *Red Dwarf*. Foundation (64) 1995, 20–31.

13787. Helling, William P.   Rita Hayworth's *The Loves of Carmen* as literary criticism. LitFQ (24:4) 1996, 445–51.

13788. Helman, Alicia; Osadnik, Wacław M.   Film and literature: historical models of film adaptation and a proposal for a (poly)system approach. CanRCL (23:3) 1996, 645–57.

13789. Hemmeter, Thomas.   Hitchcock's melodramatic silence. JFV (48:1/2) 1996, 32–40.

13790. Hendershot, Cyndy.   The possession of the male body: masculinity in *The Italian, Psycho*, and *Dressed to Kill*. See **9273**.

13791. Henderson, Mary C.   Theater in America: 250 years of plays, players, and productions. See **8554**.

13792. Hentzi, Gary.   Little cinema of horrors. FilmQ (46:3) 1993, 22–7.

13793. Herman, Jan.   A talent for trouble: the life of Hollywood's most acclaimed director, William Wyler. New York: Putnam's Sons, 1996. pp. 517, (plates) 16. Rev. by Gene D. Phillips in LitFQ (24:3) 1996, 335–6.

13794. Heston, Charlton.   In the arena: an autobiography. New York: Simon & Schuster, 1995. pp. 592. Rev. by Meryle Secrest in BkW, 15 Oct. 1995, 8.

13795. Higashi, Sumiko.   Cecil B. DeMille and American culture: the silent era. (Bibl. 1995, 12671.) Rev. by Matthew Bernstein in FilmQ (49:4) 1996, 43–4; by James Van Dyck Card in JPFT (24:1) 1996, 45–6.

13796. Higgins, John.   Event *versus* narration in *Schindler's List*. New Contrast (24:1) 1996, 49–62.

13797. Higson, Andrew.   Waving the flag: constructing a national cinema in Britain. (Bibl. 1995, 12672.) Rev. by Lester D. Friedman in FilmQ (49:4) 1996, 62–4.

13798. —— (ed.).   Dissolving views: key writings on British cinema. London; New York: Cassell, 1996. pp. viii, 264. (Rethinking British cinema.)

13799. Hildy, Franklin J.   'If you build it, they will come': the reconstruction of Shakespeare's Globe gets underway on the Bankside in London. ShB (10:3) 1992, 5–10.

13800. —— A minority report on the decisions of the Pentagram Conference. ShB (10:4) 1992, 9–12.

13801. Hilger, Michael.   From savage to nobleman: images of Native Americans in film. Lanham, MD; London: Scarecrow Press, 1995. pp. v, 289.

13802. Hill, Anthony D.   Pages from the Harlem renaissance: a chronicle of performance. New York; Frankfurt; Bern; Paris: Lang, 1996. pp. xii, 185. (Studies in African and African-American culture, 6.)

13803. Hilmes, Michele.   Hollywood and broadcasting: from radio to cable. Urbana: Illinois UP, 1990. pp. 221. (Illinois studies in communications.) Rev. by Richard B. Jewell in FilmQ (45:4) 1992, 48–9.

13804. Hirshfield, Claire.   The actress as social activist: the case of Lena Ashwell. *In* (pp. 72–86) **87**.

13805. —— The Actresses' Franchise League in peace and war: 1913–1918. NETJ (5) 1994, 35–49.

13806. —— Suffragettes onstage: women's political theatre in Edwardian England. NETJ (2) 1991, 13–26.

13807. HOFFMAN, JAMES.   Genre contention at the New Play Centre. TRC (16:1/2) 1995, 59–68. (Vancouver theatre.)

13808. HOGAN, PATRICK COLM.   Colonialism and the problem of identity in Irish literature. *See* **13128**.

13809. HOLLINGER, KAREN.   The female Oedipal drama of *Rebecca* from novel to film. QRFV (14:4) 1993, 17–30.

13810. HOLMBERG, ARTHUR.   Fallen angels at sea: Garbo, Ullman [*sic*], Richardson, and the contradictory prostitute in *Anna Christie*. EOR (20:1/2) 1996, 43–63.

13811. HOMAN, RICHARD L.   Freud's 'seduction theory' on stage: Deane's and Balderston's *Dracula*. *See* **12376**.

13812. HOPKINS, LISA.   The transference of *Clarissa*: psychoanalysis and the realm of the feminine. *See* **9300**.

13813. HORGER, J.   Derek Jarman's film adaptation of Marlowe's *Edward II*. *See* **5884**.

13814. HORN, BARBARA LEE.   Joseph Papp: a bio-bibliography. Westport, CT; London: Greenwood Press, 1992. pp. xi, 409. (Bio-bibliographies in the performing arts, 26.) Rev. by Michael J. Noble in BB (53:2) 1996, 174–5.

13815. HOUGHTON, NORRIS.   Entrances & exits: a life in and out of the theatre. (Bibl. 1993, 10160.) Rev. by Jeffrey Smart in NETJ (3) 1992, 111–13.

13816. HOULAHAN, MARK.   Cosmic Hamlets? Contesting Shakespeare in Federation space. *See* **6350**.

13817. HOWARD, JESSICA H.   *Hallelujah!*: transformation in film. *See* **3498**.

13818. HOWELL, AMANDA.   Lost boys and angry ghouls: Vietnam's undead. *In* (pp. 297–334) **9**.

13819. HUMPHREYS, DEBRA.   The discursive construction of women's sexuality and madness in mainstream cinema. *In* (pp. 64–74) **109**.

13820. HUNT, NIGEL.   The pre-text of the post-text: thoughts on play publishing by smaller Canadian presses. *See* **1058**.

13821. HYE, ALLEN E.   The moral dilemma of the scientist in modern drama: the inmost force. Lewiston, NY; Lampeter: Mellen Press, 1996. pp. 218. (Symposium, 38.)

13822. IACCINO, JAMES F.   Psychological reflections on cinematic terror: Jungian archetypes in horror films. (Bibl. 1994, 10138.) Rev. by Robert Baird in JPC (30:2) 1996, 207–8.

13823. INNESS, SHERRIE A.   The feminine en-gendering of film consumption and film technology in popular girls' serial novels, 1914–1931. JPC (29:3) 1995, 169–82.

13824. INVERSO, MARY BETH.   The gothic impulse in contemporary drama. (Bibl. 1990, 8704.) Rev. by Brian Rose in JDTC (6:1) 1991, 137–9.

13825. ISAACS, NEIL D.   *Bathgate* in the time of Coppola: a reverie. LitFQ (24:1) 1996, 109–10.

13826. —— Malle's eye for Rose's *Storyville*. LitFQ (24:2) 1996, 223–4.

13827. IVANOV, ANDREA J.   Mae West was not a man: sexual parody and genre in the plays and films of Mae West. *In* (pp. 275–97) **64**.

13828. JACK, STEVEN (ed.).   Eric Steiner: a life in the theatre. Toronto: Burgher, 1994. pp. iv, 56. Rev. by Denis Johnston in CanTR (87) 1996, 65–8.

13829. Jackson, Kathy Merlock.   Walt Disney: its persuasive products and cultural contexts. JPFT (24:2) 1996, 50–2.

13830. Jackson, Kevin (ed.).   Schrader on Schrader. London; Boston, MA: Faber & Faber, 1990. pp. xix, 235. Rev. by Scott C. Bradley in FilmQ (46:1) 1992, 48–9.

13831. Jacobs, Lea.   *An American Tragedy*: a comparison of film and literary censorship. QRFV (15:4) 1995, 87–98.

13832. —— The wages of sin: censorship and the fallen woman film, 1928–1942. (Bibl. 1992, 10900.) Rev. by E. Ann Kaplan in Signs (19:2) 1994, 550–5.

13833. Jacobson, Brooke.   Regional film: a strategic discourse in the global marketplace. JFV (43:4) 1991, 18–32.

13834. Jameson, Fredric.   Signatures of the visible. (Bibl. 1995, 12692.) Rev. by Richard Allen in FilmQ (45:4) 1992, 63–4.

13835. Jancovich, Mark.   Rational fears: American horror in the 1950s. Manchester; New York: Manchester UP, 1996. pp. vi, 324.

13836. Jansen, Ann.   Weird wet snapping sounds: the rhythms of radio drama. CanTR (75) 1993, 25–9.

13837. Jenkins, Henry, iii.   'It's not a fairy tale anymore': gender, genre, *Beauty and the Beast*. JFV (43:1/2) 1991, 90–110.

13838. Johnson, Eithne; Schaefer, Eric.   Soft-core/hard-gore: *Snuff* as a crisis in meaning. JFV (45:2/3) 1993, 40–59.

13839. Johnson, Jeffrey L. L.   The eighteenth-century ape: *Barry Lyndon* and the Darwinian pessimism of Stanley Kubrick. *See* **12472**.

13840. Johnston, Denis W.   Up the mainstream: the rise of Toronto's alternative theatres, 1968–1975. (Bibl. 1992, 10904.) Rev. by Harry Lane in CanTR (77) 1993, 79–81; by Tom Hendry in TRC (14:2) 1993, 196–8.

13841. Johnston, Ruth D.   *Committed*: feminist spectatorship and the logic of the supplement. JFV (45:4) 1993, 22–39.

13842. Jones, Christopher N.   Lessons from Hollywood: feminist film theory and the commercial theatre. PCR (2:2) 1991, 23–36.

13843. Jones, Leslie.   Strictly folklore: the view from the popular front. Australian Folklore (9) 1994, 177–80. (Baz Luhrman's *Strictly Ballroom*.)

13844. Jordan, Amy.   The portrayal of children on prime-time situation comedies. JPC (29:3) 1995, 139–47.

13845. Jordan, Chris.   Gender and class mobility in *Saturday Night Fever* and *Flashdance*. JPFT (24:3) 1996, 116–22.

13846. Jowett, Garth.   The 'facts' of the 'censored' film: theoretical and history approaches. JDTC (6:1) 1991, 159–66.

13847. Joyrich, Lynne.   Feminist Enterprise? *Star Trek: the Next Generation* and the occupation of femininity. CinJ (35:2) 1996, 61–84.

13848. Jurkiewicz, Kenneth.   Francis Coppola's secret gardens: *Bram Stoker's 'Dracula'* and the *auteur* as decadent visionary. *In* (pp. 167–71) **127**.

13849. Kahn, David; Breed, Donna.   Scriptwork: a director's approach to new play development. NETJ (7) 1996, 114–16.

13850. Kalas, Andrew; Berenstein, Rhona J.   *Woman Speaks*: representations of working women in postwar America. JFV (48:3) 1996, 30–45.

13851. Kaplan, Deborah.   Mass marketing Jane Austen: men, women, and courtship in two of the recent films. *See* **10289**.

13852. KASSEL, MICHAEL B. The American Jewish immigrant family in film and history: the historical accuracy of Barry Levinson's *Avalon*. FilmH (26:1/4) 1996, 52–60.

13853. KELLEGHAN, FIONA. Camouflage in fantastic fiction and film. Extrapolation (37:2) 1996, 109–20.

13854. KELLEY, KAROL. A modern Cinderella. JAC (17:1) 1994, 87–92. (Disney's *Cinderella*; *Pretty Woman*.)

13855. KELLEY, SUSAN M. Giggles and guns: the phallic myth in *Unforgiven*. JFV (47:1–3) 1995, 98–105.

13856. KENNEALLY, MICHAEL. The transcendent impulse in contemporary Irish drama. *In* (pp. 272–82) **49**.

13857. KENNEDY, LIAM. Alien nation: White male paranoia and imperial culture in the United States. JAStud (30:1) 1996, 87–100. (White paranoia in Hollywood film.)

13858. KERMAN, JUDITH B. (ed.). Retrofitting *Blade Runner*: issues in Ridley Scott's *Blade Runner* and Philip K. Dick's *Do Androids Dream of Electric Sheep?* (Bibl. 1992, 10915.) Rev. by Sam Unland in FilmQ (46:1) 1992, 46–8.

13859. KERR, DAVID. African theories of African theatre. SATJ (10:1) 1996, 3–23.

13860. —— The art of writing plays. SARB (8:1) 1996, 24; (8:4) 1996, 24; (8:5) 1996, 23; (8:6) 1996, 24.

13861. KERRIGAN, WILLIAM. A theory of female coyness. *See* **7563**.

13862. KERSHAW, BAZ. The politics of performance: radical theatre as cultural intervention. London; New York: Routledge, 1992. pp. viii, 281. (Cf. bibl. 1992, 10916.) Rev. by John Simon in JDTC (8:1) 1993, 202–3.

13863. KEYSSAR, HELENE (ed.). Feminist theatre and theory. Basingstoke: Macmillan; New York: St Martin's Press, 1996. pp. ix, 288. (New casebooks.)

13864. KIDD, KENNETH. Men who run with wolves, and the women who love them: child study and compulsory heterosexuality in feral child films. LU (20:1) 1996, 90–112.

13865. KIERNAN, MAUREEN. Paradise revisited: representation of the rural in Irish & Egyptian film. *In* (pp. 309–18) **60**.

13866. KINDELAN, NANCY. Shadows of realism: dramaturgy and the theories and practices of modernism. Westport, CT; London: Greenwood Press, 1996. pp. 171. (Contributions in drama and theatre studies, 68.)

13867. KING, MARGARET J. The audience in the wilderness: the Disney nature films. JPFT (24:2) 1996, 60–8.

13868. KIRKHAM, PAT; THUMIM, JANET (eds). Me Jane: masculinity, movies and women. London: Lawrence & Wishart; New York: St Martin's Press, 1995. pp. 296. Rev. by Corey Creekmur in FilmQ (48:1) 1994, 60–1.

13869. KIRKLEY, RICHARD BRUCE. A catalogue of Canadian stage plays on English Canadian television, 1952 to 1987. TRC (15:1) 1994, 96–108.

13870. —— John Hirsch and the critical mass: alternative theatre on CBC television in the 1970s. TRC (15:1) 1994, 75–95.

13871. KLEIN, JEANNE. 'Getting into the head' of the children's theatre actor. NETJ (3) 1992, 97–104.

13872. KLEIN, NORMAN M. Seven minutes: the life and death of the

American animated cartoon. (Bibl. 1995, 12710.) Rev. by Eric Porter in JPC (29:4) 1996, 239–40.

13873. KLENOTIC, JEFFREY F.   The place of rhetoric in 'new' film historiography: the discourse of corrective revisionism. *See* **2413**.

13874. KLINE, KAREN E.   *The Accidental Tourist* on page and on screen: interrogating normative theories about film adaptation. LitFQ (24:1) 1996, 70–83.

13875. KNEE, ADAM.   The compound genre film: *Billy the Kid versus Dracula* meets *The Harvey Girls*. *In* (pp. 141–56) **51**.

13876. KNIGHT, CHRISTOPHER J.   Woody Allen's *Hannah and Her Sisters*: domesticity and its discontents. LitFQ (24:4) 1996, 383–92.

13877. KNIGHTEN, MERRELL.   The triple paternity of *Forbidden Planet*. *See* **7231**.

13878. KNOWLES, RICHARD PAUL.   Stories of interest: some partial histories of Mulgrave Road groping towards a method. TRC (13:1/2) 1992, 108–19. (Contemporary Nova Scotia theatre.)

13879. —— Stratford's first young company. THC (11:1) 1990, 3–28.

13880. —— Voices (off): deconstructing the modern English-Canadian dramatic canon. *In* (pp. 91–111) **13**.

13881. KOLIN, PHILIP C.   Civil rights and the Black presence in *Baby Doll*. LitFQ (24:1) 1996, 2–11.

13882. —— An interview with Whitney J. LeBlanc. AAR (26:2) 1992, 307–17.

13883. —— (ed.).   American playwrights since 1945: a guide to scholarship, criticism, and performance. (Bibl. 1994, 10153.) Rev. by James Fisher in JDTC (6:1) 1991, 141–2.

13884. KOSZARSKI, RICHARD.   Joseph Lerner and the post-war New York film renaissance: an interview. Film History (7:4) 1995, 456–76.

13885. KRASILOVSKY, ALEXIS.   Women behind the camera: an interview with Leslie Hill. JFV (48:4) 1996, 38–53.

13886. KRASNER, DAVID.   Parody and double consciousness in the language of early Black musical theatre. AAR (29:2) 1995, 317–23.

13887. —— Whose role it it anyway? Charles Gilpin and the Harlem renaissance. AAR (29:3) 1995, 483–96.

13888. KRAUS, JOE.   The Jewish gangster: a conversation across generations. ASch (64:1) 1995, 53–65.

13889. KREIZENBECK, ALAN.   The Radio Division of the Federal Theatre Project. NETJ (2) 1991, 27–37.

13890. KRUGER, LOREN.   So what's new? Women and theater in the 'new South Africa'. Theater (25:3) 1995, 46–54.

13891. KRUTNIK, FRANK.   In a lonely street: *film noir*, genre, masculinity. (Bibl. 1995, 12721.) Rev. by Caryl Flinn in Signs (19:3) 1994, 786–91.

13892. LACEY, STEPHEN.   British realist theatre: the new wave in its context 1956–1965. (Bibl. 1995, 12724.) Rev. by Jenny S. Spencer in ConLit (37:3) 1996, 472–4.

13893. LADERMAN, DAVID.   What a trip: the road film and American culture. JFV (48:1/2) 1996, 41–57.

13894. LALLY, KEVIN.   Wilder times: the life of Billy Wilder. New York: Holt, 1996. pp. xv, 496, (plates) 16. Rev. by Gene D. Phillips in LitFQ (24:3) 1996, 335–6.

13895. LANCASTER, KURT.   Travelling among the lands of the fantastic: the imaginary worlds and simulated environments of science fiction tourism. Foundation (67) 1996, 28–47.

13896. LANDY, MARCIA.   British genres: cinema and society, 1930–1960. (Bibl. 1991, 10602.) Rev. by Kelly Boyd in JBS (34:1) 1995, 130–5.

13897. LANGDELL, CHERI DAVIS.   Pain of silence: Emily Dickinson's silences, poetic *persona* and Ada's selfhood in *The Piano. See* **10970**.

13898. LANGER, MARK.   Rethinking Flaherty: *Acoma* and Hollywood. Wide Angle (17:1–4) 1995, 239–55.

13899. LANGMAN, LARRY; FINN, DANIEL.   A guide to American crime films of the forties and fifties. Westport, CT; London: Greenwood Press, 1995. pp. xxi, 372. (Bibliographies and indexes in the performing arts, 19.)

13900. LAPALMA, MARINA DEBELLAGENTE.   Driving Doctor Ford. LitFQ (24:1) 1996, 57–62.

13901. LAPPAS, CATHERINE.   'Seeing is believing, but touching is the truth': female spectatorship and sexuality in *The Company of Wolves*. WS (25:2) 1996, 115–35.

13902. LARABEE, ANN.   Going through Harriet: ritual and theatre in the women's colleges. *See* **9765**.

13903. LAURENCE, DAN H.; GRENE, NICHOLAS (eds).   Shaw, Lady Gregory and the Abbey: a correspondence and a record. (Bibl. 1995, 12735.) Rev. by Lucy McDiarmid in Irish Literary Supplement (13:1) 1994, 4–6; by James Pethica in Yeats Annual (12) 1996, 332–8.

13904. LAWLOR, MARY.   Placing source in *Greed* and *McTeague*. *In* (pp. 93–104) **51**.

13905. LAWRENCE, ELIZABETH A.   Werewolves in psyche and cinema: man–beast transformation and paradox. JAC (19:3) 1996, 103–12.

13906. LAWSON, D. S.   Rage and remembrance: the AIDS plays. *In* (pp. 140–54) **2**.

13907. LAWSON-PEEBLES, ROBERT.   European conflict and Hollywood's reconstruction of English fiction. *See* **10293**.

13908. LAZARUS, A. L. (ed.).   A George Jean Nathan reader. (Bibl. 1992, 10933.) Rev. by Thomas F. Connolly in EOR (15:2) 1991, 119–21.

13909. LEFF, LEONARD.   A thunderous reception: Broadway, Hollywood, and *A Farewell to Arms*. HemR (15:2) 1996, 33–51.

13910. LEFF, LEONARD J.   Hollywood and the Holocaust: remembering *The Pawnbroker*. AJH (84:4) 1996, 353–76.

13911. LEFF, THOMAS.   Texts and actors: ensemble theatre in academe. NETJ (1) 1990, 101–8.

13912. LEITER, SAMUEL L.   Theatre on the home front: World War II on New York's stages, 1941–1945. JADT (5:2) 1993, 47–70.

13913. LENZ, KATJA.   Modern Scottish drama: snakes in Iceland – drama in Scotland? ZAA (44:4) 1996, 301–16.

13914. LEO, JOHN R.   Television and the narrative structures of discourse and difference. JFV (43:4) 1991, 45–55.

13915. LEVAY, JOHN.   An historical note: Margaret Anglin's last stage appearance. JADT (7:1) 1995, 74–6.

13916. —— Margaret Anglin: a stage life. *See* **9767**.

13917. LEVINE, JUDY.   Art services for the marginal: the survival of theatre for the forgotten. JAML (23:1) 1993, 37–50.

13918. LEVINE, JUNE PERRY.   The functions of the narrator's voice in literature and film: Forster and Ivory's *Maurice*. LitFQ (24:3) 1996, 309–21.

13919. LEWIS, DAVID J.   A home for Murphy Brown's son(s). CritM (7:2) 1993, 59–67.

13920. LIEBERFELD, DANIEL; SANDERS, JUDITH.   Here under false pretenses: the Marx Brothers crash the gates. ASch (64:1) 1995, 103–8.

13921. LIEBERMAN, EVAN A.   Charlie the trickster. JFV (46:3) 1994, 16–28.

13922. LINDFORS, BERNTH.   Additions and corrections to Chris Dunton's *A Bibliographic Listing of Nigerian Plays in English: 1956–1992*. JCL (30:1) 1995, 97–103. (*Adds to* bibl. 1994, 10051.)

13923. LINDROTH, COLETTE.   Spike Lee and the American tradition. LitFQ (24:1) 1996, 26–31.

13924. LINDSEY, SHELLEY STAMP.   Horror, femininity, and Carrie's monstrous puberty. JFV (43:4) 1991, 33–44.

13925. LIST, CHRISTINE.   Chicano images: refiguring ethnicity in mainstream film. New York; London: Garland, 1996. pp. vii, 182. (Garland studies in American popular history and culture.)

13926. LODGE, JACK.   The career of Herbert Brenon. Griffithiana (57/58) 1996, 5–133.

13927. LOISELLE, ANDRÉ.   Scenes from a failed marriage: a brief analytical history of Canadian and Québécois feature film adaptations of drama from 1942 to 1992. TRC (17:1) 1996, 46–66.

13928. LONEY, GLENN.   The Globe bandwagon effect: Sam Wanamaker plans ahead. ShB (10:3) 1992, 11–13.

13929. LOUAGIE, KIMBERLY.   'It belongs in a museum': the image of museums in American film, 1985–1995. JAC (19:4) 1996, 41–50.

13930. LOUNSBURY, MYRON (ed.).   The progress and poetry of the movies: a second book of film criticism. Lanham, MD; London: Scarecrow Press, 1995. pp. vii, 449.

13931. LOYO GÓMEZ, HILARIA.   Dietrich's androgyny and gendered spectatorship. *In* (pp. 317–32) **38**.

13932. LUHR, WILLIAM.   *Ordinary People*: feminist psychotherapy on a see-saw. *In* (pp. 50–60) **19**.

13933. LUNDEEN, KATHLEEN.   Heretical hoofing: strictly cinema. SCS (20) 1996, 94–100.

13934. LUNDQUIST, LYNNE.   Myth and illiteracy: Bill and Ted's explicated adventures. Extrapolation (37:3) 1996, 213–23.

13935. LUPACK, BARBARA TEPA (ed.).   Vision/re-vision: adapting contemporary American fiction by women to film. Bowling Green, OH: Bowling Green State Univ. Popular Press, 1996. pp. 250.

13936. LYONS, DONALD.   Independent visions: a critical introduction to recent independent American film. New York: Ballantine, 1994. pp. xiv, 337, (plates) 8. Rev. by S.C.B. in FilmQ (48:1) 1994, 63.

13937. —— Passionate precision: *Sense and Sensibility*. *See* **10297**.

13938. MA, SHENG-MEI.   Ang Lee's domestic tragicomedy: immigrant nostalgia, exotic/ethnic tour, global market. JPC (30:1) 1996, 191–201.

13939. —— *The Great Dictator* and *Maus*: 'the comical' before and after the Holocaust. Proteus (12:2) 1995, 47–50.

13940. McCLAREN, JOSEPH.   *Cotton Comes to Harlem*: the novel, the film and the critics. PCR (5:1) 1994, 37–46.

13941. McCONACHIE, BRUCE A.   Metaphors we act by: kinesthetics, cognitive psychology, and historical structures. JDTC (7:2) 1993, 25–45.

13942. ―― New Historicism and American theater history: toward an interdisciplinary paradigm for scholarship. *In* (pp. 265–71) **83**.

13943. McCormick, Richard W. Politics and the psyche: feminism, psychoanalysis, and film theory. Signs (18:1) 1992, 173–87 (review-article).

13944. MacDonald, Scott. Avant-garde at the Flaherty. Wide Angle (17:1–4) 1995, 257–67.

13945. ―― From zygote to global cinema *via* Su Friedrich's films. JFV (44:1/2) 1992, 30–41.

13946. McFarlane, Brian. Novel to film: an introduction to the theory of adaptation. *See* **4208**.

13947. McIlroy, Brian. When the Ulster Protestant and Unionist looks: spectatorship in (Northern) Irish cinema. IUR (26:1) 1996, 143–54.

13948. MacKenzie, Paul. Artistic truth, historical truth: the 'faction' film and the Falklands War. WLA (6:1) 1994, 41–61.

13949. Macklin, Tony. *The Grapes of Wrath*: the values of John Ford and John Steinbeck. UDR (23:3) 1996, 99–103.

13950. McLean, Adrienne L. 'I'm a Cansino': transformation, ethnicity, and authenticity in the construction of Rita Hayworth, American love goddess. JFV (44:3/4) 1992/93, 8–26.

13951. McQuade, Brett T. *Peter Pan*: Disney's adaptation of J. M. Barrie's original work. Mythlore (20:1) 1994, 5–9.

13952. McQuillan, Gene. 'Extarminate the varlets!': the reconstruction of captivity narratives in *Dances with Wolves*. *See* **8337**.

13953. Maffi, Mario. Teatro americano contemporaneo. Àcoma (5) 1995, 40–5.

13954. Malone, David, ii. A linguistic approach to the Bakhtinian hero in Steve Martin's *Roxanne*. LitFQ (24:4) 1996, 400–6.

13955. Mancoff, Debra N. Rex quondam rexque ens. *See* **3918**.

13956. Mann, George. The Sterndale Bennetts: the formative years (1910–1932). TRC (14:1) 1993, 60–89.

13957. ―― Theatre Lethbridge: a history of theatrical production in Lethbridge, Alberta (1885–1988). *See* **9773**.

13958. Mann, Karen B. The matter with mind: violence and *The Silence of the Lambs*. Criticism (38:4) 1996, 583–605.

13959. Marchalonis, Shirley. Filming the nineteenth century: *The Secret Garden* and *Little Women*. *See* **10234**.

13960. Marks, Martin. Music, drama, Warner Brothers: the cases of *Casablanca* and *The Maltese Falcon*. MichQR (35:1) 1996, 112–42.

13961. Marowitz, Charles. Alarums & excursions: our theatres in the nineties. New York: Applause, 1996. pp. xii, 306. (Applause critics circle.)

13962. Marranca, Bonnie. Ecologies of theater: essays at the century turning. Baltimore, MD; London: Johns Hopkins UP, 1996. pp. xix, 289.

13963. Marshall, Scott. Edith Wharton on film and television: a history and filmography. EWR (13:2) 1996, 15–26.

13964. Martin, Andrew. Receptions of war: Vietnam in American culture. *See* **13208**.

13965. Martin, Carol (ed.). A sourcebook of feminist theatre and performance: on and beyond the stage. London; New York: Routledge, 1996. pp. xix, 311. (Worlds of performance.)

13966. Martin, Joel W.; Ostwalt, Conrad E., Jr (eds).   Screening the sacred: religion, myth, and ideology in popular American film. (Bibl. 1995, 12774.) Rev. by Damien Chase in JAStud (30:2) 1996, 327–8.

13967. Martin, Nina K.   *Red Shoe Diaries*: sexual fantasy and the construction of the (hetero)sexual woman. JFV (46:2) 1994, 44–57.

13968. Martín Alegre, Sara.   Not Oedipus' sister: the redefinition of female rites of passage in the screen adaptation of Thomas Harris's *The Silence of the Lambs*. In (pp. 439–50) **38**.

13969. Marx, Lesley.   Underworld RSA. SATJ (10:2) 1996, 11–30. (South African gangster films.)

13970. Mason, Carol.   *Rear Window*'s Lisa Freemont: masochistic female spectator or post-war socioeconomic threat? In (pp. 109–21) **113**.

13971. Mason, Francis.   Nostalgia for the future: the end of history and postmodern 'pop' TV. JPC (29:4) 1996, 27–40.

13972. Massa, Ann.   Theatre of manners, theatre of matters: British and American theatre between the wars. In (pp. 57–74) **34**.

13973. Massood, Paula J.   Mapping the hood: the genealogy of city space in *Boyz N the Hood* and *Menace II Society*. CinJ (35:2) 1996, 85–97.

13974. Matthew-Walker, Robert.   From Broadway to Hollywood: the musical and the cinema. London: Sanctuary, 1996. pp. 225.

13975. Max, Gerry.   Richard Halliburton and Thomas Wolfe: 'when youth kept open house'. NCLR (5) 1996, 83–7, 90–3.

13976. Maxfield, James F.   'The worst part': Martin Scorsese's *Mean Streets*. LitFQ (23:4) 1995, 279–86.

13977. Maxwell, Rick.   The image is gold: value, the audience commodity, and fetishism. JFV (43:1/2) 1991, 29–45.

13978. Mazer, Cary M.   The (historical) actor and the text. *See* **5678**.

13979. Mbowa, Rose.   Theater and political repression in Uganda. RAL (27:3) 1996, 87–97.

13980. Mda, Zakes.   Theater and reconciliation in South Africa. Theater (25:3) 1995, 38–45.

13981. Metz, Walter C.   Pomp(ous) Sirk-umstance: intertextuality, adaptation, and *All That Heaven Allows*. JFV (45:4) 1993, 3–21.

13982. Mew, Diane (ed.).   Life before Stratford: the memoirs of Amelia Hall. Toronto; Oxford: Dundurn Press, 1989. pp. 264. Rev. by Paula Sperdakos in CanTR (67) 1991, 111–13.

13983. Meyer, Petra Maria.   Ästhetik des Gegenwartstheaters im technischen Zeitalter. Forum modernes Theater (11:1) 1996, 3–14.

13984. Meyer, William E. H., Jr.   From *The Sun Also Rises* to *High Noon*: the hypervisual great awakening in American literature and film. *See* **9654**.

13985. —— From *The Sun Also Rises* to *High Noon*: the hypervisual great awakening in American literature and film. *See* **9655**.

13986. Mico, Ted; Miller-Monzon, John; Rubel, David (eds).   Past imperfect: history according to the movies. New York: Holt, 1995. pp. 304. (Henry Holt reference books.) Rev. by Tom Wiener in BkW, 1 Oct. 1995, 10; by Adi Wimmer in Krieg und Literatur (1) 1995, 125–8.

13987. Mikulak, William A.   The canonization of Warner Brothers cartoons; or, How Bugs Bunny came to the Museum of Modern Art. JAC (19:1) 1996, 21–8.

13988. Miller, Mary Jane.   Turn up the contrast: CBC television drama since 1952. Vancouver: British Columbia UP, 1987. pp. ix, 429, (plates) 8. Rev. by John S. Bolin in ARCS (18:3) 1988, 408–9.

13989. MILLS, PAMELA. Wyler's version of Brontë's storms in *Wuthering Heights*. *See* **10465**.

13990. MINER, MADONNE M. 'Like a natural woman': nature, technology, and birthing bodies in *Murphy Brown*. Frontiers (16:1) 1996, 1–18.

13991. MITCHELL, KAREN S. Ever after: reading the women who read (and re-write) romances. TT (6:1) 1996, 51–69.

13992. MITCHELL, LEE CLARK. Westerns: making the man in fiction and film. Chicago; London: Chicago UP, 1996. pp. xvi, 331.

13993. MIZEJEWSKI, LINDA. Picturing the female dick: *The Silence of the Lambs* and *Blue Steel*. JFV (45:2/3) 1993, 6–23.

13994. MODLESKI, TANIA. Feminism without women: culture and criticism in a 'postfeminist' age. (Bibl. 1995, 12789.) Rev. by Janice R. Welsch in FilmQ (46:1) 1992, 31–2; by Maureen Ryan in CanL (148) 1996, 177–9.

13995. —— Our heroes have sometimes been cowgirls: an interview with Maggie Greenwald. FilmQ (49:2) 1995/96, 2–11.

13996. MOELLER, SUSAN D. The cultural construction of urban poverty: images of poverty in New York City, 1890–1917. JAC (18:4) 1995, 1–16.

13997. MOON, MICHAEL. Outlaw sex and the 'search for America': representing male prostitution and perverse desire in sixties film (*My Hustler* and *Midnight Cowboy*). QRFV (15:1) 1993, 27–40.

13998. MOORE, BARBARA; YELLIN, DAVID G. (eds). Horton Foote's three trips to Bountiful. Dallas, TX: Southern Methodist UP, 1993. pp. xii, 259.

13999. MORAN, JAMES M. Gregg Araki: guerilla film-maker for a queer generation. FilmQ (50:1) 1996, 18–26.

14000. MORDDEN, ETHAN. Medium cool: the movies of the 1960s. New York: Knopf, 1990. pp. 301. Rev. by Jon Saari in AR (49:3) 1991, 466–7.

14001. MOREY, ANNE. 'A whole book for a nickel'? L. Frank Baum as filmmaker. CLAQ (20:4) 1995/96, 155–60.

14002. MORGAN, JENNY (comp.). The film researcher's handbook: a guide to sources in North America, South America, Asia, Australasia and Africa. London; New York: Routledge, 1996. pp. xix, 452.

14003. MORRIS, CHRISTOPHER. *Psycho*'s allegory of seeing. LitFQ (24:1) 1996, 47–51.

14004. MORRIS, PETER. David Cronenberg: a delicate balance. (Bibl. 1995, 12795.) Rev. by Mark Harris in CanL (149) 1996, 140–1.

14005. MORSBERGER, ROBERT E. *East of Eden* on film. SteiQ (25:1/2) 1992, 28–42.

14006. MORTIER, JANIE. Le Unity Theatre: du front populaire à la fin de la guerre. Q/W/E/R/T/Y (6) 1996, 373–9.

14007. MORTON, DONALD. Birth of the cyberqueer. PMLA (110:3) 1995, 369–81. (Includes discussion of *Basic Instinct*.)

14008. MOSES, GAVRIEL. The nickel was for the movies: film in the novel from Pirandello to Puig. (Bibl. 1995, 12798.) Rev. by Steven G. Kellman in MFS (42:4) 1996, 921–3.

14009. MOTA, MIGUEL; TIESSEN, PAUL (eds). The cinema of Malcolm Lowry: a scholarly edition of *Tender Is the Night*. *See* **764**.

14010. MOY, JAMES S. Marginal sights: staging the Chinese in

America. (Bibl. 1995, 12799.) Rev. by Roger Daniels in AmS (36:1) 1995, 168–9.

14011.   MUCH, RITA; WILSON, ANN (eds).   Women on the Canadian stage: the legacy of Hrotsvit. Winnipeg, Man.: Blizzard, 1992. pp. xxiv, 133. Rev. by Kym Bird and Ed Nyman in CanTR (78) 1994, 65; by Sheila Rabillard in TRC (15:2) 1994, 216–18.

14012.   MULLALY, EDWARD.   W(h)ither the performance? TRC (13:1/2) 1992, 35–45. (Performance theory and theatre history.)

14013.   MULVEY, LAURA.   Fetishism and curiosity. Bloomington: Indiana UP; London: BFI, 1996. pp. xv, 188. (Perspectives.)

14014.   MUNBY, JONATHAN.   *Manhattan Melodrama*'s 'art of the weak': telling history from the other side in the 1930s talking gangster film. JAStud (30:1) 1996, 101–18.

14015.   MURPHY, BRENDA.   Tennessee Williams and Elia Kazan: a collaboration in the theatre. (Bibl. 1995, 12800.) Rev. by Thomas P. Adler in JDTC (8:1) 1993, 195–7; by Stephen A. Schrum in NETJ (5) 1994, 122–4.

14016.   MURPHY, KATHLEEN.   Jane Campion's shining: portrait of a director. *See* **11632**.

14017.   MURPHY, ROBERT.   Sixties British cinema. (Bibl. 1992, 10978.) Rev. by Kelly Boyd in JBS (34:1) 1995, 130–5.

14018.   MURRAY, TIMOTHY.   Like a film: ideological fantasy on screen, camera and canvas. (Bibl. 1995, 12805.) Rev. by Mark Harris in CanL (151) 1996, 160–1; by Peter Brunette in FilmQ (50:1) 1996, 55–6.

14019.   MYERS, NORMAN J.; SHIELDS, RONALD E.   The 'killer monologue' in contemporary American drama. NETJ (2) 1991, 99–112.

14020.   NADLER, PAUL.   Liberty censored: Black living newspapers of the Federal Theatre Project. AAR (29:4) 1995, 615–22.

14021.   NAIR, K. MOHANAN.   Existentialism in Western drama and modern Malayalam theater. WLR (1:1) 1996, 57–64.

14022.   NAREMORE, JAMES,   American *film noir*: the history of an idea. FilmQ (49:2) 1995/96, 12–27.

14023.   NEALE, STEVE.   'The story of Custer in everything but name': Colonel Thursday and *Fort Apache*. JFV (47:1–3) 1995, 26–32.

14024.   NEELY, KENT.   PRAXIS: an editorial statement. JDTC (7:2) 1993, 66–76.

14025.   NEFF, HEATHER.   Strange faces in the mirror: the ethics of diversity in children's films. LU (20:1) 1996, 50–65.

14026.   NEGRA, DIANE.   Coveting the feminine: Victor Frankenstein, Norman Bates, and Buffalo Bill. *See* **12238**.

14027.   NELSEN, PAUL.   An interview with the RSC's executive producer, Michael Attenborough. ShB (9:4) 1991, 20–3.

14028.   —— Reinventing Shakespeare's Globe? A report of design choices for ISGC Globe. ShB (10:4) 1992, 5–8.

14029.   —— Sizing up the Globe: proposed revisions to the ISGC reconstruction. ShB (11:4) 1993, 5–13.

14030.   —— Transition and revision at the Globe. ShB (12:2) 1994, 5–8.

14031.   NEWMAN, L. M. (ed.).   The correspondence of Edward Gordon Craig and Count Harry Kessler, 1903–1937. Leeds: Maney for Modern Humanities Research Assn and Inst. of Germanic Studies, Univ. of London, 1995. pp. xvi, 398, (plates) 4. (MHRA texts and dissertations, 43.) (Bithell dissertations, 21.) Rev. by John Dreyfus in BC (45:4) 1996, 576–8.

14032. NEWTON, ESTHER. Role models. *In* (pp. 39–53) **12**.

14033. NISCHIK, REINGARD M. 'Das Bild in der Fiktion': Film in Kurzprosatexten. GRM (45:2) 1995, 131–55.

14034. NOCHIMSON, MARTHA. Desire under the Douglas firs: entering the body of reality in *Twin Peaks*. FilmQ (46:2) 1992/93, 22–34.

14035. —— No end to her: soap opera and the female subject. (Bibl. 1995, 12809.) Rev. by Mary Beth Haralovich in FilmQ (47:4) 1994, 51–2; by Kathryn Dezeur in WS (25:2) 1996, 209–11.

14036. NOKES, DAVID. It isn't in the book. *See* **4229**.

14037. NOLLEN, SCOTT ALLEN. Sir Arthur Conan Doyle at the cinema. Foreword by Nicholas Meyer. *See* **11075**.

14038. NOONAN, JAMES. The making (and breaking) of a regional theatre critic: Audrey Ashley at the *Ottawa Citizen* 1961–1985. *See* **1331**.

14039. NOTHOF, ANNE. Canadian radio drama in English: prick up your ears. THC (11:1) 1990, 60–70.

14040. NOVAK, DEBORAH. The forgotten music of *Triple-A Plowed Under*, *Power*, and *One Third of a Nation*. JADT (6:2/3) 1994, 12–27.

14041. O'BOYLE, J. G. 'Be sure you're right, then go ahead': the early Disney Westerns. JPFT (24:2) 1996, 69–81.

14042. O'BRIEN, DENNIS. Shoring fragments: how CBS's *Beauty and the Beast* adapts consensus reality to shape its magical world. *In* (pp. 37–46) **36**.

14043. O'BRIEN, SHEILA RUZYCKI. Leaving behind *The Chisholm Trail* for *Red River*; or, Refiguring the female in the Western film epic. LitFQ (24:2) 1996, 183–92.

14044. O'BRIEN, TOM. The screening of America: movies and values from *Rocky* to *Rainman*. (Bibl. 1991, 10637.) Rev. by Robert P. Kolker in FilmQ (45:4) 1992, 59–60.

14045. ODABASHIAN, BARBARA. Double vision: Scorsese and Hitchcock. *In* (pp. 21–35) **113**.

14046. OHMER, SUSAN. 'That rags to riches stuff': Disney's *Cinderella* and the cultural space of animation. Film History (5:2) 1993, 231–49.

14047. OLANIYAN, TEJUMOLA. Scars of conquest/masks of resistance: the invention of cultural identities in African, African-American, and Caribbean drama. (Bibl. 1995, 12813.) Rev. by Myriam J. A. Chancy in AL (68:2) 1996, 480–1.

14048. OLDHAM, GABRIELLA. First cut: conversations with film editors. Berkeley; London: California UP, 1992. pp. ix, 417. Rev. by Stephen Prince in FilmQ (48:1) 1994, 63.

14049. OLSEN, VICKIE. The subordination of gender to race issues in the film musical *South Pacific*. *In* (pp. 345–58) **38**.

14050. O'NEILL, JOHN. Dinosaurs-R-Us: the (un)natural history of *Jurassic Park*. *In* (pp. 292–308) **72**.

14051. ORKIN, MARTIN (ed.). At the Junction: four plays by the Junction Avenue Theatre Company. Johannesburg: Witwatersrand UP, 1995. pp. 300. Rev. by Miki Flockemann in SARB (42) 1996, 5–6.

14052. ORR, JOHN. Paranoia and celebrity in American dramatic writing: 1970–90. *In* (pp. 141–58) **119**.

14053. ORVELL, MILES. Documentary film and the power of interrogation: *American Dream* and *Roger and Me*. FilmQ (48:2) 1994/95, 10–18.

14054. OSTMAN, RONALD E. Disney and its conservative critics: images *versus* realities. JPFT (24:2) 1996, 82–9.

14055. OSTROSKA, BEV. Interview with Ellen Stewart of LaMama

Experimental Theatre Club, December 9, 1989. JDTC (6:1) 1991, 99–105.

14056. Ostwalt, Conrad. *Dances with Wolves*: an American *Heart of Darkness*. LitFQ (24:2) 1996, 209–16.

14057. Pace, Patricia. Robert Bly does Peter Pan: the inner child as father to the man in Steven Spielberg's *Hook*. LU (20:1) 1996, 113–20.

14058. Pagan, Nicholas O. Decentering the subject: David Hare's *Wetherby*. In (pp. 53–63) **113**.

14059. Paige, Linda Rohrer. Wearing the red shoes: Dorothy and the power of the female imagination in *The Wizard of Oz*. JPFT (23:4) 1996, 146–53.

14060. Palmer, Gareth. *The Cosby Show* – an ideologically-based analysis. CritS (6:2) 1994, 188–94.

14061. Palmer, James; Riley, Michael. The films of Joseph Losey. (Bibl. 1993, 10232.) Rev. by Gregg Rickman in FilmQ (48:1) 1994, 63–4; by Wheeler Winston Dixon in FilmQ (50:1) 1996, 51–2.

14062. Palmer, Richard H. The critics' canon: standards of theatrical reviewing in America. (Bibl. 1989, 8100.) Rev. by James Fisher in JDTC (6:2) 1992, 160–1.

14063. Palumbo, Donald E. The politics of entropy: revolution *vs* evolution in George Pal's film version of H. G. Wells's *The Time Machine*. In (pp. 204–11) **70**.

14064. Paris, Michael. Country Blues on the screen: the Leadbelly films. *See* **3541**.

14065. —— From the Wright Brothers to *Top Gun*: aviation, nationalism and popular cinema. (Bibl. 1995, 12820.) Rev. by Stephen Constantine in JAStud (30:2) 1996, 302–3.

14066. Parker, Andrew. Praxis and performativity. WP (8:2) 1996, 265–83.

14067. Parker, Hershel. The *auteur*–author paradox: how critics of the cinema and the novel talk about flawed or even 'mutilated' texts. *See* **779**.

14068. Parkinson, David (ed.). Mornings in the dark: the Graham Greene film reader. (Bibl. 1994, 10215.) Rev. by Robert Murray Davis in WLT (69:3) 1995, 592; by Tony Williams in FilmQ (50:1) 1996, 52–3.

14069. Parshall, Peter F. Buster Keaton and the space of farce: *Steamboat Bill, Jr* versus *The Cameraman*. JFV (46:3) 1994, 29–46.

14070. Paul, William. Laughing, screaming: modern Hollywood horror and comedy. (Bibl. 1995, 12824.) Rev. by Gregory A. Waller in FilmQ (48:4) 1995, 50–1.

14071. Peake, Glenn. Icons, iconoclasts, and ideology: the strange case of Quentin Tarantino. UDR (24:1) 1996, 55–61.

14072. Pearson, Roberta E. Custer's still the hero: textual stability and transformation. JFV (47:1–3) 1995, 82–97.

14073. Pelletier, Esther. Problématique de l'enseignement du scénario comme objet de création et de construction. Études littéraires (26:2) 1993, 37–45.

14074. Pendergast, John S. A nation of Hamlets: Shakespeare and cultural politics. *See* **6432**.

14075. Pereira, John W. Opening nights: 25 years of the Manhattan Theatre Club. New York; Frankfurt; Bern; Paris: Lang, 1996. pp. x, 480. (American univ. studies, xxvi: Theatre arts, 17.)

14076. Perkins, Kathy A. (ed.). Black female playwrights:

an anthology of plays before 1950. (Bibl. 1993, 10237.) Rev. by Ann Marie McEntee in JDTC (7:1) 1992, 200–3.

14077. —— Uno, Roberta (eds). Contemporary plays by women of color: an anthology. London; New York: Routledge, 1996. pp. ix, 323.

14078. Perry, Dennis R. Imps of the perverse: discovering the Poe/Hitchcock connection. *See* **12066**.

14079. Peters, Helen. Towards Canadian postmodernism. CanTR (76) 1993, 13–17.

14080. Peterson, Jennifer. The competing tunes of *Johnny Guitar*: liberalism, sexuality, masquerade. CinJ (35:3) 1996, 3–18.

14081. Petrie, Duncan (ed.). Cinema and the realms of enchantment: lectures, seminars and essays. (Bibl. 1993, 10240.) Rev. by Neal Baker in Extrapolation (36:1) 1995, 76–9.

14082. Peucker, Brigitte. Incorporating images: film and the rival arts. Princeton, NJ; Chichester: Princeton UP, 1995. pp. xi, 227.

14083. —— Rival arts? Filming *The Age of Innocence*. EWR (13:1) 1996, 19–22.

14084. Pharr, Mary. Different shops of horrors: from Roger Corman's cult classic to Frank Oz's mainstream musical. *In* (pp. 212–19) **70**.

14085. Phelan, Peggy. Unmarked: the politics of performance. (Bibl. 1995, 12832.) Rev. by Lynda Hall in JDTC (10:2) 1996, 159–61.

14086. Phillips, Jerry; Wojcik-Andrews, Ian. Telling tales to children: the pedagogy of empire in MGM's *Kim* and Disney's *Aladdin*. LU (20:1) 1996, 66–89.

14087. Pilkington, Ace G. *Star Trek V*: the search for God. LitFQ (24:2) 1996, 169–76.

14088. Pinedo, Isabel. Recreational terror: postmodern elements of the contemporary horror film. JFV (48:1/2) 1996, 17–31.

14089. Pitt, Angela. A conversation between Deborah Warner and Angela Pitt. ERev (6:2) 1995, 10–12.

14090. Plasse, Marie A. 'Joy in repetition'? Prince's *Graffiti Bridge* and *Sign o' the Times* as sequels to *Purple Rain*. JPC (30:3) 1996, 57–65.

14091. Plo Alastrué, Ramón. Gender and genre conventions in *When Harry Met Sally*. *In* (pp. 399–418) **38**.

14092. Poe, G. Thomas. Censorship as textual ellipsis: a post-structuralist reading of the censored film. JDTC (6:1) 1991, 187–208.

14093. Pointer, Michael. Charles Dickens on the screen: the film, television, and video adaptations. *See* **10890**.

14094. Powell, Michael. Million-dollar movie: the second volume of his life in movies. (Bibl. 1995, 12842.) New York: Random House, 1995. Rev. by Joel E. Siegel in BkW, 2 Apr. 1995, 4.

14095. Prats, Armando J. Back from the sunset: the Western, the Eastwood hero, and *Unforgiven*. JFV (47:1–3) 1995, 106–23.

14096. Prats, Armando José. His master's voice(over): revisionist ethos and narrative dependence from *Broken Arrow* (1950) to *Geronimo: an American Legend* (1993). ANQ (9:3) 1996, 15–29.

14097. Prelutsky, Bert. An interview with Billy Wilder. MichQR (35:1) 1996, 65–74.

14098. Pressler, Michael. Poet and professor on the movies. GetR (4:1) 1991, 157–65.

14099. PRICE, STEVEN. American literature: the twentieth century: drama. YWES (75) 1994, 663–84.

14100. PRINCE, STEPHEN. True lies: perceptual realism, digital images, and film theory. FilmQ (49:3) 1996, 27–37.

14101. PRINSLOO, JEANNE. South African films in flux: thoughts on changes in the politics of identity in recent film productions. SATJ (10:2) 1996, 31–49.

14102. PRYLUCK, CALVIN. When is a sign not a sign? JDTC (6:2) 1992, 221–31.

14103. PURDIE, SUSAN. Film studies. YWCCT (3) 1993, 341–67.

14104. QUART, LEONARD; AUSTER, ALBERT. A novelist and screen-writer eyeballs the inner city: an interview with Richard Price. Cineaste (22:1) 1996, 12–17.

14105. QUASCHNOWITZ, DIRK. Die englische Farce im frühen 20. Jahrhundert. (Bibl. 1994, 10226.) Rev. by Ulrich Blumenbach in ZAA (43:2) 1995, 192–3.

14106. QUINE, MICHAEL. Theater audiences in Britain: a continuing research program. JAML (23:3) 1993, 225–39.

14107. QUINN, MICHAEL L. Alan Schneider's *Entrances*: auto-biography, theatre, and style in an American frame. JADT (5:3) 1993, 28–41 (review-article).

14108. —— Self-reliance and ritual renewal: anti-theatrical ideology in American method acting. JDTC (10:1) 1995, 5–20.

14109. RABINOVITZ, LAUREN. Points of resistance: women, power, and politics in the New York avant-garde cinema, 1943–71. Urbana: Illinois UP, 1991. pp. xi, 250. Rev. by Scott McDonald in FilmQ (45:4) 1992, 57–8; by Wheeler Winston Dixon in JFV (47:4) 1995/96, 46–8.

14110. RAMANATHAN, GEETHA. Sexual politics and the male playwright: the portrayal of women in ten contemporary plays. Jefferson, NC; London: McFarland, 1996. pp. x, 190.

14111. RANKIN, AUDRIE. Malcolm Lowry's *Tender Is the Night*: form, structure, spirit. MalLR (31/32) 1992/93, 85–111.

14112. RAPPAPORT, MARK. Mark Rappaport's notes on *Rock Hudson's Home Movies*. FilmQ (49:4) 1996, 16–22.

14113. RAY, NICHOLAS. I was interrupted: Nicholas Ray on making movies. Berkeley; London: California UP, 1993. pp. xlviii, 243, (plates) 12. Rev. by S.P. in FilmQ (48:1) 1994, 64.

14114. RECCHIA, EDWARD. *Film noir* and the Western. CR (40:3) 1996, 601–14.

14115. REGESTER, CHARLENE. Lynched, assaulted, and intimidated: Oscar Micheaux's most controversial films. PCR (5:1) 1994, 47–55.

14116. —— The misreading and rereading of African-American filmmaker Oscar Micheaux: a critical review of Micheaux scholarship. Film History (7:4) 1995, 426–49.

14117. —— Stepin Fetchit: the man, the image, and the African-American press. Film History (6:4) 1994, 502–21.

14118. REID, MARK A. Redefining Black film. Berkeley; London: California UP, 1993. pp. x, 170. Rev. by Eugene Levy in AHR (99:5) 1994, 1748–9; by Michael Pounds in FilmQ (48:3) 1995, 54–6.

14119. REINBERG HOLT, FAYE. Alberta plays and playwrights: Alberta Playwrights' Network catalogue. Calgary, Alta: Alberta Playwrights' Network, 1991. pp. 80. Rev. by Anne Nothof in CanTR (81) 1994, 94–5.

14120. Reinelt, Janelle. Beyond Brecht: Britain's new feminist drama. *In* (pp. 150–9) **84**.

14121. —— Is the English epic over? *In* (pp. 209–22) **119**.

14122. Reinelt, Janelle G. After Brecht: British epic theater. (Bibl. 1994, 10230.) Rev. by Robert F. Gross in JDTC (10:1) 1995, 143–5; by Jenny S. Spencer in ConLit (37:3) 1996, 474–7.

14123. Reinheimer, David. Ontological and ethical allusion: Shakespeare in *The Next Generation*. *See* **6447**.

14124. Reitinger, Douglas W. Too long in the wasteland: visions of the American West in film, 1980–1990. FilmH (26:1/4) 1996, 20–9.

14125. Remael, Aline. Censorship: cross-media cutting in 1950s–60s Britain. *See* **13280**.

14126. Ribeiro, Luisa F. *Heavenly Creatures*. FilmQ (49:1) 1995, 33–8.

14127. Richtarik, Marilynn J. Acting between the lines: the Field Day Theatre Company and Irish cultural politics, 1980–1984. (Bibl. 1995, 12855.) Rev. by Richard Jones in JDTC (11:1) 1996, 137–9; by Anthony Bradley in ConLit (37:3) 1996, 490–1; by Tom Herron in Irish Review (19) 1996, 151–3; by Michael McKinnie in Essays in Theatre (15:1) 1996, 118–20; by Ulf Dantanus in IUR (26:1) 1996, 177–9.

14128. Riegel, Henriette. Soap operas and gossip. JPC (29:4) 1996, 201–9.

14129. Roberts, Carol. The prediction of gesture: Timothy Findley and Canadian theatre. THC (12:1) 1991, 22–36.

14130. Robertson, James C. The *Casablanca* man: the cinema of Michael Curtiz. (Bibl. 1993, 10251.) Rev. by Leonard J. Leff in FilmQ (48:1) 1994, 39–40; by James Van Dyck Card in JPFT (24:1) 1996, 45.

14131. Robertson, Pamela. Camping under Western stars: Joan Crawford in *Johnny Guitar*. JFV (47:1–3) 1995, 33–49.

14132. —— 'The kinda comedy that imitates me': Mae West's identification with the feminist camp. *In* (pp. 156–72) **12**.

14133. Robinson, David. From peep show to palace: the birth of American film. New York; Chichester: Columbia UP in assn with Library of Congress, 1996. pp. xiv, 213, (plates) 16.

14134. Robinson, Marc. The other American drama. (Bibl. 1995, 12859.) Rev. by Mary Jo Sodd in JDTC (9:2) 1995, 170–3; by Marvin Carlson in Theater (25:3) 1995, 90–2.

14135. Roche, Anthony. Contemporary Irish drama: from Beckett to McGuinness. (Bibl. 1995, 12860.) Rev. by Patrick Colm Hogan in ColLit (23:3) 1996, 163–70.

14136. Rockett, Will. Jason dreams of Freddy: genre, supertext, and the production of meaning through pop-cultural literacy. *In* (pp. 179–98) **19**.

14137. Rodowick, David. The difficulty of difference: psycho-analysis, sexual difference and film theory. (Bibl. 1992, 11038.) Rev. by Linda Dittmar in NWSAJ (4:3) 1992, 359–65; by Richard W. McCormick in Signs (18:1) 1992, 173–87.

14138. Rodríguez, María Cristina. Narrators in narration in fiction and film: Ruth Prawer Jhabvala's *Heat and Dust*. CanRCL (23:3) 1996, 803–8.

14139. Rogin, Michael. Blackface, white noise: Jewish immigrants in the Hollywood melting pot. Berkeley; London: California UP, 1996. pp. xvi, 339.

14140. ROLLINS, PETER C.   Frank Capra's *Why We Fight* film series and our American dream. JAC (19:4) 1996, 81–6.

14141. ROMÁN, DAVID.   'It's my party and I'll die if I want to!': gay men, AIDS, and the circulation of camp in US theater. *In* (pp. 206–33) **12**.

14142. —— Shakespeare out of Portland: Gus Van Sant's *My Own Private Idaho*, homoneurotics, and boy actors. *In* (pp. 311–33) **30**.

14143. ROMERO, ROLANDO J.   The postmodern hybrid: do aliens dream of alien sheep? PS (16:1) 1996, 41–52.

14144. ROMERO GUILLÉN, MARÍA DOLORES.   Woman's death and patriarchal closure in Fritz Lang's *The Big Heat*. *In* (pp. 333–44) **38**.

14145. RONY, FATIMAH TOBING.   Victor Masayesva, Jr, and the politics of *Imagining Indians*. FilmQ (48:2) 1994/95, 20–33.

14146. ROSE, BRIAN.   Transformations of terror: reading changes in social attitudes through film and television adaptations of Stevenson's *Dr Jekyll and Mr Hyde*. *In* (pp. 37–52) **113**.

14147. ROSE, MARGARET.   Monologue plays for female voices: an introductory study. Turin: Tirrenia stampatori, 1995. pp. 132. (Le voci del tempo, 2.) Rev. by Elizabeth Sakellaridou in EEM (5:2) 1996, 55.

14148. ROSENBAUM, JONATHAN.   Orson Welles' memo to Universal: *Touch of Evil*. FilmQ (46:1) 1992, 2–11.

14149. —— (ed.).   This is Orson Welles. By Orson Welles and Peter Bogdanovich. (Bibl. 1993, 10255.) Rev. by John Simon in ASch (62:4) 1993, 622–6.

14150. ROSENHEIM, SHAWN.   Extraterrestrial: science fictions in *A Brief History of Time* and *The Incredible Shrinking Man*. FilmQ (48:4) 1995, 15–21.

14151. ROSENSTONE, ROBERT A.   Visions of the past: the challenge of film to our idea of history. Cambridge, MA; London: Harvard UP, 1995. pp. viii, 271.

14152. ROSOLOWSKI, TACEY A.   The chronotopic restructuring of gaze in film. AQ (52:2) 1996, 105–38.

14153. ROSS, ANDREW.   Uses of camp. *In* (pp. 54–77) **12**.

14154. ROTHMAN, STANLEY.   Is God really dead in Beverly Hills? Religion and the movies. ASch (65:2) 1996, 272–8.

14155. ROUDANÉ, MATTHEW C.   American drama since 1960: a critical history. New York: Twayne; London: Prentice Hall, 1996. pp. xv, 298. (Twayne's critical history of American drama.)

14156. —— Arthur Miller and his influence on contemporary American drama. AmDr (6:1) 1996, 1–13.

14157. ROVANO, MARCELAINE WININGER.   The angel as fantasy figure in classic and contemporary film. JFA (5:3) 1992, 58–74.

14158. RUBIN, MARTIN.   MAKE LOVE MAKE WAR: cultural confusion and the biker film cycle. Film History (6:3) 1994, 355–81.

14159. RUBY, JAY.   An anthropological critique of the films of Robert Gardner. JFV (43:4) 1991, 3–17.

14160. —— Speaking for, speaking about, speaking with, speaking alongside: an anthropological and documentary dilemma. JFV (44:1/2) 1992, 42–66.

14161. RUDAKOFF, JUDITH; MUCH, RITA (eds).   Fair play: 12 women speak: conversations with Canadian playwrights. (Bibl. 1992, 11048.) Rev. by Barbara Drennan in CanTR (70) 1992, 95–6.

14162. RUNNING-JOHNSON, CYNTHIA.   Examining critical history through theater: feminist scholarship of the 1980s and beyond. JDTC (9:1) 1994, 87–104.

14163. RUPPERT, PETER. Tracing utopia: film, spectatorship and desire. Utopian Studies (7:2) 1996, 139–52.

14164. RUSSELL, HAWLEY. Crossing games: reading Black transvestism at the movies. CritM (8:1) 1994, 109–25.

14165. RYAN, MICHAEL. Textuality and history: a response to Poe and Black. JDTC (6:1) 1991, 209–18.

14166. SABAL, ROB. Making contact: working with the White Mountain Apache on *Indian Summer*. JFV (48:4) 1996, 32–7.

14167. SADDLEMYER, ANN. Crime in literature: Canadian drama. *In* (pp. 214–30) **105**.

14168. SALTER, DENIS. The idea of a national theatre. *In* (pp. 71–90) **13**.

14169. —— On native ground: Canadian theatre historiography and the postmodernism/postcolonialism axis. TRC (13:1/2) 1992, 135–43.

14170. SAMUELS, DAVID. 'These are the stories that the dogs tell': discourses of identity and difference in ethnography and science fiction. CultA (11:1) 1996, 88–118.

14171. SANDERS, JOE. *Raising Arizona*: not quite Ozzie and Harriet meet the biker from Hell. JFA (6:2/3) 1993, 217–33.

14172. SANJEK, DAVID. Dr Hobbes' parasites: victims, victimization, and gender in David Cronenberg's *Shivers*. CinJ (36:1) 1996, 55–74.

14173. SAPERSTEIN, JEFFREY. Irony and cliché: Malamud's *The Natural* in the 1980s. LitFQ (24:1) 1996, 84–7.

14174. SARVER, STEPHANIE. Homer Simpson meets Frankenstein: cinematic influence in Nathanael West's *The Day of the Locust*. *See* **12243**.

14175. SAVAGE, STEPHANIE. Evelyn Nesbit and the film(ed) histories of the Thaw–White scandal. Film History (8:2) 1996, 159–75.

14176. SAVRAN, DAVID. Revolution ... history ... theater: the politics of the Wooster Group's second trilogy. *In* (pp. 41–55) **83**.

14177. SAWYER, DAVID. 'Yet why not say what happened?' Boundaries of the self in Raymond Carver's fiction and Robert Altman's *Short Cuts*. *In* (pp. 195–219) **8**.

14178. SCHACH, LEONARD. The flag is flying: a very personal history of theatre in the old South Africa. Cape Town: Human & Rousseau, 1996. pp. 191.

14179. SCHAEFER, ERIC. Resisting refinement: the exploitation film and self-censorship. Film History (6:3) 1994, 293–313.

14180. SCHAEFER, RICHARD J. Public television constituencies: a study in media aesthetics and intentions. JFV (43:1/2) 1991, 46–68.

14181. SCHMIDT, PAUL H. Charming pigs and mimetic desire in Quentin Tarantino's *Pulp Fiction*. UDR (24:1) 1996, 43–53.

14182. SCHMITT, NATALIE CROHN. Actors and onlookers: theater and twentieth-century scientific views of nature. (Bibl. 1995, 12883.) Rev. by Alice Rayner in JDTC (6:1) 1991, 146–9.

14183. SCHMOR, JOHN BROCKWAY. Confessional performance: postmodern culture in recent American theater. JDTC (9:1) 1994, 157–72.

14184. SCHNEIDER, ALAN. Entrances: an American director's journey. New York: Viking, 1986. pp. xv, 416, (plates) 24. Rev. by Michael L. Quinn in JADT (5:3) 1993, 28–41.

14185. SCHNIERER, PETER PAUL. Rekonventionalisierung im englischen Drama 1980–1990. (Bibl. 1994, 10252.) Rev. by Ewald

Mengel in Forum modernes Theater (10:2) 1995, 219–20; by Adolf Barth in LJGG (37:supp.) 1996, 532–6; by Manfred Beyer in Archiv (233:2) 1996, 428–30.

14186. SCHOENWALD, JONATHAN M.   Rewriting revolution: the origins, production and reception of *Viva Zapata!* Film History (8:2) 1996, 109–30.

14187. SCHROEDER, PATRICIA R.   American drama, feminist discourse, and dramatic form: in defense of critical pluralism. JDTC (7:2) 1993, 103–17.

14188. —— The feminist possibilities of dramatic realism. Madison, NJ: Fairleigh Dickinson UP; London; Toronto: Assoc. UPs, 1996. pp. 185.

14189. SCHULTE, RAINER.   Plays in translation: a profile of *PAJ* Publications/*Performing Arts Journal*. *See* **1079**.

14190. SCHULTHEISS, JOHN.   *A Season of Fear*: the blacklisted teleplays of Abraham Polonsky. LitFQ (24:2) 1996, 148–64.

14191. SCHUTH, H. WAYNE.   *Testament*: to deserve the children. *In* (pp. 146–50) **77**.

14192. SCHUTTE, XANDRA.   Tarzan, heerser van de jungle. (Tarzan, lord of the jungle.) De Gids (159:8) 1996, 688–99.

14193. SCHWARTZ, RICHARD A.   Frederick Wiseman's modernistic vision: *Central Park*. LitFQ (23:3) 1995, 223–8.

14194. SCORSESE, MARTIN; COCKS, JAY.   *The Age of Innocence*: the shooting script. Ed. by Robin Standefer. New York: Newmarket Press, 1995. pp. xi, 146. (Newmarket shooting scripts.)

14195. SELF, ROBERT T.   Redressing the law in Kathryn Bigelow's *Blue Steel*. JFV (46:2) 1994, 31–43.

14196. SELTZER, ALVIN J.   *All That Jazz*: Bob Fosse's solipsistic masterpiece. LitFQ (24:1) 1996, 99–104.

14197. SENIOR, W. A.   *Blade Runner* and cyberpunk visions of humanity. FilCr (21:1) 1996, 1–12.

14198. SEYMOUR, ANNA.   Culture and political change: British radical theatre in recent history. TRI (21:1) 1996, 8–16.

14199. SHATZKY, JOEL.   AIDS enters the American theater: *As Is* and *The Normal Heart*. *In* (pp. 131–9) **2**.

14200. SHELLARD, DOMINIC.   Harold Hobson, witness and judge: the theatre criticism of Harold Hobson. Keele: Keele UP, 1995. pp. 255. (Cf. bibl. 1993, 10278.)

14201. SHINDLER, COLIN.   Hollywood in crisis: cinema and American society, 1929–1939. London; New York: Routledge, 1996. pp. x, 258. (Cinema and society.)

14202. SHINGLER, MARTIN.   The fourth Warner Brother and her role in the war. JAStud (30:1) 1996, 127–31. (Bette Davis.)

14203. SHINN, THELMA J.   Gender images and patterns from novel to film. *In* (pp. 451–9) **38**.

14204. SHOLLE, DAVID.   Reading the audience, reading resistance: prospects and problems. JFV (43:1/2) 1991, 80–9.

14205. SHULL, MICHAEL S.; WILT, DAVID EDWARD.   Hollywood war films, 1937–1945: an exhaustive filmography of American feature-length motion pictures relating to World War II. Jefferson, NC; London: McFarland, 1996. pp. xi, 482.

14206. SIDNELL, MICHAEL J.   Used words. CanTR (75) 1993, 4–7. (Language, literature and performance.)

14207. SIEGEL, SCOTT; SIEGEL, BARBARA. American film comedy. New York; London: Prentice Hall, 1995. pp. 316.

14208. SIKOV, ED. Laughing hysterically: American screen comedy of the 1950s. New York; Chichester: Columbia UP, 1994. pp. xvii, 282, (plates) 24. (Film and culture.)

14209. SIMMON, SCOTT. Concerning the weary legs of Wyatt Earp: the classic Western according to Shakespeare. *See* **6845**.

14210. —— 'The female of the species': D. W. Griffith: father of the women's film. FilmQ (46:2) 1992/93, 8–20.

14211. —— The films of D. W. Griffith. (Bibl. 1993, 10282.) Rev. by G.R. in FilmQ (48:1) 1994, 64.

14212. SIMON, JOHN. The great gray way. TLS, 26 Apr. 1996, 17. (Contemporary American theatre.)

14213. SIMON, WILLIAM G.; SPENCE, LOUISE. Cowboy wonderland, history, and myth: 'it ain't all that different from real life'. JFV (47:1–3) 1995, 67–81.

14214. SIMONETTI, MARIE-CLAIRE. The blurring of time in *The French Lieutenant's Woman*, the novel and the film. LitFQ (24:3) 1996, 301–8.

14215. SIMPSON, MARK. 'The amateur! The amateur!': notes on *Apocalypse Now. In* (pp. 106–15) **117**.

14216. SINGER, BEN. New York, just like I pictured it … . CinJ (35:3) 1996, 104–28.

14217. SITAS, ARI. Description of a struggle: South African theatre since 1970. WLT (70:1) 1996, 83–7.

14218. SITNEY, P. ADAMS. Cinematic election and theological vanity. Raritan (11:2) 1991, 48–65.

14219. SKOLLER, JEFFREY. *The Man without a World.* FilmQ (49:1) 1995, 28–32.

14220. SLIDE, ANTHONY. The silent feminists: America's first women directors. Lanham, MD; London: Scarecrow Press, 1996. pp. xiv, 160.

14221. SMEDLEY, NICK. Fritz Lang's trilogy: the rise and fall of a European social commentator. Film History (5:1) 1993, 1–21.

14222. SMITH, ALLAN. Seeing things: race, image, and national identity in Canadian and American movies and television. ARCS (26:3) 1996, 367–90.

14223. SMITH, GREG M. Blocking *Blockade*: partisan protest, popular debate, and encapsulated texts. CinJ (36:1) 1996, 18–38.

14224. —— Silencing the new woman: ethnic and social mobility in the melodramas of Norma Talmadge. JFV (48:3) 1996, 3–16.

14225. SMITH, HARRY W. An air of the dream: Jo Mielziner, innovation, and influence, 1935–1955. JADT (5:3) 1993, 42–54.

14226. SMITH, MARY ELIZABETH. On the margins: Eastern Canadian theatre as post-colonialist discourse. TRI (21:1) 1996, 41–51.

14227. SMITH, MURRAY. Engaging characters: fiction, emotion, and the cinema. *See* **4264**.

14228. SMITH, TERRY DONOVAN. Mixing it up in the Depression: a (not-so) hidden representation of class struggle. JPFT (24:3) 1996, 124–33.

14229. SMOODIN, ERIC. Animating culture: Hollywood cartoons from the sound era. New Brunswick, NJ: Rutgers UP, 1993. pp. xvi, 216. (Communications, media, and culture.) Rev. by Susan Ohmer in Film History (6:3) 1994, 405–8; by Robert W. McEachern in JPC (29:4) 1996, 253–4; by Mark J. P. Wolf in FilmQ (50:1) 1996, 35–7.

14230. —— 'Compulsory' viewing for every citizen: *Mr Smith* and the rhetoric of reception. CinJ (35:2) 1996, 3–23.

14231. SOBCHACK, TOM.   Bakhtin's 'carnivalesque' in 1950s British comedy. JPFT (23:4) 1996, 179–85.

14232. SOBCHACK, VIVIAN.   The address of the eye: a phenomenology of film experience. Princeton, NJ; Oxford: Princeton UP, 1992. pp. xxi, 330. Rev. by Harald Stadler with response by Vivian Sobchack in JFV (46:1) 1994, 61–6.

14233. SOMERSET, J. ALAN B.   The Stratford Festival story: a catalogue-index to the Stratford, Ontario, Festival 1953–1990. (Bibl. 1994, 10269.) Rev. by Harry Lane in TRC (14:2) 1993, 204–6.

14234. SPADONI, ROBERT.   Geniuses of the systems: authorship and evidence in classical Hollywood cinema. Film History (7:4) 1995, 362–85.

14235. SPEIRS, LOGAN.   Current literature 1993: 1, New writing: drama and poetry. EngS (76:2) 1995, 156–84.

14236. SPENCER, JENNY S.   Mainstreaming British Left theater. ConLit (37:3) 1996, 471–80 (review-article).

14237. SPITTLES, BRIAN.   *Middlemarch*: TV *versus* text? *See* **11160**.

14238. SPRINGER, JOHN.   'This is a riot you're in': Hollywood and American mass culture in Nathanael West's *The Day of the Locust*. LitFQ (24:4) 1996, 439–44.

14239. STACEY, JACKIE.   Star gazing: Hollywood cinema and female spectatorship. London; New York: Routledge, 1994. pp. xiv, 282. Rev. by Rita Felski in AmLH (8:2) 1996, 391–3.

14240. STAIGER, JANET.   Interpreting films: studies in the historical reception of American cinema. (Bibl. 1992, 11073.) Rev. by Stephen Prince in FilmQ (46:2) 1992/93, 51–2; by Michael T. Isenberg in AHR (98:2) 1993, 596–7.

14241. STALYER, JANET.   Self-regulation and the classical Hollywood cinema. JDTC (6:1) 1991, 221–30.

14242. STANNARD, KATHERINE.   Technology and the female in the *Doctor Who* series: companions or competitors? *In* (pp. 64–71) **87**.

14243. STASHOWER, DANIEL.   'And here there are genuine tears': Jeremy Brett, 1935–1995. *See* **11081**.

14244. STASKOWSKI, ANDRÉA.   *Blade Runner*: the future as the past, the postmodern present; or, How to be human in the future. *In* (pp. 185–91) **117**.

14245. STEED, TONIA.   Exploring the cave: the search for a feminist mimesis in *The French Lieutenant's Woman*. TexPres (13) 1992, 71–6.

14246. STEINBERG, CAROL; PURKEY, MALCOLM.   South African theater in crisis. Theater (25:3) 1995, 24–37.

14247. STENBERG, DAVY.   The circle of life and the chain of being: Shakespearean motifs in *The Lion King*. *See* **6479**.

14248. STEPHENS, JUDITH L.   Anti-lynch plays by African-American women: race, gender, and social protest in American drama. AAR (26:2) 1992, 329–39.

14249. —— Gender ideology and dramatic convention in Progressive Era plays, 1890–1920. *In* (pp. 283–93) **84**.

14250. STETZ, MARGARET D.   *The Ghost and Mrs Muir*: laughing with the captain in the house. StudN (28:1) 1996, 93–112.

14251. STILLER, LEWIS.   *Suo gân* and *Empire of the Sun*. LitFQ (24:4) 1996, 344–7.

14252. STOCKER, SUSAN. The commercialization of *Tom Jones*. *See* **9046**.

14253. STONE, JUDY S. J. Theatre. (Bibl. 1995, 12927.) Rev. by Bruce King in WLT (69:2) 1995, 416–17.

14254. STONEBACK, H. R. Fiction into film: 'Is dying hard, daddy?' Hemingway's *Indian Camp*. *In* (pp. 93–108) **113**.

14255. STONES, BARBARA. America goes to the movies: 100 years of motion picture exhibition. North Hollywood, CA: National Assn of Theatre Owners, 1993. pp. 256. Rev. by Douglas Gomery in FilmQ (48:1) 1994, 65.

14256. STORHOFF, GARY. Icon and history in *Frances*. LitFQ (23:4) 1995, 266–72.

14257. STOWELL, SHEILA. Rehabilitating realism. JDTC (6:2) 1992, 81–8.

14258. STRAAYER, CHRIS. Lesbian narratives and queer characters in Monika Treut's *Virgin Machine*. JFV (45:2/3) 1993, 24–39.

14259. STRACZYNSKI, J. MICHAEL. The profession of science fiction: 48, Approaching Babylon. Foundation (64) 1995, 5–19. (*Babylon 5*.)

14260. STREITFELD, DAVID. But I saw the movie … . BkW, 8 Sept. 1996, 1, 15.

14261. STUDLAR, GAYLYN; DESSER, DAVID (eds). Reflections in a male eye: John Huston and the American experience. (Bibl. 1993, 10297.) Rev. by Doug K. Holm in FilmQ (47:4) 1994, 52–3.

14262. STYAN, J. L. Chekhov and American drama in the early twentieth century. AmDr (4:1) 1994, 3–20.

14263. SUÁREZ SÁNCHEZ, JUAN A. The rear view: paranoia and homosocial desire in Alfred Hitchcock's *Rear Window*. *In* (pp. 359–69) **38**.

14264. SUTHERLAND, RICHARD. The Gallimaufry and the roots of alternative theatre in Vancouver. TRC (16:1/2) 1995, 40–58.

14265. TABORSKI, BOLESŁAW. Edynburg po raz pięćdziesiąty: eksperymenty trwaja. (Edinburgh for the fiftieth time: experiments continue.) Dialog (1996:11) 185–90.

14266. TAKASHIMA, KUNIKO. America engeki kenkyu – American realism no rhetoric. (A study of American theater: the rhetoric of American realism.) Tokyo: Kokusho Kankokai, 1996. pp. 342.

14267. TANNEN, DEBORAH. Where'd all the fun go? BkW, 21 Nov. 1993, 1, 10–11.

14268. TANNER, JO A. Classical Black theatre: the Federal Theatre's all-Black *Voodoo Macbeth*. *See* **7008**.

14269. —— Dusky maidens: the odyssey of the early Black dramatic actress. *See* **9786**.

14270. TASHIRO, CHARLES. Home film and video: the case of *Who Framed Roger Rabbit?* JFV (48:1/2) 1996, 58–66.

14271. —— When history films (try to) become paintings. CinJ (35:3) 1996, 19–33.

14272. TASKER, YVONNE. Spectacular bodies: gender, genre, and the action cinema. (Bibl. 1993, 10299.) Rev. by John P. McCarthy in FilmQ (48:4) 1995, 56–7; by Elisabeth Arnold in WS (25:2) 1996, 201–3.

14273. TAYLOR, ANNETTE M.; UPCHURCH, DAVID. *Northern Exposure* and mythology of the global community. JPC (30:2) 1996, 75–85.

14274. TAYLOR, DREW HAYDEN. Alive and well: Native theatre in Canada. JCanStud (31:3) 1996, 29–37.

14275. Taylor, Hilary.   Language in their gesture: Théâtre de Complicité. EEM (2:2) 1993, 39–42. (British theatrical company.)

14276. Telotte, J. P.   Annual bibliography of film studies 1991; 1992; 1993; 1994. PS (11:3) 1992, 53–80; (12:3) 1993, 52–79; (13:3) 1994, 62–85; (14:3) 1995, 51–74.

14277. —— Definitely – falling – down: *8½*, *Falling Down*, and the death of fantasy. JPFT (24:1) 1996, 19–25.

14278. —— Fatal capers: strategy and enigma in *film noir*. JPFT (23:4) 1996, 163–70.

14279. —— In the realm of revealing: the technological double in the modern science fiction film. JFA (6:2/3) 1993, 234–52.

14280. —— Replications: a robotic history of the science fiction film. Urbana: Illinois UP, 1995. pp. 222. Rev. by Peter Ruppert in Utopian Studies (7:2) 1996, 343–4; by David Seed in JAStud (30:3) 1996, 500–1.

14281. —— *The World of Tomorrow* and the 'secret goal' of science fiction. JFV (45:1) 1993, 27–39.

14282. Thompson, Emma.   Jane Austen's *Sense and Sensibility*: the screenplay and diaries. *See* **10327**.

14283. Thomson, David.   Rosebud: the story of Orson Welles. London: Little, Brown; New York: Knopf, 1996. pp. 463.

14284. Thornham, Sue.   Feminist interventions: *Prime Suspect 1*. CritS (6:2) 1994, 226–33.

14285. Thornton, William H.   After the carnival: the filmic prosaics of *Schindler's List*. CanRCL (23:3) 1996, 701–8.

14286. Tibbets, John C.   The hole in the doughnut: the last days of Buster Keaton. JDTC (10:1) 1995, 79–99.

14287. Tiessen, Paul (ed.).   A few items culled from what started out to be a sort of preface to a film-script. MalLR (33) 1993, 48–66.

14288. Tinkcom, Matthew.   Working like a homosexual: camp visual codes and the labor of gay subjects in the MGM Freed Unit. CinJ (35:2) 1996, 24–42.

14289. Tobias, Patricia Eliot, *et al.*   A letter from *The Keaton Chronicle*. FilmQ (49:2) 1995/96, 48–51.

14290. Toles, George.   This may hurt a little: the art of humiliation in film. FilmQ (48:4) 1995, 2–4.

14291. Tompkins, Joanne.   Re-citing Shakespeare in post-colonial drama. *See* **6494**.

14292. Trushell, John.   Return of *Forbidden Planet*? Foundation (64) 1995, 82–9.

14293. Tseo, George K. Y.   *Joy Luck*: the perils of transcultural 'translation'. LitFQ (24:4) 1996, 338–43.

14294. Tucker, Stephanie.   Despair not, neither to presume: *The French Lieutenant's Woman*: a screenplay. LitFQ (24:1) 1996, 63–9.

14295. Tulloch, John; Jenkins, Henry.   Science fiction audiences: watching *Doctor Who* and *Star Trek*. London; New York: Routledge, 1995. pp. xiii, 294. (Popular fiction.) Rev. by Frances Bonner in Foundation (64) 1995, 106–10.

14296. Ukpokudu, I. Peter.   'Lest one good custom should corrupt the world': African theatre and the 'holy' canon. SATJ (9:2) 1995, 3–25.

14297. Ullyatt, Tony.   Ideology and South African radio drama in English. Textures (9) 1995, 19–31.

14298. Urbano, Cosimo.   The evil that men do: Mark Rydell's adaptation of D. H. Lawrence's *The Fox*. LitFQ (23:4) 1995, 254–61.

14299. VANDEN HEUVEL, MICHAEL. Waking the text: disorderly order in the Wooster Group's *Route 1 & 9 (the Last Act)*. JDTC (10:1) 1995, 59–78.

14300. VAN OOSTRUM, DUCO. Wim Wenders' Euro-American construction site: *Paris, Texas* or Texas, Paris. *In* (pp. 7–20) **113**.

14301. VERRIPS, JOJADA. The consumption of 'touching' images: reflections on mimetic 'wildness' in the West. Ethnologia Europaea (26:1) 1996, 51–64.

14302. VERSTRATEN, PETER. Badende cowboys. (Bathing cowboys.) De Gids (159:11/12) 1996, 937–41.

14303. VINEBERG, STEVE. Method actors: three generations of an American acting style. (Bibl. 1993, 10318.) Rev. by Kaizaad Navroze Kotwal in JDTC (7:1) 1992, 197–200.

14304. VISWANATHAN, JACQUELINE. Une écriture cinémato-graphique? Études littéraires (26:2) 1993, 9–17.

14305. VOIGT, JENNIFER. Endings. Cresset (59:3) 1996, 30–2.

14306. VORLICKY, ROBERT. Act like a man: challenging masculinities in American drama. (Bibl. 1995, 12963.) Rev. by Gary Vena in EOR (20:1/2) 1996, 148–52.

14307. WALDER, DENNIS. Interim voices: South African theatre today. *See* **6678**.

14308. WALKER, ALICE. The same river twice: honoring the difficult: a meditation on life, spirit, art, and the making of the film, *The Color Purple*, ten years later. New York: Scribner, 1996. pp. 302. Rev. by Thomas Cripps in GaHQ (80:4) 1996, 947–8.

14309. WALLACE, MICHELE. Black popular culture. Ed. by Gina Dent. Seattle: Bay Press, 1992. pp. ix, 373. (Discussions in contemporary culture, 8.) Rev. by Patricia Hill Collins in Signs (20:3) 1995, 728–32.

14310. WALLACE, ROBERT. Producing marginality: theatre and criticism in Canada. (Bibl. 1994, 10294.) Rev. by Michael J. Sidnell in THC (12:1) 1991, 104–7; Rob Nunn in CanTR (70) 1992, 93–5.

14311. WALTERS, SUZANNA DANUTA. Lives together/worlds apart: mothers and daughters in popular culture. Berkeley; London: California UP, 1992. pp. xiii, 295. Rev. by Sonya Michel in AHR (99:2) 1994, 679; by Rita Felski in AmLH (8:2) 1996, 395–6.

14312. WARD, ANNALEE P. *The Lion King*'s mythic narrative: Disney as moral educator. JPFT (23:4) 1996, 171–8.

14313. WASHBURN, TINA. Levinson's Roy: a child's hero. LitFQ (24:1) 1996, 88–91.

14314. WASSERMAN, JERRY (ed.). Modern Canadian plays. Vancouver: Talonbooks, 1993–94. 2 vols. pp. 368; 414. (Third ed.: first ed. 1985.) Rev. by Robert Nunn in CanTR (82) 1995, 90–2; by André Loiselle in TRC (16:1/2) 1995, 144–6.

14315. WEALES, GERALD. Alan Schneider on Broadway. JADT (7:3) 1995, 79–87.

14316. WELSH, JIM. Classic folly: *The Scarlet Letter*. *See* **11436**.

14317. —— Fixing *The Bridges of Madison County*. LitFQ (23:3) 1995, 154, 228.

14318. WEST, ALAN. The breath of signs: thoughts on opera and film. MichQR (35:1) 1996, 219–39.

14319. WESTFAHL, GARY. Where no market has gone before: 'the science fiction industry' and the *Star Trek* industry. Extrapolation (37:4) 1996, 291–301.

14320. Wexman, Virginia Wright.   Creating the couple: love, marriage, and Hollywood performance. Princeton, NJ; Chichester: Princeton UP, 1993. pp. xiv, 288. Rev. by Lucy Fisher in FilmQ (48:1) 1994, 43–5; by Wheeler Winston Dixon in JFV (48:4) 1996, 56–7.

14321. Whittock, Trevor.   Metaphor and film. Cambridge; New York: CUP, 1990. pp. vii, 178. (Cambridge studies in film.) Rev. by Gregg Horowitz in FilmQ (45:4) 1992, 52–4.

14322. Wilcox, Rhonda V.   Dominant female, superior male: control schemata in *Lois and Clark*, *Moonlighting*, and *Remington Steele*. JPFT (24:1) 1996, 26–33.

14323. Willemen, Paul.   Looks and frictions: essays in cultural studies and film theory. (Bibl. 1994, 10310.) Rev. by Timothy Shary in FilmQ (49:1) 1995, 53–5.

14324. Williams, Linda Ruth.   Sex in the head: visions of femininity and film in D. H. Lawrence. (Bibl. 1995, 12980.) Rev. by Christopher Orr in FilCr (21:1) 1996, 95–9.

14325. Williams, Patrick.   Imaged communities: Black British film in the eighties and nineties. CritS (8:1) 1996, 3–13.

14326. —— 'Triumph of the will?' – an interview with Eddie George. CritS (8:1) 1996, 80–3.

14327. Williamson, Catherine.   'You'll see it just as I saw it': voyeurism, fetishism, and the female spectator in *Lady in the Lake*. JFV (48:3) 1996, 17–29.

14328. Williamson, J. W.   Hillbillyland: what the movies did to the mountains and what the mountains did to the movies. *See* **3304**.

14329. Willingham, Ralph.   Science fiction and the theatre. (Bibl. 1994, 10312.) Rev. by Richard D. Erlich in Extrapolation (37:2) 1996, 174–7.

14330. Wilson, Charles, Jr.   Revolution as theme in John Oliver Killens' *Youngblood*. *In* (pp. 123–32) **113**.

14331. Winans, Linda Ford.   The lone body on stage. TexPres (14) 1993, 97–101.

14332. Witham, Barry B.   Pandemic and popular opinion: *Spirochete* in Seattle. JADT (5:2) 1993, 86–95.

14333. —— The playhouse and the committee. *In* (pp. 146–62) **83**.

14334. Woal, Linda Kowall; Woal, Michael.   Romaine Fielding's real Westerns. JFV (47:1–3) 1995, 7–25.

14335. Woal, Michael; Woal, Linda Kowall.   Chaplin and the comedy of melodrama. JFV (46:3) 1994, 3–15.

14336. Wolf, Stacy.   Politics, polyphony, and pleasure: the San Francisco Mime Troupe's *Seeing Double*. JDTC (8:1) 1993, 101–15.

14337. —— Queer performances of Mary Martin as woman and as star. WP (8:2) 1996, 225–39.

14338. Wolf, Werner.   Intermedialität als neues Paradigma der Literaturwissenschaft? Plädoyer für eine literaturzentrierte Erforschung der Grenzüberschreitungen zwischen Wortkunst und anderen Medien am Beispiel von Virginia Woolfs *The String Quartet*. AAA (21:1) 1996, 85–116.

14339. Wolfe, Alan D.   Kipling in Hollywood. KJ (70:280) 1996, 29–37.

14340. Wood, Naomi.   Domesticating dreams in Walt Disney's *Cinderella*. LU (20:1) 1996, 25–49.

14341. Woods, Jeannie Marlin.   Theatre to change men's souls: the artistry of Adrian Hall. (Bibl. 1993, 10343.) Rev. by Ed Menta in NETJ (7) 1996, 118–20.

14342. Woods, Leigh. Ethel Barrymore and the wages of vaudeville. NETJ (4) 1993, 79–95.

14343. Worden, Jason. Thirty-nine steps to immortality. AD (29:4) 1996, 453–7.

14344. Worthy, Kim. Emissaries of difference: Conrad, Coppola, and *Hearts of Darkness*. WS (25:2) 1996, 153–67.

14345. Wyatt, Justin. Cinematic/sexual transgression: an interview with Todd Haynes. FilmQ (46:3) 1993, 2–8.

14346. Yawn, Mike; Beatty, Bob. John Ford's vision of the closing West: from optimism to cynicism. FilmH (26:1/4) 1996, 6–19.

14347. Young, Elizabeth. Here comes the bride: wedding gender and race in *Bride of Frankenstein*. Feminist Studies (17:3) 1991, 403–37.

14348. Young, Kay. Hollywood, 1934: 'inventing' romantic comedy. *In* (pp. 257–74) **64**.

14349. Zakharieva, Bouriana. Frankenstein of the nineties: the composite body. *See* **12250**.

14350. Zelizer, Barbie. From home to public forum: media events and the public sphere. JFV (43:1/2) 1991, 69–79.

14351. Zettner, Maria. Tradition und Erneuerung: das Young Vic als Sproß des National Theatre in London. Forum modernes Theater (11:1) 1996, 95–102.

14352. Zimbardo, Rose. The semiotics of Restoration satire. *See* **7981**.

14353. Zimmermann, Patricia R. Midwives, hostesses, and feminist film. Wide Angle (17:1–4) 1995, 197–215.

14354. —— Reconstructing Vertov: Soviet film theory and American radical documentary. JFV (44:1/2) 1992, 80–90.

14355. Zipes, Jack. Towards a theory of the fairy-tale film: the case of *Pinocchio*. *See* **3692**.

14356. Zucker, Carole (ed.). Making visible the invisible: an anthology of original essays on film acting. (Bibl. 1991, 10724.) Rev. by Virginia Wright Wexman in FilmQ (46:2) 1992/93, 56–7.

Fiction

14357. Abraham, Julie. Are girls necessary? Lesbian writing and modern histories. New York; London: Routledge, 1996. pp. xxiv, 213. (Cf. bibl. 1991, 10137.)

14358. Acheson, James (ed.). The British and Irish novel since 1960. (Bibl. 1991, 10.) Rev. by Ansgar Nünning in ZAA (42:3) 1994, 273–5.

14359. Adams, Alice. The American short story in the cybernetic age. JSSE (17) 1991, 9–22.

14360. Adams, Jon-K. Manifest technology and the Native-American novel. Amst (41:3) 1996, 431–44.

14361. Adelman, Irving; Dworkin, Rita. The contemporary novel: a checklist of critical literature on the English language novel since 1945. (Bibl. 1973, 572.) Lanham, MD; London: Scarecrow Press, 1996. pp. xxiii, 666. (Second ed.: first ed. 1972.)

14362. Aiken, Susan Hardy, *et al.* Dialogues = *Dialogi*: literary and cultural exchanges between (ex)Soviet and American women. *See* **23**.

14363. Albert, Richard N. An annotated bibliography of jazz fiction and jazz fiction criticism. Westport, CT; London: Greenwood

Press, 1996. pp. xviii, 114. (Bibliographies and indexes in world literature, 52.)

14364. ALDISS, BRIAN.   All those big machines – the theme science fiction does not discuss. JFA (7:1) 1996, 83–91.

14365. ALLEN, CAROLYN.   Following Djuna: women lovers and the erotics of loss. Bloomington: Indiana UP, 1996. pp. 142.

14366. ALLEN, PAULA GUNN (ed.).   Voice of the turtle: American Indian literature, 1900–1970. New York: Ballantine, 1994. pp. xii, 321. Rev. by P. Jane Hafen in AICRJ (20:1) 1996, 256–9.

14367. ÁLVAREZ CALLEJA, MARÍA ANTONIA.   Realistic *vs* romantic: the imagistic world of post-war English literature. RAEI (9) 1996, 7–31.

14368. AMMONS, ELIZABETH; WHITE-PARKS, ANNETTE (eds). Tricksterism in turn-of-the-century American literature: a multicultural perspective. *See* **9791**.

14369. ANDERSON, LAVINA FIELDING.   Masks and music: recent fiction by Mormon women writers. WebS (10:3) 1993, 71–80.

14370. ANDERSON, LINDA (ed.).   Plotting change: contemporary women's fiction. (Bibl. 1992, 11127.) Rev. by Ellen Cronan Rose in Signs (18:2) 1993, 346–75.

14371. ANISFIELD, NANCY.   'Under the wheat': an analysis of options and ethical components. *In* (pp. 140–5) **77**.

14372. ANNESLEY, JAMES.   Decadence and disquiet: recent American fiction and the coming *fin de siècle*. JAStud (30:3) 1996, 365–79.

14373. ANON. (comp.).   Recent books on modern fiction. MFS (42:1) 1996, 129–32. (Bibliography.)

14374. APPLEFIELD, DAVID.   Talking with Shannon Ravenel. Frank (15) 1996, 68–70.

14375. ARLETT, ROBERT.   Epic voices: inner and global impulse in the contemporary American and British novel. Selinsgrove, PA: Susquehanna UP; London; Toronto: Assoc. UPs, 1996. pp. 192.

14376. ASKER, D. B. D.   The modern bestiary: animals in English fiction, 1880–1945. *See* **9794**.

14377. ATTEBERY, BRIAN.   The closing of the final frontier: science fiction after 1960. *In* (pp. 205–13) **36**.

14378. ATTEBERY, JENNIFER EASTMAN.   The trolls of fiction: ogres or warm fuzzies? JFA (7:1) 1996, 61–74.

14379. ATWILL, WILLIAM D.   Fire and power: the American space program as postmodern narrative. (Bibl. 1995, 13015.) Rev. by D. Quentin Miller in StudN (28:4) 1996, 592–4.

14380. ATWOOD, MARGARET; WEAVER, ROBERT (eds).   The new Oxford book of Canadian short stories in English. *See* **9795**.

14381. AWKWARD, MICHAEL.   Inspiriting influences: tradition, revision, and Afro-American women's novels. (Bibl. 1994, 10334.) Rev. by Gay Wilentz in NWSAJ (3:2) 1991, 316–20.

14382. AZIZ, NURJEHAN (ed.).   *Her Mother's Ashes*, and other stories by South Asian women in Canada and the United States. Toronto: TSAR, 1994. pp. xvii, 202. Rev. by Brinda Bose in WLT (69:3) 1995, 648–9; by Pamela McCallum in CanL (151) 1996, 178–80.

14383. BAGULEY, DAVID.   The 'lure' of the naturalist text. CanRCL (19:1/2) 1992, 273–80.

14384. BANERJEE, JACQUELINE P.   Through the northern gate: childhood and growing up in British fiction, 1719–1901. *See* **8565**.

14385. BARBIERI, DANIELE.   Simulacri, ometti, *supermen e computer*:

come la fantascienza racconta i presidenti americani. Àcoma (8) 1996, 51–8.

14386. BARR, MARLEEN S. Lost in space: probing feminist science fiction and beyond. (Bibl. 1995, 13021.) Rev. by Mária Minich Brewer in MFS (42:1) 1996, 214–19.

14387. BARROWMAN, FERGUS (ed.). The Picador book of contemporary New Zealand fiction. London: Picador, 1996. pp. xli, 470. Rev. by Howard Warner in New Zealand Books (6:1) 1996, 11; by Colm Tóibín in Landfall (4:1) 1996, 132–5; by Patrick Evans in NZList, 16 Mar. 1996, 48; by Julian Ferraro in TLS, 19 July 1996, 22.

14388. BAXTER, STEPHEN. Martian chronicles: narratives of Mars in science and SF. Foundation (68) 1996, 5–16.

14389. BECKER, ALLIENNE R. (ed.). Visions of the fantastic: selected essays from the Fifteenth International Conference of the Fantastic in the Arts. *See* **127**.

14390. BEENE, LYNNDIANNE. Guide to British prose fiction explication: nineteenth and twentieth century. *See* **9801**.

14391. BEETZ, KIRK H. (ed.). Beacham's encyclopedia of popular fiction. *See* **9802**.

14392. BENDER, BERT. The descent of love: Darwin and the theory of sexual selection in American fiction, 1871–1926. *See* **9803**.

14393. BESSIÈRE, JEAN. Enigmaticité de la littérature: pour une anatomie de la fiction au xxe siècle. Interrogation philosophique. Paris: Presses Universitaires de France, 1993. pp. xii, 239. Rev. by Iris Yaron in PT (16:4) 1995, 744–5.

14394. BETHLEHEM, LOUISE SHABAT. Simile and figurative language. *See* **2311**.

14395. BETTS, DORIS. Daughters, Southerners, and Daisy. *In* (pp. 259–76) **32**.

14396. BLACK, AYANNA (ed.). Fiery spirits: a collection of short fiction and poetry by Canadian writers of African descent. Toronto: HarperCollins, 1994. pp. xix, 231. Rev. by Cyril Dabydeen in WLT (70:2) 1996, 412–13.

14397. BLOCK, ALAN A. Anonymous toil: a re-evaluation of the American radical novel in the twentieth century. (Bibl. 1993, 10368.) Rev. by Barbara Foley in MFS (40:1) 1994, 153–4.

14398. BLOOM, CLIVE. Cult fiction: popular reading and pulp theory. Basingstoke: Macmillan; New York: St Martin's Press, 1996. pp. ix, 262.

14399. BLOOM, HAROLD (ed.). Classic science fiction writers. *See* **9805**.

14400. —— Science fiction writers of the golden age. New York: Chelsea House, 1994. pp. xii, 203. (Writers of English.) Rev. by James Gunn in Utopian Studies (7:2) 1996, 219–21.

14401. BLOOMFIELD, MAXWELL. Constitutional ideology and progressive fiction. *See* **10609**.

14402. BOEHNLEIN, JAMES M. Midwestern voices and the marginal canon: reconsidering proletarian fiction. Midamerica (22) 1995, 50–9.

14403. BOLGER, DERMOT (ed.). The Vintage book of contemporary Irish fiction. New York: Vintage, 1995. pp. xxviii, 561. (Orig. pub. as *The Picador Book of Contemporary Irish Fiction*. London: Picador, 1994.) Rev. by Michael Stephens in BkW, 17 Mar. 1996, 8.

14404. BOOKER, M. KEITH. The dystopian impulse in modern literature: fiction as social criticism. (Bibl. 1995, 13029.) Rev. by Timothy J.

Sramcik in Extrapolation (36:1) 1995, 82–3; by Richard Tuerk in JAC (19:2) 1996, 136–7; by Jerome Meckier in ANQ (9:2) 1996, 39–48.

14405. —— Literature and domination: sex, knowledge, and power in modern fiction. (Bibl. 1993, 10375.) Rev. by John Mascaro in Pynchon Notes (34/35) 1994, 188–91; by Richard Pearce in MFS (40:2) 1994, 428–30.

14406. BOOTH, ALISON (ed.). Famous last words: changes in gender and narrative closure. Afterword by U. C. Knoepflmacher. *See* **31**.

14407. BORGHI, LIANA. Sextual futures: some observations on sex and gender position in recent women's SF. Letterature d'America (55) 1994, 131–49.

14408. BOWERS, BEGE K.; BROTHERS, BARBARA (eds). Reading and writing women's lives: a study of the novel of manners. *See* **96**.

14409. BOYERS, ROBERT, *et al.* Talking about American fiction: a panel discussion with Marilynne Robinson, Russell Banks, Robert Stone, and David Rieff. Salmagundi (93) 1992, 61–77.

14410. BREINES, WINI. Sixties stories' silences: White feminism, Black feminism, Black power. NWSAJ (8:3) 1996, 101–21.

14411. BRETON, MARCELA. An annotated bibliography of selected jazz short stories. AAR (26:2) 1992, 299–306.

14412. BRINK, ANDRÉ. Reinventing a continent (revisiting history in the literature of the new South Africa: a personal testimony). *See* **9808**.

14413. BRINKLEY, DOUGLAS. Road book. AH (47:7) 1996, 56, 58–60, 62–3.

14414. BRODERICK, DAMIEN. Reading by starlight: postmodern science fiction. (Bibl. 1995, 13040.) Rev. by J. E. Steinbach in MFS (42:4) 1996, 933–5; by Michael Jackson in Utopian Studies (7:2) 1996, 224–5; by Andrew M. Butler in Foundation (66) 1996, 111–14.

14415. BROICH, ULRICH. Muted postmodernism: the contemporary British short story. ZAA (41:1) 1993, 31–9.

14416. BROOKE, STEPHEN; CAMERON, LOUISE. Anarchy in the UK? Ideas of the city and the *fin de siècle* in contemporary English film and literature. *See* **13493**.

14417. BROWN, JULIE (ed.). American women short-story writers: a collection of critical essays. *See* **3**.

14418. BROWN, RUTH. Contextualising Maori writing. New Zealand Books (6:2) 1996, 14–15.

14419. BROWN, SUSAN WINDISCH (ed.). Contemporary novelists. (Bibl. 1992, 11279.) New York: St James Press, 1996. pp. xxiv, 1173. (Contemporary writers.) (Sixth ed.: first ed. 1972.)

14420. BURKE, RUTH E. The games of poetics: ludic criticism and postmodern fiction. (Bibl. 1994, 10361.) Rev. by Steven Scott in CanRCL (23:2) 1996, 374–92.

14421. BURSTEIN, JANET. Mother at the center: Jewish American women's stories of the 1920s. *In* (pp. 182–96) **130**.

14422. BURTON, STACY. Bakhtin, temporality, and modern narrative: writing 'the whole triumphant murderous unstoppable chute'. CL (48:1) 1996, 39–64.

14423. CAIN, STEPHEN (ed.). Antipodean tales: stories from the dark side. Wellington: IPL, 1996. pp. 183.

14424. CALLAHAN, JOHN F. In the African-American grain: the pursuit of voice in twentieth-century Black fiction. (Bibl. 1991, 10776.)

Middletown, CT: Wesleyan UP, 1990. pp. 296. (Second ed.: first ed. 1988.) Rev. by Robert James Butler in AAR (26:4) 1992, 683–5.

14425. CALLOWAY, CATHERINE. Fiction: the 1930s to the 1960s. American Literary Scholarship (1993) 233–54; (1994) 279–302; (1995) 303–29.

14426. CAMPBELL, IAN. Glossing (glossing). *See* **2594**.

14427. CARR, DUANE. A question of class: the redneck stereotype in Southern fiction. Bowling Green, OH: Bowling Green State Univ. Popular Press, 1996. pp. viii, 188.

14428. CASTLE, TERRY. Marie Antoinette obsession. Representations (38) 1992, 1–38.

14429. CAWELTI, JOHN G. What rough beast – new Westerns? *See* **13541**.

14430. CECIL, HUGH. The flower of battle: how Britain wrote the Great War. (Bibl. 1995, 13050.) South Royalton, VT: Steerforth Press, 1996. pp. 440.

14431. CHAVKIN, ALLAN (ed.). English Romanticism and modern fiction: a collection of critical essays. *See* **28**.

14432. CHÉNETIER, MARC. Beyond suspicion: new American fiction since 1960. Trans. by Elizabeth A. Houlding. Liverpool: Liverpool UP; Philadelphia: Pennsylvania UP, 1996. pp. xvi, 321. (Penn studies in contemporary American fiction.) (*Trans. of* bibl. 1993, 10401.)

14433. —— Sgraffites, encres et sanguines: neuf études sur les figures de l'écriture dans la fiction américaine contemporaine. Paris: Presses de l'École Normale Supérieure, 1994. pp. 208. (Off-shore.)

14434. CLARIDGE, HENRY; PARSONS, DEBORAH. American literature: the twentieth century: fiction 1900–45. YWES (75) 1994, 631–40.

14435. CLARK, BEVERLY LYON, *et al.* Reading romance, reading ourselves. CR (40:2) 1996, 359–84.

14436. CLARKE, I. F. (ed.). The tale of the next Great War, 1871–1914: fictions of future warfare and of battles still-to-come. *See* **9817**.

14437. COATES, DONNA. The best soldiers of all: unsung heroines in Canadian women's Great War fictions. CanL (151) 1996, 66–99.

14438. COBHAM, RHONDA. Women in Jamaican literature 1900–1950. *In* (pp. 195–222) **81**.

14439. COLLINS, MICHAEL J. The body of the work of the body: physio-textuality in contemporary horror. *See* **13562**.

14440. CONDÉ, MARY. Some African-American fictional responses to *Gone with the Wind*. YES (26) 1996, 208–17.

14441. CONNOR, STEVEN. The English novel in history, 1950–1995. London; New York: Routledge, 1996. pp. vii, 260. (Novel in history.)

14442. —— Reading: the *contretemps*. *See* **9820**.

14443. CONRAD, KATHRYN. Occupied country: the negotiation of lesbianism in Irish feminist narrative. EI (31:1/2) 1996, 123–36.

14444. CORKIN, STANLEY. Realism and the birth of the modern United States: cinema, literature, and culture. *See* **13571**.

14445. CORNUT-GENTILLE D'ARCY, CHANTAL; GARCÍA LANDA, JOSÉ ÁNGEL (eds). Gender, I-deology: essays on theory, fiction and film. *See* **38**.

14446. COWLEY, JULIAN, *et al.* The twentieth century: fiction. YWES (75) 1994, 490–528.

14447. COX, MICHAEL (ed.). The Oxford book of twentieth-century ghost stories. Oxford; New York: OUP, 1996. pp. xix, 425. Rev. by Celia Wren in Cweal (123:22) 1996, 20–1; by Patricia Craig in TLS, 6 Dec. 1996, 25.

14448. CRANNY-FRANCIS, ANNE.   Feminist fiction: feminist uses of generic fiction. (Bibl. 1993, 10409.) Rev. by Susan Brown in CanRCL (20:1/2) 1993, 263–6.

14449. CREWS, BRIAN.   Anti-style and the postmodernist novel. *See* **2604**.

14450. CROFT, ANDREW.   Socialist novels from the 1930s. RT (48) 1996, 21–3.

14451. CURRIE, MARK (ed.).   Metafiction. London; New York: Longman, 1995. pp. x, 251. (Longman critical readers.) Rev. by Richard Henry in WLT (70:4) 1996, 1039.

14452. DALLAT, C. L.   After the censor had gone: the rise of the novel as a critique of de Valera's Ireland. TLS, 27 Sept. 1996, 21.

14453. DARIAS-BEAUTELL, EVA.   Displacements, self-mockery, and carnival in the Canadian postmodern. WLT (70:2) 1996, 316–20.

14454. DAVIDSON, JANE P.   Golem – Frankenstein – golem of your own. *See* **13592**.

14455. DAVIS, JANE.   South Africa: a botched civilization?. Racial conflict and identity in selected South African novels. Lanham, MD; London: UP of America, 1996. pp. xxxiv, 182.

14456. DE CAMP, L. SPRAGUE.   Rubber dinosaurs and wooden elephants: essays on literature, film, and history. *See* **13597**.

14457. DEER, GLENN.   Postmodern Canadian fiction and the rhetoric of authority. (Bibl. 1995, 13070.) Rev. by Winfried Siemerling in CanL (150) 1996, 191–3.

14458. DE GRAZIA, EDWARD.   How Justice Brennan freed novels and movies during the sixties. *See* **13601**.

14459. DE LA CONCHA, ANGELES.   The female body: a resonant voice in the multicultural scene. *In* (pp. 55–72) **38**.

14460. DEN TANDT, CHRISTOPHE.   Amazons and androgynes: over-civilization and the redefinition of gender roles at the turn of the century. *See* **9825**.

14461. DE TORO, FERNANDO.   Post-modern fiction and theatricality: simulation, deconstruction, and rhizomatic writing. *See* **13611**.

14462. DETWEILER, ROBERT.   Uncivil rites: American fiction, religion, and the public sphere. Urbana: Illinois UP, 1996. pp. x, 250. (Public expressions of religion in America.)

14463. DEVOIZE, JEANNE.   Religion in the short stories of the English-speaking Caribbean islands. JSSE (26) 1996, 26–37.

14464. DE WEEVER, JACQUELINE.   Mythmaking and metaphor in Black women's fiction. (Bibl. 1994, 10397.) Rev. by Martha J. Cutter in AAR (28:4) 1994, 665–9.

14465. D'HAEN, THEO.   Dis/coursing post-modernism: science, magic, (post)-modernity. CanRCL (23:1) 1996, 189–205.

14466. —— BERTENS, HANS (eds).   British postmodern fiction. (Bibl. 1994, 10.) Rev. by Christoph Reinfandt in LWU (29:1) 1996, 64.

14467. —— —— Postmodern fiction in Canada. (Bibl. 1994, 66.) Rev. by Jennifer Lawn in CanL (149) 1996, 150–1.

14468. DiBATTISTA, MARIA.   The lowly art of murder: Modernism and the case of the free woman. *In* (pp. 176–93) **41**.

14469. DÍZ, LUCIANO P. (ed.).   Symbiosis in prose: an anthology of short fiction. Ottawa: Split Quotation, 1995. pp. 206. Rev. by Petra Fachinger in CanL (151) 1996, 141.

14470. DOAN, LAURA L. (ed.).   Old maids to radical spinsters: unmarried women in the twentieth-century novel. Introd. by Nina Auerbach. (Bibl. 1993, 10425.) Rev. by Eileen Barrett in NWSAJ (5:1) 1993, 136–41.

14471. DORRIS, MICHAEL; ERDRICH, LOUISE.   The day after tomorrow: novelists at Armageddon. *In* (pp. 52–7) **77**.

14472. DOWNER, LESLEY.   The Beats of Edinburgh. NYTM, 31 Mar. 1996, 42–6.

14473. DOYLE, H. M.   Australian literary utopias – 1920–1950. Australian Folklore (8) 1993, 69–76.

14474. DOYLE, LAURA.   Bordering on the body: the racial matrix of modern fiction and culture. (Bibl. 1995, 13082.) Rev. by Ann Ardis in TSWL (14:2) 1995, 363–9; by Patricia Moran in MFS (42:4) 1996, 909–12; by Kimberly Drake in AAR (30:4) 1996, 684–6; by Debrah Raschke in SAtlR (61:4) 1996, 154–7.

14475. DOZOIS, GARDNER (ed.).   The year's best science fiction, twelfth annual collection. New York: St Martin's Press, 1995. pp. xlvi, 590. Rev. by Gary K. Wolfe in BkW, 27 Aug. 1995, 9.

14476. DRIVER, DOROTHY.   Transformation through art: writing, representation, and subjectivity in recent South African fiction. WLT (70:1) 1996, 45–52.

14477. DUBBER, ULRIKE.   Der englische Universitätsroman der Nachkriegszeit: ein Beitrag zur Gattungsbestimmung. Würzburg: Königshausen & Neumann, 1991. pp. 298. (Kieler Beiträge zur Anglistik und Amerikanistik, ns, 1.) Rev. by Rüdiger Imhof in ZAA (42:3) 1994, 270–2.

14478. DUCILLE, ANN.   The coupling convention: sex, text, and tradition in Black women's fiction. (Bibl. 1995, 13084.) Rev. by Gloria T. Randle in TSWL (15:2) 1996, 355–8; by Shelley Fisher Fishkin in AmQ (48:1) 1996, 142–52; by Sandra Gunning in Signs (21:2) 1996, 455–9.

14479. EAGLETON, TERRY.   Form and ideology in the Anglo-Irish novel. *In* (pp. 135–46) **60**.

14480. ELPHINSTONE, MARGARET.   Contemporary feminist fantasy in the Scottish literary tradition. *In* (pp. 84–92) **70**.

14481. EMCK, KATY.   Feminist detectives and the challenges of hardboiledness. CanRCL (21:3) 1994, 383–98.

14482. ENGEL, HOWARD.   The mystery writer: an endangered species. ARCS (18:1) 1988, 83–7.

14483. ERLICH, RICHARD D.; DUNN, THOMAS P.   Clockworks: a multi-media bibliography of works useful for the study of the human/machine interface in SF. (Bibl. 1994, 10417.) Rev. by Rob Latham in Utopian Studies (7:2) 1996, 251–3.

14484. ESSL, MONIKA.   Die Rezeption des Artusstoffes in der englischen und amerikanischen Literatur des 20. Jahrhunderts bei Thomas Berger, Marion Zimmer Bradley, E. A. Robinson, Mary Stewart und T. H. White. *See* **4856**.

14485. ESTEVES, CARMEN C.; PARAVISINI-GEBERT, LIZABETH (eds). Green cane and juicy flotsam: short stories by Caribbean women. New Brunswick, NJ: Rutgers UP, 1991. pp. xxix, 273. Rev. by Maria Helena Lima in Feminist Studies (21:1) 1995, 115–28.

14486. EVERMAN, WELCH D.   Who says this? The authority of the author, the discourse and the reader. Carbondale: Southern Illinois UP, 1988. pp. xvii, 142. (Crosscurrents/modern critiques, third series.) Rev. by Gwendolyn Sorrell Sell in LitTheol (5:1) 1991, 131–3; by Wilhelm Füger in GRM (42:3) 1992, 364–6.

14487. FADERMAN, LILLIAN.   Lesbian magazine fiction in the early twentieth century. *In* (pp. 99–120) **3**.

14488. FARIS, WENDY B.   Devastation and replenishment: New World narratives of love and nature. SHum (19:2) 1992, 171–82.

14489. FARR, MARIE T.   Freedom and control: automobiles in American women's fiction of the 70s and 80s. JPC (29:2) 1995, 157–69.

14490. FEDERMAN, RAYMOND.   Critifiction: postmodern essays. (Bibl. 1995, 13092.) Rev. by Thomas Irmer in ZAA (43:3) 1995, 284–7.

14491. FERRARO, THOMAS J.   Ethnic passages: literary immigrants in twentieth-century America. (Bibl. 1995, 13094.) Rev. by Carla Cappetti in MFS (40:2) 1994, 359–60.

14492. FILMER-DAVIES, KATH.   Chwedl gymaeg a llenyddiaeth gyfoesol. (Welsh myth and contemporary literature.) Mythlore (19:3) 1993, 53–8.

14493. FINE, DAVID; SKENAZY, PAUL (eds).   San Francisco in fiction: essays in a regional literature. *See* **108**.

14494. FLECK, RICHARD F. (ed.).   Critical perspectives on Native-American fiction. (Bibl. 1993, 10448.) Rev. by Shirley Geok-lin Lim in Signs (21:2) 1996, 494–8.

14495. FLUDERNIK, MONIKA.   Distorting language at its roots. (Late) Modernist and postmodernist experiments with narrative language. Spr (26:1) 1995, 109–26.

14496. FOLEY, BARBARA.   Radical representations: politics and form in US proletarian fiction, 1929–1941. (Bibl. 1995, 13100.) Rev. by Paula Rabinowitz in MFS (40:2) 1994, 365–7; by Craig Werner in AAR (30:1) 1996, 119–21; by Stephen Enniss in StudN (28:1) 1996, 122–3.

14497. FORTER, GREGORY.   Criminal pleasures, pleasurable crime. Style (29:3) 1995, 423–40.

14498. FRANCIS, DIANA PHARAOH.   Social robotics: constructing the ideal woman from used ideological parts. JFA (7:1) 1996, 92–101.

14499. FRANKLIN, H. BRUCE.   Fatal fiction: a weapon to end all wars. *In* (pp. 5–14) **77**.

14500. FRIEDMAN, ALAN WARREN.   Fictional death and the Modernist enterprise. (Bibl. 1995, 13103.) Rev. by Roger K. Anderson in MFS (42:1) 1996, 234–6; by Jim Barloon in ELT (39:1) 1996, 77–80; by R. J. Dingley in NQ (43:1) 1996, 118–19.

14501. FRIEDMAN, BONNIE.   Writing past dark: envy, fear, distraction, and other dilemmas in the writer's life. (Bibl. 1994, 10430.) Rev. by X. J. Kennedy in GetR (7:2) 1994, 289–303.

14502. FRIEDMAN, MELVIN J.; SIEGEL, BEN (eds).   Traditions, voices, and dreams: the American novel since the 1960s. *See* **123**.

14503. FRYE, JOANNE S.   Living stories, telling lives: women and the novel in contemporary experience. Ann Arbor: Michigan UP, 1986. pp. vii, 250. (Women and culture.) Rev. by Ellen Cronan Rose in Signs (18:2) 1993, 346–75.

14504. FULLBROOK, KATE.   Free women: ethics and aesthetics in twentieth-century women's fiction. (Bibl. 1992, 11242.) Rev. by Josephine Donovan in Signs (18:2) 1993, 476–80.

14505. FURUKAWA, HIROMI. Black eno tabiji. (A journey to the Black.) Osaka: Seseragi Shuppan, 1996. 2 vols. pp. 216; 248.

14506. GARCÍA LANDA, JOSÉ ÁNGEL. Nivel narrativo, status, persona y typología de las narraciones. *See* **8579**.

14507. GARVEY, ELLEN GRUBER. The adman in the parlor: magazines and the gendering of consumer culture, 1880s to 1910s. *See* **1270**.

14508. GASIOREK, ANDRZEJ. Post-war British fiction: realism and after. (Bibl. 1995, 13107.) Rev. by Bruce King in WLT (69:4) 1995, 803; by Pat Wheeler in CritS (8:1) 1996, 120–1.

14509. GEORGE, ROSEMARY MARANGOLY. The politics of home: postcolonial relocations and twentieth-century fiction. Cambridge; New York: CUP, 1996. pp. ix, 265. (Cf. bibl. 1993, 10461.)

14510. GESSERT, GEORGE. The angel of extinction. Northwest Review (34:3) 1996, 115–22.

14511. GESSNER-UTSCH, BETTINA. Subjektiver Roman: Studien zum Verhältnis von fiktionalen Subjektivitäts- und Wirklichkeitskonzeptionen in England vom 18. Jahrhundert bis zum Modernismus. *See* **8580**.

14512. GIFFORD, DOUGLAS. Imagining Scotlands: the return to mythology in modern Scottish fiction. *In* (pp. 17–49) **115**.

14513. GILBERT, PAMELA K. The body in question. Review (17) 1995, 65–84 (review-article).

14514. GILES, JAMES R. The naturalistic inner-city novel in America: encounters with the fat man. (Bibl. 1995, 13109.) Rev. by Heather J. Hicks in AL (68:3) 1996, 648–9; by Tim Woods in JAStud (30:3) 1996, 474–5.

14515. —— GILES, WANDA H. (eds). American novelists since World War II: fifth series. Detroit, MI; London: Gale Research, 1996. pp. xx, 379. (Dictionary of literary biography, 173.)

14516. GILYARD, KEITH. Let's flip the script: an African-American discourse on language, literature, and learning. *See* **2875**.

14517. GINDIN, JAMES. British fiction in the 1930s: the dispiriting decade. (Bibl. 1992, 11251.) Rev. by Stephan Lieske in ZAA (42:2) 1994, 187–8; by Neil Nehring in StudN (27:2) 1995, 223–6.

14518. GLAGE, LISELOTTE. Strategien der Differenz: was oder wie ist der postkoloniale Roman? ZAA (43:1) 1995, 77–90.

14519. GODIN, SETH (comp.). The encyclopedia of fictional people: the most important characters of the 20th century. *See* **13724**.

14520. GOLDEN, KENNETH L. Science fiction, myth, and Jungian psychology. *See* **9848**.

14521. GOMEZ, JEWELLE. Speculative fiction and Black lesbians. Signs (18:4) 1993, 948–55.

14522. GOODRICH, PETER. The New Age mage: Merlin as contemporary occult icon. *See* **3398**.

14523. GRÄBE, INA. Voices in contemporary South African narrative: an exploration of narrative strategies for engaging with current socio-political issues. JLS (11:2) 1996, 29–37.

14524. GREENE, GAYLE. Changing the story: feminist fiction and the tradition. (Bibl. 1992, 11260.) Rev. by Ellen Cronan Rose in Signs (18:2) 1993, 346–75.

14525. GREENE, J. LEE. Blacks in Eden: the African-American novel's first century. *See* **9852**.

14526. GREINER, DONALD J. Women without men: female bonding and the American novel of the 1980s. (Bibl. 1994, 10453.) Rev. by Liahna Babener in JAC (18:1) 1995, 114–15.

14527. GRIEM, JULIKA. Screening America: representations of television in contemporary American literature. Amst (41:3) 1996, 465–81.

14528. GRIFFIN, FARAH JASMINE. Textual healing: claiming Black women's bodies, the erotic and resistance in contemporary novels of slavery. Callaloo (19:2) 1996, 519–36.

14529. GUNN, JAMES. The worldview of science fiction. *See* **9858**.

14530. GUSS, C. R. The wound of individuality: spirits coaxed to light. GetR (9:1) 1996, 154–63 (review-article).

14531. GYSIN, FRITZ. Scandalous roots: Black and White ancestry in recent African-American fiction. SPELL (9) 1996, 169–77.

14532. HAGEMANN, SUSANNE. Introduction. *In* (pp. 7–15) **115**.

14533. —— (ed.). Studies in Scottish fiction: 1945 to the present. *See* **115**.

14534. HALL, KEN. American hard-boiled fiction and *La cabeza de la hidra* by Carlos Fuentes. UDR (24:1) 1996, 83–95.

14535. HANLEY, LYNNE. Writing war: fiction, gender, and memory. (Bibl. 1993, 10480.) Rev. by Arlene Kaplan Daniels in Signs (19:1) 1993, 285–8.

14536. HANSON, CARTER F. 1920s Yellow Peril science fiction: political appropriations of the Asian racial 'alien'. JFA (6:4) 1993, 312–29.

14537. HANTKE, STEFFEN. 'God save us from the bourgeois adventure': the figure of the terrorist in contemporary American conspiracy fiction. StudN (28:2) 1996, 219–43.

14538. HAPKE, LAURA. Daughters of the Great Depression: women, work, and fiction in the American 1930s. (Bibl. 1995, 13124.) Rev. by Caren Irr in AL (68:4) 1996, 865–7; by Katherine Capshaw Smith in DreiS (27:1) 1996, 50–3; by Martha H. Swain in GaHQ (80:4) 1996, 929–30.

14539. HARDY, STEVE. Place and identity in contemporary British fiction. Brno Studies in English (22) 1996, 107–26.

14540. HARPER, MARJORY. Adventure or exile? The Scottish emigrant in fiction. *See* **9868**.

14541. HARVIE, CHRISTOPHER. North Sea oil and Scottish culture. *In* (pp. 159–85) **115**.

14542. HAUSLADEN, GARY. Where the bodies lie: sense of place and police procedurals. JCG (16:1) 1996, 45–63.

14543. HAUT, WOODY. Pulp culture: hardboiled fiction and the Cold War. London; New York: Serpent's Tail, 1995. pp. 230. Rev. by David Seed in JAStud (30:2) 1996, 328–9.

14544. HAYLES, N. KATHERINE. The life cycle of cyborgs: writing the posthuman. *In* (pp. 152–70) **94**.

14545. HEAD, DOMINIC. The Modernist short story: a study in theory and practice. (Bibl. 1995, 13134.) Rev. by Joseph M. Flora in MFS (40:1) 1994, 210–12.

14546. HEARN, CHARLES R. F. Scott Fitzgerald and the popular magazine formula story of the twenties. *See* **1286**.

14547. HEILBRUN, CAROLYN G. The detective novel of manners. *In* (pp. 187–97) **96**.

14548. HELBIG, JÖRG. *Beyond the first syllable of recorded time*: die Prähistorie als Handlungsschauplatz in der englischen und amerikanischen Literatur. Ang (114:1) 1996, 1–23.

14549. HENDRICKSON, ROBERTA MAKASHAY. Victims and survivors: Native American women writers, violence against women, and child abuse. SAIL (8:1) 1996, 13–24.

14550. HERMAN, DAVID. Universal grammar and narrative form. *See* **2641**.

14551. HILFERTY, ROBERT. *Ready to Wear.* FilmQ (48:4) 1995, 35–8.

14552. HIRSON, DENIS; TRUMP, MARTIN (eds). The Heinemann book of South African short stories: from 1945 to the present. (Bibl. 1995, 13138.) Rev. by Robert L. Bernier in WLT (69:1) 1995, 208.

14553. HITCHCOCK, PETER. Radical writing. *In* (pp. 95–121) **33**.

14554. HOLMSTRÖM, LAKSHMI. A note on Indian short stories. *See* **9876**.

14555. HONEY, MAUREEN (ed.). Breaking the ties that bind: popular stories of the New Woman, 1915–1930. (Bibl. 1995, 13141.) Rev. by Wendy Simonds in AmP (4) 1994, 130–1; by Liahna Babener in JPC (29:4) 1996, 236–7.

14556. HOWELLS, CORAL ANN. Private and fictional words: Canadian women novelists of the 1970s and 1980s. (Bibl. 1990, 8964.) Rev. by Arnold E. Davidson in ARCS (19:2) 1989, 205–8.

14557. HUBEL, TERESA. Whose India? The independence struggle in British and Indian fiction and history. *See* **9878**.

14558. HUGGAN, GRAHAM. Territorial disputes: maps and mapping strategies in contemporary Canadian and Australian fiction. (Bibl. 1994, 10476.) Rev. by Axel Knoenagel in CanL (151) 1996, 177–8.

14559. HUKE, THOMAS. Jazz und Blues im afroamerikanischen Roman von der Jahrhundertwende bis zur Gegenwart. (Bibl. 1992, 11302.) Rev. by Wolfgang Hochbruck in LWU (29:2) 1996, 132–4.

14560. INNESS, SHERRIE. Girls will be boys and boys will be girls: cross-dressing in popular turn-of-the-century college fiction. *See* **9881**.

14561. INNESS, SHERRIE A. The feminine en-gendering of film consumption and film technology in popular girls' serial novels, 1914–1931. *See* **13823**.

14562. —— On the road and in the air: gender and technology in girls' automobile and airplane serials, 1909–1932. JPC (30:2) 1996, 47–60.

14563. IRMER, THOMAS. *Metafiction, moving pictures, moving histories*: der historische Roman in der Literatur der amerikanischen Postmoderne. (Bibl. 1995, 13151.) Rev. by Gabriele Helms in CanL (151) 1996, 163; by Jutta Zimmermann in ZAA (44:3) 1996, 283–5; by Barbara Puschmann-Nalenz in LWU (29:2) 1996, 132.

14564. IWASE, SHITSU; KAMOGAWA, TAKAHIRO; SUGA, YUKAKO (eds). Kakusareta ishou – eibeisakka no motif to souzou. (Concealed designs: motifs and creation of English and American writers.) *See* **9882**.

14565. JAMES, EDWARD. Building utopias on Mars, from Crusoe to Robinson. Foundation (68) 1996, 64–75.

14566. —— Science fiction in the twentieth century. (Bibl. 1995, 13154.) Rev. by Timothy J. Sramcik in Extrapolation (36:2) 1995, 159–60.

14567. JASON, PHILIP K. Vietnam War themes in Korean War fiction. SAtlR (61:1) 1996, 109–21.

14568. JENKINS, PHILIP. Naming the beast: contemporary apocalyptic novels. ChesR (22:4) 1996, 487–97.

14569. JUNEJA, OM P. Post-colonial novel: narratives of colonial consciousness. New Delhi: Creative Books, 1995. pp. x, 182. (Creative new literatures, 5.) Rev. by Peter Nazareth in WLT (70:3) 1996, 769–70.

14570. KANHAI, ROSANNE. 'Sensing designs in history's muddles': global feminism and the postcolonial novel. MLS (26:4) 1996, 119–30.

14571. KARLIN, WAYNE; KHUE, LE MINH; VU, TRUONG (eds). The other side of heaven: postwar fiction by Vietnamese and American writers. Willimantic, CT: Curbstone 1995. pp. xvii, 411. Rev. by Tom Wells in BkW, 31 Dec. 1995, 7.

14572. KAUL, SUVIR. Colonial figures and postcolonial reading. *See* **2410**.

14573. KEARNEY, J. A. Reading the Bambata Rebellion in South African English fiction. JLS (10:3/4) 1995, 400–24.

14574. KELLEGHAN, FIONA. Camouflage in fantastic fiction and film. *See* **13853**.

14575. KELLEY, MARGOT. Gender and genre: the case of the novel-in-stories. *In* (pp. 295–310) **3**.

14576. KELLMAN, STEVEN G. Family matters. GetR (5:4) 1992, 644–55 (review-article).

14577. —— Fighting trim. GetR (5:3) 1992, 530–8 (review-article).

14578. —— Novelists trade secrets. GetR (5:2) 1992, 345–54 (review-article).

14579. KENNEDY, J. GERALD (ed.). Modern American short story sequences: composite fictions and fictive communities. (Bibl. 1995, 32.) Rev. by Irving Malin in SSF (31:3) 1996, 160–1; by Kasia Boddy in JAStud (30:1) 1996, 165.

14580. KERMAN, JUDITH B. Uses of the fantastic in the literature of the Holocaust. JFA (5:2) 1992, 14–31.

14581. KERN, LOUIS J. American *grand guignol*: splatterpunk gore, Sadean morality and socially redemptive violence. JAC (19:2) 1996, 47–59.

14582. KERRIGAN, CATHERINE. Nationalism and gender: Scottish myths of the female. *See* **12169**.

14583. KESSLER, CAROL FARLEY (ed.). Daring to dream: utopian fiction by United States women before 1950. *See* **9889**.

14584. KLARER, MARIO. Frau und Utopie: feministische Literaturtheorie und utopischer Diskurs im anglo-amerikanischen Roman. (Bibl. 1995, 13181.) Rev. by Elfi Bettinger in Archiv (233:2) 1996, 419–21; by Jeanne Cortiel in AAA (21:1) 1996, 133–8.

14585. KLINKOWITZ, JEROME. Fiction: the 1960s to the present. American Literary Scholarship (1993) 255–80; (1994) 303–23; (1995) 331–60.

14586. —— Structuring the void: the struggle for subject in contemporary American fiction. (Bibl. 1995, 13182.) Rev. by Charles Berryman in MFS (40:1) 1994, 160–1.

14587. KLOSTERMANN, BERTHOLD. 'Blue notes – Black fiction'. Schwarze Musik in der afroamerikanischen Erzählliteratur der zwanziger und dreissiger Jahre. (Bibl. 1993, 10527.) Rev. by Thomas Huke in ZAA (43:1) 1995, 104–6.

14588. KOMAR, KATHLEEN L. Feminist curves in contemporary literary space. *In* (pp. 89–107) **97**.

14589. KRIEGEL, LEONARD. Writing the I. GetR (6:2) 1993, 239–49.

14590. KUESTER, MARTIN. Framing truths: parodic structures in contemporary English-Canadian historical novels. (Bibl. 1995, 13189.)

Rev. by Jutta Zimmermann in ZAA (42:4) 1994, 405–6; by Gabriele Helms in CanL (148) 1996, 153–5; by Cynthia Sugars in ECanW (58) 1996, 136–44.

14591. LALLA, BARBARA. Defining Jamaican fiction: *marronage* and the discourse of survival. Tuscaloosa; London: Alabama UP, 1996. pp. xi, 224.

14592. LANCASTER, KURT. Travelling among the lands of the fantastic: the imaginary worlds and simulated environments of science fiction tourism. *See* **13895**.

14593. LARSSON, CLARENCE. Identity through the other: Canadian adventure romance for adolescents. Umeå: Umeå Univ., 1996. pp. 148. (Acta Universitatis Umensis: Umeå studies in the humanities, 133.)

14594. LATHAM, ROB. The men who walked on the moon: images of America in the 'new wave' science fiction of the 1960s and 1970s. *In* (pp. 195–203) **36**.

14595. LATHAM, ROBERT A.; COLLINS, ROBERT A. (eds). Modes of the fantastic: selected essays from the Twelfth International Conference on the Fantastic in the Arts. *See* **70**.

14596. LEAVIS, L. R. Current literature 1994: 1, New writing: novels and short stories. EngS (76:6) 1995, 532–46.

14597. LEDBETTER, MARK. Victims and the postmodern narrative; or, Doing violence to the body: an ethic of reading and writing. Basingstoke: Macmillan; New York: St Martin's Press, 1996. pp. xii, 159. (Studies in literature and religion.)

14598. —— Virtuous intentions: the religious dimension of narrative. Atlanta, GA: Scholars Press, 1989. pp. 100. (American Academy of Religion academy series, 66.) Rev. by David Jasper in LitTheol (5:1) 1991, 125–6.

14599. LEPA, JACK. Historical mysteries: matters of fact *and* fiction. *See* **500**.

14600. —— Mysteries – hard boiled. *See* **501**.

14601. LEVESON, MARCIA. People of the book: images of the Jew in South African English fiction 1880–1992. *See* **9900**.

14602. LIMON, JOHN. Writing after war: American war fiction from realism to postmodernism. (Bibl. 1995, 13203.) Rev. by D. Quentin Miller in MFS (42:1) 1996, 157–9.

14603. LONG, BEVERLY WHITAKER; GRANT, CHARLES H., III. The 'surprising range of the possible': families communicating in fiction. CommEd (41:1) 1992, 89–107.

14604. LORD, GEOFFREY. Postmodernism and notions of national difference: a comparison of postmodern fiction in Britain and America. Amsterdam; Atlanta, GA: Rodopi, 1996. pp. 190. (Postmodern studies, 18.) (Cf. bibl. 1995, 14371.)

14605. LÖSCHNIGG, MARTIN. History and the search for identity: reconstructing the past in recent English novels. LWU (29:2) 1996, 103–19.

14606. LUPACK, BARBARA TEPA. Insanity as redemption in contemporary American fiction: inmates running the asylum. (Bibl. 1995, 13208.) Rev. by Carl S. Horner in AL (68:2) 1996, 488–9; by Tim Woods in JAStud (30:2) 1996, 286.

14607. —— (ed.). Vision/re-vision: adapting contemporary American fiction by women to film. *See* **13935**.

14608. McClain, Larry.   The rhetoric of regional representation: American fiction and the politics of cultural dissent. *See* **9905**.

14609. McClure, John A.   Late imperial romance. (Bibl. 1995, 13213.) Rev. by Glen Thomas in AUMLA (85) 1996, 172–4; by Andrea White in StudN (28:4) 1996, 601–4.

14610. MacDermott, Doireann.   Midnight's children come of age: some Indian novels of the past decade. RCEI (28) 1994, 11–22.

14611. McDonough, Donald.   Off with their heads: the British novel and the rise of Fascism. TPB (33) 1996, 34–42.

14612. McJannet, Tammy D.   The emphasis on the European contact situation in the American science-fiction novel's representation of culture. *In* (pp. 89–94) **127**.

14613. MacNee, Marie J.   Science fiction, fantasy and horror writers: vol. 1, A–J; vol. 2, K–Z. New York: UXL, 1995. pp. xxiv, 432. Rev. by Edward James in Utopian Studies (7:2) 1996, 298–300.

14614. Mallett, Daryl F. (ed.).   Wilderness visions: the Western theme in science-fiction literature. By David Mogen. (Bibl. 1995, 13226.) Rev. by David M. Esposito in Utopian Studies (7:1) 1996, 131–2.

14615. Maltby, Paul.   Self-reflexive fiction in the age of systemic communication. CR (40:1) 1996, 49–68.

14616. Manferlotti, Stefano.   Dopo l'impero: romanzo ed etnia in Gran Bretagna. Naples: Liguori, 1995. pp. 231. (Il leone e l'unicorno, 3.) Rev. by Elio Di Piazza in Annali anglistica (38:3) 1995, 148–50.

14617. Manguel, Alberto; Stephenson, Craig (eds).   Meanwhile, in another part of the forest: gay stories from Alice Munro to Yukio Mishima. Toronto: Knopf, 1994. pp. xxi, 682. Rev. by Helmut Reichenbächer in CanL (149) 1996, 175–6.

14618. Margolin, Uri.   Telling our story: on 'we' literary narratives. *See* **2671**.

14619. Martin, Richard.   Reading life, writing fiction: an introduction to novels by American women, 1920–1940. (Bibl. 1995, 13230.) Rev. by Catrin Gersdorf in Amst (41:2) 1996, 302–3.

14620. Mathews, Lawrence.   Calgary, canonization, and class: deciphering List B. *In* (pp. 150–66) **13**.

14621. Meckier, Jerome.   What the books were always saying. ANQ (9:2) 1996, 39–48 (review-article). (Dystopian literature.)

14622. Meyer, Martin.   Nachkriegsdeutschland im Spiegel amerikanischer Romane der Besatzungszeit 1945–1955. (Bibl. 1994, 10534.) Rev. by Axel Knönagel in CanRCL (23:4) 1996, 1264–7.

14623. Michael, Magali Cornier.   Feminism and the postmodern impulse: post-World War II fiction. Albany: New York State UP, 1996. pp. x, 275. Rev. by Amy Cowen in MFS (42:4) 1996, 931–3.

14624. Michel, Robert H.   *Floreat* Plutoria: satirical fiction about McGill. Fontanus (9) 1996, 29–45.

14625. Middleton, Jo Ann.   Fiction: 1900 to the 1930s. American Literary Scholarship (1993) 195–231; (1994) 241–78; (1995) 259–302.

14626. Milam, Michael C.   Science fiction and human nature. Humanist (55:2) 1995, 29–32.

14627. Miller, Danny L.   Wingless flights: Appalachian women in fiction. Bowling Green, OH: Bowling Green State Univ. Popular Press, 1996. pp. x, 187.

14628. Minganti, Franco.   *B.H. (Before Humphrey)*: le vicissitudini dell'*hard boiled hero* negli anni venti e trenta. Letterature d'America (36/37) 1990, 41–72.

14629. —— Updating (electronic) storytelling. *See* **1188**.

14630. MITCHELL, KAREN S. Ever after: reading the women who read (and re-write) romances. *See* **13991**.

14631. MITCHELL, LEE CLARK. Westerns: making the man in fiction and film. *See* **13992**.

14632. MOELLER, SUSAN D. The cultural construction of urban poverty: images of poverty in New York City, 1890–1917. *See* **13996**.

14633. MONTGOMERY, MAXINE LAVON. The apocalypse in African-American fiction. Gainesville: Florida UP, 1996. pp. x, 115.

14634. MOORE, JOHN. Shifting frontiers: mapping cyberpunk and the American South. Foundation (66) 1996, 59–68.

14635. MOOSMÜLLER, BIRGIT. Die experimentelle englische Kurzgeschichte der Gegenwart. Munich: Fink, 1993. pp. 384. (Munich studies in English literature, 7.) Rev. by Hilary P. Dannenberg in Archiv (233:2) 1996, 427–8.

14636. MULAS, FRANCO. The mechanical world in the Italian-American novel. *In* (pp. 395–401) **117**.

14637. MULLEN, BILL. 'A revolutionary tale': in search of African-American women's short-story writing. *In* (pp. 191–207) **3**.

14638. MUNK, ERIKA. Exiled from nowhere. *See* **9920**.

14639. MUNT, SALLY. Murder by the book? Feminism and the crime novel. (Bibl. 1994, 10548.) Rev. by Marty S. Knepper in MFS (42:1) 1996, 232–4.

14640. NATOLI, JOSEPH. Meditating on a postmodern strategy of reading. *See* **9922**.

14641. NAYLOR, GLORIA (ed.). Children of the night: the best short stories by Black writers, 1967 to the present. Boston, MA: Little, Brown, 1995. pp. xx, 569. Rev. by Ed Peaco in AR (54:3) 1996, 365–6.

14642. NEUMANN, FRITZ-WILHELM. Der englische historische Roman im 20. Jahrhundert: Gattungsgeschichte als Diskurskritik. (Bibl. 1995, 13254.) Rev. by Stephan Lieske in ZAA (43:1) 1995, 99–101; by Rudolf Beck in Archiv (233:2) 1996, 412–16.

14643. NEWMAN, JUDIE. The ballistic bard: postcolonial fictions. London; New York: Arnold, 1995. pp. xii, 202.

14644. NISCHIK, REINGARD M. 'Das Bild in der Fiktion': Film in Kurzprosatexten. *See* **14033**.

14645. —— (ed.). American and Canadian short stories. Paderborn: Schöningh, 1994. pp. 160. Rev. by Manuela Reiter in GRM (45:1) 1995, 122–3.

14646. NISCHIK, REINGARD M.; LEHR, REGINA. American and Canadian short stories: interpretations and supplementary material. Paderborn: Schöningh, 1996. pp. 184.

14647. NOLA, NINA. The migrant body: fetishing difference/differentiating the fetish. Span (42/43) 1996, 104–13.

14648. NYMAN, JOPI. Heroes in the world of rotting concrete: hard-boiled cops and detectives in American and Finnish crime fiction. Teaching & Learning (2) 1996, 39–49.

14649. OBRADOVIC, NADEZDA (ed.). African rhapsody: short stories of the contemporary African experience. Foreword by Chinua Achebe. New York: Anchor, 1994. pp. xxiii, 353. Rev. by Pamela J. Olubunmi Smith in WLT (69:2) 1995, 414.

14650. O'CALLAGHAN, EVELYN.   Interior schisms dramatised: the treatment of the 'mad' woman in the work of some female Caribbean novelists. *In* (pp. 89–109) **81**.

14651. OLDENZIEL, RUTH.   Of old and new cyborgs: feminist narratives of technology. Letterature d'America (55) 1994, 95–111.

14652. OLIPHANT, ANDRIES WALTER.   Fictions of anticipation: perspectives on some recent South African short stories in English. WLT (70:1) 1996, 59–62.

14653. OLIVER, FIONA.   The self-debasement of Scotland's post-colonial bodies. Span (42/43) 1996, 114–21.

14654. OLTEAN, STEFAN.   Free indirect discourse: some referential aspects. *See* **2554**.

14655. O'NEILL, PATRICK.   The comedy of entropy: humour, narrative, reading. (Bibl. 1995, 13260.) Rev. by Marcel Cornis-Pope in CanRCL (19:4) 1992, 664–8.

14656. OWENS, LOUIS.   Other destinies: understanding the American-Indian novel. (Bibl. 1995, 13263.) Rev. by Janet M. Cliff in JAF (106:421) 1993, 367–8; by James W. Parins in AmS (35:1) 1994, 173–4.

14657. PADOL, LISA.   Whose English? Language in the modern Arthurian novel. *See* **2689**.

14658. PALMER, PAULINA.   The city in contemporary women's fiction. *In* (pp. 315–35) **34**.

14659. PANDEY, SUDHAKAR; RAO, R. RAJ.   Introduction. *In* (pp. xi–xix) **45**.

14660. —— —— (eds).   Image of India in the Indian novel in English 1960–1985. *See* **45**.

14661. PARK, SOWON S.   Suffrage fiction: a political discourse in the marketplace. ELT (39:4) 1996, 450–61.

14662. PARKER, MICHAEL (ed.).   The hurt world: short stories of the Troubles. Belfast: Blackstaff Press, 1995. pp. 363. Rev. by John Herdman in Edinburgh Review (95) 1996, 168–9.

14663. PARKES, ADAM.   Modernism and the theater of censorship. Oxford; New York: OUP, 1996. pp. xii, 242. (Cf. bibl. 1994, 12912.)

14664. PEDERSON, JAY P. (ed.).   St James guide to science fiction writers. Detroit, MI: St James Press, 1996. pp. xxiv, 1175. Rev. by David Seed in Foundation (67) 1996, 128.

14665. PENNINGTON, JOHN.   Pierre Menard in cyberspace: the Internet as intertext. *In* (pp. 181–8) **127**.

14666. PERRET, PATTI.   The faces of fantasy. New York: TOR, 1996. pp. 235.

14667. PFITZER, GREGORY M.   The only good alien is a dead alien: science fiction and the metaphysics of Indian-hating on the high frontier. JAC (18:1) 1995, 51–67.

14668. PICKRELL, ALAN.   The mystery of mysticism: a theme for popular fiction. DNR (65:1) 1996, 3–11.

14669. PIETTE, ADAM.   Imagination at war: British fiction and poetry, 1939–1945. London: Papermac, 1995. pp. 341. Rev. by Laurence Bristow-Smith in PeakeS (4:4) 1996, 46–50.

14670. PLAIN, GILL.   Women's fiction of the Second World War: gender, power, and resistance. Edinburgh: Edinburgh UP; New York: St Martin's Press, 1996. pp. xi, 207.

14671. POLLIN, BURTON R. Poe: the 'virtual' inventor, practitioner, and inspirer of modern science fiction. *See* **12071**.

14672. PRENSHAW, PEGGY WHITMAN. Southern ladies and the Southern literary renaissance. *In* (pp. 73–88) **32**.

14673. PRESLEY, JOHN WOODROW. *Finnegans Wake, Lady Pokingham*, and Victorian erotic fantasy. *See* **9929**.

14674. PRICE HERNDL, DIANE. The dilemmas of a feminine dialogic. *In* (pp. 7–24) **33**.

14675. PRICE, THOMAS J. Spy stories, espionage and the public in the twentieth century. JPC (30:3) 1996, 81–9.

14676. PRINGLE, DAVID. Imaginary people: a who's who of fictional characters from the eighteenth century to the present day. *See* **8603**.

14677. PUGHE, THOMAS. Reading the picaresque: Mark Twain's *The Adventures of Huckleberry Finn*, Saul Bellow's *The Adventures of Augie March*, and more recent adventures. *See* **12601**.

14678. PYRHÖNEN, HETA. Murder from an academic angle: an introduction to the study of the detective narrative. (Bibl. 1995, 13278.) Rev. by Carmen Birkle in Amst (41:1) 1996, 150–1.

14679. RABINOWITZ, PAULA. Labor & desire: women's revolutionary fiction in Depression America. (Bibl. 1995, 13279.) Rev. by Rena Fraden in AmS (34:2) 1993, 155–7.

14680. RABKIN, ERIC S. The composite novel in science fiction. Foundation (66) 1996, 93–9.

14681. RAINES, GAY. 'Return' in Australian fiction. *In* (pp. 41–9) **102**.

14682. RASCHE, BERND. Der Zwang zum Erfolg: Kulturgeschichtliche Untersuchungen eines modernen Leidens an amerikanischer Kurzprosa des 20. Jahrhunderts. Stuttgart: M&P, 1991. pp. 330. Rev. by Christine Gerhardt in AAA (21:2) 1996, 315–18.

14683. RAUB, PATRICIA. A New Woman or an old-fashioned girl? The portrayal of the heroine in popular women's novels of the twenties. AmS (35:1) 1994, 109–30.

14684. REGINALD, ROBERT (ed.); BURGESS, MARY A.; MALLETT, DARYL F. (assoc. eds). Science fiction and fantasy literature, 1975–1991: a bibliography of science fiction, fantasy, and horror fiction books and nonfiction monographs. (Bibl. 1993, 10635.) Rev. by Andrew M. Butler in Foundation (63) 1995, 105–7.

14685. REHBERGER, DEAN. Vulgar fiction, impure history: the neglect of historical fiction. *See* **9933**.

14686. RIACH, ALAN. Nobody's children: orphans and their ancestors in popular Scottish fiction after 1945. *In* (pp. 51–83) **115**.

14687. ROBERTS, ROBIN. A new species: gender and science in science fiction. (Bibl. 1994, 10586.) Rev. by Kristine J. Anderson in Utopian Studies (7:1) 1996, 142–4.

14688. ROBILLARD, DOUGLAS (ed.). American supernatural fiction: from Edith Wharton to the weird tales writers. *See* **9937**.

14689. ROBINSON, KIM STANLEY (ed.). Future primitive: the new ecotopias. New York: TOR, 1994. pp. 352. Rev. by John Moore in Foundation (67) 1996, 99–102.

14690. ROBINSON, SALLY. Engendering the subject: gender and self-representation in contemporary women's fiction. (Bibl. 1993, 10640.) Rev. by Ellen Cronan Rose in Signs (18:2) 1993, 346–75.

14691. ROEMER, MICHAEL. Telling stories: postmodernism and the invalidation of traditional narrative. (Bibl. 1995, 13288.) Rev. by Ralph Flores in WLT (70:2) 1996, 483–4.

14692. Rogers, John H. (ed.).   British short-fiction writers, 1915–1945. Detroit, MI; London: Gale Research, 1996. pp. xv, 444. (Dictionary of literary biography, 162.)

14693. Roos, Henriette.   Assimilation and transformation of African and European literary traditions in the present-day South African novel. JLS (11:2) 1996, 1–14.

14694. Rose, Ellen Cronan.   American feminist criticism of contemporary women's fiction. Signs (18:2) 1993, 346–75 (review-article).

14695. Rosenberg, Roberta.   The language of power: women and literature, 1945 to the present. New York; Frankfurt; Bern; Paris: Lang, 1996. pp. xii, 273. (Writing about women, 19.)

14696. Rossen, Janice.   The university in modern fiction: when power is academic. (Bibl. 1993, 10641.) Rev. by Frank G. Novak, Jr, in StudN (28:4) 1996, 612–15.

14697. Rozett, Martha Tuck.   Constructing a world: how post-modern historical fiction reimagines the past. CLIO (25:2) 1996, 145–64.

14698. Rubenstein, Roberta.   Boundaries of the self: gender, culture, fiction. (Bibl. 1992, 11463.) Rev. by Ellen Cronan Rose in Signs (18:2) 1993, 346–75.

14699. Rubin, Louis D., Jr.   On the new North Carolina writers. See **1077**.

14700. Ruppert, James.   Mediation in contemporary Native-American fiction. (Bibl. 1995, 13291.) Rev. by Timothy Sweet in MFS (42:4) 1996, 856–8; by Laura J. Murray in AL (68:3) 1996, 658–9.

14701. Sage, Lorna.   Women in the house of fiction: post-war women novelists. (Bibl. 1994, 10595.) Rev. by Debra Bernardi in MFS (40:2) 1994, 432–4.

14702. Sage, Victor; Smith, Allan Lloyd (eds).   Modern gothic: a reader. Manchester; New York: Manchester UP, 1996. pp. vi, 202.

14703. Samuels, David.   'These are the stories that the dogs tell': discourses of identity and difference in ethnography and science fiction. See **14170**.

14704. Sargent, Pamela.   Women and science fiction. In (pp. 225–37) **38**.

14705. Sargisson, Lucy.   Contemporary feminist utopianism: practising utopia on utopia. In (pp. 238–55) **63**.

14706. Sauerberg, Lars Ole.   Fact into fiction: documentary realism in the contemporary novel. (Bibl. 1993, 10650.) Rev. by Ansgar Nünning in ZAA (41:3) 1993, 278–80.

14707. Scacchi, Anna.   Il *gadget* e l'androide: dal mito dell' apprendista stregone al simulacro. In (pp. 289–96) **117**.

14708. Schaub, Thomas Hill.   American fiction in the Cold War. (Bibl. 1995, 13297.) Rev. by Charles J. Gaspar in AmS (33:2) 1992, 136–7.

14709. Scheick, William J.   Post-nuclear holocaust re-minding. In (pp. 71–84) **77**.

14710. —— Romantic tradition in recent post-nuclear holocaust fiction. In (pp. 162–91) **28**.

14711. Schenkel, Elmar.   Cyclomanie: Fahrrad und Literatur um 1900. See **9943**.

14712. Schleifer, Ronald.   Writhing nets and goodly pearls:

The Postmodern Bible, temporal collaboration, and storytelling. CR (40:2) 1996, 385–99.

14713. SCHOLBIN, ROGER C. The artisan in modern fantasy. JFA (6:4) 1993, 285–94.

14714. —— The craving for meaning: explicit allegory in the non-implicit age. JFA (5:1) 1992, 3–12.

14715. SCHULZ, JOAN. Orphaning as resistance. *In* (pp. 89–109) **32**.

14716. SCHWAB, GABRIELE. Subjects without selves: transitional texts in modern fiction. (Bibl. 1995, 13300.) Rev. by Terry Caesar in Pynchon Notes (34/35) 1994, 192–8; by Christian Moraru in Comparatist (19) 1995, 149–51; by Michael Levenson in Modernism/Modernity (3:1) 1996, 157–9.

14717. SCHWARTZ, NINA. Dead fathers: the logic of transference in modern narrative. (Bibl. 1994, 10607.) Rev. by Nancy R. Comley in MFS (42:4) 1996, 914–16.

14718. SCHWEND, JOACHIM; DRESCHER, HORST W. (eds). Studies in Scottish fiction: twentieth century. (Bibl. 1992, 93.) Rev. by Peter Zenzinger in ZAA (42:2) 1994, 188–90.

14719. SCRUGGS, CHARLES. Sweet home: invisible cities in the Afro-American novel. (Bibl. 1994, 10609.) Rev. by Keneth Kinnamon in MFS (40:2) 1994, 364–5.

14720. SENIOR, W. A. Medieval literature and modern fantasy: toward a common metaphysic. *See* **4978**.

14721. —— *To goon on pilgrimages*: a special issue on modern fantasy and medieval literature. *See* **4979**.

14722. SENIOR, WILLIAM. Oliphaunts in the perilous realm: the function of internal wonder in fantasy. *In* (pp. 115–23) **36**.

14723. SHAFFER, BRIAN W. The blinding torch: modern British fiction and the discourse of civilization. (Bibl. 1995, 13307.) Rev. by Herbert N. Schneidau in MFS (42:1) 1996, 180–2.

14724. SHINN, THELMA J. Gender images and patterns from novel to film. *In* (pp. 451–9) **38**.

14725. —— Women shapeshifters: transforming the contemporary novel. Westport, CT; London: Greenwood Press, 1996. pp. xx, 177. (Contributions in women's studies, 156.)

14726. ŠKVORECKÝ, JOSEF. Detective stories: some notes on *Fingerprints*. *In* (pp. 231–48) **105**.

14727. SMETAK, JACQUELINE R. Sex and death in nuclear holocaust literature of the 1950s. *In* (pp. 15–26) **77**.

14728. SMIDT, KRISTIAN. T. S. Eliot's criticism of modern prose fiction. *See* **11653**.

14729. SÖDERLIND, SYLVIA. Margin/alias: language and colonization in Canadian and Québécois fiction. (Bibl. 1994, 10624.) Rev. by Sherry Simon in ECanW (55) 1995, 51–7.

14730. SOITOS, STEPHEN F. The Blues detective: a study of African-American detective fiction. Amherst: Massachusetts UP, 1996. pp. xiii, 260. Rev. by Gary Storhoff in AL (68:4) 1996, 873–4.

14731. SOLOMON, WILLIAM. Politics and rhetoric in the novel in the 1930s. *See* **2473**.

14732. SPINRAD, NORMAN. Science fiction in the real world. (Bibl. 1990, 9120.) Rev. by Jennifer Lynn Browning in Extrapolation (36:1) 1995, 70–3.

14733. STEAD, ALISTAIR.   Pastoral sexuality in British and American fiction. *In* (pp. 295–314) **34**.

14734. STEFANKO, JACQUELINE.   New ways of telling Latinas' narratives of exile and return. Frontiers (17:2) 1996, 50–69.

14735. STEVENSON, DIANE.   Landscape and race in the detective novel. SHum (19:2) 1992, 145–57.

14736. STREHLE, SUSAN.   Satire beyond the norm. ConLit (37:1) 1996, 145–54 (review-article).

14737. STREITFELD, DAVID.   But I saw the movie … . *See* **14260**.

14738. SULEIMAN, SUSAN RUBIN.   Risking who one is: encounters with contemporary art and literature. (Bibl. 1995, 13337.) Rev. by Bettina L. Knapp in WLT (69:2) 1995, 447.

14739. SULLIVAN, LARRY E.; SCHURMAN, LYDIA CUSHMAN (eds). Pioneers, passionate ladies, and private eyes: dime novels, series books, and paperbacks. *See* **1014**.

14740. SWANSON, JEAN; JAMES, DEAN.   By a woman's hand: a guide to mystery fiction by women. (Bibl. 1994, 10639.) New York: Berkley Prime Crime, 1996. pp. x, 277. (Second ed.: first ed. 1994.)

14741. SZUBERLA, GUY.   Peattie's *Precipice* and the 'settlement house' novel. *See* **12023**.

14742. TABACHNICK, STEPHEN.   A course in the graphic novel. *See* **250**.

14743. TANNEN, DEBORAH.   Where'd all the fun go? *See* **14267**.

14744. TANNER, LAURA E.   Intimate violence: reading rape and torture in twentieth-century fiction. Bloomington: Indiana UP, 1994. pp. xiii, 155. Rev. by Susan V. Donaldson in AL (68:1) 1996, 266–7; by Helen Sword in Criticism (38:4) 1996, 650–2.

14745. THOMAS, CLARA.   The other fictions. LRC (5:7) 1996, 25–6 (review-article).

14746. TIBBETTS, JOHN C.   Phantom fighters: 150 years of occult detection. *See* **9963**.

14747. TIGHMAN, CHRISTOPHER.   Where have all the fathers gone? BkW, 16 June 1996, 1, 10.

14748. TODA, HITOSHI.   Igirisu bungaku to shinwa. (English literature and myths.) *See* **6855**.

14749. URGO, JOSEPH R.   Novel frames: literature as guide to race, sex, and history in American culture. (Bibl. 1994, 10653.) Rev. by Kathy Rugoff in JAC (18:1) 1995, 121.

14750. VAN DIJCK, JOSÉ.   Imagining reproduction: feminist fictions of new reproductive technologies. *In* (pp. 484–9) **117**.

14751. VAUTHIER, SIMONE.   Reverberations: explorations in the Canadian short story. (Bibl. 1994, 10656.) Rev. by Jill Franks in CanL (150) 1996, 145.

14752. VERNON, PETER.   American literature: the twentieth century: fiction since 1945. YWES (75) 1994, 640–63.

14753. VILLA, LUISA.   La forma del nuovo: donne, decadenza, modernità, e la *short story* inglese di fine secolo. *See* **9970**.

14754. WAGENKNECHT, EDWARD.   Seven masters of supernatural fiction. *See* **9973**.

14755. WALKER, MELISSA.   Down from the mountaintop: Black women's novels in the wake of the Civil Rights Movement, 1966–1989. (Bibl. 1993, 10701.) Rev. by Elizabeth Schultz in AmS (33:2) 1992, 135; by Ellen Cronan Rose in Signs (18:2) 1993, 346–75.

14756. WALLACE, GAVIN; STEVENSON, RANDALL (eds). The Scottish novel since the seventies. (Bibl. 1995, 49.) Rev. by Robert Alan Jamieson in Edinburgh Review (92) 1994, 150–4.

14757. WALLE, ALF H. Hack writing *vs* belle letters [*sic*]: the strategic implications of literary achievement. JPC (30:3) 1996, 185–96.

14758. WALSH, RICHARD. Novel arguments: reading innovative American fiction. (Bibl. 1995, 13358.) Rev. by Steven Earnshaw in Eng (45:183) 1996, 276–81; by Val Gough in JAStud (30:2) 1996, 332–3.

14759. WARDROP, STEPHANIE. The heroine is being beaten: Freud, sadomasochism, and reading the romance. Style (29:3) 1995, 459–73.

14760. WARING, WENDY. Is this your book? Wrapping postcolonial fiction for the global market. CanRCL (22:3/4) 1995, 455–66.

14761. —— Publishers, fiction, and feminism: riding the 'second wave'. *See* **1089**.

14762. WATSON, GREER. Magic or make-believe? Acquiring conventions of witches and witchcraft. *See* **3655**.

14763. WATSON, GREGORY JOHN. A review of contemporary Australian Aboriginal literature. New Courant (5) 1996, 1–14.

14764. WEISENBURGER, STEVEN. Fables of subversion: satire and the American novel, 1930–1980. (Bibl. 1995, 13362.) Rev. by Terry Caesar in Pynchon Notes (34/35) 1994, 192–8; by Daniel Green in MidQ (37:1) 1995, 106–7; by David W. Madden in MFS (42:4) 1996, 848–51; by Susan H. Swetnam in RMRLL (50:1) 1996, 106–8; by Susan Strehle in ConLit (37:1) 1996, 145–54.

14765. WESTBROOK, DEEANNE. Ground rules: baseball & myth. Urbana: Illinois UP, 1996. pp. 348. Rev. by Melinda Kanner in AR (54:4) 1996, 490–1; by Timothy Morris in SAF (24:2) 1996, 254–5.

14766. WESTFAHL, GARY. Cosmic engineers: a study of hard science fiction. Westport, CT; London: Greenwood Press, 1996. pp. xii, 148. Rev. by Donald M. Hassler in Extrapolation (37:4) 1996, 364–6.

14767. —— Where no market has gone before: 'the science fiction industry' and the *Star Trek* industry. *See* **14319**.

14768. WHEELER, KATHLEEN. 'Modernist' women writers and narrative art. (Bibl. 1994, 10667.) Rev. by Laura Doan in MFS (42:1) 1996, 230–2.

14769. WHITE, PATTI. Gatsby's party: the system and the list in contemporary narrative. (Bibl. 1995, 13366.) Rev. by Steven G. Kellman in MFS (40:1) 1994, 161–2.

14770. WIEMER, ANNEGRET. Utopia and science fiction: a contribution to the generic description. CanRCL (19:1/2) 1992, 171–200.

14771. WILDING, MICHAEL. The modern Australian short story. CritS (6:1) 1994, 112–17.

14772. WILKINSON, JOHN. Conventions of comedies of manners and British novels of academic life. *In* (pp. 199–213) **96**.

14773. WILSON, ANNA. Death and the mainstream: lesbian detective fiction and the killing of the coming-out story. Feminist Studies (22:2) 1996, 251–78.

14774. WINTER, MICHAEL (ed.). Extremities: fiction from the Burning Rock. St John's, Nfld: Killick Press, 1994. pp. xii, 195. Rev. by Herb Wylie in CanL (149) 1996, 195–6.

14775. WITEK, JOSEPH. The dream of total war: the limits of a genre. *See* **255**.

14776. WOLFE, GARY K.   Introduction: fantasy as testimony. JFA (5:2) 1992, 3–10.

14777. WOLMARK, JENNY.   Aliens and others: science fiction, feminism and postmodernism. (Bibl. 1995, 13370.) Rev. by Mária Minich Brewer in MFS (42:1) 1996, 214–19; by Carol Baker Sapora in AL (68:1) 1996, 277–8; by Maureen T. Reddy in Signs (21:3) 1996, 782–5.

14778. WORTON, MICHAEL.   (Re)writing gay identity: fiction as theory. CanRCL (21:1/2) 1994, 9–26.

14779. YATES, NORRIS.   Gender and genre: an introduction to women writers of formula Westerns, 1900–1950. (Bibl. 1995, 13375.) Rev. by Melody Graulich in RMRLL (50:2) 1996, 212–13.

14780. ZABUS, CHANTAL.   The African palimpsest: indigenization of language in the West African Europhone novel. (Bibl. 1994, 10677.) Rev. by Ahmed Sheikh Bangura in CanRCL (20:3/4) 1993, 559–62.

14781. ZAKI, HODA M.   Phoenix renewed: the survival and mutation of utopian thought in North American science fiction, 1965–1982. (Bibl. 1989, 8430.) San Bernardino, CA: Borgo Press, 1993. pp. 112. (I. O. Evans studies in the philosophy & criticism of literature, 18.) (Revised ed.: first ed. 1988.) Rev. by Karen L. Nelson in Utopian Studies (7:2) 1996, 361–3.

14782. ZAMORA, LOIS PARKINSON.   Writing the apocalypse: historical vision in contemporary US and Latin American fiction. (Bibl. 1995, 13382.) Rev. by Charles Lock in LitTheol (5:1) 1991, 129–30.

14783. ZHANG, BENZI.   Paradox of Chinese boxes: textual heterarchy in postmodern fiction. CanRCL (20:1/2) 1993, 89–103.

14784. ZIMMERMAN, BONNIE.   The safe sea of women: lesbian fiction 1969–1989. (Bibl. 1994, 10681.) Rev. by Ellen Cronan Rose in Signs (18:2) 1993, 346–75; by Greta Gaard in Signs (18:4) 1993, 980–3.

Literature for Children

14785. ABBOTT, JEFFREY L.   Life on the edge: where mythology and reality merge. ArizEB (36:1) 1993, 12–16.

14786. ALLEN, MARJORIE N.   One hundred years of children's books in America: decade by decade. Foreword by Jane Yolen. *See* **9987**.

14787. BARLEY, JANET CRANE.   Winter in July: visits with children's authors Down Under. (Bibl. 1995, 13386.) Rev. by Stuart Hannabuss in Library Review (45:4) 1996, 65–6.

14788. BEDARD, ROGER L.; TOLCH, C. JOHN (eds).   Spotlight on the child: studies in the history of American children's theatre. *See* **13429**.

14789. BODART, JONI RICHARDS (ed.).   Booktalking the award winners: young adult retrospective volume. Bronx, NY: Wilson, 1996. pp. xiii, 375.

14790. CALLAHAN, TIM.   Censoring the world riddle. *See* **13520**.

14791. CART, MICHAEL.   From romance to realism: 50 years of growth and change in young adult literature. New York: HarperCollins, 1996. pp. 312.

14792. CASTLE, KATHRYN.   Britannia's children: reading colonialism through children's books and magazines. *See* **9988**.

14793. CHRISTIAN-SMITH, LINDA K.   Becoming a woman through romance. (Bibl. 1995, 13395.) Rev. by Anne Chandler and Deborah K. Chappel in Signs (18:3) 1993, 674–8.

14794. DIZER, JOHN T.   Researching the *Boys' Own Library*: a Street and Smith experiment. *See* **921**.

14795. Donelson, Ken. Adolescent literature and censorship, 1989–1993: a note. *See* **923**.

14796. Drotner, Kirsten. English children and their magazines, 1751–1945. *See* **1263**.

14797. Gillespie, John T.; Naden, Corinne J. The Newbery companion: booktalk and related materials for Newbery Medal and Honor books. Englewood, CO: Libraries Unlimited, 1996. pp. xv, 406.

14798. Heale, Jay. From bushveld to Biko: the growth of South African children's literature in English from 1907 to 1992 traced through 110 notable books. Grabouw, South Africa: Bookchat, 1996. pp. 48.

14799. Helbig, Alethea K.; Perkins, Agnes (eds). The Phoenix Award of the Children's Literature Association. Lanham, MD; London: Scarecrow Press, 1996. pp. xvi, 282.

14800. —— Perkins, Agnes Regan. Dictionary of American children's fiction, 1990–1994: books of recognized merit. Westport, CT; London: Greenwood Press, 1996. pp. xi, 473.

14801. Hettinga, Donald R.; Schmidt, Gary D. (eds). British children's writers, 1914–1960. Detroit, MI; London: Gale Research, 1996. pp. xv, 422. (Dictionary of literary biography, 160.)

14802. Hunt, Caroline. Young adult literature evades the theorists. CLAQ (21:1) 1996, 4–11.

14803. Hunt, Caroline C. (ed.). British children's writers since 1960: first series. Detroit, MI; London: Gale Research, 1996. pp. xvii, 394. (Dictionary of literary biography, 161.)

14804. Johnson, Dianne. Telling tales: the pedagogy and promise of African-American literature for youth. (Bibl. 1995, 13412.) Rev. by Vera R. Edwards in AAR (28:1) 1994, 153–4.

14805. Karp, Rashelle S.; Schlessinger, June H.; Schlessinger, Bernard S. Plays for children and young adults: an evaluative index and guide. Supplement 1, 1989–1994. New York; London: Garland, 1996. pp. xi, 369. (Garland reference library of social science, 926.) (*Adds to* bibl. 1991, 3131.)

14806. Lewis, David. Going along with Mr Gumpy: polysystemy & play in the modern picture book. *See* **217**.

14807. Lind, Beth Beutler. Multicultural children's literature: an annotated bibliography, grades K–8. Jefferson, NC; London: McFarland, 1996. pp. viii, 270.

14808. Locherbie-Cameron, M. A. L. Journeys through the amulet: time-travel in children's fiction. Signal (79) 1996, 45–61.

14809. Maddy, Yulisa Amadu; MacCann, Donnarae. African images in juvenile literature: commentaries on neocolonialist fiction. Jefferson, NC; London: McFarland, 1996. pp. vi, 154.

14810. Mark, Jan; Mole, John. The Signal Poetry Award. Signal (80) 1996, 79–97.

14811. Miller, Miriam Youngerman. 'Thy speech is strange and uncouth': language in the children's historical novel of the Middle Ages. *See* **2676**.

14812. Moore Kruse, Ginny; Horning, Kathleen T. (eds). Multi-cultural literature for children and young adults: a selected listing of books, 1980–1990, by and about people of color. Madison: Wisconsin Dept of Public Instruction, 1991. pp. 78. (Third ed.: first ed. 1988.) Rev. by Stan Evans in AAR (28:4) 1994, 683–5.

14813. O'SULLIVAN, EMER. The development of modern children's literature in late twentieth-century Ireland. Signal (81) 1996, 189–211.

14814. RAHN, SUZANNE. The changing language of Black child characters in American children's books. *In* (pp. 225–58) **48**.

14815. REYNOLDS, KIMBERLEY. Girls only? Gender and popular children's fiction in Britain, 1880–1910. *See* **9998**.

14816. RIFFELT-BERNERTH, HELGE. The role of parents in novels for adolescents. ArizEB (36:1) 1993, 34–7.

14817. SHAVIT, ZOHAR. Poetics of children's literature. (Bibl. 1989, 8448.) Rev. by M. Bortolussi in CanRCL (18:4) 1991, 627–30.

14818. SMITH, KAREN PATRICIA (ed.). African-American voices in young adult literature. Metuchen, NJ; London: Scarecrow Press, 1994. pp. xxxv, 405. Rev. by Philippa Hope in Library Review (45:4) 1996, 63–4.

14819. STEPHENS, JOHN. Gender, genre and children's literature. Signal (79) 1996, 17–30.

14820. STEWIG, JOHN WARREN. The witch woman: a recurring motif in recent fantasy writing for young readers. Mythlore (20:1) 1994, 48–53.

14821. SULLIVAN, C. W., III. Science fiction for young readers. (Bibl. 1993, 10756.) Rev. by Andrew Gordon in ChildLit (24) 1996, 221–5.

14822. THOMPSON, RAYMOND H. From inspiration to warning: the changing rôle of Arthurian legend in fiction for younger readers. BJRL (76:3) 1994, 237–47.

14823. TOLSON, NANCY D. Regional outreach and an evolving Black aesthetic. CLAQ (20:4) 1995/96, 183–5.

14824. WEISS, M. JERRY. Try a little tenderness. ArizEB (36:1) 1993, 41–2.

14825. WEST, MÁIRE. Kings, heroes and warriors: aspects of children's literature in Ireland in the era of emergent nationalism. *See* **10001**.

14826. YOLEN, JANE. Dark mirrors: the scholar guest of honor address from the 1993 Mythopoeic Conference. Mythlore (20:4) 1995, 38–40.

Poetry

14827. ABARRY, ABU SHARDOW. Afrocentric aesthetics in selected Harlem renaissance poetry. *In* (pp. 133–46) **55**.

14828. ABBOTT, CRAIG S. Magazine verse and Modernism: Braithwaite's anthologies. JML (19:1) 1994, 151–9.

14829. ALEXANDER, WILL. Alchemy as poetic knowing. Talisman (11) 1993, 194–8.

14830. ALLISON, JONATHAN. Beyond gentility: a note on Seamus Heaney and American poetry. CritS (8:2) 1996, 178–85.

14831. ALTIERI, CHARLES. Painterly abstraction in Modernist American poetry: the contemporaneity of Modernism. (Bibl. 1995, 13466.) Rev. by Michael J. Hoffman in AmS (33:2) 1992, 133–4.

14832. —— Some problems about agency in the theories of radical poetics. ConLit (37:2) 1996, 207–36.

14833. ÁLVAREZ CALLEJA, MARÍA ANTONIA. Realistic *vs* romantic: the imagistic world of post-war English literature. *See* **14367**.

14834. ANDREWS, BRUCE. Paradise & method: poetics & praxis.

Evanston, IL: Northwestern UP, 1996. pp. vii, 275. (Avant-garde and modernism studies.)

14835. BADARACCO, CLAIRE HOERTZ. Trading words: poetry, typography, and illustrated books in the modern literary economy. *See* **177**.

14836. BADENHAUSEN, RICHARD. Representing experience and reasserting identity: the rhetoric of combat in British literature of World War I. *See* **2304**.

14837. BALAKIAN, ANNA. The fiction of the poet: from Mallarmé to the post-Symbolist mode. (Bibl. 1992, 11611.) Rev. by Albert F. Moritz in CanRCL (23:4) 1996, 1258–61.

14838. BARBIERO, DANIEL. Avant-garde without agonism? Talisman (14) 1995, 151–60.

14839. BARRESI, DOROTHY. The world as we know it. GetR (9:1) 1996, 55–72 (review-article).

14840. BARRY, JAN. The end of art: poetry and nuclear war. *In* (pp. 85–94) **77**.

14841. BATTLE, EFFIE T., *et al.* Six poets of racial uplift. New York: G. K. Hall; London: Prentice Hall, 1996. pp. xl, 461. (African-American women writers, 1910–1940.)

14842. BAWER, BRUCE. Prophets & professors: essays on the lives and works of modern poets. Brownsville, OR: Story Line Press, 1995. pp. 351.

14843. BEACH, CHRISTOPHER. Careers in creativity: the poetry academy in the 1990s. WHR (50:1) 1996, 4–16.

14844. BEASLEY, PAUL. *Vive la différence!* Performance poetry. CritQ (38:4) 1996, 28–38.

14845. BENNETT, PAULA. Lesbian poetry in the United States, 1890–1990: a brief overview. *In* (pp. 98–110) **92**.

14846. BERCOVITCH, SACVAN (gen. ed.). The Cambridge history of American literature: vol. 8, Poetry and criticism, 1940–1995. Cambridge; New York: CUP, 1996. pp. viii, 545.

14847. BERNSTEIN, CHARLES. Community and the individual talent. Diacritics (26:3/4) 1996, 176–95.

14848. —— Poetics of the Americas. Modernism/Modernity (3:3) 1996, 1–23.

14849. BIBBY, MICHAEL. Hearts and minds: bodies, poetry, and resistance in the Vietnam era. New Brunswick, NJ: Rutgers UP, 1996. pp. xiii, 250. (Perspectives on the sixties.) (Cf. bibl. 1993, 10766.)

14850. BLACK, AYANNA (ed.). Fiery spirits: a collection of short fiction and poetry by Canadian writers of African descent. *See* **14396**.

14851. BLACKMER, CORINNE E. Writing poetry like a 'woman'. *See* **10011**.

14852. BLODGETT, E. D. The poet and the academy. In-between (1:1) 1992, 9–30.

14853. —— Towards an ethnic style. CanRCL (22:3/4) 1995, 623–38.

14854. BLY, ROBERT. American poetry: wilderness and domesticity. (Bibl. 1992, 11619.) Rev. by Harry Marten in GetR (6:2) 1993, 253–61.

14855. BORKHUIS, CHARLES. Land of the signifieds; or, Writing from inside language: late Surrealism and textual poetry in France and the US. Onthebus (3:2/4:1) 1991, 268–80.

14856. BORNHOLDT, JENNY; O'BRIEN, GREGORY (eds). My heart goes swimming: New Zealand love poems. Auckland: Godwit, 1996. pp. 127.

Rev. by Mary Raphael in NZList, 23 Mar. 1996, 55; by Anne French in New Zealand Books (6:3) 1996, 1, 3.

14857. BOURKE, EOIN.   Poetic outrage: aspects of social criticism in modern Irish poetry. *In* (pp. 88–106) **112**.

14858. BOWD, GAVIN.   La jeune poésie écossaise: le temps du renouveau. Europe (805/6) 1996, 104–6.

14859. BOWEN, ROGER.   Many histories deep: the personal landscape poets in Egypt, 1940–45. (Bibl. 1995, 13481.) Rev. by Anne R. Zahlan in SAtlR (61:1) 1996, 174–6.

14860. BOZZA, DANIELA.   Corpi, rumori, flussi, voci: musica e femminile. Annali anglistica (38:3) 1995, 61–84.

14861. BRADLEY, ANTHONY.   The politics of Irishness. *See* **13481**.

14862. BRADLEY, JERRY.   Romanticism in the 1950s: the Movement's debt to Wordsworth. *See* **12831**.

14863. BRADLEY, JOHN (ed.).   Atomic ghost: poets respond to the nuclear age. Minneapolis, MN: Coffee House Press, 1995. pp. 330. Rev. by Patricia Pollock Brodsky in WLT (69:4) 1995, 882–3.

14864. BRENNAN, RORY.   Contemporary Irish poetry: an overview. *In* (pp. 1–27) **86**.

14865. BROWN, ALLAN.   Some West Coast words. AntR (107) 1996, 11–23 (review-article).

14866. BRYAN, T. J.   Women poets of the Harlem renaissance. *In* (pp. 99–114) **37**.

14867. BUCKLEY, VINCENT (ed.).   The Faber book of modern Australian verse. (Bibl. 1991, 11153.) Rev. by Neil Powell in PN Review (18:1) 1991, 56–7.

14868. BURNS, GERALD.   Hard as rocks. Talisman (8) 1992, 86–90.

14869. CARBÓ, NICK (ed.).   Returning a borrowed tongue: poems by Filipino and Filipino-American writers. Minneapolis, MN: Coffee House Press, 1995. pp. xvi, 238. Rev. by Al Camus Palomar in WLT (70:4) 1996, 1035.

14870. CAZÉ, ANTOINE.   Penser la syntaxe de la nouvelle poésie américaine. *See* **2596**.

14871. CHAMBERLIN, J. E.   The languages of contemporary West Indian poetry. *In* (pp. 295–309) **16**.

14872. CHIPASULA, STELLA; CHIPASULA, FRANK (eds).   The Heinemann book of African women's poetry. Oxford: Heinemann, 1995. pp. xxiv, 230. (African writers.) Rev. by Charlotte H. Bruner in WLT (69:4) 1995, 848–9.

14873. CLYDE, TOM.   The echo chamber: some emerging Ulster poets. *In* (pp. 114–29) **86**.

14874. COBHAM, RHONDA.   Women in Jamaican literature 1900–1950. *In* (pp. 195–222) **81**.

14875. COLLINS, FLOYD.   Beauty and strangeness. GetR (7:3) 1994, 517–31 (review-article).

14876. —— The craft of making. GetR (6:4) 1993, 702–15 (review-article).

14877. —— Elegaic voices. GetR (5:2) 1992, 240–50 (review-article).

14878. —— Eros and Thanatos. GetR (4:4) 1991, 689–705 (review-article).

14879. —— A fine excess. GetR (9:2) 1996, 331–52 (review-article).

14880. —— Ideology and diversity in recent poetry. GetR (5:1) 1992, 146–61 (review-article).

14881. —— The living artifact. GetR (7:4) 1994, 653–67 (review-article).

14882. —— Motives for metaphor. GetR (8:2) 1995, 331–46 (review-article).

14883. —— The poetics of mutability. GetR (6:2) 1993, 342–54 (review-article).

14884. —— The sublime and the quotidian. GetR (5:3) 1992, 514–27 (review-article).

14885. —— Variations on the journey motif. GetR (4:2) 1991, 309–29 (review-article).

14886. CONTE, JOSEPH (ed.). American poets since World War II. Fourth series. Detroit, MI; London: Gale Research, 1996. pp. xviii, 377. (Dictionary of literary biography, 165.)

14887. COOK, RUFUS. Poetry and place: Wendell Berry's ecology of literature. CR (40:3) 1996, 503–16.

14888. CORKHILL, ALAN. Zum Verhältnis von deutsch- und anglo-australischer Belletristik der Kolonialperiode aus interkultureller Sicht. ZAA (41:3) 1993, 238–49.

14889. COSTELLO, BONNIE. Possibilities of paradise: myth, narrative and lyric. GetR (5:4) 1992, 725–43 (review-article).

14890. COUGHLAN, PATRICIA; DAVIS, ALEX (eds). Modernism and Ireland: the poetry of the 1930s. Cork: Cork UP, 1995. pp. 318. Rev. by Maurice Harmon in IUR (26:1) 1996, 183–5.

14891. COWAN, LAURA. The elegy and Modernism. SHum (19:1) 1992, 43–57.

14892. CRAWFORD, ROBERT, *et al.* (eds). Talking verse. St Andrews: Verse, 1995. pp. 229. (Interviews with poets.) Rev. by B.B. in TLS, 1 Mar. 1996, 29.

14893. CROTTY, PATRICK (ed.). Modern Irish poetry: an anthology. Belfast: Blackstaff Press, 1995. pp. 436. Rev. by Patricia Craig in TLS, 31 May 1996, 32.

14894. CROZIER, LORNA; LANE, PATRICK (eds). Breathing fire: Canada's new poets. Madeira Park, B.C.: Harbour, 1995. pp. 188. Rev. by Allan Brown in MalaR (115) 1996, 107–9.

14895. CURTIS, TONY (ed.). How poets work. Bridgend, Mid-Glamorgan: Seren, 1996. pp. 175.

14896. DAVIDSON, MICHAEL. The San Francisco renaissance: poetics and community at mid-century. (Bibl. 1993, 10791.) Rev. by George F. Wedge in AmS (32:2) 1991, 124–5.

14897. DAVIES, JUDE. The future of 'no future': punk rock and post-modern theory. JPC (29:4) 1996, 3–25.

14898. DAVISON, PETER. The fading smile: poets in Boston, 1955–1960 from Robert Frost to Robert Lowell to Sylvia Plath. (Bibl. 1994, 10739.) Rev. by Dana Gioia in BkW, 28 Aug. 1994, 1, 9; by Robert B. Heilman in ASch (65:1) 1996, 145–6.

14899. DAWES, KWAME. Dichotomies of reading 'street poetry' and 'book poetry'. CritQ (38:4) 1996, 3–20.

14900. DEANE, PATRICK. At home in time: forms of neo-Augustanism in modern English poetry. (Bibl. 1995, 13511.) Rev. by Terry Whalen in ESCan (22:1) 1996, 112–15.

14901. DE KOCK, LEON; TROMP, IAN (eds). The heart in exile: South African poetry in English, 1990–1995. London; Johannesburg: Penguin,

1996. pp. xxiii, 332. Rev. by Dirk Klopper in New Coin (32:2) 1996, 64–9.

14902. DELANTY, GREG; NÍ DHOMHNAILL, NUALA (eds). 'Jumping off shadows': selected contemporary Irish poets. Preface by Philip O'Leary. Cork: Cork UP, 1995. pp. xxii, 257.

14903. DESHAZER, MARY K. A poetics of resistance: women writing in El Salvador, South Africa, and the United States. (Bibl. 1994, 10742.) Rev. by Maria Roof in NWSAJ (7:3) 1995, 125–6; by Lillian S. Robinson in TSWL (15:1) 1996, 165–7.

14904. DICKIE, MARGARET; TRAVISANO, THOMAS J. (eds). Gendered Modernisms: American women poets and their readers. See **39**.

14905. DORESKI, WILLIAM. The modern voice in American poetry. (Bibl. 1995, 13522.) Rev. by Gay Sibley in AL (68:3) 1996, 653–4.

14906. DORGAN, THEO (ed.). Irish poetry since Kavanagh. Blackrock, Co. Dublin; Portland, OR: Four Courts Press, 1996. pp. 162.

14907. DOWSON, JANE (ed.). Women's poetry of the 1930s: a critical anthology. London; New York: Routledge, 1995. pp. xix, 192. Rev. by Elizabeth Maslen in CritS (8:3) 1996, 338–9.

14908. DRAGLAND, STAN. Poetry and pedagogy in the Great White North. StudCanL (21:1) 1996, 56–66.

14909. EASTHOPE, ANTONY; THOMPSON, JOHN O. (eds). Contemporary poetry meets modern theory. (Bibl. 1994, 10746.) Rev. by Dennis Brown in CritS (8:2) 1996, 228–9.

14910. EDELBERG, CYNTHIA DUBIN (ed.). Scars: American poetry in the face of violence. Tuscaloosa; London: Alabama UP, 1995. pp. xii, 214.

14911. ELDER, JOHN. Imagining the earth: poetry and the vision of nature. (Bibl. 1988, 6413.) Athens: Georgia UP, 1996. pp. xii, 246. (Second ed.: first ed. 1985.)

14912. EMIG, RAINER. Modernism in poetry: motivations, structures and limits. See **11484**.

14913. ENGEL, BERNARD F. A splendid little imperialist war. See **10025**.

14914. EZENWA-OHAETO. Bridges of orality: Nigerian pidgin poetry. See **3021**.

14915. FALLON, PETER; MAHON, DEREK (eds). The Penguin book of contemporary Irish poetry. (Bibl. 1990, 9240.) Rev. by James Keery in PN Review (17:3) 1991, 57–9.

14916. FINCH, ANNIE. The ghost of meter: culture and prosody in American free verse. (Bibl. 1995, 13532.) Rev. by Franz Meier in Ang (114:2) 1996, 292–6.

14917. FINKELSTEIN, NORMAN. Language, poetry, and the problem of the avant-garde. Talisman (9) 1992, 31–6.

14918. —— Statement and commentary. See **10027**.

14919. FLEMING, DEBORAH (ed.). Learning the trade: essays on W. B. Yeats and contemporary poetry. See **58**.

14920. FORCHÉ, CAROLYN (ed.). Against forgetting: twentieth-century poetry of witness. New York: Norton, 1993. pp. 812. Rev. by Gail Wronsky in AR (52:3) 1994, 536–7; by Peter Balakian in Agni (40) 1994, 186–93.

14921. FOSTER, EDWARD HALSEY. Understanding the Black Mountain poets. (Bibl. 1995, 13536.) Rev. by John Taggart in PLL (32:2) 1996, 213–16.

14922. France, Linda (ed.).   Sixty women poets. Newcastle upon Tyne: Bloodaxe, 1993. pp. 288. Rev. by Catherine Beeston in CritS (6:3) 1994, 387–8.

14923. Freedman, Diane P.   An alchemy of genres: cross-genre writing by American feminist poet-critics. (Bibl. 1993, 10807.) Rev. by Corinne E. Blackmer in AmLH (8:1) 1996, 130–53.

14924. Fuchs, Anne.   Turn again, Whittington! Signs of re-turn to form in the work of South African praise poets. In (pp. 139–52) **102**.

14925. Funkhouser, Christopher.   Toward a literature moving outside itself: the beginnings of hypermedia poetry. See **1155**.

14926. Furomoto, Toshi.   Contemporary poetry of Northern Ireland: recovery of political interest and social concern. In (pp. 177–81) **60**.

14927. Gery, John.   Nuclear annihilation and contemporary American poetry: ways of nothingness. Gainesville: Florida UP, 1996. pp. xi, 235.

14928. Gifford, Terry.   Green voices: understanding contemporary nature poetry. (Bibl. 1995, 13543.) Rev. by Andy Jurgis in JCSJ (15) 1996, 93–4; by Neil Griffiths in Eng (45:182) 1996, 181–6.

14929. Gilbert, Roger.   The dream of a common poetry. See **10031**.

14930. Gilbey, David.   'The dance of metaphors': notes on some new Australian poems. CritS (6:1) 1994, 43–52. (Anthony Lawrence, Caroline Caddy, Steve Evans, Donna McSkimming, Archie Weller, Gerry Turcotte.)

14931. Gregson, Ian.   Contemporary poetry and postmodernism: dialogue and estrangement. Basingstoke: Macmillan; New York: St Martin's Press, 1996. pp. x, 269.

14932. Grennan, Eamon.   The American connection: an influence on modern and contemporary Irish poetry. In (pp. 28–47) **86**.

14933. Gross, Harvey; McDowell, Robert.   Sound and form in modern poetry. (Bibl. 1968, 2417.) Ann Arbor: Michigan UP, 1996. pp. x, 348. (Second ed.: first ed. 1964.)

14934. Gu, Ming Dong.   Classical Chinese poetry: a catalytic 'other' for Anglo-American modernist poetry. CanRCL (23:4) 1996, 993–1024.

14935. Gupta, Suman.   Reinscribing nation-people in anthologies of Indian English poetry. JCL (31:2) 1996, 101–15.

14936. Gwynn, R. S. (ed.).   The advocates of poetry: a reader of American poet-critics of the Modernist era. Fayetteville: Arkansas UP, 1996. pp. xxvii, 242.

14937. Habekost, Christian.   Verbal *riddim*: the politics and aesthetics of African-Caribbean dub poetry. Amsterdam; Atlanta, GA: Rodopi, 1993. pp. vii, 262. (Cross/cultures, 10.) Rev. by Gerald Porter in JAF (107:425) 1994, 458–9; by Bruce King in RAL (26:2) 1995, 221–3.

14938. Haberkamm, Helmut.   Die Bewegung weg vom *Movement*: Studien zur britischen Gegenwartsdichtung nach 1960. Heidelberg: Winter, 1992. pp. 311. (Forum Anglistik, 9.) Rev. by Michael Hanke in LWU (29:1) 1996, 63–4.

14939. Haberstroh, Patricia Boyle.   Women creating women: contemporary Irish women poets. Syracuse, NY: Syracuse UP; Dublin: Attic, 1996. pp. xii, 250. (Irish studies.) Rev. by Clair Wills in TLS, 1 Nov. 1996, 22.

14940. Hall, Donald.   Death to the death of poetry: essays, reviews, notes, interviews. (Bibl. 1994, 10773.) Rev. by Laurence Goldstein in MichQR (35:4) 1996, 748–51.

14941. HAMILL, SAM.   Writing *re*: writing. Onthebus (4:2/5:1) 1992, 304–22.

14942. HAMILTON, IAN (ed.).   The Oxford companion to twentieth-century poetry in English. (Bibl. 1995, 13559.) Rev. by Ronald P. Draper in Archiv (233:2) 1996, 398–401.

14943. HAMPSON, ROBERT; BARRY, PETER (eds).   New British poetries: the scope of the possible. (Bibl. 1995, 13560.) Rev. by Hans-Werner Ludwig in Archiv (233:2) 1996, 404–8.

14944. HARRINGTON, JOSEPH.   Why American poetry is not American literature. AmLH (8:3) 1996, 496–515.

14945. HARRIS, JON.   An elegy for myself: British poetry and the Holocaust. Eng (41:171) 1992, 213–33.

14946. HART, KEVIN.   Australian religious poetry. LitTheol (10:3) 1996, 261–72.

14947. HARTLEY, GEORGE.   Textual politics and the Language poets. (Bibl. 1991, 11200.) Rev. by Eric Metcalf in LitTheol (5:1) 1991, 130–1.

14948. HARTMAN, CHARLES O.   Free verse: an essay on prosody. Evanston, IL: Northwestern UP, 1996. pp. 199.

14949. HASKELL, DENNIS.   Iambic pentameters and the platypus duck: trends and traditions in contemporary Australian poetry. CritS (6:1) 1994, 28–42.

14950. HEAD, ANDREW (ed.).   The path of a poet. Peterborough: Poetry Now, 1996. pp. 250.

14951. HEANEY, SEAMUS.   Keeping time: Irish poetry and contemporary society. *In* (pp. 247–62) **49**.

14952. HEUVING, JEANNE.   Poetry in our political lives. ConLit (37:2) 1996, 315–32 (review-article).

14953. HOFMANN, MICHAEL; LASDUN, JAMES (eds).   After Ovid: new metamorphoses. (Bibl. 1994, 10781.) Rev. by Warren Dwyer in NDQ (63:1) 1996, 144–9.

14954. HOOVER, PAUL (ed.).   Postmodern American poetry: a Norton anthology. (Bibl. 1995, 13564.) Rev. by Matilde Martín in Atlantis (17:1/2) 1995, 391–2.

14955. HOWE, FLORENCE (ed.).   No more masks! An anthology of twentieth-century American women poets. (Bibl. 1994, 10785.) Rev. by Nels P. Highberg in NWSAJ (6:2) 1994, 234–54.

14956. HULSE, MICHAEL.   Politics, society and the new English poetry. AntR (93/94) 1993, 217–26.

14957. HYDE, GENE.   1994 poetry slams national championship. NCLR (2:2) 1995, 162–74.

14958. JACKSON, LAURA (RIDING).   What, if not a poem, poems? DQ (31:1) 1996, 26–36.

14959. JADWIN, LISA.   Critiquing the new canon. *See* **13140**.

14960. JARMAN, MARK; MCDOWELL, ROBERT.   The *Reaper* essays. Introd. by Meg Schoerke. Brownsville, OR: Story Line Press, 1996. pp. xiv, 196.

14961. JEFFREYS, MARK.   Ideologies of lyric: a problem of genre in contemporary Anglophone poetics. PMLA (110:2) 1995, 196–205.

14962. JOHNSEN, WILLIAM A.   The treacherous years of postmodern poetry in English. *In* (pp. 75–91) **34**.

14963. JOHNSTONE, IAN M.   A visit to the Western Front: a pilgrimage tour of World War I cemeteries and memorials in northern France and Belgium August–September 1993. *See* **3351**.

14964. KALAIDJIAN, WALTER.   Marketing modern poetry and the Southern public sphere. *In* (pp. 297–319) **67**.

14965. KALAMARAS, GEORGE.   Mysticism as a social act? The possibility of the sacred in poststructuralist poetics. Talisman (16) 1996, 241–3.

14966. KAMBOURELI, SMARO.   On the edge of genre: the contemporary Canadian long poem. (Bibl. 1995, 13574.) Rev. by Heather Murray in ECanW (55) 1995, 91–7.

14967. KEEN, PAUL.   'Making strange': conversations with the Irish m/other. IUR (26:1) 1996, 75–87.

14968. KEENAN, DEBORAH; LLOYD, ROSEANN (eds).   Looking for home: women writing about exile. Minneapolis, MN: Milkweed, 1990. pp. 288. Rev. by Ann Filemyr in AR (49:1) 1991, 144–5.

14969. KELLOGG, DAVID.   'Desire pronounced and/Punctuated': Lacan and the fate of the poetic subject. AI (52:4) 1995, 405–37.

14970. KELLY, LIONEL; RIGHELATO, PAT.   American literature: the twentieth century: poetry. YWES (75) 1994, 587–631.

14971. KENNEALLY, MICHAEL (ed.).   Poetry in contemporary Irish literature. *See* **86**.

14972. KENNEDY, DAVID.   New relations: the refashioning of British poetry, 1980–1994. Bridgend, Mid-Glamorgan: Seren, 1996. pp. 293.

14973. KERN, ROBERT.   Orientalism, Modernism, and the American poem. Cambridge; New York: CUP, 1996. pp. xiii, 316. (Cambridge studies in American literature and culture, 97.)

14974. KIRBY-SMITH, H. T.   The origins of free verse. Ann Arbor: Michigan UP, 1996. pp. xiv, 304.

14975. KRAHÉ, PETER.   Stationen der englischen Dichtung des Zweiten Weltkriegs. GRM (42:2) 1992, 209–23.

14976. KROHN, FRANKLIN B.; SUAZO, FRANCES L.   Contemporary urban music: controversial messages in hip-hop and rap lyrics. *See* **2662**.

14977. LAMMON, MARTIN (ed.).   Written in water, written in stone: twenty years of *Poets on Poetry*. Foreword by David Lehman. Ann Arbor: Michigan UP, 1996. pp. xiii, 288. (Poets on poetry.)

14978. LANDAU, DEBORAH.   'How to live. What to do.' The poetics and politics of AIDS. AL (68:1) 1996, 193–225.

14979. LARRISSY, EDWARD.   Reading twentieth-century poetry: the language of gender and objects. (Bibl. 1993, 10841.) Rev. by Andrew Roberts in Eng (40:167) 1991, 174–80.

14980. LAVENDER, WILLIAM.   Disappearance of theory, appearance of praxis: Ron Silliman, L=A=N=G=U=A=G=E, and the essay. PT (17:2) 1996, 181–202. (Language poets.)

14981. LEDBETTER, KATHRYN.   Battles for Modernism and *Wheels*. *See* **1304**.

14982. LEVENSON, CHRISTOPHER (ed.).   Reconcilable differences: the changing face of poetry by Canadian men since 1970. Calgary, Alta: Bayeux Arts, 1994. pp. xx, 171. Rev. by Neil Besner in JCP (11) 1996, 170–6.

14983. LIND, L. R.   The great American epic. CML (17:1) 1996, 7–29.

14984. LONGLEY, EDNA.   'It is time that I wrote my will': anxieties of influence and succession. Yeats Annual (12) 1996, 117–62.

14985. Löschnigg, Martin. '... *a soldier's heart, / Is greater than a poet's art*': zur Problematik des Rollenverständnisses englischer und deutscher Kriegsdichter 1914–1918. GRM (45:1) 1995, 70–87.

14986. Lucas, John. The 1920s: radicals to the Right and to the Left. In-between (4:1) 1995, 3–23.

14987. —— Poetry and politics in the 1920s. EAS (49) 1996, 84–110.

14988. Lucas, Rose; McCredden, Lyn. Bridgings: readings in Australian women's poetry. Melbourne; Oxford; New York: OUP, 1996. pp. xix, 218.

14989. McAllister, Andrew (ed.). The Objectivists. Newcastle upon Tyne: Bloodaxe, 1996. pp. 159.

14990. McCarthy, Dermot. Witness poetry. LRC (5:8) 1996, 5–8 (review-article). (Canadian poetry of the Spanish Civil War.)

14991. Mahony, Christina Hunt. Poetry in modern Ireland: where postcolonial and postmodern part ways. Comparatist (20) 1996, 82–92.

14992. Maja-Pearce, Adewale (ed.). The Heinemann book of African poetry in English. (Bibl. 1991, 11224.) Rev. by Michael Hulse in PN Review (17:4) 1991, 80.

14993. Mark, Jan; Mole, John. The Signal Poetry Award. *See* **14810**.

14994. Marsland, Elizabeth A. The nation's cause: French, English and German poetry of the First World War. (Bibl. 1991, 11226.) Rev. by Martin Löschnigg in GRM (43:2) 1993, 249–52.

14995. Materer, Timothy. Poetry: 1900 to the 1940s. American Literary Scholarship (1993) 281–98; (1994) 325–43; (1995) 361–82.

14996. Meaney, Gerardine. History gasps: myth in contemporary Irish women's poetry. *In* (pp. 99–113) **86**.

14997. Meihuizen, Nicholas. New poetry: 1993–1994. English Academy Review (11) 1996, 83–95.

14998. Mishra, Sudesh. Preparing faces: modernism and Indian poetry in English. Suva, Fiji: Univ. of the South Pacific; Adelaide: CRNLE, Flinders Univ., 1995. pp. 401.

14999. Moe, Lawrence. First crops: pioneers of poetry in the Red River Valley of the North. Midamerica (22) 1995, 97–107.

15000. Monroe, Jonathan. Poetry, the university, and the culture of distraction. Diacritics (26:3/4) 1996, 3–30.

15001. Moore, Richard O. Berkeley/San Francisco poetry communities in the early 1940s. Talisman (10) 1993, 108–14.

15002. Morrisson, Mark. Performing the pure voice: elocution, verse recitation, and Modernist poetry in prewar London. *See* **1565**.

15003. Mottram, Eric. American poetry and the British poetry revival 1960–75. *In* (pp. 152–68) **34**.

15004. Murdoch, Brian. Fighting songs and warring words: popular lyrics of two world wars. (Bibl. 1992, 11733.) Rev. by Martin Löschnigg in GRM (41:2) 1991, 252–4.

15005. Nash, Susan Smith. Death, decadence, and the ironies of language poetics. Talisman (10) 1993, 201–5.

15006. Nelson, Cary. The fate of gender in modern American poetry. *In* (pp. 321–60) **67**.

15007. Niemeyer, Marc. The transatlantic cable in popular poetry. *In* (pp. 227–36) **117**.

15008. Norris, Ken. A new world: essays on poetry and poetics. Montreal: Empyreal Press, 1994. pp. 63. (Limited ed. of 500 copies.)

Rev. by Brenda Carr in CanL (150) 1996, 124–5; by Don Precosky in ECanW (58) 1996, 198–201.

15009. NOTO, JOHN. Response to the post-moderns (and the post-punkers!): a new synthesis offers April rain descending musical staffs in split-screen language televised as hands to bleed endlessly divisible orchids. Talisman (11) 1993, 183–91.

15010. O'DRISCOLL, DENNIS. Foreign relations: Irish and international poetry. *In* (pp. 48–60) **86**.

15011. OJAIDE, TANURE. Orality in recent West African poetry. *See* **2553**.

15012. O'ROURKE, DANIEL (ed.). Dream state: the new Scottish poets. Edinburgh: Polygon, 1994. pp. xliv, 231. Rev. by Charlie Orr in SLJ (supp. 42) 1995, 47–50.

15013. PAYNE, KENNETH. Cities of paradise, comrade kingdoms, and worlds of light: some versions of the Socialist utopia in the *Comrade* (1901–1905). *See* **1338**.

15014. PERELMAN, BOB. The marginalization of poetry: language writing and literary history. Princeton, NJ; Chichester: Princeton UP, 1996. pp. viii, 187.

15015. PERLOFF, MARJORIE. The dance of the intellect: studies in the poetry of the Pound tradition. Evanston, IL: Northwestern UP, 1996. pp. xii, 243. (Avant-garde and Modernism studies.)

15016. —— Radical artifice: writing poetry in the age of media. (Bibl. 1995, 13620.) Rev. by John Shoptaw in Review (16) 1994, 197–208.

15017. —— Whose new American poetry? Anthologizing in the nineties. Diacritics (26:3/4) 1996, 104–23.

15018. PETTINGELL, PHOEBE. Twentieth century blues. NewL (79:9) 1996, 30–2 (review-article).

15019. PHILLIPS, PATRICK. 'Safe house': poetic agency and 'the apex of the M'. Talisman (14) 1995, 135–50.

15020. PIETTE, ADAM. Imagination at war: British fiction and poetry, 1939–1945. *See* **14669**.

15021. PORDZIK, RALPH. Postmoderne Lyrik als Negativutopie. Untersuchungen zur Karnevalisierung der Dichtung am Beispiel des *Martian Poet* James Fenton. AAA (21:1) 1996, 33–61.

15022. POSTER, JEM. The thirties poets. (Bibl. 1993, 10875.) Rev. by Adrian Caesar in AUMLA (85) 1996, 171–2.

15023. POTTER, VILMA. Idella Purnell's *PALMS* and godfather Witter Bynner. *See* **1342**.

15024. POWELL, ANNE (ed.). The fierce light: the Battle of the Somme, July–November 1916: prose and poetry. Aberporth: Palladour, 1996. pp. xxiv, 294. Rev. by Richard Holmes in TLS, 11 Oct. 1996, 5.

15025. POYNTING, JEREMY. Prospero into Caliban: converging voices in Caribbean poetry. ERev (6:1) 1995, 12–15.

15026. PRATT, WILLIAM. Singing the chaos: madness and wisdom in modern poetry. Columbia; London: Missouri UP, 1996. pp. viii, 336. Rev. by Johanna Keller in AR (54:4) 1996, 495–6; by John L. Brown in WLT (70:4) 1996, 1039–40.

15027. PRITCHARD, WILLIAM H. Lives of the modern poets. With a new preface by the author. (Bibl. 1981, 10026.) Hanover, NH: UP of New England, 1996. pp. xvi, 316. (Revised ed.: first ed. 1980.)

15028. QUARTERMAIN, PETER. Disjunctive poetics: from Gertrude

Stein and Louis Zukofsky to Susan Howe. (Bibl. 1995, 13623.) Rev. by Elizabeth Maslen in CritS (6:3) 1994, 399–400.

15029. RAMAZANI, JAHAN.   Poetry of mourning: the modern elegy from Hardy to Heaney. (Bibl. 1995, 13624.) Rev. by Simon Curtis in CompCrit (17) 1995, 289–95.

15030. RAO, R. RAJ.   The poetry of Bombay City. JCL (31:1) 1996, 63–70.

15031. RASULA, JED.   The American poetry wax museum: reality effects, 1940–1990. Urbana, IL: National Council of Teachers of English, 1996. pp. xi, 637. (Refiguring English studies.)

15032. RICHARDS, BERNARD.   'Squeezing in a quick Hughes or a Heaney'. ERev (6:2) 1995, 13–16.

15033. RIGGS, THOMAS (ed.)   Contemporary poets. Preface by Anthony Thwaite. (Bibl. 1994, 10725.) Detroit, MI: St James Press, 1996. pp. xxiii, 1336. (Sixth ed.: first ed. 1970.)

15034. ROSENBERG, LIZ (ed.).   The invisible ladder: an anthology of contemporary American poems for young readers. New York: Holt, 1996. pp. ix, 210.

15035. ROSENTHAL, M. L.   Our life in poetry: selected essays and reviews. (Bibl. 1991, 11255.) Rev. by Harry Marten in GetR (6:2) 1993, 253–61.

15036. SCHENKEL, ELMAR.   *Sense of place*: Regionalität und Raumbewusstsein in der neueren britischen Lyrik. (Bibl. 1995, 13635.) Rev. by Götz Schmitz in Archiv (233:2) 1996, 401–4.

15037. SCHWARTZ, LEONARD.   A flicker at the edge of things: some thoughts on lyric poetry. Talisman (9) 1992, 19–30.

15038. SCHWEIK, SUSAN.   A gulf so deeply cut: American women poets and the Second World War. (Bibl. 1993, 10886.) Rev. by Corinne E. Blackmer in AmLH (8:1) 1996, 130–53.

15039. SCOTT, NATHAN A., JR.   Visions of presence in modern American poetry. (Bibl. 1995, 13636.) Rev. by David Perkins in AAR (30:2) 1996, 313–15.

15040. SHERBO, ARTHUR.   From *Shenandoah*: overlooked reviews of and poems by Eliot, Faulkner, Stevens, Hemingway, Graves, Spender, and others. *See* **1362**.

15041. SHETLEY, VERNON.   After the death of poetry: poetry and audience in contemporary America. (Bibl. 1995, 13640.) Rev. by David Baker in Kenyon Review (18:2) 1996, 170–5.

15042. SILLARS, STUART; SANSOM, IAN.   The twentieth century: poetry. YWES (75) 1994, 529–42.

15043. SMITH, LORRIE.   Against a coming extinction: W. D. Ehrhart and the evolving canon of Vietnam veterans' poetry. WLA (8:2) 1996, 1–30.

15044. SMITH, RICHARD CÁNDIDA.   Utopia and dissent: art, poetry, and politics in California. Berkeley; London: California UP, 1995. pp. xxvi, 536, (plates) 8. Rev. by Michael Orth in Utopian Studies (7:2) 1996, 338–40; by Abraham A. Davidson in AHR (101:3) 1996, 941; by Anthony W. Lee in AmQ (48:4) 1996, 708–15.

15045. SMITH, STAN.   Between hype and hyperreality: the 'New Generation' poets. In-between (4:2) 1995, 127–49.

15046. —— The language of displacement in contemporary Irish poetry. *In* (pp. 61–83) **86**.

15047. —— The things that words give a name to: the 'New Generation' poets and the politics of the hyperreal. CritS (8:3) 1996, 306–22.

15048. Smith, Steven E. An index to Poetry Book Society choices, recommendations, special commendations, and translations. BB (53:3) 1996, 219–26.

15049. Smyth, Ailbhe. Declining identities (lit. and fig.). CritS (8:2) 1996, 143–58.

15050. Sole, Kelwyn. Bird hearts taking wing: trends in contemporary South African poetry written in English. WLT (70:1) 1996, 25–31.

15051. Speirs, Logan. Current literature 1993: 1, New writing: drama and poetry. See **14235**.

15052. —— Current literature 1994: 1, New writing: poetry. EngS (77:5) 1996, 454–83.

15053. —— The new poetry. See **1083**.

15054. Steele, Timothy. Missing measures: modern poetry and the revolt against meter. (Bibl. 1993, 10895.) Rev. by Chris McCully in PN Review (17:3) 1991, 42–5.

15055. Stein, Kevin. Private poets, worldly acts: public and private history in contemporary American poetry. Athens: Ohio UP, 1996. pp. xv, 190.

15056. Stephen, Martin. The price of pity: poetry, history, and myth in the Great War. London: Cooper, 1996. pp. xv, 256.

15057. Stephens, Meic (ed.). The bright field: an anthology of contemporary poetry from Wales. (Bibl. 1991, 11268.) Rev. by Neil Powell in PN Review (18:1) 1991, 57.

15058. Stevens, Peter. Setting poetic sail for the nineties: out of the doldrums of the eighties into the open sea of the nineties. AntR (84) 1991, 21–33.

15059. Talarico, Ross. Spreading the word: poetry and the survival of community in America. (Bibl. 1995, 13655.) Rev. by John Muckle in JAStud (30:1) 1996, 180–2.

15060. Tamura, Einosuke. Genjitsu no shigaku – roman-ha to gendaishi. (Poetics of illusion and reality: Romantic and modern poetry.) See **10059**.

15061. Taylor, Andrew. A case of Romantic disinheritance. In (pp. 185–201) **47**.

15062. Thomas, Lorenzo. 'Communicating by horns': jazz and redemption in the poetry of the Beats and the Black Arts Movement. AAR (26:2) 1992, 291–8.

15063. —— Poetry: the 1940s to the present. American Literary Scholarship (1993) 299–311; (1994) 345–62; (1995) 383–400.

15064. Thompson, Clara Ann; Smith, J. Pauline; Clark, Mazie Earhart. Voices in the poetic tradition. Introd. by Mary Anne Stewart Boelcskevy. New York: G. K. Hall; London: Prentice Hall, 1996. pp. xxxvii, 246. (African-American women writers, 1910–1940.)

15065. Thwaite, Anthony. Poetry today: a critical guide to British poetry, 1960–1992. London; New York: Longman in assn with British Council, 1996. pp. xiv, 181.

15066. Tromp, Ian; De Kock, Leon. The making of *The Heart in Exile*. New Contrast (24:3) 1996, 81–94. (Anthology of South African poetry.)

15067. Tuma, Keith.   Is there a British Modernism? *In* (pp. 232–52) **34**.

15068. Vendler, Helen.   The given and the made: strategies of poetic redefinition. (Bibl. 1995, 13660.) London: Faber & Faber, 1995. Rev. by William Logan in BkW, 25 Feb. 1996, 4; by Mary Kaiser in WLT (70:3) 1996, 699–700; by James Wood in LRB (18:6) 1996, 22–3; by William T. Cotton in NOR (22:1) 1996, 114–25.

15069. —— Soul says: on recent poetry. (Bibl. 1995, 13662.) Rev. by James Wood in LRB (18:6) 1996, 22–3; by John Boening in WLT (70:3) 1996, 700–1.

15070. Vulpe, Nicola; Albari, Maha (eds).   Sealed in struggle: Canadian poetry & the Spanish Civil War: an anthology. La Laguna, Tenerife: Center for Canadian Studies, Univ. de La Laguna, 1995. pp. 269. (Canadística Canaria: Poetry, 1.) Rev. by Dermot McCarthy in LRC (5:8) 1996, 5–8.

15071. Waldrop, Rosmarie.   Form and discontent. Diacritics (26:3/4) 1996, 54–62.

15072. Walker, Cheryl.   Masks outrageous and austere: culture, psyche, and persona in modern women poets. (Bibl. 1993, 10903.) Rev. by Elaine Hedges in Signs (19:2) 1994, 507–11.

15073. Wallenstein, Barry.   JazzPoetry/jazz-poetry/ 'jazz poetry'??? AAR (27:4) 1993, 665–71 (review-article).

15074. —— Poetry and jazz: a twentieth-century wedding. BALF (25:3) 1991, 595–620.

15075. Walsh, William F.   '... to see/what was really going on'. Talisman (14) 1995, 60–9; reply by Marjorie Perloff and rejoinder (15) 1995/96, 178–80.

15076. Waniek, Marilyn Nelson.   Owning the masters. GetR (8:2) 1995, 201–9.

15077. Wilbur, Richard.   On formalism, translation, and beloved books of childhood. *See* **3218**.

15078. Wills, Clair.   Improprieties: politics and sexuality in Northern Irish poetry. (Bibl. 1995, 13673.) Rev. by Peter McDonald in Irish Review (16) 1994, 131–3; by Anthony Bradley in ConLit (37:3) 1996, 489–90.

15079. Wilson, Robert A.   Marching to a different drummer: collecting 'Beat' poets. *See* **555**.

15080. Winter, Helmut.   Alfred Stieglitz und das ästhetische Programm der amerikanischen Avantgarde: zum Verhältnis von Photographie und Literatur zwischen 1900 und 1935. GRM (46:1) 1996, 57–70.

15081. Woeber, Catharine.   'Text' and voice in recent South African poetry. Literator (17:2) 1996, 131–43.

15082. Woo, Sang-Gyun.   Hyundae youngmi sisaeui munmaek esseo bon Sylvia Plath eui bangbeob. (Sylvia Plath's method as considered in the context of the history of modern English and American poetry.) JELL (42:1) 1996, 43–64.

15083. Yorke, Liz.   Impertinent voices: subversive strategies in contemporary women's poetry. (Bibl. 1993, 10911.) Rev. by Elizabeth Maslen in CritS (6:3) 1994, 399–400.

15084. Zinsser, William.   From Natchez to Mobile, from Memphis to St Joe. ASch (63:2) 1994, 259–66.

Prose

15085. ABBEY, EDWARD. 'Mr Krutch'. *In* (pp. 105–18) **25**.

15086. APPLEGATE, EDD. Literary journalism: a biographical dictionary of writers and editors. *See* **1222**.

15087. BELL, ELIZABETH S. Dashing off to Baghdad: a sense of place in a piece of time. SAtlR (61:4) 1996, 39–52.

15088. BLAKE, DALE. Women of Labrador: realigning North from the site(s) of *métissage*. *See* **10069**.

15089. BONTA, MARCIA MYERS (ed.). American women afield: writings by pioneering women naturalists. *See* **10071**.

15090. CHRISTOPHER, ROBERT. Narrators of the Arctic: images and movements in Northland narratives. *See* **10076**.

15091. COOLEY, JOHN (ed.). Earthly words: essays on contemporary American nature and environmental writers. *See* **25**.

15092. DuPLESSIS, RACHEL BLAU. *F*-words: an essay on the essay. AL (68:1) 1996, 15–45.

15093. FOSTER, KEVIN D. Signifying the wasteland: selling the 'Falklands War'. WLA (3:1) 1991, 35–55.

15094. FRASER, ROBERT. The loneliness of the long-distance cyclist: cyclic form in Frazer and Proust. YES (26) 1996, 163–72.

15095. FREESE, PETER. 'Westward the Course of Empire takes its Way': the *translatio*-concept in popular American writing and painting. *See* **8676**.

15096. GREEN, BARBARA. Advertising feminism: ornamental bodies/docile bodies and the discourse of suffrage. *In* (pp. 191–220) **67**.

15097. HALBERSTAM, DAVID. History is their beat. BkW, 4 July 1993, 1, 8–9.

15098. HARTLEY, JENNY (ed.). Hearts undefeated: women's writing of the Second World War. (Bibl. 1995, 13687.) Rev. by Monika Hoffmann in Amst (41:2) 1996, 303–7; by Patricia Beer in LRB (18:6) 1996, 14–15.

15099. HENRÍQUEZ JIMÉNEZ, SANTIAGO. Going the distance: an analysis of modern travel writing and criticism. Barcelona: Kadle, 1995. pp. 62. Rev. by María Isabel González Cruz in Atlantis (17:1/2) 1995, 390–1.

15100. HITCHCOCK, JAMES. Murder as one of the liberal arts. ASch (63:2) 1994, 277–85.

15101. HULAN, RENÉE. Literary field notes: the influence of ethnography on representations of the North. *See* **10093**.

15102. JARNIEWICZ, JERZY. Na obrzeżach wyspy, na skraju historii: o najnowszej prozie kobiet w Wielkiej Brytanii. (On the coastline of an island, on the edge of history: on the most recent women's prose in Great Britain.) Literatura na Świecie (4) 1996, 301–13.

15103. KAMBOURELI, SMARO. Staging cultural criticism: Michael Ignatieff's *Blood and Belonging* and Myrna Kostash's *Bloodlines*. JCanStud (31:3) 1996, 166–86.

15104. KIDDER, TRACY. Facts and the nonfiction writer. *See* **2766**.

15105. KLAUS, CARL H. Embodying the self: malady and the personal essay. IowaR (25:2) 1995, 177–92.

15106. KOCHERSBERGER, ROBERT C., JR (ed.). More than a muckraker: Ida Tarbell's lifetime in journalism. Knoxville: Tennessee UP, 1994. pp. l, 242. Rev. by Beverly G. Merrick in JMCQ (73:4) 1996, 1007–8.

15107. LANE, CHRISTOPHER.   *Thoughts for the Times on War and Death*: militarism and its discontents. *See* **11676**.

15108. LAWLESS, ELAINE J.   Writing the body in the pulpit: female-sexed texts. JAF (107:423) 1994, 55–81.

15109. LEE, VALERIE.   Granny midwives and Black women writers: double-Dutched readings. London; New York: Routledge, 1996. pp. xii, 202.

15110. LEEMAN, RICHARD W. (ed.).   African-American orators: a bio-critical sourcebook. *See* **2419**.

15111. MARSHALL, IAN.   Cliff notes, foot notes, and the literary canyon: Colin Fletcher's *The Man Who Walked through Time*. Journal of the Southwest (36:2) 1994, 176–84.

15112. MAYNARD, STEVEN.   In search of 'Sodom North': the writing of lesbian and gay history in English Canada, 1970–1990. CanRCL (21:1/2) 1994, 117–32.

15113. MICHEL, ROBERT.   Diaries from the McGill University Archives – a sampling. *See* **10099**.

15114. NEMETH, DAVID J.   Irving Brown: the American Borrow? *See* **10366**.

15115. NEWQUIST, DAVID.   The violation of hospitality and the demoralization of the frontier. MidM (21) 1993, 19–28.

15116. NORRIS, KATHLEEN.   The new ICEL Psalter. CC (46:1) 1996, 97–104.

15117. POWELL, ANNE (ed.).   The fierce light: the Battle of the Somme, July–November 1916: prose and poetry. *See* **15024**.

15118. POWERS, LUKE.   'Old witch Nance and old man Beaver': gender war in Emma Bell Miles' *The Spirit of the Mountains*. TPB (32) 1995, 19–29.

15119. RANGLON, REBECCA.   Women and the great Canadian wilderness: reconsidering the wild. WS (25:5) 1996, 513–31.

15120. RILEY, SAM G. (ed.).   American magazine journalists, 1900–1960: first series. *See* **1349**.

15121. ROSENBERG, BRUCE.   The African-American sermon and literary tradition. *See* **10107**.

15122. ROY, PARAMA.   Discovering India, imagining *thuggee*. *See* **10108**.

15123. SMITH, SUSAN L.   Whitewashing womanhood: the politics of race in writing women's history. CanRCL (22:1) 1995, 93–103.

15124. SMYTHE, COLIN.   The Gregorys and Egypt, 1855–56 and 1881–82. *In* (pp. 147–53) **60**.

15125. TALLMADGE, JOHN.   Anatomy of a classic. *In* (pp. 119–34) **25**.

15126. WHEATCROFT, GEOFFREY.   Messages from a gentle Protestant. TLS, 28 June 1996, 14–15. (Hubert Butler.)

Biography and Autobiography

15127. ADAMS, TIMOTHY DOW.   Telling lies in modern American autobiography. (Bibl. 1992, 11835.) Rev. by Georg M. Gugelberger in CanRCL (19:3) 1992, 420–3; by Sidonie Smith and Camilla Stivers in Signs (18:2) 1993, 392–425; by Nancy A. Walker in AmS (34:2) 1993, 152–3.

15128. ALLISON, DOROTHY.   Skin: talking about sex, class, & literature. *See* **12923**.

15129. ALPERN, SARA, *et al.* (eds). The challenge of feminist biography: writing the lives of modern American women. Champaign: Illinois UP, 1992. pp. 210. (Women in American history.) Rev. by Winifred D. Wandersee in AHR (99:2) 1994, 676–7; by Carolyn G. Heilbrun in NWSAJ (6:1) 1994, 119–23.

15130. ANDREWS, WILLIAM L. The representation of slavery and the rise of Afro-American literary realism 1865–1920. *In* (pp. 77–89) **1**.

15131. ATLAS, JAMES. Confessing for voyeurs: the age of the literary memoir is now. NYTM, 12 May 1996, 25–7.

15132. BABENER, LIAHNA. The romance of suffering: Midwesterners remember the homestead. *See* **10124**.

15133. BELL, PETER (comp.). Victorian biography: a checklist of contemporary biographies of British men and women dying between 1851 and 1901. Introd. by Colin Matthew. *See* **10126**.

15134. BERRY, J. BILL (ed.). Home ground: Southern autobiography. *See* **43**.

15135. BLOOM, LYNN Z. Coming of age in the segregated South: autobiographies of twentieth-century childhoods, Black and White. *In* (pp. 110–22) **43**.

15136. BONTA, MARCIA MYERS (ed.). American women afield: writings by pioneering women naturalists. *See* **10071**.

15137. BRANTLEY, WILL. Feminine sense in Southern memoir: Smith, Glasgow, Welty, Hellman, Porter and Hurston. (Bibl. 1994, 10898.) Rev. by Anne Rowe in FHQ (73:2) 1994, 256–9; by Dorothy M. Scura in EGN (32) 1994, 8–9.

15138. BUSH, RONALD. James Joyce : the way he lives now. JJQ (33:4) 1996, 523–9.

15139. BUSS, HELEN M. Listening to the 'ground noise' of Canadian women settlers' memoirs: a maternal intercourse of discourses. ECanW (60) 1996, 199–214.

15140. CAROLAN-BROZY, SANDRA. 'No conventional verbal portrait': hypertextuality and synchronicity in *Red on White: the Biography of Duke Redbird*. *In* (pp. 151–75) **8**.

15141. DAVIS, ROBERT MURRAY. 'Perfection of the life or of the work': lives of Graham Greene. WLT (70:2) 1996, 329–33 (review-article).

15142. DEEDY, JOHN. The mysteries of literary lives: John Deedy interviews biographer James Mellow. Critic (48:1) 1993, 28–37.

15143. DILLARD, ANNIE; CONLEY, CORT (eds). Modern American memoirs. (Bibl. 1995, 13724.) Rev. by Madeline Marget in Cweal (123:7) 1996, 32–3.

15144. DORSEY, PETER A. Sacred estrangement: the rhetoric of conversion in modern American autobiography. (Bibl. 1995, 13726.) Rev. by Albert E. Stone in AmS (35:2) 1994, 145–6.

15145. ELIE, PAUL (ed.). A tremor of bliss: contemporary writers on the saints. New York: Harcourt Brace, 1994. pp. xxv, 325. Rev. by Anna Harrison in Cweal (122:5) 1995, 24–5.

15146. FIXMER, AUDREY METTEL. Biographies, she wrote. WD (74:3) 1994, 34–7. (Interview with Margot Peters.)

15147. FOSTER, R. F. Love, politics, and textual corruption: Mrs O'Shea's *Parnell*. *In* (pp. 197–211) **41**.

15148. FREIWALD, BINA TOLEDO. The interpellated subject lies back: Angeline Hango's *Truthfully Yours*. ECanW (58) 1996, 36–59.

15149. FRIEDMAN, AMY L.   'I say my new name': women writers of the Beat Generation. *In* (pp. 200–16) **4**.

15150. GAGNIER, REGENIA.   Feminist autobiography in the 1980s. Feminist Studies (17:1) 1991, 135–48 (review-article).

15151. GAMMEL, IRENE.   The death of the fairytale prince: feminism, postmodernism and the sexual confession. CanRCL (21:3) 1994, 281–94.

15152. GREEN, BARBARA.   Advertising feminism: ornamental bodies/docile bodies and the discourse of suffrage. *In* (pp. 191–220) **67**.

15153. HAFFENDEN, JOHN.   What the life leaves out: the biographer's tendency to put personality before poetry. TLS, 23 Feb. 1996, 14–16.

15154. HECHT, DEBORAH.   The poisoned well: Percy Lubbock and Edith Wharton. ASch (62:2) 1993, 255–9.

15155. HORNUNG, ALFRED; RUHE, ERNSTPETER (eds).   Autobiographie & Avant-garde: Alain Robbe-Grillet, Serge Doubrovsky, Rachid Boujedra, Maxine Hong Kingston, Raymond Federman, Ronald Sukenick. (Bibl. 1993, 10934.) Rev. by Thomas Irmer in ZAA (43:1) 1995, 97–9.

15156. HOROWITZ, SARA R.   Memory and testimony of women survivors of Nazi genocide. *In* (pp. 258–82) **130**.

15157. HOUGHTON, R. L.   Some remarks on MacKillop's life of F. R. Leavis. EngS (77:5) 1996, 445–53 (review-article).

15158. HOY, HELEN.   'And use the words that were hers': constructions of subjectivity in Beverly Hungry Wolf's *The Ways of My Grandmothers*. ECanW (60) 1996, 32–58.

15159. HUGHES, EAMONN.   'You need not fear that I am not amiable': reading Yeats (reading) *Autobiographies*. Yeats Annual (12) 1996, 84–116.

15160. IRMSCHER, CHRISTOPH.   Role-playing in Native-American autobiography: Charles Eastman's *From the Deep Woods to Civilization*. *In* (pp. 99–123) **8**.

15161. KADAR, MARLENE.   The discourse of ordinariness and 'multicultural history'. ECanW (60) 1996, 119–38.

15162. KIMBREL, WILLIAM W., JR.   Carlos Baker and the 'true gen'. HemR (16:1) 1996, 83–96.

15163. KORNBLUH, ANDREA TUTTLE.   'A record of their achievement': the construction of *Women of Ohio* in the 1930s. QCH (54:1) 1996, 3–12.

15164. LEE, HERMIONE.   Biomythographers: rewriting the lives of Virginia Woolf. EC (46:2) 1996, 95–114. (F. W. Bateson Memorial Lecture.)

15165. LOEB, JEFF.   Childhood's end: self-recovery in the autobiography of the Vietnam War. AmS (37:1) 1996, 95–116.

15166. LONGLEY, EDNA.   'It is time that I wrote my will': anxieties of influence and succession. *See* **14984**.

15167. MCCOOEY, DAVID.   Artful histories: modern Australian autobiography. Cambridge; New York: CUP, 1996. pp. viii, 237.

15168. MARDER, HERBERT.   The biographer and the angel. ASch (62:2) 1993, 221–31.

15169. NALBANTIAN, SUZANNE.   Aesthetic autobiography: from life to art in Marcel Proust, James Joyce, Virginia Woolf, and Anaïs Nin. (Bibl. 1995, 13742.) Rev. by John L. Brown in WLT (69:3) 1995, 658; by Morton P. Levitt in JJQ (33:4) 1996, 634–8.

15170. NEUMAN, SHIRLEY.   Introduction: reading Canadian autobiography. *See* **10145**.

15171. Paquet, Sandra Pouchet.   West Indian autobiography. *In* (pp. 196–211) **1**.

15172. Rimstead, Roxanne.   Mediated lives: oral histories and cultural memory. ECanW (60) 1996, 139–65.

15173. Riney-Kehrberg, Pamela.   'Broke in spirits': death, depression, and endurance through writing. Frontiers (17:2) 1996, 70–86.

15174. Rovit, Earl.   The lives and time of Ernest Hemingway. Review (16) 1994, 153–68 (review-article).

15175. Schiff, Stacy.   Biographer, get a life. BkW, 13 Aug. 1995, 1, 10.

15176. Sirridge, Marjorie S.; Pfannenstiel, Brenda R.   Daughters of Æsculapius: a selected bibliography of autobiographies of women medical school graduates 1849–1920. *See* **10150**.

15177. Smith, Sidonie.   Re-citing, re-siting, and re-sighting likeness: reading the family archive in Drucilla Modjeska's *Poppy*, Donna Williams' *Nobody Nowhere*, and Sally Morgan's *My Place*. MFS (40:3) 1994, 509–42.

15178. —— Subjectivity, identity, and the body: women's autobiographical practices in the twentieth century. (Bibl. 1995, 13751.) Rev. by Ergá Heller in PT (15:3) 1994, 501–2.

15179. Stone, Albert E.   After *Black Boy* and *Dusk of Dawn*: patterns in recent Black autobiography. *In* (pp. 171–95) **1**.

15180. Tattoni, Igina.   Il registratore: *autobiography: a self-recorded fiction*. *In* (pp. 284–8) **117**.

15181. Wagner-Martin, Linda.   Telling women's lives: the new biography. (Bibl. 1995, 13755.) Rev. by Françoise Lionnet in Signs (21:2) 1996, 459–63.

15182. Wain, John.   To criticize the critic. ASch (62:4) 1993, 606–11 (review-article).

15183. Wald, Gayle.   'A most disagreeable mirror': reflections on White identity in *Black like Me*. *In* (pp. 151–77) **82**.

15184. Wallace, Kathleen R.   'Roots, aren't they supposed to be buried?' The experience of place in Midwestern women's autobiographies. *In* (pp. 168–87) **66**.

Related Studies

15185. Adams, Kate.   Northamerican silences: history, identity, and witness in the poetry of Gloria Anzaldúa, Cherríe Moraga, and Leslie Marmon Silko. *In* (pp. 130–45) **59**.

15186. Alarcón, Norma.   Cognitive desires: an allegory of/for Chicana critics. *In* (pp. 260–73) **59**.

15187. Arteaga, Alfred .   An other tongue. *In* (pp. 9–33) **80**.

15188. Barblan, Paolo.   Les avatars de l'art et du discours sur l'art: de Poe aux nouvelles avant-gardes. *See* **10151**.

15189. Bartolovich, Crystal.   The work of cultural studies in the age of transnational production. MinnR (45/46) 1995/96, 117–46.

15190. Bennett, Tanya Long.   No country to call home: a study of Castillo's *Mixquiahuala Letters*. Style (30:3) 1996, 462–78.

15191. Birkerts, Sven.   'The fate of the book'. AR (54:3) 1996, 261–72.

15192. Bolter, Jay David; Grusin, Richard.   Remediation. *See* **1139**.

15193. Bruce-Novoa.   Dialogical strategies, monological goals, Chicano literature. *In* (pp. 225–45) **80**.

15194. Buell, Frederick.   National culture and the new global system. Baltimore, MD; London: Johns Hopkins UP, 1994. pp. x, 365. Rev. by Harold K. Bush, Jr, in ColLit (23:2) 1996, 181–8.

15195. Castillo, Debra A.   Borderliners: Federico Campbell and Ana Castillo. *In* (pp. 147–70) **97**.

15196. Civardi, Christian.   L'histoire et la littérature revisitées par la contre-culture du mouvement ouvrier. *See* **10156**.

15197. Cooper, B. Lee.   From *Love Letters* to *Miss You*: popular recordings, epistolary imagery, and romance during war-time, 1941–1945. JAC (19:4) 1996, 15–27.

15198. Dirlik, Arif.   The past as legacy and project: postcolonial criticism in the perspective of indigenous historicism. AICRJ (20:2) 1996, 1–31.

15199. Dorrell, Larry D.; Curtis, Dan B.; Rampal, Kuldip R.   Book-worms without books? Students reading comic books in the school house. *See* **196**.

15200. Embry, Marcus.   Cholo angels in Guadaljara: the politics and poetics of Anzaldúa's *Borderlands/La Frontera*. WP (8:2) 1996, 87–108.

15201. Esonwanne, Uzo.   'Race' and hermeneutics: paradigm shift – from scientific to hermeneutic understanding of race. AAR (26:4) 1992, 565–82.

15202. Eysturoy, Annie O.   Daughters of self-creation: the contemporary Chicana novel. Albuquerque: New Mexico UP, 1996. pp. ix, 172.

15203. Frick, Thomas.   Either/or. *See* **2022**.

15204. Gaspar de Alba, Alicia.   *Tortillerismo*: work by Chicana lesbians. Signs (18:4) 1993, 956–63.

15205. Gray, John.   Enlightenment's wake: politics and culture at the close of the modern age. London; New York: Routledge, 1995. pp. ix, 203. Rev. by R. E. Foust in NOR (22:2) 1996, 104–6.

15206. Greer, Mary K.   Women of the Golden Dawn: rebels and priestesses. Rochester, VT: Park Street Press, 1995. pp. xxi, 490. Rev. by Alex Owen in Yeats Annual (12) 1996, 339–42.

15207. Gross, Robert A.   Retribution, rehabilitation, redemption: prisoners in print. Book (36) 1995, 8–11.

15208. Gurstein, Rochelle.   Common worlds and violations: a response to Joyce Carol Oates. Salmagundi (111) 1996, 86–95.

15209. Gutiérrez-Jones, Carl.   Rethinking the borderlands: between Chicano culture and legal discourse. Berkeley; London: California UP, 1995. pp. xi, 219. (Latinos in American society and culture, 4.) Rev. by Debra A. Castillo in MFS (42:4) 1996, 854–6.

15210. Harris, Leonard (ed.).   The philosophy of Alain Locke: Harlem renaissance and beyond. Philadelphia, PA: Temple UP, 1989. pp. x, 332. Rev. by Clarence E. Walker in AAR (26:4) 1992, 675–82.

15211. Hubbard, Dolan.   Slipping into darkness: CLA and Black intellectual formation. CLAJ (40:1) 1996, 1–20.

15212. Ingebretsen, Edward J.   *Batman*: Americana with a twist – American gothic revisited. PCR (3:2) 1992, 29–37.

15213. Jones, W. Gareth (ed.).   Tolstoi and Britain. *See* **10167**.

15214. Kazin, Alfred (ed.).   A lifetime burning in every moment: from the journals of Alfred Kazin. New York: HarperCollins, 1996. pp. ix, 341.

15215. KIBERD, DECLAN. White skins, Black masks? Celticism and *Négritude?* EI (31:1/2) 1996, 163–75.

15216. LINK-HEER, URSULA. Doppelgänger und multiple Persönlichkeiten: eine Faszination der Jahrhundertwende. *See* **10170**.

15217. MARKLEY, ROBERT (ed.). Virtual realities and their discontents. *See* **1184**.

15218. MARLING, KARAL ANN. As seen on TV: the visual culture of everyday life in the 1950s. Cambridge, MA; London: Harvard UP, 1994. pp. 328. Rev. by Richard Aquila in AHR (101:1) 1996, 256–7.

15219. MORROW, RAYMOND A. The challenge of cultural studies. CanRCL (22:1) 1995, 1–20.

15220. OATES, JOYCE CAROL. Art and ethics? The (f)utility of art. Salmagundi (111) 1996, 75–85.

15221. O'DRISCOLL, SALLY. Outlaw reading: beyond queer theory. Signs (22:1) 1996, 30–51.

15222. OLANIYAN, TEJUMOLA. African-American critical discourse and the invention of cultural identities. AAR (26:4) 1992, 533–45.

15223. PATERSON, JOHN. Edwardians: London life and letters, 1901–1914. Chicago: Dee, 1996. pp. 330, (plates) 8. Rev. by Christopher Clausen in NewL (79:5) 1996, 15.

15224. PERKES, CAROLYN. Les seuils du savoir littéraire canadien: le roman québécois en traduction anglaise, 1960–90. CanRCL (23:4) 1996, 1195–1211.

15225. QUINTANA, ALVINA E. Home girls: Chicana literary voices. Philadelphia, PA: Temple UP, 1996. pp. xii, 165.

15226. SCHULTZ, APRIL. 'To lose the speakable': folklore and landscape in O. E. Rølvaag's *Giants in the Earth*. *In* (pp. 89–111) **66**.

15227. SEGAL, HOWARD P. Future imperfect: the mixed blessings of technology in America. *See* **10179**.

15228. SIEGEL, JERROLD. Boundaries: a response to Joyce Carol Oates. Salmagundi (111) 1996, 96–104.

15229. SPENCER, JON MICHAEL. The Black church and the Harlem renaissance. AAR (30:3) 1996, 453–60.

15230. SQUIER, SUSAN MERRILL. Babies in bottles: twentieth-century visions of reproductive technology. New Brunswick, NJ: Rutgers UP, 1994. pp. xiii, 270. Rev. by Kathleen Woodward in MFS (42:1) 1996, 227–30.

15231. TICHI, CECELIA. The twentieth-century television mentality. *In* (pp. 3–15) **117**.

15232. TODOROV, TZVETAN. Poetry and morality. Salmagundi (111) 1996, 68–74.

15233. WALKER, CLARENCE E. Two Black intellectuals and the burden of race. AAR (26:4) 1992, 675–82 (review-article).

15234. WOLF, HOWARD. Some roles of American studies overseas today. CanRCL (20:1/2) 1993, 209–17.

15235. WOLFF, JANET. Resident alien: feminist cultural criticism. New Haven, CT; London: Yale UP, 1995. pp. x, 156. Rev. by Renée R. Curry in RMRLL (50:1) 1996, 110–12.

15236. XIE, SHAOBO; CHEN, JOHN (ZHONG) M. Jacques Derrida and Chuang Tzu: some analogies in their deconstructionist discourse on language and truth. CanRCL (19:3) 1992, 363–76.

Literary Theory

This section is intended to contain studies **about** the literary theory, literary historiography, literary criticism, etc., produced *in* the twentieth century. For modern works **of** literary history and criticism dealing generally with this period, see under 'Twentieth Century: General Literary Studies'.

15237. ABOU-RIHAN, FADI.   Queer marks/nomadic difference: sexuality and the politics of race and ethnicity. CanRCL (21:1/2) 1994, 255–63.

15238. ADAM, IAN.   Oracy and literacy: a post-colonial dilemma? JCL (31:1) 1996, 97–109.

15239. ADAMSON, JOSEPH.   Northrop Frye: a visionary life. (Bibl. 1995, 13885.) Rev. by Leon Litvack in BJCS (11:1) 1996, 153–4.

15240. AJAYI-SOYINKA, OMOFOLABO.   Black feminist criticism and drama: thoughts on double patriarchy. *See* **13386**.

15241. ALARCÓN, NORMA.   Conjugating subjects: the heteroglossia of essence and resistance. *In* (pp. 125–38) **80**.

15242. ALDRIDGE, JOHN W.   Remembering criticism. ASch (62:4) 1993, 585–9.

15243. ALLEN, GRAHAM.   Intertextuality. YWCCT (3) 1993, 28–50.

15244. ALTIERI, CHARLES.   Some problems about agency in the theories of radical poetics. *See* **14832**.

15245. —— Whose America is *Our America*: on Walter Benn Michaels's characterizations of modernity in America. Modernism/Modernity (3:3) 1996, 107–13 (review-article).

15246. ALVAREZ, ROMÁN; VIDAL, CARMEN ÁFRICA.   What's wrong with (un)critical theory? An interview with Christopher Norris. EEM (5:2) 1996, 35–42.

15247. APPIGNANESI, RICHARD; GARRATT, CHRIS.   Postmodernism for beginners. Trumpington, Cambridge: Icon, 1995. pp. 175.

15248. ARAC, JONATHAN.   The politics of nationalism in recent American literary historiography: the case of the *New Cambridge History*. YREAL (11) 1995, 15–27.

15249. —— Post-structuralism and the contexts of history. AmS (36:1) 1995, 105–14.

15250. ARONOWITZ, STANLEY.   Dead artists, live theories, and other cultural problems. New York: Routledge, 1994. pp. xii, 323. Rev. by Timothy M. Chester in SSQ (77:2) 1996, 456–7.

15251. ARTEAGA, ALFRED .   Bonding in difference: an interview with Gayatri Chakravorty Spivak. *In* (pp. 273–85) **80**.

15252. ASANTE, MOLEFI KETE.   Locating a text: implications of Afrocentric theory. *In* (pp. 9–20) **55**.

15253. ASTON, ELAINE; CLARKE, IAN.   Feminist theory and the matriarchal soap: *EastEnders*. *See* **13402**.

15254. BADEROON, GABEBA.   Postmodernism, television, genre and narrative: extreme visibility. *See* **13410**.

15255. BAKER, WILLIAM; WOMACK, KENNETH.   Recent work in critical theory. Style (30:4) 1996, 584–692.

15256. —— —— Recent work in critical theory, 1989–1995: an annotated bibliography. Westport, CT; London: Greenwood Press, 1996. pp. xvii, 585. (Bibliographies and indexes in world literature, 51.)

15257. BAL, MIEKE; BOER, INGE E. (eds). The point of theory: practices of cultural analysis. Amsterdam: Amsterdam UP; New York: Continuum, 1994. pp. 333.

15258. BALAKIAN, ANNA. Canon harassment. CanRCL (20:1/2) 1993, 201–7.

15259. —— The snowflake on the belfry: dogma and disquietude in the critical arena. (Bibl. 1995, 13900.) Rev. by John L. Brown in WLT (69:2) 1995, 445.

15260. —— Theorizing comparison: the pyramid of similitude and difference. WLT (69:2) 1995, 263–7.

15261. BALDICK, CHRIS. Criticism and literary theory 1890 to the present. *See* **10189**.

15262. BALFOUR, IAN. Northrop Frye. (Bibl. 1990, 9419.) Rev. by Robert D. Denham in ARCS (19:2) 1989, 228–30.

15263. BALZANO, WANDA. Il *patchwork* post-coloniale irlandese. *See* **9512**.

15264. BANNET, EVE TAVOR. Structuralism and the logic of dissent: Barthes, Derrida, Foucault, Lacan. Basingstoke: Macmillan; Urbana: Illinois UP, 1989. pp. xi, 299. Rev. by Gregory Meyerson in Genre (23:4) 1990, 355–69.

15265. BARILLAS, WILLIAM. Ecocriticism and Midwestern literary studies: some points of departure (and arrival). Midamerica (22) 1995, 128–38.

15266. BARNEY, RICHARD A. Subjectivity, the novel, and the *Bildung* blocks of critical theory. *See* **4134**.

15267. BARRETT, TERRY. Critics on criticism. JAE (28:2) 1994, 71–82.

15268. BASSARD, KATHERINE CLAY. The daughters' arrival: the earliest Black women's writing community. *See* **8430**.

15269. BASTING, ANNE DAVIS. Amnesia interrupted: re-membering the living past in feminist theory and Suzanne Lacy's *Crystal Quilt*. JDTC (11:1) 1996, 55–80.

15270. BAUER, DALE M.; McKINSTRY, SUSAN JARET (eds). Feminism, Bakhtin, and the dialogic. *See* **33**.

15271. BAYARD, CAROLINE. Postmodernités européennes: *ethos* et *polis* de fin de siècle. Études littéraires (27:1) 1994, 89–112.

15272. BEHAR, RUTH; GORDON, DEBORAH A. (eds). Women writing culture. Berkeley; London: California UP, 1995. pp. xiii, 457. Rev. by Carole M. Counihan in NWSAJ (8:3) 1996, 164–5.

15273. BEINER, RONALD. Foucault's hyper-liberalism. CritR (9:3) 1995, 349–70.

15274. BELITT, BEN. The forged feature: toward a poetics of uncertainty: new and selected essays. *See* **3108**.

15275. BELL, MICHAEL, *et al.* F. R. Leavis: reminiscences and revaluations. CamQ (25:4) 1996, 303–425.

15276. BELSEY, CATHERINE. Postmodern Shakespeare. *See* **6228**.

15277. BENDER, JOHN. A new history of the Enlightenment? *In* (pp. 62–83) **91**.

15278. —— WELLBERY, DAVID E. (eds). The ends of rhetoric: history, theory, practice. *See* **2307**.

15279. BENNETT, DONNA. Conflicted vision: a consideration of canon and genre in English-Canadian literature. *In* (pp. 131–49) **13**.

15280. BENNETT, SUSAN. Feminist (theatre) historiography Canadian (feminist) theatre: a reading of some practices and theories. *See* **13433**.

15281. BENNETT, TONY.   Outside literature. (Bibl. 1994, 11015.) Rev. by Nicolas Tredell in PN Review (17:5) 1991, 57–8.

15282. BENNINGTON, GEOFFREY; DERRIDA, JACQUES.   Jacques Derrida. (Bibl. 1995, 13908.) Rev. by Christopher Norris in CL (48:1) 1996, 74–7.

15283. BENOIT, WILLIAM.   A note on Burke on 'motive'. RSQ (26:2) 1996, 67–79.

15284. BENSTOCK, SHARI.   Textualising the feminine: on the limits of genre. (Bibl. 1994, 11017.) Rev. by Lynne Huffer in MFS (40:1) 1994, 213–15.

15285. BERCOVITCH, SACVAN (gen. ed.).   The Cambridge history of American literature: vol. 8, Poetry and criticism, 1940–1995. *See* **14846**.

15286. BERGEVIN, GERALD W.   Theorizing through an ethnic lens. MLS (26:4) 1996, 13–26.

15287. BERKENKOTTER, CAROL.   Evolution of a scholarly forum: *Reader*, 1977–1988. *See* **1232**.

15288. BERNARD-DONALS, MICHAEL F.   Mikhail Bakhtin: between phenomenology and Marxism. Cambridge; New York: CUP, 1994. pp. xvii, 187. (Literature, culture, theory, 11.) (Cf. bibl. 1991, 11496.) Rev. by Michael Gardiner in Utopian Studies (7:2) 1996, 216–19.

15289. BERNSTEIN, CHARLES, *et al.*   Poetry, community, movement: a conversation. *See* **4340**.

15290. BERRESSEM, HANJO.   Negotiating the universe of discourse: the topology of hypertext. *See* **1136**.

15291. BERRY, JAY R., JR.   The significance of Darwin T. Turner's scholarship. LHR (11:2) 1992, 28–32.

15292. BERTENS, HANS.   The idea of the postmodern. London; New York: Routledge, 1995. pp. ix, 284. Rev. by David S. Gross in WLT (69:4) 1995, 883–4.

15293. BÉRUBÉ, MICHAEL.   Hybridity in the center: an interview with Houston A. Baker, Jr. AAR (26:4) 1992, 547–64.

15294. —— Public access: literary theory and American cultural politics. (Bibl. 1994, 11019.) Rev. by David S. Gross in WLT (69:2) 1995, 446; by Jim Neilson and Gregory Meyerson in MinnR (45/46) 1995/96, 263–73.

15295. BISSELL, ELIZABETH BEAUMONT.   'Something still more exact': T. S. Eliot's 'traditional claims'. Angelaki (2:2) 1996, 113–27.

15296. BIZZINI, SILVIA CAPORALE.   Power politics: literature and Foucauldian analysis. In-between (5:1) 1996, 23–39.

15297. BLACKSHIRE-BELAY, CAROL AISHA.   Afrocentricity and literary theory: the maturing imagination. *In* (pp. 3–7) **55**.

15298. BLAKE, CASEY NELSON.   Beloved community: the cultural criticism of Randolph Bourne, Van Wyck Brooks, Waldo Frank, and Lewis Mumford. (Bibl. 1994, 11025.) Rev. by David W. Noble in AmS (33:1) 1992, 133.

15299. BODE, CHRISTOPH.   Anglistische Literaturwissenschaft und/oder *Cultural Studies*? Ang (114:3) 1996, 396–424.

15300. BONNYCASTLE, STEPHEN.   In search of authority: an introductory guide to literary theory. Peterborough, Ont.: Broadview, 1996. pp. 146. (Second ed.: first ed. 1991.) Rev. by A.H. in TLS, 19 May 1996, 31.

15301. BOONE, JOSEPH A.; CADDEN, MICHAEL (eds).   Engendering men: the question of male feminist criticism. (Bibl. 1992, 11997.)

Rev. by Gregory Woods in PN Review (18:1) 1991, 60; by Marlon B. Ross in Signs (19:3) 1994, 770–7.

15302. BORDWELL, DAVID. The power of a research tradition: prospects for progress in the study of film style. *See* **13472**.

15303. BOTTOMORE, STEPHEN. Out of this world: theory, fact and film history. *See* **13473**.

15304. BOWERBANK, SYLVIA. The Greening of literary studies. CanRCL (22:3/4) 1995, 443–54.

15305. BOWERS, RICK. Bakhtin, self and other: neohumanism and communicative multiplicity. CanRCL (21:4) 1994, 565–75.

15306. BOWIE, MALCOLM. Psychoanalysis and the future of theory. Oxford; Cambridge, MA: Blackwell, 1993. pp. x, 162. (Bucknell lectures in literary theory, 9.) Rev. by Ned Lukacher in CL (48:1) 1996, 65–73.

15307. BRAUDY, LEO. Varieties of literary affection. *In* (pp. 26–41) **91**.

15308. BRIER, PETER. Howard Mumford Jones and the dynamics of liberal humanism. (Bibl. 1994, 11035.) Rev. by Paul Hansom in AL (68:1) 1996, 251–2.

15309. BRINKER-GABLER, GISELA (ed.). Encountering the other(s): studies in literature, history, and culture. Albany: New York State UP, 1995. pp. viii, 378. Rev. by Brinda Bose in WLT (69:4) 1995, 885.

15310. BRODHEAD, RICHARD H. Cultures of criticism: private confessions of a historicist critic. YREAL (11) 1995, 1–13.

15311. BROOKER, PETER; WIDDOWSON, PETER (eds). A practical reader in contemporary literary theory. London; New York: Prentice Hall/Harvester Wheatsheaf, 1996. pp. ix, 498.

15312. BROOKS, PETER. Psychoanalysis and storytelling. (Bibl. 1994, 11036.) Rev. by Ned Lukacher in CL (48:1) 1996, 65–73.

15313. BROWN, MARSHALL. Commentary. *In* (pp. 211–20) **91**.

15314. BROWN, STUART C. I. A. Richards' new rhetoric: multiplicity, instrument, and metaphor. *See* **2322**.

15315. BRUMMETT, BARRY. Speculations on the discovery of a Burkean blunder. RhR (14:1) 1995, 221–5.

15316. BRUNS, GERALD L. Along the fatal narrative turn (toward an anarchic theory of literary history). MLQ (57:1) 1996, 1–21.

15317. BRUSTER, DOUGLAS. New light on the Old Historicism: Shakespeare and the forms of historicist criticism. *See* **6250**.

15318. BUDICK, SANFORD; ISER, WOLFGANG (eds). The translatability of cultures: figurations of the space between. *See* **3113**.

15319. BURK, JULI THOMPSON. In the *I* of the storm: the problem with pluralism. *See* **13507**.

15320. BURNETT, RON (ed.). Explorations in film theory: selected essays from *Ciné-tracts*. *See* **13508**.

15321. BURNHAM, CLINT. The Jamesonian unconscious: the aesthetics of Marxist theory. (Bibl. 1995, 13933.) Rev. by Tom Moylan in Utopian Studies (7:2) 1996, 232–4; by Douglas Mao in ConLit (37:1) 1996, 161–9.

15322. BURTON, STACY. Bakhtin, temporality, and modern narrative: writing 'the whole triumphant murderous unstoppable chute'. *See* **14422**.

15323. BUSH, HAROLD K., JR. Structural America: the persistence of oppositional paradigms in American literary theory. ColLit (23:2) 1996, 181–8 (review-article).

15324. Butler, Judith.   Performative acts and gender constitution: an essay in phenomenology and feminist theory. *In* (pp. 270–82) **84**.

15325. Caminero-Santangelo, Marta.   The madwoman can't speak: postwar culture, feminist criticism, and Welty's *June Recital*. TSWL (15:1) 1996, 123–46.

15326. Candela, Giuseppe.   Aspects of realism in Auerbach and Croce. CanRCL (23:2) 1996, 485–99.

15327. Carafiol, Peter.   The American ideal: literary history as a worldly activity. (Bibl. 1994, 11046.) Rev. by Nancy A. Walker in AmS (34:2) 1993, 157–9.

15328. Carnegie, Jeniphier R.   Selected bibliography of criticism and related works. *In* (pp. 373–94) **81**.

15329. Caronia, Antonio.   Teorie del corpo e comunicazione interattiva. *In* (pp. 527–36) **117**.

15330. Carroll, Joseph.   Evolution and literary theory. (Bibl. 1995, 13941.) Rev. by John Constable in SEL (English number) 1996, 91–9.

15331. Carter, C. Allen.   Kenneth Burke and the scapegoat process. Norman; London: Oklahoma UP, 1996. pp. xxi, 169. (Oklahoma project for discourse and theory, 17.)

15332. Caruth, Cathy.   An interview with Geoffrey Hartman. *See* **10015**.

15333. —— Esch, Deborah (eds).   Critical encounters: reference and responsibility in deconstructive writing. New Brunswick, NJ: Rutgers UP, 1995. pp. vii, 305. Rev. by Rei Terada in MinnR (45/46) 1995/96, 299–309.

15334. Case, Sue-Ellen (ed.).   Performing feminisms: feminist critical theory and theatre. *See* **84**.

15335. Cavell, Stanley.   Philosophical passages: Wittgenstein, Emerson, Austin, Derrida. (Bibl. 1995, 13947.) Rev. by Martin Kevorkian in AL (68:1) 1996, 237–9.

15336. Cervo, Nathan.   The post-modernist attack on pseudo-values. NNER (16) 1992, 86–90.

15337. Chambers, Iain.   The shadow and the wound: critical reason in the epoch of the post-. Textus (4) 1991, 217–35.

15338. Champagne, Rosaria.   Feminism, essentialism, and historical context. WS (25:1) 1995, 95–108.

15339. —— The politics of survivorship: incest, women's literature, and feminist theory. *See* **9815**.

15340. Chapman, Michael.   Writing literary history in Southern Africa: the relevance of a social theory. JLS (10:3/4) 1995, 318–30.

15341. Charnes, Linda.   Styles that matter: on the discursive limits of ideology critique. SStud (24) 1996, 118–47.

15342. Chen, Xiaomei.   The poetics of 'misunderstanding': an ahistorical model of cross-cultural literary history. CanRCL (19:4) 1992, 485–506.

15343. Chénetier, Marc.   Est-il nécessaire d' 'expliquer le post-modern(ism)e aux enfants'? Études littéraires (27:1) 1994, 11–27.

15344. Chomei, Toshiko.   Shin bungaku riron no kattou. (Conflicts of new literary theories.) Tokyo: Liber Shuppan, 1996. pp. 134.

15345. Cimitile, Anna Maria.   Travel, language, identity, and the spaces in-between. Annali anglistica (38:3) 1995, 85–101.

15346. Claiborne, Corrie.   Leaving abjection: where 'Black' meets theory. MLS (26:4) 1996, 27–36.

15347. CLARK, DAVID L. Monstrosity, illegibility, denegation: de Man, bp Nichol and the resistance to postmodernism. *In* (pp. 40–71) **72**.

15348. CLAVIEZ, THOMAS. Dimensioning society: ideology, rhetoric, and criticism in the work of Sacvan Bercovitch. YREAL (11) 1995, 173–205.

15349. COHEN, JEFFREY JEROME. Monster culture (seven theses). *In* (pp. 3–25) **72**.

15350. COHEN, PAULA MARANTZ. Remembering the idea of a self: rereading Trilling. TexR (15:3/4) 1994, 41–58.

15351. COHEN, STEPHEN. New Historicism and genre: towards a historical formalism. YREAL (11) 1995, 405–23.

15352. COLDWELL, JOAN. The anxiety of influence: feminist response to father Yeats. *In* (pp. 362–8) **49**.

15353. COLLADO RODRÍGUEZ, FRANCISCO. Complexity/controversy: some aspects of contemporary Women's Studies in America. *In* (pp. 107–20) **38**.

15354. COLLINI, STEFAN (ed.). Interpretation and overinterpretation. By Umberto Eco *et al.* (Bibl. 1994, 11059.) Rev. by David Seed in Eng (41:171) 1992, 267–71.

15355. COLLINS, JEFFREY. Media studies. YWCCT (3) 1993, 233–59.

15356. CORNUT-GENTILLE D'ARCY, CHANTAL; GARCÍA LANDA, JOSÉ ÁNGEL (eds). Gender, I-deology: essays on theory, fiction and film. *See* **38**.

15357. COVI, GIOVANNA. The matrushka monster of feminist criticism. *See* **12212**.

15358. CRITCHLEY, SIMON, *et al.* Deconstruction and pragmatism. Ed. by Chantal Mouffe. London; New York: Routledge, 1996. pp. ix, 88.

15359. CRUSIUS, TIMOTHY. Neither trust nor suspicion: Kenneth Burke's rhetoric and hermeneutics. *See* **2344**.

15360. CSENGERI, KAREN (ed.). The collected writings of T. E. Hulme. (Bibl. 1995, 13971.) Rev. by Ronald Schuchard in EC (46:1) 1996, 78–87.

15361. D'ALBERTIS, DEIRDRE. Whose England? Whose English literature? Dissecting 'the corpse' of English studies. Review (17) 1995, 95–108 (review-article).

15362. DAMROSCH, LEO. Reaching mid-career in 'the eighteenth century': some personal reflections. *In* (pp. 200–10) **91**.

15363. —— (ed.). The profession of eighteenth-century literature: reflections on an institution. *See* **91**.

15364. DARLINGTON, SONYA. Reader-response: a visual and aesthetic experience. Reader (31) 1994, 11–26.

15365. DAVIDSON, CATHY N. The quest for accuracy; or, Why women's studies? EEM (3:1) 1994, 69–74.

15366. DAVIES, CAROLE BOYCE; FIDO, ELAINE SAVORY. Preface: talking it over: women, writing and feminism. *In* (pp. ix–xx) **81**.

15367. DAVIES, JUDE. The future of 'no future': punk rock and postmodern theory. *See* **14897**.

15368. DAVIS, DEANNA L. Feminist critics and literary mothers: daughters reading Elizabeth Gaskell. *See* **11255**.

15369. DAVIS, DIANE MOWERY. Breaking up (at) phallocracy: post-feminism's chortling hammer. RhR (14:1) 1995, 126–41.

15370. Davis, Robert Con; Schleifer, Ronald (eds).   Contemporary literary criticism: literary and cultural studies. (Bibl. 1990, 9464.) New York; London: Longman, 1994. pp. x, 694. (Third ed.: first ed. 1986.)

15371. Dawson, Graham.   The paradox of authority: psychoanalysis, history and cultural criticism. Angelaki (2:2) 1996, 75–102.

15372. Day, Gary.   Re-reading Leavis: culture and literary criticism. Basingstoke: Macmillan; New York: St Martin's Press, 1996. pp. xvi, 307.

15373. Daymond, M. J. (ed.).   South African feminisms: writing, theory, and criticism, 1990–1994. *See* **13031**.

15374. Dean, Paul.   Current literature 1994: II, Literary theory, history and criticism. EngS (77:1) 1996, 71–91.

15375. Dean, Tim.   Transsexual identification, gender performance theory, and the politics of the real. LitPs (39:4) 1993, 1–27.

15376. de Bolla, Peter.   Harold Bloom: towards historical rhetorics. (Bibl. 1990, 9465.) Rev. by Frederick Pollack in Salmagundi (88/89) 1990/91, 486–509.

15377. de Graef, Ortwin.   The Paul de Man affair ten years after. EEM (5:2) 1996, 31–4.

15378. Dellamora, Richard.   Responsibilities: deconstruction, feminism, and lesbian erotics. CanRCL (21:1/2) 1994, 221–42.

15379. Denham, Robert D. (ed.).   A world in a grain of sand: twenty-two interviews with Northrop Frye. (Bibl. 1995, 13979.) Rev. by Jonathan Hart in CanRCL (20:1/2) 1993, 139–71.

15380. —— Willard, Thomas (eds).   Visionary poetics: essays on Northrop Frye's criticism. (Bibl. 1995, 13980.) Rev. by Jonathan Hart in CanRCL (20:1/2) 1993, 139–71.

15381. Dews, Peter.   Logics of disintegration: post-structuralist thought and the claims of critical theory. (Bibl. 1990, 9470) Rev. by Gregory Meyerson in Genre (23:4) 1990, 355–69.

15382. D'Haen, Theo.   Dis/coursing post-modernism: science, magic, (post)-modernity. *See* **14465**.

15383. Dienst, Richard.   Still life in real time: theory after television. *See* **13620**.

15384. Dimić, Milan V.   Why study canonization? CanRCL (20:1/2) 1993, 175–86.

15385. Dimock, Wai Chee; Gilmore, Michael T. (eds).   Rethinking class: literary studies and social formations. *See* **100**.

15386. Downing, David B.; Bazargan, Susan.   Image and ideology: some preliminary histories and polemics. *In* (pp. 3–44) **44**.

15387. —— —— (eds).   Image and ideology in modern/postmodern discourse. *See* **44**.

15388. Drennan, Barbara.   Theatre history-telling: new historiography, logic and the other Canadian tradition. *See* **13630**.

15389. duCille, Ann.   The occult of true Black womanhood: critical demeanor and Black feminist studies. Signs (19:3) 1994, 591–629.

15390. DuPlessis, Rachel Blau.   Manifests. *See* **4360**.

15391. Eagleton, Mary.   Working with feminist criticism. Oxford; Cambridge, MA: Blackwell, 1996. pp. vii, 240.

15392. Eagleton, Terry; Jameson, Fredric; Said, Edward W.   Nationalism, colonialism, and literature. Introd. by Seamus Deane. (Bibl. 1994, 11097.) Rev. by Áine O'Brien in QRFV (14:3) 1993, 121–7.

15393. EAGLETON, TERRY; MILNE, DREW (eds). Marxist literary theory: a reader. Oxford; Cambridge, MA: Blackwell, 1996. pp. viii, 446.

15394. EARNSHAW, STEVEN. The direction of literary theory. Manchester: Manchester UP; New York: St Martin's Press, 1996. pp. viii, 182.

15395. ECHERUO, MICHAEL J. C. Derrida, language games and theory. Theoria (86) 1995, 99–115.

15396. EDDINS, DWIGHT (ed.). The emperor redressed: critiquing critical theory. (Bibl. 1995, 14002.) Rev. by David H. Hirsch in SAtlR (61:2) 1996, 150–4.

15397. EDMUNDSON, MARK. Lasch's Jeremiad. Raritan (11:2) 1991, 128–41 (review-article).

15398. EDWARDS, BRIAN. Figures of difference: history, historicism, and critical practice. CanRCL (19:1/2) 1992, 155–69.

15399. ELAM, DIANE. Feminism and deconstruction. London; New York: Routledge, 1994. pp. x, 154. Rev. by Shelly Gregory in TSWL (15:2) 1996, 374–6.

15400. ELAM, HELEN REGUEIRO. Introduction. See **10023**.

15401. ELAM, KEIR. The wars of the texts. See **4080**.

15402. ELDER, ARLENE A. Criticizing from the borderlands. MLS (26:4) 1996, 5–11.

15403. ENGLE, LARS. Milton, Bakhtin, and the unit of analysis. In (pp. 476–88) **98**.

15404. EPSTEIN, WILLIAM H. Professing Gray: the resumption of authority in eighteenth-century studies. In (pp. 84–94) **91**.

15405. ERENS, PATRICIA (ed.). Issues in feminist film criticism. See **13645**.

15406. ESTERHAMMER, ANGELA. Speech acts and world-creation: the dual function of the performative. See **2264**.

15407. EVERMAN, WELCH D. Who says this? The authority of the author, the discourse and the reader. See **14486**.

15408. EZELL, MARGARET J. M. Family histories, literary time. SPELL (9) 1996, 17–39.

15409. FARBER, JERRY. Aesthetic resonance: beyond the sign in literature. Reader (32) 1994, 16–33.

15410. FEAGIN, SUSAN L. Reading with feeling: the aesthetics of appreciation. Ithaca, NY; London: Cornell UP, 1996. pp. viii, 260.

15411. FELSKI, RITA. Beyond feminist aesthetics: feminist literature and social change. (Bibl. 1992, 12091.) Rev. by Ellen Cronan Rose in Signs (18:2) 1993, 346–75.

15412. —— The gender of modernity. Cambridge, MA; London: Harvard UP, 1995. pp. viii, 247. Rev. by Lynette Felber in MFS (42:4) 1996, 912–14.

15413. FERRIS, LESLEY. Absent bodies, dancing bodies, broken dishes: feminist theory, postmodernism, and the performing arts. See **13659**.

15414. FINKELSTEIN, NORMAN. Language, poetry, and the problem of the avant-garde. See **14917**.

15415. FISH, STANLEY. Professional correctness: literary studies and political change. (Bibl. 1995, 14015.) Rev. by Randy Malamud in SAtlR (61:3) 1996, 143–6.

15416. Fishlin, Daniel. Nuclear pathologies; or, No aporias, not now. *See* **13070**.

15417. Fleishman, Avrom. Changing the subject: origins and outcomes in English. SAtlR (61:2) 1996, 69–105.

15418. Fleming, Bruce E. Structure and chaos in Modernist works. New York; Frankfurt; Bern; Paris: Lang, 1996. pp. 139. (New studies in aesthetics, 27.)

15419. Flores, Ralph. A study of allegory in its historical context and relationship to contemporary theory. Lewiston, NY; Lampeter: Mellen Press, 1996. pp. 251.

15420. Fluck, Winfried. Cultures of criticism: Herman Melville's *Moby-Dick*, expressive individualism, and the New Historicism. *See* **11838**.

15421. Fludernik, Monika. Towards a 'natural' narratology. *See* **2617**.

15422. —— Towards a 'natural' narratology. *See* **2618**.

15423. Fokkema, Douwe. Orientalism, Occidentalism and the notion of discourse: arguments for a new cosmopolitanism. On Edward Said's *Orientalism* and Chen Xiaomei's *Occidentalism: a Theory of Counter-Discourse in Post-Mao China*. CompCrit (18) 1996, 227–41.

15424. Folkenflik, Robert. The heirs of Ian Watt. *See* **8578**.

15425. Frank, Marcie. The critic as performance artist: Susan Sontag's writing and gay culture. *In* (pp. 173–84) **12**.

15426. Fraser, Graham. Metcalf's criticism and the Canadian canon. ARCS (19:4) 1989, 381–95.

15427. Fraser, Kathleen. 'This phrasing unreliable except as here'. Talisman (13) 1994/95, 209–18.

15428. Fraser, Russell. A note on deconstruction. IowaR (25:1) 1995, 67–77.

15429. Freedman, Diane P.; Frey, Olivia; Zauhar, Frances Murphy (eds). The intimate critique: autobiographical literary criticism. (Bibl. 1995, 14024.) Rev. by Susanna Egan in CanL (151) 1996, 137–9.

15430. Friedman, Susan Stanford. 'Beyond' gynocriticism and gynesis: the geographics of identity and the future of feminist criticism. TSWL (15:1) 1996, 13–40.

15431. Friend, Joshua. 'Every decoding is another encoding': Morris Zapp's poststructural implications on our postmodern world. ELN (33:3) 1996, 61–7.

15432. Fulweiler, Howard W. The other missing link: Owen Barfield and the scientific imagination. Ren (46:1) 1993, 39–54.

15433. Fussell, Paul. Doing battle: the making of a skeptic. Boston, MA: Little, Brown, 1996. pp. 310. Rev. by Anthony Hecht in BkW, 29 Sept. 1996, 1, 10.

15434. Galef, David. Second thoughts: a prolegomenon to re-reading. Reader (31) 1994, 29–46.

15435. Gallop, Jane. Around 1981: academic feminist literary theory. (Bibl. 1992, 12108.) Rev. by Emily Toth in NWSAJ (5:2) 1993, 283–5.

15436. Gannett, Cinthia. Gender and the journal: diaries and academic discourse. *See* **2368**.

15437. García-Berrio, Antonio. A theory of the literary text. Trans. by Kenneth A. Horn. Berlin; NY: de Gruyter, 1992. pp. x, 544. (Research in text theory/Untersuchungen zur Texttheorie, 17.)

(Orig. pub. as *Teoría de la literatura: la construcción del significado poético.* Madrid: Cátedra, 1989.)

15438. García Landa, José Ángel. Introduction: gender, I-deology and addictive representation: the film of familiarity. *In* (pp. 13–54) **38**.

15439. Gasché, Rodolphe. Inventions of difference: on Jacques Derrida. (Bibl. 1995, 14031.) Rev. by David Thomson in CanL (151) 1996, 196–7.

15440. Gates, Henry Louis, Jr. The signifying monkey: a theory of Afro-American literary criticism. (Bibl. 1993, 11134.) Rev. by Ronald R. Butters in SECOLR (16:2) 1992, 204–7.

15441. Gebhardt, Richard C., *et al.* Symposium on peer reviewing in scholarly journals. *See* **1107**.

15442. Gerson, Carole. The canon between the wars: field-notes of a feminist archaeologist. *In* (pp. 46–56) **13**.

15443. Geyer-Ryan, Helga. Shakespeare after Derrida and Marx: death in Venice and the utopia of the open society. *See* **6309**.

15444. Gilbert, Pamela K. The body in question. *See* **14513**.

15445. Giles, Freda Scott. Disparate voices: African-American theatre critics of the 1920s. *See* **13721**.

15446. Giordano, Fedora. The anxiety of discovery: the Italian interest in Native American studies. RSAJ (5) 1994, 81–109.

15447. Glage, Liselotte. Strategien der Differenz: was oder wie ist der postkoloniale Roman? *See* **14518**.

15448. Godard, Barbara. Translating (as) woman. *See* **3141**.

15449. Goldstein, Laurence. The Harvard advocate. MichQR (35:4) 1996, 745–54 (review-article). (On Donald Hall.)

15450. Gollin, James. Cleanth Brooks remembered. ASch (64:2) 1995, 257–63.

15451. Good, Graham. Northrop Frye and liberal humanism. CanL (148) 1996, 75–91.

15452. Goodman, Kevis Bea. Making time for history: Wordsworth, the New Historicism, and the apocalyptic fallacy. *See* **12857**.

15453. Gordimer, Nadine. Across time and two hemispheres. WLT (70:1) 1996, 111–14. (Recollections of Harry Levin.)

15454. Gorman, David. Gérard Genette: an Anglo-French checklist to 1996. *See* **2630**.

15455. Grabes, Herbert. The aesthetic dimension: bliss and/or scandal. YREAL (12) 1996, 17–29.

15456. —— Errant specialisms: the recent historicist turn away from aesthetics. YREAL (11) 1995, 159–72.

15457. —— Literaturwissenschaft – Kulturwissenschaft – Anglistik. Ang (114:3) 1996, 376–95.

15458. Graham, Colin. 'Liminal spaces': post-colonial theories and Irish culture. Irish Review (16) 1994, 29–43.

15459. —— Post-colonial theory and Kiberd's 'Ireland'. Irish Review (19) 1996, 62–7.

15460. Greene, Roland. American comparative literature: reticence and articulation. WLT (69:2) 1995, 293–8.

15461. Greetham, D. C. (Textual) criticism and deconstruction. *See* **661**.

15462. Griffiths, Aled. Once more unto the breach: on the value of Derrida. EEM (4:1) 1995, 24–9. (Briefings, 10.)

15463. Grigsby, John L. The Agrarians and Ellen Douglas's

The Rock Cried Out and *Can't Quit You, Baby*: extending the tradition while expanding the canon. SoQ (34:1) 1995, 41–8.

15464. GROENING, LAURA SMYTH.   E. K. Brown: a study in conflict. (Bibl. 1995, 14054.) Rev. by Klay Dyer in JCP (10) 1995, 134–40; by Patricia Whitney in CanL (148) 1996, 194–5.

15465. GUERRA, GUSTAVO.   The critic as historian: the taming of the New Historicism. Style (30:1) 1996, 167–74 (review-article).

15466. GUILLORY, JOHN.   Literary critics as intellectuals: class analysis and the crisis of the humanities. *In* (pp. 107–49) **100**.

15467. GURPEGUI, JOSÉ ANTONIO.   An interview with Harold Bloom. RAEI (9) 1996, 165–81.

15468. GWIN, MINROSE.   Space travel: the connective politics of feminist reading. Signs (21:4) 1996, 870–905.

15469. GWYNN, R. S. (ed.).   The advocates of poetry: a reader of American poet-critics of the Modernist era. *See* **14936**.

15470. HAARBERG, JON.   Northrop Frye og den menippéiske satiren. (Northrop Frye and Menippean satire.) Skrift (8:1) 1996, 5–14.

15471. HAFFENDEN, JOHN (ed.).   The strengths of Shakespeare's shrew: essays, memoirs, and reviews. By William Empson. *See* **1409**.

15472. —— (introd.).   Three critics on one poem: Hart Crane's *Voyages III*. EC (46:1) 1996, 16–27.

15473. HALL, ANNE D.   The political wisdom of cultural poetics. MP (93:4) 1996, 423–44.

15474. HALL, GARY; WORTHAM, SIMON.   Rethinking authority: interview with Homi K. Bhabha. Angelaki (2:2) 1996, 59–63.

15475. HAMILTON, A. C.   Northrop Frye: anatomy of his criticism. (Bibl. 1992, 12127.) Rev. by Jonathan Hart in CanRCL (19:1/2) 1992, 119–54.

15476. HAMILTON, PAUL.   Historicism. London; New York: Routledge, 1996. pp. vi, 226. (New critical idiom.)

15477. HAMPTON, CHRISTOPHER.   The ideology of the text. (Bibl. 1994, 11142.) Rev. by David Pascoe in Eng (40:167) 1991, 180–6.

15478. HANDELMAN, DON.   Critiques of anthropology: literary turns, slippery bends. PT (15:3) 1994, 341–81.

15479. HANEY, WILLIAM S., II.   Presence and repetition: postmodern discourse and Vedic philosophy. SM (15:1) 1992, 48–69.

15480. HARRIS, WENDELL V.   Literary meaning: reclaiming the study of literature. Basingstoke: Macmillan; Washington Square: New York UP, 1996. pp. v, 240. Rev. by J.S. in TLS, 6 Dec. 1996, 24.

15481. —— (ed.).   Beyond poststructuralism: the speculations of theory and the experience of reading. University Park: Pennsylvania State UP, 1996. pp. xiii, 445.

15482. HART, JONATHAN.   Finding a way between: theory and practice of Ross Chambers. CanRCL (22:2) 1995, 205–11.

15483. —— Frye/about Frye. CanRCL (20:1/2) 1993, 139–71 (review-article).

15484. —— Frye's anatomizing and anatomizing Frye. CanRCL (19:1/2) 1992, 119–54 (review-article).

15485. —— Northrop Frye: the theoretical imagination. (Bibl. 1994, 11148.) Rev. by Imre Salusinszky in CanRCL (23:2) 1996, 590–3; by Michael Dolzani in Style (30:3) 1996, 519–23.

15486. —— Poetics and culture: unity, difference, and the case of Northrop Frye. ChrisL (46:1) 1996, 61–79.

15487. —— Ross Chambers: publications (1961–1995). CanRCL (22:2) 1995, 353–9.

15488. HART, RODERICK P. Modern rhetorical criticism. *See* **2392**.

15489. HARTH, DIETRICH. Vom Fetisch bis zum Drama? Anmerkungen zur Renaissance der Kulturwissenschaften. Ang (114:3) 1996, 340–75.

15490. HARTMAN, GEOFFREY. Minor prophecies: the literary essay in the culture wars. (Bibl. 1993, 11155.) Rev. by David Kaufmann in Comparatist (17) 1993, 160–2; by Mark Parker in Review (16) 1994, 93–103.

15491. HASELSTEIN, ULLA. Stephen Greenblatt's concept of a symbolic economy. YREAL (11) 1995, 347–70.

15492. HAVERKAMP, ANSELM (ed.). Deconstruction is/in America: a new sense of the political. New York: New York UP, 1995. pp. xi, 262. Rev. by Rei Terada in MinnR (45/46) 1995/96, 299–309.

15493. HAWTHORN, JEREMY. Cunning passages: New Historicism, cultural materialism, and Marxism in the contemporary literary debate. London; New York: Arnold, 1996. pp. x, 245. (Interrogating texts.)

15494. HAYLES, N. KATHERINE. Deciphering the rules of unruly disciplines: a modest proposal for literature and science. *In* (pp. 25–48) **62**.

15495. HEER, JEET. Marshall McLuhan and the politics of literary reputation. LRC (5:4) 1996, 23.

15496. HEINIMANN, DAVID. Booth, Rorty, Scarry: the Wall and the ethical age. ESCan (22:4) 1996, 461–76.

15497. HELMS, LORRAINE. Playing the woman's part: feminist criticism and Shakespearean performance. *In* (pp. 196–206) **84**.

15498. HENRY, RICHARD. Pretending and meaning: toward a pragmatic theory of fictional discourse. *See* **2640**.

15499. HERMANN, JOHN P. Why Anglo-Saxonists can't read; or, Who took the mead out of medieval studies? *See* **4616**.

15500. HIDALGO, PILAR. The New Historicism and its female discontents. *In* (pp. 131–48) **38**.

15501. HIGGINS, JOHN. Responses to Said and Taylor: critical literacy or the canon? Pretexts (5:1/2) 1995, 179–90.

15502. HIGONNET, MARGARET R. Mapping the text: critical metaphors. *In* (pp. 194–212) **97**.

15503. —— (ed.). Borderwork: feminist engagements with comparative literature. Ithaca, NY; London: Cornell UP, 1994. pp. x, 335. (Reading women writing.) Rev. by Barbara Carr in WLT (69:4) 1995, 884.

15504. HIPOLITO, T. A. Owen Barfield's *Poetic Diction*. Ren (46:1) 1993, 3–38.

15505. HIRSBRUNNER, ANNA. Which family? The gender of genre. SPELL (9) 1996, 41–51.

15506. HIRSCH, DAVID H. The deconstruction of literature: criticism after Auschwitz. (Bibl. 1993, 11163.) Rev. by Sanford Pinsker in GetR (5:3) 1992, 540–6.

15507. HITCHCOCK, PETER. Dialogics of the oppressed. (Bibl. 1993, 11165.) Rev. by Moira Ferguson in MFS (40:2) 1994, 444–6.

15508. HOF, RENATE. Engendering American studies; or, What are 'resisting readers' resisting? Amst (41:2) 1996, 195–205.

15509. Hogan, Patrick Colm.   Ethnocentrism and the very idea of literary theory. ColLit (23:1) 1996, 1–14.

15510. Hohendahl, Peter Uwe.   Reappraisals: shifting alignments in post-war critical theory. (Bibl. 1995, 14076.) Rev. by Martin Kreiswirth in MFS (40:1) 1994, 215–16.

15511. Hohne, Karen; Wussow, Helen (eds).   A dialogue of voices: feminist literary theory and Bakhtin. (Bibl. 1994, 11160.) Rev. by Penny van Toorn in CanL (149) 1996, 186.

15512. Hohnsträter, Dirk.   Homi K. Bhabhas Semiotik der Zwischenräume – eine überzeugende Konzeptualisierung interkultureller Konflikte? arcadia (31:1/2) 1996, 62–8.

15513. Hollington, Michael.   Richards and Empson in China: the recollections of Professor C. P. ('Possum') Fitzgerald. AUMLA (86) 1996, 81–92.

15514. Holub, Robert C.   Crossing borders: reception theory, poststructuralism, deconstruction. (Bibl. 1994, 11164.) Rev. by Christian Riegel in CanRCL (22:2) 1995, 365–8; by Gerd Gemünden in CL (48:1) 1996, 77–9.

15515. Horton, John.   Life, literature and ethical theory: Martha Nussbaum on the role of the literary imagination in ethical thought. In (pp. 70–97) **63**.

15516. Houghton, R. L.   Some remarks on MacKillop's life of F. R. Leavis. See **15157**.

15517. Howe, Susan.   The birth-mark: unsettling the wilderness in American literary history. See **8336**.

15518. Hyde, George M.   Climbing down Pisgah: F. R. Leavis 1895–1978. EEM (4:2) 1995, 16–18.

15519. Inglis, Fred.   Raymond Williams. (Bibl. 1995, 14087.) Rev. by Ruth Levitas in Utopian Studies (7:2) 1996, 271–2.

15520. Innes, Lyn.   Post-colonial. ERev (6:1) 1995, 6–7.

15521. Iser, Wolfgang.   On translatability: variables of interpretation. EEM (4:1) 1995, 30–8.

15522. Isernhagen, Hartwig.   Culture, fiction, literature: between the New Historicism and ethnocriticism. ZAA (41:2) 1993, 101–14.

15523. Izzo, Donatella (ed.).   Teoria della letteratura: prospettive dagli Stati Uniti. Rome: Nuova Italia Scientifica, 1996. pp. 184.

15524. Jackson, Leonard.   The dematerialisation of Karl Marx: literature and Marxist theory. (Bibl. 1995, 14091.) Rev. by Andrew R. Cooper in NQ (43:1) 1996, 119–21.

15525. Jagose, Annamarie.   Lesbian utopics. New York; London: Routledge, 1994. pp. 214. (Cf. bibl. 1993, 11182.) Rev. by Nicole Pohl in Utopian Studies (7:1) 1996, 123–4.

15526. Jahn, Manfred.   Windows of focalization: deconstructing and reconstructing a narratological concept. See **2404**.

15527. —— Nünning, Ansgar.   Narratology. EEM (2:2) 1993, 24–8.

15528. Jameson, Fredric.   The seeds of time. (Bibl. 1995, 14092.) Rev. by Tom Moylan in Utopian Studies (7:2) 1996, 230–2; by David Powelstock in Modernism/Modernity (3:1) 1996, 167–70; by Douglas Mao in ConLit (37:1) 1996, 155–75; by Geoffrey Galt Harpham in Salmagundi (111) 1996, 213–32.

15529. Jancovich, Mark.   The cultural politics of the New Criticism. (Bibl. 1993, 11184.) Rev. by John Lucas in YES (26) 1996, 337–8.

15530. —— Robert Penn Warren as New Critic: against propaganda and irresponsibility. SoLJ (24:1) 1991, 53–65.

15531. JANG, HERAN. New Historicism and Renaissance text. *See* **5576**.

15532. JAY, GREGORY. Recent fictions in theory: a reading of Jay Clayton's *Pleasures of Babel*. StudN (27:2) 1995, 197–211 (review-article).

15533. JAY, MARTIN. Modernism and the specter of psychologism. Modernism/Modernity (3:2) 1996, 93–111.

15534. JOHNSON, STEPHEN. 'Getting to' Canadian theatre history: on the tension between the new history and the nation state. *See* **9762**.

15535. JOLLY, ROSEMARY. Rehearsals of liberation: contemporary postcolonial discourse and the new South Africa. PMLA (110:1) 1995, 17–29.

15536. JONES, CHRISTOPHER N. Lessons from Hollywood: feminist film theory and the commercial theatre. *See* **13842**.

15537. JOYCE, JOYCE ANN. Warriors, conjurers and priests: defining African-centered literary criticism. Chicago: Third World, 1994. pp. 311. Rev. by Peter Nazareth in WLT (69:4) 1995, 802–3; by Madhu Dubey in AAR (30:3) 1996, 464–7.

15538. JOYNER, NANCY CAROL. Postprandial postmodernism. SAtlR (61:2) 1996, 1–7.

15539. KADAR, MARLENE. The discourse of ordinariness and 'multi-cultural history'. *See* **15161**.

15540. —— (ed.). Essays on life writing: from genre to critical practice. *See* **4194**.

15541. KADIR, DJELAL. The post of coloniality. CanRCL (22:3/4) 1995, 431–42.

15542. —— Postmodernism/postcolonialism: what are we after? WLT (69:1) 1995, 17–21.

15543. KAMINSKY, AMY. Issues for an international feminist literary criticism. Signs (19:1) 1993, 213–27.

15544. KANTAK, V. Y. In search of a valid response to literature. *See* **3885**.

15545. KAPLAN, CARLA. Reading feminist readings: recuperative reading and the silent heroine of feminist criticism. *In* (pp. 168–94) **59**.

15546. KAPLAN, CORA. Fictions of feminism: figuring the maternal. Feminist Studies (20:1) 1994, 153–67 (review-article).

15547. KAPLAN, E. ANN. Popular culture, politics, and the canon: cultural literacy in the postmodern age. *In* (pp. 12–31) **19**.

15548. KASTAN, DAVID SCOTT. Shakespeare after theory. *See* **6364**.

15549. KATZ, STEVEN B. The epistemic music of rhetoric: toward the temporal dimension of affect in reader-response and writing. *See* **2408**.

15550. KAUL, SUVIR. Colonial figures and postcolonial reading. *See* **2410**.

15551. KAZIN, ALFRED. Writing was everything. (Bibl. 1995, 14102.) Rev. by John L. Brown in WLT (70:2) 1996, 410–11; by Richard H. King in JAStud (30:2) 1996, 326–7.

15552. KEHDE, SUZANNE. Voices from the margin: bag ladies and others. *In* (pp. 25–38) **33**.

15553. KEITH, W. J. Portrait of the scholar as a young man. LRC (5:11) 1996, 18–19 (review-article). (Northrop Frye.)

15554. KELLERT, STEPHEN H. Science and literature and philosophy:

the case of chaos theory and deconstruction. Configurations (4:2) 1996, 215–32.

15555. KELLOGG, DAVID. 'Desire pronounced and/Punctuated': Lacan and the fate of the poetic subject. *See* **14969**.

15556. —— Perloff's Wittgenstein: w(h)ither poetic theory? *See* **4389**.

15557. KENNEDY, LIAM. Susan Sontag: mind as passion. (Bibl. 1995, 14107.) Rev. by Chantal Zabus in WLT (70:3) 1996, 698–9; by Joe Moran in JAStud (30:3) 1996, 475–6.

15558. KENT, THOMAS. Ethnocentrism in social-construction interpretation: a Davidsonian critique. SLI (28:2) 1995, 91–106.

15559. KERMODE, FRANK. Not entitled: a memoir. London: Harper Collins; New York: Farrar, Straus, & Giroux, 1996. pp. 263. Rev. by Michael Dirda in BkW, 26 Nov. 1995, 4–5; by Alan Ross in TLS, 7 June 1996, 29; by Bernard F. Dick in WLT (70:4) 1996, 970.

15560. KERNAN, ALVIN. Historical canons. CanRCL (20:1/2) 1993, 187–92.

15561. KEYSSAR, HELENE (ed.). Feminist theatre and theory. *See* **13863**.

15562. KIM, YOUNG HEE. Beyond dualism: the cases of Leavis and Eagleton. JELL (42:4) 1996, 923–39.

15563. KIM, YOUNG NAM. On the idea of the author in modern literary critical theories. JELLC (38:1) 1996, 175–94.

15564. KLENOTIC, JEFFREY F. The place of rhetoric in 'new' film historiography: the discourse of corrective revisionism. *See* **2413**.

15565. KNAPP, JOHN V. Striking at the joints: contemporary psychology and literary criticism. Lanham, MD; London: UP of America, 1996. pp. 302.

15566. KNEALE, J. DOUGLAS. Gentle hearts and hands: reading Wordsworth after Geoffrey Hartman. *See* **12871**.

15567. KNIGHT, CHRISTOPHER J. Defending poetry – again. *See* **4392**.

15568. KNUTSEN, KAREN PATRICK. Leaving Dr Leavis: a farewell to the Great Tradition? Margaret Drabble's *The Gates of Ivory*. EngS (77:6) 1996, 579–91.

15569. KOKOTAILO, PHILIP. Native *and* cosmopolitan: A. J. M. Smith's tradition of English-Canadian poetry. *See* **4393**.

15570. KOLODNY, ANNETTE. Rethinking frontier literary history as the stories of first cultural contact. Frontiers (17:3) 1996, 14–18.

15571. KOPELSON, KEVIN. Fake it like a man. *In* (pp. 259–67) **12**.

15572. KOSHY, SUSAN. The fiction of Asian-American literature. *See* **13160**.

15573. KOTTE, CLAUDIA. Post-colonialism or neo-imperialism? ZAA (43:3) 1995, 253–64.

15574. KRUPAT, ARNOLD (ed.). New voices in Native-American literary criticism. (Bibl. 1995, 14119.) Rev. by Robert Allen Warrior in WLT (69:1) 1995, 201–2.

15575. KUSCHEL, KARL-JOSEF. Presence of God? Towards the possibility of a theological aesthetic in an analysis of George Steiner. Trans. by Andrew Hass. LitTheol (10:1) 1996, 1–19.

15576. LADITKA, JAMES N. Language, power, and play: the dance of deconstruction and practical wisdom. RhR (15:1) 1996, 298–311.

15577. LAMARQUE, PETER. Fictional points of view. Ithaca, NY; London: Cornell UP, 1996. pp. xi, 224.

15578. LAMBROPOULOS, VASSILIS. The rise of Eurocentrism: anatomy of interpretation. (Bibl. 1995, 14124.) Rev. by Timothy J. Reiss in CanRCL (21:4) 1994, 695–703.

15579. LANDRY, DONNA. Commodity feminism. *In* (pp. 154–74) **91**.

15580. LANG, BERND-PETER. Gespaltene Modernität, verfehlte Moderne: Matthew Arnolds Kulturkritik. *See* **10199**.

15581. LANG, GEORGE. *No hay centro*: postmodernism and comparative New World criticism. CanRCL (20:1/2) 1993, 105–24 (review-article).

15582. LAUTERBACH, ANN. Misquotations from reality. *See* **4397**.

15583. LEBEAU, VICKY. Psychoanalysis. YWCCT (3) 1993, 51–69.

15584. LECERCLE, ANN. Reflections on the feminist approach to Shakespeare and Lacanian psychoanalysis. *See* **6386**.

15585. LECERCLE, JEAN-JACQUES. The current state of stylistics. *See* **2664**.

15586. —— Sentimentalism and feeling: D. H. Lawrence's *Piano* and I. A. Richards' reading of it. Études Lawrenciennes (10) 1994, 200–17.

15587. —— The 'turn' in literary studies: anthropology, or pragmatics, or both. YREAL (12) 1996, 1–15.

15588. LECHTE, JOHN (ed.). Writing and psychoanalysis: a reader. London; New York: Arnold, 1996. pp. viii, 213.

15589. LECKER, ROBERT. Canadian canons: essays in literary value. *See* **13**.

15590. LEE, ALVIN A.; DENHAM, ROBERT D. (eds). The legacy of Northrop Frye. (Bibl. 1995, 14133.) Rev. by Angela Esterhammer in ESCan (22:2) 1996, 238–40.

15591. LEHMAN, DAVID. The end of the word. GetR (4:1) 1991, 107–27.

15592. LEITCH, THOMAS M. What stories are: narrative theory and interpretation. (Bibl. 1992, 12223.) Rev. by Evelyn Cobley in CanRCL (18:1) 1991, 80–4.

15593. LEITCH, VINCENT B. Cultural criticism, literary theory, poststructuralism. (Bibl. 1995, 14137.) Rev. by Martin Donougho in Comparatist (18) 1994, 169–72.

15594. LEONARD, JERRY (ed.). Legal studies as cultural studies: a reader in (post)modern critical theory. Albany: New York State UP, 1995. pp. viii, 392. Rev. by Linda Myrsiades in ColLit (23:1) 1996, 204–16.

15595. LEVIN, RICHARD. The new and the old historicizing of Shakespeare. *See* **6390**.

15596. LINKIN, HARRIET KRAMER. Toward a theory of gendered reading. Reader (30) 1993, 1–25.

15597. LITTAU, KARIN. Deconstruction. YWCCT (3) 1993, 70–86.

15598. LITZ, A. WALTON. Florence Farr: a 'transitional' woman. *In* (pp. 85–106) **41**.

15599. LIU, ALAN. The New Historicism and the work of mourning. *See* **12875**.

15600. LONGLEY, EDNA. 'It is time that I wrote my will': anxieties of influence and succession. *See* **14984**.

15601. LORIGGIO, FRANCESCO. Comparative literature and the genres of interdisciplinarity. WLT (69:2) 1995, 256–62.

15602. LOYO GÓMEZ, HILARIA. Dietrich's androgyny and gendered spectatorship. *In* (pp. 317–32) **38**.

15603.   Lucy, Niall; McHoul, Alec.   The logical status of Searlean discourse. *See* **2277**.

15604.   Lukacher, Ned.   The third wound: Malcolm Bowie, Peter Brooks, and the myth of Actaeon. *See* **4207**.

15605.   Lusk, Linda V.   C. S. Lewis as a critic 'at the present time'. CSL (22:6/7) 1991, 1–9.

15606.   Lyne, William.   Tiger teeth around their neck: the cultural logic of the canonization of African-American literature. AQ (52:3) 1996, 99–125.

15607.   Lyons, Charles R.; Lyons, James C.   Anna Deavere Smith: perspectives on her performance within the context of critical theory. JDTC (9:1) 1994, 43–66.

15608.   Macaskill, Brian.   Figuring rupture: iconology, politics, and the image. *In* (pp. 249–71) **44**.

15609.   McCarthy, Dermot.   Early Canadian literary histories and the function of a canon. *In* (pp. 30–45) **13**.

15610.   McConachie, Bruce A.   New Historicism and American theater history: toward an interdisciplinary paradigm for scholarship. *In* (pp. 265–71) **83**.

15611.   McCoy, Richard C.   Poetry at court. *See* **5589**.

15612.   McCracken, Scott.   Postmodernism, a *Chance* to reread? *In* (pp. 267–89) **18**.

15613.   Macdonald, Michael J.   Reading material: the law of the letter in Paul de Man. CanRCL (18:4) 1991, 489–97.

15614.   McDonald, Peter.   Seamus Heaney as a critic. *In* (pp. 174–89) **86**.

15615.   McGowan, Kate.   Colonial discourse, postcolonial theory. YWCCT (3) 1993, 131–63.

15616.   Mackenthun, Gesa.   State of the art: adding empire to the study of American culture. JAStud (30:2) 1996, 263–9.

15617.   MacKenzie, Ian.   Relevance and writing. JLSem (24:2) 1995, 104–16.

15618.   MacKillop, Ian.   F. R. Leavis: a life in criticism. (Bibl. 1995, 14161.) Rev. by Michael Bell *et al.* in CamQ (25:2) 1996, 303–42; by R. L. Houghton in EngS (77:5) 1996, 445–53; by L. R. Leavis in EngS (77:5) 1996, 501–3.

15619.   Maclean, Marie.   Many hearts will understand me: Ross Chambers, Nerval, and rhizomatic criticism. CanRCL (22:2) 1995, 213–21.

15620.   McNelis, James I., iii.   The sword mightier than the pen? Hrothgar's hilt, theory, and philology. *In* (pp. 175–85) **114**.

15621.   MacPhee, Graham.   Value, tradition and the place of the present: the disputed canon in the United States. Angelaki (2:2) 1996, 65–73.

15622.   MacPike, Loralee.   Lesbian critical studies. NWSAJ (6:3) 1994, 484–8 (review-article).

15623.   Mailloux, Steven.   Persuasions good and bad: Bunyan, Iser, and Fish on rhetoric and hermeneutics in literature. *See* **2425**.

15624.   Makaryk, Irena R. (gen. ed.).   Encyclopedia of contemporary literary theory: approaches, scholars, terms. (Bibl. 1995, 14166.) Rev. by Malcolm Kelsall in CanRCL (22:2) 1995, 368–71.

15625.   Mao, Douglas.   Chill winds, cool breezes: Jameson in the nineties. ConLit (37:1) 1996, 155–75 (review-article).

15626. —— The New Critics and the text-object. ELH (63:1) 1996, 227–54.

15627. MARANTZ COHEN, PAULA. The daughter as reader: encounters between literature and life. Ann Arbor: Michigan UP, 1996. pp. 162.

15628. MARCUS, GEORGE E. On ideologies of reflexivity in contemporary efforts to remake the human sciences. PT (15:3) 1994, 383–404.

15629. MARGOLIN, URI. How to (de)construct a narrative world. CanRCL (21:3) 1994, 445–56 (review-article).

15630. MARIANI, GIORGIO (ed.). Poesia, pragmatismo e letteratura americana. Un'intervista con Richard Poirier. Àcoma (7) 1996, 85–9.

15631. MARTIN, GRAHAM. F. R. Leavis and the function of criticism. EC (46:1) 1996, 1–15.

15632. MARTINSSON, YVONNE. Eroticism, ethics and reading: Angela Carter in dialogue with Roland Barthes. Stockholm: Almqvist & Wiksell, 1996. pp. 140. (Stockholm studies in English, 86.)

15633. MATRIX, SIDNEY. Experiencing lesbian: theory, lesbian: writing, a personalist methodology. CritM (9:1) 1995, 67–78.

15634. MAYNARD, JOHN. Browning: living, hating, loving; or, Uneven developments: theory in the Browning boondocks. *See* **10527**.

15635. MEEK, MARGARET. The constructedness of critics. *See* **4313**.

15636. MELLAMPHY, DAN. YOU. Also entitled: 'The YOU-Bomb', or 'YOU-Bomb goes Kabloom': an essay on anonymity, risibility, and quantum subjectivity. CanRCL (23:2) 1996, 427–54.

15637. MEYERSON, GREGORY. Poststructuralism and the disintegration of dissent. Genre (23:4) 1990, 355–69 (review-article).

15638. MIKKONEN, KAI. Theories of metamorphosis: from metatrope to textual revision. *See* **2429**.

15639. MILLER, J. HILLIS. Derrida's Others. Skrift (8:1) 1996, 100–14.

15640. MILLS, SARA, *et al.* Feminism. YWCCT (3) 1993, 87–130.

15641. MILLS, SARA; PEARCE, LYNNE. Feminist readings/feminists reading. *See* **4222**.

15642. MITCHELL, ANGELYN (ed.). Within the circle: an anthology of African-American literary criticism from the Harlem renaissance to the present. (Bibl. 1994, 11237.) Rev. by Peter Powers in TexR (17:1/2) 1996, 122–5.

15643. MITCHELL, W. J. T. Picture theory: essays on verbal and visual representation. (Bibl. 1995, 14182.) Rev. by Jean Klucinskas in Études littéraires (28:3) 1996, 135–9.

15644. —— Why comparisons are odious. WLT (70:2) 1996, 321–4.

15645. MOGLEN, HELENE. (Un)gendering the subject: towards a feminist theory of the novel. *See* **4224**.

15646. MOHANTY, SATYA P. Colonial legacies, multicultural futures: relativism, objectivity, and the challenge of otherness. PMLA (110:1) 1995, 108–18.

15647. MONGIA, PADMINI (ed.). Contemporary postcolonial theory: a reader. London; New York: Arnold, 1996. pp. viii, 407.

15648. MONNICKENDAM, ANDREW. Lost causes: national identity and postmodernism. *See* **12176**.

15649. MONROE, JONATHAN. Syntextural investigations. Diacritics (26:3/4) 1996, 126–41.

15650. MOORE, CINDY. From new visions of self to re-visions of world: the revolutionary potential of Rachel Blau DuPlessis's *For the Etruscans.* RWT (4:1) 1996, 85–104.

15651. MOORE, DAVID CHIONI.   Anthropology is dead, long live anthropology: poststructuralism, literary studies, and anthropology's 'nervous present'. JAR (50:4) 1994, 345–65.

15652. MOORE-GILBERT, BART.   'The Bhabhal of tongues': reading Kipling, reading Bhabha. *In* (pp. 111–38) **132**.

15653. MOORE-GILBERT, BART.   Introduction: writing India, re-orienting colonial discourse analysis. *In* (pp. 1–29) **132**.

15654. MORAN, SHANE.   Self-canonizing critics: T. S. Eliot and J. M. Coetzee. JLS (10:3/4) 1995, 373–99.

15655. MORAWETZ, THOMAS.   Empathy and judgment. YJLH (8:2) 1996, 517–31 (review-article).

15656. MORGAN, W. JOHN; PRESTON, PETER (eds).   Raymond Williams: education, politics, and letters. (Bibl. 1995, 14189.) Rev. by Patrick Parrinder in YES (25) 1995, 339–40.

15657. MORRIS, DAVID B.   Samuel H. Monk and a scholar's life: humanism as praxis. *In* (pp. 175–99) **91**.

15658. MORRIS, PAM.   Literature and feminism: an introduction. (Bibl. 1994, 11239.) Rev. by Heather Kerr in AUMLA (85) 1996, 114–16.

15659. MORRISON, PAUL.   The poetics of Fascism: Ezra Pound, T. S. Eliot, Paul de Man. Oxford; New York: OUP, 1996. pp. 177.

15660. MORTON, DONALD.   Birth of the cyberqueer. *See* **14007**.

15661. MOSCOVICI, CLAUDIA.   Erotisms. Lanham, MD; London: UP of America, 1996. pp. xii, 137.

15662. MUCCI, CLARA.   The blank page as a Lacanian 'object a': silence, women's words, desire, and interpretation between literature and psychoanalysis. LitPs (38:4) 1992, 23–35.

15663. MULLALY, EDWARD.   W(h)ither the performance? *See* **14012**.

15664. MUNT, SALLY (ed.).   New lesbian criticism: literary and cultural readings. (Bibl. 1994, 11243.) Rev. by Loralee MacPike in NWSAJ (6:3) 1994, 484–8.

15665. MURPHY, PATRICK D.   Literature, nature, and other: eco-feminist critiques. (Bibl. 1995, 14195.) Rev. by Vera Norwood in WS (25:5) 1996, 541–3.

15666. MYRSIADES, LINDA.   Interdisciplinarity, law, language, and literature: a review essay. *See* **3938**.

15667. NA'ALLAH, ABOUL-RASHEED.   African literatures and post-colonialism: projections into the twenty-first century. CanRCL (22:3/4) 1995, 569–85.

15668. NARDOCCHIO, ELAINE F. (ed.).   Reader response to literature: the empirical dimension. (Bibl. 1993, 11260.) Rev. by Alison Tate in LangL (4:1) 1995, 72–4.

15669. NASH, SUSAN SMITH.   Death, decadence, and the ironies of language poetics. *See* **15005**.

15670. NATOLI, JOSEPH.   Meditating on a postmodern strategy of reading. *See* **9922**.

15671. NEFF VAN AERTSELAER, JOANNE.   Fear, desire and masculinity. *In* (pp. 73–87) **38**.

15672. NEUBAUER, JOHN.   Bakhtin *versus* Lukács: inscriptions of home-lessness in theories of the novel. PT (17:4) 1996, 531–46.

15673. NEWLYN, LUCY.   'Reading after': the anxiety of the writing subject. *See* **10045**.

15674. NEWTON, K. M. Literary theory and the Rushdie affair. Eng (41:171) 1992, 235–47.

15675. —— (ed.). Twentieth-century literary theory: a reader. (Bibl. 1989, 8826.) Rev. by James R. Bennett in CanRCL (18:1) 1991, 77–80.

15676. NIELSEN, ALDON LYNN. Black deconstruction: Russell Atkins and the reconstruction of African-American criticism. Diacritics (26:3/4) 1996, 86–103.

15677. NIERAGDEN, GÖRAN. '*Who sees when I speak?*': Neuvorschläge zur Relation von homodiegetischer Erzählung und Fokalisierung mit einer Beispielanalyse von Ian McEwans *The Child in Time*. LWU (29:3) 1996, 207–23.

15678. —— (comp.). Post-Genettian work on focalization. EEM (5:2) 1996, 49–50.

15679. NOONAN, JAMES. The making (and breaking) of a regional theatre critic: Audrey Ashley at the *Ottawa Citizen* 1961–1985. *See* **1331**.

15680. NORDQUIST, JOAN. Feminism and postmodern theory: a bibliography. Santa Cruz, CA: Reference and Research Services, 1996. pp. 60. (Social theory: a bibliographical series, 41.)

15681. NORTON, JANICE. Rhetorical criticism as ethical action: *cherchez la femme*. *See* **2436**.

15682. NOTO, JOHN. Response to the post-moderns (and the post-punkers!): a new synthesis offers April rain descending musical staffs in split-screen language televised as hands to bleed endlessly divisible orchids. *See* **15009**.

15683. NÜNNING, ANSGAR. *Gender and narratology*: Kategorien und Perspektiven einer feministischen Narrativik. ZAA (42:2) 1994, 102–21.

15684. NÜNNING, VERA; NÜNNING, ANSGAR. From thematics and formalism to aesthetics and history: phases and trends of Virginia Woolf criticism in Germany, 1946–1996. SoCR (29:1) 1996, 90–108.

15685. OCHOA, PEGGY. The historical moments of postcolonial writing: beyond colonialism's binary. TSWL (15:2) 1996, 221–9.

15686. OGEDE, ODE S. Problems of methodology and interpretation in the field of comparative African literatures. RAL (27:4) 1996, 198–204 (review-article).

15687. O'LEARY, STEPHEN D.; WRIGHT, MARK H. Psychoanalysis and Burkeian rhetorical criticism. *See* **2437**.

15688. OWENS, LOUIS. 'The song is very short': Native-American literature and literary theory. *See* **13255**.

15689. PAGE, ADRIAN. Semiotics. YWCCT (3) 1993, 19–27.

15690. PARKER, ANDREW. Praxis and performativity. *See* **14066**.

15691. PATTERSON, DAVID. The religious aspect of Bakhtin's aesthetics. Ren (46:1) 1993, 55–70.

15692. PAUL, MARY. Reading readings: some current critical debates about New Zealand literature and culture. Unpub. doct. diss., Univ. of Auckland, 1996.

15693. PEARCE, HOWARD. The play of the critic. JFA (6:4) 1993, 371–5.

15694. PENAS IBÁÑEZ, BEATRIZ. Kristeva's *Desire in Language*: a feminist semiotic perspective on language and literature. *In* (pp. 95–105) **38**.

15695. PERELMAN, BOB. Poetry in theory. *See* **4414**.

15696. PERKINS, DAVID. The *Ancient Mariner* and its interpreters: some versions of Coleridge. *See* **10695**.

15697. PERLOFF, MARJORIE.   Modernism without the Modernists: a response to Walter Benn Michaels. Modernism/Modernity (3:3) 1996, 99–105 (review-article).

15698. PETERS, HELEN.   Towards Canadian postmodernism. *See* **14079**.

15699. PFANDL-BUCHEGGER, INGRID.   David Lodge als Literaturkritiker, Theoretiker und Romanautor. (Bibl. 1993, 11295.) Rev. by Maria Zettner in AAA (21:1) 1996, 149–52.

15700. PLATE, LIEDEKE.   From reading 'against' to reading 'with': feminism and the subject of reading. Reader (30) 1993, 27–47.

15701. POLLACK, FREDERICK.   To the unknown reader. Salmagundi (88/89) 1990/91, 486–509 (review-article).

15702. PORTER, LAURENCE M.   *Larvatus prodeo*: the concept of desire in the literary criticism of Ross Chambers. CanRCL (22:2) 1995, 255–66.

15703. POSTER, MARK.   The mode of information: poststructuralism and social context. (Bibl. 1992, 12310.) Rev. by Robert Anchor in AHR (98:3) 1993, 829–30.

15704. PRICE HERNDL, DIANE.   The dilemmas of a feminine dialogic. *In* (pp. 7–24) **33**.

15705. PUGLIESE, JOSEPH.   Literary histories and the ontologies of nation. CanRCL (22:3/4) 1995, 467–86.

15706. PURDIE, SUSAN.   Film studies. *See* **14103**.

15707. RAIN, D. C.   Deconstructing Richardson: Terry Castle and *Clarissa's Ciphers*. *See* **9307**.

15708. RAITT, SUZANNE (ed.).   Volcanoes and pearl divers: essays in lesbian feminist studies. Binghamton, NY: Harrington Park Press; London: Onlywomen, 1995. pp. xvii, 292.

15709. RAJAN, TILOTTAMA; CLARK, DAVID L. (eds).   Intersections: nineteenth-century philosophy and contemporary theory. (Bibl. 1995, 14232.) Rev. by Marc Redfield in ERR (7:1) 1996, 110–14.

15710. RATCLIFFE, KRISTA.   Anglo-American feminist challenges to the rhetorical traditions: Virginia Woolf, Mary Daly, Adrienne Rich. Carbondale: Southern Illinois UP, 1996. pp. xiii, 227.

15711. RAUCH, IRMENGARD.   Deconstruction, prototype theory, and semiotics. *See* **2231**.

15712. RAYAN, KRISHNA.   Resistance in reading. *See* **9159**.

15713. REYNOLDS, CLAY.   Reviewers reviewed. PCR (4:1) 1993, 5–13.

15714. REYNOLDS, DAVID S.   The aesthetic factor in canon revision: the case of American literature. CanRCL (20:1/2) 1993, 193–200.

15715. RICCIO, BARRY D.   New York intellectual: the case of Irving Howe. JAC (19:3) 1996, 75–85.

15716. RICE, PHILIP; WAUGH, PATRICIA (eds).   Modern literary theory: a reader. (Bibl. 1995, 14235.) London; New York: Arnold, 1996. pp. x, 385. (Third ed.: first ed. 1989.)

15717. RICHETTI, JOHN.   The legacy of Ian Watt's *The Rise of the Novel*. *In* (pp. 95–112) **91**.

15718. RICHMOND, E. M.   Annotated bibliography of narrative theory and Renaissance drama. *See* **4248**.

15719. RICHMOND-GARZA, ELIZABETH M.   Twilight of the idols: poststructuralisms and the renaissance in English studies in the 1990s. CanRCL (20:1/2) 1993, 63–78.

15720. ROBBINS, BRUCE.   Less disciplinary than thou: criticism and the conflict of the faculties. MinnR (45/46) 1995/96, 95–115.

15721. ROBERTSON, DALLAS VAUGHAN.　Colin Wilson: his existential literary criticism and his novels. Unpub. doct. diss., Univ. of Auckland, 1995.

15722. ROBERTSON, ELIZABETH A.　Historicizing literacy: new directions in Anglo-Saxon criticism. *See* **4652**.

15723. ROBYNS, CLEM.　Translation and discursive identity. *See* **3192**.

15724. RODDEN, JOHN.　The opposing selves of Lionel Trilling. ModAge (38:2) 1996, 164–74.

15725. ROHR, SUSANNE.　Mimesis of the mind: literature in the context of Charles S. Peirce's semiotic epistemology. YREAL (12) 1996, 97–113.

15726. ROOCHNIK, DAVID.　Stanley Fish and the old quarrel between rhetoric and philosophy. *See* **2458**.

15727. ROSE, ELLEN CRONAN.　American feminist criticism of contemporary women's fiction. *See* **14694**.

15728. ROSELLO, MIREILLE.　The infiltrator who came in from the inside: making room in closed systems. CanRCL (22:2) 1995, 241–54.

15729. ROTH, MARTY.　Homosexual expression and homophobic censorship: the situation of the text. *In* (pp. 268–81) **12**.

15730. ROWLEY, ROBERT.　Joseph Wood Krutch: the forgotten voice of the desert. ASch (64:3) 1995, 438–43.

15731. RUDDICK, LISA.　Stein and cultural criticism in the nineties. MFS (42:3) 1996, 647–59 (review-article).

15732. RUNNING-JOHNSON, CYNTHIA.　Examining critical history through theater: feminist scholarship of the 1980s and beyond. *See* **14162**.

15733. RUPPERT, JAMES.　Theory, discourse, and the Native American literature class. *See* **13289**.

15734. RUTHVEN, K. K.　Ezra Pound as literary critic. (Bibl. 1994, 11296.) Rev. by Brendan Jackson in Eng (41:169) 1992, 87–93.

15735. RUTLAND, BARRY (ed.).　Genre, trope, gender: critical essays by Northrop Frye, Linda Hutcheon, Shirley Neuman. (Bibl. 1995, 14245.) Rev. by Andrew Heintzman in ECanW (55) 1995, 83–90.

15736. RYAN, KIERNAN (ed.).　New Historicism and cultural materialism: a reader. London; New York: Arnold, 1996. pp. xviii, 214. Rev. by Rick Waswo in EEM (5:2) 1996, 51–4.

15737. SABIN, MARGERY.　'The debate': seductions and betrayals in literary studies. Raritan (13:3) 1994, 123–46 (review-article).

15738. SADLEK, GREGORY M.　Bakhtin, the novel, and Chaucer's *Troilus and Criseyde*. *See* **4258**.

15739. SALTER, DENIS.　On native ground: Canadian theatre historiography and the postmodernism/postcolonialism axis. *See* **14169**.

15740. SALTZ, DAVID Z.　Texts in action/action in texts: a case study in critical method. *See* **6456**.

15741. SAMUELS, WILFRED D.　Soothsayer and interpreter: Darwin T. Turner and African-American literary criticism. LHR (11:2) 1992, 15–27.

15742. SAN JUAN, E., JR.　Beyond postcolonial theory: the mass line in C. L. R. James's imagination. JCL (31:1) 1996, 25–44.

15743. SANDBACH-DAHLSTROM, CATHERINE.　Virginia Woolf with and without state feminism. SoCR (29:1) 1996, 78–89.

15744. SARCHETT, BARRY W.　The joke(r) is on us: the end of popular culture studies. AQ (52:3) 1996, 71–97.

15745. Sartiliot, Claudette.   Citation and modernity: Derrida, Joyce, and Brecht. (Bibl. 1993, 11315.) Rev. by Jean-Michel Rabaté in MFS (40:2) 1994, 456–8.

15746. Scherr, Barry J.   Eagleton's flight from Lawrence and Leavis. RecL (22) 1995, 35–56.

15747. Schleifer, Ronald.   Writhing nets and goodly pearls: *The Postmodern Bible*, temporal collaboration, and storytelling. *See* **14712**.

15748. Schmidgen, Wolfram.   The principle of negative identity and the crisis of relationality in contemporary literary criticism. YREAL (11) 1995, 371–404.

15749. Schmidt, Siegfried J.   The logic of observation: an introduction to constructivism. CanRCL (19:3) 1992, 295–311.

15750. Schneidau, Herbert N.   On being the right age for theory: notes of a fellow traveler. AQ (50:1) 1994, 3–24.

15751. Schroeder, Patricia R.   American drama, feminist discourse, and dramatic form: in defense of critical pluralism. *See* **14187**.

15752. Schultz, Susan M.   'Returning to Bloom': John Ashbery's critique of Harold Bloom. ConLit (37:1) 1996, 24–48.

15753. Schwab, Gabriele.   Literary transference and the vicissitudes of culture. YREAL (12) 1996, 115–41.

15754. Schwartz, Leonard.   A flicker at the edge of things: some thoughts on lyric poetry. *See* **15037**.

15755. Scott, Nathan A., Jr; Sharp, Ronald A. (eds).   Reading George Steiner. (Bibl. 1995, 14256.) Rev. by Tony Stoneburner in CC (46:2) 1996, 269–71; by Tracy E. Martin in LitTheol (10:3) 1996, 292–4.

15756. Scott, Steven.   Playing the games we read and reading the games we play. CanRCL (23:2) 1996, 374–92 (review-article).

15757. Seaton, James.   Cultural conservatism, political liberalism: from criticism to cultural studies. Ann Arbor: Michigan UP, 1996. pp. viii, 287.

15758. Seeber, Hans Ulrich.   Literaturwissenschaft und/oder Kulturwissenschaft: Vorwort. Ang (114:3) 1996, 307–9.

15759. Segall, Jeffrey.   '*Kulturbolschewismus* is here': James Joyce and the anti-Modernist crusade in America, 1928–1944. JML (16:4) 1990, 535–62.

15760. Sellers, Susan (ed.).   Feminist criticism: theory and practice. (Bibl. 1991, 44.) Rev. by Hannah Möckel-Rieke in Signs (19:2) 1994, 519–23.

15761. Selzer, Jack.   Kenneth Burke among the moderns: *Counter-Statement* as counter statement. RSQ (26:2) 1996, 19–49.

15762. Sensibar, Judith L.; Wittenberg, Judith Bryant.   Silences in the in-between: feminist women critics and the canon. *In* (pp. 274–86) **59**.

15763. Sheff, David.   Camille Paglia. Playboy (Chicago) (42:5) 1995, 51–3, 55–8, 60–4. (Interview.)

15764. Shillingsburg, Peter L.   Text as matter, concept, and action. *See* **835**.

15765. Siebers, Tobin.   Cold War criticism and the politics of skepticism. (Bibl. 1995, 14262.) Rev. by Barbara Foley in MFS (40:2) 1994, 446–7; by Theron Britt in ColLit (23:2) 1996, 171–6.

15766. —— The ethics of criticism. (Bibl. 1992, 12356.) Rev. by Thomas Joswick in Genre (23:1) 1990, 67–70.

15767. SIELKE, SABINE. Seduced and enslaved: sexual violence in antebellum American literature and contemporary feminist discourse. *See* **9057**.

15768. SILVERMAN, HUGH J. Textualities: between hermeneutics and deconstruction. (Bibl. 1994, 11320.) Rev. by Florin Berindeanu in Comparatist (20) 1996, 196–8.

15769. SIM, STUART. Critical theory: general. YWCCT (3) 1993, 1–18.

15770. SIMPSON, DAVID. The academic postmodern and the role of literature: a report on half-knowledge. Chicago; London: Chicago UP, 1995. pp. xi, 199. Rev. by R. E. Foust in NOR (22:2) 1996, 104–5.

15771. SINGH, G. F. R. Leavis: a literary biography. With Q. D. Leavis' *Memoir*. London: Duckworth, 1995. pp. viii, 300, (plates) 8. Rev. by D. J. Taylor in TLS, 22 Mar. 1996, 14.

15772. SINGH, JYOTSNA. The influence of feminist criticism/theory on Shakespeare studies 1976–1986. *In* (pp. 381–93) **98**.

15773. SLINGERLAND, EDWARD; STATES, BERT O. Notes on the post-structural code. ASch (63:4) 1994, 631–2.

15774. SOLLORS, WERNER (ed.). The return of thematic criticism. (Bibl. 1994, 11329.) Rev. by Roger Seamon in CanL (151) 1996, 193–5.

15775. SPARGO, TAMSIN. Queer theories/cultures. YWCCT (3) 1993, 201–32.

15776. SPIVAK, GAYATRI CHAKRAVORTY. The postcolonial critic: interviews, strategies, dialogues. Ed. by Sarah Harasym. (Bibl. 1993, 11339.) Rev. by Mrinalini Sinha in Signs (17:2) 1992, 472–7.

15777. SPURLIN, WILLIAM J.; FISCHER, MICHAEL (eds). The New Criticism and contemporary literary theory: connections and continuities. New York; London: Garland, 1995. pp. xxix, 432. (Garland reference library of the humanities, 1780.) (Wellesley studies in critical theory, literary history, and culture, 9.) Rev. by Sarah Lawall in ELT (39:1) 1996, 98–102.

15778. STATES, BERT O. Notes on the poststructural code. ASch (63:1) 1994, 111–16.

15779. STEVENS, PAUL. The political ways of paradox: Renaissance literature and modern criticism. *See* **5604**.

15780. STIRLING, GRANT. Re-reading the function of language variance in post-colonial literary theory. CanRCL (22:3/4) 1995, 411–29.

15781. STOKES, ADRIAN. Theories of reading and reception. YWCCT (3) 1993, 190–200.

15782. STOLTZFUS, BEN. Lacan and literature: purloined pretexts. Albany: New York State UP, 1996. pp. xiii, 227. (SUNY series in psychoanalysis and culture.)

15783. STONUM, GARY LEE. Themes, topics, criticism. *See* **4020**.

15784. STRAUB, KRISTINA. Feminist politics and postmodernist style. *In* (pp. 274–86) **44**.

15785. STREETER, ROBERT E. Mr Outside gets the ball. Review (16) 1994, 145–52 (review-article).

15786. STURROCK, JOHN. Reading de Man. Salmagundi (88/89) 1990/91, 470–8 (review-article).

15787. SUGG, RICHARD P. (ed.). Jungian literary criticism. (Bibl. 1992, 12380.) Rev. by Chris Bullock in CanRCL (21:3) 1994, 512–15.

15788. SULLIVAN, DALE L. The epideictic character of rhetorical criticism. *See* **2481**.

15789. Surette, Leon.   Literary gamesters and critical kibitzers. CanRCL (23:2) 1996, 307–22.

15790. —— The perils of applying McLuhan. LRC (5:9) 1996, 25–6 (review-article).

15791. Sutrop, Margit.   The anthropological turn in the theory of fiction – Wolfgang Iser and Kendall Walton. YREAL (12) 1996, 81–95.

15792. Swann, Charles (ed.).   Collected essays of John Goode. Introd. by Terry Eagleton. Keele: Keele UP, 1995. pp. xvi, 491. Rev. by Pierre Coustillas in GissJ (32:4) 1996, 29–31.

15793. Swingle, L. J.   Dismantling the master's house. *See* **9957**.

15794. Swirski, Peter.   Iser's theory of aesthetic response: a brief critique. Reader (32) 1994, 1–15.

15795. Tallis, Raymond.   Newton's sleep: 2, The eunuch at the orgy. PN Review (17:4) 1991, 48–51.

15796. Taneja, G. R.   Leavis, poetry and critical practice. *See* **4436**.

15797. Tejera, Victorino.   Eco, Peirce, and interpretationism. AJSem (8:1/2) 1991, 149–68.

15798. Teres, Harvey.   Remaking Marxist criticism: *Partisan Review*'s Eliotic Leftism, 1934–1936. *In* (pp. 65–84) **41**.

15799. Todorov, Tzvetan.   Dialogism and schizophrenia. Trans. by Michael B. Smith. *In* (pp. 203–14) **80**.

15800. Tokizane, Sanae.   The politics of authorship. Tokyo: Liber Shuppan, 1996. pp. 240.

15801. Tomiyama, Takao (ed.).   Bungaku no kyoukaisen. (The borderline of literature.) Tokyo: Kenkyusha Shuppan, 1996. pp. vii, 270. (Gendai hihyou no *practice*, 4.) (The practice of modern criticism, 4.)

15802. Toomey, Deirdre.   Moran's collar: Yeats and Irish Ireland. Yeats Annual (12) 1996, 45–83.

15803. Tötösy de Zepetnek, Steven.   Readership research, cultural studies, and Canadian scholarship. Reader (35/36) 1996, 108–20.

15804. —— Systemic approaches to literature: an introduction with selected bibliographies. CanRCL (19:1/2) 1992, 21–93.

15805. —— Gunew, Sneja.   Postcolonial literatures: a selected bibliography of theory and criticism. *See* **13339**.

15806. Tratner, Michael.   The function of literature in the age of the masses. StudN (28:2) 1996, 244–53 (review-article).

15807. Tredell, Nicolas.   Bernard Bergonzi in conversation. PN Review (17:5) 1991, 29–35.

15808. —— George Steiner in conversation. PN Review (17:4) 1991, 24–31.

15809. —— Robert Hewison in conversation. PN Review (18:2) 1991, 48–53.

15810. —— Terry Eagleton in conversation. PN Review (17:6) 1991, 38–45.

15811. Trigilio, Tony.   Staring back in the classroom: genre, identity, and the power in looking. MLS (26:4) 1996, 99–107.

15812. Trilling, Diana.   The beginning of the journey: the marriage of Diana and Lionel Trilling. (Bibl. 1995, 14301.) Rev. by Sven Birkerts in BkW, 28 Nov. 1996, 11.

15813. Tschofen, Monique Y.   Post-colonial allegory and the empire of rape. CanRCL (22:3/4) 1995, 501–15.

15814. TUDEAU, MARGARET; BERRY, PHILIPPA. Knowledge of/ knowledges in the Renaissance: blindspots in recent re-visions of English Renaissance culture. *See* **5608**.

15815. TuSMITH, BONNIE. Opening up theory. MLS (26:4) 1996, 59–70.

15816. VEESER, H. ARAM (ed.). The New Historicism reader. (Bibl. 1995, 14310.) Rev. by Gustavo Guerra in Style (30:1) 1996, 167–74.

15817. VON HALLBERG, ROBERT. Literature and history: neat fits. Modernism/Modernity (3:3) 1996, 115–20 (review-article).

15818. WARE, TRACY. The contexts of Canadian criticism revisited. ARCS (20:4) 1990, 503–10 (review-article).

15819. WARING, WENDY. Publishers, fiction, and feminism: riding the 'second wave'. *See* **1089**.

15820. WATERS, LINDSAY (ed.). Critical writings, 1953–1978. By Paul de Man. (Bibl. 1992, 12414.) Rev. by John Sturrock in Salmagundi (88/89) 1990/91, 470–8.

15821. —— GODZICH, WLAD (eds). Reading de Man reading. (Bibl. 1995, 14317.) Rev. by John Sturrock in Salmagundi (88/89) 1990/91, 470–8.

15822. WEIR, LORRAINE. Normalizing the subject: Linda Hutcheon and the English-Canadian postmodern. *In* (pp. 180–95) **13**.

15823. WELSCH, JANICE. Canon (re)formation: a feminist perspective. *In* (pp. 32–49) **19**.

15824. WEST, WILLIAM N. Nothing as given: economies of the gift in Derrida and Shakespeare. *See* **7199**.

15825. WIHL, GARY. The contingency of theory: pragmatism, expressivism, and deconstruction. (Bibl. 1995, 14329.) Rev. by Robert Alexander in Criticism (38:1) 1996, 171–3.

15826. WILLIAMS, DAVID R. Critics in the wilderness: literary theory and the spiritual roots of the American wilderness tradition. *See* **4052**.

15827. WILSON, SCOTT. Historicism. YWCCT (3) 1993, 164–89.

15828. WINDERS, JAMES A. Gender, theory, and the canon. (Bibl. 1993, 11379.) Rev. by Hannah Möckel-Rieke in Signs (19:2) 1994, 519–23.

15829. WINTEROWD, W. ROSS. I. A. Richards, literary theory, and Romantic composition. *See* **2496**.

15830. WOLIN, RICHARD. The terms of cultural criticism: the Frankfurt School, existentialism, poststructuralism. (Bibl. 1995, 14336.) Rev. by John E. Toews in AHR (98:4) 1993, 1207–8.

15831. WORTHAM, SIMON. *The glasse of majesty*: reflections on New Historicism and cultural materialism. *See* **7774**.

15832. WORTON, MICHAEL. (Re)writing gay identity: fiction as theory. *See* **14778**.

15833. WYNTER, SYLVIA. Afterword: *Beyond Miranda's Meanings: Un/Silencing the 'Demonic Ground' of Caliban's 'Woman'*. *In* (pp. 355–72) **81**.

15834. XU, WENYING. Making use of European theory in the teaching of multicultural literatures. MLS (26:4) 1996, 47–58.

15835. YELVERTON, VICTOR. The dragon in the fog: play and artworlds. CanRCL (23:2) 1996, 341–71.

15836. YOUNG, ROBERT J. C. The dialectics of cultural criticism. Angelaki (2:2) 1996, 9–24.

15837. —— Torn halves: political conflict in literary and cultural theory. Manchester; New York: Manchester UP, 1996. pp. 244. Rev. by R. E. Foust in NOR (22:3/4) 1996, 186–8.

15838. YOUNGQUIST, PAUL.   Romanticism, criticism, organicity. *See* **9727**.

15839. YOUNIS, RAYMOND AARON.   Apropos the last 'post-': contemporary literature, theory and interpretation. LitTheol (10:3) 1996, 280–9.

15840. ZARETSKY, ELI.   Psychoanalysis and postmodernism. AmLH (8:1) 1996, 154–69.

15841. ZIMMERMANN, PATRICIA R.   Midwives, hostesses, and feminist film. *See* **14353**.

15842. ZONGO, OPPORTUNE.   Rethinking African literary criticism: Obioma Nnaemeka. RAL (27:2) 1996, 178–84.

AUTHORS

Edward Abbey

15843. BERGER, YVES.   The burial of Edward Abbey. Trans. and introd. by Gregory McNamee. Journal of the Southwest (35:3) 1993, 357–62.

15844. BERRY, WENDELL.   A few words in favor of Edward Abbey. *In* (pp. 19–28) **25**.

15845. FLYNN, JOHN F.   Edward Abbey on nature and moral enquiry. WebS (11:1) 1994, 69–75.

15846. HEPWORTH, JAMES R.; MCNAMEE, GREGORY (eds).   Resist much, obey little: remembering Ed Abbey. San Francisco, CA: Sierra Club, 1996. pp. xiii, 254.

15847. JIMERSON, KAY.   Edward Abbey. *In* (pp. 52–7) **121**.

15848. METTING, FRED.   Edward Abbey's unique road. SDR (34:1) 1996, 85–102.

15849. WAKOSKI, DIANE.   Edward Abbey: joining the visionary 'inhumanists'. *In* (pp. 29–36) **25**.

Peter Abrahams

15850. GREEN, MICHAEL.   History, nation, and form in Peter Abrahams's *Wild Conquest*. RAL (27:2) 1996, 1–16.

15851. LINDFORS, BERNTH.   Future returns. *In* (pp. 153–62) **102**.

Chinua Achebe

15852. FINCHAM, GAIL; HOOPER, MYRTLE (eds).   Under postcolonial eyes: Joseph Conrad after empire. Cape Town: UCT Press, 1996. pp. xxx, 216.

15853. HOCHBRUCK, WOLFGANG.   'I have spoken': fictional 'orality' in indigenous fiction. ColLit (23:2) 1996, 132–42.

15854. LESK, ANDREW.   Achebe and his critics: racism in *Heart of Darkness*. In-between (3:2) 1994, 101–10.

15855. MACKENZIE, CLAYTON G.   The metamorphosis of piety in Chinua Achebe's *Things Fall Apart*. RAL (27:2) 1996, 128–38.

15856. MOSS, LAURA.   Perceptual differences: Ngũgĩ wa Thiong'o and Chinua Achebe. In-between (2:1) 1993, 29–35.

15857. OGEDE, ODE S. Achebe and Armah: a unity of shaping visions. RAL (27:2) 1996, 112–27.

15858. OMOTOSO, KOLE. Achebe or Soyinka? A study in contrasts. London; New York: Zell, 1996. pp. xxi, 188. (New perspectives on African literature, 3.)

15859. ROSS, HESTER F. Rewriting the other: dynamic entrenchment in the colonial narrative and its reappropriation in two works by Conrad and Achebe. UES (33:2) 1995, 44–50.

15860. SPITTLES, BRIAN. Chinua Achebe's *Things Fall Apart* reconsidered. ERev (6:1) 1995, 2–5.

15861. STEWART, FRANK. A language of the people: an analysis of the use of proverbs and language in Chinua Achebe's novels. *See* **2714**.

15862. TEN KORTENAAR, NEIL. Beyond authenticity and creolization: reading Achebe writing culture. PMLA (110:1) 1995, 30–42.

15863. UDUMUKWU, ONYEMAECHI. Ideology and the dialectics of action: Achebe and Iyayi. RAL (27:3) 1996, 34–49.

15864. WILKINSON, CLAUDE H. Loaded dice: the second self in Chinua Achebe's *Chike's School Days*. NCL (26:4) 1996, 10–12.

Kathy Acker

15865. GARRETT, SHAWN-MARIE. Treasure out of treasure: Kathy Acker. Theater (26:1/2) 1995, 170–3. (Interview.)

15866. KING, NOEL. Kathy Acker on the loose. Meanjin (55:2) 1996, 334–9.

15867. LATHAM, ROB. Collage as critique and invention in the fiction of William S. Burroughs and Kathy Acker. JFA (5:3) 1992, 46–57.

15868. LATHAM, ROBERT A. Collage as critique and invention in the fiction of William S. Burroughs and Kathy Acker. *In* (pp. 29–37) **70**.

15869. SCHECTER, MARTIN. Beyond the text: s(h)ifting through postmodernism. AJSem (8:4) 1991, 173–86.

J. R. Ackerley

15870. GRAY, PIERS. Marginal men: Edward Thomas, Ivor Gurney, J. R. Ackerley. (Bibl. 1991, 11882.) Rev. by Martin Taylor in Eng (41:171) 1992, 277–83.

Peter Ackroyd

15871. ONEGA, SUSANA. Interview with Peter Ackroyd. TCL (42:2) 1996, 208–20.

15872. SERRATORE, MONICA. Barocco della rivoluzione: ovvero l'allegoria della modernità. *See* **7429**.

15873. SUÁREZ LAFUENTE, MARÍA SOCORRO. *Música Ficta, English Music* y el impulso holístico de la literatura postcolonial/postmoderna. RCEI (28) 1994, 127–38.

Harriet Stratemeyer Adams ('Carolyn Keene')

15874. NASH, ILANA. The lady and the press: Harriet Adams courts America. DNR (65:4) 1996, 111–21.

Richard Adams

15875. ANDERSON, KATHLEEN. Shaping self through spontaneous oral narration in Richard Adams' *Watership Down*. JFA (6:1) 1993, 25–33.

15876. BRIDGEMAN, JOAN.   The significance of myth in *Watership Down*. JFA (6:1) 1993, 7–24.

15877. MEYER, CHARLES A.   The Efrafran hunt for immortality in *Watership Down*. JFA (6:1) 1993, 71–88.

15878. —— Introduction. JFA (6:1) 1993, 3–6. (*Watership Down* special issue.)

15879. —— The power of myth and rabbit survival in Richard Adams' *Watership Down*. JFA (3:4) 1990 (pub. 1994), 139–50.

15880. MILTNER, ROBERT.   *Watership Down*: a genre study. JFA (6:1) 1993, 63–70.

15881. PENNINGTON, JOHN.   Shamanistic mythmaking: from civilization to wilderness in *Watership Down*. JFA (6:1) 1993, 34–50.

15882. PETERS, JOHN G.   Saturnalia and sanctuary: the role of the tale in *Watership Down*. JFA (6:1) 1993, 51–62.

Fleur Adcock

15883. STANNARD, JULIAN.   *A Surprise in the Peninsular*: a poem by Fleur Adcock. QLLSM (5) 1992, 241–7.

George Ade

15884. SZUBERLA, GUY.   George Ade at the 'Alfalfa European Hotel'. Midamerica (22) 1995, 10–24.

James Agee

15885. ANDERSON, DAVID D.   Photography and the written word: James Agee's *Let Us Now Praise Famous Men* and Sherwood Anderson's *Home Town*, and the photographs of the Historical Section of the Farm Security Administration. SSMLN (25:3) 1995, 3–7.

15886. FOLKS, JEFFREY J.   James Agee's quest for forgiveness in *Let Us Now Praise Famous Men*. SoQ (34:4) 1996, 43–52.

15887. HILGART, JOHN.   Valuable damage: James Agee's aesthetics of use. AQ (52:4) 1996, 85–114.

15888. LOWE, JAMES.   The creative process of James Agee. (Bibl. 1995, 14385.) Rev. by Victor A. Kramer in SoQ (34:2) 1996, 105–7.

15889. PECK, DAVID.   'The morning that is yours': American and British literary cultures in the thirties. *In* (pp. 214–31) **34**.

'Ai' (Florence Ogawa Anthony)

15890. 'AI'.   Movies, mom, poetry, sex and death: a self-interview. Onthebus (3:2/4:1) 1991, 240–8.

15891. LEAVITT, MICHELLE.   Ai's *Go*. Exp (54:2) 1996, 126–7.

Ama Ata Aidoo

15892. ASANTE, YAW.   (Re)discovering Europe: Ama Ata Aidoo's *Our Sister Killjoy*. In-between (2:1) 1993, 17–28.

15893. COOKE, MICHAEL G.   A rhetoric of obliquity in African and Caribbean women writers. *In* (pp. 169–84) **80**.

15894. INNES, C. L.   Reversal and return in fiction by Bessie Head and Ama Ata Aidoo. *In* (pp. 69–75) **102**.

15895. ODAMTTEN, VINCENT O.   The art of Ama Ata Aidoo: polylectics and reading against neocolonialism. (Bibl. 1994, 11426.) Rev. by Adele S. Newson in WLT (69:4) 1995, 851.

Conrad Aiken

15896. SEIGEL, CATHARINE F. The fictive world of Conrad Aiken: a celebration of consciousness. (Bibl. 1994, 11430.) Rev. by Cynthia Sugars in MalLR (33) 1993, 23–6.

15897. SUGARS, CYNTHIA S. (ed.). The letters of Conrad Aiken and Malcolm Lowry, 1929–1954. (Bibl. 1995, 14390.) Rev. by Frederick Asals in MalLR (33) 1993, 19–22.

Edward Albee

15898. ALBEE, EDWARD. On Alan Schneider and playwriting. AmDr (1:2) 1992, 77–84.

15899. BHASIN, KAMIL. 'Women, identity, and sexuality': an interview with Edward Albee. JADT (7:2) 1995, 18–40.

15900. CARDULLO, BERT. Nick in *Who's Afraid of Virginia Woolf?* NCL (25:4) 1995, 4.

15901. COLLINS, JERRE; WILSON, RAYMOND J., III. Albee's *Who's Afraid of Virginia Woolf?*: the issue of originality. AmDr (2:2) 1993, 50–75.

15902. DIAMOND, SUZANNE. Who's afraid of George and Martha's parlour? Domestic f(r)ictions and the stir-crazy gaze of Hollywood. *See* **13615**.

15903. DITSKY, JOHN. Steinbeck and Albee: affection, admiration, affinity. SteiQ (26:1/2) 1993, 13–23.

15904. EGRI, PETER. American variations on a British theme: Giles Cooper and Edward Albee. *In* (pp. 135–51) **34**.

15905. FINKELSTEIN, BONNIE BLUMENTHAL. Albee's Martha: someone's daughter, someone's wife, no one's mother. AmDr (5:1) 1995, 51–70.

15906. GEIS, DEBORAH R. Staging hypereloquence: Edward Albee and the monologic voice. AmDr (2:2) 1993, 1–11.

15907. GOLDMAN, JEFFREY. An interview with Edward Albee. StAD (6:1) 1991, 59–69.

15908. HARRIS, ANDREW B. *All Over*: defeating the expectations of the 'well-made' play. AmDr (2:2) 1992, 12–31.

15909. HUTCHINGS, WILLIAM. *All Over* again: Edward Albee's *Three Tall Women* and the later Beckett plays. TexPres (17) 1996, 30–3.

15910. LUERE, JEANE. A market for monologue? JDTC (8:1) 1993, 133–48.

15911. —— Objectivity in the growth of a Pulitzer: Edward Albee's *Three Tall Women*. JADT (7:2) 1995, 1–17.

15912. MCKELLY, JAMES C. The artist as criminal: *The Zoo Story* and *House of Games*. TexPres (12) 1991, 65–8.

15913. MASHON, LAURENCE. Edward Albee. *In* (pp. 1–23) **85**.

15914. OSTERWALDER, HANS. The battle of the sexes in the classroom: Edward Albee's *Who's Afraid of Virginia Woolf* and Arthur Miller's *After the Fall*. LWU (29:4) 1996, 293–303.

15915. —— Patriarchy *vs* matriarchy: Edward Albee's *Who's Afraid of Virginia Woolf?* and Arthur Miller's *After the Fall*. SPELL (9) 1996, 109–16.

15916. POST, ROBERT M. Salvation or damnation? Death in the plays of Edward Albee. AmDr (2:2) 1993, 32–49.

15917. ROUDANÉ, MATTHEW C. *Who's Afraid of Virginia Woolf?* Necessary fictions, terrifying realities. Boston, MA: Twayne, 1990. pp. xv, 125. (Twayne's masterwork studies, 34.) Rev. by Jeane Luere in JDTC (5:2) 1991, 235–7.

15918. SOLOMON, RAKESH H.   Crafting script into performance: Edward Albee in rehearsal. AmDr (2:2) 1993, 76–99.

Brian Aldiss

15919. BAILEY, K. V.   Mars is a district of Sheffield. Foundation (68) 1996, 81–6.

15920. FROST, R. J.   'It's alive!' *Frankenstein*: the film, the feminist novel and science fiction. *See* **12222**.

Sherman Alexie

15921. GILLAN, JENNIFER.   Reservation home movies: Sherman Alexie's poetry. AL (68:1) 1996, 91–110.

Nelson Algren

15922. CAPPETTI, CARLA.   Writing Chicago: Modernism, ethnography, and the novel. (Bibl. 1995, 14407.) Rev. by Charles Daniel Blanton in MFS (40:2) 1994, 430–2; by James Hurt in YES (26) 1996, 336–7.

15923. LEWIN, JAMES A.   Algren's outcasts: Shakespearean fools and the prophet in a neon wilderness. Midamerica (18) 1991, 97–114.

15924. —— The radical tradition of Algren's *Chicago: the City on the Make*. Midamerica (19) 1992, 106–15.

15925. SIMON, DANIEL; O'BRIEN, C. S. (eds).   Nonconformity: writings on writing. New York: Seven Stories Press, 1996. pp. 130. Rev. by Gerald Nicosia in BkW, 15 Sept. 1996, 11.

Paula Gunn Allen

15926. BOYNTON, VICTORIA.   Desire's revision: feminist appropriation of Native-American traditional stories. MLS (26:2/3) 1996, 53–71.

15927. EYSTUROY, ANNIE O.   Paula Gunn Allen. *In* (pp. 94–107) **121**.

15928. FERRELL, TRACY J. PRINCE.   Transformation, myth, and ritual in Paula Gunn Allen's *Grandmothers of the Light*. NDQ (63:1) 1996, 77–88.

15929. HERMANN, ELISABETH.   Elemente mündlichen Erzählens im erzählerischen Werk von Leslie Marmon Silko und Paula Gunn Allen. *In* (pp. 203–15) **73**.

15930. KEATING, ANALOUISE.   Women reading women writing: self-invention in Paula Gunn Allen, Gloria Anzaldúa, and Audre Lorde. Philadelphia, PA: Temple UP, 1996. pp. viii, 240.

15931. MOSS, MARIA.   We've been here before: women in creation myths and contemporary literature of the Native-American Southwest. (Bibl. 1994, 11443.) Rev. by Brigitte Georgi-Findlay in Amst (41:2) 1996, 309–11.

'Woody Allen' (Allen Stewart Konigsberg)

15932. ARIZTI MARTÍN, BÁRBARA.   Female spectatorship in *The Purple Rose of Cairo*. *In* (pp. 387–97) **38**.

15933. BROWN, DEVIN.   Powerful man gets pretty woman: style switching in *Annie Hall*. *See* **2514**.

15934. CURRY, RENÉE R. (ed.).   Perspectives on Woody Allen. *See* **13588**.

15935. FERRISS, SUZANNE.   The other in Woody Allen's *Another Woman*. *See* **13660**.

15936. Fox, Julian. Woody: movies from Manhattan. Woodstock, NY: Overlook; London: Batsford, 1996. pp. 288.

15937. Knight, Christopher J. Woody Allen's *Hannah and Her Sisters*: domesticity and its discontents. *See* **13876**.

15938. Lax, Eric. Woody Allen: a biography. (Bibl. 1994, 11448.) Rev. by Lloyd Michaels in PS (11:3) 1992, 81–2.

Phyllis Shand Allfrey

15939. Paravisini-Gebert, Lizabeth. Phyllis Shand Allfrey: a Caribbean life. New Brunswick, NJ: Rutgers UP, 1996. pp. xii, 335. Rev. by Lucretia Stewart in TLS, 25 Oct. 1996, 30.

Lisa Alther

15940. Barkhausen, Jochen. An interview with Lisa Alther. ZAA (41:2) 1993, 147–65.

Julia Alvarez

15941. Alvarez, Julia. On finding a Latino voice. BkW, 7 May 1995, 1, 10.

Kingsley Amis ('Robert Markham', 'William Tanner')

15942. Amis, Kingsley. Memoirs. (Bibl. 1995, 14420.) Rev. by Neil Powell in PN Review (18:2) 1991, 30–3.

15943. Coles, Joanna. Last of the old curmudgeon. Mail & Guardian (11:44) 1995, 3.

15944. Fussell, Paul. The anti-egotist: Kingsley Amis, man of letters. (Bibl. 1995, 14423.) Rev. by Leslie B. Mittleman in WLT (69:3) 1995, 593.

15945. Helbig, Jörg. Thema und Variation: Kingsley Amis' *The Alteration* als postmoderne Spielart des historischen Romans. GRM (42:4) 1992, 444–50.

15946. Jacobs, Eric. Kingsley Amis: a biography. (Bibl. 1995, 14424.) Rev. by Richard Jones in ASch (65:4) 1996, 624–8; by Peter Bien in WLT (70:2) 1996, 413–14.

15947. Raitala, Eija. Philip Larkin's *Lucky Jim*? A quantitative authorship study of Kingsley Amis's novel *Lucky Jim*. New Courant (6) 1996, 116–33.

15948. Woudhuysen, H. R. Sincere good wishes ... Mr Amis. TLS, 19 July 1996, 16.

Martin Amis

15949. Brown, Richard. Postmodern Americas in the fiction of Angela Carter, Martin Amis and Ian McEwan. *In* (pp. 92–110) **34**.

15950. Nash, John. Fiction may be a legal paternity: Martin Amis's *The Information*. Eng (45:183) 1996, 213–24.

15951. Wachtel, Eleanor. Eleanor Wachtel with Martin Amis: interview. MalaR (114) 1996, 43–58.

A. R. Ammons

15952. Burr, Zofia (ed.). Set in motion: essays, interviews, and dialogues. Ann Arbor: Michigan UP, 1996. pp. x, 125. (Poets on poetry.)

15953. DiCicco, Lorraine C. *Garbage*: A. R. Ammons's tape for the turn of the century. PLL (32:2) 1996, 166–88.

15954. SCHNEIDER, STEVEN P.   On sifting through A. R. Ammons's *Garbage*. NCLR (2:2) 1995, 175–82.

Berthe Amoss

15955. ISKANDER, SYLVIA PATTERSON.   Setting and local color in the young adult novels of Berthe Amoss. *In* (pp. 184–92) **65**.

Mulk Raj Anand

15956. VERMA, K. D.   Ideological confrontation and synthesis in Mulk Raj Anand's *Conversations in Bloomsbury*. JSAL (29:2) 1994, 83–111.
15957. ——— Mulk Raj Anand: a reappraisal. IndL (39:2) 1996, 150–65.

Rudolfo Anaya

15958. BOTTALICO, MICHELE (introd.).   *Message from the Inca* by Rudolfo A. Anaya. RSAJ (4) 1993, 81–96.
15959. CANDELARIA, CORDELIA CHÁVEZ.   *Différance* and the discourse of 'community' in writings in and about the ethnic other(s). *In* (pp. 185–202) **80**.
15960. CRAWFORD, JOHN.   Rudolfo Anaya. *In* (pp. 82–93) **121**.
15961. MATERASSI, MARIO.   'The cutting edge of the struggle': an interview. RSAJ (4) 1993, 66–79.

Barbara Anderson

15962. AMERY, MARK.   Lasting pleasure. Quote Unquote (42) 1996, 10. (Interview.)

Garland Anderson

15963. KREIZENBECK, ALAN.   Garland Anderson's *Appearances*: the playwright and his play. JADT (6:2/3) 1994, 28–48.

Maxwell Anderson

15964. ADAM, JULIE.   Versions of heroism in modern American drama: redefinitions by Miller, Williams, O'Neill and Anderson. (Bibl. 1991, 11929.) Rev. by Steven F. Bloom in EOR (17:1/2) 1993, 198–205.
15965. HORN, BARBARA LEE.   Maxwell Anderson: a research and production sourcebook. Westport, CT; London: Greenwood Press, 1996. pp. vi, 193. (Modern dramatists research and production sourcebooks, 10.)
15966. JONES, JENNIFER.   A fictitious injustice: the politics of conversation in Maxwell Anderson's *Gods of Lightning*. AmDr (4:2) 1995, 81–96.
15967. SPERANZA, TONY.   Renegotiating the frontier of American manhood: Maxwell Anderson's *High Tor*. AmDr (5:1) 1995, 16–35.

Poul Anderson (1926–)

15968. HELLEKSON, KAREN.   Poul Anderson's time patrol as anti-alternate history. Extrapolation (37:3) 1996, 234–44.

Robert W. Anderson (1917–)

15969. JOSELOVITZ, ERNEST.   Robert Anderson. *In* (pp. 24–47) **85**.

Sherwood Anderson

15970. ALLEN, JOHN.   Unity in *Winesburg, Ohio*: the interdependence of communication, isolation and physical description. WE (21:1) 1996, 7–10.

15971. ANDERSON, DAVID. Sherwood Anderson and the moral geography of Ohio. SSMLN (23:3) 1993, 8–16.

15972. ANDERSON, DAVID D. The dramatic landscape of Sherwood Anderson's fiction. Midamerica (20) 1993, 89–97.

15973. —— The durability of *Winesburg, Ohio*. MidM (23) 1995, 51–8.

15974. —— Photography and the written word: James Agee's *Let Us Now Praise Famous Men* and Sherwood Anderson's *Home Town*, and the photographs of the Historical Section of the Farm Security Administration. *See* **15885**.

15975. —— Sherwood Anderson, Henry Blake Fuller, James T. Farrell, and the Midwestern city as metaphor and reality. SSMLN (25:3) 1995, 16–21.

15976. —— Sherwood Anderson, *The Double Dealer*, and the New Orleans literary renaissance. Midamerica (19) 1992, 96–105.

15977. —— Sherwood Anderson and Hart Crane: a temporary friendship. SSMLN (26:2) 1996, 7–14.

15978. —— Sherwood Anderson in short: a review essay. SSMLN (23:1) 1993, 13–17.

15979. —— Sherwood Anderson's advice to young writers. SSMLN (25:2) 1995, 7–13.

15980. —— The structure of Sherwood Anderson's short-story collections. Midamerica (23) 1996, 90–8.

15981. —— Wanderers and sojourners: Sherwood Anderson and the people of Winesburg. Midamerica (22) 1995, 89–96.

15982. BLAIR, EDWIN J. Sherwood Anderson's New Orleans. WE (19:1) 1994, 6–9.

15983. BROWN, LYNDA. *Hands*: Anderson's breakthrough story. WE (19:2) 1994, 6–8.

15984. CAMPBELL, HILBERT H. The *Shadow People*: Feodor Sologub and Sherwood Anderson's *Winesburg, Ohio*. SSF (33:1) 1996, 51–8.

15985. —— Winesburg at Dartmouth. WE (17:2) 1992, 11.

15986. COATS, KAREN. Reclaiming *Mrs Wife*. WE (16:2) 1991, 9–12.

15987. CROWLEY, JOHN W. (ed.). New essays on *Winesburg, Ohio*. (Bibl. 1991, 11932.) Rev. by Kurt Müller in Amst (41:4) 1996, 708.

15988. DUNNE, ROBERT. Plainer speaking: Sherwood Anderson's non-fiction and the 'New Age'. Midamerica (19) 1992, 87–95.

15989. FISHER, JAMES. Tender men: the acquaintanceship of Eugene O'Neill and Sherwood Anderson. EOR (17:1/2) 1993, 135–47.

15990. GETZ, JOHN. Mary Wilkins Freeman and Sherwood Anderson: confluence or influence? *See* **11228**.

15991. GREASLEY, PHILIP. Sherwood Anderson's oral tradition. MidM (23) 1995, 9–16.

15992. GROVER, DORYS CROW. Four Midwestern novelists' response to French inquiries on populism. Midamerica (18) 1991, 59–68.

15993. HARRIS, RICHARD C. Sherwood Anderson and Willa Cather: fragments to shore against the ruins. WE (20:2) 1995, 9–12.

15994. HASKELL, DIANA. A Sherwood Anderson checklist 1988; 1989; 1990. WE (16:1) 1991, 16–18; (17:1) 1992, 6–8; (18:1) 1993, 10–12.

15995. HAYS, PETER L. Sherwood Anderson and *One Flew over the Cuckoo's Nest*. WE (19:2) 1994, 9–10.

15996. KULIS, MARGARET. A Sherwood Anderson checklist 1991;

1992–93; 1994. WE (19:2) 1994, 10–11; (20:1) 1995, 8–11; (21:1) 1996, 10–12.

15997. Lause, Sean.   The paradox of isolation and Sherwood Anderson's almost silent women. WE (17:2) 1992, 1–8.

15998. Lears, T. J. Jackson.   Sherwood Anderson: looking for the white spot. *In* (pp. 13–37) **88**.

15999. Lindsay, Clarence.   Another look at community in *Winesburg, Ohio*. Midamerica (20) 1993, 76–88.

16000. Lindsay, Clarence B.   The unrealized city in Sherwood Anderson's *Windy McPherson's Son* and *Marching Men*. MidM (23) 1995, 17–27.

16001. MacGowan, Christopher.   The heritage of the fathers in Sherwood Anderson's *The Man Who Became a Woman*. JSSE (21) 1993, 29–37.

16002. Miller, Paul W.   The importance of Sherwood Anderson's 'queer' brother Earl. WE (20:2) 1995, 3–8.

16003. —— Sherwood Anderson's creative distortion of his sister Stella's character in *The Memoirs*. MidM (23) 1995, 40–50.

16004. Modlin, Charles E.   Sherwood Anderson's dreams. WE (20:1) 1995, 4–8.

16005. —— Sherwood Anderson's Kentucky connections. WE (21:1) 1996, 1–5.

16006. —— (ed.).   Certain things last: the selected short stories of Sherwood Anderson. (Bibl. 1994, 11468.) Rev. by Welford D. Taylor in WE (19:1) 1994, 10–12.

16007. —— *Dive Keeper*: a new story by Sherwood Anderson. WE (19:1) 1994, 1–5.

16008. —— White, Ray Lewis (eds).   *Winesburg, Ohio*: authoritative text, backgrounds and contexts, criticism. *See* **759**.

16009. Papinchak, Robert Allen.   Sherwood Anderson: a study of the short fiction. (Bibl. 1992, 12528.) Rev. by Welford D. Taylor in WE (19:1) 1994, 10–12.

16010. Rideout, Walter B.   *Dark Laughter* revisited. WE (20:1) 1995, 1–4.

16011. —— (ed.).   Memories of Sherwood Anderson by his brother Karl. WE (16:1) 1991, 1–14.

16012. Small, Judy Jo.   A reader's guide to the short stories of Sherwood Anderson. (Bibl. 1994, 11470.) Rev. by Stephen Enniss in WE (20:1) 1995, 11–12; by Bessie Lee Fox in BB (53:2) 1996, 174.

16013. Stephens, Rebecca.   'A great many notions': patterns of perspective in *Winesburg, Ohio*. WE (17:1) 1992, 1–5.

16014. Sturgill, Mack H.   Sherwood Anderson *vs* Elizabeth Prall Anderson: Anderson seeks divorce on grounds of desertion. WE (19:2) 1994, 1–5.

16015. Szczesiul, Anthony E.   The ambiguous ending of *Winesburg, Ohio*: putting George Willard's 'departure' in perspective. WE (18:1) 1993, 2–4.

16016. Taylor, Welford D.   Progress on 'the great adventure'. WE (18:1) 1993, 6–9.

16017. Wetzel, Thomas.   'Beyond human understanding': confusion and the call in *Winesburg, Ohio*. Midamerica (23) 1996, 11–27.

16018. White, Ray Lewis.   Anderson, Faulkner, and a unique Al Jackson tale. WE (16:2) 1991, 5–8.

16019. —— Anderson and the Smith family scandal. WE (18:2) 1993, 10–12.

16020. —— Anderson's elegy for Gil Stephenson. WE (17:2) 1992, 9–10.

16021. —— Anderson's will and estate. WE (21:2) 1996, 3–5.

16022. —— (ed.).   Sherwood Anderson's secret love letters: for Eleanor, a letter a day. (Bibl. 1992, 12529.) Rev. by Welford D. Taylor in WE (17:2) 1992, 12.

16023. WIXSON, DOUGLAS.   Sherwood Anderson and Midwestern literary radicalism in the 1930s. MidM (23) 1995, 28–39.

16024. WOLFE, MARGARET RIPLEY.   Eleanor Copenhaver Anderson of the National Board of the YMCA: Appalachian feminist and author's wife. WE (18:2) 1993, 2–9.

Bruce Andrews

16025. ANDREWS, BRUCE.   Paradise & method: poetics & praxis. *See* **14834**.

16026. PERLMAN, BOB.   Building a more powerful vocabulary: Bruce Andrews and the World (Trade Center). AQ (50:4) 1994, 117–31.

V. C. Andrews

16027. HUNTLEY, E. D.   V. C. Andrews: a critical companion. Westport, CT; London: Greenwood Press, 1996. pp. xi, 153. (Critical companions to popular contemporary writers.)

Maya Angelou

16028. FOSTER, FRANCES SMITH.   Parents and children in autobiography by Southern Afro-American writers. *In* (pp. 98–109) **43**.

16029. HAGEN, LYMAN B.   Heart of a woman, mind of a writer, and soul of a poet: a critical analysis of the writings of Maya Angelou. Lanham, MD; London: UP of America, 1996. pp. 180.

16030. HENKE, SUZETTE A.   Women's life-writing and the minority voice: Maya Angelou, Maxine Hong Kingston, and Alice Walker. *In* (pp. 210–33) **123**.

16031. KENT, GEORGE E.   Maya Angelou's *I Know Why the Caged Bird Sings* and Black autobiographical tradition. *In* (pp. 162–70) **1**.

16032. LISANDRELLI, ELAINE SLIVINSKI.   Maya Angelou: more than a poet. Springfield, NJ: Enslow, 1996. pp. 128. (African-American biographies.)

16033. PETTIT, JAYNE.   Maya Angelou: journey of the heart. New York: Lodestar, 1996. pp. 70. (Rainbow biographies.)

Mary Antin

16034. SALZ, EVELYN.   The letters of Mary Antin: a life divided. AJH (84:2) 1996, 71–80.

16035. SOLLORS, WERNER (introd.).   Letter from Mary Antin to Mary Austin. RSAJ (7) 1996, 91–112.

Kofi Anyidoho

16036. EZENWA-OHAETO.   Survival strategies and the new life of orality in Nigerian and Ghanaian poetry: Osundare's *Waiting Laughters* and Anyidoho's *Earthchild*. RAL (27:2) 1996, 70–82.

Anthony Appiah

16037. APPIAH, K. ANTHONY.   Reconstructing racial identities. RAL (27:3) 1996, 68–72.

16038. AZOULAY, KATYA GIBEL.   Outside our parents' house: race, culture, and identity. *See* **13408**.

16039. KLOBAH, MAHOUMBAH, *et al.* (eds).   A conversation about Kwame Anthony Appiah's *In My Father's House: Africa in the Philosophy of Culture.* IowaR (26:3) 1996, 1–26.

16040. OYEGOKE, LEKAN.   Leaky mansion? Appiah's theory of African cultures. RAL (27:1) 1996, 143–8.

16041. SEREQUEBERHAN, TSENAY.   Reflections on *In My Father's House.* RAL (27:1) 1996, 110–18.

16042. SLAYMAKER, WILLIAM.   Agents and actors in African antifoundational aesthetics: theory and narrative in Appiah and Mudimbe. RAL (27:1) 1996, 119–28.

Ayi Kwei Armah

16043. AYIVOR, KWAME.   The African legendary tradition debunked: Ayi Kwei Armah's *Two Thousand Seasons.* ESA (39:2) 1996, 27–45.

16044. —— The Akan iconic forest of symbols: Ayi Kwei Armah's *The Healers.* ESA (39:1) 1996, 25–55.

16045. OGEDE, ODE S.   Achebe and Armah: a unity of shaping visions. *See* **15857**.

Simon Armitage

16046. O'KEEFFE, BERNARD.   Comparisons. ERev (6:2) 1995, 24–7. (Armitage, *You May Turn Over and Begin*; Duffy, *The Captain of the 1964 'Top of the Form' Team.*)

Jeannette Armstrong

16047. BEELER, KARIN.   Image, music, text: an interview with Jeannette Armstrong. StudCanL (21:2) 1996, 143–54.

16048. HOWELLS, CORAL ANN.   Disruptive geographies; or, Mapping the region of woman in contemporary Canadian women's writing in English. JCL (31:1) 1996, 115–26.

Harriette Arnow

16049. CHUNG, HAEJA K. (ed.).   Harriette Simpson Arnow: critical essays on her work. East Lansing: Michigan State UP, 1995. pp. vii, 301. Rev. by John Lang in AppalJ (24:1) 1996, 79–80.

16050. DEVERS, JAMES.   Cain and Abel in Harriette Arnow's *The Dollmaker*: a comment on war. NCL (22:3) 1992, 4–5.

John Ashbery

16051. BACHINGER, KATRINA.   Setting allegory adrift in John Ashbery's *Mountains and Rivers,* James Joyce's *Portrait of the Artist as a Young Man,* and Vincent O'Sullivan's *Let the River Stand. In* (pp. 285–93) **125**.

16052. BACIGALUPO, MASSIMO (ed.).   A poetry reading in Genoa. RSAJ (3) 1992, 23–32.

16053. BLASING, MUTLU KONUK.   Politics and form in postmodern poetry: O'Hara, Bishop, Ashbery and Merrill. Cambridge; New York: CUP, 1995. pp. x, 219. (Cambridge studies in American literature and culture, 74.)

16054. CRIVELLI, RENZO S. Ashbery and Parmigianino: alchemy *vs* technology. *In* (pp. 159–70) **117**.

16055. GRAY, JEFFREY. Ashbery's *The Instruction Manual*. Exp (54:2) 1996, 117–20.

16056. HOEPPNER, EDWARD HAWORTH. Echoes and moving fields: structure and subjectivity in the poetry of W. S. Merwin and John Ashbery. (Bibl. 1994, 11488.) Rev. by Luke Spencer in AL (68:1) 1996, 262–3.

16057. LYNCH, EDWARD. Le trasformazioni (traduzioni, tradizioni e tradimenti) di Walt Whitman, Emily Dickinson (e altri) in John Ashbery. *See* **10976**.

16058. MUELLER, ROBERT. John Ashbery and the poetry of consciousness: *Self-Portrait in a Convex Mirror*. CR (40:3) 1996, 561–72.

16059. PADDON, SEIJA. John Ashbery and Paavo Haavikko: architects of the postmodern space in mind and language. CanRCL (20:3/4) 1993, 409–16.

16060. SĀLĀGEANU, CRISTINA ILINA. John Ashbery. RomLit, 14 Feb. 1994, 20.

16061. SCHULTZ, SUSAN M. 'Returning to Bloom': John Ashbery's critique of Harold Bloom. *See* **15752**.

16062. SHOPTAW, JOHN. On the outside looking out: John Ashbery's poetry. (Bibl. 1994, 11496.) Rev. by Susan M. Schultz in AL (68:3) 1996, 655–6; by David Herd in TLS, 8 Mar. 1996, 28.

16063. SLOAN, BENJAMIN. *Houseboat Days* and *Houses Founded on the Sea*: an example of Emerson as source for Ashbery. *See* **11198**.

16064. ZINNES, HARRIET. John Ashbery: the way time feels as it passes. HC (29:3) 1992, 1–13.

Isaac Asimov

16065. GUNN, JAMES. Isaac Asimov: the foundations of science fiction. (Bibl. 1984, 9945.) Lanham, MD: Scarecrow Press, 1996. pp. ix, 276. (Revised ed.: first ed. 1982.)

16066. PALUMBO, DAVID. Psychohistory and chaos theory: *The Foundation Trilogy* and the fractal structure of Asimov's Robot/Empire/ Foundation metaseries. JFA (7:1) 1996, 23–50.

16067. SCANNAVINI, ANNA. Il *robot* e il 'piano' nel ciclo della Fondazione di Asimov. *In* (pp. 297–302) **117**.

16068. WHITE, MICHAEL. Asimov: the unauthorized life. (Bibl. 1994, 11501.) Rev. by Robert Irwin in Foundation (64) 1995, 101–3.

Gertrude Atherton

16069. MCCLURE, CHARLOTTE S. Gertrude Atherton and her San Francisco: a wayward writer and a wayward city in a wayward paradise. *In* (pp. 73–95) **108**.

16070. PENNELL, MELISSA MCFARLAND. Through the Golden Gate: madness and the Persephone myth in Gertrude Atherton's *The Foghorn*. *In* (pp. 84–98) **46**.

Margaret Atwood

16071. BERAN, CAROL L. 'At least its voice isn't mine': the concept of voice in Margaret Atwood's *Lady Oracle*. WebS (8:1) 1991, 54–71.

16072. BIESE, EIVOR. In search of voice in Margaret Atwood's *Surfacing*. New Courant (6) 1996, 26–38.

16073. Bizzini, Silvia Caporale.   Power politics: literature and Foucauldian analysis. *See* **15296**.

16074. Cheever, Leonard A.   Fantasies of sexual hell: Manuel Puig's *Pubis Angelical* and Margaret Atwood's *The Handmaid's Tale. In* (pp. 110–21) **70**.

16075. Chen, Zhongming.   Theorising about new modes of representation and ideology in the postmodern age: the practice of Margaret Atwood and Li Ang. CanRCL (21:3) 1994, 341–54.

16076. Collado Rodríguez, Francisco.   Complexity/controversy: some aspects of contemporary Women's Studies in America. *In* (pp. 107–20) **38**.

16077. Cooke, John.   The influence of painting on five Canadian writers: Alice Munro, Hugh Hood, Timothy Findley, Margaret Atwood, and Michael Ondaatje. Lewiston, NY; Lampeter: Mellen Press, 1996. pp. iv, 251. (Canadian studies, 10.)

16078. Davidson, Arnold E.   The poetics of pain in Margaret Atwood's *Bodily Harm*. ARCS (18:1) 1988, 1–10.

16079. Donaldson, Sandra.   Notes & queries. *See* **622**.

16080. Enos, Jennifer.   What's in a name? Zenia and Margaret Atwood's *The Robber Bride*. NMAS (15) 1995, 14.

16081. Florén Serrano, Celia.   A reading of Margaret Atwood's dystopia, *The Handmaid's Tale. In* (pp. 253–64) **38**.

16082. Gardner, Laurel J.   Pornography as a matter of power in *The Handmaid's Tale*. NCL (24:5) 1994, 5–7.

16083. Glasberg, Ronald P.   The dynamics of domination: Levi's *Survival in Auschwitz*, Solzhenitsyn's *Gulag Archipelago*, and Atwood's *The Handmaid's Tale*. CanRCL (21:4) 1994, 679–94.

16084. Gregory, Eileen.   Dark Persephone and Margaret Atwood's *Procedures for Underground. In* (pp. 136–52) **46**.

16085. Hite, Molly.   The other side of the story: structures and strategies of contemporary feminist narrative. Ithaca, NY; London: Cornell UP, 1989. pp. x, 172. Rev. by Ellen Cronan Rose in Signs (18:2) 1993, 346–75.

16086. Howells, Coral Ann.   Disruptive geographies; or, Mapping the region of woman in contemporary Canadian women's writing in English. *See* **16048**.

16087. —— Margaret Atwood. Basingstoke: Macmillan; New York: St Martin's Press, 1996. pp. xi, 185. (Modern novelists.)

16088. Hufnagel, Jill.   Atwood's *Variation on the Word Sleep*. Exp (54:3) 1996, 188–91.

16089. Ingersoll, Earl.   Margaret Atwood's *The Handmaid's Tale*: echoes of Orwell. JFA (5:4) 1992, 64–72.

16090. Ingersoll, Earl G.   The engendering of narrative in Doris Lessing's *Shikasta* and Margaret Atwood's *The Handmaid's Tale. In* (pp. 39–47) **127**.

16091. Johnson, Brian.   Language, power, and responsibility in *The Handmaid's Tale*: toward a discourse of literary gossip. CanL (148) 1996, 39–55.

16092. Keith, W. J.   Atwood in Oxford. LRC (5:4) 1996, 13–14 (review-article).

16093. McCombs, Judith (ed.).   Critical essays on Margaret Atwood. (Bibl. 1988, 6829.) Rev. by Arnold E. Davidson in ARCS (19:2) 1989, 204–5.

16094. MYCAK, SONIA.   Divided and dismembered: the decentered subject in Margaret Atwood's *Bodily Harm*. CanRCL (20:3/4) 1993, 469–78.

16095. NICHOLSON, COLIN (ed.).   Margaret Atwood: writing and subjectivity: new critical essays. (Bibl. 1995, 14501.) Rev. by Alice Palumbo in Signs (21:3) 1996, 767–9.

16096. NORRIS, KEN.   'The University of Denay, Nunavit': the 'historical notes' in Margaret Atwood's *The Handmaid's Tale*. ARCS (20:3) 1990, 357–64.

16097. REICHENBÄCHER, HELMUT.   Von *The Robber Bridegroom* zu *Bodily Harm*: eine analyse unveröffentlicher Entwürfe Margaret Atwoods. ZAA (41:1) 1993, 54–65.

16098. RESTUCCIA, FRANCES.   Tales of beauty: aestheticizing female melancholia. AI (53:4) 1996, 353–83.

16099. STAELS, HILDE.   Margaret Atwood's *The Handmaid's Tale*: resistance through narrating. EngS (76:5) 1995, 455–67.

16100. STEIN, KAREN.   Margaret Atwood's modest proposal: *The Handmaid's Tale*. CanL (148) 1996, 57–73.

16101. STEVEN, LAURENCE.   Margaret Atwood's 'polarities' and George Grant's polemics. ARCS (18:4) 1988, 443–54.

16102. SURETTE, LEON.   Creating the Canadian canon. *In* (pp. 17–29) **13**.

16103. THOMSON, ASHLEY; DiMARCO, DANETTE.   Current Atwood checklist, 1995. NMAS (16) 1996, 3–13.

16104. WEIN, TONI.   Margaret Atwood's historical notes. NCL (25:2) 1995, 2–3.

16105. WILSON, SHARON ROSE.   Margaret Atwood's fairy-tale sexual politics. (Bibl. 1995, 14512.) Rev. by Earl G. Ingersoll in StudN (27:4) 1995, 593–5; by Patricia Merivale in ESCan (22:3) 1996, 341–3; by Alice Palumbo in Signs (21:3) 1996, 767–9.

Louis Auchincloss

16106. GELDERMAN, CAROL.   Louis Auchincloss: a writer's life. (Bibl. 1993, 11505.) Rev. by Arthur Krystal in BkW, 10 Jan. 1996, 3, 10.

16107. TINTNER, ADELINE.   Louis Auchincloss's four 'Edith' tales: some rearrangements and reinventions of her life. EWR (13:2) 1996, 9–14.

W. H. Auden

16108. AQUIEN, PASCAL.   W. H. Auden: de l'Eden perdu au jardin des mots. Paris: L'Harmattan, 1996. pp. 285. (Critiques littéraires.)

16109. BOOTH, WAYNE; LERNER, LAURENCE.   A conversation about poetry. CPR (15:2) 1996, 28–70.

16110. BURRIS, SIDNEY.   Auden's generalizations. Shen (43:3) 1993, 5–22.

16111. CLARK, THEKLA.   Wystan and Chester: a personal memoir of W. H. Auden and Chester Kallman. Introd. by James Fenton. (Bibl. 1995, 14523.) New York: Columbia UP, 1996. pp. xii, 130, (plates) 8.

16112. CRAWFORD, ROBERT.   Exam poem. CritS (6:3) 1994, 304–11. (*The Orators*.)

16113. CURRIE, MARK.   The hectic quest for prelapsarian man: the Adamic myth in late Auden. CritS (6:3) 1994, 355–60.

16114. DAVENPORT-HINES, RICHARD. Auden. (Bibl. 1995, 14525.) Rev. by Michael Dirda in BkW, 3 Mar. 1996, 4; by Celia Wren in Cweal (123:17) 1996, 23–4; by Peter Firchow in WLT (70:4) 1996, 968–9.

16115. DUNN, DOUGLAS. Back and forth: Auden and political poetry. CritS (6:3) 1994, 325–35.

16116. FIRCHOW, P. E. Auden and Weinheber: poets of *Kirchstetten*. Salmagundi (96) 1992, 187–207.

16117. FUROMOTO, TAKETOSHI. W. H. Auden to sono nakama-tachi. (W. H. Auden and his circle.) Kyoto: Kyoto Shugakusha, 1996. pp. 210.

16118. HASHIGUCHI, MINORU. Shijin Auden. (Auden: a poet.) Tokyo: Heibonsha, 1996. pp. 310.

16119. HECHT, ANTHONY. The hidden law: the poetry of W. H. Auden. (Bibl. 1995, 14531.) Rev. by Richard Tillinghast in GetR (8:3) 1995, 423–35; by Richard Howard in BkW, 25 Apr. 1996, 4–5.

16120. HIGDON, DAVID LEON; HARPER, MARK C. Auden 'abandons' a poem: problems with eclectic texts. *See* **679**.

16121. IRIMIA, MIHAELA. The art of losing: W. H. Auden and Elizabeth Bishop. CritS (6:3) 1994, 361–5.

16122. JACOBS, ALAN. Auden at the opera. ASch (63:2) 1994, 287–95 (review-article).

16123. KERR, DOUGLAS. Disorientations: Auden and Isherwood's China. Literature and History (5:2) 1996, 53–67.

16124. MASON, DAVID. The *civitas* of sound: Auden's *Paul Bunyan* and *New Year Letter*. JML (19:1) 1994, 115–28.

16125. MAXWELL, GLYN. Notes on Auden's *Bucolics*. CritS (6:3) 1994, 351–4.

16126. MENDELSON, EDWARD. We are changed by what we change: the power politics of Auden's revisions. RR (86:3) 1995, 527–35.

16127. —— (ed.). Libretti and other dramatic writings by W. H. Auden, 1939–1973. (Bibl. 1993, 11516.) Rev. by Alan Jacobs in ASch (63:2) 1994, 287–95.

16128. O'NEILL, MICHAEL. Making and faking in some poems by W. H. Auden. CritS (6:3) 1994, 343–50.

16129. PRIESTMAN, JUDITH. An unpublished letter by W. H. Auden. *See* **408**.

16130. RUGOFF, KATHY. Auden and opera: the poet's magic flute. ArsL (6) 1992, 63–71.

16131. SHARPE, TONY. W. H. Auden and rules of disengagement. CritS (6:3) 1994, 336–42.

16132. SMITH, IAIN CRICHTON. Recollecting Auden. CritS (6:3) 1994, 301–3.

16133. SMITH, STAN. Remembering Bryden's bill: Modernism from Eliot to Auden. CritS (6:3) 1994, 312–24.

16134. WILLIAMS, DAVID G. The influence of W. H. Auden on the work of Peter Porter. Eng (41:169) 1992, 25–47.

Paul Auster

16135. ADDY, ANDREW. Narrating the self: story-telling as personal myth-making in Paul Auster's *Moon Palace*. Q/W/E/R/T/Y (6) 1996, 153–61.

16136. AUSTER, PAUL. Why write? Providence, RI: Burning Deck, 1996. pp. 58.

16137. BROOKS, CARLO. Désespoir et possibilité: le problème de l'appartenance au monde dans *Moon Palace* et *Libra*. Q/W/E/R/T/Y (6) 1996, 163–75.

16138. CÉSARI-STRICKER, FLORENCE. *Moon Palace*; ou, Les avatars du programme. Q/W/E/R/T/Y (6) 1996, 177–82.

16139. COCHOY, NATHALIE. *Moon Palace*; ou, La formation du lecteur. Q/W/E/R/T/Y (6) 1996, 183–92.

16140. DOW, WILLIAM. Never being 'this far from home': Paul Auster and picturing *Moonlight* spaces. Q/W/E/R/T/Y (6) 1996, 193–8.

16141. FLOC'H, SYLVAIN. Ascétisme et austérité dans *Moon Palace*. Q/W/E/R/T/Y (6) 1996, 199–207.

16142. HARDY, MIREILLE. Ceci n'est pas une lune: l'image–mirage de *Moon Palace*. Q/W/E/R/T/Y (6) 1996, 209–15.

16143. MAISONNAT, CLAUDE. Écriture, altérité et modernité dans *Augie Wren's Christmas Story* de Paul Auster. JSSE (20) 1993, 37–49.

16144. MICHLIN, MONICA. Bitter-sweet gravity: *Moon Palace*. Q/W/E/R/T/Y (6) 1996, 217–24.

16145. NEALON, JEFFREY T. Work of the detective, work of the writer: Paul Auster's *City of Glass*. MFS (42:1) 1996, 91–110.

16146. VALLAS, SOPHIE. *Moon Palace*: Marco autobiographie; ou, Les errances du *Bildungsroman*. Q/W/E/R/T/Y (6) 1996, 225–33.

Gayle Austin

16147. AUSTIN, GAYLE. *The Doll House Show*: a feminist theory play. JDTC (7:2) 1993, 203–7.

Mary Austin

16148. BLEND, BENAY. Building a 'house of earth': Mary Austin, environmentalist and writer. CritM (10:1) 1996, 73–89.

16149. KARELL, LINDA K. *Lost Borders* and blurred boundaries: Mary Austin as storyteller. *In* (pp. 153–66) **3**.

16150. LANIGAN, ESTHER F. (ed.). A Mary Austin reader. Tucson: Arizona UP, 1996. pp. viii, 271. Rev. by Ann Funk in AR (54:4) 1996, 493–4.

16151. SOLLORS, WERNER (introd.). Letter from Mary Antin to Mary Austin. *See* **16035**.

Avi

16152. MARKHAM, LOIS. Avi. Santa Barbara, CA: Learning Works, 1996. pp. 128. (Meet the author.)

Mark Axelrod

16153. RIMANELLI, GIOSE. Mark Axelrod's *Bombay California: a Feature Novel*. WLT (69:1) 1995, 49–50.

Alan Ayckbourn ('Roland Allen')

16154. EVANS, COLIN. Intimate exchanges: Resnais' translation/transformation of Ayckbourn in *Smoking/No Smoking*. *See* **3133**.

Jimmy Santiago Baca

16155. CRAWFORD, JOHN; EYSTUROY, ANNIE O. Jimmy Santiago Baca. *In* (pp. 180–93) **121**.

Jerome Badanes

16156. GRAUER, TRESA. 'Surprising the darkness': history, memory, and representation in Jerome Badanes' *The Final Opus of Leon Solomon*. StudAJL (15) 1996, 78–89.

Beryl Bainbridge

16157. LASSNER, PHYLLIS. 'Between the gaps': sex, class and anarchy in the British comic novel of World War II. *In* (pp. 205–19) **64**.

Nicholson Baker

16158. STATES, BERT O. On first looking into Baker's index. Salmagundi (109/110) 1996, 153–62.

James Baldwin

16159. BENITO SÁNCHEZ, JESÚS. Narrative voice and Blues expression in James Baldwin's *Sonny's Blues*. *See* **2581**.

16160. DAILEY, PETER. Jimmy. ASch (63:1) 1994, 102–10.

16161. DEGOUT, YASMIN Y. Dividing the mind: contradictory portraits of homoerotic love in *Giovanni's Room*. AAR (26:3) 1992, 425–35.

16162. HAKUTANI, YOSHINOBU; KIUCHI, TORU. The critical reception of James Baldwin in Japan: an annotated bibliography. BALF (25:4) 1991, 753–79.

16163. HAMALIAN, LEO. God's angry man. *See* **13752**.

16164. HARRIS, TRUDIER (ed.). New essays on *Go Tell It on the Mountain*. Cambridge; New York: CUP, 1996. pp. viii, 160. (American novel.)

16165. HOLMES, CAROLYN L. Reassessing African-American literature through an Afrocentric paradigm: Zora N. Hurston and James Baldwin. *In* (pp. 37–51) **55**.

16166. LEEMING, DAVID. James Baldwin: a biography. (Bibl. 1994, 11582.) Rev. by Charles Scruggs in AL (68:2) 1996, 479–80; by James Robert Payne in WLT (70:1) 1996, 193–4.

16167. MURPHY, GERALDINE. Antistalinismo sovversivo: razza e sessualità nei primi saggi di James Baldwin. Àcoma (7) 1996, 75–84.

16168. —— Subversive anti-Stalinism: race and sexuality in the early essays of James Baldwin. ELH (63:4) 1996, 1021–46.

16169. REID-PHARR, ROBERT F. Tearing the goat's flesh: homosexuality, abjection and the production of a late twentieth-century Black masculinity. StudN (28:3) 1996, 372–94.

16170. ROHY, VALERIE. Displacing desire: passing, nostalgia, and *Giovanni's Room*. *In* (pp. 218–33) **82**.

J. G. Ballard

16171. HOLLINGER, VERONICA. Travels in hyperreality: Jean Baudrillard's *America* and J. G. Ballard's *Hello America*. *In* (pp. 185–93) **36**.

16172. LATHAM, ROB. The men who walked on the moon: images of America in the 'new wave' science fiction of the 1960s and 1970s. *In* (pp. 195–203) **36**.

16173. STILLER, LEWIS. *Suo gân* and *Empire of the Sun*. *See* **14251**.

Edwin Balmer (1883–1959)

16174. OBUCHOWSKI, MARY DEJONG.   The *Indian Drum* and its authors: a reconsideration. Midamerica (22) 1995, 60–8.

Toni Cade Bambara

16175. AIKEN, SUSAN HARDY.   Telling the other('s) story; or, The blues in two languages. *In* (pp. 206–23) **23**.

16176. ALWES, DEREK.   The burden of liberty: choice in Toni Morrison's *Jazz* and Toni Cade Bambara's *The Salt Eaters*. AAR (30:3) 1996, 353–65.

16177. BROOKHART, MARY HUGHES.   Spiritual daughters of the Black American South. *In* (pp. 125–39) **32**.

16178. GRIFFIN, FARAH JASMINE.   Toni Cade Bambara: free to be anywhere in the universe. Callaloo (19:2) 1996, 229–31.

16179. KELLEY, MARGOT ANNE.   'Damballah is the first law of thermodynamics': modes of access to Toni Cade Bambara's *The Salt Eaters*. AAR (27:3) 1993, 479–93.

16180. KORENEVA, MAYA.   Children of the sixties. *In* (pp. 191–205) **23**.

Iain Banks

16181. LYALL, RODERICK J.   Postmodernist otherworld, postcalvinist purgatory: an approach to *Lanark* and *The Bridge*. Études Écossaises (2) 1993, 41–52.

16182. RIACH, ALAN.   Nobody's children: orphans and their ancestors in popular Scottish fiction after 1945. *In* (pp. 51–83) **115**.

16183. TALLARON, RICHARD.   Iain Banks. Études Écossaises (3) 1996, 141–8.

John Banville

16184. BANVILLE, JOHN.   The personae of summer. *In* (pp. 118–22) **52**.

16185. D'HAEN, THEO.   Irish regionalism, magic realism and postmodernism. *In* (pp. 59–68) **49**.

16186. IMHOF, RÜDIGER.   In search of the Rosy Grail: the creative process in the novels of John Banville. *In* (pp. 123–36) **52**.

16187. SWANN, JOSEPH.   Banville's Faust: *Doctor Copernicus, Kepler, The Newton Letter* and *Mefisto* as stories of the European mind. *In* (pp. 148–60) **112**.

Amiri Baraka (LeRoi Jones)

16188. BARAKA, IMAMU AMIRI.   Eulogies. *See* **12943**.

16189. LEE, A. ROBERT.   Black Beats: the signifying poetry of LeRoi Jones/Amiri Baraka, Ted Joans and Bob Kaufman. *In* (pp. 158–77) **4**.

16190. MACKEY, NATHANIEL.   *Other*: from noun to verb. *See* **1983**.

16191. REECE, ERIK.   Detour to the 'alltombing womb': Amiri Baraka's assault on Yeats's muse. *In* (pp. 219–35) **58**.

16192. RYAN, BRENNA J.   The (ph)allacy of Black male potency in Imamu Amiri Baraka's *The Toilet*. Ob (10:1/2) 1995, 244–63.

16193. SHANNON, SANDRA G.   Manipulating myth, magic, and legend: Amiri Baraka's *Black Mass*. CLAJ (39:3) 1996, 357–68.

16194. TURCO, LEWIS.   Amiri Baraka's Black Mountain. HC (31:3) 1994, 1–8.

16195. VANGELISTI, PAUL (ed.).   Transbluesency: the selected poems
of Amiri Baraka/LeRoi Jones, 1961–1995. New York: Marsilio, 1995.
pp. xx, 271. Rev. by Philip Heldrich in CLAJ (39:4) 1996, 510–14.

Owen Barfield

16196. DIENER, ASTRID.   An interview with Owen Barfield: *Poetic
Diction* – between conception and publication. Mythlore (20:4) 1995,
14–19.
16197. DURIEZ, COLIN.   Tolkien and the other Inklings. Mythlore
(21:2) 1996, 360–3.
16198. MEYERS, DORIS.   Breaking free: the closed universe theme in
E. M. Forster, Owen Barfield, and C. S. Lewis. Mythlore (21:3) 1996,
7–11.
16199. POTTS, DONNA L.   Howard Nemerov and objective idealism:
the influence of Owen Barfield. (Bibl. 1994, 11605.) Rev. by Jason R.
Peters in HC (32:5) 1995, 14–15.

Joan Barfoot

16200. MACPHERSON, HEIDI SLETTEDAHL.   From housewife to hermit:
fleeing the feminine mystique in Joan Barfoot's *Gaining Ground*.
StudCanL (21:1) 1996, 92–106.

Clive Barker

16201. BADLEY, LINDA.   Writing horror and the body: the fiction of
Stephen King, Clive Barker, and Anne Rice. Westport, CT; London:
Greenwood Press, 1996. pp. xiv, 183. (Contributions to the study of
popular culture, 51.)
16202. ZIEGLER, ROBERT.   Fantasy's timeless humor in Clive Barker's
The Thief of Always. NCL (24:5) 1994, 7–9.

George Barker

16203. CRAIK, ROGER.   Wanderers in the zodiac: George Barker and
L. P. Hartley. NCL (26:4) 1996, 8.

Pat Barker

16204. CAPUTO, NICOLETTA.   Storia/e al femminile: '*writing as
re-vision*'. Textus (9:1) 1996, 285–322.
16205. SHEPHARD, BEN.   Digging up the past. *See* **13302**.
16206. WEINE, STEVAN M.   The witnessing imagination: social
trauma, creative artists, and witnessing professionals. LitMed (15:2) 1996,
167–82.

Djuna Barnes

16207. ALLEN, CAROLYN.   The erotics of Nora's narrative in Djuna
Barnes's *Nightwood*. Signs (19:1) 1993, 177–200.
16208. —— Following Djuna: women lovers and the erotics of loss.
See **14365**.
16209. BROE, MARY LYNN (ed.).   Silence and power: a re-evaluation
of Djuna Barnes. With a postscript by Catharine Stimpson. (Bibl. 1992,
12644.) Rev. by Bonnie Kime Scott in Signs (18:2) 1993, 485–9.
16210. HARRIS, ANDREA L.   The third sex: figures of inversion in
Djuna Barnes's *Nightwood*. *In* (pp. 233–59) **30**.
16211. HERRING, PHILLIP.   Djuna: the life and work of Djuna Barnes.

(Bibl. 1995, 14608.) Rev. by Michael Dirda in BkW, 12 Nov. 1995, 5; in LRB (18:13) 1996, 18, 20; by Lorna Sage in TLS, 19 Apr. 1996, 4–5; by Deirdre Neilen in WLT (70:3) 1996, 702–3; by Margot Norris in StudN (28:4) 1996, 581–9.

16212. KAIVOLA, KAREN. All contraries confounded: the lyrical fiction of Virginia Woolf, Djuna Barnes, and Marguerite Duras. (Bibl. 1993, 11571.) Rev. by Jane Marcus in Signs (17:4) 1992, 806–19.

16213. NORRIS, MARGOT. Doing Djuna justice: the challenges of the Barnes biography. StudN (28:4) 1996, 581–9 (review-article).

16214. REESMAN, JEANNE CAMPBELL. 'That savage path': *Nightwood* and *The Divine Comedy*. Ren (44:2) 1992, 137–58.

16215. WILSON, DEBORAH S. Dora, Nora, and their professor: the 'talking cure', *Nightwood*, and feminist pedagogy. LitPs (42:3) 1996, 48–71.

Julian Barnes ('Dan Kavanagh')

16216. KEMPTON, ADRIAN. A Barnes-eye view of France. Franco-British Studies (22) 1996, 92–101 (review-article).

16217. SALYER, GREGORY. One good story leads to another: Julian Barnes' *A History of the World in 10 1/2 Chapters*. LitTheol (5:2) 1991, 220–33 (review-article).

Kim Barnes

16218. BARNES, KIM. In the wilderness: coming of age in unknown country. New York: Doubleday, 1996. pp. 257.

Peter Barnes

16219. DUKORE, BERNARD F. Peter Barnes on American drama. JDTC (7:1) 1992, 163–73.

Steven Barnes

16220. NEWSINGER, JOHN. 'The universe is full of warriors': masculinity, hard science and war in some novels by Larry Niven and his accomplices. Foundation (67) 1996, 47–55.

William D. Barney

16221. BARNEY, WILLIAM D. Words from a wide land. Denton: North Texas UP, 1993. pp. 194.

J. M. Barrie

16222. HOLLINDALE, PETER (ed.). The admirable Crichton; Peter Pan; When Wendy grew up; What every woman knows. (Bibl. 1995, 14626.) Rev. by J. P. Wearing in ELT (39:4) 1996, 504–7.

16223. McQUADE, BRETT T. *Peter Pan*: Disney's adaptation of J. M. Barrie's original work. *See* **13951**.

16224. PACE, PATRICIA. Robert Bly does Peter Pan: the inner child as father to the man in Steven Spielberg's *Hook*. *See* **14057**.

John Barth

16225. ADAMS, ALICE. The American short story in the cybernetic age. *See* **14359**.

16226. BARTOCCI, CLARA. From the dynamo to the computer: an ongoing challenge. Nature and technology in John Barth's *Giles Goat-Boy*. *In* (pp. 543–5) **117**.

16227. ——John Barth's *Once Upon a Time*: fiction or autobiography? RSAJ (6) 1995, 25–50.

16228. ISERNHAGEN, HARTWIG.   Technology and the body: 'post-modernism' and the voices of John Barth. *In* (pp. 563–70) **117**.

16229. KOELB, CLAYTON.   The metamorphosis of the classics: John Barth, Philip Roth, and the European tradition. *In* (pp. 108–28) **123**.

16230. NAS, LOES.   Post-structuralist notions of reading in John Barth. English Academy Review (11) 1996, 44–50.

Donald Barthelme

16231. ADAMS, ALICE.   The American short story in the cybernetic age. *See* **14359**.

16232. BERMAN, JAYE.   A quote of many colors: women and masquerade in Donald Barthelme's postmodern parody novels. *In* (pp. 123–33) **33**.

Rick Bass

16233. SLOVIC, SCOTT.   A paint brush in one hand and a bucket of water in the other: nature writing and the politics of wilderness: an interview with Rick Bass. WebS (11:3) 1994, 11–29.

Frank Baum

16234. FLYNN, RICHARD.   Imitation Oz: the sequel as commodity. *See* **13676**.

16235. FRANSON, J. KARL.   From Vanity Fair to Emerald City: Baum's debt to Bunyan. *See* **7721**.

16236. GILMAN, TODD S.   'Aunt Em: Hate you! Hate Kansas! Taking the dog. Dorothy'. Consciousness and unconscious desire in *The Wizard of Oz*. CLAQ (20:4) 1995/96, 161–7.

16237. JOHNSON, MICHAEL.   An Ozdyssey in Plato. Mythlore (19:4) 1993, 22–7.

16238. MOREY, ANNE.   'A whole book for a nickel'? L. Frank Baum as filmmaker. *See* **14001**.

16239. WESTBROOK, M. DAVID.   Readers of Oz: young and old, old and New Historicist. CLAQ (21:3) 1996, 111–19.

James K. Baxter

16240. EGGLETON, DAVID.   Oh Baxter is everywhere. NZList, 23 Mar. 1996, 52–3.

16241. MILLAR, PAUL (ed.).   Cold spring: Baxter's unpublished early collection. Auckland; New York; Oxford: OUP, 1996. pp. xxii, 74.

Stephen Baxter

16242. BAXTER, STEPHEN.   Further visions: sequels to *The Time Machine*. Foundation (65) 1995, 41–50.

16243. —— Inspiration and research. Foundation (63) 1995, 56–60. (Profession of science fiction, 47.)

Peter S. Beagle

16244. KONDRATIEV, ALEXEI.   Tales newly told: a column on current modern fantasy. Mythlore (20:1) 1994, 41, 43.

Ann Beattie

16245. CLARK, MIRIAM MARTY. Postmodernism and its children: the case of Ann Beattie's *A Windy Day at the Reservoir*. SAtlR (61:1) 1996, 77–87.

16246. PLATH, JAMES. Counternarrative: an interview with Ann Beattie. MichQR (32:3) 1993, 359–79.

Charles Beaumont

16247. PROSSER, LEE. Running from the hunter: the life and works of Charles Beaumont. San Bernardino, CA: Borgo Press, 1996. pp. 136. (Milford popular writers of today, 68.)

Mary Beckett

16248. SULLIVAN, MEGAN. Mary Beckett: an interview. Irish Literary Supplement (14:2) 1995, 10–12.

Samuel Beckett

16249. ABBOTT, H. PORTER. Beckett writing Beckett: the author in the autograph. Ithaca, NY; London: Cornell UP, 1996. pp. xii, 196.

16250. —— Consorting with spirits: the arcane craft of Beckett's later drama. *In* (pp. 91–106) **119**.

16251. ACKERLEY, CHRIS. 'Do not despair': Samuel Beckett and Robert Greene. *See* **5830**.

16252. ANSPAUGH, KELLY. 'Faith, hope, and – what was it?': Beckett reading Joyce reading Dante. JBecS (5:1/2) 1996, 18–38.

16253. —— The partially purged: Samuel Beckett's *The Calmative* as anti-comedy. CJIS (22:1) 1996, 30–41.

16254. BAKER, PHIL. Ghost stories: Beckett and the literature of introjection. JBecS (5:1/2) 1996, 39–65.

16255. —— The stamp of the father in *Molloy*. JBecS (5:1/2) 1996, 142–55.

16256. BALZANO, WANDA. Rapsodia e palinodia: un 'modo' allegorico per *How It Is* di Samuel Beckett. Textus (3:1/2) 1990, 193–223.

16257. BEAUSANG, MICHAEL. *Watt*: logic, insanity, aphasia. Trans. by Valérie Galiussi. Style (30:3) 1996, 495–513.

16258. BECKER, JOACHIM. Klangkörper und Mentalchöre – Becketts Hörspiele und das dramatische Werk. Forum modernes Theater (11:2) 1996, 170–84.

16259. BERESFORD-PLUMMER, MICHAEL. The self as an eye/I: rehearsal reflections on the playing of Samuel Beckett. JBecS (6:1) 1996, 71–9.

16260. BERNARD, MICHEL. Samuel Beckett et son sujet: une apparition évanouissante. Paris: L'Harmattan, 1996. pp. 303. (Psychanalyse et civilisations.)

16261. BERNSTEIN, STEPHEN. The gothicism of Beckett's *Murphy*. Notes on Modern Irish Literature (6) 1994, 25–30.

16262. BERSANI, LEO; DUTOIT, ULYSSE. Arts of impoverishment: Beckett, Rothko, Resnais. (Bibl. 1995, 14690.) Rev. by Craig Saper in MFS (40:2) 1994, 441–3; by Mary Ann Caws in CLS (33:4) 1996, 422–3.

16263. BISSCHOPS, RALPH. Entropie et *élan vital* chez Beckett. Samuel Beckett Today (5) 1996, 125–41.

16264. BRATER, ENOCH. The drama in the text: Beckett's late fiction.

(Bibl. 1995, 14693.) Rev. by Marshall Williams in Theater (25:2) 1994, 112–14; by Daniel Mufson in NETJ (6) 1995, 133.

16265. BREUER, ROLF. Beckett's *Film*: philosophical and poetological implications. GRM (45:4) 1995, 463–7.

16266. —— HUBER, WERNER (eds). A checklist of Beckett criticism in German. (Bibl. 1986, 11164.) Paderborn: Schöningh, 1996. pp. x, 90. (Schriften der Universität-Gesamthochschule-Paderborn: Sprach- und Literaturwissenschaft, 16.) (Second ed.: first ed. 1986.) Rev. by Oliver Kiss in LWU (29:4) 1996, 319.

16267. BRYDEN, MARY. No stars without stripes: Beckett and Dante. RR (87:4) 1996, 541–56.

16268. —— Pozzo in Samuel Beckett's *Waiting for Godot. See* **2185**.

16269. —— The schizoid space: Beckett, Deleuze, and *L'Épuisé*. Samuel Beckett Today (5) 1996, 85–93.

16270. —— Women in Samuel Beckett's prose and drama: her own other. (Bibl. 1993, 11636.) Rev. by Ann Beer in YES (26) 1996, 319–20.

16271. CARTER, STEVEN. Estragon's ancient wound: a note on *Waiting for Godot. See* **11826**.

16272. CASELLI, DANIELA. Beckett's intertextual modalities of appropriation: the case of Leopardi. JBecS (6:1) 1996, 1–24.

16273. CATANZARO, MARY F. The elemental space of passion: the *topos* of Purgatory in Beckett's *Play*. Analecta Husserliana (44) 1995, 49–57.

16274. —— Musical form and Beckett's *Lessness*. Notes on Modern Irish Literature (4) 1992, 45–50.

16275. CONNOR, STEVEN. Beckett's interdictions. *In* (pp. 313–22) **49**.

16276. COTTREAU, DEBORAH. Friel and Beckett: the politics of language. *In* (pp. 160–9) **60**.

16277. COUSINEAU, TOM. The lost father in Beckett's novels. Samuel Beckett Today (5) 1996, 73–83.

16278. CRAIG, GEORGE. By whose hand? The special case of Samuel Beckett. *See* **3121**.

16279. CRONIN, ANTHONY. Samuel Beckett: the last Modernist. London: HarperCollins, 1996. pp. ix, 645, (plates) 12. Rev. by Christopher Prendergast in LRB (18:22) 1996, 8–10; by John Taylor in TLS, 27 Sept. 1996, 3–4.

16280. DANZIGER, MARIE A. Text/countertext: postmodern paranoia in Samuel Beckett, Doris Lessing, and Philip Roth. New York; Frankfurt; Bern; Paris: Lang, 1996. pp. 120. (Studies in literary criticism and theory, 3.) (Cf. bibl. 1992, 12714.)

16281. DEN TOONDER, JEANETTE. *Compagnie*: chimère autobiographique et métatexte. Samuel Beckett Today (5) 1996, 143–53.

16282. DILLON, CYNTHIA BISHOP. Active interpretation/deconstruction play: postmodern considerations of acting in the plays of Samuel Beckett. JDTC (8:1) 1993, 27–43.

16283. DILLON MERCIER, EILÍS. Beckett's Irishness. *In* (pp. 328–35)**49**.

16284. DOHERTY, FRANCIS. Paf, hop, bing and ping. JSSE (17) 1991, 23–41.

16285. DOLL, MARY A. Ghosts of themselves: the Demeter women in Beckett. *In* (pp. 121–35) **46**.

16286. DUFFY, BRIAN. *Malone meurt*: the comfort of narrative. JBecS (6:1) 1996, 25–47.

16287. Essif, Les. Introducing the 'hyper' theatrical subject: the *mise en abyme* of empty space. JDTC (9:1) 1994, 67–86.

16288. Esslin, Martin. Beckett's German context. *In* (pp. 41–50) **119**.

16289. Foster, Verna. Buckets o' Beckett in Chicago 1996. JBecS (5:1/2) 1996, 157–65.

16290. Furlani, André. Samuel Beckett's *Molloy*: Spartan maieutics. Samuel Beckett Today (5) 1996, 105–23.

16291. Garforth, Julian A. George Tabori's Bair essentials – a perspective on Beckett staging in Germany. Forum modernes Theater (9:1) 1994, 59–75.

16292. —— Translating Beckett's translations. *See* **3136**.

16293. —— A trilingual *Godot*. *See* **3137**.

16294. Genetti, Stefano. Molto dopo Chamfort, Beckett. Quaderni di lingue e letterature (19) 1994, 163–79.

16295. Gilbert, Inger. The quotidian sublime: from language to imagination in Beckett's Three Novels and *Happy Days*. RR (84:4) 1993, 437–62.

16296. Giménez Micó, José Antonio. Le récit en direct chez Cortázar et Beckett: ces personnages qui lisent/se font lire l'histoire de leur propre devenir. CanRCL (21:4) 1994, 597–612.

16297. Gontarski, S. E. Beckett in London: winter 1996. JBecS (5:1/2) 1996, 167–75.

16298. Gordon, Lois. The world of Samuel Beckett, 1906–1946. New Haven, CT; London: Yale UP, 1996. pp. ix, 250. Rev. by John Taylor in TLS, 27 Sept. 1996, 3–4.

16299. Gray, Katherine M. Troubling the body: toward a theory of Beckett's use of the human body onstage. JBecS (5:1/2) 1996, 1–17.

16300. Gray, Katherine Martin. Beckettian interiority. Samuel Beckett Today (5) 1996, 95–103.

16301. Graziani, Luisa Laura. Ancora una '*stain upon the silence*': *Quad* di Samuel Beckett. QLLSM (3) 1989, 105–18.

16302. Green, David D. Beckett's *Dream*: more *niente* than *bel*. JBecS (5:1/2) 1996, 67–80.

16303. Gussow, Mel (ed.). Conversations with and about Beckett. London: Hern; New York: Grove Press, 1996. pp. 192. Rev. by A.H. in TLS, 18 Oct. 1996, 31.

16304. Haefner, Gerhard. Klassiker des englischen Romans im 20. Jahrhundert: Joseph Conrad, D. H. Lawrence, James Joyce, Virginia Woolf, Samuel Beckett. (Bibl. 1992, 12728.) Rev. by Rüdiger Imhof in ZAA (41:4) 1993, 371–3.

16305. Harty, John, iii. Is Beckett's 'come in' in *Finnegans Wake*? Notes on Modern Irish Literature (5) 1993, 52–6.

16306. Hoevels, Fritz Erik. Psychoanalyse und Literatur-wissenschaft: Grundlagen und Beispiele. Freiburg: Ahriman, 1996. pp. 282.

16307. Houppermans, Sjef. À cheval. Samuel Beckett Today (5) 1996, 43–55.

16308. Hutchings, William. *All Over* again: Edward Albee's *Three Tall Women* and the later Beckett plays. *See* **15909**.

16309. Jackson, Shannon. Performing the performance of power in Beckett's *Catastrophe*. JDTC (6:2) 1992, 23–41.

16310. Johnson, Toni O'Brien.   Unfamilial Beckett: unrelated voices in the plays. SPELL (9) 1996, 235–47.

16311. Juliet, Charles.   Conversations with Samuel Beckett and Bram van Velde. (Bibl. 1995, 14721.) Rev. by John Pilling in JBecS (5:1/2) 1996, 227–30.

16312. Junker, Mary.   Beckett: the Irish dimension. Dublin: Wolfhound Press, 1995. pp. 199. Rev. by Christopher Murray in IUR (26:2) 1996, 382–4.

16313. Kalb, Jonathan.   Beckett in performance. (Bibl. 1994, 11712.) Rev. by John Simon in JDTC (5:2) 1991, 223–6.

16314. Kang, Jae-Won.   Samuel Beckett eui geuk e natanan mihak. (The aesthetic in the structure of Samuel Beckett's drama.) Unpub. doct. diss., Kyungsang Univ., Korea, 1996.

16315. Katz, Daniel.   'Alone in the accusative': Beckett's narcissistic echoes. *See* **2656**.

16316. Kellman, Steven G.   J. M. Coetzee and Samuel Beckett: the translingual link. *See* **3156**.

16317. Kennedy, Andrew K.   Samuel Beckett. (Bibl. 1994, 11714.) Rev. by John Swan in JDTC (5:2) 1991, 223–6.

16318. Kenner, Hugh.   A reader's guide to Samuel Beckett. Syracuse, NY: Syracuse UP, 1996. pp. 208. (Irish studies.)

16319. Kesting, Marianne.   Ich-Figuration und Erzählerschachtelung: zur Selbstreflexion der dichterischen Imagination. *See* **10682**.

16320. Kiely, Declan D.   'The termination of this solitaire': a textual error in *Murphy*. *See* **710**.

16321. Kim, Hwa Soon.   The counterpoint of hope, obsession, and desire for death in five plays by Samuel Beckett. New York; Frankfurt; Bern; Paris: Lang, 1996. pp. xii, 104. (Currents in comparative Romance languages and literatures, 25.) (Cf. bibl. 1992, 12743.)

16322. Knowlson, James.   Damned to fame: the life of Samuel Beckett. London: Bloomsbury; New York: Simon & Schuster, 1996. pp. xxiv, 872, (plates) 32. Rev. by Christopher Prendergast in LRB (18:22) 1996, 8–10; by John Taylor in TLS, 27 Sept. 1996, 3–4; by Chris Ackerley in JBecS (6:1) 1996, 157–62.

16323. —— (gen. ed.).   The theatrical notebooks of Samuel Beckett: vol. 1, *Waiting for Godot*, with a revised text. Ed. by Dougald McMillan and James Knowlson. (Bibl. 1993, 11685.) Rev. by Christopher Prendergast in LRB (18:22) 1996, 8–10.

16324. ——   The theatrical notebooks of Samuel Beckett: vol. 2, *Endgame*, with a revised text. Ed. by S. E. Gontarski. (Bibl. 1993, 11686.) Rev. by David E. Liss in Text (Ann Arbor) (8) 1995, 496–504; by Christopher Prendergast in LRB (18:22) 1996, 8–10.

16325. —— The theatrical notebooks of Samuel Beckett: vol. 3, *Krapp's Last Tape*, with a revised text. Ed. by James Knowlson. (Bibl. 1993, 11687.) Rev. by David E. Liss in Text (Ann Arbor) (8) 1995, 496–504; by Christopher Prendergast in LRB (18:22) 1996, 8–10.

16326. Kohlhäufl, Michael.   Warten auf den Erlöser: die Umkehrung der Emmausgeschichte in Becketts *En attendant Godot*. GRM (43:4) 1993, 443–51.

16327. Kondo, Masaki.   The self vanishing into impersonal staring into the void. *In* (pp. 323–7) **49**.

16328. Krance, Charles.   The ins and outs of directing Beckett. JBecS (5:1/2) 1996, 177–88 (review-article).

16329. LAUDANDO, CARLA MARIA. Deluge of fragments: Rabelais's *Fourth Book*, Sterne's *Fragment* and Beckett's *Fizzles*. *In* (pp. 157–65) **57**.

16330. LAYIWOLA, DELE. Irish folktales and Beckett's *Molloy*: a study in tropism. *In* (pp. 78–82) **60**.

16331. LEVY, ERIC. *The Unnamable*: the metaphysics of Beckettian introspection. JBecS (5:1/2) 1996, 81–105.

16332. LEVY, SHIMON. Does Beckett 'admit the chaos'? JBecS (6:1) 1996, 81–95.

16333. LOCATELLI, CARLA. Delogocentering silence: Beckett's ultimate unwording. *In* (pp. 67–89) **119**.

16334. —— Unwording the world: Samuel Beckett's prose works after the Nobel Prize. (Bibl. 1993, 11693.) Rev. by Margherita Giulietti in Aevum (65:3) 1991, 719–21.

16335. LUERE, JEANE. A market for monologue? *See* **15910**.

16336. McCARTHY, GERRY. 'Codes from a mixed-up machine': the disintegrating actor in Beckett, Shepard, and, surprisingly, Shakespeare. *In* (pp. 171–87) **119**.

16337. MALINOWSKA, BARBARA. Beyond the Absurd: language games in the theatre of María Irene Fornés, Samuel Beckett, and Eugène Ionesco. TexPres (12) 1991, 55–60.

16338. MEHTA, XERXES. Shapes of suffering: image/narrative/impromptu in Beckett's *Ohio Impromptu*. JBecS (6:1) 1996, 97–118.

16339. MEIHUIZEN, NICHOLAS. Beckett and Coetzee: the aesthetics of insularity. Literator (17:1) 1996, 143–52.

16340. MISKINIS, STEVEN. Enduring recurrence: Samuel Beckett's nihilistic poetics. ELH (63:4) 1996, 1047–67.

16341. MORI, NAOYA. Beckett's brief dream: Dante in *Mal vu mal dit* and *Stirrings Still*. *In* (pp. 283–91) **49**.

16342. MORSE, DONALD E. Starting from the earth, starting from the stars: the fantastic in Samuel Beckett's plays and James Joyce's *Ulysses*. *In* (pp. 6–18) **112**.

16343. MURPHY, P. J. Critique of Beckett criticism: a guide to research in English, French, and German. (Bibl. 1995, 14734.) Rev. by Marshall Williams in Theater (25:2) 1994, 112–14.

16344. NISCHIK, REINGARD M. Körpersprache im Drama: ein Beitrag zur Semiotik des Dramas. *See* **6828**.

16345. O'BRIEN, EOIN; FOURNIER, EDITH (eds). Dream of fair to middling women. (Bibl. 1993, 11699.) New York: Arcade, 1993. Rev. by Denis Donoghue in BkW, 23 May 1996, 8.

16346. O'HARA, J. D. Savagely damned to fame. *See* **9325**.

16347. OPPENHEIM, LOIS (ed.). Directing Beckett. (Bibl. 1995, 14738.) Rev. by Charles Krance in JBecS (5:1/2) 1996, 177–88.

16348. —— BUNING, MARIUS (eds). Beckett on and on ——. Madison, NJ: Fairleigh Dickinson UP; London; Toronto: Assoc. UPs, 1996. pp. 259. (Papers presented to the Second International Samuel Beckett Conference, held in The Hague, Apr. 22, 1992.)

16349. PACCAUD-HUGUET, JOSIANE. En écoutant parler les sons: *Still*, de Samuel Beckett. JSSE (23) 1994, 63–76.

16350. PAPA, LEE. 'This one is enough for you?': indeterminacy and the interpretive tension between text and performance in *Waiting for Godot*. TexPres (15) 1994, 73–8.

16351. PIETTE, ADAM. Remembering and the sound of words:

Mallarmé, Proust, Joyce, Beckett. Oxford: Clarendon Press; New York: OUP, 1996. pp. 285.

16352. PULTAR, GÖNÜL.   Technique and tradition in Beckett's trilogy of novels. Lanham, MD; London: UP of America, 1996. pp. 177.

16353. RABATÉ, JEAN-MICHEL.   Beckett's ghosts and fluxions. Samuel Beckett Today (5) 1996, 23–40.

16354. ——— The ghosts of modernity. Gainesville: Florida UP, 1996. pp. xxii, 258. (Crosscurrents.) Rev. by John Pilling in JBecS (6:1) 1996, 167–70.

16355. RABINOVITZ, RUBIN.   Innovation in Samuel Beckett's fiction. (Bibl. 1995, 14743.) Rev. by Sylvie Debevec Henning in StudN (28:4) 1996, 611–12.

16356. RODRÍGUEZ-GAGO, ANTONIA.   Molly's 'happy nights' and Winnie's 'happy days'. *In* (pp. 29–40) **119**.

16357. ROSS, CIARAN.   La 'pensée de la mère': fonction et structure d'un fantasme. Samuel Beckett Today (5) 1996, 9–20.

16358. STERN, RICHARD.   Samuel Beckett. Salmagundi (90/91) 1991, 179–90.

16359. STRAUSS, WALTER,   Imagination at wit's end: Beckett's final 'trilogy'. Comparatist (15) 1991, 150–6.

16360. STURM, OLIVER.   Der letzte Satz der letzten Seite ein letztes Mal: der alte Beckett. Hamburg: Europäische Verlagsanstalt, 1994. pp. 226. (Europäische Bibliothek, 20.) Rev. by Joachim Becker in Forum modernes Theater (10:2) 1995, 221–4.

16361. TAKAHASHI, YASUNARI.   Memory inscribed in the body: *Krapp's Last Tape* and the Noh play *Izutsu*. *In* (pp. 51–65) **119**.

16362. THOMAS, MICHAEL.   Storytelling and silence in the plays of Samuel Beckett. ERev (6:4) 1996, 31–4.

16363. TÖNNIES, MERLE.   The spectator as participant: the role of integrating audience laughter in Samuel Beckett's drama. Forum modernes Theater (11:2) 1996, 185–96.

16364. VELISSARIOU, ASPASIA.   *Not I*: an aborted autobiography. JDTC (8:1) 1993, 45–59.

16365. WARNER, MARTIN.   Modes of political imagining. *In* (pp. 98–128) **63**.

16366. WOLFF, ELLEN.   Watt ... Knott ... Anglo-Ireland: Samuel Beckett's *Watt*. JBecS (5:1/2) 1996, 107–41.

Ven Begamudré

16367. COLEMAN, DANIEL.   Writing dislocation: transculturalism, gender, immigrant families. A conversation with Ven Begamudré. CanL (149) 1996, 36–51.

Louis Begley

16368. BEGLEY, LOUIS.   Reviewing his reviewers. BkW, 22 Dec. 1996, 1, 8.

Brendan Behan

16369. ELBANNA, ETAF A.   The autobiography of an Irish rebel: Brendan Behan's *Borstal Boy*. *In* (pp. 170–6) **60**.

16370. GONZALEZ, ALEXANDER G.; RHODES, ROBERT E.   Annotations for Brendan Behan's *The Hostage*. Notes on Modern Irish Literature (7:2) 1995, 36–44.

S. N. Behrman

16371. FORDYCE, WILLIAM. S. N. Behrman's *End of Summer* in the context of Molière's *Tartuffe*. AmDr (2:1) 1992, 1–25.

Clive Bell

16372. SHAFFER, BRIAN W. Civilization in Bloomsbury: Woolf's *Mrs Dalloway* and Bell's 'theory of civilization'. JML (19:1) 1994, 73–87.

Hilaire Belloc

16373. JONES, ELIZABETH. Eliot and *Tarantella*. NQ (43:4) 1996, 444–5.

16374. SHERBO, ARTHUR. Belated justice to Hilaire Belloc, versifier (1870–1953). *See* **830**.

Saul Bellow

16375. AIRAUDI, JESSE T. 'A rock of defence for human nature': philosophical and literary approaches to the causes of violence. Analecta Husserliana (49) 1996, 265–81.

16376. AMIS, MARTIN (introd.). The adventures of Augie March. London: Campbell; New York: Knopf, 1995. pp. xxxvii, 616. (Everyman's library, 215.)

16377. ANDERSON, DAVID D. Growing up in Chicago between the wars: the literary lives of Saul Bellow and Isaac Rosenfeld. SSMLN (25:3) 1995, 22–8.

16378. —— Saul Bellow and the Midwestern myth of the search. MidM (22) 1994, 46–53.

16379. —— Saul Bellow and the Midwestern myth of the search. SBJ (14:1) 1996, 19–26.

16380. —— 'Starting out in Chicago': Saul Bellow's literary apprenticeship. MidM (21) 1993, 44–56.

16381. BACH, GERHARD. Margin as center: Bellow and post-Wall Europe. SBJ (14:1) 1996, 96–107.

16382. CHAVKIN, ALLAN. The Romantic imagination of Saul Bellow. *In* (pp. 113–38) **28**.

16383. COLAKIS, MARIANTHE. Saul Bellow's *The Last Analysis* and Sophocles' *Oedipus at Colonus*. TexPres (15) 1994, 25–9.

16384. CORY, MARK. Comedic distance in Holocaust literature. JAC (18:1) 1995, 35–40.

16385. CRONIN, GLORIA L.; HALL, BLAINE H. Selected annotated critical bibliography for 1994. SBJ (14:2) 1996, 73–102.

16386. FARACI, MARY. Saul Bellow and comparative politics. SBJ (14:1) 1996, 68–83.

16387. FRIEDRICH, MARIANNE M. Character and narration in the short fiction of Saul Bellow. (Bibl. 1995, 14794.) Rev. by Sanford E. Marovitz in SBJ (14:2) 1996, 70–2.

16388. FURMAN, ANDREW. Saul Bellow's Middle East problem. SBJ (14:1) 1996, 40–67.

16389. GREENSTEIN, MICHAEL. Bellow and anthropology. SBJ (14:2) 1996, 17–27.

16390. HEER, JEET. Saul Bellow and the *schmoes*. LRC (5:6) 1996, 23.

16391. MAROVITZ, SANFORD E. The Emersonian lesson of *Humboldt's Gift. See* **11183**.

16392. Miraglia, Anne Marie.   Texts engendering texts: a Québécois writing of American novels. *In* (pp. 49–60) **51**.

16393. Newman, Judie.   Bellow's ransom tale: the Holocaust, *The Victim*, and *The Double*. SBJ (14:1) 1996, 3–18.

16394. Pughe, Thomas.   Reading the picaresque: Mark Twain's *The Adventures of Huckleberry Finn*, Saul Bellow's *The Adventures of Augie March*, and more recent adventures. *See* **12601**.

16395. Quayum, M. A.   Emerson's *Humboldt*: a probable source for Bellow's Von Humboldt Fleisher in *Humboldt's Gift*. *See* **11191**.

16396. —— Quest for equilibrium: Transcendental ideas in Bellow's *Herzog*. *See* **11192**.

16397. Reichman, Ravit.   The medical model and the wartime reading of *Dangling Man*; or, What can Joseph recover? SBJ (14:2) 1996, 28–42.

16398. Salzberg, Joel.   Malamud on Bellow, Bellow on Malamud: a correspondence and friendship. SBJ (14:2) 1996, 3–16.

16399. Siegel, Ben.   Simply not a mandarin: Saul Bellow as Jew and Jewish writer. *In* (pp. 62–88) **123**.

16400. Wilson, Raymond J., iii.   Saul Bellow's *Herzog* and Dostoevsky's *The Brothers Karamazov*. SBJ (14:1) 1996, 27–39.

16401. Yang, Kyoung-Zoo.   Ggaedaleum gwa guwon: Saul Bellow soseol eui shinbi jueui yeongu. (Enlightenment and salvation: a study of mysticism in Saul Bellow's novels.) Unpub. doct. diss., Korea Univ., Seoul, 1996.

Ludwig Bemelmans

16402. Eastman, Jackie Fisher.   Ludwig Bemelmans. New York: Twayne; London: Prentice Hall, 1996. pp. xviii, 150. (Twayne's US authors, 665.)

Stephen Vincent Benét

16403. Partenheimer, David.   Benét's *The Devil and Daniel Webster*. Exp (55:1) 1996, 37–40.

Alan Bennett

16404. Bennett, Alan.   Writing home. (Bibl. 1994, 11790.) Rev. by Lloyd Rose in BkW, 3 Sept. 1995, 2.

Arnold Bennett

16405. McDonald, Peter D.   Bringing the text to book: John Lane and the making of Arnold Bennett? *See* **966**.

16406. Marroni, Francesco.   The paradigm of negativity in *Anna of the Five Towns*. Textus (4) 1991, 97–118.

E. F. Benson

16407. Mather, Rachel R.   The heirs of Jane Austen: twentieth-century writers of the comedy of manners. *See* **10304**.

Eugene Benson

16408. Scholnick, Robert J.   'Culture' or democracy: Whitman, Eugene Benson, and the *Galaxy*. *See* **1355**.

Mary Benson

16409. BENSON, MARY.   A far cry: the making of a South African. Randburg: Ravan Press, 1996. pp. 264. (Ravan writers.) (Second ed.: first ed. 1989.)

John Berendt (1939–)

16410. BERENDT, JOHN.   Room at the top. BkW, 24 Sept. 1995, 1, 10.

John Berger

16411. MESMER, MICHAEL W.   Apostle to the techno/peasants: word and image in the work of John Berger. *In* (pp. 199–227) **44**.

Suzanne E. Berger

16412. BERGER, SUZANNE E.   Horizontal woman: the story of a body in exile. Boston, MA: Houghton Mifflin, 1996. pp. xviii, 216.

Sara Berkeley

16413. MEANEY, GERARDINE.   History gasps: myth in contemporary Irish women's poetry. *In* (pp. 99–113) **86**.

Steven Berkoff

16414. BERKOFF, STEVEN.   Free association: an autobiography. London; Boston, MA: Faber & Faber, 1996. pp. xiii, 410. Rev. by Paul Bailey in TLS, 17 May 1996, 29.

Charles Bernstein

16415. BARTHOLOMAE, DAVID, *et al.*   On poetry, language, and teaching: a conversation with Charles Bernstein. Boundary 2 (23:3) 1996, 45–66.
16416. PEQUEÑO GLAZIER, LOSS.   An autobiographical interview with Charles Bernstein. Boundary 2 (23:3) 1996, 21–43.
16417. SCHULTZ, SUSAN M.   Visions of silence in poems of Ann Lauterbach and Charles Bernstein. Talisman (13) 1994/95, 163–77.

Daniel Berrigan

16418. WAGNER, MARK.   A conversation with Daniel Berrigan. Agni (43) 1996, 1–9.

Wendell Berry

16419. COOK, RUFUS.   Poetry and place: Wendell Berry's ecology of literature. *See* **14887**.
16420. DITSKY, JOHN.   Farming Kentucky: the fiction of Wendell Berry. HC (31:1) 1994, 1–9.
16421. HICKS, JACK.   Wendell Berry's husband to the world: a place on earth. *In* (pp. 51–66) **25**.
16422. HÖNNIGHAUSEN, LOTHAR.   Ecopoetics: on poetological poems by Gary Snyder and Wendell Berry. PoetA (28:3/4) 1996, 356–67.
16423. KNOTT, JOHN.   Into the woods with Wendell Berry. ELit (23:1) 1996, 124–40.
16424. MURPHY, PATRICK D.   Penance or perception: spirituality and land in the poetry of Gary Snyder and Wendell Berry. *In* (pp. 237–49) **25**.

16425. Pennington, Vince.   Interview with Wendell Berry. KenR (13:1/2) 1996, 57–70.

16426. Weiland, Steven.   Wendell Berry resettles America: fidelity, education, and culture. *In* (pp. 37–49) **25**.

John Berryman

16427. DeFrees, Madeline.   Resolution and independence: John Berryman's ghost and the meaning of life. GetR (9:1) 1996, 9–29 (review-article).

16428. Hardy, Barbara.   Re-reading Berryman: power and solicitation. Eng (40:166) 1991, 37–46.

16429. Levine, Philip.   Mine own John Berryman. GetR (4:4) 1991, 533–52.

16430. Mariani, Paul.   Dream song: the life of John Berryman. (Bibl. 1992, 12826.) Rev. by Mark Jarman in GetR (4:4) 1991, 565–79.

16431. —— Lowell on Berryman on Lowell. GetR (4:4) 1991, 581–92.

16432. Thornbury, Charles (ed.).   Collected poems, 1937–1971. (Bibl. 1990, 9952.) Rev. by Mark Jarman in GetR (4:4) 1991, 565–79.

16433. —— Eight previously unpublished poems by John Berryman. GetR (4:4) 1991, 553–64.

Bate Besong

16434. Lindfors, Bernth.   Response to Dunton on Bate Besong. JCL (30:1) 1995, 107–8.

Ursula Bethell

16435. Brewer, Rosemary.   Mary Ursula Bethell: her women friends. Printout (11) 1996, 68–70.

Sir John Betjeman

16436. Cole, Robert.   'Good relations': Irish neutrality and the propaganda of John Betjeman, 1941–43. EI (30:4) 1995, 33–46.

Doris Betts

16437. Brown, W. Dale.   Interview with Doris Betts. SoQ (34:2) 1996, 91–104.

Helen Bevington

16438. Bevington, Helen.   The third and only way: reflections on staying alive. Durham, NC; London: Duke UP, 1996. pp. xii, 209.

Laurence Binyon

16439. Hatcher, John.   Laurence Binyon: poet, scholar of East and West. (Bibl. 1995, 14859.) Rev. by Mick Imlah in TLS, 5 July 1996, 7.

Earle Birney

16440. Cameron, Elspeth.   Earle Birney: a life. (Bibl. 1995, 14861.) Rev. by Jon Kertzer in CanL (150) 1996, 154–6; by Fred Cogswell in JCP (11) 1996, 177–8.

16441. Noonan, Gerald.   In the guts of the living: Earle Birney's words. LRC (5:5) 1996, 23.

Elizabeth Bishop

16442. BENTON, WILLIAM (ed.). Exchanging hats: paintings. New York: Farrar, Straus, & Giroux, 1996. pp. xx, 106.

16443. BLASING, MUTLU KONUK. Politics and form in postmodern poetry: O'Hara, Bishop, Ashbery and Merrill. *See* **16053**.

16444. BOLAND, EAVAN. Time, memory and obsession. PN Review (18:2) 1991, 18–24.

16445. COSTELLO, BONNIE. Elizabeth Bishop: questions of mastery. (Bibl. 1995, 14866.) Rev. by Thomas Gardner in Review (17) 1995, 287–90; by Neil Besner in CanL (150) 1996, 115.

16446. DIEHL, JOANNE FEIT. Elizabeth Bishop and Marianne Moore: the psychodynamics of creativity. (Bibl. 1995, 14869.) Rev. by Neil Besner in CanL (150) 1996, 115–16.

16447. ERKKILA, BETSY. Elizabeth Bishop, Modernism, and the Left. AmLH (8:2) 1996, 284–310.

16448. FOUNTAIN, GARY; BRAZEAU, PETER. Remembering Elizabeth Bishop: an oral biography. (Bibl. 1994, 11808.) Rev. by Thomas Gardner in Review (17) 1995, 277–80; by Barbara Page in ConLit (37:1) 1996, 119–31.

16449. GARDNER, THOMAS. Elizabeth Bishop and the powers of uncertainty. Review (17) 1995, 271–95 (review-article).

16450. GIROUX, ROBERT (ed.). One art: letters. (Bibl. 1995, 14875.) Rev. by Michael Dirda in BkW, 1 May 1994, 5; by Thomas Gardner in Review (17) 1995, 281–4; by Doris Earnshaw in WLT (69:1) 1995, 151–2; by Roberta Bienvenu in Green Mountains Review (8:2) 1995/96, 143–4; by Barbara Page in ConLit (37:1) 1996, 119–31.

16451. GOLDENSOHN, LORRIE. Elizabeth Bishop: the biography of a poetry. (Bibl. 1995, 14876.) Rev. by Thomas Gardner in Review (17) 1995, 290–3.

16452. GRAHAM, VICKI. Elizabeth Bishop's *Rainy Season; Sub-Tropics*: questions of poetic strategies. GetR (8:2) 1995, 297–309.

16453. HARRISON, VICTORIA. Elizabeth Bishop's poetics of intimacy. (Bibl. 1995, 14881.) Rev. by Thomas Gardner in Review (17) 1995, 293–5; by Neil Besner in CanL (150) 1996, 116.

16454. IRIMIA, MIHAELA. The art of losing: W. H. Auden and Elizabeth Bishop. *See* **16121**.

16455. KALSTONE, DAVID. Becoming a poet: Elizabeth Bishop with Marianne Moore and Robert Lowell. Ed. by Robert Hemenway. With a postscript by James Merrill. (Bibl. 1993, 11790.) Rev. by Thomas Gardner in Review (17) 1995, 284–7.

16456. LENSING, GEORGE S. The subtraction of emotion in the poetry of Elizabeth Bishop. GetR (5:1) 1992, 48–61.

16457. LOMBARDI, MARILYN MAY. The body and the song: Elizabeth Bishop's poetics. (Bibl. 1995, 14885.) Rev. by Gary Kerley in AL (68:1) 1996, 260–1; by Doris Earnshaw in WLT (70:2) 1996, 415.

16458. MILLIER, BRETT C. Elizabeth Bishop: life and the memory of it. (Bibl. 1995, 14889.) Rev. by X. J. Kennedy in GetR (7:2) 1994, 289–303; by David Jarraway in JCP (10) 1995, 140–6; by Thomas Gardner in Review (17) 1995, 273–7; by Corinne E. Blackmer in AmLH (8:1) 1996, 130–53; by Barbara Page in ConLit (37:1) 1996, 119–31; by Anthony Hecht in BkW, 28 Mar. 1996, 9; by Neil Besner in CanL (150) 1996, 116–17.

16459. Monteiro, George (ed.).   Conversations with Elizabeth Bishop. Jackson; London: Mississippi UP, 1996. pp. xix, 164. (Literary conversations.)

16460. Page, Barbara.   The rising figure of the poet: Elizabeth Bishop in letters and biography. ConLit (37:1) 1996, 119–31 (review-article).

16461. Siebald, Manfred.   '*Questions of travel*': die Dekonstruktion des touristischen Blicks in der Reiselyrik Elizabeth Bishops. Amst (41:4) 1996, 623–35.

16462. Spires, Elizabeth.   Elizabeth Bishop: 'The things I'd like to write'. GetR (5:1) 1992, 62–70.

16463. Stevenson, Anne.   The iceberg and the ship. MichQR (35:4) 1996, 704–19.

16464. Süssekind, Flora.   Poesia e paisagem o Brasil de Elizabeth Bishop. Letterature d'America (41/42) 1990, 211–29.

16465. Travisano, Thomas.   The Elizabeth Bishop phenomenon. *In* (pp. 217–44) **39**.

16466. —— Emerging genius: Elizabeth Bishop and *The Blue Pencil*, 1927–1930. GetR (5:1) 1992, 32–47.

16467. Upton, Lee.   Through the lens of Edward Lear: contesting sense in the poetry of Elizabeth Bishop. *See* **11761**.

16468. Wallace, Patricia.   Erasing the maternal: rereading Elizabeth Bishop. IowaR (22:2) 1992, 82–103.

16469. Zhou, Xiaojing.   Bishop's *Trouvée*. Exp (54:2) 1996, 102–5.

Algernon Blackwood

16470. Healy, Sharon.   Algernon Blackwood's gentle gothic. Romantist (9/10) 1985/86, 61–4.

Clark Blaise

16471. Lecker, Robert.   An other I: the fictions of Clark Blaise. Toronto: ECW Press, 1988. pp. 243. Rev. by Robert D. Beckett in ARCS (20:3) 1990, 391–3.

Michael Blake

16472. McQuillan, Gene.   'Extarminate the varlets!': the reconstruction of captivity narratives in *Dances with Wolves*. *See* **8337**.

16473. Ostwalt, Conrad.   *Dances with Wolves*: an American *Heart of Darkness*. *See* **14056**.

Robin Blaser

16474. Boughn, Michael.   Exody and some mechanics of splendor in Blaser and Emerson. *See* **11175**.

16475. Truitt, Samuel R.   An interview with Robin Blaser. Talisman (16) 1996, 5–25.

William Peter Blatty

16476. Geary, Robert F.   *The Exorcist*: deep horror? JFA (5:4) 1992, 55–63.

Norbert Blei

16477. Shereikis, Richard.   Scenes from the South Side: the Chicago fiction of Norbert Blei. Midamerica (18) 1991, 136–42.

Lee Blessing

16478. RICE, JOSEPH G.   An interview with Lee Blessing. AmDr (2:1) 1992, 84–100.

Edmund Blunden

16479. BOWIE, THOMAS G., JR.   An I for an eye: Edmund Blunden's war. WLA (5:2) 1993, 21–47.

Carol Bly

16480. BARTOS, EILEEN; HAYWOODE, ALYSSA; HUSSMANN, MARY. An interview with Carol Bly. IowaR (22:3) 1992, 1–17.

Robert Bly

16481. HARRIS, VICTORIA FRENKEL.   The incorporative consciousness of Robert Bly. (Bibl. 1992, 12860.) Rev. by Rosaly DeMaios Roffman in SHum (19:2) 1992, 198–202.

16482. JOHNSEN, WILLIAM A.   The treacherous years of postmodern poetry in English. *In* (pp. 75–91) **34**.

16483. LIBBY, ANTHONY.   Angels in the bone shop. *In* (pp. 281–301) **58**.

16484. MECHLING, ELIZABETH WALKER; MECHLING, JAY.   The Jung and the restless: the mythopoetic men's movement. SCJ (59:2) 1994, 97–111.

16485. SUAREZ, ERNEST.   Emerson on Vietnam: Dickey, Bly and the New Left. *See* **11200**.

Louise Bogan

16486. ROMAN, CAMILLE.   Robert Frost and three female modern poets: Amy Lowell, Louise Bogan, and Edna Millay. RFR (1995) 62–9.

Eavan Boland

16487. BOLAND, EAVAN.   Object lessons: the life of the woman and the poet in our time. (Bibl. 1995, 14924.) Rev. by Jeanne Heuving in ConLit (37:2) 1996, 317–24.

16488. —— The woman, the place, the poet. PN Review (17:3) 1991, 35–40.

16489. DENMAN, PETER.   Ways of saying: Boland, Carson, McGuckian. *In* (pp. 158–73) **86**.

16490. MAHON, ELLEN.   Eavan Boland's journey with the muse. *In* (pp. 179–94) **58**.

16491. MEANEY, GERARDINE.   History gasps: myth in contemporary Irish women's poetry. *In* (pp. 99–113) **86**.

16492. PADDON, SEIJA H.   The diversity of performance/ performance as diversity in the poetry of Laura (Riding) Jackson and Eavan Boland. ESCan (22:4) 1996, 425–39.

16493. RASCHKE, DEBRAH.   Eavan Boland's *Outside History* and *In a Time of Violence*: rescuing women, the concrete, and other things physical from the dung heap. ColbyQ (32:2) 1996, 135–42.

16494. WRIGHT, NANCY MEANS; HANNAN, DENNIS J.   Q and A with Eavan Boland. Irish Literary Supplement (10:1) 1991, 10–11. (Interview.)

Robert Bolt

16495. OTTEN, TERRY.   Historical drama and the dimensions of tragedy: *A Man for All Seasons* and *The Crucible*. AmDr (6:1) 1996, 42–60.

Ken Bolton

16496. O'BRIEN, GREGORY.   Running dog: the poetry of Ken Bolton. Sport (16) 1996, 150–60.

Edward Bond

16497. COHN, RUBY.   States of the artist: the plays of Edward Bond and Sam Shepard. *In* (pp. 169–87) **34**.

16498. HÄRTINGER, HERIBERT.   Elemente des epischen Theaters in *The War Plays* von Edward Bond. Forum modernes Theater (11:1) 1996, 70–81.

16499. KLEIN, HILDA.   Violence in the theatre of Edward Bond. In-between (4:2) 1995, 163–79.

16500. REINELT, JANELLE.   Theorizing utopia: Edward Bond's war plays. *In* (pp. 221–32) **83**.

16501. STEVENSON, MELANIE A.   Prospero back home in Milan: Bond's *Lear* as paradigm for post-imperial Britain. *See* **6973**.

16502. STUART, IAN.   Interview with Edward Bond. JDTC (8:2) 1994, 129–46.

16503. —— Politics in performance: the production work of Edward Bond, 1978–1990. New York; Frankfurt; Bern; Paris: Lang, 1996. pp. 191. (Artists and issues in the theatre, 6.) (Cf. bibl. 1992, 11081.)

Marita Bonner

16504. CHICK, NANCY.   Marita Bonner's revolutionary purple flowers: challenging the symbol of White womanhood. LHR (13:1) 1994/95, 21–32.

Arna Bontemps

16505. JAMES, CHARLES L.   Alberta Bontemps: reflections on flyleaves. LHR (13:1) 1994/95, 45–52.

16506. JONES, KIRKLAND C.   Bontemps and the old South. AAR (27:2) 1993, 179–85.

Roo Borson

16507. BARRON, GRAHAM.   The incurable beauty of the earth: an interview with Roo Borson. ECanW (55) 1995, 230–9.

Sheila Bosworth

16508. WOODLAND, J. RANDAL.   'New people in the old museum of New Orleans': Ellen Gilchrist, Sheila Bosworth, and Nancy Lemann. *In* (pp. 194–210) **65**.

David Bottoms

16509. BROWNING, DEBORAH; LIMEHOUSE, CAPERS.   The poetry receiver: an interview with David Bottoms. Atlanta Review (1:1) 1994, 20–8.

Elizabeth Bowen

16510. COATES, JOHN. Emotional need and cultural codes in *The House in Paris*. Ren (47:1) 1994, 11–29.

16511. —— False history and true in *The Little Girls*. Ren (44:2) 1992, 83–103.

16512. —— Moral choice in Elizabeth Bowen's *To the North*. Ren (43:4) 1991, 241–67.

16513. DUKES, THOMAS. Desire unsatisfied: war and love in *The Heat of the Day* and *Moon Tiger*. WLA (3:1) 1991, 75–97.

16514. GILBERT, PAUL. The idea of a national literature. *In* (pp. 198–217) **63**.

16515. GRUBGELD, ELIZABETH. Cultural autobiography and the female subject: the genre of the patrilineal history and the lifewriting of Elizabeth Bowen. Genre (27:3) 1994, 209–26.

16516. HUGHES, CLAIR. 'Hound voices': the Big House in three novels by Anglo-Irish women writers. *In* (pp. 349–55) **49**.

16517. KHOLOUSSY, SAMIA. Cracks in the edifice of national consciousness: Tawfik El Hakim's *Bird of the East* and Elizabeth Bowen's *The Last September*. *In* (pp. 266–77) **60**.

16518. WESSELS, J. A. Irish nationalism and the Anglo-Irish: historical and literary parallels to Afrikanerdom. *In* (pp. 244–51) **60**.

Neal Bowers

16519. BOWERS, NEAL. A loss for words: plagiarism and silence. ASch (63:4) 1994, 545–55.

Jane Bowles

16520. DIAMOND, ELIN. 'The garden is a mess': maternal space in Bowles, Glaspell, Robins. *In* (pp. 121–39) **119**.

16521. LACEY, R. KEVIN; POOLE, FRANCIS (eds). Mirrors on the Maghrib: critical reflections on Paul and Jane Bowles and other American writers in Morocco. *See* **13166**.

Paul Bowles

16522. BAEPLER, PAUL. Wild thing: White captivity in Paul Bowles' *A Distant Episode*. JSSE (23) 1994, 9–17.

16523. LACEY, R. KEVIN; POOLE, FRANCIS (eds). Mirrors on the Maghrib: critical reflections on Paul and Jane Bowles and other American writers in Morocco. *See* **13166**.

16524. MILLER, JEFFREY (ed.). In touch: the letters of Paul Bowles. (Bibl. 1995, 14975.) Rev. by Jack Sullivan in BkW, 14 Aug. 1994, 11.

16525. OWEN, PETER. Who is Paul Bowles? 'Anything one might want to ask about the writer is in his work'. Anaïs (12) 1994, 109–19.

16526. VETSCH, FLORIAN. Desultory correspondence: an interview with Paul Bowles on Gertrude Stein. MFS (42:3) 1996, 627–45.

Kay Boyle

16527. MELLEN, JOAN. Kay Boyle: author of herself. (Bibl. 1995, 14978.) Rev. by Deirdre Neilen in WLT (69:2) 1995, 371.

T. Coraghessan Boyle

16528. LAW, DANIELLE. Caught in the current: plotting history in *Water Music*. In-between (5:1) 1996, 41–50.

16529. SCHENKER, DANIEL.   A *samurai* in the South: cross-cultural disaster in T. Coraghessan Boyle's *East Is East.* SoQ (34:1) 1995, 70–80.

Malcolm Bradbury

16530. GENSANE, B.; MENEGALDO, G.; SHUSTERMAN, R.   An interview with Malcolm Bradbury. EEM (2:1) 1993, 39–46.

Ray Bradbury

16531. BAILEY, K. V.   Mars is a district of Sheffield. *See* **15919**.

16532. KELLEY, KEN.   Ray Bradbury. Playboy (Chicago) (43:5) 1996, 47–8, 50, 52–4, 56, 149–50. (Interview.)

16533. LOGSDON, LOREN.   Ray Bradbury's *The Kilimanjaro Device*: the need to correct the errors of time. MidM (20) 1992, 28–39.

16534. McGIVERON, RAFEEQ O.   Bradbury's *Fahrenheit 451.* Exp (54:3) 1996, 177–80.

16535. ——— What 'carried the trick'? Mass exploitation and the decline of thought in Ray Bradbury's *Fahrenheit 451.* Extrapolation (37:3) 1996, 245–56.

David Bradley

16536. GLISERMAN, MARTIN.   Psychoanalysis, language, and the body of the text. *See* **8967**.

16537. PAVLIĆ, EDWARD.   Syndetic redemption: above-underground *emergence* in David Bradley's *The Chaneysville Incident.* AAR (30:2) 1996, 165–84.

16538. REICHARDT, ULFRIED.   Writing the past: history, fiction, and subjectivity in two recent novels about slavery. YREAL (11) 1995, 283–98.

16539. WILSON, MATTHEW.   The African-American historian: David Bradley's *The Chaneysville Incident.* AAR (29:1) 1995, 97–107.

Marion Zimmer Bradley

16540. FUOG, KAREN E. C.   Imprisoned in the phallic oak: Marion Zimmer Bradley and Merlin's seductress. Quondam et Futurus (1:1) 1991, 73–88.

16541. HUGHES, MELINDA.   Dark sisters and light sisters: sister doubles and the search for sisterhood in *The Mists of Avalon* and *The White Raven.* Mythlore (19:1) 1993, 24–8.

John Braine

16542. WAGNER, HANS-PETER.   Learning to read the female body: on the function of Manet's *Olympia* in John Braine's *Room at the Top.* ZAA (42:1) 1994, 38–53.

Dionne Brand

16543. BRAND, DIONNE.   Bread out of stone: recollections, sex, recognitions, race, dreaming, politics. Toronto: Coach House Press, 1994. pp. 183.

16544. COOKE, MICHAEL G.   A rhetoric of obliquity in African and Caribbean women writers. *In* (pp. 169–84) **80**.

Edward Kamau Brathwaite

16545. BROWN, STEWART (ed.). The art of Kamau Brathwaite. Bridgend, Mid-Glamorgan: Seren, 1995. pp. 275.

16546. COOPER, CAROLYN. Race and the cultural politics of self-representation: a view from the University of the West Indies. RAL (27:4) 1996, 97–105.

16547. EZENWA-OHAETO. From a common root: revolutionary vision and social change in the poetry of Brathwaite and Chinweizu. JCS (8:1/2) 1990/91, 89–104.

16548. FRASER, ROBERT. Mental travellers: myths of return in the poetry of Walcott and Brathwaite. *In* (pp. 7–13) **102**.

16549. HOPPE, JOHN K. From Jameson to syncretism: the communal imagination of American identity in Edward Brathwaite's *The Arrivants*. WebS (9:3) 1992, 92–105.

16550. MACKEY, NATHANIEL. *Other*: from noun to verb. *See* **1983**.

16551. TEN KORTENAAR, NEIL. Where the Atlantic meets the Caribbean: Kamau Brathwaite's *The Arrivants* and T. S. Eliot's *The Waste Land*. RAL (27:4) 1996, 15–27.

16552. WILLIAMS, EMILY ALLEN. Whose words are these? Lost heritage and search for self in Edward Brathwaite's poetry. CLAJ (40:1) 1996, 104–11.

Richard Brautigan

16553. NEUSTADTER, ROGER. The astro-turf garden: pastoralism in the industrial age. PCR (2:2) 1991, 81–93.

Gerald Brenan

16554. GATHORNE-HARDY, JONATHAN. The interior castle: a life of Gerald Brenan. (Bibl. 1993, 11845.) Rev. by Jeffrey Meyers in ASch (62:4) 1993, 626–9.

16555. —— MEYERS, JEFFREY. Sex in the head. ASch (63:4) 1994, 632–5.

Christopher Brennan (1870–1932)

16556. PYM, ANTHONY. Strategies of the frontier in *fin de siècle* Australia. CL (48:1) 1996, 19–38.

Lee Breuer

16557. COCO, BILL. The dramaturgy of the dream play: monologues by Breuer, Chaikin, Shepard. *In* (pp. 159–70) **119**.

Breyten Breytenbach

16558. BREYTENBACH, BREYTEN. The terrain of the artist. BkW, 13 Nov. 1994, 1, 10.

16559. DIMITRIU, ILEANA. Translations of the self: interview with Breyten Breytenbach. Current Writing (8:1) 1996, 90–101.

16560. JOLLY, ROSEMARY JANE. Colonization, violence, and narration in White South African writing: André Brink, Breyten Breytenbach, and J. M. Coetzee. Athens: Ohio UP; Johannesburg: Witwatersrand UP, 1996. pp. xvii, 179. (Cf. bibl. 1994, 11904.)

16561. SIENAERT, MARILET. *Ut pictura poesis*? A transgressive reading of Breytenbach's poetry and painting. Current Writing (8:1) 1996, 102–12.

Sue Ellen Bridgers

16562. CARROLL, PAMELA SISSI.   Enduring values: grandmothers and granddaughters in three novels for young adults. ArizEB (36:1) 1993, 24–7.

Robert Bridges

16563. NIXON, JUDE V.   Portrait of a friendship: the unpublished letters of the Hopkins family to Robert Bridges. *See* **11493**.

16564. PHILLIPS, CATHERINE.   Robert Bridges and the English musical renaissance. *In* (pp. 89–103) **79**.

Robert Bringhurst

16565. SANGER, PETER.   Poor man's art: on the poetry of Robert Bringhurst. AntR (85/86) 1991, 151–69.

André Brink

16566. BRINK, ANDRÉ.   Reinventing a continent (revisiting history in the literature of the new South Africa: a personal testimony). *See* **9808**.

16567. HEYNS, MICHIEL.   Overtaken by history? Obsolescence-anxiety in André Brink's *An Act of Terror* and Etienne van Heerden's *Casspirs en Campari's*. English Academy Review (11) 1996, 62–72.

16568. JOLLY, ROSEMARY JANE.   Colonization, violence, and narration in White South African writing: André Brink, Breyten Breytenbach, and J. M. Coetzee. *See* **16560**.

16569. KOSSEW, SUE.   The anxiety of authorship: J. M. Coetzee's *The Master of Petersburg* (1994) and André Brink's *On the Contrary* (1993). EngA (23:1) 1996, 67–88.

R. F. Brissenden

16570. BROOKS, DAVID (ed.).   Suddenly evening: the selected poems of R. F. Brissenden. Ringwood, Vic.: McPhee Gribble; Harmondsworth: Penguin; New York: Viking Penguin, 1993. pp. xv, 157.

Vera Brittain

16571. BERRY, PAUL; BOSTRIDGE, MARK.   Vera Brittain: a life. (Bibl. 1995, 15005.) Rev. by Joyce Avrech Berkman in Albion (28:4) 1996, 723–5; by Jean McNicol in LRB (18:6) 1996, 16–18; by Russell Gollard in LitMed (15:2) 1996, 266–70.

16572. GORHAM, DEBORAH.   Vera Brittain: a feminist life. Oxford; Cambridge, MA: Blackwell, 1996. pp. x, 330. Rev. by Jean McNicol in LRB (18:6) 1996, 16–18; by Mark Bostridge in TLS, 22 Mar. 1996, 29.

Erna Brodber

16573. COOPER, CAROLYN.   Afro-Jamaican folk elements in Brodber's *Jane and Louisa Will Soon Come Home. In* (pp. 279–88) **81**.

Harold Brodkey

16574. BRODKEY, HAROLD.   This wild darkness: the story of my death. New York: Holt, 1996. pp. 177.

Louis Bromfield

16575. GROVER, DORYS CROW.   Four Midwestern novelists' response to French inquiries on populism. *See* **15992**.

William Bronk

16576. CLIPPINGER, DAVID. Luminosity, transcendence, and the certainty of not knowing. *See* **12489**.

Christine Brooke-Rose

16577. BIRCH, SARAH. Christine Brooke-Rose and contemporary fiction. (Bibl. 1994, 11921.) Rev. by Ellen G. Friedman in MFS (42:4) 1996, 893–4; by Annegret Maack in Archiv (233:2) 1996, 416–19.
16578. BROOKE-ROSE, CHRISTINE. Remaking. EEM (5:2) 1996, 12–17. (On Brooke-Rose's autobiography.)
16579. LITTLE, JUDY. The experimental self: dialogic subjectivity in Woolf, Pym, and Brooke-Rose. Carbondale: Southern Illinois UP, 1996. pp. xiii, 204. (Ad feminam.)

Anita Brookner

16580. RESTUCCIA, FRANCES. Tales of beauty: aestheticizing female melancholia. *See* **16098**.

Gwendolyn Brooks

16581. FLEISSNER, ROBERT F. 'Real cool' fire and ice: Brooks and Frost. RFR (1994) 58–62.
16582. GREASLEY, PHILIP. Gwendolyn Brooks at eighty: a retrospective. Midamerica (23) 1996, 124–35.
16583. HUBBARD, STACY CARSON. 'A splintery box': race and gender in the sonnets of Gwendolyn Brooks. Genre (25:1) 1992, 47–64.
16584. KIM, BOK-HEE. Gwendolyn Brooks eui si: euishik eui jeongchihwa. (The politicization of consciousness in Gwendolyn Brooks's poetry.) Unpub. doct. diss., Korea Univ., Seoul, 1996.
16585. LINDBERG, KATHRYNE V. Whose canon? Gwendolyn Brooks: founder at the center of the 'margins'. *In* (pp. 283–311) **39**.
16586. STANFORD, ANN FOLWELL. Dialectics of desire: war and the resistive voice in Gwendolyn Brooks's *Negro Hero* and *Gay Chaps at the Bar*. AAR (26:2) 1992, 197–211.

Brigid Brophy

16587. STEVENSON, SHERYL. Language and gender in transit: feminist extensions of Bakhtin. *In* (pp. 181–98) **33**.

Charlotte Hawkins Brown

16588. DENARD, CAROLYN C. (introd.). *Mammy: an Appeal to the Heart of the South*; and, *The Correct Thing to Do – to Say – to Wear*. New York: G. K. Hall; London: Prentice Hall, 1995. pp. xxxv, 149. (African-American women writers, 1910–1940.)

George Mackay Brown

16589. CAMPBELL, IAN. Beside Brown's ocean of time. *In* (pp. 263–74) **115**.
16590. CUDMORE, PETER. The migrant on the rock: Sir Peter Maxwell Davies, complexity, and George Mackay Brown. Edinburgh Review (92) 1994, 85–100.
16591. SCHOENE, BERTHOLD. 'I imagined nine centuries ...': narrative fragmentation and mythical closure in the shorter historical fiction of George Mackay Brown. SLJ (22:2) 1995, 41–59.

16592. —— The making of Orcadia: a narrative identity in the prose work of George Mackay Brown. (Bibl. 1995, 15039.) Rev. by Julian Meldon D'Arcy in SLJ (supp. 44) 1996, 26–9.

Larry Brown

16593. PREVOST, VERBIE LOVORN.   Larry Brown's *Dirty Work*: a study of man's responsibility for suffering. TPB (30) 1993, 21–7.

Linda Beatrice Brown (1939–)

16594. BROOKHART, MARY HUGHES.   Spiritual daughters of the Black American South. *In* (pp. 125–39) **32**.

Sterling A. Brown

16595. TIDWELL, JOHN EDGAR.   Recasting Negro life history: Sterling A. Brown and the Federal Writers' Project. LHR (13:2) 1995, 77–82.

John Brunner

16596. COLIN, VLADIMIR.   Rābdarea timpului. (The long result.) Bucharest: Nemira, 1994. pp. 200.

Dennis Brutus

16597. FOLLI, ROSE.   Dennis Brutus: erotic revolutionary. ESA (39:2) 1996, 17–25.

John Buchan

16598. DANIELL, DAVID (ed.).   Sick Heart River. (Bibl. 1995, 15046.) Rev. by Corey Coates in ELT (39:4) 1996, 514–17.
16599. GALBRAITH, WILLIAM.   The literary governor-general. LRC (5:9) 1996, 18–20 (review-article).
16600. HAGEMANN, SUSANNE.   Marginality: a bifocal approach to John Buchan's *The Three Hostages*. ZAA (44:3) 1996, 240–8.
16601. JONES, J. D. F.   Buchan papers. London: Harvill, 1996. pp. 249. Rev. by Peter Keating in TLS, 11 Oct. 1996, 28.
16602. LOWNIE, ANDREW.   John Buchan: the Presbyterian cavalier. (Bibl. 1995, 15051.) Rev. by William Galbraith in LRC (5:9) 1996, 18–20.
16603. —— MILNE, WILLIAM (eds).   John Buchan's collected poems. Aberdeen: Scottish Cultural Press, 1996. pp. xv, 232. Rev. by Peter Keating in TLS, 11 Oct. 1996, 28.
16604. WORDEN, JASON.   Thirty-nine steps to immortality. *See* **14343**.

Pearl S. Buck

16605. CONN, PETER.   Pearl S. Buck: a cultural biography. Cambridge; New York: CUP, 1996. pp. xxvi, 468.

Christopher Buckley

16606. BUCKLEY, CHRISTOPHER.   Urban scrawl. BkW, 14 July 1996, 1, 10.

Frederick Buechner

16607. BAKER, ROBERT D.   Frederick Buechner (1926–): a primary and secondary bibliography. BB (53:3) 1996, 209–18.
16608. BUECHNER, FREDERICK.   The longing for home: recollections

and reflections. San Francisco, CA: HarperSanFrancisco, 1996. pp. viii, 180.

Lois McMaster Bujold

16609. HAEHL, ANNE L. Miles Vorkosigan and the power of words: a study of Lois McMaster Bujold's unlikely hero. Extrapolation (37:3) 1996, 224–33.

Charles Bukowski

16610. MADIGAN, ANDREW J. What fame is: Bukowski's exploration of self. JAStud (30:3) 1996, 447–61.
16611. RICHMOND, STEVE. Spinning off Bukowski. Northville, MI: Sun Dog Press, 1996. pp. 141.
16612. ROBBINS, DOREN. Drinking wine in the slaughterhouse with septuagenarian stew: for Bukowski at 71. Onthebus (3:2/4:1) 1991, 282–5.
16613. ZIEGLER, ROBERT. From a Charles Bukowski reader. NCL (25:4) 1995, 13–14.

Basil Bunting

16614. ALLDRITT, KEITH. Modernism in the Second World War: the later poetry of Ezra Pound, T. S. Eliot, Basil Bunting, and Hugh MacDiarmid. New York; Frankfurt; Bern; Paris: Lang, 1989. pp. 121. Rev. by Susanne Hagemann in ZAA (41:1) 1993, 87–8.

Eugene Burdick

16615. SEED, DAVID. Military machines and nuclear accident: Burdick and Wheeler's *Fail-Safe*. WLA (6:1) 1994, 21–40.

Anthony Burgess

16616. BURGESS, ANTHONY. You've had your time; being the second part of the confessions of Anthony Burgess. (Bibl. 1991, 12300.) Rev. by Gerda Oldham in AR (49:3) 1991, 465–6.
16617. LOBDELL, JARED C. Stone pastorals: three men on the side of the horses. Extrapolation (37:4) 1996, 341–56.
16618. WALLE, ALF H. Hack writing *vs* belle letters [*sic*]: the strategic implications of literary achievement. *See* **14757**.

Linda Burgess

16619. BROWN, DIANE. In praise of gossip. Quote Unquote (37) 1996, 18–19. (Interview.)

James Lee Burke (1936–)

16620. CARNEY, ROB. Clete Purcel to the rampaging rescue: looking for the hard-boiled tradition in James Lee Burke's *Dixie City Jam*. SoQ (34:4) 1996, 121–30.
16621. WOMACK, STEVEN. A talk with James Lee Burke. AD (29:2) 1996, 138–43.

Kenneth Burke

16622. BENOIT, WILLIAM. A note on Burke on 'motive'. *See* **15283**.
16623. BRUMMETT, BARRY. Speculations on the discovery of a Burkean blunder. *See* **15315**.
16624. —— (ed.). Landmark essays on Kenneth Burke. Davis, CA:

Hermagoras Press, 1993. pp. xix, 290. (Landmark essays, 2.) Rev. by Ann L. George in RSQ (26:1) 1996, 90–3.

16625. SCHAEFFER, JOHN D.   Vico and Kenneth Burke. RSQ (26:2) 1996, 7–17.

16626. SELZER, JACK.   Kenneth Burke among the moderns: *Counter-Statement* as counter statement. *See* **15761**.

Edgar Rice Burroughs

16627. BRADY, CLARK A.   The Burroughs cyclopædia: characters, places, fauna, flora, technologies, languages, ideas, and terminologies found in the works of Edgar Rice Burroughs. Jefferson, NC; London: McFarland, 1996. pp. v, 402.

16628. DAVISON, RICHARD ALLAN.   Edgar Rice Burroughs, Tarzan, and Hemingway. NDQ (63:3) 1996, 34–9.

16629. JURCA, CATHERINE.   Tarzan, lord of the suburbs. MLQ (57:3) 1996, 479–504.

16630. McWHORTER, GEORGE T.   Each one as before will chase his favorite phantom. *See* **506**.

16631. SCHUTTE, XANDRA.   Tarzan, heerser van de jungle. (Tarzan, lord of the jungle.) *See* **14192**.

16632. WRIGHT, PETER.   Selling Mars: Burroughs, Barsoom and expedient xenography. Foundation (68) 1996, 24–46.

William Burroughs

16633. BEARD, WILLIAM.   Insect poetics: Cronenberg's *Naked Lunch*. *See* **13427**.

16634. BOCKRIS, VICTOR (comp.).   With William Burroughs: a report from the bunker. (Bibl. 1982, 10667.) New York: St Martin's Griffin, 1996. pp. xxiv, 264. (Revised ed.: first ed. 1981.)

16635. HARRIS, OLIVER (ed.).   The letters of William S. Burroughs: 1945–1959. (Bibl. 1993, 11892.) Rev. by Steven Moore in BkW, 15 Aug. 1996, 1, 14.

16636. INGRAM, DAVID.   William Burroughs and language. *In* (pp. 95–113) **4**.

16637. LATHAM, ROB.   Collage as critique and invention in the fiction of William S. Burroughs and Kathy Acker. *See* **15867**.

16638. LATHAM, ROBERT A.   Collage as critique and invention in the fiction of William S. Burroughs and Kathy Acker. *In* (pp. 29–37) **70**.

16639. McCLURE, ANDREW S.   The word, image, and addiction: language and the junk equation in William S. Burroughs' *Naked Lunch*. Dionysos (6:2) 1996, 6–19.

16640. MEYER, CHRISTOPHER.   The psychopharmacology of every-day life: W. S. Burroughs and the narcotic *régime*. AJSem (9:3) 1992, 167–84.

16641. SCARSELLA, ALESSANDRO.   'Una macchina da scrivere ad energia orgonica azionata dal boia' ovvero: paradossi tecnologici di William Burroughs. *In* (pp. 320–4) **117**.

16642. SELF, WILL.   The courage of his perversions. Mail & Guardian (11:44) 1995, 4.

Octavia Butler

16643. HELFORD, ELYCE RAE.   'Would you really rather die than bear my young?': the construction of gender, race, and species in Octavia E. Butler's *Bloodchild*. AAR (28:2) 1994, 259–71.

16644. McKible, Adam. 'These are the facts of the darky's history': thinking history and reading names in four African-American texts. AAR (28:2) 1994, 223–35.

16645. Weinhouse, Linda. Cynthia Ozick's *The Shawl* and Octavia Butler's *Kindred*: bearing witness. CEACrit (59:1) 1996, 60–7.

A. S. Byatt

16646. Bruce, Marianne. That thinking feeling. Mail & Guardian (12:27) 1996, 3. (Interview.)

16647. Buxton, Jackie. 'What's love got to do with it?' Postmodernism and *Possession*. ESCan (22:2) 1996, 199–219.

16648. Chevalier, J.-L. Entretien avec A. S. Byatt. JSSE (22) 1994, 11–27.

16649. Kelly, Kathleen Coyne. A. S. Byatt. New York: Twayne; London: Prentice Hall, 1996. pp. xviii, 158. (Twayne's English authors, 529.)

16650. Lepaludier, Laurent. The saving threads of discourse and the necessity of the reader in A. S. Byatt's *Racine and the Tablecloth*. JSSE (22) 1994, 37–48.

16651. Löschnigg, Martin. History and the search for identity: reconstructing the past in recent English novels. *See* **14605**.

16652. Maisonnat, Claude. The ghost written and the ghost writer in A. S. Byatt's story *The July Ghost*. JSSE (22) 1994, 49–62.

16653. Parlati, Maria Maddalena. Un altro libro delle inquietudini: *Possession* di A. S. Byatt. Annali anglistica (36:1–3) 1993, 111–36.

16654. Sturgess, Charlotte. Life narratives in A. S. Byatt's *'Sugar' and Other Stories*. JSSE (22) 1994, 29–35.

16655. Tredell, Nicolas. A. S. Byatt in conversation. PN Review (17:3) 1991, 24–8.

Witter Bynner

16656. Potter, Vilma. Idella Purnell's *PALMS* and godfather Witter Bynner. *See* **1342**.

James Branch Cabell

16657. Anon. Anne Virginia Bennett to James Branch Cabell: two letters. EGN (27) 1991, 6–7.

16658. MacDonald, Edgar. The final word. EGN (26) 1991, 2–10.

16659. —— James Branch Cabell and Richmond-in-Virginia. (Bibl. 1995, 15097.) Rev. by Anne E. Rowe in FHQ (73:1) 1994, 123–6.

Pat Cadigan

16660. Terranova, Tiziana. Cyber-catastrophes: the sinful technology of Pat Cadigan. *In* (pp. 516–26) **117**.

John Cage

16661. Sarratore, Steven T. Muses for a postmodern scenography: Marcel Duchamp and John Cage. NETJ (4) 1993, 19–38.

Abraham Cahan

16662. HOMBERGER, ERIC.   Some uses for Jewish ambivalence: Abraham Cahan and Michael Gold. *In* (pp. 165–80) **5**.

16663. MAROVITZ, SANFORD E.   Abraham Cahan. New York: Twayne; London: Prentice Hall, 1996. pp. xix, 203. (Twayne's US authors, 670.)

James M. Cain

16664. CASTILLE, PHILIP DUBUISSON.   Too odd for California: incest and West Virginia in James M. Cain's *The Butterfly*. AppalJ (23:2) 1996, 148–62.

16665. FINE, RICHARD.   James M. Cain and the American authors' authority. (Bibl. 1992, 12978.) Rev. by David W. Madden in MFS (40:2) 1994, 369–71.

16666. GARRETT, GREG.   The many faces of *Mildred Pierce*: a case study of adaptation and the studio system. *See* **13701**.

16667. MARLING, WILLIAM.   The American *roman noir*: Hammett, Cain, and Chandler. (Bibl. 1995, 15109.) Rev. by David W. Madden in MFS (42:4) 1996, 840–3; by Lonnie L. Willis in RMRLL (50:1) 1996, 84–5.

Erskine Caldwell

16668. BLOUNT, ROY (introd.).   Georgia boy. Athens; London: Georgia UP, 1995. pp. xiv, 239.

16669. COOK, SYLVIA JENKINS.   Erskine Caldwell and the fiction of poverty: the flesh and the spirit. (Bibl. 1994, 11980.) Rev. by John T. Matthews in MFS (40:1) 1994, 154–6.

16670. FLYNT, WAYNE.   Erskine Caldwell's poor Whites: literary realism or historical mythology? GaHQ (80:4) 1996, 835–46 (review-article).

16671. HOOD, MARY (introd.).   The sacrilege of Alan Kent. Athens; London: Georgia UP, 1995. pp. xviii, 67.

16672. KLEVAR, HARVEY L.   Erskine Caldwell: a biography. (Bibl. 1995, 15111.) Rev. by Wayne Flynt in GaHQ (80:4) 1996, 839–44.

16673. MILLER, DAN B.   Erskine Caldwell: the journey from Tobacco Road: a biography. (Bibl. 1995, 15112.) Rev. by Sylvia J. Cook in ALH (101:4) 1996, 1307–8; by Wayne Flynt in GaHQ (80:4) 1996, 840–4; by Jeffrey J. Folks in WLT (70:1) 1996, 194–5.

16674. MIXON, WAYNE.   The people's writer: Erskine Caldwell and the South. Charlottesville; London: Virginia UP, 1995. pp. xv, 213. (Minds of the new South.) Rev. by Wayne Flynt in GaHQ (80:4) 1996, 842–4.

Morley Callaghan

16675. BOIRE, GARY.   Morley Callaghan: literary anarchist. Toronto: ECW Press, 1994. pp. 131. (Canadian biography.) Rev. by John Orange in ESCan (22:4) 1996, 486–8.

16676. MICHEL, ROBERT.   The Austin 'Dink' Carroll papers in the University Archives. *See* **512**.

16677. ORANGE, JOHN.   Orpheus in winter: Morley Callaghan's *The Loved and the Lost*. Toronto: ECW Press, 1993. pp. 115. (Canadian fiction studies, 22.) Rev. by Gary Boire in ESCan (22:2) 1996, 247–9.

16678. WOODCOCK, GEORGE.   Moral predicament: Morley Callaghan's *More Joy in Heaven*. Toronto: ECW Press, 1993. pp. 71. (Canadian fiction studies, 14.) Rev. by Gary Boire in ESCan (22:2) 1996, 247–9.

Ernest Callenbach

16679. PÜTZ, MANFRED.   Ecotopia/technotopia: an interview with Ernest Callenbach on the role of technology in an ecotopian world. Amst (41:3) 1996, 381–95.

Peter Cameron

16680. WEBER, MYLES.   When a risk group is not a risk group: the absence of AIDS panic in Peter Cameron's fiction. *In* (pp. 69–75) **2**.

Bebe Moore Campbell (1950–)

16681. CAMPBELL, BEBE MOORE.   Like looking for Mr Right. BkW, 19 Mar. 1995, 1, 10.

Maria Campbell

16682. JANNETTA, A. E.   Anecdotal humour in Maria Campbell's *Halfbreed* (1973). JCanStud (31:2) 1996, 62–75.

Wilfred Campbell

16683. BOONE, LAUREL (ed.).   William Wilfred Campbell: selected poetry and essays. Waterloo, Ont.: Wilfrid Laurier UP, 1987. pp. xvi, 238. Rev. by Frank M. Tierney in ARCS (19:3) 1989, 354–5.

Dorothy Canfield (Dorothy Canfield Fisher)

16684. MADIGAN, MARK J.   A newly-discovered Robert Frost letter to Dorothy Canfield Fisher. RFR (1994) 24–5.

16685. —— Willa Cather and Dorothy Canfield Fisher: rift, reconciliation, and *One of Ours*. CathS (1) 1990, 115–29.

16686. —— (ed.).   *The Bedquilt* and other stories. Columbia; London: Missouri UP, 1996. pp. xvii, 234.

16687. —— Keeping fires night and day: selected letters of Dorothy Canfield Fisher. Foreword by Clifton Fadiman. (Bibl. 1993, 11917.) Rev. by Ida H. Washington in VH (61:4) 1993, 246–7.

16688. —— Seasoned timber. Hanover, NH; London: UP of New England, 1996. pp. xxi, 489. (Hardscrabble.)

Truman Capote

16689. ALGEO, ANN M.   The courtroom as forum: homicide trials by Dreiser, Wright, Capote, and Mailer. New York; Frankfurt; Bern; Paris: Lang, 1996. pp. 164. (Modern American literature, 1.) (Cf. bibl. 1992, 12986.)

16690. FORWARD, STEPHANIE.   *In Cold Blood*: more than just an unusual murder novel. ERev (6:4) 1996, 21–3.

Rosa Cappiello

16691. BALLYN, SUSAN.   The voice of the other: an approach to migrant writing in Australia. CritS (6:1) 1994, 91–7.

Orson Scott Card

16692. Collings, Michael R.   Orson Scott Card: an approach to mythopoeic fiction: guest of honor speech, Mythopoeic Conference xxvi. Mythlore (21:3) 1996, 36–50.

Peter Carey

16693. Ryan-Fazillau, Susan.   One-upmanship in Peter Carey's short stories. JSSE (16) 1991, 51–63.

16694. Younis, Raymond Aaron.   Apropos the last 'post-': contemporary literature, theory and interpretation. *See* **15839**.

Caleb Carr (1955–)

16695. Gonshak, Henry.   'The child is father to the man': the psychopathology of serial killing in Caleb Carr's *The Alienist*. NCL (25:1) 1995, 12–13.

Leonora Carrington

16696. Daniele, Daniela.   Corpi idealizzati, corpi smembrati: la donna come soggetto e oggetto della rappresentazione surrealista. QLLSM (7) 1995, 165–87.

James Carroll

16697. Carroll, James.   An American requiem: God, my father, and the war that came between us. Boston, MA: Houghton Mifflin, 1996. pp. 279, (plates) 8.

16698. Deedy, John.   Loose ends: John Deedy interviews James Carroll. Critic (46:3) 1992, 26–36.

Jonathan Carroll

16699. Hantke, Steffen.   Deconstructing horror: commodities in the fiction of Jonathan Carroll and Kathe Koja. JAC (18:3) 1995, 41–57.

Ciaran Carson

16700. Denman, Peter.   Ways of saying: Boland, Carson, McGuckian. *In* (pp. 158–73) **86**.

16701. McCracken, Kathleen.   Ciaran Carson: unravelling the conditional, mapping the provisional. *In* (pp. 356–72) **86**.

16702. McGrath, Niall.   Ciaran Carson: interview with Niall McGrath. Edinburgh Review (93) 1995, 61–6.

Catherine Carswell

16703. McCulloch, Margery Palmer.   'Opening the door': women, Carswell and the Scottish renaissance. Études Écossaises (supp.) 1994, 93–104.

16704. Preston, Peter.   'Under the same banner'? D. H. Lawrence and Catherine Carswell's *Open the Door!* Études Lawrenciennes (9) 1993, 111–26.

Angela Carter

16705. Bell, Mark (ed.)   The curious room: plays, film scripts and an opera. Introd. by Susannah Clapp. London: Chatto & Windus, 1996. pp. x, 510. (Collected Angela Carter.) Rev. by Charlotte Crofts in TLS, 8 Nov. 1996, 34.

16706. BROWN, RICHARD.   Postmodern Americas in the fiction of Angela Carter, Martin Amis and Ian McEwan. *In* (pp. 92–110) **34**.

16707. COLLADO RODRÍGUEZ, FRANCISCO.   Complexity/controversy: some aspects of contemporary Women's Studies in America. *In* (pp. 107–20) **38**.

16708. DUNCKER, PATRICIA.   Queer gothic: Angela Carter and the lost narratives of sexual subversion. CritS (8:1) 1996, 58–68.

16709. FALZON, ALEX R.   Angela Carter. EEM (3:1) 1994, 18–22. (Interview.)

16710. FRAILE MURLANCH, ISABEL.   The silent woman: silence as subversion in Angela Carter's *The Magic Toyshop*. *In* (pp. 239–52) **38**.

16711. HALLAB, MARY Y.   Carter and Blake: the dangers of innocence. *In* (pp. 177–83) **36**.

16712. LAPPAS, CATHERINE.   'Seeing is believing, but touching is the truth': female spectatorship and sexuality in *The Company of Wolves*. *See* **13901**.

16713. LEDWON, LENORA.   The passion of the new phallus and Angela Carter's *The Passion of New Eve*. JFA (5:4) 1992, 26–41.

16714. LONSDALE, THORUNN.   Material evidence: Angela Carter's *The Bloody Chamber*. JSSE (22) 1994, 63–70.

16715. MCLAUGHLIN, BECKY.   Perverse pleasure and fetishized text: the deathly erotics of Carter's *The Bloody Chamber*. Style (29:3) 1995, 404–22.

16716. MARTINSSON, YVONNE.   Eroticism, ethics and reading: Angela Carter in dialogue with Roland Barthes. *See* **15632**.

16717. SAGE, LORNA.   Angela Carter. Plymouth: Northcote House; London: British Council, 1996. pp. xii, 77. (Writers and their work.)

16718. SCHAUB, DANIELLE.   *Penetrating to the Heart of the Forest*: initiation according to Angela Carter. JSSE (22) 1994, 71–84.

16719. SCHOFIELD, ANN.   Lizzie Borden took an axe: history, feminism, and American culture. AmS (34:1) 1993, 91–103.

16720. WYATT, JEAN.   The violence of gendering: castration images in Angela Carter's *The Magic Toyshop*, *The Passion of New Eve*, and *Peter and the Wolf*. WS (25:6) 1996, 549–70.

Ada Jack Carver

16721. MEESE, ELIZABETH.   What the old ones know: Ada Jack Carver's Cane River stories. *In* (pp. 140–52) **65**.

Raymond Carver

16722. CAMPBELL, EWING.   Raymond Carver's therapeutics of passion. JSSE (16) 1991, 9–18.

16723. CLARK, BILLY.   Stylistic analysis and relevance theory. *See* **2598**.

16724. HORN, NICHOLAS.   Clevie Raymond, Raymond Clevie: Carver's *The Father*. JSSE (19) 1992, 25–41.

16725. KELLY, LIONEL.   Anton Chekhov and Raymond Carver: a writer's strategies of reading. YES (26) 1996, 218–31.

16726. LEHMAN, D. W.   Raymond Carver's management of symbol. JSSE (17) 1991, 43–58.

16727. MALAMET, ELLIOTT.   Raymond Carver and the fear of narration. JSSE (17) 1991, 59–74.

16728. MAXFIELD, JAMES.   Lost in the fog: the narrator of Carver's *Blackbird Pie*. JSSE (23) 1994, 51–62.

16729. NESSET, KIRK.   The stories of Raymond Carver: a critical study. (Bibl. 1995, 15161.) Rev. by Bryan D. Dietrich in AL (68:1) 1996, 267–8.

16730. PLATH, JAMES.   *After the Denim* and *After the Storm*: Raymond Carver comes to terms with the Hemingway influence. HemR (13:2) 1994, 37–51.

16731. RUNYON, RANDOLPH PAUL.   Reading Raymond Carver. (Bibl. 1993, 11956.) Rev. by Nicholas Horn in JSSE (23) 1994, 89–93; by David W. Madden in MFS (40:1) 1994, 158–9.

16732. SAWYER, DAVID.   'Yet why not say what happened?' Boundaries of the self in Raymond Carver's fiction and Robert Altman's *Short Cuts*. *In* (pp. 195–219) **8**.

16733. SCOBIE, BRIAN.   Carver country. *In* (pp. 273–87) **34**.

16734. STULL, WILLIAM L.; CARROLL, MAUREEN P. (eds).   Remembering Ray: a composite biography of Raymond Carver. (Bibl. 1993, 11957.) Rev. by Lyall Bush in SSF (33:1) 1996, 145–8.

16735. TRUSSLER, MICHAEL.   An estrangement of the real: the neo-realist short story and photography. JSSE (19) 1992, 69–82.

Joyce Cary

16736. HARVIE, CHRISTOPHER.   Garron Top to Caer Gybi: images of the inland sea. *See* **10257**.

Neal Cassady

16737. BUSH, CLIVE.   'Why do we always say angel?': Herbert Huncke and Neal Cassady. *In* (pp. 128–57) **4**.

Willa Cather

16738. ALBERTINI, VIRGIL.   Works on Cather, 1990–1991: a bibliographical essay. WCPMN (35:4) 1991/92, 35–43.

16739. —— Works on Cather, summer 1991 – summer 1992: a bibliographical essay. WCPMN (36:4) 1992/93, 47, 53–8.

16740. —— Works on Cather, summer '92 – summer '93: a bibliographical essay. WCPMN (38:1) 1994, 1–2, 4, 6, 8, 10, 12, 14–15.

16741. —— Works on Cather, summer '93 – summer '94: a bibliographical essay. WCPMN (39:1) 1995, 17–21.

16742. AMMONS, ELIZABETH.   Cather and the new canon: *The Old Beauty* and the issue of empire. CathS (3) 1996, 256–66.

16743. ANDERS, JOHN P.   Willa Cather, France, and Pierre Loti: a spirit of affiliation. WCPMN (38:4) 1995, 15–18.

16744. ARNOLD, MARILYN.   The allusive Cather. CathS (3) 1996, 137–48.

16745. —— Willa Cather's poor pitiful professors. WCPMN (35:4) 1991/92, 43–6.

16746. BAKER, BRUCE P.   Portrait of the artist by a young woman. WCPMN (37:3/4) 1993/94, 40–2.

16747. BEGLEY, ANN M.   Remembrance of America past. ASch (62:3) 1993, 455–64 (review-article).

16748. BENNETT, MILDRED R.   The world of Willa Cather. Lincoln; London: Nebraska UP, 1995. pp. xvi, 285. (New ed.: first ed. 1961.)

16749. BERKOVE, LAWRENCE I.   Rollin Mallory Daggett's *My French Friend*: a precursor of *Paul's Case*? *See* **10777**.

16750. BOXWELL, D. A.   In formation: male homosocial desire in Willa Cather's *One of Ours*. *In* (pp. 285–310) **30**.

16751. BRIGGS, CYNTHIA K.   Insulated isolation: Willa Cather's room with a view. CathS (1) 1990, 159–71.

16752. CAO, JINGHUA.   Marian Forrester, Cather's fictional portrayal of the Modernist self. WCPMN (39:1) 1995, 12–16.

16753. CARLIN, DEBORAH.   Cather, canon, and the politics of reading. (Bibl. 1994, 12039.) Rev. by M. J. McLendon in AmS (34:2) 1993, 122–3.

16754. CARRUTH, MARY C.   Cather's immortal art and *My Mortal Enemy*. WCPMN (40:1) 1996, 17–20.

16755. CASEY, THOMAS M.   Mariology and Christology in *Death Comes for the Archbishop*. WCPMN (35:3) 1991, 22–5.

16756. CHOWN, LINDA.   'It came closer than that': Willa Cather's *Lucy Gayheart*. CathS (2) 1993, 118–39.

16757. CUMBERLAND, DEBRA.   A struggle for breath: contemporary vocal theory in Cather's *The Song of the Lark*. ALR (28:2) 1996, 59–70.

16758. DENNIS, HELEN M. (ed.).   Willa Cather and European cultural influences. Lewiston, NY; Lampeter: Mellen Press, 1996. pp. x, 145. (Studies in American literature, 16.)

16759. DURYEA, POLLY.   Memories of Grand Manan. WCPMN (39:4) 1995, 60–3. (Interview.)

16760. —— Willa Cather and the Menuhin connection. WCPMN (36:2) 1992, 12–15.

16761. FABER, REBECCA J.   Some of his: Cather's use of Dr Sweeney's diary in *One of Ours*. WCPMN (37:1) 1993, 5–9.

16762. FARR, CECILIA KONCHAR.   'I too am untranslatable': failings of filming *O Pioneers! See* **13651**.

16763. FISHER-WIRTH, ANN.   Out of the mother: loss in *My Ántonia*. CathS (2) 1993, 41–71.

16764. —— Queening it: excess in *My Mortal Enemy*. WCPMN (40:2) 1996, 36–41.

16765. FISHER-WIRTH, ANN W.   Dispossession and redemption in the novels of Willa Cather. CathS (1) 1990, 36–54.

16766. FLANNIGAN, JOHN H.   Cather, Mérimée, and the problem of fanaticism in *Shadows on the Rock*. WCPMN (37:3/4) 1993/94, 29–35.

16767. —— Domenico Cimarosa: a possible source for *The Professor's House*. WCPMN (38:4) 1995, 19–20.

16768. —— Issues of gender and lesbian love: goblins in *The Garden Lodge*. CathS (2) 1993, 23–40.

16769. FUNDA, EVELYN I.   Womanhood distorted: Mrs Archie as Thea's foil in *The Song of the Lark*. WCPMN (39:2/3) 1995, 30–3.

16770. GELFANT, BLANCHE H.   The magical art of Willa Cather's *Old Mrs Harris*. WCPMN (38:3) 1994, 37–8, 40, 42, 44, 46, 48, 50.

16771. AL-GHALITH, ASAD.   Cather's use of light: an impressionistic tone. CathS (3) 1996, 267–82.

16772. —— Inroads through the desert: Willa Cather's reception in Saudi Arabia. WCPMN (36:3) 1992, 45–6.

16773. GILTROW, JANET; STOUCK, DAVID.   Lyrical measures: cohesion and sentence endings in Cather's prose. *See* **2629**.

16774. GOLDBERG, JONATHAN.   Strange brothers. StudN (28:3) 1996, 322–37.

16775. GUSTAFSON, NEIL.   On being geographically correct about Catherland. WCPMN (39:1) 1995, 21–3.

16776. HALAC, DENNIS.   Catheriana at the Bancroft. *See* **485**.

16777. HARRELL, DAVID.   Willa Cather's Mesa Verde myth. CathS (1) 1990, 130–43.

16778. HARRIS, RICHARD.   Willa Cather, Ivan Turgenev, and the novel of character. CathS (1) 1990, 172–9.

16779. HARRIS, RICHARD C.   Sherwood Anderson and Willa Cather: fragments to shore against the ruins. *See* **15993**.

16780. ——— Willa Cather, J. W. N. Sullivan, and the creative process. WCPMN (37:2) 1993, 17, 21–4.

16781. HE, ZHONGXIU.   Poverty as Myra's mortal enemy. WCPMN (35:3) 1991, 29–32.

16782. HOARE, PHILIP.   A serious pleasure: the friendship of Willa Cather and Stephen Tennant. Introd. by John Anders. WCPMN (36:2) 1992, 7–10.

16783. HOLTZ, WILLIAM.   Willa Cather and Floyd Dell. WCPMN (38:2) 1994, 34–6.

16784. HOOVER, SHARON.   Reflections of authority and community in *Sapphira and the Slave Girl*. CathS (3) 1996, 238–55.

16785. HUMPHREY, MARY JANE.   *The White Mulberry Tree* as opera. CathS (3) 1996, 51–66.

16786. JENKINS, BILL.   The accidental professor: the Kierkegaardian aesthetics in Willa Cather's *The Professor's House*. NDQ (63:1) 1996, 129–41.

16787. KEPHART, CHRISTINE.   'He turned off the lights': a study of darkness in *My Mortal Enemy*. WCPMN (37:3/4) 1993/94, 36–9.

16788. KEPPEL, TIM.   Truth and myth in Willa Cather's *My Mortal Enemy* and Katherine Anne Porter's *Old Mortality*. WCPMN (40:1) 1996, 20–4.

16789. KORT, AMY.   Coming home from Troy: Cather's journey into pessimism in *My Mortal Enemy*. WCPMN (39:2/3) 1995, 38–41.

16790. LAIRD, ROY D.   My father – Claude Wheeler? WCPMN (39:2/3) 1995, 45–7.

16791. LEDDY, MICHAEL.   'Distant and correct': the double life and *The Professor's House*. CathS (3) 1996, 182–96.

16792. LEE, HERMIONE.   Cather's bridge: Anglo-American crossings in Willa Cather. *In* (pp. 38–56) **34**.

16793. LIMBAUGH, ELAINE E.   Historicism and the sentimental: sources of power in Willa Cather's *Shadows on the Rock*. WCPMN (39:4) 1995, 63–7.

16794. LLOYD, JOANNA.   *Lucy Gayheart*: sounds and silences. WCPMN (38:4) 1995, 20–3.

16795. MADIGAN, MARK J.   Willa Cather and Dorothy Canfield Fisher: rift, reconciliation, and *One of Ours*. *See* **16685**.

16796. MARCH, JOHN.   A reader's companion to the fiction of Willa Cather. Ed. by Marilyn Arnold and Debra Lynn Thornton. (Bibl. 1995, 15185.) Rev. by Jami Lynn Hacker in ALR (28:2) 1996, 90–1.

16797. MARTIN, TERENCE.   '*Grandes communications avec Dieu*': the surrounding power of *Shadows on the Rock*. CathS (3) 1996, 31–50.

16798. MARTINEZ Y ALIRA, JEROME J. The apotheosis of Bishop Lamy: local faith perspectives. WCPMN (35:3) 1991, 19–22.

16799. MEAD, JEREMIAH P. Marsellus in the mirror: reflections of *Aeneid* VI in *The Professor's House.* WCPMN (40:2) 1996, 51–3.

16800. MESSITT, HOLLY. The internal gaze: *Coming, Aphrodite!* and the panopticon. WCPMN (36:3) 1992, 34–7.

16801. MEYERING, SHERYL L. A reader's guide to the short stories of Willa Cather. (Bibl. 1994, 12046.) Rev. by Donald D. Kummings in SSF (31:3) 1996, 157–8.

16802. MIDDLETON, JO ANN. Historical space in *Shadows on the Rock.* WCPMN (39:4) 1995, 49–53.

16803. MILLER, PAUL W. Anti-heroic theme and structure in Midwestern World War I novels from Cather to Hemingway. Midamerica (23) 1996, 99–108.

16804. MILLER, ROBERT K. Strains of blood: Myra Driscoll and the romance of the Celts. CathS (2) 1993, 169–77.

16805. MOSELEY, ANN. A New World symphony: cultural pluralism in *The Song of the Lark* and *My Ántonia.* WCPMN (39:1) 1995, 1, 7–12.

16806. —— Spatial structures and forms in *The Professor's House.* CathS (3) 1996, 197–211.

16807. MURPHY, JOHN J. An American tradition in *The Enchanted Bluff* and *Before Breakfast.* WCPMN (38:3) 1994, 47, 49.

16808. —— Cather's New World *Divine Comedy*: the Dante connection. CathS (1) 1990, 21–35.

16809. —— Gilt Diana and ivory Christ: love and Christian charity in *My Mortal Enemy.* CathS (3) 1996, 67–99.

16810. —— On the precipice of a caesura: *Death Comes for the Archbishop* and Vatican II. WCPMN (35:3) 1991, 25–9.

16811. —— *Shadows on the Rock, Maria Chapdelaine,* and the old nationalism. WCPMN (39:1) 1995, 1–6.

16812. —— The third chapter of *Sampson Speaks to the Master.* WCPMN (37:1) 1993, 1, 9–10.

16813. NETTELS, ELSA. Tradition and the woman artist: James's *The Tragic Muse* and Cather's *The Song of the Lark. See* **11635**.

16814. NEWSTROM, SCOTT L. Saying 'goonight' to 'lost' ladies: an inter-textual interpretation of allusions to *Hamlet*'s Ophelia in Cather's *A Lost Lady* and Eliot's *The Waste Land. See* **6827**.

16815. PACKER, TREVOR D. Dutch genre painting and sacramental symbolism in *Shadows on the Rock.* WCPMN (37:1) 1993, 11–14.

16816. PALLEAU-PAPIN, FRANÇOISE. The subversive language of flowers in *Sapphira and the Slave Girl.* WCPMN (39:2/3) 1995, 41–4.

16817. PASTOURMATZI, DOMNA. Willa Cather and the cult of masculinity. WCPMN (38:4) 1995, 2, 4, 6, 8, 10, 12–14.

16818. PECK, DEMAREE C. The imaginative claims of the artist in Willa Cather's fiction: 'possession granted by a different lease'. Selinsgrove, PA: Susquehanna UP; London; Toronto: Assoc. UPs, 1996. pp. 342.

16819. PETERMAN, MICHAEL. In pursuit of 'aristocracy of the spirit': Willa Cather and Robertson Davies. WCPMN (40:2) 1996, 44–9.

16820. PETRIE, PAUL R. 'Skulking escapist' *versus* 'radical editor': Willa Cather, the Left critics and *Sapphira and the Slave Girl.* SoQ (34:2) 1996, 27–37.

16821. REYNOLDS, GUY.   The ideology of Cather's Catholic progressivism: *Death Comes for the Archbishop*. CathS (3) 1996, 1–30.

16822. —— Louise Pound and Willa Cather: an intellectual network? WCPMN (39:4) 1995, 69–72.

16823. —— Willa Cather in context: progress, race, empire. Basingstoke: Macmillan; New York: St Martin's Press, 1996. pp. ix, 198. (Cf. bibl. 1992, 13038.)

16824. RIMMASCH, KRISTY.   Flux and friendship: Impressionism in *Two Friends*. WCPMN (38:2) 1994, 24, 26, 28.

16825. ROMINES, ANN.   Her mortal enemy's daughter: Cather and the writing of age. CathS (3) 1996, 100–14.

16826. —— The hermit's parish: Jeanne Le Ber and Cather's legacy from Jewett. *See* **11686**.

16827. ROSOWSKI, SUSAN J.   Cather's manifesto for art – *Coming, Aphrodite!* WCPMN (38:3) 1994, 51–6.

16828. —— Willa Cather and the imtimacy of art; or, In defense of privacy. WCPMN (36:4) 1992/93, 47–53.

16829. —— Willa Cather editing Willa Cather: from Houghton Mifflin to the house of Knopf. *See* **818**.

16830. —— Willa Cather's subverted endings and gendered time. CathS (1) 1990, 68–88.

16831. —— *et al.*   Editing Cather. *See* **819**.

16832. —— MIGNON, CHARLES W.; DANKER, KATHLEEN (eds). *O Pioneers!* With an historical essay and explanatory notes by David Stouck. (Bibl. 1993, 11972.) Rev. by Keen Butterworth in Text (Ann Arbor) (9) 1996, 442–6.

16833. SATO, HIROKO.   Willa Cather in Japan: a sequel. WCPMN (35:3) 1991, 32–3.

16834. SCHUBNELL, MATTHIAS.   The decline of America: Willa Cather's Spenglerian vision in *The Professor's House*. CathS (2) 1993, 92–117.

16835. SCHWIND, JEAN.   Fine and folk art in *The Song of the Lark*: Cather's pictorial sources. CathS (1) 1990, 89–102.

16836. —— This is a frame-up: Mother-Eve in *The Professor's House*. CathS (2) 1993, 72–91.

16837. SELL, PATRICIA.   Marian Forrester's 'fine play-acting'. WCPMN (35:2) 1991, 5–8.

16838. SHARISTANIAN, JANET.   Willa Cather and Red Cloud: an interview with Gertrude Schenck. WCPMN (36:2) 1992, 15–19.

16839. SHAW, PATRICK W.   Victorian rules and Left Bank rebellion: Willa Cather and Gertrude Stein. WCPMN (36:3) 1992, 23–7.

16840. SHERF, MARK.   The unreliable narrator and political reality in *Two Friends*. WCPMN (36:3) 1992, 40–2.

16841. SHIN, YOUNG-JA.   Willa Cather wa *lesbian feminism* yeongu. (A study of lesbian feminism in Willa Cather.) Unpub. doct. diss., Sookmyung Women's Univ., Seoul, 1996.

16842. SHIVELY, STEVE.   An interdisciplinary approach to *Neighbour Rosicky*. WCPMN (37:3/4) 1993/94, 39–40.

16843. SKAGGS, MERRILL M.   Key modulations in Cather's novels about music. WCPMN (39:2/3) 1995, 25–6, 28–30.

16844. —— Willa Cather's influence on Katherine Anne Porter's *He*. SoQ (34:2) 1996, 23–6.

16845. SKAGGS, MERRILL MAGUIRE.   After the world broke in two:

the later novels of Willa Cather. (Bibl. 1994, 12050.) Rev. by Josephine Donovan in Signs (18:2) 1993, 476–80.

16846. —— Cather's use of Parkman's histories in *Shadows on the Rock*. *See* **11995**.

16847. —— Thefts and conversation: Cather and Faulkner. CathS (3) 1996, 115–36.

16848. STEWART, HEATHER. *Shadows on the Rock*: the outsider, the disfigured, the disadvantaged, and the community. WCPMN (39:4) 1995, 54–8.

16849. STOUCK, DAVID. Willa Cather and the Russians. CathS (1) 1990, 1–20.

16850. STOUT, JANIS P. Cather's firm foundations and the rock of ages: a note. WCPMN (39:4) 1995, 59.

16851. SWIFT, JOHN N. Cather's Archbishop and the 'backward path'. CathS (1) 1990, 55–67.

16852. —— *The Old Beauty* and maternal purity. WCPMN (38:2) 1994, 17–18, 20, 22, 24.

16853. SYNNOTT, KEVIN A. Defining community in *Jack-a-Boy* and *The Best Years*. WCPMN (38:3) 1994, 41, 43, 45.

16854. —— Painting 'the tricks that shadows play': Impressionism in *Lucy Gayheart*. WCPMN (36:3) 1992, 37–9.

16855. THACKER, ROBERT. Four 'new' Cather letters to Annie Fields at the Huntington Library. CathS (3) 1996, 285–91.

16856. THOMAS, CLARA. Portraits of the artist: Thea Kronborg and Margaret Laurence's Morag Gunn. WCPMN (35:3) 1991, 15–19.

16857. TURNER, ELIZABETH A. The Willa Cather scholarly edition: texts for all readers. *See* **866**.

16858. URGO, JOSEPH R. Destinations and admonitions: Willa Cather's *Obscure Destinies*. WCPMN (40:2) 1996, 29, 31–4.

16859. —— Willa Cather and the myth of American migration. (Bibl. 1995, 15198.) Rev. by Guy Reynolds in JAStud (30:3) 1996, 494.

16860. VARDAMIS, ALEX. Two hands: Colette's *The Hand* and Cather's *Neighbour Rosicky*. WCPMN (37:3/4) 1993/94, 35–6.

16861. WASSERMAN, LORETTA. Cather in the mainstream. WCPMN (38:4) 1995, 23–4.

16862. —— *Cather in the Mainstream* – a follow-up. WCPMN (40:2) 1996, 54.

16863. —— Cather's Semitism. CathS (2) 1993, 1–22.

16864. —— *Sapphira and the Slave Girl*: Willa Cather *vs* Margaret Mitchell. WCPMN (38:1) 1994, 1, 3, 5, 7, 9, 11, 13, 15.

16865. WINTERS, LAURA. *My Mortal Enemy*: Willa Cather's ballad of exile. WCPMN (36:3) 1992, 31–4.

16866. WOLFF, CYNTHIA GRIFFIN. The artist's palette: early Cather. WCPMN (40:1) 1996, 1, 9–14.

16867. —— Time and memory in *Sapphira and the Slave Girl*: sex, abuse, and art. CathS (3) 1996, 212–37.

16868. WOODRESS, JAMES. A note on *One of Ours*. WCPMN (37:1) 1993, 1, 4.

16869. —— Willa Cather and Alphonse Daudet. CathS (2) 1993, 156–66.

16870. —— Writing Cather's biography. CathS (1) 1990, 103–14.

16871. WOOLLEY, PAULA. 'Fire and wit': storytelling and the American artist in Cather's *My Ántonia*. CathS (3) 1996, 149–81.

16872. ZETTSU, TOMOYUKI.   Slavery, song, and the South: Cather's refiguration of Stowe and Foster in *A Lost Lady*. *See* **3572**.
16873. ZITTER, EMMY STARK.   Willa Cather's early Naturalism: *A Death in the Desert*. WCPMN (38:2) 1994, 29–31.

Charles Causley

16874. WILMER, CLIVE.   Charles Causley in conversation. PN Review (17:5) 1991, 52–5.

Lorna Dee Cervantes

16875. SAVIN, ADA.   Bilingualism and dialogism: another reading of Lorna Dee Cervantes's poetry. *In* (pp. 215–23) **80**.

Joseph Chaikin (1935–)

16876. COCO, BILL.   The dramaturgy of the dream play: monologues by Breuer, Chaikin, Shepard. *In* (pp. 159–70) **119**.

Robert W. Chambers (1865–1933)

16877. SCHEICK, WILLIAM J.   Chambered intimations: *The King in Yellow* and *The Descendant*. EGN (34) 1995, 1, 4, 8–9.

Raymond Chandler

16878. BADONNEL, PATRICK; MAISONNAT, CLAUDE.   *The Big Sleep* by R. Chandler. Paris: Didier Erudition, 1995. pp. 110.
16879. BREWER, GAY.   Raymond Chandler without his knight: contracting worlds in *The Blue Dahlia* and *Playback*. *See* **13489**.
16880. CASTILLE, PHILIP DUBUISSON.   Compson and Sternwood: William Faulkner's 'Appendix' and *The Big Sleep*. *See* **13537**.
16881. CONTI, GIUSEPPE GADDA.   Dalla giungla delle orchidee alla giungla d'asfalto. Letterature d'America (36/37) 1990, 131–54.
16882. EWERT, JEANNE C.   Deep and dark waters: Raymond Chandler revisits the *fin-de-siècle*. Genre (27:3) 1994, 255–74.
16883. FORTER, GREGORY.   Criminal pleasures, pleasurable crime. *See* **14497**.
16884. KRYSTAL, ARTHUR.   No failure like success: the life of Raymond Chandler. ASch (65:3) 1996, 445–55.

Suzy McKee Charnas

16885. KING, MAUREEN.   Contemporary women writers and the 'new evil': the vampires of Anne Rice and Suzy McKee Charnas. JFA (5:3) 1992, 75–84.

Leslie Charteris

16886. BARER, BURL.   The Saint: a complete history in print, radio, film, and television of Leslie Charteris' Robin Hood of modern crime, Simon Templar, 1928–1992. *See* **13418**.

Borden Chase

16887. O'BRIEN, SHEILA RUZYCKI.   Leaving behind *The Chisholm Trail* for *Red River*; or, Refiguring the female in the Western film epic. *See* **14043**.

Bruce Chatwin

16888. CIMITILE, ANNA MARIA. Travel, language, identity, and the spaces in-between. *See* **15345**.

16889. RESCINITO, IVANA. Fra etica ed alterità: *The Songlines* di Bruce Chatwin. Annali anglistica (36:1–3) 1993, 173–90.

Nirad Chaudhuri

16890. CHAKRABARTY, DIPESH. Postcoloniality and the artifice of history: who speaks for 'Indian' pasts? Representations (37) 1992, 1–26.

Denise Chávez

16891. ANDERSON, DOUGLAS. Displaced abjection and states of grace: Denise Chávez's *The Last of the Menu Girls. In* (pp. 235–50) **3**.

16892. EYSTUROY, ANNIE O. Denise Chávez. *In* (pp. 156–69) **121**.

Paddy Chayefsky

16893. CONSIDINE, SHAUN. Mad as hell: the life and work of Paddy Chayefsky. (Bibl. 1995, 15220.) Rev. by Gerald Weales in GetR (9:2) 1996, 303–12.

16894. WEALES, GERALD. Paddy and Sidney. GetR (9:2) 1996, 303–12 (review-article).

John Cheever

16895. BLYTHE, HAL; SWEET, CHARLIE. Alcoholism and *The Swimmer*. NCL (22:4) 1992, 9–10.

16896. ———— The ironic return to the womb in Cheever's *The Swimmer*. NCL (22:1) 1992, 8–9.

16897. ———— Neddy Merrill: Cheever's contemporary Narcissus. NCL (26:5) 1996, 7–9.

16898. ———— Neddy Merrill: Cheever's failed Adam. NCL (22:4) 1992, 10–11.

16899. ———— *The Swimmer*: Cheever's building-roman. NCL (26:1) 1996, 5–6.

16900. COLLINS, JERRE; WILSON, RAYMOND J., III. Albee's *Who's Afraid of Virginia Woolf?*: the issue of originality. *See* **15901**.

16901. KURMAN, GEORGE. Escape reading: Cheever's *Falconer*, Dumas' Count, and Dr Lecter. NCL (23:3) 1993, 2–4.

16902. MAYO, WENDELL. 'I' and 'not-I': rhetoric and difference in John Cheever's *Goodbye, My Brother*. JSSE (17) 1991, 91–102.

16903. NASH, CHARLES C. Trying his wings: John Updike's reply to John Cheever's *O Youth and Beauty!* PMPA (20) 1995, 23–8.

16904. SLABEY, ROBERT M. Postmodern myth in John Cheever's *Bullet Park*. NCL (24:4) 1994, 2–3.

Susan Taylor Chehak

16905. BAKERMAN, JANE S. Timeless questions, modern phrasing: Susan Taylor Chehak, a new Midwestern voice. Midamerica (18) 1991, 153–9.

Kim Chernin

16906. CHERNIN, KIM. In my father's garden: a daughter's search for a spiritual life. Chapel Hill, NC: Algonquin Books of Chapel Hill, 1996. pp. 180.

C. J. Cherryh

16907. HYDE, PAUL NOLAN.   Dances with *dusei*: a personal response to C. J. Cherryh's *The Faded Sun*. Mythlore (18:2) 1992, 45–53.

G. K. Chesterton

16908. BERGONZI, BERNARD (ed.).   The Napoleon of Notting Hill. (Bibl. 1994, 12077.) Rev. by Kevin Morris in ChesR (22:1/2) 1996, 143–5.
16909. CARLIN, RUSSELL.   The hero who was Thursday: a modern myth. Mythlore (19:3) 1993, 27–30.
16910. CONLON, D. J. (ed.).   The collected works of G. K. Chesterton: vol. XIV, Short stories, fairy tales, mystery stories, illustrations. (Bibl. 1994, 12084.) Rev. by Stephen Medcalf in TLS, 20 Dec. 1996, 9.
16911. DARVILL, GILES.   With the Chestertons in Poland, 1927: Dorothy Collins's portfolio of the visit. ChesR (22:4) 1996, 475–85.
16912. FAULKNER, PETER (introd.).   The works of G. K. Chesterton. Ware: Wordsworth, 1995. pp. xiv, 314. (Wordsworth poetry library.)
16913. FLEMING, THOMAS.   The road from Rome. ChesR (22:3) 1996, 337–47.
16914. HEIN, ROLLAND.   G. K. Chesterton: myth, paradox, and the commonplace. SEVEN (13) 1996, 13–24.
16915. HETZLER, LEO A.   Chesterton and the realm of the unconscious. ChesR (22:3) 1996, 327–35.
16916. JOHN, CATHERINE RACHEL.   Quiller-Couch and G. K. Chesterton: some aspects of Liberalism. ChesR (22:3) 1996, 349–57.
16917. LOBDELL, JARED C.   Stone pastorals: three men on the side of the horses. *See* **16617**.
16918. MITCHELL, KEITH.   Chesterton's best book. Critic (48:4) 1994, 77–84.
16919. MORRIS, KEVIN L.   The mirror of perfection: G. K. Chesterton's interpretation of St Francis of Assisi. ChesR (22:4) 1996, 445–73.
16920. PEARCE, JOSEPH.   Wisdom and innocence: a life of G. K. Chesterton. London: Hodder & Stoughton; San Francisco, CA: Ignatius Press, 1996. pp. xiv, 522, (plates) 8. Rev. by A. N. Wilson in LRB (18:24) 1996, 22–3; by Stephen Medcalf in TLS, 20 Dec. 1996, 9.
16921. ROBSON, W. W. (ed.).   Father Brown: a selection. Oxford; New York: OUP, 1995. pp. xxvii, 555. (World's classics.) Rev. by Kevin Morris in ChesR (22:1/2) 1996, 139–43.
16922. SAWARD, JOHN.   Chesterton and Balthasar: the likeness is greater. ChesR (22:3) 1996, 301–25.
16923. WALTERS, HUGH.   Was Father Vincent McNabb a dangerous crank? ChesR (22:1/2) 1996, 101–11.
16924. WORTHINGTON, BERNARD A.   Chesterton's influence on Orwell. QLLSM (1) 1987, 233–55.

Alice Childress

16925. DRESNER, ZITA Z.   Alice Childress's *Like One of the Family*: domestic and undomesticated domestic humor. *In* (pp. 221–9) **64**.
16926. MAGUIRE, ROBERT.   Alice Childress. *In* (pp. 48–69) **85**.
16927. MARTINEZ, SAM.   Alice Childress: another hopeful soul in sorrow's kitchen. ArizEB (36:1) 1993, 46–50.

Charles Chilton

16928. JAMES, EDWARD. Journeying into space. Foundation (68) 1996, 46–57. (Profession of science fiction, 50.)

Chinweizu

16929. EZENWA-OHAETO. From a common root: revolutionary vision and social change in the poetry of Brathwaite and Chinweizu. *See* **16547**.

Ping Chong

16930. NEELY, KENT. Ping Chong's theatre of simultaneous consciousness. JDTC (6:2) 1992, 121–35.

Caryl Churchill

16931. CIONI, FERNANDO. *Scrutinizing the intruder*: figure narranti in alcuni testi teatrali inglesi contemporanei. Textus (6) 1993, 221–39.

16932. DIAMOND, ELIN. Refusing the romanticism of identity: narrative interventions in Churchill, Benmussa, Duras. *In* (pp. 92–105) **84**.

16933. GALEOTTI, ROSSELLA. Pam Gems e Caryl Churchill: due figure femminili nel teatro inglese contemporaneo. QLLSM (5) 1992, 167–77.

16934. HERMANN, ANNE. Travesty and transgression: transvestism in Shakespeare, Brecht, and Churchill. *In* (pp. 294–315) **84**.

16935. KRITZER, AMELIA HOWE. Dionysus in Bucharest: Caryl Churchill's *Mad Forest*. In-between (4:2) 1995, 151–61.

16936. —— The plays of Caryl Churchill: theatre of empowerment. (Bibl. 1994, 12109.) Rev. by Michael Swanson in JDTC (8:1) 1993, 204–6.

16937. RABILLARD, SHEILA. *Fen* and the production of a feminist ecotheater. Theater (25:1) 1994, 62–71.

16938. SILVERSTEIN, MARC. 'Make us the women we can't be': *Cloud Nine* and the female imaginary. JDTC (8:2) 1994, 7–22.

16939. SOTO-MORETTINI, DONNA. Revolution and the fatally clever smile: Caryl Churchill's *Mad Forest*. JDTC (9:1) 1994, 105–18.

Sir Winston Churchill

16940. MIEDER, WOLFGANG. 'Make hell while the sun shines': proverbial rhetoric in Winston Churchill's *The Second World War*. *See* **3332**.

Carolyn Chute

16941. BURNS, WAYNE. Triumph of the monster: a study of Carolyn Chute's *Merry Men* in relation to Steinbeck's *The Grapes of Wrath*. RecL (23) 1996, 5–32.

16942. BUTLER, EVELYN. Carolyn Chute's *Merry Men*: outside the magic circle. RecL (23) 1996, 51–60.

16943. FRUS, PHYLLIS. Regionalism, class, and anti-realism in Carolyn Chute's Maine novels: who gets read. RecL (23) 1996, 33–50.

Jill Ciment

16944. CIMENT, JILL. Half a life. New York: Crown, 1996. pp. 210.

Sandra Cisneros

16945. DOYLE, JACQUELINE.   Haunting the borderlands: La Llorona in Sandra Cisneros's *Woman Hollering Creek*. Frontiers (16:1) 1996, 53–70.

16946. GAGNIER, REGENIA.   Feminist autobiography in the 1980s. *See* **15150**.

16947. KANOZA, THERESA.   Esperanza's Mango Street: home for keeps. NCL (25:3) 1995, 9.

16948. MADSEN, D. L.   (Dis)continuous narrative: the articulation of a Chicana feminist voice in Sandra Cisneros's *The House on Mango Street*. JSSE (27) 1996, 13–28.

16949. MATCHIE, THOMAS.   Literary continuity in Sandra Cisneros's *The House on Mango Street. See* **12592**.

16950. POLLOCK, MARY S.   'A woman with one foot in this world and one foot in that': the bilingual perspective of Sandra Cisneros. JSSE (21) 1993, 53–63.

16951. RESTUCCIA, FRANCES L.   Literary representations of battered women: spectacular domestic punishment. *In* (pp. 42–71) **9**.

16952. SÁNCHEZ, REUBEN.   Remembering always to come back: the child's wished-for escape and the adult's self-empowered return in Sandra Cisneros's *House on Mango Street*. ChildLit (23) 1995, 221–41.

16953. WYATT, JEAN.   On not being La Malinche: border negotiations of gender in Sandra Cisneros's *Never Marry a Mexican* and *Woman Hollering Creek*. TSWL (14:2) 1995, 243–71.

Amy Clampitt

16954. LONGENBACH, JAMES.   Amy Clampitt's America. GetR (8:2) 1995, 220–40.

Tom Clancy

16955. GARSON, HELEN S.   Tom Clancy: a critical companion. Westport, CT; London: Greenwood Press, 1996. pp. xi, 180. (Critical companions to popular contemporary writers.)

Mary Higgins Clark

16956. WYMARD, ELLIE.   I'll be seeing you: Ellie Wymard interviews Mary Higgins Clark. Critic (48:1) 1993, 55–61.

Austin Clarke

16957. ALGOO-BAKSH, STELLA.   Austin C. Clarke: a biography. Barbados: West Indies UP; Toronto: ECW Press, 1994. pp. 234. Rev. by Andrew Salkey in WLT (69:3) 1995, 627–8; by John Clement Ball in CanL (150) 1996, 111–12; by Terry Goldie in ESCan (22:3) 1996, 357–9.

16958. HARMON, MAURICE.   Ancient lights in Austin Clarke and Thomas Kinsella. *In* (pp. 70–87) **112**.

16959. SCHIRMER, GREGORY A. (ed.).   Reviews and essays of Austin Clarke. (Bibl. 1995, 15261.) Rev. by Bernard O'Donoghue in TLS, 26 Jan. 1996, 26.

Lindsay Clarke

16960. ROWLAND, SUSAN.   The body's sacred: romance and sacrifice in religious and Jungian narratives. LitTheol (10:2) 1996, 160–70.

Helen Clarkson

16961. BRIANS, PAUL.   Nuclear family/nuclear war. *In* (pp. 151–8) **77**.

James Clavell

16962. MACDONALD, GINA.   James Clavell: a critical companion. Westport, CT; London: Greenwood Press, 1996. pp. xi, 223. (Critical companions to popular contemporary writers.)

Beverly Cleary

16963. CLEARY, BEVERLY.   My own two feet: a memoir. (Bibl. 1995, 15263.) Rev. by Nathalie op de Beeck in BkW, 10 Dec. 1995, 20.

Eldridge Cleaver

16964. REID-PHARR, ROBERT F.   Tearing the goat's flesh: homosexuality, abjection and the production of a late twentieth-century Black masculinity. *See* **16169**.

Michelle Cliff

16965. ADISA, OPAL PALMER.   Journey into speech – a writer between two worlds: an interview with Michelle Cliff. AAR (28:2) 1994, 273–81.
16966. CHANCY, MYRIAM J. A.   Exile and resistance: retelling history as a revolutionary act in the writings of Michelle Cliff and Marie Chauvet. JCS (9:3) 1993/94, 266–92.
16967. COOKE, MICHAEL G.   A rhetoric of obliquity in African and Caribbean women writers. *In* (pp. 169–84) **80**.
16968. DAVIES, CAROLE BOYCE .   Writing home: gender and heritage in the works of Afro-Caribbean/American women writers. *In* (pp. 59–73) **81**.
16969. HOVING, ISABEL.   The dark dank places of my silence: silence, sexuality, and the experience of two Caribbean women writers. JCS (9:3) 1993/94, 202–9.
16970. MIGNOLO, WALTER D.   Linguistic maps, literary geographies, and cultural landscapes: languages, languaging, and (trans)nationalism. MLQ (57:2) 1996, 181–96.

Robert M. Coates

16971. PIERCE, CONSTANCE.   Gertrude Stein and her thoroughly modern *protégé*. MFS (42:3) 1996, 607–25.

J. M. Coetzee

16972. ANON.   An interview with J. M. Coetzee. WLT (70:1) 1996, 107–10.
16973. ATTWELL, DAVID.   J. M. Coetzee: South Africa and the politics of writing. (Bibl. 1995, 15273.) Rev. by Chris Bongie in MFS (40:1) 1994, 185–7.
16974. BARTON, JUDY L.   Coetzee's *Foe*: humanitarianism in the interregnum. In-between (2:1) 1993, 37–43.
16975. BRUCE, ALASTAIR.   *In the Heart of the Country*: colonialism and temporality. Bracket (1) 1995, 38–53.
16976. COETZEE, AMPIE.   South African literature and narrating the nation. *See* **3761**.
16977. COETZEE, J. M.   Emerging from censorship. *See* **13017**.

16978. EDGECOMBE, RODNEY STENNING. A source for an incident in
J. M. Coetzee's *Life & Times of Michael K.* NCL (22:1) 1992, 7.

16979. FICK, A. C. Ways of seeing and subaltern subject positioning: scopophilia and agency in J. M. Coetzee's *Waiting for the Barbarians.*
Bracket (1) 1995, 70–84.

16980. GEERTSEMA, JOHAN. 'Traductions': J. M. Coetzee and the
violent 'invention' of the classic. *See* **3139**.

16981. GRÄBE, INA. Voices in contemporary South African
narrative: an exploration of narrative strategies for engaging with
current socio-political issues. *See* **14523**.

16982. HARRISON, JAMES. Point of view and tense in the novels of
J. M. Coetzee. JCL (30:1) 1995, 79–85.

16983. HUGGAN, GRAHAM; WATSON, STEPHEN (eds). Critical perspectives on J. M. Coetzee. Basingstoke: Macmillan; New York:
St Martin's Press, 1996. pp. xvi, 246.

16984. JOLLY, ROSEMARY JANE. Colonization, violence, and narration in White South African writing: André Brink, Breyten Breytenbach,
and J. M. Coetzee. *See* **16560**.

16985. KELLMAN, STEVEN G. J. M. Coetzee and Samuel Beckett: the
translingual link. *See* **3156**.

16986. KOSSEW, SUE. The anxiety of authorship: J. M. Coetzee's
The Master of Petersburg (1994) and André Brink's *On the Contrary* (1993).
See **16569**.

16987. LANZ, JUAN RAMÓN GALARZA. Foes in J. M. Coetzee's *Foe.*
Teaching & Learning (2) 1996, 7–14.

16988. MARAIS, MIKE. 'One of those islands without an owner': the
aesthetics of space in *Robinson Crusoe* and J. M. Coetzee's *Life and Times
of Michael K. See* **8974**.

16989. —— Places of pigs: the tension between implication and
transcendence in J. M. Coetzee's *Age of Iron* and *The Master of Petersburg.*
JCL (31:1) 1996, 83–95.

16990. MEIHUIZEN, NICHOLAS. Beckett and Coetzee: the aesthetics
of insularity. *See* **16339**.

16991. MENNECKE, ARNIM. Koloniales Bewußtsein in den Romanen
J. M. Coetzees. (Bibl. 1993, 12057.) Rev. by Erhard Reckwitz in
ZAA (42:1) 1994, 86–8.

16992. MORAN, SHANE. Self-canonizing critics: T. S. Eliot and J. M.
Coetzee. *See* **15654**.

16993. MORPHET, TONY. Stranger fictions: trajectories in the liberal
novel. WLT (70:1) 1996, 53–8.

16994. PARKER, ROBERT A. A world of ambiguities: Robert A.
Parker interviews J. M. Coetzee. Critic (46:3) 1992, 52–7.

16995. ROBERTS, SHEILA. 'City of man': the appropriation of Dante's
Inferno in J. M. Coetzee's *Age of Iron.* Current Writing (8:1) 1996, 33–44.

16996. SPAAS, LIEVE; STIMPSON, BRIAN (eds). Robinson Crusoe:
myths and metamorphoses. *See* **8986**.

16997. WENZEL, JENNIFER. Keys to the labyrinth: writing, torture,
and Coetzee's barbarian girl. TSWL (15:1) 1996, 61–71.

16998. WINNER, ANTHONY. Disorders of reading short novels and
perplexities. Kenyon Review (18:1) 1996, 117–28.

Brian Coffey

16999. MORGAN, JACK. A modern revenge poem – Brian Coffey's *Topos*. Notes on Modern Irish Literature (5) 1993, 14–18.

Leonard Cohen

17000. ADRIA, MARCO. Some comparisons of conceptions of time and space in Canada. BJCS (11:1) 1996, 125–32.

17001. FOURNIER, MICHAEL; NORRIS, KEN (eds). Take this waltz: a celebration of Leonard Cohen. Ste Anne de Bellevue, Que.: Muses, 1994. pp. 189. Rev. by Peter Cumming in CanL (150) 1996, 135; by Michael Abraham in JCP (11) 1996, 182–5.

17002. NADEL, IRA. Leonard Cohen: a life in art. Toronto: ECW Press, 1994. pp. 160. (Canadian biography.) Rev. by Peter Cumming in CanL (150) 1996, 135–6; by John Orange in ESCan (22:4) 1996, 486–8; by Michael Abraham in JCP (11) 1996, 182–5.

17003. NADEL, IRA B. Various positions: a life of Leonard Cohen. New York: Pantheon, 1996. pp. 325, (plates) 16.

17004. SCOBIE, STEPHEN. Leonard Cohen, Phyllis Webb, and the end(s) of Modernism. *In* (pp. 57–70) **13**.

17005. SIEMERLING, WINFRIED. Discoveries of the Other: alterity in the work of Leonard Cohen, Hubert Aquin, Michael Ondaatje, and Nicole Brossard. (Bibl. 1995, 15304.) Rev. by Martin Kuester in CanL (150) 1996, 158–9.

Matt Cohen

17006. IRVINE, LORNA. Crises of the legitimate: Matt Cohen and Timothy Findley. ARCS (19:1) 1989, 15–23.

Jane Candia Coleman

17007. WYMARD, ELLIE. The rhythm of the West: Ellie Wymard interviews Jane Candia Coleman. Critic (46:4) 1992, 53–9.

Merle Collins

17008. ANIM-ADDO, JOAN. Woman-centred narratives at the intersections of the oral and literary traditions in the short stories of Merle Collins. JSSE (26) 1996, 49–62.

17009. LONSDALE, THORUNN. An interview with Merle Collins. JSSE (26) 1996, 9–12.

Mary Colum

17010. GUPTA, SUMAN. Knowing Joyce and understanding *Ulysses*: Mary and Pádraic Colum. In-between (2:2) 1993, 149–56.

Pádraic Colum

17011. GUPTA, SUMAN. Knowing Joyce and understanding *Ulysses*: Mary and Pádraic Colum. *See* **17010**.

17012. SHERBO, ARTHUR. Pádraic Colum in the *Dublin Magazine*. *See* **1368**.

Marc Connelly

17013. SAUER, DAVID K. George S. Kaufman's exploitation of women (characters): dramaturgy and feminism. AmDr (4:2) 1995, 55–80.

Cyril Connolly

17014. FISHER, CLIVE.   Cyril Connolly: the life and times of England's most controversial literary critic. New York: St Martin's Press, 1996. pp. 466, (plates) 16. (Cf. bibl. 1995, 15314.)

Robert Conquest

17015. BRADLEY, JERRY.   Robert Conquest and science. RWT (4:1) 1996, 147–55.

Joseph Conrad

17016. ANTÓN-PACHECO SÁNCHEZ, LUISA.   El viaje de vuelta: del narrador al héroe en *The Shadow-Line*. EIUC (4) 1996, 149–59.

17017. ARMSTRONG, PAUL B.   Cultural differences in Conrad and James: *Under Western Eyes* and *The Ambassadors*. See **11565**.

17018. BENNETT, CARL D.   Joseph Conrad. New York: Continuum, 1991. pp. 180. (Literature and life. British writers.) Rev. by Ted Billy in Conradiana (28:3) 1996, 228–9.

17019. BERNSTEIN, STEPHEN.   Conrad and Rousseau: a note on *Under Western Eyes*. JML (19:1) 1994, 161–3.

17020. CARABINE, KEITH.   Conrad, Apollo Korzeniowski, and Dostoevsky. Conradiana (28:1) 1996, 3–25.

17021. —— The life and the art: a study of Conrad's *Under Western Eyes*. Amsterdam; Atlanta, GA: Rodopi, 1996. pp. xxx, 266, (plates) 9. (Costerus, 106.)

17022. CARAHER, BRIAN G.   A Modernist allegory of narration: Joseph Conrad's *Youth* and the ideology of the image. *In* (pp. 47–68) **44**.

17023. CASERTANO, ANGELO.   *Under Western Eyes* di Joseph Conrad: un'analisi dei motivi ricorrenti. Acme (49:2) 1996, 203–15.

17024. CIFARELLI, MARIA RITA.   Degrado metropolitano e forme della politica: *The Secret Agent* di Joseph Conrad. QLLSM (4) 1990, 123–39.

17025. CLARKE, MICHAEL TAVEL.   Reclaiming literary territory: Paule Marshall's response to Joseph Conrad. Conradiana (28:2) 1996, 138–50.

17026. CRICK, BRIAN.   Conrad's Polish joke: *The Secret Agent* as domestic art. CamQ (25:2) 1996, 124–51.

17027. CROGHAN, MARTIN J.   Swift & Conrad: gamekeepers make great poachers. *In* (pp. 208–21) **60**.

17028. DANIELS, PATSY J.   Conrad's *Heart of Darkness*. Exp (54:3) 1996, 164–5.

17029. DANOW, DAVID K.   The enigmatic faces of the *Doppelgänger*. CanRCL (23:2) 1996, 457–74.

17030. DELTCHEVA, ROUMIANA.   Destination classified: on the transformation of spatial forms in applying the narrative text to film: the case of *Heart of Darkness* and *Apocalypse Now*. See **13605**.

17031. DEVERS, JAMES.   More on symbols in Conrad's *The Secret Sharer*. Conradiana (28:1) 1996, 66–76.

17032. DiBATTISTA, MARIA.   The lowly art of murder: Modernism and the case of the free woman. *In* (pp. 176–93) **41**.

17033. EDDLEMAN, FLOYD EUGENE; HIGDON, DAVID LEON (eds). Almayer's folly: a story of an eastern river. Introd. by Ian Watt. (Bibl. 1994, 12175.) Rev. by Ted Billy in ELT (39:2) 1996, 238–41.

17034. ERDINAST-VULCAN, DAPHNA.   Joseph Conrad and the modern temper. (Bibl. 1994, 12178.) Rev. by Ruth Nadelhaft in Conradiana (28:2) 1996, 151–3.

17035. FINCHAM, GAIL; HOOPER, MYRTLE (eds). Under postcolonial eyes: Joseph Conrad after empire. *See* **15852**.

17036. GIBBONS, BRIAN. The wrong end of the telescope. *In* (pp. 141–59) **124**.

17037. GILLON, ADAM. Joseph Conrad – comparative essays. Ed. by Raymond Brebach. (Bibl. 1994, 12180.) Rev. by Marek Haltof in CanRCL (23:4) 1996, 1262–4.

17038. GOGWILT, CHRIS. Broadcasting news from nowhere: R. B. Cunninghame Graham and the geography of politics in the 1890s. *In* (pp. 235–54) **41**.

17039. GOGWILT, CHRISTOPHER. The invention of the West: Joseph Conrad and the double-mapping of Europe and Empire. (Bibl. 1995, 15352.) Rev. by Tony E. Jackson in MFS (42:4) 1996, 890–2; by Todd K. Bender in CLIO (25:4) 1996, 467–72; by Avrom Fleishman in SAtlR (61:3) 1996, 128–31.

17040. GOONETILLEKE, D. C. R. A. (ed.). Heart of darkness. (Bibl. 1995, 15354.) Rev. by Jeremy Harding in TLS, 24 May 1996, 5–6.

17041. GRIFFITH, JOHN W. Joseph Conrad and the anthropological dilemma: 'bewildered traveller'. (Bibl. 1995, 15356.) Rev. by Avrom Fleishman in ELT (39:3) 1996, 400–2.

17042. GRUESSER, JOHN. Lies that kill: Lorraine Hansberry's answer to *Heart of Darkness* in *Les Blancs*. AmDr (1:2) 1992, 1–14.

17043. HAMPSON, ROBERT. Conrad, Curle and the *Blue Peter*. *In* (pp. 89–104) **69**.

17044. ——Joseph Conrad: betrayal and identity. (Bibl. 1994, 12184.) Rev. by Vincent P. Pecora in MFS (40:1) 1994, 172–3.

17045. HARPHAM, GEOFFREY GALT. Abroad only by a fiction: creation, irony, and necessity in Conrad's *The Secret Agent*. Representations (37) 1992, 79–103.

17046. —— One of us: the mastery of Joseph Conrad. Chicago; London: Chicago UP, 1996. pp. xiv, 211.

17047. HARRISON, THOMAS. Essayism: Conrad, Musil & Pirandello. (Bibl. 1994, 12186.) Rev. by Walter A. Strauss in CLS (33:2) 1996, 225–7.

17048. HENRICKSEN, BRUCE. Nomadic voices: Conrad and the subject of narrative. (Bibl. 1995, 15359.) Rev. by Vincent P. Pecora in MFS (40:1) 1994, 171–2.

17049. HENTHORNE, TOM. 'Spinning' tales: re-telling the telling of *Heart of Darkness*. Conradiana (28:3) 1996, 206–14.

17050. HERVOUET, YVES. The French face of Joseph Conrad. (Bibl. 1995, 15360.) Rev. by Michael A. Lucas in Conradiana (28:3) 1996, 233–6.

17051. HOUSTON, GAIL. Fictions to live by: honorable intentions, authorial intentions and the intended in *Heart of Darkness*. Conradiana (28:1) 1996, 34–47.

17052. JACKSON, TONY E. The subject of Modernism: narrative alterations in the fiction of Eliot, Conrad, Woolf, and Joyce. (Bibl. 1994, 12193.) Rev. by Gary Handwerk in MFS (42:4) 1996, 865–7; by Mark Conroy in ELT (39:1) 1996, 80–5.

17053. —— Turning into Modernism: *Lord Jim* and the alteration of the narrative subject. LitPs (39:4) 1993, 65–85.

17054. JORDAN, ELAINE (ed.). Joseph Conrad. Basingstoke: Macmillan; New York: St Martin's Press, 1996. pp. ix, 227. (New casebooks.)

17055. KARL, FREDERICK R.; DAVIES, LAURENCE (eds). The collected letters of Joseph Conrad: vol. 5, 1912–1916. Cambridge; New York: CUP, 1996. pp. lx, 721.

17056. KOH, BOO EUNG. Contradictions in colonial history in *Lord Jim*. Conradiana (28:3) 1996, 163–81.

17057. KOPPER, EDWARD A., JR. The influence of *Heart of Darkness* on Scott Turow's *Pleading Guilty*. NCL (25:4) 1995, 8–9.

17058. KURTZ, R. Lloyd Fernando's *Scorpion Orchid* and Lord Jim's dilemma: another descendant, in other words. Conradiana (28:2) 1996, 115–25.

17059. LEAVIS, L. R. Marriage, murder, and morality: *The Secret Agent* and *Tess. See* **11347**.

17060. LEBDAI, BENAOUDA. The short-story teller V. S. Naipaul, the character Bobby, and the state of Africa in *In a Free State*. JSSE (26) 1996, 105–17.

17061. LEE, MI-AE. Conrad jakpum eui romancejeok yoso. (Romance elements in the works of Conrad.) Unpub. doct. diss., Seoul National Univ., 1995.

17062. LESK, ANDREW. Achebe and his critics: racism in *Heart of Darkness. See* **15854**.

17063. LONDON, BETTE. The appropriated voice: narrative authority in Conrad, Forster, and Woolf. (Bibl. 1993, 12137.) Rev. by Rachel Bowlby in Signs (19:1) 1993, 257–9.

17064. LÓPEZ, ALFRED. Meaningful paradox: the 'strange genius' of Wilson Harris. Conradiana (28:3) 1996, 190–205.

17065. LOWDEN, STEPHEN. *Heart of Darkness* revisited: the meaning of experience in *A Bend in the River*. ERev (7:2) 1996, 26–8.

17066. LUCAS, MICHAEL A. Stylistic variation in *An Anarchist. See* **2667**.

17067. McCRACKEN, SCOTT. Postmodernism, a *Chance* to reread? *In* (pp. 267–89) **18**.

17068. MAISONNAT, CLAUDE. Alterity and suicide in *An Outpost of Progress*. Conradiana (28:2) 1996, 101–14.

17069. MEYER, STEPHEN. A reading of Joseph Conrad's *Heart of Darkness*. UES (33:2) 1995, 27–32.

17070. MOORE, GENE M. Conrad items in the Dent archive in North Carolina. *See* **515**.

17071. —— A 'lost' Conrad letter rediscovered. *See* **516**.

17072. MOSER, THOMAS C. (ed.). *Lord Jim*: an authoritative text, backgrounds, sources, criticism. *See* **762**.

17073. NISHIHARA, LAVERNE. 'The fetters of that strange freedom': boundary as regulating technique in *Lord Jim*. Conradiana (28:1) 1996, 54–65.

17074. OSTWALT, CONRAD. *Dances with Wolves*: an American *Heart of Darkness. See* **14056**.

17075. PACCAUD-HUGUET, JOSIANE. *Under Western Eyes* and *Hamlet*: where angels fear to tread. *See* **6832**.

17076. PENDLETON, ROBERT. Graham Greene's Conradian masterplot: the arabesques of influence. Basingstoke: Macmillan; New York: St Martin's Press, 1996. pp. vii, 181. (Cf. bibl. 1993, 12153.)

17077. PETERS, JOHN G.   Stein's collections: order and chaos in *Lord Jim*. Conradiana (28:1) 1996, 48–53.

17078. PUTNAM, WALTER C., III.   L'aventure littéraire de Joseph Conrad et d'André Gide. (Bibl. 1993, 12155.) Rev. by Mustapha Marrouchi in CanRCL (20:1/2) 1993, 260–3.

17079. REID, S. W.   Conrad in print and on disk. *See* **807**.

17080. RHEE, SUK-KOO.   Joseph Conrad eui soseol e natanan-jegukjueui wa yeosung eokapjeok damron. (Imperialism and anti-feminist discourse in Joseph Conrad.) JELL (42:1) 1996, 66–81.

17081. ROSS, HESTER F.   Rewriting the other: dynamic entrenchment in the colonial narrative and its reappropriation in two works by Conrad and Achebe. *See* **15859**.

17082. RUDE, DONALD W.; CARROLL, CHARLES T.   Unreported Conrad manuscripts and proofs. *See* **534**.

17083. RUPPEL, RICHARD.   Yanko Goorall in the heart of darkness: *Amy Foster* as colonialist text. Conradiana (28:2) 1996, 126–32.

17084. SCANNELL, JAMES.   The method is unsound: the aesthetic dissonance of colonial justification in Kipling, Conrad, and Greene. Style (30:3) 1996, 409–32.

17085. SENS, JEAN-MARK.   *Heart of Darkness*: sub-line & sublime, the exotic immensity. CVE (44) 1996, 127–34.

17086. SHAFFER, BRIAN W.   Domestic ironies: housekeeping as man-keeping in Conrad's *The Secret Agent*. *In* (pp. 313–29) **54**.

17087. SKILLEÅS, OLE MARTIN.   Restraint in the darkness. EngS (76:1) 1995, 52–63.

17088. SMITH, THOMAS R.   The autobiography in *The 'Tremolino'*: ritual violence as fictional screen. Conradiana (28:1) 1996, 26–33.

17089. STAPE, J. H. (ed.).   The Cambridge companion to Joseph Conrad. Cambridge; New York: CUP, 1996. pp. xx, 258. (Cambridge companions to literature.)

17090. —— KNOWLES, OWEN (eds).   A portrait in letters: correspondence to and about Conrad. Amsterdam; Atlanta, GA: Rodopi, 1996. pp. xxxiii, 287. (Conradian.)

17091. TAGGE, ANNE.   The butterfly hunters. Conradiana (28:3) 1996, 182–9.

17092. TEETS, BRUCE.   Joseph Conrad: an annotated bibliography. (Bibl. 1992, 13258.) Rev. by Keith Carabine in Conradiana (28:2) 1996, 157–60.

17093. THOMAS, BRIAN.   The symbolism of textuality in Joseph Conrad's *Under Western Eyes*: Razumov as literalist of the imagination. Conradiana (28:3) 1996, 215–27.

17094. VILLA, LUISA.   L'avventura, il destino e la colpa (su *Lord Jim* e il primo Conrad). QLLSM (3) 1989, 207–79.

17095. WANG, CHULL.   Conrad eui *Eunmilhan Dongbanja* wa Dostoevsky eui *Double* eui bikyo yeongu. (Conrad's *The Secret Sharer* and Dostoevsky's *The Double*.) JELL (42:1) 1996, 83–99.

17096. WATTS, CEDRIC.   *The Ebb-Tide* and *Victory*. *See* **12359**.

17097. —— Four rather obscure allusions in *Nostromo*. Conradiana (28:1) 1996, 77–80.

17098. —— Marketing Modernism: how Conrad prospered. *In* (pp. 81–8) **69**.

17099. WHITE, ANDREA.   Joseph Conrad and the adventure tradition: constructing and deconstructing the imperial subject. (Bibl. 1995, 15415.)

Rev. by Vincent P. Pecora in MFS (40:1) 1994, 173–5; by Ansgar Nünning in ZAA (43:3) 1995, 276–8.

17100. WILLIAMS, MARY FRANCES.   Cicero's *De officiis* and Conrad's *Lord Jim*: a philosophical paradigm for the novel. CML (16:2) 1996, 131–47.

17101. WORTHY, KIM.   Emissaries of difference: Conrad, Coppola, and *Hearts of Darkness*. *See* **14344**.

17102. WORYMA, PIOTR.   A sample contrastive analysis of *The Blue Hotel* by Stephen Crane and *The Nigger of the Narcissus* by Joseph Conrad. *See* **2736**.

17103. YIM, SUNG-KYUN.   Distancing and mystifying: Conrad's narrative technique in *Amy Foster* and *The Lagoon*. JELL (42:4) 1996, 827–38.

Jack Conroy

17104. WIXSON, DOUGLAS.   Worker-writer in America: Jack Conroy and the tradition of Midwestern literary radicalism, 1898–1990. (Bibl. 1995, 15424.) Rev. by David D. Anderson in SSMLN (24:3) 1994, 15–18; by Marcus Klein in MFS (42:1) 1996, 138–40; by David Jones in Cresset (59:5) 1996, 41–2.

Pat Conroy

17105. BURNS, LANDON C.   Pat Conroy: a critical companion. Westport, CT; London: Greenwood Press, 1996. pp. xiii, 195. (Critical companions to popular contemporary writers.)

'Murray Constantine' (Katharine Burdekin)

17106. LASSNER, PHYLLIS.   The fault lines of history: dystopic novels of the Second World War by British women authors. Greyfriar (31) 1991, 14–29.

Michael Cook

17107. WALKER, CRAIG STEWART.   Elegy, mythology, and the sublime in Michael Cook's *Colour the Flesh the Colour of Dust*. TRC (15:2) 1994, 192–206.

17108. —— Ship of death: eschatology in Michael Cook's *Quiller*. TRC (16:1/2) 1995, 69–80.

Robin Cook

17109. SQUIER, SUSAN.   Conceiving difference: reproductive technology and the construction of identity in two contemporary fictions. *In* (pp. 97–115) **94**.

17110. STOOKEY, LORENA LAURA.   Robin Cook: a critical companion. Westport, CT; London: Greenwood Press, 1996. pp. xi, 210. (Critical companions to popular contemporary writers.)

Bernard Cooper

17111. COOPER, BERNARD.   Truth serum: memoirs. Boston, MA: Houghton Mifflin, 1996. pp. 225.

Giles Cooper

17112. EGRI, PETER.   American variations on a British theme: Giles Cooper and Edward Albee. *In* (pp. 135–51) **34**.

J. California Cooper

17113. MARSHALL, BARBARA J.   Kitchen table talk: J. California Cooper's use of *nommo* – female bonding and transcendence. *In* (pp. 91–102) **55**.

Jane Cooper (1924–)

17114. GUDAS, ERIC.   An interview with Jane Cooper. IowaR (25:1) 1995, 90–110.

Susan Cooper

17115. KRIPS, VALERIE.   Finding one's place in the fantastic: Susan Cooper's *The Dark Is Rising. In* (pp. 169–75) **36**.

Robert Coover

17116. CALDWELL, ROY C.   For an American *nouveau roman*: reading Coover's *Spanking the Maid*. CanRCL (18:1) 1991, 51–75.
17117. CARRATELLO, MATTIA.   Dal *flipper* alla simulazione: *The Universal Baseball Association* di Robert Coover. *In* (pp. 310–13) **117**.
17118. CHASSAY, JEAN-FRANÇOIS.   La machine en mouvement: *A Night at the Movies* de Robert Coover. Études littéraires (28:2) 1995, 45–55.
17119. DAINOTTO, ROBERTO MARIA.   Myth and carnival in Robert Coover's *The Public Burning*. RSAJ (3) 1992, 5–22.
17120. MIGUEL-ALFONSO, RICARDO.   Art and representation: thematic continuity in Robert Coover's *Whatever Happened to Gloomy Gus of the Chicago Bears?* NCL (25:5) 1995, 5–7.
17121. ZORZI, ROSELLA MAMOLI (introd.).   *Ghost Town* by Robert Coover. RSAJ (6) 1995, 93–106.

Daniel Corkery

17122. KEARNEY, COLBERT.   Daniel Corkery: a priest and his people. *In* (pp. 201–12) **106**.

Robert Cormier

17123. DEEDY, JOHN.   John Deedy interviews Robert Cormier. Critic (46:1) 1991, 57–63.
17124. HEAD, PATRICIA.   Robert Cormier and the postmodernist possibilities of young adult fiction. CLAQ (21:1) 1996, 28–33.

Frances Cornford

17125. DOWSON, JANE (ed.).   Selected poems. London: Enitharmon, 1996. pp. xxxvii, 74.

Patricia Cornwell

17126. CANTWELL, MARY.   How to make a corpse talk. NYTM, 14 July 1996, 14–17.
17127. CORNWELL, PATRICIA.   In cold blood. BkW, 31 July 1994, 1, 8.

Gregory Corso

17128. PHILIP, JIM.   Journeys in the mindfield: Gregory Corso reconsidered. *In* (pp. 61–73) **4**.

Norman Corwin

17129. KOSTELANETZ, RICHARD.   The radio dramatist Norman Corwin. AmDr (1:2) 1992, 42–60.

Douglas Coupland

17130. LAINSBURY, G. P.   *Generation X* and the end of history. ECanW (58) 1996, 229–40.

Herbert R. Coursen

17131. TURCO, LEWIS.   The protean poetry of Herbert Coursen. HC (32:3) 1995, 1–11.

Sir Noël Coward

17132. CASTLE, TERRY.   Noël Coward and Radclyffe Hall: kindred spirits. New York: Columbia UP, 1996. pp. 149.
17133. HOARE, PHILIP.   Noël Coward: a biography. (Bibl. 1995, 15444.) New York: Simon & Schuster, 1995. pp. xii, 605. Rev. by Jonathan Yardley in BkW, 18 Aug. 1996, 3.

Malcolm Cowley

17134. DOLAN, MARC.   Modern lives: a cultural re-reading of the 'Lost Generation'. West Lafayette, IN: Purdue UP, 1996. pp. x, 253.
17135. DONALDSON, SUSAN V.   Reading Faulkner reading Cowley reading Faulkner: authority and gender in the Compson appendix. FJ (7:1/2) 1991/92, 27–41.

Christine Craig (1943–)

17136. FIDO, ELAINE SAVORY .   Textures of Third World reality in the poetry of four African-Caribbean women. *In* (pp. 29–44) **81**.

Hart Crane

17137. ANDERSON, DAVID D.   Sherwood Anderson and Hart Crane: a temporary friendship. *See* **15977**.
17138. BROMWICH, DAVID.   T. S. Eliot and Hart Crane. *In* (pp. 49–64) **41**.
17139. DEAN, TIM.   Hart Crane's poetics of privacy. AmLH (8:1) 1996, 83–109.
17140. HAFFENDEN, JOHN (introd.).   Three critics on one poem: Hart Crane's *Voyages III. See* **15472**.
17141. HURLEY, PATRICK.   Aeroplane in furs: the language of masochism and the will to submit in *Cape Hatteras*. Midamerica (23) 1996, 109–13.
17142. IRWIN, JOHN T.   The triple archetype: the presence of *Faust* in *The Bridge*. AQ (50:1) 1994, 51–73.
17143. SIMON, MARC.   Eugene O'Neill's introduction to Hart Crane's *White Buildings*: why he 'would have done it in a minute but …'. EOR (15:1) 1991, 41–57.
17144. STRINGHER, BONALDA.   Hart Crane e la città. QLLSM (4) 1990, 191–205.

William Crapser (1949–)

17145. WILLIAMS, TONY.   'This guy's a 'Nam vet': Wilfred Owen in William Crapser's *Remains*. NCL (22:1) 1992, 9–10.

Robert Creeley

17146. CLARK, TOM. Robert Creeley and the genius of the American common place: together with the poet's own autobiography. (Bibl. 1993, 12228.) Rev. by Roger Gilbert in AmLH (8:2) 1996, 350–63.

Harry Crews

17147. KICH, MARTIN. Goodfellows and scar lovers (re: Harry Crews). NCL (24:3) 1994, 10–12.

Michael Crichton

17148. O'NEILL, JOHN. Dinosaurs-R-Us: the (un)natural history of *Jurassic Park. In* (pp. 292–308) **72**.
17149. STEFANELLI, MARIA ANITA. Dinosaurs in the badlands: Michael Crichton's *Jurassic Park* and Robert Kroetsch's *Badlands. In* (pp. 402–9) **117**.
17150. TREMBLEY, ELIZABETH A. Michael Crichton: a critical companion. Westport, CT; London: Greenwood Press, 1996. pp. xi, 192. Rev. by Neal Baker in Extrapolation (37:4) 1996, 368–70.

'Amanda Cross' (Carolyn G. Heilbrun)

17151. BOKEN, JULIA B. Carolyn G. Heilbrun. New York: Twayne; London: Prentice Hall, 1996. pp. xvii, 156. (Twayne's US authors, 672.)
17152. MATTHEWS, PAMELA R. Second chances: Amanda Cross's Dorinda. EGN (28) 1992, 3–4.

Gillian Cross

17153. KERTZER, ADRIENNE. Reclaiming her maternal pre-text: Little Red Riding Hood's mother and three young adult novels. *See* **3688**.

Rachel Crothers

17154. FOX, ANN. The 'sweet troubles' of a playwright: Rachel Crothers sets the stage. TexPres (17) 1996, 20–4.

Elaine Crowley (1927–)

17155. CROWLEY, ELAINE. Cowslips and chainies. Dublin: Lilliput Press, 1996. pp. 172.

Patrick Cullinan

17156. WATSON, STEPHEN (ed.). Selected poems 1961–1994. Cape Town: Snailpress, 1994. pp. 142. Rev. by Ian Tromp in New Coin Poetry (31:2) 1995, 66–8.

e. e. cummings

17157. AHEARN, BARRY (ed.). Pound/cummings: the correspondence of Ezra Pound and e. e. cummings. Ann Arbor: Michigan UP, 1996. pp. xii, 442.
17158. CHARLTON, MARYETTE. Memories of Marion. Spring (5) 1996, 18–35.
17159. CHINITZ, DAVID. cummings' challenge to academic standards. Spring (5) 1996, 78–81.
17160. COWEN, JOHN EDWIN. e. e. cummings' lyricism today. Spring (5) 1996, 82–9.

31

17161. DILWORTH, THOMAS.   *l(a.* Exp (54:3) 1996, 171–3.

17162. FRIEDMAN, NORMAN.   (Re)valuing cummings: further essays on the poet, 1962–1993. Gainesville: Florida UP, 1996. pp. xiii, 192.

17163. GILL, JOHN M.   A study of two poems. Spring (5) 1996, 105–11.

17164. HARRIS, KURT W.   A variant text of cummings' *nothing is more exactly terrible than.* Spring (5) 1996, 101–4.

17165. KENNEDY, RICHARD S.   The elusive Marion Morehouse. Spring (5) 1996, 8–17.

17166. LABRIOLA, ALBERT C.   Reader-response criticism and the poetry of e.e. cummings: *Buffalo Bill's defunct* and *in Just-.* Cithara (31:2) 1992, 38–44.

17167. LEWIS, ETHAN.   A garland for e. e. cummings. Spring (5) 1996, 71–7.

17168. MARTIN, RICHARD.   Fashion in the age of advertising. JPC (29:2) 1995, 235–54.

17169. MARTIN, W. TODD.   *The Enormous Room*: cummings' re-interpretation of John Bunyan's Doubting Castle. *See* **7727**.

17170. OLSEN, TAIMI.   e. e. cummings and the Futurist art movement. Spring (5) 1996, 155–60.

17171. PESCH, JOSEF.   Twice translated? e. e. cummings in West and East Germany. Spring (5) 1996, 138–54.

17172. POLLOCK, JOHN.   'Cambridge ladies': comments on Milton and cummings. *See* **8225**.

17173. RODRIGUEZ, RALPH E.   The foregrounded reader in e. e. cummings. SECOLR (16:2) 1992, 132–48.

17174. WEGNER, ROBERT E.   A visit with e. e. cummings: reflections and impressions. Spring (5) 1996, 59–70.

Allen Curnow

17175. BRAUNIAS, STEVE.   Sweating poesy. Metro, Apr. 1996, 76–80.

17176. DAVIE, DONALD.   Postmodernism and Allen Curnow. PN Review (17:3) 1991, 31–4.

17177. MURRAY, STUART.   Writing an island's story: the 1930s poetry of Allen Curnow. JCL (30:2) 1995, 25–43.

17178. ROBERTS, HUGH.   Accurate misquotation – a blast from the present: an appreciation of Allen Curnow. New Zealand Books (6:1) 1996, 1, 4–5.

James Oliver Curwood

17179. WEBER, RONALD.   Writing the northwoods: the short happy career of James Oliver Curwood. MichH (80:6) 1996, 52–4.

Cyril Dabydeen

17180. JOSEPH, ANNAMMA.   Cyril Dabydeen's *Dark Swirl*: a study in resistance culture. WLR (1:1) 1996, 36–47.

David Dabydeen

17181. HAND, FELICITY.   Challenging the centre: the response of British Asian writers. RCEI (28) 1994, 81–93.

Roald Dahl

17182. SATO, TSUGUSHI.   Roald Dahl ron. (Essays on Roald Dahl.) Osaka: Izumiya Shoten, 1996. pp. 206.

17183. TREGLOWN, JEREMY.   Roald Dahl: a biography. (Bibl. 1994, 12280.) Rev. by Stephen King in BkW, 10 Apr. 1994, 1, 14; by David Galef in LU (20:2) 1996, 272–4.

Janet Dailey

17184.   MASSIE, SONJA; GREENBERG, MARTIN H.   The Janet Dailey companion: a comprehensive guide to her life and novels. New York: HarperCollins, 1996. pp. xiii, 338.

Maureen Daly

17185.   CARROLL, VIRGINIA SCHAEFER.   Re-reading the romance of *Seventeenth Summer*. CLAQ (21:1) 1996, 12–19.

Robert Dana

17186.   BRUNNER, EDWARD.   From deep space: the poetry of Robert Dana. IowaR (22:3) 1992, 115–34.

Tsitsi Dangarembga

17187.   AEGERTER, LINDSAY PENTOLFE.   A dialectic of autonomy and community: Tsitsi Dangarembga's *Nervous Conditions*. TSWL (15:2) 1996, 231–40.

Sarah Daniels

17188.   HAEDICKE, SUSAN C.   Doing the dirty work: gendered versions of working-class women in Sarah Daniels' *The Gut Girls* and Israel Horovitz's *North Shore Fish*. JDTC (8:2) 1994, 77–88.

Shouri Daniels

17189.   EZEKIEL, NISSIM.   An image of India in Shouri Daniels' *A City of Children*. In (pp. 135–40) **45**.

Margaret Danner

17190.   TAFT, CLAIRE.   'Her blood sings': Margaret Danner's *Impressions of African Art Forms*. LHR (12:2) 1993, 45–9.

Edwidge Danticat

17191.   SHEA, RENEE H.   The dangerous job of Edwidge Danticat: an interview. Callaloo (19:2) 1996, 382–9.

Olive Tilford Dargan ('Fielding Burke')

17192.   ELFENBEIN, ANNA SHANNON.   A forgotten revolutionary voice: 'woman's place' and race in Olive Dargan's *Call Home the Heart*. In (pp. 193–208) **32**.

'Kamala Das' (Kamala Madhawadas)

17193.   USHA, V. T.   The private as the public: some theoretical issues in women's autobiography. WLR (1:1) 1996, 26–35.

Guy Davenport

17194.   CRANE, JOAN; NOBLE, RICHARD.   Guy Davenport: a descriptive bibliography, 1947–1995. Introd. by Hugh Kenner. Haverford, PA: Green Shade, 1996. pp. xix, 247, (plates) 12. (Limited ed. of 550 copies.)

Avram Davidson

17195. WESSELLS, HENRY.   A preliminary annotated checklist of the writings of Avram Davidson: parts I and II. BB (53:1) 1996, 23–37; (53:2) 1996, 139–51.

Donald Davidson

17196. WOOLSEY, STEPHEN A.   'The whispering in the marrow': Donald Davidson, Tennessee, and the life of words. TPB (33) 1996, 7–23.

Idris Davies

17197. JENKINS, ISLWYN.   Idris Davies of Rhymney, a personal memoir. (Bibl. 1987, 10400.) Rev. by Jeremy Hooker in PN Review (17:5) 1991, 59–60.

Robertson Davies

17198. GOLDSTEIN, LAURENCE.   Film as family history. *See* **13725**.
17199. MONK, PATRICIA.   Mud and magic shows: Robertson Davies' *Fifth Business*. (Bibl. 1992, 13333.) Rev. by Maureen F. Moran in BJCS (11:1) 1996, 148–9.
17200. PETERMAN, MICHAEL.   In pursuit of 'aristocracy of the spirit': Willa Cather and Robertson Davies. *See* **16819**.
17201. PETTIGREW, TODD.   Dunstan Ramsay's experiment in autobiography in Robertson Davies' *Fifth Business*. NCL (26:4) 1996, 2–3.

Dan Davin

17202. OVENDEN, KEITH.   A fighting withdrawal: the life of Dan Davin, writer, soldier, publisher. *See* **991**.

Frank Marshall Davis

17203. DANIELS, DOUGLAS HENRY.   A response to John Gennari. LHR (14:1/2) 1996, 34–5.
17204. GENNARI, JOHN.   'A weapon of integration': Frank Marshall Davis and the politics of jazz. LHR (14:1/2) 1996, 16–33.
17205. LESTER, CHERYL.   A response to Lawrence Rodgers. LHR (14:1/2) 1996, 13–15.
17206. —— TIDWELL, JOHN EDGAR.   Frank Marshall Davis and the Chicago Black renaissance: an introduction. LHR (14:1/2) 1996, 1–3.
17207. RODGERS, LAWRENCE R.   Richard Wright, Frank Marshall Davis and the Chicago renaissance. LHR (14:1/2) 1996, 4–12.
17208. TIDWELL, JOHN EDGAR.   'I was a weaver of jagged words': social function in the poetry of Frank Marshall Davis. LHR (14:1/2) 1996, 65–78.

H. L. Davis

17209. GROVER, DORYS CROW.   Four Midwestern novelists' response to French inquiries on populism. *See* **15992**.
17210. REKOLO, ALEC.   'Practice Standing in Death': marking time and place in *Honey in the Horn*. SDR (34:1) 1996, 63–77.

Jack Davis

17211. HODGE, BOB.   Jack Davis and the emergence of Aboriginal writing. CritS (6:1) 1994, 98–104.

Peter Davison

17212. DEEDY, JOHN. A maker of poems – and of poets: John Deedy interviews Peter Davison. Critic (50:1) 1995, 2–12.

Fielding Dawson

17213. BATHANTI, JOSEPH. Spatial and energetic: a conversation with Fielding Dawson. NCLR (2:2) 1995, 113–22.

Jean D'Costa

17214. JONES, BRIDGET. Duppies and other revenants, with particular reference to the use of the supernatural in Jean D'Costa's work. *In* (pp. 23–32) **102**.

Seamus Deane

17215. CAREY, PHYLLIS; MALLOY, CATHARINE. Making connections: an interview with Seamus Deane. Critic (48:3) 1994, 29–37.

E. M. Delafield

17216. MATHER, RACHEL R. The heirs of Jane Austen: twentieth-century writers of the comedy of manners. *See* **10304**.

Walter de la Mare

17217. SHERBO, ARTHUR. Walter de la Mare and the bibliographers. NQ (43:1) 1996, 53–4.

Shelagh Delaney

17218. BOLES, WILLIAM C. 'Have I ever laid claims to being a proper mother?': the stigma of maternity in Shelagh Delaney's *A Taste of Honey*. TexPres (17) 1996, 1–5.

Samuel R. Delany

17219. REID-PHARR, ROBERT F. Disseminating heterotopia. AAR (28:3) 1994, 347–57.
17220. SALLIS, JAMES (ed.). Ash of stars: on the writing of Samuel R. Delany. Jackson; London: Mississippi UP, 1996. pp. xviii, 224.

Don DeLillo

17221. AIRAUDI, JESSE T. 'A rock of defence for human nature': philosophical and literary approaches to the causes of violence. *See* **16375**.
17222. BONCA, CORNEL. Don DeLillo's *White Noise*: the natural language of the species. ColLit (23:2) 1996, 25–44.
17223. BROOKS, CARLO. Désespoir et possibilité: le problème de l'appartenance au monde dans *Moon Palace* et *Libra*. *See* **16137**.
17224. BRUMM, URSULA. Consensus and conspiracy in American literature. *See* **8082**.
17225. CIVELLO, PAUL. American literary Naturalism and its twentieth-century transformations: Frank Norris, Ernest Hemingway, Don DeLillo. (Bibl. 1995, 15590.) Rev. by Peter Messent in AmS (36:2) 1996, 205–6; by Mohammed Zayani in ALR (29:1) 1996, 92–4.
17226. COWART, DAVID. For whom Bell tolls: Don DeLillo's *Americana*. ConLit (37:4) 1996, 602–19.
17227. DUVALL, JOHN N. The (super)marketplace of images:

television as unmediated mediation in DeLillo's *White Noise*. AQ (50:3) 1994, 127–53.

17228. ELLIOTT, EMORY. Unnatural disasters: warnings unheeded in DeLillo's *White Noise*. Letterature d'America (39) 1990, 5–36.

17229. GERVAIS, BERTRAND. Les murmures de la machine: lire à travers le *Bruit de fond* de Don DeLillo. Études littéraires (28:2) 1995, 21–34.

17230. HANTKE, STEFFEN. 'God save us from the bourgeois adventure': the figure of the terrorist in contemporary American conspiracy fiction. *See* **14537**.

17231. JOHNSTON, JOHN. Superlinear fiction or historical diagram? Don DeLillo's *Libra*. MFS (40:2) 1994, 319–42.

17232. KEESEY, DOUGLAS. The ideology of detection in Pynchon and DeLillo. Pynchon Notes (32/33) 1993, 44–59.

17233. KITTS, THOMAS M. The individual *vs* the cult leader: Don DeLillo's *Mao II*, a novel for the 1990s. PCR (7:2) 1996, 111–27.

17234. KRONICK, JOSEPH. *Libra* and the assassination of JFK: a textbook operation. AQ (50:1) 1994, 109–32.

17235. MALTBY, PAUL. The Romantic metaphysics of Don DeLillo. ConLit (37:2) 1996, 258–77.

17236. MORRIS, DAVID B. Environment: the white noise of health. LitMed (15:1) 1996, 1–15.

17237. NADOTTI, MARIA. An interview with Don DeLillo. Salmagundi (100) 1993, 86–97.

17238. OSTEEN, MARK. Children of Godard and Coca-Cola: cinema and consumerism in Don DeLillo's early fiction. ConLit (37:3) 1996, 439–70.

17239. PEYSER, THOMAS. Globalization in America: the case of Don DeLillo's *White Noise*. CLIO (25:3) 1996, 255–72.

17240. SCANLAN, MARGARET. Writers among terrorists: Don DeLillo's *Mao II* and the Rushdie affair. MFS (40:2) 1994, 229–52.

Floyd Dell

17241. CLAYTON, DOUGLAS. Floyd Dell: the life and times of an American rebel. (Bibl. 1995, 15604.) Rev. by David Duke in AHR (101:1) 1996, 251–2; by Andrew Rosenheim in TLS, 30 Aug. 1996, 29; by Dan Jaffe in AmS (37:1) 1996, 194.

17242. HOLTZ, WILLIAM. Willa Cather and Floyd Dell. *See* **16783**.

John Del Vecchio

17243. UCHMANOWICZ, PAULINE. Vanishing Vietnam: Whiteness and the technology of memory. LitPs (41:4) 1995, 30–50.

Thomas C. Dent

17244. SALAAM, KALAMU YA. Enriching the paper trail: an interview with Tom Dent. AAR (27:2) 1993, 327–44.

August William Derleth

17245. ENG, STEVE. August Derleth: champion of fantasy poetry. Romantist (9/10) 1985/86, 47–50.

Anita Desai

17246. AFZAL-KHAN, FAWZIA. Cultural imperialism and the

Indo-English novel: genre and ideology in R. K. Narayan, Anita Desai, Kamala Markandaya, and Salman Rushdie. (Bibl. 1993, 12282.) Rev. by Susan Spearey in YES (26) 1996, 320–1.

17247. BANDE, USHA. 'Only connect' and the failure to connect: a comparative study of Anita Desai's Sita and Nella Larsen's Helga. NCL (25:2) 1995, 5–7.

17248. BRUSH, PIPPA. German, Jew, foreigner: the immigrant experience in Anita Desai's *Baumgartner's Bombay*. CritS (8:3) 1996, 277–85.

17249. GALLE, ETIENNE. '*The inky lawn*', un symbolisme dionysiaque dans une nouvelle d'Anita Desai. JSSE (24) 1995, 60–72.

17250. KARAMCHETI, INDIRA. The geographics of marginality: place and textuality in Simone Schwarz-Bart and Anita Desai. *In* (pp. 125–46) **97**.

17251. KIRPAL, VINEY. The perfect bubble: a study of Anita Desai's *In Custody*. *In* (pp. 123–34) **45**.

17252. NABAR, VRINDA. The four-dimensional reality: Anita Desai's *Clear Light of Day*. *In* (pp. 102–12) **45**.

17253. RAY, SANGEETA. Gender and the discourse of nationalism in Anita Desai's *Clear Light of Day*. *In* (pp. 96–119) **30**.

17254. SHAHANE, VASANT A. Fictional montage in Anita Desai's *Fire on the Mountain*. *In* (pp. 92–101) **45**.

17255. SWAIN, S. P. The incarcerated self and the derelict house: house imagery in Anita Desai's novels. IndL (39:5) 1996, 120–3.

17256. WANDREKAR, KALPANA. The ailing aliens: Anita Desai's *Bye Bye Blackbird* as a symptomatic study in schizophrenia. *In* (pp. 36–50) **45**.

Boman Desai

17257. BHARUCHA, NILUFER E. From behind a fine veil: a feminist reading of three Parsi novels. IndL (39:5) 1996, 132–41.

Shashi Deshpande

17258. DESHPANDE, SHASHI. Of concerns, of anxieties. IndL (39:5) 1996, 103–10.

17259. NAYAK K., KISHORI. 'The diaries of a sane housewife': Shashi Deshpande's *That Long Silence*. IndL (39:5) 1996, 111–19.

Eunice De Souza (1940–)

17260. BRADY, VERONICA. 'One long cry in the dark'? The poetry of Eunice De Souza. LitTheol (5:1) 1991, 101–23.

Peter De Vries

17261. WOOD, RALPH C. The comedy of redemption: Christian faith in four American novelists. (Bibl. 1989, 9380.) Rev. by Stephen R. Haynes in LitTheol (5:1) 1991, 126–8.

Farrukh Dhondy

17262. HAND, FELICITY. Challenging the centre: the response of British Asian writers. *See* **17181**.

Philip K. Dick ('Richard Phillips') (1928–1982)

17263. BUTLER, ANDREW M. Water, entropy and the million-year dream: Philip K. Dick's *Martian Time-Slip*. Foundation (68) 1996, 57–64.

17264. DICK, ANNE R.   The search for Philip K. Dick, 1928–1982: a memoir and biography of the science fiction writer. (Bibl. 1995, 15616.) Rev. by Michael J. Tolley in Utopian Studies (7:2) 1996, 247–8.

17265. HEER, JEET.   Philip K. Dick: from pulp gutter to literary respectability. LRC (5:8) 1996, 27.

17266. ROMERO , ROLANDO J.   The postmodern hybrid: do aliens dream of alien sheep? *See* **14143**.

17267. ROSSI, UMBERTO.   Just a bunch of words: the image of the secluded family and the problem of *logos* in P. K. Dick's *Time out of Joint*. Extrapolation (37:3) 1996, 195–211.

17268. —— P. K. Dick e la questione della tecnica (o della tecnologia). *In* (pp. 473–83) **117**.

17269. SENIOR, W. A.   *Blade Runner* and cyberpunk visions of humanity. *See* **14197**.

17270. UMLAND, SAMUEL J. (ed.).   Philip K. Dick: contemporary critical interpretations. (Bibl. 1995, 15622.) Rev. by Noel Dorman Mawer in Utopian Studies (7:1) 1996, 149–51; by Toby Widdicombe in Extrapolation (37:2) 1996, 185–7.

17271. ZHU, JIANJIONG.   Reality, fiction, and 'Wu' in *The Man in the High Castle*. JFA (5:3) 1992, 36–45.

R. A. Dick (1898–)

17272. STETZ, MARGARET D.   *The Ghost and Mrs Muir*: laughing with the captain in the house. *See* **14250**.

James Dickey

17273. GRAPES, JACK.   James Dickey: interview. Onthebus (6:1) 1993/94, 218–25.

17274. KIRSCHTEN, ROBERT.   James Dickey's *Approaching Prayer*: ritual and the shape of myth. SAtlR (61:1) 1996, 27–54.

17275. LIEBERMAN, LAURENCE.   The long cry: James Dickey's *Mercy*. TexR (15:3/4) 1994, 65–74.

17276. RICH, SUSANNA.   Dickey's *The Firebombing*. Exp (54:2) 1996, 110–13.

17277. SCHWARZ, DANIEL R.   Reconfiguring *Deliverance*: James Dickey, the modern tradition and the resistant reader. WebS (13:2) 1996, 5–19.

17278. SUAREZ, ERNEST.   Emerson on Vietnam: Dickey, Bly and the New Left. *See* **11200**.

Joan Didion

17279. ATWILL, WILLIAM D.   Through plexiglas darkly: loss of agency in Joan Didion's *Salvador*. Reader (29) 1993, 1–7.

17280. BLANKLEY, ELYSE.   Clear-cutting the Western myth: beyond Joan Didion. *In* (pp. 177–97) **108**.

17281. ELLERBY, JANET.   A psychology of terror. Reader (29) 1993, 8–13.

17282. FREGA, DONNALEE.   The struggle for verbal consciousness. Reader (29) 1993, 14–20.

17283. HISE, PAT.   The pursuit of nothingness in *Play It as It Lays*. CCTE (61) 1996, 75–84.

17284. NOLAND, DANIEL W.   Textual analysis, agency and Joan Didion's *Salvador*. Reader (29) 1993, 21–6.

17285. Schweninger, Lee.　Toward an ecofeminism. Reader (29) 1993, 27–33.

17286. Waxman, Barbara.　The Catholic Church in a world of masculine violence: a postmodern feminist response. Reader (29) 1993, 32–7.

Fatima Dike

17287. Blumberg, Marcia.　Re-evaluating otherness, building for difference: South African theatre beyond the interregnum. *See* **13460**.

Modikwe Dikobe

17288. Plakidas, George.　*The Marabi Dance*: a topology of incommensurate exchange. In-between (1:2) 1992, 141–50.

Annie Dillard

17289. Anhorn, Judy Schaaf.　Natural fact and spiritual fact in the writings of Annie Dillard. Letterature d'America (39) 1990, 37–56.

17290. Brown-Davidson, Terri.　'Choosing the given with a fierce and pointed will': Annie Dillard and risk-taking in contemporary literature. HC (30:2) 1993, 1–9.

17291. McClintock, James I.　'Pray without ceasing': Annie Dillard among the nature writers. *In* (pp. 69–86) **25**.

17292. McIlroy, Gary.　*Pilgrim at Tinker Creek* and the legacy of *Walden*. *In* (pp. 87–101) **25**.

17293. Wymard, Ellie.　Annie Dillard, living. Critic (46:2) 1991, 23–5.

'Isak Dinesen' (Karen Blixen)

17294. Mergenthal, Silvia.　Miranda and Caliban: White mistresses and Black servants in Blixen's *Out of Africa*, Lessing's *The Grass Is Singing*, and Gordimer's *July's People*. ZAA (44:3) 1996, 232–9.

17295. Rashkin, Esther.　A recipe for mourning: Isak Dinesen's *Babette's Feast*. Style (29:3) 1995, 356–74.

17296. Schleifer, Ronald.　Writhing nets and goodly pearls: *The Postmodern Bible*, temporal collaboration, and storytelling. *See* **14712**.

17297. Stambaugh, Sarah.　The witch and the goddess in the stories of Isak Dinesen: a feminist reading. (Bibl. 1994, 12329.) Rev. by J. T. Mains in CanRCL (19:3) 1992, 455–8.

Mbella Sonne Dipoko (1936–)

17298. Desroches, Dennis.　'Sweeping the arena': sites of struggle in Dipoko's *Because of Women*. In-between (3:2) 1994, 111–21.

Diane Di Prima

17299. Friedman, Amy L.　'I say my new name': women writers of the Beat Generation. *In* (pp. 200–16) **4**.

Maud Diver

17300. Sainsbury, Alison.　Married to the Empire: the Anglo-Indian domestic novel. *In* (pp. 163–87) **132**.

Thomas Dixon, Jr

17301. BLOOMFIELD, MAXWELL.   Constitutional ideology and progressive fiction. *See* **10609**.

E. L. Doctorow

17302. BRIENZA, SUSAN.   Writing as witnessing: the many voices of E. L. Doctorow. *In* (pp. 168–95) **123**.

17303. DOCTOROW, E. L.   Spring of the imagination. BkW, 17 Apr. 1994, 1, 6.

17304. HARDING, BRIAN.   Comparative metafictions of history: E. L. Doctorow and John Fowles. *In* (pp. 253–72) **34**.

17305. ISAACS, NEIL D.   *Bathgate* in the time of Coppola: a reverie. *See* **13825**.

17306. MARRANCA, RICHARD.   'Finding a historical line': an interview with E. L. Doctorow. LitR (39:3) 1996, 407–14.

17307. MORRIS, CHRISTOPHER D.   Models of misrepresentation: on the fiction of E. L. Doctorow. (Bibl. 1992, 13394.) Rev. by Michael Robertson in AmS (34:1) 1993, 167–8.

17308. PARKS, JOHN G.   E. L. Doctorow. (Bibl. 1991, 12602.) Rev. by Michael Robertson in AmS (34:1) 1993, 167–8.

17309. PERSELL, MICHELLE.   'the jews,' *Ragtime* and the politics of silence. LitPs (42:4) 1996, 1–15.

17310. SPENCER, LUKE.   A poetics of engagement in E. L. Doctorow's *Ragtime*. *See* **2711**.

17311. WUTZ, MICHAEL.   An interview with E. L. Doctorow. WebS (11:1) 1994, 6–15.

Owen Dodson

17312. HATCH, JAMES V.   Sorrow is the only faithful one: the life of Owen Dodson. Foreword by Arnold Rampersad. (Bibl. 1995, 15660.) Rev. by Barbara Lewis in AAR (29:4) 1995, 687–90.

Stephen R. Donaldson ('Reed Stephens')

17313. FIKE, MATTHEW A.   Nature as supernature: Donaldson's revision of Spenser. *See* **6030**.

17314. HENDRIX, LAUREL L.   'A world of glas': the heroine's quest for identity in Spenser's *Faerie Queene* and Stephen R. Donaldson's *Mirror of Her*. *In* (pp. 91–100) **36**.

17315. SENIOR, W. A.   Stephen R. Donaldson's *Chronicles of Thomas Covenant*: variations on the fantasy tradition. (Bibl. 1995, 15662.) Rev. by Brian W. Aldiss in Extrapolation (37:3) 1996, 274–7.

17316. SENIOR, WILLIAM.   Donaldson and Tolkien. Mythlore (18:4) 1992, 37–43.

John Donovan

17317. LIDBERG, ELIZABETH.   Donovan's legacy for young adults. ArizEB (36:1) 1993, 43–5.

Hilda Doolittle ('H.D.')

17318. ACHESON, SUSAN.   H.D. and the age of Aquarius: liturgy, astrology and gnosis in *Trilogy*. Sagetrieb (15:1/2) 1996, 133–50.

17319. ARENS, KATHERINE.   H.D.'s post-Freudian cultural analysis: Nike *versus* Oedipus. AI (52:4) 1995, 359–404.

17320. Augustine, Jane. Bisexuality in Hélène Cixous, Virginia Woolf, and H.D.: an aspect of *l'écriture féminine. In* (pp. 11–18) **109**.

17321. —— Preliminary comments on the meaning of H.D.'s *The Sword Went out to Sea*. Sagetrieb (15:1/2) 1996, 121–32.

17322. Baccolini, Raffaella. 'There was a Helen before there was a war': memory and desire in H.D.'s *Winter Love* and Pound's *Pisan Cantos*. Sagetrieb (15:1/2) 1996, 229–45.

17323. Berni, Christine. The recuperated maternal and the imposture of mastery in H.D.'s *HERmione*. WS (25:1) 1995, 51–71.

17324. Bloom, Harold (ed.). H.D. New York: Chelsea House, 1989. pp. vii, 180. (Modern critical views.) Rev. by Wolfram Donat in ZAA (41:1) 1993, 66–73.

17325. Brown, Dennis. H.D.'s *Trilogy*: modern Gnosticism? LitTheol (10:4) 1996, 351–66.

17326. Bugeja, Michael. The female masters: a look at three underrated women poets offers fresh lessons in craft. *See* **8417**.

17327. Burnett, Gary. H.D. between image and epic: the mysteries of her poetics. (Bibl. 1995, 15666.) Rev. by Wolfram Donat in ZAA (41:1) 1993, 66–73.

17328. Camboni, Marina. Il tempo in una stanza: *Bid Me to Live* di H.D. RSAJ (1) 1990, 81–98.

17329. —— (ed.). H(ilda) D(oolittle) e il suo mondo: atti della giornata di studio su H.D., Palermo, 18 ottobre 1990. Palermo: Univ. di Palermo, Facoltà di Lettere e Filosofia, 1995. pp. 123. (Studi e ricerche, 22.)

17330. —— (ed. and trans.). *Trilogia*: testo inglese a fronte. Caltanissetta: Sciascia, 1993. pp. 325. (Esperidi: collana di testi e di critica, 4.) Rev. by Roger Asselineau in EA (48:3) 1995, 369.

17331. Chisholm, Dianne. Pornopoeia, the Modernist canon, and the cultural capital of sexual literacy: the case of H.D. *In* (pp. 69–94) **39**.

17332. Crisp, Peter. Imagism's metaphors – a test case. *See* **2343**.

17333. Crown, Kathleen. 'Let us endure': atomic-age anxiety in H.D.'s *Sagesse*. Sagetrieb (15:1/2) 1996, 247–72.

17334. De Ville, Peter. Hilda Doolittle, *Eurydice* and the lost bride in D. H. Lawrence's *Bavarian Gentians*. QLLSM (5) 1992, 227–39.

17335. Donat, Wolfram. *Vindication of the scribe*: neuere H.D.-Forschung. ZAA (41:1) 1993, 66–73 (review-article).

17336. Edmunds, Susan. Out of line: history, psychoanalysis, and montage in H.D.'s long poems. (Bibl. 1994, 12341.) Rev. by Hilary Holladay in AL (68:1) 1996, 253–4.

17337. Friedman, Susan Stanford. Penelope's web: gender, modernity, H.D.'s fiction. (Bibl. 1995, 15669.) Rev. by Wolfram Donat in ZAA (41:1) 1993, 66–73.

17338. —— DuPlessis, Rachel Blau (eds). Signets: reading H.D. (Bibl. 1992, 13411.) Rev. by Wolfram Donat in ZAA (41:1) 1993, 66–73.

17339. Gavaler, Christopher P. 'I mend a break in time': an historical reconstruction of H.D.'s Wunden Eiland ceremony in *The Gift* and *Trilogy*. Sagetrieb (15:1/2) 1996, 95–120.

17340. Gregory, Eileen. H.D.'s gods: anthropology and Romantic mythography. Sagetrieb (15:1/2) 1996, 23–34.

17341. Guest, Barbara. H.D. and the conflict of Imagism. Sagetrieb (15:1/2) 1996, 13–22.

17342. HARDIN, MICHAEL. H.D.'s *Trilogy*: speaking through the margins. Sagetrieb (15:1/2) 1996, 151–60.

17343. HARRISON, VICTORIA. When a gift is poison: H.D., the Moravian, the Jew, and World War II. Sagetrieb (15:1/2) 1996, 69–93.

17344. JONES, BEN (ed.). The mystic leeway. By Frances Gregg. With an account of Frances Gregg by Oliver Marlow Wilkinson. Ottawa: Carleton UP, 1994. pp. ix, 194. (Carleton UP women's experience, 6.) Rev. by Margaret McCullough in PowJ (5) 1995, 216–19.

17345. KNUTSON, LIN. Arrested moments: *communitas* and liminality in H.D.'s *Her*. Sagetrieb (15:1/2) 1996, 35–50.

17346. LAITY, CASSANDRA. H.D., Modernism, and the transgressive sexualities of Decadent–Romantic Platonism. *In* (pp. 45–68) **39**.

17347. —— H.D. and the Victorian *fin de siècle*: gender, Modernism, Decadence. Cambridge; New York: CUP, 1996. pp. xix, 215. (Cambridge studies in American literature and culture, 104.) Rev. by Burton Hatlen in Sagetrieb (15:1/2) 1996, 273–8.

17348. LANGETEIG, KENDRA. Visions in the crystal ball: Ezra Pound, H.D., and the form of the mystical. Paideuma (25:1/2) 1996, 55–81.

17349. LUCAS, ROSE. 'Something left over': memory and desire in H.D.'s *Winter Love* and *End to Torment*. LitPs (39:4) 1993, 28–64.

17350. SWORD, HELEN. H.D.'s *Majic Ring*. TSWL (14:2) 1995, 347–62.

17351. TARLO, HARRIET. 'Ah, could they know': the place of the erotic in H.D.'s *Hymen*. Gramma (4) 1996, 89–105.

17352. —— The underworld of H.D.'s *Helen in Egypt*. Sagetrieb (15:1/2) 1996, 173–202.

17353. TWITCHELL-WAAS, JEFFREY. 'Set in eternity but lived in': H.D.'s *Vale Ave*. Sagetrieb (15:1/2) 1996, 203–27.

17354. WALKINGTON, J. W. Mystical experience in H.D. and Walt Whitman: an intertextual reading of *Tribute to the Angels* and *Song of Myself*. See **12765**.

17355. WASSERMAN, ROSANNE. H.D.'s *Helen in Egypt*: comment on the lyric. Sagetrieb (15:1/2) 1996, 161–72.

17356. WHITAKER, THOMAS R. H.D.'s *Trilogy* and the poetics of passage. *In* (pp. 269–80) **16**.

17357. WITTE, SARAH E. The archaeological context of H.D.'s *Secret Name* and *Hesperia*. Sagetrieb (15:1/2) 1996, 51–68.

17358. YAEGER, PATRICIA. The 'language of blood': toward a maternal sublime. Genre (25:1) 1992, 5–24.

17359. YOUNG, SUZANNE. Between science and the 'new psychology': an examination of H.D.'s sociohistorical consciousness. TSWL (14:2) 1995, 325–45.

Edward Dorn

17360. FREDMAN, STEPHEN; JENKINS, GRANT. First annotations to Edward Dorn's *Gunslinger*. Sagetrieb (15:3) 1996, 57–176.

17361. HATLEN, BURTON. Toward a common ground: versions of place in the poetry of Charles Olson, Edward Dorn, and Theodore Enslin. Sagetrieb (15:3) 1996, 243–61.

17362. JENKINS, GRANT. *Gunslinger*'s ethics of excess: subjectivity, community, and the politics of the could be. Sagetrieb (15:3) 1996, 207–42.

17363. Michelson, Peter. Edward Dorn, inside the outskirts. Sagetrieb (15:3) 1996, 177–206.

Michael Dorris

17364. Cowart, David. 'The rhythm of three strands': cultural braiding in Dorris's *A Yellow Raft in Blue Water*. SAIL (8:1) 1996, 1–12.
17365. Schumacher, Michael. Louise Erdrich and Michael Dorris: a marriage of minds. WD (71:6) 1991, 28–31, 59.

John Dos Passos

17366. Aaron, Daniel. *USA*. AH (47:4) 1996, 63–72.
17367. Bleu-Schwenninger, Patricia. John Dos Passos, miroir du siècle. Europe (803) 1996, 65–72.
17368. Brevda, William. How do I get to Broadway? Reading Dos Passos's *Manhattan Transfer* sign. TSLL (38:1) 1996, 79–114.
17369. Dow, William. John Dos Passos, Blaise Cendrars, and a 'squirrel cage of the meridians'. NCL (25:2) 1995, 4–5.
17370. —— John Dos Passos, Blaise Cendrars, and the 'other' Modernism. TCL (42:3) 1996, 396–415.
17371. Enniss, Stephen C. Writing war: John Dos Passos' *One Man's Initiation*. WLA (8:1) 1996, 83–96.
17372. Fink, Guido. 'Inesprimere l'esprimibile': tre romanzi americani del 1925. RSAJ (2) 1991, 37–52. (*An American Tragedy, The Great Gatsby, Manhattan Transfer*.)
17373. Ickstadt, Heinz. Reconstruire la langue: John Dos Passos entre réalisme et avant-garde. Europe (803) 1996, 99–112.
17374. Isernhagen, Hartwig. Mort-vivant entre la machine et le fox-trot: classe et culture dans *L'Eboueur* de John Dos Passos. Europe (803) 1996, 112–21.
17375. Knönagel, Axel. The interchapters in John Dos Passos's *Number One*. JML (19:2) 1995, 317–22.
17376. Landsberg, Melvin (ed.). John Dos Passos' correspondence with Arthur K. McComb; or, 'Learn to sing the carmagnole'. (Bibl. 1993, 12343.) Rev. by Neale Reinitz in AmS (35:1) 1994, 166–7.
17377. Ludington, Townsend. La réaction de John Dos Passos à l'Europe: *Manhattan Transfer* et *USA*. Trans. by Nelly Stéphane. Europe (803) 1996, 87–98.
17378. McHale, Brian. Child as ready-made: baby-talk and the language of Dos Passos's children in *USA*. *In* (pp. 202–24) **48**.
17379. Maine, Barry. Steinbeck's debt to Dos Passos. SteiQ (23:1/2) 1990, 17–26.
17380. Pavese, Cesare. Expérience et tradition. Trans. by Jean-Baptiste Para. Europe (803) 1996, 72–87.
17381. Trombold, John. Popular songs as revolutionary culture in John Dos Passos' *USA* and other early works. JML (19:2) 1995, 289–316.

Lord Alfred Douglas

17382. Giaufret, Anna. Il testo e il suo doppio: la *Salomé* di Oscar Wilde e la *Salome* di Alfred Douglas. Un'analisi comparata linguistico-stilistica. *See* **2628**.

'Ellen Douglas' (Josephine Haxton)

17383. Grigsby, John L. The Agrarians and Ellen Douglas's

The Rock Cried Out and *Can't Quit You, Baby*: extending the tradition while expanding the canon. *See* **15463**.

O. Douglas

17384. FORRESTER, WENDY.   Anna Buchan and O. Douglas. London: Maitland Press, 1995. pp. 125.

Rita Dove

17385. BOOTH, ALISON.   Abduction and other severe pleasures: Rita Dove's *Mother Love*. Callaloo (19:1) 1996, 125–30.

17386. COLAKIS, MARIANTHE.   What Jocasta knew: alternative versions of the Oedipus myth. CML (16:3) 1996, 217–29.

17387. CUSHMAN, STEPHEN.   And the Dove returned. Callaloo (19:1) 1996, 131–4.

17388. DOVE, RITA.   Who's afraid of poetry. WD (75:2) 1995, 40–3.

17389. JONES, KIRKLAND C.   Folk idiom in the literary expression of two African-American authors: Rita Dove and Yusef Komunyakaa. *In* (pp. 149–65) **55**.

17390. LOFGREN, LOTTA.   Partial horror: fragmentation and healing in Rita Dove's *Mother Love*. Callaloo (19:1) 1996, 135–42.

17391. STEFFEN, THERESE.   Movements of a marriage; or, Looking awry at US history: Rita Dove's *Thomas and Beulah*. SPELL (9) 1996, 179–96.

Coleman Dowell

17392. D'AMICO, MARIA VITTORIA (introd.).   *Willow Sheridan Rode Voltaire* by Coleman Dowell. RSAJ (5) 1994, 121–34.

Margaret Drabble

17393. KNUTSEN, KAREN PATRICK.   Leaving Dr Leavis: a farewell to the Great Tradition? Margaret Drabble's *The Gates of Ivory*. *See* **15568**.

17394. MAYA, D.   Landscape as extension of the self in Margaret Drabble's *The Realms of Gold*. WLR (1:1) 1996, 17–25.

17395. RESTUCCIA, FRANCES.   Tales of beauty: aestheticizing female melancholia. *See* **16098**.

17396. RESTUCCIA, FRANCES L.   Literary representations of battered women: spectacular domestic punishment. *In* (pp. 42–71) **9**.

17397. SKOLLER, ELEANOR HONIG.   The in-between of writing: experience and experiment in Drabble, Duras, and Arendt. (Bibl. 1995, 15717.) Rev. by Pamela L. Caughie in MFS (40:2) 1994, 435–41.

Robert Drake (1930–)

17398. DRAKE, ROBERT.   The writer as hunger artist. ModAge (34:3) 1992, 235–9.

Theodore Dreiser

17399. ALGEO, ANN M.   The courtroom as forum: homicide trials by Dreiser, Wright, Capote, and Mailer. *See* **16689**.

17400. COHEN, PHILIP.   Is there a text in this discipline? Textual scholarship and American literary studies. *See* **604**.

17401. DOWELL, RICHARD W.   'There was something mystic about it': the composition of *Sister Carrie* by Dreiser *et al*. *In* (pp. 131–59) **7**.

17402. FINK, GUIDO. 'Inesprimere l'esprimibile': tre romanzi americani del 1925. *See* **17372**.

17403. FREDERICKSON, KATHY. Dreiser's *The Girl in the Coffin*; or, What's death got to do with it? DreiS (27:1) 1996, 3–19.

17404. GAMMEL, IRENE. Sexualizing power in Naturalism: Theodore Dreiser and Frederick Philip Grove. (Bibl. 1995, 15749.) Rev. by Judy Dudar in CanL (151) 1996, 134–5.

17405. GOGOL, MIRIAM (ed.). Theodore Dreiser: beyond Naturalism. (Bibl. 1995, 15756.) Rev. by James R. Giles in Style (30:3) 1996, 523–4; by Richard Lingeman in DreiS (27:1) 1996, 43–50.

17406. HAYNE, BARRIE. Dreiser's *American Tragedy*. *In* (pp. 170–86) **105**.

17407. JACOBS, LEA. *An American Tragedy*: a comparison of film and literary censorship. *See* **13831**.

17408. MURAYAMA, KIYOHIKO. 'Two mothers were weeping and praying': a formula recycled in Theodore Dreiser's fiction. CLAJ (39:3) 1996, 380–93.

17409. OLDANI, LOUIS J. Dreiser's *Genius* in the making: composition and revision. *See* **775**.

17410. PIZER, DONALD (ed.). New essays on *Sister Carrie*. (Bibl. 1995, 15801.) Rev. by Kurt Müller in Amst (41:4) 1996, 709.

17411. RHODES, CHIP. Twenties fiction, mass culture, and the modern subject. AL (68:2) 1996, 385–404.

17412. RIGGIO, THOMAS P. Following Dreiser, seventy years later. ASch (65:4) 1996, 569–77.

17413. ROZGA, MARGARET. Sister in a quest – *Sister Carrie* and *A Thousand Acres*: the search for identity in gendered territory. MidM (22) 1994, 18–29.

17414. SCHURMAN, LYDIA CUSHMAN. Theodore Dreiser and his Street and Smith circle. DNR (65:6) 1996, 183–95.

17415. WEST, JAMES L. W., III (ed.). Dreiser's *Jennie Gerhardt*: new essays on the restored text. *See* **873**.

17416. —— Jennie Gerhardt. (Bibl. 1995, 15830.) Rev. by G. Thomas Tanselle in Text (Ann Arbor) (8) 1995, 462–9; by Philip Cohen in AmLH (8:4) 1996, 732–7; by Kurt Müller in Amst (41:2) 1996, 311–17.

17417. WOLFF, ANDREA. Dreiser constructs Russia. DreiS (27:1) 1996, 20–35.

17418. ZANINE, LOUIS J. Mechanism and mysticism: the influence of science on the thought and work of Theodore Dreiser. (Bibl. 1995, 15834.) Rev. by Brian Lloyd in AmS (36:1) 1993, 194–5.

Diane Duane

17419. KONDRATIEV, ALEXEI. Tales newly told. Mythlore (20:4) 1995, 36–7.

W. E. B. Du Bois

17420. CHANDLER, NAHUM DIMITRI. The economy of desedimentation: W. E. B. Du Bois and the discourses of the Negro. Callaloo (19:1) 1996, 78–93.

17421. LEWIS, DAVID LEVERING. W. E. B. Du Bois: biography of a race, 1868–1919. (Bibl. 1995, 15842.) Rev. by Richard Blackett in AHR (99:2) 1994, 510–11; by Nell Irvin Painter in BkW, 24 Oct. 1996, 1, 14.

17422. Roof, María.   W. E. B. Du Bois, Isabel Allende, and the empowerment of Third World women. CLAJ (39:4) 1996, 401–16.
17423. Schrager, Cynthia D.   Both sides of the veil: race, science, and mysticism in W. E. B. Du Bois. AmQ (48:4) 1996, 551–86.

Alan Duff

17424. Edwards, Denis.   Duff at the top. Quote Unquote (40) 1996, 10–12. (Interview.)
17425. Welch, Denis.   Uh, love: Alan Duff is back, more brilliant than ever. NZList, 28 Sept. 1996, 46–7.

Carol Ann Duffy

17426. O'Keeffe, Bernard.   Comparisons. See **16046**.
17427. Richards, Bernard.   Comparisons: Seamus Heaney, U. A. Fanthorpe and Carol Ann Duffy. ERev (6:4) 1996, 16–20.

Daphne Du Maurier

17428. Berglund, Birgitta.   Mrs Radcliffe and *Rebecca. See* **9270**.
17429. Hollinger, Karen.   The female Oedipal drama of *Rebecca* from novel to film. *See* **13809**.
17430. Horner, Avril; Zlosnik, Sue.   A 'disembodied spirit': the letters and fiction of Daphne Du Maurier. Prose Studies (19:2) 1996, 186–99.
17431. Iuorio, Laura.   Una scrittrice in ascolto: Daphne Du Maurier e la famiglia Brontë. *See* **10377**.
17432. Williams, Tony.   Respecting Daphne Du Maurier's *Rebecca*. NCL (26:2) 1996, 10–12.

Robert Duncan

17433. Gunn, Thom.   Adventurous song: Robert Duncan as Romantic Modernist. *See* **10516**.
17434. Mackey, Nathaniel.   From *Gassire's Lute*: Robert Duncan's Vietnam wartime poetry. Talisman (5) 1990, 86–90; (6) 1991, 141–64; (7) 1991, 141–66; (8) 1992, 189–221.
17435. Rumaker, Michael.   Robert Duncan in San Francisco. San Francisco, CA: Grey Fox Press, 1996. pp. 81.
17436. Scalapino, Leslie.   Secretion of the life experience: aspects of Robert Duncan's thought in *The H.D. Book*. Talisman (7) 1991, 15–21.

Douglas Dunn

17437. Lyon, J. M.   The art of grief: Douglas Dunn's *Elegies*. Eng (40:166) 1991, 47–67.
17438. Smalley, Rebecca.   The Englishman's Scottishman, or radical Scotsman? Reading Douglas Dunn in the light of recent reappraisal of Philip Larkin. SLJ (22:1) 1995, 74–83.

Katherine Dunn (1945–)

17439. Hill, Nancy.   The education of Katherine Dunn. WD (72:2) 1992, 34–7.

Dominick Dunne

17440. Dunne, Dominick.   A novel approaching the truth. BkW, 1 Aug. 1993, 1, 11.

John Gregory Dunne

17441. AMES, CHRISTOPHER. John Gregory Dunne's *Playland* and the Hollywood novel. NCL (26:3) 1996, 5–6.

Edward John Plunkett, Lord Dunsany

17442. JOSHI, S. T. Lord Dunsany: master of the Anglo-Irish imagination. (Bibl. 1995, 15866.) Rev. by Clinton K. Krauss in ELT (39:2) 1996, 272–5.

Christopher Durang

17443. DIECKMAN, SUZANNE BURGOYNE. Metatheatre as antitheatre: Durang's *Actor's Nightmare*. AmDr (1:2) 1992, 26–41.

Paul Durcan

17444. DALTON, MARY. Spiraling lines: Paul Durcan. Irish Literary Supplement (10:2) 1991, 23–5. (Interview.)
17445. ELLIOTT, MAURICE. Paul Durcan – Duarchain. *In* (pp. 304–28) **86**.

Lawrence Durrell

17446. BAIR, DEIRDRE. Writing as a woman: Henry Miller, Lawrence Durrell, and Anaïs Nin in the Villa Seurat. Anaïs (12) 1994, 31–8.
17447. BECKETT, WENDY. 'Art is beginning to fail us': a last visit with Lawrence Durrell. Anaïs (13) 1995, 67–71.
17448. BOONE, JOSEPH A. Vacation cruises; or, The homoerotics of Orientalism. PMLA (110:1) 1995, 89–107.
17449. KACZVINSKY, DONALD P. Classical and medieval sources for Lawrence Durrell's Livia. NCL (23:2) 1993, 11–12.
17450. PELLETIER, JACQUES. Le *Carnet noir* de Lawrence Durrell et le roman de la transition. Études littéraires (27:2) 1994, 123–33.
17451. PLO ALASTRUÉ, RAMÓN. Durrell writing about writers writing: towards a spatial definition of the *Avignon Quintet*. Misc (17) 1996, 207–25.

Geoffrey Dutton

17452. DUTTON, NINETTE. Firing. Sydney; New York: Thompson, 1995. pp. 281. (Imprint lives.) Rev. by Robert Drewe in TLS, 4 Aug. 1995, 24.

Wilma Dykeman

17453. GARNER, LINDA M. Mark McQueen: the ultimately tall man of Wilma Dykeman's *The Tall Woman*. TPB (32) 1995, 48–53.

'Bob Dylan' (Robert Zimmerman)

17454. LEDEEN, JENNY. Prophecy in the Christian era: a study of Bob Dylan's work from 1961 to 1967, emphasizing his use of enigma to teach ethics, and comparing him to Dante Alighieri and other poets. St Louis, MO: Peaceberry Press of Webster Groves, 1996. pp. 241.

Patricia Eakins

17455. CHÉNETIER, MARC. Metamorphoses of the *Metamorphoses*: Patricia Eakins, Wendy Walker, Don Webb. NLH (23:2) 1992, 383–400.

Mignon G. Eberhart

17456. FULTZ, JAY (introd.).   While the patient slept. Lincoln; London: Nebraska UP, 1995. pp. xvi, 313.

David Edgar

17457. KALSON, ALBERT.   From agitprop to SRO: the political drama of David Edgar. *In* (pp. 96–109) **19**.

Clyde Edgerton

17458. CAMPBELL, CHRISTOPHER D.   Reading, writing, and going to war: an interview with Clyde Edgerton. WLA (8:2) 1996, 133–47.

Desmond Egan

17459. KNOWLES, SEBASTIAN.   Interview with Desmond Egan. *In* (pp. 89–111) **58**.

John Ehle

17460. LANG, JOHN.   The shape of love: the motif of sacrifice in two novels by John Ehle. SoLJ (23:1) 1990, 65–78.

Lois Ehlert

17461. EHLERT, LOIS.   Under my nose. Katonah, NY: Owen, 1996. pp. 32. (Meet the author.)

W. D. Ehrhart

17462. ANDERSON, DONALD.   Darkness carried: W. D. Ehrhart's memoirs. WLA (8:2) 1996, 51–9.
17463. ANON.   A conversation with W. D. Ehrhart. WLA (8:2) 1996, 149–57.
17464. BOWIE, THOMAS G., JR.   'Every day I'm always on patrol': Bill Ehrhart's journey home. WLA (8:2) 1996, 61–8.
17465. SMITH, LORRIE.   Against a coming extinction: W. D. Ehrhart and the evolving canon of Vietnam veterans' poetry. *See* **15043**.

Loren Eiseley

17466. CARRITHERS, GALE H.   Loren Eiseley and the self as search. AQ (50:1) 1994, 75–85.
17467. FRANKE, ROBERT G.   A great stage, a great play: the theatrical and tragic in Loren Eiseley's essays. JAC (18:1) 1995, 31–4.
17468. SLOVIC, SCOTT.   Marginality, midnight optimism, and the natural cipher: an approach to Thoreau and Eiseley. *See* **12510**.

Charlotte Eliot

17469. OSER, LEE.   Charlotte Eliot and *The Love Song of J. Alfred Prufrock*. MP (94:2) 1996, 190–200.

T. S. Eliot

17470. AIRAUDI, JESSE T.   Fantasia for sewercovers and drainpipes: T. S. Eliot, Abram Tertz, and the surreal quest for *pravda*. *In* (pp. 21–7) **70**.
17471. ALEXANDER, MICHAEL.   On the dedication of *The Waste Land*. PN Review (17:5) 1991, 48–50.
17472. ALLDRITT, KEITH.   Modernism in the Second World War:

the later poetry of Ezra Pound, T. S. Eliot, Basil Bunting, and Hugh MacDiarmid. *See* **16614**.

17473. ARAKI, EIKO. Sei to shi no rhetoric – jiko wo kaku Eliot to Yeats. (Rhetoric of life and death: Eliot and Yeats – writing the self.) Tokyo: Eihosha, 1996. pp. 486.

17474. ASHER, KENNETH. T. S. Eliot and ideology. (Bibl. 1995, 15887.) Rev. by Christopher Clausen in AL (68:2) 1996, 473–4; by Stephen Medcalf in TLS, 7 June 1996, 13; by Jonathan Veitch in JAStud (30:1) 1996, 150–1.

17475. BACIGALUPO, MASSIMO. Strade rivisitate: città moderna e paesaggio simbolico in Eliot e Pound. QLLSM (4) 1990, 281–304.

17476. BADENHAUSEN, RICHARD. T. S. Eliot's parenthetical method in the Clark Lectures. SAtlR (61:4) 1996, 67–82.

17477. BARDOTTI, MARTA. *Portrait of a Lady* di T. S. Eliot: la persuasione mancata. Textus (2:1/2) 1989, 237–58.

17478. BISSELL, ELIZABETH BEAUMONT. 'Something still more exact': T. S. Eliot's 'traditional claims'. *See* **15295**.

17479. BLALOCK, SUSAN E. Guide to the secular poetry of T. S. Eliot. New York: G. K. Hall; London: Prentice Hall, 1996. pp. xxviii, 228. (Reference pubs in literature.)

17480. BRADBROOK, M. C. The Kensington Quartets. *In* (pp. 143–57) **79**.

17481. BRADSHAW, DAVID. Prufrock's muttering retreats. ERev (7:1) 1996, 6–9.

17482. —— T. S. Eliot and the Major: sources of literary anti-Semitism in the 1930s. TLS, 5 July 1996, 14–16.

17483. BROMWICH, DAVID. T. S. Eliot and Hart Crane. *In* (pp. 49–64) **41**.

17484. BROOKER, JEWEL SPEARS. Eliot in the dock. SAtlR (61:4) 1996, 107–14 (review-article).

17485. —— Mastery and escape: T. S. Eliot and the dialectic of Modernism. (Bibl. 1995, 15892.) Rev. by Jan Gorak in RMRLL (50:1) 1996, 64–6.

17486. BUZARD, JAMES. Eliot, Pound, and expatriate authority. Raritan (13:3) 1994, 106–22.

17487. CARPENTER, PETER. Modern poetry and audience: making connections. ERev (7:2) 1996, 9–11.

17488. CHANDRAN, K. NARAYANA. T. S. Eliot and Ambrose Bierce: another source for the witty rhyme in *A Cooking Egg*. *See* **10354**.

17489. CHINITZ, DAVID. T. S. Eliot and the cultural divide. PMLA (110:2) 1995, 236–47.

17490. CLEMENT, SUSAN. 'All aboard for Natchez, Cairo and St Louis': the source of a draft heading of T. S. Eliot's *Ash-Wednesday* I. NQ (43:1) 1996, 57–9.

17491. COOK, CORNELIA. The hidden apocalypse: T. S. Eliot's early work. LitTheol (10:1) 1996, 68–80.

17492. COOPER, JOHN XIROS. T. S. Eliot and the ideology of *Four Quartets*. (Bibl. 1995, 15904.) Rev. by Robert M. Jones in Eng (45:183) 1996, 271–6.

17493. COUPE, LAURENCE. Violence and the sacred: *Murder in the Cathedral*. ERev (6:2) 1995, 28–31.

17494. COYLE, MICHAEL. A present with innumerable pasts:

postmodernity and the tracing of Modernist origins. Review (18) 1996, 117–34 (review-article).

17495. —— COWAN, LAURA.   Pound and Eliot. American Literary Scholarship (1994) 127–47; (1995) 117–42.

17496. DANZER, DOROTHEA INA.   T. S. Eliot, Ezra Pound und der französische Symbolismus. (Bibl. 1994, 12432.) Rev. by Claus Daufenbach in arcadia (28:2) 1993, 211–14.

17497. DAUFENBACH, CLAUS.   Die Stadt als Kurtisane: Urbanität und dekadente Ästhetik in William Faulkners frühen New-Orleans Texten. ZAA (41:3) 1993, 227–37.

17498. DAVIE, DONALD.   'The Dry Salvages': a reconsideration. PN Review (17:5) 1991, 21–6.

17499. DEANE, PATRICK.   David Jones, T. S. Eliot, and the Modernist unfinished. Ren (47:2) 1995, 75–88.

17500. DIEPEVEEN, LEONARD.   'I can have more than enough power to satisfy me': T. S. Eliot's construction of his audience. *In* (pp. 37–60) **67**.

17501. DUDEK, JOLANTA.   T. S. Eliot a poezja polska. (T. S. Eliot and Polish poetry.) Ruch Literacki (37:3) 1996, 345–53.

17502. EDGECOMBE, RODNEY STENNING.   A source for the Christmas sermon in *Murder in the Cathedral*. NCL (26:2) 1996, 3–4.

17503. ELLIS, STEVE.   The English Eliot: design, language and landscape in *Four Quartets*. (Bibl. 1995, 15913.) Rev. by Richard Badenhausen in Review (16) 1994, 68–73.

17504. ELLMANN, MAUD.   The imaginary Jew: T. S. Eliot and Ezra Pound. *In* (pp. 84–91) **5**.

17505. EMIG, RAINER.   Modernism in poetry: motivations, structures and limits. *See* **11484**.

17506. FARROW, STEPHEN.   T. S. Eliot's communicational scepticism: a Wittgensteinian reading of *The Waste Land*. Language & Communication (16:2) 1996, 107–15.

17507. FLEISSNER, ROBERT F.   Is the 'you' in *Prufrock* a *ficelle*? NCL (23:3) 1993, 9–10.

17508. —— T. S. Eliot and the heritage of Africa: the magus and the Moor as metaphor. (Bibl. 1994, 12440.) Rev. by Richard Badenhausen in Review (16) 1994, 73–7.

17509. FROULA, CHRISTINE.   Corpse, monument, *hypocrite lecteur*: text and transference in the reception of *The Waste Land*. *See* **649**.

17510. GIULIETTI, MARGHERITA.   *The Cocktail Party* e la vocazione alla dramaturgia di T. S. Eliot. Aevum (68:3) 1994, 713–30.

17511. GRIFFITHS, ERIC.   T. S. Eliot's lost 'Hare' poems found. Mail & Guardian (12:35) 1996, 33.

17512. HARGROVE, NANCY D.; GROOTKERK, PAUL.   *The Waste Land* as a Surrealist poem. Comparatist (19) 1995, 4–19.

17513. HARTMAN, CHARLES O.   Free verse: an essay on prosody. *See* **14948**.

17514. HARWELL, THOMAS MEADE.   Porter & Eliot: *Flowering Judas* and *Burbank–Bleistein*: two essays in interpretation. Lewiston, NY; Lampeter: Mellen Press, 1996. pp. 89. (Salzburg English & American studies, 29.)

17515. HOWE, ELISABETH A.   The dramatic monologue. *See* **10519**.

17516. IRMSCHER, CHRISTOPH.   Masken der Moderne: literarische Selbststilisierung bei T. S. Eliot, Ezra Pound, Wallace Stevens und

William Carlos Williams. (Bibl. 1994, 12447.) Rev. by Herwig Friedl in Archiv (233:2) 1996, 396–8.

17517. JARMAN, MARK. Brer Rabbit and Brer Possum: the Americanness of Ezra Pound and T. S. Eliot. *In* (pp. 21–37) **34**.

17518. JAY, MARTIN. Modernism and the specter of psychologism. *See* **15533**.

17519. JEON, HONG-SHIL. *Hwangmuji* e esseoeui Ezra Pound. (Ezra Pound in *The Waste Land*.) JELLC (38:1) 1996, 5–34.

17520. JONES, ELIZABETH. Eliot and *Tarantella*. *See* **16373**.

17521. JORDAN, HEATHER BRYANT. *Ara Vos Prec*: a rescued volume. *See* **696**.

17522. JULIUS, ANTHONY. T. S. Eliot, anti-Semitism, and literary form. (Bibl. 1995, 15933.) Rev. by Tom Paulin in LRB (18:9) 1996, 13–15; by Stephen Medcalf in TLS, 7 June 1996, 13; by Jewel Spears Brooker in SAtlR (61:4) 1996, 107–14.

17523. KAPPEL, ANDREW J. Presenting Miss Moore, Modernist: T. S. Eliot's edition of Marianne Moore's *Selected Poems*. *See* **699**.

17524. KEARNS, GEORGE; KEARNS, CLEO MCNELLY. Pound and Eliot. American Literary Scholarship (1993) 101–12.

17525. LANGBAUM, ROBERT. Lawrence and the Modernists. Études Lawrenciennes (10) 1994, 145–57.

17526. LEE, CHONG-HO. Text eui mueuisik: *Prufrock eui Sarang Norae* reul jungsim euro. (The textual unconscious: a reading of *The Love Song of J. Alfred Prufrock*.) JELL (42:3) 1996, 571–90.

17527. LEGGATT, ALEXANDER. The hidden hero: Shakespeare's *Coriolanus* and Eliot's *Coriolan*. *In* (pp. 89–98) **16**.

17528. LENTRICCHIA, FRANK. Modernist quartet. (Bibl. 1995, 15942.) Rev. by Ralph Pite in CamQ (25:2) 1996, 203–5; by Mark Ford in TLS, 21 June 1996, 26; by Oliver Scheiding in ZAA (44:4) 1996, 380–1.

17529. LLOYD-KIMBREL, E. D. A condition of complete simplicity: poetic returns and Frost's *Directive*. RFR (1991) 7–17.

17530. LOUCKS, JAMES F. The exile's return: fragment of a T. S. Eliot chronology. ANQ (9:2) 1996, 16–39.

17531. MALAMUD, RANDY. T. S. Eliot's drama: a research and production sourcebook. (Bibl. 1992, 13561.) Rev. by Richard Badenhausen in Review (16) 1994, 65–8.

17532. —— Where the words are valid: T. S. Eliot's communities of drama. (Bibl. 1994, 12465.) Rev. by Jewel Spears Brooker in SAtlR (61:3) 1996, 123–7.

17533. MONTEIRO, GEORGE. Eliot and the mob: *The Waste Land*. NCL (24:1) 1994, 11–12.

17534. MOODY, A. DAVID. Thomas Stearns Eliot, poet. (Bibl. 1995, 15955.) Rev. by Stephen Medcalf in TLS, 7 June 1996, 13; by Wolfgang Wicht in ZAA (44:2) 1996, 178–80.

17535. —— Tracing T. S. Eliot's spirit: essays on his poetry and thought. Cambridge; New York: CUP, 1996. pp. xxi, 195.

17536. MOODY, ANTHONY DAVID. The Cambridge companion to T. S. Eliot. (Bibl. 1994, 12470.) Rev. by Wolfgang Wicht in ZAA (44:2) 1996, 178–80.

17537. MORAN, SHANE. Self-canonizing critics: T. S. Eliot and J. M. Coetzee. *See* **15654**.

17538. MORRISON, PAUL. The poetics of Fascism: Ezra Pound, T. S. Eliot, Paul de Man. *See* **15659**.

17539. NEWSTROM, SCOTT L.   Saying 'goonight' to 'lost' ladies: an inter-textual interpretation of allusions to *Hamlet*'s Ophelia in Cather's *A Lost Lady* and Eliot's *The Waste Land*. *See* **6827**.

17540. NORTH, MICHAEL.   The political aesthetic of Yeats, Eliot, and Pound. (Bibl. 1995, 15956.) Rev. by Wolfgang Wicht in ZAA (42:1) 1994, 74–6.

17541. OSER, LEE.   Charlotte Eliot and *The Love Song of J. Alfred Prufrock*. *See* **17469**.

17542. PALMER, MARJA.   Men and women in T. S. Eliot's early poetry. Lund: Lund UP, 1996. pp. 243. (Lund studies in English, 90.)

17543. PATTY, GABRIELLE M.   Reactionary Modernists: the literary and socio-political kinship of Stefan George and T. S. Eliot. Comparatist (15) 1991, 97–115.

17544. PELLEGRINO, JOE.   Yeats and Eliot: a hidden debt and its repercussions. Notes on Modern Irish Literature (5) 1993, 67–77.

17545. PHILLIPS, CAROLINE.   The religious quest in the poetry of T. S. Eliot. Lewiston, NY; Lampeter: Mellen Press, 1995. pp. ix, 102. (Studies in art and religious interpretation, 14.)

17546. PIZZATO, MARK.   Redressing the chaos: Nietzsche in Eliot. JRS (6:2) 1992, 1–25.

17547. RAUBICHECK, WALTER.   Jacques Maritain, T. S. Eliot, and the Romantics. *See* **9675**.

17548. RAVINDRAN, V.   Prufrock and Golyadkin: an uncanny kinship. In-between (2:2) 1993, 157–65.

17549. RAWSON, CLAUDE.   The fire and the rose. In-between (3:1) 1994, 51–4.

17550. RHEE, JOON-HAK.   T. S. Eliot eui si e natanan hoeeui eui post-modernjeok sunggyeok. (The postmodern character of skepticism in T. S. Eliot's poetry.) JELL (42:3) 1996, 591–610.

17551. RICKS, CHRISTOPHER (ed.).   Inventions of the March Hare: poems 1909–1917. London; Boston, MA: Faber & Faber, 1996. pp. xlii, 428. Rev. by Helen Vendler in LRB (18:21) 1996, 8–9.

17552. ROWLEY, STEPHEN.   Colour implications of the poetry of T. S. Eliot and D. H. Lawrence. Études Lawrenciennes (10) 1994, 159–72.

17553. RUBEL, WARREN.   Reading and rereading T. S. Eliot. Cresset (60:2/3) 1996, 12–13.

17554. RUDRUM, ALAN.   T. S. Eliot on Lancelot Andrewes's 'word within a word'. *See* **7649**.

17555. SATPATHY, SUMANYU.   The swallow in Eliot's *The Waste Land*. In-between (4:1) 1995, 41–3.

17556. SCHOENING, MARK.   T. S. Eliot meets Michael Gold: Modernism and radicalism in Depression-era American literature. Modernism/Modernity (3:3) 1996, 51–68.

17557. SCHUCHARD, RONALD.   American publishers and the transmission of T. S. Eliot's prose: a sociology of English and American editions. *In* (pp. 171–201) **69**.

17558. SCHWARTZ, JOSEPH.   T. S. Eliot's idea of the Christian poet. Ren (43:3) 1991, 215–27.

17559. SEELIG, SHARON CADMAN.   Generating texts: the progeny of seventeenth-century prose. *See* **7718**.

17560. SENA, VINOD.   *Murder in the Cathedral*: the search for a viable form. In-between (1:1) 1992, 31–56.

17561. SHARPE, TONY. T. S. Eliot and ideas of *oeuvre*. *In* (pp. 151–70) **69**.

17562. SINGH, SUKHBIR. A Shakespearean source for T. S. Eliot's 'dolphin': *The Waste Land* 2, line 96. *See* **6721**.

17563. SMIDT, KRISTIAN. T. S. Eliot's criticism of modern prose fiction. *See* **11653**.

17564. SMITH, GROVER. T. S. Eliot and the use of memory. Lewisburg, PA: Bucknell UP; London; Toronto: Assoc. UPs, 1996. pp. 186.

17565. SMITH, STAN. The origins of Modernism: Eliot, Pound, Yeats and the rhetorics of renewal. (Bibl. 1995, 15970.) Rev. by Richard Greaves in Yeats Annual (12) 1996, 347–8; by Michael Coyle in Review (18) 1996, 117–34.

17566. —— Remembering Bryden's bill: Modernism from Eliot to Auden. *See* **16133**.

17567. ŞTEFĂNESCU, VIOREL. T. S. Eliot şi modelul textual. (T. S. Eliot and the textual pattern.) RomLit, 8 Mar. 1994, 23.

17568. STROBL, GERWIN. *Quartet* and *Four Quartets*: the influence of T. S. Eliot on Paul Scott. *In* (pp. 269–84) **125**.

17569. SURETTE, LEON. The birth of Modernism: Ezra Pound, T. S. Eliot, W. B. Yeats, and the occult. (Bibl. 1995, 15973.) Rev. by Michael Coyle in Review (18) 1996, 117–34.

17570. TEN KORTENAAR, NEIL. Where the Atlantic meets the Caribbean: Kamau Brathwaite's *The Arrivants* and T. S. Eliot's *The Waste Land*. *See* **16551**.

17571. THORMÄHLEN, MARIANNE (ed.). T. S. Eliot at the turn of the century. Lund: Lund UP, 1994. pp. 244. (Lund studies in English, 86.) Rev. by Peter Corbin in Archiv (233:2) 1996, 393–6.

17572. TROMBOLD, CHRIS B. Alimentary Eliot: digestive references and metaphors in T. S. Eliot's writings. *See* **2487**.

17573. TUCKER, JOHN. *The Waste Land*, order and myth. *In* (pp. 217–27) **16**.

17574. VERMA, K. D. Ideological confrontation and synthesis in Mulk Raj Anand's *Conversations in Bloomsbury*. *See* **15956**.

17575. WARNER, MARTIN. Modes of political imagining. *In* (pp. 98–128) **63**.

17576. WHANG, CHUL-AM. Appearance and reality of 'the absolute' in the poetry of T. S. Eliot. JELLC (38:2) 1996, 133–55.

17577. WHITWORTH, MICHAEL. *Pièces d'identité*: T. S. Eliot, J. W. N. Sullivan and poetic impersonality. ELT (39:2) 1996, 149–70.

17578. WREN-LEWIS, JOHN. Communication tongued with fire: personal reflections on the eternity-vision of T. S. Eliot's *Four Quartets*. ChesR (22:4) 1996, 499–507.

17579. YONEMOTO, YOSHITAKA. *The Waste Land* ni okeru kigekisei. (Comedy in *The Waste Land*.) SEL (72:2) 1996, 227–38.

17580. ZUBIZARRETTA, JOHN. Eliot's *Gerontion* and Frost's *An Old Man's Winter Night*: counterparts of Modernism. RFR (1993) 62–9.

Stanley Elkin

17581. ELKIN, STANLEY. Politics and the novelist. BkW, 18 Apr. 1993, 1, 11.

17582. PINSKER, SANFORD. Sickness unto style. GetR (7:3) 1994, 437–45 (review-article).

Bret Easton Ellis

17583. Applegate, Nancy; Applegate, Joe. Prophet or pornographer: an evaluation of black humor in *American Psycho*. NCL (25:1) 1995, 10–12.

17584. Block, Leigh. Distancing in Bret Easton Ellis' *American Psycho*. NCL (24:1) 1994, 6–8.

17585. Irmer, Thomas. Bret Easton Ellis's *American Psycho* and its submerged references to the 1960s. ZAA (41:4) 1993, 349–56.

17586. Juchartz, Larry; Hunter, Erica. Ultraviolent metaphors for (un)popular culture: a defense of Bret Easton Ellis. PCR (7:1) 1996, 67–79.

17587. Verrips, Jojada. The consumption of 'touching' images: reflections on mimetic 'wildness' in the West. *See* **14301**.

Harlan Ellison

17588. Francavilla, Joseph. The concept of the divided self in Harlan Ellison's *I Have No Mouth and I Must Scream* and *Shatterday*. JFA (6:2/3) 1993, 107–25.

17589. Shindler, Dorman T. Hardboiled Ellison: the crime fiction of Harlan Ellison. AD (29:2) 1996, 208–11.

Ralph Ellison

17590. Allen, Caffilene. The caged bird sings: the Ellison–Dunbar connection. *See* **11090**.

17591. —— The world as possibility: the significance of Freud's *Totem and Taboo* in Ellison's *Invisible Man*. LitPs (41:1/2) 1995, 1–18.

17592. Busby, Mark. Ralph Ellison. (Bibl. 1992, 13617.) Rev. by Robert J. Butler in AAR (28:2) 1994, 321–5; by Bruce Adams in AmS (36:2) 1995, 214–15.

17593. Callahan, John F. (ed.). The collected essays of Ralph Ellison. Introd. by Saul Bellow. (Bibl. 1995, 16000.) Rev. by David Nicholson in BkW, 4 Feb. 1996, 7.

17594. Cohn, Deborah. To see or not to see: in*vis*ibility, clair*voy*ance, and re-*vis*ions of history in *Invisible Man* and *La casa de los espíritus*. CLS (33:4) 1996, 372–95.

17595. Hamalian, Leo. D. H. Lawrence and Black writers. JML (16:4) 1990, 579–96.

17596. Lee, Kun Jong. Ellison's racial variations on American themes. AAR (30:3) 1996, 421–40.

17597. McNeely, Trevor. Ideology, theory, and Ellison's *Invisible Man*. ESCan (22:2) 1996, 181–98.

17598. Marvin, Thomas F. Children of Legba: musicians at the crossroads in Ralph Ellison's *Invisible Man*. AL (68:3) 1996, 587–608.

17599. Powell, Michael. 'Pages to ripple beneath my thumb': the visible books of Ellison's *Invisible Man*. NCL (25:3) 1995, 2–3.

17600. Steele, Meíli. Democratic interpretation and the politics of difference. *See* **2712**.

17601. Warren, Kenneth W. Ralph Ellison and the reconfiguration of Black cultural politics. YREAL (11) 1995, 139–57.

James Ellroy

17602. Ellroy, James. My dark places: an L.A. crime memoir.

New York: Knopf; London: Century, 1996. pp. 351. Rev. by Paul Quinn in TLS, 22 Nov. 1996, 26.

Margaret Elphinstone

17603. Babinec, Lisa. 'Between the boundaries': an interview with Margaret Elphinstone. Edinburgh Review (93) 1995, 51–60.

Buchi Emecheta

17604. Iyer, Lisa H. The second sex three times oppressed: cultural colonization and coll(i)(u)sion in Buchi Emecheta's women. RWT (1:2) 1994, 97–114.

17605. Kenyon, Olga. Alice Walker and Buchi Emecheta rewrite the myth of motherhood. *In* (pp. 336–54) **34**.

William Empson

17606. Krautz, Joachim. Imagery and sexual connotations in William Empson's *Aubade*. ZAA (42:3) 1994, 235–42.

Marian Engel

17607. Heidenreich, Rosmarin. The bear. LRC (5:4) 1996, 20–2 (review-article).

17608. Verduyn, Christl (ed.). Dear Marian, dear Hugh: the MacLennan–Engel correspondence. (Bibl. 1995, 16019.) Rev. by John Lennox in ECanW (58) 1996, 145–50; by Rosmarin Heidenreich in LRC (5:4) 1996, 20–2.

17609. —— Lifelines: Marian Engel's writings. Montreal; London: McGill–Queen's UP, 1995. pp. viii, 278. Rev. by Rosmarin Heidenreich in LRC (5:4) 1996, 20–2.

George Allan England (1877–1936)

17610. Pittenger, Mark. Imagining genocide in the progressive era: the socialist science fiction of George Allan England. AmS (35:1) 1994, 91–108.

Paul Engle

17611. Engle, Paul. A lucky American childhood. Foreword by Albert E. Stone. Iowa City: Iowa UP, 1996. pp. xxiv, 192. (Singular lives.)

Elizabeth Engstrom

17612. Schofield, Ann. Lizzie Borden took an axe: history, feminism, and American culture. *See* **16719**.

D. J. Enright

17613. Enright, D. J. Interplay: a kind of commonplace book. (Bibl. 1995, 16020.) Rev. by William Fiennes in TLS, 26 Jan. 1996, 25.

Theodore Enslin

17614. Foster, Edward. An interview with Theodore Enslin. Talisman (12) 1994, 25–36.

17615. Hatlen, Burton. Toward a common ground: versions of place in the poetry of Charles Olson, Edward Dorn, and Theodore Enslin. *See* **17361**.

17616. NOWAK, MARK.   Mnemones and the ancestors: Theodore
Enslin's practice. Talisman (12) 1994, 74–81.

Leslie Epstein

17617. YOGEV, MICHAEL P.   The fantastic in Holocaust literature:
writing and unwriting the unbearable. JFA (5:2) 1992, 32–49.

Louise Erdrich

17618. BARAK, JULIE.   Blurs, blends, berdaches: gender mixing in the
novels of Louise Erdrich. SAIL (8:3) 1996, 49–62.

17619. BREHM, VICTORIA.   The metamorphoses of an Ojibwa *manido*.
AL (68:4) 1996, 677–706.

17620. BURDICK, DEBRA A.   Louise Erdrich's *Love Medicine, The Beet
Queen,* and *Tracks*: an annotated survey of criticism through 1994. AICRJ
(20:3) 1996, 137–66.

17621. CASTILLO, SUSAN.   Women aging into power: fictional
representations of power and authority in Louise Erdrich's female
characters. SAIL (8:4) 1996, 13–20.

17622. DALE, CORINNE H.   Reconstructing the Native-American
woman: Louise Erdrich's *Fleur*. JSSE (27) 1996, 113–30.

17623. DANIELE, DANIELA.   Transactions in a native land: mixed-
blood identity and Indian legacy in Louise Erdrich's writing. RSAJ (3)
1992, 43–58.

17624. HAFEN, P. JANE.   Sacramental language: ritual in the poetry
of Louise Erdrich. GPQ (16:3) 1996, 147–55.

17625. QUEHENBERGER-DOBBS, LINDA.   Literature, the imagination
and survival: Louise Erdrich's *Love Medicine*. AAA (21:2) 1996, 255–65.

17626. RUPPERT, JAMES.   Mediation in contemporary Native-
American writing. Genre (25:4) 1992, 321–37.

17627. SCHUMACHER, MICHAEL.   Louise Erdrich and Michael Dorris:
a marriage of minds. *See* **17365**.

17628. SECCO, ANNA.   The search for origins through storytelling in
Native-American literature: Momaday, Silko, Erdrich. RSAJ (3) 1992,
59–71.

17629. SLOBODA, NICHOLAS.   Beyond the iconic subject: re-visioning
Louise Erdrich's *Tracks*. SAIL (8:3) 1996, 63–79.

Clayton Eshleman

17630. TUMA, KEITH.   An interview with Clayton Eshleman.
ConLit (37:2) 1996, 179–206.

Loren D. Estleman

17631. HYNES, JOSEPH.   Looking for endings: the fiction of Loren D.
Estleman. JPC (29:3) 1995, 121–7.

Caradoc Evans

17632. HOPKINS, CHRIS.   Translating Caradoc Evans's Welsh
English. *See* **2646**.

William Everson ('Brother Antoninus')

17633. EVERSON, WILLIAM.   Prodigious thrust. Afterword by Allan
Campo. Santa Rosa, CA: Black Sparrow Press, 1996. pp. 325.

Nissim Ezekiel

17634. MOHANTY, NIRANJAN. Irony in the poetry of Nissim Ezekiel. WLT (69:1) 1995, 51–5.

17635. PANDEYA, PRABHAT KUMAR. Eros and literature: Nissim Ezekiel in conversation. IndL (39:3) 1996, 156–9.

Sarah Webster Fabio

17636. WARD, JERRY W., JR. Reading South: poets mean & poems signify – a note on origins. AAR (27:1) 1993, 125–6.

A. R. D. Fairburn

17637. JACKSON, MAC. To the editor. NZList, 23 Mar. 1996, 54–5.

17638. —— (ed.). Selected poems. (Bibl. 1995, 16053.) Rev. by Michele Leggott in NZList, 23 Mar. 1996, 54; by Denys Trussell in Quote Unquote (34) 1996, 27–8.

17639. STAFFORD, JANE. Masculinism and poetry: a note of warning. Landfall (4:2) 1996, 261–70.

Mary Fallon

17640. JAGOSE, ANNAMARIE. Lesbian utopics. *See* **15525**.

Peter Fallon

17641. JOHNSTON, DILLON. 'My feet on the ground': an interview with Peter Fallon. *See* **1062**.

17642. LINCECUM, JERRY B. Peter Fallon: contemporary Irish poet, editor and publisher. *See* **1066**.

U. A. Fanthorpe

17643. RICHARDS, BERNARD. Comparisons: Seamus Heaney, U. A. Fanthorpe and Carol Ann Duffy. *See* **17427**.

Nuruddin Farah

17644. NGABOH-SMART, FRANCIS. Dimensions of gift-giving in Nuruddin Farah's *Gifts*. RAL (27:4) 1996, 144–56.

Richard Fariña

17645. McCARRON, WILLIAM. Fariña and Pynchon. NCL (22:4) 1992, 11–12.

Florence Farr

17646. LITZ, A. WALTON. Florence Farr: a 'transitional' woman. *In* (pp. 85–106) **41**.

Fiona Farrell

17647. EARL, VICKI. One clever girl. Quote Unquote (42) 1996, 10. (Interview.)

17648. REWI, ADRIENNE. Fiona Farrell. Pacific Way, Oct. 1996, 40–2.

J. G. Farrell

17649. STROBL, GERWIN. The challenge of cross-cultural interpretation in the Anglo-Indian novel: the Raj revisited: a comparative study of three Booker Prize authors: Paul Scott, The Raj Quartet;

J. G. Farrell, *The Siege of Krishnapur*; Ruth Prawer Jhabvala, *Heat and Dust*. Lewiston, NY; Lampeter: Mellen Press, 1995. pp. 278. (Salzburg English & American studies, 3.)

James T. Farrell

17650. ANDERSON, DAVID D.   Sherwood Anderson , Henry Blake Fuller, James T. Farrell, and the Midwestern city as metaphor and reality. *See* **15975**.

17651. BRANCH, EDGAR M.   Studs Lonigan's neighborhood and the making of James T. Farrell. Newton, MA: Arts End, 1996. pp. ii, 103.

17652. EBEST, RON.   The Irish Catholic schooling of James T. Farrell, 1914–23. EI (30:4) 1995, 18–32.

17653. GROVER, DORYS CROW.   Four Midwestern novelists' response to French inquiries on populism. *See* **15992**.

17654. SMITH, GENE.   The Lonigan curse. AH (46:2) 1995, 150–1.

Howard Fast ('E. V. Cunningham')

17655. FONER, ERIC (introd.).   Freedom Road. Armonk, NY; London: Sharpe, 1995. pp. xviii, 275. (American history through literature.)

17656. MACDONALD, ANDREW.   Howard Fast: a critical companion. Westport, CT; London: Greenwood Press, 1996. pp. xi, 201. (Critical companions to popular contemporary writers.)

William Faulkner

17657. ALTMAN, MERYL.   The bug that dare not speak its name: sex, art, Faulkner's worst novel, and the critics. FJ (9:1/2) 1993/94, 43–68.

17658. ANDREWS, KAREN M.   Toward a 'culturalist' approach to Faulkner studies: making connections in *Flags in the Dust*. FJ (7:1/2) 1991/92, 13–26.

17659. ANON.   Bibliography: a Latin American Faulkner. FJ (11:1/2) 1995/96, 185–94.

17660. ARNOLD, EDWIN T.; TROUARD, DAWN.   Reading Faulkner. *Sanctuary*: glossary and commentary. Jackson; London: Mississippi UP, 1996. pp. xviii, 280. (Reading Faulkner.)

17661. BALDWIN, MARC D.   Faulkner's cartographic method: producing the *land* through cognitive mapping. FJ (7:1/2) 1991/92, 193–214.

17662. BENOIT, RAYMOND.   Archetypes and ecotones: the tree in Faulkner's *The Bear* and Irving's *Rip Van Winkle*. *See* **11538**.

17663. BESSIÈRE, JEAN.   Carlos Fuentes vis-à-vis William Faulkner: novel, tragedy, history. Trans. by Evelyn Tavarelli. FJ (11:1/2) 1995/96, 33–42.

17664. BOKER, PAMELA A.   '*How can he be so nothungry?*': fetishism, anorexia, and the disavowal of the cultural 'I' in *Light in August*. FJ (7:1/2) 1991/92, 175–91.

17665. BOON, KEVIN A.   Temple defiled: the brainwashing of Temple Drake in Faulkner's *Sanctuary*. FJ (6:2) 1991, 33–50.

17666. BOYD, MOLLY.   William Faulkner's *Doctor Martino*. SoQ (34:2) 1996, 39–49.

17667. BURGESS, M. J.   Watching (Jefferson) watching: *Light in August* and the aestheticization of gender. FJ (7:1/2) 1991/92, 95–114.

17668. BURNS, MARGIE.   A good rose is hard to find: Southern gothic as signs of social dislocation in Faulkner and O'Connor. *In* (pp. 105–23) **44**.

17669. BURTON, STACY.   Bakhtin, temporality, and modern narrative: writing 'the whole triumphant murderous unstoppable chute'. *See* **14422**.

17670. CARPENTER, LUCAS.   Floyd Collins and the Sand Cave tragedy: a possible source for Faulkner's *As I Lay Dying*. KenR (12:3) 1995, 3–18.

17671. CASTILLE, PHILIP DUBUISSON.   Compson and Sternwood: William Faulkner's 'Appendix' and *The Big Sleep*. *See* **13537**.

17672. CHABRIER, GWENDOLYNE.   Faulkner's families: a Southern saga. New York: Gordian Press, 1993. pp. xii, 305.

17673. CHAPDELAINE, ANNICK.   Faulkner in French: humor obliterated. Trans. by Michael Gilson. FJ (7:1/2) 1991/92, 43–60.

17674. ——— Translating the comic: a case study of *Sanctuaire*. Trans. by Michael Gilson. FJ (8:2) 1993, 67–83.

17675. CLARK, KEITH.   Man on the margin: Lucas Beauchamp and the limitations of space. FJ (6:1) 1990, 67–79.

17676. COHEN, PHILIP.   Faulkner. American Literary Scholarship (1994) 149–65; (1995) 143–72.

17677. COX, JAMES M.   Beneath my father's name. *In* (pp. 13–30) **43**.

17678. DAUFENBACH, CLAUS.   Die Stadt als Kurtisane: Urbanität und dekadente Ästhetik in William Faulkners frühen New-Orleans Texten. *See* **17497**.

17679. DELAY, FLORENCE; DE LABRIOLLE, JACQUELINE.   Is García Márquez the Colombian Faulkner? Trans. by Arthur W. Wilhelm. FJ (11:1/2) 1995/96, 119–38.

17680. DIMINO, ANDREA.   From goddess to 'galmeat': narrative politics and narrative desire in Faulkner's novels. FJ (10:2) 1995, 65–80.

17681. DONALDSON, SUSAN V.   Faulkner and sexuality. FJ (9:1/2) 1993/94, 3–12.

17682. ——— Reading Faulkner reading Cowley reading Faulkner: authority and gender in the Compson appendix. *See* **17135**.

17683. DONLON, JOCELYN HAZELWOOD.   Porches: stories: power: spatial and racial intersections in Faulkner and Hurston. JAC (19:4) 1996, 95–110.

17684. DUNLEAVY, LINDA.   *Sanctuary*, sexual difference, and the problem of rape. SAF (24:2) 1996, 171–91.

17685. DUVALL, JOHN N.   Faulkner's marginal couple: invisible, outlaw, and unspeakable communities. (Bibl. 1995, 16094.) Rev. by Jean Mullin Yonke in AmS (32:2) 1991, 122.

17686. DWYER, JUNE.   Feminization, masculinization, and the role of the woman patriot in *The Unvanquished*. FJ (6:2) 1991, 55–64.

17687. FABIJANCIC, TONY.   Reification, dereification, subjectivity: towards a Marxist reading of William Faulkner's poor-White topography. FJ (10:1) 1994, 75–94.

17688. FOWLER, DOREEN.   'I am dying': Faulkner's Hightower and the Oedipal moment. FJ (9:1/2) 1993/94, 139–48.

17689. ——— 'You cant beat a woman': the preoedipal mother in *Light in August*. FJ (10:2) 1995, 55–64.

17690. FRISCH, MARK.   Nature, postmodernity, and real marvelous: Faulkner, Quiroga, Mallea, Rulfo, Carpentier. FJ (11:1/2) 1995/96, 67–82.

17691. FUENTES, CARLOS. The novel as tragedy: William Faulkner. Trans. by Trude Stern; revised by Evelyn Tavarelli. FJ (11:1/2) 1995/96, 13–31.

17692. GARTNER, CAROL B. Faulkner in context: seeing *That Evening Sun* through the Blues. SoQ (34:2) 1996, 50–8.

17693. GEOFFROY, ALAIN. William Faulkner's *The Leg*: the printed story of an 'unprintable phrase'. JSSE (20) 1993, 27–36.

17694. GILES, RONALD K. Dialogue in Faulkner's *Dr Martino*. TPB (30) 1993, 15–21.

17695. GLISSANT, EDOUARD. Faulkner, Mississippi. Paris: Stock, 1996. pp. 357. (Échanges.)

17696. GODDEN, RICHARD. *Absalom, Absalom!* and Rosa Coldfield; or, What *is* in the dark house? FJ (8:2) 1993, 31–66.

17697. GRAY, RICHARD. The life of William Faulkner: a critical biography. (Bibl. 1995, 16097.) Rev. by Cathy Chance Harvey in AL (68:1) 1996, 258–9; by Ian Jackson in NQ (43:2) 1996, 240–1; by Richard H. King in JAStud (30:1) 1996, 143–6.

17698. GUTTING, GABRIELE. The mysteries of the map-maker: Faulkner, *If I Forget Thee, Jerusalem*, and the secret of a map. FJ (8:2) 1993, 85–93.

17699. GWIN, MINROSE C. The feminine and Faulkner: reading (beyond) sexual difference. (Bibl. 1995, 16099.) Rev. by Jean Mullin Yonke in AmS (33:1) 1992, 137–8.

17700. —— *Mosquitoes'* missing bite: the four deletions. *See* **666**.

17701. HANNON, CHARLES. Signification, simulation, and containment in *If I Forget Thee, Jerusalem*. FJ (7:1/2) 1991/92, 133–50.

17702. HANSON, PHILIP J. The logic of anti-capitalism in *The Sound and the Fury*. FJ (10:1) 1994, 3–27.

17703. HERNÁNDEZ, MARÍA DEL CARMEN; URGO, JOSEPH; VEGH, BEATRIZ. An interview with Ricardo Piglia. Trans. by Trude Stern. FJ (11:1/2) 1995/96, 43–50.

17704. HINES, THOMAS S. William Faulkner and the tangible past: the architecture of Yoknapatawpha. Berkeley; London: California UP, 1996. pp. xiv, 164.

17705. HOLMES, CATHERINE D. Annotations to William Faulkner's *The Hamlet*. New York; London: Garland, 1996. pp. xiii, 221. (William Faulkner, annotations to the novels.) (Cf. bibl. 1995, 16108.)

17706. HÖNNIGHAUSEN, LOTHAR. Thomas Mann's *Buddenbrooks* and William Faulkner's *Sartoris* as family novels. FJ (6:1) 1990, 33–45.

17707. HORTON, MERRILL. Annotations to William Faulkner's *The Town*. New York; London: Garland, 1996. pp. xi, 274. (William Faulkner, annotations to the novels.)

17708. —— Thackeray in Faulkner. *See* **12470**.

17709. INGE, M. THOMAS. Mo Yan and William Faulkner: influences and confluences. FJ (6:1) 1990, 14–24.

17710. IRWIN, JOHN T. Doubling and incest/repetition and revenge: a speculative reading of Faulkner. (Bibl. 1979, 10737.) Baltimore, MD; London: Johns Hopkins UP, 1996. pp. 245. (Expanded ed.: first ed. 1975.)

17711. KANG, HEE. A new configuration of Faulkner's feminine: Linda Snopes Kohl in *The Mansion*. FJ (8:1) 1992, 21–41.

17712. KARTIGANER, DONALD M.; ABADIE, ANN J. (eds). Faulkner and gender: Faulkner and Yoknapatawpha, 1994. Jackson; London: Mississippi UP, 1996. pp. xxii, 302.

17713. ———— Faulkner and the artist: Faulkner and Yoknapatawpha, 1993. Jackson; London: Mississippi UP, 1996. pp. xxvii, 344.

17714. KINNEY, ARTHUR F. *Go Down, Moses*: the miscegenation of time. New York: Twayne; London: Prentice Hall, 1996. pp. xxi, 181. (Twayne's masterwork studies, 148.)

17715. ——BERMAN, DAVID. Senator John Sharp Williams, Phil Stone, and a postmaster's job for Faulkner. FJ (8:2) 1993, 95–8.

17716. KINNEY, ARTHUR F. (ed.). Critical essays on William Faulkner: the Sutpen family. New York: G. K. Hall; London: Prentice Hall, 1996. pp. xvii, 289, (plates) 16. (Critical essays on American literature.)

17717. KIRCHDORFER, ULF. *Sanctuary*: Temple as a parrot. FJ (6:2) 1991, 51–3.

17718. KLEPPE, SANDRA LEE. The curse of God in Faulkner's *Go Down, Moses*. LitTheol (10:4) 1996, 361–9.

17719. LADD, BARBARA. Nationalism and the color line in George W. Cable, Mark Twain, and William Faulkner. *See* **10577**.

17720. LAHEY, MICHAEL E. Film, fantasy and assault: accusation and esteem in Faulkner's *Dry September*. JSSE (19) 1992, 43–52.

17721. LALONDE, CHRIS. *New Orleans* and an aesthetics of indeterminacy. FJ (8:2) 1993, 13–29.

17722. —— 'To rave notices': William Faulkner's *Requiem for a Nun* at the Royal Court Theatre. JADT (7:1) 1995, 64–73.

17723. LALONDE, CHRISTOPHER A. William Faulkner and the rites of passage. Macon, GA: Mercer UP, 1996. pp. 178.

17724. LIU, XIAN. Echoing *Pantaloon in Black* in Chinese. FJ (10:1) 1994, 57–74.

17725. McMILLEN, NEIL R.; POLK, NOEL. Faulkner on lynching. FJ (8:1) 1992, 3–14.

17726. MÁRQUEZ, ANTONIO C. Faulkner in Latin America. FJ (11:1/2) 1995/96, 83–100.

17727. MARSHALL, ALEXANDER J., III. Faulkner. American Literary Scholarship (1993) 113–24.

17728. MARTIN, REGINALD. Faulkner's Southern reflections: the Black on the back of the mirror in *Ad Astra*. AAR (27:1) 1993, 53–7.

17729. MATERASSI, MARIO. From *Light in August* to *Luce d'agosto*: Elio Vittorini's literary offences. RSAJ (6) 1995, 5–23.

17730. MATTHEWS, JOHN T. Faulkner and cultural studies. FJ (7:1/2) 1991/92, 5–12.

17731. MEYER, WILLIAM E. H., JR. Culture-wars/gender-scars: Faulkner's South *vs* America. JAC (18:4) 1995, 33–41.

17732. MILLGATE, MICHAEL. Undue process: William Faulkner's *Sanctuary*. *In* (pp. 157–69) **105**.

17733. MUMBACH, MARY. The figural action of sacrifice in *Go Down, Moses*. *In* (pp. 247–72) **29**.

17734. NICOLAISEN, PETER. 'Because we were forever free': slavery and emancipation in *The Unvanquished*. FJ (10:2) 1995, 81–91.

17735. O'DONNELL, PATRICK. Between the family and the state: nomadism and authority in *As I Lay Dying*. FJ (7:1/2) 1991/92, 83–94.

17736. PEARCE, RICHARD. The politics of narration: James Joyce,

William Faulkner, and Virginia Woolf. (Bibl. 1994, 12590.) Rev. by Cheryl Lester in MFS (40:2) 1994, 434–5.

17737. PEPPERS, CATHY.   What does Faulkner want? *Light in August* as a hysterical male text. FJ (9:1/2) 1993/94, 125–37.

17738. PETERS, JOHN G.   Repudiation, wilderness, birthright: reconciling conflicting views of Faulkner's Ike McCaslin. ELN (33:3) 1996, 39–46.

17739. POLK, NOEL.   Children of the dark house: text and context in Faulkner. Jackson; London: Mississippi UP, 1996. pp. xv, 288.

17740. POTHIER, JACQUES.   Voices from the South, voices of the souths: Faulkner, García Márquez, Vargas Llosa, Borges. FJ (11:1/2) 1995/96, 101–18.

17741. PREGO, OMAR.   William Faulkner and Juan Carlos Onetti: revisiting some critical approaches about a literary affinity. Trans. by Trude Stern. FJ (11:1/2) 1995/96, 139–47.

17742. RADO, LISA.   'A perversion that builds Chartres and invents Lear is a pretty good thing': *Mosquitoes* and Faulkner's androgynous imagination. FJ (9:1/2) 1993/94, 13–30.

17743. RAILEY, KEVIN.   Paternalism and liberalism: contending ideologies in *Absalom, Absalom!* FJ (7:1/2) 1991/92, 115–32.

17744. REID, GREGORY.   Wind in August: *Les Fous de Bassan*'s reply to Faulkner. StudCanL (16:2) 1991/92, 112–27.

17745. ROBERTS, DIANE.   Faulkner and Southern womanhood. (Bibl. 1995, 16132.) Rev. by Cheryl Lester in AmS (36:2) 1995, 207–8.

17746. RODMAN, ISAAC.   Irony and isolation: narrative distance in Faulkner's *A Rose for Emily*. FJ (8:2) 1993, 3–12.

17747. ROSS, STEPHEN M.; POLK, NOEL.   Reading Faulkner. *The Sound and the Fury*: glossary and commentary. Jackson; London: Mississippi UP, 1996. pp. xi, 196. (Reading Faulkner.)

17748. SAAD, GABRIEL.   An interview with Juan José Saer. Trans. by Evelyn Tavarelli. FJ (11:1/2) 1995/96, 59–65.

17749. SAMWAY, PATRICK.   Intertextual observations concerning Faulkner's *Mistral*. JSSE (16) 1991, 65–80.

17750. SASS, KAREN R.   At a loss for words: Addie and language in *As I Lay Dying*. FJ (6:2) 1991, 9–21.

17751. SAUNDERS, REBECCA.   On lamentation and the redistribution of possessions: Faulkner's *Absalom, Absalom!* and the new South. MFS (42:4) 1996, 730–62.

17752. SAYRE, ROBERT.   Romanticism and the Faulknerian short story of the early 1930s. JSSE (20) 1993, 65–80.

17753. SCHREIBER, EVELYN JAFFE.   What's love got to do with it? Desire and subjectivity in Faulkner's Snopes Trilogy. FJ (9:1/2) 1993/94, 83–98.

17754. SCOBLIONKO, ANDREW.   Subjectivity and homelessness in *Soldiers' Pay*. FJ (8:1) 1992, 61–71.

17755. SKAGGS, MERRILL MAGUIRE.   Thefts and conversation: Cather and Faulkner. *See* **16847**.

17756. SKINFILL, MAURI.   Faulkner, Franklin, and the sons of the father. *See* **9060**.

17757. —— Reconstructing class in Faulkner's late novels: *The Hamlet* and the discovery of capital. SAF (24:2) 1996, 151–69.

17758. SLAUGHTER, CAROLYN NORMAN.   *Absalom, Absalom!*: 'fluid cradle of events (time)'. FJ (6:2) 1991, 65–84.

17759. Strong, Amy Lovell. Machines and machinations: controlling desires in Faulkner's *Sanctuary*. FJ (9:1/2) 1993/94, 69–81.

17760. Tarquini, Francesco. Dalla saga di Yoknapatawpha al mito di Santa Maria. Letterature d'America (41/42) 1990, 139–79.

17761. Taylor, Nancy Dew. *Go Down, Moses* and the literature of the New World commemoration. FJ (6:1) 1990, 25–32.

17762. Towner, Theresa M. 'How can a Black man ask?': race and self-representation in Faulkner's later fiction. FJ (10:2) 1995, 3–21.

17763. Tribak, Nabila. Money, incest, and the double in Faulkner's *Go Down, Moses*. Letterature d'America (50) 1993, 89–103.

17764. Ujiie, Harumi. W. Faulkner: bunka no fuukei. (W. Faulkner: cultural landscapes.) Tokyo: Kobian Shobo, 1996. pp. 238.

17765. Urgo, Joseph. Deep breathing: Faulknerian reflections on Ricardo Piglia's *Artificial Respiration*. FJ (11:1/2) 1995/96, 51–8.

17766. Valente, Luiz Fernando. Marriages of speaking and hearing: mediation and response in *Absalom, Absalom!* and *Grande Sertão: Veredas*. FJ (11:1/2) 1995/96, 149–64.

17767. Vegh, Beatriz. Introduction: a Latin American Faulkner. FJ (11:1/2) 1995/96, 5–10.

17768. —— *The Wild Palms* and *Las palmeras salvajes*: the southern counterpoint Faulkner/Borges. FJ (11:1/2) 1995/96, 165–79.

17769. —— William Faulkner's works translated into Spanish. FJ (11:1/2) 1995/96, 181–4.

17770. Visser, Irene. Knowing and remembering: *Light in August* as readerly/writerly text. RWT (1:2) 1994, 35–66.

17771. Wall, Carey. *Go Down, Moses*: the collective action of redress. FJ (7:1/2) 1991/92, 151–74.

17772. Watson, James G. Two letters about William Faulkner, 1918. FJ (8:1) 1992, 15–19.

17773. —— (ed.). Thinking of home: William Faulkner's letters to his mother and father, 1918–1925. (Bibl. 1994, 12610.) Rev. by María Eugenia Díaz Sánchez in Atlantis (17:1/2) 1995, 397–9.

17774. Watson, Jay. The failure of forensic storytelling in *Sanctuary*. FJ (6:1) 1990, 47–66.

17775. —— Overdoing masculinity in *Light in August*; or, Joe Christmas and the gender guard. FJ (9:1/2) 1993/94, 149–77.

17776. Watson, Neil. The 'incredibly loud … miss-fire': a sexual reading of *Go Down, Moses*. FJ (9:1/2) 1993/94, 113–23.

17777. Weinstein, Philip M. Diving into the wreck: Faulknerian practice and the imagination of slavery. FJ (10:2) 1995, 23–53.

17778. —— Faulkner's subject: a cosmos no one owns. (Bibl. 1995, 16150.) Rev. by Jean Mullin Yonke in AmS (34:2) 1993, 132–3.

17779. White, Ray Lewis. Anderson , Faulkner, and a unique Al Jackson tale. *See* **16018**.

17780. Williamson, Joel. William Faulkner and Southern history. (Bibl. 1995, 16153.) Rev. by Cheryl Lester in AmS (35:2) 1994, 139–41; by Jonathan Yardley in BkW, 22 Aug. 1996, 3.

17781. Wilmeth, Thomas L. You hope to learn: Flem's self-empowerment through silence in Faulkner's Snopes Trilogy. SECOLR (16:2) 1992, 165–78.

17782. Wilson, Deborah. 'A shape to fill a lack': *Absalom, Absalom!* and the pattern of history. FJ (7:1/2) 1991/92, 61–81.

17783. Wolff, Sally; Watkins, Floyd C. Talking about William

Faulkner: interviews with Jimmy Faulkner and others. Baton Rouge; London: Louisiana State UP, 1996. pp. xviii, 196. (Southern literary studies.)

17784. Wondra, Janet. 'Play' within a play: gaming with language in *Requiem for a Nun*. FJ (8:1) 1992, 43–59.

17785. Wood, Amy Louise. Feminine rebellion and mimicry in Faulkner's *As I Lay Dying*. FJ (9:1/2) 1993/94, 99–112.

17786. Woodbery, Bonnie. The abject in Faulkner's *As I Lay Dying*. LitPs (40:3) 1994, 26–42.

17787. Yarup, Robert L. Faulkner's *The Sound and the Fury*. Exp. (55:1) 1996, 34–7.

17788. Yerkes, David. The reporter's name in *Pylon* and why that's important. FJ (6:2) 1991, 3–8.

17789. Yorifuji, Michio. Faulkner no sekai – sono root. (Faulkner's world: its roots.) Tokyo: Seibido, 1996. pp. 280.

17790. Yunis, Susan S. The narrator of Faulkner's *Barn Burning*. FJ (6:2) 1991, 23–31.

Jessie Fauset

17791. McCaskill, Barbara. The folklore of the coasts in Black women's fiction of the Harlem renaissance. *See* **3293**.

17792. McCoy, Beth A. 'Is this really what you wanted me to be?': the daughter's disintegration in Jessie Redmon Fauset's *There Is Confusion*. MFS (40:1) 1994, 101–17.

17793. McLendon, Jacquelyn Y. The politics of color in the fiction of Jessie Fauset and Nella Larsen. (Bibl. 1995, 16156.) Rev. by Kimberley J. Roberts in TSWL (15:1) 1996, 163–4; by Beverly Lanier Skinner in AL (68:2) 1996, 477–8.

17794. Miller, Nina. Femininity, publicity, and the class division of cultural labor: Jessie Redmon Fauset's *There Is Confusion*. AAR (30:2) 1996, 205–20.

17795. Sisney, Mary F. The view from the outside: Black novels of manners. *In* (pp. 171–85) **96**.

Kenneth Fearing

17796. Barnard, Rita. The Great Depression and the culture of abundance: Kenneth Fearing, Nathanael West, and mass culture in the 1930s. (Bibl. 1995, 16163.) Rev. by Walter Kalaidjian in MFS (42:4) 1996, 837–40; by Jonathan Veitch in AL (68:4) 1996, 864–5.

Raymond Federman

17797. Federman, Raymond. Eine Version meines Lebens: die frühen Jahre. Trans. by Peter Torberg. Augsburg: Maro, 1993. (Toller Bücher, 3.) Rev. by Thomas Irmer in ZAA (42:1) 1994, 82–4.

17798. Hartl, Thomas. Raymond Federman's real fictitious discourses: formulating yet another paradox. Lewiston, NY; Lampeter: Mellen Press, 1995. pp. 158. (Salzburg English & American studies, 19.)

17799. Hartman, Geoffrey. Public memory and its discontents. *See* **13116**.

David Feldshuh

17800. Appler, Keith. Multicultural theater and the White physician. AmDr (5:2) 1996, 57–75.

James Fenton

17801. PORDZIK, RALPH. Postmoderne Lyrik als Negativutopie. Untersuchungen zur Karnevalisierung der Dichtung am Beispiel des *Martian Poet* James Fenton. *See* **15021**.

Lawrence Ferlinghetti

17802. WISKER, ALISTAIR. An anarchist among the floorwalkers: the poetry of Lawrence Ferlinghetti. *In* (pp. 74–94) **4**.

Roberto Fernández

17803. FEBLES, JORGE. A character's indictment of authorial subterfuge: the parody of texts in Roberto G. Fernández. *In* (pp. 21–35) **51**.

Lloyd Fernando

17804. KURTZ, R. Lloyd Fernando's *Scorpion Orchid* and Lord Jim's dilemma: another descendant, in other words. *See* **17058**.

Thomas Hornsby Ferril

17805. BARON, ROBERT C.; LEONARD, STEPHEN J.; NOEL, THOMAS J. (eds). Thomas Hornsby Ferril and the American West. Golden, CO: Fulcrum; Boulder, CO: Center of the American West, Univ. of Colorado at Boulder, 1996. pp. x, 166.

Robert Ferro

17806. DEWEY, JOSEPH. Music for a closing: responses to AIDS in three American novels. *In* (pp. 23–38) **2**.

Padraic Fiacc

17807. DAWE, GERALD; MAC PÓILIN, AODÁN (eds). Ruined pages: selected poems. Belfast: Blackstaff Press, 1994. pp. 171. Rev. by Des O'Rawe in Irish Review (16) 1994, 138–9.

Darrell Figgis

17808. DEANE, PAUL. The death of greatness: Darrell Figgis's *The Return of the Hero*. Notes on Modern Irish Literature (3) 1991, 30–6.
17809. —— Paganism *vs* Christianity: images of priests in contemporary Irish literature. Notes on Modern Irish Literature (8) 1996, 19–24.

Timothy Findley

17810. BAILEY, ANNE GEDDES. Misrepresentations of Vanessa Van Horne: intertextual clues in Timothy Findley's *The Telling of Lies*. ECanW (55) 1995, 191–213.
17811. COOKE, JOHN. The influence of painting on five Canadian writers: Alice Munro, Hugh Hood, Timothy Findley, Margaret Atwood, and Michael Ondaatje. *See* **16077**.
17812. CUDE, WILF. Truth slips in: Timothy Findley's doors of fiction. AntR (105) 1996, 75–90.
17813. FINDLEY, TIMOTHY. Everything I tell you is the truth – except the lies. JCanStud (31:2) 1996, 154–65.
17814. IRVINE, LORNA. Crises of the legitimate: Matt Cohen and Timothy Findley. *See* **17006**.

17815. KRÖLLER, EVA-MARIE. 'Sur les rivages d'un autre âge': Timothy Findley et Evelyn Waugh. Études littéraires (27:1) 1994, 29–41.

17816. KRUK, LAURIE. I want edge: an interview with Timothy Findley. CanL (148) 1996, 115–29.

17817. MARTELL, CECILIA. Unpacking the baggage: 'camp' humour in Timothy Findley's *Not Wanted on the Voyage*. CanL (148) 1996, 96–111.

17818. PENNEE, DONNA. Moral metafiction: counterdiscourse in the novels of Timothy Findley. (Bibl. 1995, 16183.) Rev. by Catherine Hunter in ECanW (55) 1995, 140–6.

17819. ROBERTS, CAROL. The prediction of gesture: Timothy Findley and Canadian theatre. *See* **14129**.

17820. —— Timothy Findley: stories from a life. (Bibl. 1995, 16184.) Rev. by David Ingham in ESCan (22:2) 1996, 244–5.

17821. YORK, LORRAINE M. Front lines: the fiction of Timothy Findley. (Bibl. 1992, 13742.) Rev. by Catherine Hunter in ECanW (55) 1995, 140–6.

17822. —— The other side of dailiness: photography in the works of Alice Munro, Timothy Findley, Michael Ondaatje, and Margaret Laurence. Toronto: ECW Press, 1988. pp. 172, (plates) 6. (Cf. bibl. 1986, 10451.) Rev. by Lorna Irvine in ARCS (18:3) 1988, 399–401.

17823. —— 'The things that are seen in the flashes': Timothy Findley's *Inside Memory* as photographic life writing. MFS (40:3) 1994, 643–56.

Ian Hamilton Finlay

17824. MILNE, DREW. *Adorno's Hut*: Ian Hamilton Finlay's neo-classical rearmament programme. SLJ (23:2) 1996, 69–79.

William Finn

17825. SMART, JEFFREY. Labels are not characters: critical mis-perception of *Falsettoland*. JDTC (10:2) 1996, 61–74.

Jack Finney

17826. HAMPTON, HOWARD. Return of the body snatchers. *See* **13756**.

Ronald Firbank

17827. CLARK, WILLIAM LANE. Degenerate personality: deviant sexuality and race in Ronald Firbank's novels. *In* (pp. 134–55) **12**.

17828. MOORE, STEVEN. Ronald Firbank: an annotated bibliography of secondary materials, 1905–1995. Normal, IL: Dalkey Archive Press, 1996. pp. ix, 154. (Dalkey Archive bibliography, 3.)

Gary Fisher (1962?–1994)

17829. SEDGWICK, EVE KOSOFSKY (ed.). Gary in your pocket: stories and notebooks of Gary Fisher. Introd. by Don Belton. Durham, NC; London: Duke UP, 1996. pp. xii, 291. (Series Q.)

Roy Fisher

17830. SHEPPARD, ROBERT. De-Anglicising the Midlands: the European context of Roy Fisher's *City*. Eng (41:169) 1992, 49–70.

F. Scott Fitzgerald

17831. ACKERLEY, CHRIS. Notes towards Lowry's screenplay of *Tender Is the Night. See* **13380**.

17832. ANASTAS, BENJAMIN. Three ways of being modern: the 'Lost Generation' Trilogy by James R. Mellow. IowaR (23:1) 1993, 161–74.

17833. ANON. (comp.). F. Scott Fitzgerald: centenary exhibition, September 24, 1896 – September 24, 1996: the Matthew J. and Arlyn Bruccoli Collection, the Thomas Cooper Library. *See* **445**.

17834. BAUMGARTEN, MURRAY. Seeing double: Jews in the fiction of F. Scott Fitzgerald, Charles Dickens, Anthony Trollope, and George Eliot. *In* (pp. 44–61) **5**.

17835. BERMAN, RONALD. *The Great Gatsby* and modern times. (Bibl. 1995, 16194.) Rev. by Robert M. Luscher in AL (68:3) 1996, 649–50.

17836. BESSIÈRE, JEAN. F. S. Fitzgerald, univers littéraire, univers américain. Europe (803) 1996, 8–22.

17837. BROOKS, NIGEL. Fitzgerald's *The Great Gatsby* and Glyn's *Three Weeks*. Exp (54:4) 1996, 233–6.

17838. BRUCCOLI, MATTHEW J. Fitzgerald and Hemingway: a dangerous friendship. (Bibl. 1994, 12640.) London: Deutsch, 1996. Rev. by Joyce Carol Oates in TLS, 5 Jan. 1996, 3–4.

17839. —— (ed.). The love of the last tycoon: a western. (Bibl. 1994, 12641.) Rev. by Philip Cohen in AmLH (8:4) 1996, 737–9; by Edward Margolies in EngS (77:3) 1996, 297–8; by Joyce Carol Oates in TLS, 5 Jan. 1996, 3–4.

17840. BRUCCOLI, MATTHEW J.; BAUGHMAN, JUDITH S. Reader's companion to F. Scott Fitzgerald's *Tender Is the Night*. Columbia: South Carolina UP, 1996. pp. xi, 263.

17841. —— —— (eds). F. Scott Fitzgerald on authorship. Columbia: South Carolina UP, 1996. pp. 203.

17842. BRYER, JACKSON R. (ed.). New essays on F. Scott Fitzgerald's neglected stories. Columbia; London: Missouri UP, 1996. pp. xi, 367.

17843. CALLAHAN, JOHN F. F. Scott Fitzgerald's evolving American dream: the 'pursuit of happiness' in *Gatsby, Tender Is the Night*, and *The Last Tycoon*. TCL (42:3) 1996, 374–95.

17844. CAMPI DE CASTRO, NANCY. The archetype of the house in *The Great Gatsby*. Analecta Husserliana (44) 1995, 71–9.

17845. CHÉNETIER, MARC. L'enfer du paradis. Europe (803) 1996, 3–7.

17846. COHEN, PHILIP. Is there a text in this discipline? Textual scholarship and American literary studies. *See* **604**.

17847. DEFAZIO, ALBERT J., III. Fitzgerald and Hemingway. American Literary Scholarship (1993) 125–42; (1994) 167–83; (1995) 173–90.

17848. DIXSAUT, CLAIRE. La galaxie Gatsby. Europe (803) 1996, 23–32.

17849. DOLAN, MARC. Modern lives: a cultural re-reading of the 'Lost Generation'. *See* **17134**.

17850. DONALDSON, SCOTT. A death in Hollywood: F. Scott Fitzgerald remembered. IowaR (26:1) 1996, 105–12.

17851. ERWIN, ROBERT. The good boy. TexR (17:1/2) 1996, 64–79.

17852. FINK, GUIDO. 'Inesprimere l'esprimibile': tre romanzi americani del 1925. *See* **17372**.

17853. HAGEN, BILL.   Malcolm Lowry's 'adjustable blueprint': the screenplay of *Tender Is the Night*. See **13747**.

17854. HEARN, CHARLES R.   F. Scott Fitzgerald and the popular magazine formula story of the twenties. See **1286**.

17855. HEWITT, JESSICA L.   'Owl Eyes' in *The Great Gatsby*. ANQ (9:1) 1996, 26–7.

17856. INTISSAR-ZAUGG, BRIGITTE.   *Tendre est la nuit* ou le rêve d'un ailleurs. Europe (803) 1996, 44–54.

17857. KERR, FRANCES.   Feeling 'half feminine': Modernism and the politics of emotion in *The Great Gatsby*. AL (68:2) 1996, 405–31.

17858. LANAHAN, ELEANOR.   Scottie, the daughter of —: the life of Frances Scott Fitzgerald Lanahan Smith. (Bibl. 1995, 16211.) Rev. by Andy Solomon in BkW, 20 Aug. 1995, 4–5; by Edward J. Rielly in JPC (30:1) 1996, 278–80.

17859. LASALLE, PETER.   The last book. AR (54:1) 1996, 5–19.

17860. LE VOT, ANDRÉ.   Les intermittences du baiser: Fitzgerald et *La Recherche du temps perdu*. Europe (803) 1996, 33–43.

17861. LOZANO, MARIA.   Les voies du silence: à propos de quelques nouvelles de F. S. Fitzgerald. Trans. by Marc Chénetier. Europe (803) 1996, 55–64.

17862. MEYERS, JEFFREY.   Scott Fitzgerald: a biography. (Bibl. 1995, 16212.) Rev. by Joyce Carol Oates in TLS, 5 Jan. 1996, 3–4.

17863. MIRAGLIA, ANNE MARIE.   Texts engendering texts: a Québécois writing of American novels. *In* (pp. 49–60) **51**.

17864. MORELAND, KIM.   The medievalist impulse in American literature: Twain, Adams, Fitzgerald, and Hemingway. See **10216**.

17865. MORTIMER, ROGER.   The Matthew J. and Arlyn Bruccoli collection of F. Scott Fitzgerald. See **518**.

17866. MOTA, MIGUEL; TIESSEN, PAUL (eds).   The cinema of Malcolm Lowry: a scholarly edition of *Tender Is the Night*. See **764**.

17867. NAGAOKA, SADAO.   Tokkou Fitzgerald. (A special lecture on Fitzgerald.) Tokyo: Kobian Shobo, 1996. pp. 300.

17868. O'HARA, KIERON.   'You do not know *why* you dance': comedy in *Under the Volcano*, *Through the Panama*, and *Tender Is the Night*. MalLR (31/32) 1992/93, 68–84.

17869. O'KEEFFE, BERNARD.   On the road. ERev (6:3) 1996, 6–11. (Images of cars in Fitzgerald, Miller, Kerouac.)

17870. RAND, WILLIAM E.   The structure of the outsider in the short fiction of Richard Wright and F. Scott Fitzgerald. CLAJ (40:2) 1996, 230–45.

17871. RANKIN, AUDRIE.   Malcolm Lowry's *Tender Is the Night*: form, structure, spirit. See **14111**.

17872. ROBERTS, DIANE.   Scott Fitzgerald and the Jazz Age. ERev (5:3) 1995, 23–6.

17873. ROULSTON, ROBERT; ROULSTON, HELEN H.   The winding road to West Egg: the artistic development of F. Scott Fitzgerald. (Bibl. 1995, 16216.) Rev. by Kate Rhodes in JAStud (30:2) 1996, 305–6.

17874. SEED, DAVID.   Party-going: the Jazz Age novels of Evelyn Waugh, Wyndham Lewis, F. Scott Fitzgerald and Carl Van Vechten. *In* (pp. 117–34) **34**.

17875. SHIFFMAN, DAN.   'Let's go to Coney Island, old sport': the ethnic sensibility of F. Scott Fitzgerald. PCR (6:1) 1995, 87–96.

17876. SILHOL, ROBERT.   *Tender Is the Night*; or, The rape of the child. LitPs (40:4) 1994, 40–63.

17877. TIESSEN, PAUL (ed.).   A few items culled from what started out to be a sort of preface to a film-script. *See* **14287**.

17878. TUCKER, KENNETH.   Important brush strokes: the significance of two biblical episodes in Fitzgerald's *Tender Is the Night*. ANQ (9:4) 1996, 44–8.

17879. VATANPOUR, SINA.   The American dream and the meretricious game of money and love in Fitzgerald's *The Great Gatsby*. Letterature d'America (50) 1993, 71–87.

17880. WESTBROOK, ROBERT.   Intimate lies: F. Scott Fitzgerald and Sheilah Graham: her son's story. (Bibl. 1995, 16221.) Rev. by Andy Solomon in BkW, 20 Aug. 1995, 4–5.

Zelda Fitzgerald

17881. ANASTAS, BENJAMIN.   Three ways of being modern: the 'Lost Generation' Trilogy by James R. Mellow. *See* **17832**.

17882. KRAMER, PETER D.   How crazy was Zelda? NYTM, 1 Dec. 1996, 106–9.

17883. LANAHAN, ELEANOR (ed.).   Zelda, an illustrated life: the private world of Zelda Fitzgerald. With essays by Peter Kurth and Jane S. Livingston. New York: Abrams, 1996. pp. 127.

17884. NANNEY, LISA.   Zelda Fitzgerald's *Save Me the Waltz* as Southern novel and *Künstlerroman*. *In* (pp. 220–32) **32**.

George Fitzmaurice

17885. DEANE, PAUL.   Paganism *vs* Christianity: images of priests in contemporary Irish literature. *See* **17809**.

Janet Flanner ('Genêt')

17886. KAMENISH, PAULA K.   Naming the crime: responses to the Papin murders from Lacan, Beauvoir, and Flanner. Comparatist (20) 1996, 93–110.

Ian Fleming

17887. LYCETT, ANDREW.   Ian Fleming: the man behind James Bond. (Bibl. 1995, 16225.) Atlanta, GA: Turner, 1995. pp. x, 486, (plates) 16.

17888. PENZLER, OTTO.   Collecting mystery fiction: Ian Fleming's James Bond. *See* **524**.

17889. RIACH, ALAN.   Nobody's children: orphans and their ancestors in popular Scottish fiction after 1945. *In* (pp. 51–83) **115**.

John Gould Fletcher

17890. RUDOLPH, LEIGHTON; CARPENTER, LUCAS; SIMPSON, ETHEL C. (eds).   Selected letters of John Gould Fletcher. Fayetteville: Arkansas UP, 1996. pp. xxvii, 279. (John Gould Fletcher, 7.)

Homer Eon Flint

17891. BIRKEN, LAWRENCE.   *The Blind Spot* in science fiction: a reconsideration. Extrapolation (37:2) 1996, 139–50.

Michael Foley

17892.   MARKEN, RON.   Michael Foley, Robert Johnstone and Frank Ormsby: three Ulster poets in the *GO* situation. *In* (pp. 130–43) **86**.

Barbara Newhall Follett

17893.   MYERS, MITZI.   Of mimicry and (wo)man: *infans* or forked tongue? *See* **11106**.

17894.   WOOD, NAOMI J.   Who writes and who is written? Barbara Newhall Follett and typing the natural child. ChildLit (23) 1995, 45–65.

Horton Foote

17895.   MOORE, BARBARA; YELLIN, DAVID G. (eds).   Horton Foote's three trips to Bountiful. *See* **13998**.

17896.   PORTER, LAURIN R.   An interview with Horton Foote. StAD (6:2) 1991, 177–94.

17897.   WATSON, CHARLES S.   Beyond the commercial media: Horton Foote's procession of defeated men. StAD (8:2) 1993, 175–87.

Carolyn Forché

17898.   BEDIENT, CALVIN.   Poetry and silence at the end of the century. Salmagundi (111) 1996, 195–207.

17899.   HELLE, ANITA.   Elegy as history: three women poets 'by the century's deathbed'. SAtlR (61:2) 1996, 51–68.

'Ford Madox Ford' (Ford Madox Hueffer)

17900.   CHOUDHURY, SHEILA LAHIRI.   D. H. Lawrence and Ford Madox Ford: a brief encounter. Études Lawrenciennes (9) 1993, 97–109.

17901.   FORTUNATI, VITA.   The visual arts and the novel: the contrasting cases of Ford Madox Ford and D. H. Lawrence. Études Lawrenciennes (10) 1994, 129–43.

17902.   MONTEIRO, GEORGE.   'There *is* a figure in the carpet': James, Hueffer, and Garnett. *See* **11631**.

17903.   MORRISSON, MARK.   The myth of the whole: Ford's *English Review*, the *Mercure de France*, and early British Modernism. *See* **1325**.

17904.   ROSSI, UMBERTO.   No sense of an ending: the difficulty of ending a (hi)story in European and American World War I narratives. Krieg und Literatur (1) 1995, 79–99.

17905.   SAUNDERS, MAX.   Ford Madox Ford: a dual life: vol. 1, The world before the war. Oxford; New York: OUP, 1996. pp. xvii, 632, (plates) 8. Rev. by Ian Hamilton in LRB (18:12) 1996, 10; by Tony Tanner in TLS, 16 Feb. 1996, 3–4.

17906.   —— Ford Madox Ford: a dual life: vol. 2, The after-war world. Oxford; New York: OUP, 1996. pp. xiv, 696, (plates) 8. Rev. by John Taylor in TLS, 1 Nov. 1996, 4–5.

17907.   STANG, SONDRA J.; COCHRAN, KAREN (eds).   The correspondence of Ford Madox Ford and Stella Bowen. (Bibl. 1995, 16237.) Rev. by Joseph Wiesenfarth in Review (17) 1995, 85–94.

17908.   WIESENFARTH, JOSEPH.   The Ford–Bowen correspondence. Review (17) 1995, 85–94 (review-article).

17909.   —— 'Schreibe, wie du sprichst': *Ford Madox Ford's fiction. In* (pp. 137–48) **73**.

Jesse Hill Ford

17910. CHENEY, ANNE. The life and letters of Jesse Hill Ford, Southern writer: with annotations and commentary. Lewiston, NY; Lampeter: Mellen Press, 1996. pp. liv, 485. (Studies in American literature, 19.) Rev. by Ray Browne in JPC (30:3) 1996, 263–4; by Madison Jones in SAtlR (61:4) 1996, 141–3.

Richard Ford (1944–)

17911. BÉRUBÉ, RENALD. L'écrivain comme journaliste sportif (ou vice versa): *The Sportswriter* de Richard Ford. Études littéraires (28:2) 1995, 81–94.
17912. DUPUY, EDWARD. The confessions of an ex-suicide: relenting and recovering in Richard Ford's *The Sportswriter*. SoLJ (23:1) 1990, 93–103.

Richard Foreman

17913. AHRENDS, GÜNTER. The nature and function of cruelty in the theatre of Artaud and Foreman. Forum modernes Theater (9:1) 1994, 3–12.
17914. FUCHS, ELINOR. Today I am a fountain pen: an interview with Richard Foreman. Theater (25:1) 1994, 82–6.
17915. MARRANCA, BONNIE. Teatr ontologiczno-histeryczny Richarda Foremana. (Richard Foreman's ontological-hysterical theatre.) Dialog (1996:8) 61–70.

María Irene Fornés

17916. CUMMINGS, SCOTT T. Fornés's odd couple: *Oscar and Bertha* at the Magic Theatre. JDTC (8:2) 1994, 147–56.
17917. KENT, ASSUNTA. *And What of the Night?*: Fornés' apocalyptic vision of American greed and poverty. JDTC (7:2) 1993, 133–47.
17918. KENT, ASSUNTA BARTOLOMUCCI. María Irene Fornés and her critics. Westport, CT; London: Greenwood Press, 1996. pp. xi, 230. (Contributions in drama and theatre studies, 70.)
17919. MALINOWSKA, BARBARA. Beyond the Absurd: language games in the theatre of María Irene Fornés, Samuel Beckett, and Eugène Ionesco. *See* **16337**.
17920. MOROFF, DIANE LYNN. Fornés: theater in the present tense. Ann Arbor: Michigan UP, 1996. pp. 155. (Cf. bibl. 1993, 12615.)
17921. ROSSINI, JON. Fighting passions, fighting ethnicities: another look at *Sarita*. TexPres (16) 1995, 85–9.

Leon Forrest

17922. DUBEY, MADHU. The mythos of gumbo: Leon Forrest talks about *Divine Days*. Callaloo (19:3) 1996, 588–602.

E. M. Forster

17923. BAKSHI, PARMINDER KAUR. Distant desire: homoerotic codes and the subversion of the English novel in E. M. Forster's fiction. New York; Frankfurt; Bern; Paris: Lang, 1996. pp. xii, 250. (Sexuality and literature, 5.)
17924. BEAUMAN, NICOLA. Morgan: a biography of E. M. Forster. (Bibl. 1994, 12675.) Rev. by Dennis Drabelle in BkW, 3 Apr. 1994, 8, 12.

17925. Buck, R. A.   Reading Forster's style: face actions and social scripts in *Maurice. See* **2592**.

17926. Burnett, A. D.   A literary ghost: William Plomer's proposed biographical account of E. M. Forster. RES (47:185) 1996, 53–8.

17927. Caporaletti, Silvana.   Il lato oscuro della scienza in *The Machine Stops* di E. M. Forster. Textus (8:1) 1995, 153–72.

17928. Childs, Peter.   'One may as well begin with Helen's letters ...': corresponding but not connecting in the writings of E. M. Forster. Prose Studies (19:2) 1996, 200–10.

17929. Das, Prasanta.   'The Common Iora' in *A Passage to India.* NQ (43:1) 1996, 54–5.

17930. Doloff, Steven.   Forster's *The Road from Colonus.* Exp (54:4) 1996, 229–30.

17931. Dorland, Tamera.   'Contrary to the prevailing current'? Homoeroticism and the voice of maternal law in Forster's *The Other Boat.* Style (29:3) 1995, 474–97.

17932. Enos, Michael R.   'The head of Eros': same-sex desire, self-surveillance, and the male body. Études Lawrenciennes (12) 1995/96, 137–68. (D. H. Lawrence, E. M. Forster, Thomas Mann.)

17933. Foata, Anne.   The knocking at the door: a fantasy on fate, Forster and Beethoven's Fifth. CVE (44) 1996, 135–45.

17934. Freedgood, Elaine.   E. M. Forster's queer nation: taking the closet to the colony in *A Passage to India. In* (pp. 123–44) **9**.

17935. Gilchrist, Susan Y.   D. H. Lawrence and E. M. Forster: a failed friendship. Études Lawrenciennes (9) 1993, 127–38.

17936. Kerman, Joseph.   Representing a relationship: notes on a Beethoven concerto. Representations (39) 1992, 80–101.

17937. Lago, Mary.   E. M. Forster: a literary life. (Bibl. 1995, 16257.) Rev. by Judith Scherer Herz in ELT (39:2) 1996, 225–8.

17938. Lane, Christopher.   Volatile desire: ambivalence and distress in Forster's colonial narratives. *In* (pp. 188–212) **132**.

17939. Lavin, Audrey A. P.   Aspects of the novelist: E. M. Forster's pattern and rhythm. (Bibl. 1995, 16259.) Rev. by Alistair M. Duckworth in ELT (39:4) 1996, 494–7.

17940. Levine, June Perry.   The functions of the narrator's voice in literature and film: Forster and Ivory's *Maurice. See* **13918**.

17941. Loney, Douglas.   C. S. Lewis' debt to E. M. Forster's *'The Celestial Omnibus' and Other Stories.* Mythlore (21:1) 1995, 14–22.

17942. May, Brian.   Modernism and other modes in Forster's *The Longest Journey.* TCL (42:2) 1996, 234–57.

17943. Meyers, Doris.   Breaking free: the closed universe theme in E. M. Forster, Owen Barfield, and C. S. Lewis. *See* **16198**.

17944. Papazoglou, Dimitra.   'The fever of Hellenism': the influence of Ancient Greece on the work of E. M. Forster. Athens: Parousia, 1995. pp. vi, 278. (Parousia, 34.) (Cf. bibl. 1995, 16261.)

17945. Rapport, Nigel.   The prose and the passion: anthropology, literature, and the writing of E. M. Forster. (Bibl. 1995, 16262.) Rev. by Michael Bell in YES (26) 1996, 310–12.

17946. Stern, Michael Lynn.   'It has been itself a dream': the oneiric plot of *Howards End.* LitPs (41:1/2) 1995, 19–36.

17947. Tambling, Jeremy (ed.).   E. M. Forster. (Bibl. 1995, 16267.) Rev. by J. H. Stape in ELT (39:1) 1996, 88–91; by Kathleen Watson in NQ (43:4) 1996, 490–1.

David Foster

17948. RIEMER, A. P.   Maverick voices: the novels of David Foster and Robin Wallace-Crabbe. CritS (6:1) 1994, 125–32.

John Fowles

17949. ARLETT, ROBERT.   Epic voices: inner and global impulse in the contemporary American and British novel. *See* **14375**.

17950. AUBREY, JAMES R.   Jungian 'synchronicity' and John Fowles's *The Magus*. NCL (24:2) 1994, 11–12.

17951. BALSAMO, GIAN.   The narrative text as historical artifact: the case of John Fowles. *In* (pp. 127–52) **44**.

17952. BEVIS, RICHARD.   Actaeon's sin: the 'previous iconography' of Fowles's *The Ebony Tower*. TCL (42:1) 1996, 114–23.

17953. BRANDT, PETER.   Somewhere else in the forest. TCL (42:1) 1996, 145–64. (*Daniel Martin*.)

17954. BROICH, ULRICH.   Muted postmodernism: the contemporary British short story. *See* **14415**.

17955. FABER, PAMELA; WALLHEAD, CELIA.   The lexical field of visual perception in *The French Lieutenant's Woman* by John Fowles. *See* **2612**.

17956. FOWLES, JOHN.   Behind *The Magus*. TCL (42:1) 1996, 58–68.

17957. —— VIPOND, DIANNE.   'An unholy inquisition'. TCL (42:1) 1996, 12–28. (Interview.)

17958. GRIGORESCU, DAN (postscr.).   Iubita locotenentului francez. (The French lieutenant's woman.) Bucharest: Univers, 1994. pp. 560.

17959. HARDING, BRIAN.   Comparative metafictions of history: E. L. Doctorow and John Fowles. *In* (pp. 253–72) **34**.

17960. LANDRUM, DAVID.   Rewriting Marx: emancipation and restoration in *The French Lieutenant's Woman*. TCL (42:1) 1996, 103–13.

17961. LOE, THOMAS.   Design and meaning in *The Ebony Tower*. JSSE (25) 1995, 32–47.

17962. LORENZ, PAUL H.   Heraclitus against the barbarians: John Fowles's *The Magus*. TCL (42:1) 1996, 69–87.

17963. LÖSCHNIGG, MARTIN.   History and the search for identity: reconstructing the past in recent English novels. *See* **14605**.

17964. MARTÍNEZ, MARÍA JESÚS.   Astarte's game: variations in John Fowles's *The Enigma*. TCL (42:1) 1996, 124–44.

17965. NEARY, JOHN.   Something and nothingness: the fiction of John Updike & John Fowles. (Bibl. 1993, 12661.) Rev. by George J. Searles in MFS (40:2) 1994, 379–80.

17966. ONEGA, SUSANA.   Self, world, and art in the fiction of John Fowles. TCL (42:1) 1996, 29–56.

17967. SIBLEY, JOAN M.   The John Fowles papers at the Harry Ransom Humanities Research Center, the University of Texas at Austin. *See* **539**.

17968. SIMONETTI, MARIE-CLAIRE.   The blurring of time in *The French Lieutenant's Woman*, the novel and the film. *See* **14214**.

17969. STEED, TONIA.   Exploring the cave: the search for a feminist mimesis in *The French Lieutenant's Woman*. *See* **14245**.

17970. TARBOX, KATHERINE.   *The French Lieutenant's Woman* and the evolution of narrative. TCL (42:1) 1996, 88–102.

17971. TUCKER, STEPHANIE.   Despair not, neither to presume: *The French Lieutenant's Woman*: a screenplay. *See* **14294**.

17972. WARBURTON, EILEEN.   Ashes, ashes, we all fall down: *Ourika, Cinderella,* and *The French Lieutenant's Woman.* TCL (42:1) 1996, 165–86.

17973. WILSON, RAYMOND J., III.   '*Et in Arcadia ego*' in John Fowles's *A Maggot*: postmodern utopia. Analecta Husserliana (44) 1995, 367–78.

17974. ZANDER, ANDELA.   '*Spot the source*': Wilkie Collins' *The Moonstone* und John Fowles' *The French Lieutenant's Woman. See* **10723**.

Paula Fox

17975. GENUNG, JEANNE.   Persistence of vision? ArizEB (36:1) 1993, 28–33.

Janet Frame

17976. HANSSON, KARIN.   The unstable manifold: Janet Frame's challenge to determinism. Lund: Lund UP, 1996. pp. 149. (Lund studies in English, 87.)

17977. PANNY, JUDITH DELL.   I have what I gave: the fiction of Janet Frame. (Bibl. 1993, 12683.) Rev. by Marion Spies in ZAA (42:3) 1994, 278–80.

17978. REIF-HÜLSER, MONIKA.   'Glass beads of fantasy' – Janet Frame's *Faces in the Water*; or, The enigma of identity. YREAL (12) 1996, 179–202.

Kathleen Fraser

17979. KINNAHAN, LINDA A.   Poetics of the feminine: authority and literary tradition in William Carlos Williams, Mina Loy, Denise Levertov, and Kathleen Fraser. (Bibl. 1994, 12714.) Rev. by Corinne E. Blackmer in AmLH (8:1) 1996, 130–53.

David French

17980. NUNN, ROBERT.   The subjects of *Salt-Water Moon.* THC (12:1) 1991, 3–21.

Marilyn French

17981. BIZZINI, SILVIA CAPORALE.   Power politics: literature and Foucauldian analysis. *See* **15296**.

Philip Freund

17982. COLAKIS, MARIANTHE.   What Jocasta knew: alternative versions of the Oedipus myth. *See* **17386**.

Kinky Friedman

17983. MULLER, ADRIAN.   The Kinkster writes again: an interview with Kinky Friedman. AD (29:1) 1996, 38–42.

Brian Friel

17984. ANDREWS, ELMER.   The art of Brian Friel: neither reality nor dreams. (Bibl. 1995, 16290.) Rev. by Anthony Roche in IUR (26:1) 1996, 179–81.

17985. BONACCORSO, RICHARD.   Personal devices: two representative stories by Brian Friel. ColbyQ (32:2) 1996, 93–9.

17986. BRESLIN, JOHN.   Brian Friel: dancing from Philadelphia to Lughnasa. Critic (46:1) 1991, 74–80.

17987. BURKE, PATRICK. 'Both heard and imagined': music as structuring principle in the plays of Brian Friel. *In* (pp. 43–52) **112**.

17988. CAVE, RICHARD ALLEN. The city *versus* the village. *In* (pp. 281–96) **60**.

17989. CIONI, FERNANDO. *Scrutinizing the intruder*: figure narranti in alcuni testi teatrali inglesi contemporanei. *See* **16931**.

17990. COTTREAU, DEBORAH. Friel and Beckett: the politics of language. *In* (pp. 160–9) **60**.

17991. CULLINGFORD, ELIZABETH BUTLER. British Romans and Irish Carthaginians: anticolonial metaphor in Heaney, Friel, and McGuinness. PMLA (111:2) 1996, 222–39.

17992. FRIEL, JUDY. Living with Lughnasa. Critic (47:4) 1993, 2–15.

17993. KENNEALLY, MICHAEL. The transcendent impulse in contemporary Irish drama. *In* (pp. 272–82) **49**.

17994. LANTERS, JOSÉ. Violence and sacrifice in Brian Friel's *The Gentle Island* and *Wonderful Tennessee*. IUR (26:1) 1996, 163–76.

17995. MAZHAR, AMAL ALY. The symbolic significance of place in Brian Friel's *Philadelphia, Here I Come* and Mahmoud Diab's *A Messenger from the Village of Temira*. *In* (pp. 345–57) **60**.

17996. MOLINO, MICHAEL R. The net of language: marginalization, resistance, and difference in contemporary Irish literature. AJSem (11:1/2) 1994, 197–213.

17997. REGAN, STEPHEN. *Translations* by Brian Friel. ERev (6:1) 1995, 38–41.

17998. RETTBERG, SCOTT. The new frontier as a vast restless place: the Irish narrative of the American dream in Brian Friel's *Philadelphia, Here I Come*, Tom Murphy's *Conversations on a Homecoming*, and Joseph O'Connor's *Red Roses and Petrol*. TexPres (17) 1996, 58–64.

17999. SULLIVAN, HANNAH. The role of the Classics in Brian Friel's *Translations*. ERev (7:2) 1996, 16–19.

Robert Frost

18000. ABSHEAR-SEALE, LISA. A lifetime of thinking aloud: reassessing Robert Frost's public talks and readings. RFR (1995) 36–44.

18001. —— 'What Catullus means by *mens animi*': Robert Frost's *Kitty Hawk*. RFR (1993) 37–46.

18002. ANGYAL, ANDREW J. From Swedenborg to William James: the shaping of Frost's religious beliefs. RFR (1994) 69–81.

18003. BAGBY, GEORGE F. Frost and the book of nature. (Bibl. 1994, 12730.) Rev. by Donald J. Greiner in RFR (1994) 110–12; by George Monteiro in Review (18) 1996, 209–15.

18004. BAKER, CHRISTOPHER. Frost's *After Apple-Picking* as hypnotic vision. RFR (1994) 28–32.

18005. BENSON, JACKSON J. A friendship with consequences: Robert Frost and Wallace Stegner. SDR (34:2) 1996, 7–23.

18006. BENTLEY, LOUISE. Robert Frost: a man of many reasons. TPB (30) 1993, 6–14.

18007. —— You think the talk is all (Robert Frost's poetic conversational power). RFR (1992) 52–7.

18008. BRANNON, BARBARA. Robert Frost and the Conklings: an added chapter of 'the Frost story'. RFR (1996) 71–87.

18009. Brodsky, Joseph; Heaney, Seamus; Walcott, Derek. Homage to Robert Frost. New York: Farrar, Straus, & Giroux, 1996. pp. 117.

18010. Brogunier, Joseph.   Walking my dog in *Sand Dunes*. *See* **10932**.

18011. Brooks, Cleanth.   The humanities: liberator of mind and spirit. *In* (pp. 162–75) **79**.

18012. Bush, Harold K., Jr.   Robert Frost writing the myth of America: rereading *The Gift Outright*. RFR (1995) 45–55.

18013. Cappeluti, Jo-Anne.   For once, then, something: the sublime reality of fiction in Robert Frost. RFR (1993) 86–92.

18014. Cooper, David D.   Looking beyond the picture: Robert Frost's *For Once, Then, Something*. RFR (1993) 47–9.

18015. Cramer, Jeffrey S.   Forgotten Frost: a study of the uncollected and unpublished poetry of Robert Frost. RFR (1992) 1–27.

18016. ⸻ Robert Frost among his poems: a literary companion to the poet's own biographical contexts and associations. Jefferson, NC; London: McFarland, 1996. pp. viii, 296. Rev. by Earl J. Wilcox in RFR (1996) 99–100.

18017. Doyle, T. Douglas.   The cold in New England narrative: *sangfroid* in Frost's *Out, Out —*. RFR (1995) 71–2.

18018. Dubinsky, James Michael.   War and rumors of war in Frost. RFR (1995) 1–22.

18019. Ellis, John.   Robert Frost's four types of belief in *Birches*. RFR (1993) 70–4.

18020. Fleissner, Robert F.   Frost's road taken. New York; Frankfurt; Bern; Paris: Lang, 1996. pp. xv, 250. (Modern American literature, 7.)

18021. ⸻ 'Real cool' fire and ice: Brooks and Frost. *See* **16581**.

18022. ⸻ The road elected: a Wordsworthian–Frost synthesis by Grace Noll Crowell. *See* **12849**.

18023. ⸻ 'Spot of time' in Frost: Beddoès, Vaughan – or Wordsworth in *Stopping by the Woods*? *See* **8381**.

18024. Francis, Lesley Lee.   The Frost family's adventure in poetry: sheer morning gladness at the brim. (Bibl. 1995, 16313.) Rev. by George Monteiro in RFR (1994) 106–10; by Lewis Klausner in AL (68:1) 1996, 255–6.

18025. ⸻ Robert Frost and Helen Thomas revisited. RFR (1993) 77–85.

18026. Frattali, Steven V.   Frost's critique of humanism: a rereading of *Directive*. RFR (1994) 94–100.

18027. Gerber, Philip.   Frost to Mrs Boyle: a 'lost' holograph recovered. RFR (1996) 36–46.

18028. Hall, Dorothy Judd.   Robert Frost's hidden *figura*. RFR (1992) 29–32.

18029. Heaney, Seamus.   Above the brim: on Robert Frost. Salmagundi (88/89) 1990/91, 275–94.

18030. Hoffman, Daniel.   Robert Frost: the symbols a poem makes. GetR (7:1) 1994, 101–12.

18031. Horton, Merrill.   Anthropomorphism in the poetry of Robert Frost. RFR (1994) 63–7.

18032. Iadonisi, Richard A.   (In)felicitous space: the interior landscape of *Snow*. RFR (1996) 47–53.

18033. INGEBRETSEN, ED. Robert Frost's star in a stone boat: a grammar of belief. San Francisco, CA: Catholic Scholars Press, 1994. pp. vii, 300. Rev. by Peter J. Stanlis in RFR (1996) 94–8.

18034. INGEBRETSEN, EDWARD J. 'Design of darkness to appall': religious terror in the poetry of Robert Frost. RFR (1993) 50–7.

18035. ISITT, LARRY. Dark climber: Robert Frost's spiritual ambivalence in *Birches*. RFR (1994) 13–16.

18036. JACKSON, SARAH R. Frost in Texas: lecture tour 1933. RFR (1995) 26–35.

18037. —— Sounds and sights of home from Robert Frost and Andrew Wyeth: the sounds and sights of New England. RFR (1993) 29–36.

18038. KATZ, SANDRA L. Robert Frost, humorist. RFR (1991) 24–9.

18039. KEARNS, KATHERINE. Robert Frost and a poetics of appetite. (Bibl. 1995, 16316.) Rev. by Judith Oster in RFR (1994) 118–21; by Stephen Matterson in YES (26) 1996, 334.

18040. LAKRITZ, ANDREW M. Modernism and the Other in Stevens, Frost, and Moore. Gainesville: Florida UP, 1996. pp. xi, 218.

18041. LeVAY, JOHN. Frost's *The Black Cottage*. Exp (54:2) 1996, 91–2.

18042. LIEBMAN, SHELDON W. Robert Frost, romantic. TCL (42:4) 1996, 417–37.

18043. LLOYD-KIMBREL, E. D. A condition of complete simplicity: poetic returns and Frost's *Directive*. See **17529**.

18044. McGAVRAN, DOROTHY H. Building community: houses and other structures in the poetry of Frost and Ransom. RFR (1994) 1–12.

18045. MADIGAN, MARK J. A newly-discovered Robert Frost letter to Dorothy Canfield Fisher. See **16684**.

18046. MARKS, ANDREW R. The rabbi and the poet: Victor Reichert and Robert Frost. Alton, NH: Andover Green, 1994. pp. xiii, 48. Rev. by Earl J. Wilcox in RFR (1996) 99–100.

18047. MEYERS, JEFFREY. An earring for erring: Robert Frost and Kay Morrison. ASch (65:2) 1996, 219–41.

18048. —— Robert Frost: a biography. Boston, MA: Houghton Mifflin; London: Constable, 1996. pp. xvi, 424, (plates) 16. Rev. by Helen Vendler in LRB (18:13) 1996, 3, 5–6; by David Herd in TLS, 30 Aug., 1996, 4–5.

18049. MIEDER, WOLFGANG. Good proverbs make good Vermonters: a study of regional proverbs in the United States. See **3329**.

18050. MILLER, LEWIS H., JR. *Snow*: Frost's drama of little people. RFR (1994) 47–51.

18051. MONTEIRO, GEORGE. Frost organized. Review (18) 1996, 209–15 (review-article).

18052. —— A pre-publication version of Robert Frost's *November*. RFR (1991) 5–6.

18053. —— (ed.). For glory and for use: Robert Frost at Brown University. GetR (7:1) 1994, 89–99.

18054. NATHAN, RHODA. 'Perfect and upright'? Frost's fidelity to Hebrew scripture in *A Masque of Reason*. SHum (19:1) 1992, 58–67.

18055. OSTER, JUDITH. Toward Robert Frost: the reader and the poet. (Bibl. 1992, 13892.) Rev. by Earl J. Wilcox in RFR (1992) 69–71; by William H. Pritchard in ASch (62:3) 1993, 464–6.

18056. OSTER, JUDY. Whose Frost? The biographer, the poet, and the reader. RFR (1996) 1–11.

18057. Parfitt, Matthew.   Robert Frost's *Modern Georgics*. RFR (1996) 54–70.

18058. Pellegrino, Joe.   Frost, Schopenhauer, and *The Trial by Existence*. RFR (1993) 93–100.

18059. Perrine, Laurence.   Provide, provide. RFR (1992) 33–9.

18060. Poirier, Richard; Richardson, Mark (eds).   Collected poems, prose & plays. New York: Library of America, 1995. pp. 1036. (Library of America, 81.) Rev. by Helen Vendler in LRB (18:13) 1996, 3, 5–6.

18061. Richardson, Mark.   Frost's *Closed for Good*: editorial and interpretive problems. RFR (1996) 23–35.

18062. —— The misdating of a 1936 letter from Robert Frost to Leonidas W. Payne, Jr. RFR (1995) 23–5.

18063. —— Parables of vocation: Frost and Pound in the villages of (Gingrich's?) America. ELit (23:1) 1996, 99–123.

18064. Roman, Camille.   Robert Frost and three female modern poets: Amy Lowell, Louise Bogan, and Edna Millay. *See* **16486**.

18065. Roth, Elizabeth Elam.   Terror and tragedy: divergent roads in the poetry of Robert Frost and Joseph Brodsky. CCTE (61) 1996, 9–18.

18066. Sanders, David A.   Looking through the glass: Frost's *After Apple-Picking* and Paul's 1 Corinthians. RFR (1996) 12–22.

18067. Scott, Mark.   Andrew Lang's *Scythe Song* becomes Robert Frost's *Mowing*: Frost's practice of poetry. *See* **11756**.

18068. Sheehy, Donald G.   The correspondence of Robert Frost and Marie A. Hodge (1913–16). RFR (1994) 82–93.

18069. —— Measure for measure: the Frostian classicism of Timothy Steele. RFR (1995) 73–97.

18070. Stanlis, Peter J.   Dualism: the basis of Robert Frost's philosophy. RFR (1994) 33–46.

18071. Summerlin, Charles Timothy.   The Romantic absolute in Frost's *Home Burial*. RFR (1994) 53–7.

18072. Tuten, Nancy L.   *The Seekonk Woods*: Kinnell's Frostian 'Directive' to the wilderness. RFR (1992) 45–51.

18073. Vandenberg, Peter.   Prosody as meaning in *To the Thawing Wind* and *Home Burial*. RFR (1994) 17–22.

18074. Wakefield, Richard.   Making snug in the limitless: Frost's *Time Out*. RFR (1995) 56–61.

18075. Walsh, John Evangelist.   Into my own: the English years of Robert Frost, 1912–1915. (Bibl. 1989, 9709.) Rev. by Earl J. Wilcox in RFR (1992) 68–9.

18076. Ware, Tracy.   A Canadian source for Frost's *Design*? *See* **12098**.

18077. Watterson, William Collins.   Gerontion as jokester: humor and anxiety in Robert Frost's *Directive*. *See* **12511**.

18078. Zubizarretta, John.   Eliot's *Gerontion* and Frost's *An Old Man's Winter Night*: counterparts of Modernism. *See* **17580**.

Christopher Fry

18079. Bak, John S.   'little death-watch beetle': Nicholas Devize as the Devil in Christopher Fry's *The Lady's Not for Burning*. NCL (23:5) 1993, 6–8.

Northrop Frye

18080. DENHAM, ROBERT D. Northrop Frye: letters and notebooks, a selection. Shen (44:3) 1994, 26–53.

18081. HART, JONATHAN. Poetics and culture: unity, difference, and the case of Northrop Frye. *See* **15486**.

Athol Fugard

18082. COLLERAN, JEANNE. Re-situating Fugard, re-thinking revolutionary theatre. *See* **13560**.

18083. FUGARD, ATHOL. Cousins: a memoir. Johannesburg: Witwatersrand UP, 1994. pp. 106. Rev. by Dennis Walder in SARB (42) 1996, 15–16.

18084. McCOY, JAMES A. Potatoes, beets and *radishes?*: a divergence of critical opinion concerning imagery and the character of Marius as symbol in Fugard's *The Road to Mecca*. NCL (24:2) 1994, 2–3.

18085. RAGUZ, JENNIFER. Cut that speech or starve! Techniques for avoidance of South African state censorship in Athol Fugard's *My Children! My Africa!* and Zakes Mda's *Banned*. TexPres (16) 1995, 80–4.

18086. RUSSO, BRIAN C. Efficacy *versus* representation: segregated dramatic traditions under apartheid. TexPres (12) 1991, 83–7.

18087. SUTTON, BRIAN. Fugard's *Master Harold ... and the Boys*. Exp (54:2) 1996, 120–3.

Michiyo Fukaya (1953–1987)

18088. SHERVINGTON, GWENDOLYN L. (ed.). A fire is burning, it is in me: the life and writings of Michiyo Fukaya. Norwich, VT: New Victoria, 1996. pp. 181.

William Fulford

18089. SIMPSON, ROGER. William Fulford: an Arthurian reclaimed. *See* **5257**.

Henry Blake Fuller

18090. ANDERSON, DAVID D. Sherwood Anderson , Henry Blake Fuller, James T. Farrell, and the Midwestern city as metaphor and reality. *See* **15975**.

18091. BURNS, WILLIAM D. *The Chevalier of Pensieri-Vani*: Henry Fuller's not-so-elusive anatomy. RMRLL (50:2) 1996, 147–63.

Roy Fuller

18092. FULLER, ROY. Spanner and pen: post-war memoirs. (Bibl. 1991, 13055.) Rev. by Neil Powell in PN Review (18:2) 1991, 30–3.

18093. POWELL, NEIL. Roy Fuller: writer and society. (Bibl. 1995, 16333.) Rev. by Ian Sansom in TLS, 26 Jan. 1996, 24.

18094. SMITH, STEVEN E. Roy Fuller: a bibliography. Aldershot: Scolar Press; Brookfield, VT: Ashgate, 1996. pp. xiv, 216.

Alice Fulton

18095. PETOSKEY, BARBARA J. Alice Fulton's powers of poetry. WD (71:9) 1991, 36–9.

William Gaddis

18096. BRUNEL, JEAN-LOUIS. *Carpenter's Gothic*; ou, Le temps des faussaires. Études littéraires (28:2) 1995, 57–65.

18097. COMNES, GREGORY. The ethics of indeterminacy in the novels of William Gaddis. (Bibl. 1995, 16335.) Rev. by Peter Wolfe in MFS (40:2) 1994, 375–7; by Susan Strehle in ConLit (37:1) 1996, 145–54.

18098. KIHARA, YOSHIHIKO. 'A patchwork of conceits, borrowings, deceptions': style in William Gaddis's *Carpenter's Gothic. See* **2658**.

18099. STREHLE, SUSAN. Satire beyond the norm. *See* **14736**.

Ernest J. Gaines

18100. BEAVERS, HERMAN. Wrestling angels into song: the fictions of Ernest J. Gaines and James Alan McPherson. (Bibl. 1995, 16340.) Rev. by Frank W. Shelton in SoQ (34:3) 1996, 149–51.

18101. DOYLE, MARY ELLEN. The best of *Bloodline*: 'camcorder' narration in two stories by Ernest Gaines. JSSE (18) 1992, 63–70.

18102. FOLKS, JEFFREY J. Ernest Gaines and the New South. SoLJ (24:1) 1991, 32–46.

18103. GAUDET, MARCIA. The failure of traditional religion in Ernest Gaines' short stories. JSSE (18) 1992, 81–9.

18104. LOWE, JOHN (ed.). Conversations with Ernest Gaines. (Bibl. 1995, 16344.) Rev. by Frank W. Shelton in SoQ (34:3) 1996, 149–51.

18105. LUSCHER, ROBERT M. The visionary in Ernest Gaines's *Bloodline*. JSSE (18) 1992, 71–80.

18106. PAPA, LEE. 'His feet on your neck': the new religion in the works of Ernest J. Gaines. AAR (27:2) 1993, 187–93.

Zona Gale

18107. RHOADES, LYNN. Maid or writer? The rhetoric of conformity and rebellion in *Miss Lulu Bett*. Midamerica (23) 1996, 73–89.

Tess Gallagher

18108. LEVINE-KEATING, HELANE. The bright shadow: images of the double in women's poetry. *In* (pp. 166–84) **109**.

18109. TANNEHILL, ARLENE. 'No saint or hero ... / Brings dangerous tokens to the new era': Derek Mahon and Tess Gallagher's revisions of Yeats's *The Magi. In* (pp. 47–69) **58**.

Mavis Gallant

18110. BESNER, NEIL K. The light of imagination: Mavis Gallant's fiction. (Bibl. 1988, 7553.) Rev. by John Hoey in ARCS (18:4) 1988, 497–9.

18111. LEITH, LINDA. The scream: Mavis Gallant's *A Fairly Good Time*. ARCS (18:2) 1988, 213–21.

Janice Galloway

18112. BELL, IAN A. Imagine living there: form and ideology in contemporary Scottish fiction. *In* (pp. 217–33) **115**.

18113. MARINELLI, SARA. Desiderio d'identità: *The Trick Is to Keep Breathing* di Janice Galloway. Annali anglistica (38:3) 1995, 29–36.

18114. PACCAUD-HUGUET, JOSIANE. Breaking through cracked mirrors: the short stories of Janice Galloway. Études Écossaises (2) 1993, 5–29.

John Galsworthy

18115. HARVEY, GEOFFREY.   Reading *The Forsyte Saga*. YES (26) 1996, 127–34.

James Galvin

18116. BARRETT, FAITH; YOUNG, BRIAN.   An interview with James Galvin. IowaR (24:1) 1994, 109–27.

Cristina Garcia

18117. MITCHELL, DAVID T.   National families and familial nations: *communista* Americans in Cristina Garcia's *Dreaming in Cuban*. TSWL (15:1) 1996, 51–60.

Erle Stanley Gardner

18118. BOUNDS, J. DENNIS.   Perry Mason: the authorship and reproduction of a popular hero. *See* **13474**.

18119. WALLE, ALF H.   Hack writing *vs* belle letters [*sic*]: the strategic implications of literary achievement. *See* **14757**.

John Gardner

18120. JOHNSON, CHARLES.   John Gardner as mentor. AAR (30:4) 1996, 619–24.

18121. O'NAN, STEWART (ed.).   On writers and writing. Introd. by Charles Johnson. (Bibl. 1995, 16360.) Rev. by Jonathan Yardley in BkW, 17 Apr. 1994, 3.

18122. PAYNE, CRAIG.   The cycle of the zodiac in John Gardener's [*sic*] *Grendel*. Mythlore (18:4) 1992, 61–5.

18123. —— The redemption of Cain in John Gardner's *Grendel*. Mythlore (18:2) 1992, 12–16.

18124. VENTURA, SALLY.   Gardner's dialogue with the Book of Job. MidQ (37:1) 1995, 80–91.

Leon Garfield

18125. NATOV, RONI.   Leon Garfield. (Bibl. 1994, 12774.) Rev. by Jack Zipes in ChildLit (24) 1996, 226–8; by John Stephens in CLAQ (21:1) 1996, 47–8.

18126. SIMPSON, ELIZABETH.   Rediscovering Leon Garfield. ArizEB (36:1) 1993, 21–3.

Hamlin Garland

18127. BROWN, BILL.   The popular, the populist, and the populace: locating Hamlin Garland in the politics of culture. AQ (50:3) 1994, 89–110.

18128. McCULLOUGH, JOSEPH B. (introd.).   Main-travelled roads. Lincoln; London: Nebraska UP, 1995. pp. xxi, 247.

18129. MARTIN, QUENTIN E.   Hamlin Garland's *The Return of a Private* and *Under the Lion's Paw* and the monopoly of money in post-Civil War America. ALR (29:1) 1996, 62–77.

18130. NEWLIN, KEITH.   Hamlin Garland and the 'Illegitimacy Bill' of 1913. ALR (29:1) 1996, 78–88.

18131. Sutton, John L.   The regional form as a commodified site in Hamlin Garland's *Main-Travelled Roads*. Midamerica (23) 1996, 56–63.

Raymond Garlick

18132. Dale-Jones, Don.   Raymond Garlick. Cardiff: UP of Wales, 1996. pp. 121. (Writers of Wales.)

Alan Garner

18133. Beach, Sarah.   Breaking the pattern: Alan Garner's *The Owl Service* and the *Mabinogion*. Mythlore (20:1) 1994, 10–14.

Edward Garnett

18134. Monteiro, George.   'There *is* a figure in the carpet': James, Hueffer, and Garnett. *See* **11631**.

Ken Garnhum

18135. Wilson, Ann.   Laughter in the theatre of mourning: the politics of Ken Garnhum's *Beuys Buoys Boys*. CanTR (77) 1993, 13–20.

William Gass

18136. Bush, Laurel.   Desire and language in William Gass's *Omensetter's Luck*. New Courant (6) 1996, 145–61.

18137. —— Midwestern literature as the ground for parody in William Gass's *In the Heart of the Heart of the Country*. Midamerica (20) 1993, 118–26.

18138. Gass, William H.   Finding a form. *See* **2624**.

18139. —— In other words. *See* **3138**.

William Allen Gaston (1953–)

18140. Tremblay, Tony.   Tall tales from a genteel hoodlum: the artful exaggerations of Bill Gaston. StudCanL (16:2) 1991/92, 197–215. (Interview.)

'John Gawsworth' (Terence Ian Fytton Armstrong)

18141. Wolf, Rose.   Dancing on diamonds: the artistry of John Gawsworth's *Toreros*. Romantist (9/10) 1985/86, 55–6.

David Geary

18142. Young, Stuart.   'So much more the man': *Lovelock's Dream Run* and the refashioning of masculinity in New Zealand drama. Landfall (4:2) 1996, 292–310.

Maurice Gee

18143. Amery, Mark.   Territorial imperative. Quote Unquote (36) 1996, 12–13. (Interview.)

18144. Dugdale, Sarah.   A post-colonial body? Maurice Gee in the 1990s. Span (42/43) 1996, 30–41.

Joseph Geha

18145. Robb, Kenneth A.   The fading narrator in Joseph Geha's *Through and Through*. NCL (22:3) 1992, 9–11.

Martha Gellhorn

18146. ROLLYSON, CARL. Nothing ever happens to the brave: the story of Martha Gellhorn. (Bibl. 1991, 13101.) Rev. by Patricia Rice in GateH (12:3) 1991, 75–6.

Pam Gems

18147. GALEOTTI, ROSSELLA. Pam Gems e Caryl Churchill: due figure femminili nel teatro inglese contemporaneo. *See* **16933**.
18148. PERKINS, SALLY J. The dilemma of identity: theatrical portrayals of a 16th-century feminist. SCJ (59:3) 1994, 205–14.

Jean Craighead George

18149. CARY, ALICE. Jean Craighead George. Santa Barbara, CA: Learning Works, 1996. pp. 136. (Meet the author.)

William Gerhardie

18150. CRAIG, RANDALL. Evelyn Waugh and William Gerhardie. JML (16:4) 1990, 597–614.
18151. LOWENSTEIN, ANDREA FREUD. The protection of masculinity: Jews as projective pawns in the texts of William Gerhardi [*sic*] and George Orwell. *In* (pp. 145–64) **5**.

Amitav Ghosh

18152. DIXON, ROBERT. 'Travelling in the West': the writing of Amitav Ghosh. JCL (31:1) 1996, 3–24.
18153. MAJEED, JAVED. Amitav Ghosh's *In an Antique Land*: the ethnographer-historian and the limits of irony. JCL (30:2) 1995, 45–55.

'Lewis Grassic Gibbon' (James Leslie Mitchell)

18154. D'ARCY, JULIAN MELDON. Chris Guthrie, Ellen Johns and the two Ewan Tavendales: significant parallels in *A Scots Quair*. SLJ (23:1) 1996, 42–9.
18155. DIXON, KEITH. Letting the side down: some remarks on James Leslie Mitchell's vision of history. Études Écossaises (1) 1992, 273–81.
18156. MCCULLOCH, MARGERY PALMER. 'Opening the door': women, Carswell and the Scottish renaissance. *See* **16703**.
18157. MCKENNA, BRIAN. The British Communist novel of the 1930s and 1940s: a 'party of equals'? (And does that matter?) RES (47:187) 1996, 369–85.
18158. WATSON, RODERICK. Visions of Alba: the construction of Celtic roots in modern Scottish literature. *See* **13356**.
18159. ZAGRATSKI, UWE. Lewis Grassic Gibbon's Scottish narratives: a homage to the free spirit. Études Écossaises (3) 1996, 149–58.

Kaye Gibbons

18160. BARNES, LINDA ADAMS. Telling yourself into existence: the fiction of Kaye Gibbons. TPB (30) 1993, 28–35.
18161. WYMARD, ELLIE. A demanding voice: Ellie Wymard interviews Kaye Gibbons. Critic (46:3) 1992, 46–51.

William Gibson

18162. BOOKER, M. KEITH.   Technology, history, and the post-modern imagination: the cyberpunk fiction of William Gibson. AQ (50:4) 1994, 63–87.

18163. HICKS, HEATHER J.   'Whatever it is that she's since become': writing bodies of text and bodies of women in James Tiptree, Jr's *The Girl Who Was Plugged In* and William Gibson's *The Winter Market*. ConLit (37:1) 1996, 62–93.

18164. LINDBERG, KATHRYNE V.   Prosthetic mnemonics and prophylactic politics: William Gibson among the subjectivity mechanisms. Boundary 2 (23:2) 1996, 47–83.

18165. RUDDICK, NICHOLAS.   Putting the bits together: information theory, *Neuromancer*, and science fiction. JFA (3:4) 1990 (pub. 1994), 84–92.

18166. SPONSLER, CLAIRE.   William Gibson and the death of cyberpunk. *In* (pp. 47–55) **70**.

18167. STEVENS, TYLER.   'Sinister fruitiness': *Neuromancer*, Internet sexuality and the Turing Test. StudN (28:3) 1996, 414–33.

18168. VISTARCHI, ANGELA.   Cyberpunk in Gibson's Sprawl Trilogy. *In* (pp. 509–15) **117**.

Jack Gilbert

18169. ADAMO, RALPH; BIGUENET, JOHN.   An interview with Jack Gilbert. NOR (22:3/4) 1996, 152–76.

Sandra M. Gilbert

18170. CLARK, KEVIN.   Learning to read the mother tongue: on Sandra Gilbert's *Blood Pressure*. IowaR (22:1) 1992, 212–20.

Ellen Gilchrist

18171. WOODLAND, J. RANDAL.   'New people in the old museum of New Orleans': Ellen Gilchrist, Sheila Bosworth, and Nancy Lemann. *In* (pp. 194–210) **65**.

Frances Gillmor (1903–)

18172. JOHNSON, DAVID.   Frances Gillmor. *In* (pp. 26–39) **121**.

Charlotte Perkins Gilman (Mrs Stetson)

18173. CEPLAIR, LARRY (ed.).   Charlotte Perkins Gilman: a nonfiction reader. (Bibl. 1992, 13965.) Rev. by Mary N. Moynihan in NWSAJ (4:3) 1992, 395–8.

18174. CREWE, JONATHAN.   Queering *The Yellow Wallpaper*? Charlotte Perkins Gilman and the politics of form. TSWL (14:2) 1995, 273–93.

18175. DOCK, JULIE BATES.   'But one expects that': Charlotte Perkins Gilman's *The Yellow Wallpaper* and the shifting light of scholarship. *See* **621**.

18176. DOSKOW, MINNA.   *Herland*: utopic in a different voice. *In* (pp. 53–63) **87**.

18177. GOLDEN, CATHERINE.   'Light of the Home', light of the world: the presentation of motherhood in Gilman's short fiction. MLS (26:2/3) 1996, 135–47.

18178. —— (ed.).   The captive imagination: a casebook on

The Yellow Wallpaper. (Bibl. 1992, 13970.) Rev. by Lillian S. Robinson in NWSAJ (5:1) 1993, 120–2.

18179. KESSLER, CAROL FARLEY. Charlotte Perkins Gilman: her progress toward utopia with selected writings. (Bibl. 1995, 16399.) Rev. by Val Gough in Utopian Studies (7:2) 1996, 274–5; by Dale Bauer in AL (68:1) 1996, 248–9; by Ann J. Lane in ALH (101:4) 1996, 1292–3; by Gary Scharnhorst in StudN (28:4) 1996, 594–6.

18180. KNIGHT, DENISE D. 'With the first grass-blade': Whitman's influence on the poetry of Charlotte Perkins Gilman. *See* **12698**.

18181. —— (ed.). The diaries of Charlotte Perkins Gilman: vol. 1, 1879–87; vol. 2, 1890–1935. Charlottesville; London: Virginia UP, 1994. pp. xxviii, 943.

18182. OLIVER, LAWRENCE J.; SCHARNHORST, GARY. Charlotte Perkins Gilman *v.* Ambrose Bierce: the literary politics of gender in *fin-de-siècle* California. *See* **10359**.

18183. RUDNICK, LOIS. Feminist utopian visions and the 'New Woman': Jane Addams and Charlotte Perkins Gilman. *In* (pp. 181–93) **38**.

18184. SHULMAN, ROBERT (ed.). *The Yellow Wall-Paper* and other stories. Oxford; New York: OUP, 1995. pp. xli, 332. (World's classics.)

Dorothy Gilman (1923–)

18185. GIFFONE, TONY. Disoriented in the Orient: the representation of the Chinese in two contemporary mystery novels. *In* (pp. 143–51) **19**.

Beryl Gilroy

18186. GYSSELS, KATHLEEN. L'identité féminine et l'espace clos dans le roman caribéen: l'oeuvre de Simone et André Schwarz-Bart et de Beryl Gilroy. CanRCL (22:3/4) 1995, 787–801.

Allen Ginsberg

18187. MORGAN, BILL. The response to Allen Ginsberg, 1926–1994: a bibliography of secondary sources. Foreword by Allen Ginsberg. Westport, CT; London: Greenwood Press, 1996. pp. xv, 505. (Bibliographies and indexes in American literature, 23.)

18188. MUCKLE, JOHN. The names: Allen Ginsberg's writings. *In* (pp. 10–36) **4**.

Dana Gioia

18189. CARTWRIGHT, ISABELLE. Dana Gioia. Irish Review (16) 1994, 109–22. (Interview.)

Nikki Giovanni

18190. FOWLER, VIRGINIA C. Nikki Giovanni. (Bibl. 1993, 12781.) Rev. by Ann Folwell Stanford in AAR (28:3) 1994, 481–4.

18191. —— (ed.). Conversations with Nikki Giovanni. (Bibl. 1992, 13985.) Rev. by Mozella G. Mitchell in AAR (29:1) 1995, 155–7.

Todd Gitlin

18192. BELL, ELIZABETH S. He's relatively familiar: Albert Einstein in contemporary American fiction. JAC (19:2) 1996, 119–25.

Ellen Glasgow

18193. ABBOTT, REGINALD.   Tea and sophistication: a note on Ellen Glasgow and Frances Newman. EGN (31) 1993, 5, 8–9, 12–13.

18194. ANON.   Recent scholarship on Ellen Glasgow. EGN (28) 1992, 13–14; (29) 1992, 15.

18195. —— Recent scholarship. EGN (32) 1994, 12.

18196. BAUER, MARGARET D.   Echoes of barren ground in *Gone with the Wind*: a p(re). s(cript). EGN (29) 1992, 8–14.

18197. —— Secondary sources on Ellen Glasgow, 1986–1990. EGN (26) 1991, 10–19.

18198. BEARSS, SARA B. (ed.).   'It is always a lonely thing to be a queen': letters from Marie of Rumania to Henry W. Anderson, 1919–1920. EGN (30) 1993, 5–10; (31) 1993, 6–8.

18199. —— (introd.).   Life is far from sweet: a letter from Queen Marie of Rumania. EGN (28) 1992, 4–6.

18200. BRANSON, STEPHANIE.   'A plant for women's troubles': rue in Marie de France's *Eliduc* and Ellen Glasgow's *The Past*. EGN (33) 1994, 1, 4–5.

18201. —— Ripe fruit: fantastic elements in the short fiction of Ellen Glasgow, Edith Wharton, and Eudora Welty. *In* (pp. 61–71) **3**.

18202. COOK, MARTHA E.   Miss Ellen and Miss Lucy: the Richmond–Nordhausen connection. EGN (30) 1993, 13–15.

18203. DUKE, JANE TAYLOR.   Golfing with genius. Preface by Ray Bonis. EGN (35) 1995, 3–4.

18204. GODBOLD, E. STANLEY, JR.   A biography and a biographer. EGN (32) 1994, 4–5.

18205. GOODMAN, SUSAN.   Ellen Glasgow: Calvinism and a religious odyssey. APJPH (74:1) 1996, 31–42.

18206. GULLETTE, MARGARET MORGANROTH.   Inventing the 'post-maternal' woman, 1898–1927: idle, unwanted, and out of a job. Feminist Studies (21:2) 1995, 221–53.

18207. HOAGWOOD, TERENCE ALLAN.   A feminist intertext for Ellen Glasgow's poetry. EGN (34) 1995, 1, 3–4.

18208. —— Glasgow's *A Plea*. EGN (29) 1992, 7–8.

18209. LURIE, MARK; WILSON, SHANON (eds).   The eyes of the sphinx: selections from Rebe Glasgow's travel journal of 1899. EGN (35) 1995, 1, 7–10; (36) 1996, 3, 9–15; (37) 1996, 3, 5–9.

18210. MACDONALD, EDGAR.   The final word. *See* **16658**.

18211. MACDONALD, EDGAR A.   'Remembering Ellen Glasgow' – and Elizabeth Branch Bowie. EGN (32) 1994, 1, 3, 6–7.

18212. MATTHEWS, PAMELA R.   Ellen Glasgow and a woman's traditions. (Bibl. 1995, 16423.) Rev. by Dorothy M. Scura in EGN (34) 1995, 5–6; by Susan Goodman in MFS (42:1) 1996, 145–7; by Beverly Spears in TexR (17:1/2) 1996, 132–3.

18213. —— Second chances: Amanda Cross's Dorinda. *See* **17152**.

18214. NEARY, GWEN M.   Glasgow's ghost stories and the 'pattern of society'. EGN (36) 1996, 1, 6–8.

18215. PEASLEE, CATHERINE G.   A poem for a dear friend from Castle Hill. EGN (33) 1994, 6–7.

18216. PEASLEE, KAY.   Jerdone Castle: Ellen Glasgow's idyllic inspiration. EGN (37) 1996, 1, 4–5.

18217. SAUNDERS, FRANCES W.   Glasgow's secret love: 'Gerald B.' or 'William T.'? EGN (31) 1993, 1, 3–4.

18218. SCHEICK, WILLIAM J. Chambered intimations: *The King in Yellow* and *The Descendant*. *See* **16877**.

18219. —— The narrative ethos of Glasgow's *A Point in Morals*. EGN (30) 1993, 1, 3–4.

18220. SCURA, DOROTHY M. (ed.). Ellen Glasgow: new perspectives. (Bibl. 1995, 16428.) Rev. by Linda Kornasky in EGN (36) 1996, 4–5, 16; by E. Stanley Godbold, Jr, in SAtlR (61:3) 1996, 136–8; by Barbara C. Ewell in SoQ (34:2) 1996, 154–6.

Susan Glaspell

18221. BEN-ZVI, LINDA. O'Neill's cape(d) compatriot. EOR (19:1/2) 1995, 129–38.

18222. —— (ed.). Susan Glaspell: essays on her theater and fiction. (Bibl. 1995, 16433.) Rev. by Bette Mandl in EOR (20:1/2) 1996, 153–5.

18223. DIAMOND, ELIN. 'The garden is a mess': maternal space in Bowles, Glaspell, Robins. *In* (pp. 121–39) **119**.

18224. KATTWINKEL, SUSAN. Absence as a site for debate: modern feminism and Victorianism in the plays of Susan Glaspell. NETJ (7) 1996, 37–55.

18225. MAKOWSKY, VERONICA. Susan Glaspell's century of American women: a critical interpretation of her work. (Bibl. 1995, 16434.) Rev. by Yvonne Shafer in JDTC (8:2) 1994, 230–3; by Kim Marra in NETJ (5) 1994, 115–17.

18226. NOE, MARCIA A. Reconfiguring the subject/recuperating realism: Susan Glaspell's unseen woman. AmDr (4:2) 1995, 36–54.

18227. PAPKE, MARY E. Susan Glaspell: a research and production sourcebook. (Bibl. 1994, 12820.) Rev. by Yvonne Shafer in JDTC (8:2) 1994, 230–3.

18228. WEST, ROBIN. Invisible victims: a comparison of Susan Glaspell's *Jury of Her Peers*, and Herman Melville's *Bartleby the Scrivener*. *See* **11903**.

John Glassco

18229. DELLAMORA, RICHARD. Queering Modernism: a Canadian in Paris. ECanW (60) 1996, 256–73.

18230. KOKOTAILO, PHILIP. John Glassco's richer world: memoirs of Montparnasse. (Bibl. 1988, 7571.) Rev. by Timothy Dow Adams in ARCS (18:4) 1988, 499–500.

Denis Glover

18231. MANHIRE, BILL (ed.) Selected poems. (Bibl. 1995, 16439.) Rev. by Michele Leggott in NZList, 23 Mar. 1996, 53–4; by Bede Scott in Quote Unquote (34) 1996, 28.

18232. STAFFORD, JANE. Masculinism and poetry: a note of warning. *See* **17639**.

Louise Glück

18233. HIX, H. L. The triumph of Louise Glück's *Achilles*. NCL (22:2) 1992, 3–6.

18234. TOWNSEND, ANN. The problem of sincerity: the lyric plain style of George Herbert and Louise Glück. *See* **7958**.

Elinor Glyn

18235. BROOKS, NIGEL.   Fitzgerald's *The Great Gatsby* and Glyn's *Three Weeks*. *See* **17837**.

Rumer Godden

18236. ROSENTHAL, LYNNE M.   Rumer Godden revisited. New York: Twayne; London: Prentice Hall, 1996. pp. xvii, 142. (Twayne's English authors, 519.) (Children's literature.)

Gail Godwin

18237. JONES, SUZANNE W.   Dismantling stereotypes: interracial friendships in *Meridian* and *A Mother and Two Daughters*. *In* (pp. 140–57) **32**.

18238. KISSEL, SUSAN S.   Moving on: the heroines of Shirley Ann Grau, Anne Tyler, and Gail Godwin. Bowling Green, OH: Bowling Green State Univ. Popular Press, 1996. pp. x, 232.

'Michael Gold' (Irwin Granich)

18239. HOMBERGER, ERIC.   Some uses for Jewish ambivalence: Abraham Cahan and Michael Gold. *In* (pp. 165–80) **5**.

18240. SCHOENING, MARK.   T. S. Eliot meets Michael Gold: Modernism and radicalism in Depression-era American literature. *See* **17556**.

William Golding

18241. MCCARRON, KEVIN.   The coincidence of opposites: William Golding's later fiction. Sheffield: Sheffield Academic Press, 1995. pp. 206. (Cf. bibl. 1993, 12800.) Rev. by Betty J. Ring in CritS (8:3) 1996, 339–40.

18242. SPAAS, LIEVE; STIMPSON, BRIAN (eds).   Robinson Crusoe: myths and metamorphoses. *See* **8986**.

18243. TANZMAN, LEA.   Poe's *A Tale of the Ragged Mountains* as a source for Golding's post-mortem consciousness technique in *Pincher Martin*. *See* **12082**.

18244. TIMMONS, DANIEL.   Sub-creation in William Golding's *The Inheritors*. ESCan (22:4) 1996, 399–412.

Lorna Goodison

18245. FIDO, ELAINE SAVORY .   Textures of Third World reality in the poetry of four African-Caribbean women. *In* (pp. 29–44) **81**.

Paul Goodman

18246. VINCENT, BERNARD.   Paul Goodman: an Edenic voice in the technological *inferno*. *In* (pp. 372–7) **117**.

Nadine Gordimer

18247. BAZIN, NANCY TOPPING.   Southern Africa and the theme of madness: novels by Doris Lessing, Bessie Head, and Nadine Gordimer. *In* (pp. 137–49) **50**.

18248. BLACK, WILLIAM.   Necessary excesses: on writers in search of literature's relevance. BWR (23:1) 1996, 141–55.

18249. BOYERS, ROBERT.   The art of Nadine Gordimer. Salmagundi (93) 1992, 188–203 (review-article).

18250. ECHERUO, MICHAEL J. C.   Shakespeare and the boundaries of kinship. *See* **6289**.

18251. ETTIN, ANDREW V.   Betrayals of the body politic: the literary commitments of Nadine Gordimer. (Bibl. 1995, 16470.) Rev. by Chris Bongie in MFS (40:1) 1994, 185–7.

18252. GORDIMER, NADINE.   Across time and two hemispheres. *See* **15453**.

18253. —— Writing and being. (Bibl. 1995, 16473.) Rev. by Carol Ludtke Prigan in WLT (70:1) 1996, 227.

18254. HEAD, DOMINIC.   Nadine Gordimer. (Bibl. 1995, 16476.) Rev. by Stephen Clingman in MFS (42:4) 1996, 906–8.

18255. MACASKILL, BRIAN.   Figuring rupture: iconology, politics, and the image. *In* (pp. 249–71) **44**.

18256. MERGENTHAL, SILVIA.   Miranda and Caliban: White mistresses and Black servants in Blixen's *Out of Africa*, Lessing's *The Grass Is Singing*, and Gordimer's *July's People*. *See* **17294**.

18257. MORPHET, TONY.   Stranger fictions: trajectories in the liberal novel. *See* **16993**.

18258. QUAYUM, M. A.   *July's People*: Gordimer's radical critique of White 'liberal' attitude. ESA (39:1) 1996, 13–24.

18259. WINNER, ANTHONY.   Disorders of reading short novels and perplexities. *See* **16998**.

18260. YELIN, LOUISE.   Problems of Gordimer's poetics: dialogue in *Burger's Daughter*. *In* (pp. 219–38) **33**.

Caroline Gordon

18261. FRITZ-PIGGOTT, JILL.   The dominant chord and the different voice: the sexes in Gordon's stories. *In* (pp. 209–19) **32**.

18262. HENDERSON, KATHLEEN.   Caroline Gordon's *Green Centuries*: the end of the epic journey. *In* (pp. 273–97) **29**.

18263. HENDERSON, KATHLEEN BURK.   Sketches for an unfinished portrait: autobiography and fiction in Caroline Gordon's last published stories. JSSE (18) 1992, 91–102.

18264. JONZA, NANCYLEE NOVELL.   The underground stream: the life and art of Caroline Gordon. (Bibl. 1995, 16488.) Rev. by Veronica Makowsky in SoQ (34:1) 1995, 154–5; by Brian Abel Ragen in AL (68:1) 1996, 257–8; by Nancy A. Walker in AmS (37:1) 1996, 196.

18265. SULLIVAN, WALTER.   Strange children: Caroline Gordon and Allen Tate. *In* (pp. 123–30) **43**.

18266. WHITE, MARY WHEELING.   *The Captive* who can never be free: the irony of Caroline Gordon's 'traditional' narrative. JSSE (19) 1992, 83–92.

John Gordon (1925–)

18267. PARDOE, RO.   An interview with John Gordon. Ghosts and Scholars (21) 1996, 1–5.

Mary Gordon (1949–)

18268. BENNETT, ALMA.   Mary Gordon. New York: Twayne; London: Prentice Hall, 1996. pp. xiv, 220. (Twayne's US authors, 671.)

18269. GORDON, MARY.   The shadow man. New York: Random House, 1996. pp. xxiv, 274. Rev. by Sara Maitland in Cweal (123:10) 1996, 17–18.

18270. LABRIE, ROSS. Women and the Catholic Church in the fiction of Mary Gordon. ESCan (22:2) 1996, 167–79.

Edward Gorman

18271. CHASE, ROBERT DAVID. Ed Gorman. AD (29:1) 1996, 31–2. (Interview.)

Sir Edmund Gosse

18272. MANARIN, KAREN HEATON. 'The flower-like thought of our departed': the mother in *Father and Son*. ESCan (22:1) 1996, 59–70.

Hiromi Goto

18273. BEAUREGARD, GUY. Hiromi Goto's *Chorus of Mushrooms* and the politics of writing diaspora. WCL (29:3) 1995/96, 47–62.

Katherine Govier (1948–)

18274. McCARTHY, DERMOT. The true and false guide: character-ization in Katherine Govier's *Between Men*. StudCanL (21:1) 1996, 107–30.

Elsie Park Gowan

18275. DAY, MOIRA. Elsie Park Gowan's (re-)*Building of Canada* (1937–1938): revisioning the historical radio series through feminist eyes. TRC (14:1) 1993, 3–19.
18276. —— (ed.). The hungry spirit: selected plays and prose. Edmonton, Alta: NeWest Press, 1992. pp. 328. (Prairie plays, 11.) Rev. by Joyce Doolittle in TRC (13:1/2) 1992, 194–6.

William Goyen

18277. PHILLIPS, ROBERT. A way of life: some letters by William Goyen. Shen (44:3) 1994, 93–110.

Sue Grafton

18278. RABINOWITZ, PETER J. 'Reader, I blew him away': conven-tion and transgression in Sue Grafton. *In* (pp. 326–44) **31**.

Jorie Graham

18279. HUDGINS, ANDREW. 'The honest work of the body': Jorie Graham's *Erosion*. Shen (46:2) 1996, 48–59.

R. B. Cunninghame Graham

18280. GOGWILT, CHRIS. Broadcasting news from nowhere: R. B. Cunninghame Graham and the geography of politics in the 1890s. *In* (pp. 235–54) **41**.
18281. HUBBARD, TOM. Ordered south? Scottish artists in the Mediterranean, 1864–1927. *See* **12335**.

Kenneth Grahame

18282. STEVENSON, DEBORAH. The river bank redux? Kenneth Grahame's *The Wind in the Willows* and William Harwood's *The Willows in Winter*. CLAQ (21:3) 1996, 126–32.
18283. WYTENBROEK, J. R. Natural mysticism in Kenneth Grahame's *The Wind in the Willows*. Mythlore (21:2) 1996, 431–4.

Judy Grahn

18284. BACKUS, MARGOT GAYLE. Judy Grahn and the lesbian invocational elegy: testimonial prophetic responses to social death in *A Woman Is Talking to Death*. Signs (18:4) 1993, 815–37.

Martin Allerdale Grainger

18285. DEAN, MISAO. The construction of masculinity in Martin Allerdale Grainger's *Woodsmen of the West*. CanL (149) 1996, 74–87.

Harley Granville-Barker

18286. SYDENSTRICKER, GLÓRIA. The Shaw/Maeterlinck touch in Granville-Barker's drama. IndS (34:1/2) 1996, 13–16.

Shirley Ann Grau

18287. KISSEL, SUSAN S. Moving on: the heroines of Shirley Ann Grau, Anne Tyler, and Gail Godwin. *See* **18238**.
18288. OLEKSY, ELZBIETA. The keepers of the house: Scarlett O'Hara and Abigail Howland. *In* (pp. 168–82) **65**.

Robert Graves

18289. CARTER, NICHOLAS. The First World War and the poetry of Robert Graves. GRM (41:1) 1991, 82–94.
18290. FIOL, JOAN M. The perfect guest: the poet and the island – a lasting affair. Gravesiana (1:1) 1996, 63–74.
18291. GRAVES, BERYL; WARD, DUNSTAN (eds). Complete poems: vol. 1. (Bibl. 1995, 16523.) Rev. by Patrick Campbell in Gravesiana (1:1) 1996, 75–80.
18292. GRAVES, LUCIA (ed.). Complete short stories. (Bibl. 1995, 16524.) Rev. by Patrick Campbell in Gravesiana (1:1) 1996, 75–80.
18293. GRAVES, RICHARD PERCEVAL. Robert Graves and the white goddess, 1940–85. (Bibl. 1995, 16525.) Rev. by John Smeds in Gravesiana (1:1) 1996, 85–91; by Michael Dirda in BkW, 25 Aug. 1996, 6.
18294. KNOWLES, SEBASTIAN D. G. Men of reality: Owen, Sassoon, and Graves. Review (18) 1996, 59–80 (review-article).
18295. LEONARD, JOHN. 'At what vantage-point': cultural relativism and the novels of Robert Graves. AUMLA (85) 1996, 15–27.
18296. MACCOBY, HYAM. Robert Graves and *The Nazarene Gospel Restored*. Gravesiana (1:1) 1996, 46–51.
18297. MANGLINIS, ELIAS. Yia ton Robert Graves: 'S'efcharisto Thee mou. Den eimai o T. S. Eliot.' (On Robert Graves: 'Thank you, God. I am not T. S. Eliot.') Diavazo (365) 1996, 54–6.
18298. O'PREY, PAUL (ed.). Collected writings on poetry. (Bibl. 1995, 16527.) Rev. by Patrick Campbell in Gravesiana (1:1) 1996, 75–80; by Rikky Rooksby in NQ (43:3) 1996, 370.
18299. PAINTER, ANDREW. On metaphor in the early poetry of Robert Graves: anticipating an alternative poetics. *See* **2442**.
18300. PHARAND, MICHEL. 'A great deal to be grateful for': Robert Graves and Edward Marsh. Gravesiana (1:1) 1996, 52–8.
18301. POWELL, ANNE. Two centenary salutes: Charles Hamilton Sorley and Robert Graves. Gravesiana (1:1) 1996, 21–32.
18302. PRESLEY, JOHN W. *The Owl*: an extended bibliographic note. *See* **1344**.

18303.   QUINN, PATRICK (ed.).   The centenary selected poems.
(Bibl. 1995, 16529.) Rev. by Patrick Campbell in Gravesiana (1:1) 1996,
75–80; by Rikky Rooksby in NQ (43:3) 1996, 369–70.

18304.   QUINN, PATRICK J.   The Great War and the missing muse:
the early writings of Robert Graves and Siegfried Sassoon. (Bibl. 1995,
16530.) Rev. by Sebastian D. G. Knowles in Review (18) 1996, 59–80;
by Bernard Bergonzi in YES (26) 1996, 309–10.

18305.   ROSSI, UMBERTO.   No sense of an ending: the difficulty of
ending a (hi)story in European and American World War I narratives.
See **17904**.

18306.   SARNER, HARVEY; HAHN, CARL.   A collection of the works
of Robert Graves: with bibliographic comments, corrections, and
additions. Cathedral City, CA: Brunswick Press, 1995. pp. 100. Rev. by
John Woodrow Presley in Gravesiana (1:1) 1996, 80–2.

18307.   SEYMOUR, MIRANDA.   Riding and Graves: partnership as theft.
Gravesiana (1:1) 1996, 6–10.

18308.   —— Robert Graves: life on the edge. (Bibl. 1995, 16531.)
Rev. by John Smeds in Gravesiana (1:1) 1996, 85–91.

18309.   SEYMOUR-SMITH, MARTIN.   Robert Graves: his life and work.
(Bibl. 1984, 11177.) London: Bloomsbury, 1995. pp. xxiii, 600. (Revised
ed.: first ed. 1982.)

Alasdair Gray

18310.   BELL, IAN A.   Imagine living there: form and ideology in contemporary Scottish fiction. *In* (pp. 217–33) **115**.

18311.   DALY, MACDONALD.   Concplags and totplag: *Lanark* exposed.
Edinburgh Review (93) 1995, 167–200.

18312.   KLAUS, H. GUSTAV.   1984 Glasgow: Alasdair Gray, Tom
Leonard, James Kelman. Études Écossaises (2) 1993, 31–40.

18313.   LYALL, RODERICK J.   Postmodernist otherworld, postcalvinist
purgatory: an approach to *Lanark* and *The Bridge. See* **16181**.

18314.   PITTIN, MARIE ODILE.   Alasdair Gray: a strategy of ambiguity. *In* (pp. 199–215) **115**.

18315.   STENHOUSE, DAVID.   A wholly healthy Scotland: a Reichian
reading of *1982, Janine.* Edinburgh Review (95) 1996, 113–22.

18316.   WHYTE, CHRISTOPHER.   Unspeakable heterosexuality.
Edinburgh Review (95) 1996, 123–34.

Arthur Gray

18317.   PARDOE, ROSEMARY.   Arthur Gray. Ghosts and Scholars (13)
1991, 29–31. (Writers in the James tradition, 10.)

Simon Gray

18318.   HUTCHINGS, WILLIAM.   Dramaturgies of quiet 'madness':
David Storey's *Stages* and Simon Gray's *Melon.* TexPres (15) 1994, 43–6.

Spalding Gray

18319.   BREWER, GAY.   Talking his way back to life: Spalding Gray
and the embodied voice. ConLit (37:2) 1996, 237–57.

18320.   JONES, JENNIFER.   Climbing into their graves: intertextual
quotation in Gregory Mosher's *Our Town.* NETJ (5) 1994, 51–63.

18321.   KING, W. D.   Dramaturgical text and historical record in the
new theatre: the case of *Rumstick Road.* JDTC (7:1) 1992, 71–87.

Andrew Greeley

18322. SHAFER, INGRID.   Shusaku Endo and Andrew Greeley: Catholic imagination East and West. Midamerica (18) 1991, 160–73.

'Henry Green' (Henry Vincent Yorke)

18323. HITCHCOCK, PETER.   Passing: Henry Green and working-class identity. MFS (40:1) 1994, 1–31.

18324. YORKE, MATTHEW (ed.).   Surviving: the uncollected works of Henry Green. Introd. by John Updike. (Bibl. 1992, 14059.) New York: Knopf, 1993. Rev. by Michael Dirda in BkW, 28 Feb. 1996, 5.

Alvin Greenberg

18325. BELLMAN, SAMUEL J.   A peculiar method of literary transformation: 'defamiliarization' in the cowboy-novel serial. PCR (2:2) 1991, 1–7.

Graham Greene

18326. ALBA PELAYO, Mᴬ ASUNCIÓN.   Unamuno y Greene: un estudio comparativo. Alicante: Univ. de Alicante, 1989. pp. 212. Rev. by María Dolores García Flores in RCEI (28) 1994, 207–11.

18327. ATKINSON, WILLIAM R.   The lives of Graham Greene. SAtlR (61:3) 1996, 113–20 (review-article).

18328. CHOI, JAE-SUCK.   A trio of hope: Graham Greene's *The Honorary Consul*. JELL (42:4) 1996, 839–53.

18329. DAVIS, ROBERT MURRAY.   'Perfection of the life or of the work': lives of Graham Greene. *See* **15141**.

18330. DEGAN, JAMES.   Memory and automythography in Graham Greene's *Under the Garden*. LitPs (40:1/2) 1994, 81–107.

18331. GARCÍA FLORES, MARÍA DOLORES.   Reflexiones sobre el libro *Unamuno y Greene* de Asunción Alba. RCEI (28) 1994, 207–11 (review-article).

18332. GREENE, GRAHAM.   A world of my own: a dream diary. (Bibl. 1995, 16565.) Rev. by John F. Desmond in WLT (69:2) 1995, 372.

18333. KUNKEL, FRANCIS L.   Graham Greene: the staying power and the glory. Critic (45:4) 1991, 48–55.

18334. MALAMET, ELLIOTT.   The uses of delay in *The Power and the Glory*. Ren (46:4) 1994, 211–23.

18335. MARTÍNEZ LORENTE, JOAQUÍN.   Blurring focalization: psychological expansions of point of view and modality. *See* **4215**.

18336. PENDLETON, ROBERT.   Graham Greene's Conradian masterplot: the arabesques of influence. *See* **17076**.

18337. SCANNELL, JAMES.   The method is unsound: the aesthetic dissonance of colonial justification in Kipling, Conrad, and Greene. *See* **17084**.

18338. SHELDEN, MICHAEL.   Graham Greene: the man within. (Bibl. 1995, 16571.) Rev. by Robert Murray Davis in WLT (70:2) 1996, 329–33.

18339. SHERRY, NORMAN.   The life of Graham Greene: vol. 2, 1939–1955. (Bibl. 1995, 16572.) New York: Viking, 1995. Rev. by Michael Newshaw in BkW, 12 Feb. 1995, 4; by Robert Murray Davis in WLT (70:2) 1996, 329–33.

18340. TOBIN, LEE ANN.   Give the saint her due: hagiographical values for Chaucer's Second Nun's Tale and Graham Greene's *The End of the Affair*. *See* **5461**.

18341. WHITFIELD, STEPHEN J. Limited engagement: *The Quiet American* as history. JAStud (30:1) 1996, 65–86.

18342. ZARIFOPOL-JOHNSTON, ILINCA. The parody of influence: *The Heart of the Matter* in Robbe-Grillet's *La Jalousie*. Comparatist (15) 1991, 64–77.

Augusta, Lady Gregory

18343. McDIARMID, LUCY. The demotic Lady Gregory. *In* (pp. 212–34) **41**.

18344. MacDONOGH, CAROLINE. Augusta Gregory: a portrait of a lady. *In* (pp. 109–20) **106**.

18345. PETHICA, JAMES (ed.). Lady Gregory's diaries, 1892–1902. Gerrards Cross: Smythe; New York: OUP, 1996. pp. xxxviii, 346, (plates) 16. Rev. by Aisling Foster in TLS, 27 Sept. 1996, 31.

18346. TALLONE, GIOVANNA. *Odi et amo*: Deirdre, Grania and Lady Gregory. *In* (pp. 117–24) **60**.

18347. TOOMEY, DEIRDRE. Moran's collar: Yeats and Irish Ireland. *See* **15802**.

Zane Grey

18348. GREY, LOREN (introd.). Betty Zane. Lincoln; London: Nebraska UP, 1995. pp. 291. (Zane Grey's new western series.)

18349. JACKSON, CARLTON. Zane Grey. Boston, MA: Twayne, 1989. pp. xiv, 173. (Twayne's US authors, 218.) (Revised ed.: first ed., 1973.) Rev. by Frederick Manfred in NDQ (60:3) 1992, 201–2.

18350. KIMBALL, ARTHUR G. Ace of hearts: the Westerns of Zane Grey. (Bibl. 1993, 12864.) Rev. by M. D. Butler in AmS (37:1) 1996, 188–9.

18351. LUTMAN, RICHARD A. A woman to live in your heart forever: the women of Zane Grey's West. JWest (32:1) 1993, 62–8.

Linda Griffiths

18352. PERREAULT, JEANNE. Writing Whiteness: Linda Griffiths's raced subjectivity in *The Book of Jessica*. ECanW (60) 1996, 14–31.

Angelina Weld Grimké

18353. HEBEL, UDO J. '*Sweet world of motherhood*'? Angelina Weld Grimkés *Rachel* (1916): afroamerikanisches Melodrama zwischen artistischer Innovation und politischer Propaganda. Amst (41:2) 1996, 239–63.

18354. HIRSCH, DAVID A. HEDRICH. Speaking silences in Angelina Weld Grimké's *The Closing Door* and *Blackness*. AAR (26:3) 1992, 459–74.

18355. HUXMAN, SUSAN SCHULTZ. Mary Wollstonecraft, Margaret Fuller, and Angelina Grimké: symbolic convergence and a nascent rhetorical vision. *See* **9499**.

18356. STORM, WILLIAM. Reactions of a 'highly-strung girl': psychology and dramatic representation in Angelina W. Grimké's *Rachel*. AAR (27:3) 1993, 461–71.

John Grisham

18357. STREET, ROBIN. The Grisham brief. WD (73:7) 1993, 32–4.

Frederick Philip Grove

18358. MARTENS, KLAUS.	Nixe on the river: Felix Paul Greve in Bonn (1898–1901). CanL (151) 1996, 10–43.

Johnny Gruelle

18359. HALL, PATRICIA.	Johnny Gruelle, creator of Raggedy Ann and Andy. Gretna, LA: Pelican, 1993. pp. 221. Rev. by William F. Touponce in ChildLit (24) 1996, 217–20.

Doris Grumbach

18360. GILMOUR, PETER.	Peter Gilmour reflects on Doris Grumbach's memoir: *Extra Innings*. Critic (48:3) 1994, 45–50.

18361. GRUMBACH, DORIS.	Extra innings: a memoir. (Bibl. 1995, 16590.) Rev. by Diana O'Hehir in BkW, 24 Oct. 1996, 5.

18362.	—— Life in a day. Boston, MA: Beacon Press, 1996. pp. 140.

John Guare

18363. GROSS, ROBERT F.	Life in a silken net: mourning the beloved monstrous in *Lydie Breeze*. JDTC (9:1) 1994, 21–42.

18364. ROSE, LLOYD.	John Guare. *In* (pp. 70–85) **85**.

Barbara Guest

18365. HILLMAN, BRENDA.	The artful dare: Barbara Guest's *Selected Poems*. Talisman (16) 1996, 207–20 (review-article).

Romesh Gunesekera

18366. PERERA, WALTER.	Images of Sri Lanka through expatriate eyes: Romesh Gunesekera's *Reef*. JCL (30:1) 1995, 63–78.

Bill Gunn

18367. WILLIAMS, JOHN.	Bill Gunn (1929–1989): a checklist of his films, dramatic works, and novels. BALF (25:4) 1991, 781–7.

Neil M. Gunn

18368. CURTIS, JAN.	The Celtic tradition of the winged poet and the mythical salmon of wisdom in Neil Gunn's *Highland River*. SLJ (22:2) 1995, 60–75.

18369. DIXON, KEITH.	Scottish spirit(s): a discussion of Neil Gunn's *Whisky and Scotland*. Études Écossaises (2) 1993, 195–204.

18370. McCULLOCH, MARGERY.	Neil M. Gunn and the historical novel. Études Écossaises (1) 1992, 243–51.

18371. McCULLOCH, MARGERY PALMER.	'Opening the door': women, Carswell and the Scottish renaissance. *See* **16703**.

18372. MACK, DOUGLAS S.	Culloden and after: Scottish Jacobite novels. *See* **11466**.

18373. PRICE, RICHARD.	Choosing a play: a critical survey of Neil M. Gunn's drama. SSL (29) 1996, 95–117.

18374.	—— STOKOE, C. J. L.	*A Bibliography of the Works of Neil M. Gunn*: an addendum. SLJ (22:2) 1995, 76–93.

18375. WATSON, RODERICK.	Visions of Alba: the construction of Celtic roots in modern Scottish literature. *See* **13356**.

Thom Gunn

18376. MICHELUCCI, STEFANIA. Cole Street, San Francisco: a conversation with Thom Gunn. *See* **3927**.

A. R. Gurney

18377. COLAKIS, MARIANTHE. Tragedy into comedy-drama: A. R. Gurney's *Another Antigone*. TexPres (12) 1991, 1–5.

18378. LAING, JEFFREY M. Missed connections in A. R. Gurney's *Love Letters*. NCL (25:2) 1995, 3–4.

18379. SPONBERG, ARVID E. A. R. Gurney. *In* (pp. 86–101) **85**.

Ivor Gurney

18380. THORNTON, R. K. R.; WALTER, GEORGE (eds). Best poems; and, *The Book of Five Makings*. (Bibl. 1995, 16603.) Rev. by M.I. in TLS, 1 Mar. 1996, 29.

David Guterson

18381. KÖPF, GERHARD. Über den Schneefall als Kulturkonflikt. Anmerkungen zu David Guterson: *Snow Falling on Cedars*. arcadia (31:1/2) 1996, 217–22.

Don Gutteridge

18382. DICKINSON, PETER. Documenting 'North' in Canadian poetry and music. *See* **8672**.

Marilyn Hacker

18383. CAMPO, RAFAEL. About Marilyn Hacker. Ploughshares (22:1) 1996, 195–9.

18384. JAGOSE, ANNAMARIE. Lesbian utopics. *See* **15525**.

Pamela White Hadas

18385. CUMMINS, ELIZABETH. The PHairy tales: Pamela Hadas and Patty Hearst. PMPA (16) 1991, 85–92.

Rachel Hadas

18386. HELLE, ANITA. Elegy as history: three women poets 'by the century's deathbed'. *See* **17899**.

Jessica Hagedorn

18387. COVI, GIOVANNA. The post-colonial cyborg: Jessica Hagedorn's *Dogeaters*. *In* (pp. 499–508) **117**.

John Haines (1924–)

18388. BEZNER, KEVIN; WALZER, KEVIN (eds). The wilderness of vision: on the poetry of John Haines. Brownsville, OR: Story Line Press, 1996. pp. ix, 242.

18389. HAINES, JOHN. The writing of *The Wall*. WD (73:7) 1993, 38–9.

18390. HAINES, JOHN MEADE. Fables and distances: new and selected essays. Saint Paul, MN: Graywolf Press, 1996. pp. xiv, 269.

Janet Campbell Hale

18391. HALE, FREDERICK. In the tradition of Native-American autobiography? Janet Campbell Hale's *Bloodlines*. SAIL (8:1) 1996, 68–80 (review-article).

18392.   HALE, JANET CAMPBELL.   Bloodlines: odyssey of a native daughter. New York: Random House, 1993. pp. xxxiii, 187. Rev. by Frederick Hale in SAIL (8:1) 1996, 68–80.

Alex Haley

18393.   AZOULAY, KATYA GIBEL.   Outside our parents' house: race, culture, and identity. *See* **13408**.

18394.   GRIFFIN, CHRISTOPHER O.   *Roots*, violence, and the context of intention. Griot (15:1) 1996, 1–14.

'Adam Hall' (Elleston Trevor)

18395.   TOLSTIAKOV, GEORGE.   The man who was Quiller. AD (29:1) 1996, 80–4.

Austin Hall

18396.   BIRKEN, LAWRENCE.   *The Blind Spot* in science fiction: a reconsideration. *See* **17891**.

Donald Hall

18397.   HALL, DONALD.   Life work. (Bibl. 1995, 16614.) Rev. by X. J. Kennedy in GetR (7:2) 1994, 289–303; by Scott Donaldson in BkW, 12 Sept. 1996, 4–5; by Laurence Goldstein in MichQR (35:4) 1996, 751–4.

Lynn Hall

18398.   STAN, SUSAN.   Presenting Lynn Hall. New York: Twayne; London: Prentice Hall, 1996. pp. xii, 125. (Twayne's US authors, 659.)

Radclyffe Hall

18399.   BACKUS, MARGOT GAYLE.   Sexual orientation in the (post)imperial nation: Celticism and inversion theory in Radclyffe Hall's *The Well of Loneliness*. TSWL (15:2) 1996, 253–66.

18400.   CASTLE, TERRY.   Noël Coward and Radclyffe Hall: kindred spirits. *See* **17132**.

18401.   SCANLON, JOAN.   Bad language *vs* bad prose? *Lady Chatterley* and *The Well*. *See* **1972**.

Roger Hall

18402.   MARTYN, TAMARA.   Roger Hall – the funny side of serious. Pacific Way, May 1996, 36–8.

Marion Halligan

18403.   RAHBEK, ULLA.   Tales of love, lust, jealousy and revenge: intertextuality in Marion Halligan's *Spidercup*. *See* **7334**.

Pete Hamill

18404.   CALLAHAN, TOM.   'I have to give it everything I have'. WD (73:9) 1993, 44–7, 76.

Cicely Hamilton

18405.   HIRSHFIELD, CLAIRE.   Suffragettes onstage: women's political theatre in Edwardian England. *See* **13806**.

Patrick Hamilton

18406. McKenna, Brian.   The British Communist novel of the 1930s and 1940s: a 'party of equals'? (And does that matter?) *See* **18157**.

Virginia Hamilton

18407. Sobat, Gail Sidonie.   If the ghost be there, then am I crazy? An examination of ghosts in Virginia Hamilton's *Sweet Whispers, Brother Rush* and Toni Morrison's *Beloved*. CLAQ (20:4) 1995/96, 168–74.

Dashiell Hammett

18408. Abrahams, Paul P.   On re-reading *The Maltese Falcon*. JAC (18:1) 1995, 97–107.
18409. Casillo, Robert.   The idea of society in Dashiell Hammett. Letterature d'America (36/37) 1990, 73–105.
18410. Forter, Gregory.   Criminal pleasures, pleasurable crime. *See* **14497**.
18411. Gale, Steven H.   *The Maltese Falcon*: melodrama or *film noir*? *See* **13697**.
18412. Mellen, Joan.   Hellman and Hammett: the legendary passion of Lillian Hellman and Dashiell Hammett. New York: HarperCollins, 1996. pp. xix, 572, (plates) 32.
18413. Metress, Christopher (ed.).   The critical response to Dashiell Hammett. (Bibl. 1994, 12916.) Rev. by Scott Yarbrough in SAtlR (61:2) 1996, 180–2.
18414. Miller, R. H.   Hammett's *The Maltese Falcon*. Exp (54:3) 1996, 173–4.
18415. Skenazy, Paul .   The 'heart field': Dashiell Hammett's anonymous territory. *In* (pp. 96–110) **108**.

Patricia Hampl (1946–)

18416. Bartkevicius, Jocelyn; Hamilton, David; Hussmann, Mary.   A conversation with Patricia Hampl. IowaR (23:3) 1993, 1–25.

Christopher Hampton

18417. Peterson, William.   Commodifying and subduing the body on the Singaporean stage. Span (42/43) 1996, 124–36.

Elizabeth Hand

18418. Kondratiev, Alexei.   Tales newly told: a column on current modern fantasy. Mythlore (19:1) 1993, 15, 21.

Davoren Hanna

18419. Hanna, Jack.   The friendship tree: the life and poems of Davoren Hanna. Dublin: New Island, 1996. pp. iv, 222.

Barbara Hanrahan

18420. Lindsay, Elaine.   On first looking into Barbara Hanrahan's diaries: 'the terrible creative task'. LitTheol (10:3) 1996, 230–7.

Lorraine Hansberry

18421. Blair, John G.   Representations of the family in modern American drama: media implications for the theatre, film and television. *See* **13453**.

18422. GRUESSNER, JOHN.   Lies that kill: Lorraine Hansberry's answer to *Heart of Darkness* in *Les Blancs*. *See* **17042**.

18423. HURD, MYLES RAYMOND.   Hansberry's Mrs Johnson and a restored scene in *A Raisin in the Sun*. NCL (24:3) 1994, 8–10.

18424. SEATON, SANDRA.   *A Raisin in the Sun*: a study in Afro-American culture. MidM (20) 1992, 40–9.

18425. WILKERSON, MARGARET B.   *A Raisin in the Sun*: anniversary of an American classic. *In* (pp. 119–30) **84**.

David Hare

18426. DEVINNEY, KAREN.   Transmitting the *Bildungsroman* to the small screen: David Hare's *Dreams of Leaving* and *Heading Home*. *See* **13614**.

18427. DONESKY, FINLAY.   David Hare: moral and historical perspectives. Westport, CT; London: Greenwood Press, 1996. pp. 214. (Contributions in drama and theatre studies, 75.)

18428. FRASER, SCOTT.   A politic theatre: the drama of David Hare. Amsterdam; Atlanta, GA: Rodopi, 1996. pp. 208. (Costerus, 105.)

18429. HOMDEN, CAROL.   The plays of David Hare. (Bibl. 1995, 16639.) Rev. by Jenny S. Spencer in ConLit (37:3) 1996, 478–80; by Sheila Rabillard in Essays in Theatre (15:1) 1996, 122–4.

18430. OLIVA, JUDY LEE.   David Hare: theatricalizing politics. (Bibl. 1993, 12897.) Rev. by Susan Bennett in JDTC (6:1) 1991, 139–41.

18431. PAGAN, NICHOLAS O.   Decentering the subject: David Hare's *Wetherby*. *In* (pp. 53–63) **113**.

18432. SPENCER, JENNY S.   Mainstreaming British Left theater. *See* **14236**.

Donald Harington

18433. HUGHES, LINDA K.   Staying more in the world of Donald Harington. PMPA (16) 1991, 1–7.

18434. LUND, MICHAEL.   Donald Harington's continuing story. PMPA (16) 1991, 8–15.

18435. VONALT, LARRY.   Donald Harington's enchanted hunters. PMPA (16) 1991, 24–9.

Joy Harjo

18436. COLTELLI, LAURA (ed.).   The spiral of memory: interviews. Ann Arbor: Michigan UP, 1996. pp. 142. (Poets on poetry.)

18437. CRAWFORD, JOHN; SMITH, PATRICIA CLARK.   Joy Harjo. *In* (pp. 170–9) **121**.

Frances Ellen Watkins Harper

18438. McCASKILL, BARBARA.   The folklore of the coasts in Black women's fiction of the Harlem renaissance. *See* **3293**.

Claire Harris

18439. RUDY, SUSAN.   'What there is teasing beyond the edges': Claire Harris's liminal autobiography. ECanW (60) 1996, 78–99.

Thomas Harris

18440. BORCHARDT, EDITH.   Criminal artists and artisans in mysteries by E. T. A. Hoffman, Dorothy Sayers, Ernesto Sábato, Patrick Süskind, and Thomas Harris. *In* (pp. 125–34) **36**.

18441. DeVine, Kelly M.   *The Silence of the Lambs*: a sheep in wolf's clothing? *See* **13613**.

18442. Fowler, Douglas.   The aesthete as serial killer: Dr Lecter. NCL (25:1) 1995, 2–3.

18443. Kurman, George.   Escape reading: Cheever's *Falconer*, Dumas' Count, and Dr Lecter. *See* **16901**.

18444. McCarron, Bill.   *The Silence of the Lambs* as secular eucharist. NCL (25:1) 1995, 5–6.

18445. Mann, Karen B.   The matter with mind: violence and *The Silence of the Lambs*. *See* **13958**.

18446. Martínz Alegre, Sara.   Not Oedipus' sister: the redefinition of female rites of passage in the screen adaptation of Thomas Harris's *The Silence of the Lambs*. *In* (pp. 439–50) **38**.

18447. Simpson, Philip.   The contagion of murder: Thomas Harris' *Red Dragon*. NCL (25:1) 1995, 6–8.

18448. Williams, Tony.   Through a dark mirror: red dragon's gaze. NCL (25:1) 1995, 8–10.

18449. Ziegler, Robert.   Incorporation and rebirth in *The Silence of the Lambs*. NCL (23:2) 1993, 7–9.

Wilson Harris

18450. Harris, Wilson.   Living absences and presences. *In* (pp. 1–5) **102**.

18451. López, Alfred.   Meaningful paradox: the 'strange genius' of Wilson Harris. *See* **17064**.

18452. Simon, Louis.   The politics of complex faith: Wilson Harris's *Resurrection at Sorrow Hill*. JCL (31:2) 1996, 75–86.

18453. Stewart, Joyce.   Woman as life or 'spirit of place': Wilson Harris's *Companions of the Day and Night*. *In* (pp. 237–47) **81**.

18454. Webb, Barbara J.   Myth and history in Caribbean fiction: Alejo Carpentier, Wilson Harris, and Edouard Glissant. (Bibl. 1993, 12912.) Rev. by Marc Zimmerman in MFS (40:1) 1994, 168–9.

Jim Harrison

18455. Reilly, Edward C.   Jim Harrison. New York: Twayne; London: Prentice Hall, 1995. pp. xvi, 222. (Twayne's US authors, 664.)

Kathryn Harrison

18456. Ziegler, Robert.   The body in pictures in Kathryn Harrison's *Exposure*. NCL (26:5) 1996, 6–7.

Tony Harrison

18457. Astley, Neil (ed.).   Tony Harrison. (Bibl. 1991, 13252.) Rev. by Keith Silver in PN Review (18:1) 1991, 58–9.

18458. Haberkamm, Helmut.   '*The* versuses *of life*': der britische Dichter Tony Harrison und seine soziale Elegie *V*. LWU (29:1) 1996, 17–28.

18459. Wilmer, Clive.   Tony Harrison in conversation. PN Review (18:1) 1991, 28–31.

Carla Harryman

18460. SIMPSON, MEGAN. An interview with Carla Harryman. ConLit (37:4) 1996, 511–32.

L. P. Hartley

18461. CRAIK, ROGER. Wanderers in the zodiac: George Barker and L. P. Hartley. *See* **16203**.

18462. JURICH, MARILYN. 'A woman's a two-faced' or the *Doppelgangerin* unveiled. JFA (6:2/3) 1993, 143–65.

18463. SHAYER, DAVID. Perturbation in *The Go-Between*. ERev (7:1) 1996, 37–9.

18464. WRIGHT, ADRIAN. Foreign country: the life of L. P. Hartley. London: Deutsch, 1996. pp. xi, 304. Rev. by John Bayley in LRB (18:8) 1996, 26–7; by Peter Parker in TLS, 16 Feb. 1996, 4–5.

John Harvey (1938–)

18465. SILET, CHARLES L. P. Nottingham *noir*: an interview with John Harvey. AD (29:3) 1996, 272–9.

Gwen Harwood ('Francis Geyer', 'T. F. Kline', 'Walter Lehmann', 'Miriam Stone')

18466. STRAUSS, JENNIFER. Boundary conditions: the poetry of Gwen Harwood. (Bibl. 1993, 12922.) St Lucia: Queensland UP, 1996. pp. 249. (Second ed.: first ed. 1992.) (UQP studies in Australian literature.)

18467. —— Playing in time: the poetry of Gwen Harwood. CritS (6:1) 1994, 81–7.

Ronald Harwood

18468. PARKER, R. B. *King Lear*, Sir Donald Wolfit, and *The Dresser*. *In* (pp. 99–109) **16**.

Robert Hass

18469. MARSHALL, TOD. The provinces of poetry. Northwest Review (34:2) 1996, 121–43.

Jon Hassler

18470. DOWD, DICK. Pulled along by stories: Dick Dowd interviews Jon Hassler. Critic (49:4) 1995, 18–28.

18471. LOW, ANTHONY. Jon Hassler: Catholic realist. Ren (47:1) 1994, 59–70.

John Hawkes

18472. FERRARI, RITA. Innocence, power, and the novels of John Hawkes. Philadelphia: Pennsylvania UP, 1996. pp. vi, 220. (Penn studies in contemporary American fiction.) (Cf. bibl. 1992, 14154.)

18473. SCHMUNDT-THOMAS, GEORG. *Time*, *Life*, and John Hawkes' *Cannibal*. NCL (22:2) 1992, 10–11.

John MacDougall Hay

18474. DUNNE, ROBERT. Dueling ideologies of America in *The Bread-Winners* and *The Money-Makers*. *See* **11730**.

Ernest Haycox (1899–1950)

18475. TANNER, STEPHEN L.   Ernest Haycox. New York: Twayne;
London: Prentice Hall, 1996. pp. xii, 150. (Twayne's US authors, 666.)

Robert Hayden

18476. CHAMBLEE, ANGELA E.   Frederick Douglass in the painting of
Jacob Lawrence and the poetry of Robert Hayden. *See* **11026**.

Sian Hayton

18477. WHYTE, CHRISTOPHER.   Postmodernism, gender and belief in
recent Scottish fiction. SLJ (23:1) 1996, 50–64.

Samuel Hazo

18478. SOKOLOWSKI, DAVID.   An interview with Samuel Hazo.
Ren (43:3) 1991, 163–93.

Shirley Hazzard

18479. McDOUGALL, RUSSELL.   Beyond humanism? The black drop
of Shirley Hazzard's *The Transit of Venus*. JCL (30:2) 1995, 119–33.

Bessie Head

18480. BAZIN, NANCY TOPPING.   Southern Africa and the theme of
madness: novels by Doris Lessing, Bessie Head, and Nadine Gordimer.
In (pp. 137–49) **50**.
18481. COETZEE, PAULETTE; MACKENZIE, CRAIG.   Bessie Head: rediscovered early poems. *See* **603**.
18482. COUNDOURIOTIS, ELENI.   Authority and invention in the
fiction of Bessie Head. RAL (27:2) 1996, 17–32.
18483. CROUS, MARIUS.   Dikledi's revenge: a reading of Bessie Head's
The Collector of Treasures. Literator (17:1) 1996, 133–42.
18484. GAGIANO, ANNIE.   Finding foundations for change in Bessie
Head's *The Cardinals*. JCL (31:2) 1996, 47–60.
18485. IBRAHIM, HUMA.   Bessie Head: subversive identities in exile.
Charlottesville; London: Virginia UP, 1996. pp. ix, 252.
18486. INGERSOLL, EARL G.   Sexuality in the stories of Bessie Head.
CLAJ (39:4) 1996, 458–67.
18487. INNES, C. L.   Reversal and return in fiction by Bessie Head
and Ama Ata Aidoo. *In* (pp. 69–75) **102**.
18488. LEWIS, DESIREE.   *The Cardinals* and Bessie Head's allegories of
self. WLT (70:1) 1996, 73–7.
18489. NEWELL, STEPHANIE.   Conflict and transformation in Bessie
Head's *A Question of Power*, *Serowe: Village of the Rain Wind*, and *A Bewitched
Crossroad*. JCL (30:2) 1995, 64–83.
18490. TAYLOR, CAROLE ANNE.   Tragedy reborn(e): *A Question of
Power* and the soul-journeys of Bessie Head. Genre (26:2/3) 1993, 331–51.

Seamus Heaney

18491. ALLISON, JONATHAN.   Beyond gentility: a note on Seamus
Heaney and American poetry. *See* **14830**.
18492. —— Imagining the community: Seamus Heaney in 1966.
Notes on Modern Irish Literature (4) 1992, 27–34.
18493. ANDREWS, ELMER (ed.).   Seamus Heaney: a collection of

critical essays. (Bibl. 1993, 12950.) Rev. by Neil Sammells in CritS (6:2) 1994, 282–4.

18494. ARROYO, RANE RAMÓN. The haunting of Seamus Heaney: on *Station Island*. Notes on Modern Irish Literature (8) 1996, 5–11.

18495. BLACK, WILLIAM. Necessary excesses: on writers in search of literature's relevance. *See* **18248**.

18496. BRESLIN, JOHN. Seeing things: John Breslin interviews Seamus Heaney. Critic (46:2) 1991, 26–35.

18497. BROWN, TERENCE. The new Nobel laureate. EEM (4:2) 1995, 11.

18498. BURRIS, SIDNEY. Pastoral nostalgia and the poetry of W. B. Yeats and Seamus Heaney. *In* (pp. 195–201) **58**.

18499. COLLINS, FLOYD. Seamus Heaney: the crisis of identity. GetR (6:1) 1993, 140–59 (review-article).

18500. COSGROVE, BRIAN. 'Between politics and transcendence': history and utopian possibility in the work of Seamus Heaney. *In* (pp. 305–18) **125**.

18501. CULLINGFORD, ELIZABETH BUTLER. British Romans and Irish Carthaginians: anticolonial metaphor in Heaney, Friel, and McGuinness. *See* **17991**.

18502. DONNER, IRA. Interview with Seamus Heaney. New Courant (6) 1996, 50–67.

18503. DOUGLASS, THOMAS E. 'Time and the smell of the earth': Seamus Heaney returns to the land of Henry Pearson. NCLR (5) 1996, 26–44.

18504. FUMAGALLI, MARIA CRISTINA. *Station Island*: Seamus Heaney's *Divina commedia*. IUR (26:1) 1996, 127–42.

18505. GENET, JACQUELINE; HELLEGOUARC'H, ÉLISABETH (eds). Seamus Heaney et la création poétique. Caen: Presses Universitaires de Caen, 1995. pp. 119.

18506. HABERKAMM, HELMUT. Die Bewegung weg vom *Movement*: Studien zur britischen Gegenwartsdichtung nach 1960. *See* **14938**.

18507. HARMON, MAURICE. Seamus Heaney and the gentle flame. *In* (pp. 17–29) **52**.

18508. HART, HENRY. Heaney among the deconstructionists. JML (16:4) 1990, 461–92.

18509. HEANEY, SEAMUS. Crediting poetry. *See* **4376**.

18510. —— *Crediting Poetry*: the 1995 Nobel Lecture. *See* **4377**.

18511. —— *Crediting Poetry*: the Nobel lecture. *See* **4378**.

18512. —— The frontier of writing. *In* (pp. 3–16) **52**.

18513. —— Keeping time: Irish poetry and contemporary society. *In* (pp. 247–62) **49**.

18514. HOBBS, JOHN. 'Old father, mother's son': Seamus Heaney on James Joyce. Notes on Modern Irish Literature (8) 1996, 47–51.

18515. —— Seamus Heaney's 'tentative art': the poem as political mediation. Notes on Modern Irish Literature (7:1) 1995, 18–23.

18516. HONG, SUNG-SOOK. Seamus Heaney si e jeonge. (The development of Seamus Heaney's poetry.) JELLC (38:2) 1996, 101–31.

18517. HUFSTADER, JONATHAN. 'Coming to consciousness by jumping in graves': Heaney's bog poems and the politics of *North*. IUR (26:1) 1996, 61–74.

18518. JARNIEWICZ, JERZY. Seamus Heaney: poezja i archeologia.

(Seamus Heaney: poetry and archaeology.) Tygiel Kultury, Jan. 1996, 40–3.

18519. JENKINS, NICHOLAS.   Walking on air: travel and release in Seamus Heaney. TLS, 5 July 1996, 10–12.

18520. JOHNSEN, WILLIAM A.   The treacherous years of postmodern poetry in English. *In* (pp. 75–91) **34**.

18521. KEEN, SUZANNE.   Catching the heart off guard: the generous vision of Seamus Heaney. Cweal (123:10) 1996, 10–12, 14.

18522. KOCH, STEFAN.   Dichtung als Archäologie: die Lyrik Seamus Heaneys. (Bibl. 1995, 16710.) Rev. by Robert F. Garratt in ZAA (42:1) 1994, 76–8.

18523. LONGLEY, EDNA.   'A foreign oasis'? English literature, Irish studies and Queen's University. Irish Review (17/18) 1995, 26–39.

18524. McCANN, HUGO.   Poetic governing of the tongue: the poetry of Seamus Heaney, Nobel Laureate for Literature 1995. Takahe (25) 1996, 38–43.

18525. McDONALD, PETER.   The poet and 'the finished man': Heaney's Oxford lectures. Irish Review (19) 1996, 98–108.

18526.   —— Seamus Heaney as a critic. *In* (pp. 174–89) **86**.

18527.   —— Yeats, form and Northern Irish poetry. Yeats Annual (12) 1996, 213–42.

18528. McGINLEY, CHRISTOPHER J.   'The boundaries of the land': sectarian division and the politicization of space in the poetry of Seamus Heaney. ColbyQ (32:2) 1996, 125–34.

18529. MALLOY, CATHARINE.   Seamus Heaney's *Station Island*: questioning orthodoxy and commitment. Notes on Modern Irish Literature (4) 1992, 22–6.

18530.   —— Silence as liberator in Seamus Heaney's *The Underground*. Notes on Modern Irish Literature (5) 1993, 19–22.

18531.   —— CAREY, PHYLLIS (eds).   Seamus Heaney: the shaping spirit. Newark: Delaware UP; London; Toronto: Assoc. UPs, 1996. pp. 199. (Cf. bibl. 1993, 12957.)

18532. MALONE, CHRISTOPHER.   Poetic authority and accountability: what we expect of Seamus Heaney. ELit (23:2) 1996, 277–91.

18533. MOLINO, MICHAEL R.   The net of language: marginalization, resistance, and difference in contemporary Irish literature. *See* **17996**.

18534.   —— Questioning tradition, language, and myth: the poetry of Seamus Heaney. (Bibl. 1994, 12966.) Rev. by Rosemary Thomas in IUR (26:1) 1996, 186–7.

18535. O'DONOGHUE, BERNARD.   Seamus Heaney and the language of poetry. (Bibl. 1994, 12968.) Rev. by R. P. Draper in Archiv (233:2) 1996, 409–11.

18536. OSTERWALDER, HANS.   From the peatbog to the Golden Bough: Seamus Heaney's poetic development. ZAA (44:4) 1996, 289–300.

18537. POTTS, DONNA L.   'Not in the aiming but the opening hand': Seamus Heaney's *Seeing Things*. Notes on Modern Irish Literature (7:1) 1995, 11–17.

18538. PRATT, WILLIAM.   The great Irish elk: Seamus Heaney's personal Helicon. WLT (70:2) 1996, 261–6.

18539. QUINLAN, KIERAN.   Tracing Seamus Heaney. WLT (69:1) 1995, 63–8.

18540. RAIZIS, MARIOS BYRON.   He diachronike glossa tou Seamus

Heaney. (The diachronic language of Seamus Heaney.) Nea Hestia (140:1646) 1996, 167–76.

18541. RICHARDS, BERNARD.   Comparisons: Seamus Heaney, U. A. Fanthorpe and Carol Ann Duffy. *See* **17427**.

18542. SAILER, SUSAN SHAW.   Time against time: myth and the poetry of Yeats and Heaney. *In* (pp. 202–17) **58**.

18543. SANDY, STEPHEN.   Seeing things: the visionary ardor of Seamus Heaney. Salmagundi (100) 1993, 207–25.

18544. SEMINO, ELENA.   Schema theory and the analysis of text worlds in poetry. *See* **2704**.

18545. TANIGAWA, FUYUJI.   The deconstructive impulse: Seamus Heaney's poetics in 'kinship'. *In* (pp. 263–71) **49**.

18546. TINKLER-VILLANI, VALERIA.   The poetry of Hell and the poetry of Paradise: food for thought for translators, critics, poets and other readers. *See* **3209**.

18547. TRACY, ROBERT.   Into an Irish Free State: Heaney, Sweeney and clearing away. *In* (pp. 238–62) **86**.

Nathan C. Heard

18548. BEAUMONT, ERIC.   The Nathan Heard interviews. AAR (28:3) 1994, 395–410.

James Hearst

18549. LANTER, WAYNE.   Threshing time: a tribute to James Hearst. Freeburg, IL: River King Press, 1996. pp. 104.

Roy A. K. Heath

18550. MCWATT, MARK A.   Wives and other victims: women in the novels of Roy A. K. Heath. *In* (pp. 223–35) **81**.

John Heath-Stubbs

18551. HEATH-STUBBS, JOHN.   The folklore I grew up with. *See* **3287**.

Anthony Hecht

18552. CASEY, ELLEN MILLER.   Hecht's *More Light! More Light!* Exp (54:2) 1996, 113–15.

18553. STRAND, MARK.   Views of the mysterious hill: the appearance of Parnassus in American poetry. *See* **11004**.

Thomas Heggen

18554. BEIDLER, PHILIP D.   *Mr Roberts* and American remembering; or, Why Major Major Major Major looks like Henry Fonda. JAStud (30:1) 1996, 47–64.

Florence Parry Heide

18555. HUNT, CAROLINE C.   Dwarf, small world, shrinking child: three versions of miniature. ChildLit (23) 1995, 115–36.

Robert A. Heinlein

18556. BLACKMORE, TIM.   Talking with *Strangers*: interrogating the many texts that became Heinlein's *Stranger in a Strange Land*. *See* **576**.

18557. PARKIN-SPEER, DIANE.   Almost a feminist: Robert A. Heinlein. Extrapolation (36:2) 1995, 113–25.

18558. RENO, SHAUN.   The Zuni Indian tribe: a model for *Stranger in a Strange Land*'s Martian culture. Extrapolation (36:2) 1995, 151–8.
18559. SLUSSER, GEORGE.   Heinlein's fallen futures. Extrapolation (36:2) 1995, 96–112.
18560. WESTFAHL, GARY.   The dark side of the moon: Robert A. Heinlein's *Project Moonbase*. Extrapolation (36:2) 1995, 126–35.

Lyn Hejinian

18561. ALTIERI, CHARLES.   Some problems about agency in the theories of radical poetics. *See* **14832**.
18562. SPAHR, JULIANA.   Resignifying autobiography: Lyn Hejinian's *My Life*. AL (68:1) 1996, 139–59.

Joseph Heller

18563. BEIDLER, PHILIP D.   *Mr Roberts* and American remembering; or, Why Major Major Major Major looks like Henry Fonda. *See* **18554**.
18564. BERTONNEAU, THOMAS F.   The mind bound round: language and reality in Heller's *Catch-22*. StudAJL (15) 1996, 29–41.
18565. CRAIG, DAVID M.   From Avignon to *Catch-22*. WLA (6:2) 1994, 27–54.
18566. —— Rewriting a classic and thinking about life: Joseph Heller's *Closing Time*. CEACrit (58:3) 1996, 15–30.
18567. GREEN, DANIEL.   A world worth laughing at: *Catch-22* and the humor of black humor. StudN (27:2) 1995, 186–96.
18568. MALLORY, CAROLE.   The Joe and Kurt show. Playboy (Chicago) (39:5) 1992, 86–8, 130–5. (Interview.)
18569. MARTIN, ROBERT A.   Joseph Heller's *Something Happened*. NCL (22:3) 1992, 11–12.
18570. MOORE, MICHAEL.   Pathological communication patterns in Heller's *Catch-22*. *See* **2678**.
18571. NAGEL, JAMES.   The early composition history of *Catch-22*. *In* (pp. 262–90) **7**.
18572. SCOTT, GRANT F.   *Going after Cacciato* and the problem of teleology. *See* **10767**.

Michael Heller

18573. FINKELSTEIN, NORMAN.   *Di-yanu*: Michael Heller's *Bialystok Stanzas*. Talisman (11) 1993, 77–80.
18574. FOSTER, EDWARD.   An interview with Michael Heller. Talisman (11) 1993, 48–64.
18575. FRYE, RICHARD.   The poet as phenomenologist. Talisman (11) 1993, 90–1.
18576. GARDNER, THOMAS.   'Speaking the estranged of things': on Michael Heller. Talisman (11) 1993, 92–5.
18577. GÉFIN, LASZLO K.   Michael Heller's personae. Talisman (11) 1993, 81–5.
18578. KIMMELMAN, BURT.   The autobiography of poetics: Michael Heller's living root. Talisman (11) 1993, 67–76.
18579. PETERSON, JEFFREY.   The builder's art of Michael Heller. Talisman (11) 1993, 96–9.
18580. RIEMER, RUBY.   Michael Heller: a poet's quest. Talisman (11) 1993, 100–2.

18581. Schwerner, Armand. 'Taking up the thread' (*Father Studies*): on the poetry of Michael Heller. Talisman (11) 1993, 65–6.
18582. Tarn, Nathaniel. A letter to Michael Heller. Talisman (11) 1993, 86–9.
18583. Weber, Marc. Heller's realm: the overlook. Talisman (11) 1993, 103–4.
18584. Weinfield, Henry. Fragment of an imaginary dialogue with Michael Heller on *In the Builded Place*. Talisman (11) 1993, 110–12.

Lillian Hellman

18585. Hays, Peter L. O'Neill and Hellman. EOR (18:1/2) 1994, 189–92.
18586. Hedderel, Vance Philip. Sibling rivalry in *Mourning Becomes Electra* and *The Little Foxes*. EOR (17:1/2) 1993, 60–5.
18587. Mellen, Joan. Hellman and Hammett: the legendary passion of Lillian Hellman and Dashiell Hammett. *See* **18412**.

Ernest Hemingway

18588. Anastaplo, George. Can beauty 'hallow even the bloodiest tomahawk'? Critic (48:2) 1993, 2–18.
18589. Anastas, Benjamin. Three ways of being modern: the 'Lost Generation' Trilogy by James R. Mellow. *See* **17832**.
18590. Anon. (ed.). The unpublished opening of *The Sun Also Rises*. Antaeus (75/76) 1994, 388–95.
18591. Barton, Edwin J. The story as it should be: epistemological uncertainty in *Cat in the Rain*. HemR (14:1) 1994, 72–8.
18592. Beistle, Donald. Ernest Hemingway's ETO chronology. HemR (14:1) 1994, 1–17.
18593. Benson, Jackson J. (ed.). New critical approaches to the short stories of Ernest Hemingway. (Bibl. 1995, 16734.) Rev. by Linda Wagner-Martin in AmS (32:2) 1991, 123–4.
18594. Boker, Pamela A. The grief taboo in American literature: loss and prolonged adolescence in Twain, Melville, and Hemingway. *See* **11820**.
18595. —— Negotiating the heroic paternal ideal: historical fiction as transference in Hemingway's *For Whom the Bell Tolls*. LitPs (41:1/2) 1995, 85–112.
18596. Brogan, Jacqueline Vaught. Parody or parity? A brief note on Gertrude Stein and *For Whom the Bell Tolls*. HemR (15:2) 1996, 89–95.
18597. Bruccoli, Matthew J. (ed.); Trogdon, Robert W. (asst ed.). The only thing that counts: the Ernest Hemingway/Maxwell Perkins correspondence 1925–1947. New York: Scribner, 1996. pp. 367. Rev. by James Campbell in TLS, 8 Nov. 1996, 30.
18598. Burwell, Rose Marie. Hemingway: the postwar years and the posthumous novels. Cambridge; New York: CUP, 1996. pp. xxvii, 250. (Cambridge studies in American literature and culture, 96.) Rev. by Carl Eby in HemR (15:2) 1996, 108–12.
18599. Buske, Morris. The soldier's home again. HemR (15:2) 1996, 104–7.
18600. Carter, Steven. 'Hail nothing full of nothing': a note on Hemingway and Tolstoy. LMN (19) 1995, 7–10.
18601. Cartosio, Bruno. Modi di produzione: Hemingway e Hawks. *See* **13536**.

18602. CHEATHAM, GEORGE.   Androgyny and *In Our Time*, Chapter VII. HemR (14:1) 1994, 67–71.

18603. CIVELLO, PAUL.   Hemingway's 'primitivism': archetypal patterns in *Big Two-Hearted River*. HemR (13:1) 1993, 1–16.

18604. CLIFFORD, STEPHEN.   Hemingway's fragmentary novel: readers writing the hero in *In Our Time*. HemR (13:2) 1994, 12–23.

18605. COMLEY, NANCY R.; SCHOLES, ROBERT.   Hemingway's genders: rereading the Hemingway text. (Bibl. 1995, 16742.) Rev. by Jamie Barlow in HemR (14:1) 1994, 84–7; by Tom Strychacz in MFS (42:1) 1996, 147–9; by D. Quentin Miller in StudN (28:2) 1996, 258–60.

18606. CROFT, STEVEN.   Karl Jasper's ideas on tragedy and Hemingway's *The Old Man and the Sea*. NCL (25:3) 1995, 7–8.

18607. DAVISON, RICHARD ALLAN.   Edgar Rice Burroughs, Tarzan, and Hemingway. *See* **16628**.

18608. DEFAZIO, ALBERT J., III.   Current bibliography. HemR (13:1) 1993, 113–19; (13:2) 1994, 114–19; (14:1) 1994, 91–8.

18609. —— Current bibliography: annotated. HemR (15:2) 1996, 119–28; (16:1) 1996, 124–37.

18610. —— Fitzgerald and Hemingway. *See* **17847**.

18611. DEVOST, NADINE.   Hemingway's girls: unnaming and re-naming Hemingway's female characters. *See* **2133**.

18612. DOLAN, MARC.   Modern lives: a cultural re-reading of the 'Lost Generation'. *See* **17134**.

18613. DONALDSON, SCOTT (ed.).   The Cambridge companion to Hemingway. Cambridge; New York: CUP, 1996. pp. xii, 321. (Cambridge companions to literature.) Rev. by Kim Moreland in HemR (16:1) 1996, 108–12.

18614. —— New essays on *A Farewell to Arms*. (Bibl. 1995, 16750.) Rev. by Kurt Müller in Amst (41:4) 1996, 708.

18615. DOYLE-ANDERSON, ANN; HOUSTON, NEAL B.   The letters of Adriana Ivancich to Ernest Hemingway. HemR (13:1) 1993, 63–75.

18616. FLEMING, ROBERT E.   The face in the mirror: Hemingway's writers. (Bibl. 1995, 16755.) Rev. by Robert Gajdusek in HemR (13:2) 1994, 101–6.

18617. —— The fun also rises: a tribute to Jim Hinkle. HemR (13:1) 1993, 90–1.

18618. FLORA, JOSEPH M.   *Today Is Friday* and the pattern of *Men without Women*. HemR (13:1) 1993, 17–35.

18619. GAJDUSEK, ROBERT E.   The oxymoronic compound and the ambiguous noun: paradox as paradigm in *A Farewell to Arms*. *See* **2367**.

18620. HAMPTON, HOWARD.   Return of the body snatchers. *See* **13756**.

18621. HARRINGTON, GARY.   'A plague of all cowards': *Macomber* and *Henry IV*. *See* **6869**.

18622. HASEGAWA, HIROKAZU.   Hemingway to 'dansei taishuushi' to iu shisou – *Esquire*, dokusha, soshite 1930 nendai. (Hemingway and the ideology of the 'magazine for men': *Esquire*, the readers, and the 1930s.) *See* **1285**.

18623. HEMINGWAY, LEICESTER.   My brother, Ernest Hemingway. (Bibl. 1963, 5971.) Sarasota, FL: Pineapple Press, 1996. pp. 327. (Fourth ed.: first ed. 1962.)

18624. HILY-MANE, GENEVIÈVE.   Ernest Hemingway in France, 1926–1994: a comprehensive bibliography. Reims: CIRLEP, UFR

Lettres et Sciences Humaines, 1995. pp. 190. Rev. by Albert J. DeFazio, III, in HemR (16:1) 1996, 120–1.

18625. Hurley, C. Harold. Baseball in Hemingway's *The Three-Day Blow*: the way it really was in the fall of 1916. HemR (16:1) 1996, 43–55.

18626. —— (ed.). Hemingway's debt to baseball in *The Old Man and the Sea*: a collection of critical readings. (Bibl. 1992, 14231.) Rev. by Luis A. Losada in HemR (13:1) 1993, 106–8.

18627. Imamura, Tateo. *Soldier's Home*: another story of a broken heart. HemR (16:1) 1996, 102–7.

18628. Jobst, Jack; Williamson, W. J. Hemingway and Maupassant: more light on *The Light of the World*. HemR (13:2) 1994, 52–61.

18629. Josephs, Allen. *For Whom the Bell Tolls*: Ernest Hemingway's undiscovered country. (Bibl. 1995, 16766.) Rev. by Rena Sanderson in HemR (14:1) 1994, 87–90.

18630. —— How did Hemingway write? NDQ (63:3) 1996, 50–64.

18631. Junkins, Donald. 'Oh, give the bird a chance': nature and vilification in Hemingway's *The Torrents of Spring*. NDQ (63:3) 1996, 65–80.

18632. Kerner, David. Hemingway's attention to *A Clean Well-Lighted Place*. HemR (13:1) 1993, 48–62.

18633. Kimbrel, William W., Jr. Carlos Baker and the 'true gen'. *See* **15162**.

18634. Kolin, Philip C. Tennessee Williams, Ernest Hemingway, and Fidel Castro. NCL (26:1) 1996, 6–7.

18635. Lamb, Robert Paul. Hemingway and the creation of twentieth-century dialogue. TCL (42:4) 1996, 453–80.

18636. —— Hemingway's critique of anti-Semitism: semiotic confusion in *God Rest You Merry, Gentlemen*. SSF (33:1) 1996, 25–34.

18637. —— Observations on Hemingway, suggestiveness, and the modern short story. MidQ (37:1) 1995, 11–26.

18638. Leff, Leonard. A thunderous reception: Broadway, Hollywood, and *A Farewell to Arms*. *See* **13909**.

18639. Leonard, John. *A Man of the World* and *A Clean, Well-Lighted Place*: Hemingway's unified view of old age. HemR (13:2) 1994, 62–73.

18640. Losada, Luis A. George Sisler, Manolin's age, and Hemingway's use of baseball. HemR (14:1) 1994, 79–83.

18641. Mandel, Miriam. Ferguson and lesbian love: unspoken subplots in *A Farewell to Arms*. HemR (14:1) 1994, 18–24.

18642. Mandel, Miriam B. *Across the River and into the Trees*: reading the Brusadelli stories. JML (19:2) 1995, 334–45.

18643. Martin, Robert A. Robert Jordan and the Spanish country: learning to live in it 'truly and well'. HemR (16:1) 1996, 56–64.

18644. Mellow, James R. Hemingway: a life without consequences. (Bibl. 1992, 14247.) Rev. by Earl Rovit in Review (16) 1994, 159–61.

18645. Meredith, James H. The eyewitness narrator in Hemingway's *Collier's* dispatches and *Black Ass at the Cross Roads*. WLA (7:1) 1995, 43–59.

18646. —— The Rapido River and Hürtgen Forest in *Across the River and into the Trees*. HemR (14:1) 1994, 60–6.

18647. Messent, Peter. Ernest Hemingway. (Bibl. 1995, 16781.) Rev. by Rose Marie Burwell in HemR (13:1) 1993, 100–3.

18648. MILLER, PAUL W.   Anti-heroic theme and structure in Midwestern World War I novels from Cather to Hemingway. *See* **16803**.

18649. —— French criticism of Ernest Hemingway: a brief survey (1932–89). Midamerica (18) 1991, 69–79.

18650. —— Hemingway's art of self-exculpation in life and in *The Garden of Eden*. Midamerica (19) 1992, 27–35.

18651. —— Hemingway's posthumous fiction, 1961–87: a Rorschach test for critics. Midamerica (20) 1993, 98–107.

18652. MONTEIRO, GEORGE.   Ernest Hemingway's *A Farewell to Arms* – the first sixty-five years: a checklist of criticism, scholarship, and commentary. BB (53:4) 1996, 273–92.

18653. MORELAND, KIM.   The medievalist impulse in American literature: Twain, Adams, Fitzgerald, and Hemingway. *See* **10216**.

18654. MORRIS, DANIEL.   Hemingway and *Life*: consuming revolutions. *See* **1323**.

18655. MURPHY, CHARLENE M.   Hemingway, Winslow Homer, and *Islands in the Stream*: influence and tribute. HemR (13:1) 1993, 76–85.

18656. NAGEL, JAMES.   Ernest Hemingway: the Oak Park legacy. Tuscaloosa; London: Alabama UP, 1996. pp. x, 231. (Essays presented at a conference held July 17–21, 1993, in Oak Park, IL.)

18657. NELSON, CARY.   Hemingway, the American Left, and the Soviet Union: some forgotten episodes. HemR (14:1) 1994, 36–45.

18658. —— Milton Wolff, Ernest Hemingway, and historical memory: the Spanish Civil War sixty years later. NDQ (63:3) 1996, 81–9.

18659. NOLAN, CHARLES J., JR.   *Ten Indians* and the pleasures of close reading. HemR (15:2) 1996, 67–78.

18660. O'ROURKE, SEAN.   Evan Shipman and *The Gambler, the Nun, and the Radio*. HemR (13:1) 1993, 86–9.

18661. PARNELL, DAVID.   A Hawthornian analysis of Hemingway's *For Whom the Bell Tolls*. *See* **11423**.

18662. PENAS IBÁÑEZ, BEATRIZ.   A Hemingway–Vallejo analogue. HemR (13:2) 1994, 87–96.

18663. PFEIFFER, GERHARD; KÖNIG, MARTINA.   'The bill always came': Hemingway's use of the Epiphany in *Cross-Country Snow*. HemR (16:1) 1996, 97–101.

18664. —— Die Epiphanie und ihre Funktion in Hemingways Kurzgeschichte *Cross-Country Snow*. GRM (46:1) 1996, 108–10.

18665. PHILBRICK, NATHANIEL.   A window on the prey: the hunter sees a human face in Hemingway's *After the Storm* and Melville's *The Grand Armada*. *See* **11874**.

18666. PHILLIPS, DANA.   Is nature necessary? Raritan (13:3) 1994, 78–100.

18667. PLATH, JAMES.   *After the Denim* and *After the Storm*: Raymond Carver comes to terms with the Hemingway influence. *See* **16730**.

18668. —— Santiago at the plate: baseball in *The Old Man and the Sea*. HemR (16:1) 1996, 65–82.

18669. POWELL, TAMARA M.   Lilith started it! Catherine as Lilith in *The Garden of Eden*. HemR (15:2) 1996, 79–88.

18670. PRESSMAN, RICHARD S.   Individualists or collectivists: Steinbeck's *In Dubious Battle* and Hemingway's *To Have and Have Not*. SteiQ (25:3/4) 1992, 119–33.

18671. PUTNAM, ANN. Across the river and into the stream: journey of the divided heart. NDQ (63:3) 1996, 90–8.

18672. RAY, NINA M. The endorsement potential also rises: the merchandising of Ernest Hemingway. HemR (13:2) 1994, 74–86.

18673. REYNOLDS, MICHAEL. Hemingway: the American homecoming. (Bibl. 1995, 16794.) Rev. by Earl Rovit in Review (16) 1994, 162–5.

18674. REYNOLDS, THOMAS J. Hemingway and basic writers: a computer-based reader-response study. Reader (28) 1992, 52–68.

18675. ROSEN, KENNETH (ed.). Hemingway repossessed. (Bibl. 1994, 13011.) Rev. by Linda Patterson in HemR (13:2) 1994, 107–10; by Thomas K. Meier in SSF (31:3) 1996, 159–60.

18676. ROSSI, UMBERTO. No sense of an ending: the difficulty of ending a (hi)story in European and American World War I narratives. *See* **17904**.

18677. ROVIT, EARL. The lives and time of Ernest Hemingway. *See* **15174**.

18678. RUDAT, WOLFGANG E. H. Macho posturing in *For Whom the Bell Tolls*: the role of Andrés of Villaconejos. ANQ (9:1) 1996, 27–31.

18679. RYAN, DENNIS. 'A divine gesture': Hemingway's complex parody of the modern. HemR (16:1) 1996, 1–17.

18680. SCOTT, GRANT F. *Going after Cacciato* and the problem of teleology. *See* **10767**.

18681. SMITH, CLAUDE CLAYTON. Hemingway's *The Sun Also Rises*. Exp (54:4) 1996, 236–7.

18682. SPILKA, MARK. Hemingway's quarrel with androgyny. (Bibl. 1995, 16807.) Rev. by Peter L. Hays in AmS (32:2) 1991, 122–3.

18683. STONEBACK, H. R. Fiction into film: 'Is dying hard, daddy?' Hemingway's *Indian Camp. In* (pp. 93–108) **113**.

18684. —— 'I should have kissed him': Hemingway's last war – ringing the changes. NDQ (63:3) 1996, 99–114.

18685. STRONG, AMY. Screaming through silence: the violence of race in *Indian Camp* and *The Doctor and the Doctor's Wife*. HemR (16:1) 1996, 18–32.

18686. STRYCHACZ, THOMAS. Trophy-hunting as a trope of manhood in Ernest Hemingway's *Green Hills of Africa*. HemR (13:1) 1993, 36–47.

18687. SUGIYAMA, MICHELLE SCALISE. What's love got to do with it? An evolutionary analysis of *The Short Happy Life of Francis Macomber*. HemR (15:2) 1996, 15–32.

18688. SVOBODA, FREDERIC J. Landscapes real and imagined: *Big Two-Hearted River*. HemR (16:1) 1996, 33–42.

18689. THOREEN, DAVID. Poor Ernest's almanac: the petty economies of *Fifty Grand*'s Jack Brennan. HemR (13:2) 1994, 24–36.

18690. TROGDON, ROBERT W. 'Forms of combat': Hemingway, the critics, and *Green Hills of Africa*. HemR (15:2) 1996, 1–14.

18691. TYLER, LISA. Ernest Hemingway's date-rape story: sexual trauma in *Up in Michigan*. HemR (13:2) 1994, 1–11.

18692. WATSON, WILLIAM BRAASCH. Hemingway in Bimini: an introduction. NDQ (63:3) 1996, 130–44.

18693. WILSON, ANDREW. Bidding goodbye to the plumed troop and the big wars: the presence of *Othello* in *A Farewell to Arms*. *See* **7112**.

18694. WOLTER, JÜRGEN C.   Caesareans in an Indian camp. HemR (13:1) 1993, 92–4.

18695. YUTAI, LU.   Hemingway: a star in China. HemR (13:2) 1994, 97–100.

18696. ZIVLEY, SHERRY LUTZ.   Hemingway's 'pretty' illusions in American fiction. NCL (22:1) 1992, 11–12.

Alice Corbin Henderson

18697. BLEND, BENAY.   'I have heard the spinning woman of the sky': Alice Corbin, poet and art critic (1881–1949). *In* (pp. 128–42) **37**.

Beth Henley

18698. KULLMAN, COLBY H.   Beth Henley's marginalized heroines. StAD (8:1) 1993, 21–8.

18699. WIMMER-MOUL, CYNTHIA.   Beth Henley. *In* (pp. 102–22) **85**.

'O. Henry' (William Sydney Porter)

18700. CURRENT-GARCIA, EUGENE.   O. Henry: a study of the short fiction. (Bibl. 1993, 13029.) Rev. by Robert M. Luscher in SSF (31:3) 1996, 161–3.

Caroline Lee Hentz

18701. WIMSATT, MARY ANN.   Caroline Hentz's balancing act. *In* (pp. 161–75) **32**.

Frank Herbert

18702. MULCAHY, KEVIN.   *The Prince* on Arrakis: Frank Herbert's dialogue with Machiavelli. Extrapolation (37:1) 1996, 22–36.

W. N. Herbert

18703. SKOBLOW, JEFFREY.   Herbert's *Horse Island*: perverse pleasures in the archive. SLJ (23:2) 1996, 80–8.

Josephine Herbst

18704. ROBERTS, NORA RUTH.   Three radical women writers: class and gender in Meridel Le Sueur, Tillie Olsen, and Josephine Herbst. New York; London: Garland, 1996. pp. xi, 209. (Garland reference library of the humanities, 1452.) (Gender & genre in literature. 6.) (Cf. bibl. 1995, 16824.)

James Leo Herlihy

18705. MOON, MICHAEL.   Outlaw sex and the 'search for America': representing male prostitution and perverse desire in sixties film (*My Hustler* and *Midnight Cowboy*). *See* **13997**.

John Hersey

18706. TURNER, CATHERINE.   The angel of the shelter: American women and the atomic bomb. *See* **1382**.

Dorothy Hewett

18707. NEWMAN, JOAN.   Dealing it out: Dorothy Hewett's *Wild Card*. CritS (6:1) 1994, 133–9.

18708. SCHAFER, ELIZABETH. Golden girls and bad girls: the plays of Dorothy Hewett. CritS (6:1) 1994, 140–5.

John Hewitt

18709. DE LA VARS, GORDON J. Contrasting landscapes: John Hewitt's rural vision and Yeats's Irish world. *In* (pp. 39–45) **58**.

18710. HARVIE, CHRISTOPHER. Garron Top to Caer Gybi: images of the inland sea. *See* **10257**.

18711. LONGLEY, EDNA. 'A foreign oasis'? English literature, Irish studies and Queen's University. *See* **18523**.

18712. MACDONALD, MURDO. The outlook tower: Patrick Geddes in context: glossing Lewis Mumford in the light of John Hewitt. Irish Review (16) 1994, 53–73.

18713. OLINDER, BRITTA. Hewitt's region in a post-colonial perspective. *In* (pp. 301–10) **49**.

18714. PATTEN, EVE (ed.). Returning to ourselves: second volume of papers from the John Hewitt International Summer School. Belfast: Lagan Press, 1995. pp. xv, 395.

Carl Hiaasen

18715. KATZ, IAN. The king of Miami spice. Mail & Guardian (12:7) 1996, 2.

18716. PHILLIPS, DANA. Is nature necessary? *See* **18666**.

18717. SILET, CHARLES L. P. Sun, sand and tirades: an interview with Carl Hiaasen. AD (29:1) 1996, 9–18.

Aidan Higgins

18718. IMHOF, RÜDIGER. The prose works of Aidan Higgins: fiction, fictionalised autobiography, travelogue. Ang (114:1) 1996, 57–90.

George V. Higgins

18719. DEEDY, JOHN. Dynamite dialogue and thriller plots: John Deedy interviews crime novelist George V. Higgins. Critic (49:1) 1994, 15–28.

Patricia Highsmith ('Claire Morgan')

18720. CALANCHI, ALESSANDRA. 'Put it into words': insular dream and nightmarish insularity in *Edith's Diary* by Patricia Highsmith. Letterature d'America (55) 1994, 53–72.

Geoffrey Hill

18721. JOHNSEN, WILLIAM A. The treacherous years of postmodern poetry in English. *In* (pp. 75–91) **34**.

18722. PORDZIK, RALPH. Die Postmoderne als eine Ästhetik des Erhabenen: barocke Elemente in Geoffrey Hills Sonettzyklus *Lachrimae; or, Seven Tears Figured in Seven Passionate Pavans*. ZAA (44:1) 1996, 11–26.

18723. WEISMAN, KAREN A. Romantic constructions and epic subversions in Geoffrey Hill's *Mercian Hymns*. MLQ (57:1) 1996, 37–49.

Tony Hillerman

18724. BERNELL, SUE; KARNI, MICHAELA. Tony Hillerman. *In* (pp. 40–51) **121**.

18725. KNEPPER, PAUL; PUCKETT, MICHAEL B.   The historicity of Tony Hillerman's Indian police. JWest (34:1) 1995, 13–18.

18726. REILLY, JOHN M.   Tony Hillerman: a critical companion. Westport, CT; London: Greenwood Press, 1996. pp. xiii, 218. (Critical companions to popular contemporary writers.)

18727. SOBOL, JOHN.   Tony Hillerman: a public life. Toronto: ECW Press, 1994. pp. 128.

James Hilton

18728. RICHARDS, THOMAS.   Archive and utopia. Representations (37) 1992, 104–35. (*Kim, Lost Horizon.*)

Chester Himes

18729. COCHRAN, DAVID.   So much nonsense must make sense: the Black vision of Chester Himes. MidQ (38:1) 1996, 11–30.

18730. McCLAREN, JOSEPH.   *Cotton Comes to Harlem*: the novel, the film and the critics. *See* **13940**.

18731. SIEGEL, JEFF.   Lonely crusader: a few words about Chester Himes. AD (29:4) 1996, 406–9.

18732. WALTERS, WENDY W.   Limited options: strategic maneuverings in Himes's Harlem. AAR (28:4) 1994, 615–31.

Russell Hoban

18733. BRANSCOMB, JACK.   Knowledge and understanding in *Riddley Walker. In* (pp. 106–13) **77**.

18734. MALEKIN, PETER.   Re-membering: time and myth in *Kleinzeit* and *The Medusa Frequency. In* (pp. 189–95) **127**.

Alice Hoffman

18735. DEWEY, JOSEPH.   Music for a closing: responses to AIDS in three American novels. *In* (pp. 23–38) **2**.

18736. PASTORE, JUDITH LAURENCE.   Suburban AIDS: Alice Hoffman's *At Risk. In* (pp. 39–49) **2**.

William Hoffman

18737. SHATZKY, JOEL.   AIDS enters the American theater: *As Is* and *The Normal Heart. In* (pp. 131–9) **2**.

18738. VAN NESS, GORDON.   'Something very much like courage': the Agrarian tradition and William Hoffman's *The Land that Drank the Rain.* Shen (41:2) 1991, 91–107.

Desmond Hogan

18739. DEANE, PAUL.   The great chain of Irish being reconsidered: Desmond Hogan's *A Curious Street.* Notes on Modern Irish Literature (6) 1994, 39–48.

18740. D'HAEN, THEO.   Irish regionalism, magic realism and post-modernism. *In* (pp. 59–68) **49**.

Linda Hogan

18741. SMITH, PATRICIA CLARK.   Linda Hogan. *In* (pp. 140–55) **121**.

18742. STEINBERG, MARC H.   Linda Hogan's *Mean Spirit*: the wealth, value, and worth of the Osage tribe. NCL (25:2) 1995, 7–8.

Michael Hollingsworth

18743. McKinnie, Michael. King-maker: reading theatrical presentations of Canadian political history. TRC (15:2) 1994, 165–90.

John Clellon Holmes

18744. Hamilton, Cynthia S. The prisoner of self: the work of John Clellon Holmes. *In* (pp. 114–27) **4**.

William Douglas Home

18745. Fraser, David. Will: a portrait of William Douglas Home. London: Deutsch, 1995. pp. x, 262, (plates) 16.

Hugh Hood

18746. Cooke, John. The influence of painting on five Canadian writers: Alice Munro, Hugh Hood, Timothy Findley, Margaret Atwood, and Michael Ondaatje. *See* **16077**.

18747. Copoloff-Mechanic, Susan. Pilgrim's progress: a study of the short stories of Hugh Hood. Toronto: ECW Press, 1988. pp. 155. Rev. by John Ferres in ARCS (19:1) 1989, 123–5.

18748. Vauthier, Simone. Tableaux imaginaires dans un roman de Hugh Hood. Études littéraires (28:3) 1996, 77–90.

A. D. Hope

18749. Auster, Martin. The Celtic imagination in exile. *See* **11788**.

18750. Bowers, Neal. Form as substance in the poetry of A. D. Hope. Shen (44:1) 1994, 68–80.

Paul Horgan

18751. Zinsser, William. A visit with Paul Horgan. ASch (64:1) 1995, 119–24.

E. W. Hornung

18752. Bloom, Clive (introd.). The collected Raffles stories. Oxford; New York: OUP, 1996. pp. xxi, 408. (Oxford popular fiction.)

18753. Goodman, Jonathan. Museum piece. AD (29:4) 1996, 416–17.

Israel Horovitz

18754. Haedicke, Susan C. Doing the dirty work: gendered versions of working-class women in Sarah Daniels' *The Gut Girls* and Israel Horovitz's *North Shore Fish*. *See* **17188**.

18755. Kane, Leslie (ed.). Israel Horovitz: a collection of critical essays. (Bibl. 1995, 16860.) Rev. by Mark S. P. Turvin in NETJ (6) 1995, 134.

William Horwood

18756. Stevenson, Deborah. The river bank redux? Kenneth Grahame's *The Wind in the Willows* and William Harwood's *The Willows in Winter*. *See* **18282**.

Janette Turner Hospital

18757. Bowen, Deborah. Borderline magic: Janette Turner

Hospital and transfiguration by photography. StudCanL (16:2) 1991/92, 182–96.

18758. CALLAHAN, DAVID.   Acting in the public sphere and the politics of memory in Janette Turner Hospital. TSWL (15:1) 1996, 73–81.

Claude Houghton

18759. McCARTHY, PATRICK A.   Claude Houghton and Flann O'Brien on Hell: *Julian Grant Loses His Way* and *The Third Policeman*. Notes on Modern Irish Literature (7:1) 1995, 5–10.

A. E. Housman

18760. EFRATI, CAROL.   The horses and the reins. VP (34:1) 1996, 53–71.

18761. HOAGWOOD, TERENCE ALLAN.   A. E. Housman revisited. New York; Twayne; London: Prentice Hall, 1995. pp. xvii, 130. (Twayne's English authors, 514.)

18762. NAIDITCH, P. G.   A. E. Housman's *Prosody and Method*. NQ (43:1) 1996, 55.

18763. —— Problems in the life and writings of A. E. Housman. (Bibl. 1995, 16878.) Rev. by J.H.C.L. in TLS, 13 Sept. 1996, 32.

18764. ROBBINS, RUTH.   'A very curious construction': masculinity and the poetry of A. E. Housman and Oscar Wilde. *In* (pp. 137–59) **18**.

James D. Houston

18765. CHEUSE, ALAN.   Double wonder: the novelistic achievement of James D. Houston. *In* (pp. 144–59) **108**.

Velina Houston

18766. HAEDICKE, SUSAN.   'Suspended between two worlds': inter-culturalism and the rehearsal process for Horizons Theatre's production of Velina Hasu Houston's *Tea*. TT (4:1) 1994, 89–103.

Robert E. Howard (1906–36)

18767. DITOMMASO, LORENZO.   Robert E. Howard's Hyborian tales and the question of race in fantastic literature. Extrapolation (37:2) 1996, 151–70.

18768. HERRON, DON.   Swords at the academy gates; or, Robert E. Howard is there, where are the critics? Romantist (9/10) 1985/86, 37–41.

Susan Howatch

18769. WAHL, BILL.   A wondrous novel: *Wheel of Fortune*. *In* (pp. 351–64) **125**.

Susan Howe

18770. HOWARD, W. SCOTT.   'Writing ghost writing', a discursive poetics of history; or, Howes 'hau' in Susan Howe's *A Bibliography of the King's Book; or, 'Eikon basilike'*. Talisman (14) 1995, 108–30.

18771. NICHOLLS, PETER.   Unsettling the wilderness: Susan Howe and American history. ConLit (37:4) 1996, 586–601.

Tina Howe

18772. JOHNSON, KENNETH E. Tina Howe and feminine discourse. AmDr (1:2) 1992, 15–25.

18773. MYERS, NORMAN J.; SHIELDS, RONALD E. The 'killer monologue' in contemporary American drama. *See* **14019**.

18774. SMITH, CAROLYN H. Painting over gender codes in Tina Howe's *Painting Churches*. TexPres (12) 1991, 89–93.

David Huddle (1942–)

18775. STANLEY, TAL. Interview: David Huddle. AppalJ (23:2) 1996, 174–87.

Andrew Hudgins

18776. HUDGINS, ANDREW. An autobiographer's lies. ASch (65:4) 1996, 541–53.

Langston Hughes

18777. BAXTER, KAREN. An on-going dialogue with George Bass. LHR (9:1/2)/(10:1/2) 1990/91, 69–81.

18778. BEAVERS, HERMAN. Dead rocks and sleeping men: aurality in the aesthetic of Langston Hughes. LHR (11:1) 1992, 1–5.

18779. BERTSCHMAN, DON. Jesse B. Simple and the racial mountain: a bibliographic essay. LHR (13:2) 1995, 29–44.

18780. BIENVENU, GERMAIN J. Intracaste prejudice in Langston Hughes's *Mulatto*. AAR (26:2) 1992, 341–53.

18781. BOGUMIL, MARY L. Voice, dialogue, and community: in search of the 'Other' in African-American texts. *See* **12971**.

18782. BORDEN, ANNE. Heroic 'hussies' and 'brilliant queers': genderracial resistance in the works of Langston Hughes. AAR (28:3) 1994, 333–45.

18783. BOURNE, ST CLAIR. George Houston Bass on Langston Hughes. LHR (9:1/2)/(10:1/2) 1990/91, 92–102. (Interview.)

18784. BOYD, LISA. The folk, the Blues, and the problems of *Mule Bone*. LHR (13:1) 1994/95, 33–44.

18785. BURKHARDT, BARBARA. The Blues in Langston Hughes's *Not without Laughter*. Midamerica (23) 1996, 114–23.

18786. CHINITZ, DAVID. Literacy and authenticity: the Blues poems of Langston Hughes. Callaloo (19:1) 1996, 177–92.

18787. DAVIS, THADIOUS M. Reading the woman's face in Langston Hughes's and Roy De Carava's *Sweet Flypaper of Life*. LHR (12:1) 1993, 22–8.

18788. DESANTIS, CHRISTOPHER C. Rage, repudiation, and endurance: Langston Hughes's radical writings. LHR (12:1) 1993, 31–9.

18789. ETHERIDGE, SHARYNN O. Langston Hughes: an annotated bibliography (1977–1986). LHR (11:1) 1992, 41–57.

18790. FERRELL, TRACY J. PRINCE. *Theme for English B* and the dreams of Langston Hughes. ERev (6:1) 1995, 36–7.

18791. FORD, KAREN JACKSON. Making poetry pay: the commodification of Langston Hughes. *In* (pp. 275–96) **67**.

18792. HALE, ROBERT C. Revolution and the 'low-down folk': poetic strategies for the masses in William Wordsworth's *Lyrical Ballads* and Langston Hughes' *Fine Clothes to the Jew*. *See* **12859**.

18793. HAMALIAN, LEO.   D. H. Lawrence and Black writers. *See* **17595**.

18794. HARPER, DONNA AKIBA SULLIVAN.   Not so simple: the 'Simple' stories by Langston Hughes. (Bibl. 1995, 16895.) Rev. by John McCluskey, Jr, in AL (68:2) 1996, 478–9.

18795. HERNTON, CALVIN.   The poetic consciousness of Langston Hughes from affirmation to revolution. LHR (12:1) 1993, 2–9.

18796. HUBBARD, DOLAN.   Symbolizing America in Langston Hughes's *Father and Son*. LHR (11:1) 1992, 14–20.

18797. HUDSON, THEODORE R.   The duke and the laureate: loose connections. LHR (11:1) 1992, 28–35.

18798. IGNATOW, DAVID.   Memories of Langston Hughes. LHR (13:2) 1995, 5–11.

18799. JARRAWAY, DAVID R.   Montage of an Otherness deferred: dreaming subjectivity in Langston Hughes. AL (68:4) 1996, 819–47.

18800. KELLNER, BRUCE.   Langston Hughes's *Nigger Heaven* Blues. LHR (11:1) 1992, 21–7.

18801. MAYBERRY, SUSAN NEAL.   Ask your mama: women in Langston Hughes's *The Ways of White Folks*. LHR (13:2) 1995, 12–25.

18802. MOORE, DAVID CHIONI.   Local color, global 'color': Langston Hughes, the Black Atlantic, and Soviet Central Asia, 1932. RAL (27:4) 1996, 49–70.

18803. OESTREICH, ALAN E.   'Another Harlem [radiology] specialist' in Langston Hughes' *The Big Sea*. LHR (13:2) 1995, 26–8.

18804. OSOFSKY, AUDREY.   Free to dream: the making of a poet: Langston Hughes. New York: Lothrop, Lee & Shepard, 1996. pp. 112.

18805. SANDERS, LESLIE CATHERINE.   'Also own the theatre': representation in the comedies of Langston Hughes. LHR (11:1) 1992, 6–13.

18806. SAZ, SARA M.   Alfonso Sastre: on the genesis of *Mulatto*. LHR (12:2) 1993, 16–23. (Interview.)

18807. SCHEVILL, JAMES.   An interview with George H. Bass. LHR (9:1/2)/(10:1/2) 1990/91, 14–27.

18808. SHIELDS, JOHN P.   'Never cross the divide': reconstructing Langston Hughes's *Not without Laughter*. AAR (28:4) 1994, 601–13.

18809. TRACY, STEVEN C.   Blues to live by: Langston Hughes's *The Blues I'm Playing*. LHR (12:1) 1993, 12–18.

18810. WALKER, CAROLYN P.   Liberating Christ: Sargeant's metamorphosis in Langston Hughes's *On the Road*. BALF (25:4) 1991, 745–52.

18811. WHITE, JEANNETTE S.; WHITE, CLEMENT A.   Langston Hughes' *On the Road*: no path to freedom. LHR (14:1/2) 1996, 97–103.

18812. ———— Two nations, one vision: America's Langston Hughes and Cuba's Nicolás Guillén: poetry of affirmation: a revision. LHR (12:1) 1993, 42–50.

Ted Hughes

18813. HABERKAMM, HELMUT.   Die Bewegung weg vom *Movement*: Studien zur britischen Gegenwartsdichtung nach 1960. *See* **14938**.

18814. MALCOLM, JANET.   The silent woman: Sylvia Plath & Ted Hughes. (Bibl. 1995, 16906.) Rev. by Marie Arana-Ward in BkW, 27 Mar. 1994, 1, 8; by Terry Whalen in AntR (104) 1996, 67–73.

T. E. Hulme

18815. WHITWORTH, MICHAEL.   T. E. Hulme's quotations from Milton and Ireton. *See* **7616**.

Herbert Huncke

18816. BUSH, CLIVE.   'Why do we always say angel?': Herbert Huncke and Neal Cassady. *In* (pp. 128–57) **4**.

Violet Hunt

18817. WIESENFARTH, JOSEPH.   The Ford–Bowen correspondence. *See* **17908**.

Fannie Hurst

18818. KOPPELMAN, SUSAN.   Fannie Hurst's short stories of working women – *Oats for the Woman, Sob Sister*, and contemporary reader responses: a meditation. *In* (pp. 137–52) **3**.

Zora Neale Hurston

18819. ASHE, BERTRAM D.   'Why don't he like my hair?' Constructing African-American standards of beauty in Toni Morrison's *Song of Solomon* and Zora Neale Hurston's *Their Eyes Were Watching God*. AAR (29:4) 1995, 579–92.

18820. AWKWARD, MICHAEL (ed.).   New essays on *Their Eyes Were Watching God*. (Bibl. 1991, 13458.) Rev. by Missy Dehn Kubitschek in AAR (28:2) 1994, 305–9.

18821. BOI, PAOLA.   A train of words: techn-ique and the dis-closure of knowledge in *Jonah's Gourd Vine* by Zora Neale Hurston. *In* (pp. 417–27) **117**.

18822. BOXWELL, D. A.   'Sis Cat' as ethnographer: self-presentation and self-inscription in Zora Neale Hurston's *Mules and Men*. AAR (26:4) 1992, 605–17.

18823. BOYD, LISA.   The folk, the Blues, and the problems of *Mule Bone*. *See* **18784**.

18824. BRANTLEY, WILL.   O'Connor, Porter, and Hurston on the state of the world. ConLit (37:1) 1996, 132–44 (review-article).

18825. CANDELARIA, CORDELIA CHÁVEZ.   *Différance* and the discourse of 'community' in writings in and about the ethnic other(s). *In* (pp. 185–202) **80**.

18826. CAPPETTI, CARLA.   Zora Neale Hurston: la mitologia e la storia. Àcoma (4) 1995, 76–87.

18827. COOPER, CAROLYN.   Race and the cultural politics of self-representation: a view from the University of the West Indies. *See* **16546**.

18828. COOPER, JAN.   Zora Neale Hurston was always a Southerner too. *In* (pp. 57–69) **32**.

18829. CURREN, ERIK D.   Should their eyes have been watching God? Hurston's use of religious experience and gothic horror. AAR (29:1) 1995, 17–25.

18830. DANIEL, JANICE.   'De understandin' to go 'long wid it': realism and romance in *Their Eyes Were Watching God*. SoLJ (24:1) 1991, 66–76.

18831. DAVIES, KATHLEEN.   Zora Neale Hurston's poetics of embalmment: articulating the rage of Black women and narrative self-defense. AAR (26:1) 1992, 147–59.

18832. Donlon, Jocelyn Hazelwood.   Porches: stories: power: spatial and racial intersections in Faulkner and Hurston. *See* **17683**.

18833. Dubek, Laura.   The social geography of race in Hurston's *Seraph on the Suwanee*. AAR (30:3) 1996, 341–51.

18834. Eisen, Kurt.   Blues speaking women: performing cultural change in *Spunk* and *Ma Rainey's Black Bottom*. TexPres (14) 1993, 21–6.

18835. Foster, Frances Smith.   Parents and children in autobiography by Southern Afro-American writers. *In* (pp. 98–109) **43**.

18836. Glassman, Steve; Seidel, Kathryn Lee (eds).   Zora in Florida. (Bibl. 1993, 13094.) Rev. by Charlotte D. Hunt in FHQ (70:4) 1992, 498–500.

18837. Hale, Anthony R.   Framing the folk: Zora Neale Hurston, John Millington Synge, and the politics of aesthetic ethnography. Comparatist (20) 1996, 50–61.

18838. Harris, Trudier.   The power of the porch: the storyteller's craft in Zora Neale Hurston, Gloria Naylor, and Randall Kenan. Athens; London: Georgia UP, 1996. pp. xiv, 152. (Mercer Univ. Lamar memorial lectures, 39.)

18839. Hayes, Elizabeth T.   'Like seeing you buried': Persephone in *The Bluest Eye*, *Their Eyes Were Watching God*, and *The Color Purple*. *In* (pp. 170–94) **46**.

18840. Hill, Lynda Marion.   Social rituals and the verbal art of Zora Neale Hurston. Washington, DC: Howard UP, 1996. pp. xxxii, 269.

18841. Holmes, Carolyn L.   Reassessing African-American literature through an Afrocentric paradigm: Zora N. Hurston and James Baldwin. *In* (pp. 37–51) **55**.

18842. Hruby, George G.   Zora Neale Hurston as proto-existentialist in hot pursuit of the American dream. LHR (13:2) 1995, 45–53.

18843. Hubbard, Dolan.   '… Ah said Ah'd save de text for you': recontextualizing the sermon to tell (her)story in Zora Neale Hurston's *Their Eyes Were Watching God*. AAR (27:2) 1993, 167–78.

18844. Hurd, Myles Raymond.   What goes around comes around: characterization, climax, and closure in Hurston's *Sweat*. LHR (12:2) 1993, 7–15.

18845. Jones, Evora.   Ascent and immersion: narrative expression in *Their Eyes Were Watching God*. CLAJ (39:3) 1996, 369–79.

18846. Kaplan, Carla.   The erotics of talk: women's writing and feminist paradigms. *See* **10418**.

18847. Knudsen, Janice L.   The tapestry of living: a journey of self-discovery in Hurston's *Their Eyes Were Watching God*. CLAJ (40:2) 1996, 214–29.

18848. Lemke, Sieglinde.   Blurring generic boundaries. Zora Neale Hurston: a writer of fiction and anthropologist. YREAL (12) 1996, 163–77.

18849. Lionnet, Françoise.   Autoethnography: the an-archic style of *Dust Tracks on a Road*. *In* (pp. 113–37) **1**.

18850. Lowe, John.   Jump at the sun: Zora Neale Hurston's cosmic comedy. (Bibl. 1995, 16946.) Rev. by Anna Lillios in SoQ (34:1) 1995, 153–4; by Cyrena N. Pondrom in MFS (42:1) 1996, 149–52; by Jennifer Jordan in TSWL (15:2) 1996, 358–9; by Will Brantley in ConLit (37:1) 1996, 141–4; by Debra Walker King in AAR (30:3) 1996, 481–2; by Kathryn Lee Seidel in FHQ (74:3) 1996, 363–4.

18851. Lyons, Mary E. Sorrow's kitchen: the life and folklore of Zora Neale Hurston. (Bibl. 1993, 13099.) Rev. by Mildred A. Hill-Lubin in FHQ (70:3) 1992, 391–2.

18852. McCaskill, Barbara. The folklore of the coasts in Black women's fiction of the Harlem renaissance. *See* **3293**.

18853. Mackey, Nathaniel. *Other*: from noun to verb. *See* **1983**.

18854. Meisenhelder, Susan. Conflict and resistance in Zora Neale Hurston's *Mules and Men*. *See* **3425**.

18855. —— 'Eating cane' in Gloria Naylor's *The Women of Brewster Place* and Zora Neale Hurston's *Sweat*. NCL (23:2) 1993, 5–7.

18856. Monroe, Barbara. Courtship, comedy, and African-American expressive culture in Zora Neale Hurston's fiction. *In* (pp. 173–88) **64**.

18857. Moore, Opal. The problem of (Black) art. *In* (pp. 177–93) **8**.

18858. Nathiri, N. Y. (ed.). Zora! Zora Neale Hurston, a woman and her community. (Bibl. 1992, 14370.) Rev. by George T. Johnson in AR (49:3) 1991, 465.

18859. Patterson, Gordon. Hurston goes to war: the Army Signal Corps in Saint Augustine. FHQ (74:2) 1995, 166–83.

18860. Plant, Deborah G. Every tub must sit on its own bottom: the philosophy and politics of Zora Neale Hurston. (Bibl. 1995, 16954.) Rev. by Jennifer Jordan in TSWL (15:2) 1996, 359–60; by Darden Asbury Pyron in FHQ (75:2) 1996, 211–13.

18861. Potter, Rich. Zora Neale Hurston and African-American folk identity in *Their Eyes Were Watching God*. Griot (15:1) 1996, 15–26.

18862. Racine, Maria J. Voice and interiority in Zora Neale Hurston's *Their Eyes Were Watching God*. AAR (28:2) 1994, 283–92.

18863. Roark, Chris. Hurston's Shakespeare: 'something like a king, bigger and better!' *See* **6969**.

18864. Stein, Rachel. Remembering the sacred tree: Black women, nature and voodoo in Zora Neale Hurston's *Tell My Horse* and *Their Eyes Were Watching God*. WS (25:5) 1996, 465–82.

18865. Turner, Darwin T. Zora Neale Hurston: one more time. LHR (11:2) 1992, 34–7.

18866. Urgo, Joseph R. 'The tune is the unity of the thing': power and vulnerability in Zora Neale Hurston's *Their Eyes Were Watching God*. SoLJ (23:2) 1991, 40–54.

18867. Woodson, Jon. Zora Neale Hurston's *Their Eyes Were Watching God* and the influence of Jens Peter Jacobsen's *Marie Grubbe*. AAR (26:4) 1992, 619–35.

Aldous Huxley

18868. Attarian, John. *Brave New World* and the flight from God. ModAge (38:4) 1996, 332–42.

18869. Baker, Robert S. Aldous Huxley: history and science between the wars. CLIO (25:3) 1996, 293–300 (review-article).

18870. Bradshaw, David. The best of companions: J. W. N. Sullivan, Aldous Huxley, and the new physics. RES (47:186) 1996, 188–206; (47:187) 1996, 352–68.

18871. —— (ed.). Between the wars: essays and letters. Chicago: Dee, 1994. pp. xxvi, 255. Rev. by Robert S. Baker in CLIO (25:3) 1996, 293–300.

18872. —— The hidden Huxley: contempt and compassion for the masses, 1920–36. (Bibl. 1994, 13143.) Rev. by Jerome Meckier in Utopian Studies (7:2) 1996, 206–12.

18873. DEERY, JUNE.   Aldous Huxley and the mysticism of science. Basingstoke: Macmillan; New York: St Martin's Press, 1996. pp. xi, 231.

18874. MECKIER, JEROME.   Aldous Huxley: dystopian essayist of the 1930s. Utopian Studies (7:2) 1996, 196–212 (review-article).

18875. ——— (ed.).   Critical essays on Aldous Huxley. New York: G. K. Hall; London: Prentice Hall, 1996. pp. xi, 237. (Critical essays on British literature.)

18876. NUGEL, BERNFRIED (ed.).   Now more than ever: proceedings of the Aldous Huxley Centenary Symposium, Münster, 1994. New York; Frankfurt; Bern; Paris: Lang, 1995. pp. xv, 379.

18877. SEXTON, JAMES (ed.).   Aldous Huxley's Hearst essays. (Bibl. 1994, 13151.) Rev. by Jerome Meckier in Utopian Studies (7:2) 1996, 196–206; by Robert S. Baker in CLIO (25:3) 1996, 292–300.

18878. SÖRING, JÜRGEN.   Provozierte 'Gewalt' – zur Poetologie des Drogenrauschs. *See* **10706**.

18879. SQUIER, SUSAN M.   Embryologies of Modernism. Modernism/Modernity (3:3) 1996, 145–53.

Elspeth Huxley

18880. CROSS, ROBERT; PERKIN, MICHAEL.   Elspeth Huxley: a bibliography. Foreword by Elspeth Huxley. Winchester: St Paul's Bibliographies; New Castle, DE: Oak Knoll Press, 1996. pp. xix, 187. (Winchester bibliographies of 20th-century writers.) Rev. by B.C.B. in TLS, 14 June 1996, 30.

18881. FLANAGAN, KATHLEEN.   African folk tales as disruptions of narrative in the works of Grace Ogot and Elspeth Huxley. WS (25:4) 1996, 371–84.

David Henry Hwang

18882. FROCKT, DEBORAH.   David Henry Hwang. *In* (pp. 123–46) **85**.

18883. HAEDICKE, JANET V.   David Henry Hwang's *M. Butterfly*: the eye on the wing. JDTC (7:1) 1992, 27–44.

18884. MA, RUIQI.   The ideology of cultural and gender misunderstanding in D. H. Hwang's *M. Butterfly*. CanRCL (23:4) 1996, 1053–63.

Douglas Hyde

18885. KIBERD, DECLAN.   Decolonizing the mind: Douglas Hyde and Irish Ireland. *In* (pp. 121–37) **106**.

'Robin Hyde' (Iris Guiver Wilkinson)

18886. NEWNHAM, TOM.   New Zealand women in China. Auckland: Graphic, 1995. pp. 129.

Witi Ihimaera

18887. SIMMS, NORMAN.   Mythic grandeur or pastoral naïveté in *Tangi* by Witi Ihimaera. RecL (20) 1994, 5–22.

William Inge

18888. COURANT, JANE.   Social and cultural prophecy in the works of William Inge. StAD (6:2) 1991, 135–51.

18889. SAMPSON, GRANT. Comedy as epic action: structural variants in *Pericles*, *Plain-Dealer*, and *Picnic*. *See* **7120**.

Alootook Ipellie (1951–)

18890. KENNEDY, MICHAEL P. J. Alootook Ipellie: the voice of an Inuk artist. StudCanL (21:2) 1996, 155–64. (Interview.)

R. R. (Robert R.) Irvine

18891. MILLER, JOAN DRUMMOND. Pillar of fire: an interview with Robert Irvine, creator of the Moroni Traveler mysteries. AD (29:2) 1996, 160–4.

John Irving

18892. IRVING, JOHN. The imaginary girlfriend. London: Bloomsbury; Toronto: Knopf, 1996. pp. 148. (Memoir.) Rev. by Andrew Rosenheim in TLS, 22 Mar. 1996, 30.
18893. SYKES, JOHN. Christian apologetic uses of the grotesque in John Irving and Flannery O'Connor. LitTheol (10:1) 1996, 58–67.

Christopher Isherwood

18894. BUCKNELL, KATHERINE (ed.). Diaries: vol. 1, 1939–1960. London; New York: Methuen, 1996. pp. liv, 1048.
18895. KANE, RICHARD C. Ceremony as camouflage: form and ritual in the life and work of Christopher Isherwood. JRS (8:1) 1994, 27–51.
18896. KAPLAN, FRED. Pleased to have been your contemporary: the letters of Christopher Isherwood and Gore Vidal. TLS, 20 Dec. 1996, 14–15.
18897. KERR, DOUGLAS. Disorientations: Auden and Isherwood's China. *See* **16123**.

Kazuo Ishiguro

18898. MANFERLOTTI, STEFANO. Dopo l'impero: romanzo ed etnia in Gran Bretagna. *See* **14616**.
18899. O'BRIEN, SUSIE. Serving a new world order: postcolonial politics in Kazuo Ishiguro's *The Remains of the Day*. MFS (42:4) 1996, 787–806.

Arturo Islas

18900. SKENAZY, PAUL. Borders and bridges, doors and drugstores: toward a geography of time. *In* (pp. 198–216) **108**.

Festus Iyayi

18901. UDUMUKWU, ONYEMAECHI. Ideology and the dialectics of action: Achebe and Iyayi. *See* **15863**.

Charles Jackson

18902. MCCARTHY, PATRICK A. Lowry and *The Lost Weekend*. MalLR (33) 1993, 38–47.

Shirley Jackson

18903. BOBBITT, RANDY. The spiral of silence: a sociological interpretation of Shirley Jackson's *The Lottery*. NCL (24:1) 1994, 8–9.

18904. HALL, JOAN WYLIE.   Fallen Eden in Shirley Jackson's *The Road through the Wall*. Ren (46:4) 1994, 261–70.

18905. RUBENSTEIN, ROBERTA.   House mothers and haunted daughters: Shirley Jackson and female gothic. TSWL (15:2) 1996, 309–31.

W. W. Jacobs

18906. CLOY, JOHN D.   Pensive jester: the literary career of W. W. Jacobs. Lanham, MD; London: UP of America, 1996. pp. vii, 158.

John Jakes

18907. JONES, MARY ELLEN.   John Jakes: a critical companion. Westport, CT; London: Greenwood Press, 1996. pp. xi, 225. (Critical companions to popular contemporary writers.)

C. L. R. James

18908. GRIMSHAW, ANNA (ed.).   Special delivery: the letters of C. L. R. James to Constance Webb, 1939–1948. Oxford; Cambridge, MA: Blackwell, 1996. pp. 393.

M. R. James

18909. HOWARD, JOHN.   M. R. James's New England reading. Ghosts and Scholars (21) 1996, 6–7.

18910. LOUVEL, LILIANE.   *The Mezzotint* de Montague Rhodes James: la manière noire ou l'interposition de la forme. JSSE (23) 1994, 35–50.

18911. MACCULLOCH, SIMON.   The toad in the study: M. R. James, H. P. Lovecraft and forbidden knowledge: part two; part three. Ghosts and Scholars (21) 1996, 37–42; (22) 1996, 40–6.

18912. MICHALSKI, ROBERT.   The malice of inanimate objects: exchange in M. R. James's ghost stories. Extrapolation (37:1) 1996, 46–62.

18913. PARDOE, ROSEMARY, *et al.*   *Stories I Have Tried to Write*: annotations. Ghosts and Scholars (22) 1996, 31–4.

18914. SIMPSON, JACQUELINE.   Ghosts & posts. Ghosts and Scholars (22) 1996, 46–7.

P. D. James

18915. KENNEDY, THOMAS D.   An interview with P. D. James. Cresset (59:3) 1996, 5–10.

Storm Jameson

18916. LASSNER, PHYLLIS.   The fault lines of history: dystopic novels of the Second World War by British women authors. *See* **17106**.

Percy Janes

18917. SHORROCKS, GRAHAM.   Language in Percy Janes's novella, *The Picture on the Wall*. *See* **2705**.

Randall Jarrell

18918. GRISWOLD, JEROME.   The children's books of Randall Jarrell. Introd. by Mary Jarrell. Athens; London: Georgia UP, 1988. pp. xvii, 145. Rev. by Richard Flynn in CLAQ (16:2) 1991, 87–8.

18919. JARRELL, MARY. Randall Jarrell and kitten. NCLR (5) 1996, 132–3.

18920. LONGENBACH, JAMES. Randall Jarrell's semifeminine mind. SRev (81:3) 1996, 368–86.

18921. PRITCHARD, WILLIAM H. Randall Jarrell: a literary life. (Bibl. 1995, 17026.) Rev. by Mark Jarman in GetR (4:4) 1991, 565–79.

18922. —— (ed.). Selected poems. (Bibl. 1992, 14412.) Rev. by Mark Jarman in GetR (4:4) 1991, 565–79.

Robinson Jeffers

18923. BEERS, TERRY. A thousand graceful subtleties: rhetoric in the poetry of Robinson Jeffers. (Bibl. 1995, 17027.) Rev. by Arthur B. Coffin in RMRLL (50:2) 1996, 214–24.

18924. BROPHY, ROBERT (ed.). Robinson Jeffers: dimensions of a poet. New York: Fordham UP, 1995. pp. xvii, 248. Rev. by Arthur B. Coffin in RMRLL (50:2) 1996, 214–24.

18925. HUNT, TIM. Double the *Axe*, double the fun: is there a final version of Jeffers's *The Double Axe*? See **686**.

18926. PORTER, J. S. Robinson Jeffers and the poetry of the end. AntR (92) 1993, 25–31.

18927. WHITE, FRED D. 'The sun proceeds unmoved': Dickinson's circumference as a context of Jeffers' inhumanism. See **11012**.

'Gish Jen' (Lillian Gen)

18928. TUSMITH, BONNIE. Success Chinese-American style: Gish Jen's *Typical American*. Proteus (11:2) 1994, 21–6.

Louis Jenkins (1942–)

18929. NELSON, HOWARD. The work of Louis Jenkins. HC (30:5) 1993, 1–9.

Robin Jenkins

18930. MALZAHN, MANFRED. 'Yet at the start of every season hope springs up': Robin Jenkins's *The Thistle and the Grail* (1954). *In* (pp. 85–96) **115**.

18931. SELLIN, BERNARD. Commitment and betrayal: Robin Jenkins' *A Very Scotch Affair*. *In* (pp. 97–108) **115**.

18932. —— Histoire personelle et histoire collective dans les romans de Robin Jenkins. Études Écossaises (1) 1992, 315–22.

18933. SMITH, IAIN CRICHTON. Robin Jenkins's *The Cone-Gatherers*. Aberdeen: Assn for Scottish Literary Studies, 1995. pp. 45. (Scotnotes, 10.)

Elizabeth Jennings

18934. COELSCH-FOISNER, SABINE. Denying Eros: reading women's poetry of the mid-twentieth century. Gramma (4) 1996, 55–76.

Ruth Prawer Jhabvala

18935. NEWMAN, JUDIE. Postcolonial gothic: Ruth Prawer Jhabvala and the Sobhraj case. MFS (40:1) 1994, 85–100.

18936. RODRÍGUEZ, MARÍA CRISTINA. Narrators in narration in fiction and film: Ruth Prawer Jhabvala's *Heat and Dust*. See **14138**.

18937. Strobl, Gerwin. The challenge of cross-cultural interpretation in the Anglo-Indian novel: the Raj revisited: a comparative
study of three Booker Prize authors: Paul Scott, The Raj Quartet; J. G.
Farrell, *The Siege of Krishnapur*; Ruth Prawer Jhabvala, *Heat and Dust*.
See **17649**.

18938. Urstad, Tone Sundt. Protecting one's inner self: Ruth
Prawer Jhabvala's *Rose Petals*. SSF (33:1) 1996, 43–9.

Paulette Jiles

18939. Brown, Susan. Paulette Jiles's transnational railway ride:
generic change and economic exchange in *Sitting in the Club Car Drinking
Rum and Karma-Kola*. ARCS (26:3) 1996, 391–403.

Ted Joans

18940. Lee, A. Robert. Black Beats: the signifying poetry of LeRoi
Jones/Amiri Baraka, Ted Joans and Bob Kaufman. *In* (pp. 158–77) **4**.

Rita Joe

18941. Joe, Rita; Henry, Lynn. Song of Rita Joe: autobiography
of a Mi'kmaq poet. Lincoln; London: Nebraska UP, 1996. pp. 191.

B. S. Johnson

18942. Crews, Brian. Anti-style and the postmodernist novel.
See **2604**.

Charles Johnson (1948–)

18943. Anon. A selected checklist of works by and about Charles
Johnson. AAR (30:4) 1996, 675.

18944. Boccia, Michael. An interview with Charles Johnson.
AAR (30:4) 1996, 611–18.

18945. Byrd, Rudolph P. *Oxherding Tale* and *Siddhartha*: philosophy,
fiction, and the emergence of a hidden tradition. AAR (30:4) 1996,
549–58.

18946. Coleman, James W. Charles Johnson's quest for Black
freedom in *Oxherding Tale*. AAR (29:4) 1995, 631–44.

18947. Fagel, Brian. Passages from the middle: coloniality and
postcoloniality in Charles Johnson's *Middle Passage*. AAR (30:4) 1996,
625–34.

18948. Gleason, William. The liberation of perception: Charles
Johnson's *Oxherding Tale*. BALF (25:4) 1991, 705–28.

18949. Goudie, S. X. 'Leavin' a mark on the wor(l)d': marksmen
and marked men in *Middle Passage*. AAR (29:1) 1995, 109–22.

18950. Griffiths, Frederick T. 'Sorcery is dialectical': Plato and
Jean Toomer in Charles Johnson's *The Sorcerer's Apprentice*. AAR (30:4)
1996, 527–38.

18951. Hayward, Jennifer. Something to serve: constructs of the
feminine in Charles Johnson's *Oxherding Tale*. BALF (25:4) 1991,
689–703.

18952. Little, Jonathan. From the comic book to the comic:
Charles Johnson's variations on creative expression. AAR (30:4) 1996,
579–601.

18953. Muther, Elizabeth. Isadora at sea: misogyny as comic
capital in Charles Johnson's *Middle Passage*. AAR (30:4) 1996, 649–58.

18954. O'KEEFE, VINCENT A. Reading *rigor mortis*: offstage violence and excluded middles 'in' Johnson's *Middle Passage* and Morrison's *Beloved*. AAR (30:4) 1996, 635–47.

18955. REICHARDT, ULFRIED. Writing the past: history, fiction, and subjectivity in two recent novels about slavery. *See* **16538**.

18956. RUSHDY, ASHRAF H. A. The phenomenology of the Allmuseri: Charles Johnson and the subject of the narrative of slavery. AAR (26:3) 1992, 373–94.

18957. —— The properties of desire: forms of slave identity in Charles Johnson's *Middle Passage*. AQ (50:2) 1994, 73–108.

18958. SCOTT, DANIEL M., III. Interrogating identity: appropriation and transformation in *Middle Passage*. AAR (29:4) 1995, 645–55.

18959. SMITH, VIRGINIA WHATLEY. Sorcery, double-consciousness, and warring souls: an intertextual reading of *Middle Passage* and *Captain Blackman*. AAR (30:4) 1996, 659–74.

18960. STORHOFF, GARY. The artist as universal mind: Berkeley's influence on Charles Johnson. AAR (30:4) 1996, 539–48.

18961. TRAVIS, MOLLY ABEL. Reading in the middle passage: inter-textuality, intersubjectivity, and intercultural conversation. Reader (27) 1992, 12–20.

18962. WALBY, CELESTIN. The African sacrificial kingship ritual and Johnson's *Middle Passage*. AAR (29:4) 1995, 657–69.

Colin Johnson (Mudrooroo Narogin)

18963. PERRETT, BILL. The novels of Mudrooroo. CritS (6:1) 1994, 105–11.

18964. RAINES, GAY. 'Return' in Australian fiction. *In* (pp. 41–9) **102**.

Curt Johnson (1928–)

18965. SAUTTER, R. CRAIG. Curt Johnson: Chicago novelist and publisher. Midamerica (20) 1993, 108–17.

Denis Johnson

18966. BLANKLEY, ELYSE. Clear-cutting the Western myth: beyond Joan Didion. *In* (pp. 177–97) **108**.

18967. LENZ, MILLICENT. Reinventing a world: myth in Denis Johnson's *Fiskadoro*. *In* (pp. 114–22) **77**.

Fenton Johnson

18968. HARRINGTON, JOSEPH. A response to Lisa Woolley. LHR (14:1/2) 1996, 49–51.

18969. WOOLLEY, LISA. From Chicago renaissance to Chicago renaissance: the poetry of Fenton Johnson. LHR (14:1/2) 1996, 36–48.

James Weldon Johnson

18970. CLARKE, CHERYL. Race, homosocial desire, and 'Mammon' in *Autobiography of an Ex-Coloured Man*. *In* (pp. 84–97) **92**.

18971. GOELLNICHT, DONALD C. Passing as autobiography: James Weldon Johnson's *The Autobiography of an Ex-Coloured Man*. AAR (30:1) 1996, 17–33.

18972. KAWASH, SAMIRA. *The Autobiography of an Ex-Coloured Man*: (passing for) Black passing for White. *In* (pp. 59–74) **82**.

18973. PFEIFFER, KATHLEEN.   Individualism, success, and American identity in *The Autobiography of an Ex-Colored Man*. AAR (30:3) 1996, 403–19.

Stephanie Johnson

18974. EDWARDS, DENIS.   She's got attitude. Quote Unquote (33) 1996, 12–13. (Interview.)

Denis Johnston

18975. RONSLEY, JOSEPH.   Initial response to Denis Johnston's *The Moon in the Yellow River*. In (pp. 235–46) **49**.

Jennifer Johnston

18976. FRANKOVÁ, MILADA.   The unbridgeable gulf: the sense of division in Jennifer Johnston's *The Railway Station Man*. Brno Studies in English (22) 1996, 97–106.

18977. MURSI, WAFFIA.   The Big House in Mahfouz's *The Count Down* and Jennifer Johnston's *Fool's Sanctuary*. In (pp. 23–36) **60**.

18978. WINNER, ANTHONY.   Disorders of reading short novels and perplexities. See **16998**.

Robert Johnstone

18979. MARKEN, RON.   Michael Foley, Robert Johnstone and Frank Ormsby: three Ulster poets in the *GO* situation. *In* (pp. 130–43) **86**.

David Jones

18980. CAMPBELL, ANDREW.   Strata and bedrock in David Jones' *Anathémata*. Ren (46:2) 1994, 117–31.

18981. CUNNINGHAM, ADRIAN.   Primary things: land, work, and sign. ChesR (22:1/2) 1996, 73–87.

18982. DAVENPORT, GUY.   Stanley Spencer and David Jones. *In* (pp. 259–68) **16**.

18983. DEANE, PATRICK.   David Jones, T. S. Eliot, and the Modernist unfinished. See **17499**.

18984. DILWORTH, THOMAS.   David Jones's *The Deluge*: engraving the structure of the modern long poem. See **194**.

18985. —— *In Parenthesis*: the displacement of chronicle. *In* (pp. 229–40) **16**.

18986. —— Liturgical echoes: David Jones on Shakespeare's *Richard III*, v, iii. See **7147**.

18987. GOLDPAUGH, TOM.   On the traverse of the wall: the lost long poem of David Jones. JML (19:1) 1994, 31–53.

18988. GRENNEN, JOSEPH E.   The 'making of works': David Jones and medieval drama. See **5028**.

18989. HYNE, ANTHONY (sel.).   David Jones, a fusilier at the Front: his records of the Great War in word and image. Bridgend, Mid-Glamorgan: Seren, 1995. pp. 183.

18990. KEITH, W. J.   'Intermixed lingo': listening to David Jones. *In* (pp. 251–8) **16**.

18991. MATTHIAS, JOHN (ed.).   David Jones: man and poet. Orono: National Poetry Foundation, Univ. of Maine, 1989. pp. 580, (plates) 32. Rev. by Jeremy Hooker in PN Review (17:3) 1991, 69.

18992. ROSSI, UMBERTO.   No sense of an ending: the difficulty of ending a (hi)story in European and American World War I narratives. *See* **17904**.

18993. SHERRY, VINCENT. David Jones and literary Modernism: the use of the dramatic monologue. *In* (pp. 241–9) **16**.

Diana Wynne Jones

18994. KONDRATIEV, ALEXEI. Tales newly told: a column on current modern fantasy. Mythlore (19:2) 1993, 34, 44.

Gayl Jones

18995. BASU, BIMAN. Public and private discourses and the Black female subject: Gayl Jones' *Eva's Man*. Callaloo (19:1) 1996, 193–208.

18996. DAVISON, CAROL MARGARET. 'Love 'em and lynch 'em': the castration motif in Gayl Jones's *Eva's Man*. AAR (29:3) 1995, 393–410.

18997. GOTTFRIED, AMY S. Angry arts: silence, speech, and song in Gayl Jones's *Corregidora*. AAR (28:4) 1994, 559–70.

18998. KESTER, GUNILLA THEANDER. The forbidden fruit and female disorderly eating: three versions of Eve. *In* (pp. 231–8) **24**.

18999. MCKIBLE, ADAM. 'These are the facts of the darky's history': thinking history and reading names in four African-American texts. *See* **16644**.

19000. WILCOX, JANELLE. Resistant silence, resistant subject: (re)reading Gayl Jones's *Eva's Man*. *In* (pp. 72–96) **9**.

19001. WILENTZ, GAY. Gayl Jones's oraliterary explorations. *See* **13367**.

James Jones

19002. CHAMPION, LAURIE. Jones's *From Here to Eternity*. Exp (54:4) 1996, 242–4.

Rodney Jones (1950–)

19003. MCKAY, ROBERT. A conversation with Rodney Jones. BWR (22:2) 1996, 25–32.

Thom Jones

19004. TRUCKS, ROB. A conversation with Thom Jones. BWR (22:1) 1995, 143–62.

Erica Jong

19005. JADWIN, LISA. Critiquing the new canon. *See* **13140**.

19006. JONG, ERICA. Fear of fifty: a midlife memoir. (Bibl. 1994, 13203.) Rev. by Lynn Freed in BkW, 31 July 1994, 5.

19007. TEMPLIN, CHARLOTTE. Feminism and the politics of literary reputation: the example of Erica Jong. (Bibl. 1995, 17079.) Rev. by Mary Anne Ferguson in TSWL (15:1) 1996, 173–5; by Lisa Jadwin in ColLit (23:3) 1996, 171–7.

June Jordan

19008. SPLAWN, P. JANE. New World consciousness in the poetry of Ntozake Shange and June Jordan: two African-American women's response to expansionism in the Third World. CLAJ (39:4) 1996, 417–31.

Allison Joseph

19009. HAMILTON, KENDRA.   An interview with Allison Joseph. Callaloo (19:2) 1996, 461–72.

Jenny Joseph

19010. COELSCH-FOISNER, SABINE.   Epiphanies and polyphonies: '*Ghosts' and Other Stories* by Jenny Joseph. Poet's Voice (3:1) 1996, 102–7.

Arun Joshi

19011. DHAWAN, R. K.   Destiny of a nation: Arun Joshi's *The Apprentice. In* (pp. 51–60) **45**.

Gabriel Josipovici

19012. JOSIPOVICI, GABRIEL.   *The Big Glass*: a note. Salmagundi (88/89) 1990/91, 333–8.

Elsa Joubert

19013. GREADY, PAUL.   The witness: Rian Malan's *My Traitor's Heart* and Elsa Joubert's *Poppie*. Current Writing (7:1) 1995, 88–104.

James Joyce

19014. ACHILLES, JOCHEN.   Funktionen der Religion in der irischen Kultur der Jahrhundertwende: Moore, Shaw, Yeats and Joyce. LJGG (37) 1996, 193–210.

19015. ANSPAUGH, KELLY.   'Faith, hope, and – what was it?': Beckett reading Joyce reading Dante. *See* **16252**.

19016. —— Flann O'Brien: postmodern Judas. Notes on Modern Irish Literature (4) 1992, 11–16.

19017. —— The metempsychosis of Ajax: Leopold Bloom as excremental hero. MS (90:2) 1996, 139–53.

19018. —— 'When lovely wooman stoops to conk him': Virginia Woolf in *Finnegans Wake*. JSA (7) 1996, 176–91.

19019. ARKINS, BRIAN.   Joyce and Greek. NQ (43:4) 1996, 444.

19020. ARMSTRONG, PAUL B.   James Joyce and the politics of reading: power, belief, and justice in *Ulysses*. YREAL (11) 1995, 325–45.

19021. ATTRIDGE, DEREK (ed.).   The Cambridge companion to James Joyce. (Bibl. 1995, 17087.) Rev. by Wolfgang Wicht in ZAA (41:1) 1993, 85–7.

19022. BACHINGER, KATRINA.   Setting allegory adrift in John Ashbery's *Mountains and Rivers*, James Joyce's *Portrait of the Artist as a Young Man*, and Vincent O'Sullivan's *Let the River Stand. In* (pp. 285–93) **125**.

19023. BALLESTEROS GONZÁLEZ, ANTONIO.   Digression and inter-textual parody in Thomas Nashe, Laurence Sterne and James Joyce. *In* (pp. 55–64) **57**.

19024. BARTA, PETER I.   Bely, Joyce, and Döblin: peripatetics in the city novel. Gainesville: Florida UP, 1996. pp. xv, 119. (Florida James Joyce.)

19025. BARTLETT, SALLY A.   Spectral thought and psychological mimesis in *A Portrait of the Artist as a Young Man*. Notes on Modern Irish Literature (5) 1993, 57–66.

19026. BAŠIĆ, SONJA.   A book of many uncertainties: Joyce's *Dubliners*. Style (25:3) 1991, 351–77.

19027. Baucom, Ian. Mournful histories: narratives of postimperial melancholy. *See* **3714**.

19028. Baxter, Charles. Rhyming action. *See* **4338**.

19029. Beekman, E. M. The verbal empires of Simon Vestdijk and James Joyce. *See* **2579**.

19030. Beja, Morris; Norris, David (eds). Joyce in the Hibernian metropolis: essays. Columbus: Ohio State UP, 1996. pp. xx, 312. (13th International James Joyce Symposium, Dublin, June 1992.)

19031. Benstock, Bernard. Narrative con/texts in *Ulysses*. (Bibl. 1993, 13176.) Rev. by Garry Leonard in MFS (40:2) 1994, 409–11.

19032. Billi, Mirella; Bini, Benedetta; Splendore, Paola (eds). Intorno a Joyce: cinquant'anni dopo. Viterbo, 10–11 dicembre 1991: atti del convegno. Bologna: Cosmopoli, 1995. pp. 125.

19033. Black, Martha Fodaski. Shaw and Joyce: the last word in stolentelling. (Bibl. 1995, 17097.) Rev. by Scott W. Klein in MFS (42:4) 1996, 886–7; by Norman L. Lofland in ELN (34:1) 1996, 90–1.

19034. Blades, John. How to study James Joyce. Basingstoke: Macmillan, 1996. pp. 168. (How to study literature.)

19035. Blamires, Harry. The new Bloomsday book: a guide through *Ulysses*. (Bibl. 1968, 9773.) London; New York: Routledge, 1996. pp. xvi, 253. (Third ed.: first ed. 1966.)

19036. Bloomer, Jennifer. Architecture and the text: the scrypts of Joyce and Piranesi. (Bibl. 1995, 17099.) Rev. by Kevin J. H. Dettmar in JJQ (33:3) 1996, 459–61.

19037. Bluemel, Kristin. The feminine laughter of no return: James Joyce and Dorothy Richardson. *In* (pp. 161–71) **64**.

19038. Blumenbach, Ulrich. Irish views on British wars: Joyce's Museyroom memorial: metaphors of memory and recollection. ZAA (44:1) 1996, 44–50.

19039. —— Joyce's handiwork on myth. ZAA (41:4) 1993, 331–40.

19040. Blythe, Hal; Sweet, Charlie. Diptych in *Araby*: the key to understanding the boy's 'anguish and anger'. Notes on Modern Irish Literature (6) 1994, 16–18.

19041. Boldrini, Lucia. *The Sisters* and the *Inferno*: an intertextual network. Style (25:3) 1991, 453–65.

19042. Boscagli, Maurizia; Duffy, Enda. Joyce's face. *In* (pp. 133–59) **67**.

19043. Brammer, Marsanne. Joyce's *hallucinian via*: mysteries, gender, and the staging of 'Circe'. JSA (7) 1996, 86–124.

19044. Brian, Michael. 'A very fine piece of writing': an etymological, Dantean, and gnostic reading of Joyce's *Ivy Day in the Committee Room*. *See* **2590**.

19045. Briggs, Austin. The full stop at the end of 'Ithaca': thirteen ways – and then some – of looking at a black dot. *See* **588**.

19046. Brockman, William S. Current JJ checklist: 72; 73; 74. JJQ (33:2) 1996, 245–54; (33:3) 1996, 429–40; (33:4) 1996, 605–15.

19047. Buckwald, Craig. Journeying westward: Romantic nature rhetoric and lyric structure for Joyce's *The Dead*. *In* (pp. 7–37) **28**.

19048. Burrell, Harry. Chemistry and physics in *Finnegans Wake*. JSA (7) 1996, 192–218.

19049. —— Narrative design in *Finnegans Wake*: the *Wake* lock picked. Gainesville: Florida UP, 1996. pp. xiii, 226. (Florida James Joyce.)

19050. BUSH, RONALD.   James Joyce: the way he lives now. *See* **15138**.

19051. ——James Joyce and Oscar Wilde. *See* **12779**.

19052. CAHALAN, JAMES M.   'The guilty forgiving the innocent': Stanislaus, Shaun, and Shem in *Finnegans Wake*. Notes on Modern Irish Literature (6) 1994, 5–11.

19053. CANEDA CABRERA, M. TERESA.   *Ulysses* and heteroglossia: a Bakhtinian reading of the 'Nausicaa' episode. *See* **2595**.

19054. CARRIKER, KITTI.   Neologisms and hypograms in the language of Stephen Dedalus: a Riffaterrean reading of *Portrait. See* **1825**.

19055. CATO, BOB; VITIELLO, GREG (eds).   Joyce images. Introd. by Anthony Burgess. (Bibl. 1995, 17116.) Rev. by Stephen Watt in JJQ (33:3) 1996, 462–5.

19056. CHENG, VINCENT J.   Joyce, race, and Empire. (Bibl. 1995, 17118.) Rev. by Tracey Teets Schwarze in MFS (42:4) 1996, 873–83; by Tony Crowley in NQ (43:2) 1996, 239–40; by Ronan McDonald in TLS, 20 Dec. 1996, 12.

19057. —— MARTIN, TIMOTHY (eds).   Joyce in context. (Bibl. 1995, 17119.) Rev. by R. Brandon Kershner in MFS (40:1) 1994, 179–80.

19058. CHESNEY, THOM D.   Joyce and O'Faolain: when 'talking trees' speak two authors' names. Notes on Modern Irish Literature (7:1) 1995, 50–4.

19059. CHISHOLM, DIANNE.   Feminist deleuzions: James Joyce and the politics of 'becoming-woman'. CanRCL (19:1/2) 1992, 201–24.

19060. CIANCI, GIOVANNI.   Sperimentando: la Dublino simultanea di Joyce. QLLSM (4) 1990, 239–57.

19061. CIXOUS, HÉLÈNE.   'Mamãe, disse ele'; or, Joyce's second hand. PT (17:3) 1996, 339–66.

19062. CONDE-PARRILLA, Mᴬ ÁNGELES.   James Joyce's *Ulysses*: the obscene nature of Molly's soliloquy and two Spanish translations. JJQ (33:2) 1996, 211–36.

19063. CONELY, JAMES.   Sounding the sirens again: an evaluation of musical structure in the 'Sirens' chapter of James Joyce's *Ulysses*. ArsL (7) 1993, 107–16.

19064. CONNOR, JAMES A.   RADIOfree JOYCE: *Wake* language and the experience of radio. Critic (48:3) 1994, 3–15.

19065. CONNOR, STEVEN.   James Joyce. Plymouth: Northcote House; London: British Council, 1996. pp. ix, 110. (Writers and their work.)

19066. CORCORAN, MARLENA G.   Language, character, and gender in the direct discourse of *Dubliners. See* **2602**.

19067. COSGROVE, BRIAN.   Male sexuality and female rejection: persistent irony in Joyce's *The Dead*. IUR (26:1) 1996, 37–47.

19068. COSTELLO, PETER.   James Joyce: the years of growth, 1882–1915: a biography. (Bibl. 1995, 17127.) Rev. by John Kidd in BkW, 23 May 1996, 9.

19069. CULLETON, CLAIRE A.   Names and naming in Joyce. *See* **2131**.

19070. DAVISON, NEIL R.   'Cyclops', Sinn Féin, and 'the Jew': an historical reconsideration. JML (19:2) 1995, 245–57.

19071. —— James Joyce, *Ulysses* and the construction of Jewish identity: culture, biography and 'the Jew' in Modernist Europe. Cambridge; New York: CUP, 1996. pp. xi, 305. (Cf. bibl. 1994, 13251.) Rev. by Bryan Cheyette in TLS, 11 Oct. 1996, 29.

19072. DETTMAR, KEVIN J. H.   The illicit Joyce of postmodernism:

reading against the grain. Madison; London: Wisconsin UP, 1996. pp. xv, 276. (Bibl. 1991, 13578.)

19073. DIMENT, GALYA. The autobiographical novel of co-consciousness: Goncharov, Woolf, and Joyce. (Bibl. 1994, 13258.) Rev. by Steven Trout in ELT (39:2) 1996, 259–63; by Neil Cornwell in JJQ (33:4) 1996, 639–41.

19074. DOHERTY, FRANCIS. William Trevor's *A Meeting in Middle Age* and romantic irony. JSSE (16) 1991, 19–28.

19075. DOLOFF, STEVEN. Rousseau and the confessions of *Araby*. JJQ (33:2) 1996, 255–8.

19076. DUFFY, ENDA. The subaltern *Ulysses*. (Bibl. 1995, 17139.) Rev. by Scott W. Klein in MFS (42:4) 1996, 883–6.

19077. ECHERUO, MICHAEL J. C. Joyce's 'epical equidistance'. *See* **2609**.

19078. —— Modernism, Blackface, and the postcolonial condition. *See* **13057**.

19079. ERZGRÄBER, WILLI. Mündlich tradiertes Wissen in *Finnegans Wake. In* (pp. 149–69) **73**.

19080. —— The Wife of Bath and Molly Bloom: self-portrait of two women. *In* (pp. 75–82) **11**.

19081. FAIRHALL, JAMES. James Joyce and the question of history. (Bibl. 1994, 13265.) Rev. by Mark Osteen in MFS (40:2) 1994, 404–6; by Wolfgang Wicht in ZAA (42:4) 1994, 411–12; by Brian W. Shaffer in ELT (39:1) 1996, 95–8; by Andrew Gibson in Eng (45:182) 1996, 166–70; by Fred Radford in JJQ (33:2) 1996, 272–9; by Patrick Parrinder in YES (26) 1996, 314–15.

19082. FARGNOLI, A. NICHOLAS; GILLESPIE, MICHAEL PATRICK. James Joyce A to Z: the essential reference to the life and work. (Bibl. 1995, 17146.) London: Bloomsbury, 1996. Rev. by J.C. in TLS, 12 Jan. 1996, 28.

19083. FELTON, SHARON. Portraits of the artists as young defiers: James Joyce and Muriel Spark. TPB (33) 1996, 24–33.

19084. FERRER, DANIEL. Joyce's notebooks: publicizing the private sphere of writing. *In* (pp. 202–22) **69**.

19085. —— GRODEN, MICHAEL. Post-genetic Joyce. RR (86:3) 1995, 501–12.

19086. FERRIS, KATHLEEN. James Joyce & the burden of disease. (Bibl. 1995, 17147.) Rev. by Patrick A. McCarthy in ELT (39:2) 1996, 250–3; by Ronan McDonald in TLS, 20 Dec. 1996, 12; by Joseph Kelly in JJQ (33:4) 1996, 626–34.

19087. FESHBACH, SIDNEY. The magic lantern of tradition on *A Portrait of the Artist as a Young Man.* JSA (7) 1996, 3–66.

19088. FINNERAN, RICHARD J. 'That word known to all men' in *Ulysses*: a reconsideration. *See* **643**.

19089. FLEISCHMANN, RUTH. Knowledge of the world as the forbidden fruit: Canon Sheehan and Joyce on the *sacrificium intellectus. In* (pp. 127–37) **112**.

19090. FRIEDMAN, SUSAN STANFORD (ed.). Joyce: the return of the repressed. (Bibl. 1995, 17148.) Rev. by Michael Patrick Gillespie in CLIO (25:1) 1995, 83–94.

19091. FROULA, CHRISTINE. Modernism's body: sex, culture, and Joyce. New York: Columbia UP, 1996. pp. xvi, 316.

19092. FÜGER, WILHELM. James Joyce: Epoche, Werk, Wirkung.

Munich: Beck, 1994. pp. 352. (Arbeitsbücher zur Literaturgeschichte.) Rev. by Wolfgang Wicht in ZAA (43:4) 1995, 366–8.

19093. GABLER, HANS WALTER.   Optionen und Lösungen: zur kritischen und synoptischen Edition von James Joyces *Ulysses. See* **650**.

19094. GARCIA-LEON, RAFAEL I.   'Threemaster': a note on the last line of the 'Telemachia' of *Ulysses*. Notes on Modern Irish Literature (3) 1991, 49–51.

19095. GIBSON, ANDREW (ed.).   Joyce's 'Ithaca'. Amsterdam; Atlanta, GA: Rodopi, 1996. pp. 267. (European Joyce Studies, 6.)

19096. GILLESPIE, GERALD.   The city of wo/man: labyrinth, wilderness, garden. *See* **3834**.

19097. GILLESPIE, MICHAEL PATRICK.   'It seems history is to blame': interpretive subjectivity in Joyce and his critics. CLIO (25:1) 1995, 83–94 (review-article).

19098. GIOVANNANGELI, JEAN-LOUIS.   La rupture des pactes dans *Ulysses*. CVE (44) 1996, 167–83.

19099. GOODWYN, ANDREW (ed.).   Dubliners. Cambridge; New York: CUP, 1995. pp. 240. (Cambridge literature.)

19100. GORDON, JOHN.   The *Golden Ass* in *Finnegans Wake*. Notes on Modern Irish Literature (3) 1991, 45–8.

19101. —— *Joyce egg* and *claddagh ring*: Joycean artifacts in *Ulysses* and *Finnegans Wake. See* **1840**.

19102. —— Some Joyce skies. JJQ (33:3) 1996, 411–27.

19103. GOTTFRIED, ROY.   Joyce's iritis and the irritated text: the dislexic *Ulysses*. (Bibl. 1995, 17161.) Rev. by M. Keith Booker in SAtlR (61:4) 1996, 118–21.

19104. GRAFF, AGNIESZKA.   Dipping into the riverrun: a foreigner's reading of *Finnegans Wake*. AP (23) 1996, 83–94.

19105. GRAYSON, JANET.   The consecration of Stephen Dedalus. ELN (34:1) 1996, 55–63.

19106. GREGORY, SHELLY.   ReWaking the mother tongue in *Finnegans Wake*: a Kristevan interpretation. *See* **2633**.

19107. GUNN, DANIEL P.   Beware of imitations: advertisement as reflexive commentary in *Ulysses*. TCL (42:4) 1996, 481–93.

19108. GUPTA, SUMAN.   Knowing Joyce and understanding *Ulysses*: Mary and Pádraic Colum. *See* **17010**.

19109. HART, MICHAEL.   'Many planes of narrative': a comparative perspective on Sterne and Joyce. *In* (pp. 65–80) **57**.

19110. HARTY, JOHN.   'Cyclops': a drunken nightmare of Irish history. Notes on Modern Irish Literature (7:2) 1995, 16–21.

19111. —— The doubling of Dublin messages in *The Sisters*. Notes on Modern Irish Literature (4) 1992, 42–4.

19112. —— James Joyce and P. T. Barnum. Notes on Modern Irish Literature (8) 1996, 41–6.

19113. HARTY, JOHN, III.   *FW* 26.25–36: 'Belly the First'. Notes on Modern Irish Literature (6) 1994, 12–15.

19114. —— Is Beckett's 'come in' in *Finnegans Wake*? *See* **16305**.

19115. HASHEM, EVINE.   The re-enactment of colonialism in James Joyce's *A Portrait of the Artist as a Young Man*. *In* (pp. 235–43) **60**.

19116. HAYMAN, DAVID.   Attitudinal dynamics in narrative: Flaubert, Lawrence, Joyce. JML (19:2) 1995, 201–14.

19117. HEDBERG, JOHANNES.   Hans Kraus, Jan Parandowski, and James Joyce. JJQ (33:3) 1996, 441–6.

19118. HERMAN, DAVID. Universal grammar and narrative form. *See* **2641**.

19119. HERRING, PHILLIP F. Joyce's uncertainty principle. (Bibl. 1987, 11252.) Rev. by Joseph Valente in Style (25:3) 1991, 506–13.

19120. HOBBS, JOHN. 'Old father, mother's son': Seamus Heaney on James Joyce. *See* **18514**.

19121. HOFHEINZ, THOMAS C. Joyce and the invention of Irish history: *Finnegans Wake* in context. (Bibl. 1995, 17174.) Rev. by Tracey Teets Schwarze in MFS (42:4) 1996, 873–83; by Mary Lowe-Evans in ELT (39:3) 1996, 389–93.

19122. JAMES, LAWRENCE L. 'Hearasay in/paradox lust': dissemination, desire and Joyce's (hyper)textual apparatus. Litteraria Pragensia (6:11) 1996, 91–100.

19123. JEDYNAK, STANLEY L. Joyce's Dante and *The Dead*. Greyfriar (31) 1991, 3–13.

19124. JOCKERS, MATTHEW L. Another 'word known to all men' in Joyce's *Ulysses*. Notes on Modern Irish Literature (8) 1996, 38–40.

19125. JOHNSON, JERI (ed.). Ulysses. (Bibl. 1995, 17181.) Rev. by Richard Aczel in EEM (3:2) 1994, 84–5.

19126. KEMENY, TOMASO (ed.). Differences similar: more jottings on Joyce. Udine: Campanotto, 1990. pp. 109.

19127. KERSHNER, R. B. (ed.). Joyce and popular culture. Gainesville: Florida UP, 1996. pp. 223. (Florida James Joyce.)

19128. KIRCHHOFER, ANTON. The text in the closet: concealment and disclosure in James Joyce's *Ulysses*. *See* **12790**.

19129. KLEIN, SCOTT W. The fictions of James Joyce and Wyndham Lewis: monsters of nature and design. Cambridge; New York: CUP, 1994. pp. xiii, 260. (Cf. bibl. 1991, 13622.) Rev. by Michael Wutz in MFS (42:1) 1996, 189–92; by Jesse Matz in Modernism/Modernity (3:2) 1996, 119–21; by John Gordon in ELT (39:3) 1996, 386–9; by Timothy Materer in JJQ (33:4) 1996, 646–9; by Kelly Anspaugh in CLIO (25:3) 1996, 338–41.

19130. LANG, FREDERICK K. *Ulysses* and the Irish god. (Bibl. 1994, 13299.) Rev. by Daniel Schenker in StudN (27:2) 1995, 226–8; by Bruce Bradley in JJQ (33:2) 1996, 300–5.

19131. LEHAN, RICHARD. James Joyce: the limits of Modernism and the realms of the literary text. AQ (50:1) 1994, 87–108.

19132. LEONARD, GARRY M. Reading *Dubliners* again: a Lacanian perspective. (Bibl. 1995, 17198.) Rev. by Hilary Clark in JJQ (33:2) 1996, 318–23.

19133. LERNOUT, GEERT. The real 'scandal' of *Ulysses*. *See* **721**.

19134. —— (ed.). *Finnegans Wake*: fifty years. (Bibl. 1993, 13292.) Rev. by Wolfgang Wicht in ZAA (41:2) 1993, 184–5.

19135. LEWIECKI-WILSON, CYNTHIA. Writing against the family: gender in Lawrence and Joyce. (Bibl. 1995, 17201.) Rev. by Earl G. Ingersoll in StudN (28:2) 1996, 263–6.

19136. LOLL, UDO. James Joyce: Genie im Patriarchat. Stuttgart: Metzler, 1992. pp. 340. Rev. by Wilhelm Füger in GRM (43:3) 1993, 360–3.

19137. LOSS, ARCHIE. The censor swings: Joyce's work and the new censorship. *See* **1068**.

19138. LOWE-EVANS, MARY. Sex and confession in the Joyce canon: some historical parallels. JML (16:4) 1990, 563–76.

19139. LYONS, J. B.   The drinking days of Joyce and Lowry. MalLR (31/32) 1992/93, 112–21.

19140. McBRIDE, MARGARET.   *Finnegans Wake*: the issue of Issy's schizophrenia. JSA (7) 1996, 145–75.

19141. McLUHAN, ERIC.   Joyce and McLuhan. AntR (106) 1996, 157–65.

19142. McMAHON, TIMOTHY G.   Cultural nativism and Irish-Ireland: the *Leader* as a source for Joyce's *Ulysses*. See **1315**.

19143. MALLOY, CATHARINE.   Seamus Heaney's *Station Island*: questioning orthodoxy and commitment. See **18529**.

19144. MARCHI, DUDLEY M.   Participatory aesthetics: reading Mallarmé and Joyce. Comparatist (19) 1995, 76–96.

19145. METRESS, CHRIS.   Peter Taylor's Tennessee *Dubliners*: paralysis and silence in '*A Long Fourth' and Other Stories*. JSSE (18) 1992, 103–14.

19146. MOLINO, MICHAEL R.   The net of language: marginalization, resistance, and difference in contemporary Irish literature. See **17996**.

19147. MORSE, DONALD E.   Starting from the earth, starting from the stars: the fantastic in Samuel Beckett's plays and James Joyce's *Ulysses*. In (pp. 6–18) **112**.

19148. MOSHER, HAROLD F., JR.   Clichés and repetition in *Dubliners*: the example of *A Little Cloud*. Style (25:3) 1991, 378–92.

19149. MULLER, JILL.   John Henry Newman and the education of Stephen Dedalus. See **11969**.

19150. NOLAN, EMER.   James Joyce and Nationalism. (Bibl. 1995, 17227.) Rev. by Tracey Teets Schwarze in MFS (42:4) 1996, 873–83; by Susan Shaw Sailer in ELT (39:2) 1996, 253–8; by Brian G. Caraher in Irish Review (19) 1996, 140–6; by Ronan McDonald in TLS, 20 Dec. 1996, 12.

19151. NORRIS, MARGOT.   Joyce's web: the social unraveling of Modernism. (Bibl. 1995, 17230.) Rev. by Michael Patrick Gillespie in CLIO (25:1) 1995, 83–94.

19152. O'NEILL, CHRISTINE.   Too fine a point: a stylistic analysis of the 'Eumaeus' episode in James Joyce's *Ulysses*. Trier: WVT, 1996. pp. 177. (Horizonte, 20.)

19153. ONO, MOTOKO.   Portraits of a mask: Wilde, Joyce and Mishima. In (pp. 112–16) **60**.

19154. OSTEEN, MARK.   The economy of *Ulysses*: making both ends meet. (Bibl. 1995, 17232.) Rev. by Tracey Teets Schwarze in MFS (42:4) 1996, 873–83; by Gregory Castle in ELT (39:4) 1996, 510–14.

19155. —— The treasure-house of language: managing symbolic economies in Joyce's *Portrait*. See **2688**.

19156. PARRINDER, PATRICK.   On Geert Lernout's *The Real 'Scandal' of 'Ulysses'*. See **781**.

19157. PATELLANI, MASSIMO.   'Attualità' di Nietzsche e 'inattualità' di Joyce: il problema della storia in 'Nestor'. QLLSM (5) 1992, 99–126.

19158. PEARCE, RICHARD (ed.).   Molly Blooms: a polylogue on 'Penelope' and cultural studies. (Bibl. 1995, 17235.) Rev. by Michael Patrick Gillespie in CLIO (25:1) 1995, 83–94.

19159. PIETTE, ADAM.   *Finnegans Wake* and familial memory. SPELL (9) 1996, 249–55.

19160. —— Remembering and the sound of words: Mallarmé, Proust, Joyce, Beckett. See **16351**.

19161. Pillonca, Giovanni. Wilde in *Ulysses*: il valore di una presenza. *See* **12800**.

19162. Presley, John Woodrow. *Finnegans Wake, Lady Pokingham,* and Victorian erotic fantasy. *See* **9929**.

19163. Rademacher, Jörg. '*James Joyce's own image*'. Über die allmähliche Verfertigung der Begriffe '*image*' und '*imagination*' beim Schreiben in *A Portrait* und *Ulysses*. (Bibl. 1993, 13349.) Rev. by Wolfgang Wicht in ZAA (43:1) 1995, 101–2.

19164. Rademacher, Jörg W. Totalized (auto-)biography as fragmented intertextuality: Shakespeare – Sterne – Joyce. *In* (pp. 81–6) **57**.

19165. Radford, Fred. Anticipating *Finnegans Wake*: the *United Irishman* and La Belle Iseult. *See* **1345**.

19166. —— James Joyce and the question of historicist desire. JJQ (33:2) 1996, 271–91 (review-article).

19167. Rado, Lisa. *Hypsos* or *spadia*? Rethinking androgyny in *Ulysses* with help from Sacher-Masoch. TCL (42:2) 1996, 193–207.

19168. Rainey, Lawrence. Consuming investments: Joyce's *Ulysses*. *See* **1075**.

19169. Rainsford, Dominic. Pity in Joyce: the significance of the blind stripling. ELN (34:1) 1996, 47–55.

19170. Reizbaum, Marilyn. A nightmare of history: Ireland's Jews and Joyce's *Ulysses*. *In* (pp. 102–13) **5**.

19171. Rice, Thomas Jackson. The geometry of meaning in *Dubliners*: a Euclidian approach. Style (25:3) 1991, 393–404.

19172. Richards, Bernard. Epiphany. *See* **12119**.

19173. Rickard, John S. Chiromancy in *Ulysses*. JJQ (33:3) 1996, 446–7.

19174. Riquelme, J. P. Joyce's *The Dead*: the dissolution of the self and the police. Style (25:3) 1991, 488–505.

19175. Robinson, Peter. Joyce's lyric poetry. *In* (pp. 151–8) **49**.

19176. Rocco, John. Drinking *Ulysses*: Joyce, Bass ale, and the typography of Cubism. JJQ (33:3) 1996, 399–409.

19177. Rodríguez-Gago, Antonia. Molly's 'happy nights' and Winnie's 'happy days'. *In* (pp. 29–40) **119**.

19178. Romine, Scott. Poetry and parody: James Joyce and his *Little Cloud*. Notes on Modern Irish Literature (5) 1993, 5–13.

19179. Rose, Danis. The textual diaries of James Joyce. Dublin: Lilliput Press, 1995. pp. x, 198. Rev. by Brian G. Caraher in Irish Review (19) 1996, 140–6; by Hans Walter Gabler in JJQ (33:4) 1996, 621–5.

19180. Ross, Míceál. Androgynous Bloom: forerunners in Irish and Egyptian folk tradition. *In* (pp. 83–90) **60**.

19181. Rossi, Umberto. No sense of an ending: the difficulty of ending a (hi)story in European and American World War I narratives. *See* **17904**.

19182. Sandquist, Brigitte L. The tree wedding in 'Cyclops' and the ramifications of cata-logic. JJQ (33:2) 1996, 195–209.

19183. Sarbu, Aladár. Romantic and modern: vision and form in Yeats, Shaw and Joyce. *In* (pp. 19–27) **112**.

19184. Schneider, Ulrich. Titles in *Dubliners*. Style (25:3) 1991, 405–15.

19185. Schoening, Mark. T. S. Eliot meets Michael Gold:

Modernism and radicalism in Depression-era American literature. *See* **17556**.

19186. Scholes, Robert.   In the brothel of Modernism: Picasso and Joyce. AJSem (8:1/2) 1991, 5–25.

19187. Schwarz, Daniel R.   Searching for Modernism's genetic code: Picasso, Joyce, and Stevens as cultural configuration. WebS (10:1) 1993, 67–86.

19188. —— (ed.).   *The Dead*: complete, authoritative text with biographical and historical contexts, critical history, and essays from five contemporary critical perspectives. (Bibl. 1995, 17257.) Rev. by John Whittier-Ferguson in JJQ (33:4) 1996, 641–6.

19189. Scott, Bonnie Kime.   Joyce's post-modern return to Ireland. *In* (pp. 123–34) **49**.

19190. Segall, Jeffrey.   Joyce in America: cultural politics and the trials of *Ulysses*. (Bibl. 1994, 13355.) Rev. by Garry Leonard in MFS (40:2) 1994, 406–9; by Michael Patrick Gillespie in CLIO (25:1) 1995, 83–94.

19191. —— '*Kulturbolschewismus* is here': James Joyce and the anti-Modernist crusade in America, 1928–1944. *See* **15759**.

19192. Senn, Fritz.   Inductive scrutinies: focus on Joyce. Ed. by Christine O'Neill. (Bibl. 1995, 17261.) Rev. by Tracey Teets Schwarze in MFS (42:4) 1996, 873–83; by Brian G. Caraher in Irish Review (19) 1996, 140–6.

19193. Sherry, Vincent.   James Joyce, *Ulysses*. (Bibl. 1994, 13362.) Rev. by David Kadlec in Modernism/Modernity (3:1) 1996, 159–60; by Michael Patrick Gillespie in JJQ (33:3) 1996, 469–71.

19194. Simmerman, Stephen K.   Joycean liminality: Gabriel Conroy and Stephen Dedalus on the verge of becoming artists. TPB (33) 1996, 43–52.

19195. Spoo, Robert.   James Joyce and the language of history: Dedalus's nightmare. (Bibl. 1995, 17267.) Rev. by Michael Patrick Gillespie in CLIO (25:1) 1995, 83–94; by Derek Attridge in MFS (42:4) 1996, 888–90; by Susan Swartzlander in ELT (39:2) 1996, 258–9; by Ronan McDonald in TLS, 20 Dec. 1996, 12; by Fred Radford in JJQ (33:2) 1996, 279–84; by Susan C. Harris in StudN (28:2) 1996, 271–3.

19196. Stanzel, F. K.   'A naval Siberia': James Joyce in Pola 1904–5. GRM (46:3) 1996, 302–14.

19197. Strub, Christian.   Odysseus hört Argonautenmusik; oder, Warum die Sirenen nicht singen. Zur Handlungsstruktur im 'Sirens'-Kapitel des *Ulysses*. ZAA (41:4) 1993, 318–30.

19198. Suzuki, Takashi.   Regionalism in *Ulysses*: a trap. *In* (pp. 115–22) **49**.

19199. Swinson, Ward.   Notes on *Ulysses*. JJQ (33:2) 1996, 258–66.

19200. Theall, Donald F.   Beyond the word: reconstructing sense in the Joyce era of technology, culture, and communication. Toronto; Buffalo, NY; London: Toronto UP, 1995. pp. xxi, 328. Rev. by Leon Surette in LRC (5:9) 1996, 25–6.

19201. Theoharis, Theoharis Constantine.   Making much of nothing. JJQ (33:4) 1996, 583–91.

19202. Tiffany, Grace.   *Our Mutual Friend* in 'Eumaeus': Joyce appropriates Dickens. *See* **10919**.

19203. Ungar, András P.   Ulysses in *Ulysses*: what the Nolan said. *In* (pp. 138–47) **112**.

19204. Valente, Joseph. Examining uncertainty. Style (25:3) 1991, 506–13 (review-article).

19205. ——— James Joyce and the problem of justice: negotiating sexual and colonial difference. (Bibl. 1995, 17285.) Rev. by Zack Bowen in ELT (39:4) 1996, 507–10.

19206. Walton, James. Weaving the wind: Stephen Dedalus, Joseph Joubert, and the conditions of art. Comparatist (16) 1992, 69–100.

19207. Watson, George J. Irish identity and the literary revival: Synge, Yeats, Joyce, and O'Casey. (Bibl. 1995, 17290.) Rev. by Patrick Colm Hogan in ColLit (23:3) 1996, 163–70.

19208. Welch, Robert. 'He rests. He has travelled.' Movement in Joyce. In (pp. 135–50) **49**.

19209. Wheatley-Lovoy, Cynthia D. The rebirth of tragedy: Nietzsche and Narcissus in *A Painful Case* and *The Dead*. JJQ (33:2) 1996, 177–93.

19210. Whittaker, Stephen. A Joycean permutation. *See* **875**.

19211. Williams, Trevor. 'Brothers of the great white lodge': Joyce and the critique of imperialism. JJQ (33:3) 1996, 377–97.

19212. Williams, Trevor L. No cheer for the 'gratefully oppressed' in Joyce's *Dubliners*. Style (25:3) 1991, 416–38.

19213. Yun, Hee-Whan. Illuminating darkness of *Araby*: a boy's self-discovery. EngSt (20) 1996, 123–44.

19214. Ziaukas, Tim. 'Indispensable wires': Joyce's *Ulysses* and the origins of public relations. EI (31:3/4) 1996, 176–88.

Donald Justice

19215. McCoy, James A. 'Black flowers, black flowers': meta-criticism in Donald Justice's *Bus Stop*. NCL (26:5) 1996, 9–10.

19216. Turco, Lewis. The progress of Donald Justice. HC (29:4) 1992, 1–7.

Roberta Kalechofsky

19217. Materassi, Mario (introd.). *Myra Is Dying* by Roberta Kalechofsky. RSAJ (3) 1992, 113–29.

Smaro Kamboureli

19218. Rao, Eleonora. Customs and immigration: Smaro Kamboureli *in the second person* and the airport of language. Textus (6) 1993, 241–58.

Sarah Kane

19219. Sellar, Tom. Truth and dare: Sarah Kane's *Blasted*. Theater (27:1) 1996, 29–34.

Welwyn Wilton Katz

19220. Wytenbroek, J. R. Cetacean consciousness in Katz's *Whalesinger* and L'Engle's *A Ring of Endless Light*. Mythlore (21:2) 1996, 435–8.

Janet Kauffman

19221. Hinnefeld, Joyce. For the collaborators (thoughts on narrative, on the works of Janet Kauffman, on I and she, on autobiography, on suicide or not). DQ (31:2) 1996, 70–8.

Bob Kaufman

19222. LEE, A. ROBERT . Black Beats: the signifying poetry of LeRoi Jones/Amiri Baraka, Ted Joans and Bob Kaufman. *In* (pp. 158–77) **4**.

19223. LINDBERG, KATHRYNE V. Bob Kaufman, Sir Real, and his rather surreal self-presentation. Talisman (11) 1993, 167–82.

George S. Kaufman

19224. SAUER, DAVID K. George S. Kaufman's exploitation of women (characters): dramaturgy and feminism. *See* **17013**.

'Anna Kavan' (Helen Woods Edmonds)

19225. CALLARD, D. A. The case of Anna Kavan: a biography. (Bibl. 1993, 13413.) Rev. by Doris Earnshaw in WLT (69:2) 1995, 370.

19226. GARRITY, JANE. Nocturnal transgressions in *The House of Sleep*: Anna Kavan's maternal registers. MFS (40:2) 1994, 253–77.

19227. RAO, ELEONORA. The 'black sun': Anna Kavan's narratives of abjection. Textus (4) 1991, 119–45.

Patrick Kavanagh (1905–1967)

19228. ALLISON, JONATHAN. Patrick Kavanagh: a reference guide. New York: G. K. Hall; London: Prentice Hall, 1996. pp. xxviii, 218. (Reference guide to literature.)

19229. HARMON, MAURICE. Kavanagh's old peasant. *In* (pp. 213–22) **106**.

19230. HOLLIDAY, SHAWN. Sex and comedy in Patrick Kavanagh's *The Great Hunger*. Notes on Modern Irish Literature (7:1) 1995, 34–40.

John B. Keane

19231. DEANE, PAUL. John B. Keane: the writer as Irishman. Notes on Modern Irish Literature (7:1) 1995, 24–33.

19232. QUINTELLI-NEARY, MARGUERITE. Traditional satire in the novels of John B. Keane. Notes on Modern Irish Literature (7:2) 1995, 29–35.

Molly Keane ('M. J. Farrell')

19233. DEANE, PAUL. The Big House revisited: Molly Keane's *Time after Time*. Notes on Modern Irish Literature (3) 1991, 37–44.

19234. HUGHES, CLAIR. 'Hound voices': the Big House in three novels by Anglo-Irish women writers. *In* (pp. 349–55) **49**.

Janice Kulyk Keefer

19235. MÄRALD, ELISABETH. In transit: aspects of transculturalism in Janice Kulyk Keefer's travels. Umeå: Umeå Univ., 1996. pp. ii, 182. (Acta Universitatis Umensis: Umeå studies in the humanities, 130.)

Garrison Keillor

19236. COGNARD-BLACK, JENNIFER A. Garrison Keillor's Wobegon heroes. PCR (6:1) 1995, 107–19.

19237. OSTREM, WILLIAM. Nietzsche, Keillor and the religious heritage of Lake Wobegon. Midamerica (18) 1991, 115–23.

19238. SCHOLL, PETER A. Garrison Keillor. (Bibl. 1993, 13423.) Iowa City: Iowa UP, 1996. pp. 248. Rev. by Ray B. Browne in JAC (18:3)

1995, 111; by Bruce Michelson in AmS (36:2) 1995, 221–2; by B.K. in TLS, 24 May 1996, 36.

Helen Keller

19239. WHITTY, PAM.   Helen Keller: words, worlds and literacies. Signal (78) 1995, 193–206.

Myra Kelly

19240. RICO, BARBARA ROCHE.   Cross-cultural encounters in Myra Kelly's short fiction. Notes on Modern Irish Literature (6) 1994, 31–8.

James Kelman

19241. BAKER, SIMON.   'Wee stories with a working-class theme': the reimagining of urban realism in the fiction of James Kelman. *In* (pp. 235–50) **115**.
19242. BELL, IAN A.   Imagine living there: form and ideology in contemporary Scottish fiction. *In* (pp. 217–33) **115**.
19243. KLAUS, GUSTAV.   Kelman for beginners. JSSE (22) 1994, 127–35.
19244. KLAUS, H. GUSTAV.   1984 Glasgow: Alasdair Gray, Tom Leonard, James Kelman. *See* **18312**.
19245. MACARTHUR, J. D.   The narrative voice in James Kelman's *The Burn*. SEL (72:2) 1996, 181–95.
19246. MALEY, WILLY.   Swearing blind: Kelman and the curse of the working classes. Edinburgh Review (95) 1996, 105–12.
19247. MONNICKENDAM, ANDREW.   Historicity and representation in the Scottish novel. *See* **11468**.
19248. SELLIN, BERNARD.   James Kelman, *The Busconductor Hines* et la réalité ouvrière. Études Écossaises (3) 1996, 129–39.

Randall Kenan

19249. HARRIS, TRUDIER.   The power of the porch: the storyteller's craft in Zora Neale Hurston, Gloria Naylor, and Randall Kenan. *See* **18838**.
19250. HUNT, V.   A conversation with Randall Kenan. AAR (29:3) 1995, 411–20.

Thomas Keneally

19251. EDWARDS, VANESSA.   Keneally's republican push and the Irish influence. *See* **3234**.
19252. HIGGINS, JOHN.   Event *versus* narration in *Schindler's List*. *See* **13796**.
19253. KENEALLY, THOMAS.   Faithful in his fashion. BkW, 12 Nov. 1995, 1, 10.

Adrienne Kennedy

19254. BARNETT, CLAUDIA.   Adrienne Kennedy and Shakespeare's sister. AmDr (5:2) 1996, 44–56.
19255. BRYANT-JACKSON, PAUL K.; OVERBECK, LOIS MORE (eds). Intersecting boundaries: the theatre of Adrienne Kennedy. (Bibl. 1993, 13431.) Rev. by John Williams in AAR (27:3) 1993, 495–500.
19256. CARBONE, MELISSA.   The concomitant forces of placement:

re-placing the African-American woman in Adrienne Kennedy's *Funnyhouse of a Negro* and *Ohio State Murders*. TexPres (14) 1993, 5–9.

19257. GAGNIER, REGENIA.   Feminist autobiography in the 1980s. *See* **15150**.

19258. KENNEDY, ADRIENNE.   People who led to my plays. (Bibl. 1988, 7925.) Rev. by Regenia Gagnier in Feminist Studies (17:1) 1991, 138–40.

19259. KOLIN, PHILIP C.   Color connections in Adrienne Kennedy's *She Talks to Beethoven*. NCL (24:2) 1994, 4–6.

19260. —— Orpheus ascending: music, race, and gender in Adrienne Kennedy's *She Talks to Beethoven*. AAR (28:2) 1994, 293–304.

19261. ZINMAN, TOBY SILVERMAN.   'In the presence of mine enemies': Adrienne Kennedy's *An Evening with Dead Essex*. StAD (6:1) 1991, 3–13.

Anne Kennedy

19262. SUÁREZ LAFUENTE, MARÍA SOCORRO.   *Música Ficta, English Music* y el impulso holístico de la literatura postcolonial/postmoderna. *See* **15873**.

Leo Kennedy

19263. MORLEY, PATRICIA.   As though life mattered: Leo Kennedy's story. (Bibl. 1995, 17337.) Rev. by Maureen Ryan in CanL (148) 1996, 177–9; by George L. Parker in ESCan (22:3) 1996, 354–5.

William Kennedy

19264. REILLY, EDWARD C.   A William Kennedy bibliography. BB (48:2) 1991, 61–74.

19265. SMITH, TOM.   Very bountiful bones: an interview with William Kennedy. WebS (10:1) 1993, 21–44.

Brendan Kennelly

19266. BROWN, TERENCE.   Telling tales: Kennelly's *Cromwell*, Muldoon's *The More a Man Has the More a Man Wants*. *In* (pp. 144–57) **86**.

19267. PERSSON, ÅKE.   Betraying the age: Brendan Kennelly's mission. IUR (26:1) 1996, 118–26.

19268. —— The heroic ideal in Brendan Kennelly's poetry. *In* (pp. 97–104) **60**.

19269. —— (ed.).   This fellow with the fabulous smile: a tribute to Brendan Kennelly. Newcastle upon Tyne: Bloodaxe, 1996. pp. 128.

Jack Kerouac

19270. CHARTERS, ANN (ed.).   Jack Kerouac: selected letters, 1940–1956. (Bibl. 1995, 17345.) Rev. by Joyce Johnson in BkW, 12 Mar. 1995, 1, 14.

19271. ELLIS, R. J.   'I am only a jolly storyteller': Jack Kerouac's *On the Road* and *Visions of Cody*. *In* (pp. 37–60) **4**.

19272. KOWALEWSKI, MICHAEL.   Jack Kerouac and the Beats in San Francisco. *In* (pp. 126–43) **108**.

19273. LE PELLEC, YVES.   Jack Kerouac, *pícaro* de l'âme. Études littéraires (26:3) 1993/94, 45–57.

19274. McNEIL, HELEN.   The archaeology of gender in the Beat Movement. *In* (pp. 178–99) **4**.

19275. MIRAGLIA, ANNE MARIE.   Texts engendering texts: a Québécois writing of American novels. *In* (pp. 49–60) **51**.

19276. O'KEEFFE, BERNARD. On the road. *See* **17869**.
19277. SINCLAIR, IAIN. Off-beat. LRB (18:11) 1996, 12–13.

Ken Kesey

19278. HAGUE, THEODORA-ANN. Gendered irony in Ken Kesey's *One Flew over the Cuckoo's Nest*. Cithara (33:1) 1993, 27–34.
19279. HAYS, PETER L. Sherwood Anderson and *One Flew over the Cuckoo's Nest*. *See* **15995**.
19280. NEUSTADTER, ROGER. The astro-turf garden: pastoralism in the industrial age. *See* **16553**.
19281. SEMINO, ELENA; SWINDLEHURST, KATE. Metaphor and mind style in Ken Kesey's *One Flew over the Cuckoo's Nest*. *See* **2467**.
19282. TANNER, STEPHEN L. The Western American context of *One Flew over the Cuckoo's Nest*. *In* (pp. 291–320) **7**.
19283. WAXLER, ROBERT P. The mixed heritage of the chief: revisiting the problem of manhood in *One Flew over the Cuckoo's Nest*. JPC (29:3) 1995, 225–35.

Jessie Kesson

19284. MONNICKENDAM, ANDREW. Beauty or beast? Landscape in the fiction of Jessie Kesson. *In* (pp. 109–23) **115**.

Benedict Kiely

19285. KERSNOWSKI, FRANK. An interview with Benedict Kiely. JSSE (21) 1993, 39–52.

John Oliver Killens

19286. WILSON, CHARLES, JR. Revolution as theme in John Oliver Killens' *Youngblood*. *In* (pp. 123–32) **113**.

Thomas Kilroy

19287. KILROY, THOMAS. From page to stage. *In* (pp. 55–62) **52**.
19288. MURRAY, CHRISTOPHER. Thomas Kilroy's world elsewhere. *In* (pp. 63–77) **52**.

Jamaica Kincaid

19289. CHICK, NANCY. The broken clock: time, identity, and autobiography in Jamaica Kincaid's *Lucy*. CLAJ (40:1) 1996, 90–103.
19290. COVI, GIOVANNA. Jamaica Kincaid and the resistance to canons. *In* (pp. 345–54) **81**.
19291. DAVIES, CAROLE BOYCE . Writing home: gender and heritage in the works of Afro-Caribbean/American women writers. *In* (pp. 59–73) **81**.
19292. FERGUSON, MOIRA. Jamaica Kincaid: where the land meets the body. (Bibl. 1994, 13426.) Rev. by Lynda Koolish in AL (68:1) 1996, 268–9.
19293. LIMA, MARIA HELENA. Decolonizing genre: Jamaica Kincaid and the *Bildungsroman*. Genre (26:4) 1993, 431–59.
19294. LOE, THOMAS. Jamaica Kincaid's *Lucy* as a short-story sequence. NCL (26:1) 1996, 2–3.
19295. NAGEL, JAMES. Desperate hopes, desperate lives: depression and self-realization in Jamaica Kincaid's *Annie John* and *Lucy*. *In* (pp. 237–53) **123**.

19296. WACHTEL, ELEANOR.   Eleanor Wachtel with Jamaica Kincaid: interview. MalaR (116) 1996, 55–71.

Larry King

19297. MONDELLO, BOB.   Larry L. King. *In* (pp. 147–67) **85**.

Stephen King ('Richard Bachman')

19298. ABBOTT, JOE.   Why is Stephen King so popular? Or, Meditations on the 'domestic monsterdrama'. PCR (6:2) 1995, 27–43.

19299. BADLEY, LINDA.   Writing horror and the body: the fiction of Stephen King, Clive Barker, and Anne Rice. *See* **16201**.

19300. CASEBEER, EDWIN F.   The ecological system of Stephen King's *The Dark Half*. JFA (6:2/3) 1993, 126–42.

19301. DE ANGELIS, VALERIO MASSIMO.   L'automobile: le macchine della narrazione di Stephen King. *In* (pp. 277–83) **117**.

19302. KEYISHIAN, AMY; KEYISHIAN, MARJORIE.   Stephen King. New York: Chelsea House, 1996. pp. 127. (Pop culture legends.)

19303. MUSTAZZA, LEONARD.   The power of symbols and the failure of virtue: Catholicism in Stephen King's *Salem's Lot*. JFA (3:4) 1990 (pub. 1994), 107–19.

19304. POLLIN, BURTON R.   Stephen King's fiction and the legacy of Poe. *See* **12073**.

19305. RUSSELL, SHARON A.   Stephen King: a critical companion. Westport, CT; London: Greenwood Press, 1996. pp. xi, 171. (Critical companions to popular contemporary writers.)

19306. SCHROEDER, NATALIE.   Stephen King's *Misery*: Freudian sexual symbolism and the battle of the sexes. JPC (30:2) 1996, 137–48.

19307. STEIN, LEON.   A Holocaust education in reverse: Stephen King's *The Summer of Corruption: Apt Pupil*. JFA (5:2) 1992, 61–80.

19308. STROBY, W. C.   Digging up stories with Stephen King. WD (72:3) 1992, 22–7.

Thomas King

19309. MATCHIE, THOMAS; LARSON, BRETT.   Coyote fixes the world: the power of myth in Thomas King's *Green Grass, Running Water*. NDQ (63:2) 1996, 153–68.

Margaret Kingery

19310. GENTRY, MARSHALL BRUCE.   An interview with Margaret Kingery. SDR (34:2) 1996, 117–28.

Barbara Kingsolver

19311. RYAN, MAUREEN.   Barbara Kingsolver's lowfat fiction. JAC (18:4) 1995, 77–82.

Maxine Hong Kingston

19312. FURTH, ISABELLA.   Bee-e-een! Nation, transformation and the hyphen of ethnicity in Kingston's *Tripmaster Monkey*. MFS (40:1) 1994, 33–49.

19313. GAO, YAN.   The art of parody: Maxine Hong Kingston's use of Chinese sources. New York; Frankfurt; Bern; Paris: Lang, 1996. pp. x, 178. (Many voices: ethnic literatures of the Americas, 2.)

19314. GOLDMAN, MARLENE.   Naming the unspeakable: the mapping of female identity in Maxine Hong Kingston's *The Woman Warrior*. *In* (pp. 223–32) **50**.

19315. HENKE, SUZETTE A. Women's life-writing and the minority voice: Maya Angelou, Maxine Hong Kingston, and Alice Walker. *In* (pp. 210–33) **123**.

19316. MONSMA, BRADLEY JOHN. 'Active readers … obverse tricksters': trickster texts and cross-cultural reading. MLS (26:4) 1996, 83–98.

19317. OCHOA, PEGGY. The historical moments of postcolonial writing: beyond colonialism's binary. *See* **15685**.

19318. SESHACHARI, NEILA C. Reinventing peace: conversations with tripmaster Maxine Hong Kingston: an interview. WebS (12:1) 1995, 7–26.

19319. SKENAZY, PAUL. Borders and bridges, doors and drugstores: toward a geography of time. *In* (pp. 198–216) **108**.

19320. SMITH, JEANNE R. Rethinking American culture: Maxine Hong Kingston's cross-cultural *Tripmaster Monkey*. MLS (26:4) 1996, 71–81.

19321. YU, NING. A strategy against marginalization: the 'high' and 'low' cultures in Kingston's *China Men*. ColLit (23:3) 1996, 73–87.

Galway Kinnell

19322. LIBBY, ANTHONY. Angels in the bone shop. *In* (pp. 281–301) **58**.

19323. MACEIRA, KAREN. Galway Kinnell: a voice to lead us. HC (32:4) 1995, 1–14.

19324. TUTEN, NANCY L. *The Seekonk Woods*: Kinnell's Frostian 'Directive' to the wilderness. *See* **18072**.

19325. TUTEN, NANCY LEWIS. The language of sexuality: Walt Whitman and Galway Kinnell. *See* **12762**.

19326. ZIMMERMAN, LEE. Self-delighting souls, self-enclosed egos: Yeats and Galway Kinnell. *In* (pp. 265–79) **58**.

Thomas Kinsella

19327. ABBATE BADIN, DONATELLA. Thomas Kinsella. New York: Twayne; London: Prentice Hall, 1996. pp. xv, 226. (Twayne's English authors, 527.)

19328. DAWE, GERALD. Poetry as example: Kinsella's Peppercanister poems. *In* (pp. 204–15) **86**.

19329. HARMON, MAURICE. Ancient lights in Austin Clarke and Thomas Kinsella. *In* (pp. 70–87) **112**.

19330. JACKSON, THOMAS. 'Get the fresh rain down!' – Thomas Kinsella and translation. *See* **3152**.

19331. JOHN, BRIAN. Reading the ground: the poetry of Thomas Kinsella. Washington, DC: Catholic Univ. of America Press, 1996. pp. xii, 275.

19332. MURSI, NAWAL. Death in urban and rural poems of Thomas Kinsella. *In* (pp. 297–308) **60**.

W. P. Kinsella

19333. COOPER, CAROLINE M. *Field of Dreams*: a favorite of President Clinton – but a typical Reaganite film. *See* **13569**.

Rudyard Kipling

19334. ASCHE, AUSTIN.   Sticks and stones: Kipling and the Marconi scandal. KJ (70:280) 1996, 12–28.

19335. BROWN, ROBIN.   Edgar Wallace and Kiplings *manqués*. KJ (70:279) 1996, 41–6.

19336. CIHA, KAREN; JOSEPH, JANET; MARTIN, TERRY J.   Racism in Walt Disney's *The Jungle Book. See* **13550**.

19337. DI PIAZZA, ÉLIO.   Il socialdarvinismo di Kipling nei *Plain Tales*. Textus (8:1) 1995, 127–51.

19338. DUNHAM, WOLCOTT B., JR.   Not Roosevelt but Dunham. KJ (70:277) 1996, 37–8. (Correction of error in Lord Birkenhead's biography of Kipling.)

19339. FURNAS, J. C.   Transatlantic twins: Rudyard Kipling and Owen Wister. ASch (64:4) 1995, 599–606.

19340. HAEFS, GISBERT.   *Captains Courageous* in German. KJ (70:279) 1996, 36–9.

19341. HOPKIRK, PETER.   Quest for Kim: in search of Kipling's Great Game. London: Murray, 1996. pp. 274. Rev. by T. J. Binyon in TLS, 8 Nov. 1996, 29.

19342. JACKSON, PETER; KOBAYASHI, AUDREY.   Narratives of empire: British and Canadian readings of Kipling's colonial fiction. BJCS (11:2) 1996, 299–306.

19343. KEMP, SANDRA; LEWIS, LISA (eds).   Writings on writing by Rudyard Kipling. Cambridge; New York: CUP, 1996. pp. xxviii, 213.

19344. LAL, MALASHRI.   Questioning otherness: racial indeterminacy in Kipling, Tagore and Paul Scott. In-between (3:1) 1994, 3–13.

19345. LITTLEWOOD, IAN.   Kipling and Japan, with particular reference to Kipling's first visit, in 1889. KJ (70:278) 1996, 11–20.

19346. LOW, GAIL CHING-LIANG.   White skins/Black masks: representation and colonialism. *See* **9641**.

19347. MENAND, LOUIS.   Kipling in the history of forms. *In* (pp. 148–65) **41**.

19348. MERTNER, EDGAR.   'Rudderless Ruddy': Kipling and the women in his life. ZAA (44:3) 1996, 220–31.

19349. —— Rudyard Kipling: women in his work and the *conditio humana*. LWU (29:4) 1996, 271–85.

19350. MOORE-GILBERT, B. J.   Cultural transfer in Kipling's writing. KJ (70:277) 1996, 11–18.

19351. MOORE-GILBERT, BART .   'The Bhabhal of tongues': reading Kipling, reading Bhabha. *In* (pp. 111–38) **132**.

19352. PAXTON, NANCY L.   Secrets of the colonial harem: gender, sexuality, and the law in Kipling's novels. *In* (pp. 139–62) **132**.

19353. PHILLIPS, JERRY; WOJCIK-ANDREWS, IAN.   Telling tales to children: the pedagogy of empire in MGM's *Kim* and Disney's *Aladdin. See* **14086**.

19354. PINNEY, THOMAS (ed.).   The letters of Rudyard Kipling: vol. 3, 1900–10. Basingstoke: Macmillan; Iowa City: Iowa UP, 1996. pp. xii, 482. Rev. by Miranda Seymour in TLS, 10 May 1996, 26.

19355. PRAKASH, GYAN.   Science 'gone native' in colonial India. Representations (40) 1992, 153–78.

19356. RICHARDS, THOMAS.   Archive and utopia. *See* **18728**.

19357. RICKETTS, HARRY.   Was Kipling gay? (Does it matter?) New Zealand Books (6:5) 1996, 11.

19358. SCANNELL, JAMES. The method is unsound: the aesthetic dissonance of colonial justification in Kipling, Conrad, and Greene. *See* **17084**.

19359. STAMERS-SMITH, EILEEN. Kipling and Bermuda. KJ (70:277) 1996, 21–36.

19360. SULLIVAN, ZOHREH T. Narratives of Empire: the fictions of Rudyard Kipling. (Bibl. 1995, 17425.) Rev. by John McClure in StudN (28:1) 1996, 130–2.

19361. VAN BOHEEMEN, CHRISTEL. Kipling, koloniale identiteit en het djungelgevoel. (Kipling, colonial identity and the jungle feeling.) De Gids (159:8) 1996, 601–7.

19362. WOLFE, ALAN D. Kipling in Hollywood. *See* **14339**.

Russell Kirk

19363. NELSON, DALE J. Russell Kirk and Basil Smith. Ghosts and Scholars (20) 1995, 46–8. (Writers in the James tradition, 17.)

A. M. Klein

19364. CAPLAN, USHER; STEIN, M. W. (eds). Literary essays and reviews. (Bibl. 1989, 10209.) Rev. by Linda Rozmovits in ARCS (18:4) 1988, 494–5.

19365. LEMM, RICHARD. Izak and Ishmael: A. M. Klein's Zionist poetry and the Palestinian conflict. StudCanL (16:2) 1991/92, 54–78.

19366. POLLOCK, ZAILIG. A. M. Klein: the story of the poet. (Bibl. 1994, 13486.) Rev. by Jon Kertzer in CanL (151) 1996, 175–7; by P. K. Page in JCP (11) 1996, 191–3; by Irving Massey in Criticism (38:2) 1996, 342–7.

William Kloefkorn

19367. SAUCERMAN, JAMES R. Poems of popular common ground: four voices of the Midwest. MidM (22) 1994, 9–17.

Etheridge Knight

19368. ANAPORTE-EASTON, JEAN. Etheridge Knight, poet and prisoner: an introduction. Callaloo (19:4) 1996, 941–6.

19369. ROWELL, CHARLES H. An interview with Etheridge Knight. Callaloo (19:4) 1996, 967–81.

Elizabeth Knox

19370. AMERY, MARK. Family affairs. Quote Unquote (39) 1996, 16–17. (Interview.)

C. J. Koch

19371. FARNSWORTH, RODNEY. An Australian cultural synthesis: *Wayang*, the Hollywood romance, and *The Year of Living Dangerously*. *See* **13650**.

Kenneth Koch

19372. KOCH, KENNETH. The art of poetry: poems, parodies, interviews, essays and other work. Ann Arbor: Michigan UP, 1996. pp. vi, 214. (Poets on poetry.)

Joy Kogawa

19373. CHEUNG, KING-KOK.   Attentive silence in Joy Kogawa's *Obasan. In* (pp. 113–29) **59**.

19374. KANEFSKY, RACHELLE.   Debunking a postmodern conception of history: a defence of humanist values in the novels of Joy Kogawa. CanL (148) 1996, 11–36.

Frederick Kohner

19375.   O'BRIEN, KEVIN.   *Gidget*: surfing the illusory wave of change. PCR (6:2) 1995, 83–91.

Kathe Koja

19376.   HANTKE, STEFFEN.   Deconstructing horror: commodities in the fiction of Jonathan Carroll and Kathe Koja. *See* **16699**.

Yusef Komunyakaa

19377.   AUBERT, ALVIN.   Yusef Komunyakaa: the unified vision – canonization and humanity. AAR (27:1) 1993, 119–23.

19378.   FABRE, MICHEL.   On Yusef Komunyaka [*sic*]. SoQ (34:2) 1996, 5–8.

19379.   JONES, KIRKLAND C.   Folk idiom in the literary expression of two African-American authors: Rita Dove and Yusef Komunyakaa. *In* (pp. 149–65) **55**.

Dean Koontz

19380.   KOTKER, JOAN G.   Dean Koontz: a critical companion. Westport, CT; London: Greenwood Press, 1996. pp. xi, 184. (Critical companions to popular contemporary writers.)

Ted Kooser

19381.   SAUCERMAN, JAMES R.   Poems of popular common ground: four voices of the Midwest. *See* **19367**.

Arthur Kopit

19382.   ZINS, DANIEL F.   Waging nuclear war rationally: strategic 'thought' in Arthur Kopit's *End of the World. In* (pp. 129–39) **77**.

Jerzy Kosinski

19383.   CORY, MARK.   Comedic distance in Holocaust literature. *See* **16384**.

19384.   HAWTHORNE, MARK D.   Allusions to Robert Browning in Jerzy Kosinski's *The Hermit of 69th Street. See* **10518**.

19385.   —— Author as text: Kosinski's *The Hermit of 69th Street.* StudAJL (15) 1996, 17–28.

19386.   MEEHAN, WILLIAM F., III.   Towards understanding Jerzy Kosinski's *Being There.* NCL (25:5) 1995, 9–11.

19387.   SLOAN, JAMES PARK.   Jerzy Kosinski: a biography. New York: Dutton, 1996. pp. 505, (plates) 16. Rev. by Jonathan Yardley in BkW, 3 Mar. 1996, 3.

Eric Kraft

19388.   COLLADO RODRÍGUEZ, FRANCISCO.   Insulation *vs* dissolution? An interview with Eric Kraft. Misc (15) 1994, 95–109.

Larry Kramer

19389. BERGMAN, DAVID.   Larry Kramer and the rhetoric of AIDS. *In* (pp. 175–86) **2**.

19390. SHATZKY, JOEL.   AIDS enters the American theater: *As Is* and *The Normal Heart. In* (pp. 131–9) **2**.

David Kranes

19391. CARLSON, RON.   Fierce and fostering: David Kranes in an interview. WebS (10:2) 1993, 29–40.

Robert Kroetsch

19392. CAMPBELL, WANDA.   Strange plantings: Robert Kroetsch's *Seed Catalogue.* StudCanL (21:1) 1996, 17–36.

19393. CREELMAN, DAVID.   Robert Kroetsch: criticism in the middle ground. StudCanL (16:1) 1991, 63–81.

19394. CUMMING, PETER.   'The prick and its vagaries': men, reading, Kroetsch. ECanW (55) 1995, 115–39.

19395. DORSCHT, SUSAN RUDY.   Women, reading, Kroetsch: telling the difference. (Bibl. 1993, 13529.) Rev. by Stan Dragland in ECanW (55) 1995, 98–114.

19396. DRAGLAND, STAN.   Potatoes and the moths of just history. ECanW (55) 1995, 98–114 (review-article).

19397. FLORBY, GUNILLA.   Robert Kroetsch's *What the Crow Said*: a post-colonial protest. Annales de l'Université de Savoie (21) 1996, 113–21.

19398. JACKMAN, CHRISTINE.   *What the Crow Said*: a *topos* of excess. StudCanL (16:2) 1991/92, 79–92.

19399. JEWINSKI, ED.   Mr Canadian postmodern. LRC (5:8) 1996, 12–13 (review-article).

19400. KROETSCH, ROBERT.   A likely story: the writing life. Red Deer, Alta: Red Deer College Press, 1995. pp. 223. Rev. by Ed Jewinski in LRC (5:8) 1996, 12–13.

19401. STEFANELLI, MARIA ANITA.   Dinosaurs in the badlands: Michael Crichton's *Jurassic Park* and Robert Kroetsch's *Badlands. In* (pp. 402–9) **117**.

19402. SURETTE, LEON.   Creating the Canadian canon. *In* (pp. 17–29) **13**.

19403. TIEFENSEE, DIANNE.   The old dualities: deconstructing Robert Kroetsch and his critics. (Bibl. 1994, 13504.) Rev. by Susan Rudy Dorscht in CanL (150) 1996, 140–2; by Ed Jewinski in LRC (5:8) 1996, 12–13.

19404. WHETTER, DARRYL.   The birds, the bees, and Kristeva: an examination of sexual desire in the nature poetry of Daphne Marlatt, Robert Kroetsch, and Tim Lilburn. StudCanL (21:2) 1996, 37–48.

19405. WILLIAMS, DAVID.   Cyberwriting and the borders of identity: 'what's in a name' in Kroetsch's *The Puppeteer* and Mistry's *Such a Long Journey? See* **2169**.

Stanley Kunitz

19406. STITT, PETER.   An interview with Stanley Kunitz. GetR (5:2) 1992, 193–209.

Hanif Kureishi

19407. HAND, FELICITY.   Challenging the centre: the response of British Asian writers. *See* **17181**.

19408. MANFERLOTTI, STEFANO.   Dopo l'impero: romanzo ed etnia in Gran Bretagna. *See* **14616**.

19409. NARANJO ACOSTA, ISAÍAS.   Pilgrimage: on Hanif Kureishi's *The Buddha of Suburbia*. RCEI (28) 1994, 53–63.

19410. WALLHEAD, CELIA M.   Paradigms of diversity in Hanif Kureishi's *The Buddha of Suburbia*. RCEI (28) 1994, 65–79.

19411. YOUSAF, NAHEM.   Hanif Kureishi and 'the brown man's burden'. CritS (8:1) 1996, 14–25.

Tony Kushner

19412. KIEFER, DANIEL.   *Angels in America* and the failure of revelation. AmDr (4:1) 1994, 21–38.

19413. MÜLLER, ULRICH.   Modern morality plays of Broadway: *Jelly's Last Jam* and *Angels in America*. *In* (pp. 375–84) **125**.

19414. POSNOCK, ROSS.   Roy Cohn in America. Raritan (13:3) 1994, 64–77.

Greg Kuzma

19415. SAUCERMAN, JAMES R.   Poems of popular common ground: four voices of the Midwest. *See* **19367**.

Joanne Kyger

19416. FRIEDMAN, AMY L.   'I say my new name': women writers of the Beat Generation. *In* (pp. 200–16) **4**.

Suzanne Lacy

19417. BASTING, ANNE DAVIS.   Amnesia interrupted: re-membering the living past in feminist theory and Suzanne Lacy's *Crystal Quilt*. *See* **15269**.

Alex La Guma

19418. GOVER, DANIEL.   Alex La Guma's angry young men. ESA (39:2) 1996, 47–54.

George Lamming

19419. NAIR, SUPRIYA.   Caliban's curse: George Lamming and the revisioning of history. Ann Arbor: Michigan UP, 1996. pp. viii, 171. (Cf. bibl. 1993, 13543.)

Patrick Lane

19420. CARTER, ADAM.   'How struggle roots itself in ritual': a Marxist reading of the poetry of Patrick Lane. ECanW (55) 1995, 1–21.

Rose Wilder Lane

19421. HOLTZ, WILLIAM.   Ghost and host in the Little House books. *See* **683**.

19422. ——— The ghost in the Little House: a life of Rose Wilder Lane. (Bibl. 1995, 17477.) Rev. by Robert Ellis Hosmer, Jr, in BkW, 13 June 1996, 10.

19423. MILLER, JOHN E.   Rose Wilder Lane and Thomas Hart

Benton: a turn toward history during the 1930s. AmS (37:2) 1996, 83–101.

Mandla Langa

19424. GEVISSER, MARK.   Author in need of healing. Mail & Guardian (12:35) 1996, 16.

Gerrit Lansing

19425. PODGURSKI, ROBERT.   *Anagnorisis* and the magical ground of *Heavenly Tree/Soluble Forest.* Talisman (15) 1995/96, 42–7.
19426. SCHELB, EDWARD.   'Of sea-stoned attitudes the constelled swing': on the poetry of Gerrit Lansing. Talisman (15) 1995/96, 16–26.
19427. STEIN, CHARLES.   For Gerrit Lansing and his *Soluble Forest.* Talisman (15) 1995/96, 41.
19428. STROFFOLINO, CHRIS.   The simplicity of two: Gerrit Lansing's *Filthy Lucre.* Talisman (15) 1995/96, 30–5.

James Lapine

19429. SMART, JEFFREY.   Labels are not characters: critical misperception of *Falsettoland. See* **17825**.

Ring Lardner (1885–1933)

19430. BOOMHOWER, RAY.   Covering the bases. MichH (80:3) 1996, 20–7.
19431. HEWITT, JESSICA L.   'Owl Eyes' in *The Great Gatsby. See* **17855**.
19432. HILTON, GEORGE W. (ed.).   The annotated baseball stories of Ring W. Lardner, 1914–1919. Stanford, CA: Stanford UP, 1995. pp. xii, 631. Rev. by Douglas A. Noverr in JPC (30:2) 1996, 206–7.

Philip Larkin

19433. BOOTH, JAMES.   Philip Larkin: writer. (Bibl. 1993, 13553.) Rev. by Terry Whalen in AntR (93/94) 1993, 79–86.
19434. CARPENTER, PETER.   Modern poetry and audience: making connections. *See* **17487**.
19435. CRAIK, ROGER.   Changing places: Philip Larkin as train traveler. UDR (24:1) 1996, 63–81.
19436. —— Larkin's *This Be the Verse.* Exp (55:1) 1996, 48–9.
19437. CRAIK, ROGER J.   A little-known source for Philip Larkin's *Next, Please.* NCL (26:1) 1996, 9–10.
19438. —— *The Mower*: Philip Larkin's struggle against stagnation. NCL (25:4) 1995, 2–3.
19439. HASSAN, SALEM K.   Women in Philip Larkin. EngS (77:2) 1996, 142–54.
19440. KWON, YOUNG-TAK.   Philip Larkin eui 'yeomsejueui' yeongu. (A study of Philip Larkin's 'pessimism'.) Unpub. doct. diss., Korea Univ., Seoul, 1995.
19441. LEGGETT, B. J.   Larkin's Blues: jazz and modernism. TCL (42:2) 1996, 258–76.
19442. MOTION, ANDREW.   Philip Larkin: a writer's life. (Bibl. 1995, 17487.) Rev. by Terry Whalen in AntR (93/94) 1993, 79–86; by X. J. Kennedy in GetR (7:2) 1994, 289–303; by Dana Gioia in BkW, 15 Aug. 1996, 1, 9.

19443. Newman, Cathy.   'Something that'll sound like real life'. ERev (6:3) 1996, 35–7.

19444. O'Donoghue, Bernard.   Comparisons. *See* **5985**.

19445. Osterwalder, Hans.   The Little Englander's myth-kitty: the cyclic concept of time in Philip Larkin's poetry. ZAA (42:2) 1994, 139–47.

19446. Pickering, Outi.   Tennyson's *Mariana* and Larkin's *The Whitsun Weddings*. *See* **12444**.

19447. Raitala, Eija.   Philip Larkin's *Lucky Jim*? A quantitative authorship study of Kingsley Amis's novel *Lucky Jim*. *See* **15947**.

19448. Rawson, Claude.   Larkin's desolate attics. Raritan (11:2) 1991, 25–47.

19449. Smalley, Rebecca.   The Englishman's Scottishman, or radical Scotsman? Reading Douglas Dunn in the light of recent re-appraisal of Philip Larkin. *See* **17438**.

19450. Swarbrick, Andrew.   Out of reach: the poetry of Philip Larkin. (Bibl. 1995, 17493.) Rev. by Henry Hart in ANQ (9:4) 1996, 58–61.

19451. Thwaite, Anthony (ed.).   Selected letters of Philip Larkin, 1940–1985. (Bibl. 1995, 17494.) New York: Farrar, Straus, & Giroux, 1993. Rev. by Terry Whalen in AntR (93/94) 1993, 79–86; by John Simon in BkW, 12 Dec. 1996, 1, 11.

19452. Whalen, Terry.   'Remorseless scrutiny': Philip Larkin's life and letters. AntR (93/94) 1993, 79–86 (review-article).

19453. ——— 'Strangeness made sense': Philip Larkin in Ireland. AntR (107) 1996, 157–69.

Nella Larsen

19454. Bande, Usha.   'Only connect' and the failure to connect: a comparative study of Anita Desai's Sita and Nella Larsen's Helga. *See* **17247**.

19455. Beemyn, Brett.   A bibliography of works by and about Nella Larsen. AAR (26:1) 1992, 183–8.

19456. Blackmore, David L.   'That unreasonable restless feeling': the homosexual subtexts of Nella Larsen's *Passing*. AAR (26:3) 1992, 475–84.

19457. Cutter, Martha J.   Sliding significations: passing as a narrative and textual strategy in Nella Larsen's fiction. *In* (pp. 75–100) **82**.

19458. Davis, Thadious M.   Nella Larsen, novelist of the Harlem renaissance: a woman's life unveiled. (Bibl. 1995, 17496.) Rev. by Bruce Adams in AmS (36:2) 1995, 206–7; by Anne Stavney in TSWL (15:1) 1996, 161–2; by Jacquelyn Y. McLendon in AAR (30:3) 1996, 478–81.

19459. Elkins, Marilyn.   Expatriate Afro-American women as exotics. *In* (pp. 264–73) **50**.

19460. Larson, Charles R.   Invisible darkness: Jean Toomer and Nella Larsen. (Bibl. 1994, 13544.) Rev. by Rudolph P. Byrd in AAR (30:1) 1996, 127–30.

19461. Little, Jonathan.   Nella Larsen's *Passing*: irony and the critics. AAR (26:1) 1992, 173–82.

19462. McCaskill, Barbara.   The folklore of the coasts in Black women's fiction of the Harlem renaissance. *See* **3293**.

19463. Silverman, Debra B.   Nella Larsen's *Quicksand*: untangling the webs of exoticism. AAR (27:4) 1993, 599–614.

19464. SISNEY, MARY F.   The view from the outside: Black novels of manners. *In* (pp. 171–85) **96**.

Marghanita Laski

19465. LASSNER, PHYLLIS.   'Between the gaps': sex, class and anarchy in the British comic novel of World War II. *In* (pp. 205–19) **64**.

James Laughlin

19466. SANGIACOMO, MARCO.   James Laughlin, poeta minore e maggiore. QLLSM (8) 1996, 225–32.

Margaret Laurence

19467. CAROLAN-BROZY, SANDRA; HAGEMANN, SUSANNE.   'There is such a place' – is there? Scotland in Margaret Laurence's *The Diviners*. *In* (pp. 145–58) **115**.

19468. COGER, GRETA M. K. MCCORMICK (ed.).   New perspectives on Margaret Laurence: poetic narrative, multiculturalism, and feminism. Westport, CT; London: Greenwood Press, 1996. pp. xxviii, 232. (Contributions in women's studies, 154.)

19469. DRUMMOND, DENNIS.   Florentine Lacasse, Rachel Cameron, and existential anguish. ARCS (19:4) 1989, 397–406.

19470. KERTZER, JONATHAN.   'That house in Manawaka': Margaret Laurence's *A Bird in the House*. (Bibl. 1994, 13549.) Rev. by Nora Foster Stovel in ARCS (26:1) 1996, 135–7.

19471. KUESTER, HILDEGARD.   The crafting of chaos: narrative structure in Margaret Laurence's *The Stone Angel* and *The Diviners*. (Bibl. 1994, 13550.) Rev. by Beverly J. Rasporich in CanL (150) 1996, 183–4; by Peter Cumming in ECanW (58) 1996, 65–70; by Kathryn Carter in ZAA (44:2) 1996, 190–2.

19472. LENNOX, JOHN.   A compelling continuum. ECanW (58) 1996, 145–50 (review-article).

19473. MORLEY, PATRICIA.   Margaret Laurence: the long journey home. Montreal; London: McGill–Queen's UP, 1991. pp. 195. Rev. by Donez Xiques in AntR (92) 1993, 45–6.

19474. NICHOLSON, COLIN (ed.).   Critical approaches to the fiction of Margaret Laurence. (Bibl. 1993, 13576.) Rev. by Donez Xiques in AntR (92) 1993, 46–8.

19475. POWELL, BARBARA.   The conflicting inner voices of Rachel Cameron. StudCanL (16:1) 1991, 22–35.

19476. STOVEL, NORA.   Rachel's children: Margaret Laurence's *A Jest of God*. (Bibl. 1994, 13556.) Rev. by Lorraine M. York in ESCan (22:1) 1996, 107–8.

19477. SURETTE, LEON.   Creating the Canadian canon. *In* (pp. 17–29) **13**.

19478. TEN KORTENAAR, NEIL.   The trick of divining a postcolonial Canadian identity: Margaret Laurence between race and nation. CanL (149) 1996, 11–33.

19479. THOMAS, CLARA.   Portraits of the artist: Thea Kronborg and Margaret Laurence's Morag Gunn. *See* **16856**.

19480. VERDUYN, CHRISTL (ed.).   Margaret Laurence: an appreciation. Peterborough, Ont.; Lewiston, NY: Broadview Press, 1988. pp. 265. Rev. by Donez Xiques in ARCS (20:1) 1990, 131–4.

19481. VINCENT, KERRY.   Decoding the hieroglyphics: naming and meaning in *The Prophet's Camel Bell.* JCL (30:1) 1995, 29–44.

19482. WAINWRIGHT, J. A. (ed.).   A very large soul: selected letters from Margaret Laurence to Canadian writers. Dunvegan, Ont.: Cormorant, 1995. pp. xxi, 264. Rev. by Deborah Dudek in CanL (151) 1996, 135–6; by John Lennox in ECanW (58) 1996, 145–50; by Donez Xiques in AntR (106) 1996, 63–7; by the same in ARCS (26:1) 1996, 127–30.

19483. WARWICK, SUSAN J.   River of now and then: Margaret Laurence's *The Diviners.* (Bibl. 1995, 17517.) Rev. by Lorraine M. York in ESCan (22:1) 1996, 107–8.

19484. YORK, LORRAINE M.   The other side of dailiness: photography in the works of Alice Munro, Timothy Findley, Michael Ondaatje, and Margaret Laurence. *See* **17822**.

Ann Lauterbach

19485. SCHULTZ, SUSAN M.   Visions of silence in poems of Ann Lauterbach and Charles Bernstein. *See* **16417**.

Emmet Lavery (1902–)

19486. GENDRE, CLAUDE.   The literary destiny of the sixteen Carmelite martyrs of Compiègne and the role of Emmet Lavery. Ren (48:1) 1995, 37–60.

Mary Lavin

19487. NEARY, MICHAEL.   Flora's answer to the Irish Question: a study of Mary Lavin's *The Becker Wives.* TCL (42:4) 1996, 516–25.

19488. SHUMAKER, JEANETTE.   The Madonna ideal in Mary Lavin's short stories: a Kristevan perspective. JSSE (20) 1993, 81–8.

D. H. Lawrence

19489. ALLDRITT, KEITH.   The Europeans of D. H. Lawrence. Études Lawrenciennes (9) 1993, 11–19.

19490. ARAI, HIDENAGA.   The invisible core of resistance: the anti-aesthetic and anti-organic tendency in *Aaron's Rod.* SEL (72:2) 1996, 255–68.

19491. ASCHERMANN, ULRIKE.   D. H. Lawrence. Rezeption im deutschen Sprachraum. Eine deskriptive Übersetzungsanalyse von *Lady Chatterley's Lover.* New York; Frankfurt; Bern; Paris: Lang, 1995. pp. 267. (Cf. bibl. 1994, 13562.) Rev. by Dieter Mehl in Archiv (233:1) 1996, 233–4.

19492. ATKINS, A. R.   A bibliographical analysis of the manuscript of D. H. Lawrence's *The White Peacock. See* **334**.

19493. ATKINS, ANTONY R.   Masculinity and the reproduction of mothering in *The White Peacock.* Études Lawrenciennes (12) 1995/96, 27–43.

19494. BALLIN, MICHAEL.   Sexuality, society and individual growth in D. H. Lawrence's *Women in Love.* Études Lawrenciennes (12) 1995/96, 61–78.

19495. BARON, HELEN V.   The surviving galley proofs of Lawrence's *Sons and Lovers. See* **569**.

19496. BECKET, FIONA.   The reception of Lawrence in Poland: towards a Polish response. Études Lawrenciennes (9) 1993, 167–79.

19497. BELL, MICHAEL. D. H. Lawrence: language and being. (Bibl. 1995, 17527.) Rev. by Jean-Jacques Lecercle in Études Lawrenciennes (10) 1994, 237; by Lydia Blanchard in MFS (40:2) 1994, 402–4; by Margaret Masson in LitTheol (10:2) 1996, 197–8.

19498. —— D. H. Lawrence and Thomas Mann: *unbewusste Brüderschaft*. Études Lawrenciennes (10) 1994, 187–97.

19499. —— Lawrence, language and relatedness. *See* **2580**.

19500. BJÖRKÉN, CECILIA. Into the isle of self: Nietzschean patterns and contrasts in D. H. Lawrence's *The Trespasser*. Lund: Lund UP, 1996. pp. 247. (Lund studies in English, 89.)

19501. BLYTHE, JOAN. Escape to reality: the ecocritical symbiosis of D. H. Lawrence and Mabel Dodge Luhan. ANQ (9:3) 1996, 40–61.

19502. BORGES, STEPHANY. Rebels and old maids: the contradiction between a socially and a biological constituted gender identity in *The Lost Girl*. Études Lawrenciennes (12) 1995/96, 91–117.

19503. BOULTON, JAMES T. Editing D. H. Lawrence's letters: the editor's creative role. *See* **581**.

19504. BROWN, ASHLEY. Prose into poetry: D. H. Lawrence's *The Rainbow*. In (pp. 133–42) **79**.

19505. BUMP, JEROME. D. H. Lawrence and family systems theory. Ren (44:1) 1991, 61–80.

19506. BYRNE, JANET. A genius for living: a biography of Frieda Lawrence. (Bibl. 1995, 17537.) London: Bloomsbury, 1995. pp. viii, 504, (plates) 16.

19507. CARPENTER, REBECCA. Can I be a feminist and still like *The Plumed Serpent*? Études Lawrenciennes (12) 1995/96, 119–35.

19508. CECCARINI, MICHELA. '*The long, long African process*': il tema dell'arte tribale in *Women in Love* di D. H. Lawrence. QLLSM (6) 1993, 151–80.

19509. CERAMELLA, NICOLA. Monistic mankind–nature relations in Lawrence. Études Lawrenciennes (13) 1996, 123–40.

19510. CHOUDHURY, SHEILA LAHIRI. D. H. Lawrence and Ford Madox Ford: a brief encounter. *See* **17900**.

19511. CLARKE, IAN. Lawrence and the drama of his European contemporaries. Études Lawrenciennes (10) 1994, 173–86.

19512. COMELLINI, CARLA. D. H. Lawrence: a study on mutual and cross-references and interferences. Bologna: CLUEB, 1995. pp. 154. (Mosaici, 2.)

19513. CUSHMAN, KEITH. Lawrence, Compton Mackenzie, and the 'semi-literary cats' of Capri. Études Lawrenciennes (9) 1993, 139–53.

19514. DE VILLE, PETER. Hilda Doolittle, *Eurydice* and the lost bride in D. H. Lawrence's *Bavarian Gentians*. *See* **17334**.

19515. —— The Italian Lawrence and *Sea and Sardinia*. QLLSM (3) 1989, 89–104.

19516. DIAMOND, SUZANNE. Mothers in the margins: Thomas Hardy, D. H. Lawrence, and suffragism's discontents. *See* **11324**.

19517. DÍEZ-MEDRANO, CONCHITA. Breaking moulds, smashing mirrors: the intertextual dynamics of D. H. Lawrence's *The Lovely Lady*. RAEI (9) 1996, 91–103.

19518. DOHERTY, GERALD. The art of appropriation: the rhetoric of sexuality in D. H. Lawrence. *See* **2349**.

19519. —— Metaphor and mental disturbance: the case of *Lady Chatterley's Lover*. *See* **2350**.

19520. DRAPER, R. P.   Take me south again. Études Lawrenciennes (9) 1993, 21–34.

19521. ECKER, MICHAEL.   The serpent of the sun: D. H. Lawrence's moral ego revisited. Lewiston, NY; Lampeter: Mellen Press, 1995. pp. 118. (Salzburg English & American studies, 27.)

19522. EGGERT, PAUL.   Document or process as the site of authority: establishing chronology of revision in competing typescripts of Lawrence's *The Boy in the Bush. See* **631**.

19523. —— (ed.).   *Twilight in Italy* and other essays. (Bibl. 1995, 17551.) Rev. by Ronald G. Walker in ELT (39:1) 1996, 91–5; by Hilary Simpson in NQ (43:3) 1996, 368–9.

19524. —— WORTHEN, JOHN (eds).   Lawrence and comedy. Cambridge; New York: CUP, 1996. pp. xiv, 216.

19525. ELLIS, DAVID.   D. H. Lawrence and the female body. EC (46:2) 1996, 136–52.

19526. ENOS, MICHAEL R.   'The head of Eros': same-sex desire, self-surveillance, and the male body. *See* **17932**.

19527. FERNANDES, ISABEL; FERREIRA, MARIA ALINE; BIRRENTO, ANA CLARA.   A first approach to a Portuguese D. H. Lawrence bibliography. Études Lawrenciennes (9) 1993, 191–206.

19528. FERTILE, CANDACE.   Triangular relationships in *Mother and Daughter*. Études Lawrenciennes (12) 1995/96, 17–26.

19529. FORTUNATI, VITA.   The visual arts and the novel: the contrasting cases of Ford Madox Ford and D. H. Lawrence. *See* **17901**.

19530. FUJIWARA, MASUKO.   Lawrence no Italia. (Lawrence's Italy.) Kyoto: Kyoto Shugakusha, 1996. pp. 118.

19531. GAMACHE, LAWRENCE B.   D. H. Lawrence and religious conflict–dualism. Études Lawrenciennes (10) 1994, 9–25.

19532. GIFFORD, TERRY.   'Anotherness' as a construction of nature in *Birds, Beasts and Flowers*. Études Lawrenciennes (12) 1995/96, 7–16.

19533. GILBERT, SANDRA M.   Feminism and D. H. Lawrence: some notes toward a vindication of his rites. Anaïs (9) 1991, 92–100.

19534. GILCHRIST, SUSAN Y.   D. H. Lawrence and E. M. Forster: a failed friendship. *See* **17935**.

19535. GOUIRAND, JACQUELINE.   Birkin and the new ethic of human relationships (with reference to the pre-texts). Études Lawrenciennes (12) 1995/96, 45–59.

19536. —— Star-equilibrium: the evolution of the 'Mino' chapter in *Women in Love. See* **655**.

19537. —— Viennese Modernists and D. H. Lawrence (1913–1919): a convergence of sensibilities. Études Lawrenciennes (10) 1994, 59–78.

19538. HAMALIAN, LEO.   Beyond the paleface: D. H. Lawrence and Gary Snyder. Talisman (7) 1991, 50–5.

19539. —— D. H. Lawrence and Black writers. *See* **17595**.

19540. —— D. H. Lawrence and nine women writers. *See* **13110**.

19541. —— A spy in the house of Lawrence: tracing the signposts of Anaïs Nin's development as a writer. Anaïs (13) 1995, 14–26.

19542. HARRISON, ANDREW; HIBBITT, RICHARD.   D. H. Lawrence and Thomas Mann. NQ (43:4) 1996, 443.

19543. HAYMAN, DAVID.   Attitudinal dynamics in narrative: Flaubert, Lawrence, Joyce. *See* **19116**.

19544. HOLLINGTON, MICHAEL.   Simultaneous orgasm and other temporal aspects of *Lady Chatterley's Lover* and other late writings of D. H. Lawrence. Études Lawrenciennes (12) 1995/96, 169–87.

19545. —— Simultaneous orgasm in late Lawrence: reflections on Feinstein's *Lawrence's Women.* EEM (5:1) 1996, 25–9.

19546. HOWARD, ROSEMARY.   Intimations of wonder in Wittgenstein and Lawrence. *See* **2647**.

19547. —— Lawrence and Russell. Études Lawrenciennes (10) 1994, 43–57.

19548. HYDE, VIRGINIA.   'Lost' girls: D. H. Lawrence's versions of Persephone. *In* (pp. 99–120) **46**.

19549. —— The risen Adam: D. H. Lawrence's revisionist typology. (Bibl. 1994, 13600.) Rev. by Margaret Masson in LitTheol (10:2) 1996, 198–9.

19550. IIDA, TAKEO.   Nature deities: reawakening blood-consciousness in the Europeans. Études Lawrenciennes (10) 1994, 27–42.

19551. INGERSOLL, EARL G.   Gender and language in *Sons and Lovers.* MidQ (37:4) 1996, 434–7.

19552. JACKSON, ROSIE.   Frieda Lawrence: including, *Not I, but the Wind,* and other autobiographical writings. (Bibl. 1994, 13605.) Rev. by Marion Shaw in CritS (8:1) 1996, 128–9.

19553. JANSOHN, CHRISTA.   Die D. H. Lawrence-Ausgabe der Cambridge University Press. *See* **692**.

19554. KALNINS, MARA (ed.).   Aaron's rod. Introd. and notes by Steven Vine. London; New York: Penguin, 1995. pp. xxxviii, 323. (Penguin twentieth-century classics.)

19555. KATZ-ROY, GINETTE.   'This may be a withering tree this Europe': Bachelard, Deleuze and Guattari on D. H. Lawrence's poetic imagination. Études Lawrenciennes (10) 1994, 219–35.

19556. KINKEAD-WEEKES, MARK.   D. H. Lawrence: triumph to exile, 1912–1922. Cambridge; New York: CUP, 1996. pp. xlv, 943, (plates) 32. (Cambridge biography: D. H. Lawrence, 1885–1930.) Rev. by Tony Tanner in TLS, 23 Aug. 1996, 3–4.

19557. KOGA, MASAKAZU.   Lawrence kenkyu – seiyou bunmei wo koete. (A study of Lawrence: beyond Western civilization.) Osaka: Osaka Kyoiku Tosho, 1996. pp. 340.

19558. KONDO, KYOKO KAY.   Colours, images and related adjectives in *Women in Love. See* **2661**.

19559. LACHAPELLE, DOLORES.   D. H. Lawrence: future primitive. Introd. by Thomas J. Lyon. Denton: North Texas UP, 1996. pp. xix, 223. (Philosophy and the environment, 5.)

19560. LANGBAUM, ROBERT.   Lawrence and the Modernists. *See* **17525**.

19561. LECERCLE, JEAN-JACQUES.   Sentimentalism and feeling: D. H. Lawrence's *Piano* and I. A. Richards' reading of it. *See* **15586**.

19562. LEE BRYANT, BRENDA.   The arch of the rainbow: D. H. Lawrence's vision of relationships. Études Lawrenciennes (12) 1995/96, 79–89.

19563. McVEA, DEBORAH.   The Eastwood dialect: an error in the Cambridge edition of D. H. Lawrence's *The White Peacock. See* **748**.

19564. MEHL, DIETER; JANSOHN, CHRISTA (eds).   *The Woman Who Rode Away* and other stories. (Bibl. 1995, 17587.) Rev. by Judith Ruderman in ELT (39:4) 1996, 478–82.

19565. MENDELSON, EDWARD.   How Lawrence corrected Wells; how Orwell refuted Lawrence. *In* (pp. 166–75) **41**.

19566. MERLINI, MADELINE.   D. H. Lawrence and the Italian political scene. Études Lawrenciennes (9) 1993, 63–74.

19567. MONTGOMERY, ROBERT E.   The visionary D. H. Lawrence: beyond philosophy and art. (Bibl. 1995, 17591.) Rev. by James C. Cowan in MFS (42:4) 1996, 870–3.

19568. MORGAN, JAMES.   'Thrice adream': father, son, and masculinity in Lawrence's *Snake*. LitPs (39:1/2) 1993, 97–111.

19569. NICOLAJ, RINA.   D. H. Lawrence as interpreter and translator of Giovanni Verga. Études Lawrenciennes (10) 1994, 107–25.

19570. OHIRA, AKIRA.   Lawrence bungaku no politics. (The politics of Lawrence's literature.) Tokyo: Kinseido, 1996. pp. vi, 176

19571. PACCAUD-HUGUET, JOSIANE.   Narrative as a symbolic act: the historicity of Lawrence's modernity. Études Lawrenciennes (9) 1993, 75–94.

19572. —— *Women in Love*: de la tentation perverse à l'écriture. (Bibl. 1993, 13655.) Rev. by Jacqueline Gouirand in Études Lawrenciennes (10) 1994, 239–40.

19573. PARK, CHANG-DO.   D. H. Lawrence eui *Mujige* yeongu: ingan jonje yangshik eui tamgu. (A study on the form of being in D. H. Lawrence's *The Rainbow*.) JELL (42:1) 1996, 101–18.

19574. PHELPS, JAMES M.   Innocence and experience in the classroom: D. H. Lawrence's school poems. ESA (38:1) 1995, 19–34.

19575. PHILIPPRON, GUY.   The reception of D. H. Lawrence's fiction in France in the 1930s: the *NRF*'s support. Études Lawrenciennes (9) 1993, 157–66.

19576. PITCHER, E. W.   Another approach to Lawrence's *The Horse-Dealer's Daughter*. JSSE (19) 1992, 53–68.

19577. POPLAWSKI, PAUL.   D. H. Lawrence: a reference companion. With a biography by John Worthen. Westport, CT; London: Greenwood Press, 1996. pp. xxi, 714.

19578. —— Language, art and reality in D. H. Lawrence's *St Mawr*. Lewiston, NY; Lampeter: Mellen Press, 1996. pp. 292.

19579. PRESTON, PETER.   'Under the same banner'? D. H. Lawrence and Catherine Carswell's *Open the Door! See* **16704**.

19580. PUGH, BRIDGET L.   D. H. Lawrence: some Russian parallels. Études Lawrenciennes (10) 1994, 81–91.

19581. ROMANSKI, PHILIPPE.   'Europe is a lost name': entropy in the first two chapters of *Women in Love*. Études Lawrenciennes (9) 1993, 51–60.

19582. ROWLEY, STEPHEN.   Colour implications of the poetry of T. S. Eliot and D. H. Lawrence. *See* **17552**.

19583. —— Darkness – the blind man's third eye. Études Lawrenciennes (13) 1996, 41–57.

19584. RYLANCE, RICK (ed.).   Sons and lovers. Basingstoke: Macmillan; New York: St Martin's Press, 1996. pp. ix, 213. (New casebooks.)

19585. SCANLON, JOAN.   Bad language *vs* bad prose? *Lady Chatterley* and *The Well. See* **1972**.

19586. SCHERR, BARRY J.   D. H. Lawrence's response to Plato: a Bloomian interpretation. New York; Frankfurt; Bern; Paris:

Lang, 1995. pp. 191. (American univ. studies, IV: English language and literature, 179.)

19587. ⸺ Eagleton's flight from Lawrence and Leavis. *See* **15746**.

19588. ⸺ 'Love battle' in *Aaron's Rod*. RecL (20) 1994, 23–45.

19589. ⸺ Two essays on D. H. Lawrence's 'darkness': 1, The 'fecund darkness' of *The Rainbow*; II, The 'body of darkness' in *Women in Love*. RecL (18) 1991/92, 8–40.

19590. SKLENICKA, CAROL; SPILKA, MARK. A womb of his own: Lawrence's passional/paternal view of childhood. *In* (pp. 164–83) **48**.

19591. SÖRING, JÜRGEN. Provozierte 'Gewalt' – zur Poetologie des Drogenrauschs. *See* **10706**.

19592. STEELE, BRUCE (ed.). *England, My England* and other stories. Introd. and notes by Michael Bell. London; New York: Penguin, 1995. pp. xl, 241.

19593. ⸺ Kangaroo. (Bibl. 1995, 17609.) Rev. by Hilary Simpson in NQ (43:3) 1996, 368–9.

19594. STEWART, JACK. Linguistic incantation and parody in *Women in Love*. *See* **2715**.

19595. STOVEL, NORA FOSTER. The woman in the moon: metaphor, myth and marriage in *The Rainbow* and *Women in Love*. *See* **2478**.

19596. TEMPLETON, WAYNE. Resisting evaluation: canonization and *The Rocking-Horse Winner*. JSSE (21) 1993, 79–94.

19597. THORNTON, WELDON. D. H. Lawrence: a study of the short fiction. (Bibl. 1995, 17620.) Rev. by Brian Murray in SSF (31:3) 1996, 163–5.

19598. URBANO, COSIMO. The evil that men do: Mark Rydell's adaptation of D. H. Lawrence's *The Fox*. *See* **14298**.

19599. VENTER, J. J. Conceiving conflict/competition – gripped by a world picture: C. Darwin, D. H. Lawrence and F. A. von Hayek. Analecta Husserliana (48) 1996, 205–48.

19600. VICHY, THÉRÈSE. Lawrence's Bavarian heights. Études Lawrenciennes (9) 1993, 35–50.

19601. VIINIKKA, ANJA. D. H. Lawrence and Finland. Études Lawrenciennes (9) 1993, 181–9.

19602. WEXLER, JOYCE. Selling sex as art. *In* (pp. 91–108) **67**.

19603. WIDMER, KINGSLEY. Defiant desire: some dialectical legacies of D. H. Lawrence. (Bibl. 1995, 17628.) Rev. by Lydia Blanchard in MFS (40:2) 1994, 402–4.

19604. WORTHEN, JOHN. D. H. Lawrence and the 'expensive edition business'. *In* (pp. 105–23) **69**.

19605. ZYTARUK, GEORGE J. Lawrence and Rozanov: clarifying the phallic vision. Études Lawrenciennes (10) 1994, 93–103.

Jerome Lawrence

19606. COE, RICHARD L. Jerome Lawrence. *In* (pp. 168–81) **85**.

19607. COUCH, NENA. An interview with Jerome Lawrence and Robert E. Lee. StAD (7:1) 1992, 3–18.

19608. WINCHESTER, MARK D. Jerome Lawrence and Robert E. Lee: a classified bibliography. StAD (7:1) 1992, 88–160.

T. E. Lawrence

19609. BOONE, JOSEPH A. Vacation cruises; or, The homoerotics of Orientalism. *See* **17448**.

19610. CRAWFORD, FRED D.; BERTON, JOSEPH A.   How well did Lowell Thomas know Lawrence of Arabia? ELT (39:3) 1996, 298–318.
19611. MENGAY, DONALD H.   Arabian rites: T. E. Lawrence's *Seven Pillars of Wisdom* and the erotics of empire. Genre (27:4) 1994, 395–416.
19612. ORLANS, HAROLD (ed.).   Lawrence of Arabia, strange man of letters: the literary criticism and correspondence of T. E. Lawrence. (Bibl. 1994, 13654.) Rev. by Stephen E. Tabachnick in ELT (39:1) 1996, 128–30.
19613. WILSON, JEREMY.   Lawrence of Arabia: the authorised biography of Lawrence of Arabia. (Bibl. 1995, 17644.) Rev. by Janice J. Terry in AHR (96:5) 1991, 1587–8.

Robert Lax
19614. UEBBING, JAMES.   The poet who fell off the map: Robert Lax on the island of Patmos. Cweal (123:8) 1996, 13–17.

A. L. Lazarus ('Leslie Arnold', 'A. L. Leslie')
19615. HOOKER, JEREMY.   Les Arnold: poet and teacher. PN Review (20:3) 1994, 6–7.

Stephen Leacock
19616. BINNIE, IAN.   The Leacock Mission Statement. Fontanus (7) 1994, 33–9.
19617. CAYA, MARCEL.   Leacock enters McGill. Fontanus (7) 1994, 149–52.
19618. DÜRTÖSI, KATALIN.   The alternative theatre adaptation of Leacock's *Sorrows of a Super Soul* in Hungary. THC (11:1) 1990, 86–93.
19619. LYNCH, GERALD.   Stephen Leacock: humour and humanity. (Bibl. 1990, 11400.) Rev. by Ronald M. Meldrum in ARCS (20:3) 1990, 393–5.
19620. MÖLLER, HANS; VIRR, RICHARD.   Stephen Leacock and his books. *See* **225**.
19621. WHITEMAN, BRUCE.   Leacock remains at McGill: some notes on the Stephen Leacock collection. *See* **553**.

'John le Carré' (David John Cornwell)
19622. BUZARD, JAMES M.   Faces, photos, mirrors: image and ideology in the novels of John le Carré. *In* (pp. 153–79) **44**.

John Moalusi Ledwaba
19623. GEVISSER, MARK.   Writing for the man in the street: an interview with John Ledwaba. Theater (25:3) 1995, 19–23.

Andrea Lee (1953–)
19624. ELKINS, MARILYN.   Expatriate Afro-American women as exotics. *In* (pp. 264–73) **50**.

Harper Lee
19625. BAINES, LAWRENCE.   From page to screen: when a novel is interpreted for film, what gets lost in the translation? *See* **10449**.
19626. HESS, NATALIE.   Code-switching and style-shifting as markers of liminality in literature. *See* **2643**.

19627. Jones, Carolyn.   Atticus Finch and the mad dog: Harper Lee's *To Kill a Mockingbird*. SoQ (34:4) 1996, 53–63.
19628. Witt, Margaret E.   Flannery O'Connor and the child's book: an unusual coupling. NCL (22:4) 1992, 4–5.

Helen Elaine Lee

19629. Davis, Thulani.   An interview with Helen Elaine Lee. Callaloo (19:2) 1996, 266–75.

Li-Young Lee (1957–)

19630. Bresnahan, Roger J.   The Midwest as metaphor: four Asian writers. Midamerica (19) 1992, 138–44.
19631. Engles, Tim.   Lee's *Persimmons*. Exp (54:3) 1996, 191–2.
19632. Hesford, Walter A.   *The City in Which I Love You*: Li-Young Lee's excellent song. ChrisL (46:1) 1996, 37–60.

Robert E. Lee

19633. Couch, Nena.   An interview with Jerome Lawrence and Robert E. Lee. *See* **19607**.
19634. Fink, Larry.   Creating a new Broadway: the American Playwrights Theatre production of *The Night Thoreau Spent in Jail; or, What Is Henry David Thoreau Doing in Campus Riots and Nixon's Hometown?* JADT (7:1) 1995, 40–9.
19635. Winchester, Mark D.   Jerome Lawrence and Robert E. Lee: a classified bibliography. *See* **19608**.

Ursula K. Le Guin

19636. Attebery, Brian.   Gender, fantasy, and the authority of tradition. JFA (7:1) 1996, 51–60.
19637. Feimer, Joel N.   Biblical typology in Le Guin's *The Eye of the Heron*: character, structure and theme. Mythlore (19:4) 1993, 13–19.
19638. Franko, Carol.   Acts of attention at the borderlands: Le Guin's *The Beginning Place* revisited. Extrapolation (37:4) 1996, 302–15.
19639. Malkki, Tarya.   The marriage metaphor in the works of Ursula K. Le Guin. *In* (pp. 100–9) **70**.
19640. Maslen, Robert.   'Towards an archaeology of the present': Theodora Kroeber and Ursula K. Le Guin. Foundation (67) 1996, 62–74.
19641. Mironov, Alexandru (postscr.).   Mîna stîngā a întunericu-lui. (The left hand of darkness.) Bucharest: Nemira, 1994. pp. 240.
19642. Moore, John.   An archaeology of the future: Ursula Le Guin and anarcho-primitivism. Foundation (63) 1995, 32–9.
19643. Nodelman, Perry.   Reinventing the past: gender in Ursula K. Le Guin's *Tehanu* and the Earthsea Trilogy. ChildLit (23) 1995, 179–201.
19644. Rochelle, Warren.   The story, Plato, and Ursula K. Le Guin. Extrapolation (37:4) 1996, 316–29.
19645. Scheiding, Oliver.   An archeology of the future: post-modern strategies of boundary transitions in Ursula K. Le Guin's *Always Coming Home* (1985). Amst (41:4) 1996, 637–56.
19646. Sobat, Gail Sidonie.   The night in her own country: the heroine's quest for self in Ursula K. Le Guin's *The Tombs of Atuan*. Mythlore (21:3) 1996, 24–32.

19647. Webb, Sarah Jo.   Culture as spiritual metaphor in Le Guin's *Always Coming Home*. *In* (pp. 155–60) **36**.

Fritz Leiber

19648. Lovett-Graff, Bennett.   Parodying the theater of religion in the fantasy of Fritz Leiber. SAH (3:3) 1996, 66–81.

19649. Pardoe, Ro; Howard, John.   Fritz Leiber's *Our Lady of Darkness*: annotations. Ghosts and Scholars (21) 1996, i–xii.

19650. Pardoe, Rosemary.   Fritz Leiber's *The Button Molder*: a Jamesian story? Ghosts and Scholars (22) 1996, 52–6.

Mary Leland

19651. Morrison, Kristin.   Child murder as metaphor of colonial exploitation in Toni Morrison's *Beloved*, *The Silence in the Garden*, and *The Killeen*. *In* (pp. 292–300) **49**.

Nancy Lemann

19652. Woodland, J. Randal.   'New people in the old museum of New Orleans': Ellen Gilchrist, Sheila Bosworth, and Nancy Lemann. *In* (pp. 194–210) **65**.

Madeleine L'Engle

19653. Hammond, Wayne G.   Seraphim, cherubim, and virtual unicorns: order and being in Madeline [*sic*] L'Engle's Time Quartet. Mythlore (20:4) 1995, 41–5.

19654. Wytenbroek, J. R.   Cetacean consciousness in Katz's *Whalesinger* and L'Engle's *A Ring of Endless Light*. *See* **19220**.

Elmore Leonard

19655. Grobel, Lawrence.   Pulp fiction. Playboy (Chicago) (42:5) 1995, 122–4, 140–2.

Tom Leonard

19656. Klaus, H. Gustav.   1984 Glasgow: Alasdair Gray, Tom Leonard, James Kelman. *See* **18312**.

Laurence Lerner

19657. Booth, Wayne; Lerner, Laurence.   A conversation about poetry. *See* **16109**.

Doris Lessing ('Jane Somers')

19658. Altman, Meryl.   Before we said 'we' (and after): bad sex and personal politics in Doris Lessing and Simone de Beauvoir. CritQ (38:3) 1996, 14–29.

19659. Arlett, Robert.   Epic voices: inner and global impulse in the contemporary American and British novel. *See* **14375**.

19660. Bazin, Nancy Topping.   Southern Africa and the theme of madness: novels by Doris Lessing, Bessie Head, and Nadine Gordimer. *In* (pp. 137–49) **50**.

19661. Danziger, Marie A.   Text/countertext: postmodern paranoia in Samuel Beckett, Doris Lessing, and Philip Roth. *See* **16280**.

19662. Gardiner, Judith Kegan.   Rhys, Stead, Lessing, and the politics of empathy. (Bibl. 1994, 13691.) Rev. by Evelyne Keitel in Signs

(18:3) 1993, 736–9; by Cora Kaplan in Feminist Studies (20:1) 1994, 160–5.

19663. GREENE, GAYLE. Doris Lessing: the poetics of change. (Bibl. 1994, 13693.) Rev. by Betsy Draine in MFS (42:1) 1996, 194–8.

19664. HITE, MOLLY. The other side of the story: structures and strategies of contemporary feminist narrative. See **16085**.

19665. HOOPER, MYRTLE. Madness and the store: representations of Settler society in Doris Lessing's *The Grass Is Singing* and Daphne Rooke's *A Grove of Fever Trees*. Current Writing (8:1) 1996, 61–74.

19666. HYNES, JOSEPH. Doris Lessing's *Briefing* as structural life and death. Ren (46:4) 1994, 225–45.

19667. INGERSOLL, EARL G. The engendering of narrative in Doris Lessing's *Shikasta* and Margaret Atwood's *The Handmaid's Tale*. In (pp. 39–47) **127**.

19668. —— Writing for balance: a conversation with Doris Lessing. OntR (40) 1994, 46–58.

19669. KAPLAN, CORA. Fictions of feminism: figuring the maternal. See **15546**.

19670. MERGENTHAL, SILVIA. Miranda and Caliban: White mistresses and Black servants in Blixen's *Out of Africa*, Lessing's *The Grass Is Singing*, and Gordimer's *July's People*. See **17294**.

19671. ROWE, MARGARET MOAN. Doris Lessing. (Bibl. 1995, 17676.) Rev. by Betsy Draine in MFS (42:1) 1996, 194–8; by Mara Kalnins in NQ (43:1) 1996, 113–14.

19672. SAXTON, RUTH; TOBIN, JEAN (eds). Woolf and Lessing: breaking the mold. Basingstoke: Macmillan; New York: St Martin's Press, 1994. pp. xiii, 208. Rev. by Diane Gillespie in RMRLL (50:2) 1996, 169–78; by Mary Lou Emery in ELT (39:1) 1996, 123–8.

19673. SCHNEIDER, KAREN. A different war story: Doris Lessing's great escape. JML (19:2) 1995, 259–72.

19674. VELCIC, VLATKA. Doris Lessing's Alice: good house-mother and bad terrorist. TPB (33) 1996, 63–72.

19675. YU, JE-BOON. Utopiajeok sangsangryeok gwa *feminism*: Doris Lessing eui *Sadaemun eui dosi*. (Utopian imagination and feminism: Doris Lessing's *The Four-Gated City*.) JELL (42:2) 1996, 345–62.

Meridel Le Sueur

19676. COINER, CONSTANCE. Better red: the writing and resistance of Tillie Olsen and Meridel Le Sueur. (Bibl. 1995, 17685.) Rev. by Lillian S. Robinson in TSWL (14:2) 1995, 370–4; by Michael Thurston in MFS (42:4) 1996, 844–6; by Barbara Foley in AL (68:2) 1996, 485–6; by Douglas Wixson in Cresset (60:1) 1996, 30–1.

19677. ROBERTS, NORA RUTH. Three radical women writers: class and gender in Meridel Le Sueur, Tillie Olsen, and Josephine Herbst. See **18704**.

19678. SIPPLE, SUSAN. 'Witness [to] the suffering of women': poverty and sexual transgression in Meridel Le Sueur's *Women on the Breadlines*. In (pp. 135–53) **33**.

Ada Leverson

19679. ROHSE, CORINNA SUNDARARAJAN. The sphinx goes wild(e): Ada Leverson, Oscar Wilde, and the gender equipollence of parody. In (pp. 119–36) **64**.

19680. SPEEDIE, JULIE. Wonderful sphinx: the biography of Ada Leverson. (Bibl. 1995, 17689.) Rev. by Gary Schmidgall in Review (17) 1995, 330–1.

Denise Levertov

19681. CRAMER, TIMOTHY R. Levertov's 'line still taut' between her past and present. NCL (22:2) 1992, 11–12.

19682. LEVERTOV, DENISE. Tesserae: memories & suppositions. (Bibl. 1995, 17695.) Rev. by Rita D. Jacobs in WLT (70:1) 1996, 195.

19683. LEVINE-KEATING, HELANE. The bright shadow: images of the double in women's poetry. *In* (pp. 166–84) **109**.

19684. RODRÍGUEZ HERRERA, JOSÉ. Eros at the temple stream: eroticism in the poetry of Denise Levertov. Gramma (4) 1996, 119–27.

Sonya Levien

19685. CEPLAIR, LARRY. A great lady: a life of the screenwriter Sonya Levien. Lanham, MD; London: Scarecrow Press, 1996. pp. x, 160. (Filmmakers, 50.)

Miriam Levine

19686. LEVINE, MIRIAM. Food, sex, and betrayal. AL (68:1) 1996, 85–90.

Norman Levine

19687. MARTIN, RANDALL. Norman Levine's *Canada Made Me*. CanL (148) 1996, 200–3.

Philip Levine

19688. LEVINE, PHILIP. The bread of time: toward an autobiography. (Bibl. 1995, 17697.) Rev. by Mary Kaiser in WLT (69:2) 1995, 371–2.

Benn Levy

19689. RUSINKO, SUSAN. The plays of Benn Levy: between Shaw and Coward. (Bibl. 1995, 17698.) Rev. by Stanley Weintraub in Shaw (16) 1996, 226–8.

C. S. Lewis

19690. AUSTER, MARTIN. The Celtic imagination in exile. *See* **11788**.

19691. BARBIERO, JOE. Notes on *The Pilgrim's Regress*. CSL (23:5) 1992, 4–5.

19692. BEACH, CHARLES FRANKLYN. C. S. Lewis, courtly love, and Chaucer's *Troilus and Criseyde*. *See* **5470**.

19693. —— Courtesy and self in the thought of Charles Williams and C. S. Lewis. CSL (25:3/4) 1994, 1–11.

19694. —— Pilgrimage in the writings of C. S. Lewis. CSL (27:13/14) 1996, 1–12.

19695. BRAMLETT, PERRY C. C. S. Lewis: life at the center. Macon, GA: Peake Road, 1996. pp. viii, 87.

19696. BRANSON, DAVID A. Arthurian elements in *That Hideous Strength*. Mythlore (19:4) 1993, 20–1.

19697. BROWN, DEVIN G.; ROBSON, WILLIAM LANE M. Seeing clearly in *The Silver Chair*. CSL (27:9/10) 1996, 1–8.

19698. CARNELL, CORBIN SCOTT.   Echoes of George MacDonald's *Lilith* in the works of C. S. Lewis. *See* **11789**.

19699. CHRISTOPHER, JOE R.   C. S. Lewis' linguistic myth. Mythlore (21:1) 1995, 41–50.

19700. ——— A catalogue, two notebooks, and an exercise book. Mythprint (31:4) 1994, 2–4, 8.

19701. ———A literary friendship: C. S. Lewis and J. R. R. Tolkien. Mythprint (30:8) 1993, 7–9.

19702. ——— No fish for the phoenix. CSL (23:9) 1992, 1–7.

19703. ———HAMMOND, WAYNE G. (comps).   An Inklings bibliography. Mythlore (18:2) 1992, 28–33, 39–40; (18:3) 1992, 49–53; (18:4) 1992, 49–50, 52; (19:1) 1993, 56–64; (19:2) 1993, 61–5; (19:3) 1993, 59–65; (19:4) 1993, 60–5; (20:1) 1994, 59–62; (20:2) 1994, 32–4; (20:4) 1995, 61–5; (21:1) 1995, 61–5; (21:3) 1996, 59–65.

19704. COMO, JAMES.   The centrality of rhetoric to an understanding of C. S. Lewis. *See* **2339**.

19705. ——— Mere Lewis. CSL (26:9/10) 1995, 2–10.

19706. ——— *Shadowlands* IV. *See* **13563**.

19707. CUTSINGER, JAMES S.   Angels and Inklings. Mythlore (19:2) 1993, 57–60.

19708. DURIEZ, COLIN.   Tolkien and the other Inklings. *See* **16197**.

19709. GATLING, CLOVER HOLLY.   Echoes of epic in Lewis's *The Great Divorce*. CSL (26:3) 1995, 1–8.

19710. GLASPEY, TERRY.   Not a tame lion: the spiritual legacy of C. S. Lewis. Nashville, TN: Cumberland House, 1996. pp. 243. (Leaders in action.)

19711. GOFFAR, JANINE (ed.).   C. S. Lewis index: rumours from the sculptor's shop. Riverside, CA: La Sierra UP, 1995. pp. xiv, 678. Rev. by Wayne Martindale in SEVEN (13) 1996, 103–4.

19712. GOODMAN, MARGARET.   Posthumous journeys: *The Great Divorce* and other travels to eternity. *See* **11410**.

19713. GRIFFIN, WILLIAM.   In search of the real C. S. Lewis. CSL (25:9–11) 1994, 18–26.

19714. GUSSMAN, NEIL.   Translations of Latin, Greek and French phrases from *Studies in Medieval and Renaissance Literature* and from *The Pilgrim's Regress*. CSL (25:12) 1994, 1–5.

19715. GUSSMAN, NEIL G.   *Till We Have Faces*: a key-word concordance. CSL (23:10/11) 1992, 11–16; (23:12/24:1) 1992/93, 11–16.

19716. HANNAY, MARGARET.   The mythology of *Out of the Silent Planet*. Mythlore (20:2) 1994, 20–2.

19717. HERRICK, JIM.   C. S. Lewis and narrative argument in *Out of the Silent Planet*. Mythlore (18:4) 1992, 15–22.

19718. HONDA, MINEKO.   C. S. Lewis and liberal Christianity. CSL (27:5/6) 1996, 2–12.

19719. HOOPER, WALTER.   C. S. Lewis: a companion & guide. San Francisco, CA: HarperSanFrancisco, 1996. pp. xvi, 940.

19720. HOPKINS, LISA.   Female authority figures in the works of Tolkien, C. S. Lewis and Charles Williams. Mythlore (21:2) 1996, 364–6.

19721. JOECKEL, SAMUEL.   Lewis and Samuel Johnson's *Rasselas*: hearing the call of the *Sehnsucht*. *See* **9146**.

19722. JURICH, MARILYN.   'A woman's a two-faced' or the *Doppelgangerin* unveiled. *See* **18462**.

19723. KASTOR, FRANK S.   C. S. Lewis's John Milton: influence, presence, and beyond. *See* **8189**.

19724. KNECHT, WILLIAM L.   C. S. Lewis and apotheosis. CSL (23:8) 1992, 1–4.

19725. KOTERSKI, JOSEPH W.   C. S. Lewis and the natural law. CSL (26:6) 1995, 1–7.

19726. LAMBARSKI, TIM.   Homeliness, strangeness and receptivity: paths to Aslan's country in *The Voyage of the 'Dawn Treader'*. CSL (25:5/6) 1994, 6–11.

19727. LAURENT, JOHN.   C. S. Lewis and animal rights. Mythlore (19:1) 1993, 46–51.

19728. LINDSKOOG, KATHRYN.   Light in the shadow lands: protecting the real C. S. Lewis. Sisters, OR: Multnomah, 1994. pp. xxv, 345. Rev. by David Bratman in Mythprint (31:11/12) 1994, 7–8.

19729. LINDVALL, TERRY.   Surprised by laughter. Nashville, TN: Nelson, 1996. pp. 422.

19730. LONEY, DOUGLAS.   C. S. Lewis' debt to E. M. Forster's *'The Celestial Omnibus' and Other Stories*. *See* **17941**.

19731. LUSK, LINDA V.   C. S. Lewis as a critic 'at the present time'. *See* **15605**.

19732. McGOVERN, EUGENE.   Lewis, Columbus, and the discovery of new worlds. CSL (23:12/24:1) 1992/93, 1–7.

19733. —— Lewis and modern Christian novels. CSL (23:5) 1992, 5–8.

19734. —— Notes on a few misprints and such in Lewis's works. *See* **741**.

19735. McGREW, LYDIA M.   Action and the passionate patient in *That Hideous Strength*. CSL (23:7) 1992, 1–6.

19736. McKIM, MARK G.   C. S. Lewis on the disappearance of the individual. CSL (23:5) 1992, 1–3.

19737. —— The poison brewed in the west. CSL (26:11/12) 1995, 1–6.

19738. —— Secularism, the academy, the arts and C. S. Lewis. CSL (22:5) 1991, 1–5.

19739. McLAUGHLIN, SARA.   *The City of God* revisited: C. S. Lewis's debt to Saint Augustine. CSL (23:6) 1992, 1–9.

19740. —— Reality personified: how Aslan embodies all that is real. CSL (22:9) 1991, 1–4.

19741. McLAUGHLIN, SARA PARK.   A legacy of truth: the influence of George MacDonald's *Unspoken Sermons* on C. S. Lewis's *Mere Christianity*. *See* **11793**.

19742. MARTIN, JOHN.   C. S. Lewis and animals: the road to Whipsnade. CSL (24:11) 1993, 1–7.

19743. MERCHANT, ROBERT.   Pope, council, Bible and/or self: Lewis and the question of authority. CSL (23:10/11) 1992, 1–10.

19744. MEYERS, DORIS.   Breaking free: the closed universe theme in E. M. Forster, Owen Barfield, and C. S. Lewis. *See* **16198**.

19745. MILWARD, PETER.   A challenge to C. S. Lewis. Madison–Teaneck, NJ: Fairleigh Dickinson UP; London; Toronto: Assoc. UPs, 1995. pp. 138. Rev. by James Tetreault in CSL (27:7/8) 1996, 1–7.

19746. MORRISON, JOHN.   How to go to Heaven, not how the heavens go. CSL (26:7/8) 1995, 1–11.

19747. MYERS, DORIS E.   Law and disorder: two settings in *That Hideous Strength*. Mythlore (19:1) 1993, 9–14.

19748. MYERS, DORIS T.   C. S. Lewis in context. (Bibl. 1995, 17717.)

Rev. by Nancy-Lou Patterson in Mythlore (21:1) 1995, 57–9; by Susan Butvin in Extrapolation (36:2) 1995, 165–8; by Donald Stucky in Utopian Studies (7:1) 1996, 137–8.

19749. NEUHOUSER, DAVID L.   Higher dimensions: C. S. Lewis and mathematics. SEVEN (13) 1996, 45–63.

19750. NICHOLSON, MERVYN.   Bram Stoker and C. S. Lewis: *Dracula* as a source for *That Hideous Strength*. See **12379**.

19751. PHEMISTER, WILLIAM.   Fantasy set to music: Donald Swann, C. S. Lewis and J. R. R. Tolkien. SEVEN (13) 1996, 65–82.

19752. PROTHERO, JAMES.   Lewis's poetry: a preliminary exploration. CSL (25:5/6) 1994, 2–6.

19753. SHAW, LUCI N.   Looking back to Eden: the poetry of C. S. Lewis. CSL (23:4) 1992, 1–7.

19754. SKOOG, KATHRYN LIND.   C. S. Lewis and Sadu Sundar Singh. CSL (22:3) 1991, 1–6.

19755. SQUIZZATO, LUCIANO (ed.).   Una gioia insolita: lettere tra un prete cattolico e un laico anglicano. Trans. by Patrizia Morelli. Milan: Jaca, 1995. pp. 307. (Già e non ancora.) (Letters between C. S. Lewis and Giovanni Calabria.) Rev. by Barbara Reynolds in SEVEN (13) 1996, 104–6.

19756. STAUFER, AMY N.   Do angels have wings? CSL (24:7/8) 1993, 6–8.

19757. TOTARO, REBECCA.   Regaining perception: the Ransom Trilogy as a re-embodiment of the Neoplatonic model. CSL (22:10) 1991, 1–11.

19758. WASHICK, JAMES.   The framed narrative in *Perelandra*. CSL (25:7/8) 1994, 1–4.

19759. WATSON, THOMAS RAMEY.   Enlarging Augustinian systems: C. S. Lewis' *The Great Divorce* and *Till We Have Faces*. Ren (46:3) 1994, 163–74.

19760. YANDELL, STEPHEN.   'A pattern which our nature cries out for': the medieval tradition of the ordered four in the fiction of J. R. R. Tolkien. Mythlore (21:2) 1996, 375–92.

Saunders Lewis

19761. JONES, DARRYL.   'I failed utterly': Saunders Lewis and the cultural politics of Welsh Modernism. Irish Review (19) 1996, 22–43.

Sinclair Lewis

19762. EBY, CLARE VIRGINIA.   *Babbitt* as Veblenian critique of manliness. AmS (34:2) 1993, 5–23.

19763. HEBEL, UDO J.   *The whole evanescent context*? Möglichkeiten und Grenzen synchroner Kulturpolitik am Beispiel von Sinclair Lewis' *Main Street* (1920). LJGG (37) 1996, 261–82.

19764. HUTCHISSON, JAMES M.   The rise of Sinclair Lewis, 1920–1930. University Park: Pennsylvania State UP, 1996. pp. xii, 276. (Penn State series in the history of the book.)

19765. MOREFIELD, KENNETH R.   Searching for the fairy child: a psychoanalytic study of *Babbitt*. MidQ (37:4) 1996, 448–58.

19766. PARRY, SALLY E.   Gopher Prairie, Zenith, and Grand Republic: nice places to visit, but would even Sinclair Lewis want to live there? MidM (20) 1992, 15–27.

19767. REITINGER, D. W.   A source for Tanis Judique in Sinclair Lewis's *Babbitt*. NCL (23:5) 1993, 3–4.

Wyndham Lewis

19768. ANSPAUGH, KELLY.   Getting even with Uncle Ez: Wyndham Lewis's *Doppelgänger*. JML (19:2) 1995, 235–43.

19769. CARACCIOLO, PETER L.   The metamorphoses of Wyndham Lewis's *The Human Age*: medium, intertextuality, genre. *In* (pp. 258–86) **69**.

19770. EDWARDS, PAUL (ed.).   Time and Western man. Santa Rosa, CA: Black Sparrow, 1993. pp. xix, 617. Rev. by Dennis Brown in CritS (7:1) 1995, 88–90; by C. J. Fox in JJQ (33:2) 1996, 323–9.

19771. FOSHAY, TOBY.   Wyndham Lewis and the avant-garde: the politics of the intellect. (Bibl. 1994, 13753.) Rev. by Reed Way Dasenbrock in MFS (40:1) 1994, 180–1; by Tony Tremblay in ESCan (22:1) 1996, 110–12.

19772. KLEIN, SCOTT W.   The fictions of James Joyce and Wyndham Lewis: monsters of nature and design. *See* **19129**.

19773. NICHOLLS, PETER.   Literature and politics: the importance of Wyndham Lewis. QLLSM (8) 1996, 205–23.

19774. PERRINO, MARK.   The poetics of mockery: Wyndham Lewis's *The Apes of God* and the popularization of Modernism. Leeds: Maney for Modern Humanities Research Assn, 1995. pp. 170. (Texts and dissertations, 40.) (Cf. bibl. 1992, 14938.)

19775. SEED, DAVID.   Party-going: the Jazz Age novels of Evelyn Waugh, Wyndham Lewis, F. Scott Fitzgerald and Carl Van Vechten. *In* (pp. 117–34) **34**.

19776. SHERRY, VINCENT.   Ezra Pound, Wyndham Lewis, and radical Modernism. (Bibl. 1995, 17739.) Rev. by Joe Hall in ChrisL (46:1) 1996, 92–3; by Michael Tratner in StudN (28:2) 1996, 244–53.

19777. STOCKTON, SHARON.   Aesthetics, politics, and the staging of the world: Wyndham Lewis and the Renaissance. *See* **6482**.

Maria Lewitt

19778. BALLYN, SUSAN.   The voice of the other: an approach to migrant writing in Australia. *See* **16691**.

Mark Leyner

19779. LITTLE, WILLIAM G.   Figuring out Mark Leyner: a waste of time. AQ (52:4) 1996, 135–63.

Lyn Lifshin

19780. LIFSHIN, LYN.   The writing of *Mint Leaves at Yaddow*. WD (74:9) 1994, 26–9.

Alan P. (Alan Paige) Lightman (1948–)

19781. BELL, ELIZABETH S.   He's relatively familiar: Albert Einstein in contemporary American fiction. *See* **18192**.

Tim Lilburn (1950–)

19782. WHETTER, DARRYL.   The birds, the bees, and Kristeva: an examination of sexual desire in the nature poetry of Daphne Marlatt, Robert Kroetsch, and Tim Lilburn. *See* **19404**.

Shirley Lim

19783. LIM, SHIRLEY GEOK-LIN.   Among the white moon faces: an Asian-American memoir of homelands. New York: Feminist Press at the City Univ. of New York, 1996. pp. 232. (Cross-cultural memoirs.)

Anne Morrow Lindbergh

19784. BELL, ELIZABETH S.   The Odyssey and the Argonautica: Charles and Anne Lindbergh's voyages of discovery. WebS (9:3) 1992, 66–80.

David Lindsay (1876–1945)

19785. KEGLER, ADELHEID.   Encounter darkness: the black Platonism of David Lindsay. Mythlore (19:2) 1993, 24–33.

Joan Lindsay

19786. HALTOF, MAREK.   The spirit of Australia in *Picnic at Hanging Rock*: a case study in film adaptation. *See* **13751**.

Vachel Lindsay

19787. HORGAN, PAUL.   Vachel Lindsay and *The Book of the Dead*. ASch (62:4) 1993, 565–70.
19788. LOUNSBURY, MYRON (ed.).   The progress and poetry of the movies: a second book of film criticism. *See* **13930**.
19789. PRESSLER, MICHAEL.   Poet and professor on the movies. *See* **14098**.
19790. WENTWORTH, MICHAEL.   'A walk through the paradise garden': Vachel Lindsay's idea of Kansas in *Adventures while Preaching the Gospel of Beauty*. Midamerica (20) 1993, 26–39.
19791. WOOLLEY, LISA.   Vachel Lindsay's crusade for cultural literacy. Midamerica (22) 1995, 83–8.

Penelope Lively

19792. BURTON, STACY.   Bakhtin, temporality, and modern narrative: writing 'the whole triumphant murderous unstoppable chute'. *See* **14422**.
19793. DUKES, THOMAS.   Desire unsatisfied: war and love in *The Heat of the Day* and *Moon Tiger*. *See* **16513**.
19794. JACKSON, TONY E.   The consequences of chaos: *Cleopatra's Sister* and postmodern historiography. MFS (42:2) 1996, 397–417.

Douglas Livingstone

19795. CHAPMAN, MICHAEL.   Douglas Livingstone 1932–1996. Current Writing (8:1) 1996, i–ii.
19796. CONNELL, ALLAN.   *In memoriam*: Dr Douglas Livingstone – the scientist. New Contrast (24:2) 1996, 14–17.
19797. GRAY, STEPHEN.   A gap in our horizon. Mail & Guardian (12:8) 1996, 38.
19798. HOPE, CHRISTOPHER.   *In memoriam*: Douglas Livingstone. New Contrast (24:2) 1996, 7–13.

Caroline Lockhart

19799. Furman, Necah Stewart.   Caroline Lockhart: her life and legacy. Introd. by Annette Kolodny. (Bibl. 1994, 13775.) Rev. by Priscilla Leder in Legacy (13:1) 1996, 82–4.

Ross Lockridge

19800. Weales, Gerald.   A return to Raintree County. GetR (9:1) 1996, 168–76 (review-article).

David Lodge

19801. Arizti Martín, Bárbara.   Shortcircuiting death: the ending of *Changing Places* and the death of the novel. Misc (17) 1996, 39–50.
19802. Bergonzi, Bernard.   David Lodge. Plymouth: Northcote House; London: British Council, 1995. pp. ix, 68. (Writers and their work.)
19803. —— A religious romance: David Lodge in conversation. Critic (47:1) 1992, 68–73.
19804. Coelsch-Foisner, Sabine.   Sex-maniacs, errant knights and lady professors: romance and satire in Lodge's university novels. *In* (pp. 333–49) **125**.
19805. Friend, Joshua.   'Every decoding is another encoding': Morris Zapp's poststructural implications on our postmodern world. *See* **15431**.
19806. Schmeling, Max.   Narrative, perspective and cultural otherness. *See* **2701**.

Jack London

19807. Auerbach, Jonathan.   Male call: becoming Jack London. Durham, NC; London: Duke UP, 1996. pp. x, 289. (New Americanists.)
19808. Berkove, Lawrence I.   London's developing conceptions of masculinity. JLJ (3) 1996, 117–26.
19809. Cassuto, Leonard; Reesman, Jeanne Campbell (eds). Rereading Jack London. Afterword by Earle Labor. Stanford, CA: Stanford UP, 1996. pp. xvii, 287.
19810. Fine, David.   Jack London's Sonoma Valley: finding the way home. *In* (pp. 56–72) **108**.
19811. Gatti, Susan Irvin.   Stone hearths and marble babies: Jack London and the domestic ideal. JLJ (3) 1996, 43–56.
19812. Labor, Earle; Leitz, Robert C., iii; Shepard, I. Milo (eds). The complete short stories of Jack London. (Bibl. 1995, 17776.) Rev. by Charles L. Crow in JAC (18:2) 1995, 99; by R. W. (Herbie) Butterfield in YES (26) 1996, 318–19.
19813. ——Reesman, Jeanne Campbell.   Jack London. (Bibl. 1995, 17777.) Rev. by Bennett Lovett-Graff in Utopian Studies (7:1) 1996, 126–8.
19814. Lovett-Graff, Bennett.   Prehistory as posthistory: the socialist science fiction of Jack London. JLJ (3) 1996, 88–104.
19815. Nuernberg, Susan M. (ed.).   The critical response to Jack London. Westport, CT; London: Greenwood Press, 1995. pp. xxxix, 291. (Critical responses in arts and letters, 19.)
19816. Okun, Peter T.   John Barleycorn's body. AQ (52:3) 1996, 63–86.
19817. Petersen, Per Serritslev.   The Dr Jekyll and Mr Hyde

motif in Jack London's science fiction: formula and intertextuality in *When the World Was Young*. See **12351**.

19818. Poole, Gordon. The drunken Scheherazade: self-reflection in Jack London's *The Road, Martin Eden* and *John Barleycorn*. RSAJ (1) 1990, 69–80.

19819. Stasz, Clarice. Jack London's delayed discovery of fatherhood. JLJ (3) 1996, 146–61.

19820. —— (ed.). Joan London to Jack London: a selection of letters. JLJ (3) 1996, 162–8.

19821. White, Bruce. Jack London on Elbert Hubbard: from 'splendid character' to cad. *See* **11528**.

19822. Williams, Tony. Jack London and Carl G. Jung: an alternative reading. JLJ (3) 1996, 127–45.

Michael Longley

19823. Longley, Michael. Tuppenny stung: autobiographical chapters. Belfast: Lagan Press, 1994. pp. 82. Rev. by Sean Dunne in Irish Review (16) 1994, 133–4.

19824. Lyon, John. Michael Longley's lists. Eng (45:183) 1996, 228–46.

19825. McDonald, Peter. Yeats, form and Northern Irish poetry. *See* **18527**.

19826. Peacock, Alan. Michael Longley: poet between worlds. *In* (pp. 263–79) **86**.

Barry Lopez

19827. Ruckert, William H. Barry Lopez and the search for a dignified and honorable relationship with nature. *In* (pp. 137–64) **25**.

Audre Lorde (Gamba Adisa)

19828. Adams, Alice. Out of the womb: the future of the uterine metaphor. Feminist Studies (19:2) 1993, 269–89.

19829. Davies, Carole Boyce. Writing home: gender and heritage in the works of Afro-Caribbean/American women writers. *In* (pp. 59–73) **81**.

19830. Gagnier, Regenia. Feminist autobiography in the 1980s. *See* **15150**.

19831. Keating, AnaLouise. Women reading women writing: self-invention in Paula Gunn Allen, Gloria Anzaldúa, and Audre Lorde. *See* **15930**.

19832. McRuer, Robert. Boys' own stories and new spellings of my name: coming out and other myths of queer positionality. *In* (pp. 260–84) **30**.

19833. Oldfield, Sybil. The news from the confessional – some reflections on recent autobiographical writing by women and its areas of taboo. *See* **4495**.

19834. Sánchez Calle, M. Pilar. The maternal, the lesbian and the political: explorations of the erotic in Audre Lorde's poetry. Gramma (4) 1996, 107–17.

H. P. Lovecraft

19835. Joshi, S. T. H. P. Lovecraft: a life. West Warwick, RI: Necronomicon Press, 1996. pp. xii, 704.

19836. MacCulloch, Simon.   The toad in the study: M. R. James, H. P. Lovecraft and forbidden knowledge: part two; part three. *See* **18911**.

19837. Wohleber, Curt.   The man who can scare Stephen King. AH (46:8) 1995, 82–90.

Amy Lowell

19838. Roman, Camille.   Robert Frost and three female modern poets: Amy Lowell, Louise Bogan, and Edna Millay. *See* **16486**.

Robert Lowell

19839. Doreski, William E.   The sudden bridegroom: the dialectic of *Lord Weary's Castle*. MP (93:3) 1996, 352–70.

19840. Estrin, Barbara L.   Lowelling and laureling: revising gender and genre in Robert Lowell's *Day by Day*. MLQ (57:1) 1996, 77–105.

19841. Greene, Michael.   'More consciously mistaken': confessional crisis and self-revision in Robert Lowell's *Day by Day*. CEACrit (58:3) 1996, 1–14.

19842. Hart, Henry.   Robert Lowell and the sublime. Foreword by Jay Parini. (Bibl. 1995, 17831.) Rev. by William V. Davis in AL (68:3) 1996, 654–5.

19843. Herbert, Gary B.   Master and slave in Robert Lowell's *Benito Cereno*. Ren (43:4) 1991, 292–302.

19844. Hoffman, Daniel.   Afternoon with Robert Lowell. GetR (6:3) 1993, 480–9.

19845. James, Stephen.   Revision as redress? Robert Lowell's manuscripts. *See* **691**.

19846. Labrie, Ross.   Reassessing Robert Lowell's Catholic poetry. Ren (47:2) 1995, 117–33.

19847. Mariani, Paul.   Lost puritan: a life of Robert Lowell. (Bibl. 1995, 17836.) Rev. by Bruce Bawer in BkW, 2 Oct. 1994, 4–5; by Ashley Brown in WLT (70:3) 1996, 703–4.

19848. —— Lowell on Berryman on Lowell. *See* **16431**.

19849. —— Robert Lowell and Jean Stafford. GetR (6:3) 1993, 457–74.

19850. Mulas, Francesco.   Un altra '*imitation*' di Robert Lowell. RSAJ (1) 1990, 99–106.

19851. Nohrnberg, Peter C. L.   The book the poet makes: collection and re-collection in W. B. Yeats' *The Tower* and Robert Lowell's *Life Studies*. Cambridge, MA: Dept of English and American Literature and Language, Harvard Univ., 1995. pp. ii, 102. (LeBaron Russell Briggs prize honors essays in English, 1993.)

19852. Witek, Terri.   The boy with the rapsberry sherbert heart. Shen (43:2) 1993, 107–20.

Susan Lowell (1950–)

19853. Olson, Peter.   A weaver's pathway: the text(ile) of metaphor, children, and identity in Susan Lowell's *Ganado Red*. Journal of the Southwest (38:2) 1996, 139–61.

Lois Lowry

19854. Kertzer, Adrienne.   Reclaiming her maternal pre-text: Little Red Riding Hood's mother and three young adult novels. *See* **3688**.

Malcolm Lowry

19855. ACKERLEY, CHRIS.   Notes towards Lowry's screenplay of *Tender Is the Night. See* **13380**.

19856. AMOR, NORMAN (comp.).   Malcolm Lowry: a checklist: a bibliographic supplement to W. H. New's *Malcolm Lowry: a Reference Guide* and J. H. Woolmer's *Malcolm Lowry: a Bibliography*. MalLR (34/35) 1994, 5–210.

19857. —— Supplement no. 1 to *Malcolm Lowry, a Checklist* (1994). MalLR (38/39) 1996, 118–37.

19858. —— Supplement no. 11 to W. H. New's *Malcolm Lowry: a Reference Guide*, 1978. MalLR (28) 1991, 50–70.

19859. —— Supplement no. 12 to W. H. New's *Malcolm Lowry: a Reference Guide*, 1978. MalLR (29/30) 1991/92, 103–21.

19860. ASALS, FREDERICK.   Introduction to *The 1940 'Under the Volcano'* (1994). MalLR (38/39) 1996, 53–78.

19861. BOWKER, GORDON.   Pursued by Furies: a life of Malcolm Lowry. (Bibl. 1994, 13805.) Rev. by Cynthia Sugars in MalLR (36/37) 1995, 11–15; by Patrick A. McCarthy in MalLR (36/37) 1995, 16–24; by Paul Tiessen in MalLR (36/37) 1995, 25–34; by Frederick Asals in MalLR (36/37) 1995, 45–51; by Richard Hauer Costa in MalLR (36/37) 1995, 52–5; by W. M. Hagen in WLT (70:4) 1996, 968; by Blake Bailey in NOR (22:1) 1996, 112–14.

19862. —— *Pursued by Furies: a Life of Malcolm Lowry* (4): response to Sugars, McCarthy and Tiessen. MalLR (36/37) 1995, 35–44.

19863. —— *Sursum Corda!* and the biographical waters. MalLR (38/39) 1996, 27–43.

19864. CHEN, JOHN (ZHONG) MING; XIE, SHAOBO.   Malcolm Lowry and the Tao. CanRCL (20:3/4) 1993, 356–80.

19865. DOYLE, JAMES.   The politics of Lowry's 'alcoholic tale': the Marxist response to *Under the Volcano*. MalLR (38/39) 1996, 46–52.

19866. DUPLAY, MATHIEU.   Poétique de la dette: *Under the Volcano* et la tradition. RANAM (29) 1996, 145–64.

19867. EGGLESTON, WILFRID.   *Writer's Notebook*: Wilfrid Eggleston on Malcolm Lowry. MalLR (29/30) 1991/92, 78–102.

19868. FILIPCZAK, DOROTA.   *Léviathan ou la Traversée inutile* and the death of the old self in *Through the Panama*. MalLR (31/32) 1992/93, 45–57.

19869. FOX, STANLEY.   Stanley Fox on Malcolm Lowry. MalLR (29/30) 1991/92, 27–30.

19870. GRACE, SHERRILL.   Thoughts towards the archeology of editing: *Caravan of Silence. See* **656**.

19871. —— (ed.).   Swinging the maelstrom: new perspectives on Malcolm Lowry. (Bibl. 1995, 17848.) Rev. by Miguel Mota in MalLR (31/32) 1992/93, 22–9.

19872. GRACE, SHERRILL E. (ed.).   Sursum corda! The collected letters of Malcolm Lowry: vol. 1, 1926–1946. (Bibl. 1995, 17849.) Rev. by Patrick A. McCarthy in MalLR (38/39) 1996, 19–26.

19873. HAGEN, BILL.   Malcolm Lowry's 'adjustable blueprint': the screenplay of *Tender Is the Night. See* **13747**.

19874. HORGAN, MARK J.   He lived, nightly. With a response by Kathleen Scherf. MalLR (31/32) 1992/93, 41–4.

19875. KELM, REBECCA STURM.   The skeleton within: American attractions of Mexico's 'Days of the Dead'. MalLR (38/39) 1996, 107–17.

19876. Lyons, J. B.   The drinking days of Joyce and Lowry. *See* **19139**.

19877. —— Malcolm Lowry's love notes. MalLR (28) 1991, 40–9.

19878. McAlice, Edward.   A Cocteau allusion in Lowry's *Lunar Caustic*. NCL (25:3) 1995, 6–7.

19879. McCarthy, Patrick A.   Forests of symbols: world, text & self in Malcolm Lowry's fiction. (Bibl. 1995, 17851.) Rev. by Miguel Mota in MalLR (38/39) 1996, 15–18.

19880. —— Lowry and *The Lost Weekend*. *See* **18902**.

19881. —— Lowry's forest of symbols: reading in *Under the Volcano*. JML (19:1) 1994, 55–72.

19882. —— The *La Mordida* drafts and notes at UBC. MalLR (28) 1991, 6–12.

19883. MacGregor, Catherine.   Something else new about hellfire: Hugh's co-dependency in *Under the Volcano*. MalLR (28) 1991, 13–33.

19884. Mota, Miguel.   Authoring Lowry: the role of the paratext in the fiction of Malcolm Lowry. ESCan (22:4) 1996, 413–24.

19885. —— Tiessen, Paul (eds).   The cinema of Malcolm Lowry: a scholarly edition of *Tender Is the Night*. *See* **764**.

19886. Newton, Norman.   Malcolm Lowry and the radiophonic imagination. MalLR (36/37) 1995, 56–95.

19887. —— The myth of America in *Under the Volcano*. MalLR (38/39) 1996, 86–106.

19888. O'Hara, Kieron.   'You do not know *why* you dance': comedy in *Under the Volcano, Through the Panama*, and *Tender Is the Night*. *See* **17868**.

19889. Rankin, Audrie.   Malcolm Lowry's *Tender Is the Night*: form, structure, spirit. *See* **14111**.

19890. Scherf, Kathleen (ed.).   The collected poetry of Malcolm Lowry. Annotations by Chris Ackerley. (Bibl. 1995, 17855.) Rev. by Frederick Asals in MalLR (31/32) 1992/93, 12–21.

19891. Seigel, Cathy.   The voice crying from Quauhnahuac. MalLR (31/32) 1992/93, 58–67.

19892. Slide, Anthony.   The film career of Margerie Bonner Lowry. MalLR (29/30) 1991/92, 20–6.

19893. Sugars, Cynthia.   Lowry's keepers: Victor MacLean and A. B. Carey. MalLR (28) 1991, 34–9.

19894. Tiessen, Paul (ed.).   A few items culled from what started out to be a sort of preface to a film-script. *See* **14287**.

19895. —— (introd.).   *Moby-Dick* adapted (1945). *See* **11895**.

Mina Loy

19896. Burke, Carolyn.   Becoming modern: the life of Mina Loy. New York: Farrar, Straus, & Giroux, 1996. pp. ix, 493. Rev. by Thom Gunn in TLS, 30 Aug. 1996, 3–4.

19897. Conover, Roger L. (ed.).   The lost lunar Baedeker: poems. New York: Farrar, Straus, & Giroux, 1996. pp. xx, 236. Rev. by Thom Gunn in TLS, 30 Aug. 1996, 304.

19898. Ress, Lisa.   From Futurism to feminism: the poetry of Mina Loy. *In* (pp. 115–27) **37**.

19899. Shreiber, Maeera.   'Love is a lyric / Of bodies': the negative aesthetics of Mina Loy's *Love Songs to Joannes*. Genre (27:1/2) 1994, 143–63.

Clare Boothe Luce

19900. HAMILTON, JOAN T. Visible power and invisible men in Clare Boothe's *The Women*. AmDr (3:1) 1993, 31–53.

Charles F. Lummis

19901. PADGET, MARTIN. Travel, exoticism, and the writing of region: Charles Fletcher Lummis and the 'creation' of the Southwest. Journal of the Southwest (37:3) 1995, 421–49.

Alison Lurie

19902. KRUSE, HORST. Alison Lurie's *Only Children*: an intertextual portrait of the artist as a young girl. LWU (29:2) 1996, 97–102.
19903. NEWMAN, JUDIE. Paleface into Redskin: cultural transformations in Alison Lurie's *Foreign Affairs*. In (pp. 188–205) **34**.
19904. PEARLMAN, MICKEY. Alison Lurie: interview. Onthebus (3:2/4:1) 1991, 250–4.

John Lutz (1939–)

19905. HARRIS, ELLEN. On duty with John Lutz: an interview. AD (29:4) 1996, 458–60.

George Ella Lyon

19906. LYON, GEORGE ELLA. A wordful child. Katonah, NY: Owen, 1996. pp. 32. (Meet the author.)

Lindiwe Mabuza

19907. UPTON, ELAINE MARIA. Born to the struggle, learning to write: an interview with Lindiwe Mabuza, poet and chief representative of the African National Congress (of South Africa) in the United States. Feminist Studies (21:3) 1995, 615–27.

Rose Macaulay

19908. CRAWFORD, ALICE. Paradise pursued: the novels of Rose Macaulay. (Bibl. 1995, 17865.) Rev. by Daphne Patai in Utopian Studies (7:2) 1996, 243–5; by Valerie Grosvenor Myer in NQ (43:1) 1996, 112–13.

James McAuley

19909. McCREDDEN, LYN. Mastering Romanticism: the struggle for vocation in the texts of James McAuley. In (pp. 265–73) **47**.

Paul J. McAuley

19910. BAILEY, K. V. Mars is a district of Sheffield. *See* **15919**.

'Ed McBain' (Evan Hunter)

19911. HUNTER, EVAN. The writing life: you just can't fake it. BkW, 25 Feb. 1996, 1, 10.
19912. SCHOFIELD, ANN. Lizzie Borden took an axe: history, feminism, and American culture. *See* **16719**.

Anne McCaffrey

19913. ROBERTS, ROBIN.   Anne McCaffrey: a critical companion. Westport, CT; London: Greenwood Press, 1996. pp. xi, 186. (Critical companions to popular contemporary writers.)

Norman MacCaig

19914. DEGOTT-REINHARDT, ANETTE.   Norman MacCaigs lyrisches Werk. Eine form-analytische Untersuchung. (Bibl. 1994, 13822.) Rev. by Andrea Heilmann in SSL (29) 1996, 304–8; by Bart Eeckhout in EngS (77:2) 1996, 201–3.

Charles McCarry

19915. McCARRY, CHARLES.   Between the real and the believable. BkW, 11 Dec. 1994, 1, 7.

Anthony McCarten

19916. TYLER, JANET.   Froth bite. Quote Unquote (31) 1996, 12–13. (Interview.)

Cormac McCarthy

19917. BARTLETT, ANDREW.   From voyeurism to archaeology: Cormac McCarthy's *Child of God*. SoLJ (24:1) 1991, 3–15.
19918. GUNN, SUSAN C.   McCarthy's *All the Pretty Horses*. Exp (54:4) 1996, 250–1.
19919. HALL, WADE; WALLACH, RICK (eds).   Sacred violence: a reader's companion to Cormac McCarthy: selected essays from the First McCarthy Conference, Bellarmine College, Louisville, Kentucky, October 15–17, 1993. El Paso: Univ. of Texas at El Paso, 1995. pp. xxi, 200. Rev. by John Wegner in TexR (17:1/2) 1996, 137–8.
19920. PHILLIPS, DANA.   History and the ugly facts of Cormac McCarthy's *Blood Meridian*. AL (68:2) 1996, 433–60.
19921. SEPICH, JOHN EMIL.   The dance of history in Cormac McCarthy's *Blood Meridian*. SoLJ (24:1) 1991, 16–31.
19922. SNODGRASS, W. D.   Shapes merging and emerging. Shen (41:4) 1991, 58–83.
19923. WITEK, TERRI.   'He's hell when he's well': Cormac McCarthy's rhyming dictions. Shen (41:3) 1991, 51–66.

Mary McCarthy

19924. BRIGHTMAN, CAROL.   Mary McCarthy: at home with Edmund Wilson. Salmagundi (90/91) 1991, 107–29.
19925. —— Writing dangerously: Mary McCarthy and her world. (Bibl. 1994, 13824.) Rev. by John Wain in ASch (62:4) 1993, 606–11.
19926. KRAUS, BARBARA.   Reliable narrators and unreliable memories: the case of Mary McCarthy's *Memories of a Catholic Girlhood*. *In* (pp. 141–50) **8**.
19927. STWERTKA, EVE; VISCUSI, MARGO (eds).   Twenty-four ways of looking at Mary McCarthy: the writer and her work. Westport, CT; London: Greenwood Press, 1996. pp. xii, 224. (Contributions to the study of world literature, 70.)
19928. WAIN, JOHN.   To criticize the critic. *See* **15182**.

Sue McCauley

19929. WILSON, TIM.   On the margins. Quote Unquote (38) 1996, 12–14. (Interview.)

Nellie L. McClung

19930. WARNE, RANDI R.   Literature as pulpit: the Christian social activism of Nellie L. McClung. (Bibl. 1995, 17876.) Rev. by Susanne Goodison in CanL (149) 1996, 134–5.

John McCluskey

19931. ROWELL, CHARLES H.   An interview with John McCluskey, Jr. Callaloo (19:4) 1996, 911–28.

Fionn Mac Colla ('Tom MacDonald')

19932. POGGI, VALENTINA.   History and the reconstructive imagination in Fionn Mac Colla's work. Études Écossaises (1) 1992, 265–72.

James McConkey

19933. ANDERSON, DONALD.   Court of memory: an interview. Epoch (43:3) 1994, 273–88.
19934. McCONKEY, JAMES M.   Poetry in the violent days: the artist and social responsibility. Epoch (43:3) 1994, 289–91.

Jill McCorkle

19935. WALKER, ELINOR ANN.   Celebrating voice and self in Jill McCorkle's *Crash Diet*. NCL (23:1) 1993, 11–12.

Carson McCullers

19936. CHAMPION, LAURIE.   Black and White Christs in Carson McCullers's *The Heart Is a Lonely Hunter*. SoLJ (24:1) 1991, 47–52.
19937. DAVIS, KATHERINE.   'A thing known and not spoken': sexual difference in Carson McCullers' *Member of the Wedding*. TexPres (16) 1995, 39–42.
19938. FREEMAN, ELIZABETH.   'The we of me': *The Member of the Wedding*'s novel alliances. WP (8:2) 1996, 111–35.
19939. HANNON, CHARLES.   *The Ballad of the Sad Café* and other stories of women's wartime labor. *In* (pp. 97–119) **9**.
19940. STAFFORD, TONY J.   'Gray eyes is glass': image and theme in *The Member of the Wedding*. AmDr (3:1) 1993, 54–66.
19941. VANDE KIEFT, RUTH M.   The love ethos of Porter, Welty, and McCullers. *In* (pp. 235–58) **32**.

Colleen McCullough

19942. DeMARR, MARY JEAN.   Colleen McCullough: a critical companion. Westport, CT; London: Greenwood Press, 1996. pp. xiii, 187. (Critical companions to popular contemporary writers.)

Val McDermid

19943. SYKES, JERRY.   An interview with Val McDermid. AD (29:3) 1996, 312–15.

Alice McDermott

19944. McDermott, Alice.   Books and babies. BkW, 9 May 1993, 1, 7.

19945. Wymard, Ellie.   Everything is memory: Ellie Wymard interviews Alice McDermott. Critic (47:1) 1992, 63–7.

Beverly Brodsky McDermott

19946. Frongia, Teri.   Tales of old Prague: of ghettos, Passover, and the blood of libel. JFA (7:2/3) 1996, 146–62.

'Hugh MacDiarmid' (C. M. Grieve)

19947. Alldritt, Keith.   Modernism in the Second World War: the later poetry of Ezra Pound, T. S. Eliot, Basil Bunting, and Hugh MacDiarmid. *See* **16614**.

19948. Fournier, Jean-Marie.   Poésie et historicité chez Mac-Diarmid. Études Écossaises (1) 1992, 333–41.

19949. McCulloch, Margery Palmer.   'Opening the door': women, Carswell and the Scottish renaissance. *See* **16703**.

19950. Milton, Colin.   'Shibboleths o the Scots': Hugh Mac-Diarmid and Jamieson's *Etymological Dictionary of the Scottish Language*. *See* **2053**.

19951. Stanforth, Susan M.   New light on the text of Mac-Diarmid's *The Nature of a Bird's World*. *See* **842**.

19952. Watson, Roderick.   Visions of Alba: the construction of Celtic roots in modern Scottish literature. *See* **13356**.

19953. Whyte, Christopher.   Unspeakable heterosexuality. *See* **18316**.

Ann-Marie MacDonald

19954. Fortier, Mark.   Two-voiced, delicate monster: *The Tempest*, romance, and post-colonialism. *See* **7221**.

Betty MacDonald

19955. Gainor, J. Ellen.   'The slow-eater-tiny-bite-taker': an eating disorder in Betty MacDonald's *Mrs Piggle-Wiggle*. *In* (pp. 29–41) **24**.

Cynthia MacDonald

19956. Bowers, Susan R.   The witch's garden: the feminist grotesque. *In* (pp. 19–36) **109**.

'Ross Macdonald' (Kenneth Millar)

19957. Albert, Neil.   Ross Macdonald: an appreciation. AD (29:3) 1996, 290–5.

Joseph McElroy

19958. Hantke, Steffen.   'God save us from the bourgeois adventure': the figure of the terrorist in contemporary American conspiracy fiction. *See* **14537**.

Ian McEwan

19959. Brown, Richard.   Postmodern Americas in the fiction of Angela Carter, Martin Amis and Ian McEwan. *In* (pp. 92–110) **34**.

19960. DELVILLE, MICHEL. Marsilio Ficino and political syncretism in Ian McEwan's *Black Dogs*. NCL (26:3) 1996, 11–12.

19961. NIERAGDEN, GÖRAN. '*Who sees when I speak?*': Neuvorschläge zur Relation von homodiegetischer Erzählung und Fokalisierung mit einer Beispielanalyse von Ian McEwans *The Child in Time*. *See* **15677**.

19962. REYNIER, CHRISTINE. Psychic journey into artistic creation: a reading of Ian McEwan's *Reflections of a Kept Ape*. JSSE (22) 1994, 115–25.

19963. RYAN, KIERNAN. Ian McEwan. Plymouth: Northcote House; London: British Council, 1996. pp. viii, 72. (Writers and their work.)

19964. SLAY, JACK, JR. The absurdity of love: parodic relationships in Ian McEwan's *Reflections of a Kept Ape* and *Dead as They Come*. NCL (25:3) 1995, 4–6.

19965. —— Ian McEwan. New York; Twayne; London: Prentice Hall, 1996. pp. xiv, 165. (Twayne's English authors, 518.)

Gwendolyn MacEwen

19966. GERRY, THOMAS M. F. 'Green yet free of seasons': Gwendolyn MacEwen and the mystical tradition of Canadian poetry. *See* **8776**.

19967. ROSENBLATT, JOE. Gwen's magic. LRC (5:6) 1996, 15–17 (review-article).

19968. SULLIVAN, ROSEMARY. Shadow maker: the life of Gwendolyn MacEwen. Toronto: HarperCollins, 1995. pp. xvi, 416. Rev. by Joe Rosenblatt in LRC (5:6) 1996, 15–17.

John McGahern

19969. CRONIN, JOHN. John McGahern: a new image? *In* (pp. 110–17) **52**.

19970. McGAHERN, JOHN. Reading and writing. *In* (pp. 103–9) **52**.

19971. SAMPSON, DENIS. Outstaring nature's eye: the fiction of John McGahern. (Bibl. 1995, 17912.) Rev. by Ninian Mellamphy in ESCan (22:2) 1996, 233–6.

Roger McGough

19972. HABERKAMM, HELMUT. Die Bewegung weg vom *Movement*: Studien zur britischen Gegenwartsdichtung nach 1960. *See* **14938**.

Thomas McGrath

19973. STEIN, JULIA. Thomas McGrath: interview. Onthebus (3:2/4:1) 1991, 256–66.

Thomas McGreevy

19974. DAVIS, ALEX. Irish poetic modernisms: a reappraisal. CritS (8:2) 1996, 186–97.

Fiona McGregor (1965–)

19975. McGREGOR, FIONA. I am not a lesbian. Meanjin (55:1) 1996, 31–40.

Medbh McGuckian

19976. BOHMAN, KIMBERLY S. Surfacing: an interview with Medbh McGuckian. Irish Review (16) 1994, 95–108.

19977. DENMAN, PETER.   Ways of saying: Boland, Carson, McGuckian. *In* (pp. 158–73) **86**.

19978. EBERLE, WENDY J.   Painting a pictographic language, beyond sound boundaries: Medbh McGuckian's poetic making. CJIS (22:1) 1996, 61–70.

19979. GRAY, CECILE.   Medbh McGuckian: imagery wrought to its uttermost. *In* (pp. 165–77) **58**.

19980. MURPHY, SHANE.   Obliquity in the poetry of Paul Muldoon and Mebdh McGuckian. EI (31:3/4) 1996, 76–101.

19981. O'CONNOR, MARY.   'Rising out': Medbh McGuckian's de-stabilizing poetics. EI (30:4) 1995, 154–72.

19982. PORTER, SUSAN.   The 'imaginative space' of Medbh McGuckian. *In* (pp. 86–101) **50**.

19983. WILLS, CLAIR.   Voices from the nursery: Medbh McGuckian's plantation. *In* (pp. 373–99) **86**.

Frank McGuinness

19984. CULLINGFORD, ELIZABETH BUTLER.   British Romans and Irish Carthaginians: anticolonial metaphor in Heaney, Friel, and McGuinness. *See* **17991**.

19985. GLEITMAN, CLAIRE.   'Like father like son': *Someone Who'll Watch over Me* and the geopolitical family drama. EI (31:1/2) 1996, 78–88.

19986. PINE, RICHARD.   Frank McGuinness: a profile. Irish Literary Supplement (10:1) 1991, 29–30. (Interview.)

William MacHarg (1872–1951)

19987. OBUCHOWSKI, MARY DEJONG.   The *Indian Drum* and its authors: a reconsideration. *See* **16174**.

Arthur Machen

19988. COULOMBE, CHARLES A.   Hermetic imagination: the effect of the Golden Dawn on fantasy literature. Mythlore (21:2) 1996, 345–55.

19989. VILLA, LUISA.   Verso/attraverso *The Hill of Dreams*: Walter Pater, Arthur Machen, l'oggetto estetico e la decadenza. *See* **12011**.

Heather McHugh

19990. McHUGH, HEATHER.   Broken English: poetry and partiality. (Bibl. 1993, 13834.) Rev. by John Palattella in DQ (31:1) 1996, 68–78.

William McIlvanney

19991. DIXON, KEITH.   'No fairies. No monsters. Just people.' Resituating the work of William McIlvanney. *In* (pp. 187–98) **115**.

Jay McInerney

19992. GIRARD, STEPHANIE.   'Standing at the corner of Walk and Don't Walk': Vintage Contemporaries, *Bright Lights, Big City*, and the problems of betweenness. *See* **1053**.

Claude McKay

19993. COOPER, CAROLYN.   Race and the cultural politics of self-representation: a view from the University of the West Indies. *See* **16546**.

19994. HAMALIAN, LEO.   D. H. Lawrence and Black writers. *See* **17595**.

19995. KELLER, JAMES R.   'A chafing savage, down the decent street': the politics of compromise in Claude McKay's protest sonnets. AAR (28:3) 1994, 447–56.

19996. TILLERY, TYRONE.   Claude McKay: a Black poet's struggle for identity. (Bibl. 1993, 13838.) Rev. by Cary D. Wintz in AHR (98:2) 1993, 568–9.

Don McKay

19997. BUSHELL, KEVIN.   Don McKay and metaphor: stretching language toward wilderness. StudCanL (21:1) 1996, 37–55.

Percy MacKaye

19998. ANGELL, GEORGE W.   Theatre, history, and myth on the New England coast. NETJ (1) 1990, 79–91.

19999. POTTER, VILMA RASKIN.   Percy MacKaye's Caliban for a democracy. JAC (19:4) 1996, 71–9.

Sir Compton Mackenzie

20000. CUSHMAN, KEITH.   Lawrence, Compton Mackenzie, and the 'semi-literary cats' of Capri. *See* **19513**.

20001. HAGEMANN, SUSANNE.   Performative parodies: Scots and Americans in Compton Mackenzie's *The Monarch of the Glen. In* (pp. 125–39) **8**.

Nathaniel Mackey

20002. DONAHUE, JOSEPH.   Sprung polity: on Nathaniel Mackey's recent work. Talisman (9) 1992, 62–5.

20003. FOSTER, EDWARD.   An interview with Nathaniel Mackey. Talisman (9) 1992, 48–61.

20004. FRANCO, MICHAEL.   Bedouin hornbook. Talisman (9) 1992, 71–3.

20005. MOBILIO, ALBERT.   On Mackey's *Bedouin Hornbook*: hearing voices. Talisman (9) 1992, 69–70.

20006. MULLEN, HARRYETTE.   Phantom pain: Nathaniel Mackey's *Bedouin Hornbook*. Talisman (9) 1992, 37–43.

20007. NIELSEN, ALDON L.   Gassire's lute. Talisman (9) 1992, 66–8.

20008. SCROGGINS, MARK.   The master of speech and speech itself: Nathaniel Mackey's *Septet for the End of Time*. Talisman (9) 1992, 44–7.

Robin McKinley

20009. CADDEN, MICHAEL.   The illusion of control: narrative authority in Robin McKinley's *Beauty* and *The Blue Sword*. Mythlore (20:2) 1994, 16–19, 31.

Patricia MacLachlan

20010. TRITES, ROBERTA SEELINGER.   Is flying extraordinary? Patricia MacLachlan's use of aporia. *See* **2486**.

Mary MacLane

20011. HALVERSON, CATHRYN.   Mary MacLane's story. AQ (50:4) 1994, 31–61.

20012. Pruitt, Elisabeth (ed.).   Tender darkness: a Mary MacLane anthology. Belmont, CA: Abernathy & Brown, 1993. pp. 204. Rev. by Priscilla Leder in Legacy (13:1) 1996, 82–4.

Archibald MacLeish

20013. Donaldson, Scott; Winnick, R. H.   Archibald MacLeish: an American life. (Bibl. 1995, 17941.) Rev. by John P. Sisk in ASch (62:1) 1993, 145–50.

Hugh MacLennan

20014. Gareau-Des Bois, Louise.   Hugh MacLennan as I knew him. Fontanus (7) 1994, 113–26.
20015. Heidenreich, Rosmarin.   The bear. *See* **17607**.
20016. Lennox, John.   A compelling continuum. *See* **19472**.
20017. Metraux, Daniel A.   The political fiction of Hugh MacLennan and the politics of Québec nationalism. CanRCL (23:4) 1996, 1158–71.
20018. Tierney, Frank M. (ed.).   Hugh MacLennan. Ottawa: Ottawa UP, 1994. pp. vi, 210. (Re-appraisals: Canadian writers, 19.) Rev. by Julie Beddoes in ESCan (22:2) 1996, 246–7.
20019. Turpin, Rosemary.   Isabella Christine MacLennan. Fontanus (8) 1995, 27–47.

Alistair MacLeod

20020. Berces, Francis.   Existential maritimer: Alistair MacLeod's *The Lost Salt Gift of Blood*. StudCanL (16:1) 1991, 114–28.

'Fiona Macleod' (William Sharp)

20021. Meyers, Terry L.   The sexual tensions of William Sharp: a study of the birth of Fiona Macleod, incorporating two lost works, *Ariadne in Naxos* and *Beatrice*. New York; Frankfurt; Bern; Paris: Lang, 1996. pp. 126. (Studies in nineteenth-century British literature, 2.)

Seumas MacManus

20022. Deane, Paul.   Paganism *vs* Christianity: images of priests in contemporary Irish literature. *See* **17809**.

Wesley McNair

20023. Davies, Linda.   Running in place: an interview with Wesley McNair. Green Mountains Review (8:2) 1995/96, 15–26.

Terrence McNally

20024. Drukman, Steven.   Gay-gazing at *The Lisbon 'Traviata'*; or, How are things in *Tosca, Norma*? TT (5:1) 1995, 23–34.
20025. Zinoman, Joy.   Terrence McNally. *In* (pp. 182–204) **85**.

'Brinsley MacNamara' (John Weldon)

20026. Gonzalez, Alexander G.   Theme and structure in Brinsley MacNamara's *The Mirror in the Dust*. SAtlR (61:4) 1996, 53–65.

Desmond MacNamara

20027. Quintelli-Neary, Marguerite.   Desmond MacNamara's intrusions and invasions. Notes on Modern Irish Literature (8) 1996, 25–30.

Louis MacNeice

20028. ENGLE, JOHN. A modest refusal: Yeats, MacNeice, and Irish poetry. *In* (pp. 71–88) **58**.

20029. HEUSER, ALAN (ed.). Selected prose of Louis MacNeice. (Bibl. 1994, 13875.) Rev. by Robyn Marsack in PN Review (17:5) 1991, 59.

20030. —— McDONALD, PETER (eds). Selected plays of Louis MacNeice. (Bibl. 1995, 17957.) Rev. by Michael J. Sidnell in ESCan (22:1) 1996, 115–17.

20031. STALLWORTHY, JON. Louis MacNeice. (Bibl. 1995, 17960.) Rev. by Michael Shelden in BkW, 23 July 1995, 4.

D'Arcy McNickle

20032. DUANE, DANIEL. Mixed intentions in D'Arcy McNickle's *Wind from an Enemy Sky*. SAIL (8:1) 1996, 25–43.

20033. PURDY, JOHN LLOYD (ed.). The legacy of D'Arcy McNickle: writer, historian, activist. Norman; London: Oklahoma UP, 1996. pp. xv, 264. (American Indian literature and critical studies, 21.)

20034. RUPPERT, JAMES. Mediation in contemporary Native-American writing. *See* **17626**.

John McPhee

20035. BAILEY, THOMAS C. John McPhee: the making of a meta-naturalist. *In* (pp. 195–213) **25**.

20036. GIDDENS, ELIZABETH. An epistemic case study: identification and attitude change in John McPhee's *Coming into the Country*. *See* **2371**.

20037. TURNER, BRIAN. Giving good reasons: environmental appeals in the non-fiction of John McPhee. *See* **2488**.

Sandra McPherson

20038. BROWN-DAVIDSON, TERRI. The belabored scene, the subtlest detail: how craft affects heat in the poetry of Sharon Olds and Sandra McPherson. HC (29:1) 1992, 1–9.

Derek Mahon

20039. BROWN, TERENCE (ed.). Journalism: selected prose, 1970–1995. Oldcastle, Co. Meath: Gallery, 1996. pp. 241.

20040. LONGLEY, EDNA. Derek Mahon: extreme religion of art. *In* (pp. 280–303) **86**.

20041. McDONALD, PETER. Yeats, form and Northern Irish poetry. *See* **18527**.

20042. MURPHY, JAMES J.; McDIARMID, LUCY; DURKAN, MICHAEL J. Q and A with Derek Mahon. Irish Literary Supplement (10:2) 1991, 27–8. (Interview.)

20043. RÁCZ, ISTVÁN D. Mask lyrics in the poetry of Paul Muldoon and Derek Mahon. *In* (pp. 107–18) **112**.

20044. TANNEHILL, ARLENE. 'No saint or hero … / Brings danger-ous tokens to the new era': Derek Mahon and Tess Gallagher's revisions of Yeats's *The Magi*. *In* (pp. 47–69) **58**.

Margaret Mahy

20045. LAWRENCE-PIETRONI, ANNA. *The Tricksters, The Changeover*, and the fluidity of adolescent literature. CLAQ (21:1) 1996, 34–9.

Norman Mailer

20046. ALGEO, ANN M. The courtroom as forum: homicide trials by Dreiser, Wright, Capote, and Mailer. *See* **16689**.

20047. ARLETT, ROBERT. Epic voices: inner and global impulse in the contemporary American and British novel. *See* **14375**.

20048. BOONE, JOSEPH A. Vacation cruises; or, The homoerotics of Orientalism. *See* **17448**.

20049. CAFAGNA, DIANNE. Mailer's moon over *An American Dream*. NCL (22:5) 1992, 3–4.

20050. MELLARD, JAMES M. Origins, language, and the constitution of reality: Norman Mailer's *Ancient Evenings*. *In* (pp. 131–49) **123**.

20051. MONTEIRO, GEORGE. *Moby-Dick* and *The Naked and the Dead* reviewed in the *Fourth International*. *See* **11865**.

20052. MYLAN, SHERYL A. Love in the trenches: images of woman in Mailer's *The Naked and the Dead*. WLA (6:1) 1994, 75–85.

20053. NEUSTADTER, ROGER. The astro-turf garden: pastoralism in the industrial age. *See* **16553**.

20054. SCOTT, GRANT F. *Going after Cacciato* and the problem of teleology. *See* **10767**.

20055. THORNTON, WILLIAM H. Stranded in the sixties: the politics of Norman Mailer's *Armies of the Night*. PCR (5:1) 1994, 95–105.

20056. TURNER, CATHERINE. The angel of the shelter: American women and the atomic bomb. *See* **1382**.

20057. VAN ZYL, SUSAN; SEY, JAMES. The compulsion to confess. Literator (17:3) 1996, 77–92.

20058. YAEGER, PATRICIA. The 'language of blood': toward a maternal sublime. *See* **17358**.

Geoff Mains

20059. WRIGHT, LES. Gay genocide as literary trope. *In* (pp. 50–68) **2**.

Roger Mais

20060. MIDDLETON, DARREN J. N. Christ recrucified: the portrayal of Rastaman in Roger Mais's *Brother Man*. NCL (25:2) 1995, 10–12.

Clarence Major

20061. BELL, BERNARD W. Clarence Major's homecoming voice in *Such Was the Season*. AAR (28:1) 1994, 89–94.

20062. —— Introduction: Clarence Major's double consciousness as a Black postmodernist artist. AAR (28:1) 1994, 5–9.

20063. COLEMAN, JAMES W. Clarence Major's *All-Night Visitors*: Calabanic discourse and Black male expression. AAR (28:1) 1994, 95–108.

20064. HAYWARD, STEVE. Against commodification: Zuni culture in Clarence Major's Native-American texts. AAR (28:1) 1994, 109–20.

20065. KLAWANS, STUART. 'I was a weird example of art': *My Amputations* as Cubist confession. AAR (28:1) 1994, 77–87.

20066. KLINKOWITZ, JEROME. Clarence Major's innovative fiction. AAR (28:1) 1994, 57–63.

20067. McCAFFERY, LARRY; KUTNIK, JERZY. 'I follow my eyes': an interview with Clarence Major. AAR (28:1) 1994, 121–38.

20068. MAJOR, CLARENCE; WEIXLMANN, JOE. A checklist of books by Clarence Major. AAR (28:1) 1994, 139–40.

20069. RONEY, LISA C. The double vision of Clarence Major, painter and writer. AAR (28:1) 1994, 65–75.

Bernard Malamud

20070. ABRAMSON, EDWARD A. Experiments in theme and form: five Malamud apprenticeship stories. StudAJL (15) 1996, 49–60.

20071. ANON. (ed.). America tampen shousetsu wo yomi naosu – josei, kazoku, ethnicity. (Re-reading American short stories: women, family and ethnicity.) Tokyo: Hokuseido Shoten, 1996. pp. xii, 390.

20072. CHEUSE, ALAN; DELBANCO, NICHOLAS. Talking horse: Bernard Malamud on life and work. New York; Chichester: Columbia UP, 1996. pp. xxiv, 220.

20073. KRETZER, BIRGIT ERIKA. Zwischen Kulturprotest und Flucht: der jüdisch-amerikanische Roman von 1920 bis Ende der 70er Jahre: eine Analyse an ausgewählten Beispielen. (Bibl. 1995, 17995.) Rev. by Susanne Opfermann in Ang (114:2) 1996, 296–8.

20074. PURCELL, WILLIAM F. The demands of love: the ending of Bernard Malamud's *The Assistant*. NCL (23:5) 1993, 4–5.

20075. SALZBERG, JOEL. Malamud on Bellow, Bellow on Malamud: a correspondence and friendship. See **16398**.

20076. SAPERSTEIN, JEFFREY. Irony and cliché: Malamud's *The Natural* in the 1980s. See **14173**.

20077. WASHBURN, TINA. Levinson's Roy: a child's hero. See **14313**.

20078. WATTS, EILEEN H. The art of racism: Blacks, Jews and language in *The Tenants*. StudAJL (15) 1996, 42–8.

'Lucas Malet' (Mary St Leger Kingsley Harrison)

20079. SCHAFFER, TALIA. Some chapter of some other story: Henry James, Lucas Malet, and the real past of *The Sense of the Past*. See **11647**.

20080. SREBRNIK, PATRICIA. The re-subjection of 'Lucas Malet': Charles Kingsley's daughter and the response to muscular Christianity. *In* (pp. 194–214) **74**.

Manohar Malgonkar

20081. MADGE, V. M. Rise of the *demos*: a study of Malgonkar's *The Princes*. *In* (pp. 12–20) **45**.

'Ern Malley' (James McAuley and Harold Stewart)

20082. HEYWARD, MICHAEL. The Ern Malley affair. (Bibl. 1993, 13883.) Rev. by David Lehman in BkW, 6 Mar. 1994, 1, 10.

20083. KANE, PAUL. An Australian hoax. Raritan (11:2) 1991, 82–98.

David Malouf

20084. BINDELLA, MARIA TERESA. Crossing boundaries in David Malouf's *Antipodes*. Quaderni di lingue e letterature (19) 1994, 109–23.

20085. TAYLOR, ANDREW. Postmodern Romantic: the imaginary in David Malouf's *An Imaginary Life*. *In* (pp. 275–90) **47**.

20086. WINNER, ANTHONY.   Disorders of reading short novels and perplexities. *See* **16998**.

20087. YOUNIS, RAYMOND AARON.   Apropos the last 'post-': contemporary literature, theory and interpretation. *See* **15839**.

Karen Malpede

20088. KRAMER, RICHARD E.   An interview with Karen Malpede. StAD (8:1) 1993, 45–60.

20089. PAVLIDES, MEROPE.   Poetics of women's writing: dramatic tragedy. *In* (pp. 11–21) **37**.

20090. WEINE, STEVAN M.   The witnessing imagination: social trauma, creative artists, and witnessing professionals. *See* **16206**.

David Mamet

20091. BREWER, GAY.   David Mamet and film: illusion/disillusion in a wounded land. (Bibl. 1993, 10058.) Rev. by Scott C. Bradley in FilmQ (48:1) 1994, 61.

20092. CULLICK, JONATHAN S.   'Always be closing': completeness and the discourse of closure in David Mamet's *Glengarry Glen Ross*. JDTC (8:2) 1994, 23–36.

20093. FOSTER, VERNA.   Sex, power, and pedagogy in Mamet's *Oleanna* and Ionesco's *The Lesson*. AmDr (5:1) 1995, 36–50.

20094. GOIST, PARK DIXON.   Ducks and sex in David Mamet's *Chicago*. Midamerica (18) 1991, 143–52.

20095. GOLDONI, ANNALISA.   Mamet and money: *American Buffalo*. Letterature d'America (50) 1993, 105–13.

20096. KANE, LESLIE (ed.).   David Mamet's *Glengarry Glen Ross*: text and performance. New York; London: Garland, 1996. pp. xxxii, 278. (Garland reference library of the humanities, 1817.) (Studies in modern drama, 8.)

20097. KIM, SO-IM.   Sexual myths in David Mamet: *Sexual Perversity in Chicago* and *Edmond*. JELL (42:4) 1996, 899–922.

20098. LAING, JEFFREY M.   The failure of language in David Mamet's *Oleanna*. NCL (24:4) 1994, 12.

20099. LAPALMA, MARINA DEBELLAGENTE.   Driving Doctor Ford. *See* **13900**.

20100. McKELLY, JAMES C.   The artist as criminal: *The Zoo Story* and *House of Games*. *See* **15912**.

20101. NELSON, JEANNE-ANDRÉE.   So close to closure: the selling of desire in *Glengarry Glen Ross*. Essays in Theatre (14:2) 1996, 107–16.

20102. NORMAN, GEOFFREY; REZEK, JOHN.   David Mamet. Playboy (Chicago) (42:4) 1995, 51–3, 56, 58–60, 148–50. (Interview.)

20103. RADAVICH, DAVID.   Collapsing male myths: Rabe's tragicomic *Hurlyburly*. AmDr (3:1) 1993, 1–16.

20104. —— Man among men: David Mamet's homosocial order. AmDr (1:1) 1991, 46–60.

Matsemela Manaka

20105. DAVIS, GEOFFREY V.   'When it's all over, and we all return': Matsemela Manaka's play *Ekhaya – Going Home*. *In* (pp. 123–38) **102**.

20106. RUSSO, BRIAN C.   Efficacy *versus* representation: segregated dramatic traditions under apartheid. *See* **18086**.

Eli Mandel

20107. STUBBS, ANDREW. Myth, origins, magic: a study of form in Eli Mandel's writing. (Bibl. 1995, 18016.) Rev. by Donald G. Stephens in JCP (10) 1995, 146–8.

Christine Mangala

20108. FROST, CHRISTINE MANGALA. 'Fleshing the bones': conducting inter-faith dialogue in fiction. LitTheol (10:3) 1996, 216–23.

Bill Manhire

20109. SHARP, IAIN. Triple Bill. Quote Unquote (34) 1996, 11–13.

Emily Mann

20110. HAMLIN, SCOTT. Out of danger. Theater (27:1) 1996, 99–101.

'Katherine Mansfield'
(Kathleen Mansfield Beauchamp, 'Julian Mark')

20111. ALONSO RODRÍGUEZ, PILAR. The role of intersentential connectives in complex narrative discourse: Katherine Mansfield's *The Garden Party. See* **2575**.

20112. BODDY, GILLIAN (ed.). Katherine Mansfield: a 'do you remember' life. Four stories with an illustrated introduction. Wellington: Victoria UP; Katherine Mansfield Birthplace Soc., 1996. pp. 143. (*A Birthday, The Wind Blows, Prelude, The Doll's House.*)

20113. BURGAN, MARY. The 'feminine' short story in America: historicizing epiphanies. *In* (pp. 267–80) **3**.

20114. —— Illness, gender, and writing: the case of Katherine Mansfield. (Bibl. 1995, 18027.) Rev. by Rhoda Nathan in MFS (42:1) 1996, 192–4.

20115. CLARK, JOHN R. Mansfield makes an end of permanent *Bliss*. NCL (24:4) 1994, 3–6.

20116. GONG, SHIFEN. Katherine Mansfield in Chinese translations. JCL (31:2) 1996, 117–37.

20117. KAPLAN, SYDNEY JANET. Katherine Mansfield and the origins of Modernist fiction. (Bibl. 1995, 18029.) Rev. by Anne Herrmann in Signs (18:3) 1993, 727–31.

20118. MORAN, PATRICIA. Unholy meanings: maternity, creativity, and orality in Katherine Mansfield. Feminist Studies (17:1) 1991, 105–25.

20119. —— Word of mouth: body language in Katherine Mansfield and Virginia Woolf. Charlottesville; London: Virginia UP, 1996. pp. xiv, 208. (Feminist issues.)

20120. NASORRI, CAROLA. Scrittura femminile e *short story* modernista: il caso di Katherine Mansfield. QLLSM (7) 1995, 273–90.

20121. NIERAGDEN, GÖRAN. Action, speech and thought: (de)constructing gender stereotypes in Katherine Mansfield's *A Birthday* and *The Escape* from a systemic grammar perspective. *See* **2680**.

20122. O'SULLIVAN, VINCENT; SCOTT, MARGARET (eds). The collected letters of Katherine Mansfield: vol. 4, 1920–1921. Oxford; New York: OUP, 1996. pp. xix, 372. Rev. by Dennis McEldowney in NZList, 7 Sept. 1996, 44; by Sarah Sandley in Quote Unquote (40) 1996, 27–8.

20123. PILDITCH, JAN (ed.). The critical response to Katherine Mansfield. Westport, CT; London: Greenwood Press, 1996. pp. xxx,

249. (Critical responses in arts and letters, 21.) Rev. by Ana Belén López Pérez in RAEI (9) 1996, 184–7.

20124. SCOTT, MARGARET.   The early notebooks of Katherine Mansfield. TLR (29) 1996, 79–84.

20125. ZIVLEY, SHERRY LUTZ.   Laura, Laurie, and language in Mansfield's *Garden Party*. JSSE (25) 1995, 71–7.

Maishe Maponya

20126. FRIEDMAN, HAZEL.   Recapturing the vision. Mail & Guardian (12:38) 1996, 30. (Interview.)

20127. STEADMAN, IAN (introd.).   Doing plays for a change. Johannesburg: Witwatersrand UP, 1995. pp. xxiii, 148. Rev. by Miki Flockemann in SARB (42) 1996, 5–6.

Lee Maracle

20128. SÁNCHEZ-PARDO GONZÁLEZ, ESTHER.   Rewriting history, post-coloniality and feminism: Lee Maracle's autobiographical works. RCEI (28) 1994, 161–76.

20129. WARLEY, LINDA.   Reviewing past and future: postcolonial Canadian autobiography and Lee Maracle's *Bobbi Lee, Indian Rebel*. ECanW (60) 1996, 59–77.

Dambudzo Marechera

20130. GRAY, STEPHEN.   A skeleton in his own cupboard. Mail & Guardian (11:15) 1995, 38.

Donald Margulies

20131. SCHLUETER, JUNE.   Ways of seeing in Donald Margulies' *Sight Unseen*. StAD (8:1) 1993, 3–11.

Richard Marius

20132. VIERA, CARROLL.   Two journeys in search of Arcadia: Richard Marius and *Bound for the Promised Land*. TPB (30) 1993, 36–42.

'Kamala Markandaya' (Kamala Purnaiya Taylor)

20133. SINGH, R. S.   West meets East: a study of Kamala Markandaya's *Possession*. In (pp. 21–35) **45**.

Daphne Marlatt

20134. BROSSARD, NICOLE; MARLATT, DAPHNE.   Only a body to measure reality by: writing the in-between. JCL (31:2) 1996, 5–17.

20135. RAO, ELEONORA.   Daphne Marlatt's liminal method: *Ana Historic* between fact and fiction. BJCS (11:2) 1996, 307–22.

20136. SCHEEL, KATHLEEN M.   Freud and Frankenstein: the monstered language of *Ana Historic*. ECanW (58) 1996, 93–114.

20137. WHETTER, DARRYL.   The birds, the bees, and Kristeva: an examination of sexual desire in the nature poetry of Daphne Marlatt, Robert Kroetsch, and Tim Lilburn. *See* **19404**.

Charles Marowitz

20138. BULMAN, JAMES C.   On being unfaithful to Shakespeare: Miller, Marowitz, and Wesker. *See* **6547**.

20139. PICKER, JOHN M.   Shakespeare divided: revision and transformation in Marowitz's *Variations on 'The Merchant of Venice'* and Wesker's *Shylock*. *See* **7036**.

Ngaio Marsh

20140. ACHESON, CAROLE; LIDGARD, CAROLYN (eds).   Return to black beech: papers from a centenary symposium on Ngaio Marsh. Christchurch: Centre for Continuing Education, Univ. of Canterbury, 1996. pp. 104.

Paule Marshall

20141. BROOKHART, MARY HUGHES.   Spiritual daughters of the Black American South. *In* (pp. 125–39) **32**.

20142. CLARKE, MICHAEL TAVEL.   Reclaiming literary territory: Paule Marshall's response to Joseph Conrad. *See* **17025**.

20143. DAVIES, CAROLE BOYCE .   Writing home: gender and heritage in the works of Afro-Caribbean/American women writers. *In* (pp. 59–73) **81**.

20144. ELAM, ANGELA.   To be in the world: an interview conducted with Paule Marshall. New Letters (62:4) 1996, 96–105.

20145. MIDOLO, CHIARA.   'Machines come natural to your kind': the machine and the body in Paule Marshall's *The Chosen Place, the Timeless People*. *In* (pp. 410–16) **117**.

20146. NIESEN DE ABRUÑA, LAURA.   The ambivalence of mirroring and female bonding in Paule Marshall's *Brown Girl, Brownstones*. *In* (pp. 245–52) **50**.

20147. PETTIS, JOYCE.   'Talk' as defensive artifice: Merle Kinbona in *The Chosen Place, the Timeless People*. AAR (26:1) 1992, 109–17.

20148. —— Toward wholeness in Paule Marshall's fiction. Charlottesville; London: Virginia UP, 1995. pp. x, 173. Rev. by Shirley C. Parry in AL (68:4) 1996, 872–3.

Troy Kennedy Martin

20149. SANDERS, JOE.   *Edge of Darkness* as transhuman thriller. JFA (5:4) 1992, 83–91.

Valerie Martin

20150. PENNINGTON, JOHN.   Textual doubling and divided selves: the strange case of Dr Jekyll and Mary Reilly. *See* **12350**.

20151. SMITH, R. McCLURE.   *A Recent Martyr*: the masochistic aesthetic of Valerie Martin. ConLit (37:3) 1996, 391–415.

Edward Martyn

20152. RIYADH, MUSTAFA.   The provincial scene in Edward Martyn's *The Heather Field* and *Maeve*. *In* (pp. 319–26) **60**.

John Masefield

20153. DODDS, DAVID LLEWELLYN (ed.).   John Masefield. (Bibl. 1994, 13944.) Rev. by Rebecca A. Umland in Arthuriana (6:2) 1996, 111–13.

20154. NOBLE, PETER.   Arthur, anti-Fascist or pirate king? Quondam et Futurus (3:3) 1993, 46–54.

Bobbie Ann Mason

20155. BLYTHE, HAL; SWEET, CHARLIE.   Bird imagery in Mason's *Shiloh*. NCL (25:5) 1995, 2–3.

20156. —————— Mason's *Shiloh*: another Civil War. NCL (25:4) 1995, 5–6.

20157. BOOTH, DAVID.   Sam's quest, Emmett's wound: Grail motifs in Bobbie Ann Mason's portrait of America after Vietnam. SoLJ (23:2) 1991, 98–109.

20158. GUNN, DREWEY WAYNE.   Initiation, individuation, *In Country*. MidQ (38:1) 1996, 59–72.

20159. UCHMANOWICZ, PAULINE.   Vanishing Vietnam: Whiteness and the technology of memory. *See* **17243**.

Philip Mason ('Philip Woodruff')

20160. SARJEANT, WILLIAM ANTONY SWITHIN.   A forgotten children's fantasy: Philip Woodruff's *The Sword of Northumbria*. Mythlore (20:4) 1995, 30–5.

John Masters

20161. ROY, PARAMA.   Discovering India, imagining *thuggee*. *See* **10108**.

William Matthews

20162. TAYLOR, HENRY.   Memory like a prayer. Shen (43:3) 1993, 65–74.

Peter Matthiessen

20163. COOLEY, JOHN.   Matthiessen's voyages on the River Styx: deathly waters, endangered peoples. *In* (pp. 167–92) **25**.

W. Somerset Maugham

20164. ARCHER, STANLEY.   W. Somerset Maugham: a study of the short fiction. (Bibl. 1994, 13951.) Rev. by Dean Baldwin in SSF (31:3) 1996, 165–7.

20165. HEIL, DOUGLAS.   The construction of racism through narrative and cinematography in *The Letter*. *See* **13785**.

20166. HOLDEN, PHILIP.   Orienting masculinity, orienting nation: W. Somerset Maugham's exotic fiction. Westport, CT; London: Greenwood Press, 1996. pp. 168. (Contributions to the study of world literature, 68.) (Cf. bibl. 1995, 18067.)

20167. ROGAL, SAMUEL J.   A companion to the characters in the fiction and drama of W. Somerset Maugham. Westport, CT; London: Greenwood Press, 1996. pp. xvii, 468.

20168. TAKANA, ICHIRO.   Himitsu chouhouin Somerset Maugham. (Somerset Maugham: an intelligence officer.) Tokyo: Kawade Shobo Shinsha, 1996. pp. 318.

William Maxwell (1908–)

20169. STEINMAN, MICHAEL (ed.).   The happiness of getting it down right: letters of Frank O'Connor and William Maxwell, 1945–1966. New York: Knopf, 1996. pp. xiii, 282, (plates) 8.

Harry Mazer

20170. Reed, Arthea J. S.   Presenting Harry Mazer. New York: Twayne; London: Prentice Hall, 1996. pp. xvi, 153. (Twayne's US authors, 673) (Young adult authors.)

Zakes Mda

20171. Raguz, Jennifer.   Cut that speech or starve! Techniques for avoidance of South African state censorship in Athol Fugard's *My Children! My Africa!* and Zakes Mda's *Banned. See* **18085**.

Kat Meads

20172. Meads, Kat.   Born southern and restless. Pittsburgh, PA: Duquesne UP, 1996. pp. vii, 224. (Emerging writers in creative nonfiction.)

Mark Medoff

20173. Gage, Nancy.   Mark Medoff. *In* (pp. 108–17) **121**.
20174. Gladstein, Mimi.   An interview with Mark Medoff. StAD (8:1) 1993, 61–83.

Charles L. Mee

20175. Andreach, Robert J.   Charles L. Mee's *Orestes*: a Euripidean tragedy as contemporary transvaluation. CML (16:3) 1996, 191–202.

Paula Meehan

20176. Brain, Tracy.   Dry socks and floating signifiers: Paula Meehan's poems. CritS (8:1) 1996, 110–17.
20177. Carney, Rob.   An interview with Paula Meehan. Atlanta Review (2:2) 1995, 49–58.

Rama Mehta

20178. Chindhade, Shirish V.   The triumph of timeless India: Rama Mehta's *Inside the Haveli. In* (pp. 84–91) **45**.

Pauline Melville

20179. Condé, Mary.   McGregor as Orpheus: Pauline Melville's *McGregor's Journey.* JSSE (26) 1996, 63–74.

Samuel Menashe

20180. Ahearn, Barry.   Poetry and synthesis: the art of Samuel Menashe. TCL (42:2) 1996, 294–308.

H. L. Mencken

20181. Grant, Thomas.   The *American Spectator*'s R. Emmett Tyrrell, Jr: Chicken McMencken. *See* **1277**.
20182. Harrison, S. L.   Mencken: magnificent anachronism: bibliographic essay. AmJ (13:1) 1996, 60–78.
20183. Hobson, Fred.   Mencken: a life. (Bibl. 1995, 18076.) Rev. by Bruce Bawer in BkW, 1 May 1994, 4–5; by Charles Scruggs in AL (68:4) 1996, 861–2; by Douglas C. Stenerson in SAtlR (61:3) 1996, 164–6.
20184. Martin, Edward A. (ed.).   In defense of Marion: the love of Marion Bloom & H. L. Mencken. Athens; London: Georgia UP, 1996. pp. lii, 397.

20185. SANDERS, JACK (ed.).   Do you remember? The whimsical letters of H. L. Mencken and Philip Goodman. Baltimore: Maryland Historical Soc., 1996. pp. xv, 189.

20186. YARDLEY, JONATHAN (ed.).   My life as author and editor. (Bibl. 1994, 13975.) Rev. by X. J. Kennedy in GetR (7:2) 1994, 289–303; by Daniel Aaron in BkW, 17 Jan. 1996, 6.

Judith Merril ('Rose Sharon', 'Eric Thorstein')

20187. BRIANS, PAUL.   Nuclear family/nuclear war. *In* (pp. 151–8) **77**.

James Merrill

20188. ADAMS, DON.   Heroes without name or origin: James Merrill's poetry of loss. NCL (26:3) 1996, 2–4.

20189. —— Merrill's *A Prism*. Exp (54:3) 1996, 185–7.

20190. BLASING, MUTLU KONUK.   Politics and form in postmodern poetry: O'Hara, Bishop, Ashbery and Merrill. *See* **16053**.

20191. MARIANI, ANDREA.   James Merrill: a postmodern poet? Yes & no (with a new poem by James Merrill). RSAJ (4) 1993, 31–56.

20192. MERRILL, JAMES.   A different person: a memoir. (Bibl. 1995, 18088.) Rev. by David Lehman in BkW, 12 Sept. 1996, 4.

20193. ROTELLA, GUY (ed.).   Critical essays on James Merrill. New York: G. K. Hall, 1996. pp. ix, 251. (Critical essays on American literature.)

20194. SMITH, EVANS LANSING.   Merrill's *The Changing Light at Sandover*. Exp (55:1) 1996, 51–3.

20195. WHITE, HEATHER.   An interview with James Merrill. Ploughshares (21:4) 1995/96, 190–5.

Thomas Merton

20196. CALLAHAN, ANNICE.   The development of Thomas Merton's Christ-consciousness. ABR (47:1) 1996, 99–113.

20197. DEFREES, MADELINE.   *Monks Pond* and the slough of despond: crisis in the cloister and the flight from the feminine. Critic (46:2) 1991, 2–14.

20198. GRZYBOWSKI, WACŁAW.   Epistemology, poetics and mysticism in Thomas Merton's theory of poetry. ZNWO (8) 1996, 105–27.

20199. KRAMER, VICTOR A. (ed.).   Turning toward the world: the pivotal years. San Francisco, CA: HarperSanFrancisco, 1996. pp. xix, 360. (Journals of Thomas Merton, 4.)

20200. LANE, BELDEN C.   Prayer without language in the apophatic tradition: knowing God as 'inaccessible mountain' – 'marvelous desert'. *See* **2416**.

20201. O'CONNELL, PATRICK F.   Thomas Merton and the multi-culturalism debate: cultural diversity or transcultural consciousness? Cithara (34:2) 1995, 27–36.

Samuel Merwin (1874–1936)

20202. BLOOMFIELD, MAXWELL.   Constitutional ideology and pro-gressive fiction. *See* **10609**.

W. S. Merwin

20203. COLLINS, FLOYD.   From open to closed: the poetry of W. S. Merwin. GetR (7:1) 1994, 144–62.

20204. FRAZIER, JANE. Writing outside the self: the disembodied narrators of W. S. Merwin. Style (30:2) 1996, 341–50.

20205. LIBBY, ANTHONY. Angels in the bone shop. *In* (pp. 281–301) **58**.

Paul Metcalf (1917–)

20206. ALEXANDER, CHRISTY. Paul Metcalf: an introduction. NCLR (2:2) 1995, 142–5.

Livi Michael

20207. MONTEITH, SHARON. On the streets and in the tower blocks: Ravinder Randhawa's *A Wicked Old Woman* (1987) and Livi Michael's *Under a Thin Moon* (1992). CritS (8:1) 1996, 26–36.

Barbara Michaels (1927–)

20208. FOXWELL, ELIZABETH. Novels of many shadows: the messages of Barbara Michaels. AD (29:3) 1996, 330–3.

Oscar Micheaux

20209. REGESTER, CHARLENE. Lynched, assaulted, and intimidated: Oscar Micheaux's most controversial films. *See* **14115**.

20210. —— The misreading and rereading of African-American filmmaker Oscar Micheaux: a critical review of Micheaux scholarship. *See* **14116**.

James A. Michener

20211. ANDERSON, DAVID D. East and Midwest in James Michener's tales of the Pacific War. SSMLN (26:1) 1996, 12–16.

20212. ARTHUR, ANTHONY. Avoiding nostalgia: James Michener's *The Bridge at Andau*. WLA (5:1) 1993, 47–53.

20213. MICHENER, JAMES. Lessons of a lifetime. BkW, 3 Oct. 1993, 1, 6.

20214. SEVERSON, MARILYN S. James A. Michener: a critical companion. Westport, CT; London: Greenwood Press, 1996. pp. xi, 199. (Critical companions to popular contemporary writers.)

Edna St Vincent Millay ('Nancy Boyd')

20215. CLARK, SUZANNE. *Jouissance* and the sentimental daughter: Edna St Vincent Millay. *In* (pp. 143–69) **39**.

20216. ROMAN, CAMILLE. Robert Frost and three female modern poets: Amy Lowell, Louise Bogan, and Edna Millay. *See* **16486**.

20217. WALKER, CHERYL. Antimodern, modern, and postmodern Millay: contexts of revaluation. *In* (pp. 170–88) **39**.

Arthur Miller

20218. BABCOCK, GRANGER. 'What's the secret?': Willy Loman as desiring machine. AmDr (2:1) 1992, 59–83.

20219. BALAKIAN, JAN. An interview with Arthur Miller. StAD (6:1) 1991, 29–47.

20220. BLOOM, HAROLD (ed.). Arthur Miller's *Death of a Salesman*. New York: Chelsea House, 1996. pp. 72. (Bloom's notes.)

20221. BOGARD, TRAVIS; BRYER, JACKSON R. (eds). 'A comradeship-in-arms': a letter from Eugene O'Neill to Arthur Miller. EOR (17:1/2) 1993, 121–3.

20222. CARUSO, CRISTINA C. 'One finds what one seeks': Arthur Miller's *The Crucible* as a regeneration of the American myth of violence. JADT (7:3) 1995, 30–42.

20223. CENTOLA, STEVEN R. 'How to contain the impulse of betrayal': a Sartrean reading of *The Ride down Mount Morgan*. AmDr (6:1) 1996, 14–28.

20224. —— 'Just looking for a home': a conversation with Arthur Miller. AmDr (1:1) 1991, 85–99.

20225. —— The last Yankee: an interview with Arthur Miller. AmDr (5:1) 1995, 78–98.

20226. COUPE, LAURENCE. What's wrong with Willy Loman? ERev (5:4) 1995, 16–19.

20227. GRIFFIN, ALICE. Understanding Arthur Miller. Columbia: South Carolina UP, 1996. pp. xii, 208. (Understanding contemporary American literature.)

20228. ISAAC, DAN. Founding father: O'Neill's correspondence with Arthur Miller and Tennessee Williams. EOR (17:1/2) 1993, 124–33.

20229. KANE, LESLIE. Dreamers and drunks: moral and social consciousness in Arthur Miller and Sam Shepard. AmDr (1:1) 1991, 27–45.

20230. MARTIN, ROBERT A. Arthur Miller's *After the Fall*: 'a play about a theme'. AmDr (6:1) 1996, 73–88.

20231. —— The nature of tragedy in Arthur Miller's *Death of a Salesman*. SAtlR (61:4) 1996, 97–106.

20232. —— CENTOLA, STEVEN R. (eds). The theater essays of Arthur Miller. Foreword by Arthur Miller. (Bibl. 1979, 11882.) New York: Da Capo Press, 1996. pp. liv, 628. (Revised and expanded ed.: first ed. 1978.)

20233. MARTINE, JAMES J. *The Crucible*: politics, property, and pretense. (Bibl. 1993, 13963.) Rev. by Steven R. Centola in Cithara (34:2) 1995, 52–3.

20234. MILLER, ARTHUR. Timebends: a life. (Bibl. 1992, 15231.) Rev. by Gabriel Miller in AmDr (1:1) 1991, 61–84.

20235. MORINO, KAZUYA. The body of a salesman: Arthur Miller's *Death of a Salesman*. StAL (33) 1996, 51–63.

20236. MURPHY, BRENDA. *The Man Who Had All the Luck*: Miller's answer to *The Master Builder*. AmDr (6:1) 1996, 29–41.

20237. —— Miller: *Death of a Salesman*. (Bibl. 1995, 18115.) Rev. by Neil Carson in Essays in Theatre (15:1) 1996, 103–4.

20238. O'KEEFFE, BERNARD. On the road. *See* **17869**.

20239. OSTERWALDER, HANS. The battle of the sexes in the classroom: Edward Albee's *Who's Afraid of Virginia Woolf?* and Arthur Miller's *After the Fall*. *See* **15914**.

20240. —— Patriarchy *vs* matriarchy: Edward Albee's *Who's Afraid of Virginia Woolf?* and Arthur Miller's *After the Fall*. *See* **15915**.

20241. OTTEN, TERRY. Historical drama and the dimensions of tragedy: *A Man for All Seasons* and *The Crucible*. *See* **16495**.

20242. PEARSON, MICHELLE I. John Proctor and the crucible of individuation in Arthur Miller's *The Crucible*. StAD (6:1) 1991, 15–27.

20243. PETHER, PENELOPE. Jangling the keys to the kingdom: some reflections on *The Crucible*, on an American constitutional paradox, and on Australian judicial review. CSLL (8:2) 1996, 317–37.

20244. PHELPS, H. C. The fat and lean years of Biff and Bernard: an overlooked parallelism in *Death of a Salesman*. NCL (25:4) 1995, 9–11.

20245. PORTER, THOMAS E. Strong gods and sexuality: guilt and responsibility in the later plays of Arthur Miller. AmDr (6:1) 1996, 89–112.

20246. ROUDANÉ, MATTHEW C. Arthur Miller and his influence on contemporary American drama. *See* **14156**.

20247. TUTTLE, JON. The efficacy of work: Arthur Miller and Albert Camus' *The Myth of Sisyphus*. AmDr (6:1) 1996, 61–72.

20248. WEALES, GERALD. Arthur Miller takes the air. AmDr (5:1) 1995, 1–15.

20249. ZEIFMAN, HERSH. All my sons after the Fall: Arthur Miller and the rage for order. *In* (pp. 107–20) **119**.

Henry Miller

20250. BAIR, DEIRDRE. Writing as a woman: Henry Miller, Lawrence Durrell, and Anaïs Nin in the Villa Seurat. *See* **17446**.

20251. BALLIET, GAY LOUISE. Henry Miller and Surrealist metaphor: 'riding the ovarian trolley'. New York; Frankfurt; Bern; Paris: Lang, 1996. pp. xiv, 187. (Modern American literature, 3.) (Cf. bibl. 1995, 18123.)

20252. BRASSAÏ. Henry Miller, the Paris years. New York: Arcade, 1995. pp. 224, (plates) 16.

20253. FERGUSON, ROBERT. Henry Miller: a life. (Bibl. 1991, 14318.) Rev. by Dominic Bevan in PN Review (17:6) 1991, 68–9.

20254. MANNING, HUGO. The wider purpose of Henry Miller: - literature as experience and revelation. Anaïs (8) 1990, 98–106.

20255. NANDYAL, RANGANATH. Henry Miller in the light of Eastern thought. New Delhi: Arnold, 1991. pp. 99. Rev. by Gay Wilson Allen in WWQR (13:1/2) 1995, 96–7.

20256. SMITH, MEL. Ten letters on death, dying, and condolences. *See* **9264**.

20257. STUHLMANN, GUNTHER. What Emil knew: Henry Miller writes to his best friend in America. Anaïs (8) 1990, 107–14.

20258. —— Who is H. V. Miller and how did he get that way? Approaching the man and his work on the centenary of his birth. Anaïs (10) 1992, 111–18.

Perry Miller

20259. WERTHEIMER, ERIC. 'To spell out each other': Roger Williams, Perry Miller, and the Indian. *See* **8410**.

Walter M. Miller, Jr

20260. GARVEY, JOHN. A canticle for Leibowitz: a eulogy for Walt Miller. Cweal (123:7) 1996, 7–8.

20261. SEED, DAVID. Recycling the texts of the culture: Walter M. Miller's *A Canticle for Leibowitz*. Extrapolation (37:3) 1996, 257–71.

Kate Millett

20262. MOLINA, CAROLINE. Paranoid discourse in the lesbian text: Kate Millett's *Sita*. LitPs (40:1/2) 1994, 108–17.

Steven Millhauser

20263. KINZIE, MARY.   Succeeding Borges, escaping Kafka: on the fiction of Steven Millhauser. Salmagundi (92) 1991, 115–44.

Joseph Mills

20264. FOURTINA, HERVÉ.   'Gloire de la non-essence': le commandement fait à l'Écossais dans *Watch Out, the World Is Behind You* de Joseph Mills. Études Écossaises (2) 1993, 53–61.

A. A. Milne

20265. MELROSE, A. R.   The Pooh bedside reader. New York: Dutton, 1996. pp. ix, 164.

Rohinton Mistry

20266. BHARUCHA, NILUFER E.   From behind a fine veil: a feminist reading of three Parsi novels. *See* **17257**.
20267. —— 'When old tracks are lost': Rohinton Mistry's fiction as diasporic discourse. JCL (30:2) 1995, 57–63.
20268. WILLIAMS, DAVID.   Cyberwriting and the borders of identity: 'what's in a name' in Kroetsch's *The Puppeteer* and Mistry's *Such a Long Journey? See* **2169**.

Joseph Mitchell

20269. ZINSSER, WILLIAM.   Journeys with Joseph Mitchell. ASch (62:1) 1993, 132–8.

Margaret Mitchell

20270. BAUER, MARGARET D.   Echoes of barren ground in *Gone with the Wind*: a p(re). s(cript). *See* **18196**.
20271. CONDÉ, MARY.   Some African-American fictional responses to *Gone with the Wind*. *See* **14440**.
20272. MOORE, EARL.   Auction trends. *See* **514**.
20273. OLEKSY, ELZBIETA.   The keepers of the house: Scarlett O'Hara and Abigail Howland. *In* (pp. 168–82) **65**.
20274. WASSERMAN, LORETTA.   *Sapphira and the Slave Girl*: Willa Cather *vs* Margaret Mitchell. *See* **16864**.

Naomi Mitchison

20275. LASSNER, PHYLLIS.   The fault lines of history: dystopic novels of the Second World War by British women authors. *See* **17106**.

Nancy Mitford

20276. McDONOUGH, DONALD.   Off with their heads: the British novel and the rise of Fascism. *See* **14611**.

Wendy Mnookin

20277. ALAMA, PAULINE J.   A woman in King Arthur's court: Wendy Mnookin's *Guenever Speaks*. Quondam et Futurus (2:2) 1992, 81–8.

Timothy Mo

20278. DAVIES, J. M. Q.   Refractions: fiction, historiography, and Mo's *The Redundancy of Courage*. CanRCL (23:4) 1996, 983–92.

20279. Ho, ELAINE YEE LIN. Satire and the national body: Timothy Mo's *The Redundancy of Courage*. Span (42/43) 1996, 76–85.

20280. MANFERLOTTI, STEFANO. Dopo l'impero: romanzo ed etnia in Gran Bretagna. *See* **14616**.

Nicholasa Mohr

20281. DWYER, JUNE. The wretched refuse at the golden door: Nicholasa Mohr's *The English Lesson* and America's persistent patronizing of immigrants. Proteus (11:2) 1994, 45–8.

Ursule Molinaro

20282. COLAKIS, MARIANTHE. What Jocasta knew: alternative versions of the Oedipus myth. *See* **17386**.

N. Scott Momaday

20283. FIORENTINO, DANIELE. The American Indian writer as cultural broker: an interview with N. Scott Momaday. SAIL (8:4) 1996, 61–72.

20284. LANDRUM, LARRY. The shattered modernism of Momaday's *House Made of Dawn*. MFS (42:4) 1996, 763–86.

20285. OWENS, LOUIS. N. Scott Momaday. *In* (pp. 58–69) **121**.

20286. RUPPERT, JAMES. Mediation in contemporary Native-American writing. *See* **17626**.

20287. SECCO, ANNA. The search for origins through storytelling in Native-American literature: Momaday, Silko, Erdrich. *See* **17628**.

20288. VIZENOR, GERALD. Native-American Indian identities: autoinscriptions and the cultures of names. *See* **2168**.

20289. WALLACE, KAREN L. Liminality and myth in Native-American fiction: *Ceremony* and *The Ancient Child*. AICRJ (20:4) 1996, 91–119.

Geraldine Monk

20290. KINNAHAN, LINDA A. Experimental poetics and the lyric in British women's poetry: Geraldine Monk, Wendy Mulford, and Denise Riley. ConLit (37:4) 1996, 620–70.

Harriet Monroe

20291. ATLAS, MARILYN J. Tone and technology in Harriet Monroe's *The Turbine*. Midamerica (22) 1995, 69–82.

John Montague

20292. CAVE, RICHARD ALLEN. John Montague: poetry of the depersonalised self. *In* (pp. 216–37) **86**.

20293. GARDINER, DAVID. 'Campaigning against memory's mortmain': Benjaminian allegory in John Montague's *The Rough Field*. Notes on Modern Irish Literature (8) 1996, 12–18.

20294. MARTIN, AUGUSTINE. John Montague: passionate contemplative. *In* (pp. 37–51) **52**.

20295. MOLINO, MICHAEL R. The net of language: marginalization, resistance, and difference in contemporary Irish literature. *See* **17996**.

20296. MONTAGUE, JOHN. The sweet way. *In* (pp. 30–6) **52**.

L. M. Montgomery

20297. BRENNAN, JOSEPH GERARD.   The story of a classic: Anne and after. ASch (64:2) 1995, 247–56.

20298. EPPERLY, ELIZABETH ROLLINS.   The fragrance of sweet-grass: L. M. Montgomery's heroines and the pursuit of romance. (Bibl. 1994, 14029.) Rev. by Jennie Rubio in ECanW (55) 1995, 161–8.

20299. LANDAW, JEFFREY M.; BRENNAN, JOSEPH GERARD.   The story of a classic. ASch (64:3) 1995, 478.

20300. RUBIO, MARY HENLEY (ed.).   Harvesting thistles: the textual garden of L. M. Montgomery: essays on her novels and journals. Guelph, Ont.: Canadian Children's Press, 1994. pp. xi, 185. Rev. by Judy Dudar in CanL (151) 1996, 133–5.

Michael Moorcock

20301. BAXTER, STEPHEN.   Further visions: sequels to *The Time Machine. See* **16242**.

Brian Moore ('Michael Bryan')

20302. ARBLASTER, ANTHONY.   Literature and moral choice. *In* (pp. 129–44) **63**.

20303. NIEL, RUTH.   Speech and silence: beyond the religious in Brian Moore's novels. *In* (pp. 161–74) **112**.

20304. SULLIVAN, ROBERT.   A matter of faith: the fiction of Brian Moore. Westport, CT; London: Greenwood Press, 1996. pp. xvi, 137. (Contributions to the study of world literature, 69.)

George Moore

20305. ACHILLES, JOCHEN.   Funktionen der Religion in der irischen Kultur der Jahrhundertwende: Moore, Shaw, Yeats and Joyce. *See* **19014**.

20306. DEANE, PAUL.   Conversion to doubt: George Moore's *The Lake*. Notes on Modern Irish Literature (4) 1992, 35–41.

20307. FREITAG, BARBARA.   *The Untilled Field*: harvesting the seeds of discontent. *In* (pp. 327–34) **60**.

20308. GRAY, TONY.   A peculiar man: a life of George Moore. London: Sinclair-Stevenson, 1996. pp. 344, (plates) 8. Rev. by E. S. Turner in LRB (18:11) 1996, 17; by Penelope Fitzgerald in TLS, 26 Apr. 1996, 22.

20309. MITCHELL, JUDITH.   Naturalism in George Moore's *A Mummer's Wife* (1885). *In* (pp. 159–79) **75**.

20310. O'TOOLE, TESS.   The servant's body: the Victorian wet-nurse and George Moore's *Esther Waters*. WS (25:4) 1996, 329–49.

Marianne Moore

20311. ERICKSON, DARLENE WILLIAMS.   Illusion is more precise than precision: the poetry of Marianne Moore. (Bibl. 1993, 14005.) Rev. by Lisa R. Myers in Review (16) 1994, 135–44.

20312. KAPPEL, ANDREW J.   Presenting Miss Moore, Modernist: T. S. Eliot's edition of Marianne Moore's *Selected Poems. See* **699**.

20313. LAKRITZ, ANDREW M.   Modernism and the Other in Stevens, Frost, and Moore. *See* **18040**.

20314. LEAVELL, LINDA.   Marianne Moore and the visual arts:

prismatic color. (Bibl. 1995, 18179.) Rev. by David Bergman in AL (68:1) 1996, 260; by Rachel Potter in JAStud (30:2) 1996, 333–5.

20315. MILLER, CRISTANNE.   Marianne Moore: questions of authority. (Bibl. 1995, 18180.) Rev. by Celeste Goodridge in AL (68:2) 1996, 487–8; by Fiona Green in TLS, 30 Aug. 1996, 28; by Rachel Potter in JAStud (30:2) 1996, 333–5.

20316. MYERS, LISA R.   Precision and illusion: the objects of Marianne Moore's affections. Review (16) 1994, 135–44 (review-article).

20317. SCHULZE, ROBIN G.   The web of friendship: Marianne Moore and Wallace Stevens. (Bibl. 1995, 18183.) Rev. by Fiona Green in TLS, 30 Aug. 1996, 28.

20318. SCHULZE, ROBIN GAIL.   *The Frigate Pelican*'s progress: Marianne Moore's multiple versions and Modernist practice. *In* (pp. 117–39) **39**.

20319. STEINMAN, LISA M.   'So as to be one having some way of being one having some way of working': Marianne Moore and literary tradition. *In* (pp. 97–116) **39**.

Nicholas Moore

20320. RILEY, PETER (ed.).   Longings of the acrobats: selected poems. Manchester: Carcanet, 1990. pp. 87. Rev. by James Keery in PN Review (17:6) 1991, 65–7.

Thomas Sturge Moore

20321. POWELL, GROSVENOR.   T. Sturge Moore and Yeats's golden bird. *In* (pp. 104–16) **79**.

Frank Moorhouse

20322. RAINES, GAY.   'Return' in Australian fiction. *In* (pp. 41–9) **102**.

Pat Mora

20323. REBOLLEDO, TEY DIANA.   Pat Mora. *In* (pp. 128–39) **121**.

Edwin Morgan

20324. FAZZINI, MARCO.   Edwin Morgan: two interviews. SSL (29) 1996, 45–57.

20325. HOUSTON, AMY.   New lang syne: *Sonnets from Scotland* and restructured time. SLJ (22:1) 1995, 66–73.

20326. WHYTE, CHRISTOPHER.   Unspeakable heterosexuality. *See* **18316**.

Robert Morgan

20327. LANG, JOHN.   'Coming out from under Calvinism': religious motifs in Robert Morgan's poetry. Shen (42:2) 1992, 46–60.

20328. STANLEY, TAL.   Interview: Robert Morgan. AppalJ (23:3) 1996, 276–92.

Sally Morgan

20329. SMITH, SIDONIE.   Re-citing, re-siting, and re-sighting likeness: reading the family archive in Drucilla Modjeska's *Poppy*, Donna Williams' *Nobody Nowhere*, and Sally Morgan's *My Place*. *See* **15177**.

Ronald Hugh Morrieson

20330. Millen, Julia.   Ronald Hugh Morrieson: a biography. Auckland: Ling, 1996. pp. 246. Rev. by David Hill in NZList, 2 Nov. 1996, 46–7.

Herbert Morris

20331. Guinee, Trudy.   Dream palaces and crystal cages: dialogue between the work of Herbert Morris and Joseph Cornell. DQ (30:3) 1996, 105–19.

Wright Morris

20332. Hollander, John.   The figure on the page: words and images in Wright Morris's *The Home Place*. See **207**.

20333. Trachtenberg, Alan.   Wright Morris's 'photo-texts'. See **252**.

20334. Wydeven, Joseph J.   Myth and melancholy: Wright Morris's stories of old age. WebS (12:1) 1995, 36–47.

20335. —— Visual artistry in Wright Morris's *Plains Song for Female Voices*. Midamerica (19) 1992, 116–26.

Jim Morrison

20336. Lisciandro, Frank; Reid, Rebecca.   Stumbling in the neon groves: the art & life of James Douglas Morrison. Frank (15) 1996, 20–2.

20337. Thomas, Tony.   Jim Morrison … speaking live. Frank (15) 1996, 23–7. (Interview recorded 1970; not previously published.)

Toni Morrison

20338. Aguiar, Sarah Appleton.   'Everywhere and nowhere': *Beloved*'s 'Wild' legacy in Toni Morrison's *Jazz*. NCL (25:4) 1995, 11–12.

20339. Alwes, Derek.   The burden of liberty: choice in Toni Morrison's *Jazz* and Toni Cade Bambara's *The Salt Eaters*. See **16176**.

20340. Ashe, Bertram D.   'Why don't he like my hair?' Constructing African-American standards of beauty in Toni Morrison's *Song of Solomon* and Zora Neale Hurston's *Their Eyes Were Watching God*. See **18819**.

20341. Atlas, Marilyn J.   Cracked psyches and verbal putty: geography and integrity in Toni Morrison's *Jazz*. MidM (24) 1996, 63–76.

20342. Badt, Karin Luisa.   The roots of the body in Toni Morrison: a *mater* of 'ancient properties'. AAR (29:4) 1995, 567–77.

20343. Basu, Biman.   The Black voice and the language of the text: Toni Morrison's *Sula*. ColLit (23:3) 1996, 88–103.

20344. Bell, Bernard W.   *Beloved*: a womanist neo-slave narrative; or, Multivocal remembrances of things past. AAR (26:1) 1992, 7–15

20345. Bender, Eileen T.   Repossessing *Uncle Tom's Cabin*: Toni Morrison's *Beloved*. *In* (pp. 129–42) **19**.

20346. Bergenholtz, Rita A.   Toni Morrison's *Sula*: a satire on binary thinking. AAR (30:1) 1996, 89–98.

20347. Berger, James.   Ghosts of liberalism: Morrison's *Beloved* and the Moynihan Report. PMLA (111:3) 1996, 408–20.

20348. Bosenberg, Eva.   Das Überleben der Sprache in der Stille: zur Adaptation mündlicher Erzähltraditionen in drei Werken zeitgenössischer afro-amerikanischer Autorinnen. *In* (pp. 229–50) **73**.

20349. BRANCH, ELEANOR. Through the maze of the Oedipal: Milkman's search for self in *Song of Solomon*. LitPs (41:1/2) 1995, 52–84.

20350. BROAD, ROBERT L. Giving blood to the scraps: haints, history, and Hosea in *Beloved*. AAR (28:2) 1994, 189–96.

20351. CORTI, LILIAN. *Medea* and *Beloved*: self-definition and abortive nurturing in literary treatments of the infanticidal mother. *In* (pp. 61–77) **24**.

20352. DEMATRAKOPOULOS, STEPHANIE A. Maternal bonds as devourers of women's individuation in Toni Morrison's *Beloved*. AAR (26:1) 1992, 51–9.

20353. DI LORETO, SONIA. Dogane: *The Custom House* e *Beloved*. *See* **11402**.

20354. EK, AULI. 'Not American, not Black, just *me*': redefining Black female identity in the novels of Toni Morrison. New Courant (6) 1996, 138–44.

20355. ELKINS, MARILYN. Expatriate Afro-American women as exotics. *In* (pp. 264–73) **50**.

20356. FILS-AIMÉ, HOLLY W. The sweet scent of ginger: understanding the roots of *Song of Solomon* and *Mama Day*. Griot (15:1) 1996, 27–33.

20357. FUJIHIRA, IKUKO. Carnival iro no patchwork quilt – Toni Morrison no bungaku. (A patchwork quilt of carnival color: the literature of Toni Morrison.) Tokyo: Gakugei Shorin, 1996. pp. 318.

20358. FULWEILER, HOWARD W. Belonging and freedom in Morrison's *Beloved*: slavery, sentimentality, and the evolution of consciousness. CR (40:2) 1996, 331–58.

20359. GOLDSTEIN-SHIRLEY, DAVID. Race/[gender]: Toni Morrison's *Recitatif*. JSSE (27) 1996, 83–96.

20360. HAMILTON, CYNTHIA S. Revisions, rememories and exorcisms: Toni Morrison and the slave narrative. *See* **10138**.

20361. HARDING, WENDY; MARTIN, JACKY. A world of difference: an inter-cultural study of Toni Morrison's novels. (Bibl. 1994, 14066.) Rev. by Denise Heinze in AAR (30:3) 1996, 483–4.

20362. HARRIS, TRUDIER. Fiction and folklore: the novels of Toni Morrison. (Bibl. 1993, 14038.) Rev. by Barbara J. Wilcots in AAR (26:4) 1992, 691–4.

20363. HARTMAN, GEOFFREY. Public memory and its discontents. *See* **13116**.

20364. HAYES, ELIZABETH T. 'Like seeing you buried': Persephone in *The Bluest Eye*, *Their Eyes Were Watching God*, and *The Color Purple*. *In* (pp. 170–94) **46**.

20365. HEYMAN, RICHARD. Universalization and its discontents: Morrison's *Song of Solomon* – a (w)hol(e)y Black text. AAR (29:3) 1995, 381–92.

20366. HUNT, PATRICIA. War and peace: transfigured categories and the politics of *Sula*. AAR (27:3) 1993, 443–59.

20367. JONES, CAROLYN M. *Sula* and *Beloved*: images of Cain in the novels of Toni Morrison. AAR (27:4) 1993, 615–26.

20368. KIM, MYUNG-JA. Morrison eui *Sula*: jeontong yeosungsang eui haechae. (Morrison's *Sula*: deconstruction of the images of traditional womanhood.) JELL (42:2) 1996, 363–80.

20369. Koolish, Lynda.   Fictive strategies and cinematic representations in Toni Morrison's *Beloved*: postcolonial theory/postcolonial text.
AAR (29:3) 1995, 421–38.

20370. Krumholz, Linda.   The ghosts of slavery: historical recovery
in Toni Morrison's *Beloved*. AAR (26:3) 1992, 395–408.

20371. Kuenz, Jane.   *The Bluest Eye*: notes on history, community,
and Black female subjectivity. AAR (27:3) 1993, 421–31.

20372. Ledbetter, Mark.   Victims and the postmodern narrative;
or, Doing violence to the body: an ethic of reading and writing.
See **14597**.

20373. Lee, Rachel.   Missing peace in Toni Morrison's *Sula* and
Beloved. AAR (28:4) 1994, 571–83.

20374. Lee, Seung-Eun.   Heukin ueosung eui jaah jeongchaesung
gwa geu hursang: Toni Morrison eui *Tar Baby*. (A Black woman's self-
identity and its illusion: Toni Morrison's *Tar Baby*.) JELL (42:2) 1996,
397–418.

20375. McKee, Patricia.   Spacing and placing experience in Toni
Morrison's *Sula*. MFS (42:1) 1996, 1–30.

20376. McKible, Adam.   'These are the facts of the darky's history':
thinking history and reading names in four African-American texts.
See **16644**.

20377. Martin, William.   Linear and non-linear concepts of time
in Toni Morrison's *Song of Solomon*. NCL (26:3) 1996, 9–11.

20378. Maszewska, Jadwiga.   Home and homelessness in Toni
Morrison's *Beloved*. LWU (29:4) 1996, 287–92.

20379. Mock, Michele.   Spitting out the seed: ownership of mother,
child, breasts, milk, and voice in Toni Morrison's *Beloved*. ColLit (23:3)
1996, 117–26.

20380. Morrison, Kristin.   Child murder as metaphor of colonial
exploitation in Toni Morrison's *Beloved*, *The Silence in the Garden*, and
The Killeen. *In* (pp. 292–300) **49**.

20381. Morrison, Toni.   The dancing mind: speech upon acceptance of the National Book Foundation Medal for Distinguished
Contribution to American Letters on the sixth of November, nineteen
hundred and ninety-six. New York: Knopf, 1996. pp. 17.

20382. Ohkoso, Toshiko.   Toni Morrison – sozou to kaihou no
bungaku. (Toni Morrison: literature of creation and liberation.) Tokyo:
Heibonsha, 1996. pp. 314.

20383. O'Keefe, Vincent A.   Reading *rigor mortis*: offstage violence
and excluded middles 'in' Johnson's *Middle Passage* and Morrison's
Beloved. *See* **18954**.

20384. O'Reilly, Andrea.   In search of my mother's garden,
I found my own: mother-love, healing, and identity in Toni Morrison's
Jazz. AAR (30:3) 1996, 367–79.

20385. Osagie, Iyunolu.   Is Morrison also among the prophets?
'Psychoanalytic' strategies in *Beloved*. AAR (28:3) 1994, 423–40.

20386. Page, Philip.   Circularity in Toni Morrison's *Beloved*.
AAR (26:1) 1992, 31–9.

20387. —— Dangerous freedom: fusion and fragmentation in Toni
Morrison's novels. Jackson; London: Mississippi UP, 1995. pp. 231.

20388. —— Traces of Derrida in Toni Morrison's *Jazz*. AAR (29:1)
1995, 55–66.

20389. PEREIRA, MALIN WALTHER. Be(e)ing and 'truth': *Tar Baby*'s signifying on Sylvia Plath's bee poems. TCL (42:4) 1996, 526–34.

20390. PERRY, CAROLYN; MADDOX, TONYA. Repetition and revision in Toni Morrison's *Jazz*. PMPA (21) 1996, 62–8.

20391. PESCH, JOSEF. *Beloved*: Toni Morrison's post-apocalyptic novel. CanRCL (20:3/4) 1993, 395–408.

20392. PESSONI, MICHELE. 'She was laughing at their God': discovering the Goddess within in *Sula*. AAR (29:3) 1995, 439–51.

20393. PORTELLI, ALESSANDRO. Figlie e padri, scrittura e assenza in *Beloved* di Toni Morrison. Àcoma (5) 1995, 72–84.

20394. PRINGLE, MARY BETH. On a jet plane: Jadine's search for identity through place in Toni Morrison's *Tar Baby*. MidM (24) 1996, 37–50.

20395. RICE, HERBERT WILLIAM. Toni Morrison and the American tradition: a rhetorical reading. New York; Frankfurt; Bern; Paris: Lang, 1996. pp. viii, 155. (American univ. studies, XXIV: American literature, 60.) (Cf. bibl. 1993, 14071.)

20396. ROHRKEMPER, JOHN. 'The site of memory': narrative and meaning in Toni Morrison's *Beloved*. MidM (24) 1996, 51–62.

20397. SALE, MAGGIE. Call and response as critical method: African-American oral traditions and *Beloved*. AAR (26:1) 1992, 41–50.

20398. SCARPA, GIULIA. Toni Morrison: la memoria, i fantasmi e la scrittura. Àcoma (1) 1994, 68–77.

20399. SCHMUDDE, CAROL E. The haunting of 124. AAR (26:3) 1992, 409–16.

20400. SCHREIBER, EVELYN JAFFE. Reader, text, and subjectivity: Toni Morrison's *Beloved* as Lacan's gaze *qua* object. Style (30:3) 1996, 445–61.

20401. SCOTT, LYNN. Beauty, virtue, and disciplinary power: a Foucauldian reading of Toni Morrison's *The Bluest Eye*. MidM (24) 1996, 9–23.

20402. SEIDEL, KATHRYN LEE. The Lilith figure in Toni Morrison's *Sula* and Alice Walker's *The Color Purple*. WebS (10:2) 1993, 85–94.

20403. SITTER, DEBORAH AYER. The making of a man: dialogic meaning in *Beloved*. AAR (26:1) 1992, 17–29.

20404. SMITH, CYNTHIA J. Intertextuality as agent of representation in Toni Morrison's *Tar Baby*. Genre (27:3) 1994, 165–81.

20405. SOBAT, GAIL SIDONIE. If the ghost be there, then am I crazy? An examination of ghosts in Virginia Hamilton's *Sweet Whispers, Brother Rush* and Toni Morrison's *Beloved*. *See* **18407**.

20406. STOCKTON, KATHRYN BOND. Prophylactics and brains: *Beloved* in the cybernetic age of AIDS. StudN (28:3) 1996, 434–65.

20407. VEGA GONZÁLEZ, SUSANA. From emotional orphanhood to cultural orphanhood: spiritual death and re-birth in two novels by Toni Morrison. RAEI (9) 1996, 143–51. (*Sula, Tar Baby*.)

20408. WILENTZ, GAY. Civilizations underneath: African heritage as cultural discourse in Toni Morrison's *Song of Solomon*. AAR (26:1) 1992, 61–76.

20409. WILSON, MICHAEL. Affirming characters, communities, and change: dialogism in Toni Morrison's *Sula*. MidM (24) 1996, 24–36.

20410. YATES, KIMBERLEY A. Power and resistance: Sula and Nel in Toni Morrison's *Sula*. Bracket (1) 1995, 115–30.

Daniel David Moses (1952–)

20411. APPLEFORD, ROB.   The desire to crunch bone: Daniel David Moses and the 'true real Indian'. CanTR (77) 1993, 21–6.

Thylias Moss

20412. DOUGHERTY, SEAN THOMAS.   Thylias Moss: interview. Onthebus (4:2/5:1) 1992, 296–301.

Erin Mouré

20413. WILLIAMSON, JANICE.   Sexing the prairie: an interview with Erin Mouré. WCL (30:2) 1996, 114–23.

Mourning Dove

20414. WILSON, MICHAEL.   Writing a friendship dance: orality in Mourning Dove's *Cogewea*. AICRJ (20:1) 1996, 27–41.

Es'kia Mphahlele

20415. LINDFORS, BERNTH.   Future returns. *In* (pp. 153–62) **102**.
20416. MUNNICK, JAMES.   Back to the roots: Mphahlele's return to South Africa. *In* (pp. 101–9) **102**.

Lavonne Mueller

20417. CONSTANTINIDIS, STRATOS E.   Playwriting and oral history: an interview with playwright Lavonne Mueller. JDTC (9:1) 1994, 145–55.

Edwin Muir

20418. O'DONOGHUE, NOEL DERMOT.   Edwin Muir: the untutored music. SM (ns 1) 1995, 193–202.

Willa Muir

20419. KERRIGAN, CATHERINE.   Nationalism and gender: Scottish myths of the female. *See* **12169**.

Bharati Mukherjee

20420. BRESNAHAN, ROGER J.   The Midwest as metaphor: four Asian writers. *See* **19630**.
20421. —— 'This country has so many ways of humiliating': Bharati Mukherjee's depiction of Midwestern community values. Midamerica (22) 1995, 122–7.
20422. COLLADO RODRÍGUEZ, FRANCISCO.   Naming female multiplicity: an interview with Bharati Mukherjee. Atlantis (17:1/2) 1995, 293–306.
20423. D'SOUZA-DELEURY, FLORENCE.   Crossing borders in Bharati Mukherjee's *'The Middleman' and Other Stories*. JSSE (27) 1996, 68–82.
20424. KEHDE, SUZANNE.   Colonial discourse and female identity: Bharati Mukherjee's *Jasmine*. *In* (pp. 70–7) **50**.
20425. MORTON-MOLLO, SHERRY.   Cultural collisions: dislocation, reinvention, and resolution in Bharati Mukherjee. Proteus (11:2) 1994, 35–8.

Paul Muldoon

20426. ALLISON, JONATHAN.   Questioning Yeats: Paul Muldoon's *7, Middagh Street*. *In* (pp. 3–20) **58**.

20427. Brown, Terence. Telling tales: Kennelly's *Cromwell*, Muldoon's *The More a Man Has the More a Man Wants*. *In* (pp. 144–57) **86**.

20428. Kendall, Tim. Paul Muldoon. Chester Springs, PA: Dufour, 1996. pp. 258.

20429. McDonald, Peter. Yeats, form and Northern Irish poetry. *See* **18527**.

20430. Murphy, Shane. Obliquity in the poetry of Paul Muldoon and Mebdh McGuckian. *See* **19980**.

20431. O'Donoghue, Bernard. 'The half-said thing to them is dearest': Paul Muldoon. *In* (pp. 400–18) **86**.

20432. Putzel, Steven D. Fluid disjunction in Paul Muldoon's *Immram* and *The More a Man Has the More a Man Wants*. PLL (32:1) 1996, 85–108.

20433. Rácz, István D. Mask lyrics in the poetry of Paul Muldoon and Derek Mahon. *In* (pp. 107–18) **112**.

20434. Wills, Clair. Paul Muldoon: *The Annals of Chile*. EAS (49) 1996, 111–39.

20435. Wilson, William A. Yeats, Muldoon, and heroic history. *In* (pp. 21–38) **58**.

Clarence E. Mulford

20436. Nevins, Francis M., Jr. Bar-20: the life of Clarence E. Mulford, creator of Hopalong Cassidy, with seven original stories reprinted. Foreword by John Tuska. (Bibl. 1994, 14122.) Rev. by Garyn Roberts in JPC (30:2) 1996, 214–15.

Wendy Mulford

20437. Kinnahan, Linda A. Experimental poetics and the lyric in British women's poetry: Geraldine Monk, Wendy Mulford, and Denise Riley. *See* **20290**.

Harryette Mullen

20438. Bedient, Calvin. The solo mysterioso blues: an interview with Harryette Mullen. Callaloo (19:3) 1996, 651–69.

20439. Monroe, Jonathan. Syntextural investigations. *See* **15649**.

Alice Munro

20440. Blodgett, E. D. Alice Munro. Boston, MA: Twayne, 1988. pp. 179. (Twayne's world authors, 800.) Rev. by Ildikó de Papp Carrington in ARCS (19:1) 1989, 121–3.

20441. Canitz, A. E. Christa; Seamon, Roger. The rhetoric of fictional realism in the stories of Alice Munro. CanL (150) 1996, 67–80.

20442. Carrington, Ildikó de Papp. Controlling the uncontrollable: the fiction of Alice Munro. (Bibl. 1992, 15368.) Rev. by Lorna Irvine in ARCS (20:2) 1990, 252–4.

20443. —— Double-talking devils: Alice Munro's *A Wilderness Station*. ECanW (58) 1996, 71–92.

20444. Carscallen, James. The other country: patterns in the writing of Alice Munro. Toronto: ECW Press, 1993. pp. x, 581. Rev. by Maureen F. Moran in BJCS (11:1) 1996, 145–7; by Christine Somerville in CanL (148) 1996, 180–1; by Gerald A. Noonan in ESCan (22:1) 1996, 97–9.

20445. CLARK, MIRIAM MARTY.   Allegories of reading in Alice Munro's *Carried Away*. ConLit (37:1) 1996, 49–61.

20446. COOKE, JOHN.   The influence of painting on five Canadian writers: Alice Munro, Hugh Hood, Timothy Findley, Margaret Atwood, and Michael Ondaatje. *See* **16077**.

20447. GARSON, MARJORIE.   I would try to make lists: the catalogue in *Lives of Girls and Women*. CanL (150) 1996, 45–63.

20448. GOODMAN, CHARLOTTE.   Cinderella in the classroom: (mis)reading Alice Munro's *Red Dress – 1946*. Reader (30) 1993, 49–64.

20449. HEBLE, AJAY.   The tumble of reason: Alice Munro's discourse of absence. Toronto; Buffalo, NY; London: Toronto UP, 1994. pp. xi, 210. (Cf. bibl. 1991, 14407.) Rev. by Barbara Godard in MFS (42:1) 1996, 164–7; by Beverly J. Rasporich in CanL (150) 1996, 184–5; by Louis K. MacKendrick in ESCan (22:4) 1996, 481–3.

20450. MARS-JONES, ADAM.   Histories of American marriage. TLS, 8 Nov. 1996, 26.

20451. SOMACARRERA, PILAR.   Exploring the impenetrability of narrative: a study of linguistic modality in Alice Munro's early fiction. *See* **2710**.

20452. YORK, LORRAINE M.   'Distant parts of myself': the topography of Alice Munro's fiction. ARCS (18:1) 1988, 33–8.

20453. —— The other side of dailiness: photography in the works of Alice Munro, Timothy Findley, Michael Ondaatje, and Margaret Laurence. *See* **17822**.

David Mura

20454. ROSSI, LEE.   David Mura. Onthebus (2:2/3:1) 1990/91, 263–73. (Interview.)

Iris Murdoch

20455. ANTONACCIO, MARIA; SCHWEIKER, WILLIAM (eds).   Iris Murdoch and the search for human goodness. Chicago; London: Chicago UP, 1996. pp. xx, 266.

20456. BYATT, A. S.   Degrees of freedom: the early novels of Iris Murdoch. (Bibl. 1967, 9257.) London: Vintage, 1994. pp. x, 358. (Second ed.: first ed. 1965.)

20457. GONZALEZ, ALEXANDER G.   The problem of gender in Iris Murdoch's *Something Special*. JSSE (21) 1993, 19–27.

20458. HOOKS, SUSAN LUCK.   Development of identity: Iris Murdoch's *Under the Hat*. NCL (23:4) 1993, 6–8.

20459. O'CONNOR, PATRICIA J.   To love the good: the moral philosophy of Iris Murdoch. New York; Frankfurt; Bern; Paris: Lang, 1996. pp. viii, 297. (American univ. studies, v: Philosophy, 136.)

Richard Murphy

20460. BRANDES, RAND.   A shaping music: Richard Murphy's *The Price of Stone*. *In* (pp. 190–203) **86**.

20461. DEWSNAP, TERENCE.   Richard Murphy's *Apologia*: the price of stone. CJIS (22:1) 1996, 71–86.

Thomas Murphy (1935–)

20462. EL-HALAWANY, MONA.   The spatial role of the village and the city in Thomas Murphy's *Bailegangaire* and Yussuf Idris's *Al-Naddaha*. *In* (pp. 358–70) **60**.

20463. HENDERSON, LYNDA.   Men, women and the life of the spirit in Tom Murphy's plays. *In* (pp. 87–99) **52**.

20464. KENNEALLY, MICHAEL.   The transcendent impulse in contemporary Irish drama. *In* (pp. 272–82) **49**.

20465. MURPHY, TOM.   The creative process. *In* (pp. 78–86) **52**.

20466. RETTBERG, SCOTT.   The new frontier as a vast restless place: the Irish narrative of the American dream in Brian Friel's *Philadelphia, Here I Come*, Tom Murphy's *Conversations on a Homecoming*, and Joseph O'Connor's *Red Roses and Petrol. See* **17998**.

Albert Murray

20467. CARSON, WARREN.   Albert Murray: literary reconstruction of the vernacular community. AAR (27:2) 1993, 287–95.

Les A. Murray

20468. BEURSKENS, HUUB.   Alle ik doen de brul: bij een gedicht van Les Murray. De Gids (159:1) 1996, 38–9.

T. C. Murray

20469. HOGAN, ROBERT.   The brave timidity of T. C. Murray. IUR (26:1) 1996, 155–62.

Susan Musgrave

20470. MUSGRAVE, SUSAN.   Musgrave landing: musings on the writing life. Toronto: Stoddart, 1994. pp. xiv, 127. Rev. by Brenda Carr in CanL (150) 1996, 125.

Edward Myers

20471. KONDRATIEV, ALEXEI.   Tales newly told: a column on current modern fantasy. Mythlore (18:3) 1992, 59–60.

Walter Dean Myers

20472. PATRICK-WEXLER, DIANE.   Walter Dean Myers. Austin, TX: Raintree Steck-Vaughn, 1996. pp. 48. (Contemporary African Americans.)

Vladimir Nabokov

20473. BAXTER, CHARLES.   Rhyming action. *See* **4338**.

20474. BERDJIS, NASSIM WINNIE.   Imagery in Vladimir Nabokov's last Russian novel (*Dar*), its English translation (*The Gift*), and other prose works of the 1930s. New York; Frankfurt; Bern; Paris: Lang, 1995. pp. 396. (Mainzer Studien zur Amerikanistik, 31.)

20475. BEURSKENS, HUUB.   Autorijschool Rilke. (Rilke Driving School.) De Gids (159:9) 1996, 713–23.

20476. BICK, ILSA J.   'That hurts!': humor and sadomasochism in *Lolita. See* **13446**.

20477. BOYD, BRIAN.   Nabokov's *Bend Sinister*. Shen (41:1) 1991, 12–28.

20478. BRONFEN, ELISABETH.   Exil in der Literatur: zwischen Metapher und Realität. arcadia (28:2) 1993, 167–83.

20479. BRUHM, STEVEN.   Queer, queer Vladimir. AI (53:4) 1996, 281–306.

20480. DESCARGUES, MADELEINE.   Sterne, Nabokov and the happy (non)ending of biography. *In* (pp. 167–78) **57**.

20481. FOSTER, JOHN BURT, JR.   Nabokov's art of memory and European Modernism. (Bibl. 1995, 18362.) Rev. by Leona Toker in CanRCL (23:2) 1996, 606–9; by Brian Boyd in MFS (42:1) 1996, 203–5.

20482. —— Starting with Dostoevsky's double: Bakhtin and Nabokov as intertextualists. *In* (pp. 9–20) **51**.

20483. FURLANI, ANDRE.   'Elenctic tones': Socratic method in *The Real Life of Sebastian Knight*. ESCan (22:3) 1996, 283–96.

20484. GABBARD, KRIN.   The circulation of sadomasochistic desire in the *Lolita* texts. *See* **13695**.

20485. GRABES, HERBERT.   Ethics and aesthetics in the reception of literary character: the case of Nabokov's *Lolita*. EIUC (4) 1996, 23–40.

20486. HENNARD, MARTINE.   Playing a game of worlds in Nabokov's *Pale Fire*. MFS (40:2) 1994, 299–317.

20487. LANGE, BERND-PETER.   Chess as text: Nabokov's *Pale Fire*. Brno Studies in English (22) 1996, 127–42.

20488. LINETSKI, VADIM.   The mechanism of the production of ambiguity: Freud's *Dora* and Nabokov's *Lolita*. CanRCL (23:2) 1996, 531–46.

20489. MARTIN, TERRY J.   Ways of knowing in Nabokov's *Signs and Symbols*. JSSE (17) 1991, 75–89.

20490. MEYERS, JEFFREY.   The bulldog and the butterfly: the friendship of Edmund Wilson and Vladimir Nabokov. ASch (63:3) 1994, 379–99.

20491. NAKATANI, HITOMI.   The Veen's three swans and incest's artful guise: Vladimir Nabokov's *Ada* (1969). SEL (English number) 1996, 67–80.

20492. RAGUET-BOUVARD, CHRISTINE.   *Lolita*: un royaume au-delà des mers. Bordeaux: Presses Universitaires de Bordeaux, 1996. pp. 313. (Images.)

20493. SCHUMAN, SAMUEL.   Inventing Nabokov. NCL (22:3) 1992, 7–9.

20494. THEWELEIT, KLAUS.   Vladimir Nabokov: Tsjorbs terugkomst. (Vladimir Nabokov: Tsjorb's coming back.) De Gids (159:11/12) 1996, 952–66.

20495. WOOD, MICHAEL.   The magician's doubts: Nabokov and the risks of fiction. (Bibl. 1995, 18393.) Rev. by John Crowley in BkW, 19 Nov. 1995, 1, 11.

Sarojini Naidu

20496. MARX, EDWARD.   Sarojini Naidu: the nightingale as nationalist. JCL (31:1) 1996, 45–62.

V. S. Naipaul

20497. BAUCOM, IAN.   Mournful histories: narratives of postimperial melancholy. *See* **3714**.

20498. FIRTH, KATHLEEN.   V. S. Naipaul: East Indian–West Indian. RCEI (28) 1994, 95–108.

20499. KING, BRUCE.   V. S. Naipaul. (Bibl. 1994, 14194.) Rev. by Feroza Jussawalla in WLT (69:1) 1995, 213.

20500. LEBDAI, BENAOUDA.   The short-story teller V. S. Naipaul, the character Bobby, and the state of Africa in *In a Free State*. *See* **17060**.

20501. LOUVEL, LILIANE. *The Night Watchman's Occurrence Book*: V. S. Naipaul; or, The narrator in spite of himself. JSSE (26) 1996, 118–35.
20502. LOWDEN, STEPHEN. *Heart of Darkness* revisited: the meaning of experience in *A Bend in the River*. See **17065**.
20503. PRESCOTT, LYNDA. Landscapes and language in the work of V. S. Naipaul. ERev (6:1) 1995, 16–18.
20504. WEISS, TIMOTHY. Invisible forces of the postcolonial world: a reading of Naipaul's *Tell Me Who to Kill*. JSSE (26) 1996, 94–104.
20505. WISE, CHRISTOPHER. The garden trampled; or, The liquidation of African culture in V. S. Naipaul's *A Bend in the River*. ColLit (23:3) 1996, 58–72.

R. K. Narayan

20506. BHARUCHA, NILUFER E. R. K. Narayan's Malgudiscape. ERev (6:1) 1995, 29–32.
20507. DNYATE, RAMESH. The hothouse cactus: a note on R. K. Narayan's *The Painter of Signs*. In (pp. 61–8) **45**.
20508. NAIK, M. K. Waiting for the meaning: second thoughts on R. K. Narayan's *Waiting for the Mahatma*. In-between (3:1) 1994, 41–9.

Bill Naughton

20509. ALDGATE, TONY. *Alfie*: Tony Aldgate looks at how a 60s film about a Cockney Lothario dealt with sex, censorship and angry/cynical young men. See **13388**.
20510. HARTE, LIAM. Migrant memory: the recovery of self in the autobiography of Bill Naughton. CritS (8:2) 1996, 168–77.
20511. NAUGHTON, BILL. Neither use nor ornament: a memoir of Bolton, 1920s. Newcastle upon Tyne: Bloodaxe, 1995. pp. 207.

Gloria Naylor

20512. BANDE, USHA. Murder as social revenge in *The Street* and *The Women of Brewster Place*. NCL (23:1) 1993, 4–5.
20513. BOSENBERG, EVA. Das Überleben der Sprache in der Stille: zur Adaptation mündlicher Erzähltraditionen in drei Werken zeitgenössischer afro-amerikanischer Autorinnen. In (pp. 229–50) **73**.
20514. FILS-AIMÉ, HOLLY W. The sweet scent of ginger: understanding the roots of *Song of Solomon* and *Mama Day*. See **20356**.
20515. FOWLER, VIRGINIA C. Gloria Naylor: in search of sanctuary. New York: Twayne; London: Prentice Hall, 1996. pp. xiii, 181. (Twayne's US authors, 660.)
20516. HARRIS, TRUDIER. The power of the porch: the storyteller's craft in Zora Neale Hurston, Gloria Naylor, and Randall Kenan. See **18838**.
20517. MEISENHELDER, SUSAN. 'Eating cane' in Gloria Naylor's *The Women of Brewster Place* and Zora Neale Hurston's *Sweat*. See **18855**.
20518. —— 'The whole picture' in Gloria Naylor's *Mama Day*. AAR (27:3) 1993, 405–19.
20519. MONTGOMERY, MAXINE LAVON. Authority, multivocality, and the new world order in Gloria Naylor's *Bailey's Cafe*. AAR (29:1) 1995, 27–33.
20520. O'CONNOR, MARY. Subject, voice, and women in some contemporary Black American women's writing. In (pp. 199–217) **33**.

20521. PAGE, PHILIP.   Living with the abyss in Gloria Naylor's *Bailey's Cafe*. CLAJ (40:1) 1996, 21–45.

20522. RESTUCCIA, FRANCES L.   Literary representations of battered women: spectacular domestic punishment. *In* (pp. 42–71) **9**.

20523. SISNEY, MARY F.   The view from the outside: Black novels of manners. *In* (pp. 171–85) **96**.

20524. STORHOFF, GARY.   'The only voice is your own': Gloria Naylor's revision of *The Tempest*. *See* **7238**.

20525. TUCKER, LINDSEY.   Recovering the conjure woman: texts and contexts in Gloria Naylor's *Mama Day*. AAR (28:2) 1994, 173–88.

20526. WOOD, REBECCA S.   'Two warring ideals in one dark body': universalism and nationalism in Gloria Naylor's *Bailey's Cafe*. AAR (30:3) 1996, 381–95.

Peter Nazareth

20527. SCHECKTER, JOHN.   Peter Nazareth and the Ugandan expulsion: pain, distance, narration. RAL (27:2) 1996, 83–93.

John G. Neihardt

20528. HOCHBRUCK, WOLFGANG.   *'Black Elk speaks'*: Ansprüche und Grenzen bei der Verwendung indianischen mündlichen Wissens in literarischen Texten. *In* (pp. 185–201) **73**.

John Shaw Neilson

20529. GRAY, ROBERT (ed.).   Selected poems. Pymble, NSW: Angus & Robertson; London: HarperCollins, 1993. pp. 147. (A&R modern poets.)

20530. HASKELL, DENNIS.   Landscape at the edge of a promise: Australian Romanticism and John Shaw Neilson. *In* (pp. 203–15) **47**.

Howard Nemerov

20531. NEMEROV, ALEXANDER.   Modeling my father. ASch (62:4) 1993, 551–61.

E. Nesbit

20532. RUSSELL, W. M. S.   Time before and after *The Time Machine*. *See* **10607**.

Frances Newman

20533. ABBOTT, REGINALD.   Tea and sophistication: a note on Ellen Glasgow and Frances Newman. *See* **18193**.

Fae Myenne Ng (1956–)

20534. SAINT-MARTIN, LORI.   'Ta mère est dans tes os': Fae Myenne Ng et Amy Tan; ou, Le passage des savoirs entre la Chine et l'Amérique. Études littéraires (28:2) 1995, 67–80.

Mbongeni Ngema

20535. GULDIMANN, COLETTE.   The (Black) male gaze: Mbongeni Ngema's *Sarafina*. SATJ (10:2) 1996, 85–99.

20536. UNO, ROBERTA.   Mbongeni Ngema: a theater of the ancestors. TT (4:1) 1994, 15–30.

Ngũgĩ wa Thiong'o

20537. FINCHAM, GAIL; HOOPER, MYRTLE (eds). Under postcolonial eyes: Joseph Conrad after empire. *See* **15852**.

20538. MOSS, LAURA. Perceptual differences: Ngũgĩ wa Thiong'o and Chinua Achebe. *See* **15856**.

20539. NGŨGĨ WA THIONG'O. Literature and politics: transcending borders. In-between (5:2) 1996, 115–22.

20540. NICHOLLS, BRENDON. The production of 'woman' in Ngũgĩ's *The River Between*. Bracket (1) 1995, 98–114.

20541. USKALIS, ĒRIKS. Exchange and language in public spheres: constructions of democracy and citizenship in Ngũgĩ's *Devil on the Cross*. CritS (8:3) 1996, 286–95.

bp Nichol

20542. CLARK, DAVID L. Monstrosity, illegibility, denegation: de Man, bp Nichol and the resistance to postmodernism. *In* (pp. 40–71) **72**.

20543. JAEGER, PETER. 'contradiction … contains the diction': translation strategies in bp Nichol's *The Martyrology* and *Selected Organs*. WCL (29:3) 1995/96, 37–46.

20544. NIECHODA, IRENE. A sourcery for Books 1 and 2 of bp Nichol's *The Martyrology*. (Bibl. 1995, 18443.) Rev. by Susan Billingham in BJCS (11:1) 1996, 152–3.

John Nichols (1940–)

20545. BRUCE-NOVOA, JUAN. There's many a slip between good intentions and script: *The Milagro Beanfield War. See* **13499**.

20546. GUNN, SUSAN C. Nichols's *The Milagro Beanfield War*. Exp (55:1) 1996, 57–9.

20547. OSTERMANN, ROBERT. John Nichols: defying description. Critic (49:2) 1994, 56–68.

20548. THOMPSON, PHYLLIS. John Nichols. *In* (pp. 118–27) **121**.

William Nicholson

20549. MOSS, ELAINE. Clever Bill: William Nicholson, children & picture books. *See* **227**.

Eiléan Ní Chuilleanáin

20550. CONSALVO, DEBORAH McWILLIAMS. An interview with Eiléan Ní Chuilleanáin. Irish Literary Supplement (12:1) 1993, 15–17.

20551. MEANEY, GERARDINE. History gasps: myth in contemporary Irish women's poetry. *In* (pp. 99–113) **86**.

20552. RAY, KEVIN. Interview with Eiléan Ní Chuilleanáin. EI (31:1/2) 1996, 62–73.

Lorine Niedecker

20553. DAVIE, DONALD. Postmodernism and Lorine Niedecker. PN Review (18:2) 1991, 43–5.

20554. PENBERTHY, JENNY (ed.). Lorine Niedecker: woman and poet. Orono: National Poetry Foundation, Univ. of Maine, 1996. pp. 439. (Man/woman and poet.)

Don Nigro

20555. CONSTANTINIDIS, STRATOS E. Playwriting and the masks of history: an interview with playwright Don Nigro. JDTC (8:1) 1993, 149–56.

Anaïs Nin

20556. ANON. (ed.).   Talking about *The Diary* in 1966: from a taped interview with a Swedish journalist. Anaïs (13) 1995, 72–8.

20557. —— Under the star of writing: letters about and to Gore Vidal, 1946–1961. Anaïs (14) 1996, 42–54.

20558. BAIR, DEIRDRE.   Anaïs Nin: a biography. (Bibl. 1995, 18450.) Rev. by Bettina L. Knapp in WLT (69:4) 1995, 803–4.

20559. —— Writing as a woman: Henry Miller, Lawrence Durrell, and Anaïs Nin in the Villa Seurat. *See* **17446**.

20560. BRADFORD, JEAN.   Venus rising on a full shell: the web of archetypal connections in the work of Anaïs Nin. Anaïs (13) 1995, 114–23.

20561. BURFORD, WILLIAM.   The art of Anaïs Nin: an introduction to the pamphlet *On Writing*. Anaïs (8) 1990, 40–4.

20562. CHRISTMASS, PHILIPPA.   A mother to us all? Feminism and *The Diary of Anaïs Nin* – thirty years later. Anaïs (14) 1996, 35–41.

20563. DuBow, WENDY M.   The elusive text: reading *The Diary of Anaïs Nin, Volume 1, 1931–1934*. Anaïs (11) 1993, 22–36.

20564. FAY, MARION.   Selfhood and social conscience: on reading some stories in *Under a Glass Bell*. Anaïs (13) 1995, 100–8.

20565. FELBER, LYNETTE.   The three faces of June: Anaïs Nin's appropriation of feminine writing. TSWL (14:2) 1995, 309–24.

20566. FRANKLIN, BENJAMIN (ed.).   Recollections of Anaïs Nin by her contemporaries. Athens: Ohio UP, 1996. pp. x, 173.

20567. FRIEDMAN, ELLEN G.   Escaping from the house of incest: on Anaïs Nin's efforts to overcome patriarchal constraints. Anaïs (10) 1992, 39–45.

20568. HAMALIAN, LEO.   A spy in the house of Lawrence: tracing the signposts of Anaïs Nin's development as a writer. *See* **19541**.

20569. HENKE, SUZETTE.   A confessional narrative: maternal anxiety and daughter loss in Anaïs Nin's *Journal of Love: Incest*. Anaïs (14) 1996, 71–7.

20570. JASON, PHILIP K.   Anaïs Nin and her critics. (Bibl. 1993, 14224.) Rev. by Wendy M. DuBow in Anaïs (12) 1994, 105–8.

20571. —— A delicate battle cry: Anaïs Nin's pamphlets of the 1940s. Anaïs (8) 1990, 30–4.

20572. —— (ed.).   The critical response to Anaïs Nin. Westport, CT; London: Greenwood Press, 1996. pp. xviii, 271. (Critical responses in arts and letters, 23.)

20573. JONG, ERICA.   A story never told before: reading the new, unexpurgated diaries of Anaïs Nin. Anaïs (12) 1994, 15–25.

20574. KELLER, JANE EBLEN.   Reinventing lives: Anaïs Nin and Georges Simenon: feminine and masculine versions of much the same story. Anaïs (14) 1996, 96–110.

20575. KRIZAN, KIM.   Illusion and the art of survival: tracing the origins of Anaïs Nin's creativity. Anaïs (10) 1992, 18–28.

20576. MASON, GREGORY H.   Arrows of longing: the correspondence between Anaïs Nin and Felix Pollak. Anaïs (14) 1996, 78–95.

20577. MERCHANT, HOSHANG.   Out of and into the labyrinth: approaching the aesthetics of Anaïs Nin. Anaïs (8) 1990, 51–9.

20578. MILLETT, KATE. Anaïs – a mother to us all: the birth of the artist as a woman. Anaïs (9) 1991, 3–8.

20579. NALBANTIAN, SUZANNE. Into the house of myth: from the real to the universal, from singleness to a variety of selfhood. Anaïs (11) 1993, 12–15.

20580. PAPACHRISTOU, SOPHIA. The body in the diary: on Anaïs Nin's first erotic writings. Anaïs (9) 1991, 58–66.

20581. PINEAU, ELYSE LAMM. The performing self: an alternative reading of *Seduction of the Minotaur*. Anaïs (12) 1994, 65–73.

20582. PODNIEKS, ELIZABETH. The theater of *Incest*: enacting Artaud, Mirbeau and Rimbaud in the pages of the *Diary*. Anaïs (13) 1995, 39–52.

20583. RIBERA I GÓRRIZ, NÚRIA. Proust, Rimbaud, and the Surrealists: on the development of Anaïs Nin's artistic theories. Anaïs (12) 1994, 44–55.

20584. —— Regarding *The Voice*: some comments on one of Anaïs Nin's pivotal fictions. Anaïs (14) 1996, 111–20.

20585. RICHARD-ALLERDYCE, DIANE. Narrative and authenticity: strategies of evasion in the diaries of Anaïs Nin: then and now. Anaïs (13) 1995, 79–94.

20586. ROCK, JOANNE. The birth of 'savage': savagery as a metaphor for Anaïs Nin's developing feminist awareness. Anaïs (14) 1996, 65–70.

20587. —— Her father's daughter: re-evaluating an incestuous relationship. Anaïs (13) 1995, 29–38.

20588. SALBER, LINDE. Artists – the third sex: a few thoughts on the psychology of the creative urge. Anaïs (11) 1993, 59–68.

20589. —— Life as provocation: on writing a biography of Anaïs Nin. Anaïs (12) 1994, 26–30.

20590. —— Two lives, one experiment: Lou Andreas-Salomé and Anaïs Nin. Anaïs (9) 1991, 78–91.

20591. SEYBERT, GISLINDE. Between love and passion: some notes on the physical in *Henry & June*. Anaïs (9) 1991, 67–74.

20592. STUHLMANN, GUNTHER. Discretion and revelation: the difficulties of a secret life, Anaïs Nin at ninety. Anaïs (11) 1993, 119–24.

20593. —— From 'Jim' to 'Jamie': tracing a friendship in Anaïs Nin's *Diary*. Anaïs (12) 1994, 120–4.

20594. —— (ed.). Nearer the moon: from *A Journal of Love: the Unexpurgated Diary of Anaïs Nin, 1937–1939*. Preface by Rupert Pole. New York: Harcourt Brace, 1996. pp. xiii, 396.

20595. WOOD, LORI A. Between creation and destruction: toward a new concept of the female artist. Anaïs (8) 1990, 15–26.

Larry Niven

20596. NEWSINGER, JOHN. 'The universe is full of warriors': masculinity, hard science and war in some novels by Larry Niven and his accomplices. *See* **16220**.

Joan Lowery Nixon

20597. PAVONETTI, LINDA M. Joan Lowery Nixon: the *grande dame* of young adult mystery. JAAL (39:6) 1996, 454–61.

Lewis Nkosi

20598. HARRIS, JANICE. On tradition, madness, and South Africa: an interview with Lewis Nkosi. WebS (11:2) 1994, 25–37.

20599. ROBB, KENNETH A.; VASUDEVA, HARENDER. Jackson 'Pollock' Moloi in Lewis Nkosi's *Under the Shadow of the Guns*. NCL (25:3) 1995, 3–4.

Marguerite Noble (1910–)

20600. KEHL, D. G.   The Southwest viewed from the inside out: a conversation with Marguerite Noble. Journal of the Southwest (36:2) 1994, 131–47.

Michael Noonan

20601. NOONAN, MICHAEL.   In with the tide: memoirs of a storyteller. St Lucia: Queensland UP, 1996. pp. viii, 300, (plates) 16.

Lewis Nordan

20602. MAHER, BLAKE.   An interview with Lewis Nordan. SoQ (34:1) 1995, 113–23.

Gurney Norman

20603. COVENEY, NANCY COMAN; URCH, KAKIE; SHENEFELT, LORI. Divine Right's trip redux: feminists read the Southern sixties. SoQ (34:3) 1996, 21–45.

20604. WILLIAMSON, J. W.   Go ahead on: an interview with Gurney Norman. SoQ (34:3) 1996, 9–20.

Marsha Norman

20605. BROWN, LINDA GINTER (ed.).   Marsha Norman: a casebook. New York; London: Garland, 1996. pp. xvi, 242. (Garland reference library of the humanities, 1750.) (Casebooks on modern dramatists, 19.)

20606. JONES, CHRISTOPHER N.   Lessons from Hollywood: feminist film theory and the commercial theatre. *See* **13842**.

20607. KARTER, M. JOSHUA.   Back from the Nikitsky Gates Theater: reflections on cross-cultural concerns in the staging of Marsha Norman's *'night, Mother* in Moscow. TT (4:1) 1994, 75–88.

Frank Norris

20608. ARIMA, KEN'ICHI.   Frank Norris to San Francisco – America shizenshugi shousetsuron. (Frank Norris and San Francisco: a study of American Naturalistic fiction.) Tokyo: Kirihara Shoten, 1996. pp. 234.

20609. BOWER, STEPHANIE.   Dangerous liaisons: prostitution, disease, and race in Frank Norris's fiction. MFS (42:1) 1996, 31–60.

20610. CIVELLO, PAUL.   Evolutionary feminism, popular romance, and Frank Norris's 'man's woman'. SAF (24:1) 1996, 23–41.

20611. JOHANNINGSMEIER, CHARLES.   'Rediscovering' Frank Norris's *A Salvation Boom in Matabeleland*. FNS (22) 1996, 1–6.

20612. JONES, GWENDOLYN.   Frank Norris's *The Pit*: 'A Romance of Chicago' and 'A Story of Chicago'. FNS (21) 1996, 1–8.

20613. LAWLOR, MARY.   Placing source in *Greed* and *McTeague*. *In* (pp. 93–104) **51**.

20614. LEITZ, ROBERT C., III.   Norris in cyberspace. *See* **1305**.

20615. LOVING, JEROME (ed.).   McTeague: a story of San Francisco. Oxford; New York: OUP, 1995. pp. xxxiii, 338. (World's classics.)

20616. MCELRATH, JOSEPH R., JR.   Beyond San Francisco: Frank Norris's invention of Northern California. *In* (pp. 35–55) **108**.

20617. —— Frank Norris: a descriptive bibliography. (Bibl. 1995, 18472.) Rev. by Craig S. Abbott in Review (16) 1994, 21–30.

20618. MURPHY, BRENDA. McTeague's dream and *The Emperor Jones*: O'Neill's move from Naturalism to Modernism. EOR (17:1/2) 1993, 21–9.

Kathleen Norris

20619. BALAY, ANNE G. 'Hands full of living': birth control, nostalgia, and Kathleen Norris. AmLH (8:3) 1996, 471–95.

20620. GULLETTE, MARGARET MORGANROTH. Inventing the 'post-maternal' woman, 1898–1927: idle, unwanted, and out of a job. *See* **18206**.

Ken Norris

20621. PRECOSKY, DON. The insecurities of Ken Norris. ECanW (58) 1996, 198–201 (review-article).

Arthur Nortje

20622. BUNN, DAVID. 'Some alien native land': Arthur Nortje, literary history, and the body in exile. WLT (70:1) 1996, 33–44.

Mary Norton

20623. HUNT, CAROLINE C. Dwarf, small world, shrinking child: three versions of miniature. *See* **18555**.

Alice Notley (1945–)

20624. DuCHARME, MARK. Alice Notley: interview. Onthebus (4:2/5:1) 1992, 284–95.

Craig Nova

20625. NOVA, CRAIG. His father's story. BkW, 20 June 1993, 1, 10.

Louis Nowra

20626. MAKEHAM, PAUL. The black hole in our history: a conversation with Louis Nowra. CanTR (74) 1993, 27–31.

Peter Nwankwo

20627. EZENWA-OHAETO. Critical realism and the thriller tradition in Nigerian fiction: Williams, Nwankwo and Uzoatu. Ob (10:1/2) 1995, 205–17.

Flora Nwapa

20628. COOKE, MICHAEL G. A rhetoric of obliquity in African and Caribbean women writers. *In* (pp. 169–84) **80**.

Naomi Shihab Nye

20629. ELLIOTT, DAVID L. Home keeps getting bigger: a conversation with Naomi Shihab Nye. Tampa Review (12) 1996, 25–9.

20630. WYMARD, ELLIE. Borderless skins: Ellie Wymard interviews Naomi Shihab Nye. Critic (48:4) 1994, 85–94.

Joyce Carol Oates

20631. DALY, BRENDA O. The central nervous system of America:

the writer as/in the crowd of Joyce Carol Oates's *Wonderland. In* (pp. 155–80) **33**.

20632. —— Lavish self-divisions: the novels of Joyce Carol Oates. Jackson; London: Mississippi UP, 1996. pp. xxiv, 278.

20633. DEAN, SHARON.   Literature and composition theory: Joyce Carol Oates' journal stories. *See* **2347**.

20634. GROBEL, LAWRENCE.   Joyce Carol Oates. Playboy (Chicago) (40:11) 1993, 63–4, 66–70, 72–4, 76. (Interview.)

20635. PEARLMAN, MICKEY.   Joyce Carol Oates. Onthebus (2:2/3:1) 1990/91, 255–62.

20636. ROZGA, MARGARET.   Joyce Carol Oates: reimagining the masters; or, A woman's place is in her own fiction. *In* (pp. 281–94) **3**.

20637. TODD, DAVID Y.   An interview with Joyce Carol Oates. GetR (6:2) 1993, 291–9.

20638. WAGNER-MARTIN, LINDA.   Panoramic, unpredictable, and human: Joyce Carol Oates's recent novels. *In* (pp. 196–209) **123**.

Patrick O'Brian

20639. KING, DEAN; HATTENDORF, JOHN B.   Harbors and high seas: an atlas and geographical guide to the Aubrey–Maturin novels of Patrick O'Brian. New York: Holt, 1996. pp. xvi, 219.

20640. LOWDEN, STEPHEN.   Patrick O'Brian. ERev (7:1) 1996, 40–1.

20641. WHEELER, EDWARD T.   Ahoy! Patrick O'Brian sails again. Cweal (123:19) 1996, 9–10.

Conor Cruise O'Brien

20642. AKENSON, DONALD HARMAN.   Conor: a biography of Conor Cruise O'Brien. (Bibl. 1995, 18497.) Rev. by John Kenneth Galbraith in BkW, 25 Dec. 1994, 4–5.

20643. —— *Conor: a Biography of Conor Cruise O'Brien*: anthology. Ithaca, NY; London: Cornell UP, 1994. pp. xiii, 356. Rev. by John Kenneth Galbraith in BkW, 25 Dec. 1994, 4–5.

Edna O'Brien

20644. HUBER, WERNER.   Myth and motherland: Edna O'Brien's *Mother Ireland. In* (pp. 175–81) **112**.

'Flann O'Brien' (Brian O'Nolan, 'Myles na gCopaleen')

20645. ANSPAUGH, KELLY.   Flann O'Brien: postmodern Judas. *See* **19016**.

20646. DEL RÍO ÁLVARO, CONSTANZA.   Misogyny in Flann O'Brien's *The Third Policeman. In* (pp. 207–24) **38**.

20647. HAFEZ, AZIZA S.   The use of myth, parable and folk tale in Flann O'Brien's *At Swim-Two-Birds* and Etedal Othman's *The Sun's Tattoo. In* (pp. 62–72) **60**.

20648. HOPPER, KEITH.   Flann O'Brien: a portrait of the artist as a young post-modernist. Cork: Cork UP, 1995. pp. 292. Rev. by Joseph McMinn in Irish Review (17/18) 1995, 185–7.

20649. JACQUIN, DANIELLE.   '*Cerveaux lucides* is good begob': Flann O'Brien and the world of peasants. *In* (pp. 223–34) **106**.

20650. MCCARTHY, PATRICK A.   Claude Houghton and Flann O'Brien on Hell: *Julian Grant Loses His Way* and *The Third Policeman. See* **18759**.

20651. Quintelli-Neary, Marguerite.　Desmond MacNamara's intrusions and invasions. *See* **20027**.

Kate O'Brien

20652. Hogan, Desmond (introd.).　That lady: a novel. London: Virago Press, 1985. pp. xiv, 378. (Virago modern classics, 168.)
20653. Kiely, Benedict.　Lore and pain and parting: the novels of Kate O'Brien. HC (29:2) 1992, 1–10.

Tim O'Brien

20654. Griffith, James.　A walk through history: Tim O'Brien's *Going after Cacciato*. WLA (3:1) 1991, 1–34.
20655. Loeb, Jeff.　Childhood's end: self-recovery in the autobiography of the Vietnam War. *See* **15165**.
20656. McNerney, Brian C.　Responsibly inventing history: an interview with Tim O'Brien. WLA (6:2) 1994, 1–26.
20657. Palm, Edward F.　Falling in and out: military idiom as metaphoric motif in *Going after Cacciato*. NCL (22:5) 1992, 8.
20658. Schweninger, Lee.　Ecofeminism, nuclearism, and O'Brien's *The Nuclear Age. In* (pp. 177–85) **77**.
20659. Scott, Grant F.　*Going after Cacciato* and the problem of teleology. *See* **10767**.
20660. Uchmanowicz, Pauline.　Vanishing Vietnam: Whiteness and the technology of memory. *See* **17243**.

Sean O'Casey

20661. Ayling, Ronald.　Sean O'Casey's editions: a note on their publishing history. *See* **564**.
20662. Kosok, Heinz.　Ta-ra-ra-boom-dee-ay *vs* the *Noh*: Sean O'Casey and William Butler Yeats. *In* (pp. 211–27) **49**.
20663. Schrank, Bernice.　'Death is here and death is there, death is busy everywhere': temporality and the desire for transcendence in O'Casey's *The Shadow of a Gunman. In* (pp. 53–60) **112**.
20664. —— Sean O'Casey: a research and production sourcebook. Westport, CT; London: Greenwood Press, 1996. pp. viii, 298. (Modern dramatists research and production sourcebooks, 11.)

Flannery O'Connor

20665. Anastaplo, George.　Can beauty 'hallow even the bloodiest tomahawk'? *See* **18588**.
20666. Bacon, Jon Lance.　Flannery O'Connor and Cold War culture. (Bibl. 1994, 14291.) Rev. by Thomas Schaub in MFS (40:2) 1994, 373–5; by Will Brantley in ConLit (37:1) 1996, 133–7; by Sebastian D. G. Knowles in YES (26) 1996, 315–16.
20667. Benoit, Raymond.　The existential intuition of Flannery O'Connor in *The Violent Bear It Away*. NCL (23:4) 1993, 2–3.
20668. Blythe, Hal; Sweet, Charlie.　O'Connor's *A Good Man Is Hard to Find*. Exp (55:1) 1996, 49–51.
20669. —— The misfit: O'Connor's 'family' man as serial killer. NCL (25:1) 1995, 3–5.
20670. Brantley, Will.　O'Connor, Porter, and Hurston on the state of the world. *See* **18824**.

20671. Burke, William.   Fetishism in the fiction of Flannery O'Connor. FOB (22) 1993/94, 45–52.

20672. Burns, Margie.   A good rose is hard to find: Southern gothic as signs of social dislocation in Faulkner and O'Connor. *In* (pp. 105–23) **44**.

20673. Cash, Jean.   O'Connor in the Iowa Writers' Workshop. FOB (24) 1995/96, 67–75.

20674. Corn, Alfred.   An encounter with O'Connor and *Parker's Back*. FOB (24) 1995/96, 104–18.

20675. Desmond, John.   Flannery O'Connor and the idolatrous mind. ChrisL (46:1) 1996, 25–35.

20676. Di Renzo, Anthony.   American gargoyles: Flannery O'Connor and the medieval grotesque. (Bibl. 1994, 14297.) Rev. by Margaret Bauer in SM (ns 2) 1996, 272–4.

20677. Donahoo, Ronald.   O'Connor's ancient comedy: form in *A Good Man Is Hard to Find*. JSSE (16) 1991, 29–40.

20678. Edmunds, Susan.   Through a glass darkly: visions of integrated community in Flannery O'Connor's *Wise Blood*. ConLit (37:4) 1996, 559–85.

20679. Foran, Donald J.   Flannery O'Connor's anagogical way of seeing. Critic (48:4) 1994, 113–17.

20680. Fowler, Doreen.   Deconstructing racial difference: O'Connor's *The Artificial Nigger*. FOB (24) 1995/96, 22–32.

20681. Gillespie, Michael Patrick.   Baroque Catholicism in Southern fiction: Flannery O'Connor, Walker Percy, and John Kennedy Toole. *In* (pp. 25–47) **123**.

20682. Grimshaw, James A., Jr.   Onomastics in Flannery O'Connor's *Parker's Back*. *See* **2143**.

20683. Hannon, Jane.   The wide world her parish: O'Connor's all-embracing vision of church. FOB (24) 1995/96, 1–21.

20684. Hurd, Myles Raymond.   The misfit as parricide in Flannery O'Connor's *A Good Man Is Hard to Find*. NCL (22:4) 1992, 5–7.

20685. Janowski, Lawrence.   Flannery O'Connor: for the deaf, for the blind. Critic (48:4) 1994, 3–14.

20686. Kreyling, Michael (ed.).   New essays on *Wise Blood*. (Bibl. 1995, 18542.) Rev. by Peter Rawlings in JAStud (30:3) 1996, 471–2; by Irving Malin in SoQ (34:3) 1996, 164–5.

20687. Larsen, Val.   A tale of tongue and pen: orality and literacy in *The Barber*. FOB (22) 1993/94, 25–44.

20688. McMullen, Joanne Halleran.   Writing against God: language as message in the literature of Flannery O'Connor. Macon, GA: Mercer UP, 1996. pp. viii, 152. (Cf. bibl. 1991, 14629.) Rev. by Marshall Bruce Gentry in FOB (24) 1995/96, 129–32.

20689. Mayer, David R.   Drooping sun, coy moon: essays on Flannery O'Connor. Kyoto: Yamaguchi Shoten, 1996. pp. viii, 176.

20690. Niland, Kurt R.; Evans, Robert C.   *A Memoir of Mary Ann* and *Everything That Rises Must Converge*. FOB (22) 1993/94, 55–73.

20691. Prunty, Wyatt.   The figure of vacancy. Shen (46:3) 1996, 38–55.

20692. Quinn, John J. (ed.).   Flannery O'Connor: a memorial. (Bibl. 1995, 18549.) Rev. by Sura Rath in FOB (24) 1995/96, 138–40.

20693. Rath, Sura P.; Shaw, Mary Neff (eds). Flannery O'Connor: new perspectives. Athens; London: Georgia UP, 1996. pp. viii, 225. Rev. by Virginia Wray in FOB (24) 1995/96, 133–7.

20694. Russell, Henry M. W. Racial integration in a disintegrating society: O'Connor and European Catholic thought. FOB (24) 1995/96, 33–45.

20695. Saunders, J. R. The fallacies of guidance and light in Flannery O'Connor's *The Artificial Nigger*. JSSE (17) 1991, 103–13.

20696. Spivey, Ted R. Flannery O'Connor: the woman, the thinker, the visionary. (Bibl. 1995, 18552.) Rev. by Marshall Bruce Gentry in SoQ (34:2) 1996, 149–50.

20697. Stephenson, Will; Stephenson, Mimosa. Ruby Turpin: O'Connor's travesty of the ideal woman. FOB (24) 1995/96, 57–66.

20698. Streight, Irwin Howard. Is there a text in this man? A semiotic reading of *Parker's Back*. FOB (22) 1993/94, 1–11.

20699. Sykes, John. Christian apologetic uses of the grotesque in John Irving and Flannery O'Connor. *See* **18893**.

20700. Thiemann, Fred R. Usurping the *logos*: clichés in O'Connor's *Good Country People*. FOB (24) 1995/96, 46–56.

20701. Westling, Louise. Fathers and daughters in Welty and O'Connor. *In* (pp. 110–24) **32**.

20702. —— Flannery O'Connor's hilarious rage. FOB (22) 1993/94, 119–32.

20703. Whitt, Margaret Earley. Understanding Flannery O'Connor. (Bibl. 1995, 18554.) Rev. by John F. Desmond in AL (68:4) 1996, 871–2; by Marshall Bruce Gentry in SoQ (34:2) 1996, 149–50.

20704. Witt, Jonathan. *Wise Blood* and the irony of redemption. FOB (22) 1993/94, 12–24.

20705. Witt, Margaret E. Flannery O'Connor and the child's book: an unusual coupling. *See* **19628**.

20706. Wood, Ralph C. Where is the voice coming from? Flannery O'Connor on race. FOB (22) 1993/94, 99–118.

20707. Wray, Virginia. The importance of home to the fiction of Flannery O'Connor. Ren (47:2) 1995, 103–15.

20708. York, Lamar. Breakfast at Flannery's. ModAge (38:3) 1996, 245–52.

'Frank O'Connor' (Michael O'Donovan)

20709. Steinman, Michael (ed.). The happiness of getting it down right: letters of Frank O'Connor and William Maxwell, 1945–1966. *See* **20169**.

Joseph O'Connor (1963–)

20710. Rettberg, Scott. The new frontier as a vast restless place: the Irish narrative of the American dream in Brian Friel's *Philadelphia, Here I Come*, Tom Murphy's *Conversations on a Homecoming*, and Joseph O'Connor's *Red Roses and Petrol*. *See* **17998**.

Clifford Odets

20711. Gibson, William (introd.). The time is ripe: the 1940 journal of Clifford Odets. (Bibl. 1988, 8413.) Rev. by Gabriel Miller in AmDr (1:1) 1991, 61–84.

Julia O'Faolain

20712. DAMLOS-KINZEL, CHRISTIANE. '*Women's role in our troubled times …* '. Eine Untersuchung zum literarischen Werk Julia O'Faolains. Würzburg: Königshausen & Neumann, 1994. pp. 254. (Kieler Beiträge zur Anglistik und Amerikanistik, 7.) Rev. by Rüdiger Imhof in LWU (29:2) 1996, 126–7.

Sean O'Faolain

20713. ARNDT, MARIE. Sean O'Faolain: an advocate for women? *In* (pp. 356–61) **49**.

20714. CHESNEY, THOM D. Joyce and O'Faolain: when 'talking trees' speak two authors' names. *See* **19058**.

20715. FAHIM, SHADIA S. The city and the crisis of identity in the *Bildungsromane* of Mahfouz and O'Faolain. *In* (pp. 335–44) **60**.

20716. KENNY, HERBERT A. Sean O'Faolain: this man is Ireland. Critic (46:1) 1991, 51–6.

20717. ROSKOSKI, MARK. The cycle of time in Sean O'Faolain's *The Silence of the Valley*. Notes on Modern Irish Literature (6) 1994, 19–24.

20718. SHERBO, ARTHUR. More periodical grubbings: Sean O'Faolain's contributions to the *Bell*. *See* **1367**.

Sidney Offit

20719. OFFIT, SIDNEY. Memoir of the bookie's son. New York: St Martin's Press, 1996. pp. vii, 165.

Liam O'Flaherty

20720. DEANE, PAUL. The ambiguous rebel: Liam O'Flaherty's *The Martyr*. Notes on Modern Irish Literature (7:2) 1995, 22–8.

20721. FRIBERG, HEDDA. An old order and a new: the split world of Liam O'Flaherty's novels. Uppsala: Almqvist & Wiksell, 1996. pp. 266. (Acta Universitatis Upsaliensis: Studia Anglistica Upsaliensia, 95.)

Grace Ogot

20722. FLANAGAN, KATHLEEN. African folk tales as disruptions of narrative in the works of Grace Ogot and Elspeth Huxley. *See* **18881**.

Desmond O'Grady (1935–)

20723. MOLONEY, KAREN MARGUERITE. Re-envisioning Yeats's *The Second Coming*: Desmond O'Grady and the Charles River. *In* (pp. 135–47) **58**.

Wale Ogunyemi

20724. ADELUGBA, DAPO (ed.). Chief Wale Ogunyemi at fifty: essays in honour of a Nigerian actor-dramatist. Ibadan: End-Time in assn with Lace Occasional, 1993. pp. v, 139. Rev. by Chris Dunton in RAL (26:1) 1995, 160–2.

Howard O'Hagan

20725. CARDINAL, JACQUES. Le récit salvateur: messianisme amér-indien dans *Ahini* d'Yves Thériault et *Tay John* de Howard O'Hagan. CanRCL (23:4) 1996, 1173–94.

Frank O'Hara

20726. ALLEN, DONALD (ed.).   The selected poems of Frank O'Hara. (Bibl. 1991, 14656.) Rev. by Michael Leddy in WLT (70:2) 1996, 409–10.
20727. BLASING, MUTLU KONUK.   Politics and form in postmodern poetry: O'Hara, Bishop, Ashbery and Merrill. *See* **16053**.
20728. ELLEDGE, JIM.   Frank O'Hara: to be true to a city. Ann Arbor: Michigan UP, 1990. pp. xii, 399. (Under discussion.) Rev. by Ann Filemyr in AR (49:1) 1991, 149.
20729. GOOCH, BRAD.   City poet: the life and times of Frank O'Hara. (Bibl. 1995, 18576.) Rev. by Walter Clemons in BkW, 29 Aug. 1996, 5, 13.

John O'Hara

20730. ABSHIRE, KREG.   At home in Hollywood: *Hope of Heaven* as cultural history, autobiography, and fiction. ColbyQ (32:3) 1996, 151–60.
20731. BASSETT, CHARLES.   *A Rage to Live*: gender roles in O'Hara's post-WW II fiction. ColbyQ (32:3) 1996, 161–8.
20732. BECKER, MARSHALL JOSEPH.   John O'Hara as an ethnographer of complex society: social class and ethnic tradition in southeastern Pennsylvania. ColbyQ (32:3) 1996, 169–89.
20733. BERNER, R. THOMAS.   The doctor's son covers a euthanasia trial: John O'Hara the journalist. AmJ (13:2) 1996, 111–25.
20734. EPPARD, PHILIP B.   Julian English outside of *Samarra*. ColbyQ (32:3) 1996, 190–5.
20735. GOLDLEAF, STEVEN.   'When I couldn't write': John O'Hara's lack of productivity during World War II. ColbyQ (32:3) 1996, 196–206.
20736. PLESNAR, A. M.   D.D.S.: dental details in *Samarra*. ColbyQ (32:3) 1996, 207–11.

Seumas O'Kelly

20737. MARTIN, AUGUSTINE.   The past and the peasant in the stories of Seumas O'Kelly. *In* (pp. 185–200) **106**.

Ben Okri

20738. CEZAIR-THOMPSON, MARGARET.   Beyond the postcolonial novel: Ben Okri's *The Famished Road* and its '*abiku*' traveller. JCL (31:2) 1996, 33–45.

Sharon Olds

20739. BEDIENT, CALVIN.   Sentencing Eros. Salmagundi (97) 1993, 169–81 (review-article).
20740. BROWN-DAVIDSON, TERRI.   The belabored scene, the subtlest detail: how craft affects heat in the poetry of Sharon Olds and Sandra McPherson. *See* **20038**.
20741. KICH, MARTIN.   A note on two poems by Sharon Olds. NCL (26:2) 1996, 6–7.
20742. OLDFIELD, SYBIL.   The news from the confessional – some reflections on recent autobiographical writing by women and its areas of taboo. *See* **4495**.
20743. PEARLMAN, MICKEY.   Sharon Olds: interview. Onthebus (5:2) 1993, 238–44.
20744. YAEGER, PATRICIA.   The 'language of blood': toward a maternal sublime. *See* **17358**.

Mary Oliver

20745. Burton-Christie, Douglas.   Nature, spirit, and imagination in the poetry of Mary Oliver. CC (46:1) 1996, 77–87.

20746. Fast, Robin Riley.   The Native-American presence in Mary Oliver's poetry. KenR (12:1/2) 1993, 59–68.

20747. Yaeger, Patricia.   The 'language of blood': toward a maternal sublime. *See* **17358**.

Robert Olmstead

20748. Olmstead, Robert.   Heart's blood. AL (68:1) 1996, 187–92.

20749. —— Stay here with me: a memoir. New York: Metropolitan, 1996. pp. 207. Rev. by Scott Bradfield in TLS, 30 Aug. 1996, 28.

20750. Zenowich, Christopher.   An interview with Robert Olmstead. WebS (13:3) 1996, 13–26.

Tillie Olsen

20751. Aiken, Susan Hardy.   Stages of dissent: Olsen, Grekova, and the politics of creativity. *In* (pp. 120–40) **23**.

20752. Coiner, Constance.   'No one's private ground': a Bakhtinian reading of Tillie Olsen's *Tell Me a Riddle*. *In* (pp. 71–93) **59**.

20753. Dizard, Robin.   Filling in the silences: Tillie Olsen's reading lists. *In* (pp. 295–309) **59**.

20754. Faulkner, Mara.   Protest and possibility in the writing of Tillie Olsen. (Bibl. 1995, 18596.) Rev. by Lillian S. Robinson in TSWL (14:2) 1995, 370–4.

20755. Fishkin, Shelley Fisher.   Reading, writing, and arithmetic: the lessons *Silences* has taught us. *In* (pp. 23–48) **59**.

20756. Hedges, Elaine; Fishkin, Shelley Fisher (eds).   Listening to silences: new essays in feminist criticism. *See* **59**.

20757. Materassi, Mario.   An interview with Tillie Olsen. RSAJ (2) 1991, 85–98.

20758. Middlebrook, Diane.   Circle of women artists: Tillie Olsen and Anne Sexton at the Radcliffe Institute. *In* (pp. 17–22) **59**.

20759. Oldfield, Sybil.   The news from the confessional – some reflections on recent autobiographical writing by women and its areas of taboo. *See* **4495**.

20760. Orr, Elaine.   Rethinking the father: maternal recursion in Tille Olsen's *Requa*. JSSE (20) 1993, 51–63.

20761. Roberts, Nora Ruth.   Three radical women writers: class and gender in Meridel Le Sueur, Tillie Olsen, and Josephine Herbst. *See* **18704**.

20762. Rosenfelt, Deborah Silverton.   Rereading *Tell Me a Riddle* in the age of deconstruction. *In* (pp. 49–70) **59**.

20763. Stetsenko, Ekaterina .   Revolutions from within. *In* (pp. 141–57) **23**.

20764. Wilson, Christopher P.   Unlimn'd they disappear: recollecting *Yonnondio: from the Thirties*. *In* (pp. 39–63) **88**.

20765. Wolfe, Kathy.   'Coming to writing' through the impressionistic fiction of Tillie Olsen. MidM (21) 1993, 57–67.

Charles Olson

20766. Hatlen, Burton.   Toward a common ground: versions of place in the poetry of Charles Olson, Edward Dorn, and Theodore Enslin. *See* **17361**.

20767. MAUD, RALPH.   Charles Olson's reading: a biography. Carbondale: Southern Illinois UP, 1996. pp. x, 372.

20768. PATTERSON, TOM.   The success of its own accident: an opinionated, encapsulated history of Black Mountain College. NCLR (2:2) 1995, 17–30.

20769. RUMAKER, MICHAEL.   Meeting Charles Olson at Black Mountain. NCLR (2:2) 1995, 56–66.

20770. SHACKLETON, MARK.   The myth of America and the spirit of place: Charles Olson's sense of the place of America in the history of the Western imagination. New Courant (6) 1996, 89–94.

Michael Ondaatje

20771. BARBOUR, DOUGLAS.   Michael Ondaatje. (Bibl. 1995, 18611.) Rev. by Gerald Lynch in JCP (10) 1995, 131–4.

20772. CLARKE, GEORGE ELLIOTT.   Michael Ondaatje and the production of myth. StudCanL (16:1) 1991, 1–21.

20773. COOKE, JOHN.   The influence of painting on five Canadian writers: Alice Munro, Hugh Hood, Timothy Findley, Margaret Atwood, and Michael Ondaatje. *See* **16077**.

20774. DAVIS, ROCÍO G.   Imaginary homelands revisited in Michael Ondaatje's *Running in the Family*. EngS (77:3) 1996, 266–74.

20775. ELLIS, SUSAN.   Trade and power, money and war: rethinking masculinity in Michael Ondaatje's *The English Patient*. StudCanL (21:2) 1996, 22–36.

20776. JEWINSKI, ED.   Michael Ondaatje: express yourself beautifully. Toronto: ECW Press, 1994. pp. 144. (Canadian biography.) Rev. by Susan Billingham in BJCS (11:1) 1996, 149–50; by David Ingham in ESCan (22:2) 1996, 243–4; by Michael Abraham in JCP (11) 1996, 182–5.

20777. KLIMAN, TODD.   Michael Ondaatje: cat burglar in the house of fiction. HC (31:5) 1994, 1–13.

20778. LÖNNECKE, ANNETTE.   Breaking through windows: the possibility of postmodernism as a new frontier in Michael Ondaatje's *Coming through Slaughter*. LWU (29:1) 1996, 33–40.

20779. PRESSON, REBEKAH.   Fiction as opposed to fact: an interview with Michael Ondaatje. New Letters (62:3) 1996, 80–90.

20780. SCHUMACHER, ROD.   Patrick's quest: narration and subjectivity in Michael Ondaatje's *In the Skin of a Lion*. StudCanL (21:2) 1996, 1–21.

20781. SIEMERLING, WINFRIED.   Das andere Toronto: mündliches Wissen in Michael Ondaatjes *In the Skin of a Lion*. In (pp. 171–83) **73**.

20782. SPEAREY, SUSAN.   Cultural crossings: the shifting subjectivities and stylistics of Michael Ondaatje's *Running in the Family* and *In the Skin of a Lion*. BJCS (11:1) 1996, 133–41.

20783. YORK, LORRAINE M.   The other side of dailiness: photography in the works of Alice Munro, Timothy Findley, Michael Ondaatje, and Margaret Laurence. *See* **17822**.

Eugene O'Neill

20784. ABBOTT, MICHAEL.   The curse of the misbegotten: the wanton son in the plays of Eugene O'Neill and Sam Shepard. EOR (18:1/2) 1994, 193–8.

20785. ADLER, THOMAS P.   The legacy of Eugene O'Neill according to Stark Young. EOR (20:1/2) 1996, 64–71.

20786. ALEXANDER, DORIS.   Eugene O'Neill's creative struggle: the decisive decade, 1924–1933. (Bibl. 1995, 18621.) Rev. by Steven F. Bloom in EOR (17:1/2) 1993, 193–6.

20787. BAK, JOHN S.   Eugene O'Neill and John Reed: recording the body politic, 1913–1922. EOR (20:1/2) 1996, 17–35.

20788. BARLOW, JUDITH E.   No he-men need apply: a look at O'Neill's heroes. EOR (19:1/2) 1995, 111–22.

20789. BASILE, MICHAEL.   Semiotic transformability in *All God's Chillun Got Wings*. EOR (16:1) 1992, 25–37.

20790. BEN-ZVI, LINDA.   O'Neill's cape(d) compatriot. *See* **18221**.

20791. BERLIN, NORMAND.   O'Neill's Shakespeare. (Bibl. 1994, 14361.) Rev. by Frederick C. Wilkins in EOR (17:1/2) 1993, 196–7; by W. L. Godschalk in AmDr (3:2) 1994, 94–100; by Don B. Wilmeth in Review (18) 1996, 255–70.

20792. —— Olivier's Tyrone. EOR (18:1/2) 1994, 135–42.

20793. BLACK, STEPHEN A.   Eugene O'Neill in mourning. EOR (18:1/2) 1994, 171–88.

20794. —— O'Neill and the old ham. EOR (17:1/2) 1993, 77–81.

20795. —— O'Neill's early recklessness. EOR (20:1/2) 1996, 11–16.

20796. —— On Jason Robards as O'Neill's Nietzschean Iceman. EOR (17:1/2) 1993, 149–56.

20797. —— Reality and its vicissitudes: the problem of understanding in *Long Day's Journey into Night*. EOR (16:2) 1992, 57–72.

20798. BLOOM, STEVEN F.   The lingering (comic?) legacy of Eugene O'Neill. EOR (20:1/2) 1996, 139–46.

20799. BOGARD, TRAVIS.   Alice and Alla. EOR (18:1/2) 1994, 65–77.

20800. —— BRYER, JACKSON R. (eds).   'A comradeship-in-arms': a letter from Eugene O'Neill to Arthur Miller. *See* **20221**.

20801. BOWER, MARTHA.   Regionalism and cultural marginalism: the New England Irish in O'Neill's late plays. *In* (pp. 154–9) **60**.

20802. BOWER, MARTHA GILMAN.   Carlotta Monterey and Eugene O'Neill: a spectacular collaboration. EOR (19:1/2) 1995, 139–49.

20803. —— Eugene O'Neill's unfinished threnody and process of invention in four cycle plays. (Bibl. 1993, 14340.) Rev. by Steven A. Black in EOR (19:1/2) 1995, 150–2.

20804. —— Upstairs/downstairs: dueling triangles in *A Touch of the Poet*. EOR (20:1/2) 1996, 97–101.

20805. BRUCHER, RICHARD.   O'Neill, Othello and Robeson. *See* **6544**.

20806. BRYAN, GEORGE B.; MIEDER, WOLFGANG (comps).   The proverbial Eugene O'Neill: an index to proverbs in the works of Eugene Gladstone O'Neill. *See* **3315**.

20807. CAHILL, GLORIA.   Mothers and whores: the process of integration in the plays of Eugene O'Neill. EOR (16:1) 1992, 5–23.

20808. CARDULLO, BERT.   Dreams of journey. ELN (34:1) 1996, 86–9. (*Long Day's Journey into Night*.)

20809. —— Dreams of journey. EOR (18:1/2) 1994, 132–4.

20810. —— Dreams of journey: Eugene O'Neill's *Long Day's Journey into Night*. NCL (26:1) 1996, 3–5.

20811. COMBS, ROBERT.   O'Neill's (and others') characters as others. EOR (20:1/2) 1996, 118–25.

20812. CONNOLLY, THOMAS F.   Was good old Nathan reliable? EOR (20:1/2) 1996, 72–9.

20813. COOPERMAN, ROBERT.   Unacknowledged familiarity: Jean Toomer and Eugene O'Neill. EOR (16:1) 1992, 39–48.

20814. CORDARO, JOSEPH.   Long day's journey into *Frankenstein*. *See* **12211**.

20815. CUNNINGHAM, FRANK R.   Eugene O'Neill in our time: overcoming student resistance. EOR (16:2) 1992, 45–55.

20816. —— O'Neill's beginnings and the birth of Modernism in American drama. EOR (17:1/2) 1993, 11–20.

20817. DALLETT, ATHENAIDE.   Old beauty and gutter tramps: O'Neill on stage. EOR (18:1/2) 1994, 13–20.

20818. DAWES, JAMES R.   Drama and ethics, grief and privacy: the case of Eugene O'Neill. EOR (17:1/2) 1993, 83–92.

20819. DOUGHERTY, DRU; VILCHES DE FRUTOS, MARÍA FRANCISCA. Eugene O'Neill in Madrid, 1918–1936. EOR (17:1/2) 1993, 157–64.

20820. EISEN, KURT.   The inner strength of opposites: O'Neill's novelistic drama and the melodramatic imagination. (Bibl. 1995, 18623.) Rev. by Michael Manheim in EOR (19:1/2) 1995, 153–6; by Don B. Wilmeth in Review (18) 1996, 255–70.

20821. ELLIOTT, THOMAS S.   Altar ego: O'Neill's sacrifice of self and character in *The Great God Brown*. EOR (18:1/2) 1994, 59–64.

20822. ESTRIN, MARK W. (ed.).   Conversations with Eugene O'Neill. Jackson; London: Mississippi UP, 1990. pp. xxxv, 242. (Literary conversations.) Rev. by Frederick C. Wilkins in EOR (15:1) 1991, 105–6.

20823. FIELD, BRAD.   Characterization in O'Neill: self-doubt as an aid to art. EOR (20:1/2) 1996, 126–31.

20824. —— Corrections in O'Neill. EOR (17:1/2) 1993, 93–105.

20825. FISHER, JAMES.   Tender men: the acquaintanceship of Eugene O'Neill and Sherwood Anderson. *See* **15989**.

20826. FRANK, GLENDA.   The tiger as daddy's girl. EOR (19:1/2) 1995, 55–65.

20827. FULFORD, ROBERT.   A theatrical journey into long-lost lingo. EOR (18:1/2) 1994, 129–31.

20828. GALLUP, DONALD (ed.).   *Greed of the Meek*: O'Neill's scenario for Act One of the first play of his eight-play cycle. EOR (16:2) 1992, 5–11.

20829. —— O'Neill's original 'Epilogue' for *A Touch of the Poet*. EOR (15:2) 1991, 93–107.

20830. GARVEY, SHEILA HICKEY.   Anna Christie and the 'fallen woman genre'. EOR (19:1/2) 1995, 66–80.

20831. GAUSS, REBECCA B.   O'Neill, Gruenberg and *The Emperor Jones*. EOR (18:1/2) 1994, 38–44.

20832. GELB, BARBARA.   Interviewing ghosts. EOR (18:1/2) 1994, 9–12.

20833. GRAM, JULIE M.   *Tomorrow*: from whence *The Iceman Cometh*. EOR (15:1) 1991, 79–92.

20834. HALL, ANN C.   'A kind of Alaska': women in the plays of O'Neill, Pinter and Shepard. (Bibl. 1995, 18626.) Rev. by Bette Mandl in EOR (17:1/2) 1993, 205–6.

20835. HAMMERMAN, HARLEY J.   On collecting O'Neill. *See* **488**.

20836. HANSON, PHILIP J.   *The Emperor Jones*: Naturalistic tragedy in hemispheric perspective. AmDr (5:2) 1996, 23–43.

20837. HAYS, PETER L.   O'Neill and Hellman. *See* **18585**.

20838. HEDDEREL, VANCE PHILIP.   Sibling rivalry in *Mourning Becomes Electra* and *The Little Foxes*. *See* **18586**.

20839. HOLMBERG, ARTHUR.   Fallen angels at sea: Garbo, Ullman [*sic*], Richardson, and the contradictory prostitute in *Anna Christie*. *See* **13810**.

20840. HOLTON, DEBORAH WOOD.   Revealing blindness, revealing vision: interpreting O'Neill's Black female characters in *Moon of the Caribbees, The Dreamy Kid* and *All God's Chillun Got Wings*. EOR (19:1/2) 1995, 29–44.

20841. HORI, MARIKO.   Aspects of *Noh* theatre in three late O'Neill plays. EOR (18:1/2) 1994, 143–8.

20842. HOUCHIN, JOHN H. (ed.).   The critical response to Eugene O'Neill. Westport, CT; London: Greenwood Press, 1993. pp. xxii, 319. (Critical responses in arts and letters, 5.) Rev. by Glenda Frank in EOR (17:1/2) 1993, 211–14.

20843. ISAAC, DAN.   Founding father: O'Neill's correspondence with Arthur Miller and Tennessee Williams. *See* **20228**.

20844. KEHL, D. G.   The 'big subject' in *The Hairy Ape*: a new look at Scene Five. EOR (17:1/2) 1993, 39–43.

20845. KELLER, JAMES R.   Rage against order: O'Neill's Yank and Milton's Satan. *See* **8191**.

20846. KRASNER, DAVID.   Whose role it it anyway? Charles Gilpin and the Harlem renaissance. *See* **13887**.

20847. LAPISARDI, FREDERICK S.   Not-so-random notes on masks in Yeats & O'Neill. EOR (20:1/2) 1996, 132–8.

20848. LEWIS, WARD B.   Eberhard Brüning, *Eugene O'Neill and the Coming of Age of the American Theater*. EOR (20:1/2) 1996, 158–62.

20849. LIU, HAIPING.   The invisible: a study of Eugene O'Neill's off-stage characters. EOR (18:1/2) 1994, 149–61.

20850. —— SWORTZELL, LOWELL (eds).   Eugene O'Neill in China: an international centenary celebration. (Bibl. 1995, 18630.) Rev. by Martha Bower in EOR (17:1/2) 1993, 208–11.

20851. McCOWN, CYNTHIA.   *The Great God Brown*: a diagnostic of commercialism's ills. EOR (17:1/2) 1993, 53–9.

20852. McDONOUGH, EDWIN J.   Quintero directs O'Neill. Chicago: A Cappella, 1991. pp. xii, 305. Rev. by Frederick C. Wilkins in EOR (15:2) 1991, 121–3.

20853. MANDL, BETTE.   Gender as design in Eugene O'Neill's *Strange Interlude*. EOR (19:1/2) 1995, 123–8.

20854. MANHEIM, MICHAEL.   At home with the Harfords. EOR (20:1/2) 1996, 102–9.

20855. MANN, BRUCE J.   An FBI memorandum on O'Neill. EOR (15:1) 1991, 58–63.

20856. MAUFORT, MARC.   Songs of American experience: the vision of O'Neill and Melville. *See* **11862**.

20857. —— (ed.).   Eugene O'Neill and the emergence of American drama. (Bibl. 1993, 14355.) Rev. by Bette Mandl in EOR (15:1) 1991, 107–9.

20858. MEADE, ROBERT.   Incest fantasy and the hero in *A Touch of the Poet*. EOR (18:1/2) 1994, 79–94.

20859. MILIORA, MARIA T.   Narcissistic fantasies in *A Touch of the Poet*: a self-psychological study. EOR (18:1/2) 1994, 95–107.

20860. MILLER, EILEEN. The Turks on O'Neill: putting the iceman on ice. EOR (20:1/2) 1996, 88–96.

20861. MONTEIRO, GEORGE. Jorge de Sena, Eugene O'Neill's critic and translator. EOR (17:1/2) 1993, 165–6.

20862. MURPHY, BRENDA. Fetishizing the dynamo: Henry Adams and Eugene O'Neill. *See* **10217**.

20863. —— McTeague's dream and *The Emperor Jones*: O'Neill's move from Naturalism to Modernism. *See* **20618**.

20864. MURRAY, DAVID AARON. O'Neill's transvaluation of pessimism in *The Iceman Cometh*. EOR (16:2) 1992, 73–9.

20865. PETERSON, WILLIAM M. O'Neill's divided agonists. EOR (20:1/2) 1996, 110–18.

20866. —— A portrait of O'Neill's Electra. EOR (17:1/2) 1993, 66–75.

20867. PFISTER, JOEL. Staging depth: Eugene O'Neill and the politics of psychological discourse. (Bibl. 1995, 18633.) Rev. by Robert Combs in EOR (20:1/2) 1996, 147–8.

20868. POOLE, GABRIELE. 'Blarsted niggers!': *The Emperor Jones* and Modernism's encounter with Africa. EOR (18:1/2) 1994, 21–37.

20869. PORTER, LAURIN R. The banished prince revisited: a feminist reading of *More Stately Mansions*. EOR (19:1/2) 1995, 7–28.

20870. —— Modern and postmodern wastelands: *Long Day's Journey into Night* and Shepard's *Buried Child*. EOR (17:1/2) 1993, 106–19.

20871. —— Self and other: the problem of possession in O'Neill's historical cycle. EOR (18:1/2) 1994, 109–15.

20872. RICE, JOSEPH. The blinding of Mannon house: O'Neill, Electra, and Oedipus. TexPres (13) 1992, 45–51.

20873. ROBINSON, JAMES A. The masculine primitive and *The Hairy Ape*. EOR (19:1/2) 1995, 95–110.

20874. ROGALUS, PAUL W. Shepard's *Tooth of Crime*, O'Neill's *Emperor Jones*, and the contemporary American tragic hero. NCL (22:2) 1992, 2–3.

20875. SAIZ, PETER R. The colonial story in *The Emperor Jones*. EOR (17:1/2) 1993, 31–8.

20876. SCHVEY, HENRY I. The master and his double: Eugene O'Neill and Sam Shepard. JDTC (5:2) 1991, 49–60.

20877. SHAFER, YVONNE. A Berlin diary: *The Iceman Cometh*. EOR (16:2) 1992, 80–103.

20878. SHAUGHNESSY, EDWARD L. Brutus in the heartland: *The Emperor Jones* in Indianapolis, 1921. EOR (20:1/2) 1996, 36–42.

20879. —— Down the nights and down the days: Eugene O'Neill's Catholic sensibility. Notre Dame, IN: Notre Dame UP, 1996. pp. xii, 226. (Irish in America.)

20880. —— Ella, James, and Jamie O'Neill: 'My name is might-have-been'. EOR (15:2) 1991, 5–92.

20881. —— Ella O'Neill and the imprint of faith. EOR (16:2) 1992, 29–43.

20882. —— O'Neill's Catholic dilemma in *Days without End*. EOR (15:1) 1991, 5–26.

20883. SHEA, LAURA. A note on O'Neill's *Long Day's Journey into Night*. NCL (23:3) 1993, 4–5.

20884. SIMON, MARC. Eugene O'Neill's introduction to Hart Crane's *White Buildings*: why he 'would have done it in a minute but ... '. *See* **17143**.

20885. SMITH, MADELINE C.; EATON, RICHARD.   Everything's up to date in Kansas City. EOR (16:1) 1992, 71–84.
20886. ————— More roads to Xanadu. EOR (15:1) 1991, 27–39.
20887. ————— The O'Neill–Komroff connection: thirteen letters from Eugene O'Neill. EOR (16:2) 1992, 12–28.
20888. ————— The truth about Hogan. EOR (18:1/2) 1994, 163–70.
20889. SMITH, SUSAN HARRIS.   Inscribing the body: Lavinia Mannon as the site of struggle. EOR (19:1/2) 1995, 45–54.
20890. THERIOT, IBRY G.-F.   The bitch archetype. JDTC (9:1) 1994, 119–33.
20891. TITCOMB, CALDWELL.   'O'Neill's people'. EOR (18:1/2) 1994, 5–8.
20892. TÖRNQVIST, EGIL.   Strindberg, O'Neill, Norén: a Swedish-American triangle. EOR (15:1) 1991, 64–78.
20893. ———— To speak the unspoken: audible thinking in O'Neill's plays. EOR (16:1) 1992, 55–70.
20894. VOGLINO, BARBARA.   'Games' the Tyrones play. EOR (16:1) 1992, 91–103.
20895. VORLICKY, ROBERT.   'No use gabbin' here all night': male talk and silence in *Hughie*. EOR (19:1/2) 1995, 81–94.
20896. VORLICKY, ROBERT H.   O'Neill's first play: *A Wife for a Life*. EOR (20:1/2) 1996, 5–10.

Joel Oppenheimer

20897. GILMORE, LYMAN.   'Don't touch the poet'. NCLR (2:2) 1995, 68–83.

Frank Ormsby

20898. MARKEN, RON.   Michael Foley, Robert Johnstone and Frank Ormsby: three Ulster poets in the *GO* situation. *In* (pp. 130–43) **86**.

Joe Orton

20899. BOONE, JOSEPH A.   Vacation cruises; or, The homoerotics of Orientalism. *See* **17448**.
20900. KELLER, JAMES R.   Tennessee Williams' *Orpheus Descending* and Joe Orton's *Entertaining Mr Sloane*. NCL (22:2) 1992, 8–10.
20901. NIERAGDEN, GÖRAN.   Comedy and menace: a Gricean look at the dialogue in Joe Orton's *Loot*. *See* **2681**.
20902. RUSINKO, SUSAN.   Joe Orton. (Bibl. 1995, 18646.) Rev. by Bernard F. Dick in WLT (70:3) 1996, 699.

'George Orwell' (Eric Blair)

20903. BYRNE, KATHARINE.   Not all books are created equal: George and his animals at fifty. Cweal (123:10) 1996, 14, 16.
20904. CHARLES, J. DARYL.   The new verbal order. ModAge (38:4) 1996, 321–31.
20905. CLYMER, WESLEY.   Collective madness, collective solipsism in Orwell's *Nineteen Eighty-Four*. NNER (16) 1992, 71–6.
20906. DAVISON, PETER.   George Orwell: a literary life. Basingstoke: Macmillan; New York: St Martin's Press, 1996. pp. xxvii, 175. (Literary lives.)
20907. HOEVELS, FRITZ ERIK.   Psychoanalyse und Literaturwissenschaft: Grundlagen und Beispiele. *See* **16306**.

20908. INGERSOLL, EARL. Margaret Atwood's *The Handmaid's Tale*: echoes of Orwell. *See* **16089**.

20909. INGLE, STEPHEN. The anti-imperialism of George Orwell. *In* (pp. 218–37) **63**.

20910. KEARNEY, ANTHONY. Orwell's *Animal Farm* and *1984*. Exp (54:4) 1996, 238–40.

20911. LOBDELL, JARED C. Stone pastorals: three men on the side of the horses. *See* **16617**.

20912. LOWENSTEIN, ANDREA FREUD. The protection of masculinity: Jews as projective pawns in the texts of William Gerhardi [*sic*] and George Orwell. *In* (pp. 145–64) **5**.

20913. MENDELSON, EDWARD. How Lawrence corrected Wells; how Orwell refuted Lawrence. *In* (pp. 166–75) **41**.

20914. OHI, YASUO. Burma no exile – Orwell to Takami Jun. (Exiles in Burma: Orwell and Jun Takami.) Tokyo: Kindai Bungeisha, 1996. pp. 280.

20915. PECK, DAVID. 'The morning that is yours': American and British literary cultures in the thirties. *In* (pp. 214–31) **34**.

20916. ROSS, WILLIAM T. Pacifism *vs* patriotism: the case of George Orwell. WebS (12:2) 1995, 54–66.

20917. RUHL, CHARLES. Orwell's problem, autonomy, and lexical meaning. SECOLR (16:2) 1992, 149–64.

20918. SCHERER, THOMAS. Die Geschichte des O: die pornographische Dimension von George Orwells *Nineteen Eighty-Four*. ZAA (43:2) 1995, 145–60.

20919. SEATON, JAMES. Trilling's *Homage to Catalonia*. Salmagundi (94/95) 1992, 142–56.

20920. WORTHINGTON, BERNARD A. Chesterton's influence on Orwell. *See* **16924**.

John Osborne

20921. BEYER, MANFRED. John Osborne: Traditionsstifter einer Dramaturgie des Zorns. ZAA (42:3) 1994, 198–215.

Micheal O'Siadhail

20922. SCHRICKER, GALE C. From Yeats's *Great Wheel* to O'Siadhail's *Image Wheel*. *In* (pp. 149–64) **58**.

Philip Osment

20923. BENNETT, SUSAN. Rehearsing *The Tempest*, directing the postcolonial body: disjunctive identity in Philip Osment's *This Island's Mine*. Essays in Theatre (15:1) 1996, 35–44.

Femi Osofisan ('Okinba Launko')

20924. RICHARDS, SANDRA L. Ancient songs set ablaze: the theatre of Femi Osofisan. Washington, DC: Howard UP, 1996. pp. xxvi, 210.

Alicia Ostriker

20925. HELLER, JANET RUTH. Exploring the depths of relationships in Alicia Ostriker's poetry. LitPs (38:1/2) 1992, 71–83.

Vincent O'Sullivan

20926. BACHINGER, KATRINA. Setting allegory adrift in John

Ashbery's *Mountains and Rivers*, James Joyce's *Portrait of the Artist as a Young Man*, and Vincent O'Sullivan's *Let the River Stand. In* (pp. 285–93) **125**.

Niyi Osundare

20927. EZENWA-OHAETO.   Survival strategies and the new life of orality in Nigerian and Ghanaian poetry: Osundare's *Waiting Laughters* and Anyidoho's *Earthchild. See* **16036**.

Wilfred Owen

20928. COMER, KEITH V.   Strange meetings: Walt Whitman, Wilfred Owen and poetry of war. *See* **12667**.

20929. KEDZIERSKA, ALEKSANDRA.   Space of unfreedom in the Great War poems of Wilfred Owen and Isaac Rosenberg. Annales UMCS (12/13:2) 1994/95, 13–33.

20930. KERR, DOUGLAS.   Wilfred Owen's voices: language and community. (Bibl. 1995, 18678.) Rev. by Sebastian D. G. Knowles in Review (18) 1996, 59–80.

20931. KNOWLES, SEBASTIAN D. G.   Men of reality: Owen, Sassoon, and Graves. *See* **18294**.

20932. PLASA, CARL.   Fantasias of war: language, intertextuality and gender in *Dulce et Decorum Est*. Krieg und Literatur (1) 1995, 61–78.

20933. RAMAZANI, JAHAN.   Wilfred Owen: 'elegies in no sense consolatory'. Genre (23:1) 1990, 15–32.

20934. WILLIAMS, TONY.   'This guy's a 'Nam vet': Wilfred Owen in William Crapser's *Remains. See* **17145**.

Rochelle Owens

20935. NASH, SUSAN SMITH.   An immense and continuous splendor: thoughts on the poetry of Rochelle Owens. Talisman (12) 1994, 129–40.

Cynthia Ozick

20936. BAUMGARTEN, MURRAY.   Reading Cynthia Ozick: imagining Jewish writing. ConLit (37:2) 1996, 307–14 (review-article).

20937. COHEN, SARAH BLACHER.   Cynthia Ozick: prophet for parochialism. *In* (pp. 283–98) **130**.

20938. —— Cynthia Ozick's comic art: from levity to liturgy. (Bibl. 1995, 18683.) Rev. by Elaine B. Safer in SAH (3:2) 1995, 116–19; by Elaine M. Kauvar in StudN (27:4) 1995, 570–1; by Murray Baumgarten in ConLit (37:2) 1996, 308–9.

20939. DE MARCO, FRANCESCA.   Rosa, una Ebrea Errante a Miami: *The Shawl* di Cynthia Ozick. Letterature d'America (55) 1994, 73–93.

20940. DOKOU, CHRISTINA; WALDEN, DANIEL.   The pagan condemnation and orthodox redemption of Rabbi Isaac Kornfeld. StudAJL (15) 1996, 6–16.

20941. FRIEDMAN, LAWRENCE S.   Understanding Cynthia Ozick. (Bibl. 1992, 15657.) Rev. by Amy Gottfried in StudAJL (15) 1996, 130–1.

20942. GORDON, ANDREW.   Cynthia Ozick's *The Shawl* and the transitional object. LitPs (40:1/2) 1994, 1–9.

20943. KAUVAR, ELAINE M.   Cynthia Ozick's fiction: tradition & invention. (Bibl. 1994, 14424.) Rev. by Hans Borchers in MFS (42:1) 1996, 159–61; by Murray Baumgarten in ConLit (37:2) 1996, 310–11.

20944. —— Notes toward editing a contemporary writer's letters. *See* **701**.

20945. KESSNER, CAROLE S. Matrilineal dissent: the rhetoric of zeal in Emma Lazarus, Marie Syrkin, and Cynthia Ozick. *In* (pp. 197–215) **130**.

20946. KREMER, S. LILLIAN. Holocaust survivors. Proteus (12:2) 1995, 27–31.

20947. KRUPNICK, MARK. Jewish Jacobites: Henry James's presence in the fiction of Philip Roth and Cynthia Ozick. *In* (pp. 89–107) **123**.

20948. MATERASSI, MARIO. Imagination unbound: an interview with Cynthia Ozick. Salmagundi (94/95) 1992, 85–113.

20949. STRANDBERG, VICTOR. Greek mind/Jewish soul: the conflicted art of Cynthia Ozick. (Bibl. 1995, 18692.) Rev. by Elaine M. Kauvar in StudN (27:4) 1995, 571–3; by Murray Baumgarten in ConLit (37:2) 1996, 309–10.

20950. WEINHOUSE, LINDA. Cynthia Ozick's *The Shawl* and Octavia Butler's *Kindred*: bearing witness. *See* **16645**.

Joy Packer

20951. STOTESBURY, JOHN A. Apartheid, liberalism and romance: a critical investigation of the writing of Joy Packer. Umeå: Umeå Univ., 1996. pp. iv, 247. (Acta Universitatis Umensis: Umeå studies in the humanities, 128.)

Ron Padgett

20952. FOSTER, EDWARD. An interview with Ron Padgett. Talisman (7) 1991, 68–81.

20953. SHAPIRO, DAVID. A night painting of Ron Padgett. Talisman (7) 1991, 82–7.

Myra Page

20954. BAKER, CHRISTINA LOOPER. In a generous spirit: a first-person biography of Myra Page. Foreword by Alice Kessler-Harris; afterword by Mary Frederickson. Urbana: Illinois UP, 1996. pp. xxiii, 273. (Women in American history.)

P. K. Page

20955. DJWA, SANDRA. P. K. Page: a biograpical interview. MalaR (117) 1996, 33–54.

20956. ELLIS, SARAH. Seeing the sea: the fairytales of P. K. Page. MalaR (117) 1996, 68–71.

20957. FISHER, DON. Eastern perspectives in the work of P. K. Page. MalaR (117) 1996, 129–34.

20958. KILLIAN, LAURA. Poetry and the modern woman: P. K. Page and the gender of impersonality. CanL (150) 1996, 86–105.

20959. PAGE, P. K. Australian journal, 1953–1956. MalaR (117) 1996, 6–28.

20960. PAUL, NANCY. 'Redressing the balance': female and male in the early poetry of P. K. Page. ECanW (58) 1996, 115–35.

20961. ROOKE, CONSTANCE. Consoeur. MalaR (117) 1996, 145–50.

20962. ROOKE, LEON. Legend of the flaming moths: a tribute to P. K. Page. MalaR (117) 1996, 29–32.

20963. SULLIVAN, ROSEMARY. Hologram. MalaR (117) 1996, 121–8.

Grace Paley

20964. ACCARDO, ANNALUCIA.   Grace Paley: la difficoltà di ascoltare e l'impossibilità di tacere. Àcoma (5) 1995, 52–7.

20965. PEARLMAN, MICKEY.   Grace Paley: interview. Onthebus (5:2) 1993, 228–37.

Morris Panych

20966. GILBERT, REID.   The theatrical stories of Morris Panych. CanTR (67) 1991, 5–11.

Sara Paretsky

20967. BIAMONTE, GLORIA A.   Funny isn't it? Testing the boundaries of gender and genre in women's detective fiction. *In* (pp. 231–54) **64**.

20968. SZUBERLA, GUY.   Paretsky, Turow, and the importance of symbolic ethnicity. Midamerica (18) 1991, 124–35.

Dorothy Parker

20969. JOHNSON, KEN.   Dorothy Parker's perpetual motion. *In* (pp. 251–65) **3**.

20970. SIMPSON, AMELIA.   Black on blonde: the Africanist presence in Dorothy Parker's *Big Blonde*. ColLit (23:3) 1996, 105–16.

Pat Parker

20971. MANGLINIS, ELIAS.   Pat Parker: 'M'endiaferoun oi synepeies ton historikon gegonoton stis anthropines zoes.' (Pat Parker: 'I am interested in the effects of historic events on human lives.') Diavazo (366) 1996, 96–111.

Stewart Parker

20972. KENNEALLY, MICHAEL.   The transcendent impulse in contemporary Irish drama. *In* (pp. 272–82) **49**.

20973. KURDI, MÁRIA.   The ways of twoness: pairs, parallels and contrasts in Stewart Parker's *Spokesong*. *In* (pp. 61–9) **112**.

Suzan-Lori Parks

20974. BEN-ZVI, LINDA.   'Aroun the worl': the signifyin(g) theater of Suzan-Lori Parks. *In* (pp. 189–208) **119**.

20975. JIGGETTS, SHELBY.   Interview with Suzan-Lori Parks. Callaloo (19:2) 1996, 309–17.

Vernon Louis Parrington

20976. HALL, H. LARK.   V. L. Parrington: through the avenue of art. (Bibl. 1995, 18705.) Rev. by Michael Kammen in AmS (36:1) 1995, 186–7.

Alan Paton

20977. ALEXANDER, PETER.   Alan Paton: a biography. (Bibl. 1995, 18711.) Rev. by Jay Tolson in BkW, 27 Nov. 1994, 4, 10; by Robert L. Berner in WLT (69:2) 1995, 421–2.

20978. JORDAN, JOHN O.   Alan Paton and the novel of South African liberalism: *Too Late the Phalarope*. MFS (42:4) 1996, 681–706.

20979. KOHLER, PETER (ed.).   Songs of Africa: collected poems.

(Bibl. 1995, 18712.) Rev. by Christo Doherty in New Coin (32:1) 1996, 72–6; by Colin Gardner in SARB (41) 1996, 18–19.

20980. LENTA, MARGARET. Rereading Rooke and Paton: *Mittee* and *Too Late the Phalarope*. EngA (23:1) 1996, 89–104.

20981. McGOVERN, EUGENE. Lewis and modern Christian novels. *See* **19733**.

20982. MORPHET, TONY. Stranger fictions: trajectories in the liberal novel. *See* **16993**.

20983. PRINSLOO, JEANNE. South African films in flux: thoughts on changes in the politics of identity in recent film productions. *See* **14101**.

20984. WILLIAMS, KEMP. The style of paradox: thematic and linguistic duality in *Cry, the Beloved Country*. *See* **2732**.

Glenn Patterson

20985. McGRATH, NIALL. Glenn Patterson: interview with Niall McGrath. Edinburgh Review (93) 1995, 41–50.

Tom Paulin

20986. ANDREWS, ELMER. Tom Paulin: underground resistance fighter. *In* (pp. 329–43) **86**.

20987. PORDZIK, RALPH. Lyrik als Geschichtspoetik: über einige Aspekte des *New Historicism* im Werk Tom Paulins. GRM (46:2) 1996, 216–30.

Gary Paulsen

20988. SALVNER, GARY M. Presenting Gary Paulsen. New York: Twayne; London: Prentice Hall, 1996. pp. xix, 171. (Twayne's US authors, 657.) (Young adult authors.)

Diana L. Paxson

20989. HUGHES, MELINDA. Dark sisters and light sisters: sister doubles and the search for sisterhood in *The Mists of Avalon* and *The White Raven*. *See* **16541**.

20990. KONDRATIEV, ALEXEI. Tales newly told: a column on current modern fantasy. Mythlore (19:3) 1993, 31–2.

Okot p'Bitek

20991. OFUANI, OGO A. Old wine in new skins? An exploratory review of Okot p'Bitek's *White Teeth: a Novel*. RAL (27:2) 1996, 185–93.

Mervyn Peake

20992. BISENIEKS, DAINIS. How not to edit Mervyn Peake. *See* **574**.

20993. HINDLE, ROB. Elysian fields, Hadean glooms: Titus Groan's mythical quest. PeakeS (4:4) 1996, 7–20.

20994. MASON, DESMOND. Peake and Son Ltd: a review of an audience with Sebastian Peake and Brian Sibley. PeakeS (4:4) 1996, 39–42.

20995. SHAYER, DAVID. Invitation to Derrible: the Pye project. PeakeS (4:4) 1996, 21–6.

Robert Newton Peck

20996. BURNS, ANN ELIZABETH. Humor *du jour*: a look at Robert Newton Peck's use of humor in the Soup series. ArizEB (36:1) 1993, 38–40.

Walker Percy

20997. BERTONNEAU, THOMAS.   The view from the stylite's tower: the vindication of the self in Walker Percy's *The Thanatos Syndrome*. NDQ (63:2) 1996, 113–36.

20998. BIZUP, JOSEPH.   Hopkins' influence on Percy's *Love in the Ruins*. *See* **11478**.

20999. DESMOND, JOHN F.   Walker Percy and the little way. Ren (43:4) 1991, 283–91.

21000. ——— Walker Percy's triad: science, literature, and religion. Ren (47:1) 1994, 3–9.

21001. DUPUY, ÉDWARD J.   Autobiography in Walker Percy: repetition, recovery, and redemption. Baton Rouge; London: Louisiana State UP, 1996. pp. xiii, 171. (Southern literary studies.) (Cf. bibl. 1992, 3994.) Rev. by Jeffrey J. Folks in SAtlR (61:4) 1996, 131–2.

21002. GILLESPIE, MICHAEL PATRICK.   Baroque Catholicism in Southern fiction: Flannery O'Connor, Walker Percy, and John Kennedy Toole. *In* (pp. 25–47) **123**.

21003. HAYNES, STEPHEN.   Theology as fiction and fiction as theology: Karl Barth and Walker Percy on 'the Jews'. LitTheol (5:4) 1991, 388–407.

21004. LAUDER, ROBERT E.   Walker Percy: prophetic, existentialist, Catholic storyteller. Foreword by Robert Coles. New York; Frankfurt; Bern; Paris: Lang, 1996. pp. x, 127. (New connections, 12.)

21005. LAWSON, LEWIS.   Tom More's 'Nobel Prize complex'. Ren (44:3) 1992, 175–82.

21006. LAWSON, LEWIS A.   Still following Percy. Jackson; London: Mississippi UP, 1996. pp. xv, 257.

21007. LINK, ERIC CARL.   An impotent savior: the messiah complex in Walker Percy's *Love in the Ruins*. SoQ (34:1) 1995, 24–31.

21008. MCQUILLAN, GENE.   Mont Blanc, Romantic tourism, and the legacy of travel writing. *See* **12279**.

21009. MARTIN, RICHARD T.   Language specificity as pattern of redemption in *The Thanatos Syndrome*. Ren (48:3) 1996, 209–23.

21010. MILLS, HENRY P.   An essential Walker Percy bibliography. SoQ (34:2) 1996, 129–39.

21011. NEWKIRK, TERRYE.   *Via negativa* and the little way: the hidden God of *The Moviegoer*. Ren (44:3) 1992, 183–202.

21012. PRIDGEN, ALLEN.   The Brownian leaves: sacramental presence in Walker Percy's *The Last Gentleman*. Ren (48:4) 1996, 297–308.

21013. ——— Up in his head: orbit and sacrament in Walker Percy's *The Thanatos Syndrome*. SoQ (34:1) 1995, 32–8.

21014. PROCHASKA, BERNADETTE.   The elemental passion of home and Walker Percy's Lancelot. Analecta Husserliana (44) 1995, 81–7.

21015. QUINLAN, KIERAN.   Walker Percy: the last Catholic novelist. Baton Rouge; London: Louisiana State UP, 1996. pp. xi, 242. (Southern literary studies.)

21016. RUBIN, LOUIS D., JR.   Walker Percy, 1916–1990. SoLJ (23:1) 1990, 5–7.

21017. SAMWAY, PATRICK.   Gaps and codes: Walker Percy's *Carnival in Gentilly*. Shen (43:1) 1993, 47–56.

21018. SAMWAY, PATRICK H. (ed.).   A thief of Peirce: the letters of Kenneth Laine Ketner and Walker Percy. Jackson; London:

Mississippi UP, 1995. pp. xix, 328. Rev. by Gary M. Ciuba in SoQ (34:4) 1996, 146–8.

21019. Schwalm, Gisela. *First person possessive*: Determination als Stilmittel in Walker Percys *Lancelot. See* **1980**.

21020. Stephenson, Will; Stephenson, Mimosa. Abraham of the Ur-Plain in Percy's *The Last Gentleman*. NCL (23:4) 1993, 5–6.

21021. —— Dr Gamow and Dr Duk: the inadequacy of science in Walker Percy's novels. NCL (23:3) 1993, 7–8.

21022. —— Father Boomer as Boanerges in Walker Percy's *The Last Gentleman*. NCL (22:3) 1992, 2–3.

21023. —— A Keats allusion in Walker Percy's *The Last Gentleman. See* **11724**.

21024. Taylor, L. Jerome, Jr. The movement to selfhood: Will Barrett's second coming. Ren (44:3) 1992, 163–74.

21025. Tolson, Jay. Pilgrim in the ruins: a life of Walker Percy. (Bibl. 1995, 18750.) Rev. by John P. Sisk in Salmagundi (100) 1993, 226–31.

21026. Werning, David Hugh. The museum scene in Walker Percy's *The Last Gentleman*. Ren (44:3) 1992, 203–15.

21027. Westarp, Karl-Heinz. Message to the lost self: Percy's analysis of the human situation. Ren (44:3) 1992, 216–24.

21028. Wyatt-Brown, Bertram. The house of Percy: honor, melancholy and imagination in a Southern family. (Bibl. 1995, 18752.) Rev. by Jonathan Yardley in BkW, 30 Oct. 1994, 3; by Gary M. Ciuba in SoQ (34:1) 1995, 145–6; by William A. Percy, III, in AlaR (49:2) 1996, 126–30.

21029. —— The literary Percys: family history, gender, and the Southern imagination. (Bibl. 1995, 18753.) Rev. by Jonathan Yardley in BkW, 30 Oct. 1994, 3; by William A. Percy, III, in AlaR (49:2) 1996, 126–30; by Elizabeth Moss in AHR (101:3) 1996, 913–14.

Maxwell Perkins

21030. Bruccoli, Matthew J. (ed.); Trogdon, Robert W. (asst ed.). The only thing that counts: the Ernest Hemingway/Maxwell Perkins correspondence 1925–1947. *See* **18597**.

'Ellis Peters' (Edith Pargeter)

21031. Feder, Sue. Edith Pargeter 1913–1995 Ellis Peters: beloved creator of 'Brother Cadfael'. AD (29:1) 1996, 34–6.

21032. Sarjeant, William A. S. *Black Is the Colour of My True Love's Heart*: a crime novel with a folk-song theme. *See* **3559**.

Paul Peters

21033. Redd, Tina. *Stevedore* in Seattle: a case study in the politics of presenting race on stage. JADT (7:2) 1995, 66–87.

Ann Petry

21034. Bande, Usha. Murder as social revenge in *The Street* and *The Women of Brewster Place. See* **20512**.

21035. Clark, Keith. A distaff dream deferred? Ann Petry and the art of subversion. AAR (26:3) 1992, 495–505.

21036. Holladay, Hilary. Ann Petry. New York: Twayne; London: Prentice Hall, 1996. pp. xiii, 149. (Twayne's US authors, 667.)

Audrey Petty

21037. Paylor, Diane.   An interview with Audrey Petty. Callaloo (19:2) 1996, 431–41.

Marlene Nourbese Philip

21038. Hoving, Isabel.   The dark dank places of my silence: silence, sexuality, and the experience of two Caribbean women writers. *See* **16969**.

21039. Philip, Marlene Nourbese.   The absence of writing; or, How I almost became a spy. *In* (pp. 271–8) **81**.

Caryl Phillips

21040. Galván, Fernando.   La obra narrativa de Caryl Phillips: tras las huellas de una tradición dual. RCEI (28) 1994, 109–26.

21041. Ledent, Bénédicte.   'Overlapping territories, intertwined histories': cross-culturality in Caryl Phillips's *Crossing the River*. JCL (30:1) 1995, 55–62.

Esther Phillips

21042. Fido, Elaine Savory .   Textures of Third World reality in the poetry of four African-Caribbean women. *In* (pp. 29–44) **81**.

Jayne Anne Phillips

21043. Barker, Adele Marie .   The world of our mothers. *In* (pp. 253–65) **23**.

21044. Koreneva, Maya.   Hopes and nightmares of the young. *In* (pp. 266–78) **23**.

21045. Phillips, Jayne Anne.   The writer as outlaw. BkW, 16 Oct. 1994, 1, 12.

21046. Willis, Meredith Sue.   Witness in the nightmare country: Jayne Anne Phillips. AppalJ (24:1) 1996, 44–51.

Ovid Williams Pierce

21047. McMillan, Douglas J.   Folk belief in some of Ovid Williams Pierce's early short stories. *See* **3640**.

Marge Piercy

21048. Adams, Alice.   Out of the womb: the future of the uterine metaphor. *See* **19828**.

21049. Afnan, Elham.   Chaos and utopia: social transformation in *Woman on the Edge of Time*. Extrapolation (37:4) 1996, 330–40.

21050. Caporale Bizzini, Silvia.   Narrating the exclusion: *Woman on the Edge of Time*. EIUC (4) 1996, 91–104.

21051. Palmer, Paulina.   The city in contemporary women's fiction. *In* (pp. 315–35) **34**.

21052. Sautter, Diane.   Erotic and existential paradoxes of the golem: Marge Piercy's *He, She, and It*. JFA (7:2/3) 1996, 255–68.

Harold Pinter

21053. Billington, Michael.   The life and work of Harold Pinter. London; Boston, MA: Faber & Faber, 1996. pp. x, 414. Rev. by Michael Wood in LRB (18:22) 1996, 11–12; by Lachlan Mackinnon in TLS, 25 Oct. 1996, 20.

21054. BURKMAN, KATHERINE H.; KUNDERT-GIBBS, JOHN L. (eds).
Pinter at sixty. (Bibl. 1994, 14494.) Rev. by Marya Bednerik in JDTC
(10:2) 1996, 162–3.
21055. GUSSOW, MEL. Conversations with Pinter. (Bibl. 1995, 18780.)
Rev. by Karen C. Blansfield in NETJ (6) 1995, 131–2.
21056. KNOWLES, RONALD. *A Kind of Alaska*: Pinter and Pygmalion.
CML (16:3) 1996, 231–40.
21057. ——— Theorizing Pinter's plays. EP (21) 1996, 161–73.
21058. MILLER, LOUISE M. Demonising the domestic: the menacing
objects of *The Caretaker*. Q/W/E/R/T/Y (6) 1996, 147–52.
21059. NISCHIK, REINGARD M. Körpersprache im Drama: ein
Beitrag zur Semiotik des Dramas. *See* **6828**.
21060. NORRICK, NEAL R.; BAKER, WILLIAM. Metalingual humor in
Pinter's early plays. *See* **2682**.
21061. OH, SAE-A. Harold Pinter geuk e natanan pokryeok gwa
bupae mitt yeosung eui yeokhwal. (Pinter's female characters: closed
women *versus* open women in patriarchal society.) JELLC (38:1) 1996,
219–56.
21062. PEARCE, HOWARD. The doll house in Harold Pinter's *Betrayal*.
TexPres (17) 1996, 46–52.
21063. PRENTICE, PENELOPE. Madness in Harold Pinter's plays and
filmscripts: the public consequences of private madness. Cithara (32:1)
1992, 31–8.
21064. ——— The Pinter ethic. (Bibl. 1994, 14501.) Rev. by James J.
Martine in Cithara (34:1) 1994, 54–6.
21065. SCHREIBER, EVELYN. Stream-of-consciousness and Freud's
primary process: comprehending Pinter's *Old Times*. LitPs (40:1/2) 1994,
71–80.
21066. TUCKER, STEPHANIE. Despair not, neither to presume:
The French Lieutenant's Woman: a screenplay. *See* **14294**.
21067. VISSER, DIRK. Communicating torture: the dramatic
language of Harold Pinter. *See* **2726**.

Ruth Pitter

21068. COELSCH-FOISNER, SABINE. Denying Eros: reading women's
poetry of the mid-twentieth century. *See* **18934**.

Sol T. Plaatje

21069. FINCHAM, GAIL; HOOPER, MYRTLE (eds). Under postcolonial
eyes: Joseph Conrad after empire. *See* **15852**.
21070. JOHNSON, DAVID. Literature for the Rainbow Nation: the case
of Sol Plaatje's *Mhudi*. JLS (10:3/4) 1995, 345–58.
21071. MPE, PHASWANE. 'Naturally these stories lost nothing by
repetition': Plaatje's mediation of oral history in *Mhudi*. Current Writing
(8:1) 1996, 75–89.
21072. WILLAN, BRIAN (ed.). Sol Plaatje: selected writings.
Johannesburg: Witwatersrand UP, 1996; Athens: Ohio UP, 1996.
pp. xvi, 483. Rev. by Stephen Gray in Mail & Guardian (12:47) 1996, 33.

Sylvia Plath

21073. ALEXANDER, PAUL. Rough magic: a biography of Sylvia
Plath. (Bibl. 1992, 15727.) Rev. by Richard Tallinghast in GetR (6:1)
1993, 124–35.

21074. GREENE, SALLY. A flare of resistance in Plath's *Nick and the Candlestick*. NCL (24:1) 1994, 4–6.

21075. HAMPL, PATRICIA. The smile of accomplishment: Sylvia Plath's ambition. IowaR (25:1) 1995, 1–28.

21076. HARGROVE, NANCY D. The chronology of Sylvia Plath's poems: 1956–1959. SB (45) 1992, 265–91.

21077. —— The journey toward *Ariel*: Sylvia Plath's poems of 1956–1959. (Bibl. 1995, 18803.) Rev. by Rebecca N. Viney in MidQ (37:1) 1995, 107–8; by Joanna Montgomery Byles in Archiv (233:2) 1996, 408–9.

21078. HAYMAN, RONALD. The death and life of Sylvia Plath. (Bibl. 1992, 15733.) Rev. by Eavan Boland in PN Review (18:2) 1991, 54.

21079. LINDBERG-SEYERSTED, BRITA. Dramatizations of 'visionary events' in Sylvia Plath's poetry. SN (68:2) 1996, 205–15.

21080. McCULLOUGH, FRANCES; HUGHES, TED (eds). The journals of Sylvia Plath. (Bibl. 1983, 12961.) Rev. by Joan N. Burstyn in NWSAJ (6:2) 1994, 234–54.

21081. MANNERS, MARILYN. The doxies of daughterhood: Plath, Cixous, and the father. CL (48:2) 1996, 150–71.

21082. PEREIRA, MALIN WALTHER. Be(e)ing and 'truth': *Tar Baby*'s signifying on Sylvia Plath's bee poems. *See* **20389**.

21083. PHELPS, H. C. Sylvia Plath's 'Polack friend': the ambiguous geography, history, and ethnic hierarchies of *Daddy*. NCL (26:1) 1996, 7–8.

21084. PUNTER, DAVID. Towards a homeopathic erotics: Sylvia Plath's *Nick and the Candlestick*. Gramma (4) 1996, 41–54.

21085. ROSE, JACQUELINE. The haunting of Sylvia Plath. (Bibl. 1994, 14523.) Rev. by Eavan Boland in PN Review (18:2) 1991, 54; by Janet Thormann in LitPs (40:3) 1994, 65–9.

21086. SEMINO, ELENA. Schema theory and the analysis of text worlds in poetry. *See* **2704**.

21087. STEINERT, MONIKA. Mythos in den Gedichten Sylvia Plaths. New York; Frankfurt; Bern; Paris: Lang, 1995. pp. 302. (Neue Studien zur Anglistik und Amerikanistik, 65.) (Cf. bibl. 1994, 14524.) Rev. by Carmen Birkle in Amst (41:2) 1996, 317–19.

21088. STEVENSON, ANNE. Bitter fame: a life of Sylvia Plath. (Bibl. 1995, 18810.) Rev. by Richard Tallinghast in GetR (6:1) 1993, 124–35.

21089. STRANGEWAYS, AL. 'The boot in the face': the problem of the Holocaust in the poetry of Sylvia Plath. ConLit (37:3) 1996, 370–90.

21090. TRIPP, ANNA. Sylvia Plath's *Words*. ERev (5:3) 1995, 20–2.

21091. WOO, SANG-GYUN. Hyundae youngmi sisaeui munmaek esseo bon Sylvia Plath eui bangbeob. (Sylvia Plath's method as considered in the context of the history of modern English and American poetry.) *See* **15082**.

William Plomer

21092. BURNETT, A. D. A literary ghost: William Plomer's proposed biographical account of E. M. Forster. *See* **17926**.

21093. FINCHAM, GAIL; HOOPER, MYRTLE (eds). Under postcolonial eyes: Joseph Conrad after empire. *See* **15852**.

Frederik Pohl

21094. BAILEY, K. V. Spindly mazes: dead men and doppels: Frederik Pohl's Gateway creations. Foundation (63) 1995, 40–55.

Stephen Poliakoff

21095. MIDDEKE, MARTIN. Stephen Poliakoff: Drama und Dramaturgie in der abstrakten Gesellschaft. Paderborn: Schöningh, 1994. pp. 326. (Schriften der Universität-Gesamthochschule-Paderborn: Sprach- und Literaturwissenschaft, 14.) Rev. by Raimund Schäffner in Forum modernes Theater (10:2) 1995, 215–18; by Bernhard Reitz in ZAA (44:2) 1996, 180–2.

Rachel Pollack

21096. KONDRATIEV, ALEXEI. Tales newly told: a column on current modern fantasy. *See* **20471**.

Sharon Pollock

21097. HOLDER, HEIDI J. Broken toys: the destruction of the national hero in the early history plays of Sharon Pollock. Essays in Theatre (14:2) 1996, 131–45.
21098. SCHOFIELD, ANN. Lizzie Borden took an axe: history, feminism, and American culture. *See* **16719**.

Abraham Polonsky

21099. SCHULTHEISS, JOHN. *A Season of Fear*: the blacklisted teleplays of Abraham Polonsky. *See* **14190**.

Jack Popplewell

21100. MERINO ÁLVAREZ, RAQUEL. *¡Vengan corriendo que les tengo un muerto!* (*Busybody*): prototipo de versión española de una obra de teatro comercial. *See* **3168**.

Katherine Anne Porter

21101. BLAIR, JOHN. South by Southwest: Texas and the Deep South in the stories of Katherine Anne Porter. Journal of the Southwest (37:3) 1995, 495–502.
21102. BRANTLEY, WILL. O'Connor, Porter, and Hurston on the state of the world. *See* **18824**.
21103. BRINKMEYER, ROBERT H., JR. Katherine Anne Porter's artistic development: primitivism, traditionalism, and totalitarianism. (Bibl. 1995, 18815.) Rev. by Janis P. Stout in MFS (40:2) 1994, 367–9; by Mary Titus in StudN (27:4) 1995, 568–70; by Sebastian D. G. Knowles in YES (26) 1996, 327–8.
21104. BURGAN, MARY. The 'feminine' short story in America: historicizing epiphanies. *In* (pp. 267–80) **3**.
21105. CIUBA, GARY M. One singer left to mourn: death and discourse in Porter's *Pale Horse, Pale Rider*. SAtlR (61:1) 1996, 55–76.
21106. FERRARI, RITA. Masking, revelation, and fiction in Katherine Anne Porter's *Flowering Judas* and *Pale Horse, Pale Rider*. JSSE (25) 1995, 9–19.
21107. FERRUGGIA, GABRIELLA. '*This Sphynx of countries*': il Messico di Katherine Anne Porter. Letterature d'America (41/42) 1990, 31–59.
21108. FREDERICK, JOAN. Order from chaos: war, pestilence, and the

near-death experience in Katherine Anne Porter's *Pale Horse, Pale Rider*. *In* (pp. 25–31) **127**.

21109. GIVNER, JOAN.   Letters to Lodwick: uncovering the hidden life of Katherine Anne Porter. SRev (81:1) 1996, 11–27.

21110. HARWELL, THOMAS MEADE.   Porter & Eliot: *Flowering Judas* and *Burbank–Bleistein*: two essays in interpretation. *See* **17514**.

21111. HINZE, DIANA.   Texas and Berlin: images of Germany in Katherine Anne Porter's prose. SoLJ (24:1) 1991, 77–87.

21112. JONES, SUZANNE W.   Reading the endings in Katherine Anne Porter's *Old Mortality*. *In* (pp. 280–99) **31**.

21113. KEPPEL, TIM.   Truth and myth in Willa Cather's *My Mortal Enemy* and Katherine Anne Porter's *Old Mortality*. *See* **16788**.

21114. SKAGGS, MERRILL.   The Louisianas of Katherine Anne Porter's mind. *In* (pp. 154–67) **65**.

21115. SKAGGS, MERRILL M.   Willa Cather's influence on Katherine Anne Porter's *He*. *See* **16844**.

21116. STOUT, JANIS P.   Katherine Anne Porter: a sense of the times. (Bibl. 1995, 18818.) Rev. by Louis T. Rubin, Jr, in BkW, 20 Aug. 1995, 4; by Debra A. Moddelmog in AL (68:3) 1996, 651–2; by Thomas Austenfeld in RMRLL (50:1) 1996, 97–9; by Will Brantley in ConLit (37:1) 1996, 137–41; by Phyllis Richardson in TLS, 5 Jan. 1996, 6–7; by Laurie Champion in SoQ (34:3) 1996, 161–2.

21117. TITUS, MARY.   'A little stolen holiday': Katherine Anne Porter's narrative of the woman artist. WS (25:1) 1995, 73–93.

21118. TITUS, MARY E.   The 'booby trap' of love: artist and sadist in Katherine Anne Porter's Mexico fiction. JML (16:4) 1990, 617–34.

21119. VANDE KIEFT, RUTH M.   The love ethos of Porter, Welty, and McCullers. *In* (pp. 235–58) **32**.

21120. WALSH, THOMAS.   'That deadly female accuracy of vision': Katherine Anne Porter and *El Heraldo de Mexico*. JML (16:4) 1990, 635–43.

Peter Porter

21121. WILLIAMS, DAVID G.   The influence of W. H. Auden on the work of Peter Porter. *See* **16134**.

Beatrix Potter

21122. AVERY, GILLIAN.   Beatrix Potter and social comedy. BJRL (76:3) 1994, 185–200.

21123. SIEBERT, GILLIAN.   Tales about tails: a glance at the lasting legacies of Beatrix Potter. Textures (10) 1996, 57–61.

21124. TAYLOR, JUDY.   Beatrix Potter: artist, storyteller, and country-woman. (Bibl. 1988, 8534.) London; New York: Warne, 1996. pp. 224, (plates) 13. (Revised ed.: first ed. 1986.)

21125. —— (ed.).   Beatrix Potter: a holiday diary: with a short history of the Warne family. London: Beatrix Potter Soc., 1996. pp. 80.

Dennis Potter

21126. COOK, JOHN R.   Dennis Potter: a life on screen. (Bibl. 1995, 18827.) Rev. by Peter Kemp in TLS, 26 Apr. 1996, 11–12.

21127. GILBERT, W. STEPHEN.   Fight and kick and bite: the life and work of Dennis Potter. (Bibl. 1995, 18828.) Rev. by Peter Kemp in TLS, 26 Apr. 1996, 11–12.

Ezra Pound

21128. AHEARN, BARRY (ed.). Pound/Cummings: the correspondence of Ezra Pound and e. e. cummings. *See* **17157**.

21129. ALLDRITT, KEITH. Modernism in the Second World War: the later poetry of Ezra Pound, T. S. Eliot, Basil Bunting, and Hugh MacDiarmid. *See* **16614**.

21130. ANON. (ed.). On criticism in general. By Ezra Pound. Paideuma (25:3) 1996, 107–24.

21131. ARDIZZONE, MARIA LUISA (ed.). Machine art and other writings: the lost thought of the Italian years: essays. Durham, NC; London: Duke UP, 1996. pp. xi, 174.

21132. BACCOLINI, RAFFAELLA. 'There was a Helen before there was a war': memory and desire in H.D.'s *Winter Love* and Pound's *Pisan Cantos*. *See* **17322**.

21133. BACIGALUPO, MASSIMO. Strade rivisitate: città moderna e paesaggio simbolico in Eliot e Pound. *See* **17475**.

21134. —— 'I wish he would explain his explanation': authorial explication in Wallace Stevens and Ezra Pound. RSAJ (7) 1996, 63–78.

21135. BAECHLER, LEA; LITZ, A. WALTON; LONGENBACH, JAMES (comps). Ezra Pound's poetry and prose: contributions to periodicals: in ten volumes. (Bibl. 1993, 14496.) Rev. by Ronald Bush in Text (Ann Arbor) (7) 1994, 538–43.

21136. BARTON, EDWIN J. Of labyrinths and vacuum tubes: Pound, McLuhan, and Canto LXXXII. Paideuma (25:1/2) 1996, 191–202.

21137. BORNSTEIN, GEORGE. The end(s) of Modernist editing. *See* **580**.

21138. BUSH, RONALD. 'Unstill, ever turning': the composition of Ezra Pound's *Drafts & Fragments*. *See* **595**.

21139. BUZARD, JAMES. Eliot, Pound, and expatriate authority. *See* **17486**.

21140. CAPPS, KATHLEEN. The François Villon–Ezra Pound connection: from *The Testament* to *The Cantos*. Paideuma (25:1/2) 1996, 205–16.

21141. COLE, THOMAS. Further notes on Pound and his poetry. Paideuma (25:1/2) 1996, 217–20.

21142. COYLE, MICHAEL. Ezra Pound, popular genres, and the discourse of culture. (Bibl. 1995, 18837.) Rev. by William Pratt in AL (68:2) 1996, 472–3; by Joseph G. Kronick in ELT (39:3) 1996, 393–6; by Tyler Hoffman in SAtlR (61:2) 1996, 154–7.

21143. —— A present with innumerable pasts: postmodernity and the tracing of Modernist origins. *See* **17494**.

21144. —— COWAN, LAURA. Pound and Eliot. *See* **17495**.

21145. CRISP, PETER. Imagism's metaphors – a test case. *See* **2343**.

21146. —— Pound – millenarian or utopian? Paideuma (25:1/2) 1996, 117–37.

21147. DASENBROCK, REED WAY. Ezra Pound, the last Ghibelline. JML (16:4) 1990, 511–33.

21148. DENNIS, HELEN MAY. A new approach to the poetry of Ezra Pound: through the medieval Provençal aspect. Lewiston, NY; Lampeter: Mellen Press, 1996. pp. xvi, 487. (Studies in American literature, 21.)

21149. DILWORTH, THOMAS. The other 'person of some interest' in Pound's *Portrait d'une femme*. Paideuma (25:1/2) 1996, 221–3.

21150. DONOVAN, STEWART.   Writers and politics: Ezra Pound back in the dock. AntR (93/94) 1993, 47–55.

21151. ELLMANN, MAUD.   The imaginary Jew: T. S. Eliot and Ezra Pound. *In* (pp. 84–91) **5**.

21152. EMIG, RAINER.   Modernism in poetry: motivations, structures and limits. *See* **11484**.

21153. FINDLEY, TIMOTHY.   Everything I tell you is the truth – except the lies. *See* **17813**.

21154. GEORGE, ANITA.   The Pisan mysteries: sex, death and rebirth in *The Pisan Cantos*. Paideuma (25:1/2) 1996, 139–60.

21155. GUENZI, CRISTINA.   Music and poetry which evoke nature: David Sylvian and Ezra Pound. Paideuma (25:1/2) 1996, 83–115.

21156. GUNN, THOM.   Adventurous song: Robert Duncan as Romantic Modernist. *See* **10516**.

21157. HATCHER, LESLIE; WITEMEYER, HUGH.   Lord Palmerston as factive hero in *The Cantos*. Paideuma (25:1/2) 1996, 225–33.

21158. HATLEN, BURTON.   Pound and nature: a reading of Canto XXIII. Paideuma (25:1/2) 1996, 161–88.

21159. HOWE, ELISABETH A.   The dramatic monologue. *See* **10519**.

21160. JARMAN, MARK.   Brer Rabbit and Brer Possum: the Americanness of Ezra Pound and T. S. Eliot. *In* (pp. 21–37) **34**.

21161. JEON, HONG-SHIL.   *Hwangmuji e esseoeui Ezra Pound*. (Ezra Pound in *The Waste Land*.) *See* **17519**.

21162. KEARNS, GEORGE; KEARNS, CLEO MCNELLY.   Pound and Eliot. *See* **17524**.

21163. KYBURZ, MARK.   *Voi altri pochi*: Ezra Pound and his audience, 1908–1925. Basel; Boston, MA: Birkhäuser, 1996. pp. 181. (ICSELL, 5.)

21164. LANGBAUM, ROBERT.   Lawrence and the Modernists. *See* **17525**.

21165. LANGETEIG, KENDRA.   Visions in the crystal ball: Ezra Pound, H.D., and the form of the mystical. *See* **17348**.

21166. LIEBREGTS, PETER TH. M. G.   Ezra Pound's *An Idyl for Glaucus*. JML (19:1) 1994, 171–8.

21167. —— Yeatsian moods and Plotinian ecstasy: the question of the self in Ezra Pound's *A lume spento*. Paideuma (25:1/2) 1996, 7–54.

21168. MCNAUGHTON, WILLIAM.   Pound's *usura* and the Islamic concept of *riba*. Paideuma (25:3) 1996, 9–58.

21169. MATERER, TIMOTHY.   Make it sell! Ezra Pound advertises Modernism. *In* (pp. 17–36) **67**.

21170. —— (ed.).   The selected letters of Ezra Pound to John Quinn, 1915–1924. (Bibl. 1993, 14572.) Rev. by William Pratt in WLT (69:2) 1995, 372–3.

21171. MOODY, A. DAVID.   'They dug him up out of sepulture': Pound, Erigena and Fiorentino. Paideuma (25:1/2) 1996, 241–7.

21172. MORRISON, PAUL.   The poetics of Fascism: Ezra Pound, T. S. Eliot, Paul de Man. *See* **15659**.

21173. PERLOFF, MARJORIE.   The dance of the intellect: studies in the poetry of the Pound tradition. *See* **15015**.

21174. QIAN, ZHAOMING.   Orientalism and Modernism: the legacy of China in Pound and Williams. (Bibl. 1995, 18874.) Rev. by Jacqueline Kaye in JAStud (30:2) 1996, 324–5.

21175. RAINEY, LAWRENCE.   The letters and the spirit: Pound's correspondence and the concept of Modernism. *See* **801**.

21176. READ, RICHARD. Art criticism *versus* poetry: an introduction to Adrian Stokes's *Pisanello*. *See* **12009**.

21177. RICHARDSON, MARK. Parables of vocation: Frost and Pound in the villages of (Gingrich's?) America. *See* **18063**.

21178. ROGERS, SHEF. How many *T*s had Ezra Pound's printer? *See* **308**.

21179. SPARROW, NED. Pound's ideogrammic legacy. Paideuma (25:3) 1996, 103–6.

21180. TAYLOR, RICHARD. Towards a textual biography of *The Cantos*. *In* (pp. 223–57) **69**.

21181. USHER, M. D. The strange case of Dr Syntax and Mr Pound. CML (16:2) 1996, 95–106.

21182. WACKER, NORMAN. Ezra Pound and the visual: notations for new subjects in *The Cantos*. *In* (pp. 85–104) **44**.

21183. WELLEN, PAUL. Analytic dictionary of Ezra Pound's Chinese characters. Paideuma (25:3) 1996, 59–100.

21184. WILHELM, J. J. Ezra Pound: the tragic years, 1925–1972. (Bibl. 1995, 18891.) Rev. by Michael Coyle in Review (18) 1996, 117–34.

Jerry Pournelle

21185. NEWSINGER, JOHN. 'The universe is full of warriors': masculinity, hard science and war in some novels by Larry Niven and his accomplices. *See* **16220**.

Anthony Powell

21186. MONAGAN, JOHN S. A visit with Anthony Powell: time's musician. ASch (65:3) 1996, 433–40.

21187. POWELL, VIOLET (introd.). Journals 1987–1989. London: Heinemann, 1996. pp. x, 239. Rev. by Jonathan Keates in TLS, 26 July 1996, 23.

Patricia Powell

21188. SMITH, FAITH. An interview with Patricia Powell. Callaloo (19:2) 1996, 324–9.

Tim Powers

21189. KONDRATIEV, ALEXEI. Tales newly told: a column on current modern fantasy. Mythlore (18:4) 1992, 26–7.

21190. WEBB, JANEEN. Simmons and Powers: postmodernism to postromanticism. *In* (pp. 139–46) **127**.

John Cowper Powys

21191. AUSTER, MARTIN. The Celtic imagination in exile. *See* **11788**.

21192. KRISSDOTTIR, MORINE (ed.). Petrushka and the dancer: the diaries of John Cowper Powys, 1929–1939. (Bibl. 1995, 18910.) Rev. by Harold Fromm in ASch (65:3) 1996, 475–7.

T. F. Powys

21193. AHRENS, HENNING. *The outcast monk type*: zum Werk von Theodore Francis Powys. ZAA (44:2) 1996, 134–41.

21194. GERVAIS, DAVID. T. F. Powys: invention and myth. Eng (45:181) 1996, 62–78.

Terry Pratchett

21195. Butler, Andrew M.   Terry Pratchett and the comedic *Bildungsroman*. Foundation (67) 1996, 56–62.

21196. Stephens, John.   Gender, genre and children's literature. *See* **14819**.

E. J. Pratt

21197. Gingell, Susan (ed.).   Pursuits amateur and academic: the selected prose of E. J. Pratt. Toronto; Buffalo, NY; London: Toronto UP, 1995. pp. xxxvii, 373. (Collected works of E.J. Pratt.)

Minnie Bruce Pratt

21198. Gilmore, Leigh; Aldrich, Marcia.   Writing home: 'home' and lesbian representation in Minnie Bruce Pratt. Genre (25:1) 1992, 25–46.

John Preston

21199. Antoniou, Laura (ed.).   Looking for Mr Preston. New York: Masquerade, 1995. pp. 298.

Reynolds Price

21200. Ciuba, Gary M.   Price's *Love and Work*: discovering the 'perfect story'. Ren (44:1) 1991, 45–60.

21201. Price, Reynolds.   Of love and death. BkW, 18 June 1995, 1, 10.

21202. —— A whole new life. (Bibl. 1995, 18922.) Rev. by Geoffrey Wolff in BkW, 12 June 1994, 1, 10.

21203. Schiff, James A.   Understanding Reynolds Price. Columbia: South Carolina UP, 1996. pp. 217. (Understanding contemporary American literature.)

Richard Price (1949–)

21204. Quart, Leonard; Auster, Albert.   A novelist and screenwriter eyeballs the inner city: an interview with Richard Price. *See* **14104**.

Christopher Priest

21205. Baxter, Stephen.   Further visions: sequels to *The Time Machine*. *See* **16242**.

F. T. Prince

21206. Kirkham, Michael.   The high Modernism of F. T. Prince. *In* (pp. 281–94) **16**.

V. S. Pritchett

21207. Theoharis, Theoharis C.   What happens in V. S. Pritchett's stories. JSSE (22) 1994, 85–92.

E. Annie Proulx

21208. Else, Barbara.   'Give me a plumber any day.' Quote Unquote (35) 1996, 10–11. (Interview.)

James Purdy

21209. LONG, BEVERLY WHITAKER; GRANT, CHARLES H., III. The 'surprising range of the possible': families communicating in fiction. *See* **14603**.

Barbara Pym

21210. BELLRINGER, ALAN W. A fistful of Pyms: Barbara Pym's use of cross-over characters. YES (26) 1996, 199–207.

21211. BROTHERS, BARBARA. Love, marriage, and manners in the novels of Barbara Pym. *In* (pp. 153–70) **96**.

21212. FULTON, JOE B. Mildred's mad tea party: carnival in Barbara Pym's *Excellent Women*. Dionysos (6:2) 1996, 25–37.

21213. LITTLE, JUDY. The experimental self: dialogic subjectivity in Woolf, Pym, and Brooke-Rose. *See* **16579**.

21214. MCINNIS, JUDY B. Communal rites: tea, wine and Milton in Barbara Pym's novels. *See* **8210**.

21215. NEROZZI, PATRIZIA; CORSO, GRAZIELLA (eds). Saggi italiani su Barbara Pym. Milan: Marcos y Marcos, 1996. pp. 253.

Thomas Pynchon

21216. ADAMS, ALICE. The American short story in the cybernetic age. *See* **14359**.

21217. ALLBAUGH, TOM. Dr Hilarius as a reader in Pynchon's *The Crying of Lot 49*. NCL (26:5) 1996, 2–3.

21218. ANDRIANO, JOSEPH. The masks of Gödel: math and myth in Thomas Pynchon's *Gravity's Rainbow*. *In* (pp. 14–20) **70**.

21219. ANON. Bibliography (–1996). Pynchon Notes (32/33) 1993, 205–18; (34/35) 1994, 209–22.

21220. ARLETT, ROBERT. Epic voices: inner and global impulse in the contemporary American and British novel. *See* **14375**.

21221. BAKER, JEFFREY S. A democratic Pynchon: counterculture, counterforce and participatory democracy. Pynchon Notes (32/33) 1993, 99–131.

21222. BERGH, MAGNUS. The courier's tragedy: Thomas Pynchon and Salman Rushdie in tune with each other. Pynchon Notes (32/33) 1993, 188–92.

21223. BERRESSEM, HANJO. Pynchon's poetics: interfacing theory and text. (Bibl. 1994, 14652.) Rev. by Judith Chambers in Pynchon Notes (32/33) 1993, 196–200; by Bernard Duyfhuizen in MFS (40:1) 1994, 163–4.

21224. —— Strangely attractive: the topology of psychic and social space in *Vineland*. Pynchon Notes (34/35) 1994, 38–55.

21225. BLUMBERG, DAVID. Umlauts and Oz: signifiers within the textual zone of Pynchon's *Gravity's Rainbow*. AJSem (9:4) 1992, 69–76.

21226. CARTER, STEVEN. Avatars of the third other. *See* **11825**.

21227. CASSIDY, ERIC. Cyberotics: markets, materialism and method in Pynchon and Deleuze. Pynchon Notes (34/35) 1994, 107–28.

21228. CELMER, PAUL W., JR. Pynchon's *V.* and the rhetoric of the Cold War. Pynchon Notes (32/33) 1993, 5–32.

21229. CLARKE, BRUCE. Allegories of Victorian thermodynamics. *See* **2335**.

21230. CONNER, MARC C. Postmodern exhaustion: Thomas

Pynchon's *Vineland* and the aesthetic of the beautiful. SAF (24:1) 1996, 65–85.

21231. DAS, PRASANTA.   Oedipa's night journey in Pynchon's *The Crying of Lot 49*. NCL (23:2) 1993, 4–5.

21232. DUYFHUIZEN, BERNARD.   Critiquing the cartel: anti-capitalism, Walter Rathenau and *Gravity's Rainbow*. Pynchon Notes (34/35) 1994, 88–106.

21233. EDWARDS, BRIAN.   Rigged play: Pynchon's *Gravity's Rainbow* as decentered text. CanRCL (23:2) 1996, 277–305.

21234. FACTOR, T. R. (ed.).   The letters of Wanda Tinasky. Foreword by Steven Moore. Introd. by Bruce Anderson. Portland, OR: Vers Libre Press, 1996. pp. xviii, 224.

21235. GOCHENOUR, PHILLIP.   The history written on the body: photography, history and memory in Pynchon's *Vineland*. Pynchon Notes (32/33) 1993, 169–80.

21236. GRANT, J. KERRY.   A companion to *The Crying of Lot 49*. (Bibl. 1994, 14661.) Rev. by David Seed in JAStud (30:1) 1996, 182–3.

21237. HASSAN, WAÏL.   This is not a novel: *The Crying of Lot 49*. Pynchon Notes (32/33) 1993, 86–98.

21238. HERMAN, LUC.   Enzian's meditation on technology in *Gravity's Rainbow*. *In* (pp. 556–62) **117**.

21239. JÄRVI, SAMI.   Postmodern demonology: Maxwell's Demon in Thomas Pynchon's *The Crying of Lot 49*. New Courant (6) 1996, 68–88.

21240. JOHNSTON, JOHN.   An American Book of the Dead: media and the unconscious in *Vineland*. Pynchon Notes (34/35) 1994, 20–37.

21241. KARPINSKI, EVA C.   From *V.* to *Vineland*: Pynchon's utopian moments. Pynchon Notes (32/33) 1993, 33–43.

21242. KEESEY, DOUGLAS.   The ideology of detection in Pynchon and DeLillo. *See* **17232**.

21243. KUZNETSOV, SERGEY.   Vassily Aksyonov's parody of *V.* Pynchon Notes (32/33) 1993, 181–5.

21244. McCARRON, WILLIAM.   Fariña and Pynchon. *See* **17645**.

21245. —— Pynchon and Zwitterions in *Gravity's Rainbow*. NCL (26:3) 1996, 4–5.

21246. McCONNELL, WILL.   Pynchon, Foucault, power, and strategies of resistance. Pynchon Notes (32/33) 1993, 152–68.

21247. MARTÍNEZ MARTÍNEZ, MARÍA ÁNGELES.   Function and linguistic organization: an analysis of character and setting in Thomas Pynchon's *Under the Rose* rewritten in *V. See* **2672**.

21248. MENDELSON, EDWARD.   Oedipa and the *cristeros*. Pynchon Notes (32/33) 1993, 186–7.

21249. MOULTHROP, STUART; McDAID, JOHN.   'Not yet blindingly one': *Gravity's Rainbow* and the hypertextualists. Pynchon Notes (32/33) 1993, 132–51.

21250. O'DONNELL, PATRICK (ed.).   New essays on *The Crying of Lot 49*. (Bibl. 1994, 14674.) Rev. by Kurt Müller in Amst (41:4) 1996, 709–10.

21251. O'HARA, DAN.   On the line of flight: Pynchon's entropy machine. Pynchon Notes (34/35) 1994, 56–69.

21252. PÉREZ-LLANTADA AURÍA, CARMEN.   On fractal geometry and meaning dissemination: re-thinking Pynchon's *The Crying of Lot 49*. Atlantis (17:1/2) 1995, 229–43.

21253. PORUSH, DAVID.   'The hacker we call God': transcendent writing machines in Kafka and Pynchon. Pynchon Notes (34/35) 1994, 129–47.

21254. ROSENBERG, MARTIN E.   Portals in Duchamp and Pynchon. Pynchon Notes (34/35) 1994, 148–75.

21255. SAFER, ELAINE.   Dreams and nightmares: 'high-tech paranoia' and the Jamesonian sublime – an approach to Thomas Pynchon's postmodernism. *In* (pp. 279–97) **123**.

21256. SCHACHTERLE, LANCE.   Information entropy in Pynchon's fiction. Configurations (4:2) 1996, 185–214.

21257. SHERARD, TRACEY.   The birth of the female subject in *The Crying of Lot 49*. Pynchon Notes (32/33) 1993, 60–74.

21258. SORFA, DAVID.   'Small comfort': significance and the uncanny in *The Crying of Lot 49*. Pynchon Notes (32/33) 1993, 75–85.

21259. STONEHILL, BRIAN.   Pynchon's prophecies of cyberspace. Pynchon Notes (34/35) 1994, 11–19.

21260. THIGPEN, KENNETH A.   Thomas Pynchon e gli alligatori nelle fogne: letteratura e folklore urbano. *See* **3456**.

21261. WEISENBURGER, STEVEN.   Hyper-embedded narration in *Gravity's Rainbow*. Pynchon Notes (34/35) 1994, 70–87.

Sir Arthur Quiller-Couch ('Q.')

21262. JOHN, CATHERINE RACHEL.   Quiller-Couch and G. K. Chesterton: some aspects of Liberalism. *See* **16916**.

Anna Quindlen

21263. BAUMANN, PAUL.   An editor's notebook: Anna Quindlen's church, objections from a mad hatter. Cweal (119:4) 1992, 5–6.

21264. SANTORA, ALEXANDER M.   Anna Quindlen: from the '60s to the '90s. Cweal (119:3) 1992, 9–13.

21265. WYMARD, ELLIE.   Ellie Wymard interviews Anna Quindlen. Critic (45:4) 1991, 61–5.

David Rabe

21266. BIENEN, LEIGH.   Playwrighting as an evolving process: an interview with David Rabe on *Those the River Keeps*. NETJ (5) 1994, 65–79.

21267. RADAVICH, DAVID.   Collapsing male myths: Rabe's tragicomic *Hurlyburly*. *See* **20103**.

21268. STAFFORD, TONY J.   The metaphysics of Rabe's *Hurlyburly*: 'staring into the eyes of Providence'. AmDr (1:2) 1992, 61–76.

Kathleen Raine

21269. RUSSELL, PETER.   A note on Kathleen Raine. NDQ (63:1) 1996, 49–63.

Carl Rakosi

21270. PERLOFF, MARJORIE.   Looking for the real Carl Rakosi: collecteds and selecteds. JAStud (30:2) 1996, 271–83 (review-article).

A. K. Ramanujan

21271. BRESNAHAN, ROGER J.   The Midwest as metaphor: four Asian writers. *See* **19630**.

21272. NAQVI, ROOMY.   A poetics of space. IndL (39:3) 1996, 145–6.

Ayn Rand

21273. BERLINER, MICHAEL S. (ed.).   The letters of Ayn Rand. Introd. by Leonard Peikoff. (Bibl. 1995, 18984.) London: Penguin, 1995. Rev. by Jeffrey A. Frank in BkW, 9 July 1995, 4–5.

21274. MAYHEW, ROBERT (ed.).   Ayn Rand's marginalia: her critical comments on the writings of over 20 authors. New Milford, CT: Second Renaissance, 1995. pp. viii, 231.

Margaret Randall

21275. CRAWFORD, JOHN; SMITH, PATRICIA CLARK.   Margaret Randall. *In* (pp. 70–81) **121**.

Ravinder Randhawa

21276. MONTEITH, SHARON.   On the streets and in the tower blocks: Ravinder Randhawa's *A Wicked Old Woman* (1987) and Livi Michael's *Under a Thin Moon* (1992). *See* **20207**.

John Crowe Ransom

21277. ABBOTT, CRAIG S.   John Crowe Ransom's ghosts. *See* **881**.

21278. COULTHARD, A. R.   Ransom's *Bells for John Whiteside's Daughter*. Exp (54:2) 1996, 94–5.

21279. McGAVRAN, DOROTHY H.   Building community: houses and other structures in the poetry of Frost and Ransom. *See* **18044**.

Raja Rao

21280. CLERFEUILLE, MICHEL.   The parable of the cow: an essay on a short story by Raja Rao. JSSE (24) 1995, 42–51.

21281. FROST, CHRISTINE MANGALA.   'Fleshing the bones': conducting inter-faith dialogue in fiction. *See* **20108**.

21282. MORSE, RUTH.   Raja Rao and the return of the oppressed. JSSE (24) 1995, 52–9.

21283. PARANJAPE, MAKARAND.   Critique of Communism in Raja Rao's *Comrade Kirillov*. *In* (pp. 69–83) **45**.

21284. SANKARAN, CHITRA.   Misogyny in Raja Rao's *The Chessmaster and His Moves*. JCL (30:1) 1995, 87–95.

21285. SHIRWADKAR, K. R.   Literature as ideology: Raja Rao's *The Serpent and the Rope*. *In* (pp. 1–11) **45**.

Terence Rattigan

21286. COLLINS, JERRE; WILSON, RAYMOND J., III.   Albee's *Who's Afraid of Virginia Woolf?*: the issue of originality. *See* **15901**.

21287. WANSELL, GEOFFREY.   Terence Rattigan. (Bibl. 1995, 18989.) Rev. by John Bayley in LRB (18:2) 1996, 17–18.

Simon Raven

21288. BARBER, MICHAEL.   The captain: the life and times of Simon Raven. London: Duckworth, 1996. pp. vi, 250, (plates) 8. Rev. by Alan Ross in TLS, 28 June 1996, 33.

Beatrice Ravenel

21289. DONALDSON, SUSAN V.   Songs with a difference: Beatrice Ravenel and the detritus of Southern history. *In* (pp. 176–92) **32**.

Marjorie Kinnan Rawlings

21290.　TARR, RODGER L.　Marjorie Kinnan Rawlings: a descriptive bibliography. Pittsburgh, PA: Pittsburgh UP, 1996. pp. xix, 283. (Pittsburgh series in bibliography.)

Piers Paul Read

21291.　HARTILL, ROSEMARY.　A married man: Piers Paul Read revealed. Critic (46:4) 1992, 35–50.

James Reaney

21292.　CAMPBELL, WANDA.　Alchemy in Ontario: Reaney's *Twelve Letters to a Small Town*. CanL (151) 1996, 102–17.

21293.　PARKER, GERALD D.　How to play: the theatre of James Reaney. (Bibl. 1994, 14700.) Rev. by Jerry Wasserman in TRC (13:1/2) 1992, 201–3.

Ishmael Reed

21294.　BROWNING, BARBARA.　Babaluaiyé: searching for the text of a pandemic. *In* (pp. 76–87) **2**.

21295.　CÔTÉ, JEAN-FRANÇOIS.　The North American novel in the United States: Ishmael Reed's Canada. ARCS (26:3) 1996, 469–80.

21296.　LINDROTH, JAMES.　Images of subversion: Ishmael Reed and the hoodoo trickster. AAR (30:2) 1996, 185–96.

21297.　MONSMA, BRADLEY JOHN.　'Active readers … obverse tricksters': trickster texts and cross-cultural reading. *See* **19316**.

John Reed

21298.　BAK, JOHN S.　Eugene O'Neill and John Reed: recording the body politic, 1913–1922. *See* **20787**.

Mary Renault

21299.　HOBERMAN, RUTH.　Masquing the phallus: genital ambiguity in Mary Renault's historical novels. TCL (42:2) 1996, 277–93.

Ruth Rendell ('Barbara Vine')

21300.　GIFFONE, TONY.　Disoriented in the Orient: the representation of the Chinese in two contemporary mystery novels. *In* (pp. 143–51) **19**.

Renée (Renée Taylor)

21301.　SAYER, SUSAN.　Empire and nation, home and family: Renée's *Does This Make Sense to You?* Span (42/43) 1996, 162–73.

Kenneth Rexroth

21302.　GUTIERREZ, DONALD.　The age of gold *versus* the age of iron: Kenneth Rexroth's *The Dragon and the Unicorn*. NDQ (63:2) 1996, 189–205.

21303.　—— The holiness of the real: the short verse of Kenneth Rexroth. Madison, NJ: Fairleigh Dickinson UP; London; Toronto: Assoc. UPs, 1996. pp. 276.

Mack Reynolds

21304. SMITH, CURTIS C.   The legacy of Mack Reynolds. JFA (5:4) 1992, 73–82.

Jewell Parker Rhodes

21305. RHODES, BARBARA C.; RAMSEY, ALLEN.   An interview with Jewell Parker Rhodes. AAR (29:4) 1995, 593–603.

Jean Rhys

21306. ALEXANDER, ROBYN.   Mirrors, madness, and the mother figure in Jean Rhys's *Wide Sargasso Sea*. Bracket (1) 1995, 4–12.

21307. BARNES, FIONA R.   Dismantling the master's houses: Jean Rhys and West Indian identity. *In* (pp. 150–61) **50**.

21308. BAUCOM, IAN.   Mournful histories: narratives of postimperial melancholy. *See* **3714**.

21309. BERRY, BETSY.   'Between dog and wolf': Jean Rhys's version of Naturalism in *After Leaving Mr Mackenzie*. StudN (27:4) 1995, 544–62.

21310. CARR, HELEN.   Jean Rhys. Plymouth: Northcote House; London: British Council, 1996. pp. xiv, 112. (Writers and their work.)

21311. EMERY, MARY LOU.   Jean Rhys at 'world's end': novels of colonial and sexual exile. Austin: Texas UP, 1990. pp. xvi, 219. Rev. by Mrinalini Sinha in Signs (17:2) 1992, 472–7.

21312. FILS-AIMÉ, HOLLY W.   *Coulibri* and *libellule*: tradition empowering women in novels by Jean Rhys and Simone Schwarz-Bart. JCS (9:3) 1993/94, 164–76.

21313. GREGG, VERONICA MARIE.   Jean Rhys's historical imagination: reading and writing the creole. (Bibl. 1995, 19017.) Rev. by Sheila Kineke in MFS (42:4) 1996, 895–6.

21314. HEAD, KEN.   *Wide Sargasso Sea*: a devil of a book. ERev (5:4) 1995, 26–8.

21315. HITE, MOLLY.   The other side of the story: structures and strategies of contemporary feminist narrative. *See* **16085**.

21316. JORDIS, CHRISTINE.   Jean Rhys, la prisonnière. Paris: Stock, 1996. pp. 263. (Échanges.)

21317. KAPLAN, CORA.   Fictions of feminism: figuring the maternal. *See* **15546**.

21318. LE GALLEZ, PAULA.   The Rhys woman. (Bibl. 1991, 15160.) Rev. by Mrinalini Sinha in Signs (17:2) 1992, 472–7.

21319. LONSDALE, THORUNN.   Reconstructing Dominica: Jean Rhys's *Pioneers, Oh Pioneers*. JSSE (26) 1996, 75–86.

21320. MADDEN, DEANNA.   Wild child, tropical flower, mad wife: female identity in Jean Rhys's *Wide Sargasso Sea*. *In* (pp. 162–74) **50**.

21321. MALCOLM, CHERYL ALEXANDER; MALCOLM, DAVID.   Jean Rhys: a study of the short fiction. New York: Twayne; London: Prentice Hall, 1996. pp. xix, 144. (Twayne's studies in short fiction, 61.)

21322. PIELA, CATHERINE HORBURY.   Finding order: a note on Rhys' *Wide Sargasso Sea*. NCL (24:2) 1994, 9–11.

21323. RODY, CAROLINE.   Burning down the house: the revisionary paradigm of Jean Rhys's *Wide Sargasso Sea*. *In* (pp. 300–26) **31**.

21324. YOON, JUNGGIL.   Yeokap batneun jah eui 'gwanggi': Jean Rhys eui *Gwanghwalhan Sargasso Sea* yeongu. (The 'madness' of the oppressed: Jean Rhys's *Wide Sargasso Sea*.) JELL (42:1) 1996, 119–39.

Anne Rice ('Anne Rampling', 'A. N. Roquelaure')

21325. BADLEY, LINDA. Writing horror and the body: the fiction of Stephen King, Clive Barker, and Anne Rice. *See* **16201**.

21326. BEAHM, GEORGE (ed.). The unauthorized Anne Rice companion. Kansas City, MO: Andrews and McMeel, 1996. pp. xvii, 246.

21327. BRANSON, STEPHANIE R. The 'curse of immortality': some philosophical implications of Bram Stoker's *Dracula* and Anne Rice's *Interview with the Vampire*. *See* **12366**.

21328. DIEHL, DIGBY. Anne Rice. Playboy (Chicago) (40:3) 1993, 53–4, 56, 58–64. (Interview.)

21329. HOPPENSTAND, GARY; BROWNE, RAY B. (eds). The gothic world of Anne Rice. Bowling Green, OH: Bowling Green State Univ. Popular Press, 1996. pp. 261.

21330. KING, MAUREEN. Contemporary women writers and the 'new evil': the vampires of Anne Rice and Suzy McKee Charnas. *See* **16885**.

21331. RAMSLAND, KATHERINE. The Roquelaure reader: a companion to Anne Rice's erotica. New York: Plume, 1996. pp. x, 244.

21332. RILEY, MICHAEL. Conversations with Anne Rice. New York: Ballantine, 1996. pp. xvii, 296.

21333. ROBERTS, BETTE B. Anne Rice. New York: Twayne; Toronto; Oxford: Maxwell Macmillan, 1994. pp. xii, 173. Rev. by G. Warlock Vance in Extrapolation (37:2) 1996, 178–80.

21334. ROUT, KAY KINSELLA. The least of these: exploitation in Anne Rice's Mayfair Trilogy. JAC (19:4) 1996, 87–93.

21335. SMITH, JENNIFER. Anne Rice: a critical companion. Westport, CT; London: Greenwood Press, 1996. pp. xi, 193. (Critical companions to popular contemporary writers.)

21336. TOMC, SANDRA. Dieting and damnation: Anne Rice's *Interview with the Vampire*. ESCan (22:4) 1996, 441–60.

Elmer Rice

21337. WITHAM, BARRY. *Between Two Worlds*: Elmer Rice chairs the thirties debate. AmDr (4:2) 1995, 1–16.

Adrienne Rich

21338. CRAWFORD, AUDREY. 'Handing the power-glasses back and forth': women and technology in poems by Adrienne Rich. NWSAJ (7:3) 1995, 35–53.

21339. DESHAZER, MARY K. 'The end of a century': feminist millennial vision in Adrienne Rich's *Dark Fields of the Republic*. NWSAJ (8:3) 1996, 36–62.

21340. ELIAS, KAREN. The pain of the body's world: women, poetry, and society in the work of Adrienne Rich. *In* (pp. 115–26) **109**.

21341. ESTRIN, BARBARA L. Space-off and voice-over: Adrienne Rich and Wallace Stevens. WS (25:1) 1995, 23–46.

21342. HEDLEY, JANE. 'Old songs with new words': the achievement of Adrienne Rich's *Twenty-One Love Poems*. Genre (23:4) 1990, 325–54.

21343. HELLE, ANITA. Elegy as history: three women poets 'by the century's deathbed'. *See* **17899**.

21344. HUSSMANN, MARY. On Adrienne Rich. IowaR (22:1) 1992, 221–5.

21345. NILAND, KURT R.   Moulsworth and recent feminist theory: the example of Adrienne Rich. *See* **8292**.

21346. PATTERSON, KATHERINE.   Out of a convention of awakening: defining a space beyond awareness. *See* **10628**.

21347. RATCLIFFE, KRISTA.   Anglo-American feminist challenges to the rhetorical traditions: Virginia Woolf, Mary Daly, Adrienne Rich. *See* **15710**.

21348. SCHÄFER, HEIKE.   The poet's poet: Adrienne Rich and Emily Dickinson. *See* **10996**.

21349. TEMPLETON, ALICE.   The dream and the dialogue: Adrienne Rich's feminist poetics. (Bibl. 1994, 14754.) Rev. by Suzanne Juhasz in TSWL (14:2) 1995, 375–6; by Gertrude Reif Hughes in AL (68:1) 1996, 261–2; by Terence Diggory in ColLit (23:2) 1996, 190–2.

21350. TRUCHLAR, LEO.   Wozu lese und schreibe ich? Notizen aus Anlass meiner Lektüren von Adrienne Rich und Friederike Mayröcker. *In* (pp. 3–14) **125**.

David Adams Richards

21351. MACDONALD, FRANCES.   War of the worlds: David Adams Richards and modern times. AntR (104) 1996, 17–24.

Dorothy Richardson

21352. BLUEMEL, KRISTIN.   The feminine laughter of no return: James Joyce and Dorothy Richardson. *In* (pp. 161–71) **64**.

21353. ——— Missing sex in Dorothy Richardson's *Pilgrimage*. ELT (39:1) 1996, 20–38.

21354. FROMM, GLORIA G. (ed.).   Windows on Modernism: selected letters of Dorothy Richardson. (Bibl. 1995, 19046.) Rev. by Lynette Felber in ELT (39:1) 1996, 73–7.

21355. ROSE, JACQUELINE.   Dorothy Richardson and the Jew. *In* (pp. 114–28) **5**.

21356. THOMSON, GEORGE H.   Dorothy Richardson's Foreword to *Pilgrimage*. TCL (42:3) 1996, 344–59.

21357. ——— A reader's guide to Dorothy Richardson's *Pilgrimage*. Greensboro, NC: ELT Press; Gerrards Cross: Smythe, 1996. pp. xiv, 169. (1880–1920 British authors, 11.)

21358. WITTMANN, LIVIA KÄTHE.   Desire in feminist narration: reading Margit Kaffka and Dorothy Richardson. CanRCL (21:3) 1994, 399–415.

Willis Richardson (1889–)

21359. GILES, FREDA SCOTT.   Willis Richardson and Eulalie Spence: dramatic voices of the Harlem renaissance. AmDr (5:2) 1996, 1–22.

Mordecai Richler

21360. HOWELLS, ROBIN.   Babel and parody: discourses in Mordecai Richler's *Duddy Kravitz*. BJCS (11:2) 1996, 323–38.

Laura Riding (Laura (Riding) Jackson)

21361. FRIEDMANN, ELIZABETH; NYE, ROBERT.   Laura (Riding) Jackson at 90. PN Review (17:4) 1991, 57–76.

21362. HEUVING, JEANNE.   Laura (Riding) Jackson's 'really new' poem. *In* (pp. 191–213) **39**.

21363. Lowden, Stephen.   *The Wind Suffers* by Laura Riding. ERev (6:3) 1996, 18–19.

21364. Paddon, Seija H.   The diversity of performance/performance as diversity in the poetry of Laura (Riding) Jackson and Eavan Boland. *See* **16492**.

21365. Seymour, Miranda.   Riding and Graves: partnership as theft. *See* **18307**.

Sharon Riis

21366. Robinson, Jack.   Sharon Riis: 'The reality is the present tense'. StudCanL (16:1) 1991, 129–41. (Interview.)

Denise Riley

21367. Kinnahan, Linda A.   Experimental poetics and the lyric in British women's poetry: Geraldine Monk, Wendy Mulford, and Denise Riley. *See* **20290**.

Mary Roberts Rinehart

21368. Biamonte, Gloria A.   Funny isn't it? Testing the boundaries of gender and genre in women's detective fiction. *In* (pp. 231–54) **64**.

Faith Ringgold

21369. Graulich, Melody; Witzling, Mara.   The freedom to say what she pleases: a conversation with Faith Ringgold. NWSAJ (6:1) 1994, 1–27.

Jose Rivera

21370. Jacobson, Lynn.   An interview with Jose Rivera. StAD (6:1) 1991, 49–58.

21371. Rivera, Jose.   Poverty and magic in *Each Day Dies with Sleep*. StAD (7:2) 1992, 163–6.

Amélie Rives

21372. Peaslee, Catherine G.   A poem for a dear friend from Castle Hill. *See* **18215**.

Michèle Roberts

21373. Rowland, Susan.   The body's sacred: romance and sacrifice in religious and Jungian narratives. *See* **16960**.

21374. Stowers, Cath.   'No legitimate place, no land, no fatherland': communities of women in the fiction of Roberts and Winterson. CritS (8:1) 1996, 69–79.

Morley Roberts

21375. Coustillas, Pierre.   A letter from the Western Avernus: Morley Roberts to his sister Ida. *See* **11288**.

Don Robertson

21376. Anderson, David D.   Don Robertson's Cleveland Trilogy. MidM (20) 1992, 50–6.

Elizabeth Robins ('C. E. Raimond')

21377. DIAMOND, ELIN.   'The garden is a mess': maternal space in Bowles, Glaspell, Robins. *In* (pp. 121–39) **119**.

21378. GATES, JOANNE E.   Elizabeth Robins, 1862–1952: actress, novelist, feminist. (Bibl. 1995, 19065.) Rev. by J. O. Baylen in ELT (39:4) 1996, 487–90; by Elsa Nettels in Legacy (13:1) 1996, 76–7.

21379. HIRSHFIELD, CLAIRE.   Suffragettes onstage: women's political theatre in Edwardian England. *See* **13806**.

21380. JOHN, ANGELA V.   Elizabeth Robins: staging a life, 1862–1952. (Bibl. 1995, 19066.) Rev. by Patricia W. Romero in ALH (101:5) 1996, 1545–6; by Kali Israel in Albion (28:3) 1996, 526–7; by J. O. Baylen in ELT (39:4) 1996, 487–90.

Edwin Arlington Robinson

21381. BRANSCOMB, JACK.   Edwin Arlington Robinson's wretched wight: *Miniver Cheevy* and *La Belle Dame sans Merci*. *See* **11695**.

21382. MOISE, EDWIN.   Robinson's *The Sheaves*. Exp (54:4) 1996, 226–9.

21383. STRAND, MARK.   Views of the mysterious hill: the appearance of Parnassus in American poetry. *See* **11004**.

Kim Stanley Robinson

21384. BAILEY, K. V.   Mars is a district of Sheffield. *See* **15919**.

21385. FOOTE, BUD.   Assuming the present in SF: Sartre in a new dimension. *In* (pp. 161–7) **36**.

21386. SEED, DAVID.   The Mars Trilogy: an interview. Foundation (68) 1996, 75–80.

Marilynne Robinson

21387. BARTOS, EILEEN; JACOBSON, CAROLYN.   Mostly on mother country. IowaR (22:1) 1992, 8–21. (Interview.)

21388. CAVER, CHRISTINE.   Nothing left to lose: *Housekeeping*'s strange freedoms. AL (68:1) 1996, 111–37.

21389. HEDRICK, TACE.   On influence and appropriation. IowaR (22:1) 1992, 1–7. (Interview.)

21390. KING, KRISTIN.   Resurfacings of *the deeps*: semiotic balance in Marilynne Robinson's *Housekeeping*. StudN (28:4) 1996, 565–80.

21391. LISCIO, LORRAINE.   Marilynne Robinson's *Housekeeping*: misreading *The Prelude*. *In* (pp. 139–62) **28**.

21392. MASZEWSKA, JADWIGA.   Ecofeminist themes in Marilynne Robinson, *Housekeeping*. AMSS (28) 1995, 63–70.

21393. SCHAUB, THOMAS.   Lingering hopes, faltering dreams: Marilynne Robinson and the politics of contemporary American fiction. *In* (pp. 298–321) **123**.

21394. VOSS, ANNE E.   Portrait of Marilynne Robinson. IowaR (22:1) 1992, 21–8. (Interview.)

Joseph Roccasalvo

21395. GILMOUR, PETER.   Writing as an act of faith: Peter Gilmour interviews Joseph Roccasalvo. Critic (49:4) 1995, 56–71.

John Rodker

21396. CROZIER, ANDREW (ed.).   Poems and *Adolphe* 1920. Manchester: Carcanet, 1996. pp. xxiv, 188. Rev. by Mark Ford in TLS, 5 July 1996, 5–6.

Richard Rodriguez

21397. SKENAZY, PAUL.   Borders and bridges, doors and drugstores: toward a geography of time. *In* (pp. 198–216) **108**.

Theodore Roethke

21398. BENOIT, RAYMOND.   *Moss-Picking*: an undergraduate theme of Theodore Roethke. ELN (33:3) 1996, 47–51.
21399. LENSE, EDWARD.   An influence survived: Roethke and Yeats. *In* (pp. 253–64) **58**.

Will Rogers

21400. ROBINSON, RAY.   American original: a life of Will Rogers. Oxford; New York: OUP, 1996. pp. xii, 288, (plates) 16.

Daphne Rooke

21401. HOOPER, MYRTLE.   Madness and the store: representations of Settler society in Doris Lessing's *The Grass Is Singing* and Daphne Rooke's *A Grove of Fever Trees*. *See* **19665**.
21402. KEARNEY, J. A.   A comparative study of the narrators in Daphne Rooke's first four novels. JCL (30:2) 1995, 99–117.
21403. LENTA, MARGARET.   Rereading Rooke and Paton: *Mittee* and *Too Late the Phalarope*. *See* **20980**.

Wendy Rose ('Bronwen Elizabeth Edwards', 'Chiron Khanshendal')

21404. GIORDANO, FEDORA.   Wendy Rose: le parole dell'assenza. RSAJ (2) 1991, 73–84.
21405. TONGSON-McCALL, KAREN.   The nether world of neither world: hybridization in the literature of Wendy Rose. AICRJ (20:4) 1996, 1–40.

Isaac Rosenberg

21406. KEDZIERSKA, ALEKSANDRA.   Nature and war in the trench poems of Isaac Rosenberg. LMN (19) 1995, 21–35.
21407. —— Space of unfreedom in the Great War poems of Wilfred Owen and Isaac Rosenberg. *See* **20929**.
21408. ROBERTS, BETH ELLEN.   The female God of Isaac Rosenberg: a muse for wartime. ELT (39:3) 1996, 319–32.

Joe Rosenblatt (1933–)

21409. KIRKWOOD, HILDA.   The merman. LRC (5:9) 1996, 14–15 (review-article).

Isaac Rosenfeld

21410. ANDERSON, DAVID D.   Growing up in Chicago between the wars: the literary lives of Saul Bellow and Isaac Rosenfeld. *See* **16377**.

Ishbel Ross (1897–)

21411. MERRICK, BEVERLY G.   Ishbel Ross, from Bonar Bridge to Manhattan: the Gaelic beginning of an American reporter. AmJ (13:4) 1996, 440–55.

Henry Roth

21412. CANDELARIA, CORDELIA CHÁVEZ.   *Différance* and the discourse of 'community' in writings in and about the ethnic other(s). *In* (pp. 185–202) **80**.

21413. MATERASSI, MARIO (ed.).   *Trolley Car Runs* di Henry Roth. RSAJ (1) 1990, 107–19.

21414. SCHOENING, MARK.   T. S. Eliot meets Michael Gold: Modernism and radicalism in Depression-era American literature. *See* **17556**.

Philip Roth

21415. AUBERT, DIDIER.   Baseballogie: sur trois romans de Philip Roth. Europe (805/6) 1996, 186–90.

21416. BUDICK, EMILY MILLER.   Philip Roth's Jewish family Marx and the defense of faith. AQ (52:2) 1996, 55–70.

21417. CHEYETTE, BRYAN.   Philip Roth and Clive Sinclair: representations of an 'imaginary homeland' in postwar British and American-Jewish literature. *In* (pp. 355–73) **34**.

21418. COOPER, ALAN.   Philip Roth and the Jews. Albany: New York State UP, 1996. pp. xiv, 319. (SUNY series in modern Jewish literature and culture.)

21419. DANZIGER, MARIE A.   Text/countertext: postmodern paranoia in Samuel Beckett, Doris Lessing, and Philip Roth. *See* **16280**.

21420. DOYLE, T. DOUGLAS.   The buck stops here: Brenda in *Goodbye, Columbus*. NCL (24:1) 1994, 2–3.

21421. KOELB, CLAYTON.   The metamorphosis of the classics: John Barth, Philip Roth, and the European tradition. *In* (pp. 108–28) **123**.

21422. KRUPNICK, MARK.   Jewish Jacobites: Henry James's presence in the fiction of Philip Roth and Cynthia Ozick. *In* (pp. 89–107) **123**.

21423. ROSENTHAL, REGINE.   Still restlessly roaming: versions of the Wandering Jew in two contemporary Jewish novels. ZAA (43:2) 1995, 161–76. (Stefan Heym, *Ahasver*; Philip Roth, *The Counterlife*.)

21424. SOLINGER, JASON D.   Philip Roth: an annotated bibliography of uncollected criticism 1989–1994. StudAJL (15) 1996, 61–72.

21425. WADE, STEPHEN.   The imagination in transit: the fiction of Philip Roth. Sheffield: Sheffield Academic Press, 1996. pp. 140.

Abraham Rothberg

21426. CHRISTENSEN, PETER G.   Abraham Rothberg's *The Sword of the Golem*: the use of the fantastic in defense of Judaism. JFA (7:2/3) 1996, 163–76.

Ola Rotimi

21427. MONYE, AMBROSE A.   The use of proverbs in Ola Rotimi's *The Gods Are Not to Blame*. *See* **3335**.

Marty Rubin

21428. WRIGHT, LES. Gay genocide as literary trope. *In* (pp. 50–68) **2**.

Muriel Rukeyser

21429. DANIELS, KATE. Muriel Rukeyser and her literary critics. *In* (pp. 247–63) **39**.

21430. FLYNN, RICHARD. 'The buried life and the body of waking': Muriel Rukeyser and the politics of literary history. *In* (pp. 264–79) **39**.

21431. WRIGHT, ANDREA ROHLFS. Masks uncovered: (fe)male language in the poetry of Muriel Rukeyser. CCTE (61) 1996, 34–40.

Salman Rushdie

21432. AIRAUDI, JESSE T. 'A rock of defence for human nature': philosophical and literary approaches to the causes of violence. *See* **16375**.

21433. BERGH, MAGNUS. The courier's tragedy: Thomas Pynchon and Salman Rushdie in tune with each other. *See* **21222**.

21434. DAVIES, J. M. Q. Aspects of the grotesque in Rushdie's *The Satanic Verses*. AUMLA (85) 1996, 29–37.

21435. DESAI, ANITA (introd.). Midnight's children. London: Campbell, 1995. pp. xxxi, 589. (Everyman's library, 217.)

21436. D'SOUZA, FRANCES. A world without censorship? *See* **1050**.

21437. FLETCHER, M. D. (ed.). Reading Rushdie: perspectives on the fiction of Salman Rushdie. Amsterdam; Atlanta, GA: Rodopi, 1994. pp. ix, 400. (Cross/cultures: readings in the post/colonial literatures in English, 16.) Rev. by J. M. Q. Davies in AUMLA (86) 1996, 123–4; by Christoph Reinfandt in LWU (29:4) 1996, 318–19; by Don L. F. Nilsen in SCS (20) 1996, 165–72.

21438. FORSYTH, NEIL; HENNARD, MARTINE. 'Mr Mustapha Aziz and Fly': defamiliarization of 'family' in Salman Rushdie's *Midnight's Children*. SPELL (9) 1996, 197–206.

21439. GÖBEL, WALTER; GRINT, DAMIAN. Salman Rushdie's silver medal. *In* (pp. 87–98) **57**.

21440. HAND, FELICITY. Challenging the centre: the response of British Asian writers. *See* **17181**.

21441. JOHNSON, STEPHANIE. Indian ink. Quote Unquote (32) 1996, 12–14. (Interview.)

21442. JUSSAWALLA, FEROZA. Rushdie's *dastan-e-dilruba*: *The Satanic Verses* as Rushdie's love letter to Islam. Diacritics (26:1) 1996, 50–73.

21443. KANE, JEAN M. The migrant intellectual and the body of history: Salman Rushdie's *Midnight's Children*. ConLit (37:1) 1996, 94–118.

21444. KUNDERA, MILAN. The day Panurge no longer makes people laugh. CritQ (38:2) 1996, 33–50.

21445. LANGELAND, AGNES SCOTT. Rushdie's language. *See* **2663**.

21446. LUZ GONZÁLEZ, MARÍA. Subversion of history and the creation of alternative realities in Salman Rushdie. RCEI (28) 1994, 41–51.

21447. MACCABE, COLIN. Salman Rushdie talks to the London Consortium about *The Satanic Verses*. CritQ (38:2) 1996, 51–70. (Interview.)

21448. MANFERLOTTI, STEFANO. Dopo l'impero: romanzo ed etnia in Gran Bretagna. *See* **14616**.

21449. MATHUR, O. P.   A metaphor of reality: a study of the protagonist of *Midnight's Children*. *In* (pp. 113–22) **45**.

21450. MOKA-DIAS, BRUNDA.   'The stuff that dreams are made of': interpreting dreams in Salman Rushdie's *The Satanic Verses*. JFA (7:4) 1996, 60–73.

21451. NEWTON, K. M.   Literary theory and the Rushdie affair. *See* **15674**.

21452. NOOR, RONNY.   Misrepresentation of history in Salman Rushdie's *Midnight's Children*. NCL (26:2) 1996, 7–8.

21453. —— Recalling 'Mahound': an intention misunderstood? NCL (22:3) 1992, 5–6.

21454. OLIVA, JUAN IGNACIO.   El lenguaje de las novelas indostanas de Salman Rushdie. *See* **2684**.

21455. PARNELL, TIM.   Salman Rushdie: from colonial politics to postmodern poetics. *In* (pp. 236–62) **132**.

21456. PETERSSON, MARGARETA.   Unending metamorphoses: myth, satire and religion in Salman Rushdie's novels. Lund: Lund UP, 1996. pp. 357. (Litteratur, teater, film, 14.)

21457. PIWINSKI, DAVID J.   Losing Eden in modern Bombay: Rushdie's *Midnight's Children*. NCL (23:3) 1993, 10–12.

21458. PORÉE, MARC; MASSERY, ALEXIS.   Salman Rushdie. Paris: Seuil, 1996. pp. 221. (Contemporains, 20.)

21459. AL-RAHEB, HANI.   Religious satire in Rushdie's *Satanic Verses*. JFA (6:4) 1993, 330–40.

21460. ROBINSON, ROGER.   To be a fugitive. NZList, 6 Jan. 1996, 46.

21461. SANTAOLALLA, ISABEL.   A fictitious return to the past: Saleem Sinai's autobiographical journey in *Midnight's Children*. *In* (pp. 163–70) **102**.

21462. SCANLAN, MARGARET.   Writers among terrorists: Don DeLillo's *Mao II* and the Rushdie affair. *See* **17240**.

21463. SHEFF, DAVID.   Salman Rushdie. Playboy (Chicago) (43:4) 1996, 49–52, 54, 58–60, 62, 165. (Interview.)

21464. TANEJA, G. R.   Facts of fiction: Rushdie's *Haroun*. In-between (1:1) 1992, 77–87.

Joanna Russ

21465. GARDINER, JUDITH KEGAN.   Empathic ways of reading: narcissism, cultural politics, and Russ's *Female Man*. Feminist Studies (20:1) 1994, 87–111.

21466. WILLS, DEBORAH.   The madwoman in the matrix: Joanna Russ's *The Two of Them* and the psychiatric postmodern. *In* (pp. 93–9) **70**.

George William Russell ('Æ')

21467. DEANE, PAUL.   Æ and the great chain of Irish being. Notes on Modern Irish Literature (5) 1993, 34–42.

Peter Russell

21468. REISINGER, WOLFGANG.   Ancient myth and philosophy in Peter Russell's *Agamemnon in Hades*. Lewiston, NY; Lampeter: Mellen Press, 1996. pp. vii, 256. (Salzburg studies in English literature: Poetic drama & poetic theory, 121.)

Rafael Sabatini

21469. KNIGHT, JESSE F.   Rafael Sabatini: the swashbuckler as serious artist. Romantist (9/10) 1985/86, 1–17.

V. Sackville-West

21470. BELL, ELIZABETH S.   Dashing off to Baghdad: a sense of place in a piece of time. *See* **15087**.

21471. CHIAVETTA, ELEONORA.   From biography to autobiography: female portraits by Vita Sackville-West. Textus (9:1) 1996, 223–42.

21472. LASSNER, PHYLLIS.   The fault lines of history: dystopic novels of the Second World War by British women authors. *See* **17106**.

21473. LEASKA, MITCHELL A.; PHILLIPS, JOHN (eds).   Violet to Vita: the letters of Violet Trefusis to Vita Sackville-West, 1910–21. (Bibl. 1989, 11056.) Rev. by Clare MacCulloch in AntR (84) 1991, 39–49.

21474. RAITT, SUZANNE.   Vita and Virginia: the work and friendship of V. Sackville-West and Virginia Woolf. (Bibl. 1995, 19149.) Rev. by Vera Nünning in ZAA (42:1) 1994, 88–90; by Ruth Freifrau von Ledebur in Archiv (233:1) 1996, 183–8.

Nayantara Sahgal

21475. MADAN, V. MOHINI.   The genre of neo-sociopolitical novel: novels of Nayantara Sahgal. IndL (39:5) 1996, 124–31.

21476. SAHGAL, NAYANTARA.   The myth reincarnated. JCL (30:1) 1995, 23–8.

21477. SALGADO, MINOLI.   Myths of the nation and female (self)sacrifice in Nayantara Sahgal's narratives. JCL (31:2) 1996, 61–73.

J. R. Salamanca

21478. ROBB, KENNETH A.   Aberrant place and time in J. R. Salamanca's *Lilith*. NCL (22:5) 1992, 6–7.

J. D. Salinger

21479. MATCHIE, THOMAS.   Literary continuity in Sandra Cisneros's *The House on Mango Street*. *See* **12592**.

21480. TAFANI, CINZIA.   L''autobiografia sognata' di J. D. Salinger: i racconti della famiglia Glass. QLLSM (1) 1987, 177–96.

21481. TANAKA, KEISHI.   *Mysterious Salinger* – kakusareta monogatari. (Mysterious Salinger: hidden stories.) Tokyo: Nan'undo, 1996. pp. 298.

Sonia Sanchez

21482. DE LANCEY, FRANZELLA ELAINE.   Refusing to be boxed in: Sonia Sanchez's transformation of the haiku form. *In* (pp. 21–36) **55**.

21483. JENNINGS, REGINA B.   The blue/black poetics of Sonia Sanchez. *In* (pp. 119–32) **55**.

Carl Sandburg

21484. DORESKI, C. K.   From news to history: Robert Abbott and Carl Sandburg read the 1919 Chicago riot. AAR (26:4) 1992, 637–50.

21485. LUTZ, STUART; REZNIKOFF, JOHN.   Presidential press(ures). MSS (47:2) 1995, 112–22.

21486. MIEDER, WOLFGANG.   Good proverbs make good Vermonters: a study of regional proverbs in the United States. *See* **3329**.

Mari Sandoz

21487. DeMarr, Mary Jean.   A historian's fiction: uses of stereotype in Mari Sandoz's *Son of the Gamblin' Man*. MidM (21) 1993, 29–43.

21488. Downey, Betsy.   'She does not write like a historian': Mari Sandoz and the old and new Western history. GPQ (16:1) 1996, 9–28.

21489. Farnsley, Kathy Wolfe.   From life to art: the short fiction of Mari Sandoz. MidM (22) 1994, 30–5.

21490. Lindell, Lisa R.   Recasting epic tradition: the dispossessed as hero in Sandoz's *Crazy Horse* and *Cheyenne Autumn*. GPQ (16:1) 1996, 43–53.

21491. Riley, Glenda.   Mari Sandoz's *Slogum House*: greed as woman. GPQ (16:1) 1996, 29–41.

21492. Rippey, Barbara; Wunder, John R.   An introduction. GPQ (16:1) 1996, 3–7.

21493. Stauffer, Helen Winter.   Mari Sandoz's portrait of an artist's youth: Robert Henri's Nebraska years. GPQ (16:1) 1996, 54–66.

George Santayana

21494. Cruz Hernández, Juan José.   *The Genteel Tradition in American Philosophy* as a valedictory indictment of the United States. *See* **11672**.

Bienvenido N. Santos

21495. Bresnahan, Roger J.   The Midwest as metaphor: four Asian writers. *See* **19630**.

Pamela Sargent

21496. Clarke, Boden (ed.).   The work of Pamela Sargent: an annotated bibliography & literary guide. By Jeffrey M. Elliot. San Bernardino, CA: Borgo Press, 1996. pp. 144. (Second ed.: first ed. 1990.) (Bibliographies of modern authors, 13.)

21497. Webb, Janeen.   Great SF short fiction: 1, *Danny Goes to Mars* by Pamela Sargent. Foundation (68) 1996, 105–7.

Frank Sargeson

21498. King, Michael.   Frank Sargeson: a life. (Bibl. 1995, 19162.) Rev. by C. K. Stead in Landfall (4:1) 1996, 127–32.

21499. Williams, Mark.   Frank Sargeson: apostle of love. Landfall (4:2) 1996, 209–21.

Ken Saro-Wiwa

21500. Jarniewicz, Jerzy.   Fajka Kena. (Ken's pipe.) Tygiel Kultury, Feb. 1996, 5–12. (Reminiscence.)

21501. Ogbowei, G. 'Ebinyo; Bell-Gam, Ibiere.   *Sozaboy*: language and a disordered world. *See* **2161**.

William Saroyan

21502. Haslan, Gerald.   William Saroyan and San Francisco: emergence of a genius (self-proclaimed). *In* (pp. 111–25) **108**.

21503. Kouymjian, Dickran.   Whitman and Saroyan: singing the song of America. *See* **12699**.

21504. Reynolds, Steven C.   Communication between director and playwright: a lesson from Robert Lewis and William Saroyan. NETJ (4) 1993, 65–77.

May Sarton

21505. KALLET, MARILYN (ed.). A house of gathering: poets on May Sarton's poetry. (Bibl. 1993, 14891.) Rev. by Phyllis F. Mannocchi in NWSAJ (7:1) 1995, 131–7.

21506. MALPEZZI, FRANCES R. 'Clear geometric praise': two ekphrastic poems of May Sarton. Cithara (35:2) 1996, 18–26.

21507. MANNOCCHI, PHYLLIS F. May Sarton. NWSAJ (7:1) 1995, 131–7 (review-article).

21508. SARTON, MAY. At eighty-two: a journal. New York; London: Norton, 1996. pp. 350.

21509. —— Encore: a journal of the eightieth year. (Bibl. 1993, 14892.) Rev. by Phyllis F. Mannocchi in NWSAJ (7:1) 1995, 131–7.

21510. SESHACHARI, NEILA C. 'I see myself as a builder of bridges': May Sarton at eighty: an interview with May Sarton. WebS (9:2) 1992, 16–32.

21511. SWARTZLANDER, SUSAN; MUMFORD, MARILYN R. (eds). That great sanity: critical essays on May Sarton. (Bibl. 1992, 16071.) Rev. by Phyllis F. Mannocchi in NWSAJ (7:1) 1995, 131–7.

Siegfried Sassoon

21512. CAMPBELL, PATRICK. Sassoon's *To Any Dead Officer*. Exp (54:2) 1996, 92–4.

21513. KNOWLES, SEBASTIAN D. G. Men of reality: Owen, Sassoon, and Graves. *See* **18294**.

John Saul

21514. BAIL, PAUL. John Saul: a critical companion. Westport, CT; London: Greenwood Press, 1996. pp. xiii, 203. (Critical companions to popular contemporary writers.)

Dorothy L. Sayers

21515. BEACH, SARAH. Harriet in rehearsal: Hilary Thorpe in *The Nine Tailors*. Mythlore (19:3) 1993, 37–9, 65.

21516. BORCHARDT, EDITH. Criminal artists and artisans in mysteries by E. T. A. Hoffman, Dorothy Sayers, Ernesto Sábato, Patrick Süskind, and Thomas Harris. *In* (pp. 125–34) **36**.

21517. BUCHANAN, COLIN. Dorothy L. Sayers's *Worship in the Anglican Church*: an Anglican response. SEVEN (13) 1996, 91–5.

21518. CHRISTOPHER, JOE R. Dorothy L. Sayers as a mythopoeic writer. Mythprint (30:5/6) 1993, 15–16.

21519. —— The fragmentary Lord Peter. Mythlore (19:3) 1993, 23–6.

21520. DALE, ALZINA STONE (ed.). Dorothy L. Sayers: the centenary celebration. (Bibl. 1994, 14856.) Rev. by Nancy-Lou Patterson in Mythlore (20:1) 1994, 57–8.

21521. DOUGHAN, DAVID. Tolkien, Sayers, sex and gender. Mythlore (21:2) 1996, 356–9.

21522. GILLESPIE, GERALD. The city of wo/man: labyrinth, wilderness, garden. *See* **3834**.

21523. LOADES, ANN (ed.). Spiritual writings. Cambridge, MA: Cowley, 1993. pp. 184. Rev. by Patricia A. Ward in SEVEN (13) 1996, 107–8.

21524. NOLL, MARK A. Dorothy L. Sayers's *Worship in the Anglican Church*: a Presbyterian response. SEVEN (13) 1996, 84–91.

21525. PATTERSON, NANCY-LOU.   'A Bloomsbury blue-stocking': Dorothy L. Sayers' Bloomsbury years in their 'spatial and temporal content'. Mythlore (19:3) 1993, 6–15.

21526. REYNOLDS, BARBARA.   Dorothy L. Sayers: her life and soul. (Bibl. 1995, 19180.) Rev. by Daniel Patrick King in WLT (69:1) 1995, 150–1; by Godfrey Hodgson in BkW, 22 Aug. 1996, 6.

21527. —— (ed.).   The letters of Dorothy L. Sayers, 1899–1936: the making of a detective novelist. Pref. by P. D. James. (Cf. bibl. 1995, 19181.) Rev. by Catherine Aird in SEVEN (13) 1996, 108–10.

Leslie Scalapino

21528. CAMPBELL, BRUCE.   Neither in nor out: the poetry of Leslie Scalapino. Talisman (8) 1992, 53–60.

21529. ELLIS, STEPHEN.   Lock-step chaos: Leslie Scalapino's multiples of time. Talisman (8) 1992, 63–6.

21530. FOSTER, EDWARD.   An interview with Leslie Scalapino. Talisman (8) 1992, 32–41.

21531. FROST, ELISABETH A.   An interview with Leslie Scalapino. ConLit (37:1) 1996, 1–23.

21532. NASH, SUSAN SMITH.   Magic and mystery in poetic language: a response to the writings of Leslie Scalapino. Talisman (14) 1995, 90–100.

21533. WATTEN, BARRETT.   Political economy and the avant-garde: a note on Haim Steinbach and Leslie Scalapino. Talisman (8) 1992, 48–52.

Dorothy Scarborough

21534. INNESS, SHERRIE A.   'Good enough for a man or a dog, but no place for a woman or a cat': the myth of the heroic frontier woman in Dorothy Scarborough's *The Wind*. ALR (28:2) 1996, 25–40.

Jack Schaefer

21535. FLORA, JOSEPH M.   *Shane* (novel and film) at century's end. *See* **13675**.

Susan Fromberg Schaeffer

21536. KREMER, S. LILLIAN.   Holocaust survivors. *See* **20946**.

21537. UCHMANOWICZ, PAULINE.   Vanishing Vietnam: Whiteness and the technology of memory. *See* **17243**.

Joan Schenkar

21538. PATRAKA, VIVIAN M.   Feminism and the Jewish subject in the plays of Sachs, Atlan, and Schenkar. *In* (pp. 160–74) **84**.

Robert Schenkkan (1917–)

21539. COLAKIS, MARIANTHE.   Aeschylean elements in Robert Schenkkan's *The Kentucky Cycle*. TexPres (16) 1995, 19–23.

Michael Schmidt

21540. HULSE, MICHAEL.   Michael Schmidt in conversation. *See* **1057**.

Diane Schoemperlen

21541. WHETTER, DARRYL.   In the language of Schoemperlen. StudCanL (21:1) 1996, 131–40. (Interview.)

George Schuyler

21542. HILL, ROBERT A.; RASMUSSEN, R. KENT (eds).   Black empire. Foreword by John A. Williams. Boston, MA: Northeastern UP, 1991. pp. xx, 347. (Northeastern library of Black literature.) Rev. by John C. Gruesser in AAR (27:4) 1993, 679–86.

James Schuyler

21543. LITTLE, CARL.   An interview with James Schuyler. Talisman (9) 1992, 176–80.

Delmore Schwartz

21544. BAUER, DALE.   The figure of the film critic as virile poet: Delmore Schwartz at the *New Republic* in the 1930s. *In* (pp. 110–19) **19**.

Lynne Sharon Schwartz

21545. SCHWARTZ, LYNNE SHARON.   Ruined by reading: a life in books. Boston, MA: Beacon Press, 1996. pp. 128.

Armand Schwerner

21546. LAVAZZI, TOM.   Editing Schwerner: versions of Armand Schwerner's 'design-tablet'. *See* **719**.

Alexander Scott (1920–)

21547. ROBB, DAVID S. (ed.).   The collected poems of Alexander Scott. Edinburgh: Mercat Press, 1994. pp. xxiv, 260. Rev. by Carol Gow in SLJ (supp. 42) 1995, 21–4; by G. Ross Roy in WLT (69:4) 1995, 801–2.

Duncan Campbell Scott

21548. BENTLEY, D. M. R.   Duncan Campbell Scott and Maurice Maeterlinck. StudCanL (21:2) 1996, 104–19.

21549. DRAGLAND, STAN.   Floating voice: Duncan Campbell Scott and the literature of Treaty 9. Concord, Ont.: Anansi, 1994. pp. xi, 289. Rev. by Tracy Ware in ESCan (22:4) 1996, 477–9.

21550. SALEM-WISEMAN, LISA.   'Verily, the White man's ways were the best': Duncan Campbell Scott, native culture, and assimilation. StudCanL (21:2) 1996, 120–42.

'Eleanor Scott' (Helen M. Leys)

21551. DALBY, RICHARD.   Eleanor Scott. Ghosts and Scholars (17) 1994, 37–41. (Writers in the James tradition, 14.)

21552. —— (introd.).   Randalls round. Penyffordd, Chester: Ash-Tree Press, 1996. pp. xvi, 139. (500 numbered copies.) Rev. by Jan Arter in Ghosts and Scholars (22) 1996, 57.

F. R. Scott

21553. DJWA, SANDRA.   The politics of the imagination: a life of F. R. Scott. (Bibl. 1989, 11076.) Rev. by Christopher M. Armitage in ARCS (18:3) 1988, 387–8.

Frederick George Scott

21554. YARDLEY, M. JEANNE.   'The bitterness and the greatness': reading F. G. Scott's war. StudCanL (16:1) 1991, 82–101.

Jody Scott

21555. HOLLINGER, VERONICA.   The vampire and/as the alien. *See* **12375**.

Kim Scott (1957–)

21556. BRADY, VERONICA.   Aboriginal spirituality. LitTheol (10:3) 1996, 242–51.

Lawrence Scott

21557. DUBOIS, DOMINIQUE.   *Ballad for the New World*; or, The remembrance of a lost world. JSSE (26) 1996, 87–93.

Paul Scott

21558. COLWELL, DANNY.   'I am your Mother and your Father': Paul Scott's Raj Quartet and the dissolution of imperial identity. *In* (pp. 213–35) **132**.

21559. LAL, MALASHRI.   Questioning otherness: racial indeterminacy in Kipling, Tagore and Paul Scott. *See* **19344**.

21560. SHARMA, J. N.   The Bibighar episode: narration in the Raj Quartet. In-between (5:1) 1996, 51–63.

21561. STROBL, GERWIN.   The challenge of cross-cultural interpretation in the Anglo-Indian novel: the Raj revisited: a comparative study of three Booker Prize authors: Paul Scott, The Raj Quartet; J. G. Farrell, *The Siege of Krishnapur*; Ruth Prawer Jhabvala, *Heat and Dust*. *See* **17649**.

21562. —— *Quartet* and *Four Quartets*: the influence of T. S. Eliot on Paul Scott. *In* (pp. 269–84) **125**.

Rosie Scott

21563. O'NEILL, ROB.   Passion and politics. Quote Unquote (38) 1996, 26. (Interview.)

E. J. Scovell

21564. COELSCH-FOISNER, SABINE.   Denying Eros: reading women's poetry of the mid-twentieth century. *See* **18934**.

Carolyn See

21565. GARRETT, GEORGE.   A letter to Carolyn See. MichQR (32:2) 1993, 296–301.

Erich Segal

21566. WILLSON, ROBERT F., JR.   Franco Zeffirelli's *Romeo and Juliet* and the uses of cultural translation. *See* **6685**.

Samuel Selvon

21567. CLARKE, AUSTIN.   A passage back home: a personal reminiscence of Samuel Selvon. Toronto: Exile, 1994. pp. 143. Rev. by John Clement Ball in CanL (150) 1996, 112–13.

21568. LOOKER, MARK.   Atlantic passages: history, community, and language in the fiction of Sam Selvon. New York; Frankfurt; Bern; Paris: Lang, 1996. pp. x, 243. (Studies of world literature in English, 7.)

21569. WYKE, CLEMENT H. Sam Selvon's dialectal style and fictional strategy. (Bibl. 1994, 14870.) Rev. by Swift Stiles Dickison in CanRCL (21:4) 1994, 749–52.

Richard Selzer

21570. STRIPLING, MAHALA YATES. A dialogic/rhetorical analysis of Richard Selzer's *Smoking* from *Mortal Lessons* (1974). RWT (4:1) 1996, 105–18.

Maurice Sendak

21571. ANON. Sendak in Asia: exhibition and sale of original artwork. Tokyo: Maruzen; Kingston, NY: Battledore, 1996. 1 vol. (unpaged). (Catalogue of an exhibition held in Tokyo, Oct. 21 – Nov. 2, 1996.)

21572. BROWN-DAVIDSON, TERRI. Inside literature's weird, wonderful night kitchen: the picture books of Maurice Sendak. *See* **185**.

21573. CECH, JOHN. Angels and wild things: the archetypal poetics of Maurice Sendak. (Bibl. 1995, 19215.) Rev. by Nathalie op de Beeck in BkW, 10 Dec. 1995, 20; by George R. Bodmer in LU (20:2) 1996, 280–2; by Elizabeth N. Goodenough in ChildLit (24) 1996, 235–40; by Hugh T. Keenan in SAtlR (61:4) 1996, 143–5.

Olive Senior

21574. DONNELL, ALISON. Hybrid bodies: theorizing the body that will not fit in Olive Senior's short stories. JSSE (26) 1996, 38–48.

21575. DUBOIS, DOMINIQUE; DEVOIZE, JEANNE. An interview of Olive Senior. JSSE (26) 1996, 13–25.

21576. FIDO, ELAINE SAVORY . Textures of Third World reality in the poetry of four African-Caribbean women. *In* (pp. 29–44) **81**.

Sipho Sepamla

21577. NGWENYA, THENGANI H. Interview with Sipho Sepamla: 2 September 1993. English Academy Review (11) 1996, 73–82.

Rod Serling (1924–1975)

21578. WINCHELL, MARK ROYDEN. Rod Serling's *Requiem for a Heavyweight*: a drama for its time. StAD (8:1) 1993, 13–20.

Mary Lee Settle

21579. DYER, JOYCE. The historical dimensions of Mary Lee Settle's *The Scapegoat*: Appalachia, labor, and Mother Jones. *In* (pp. 166–84) **87**.

21580. ROSENBERG, BRIAN. Mary Lee Settle's Beulah Quintet: the price of freedom. (Bibl. 1995, 19221.) Rev. by Gordon Simmons in WVH (51) 1992, 101–3.

'Dr Seuss' (Theodore Seuss Geisel)

21581. WOLF, TIM. Imagination, rejection, and rescue: recurrent themes in Dr Seuss. ChildLit (23) 1995, 137–64.

Anne Sexton

21582. BOWERS, SUSAN R.   The witch's garden: the feminist grotesque. *In* (pp. 19–36) **109**.

21583. COLBURN, STEVEN E.   Anne Sexton: a supplemental bibliography. BB (48:2) 1991, 109–15.

21584. DAVANI, MARIA CARMELA COCO.   Anne Sexton: the scene of the disordered senses. RSAJ (2) 1991, 53–71.

21585. HRUSCHKA, JOHN.   Anne Sexton and anima *Transformations*: *Transformations* as a critique of the psychology of love in Grimm's fairy tales. Mythlore (20:1) 1994, 45–7.

21586. LONG, MIKHAIL ANN.   As if day had rearranged into night: suicidal tendencies in the poetry of Anne Sexton. LitPs (39:1/2) 1993, 26–41.

21587. MIDDLEBROOK, DIANE.   Circle of women artists: Tillie Olsen and Anne Sexton at the Radcliffe Institute. *In* (pp. 17–22) **59**.

21588. MIDDLEBROOK, DIANE WOOD.   Anne Sexton: a biography. (Bibl. 1995, 19230.) Rev. by George Monteiro in NCL (24:3) 1994, 4–6.

21589. MONTEIRO, GEORGE.   Anne Sexton's radio days. NCL (25:5) 1995, 4–5.

21590. OLDFIELD, SYBIL.   The news from the confessional – some reflections on recent autobiographical writing by women and its areas of taboo. *See* **4495**.

21591. SEXTON, LINDA GRAY; AMES, LOIS (eds).   Anne Sexton: a self-portrait in letters. Boston, MA: Houghton Mifflin, 1991. pp. xxi, 433. Rev. by Jennifer Horne in SAtlR (61:1) 1996, 139–42.

21592. SKORCZEWSKI, DAWN.   What prison is this? Literary critics cover incest in Anne Sexton's *Briar Rose*. Signs (21:2) 1996, 309–35.

Maurice Shadbolt

21593. HUBBARD, ANTHONY.   A subversive pen. NZList, 10 Feb. 1996, 27.

Peter Shaffer

21594. AKSTENS, THOMAS.   Redression as a structured imperative in Shaffer's *Equus*. JDTC (6:2) 1992, 89–98.

21595. GIANAKARIS, C. J.   Peter Shaffer: a casebook. (Bibl. 1993, 14937.) Rev. by James Fisher in JDTC (7:2) 1993, 79–81.

21596. —— Peter Shaffer and the dilemma of adapting for film. *See* **13711**.

21597. NÜNNING, ANSGAR.   *Be my confessors!* Formen und Funktionen epischer Kommunikationsstrukturen in Peter Shaffers *Amadeus*. Forum modernes Theater (9:2) 1994, 141–59.

21598. OSTERWALDER, HANS.   Zwischen epischem und totalem Theater: Peter Shaffers Suche nach dem Numinosen. ZAA (43:3) 1995, 234–43.

Ntozake Shange

21599. ANDERLINI, SERENA.   Drama as performance art: an interview with Ntozake Shange. JDTC (6:1) 1991, 85–97.

21600. BÖSCH, SUSANNA A.   *Colored girls* as mothers: Ntozake Shange's independent women. AAA (21:2) 1996, 287–302.

21601. BOSENBERG, EVA.   Das Überleben der Sprache in der Stille:

zur Adaptation mündlicher Erzähltraditionen in drei Werken zeitgenössischer afro-amerikanischer Autorinnen. *In* (pp. 229–50) **73**.

21602. ELDER, ARLENE. *Sassafrass, Cypress & Indigo*: Ntozake Shange's neo-slave/Blues narrative. AAR (26:1) 1992, 99–107.

21603. KENT, ASSUNTA. The rich multiplicity of *Betsey Brown*. JDTC (7:1) 1992, 151–61.

21604. LeSEUR, GETA. From nice colored girl to womanist: an explanation of development in Ntozake Shange's writings. *In* (pp. 167–80) **55**.

21605. LESTER, NEAL A. Shange's men: *for colored girls* revisited, and movement beyond. AAR (26:2) 1992, 319–28.

21606. O'CONNOR, MARY. Subject, voice, and women in some contemporary Black American women's writing. *In* (pp. 199–217) **33**.

21607. PAVLIDES, MEROPE. Poetics of women's writing: dramatic tragedy. *In* (pp. 11–21) **37**.

21608. QURESHI, AMBER. Where the womanisms grow: ritual and romanticism in *for colored girls who have considered suicide*. NCL (26:4) 1996, 6–8.

21609. RANKOVIC, CATHERINE. An interview with Ntozake Shange. GateH (16:3) 1995/96, 38–43.

21610. SHANGE, NTOZAKE. When the rainbow is enough. BkW, 31 Mar. 1996, 1, 11.

21611. SPLAWN, P. JANE. New World consciousness in the poetry of Ntozake Shange and June Jordan: two African-American women's response to expansionism in the Third World. *See* **19008**.

21612. WASHINGTON, MARY HELEN. Ntozake Shange. *In* (pp. 205–20) **85**.

Alan Shapiro

21613. SHAPIRO, ALAN. The last happy occasion. Chicago; London: Chicago UP, 1996. pp. x, 229.

David Shapiro

21614. FINK, THOMAS. Tracing David Shapiro's *The Seasons*. ConLit (37:3) 1996, 416–38.

Karl Shapiro

21615. ENGLES, TIM. Shapiro's *The Fly*. Exp (55:1) 1996, 41–3.

Tom Sharpe

21616. GUTIERREZ, ANA MOYA. Tom Sharpe and *Wilt*. EEM (2:2) 1993, 12–17. (Interview.)

George Bernard Shaw

21617. ACHILLES, JOCHEN. Funktionen der Religion in der irischen Kultur der Jahrhundertwende: Moore, Shaw, Yeats and Joyce. *See* **19014**.

21618. BARTLETT, SALLY A. Fantasy as internal mimesis in Bernard Shaw's *Saint Joan*. Notes on Modern Irish Literature (3) 1991, 5–12.

21619. BERST, CHARLES A. *Pygmalion*: Shaw's spin on myth and Cinderella. (Bibl. 1995, 19253.) Rev. by Frederick P. W. McDowell in ELT (39:3) 1996, 379–80.

21620. BERTOLINI, JOHN A.   The playwrighting self of Bernard Shaw. (Bibl. 1995, 19254.) Rev. by David Schulz in JDTC (6:2) 1992, 150–2.

21621. CAVE, RICHARD ALLEN.   The city *versus* the village. *In* (pp. 281–96) **60**.

21622. DAVIS, TRACY C.   George Bernard Shaw and the Socialist theatre. (Bibl. 1995, 19262.) Rev. by Ted Bain in NETJ (6) 1995, 126–8; by Frederick P. W. McDowell in Shaw (16) 1996, 229–31.

21623. DEKKERS, ODIN.   Robertson and Shaw: an 'unreasonable friendship'. ELT (39:4) 1996, 431–49.

21624. DIETRICH, RICHARD FARR.   Bernard Shaw's novels: portraits of the artist as man and superman. Gainesville: Florida UP, 1996. pp. xviii, 203. Rev. by John Koontz in IndS (34:3) 1996, 67–9.

21625. GAINOR, J. ELLEN.   Bernard Shaw and the drama of imperialism. *In* (pp. 56–74) **83**.

21626. —— G.B.S. and the New Woman. NETJ (1) 1990, 1–17.

21627. —— Shaw's daughters: dramatic and narrative constructions of gender. (Bibl. 1993, 14957.) Rev. by Don B. Wilmeth in NETJ (4) 1993, 108–13.

21628. GAREBIAN, KEITH.   George Bernard Shaw and Christopher Newton: explorations of Shavian theatre. (Bibl. 1995, 19271.) Rev. by Richard Plant in CanTR (79/80) 1994, 154–7; by J. Percy Smith in TRC (15:1) 1994, 114–15.

21629. GIBBS, A. M.   'Giant brain … no heart': Bernard Shaw's reception in criticism and biography. IUR (26:1) 1996, 15–36.

21630. —— *Heartbreak House*: preludes of apocalypse. New York: Twayne; Toronto; Oxford: Maxwell Macmillan, 1994. pp. xvii, 149. (Twayne's masterwork studies, 136.) Rev. by John A. Bertolini in Shaw (16) 1996, 223–5.

21631. GRENE, NICHOLAS.   The Edwardian Shaw; or, The Modernist that never was. *In* (pp. 135–47) **41**.

21632. —— Shaw, Egypt and the Empire. *In* (pp. 201–7) **60**.

21633. HAVELY, CICELY PALSER.   Happy ever after? The ending of Shaw's *Pygmalion*. ERev (7:1) 1996, 26–9.

21634. HOLROYD, MICHAEL.   Bernard Shaw: vol. 3, 1918–1950: The lure of fantasy. (Bibl. 1995, 19274.) Rev. by Lucy McDiarmid in Irish Literary Supplement (11:1) 1992, 21–4.

21635. —— Bernard Shaw: vol. 4, 1950–1991: The last laugh. (Bibl. 1995, 19275.) Rev. by Don B. Wilmeth in NETJ (4) 1993, 108–13.

21636. JOYCE, STEVEN.   The worldbetterers: philanthropists in George Bernard Shaw's *Buoyant Billions* and Thomas Bernhard's *Der Weltverbesserer*. Comparatist (15) 1991, 78–85.

21637. KNOLL, ELISABETH.   Produktive Mißverständnisse: George Bernard Shaw und sein deutscher Übersetzer Siegfried Trebitsch. (Bibl. 1995, 19279.) Rev. by Britta Goerke in ZAA (44:4) 1996, 378–80.

21638. KOHL, NORBERT H.   Bernard Shaws viktorianisches Erbe. (Bibl. 1995, 19280.) Rev. by Britta Goerke in ZAA (44:3) 1996, 274–7.

21639. LAURENCE, DAN H. (ed.).   Theatrics. (Bibl. 1995, 19283.) Rev. by Richard Nickson in IndS (34:1/2) 1996, 39–41; by Elsie B. Adams in ELT (39:4) 1996, 501–4; by Lisbie Rae in CanTR (87) 1996, 70–1.

21640. —— LEARY, DANIEL J. (eds).   The complete prefaces: vol. 2, 1914–1929. (Bibl. 1995, 19285.) Rev. by Rhoda Nathan in IndS (34:1/2) 1996, 41–4.

21641. —— PETERS, MARGOT (eds). Unpublished Shaw. *See* **717**.

21642. NISCHIK, REINGARD M. Körpersprache im Drama: ein Beitrag zur Semiotik des Dramas. *See* **6828**.

21643. Ó H-EIDIRSCEOIL, SEÁN. A Shavian interlude. *In* (pp. 180–8) **49**.

21644. PETERS, SALLY. Bernard Shaw: the ascent of the superman. New Haven, CT; London: Yale UP, 1996. pp. xvi, 328. Rev. by Daniel Leary in IndS (34:1/2) 1996, 35–9; by A. N. Wilson in LRB (18:12) 1996, 11; by John Sutherland in TLS, 3 May 1996, 26.

21645. —— Ingrid Bergman, *Saint Joan*, and G.B.S. IndS (34:1/2) 1996, 9–11.

21646. PFEIFFER, JOHN R. A continuing checklist of Shaviana. Shaw (16) 1996, 233–45.

21647. PHARAND, MICHEL W. From Shavian warrior to Gallic waif: Bernard Shaw's *Saint Joan* on the French stage. TexPres (12) 1991, 75–81.

21648. PINKSY, MIKE. The mistaken mistake: permutations of the golem legend. JFA (7:2/3) 1996, 215–27.

21649. SARBU, ALADÁR. Romantic and modern: vision and form in Yeats, Shaw and Joyce. *In* (pp. 19–27) **112**.

21650. SHERBO, ARTHUR. Shaw's forgotten lecture (and other matters Shavian). *See* **1369**.

21651. —— Two overlooked reviews of Shaw. NQ (43:1) 1996, 55–6.

21652. SHINKUMA, KIYOSHI. Bernard Shaw kenkyu – engeki ron. (A study of Bernard Shaw: his plays.) Tokyo: Bunka Shobo Hakubunsha, 1996. pp. 290.

21653. SMITH, MEL. Ten letters on death, dying, and condolences. *See* **9264**.

21654. SOLOMONSON, MICHAEL. *Man and Superman*: the Shavianizing of Friedrich Nietzsche. IndS (34:3) 1996, 54–9.

21655. SYDENSTRICKER, GLÓRIA. The Shaw/Maeterlinck touch in Granville-Barker's drama. *See* **18286**.

21656. WEALES, GERALD. Shaw's American inheritors. JADT (6:2/3) 1994, 1–11.

21657. WEINTRAUB, STANLEY. Bernard Shaw: a guide to research. (Bibl. 1994, 14916.) Rev. by Don B. Wilmeth in NETJ (4) 1993, 108–13.

21658. —— 'The Hibernian School': Oscar Wilde and Bernard Shaw. *In* (pp. 169–79) **49**.

Robert Shaw (1927–)

21659. CORY, MARK. Comedic distance in Holocaust literature. *See* **16384**.

Wallace Shawn

21660. BREWER, GAY. He's still falling: Wallace Shawn's problem of morality. AmDr (2:1) 1992, 26–58.

21661. KING, W. D. Beyond 'a certain chain of reasoning': Wallace Shawn's *Aunt Dan and Lemon*. JADT (6:1) 1994, 61–78.

Edward R. F. Sheehan

21662. DEEDY, JOHN. A bittersweet romance – with words and Church: John Deedy interviews Edward R. F. Sheehan. Critic (46:4) 1992, 12–22.

Farhana Sheikh

21663. WILLIAMS, PATRICK.   Inter-nationalism: diaspora and gendered identity in Farhana Sheikh's *The Red Box*. JCL (30:1) 1995, 45–54.

Sam Shepard

21664. ABBOTT, MICHAEL.   The curse of the misbegotten: the wanton son in the plays of Eugene O'Neill and Sam Shepard. *See* **20784**.

21665. BASSAN, MAURICE.   The 'true West' of Sam Shepard and Stephen Crane. *See* **10753**.

21666. COCO, BILL.   The dramaturgy of the dream play: monologues by Breuer, Chaikin, Shepard. *In* (pp. 159–70) **119**.

21667. COHN, RUBY.   States of the artist: the plays of Edward Bond and Sam Shepard. *In* (pp. 169–87) **34**.

21668. KANE, LESLIE.   Dreamers and drunks: moral and social consciousness in Arthur Miller and Sam Shepard. *See* **20229**.

21669. LANIER, GREGORY W.   *True West?*: Sam Shepard's mythic misdirection. TexPres (12) 1991, 49–54.

21670. MCCARTHY, GERRY.   'Codes from a mixed-up machine': the disintegrating actor in Beckett, Shepard, and, surprisingly, Shakespeare. *In* (pp. 171–87) **119**.

21671. MCDONOUGH, CARLA J.   The politics of stage space: women and male identity in Sam Shepard's family plays. JDTC (9:2) 1995, 65–83.

21672. NISCHIK, REINGARD M.   Film as theme and technique in Sam Shepard's plays. ZAA (43:1) 1995, 60–76.

21673. PETERSON, JANE T.   Psychic geography in *True West*. NCL (23:1) 1993, 5–7.

21674. PORTER, LAURIN R.   Modern and postmodern wastelands: *Long Day's Journey into Night* and Shepard's *Buried Child. See* **20870**.

21675. RAMSEY, ALLEN.   The semiology of the imagination in *Fool for Love*. SHum (18:1) 1991, 78–81.

21676. ROGALUS, PAUL W.   Shepard's *Tooth of Crime*, O'Neill's *Emperor Jones*, and the contemporary American tragic hero. *See* **20874**.

21677. SCHVEY, HENRY I.   The master and his double: Eugene O'Neill and Sam Shepard. *See* **20876**.

21678. WOLTER, JÜRGEN C.   Sam Shepard in German-speaking countries: a classified bibliography. StAD (6:2) 1991, 195–225.

Delia Sherman

21679. ATTEBERY, BRIAN.   Gender, fantasy, and the authority of tradition. *See* **19636**.

R. C. Sherriff

21680. SONNEGA, WILLIAM.   Infiltrating the ranks: the silence of women in plays by First World War soldiers. TexPres (14) 1993, 91–5.

21681. TROUT, STEVEN.   'Glamorous melancholy': R. C. Sherriff's *Journey's End*. WLA (5:2) 1993, 1–19.

Carol Shields

21682. BURGESS, LINDA.   Reflecting women. Quote Unquote (32) 1996, 15–17. (Interview.)

21683. HAMMILL, FAYE.   Carol Shields's 'native genre' and the figure of the Canadian author. JCL (31:2) 1996, 87–99.

21684. LÉGER, BENOIT.   Traduction littéraire et polyphonie dans *Mrs Turner Cutting the Grass* de Carol Shields. StudCanL (20:1) 1995, 16–28.

Ted Shine

21685. LEBLANC, WHITNEY J.   An interview with Ted Shine. StAD (8:1) 1993, 29–43.

'Nevil Shute' (Nevil Shute Norway)

21686. ERISMAN, FRED.   The technological utopias of Thorstein Veblen and Nevil Shute. WebS (11:2) 1994, 117–26.

Nina Sibal

21687. CONDÉ, MARY.   Tourists and pilgrims in Nina Sibal's short story collection *The Secret Life of Gujjar Mal*. JSSE (24) 1995, 73–81.

Bapsi Sidhwa

21688. BHARUCHA, NILUFER E.   From behind a fine veil: a feminist reading of three Parsi novels. *See* **17257**.

Leslie Marmon Silko

21689. ADAMS, KATE.   Northamerican silences: history, identity, and witness in the poetry of Gloria Anzaldúa, Cherríe Moraga, and Leslie Marmon Silko. *In* (pp. 130–45) **59**.

21690. BARKER, ADELE MARIE .   Crossings. *In* (pp. 340–53) **23**.

21691. BOYNTON, VICTORIA.   Desire's revision: feminist appropriation of Native-American traditional stories. *See* **15926**.

21692. COHEN, ROBIN.   Landscape, story, and time as elements of reality in Silko's *Yellow Woman*. WebS (12:3) 1995, 141–7.

21693. COLTELLI, LAURA.   Leslie Marmon Silko's *Sacred Water*. SAIL (8:4) 1996, 21–9.

21694. —— Le *sacred waters* di Leslie Marmon Silko. RSAJ (4) 1993, 57–65.

21695. DONNELLY, DARIA.   *Almanac of the Dead* di Leslie Silko: un intrattenimento rivoluzionario. Àcoma (5) 1995, 58–66.

21696. GROSS, KONRAD.   Mündliches Wissen in Leslie Silkos *Storyteller*. *In* (pp. 217–27) **73**.

21697. HERMANN, ELISABETH.   Elemente mündlichen Erzählens im erzählerischen Werk von Leslie Marmon Silko und Paula Gunn Allen. *In* (pp. 203–15) **73**.

21698. HOCHBRUCK, WOLFGANG.   'I have spoken': fictional 'orality' in indigenous fiction. *See* **15853**.

21699. JASKOSKI, HELEN.   Thinking woman's children and the bomb. *In* (pp. 159–76) **77**.

21700. LYNCH, TOM.   What Josiah said: Uncle Josiah's role in *Ceremony*. NDQ (63:2) 1996, 138–52.

21701. MARIANI, GIORGIO.   Technology and storytelling: Leslie Silko's *Ceremony* as world epic. *In* (pp. 451–8) **117**.

21702. MORRIS, ROMA HEILLIG.   The whole story: nature, healing, and narrative in the Native-American wisdom tradition. LitMed (15:1) 1996, 94–111.

21703. RAINWATER, CATHERINE. The semiotics of dwelling in Leslie Marmon Silko's *Ceremony*. AJSem (9:3) 1992, 219–40.

21704. RUOFF, A. LaVONNE BROWN. Ritual and renewal: Keres traditions in the short fiction of Leslie Silko. *In* (pp. 167–89) **3**.

21705. RUPPERT, JAMES. Mediation in contemporary Native-American writing. *See* **17626**.

21706. SECCO, ANNA. The search for origins through storytelling in Native-American literature: Momaday, Silko, Erdrich. *See* **17628**.

21707. STETSENKO, EKATERINA . Retelling the legends. *In* (pp. 327–39) **23**.

21708. WALLACE, KAREN L. Liminality and myth in Native-American fiction: *Ceremony* and *The Ancient Child*. *See* **20289**.

Ron Silliman

21709. LAVENDER, WILLIAM. Disappearance of theory, appearance of praxis: Ron Silliman, L=A=N=G=U=A=G=E, and the essay. *See* **14980**.

Alan Sillitoe

21710. HUTCHINGS, WILLIAM. Proletarian Byronism: Alan Sillitoe and the Romantic tradition. *In* (pp. 83–112) **28**.

Clifford D. Simak

21711. DeMARR, MARY JEAN. Clifford D. Simak's use of the Midwest in science fiction. Midamerica (22) 1995, 108–21.

Charles Simic

21712. HEANEY, SEAMUS. Shorts for Simic. Agni (44) 1996, 202–8.

21713. LIMEHOUSE, CAPERS; SEXTON, MEGAN. Visionary sceptic: an interview with Charles Simic. Atlanta Review (2:1) 1995, 23–36.

21714. SIMIC, CHARLES. New York days, 1958–1964. GetR (9:2) 1996, 373–84.

21715. WRIGHT, CHARLES. Improvisations: narrative of the image (a correspondence with Charles Simic). GetR (8:1) 1995, 9–21.

Dan Simmons

21716. WEBB, JANEEN. Simmons and Powers: postmodernism to postromanticism. *In* (pp. 139–46) **127**.

Neil Simon

21717. BRYER, JACKSON R. An interview with Neil Simon. StAD (6:2) 1991, 153–76.

21718. —— Neil Simon. *In* (pp. 221–40) **85**.

21719. SIMON, NEIL. Rewrites: a memoir. New York: Simon & Schuster, 1996. pp. 397, (plates) 16.

Louis Simpson

21720. MORAN, RONALD. Louis Simpson: an interview. FiveP (1:1) 1996, 45–63.

Bertrand William Sinclair (1878–)

21721. LANE, RICHARD. British Columbia's war of two worlds:

the birth of the modern age in Bertrand Sinclair's fiction. JCL (31:1) 1996, 71–81.

Clive Sinclair

21722. CHEYETTE, BRYAN.   Philip Roth and Clive Sinclair: representations of an 'imaginary homeland' in postwar British and American-Jewish literature. *In* (pp. 355–73) **34**.

Iain Sinclair

21723. HLAVIZNA, IVO.   Within an ontological whirl: the London carnival of Iain Sinclair. Litteraria Pragensia (3:6) 1993, 70–7.

Upton Sinclair

21724. GROVER, DORYS CROW.   Upton Sinclair: never forgotten. Midamerica (22) 1995, 41–9.

C. H. Sisson

21725. TINKLER-VILLANI, VALERIA.   The poetry of Hell and the poetry of Paradise: food for thought for translators, critics, poets and other readers. *See* **3209**.

The Sitwells

21726. LEDBETTER, KATHRYN.   Battles for Modernism and *Wheels*. *See* **1304**.

Edith Sitwell

21727. RITCHIE, NEIL.   Footnote to *Façade*. BC (45:2) 1996, 261–2. (Note 557.)

Sacheverell Sitwell

21728. BRADFORD, SARAH.   Splendours and miseries: a life of Sacheverell Sitwell. (Bibl. 1995, 19363.) Rev. by Michael Shelden in BkW, 23 Jan. 1994, 8–9.

Peter Skrzynecki

21729. BALLYN, SUSAN.   The voice of the other: an approach to migrant writing in Australia. *See* **16691**.

Elizabeth Smart

21730. HORNE, DEE.   Elizabeth Smart's novel-journal. StudCanL (16:2) 1991/92, 128–46.

Jane Smiley

21731. BAKERMAN, JANE S.   'The gleaming obsidian shard': Jane Smiley's *A Thousand Acres*. Midamerica (19) 1992, 127–37.
21732. HOLSTAD, SCOTT C.   Jane Smiley's *A Thousand Acres*. NCL (26:2) 1996, 5–6.
21733. ROZGA, MARGARET.   Sister in a quest – *Sister Carrie* and *A Thousand Acres*: the search for identity in gendered territory. *See* **17413**.
21734. WEEN, LORI.   Family sagas of the Americas: *Los Sangurimas* and *A Thousand Acres*. Comparatist (20) 1996, 111–25.

A. J. M. Smith

21735. COMPTON, ANNE.   A. J. M. Smith: Canadian metaphysical. Toronto: ECW Press, 1994. pp. 262. (Cf. bibl. 1989, 11154.) Rev. by Deborah Bowen in JCP (11) 1996, 179–82; by George L. Parker in ESCan (22:3) 1996, 355–7.

21736. PRECOSKY, DON.   'Like that old king': A. J. M. Smith in Vagabondia. ECanW (58) 1996, 176–84.

Anna Deavere Smith

21737. LYONS, CHARLES R.; LYONS, JAMES C.   Anna Deavere Smith: perspectives on her performance within the context of critical theory. *See* **15607**.

Basil Smith

21738. NELSON, DALE J.   Russell Kirk and Basil Smith. *See* **19363**.

Charlie Smith (1947–)

21739. HIERS, JOHN T.   Charlie Smith's elephant graveyard. NCL (24:1) 1994, 3–4.

Dave Smith ('Smith Cornwell')

21740. SUAREZ, ERNEST.   An interview with Dave Smith. ConLit (37:3) 1996, 349–69.

Dodie Smith

21741. GROVE, VALERIE.   Dear Dodie: the life of Dodie Smith. London: Chatto & Windus, 1996. pp. xi, 339, (plates) 8. Rev. by Claire Harman in TLS, 2 Feb. 1996, 27.

21742. —— (introd.).   I capture the castle. London: Virago Press, 1996. pp. xi, 342. (Virago modern classics, 410.)

Iain Crichton Smith

21743. BERTON, JEAN.   Le degré d'historicité dans *Consider the Lilies* de Iain Crichton Smith. Études Écossaises (1) 1992, 323–31.

Lee Smith

21744. MANNING, MICHELLE.   The Southern voice of Lee Smith: an annotated bibliography. BB (53:2) 1996, 161–72.

21745. PERKINS, JAMES A.   Hallucination, allusions and illusions in *The Last Day the Dogbushes Bloomed*. SoQ (34:2) 1996, 81–6.

21746. REILLY, ROSALIND B.   *Oral History*: the enchanted circle of narrative and dream. SoLJ (23:1) 1990, 79–92.

21747. WYMARD, ELLIE.   The Devil's dream: Ellie Wymard interviews Lee Smith. Critic (48:2) 1993, 44–51.

Lillian Smith

21748. GLADNEY, MARGARET ROSE (ed.).   How am I to be heard? Letters of Lillian Smith. Chapel Hill; London: North Carolina UP, 1993. pp. xx, 384. (Gender and American culture.) Rev. by Emily Toth in BkW, 22 Aug. 1993, 3, 12.

Martin Cruz Smith ('Simon Quinn', 'Nick Carter')

21749. JASKOSKI, HELEN.   Thinking woman's children and the bomb. *In* (pp. 159–76) **77**.

Pauline Smith

21750. PEREIRA, ERNEST (ed.).   The unknown Pauline Smith: unpublished and out of print stories, diaries and other prose writings (including her Arnold Bennett memoir). (Bibl. 1994, 14970.) Rev. by Michael Cosser in EngA (23:2) 1996, 85–102.

21751. TORLESSE, ANN; SCHOLTEN, SHEILA (eds).   Pauline Smith letters. EngA (23:2) 1996, 1–84.

Ray Smith

21752. ZICHY, FRANCIS.   'Aestheticism with guts': the neorealism of Ray Smith's *A Night at the Opera*. ECanW (58) 1996, 206–28.

Stevie Smith

21753. LASSNER, PHYLLIS.   'The milk of our mother's kindness has ceased to flow': Virginia Woolf, Stevie Smith, and the representation of the Jew. *In* (pp. 129–44) **5**.

21754. PICCHIONI, PAOLA.   Eco come figura retorica e mitologica in *Loin de l'Être* di Stevie Smith. *See* **2447**.

Wilbur Smith

21755. STOTESBURY, JOHN A.   Popularizing late-apartheid South Africa: an interview with Wilbur Smith. Teaching & Learning (2) 1996, 73–88.

Steve Sneyd

21756. MINTZ, CATHERINE.   Poetry, poets, and the rest of the world: an interview with Steve Sneyd. Foundation (63) 1995, 68–73.

W. D. Snodgrass

21757. TURCO, LEWIS.   The poetics of W. D. Snodgrass. HC (30:3) 1993, 1–9.

21758. WEES, COREEN DWYER.   The strength of departure in Snodgrass's *Leaving the Motel*. NCL (24:2) 1994, 3–4.

C. P. Snow

21759. PORTER, ROY.   The two cultures revisited. Boundary 2 (23:2) 1996, 1–17.

21760. TALLIS, RAYMOND.   Newton's sleep: 2, The eunuch at the orgy. *See* **15795**.

Gary Snyder

21761. FOLSOM, ED.   Gary Snyder's descent to Turtle Island: searching for fossil love. *In* (pp. 217–36) **25**.

21762. HAMALIAN, LEO.   Beyond the paleface: D. H. Lawrence and Gary Snyder. *See* **19538**.

21763. HÖNNIGHAUSEN, LOTHAR.   Ecopoetics: on poetological poems by Gary Snyder and Wendell Berry. *See* **16422**.

21764. MURPHY, PATRICK D.   Penance or perception: spirituality and land in the poetry of Gary Snyder and Wendell Berry. *In* (pp. 237–49) **25**.

Gustaf Sobin

21765. ENGLISH, ZOË.   Essence, absence, and Sobin's *Venus Blue*. Talisman (10) 1993, 60–2.

21766. FOSTER, EDWARD.   An interview with Gustaf Sobin. Talisman (10) 1993, 26–40.

21767. JANUZZI, MARISA.   Luminous cargo: Gustaf Sobin, *A Portrait of the Self as Instrument of its Syllables*. Talisman (10) 1993, 69–72.

21768. LUTKUS, TONY.   On Gustaf Sobin. Talisman (10) 1993, 66–8.

21769. MA, MING-QIAN.   The dialectic of 'saying so little': Gustaf Sobin's poetics of 'toward'. Talisman (10) 1993, 54–9.

21770. NASH, SUSAN SMITH.   Gustaf Sobin and a consolation of *Imagerie*. Talisman (10) 1993, 52–3.

21771. TRITICA, JOHN.   At each instant's extremity: the tentative edges of a practice. Talisman (10) 1993, 63–5.

Roland Sodowsky

21772. AL-GHALITH, ASAD.   A paradigm of power relations: Roland Sodowsky's Nigerian *Squashgirl*. NCL (23:2) 1993, 9–10.

'Somerville and Ross'
(Edith Somerville and Violet Martin)

21773. HUGHES, CLAIR.   'Hound voices': the Big House in three novels by Anglo-Irish women writers. *In* (pp. 349–55) **49**.

John Sommerfield

21774. MCKENNA, BRIAN.   The British Communist novel of the 1930s and 1940s: a 'party of equals'? (And does that matter?) *See* **18157**.

Cathy Song

21775. MORSE, JONATHAN.   Some of the things we mean when we say 'New England'. *See* **2184**.

Susan Sontag

21776. FRANK, MARCIE.   The critic as performance artist: Susan Sontag's writing and gay culture. *In* (pp. 173–84) **12**.

21777. ROLLYSON, CARL.   *AIDS and Its Metaphors*: Susan Sontag and gay rage. PCR (7:2) 1996, 3–8.

Charles Hamilton Sorley

21778. POWELL, ANNE.   Two centenary salutes: Charles Hamilton Sorley and Robert Graves. *See* **18301**.

Gilbert Sorrentino

21779. BUZZARD, SHARON.   The mirror of the text: reading Gilbert Sorrentino's *Mulligan Stew*. Reader (26) 1991, 65–77.

21780. MONTRESSOR, JAYE BERMAN.   The artist as accidental tourist in Gilbert Sorrentino's *Blue Pastoral*. SAH (3:1) 1994, 95–103.

Ellease Southerland

21781. BROOKHART, MARY HUGHES. Spiritual daughters of the Black American South. *In* (pp. 125–39) **32**.

Wole Soyinka

21782. BISSIRI, AMADOU. Aspects of Africanness in August Wilson's drama: reading *The Piano Lesson* through Wole Soyinka's drama. AAR (30:1) 1996, 99–113.

21783. CONRADIE, P. J. Debates surrounding an approach to African tragedy. *See* **13567**.

21784. GALLE, ETIENNE. Soyinka's twisted circle: a return with a difference. *In* (pp. 77–84) **102**.

21785. GIBBS, JAMES. 'Marshal Ky of African culture' or 'heir to the tradition'? Wole Soyinka's position on his return to Nigeria in 1960. *In* (pp. 85–99) **102**.

21786. LAYIWOLA, DELE. The philosophy of Wole Soyinka's art. JDTC (10:2) 1996, 19–42.

21787. OJAIDE, TANURE. The poetry of Wole Soyinka. (Bibl. 1995, 19408.) Rev. by Michael Thorpe in WLT (69:4) 1995, 858.

21788. OMOTOSO, KOLE. Achebe or Soyinka? A study in contrasts. *See* **15858**.

21789. QUAYSON, ATO. Wole Soyinka and autobiography as political unconscious. JCL (31:2) 1996, 19–32.

21790. SOYINKA, WOLE. Ibadan: the Penkelemes years: a memoir, 1946–1965. (Bibl. 1995, 19409.) Rev. by James Gibbs in WLT (69:2) 1995, 420.

21791. THOMSON, JEFF. The politics of the shuttle: Wole Soyinka's poetic space. RAL (27:2) 1996, 94–101.

21792. TIDJANI-SERPOS, NOURÉINI. The postcolonial condition: the archeology of African knowledge: from the feat of Ogun and Sango to the postcolonial creativity of Obatala. RAL (27:1) 1996, 3–18.

Muriel Spark

21793. CRAIG, CAIRNS. Doubtful imaginings: the sceptical art of Muriel Spark. Études Écossaises (2) 1993, 63–78.

21794. EDGECOMBE, RODNEY STENNING. Muriel Spark, Cardinal Newman and an aphorism in *Memento Mori*. *See* **11966**.

21795. FELTON, SHARON. Portraits of the artists as young defiers: James Joyce and Muriel Spark. *See* **19083**.

21796. HYNES, JOSEPH (ed.). Critical essays on Muriel Spark. (Bibl. 1992, 16261.) Rev. by Joan Leonard in SSL (29) 1996, 324–7.

21797. McCULLOCH, MARGERY PALMER. Calvinism and narrative form in *The Prime of Miss Jean Brodie*. ERev (6:1) 1995, 19–22.

21798. MACLACHLAN, CHRISTOPHER. Muriel Spark and gothic. *In* (pp. 125–44) **115**.

21799. SPARK, MURIEL. Curriculum vitae: autobiography. (Bibl. 1995, 19413.) Boston, MA: Houghton Mifflin, 1993. Rev. by Nina King in BkW, 6 June 1996, 5; by X. J. Kennedy in GetR (7:2) 1994, 289–303.

Eulalie Spence (1884–1981)

21800. GILES, FREDA SCOTT. Willis Richardson and Eulalie Spence: dramatic voices of the Harlem renaissance. *See* **21359**.

Bernard Spencer

21801. BOLTON, JONATHAN. 'The historian with his spade': landscape and historical continuity in the poetry of Bernard Spencer. JML (19:2) 1995, 273–87.

Elizabeth Spencer

21802. DALE, CORINNE H.; GIRARD, ANNE-MARIE; PAINE, J. H. E. An interview with Elizabeth Spencer. JSSE (18) 1992, 13–34.
21803. PRENSHAW, PEGGY WHITMAN. The persisting South in the fiction of Elizabeth Spencer. JSSE (18) 1992, 35–42.

Art Spiegelman

21804. DOHERTY, THOMAS. Art Spiegelman's *Maus*: graphic art and the Holocaust. AL (68:1) 1996, 69–84.
21805. GORDON, JOAN. Surviving the survivor: Art Spiegelman's *Maus*. JFA (5:2) 1992, 81–9.
21806. MA, SHENG-MEI. *The Great Dictator* and *Maus*: 'the comical' before and after the Holocaust. *See* **13939**.

Mickey Spillane

21807. SILET, CHARLES L. P. The first angry White male: Mickey Spillane's Mike Hammer. AD (29:2) 1996, 194–9.
21808. —— I, Mickey Spillane: an interview with Mike Hammer's creator. AD (29:2) 1996, 200–1.
21809. WALLE, ALF H. Hack writing *vs* belle letters [*sic*]: the strategic implications of literary achievement. *See* **14757**.

H. de Vere Stacpoole

21810. HARDIN, RICHARD F. The man who wrote *The Blue Lagoon*: Stacpoole's pastoral center. ELT (39:2) 1996, 205–20.

Jean Stafford

21811. GOODMAN, CHARLOTTE MARGOLIS. Jean Stafford: the savage heart. (Bibl. 1991, 15428.) Rev. by Evelyn Toynton in Salmagundi (92) 1991, 238–44.
21812. HULBERT, ANN. The interior castle: the art and life of Jean Stafford. (Bibl. 1995, 19417.) Rev. by Ingrid Winther Scobie in AHR (98:5) 1993, 1695–6.
21813. MARIANI, PAUL. Robert Lowell and Jean Stafford. *See* **19849**.
21814. ROBINSON, FORREST G. Innocence, irony and art: notes on Jean Stafford's *The Mountain Lion*. SoQ (34:1) 1995, 63–9.

William Stafford

21815. ANDERSON, ERLAND G. Stafford's *Ask Me*. Exp (54:3) 1996, 175–7.
21816. —— Stafford's *Father and Son*. Exp (54:2) 1996, 105–7.
21817. ANDREWS, TOM (ed.). On William Stafford: the worth of local things. (Bibl. 1993, 15081.) Rev. by John Kennedy in AR (53:3) 1995, 496.
21818. HOLDEN, JONATHAN. Remembering William Stafford. CimR (114) 1996, 118–23.
21819. RUGGIERI, HELEN. Stafford's *Alexis Christa Von Hartmann*. Exp (55:1) 1996, 45–7.

21820. STAFFORD, WILLIAM.   The writing of *Bees*. WD (72:2) 1992, 28–9.

Donald E. Stanford (1913–)

21821. MIDDLETON, DAVID.   The classic mind restored: the achievement of Donald Stanford – poet, editor, mentor. *In* (pp. 192–211) **79**.

Olaf Stapledon

21822. CROSSLEY, ROBERT.   Olaf Stapledon: speaking for the future. (Bibl. 1995, 19420.) Rev. by Paul Marrow in Foundation (65) 1995, 123–5; by Donald M. Hassler in Extrapolation (37:1) 1996, 96–7.

Barrie Stavis

21823. GOLDSTEIN, EZRA.   An interview with Barrie Stavis. StAD (6:1) 1991, 71–113.

21824. LARNER, DANIEL.   Anywhere but home: the life and work of Barrie Stavis. AmDr (4:1) 1994, 39–61.

21825. —— An interview with Barrie Stavis. AmDr (4:1) 1994, 62–91.

Christina Stead

21826. BLAKE, ANN.   An ocean of story: the novels of Christina Stead. CritS (6:1) 1994, 118–24.

21827. KAPLAN, CORA.   Fictions of feminism: figuring the maternal. *See* **15546**.

21828. ROWLEY, HAZEL.   Christina Stead: a biography. (Bibl. 1994, 15028.) New York: Henry Holt, 1994. Rev. by Elizabeth Ward in BkW, 2 Oct. 1994, 4.

Flora Annie Steel

21829. PAXTON, NANCY L.   Mobilizing chivalry: rape in Flora Annie Steel's *On the Face of the Waters* (1896) and other British novels about the Indian uprising of 1857. *In* (pp. 247–75) **75**.

Max Steele

21830. JENKINS, JOE.   A talk with Max Steele. Frank (15) 1996, 77–82.

Timothy Steele

21831. SHEEHY, DONALD G.   Measure for measure: the Frostian classicism of Timothy Steele. *See* **18069**.

John Steffler

21832. MCCONNELL, KATHLEEN.   Textile tropes in *The Afterlife of George Cartwright*. *See* **2422**.

Wallace Stegner

21833. BENSON, JACKSON J.   A friendship with consequences: Robert Frost and Wallace Stegner. *See* **18005**.

21834. —— Wallace Stegner: his life and work. New York: Viking, 1996. pp. xx, 472, (plates) 8. Rev. by Michael Shelden in BkW, 22 Dec. 1996, 4–5.

21835. COOK-LYNN, ELIZABETH.   *Why I Can't Read Wallace Stegner* and other essays: a tribal voice. Madison; London: Wisconsin UP, 1996. pp. xiv, 158.

21836.   MAGUIRE, JAMES H.   *Cœur d'Alene* and *Angle of Repose*: justice and the quality of mercy. *See* **11225**.

21837.   NELSON, NANCY OWEN.   Land lessons in an 'unhistoried' West: Wallace Stegner's California. *In* (pp. 160–76) **108**.

21838.   OCCHINO, JANET.   Inside out: the West of Wallace Stegner's *Angle of Repose*. ANQ (9:3) 1996, 30–9.

21839.   RANKIN, CHARLES E. (ed.).   Wallace Stegner: man and writer. Foreword by Stewart L. Udall. Albuquerque: New Mexico UP, 1996. pp. xvi, 280.

21840.   STEGNER, PAGE; STEGNER, MARY (eds).   The geography of hope: a tribute to Wallace Stegner. San Francisco, CA: Sierra Club, 1996. pp. 140.

21841.   STEGNER, WALLACE; ETULAIN, RICHARD W.   Conversations with Wallace Stegner on Western history and literature. (Cf. bibl. 1987, 12568.) Salt Lake City: Utah UP, 1990. pp. xxix, 207. (Revised ed.: first ed. 1983.) Rev. by Robert C. Steensma in WebS (8:1) 1991, 99–100.

Gertrude Stein

21842.   ABRAHAM, JULIE.   'We are Americans': Gertrude, *Brewsie and Willie*. MFS (42:3) 1996, 508–27.

21843.   ALBRINCK, MEG.   'How can a sister see Saint Therese suitably': difficulties in staging Gertrude Stein's *Four Saints in Three Acts*. WS (25:1) 1995, 1–22.

21844.   ANASTAS, BENJAMIN.   Three ways of being modern: the 'Lost Generation' Trilogy by James R. Mellow. *See* **17832**.

21845.   BERNSTEIN, CHARLES.   Stein's identity. MFS (42:3) 1996, 485–8.

21846.   BERRY, ELLEN E.   Curved thought and textual wandering: Gertrude Stein's postmodernism. (Bibl. 1995, 19431.) Rev. by Charles Caramello in MFS (40:1) 1994, 149–52.

21847.   BLACKMER, CORINNE E.   Selling taboo subjects: the literary commerce of Gertrude Stein and Carl Van Vechten. *In* (pp. 221–52) **67**.

21848.   BROGAN, JACQUELINE VAUGHT.   Parody or parity? A brief note on Gertrude Stein and *For Whom the Bell Tolls*. *See* **18596**.

21849.   BUCKHAM, DAVID.   The art of repetition: Gertrude Stein's *Melanctha*. Bracket (1) 1995, 55–69.

21850.   BURNS, EDWARD M.; DYDO, ULLA E.; RICE, WILLIAM (eds). The letters of Gertrude Stein and Thornton Wilder. New Haven, CT; London: Yale UP, 1996. pp. xxx, 452. (Henry McBride series in Modernism and modernity.)

21851.   CARAMELLO, CHARLES.   Henry James, Gertrude Stein, and the biographical act. *See* **11581**.

21852.   CONRAD, BRYCE.   Gertrude Stein in the American marketplace. JML (19:2) 1995, 215–33.

21853.   CURNUTT, KIRK.   Parody and pedagogy: teaching style, voice, and authorial intent in the works of Gertrude Stein. ColLit (23:2) 1996, 1–24.

21854.   DAMON, MARIA.   Gertrude Stein's Jewishness, Jewish social scientists, and the 'Jewish question'. MFS (42:3) 1996, 489–506.

21855.   DEKOVEN, MARIANNE.   Introduction: transformations of Gertrude Stein. MFS (42:3) 1996, 469–83.

21856. DICKIE, MARGARET. Recovering the repression in Stein's erotic poetry. *In* (pp. 3–25) **39**.

21857. FIFER, ELIZABETH. Rescued readings: a reconstruction of Gertrude Stein's difficult texts. (Bibl. 1995, 19438.) Rev. by Charles Caramello in MFS (40:1) 1994, 149–52.

21858. FRIEDL, HERWIG. Ontography and ontology: Gertrude Stein writing and thinking. Amst (41:4) 1996, 575–91.

21859. GUERRA DE LA TORRE, JUANA T. Fractals in Gertrude Stein's 'word-system': natural reality and/or verbal reality. *See* **2635**.

21860. HOFFMANN, MONIKA. Gertrude Steins Autobiographien: *The Autobiography of Alice B. Toklas* und *Everybody's Autobiography*. New York; Frankfurt; Bern; Paris: Lang, 1992. pp. 346. (Mainzer Studien zur Amerikanistik, 25.) Rev. by Franziska Gygax in Amst (41:3) 1996, 521–2.

21861. HOVEY, JAIME. Sapphic primitivism in Gertrude Stein's *Q.E.D.* MFS (42:3) 1996, 547–68.

21862. JOHNSTON, GEORGIA. Narratologies of pleasure: Gertrude Stein's *The Autobiography of Alice B. Toklas*. MFS (42:3) 1996, 590–606.

21863. LOEFFELHOLZ, MARY. History as conjugation: Stein's *Stanzas in Meditation* and the literary history of the Modernist long poem. *In* (pp. 26–42) **39**.

21864. MIX, DEBORAH M. Gertrude Stein: a selected bibliography. MFS (42:3) 1996, 661–80.

21865. MONROE, JONATHAN. Syntextural investigations. *See* **15649**.

21866. PERKINS, PRISCILLA. 'A little body with a very large head': composition, psychopathology, and the making of Stein's normal self. MFS (42:3) 1996, 529–46.

21867. PIERCE, CONSTANCE. Gertrude Stein and her thoroughly modern *protégé*. *See* **16971**.

21868. POST, ROBERT M. 'An audience is an audience': Gertrude Stein addresses the five hundred. KenR (13:1/2) 1996, 71–83.

21869. REHLING, NICOLA. Taking patriarchy out of poetry: eroticism and subversion in Gertrude Stein's *Lifting Belly*. Gramma (4) 1996, 77–87.

21870. ROHR, SUSANNE. 'Everybody sees, and everybody says they do': another guess at Gertrude Stein's *Blood on the Dining-Room Floor*. Amst (41:4) 1996, 593–602.

21871. RUDDICK, LISA. Stein and cultural criticism in the nineties. *See* **15731**.

21872. RUST, MARTHA DANA. Stop the world, I want to get off! Identity and circularity in Gertrude Stein's *The World Is Round*. *See* **2700**.

21873. SCHILLER, GEORG. Symbolische Erfahrung und Sprache im Werk von Gertrude Stein. New York; Frankfurt; Bern; Paris: Lang, 1996. pp. viii, 222. (Düsseldorfer Beiträge aus Anglistik und Amerikanistik, 5.) Rev. by Monika Hoffmann in Amst (41:4) 1996, 715–17.

21874. SHAW, PATRICK W. Victorian rules and Left Bank rebellion: Willa Cather and Gertrude Stein. *See* **16839**.

21875. SMEDMAN, LORNA J. 'Cousin to cooning': relation, difference, and racialized language in Stein's nonrepresentational texts. *See* **2709**.

21876. SOUHAMI, DIANA. Gertrude and Alice. (Bibl. 1992, 16313.) Rev. by Anne Charles in NWSAJ (5:2) 1993, 270–3.

21877. VAN DUSEN, WANDA. Portrait of a national fetish: Gertrude Stein's *Introduction to the Speeches of Maréchal Pétain* (1942). Modernism/Modernity (3:3) 1996, 69–92.

21878. VETSCH, FLORIAN.   Desultory correspondence: an interview with Paul Bowles on Gertrude Stein. *See* **16526**.

21879. WAGNER-MARTIN, LINDA.   Favored strangers: Gertrude Stein and her family. (Bibl. 1995, 19461.) Rev. by Marianne DeKoven in AL (68:4) 1996, 862–4; by Christopher Benfey in TLS, 2 Feb. 1996, 25–6.

John Steinbeck

21880. ARISS, BRUCE.   Inside Cannery Row: sketches from the Steinbeck era in words and pictures. Ed. by Laurie Cohn and Mike Witter. San Francisco, CA: Lexikos, 1988. pp. viii, 119. Rev. by Beverly K. Simpson in SteiQ (23:1/2) 1990, 46–9.

21881. BAINES, LAWRENCE.   From page to screen: when a novel is interpreted for film, what gets lost in the translation? *See* **10449**.

21882. BELNAREK, JANET R. DALY.   An historian's view of *The Grapes of Wrath*. UDR (23:3) 1996, 83–8.

21883. BENSON, JACKSON J.   Looking for Steinbeck's ghost. (Bibl. 1993, 15103.) Rev. by John H. Timmerman in SteiQ (23:1/2) 1990, 51–3.

21884. —— Steinbeck's *Cannery Row*: a reconsideration. Muncie, IN: Steinbeck Research Inst., Ball State Univ., 1991. pp. 29. (Steinbeck essays, 4.) Rev. by John H. Timmerman in SteiQ (25:1/2) 1992, 62–3.

21885. —— (ed.).   The short novels of John Steinbeck: critical essays with a checklist to Steinbeck criticism. Durham, NC; London: Duke UP, 1990. pp. x, 349. Rev. by Christopher S. Busch in SteiQ (24:3/4) 1991, 108–11.

21886. BEYER, PRESTON (comp.).   Essays on collecting John Steinbeck books. *See* **455**.

21887. BLOOM, HAROLD (ed.).   John Steinbeck. New York: Chelsea House, 1987. pp. viii, 172. (Modern critical views.) Rev. by Barbara Heavilin in SteiQ (23:3/4) 1990, 96–102.

21888. —— John Steinbeck's *Of Mice and Men*. New York: Chelsea House, 1996. pp. 64. (Bloom's notes.)

21889. —— John Steinbeck's *The Grapes of Wrath*. New York: Chelsea House, 1996. pp. 72. (Bloom's notes.)

21890. BURNS, WAYNE.   Triumph of the monster: a study of Carolyn Chute's *Merry Men* in relation to Steinbeck's *The Grapes of Wrath*. *See* **16941**.

21891. BUSCH, CHRISTOPHER S.   A historical bibliographical survey of the Steinbeck Monograph Series (1971–91) and the Steinbeck Essay Series (1986–91). *See* **136**.

21892. —— Longing for the lost frontier: Steinbeck's vision of cultural decline in *The White Quail* and *The Chrysanthemums*. SteiQ (26:3/4) 1993, 81–90.

21893. —— Steinbeck's *The Wayward Bus*: an affirmation of the Frontier myth. SteiQ (25:3/4) 1992, 98–108.

21894. COERS, DONALD V.   John Steinbeck as propagandist: *The Moon Is Down* goes to war. (Bibl. 1992, 16315.) Rev. by John Ditsky in SteiQ (25:1/2) 1992, 52–3; by Donald R. Noble in SAtlR (61:1) 1996, 152–6.

21895. DeMOTT, ROBERT.   *East of Eden*: a bibliographical checklist. SteiQ (25:1/2) 1992, 14–28.

21896. —— 'A truly American book': pressing *The Grapes of Wrath*. *In* (pp. 187–225) **7**.

21897. —— (ed.).   Working days: the journals of *The Grapes of Wrath*, 1938–1941. (Bibl. 1991, 15454.) Rev. by Barbara Heavilin in SteiQ (23:1/2) 1990, 42–4.
21898. DeMott, Robert (introd.).   The grapes of wrath. London; New York: Penguin, 1992. pp. l, 619. (Penguin twentieth-century classics.)
21899. Dewey, Joseph.   'There was a seedy grandeur about the man': rebirth and recovery in *Travels with Charley*. SteiQ (24:1/2) 1991, 22–30.
21900. Dircks, Phyllis T.   Steinbeck's statement on the inner –chapters of *The Grapes of Wrath*. SteiQ (24:3/4) 1991, 86–94.
21901. Ditsky, John.   The Devil in music: unheard themes in Steinbeck's fiction. SteiQ (25:3/4) 1992, 80–6.
21902. —— John Steinbeck – yesterday, today, and tomorrow. SteiQ (23:1/2) 1990, 5–16.
21903. —— Steinbeck and Albee: affection, admiration, affinity. *See* **15903**.
21904. —— (ed.).   Critical essays on Steinbeck's *The Grapes of Wrath*. Boston, MA: G. K. Hall, 1989. pp. viii, 168. (Critical essays on American literature.) Rev. by Thomas Fensch in SteiQ (23:3/4) 1990, 105–8.
21905. Enea, Sparky.   With Steinbeck in the Sea of Cortez: a memoir of the Steinbeck/Ricketts expedition as told to Audry Lynch. Los Osos, CA: Sand River, 1991. pp. v, 82. Rev. by Maurice Dunbar in SteiQ (25:1/2) 1992, 53–4.
21906. French, Warren.   John Steinbeck's fiction revisited. (Bibl. 1994, 15053.) Rev. by Charles G. Masinton in AmS (36:2) 1995, 213.
21907. —— John Steinbeck's nonfiction revisited. New York: Twayne; London: Prentice Hall, 1996. pp. xviii, 148. (Twayne's US authors, 662.)
21908. Gaither, Gloria.   John Steinbeck: from the tidal pool to the stars: connectedness, is-thinking, and breaking through – a reconsideration. SteiQ (25:1/2) 1992, 42–52.
21909. Gladstein, Mimi R.   *Cannery Row*: a male world and the female reader. SteiQ (25:3/4) 1992, 87–97.
21910. —— The strong female principle of good – or evil: the women of *East of Eden*. SteiQ (24:1/2) 1991, 30–40.
21911. Hadella, Charlotte.   New critical approaches to Steinbeck's fiction: an introduction. SteiQ (25:3/4) 1992, 78–9.
21912. Harmon, Robert B.   John Steinbeck: an annotated guide to biographical sources. Lanham, MD; London: Scarecrow Press, 1996. pp. xviii, 288.
21913. —— Early, John F. (comps).   *The Grapes of Wrath*: a fifty-year bibliographic survey. San Jose, CA: Steinbeck Research Center, San Jose State Univ., 1990. pp. ix, 325. Rev. by Dean H. Keller in SteiQ (24:1/2) 1991, 50.
21914. Hayashi, Tetsumaro.   John Steinbeck and Adlai E. Stevenson: their moral and political vision. SteiQ (24:3/4) 1991, 94–107.
21915. —— Steinbeck's American in *Travels with Charley*. SteiQ (23:3/4) 1990, 88–95.
21916. —— (ed.).   John Steinbeck: the years of greatness, 1936–1939. Introd. by John H. Timmerman. (Bibl. 1994, 15054.) Rev. by Donald R. Noble in SAtlR (61:1) 1996, 152–6.
21917. —— Steinbeck's literary dimension: a guide to comparative

studies: series II. (Bibl. 1992, 16317.) Rev. by Gloria L. Gaither in SteiQ (25:3/4) 1992, 133–4.

21918. —— Steinbeck's short stories in *The Long Valley*: essays in criticism. (Bibl. 1993, 15108.) Rev. by Barbara Heavilin in SteiQ (25:1/2) 1992, 54–8.

21919. —— Steinbeck's *The Grapes of Wrath*: essays in criticism. Muncie, IN: Steinbeck Research Inst., Ball State Univ., 1990. pp. ix, 77. (Steinbeck essay ser., 3.) Rev. by Thomas Koontz in SteiQ (24:1/2) 1991, 51–2.

21920. HEARLE, KEVIN. The pastures of contested pastoral discourse. SteiQ (26:1/2) 1993, 38–45.

21921. HEAVILIN, BARBARA. Judge, observer, prophet: the American Cain and Steinbeck's shifting perspective. SDR (34:2) 1996, 192–205.

21922. HEAVILIN, BARBARA A. Steinbeck's exploration of good and evil: structural and thematic unity in *East of Eden*. SteiQ (26:3/4) 1993, 90–100.

21923. HESS, NATALIE. Code-switching and style-shifting as markers of liminality in literature. *See* **2643**.

21924. HODGES, LAURA F. Steinbeck's adaptation of Malory's Launcelot: a triumph of realism over supernaturalism. *See* **5245**.

21925. HUGHES, R. S. John Steinbeck: a study of the short fiction. Boston, MA: Twayne, 1989. pp. xii, 218. (Twayne's studies in short fiction, 5). Rev. by George Spies in SteiQ (23:3/4) 1990, 115–16.

21926. HUGHES, ROBERT S., JR. What went wrong? How a 'vintage' Steinbeck short story became the flawed *Winter of Our Discontent*. SteiQ (26:1/2) 1993, 7–12.

21927. KIM, YOON-HEE. John Steinbeck eui jakpum e natanan *realism* mihak e gwanhan yeongu. (A study of the aesthetics of realism in John Steinbeck's works.) Unpub. doct. diss., Myong Ji Univ., Seoul, 1996.

21928. LEWIS, CLIFF. John Steinbeck's alternative to internment camps: a policy for the President, December 15, 1941. JWest (34:1) 1995, 55–61.

21929. L'HEUREUX, CONRAD E. Life's journey and *The Grapes of Wrath*. UDR (23:3) 1996, 89–97.

21930. MCELRATH, JOSEPH R, JR; CRISLER, JESSE S.; SHILLINGLAW, SUSAN (eds). John Steinbeck: the contemporary reviews. Cambridge; New York: CUP, 1996. pp. xxiv, 562. (American critical archives, 8.)

21931. MACKLIN, TONY. *The Grapes of Wrath*: the values of John Ford and John Steinbeck. *See* **13949**.

21932. MAINE, BARRY. Steinbeck's debt to Dos Passos. *See* **17379**.

21933. MEYER, MICHAEL J. Transforming evil to good: the image of Iscariot in *The Winter of Our Discontent*. SteiQ (26:3/4) 1993, 101–11.

21934. MORSBERGER, ROBERT E. *East of Eden* on film. *See* **14005**.

21935. MULDER, STEVEN. The reader's story: *East of Eden* as postmodernist metafiction. SteiQ (25:3/4) 1992, 109–18.

21936. NAKAYAMA, KIYOSHI. Nihon ni okeru Steinbeck bunken shoshi. (A bibliography of Japanese studies of Steinbeck.) (Bibl. 1992, 16321.) Rev. by Kozen Nakachi in SteiQ (26:3/4) 1993, 131–4.

21937. OWENS, LOUIS. A garden of my land: landscape and dreamscape in John Steinbeck's fiction. SteiQ (23:3/4) 1990, 78–87.

21938. PARINI, JAY. John Steinbeck: a biography. (Bibl. 1995, 19476.) Rev. by Mark Schechner in BkW, 12 Feb. 1995, 4–5; by Robert Murray

Davis in WLT (69:3) 1995, 592; by Stephen Allison in AR (54:2) 1996, 245.

21939. PRESSMAN, RICHARD S.   Individualists or collectivists: Steinbeck's *In Dubious Battle* and Hemingway's *To Have and Have Not*. *See* **18670**.

21940. RAILSBACK, BRIAN.   Darwin and Steinbeck: the 'older method' and *Sea of Cortez*. SteiQ (23:1/2) 1990, 27–33.

21941. REEF, CATHERINE.   John Steinbeck. New York: Clarion, 1996. pp. 163.

21942. SCHOENWALD, JONATHAN M.   Rewriting revolution: the origins, production and reception of *Viva Zapata! See* **14186**.

21943. SIMMONDS, ROY.   John Steinbeck: the war years, 1939–1945. Lewisburg, PA: Bucknell UP; London; Toronto: Assoc. UPs, 1996. pp. xvi, 348.

21944. SMITH, MEL.   Steinbeck on politics. MSS (47:4) 1995, 301–7.

21945. STONEBACK, H. R.   Songs of 'anger and survival': John Steinbeck on Woody Guthrie. *See* **3563**.

21946. TIMMERMAN, JOHN H.   The dramatic landscape of Steinbeck's short stories. (Bibl. 1994, 15061.) Rev. by Brian Railsback in SteiQ (24:3/4) 1991, 123–5.

21947. VALENTI, PETER.   Steinbeck's geographical seasons: *The Winter of Our Discontent*. SteiQ (26:3/4) 1993, 111–17.

21948. WYATT, DAVID (ed.).   New essays on *The Grapes of Wrath*. (Bibl. 1990, 12303.) Rev. by Christopher S. Busch in SteiQ (24:3/4) 1991, 111–13; by Kurt Müller in Amst (41:4) 1996, 708–9.

George Steiner

21949. KNIGHT, CHRISTOPHER J.   George Steiner's religion of abstraction. ReLit (28:1) 1996, 49–84.

James Stephens

21950. KULLMANN, THOMAS.   Irish mythology, Eastern philosophy and literary Modernism in James Stephens' *The Crock of Gold. In* (pp. 53–61) **60**.

21951. LENNON, JOSEPH.   James Stephens's diminutive national narratives: imagining an Irish nation based on the 'Orient'. Comparatist (20) 1996, 62–81.

Bruce Sterling

21952. MOORE, JOHN.   Shifting frontiers: mapping cyberpunk and the American South. *See* **14634**.

George Sterling

21953. ERBENTRAUT, EDWIN BERT.   Levels of meaning in Sterling's *Three That Knew Helen*. Romantist (9/10) 1985/86, 65–7.

Richard Stern

21954. STERN, RICHARD G.   A sistermony. New York: Fine, 1995. pp. 121.

Wallace Stevens

21955. AUSUBEL, JONATHAN.   'This hot, dependent orator': shifting narrative stance and the collision of speaker and reader in *Notes toward a Supreme Fiction*. TCL (42:3) 1996, 360–73.

21956. BACIGALUPO, MASSIMO. 'I wish he would explain his explanation': authorial explication in Wallace Stevens and Ezra Pound. *See* **21134**.

21957. BALFOUR, IAN. The uncommonplaces of writing: Wallace Stevens's *Description without Place*. Genre (26:2/3) 1993, 311–30.

21958. BOOKER, M. KEITH. Notes toward a Lacanian reading of Wallace Stevens. JML (16:4) 1990, 493–509.

21959. CAPPUCCI, PAUL R. Stevens' *God Is Good. It Is a Beautiful Night*. Exp (55:1) 1996, 32–4.

21960. COULTHARD, A. R. Stevens' *Anecdote of the Jar*: art as entrapment. NCL (25:5) 1995, 8–9.

21961. ESTRIN, BARBARA L. Space-off and voice-over: Adrienne Rich and Wallace Stevens. *See* **21341**.

21962. FILREIS, ALAN. Modernism from Right to Left: Wallace Stevens, the thirties & literary radicalism. (Bibl. 1994, 15077.) Rev. by David H. Hesla in AL (68:1) 1996, 254–5; by Ralph Pite in CamQ (25:2) 1996, 201–3.

21963. FRASER, KATHLEEN. 'Things that do not exist without words'. Talisman (9) 1992, 144–9.

21964. HALLIDAY, MARK. Stevens and the interpersonal. (Bibl. 1994, 15083.) Rev. by William H. Pritchard in ASch (62:3) 1993, 464–6.

21965. JARRAWAY, DAVID R. 'The novel that took the place of a poem': Wallace Stevens and queer discourse. ESCan (22:4) 1996, 377–97.

21966. —— Wallace Stevens and the question of belief: metaphysician in the dark. (Bibl. 1995, 19508.) Rev. by Barbara M. Fisher in Review (17) 1995, 297–313.

21967. LAKRITZ, ANDREW M. Modernism and the Other in Stevens, Frost, and Moore. *See* **18040**.

21968. LECKIE, ROSS. Reading *The Snow Man*: Stevens's structures of undecidability. WebS (13:2) 1996, 47–54.

21969. LENSING, GEORGE S. The early readers of Wallace Stevens. *In* (pp. 49–73) **79**.

21970. LOMBARDI, THOMAS FRANCIS. Wallace Stevens and the Pennsylvania keystone: the influence of origins on his life and poetry. Selinsgrove, PA: Susquehanna UP; London; Toronto: Assoc. UPs, 1996. pp. 290.

21971. MACLEOD, GLEN. Wallace Stevens and modern art: from the Armory Show to abstract expressionism. (Bibl. 1994, 15098.) Rev. by Barbara M. Fisher in Review (17) 1995, 297–313; by Dean Rader in PT (17:2) 1996, 266–9.

21972. MOON, HYE-YOUNG. Wallace Stevens eui shiljaegwan. (Wallace Stevens's changing attitude towards reality.) Unpub. doct. diss., Hankuk Univ. of Foreign Studies, Seoul, 1996.

21973. ROSU, ANCA. The metaphysics of sound in Wallace Stevens. Tuscaloosa; London: Alabama UP, 1995. pp. xv, 180.

21974. SCHWARZ, DANIEL R. Searching for Modernism's genetic code: Picasso, Joyce, and Stevens as cultural configuration. *See* **19187**.

21975. STRAND, MARK. Views of the mysterious hill: the appearance of Parnassus in American poetry. *See* **11004**.

Mary Stewart

21976. DEAN, CHRISTOPHER. The metamorphosis of Merlin: an examination of the protagonist of *The Crystal Cave* and *The Hollow Hills*. *In* (pp. 63–75) **15**.

James Still

21977. RUNYON, RANDOLPH PAUL. Looking the story in the eye: James Still's *Rooster*. SoLJ (23:2) 1991, 55–64.

Dal Stivens (1911–)

21978. HOOPER, S.; MURPHY, R.; RYAN, J. S. Towards a Dal Stivens bibliography. *See* **3237**.

21979. HOOPER, S.; RAINEY, P. Dal Stivens: a neglected Australian folklorist. *See* **3238**.

21980. HOOPER, STEPHEN. Dal Stivens as Australian cultural critic: Australian landscape, folklore and comic strips. *See* **210**.

Adrian Stokes

21981. READ, RICHARD. Art criticism *versus* poetry: an introduction to Adrian Stokes's *Pisanello*. *See* **12009**.

Robert Stone

21982. FREDRICKSON, ROBERT S. Robert Stone's decadent Leftists. PLL (32:3) 1996, 315–34.

21983. TAGER, MICHAEL. Cynicism in Robert Stone's *A Hall of Mirrors*. MidQ (37:1) 1995, 52–66.

Ruth Stone

21984. BARKER, WENDY; GILBERT, SANDRA M. (eds). The house is made of poetry: the art of Ruth Stone. Carbondale: Southern Illinois UP, 1996. pp. xiii, 214. (Ad feminam.)

Tom Stoppard

21985. BLÜGGEL, BEATE. Tom Stoppard: Metadrama und Postmoderne. (Bibl. 1992, 16397.) Rev. by Ulrich Blumenbach in ZAA (43:3) 1995, 283–4; by Norbert Greiner in AAA (21:1) 1996, 120–2.

21986. CIONI, FERNANDO. *Scrutinizing the intruder*: figure narranti in alcuni testi teatrali inglesi contemporanei. *See* **16931**.

21987. FREEMAN, JOHN. Holding up the mirror to mind's nature: reading *Rosencrantz* 'beyond Absurdity'. MLR (91:1) 1996, 20–39.

21988. GUASPARI, DAVID. Stoppard's *Arcadia*. AR (54:2) 1996, 222–38.

21989. GUSSOW, MEL. Conversations with Stoppard. (Bibl. 1995, 19559.) Rev. by Susan Rusinko in WLT (70:1) 1996, 193.

21990. MITCHELL, CHARLIE. 'Put your discourse into some frame': replacing the idea with the actual in CSF's *Rosencrantz and Guildenstern Are Dead*. OnS (19) 1996, 144–59.

21991. STOPPARD, TOM. Stoppard o sobie. (Stoppard on himself.) Dialog (1996:3) 176–8.

21992. TAN, PETER K. W. A stylistics of drama: with special focus on Stoppard's *Travesties*. *See* **2717**.

David Storey

21993. HUTCHINGS, WILLIAM.   Dramaturgies of quiet 'madness': David Storey's *Stages* and Simon Gray's *Melon*. *See* **18318**.

21994. LIEBMAN, HERBERT.   The dramatic art of David Storey: the journey of a playwright. Westport, CT; London: Greenwood Press, 1996. pp. 183. (Contributions in drama and theatre studies, 71.) (Cf. bibl. 1995, 19563.)

Rex Stout

21995. PENZLER, OTTO.   Collecting mystery fiction: Rex Stout: part I. *See* **525**.

Lytton Strachey

21996. ALTICK, RICHARD D.   Eminent Victorianism: what Lytton Strachey hath wrought. ASch (64:1) 1995, 81–9.

Mark Strand

21997. COLES, KATHARINE.   In the presence of America: a conversation with Mark Strand: an interview. WebS (9:3) 1992, 8–28.

21998. STRAND, MARK.   Views of the mysterious hill: the appearance of Parnassus in American poetry. *See* **11004**.

Sharan Strange

21999. DERRICOTTE, TOI.   An interview with Sharan Strange. Callaloo (19:2) 1996, 291–8.

Edward Stratemeyer ('Franklin W. Dixon')

22000. CHAMBERLAIN, KATHLEEN.   The search for Stratemeyer: twenty minutes in the archives. *See* **462**.

22001. DIZER, JOHN T.   The search for Stratemeyer: the Rosetta Stone. DNR (65:4) 1996, 122–4.

22002. DYER, CAROLYN STEWART; ROMALOV, NANCY TILLMAN (eds). Rediscovering Nancy Drew. (Bibl. 1995, 19571.) Rev. by Sherrie A. Inness in JPC (30:3) 1996, 246–7; by the same in NWSAJ (8:3) 1996, 144–53.

22003. JOHNSON, DEIDRE.   Edward Stratemeyer and the Stratemeyer Syndicate. (Bibl. 1995, 19572.) Rev. by Ray Browne in JPC (29:4) 1996, 238–9.

22004. JOHNSON, DEIDRE A.   The search for Stratemeyer: Stratemeyer Syndicate archives box 7856; or, What the NYPL archives revealed. *See* **493**.

22005. NASH, ILANA.   The lady and the press: Harriet Adams courts America. *See* **15874**.

Allan Stratton

22006. MCKINNIE, MICHAEL.   King-maker: reading theatrical presentations of Canadian political history. *See* **18743**.

T. S. Stribling

22007. PIACENTINO, ED.   Through a lens darkly: T. S. Stribling's representations of the past in his Alabama Trilogy. SoLJ (23:1) 1990, 21–9.

Eithne Strong

22008. WRIGHT, NANCY MEANS; HANNAN, DENNIS. An interview with Eithne Strong. Irish Literary Supplement (13:1) 1994, 13–15.

Jonathan Strong

22009. STRONG, JONATHAN. Books and silence. AL (68:1) 1996, 9–13.

Lucien Stryk

22010. PORTERFIELD, SUSAN. Portrait of a poet as a young man: Lucien Stryk. MidM (22) 1994, 36–45.

Francis Stuart

22011. McCARTNEY, ANNE. 'The impact of reality': Francis Stuart's narrative theology. ReLit (28:2/3) 1996, 165–84.

William Styron

22012. ALLEN, JOE. Blues in *The Confessions of Nat Turner*. NCL (24:5) 1994, 2–3.

22013. CALDER, J. KENT. Ordeal and renewal: David Laurance Chambers, Hiram Haydn, and *Lie Down in Darkness*. See **908**.

22014. CHINN, NANCY. Games and tragedy: unidentified quotations in William Styron's *Sophie's Choice*. ELN (33:3) 1996, 51–61.

22015. COHEN, PHILIP. Is there a text in this discipline? Textual scholarship and American literary studies. See **604**.

22016. COLOGNE-BROOKES, GAVIN. The novels of William Styron: from harmony to history. (Bibl. 1995, 19586.) Rev. by Christopher Metress in MFS (42:1) 1996, 152–4.

22017. HADALLER, DAVID. Gynicide: women in the novels of William Styron. Madison, NJ: Fairleigh Dickinson UP; London; Toronto: Assoc. UPs, 1996. pp. 218. (Cf. bibl. 1994, 15141.)

22018. LAW, RICHARD G. The reach of fiction: narrative technique in Styron's *Sophie's Choice*. SoLJ (23:1) 1990, 45–64.

22019. ROSS, DANIEL W. (ed.). The critical response to William Styron. Westport, CT; London: Greenwood Press, 1995. pp. xvii, 285. (Critical responses in arts and letters, 22.)

22020. STEWART, ANTHONY. William Turnergraystyron, novelist(s): reactivating state power in *The Confessions of Nat Turner*. StudN (27:2) 1995, 169–85.

22021. WEST, JAMES L. W., III. Inheritance of night: early drafts of *Lie Down in Darkness*. (Bibl. 1994, 15144.) Rev. by Philip Cohen in AmLH (8:4) 1996, 739–42.

22022. —— Voices interior and exterior: William Styron's narrative personae. *In* (pp. 48–61) **123**.

Ruth Suckow

22023. DeMARR, MARY JEAN. An Iowa woman's life: Ruth Suckow's *Cora*. Midamerica (18) 1991, 80–96.

22024. —— Sexual stereotypes in Ruth Suckow's *The Kramer Girls*. Midamerica (19) 1992, 61–73.

Rodie Sudbery

22025. SUDBERY, RODIE. Let me involve you in this curious tale. Signal (79) 1996, 31–44.

Rosemary Sutcliff

22026. WITHRINGTON, JOHN.   An interview with Rosemary Sutcliff. Quondam et Futurus (1:4) 1991, 53–60.

Susan Swan

22027. KAMBOURELI, SMARO.   *The Biggest Modern Woman of the World*: Canada as the absent spouse. StudCanL (16:2) 1991/92, 1–16.

May Swenson

22028. SWENSON, PAUL.   May in October: life and death as existential riddles in May Swenson's poetry. WebS (8:1) 1991, 18–31.

22029. WILBUR, RICHARD.   May Swenson: a memorial tribute. GetR (5:2) 1992, 81–5.

Graham Swift

22030. BROICH, ULRICH.   Muted postmodernism: the contemporary British short story. *See* **14415**.

22031. COOPER, PAMELA.   Imperial topographies: the spaces of history in *Waterland*. MFS (42:2) 1996, 371–96.

22032. HARTUNG-BRÜCKNER, HEIKE.   'Historionics': Varianten und Implikationen der Auseinandersetzung mit Geschichte im erzähler- ischen Werk von Graham Swift – Gestützt auf ein Interview mit dem Autor. GRM (46:4) 1996, 463–72.

22033. LÖSCHNIGG, MARTIN.   History and the search for identity: reconstructing the past in recent English novels. *See* **14605**.

Rob Swigart

22034. MINGANTI, FRANCO.   Hypertextually, maybe? Rob Swigart's interactive fiction: *Portal. In* (pp. 84–93) **117**.

Julian Symons

22035. PRITCHARD, WILLIAM H.   The last man of letters: Julian Symons. ASch (65:1) 1996, 107–13.

J. M. Synge

22036. AGOSTINI, RENÉ.   J. M. Synge's 'celestial peasants'. *In* (pp. 159–73) **106**.

22037. BROWN, MAVIS.   Christy's two fathers. CJIS (22:1) 1996, 42–60.

22038. CLARKE, IAN.   Lawrence and the drama of his European contemporaries. *See* **19511**.

22039. DEVLIN, JOSEPH.   The source of Synge's *Playboy of the Western World. See* **3385**.

22040. GONZALEZ, ALEXANDER G. (ed.).   Assessing the achievement of J. M. Synge. Westport, CT; London: Greenwood Press, 1996. pp. xiii, 197. (Contributions in drama and theatre studies, 73.)

22041. HALE, ANTHONY R.   Framing the folk: Zora Neale Hurston, John Millington Synge, and the politics of aesthetic ethnography. *See* **18837**.

22042. KIELY, DAVID M.   John Millington Synge: a biography. Dublin: Gill & Macmillan, 1994; New York: St Martin's Press, 1995. pp. xiii, 305, (plates) 16.

22043. SADDLEMYER, ANN. Vision and design in *The Playboy of the Western World. In* (pp. 203–16) **16**.

22044. —— (ed.). *The Playboy of the Western World* and other plays. (Bibl. 1995, 19613.) Rev. by J. P. Wearing in ELT (39:4) 1996, 504–7.

Netta Syrett

22045. ARDIS, ANN. Toward a redefinition of 'experimental writing': Netta Syrett's realism, 1908–12. *In* (pp. 259–79) **31**.

Marie Syrkin (1900–)

22046. KESSNER, CAROLE S. Matrilineal dissent: the rhetoric of zeal in Emma Lazarus, Marie Syrkin, and Cynthia Ozick. *In* (pp. 197–215) **130**.

Rabindranath Tagore

22047. DUTTA, KRISHNA; ROBINSON, ANDREW. Rabindranath Tagore: the myriad-minded man. (Bibl. 1995, 19618.) Rev. by John Coates in ChesR (22:1/2) 1996, 164–7.

22048. LAL, MALASHRI. Questioning otherness: racial indeterminacy in Kipling, Tagore and Paul Scott. *See* **19344**.

22049. MAHAPATRA, U. Gurudev and Allama. IndL (39:3) 1996, 171–6. (Tagore and Iqbal.)

22050. RADICE, WILLIAM. Small lives, humble distress: Tagore, Bibhutibhushan and the Bengali short story. JSSE (24) 1995, 23–41.

22051. RAY, SITANSU. The *asrama*-anthem: Tagore's passion for Santiniketan. Analecta Husserliana (44) 1995, 45–7.

22052. —— European scholars on Indian music. Analecta Husserliana (49) 1996, 311–27.

22053. —— *Shesher Kabita*: Tagorean ideals towards the man–woman relationship. Analecta Husserliana (49) 1996, 165–74.

22054. —— Tagore, Freud and Jung on artistic creativity: a psycho-phenomenological study. Analecta Husserliana (48) 1996, 329–41.

22055. —— The Tagore–Einstein conversations: reality and the human world, causality and chance. Analecta Husserliana (47) 1995, 59–65.

Amy Tan

22056. BOLDT, CHRIS. Why is the Moon Lady in Amy Tan's *The Joy Luck Club* revealed to be a man? NCL (24:4) 1994, 9–10.

22057. DAVIS, ROCÍO G. Amy Tan's *The Kitchen God's Wife*: an American dream come true – in China. NCL (24:5) 1994, 3–5.

22058. KRAMER, BARBARA. Amy Tan, author of *The Joy Luck Club*. Springfield, NJ: Enslow, 1996. pp. 112. (People to know.)

22059. SAINT-MARTIN, LORI. 'Ta mère est dans tes os': Fae Myenne Ng et Amy Tan; ou, Le passage des savoirs entre la Chine et l'Amérique. *See* **20534**.

22060. SHEN, GLORIA. Born of a stranger: mother–daughter relationships and storytelling in Amy Tan's *The Joy Luck Club. In* (pp. 233–44) **50**.

22061. TSEO, GEORGE K. Y. *Joy Luck*: the perils of transcultural 'translation'. *See* **14293**.

22062. WYMARD, ELLIE. Live, on stage with Amy Tan. Critic (47:2) 1992, 77–83.

Luci Tapahonso (1953–)

22063. CRAWFORD, JOHN; EYSTUROY, ANNIE O.   Luci Tapahonso. *In* (pp. 194–202) **121**.

22064. PENNER, ANDREA M.   The moon is so far away: an interview with Luci Tapahonso. SAIL (8:3) 1996, 1–12.

Nathaniel Tarn

22065. GIORDANO, FEDORA (ed.).   *Bartok in Udaipur* di Nathaniel Tarn. RSAJ (2) 1991, 99–105.

Allen Tate

22066. HUFF, PETER A.   Allen Tate and the Catholic revival: trace of the fugitive gods. New York: Paulist Press, 1996. pp. xv, 159. (Isaac Hecker studies.) (Cf. bibl. 1995, 19632.)

22067. SIMPSON, LEWIS P.   The autobiographical impulse in the South. *In* (pp. 63–84) **43**.

22068. SULLIVAN, WALTER.   Strange children: Caroline Gordon and Allen Tate. *In* (pp. 123–30) **43**.

Elizabeth Taylor

22069. HANSON, CLARE.   'Katherine Mansfield's journal covered with dust': the postmodern short fiction of Elizabeth Taylor. JSSE (22) 1994, 93–103.

Mildred D. Taylor

22070. BOSMAJIAN, HAMIDA.   Mildred Taylor's story of Cassie Logan: a search for law and justice in a racist society. ChildLit (24) 1996, 141–60.

Peter Taylor

22071. CHAPPELL, FRED.   Peter Taylor: the genial mentor. NCLR (5) 1996, 45–54.

22072. DUNNE, SARA LEWIS.   Peter Taylor's book of practical ghosts. TPB (32) 1995, 30–7.

22073. KUEHL, LINDA KANDEL.   Public occasions and private evasions in the plays of Peter Taylor. SoQ (34:1) 1995, 49–62.

22074. KURTZ, RICHARD L.   Freud checks in: the 'Oedipus' in Peter Taylor's *Reservations*. NCLR (5) 1996, 55–7.

22075. LOYD, DENNIS.   Peter Taylor's Tennessee. TPB (32) 1995, 54–61.

22076. METRESS, CHRIS.   Peter Taylor's Tennessee *Dubliners*: paralysis and silence in *'A Long Fourth' and Other Stories. See* **19145**.

22077. PRUNTY, WYATT.   The figure of vacancy. *See* **20691**.

Simon Taylor

22078. WHYTE, CHRISTOPHER.   Postmodernism, gender and belief in recent Scottish fiction. *See* **18477**.

Kylie Tennant

22079. CAIRA, DIANA.   Kylie Tennant's ear for the people's voices. *See* **3227**.

Sheri S. Tepper

22080. ATTEBERY, BRIAN. Gender, fantasy, and the authority of tradition. *See* **19636**.

22081. PRICE, BEVERLY. Sheri S. Tepper and feminism's future. Mythlore (18:2) 1992, 41–4.

Studs Terkel

22082. PARKER, TONY. Studs Terkel: a life in words. New York: Holt, 1996. pp. xviii, 237.

'Josephine Tey'
('Gordon Daviot', Elizabeth Mackintosh)

22083. MARTIN, CHRISTINA R. Josephine Tey: Scottish detective novelist. SSL (29) 1996, 191–204.

Shashi Tharoor

22084. CHOWDHURY, KANISHKA. Revisioning history: Shashi Tharoor's *Great Indian Novel*. WLT (69:1) 1995, 41–8.

Jean Thesman

22085. KERTZER, ADRIENNE. Reclaiming her maternal pre-text: Little Red Riding Hood's mother and three young adult novels. *See* **3688**.

Angela Thirkell

22086. MATHER, RACHEL R. The heirs of Jane Austen: twentieth-century writers of the comedy of manners. *See* **10304**.

Audrey Thomas

22087. BUCKMAN, JACQUELINE. Questions of identity and subjectivity: Audrey Thomas's *Intertidal Life*. ESCan (22:1) 1996, 71–87.

D. M. Thomas

22088. CASADEMONT, ROSA GONZÁLEZ. Art and the unseen pattern in the universe: an interview with D. M. Thomas. EEM (3:2) 1994, 7–12.

22089. HIGDON, DAVID LEON. Solomon's fair Shulamite in D. M. Thomas' *The White Hotel*. JML (19:2) 1995, 328–33.

22090. MACINNES, JOHN. The case of Anna G.: *The White Hotel* and acts of understanding. Soundings (77) 1994, 253–69.

22091. TORI, SIMONA. *The White Hotel*: romanzo a più voci. Textus (4) 1991, 147–69.

22092. WREN, JAMES A. Thomas's *The White Hotel*. Exp (54:2) 1996, 123–6.

Dylan Thomas

22093. ACKERMAN, JOHN. Dylan Thomas: his life and work. New York: St Martin's Press, 1996. pp. xxxv, 201. (Cf. bibl. 1991, 15582.)

22094. —— (ed.). Dylan Thomas: the filmscripts. *See* **13381**.

22095. BALAKIER, JAMES J. The ambiguous reversal of Dylan Thomas's *In Country Sleep*. PLL (32:1) 1996, 21–44.

22096. BIGLIAZZI, SILVIA. Fable *versus* fact: Hamlet's ghost in Dylan Thomas's early poetry. *See* **6788**.

22097. CARSON, RICKS. Thomas's *A Refusal to Mourn the Death, by Fire, of a Child in London.* Exp (54:4) 1996, 240–1.

22098. DAVIES, WALFORD; MAUD, RALPH (eds). Under milk wood: a play for voices. London: Dent; Rutland, VT: Tuttle, 1995. pp. xlviii, 104.

22099. HEANEY, SEAMUS. Dylan the durable? On Dylan Thomas. Salmagundi (100) 1993, 66–85.

Edward Thomas

22100. JAMES, NORMAN G. BRETT, *et al.* On Edward Thomas. Yoxford, Suffolk: Demeter, 1995. pp. 29.

22101. LONGLEY, EDNA. 'The business of the earth': Edward Thomas and ecocentrism. *In* (pp. 107–31) **41**.

22102. THOMAS, R. GEORGE (ed.). Selected letters. (Bibl. 1995, 19662.) Rev. by Penelope Fitzgerald in LRB (18:13) 1996, 7; by Andrew Motion in TLS, 5 July 1996, 6.

Ethel Thomas (1870–1970)

22103. KRATT, MARY. Aunt Becky's way. NCLR (5) 1996, 154–9, 162–7.

R. S. Thomas

22104. LLOYD, DAVID. Through the looking-glass: R. S. Thomas's *The Echoes Return Slow* as poetic autobiography. TCL (42:4) 1996, 438–52.

22105. SHEPHERD, ELAINE. R. S. Thomas: conceding an absence: images of God explored. New York: St Martin's Press; Basingstoke: Macmillan, 1996. pp. xiii, 216.

Earl Thompson

22106. PAGE, TOM. The case of Earl Thompson. SSMLN (24:1) 1994, 6–11.

Jim Thompson

22107. HENDERSHOT, CYNDY. Imaginary imagery and Oedipal tyranny: Jim Thompson's *A Swell-Looking Babe.* NCL (23:2) 1993, 2–4.

22108. PAYNE, KENNETH. Misogyny and Oedipal fixation in Jim Thompson's *A Hell of a Woman.* NCL (26:3) 1996, 7–9.

22109. POLITO, ROBERT. Savage art: a biography of Jim Thompson. (Bibl. 1995, 19669.) Rev. by William Heffernan in BkW, 24 Dec. 1995, 5; by Christopher Hawtree in TLS, 30 Aug. 1996, 29.

Judith Thompson

22110. DUCHESNE, SCOTT; FLETCHER, JENNIFER. *Sled*: a workshop diary. CanTR (89) 1996, 33–8.

22111. FLETCHER, JENNIFER. The last thing in the *Sled*: an interview with Judith Thompson. CanTR (89) 1996, 39–41.

22112. HARVIE, JENNIFER. Constructing fictions of an essential reality; or, 'This pickshur is niiice': Judith Thompson's *Lion in the Streets.* TRC (13:1/2) 1992, 81–93.

22113. HONG, AHNES. Judith Thompson: a bibliography. CanTR (89) 1996, 42–4.

22114. LANE, HARRY. Redefining the comfort zone: Nancy Palk, on acting Judith Thompson. CanTR (89) 1996, 19–21.

22115. Nunn, Robert. Strangers to ourselves: Judith Thompson's *Sled*. CanTR (89) 1996, 29–32.
22116. Thompson, Judith. Epilepsy and the snake: fear and the creative process. CanTR (89) 1996, 4–7.
22117. Wilson, Ann. Canadian grotesque: the reception of Judith Thompson's plays in London. CanTR (89) 1996, 25–8.

Sam Thompson

22118. Pilkington, Lionel. Theatre and cultural politics in Northern Ireland: the *Over the Bridge* controversy, 1959. EI (30:4) 1995, 76–93.

Lawrence Thornton

22119. Gilmour, Peter. Bearing witness: Peter Gilmour interviews Lawrence Thornton. Critic (47:2) 1992, 84–94.

James Thurber

22120. Grauer, Neil A. Remember laughter: a life of James Thurber. (Bibl. 1995, 19674.) Rev. by Stephen L. Tanner in AmS (36:2) 1995, 213–14; by R. Thomas Berner in JMCQ (73:4) 1996, 1005–6.
22121. Kinney, Harrison. James Thurber: his life and times. (Bibl. 1995, 19675.) Rev. by Heywood Hale Broun in BkW, 31 Dec. 1995, 5; by R. Thomas Berner in JMCQ (73:4) 1996, 1005–6; by Janet Overmyer in OhioanaQ (39:1) 1996, 13–14.
22122. Sun, Douglas. Thurber's *Fables for Our Time*: a case study in satirical use of Great Chain metaphor. SAH (3:1) 1994, 51–61.
22123. Tanner, Stephen L. The art of self-deprecation in American literary humor. *See* **12618**.

Wallace Thurman

22124. Dickson-Carr, Darryl. Signs of adolescence: problems of group identity in Wallace Thurman's *Infants of the Spring*. SCS (20) 1996, 145–59.
22125. Giles, Freda Scott. Glitter, glitz, and race: the production of *Harlem*. JADT (7:3) 1995, 1–12.

'James Tiptree, Jr'
(Alice Sheldon, 'Raccoona Sheldon')

22126. Boulter, Amanda. Alice James Raccoona Tiptree Sheldon, Jr: textual personas in the short fiction of Alice Sheldon. Foundation (63) 1995, 5–31.
22127. Hicks, Heather J. 'Whatever it is that she's since become': writing bodies of text and bodies of women in James Tiptree, Jr's *The Girl Who Was Plugged In* and William Gibson's *The Winter Market*. *See* **18163**.
22128. Vallorani, Nicoletta. La rappresentazione imperfetta: tecnologia, corpo e linguaggio in *The Girl Who Was Plugged In* di James Tiptree Jr. *In* (pp. 490–8) **117**.

Miriam Tlali

22129. Gqola, Pumla. Contradiction and refusal in Miriam Tlali's work. Bracket (1) 1995, 85–97.

J. R. R. Tolkien

22130. AGØY, NILS-IVAR.   *Quid Hinieldus cum Christo?*: new perspectives on Tolkien's theological dilemma and his sub-creation theory. Mythlore (21:2) 1996, 31–8.

22131. ANON.   Realms of Tolkien: images of Middle-earth. *See* **175**.

22132. ARMSTRONG, HELEN.   Good guys, bad guys, fantasy and reality. Mythlore (21:2) 1996, 247–52.

22133. BARKLEY, CHRISTINE.   Point of view in Tolkien. Mythlore (21:2) 1996, 256–62.

22134. —— The realm of faërie. Mythlore (21:2) 1996, 253–5.

22135. BEACH, SARAH, *et al.*   Artists' comments. Mythlore (19:1) 1993, 22–3, 34–5.

22136. BRATMAN, DAVID.   J. R. R. Tolkien: a centenary survey. Mythprint (29:1) 1992, 11–13; (29:2) 1992, 9–12.

22137. BURNS, MARJORIE.   Eating, devouring, sacrifice and ultimate just desserts. Mythlore (21:2) 1996, 108–14.

22138. CALLAHAN, BONNIE, *et al.*   Artists' comments. Mythlore (18:3) 1992, 4, 26, 40–1, 53; (18:4) 1992, 8, 51.

22139. CHANCE, JANE.   Power and knowledge in Tolkien: the problem of difference in 'the birthday party'. Mythlore (21:2) 1996, 115–20.

22140. CHRISTOPHER, JOE R.   J. R. R. Tolkien and the clerihew. Mythlore (21:2) 1996, 263–71.

22141. —— A literary friendship: C. S. Lewis and J. R. R. Tolkien. *See* **19701**.

22142. —— The moral epiphanies in *The Lord of the Rings*. Mythlore (21:2) 1996, 121–5.

22143. ——HAMMOND, WAYNE G. (comps).   An Inklings bibliography. *See* **19703**.

22144. COOMBS, JENNY; READ, MARC.   A physics of Middle-Earth. Mythlore (21:2) 1996, 323–9.

22145. COULOMBE, CHARLES A.   Hermetic imagination: the effect of the Golden Dawn on fantasy literature. *See* **19988**.

22146. CROWE, EDITH L.   Power in Arda: sources, uses and misuses. Mythlore (21:2) 1996, 272–7.

22147. CURRY, PATRICK.   'Less noise and more green': Tolkien's ideology for England. Mythlore (21:2) 1996, 126–38.

22148. CUTSINGER, JAMES S.   Angels and Inklings. *See* **19707**.

22149. DE ARMAS, FREDERICK A.   Gyges' ring: invisibility in Plato, Tolkien and Lope de Vega. JFA (3:4) 1990 (pub. 1994), 120–38.

22150. DOUGHAN, DAVID.   Tolkien, Sayers, sex and gender. *See* **21521**.

22151. DURIEZ, COLIN.   Tolkien and the other Inklings. *See* **16197**.

22152. FENWICK, MAC.   Breastplates of silk: Homeric women in *The Lord of the Rings*. Mythlore (21:3) 1996, 17–23, 51.

22153. FLIEGER, VERLYN.   Tolkien's experiment with time: *The Lost Road*, *The Notion Club Papers*, and J. W. Dunne. Mythlore (21:2) 1996, 39–44.

22154. FUNK, DAVID A.   Explorations into the psyche of dwarves. Mythlore (21:2) 1996, 330–3.

22155. GILLIVER, PETER M.   At the wordface: J. R. R. Tolkien's work on the *Oxford English Dictionary*. *See* **2046**.

22156. GILSON, CHRISTOPHER; WYNNE, PATRICK. The growth of grammar in the elven tongues. Mythlore (21:2) 1996, 187–94.

22157. GOODKNIGHT, GLEN H. J. R. R. Tolkien in translation. Mythlore (18:3) 1992, 61–9. (Updated version of bibl. 1982, 13667.)

22158. GORMAN, ANITA G. J. R. R. Tolkien's *Leaf by Niggle*: word pairs and paradoxes. Mythlore (20:4) 1995, 52–5.

22159. GRAFF, ERIC S. The three faces of faërie in Tolkien's shorter fiction: Niggle, Smith and Giles. Mythlore (18:3) 1992, 15–19.

22160. GREENE, DEIRDRE. Higher argument: Tolkien and the tradition of vision, epic and prophecy. *See* **6033**.

22161. —— Tolkien's dictionary poetics: the influence of the *OED*'s defining style on Tolkien's fiction. *See* **2049**.

22162. GREENMAN, DAVID. Aeneidic and Odyssean patterns of escape and return in Tolkien's 'The Fall of Gondolin' and *The Return of the King*. Mythlore (18:2) 1992, 4–9.

22163. GRUSHETSKIY, VLADIMIR. How Russians see Tolkien. Mythlore (21:2) 1996, 221–5.

22164. HAMMOND, WAYNE G. The critical response to Tolkien's fiction. Mythlore (21:2) 1996, 226–32.

22165. HOOD, GWENYTH. The Earthly Paradise in Tolkien's *The Lord of the Rings*. Mythlore (21:2) 1996, 139–44.

22166. HOOD, GWYNETH. Nature and technology: angelic and sacrificial strategies in Tolkien's *The Lord of the Rings*. Mythlore (19:4) 1993, 6–12.

22167. HOPKINS, CHRIS. Tolkien and Englishness. Mythlore (21:2) 1996, 278–80.

22168. HOPKINS, LISA. Female authority figures in the works of Tolkien, C. S. Lewis and Charles Williams. *See* **19720**.

22169. HOSTETTER, CARL F.; SMITH, ARDEN R. A mythology for England. Mythlore (21:2) 1996, 281–90.

22170. ——WYNNE, PATRICK. Stone towers. Mythlore (19:4) 1993, 47–55, 65.

22171. HOUGHTON, JOHN. Augustine and the *Ainulindale*. Mythlore (21:1) 1995, 4–8.

22172. HYDE, PAUL NOLAN. The 'Gondolinic runes': another picture. Mythlore (18:3) 1992, 20–5.

22173. —— Snuffling out footsteps: a translation at risk. Mythlore (18:2) 1992, 23–7.

22174. JUHREN, MARCELLA. The ecology of Middle-Earth. Mythlore (20:2) 1994, 5–9.

22175. KEENE, LOUISE E. The restoration of language in Middle-Earth. Mythlore (20:4) 1995, 6–13.

22176. KONDRATIEV, ALEXEI. Tales newly told: a column on current modern fantasy. Mythlore (18:2) 1992, 10–11.

22177. LEWIS, ALEX. Historical bias in the making of *The Silmarillion*. Mythlore (21:2) 1996, 158–66.

22178. LULING, VIRGINIA. An anthropologist in Middle-Earth. Mythlore (21:2) 1996, 53–7.

22179. McCOMAS, ALAN. Negating and affirming spirit through language: the integration of character, magic, and story in *The Lord of the Rings*. Mythlore (19:2) 1993, 4–14; (19:3) 1993, 40–9.

22180. MANGANIELLO, DOMINIC. The neverending story: textual happiness in *The Lord of the Rings*. Mythlore (18:3) 1992, 5–14.

22181. MARTSCH, NANCY.   A Tolkien chronology. Mythlore (21:2) 1996, 291–7.

22182. MATHEWS, RICHARD.   The edges of reality in Tolkien's tale of Aldarion and Erendis. Mythlore (18:3) 1992, 27–31.

22183. MITCHELL, BRUCE.   J. R. R. Tolkien and Old English studies: an appreciation. *See* **4636**.

22184. MURRAY, ROBERT.   Sermon at Thanksgiving Service, Keble College Chapel, 23rd August 1992. Mythlore (21:2) 1996, 17–20.

22185. NAGEL, RAINER.   Normenvorgabe in der literarischen Übersetzung: illustriert an den Eigennamen in J. R. R. Tolkiens *The Lord of the Rings*. *See* **2156**.

22186. NELSON, CHARLES W.   But who is Rose Cotton? Love and romance in *The Lord of the Rings*. JFA (3:3) 1990 (pub. 1994), 6–20.

22187. NOAD, CHARLES E.   Frodo and his spectre: Blakean resonances in Tolkien. *See* **8818**.

22188. OBERTINO, JAMES.   Tolkien's *The Fellowship of the Ring*. Exp (54:4) 1996, 230–3.

22189. O'BRIEN, DONALD.   Natural functions in Arda. Mythprint (28:2) 1991, 8–9.

22190. OLSZAŃSKI, ANDRZEJ.   Evil and the Evil One in Tolkien's theology. Trans. by Agnieszka Sylwanowicz. Mythlore (21:2) 1996, 298–300.

22191. PAVLAC, DIANA LYNNE.   More than a bandersnatch: Tolkien as a collaborative writer. Mythlore (21:2) 1996, 367–74.

22192. PHEMISTER, WILLIAM.   Fantasy set to music: Donald Swann, C. S. Lewis and J. R. R. Tolkien. *See* **19751**.

22193. RAWLS, MELANIE A.   The verse of J. R. R. Tolkien. Mythlore (19:1) 1993, 4–8.

22194. REYNOLDS, PATRICIA.   Funeral customs in Tolkien's fiction. Mythlore (19:2) 1993, 45–53.

22195. ST CLAIR, GLORIANA.   An overview of the Northern influences on Tolkien's works. Mythlore (21:2) 1996, 63–7.

22196. —— Tolkien as reviser: a case study. Mythlore (21:2) 1996, 145–50.

22197. —— *Volsunga Saga* and Narn: some analogies. Mythlore (21:2) 1996, 68–72.

22198. SARJEANT, WILLIAM ANTONY SWITHIN.   The geology of Middle-Earth. Mythlore (21:2) 1996, 334–9.

22199. —— Where did the dwarves come from? Mythlore (19:1) 1993, 43, 64.

22200. SAWA, HUBERT.   Short history of the territorial development of the dwarves' kingdoms in the second and third ages of Middle-Earth. Trans. by Paulina Braiter. Mythlore (21:2) 1996, 396–410.

22201. SAYER, GEORGE.   Recollections of J. R. R. Tolkien. Mythlore (21:2) 1996, 21–5.

22202. SCHWEICHER, ERIC.   Aspects of the Fall in *The Silmarillion*. Mythlore (21:2) 1996, 167–71.

22203. SCULL, CHRISTINA.   Open minds, closed minds in *The Lord of the Rings*. Mythlore (21:2) 1996, 151–6.

22204. SEEMAN, CHRIS.   Tolkien's revision of the Romantic tradition. *See* **10705**.

22205. SENIOR, WILLIAM.   Donaldson and Tolkien. *See* **17316**.

22206. SHIPPEY, TOM.   Tolkien and the *Gawain*-poet. *See* **5524**.

22207. —— Tolkien as a post-war writer. Mythlore (21:2) 1996, 84–93.

22208. SIMONS, LESTER E. Writing and allied technologies in Middle-Earth. Mythlore (21:2) 1996, 340–3.

22209. STANTON, MICHAEL N. 'Advice is a dangerous gift': (pseudo)proverbs in *The Lord of the Rings*. See **3348**.

22210. STENSTRÖM, ANDERS. A mythology? For England? Mythlore (21:2) 1996, 310–14.

22211. STODDARD, WILLIAM H. Law and institutions in the Shire. Mythlore (18:4) 1992, 4–8.

22212. SULLIVAN, C. W., III. Tolkien and the telling of a traditional narrative. JFA (7:1) 1996, 75–82.

22213. SURTEES, ANGELA; GARDNER, STEVE. The mechanics of dragons: an introduction to the study of their 'ologies. See **4027**.

22214. TALBOT, NORMAN. Where do elves go to? Tolkien and a fantasy tradition. Mythlore (21:2) 1996, 94–106.

22215. THOMPSON, RICKY L. Tolkien's word-hord *onlēac*. See **4790**.

22216. THORPE, DWAYNE. Tolkien's elvish craft. Mythlore (21:2) 1996, 315–21.

22217. TIMMONS, DANIEL. Sub-creation in William Golding's *The Inheritors*. See **18244**.

22218. UNWIN, RAYNER. Publishing Tolkien. See **1023**.

22219. VANHECKE, JOHAN. Tolkien in Dutch: a study of the reception of Tolkien's work in Belgium and The Netherlands. Mythlore (18:4) 1992, 53–60.

22220. VAN ROSSENBERG, RENÉ. Tolkien's exceptional visit to Holland: a reconstruction. Mythlore (21:2) 1996, 301–9.

22221. WYNNE, PATRICK; DISANTE, PAULA; BEACH, SARAH. Artists' comments. Mythlore (20:1) 1994, 42–3.

22222. WYNNE, PATRICK, *et al.* Joint artists' project. Mythlore (18:2) 1992, 34–6, 54.

22223. YANDELL, STEPHEN. 'A pattern which our nature cries out for': the medieval tradition of the ordered four in the fiction of J. R. R. Tolkien. See **19760**.

22224. YATES, JESSICA. Tolkien the anti-totalitarian. Mythlore (21:2) 1996, 233–45.

22225. ZIMMER, PAUL EDWIN. Another opinion of *The Verse of J. R. R. Tolkien*. Mythlore (19:2) 1993, 16–23.

Melvin B. Tolson

22226. NIELSEN, ALDON L. Melvin B. Tolson and the deterritorialization of Modernism. AAR (26:2) 1992, 241–55.

Charles Tomlinson

22227. HENNESSY, MICHAEL. Louis Zukofsky, Charles Tomlinson, and the 'objective tradition'. ConLit (37:2) 1996, 333–45 (review-article).

22228. SWIGG, RICHARD. Charles Tomlinson and the objective tradition. Lewisburg, PA: Bucknell UP; London; Toronto: Assoc. UPs, 1994. pp. 271. Rev. by Michael Hennessy in ConLit (37:2) 1996, 340–5.

John Kennedy Toole

22229. BRITTON, WESLEY. Two visions of medievalism and determinism: Mark Twain and John Kennedy Toole's *A Confederacy of Dunces*. See **12550**.

22230. GARDNER, PAT.   Midst great laughter. SoQ (34:2) 1996, 87–90.
22231. GILLESPIE, MICHAEL PATRICK.   Baroque Catholicism in Southern fiction: Flannery O'Connor, Walker Percy, and John Kennedy Toole. *In* (pp. 25–47) **123**.

Jean Toomer

22232. COOPERMAN, ROBERT.   Unacknowledged familiarity: Jean Toomer and Eugene O'Neill. *See* **20813**.
22233. FOLEY, BARBARA.   Jean Toomer's Washington and the politics of class: from 'blue veins' to Seventh-Street rebels. MFS (42:2) 1996, 289–321.
22234. GRIFFITHS, FREDERICK T.   'Sorcery is dialectical': Plato and Jean Toomer in Charles Johnson's *The Sorcerer's Apprentice*. *See* **18950**.
22235. JONES, ROBERT B.   Jean Toomer and the prison-house of thought: a phenomenology of the spirit. (Bibl. 1994, 15234.) Rev. by George Hutchinson in AAR (30:1) 1996, 131–3.
22236. KERMAN, CYNTHIA EARL; ELDRIDGE, RICHARD.   The lives of Jean Toomer: a hunger for wholeness. (Bibl. 1990, 12457.) Rev. by R. Baxter Miller in LHR (11:1) 1992, 36–40.
22237. PICCINATO, STEFANIA.   Le metafore del dissidio: paesaggi e immaginario urbano in *Cane* di Jean Toomer. Letterature d'America (39) 1990, 57–90.

Honor Tracy

22238. KHALLAF, NADIA.   Colonialism in Honor Tracy's 'Irish' novel, *A Number of Things*. *In* (pp. 222–7) **60**.

'B. Traven' (Ret Marut, Albert Otto Max Feige)

22239. GUTHKE, KARL S.   Eine pseudo-Travensche Kurzgeschichte. GRM (44:2) 1994, 215–17.
22240. PAYNE, KENNETH.   B. Traven's Mexican Indian utopias. AntR (104) 1996, 129–40.
22241. ZOGBAUM, HEIDI.   B. Traven: a vision of Mexico. (Bibl. 1992, 16542.) Rev. by Karl S. Guthke in GGA (245:3/4) 1993, 309–14.

Sophie Treadwell

22242. CHIRICO, MIRIAM M.   *Machinal*: Sophie Treadwell's expressionist reply. TexPres (17) 1996, 6–12.
22243. FOX, ANN M.   Variations on a theme: *For Saxophone* by Sophie Treadwell. TexPres (14) 1993, 41–5.

Violet Trefusis

22244. ZAMORANO, ANA.   'Adrift on an unknown sea': androgyny and writing with particular reference to *Echo* by Violet Trefusis. *In* (pp. 195–206) **38**.

Natasha Trethewey

22245. PETTY, JILL.   An interview with Natasha Trethewey. Callaloo (19:2) 1996, 364–75.

William Trevor

22246. CORE, GEORGE.   Belonging nowhere, seeing everywhere: William Trevor and the art of distance. HC (30:4) 1993, 1–9.

22247. DOHERTY, FRANCIS.   William Trevor's *A Meeting in Middle Age* and romantic irony. *See* **19074**.

22248. FITZGERALD-HOYT, MARY.   De-colleenizing Ireland: William Trevor's *Family Sins*. Notes on Modern Irish Literature (5) 1993, 28–33.

22249. LASDUN, JAMES.   A genius for misery: William Trevor and the art of the short story. TLS, 27 Sept. 1996, 23.

22250. MORRISON, KRISTIN.   Child murder as metaphor of colonial exploitation in Toni Morrison's *Beloved, The Silence in the Garden*, and *The Killeen*. *In* (pp. 292–300) **49**.

Lionel Trilling

22251. SEATON, JAMES.   Trilling's *Homage to Catalonia*. *See* **20919**.

Valerie Tripp (1951–)

22252. TRIPP, VALERIE.   Writing for children: quirks, foibles, and curiosity. BkW, 9 May 1993, 17.

Joanna Trollope ('Caroline Harvey')

22253. ALLAN, JAMES.   Strangely soothing. Quote Unquote (41) 1996, 10–11. (Interview.)

22254. WICHTEL, DIANA.   A class of her own. NZList, 26 Oct. 1996, 34–5.

Jim Tully

22255. ANDERSON, DAVID D.   The painful memories of an Ohio boyhood in Jim Tully's fiction. SSMLN (24:3) 1994, 8–14.

Scott Turow

22256. KOPPER, EDWARD A., JR.   The influence of *Heart of Darkness* on Scott Turow's *Pleading Guilty*. *See* **17057**.

22257. SZUBERLA, GUY.   Paretsky, Turow, and the importance of symbolic ethnicity. *See* **20968**.

22258. TUROW, SCOTT.   The burden of race. *See* **13343**.

Hone Tuwhare

22259. DERBY, MARK.   Sharing riches. Quote Unquote (41) 1996, 25.

22260. SHARP, IAIN.   When a poem kicks: Tuwhare's river talk. Landfall (4:1) 1996, 50–61.

Anne Tyler

22261. ALMOND, BARBARA R.   The accidental therapist: intrapsychic change in a novel. LitPs (38:1/2) 1992, 84–104.

22262. CUNINGHAM, HENRY.   An accidental tourist's best friend: Edward as four-legged literary device. NCL (23:4) 1993, 10–12.

22263. KISSEL, SUSAN S.   Moving on: the heroines of Shirley Ann Grau, Anne Tyler, and Gail Godwin. *See* **18238**.

22264. KLINE, KAREN E.   *The Accidental Tourist* on page and on screen: interrogating normative theories about film adaptation. *See* **13874**.

22265. SALWAK, DALE (ed.).   Anne Tyler as novelist. (Bibl. 1994, 15242.) Rev. by Judie Newman in JAStud (30:2) 1996, 323.

22266. SWEENEY, SUSAN ELIZABETH.   Anne Tyler's invented games: *The Accidental Tourist* and *Breathing Lessons*. SoQ (34:1) 1995, 81–97.

Katharine Tynan

22267. REVIE, LINDA L.   The little red fox, emblem of the Irish peasant in poems by Yeats, Tynan and Ní Dhomhnaill. *In* (pp. 113–33) **58**.

Sir Gerald Hugh Tyrwhitt-Wilson,
Fourteenth Baron Berners

22268. COWLEY, JULIAN.   The neglected satirical fiction of Lord Berners. JML (19:2) 1995, 187–200.

John Updike

22269. BROER, LAWRENCE R.   The heart of Harry Angstrom: dream visions in Updike's Rabbit tetralogy. JFA (7:4) 1996, 84–101.

22270. CALINESCU, MATEI.   Secrecy in fiction: textual and inter-textual secrets in Hawthorne and Updike. *See* **11398**.

22271. DEBELLIS, JACK.   'It captivates … it hypnotizes': Updike goes to the movies. *See* **13596**.

22272. KLINKOWITZ, JEROME.   Toward a new American mainstream: John Updike and Kurt Vonnegut. *In* (pp. 150–67) **123**.

22273. LUSCHER, ROBERT M.   John Updike: a study of the short fiction. (Bibl. 1994, 15251.) Rev. by George J. Searles in MFS (40:2) 1994, 380–1.

22274. MITSCH, RUTHMARIE H.   Updike's *Tristan and Iseult*. Exp (54:4) 1996, 247–9.

22275. NASH, CHARLES C.   Trying his wings: John Updike's reply to John Cheever's *O Youth and Beauty! See* **16903**.

22276. PLATH, JAMES (ed.).   Conversations with John Updike. (Bibl. 1994, 15253.) Rev. by George J. Searles in MFS (40:2) 1994, 384–5.

22277. SETHURAMAN, RAMCHANDRAN.   Updike's *The Centaur*: on aphanisis, gaze, eyes, and the death drive. LitPs (39:3) 1993, 38–65.

22278. TRACHTENBERG, STANLEY (ed.).   New essays on *Rabbit, Run*. (Bibl. 1995, 19740.) Rev. by Marianne DeKoven in MFS (40:2) 1994, 399–400; by Kurt Müller in Amst (41:4) 1996, 710.

22279. TRANQUILLA, RONALD.   John Updike's *Toward Evening*: hoodwinked. ARCS (26:1) 1996, 67–82.

22280. VIDAL, GORE.   Rabbit's own burrow: the comfortable patriotism of John Updike and his fiction. TLS, 26 Apr. 1996, 3–7.

Jean Ure

22281. STEPHENS, JOHN.   Gender, genre and children's literature. *See* **14819**.

Jane Urquhart

22282. COMPTON, ANNE.   Meditations on the house: the poetics of space in Jane Urquhart's *Changing Heaven* and *The Whirlpool*. CanL (150) 1996, 10–21.

22283. GOLDMAN, MARLENE.   Translating the sublime: Jane Urquhart's *The Whirlpool*. CanL (150) 1996, 23–42.

Pieter-Dirk Uys

22284. RAGUŽ, JENNIFER M.   What the eye does not see, the heart … . Seeing and blindness in Pieter-Dirk Uys's play *Panorama*. TexPres (17) 1996, 53–7.

Uzor Maxim Uzoatu

22285. Ezenwa-Ohaeto. Critical realism and the thriller tradition in Nigerian fiction: Williams, Nwankwo and Uzoatu. *See* **20627**.

Chris Van Allsburg

22286. Stanton, Joseph. The dreaming picture books of Chris Van Allsburg. *See* **248**.

Jack Vance

22287. Temianka, Daniel. The king of wordsmiths. *See* **1877**.

Guy Vanderhaeghe

22288. Horava, Tony. Guy Vanderhaeghe: a bibliography. ECanW (58) 1996, 241–66.

Mona Van Duyn

22289. Shaw, Robert B. Life work. Shen (44:1) 1994, 38–48.

John C. Van Dyke

22290. Ingham, Zita; Wild, Peter. The preface as illumination: the curious (if not tricky) case of John C. Van Dyke. RhR (9:2) 1991, 328–39.
22291. Wild, Peter. How a London madman painted our deserts. NDQ (63:2) 1996, 5–17.
22292. ——— A new look at our foremost desert classic. NDQ (63:1) 1996, 116–27.

Sutton Vane

22293. Goodman, Margaret. Posthumous journeys: *The Great Divorce* and other travels to eternity. *See* **11410**.

Aritha Van Herk

22294. Beautell, Eva Darias. Panties and roads: woman, fiction and cartography in Aritha Van Herk's *No Fixed Address*. RCEI (28) 1994, 151–9.
22295. Howells, Coral Ann. Disruptive geographies; or, Mapping the region of woman in contemporary Canadian women's writing in English. *See* **16048**.
22296. Neuman, Shirley. Writing the reader, writing the self in Aritha Van Herk's *Places Far from Ellesmere*. ECanW (60) 1996, 215–34.
22297. Van Herk, Aritha. The map's temptation; or, The search for a secret book. JCL (31:1) 1996, 129–36.

Jean-Claude van Itallie

22298. Plunka, Gene A. Artaud's theatre of cruelty on Route 666: Jean-Claude van Itallie's *Motel*. SAtlR (61:1) 1996, 89–108.
22299. ——— Jean-Claude van Itallie. *In* (pp. 241–56) **85**.

Carl Van Vechten

22300. Blackmer, Corinne E. Selling taboo subjects: the literary commerce of Gertrude Stein and Carl Van Vechten. *In* (pp. 221–52) **67**.
22301. Kellner, Bruce. Langston Hughes's *Nigger Heaven* Blues. *See* **18800**.
22302. Seed, David. Party-going: the Jazz Age novels of Evelyn

Waugh, Wyndham Lewis, F. Scott Fitzgerald and Carl Van Vechten. *In* (pp. 117–34) **34**.

22303. WORTH, ROBERT F.   *Nigger Heaven* and the Harlem renaissance. AAR (29:3) 1995, 461–73.

M. G. Vassanji

22304. BARDOLPH, JACQUELINE.   M. G. Vassanji's *Uhuru Street*: a short story sequence by a Canadian-African-Asian. JSSE (24) 1995, 82–93.

Elizabeth Dewberry Vaughn

22305. CRONIN, GLORIA L.   Fundamentalist views and feminist dilemmas: Elizabeth Dewberry Vaughn's *Many Things Have Happened Since He Died* and *Break the Heart of Me*. *In* (pp. 254–78) **123**.

Gore Vidal

22306. ANON. (ed.).   Under the star of writing: letters about and to Gore Vidal, 1946–1961. *See* **20557**.

22307. FLETCHER, M. D.; FEROS, KATE.   Gore Vidal's satire. SCS (20) 1996, 160–4.

22308. GOLDSTEIN, LAURENCE.   Film as family history. *See* **13725**.

22309. KAPLAN, FRED.   Pleased to have been your contemporary: the letters of Christopher Isherwood and Gore Vidal. *See* **18896**.

22310. PARINI, JAY (ed.).   Gore Vidal: writer against the grain. (Bibl. 1992, 16582.) Rev. by Robert J. Corber in MFS (40:2) 1994, 377–8; by Marvin J. LaHood in WLT (70:1) 1996, 191–2; by Joe Moran in JAStud (30:1) 1996, 160–1.

22311. VIDAL, GORE.   Palimpsest: a memoir. (Bibl. 1995, 19758.) Rev. by Jonathan Yardley in BkW, 8 Oct. 1995, 3; by Marvin J. LaHood in WLT (70:3) 1996, 704.

Joan D. Vinge

22312. SANDERS, JOE.   Private *psi*: Joan D. Vinge's *Catspaw*. Extrapolation (37:2) 1996, 121–6.

Elfrida Vipont

22313. SCRAGG, BRENDA J.   Elfrida Vipont: Quaker children's writer. BJRL (76:3) 1994, 249–65.

Helena María Viramontes

22314. CAMINERO-SANTANGELO, MARTA.   Beyond otherness: negotiated identities and Viramontes' *The Cariboo Cafe*. JSSE (27) 1996, 29–42.

Sean Virgo (1940–)

22315. FROELICH, VERA P.   Theme and symbol in Sean Virgo's *Home and Native Land*. NCL (25:2) 1995, 8–10.

Gerald Vizenor

22316. BLAESER, KIMBERLY M.   Gerald Vizenor: writing in the oral tradition. Norman; London: Oklahoma UP, 1996. pp. xii, 260.

22317. HAUSS, JON.   Real stories: memory, violence, and enjoyment in Gerald Vizenor's *Bearheart*. LitPs (41:4) 1995, 1–16.

22318. ISERNHAGEN, HARTWIG.   'Historical in a world of postmodern survivance' – an excerpt from an interview with Gerald Vizenor. ZAA (43:4) 1995, 336–50.

22319. MONSMA, BRADLEY JOHN. 'Active readers ... obverse tricksters': trickster texts and cross-cultural reading. *See* **19316**.

22320. RODRIGUEZ, JUANA MARIA. Gerald Vizenor's shadow plays: narrative mediations and multiplicities of power. Genre (25:4) 1992, 421–9.

22321. RUPPERT, JAMES. Mediation in contemporary Native-American writing. *See* **17626**.

22322. VELIE, ALAN. The Indian historical novel. Genre (25:4) 1992, 391–406.

22323. VIZENOR, GERALD. Native-American Indian identities: autoinscriptions and the cultures of names. *See* **2168**.

Herman Voaden

22324. WAGNER, ANTON (ed.). A vision of Canada: Herman Voaden's dramatic works, 1928–1945. (Bibl. 1995, 19766.) Rev. by Richard Plant in CanTR (79/80) 1994, 154–7; by Don Perkins in TRC (15:2) 1994, 223–5.

Cynthia Voigt

22325. CARROLL, PAMELA SISSI. Enduring values: grandmothers and granddaughters in three novels for young adults. *See* **16562**.

22326. STEPHENS, JOHN. Gender, genre and children's literature. *See* **14819**.

Kurt Vonnegut, Jr

22327. BĂLU, ANDI. Kurt Vonnegut Jr şi romanul parabolă. (Kurt Vonnegut, Jr, and the parable novel.) Steaua (45:1/2) 1994, 52.

22328. BLAND, MICHAEL. A game of black humor in Vonnegut's *Cat's Cradle*. NCL (24:4) 1994, 8–9.

22329. BOON, KEVIN A. The problem with Pilgrim in Kurt Vonnegut's *Slaughterhouse Five*. NCL (26:2) 1996, 8–10.

22330. GOCH, MARTIN. Darwin und die postmoderne Literatur: der Kampf der Prätexte in Kurt Vonneguts *Galápagos* (1985). GRM (45:2) 1995, 204–20.

22331. HEARRON, TOM. The theme of guilt in Vonnegut's cataclysmic novels. *In* (pp. 186–92) **77**.

22332. HUGHES, JOSEPH J. Echoes of *Gilgamesh* in Vonnegut's *Breakfast of Champions*. PMPA (16) 1991, 93–7.

22333. KLINKOWITZ, JEROME. Kurt Vonnegut's ultimate. *In* (pp. 193–8) **77**.

22334. —— Toward a new American mainstream: John Updike and Kurt Vonnegut. *In* (pp. 150–67) **123**.

22335. LEEDS, MARC. The Vonnegut encyclopedia: an authorized compendium. Foreword by Kurt Vonnegut. (Bibl. 1995, 19775.) Rev. by Arthur O. Lewis in Utopian Studies (7:2) 1996, 286–8; by Todd Davis in Style (30:2) 1996, 351–4; by Michael Schoenecke in JPC (30:2) 1996, 209–10.

22336. MALLORY, CAROLE. The Joe and Kurt show. *See* **18568**.

22337. MUSTAZZA, LEONARD (ed.). The critical response to Kurt Vonnegut. (Bibl. 1994, 15283.) Rev. by Wallace Austin Flanders in

Utopian Studies (7:1) 1996, 136–7; by Todd Davis in Style (30:2) 1996, 351–4.

22338. NORRMAN, RALF.   Thanks a million: gratitude in Kurt Vonnegut's world. *In* (pp. 193–209) Natalia Baschmakoff, Arja Rosenholm, Hannu Tommola (eds), Aspekteja. Tampere: Univ. of Tampere, 1996. pp. i, 381. (Slavica Tamperensia, 5.)

22339. PISAPIA, BIANCAMARIA.   Kurt Vonnegut, il *computer*, ovvero l'epica tenzone tra il racconto e la cibernetica (in due assalti). *In* (pp. 265–8) **117**.

22340. REED, PETER J.; LEEDS, MARC (eds).   The Vonnegut chronicles: interviews and essays. Westport, CT; London: Greenwood Press, 1996. pp. 257. (Contributions to the study of world literature, 65.)

22341. UCHMANOWICZ, PAULINE.   Vanishing Vietnam: Whiteness and the technology of memory. *See* **17243**.

Helen Waddell

22342. LOCKLEAR, GLORIANNA.   Delicious poison: Heloise and Abelard out of time. *See* **9250**.

Fred Wah

22343. DERKSEN, JEFF.   Making race opaque: Fred Wah's poetics of opposition and differentiation. WCL (29:3) 1995/96, 63–76.

Diane Wakoski

22344. WAKOSKI, DIANE.   The writing of *The Photos*. WD (71:11) 1991, 38–41.

Derek Walcott

22345. BAER, WILLIAM (ed.).   Conversations with Derek Walcott. Jackson; London: Mississippi UP, 1996. pp. xv, 211. (Literary conversations.)

22346. DAVIS, C. B.   'There is no *l* after the eye.' The Cyclops as dramatized by Euripides and Derek Walcott. TexPres (16) 1995, 32–8.

22347. FRASER, ROBERT.   Mental travellers: myths of return in the poetry of Walcott and Brathwaite. *In* (pp. 7–13) **102**.

22348. GIDMARK, JILL B.; HUNT, ANTHONY.   Catherine Weldon: Derek Walcott's visionary telling of history. CEACrit (59:1) 1996, 8–20.

22349. MACPHEE, GRAHAM.   Value, tradition and the place of the present: the disputed canon in the United States. *See* **15621**.

22350. RIGHETTI, ANGELO (introd.).   Sul mare non si costruiscono castelli: intervista a Derek Walcott di Hella Boschmann. Trans. by Sabrina Delucca. Quaderni di lingue e letterature (19) 1994, 265–71. (Italian trans. of *Die Welt* interview, 1994.)

22351. SPAAS, LIEVE; STIMPSON, BRIAN (eds).   Robinson Crusoe: myths and metamorphoses. *See* **8986**.

Anne Waldman (1945–)

22352. BAMBERGER, W. C.   Emptiness inside the compound: the architecture of Anne Waldman's reality. Talisman (13) 1994/95, 130–6.

22353. FOSTER, EDWARD.   An interview with Anne Waldman. Talisman (13) 1994/95, 62–78.

22354. FRIEDMAN, AMY L.   'I say my new name': women writers of the Beat Generation. *In* (pp. 200–16) **4**.

22355. PREVALLET, KRISTIN. Avenging Mars on Anne Waldman's *Field of Opposition.* Talisman (13) 1994/95, 137–9.

22356. RITKES, DAN. Anne Waldman: interview. Onthebus (3:2/4:1) 1991, 232–9.

Rosmarie Waldrop

22357. FOSTER, EDWARD. An interview with Rosmarie Waldrop. Talisman (6) 1991, 27–39.

Alice Walker

22358. APPLEGATE, NANCY. Feminine sexuality in Alice Walker's *Possessing the Secret of Joy.* NCL (24:4) 1994, 11.

22359. BRAENDLIN, BONNIE. Alice Walker's *The Temple of My Familiar* as pastiche. AL (68:1) 1996, 47–67.

22360. BUCKMAN, ALYSON R. The body as a site of colonization: Alice Walker's *Possessing the Secret of Joy.* JAC (18:2) 1995, 89–94.

22361. BUTLER, ROBERT JAMES. Alice Walker's vision of the South in *The Third Life of Grange Copeland.* AAR (27:2) 1993, 195–204.

22362. CHRISTIAN, BARBARA T. (ed.). Everyday use. New Brunswick, NJ: Rutgers UP, 1994. pp. vi, 229. Rev. by Martha Sledge in SoQ (34:2) 1996, 156.

22363. CROSLAND, ANDY. Alice Walker's *Nineteen Fifty-Five*: fiction and fact. ELN (34:2) 1996, 59–63.

22364. DIEKE, IKENNA. Toward a monastic idealism: the thematics of Alice Walker's *The Temple of My Familiar.* AAR (26:3) 1992, 507–14.

22365. DOLE, CAROL M. The return of the father in Spielberg's *The Color Purple. See* **13628**.

22366. ELSLEY, JUDY. 'Nothing can be sole or whole that has not been rent': fragmentation in the quilt and *The Color Purple.* WebS (9:2) 1992, 71–81.

22367. GOURDINE, ANGELETTA K. M. Postmodern ethnography and the womanist mission: postcolonial sensibilities in *Possessing the Secret of Joy.* AAR (30:2) 1996, 237–44.

22368. HALL, JAMES C. Towards a map of mis(sed) reading: the presence of absence in *The Color Purple.* AAR (26:1) 1992, 89–97.

22369. HAYES, ELIZABETH T. 'Like seeing you buried': Persephone in *The Bluest Eye, Their Eyes Were Watching God,* and *The Color Purple. In* (pp. 170–94) **46**.

22370. HENKE, SUZETTE A. Women's life-writing and the minority voice: Maya Angelou, Maxine Hong Kingston, and Alice Walker. *In* (pp. 210–33) **123**.

22371. HITE, MOLLY. The other side of the story: structures and strategies of contemporary feminist narrative. *See* **16085**.

22372. HUBBARD, DOLAN. Society and self in Alice Walker's *In Love and Trouble. In* (pp. 209–33) **3**.

22373. JACKSON, TOMMIE L. Orphanage in Simone Schwartz-Bart's *The Bridge of Beyond* and Alice Walker's *The Third Life of Grange Copeland.* Griot (15:2) 1996, 7–13.

22374. JOHNSON, MARIA V. 'You *just* can't keep a good woman down': Alice Walker sings the Blues. AAR (30:2) 1996, 221–36.

22375. JONES, SUZANNE W. Dismantling stereotypes: interracial friendships in *Meridian* and *A Mother and Two Daughters. In* (pp. 140–57) **32**.

22376. KAPLAN, CARLA.   The erotics of talk: women's writing and feminist paradigms. *See* **10418**.

22377. KENYON, OLGA.   Alice Walker and Buchi Emecheta rewrite the myth of motherhood. *In* (pp. 336–54) **34**.

22378. LOEB, MONICA.   Walker's *The Flowers*. Exp (55:1) 1996, 60–2.

22379. MARVIN, THOMAS F.   'Preachin' the Blues': Bessie Smith's secular religion and Alice Walker's *The Color Purple*. AAR (28:3) 1994, 411–21.

22380. MOORE, OPAL.   The problem of (Black) art. *In* (pp. 177–93) **8**.

22381. O'CONNOR, MARY.   Subject, voice, and women in some contemporary Black American women's writing. *In* (pp. 199–217) **33**.

22382. PIFER, LYNN.   Coming to voice in Alice Walker's *Meridian*: speaking out for the revolution. AAR (26:1) 1992, 77–88.

22383. PREBLE-NIEMI, ORALIA.   Magical realism and the great goddess in two novels by Alejo Carpentier and Alice Walker. Comparatist (16) 1992, 101–14.

22384. RESTUCCIA, FRANCES L.   Literary representations of battered women: spectacular domestic punishment. *In* (pp. 42–71) **9**.

22385. SEIDEL, KATHRYN LEE.   The Lilith figure in Toni Morrison's *Sula* and Alice Walker's *The Color Purple*. *See* **20402**.

22386. SELZER, LINDA.   Race and domesticity in *The Color Purple*. AAR (29:1) 1995, 67–82.

22387. SMITH, FELIPE.   Alice Walker's redemptive art. AAR (26:3) 1992, 437–51.

22388. WALKER, ALICE.   The same river twice: honoring the difficult: a meditation on life, spirit, art, and the making of the film, *The Color Purple*, ten years later. *See* **14308**.

22389. WESTON, RUTH D.   Who touches this touches a woman: the naked self in Alice Walker. WebS (9:2) 1992, 49–60.

22390. WINCHELL, DONNA HAISTY.   Alice Walker. (Bibl. 1992, 16626.) Rev. by Martha J. Cutter in AAR (28:4) 1994, 665–9; by Cedric Gael Bryant in MFS (40:1) 1994, 156–7.

Margaret Walker

22391. GRAHAM, MARYEMMA.   The fusion of ideas: an interview with Margaret Walker Alexander. AAR (27:2) 1993, 279–86.

Mildred Walker

22392. HUGO, RIPLEY (introd.).   The quarry. Lincoln; London: Nebraska UP, 1995. pp. xii, 339.

Wendy Walker

22393. CHÉNETIER, MARC.   Metamorphoses of the *Metamorphoses*: Patricia Eakins, Wendy Walker, Don Webb. *See* **17455**.

David Foster Wallace

22394. BRUNI, FRANK.   The grunge American novelist. NYTM, 24 Mar. 1996, 40–1.

Edgar Wallace

22395. BROWN, ROBIN.   Edgar Wallace and Kiplings *manqués*. *See* **19335**.

Robin Wallace-Crabbe

22396. RIEMER, A. P.	Maverick voices: the novels of David Foster and Robin Wallace-Crabbe. *See* **17948**.

Robert James Waller (1939–)

22397. WELSH, JIM.	Fixing *The Bridges of Madison County*. *See* **14317**.

Irvine Walsh

22398. MONNICKENDAM, ANDREW.	Lost causes: national identity and postmodernism. *See* **12176**.

Michael Walsh (1897–1938)

22399. KIELY, BENEDICT (introd.).	Collected poems. Dublin: Walsh, 1996. pp. 143.

Anna Lee Walters (1946–)

22400. AIGNER-ALVAREZ, ERIKA.	Artifact and written history: freeing the terminal Indian in Anna Lee Walters' *Ghost Singer*. SAIL (8:1) 1996, 45–59.

Ania Walwicz

22401. BALLYN, SUSAN.	The fragmented self and strategies of subversive construction: Ania Walwicz and Rosa Cappiello. RCEI (28) 1994, 139–49.
22402. —— The voice of the other: an approach to migrant writing in Australia. *See* **16691**.

Marina Warner

22403. CAPUTO, NICOLETTA.	Storia/e al femminile: '*writing as re-vision*'. *See* **16204**.
22404. CONDÉ, MARY.	Finding a voice for Martha: Marina Warner's *Mary Takes the Better Part*. JSSE (22) 1994, 105–13.
22405. KORTE, BARBARA.	Kulturwissenschaft *in* der Literaturwissenschaft: am Beispiel von Marina Warners Roman *Indigo*. Ang (114:3) 1996, 425–45.

Sylvia Townsend Warner

22406. BAXTER, CHARLES.	Rhyming action. *See* **4338**.
22407. McKENNA, BRIAN.	The British Communist novel of the 1930s and 1940s: a 'party of equals'? (And does that matter?) *See* **18157**.

Robert Penn Warren

22408. BROOKS, CLEANTH.	The humanities: liberator of mind and spirit. *In* (pp. 162–75) **79**.
22409. CLARK, WILLIAM BEDFORD.	The American vision of Robert Penn Warren. (Bibl. 1993, 15353.) Rev. by Victor Strandberg in GetR (5:3) 1992, 480–97.
22410. —— Whitman, Warren, and the literature of discovery. *See* **12664**.
22411. CORE, GEORGE.	Life's bright parenthesis: Warren's example and one man's pedagogy. *In* (pp. 48–60) **43**.
22412. CULLICK, JONATHAN S.	Levels of historical representation in *All the King's Men*. SoQ (34:2) 1996, 59–64.

22413. JANCOVICH, MARK.   Robert Penn Warren as New Critic: against propaganda and irresponsibility. *See* **15530**.

22414. JUSTUS, JAMES H.   Warren in the 1900s and the prospects for Southern writers. SoCR (29:1) 1996, 179–86.

22415. KOPPELMAN, ROBERT S.   Robert Penn Warren's Modernist spirituality. (Bibl. 1995, 19846.) Rev. by James A. Grimshaw, Jr, in SoQ (34:3) 1996, 156–7.

22416. MCDONALD, JOYCE.   Lacan's mirror stage as symbolic metaphor in *All the King's Men*. SoQ (34:4) 1996, 73–9.

22417. MILLICHAP, JOSEPH R.   'A special kind of complex Eden': Robert Penn Warren's Italy. SoQ (34:2) 1996, 65–71.

22418. OLNEY, JAMES.   Parents and children in Robert Penn Warren's autobiography. *In* (pp. 31–47) **43**.

22419. PERKINS, DAVID.   The *Ancient Mariner* and its interpreters: some versions of Coleridge. *See* **10695**.

22420. RUNYON, RANDOLPH PAUL.   The braided dream: Robert Penn Warren's late poetry. (Bibl. 1995, 19849.) Rev. by Victor Strandberg in GetR (5:3) 1992, 480–97.

22421. —— The taciturn text: the fiction of Robert Penn Warren. (Bibl. 1994, 15335.) Rev. by Victor Strandberg in GetR (5:3) 1992, 480–97.

22422. RUPPERSBURG, HUGH.   Robert Penn Warren and the American imagination. (Bibl. 1995, 19850.) Rev. by Victor Strandberg in GetR (5:3) 1992, 480–97.

22423. STRANDBERG, VICTOR.   Robert Penn Warren and the search for design. GetR (5:3) 1992, 480–97 (review-article).

22424. THIEMANN, FRED R.   Politics and the self in Robert Penn Warren's poetry. SAtlR (61:4) 1996, 83–96.

22425. WATKINS, FLOYD C.; HIERS, JOHN T.; WEAKS, MARY LOUISE (eds).   Talking with Robert Penn Warren. (Bibl. 1995, 19853.) Rev. by Victor Strandberg in GetR (5:3) 1992, 480–97.

Emma Lee Warrior

22426. FACHINGER, PETRA.   Cross-dressing as appropriation in the short stories of Emma Lee Warrior. SAIL (8:3) 1996, 36–48.

Booker T. Washington

22427. ANDREWS, WILLIAM L.   Booker T. Washington, Belle Kearney, and the Southern patriarchy. *In* (pp. 85–97) **43**.

Wendy Wasserstein

22428. DOUTHIT, LUE MORGAN.   Reconsidering the feminism of 'Heidi': a look at the comic structure in *The Heidi Chronicles*. TexPres (14) 1993, 11–19.

22429. JACOBSON, LESLIE.   Wendy Wasserstein. *In* (pp. 257–76) **85**.

22430. WASSERSTEIN, WENDY.   The holiday chronicles. BkW, 17 Dec. 1995, 1, 10.

Judah Waten

22431. BALLYN, SUSAN.   The voice of the other: an approach to migrant writing in Australia. *See* **16691**.

Frank Waters

22432. ADAMS, CHARLES. Frank Waters. *In* (pp. 14–25) **121**.
22433. —— Invitation to the dance: the 'deep ecology' of Frank Waters. PCR (3:1) 1992, 33–40.

Sheila Watson

22434. KUESTER, MARTIN. (Post-)modern *bricolage*: Classical mythology in Sheila Watson's short stories. ZAA (42:3) 1994, 225–34.
22435. VENTURA, HÉLIANE. 'The energy of reiteration': Sheila Watson's *Antigone*. RANAM (29) 1996, 183–98.

Evelyn Waugh

22436. CRAIG, RANDALL. Evelyn Waugh and William Gerhardie. *See* **18150**.
22437. HASTINGS, SELINA. Evelyn Waugh: a biography. (Bibl. 1995, 19876.) Rev. by Michael Dirda in BkW, 30 Apr. 1995, 6; by Robert Murray Davis in WLT (69:4) 1995, 804–5; by the same in Cweal (122:10) 1996, 35–7.
22438. HEINIMANN, DAVID. An ethical critique of Waugh's Guy Crouchback. Ren (46:3) 1994, 175–85.
22439. JOHNSON, R. NEILL. Shadowed by the gaze: Evelyn Waugh's *Vile Bodies* and *The Ordeal of Gilbert Pinfold*. MLR (91:1) 1996, 9–19.
22440. KRÖLLER, EVA-MARIE. 'Sur les rivages d'un autre âge': Timothy Findley et Evelyn Waugh. *See* **17815**.
22441. LASSNER, PHYLLIS. 'Between the gaps': sex, class and anarchy in the British comic novel of World War II. *In* (pp. 205–19) **64**.
22442. MOONEYHAM, LAURA. The triple conversions of *Brideshead Revisited*. Ren (45:4) 1993, 225–35.
22443. ROBINSON, DANIEL. Evelyn Waugh in 'the best of all possible worlds': *Decline and Fall*, a comedy of theodicy. ELN (34:1) 1996, 77–86.
22444. SEED, DAVID. Party-going: the Jazz Age novels of Evelyn Waugh, Wyndham Lewis, F. Scott Fitzgerald and Carl Van Vechten. *In* (pp. 117–34) **34**.

Don Webb

22445. CHÉNETIER, MARC. Metamorphoses of the *Metamorphoses*: Patricia Eakins, Wendy Walker, Don Webb. *See* **17455**.

Phyllis Webb

22446. SCOBIE, STEPHEN. Leonard Cohen, Phyllis Webb, and the end(s) of Modernism. *In* (pp. 57–70) **13**.

Bruce Weigl

22447. STEPHENS, MICHAEL. A bad and green dream: Bruce Weigl's many voices and landscapes. HC (31:2) 1994, 1–11.

Denton Welch

22448. HALL, THOMAS C. The uncensored novels of Denton Welch: an excavation of intent. RecL (22) 1995, 6–21.

Don Welch

22449. SAUCERMAN, JAMES R. Poems of popular common ground: four voices of the Midwest. *See* **19367**.

James Welch

22450. BEVIS, WILLIAM.   Wylie tales: an interview with James Welch. WebS (12:3) 1995, 15–31.

22451. FITZ, KARSTEN.   Bridging the gap: strategies of survival in James Welch's novels. AICRJ (20:1) 1996, 131–46.

22452. VELIE, ALAN.   The Indian historical novel. *See* **22322**.

Fay Weldon

22453. HEBERT, ANN MARIE.   Rewriting the feminine script: Fay Weldon's wicked laughter. CritM (7:1) 1993, 22–40.

22454. SQUIER, SUSAN.   Conceiving difference: reproductive technology and the construction of identity in two contemporary fictions. *In* (pp. 97–115) **94**.

Michael Weller

22455. WELLER, MICHAEL.   Helen Weinberger Address. AmDr (1:1) 1991, 1–15.

Paul O'M. Welles

22456. WRIGHT, LES.   Gay genocide as literary trope. *In* (pp: 50–68) **2**.

Carolyn Wells

22457. HALL, JOAN WYLIE.   Legacy profile: Carolyn Wells (1862–1942). Legacy (13:2) 1996, 142–51.

H. G. Wells

22458. ALLETT, JOHN.   The ambivalent feminism of *Ann Veronica*. SHum (20:1) 1993, 63–75.

22459. BAILEY, K. V.   Mars is a district of Sheffield. *See* **15919**.

22460. BAXTER, STEPHEN.   Further visions: sequels to *The Time Machine*. *See* **16242**.

22461. COREN, MICHAEL.   The invisible man: the life and liberties of H. G. Wells. (Bibl. 1995, 19917.) Rev. by Andrew Motion in BkW, 22 Aug. 1996, 8–9.

22462. DALY, MACDONALD (ed.).   The invisible man: a grotesque romance. London: Dent; Rutland, VT: Tuttle, 1995. pp. xli, 181. (Everyman library.)

22463. DERRY, STEPHEN.   *The Island of Doctor Moreau* and Stevenson's *The Ebb-Tide*. *See* **12333**.

22464. —— The Time Traveller's utopian books and his reading of the future. *See* **10351**.

22465. FOOT, MICHAEL.   H.G.: the history of Mr Wells. (Bibl. 1995, 19920.) Rev. by Stephen Baxter in Foundation (65) 1995, 103–8; by W. Warren Wagar in BkW, 7 Jan. 1996, 6.

22466. GAILOR, DENIS.   Wells's *War of the Worlds*, the 'invasion story' and Victorian moralism. CritS (8:3) 1996, 270–6.

22467. HENDERSHOT, CYNDY.   The animal without: masculinity and imperialism in *The Island of Doctor Moreau* and *The Adventure of the Speckled Band*. *See* **11064**.

22468. HUNTINGTON, JOHN.   *The Time Machine* and Wells's social trajectory. Foundation (65) 1995, 6–15.

22469. KEMP, PETER.   H. G. Wells and the culminating ape:

biological imperatives and imaginative obsessions. Basingstoke: Macmillan; New York: St Martin's Press, 1996. pp. 232. (Repr. of bibl. 1985, 13398, with alterations including a new postscript.)

22470. KUMAR, KRISHAN (ed.).   A modern Utopia. London: Everyman, 1994. pp. xlii, 270.

22471. MACDONALD, ALEX.   'Passionate intensity' in Wells's *The Island of Doctor Moreau* and Yeats's *The Second Coming*: constructing an echo. ANQ (9:4) 1996, 40–3.

22472. MENDELSON, EDWARD.   How Lawrence corrected Wells; how Orwell refuted Lawrence. *In* (pp. 166–75) **41**.

22473. PALUMBO, DONALD E.   The politics of entropy: revolution *vs* evolution in George Pal's film version of H. G. Wells's *The Time Machine*. *In* (pp. 204–11) **70**.

22474. PARRINDER, PATRICK.   Shadows of the future: H. G. Wells, science fiction, and prophecy. (Bibl. 1995, 19931.) Rev. by Stephen Baxter in Foundation (65) 1995, 103–8; by Howard Canaan in Utopian Studies (7:2) 1996, 314–16; by John Huntington in ELT (39:3) 1996, 351–3.

22475. RUSSELL, W. M. S.   Time before and after *The Time Machine*. *See* **10607**.

22476. SCHEICK, WILLIAM J. (ed.).   The critical response to H. G. Wells. (Bibl. 1995, 19932.) Rev. by Darren Harris-Fain in Extrapolation (37:3) 1996, 279–83.

22477. SQUIER, SUSAN M.   Embryologies of Modernism. *See* **18879**.

22478. STOVER, LEON (ed.).   *The Island of Doctor Moreau*: a critical text of the 1896 London first edition, with an introduction and appendices. *See* **844**.

22479. —— *The Time Machine: an Invention*: a critical text of the 1895 London first edition, with an introduction and appendices. *See* **845**.

22480. WASHICK, JAMES.   The framed narrative in *Perelandra*. *See* **19758**.

Irvine Welsh

22481. FREEMAN, ALAN.   Ghosts in sunny Leith: Irvine Welsh's *Trainspotting*. *In* (pp. 251–62) **115**.

22482. —— Ourselves as others: *Marabou Stork Nightmares*. Edinburgh Review (95) 1996, 135–41.

22483. O'KEEFFE, BERNARD.   The language of *Trainspotting*. *See* **2683**.

Eudora Welty

22484. ANON.   Works by Welty: a continuing checklist. EWeltyN (19:2) 1995, 7.

22485. BENZEL, MICHAEL.   Textual variants in *A Note on Jane Austen/Jane Austen*. *See* **572**.

22486. BIXBY, GEORGE.   Addendum to Polk's bibliography of Welty. EWeltyN (19:1) 1995, 12–13. (*Adds to* bibl. 1995, 19951.)

22487. BRANSON, STEPHANIE.   Ripe fruit: fantastic elements in the short fiction of Ellen Glasgow, Edith Wharton, and Eudora Welty. *In* (pp. 61–71) **3**.

22488. BURGAN, MARY.   The 'feminine' short story in America: historicizing epiphanies. *In* (pp. 267–80) **3**.

22489. CAMINERO-SANTANGELO, MARTA.   The madwoman can't speak: postwar culture, feminist criticism, and Welty's *June Recital*. *See* **15325**.

22490. CHENGGES, CATHERINE H.   Substantive variants in *The Bride of the Innisfallen*. *See* **600**.

22491. DEVLIN, ALBERT J.   The making of *Delta Wedding*; or, Doing 'something Diarmuid thought I could do'. *In* (pp. 226–61) **7**.

22492. DEVOIZE, JEANNE.   Some narrative variations in Eudora Welty's *The Golden Apples*. JSSE (18) 1992, 53–62.

22493. DIRENC, DILEK.   Eudora Welty on writing an American quilt: justifying women's work in the American literary canon. CR (40:3) 1996, 587–600.

22494. GARDNER, JOSEPH H.   Errands of love: a study in black and white. KenR (12:1/2) 1993, 69–78.

22495. GIBLEY, KEVIN CHARLES.   'Half-concealed and half-sought for': Eudora Welty's *A Still Moment* as aesthetic allegory. JSSE (18) 1992, 43–51.

22496. GRETLUND, JAN NORDBY.   Eudora Welty's aesthetics of place. (Bibl. 1995, 19942.) Rev. by Thomas E. Kennedy in HC (32:5) 1995, 12–14; by Betty J. Cortright in AL (68:1) 1996, 264.

22497. GYGAX, FRANZISKA.   Serious daring from within: female narrative strategies in Eudora Welty's novels. (Bibl. 1991, 15771.) Rev. by Rebecca Mark in Signs (18:2) 1993, 443–7.

22498. HANKINS, LESLIE K.   The thwarting of the artist as a young woman: gender and class acts in Eudora Welty's *The Golden Apples*. *In* (pp. 158–65) **87**.

22499. LEPALUDIER, LAURENT.   Womanhood in Eudora Welty's *Moon Lake*. JSSE (21) 1993, 63–77.

22500. MCCADDON, BEAUVAIS.   Making the grade in Eudora Welty's class: a creative writing workshop in the 1960s. SoQ (34:4) 1996, 99–108.

22501. MCDONALD, W. U., JR.   Textual variants in *Going to Naples*. *See* **733**.

22502. —— Textual variants in *No Place for You, My Love*. *See* **734**.

22503. —— Textual variants in *Spring/Ladies in Spring*. *See* **735**.

22504. —— Works by Welty: a continuing checklist. EWeltyN (19:1) 1995, 13; (20:1) 1996, 8; (20:2) 1996, 7–9.

22505. MCHANEY, PEARL A.   A checklist of Welty scholarship, 1994–95. EWeltyN (19:2) 1995, 9–15.

22506. —— Checklist of Welty scholarship, 1995–96. EWeltyN (20:2) 1996, 11–15.

22507. MARK, REBECCA.   The dragon's blood: feminist intertextuality in Eudora Welty's *The Golden Apples*. (Bibl. 1995, 19948.) Rev. by Peggy Whitman Prenshaw in Signs (21:3) 1996, 779–82.

22508. MONTGOMERY, MATT.   Welty for the birds. EWeltyN (20:1) 1996, 1–4.

22509. MORTIMER, GAIL L.   Daughter of the swan: love and knowledge in Eudora Welty's fiction. (Bibl. 1995, 19949.) Rev. by Peggy Whitman Prenshaw in MFS (42:1) 1996, 155–7.

22510. PINGATORE, DIANE R.   A reader's guide to the short stories of Eudora Welty. New York: G. K. Hall; London: Prentice Hall, 1996. pp. xxi, 421. (Reference pubs in literature.)

22511. POLK, NOEL.   Welty, Hawthorne, and Poe: men of the crowd and the landscape of alienation. *See* **11426**.

22512. POLLACK, HARRIET. Story-making in *The Golden Apples*: point of view, gender and the importance of Cassie Morrison. SoQ (34:2) 1996, 75–80.

22513. PRENSHAW, PEGGY WHITMAN (ed.). More conversations with Eudora Welty. Jackson; London: Mississippi UP, 1996. pp. xxi, 304. (Literary conversations.)

22514. RANDISI, JENNIFER L. Eudora Welty and the fairy tale. SoLJ (23:1) 1990, 30–44.

22515. SEAMAN, GERDA; WALKER, ELLEN L. 'It's all in a way of speaking': a discussion of *The Ponder Heart*. SoLJ (23:2) 1991, 65–76.

22516. THORNTON, NAOKO FUWA. Sideshadows of life: '*The Bride of the Innisfallen' and Other Stories* and 'other' stories. StAL (33) 1996, 19–34.

22517. VANDE KIEFT, RUTH M. The love ethos of Porter, Welty, and McCullers. *In* (pp. 235–58) **32**.

22518. WESTLING, LOUISE. Fathers and daughters in Welty and O'Connor. *In* (pp. 110–24) **32**.

22519. WESTON, RUTH D. Gothic traditions and narrative techniques in the fiction of Eudora Welty. (Bibl. 1995, 19955.) Rev. by Benjamin F. Fisher in Review (18) 1996, 249–53; by Kate Rhodes in JAStud (30:1) 1996, 139–40.

Patricia Wentworth

22520. ROBBINS, JOAN HAMERMAN. A re(de)fined sensibility: raising consciousness about women's issues in Maud Silver's world. AD (29:4) 1996, 430–5.

Timberlake Wertenbaker

22521. DAHL, MARY KAREN. Constructing the subject: Timberlake Wertenbaker's *The Grace of Mary Traverse*. JDTC (7:2) 1993, 149–59.

22522. SONCINI, SARA. *The Love of the Nightingale* (1988) di Timberlake Wertenbaker: la riscrittura del mito alla ricerca di un nuovo linguaggio. Acme (49:3) 1996, 273–85.

22523. THOMAS, MICHAEL. *Our Country's Good*: from 'canting slang' to 'refined, literate language'. *See* **2719**.

Arnold Wesker

22524. BULMAN, JAMES C. On being unfaithful to Shakespeare: Miller, Marowitz, and Wesker. *See* **6547**.

22525. PICKER, JOHN M. Shakespeare divided: revision and transformation in Marowitz's *Variations on the 'Merchant of Venice'* and Wesker's *Shylock*. *See* **7036**.

Dorothy West

22526. DALSGÅRD, KATRINE. Alive and well and living on the island of Martha's Vineyard: an interview with Dorothy West, October 29, 1988. LHR (12:2) 1993, 28–44.

22527. RODGERS, LAWRENCE R. Dorothy West's *The Living Is Easy* and the ideal of Southern folk community. AAR (26:1) 1992, 161–72.

Mae West

22528. IVANOV, ANDREA J. Mae West was not a man: sexual parody and genre in the plays and films of Mae West. *In* (pp. 275–97) **64**.

22529.   ROBERTSON, PAMELA.   'The kinda comedy that imitates me': Mae West's identification with the feminist camp. *In* (pp. 156–72) **12**.

'Nathanael West' (Nathan Wallenstein Weinstein)

22530.   MERRILL, CATHERINE.   Defining the fantastic grotesque: Nathanael West's *The Dream Life of Balso Snell*. *In* (pp. 64–73) **70**.

22531.   —— The flesh made word: *Miss Lonelyhearts*' sublime grotesque. *In* (pp. 33–8) **127**.

22532.   ROBERTS, MATHEW.   Bonfire of the avant-garde: cultural rage and readerly complicity in *The Day of the Locust*. MFS (42:1) 1996, 61–90.

22533.   ST CLAIR, JANET.   Timid defender of the faith: the prophetic vision of *Miss Lonelyhearts*. Ren (46:3) 1994, 147–61.

22534.   SARVER, STEPHANIE.   Homer Simpson meets Frankenstein: cinematic influence in Nathanael West's *The Day of the Locust*. *See* **12243**.

22535.   SPRINGER, JOHN.   'This is a riot you're in': Hollywood and American mass culture in Nathanael West's *The Day of the Locust*. *See* **14238**.

Paul West

22536.   MADDEN, DAVID W.   Understanding Paul West. (Bibl. 1993, 15450.) Rev. by Arthur M. Saltzman in MFS (40:2) 1994, 386–7.

'Rebecca West' (Mrs H. M. Andrews)

22537.   ROLLYSON, CARL.   Rebecca West: a life. New York: Scribner, 1996. pp. 511.

22538.   THOMAS, SUE.   Some more Rebecca West articles and letters to the editor. ELN (33:3) 1996, 38–9.

Robert Westall

22539.   NEWSINGER, JOHN.   Futuretracks: the juvenile science fiction of Robert Westall. Foundation (63) 1995, 61–7.

Donald Westlake

22540.   SILET, CHARLES L. P.   What's the worst that could happen? An interview with Donald Westlake. AD (29:4) 1996, 394–401.

Stanley J. Weyman

22541.   TARR, C. ANITA.   A twisted romance: abduction and rape in Stanley John Weyman's *The Castle Inn*. ELT (39:1) 1996, 63–72.

Edith Wharton

22542.   BALESTRA, GIANFRANCA.   A backward glance over travelled roads: Edith Wharton and expatriation. RSAJ (5) 1994, 51–64.

22543.   —— Edith Wharton, Henry James, and 'the proper vehicle of passion'. *In* (pp. 595–604) **117**.

22544.   —— 'For the use of the magazine morons': Edith Wharton rewrites the tale of the fantastic. SSF (33:1) 1996, 13–24.

22545.   BAUER, DALE M.   Edith Wharton's brave new politics. (Bibl. 1995, 19977.) Rev. by Jean Rohloff in HJR (17:3) 1996, 308–9; by Judith E. Funston in AL (68:3) 1996, 647–8; by Kasia Boddy in JAStud (30:2) 1996, 317–18; by Stephanie Batcos in SAF (24:2) 1996, 249–51.

22546.   BEER, JANET.   American literature to 1900: American literature 1865 to 1900. *See* **9517**.

22547. BELL, MILLICENT (ed.). The Cambridge companion to Edith Wharton. (Bibl. 1995, 19978.) Rev. by Kasia Boddy in JAStud (30:2) 1996, 317–18.

22548. BENERT, ANNETTE LARSON. Edith Wharton at war: civilized space in troubled times. TCL (42:3) 1996, 322–43.

22549. BENSTOCK, SHARI. No gifts from chance: a biography of Edith Wharton. (Bibl. 1995, 19980.) Rev. by Daniel Mark Fogel in BkW, 31 July 1994, 3; by Christine Hendrick in WLT (69:2) 1995, 369–70; by Janet Sharistanean in AmS (36:1) 1995, 188–90; by Helen Killoran in SSF (31:3) 1996, 152–4.

22550. —— 'The word which made all clear': the silent close of *The House of Mirth. In* (pp. 230–58) **31**.

22551. BRANSON, STEPHANIE. Ripe fruit: fantastic elements in the short fiction of Ellen Glasgow, Edith Wharton, and Eudora Welty. *In* (pp. 61–71) **3**.

22552. BROOKS, KRISTINA. New Woman, fallen woman: the crisis of reputation in turn-of-the-century novels by Pauline Hopkins and Edith Wharton. *See* **11505**.

22553. CLUBBE, JOHN. Interiors and the interior life in Edith Wharton's *The House of Mirth.* StudN (28:4) 1996, 543–64.

22554. COULOMBE, JOSEPH. Man or mannequin? Lawrence Selden in *The House of Mirth.* EWR (13:2) 1996, 3–8.

22555. DWIGHT, ELEANOR. Edith Wharton: an extraordinary life. (Bibl. 1995, 19987.) Rev. by Daniel Mark Fogel in BkW, 31 July 1994, 3; by Mary Ignatius Kaiser in WLT (69:1) 1995, 149–50.

22556. EDMONDS, MARY K. 'A theatre with all the lustres blazing': customs, costumes, and customers in *The Custom of the Country.* ALR (28:3) 1996, 1–18.

22557. ERLICH, GLORIA C. The sexual education of Edith Wharton. (Bibl. 1995, 19990.) Rev. by Gayle Graham Yates in MFS (40:1) 1994, 147–9; by Annette Larson Benert in ALR (28:2) 1996, 91–2.

22558. FARLAND, MARIA MAGDALENA. *Ethan Frome* and the 'springs' of masculinity. MFS (42:4) 1996, 707–29.

22559. FRACASSO, EVELYN E. Edith Wharton's *Prisoners of Consciousness*: a study of theme and technique in the tales. (Bibl. 1994, 15424.) Rev. by Samuel Irving Bellman in SSF (31:3) 1996, 154–7.

22560. —— The evolution of theme and technique in selected tales of Edith Wharton. JSSE (16) 1991, 41–50.

22561. GAVIOLI, DAVIDA. A reversal of perspective: the mother's voice in Edith Wharton's *The Mother's Recompense.* RSAJ (5) 1994, 65–80.

22562. GOODMAN, SUSAN. Edith Wharton's *Sketch of an Essay on Walt Whitman. See* **12682**.

22563. —— Edith Wharton's women: friends and rivals. (Bibl. 1994, 15429.) Rev. by Josephine Donovan in Signs (18:2) 1993, 476–80.

22564. GOODWYN, JANET BEER (ed.). The age of innocence. Cambridge; New York: CUP, 1995. pp. 320. (Cambridge literature.)

22565. HECHT, DEBORAH. The poisoned well: Percy Lubbock and Edith Wharton. *See* **15154**.

22566. HOELLER, HILDEGARD. The gains and losses of 'sentimental economies' in Edith Wharton's *The Dilettante.* ALR (28:3) 1996, 19–29.

22567. HUH, JEONG-AE. Edith Wharton eui jakpum e natanan 'shinyeosung' eui banhang gwa jwajeol. (Rebellion and frustration:

Edith Wharton's 'New Woman'.) Unpub. doct. diss., Hankuk Univ. of Foreign Studies, Seoul, 1996.

22568. HUMMEL, WILLIAM E.   My 'dull-witted enemy': symbolic violence and abject maleness in Edith Wharton's *Summer*. SAF (24:2) 1996, 215–36.

22569. JOSLIN, KATHERINE; PRICE, ALAN (eds).   Wretched exotic: essays on Edith Wharton in Europe. (Bibl. 1994, 15433.) Rev. by Jean Gooder in CamQ (25:2) 1996, 190–6; by Janet Beer Goodwyn in YES (26) 1996, 335–6.

22570. JURECIC, ANN.   The fall of the knowledgeable woman: the diminished female healer in Edith Wharton's *The Fruit of the Tree*. ALR (29:1) 1996, 29–53.

22571. KABEL, HANNO.   Money, alienation, and the leisure class: Henry James, Edith Wharton, Thorstein Veblen. *See* **11609**.

22572. KILLORAN, HELEN.   Edith Wharton: art and allusion. Tuscaloosa; London: Alabama UP, 1996. pp. xiii, 223.

22573. —— Sexuality and abnormal psychology in Edith Wharton's *The Lady's Maid's Bell*. CEACrit (58:3) 1996, 41–9.

22574. —— *Xingu*: Edith Wharton instructs literary critics. SAH (3:3) 1996, 1–13.

22575. KOPRINCE, SUSAN.   Edith Wharton, Henry James, and *Roman Fever*. *See* **11618**.

22576. LEVINE, JESSICA.   Discretion and self-censorship in Wharton's fiction: *The Old Maid* and the politics of publishing. *See* **962**.

22577. MACCOMB, DEBRA ANN.   New wives for old: divorce and the leisure-class marriage market in Edith Wharton's *The Custom of the Country*. AL (68:4) 1996, 765–97.

22578. MARSHALL, SCOTT.   Edith Wharton on film and television: a history and filmography. *See* **13963**.

22579. NETTELS, ELSA.   New England indigestion and its victims. *In* (pp. 167–84) **24**.

22580. PEUCKER, BRIGITTE.   Rival arts? Filming *The Age of Innocence*. *See* **14083**.

22581. PRICE, ALAN.   The end of the age of innocence: Edith Wharton and the First World War. London: Hale; New York: St Martin's Press, 1996. pp. xvii, 238.

22582. RAPHAEL, LEV.   Edith Wharton at Pavillon Colombe; or, A house is not always a home. SHum (18:1) 1991, 69–77.

22583. —— Edith Wharton's prisoners of shame: a new perspective on her neglected fiction. Introd. by Cynthia Griffin Wolff. (Bibl. 1993, 15475.) Rev. by Elaine Hedges in Signs (19:2) 1994, 507–11.

22584. SCORSESE, MARTIN; COCKS, JAY.   *The Age of Innocence*: the shooting script. Ed. by Robin Standefer. *See* **14194**.

22585. SHOWALTER, ELAINE (ed.).   Ethan Frome. Oxford; New York: OUP, 1996. pp. xxxiii, 122. (World's classics.)

22586. SINGLEY, CAROL J.   Edith Wharton: matters of mind and spirit. (Bibl. 1995, 20008.) Rev. by Susan Goodman in MFS (42:4) 1996, 836–7; by Mary Suzanne Schriber in AL (68:2) 1996, 470–1; by Anneke Leenhouts in JAStud (30:3) 1996, 472–3; by Stephanie Batcos in SAF (24:2) 1996, 249–51.

22587. SPRINGER, MARLENE.   *Ethan Frome*: a nightmare of need. New York: Twayne; Toronto; Oxford: Maxwell Macmillan, 1993.

pp. xiv, 130. (Twayne's masterwork studies, 121.) Rev. by Samuel Irving Bellman in SSF (31:3) 1996, 154–7.

22588. TINTNER, ADELINE. Louis Auchincloss's four 'Edith' tales: some rearrangements and reinventions of her life. *See* **16107**.

22589. VITA-FINZI, PENELOPE. Italian background: Edith Wharton's debt to Vernon Lee. *See* **11762**.

22590. WAID, CANDACE. Building *The House of Mirth*. *In* (pp. 160–86) **7**.

22591. —— Edith Wharton's letters from the underworld: fictions of women and writing. (Bibl. 1995, 20013.) Rev. by Josephine Donovan in Signs (18:2) 1993, 476–80.

22592. WOLFF, CYNTHIA GRIFFIN. Edith Wharton and the ladies' matinee. EWR (13:1) 1996, 38–40.

22593. WRIGHT, SARAH BIRD. Refracting the odyssey: Edith Wharton's travel writing as the cultural capital of her fiction. EWR (13:1) 1996, 23–30.

22594. YOUNG, JUDY HALE. The repudiation of sisterhood in Edith Wharton's *Pomegranate Seed*. SSF (33:1) 1996, 1–11.

Harvey Wheeler

22595. SEED, DAVID. Military machines and nuclear accident: Burdick and Wheeler's *Fail-Safe*. *See* **16615**.

Claire Nicolas White (1925–)

22596. PETERNEL, JOAN. Claire White's Catholic poems. Critic (49:2) 1994, 90–5.

E. B. White

22597. HUNT, CAROLINE C. Dwarf, small world, shrinking child: three versions of miniature. *See* **18555**.

22598. NEUMEYER, PETER F. (introd. and notes). The annotated *Charlotte's Web*. (Bibl. 1994, 15446.) Rev. by Judy K. Morris in BkW, 4 Dec. 1994, 18.

22599. TANNER, STEPHEN L. The art of self-deprecation in American literary humor. *See* **12618**.

Edmund White

22600. MCRUER, ROBERT. Boys' own stories and new spellings of my name: coming out and other myths of queer positionality. *In* (pp. 260–84) **30**.

Kenneth White

22601. MCMANUS, TONY. From the centred complex: an interview with Kenneth White, July 1993. Edinburgh Review (92) 1994, 122–30.

22602. WATSON, RODERICK. Visions of Alba: the construction of Celtic roots in modern Scottish literature. *See* **13356**.

Patrick White

22603. BEN-BASSAT, HEDDA. Marginal existence and communal consensus in *The Scarlet Letter* & *A Fringe of Leaves*. *See* **11387**.

22604. BRADY, VERONICA. Towards an Australian spirituality. SSp (6) 1996, 289–300.

22605. COAD, DAVID.   Platonic return in Patrick White's *The Eye of the Storm*. *In* (pp. 51–5) **102**.

22606. DURING, SIMON.   Patrick White. Melbourne; New York; Oxford: OUP, 1996. pp. 106. (Australian writers.) Rev. by David Coad in WLT (70:4) 1996, 1025.

22607. EDGECOMBE, RODNEY STENNING.   Patrick White and Dickens: two points of contact. *See* **10839**.

22608. GIFFIN, MICHAEL.   Arthur's dream: the religious imagination in the fiction of Patrick White. Paddington, N.S.W.: Spaniel, 1996. pp. xi, 268. Rev. by Jeremy Hall in LitTheol (10:4) 1996, 388–9.

22609. LEONARD, JOHN STUART.   Craven on During, During on White. Meanjin (55:2) 1996, 267–75.

22610. MÄKINEN, ANTTI.   On Patrick White's language in general and in *Riders in the Chariot* in particular. *See* **2670**.

22611. MARR, DAVID (ed.).   Letters. (Bibl. 1995, 20033.) Chicago: Chicago UP, 1996.

22612. RIIKONEN, H. K.   The life of an author: on reading David Marr's *Patrick White*. New Courant (5) 1996, 66–74.

22613. WATT, GEORGE.   Patrick White: novelist as prophet. LitTheol (10:3) 1996, 273–9.

T. H. White

22614. ADDERLEY, C. M.   The best thing for being sad: education and educators in T. H. White's *The Once and Future King*. Quondam et Futurus (2:1) 1992, 55–68.

22615. BREWER, ÉLISABETH.   T. H. White's *The Once and Future King*. (Bibl. 1995, 20034.) Rev. by T. A. Shippey in YES (26) 1996, 312–13.

22616. KELLMAN, MARTIN.   T. H. White's Merlyn: a flawed prophet. *In* (pp. 55–61) **15**.

22617. SANDLER, FLORENCE FIELD.   Family romance in *The Once and Future King*. Quondam et Futurus (2:2) 1992, 73–80.

22618. SERRANO, AMANDA.   T. H. White's defence of Guenever: portrait of a 'real' person. Mythlore (21:1) 1995, 9–13.

22619. SMITH, EVANS LANSING.   The narrative structure of T. H. White's *The Once and Future King*. Quondam et Futurus (1:4) 1991, 39–52.

Walter White

22620. JANKEN, KENNETH R.   Civil rights and socializing in the Harlem renaissance: Walter White and the fictionalization of the 'New Negro' in Georgia. GaHQ (80:4) 1996, 817–34.

George Whitmore

22621. DEWEY, JOSEPH.   Music for a closing: responses to AIDS in three American novels. *In* (pp. 23–38) **2**.

Zoë Wicomb

22622. DRIVER, DOROTHY.   Transformation through art: writing, representation, and subjectivity in recent South African fiction. *See* **14476**.

John Edgar Wideman

22623. LUSTIG, JESSICA.   Home: an interview with John Edgar Wideman. AAR (26:3) 1992, 453–7.

22624. SAUNDERS, JAMES ROBERT.　Exorcising the demons: John Edgar Wideman's literary response. HC (29:5) 1992, 1–9.

Rudy Wiebe

22625. DUFFY, DENNIS.　Wiebe's real Riel? *The Scorched-Wood People* and its audience. *In* (pp. 200–13) **105**.

Elie Wiesel

22626. DAVIS, COLIN.　Elie Wiesel's secretive texts. Gainesville: Florida UP, 1994. pp. 201. Rev. by Miriyam Glazer in AL (68:1) 1996, 280–1.

22627. FRONGIA, TERI.　Tales of old Prague: of ghettos, Passover, and the blood of libel. *See* **19946**.

Marianne Wiggins

22628. SCHUMACHER, MICHAEL.　The breakthrough of Marianne Wiggins. WD (71:2) 1991, 38–40, 62.

Richard Wilbur

22629. BISHOP, JONATHAN.　The individual thing. Ren (45:1/2) 1992/93, 17–33.

22630. CIUBA, GARY M.　Richard Wilbur: the poetry of real presences. Ren (45:1/2) 1992/93, 49–64.

22631. EDGECOMBE, RODNEY STENNING.　Wilbur's *Ceremony*. Exp (54:2) 1996, 107–10.

22632. GATTA, JOHN.　Richard Wilbur's poetry of love. Ren (45:1/2) 1992/93, 3–15.

22633. HARDY, JOHN EDWARD.　Faunal presences in the poetry of Richard Wilbur. Ren (45:1/2) 1992/93, 97–113.

22634. HAZO, SAMUEL.　One definite Mozart. Ren (45:1/2) 1992/93, 81–96.

22635. MIKOLAJCZAK, MICHAEL ALLEN.　Inscriptions of wonder: the poetry of Richard Wilbur. Ren (45:1/2) 1992/93, 115–25.

22636. PAYNE, MARJORY.　Richard Wilbur's religious vision in his later poems. Ren (45:1/2) 1992/93, 65–80.

22637. RULEMAN, WILLIAM.　Notes on the making of Richard Wilbur's *Love Calls Us to the Things of This World*. NCL (26:4) 1996, 9–10.

22638. SCHWARTZ, JOSEPH.　The concept of historical form in the poetry of Richard Wilbur. Ren (45:1/2) 1992/93, 35–48.

22639. SUTTON, BRIAN.　Wilbur's *A Summer Morning*. Exp (54:3) 1996, 180–2.

22640. WAI, ISABELLA.　Wilbur's *A Baroque Wall-Fountain in the Villa Sciarra*. Exp (54:4) 1996, 244–7.

22641. —— Wilbur's *Cottage Street*, 1953. Exp (54:3) 1996, 183–4.

Laura Ingalls Wilder

22642. ANDERSON, WILLIAM.　The Little House guidebook. New York: HarperCollins, 1996. pp. 96. (Little House.)

22643. FELLMAN, ANITA CLAIR.　'Don't expect to depend on anybody else': the frontier as portrayed in the Little House books. ChildLit (24) 1996, 101–16.

22644. HOLTZ, WILLIAM.　Ghost and host in the Little House books. *See* **683**.

22645. MILLER, JOHN E.   Laura Ingalls Wilder's little town: where history and literature meet. (Bibl. 1995, 20055.) Rev. by Diane D. Quantic in AmS (36:2) 1996, 206–7.

22646. MILLS, CLAUDIA.   From obedience to autonomy: moral growth in the Little House books. ChildLit (24) 1996, 127–40.

22647. RAHN, SUZANNE.   What really happens in the Little Town on the Prairie. ChildLit (24) 1996, 117–26.

22648. WILKINSON, ALAN.   Miseries of the Old West: what the *Little House* books left out. TLS, 23 Aug. 1996, 16.

Thornton Wilder

22649. BLAIR, JOHN G.   Representations of the family in modern American drama: media implications for the theatre, film and television. *See* **13453**.

22650. BLANK, MARTIN (ed.).   Critical essays on Thornton Wilder. New York: G. K. Hall; London: Prentice Hall, 1996. pp. xv, 160. (Critical essays on American literature.)

22651. BURNS, EDWARD M.; DYDO, ULLA E.; RICE, WILLIAM (eds). The letters of Gertrude Stein and Thornton Wilder. *See* **21850**.

22652. CARDULLO, BERT.   Whose town? NCL (26:4) 1996, 3–5.

22653. GAJLEWICZ, JOANNA.   Illusion and reality in Pirandello's *Six Characters in Search of an Author* and Wilder's *The Skin of Our Teeth*. Anglica Wratislaviensia (30) 1996, 7–22.

22654. JONES, JENNIFER.   Climbing into their graves: intertextual quotation in Gregory Mosher's *Our Town*. *See* **18320**.

22655. LEWIS, WARD B.   The reception of Thornton Wilder during the Weimar Republic. GRM (41:4) 1991, 413–22.

Anne Wilkinson

22656. COLDWELL, JOAN (ed.).   The tightrope walker: auto-biographical writings of Anne Wilkinson. (Bibl. 1993, 15519.) Rev. by Susan Billingham in BJCS (11:1) 1996, 151–2.

Bayo Williams

22657. EZENWA-OHAETO.   Critical realism and the thriller tradition in Nigerian fiction: Williams, Nwankwo and Uzoatu. *See* **20627**.

Charles Williams

22658. ADDERLEY, C. M.   Preliminary matters: the neglected preludes to Charles Williams' Arthuriad. Mythlore (21:1) 1995, 23–8.

22659. BEACH, CHARLES.   'Courtesy' in Charles Williams' *The Greater Trumps*. Mythlore (19:1) 1993, 16–21.

22660. BEACH, CHARLES FRANKLYN.   Courtesy and self in the thought of Charles Williams and C. S. Lewis. *See* **19693**.

22661. BEACH, SARAH, *et al.*   Artists' comments. *See* **22135**.

22662. BOSKY, BERNADETTE.   Charles Williams: occult fantasies/occult fact. *In* (pp. 176–85) **70**.

22663. CAVALIERO, GLEN (introd. and notes).   Letters to Lalage: the letters of Charles Williams to Lois Lang-Sims. With commentary by Lois Lang-Sims. (Bibl. 1993, 15522.) Rev. by Maureen Fries in Quondam et Futurus (1:2) 1991, 92–5.

22664. CHRISTOPHER, JOE R.; HAMMOND, WAYNE G. (comps).   An Inklings bibliography. *See* **19703**.

22665. Coulombe, Charles A.   Hermetic imagination: the effect of the Golden Dawn on fantasy literature. *See* **19988**.

22666. Curtis, Jan.   Byzantium and the matter of Britain: the narrative framework of Charles Williams's later Arthurian poems. Quondam et Futurus (2:1) 1992, 28–54.

22667. —— Charles Williams's *The Sister of Percivale*: towards a theology of *Theotokos*. Quondam et Futurus (2:4) 1992, 56–72.

22668. —— A confluence of pagan-Celtic and Christian traditions in Charles Williams's *Bors to Elayne: the Fish of Broceliande*. Arthuriana (6:1) 1996, 96–111.

22669. Cutsinger, James S.   Angels and Inklings. *See* **19707**.

22670. Dodds, David Llewellyn (ed.).   Charles Williams. (Bibl. 1992, 16836.) Rev. by Charles Moorman in Quondam et Futurus (2:2) 1992, 89–91.

22671. Duriez, Colin.   Tolkien and the other Inklings. *See* **16197**.

22672. Hopkins, Lisa.   Female authority figures in the works of Tolkien, C. S. Lewis and Charles Williams. *See* **19720**.

22673. Horne, Brian (ed.).   Charles Williams: a celebration. Leominster: Gracewing, 1995. pp. xiv, 283. Rev. by Judith J. Kollman in SEVEN (13) 1996, 113–14; by Nancy-Lou Patterson in Mythlore (21:3) 1996, 54–6.

22674. Huttar, Charles A.; Schakel, Peter (eds).   The rhetoric of vision: essays on Charles Williams. Foreword by John Heath-Stubbs. Lewisburg, PA: Bucknell UP; London; Toronto: Assoc. UPs, 1996. pp. 356. Rev. by Adam Schwartz in ChrisL (46:1) 1996, 94–6.

22675. Kollmann, Judith.   *Eros, philia*, and *agape* in Charles Williams' Arthuriad. Mythlore (18:4) 1992, 9–14.

22676. McGrew, Lydia M.   Action and the passionate patient in *That Hideous Strength*. *See* **19735**.

22677. Peckham, Robert W.   Rhetoric and the supernatural in the novels of Charles Williams. Ren (45:4) 1993, 237–46.

22678. Russell, W. M. S.   Time before and after *The Time Machine*. *See* **10607**.

22679. Smith, Evans Lansing.   The mythical method of *Descent into Hell*. Mythlore (20:2) 1994, 10–15.

22680. Tilley, Elizabeth S.   Language in Charles Williams' *All Hallows' Eve*. Ren (44:4) 1992, 303–19.

22681. Yandell, Stephen.   'A pattern which our nature cries out for': the medieval tradition of the ordered four in the fiction of J. R. R. Tolkien. *See* **19760**.

Florence Williams

22682. Fisher-Wirth, Ann.   The allocations of desire: *This Is Just to Say* and Flossie Williams's *Reply*. WCWR (22:2) 1996, 47–56.

Garth Williams

22683. Sollors, Werner.   Can rabbits have interracial sex? SPELL (9) 1996, 143–67.

John A. Williams

22684. Smith, Virginia Whatley.   Sorcery, double-consciousness, and warring souls: an intertextual reading of *Middle Passage* and *Captain Blackman*. *See* **18959**.

Jonathan Williams (1929–)

22685. SMITH, LEVERETT T.   Twenty-seven batting-practice pitches for the John Kruk of American letters: an interview with Jonathan Williams. NCLR (2:2) 1995, 98–111.

Miller Williams

22686. WILLIAMS, MILLER.   The writing of *Adjusting to the Light* and *Any August Evening outside of Nashville*. WD (73:4) 1993, 43–5.

Sherley Anne Williams

22687. McKIBLE, ADAM.   'These are the facts of the darky's history': thinking history and reading names in four African-American texts. *See* **16644**.

22688. RUSHDY, ASHRAF H. A.   Reading mammy: the subject of relation in Sherley Anne Williams' *Dessa Rose*. AAR (27:3) 1993, 365–89.

Tad Williams

22689. COWAN, S. A.   Eatbugs, Edgar, and Odin: the influence of Shakespeare and Northern mythology on Williams's *Tailchaser's Song*. *See* **6942**.

Tennessee Williams

22690. BRUHM, STEVEN.   Blond ambition: Tennessee Williams's homographesis. Essays in Theatre (14:2) 1996, 97–105.

22691. CLINTON, CRAIG.   The reprise of Tennessee Williams' *Vieux Carré*: an interview with director Keith Hack. StAD (7:2) 1992, 265–75.

22692. COLANZI, RITA M.   Tennessee Williams's revision of *Suddenly Last Summer*. *See* **606**.

22693. CRANDELL, GEORGE W. (ed.).   The critical response to Tennessee Williams. Westport, CT; London: Greenwood Press, 1996. pp. xxxix, 307. (Critical responses in arts and letters, 24.)

22694. DANIEL, LaNELLE.   Mirrors and curses: Blanche DuBois and the Lady of Shalott. *See* **12428**.

22695. GRIFFIN, ALICE.   Understanding Tennessee Williams. (Bibl. 1995, 20074.) Rev. by Philip C. Kolin in JDTC (10:2) 1996, 133–6; by Pearl A. McHaney in SoQ (34:3) 1996, 153–5.

22696. GRONBECK-TEDESCO, JOHN L.   Absence and the actor's body: Marlon Brando's performance in *A Streetcar Named Desire* on stage and film. *See* **13743**.

22697. HALE, ALLEAN.   *Noh* and *Kabuki* in the drama of Tennessee Williams. TexPres (15) 1994, 37–41.

22698. HARRIS, LAURILYN J.   *Menagerie* in Manila and other cross-cultural affinities: the relevance of the plays of Tennessee Williams on the Filipino stage. StAD (8:2) 1993, 163–74.

22699. HAYMAN, RONALD.   Tennessee Williams: everyone else is an audience. (Bibl. 1994, 15488.) Rev. by Angel Luis Pujante in Atlantis (17:1/2) 1995, 388–9; by James Fisher in JDTC (9:2) 1995, 181–3; by Stephen Grecco in WLT (69:1) 1995, 150.

22700. ISAAC, DAN.   Founding father: O'Neill's correspondence with Arthur Miller and Tennessee Williams. *See* **20228**.

22701. KELLER, JAMES R.   A fellowship of madness: Williams' Blanche Dubois and Zindel's Anna Reardon. NCL (23:5) 1993, 2–3.

22702. —— Tennessee Williams' *Orpheus Descending* and Joe Orton's *Entertaining Mr Sloane. See* **20900**.

22703. KOLIN, PHILIP C. Black and multi-racial productions of Tennessee Williams's *The Glass Menagerie.* JDTC (9:2) 1995, 97–128.

22704. —— Bonaparte Kowalski; or, What Stanley and Napoleon have in common (and what they don't) in *A Streetcar Named Desire.* NCL (24:4) 1994, 6–8.

22705. —— Civil rights and the Black presence in *Baby Doll. See* **13881**.

22706. —— Cleopatra of the Nile and Blanche DuBois of the French Quarter: *Antony and Cleopatra* and *A Streetcar Named Desire. See* **6712**.

22707. —— The existential nightmare in Tennessee Williams's *The Chalky White Substance.* NCL (23:1) 1993, 8–11.

22708. —— The first critical assessments of *A Streetcar Named Desire*: the *Streetcar* tryouts and the reviewers. JDTC (6:1) 1991, 45–67.

22709. —— The function of Susie in Tennessee Williams's *Period of Adjustment.* NCL (25:3) 1995, 10–11.

22710. —— 'Rutting' in *A Streetcar Named Desire.* NCL (22:1) 1992, 2–3.

22711. —— Sleeping with Caliban: the politics of race in Tennessee Williams' *Kingdom of Earth.* StAD (8:2) 1993, 140–62.

22712. —— Tennessee Williams, Ernest Hemingway, and Fidel Castro. *See* **18634**.

22713. —— (ed.). Confronting Tennessee Williams' *A Streetcar Named Desire*: essays in critical pluralism. (Bibl. 1995, 20076.) Rev. by James Fisher in JDTC (7:2) 1993, 79–81; by the same in JDTC (9:2) 1995, 181–3.

22714. LEVERICH, LYLE. Tom: the unknown Tennessee Williams. (Bibl. 1995, 20077.) Rev. by Wendy Smith in BkW, 12 Nov. 1995, 4, 6; by Melinda Kanner in AR (54:2) 1996, 247; by Mark Childress in TLS, 5 Jan. 1996, 5–6; by Stephen Grecco in WLT (70:3) 1996, 703; by Robert Bray in SAtlR (61:3) 1996, 121–3.

22715. MONTEIRO, GEORGE. The seahorse in *A Streetcar Named Desire.* NCL (23:3) 1993, 9.

22716. MORROW, LAURA; MORROW, EDWARD. Humpty-Dumpty lives! Complexity theory as an alternative to the omelet scenario in *The Glass Menagerie.* StAD (8:2) 1993, 127–39.

22717. NEUMANN, CLAUS-PETER. Tennessee Williams's plastic theatre: *Camino Real.* JADT (6:2/3) 1994, 93–111.

22718. THERIOT, IBRY G.-F. The bitch archetype. *See* **20890**.

22719. ZHU, LIAN QUN. A bibliography of Tennessee Williams in China, 1975–1992. StAD (8:2) 1993, 214–16.

William Carlos Williams

22720. AHEARN, BARRY. William Carlos Williams and alterity: the early poetry. (Bibl. 1995, 20086.) Rev. by Edward Margolies in EngS (77:3) 1996, 294–6.

22721. CAWS, MARY ANN. William Carlos Williams and René Char: two poets injured in the street. WCWR (22:1) 1996, 75–9.

22722. CORONITI, JOSEPH. 'An assembled order': William Carlos Williams' music of the imagination. AntR (92) 1993, 83–90.

22723. CRAWFORD, T. HUGH. Modernism, medicine & William Carlos Williams. (Bibl. 1995, 20094.) Rev. by Sara Lundquist in AL (68:1) 1996, 256–7.

22724. —— *Paterson*, memex, and hypertext. *See* **1146**.

22725. DANIELE, DANIELA.   Travelogues in a broken landscape: Robert Smithson's mixed-medial tribute to William Carlos Williams. *In* (pp. 94–105) **117**.

22726. DIGGORY, TERENCE.   The geometry of dreams: projecting the place of Surrealism in Williams's poetics. WCWR (22:1) 1996, 45–62.

22727. —— William Carlos Williams's early 'references to Freud': 1917–1930. WCWR (22:2) 1996, 3–17.

22728. DOLIN, SHARON.   'Bitter and delicious relations': the transitional object in Williams's poetry. WCWR (22:2) 1996, 19–28.

22729. EBY, CARL.   *The Ogre* and the 'Beautiful Thing': voyeurism, exhibitionism, and the image of 'woman' in the poetry of William Carlos Williams. WCWR (22:2) 1996, 29–45.

22730. FISHER-WIRTH, ANN.   The allocations of desire: *This Is Just to Say* and Flossie Williams's *Reply*. *See* **22682**.

22731. HARTMAN, CHARLES O.   Free verse: an essay on prosody. *See* **14948**.

22732. KLOTZ, K. H.   Poetic theory in the Depression years: language, objectivity, and image in the poems of William Carlos Williams and Bertolt Brecht. Comparatist (20) 1996, 126–52.

22733. MACGOWAN, CHRISTOPHER.   'Sparkles of understanding': Williams and Nicolas Calas. WCWR (22:1) 1996, 81–98.

22734. MEYER, KINERETH.   Possessing America: William Carlos Williams's *Paterson* and the politics of appropriation. *In* (pp. 152–67) **66**.

22735. MILLER, TYRUS.   Poetic contagion: Surrealism and Williams's *A Novelette*. WCWR (22:1) 1996, 17–27.

22736. MORRIS, DANIEL.   A taste of fortune: *In the Money* and Williams's New Directions phase. *In* (pp. 161–87) **67**.

22737. —— The writings of William Carlos Williams: publicity for the self. (Bibl. 1995, 20113.) Rev. by Clive Meachen in JAStud (30:2) 1996, 294–5.

22738. PETERSON, JEFFREY.   'A laboratory … for dissociations': approaching Williams's automatic writing. WCWR (22:1) 1996, 29–44.

22739. SAYRE, HENRY M.   The enchained dragon: Williams and the optical unconscious. WCWR (22:1) 1996, 63–74.

22740. TASHJIAN, DICKRAN.   Williams and automatic writing: against the presence of Surrealism. WCWR (22:1) 1996, 5–16.

22741. ULRICH, JOHN.   Giving Williams some credit: money and language in *Paterson*, Book Four, Part II. *In* (pp. 121–9) **71**.

22742. ZETTSU, TOMOYUKI.   In quest of the 'beautiful thing': *Paterson* and *Moby-Dick*. *See* **11908**.

David Williamson

22743. KIERNAN, BRIAN.   The ways we live now: David Williamson's recent plays. CritS (6:1) 1994, 146–52.

22744. MCGILLICK, PAUL.   Heresy. Meanjin (55:2) 1996, 258–66.

Angus Wilson

22745. DRABBLE, MARGARET.   Angus Wilson: a biography. (Bibl. 1995, 20131.) New York: St Martin's Press, 1996. Rev. by Dennis Drabelle in BkW, 2 June 1996, 4.

22746. ERZGRÄBER, WILLI.   Zwischen Viktorianismus und Moderne: zu Angus Wilsons Roman *No Laughing Matter*. GRM (45:1) 1995, 88–103.

August Wilson

22747. BISSIRI, AMADOU. Aspects of Africanness in August Wilson's drama: reading *The Piano Lesson* through Wole Soyinka's drama. *See* **21782**.

22748. EISEN, KURT. Blues speaking women: performing cultural change in *Spunk* and *Ma Rainey's Black Bottom*. *See* **18834**.

22749. ELAM, HARRY J. *Ma Rainey's Black Bottom*: singing Wilson's Blues. AmDr (5:2) 1996, 76–99.

22750. GRANT, NATHAN L. Men, women, and culture: a conversation with August Wilson. AmDr (5:2) 1996, 100–22.

22751. MYERS, NORMAN J.; SHIELDS, RONALD E. The 'killer monologue' in contemporary American drama. *See* **14019**.

22752. PEREIRA, KIM. August Wilson and the African-American odyssey. (Bibl. 1995, 20133.) Rev. by Josephine Lee in AL (68:2) 1996, 481–2; by Mike Pederson in NETJ (7) 1996, 130–1.

22753. PLUM, JAY. Blues, history, and the dramaturgy of August Wilson. AAR (27:4) 1993, 561–7.

22754. SAUNDERS, JAMES ROBERT. Essential ambiguities in the plays of August Wilson. HC (32:5) 1995, 1–11.

22755. SHANNON, SANDRA G. Blues, history, and dramaturgy: an interview with August Wilson. AAR (27:4) 1993, 539–59.

22756. WANG, QUN. Towards the poetization of the 'field of manners'. AAR (29:4) 1995, 605–13.

Colin Wilson

22757. HOLLINGER, VERONICA. The vampire and/as the alien. *See* **12375**.

22758. ROBERTSON, DALLAS VAUGHAN. Colin Wilson: his existential literary criticism and his novels. *See* **15721**.

Edmund Wilson

22759. BRIGHTMAN, CAROL. Mary McCarthy: at home with Edmund Wilson. *See* **19924**.

22760. DABNEY, LEWIS M. (ed.). The sixties: the last journal, 1960–1972. (Bibl. 1995, 20134.) Rev. by Melvin Landsberg in AmS (36:2) 1995, 139–47; by Michael Dirda in BkW, 4 July 1996, 1, 10.

22761. GROTH, JANET; CASTRONOVO, DAVID (eds). From the uncollected Edmund Wilson. (Bibl. 1995, 20136.) Rev. by John L. Brown in WLT (70:3) 1996, 705–6.

22762. MEYERS, JEFFREY. The bulldog and the butterfly: the friendship of Edmund Wilson and Vladimir Nabokov. *See* **20490**.

22763. —— Edmund Wilson: a biography. (Bibl. 1995, 20137.) Rev. by Bruce Bawer in BkW, 2 July 1995, 4–5; by Daniel Patrick King in WLT (70:4) 1996, 969–70.

22764. RAFFEL, BURTON. From the uncollected Edmund Wilson. LitR (39:3) 1996, 428–34.

Ethel Wilson

22765. STOUCK, DAVID (ed.). Ethel Wilson: stories, essays, letters. (Bibl. 1989, 11559.) Rev. by Gordon Johnston in ARCS (18:3) 1988, 396–8.

Harry Leon Wilson

22766. RHODES, CHIP. Twenties fiction, mass culture, and the modern subject. *See* **17411**.

Lanford Wilson

22767. BRYER, JACKSON R . Lanford Wilson. *In* (pp. 277–96) **85**.

22768. FINK, LARRY. From 'madness' to 'the cosmos': gay/lesbian characters in the plays of Lanford Wilson. JADT (7:2) 1995, 57–65.

22769. TIBBETS, JOHN C. An interview with Lanford Wilson. JDTC (5:2) 1991, 175–80.

Robert Wilson (1941–)

22770. GRAFF, BERND. Das Geheimnis der Oberfläche: der Raum der Postmoderne und die Bühnenkunst Robert Wilsons. Tübingen: Niemeyer, 1994. pp. ix, 330. (Theatron, 9.) Rev. by Jörg Wiesel in Forum modernes Theater (10:2) 1995, 224–6.

22771. ROMERO, LAURENCE. Dichter aus einer anderen Welt: Robert Wilson in Frankreich. Forum modernes Theater (9:2) 1994, 126–40.

Chris Wiltz

22772. FRANCIS, WILLIAM A. An interview with New Orleans novelist Chris Wiltz. SoQ (34:4) 1996, 109–19.

Donald Windham

22773. KELLNER, BRUCE. Donald Windham: a bio-bibliography. With a footnote by Donald Windham. (Bibl. 1992, 16913.) Rev. by Harold Hatt in JAC (19:2) 1996, 150.

Jeanette Winterson

22774. ASENSIO ARÓSTEGUI, MARÍA DEL MAR. Subversion of sexual identity in Jeanette Winterson's *The Passion*. *In* (pp. 265–79) **38**.

22775. BURNS, CHRISTY L. Fantastic language: Jeanette Winterson's recovery of the postmodern word. ConLit (37:2) 1996, 278–306.

22776. GONZÁLEZ ÁBALOS, SUSANA. Winterson's *Sexing the Cherry*: rewriting 'woman' through fantasy. *In* (pp. 281–95) **38**.

22777. LAINSBURY, G. P. Hubris and the young author: the problem of the introduction to *Oranges Are Not the Only Fruit*. NCL (22:4) 1992, 2–3.

22778. ONEGA, SUSANA. 'Self' and 'other' in Jeanette Winterson's *The Passion*. RCEI (28) 1994, 177–93.

22779. ONEGA JAÉN, SUSANA. Jeanette Winterson's politics of uncertainty in *Sexing the Cherry*. *In* (pp. 297–313) **38**.

22780. STOWERS, CATH. 'No legitimate place, no land, no fatherland': communities of women in the fiction of Roberts and Winterson. *See* **21374**.

Mildred Wirt

22781. HEILBRUN, CAROLYN G. Nancy Drew: a moment in feminist history. AD (29:1) 1996, 62–7.

Adele Wiseman

22782. KERTZER, J. M. Beginnings and endings: Adele Wiseman's *Crackpot*. ECanW (58) 1996, 15–35.

22783. PENNEE, DONNA PALMATEER. 'The hand of a murderer, hero,

artist, the hand of a man': rereading Adele Wiseman's *The Sacrifice*.
ECanW (58) 1996, 1–14.

Owen Wister

22784. FURNAS, J. C. Transatlantic twins: Rudyard Kipling and
Owen Wister. *See* **19339**.

P. G. Wodehouse

22785. RING, TONY; JAGGARD, GEOFFREY. Wodehouse in the club-
house. Maidenhead: Porpoise, 1994. pp. xvi, 153. (Millennium
Wodehouse concordance, 1.)

Larry Woiwode

22786. BLOCK, ED. Larry Woiwode. Critic (47:4) 1993, 57–65.
22787. BLOCK, ED, JR. An interview with Larry Woiwode. Ren (44:1)
1991, 17–30.

David Wojahn

22788. STEIN, KEVIN. Manipulating cultural assumptions: transgression and obedience in David Wojahn's rock 'n' roll sonnets.
ColLit (23:2) 1996, 45–61.

Gene Wolfe

22789. ANDRE-DRIUSSI, MICHAEL. Gene Wolfe at the Lake of Birds.
Foundation (66) 1996, 5–12.
22790. —— Lexicon Urthus: a dictionary for the Urth Cycle. San
Francisco, CA: Sirius, 1994. pp. xvi, 280. Rev. by Neal Baker in
Extrapolation (37:1) 1996, 102–4.
22791. —— Posthistory 101. Extrapolation (37:2) 1996, 127–38.
22792. CHRISTOPHER, JOE R. A second view of *Castleview*. Quondam
et Futurus (3:3) 1993, 66–76.
22793. HELDRETH, LILLIAN M. The mercy of the torturer: the paradox of compassion in Gene Wolfe's world of the new sun. *In* (pp.
186–94) **70**.
22794. KONDRATIEV, ALEXEI. Tales newly told: a column on current
modern fantasy. Mythlore (19:4) 1993, 30–1.
22795. WRIGHT, PETER. God-games: cosmic conspiracies and narrative sleights in Gene Wolfe's *The Fictions of the New Sun*. Foundation (66)
1996, 13–39.
22796. —— Grasping the god-games: metafictional keys to the interpretation of Gene Wolfe's *The Fictions of the New Sun*. Foundation (66)
1996, 39–59.

George C. Wolfe

22797. EISEN, KURT. Blues speaking women: performing cultural
change in *Spunk* and *Ma Rainey's Black Bottom*. *See* **18834**.
22798. MÜLLER, ULRICH. Modern morality plays of Broadway:
Jelly's Last Jam and *Angels in America*. *In* (pp. 375–84) **125**.

Thomas Wolfe (1900–1938)

22799. BASSETT, JOHN E. Thomas Wolfe: an annotated critical
bibliography. Lanham, MD; London: Scarecrow Press, 1996. pp. xxv,
432. (Scarecrow author bibliographies, 96.)

22800. BONNER, THOMAS, JR.   Thomas Wolfe and the Civil War. WLA (8:1) 1996, 75–82.

22801. CLARK, JAMES W., JR.   Getting Dick Prosser right. TWR (20:2) 1996, 21–33.

22802. EDMINSTER, WARREN.   A portrait of an American artist: the implied author/protagonist relationship in Wolfe's *Look Homeward, Angel*. TWR (20:2) 1996, 37–43.

22803. GEORGE, AMY C.   The play's the thing: catching the conscience of Thomas Wolfe's *Mannerhouse*. TWR (20:2) 1996, 53–9.

22804. GILL, JOHN M.   'Carrying the torch': Fred Wolfe counterpunches Bernard DeVoto. TWR (20:1) 1996, 33–55.

22805. IDOL, JOHN L., JR.   The town square in Thomas Wolfe's writings: a representative look. TWR (20:2) 1996, 44–52.

22806. JOHNSTON, CAROL INGALLS.   Of time and the artist: Thomas Wolfe, his novels, and the critics. Columbia, SC: Camden House, 1996. pp. 221. (Studies in English and American literature, linguistics, and culture.)

22807. KENNEDY, RICHARD S. (ed.).   The Starwick episodes. (Bibl. 1995, 20165.) Rev. by John Halberstadt in ASch (64:4) 1995, 624–7; by James W. Clark, Jr, in NCLR (2:2) 1995, 217–19.

22808. LAKE, INEZ HOLLANDER.   A tale of two cities: an analogy between Thomas Wolfe's exile in the American and European city. TWR (20:1) 1996, 71–7.

22809. MAX, GERRY.   Richard Halliburton and Thomas Wolfe: 'when youth kept open house'. *See* **13975**.

22810. MILLS, JERRY LEATH.   The Williams–Greenlaw axis in the young Wolfe's search for form. TWR (20:1) 1996, 59–70.

22811. MITCHELL, TED.   'Two tons of manuscript': Thomas Wolfe archives. *See* **513**.

22812. —— Windows of the heart: the letters of Margaret Roberts to Thomas Wolfe. TWR (20:2) 1996, 2–20.

22813. NISHIMURA, YORIO.   Thomas Wolfe no shuugyou jidai. (Thomas Wolfe's days of literary training.) Tokyo: Eihosha, 1996. pp. 208.

22814. PETERSON, MARVIN V.   Thomas Wolfe's *The Child by Tiger*: a historical allusion. TWR (20:2) 1996, 34–6.

22815. PHILLIPSON, JOHN S.   Thomas Wolfe as a writer on travel. TWR (20:1) 1996, 25–31.

22816. STEPHENSON, SHELBY.   Elements of lyricism in *Look Homeward, Angel*. TWR (20:1) 1996, 79–86.

22817. STUTMAN, SUZANNE; IDOL, JOHN L., JR (eds).   The party at Jack's. Chapel Hill; London: North Carolina UP, 1995. pp. xxxii, 242. Rev. by John Halberstadt in ASch (64:4) 1995, 624–7.

Tom Wolfe (1931–)

22818. LUND, MICHAEL.   The nineteenth-century periodical novel continued: *Bonfire of the Vanities* in *Rolling Stone*. AmP (3) 1993, 51–61.

22819. MUSTAZZA, LEONARD.   The limits of narcissism: self and society in Tom Wolfe's *The Bonfire of the Vanities*. PCR (3:2) 1992, 3–18.

22820. REILLY, CHARLIE.   Tom Wolfe: interview. Onthebus (6:1) 1993/94, 226–9.

Martha Wolfenstein (1869–1906)

22821. SHOLLAR, BARBARA. Martha Wolfenstein's *Idyls of the Gass* and the dilemma of ethnic self-representation. *In* (pp. 121–36) **3**.

Ruth Wolff

22822. PERKINS, SALLY J. The dilemma of identity: theatrical portrayals of a 16th-century feminist. *See* **18148**.

Tobias Wolff

22823. HANNAH, JAMES. Tobias Wolff: a study of the short fiction. New York: Twayne; London: Prentice Hall, 1996. pp. xviii, 187. (Twayne's studies in short fiction.)

George Woodcock

22824. WOODCOCK, GEORGE. Walking through the valley: an autobiography. Toronto: ECW Press, 1994. pp. 213. Rev. by John Moss in CanL (149) 1996, 161–2; by Douglas Freake in ESCan (22:2) 1996, 241–2.

Christopher Woodforde

22825. DALBY, RICHARD. Christopher Woodforde. Ghosts and Scholars (14) 1992, 36–8. (Writers in the James tradition, 11.)

Leonard Woolf

22826. MARCUS, LAURA. Virginia Woolf and the Hogarth Press. *In* (pp. 124–50) **69**.

Virginia Woolf

22827. ABEL, ELIZABETH. Virginia Woolf and the fictions of psychoanalysis. (Bibl. 1993, 15601.) Rev. by Cora Kaplan in Feminist Studies (20:1) 1994, 155–60.
22828. ANSPAUGH, KELLY. 'When lovely wooman stoops to conk him': Virginia Woolf in *Finnegans Wake*. *See* **19018**.
22829. AUGUSTINE, JANE. Bisexuality in Hélène Cixous, Virginia Woolf, and H.D.: an aspect of *l'écriture féminine*. *In* (pp. 11–18) **109**.
22830. BANKS, JOANNE TRAUTMANN (ed.). Congenial spirits: the selected letters of Virginia Woolf. (Bibl. 1990, 12718.) Rev. by Clare MacCulloch in AntR (85/86) 1991, 229–35.
22831. BARTKEVICIUS, JOCELYN. A form of one's own: Virginia Woolf's art of the portrait essay. IowaR (22:1) 1992, 123–34.
22832. BARZILAI, SHULI. The politics of quotation in *To the Lighthouse*: Mrs Woolf resites Mr Tennyson and Mr Cowper. *See* **8938**.
22833. BATCHELOR, JOHN. Virginia Woolf: the major novels. (Bibl. 1993, 15604.) Rev. by Jane Marcus in Signs (17:4) 1992, 806–19.
22834. BEER, GILLIAN. Virginia Woolf: the common ground. Ann Arbor: Michigan UP, 1996. pp. 183.
22835. BEZRUCKA, YVONNE. Assenza, violenza, proliferazione dei sensi in *Between the Acts* di Virginia Woolf. Quaderni di lingue e letterature (19) 1994, 97–107.
22836. —— L'estetica di *To the Lighthouse*: la tentazione della bellezza astratta e il rifiuto delle 'strane indicazioni'. QLLSM (7) 1995, 291–315.
22837. BRIGGS, JULIA. Editing Woolf for the nineties. *See* **589**.
22838. CARAMAGNO, THOMAS C. The flight of the mind: Virginia

Woolf's art and manic-depressive illness. (Bibl. 1994, 15605.) Rev. by Jane Marcus in Signs (17:4) 1992, 806–19.

22839. CAUGHIE, PAMELA L.   Virginia Woolf and postmodernism: literature in quest & question of itself. (Bibl. 1994, 15606.) Rev. by Jane Marcus in Signs (17:4) 1992, 806–19; by Bonnie Kime Scott in MFS (40:1) 1994, 176–8.

22840. CRATER, THERESA L.   Lily Briscoe's vision: the articulation of silence. RMRLL (50:2) 1996, 121–36.

22841. CUDDY-KEANE, MELBA; KI, KAY.   Passage to China: East and West and Woolf. SoCR (29:1) 1996, 132–49.

22842. DAUGHERTY, BETH RIGEL; BARRETT, EILEEN (eds).   Virginia Woolf: texts and contexts: selected papers from the Fifth Annual Conference on Virginia Woolf, Otterbein College, Westerville, Ohio, June 15–18, 1995. Lanham, MD: UP of America; New York; London: Pace UP, 1996. pp. xxix, 315. Rev. by Diane Gillespie in RMRLL (50:2) 1996, 169–78.

22843. DEGLI-ESPOSTI, CRISTINA.   Sally Potter's *Orlando* and the neo-baroque scopic regime. *See* **13600**.

22844. DOYLE, LAURA.   Sublime barbarians in the narrative of empire; or, Longinus at sea in *The Waves*. MFS (42:2) 1996, 323–47.

22845. ENDER, EVELYNE.   A writer's birthpains: Virginia Woolf and the mother's share. SPELL (9) 1996, 257–72.

22846. ENDO, FUHITO.   'Perhaps poetry grew from mud': a reading of 'the hollow' in *Between the Acts*. SEL (72:2) 1996, 209–25.

22847. ENGLER, BERND.   Imagining her-story: Virginia Woolf's *The Journal of Mistress Joan Martyn* as historiographical metafiction. JSSE (20) 1993, 9–26.

22848. ERZGRÄBER, WILLI.   Virginia Woolf: eine Einführung. Tübingen: Francke, 1993. pp. 223. (Second ed.: first ed. 1982.) Rev. by Ruth Freifrau von Ledebur in Archiv (233:1) 1996, 183–8.

22849. FERRER, DANIEL.   Virginia Woolf and the madness of language. Trans. by Geoffrey Bennington and Rachel Bowlby. (Bibl. 1993, 15622.) Rev. by Jane Marcus in Signs (17:4) 1992, 806–19.

22850. FLINT, KATE.   Reading uncommonly: Virginia Woolf and the practice of reading. YES (26) 1996, 187–98.

22851. FRIEDMAN, SUSAN STANFORD.   Uncommon readings: seeking the geopolitical Woolf. SoCR (29:1) 1996, 24–44.

22852. FROULA, CHRISTINE.   Modernism, genetic texts, and literary authority in Virginia Woolf's portraits of the artist as the audience. RR (86:3) 1995, 513–26.

22853. GIDDEY, ERNEST.   Rocks and waves: Virginia Woolf, Leslie Stephen, and Byron. *In* (pp. 295–304) **125**.

22854. GLISERMAN, MARTIN.   Psychoanalysis, language, and the body of the text. *See* **8967**.

22855. GOODENOUGH, ELIZABETH.   'We haven't the words': the silence of children in the novels of Virginia Woolf. *In* (pp. 184–201) **48**.

22856. HANSON, CLARE.   Virginia Woolf. (Bibl. 1994, 15633.) Rev. by Diane Gillespie in RMRLL (50:2) 1996, 169–78.

22857. HARRISON, BERNARD.   Virginia Woolf and 'the true reality'. WHR (50:2) 1996, 100–22.

22858. HAULE, JAMES M.   Virginia Woolf's revisions of *The Voyage Out*: some new evidence. *See* **677**.

22859. HERMAN, DAVID. Universal grammar and narrative form. *See* **2641**.

22860. HUSSEY, MARK. 'I' rejected, 'we' substituted: self and society in *Between the Acts*. *In* (pp. 141–52) **96**.

22861. —— Virginia Woolf A to Z: a comprehensive reference for students, teachers, and common readers to her life, work, and critical reception. (Bibl. 1995, 20213.) Rev. by Diane Gillespie in RMRLL (50:2) 1996, 169–78; by Mark A. Graves in ELT (39:3) 1996, 384–6.

22862. JARNIEWICZ, JERZY. Orlando, Orlanda i to trzecie. (Orlando, Orlanda and the third one.) Literatura na Świecie (4) 1996, 323–33.

22863. KAPLAN, CORA. Fictions of feminism: figuring the maternal. *See* **15546**.

22864. KING, JAMES. Virginia Woolf. (Bibl. 1995, 20220.) New York: Norton, 1995. Rev. by Roberta Rubenstein in BkW, 2 Apr. 1995, 4–5; by Diane Gillespie in RMRLL (50:2) 1996, 169–78.

22865. LASSNER, PHYLLIS. 'The milk of our mother's kindness has ceased to flow': Virginia Woolf, Stevie Smith, and the representation of the Jew. *In* (pp. 129–44) **5**.

22866. LAURENCE, PATRICIA. Women's silence as a ritual of truth: a study of literary expressions in Austen, Brontë, and Woolf. *In* (pp. 156–67) **59**.

22867. LAURENCE, PATRICIA ONDEK. The reading of silence: Virginia Woolf in the English tradition. (Bibl. 1993, 15643.) Rev. by Rachel Bowlby in Signs (19:1) 1993, 257–9; by Bonnie Kime Scott in MFS (40:1) 1994, 176–8.

22868. LEASKA, MITCHELL A. (ed.). A passionate apprentice: the early journals, 1897–1909. (Bibl. 1991, 15972.) Rev. by Jane Marcus in Signs (17:4) 1992, 806–19.

22869. LEE, HERMIONE. Biomythographers: rewriting the lives of Virginia Woolf. *See* **15164**.

22870. —— Virginia Woolf. London: Chatto & Windus, 1996. pp. xi, 892, (plates) 24. Rev. by Helen Simpson in TLS, 20 Sept. 1996, 28–9.

22871. LINLEY, MARGARET. Sappho's conversions in Felicia Hemans, Letitia Landon, and Christina Rossetti. *See* **11452**.

22872. LITTLE, JUDY. The experimental self: dialogic subjectivity in Woolf, Pym, and Brooke-Rose. *See* **16579**.

22873. LOVISA, MANUELA. Reality, identity, and time in the experimental novels of Virginia Woolf. Textures (10) 1996, 34–8.

22874. McWHIRTER, DAVID. Feminism/gender/comedy: Meredith, Woolf, and the reconfiguration of comic distance. *In* (pp. 189–204) **64**.

22875. MARCUS, JANE. Pathographies: the Virginia Woolf soap opera. Signs (17:4) 1992, 806–19 (review-article).

22876. —— Registering objections: grounding feminist alibis. *In* (pp. 171–93) **97**.

22877. —— Wrapped in the stars and stripes: Virginia Woolf in the USA. SoCR (29:1) 1996, 17–23.

22878. MARCUS, LAURA. Virginia Woolf and the Hogarth Press. *In* (pp. 124–50) **69**.

22879. MORAN, PATRICIA. Word of mouth: body language in Katherine Mansfield and Virginia Woolf. *See* **20119**.

22880. MOSES, JOHN W. Orlando's 'caricature value': Virginia Woolf's portrait of the artist as a Romantic poet. *In* (pp. 39–81) **28**.

22881. MÜLLER, MARLENE. Woolf mit Lacan: der Signifikant in den Wellen. Bielefeld: Aisthesis, 1993. pp. 227. Rev. by Ruth Freifrau von Ledebur in Archiv (233:1) 1996, 183–8.

22882. NEWMAN, HERTA. Virginia Woolf and Mrs Brown: toward a realism of uncertainty. New York; London: Garland, 1996. pp. xiv, 149. (Garland reference library of the humanities, 1328.) (Origins of Modernism, 3.)

22883. NÜNNING, VERA; NÜNNING, ANSGAR. From thematics and formalism to aesthetics and history: phases and trends of Virginia Woolf criticism in Germany, 1946–1996. *See* **15684**.

22884. OLDFIELD, SYBIL. Virginia Woolf and Antigone – thinking against the current. SoCR (29:1) 1996, 45–57.

22885. PADDON, SEIJA. Virginia Woolf's *Between the Acts*: a novel on the edge of a narrative crash? New Courant (6) 1996, 107–15.

22886. PEARCE, RICHARD. Virginia Woolf's struggle with author-ity. *In* (pp. 69–83) **44**.

22887. PHILLIPS, KATHY J. Virginia Woolf against Empire. (Bibl. 1994, 15659.) Rev. by Ellen Bayuk Rosenman in MFS (42:1) 1996, 176–8; by Jennifer T. Kennedy in Modernism/Modernity (3:2) 1996, 123–4; by Diane Gillespie in RMRLL (50:2) 1996, 169–78; by Mark Gaipa in ELT (39:1) 1996, 119–23; by Vincent Sherry in TLS, 30 Aug. 1996, 6.

22888. POOLE, ROGER. The unknown Virginia Woolf. (Bibl. 1991, 15982.) Cambridge; New York: CUP, 1995. pp. vii, 285. (Fourth ed.: first ed. 1978.)

22889. POSTER, JEM. A combination of interest: Virginia Woolf's *To the Lighthouse*. CritS (8:2) 1996, 210–15.

22890. RATCLIFFE, KRISTA. Anglo-American feminist challenges to the rhetorical traditions: Virginia Woolf, Mary Daly, Adrienne Rich. *See* **15710**.

22891. —— A rhetoric of textual feminism: (re)reading the emotional in Virginia Woolf's *Three Guineas*. *See* **2453**.

22892. REESE, JUDY S. Recasting social values in the work of Virginia Woolf. Selinsgrove, PA: Susquehanna UP; London; Toronto: Assoc. UPs, 1996. pp. 168. (Cf. bibl. 1994, 15664.)

22893. REID, PANTHEA. Art and affection: a life of Virginia Woolf. Oxford; New York: OUP, 1996. pp. xxii, 570.

22894. REYNIER, CHRISTINE. Les nouvelles de Virginia Woolf et l'art pictural. CVE (44) 1996, 147–66.

22895. —— Writing in the making in Virginia Woolf's short stories. JSSE (23) 1994, 77–88.

22896. RUHEMANN, LINDA. Virginia Woolf as a 'woman writer'. ERev (5:4) 1995, 38–41.

22897. SALVANESCHI, ENRICA; STRINGHER, BONALDA. Virginia Woolf: 'la signora nello specchio'. Una riflessione a due voci. QLLSM (7) 1995, 317–36.

22898. SANDBACH-DAHLSTROM, CATHERINE. Virginia Woolf with and without state feminism. *See* **15743**.

22899. SAXTON, RUTH; TOBIN, JEAN (eds). Woolf and Lessing: breaking the mold. *See* **19672**.

22900. SCANLON, JOAN. Bad language *vs* bad prose? *Lady Chatterley* and *The Well*. See **1972**.

22901. SCHRÖDER, LEENA KORE. The politics of Englishness in *Mrs Dalloway*. ERev (6:3) 1996, 28–31.

22902. Schroeder, Steven.   Virginia Woolf's subject and the subject of ethics: notes toward a poetics of persons. Lewiston, NY; Lampeter: Mellen Press, 1996. pp. 248.

22903. Seeley, Tracy.   (Un)weaving the shroud of the fathers: 'a woman's sentence' in *Between the Acts*. CritM (7:1) 1993, 81–97.

22904. Selboe, Tone.   'A novel about silence'? Virginia Woolf's debutroman *The Voyage Out*. Edda (1996:4) 317–27.

22905. Shaffer, Brian W.   Civilization in Bloomsbury: Woolf's *Mrs Dalloway* and Bell's 'theory of civilization'. *See* **16372**.

22906. Shaw, Marion.   From *A Room of One's Own* to a literature of one's own. SoCR (29:1) 1996, 58–66.

22907. Squier, Susan M.   Embryologies of Modernism. *See* **18879**.

22908. Stansky, Peter.   On or about December 1910: early Bloomsbury and its intimate world. *See* **13318**.

22909. Stape, J. H. (ed.).   Virginia Woolf: interviews and recollections. (Bibl. 1995, 20253.) Rev. by Judy Little in ELT (39:2) 1996, 236–8.

22910. Stevenson, Randall; Goldman, Jane.   'But what? Elegy?': Modernist reading and the death of Mrs Ramsay. YES (26) 1996, 173–86.

22911. Terentowicz, Urszula.   The world and the word in *The Waves* by Virginia Woolf. LMN (19) 1995, 49–64.

22912. Tremper, Ellen.   'The earth of our earliest life': Mr Carmichael in *To the Lighthouse*. JML (19:1) 1994, 163–71.

22913. Vandivere, Julie.   Waves and fragments: linguistic construction as subject formation in Virginia Woolf. *See* **2724**.

22914. Villeneuve, Pierre-Eric.   Virginia Woolf and the French reader: an overview. SoCR (29:1) 1996, 109–21.

22915. Vlasopolos, Anca.   Staking claims for no territory: the sea as woman's space. *In* (pp. 72–88) **97**.

22916. Webb, Caroline.   Life after death: the allegorical progress of *Mrs Dalloway*. MFS (40:2) 1994, 279–98.

22917. Whelan, P. T.   Women's domestic quest: minimal journeys and their frames in the *Thousand and One Nights*, *The Mark on the Wall* and *The Man with the Buttons*. Comparatist (18) 1994, 150–63.

22918. Whitworth, Michael.   Virginia Woolf and the 'mouse which turns for ever'. NQ (43:1) 1996, 56–7.

22919. Wicke, Jennifer.   Coterie consumption: Bloomsbury, Keynes, and Modernism as marketing. *In* (pp. 109–32) **67**.

22920. Wiley, Catherine.   Making history unrepeatable in Virginia Woolf's *Between the Acts*. CLIO (25:1) 1995, 3–20.

22921. Wilson, Jean Moorcroft.   Conceived with kindness: the Woolf family perspective. SoCR (29:1) 1996, 5–16.

22922. Wolf, Werner.   Intermedialität als neues Paradigma der Literaturwissenschaft? Plädoyer für eine literaturzentrierte Erforschung der Grenzüberschreitungen zwischen Wortkunst und anderen Medien am Beispiel von Virginia Woolfs *The String Quartet*. *See* **14338**.

22923. Yoshioka, Chiharu.   It takes two to make a daughter's story: the double bind structure of *To the Lighthouse*. SEL (72:2) 1996, 239–54.

22924. Zamorano, Ana.   'Adrift on an unknown sea': androgyny and writing with particular reference to *Echo* by Violet Trefusis. *In* (pp. 195–206) **38**.

Persia Woolley

22925. ANDRESEN, OLIVER; MARIN, GLENN.   An analysis of *Queen of the Summer Stars* by use of the literary profundity scale. Quondam et Futurus (2:1) 1992, 82–97.

Joseph Wortis

22926. WEISS, GERHARD.   'Tricky Dick': *Struwwelpeter* and American politics. LU (20:2) 1996, 217–29.

Herman Wouk

22927. SHAPIRO, EDWARD S.   The Jew as patriot: Herman Wouk and American Jewish identity. AJH (84:4) 1996, 333–51.

Charles Wright

22928. BEDIENT, CALVIN.   Poetry and silence at the end of the century. *See* **17898**.
22929. COLLINS, FLOYD.   Metamorphosis within the poetry of Charles Wright. GetR (4:3) 1991, 464–79 (review-article).
22930. COOPERMAN, MATTHEW.   An interview with Charles Wright. Field (52) 1995, 34–44.
22931. WRIGHT, CHARLES.   Improvisations: narrative of the image (a correspondence with Charles Simic). *See* **21715**.
22932. —— Miseducation of the poet. GetR (6:1) 1993, 73–84.

David Wright

22933. ANON.   Obituary: David Wright (1920–1994). Current Writing (6:2) 1994, 181.

James Wright (1927–1980)

22934. BROWNE, MICHAEL DENNIS.   My James Wright. GetR (6:2) 1993, 306–17.
22935. DAVIS, WILLIAM V.   'Dreaming of heroes', 'dying for love': *Autumn Begins in Martin's Ferry, Ohio,* James Wright's *cogito*. NCL (23:1) 1993, 3–4.
22936. —— 'To step lightly, lightly, all the way through your ruins': James Wright's Ohio. MidQ (37:4) 1996, 353–64.
22937. HOROWITZ, STEVEN.   W. B. Yeats's Ireland and James Wright's Ohio. *In* (pp. 237–51) **58**.
22938. MALEY, SAUNDRA ROSE.   Solitary apprenticeship: James Wright and German poetry. Lewiston, NY; Lampeter: Mellen Press, 1996. pp. ii, 710. (Cf. bibl. 1995, 20269.)
22939. YATCHISIN, GEORGE.   A listening to Walt Whitman and James Wright. *See* **12772**.

Judith Wright

22940. BRADY, VERONICA.   Towards an Australian spirituality. *See* **22604**.
22941. STRAUSS, JENNIFER.   Judith Wright. (Bibl. 1995, 20273.) Rev. by Simon Sorensen in WLT (70:4) 1996, 1026–7.

Richard Wright (1908–1960)

22942. ALGEO, ANN M.   The courtroom as forum: homicide trials by Dreiser, Wright, Capote, and Mailer. *See* **16689**.

22943. BARNES, DEBORAH. 'I'd rather be a lamppost in Chicago': Richard Wright and the Chicago renaissance of African-American literature. LHR (14:1/2) 1996, 52–61.

22944. BLAKE, CAESAR R. On Richard Wright's *Native Son. In* (pp. 187–99) **105**.

22945. CARON, TIMOTHY B. 'The Reds are in the Bible room': political activism and the Bible in Richard Wright's *Uncle Tom's Children.* SAF (24:1) 1996, 45–64.

22946. COX, JAMES M. Beneath my father's name. *In* (pp. 13–30) **43**.

22947. DAVIS, CHARLES T. From experience to eloquence: Richard Wright's *Black Boy* as art. *In* (pp. 138–50) **1**.

22948. FABRE, MICHEL. The unfinished quest of Richard Wright. Trans. by Isabel Barzun. (Bibl. 1995, 20285.) Rev. by Edward Margolies in AAR (29:3) 1995, 525–7.

22949. GATES, HENRY LOUIS, JR; APPIAH, K. A. (eds). Richard Wright: critical perspectives past and present. New York: Amistad, 1993. pp. 492. Rev. by Yoshinobu Hakutani in AAR (29:4) 1995, 683–7.

22950. HAKUTANI, YOSHINOBU. Richard Wright and racial discourse. Columbia; London: Missouri UP, 1996. pp. xiii, 312.

22951. —— Richard Wright's *The Long Dream* as racial and sexual discourse. AAR (30:2) 1996, 267–80.

22952. HAMALIAN, LEO. D. H. Lawrence and Black writers. *See* **17595**.

22953. KINNAMON, KENETH; FABRE, MICHEL (eds). Conversations with Richard Wright. (Bibl. 1995, 20293.) Rev. by Robert J. Butler in AAR (29:1) 1995, 131–4.

22954. LESTER, CHERYL. A response to Lawrence Rodgers. *See* **17205**.

22955. LYNCH, MICHAEL F. Haunted by innocence: the debate with Dostoevsky in Wright's 'other novel', *The Outsider.* AAR (30:2) 1996, 255–66.

22956. McCARTHY, B. EUGENE. Models of history in Richard Wright's *Uncle Tom's Children.* BALF (25:4) 1991, 729–43.

22957. MASON, THEODORE O., JR. 'Mapping' Richard Wright: a response to Deborah Barnes' *I'd Rather Be a Lamppost in Chicago*: Richard Wright and the Chicago renaissance of African-American literature. LHR (14:1/2) 1996, 62–4.

22958. PETERSON, DALE E. Richard Wright's long journey from Gorky to Dostoevsky. AAR (28:3) 1994, 375–87.

22959. RAND, WILLIAM E. The structure of the outsider in the short fiction of Richard Wright and F. Scott Fitzgerald. *See* **17870**.

22960. RODGERS, LAWRENCE R. Richard Wright, Frank Marshall Davis and the Chicago renaissance. *See* **17207**.

S. Fowler Wright

22961. BURGESS, MICHAEL (ed.). Sermons in science fiction: the novels of S. Fowler Wright. By Mary S. Weinkauf. San Bernardino, CA: Borgo Press, 1994. pp. 128. (Milford popular writers of today, 51.) Rev. by David M. Esposito in Utopian Studies (7:1) 1996, 155–6.

Patricia Wrightson

22962. Murray, John.   Inheriting the land? Some literary and ethical issues in the use of indigenous material by an Australian children's writer, 1960–1990. LitTheol (10:3) 1996, 252–60.

Philip Wylie

22963. Obuchowski, Mary DeJong.   The *Indian Drum* and its authors: a reconsideration. *See* **16174**.

Sylvia Wynter

22964. Liddell, Janice Lee.   The narrow enclosure of motherdom/martyrdom: a study of Gatha Randall Barton in Sylvia Wynter's *The Hills of Hebron*. *In* (pp. 321–30) **81**.

Hisaye Yamamoto

22965. Sugiyama, Naoko.   *Issei* mothers' silence, *nisei* daughters' stories: the short fiction of Hisaye Yamamoto. CLS (33:1) 1996, 1–14.
22966. Wang, Veronica C.   The transgression of gender roles: Hisaye Yamamoto's disobedient women. JSSE (27) 1996, 43–54.

Richard Yates

22967. Castronovo, David; Goldleaf, Steven.   Richard Yates. New York: Twayne; London: Prentice Hall, 1996. pp. xii, 162. (Twayne's US authors, 669.)

Jack B. Yeats

22968. Connelly, Joseph F.   The amalgam of traditions in J. B. Yeats's *Harlequin's Positions*. Notes on Modern Irish Literature (8) 1996, 31–7.
22969. —— J. B. Yeats's imaginative forays into writing: memory, moment and creative impulse. Notes on Modern Irish Literature (7:1) 1995, 41–9.
22970. McNamara, Leo.   The plays of Jack B. Yeats. *In* (pp. 228–34) **49**.

W. B. Yeats

22971. Achilles, Jochen.   Funktionen der Religion in der irischen Kultur der Jahrhundertwende: Moore, Shaw, Yeats and Joyce. *See* **19014**.
22972. Allison, Jonathan.   Questioning Yeats: Paul Muldoon's *7, Middagh Street*. *In* (pp. 3–20) **58**.
22973. —— (ed.).   Yeats's political identities: selected essays. Ann Arbor: Michigan UP, 1996. pp. viii, 352.
22974. Altieri, Charles.   The values of articulation: aesthetics after the aesthetic ideology. *In* (pp. 66–89) **6**.
22975. Araki, Eiko.   Sei to shi no rhetoric – jiko wo kaku Eliot to Yeats. (Rhetoric of life and death: Eliot and Yeats – writing the self.) *See* **17473**.
22976. Bornstein, George (ed.).   *The Wanderings of Oisin*, and other early poems to 1895. (Bibl. 1995, 20315.) Rev. by Peter McDonald in TLS, 27 Sept. 1996, 10–11.
22977. Brooks, Cleanth.   The humanities: liberator of mind and spirit. *In* (pp. 162–75) **79**.

22978. Burris, Sidney. Pastoral nostalgia and the poetry of W. B. Yeats and Seamus Heaney. *In* (pp. 195–201) **58**.

22979. Chadwick, Joseph. Yeats: colonialism and responsibility. *In* (pp. 107–14) **49**.

22980. Cho, Yong-Hea. A study of aesthetic development from Brahmanism to Daimonism in W. B. Yeats. JELLC (38:2) 1996, 49–99.

22981. Coldwell, Joan. The anxiety of influence: feminist response to father Yeats. *In* (pp. 362–8) **49**.

22982. Coulombe, Charles A. Hermetic imagination: the effect of the Golden Dawn on fantasy literature. *See* **19988**.

22983. Coyle, Michael. A present with innumerable pasts: post-modernity and the tracing of Modernist origins. *See* **17494**.

22984. Cullingford, Elizabeth Butler. Gender and history in Yeats's love poetry. (Bibl. 1995, 20323.) Rev. by Edna Longley in Yeats Annual (12) 1996, 324–7; by Carolyn Holdsworth in YES (26) 1996, 313–14.

22985. D'Ambrosio, John. William Butler Yeats' evolving drama of self-analysis: the psychoanalytic process of *On Baile's Strand* and *Purgatory*. LitPs (39:1/2) 1993, 42–51.

22986. Davis, Alex. Irish poetic modernisms: a reappraisal. *See* **19974**.

22987. Deane, Paul. Paganism *vs* Christianity: images of priests in contemporary Irish literature. *See* **17809**.

22988. De La Vars, Gordon J. Contrasting landscapes: John Hewitt's rural vision and Yeats's Irish world. *In* (pp. 39–45) **58**.

22989. Devy, Ganesh N. The Indian Yeats. *In* (pp. 93–106) **49**.

22990. Eaton, Heather Louise. Yeats's *Among School Children*. Exp (54:3) 1996, 165–8.

22991. Emig, Rainer. Modernism in poetry: motivations, structures and limits. *See* **11484**.

22992. Engle, John. A modest refusal: Yeats, MacNeice, and Irish poetry. *In* (pp. 71–88) **58**.

22993. Finneran, Richard J. *The Collected Letters of W. B. Yeats*: a project in disarray. *See* **642**.

22994. Fitz Gerald, Joan. Yeats's Irish traditions. Textus (2:1/2) 1989, 17–39.

22995. Flannery, James W. Staging the phantasmagorical: the theatrical challenges and rewards of W. B. Yeats. IUR (26:1) 1996, 92–106.

22996. —— Staging the phantasmagorical: the theatrical challenges and rewards of William Butler Yeats. *In* (pp. 149–65) **127**.

22997. Fleming, Deborah (ed.). Learning the trade: essays on W. B. Yeats and contemporary poetry. *See* **58**.

22998. Foster, John Wilson. Getting the North: Yeats and Northern nationalism. Yeats Annual (12) 1996, 180–212.

22999. Foster, R. F. 'When the newspapers have forgotten me': Yeats, obituarists, and Irishness. *See* **1268**.

23000. Foster, Roy. The poet of the coming times: Yeats's progress from the twilight of the Ascendancy to the new nation. TLS, 27 Sept. 1996, 9–10.

23001. Genet, Jacqueline. Yeats and the myth of rural Ireland. *In* (pp. 139–57) **106**.

23002. GORSKI, WILLIAM T.   Yeats and alchemy. Albany: New York State UP, 1996. pp. xv, 223. (SUNY series in Western esoteric traditions.)

23003. GOULD, WARWICK.   'Playing at treason with Miss Maud Gonne': Yeats and his publishers in 1900. *In* (pp. 36–80) **69**.

23004. —— KELLY, JOHN; TOOMEY, DEIRDRE (eds).   The collected letters of W. B. Yeats: vol. 2, 1896–1900. Oxford: Clarendon Press; New York: OUP, 1996. pp. lxxi, 790.

23005. HARDWICK, JOAN.   The Yeats sisters: a biography of Susan and Elizabeth Yeats. *See* **942**.

23006. HARPER, GEORGE MILLS (gen. ed.); HARPER, MARY JANE (asst ed.).   Yeats's *Vision* papers: vol. 1, The automatic script: 5 November 1917 – 18 June 1918. Ed. by Steve L. Adams, Barbara J. Frieling and Sandra L. Sprayberry. London: Macmillan; Iowa City: Iowa UP, 1992. pp. xiv, 565. Rev. by Deirdre Toomey in Yeats Annual (10) 1993, 267–73; by K. P. S. Jochum in ELT (36:3) 1993, 323–36; by David Holdeman in Text (Ann Arbor) (8) 1995, 469–77; by Elizabeth Bergmann Loizeaux in Review (18) 1996, 217–24.

23007. ——— Yeats's *Vision* papers: vol. 2, The automatic script: 25 June 1918 – 29 March 1920. Ed. by Steve L. Adams, Barbara J. Frieling and Sandra L. Sprayberry. London: Macmillan; Iowa City: Iowa UP, 1992. pp. xiii, 596. Rev. by Deirdre Toomey in Yeats Annual (10) 1993, 267–73; by K. P. S. Jochum in ELT (36:3) 1993, 323–36; by David Holdeman in Text (Ann Arbor) (8) 1995, 469–77; by Elizabeth Bergmann Loizeaux in Review (18) 1996, 217–24.

23008. ——— Yeats's *Vision* papers: vol. 3, Sleep and dream notebooks, *Vision* notebooks 1 and 2, card file. Ed. by Robert Anthony Martinich and Margaret Mills. London: Macmillan; Iowa City: Iowa UP, 1992. pp. xiii, 444. Rev. by Deirdre Toomey in Yeats Annual (10) 1993, 267–73; by K. P. S. Jochum in ELT (36:3) 1993, 323–36; by David Holdeman in Text (Ann Arbor) (8) 1995, 469–77; by Elizabeth Bergmann Loizeaux in Review (18) 1996, 217–24.

23009. HARVIE, CHRISTOPHER.   Garron Top to Caer Gybi: images of the inland sea. *See* **10257**.

23010. HOLDEMAN, DAVID.   Interpreting textual processes: the case of Yeats's *In the Seven Woods*. *See* **682**.

23011. HOLSTAD, SCOTT C.   Yeats's *Leda and the Swan*: psycho-sexual therapy in action. Notes on Modern Irish Literature (7:2) 1995, 45–52.

23012. HOROWITZ, STEVEN.   W. B. Yeats's Ireland and James Wright's Ohio. *In* (pp. 237–51) **58**.

23013. HOWE, ELISABETH A.   Voice of language or language of voice: Valéry, Yeats, and French Symbolism. Comparatist (15) 1991, 86–96.

23014. HOWES, MARJORIE.   Yeats' nations: gender, class, and Irishness. Cambridge; New York: CUP, 1996. pp. 250. (Cf. bibl. 1991, 16098.)

23015. HUGHES, EAMONN.   'You need not fear that I am not amiable': reading Yeats (reading) *Autobiographies*. *See* **15159**.

23016. JEFFARES, A. NORMAN.   W. B. Yeats: man and poet. (Bibl. 1962, 7956.) London: Cathie; New York: St Martin's Press, 1996. pp. x, 338. (Third ed.: first ed. 1949.)

23017. JOHNSON, ANTHONY L.   W. B. Yeats: the automatic script as a source for his plays and poems. Textus (2:1/2) 1989, 3–16.

23018. KELLY, JOHN; SCHUCHARD, RONALD (eds).   The collected letters of W. B. Yeats: vol. 3, 1901–1904. Oxford: Clarendon Press; New York: OUP, 1994. pp. liv, 777. Rev. by Denis Donoghue in TLS, 24 June 1994, 15–16; by Terry Eagleton in LRB (16:13) 1994, 8–9; by Nicholas Grene in NQ (42:4) 1995, 517–19; by K. P. S. Jochum in ELT (38:4) 1995, 507–10; by Michael J. Sidnell in Yeats Annual (12) 1996, 267–78; by Richard J. Finneran in Review (18) 1996, 45–58; by Thomas Kilroy in Irish Review (19) 1996, 138–40; by S. J. Caterson in EngS (77:3) 1996, 292–3.

23019. KIBERD, DECLAN.   Yeats and the national longing for form. In (pp. 185–200) **60**.

23020. KIRSCHNER, PAUL; STILLMARK, ALEXANDER (eds).   Between time and eternity: nine essays on W. B. Yeats and his contemporaries Hofmannsthal and Blok. (Bibl. 1995, 20354.) Rev. by Richard Greaves in Yeats Annual (12) 1996, 345–6.

23021. KOSOK, HEINZ.   Ta-ra-ra-boom-dee-ay *vs* the *Noh*: Sean O'Casey and William Butler Yeats. In (pp. 211–27) **49**.

23022. LAPISARDI, FREDERICK S.   Not-so-random notes on masks in Yeats & O'Neill. *See* **20847**.

23023. LARRISSY, EDWARD.   Yeats the poet: the measures of difference. (Bibl. 1995, 20356.) Rev. by Deirdre Toomey in Yeats Annual (12) 1996, 356–64.

23024. LENSE, EDWARD.   An influence survived: Roethke and Yeats. In (pp. 253–64) **58**.

23025. LIBBY, ANTHONY.   Angels in the bone shop. In (pp. 281–301) **58**.

23026. LIEBREGTS, P. TH. M. G.   Centaurs in the twilight: W. B. Yeats's use of the Classical tradition. (Bibl. 1993, 15742.) Rev. by A. Norman Jeffares in Yeats Annual (12) 1996, 349–52.

23027. LIEBREGTS, PETER TH. M. G.   Yeatsian moods and Plotinian ecstasy: the question of the self in Ezra Pound's *A lume spento*. *See* **21167**.

23028. LOIZEAUX, ELIZABETH BERGMANN.   Yeats's spirits: *Vision* papers, Maud Gonne, and the theatre. *See* **725**.

23029. LONGLEY, EDNA.   Introductory reflections. Yeats Annual (12) 1996, 3–28.

23030. —— 'It is time that I wrote my will': anxieties of influence and succession. *See* **14984**.

23031. MACDONALD, ALEX.   'Passionate intensity' in Wells's *The Island of Doctor Moreau* and Yeats's *The Second Coming*: constructing an echo. *See* **22471**.

23032. McDONALD, PETER.   Yeats, form and Northern Irish poetry. *See* **18527**.

23033. MARCUS, PHILLIP L.   Yeats and artistic power. (Bibl. 1994, 15725.) Rev. by Richard Greaves in Yeats Annual (12) 1996, 343–5.

23034. MEIHUIZEN, NICHOLAS.   The nature of the beast: Yeats and the shadow. In (pp. 105–11) **60**.

23035. MOLONEY, KAREN MARGUERITE.   Re-envisioning Yeats's *The Second Coming*: Desmond O'Grady and the Charles River. In (pp. 135–47) **58**.

23036. MURPHY, WILLIAM M.   Family secrets: William Butler Yeats and his relatives. (Bibl. 1995, 20369.) Rev. by Helen Vendler in BkW, 5 Mar. 1995, 1, 10; by Richard J. Finneran in ELT (39:2) 1996, 231–5.

23037. NEEPER, L. LAYNE.   Yeats and the poetics of crisis. Notes on Modern Irish Literature (3) 1991, 13–21.

23038. NITSCH, JESSICA M.-E.; PARRY, MONICA I.   Yeats's view of power in *Leda and the Swan*. NCL (22:5) 1992, 9–12.

23039. NOHRNBERG, PETER C. L.   The book the poet makes: collection and re-collection in W. B. Yeats' *The Tower* and Robert Lowell's *Life Studies. See* **19851**.

23040. NOONAN, GERALD.   W. B. Yeats in St Catharines. LRC (5:9) 1996, 27.

23041. OPPEL, FRANCES NESBITT.   Thinking about tragedy: Yeats's *Purgatory* and modern tragic theory. Genre (23:1) 1990, 33–46.

23042. PATTEN, EVE.   A 'general crowd of small singers': Yeats and Dowden reassessed. *See* **11041**.

23043. PELLEGRINO, JOE.   Yeats and Eliot: a hidden debt and its repercussions. *See* **17544**.

23044. PIERCE, DAVID.   Yeats's worlds: Ireland, England and the poetic imagination. New Haven, CT; London: Yale UP, 1995. pp. xiv, 346. Rev. by Wiliam Gorski in SAtlR (61:4) 1996, 132–5.

23045. POWELL, GROSVENOR.   T. Sturge Moore and Yeats's golden bird. *In* (pp. 104–16) **79**.

23046. PURDY, DWIGHT H.   Biblical echo and allusion in the poetry of W. B. Yeats: poetics and the art of God. (Bibl. 1995, 20376.) Rev. by A. Norman Jeffares in Yeats Annual (12) 1996, 353–5.

23047. RAIZIS, MARIUS BYRON.   Yeats's preoccupation with spiritualism and his Byzantium poems. *In* (pp. 119–26) **112**.

23048. REECE, ERIK.   Detour to the 'alltombing womb': Amiri Baraka's assault on Yeats's muse. *In* (pp. 219–35) **58**.

23049. REGAN, STEPHEN.   W. B. Yeats and Irish cultural politics in the 1890s. *In* (pp. 66–84) **18**.

23050. REVIE, LINDA L.   The little red fox, emblem of the Irish peasant in poems by Yeats, Tynan and Ní Dhomhnaill. *In* (pp. 113–33) **58**.

23051. RICHMAN, DAVID.   Yeats, personality, and *Cathleen ni Houlihan*. NETJ (5) 1994, 81–92.

23052. ROMINE, SCOTT.   Ella Wheeler Wilcox as a source for W. B. Yeats's *The Choice. See* **12775**.

23053. ROSENTHAL, M. L.   Running to paradise: Yeats's poetic art. (Bibl. 1995, 20380.) Rev. by Jonathan Allison in ANQ (9:1) 1996, 45–7.

23054. SADDLEMYER, ANN.   Reading Yeats's *A Prayer for My Daughter* – yet again. *In* (pp. 69–81) **49**.

23055. SAILER, SUSAN SHAW.   Time against time: myth and the poetry of Yeats and Heaney. *In* (pp. 202–17) **58**.

23056. SARBU, ALADÁR.   Romantic and modern: vision and form in Yeats, Shaw and Joyce. *In* (pp. 19–27) **112**.

23057. SCHRICKER, GALE C.   From Yeats's *Great Wheel* to O'Siadhail's *Image Wheel. In* (pp. 149–64) **58**.

23058. SCOTT, PETER DALE.   Alone on Ararat: Scott, Blake, Yeats, and apocalyptic. *See* **8833**.

23059. SIDNELL, MICHAEL J.   Yeats's poetry and poetics. Basingstoke: Macmillan; New York: St Martin's Press, 1996. pp. xvi, 192.

23060. SMYTHE, COLIN.   A. L. Burt's 1898 edition of *Irish Fairy and Folk Tales* 'edited by W. B. Yeats'. *See* **153**.

23061. —— W. B. Yeats, Austin Spare and *Eight Poems* (*Wade* 114). *See* **154**.

23062. SPENTZOU, EFFIE.   Helen of Troy and the poetics of innocence: from ancient fiction to modern metafiction. *See* **12081**.

23063. SUZUKI, AKIRA.   Shumatsu no vision – W. B. Yeats to Europe kindai. (The final vision: W. B. Yeats and modern Europe.) Tokyo: Kashiwa Shobo, 1996. pp. 318.

23064. SWAIN, STELLA.   The problem of belief in Yeats' *A Vision*: text and context. LitTheol (5:2) 1991, 198–219.

23065. TANNEHILL, ARLENE.   'No saint or hero … / Brings dangerous tokens to the new era': Derek Mahon and Tess Gallagher's revisions of Yeats's *The Magi*. *In* (pp. 47–69) **58**.

23066. THOMPSON, J. B.   Crazy Jane's reconciliation of the 'swordsman' and the 'saint'. EngS (77:3) 1996, 255–65.

23067. TOOMEY, DEIRDRE.   Moran's collar: Yeats and Irish Ireland. *See* **15802**.

23068. WHITE, ANNA MACBRIDE; JEFFARES, A. NORMAN (eds).   The Gonne–Yeats letters, 1893–1938: always your friend. (Bibl. 1995, 20396.) Rev. by John P. Sisk in ASch (62:4) 1993, 616–19; by David Krause in Irish Literary Supplement (14:2) 1995, 21–3; by Elizabeth Bergmann Loizeaux in Review (18) 1996, 224–9; by Daniel Patrick King in WLT (70:2) 1996, 411–12; by Thomas Flanagan in BkW, 14 Feb. 1996, 1, 11.

23069. WILSON, WILLIAM A.   Yeats, Muldoon, and heroic history. *In* (pp. 21–38) **58**.

23070. YAMAZAKI, HIROYUKI.   Yeats and Orientalism. *In* (pp. 82–92) **49**.

23071. —— Yeats to Orientalizm – kaishakugaku-teki tachiba kara. (Yeats and Orientalism: an interpretation.) Tokyo: Kindai Bungeisha, 1996. pp. 470.

23072. YOON, KIHO.   Yeats yeongeuk eseo sigakyesul eui hwalyong e gwanhan yeongu. (A study of the visual arts applied to Yeats's drama.) JELLC (38:1) 1996, 257–71.

23073. ZIMMERMAN, LEE.   Self-delighting souls, self-enclosed egos: Yeats and Galway Kinnell. *In* (pp. 265–79) **58**.

Anzia Yezierska

23074. SCHOENING, MARK.   T. S. Eliot meets Michael Gold: Modernism and radicalism in Depression-era American literature. *See* **17556**.

23075. WEXLER, LAURA.   Looking at Yezierska. *In* (pp. 153–81) **130**.

Jose Yglesias

23076. MELONE, MARY JO.   Remembering Jose Yglesias. Tampa Review (12) 1996, 15–23.

Jane Yolen

23077. BRATMAN, DAVID.   A Jane Yolen bibliography. Mythprint (30:7) 1993, 11–13.

23078. WEIL, ELLEN R.   The door to Lilith's cave: memory and imagination in Jane Yolen's Holocaust novels. JFA (5:2) 1992, 90–104.

Marguerite Young

23079. FUCHS, MIRIAM (ed.).   Marguerite Young, our darling: tributes and essays. Normal, IL: Dalkey Archive, 1994. pp. xiv, 143. Rev. by Gregory Feeley in BkW, 14 Aug. 1994, 5.

Ray A. Young Bear

23080. PARKER, ROBERT DALE.   To be there, no authority to anything: ontological desire and cultural and poetic authority in the poetry of Ray A. Young Bear. AQ (50:4) 1994, 89–115.

Paul Zimmer

23081. GERY, JOHN.   The atomic test poems of Paul Zimmer. WLA (6:1) 1994, 1–19.

Paul Zindel

23082. KELLER, JAMES R.   A fellowship of madness: Williams' Blanche Dubois and Zindel's Anna Reardon. *See* **22701**.

23083. LOOMIS, JEFFREY B.   Female freedoms, Dantesque dreams, and Paul Zindel's anti-sexist *The Effect of Gamma Rays on Man-in-the-Moon Marigolds*. StAD (6:2) 1991, 123–33.

Louis Zukofsky

23084. HENNESSY, MICHAEL.   Louis Zukofsky, Charles Tomlinson, and the 'objective tradition'. *See* **22227**.

23085. SCROGGINS, MARK.   'To breath the literal meaning': Zukofsky's *Catullus*. Talisman (6) 1991, 42–4.

23086. STANLEY, SANDRA KUMAMOTO.   Louis Zukofsky and the transformation of a modern American poetics. (Bibl. 1994, 15769.) Rev. by Michael Hennessy in ConLit (37:2) 1996, 335–45.

INDEXES

INDEX OF AUTHORS AND SUBJECTS

This index consists mainly of author's names, titles and subjects which appear as
headings in the main body of the work, with some explanatory additions, cross-
references, etc. For a breakdown by genre, of the various periods within the 'English
Literature' section, see the Table of Contents.

INDEX OF SCHOLARS

including compilers, critics, editors, and translators.
Reviewers are included only when the item has been counted as a review-article.

d'Albertis, Deirdre, 10407,
  15361
Dalby, Richard, 21551–2,
  22825
Dale, Alzina Stone, 21520
— Corinne H., 17622,
  21802
— Peter Allan, 9556
Dale-Jones, Don, 18132
Daley, A. Stuart, 6732
Dallat, C. L., 14452
Dallett, Athenaide, 20817
Dalrymple, Scott, 12560
Dalsgård, Katrine, 22526
Dalsimer, Adele M., 11733
Dalton, Mary, 17444
Dalton-Puffer, Christiane,
  1628
Daly, Brenda O., 20631–2
— Macdonald, 18311,
  22462
— Peter M., 190, 209
Dalzell, Tom, 2090
Dalziel, Pamela, 191,
  10596, 11322
D'Ambrosio, John, 22985
Dame, Frederick William,
  8450
Damian-Grint, Peter,
  5063–4
D'Amico, Maria Vittoria,
  17392
Damlos-Kinzel,
  Christiane, 20712
Damon, Maria, 21854
Damon-Moore, Helen,
  1254
Damrosch, Leo, 91, 8451
Danahay, Martin A.,
  10832
Dane, Joseph A., 266–7,
  610–12
D'Angelo, Frank, 2346
Daniel, Clay, 9236
— Douglass K., 13590
— Janice, 18830
— LaNelle, 12428
Daniele, Daniela, 10228,
  16696, 17623, 22725
Daniell, David, 6094,
  16598
Daniels, Bruce C., 7628
— Douglas Henry, 17203
— Kate, 21429
— Patsy J., 17028
— Peter T., 1594
Danielson, Dennis, 7720
Danker, Kathleen, 16832
Danow, David K., 17029
Danzer, Dorothea Ina,
  17496
Danziger, Marie A., 16280
Daphinoff, Dimiter, 7916
Darby, Trudi Laura, 268
— William, 13591

D'Arcy, Julian Meldon,
  18154
Dardis, Tom, 918
Darias-Beautell, Eva,
  14453
Darlington, Sonya, 15364
— Wilf, 3582
Darnell, Donald, 10728
Darnton, Robert, 137
Darvill, Giles, 16911
Das, Prasanta, 17929,
  21231
— Sisir Kumar, 3778
Dasenbrock, Reed Way,
  21147
Dasgupta, Probal, 2979
Daskalova, Krassimira,
  137
Dathorne, O. R., 4517
Dauber, Kenneth, 8453
Daufenbach, Claus, 17497
Daugherty, Beth Rigel,
  22842
— Sarah B., 11518
Dautermann, Jennie, 2522
Davani, Maria Carmela
  Coco, 21584
D'Avanzo, Mario L.,
  10020
Davenport, Edwin, 5755
— Guy, 18982
Davenport-Hines,
  Richard, 16114
Davey, Frank, 13026
— Gwenda Beed, 3229,
  3278
David, Deirdre, 10716
Davidhazi, Peter, 6374
Davidson, Arnold E., 3779,
  4163, 16078
— Cathy N., 3780, 15365
— Clifford, 5020–1
— Edward H., 9222
— George, 1668
— Jane P., 13592
— Keith, 2939, 2995
— Michael, 14896
Davie, Donald, 8641,
  9477–8, 17176, 17498,
  20553
— Sharon, 11549
Davies, Anthony, 6564
— Carole Boyce, 81, 3279,
  13027–8, 15366, 16968
— Damian Walford, 613,
  7801, 8778, 11096,
  12839
— Gwendolyn, 4371
— J. M. Q., 8147, 20278,
  21434
— Jude, 14897
— Kathleen, 18831
— Laurence, 17055
— Linda, 20023
— Marion, 3619

— Owen, 3620
— Richard A., 11316
— Stevie, 7802, 10383
— Walford, 22098
Davis, Adam, 4591
— Alex, 14890, 19974
— Amy, 3583
— C. B., 22346
— Caroline, 601
— Charles T., 22947
— Chester L., Sr, 12562
— Clark, 11833
— Colin, 22626
— Craig, 4751
— Cynthia J., 3781, 11991
— Daniel R., 2200
— Davie S., 10457
— Deanna L., 11255
— Deborah R., 3621
— Diane Mowery, 15369
— Geoffrey V., 13593,
  20105
— Hayley, 2523
— J. Madison, 2091
— Jane, 14455
— Katherine, 19937
— Lennard J., 7684
— Linda H., 10756
— Mike, 8798
— Natalie Zemon, 42
— Paul, 10833
— Philip, 6276
— R., 10081
— Robert Con, 15370
— Robert Murray, 9822,
  15141
— Rocío G., 20774, 22057
— Thadious M., 9558,
  18787, 19458
— Thulani, 19629
— Tom, 614
— Tracy C., 9750, 21622
— W. Eugene, 11323
— Walter R., 5719
— William V., 22935–6
Davis-Goff, Annabel, 3782
Davison, Carol Margaret,
  18996
— Neil R., 19070–1
— Peter, 6135, 14898,
  20906
— Richard Allan, 16628
Davlin, Mary Clemente,
  5181
d'Avray, D. L., 5065
Dawe, Gerald, 17807,
  19328
Dawes, James R., 20818
— Kwame, 14899
Dawidoff, Robert, 10213
Dawney, Michael, 3484
Dawson, Carl, 11444
— Graham, 15371
— P. M. S., 10645–6,
  10648

42

— Donald, 8901
— Gail Ching-Liang, 9641
— Lisa, 7564
Lowance, Mason I., Jr, 2420, 9001
Lowden, Stephen, 17065, 20640, 21363
Lowe, James, 15888
— John, 18104, 18850
— Lisa, 13192
Lowe-Evans, Mary, 6003, 19138
Lowenberg, Carlton, 10975
— Peter H., 3007
Lowenstein, Andrea Freud, 18151
Lownie, Andrew, 16602–3
Lowry, Richard S., 12588
Loyd, Dennis, 22075
Loyo Gómez, Hilaria, 13931
Lozano, Maria, 17861
Lu, Weiping, 4556
Lubbers, Klaus, 8494
Lubitz, Rita, 10875
Lucas, Angela M., 4922
— Elona K., 5165
— John, 10642, 14986–7
— Michael A., 2667
— Peter J., 385
— Rose, 14988, 17349
Lucking, David, 6760
Lucko, Peter, 2803
Luckyj, Christina, 8401
Lucy, Niall, 2277
Ludington, Townsend, 17377
Lueck, Beth, 11435
Luere, Jeane, 15910–11
Luftig, Victor, 9642
Luhr, William, 13932
Lukacher, Ned, 4207, 6394
Luling, Virginia, 22178
Lund, Michael, 9904, 18434, 22818
Lundeen, Kathleen, 13933
Lundgren, Tim, 3517
Lundin, Anne, 11308
Lundquist, Lynne, 13934
Lung, Eve, 3241
Lupack, Barbara Tepa, 13935, 14606
Lurbe, Eve D., 5850
Lurie, Alison, 3417
— Mark, 18209
Lusardi, James P., 7493
Luscher, Robert M., 18105, 22273
Luscombe, D. E., 5088
Lusk, Linda V., 15605
Lussier, Mark S., 7695, 8813–14
Lustig, Irma S., 8857
— Jessica, 22623

— T. J., 11625
Lutkus, Tony, 21768
Lutman, Richard A., 18351
Lutwack, Leonard, 3913
Lutz, Hartmut, 13193
— Stuart, 21485
— Tom, 13194
Luxon, Thomas H., 7402, 8208
Luz González, María, 21446
Lyall, Francis, 8593
— Roderick, 5736
— Roderick J., 2421, 5911, 16181
Lycett, Andrew, 17887
Lyle, Emily, 3518
Lynch, Deirdre, 8744
— Edward, 10976
— Gerald, 19619
— Kathleen, 8023
— Michael F., 22955
— Tom, 21700
Lyne, William, 15606
Lynn, Ruth Nadelman, 4309
Lyon, George Ella, 19906
— J. M., 17437
— John, 19824
— Thomas J., 19559
Lyons, Charles R., 4099, 15607
— Donald, 10297, 13936
— J. B., 19139, 19877
— James C., 15607
— Mary E., 18851

Ma, Ming-Qian, 21769
— RuiQi, 18884
— Sheng-mei, 13938–9
Mabee, Carleton, 12538
Mabey, Richard, 4460
McAdam, Ian, 5891
Macafee, C. I., 2102
McAleer, Joseph, 965
McAlice, Edward, 19878
McAlindon, T., 5892
McAllister, Andrew, 14989
— Robin, 12055
McAlpine, Kaye, 3519–20
Mac Aoidh, Caoimhín, 3521
McArthur, Feri, 1413
Macarthur, J. D., 19245
McArthur, Roshan, 1412, 1855
— Tom, 1412–13
Macaskill, Brian, 15608
Macaulay, Ronald K. S., 2835
MacBain, Danielle Morgan, 5250
McBride, Margaret, 19140

MacCabe, Colin, 21447
McCaddon, Beauvais, 22500
McCaffery, Larry, 20067
McCallum, Heather, 4100
McCalman, Iain, 8878
MacCann, Donnarae, 14809
McCann, Hugo, 18524
McCarron, Bill, 18444
— Kevin, 9643, 18241
— William, 17645, 21245
McCarry, Charles, 19915
McCarthy, B. Eugene, 22956
— Dermot, 10202, 14990, 18274
— Fiona, 11953–4
— Gerry, 6395
— Kevin M., 13195
— Patrick A., 18759, 18902, 19879, 19881–2
— Thomas J., 8902
— William Bernard, 3418, 3522
McCartney, Anne, 22011
McCaskill, Barbara, 3293, 10097
McCauley, Barbara Lynne, 5089
McCausland, Elizabeth D., 11266
McClain, Larry, 9905
McClaren, Joseph, 13940
McClellan, Rachel, 8855
— William, 386–7, 731
McClintock, James I., 17291
McCluney-Criswell, Samantha, 3419
McClure, Andrew S., 16639
— Charlotte S., 16069
— John A., 14609
Maccoby, Hyam, 18296
McComas, Alan, 22179
MacComb, Debra, 11626
— Debra Ann, 22577
McCombs, Judith, 16093
McConachie, Bruce A., 9769–70, 13941–2
McConchie, R. W., 218
McConkey, James M., 19934
McConnell, Frank, 2768
— Kathleen, 2422
— Will, 21246
McCooey, David, 15167
McCorison, Marcus A., 293
McCormack, K., 1310
— W. J., 146, 1311, 8495
McCormick, Catherine M., 2103
— Frank, 8379

43

Rosso, George Anthony, Jr, 8829
— Stefano, 13285
Roston, Murray, 9680
Røstvig, Maren-Sofie, 5743, 8237
Rosu, Anca, 21973
Rot, Sándor, 1786
Rotella, Guy, 20193
Roth, Barry, 10314–15
— Elizabeth Elam, 18065
— Marty, 4253, 15729
Rothenberg, Molly Anne, 8830–1
Rothman, Barbara Katz, 4004
— Irving N., 820
— Stanley, 14154
Rothwell, W., 1910
Roudané, Matthew C., 14155–6, 15917
Roulston, Helen H., 17873
— Robert, 17873
Round, Phillip, 9061
Rousseau, Constance M., 5298
Rout, Kay Kinsella, 21334
Rovang, Paul R., 5256
Rovano, Marcelaine Wininger, 14157
Rovit, Earl, 15174
Rowbotham, Judith, 9938
Rowe, M. W., 10701
— Margaret Moan, 19671
Rowell, Charles H., 4254, 19369, 19931
Rowen, Norma, 3447
Rowland, Jon, 8929
— Peter, 8951
— Susan, 16960
— William G., Jr, 10053
Rowley, Hazel, 21828
— Robert, 15730
— Stephen, 17552, 19583
Rowlinson, Matthew, 10899, 12447
Rowsell, Jennifer, 8309
Rowson, Martin, 241
Roy, G. Ross, 8660, 8913
— Parama, 10108
Royer, Daniel J., 2459, 11037
Royot, Daniel, 3980–1
Rozett, Martha Tuck, 14697
Rozga, Margaret, 17413, 20636
Rozik, Eli, 2286
Rubel, David, 13986
— Warren, 17553
Rubenstein, Roberta, 14698, 18905
Rubidge, Bradley, 6193
Rubik, Margarete, 9209, 11986

Rubin, Deborah, 7952
— Donald L., 2460
— Joan Shelley, 1002
— Louis D., Jr, 1077, 13287, 21016
— Martin, 14158
Rubio, Mary Henley, 20300
Ruby, Jay, 14159–60
Ruckert, William H., 19827
Rudakoff, Judith, 14161
Rudanko, Juhani, 1737, 1800, 2287
Rudat, Wolfgang E. H., 5448–50, 18678
Rudd, Gillian, 4971–3, 5197–8
Ruddick, Lisa, 15731
— Nicholas, 18165
Rude, Donald W., 534
Rudnick, Lois, 10221
Rudolph, Leighton, 17890
Rudrum, Alan, 7649, 8384
Rudy, John G., 12893
— Stephen, 2693
— Susan, 18439
Ruesga, G. Albert, 4255
Ruff, Loren K., 10494
Ruggieri, Helen, 21819
Ruggiers, Paul G., 5451
Rugoff, Kathy, 16130
Ruhe, Ernstpeter, 15155
Ruhemann, Linda, 22896
Ruhl, Charles, 1989, 20917
Ruland, Richard, 3982
Ruleman, William, 22637
Rulewicz, Wanda, 10468
Rullmann, Hotze, 1918
Rulon-Miller, Nina, 7106
Rumaker, Michael, 17435, 20769
Rumble, Alexander R., 414
Rumbold, Valerie, 9180
Rumrich, John, 8238–9
— John P., 8240
Runda, Todd, 4786
Rundell, Michael, 2561
Rundle, Vivienne, 10506
Runge, Laura L., 4256
Running-Johnson, Cynthia, 14162
Runyon, Randolph Paul, 16731, 21977, 22420–1
Runzo, Sandra, 10992
Ruoff, A. Lavonne Brown, 9681, 13288, 21704
Rupp, Katrin, 4657
Ruppel, Richard, 17083
Ruppersburg, Hugh, 22422
Ruppert, James, 13289, 14700, 17626
— Peter, 4257, 14163

Rupp-Serano, Karen, 1200
Rusche, Philip G., 415
Rushdy, Ashraf H. A., 18956–7, 22688
Rusinko, Susan, 19689, 20902
Russ, Joanna, 3983
Russell, Charles G., 2236
— Hawley, 14164
— Henry M. W., 20694
— Henry W., 5990
— Peter, 21269
— Sharon A., 19305
— W. M. S., 10607
Russo, Brian C., 18086
— John Paul, 11990
— Paola, 11885
Rust, Marion, 9012
— Martha Dana, 2700
Ruthven, K. K., 15734
Rutland, Barry, 15735
Ruud, Jay, 5160
Ruvin, Louis D., Jr, 4191
Ryals, Clyde de L., 9682, 10531, 10583–5
Ryan, Brenna J., 16192
— Dennis, 18679
— Francis J., 12609
— J. S., 3237, 3448, 11531
— Judith, 13290
— Kiernan, 6455, 15736, 19963
— Maureen, 19311
— Michael, 14165
Ryan-Fazillau, Susan, 16693
Ryden, Kent C., 3300
Rydland, Kurt, 1574
Rylance, Rick, 19584
Rymes, Betsy, 2163
Ryskamp, Charles, 8936–7

Saad, Gabriel, 17748
Saameño, Emilio, 1767
Saar, Doreen Alvarez, 8607
Sabal, Rob, 14166
Sabbadini, Silvano, 7276, 7299
Sabin, Margery, 10149, 15737
— Roger, 10726
Sabine, Maureen, 7768, 7840
Sabino, Robin, 1575, 3029
Sabor, Peter, 8891
Saccamano, Neil, 8771
Sachithanandan, V., 10702
Sachs, Viola, 3984
Saddlemyer, Ann, 9781, 14167, 22043–4, 23054
Sadleir, Michael, 12530

SCHOLARS

Streeter, Robert E., 15785
Strehle, Susan, 14736
Streight, Irwin Howard,
  20698
Streitfeld, David, 14260
Streitmatter, Rodger,
  1374, 4508
Strier, Richard, 5605, 5707
String, Tatiana C., 249
Stringer, Gary A., 7857
— Jenny, 13324
Stringher, Bonalda, 17144,
  22897
Stripling, Mahala Yates,
  21570
Strobl, Gerwin, 17568,
  17649
Stroby, W. C., 19308
Stroffolino, Chris, 19428
Strommer, Jean Theresa,
  7858
— Joan Elizabeth, 7858
Strong, Amy, 18685
— Amy Lovell, 17759
— Jonathan, 22009
Stroupe, John H., 5020–1
Strub, Christian, 19197
Struve, Laura, 11958
Strychacz, Thomas, 11656,
  18686
Stuart, Christopher, 4995
— Elaine Potts, 8296
— Ian, 16502–3
Stubbs, Andrew, 20107
— Michael, 1208
Studing, Richard, 6483
Studlar, Gaylyn, 14261
Stuhlmann, Gunther,
  20257–8, 20592–4
Stull, William L., 16734
Stump, Gregory T., 1624
Sturges, Robert S., 4996
Sturgess, Charlotte, 16654
Sturgill, Mack H., 16014
Sturm, Oliver, 16360
Sturman, Christopher,
  846
Sturrock, John, 13325,
  15786
Stutman, Suzanne, 22817
Stwertka, Eve, 19927
Styan, J. L., 4113, 14262
Suarez, Ernest, 11200,
  21740
— Michael F., 1013
Suárez Lafuente, María
  Socorro, 15873
Suárez Sánchez, Juan A.,
  14263
Suazo, Frances L., 2662
Subbiondo, Joseph L., 1511
Suchoff, David, 4498
Suchy, Patricia A., 4114
Sudan, Rajani, 10801
Sudbery, Rodie, 22025

Suerbaum, Ulrich, 6484
Suga, Yukako, 9882
Sugars, Cynthia, 13326,
  19893
— Cynthia S., 15897
Sugg, Richard P., 15787
Suggs, Henry Lewis, 1375
Sugiyama, Michelle
  Scalise, 18687
— Naoko, 22965
Suhamy, Henri, 6485,
  12189
Sujaku, Shigeko, 6722
Suksang, Duangrudi,
  11754
Suleiman, Susan Rubin,
  14738
Suleri, Sara, 2480
Sullens, Idelle, 5265
Sullivan, Brad, 12111
— C. W., III, 4023, 14821,
  22212
— Ceri, 5606, 5905, 7859
— Dale L., 2481
— David, 11005–7
— Ernest W., II, 426, 847
— Hannah, 17999
— Larry E., 1014
— Laura L., 2292
— Matthew, 5155
— Megan, 16248
— Robert, 20304
— Rosemary, 19968,
  20963
— Walter, 18265
— William L., 11926
— Zohreh T., 19360
Sumida, Stephen H., 4024,
  13130
Summerfield, Geoffrey,
  10640
Summerlin, Charles
  Timothy, 18071
Summers, Claude J., 128,
  4025, 5906
— Joseph H., 5746
Summit, Jennifer, 5124,
  5821
Sun, Douglas, 22122
Sundby, Bertil, 1485
Sundquist, Eric J., 4026,
  11040
Sung, Eun-Ae, 10912–13
Sunstein, Emily W., 9080
Surette, Leon, 15789–90,
  16102, 17569
Surtees, Angela, 4027
Süssekind, Flora, 16464
Sussman, Herbert, 9703
Sutcliffe, Chris, 5773
Sutherland, Eileen, 10326
— John, 1015, 9956,
  12190, 12530, 12625,
  13324
— Richard, 14264

— Zena, 4301
Sutrop, Margit, 15791
Sutton, Anne F., 5108
— Brian, 18087, 22639
— John L., 18131
— Walter, 1376
Suvin, Darko, 4432
Suzman, Janet, 6668
Suzuki, Akira, 23063
— Mihoko, 5818
— Sachiko, 12482
— Seiichi, 1528, 4433,
  4789
— Takashi, 19198
— Zenzo, 4028
Svartvik, Jan, 2069
Svilpis, Jānis, 8989
Svoboda, Frederic J.,
  18688
Swaim, Kathleen M., 7729
Swain, S. P., 17255
— Stella, 23064
Swander, Homer, 7007
Swanepoel, C. F., 3831
Swann, Charles, 8076,
  10595, 11161–2, 15792
— Joan, 1446
— Joseph, 16187
— Marjorie, 7740
Swanson, Jean, 14740
Swanton, Michael, 4669
Swarbrick, Andrew, 19450
Swartz, Omar, 2482
Swartzlander, Susan, 21511
Swearingen, C. Jan, 2483
Sweeney, Susan Elizabeth,
  22266
Sweet, Charlie, 16895–9,
  19040, 20155–6,
  20668–9
Sweeting, Adam W., 9704
Swenson, Paul, 22028
Swiderski, Richard M.,
  1486
Swift, John N., 16851–2
— Rebecca, 4149
Swigg, Richard, 22228
Swindlehurst, Kate, 2467
Swingle, L. J., 9957
Swinson, Ward, 19199
Swirski, Peter, 15794
Swisher, Clarice, 11431
Swiss, Margo, 40, 7862
Sword, Helen, 17350
Swortzell, Lowell, 20850
Sydenstricker, Glória,
  18286
Sykes, Jerry, 19943
— John, 18893
Sylvester, Louise, 1876,
  1914
Sylwanowicz, Agnieszka,
  22190
Symons, Julian, 4267,
  13327

Wang, Chull, 17095
— Qun, 22756
— Veronica C., 22966
— William S.-Y., 1641
Waniek, Marilyn Nelson, 15076
Wansell, Geoffrey, 21287
Warburton, Eileen, 17972
Ward, Annalee P., 14312
— Bernadette, 11499
— Candace, 10532
— Douglas B., 1026
— Dunstan, 18291
— Gregory, 2508
— Ian, 4041
— Jerry W., Jr, 9681, 13355, 17636
— Laviece C., 437
— Maryanne C., 9974
— Patricia H., 5049, 6860
Wardrop, Daneen, 11011
— Stephanie, 14759
Ware, Tracy, 12098, 15818
Wareham, John, 10652
Warhol, Robyn R., 10444
Waring, Wendy, 1089, 14760
Warkentin, Germaine, 6082
Warley, Linda, 20129
Warminski, Andrzej, 8440
Warne, Randi R., 19930
Warner, Anthony R., 1758
— John M., 8992
— Marina, 3460
— Martin, 9453
— Michael, 1027, 7441
Warnicke, Retha, 7646
Warren, Beatrice, 2247
— James Perrin, 12766
— Joyce W., 9716, 11213–14
— Kenneth W., 17601
— Roger, 6199, 6679
Wartofsky, Steven A., 12767
Warwick, Alexandra, 9975
— Claire, 7769
— Susan J., 19483
Washburn, Tina, 14313
Washick, James, 19758
Washington, Edward T., 7130
— Mary Helen, 21612
Wasilewska, Anna, 12776
Wasow, Thomas, 2913
Wasserman, Jerry, 14314
— Julian N., 5493
— Loretta, 16861–4
— Renata R. Mautner, 9717
— Rosanne, 17355
Wasserstein, Wendy, 22430
Wasson, John, 6976

Waswo, Richard, 1492, 5792
Watanabe, Toshio, 4042
Watarai, Yoshiichi, 11450
Water, Bill Vande, 11084
Waterhouse, Ruth, 4793
Waters, D. Douglas, 6500, 7176
— Lindsay, 15820–1
Watkins, Floyd C., 17783, 22425
Watkiss, Leslie, 5112
Watson, Charles S., 12314, 17897
— George J., 19207
— Greer, 3655
— Gregory John, 14763
— J. R., 11275
— James G., 17772–3
— Jay, 17774–5
— John, 12484
— Julia, 4504
— Marsha, 9486
— Neil, 17776
— Nicholas, 5161, 5272
— Nicola J., 8617
— Paula D., 550
— Ritchie Devon, Jr, 9976
— Robert N., 5610
— Roderick, 4438, 13356
— Stephen, 13357, 16983, 17156
— Thomas Ramey, 19759
— William Braasch, 18692
Watt, George, 22613
— Ian, 8993, 17033
— Milton, 3217
— R. J. C., 1215, 6200
— Stephen, 67
Watten, Barrett, 21533
Watters, David H., 9001
Watterson, William Collins, 7110, 12511
Watts, Carol, 9405
— Cedric, 1028, 12359, 17097
— Eileen H., 20078
— Steven, 10485
— William, 5488
Waugh, Linda R., 1880
— Patricia, 15716
Wawia, Dolores Nawagesic, 12973
Waxler, Robert P., 19283
Waxman, Barbara, 17286
Wayne, Valerie, 6092
Weaks, Mary Louise, 22425
Weales, Gerald, 14315, 16894, 19800, 20248, 21656
Weatherby, H. L., 6083
— Harold L., 6084–5
Weatherford, Kathleen Jeannette, 10635

Weatherly, Joan, 2249
Weaver, Robert, 9795
Webb, Barbara J., 18454
— Caroline, 22916
— Janeen, 21190, 21497
— Sarah Jo, 19647
Webber, Teresa, 438
Weber, A. S., 6725
— Alfred, 11435
— Harold, 90, 5595, 8333
— Horst, 13358
— Jean Jacques, 2729
— Marc, 18583
— Myles, 16680
— Ronald, 17179
Webster, Alison, 8758
— Jack, 3570
Wechselblatt, Martin, 9173
Wee, C. J. W.-L, 11741
Weedon, Alexis, 324
Weekes, Ann Owens, 9977
Ween, Lori, 21734
Wees, Coreen Dwyer, 21758
Wegemer, Gerard, 5927
Wegener, Frederick, 11668
Wegner, J. P., 325
— Pamela S., 11458
— Robert E., 17174
Weier, Gary M., 6923
Weikert, Heidrun-Edda, 10533, 12135
Weil, Ellen R., 23078
Weiland, Steven, 16426
Weimann, Robert, 5611, 6680
Wein, Toni, 16104
Weinauer, Ellen M., 10116
Weinberg, Louise, 12535
— S. C., 5213
Weinbrot, Howard D., 7442, 9174
Weine, Stevan M., 16206
Weinfield, Henry, 18584
Weinhouse, Linda, 16645
Weinig, Edelbert, 6924
Weinkauf, Mary S., 22961
Weinsheimer, Joel C., 8765
Weinstein, Arnold, 4271, 9978
— Charles E., 6681
— Cindy, 9979
— Philip M., 17777–8
Weinstock, Alexander, 1424
— Carola, 1424
— Constanze, 1424
— Horst, 1529
Weintraub, Stanley, 11019, 12816, 21657
Weir, Lorraine, 15822
Weisberg, Richard, 4044
Weisbuch, Robert, 10987